The TEAM BY TEAM Encyclopedia of Major League BASEBALL

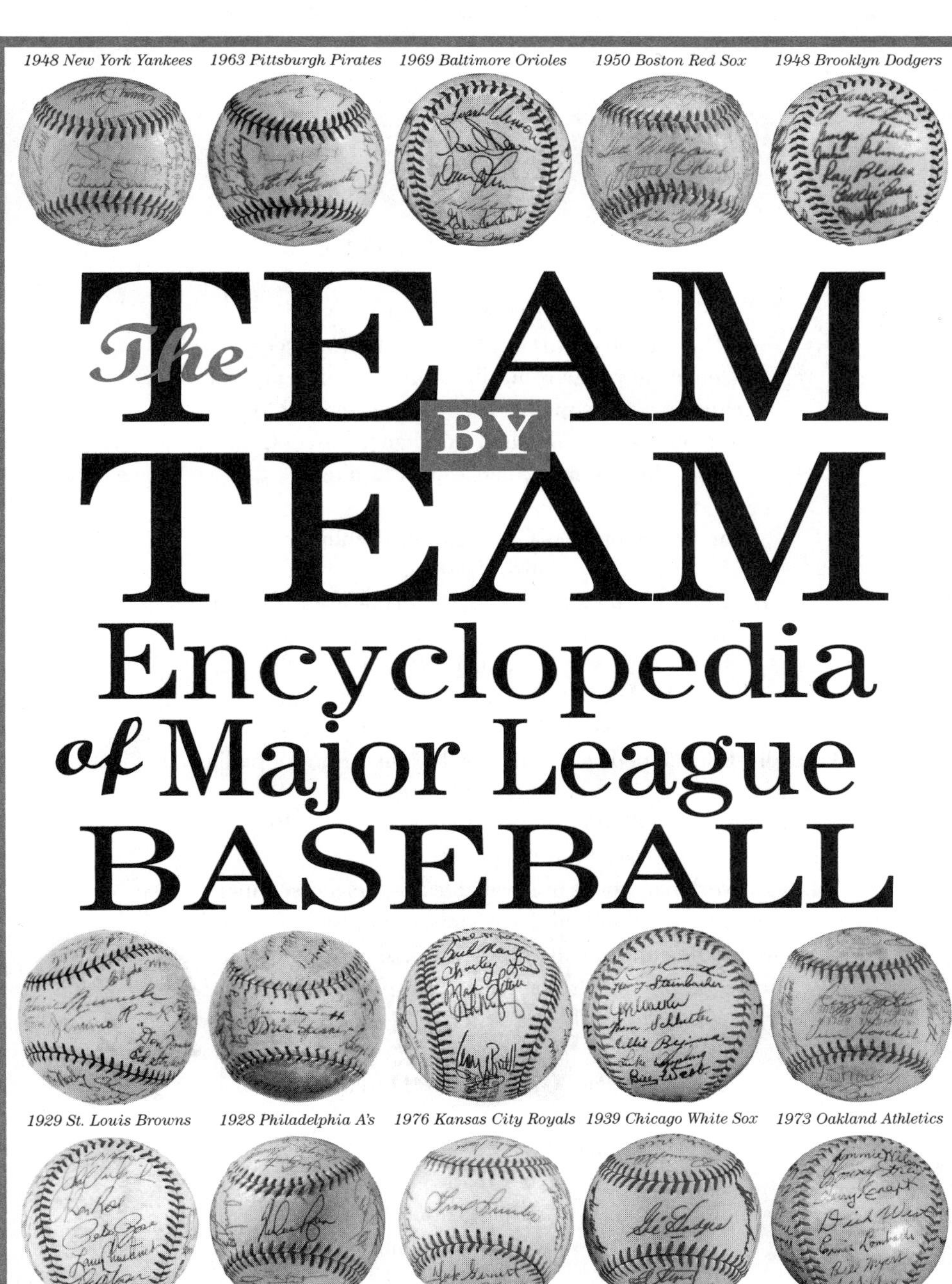

The TEAM BY TEAM Encyclopedia of Major League BASEBALL

by Dennis Purdy

Foreword by Tony LaRussa

Workman Publishing • New York

Library of Congress Cataloging-in-Publication Data
Purdy, Dennis.
The team by team encyclopedia of major league baseball /
by Dennis Purdy; foreword by Tony LaRussa.
p. cm.
ISBN-13: 978-0-7611-3943-0 (alk. paper)
ISBN-10: 0-7611-3943-5 (alk. paper)
1. Baseball—Encyclopedias. 2. Baseball teams—Encyclopedias. I. Title.
GV862.3.P87 2006
796.357'64097303—dc22 2006045047

Workman books are available at special discounts
when purchased in bulk for premiums and sales promotions
as well as for fund-raising or educational use. Special editions
of book excerpts can also be created to specification. For details,
contact the Special Sales Director at the address below.

Design by Paul Gamarello and Orlando Adiao

WORKMAN PUBLISHING COMPANY, INC.
708 Broadway
New York, NY 10003-9555
www.workman.com

Printed in U.S.A.
First printing June 2006

10 9 8 7 6 5 4 3 2 1

ACKNOWLEDGMENTS

The risk of offending anyone by forgetting to thank them for their help in reaching a long-contemplated goal like this one is not small, but here goes.

First, I'd like to thank my mother, Beverly Joan Clayton, who worked at one time for *Look* magazine. She was dealt many tough hands in her life, but she never once complained about any of them. She fostered my desire to read and write early in my life, and she reinforced it through the writings of hers that I discovered after her death.

I'd like to thank her sister, my Aunt Marjorie Smith, a long-time freelance writer and newspaper editor, who kept the writing desire alive in me. She never failed to kick me when I needed kicking.

I'd like to thank my brother, William Purdy, who now is an Assistant U.S. Attorney, but 37 years ago was "Billy, of the [accursed] Yankees," and my constant opponent when we played a million games of Wiffleball against the barn in Tama, Iowa, sometimes until well after dark. Our home runs were fly balls that landed on the first three rows of shingles on the barn's roof (fourth row and higher were outs); our triples were balls that hit the rain barrel; our doubles were liners off the siding between two windows; our singles were grounders against the siding; outs were fly balls and grounders fielded cleanly; and if you hit a ball through the open barn window and the ball landed in the manure pile, well, *that* was a triple play, and deservedly so. Nearly four decades later, those still remain some of the happiest memories of my youth.

When I was 15 years old, I began the habit of writing down baseball statistics, records, and standings in spiral notebooks for my own enjoyment. This was a year or two before Macmillan's *Baseball Encyclopedia* came out. One day in 1969, as I was studying (or more likely, girl watching) in the library of South Tama County High School, I was summoned to the office by the school's vice-principal, Mr. Watkins, a stern, no-nonsense administrator if ever there was one, whose sole purpose in life seemed to be the administering of punishments of one kind or another. I had no idea what I'd done to warrant a trip to his dungeon.

He gruffly told me to come into his inner office, closed the door behind me, and held up one of my spiral notebooks filled with baseball statistics that I had apparently lost somewhere along the line. "Is this yours?"

So that was the crime in question. I admitted the notebook was mine, bowed my head, and awaited my punishment.

"Well," Vice-principal Watkins said, "it's very interesting. Fascinating, actually. I wish more young men would take an interest in such things." He then gave me back the spiral notebook and we had a wonderful conversation about baseball, my future plans, and my Vietnam War draft status, after which he slapped me on the back and told me to keep up the good work on "the baseball stuff," but not to forget about my algebra.

Well, Mr. Watkins, here it is, 37 years later. As you can see, I took your advice. On the baseball stuff, that is.

I'm indebted to my literary agent, Evelyn Fazio. When I first sent a proposal letter to her agency, I was actually seeking representation for a novel I had written, but after a three-hour conversation that involved my interest and background in baseball, she asked me why I wasn't presenting her with a book about some aspect of *that.* After a couple of weeks and at Evelyn's urging, I came up with the idea for the book that you now hold in your hands. So here's a big thanks to Evelyn and her partner, Pam Brodowsky.

A mammoth project such as this book requires a lot of fact-checking and proofreading. For this I drew upon those closest to me: My daughter, Dennika, and my son, Dakota, spent many hours double-checking batting records, attendance figures, 20-game winners, and much, much more. And considering they're teenagers, they didn't mind too much, especially when they discovered they would get school credit for it as "a life experience project."

I would also like to thank Kathy, my muse, who spent a lot of hours on the calculator compiling and verifying statistics. In baseball terms, she's a game-winning grand slam.

I'm indebted to photo editors Leora Kahn and Kristy Ramsammy, and book designers Paul Gamarello and Orlando Adiao, for making this so visually beautiful a book. Baseball reference books are normally so humble looking.

Finally, a project like this requires massive work on the editorial side. Maybe I had to write it all, but someone else had to read it all and make corrections, suggestions, and generally fine-tune a document that was 1,631 pages—single-spaced! That someone was Richard Rosen, senior editor at Workman Publishing. I don't know what this project would have been like without Richard as my editor, but I'm glad I didn't have to find out. His love of baseball is equal to my own, and his passion for the sport and this book helped make it what it is. For that I am truly grateful, and I'm already looking forward to working with him on our next book, and hopefully many more.

PHOTO CREDITS

We would like to thank the following people for their photo contribution:
Gar Miller, Mike Gutierrez and **Hunt Auctions.**

AP Wide World Photos - pages: 2, 3, 14, 16 top & btm, 19, 34, 48, 56, 66, 67, 69, 73, 89, 98 top & btm, 100 btm, 101, 102, 103, 104, 111, 112, 113, 117, 138, 139 top & btm, 140, 143, 145, 148 btm, 149, 150 top, 153, 160, 162, 171, 189, 199, 204 btm, 206, 212, 213, 214, 218, 249, 291, 300, 304 top, 308, 311, 314, 316, 342, 345, 346, 353, 354, 357 top, 362, 367, 378 btm, 391, 417, 420 top & btm, 421, 422, 423, 428 btm, 432, 433, 446 btm, 454, 483, 488, 504, 507 mid, 510, 511, 518, 531 top, 534 btm, 538 btm, 539 top, 540, 544, 573, 575 top & btm, 577 top, 580 btm, 583 top & btm, 584, 592, 596, 597, 601, 613, 623, 649, 651, 652 top, 656, 659, 661, 665, 666 top, 671, 685, 686 top & btm, 691, 693, 694, 696, 698, 698, 700, 701, 705, 728, 730, 732 top, 734 top & btm, 736 top & btm, 737, 738, 741, 743 btm, 744, 747, 750, 751, 756, 778, 782, 783 top & btm, 785, 786, 787 top, 792, 796, 797, 824, 825 btm, 827, 830 top, 831 top, 832, 834, 837, 838, 872, 893, 895, 903, 928, 933, 946, 947, 950, 951, 967, 974, 977, 978, 979, 980 left & right, 985, 1008 top & btm, 1016 top, 1032 , 1034, 1035, 1037, 1051, 1053 btm, 1054, 1055 top, 1056 btm, 1057 btm, 1060, 1062, 1073 btm, 1076, 1077, 1085, 1101 top & btm, 1111, 1113, 1115, 1131, 1136, 1138 top, 1139 btm, 1143, 1156; Bricol Sports- pages: 449; **The Carnegie Library of Pittsburgh** - page: 836, 888 btm; **Cincinnati Historical Society Library** - pages: 261, 263; **Library of Congress** - pages: xvii top, 51 top & btm, 55 top & btm, 57, 59 btm, 62, 63 top & btm, 64, 106 btm, 107, 150 btm, 157 btm, 168, 190, 192, 193, 194 top & btm, 195 btm, 197, 201, 202, 226, 241, 243, 245, 247, 255, 256 top & btm, 276, 295, 296 top, 304 btm, 350, 351 btm, 410 top, 411, 414, 425, 430, 545, 574 top, 581, 588 top, 589, 593, 616, 622, 652 btm, 653 btm, 657, 739 top, 744, 746, 776, 777 top, 781 top & btm, 787 btm, 795, 822 btm, 826 top & btm, 828 top & btm, 830 btm, 833 top, 869, 870 top & btm, 874, 879, 880 btm, 882, 886 top, 890, 927, 929, 932 top, 1009, 1010 top & btm, 1011, 1014 top, 1015, 1017, 1021, 1022 btm, 1025, 1028 top & btm, 1029, 1030, 1031 top; **Minnesota Historical Society** - page: 628; **National Baseball Hall of Fame and Museum Inc.** - pages: 18, 21, 47, 161, 162, 191, 320, 343, 380, 381, 752, 821, 892, 976; **Zuma Press** - pages: 315 (top) The Sporting News, 382 The Sporting News, 386 The Sporting News, 450 Malcolm Emmons, 451, 482 Karl Mondon, 546 Karl Mondon, 551 The Sporting News, 664 Louis Requena, 894 TSN Archives, 900 The Sporting News, 1127, 1136.

TABLE OF CONTENTS

FOREWORD

by Tony LaRussa

You are in for a treat. In a world with no shortage of baseball reference books, Dennis Purdy has created something new: an encyclopedia of major league franchises that is both historical and statistical. Using numbers, narrative, and an encyclopedic knowledge of the game's history, Purdy conjures up the entire existence of every current major league team.

Like a good baseball team, Purdy's book is strong in all phases. It has power: Nowhere else can you find such a wealth of individual and team stats organized like this—by team. *The Team-By-Team Encyclopedia of Major League Baseball* has depth, with its astute and concise histories of each franchise and its mini-biographies of every "franchise player"—tracing the lives of all the great ones, with their larger-than-life talents and their sometimes larger-than-life foibles, from their glory days to their often humble denouements. And thanks to Purdy's taste for oddity and irony, this book will never bore you for a minute. Like any winning baseball team, this book does all the little things well: It gives you the principal starting lineup for each team for every year of its existence, each franchise's all-time win-loss record against all opponents, who managed and when, no-hitters pitched, all its Gold Glove winners, Hall of Fame members, you name it.

Purdy's gone back through more than a century of dusty baseball records and newspaper accounts and mined them for every fascinating anecdote and marvelous bit of statistical trivia he could find. I was impressed by all the delightful stories I'd never heard, and surprised to learn more about the famous ones I had. If you want to know what Babe Ruth told Lou Gehrig (with whom he was barely speaking) as he crossed home plate after hitting his controversial "called shot" home run at Wrigley Field in the 1932 World Series, you'll find it in here. And pretty much only here. You'll also find the tragic story of Cincinnati catcher Ernie Lombardi, the unbelievable tale of Philadelphia Athletics great Rube Waddell, and the poignant story of Johnny Evers and Joe Tinker, the former Cubs double-play combo, sobbing in each other's arms when reunited after 30 years of not speaking to each other. If you ever wondered where the saying "It ain't braggin' if you can do it," originated, here's your chance to find out (hint: the source was a vertiginous Redbird).

I've been a baseball fanatic since I was five years old and I've worked in professional baseball for more than 40 years, including field managing since 1978. Early on I never imagined there was so much baseball to learn. It's much later, and I'm still learning. Purdy's book keeps the process going.

In a reference-book version of team chemistry, *The Team-By-Team Encyclopedia of Major League Baseball* is more than the sum of its parts. By showing you every team from so many different angles—the historical, the purely statistical, the personalities that made the franchises, and the trends and idiosyncrasies that helped define them—Purdy achieves something that raises this book far above other references. It makes the franchises come alive, as living, breathing institutions that wrote the history of our national pastime, and therefore helped write the history of America.

INTRODUCTION

Another book on baseball? Why? Because this one's different. It's not simply a record book. It's not simply a book filled with statistics or biographies. It's not a trivia book. It is all of these rolled into one, with baseball history and little-known anecdotes thrown in as well.

Another difference is that I've organized this book by team. Baseball is, after all, a team sport, and the stories of major league franchises—their origins, evolution, many great protagonists, and statistics—will bring you closer to the soul of the game than any one- or two-dimensional reference book. Each of the chapters will leave you with the most detailed snapshot available of one of our national pastime's franchises. This book was not designed as a standard reference work that gives you the answer to a specific statistical question and then gets put back on the shelf until the next person asks you, "Who had the most home runs in his first three seasons?" Think of this book instead as a gourmet buffet for the baseball connoisseur. Help yourself, consume at your leisure, then go back for seconds. I've tried to make each chapter a satisfying mix of history, trivia, anecdotes, records, and biographies.

It was inevitable that my passion for baseball would finally express itself as this book. During my early high-school days, I was the guy in class who, just for his own enjoyment, compulsively recorded the final standings, league leaders, and certain record holders for each year in baseball history in spiral notebooks. As a kid in Tama, Iowa, I played "barn baseball" with my brothers, sandlot baseball with the neighborhood kids, and organized ball in high school.

After graduating I moved on to fast-pitch softball and then semipro baseball, where I was discovered in 1976 pitching for the Nevada, Iowa, team by a scout for the Minnesota Twins. At my two-day tryout in Metropolitan Stadium in Bloomington, Minnesota, I had a chance to work out with major league players. It was an unforgettable experience—although at times I wish I could forget it, since I was knocked around like a kite in a hurricane by backup outfielder Steve Brye. The record books list Brye as having hit only two home runs and 11 doubles in 1976, so they obviously aren't including the seven home runs and 15 doubles he hit off me that June day. When the conditioning coach told me I had to run a 50-yard dash in six seconds flat or faster just to be considered further, I remember asking him if Mickey Lolich could run it in six seconds. He pointed out—and I'm cleaning up his language here—that I wasn't Mickey Lolich.

As an adult, playing baseball gradually gave way entirely to contemplating and promoting it. In 1978 I developed a powerful baseball wagering system that ultimately became so widely used by baseball bettors that Las Vegas oddsmakers eventually had to change their daily odds to reflect the system's popular use. In 1987 I created my syndicated feature, "Baseball Trivia Game," which I self-syndicated to about two dozen newspapers around the country for several years.

In 1990 I began my baseball-card trade show promotion business in Tacoma, Washington, sponsoring a baseball-card show nearly every weekend somewhere in Washington, Oregon, Idaho, or California for the next decade—something I still do four times a year. In 1991 I displayed at my shows, for the first time, my Traveling Baseball Card Museum. Over the years the museum increased in size and stature, eventually containing significant baseball cards dating back to the 1860s, some of which were one-of-a-kind and valued at upwards of $10,000. By 1994 I added a History of Baseball Exhibit to the shows.

While at one of my weekend shows in Puyallup, Washington, I was approached by the Dean of Continuing Education for Tacoma Community College, who was impressed with the museum. After talking to the dean for an hour or so, she invited me to teach baseball history at TCC, which I did for several years in the early 1990s. After discovering how much I liked teaching baseball history, I decided to blend my love of writing, baseball, and baseball cards by publishing my own magazine. In 1995 I unveiled *The Vintage & Classic Baseball Collector Magazine,* a journal devoted to both baseball history and the sport's rare collectibles. After a six-year run, I sold the magazine in 2000 to pursue my dream of writing books.

Over the years I have accumulated many hundreds of books in my baseball library, including a complete set of all the *Spalding, Reach, Sporting News,* and other annual guides dating back to 1876. These were instrumental in the preparation of this book. You'll find an example of the type of anecdote I was able to unearth for this book—this one from the 1933 Spalding Guide—in the Babe Ruth bio in the New York Yankees chapter, which describes a *second* "called shot" in the 1932 World Series.

Another source of original material for this book is the wealth of personal conversations I've had over the years with hundreds of former and current players through my baseball card show business. Driving them to and from the airport for their appearances during their autograph sessions, I heard from the ultimate sources the stories behind some of baseball's most hallowed events. It was thrilling, for example, to hear from Hall of Famer Enos Slaughter himself that he never would have tried his "mad dash home" in the 1946 World Series had Dom DiMaggio not been injured and replaced in center field the inning before. I've also witnessed firsthand the strained relationship between former teammates Pete Rose and Joe Morgan, who sat together for half an hour in the backroom at one of my autograph shows signing items without once speaking to each other. I learned firsthand why some players have the reputation for being jerks (Frank Robinson, Warren Spahn, Ryan Klesko, and particularly Orlando Cepeda come to mind), oddballs (Jimmy Piersall, Dock Ellis, and Denny McLain), or first-class men (about 600 others, although Steve Garvey, Jim Palmer, Yogi Berra, Don Drysdale, Andy Pafko, Bobby Richardson, and Bill Mazeroski stand out as the best of the best). Many of this book's biographies reflect my privileged contact with these and other men who played the game.

—Dennis Purdy
Tacoma, Washington
January 2006

THE GROUND RULES

The Team-By-Team Encyclopedia of Major League Baseball is a unique book. In some ways, books are like ballparks, each with nuances, corners, and characteristics all their own. In that regard, this book has some ground rules all its own, and understanding them will give you a better appreciation of the information contained in these pages

DEFINITION OF A "FRANCHISE"

The book is divided into 30 chapters, one for each current baseball franchise. The term *franchise,* as used in this book, refers to the current team and any and all cities and leagues through which the current franchise can be traced with a chain of ownership. The chain continues and the entity remains the same, with an essentially unchanged lineup from one year to the next, even when the franchise shifts to another city or league. It's the same organization even if the team's name changes. Let me provide several examples.

The Los Angeles Dodgers of today can be traced back to their days in Brooklyn, when the team—unbroken and unchanged—moved from New York to California in 1957. The Dodgers can be traced back even farther, to the time they transferred from the American Association to the National League following the 1889 season, again, unbroken and unchanged. Thus, for the purposes of this book, all records and statistics pertaining to the Dodgers are drawn from their inception in the American Association in 1884 to today.

For a second example, let's consider the San Francisco Giants. Like the Dodgers, the Giants franchise moved to the West Coast from New York in time for the 1958 season. Their lineage can be traced back to 1883, the first year the team played in New York City. Some historians (and record books), however, consider the Giants to have existed in Troy, New York, through 1882 before the team was transferred to New York. I do not. The reason I don't connect the lineage from Troy to New York is that only part of the team went from Troy to New York. The Troy team's charter was revoked by the National League for a number of reasons, and, after the Troy team was auctioned off, the winning bidder (who already owned two teams, the new Gothams franchise in New York and the Metropolitans franchise of the American Association, also in New York) split the Troy players he wanted to keep between his two New York teams. Therefore, although the New York Gothams (later the Giants) replaced the Troy Trojans, they did not move from one city to another with essentially the same lineup, my condition for franchise continuity. The New York Gothams was a brand new franchise in 1883 that replaced the disbanded Troy Trojans.

A third example of franchise continuity would be cases like the Minnesota Twins and Washington Nationals of today. Both teams played in different cities (the Twins were in Washington as the Senators, and the Nationals were in Montreal as the Expos), but when they moved they changed their team names. Nonetheless, these types of transfers maintain the continuity of the franchise because the entire team transferred to a new city, *unbroken and essentially unchanged,* for the following season.

As a final example, consider the Milwaukee Brewers of today. They started out as the Seattle Pilots in 1969, then transferred to Milwaukee and became the Brewers in 1970. Still later (1998), they transferred from the American League to the National League, but did so without missing a season and while maintaining essentially the same roster. Thus, in this book, the Milwaukee Brewers records and statistics include time in both leagues and in both Seattle and Milwaukee. In the front of this book I have included, for your convenience, a chart that illustrates the lineage of all the current 30 major league franchises.

PRIMARY PITCHING STAFFS

In the "Primary Pitching Staff" section, the starting pitchers are not listed in any particular order of significance, such as innings pitched, starts, etc. They are listed merely for convenience's sake, mostly in an attempt to maintain the continuity of a pitcher's career with that franchise. The same applies to "The Bullpen" portion of this section. Also, not every pitcher who played with a particular franchise in a particular year is listed, only the primary pitchers, up to five starters and four relievers.

Occasionally you will notice that there are gaps in the primary pitching staffs, especially in the 19th and early 20th-century years, when franchises didn't *have* any more pitchers. It was common during this era for a team to have two or three workhorses who pitched 200-500 innings each, and only a couple more who pitched less than 15 innings each. As to the "closer" role, the pitcher listed is the one who had the most saves or, if applicable, the most games finished for the team in that year. Before the 1960s, baseball strategy was different in a number of ways than it is today, so in most cases teams didn't have designated closers, as they do today.

CAREER STATS

The career stats listed for a player in his bio or in the Top 10 listings represents the career stats earned *only* with the team in question, *not* his entire major league career if he played for more than one team.

QUALIFYING STATS

In the Top 10 listings, pitchers needed at least 500 innings to qualify for inclusion in the career records. I had to make several exceptions, however, for a few teams which haven't been around very long. For example, the Florida Marlins, who began play only in 1993, haven't been around long enough for their pitchers to compile substantial career statistics. Because Florida doesn't have 10 pitchers who've accumulated at least 500 innings with the team, I relaxed the qualifying innings total to 400. In the case of Tampa Bay, which began play in 1998, the requirement is only 300 innings. Similar allowances were made for Arizona and Colorado. Commensurate allowances were made for their hitters as well in the career hitting categories.

A SEASON IS A SEASON

Over the history of major league baseball, the regular season has varied anywhere from a high of 162 games (as it's been since 1962) to as few as 60 or so in the 1870s (the Cubs played only 59 games in 1877, for example). In between we've seen major league regular-season schedules of 84, 98, 112, 124, 132, 136, 140, 144, and 154 games. In addition, we've had numerous shortened seasons due to player strikes and wars. So rather than drive you crazy with asterisks, I have considered a season a season, regardless of how many games were played.

Besides, all this was settled years ago when Roger Maris broke Babe Ruth's single-season home-run record—but he did so over the course of a season that lasted 162 games, in contrast to the Babe, who did it in only 154 games. Initially, an (*) was placed after Maris's name in the record books, but eventually everyone got tired of making the distinction and the (*) was dropped. Major League Baseball officially declared, "A season is a season, and no distinction of the number of games played will be made."

PRE-1900 RECORDS

Some record books differentiate between pre- and post-1900 records, as if some earth-shattering change transformed the way baseball was played after 1900. Well, it didn't. Yes, there were times in the 19th century when significant rules changes were adopted, but essentially it's been the same game since 1871, when the first professional league, the National Association, began play. For example, it hasn't always been the case that four balls produces a walk and three strikes equals a strikeout. At different times, batters were given five balls, and seven balls, and nine balls before walking. For a time, batters couldn't be walked at all, but had to stay in the batter's box until they struck a fair ball. For a time, batters weren't awarded first base when hit by a pitch. For a time, a third foul ball constituted an out. For a time, balls that started in fair territory but bounded foul before reaching first or third base were considered fair balls, and all sorts of crazy batting styles developed until it was outlawed. For a time, infielders stood on their bags rather than playing in between them. For a time, the pitcher's mound (a slab, really) was only 50 feet away from home plate instead of the current 60' 6". For a time, pitchers were required to pitch underhanded.

There are literally scores and scores of additional rules/strategy/playing changes that have taken place over the years, rendering any attempt to differentiate eras of the game by year rather arbitrary. As an example, some record books rationalize the segregation of pre-1900 pitching records from post-1900 pitching records because, among other things, pitchers routinely pitched complete games. But, by that logic, why wouldn't we also segregate pitching stats from 1969 on, when saves increased dramatically because of the way major league managers altered their pitching strategy with larger bullpens? It's not uncommon today to see a reliever collect 40–50 saves in a season. In 1919, the year of the infamous Black Sox scandal, the National League leader in saves had four, and five led the American League.

The same logic could be applied to home runs. Before 1920 the major leagues were playing with what we now call a "dead ball"; post-1920 home-run totals skyrocketed because of the newer, tightly wound baseballs. Shouldn't we discriminate among various home-run records because of the type of ball used? Consider also the difference in playing fields. For decades, hitters in the majors profited from playing in many parks with short fences that have since been outlawed; some were closer than 300 feet away from home plate. Should we then adjust all extra-base and home-run records according to the parks in which each hit occurred? Should we adjust team batting records since the implementation of the designated hitter rule?

Even the best of the current sabermetrician and baseball performance analysts can't begin to account for all the variables. For the purposes of this book, a season is a season, a category is a category, and a record is a record. Period.

Hall of Fame Members—Players (and Managers)

You will notice that most teams have a number of players and managers listed in their Hall of Fame section. The players and managers listed did not necessarily (and in most cases did NOT) get named to the Hall of Fame based on their record with the listed team. The Hall of Fame Members list in this book is merely a list of all Hall of Famers who happened to play or manage for that team, however briefly. For example, in the Oakland A's chapter, you will notice that Tommy Lasorda is listed as playing 19 games with the franchise when it was in Kansas City in 1956. Obviously, Lasorda did not get elected to Cooperstown based on these 19 games. He got elected for his 20+ years as a manager of the Los Angeles Dodgers. I just felt it would be interesting to readers to see which Hall of Famers spent time with each team.

Number of Times League Champions

In the "Team Records—Miscellaneous" section of each chapter, you will notice this category. The number listed reflects all championships won, regardless of which league the team was in. For example, in the chapter on the St. Louis Cardinals, you will notice that they have won 20 league titles. Besides their 16 National League pennants, the Cardinals won four American Association pennants before they transferred to the National League in 1892.

YEARLY RECORD/FINISH/ ATTENDANCE

The number listed under the DIV/LG Finish represents the team's finish in its division since 1969, their finish in the league for all previous years.

TEAM STADIUM HISTORY

Many ballparks actually went by two or three different names at the same time, and this has led to considerable confusion in ascertaining the correct dates for the lifespan of some parks. For a recent example, when the Los Angeles Angels began play in 1961, they played for a year at Wrigley Field before moving to Dodger Stadium from 1962–1965. But when the Angels played their home games in Dodger Stadium, they referred to it as Chavez Ravine. So for the years 1962–1965, you can find references to the facility calling it either Dodger Stadium or Chavez Ravine. This type of situation was typical in the 19th century and early 20th century. In the early 1930s, for example, Cleveland's Municipal Stadium was also called Lakefront Stadium at the same time. Either name was correct. To further complicate matters, from the 1870s to the 1910s, wooden ballpark fires were common, and when the park was rebuilt or replaced, sometimes the name stayed the same, sometimes it was given a new name, and sometimes it was referred to by both names.

Because reference books don't always agree on some of the names, I cannot be certain that every name listed in this book is 100 percent accurate, but I believe I've come closer to the truth than previous accounts.

TEAM NAME HISTORY

As with stadium names, it is impossible to say with certainty what every team was called in every year of its existence. Often a team was known by two or three names at the same time. In 1902 Cleveland was officially called the Bluebirds, but some players and fans referred to the team as the Blues, both because there was a previous Cleveland Blues team and because Blues sounded manlier than Bluebirds. But some of the players balked at being called either the Blues or the Bluebirds and referred to themselves as the Broncos, a still more macho name. The confusion prompted a local newspaper in 1903 to run a "name our team" contest, the winner of which was the Naps, after new team captain Napoleon Lajoie. Go figure. To further add to the confusion, many of the baseball guides and newspapers of the day refer to the team as the Cleveland Americans, meaning the Cleveland franchise of the American League.

While not such a big deal in Cleveland, which had only one major league team at a time, the name game caused havoc in cities with two or three teams, like Philadelphia, New York, St. Louis, Boston, and Chicago. In 1914 and 1915, for example, Chicago had three major league teams, the White Sox, the Cubs, and the Whales (Federal League). To minimize confusion, the teams were often referred to with their league affiliations. Again, as with the stadium names, it's almost impossible to say that every team name listed in this book is correct for every year, because there is a lot of bad information out there, but I believe I've improved on my predecessors in this area.

ALL-TIME WIN-LOSS RECORDS

For National League teams, I didn't go back past 1900 for several reasons, primarily because of the large number of 19th-century teams that jumped from city to city with alarming frequency and the large number of teams that folded with great regularity, sometimes in midseason. From 1900 on, however, both major leagues witnessed great stability in terms of their franchises, with no franchise shifts at all from 1903 to 1953.

20-Game Winners

In this section I included pitchers who won 20 or more games with a particular franchise in a season. What you won't find, for example, is a case like Rick Sutcliffe in 1984. Although he went 20-6 on the season, he was 4-5 for Cleveland before being traded to the Cubs, where he went 16-1. Since he didn't win 20 or more for one franchise, he isn't listed with the Cubs as a 20-game winner, as he is in many other reference books.

Innings Pitched

Whenever you see a number reflecting innings pitched, it will either be a whole number, such as 243, or it will end in ".0", ".3" or ".7". The ".3" represents one-third of an inning, the ".7" represents two-thirds of an inning, and the ".0" represents a full inning.

Significant Players

My choices for each franchise's significant players were, of course, personal, based on who I thought had a significant impact on a particular franchise relative to all of the other players who played for it.

For example, Hank Aaron was a significant player for the Braves (and his bio accordingly is included in the Braves chapter), but he is not covered in the Milwaukee Brewers chapter even though he spent two years with the team at the end of his career—years during which he was truly just hanging on, averaging only 11 homers with a .230 batting average. Babe Ruth, on the other hand, was a significant player for both the Red Sox and Yankees, so his career with each team is covered in both chapters. Finally, I didn't consider as significant any player who had a brief "flash in the pan" career, such as Mark Fidrych of Detroit, no matter how much publicity they generated.

World Series MVP Awards

There are two major World Series MVP Awards: the Babe Ruth Award and the *Sport* Magazine Award. The Babe Ruth Award began in 1949, a year after Ruth's death, and is awarded annually by the New York chapter of the Baseball Writers' Association of America. The *Sport* Magazine Award began in 1955, awarded first by the magazine's editors, then later by a panel of various sports writers and officials (the magazine folded in 2000). The award is now sanctioned by Major League Baseball and is considered the more prestigious of the two. Hence, in this book, I list as World Series MVPs those players selected for the Babe Ruth Award from 1949 to 1954, and then those who won the *Sport* Magazine Award from 1955 on.

FRANCHISE TIMELINE

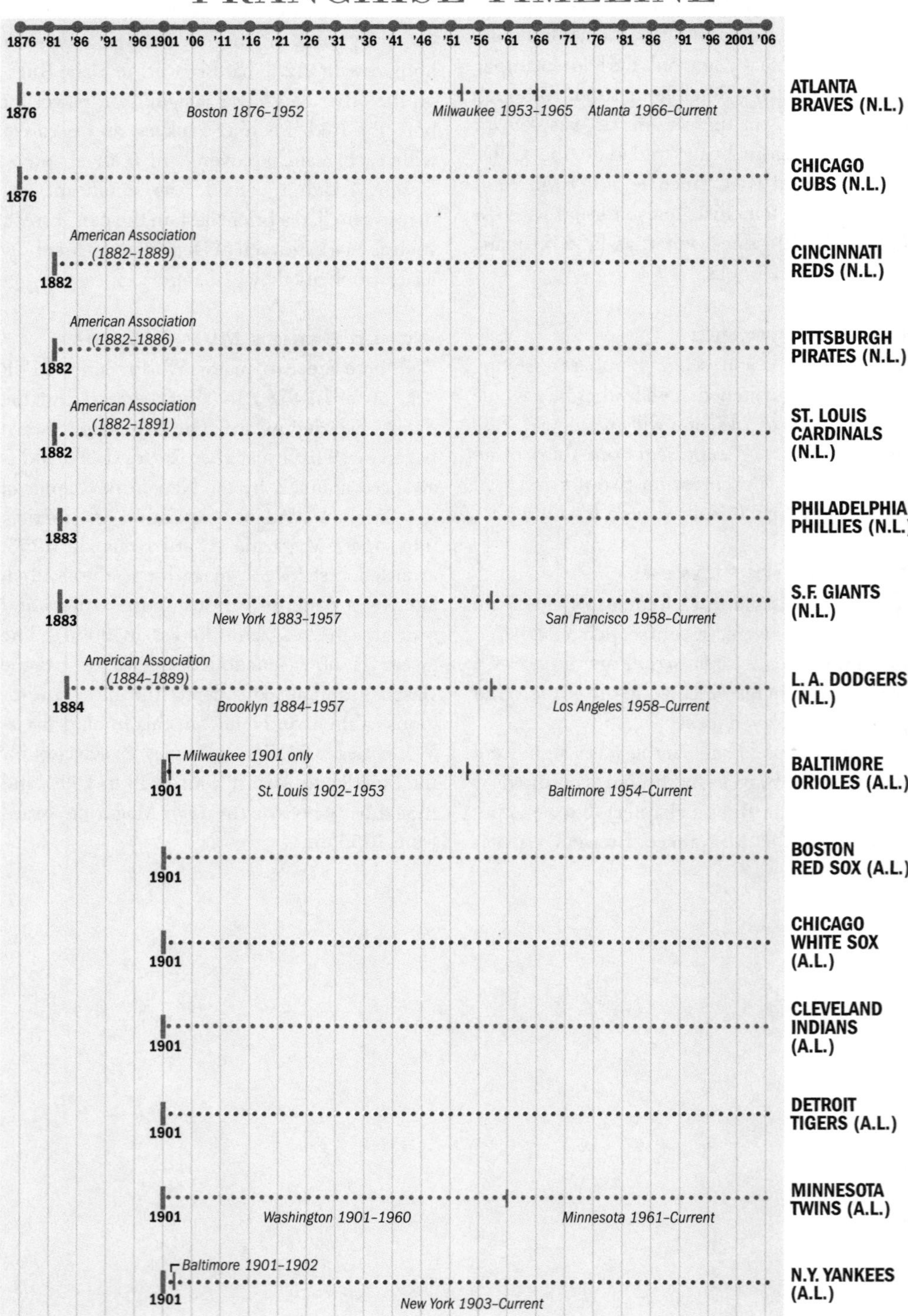

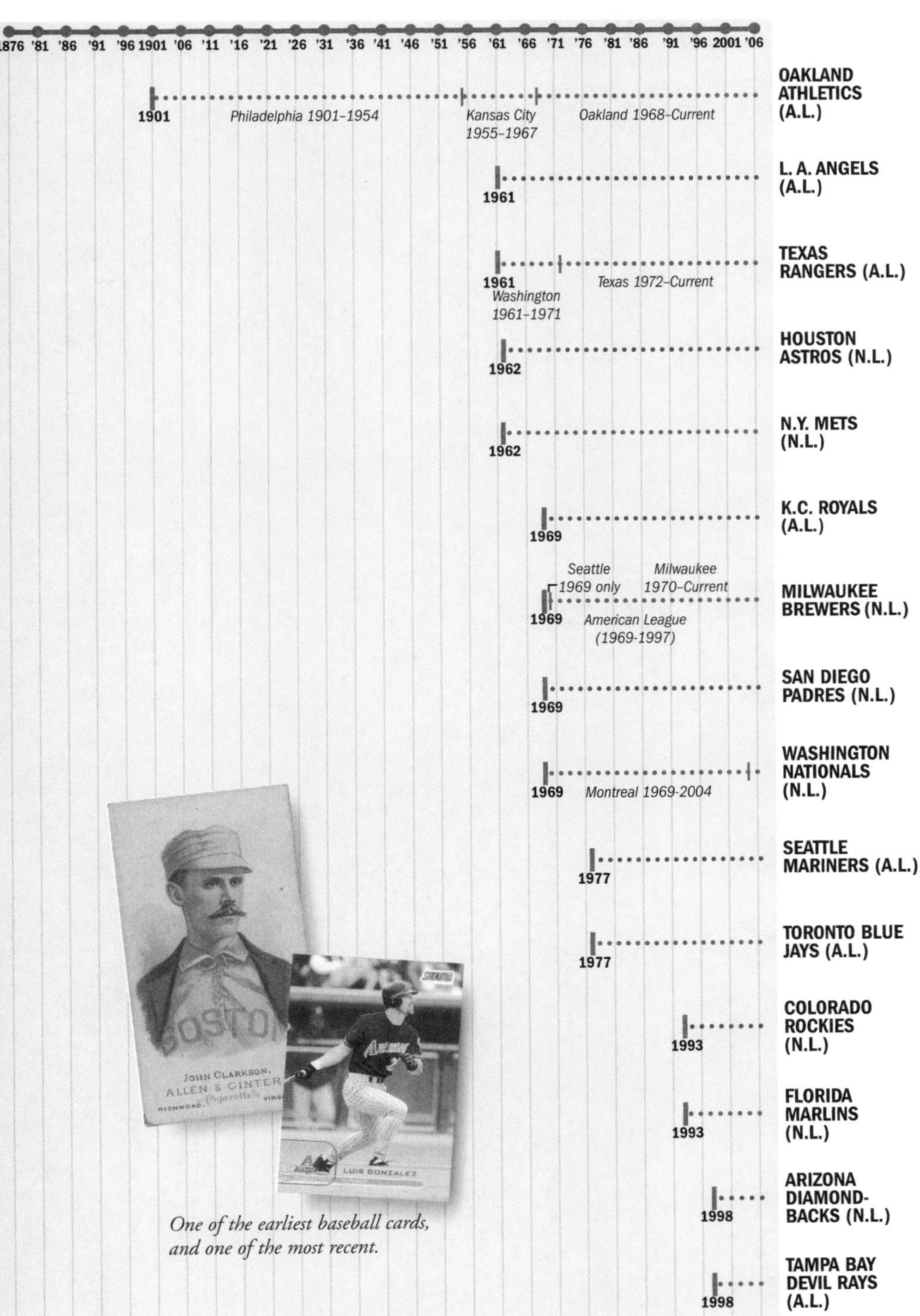

One of the earliest baseball cards, and one of the most recent.

Arizona Diamondbacks

Since 1998

1998 Team Ball

1999 In just their second season, the Diamondbacks win 100 games (35 more than in their first year) and the National League Western Division title. The 35-game turnaround represents the greatest improvement from one year to the next in the 20th century.... **2001** In Game 6 of the World Series, the Diamondbacks defeat the Yankees 15–2, the worst drubbing suffered by the Yankees in their 293 World Series games up to this point.... **2002** Only five 15-strikeout games are pitched in the majors this season—all by Diamondbacks. Randy Johnson has four and Curt Schilling has the other.

FRANCHISE HISTORY

The Arizona Diamondbacks came into being on March 9, 1995, when baseball's owners unanimously approved expansion into Phoenix and Tampa Bay. Both teams began play three years later in 1998. Jerry Colangelo, the owner of the NBA's Phoenix Suns, headed the ownership group that purchased the franchise for a whopping $130 million expansion fee. Other original investor/ owners included John Teets of Dial Corp. of America; Phil Knight of Nike; comedian Billy Crystal; Phoenix Newspapers, Inc.; Bank of America; Pulitzer Publishing Company; and NBA star Danny Manning. The team's first general manager was Joe Garagiola Jr., son of former major leaguer and longtime television announcer Joe Garagiola. The Diamondbacks shelled out more than $5 million to the Phoenix Firebirds of the Pacific Coast League as compensation for taking over their AAA territory.

In 1998, the team started off in typical new-franchise fashion, compiling a 65–97 record and finishing last in the NL West, 33 games behind the San Diego Padres. In 1999, however, the Diamondbacks performed like anything but an expansion team. After spending big money in the offseason on free agents, primarily pitching ace Randy Johnson, the Diamondbacks accomplished the best one-season turnaround in the 20th century and won 100 games and the division title. Although the Diamondbacks were quickly dispatched in the playoffs by the New York Mets, they rebounded in 2001 by winning it all. Led by slugger Luis Gonzalez, Johnson, and newly acquired free-agent ace Curt Schilling, Arizona climaxed its fourth season in the league by defeating the New York Yankees in one of the most exciting World Series in recent history. In 2002, the team won its third division title in four years, but after letting some of their top stars exit via free agency, the Diamondbacks slid back into the cellar by 2004. In early 2004, a group of minority owners bought out the managing partners of the Diamondbacks, including Jerry Colangelo, pledging to raise nearly $100 million to once again make the team competitive.

Of the 14 expansion teams to begin play since 1961, Arizona is the only one with a winning record: 652–644 (.503 winning percentage).

After many mediocre seasons elsewhere, Luis Gonzalez found his sweet spot in Arizona.

TEAM NAME HISTORY

Official Names

Diamondbacks (1998–current)

Unofficial Names/Nicknames

D'backs

STADIUM HISTORY

Bank One Ballpark ("the Bob"; 1998–2005)
Chase Field (beginning in 2006)
(Bank One Ballpark renamed)

YEARLY RECORD, FINISH, & ATTENDANCE FIGURES

Year	League	Record	DIV/LG Finish	Attendance	Avg/Gm
2005	NL West	77–85	2	2,059,424	25,425
2004	NL West	51–111	5	2,519,560	31,106
2003	NL West	84–78	3	2,805,542	34,636
2002	NL West	98–64	1	3,198,977	39,494
2001	NL West	92–70	1	2,736,451	33,783
2000	NL West	85–77	3	2,942,251	36,324
1999	NL West	100–62	1	3,019,654	37,280
1998	NL West	65–97	5	3,610,290	44,571

MANAGER HISTORY

Manager	Years	W–L	Win %
Buck Showalter	1998–2001	250–236	.514
Bob Brenly	2001–2004	303–262	.536
Al Pedrique	2004	22–61	.265
Bob Melvin	2005	66–96	.407

ALL-TIME WIN-LOSS RECORDS VS. ALL OPPONENTS

Opponent	W–L
ALL-TIME	652–644
Angels	7–5
Astros	30–25
Athletics	3–9
Blue Jays	3–3
Braves	23–36
Brewers	30–27
Cardinals	21–36
Cubs	38–26
Devil Rays	0–3
Dodgers	63–69
Giants	55–76
Indians	4–5
INTERLEAGUE	61–66
Mariners	5–7
Marlins	34–24
Mets	29–31
Nationals	25–32
Orioles	4–2
Padres	73–60
Phillies	33–27
Pirates	34–22
Rangers	6–10
Reds	30–28
Red Sox	3–0
Rockies	73–59
Royals	5–4
Tigers	11–7
Twins	4–5
White Sox	4–2
Yankees	2–4

The right-field pool at Bank One Ballpark

Franchise Highlights, Low Points, and Strange Distinctions

1998 Andy Benes's 14 wins were the most ever by a pitcher on a National League expansion team's inaugural season. Benes is tied for the major league record in this category with Tampa Bay's Rolando Arrojo, who duplicated the feat in the American League in the same year.

Outfielder Devon White became the first expansion team player to hit at least 20 homers and steal 20 bases in the same season.

....

1999 In 1999, just their second season, the Diamondbacks won 100 games and the National League Western Division title. This 35-game turnaround from the previous season represents the greatest improvement from one year to the next in the twentieth century. No other expansion team has ever made the playoffs so soon after its founding. Amazingly, four Arizona players scored 100 or more runs and four players had 100 or more RBIs. When Arizona won the World Series in 2001, in only their fourth year in existence, it was the fastest an expansion team had ever won the Fall Classic.

The Arizona record for most runs scored in a single game is 17 (performed four times). The team racked up this score against St. Louis in three consecutive years: 1999, 2000, and 2001.

....

2000 Starting pitcher Brian Anderson had 14 no-decisions in 2000, including 10 starts in which he allowed two or fewer runs.

2001 Randy Johnson's 372 strikeouts in 2001 rank as the third highest single-season total in major league history. In 2002, Johnson became the first pitcher ever to record 300-plus strikeouts in five consecutive seasons.

Arizona is the only team in history to win the World Series in November.

Bob Brenly became the first rookie manager in 40 years to win the World Series when the Diamondbacks won it all in 2001. The last one to do so was Ralph Houk in 1961.

Of the 14 expansion teams to begin play since 1961, Arizona is the only one with a winning record: 652–644 (.503 winning percentage).

....

2002 In 2002, the Diamondbacks won their third division title in only their fifth year of existence.

....

2004 On May 18, 2004, Randy Johnson became the oldest pitcher to hurl a perfect game when he defeated the Atlanta Braves 2–0, fanning 13 in the process. This was just the 17th nine-inning perfect game in major league history.

Later that season, on June 29, 2004, Randy Johnson became the fourth pitcher in history to amass 4,000 career strikeouts. In 2004, Arizona led the major leagues in 10-strikeout games with 13, and Randy Johnson accounted for all of them. Amazingly, Johnson had more 10-strikeout games than all the pitchers on 15 other teams combined.

Special Achievements

World Series Results

Year	Opponent	Result	Games
2001	NY Yankees	Won	4–3

World Series Managerial Records

Manager	Series Record	Games Record
Bob Brenly	1–0	4–3

All-Time Postseason Record

Divisional Playoffs	4–5
League Championship Series	4–1
World Series	4–3

All-Star Games at Bank One Ballpark

None

Hall of Famers Who Played Team

None

Hall of Famers Who Managed Team

None

MVP Award Winners

None

Cy Young Award Winners

Pitcher	Year	W–L	ERA
Randy Johnson	1999	17–9	2.48
Randy Johnson	2000	19–7	2.64
Randy Johnson	2001	21–6	2.49
Randy Johnson	2002	24–5	2.32

Rookie of the Year Award Winners

None

Gold Glove Winners

Year	Position	Player
1999	OF	Steve Finley
2000	OF	Steve Finley
2004	OF	Steve Finley

Triple Crown Winners

None

Fireman of the Year Award Winners

None

World Series MVP

Randy Johnson	2001
Curt Schilling	2001
(Cochampions)	

League Championship Series MVP

Craig Counsell	2001

All-Star Game MVP

None

Manager of the Year Award Winners

None

Batting Champions

None

Nine-Inning No-Hitters Pitched

Year	Pitcher	Opp.	Score
2004	Randy Johnson	ATL	2–0

20-Game Winners

Year	Pitcher	W–L
2001	Curt Schilling	22–6
	Randy Johnson	21–6
2002	Randy Johnson	24–5
	Curt Schilling	23–7

Retired Uniform Numbers

None

Team Records—Wins & Losses

- Games won in a season: 100 in 1999
- Games lost in a season: 111 in 2004
- Games won in a month: 22 in August 1998
- Games lost in a month: 23 in July 2004
- Consecutive games won: 12 in 2003
- Consecutive games lost: 14 in 2004
- Biggest shutout victory: 12–0 over San Diego on July 26, 2002
- Biggest shutout loss: 12–0 to San Diego on Sept. 3, 2003

- Highest winning percentage: .617 in 1999 (100–62)
- Lowest winning percentage: .315 in 2004 (51–111)

TEAM RECORDS—BATTING

- Highest team batting average: .277 in 1999
- Lowest team batting average: .246 in 1998
- Highest team slugging average: .459 in 1999
- Highest team on-base percentage: . 347 in 1999
- Total hits: 1,566 in 1999
- Extra-base hits: 551 in 1999
- Hits in a single game: 21 vs. Dodgers on April 13, 1999 (16 innings)
- Longest individual hitting streak: 30, Luis Gonzalez, 1999
- Most .300 hitters in a single season: 2 in 1999 and 2005
- Home runs: 216 in 1999
- Home runs in a month: 13, Luis Gonzalez, April 2001
- Home runs in a game: 5 (accomplished many times)
- Home runs by a rookie: 22, Travis Lee, 1998
- Home runs by a right-hander: 38, Jay Bell, 1999
- Home runs by a left-hander: 57, Luis Gonzalez, 2001
- Home runs by a switch-hitter: 30, Tony Clark, 2005
- Grand slams: 9 in 2001
- Grand slams (individual; single season): 2 (accomplished by four different players)
- Grand slams (individual; career): 7, Matt Williams
- Triples: 47 in 2003
- Doubles: 303 in 2003
- Singles: 1,015 in 1999
- Walks: 643 in 2002
- Runs scored: 908 in 1999
- Runs scored in a game: 17 (accomplished four times)
- Runs scored in an inning: 8 (accomplished four times)
- Most batters hit by a pitch: 64 in 1998
- Times shut out: 16 in 1998
- Grounded into double plays: 137 in 2004
- Fewest grounded into double plays: 94 in 1999
- Runners left on base: 1,247 in 2005

TEAM RECORDS—BASERUNNING

- Stolen bases: 137 in 1999
- Caught stealing: 46 in 2002

TEAM RECORDS—PITCHING

- Lowest earned run average: 3.77 in 1999
- Complete games: 16 in 1999 and 2000
- Saves: 45 in 2005
- Strikeouts: 1,303 in 2002
- Shutouts: 13 in 2001
- Walks: 668 in 2004
- Hit batsmen: 75 in 2004
- Wild pitches: 71 in 2004
- Consecutive wins (individual): 9, Curt Schilling, 2002
- Consecutive losses (individual): 9, Edgar Gonzalez, 2004
- Strikeouts in a game (individual): 20, Randy Johnson, May 8, 2001
- Most runs allowed in a game: 20 vs. Colorado, September 28, 2002

TEAM RECORDS—FIELDING

- Fielding average: .986 in 2001
- Most errors committed: 139 in 2004
- Fewest errors committed: 84 in 2001
- Most double plays turned: 159 in 2005
- Fewest double plays turned: 116 in 2002

TEAM RECORDS—MISCELLANEOUS

- Number of times league champions: 1
- Number of times finishing last in league: 1
- Largest attendance, single game: 48,389 vs. Seattle, June 27, 1998
- Team has never played a doubleheader at home
- Players used in a season: 52 in 2004
- Seasons played: 7, Luis Gonzalez

PRIMARY PITCHING STAFFS

Year	Starter	Starter	Starter	Starter	Starter	Closer	Bullpen	Bullpen	Bullpen
2005	Vazquez	Webb	Halsey	Ortiz	Estes	Valverde	Cormier	Bruney	Koplove
2004	Johnson	Webb	Fossum	Sparks	Daigle	Aquino	Koplove	Choate	Randolph
2003	Johnson	Schilling	Dessens	Batista	Webb	Mantei	Villarreal	Myers	Valverde
2002	Johnson	Schilling	Anderson	Batista	Helling	Kim	Koplove	Myers	Swindell
2001	Johnson	Schilling	Anderson	Batista	Ellis	Kim	Brohawn	Prinz	Swindell
2000	Johnson	Reynoso	Anderson	Stottlemyre	Daal	Mantei	Plesac	Kim	Swindell
1999	Johnson	Reynoso	Anderson	Benes	Daal	Mantei	Olson	Holmes	Swindell
1998	Blair	Telemaco	Anderson	Benes	Daal	Olson	Sodowsky	Rodriguez	Embree

PRIMARY STARTING LINEUPS

Year	C	1B	2B	3B	SS	LF	CF	RF
2005	Snyder	Clark	Counsell	Glaus	Clayton	Gonzalez	Terrero	Green
2004	Brito	Hillenbrand	Hairston	Tracy	Cintron	Gonzalez	Finley	Bautista
2003	Barajas	Overbay	Spivey	Counsell	Cintron	Gonzalez	Finley	Bautista
2002	Miller	Grace	Spivey	Counsell	Womack	Gonzalez	Finley	McCracken
2001	Miller	Grace	Bell	Williams	Womack	Gonzalez	Finley	Sanders
2000	Miller	Colbrunn	Bell	Williams	Womack	Gonzalez	Finley	Bautista
1999	Miller	Lee	Bell	Williams	Fox	Gonzalez	Finley	Womack
1998	Stinnett	Lee	Stankiewicz	Williams	Bell	Dellucci	White	Garcia

Top 10 Batting Leaders, Single Season & Career with Team

GAMES PLAYED: CAREER WITH TEAM

Player	G	PA
1. Luis Gonzalez	1,041	4,578
2. Steve Finley	849	3,449
3. Tony Womack	629	2,744
4. Jay Bell	616	2,547
5. Matt Williams	595	2,462
6. Craig Counsell	559	2,219
7. David Dellucci	503	1,322
8. Damian Miller	467	1,632
9. Danny Bautista	456	1,595
10. Alex Cintron	439	1,545

AT-BATS: SEASON

Player	AB	Year
1. Matt Williams	627	1999
2. Luis Gonzalez	618	2000
3. Tony Womack	617	2000
4. Luis Gonzalez	614	1999
Tony Womack	614	1999
6. Luis Gonzalez	609	2001
7. Steve Finley	590	1999
Tony Womack	590	2002
9. Jay Bell	589	1999
10. Shawn Green	581	2005

AT-BATS: CAREER WITH TEAM

Player	AB	PA
1. Luis Gonzalez	3,902	4,578
2. Steve Finley	3,049	3,449
3. Tony Womack	2,521	2,744
4. Matt Williams	2,265	2,462
5. Jay Bell	2,180	2,547
6. Craig Counsell	1,927	2,219
7. Damian Miller	1,465	1,632
8. Danny Bautista	1,461	1,595
9. Alex Cintron	1,425	1,545
10. David Dellucci	1,186	1,322

BATTING AVERAGE: SEASON

Player	BA	Year
1. Luis Gonzalez	.336	1999
2. Luis Gonzalez	.325	2001
3. Alex Cintron	.317	2003
4. Greg Colbrunn	.313	2000
5. Luis Gonzalez	.311	2000
6. Shea Hillenbrand	.310	2004
7. Quinton McCracken	.309	2002
8. Chad Tracy	.308	2005
9. Luis Gonzalez	.304	2003
Tony Clark	.304	2005

BATTING AVERAGE: CAREER WITH TEAM

Player	BA	PA
1. Luis Gonzalez	.302	4,578
2. Danny Bautista	.296	1,595
3. Alex Cintron	.279	1,545
Junior Spivey	.279	1,229
5. Steve Finley	.278	3,449
Matt Williams	.278	2,462
7. David Dellucci	.272	1,322
8. Tony Womack	.269	2,744
Damian Miller	.269	1,632
10. Craig Counsell	.268	2,219

TOTAL HITS: SEASON

Player	H	Year
1. Luis Gonzalez	206	1999
2. Luis Gonzalez	198	2001
3. Luis Gonzalez	192	2000
4. Matt Williams	190	1999
5. Luis Gonzalez	176	2003
6. Shea Hillenbrand	174	2004

7. Jay Bell	170	1999
Tony Womack	170	1999
9. Tony Womack	167	2000
10. Shawn Green	166	2005

TOTAL HITS: CAREER WITH TEAM

Player	H	PA
1. Luis Gonzalez	1,178	4,578
2. Steve Finley	847	3,449
3. Tony Womack	677	2,744
4. Matt Williams	629	2,462
5. Jay Bell	573	2,547
6. Craig Counsell	516	2,219
7. Danny Bautista	432	1,595
8. Alex Cintron	398	1,545
9. Damian Miller	394	1,632
10. David Dellucci	322	1,322

HOME RUNS: SEASON

Player	HR	Year
1. Luis Gonzalez	57	2001
2. Jay Bell	38	1999
3. Troy Glaus	37	2005
4. Steve Finley	35	2000
Matt Williams	35	1999
6. Steve Finley	34	1999
7. Reggie Sanders	33	2001
8. Luis Gonzalez	31	2000
9. Tony Clark	30	2005
10. Luis Gonzalez	28	2002

HOME RUNS: CAREER WITH TEAM

Player	HR	PA
1. Luis Gonzalez	209	4,578
2. Steve Finley	153	3,449
3. Matt Williams	99	2,462
4. Jay Bell	91	2,547
5. Damian Miller	48	1,632
6. Erubiel Durazo	47	901
7. Travis Lee	39	1,316
Kelly Stinnett	39	1,043
9. Troy Glaus	37	634
10. Chad Tracy	35	1,085

TRIPLES: SEASON

Player	3B	Year
1. Tony Womack	14	2000
2. David Dellucci	12	1998
3. Steve Finley	10	1999
Steve Finley	10	2003
Tony Womack	10	1999
6. Karim Garcia	8	1998
Quinton McCracken	8	2002
8. Danny Bautista	7	2000
Alex Cintron	7	2004
Luis Gonzalez	7	2001

TRIPLES: CAREER WITH TEAM

Player	3B	PA
1. Tony Womack	37	2,744
2. Steve Finley	34	3,449
3. Luis Gonzalez	25	4,578
4. David Dellucci	20	1,322
5. Jay Bell	18	2,547
6. Alex Cintron	16	1,545
7. Danny Bautista	15	1,595
8. Quinton McCracken	14	1,044
9. Craig Counsell	12	2,219
10. Junior Spivey	11	1,229

DOUBLES: SEASON

Player	2B	Year
1. Luis Gonzalez	47	2000
2. Luis Gonzalez	46	2003
3. Luis Gonzalez	45	1999
4. Luis Gonzalez	37	2005
Matt Williams	37	1999
Shawn Green	37	2005
7. Luis Gonzalez	36	2001
Shea Hillenbrand	36	2004
9. Junior Spivey	34	2002
Craig Counsell	34	2005
Chad Tracy	34	2005

DOUBLES: CAREER WITH TEAM

Player	2B	PA
1. Luis Gonzalez	258	4,578
2. Steve Finley	150	3,449
3. Matt Williams	127	2,462
4. Jay Bell	116	2,547
5. Damian Miller	98	1,632
Tony Womack	98	2,744
7. Craig Counsell	92	2,219
8. Alex Cintron	82	1,545
9. Danny Bautista	75	1,595
10. Chad Tracy	63	1,085

EXTRA-BASE HITS: SEASON

Player	XBH	Year
1. Luis Gonzalez	100	2001
2. Luis Gonzalez	80	2000
3. Jay Bell	76	1999
Steve Finley	76	1999
Luis Gonzalez	76	2003
6. Luis Gonzalez	75	1999
7. Matt Williams	74	1999
8. Steve Finley	67	2000
Troy Glaus	67	2005
10. Chad Tracy	65	2005

EXTRA-BASE HITS: CAREER WITH TEAM

Player	XBH	PA
1. Luis Gonzalez	492	4,578
2. Steve Finley	337	3,449
3. Matt Williams	233	2,462
4. Jay Bell	225	2,547
5. Tony Womack	156	2,744
6. Damian Miller	148	1,632
7. Craig Counsell	124	2,219
8. Danny Bautista	123	1,595
Alex Cintron	123	1,545
10. Junior Spivey	107	1,229

TOTAL BASES: SEASON

Player	TB	Year
1. Luis Gonzalez	419	2001
2. Luis Gonzalez	337	1999
3. Luis Gonzalez	336	2000
Matt Williams	336	1999
5. Jay Bell	328	1999
6. Steve Finley	310	1999
7. Luis Gonzalez	308	2003
8. Steve Finley	293	2000
9. Troy Glaus	281	2005
10. Chad Tracy	278	2005

TOTAL BASES: CAREER WITH TEAM

Player	TB	PA
1. Luis Gonzalez	2,113	4,578
2. Steve Finley	1,524	3,449
3. Matt Williams	1,067	2,462
4. Jay Bell	998	2,547
5. Tony Womack	912	2,744
6. Craig Counsell	692	2,219
7. Damian Miller	640	1,632
8. Danny Bautista	636	1,595
9. Alex Cintron	587	1,545
10. David Dellucci	498	1,322

RUNS BATTED IN: SEASON

Player	RBI	Year
1. Luis Gonzalez	142	2001
Matt Williams	142	1999

3. Luis Gonzalez	114	2000
4. Jay Bell	112	1999
5. Luis Gonzalez	111	1999
6. Luis Gonzalez	104	2003
7. Steve Finley	103	1999
Luis Gonzalez	103	2002
9. Troy Glaus	97	2005
10. Steve Finley	96	2000

RUNS BATTED IN: CAREER WITH TEAM

Player	RBI	PA
1. Luis Gonzalez	701	4,578
2. Steve Finley	479	3,449
3. Matt Williams	381	2,462
4. Jay Bell	304	2,547
5. Tony Womack	200	2,744
6. Danny Bautista	197	1,595
7. Damian Miller	194	1,632
8. Craig Counsell	163	2,219
9. Travis Lee	162	1,316
10. David Dellucci	156	1,322

RUNS SCORED: SEASON

Player	R	Year
1. Jay Bell	132	1999
2. Luis Gonzalez	128	2001
3. Luis Gonzalez	112	1999
4. Tony Womack	111	1999
5. Luis Gonzalez	106	2000
6. Junior Spivey	103	2002
7. Steve Finley	100	1999
Steve Finley	100	2000
9. Matt Williams	98	1999
10. Tony Womack	95	2000

RUNS SCORED: CAREER WITH TEAM

Player	R	PA
1. Luis Gonzalez	687	4,578
2. Steve Finley	491	3,449
3. Tony Womack	392	2,744
4. Jay Bell	360	2,547
5. Matt Williams	317	2,462
6. Craig Counsell	287	2,219
7. Junior Spivey	188	1,229
8. Danny Bautista	186	1,595
9. Damian Miller	180	1,632
10. Alex Cintron	173	1,545

WALKS: SEASON

Player	BB	Year
1. Luis Gonzalez	100	2001
2. Luis Gonzalez	97	2002
3. Luis Gonzalez	94	2003
4. Troy Glaus	84	2005
5. Jay Bell	82	1999
6. Jay Bell	81	1998
7. Luis Gonzalez	78	2000
Luis Gonzalez	78	2005
Craig Counsell	78	2005
10. Jay Bell	70	2000

WALKS: CAREER WITH TEAM

Player	BB	PA
1. Luis Gonzalez	581	4,578
2. Steve Finley	337	3,449
3. Jay Bell	303	2,547
4. Craig Counsell	245	2,219
5. Matt Williams	163	2,462
6. Tony Womack	159	2,744
7. Travis Lee	150	1,316
8. Damian Miller	139	1,632
9. Erubiel Durazo	137	901
10. Mark Grace	129	1,056

STRIKEOUTS: SEASON

Player	SO	Year
1. Troy Glaus	145	2005
2. Jay Bell	132	1999
3. Jay Bell	129	1998
4. Reggie Sanders	126	2001
5. Travis Lee	123	1998
6. Royce Clayton	105	2005
7. David Dellucci	103	1998
8. Devon White	102	1998
Matt Williams	102	1998
10. Junior Spivey	100	2002

STRIKEOUTS: CAREER WITH TEAM

Player	SO	PA
1. Luis Gonzalez	522	4,578
2. Steve Finley	467	3,449
3. Jay Bell	437	2,547
4. Matt Williams	383	2,462
5. Damian Miller	363	1,632
6. Tony Womack	303	2,744
7. David Dellucci	288	1,322
8. Craig Counsell	247	2,219
9. Kelly Stinnett	245	1,043
10. Junior Spivey	242	1,229

SLUGGING PERCENTAGE: SEASON

Player	SLG	Year
1. Luis Gonzalez	.688	2001
2. Tony Clark	.636	2005
3. Jay Bell	.557	1999
4. Chad Tracy	.553	2005
5. Luis Gonzalez	.549	1999
Reggie Sanders	.549	2001
7. Luis Gonzalez	.544	2000
Steve Finley	.544	2000
9. Matt Williams	.536	1999
10. Luis Gonzalez	.532	2003

SLUGGING PERCENTAGE: CAREER WITH TEAM

Player	SLG	PA
1. Luis Gonzalez	.542	4,578
2. Steve Finley	.500	3,449
3. Matt Williams	.471	2,462
4. Jay Bell	.458	2,547
5. Junior Spivey	.453	1,229
6. Damian Miller	.437	1,632
7. Danny Bautista	.435	1,595
8. David Dellucci	.420	1,322
9. Alex Cintron	.412	1,545
10. Travis Lee	.401	1,316

ON-BASE PERCENTAGE: SEASON

Player	OBP	Year
1. Luis Gonzalez	.429	2001
2. Greg Colbrunn	.405	2000
3. Luis Gonzalez	.403	1999
4. Luis Gonzalez	.402	2003
5. Luis Gonzalez	.400	2002
6. Carlos Baerga	.396	2003
7. Luis Gonzalez	.392	2000
8. Junior Spivey	.389	2002
9. Mark Grace	.386	2001
10. Jay Bell	.374	1999

ON-BASE PERCENTAGE: CAREER WITH TEAM

Player	OBP	PA
1. Luis Gonzalez	.396	4,578
2. Junior Spivey	.363	1,229
3. Jay Bell	.355	2,547
4. Craig Counsell	.352	2,219
5. Steve Finley	.351	3,449
6. Danny Bautista	.344	1,595
7. David Dellucci	.341	1,322
8. Damian Miller	.336	1,632
Travis Lee	.336	1,316
10. Matt Williams	.327	2,462

OPS (On-Base Percentage + Slugging Percentage): Season

Player	OPS	Year
1. Luis Gonzalez	1.117	2001
2. Tony Clark	1.003	2005
3. Luis Gonzalez	.952	1999
4. Luis Gonzalez	.935	2000
5. Luis Gonzalez	.934	2003
6. Jay Bell	.931	1999
7. Greg Colbrunn	.928	2000
8. Chad Tracy	.911	2005
9. Steve Finley	.904	2000
10. Luis Gonzalez	.896	2002

OPS (On-Base Percentage + Slugging Percentage): Career with Team

Player	OPS	PA
1. Luis Gonzalez	.938	4,578
2. Steve Finley	.851	3,449
3. Junior Spivey	.816	1,229
4. Jay Bell	.812	2,547
5. Matt Williams	.798	2,462
6. Danny Bautista	.779	1,595
7. Damian Miller	.773	1,632
8. David Dellucci	.761	1,322
9. Travis Lee	.737	1,316
10. Alex Cintron	.732	1,545

Stolen Bases: Season

Player	SB	Year
1. Tony Womack	72	1999
2. Tony Womack	45	2000
3. Tony Womack	29	2002
4. Tony Womack	28	2001
5. Craig Counsell	26	2005
6. Devon White	22	1998
7. Travis Lee	17	1999
8. Steve Finley	16	2002
9. Steve Finley	15	2003
10. Andy Fox	14	1998
Reggie Sanders	14	2001

Stolen Bases: Career with Team

Player	SB	PA
1. Tony Womack	182	2,744
2. Steve Finley	70	3,449
3. Craig Counsell	53	2,219
4. Luis Gonzalez	32	4,578
5. Travis Lee	30	1,316
6. Devon White	22	627
7. Danny Bautista	21	1,595
8. Andy Fox	20	974
9. David Dellucci	18	1,322
Junior Spivey	18	1,229

Sacrifice Hits: Season

Player	Sac	Year
1. Curt Schilling	14	2001
2. Quinton McCracken	13	2002
Brandon Webb	13	2005
4. Alex Cintron	12	2004
5. Andy Benes	10	1998
Andy Benes	10	1999
Elmer Dessens	10	2003
Royce Clayton	10	2005
9. Brian Anderson	9	2000
Tony Womack	9	1999

Sacrifice Hits: Career with Team

Player	Sac	PA
1. Curt Schilling	33	293
2. Randy Johnson	30	511
3. Quinton McCracken	26	1,044
4. Tony Womack	25	2,744
5. Brandon Webb	24	206
6. Jay Bell	23	2,547
7. Alex Cintron	22	1,545
8. Brian Anderson	21	284
9. Andy Benes	20	155
10. Armando Reynoso	18	128

Hit by Pitch: Season

Player	HBP	Year
1. Andy Fox	18	1998
2. Junior Spivey	16	2002
3. Luis Gonzalez	14	2001
4. Luis Gonzalez	12	2000
Shea Hillenbrand	12	2004
6. Luis Gonzalez	11	2005
7. Greg Colbrunn	10	2000
8. Andy Fox	9	1999
Devon White	9	1998
10. Steve Finley	8	2000
Craig Counsell	8	2005
Chad Tracy	8	2005

Hit by Pitch: Career with Team

Player	HBP	PA
1. Luis Gonzalez	54	4,578
2. Andy Fox	27	974
3. Junior Spivey	25	1,229
4. Steve Finley	22	3,449
5. Jay Bell	19	2,547
Tony Womack	19	2,744
7. Greg Colbrunn	18	861
Kelly Stinnett	18	1,043
9. Craig Counsell	15	2,219
10. Shea Hillenbrand	14	958

Top 10 Pitching Leaders, Single Season & Career with Team

Games Pitched: Season

Player	GP	Year
1. Oscar Villarreal	86	2003
2. Byung-Hyun Kim	78	2001
3. Mike Koplove	76	2004
4. Randy Choate	74	2004
5. Byung-Hyun Kim	72	2002
6. Mike Myers	69	2002
7. Lance Cormier	67	2005
8. Mike Myers	64	2003
Gregg Olson	64	1998
Greg Swindell	64	2000
Greg Swindell	64	2001

Games Pitched: Career with Team

Player	GP	IP
1. Byung-Hyun Kim	243	323.0
2. Greg Swindell	225	227.3
3. Mike Koplove	215	245.7
4. Randy Johnson	193	1389.7

5. Matt Mantei	178	173.7
6. Brian Anderson	160	840.7
7. Jose Valverde	144	146.3
8. Mike Myers	133	73.3
9. Gregg Olson	125	129.3
10. Miguel Batista	120	517.3
Mike Morgan	120	173.7

INNINGS PITCHED: SEASON

Player	IP	Year
1. Randy Johnson	271.7	1999
2. Randy Johnson	260.0	2002
3. Curt Schilling	259.3	2002
4. Curt Schilling	256.7	2001
5. Randy Johnson	249.7	2001
6. Randy Johnson	248.7	2000
7. Randy Johnson	245.7	2004
8. Andy Benes	231.3	1998
9. Brandon Webb	229.0	2005
10. Javier Vazquez	215.7	2005

INNINGS PITCHED: CAREER WITH TEAM

Player	IP
1. Randy Johnson	1,389.7
2. Brian Anderson	840.7
3. Curt Schilling	781.7
4. Brandon Webb	617.7
5. Miguel Batista	517.3
6. Omar Daal	473.3
7. Andy Benes	429.7
8. Armando Reynoso	386.0
9. Byung-Hyun Kim	323.0
10. Elmer Dessens	261.0

BATTERS FACED: SEASON

Player	BF	Year
1. Randy Johnson	1,079	1999
2. Randy Johnson	1,035	2002
3. Curt Schilling	1,021	2001
4. Curt Schilling	1,017	2002
5. Randy Johnson	1,001	2000
6. Randy Johnson	994	2001
7. Andy Benes	979	1998
8. Randy Johnson	964	2004
9. Brandon Webb	943	2005
10. Brandon Webb	933	2004

BATTERS FACED: CAREER WITH TEAM

Player	BF	IP
1. Randy Johnson	5,562	1,389.7
2. Brian Anderson	3,500	840.7
3. Curt Schilling	3,099	781.7
4. Brandon Webb	2,626	617.7
5. Miguel Batista	2,193	517.3
6. Omar Daal	2,019	473.3
7. Andy Benes	1,865	429.7
8. Armando Reynoso	1,676	386.0
9. Byung-Hyun Kim	1,357	323.0
10. Elmer Dessens	1,167	261.0

GAMES STARTED: SEASON

Player	GS	Year
1. Randy Johnson	35	1999
Randy Johnson	35	2000
Randy Johnson	35	2002
Randy Johnson	35	2004
Curt Schilling	35	2001
Curt Schilling	35	2002
Brandon Webb	35	2004
8. Andy Benes	34	1998
Randy Johnson	34	2001
10. Javier Vazquez	33	2005
Brandon Webb	33	2005

GAMES STARTED: CAREER WITH TEAM

Player	GS	IP
1. Randy Johnson	192	1,389.7
2. Brian Anderson	129	840.7
3. Curt Schilling	107	781.7
4. Brandon Webb	96	617.7
5. Miguel Batista	76	517.3
6. Omar Daal	71	473.3
7. Andy Benes	66	429.7
Armando Reynoso	66	386.0
9. Elmer Dessens	39	261.0
Todd Stottlemyre	39	217.0

COMPLETE GAMES: SEASON

Player	CG	Year
1. Randy Johnson	12	1999
2. Randy Johnson	8	2000
Randy Johnson	8	2002
4. Curt Schilling	6	2001
5. Curt Schilling	5	2002
6. Randy Johnson	4	2004
Curt Schilling	4	2000
8. Omar Daal	3	1998
Randy Johnson	3	2001
Curt Schilling	3	2003
Javier Vazquez	3	2005

COMPLETE GAMES: CAREER WITH TEAM

Player	CG	IP
1. Randy Johnson	36	1,389.7
2. Curt Schilling	18	781.7
3. Brian Anderson	7	840.7
4. Omar Daal	5	473.3
5. Miguel Batista	3	517.3
Javier Vazquez	3	215.7
Brandon Webb	3	617.7
8. Albie Lopez	2	81.0
Armando Reynoso	2	386.0
Shawn Estes	2	123.7

GAMES WON: SEASON

Player	W	Year
1. Randy Johnson	24	2002
2. Curt Schilling	23	2002
3. Curt Schilling	22	2001
4. Randy Johnson	21	2001
5. Randy Johnson	19	2000
6. Randy Johnson	17	1999
7. Omar Daal	16	1999
Randy Johnson	16	2004
9. Andy Benes	14	1998
Brandon Webb	14	2005

GAMES WON: CAREER WITH TEAM

Player	W	IP
1. Randy Johnson	103	1,389.7
2. Curt Schilling	58	781.7
3. Brian Anderson	41	840.7
4. Brandon Webb	31	617.7
5. Miguel Batista	29	517.3
6. Andy Benes	27	429.7
7. Omar Daal	26	473.3
8. Armando Reynoso	22	386.0
9. Byung-Hyun Kim	21	323.0
10. Todd Stottlemyre	15	217.0
Mike Koplove	15	245.7

GAMES LOST: SEASON

Player	L	Year
1. Brandon Webb	16	2004
2. Willie Blair	15	1998

Casey Fossum	15	2004
Javier Vazquez	15	2005
5. Randy Johnson	14	2004
6. Brian Anderson	13	1998
Andy Benes	13	1998
8. Andy Benes	12	1999
Omar Daal	12	1998
Rick Helling	12	2002
Armando Reynoso	12	2000
Brad Halsey	12	2005
Brandon Webb	12	2005

Games Lost: Career with Team

Player	L	IP
1. Randy Johnson	49	1,389.7
2. Brian Anderson	42	840.7
3. Brandon Webb	37	617.7
4. Omar Daal	31	473.3
5. Curt Schilling	28	781.7
6. Miguel Batista	26	517.3
7. Andy Benes	25	429.7
8. Armando Reynoso	24	386.0
9. Byung-Hyun Kim	22	323.0
10. Willie Blair	15	146.7
Casey Fossum	15	142.0
Javier Vazquez	15	215.7

Winning Percentage: Season

Player	W%	Year
1. Randy Johnson	.828	2002
2. Curt Schilling	.786	2001
3. Randy Johnson	.778	2001
4. Curt Schilling	.767	2002
5. Randy Johnson	.731	2000
6. Randy Johnson	.654	1999
7. Omar Daal	.640	1999
8. Armando Reynoso	.625	1999
9. Brian Anderson	.611	2000
10. Oscar Villarreal	.588	2003

Winning Percentage: Career with Team

Player	W%	IP
1. Mike Koplove	.682	196.0
2. Randy Johnson	.678	1,389.7
3. Curt Schilling	.674	781.7
4. Todd Stottlemyre	.577	217.0
5. Miguel Batista	.527	517.3
6. Andy Benes	.519	429.7
7. Brian Anderson	.494	840.7
8. Byung-Hyun Kim	.488	323.0
9. Armando Reynoso	.478	386.0
10. Omar Daal	.456	473.3
Brandon Webb	.456	617.7

Shutouts: Season

Player	SHO	Year
1. Randy Johnson	4	2002
2. Randy Johnson	3	2000
3. Randy Johnson	2	1999
Randy Johnson	2	2001
Randy Johnson	2	2004
Albie Lopez	2	2001
Curt Schilling	2	2003
8. 11 tied with . . .	1	—

Shutouts: Career with Team

Player	SHO	IP
1. Randy Johnson	14	1,389.7
2. Curt Schilling	5	781.7
3. Brian Anderson	2	840.7
Omar Daal	2	473.3
Albie Lopez	2	81.0
6. Miguel Batista	1	517.3
Brandon Webb	1	388.7
Javier Vazquez	1	215.7

ERA: Season

Player	ERA	Year
1. Randy Johnson	2.32	2002
2. Randy Johnson	2.48	1999
3. Randy Johnson	2.49	2001
4. Randy Johnson	2.60	2004
5. Randy Johnson	2.64	2000
6. Brandon Webb	2.84	2003
7. Omar Daal	2.88	1998
8. Curt Schilling	2.95	2003
9. Curt Schilling	2.98	2001
10. Curt Schilling	3.23	2002

ERA: Career with Team

Player	ERA	IP
1. Randy Johnson	2.65	1,389.7
2. Curt Schilling	3.14	781.7
3. Byung-Hyun Kim	3.26	323.0
4. Brandon Webb	3.35	617.7
5. Miguel Batista	3.76	517.3
Greg Swindell	3.76	227.3
7. Mike Koplove	3.77	245.7
8. Omar Daal	4.11	473.3
9. Andy Benes	4.36	429.7
10. Brian Anderson	4.52	840.7

Earned Runs Allowed: Season

Player	ER	Year
1. Andy Benes	106	1999
Javier Vazquez	106	2005
3. Casey Fossum	105	2004
4. Andy Benes	102	1998
5. Brian Anderson	100	1998
Armando Reynoso	100	2000
7. Elmer Dessens	99	2003
8. Brian Anderson	96	2000
9. Curt Schilling	93	2002
10. Brandon Webb	90	2005

Earned Runs Allowed: Career with Team

Player	ER	IP
1. Brian Anderson	422	840.7
2. Randy Johnson	409	1,389.7
3. Curt Schilling	273	781.7
4. Brandon Webb	230	617.7
5. Miguel Batista	216	517.3
Omar Daal	216	473.3
7. Armando Reynoso	214	386.0
8. Andy Benes	208	429.7
9. Elmer Dessens	144	261.0
10. Byung-Hyun Kim	117	323.0

Strikeouts: Season

Player	K	Year
1. Randy Johnson	372	2001
2. Randy Johnson	364	1999
3. Randy Johnson	347	2000
4. Randy Johnson	334	2002
5. Curt Schilling	316	2002
6. Curt Schilling	293	2001
7. Randy Johnson	290	2004
8. Curt Schilling	194	2003
9. Javier Vazquez	192	2005
10. Brandon Webb	172	2003
Brandon Webb	172	2005

Strikeouts: Career with Team

Player	K	IP
1. Randy Johnson	1,832	1,389.7
2. Curt Schilling	875	781.7
3. Brandon Webb	508	617.7
4. Brian Anderson	410	840.7
5. Byung-Hyun Kim	380	323.0

6. Miguel Batista	344	517.3
7. Omar Daal	325	473.3
8. Andy Benes	305	429.7
9. Matt Mantei	221	173.7
10. Javier Vazquez	192	215.7

Strikeouts Per Nine IP: Season

Player	K/9	Year
1. Randy Johnson	13.41	2001
2. Randy Johnson	12.56	2000
3. Randy Johnson	12.06	1999
4. Randy Johnson	11.56	2002
5. Curt Schilling	10.97	2002
6. Randy Johnson	10.62	2004
7. Curt Schilling	10.39	2003
8. Curt Schilling	10.27	2001
9. Brandon Webb	8.57	2003
10. Javier Vazquez	8.01	2005

Strikeouts Per Nine IP: Career with Team

Player	K/9	IP
1. Randy Johnson	11.86	1,389.7
2. Byung-Hyun Kim	10.59	323.0
3. Curt Schilling	10.07	781.7
4. Brandon Webb	7.40	388.7
5. Greg Swindell	7.13	227.3
6. Todd Stottlemyre	6.72	217.0
7. Andy Benes	6.39	429.7
8. Mike Koplove	6.23	245.7
9. Omar Daal	6.18	473.3
10. Miguel Batista	5.98	517.3

Hits Allowed: Season

Player	HA	Year
1. Curt Schilling	237	2001
2. Brandon Webb	229	2005
3. Brian Anderson	226	2000
4. Javier Vazquez	223	2005
5. Brian Anderson	221	1998
Andy Benes	221	1998
7. Curt Schilling	218	2002
8. Andy Benes	216	1999
9. Elmer Dessens	212	2003
10. Randy Johnson	207	1999

Hits Allowed: Career with Team

Player	HA	IP
1. Randy Johnson	1,089	1,389.7
2. Brian Anderson	921	840.7
3. Curt Schilling	693	781.7
4. Brandon Webb	563	617.7
5. Miguel Batista	482	517.3
6. Omar Daal	461	473.3
7. Andy Benes	437	429.7
8. Armando Reynoso	418	386.0
9. Elmer Dessens	319	261.0
10. Todd Stottlemyre	230	217.0

Hits Allowed Per Nine IP: Season

Player	H/9	Year
1. Randy Johnson	6.48	2004
2. Randy Johnson	6.52	2001
3. Randy Johnson	6.82	2002
4. Randy Johnson	6.86	1999
5. Brandon Webb	6.97	2003
6. Randy Johnson	7.31	2000
7. Curt Schilling	7.57	2002
8. Curt Schilling	7.71	2003
9. Omar Daal	7.88	1999
10. Omar Daal	8.08	1998

Hits Allowed Per Nine IP: Career with Team

Player	H/9	IP
1. Byung-Hyun Kim	6.35	323.0
2. Randy Johnson	7.05	1,389.7
3. Curt Schilling	7.98	781.7
4. Mike Koplove	8.06	245.7
5. Brandon Webb	8.20	617.7
6. Miguel Batista	8.39	517.3
7. Greg Swindell	8.47	227.3
8. Omar Daal	8.77	473.3
9. Andy Benes	9.15	429.7
10. Todd Stottlemyre	9.54	217.0

Walks Allowed: Season

Player	BB	Year
1. Brandon Webb	119	2004
2. Andy Benes	82	1999
3. Omar Daal	79	1999
4. Randy Johnson	76	2000
Stephen Randolph	76	2004
6. Andy Benes	74	1998
7. Randy Johnson	71	2001
Randy Johnson	71	2002
9. Miguel Batista	70	2002
Randy Johnson	70	1999

Walks Allowed: Career with Team

Player	BB	IP
1. Randy Johnson	359	1,389.7
2. Brandon Webb	246	617.7
3. Miguel Batista	190	517.3
4. Omar Daal	172	473.3
5. Andy Benes	156	429.7
6. Brian Anderson	153	840.7
7. Byung-Hyun Kim	151	323.0
8. Armando Reynoso	133	386.0
9. Stephen Randolph	119	141.7
10. Curt Schilling	117	781.7

Walks Allowed Per Nine IP: Season

Player	BB/9	Year
1. Brian Anderson	1.04	1998
2. Curt Schilling	1.15	2002
3. Curt Schilling	1.37	2001
4. Randy Johnson	1.61	2004
5. Brian Anderson	1.65	2000
6. Curt Schilling	1.71	2003
7. Javier Vazquez	1.92	2005
8. Brandon Webb	2.32	2005
Randy Johnson	2.32	1999
10. Randy Johnson	2.46	2002

Walks Allowed Per Nine IP: Career with Team

Player	BB/9	IP
1. Curt Schilling	1.35	781.7
2. Brian Anderson	1.64	840.7
3. Greg Swindell	2.14	227.3
4. Randy Johnson	2.33	1,389.7
5. Elmer Dessens	2.76	261.0
6. Armando Reynoso	3.10	386.0
7. Andy Benes	3.26	429.7
8. Omar Daal	3.27	473.3
9. Miguel Batista	3.31	517.3
10. Todd Stottlemyre	3.44	217.0

WHIP (Walks + Hits Per Nine IP): Season

Player	WHIP	Year
1. Randy Johnson	0.900	2004

Player	WHIP	Year
2. Curt Schilling	0.968	2002
3. Randy Johnson	1.009	2001
4. Randy Johnson	1.020	1999
5. Randy Johnson	1.031	2002
6. Curt Schilling	1.048	2003
7. Curt Schilling	1.075	2001
8. Randy Johnson	1.118	2000
9. Brandon Webb	1.151	2003
10. Brian Anderson	1.178	1998

WHIP (Walks + Hits Per Nine IP): Career with Team

Player	WHIP	IP
1. Curt Schilling	1.036	781.7
2. Randy Johnson	1.042	1,389.7
3. Byung-Hyun Kim	1.173	323.0
4. Greg Swindell	1.179	227.3
5. Brian Anderson	1.278	840.7
6. Mike Koplove	1.280	245.7
7. Miguel Batista	1.299	517.3
8. Brandon Webb	1.310	617.7
9. Omar Daal	1.338	473.3
10. Andy Benes	1.380	429.7

Home Runs Allowed: Season

Player	HRA	Year
1. Brian Anderson	39	1998
2. Brian Anderson	38	2000
3. Curt Schilling	37	2001
4. Javier Vazquez	35	2005
5. Andy Benes	34	1999
6. Casey Fossum	31	2004
Rick Helling	31	2002
8. Randy Johnson	30	1999
9. Curt Schilling	29	2002
10. Willie Blair	27	1998

Home Runs Allowed: Career with Team

Player	HRA	IP
1. Brian Anderson	143	840.7
2. Randy Johnson	132	1,389.7
3. Curt Schilling	93	781.7
4. Andy Benes	59	429.7
5. Armando Reynoso	55	386.0
6. Omar Daal	50	473.3
Brandon Webb	50	617.7
8. Miguel Batista	38	517.3
9. Greg Swindell	36	227.3
10. Javier Vazquez	35	215.7

Saves: Season

Player	SV	Year
1. Byung-Hyun Kim	36	2002
2. Gregg Olson	30	1998
3. Matt Mantei	29	2003
4. Matt Mantei	22	1999
5. Byung-Hyun Kim	19	2001
6. Matt Mantei	17	2000
7. Greg Aquino	16	2004
8. Jose Valverde	15	2005
9. Byung-Hyun Kim	14	2000
Gregg Olson	14	1999
Brandon Lyon	14	2005

Saves: Career with Team

Player	SV	IP
1. Matt Mantei	74	173.7
2. Byung-Hyun Kim	70	323.0
3. Gregg Olson	44	129.3
4. Jose Valverde	33	146.3
5. Greg Aquino	17	66.7
6. Brandon Lyon	14	29.3
7. Brian Bruney	12	77.3
8. Bret Prinz	9	55.3
9. Mike Morgan	5	173.7
Felix Rodriguez	5	44.0

Wild Pitches: Season

Player	WP	Year
1. Brandon Webb	17	2004
2. Brandon Webb	14	2005
3. Andy Benes	10	1999
4. Miguel Batista	9	2002
Andy Benes	9	1998
Brandon Webb	9	2003
7. Randy Johnson	8	2001
8. Miguel Batista	7	2003
Rick Helling	7	2002
Armando Reynoso	7	1999
Javier Vazquez	7	2005

Wild Pitches: Career with Team

Player	WP	IP
1. Brandon Webb	40	617.7
2. Randy Johnson	24	1,389.7
3. Miguel Batista	22	517.3
4. Andy Benes	19	429.7
5. Byung-Hyun Kim	14	323.0
Curt Schilling	14	781.7
7. Armando Reynoso	12	386.0
8. Matt Mantei	11	173.7
9. Mike Fetters	10	43.3
10. Jose Valverde	9	146.3

Hit Batsmen: Season

Player	HB	Year
1. Randy Johnson	18	2001
2. Randy Johnson	13	2002
Brandon Webb	13	2003
4. Brandon Webb	11	2004
5. Miguel Batista	10	2001
Casey Fossum	10	2004
Randy Johnson	10	2004
8. Randy Johnson	9	1999
Byung-Hyun Kim	9	2000
Brad Halsey	9	2005

Hit Batsmen: Career with Team

Player	HB	IP
1. Randy Johnson	64	1,389.7
2. Byung-Hyun Kim	32	323.0
3. Brandon Webb	26	617.7
4. Miguel Batista	24	517.3
5. Mike Koplove	18	245.7
6. Omar Daal	17	473.3
7. Armando Reynoso	16	386.0
8. Mike Myers	13	73.3
9. Brian Anderson	10	840.7
Andy Benes	10	429.7
Casey Fossum	10	142.0

Games Finished: Season

Player	GF	Year
1. Byung-Hyun Kim	66	2002
2. Gregg Olson	49	1998
3. Byung-Hyun Kim	44	2001
Matt Mantei	44	2003
5. Matt Mantei	38	2000
6. Gregg Olson	36	1999
7. Jose Valverde	34	2005
8. Jose Valverde	33	2003
9. Byung-Hyun Kim	30	2000
10. Matt Mantei	28	1999

Games Finished: Career with Team

Player	GF	IP
1. Byung-Hyun Kim	150	323.0
2. Matt Mantei	132	173.7
3. Jose Valverde	87	146.3
4. Gregg Olson	85	129.3
5. Greg Swindell	59	227.3
6. Mike Koplove	56	245.7
7. Greg Aquino	37	66.7
8. Brian Bruney	35	77.3
9. Mike Morgan	33	173.7
10. Mike Myers	32	73.3
Russ Springer	32	112.3

Significant Diamondbacks

FINLEY, STEVE (OF)
(1999–2004)

While not spectacular, Steve Finley has been a solid outfielder his entire career, winning three Gold Gloves with Arizona (and five overall). Coming to Arizona as a free agent after leaving San Diego, Finley is at or near the top of the list of many all-time Diamondback hitting categories. He received one selection to the All-Star team as a Diamondback (2000).

CAREER DIAMONDBACKS RECORD:

Games	AB	Hits	Runs
849	3,049	847	491

Avg	HR	RBI	SB
.278	153	479	70

GONZALEZ, LUIS (OF)
(1999–2005)

If any one hitter could be called "Mr. Diamondback," it would be Luis Gonzalez. Gonzalez holds many of Arizona's all-time hitting records. After nine mediocre years with the Astros, Cubs, and Tigers—never hitting more than 23 homers, 79 RBIs, or 84 runs in a season—Gonzalez came into his own after joining the Diamondbacks in 1999 in a trade from Detroit for outfielder Karim Garcia. In his first five seasons with the Diamondbacks, Gonzalez averaged 34 homers, 115 RBIs, and 105 runs scored. He had his best year in 2001, when he led the Diamondbacks to the World Series title, slugging 57 homers, racking up 142 RBIs, and finishing with a .325 average. As a member of the Diamondbacks, Gonzalez was named to the National League All-Star team five times and won a Silver Slugger Award in 2001.

CAREER DIAMONDBACKS RECORD:

Games	AB	Hits	Runs
1,041	3,902	1,178	687

Avg	HR	RBI	SB
.302	209	701	32

JOHNSON, RANDY (SP)
(1999–2004)

One of the most feared pitchers in all of baseball, the 6'10" Johnson sported a fastball that usually approached 100 mph. While right-handed batters found it difficult at best to hit against the southpaw, left-handed hitters found it almost impossible. Signed as a free agent after the 1998 season, Johnson won the National League's Cy Young Award four times during his six-year stint in Arizona and led the team to its only World Series title in 2001 in a thrilling victory over the Yankees. In 2004, Johnson pitched a perfect game against the Braves, defeating them 2–0. It is the only no-hitter in Arizona's history. After the 2004 season, Johnson left the Diamondbacks, signing a huge free-agent contract with the New York Yankees. *(See Mariners bio.)*

CAREER DIAMONDBACKS RECORD:

W	L	W%	ERA	SV
103	49	.678	2.65	0

K	BB	SHO	IP
1,832	359	14	1,389.7

SCHILLING, CURT (SP)
(2000–2003)

From 2000 to 2003, the Arizona Diamondbacks possessed perhaps the best one-two pitching punch in the major leagues. Arizona traded four players to the Phillies on July 26, 2000, in order to secure Schilling as a second ace for its pitching staff. As a Diamondback, the savvy, gritty Schilling averaged 10 strikeouts for every nine innings pitched and was a major factor in the Diamondbacks' win over the Yankees in the 2001 World Series. He struck out 26 batters in 21 innings and held the Yankees in check with a 1.69 ERA for the Series. With Arizona, Schilling twice won more than 20 games in a season and twice was selected to the All-Star team. Following the 2001 season, Schilling won an armload of awards, including the Branch Rickey Award, the Hutch Award, and the Roberto Clemente Award; he was also co-winner of the World Series MVP Award with Randy Johnson. After the 2003 season, Schilling opted for free agency and signed with the Red Sox, where his fine season and gutsy postseason helped Boston win its first World Series since 1918. *(See Phillies bio.)*

CAREER DIAMONDBACKS RECORD:

W	L	W%	ERA	SV
58	28	.674	3.14	0

K	BB	SHO	IP
875	117	5	781.7

Atlanta Braves

Since 1876

1965 Team Ball

1892 The Boston Beaneaters become the first major league team ever to win 100 games in a season, finishing the year at 102–48.... **1935** The 1935 Boston Braves are so bad (38–115) that they finish 26 games behind the *seventh-place* Philadelphia Phillies in the eight-team league.... **1952–1966** Eddie Mathews of the Boston/Milwaukee/Atlanta Braves becomes the only regular position player in major league history to play for the same franchise in three different cities.... **1991** The Atlanta Braves become the first National League team to go from worst in the league one year to NL champs the next.... **2001** The Braves become the first professional sports franchise to win 10 consecutive division titles. By 2005, the streak is still intact with 14 straight seasons as division champions.

FRANCHISE HISTORY

The Atlanta Braves—not the Cincinnati Reds, as many believe—can lay claim to being the oldest continuous professional franchise in all of baseball. The team that would become known as the Braves in 1912 got its start just after the Civil War as the Cincinnati Red Stockings, a top-notch amateur team. In 1868 attorney-entrepreneur Aaron Burr Champion reorganized the team, stocking it with four paid players. By 1869 Champion, through his manager Harry Wright, had completed his search for the best Eastern players money could buy, accumulating a whole team of salaried players, all with outside jobs. The 1869–1870 Red Stockings toured the country, playing exhibition games for money, taking on—and destroying—all challengers for most of two years. Newspaper accounts are a bit sketchy, but it appears that the team won about 130 consecutive games over two seasons, with only one tie marring their record before they suffered their first loss at the hands of the Brooklyn Atlantics on June 14, 1870, in front of 9,000 fans. (The game had been tied at 5–5 after nine innings, before the Red Stockings scored two runs in the top of the 11th, but Brooklyn came back with three runs in the bottom of the inning to hand Cincinnati its first-ever loss.)

Over the remainder of the 1870 season, the Red Stockings lost five more games and the wild interest that had followed the team while they remained undefeated soon faded away—and their cash receipts dwindled along with the crowds. New team president A.P. Bronte announced that the team would not be brought back for the 1871 season due to high salary demands, so the majority of the team's members moved to Boston and joined the new National Association, playing as the Boston Red Stockings. One of the owners of the Cincinnati Red Stockings later admitted that Bronte's announcement not to bring the team back in 1871 had actually been a bluff in order to drive down player salaries, but the strategy backfired and they lost their powerful team.

During the 1890s, pitcher Kid Nichols of the Beaneaters won 297 games, more than any other pitcher ever won in any decade.

The 1914 Boston Braves

Hank Aaron. April 8, 1974. Number 715. Enough said.

The National Association, the first professional baseball league, operated from 1871 to 1875 and was beset by chaos, bankruptcy, and organizational nightmares. The transplanted Boston Red Stockings won four pennants in their five years (1872–1875) in the NA, dominating the competition. When the dysfunctional league folded up shop following the 1875 season, the Boston Red Stockings joined the new National League as one of the charter members and changed their official name to the Red Caps, although many fans continued to refer to them as the Red Stockings. The team's first significant owner in the National League was Arthur Soden, a man who had acquired his fortune in the roofing business. He was originally a minority owner, purchasing three shares of stock in 1876 for $15. He aggressively bought up as many outstanding shares as he could and soon became the controlling partner. Soden controlled the team for 30 years, overseeing eight pennants during the 19th century (the last in 1898) despite being one of the most notorious penny-pinchers in the league. During his tenure, the team changed its name in 1883 to the Boston Beaneaters.

Soden sold out following the 1906 season to brothers George and John Dovey, whose family had made some money in the Kentucky coal business before it went bad. George then accumulated new wealth from his successful trolley car business in St. Louis. After the brothers took over, they changed the team's name to the Boston Doves, in their own honor. The Doveys had become interested in the baseball business through their friend from Kentucky, Barney Dreyfuss, who had formerly owned the Louisville franchise before buying the Pittsburgh Pirates. The Doveys proved to be as ineffective at owning the team as their players did at playing on it, and they quickly lost interest—and a lot of money. When George died suddenly in June 1909, the team was left to John, the less effective of the brothers. In mid-1910 he sold the team for $100,000 to an investment group headed by William Hepburn Russell.

Russell, who changed the team name to the Rustlers (in his own honor) in mid-1910, was a Boston attorney who had his hands in a number of business ventures, including construction. A native Missourian, Russell was also active in Boston politics and had at one time been the editor of the *Hannibal Morning Journal.* While in Hannibal in his earlier life, Russell had been a boyhood friend of Samuel Clemens (Mark Twain) and had become interested enough in baseball to play for the Hannibal team, said by some to be the best amateur team in Missouri at the time. After the 1911 season, Russell, looking to make a quick buck (75,000 bucks, actually), sold the team for $175,000 to an investment group headed by James Gaffney.

Gaffney, a Tammany Hall–connected businessman, was a former police officer who made his fortune after getting the contract to excavate the Pennsylvania Railroad and tunnel station in New York. He also had a hand in building many of the New York docks. Gaffney had been encouraged to buy out Russell by his friend Frank Farrell, owner of the New York Highlanders (now Yankees). In 1912 Gaffney, who changed the team's name to the Braves, bought out his two investment partners, taking sole possession of the controlling interest formerly held by Russell. Gaffney was a personable man who helped settle the Federal League war, and who made a $300,000 profit in 1914 alone when the "Miracle Braves" came back from last place to win the pennant and the World Series. Due to illness, and a desire to leave the game with a handsome profit, Gaffney sold the team in early 1916 to Percy Haughton, a front man for Miller, Roe & Haggen, the investment banking firm that had financed the deal. They also had financed the construction of Braves Field in 1915. The group also included team manager George Stallings and several local politicians.

The 1982 Atlanta Braves hold the major league record for most consecutive wins from the start of a season with 13. The Cincinnati Reds ended the streak on April 22 with a 2–1 victory, which started the Braves on a five-game losing streak.

Three years later, in 1919, the Haughton group sold the team for $400,000 to a New York investment group headed by George Washington Grant. Grant had made his fortune in the motion picture industry in England before selling his interests in 1917. A huge baseball fan in his earlier days in Cincinnati, Grant had also been a fight manager, and was a close friend of Charles Murphy, former owner of the Cubs. Grant oversaw four dismal seasons before selling his interest in the Braves to his investment partner, Judge Emil Fuchs, in 1922. Fuchs was actually an attorney, not a judge, who brought in various celebrity minority owners (such as Christy Mathewson and Babe Ruth) in an effort to boost attendance, but it was all for naught as Fuchs labored under the strain of financial losses year after year. Eventually the National League had to take control of the team's stadium lease. In August 1935, Fuchs was forced to sell the financially strapped team, and successful businessman Charles Adams stepped in and bought it.

Adams was a pure business speculator who cared little about baseball or the Braves, and in his first year of ownership, the team changed its name—again—to the Boston Bees in a marketing effort to boost poor attendance. Adams, who had been responsible for bringing professional hockey to Boston, also owned Suffolk Downs Racetrack. He found himself continually at odds with Commissioner Landis because of the baseball czar's noted opposition to mixing baseball and horse racing. Eventually, Adams tired of his continual battles with Landis and sold the team in 1941 to an investment group headed

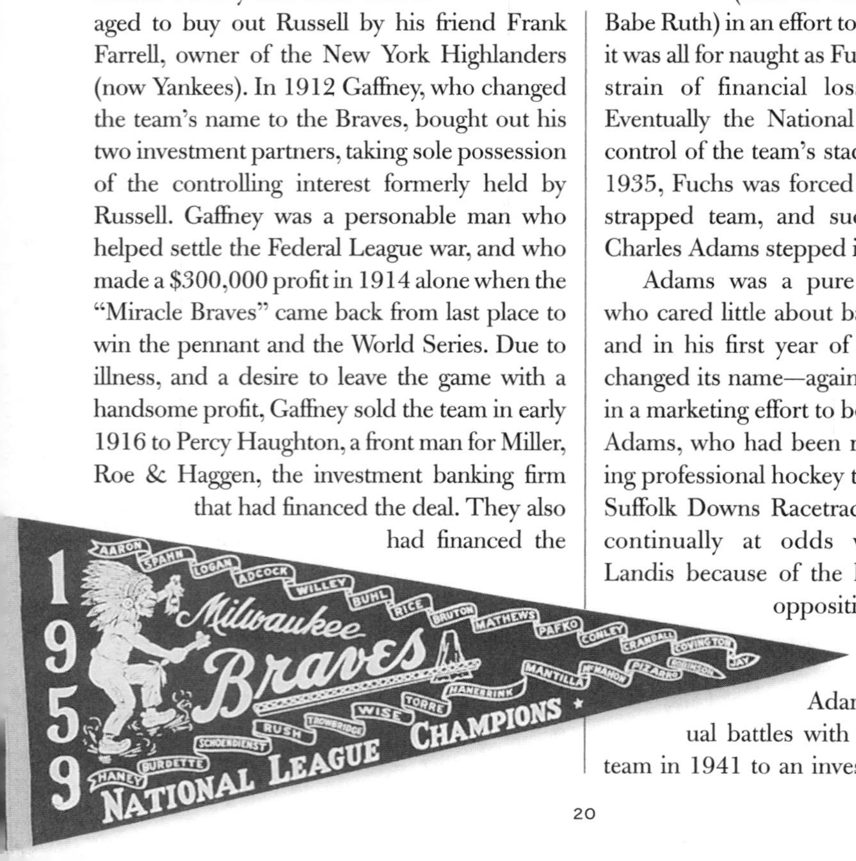

Tom Glavine

Perini, a construction magnate who had made his fortune during World War II. Over the years, Perini, who changed the team name back to the Braves, bought out virtually all the other minority investors and took sole possession of the team by 1952, the team's last year in Boston. During Pirini's reign, the Braves won their first pennant in 34 years in 1948, though they lost the Series to the Indians in six games.

When the Braves won the pennant in 1948, their season attendance was 1.45 million. In 1949 it fell to 1.1 million, then to 844,000 in 1950. The slide continued in 1951, falling to 487,000, before plummeting still further in 1952, when the team drew a mere 281,000 fans. That produced a whopping $600,000 loss in 1952 alone, the largest single-season loss in major league history up to that time. The average attendance in 1952 was just over 3,600 per game. The Braves were no longer able to compete in the Boston market with the more popular (and successful) Red Sox. Perini agonized all winter over what to do. He debated moving the team to Montreal, Denver, Toronto, Houston, or Dallas, when Milwaukee suddenly and unexpectedly entered the picture during spring training. Milwaukee city officials lobbied hard, armed with their brand-new 35,000-seat stadium, which had just been completed for their Triple-A team. Perini received permission from the National League to move the club to Milwaukee. Commissioner Ford Frick then intervened and announced on March 7, 1953, that he would not allow a franchise shift so late in spring training. When Perini announced the move was off, Wisconsin state officials threatened to reopen the just-concluded Congressional investigation into baseball's antitrust exemption if Perini wasn't allowed to move the team to Milwaukee. A few days later, Frick backed down and allowed the move, which was announced on Friday, March 13, 1953 (a day which became known as Black Friday to the few remaining Braves fans in Boston), just a few weeks before the season was to open. On March 18th, the team left Boston after 79 years in the city. With the arrival of the Braves, Milwaukee's Triple-A team moved to Toledo, Ohio.

The move paid off both financially and in the standings, as the team drew 1.8 million paying fans its first year (outdrawing the Braves' entire 1952 season in just the first 13 games), and finished in second place. With renewed finances, energy, and fans, as well as some exciting young players like Hank Aaron and Eddie Mathews, the Milwaukee Braves flourished, finishing second three times in their first four years in Milwaukee. In 1957 they got over the hump and won both the NL pennant and the World Series. The Braves repeated as NL champs in 1958, losing to the Yankees in the Series, then finished second again in 1959 (after losing a three-game playoff to the Dodgers) as well as in 1960. Attendance in each of the first seven years in Milwaukee was between 1.8 and 2.2 million, but starting in 1961, the arrival of the Minnesota Twins in the upper Midwest started eating into the Braves' market. Attendance first slipped in 1961 to 1.5 million, then tumbled in 1962 to 1.1 million. Perini was either clairvoyant or still feeling the pain of the Boston attendance massacre, so he sold the team in 1962 to the LaSalle Corporation, an investment group headed by Bill Bartholomay.

Bartholomay and his group had purchased the 46 percent interest held in the Chicago White Sox by Chuck Comiskey (son of Lou Comiskey and grandson of Charles Comiskey) with the understanding that they would eventually be able to purchase the remaining 54 percent held by the Allyn brothers. When that proved not to be the case, the Bartholomay group bought the Braves and sold their interest in the White Sox to the Allyns in 1962. The Bartholomay group watched helplessly as the attendance fade worsened, falling to 770,000 in both 1962 and 1963. It rebounded a bit in 1964 to 911,000, but the financial handwriting was on the wall. Bartholomay decided to move the team to Atlanta for the 1965 season, making a public announcement in October 1964. The move was blocked in court, however, and the presiding judge ultimately ruled that the Braves had to play one more season in Milwaukee because of various contractual agreements. As a lame-duck team in 1965, Milwaukee's attendance sagged to an all-time low of 555,000.

The mercurial attendance problems continued in Atlanta. After drawing 1.5 million fans in their first year, the Braves' attendance steadily declined to 535,000 in 1975. In all the years the Bartholomay group owned the team, the Braves won only a single division title (1969). Finally deciding that they too had had enough, the Bartholomay group sold out to television magnate Ted Turner in 1976. Turner had become wealthy through his Miami television station, Channel 17, and multiplied that wealth through cable TV's Superstation, WTBS, until he became a bonafide billionaire. Turner was a colorful playboy who liked being rich and buying expensive toys, and the Atlanta Braves were his newest gadget. In 1977, his second year of ownership, Turner, upset at his toy's performance, decided he could do a better job of managing than his manager. He moved to the dugout, lost the only game he managed, and generally made a loudmouthed ass of himself in the media circus that he created. Commissioner Bowie Kuhn stepped in and banned Turner from ever managing again. Relieved of his managing fantasies, he proceeded to spend his time acquiring a movie studio, a movie-star wife, the NBA's Atlanta Hawks—and 14 straight division titles since 1991, missing only in 1994 because of the players' strike, which ended the year without division champions or a postseason. After winning those 14 division titles, the Braves have typically played poorly in subsequent playoff rounds, capturing only five NL pennants and one World Series title, in 1995.

TEAM NAME HISTORY

Official Names

Boston Red Caps (1876–1882)
Boston Beaneaters (1883–1906)
Boston Doves (1907–1910)
Boston Rustlers (1910–1911)
Boston Braves (1912–1935)
Boston Bees (1936–1940)
Boston Braves (1941–1952)
Milwaukee Braves (1953–1965)
Atlanta Braves (1966–current)

Unofficial Names/Nicknames

Bostons, Red Stockings, Reds, Nationals, Pilgrims

STADIUM HISTORY

South End Grounds	1876–May 15, 1894
Congress Street Park	May 16, 1894–July 19, 1894 (while fire damage was being repaired to South End Grounds)
South End Grounds	July 20, 1894–June 3, 1915
Fenway Park	1914 World Series; June 22, 1915–July 26, 1915; 1946 (some games)

Braves Field	August 18, 1915–1952	Atlanta-Fulton	
County Stadium	1953–1965	County Stadium	1966–1996
		Turner Field	1997–current

YEARLY RECORD, FINISH, & ATTENDANCE FIGURES

Year	League	Record	DIV/LG Finish	Attendance	Avg/Gm
2005	NL East	90–72	1	2,521,167	31,126
2004	NL East	96–66	1	2,327,565	28,735
2003	NL East	101–61	1	2,401,084	29,643
2002	NL East	101–59	1	2,603,484	32,142
2001	NL East	88–74	1	2,823,530	34,858
2000	NL East	95–67	1	3,234,304	39,930
1999	NL East	103–59	1	3,284,897	40,554
1998	NL East	106–56	1	3,360,860	41,492
1997	NL East	101–61	1	3,464,488	42,771
1996	NL East	96–66	1	2,901,242	35,818
1995	NL East	90–54	1	2,561,831	35,581
1994	NL East	68–46	2	2,539,240	46,168
1993	NL West	104–58	1	3,884,720	47,960
1992	NL West	98–64	1	3,077,400	37,993
1991	NL West	94–68	1	2,140,217	26,422
1990	NL West	65–97	6	980,129	12,100
1989	NL West	63–97	6	984,930	12,467
1988	NL West	54–106	6	848,089	10,735
1987	NL West	69–92	5	1,217,402	15,030
1986	NL West	72–89	6	1,387,181	17,126
1985	NL West	66–96	5	1,350,137	16,668
1984	NL West	80–82	3	1,724,892	21,295
1983	NL West	88–74	2	2,119,935	26,499
1982	NL West	89–73	1	1,801,985	22,247
1981	NL West	50–56	4/5	535,418	10,708
1980	NL West	81–80	4	1,048,411	13,105
1979	NL West	66–94	6	769,465	9,740
1978	NL West	69–93	6	904,494	11,167
1977	NL West	61–101	6	872,464	10,771
1976	NL West	70–92	6	818,179	10,101
1975	NL West	67–94	5	534,672	6,683
1974	NL West	88–74	3	981,085	12,112
1973	NL West	76–85	5	800,655	9,885
1972	NL West	70–84	4	752,973	9,654
1971	NL West	82–80	3	1,006,320	12,272
1970	NL West	76–86	5	1,078,848	13,319
1969	NL West	93–69	1	1,458,320	18,004
1968	NL	81–81	5	1,126,540	13,908
1967	NL	77–85	7	1,389,222	17,151
1966	NL	85–77	5	1,539,801	18,778
1965	NL	86–76	5	555,584	6,859
1964	NL	88–74	5	910,911	11,246
1963	NL	84–78	6	773,018	9,427
1962	NL	86–76	5	766,921	9,468
1961	NL	83–71	4	1,101,441	14,304
1960	NL	88–66	2	1,497,799	19,452

YEARLY RECORD, FINISH, & ATTENDANCE FIGURES (CONT.)

Year	League	Record	DIV/LG Finish	Attendance	Avg/Gm
1959	NL	86–70	2	1,749,112	22,141
1958	NL	92–62	1	1,971,101	25,599
1957	NL	95–59	1	2,215,404	28,403
1956	NL	92–62	2	2,046,331	26,576
1955	NL	85–69	2	2,005,836	26,050
1954	NL	89–65	3	2,131,388	27,680
1953	NL	92–62	2	1,826,397	23,119
1952	NL	64–89	7	281,278	3,653
1951	NL	76–78	4	487,475	6,250
1950	NL	83–71	4	944,391	11,954
1949	NL	75–79	4	1,081,795	14,049
1948	NL	91–62	1	1,455,439	19,151
1947	NL	86–68	3	1,277,361	16,589
1946	NL	81–72	4	969,673	12,593
1945	NL	67–85	6	374,178	4,989
1944	NL	65–89	6	208,691	2,676
1943	NL	68–85	6	271,289	3,523
1942	NL	59–89	7	285,332	4,019
1941	NL	62–92	7	263,680	3,469
1940	NL	65–87	7	241,616	3,222
1939	NL	63–88	7	285,994	3,918
1938	NL	77–75	5	341,149	4,549
1937	NL	79–73	5	385,339	5,070
1936	NL	71–83	6	340,585	4,311
1935	NL	38–115	8	232,754	3,103
1934	NL	78–73	4	303,205	4,043
1933	NL	83–71	4	517,803	6,725
1932	NL	77–77	5	507,606	6,592
1931	NL	64–90	7	515,005	6,603
1930	NL	70–84	6	464,835	6,037
1929	NL	56–98	8	372,351	4,836
1928	NL	50–103	7	227,001	2,987
1927	NL	60–94	7	288,685	3,901
1926	NL	66–86	7	303,598	3,943
1925	NL	70–83	5	313,528	4,125
1924	NL	53–100	8	177,478	2,335
1923	NL	54–100	7	227,802	2,958
1922	NL	53–100	8	167,965	2,210
1921	NL	79–74	4	318,627	4,306
1920	NL	62–90	7	162,483	2,196
1919	NL	57–82	6	167,401	2,462
1918	NL	53–71	7	84,938	1,633
1917	NL	72–81	6	174,253	2,263
1916	NL	89–63	3	313,495	4,019
1915	NL	83–69	2	376,283	4,824
1914	NL	94–59	1	382,913	4,847
1913	NL	69–82	5	208,000	2,701
1912	NL	52–101	8	121,000	1,532
1911	NL	44–107	8	116,000	1,547
1910	NL	53–100	8	149,027	1,911
1909	NL	45–108	8	195,188	2,568

Yearly Record, Finish, & Attendance Figures (cont.)

Year	League	Record	DIV/LG Finish	Attendance	Avg/Gm
1908	NL	63–91	6	253,750	3,253
1907	NL	58–90	7	203,221	2,746
1906	NL	49–102	8	143,280	1,885
1905	NL	51–103	7	150,003	1,974
1904	NL	55–98	7	140,694	1,781
1903	NL	58–80	6	143,155	2,105
1902	NL	73–64	3	116,960	1,624
1901	NL	69–69	5	146,502	2,093
1900	NL	66–72	4	202,000	2,845
1899	NL	95–57	2	200,384	2,619
1898	NL	102–47	1	229,275	3,017
1897	NL	93–39	1	334,800	4,960
1896	NL	74–57	4	240,000	3,636
1895	NL	71–60	6	242,000	3,667
1894	NL	83–49	3	152,800	2,298
1893	NL	86–43	1	193,300	2,951
1892	NL	102–48	1	146,421	1,927
1891	NL	87–51	1	184,472	2,635
1890	NL	76–57	5	147,539	2,202
1889	NL	83–45	2	N/A	N/A
1888	NL	70–64	4	N/A	N/A
1887	NL	61–60	5	N/A	N/A
1886	NL	56–61	5	N/A	N/A
1885	NL	46–66	5	N/A	N/A
1884	NL	73–38	2	N/A	N/A
1883	NL	63–35	1	N/A	N/A
1882	NL	45–39	4	N/A	N/A
1881	NL	38–45	6	N/A	N/A
1880	NL	40–44	6	N/A	N/A
1879	NL	54–30	2	N/A	N/A
1878	NL	41–19	1	N/A	N/A
1877	NL	42–18	1	N/A	N/A
1876	NL	39–31	4	N/A	N/A

Manager History

Manager	Years	W–L	Win %
Harry Wright	1876–1881	254–187	.576
John Morrill	1882, 1883–1886, 1887–1888	335–296	.531
Jack Burdock	1883	30–24	.556
King Kelly	1887	49–43	.533
Jim Hart	1889	83–45	.648
Frank Selee	1890–1901	1,004–649	.607
Al Buckenberger	1902–1904	186–242	.435
Fred Tenney	1905–1907, 1911	202–402	.334
Joe Kelley	1908	63–91	.409
Frank Bowerman	1909	22–54	.289
Harry Smith	1909	23–54	.299
Fred Lake	1910	53–100	.346
Johnny Kling	1912	52–101	.340

MANAGER HISTORY (CONT.)

Manager	Years	W–L	Win %
George Stallings	1913–1920	579–597	.492
Fred Mitchell	1921–1923	186–274	.404
Dave Bancroft	1924–1927	249–363	.407
Jack Slattery	1928	11–20	.355
Rogers Hornsby	1928	39–83	.320
Emil Fuchs	1929	56–98	.364
Bill McKechnie	1930–1937	560–666	.457
Casey Stengel	1938–1943	373–491	.432
Bob Coleman	1943, 1944–1945	128–165	.437
Del Bissonette	1945	25–34	.424
Billy Southworth	1946–1951	424–358	.542
Tommy Holmes	1951–1952	61–69	.469
Charlie Grimm	1952–1956	341–285	.545
Fred Haney	1956–1959	341–231	.596
Chuck Dressen	1960–1961	159–124	.562
Birdie Tebbetts	1961–1962	98–89	.524
Bobby Bragan	1963–1966	310–287	.519
Billy Hitchcock	1966–1967	110–100	.524
Ken Silvestri	1967	0–3	.000
Lum Harris	1968–1972	379–373	.504
Eddie Mathews	1972–1974	149–161	.481
Clyde King	1974–1975	96–101	.487
Connie Ryan	1975	9–18	.333
Dave Bristol	1976–1977	131–192	.406
Ted Turner	1977	0–1	.000
Bobby Cox	(see below)		
Joe Torre	1982–1984	257–229	.529
Eddie Haas	1985	50–71	.413
Bobby Wine	1985	16–25	.390
Chuck Tanner	1986–1988	153–208	.424
Russ Nixon	1988–1990	130–216	.376
Bobby Cox	1978–1981, 1990–2005	1,737–1,311	.570

ALL-TIME WIN-LOSS RECORDS VS. ALL OPPONENTS (SINCE 1900)

ALL-TIME	7,913–8,453
Angels	1–2
Astros	353–304
Athletics	3–3
Blue Jays	6–9
Brewers	37–18
Cardinals	863–1,003
Cubs	844–1,018
Devil Rays	11–4
Diamondbacks	36–23
Dodgers	907–1,090
Giants	905–1,086
Indians	1–2
INTERLEAGUE	86–65
Mariners	1–2
Marlins	110–83
Mets	328–271
Nationals	252–223
Orioles	14–10
Padres	301–236
Phillies	1,009–932
Pirates	854–1,003
Rangers	7–2
Reds	953–1,057
Red Sox	23–13
Rockies	75–41
Royals	1–2
Tigers	4–5
Twins	2–1
White Sox	4–2
Yankees	8–8

Franchise Highlights, Low Points, and Strange Distinctions

1890s Pitcher Kid Nichols of the Beaneaters won 297 games, more than any other pitcher ever won in any decade.

• • • •

1894 Outfielder Hugh Duffy batted .440 for the Beaneaters, the highest single-season batting average in major league history.

• • • •

1900 The first shortstop ever to win a league home run title was Herman Long of the Beaneaters in 1900 when he smacked 12 to lead the National League.

• • • •

1905 The Beaneaters were the first team in major league history to have four 20-game losers in the same year. Hall of Famer Vic Willis led the way with 29 defeats, followed by Chick Fraser and Kaiser Wilhelm with 22 each, and rookie Irv Young with 21. The next year Boston again had four 20-game losers (Irv Young and Gus Dorner, 25 each; Viv Lindaman, 23; and Jeff Pfeffer, 22) as the Beaneaters finished 54½ games out of first.

• • • •

1907 Third baseman Dave Brain of the Braves led the National League in homers with 10, but never hit another homer in his career.

1914 The Braves got off to a 4–18 start and were still in last place on July 4th. After putting together a 19–6 record in August and 26–5 in September, the "Miracle Braves" came all the way back to romp to the National League pennant by 10½ games over the New York Giants.

• • • •

1918 On August 1, Art Nehf of the Braves pitched 20 scoreless innings against the Pirates before losing 2–0 in the 21st inning.

• • • •

1929 When first baseman George Sisler ended the 1929 season with 205 hits, he became the first player in major league history to collect 200 hits in both the American and National Leagues.

• • • •

1937 Only one 20th-century team ever had two rookie 20-game winners on its roster: the 1937 Boston Bees. Lou Fette was 20–10 with a 2.88 ERA, while Jim Turner went 20–11 with a 2.38 ERA. Even more amazing is the fact that both of them were late bloomers (Fette was 30, Turner 33), having spent long careers in the minor leagues. In 1938 they both suffered from the sophomore jinx, with Turner going 14–18 and Fette finishing 11–13.

1939 Outfielder Johnny Cooney played in the major leagues for 20 years, 15 of them for Boston. He only hit two home runs in his entire career, and—incredibly—they were on consecutive days while playing with the Boston Bees.

••••

1943 The Braves were lucky to finish sixth instead of in the cellar, given the performances of three of their starting infielders. Second baseman Connie Ryan hit .212 with 24 RBIs, third baseman Eddie Joost hit .185 with 20 RBIs, and shortstop Whitey Wietelmann hit .215 with 39 RBIs.

••••

1944 On August 10, Braves hurler Red Barrett pitched a complete game, 2–0 shutout of the Cincinnati Reds, using a major league record-low 58 pitches.

••••

1945 Outfielder Tommy Holmes became the only player ever to lead the National League in both home runs (28) and fewest strikeouts (9) in the same season when he accomplished the near-impossible feat in 1945.

••••

1953 Max Surkont of the Milwaukee Braves became the first 20th-century pitcher to strike out eight consecutive hitters in a game when he accomplished the feat against the Cincinnati Reds on May 25.

••••

1955 When outfielder Bill Bruton of the Braves stole 25 bases, he became the first National League player ever to lead the league in stolen bases his first three years in the league.

••••

1957 Lew Burdette won three games in the 1957 World Series against the Yankees, including two shutouts, marking the first time a pitcher had thrown two shutouts in one World Series since Christy Mathewson tossed three in the 1905 Series for the Giants against the Athletics.

••••

1961 On July 13, in his major league debut, Mack Jones collected four hits for the Milwaukee Braves.

Warren Spahn became the first National League left-hander to win 300 games. His 21 wins also led the league for a major league record ninth time. Two years later, in 1963, Spahn won 23 games at the age of 42, becoming the oldest 20-game winner in history.

••••

1966 Matty Alou of the Pirates won the NL batting title with a .342 average, while brother Felipe Alou of the Braves finished second at .327, marking the only time in history that two brothers finished 1–2 in a batting race.

The first time a National League player hit two grand slams in the same game was on July 3, the NL's 91st year in existence. The celebrated slugger was—GULP!—pitcher Tony Cloninger!

••••

1976 Outfielder Jim Wynn led the Braves in homers, RBIs, and runs scored, even though he hit just .207 on the season.

1979 When Phil Niekro finished the season with a 21–20 record, he became the first pitcher since Jim Whitney in 1881 to lead his league in both wins and losses in the same season. Whitney pitched for the Boston Red Caps, who eventually became the Boston Braves, who eventually became the Atlanta Braves, the team Niekro pitched for in 1979. That same year, Phil's brother Joe Niekro also won 21 games for the Astros.

• • • •

1982 The 1982 Atlanta Braves hold the major league record for most consecutive wins from the start of a season with 13. The Cincinnati Reds ended the streak on April 22 with a 2–1 victory, which started the Braves on a five-game losing streak.

• • • •

1985 Steve Bedrosian of the Atlanta Braves set a new major league record by starting 37 games and not completing any of them.

• • • •

1986 On July 6, the Montreal Expos beat Atlanta 11–8, a game in which Bob Horner of the Braves became the first 20th-century player to hit four homers in a game his team lost.

• • • •

1991 When Kent Mercker, Mark Wohlers, and Alejandro Pena combined for their no-hitter against San Diego on September 11, it was the first combined no-hitter in National League history.

1994 The Braves set a modern National League record by winning their first seven road games to start the season.

• • • •

1995 Pitcher Greg Maddux set a major league record by winning 18 consecutive road games. He also became the first major league pitcher since Walter Johnson in 1918 and 1919 to post an ERA under 1.80 in consecutive seasons.

• • • •

1998 The Braves set a new National League record by hitting at least one homer in 25 consecutive games. The Cardinals ended the streak on May 14.

• • • •

1999 When third baseman Chipper Jones slugged 45 home runs, it established a new National League record for switch-hitters. In 2001, Chipper Jones became the first third baseman in major league history to drive in at least 100 runs in six straight seasons when he finished the campaign with 102 RBIs.

• • • •

2005 Less than two months shy of his 47th birthday, Julio Franco became the oldest player in major league history to hit a pinch-hit grand slam when he delivered in a 7–2 win over Florida on June 27.

When John Smoltz took the loss in the 2005 All-Star Game, he became the first pitcher in history to record an All-Star decision in three different decades. He was the loser in 1989 and the winner in 1996.

Special Achievements

World Series Results

Year	Opponent	Result	Games
1914	Philadelphia A's	Won	4–0
1948	Cleveland Indians	Lost	2–4
1957	New York Yankees	Won	4–3
1958	New York Yankees	Lost	3–4
1991	Minnesota Twins	Lost	3–4
1992	Toronto Blue Jays	Lost	2–4
1995	Cleveland Indians	Won	4–2
1996	New York Yankees	Lost	2–4
1999	New York Yankees	Lost	0–4

World Series Managerial Records

Manager	Series Record	Games Record
George Stallings	1–0	4–0
Billy Southworth	0–1	2–4
Fred Haney	1–1	7–7
Bobby Cox	1–4	11–18

All-Time Postseason Record

Divisional Playoffs	25–19
League Championship Series	27–33
World Series	24–29

All-Star Games at Boston (when NL was home team), Milwaukee & Atlanta

Year	Date	Winner	Score	Stadium
1936	July 7	National	4–3	Braves Field
1955	July 12	National	6–5	County Stadium
1972	July 25	National	4–3	Atlanta-Fulton County Stadium
2000	July 11	American	6–3	Turner Field

Hall of Famers Who Played for Team

	Position	Years	Games with Boston/ Milwaukee/ Atlanta
Hank Aaron	OF/1B	1954–1974	3,076
Earl Averill	OF	1941	8
Dave Bancroft	SS	1924–1927	445
Dan Brouthers	1B	1889	126
Orlando Cepeda	1B	1969–1972	401
John Clarkson	SP	1888–1892	244
Jimmy Collins	3B	1895–1900	674
Hugh Duffy	OF	1892–1900	1,152
Johnny Evers	2B	1914–1917, 1929	318
Burleigh Grimes	SP	1930	11
Billy Hamilton	OF	1896–1901	690
Billy Herman	2B/1B	1946	75
Rogers Hornsby	2B	1928	140
Joe Kelley	OF/1B	1891, 1908	85
King Kelly	OF/C/2B	1887–1889, 1891–1892	442
Ernie Lombardi	C	1942	105
Al Lopez	C	1936–1940	471
Rabbit Maranville	SS	1912–1920, 1929–1933, 1935	1,795
Rube Marquard	SP/RP	1922–1925	109
Eddie Mathews	3B	1952–1966	2,223
Tommy McCarthy	OF	1885, 1892–1895	552
Bill McKechnie	OF	1913	1
Joe Medwick	OF/1B	1945	66
Kid Nichols	SP	1890–1901	584
Phil Niekro	SP/RP	1964–1983, 1987	742
Jim O'Rourke	OF	1876–1880	277
Gaylord Perry	SP	1981	24
Charles Radbourn	SP	1886–1889	176
Babe Ruth	OF	1935	28
Red Schoendienst	2B	1957–1960	272
Al Simmons	OF	1939	93
George Sisler	1B	1928–1930	388
Enos Slaughter	PH/OF	1959	11
Warren Spahn	SP/RP	1942, 1946–1964	746
Casey Stengel	OF	1924–1925	143
Ed Walsh	SP/RP	1917	4
Lloyd Waner	OF	1941	19
Paul Waner	OF	1941–1942	209
Hoyt Wilhelm	RP	1969–1971	61
Vic Willis	SP	1898–1905	338
George Wright	SS/2B	1876–1878, 1880–1881	198
Harry Wright	OF	1876–1877	2
Cy Young	SP	1911	11

Hall of Famers Who Managed Team

	Years	Games with Boston/ Milwaukee/Atlanta
Dave Bancroft	1924–1927	615
Rogers Hornsby	1928	122
Joe Kelley	1908	156
King Kelly	1887	95
Eddie Mathews	1972–1974	311
Bill McKechnie	1930–1937	1,235
Frank Selee	1890–1901	1,677
Casey Stengel	1938–1943	870
Harry Wright	1876–1881	444

MVP Award Winners

Bob Elliott	3B	1947
Hank Aaron	OF	1957
Dale Murphy	OF	1982
Dale Murphy	OF	1983
Terry Pendleton	3B	1991
Chipper Jones	3B	1999

Cy Young Award Winners

Pitcher	Year	W–L	SV	ERA
Warren Spahn	1957	21–11	3	2.69
Tom Glavine	1991	20–11	0	2.55
Greg Maddux	1993	20–10	0	2.36
Greg Maddux	1994	16–6	0	1.56
Greg Maddux	1995	19–2	0	1.63
John Smoltz	1996	24–8	0	2.94
Tom Glavine	1998	20–6	0	2.47

Rookie of the Year Award Winners

Alvin Dark	SS	1948
Sam Jethroe	OF	1950
Earl Williams	C	1971
Bob Horner	3B	1978
David Justice	OF	1990
Rafael Furcal	SS	2000

Gold Glove Winners

Year	Position	Player
1958	C OF	Del Crandall Hank Aaron
1959	C OF	Del Crandall Hank Aaron
1960	C OF	Del Crandall Hank Aaron
1962	C	Del Crandall
1965	C	Joe Torre
1969	1B 3B	Felix Milan Clete Boyer
1972	1B	Felix Milan
1978	SP	Phil Niekro
1979	SP	Phil Niekro
1980	SP	Phil Niekro
1982	SP OF	Phil Niekro Dale Murphy
1983	SP OF	Phil Niekro Dale Murphy
1984	OF	Dale Murphy
1985	OF	Dale Murphy
1986	OF	Dale Murphy
1992	3B	Terry Pendleton
1993	SP	Greg Maddux
1994	SP	Greg Maddux
1995	SP OF	Greg Maddux Marquis Grissom
1996	SP OF	Greg Maddux Marquis Grissom
1997	SP	Greg Maddux
1998	SP OF	Greg Maddux Andruw Jones
1999	SP OF	Greg Maddux Andruw Jones
2000	SP OF	Greg Maddux Andruw Jones
2001	SP OF	Greg Maddux Andruw Jones
2002	SP OF	Greg Maddux Andruw Jones
2003	SP OF	Mike Hampton Andruw Jones
2004	OF	Andruw Jones
2005	OF	Andruw Jones

Triple Crown Winners

Player	Year	Avg	HR	RBI
Hugh Duffy	1894	.440	18	145

Fireman of the Year Award Winners

John Smoltz	2002

World Series MVP

Lew Burdette	1957
Tom Glavine	1995

League Championship Series MVP

Steve Avery	1991
John Smoltz	1992
Mike Devereaux	1995
Javier Lopez	1996
Eddie Perez	1999

All-Star Game MVP

Fred McGriff	1994

Manager of the Year Award Winners

Bobby Cox	1991
Bobby Cox	2004
Bobby Cox	2005

Batting Champions

Player	Year	Avg
Deacon White	1877	.387
Dan Brouthers	1889	.373
Hugh Duffy	1893	.363
Hugh Duffy	1894	.440
Rogers Hornsby	1928	.387

Ernie Lombardi	1942	.330
Hank Aaron	1956	.328
Hank Aaron	1959	.353
Rico Carty	1970	.366
Ralph Garr	1974	.353
Terry Pendleton	1991	.319

Nine-Inning No-Hitters Pitched

Year	Pitcher	Opp.	Score
1892	Jack Stivetts	BRK	11–0
1907	Frank Pfeffer	CIN	6–0
1914	George Davis	PHI	7–0
1916	Tom Hughes	PIT	2–0
1944	Jim Tobin	BRK	2–0
1950	Vern Bickford	BRK	7–0
1954	Jim Wilson	PHI	2–0
1960	Lew Burdette	PHI	1–0
	Warren Spahn	PHI	4–0
1961	Warren Spahn	SF	1–0
1973	Phil Niekro	SD	9–0
1991	Kent Mercker/		
	Mark Wohlers/		
	Alejandro Pena	SD	1–0
1994	Kent Mercker	LA	6–0

20-Game Winners

Year	Pitcher	W–L
1877	Tommy Bond	40–17
1878	Tommy Bond	40–19
1879	Tommy Bond	43–19
1880	Tommy Bond	26–29
1881	Jim Whitney	31–33
1882	Jim Whitney	24–21
1883	Jim Whitney	37–21
	Charlie Buffinton	25–14
1884	Charlie Buffinton	48–16
	Jim Whitney	23–14
1885	Charlie Buffinton	22–27
1886	Charles Radbourn	27–31
	Bill Stemmeyer	22–18
1887	Charles Radbourn	24–23
	Michael Madden	21–14
1888	John Clarkson	33–20
1889	John Clarkson	49–19
	Charles Radbourn	20–11
1890	Kid Nichols	27–19
	John Clarkson	26–18
	Charlie Getzien	23–17
1891	John Clarkson	33–19
	Kid Nichols	30–17
	Harry Staley	20–8
1892	Kid Nichols	35–16
	Jack Stivetts	35–16
	Harry Staley	22–10
1893	Kid Nichols	34–14
	Jack Stivetts	20–12
1894	Kid Nichols	32–13
	Jack Stivetts	26–14
1895	Kid Nichols	26–16
1896	Kid Nichols	30–14
	Jack Stivetts	22–14
1897	Kid Nichols	31–11
	Fred Klobedanz	26–7
	Ted Lewis	21–12
1898	Kid Nichols	31–12
	Ted Lewis	26–8
	Vic Willis	25–13
1899	Vic Willis	27–8
	Kid Nichols	21–19
1900	Bill Dineen	20–14
1901	Vic Willis	20–17
1902	Togie Pittinger	27–16
	Vic Willis	27–20
1905	Irv Young	20–21
1914	Bill James	26–7
	Dick Rudolph	26–10
1915	Dick Rudolph	22–19
1921	Joe Oeschger	20–14
1933	Ben Cantwell	20–10
1937	Lou Fette	20–10
	Jim Turner	20–11
1946	Johnny Sain	20–14
1947	Warren Spahn	21–10
	Johnny Sain	21–12
1948	Johnny Sain	24–15
1949	Warren Spahn	21–14
1950	Warren Spahn	21–17
	Johnny Sain	20–13
1951	Warren Spahn	22–14
1953	Warren Spahn	23–7
1954	Warren Spahn	21–12
1956	Warren Spahn	20–11
1957	Warren Spahn	21–11
1958	Warren Spahn	22–11
	Lew Burdette	20–10
1959	Lew Burdette	21–15
	Warren Spahn	21–15
1960	Warren Spahn	21–10
1961	Warren Spahn	21–13
1963	Warren Spahn	23–7
1965	Tony Cloninger	24–11
1969	Phil Niekro	23–13
1974	Phil Niekro	20–13
1979	Phil Niekro	21–20
1991	Tom Glavine	20–11
1992	Tom Glavine	20–8
1993	Tom Glavine	22–6
	Greg Maddux	20–10
1997	Denny Neagle	20–5
1998	Tom Glavine	20–6
2000	Tom Glavine	21–9
2003	Russ Ortiz	21–7

RETIRED UNIFORM NUMBERS

Number	Player	Position
3	Dale Murphy	OF
21	Warren Spahn	SP
35	Phil Niekro	SP
41	Eddie Mathews	3B
44	Hank Aaron	OF

TEAM RECORDS—WINS & LOSSES

- Games won in a season: 106 in 1998
- Games lost in a season: 115 in 1935
- Games won in a month: 26 in September 1914
- Games lost in a month: 25 in September 1928 and September 1935
- Consecutive games won: 18 in 1891
- Consecutive games lost: 19 in 1906
- Biggest shutout victory: 18–0 over Buffalo on October 3, 1885 and Florida on October 3, 1999
- Biggest shutout loss: 19–0 to Montreal Expos on July 30, 1978
- Highest winning percentage: .705 in 1897 (93–39)
- Lowest winning percentage: .248 in 1935 (38–115)

TEAM RECORDS—BATTING

- Highest team batting average: .292 in 1925
- Lowest team batting average: .223 in 1909
- Highest team slugging average: .475 in 2003
- Highest team on-base percentage: .401 in 1894
- Total hits: 1,608 in 2003
- Extra-base hits: 587 in 2003
- Hits in a single game: 32 vs. St. Louis on September 3, 1896 (first game)
- Longest individual hitting streak: 37, Tommy Holmes, 1945
- Most .300 hitters in a single season: 8 in 1953
- Home runs: 235 in 2003
- Home runs in a month: 15, Joe Adcock, July 1956
- Home runs in a game: 8 vs. Pittsburgh on August 30, 1953 (first game)
- Home runs by a rookie: 38, Wally Berger, 1930
- Home runs by a righthander: 51, Andruw Jones, 2005
- Home runs by a lefthander: 47, Eddie Mathews, 1953
- Home runs by a switch-hitter: 45, Chipper Jones, 1999
- Grand slams: 12 in 1997
- Grand slams (individual; single season): 4, Sid Gordon, 1950
- Grand slams (individual; career): 16, Hank Aaron
- Triples: 100 in 1921
- Doubles: 321 in 2003
- Singles: 1,196 in 1925
- Walks: 684 in 1949
- Runs scored: 1,220 in 1894
- Runs scored in a game: 30 vs. Detroit on June 9, 1883
- Runs scored in an inning: 16 vs. Baltimore on June 18, 1894 (first inning)
- Most batters hit by a pitch: 61 in 1998
- Times shut out: 28 in 1906
- Grounded into double plays: 154 in 1985
- Fewest grounded into double plays: 82 in 1992
- Runners left on base: 1,255 in 1948

TEAM RECORDS—BASERUNNING

- Stolen bases: 373 in 1887
- Caught stealing: 100 in 1921

TEAM RECORDS—PITCHING

- Lowest earned run average: 2.15 in 1877
- Complete games: 142 in 1892
- Saves: 57 in 2002
- Strikeouts: 1,245 in 1996
- Shutouts: 24 in 1992
- Walks: 672 in 1911
- Hit batsmen: 69 in 1899
- Wild pitches: 95 in 1886
- Consecutive wins (individual): 14, John Smoltz, 1996
- Consecutive losses (individual): 18, Cliff Curtis, 1910
- Strikeouts in a game (individual): 18, Warren Spahn, June 14, 1952 (15 innings); 9 innings: 15, Warren Spahn, September 16, 1960 and John Smoltz, May 24, 1992
- Most runs allowed in a game: 27 vs. Pittsburgh on June 6, 1894

TEAM RECORDS—FIELDING

- Best fielding average: .986 in 2005
- Most errors committed: 522 in 1887
- Fewest errors committed: 86 in 2005
- Most double plays turned: 197 in 1985
- Fewest double plays turned: 101 in 1935

TEAM RECORDS—MISCELLANEOUS

- Number of times league champions: 17
- Number of times finishing last in league: 13
- Largest attendance, single game: 53,775 vs. Los Angeles Dodgers, April 8, 1974
- Largest attendance, doubleheader: 50,597 vs. Chicago Cubs, July 4, 1972
- Players used in a season: 48 in 1946
- Seasons played: 19 by Phil Niekro

Frank Torre jumps on Lew Burdette after the Braves shut out the Yankees in game 7 of the 1957 World Series.

PRIMARY PITCHING STAFFS

Year	Starter	Starter	Starter	Starter	Starter	Closer	Bullpen	Bullpen	Bullpen
2005	Smoltz	Ramirez	Hudson	Sosa	Thomson	Reitsma	Kolb	Foster	Boyer
2004	Ortiz	Wright	Hampton	Byrd	Thomson	Smoltz	Reitsma	Alfonseca	Gryboski
2003	Ortiz	Maddux	Hampton	Reynolds	Ramirez	Smoltz	King	Hernandez	Gryboski
2002	Glavine	Maddux	Millwood	Moss	Marquis	Smoltz	Remlinger	Hammond	Gryboski
2001	Glavine	Maddux	Millwood	Burkett	Marquis	Rocker	Remlinger	Cabrera	Drabowsky
2000	Glavine	Maddux	Millwood	Burkett	Mulholland	Rocker	Remlinger	Kamieniecki	Ligtenberg
1999	Glavine	Maddux	Millwood	Smoltz	Perez	Rocker	Remlinger	McGlinchy	Seanez
1998	Glavine	Maddux	Millwood	Smoltz	Neagle	Ligtenberg	Martinez	Rocker	Cather
1997	Glavine	Maddux	Wade	Smoltz	Neagle	Wohlers	Embree	Clontz	Bielecki
1996	Glavine	Maddux	Avery	Smoltz	Schmidt	Wohlers	McMichael	Clontz	Wade
1995	Glavine	Maddux	Avery	Smoltz	Mercker	Wohlers	McMichael	Clontz	Borbon
1994	Glavine	Maddux	Avery	Smoltz	Mercker	McMichael	Wohlers	Stanton	Bedrosian
1993	Glavine	Maddux	Avery	Smoltz	Smith	Stanton	McMichael	Howell	Bedrosian
1992	Glavine	Leibrandt	Avery	Smoltz	Bielecki	Pena	Stanton	Freeman	Mercker
1991	Glavine	Leibrandt	Avery	Smoltz	Smith	Berenguer	Stanton	Freeman	Mercker
1990	Glavine	Leibrandt	Avery	Smoltz	Clary	Boever	Castillo	Luecken	Mercker
1989	Glavine	Lilliquist	Smith	Smoltz	Clary	Boever	Acker	Assenmacher	Eichhorn
1988	Glavine	Mahler	Smith	Smoltz	Smith	Sutter	Alvarez	Assenmacher	Puleo
1987	Palmer	Mahler	Alexander	Puleo	Smith	Acker	Dedmon	Assenmacher	Garber
1986	Palmer	Mahler	Alexander	Johnson	Smith	Garber	Dedmon	Assenmacher	Olwine
1985	Bedrosian	Mahler	Perez	Barker	Smith	Sutter	Dedmon	Camp	Garber
1984	McMurtry	Mahler	Perez	Barker	Camp	Moore	Dedmon	Bedrosian	Garber
1983	McMurtry	Niekro	Perez	Dayley	Camp	Bedrosian	Forster	Moore	Garber
1982	Mahler	Niekro	Walk	Dayley	Camp	Garber	Bedrosian	Hrabosky	McWilliams
1981	Mahler	Niekro	Boggs	Perry	Montefusco	Camp	Garber	Hrabosky	Bradford
1980	Alexander	Niekro	Boggs	McWilliams	Matula	Camp	Garber	Hrabosky	Bradford
1979	Solomon	Niekro	Brizzolara	Mahler	Matula	Garber	Skok	Devine	McLaughlin
1978	Hanna	Niekro	McWilliams	Mahler	Ruthven	Garber	Skok	Campbell	Camp
1977	Capra	Niekro	Solomon	Messersmith	Ruthven	Campbell	Collins	Leon	Camp
1976	Morton	Niekro	LaCorte	Messersmith	Ruthven	Devine	Dal Canton	Leon	Torrealba
1975	Morton	Niekro	Easterly	Capra	Reed	House	Sosa	Leon	Beard
1974	Morton	Niekro	Harrison	Capra	Reed	House	Frisella	Leon	Krausse
1973	Morton	Niekro	Harrison	Schueler	Reed	Frisella	House	Devine	Panther
1972	Stone	Niekro	Kelley	Schueler	Reed	Upshaw	Jarvis	Hardin	Hoerner
1971	Stone	Niekro	Kelley	Jarvis	Reed	Upshaw	Priddy	Barber	Nash
1970	Stone	Niekro	Nash	Jarvis	Reed	Wilhelm	Priddy	McQueen	Navarro
1969	Stone	Niekro	Pappas	Jarvis	Reed	Upshaw	Doyle	Raymond	Neibauer
1968	Johnson	Niekro	Pappas	Jarvis	Reed	Upshaw	Britton	Raymond	Kelley
1967	Johnson	Niekro	Lemaster	Jarvis	Cloninger	Upshaw	Ritchie	Hernandez	Carroll
1966	Johnson	Kelley	Lemaster	Blasingame	Cloninger	Carroll	Olivo	Abernathy	Niekro
1965	Johnson	Fischer	Lemaster	Blasingame	Cloninger	O'Dell	Osinski	Sadowski	Niekro
1964	Spahn	Fischer	Lemaster	Sadowski	Cloninger	Tiefenauer	Hoeft	Olivo	Blasingame
1963	Spahn	Hendley	Lemaster	Sadowski	Cloninger	Shaw	Raymond	Piche	Fischer
1962	Spahn	Hendley	Shaw	Burdette	Cloninger	Raymond	Nottebart	Curtis	Willey
1961	Spahn	Hendley	Buhl	Burdette	Willey	McMahon	Nottebart	Cloninger	Drabowsky
1960	Spahn	Pizarro	Buhl	Burdette	Willey	McMahon	Piche	Jay	Brunet
1959	Spahn	Jay	Buhl	Burdette	Willey	McMahon	Rush	Pizarro	Trowbridge
1958	Spahn	Jay	Rush	Burdette	Willey	McMahon	Conley	Robinson	Trowbridge
1957	Spahn	Buhl	Conley	Burdette	Trowbridge	McMahon	Johnson	Phillips	Pizarro
1956	Spahn	Buhl	Conley	Burdette	Crone	Jolly	Johnson	Phillips	Sleater
1955	Spahn	Buhl	Conley	Burdette	Nichols	Johnson	Jolly	Crone	
1954	Spahn	Wilson	Conley	Burdette	Nichols	Jolly	Johnson	Buhl	Crone
1953	Spahn	Wilson	Antonelli	Surkont	Buhl	Burdette	Johnson	Liddle	Jolly

PRIMARY PITCHING STAFFS (CONT.)

Year	Starter	Starter	Starter	Starter	Starter	Closer	Bullpen	Bullpen	Bullpen
1952	Spahn	Wilson	Bickford	Surkont	Johnson	Burdette	Jones	Chipman	Cole
1951	Spahn	Sain	Bickford	Surkont	Nichols	Estock	Chipman	Cole	
1950	Spahn	Sain	Bickford	Surkont	Chipman	Hogue	Hall	Antonelli	Roy
1949	Spahn	Sain	Bickford	Voiselle	Antonelli	Potter	Hall	Hogue	Barrett
1948	Spahn	Sain	Bickford	Voiselle	Barrett	Shoun	Hogue	Potter	
1947	Spahn	Sain	Johnson	Voiselle	Barrett	Shoun	Lanfranconi	Karl	
1946	Spahn	Sain	Cooper	Lee	Wright	Johnson	Wallace	Barrett	
1945	Logan	Tobin	Andrews	Lee	Javery	Hutchings	Hendrickson		Cooper
1944	Barrett	Tobin	Andrews	Hutchinson	Javery	Hutchings	Klopp	Cardoni	
1943	Barrett	Tobin	Andrews	Salvo	Javery	Odom	MacFayden	Cardoni	
1942	Tost	Tobin	Earley	Salvo	Javery	Sain	Donovan	Errickson	Hutchings
1941	Errickson	Tobin	Johnson	Salvo	Javery	LaManna	Earley	Hutchings	
1940	Errickson	Posedel	Sullivan	Salvo	Strincevich	Coffman	Javery	Piechota	
1939	MacFayden	Posedel	Fette	Turner	Shoffner	Lanning	Sullivan	Errickson	
1938	MacFayden	Lanning	Fette	Turner	Shoffner	Errickson	Hutchinson	Reis	
1937	MacFayden	Lanning	Fette	Turner	Bush	Hutchinson	Gabler	Smith	
1936	MacFayden	Lanning	Chaplin	Benge	Cantwell	Smith	Reis	Bush	Weir
1935	MacFayden	Frankhouse	Brandt	Smith	Cantwell	Betts	Benton	Brown	
1934	Betts	Frankhouse	Brandt	Rhem	Cantwell	Smith	Mangum	Brown	
1933	Betts	Frankhouse	Brandt	Zachary	Cantwell	Smith	Mangum	Seibold	
1932	Betts	Brown	Brandt	Zachary	Seibold	Frankhouse	Cantwell	Cunningham	
1931	Sherdel	Cantwell	Brandt	Zachary	Seibold	Frankhouse	Haid	Cunningham	
1930	Sherdel	Cantwell	Smith	Zachary	Seibold	Frankhouse	Brandt	Cunningham	
1929	Jones	Cantwell	Smith	Brandt	Seibold	Leverett	Delaney	Cunningham	
1928	Greenfield	Delaney	Smith	Brandt	Genewich	Cooney	Cantwell	Edwards	
1927	Greenfield	Robertson	Smith	Werts	Genewich	Goldsmith	Mogridge	Edwards	
1926	Benton	Goldsmith	Smith	Werts	Genewich	Hearn	Mogridge	Cooney	
1925	Benton	Cooney	Barnes	Graham	Genewich	Ryan	Marquard	Kamp	
1924	Benton	Cooney	Barnes	McNamara	Genewich	Yeargin	Lucas	Stryker	
1923	Marquard	Oeschger	Barnes	McNamara	Genewich	Fillingim	Benton	Cooney	
1922	Marquard	Oeschger	Watson	Miller	McQuillan	Fillingim	Braxton	McNamara	
1921	Scott	Oeschger	Watson	Fillingim	McQuillan	Morgan	Braxton	Cooney	
1920	Scott	Oeschger	Rudolph	Fillingim	McQuillan	Watson	Hearn	Eayrs	
1919	Nehf	Demaree	Rudolph	Fillingim	Keating	Scott	McQuillan	Northrop	
1918	Nehf	Ragan	Rudolph	Fillingim	Hearn	Canavan	George	Northrop	
1917	Nehf	Barnes	Rudolph	Tyler	Allen	Ragan	Hughes	Scott	
1916	Ragan	Barnes	Rudolph	Tyler	Hughes	Nehf	Reulbach	Allen	
1915	Ragan	Nehf	Rudolph	Tyler	Hughes	Davis	Crutcher	James	
1914	James	Crutcher	Rudolph	Tyler	Hess	Strand	Cocreham	Perdue	
1913	Perdue	Dickson	Rudolph	Tyler	Hess	James	Noyes	Quinn	
1912	Perdue	Dickson	Brown	Tyler	Hess	Donnelly	Hogg	McTigue	
1911	Perdue	Mattern	Brown	Tyler	Weaver	Pfeffer	Griffin	McTigue	
1910	Curtis	Mattern	Brown	Frock	Ferguson	Burke	Evans	Parson	
1909	White	Mattern	Brown	Richie	Ferguson	Tuckey	Lindaman	More	
1908	Flaherty	Lindaman	Dorner	Young	Ferguson	Boultes	McCarthy	Chappelle	
1907	Flaherty	Lindaman	Dorner	Young	Pfeffer	Boultes			
1906		Lindaman	Dorner	Young	Pfeffer	Witherup			
1905	Willis	Fraser	Wilhelm	Young		Harley			
1904	Willis	Pittinger	Wilhelm	Fisher	McNichol				
1903	Willis	Pittinger	Malarkey	Piatt	Williams	Carney			
1902	Willis	Pittinger	Malarkey	Eason	Hale				
1901	Willis	Pittinger	Nichols	Dineen		Lawson			
1900	Willis	Pittinger	Nichols	Dineen	Lewis	Cuppy			

PRIMARY PITCHING STAFFS (CONT.)

Year	Starter	Starter	Starter	Starter	Starter	Closer	Bullpen	Bullpen	Bullpen
1899	Willis	Meekin	Nichols	Killen	Lewis	Bailey	Hickman		
1898	Willis	Klobedanz	Nichols		Lewis		Hickman		
1897	Stivetts	Klobedanz	Nichols	Sullivan	Lewis				
1896	Stivetts	Klobedanz	Nichols	Sullivan		Mains	Lewis	Dolan	
1895	Stivetts	Dolan	Nichols	Sullivan	Wilson	Sexton			
1894	Stivetts	Staley	Nichols	Lovett	Hodson				
1893	Stivetts	Staley	Nichols	Gastright					
1892	Stivetts	Staley	Nichols	Clarkson					
1891	Getzein	Staley	Nichols	Clarkson					
1890	Getzein		Nichols	Clarkson					
1889	Radbourn	Madden	Daley	Clarkson		Sowders			
1888	Radbourn	Madden	Sowders	Clarkson	Conway				
1887	Radbourn	Madden	Stemmeyer		Conway				
1886	Radbourn	Buffinton	Stemmeyer						
1885	Whitney	Buffinton	Davis						
1884	Whitney	Buffinton	Connor			Morrill			
1883	Whitney	Buffinton							
1882	Whitney	Mathews	Buffinton						
1881	Whitney	Fox	Bond		Mathews				
1880	Bond	Foley		Morrill					
1879	Bond	Foley	Tyng						
1878	Bond			Manning					
1877	Bond	White							
1876	Borden	Bradley	Manning						

PRIMARY STARTING LINEUPS

Year	C	1B	2B	3B	SS	LF	CF	RF
2005	Estrada	LaRoche	Giles	Jones	Furcal	Johnson	Jones	Francoeur
2004	Estrada	LaRoche	Giles	Jones	Furcal	Thomas	Jones	Drew
2003	Lopez	Fick	Giles	Castilla	Furcal	Jones	Jones	Sheffield
2002	Lopez	Franco	Lockhart	Castilla	Furcal	Jones	Jones	Sheffield
2001	Lopez	Helms	Veras	Jones	Furcal	Surhoff	Jones	Jordan
2000	Lopez	Galarraga	Veras	Jones	Furcal	Sanders	Jones	Jordan
1999	Perez	Hunter	Boone	Jones	Weiss	Williams	Jones	Jordan
1998	Lopez	Galarraga	Lockhart	Jones	Weiss	Klesko	Jones	Tucker
1997	Lopez	McGriff	Lemke	Jones	Blauser	Klesko	Lofton	Tucker
1996	Lopez	McGriff	Lemke	Jones	Blauser	Klesko	Grissom	Dye
1995	Lopez	McGriff	Lemke	Jones	Blauser	Klesko	Grissom	Justice
1994	Lopez	McGriff	Lemke	Pendleton	Blauser	Klesko	Kelly	Justice
1993	Berryhill	Bream	Lemke	Pendleton	Blauser	Gant	Nixon	Justice
1992	Olson	Bream	Lemke	Pendleton	Belliard	Gant	Nixon	Justice
1991	Olson	Bream	Lemke	Pendleton	Belliard	Smith	Gant	Justice
1990	Olson	Justice	Treadway	Presley	Blauser	Smith	Gant	Murphy
1989	Davis	Perry	Treadway	Blauser	Thomas	Smith	Murphy	Gregg
1988	Virgil	Perry	Gant	Oberkfell	Thomas	James	Hall	Murphy
1987	Virgil	Perry	Hubbard	Oberkfell	Thomas	Griffey	James	Murphy
1986	Virgil	Horner	Hubbard	Oberkfell	Thomas	Griffey	Murphy	Moreno
1985	Cerone	Horner	Hubbard	Oberkfell	Ramirez	Harper	Murphy	Washington
1984	Benedict	Chambliss	Hubbard	Johnson	Ramirez	Perry	Murphy	Washington
1983	Benedict	Chambliss	Hubbard	Horner	Ramirez	Butler	Murphy	Washington
1982	Benedict	Chambliss	Hubbard	Horner	Ramirez	Linares	Murphy	Washington

PRIMARY STARTING LINEUPS (CONT.)

Year	C	1B	2B	3B	SS	LF	CF	RF
1981	Benedict	Chambliss	Hubbard	Horner	Ramirez	Linares	Murphy	Washington
1980	Benedict	Chambliss	Hubbard	Horner	Gomez	Burroughs	Murphy	Matthews
1979	Benedict	Murphy	Hubbard	Horner	Frias	Burroughs	Office	Matthews
1978	Pocoroba	Murphy	Royster	Horner	Chaney	Burroughs	Office	Matthews
1977	Pocoroba	Montanez	Gilbreath	Moore	Rockett	Matthews	Office	Burroughs
1976	Correll	Montanez	Gilbreath	Royster	Chaney	Wynn	Office	Henderson
1975	Correll	Williams	Perez	Evans	Blanks	Garr	Office	Baker
1974	Oates	Johnson	Perez	Evans	Robinson	Garr	Office	Baker
1973	Oates	Lum	Johnson	Evans	Perez	Aaron	Baker	Garr
1972	Williams	Aaron	Millan	Evans	Perez	Carty	Baker	Lum
1971	Williams	Aaron	Millan	Evans	Perez	Garr	Jackson	Lum
1970	Tillman	Cepeda	Millan	Boyer	Jackson	Carty	Gonzalez	Aaron
1969	Didier	Cepeda	Millan	Boyer	Jackson	Carty	Alou	Aaron
1968	Torre	Johnson	Millan	Boyer	Jackson	Lum	Alou	Aaron
1967	Torre	Alou	Woodward	Boyer	Menke	Carty	Jones	Aaron
1966	Torre	Alou	Woodward	Mathews	Menke	Carty	Jones	Aaron
1965	Torre	Alou	Bolling	Mathews	Woodward	Carty	Jones	Aaron
1964	Torre	Oliver	Bolling	Mathews	Menke	Carty	Maye	Aaron
1963	Torre	Oliver	Bolling	Mathews	McMillan	Dillard	Maye	Aaron
1962	Crandall	Adcock	Bolling	Mathews	McMillan	Bell	Aaron	Jones
1961	Torre	Adcock	Bolling	Mathews	McMillan	Thomas	Cimoli	Aaron
1960	Crandall	Adcock	Cottier	Mathews	Logan	Spangler	Bruton	Aaron
1959	Crandall	Adcock	Mantilla	Mathews	Logan	Covington	Bruton	Aaron
1958	Crandall	Torre	Schoendienst	Mathews	Logan	Covington	Bruton	Aaron
1957	Crandall	Torre	Schoendienst	Mathews	Logan	Covington	Bruton	Aaron
1956	Crandall	Adcock	O'Connell	Mathews	Logan	Thomson	Bruton	Aaron
1955	Crandall	Crowe	O'Connell	Mathews	Logan	Thomson	Bruton	Aaron
1954	Crandall	Adcock	O'Connell	Mathews	Logan	Aaron	Bruton	Pafko
1953	Crandall	Adcock	Dittmer	Mathews	Logan	Gordon	Bruton	Pafko
1952	Cooper	Torgeson	Dittmer	Mathews	Logan	Gordon	Jethroe	Daniels
1951	Cooper	Torgeson	Hartsfield	Elliott	Kerr	Gordon	Jethroe	Marshall
1950	Cooper	Torgeson	Hartsfield	Elliott	Kerr	Gordon	Jethroe	Holmes
1949	Crandall	Fletcher	Stanky	Elliott	Dark	Rickert	Russell	Holmes
1948	Masi	Torgeson	Stanky	Elliott	Dark	Heath	Russell	Holmes
1947	Masi	Torgeson	Ryan	Elliott	Culler	Rowell	Hopp	Holmes
1946	Masi	Sanders	Ryan	Fernandez	Culler	Rowell	Gillenwater	Holmes
1945	Masi	Shupe	Wietelmann	Workman	Culler	Nieman	Gillenwater	Holmes
1944	Masi	Etchison	Ryan	Phillips	Wietelmann	Nieman	Holmes	Workman
1943	Masi	McCarthy	Ryan	Joost	Wietelmann	Nieman	Holmes	Workman
1942	Lombardi	West	Sisti	Fernandez	Miller	Ross	Holmes	Waner
1941	Berres	Hassett	Rowell	Sisti	Miller	West	Cooney	Moore
1940	Berres	Hassett	Rowell	Sisti	Miller	Ross	Cooney	Moore
1939	Lopez	Hassett	Cuccinello	Majeski	Miller	Simmons	Cooney	Garms
1938	Mueller	Fletcher	Cuccinello	Stripp	Warstler	West	DiMaggio	Cooney
1937	Lopez	Fletcher	Cuccinello	English	Warstler	Garms	DiMaggio	Moore
1936	Lopez	Jordan	Cuccinello	Coscarart	Urbanski	Lee	Berger	Moore
1935	Spohrer	Jordan	Mallon	Whitney	Urbanski	Lee	Berger	Moore
1934	Spohrer	Jordan	McManus	Whitney	Urbanski	Lee	Berger	Thompson
1933	Hogan	Jordan	Maranville	Whitney	Urbanski	Lee	Berger	Moore
1932	Spohrer	Shires	Maranville	Knothe	Urbanski	Worthington	Berger	Schulmerich
1931	Spohrer	Sheely	Maguire	Urbanski	Maranville	Worthington	Berger	Schulmerich
1930	Spohrer	Sisler	Maguire	Chatham	Maranville	Berger	Welsh	Richbourg
1929	Spohrer	Sisler	Maguire	Bell	Maranville	Harper	Clark	Richbourg

PRIMARY STARTING LINEUPS (CONT.)

Year	C	1B	2B	3B	SS	LF	CF	RF
1928	Taylor	Sisler	Hornsby	Bell	Farrell	Brown	Smith	Richbourg
1927	Hogan	Fournier	Gautreau	High	Bancroft	Brown	Welsh	Richbourg
1926	Taylor	Burrus	Gautreau	High	Bancroft	Wilson	Brown	Welsh
1925	Gibson	Burrus	Gautreau	Marriott	Bancroft	Harris	Neis	Welsh
1924	O'Neil	McInnis	Tierney	Padgett	Smith	Cunningham	Felix	Stengel
1923	O'Neil	McInnis	Ford	Boeckel	Smith	Felix	Powell	Southworth
1922	O'Neil	Holke	Kopf	Boeckel	Ford	Nixon	Powell	Cruise
1921	O'Neil	Holke	Ford	Boeckel	Barbare	Cruise	Powell	Southworth
1920	O'Neil	Holke	Pick	Boeckel	Maranville	Mann	Powell	Cruise
1919	Gowdy	Holke	Herzog	Boeckel	Maranville	Mann	Riggert	Powell
1918	Wilson	Konetchy	Herzog	Smith	Rawlings	Kelly	Powell	Wickland
1917	Tragesser	Konetchy	Rawlings	Smith	Maranville	Kelly	Powell	Rehg
1916	Gowdy	Konetchy	Evers	Smith	Maranville	Magee	Snodgrass	Wilhoit
1915	Gowdy	Schmidt	Evers	Smith	Maranville	Connolly	Magee	Moran
1914	Gowdy	Schmidt	Evers	Deal	Maranville	Connolly	Mann	Gilbert
1913	Rariden	Myers	Sweeney	Devlin	Maranville	Connolly	Mann	Titus
1912	Kling	Houser	Sweeney	McDonald	O'Rourke	Jackson	Campbell	Titus
1911	Kling	Tenney	Sweeney	Ingerton	Herzog	Jackson	Donlin	Miller
1910	Graham	Sharpe	Shean	Herzog	Sweeney	Collins	Beck	Miller
1909	Graham	Stem	Shean	Sweeney	Coffey	Thomas	Beaumont	Becker
1908	Bowerman	McGann	Ritchey	Sweeney	Dahlen	Bates	Beaumont	Browne
1907	Needham	Tenney	Ritchey	Brain	Bridwell	Randall	Beaumont	Bates
1906	Needham	Tenney	Strobel	Brain	Bridwell	Howard	Bates	Dolan
1905	Moran	Tenney	Raymer	Wolverton	Abbaticchio	Delahanty	Cannell	Dolan
1904	Needham	Tenney	Raymer	Delahanty	Abbaticchio	Cooley	Geier	Cannell
1903	Moran	Tenney	Abbaticchio	Gremminger	Aubrey	Cooley	Dexter	Carney
1902	Kittridge	Tenney	DeMontreville	Gremminger	Long	Cooley	Lush	Carney
1901	Kittridge	Tenney	DeMontreville	Lowe	Long	Murphy	Hamilton	Slagle
1900	Clarke	Tenney	Lowe	Collins	Long	Duffy	Hamilton	Freeman
1899	Bergen	Tenney	Lowe	Collins	Long	Duffy	Hamilton	Stahl
1898	Bergen	Tenney	Lowe	Collins	Long	Duffy	Hamilton	Stahl
1897	Bergen	Tenney	Lowe	Collins	Long	Duffy	Hamilton	Stahl
1896	Bergen	Tucker	Lowe	Collins	Long	Duffy	Hamilton	Bannon
1895	Ganzel	Tucker	Lowe	Nash	Long	McCarthy	Duffy	Bannon
1894	Ganzel	Tucker	Lowe	Nash	Long	McCarthy	Duffy	Bannon
1893	Bennett	Tucker	Lowe	Nash	Long	McCarthy	Duffy	Carroll
1892	Kelly	Tucker	Quinn	Nash	Long	Lowe	Duffy	McCarthy
1891	Bennett	Tucker	Quinn	Nash	Long	Lowe	Brodie	Stovey
1890	Bennett	Tucker	Smith	McGarr	Long	Sullivan	Hines	Brodie
1889	Bennett	Brouthers	Richardson	Nash	Quinn	Brown	Johnston	Kelly
1888	Kelly	Morrill	Quinn	Nash	Wise	Hornung	Johnston	Brown
1887	Tate	Morrill	Burdock	Nash	Wise	Hornung	Johnston	Kelly
1886	Daily	Wise	Burdock	Nash	Morrill	Hornung	Johnston	Poorman
1885	Gunning	Morrill	Burdock	Sutton	Wise	McCarthy	Manning	Poorman
1884	Hackett	Morrill	Burdock	Sutton	Wise	Hornung	Manning	Crowley
1883	Hines	Morrill	Burdock	Sutton	Wise	Hornung	Smith	Radford
1882	Deasley	Morrill	Burdock	Sutton	Wise	Hornung	Hotaling	Rowen
1881	Snyder	Morrill	Burdock	Sutton	Barnes	Hornung	Crowley	Lewis
1880	Powers	Morrill	Burdock	O'Rourke	Sutton	Jones	O'Rourke	Foley
1879	Snyder	Cogswell	Burdock	Morrill	Sutton	Jones	O'Rourke	Houck
1878	Snyder	Morrill	Burdock	Sutton	Wright	Leonard	O'Rourke	Manning
1877	Brown	White	Wright	Morrill	Sutton	Leonard	O'Rourke	Schafer
1876	Brown	Murnane	Morrill	Schafer	Wright	Leonard	O'Rourke	Manning

Top 10 Batting Leaders, Single Season & Career with Team

Games Played: Career with Team

Player	G	PA
1. Hank Aaron	3,076	13,089
2. Eddie Mathews	2,223	9,533
3. Dale Murphy	1,926	8,094
4. Rabbit Maranville	1,795	7,537
5. Fred Tenney	1,737	7,682
6. Chipper Jones	1,651	7,066
7. Herman Long	1,646	7,497
8. Andruw Jones	1,451	5,948
9. Bobby Lowe	1,410	6,184
10. Del Crandall	1,394	5,083

At-Bats: Season

Player	AB	Year
1. Marquis Grissom	671	1996
2. Ralph Garr	668	1973
3. Felipe Alou	666	1966
4. Rafael Furcal	664	2003
5. Felipe Alou	662	1968
6. Andruw Jones	656	2000
7. Felix Millan	652	1969
8. Herman Long	646	1892
9. Terry Pendleton	640	1992
10. Ralph Garr	639	1971

At-Bats: Career with Team

Player	AB	PA
1. Hank Aaron	11,628	13,089
2. Eddie Mathews	8,049	9,533
3. Dale Murphy	7,098	8,094
4. Herman Long	6,777	7,497
5. Rabbit Maranville	6,724	7,537
6. Fred Tenney	6,637	7,682
7. Chipper Jones	5,974	7,066
8. Bobby Lowe	5,617	6,184
9. Andruw Jones	5,271	5,948
10. Tommy Holmes	4,956	5,525

Batting Average: Season

Player	BA	Year
1. Hugh Duffy	.440	1894
2. Rogers Hornsby	.387	1928
3. Dan Brouthers	.373	1889
4. Billy Hamilton	.369	1898
5. Rico Carty	.366	1970
6. Billy Hamilton	.365	1896
7. Hugh Duffy	.362	1893
8. Hank Aaron	.355	1959
9. Chick Stahl	.354	1897
10. Ralph Garr	.353	1974

Batting Average: Career with Team

Player	BA	PA
1. Billy Hamilton	.338	3,206
2. Hugh Duffy	.332	5,214
3. Chick Stahl	.327	2,302
4. Rico Carty	.317	3,098
Ralph Garr	.317	3,447
6. Lance Richbourg	.311	2,660
7. Hank Aaron	.310	13,089
8. Jimmy Collins	.309	2,935
9. Wally Berger	.304	4,549
10. Tommy Holmes	.303	5,525

Total Hits: Season

Player	H	Year
1. Hugh Duffy	237	1894
2. Tommy Holmes	224	1945
3. Hank Aaron	223	1959
4. Ralph Garr	219	1971
5. Felipe Alou	218	1966
6. Ralph Garr	214	1974
7. Bobby Lowe	212	1894
8. Felipe Alou	210	1968
9. Fred Tenney	209	1899
10. Marquis Grissom	207	1996

Total Hits: Career with Team

Player	H	PA
1. Hank Aaron	3600	13,089
2. Eddie Mathews	2201	9,533
3. Fred Tenney	1994	7,682
4. Dale Murphy	1901	8,094
5. Herman Long	1900	7,497
6. Chipper Jones	1811	7,066
7. Rabbit Maranville	1696	7,537
8. Bobby Lowe	1606	6,184
9. Hugh Duffy	1544	5,214
10. Tommy Holmes	1503	5,525

Home Runs: Season

Player	HR	Year
1. Andruw Jones	51	2005
2. Hank Aaron	47	1971
Eddie Mathews	47	1953
4. Eddie Mathews	46	1959
5. Hank Aaron	45	1962
Chipper Jones	45	1999
7. Hank Aaron	44	1957
Hank Aaron	44	1963
Hank Aaron	44	1966
Hank Aaron	44	1969
Andres Galarraga	44	1998
Dale Murphy	44	1987

Home Runs: Career with Team

Player	HR	PA
1. Hank Aaron	733	13,089
2. Eddie Mathews	493	9,533
3. Dale Murphy	371	8,094
4. Chipper Jones	331	7,066
5. Andruw Jones	301	5,948
6. Joe Adcock	239	4,696
7. Bob Horner	215	3,966
8. Javier Lopez	214	4,368
9. Wally Berger	199	4,549
10. Del Crandall	170	5,083

Triples: Season

Player	3B	Year
1. Dick Johnston	20	1887
Harry Stovey	20	1891
3. Chick Stahl	19	1899
4. Dick Johnston	18	1888
Ray Powell	18	1921
6. Ralph Garr	17	1974
Fred Tenney	17	1899
Sam Wise	17	1887
9. Hugh Duffy	16	1894
John Morrill	16	1883
Billy Southworth	16	1923
Chick Stahl	16	1900

Triples: Career with Team

Player	3B	PA
1. Rabbit Maranville	103	7,537
2. Hank Aaron	96	13,08[illegible]

Player		
3. Herman Long	91	7,497
4. John Morrill	80	5,088
5. Bill Bruton	79	4,442
6. Fred Tenney	74	7,682
7. Hugh Duffy	73	5,214
8. Bobby Lowe	71	6,184
Sam Wise	71	3,009
10. Eddie Mathews	70	9,533

Doubles: Season

Player	2B	Year
1. Hugh Duffy	51	1894
2. Marcus Giles	49	2003
3. Tommy Holmes	47	1945
4. Hank Aaron	46	1959
5. Marcus Giles	45	2005
6. Wally Berger	44	1931
Lee Maye	44	1964
8. Tommy Holmes	42	1944
Rogers Hornsby	42	1928
10. Dick Burrus	41	1925
Chipper Jones	41	1997
Chipper Jones	41	1999
King Kelly	41	1889

Doubles: Career with Team

Player	2B	PA
1. Hank Aaron	600	13,089
2. Chipper Jones	355	7,066
3. Eddie Mathews	338	9,533
4. Dale Murphy	306	8,094
5. Herman Long	295	7,497
6. Tommy Holmes	291	5,525
7. Andruw Jones	274	5,948
8. Wally Berger	248	4,549
9. Rabbit Maranville	244	7,537
10. Fred Tenney	242	7,682

Extra-Base Hits: Season

Player	XBH	Year
1. Hank Aaron	92	1959
2. Chipper Jones	87	1999
3. Eddie Mathews	86	1953
4. Hugh Duffy	85	1894
5. Hank Aaron	83	1961
6. Tommy Holmes	81	1945
7. Hank Aaron	79	1962
Hank Aaron	79	1967
Wally Berger	79	1930
10. Andruw Jones	78	2000
Andruw Jones	78	2005
Gary Sheffield	78	2003

Extra-Base Hits: Career with Team

Player	XBH	PA
1. Hank Aaron	1429	13,089
2. Eddie Mathews	901	9,533
3. Dale Murphy	714	8,094
4. Chipper Jones	713	7,066
5. Andruw Jones	607	5,948
6. Wally Berger	499	4,549
7. Herman Long	474	7,497
8. Joe Adcock	458	4,696
9. Tommy Holmes	426	5,525
10. Javier Lopez	418	4,368

Total Bases: Season

Player	TB	Year
1. Hank Aaron	400	1959
2. Hugh Duffy	374	1894
3. Hank Aaron	370	1963
4. Hank Aaron	369	1957
5. Tommy Holmes	367	1945
6. Hank Aaron	366	1962
7. Eddie Mathews	363	1953
8. Chipper Jones	359	1999
9. Hank Aaron	358	1961
10. Felipe Alou	355	1966
Andruw Jones	355	2000

Total Bases: Career with Team

Player	TB	PA
1. Hank Aaron	6,591	13,089
2. Eddie Mathews	4,158	9,533
3. Dale Murphy	3,394	8,094
4. Chipper Jones	3,213	7,066
5. Andruw Jones	2,649	5,948
6. Herman Long	2,641	7,497
7. Fred Tenney	2,435	7,682
8. Rabbit Maranville	2,215	7,537
9. Wally Berger	2,212	4,549
10. Joe Adcock	2,164	4,696

Runs Batted In: Season

Player	RBI	Year
1. Hugh Duffy	145	1894
2. Eddie Mathews	135	1953
3. Hank Aaron	132	1957
Jimmy Collins	132	1897
Gary Sheffield	132	2003
6. Hank Aaron	130	1963
Wally Berger	130	1935
8. Hugh Duffy	129	1897
9. Hank Aaron	128	1962
Andruw Jones	128	2005

Runs Batted In: Career with Team

Player	RBI	PA
1. Hank Aaron	2202	13,089
2. Eddie Mathews	1388	9,533
3. Dale Murphy	1143	8,094
4. Chipper Jones	1111	7,066
5. Herman Long	964	7,497
6. Hugh Duffy	927	5,214
7. Andruw Jones	894	5,948
8. Bobby Lowe	872	6,184
9. Billy Nash	809	5,194
10. Joe Adcock	760	4,696

Runs Scored: Season

Player	R	Year
1. Hugh Duffy	160	1894
2. Bobby Lowe	158	1894
3. Billy Hamilton	152	1896
Billy Hamilton	152	1897
5. Herman Long	149	1893
6. Hugh Duffy	147	1893
7. Herman Long	136	1894
8. Billy Nash	132	1894
9. Dale Murphy	131	1983
10. Jimmy Bannon	130	1894
Hugh Duffy	130	1897
Rafael Furcal	130	2003
Bobby Lowe	130	1893

Runs Scored: Career with Team

Player	R	PA
1. Hank Aaron	2,107	13,089
2. Eddie Mathews	1,452	9,533
3. Herman Long	1,291	7,497
4. Fred Tenney	1,134	7,682
5. Dale Murphy	1,103	8,094
6. Chipper Jones	1,101	7,066
7. Bobby Lowe	999	6,184
8. Hugh Duffy	996	5,214
9. Andruw Jones	855	5,948
Billy Nash	855	5,194

Walks: Season

Player	BB	Year
1. Bob Elliott	131	1948
2. Jimmy Wynn	127	1976
3. Darrell Evans	126	1974
Chipper Jones	126	1999
5. Darrell Evans	124	1973

Eddie Mathews	124	1963
7. Earl Torgeson	119	1950
8. J.D. Drew	118	2004
9. Jeff Burroughs	117	1978
10. Dale Murphy	115	1987

Walks: Career with Team

Player	BB	PA
1. Eddie Mathews	1,376	9,533
2. Hank Aaron	1,297	13,089
3. Chipper Jones	1,009	7,066
4. Dale Murphy	912	8,094
5. Fred Tenney	750	7,682
6. Billy Nash	598	5,194
7. Andruw Jones	565	5,948
8. Darrell Evans	563	3,522
9. Rabbit Maranville	561	7,537
10. Billy Hamilton	545	3,206

Strikeouts: Season

Player	SO	Year
1. Andruw Jones	147	2004
2. Andres Galarraga	146	1998
3. Dale Murphy	145	1978
4. Andruw Jones	142	2001
Dale Murphy	142	1989
6. Dale Murphy	141	1985
Dale Murphy	141	1986
8. Dale Murphy	136	1987
9. Andruw Jones	135	2002
10. Vince DiMaggio	134	1938
Dale Murphy	134	1982
Dale Murphy	134	1984

Strikeouts: Career with Team

Player	SO	PA
1. Dale Murphy	1,581	8,094
2. Eddie Mathews	1,387	9,533
3. Hank Aaron	1,294	13,089
4. Andruw Jones	1,129	5,948
5. Chipper Jones	933	7,066
6. Jeff Blauser	792	4,598
7. Joe Adcock	732	4,696
8. Javier Lopez	728	4,368
9. John Morrill	632	5,088
10. Ron Gant	600	3,546

Slugging Percentage: Season

Player	SLG	Year
1. Hugh Duffy	.694	1894
2. Javier Lopez	.687	2003
3. Hank Aaron	.669	1971
4. Hank Aaron	.643	1973
5. Hank Aaron	.636	1959
6. Chipper Jones	.633	1999
7. Rogers Hornsby	.632	1928
8. Eddie Mathews	.627	1953
9. Fred McGriff	.623	1994
10. Hank Aaron	.618	1962

Slugging Percentage: Career with Team

Player	SLG	PA
1. Hank Aaron	.567	13,089
2. Chipper Jones	.538	7,066
3. Wally Berger	.533	4,549
4. Ryan Klesko	.525	2,772
5. Eddie Mathews	.517	9,533
6. Fred McGriff	.516	2,705
7. Joe Adcock	.511	4,696
8. Bob Horner	.508	3,966
9. Andruw Jones	.503	5,948
10. Javier Lopez	.502	4,368

On-Base Percentage: Season

Player	OBP	Year
1. Hugh Duffy	.502	1894
2. Rogers Hornsby	.498	1928
3. Billy Hamilton	.480	1898
4. Billy Hamilton	.477	1896
5. Dan Brouthers	.462	1889
6. Billy Hamilton	.461	1897
7. Rico Carty	.454	1970
8. Billy Hamilton	.449	1900
9. Chipper Jones	.441	1999
10. J.D. Drew	.436	2004

On-Base Percentage: Career with Team

Player	OBP	PA
1. Billy Hamilton	.456	3,206
2. Chipper Jones	.401	7,066
3. Bob Elliott	.398	3,047
4. Hugh Duffy	.394	5,214
5. Rico Carty	.388	3,098
6. Chick Stahl	.387	2,302
7. Earl Torgeson	.385	2,993
Sid Gordon	.385	2,350
9. Tommy McCarthy	.382	2,528
10. Eddie Mathews	.379	9,533

OPS (On-Base Percentage + Slugging Percentage): Season

Player	OPS	Year
1. Hugh Duffy	1.196	1894
2. Rogers Hornsby	1.130	1928
3. Hank Aaron	1.079	1971
4. Chipper Jones	1.074	1999
5. Javier Lopez	1.065	2003
6. Hank Aaron	1.045	1973
7. Rico Carty	1.037	1970
Hank Aaron	1.037	1959
9. Eddie Mathews	1.033	1953
10. Chipper Jones	1.032	2001

OPS (On-Base Percentage + Slugging Percentage): Career with Team

Player	OPS	PA
1. Hank Aaron	.944	13,089
2. Chipper Jones	.939	7,066
3. Eddie Mathews	.896	9,533
4. Wally Berger	.894	4,549
5. Ryan Klesko	.886	2,772
Sid Gordon	.886	2,350
7. Fred McGriff	.885	2,705
8. Rico Carty	.884	3,098
9. Bob Elliott	.883	3,047
10. David Justice	.873	3,349

Stolen Bases: Season

Player	SB	Year
1. King Kelly	84	1887
2. Billy Hamilton	83	1896
3. Otis Nixon	72	1991
4. King Kelly	68	1889
5. Billy Hamilton	66	1897
6. Tom Brown	63	1889
7. Herman Long	60	1891
8. Herman Long	57	1892
Hap Myers	57	1913
Harry Stovey	57	1891

Stolen Bases: Career with Team

Player	SB	PA
1. Herman Long	431	7,497
2. Hugh Duffy	331	5,214
3. Billy Hamilton	274	3,206

Player	Sac	PA
4. Bobby Lowe	260	6,184
Fred Tenney	260	7,682
6. Hank Aaron	240	13,089
7. King Kelly	238	1,968
8. Billy Nash	232	5,194
9. Rabbit Maranville	194	7,537
10. Rafael Furcal	189	3,649

SACRIFICE HITS: SEASON

Player	Sac	Year
1. Stuffy McInnis	37	1923
2. Beals Becker	35	1909
Billy Southworth	35	1921
4. Bill Sweeney	33	1912
5. Jimmy Welsh	32	1926
6. Johnny Evers	31	1914
Johnny Logan	31	1956
Freddie Maguire	31	1931
9. Fred Tenney	29	1902
10. Jimmy Welsh	28	1927

SACRIFICE HITS: CAREER WITH TEAM

Player	Sac	PA
1. Fred Tenney	242	7,682
2. Rabbit Maranville	220	7,537
3. Tom Glavine	168	1,265
4. Herman Long	138	7,497
5. Phil Niekro	129	1,707
6. Johnny Logan	121	5,538
7. John Smoltz	104	988
8. Red Smith	103	2,850
9. Bill Sweeney	101	3,701
10. Greg Maddux	98	897

HIT BY PITCH: SEASON

Player	HBP	Year
1. Tommy Tucker	29	1891
2. Tommy Tucker	26	1892
3. Andres Galarraga	25	1998
Tommy Tucker	25	1890
5. Jeff Blauser	20	1997
Tommy Tucker	20	1893
7. Dan McGann	19	1908
Tommy Tucker	19	1895
9. Andres Galarraga	17	2000
Tommy Tucker	17	1894

HIT BY PITCH: CAREER WITH TEAM

Player	HBP	PA
1. Tommy Tucker	150	4,045
2. Jeff Blauser	75	4,598
3. Andruw Jones	62	5,948
4. Bobby Lowe	57	6,184
5. Fred Tenney	53	7,682
6. Javier Lopez	51	4,368
7. Herman Long	46	7,497
8. Jimmy Collins	45	2,935
9. Andres Galarraga	42	1,196
Mack Jones	42	2,318

Top 10 Pitching Leaders, Single Season & Career with Team

GAMES PITCHED: SEASON

Player	GP	Year
1. Chris Reitsma	84	2004
2. Brad Clontz	81	1996
3. Ray King	80	2003
4. Antonio Alfonseca	79	2004
5. Rick Camp	77	1980
Mark Wohlers	77	1996
7. Chris Reitsma	76	2005
8. Kerry Ligtenberg	75	1998
John Smoltz	75	2002
10. Greg McMichael	74	1993
Mike Remlinger	74	2001
John Rocker	74	1999
Mike Stanton	74	1991

GAMES PITCHED: CAREER WITH TEAM

Player	GP	IP
1. Phil Niekro	740	4,622.7
2. Warren Spahn	714	5,046.0
3. John Smoltz	635	2,929.3
4. Gene Garber	557	856.0
5. Kid Nichols	556	4,538.0
6. Tom Glavine	505	3,344.7
7. Lew Burdette	468	2,638.0
8. Rick Camp	414	942.3
9. Mark Wohlers	388	386.3
10. Greg Maddux	363	2,526.7

INNINGS PITCHED: SEASON

Player	IP	Year
1. John Clarkson	620.0	1889
2. Charlie Buffinton	587.0	1884
3. Tommy Bond	555.3	1879
4. Jim Whitney	552.3	1881
5. Tommy Bond	532.7	1878
6. Tommy Bond	521.0	1877
7. Jim Whitney	514.0	1883
8. Charles Radbourn	509.3	1886
9. Tommy Bond	493.0	1880
10. John Clarkson	483.3	1888

INNINGS PITCHED: CAREER WITH TEAM

Player	IP
1. Warren Spahn	5,046.0
2. Phil Niekro	4,622.7
3. Kid Nichols	4,538.0
4. Tom Glavine	3,344.7
5. John Smoltz	2,929.3
6. Lew Burdette	2,638.0
7. Vic Willis	2,575.0
8. Greg Maddux	2,526.7
9. Jim Whitney	2,263.7
10. Tommy Bond	2,127.3

BATTERS FACED: SEASON

Player	BF	Year
1. John Clarkson	2,736	1889
2. Charlie Buffinton	2,383	1884
3. Jim Whitney	2,301	1881
4. Tommy Bond	2,189	1879
5. Tommy Bond	2,165	1877
6. Charles Radbourn	2,162	1886
7. Tommy Bond	2,159	1878
8. Jim Whitney	2,101	1883
9. Tommy Bond	2,082	1880
10. John Clarkson	2,029	1888

BATTERS FACED: CAREER WITH TEAM

Player	BF	IP
1. Warren Spahn	20,701	5,046.0
2. Phil Niekro	19,238	4,622.7
3. Kid Nichols	19,109	4,538.0
4. Tom Glavine	14,030	3,344.7

5. John Smoltz	11,997	2,929.3
6. Lew Burdette	10,931	2,638.0
7. Greg Maddux	10,081	2,526.7
8. Jim Whitney	9,375	2,263.7
9. Tommy Bond	8,708	2,127.3
10. Dick Rudolph	8,220	2,035.0

Games Started: Season

Player	GS	Year
1. John Clarkson	72	1889
2. Charlie Buffinton	67	1884
3. Tommy Bond	64	1879
4. Jim Whitney	63	1881
5. Tommy Bond	59	1878
6. Tommy Bond	58	1877
Charles Radbourn	58	1886
8. Tommy Bond	57	1880
9. Jim Whitney	56	1883
10. John Clarkson	54	1888

Games Started: Career with Team

Player	GS	IP
1. Warren Spahn	635	5,046.0
2. Phil Niekro	595	4,622.7
3. Tom Glavine	505	3,344.7
4. Kid Nichols	501	4,538.0
5. John Smoltz	394	2,929.3
6. Greg Maddux	363	2,526.7
7. Lew Burdette	330	2,638.0
8. Vic Willis	302	2,575.0
9. Jim Whitney	254	2,263.7
10. Tommy Bond	241	2,127.3

Complete Games: Season

Player	CG	Year
1. John Clarkson	68	1889
2. Charlie Buffinton	63	1884
3. Tommy Bond	59	1879
4. Tommy Bond	58	1877
5. Tommy Bond	57	1878
Charles Radbourn	57	1886
Jim Whitney	57	1881
8. Jim Whitney	54	1883
9. John Clarkson	53	1888
10. Jim Whitney	50	1885

Complete Games: Career with Team

Player	CG	IP
1. Kid Nichols	475	4,538.0
2. Warren Spahn	374	5,046.0
3. Vic Willis	268	2,575.0
4. Jim Whitney	242	2,263.7
5. John Clarkson	226	2,092.7
Phil Niekro	226	4,622.7
7. Tommy Bond	225	2,127.3
8. Jack Stivetts	176	1,798.7
9. Dick Rudolph	171	2,035.0
10. Charlie Buffinton	166	1,547.3

Games Won: Season

Player	W	Year
1. John Clarkson	49	1889
2. Charlie Buffinton	48	1884
3. Tommy Bond	43	1879
4. Tommy Bond	40	1877
Tommy Bond	40	1878
6. Jim Whitney	37	1883
7. Kid Nichols	35	1892
Jack Stivetts	35	1892
9. Kid Nichols	34	1893
10. John Clarkson	33	1888
John Clarkson	33	1891

Games Won: Career with Team

Player	W	IP
1. Warren Spahn	356	5,046.0
2. Kid Nichols	329	4,538.0
3. Phil Niekro	268	4,622.7
4. Tom Glavine	242	3,344.7
5. Greg Maddux	194	2,526.7
6. Lew Burdette	179	2,638.0
7. John Smoltz	177	2,929.3
8. Vic Willis	151	2,575.0
9. Tommy Bond	149	2,127.3
John Clarkson	149	2,092.7

Games Lost: Season

Player	L	Year
1. Jim Whitney	33	1881
2. Jim Whitney	32	1885
3. Charles Radbourn	31	1886
4. Tommy Bond	29	1880
Vic Willis	29	1905
6. Charlie Buffinton	27	1885
7. Ben Cantwell	25	1935
Gus Dorner	25	1906
Vic Willis	25	1904
Irv Young	25	1906

Games Lost: Career with Team

Player	L	IP
1. Phil Niekro	230	4,622.7
2. Warren Spahn	229	5,046.0
3. Kid Nichols	183	4,538.0
4. Vic Willis	147	2,575.0
5. Tom Glavine	143	3,344.7
6. John Smoltz	128	2,929.3
7. Jim Whitney	121	2,263.7
8. Lew Burdette	120	2,638.0
Bob Smith	120	1,813.3
10. Ed Brandt	119	1,761.7

Winning Percentage: Season

Player	W%	Year
1. Greg Maddux	.905	1995
2. John Smoltz	.850	1998
3. Tom Hughes	.842	1916
4. Greg Maddux	.826	1997
5. Jorge Sosa	.812	2005
6. Phil Niekro	.810	1982
7. Denny Neagle	.800	1997
8. Bill James	.788	1914
Fred Klobedanz	.788	1897
10. Tom Glavine	.786	1993

Winning Percentage: Career with Team

Player	W%	IP
1. Greg Maddux	.688	2,526.7
2. Fred Klobedanz	.679	702.0
3. Harry Staley	.655	1,023.7
4. John Clarkson	.645	2,092.7
5. Kid Nichols	.643	4,538.0
6. Tommy Bond	.631	2,127.3
7. Tom Glavine	.629	3,344.7
8. Jack Stivetts	.627	1,798.7
9. Ted Lewis	.624	1,088.7
10. Kevin Millwood	.620	1,004.3

Shutouts: Season

Player	SHO	Year
1. Tommy Bond	11	1879
2. Tommy Bond	9	1878
3. Charlie Buffinton	8	1884
John Clarkson	8	1889
5. Kid Nichols	7	1890
Togie Pittinger	7	1902
Warren Spahn	7	1947
Warren Spahn	7	1951
Warren Spahn	7	1963
Irv Young	7	1905

Shutouts: Career with Team

Player	SHO	IP
1. Warren Spahn	63	5,046.0
2. Kid Nichols	44	4,538.0

3. Phil Niekro	43	4,622.7
4. Lew Burdette	30	2,638.0
5. Tommy Bond	29	2,127.3
6. Dick Rudolph	27	2,035.0
7. Vic Willis	26	2,575.0
8. Tom Glavine	22	3,344.7
Lefty Tyler	22	1,687.7
10. Greg Maddux	21	2,526.7

ERA: Season

Player	ERA	Year
1. Greg Maddux	1.56	1994
2. Greg Maddux	1.63	1995
3. Phil Niekro	1.87	1967
4. Bill James	1.90	1914
5. Tommy Bond	1.96	1879
6. Lefty Tyler	2.02	1916
7. Tommy Bond	2.06	1878
8. Bill Sowders	2.07	1888
9. Pat Ragan	2.08	1916
10. Jim Whitney	2.09	1884

ERA: Career with Team

Player	ERA	IP
1. Tommy Bond	2.21	2,127.3
2. Tom Hughes	2.22	550.7
3. Bill James	2.28	541.7
4. Jim Whitney	2.49	2,263.7
5. Art Nehf	2.52	885.7
6. Dick Rudolph	2.62	2,035.0
7. Greg Maddux	2.63	2,526.7
8. Pat Ragan	2.74	775.7
9. John Clarkson	2.82	2,092.7
Vic Willis	2.82	2,575.0

Earned Runs Allowed: Season

Player	ER	Year
1. Kid Nichols	215	1894
Charles Radbourn	215	1887
3. John Clarkson	188	1889
4. Jack Stivetts	184	1894
5. Charles Radbourn	170	1886
6. Kid Nichols	166	1893
7. Fred Klobedanz	158	1897
Harry Staley	158	1894
9. Jim Whitney	152	1881
10. Harry Staley	150	1893
Jack Stivetts	150	1895
Jack Stivetts	150	1896

Earned Runs Allowed: Career with Team

Player	ER	IP
1. Warren Spahn	1,710	5,046.0
2. Phil Niekro	1,645	4,622.7
3. Kid Nichols	1,511	4,538.0
4. Tom Glavine	1,252	3,344.7
5. John Smoltz	1,060	2,929.3
6. Lew Burdette	1,036	2,638.0
7. Jack Stivetts	823	1,798.7
8. Bob Smith	818	1,813.3
9. Vic Willis	808	2,575.0
10. Ed Brandt	785	1,761.7

Strikeouts: Season

Player	K	Year
1. Charlie Buffinton	417	1884
2. Jim Whitney	345	1883
3. John Clarkson	284	1889
4. John Smoltz	276	1996
5. Jim Whitney	270	1884
6. Phil Niekro	262	1977
7. Phil Niekro	248	1978
8. Charlie Buffinton	242	1885
9. John Smoltz	241	1997
10. Kid Nichols	240	1891

Strikeouts : Career with Team

Player	K	IP
1. Phil Niekro	2,912	4,622.7
2. John Smoltz	2,567	2,929.3
3. Warren Spahn	2,493	5,046.0
4. Tom Glavine	2,054	3,344.7
5. Greg Maddux	1,828	2,526.7
6. Kid Nichols	1,667	4,538.0
7. Vic Willis	1,161	2,575.0
8. Jim Whitney	1,157	2,263.7
9. Lew Burdette	923	2,638.0
10. Charlie Buffinton	911	1,547.3

Strikeouts Per Nine IP: Season

Player	K/9	Year
1. John Smoltz	9.79	1996
2. John Smoltz	9.29	1998
3. John Smoltz	9.02	1995
4. John Smoltz	8.47	1997
5. Kevin Millwood	8.41	1998
6. Kevin Millwood	8.09	1999
7. John Smoltz	7.84	1992
8. Greg Maddux	7.77	1995
9. John Smoltz	7.68	1993
Jaret Wright	7.68	2004

Strikeouts Per Nine IP: Career with Team

Player	K/9	IP
1. John Smoltz	7.89	2929.3
2. Kevin Millwood	7.53	1004.3
3. Kent Mercker	7.32	532.7
4. Steve Bedrosian	7.23	696.0
5. Denny Lemaster	7.03	1077.3
6. Greg Maddux	6.51	2526.7
7. Tony Cloninger	6.18	1215.3
8. Steve Avery	6.00	1222.3
9. Pete Smith	5.84	663.7
10. Gene Garber	5.68	856.0

Hits Allowed: Season

Player	HA	Year
1. John Clarkson	589	1889
2. Tommy Bond	571	1878
3. Tommy Bond	559	1880
4. Jim Whitney	548	1881
5. Tommy Bond	543	1879
6. Tommy Bond	530	1877
7. Charles Radbourn	521	1886
8. Charlie Buffinton	506	1884
9. Charles Radbourn	505	1887
10. Jim Whitney	503	1885

Hits Allowed: Career with Team

Player	HA	IP
1. Warren Spahn	4,620	5,046.0
2. Kid Nichols	4,434	4,538.0
3. Phil Niekro	4,224	4,622.7
4. Tom Glavine	3,174	3,344.7
5. Lew Burdette	2,698	2,638.0
6. John Smoltz	2,537	2,929.3
7. Vic Willis	2,386	2,575.0
8. Greg Maddux	2,273	2,526.7
9. Tommy Bond	2,243	2,127.3
10. Jim Whitney	2,219	2,263.7

Hits Allowed Per Nine IP: Season

Player	H/9	Year
1. Greg Maddux	6.31	1995
2. Kevin Millwood	6.63	1999
3. Tom Hughes	6.68	1915
Greg Maddux	6.68	1994

5. Buzz Capra	6.76	1974
6. John Smoltz	6.92	1989
7. Damian Moss	7.04	2002
8. John Smoltz	7.06	1996
9. Bill James	7.07	1914
Pat Ragan	7.07	1916

Hits Allowed Per Nine IP: Career with Team

Player	H/9	IP
1. Tom Hughes	6.77	550.7
2. Kent Mercker	7.69	532.7
Steve Bedrosian	7.69	696.0
4. Bill James	7.79	541.7
John Smoltz	7.79	2,929.3
6. Lefty Tyler	8.00	1,687.7
7. Art Nehf	8.05	885.7
8. Greg Maddux	8.10	2,526.7
9. Bob Buhl	8.11	1,599.7
10. Gus Dorner	8.13	785.7

Walks Allowed: Season

Player	BB	Year
1. John Clarkson	203	1889
2. Jack Stivetts	171	1892
3. Phil Niekro	164	1977
4. John Clarkson	154	1891
5. Chick Fraser	149	1905
6. Vic Willis	148	1898
7. Togie Pittinger	144	1904
Bill Stemmeyer	144	1886
9. Togie Pittinger	143	1903
10. John Clarkson	140	1890

Walks Allowed: Career with Team

Player	BB	IP
1. Phil Niekro	1,458	4,622.7
2. Warren Spahn	1,378	5,046.0
3. Kid Nichols	1,159	4,538.0
4. Tom Glavine	1,140	3,344.7
5. John Smoltz	882	2,929.3
6. Vic Willis	854	2,575.0
7. Bob Buhl	782	1,599.7
8. Lefty Tyler	678	1,687.7
9. John Clarkson	676	2,092.7
10. Jack Stivetts	651	1,798.7

Walks Allowed Per Nine IP: Season

Player	BB/9	Year
1. Tommy Bond	0.39	1879
2. Tommy Bond	0.56	1878
3. Jim Whitney	0.61	1883
4. Tommy Bond	0.62	1877
5. Bobby Mathews	0.69	1882
6. Jim Whitney	0.72	1884
7. Jim Whitney	0.75	1885
8. Greg Maddux	0.77	1997
9. Tommy Bond	0.82	1880
10. Foghorn Bradley	0.83	1876

Walks Per Nine IP: Career with Team

Player	BB/9	IP
1. Tommy Bond	0.59	2,127.3
2. Jim Whitney	0.91	2,263.7
3. Greg Maddux	1.36	2,526.7
4. Charlie Buffinton	1.70	1,547.3
5. Dick Rudolph	1.77	2,035.0
6. Ken Johnson	1.81	769.7
7. Huck Betts	1.85	836.3
8. Lew Burdette	1.90	2,638.0
9. Jesse Barnes	1.95	1,182.7
Irv Young	1.95	1,066.7

WHIP (Walks + Hits Per Nine IP): Season

Player	WHIP	Year
1. Greg Maddux	0.811	1995
2. Jim Whitney	0.890	1884
3. Greg Maddux	0.896	1994
4. Greg Maddux	0.946	1997
5. Tom Hughes	0.949	1915
6. Dick Rudolph	0.974	1916
7. Greg Maddux	0.980	1998
8. Pat Jarvis	0.984	1968
9. Charlie Buffinton	0.991	1884
10. Kevin Millwood	0.996	1999

WHIP (Walks + Hits Per IP): Career with Team

Player	WHIP	IP
1. Tom Hughes	1.022	550.7
2. Greg Maddux	1.051	2,526.7
3. Jim Whitney	1.082	2,263.7
4. Art Nehf	1.116	885.7
5. Tommy Bond	1.120	2,127.3
6. Dick Rudolph	1.154	2,035.0
7. John Smoltz	1.167	2,929.3
8. Ken Johnson	1.171	769.7
9. Charlie Buffinton	1.179	1,547.3
10. Pat Ragan	1.180	775.7

Home Runs Allowed: Season

Player	HRA	Year
1. Phil Niekro	41	1979
2. Phil Niekro	40	1970
3. Lew Burdette	38	1959
4. Johnny Sain	34	1950
5. Lew Burdette	31	1961
Horacio Ramirez	31	2005
7. Denny Lemaster	30	1963
Phil Niekro	30	1980
Tony Cloninger	29	1966
Phil Niekro	29	1975
Warren Spahn	29	1958

Home Runs Allowed: Career with Team

Player	HRA	IP
1. Warren Spahn	408	5,046.0
2. Phil Niekro	392	4,622.7
3. Lew Burdette	251	2,638.0
4. Tom Glavine	247	3,344.7
5. John Smoltz	234	2,929.3
6. Greg Maddux	152	2,526.7
7. Kid Nichols	151	4,538.0
8. Rick Mahler	132	1,558.7
9. Bob Buhl	130	1,599.7
10. Tony Cloninger	125	1,215.3
Denny Lemaster	125	1,077.3

Saves: Season

Player	SV	Year
1. John Smoltz	55	2002
2. John Smoltz	45	2003
3. John Smoltz	44	2004
4. Mark Wohlers	39	1996
5. John Rocker	38	1999
6. Mark Wohlers	33	1997
7. Gene Garber	30	1982
Kerry Ligtenberg	30	1998
9. Mike Stanton	27	1993
Cecil Upshaw	27	1969

Saves: Career with Team

Player	SV	IP
1. John Smoltz	154	2,929.3
2. Gene Garber	141	856.0
3. Mark Wohlers	112	386.3
4. John Rocker	83	195.3
5. Cecil Upshaw	78	409.7
6. Rick Camp	57	942.3
7. Mike Stanton	55	289.7

8. Don McMahon	50	344.7
9. Kerry Ligtenberg	44	266.7
Greg McMichael	44	334.0

Wild Pitches: Season

Player	WP	Year
1. Bill Stemmeyer	63	1886
2. Jim Whitney	46	1881
3. Jim Whitney	37	1883
4. John Clarkson	33	1888
5. Jim Whitney	32	1885
6. Kid Nichols	30	1890
7. Jim Whitney	29	1882
8. Charlie Buffinton	28	1885
9. Tony Cloninger	27	1966
10. Tommy Bond	24	1880
Charlie Buffinton	24	1884
Kid Nichols	24	1892

Wild Pitches: Career with Team

Player	WP	IP
1. Phil Niekro	200	4,622.7
2. Jim Whitney	162	2,263.7
3. Kid Nichols	156	4,538.0
4. John Smoltz	130	2,929.3
5. Tony Cloninger	91	1,215.3
6. John Clarkson	89	2,092.7
7. Charlie Buffinton	80	1,547.3

8. Warren Spahn	79	5,046.0
9. Bill Stemmeyer	77	479.0
10. Vic Willis	74	2,575.0

Hit Batsmen: Season

Player	HB	Year
1. Vic Willis	30	1898
Vic Willis	30	1899
3. Fred Klobedanz	23	1897
4. Kid Madden	20	1887
5. John Clarkson	17	1889
Kid Nichols	17	1891
Togie Pittinger	17	1903
8. Gus Dorner	16	1906
Kid Madden	16	1889
Kid Nichols	16	1893
Big Jeff Pfeffer	16	1906
Togie Pittinger	16	1902

Hit Batsmen: Career with Team

Player	HB	IP
1. Vic Willis	134	2,575.0
2. Kid Nichols	122	4,538.0
3. Phil Niekro	108	4,622.7
4. Greg Maddux	65	2,526.7
5. Togie Pittinger	63	1,471.7
6. Lefty Tyler	59	1,687.7
7. Kid Madden	51	664.0
8. Tom Glavine	50	3,344.7

9. Gus Dorner	48	785.7
10. John Smoltz	41	2,929.3

Games Finished: Season

Player	GF	Year
1. John Smoltz	68	2002
2. Mark Wohlers	64	1996
3. John Rocker	61	1999
John Smoltz	61	2004
5. Gene Garber	56	1982
Kerry Ligtenberg	56	1998
7. Gene Garber	55	1979
John Smoltz	55	2003
Mark Wohlers	55	1997
10. Joe Boever	53	1989

Games Finished: Career with Team

Player	GF	IP
1. Gene Garber	388	856.0
2. Mark Wohlers	233	386.3
3. John Smoltz	204	2,929.3
4. Cecil Upshaw	176	409.7
5. Rick Camp	170	942.3
6. Don McMahon	157	344.7
7. John Rocker	146	195.3
8. Steve Bedrosian	143	696.0
9. Kerry Ligtenberg	133	266.7
10. Bob Smith	132	1,813.3

Warren Spahn

Significant Braves

AARON, HANK (OF)
(1954–1974)

Hank Aaron began his professional ballplaying career in 1952 as a member of the barnstorming Indianapolis Clowns, baseball's equivalent of the Harlem Globetrotters. After eating in a Washington, D.C., restaurant while in town for some exhibition games, Aaron and the other players got up to leave when they heard the sound of breaking glass coming from the kitchen. Restaurant personnel were breaking all the dishes the black players had just eaten off of because the forks and spoons that they had placed in their mouths had touched the dishes. The bitter irony of playing in the capital city of the land of freedom and equality while enduring such prejudice remained with Aaron for the rest of his life and dictated his future actions.

When a Braves scout saw Aaron play with the Clowns, he convinced the Braves owner to quickly purchase Aaron's contract for $7,500. At the close of spring training in 1954, the Braves and Dodgers toured together on their way north prior to the season. Aaron made a habit of hanging around Jackie Robinson's room, a nightly gathering spot for all the black players on the two teams, including Roy Campanella, Joe Black, Jim Gilliam, Don Newcombe, Robinson, and Aaron. The young slugger was a good listener, soaking in what the veterans had to say regarding matters on the field as well as how to handle racially sensitive issues. "Those hotel rooms were my college," Aaron would later say. Aaron felt that black players were better than white players in the 1950s and '60s because they had to be—and they knew they had to be.

During his career, Aaron hit over .300 14 times, scored 100+ runs 15 times, drove in more than 100 RBIs 11 times, hit 20 or more homers in 20 straight years, and made the All-Star Game 21 consecutive years. He won two batting titles (1956 and 1959), three Gold Gloves (1958–1960), and the 1957 NL MVP Award. His main claim to fame, of course, was breaking Babe Ruth's career record of 714 homers, a total once considered unbeatable. In 1969 Aaron was starting to think of retirement, but baseball historian Lee Allen convinced him to play as long as he could so that he could break many of baseball's important records, thereby giving him the recognition he craved, as well as the credibility and the platform to air his concerns about racial inequality. Aaron accepted Allen's challenge and continued to play with a fierce determination. His pursuit of Ruth became an obsession. Aaron not only joined the 3,000-hit club, he amassed 3,771 career hits. He still holds the career records for home runs (755), RBIs (2,297), extra-base hits (1,477), and total bases (6,856). He is tied with Babe Ruth for second in runs scored with 2,174, trailing only Ty Cobb.

When Aaron began to close in on Ruth's 714 career home runs, the hate mail began in earnest. While he and his family received many death threats, Aaron received so many letters of encouragement (930,000) that the U.S. Post Office awarded him a plaque for having received the most mail of any non-politician in America. He finished the 1973 campaign with 713 homers, one behind Ruth. Just before the 1974 season began, a controversy arose. The Atlanta Braves were scheduled to start the season on the road with three games at Cincinnati. Braves management wanted Aaron to tie and break the record at home, so it was announced he would sit out the first three games of the season. Many sportswriters of the day felt that such an action would be a travesty and loudly voiced their protests in the media. Commissioner Bowie Kuhn agreed and ordered Aaron to play at least two of the three games in Cincinnati. Aaron complied, hitting a home run in his first at-bat of the season to tie Ruth. He sat out the second game, then went 0-for-3 in the third game. In the next series, at home against the Dodgers, Aaron broke Ruth's record with a home run off Al Downing. He finished the year with 733 career homers and was promptly traded to the Milwaukee Brewers, where he hit 22 more for a career total of 755. Aaron later said that he believed the reason he was chosen to break Ruth's record was so that he could carry on where Jackie Robinson left off. Hank Aaron was elected to the Hall of Fame in 1982.

CAREER BRAVES RECORD:

Games	AB	Hits	Runs
3,076	11,628	3,600	2,107
Avg	**HR**	**RBI**	**SB**
.310	733	2,202	240

BERGER, WALLY (OF)
(1930–1937)

The greatest slugger to wear a Braves uniform until the arrival of Hank Aaron and Eddie Mathews, Wally Berger once played on the same high school team as Hall of Famer Joe Cronin. Originally in the Cubs' minor league organization, Berger was traded to the Boston Braves just before the 1930 season. He exploded with a debut unlike any other rookie in major league history, batting .310 with a rookie record 38 homers and 119 RBIs. Although Frank Robinson tied his rookie home-run record in 1956, it wasn't broken until 1987, when Mark McGwire hit 49 dingers. Berger batted over .300 and had 100+ RBIs four times each during his 11-year career, and was the only legitimate home run threat the Braves had at the time. The fact that he hit 25 or more home runs in five of his first seven seasons with Boston is made even more impressive when you consider that he had no one to protect him in the lineup; pitchers could routinely pitch around him. (Gene Moore hit 13 homers in 1936, the most by any other Brave during those seven years, and on only two other occasions did a Brave hit 10 or more home runs during that span.) Berger also had to contend with playing in one of the largest parks in the major leagues. When Berger led the NL in homers in 1935 with 34, Babe Ruth was second on the team with six. After suffering a shoulder injury, Berger, who played in baseball's first four All-Star Games from 1933 to 1936, was traded to the New York Giants in 1937 and helped them win the pennant. In 1938 he was sent to Cincinnati, where he helped the Reds win the pennant the following year. When Cincinnati released him after the season, Berger signed with the Phillies, but played only 20 games before retiring.

CAREER BRAVES RECORD:

Games	AB	Hits	Runs
1,057	4,153	1,263	651
Avg	**HR**	**RBI**	**SB**
.304	199	746	29

BOND, TOMMY (SP)
(1877–1881)

Tommy Bond spent two seasons in the National Association (predecessor to the National League) from 1874 to 1875, winning 22 and 19 games respectively for Brooklyn and Hartford. When Hartford shifted to the NL in 1876, Bond became one of the new league's stars, winning 31 games. He joined Boston in 1877 and raised his game to another level, collecting 40, 40, and 43 wins the next three years with ERAs of 2.11, 2.06, and 1.96. In so doing, Bond became the last major league pitcher to win 40 or more games in three consecutive years. In 1880 he slipped to 26–29 and, after starting the 1881 campaign 0–3, he was replaced in the starting lineup, his career effectively over at the age of 25, another of baseball's many victims of overuse. Over the next three seasons, Bond pitched briefly for Indianapolis of the American Association and Boston of the Union Association before ending his playing career. Bond spent a short time managing and umpiring before becoming the coach at Harvard, where two of his players included John Clarkson and Tim Keefe, both future Hall of Famers.

CAREER BRAVES RECORD:

W	L	W%	ERA	SV
149	87	.631	2.21	0
K	**BB**	**SHO**	**IP**	
627	140	29	2,127.3	

BURDETTE, LEW (SP/RP)
(1951–1963)

The New York Yankees signed Lew Burdette as an amateur free agent in April 1947; they brought him to the majors for two appearances in 1950 before trading him to the Braves in August 1951. Burdette was primarily a reliever from 1951 to 1953, compiling a 21–16 record with 15 saves, before joining the starting rotation in 1954. He had a winning record over the next nine years as a starter, including two 20-win seasons in 1958 and 1959. Burdette's greatest glory came in the 1957 World Series when he beat the Yankees three times, throwing two shutouts as the Braves defeated New York in seven games. His third win in Game 7 came with just two days' rest, and for his efforts he was honored with the World Series MVP Award. Burdette was often accused of throwing a spitter—a writer once said that if Burdette ever won a Cy Young Award it should come in the form of a spittoon—but he always denied the charge. In 1959 Burdette was the winner in one of baseball's most famous games, a 1–0 complete-game affair in which Harvey Haddix of the Pirates pitched a perfect game against the Braves for 12 innings before the Braves won in the 13th. On August 18, 1960, Burdette just missed a perfect game himself when he allowed only one walk in a no-hitter over the Phillies. After being traded to the Cardinals in mid-1963, Burdette, a two-time All-Star, bounced around for four-plus years with four different teams before retiring in 1967 to work for a cable television company.

CAREER BRAVES RECORD:

W	L	W%	ERA	SV
179	120	.599	3.53	23
K	**BB**	**SHO**	**IP**	
923	557	30	2,638.0	

CLARKSON, JOHN (SP)
(1888–1892)

After arriving from Chicago for the record-tying price of $10,000 (the same amount paid for King Kelly a year earlier), Clarkson enjoyed four-plus fine seasons with Boston. He won 33 games in 1888 before winning pitching's Triple Crown in 1889 with 49 wins, 284 strikeouts, and a 2.73 ERA. He also pitched an incredible 620 innings with 68 complete games that season, but the overuse would come back to haunt him later; 1889 turned out to be the last year he led the league in any major pitching category. Though his numbers were beginning to slip, Clarkson still won 26 games in 1890 and 33 in 1891 before being traded to Cleveland after starting the 1892 season with an 8–6 record. Clarkson finished his career with 49 wins combined in three years with the Cleveland Spiders. He retired at the age of 32, but his pitching arm had preceded him, victimized by overuse, a common fate suffered by many 19th- and early 20th-century pitchers. Three times he had pitched over 500 innings in a season, and twice over 600. He died at the age of 47 from pneumonia. Clarkson was elected to the Hall of Fame in 1963. *(See Cubs bio.)*

CAREER BRAVES RECORD:

W	L	W%	ERA	SV
149	82	.645	2.82	4

K	BB	SHO	IP
834	676	20	2,092.7

DUFFY, HUGH (OF)
(1892–1900)

Originally a mill worker who made a few extra bucks by playing ball on the weekends, Hugh Duffy played four seasons for three different teams before joining the Beaneaters in 1892. In the 1890s Duffy put together one of the best decades by a ballplayer during his or any other era of baseball history. During that time he had 100+ runs and RBIs eight times each, and twice scored over 160 runs. He stole 40 or more bases seven times, including one year with 78 and another with 85. Duffy also had 180+ hits seven times during that same span. All of these numbers are even more remarkable considering that the major league season was 20–30 games shorter during most of the 1890s as compared to today. Duffy's crowning year was 1894, when he won the Triple Crown, batting .440 (the highest single-season average ever) with 18 homers and 145 RBIs. He also laced 51 doubles and 16 triples among his 237 hits in just 125 games. During the season he had 12 four-hit games and two five-hit games. Before the 1901 season, he jumped for big bucks to Milwaukee of the new American League. When the club moved to St. Louis after the season and became the Browns, Duffy stayed behind and managed the Western League's new Milwaukee franchise for two years. From 1904 to 1906, he was the player-manager of the Phillies and from 1910 to 1911, he managed the White Sox before returning again to manage Milwaukee, now in the American

Association. Duffy bounced around between coaching, scouting, and minor league managing before returning to the majors again in 1921 to manage the Red Sox for two years. After leaving the managing job, Duffy remained a scout and coach with the Red Sox for 32 years until he died in 1954. He was elected to the Hall of Fame in 1945.

CAREER BRAVES RECORD:

Games	AB	Hits	Runs
1,152	4,656	1,544	996
Avg	**HR**	**RBI**	**SB**
.332	69	927	331

GLAVINE, TOM (SP)
(1987–2002)

The Braves drafted Tom Glavine in the second round of the June 1984 amateur draft and brought him to Atlanta in time to play with some of the worst Braves teams in the last 50 years. Glavine struggled in his first four years, finishing with a losing record three times. By 1991 Glavine had been joined by Steve Avery and John Smoltz, and the Braves' fortunes turned dramatically, as they won the first of 14 straight division titles. Glavine was an integral part of five National League pennant-winning teams, including the 1995 Braves (for whom he won 16 games in the strike-shortened season), who won the World Series over Cleveland as Glavine took home the World Series MVP trophy after combining with Mark Wohlers on a 1–0, one-hit victory in the deciding sixth game. During Glavine's 16-year Braves career, he captured two Cy Youngs (1991 and 1998), four Silver Slugger Awards, and made the NL All-Star team eight times. Glavine's 1992 campaign was—statistically—better than his Cy Young season of 1991, as he won 20 games and allowed only six home runs all year, but he finished second to Greg Maddux of the Cubs. Glavine led the NL in victories five times, each time winning 20 or more games. He left the Braves via free agency after the 2002 season and landed with the Mets, but after three years in the Big Apple, he has yet to post a winning season.

CAREER BRAVES RECORD:

W	L	W%	ERA	SV
242	143	.629	3.37	0
K	**BB**	**SHO**	**IP**	
2,054	1,140	22	3,344.7	

HOLMES, TOMMY (OF)
(1942–1951)

Tommy Holmes' dad raised his son to be a professional boxer, but after he fell in love with baseball, he put his father's dreams on hold and set out after his own. The Yankees signed him in 1937 and he performed admirably in the minors, but the Yanks were loaded in the outfield with DiMaggio, Henrich, Keller, and Selkirk. Following the 1941 season, Holmes was traded to the Braves and he got his chance to play, becoming a starting outfielder right out of the gate in 1942. After three decent seasons patrolling Boston's outfield, Holmes became a fan favorite and had his career year in 1945, barely missing a Triple Crown. He led the league with 28 home runs, finished second in the batting race by three points with a .352 average, and was second in RBIs with 117, just seven short of leading the category. He also led the league with 47 doubles, 224 hits, and a .577 slugging average. Amazingly, Holmes struck out only nine times all year in 636 at-bats. Along the way he put together a 37-game hitting streak, the third longest in NL history, behind only Wee Willie Keeler's 44-game masterpiece and Bill Dahlen's 42-game skein. Incredibly, Holmes did not win the NL MVP Award that year, coming in second to Chicago's Phil Cavarretta, even though Holmes blew the Cub away in every category except batting average. Later in his career, Holmes would put together two more hitting streaks of 20 games each. In 1948 he hit .325 as the Braves won the NL pennant, but lost the Series to Cleveland. Holmes, who struck out only 122 times in nearly 5,000 at-bats, broke up three no-hitters, getting the only Braves hit in the games. After 10 years with the Braves, Holmes' numbers began to decline and he was released in 1951. He came back later that year to manage the club for parts of 1951 and 1952 before being released again. Brooklyn picked him up in the middle of 1952, but after he hit only .111 in 36 games, they, too, dropped him, and his playing career was over. Holmes spent a lot of time shuttling around the minors in various managing jobs before becoming a scout for the Dodgers in 1958. He later became the director of the Greater New York Sandlot Baseball Foundation. In 1973, after a time as a salesman, Holmes became the community relations director of the Mets' youth baseball program, which over the years sent 65 players to the major leagues.

CAREER BRAVES RECORD:

Games	AB	Hits	Runs
1,289	4,956	1,503	696
Avg	**HR**	**RBI**	**SB**
.303	88	580	40

JONES, ANDRUW (OF)
(1996–2005)

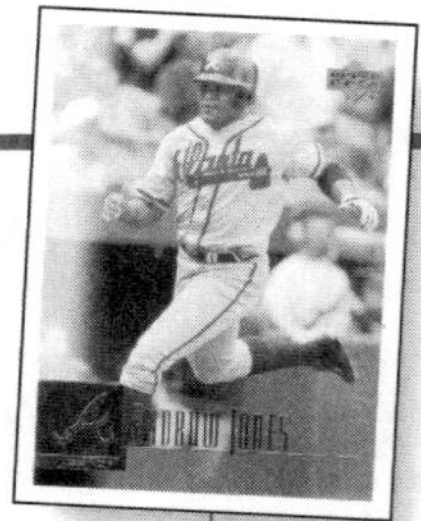

Simply put, Andruw Jones is on a path to become one of the best players in major league history. He broke in at the major league level at age 19 after being signed as a 16-year-old amateur free agent in 1993. By 1997 he had become a regular in the Atlanta outfield, and since that time has missed fewer than 40 games over nine seasons. While he has never been a particularly high-average hitter (he's topped .300 only once), he has been a very productive run producer, averaging 30+ homers over that span with nearly 100 runs and RBIs per season. Jones, who won't be 29 until a month into the 2006 season, has already passed the 300 plateau in career homers, and is only about 40 behind Hank Aaron at the same point in his career. Jones, a four-time All-Star, is also an excellent defensive center fielder, winning his eighth straight Gold Glove in 2005. Barring injury or an otherwise shortened career, Jones should be threatening many major league records in about 8–10 years.

CAREER BRAVES RECORD:

Games	AB	Hits	Runs
1,451	5,271	1,408	855
Avg	**HR**	**RBI**	**SB**
.267	301	894	129

JONES, CHIPPER (3B/OF)
(1993, 1995–2005)

Larry "Chipper" Jones was the first pick of the first round of the June 1990 amateur draft. After a brief 1993 appearance, the switch-hitting Jones arrived in Atlanta for good in 1995 and has been a terrific source of run production ever since. Jones has never hit fewer than 20 homers in any of his 11 full major league seasons, and has hit better than .300 seven times. Jones had eight consecutive years of 100+ RBIs from 1996 to 2003, along with seven years of 100+ runs scored. The five-time All-Star has also won two Silver Slugger Awards as the NL's best-hitting third baseman (1999 and 2000), and was the National League's MVP in 1999, as he sparked the Braves to the NL pennant. Jones has played in 11 consecutive post-seasons.

CAREER BRAVES RECORD:

Games	AB	Hits	Runs
1,651	5,974	1,811	1,101
Avg	**HR**	**RBI**	**SB**
.303	331	1,111	123

LONG, HERMAN (SS) (1890–1902)

After one season in the American Association with the Kansas City Cowboys, shortstop Herman Long was sold to the Boston Beaneaters, where he remained a dominant force on both offense and defense for the next 13 years. Long was the Ozzie Smith of his day, routinely making spectacular fielding plays. Once he fielded a ball with his foot, deflecting it into the air where he caught it and threw the runner out. Long was once described as playing like a man on a flying trapeze. The record books don't do him justice because he probably made more errors than any other shortstop in history, but many of those errors were on balls no one else would have reached. Moreover, balls in his era were usually lopsided, the grounds were little better than pulverized gravel, and gloves were either not used at all or were little more than clumsy hand pads. Finally, the official scorers of the day would give a fielder an error for any ball he touched that he did not turn into an out, brutally unfair by today's standards. Long was also an offensive threat who helped the Beaneaters to three consecutive National League championships from 1891–1893, often finishing in the top 10 in doubles, steals, and homers. He was adept at the hit-and-run, something Boston developed in the 1890s, as well as stealing signs. His best season was 1896 when he hit .343 with 105 runs, 100 RBIs, and 36 stolen bases. Long retired as a player in 1904 and spent time managing in the minors, but after contracting tuberculosis, he moved to Colorado, where he died of the disease in 1909 at the age of 43.

CAREER BRAVES RECORD:

Games	AB	Hits	Runs
1,646	6,777	1,900	1,291
Avg	**HR**	**RBI**	**SB**
.280	88	964	431

LOWE, BOBBY (2B/OF/3B) (1890–1901)

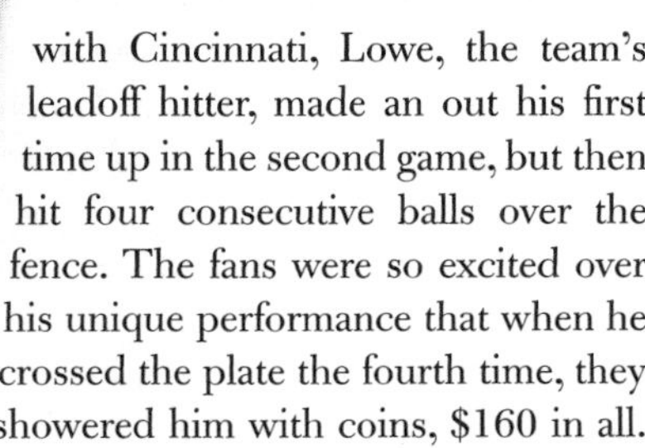

For more than a decade, Bobby Lowe was a fixture on the great Beaneaters teams of the 1890s. He was originally an outfielder, but was moved to second base in 1893 and became half of the best defensive middle infield of the era, teaming with shortstop Herman Long. Lowe's main claim to fame, however, stems from a game on May 30, 1894, when he became the first player in major league history to hit four home runs in one game. After going 0-for-6 in the first game of a doubleheader with Cincinnati, Lowe, the team's leadoff hitter, made an out his first time up in the second game, but then hit four consecutive balls over the fence. The fans were so excited over his unique performance that when he crossed the plate the fourth time, they showered him with coins, $160 in all. According to the Boston Globe, all four home runs were "line drives far over the fence . . . good for four bases on open prairie." In his next trip to the plate, Lowe hit a single, giving him a major league record 17 total bases for the game, a record that stood until Joe Adcock eclipsed it in 1954 with 18 (four homers and a double). Earlier in his career, Lowe had a six-hit game, and in 1894 he scored 158 runs, still in the NL's top 10 all-time. In 1895 he set a major league record by scoring six runs in a game, something that has never been exceeded. After 12 years in Boston, Lowe was traded to Chicago. Two years later he was sold to Pittsburgh, but after just one game he was sold to Detroit, where he spent his last three years. Upon retiring as a player, Lowe worked for the Department of Public Works for many years.

CAREER BRAVES RECORD:

Games	AB	Hits	Runs
1,410	5,617	1,606	999
Avg	HR	RBI	SB
.286	70	872	260

MADDUX, GREG (SP)
(1993–2003)

The Chicago Cubs drafted Greg Maddux in the second round of the June 1984 amateur draft and brought him up to the big leagues at the end of 1986. For the next 19 years he provided baseball fans with an example of what a great pitcher really is. For 17 consecutive years from 1988 to 2004, Maddux won at least 15 games every year. He twice won 20 games (1992–1993) and five times won 19 games along the way to capturing four consecutive National League Cy Young Awards (1992–1995). Maddux has consistently been among the league leaders in many categories, leading the league five times in shutouts, four times in ERA, and seven times in starts. A control specialist, Maddux has led the league seven times in fewest walks per nine innings pitched. An eight-time All-Star, Maddux had his string of consecutive years with 15 or more wins snapped in 2005 when he finished 13–15, his first losing season since 1987. Maddux spent his first seven years with the Cubs before leaving via free agency for Atlanta, where he spent 11 seasons. In 2004 he returned to Chicago, again through free agency. With 318 career victories and 3,000+ strikeouts heading into the 2006 season, Maddux is a sure first-ballot Hall of Famer.

CAREER BRAVES RECORD:

W	L	W%	ERA	SV
194	88	.688	2.63	0
K	BB	SHO	IP	
1,828	383	21	2,526.7	

MARANVILLE, RABBIT (SS/2B) (1912–1920, 1929–1933, 1935)

At just 5'5" and 155 pounds, Walter "Rabbit" Maranville was one of the smallest men ever to play the game. He was also a defensive wizard, setting many shortstop records for putouts, assists, and total chances, while leading the league four times in fielding percentage. Maranville might also be the all-time leader in practical jokes, some of which drove his fellow players and managers so crazy that it likely contributed to his peripatetic career with five different teams. Maranville, a notorious violator of team curfews, was once forced to room with his manager so the skipper could keep an eye on him. On the first night of the new experiment, the manager went out for a movie and returned by 10 P.M., pleased to find Maranville and roommate Chief Yellowhorse fast asleep. When the manager got undressed and opened the closet door to put his clothes away, a flock of pigeons flew out in his face. The commotion awoke the two players, to which Maranville told his manager, "You just let out the Chief's pigeons. Mine are in the other closet, so don't open the door." On another occasion, Maranville, a heavy drinker himself, wouldn't give teammate Jim Thorpe a drink of his liquor, so Thorpe grabbed the diminutive shortstop by his ankles and held him out the hotel window until he agreed to give him a drink.

On still another occasion, Maranville was demonstrating a hook slide on the stage of a vaudeville act when he overshot the stage and crashed into the orchestra pit, knocking instruments and musicians in all directions. Finally, during a particularly vicious baseball brawl that was threatening to turn into a full-fledged riot, the tiny Maranville tried several times to jump into the fray, but kept getting shoved aside. Not to be denied, he went to the unoccupied first-base coaching box and began to shadowbox. The fans and other players stopped their fighting to watch Maranville, eventually breaking out in laughter. He then gave himself an uppercut and pretended to knock himself out. The fans and players went nuts and the brawl abruptly ended. The next day, Commissioner Kenesaw Mountain Landis summoned Maranville to his office to thank him for preventing a riot.

After shattering his leg in an attempted steal of home in 1933, Maranville sat out all of 1934 before making an abbreviated comeback in 1935. After spending 15 of his 23 seasons with the Braves, Maranville retired at the age of 43. Following a number of minor league managing jobs, Maranville took a position running a series of baseball clinics for the Hearst newspapers. He was elected to the Hall of Fame in 1954, just months after his death.

CAREER BRAVES RECORD:

Games	AB	Hits	Runs
1,795	6,724	1,696	801
Avg	**HR**	**RBI**	**SB**
.252	23	558	194

MATHEWS, EDDIE (3B)
(1952–1966)

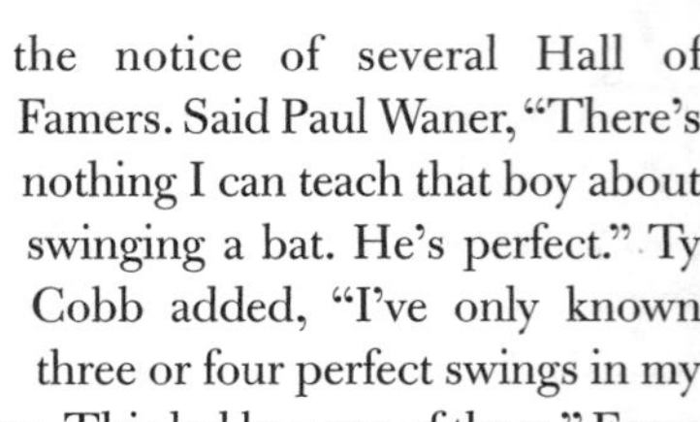

The Boston Braves signed Eddie Mathews as an amateur free agent before the 1949 season for a bonus of $5,999 (bonus baby rules in effect at the time required any player getting a bonus of $6,000 or more to remain in the majors for at least two years, but Mathews and his father knew that Eddie would benefit from some time in the minors). A number of teams had offered Mathews a bonus, with the largest offer dangled by the Dodgers ($30,000), but after Eddie and his father reviewed the rosters of the teams involved, they felt that they should go with the Braves, since their third baseman, Bob Elliott, was currently the oldest one among the teams who'd made an offer. Mathews performed well in the Southern Association in 1950 and then enlisted in the Navy since he was going to be drafted. After just a few weeks, Mathews was given a dependency discharge when his father was diagnosed with tuberculosis. Mathews came up to Boston in 1952 and slugged 25 homers, then a record for rookies. He also hit three homers in one game that year, the first rookie ever to accomplish the feat.

The Braves moved to Milwaukee in 1953 and Mathews hit 47 homers to lead the league, the first of three straight 40+ homer, 100-RBI seasons. His swing was so perfect that it drew the notice of several Hall of Famers. Said Paul Waner, "There's nothing I can teach that boy about swinging a bat. He's perfect." Ty Cobb added, "I've only known three or four perfect swings in my time. This lad has one of them." From 1952 to 1959, Mathews hit 299 homers, tops among all major leaguers. A nine-time All-Star, Mathews suffered a severe shoulder injury after taking a swing in a 1962 game against the Colt .45s and was never the same again. He continued to play for six more seasons, but was clearly in a state of decline, particularly in batting average. After the 1966 season, Mathews was traded to Houston and in midseason was traded again, this time to Detroit, where he finished his career early into the 1967 season. Following his career as a player, Mathews spent several years as a coach for Atlanta before taking over the managing reins in 1972, lasting until mid-1974. Mathews, elected to the Hall of Fame in 1978, was baseball's greatest slugging third baseman until the arrival of Mike Schmidt.

CAREER BRAVES RECORD:

Games	AB	Hits	Runs
2,223	8,049	2,201	1,452
Avg	**HR**	**RBI**	**SB**
.273	493	1,388	66

MURPHY, DALE (OF/1B) (1976–1990)

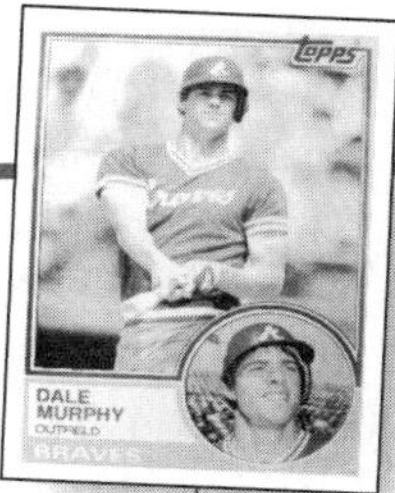

The Atlanta Braves selected Dale Murphy as the fifth pick of the first round of the June 1974 amateur draft and brought him up to the majors in late 1976. He began his career as a catcher, but eventually moved to first base (1979) and then the outfield (1980) to take advantage of his powerful throwing arm. As an outfielder, Murphy won five Gold Gloves and four Silver Slugger Awards. He became the youngest player ever to win consecutive MVP Awards, receiving back-to-back National League MVP honors in 1982 and 1983. In 1983 he became baseball's sixth-ever 30–30 man, hitting 36 homers and stealing 30 bases. Murphy was a devout Mormon who rarely missed a game, putting together a 740-game streak from 1982 to 1986. A five-time 100-RBI producer who also scored 100+ runs four times, Murphy had the second-most home runs and RBIs during the 1980s with 308 and 929, respectively, while playing in 1,537 of Atlanta's 1,557 games during the decade. A very well liked player by fans and opponents alike, Murphy was traded to Philadelphia after spending 15 years in a Braves uniform. After two-plus seasons with the Phillies (hitting only .161 in 1992), Murphy was released in 1993 and signed with Colorado. After hitting only .143 in 26 games with the Rockies, Murphy retired rather than continue to embarrass himself. His career numbers of .265 with 398 homers and around 1,100 runs and RBIs make him questionable for the Hall of Fame.

CAREER BRAVES RECORD:

Games	AB	Hits	Runs
1,926	7,098	1,901	1,103
Avg	**HR**	**RBI**	**SB**
.268	371	1,143	160

NICHOLS, KID (SP/RP) (1890–1901)

Following the 1889 season, Manager Frank Selee of the Omaha team in the Western Association was hired to manage the National League's Boston Beaneaters, so he took his team's 36-game winner, Kid Nichols, with him. Nichols spent a dozen years with the Beaneaters, including all of the 1890s, and was baseball's winningest pitcher during that time, surpassing even the great Cy Young by 30 wins. With pinpoint control, Nichols used only a fastball to lead Boston to five pennants during the decade. Nichols won 30 or more games in seven of eight seasons from 1891 to 1898, missing only in 1895, when he won 26 games. In 1892 the National League went to a two-half format in which the winner of the first half played the winner of the second half in the World Series. Boston, winner of the first half, played Cleveland, winner of the second half, and won five games to none with one tie, to take the title. When the pitching mound was moved back from 50 feet to 60 feet 6 inches in 1893, many pitchers were adversely affected, but Nichols hardly missed a beat, winning 34 games as he led the Beaneaters to their third straight NL title. The Beaneaters won the championship again in both 1897 and 1898, Nichols winning 31 games each year. After falling to 21–19 in 1899, Nichols slumped to 13–16 in 1900, the first losing record of his career.

In 1901 many of Nichols' teammates jumped to the new American League, but Nichols did not, winning 19 games for the weakened Beaneaters before being released at the end of the season. For the next two years, Nichols was the player-manager of the Kansas City team of the Western League, collecting 48 pitching wins in 1902 and 1903. In 1904 he returned to the National League as the player-manager of the St. Louis Cardinals, compiling a 21–13 record for the fifth-place team. In 1905 he was fired as manager but kept on as a pitcher; however, when vindictive owner Stanley Robison ordered him to be a gate attendant on a day when he didn't pitch, Nichols refused and was released. During his career, Nichols started 561 games and completed an astounding 531 of them. His 361 career victories place him sixth all time. After leaving the game, Nichols teamed up with former Cubs shortstop Joe Tinker, opening a group of bowling alleys in the Kansas City area, then later became involved in the real estate and movie businesses. In 1949 Nichols was inducted into the Baseball Hall of Fame in Cooperstown.

CAREER BRAVES RECORD:

W	L	W%	ERA	SV
329	183	.643	3.00	16
K	**BB**	**SHO**	**IP**	
1,667	1,159	44	4,538.0	

NIEKRO, PHIL (SP/RP)
(1964–1983, 1987)

The Milwaukee Braves signed Phil Niekro as an amateur free agent in July 1958, and it took six years for the young knuckleballer to make it to the majors. Niekro's father was playing catch with him one day and threw him a knuckleball as a joke. The fluttering pitch so fascinated the young Niekro that he worked hard to perfect one of his own. By the time he was in high school, Niekro threw such a good knuckleball that few could catch it. Niekro was primarily a reliever in his first four major league seasons, finally making the conversion to full-time starter in 1968, when he was 29 years old. In 1969 Niekro, who was selected to the first of his five All-Star Games, won 23 games to lead the Braves to the first-ever NL West title. Niekro pitched masterfully, throwing a no-hitter against San Diego in 1973, but the Braves were a poor hitting team that gave him little support.

On July 29, 1977, Niekro became the ninth pitcher in history to strike out four batters in an inning. In 1979 Niekro won 21 games for the last-place Braves, becoming the last major league pitcher to win 20 for a cellar dweller. Of course, he also lost 20 games that year, becoming the first pitcher since George Mullin in 1905 to both win and lose at least 20 games in a season. Niekro was also a fine fielder, winning five Gold Gloves during his career. After 20 years with the Braves, Niekro was released and signed with the Yankees, for whom he won 16 games in both 1984 and 1985. After a season in Cleveland and one more campaign split between the Indians, Blue Jays, and Braves again, Niekro retired at the age of 48, having won 121 games after turning 40. He also retired with the National League record for wild pitches with 200, and worst Opening Day record in major league history (0–7). After retiring, Niekro took the coaching job of the Colorado Silver Bullets, a women's professional baseball team. Cooperstown finally called in 1997, inducting him in his fifth year of eligibility.

CAREER BRAVES RECORD:

W	L	W%	ERA	SV
268	230	.538	3.20	29
K	**BB**	**SHO**	**IP**	
2,912	1,458	43	4,622.7	

SMOLTZ, JOHN (SP/RP)
(1988–1999, 2001–2005)

In 1987 the Atlanta Braves traded veteran Doyle Alexander to the Detroit Tigers for minor leaguer John Smoltz in a swap of pitchers that resulted in one playoff appearance for the Tigers and—so far—14 for the Braves. Smoltz became the second of Atlanta's big four pitchers (Tom Glavine had arrived the year before, followed later by Steve Avery and Greg Maddux) to join the lowly Braves and transform the team from doormat to dynasty. Smoltz won the NLCS MVP Award in 1992 as he led the Braves over the Pirates and into the World Series against the Blue Jays. Smoltz, who seemed to improve as the years went by, finally put it all together in 1996 when he went 24–8 with a 2.94 ERA to capture the NL Cy Young Award.

After suffering an arm injury in 1999, Smoltz underwent surgery that left his future playing ability in question. After sitting out the entire 2000 season, Smoltz returned as a closer, a position the Braves wanted him to fill in order to keep his inning count down and reduce the strain on his elbow. He performed so well as the team's stopper in 2001 that the Braves left him there, and Smoltz collected 144 saves over the next three seasons, rivaling Eric Gagne of the Dodgers as the best closer in the National League. However, he always expressed a desire to return to the starting rotation and, in 2005, the seven-time All-Star got his wish. Although the 38-year old finished 14–7, he won fewer games than he should have because—alas—the new and various Braves closers blew a gaggle of games in which he left holding a lead. Smoltz has been particularly tough in the postseason, as his 15–4 career record attests.

CAREER BRAVES RECORD:

W	L	W%	ERA	SV
177	128	.580	3.26	154
K	**BB**	**SHO**	**IP**	
2,567	882	15	2,929.3	

SPAHN, WARREN (SP/RP)
(1942, 1946–1964)

The Boston Bees signed Warren Spahn as an amateur free agent before the 1940 season and brought him up for a taste of major league play at the start of the 1942 season before demoting him back to the minors for refusing Casey Stengel's order to throw a brushback pitch at Pee Wee Reese. Pitching for Hartford of the Eastern League, Spahn went 17–12 with a 1.96 ERA, but always regretted his decision not to throw at Reese, admitting later in his career that it was the biggest mistake he ever made. Spahn was drafted in 1943 and served with the U.S. Army in Europe, fighting in the Battle of the Bulge and taking part in the famous battle for the bridge at Remagen, winning a Bronze Star, a Purple Heart, and a battlefield commission. After being discharged in mid-1946,

Spahn returned to the Braves in July and finished the season 8–5. In 1947 he went 21–10, the first of 13 20-win seasons, a mark equaled only by Christy Mathewson of the Giants. During his career he pitched 67 shutouts, more than any other left-hander in NL history.

A 14-time All-Star, Spahn won the 1957 Cy Young Award after leading the Milwaukee Braves to the NL pennant. As good as he was, Spahn didn't pitch a no-hitter until he was 39 years old, when he shut down the Phillies for his 20th win of the 1960 season. In 1961 he pitched his second no-hitter at the age of 40, a 1–0 gem over the Giants. Spahn was also one of the best hitting pitchers in baseball history, socking 35 career homers, fourth best all time. In 1958 he performed the rare feat of winning 20 games and hitting over .300 in the same season. Following the 1964 season, after 20 years with the Braves, Spahn was sold to the Mets, where he performed as a pitcher-coach for Casey Stengel for one season. Teaming up with player-coach Yogi Berra, the two aging players comprised a historic battery. "I don't know if we're the oldest battery ever," said Berra, "but we're certainly the ugliest." On July 22, 1965, the Mets released Spahn and he signed the same day with the Giants, finishing the year and his career with them. Following his playing career, Spahn spent time as a pitching coach in Mexico, Japan, and Cleveland, three foreign lands desperate for great pitching.

CAREER BRAVES RECORD:

W	L	W%	ERA	SV
356	229	.609	3.05	29

K	BB	SHO	IP
2,493	1,378	63	5,046.0

SUTTON, EZRA (3B/SS)
(1877–1888)

After six years with the Cleveland Forest Citys and Philadelphia Athletics, "Uncle" Ezra Sutton joined the Boston Beaneaters in 1877 and was a mainstay in the infield for the next dozen years, helping Boston win championships in 1877, 1878, and 1883. As one of baseball's early professional pioneers, Sutton took part in a number of historic moments in the game. He played in the National Association's first game on May 4, 1871, at Fort Wayne, Indiana. Four days later he hit the first home run in professional league history, then later in the game added the second. He made the first error in National League history in 1876, and later that year, on June 14, he and teammate George Hall both hit three triples in a game, becoming the first players ever to do so. On August 27, 1887, he scored six runs in one game. Sutton hit over .300 seven times in his major league career, with his best season being his first, .352 in 1871. Following his playing career, Sutton's life was marked by a series of tragedies. He used his savings to open a sawmill that failed miserably. In 1890 an accident left him paralyzed for life. In 1906 his loving, long-suffering wife died after a lamp exploded and set her afire. A year later Sutton died as well.

CAREER BRAVES RECORD:

Games	AB	Hits	Runs
977	4,045	1,161	694

Avg	HR	RBI	SB
.287	20	487	45

TENNEY, FRED (1B)
(1894–1907, 1911)

Though left-handed, Fred Tenney was a star catcher at Brown University who was signed directly out of college and sent to the major leagues. Although a good hitter, Tenney mostly sat on the bench his first two years in Boston because the Braves had no place to put him, letting him catch and play the outfield on occasion. He gained playing time in 1896, and by the next year he was a regular, holding down the first-base spot. He turned out to be a very good fielder, eventually becoming the best in the league. Teamed with Herman Long, Bobby Lowe, and Jimmy Collins, Tenney helped form the best defensive infield of the 19th century, one that carried the team to back-to-back championships in 1897 and 1898. By 1905, however, many of the team's stars had either retired or jumped to the new American League and Boston fell into also-ran status. Tenney was named the team's player-manager that year and given a contract laden with incentives—not so much to win as to turn a profit. Tenney would go so far as to jump into the stands to retrieve foul balls to keep costs down. In 1907 he helped broker the sale of the team to the Dovey brothers, and for his efforts he was given a share of the team. By the end of the season, however, he and the Dovey brothers had a falling out and Tenney was traded to the New York Giants and became their first baseman. Late in the 1908 season, Tenney suffered an injury that would keep him out of the lineup one day and allow his replacement, Fred Merkle, to play an active role in one of baseball's most famous incidents, "Merkle's Boner," a baserunning mistake that cost the Giants the 1908 pennant. After one more stab as Boston's player-manager (now called the Rustlers) in 1911—a year in which he hit just .263 and guided the team to a last-place finish—Tenney retired from baseball.

CAREER BRAVES RECORD:

Games	AB	Hits	Runs
1,737	6,637	3,600	1,994
Avg	**HR**	**RBI**	**SB**
.300	17	609	260

WHITNEY, JIM (SP)
(1881–1885)

Like Babe Ruth later, Jim Whitney was an ace pitcher who, when not pitching, often played the outfield, usually batting cleanup. In 1881 he had the distinction of both winning and losing 30 games in a season when he finished the year at 31–33—both league-leading totals—while starting 66 of the team's 83 games that season. Although he was known to be wild early in his career, Whitney eventually developed a relationship with the strike zone that has seldom been equaled. From 1882–1885 he walked fewer than one batter for every nine innings pitched. In 1882 he finished with 24 wins while batting .323 with a .510 slugging average, good for fifth and third places respectively in the National League. In 1883 Whitney became one of the few major leaguers ever to score six runs in a game. From 1886 to 1890, Whitney bounced around with four different teams, recording only one winning season. In 1890 he was hit in the chest by a line drive, an injury that later developed into tuberculosis, from which he died a year later.

CAREER BRAVES RECORD:

W	L	W%	ERA	SV
133	121	.524	2.49	2

K	BB	SHO	IP
1,157	230	18	2,263.7

WILLIS, VIC (SP)
(1898–1905)

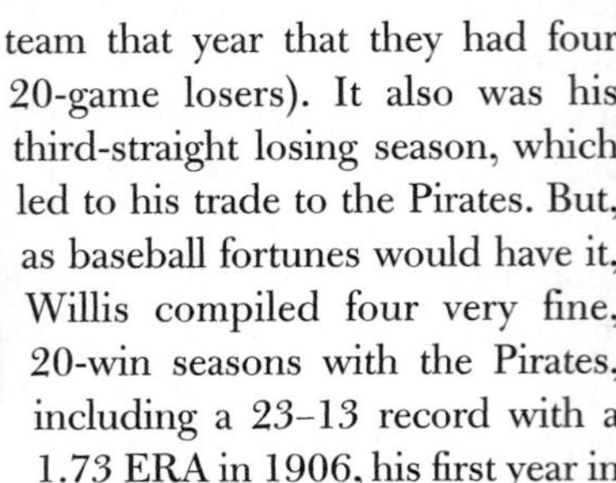

After three years in the minor leagues, Vic Willis arrived in Boston in 1898 and used his killer curveball to compile a 25–13 record in his rookie season. In 1899 he went 27–8 with a 2.50 ERA, tossing a no-hitter against Washington on August 7. In 1902 he set the 20th century's major league record with 45 complete games on his way to another 27-win season. Strangely, Willis's yearly record during his 13-year career was one of either feast or famine. Eight times he won 20 or more games. In the other five years his records were 10–17, 12–18, 18–25, 12–29, and 9–12. When he lost 29 games in 1905, it established a 20th-century record for most losses in a season (though it should be stated that the Beaneaters were such a poor team that year that they had four 20-game losers). It also was his third-straight losing season, which led to his trade to the Pirates. But, as baseball fortunes would have it, Willis compiled four very fine, 20-win seasons with the Pirates, including a 23–13 record with a 1.73 ERA in 1906, his first year in a Pirate uniform. In 1910 the Pirates sold him to the Cardinals, where he finished his career with a 9–12 season. In 1995 he was enshrined in the Hall of Fame.

CAREER BRAVES RECORD:

W	L	W%	ERA	SV
151	147	.507	2.82	5

K	BB	SHO	IP
1,161	854	26	2,575.0

Baltimore Orioles

Since 1901

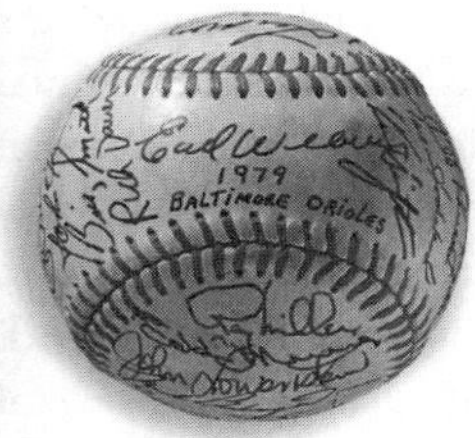

1979 Team Ball

1906 St. Louis Browns rookie catcher Branch Rickey becomes the first player in the team's history to hit two home runs in a game. Amazingly, he hits only one other in his entire four-year career.... **1944** The Browns win the American League pennant for the first time in their history, ending a record 43-year drought. It will be their only pennant while in St. Louis.... **1971** The Orioles become just the second team in major league history (joining the 1920 White Sox) to boast four 20-game winners in one season: Dave McNally (with 21 wins) and Jim Palmer, Pat Dobson, and Mike Cuellar with 20 each. The feat hasn't been accomplished since in the American League and has never been performed in the National League.... **1996** The Orioles set the record for home runs in a season when they hit 257, eclipsing the 1961 Yankees' mark of 241. The O's also become the first team ever to field a starting nine in which every member of the team has at least 20 homers.

FRANCHISE HISTORY

When the Western League changed its name to the American League in 1900, and took on major league status in 1901, part of Ban Johnson's grand scheme was to compete with the National League in as many of that league's cities as possible. One of those cities was St. Louis, which was home to the NL's Cardinals. Johnson had been handpicking many of the American League owners/investors, and for St. Louis he had solicited Zachary Tinker, owner of a Milwaukee brewery. The Western League's Milwaukee Brewers franchise was owned by Matt and Tim Killilea, a couple of entrepreneurs of modest means who wanted to sell the team. Johnson was trying to orchestrate the sale because he wanted someone with more financial backing, like Tinker, as the owner—he knew that once the American League went to war with the National League, it would take deep pockets to survive it. Tinker originally agreed to a deal with the Killileas, but backed out at the last minute, just before the team was to transfer from Milwaukee to St. Louis. Rather than moving the team as planned for the 1901 season—in the midst of the resulting chaos created by Tinker's 11th-hour defection and still saddled with owners that lacked the necessary capital to withstand a potential financial bloodbath with the National League—Johnson decided to leave the team in Milwaukee until a buyer could be found. After securing financial backing from several of his wealthy friends, Johnson took over the Milwaukee franchise himself in 1901, presiding over the team's dismal 48–89 record in their first American League season.

The first MVP Award presented by the American League, not a private sponsor, was given out in 1922 to George Sisler of the Browns.

Brooks Robinson, Andy Etchebarren, and Dave McNally celebrate 1–0 victory that gave Baltimore a World Series sweep of Dodgers on October 9, 1966.

Cal Ripken Jr. warms up after breaking Lou Gehrig's consecutive-game record, September 6, 1995.

In 1902, having had a year to prepare, Johnson moved the team to St. Louis, a much larger market than Milwaukee, with only one competing team (the Cardinals) rather than two (the Cubs and White Sox were just 90 miles south of Milwaukee). It also allowed him to build a franchise that would be more desirable for a suitable buyer. That suitable buyer turned out to be Robert Hedges, the owner of Banner Buggies, an early automobile. Johnson and Hedges had known each other in Cincinnati in the 1880s when Johnson was still a newspaper reporter. Hedges, in turn, lured Branch Rickey back into baseball from his failing law practice to be his GM. Hedges owned the team until 1915, when failing health forced him to sell out to Phillip Ball and Otto Seifel for $750,000.

Ball and Seifel were very wealthy men who had owned the St. Louis Terriers of the Federal League, which folded in 1915. Seifel was a brewer and Ball had made his fortune as a manufacturer of ice machines and cold-storage facilities. Ball controlled the club until he died in 1933, losing over $300,000 during his tenure. Ball's 87 percent interest passed to his widow and two children. Louis Von Weise, Ball's attorney, ran the club for the next three years until he could find a buyer. Von Weise and Ball's relatives knew or cared nothing about baseball. He tried, unsuccessfully, to interest Branch Rickey, the team's GM, in purchasing the team, but Rickey did find a buyer for the team. Rickey's assistant, Bill DeWitt, had risen from ballpark vendor to assistant vice president of the Browns. He and his father-in-law, Don Barnes, a wealthy investment banker, bought the Browns in 1936 for $375,000, which included $150,000 of Barnes' own money. The purchase price also included the San Antonio franchise of the Texas League. Barnes raised some of the money by selling 20,000 shares of stock at $5 per share. He also brought on board minority investors Al Curtis and International Shoe for $25,000 each. The American League also loaned the team $50,000 to help with operating expenses.

Barnes controlled the Browns until 1945, when he sold his 56 percent interest of 50,000 shares for $200,000 to Richard Muckerman, a prominent St. Louis businessman who was heir to the St. Louis City Ice & Fuel Company fortune. While Muckerman spent a lot of money in an effort to improve the ballpark, he spent virtually nothing on obtaining better players. After four years of losing money on the team, Muckerman sold out to Bill DeWitt and his brother in 1949, who in turn sold the club to Bill Veeck in 1951. Veeck lost $400,000 on the team in his first year alone. He tried to move the club back to Milwaukee, but was beaten to the punch by the Boston Braves, who relocated there themselves in 1953. Due to financial problems, Veeck was forced to sell the team in 1953. The principal buyer was Baltimore brewer Jerrold C. Hoffberger, who headed a group that paid almost $2.5 million

From 1935 to 1939, the St. Louis Browns recorded the highest ERA in the American League all five years, including an all-time AL worst 6.24 in 1936.

for the team, but not before getting approval from the American League to relocate the team to Baltimore.

Hoffberger owned National Brewery Company. The main minority partner was Clarence Miles, a Baltimore attorney. (Hoffberger had once failed in a bid to purchase the Detroit Tigers with Bill Veeck, hence the connection between the two.) Hoffberger had served in WWII, and after the war became the general manager of the brewery while just 26 years old. The following year he became the president of the brewery, a position he maintained for nearly 30 years. Over the next 25 years, Hoffberger continued to buy up more and more of the Orioles stock until he owned controlling interest in 1963. He put the club up for sale in 1974, but took it off the market the next year. In August 1979, Hoffberger finally sold the Orioles to longtime friend and business associate, attorney Edward Bennett Williams. Williams paid $12 million for the team, knowing he likely wouldn't turn a profit on a yearly basis, but hoping at the very least not to lose money. (He bought out the public shares that Barnes had sold back in 1936 for an extremely nice return on their owners' original $5-per-share investments.) When Williams died of cancer, his law partner, Larry Lucchino, took over the club until its sale could be arranged in 1988.

The Yankees and Orioles set a record after the 1954 season when they completed an 18-player trade. This was the trade that brought perfect-game pitcher Don Larsen to the Yankees.

The investment group that purchased the Orioles was led by financial investor Eli Jacob, who purchased an 87 percent stake for $70 million. Larry Lucchino and Sargent Shriver, the Democratic vice-presidential candidate in 1980, were minority shareholders. Jacob tried to turn a quick profit and sell the club for $200 million, but failed. In 1991 Jacob was estimated to be worth $500 million, but bad investments were rapidly shrinking his fortune. He was also reeling from creditors accusing him of trying to default on $44 million in loans. In April 1993, Jacob declared bankruptcy and was forced to sell the team. Attorney Peter Angelos led the investment group that bought the Orioles at a spirited bankruptcy auction in which three groups were bidding. Besides Angelos, who made his billion-dollar fortune as a trial lawyer suing deep-pocketed defendants, other minor partners were tennis star Pam Shriver, broadcaster Jim McKay, author Tom Clancy, director Barry Levinson, and Cincinnati businessman William DeWitt, whose father had owned the St. Louis Browns in the 1940s. Angelos remains the current owner.

When Brooks Robinson played his 23rd consecutive season with the Orioles in 1977, he set a new record for playing the most years with the same ball club.

On the field, the team was lousy in its one year in Milwaukee and just plain terrible in St. Louis for half a century. The Browns won just one pennant in 53 years, in the talent-depleted year of 1944, when their entire infield was classified 4-F for the military. Though they thrilled the hearts of their faithful few by winning the pennant, they lost the World Series in six games to their crosstown rivals, the St. Louis Cardinals. They did challenge the Yankees in 1922, finishing just a game behind. Other than that, zip.

Things went better in Baltimore. In 1966 the Orioles (the team name derived from the Maryland state bird) won their first of six pennants and swept Sandy Koufax's Dodgers in the World Series. For three consecutive seasons, 1969–1971, the O's won more than 100 games. They swept their opponents in the LCS all three years to capture the pennant. In 1970 they won the Series in five games over the Reds, but in both 1969 and 1971 they were upset as heavy favorites, losing to the Miracle

The St. Louis Browns shared Sportsman's Park with the Cardinals until 1953.

Mets and the Pittsburgh Pirates. Throughout the 1970s, the Orioles continued to be a strong team, winning their division in 1973, 1974, and 1979. The powerful Oakland A's eliminated the O's in the LCS in both 1973 and 1974. In 1979 they defeated the Angels in the LCS and led the Pirates three games to one in the World Series before the Pirates stormed back to take the Series. The O's won their last World Series in 1983, defeating the Phillies in five games. In the last 22 years, however, the Orioles have fallen on hard times, making the playoffs only twice with no World Series appearances. On the bright side, however, when Camden Yards opened for play in 1992, it sparked a huge surge in attendance for the Orioles and ushered in the era of retro ballparks.

Cal Ripken Jr.'s incredible consecutive games streak ended at 2,632 on September 20, 1998, when he took himself out of the lineup.

TEAM NAME HISTORY

Official Names

Brewers, 1901 (Milwaukee)
Browns, 1902–1953 (St. Louis)
Orioles, 1954–current (Baltimore)

Unofficial Names/Nicknames

While in St. Louis: St. Louis Americans, Brownies, Pixies, Elves
While in Baltimore: O's, Birds

STADIUM HISTORY

In Milwaukee

Milwaukee Park (also known as Lloyd Street Park)	1901

In St. Louis

Sportsman's Park	1902–1953

In Baltimore

Memorial Stadium	1954–1991
Oriole Park at Camden Yards	1992–current

YEARLY RECORD, FINISH, & ATTENDANCE FIGURES

Year	League	Record	DIV/LG Finish	Attendance	Avg/Gm
2005	AL East	74–88	4	2,624,740	32,404
2004	AL East	78–84	3	2,744,018	33,877
2003	AL East	71–91	4	2,454,523	30,303
2002	AL East	67–95	4	2,682,439	33,117
2001	AL East	63–98	4	3,094,841	38,686
2000	AL East	74–88	4	3,297,031	40,704
1999	AL East	78–84	4	3,433,150	42,385
1998	AL East	79–83	4	3,684,650	45,490
1997	AL East	98–64	1	3,711,132	45,816
1996	AL East	88–74	2	3,646,950	44,475
1995	AL East	71–73	3	3,098,475	43,034
1994	AL East	63–49	2	2,535,359	46,097
1993	AL East	85–77	3	3,644,965	45,000
1992	AL East	89–73	3	3,567,819	44,047
1991	AL East	67–95	6	2,552,753	31,515
1990	AL East	76–85	5	2,415,189	30,190
1989	AL East	87–75	2	2,535,208	31,299
1988	AL East	54–107	7	1,660,738	20,759
1987	AL East	67–95	6	1,835,692	22,386
1986	AL East	73–89	7	1,973,176	24,977
1985	AL East	83–78	4	2,132,387	26,326
1984	AL East	85–77	5	2,045,784	25,257
1983	AL East	98–64	1	2,042,071	25,211
1982	AL East	94–68	2	1,613,031	19,671
1981	AL East	59–46	2/4	1,024,247	18,623
1980	AL East	100–62	2	1,797,438	22,191
1979	AL East	102–57	1	1,681,009	21,279
1978	AL East	90–71	4	1,051,724	12,984
1977	AL East	97–64	2	1,195,769	14,763
1976	AL East	88–74	2	1,058,609	13,069
1975	AL East	90–69	2	1,002,157	13,015
1974	AL East	91–71	1	962,572	11,884
1973	AL East	97–65	1	958,667	11,835
1972	AL East	80–74	3	899,950	11,688
1971	AL East	101–57	1	1,023,037	13,286
1970	AL East	108–54	1	1,057,069	13,050
1969	AL East	109–53	1	1,062,069	13,112
1968	AL	91–71	2	943,977	11,800
1967	AL	76–85	7	955,053	12,403
1966	AL	97–63	1	1,203,366	15,232
1965	AL	94–68	3	781,649	9,894
1964	AL	97–65	3	1,116,215	13,612
1963	AL	86–76	4	774,343	9,560
1962	AL	77–85	7	790,254	9,637
1961	AL	95–67	3	951,089	11,599
1960	AL	89–65	2	1,187,849	15,427
1959	AL	74–80	6	891,926	11,435
1958	AL	74–79	6	829,991	10,641
1957	AL	76–76	5	1,029,581	13,371
1956	AL	69–85	6	901,201	11,704
1955	AL	57–97	7	852,039	10,785

Yearly Record, Finish, & Attendance Figures (cont.)

Year	League	Record	DIV/LG Finish	Attendance	Avg/Gm
1954	AL	54–100	7	1,060,910	13,778
1953	AL	54–100	8	297,238	3,860
1952	AL	64–90	7	518,796	6,651
1951	AL	52–102	8	293,790	3,815
1950	AL	58–96	7	247,131	3,340
1949	AL	53–101	7	270,936	3,519
1948	AL	59–94	6	335,564	4,415
1947	AL	59–95	8	320,474	4,162
1946	AL	66–88	7	526,435	6,837
1945	AL	81–70	3	482,986	6,355
1944	AL	89–65	1	508,644	6,606
1943	AL	72–80	6	214,392	2,784
1942	AL	82–69	3	255,617	3,320
1941	AL	70–84	7	176,240	2,231
1940	AL	67–87	6	239,591	3,112
1939	AL	43–111	8	109,159	1,399
1938	AL	55–97	7	130,417	1,694
1937	AL	46–108	8	123,121	1,578
1936	AL	57–95	7	93,267	1,211
1935	AL	65–87	7	80,922	1,065
1934	AL	67–85	6	115,305	1,517
1933	AL	55–96	8	88,113	1,144
1932	AL	63–91	6	112,558	1,501
1931	AL	63–91	5	179,126	2,326
1930	AL	64–90	6	152,088	1,950
1929	AL	79–73	4	280,697	3,645
1928	AL	82–72	3	339,497	4,409
1927	AL	59–94	7	247,879	3,178
1926	AL	62–92	7	283,986	3,595
1925	AL	82–71	3	462,898	5,935
1924	AL	74–78	4	533,349	6,838
1923	AL	74–78	5	430,296	5,517
1922	AL	93–61	2	712,918	9,259
1921	AL	81–73	3	355,978	4,623
1920	AL	76–77	4	419,311	5,376
1919	AL	67–72	5	349,350	4,991
1918	AL	58–64	5	122,076	2,303
1917	AL	57–97	7	210,486	2,699
1916	AL	79–75	5	335,740	4,250
1915	AL	63–91	6	150,358	1,978
1914	AL	71–82	5	244,714	3,021
1913	AL	57–96	8	250,330	3,251
1912	AL	53–101	7	214,070	2,710
1911	AL	45–107	8	207,984	2,666
1910	AL	47–107	8	249,889	3,163
1909	AL	61–89	7	366,274	4,636
1908	AL	83–69	4	618,947	7,935
1907	AL	69–83	6	419,025	5,513
1906	AL	76–73	5	389,157	5,120
1905	AL	54–99	8	339,112	4,293
1904	AL	65–87	6	318,108	4,078

YEARLY RECORD, FINISH, & ATTENDANCE FIGURES (CONT.)

Year	League	Record	DIV/LG Finish	Attendance	Avg/Gm
1903	AL	65–74	6	380,405	5,434
1902	AL	78–58	2	272,283	3,730
1901	AL	48–89	8	139,034	1,986

MANAGER HISTORY

Manager	Years	W–L	Win %
Hugh Duffy	1901	48–89	.350
Jimmy McAleer	1902–1909	551–632	.466
Jack O'Connor	1910	47–107	.305
Bobby Wallace	1911–1912	57–134	.298
George Stovall	1912–1913	91–158	.365
Branch Rickey	1913–1915	139–179	.437
Fielder Jones	1916–1918	158–196	.446
Jimmy Austin	1913, 1918, 1923	31–44	.413
Jimmy Burke	1918–1920	172–180	.489
Lee Fohl	1921–1923	226–183	.553
George Sisler	1924–1926	218–241	.475
Dan Howley	1927–1929	220–239	.479
Bill Killefer	1930–1933	224–339	.398
Al Sothoron	1933	2–6	.250
Rogers Hornsby	1933–1937, 1952	255–381	.401
Jim Bottomley	1937	21–56	.273
Gabby Street	1938	55–97	.362
Fred Haney	1939–1941	125–227	.355
Luke Sewell	1941–1946	432–410	.513
Zack Taylor	1946, 1948–1951	235–410	.364
Marty Marion	1952–1953	96–161	.374
Jimmie Dykes	1954	54–100	.351
Paul Richards	1955–1961	517–539	.490
Lum Harris	1961	17–10	.630
Billy Hitchcock	1962–1963	163–161	.503
Hank Bauer	1964–1968	407–318	.561
Earl Weaver	1968–1982, 1985–1986	1,480–1,060	.583
Joe Altobelli	1983–1985	212–167	.559
Cal Ripken Sr.	1987–1988	68–101	.402
Frank Robinson	1988–1991	230–285	.447
Johnny Oates	1991–1994	362–343	.513
Phil Regan	1995	71–73	.493
Davey Johnson	1996–1997	186–138	.574
Ray Miller	1998–1999	157–167	.485
Mike Hargrove	2000–2003	275–372	.425
Lee Mazzilli	2004–2005	129–140	.480
Sam Perlozzo	2005–current	23–32	.418

ALL-TIME WIN-LOSS RECORDS VS. ALL OPPONENTS (SINCE 1901)

Opponent	Record
ALL-TIME	7,742–8,484
Angels	317–248
Astros	3–3
Athletics	907–950
Blue Jays	191–206
Braves	10–14
Brewers	227–162
Cardinals	1–2
Cubs	1–2
Devil Rays	69–62
Diamondbacks	2–4
Dodgers	1–2
Giants	3–3
Indians	822–1,088
INTERLEAGUE	64–93
Mariners	174–143
Marlins	4–11
Mets	5–11
Nationals	6–9
Padres	2–1
Phillies	19–20
Pirates	1–2
Rangers	346–216
Reds	1–2
Red Sox	902–1,077
Rockies	3–3
Royals	221–174
Tigers	918–1,009
Twins	931–910
White Sox	845–973
Yankees	810–1,177

Mike Cuellar and Brooks Robinson celebrate the franchise's 2nd World Series Championship on October 15, 1970.

Franchise Highlights, Low Points, and Strange Distinctions

1910 Pitcher Bill Bailey was 2–1 as a reliever for the Browns in 1910, but 0–17 as a starter.

••••

1914 Frank Crossing of the Browns became the only catcher in major league history to perform two unassisted double plays in a season—an even more remarkable feat considering that he played in only 41 games that year.

••••

1917 After earning a save in the first game of a doubleheader on May 6, Browns pitcher Bob Groom started the second game and threw a no-hitter against the White Sox.

••••

1920 When George Sisler won the AL batting title with a .407 average, he recorded 257 base hits, the all-time record until it was broken by Ichiro Suzuki of the Mariners, who collected 262 hits in 2004.

••••

1922 When Browns outfielder Ken Williams led the American League in home runs with 39, he slugged an amazing 32 of them at Sportsman's Park in St. Louis. That same season, the Browns became the first team in major league history to have four 100-RBI men (Williams led the AL with 155). The three teammates who joined him in the 100-RBI circle were second baseman Marty McManus with 109, first baseman George Sisler with 105, and outfielder Baby Doll Jacobson with 102.

The first MVP Award presented by the American League, not a private sponsor, was given out to George Sisler of the Browns.

••••

1925 The Browns were the first team in history to have at least six players hit 10 or more homers in a season.

••••

1926 On September 26, the last day of the season, the Browns and Yankees hooked up in a doubleheader in Sportsman's Park. The Browns swept the AL champion Yanks, 6–1 and 6–2. As if that wasn't enough, they performed the incredible sweep in just two hours and seven minutes . . . for both games! One of the games took just 55 minutes, still the record for the shortest time taken to play a nine-inning game.

••••

1935-39 From 1935 to 1939, the St. Louis Browns recorded the highest ERA in the American League all five years, including an all-time AL worst 6.24 in 1936.

••••

1938 Bobo Newsom of the Browns finished with a 20–16 record. There were two amazing things about this. First, the Browns went 55–97 that season. Second, Newsom's ERA on the year was 5.08, the worst in history by a 20-game winner. He also led the league in complete games and innings pitched that year.

1951 The Browns finished last in the AL with a 52–102 record, but pitcher Ned Garver somehow compiled a 20–12 record with a 3.73 ERA.

••••

1953 On May 6, pitcher Bobo Holloman of the Browns became the only pitcher in the 20th century to hurl a no-hitter in his first major league start, defeating the Philadelphia A's 6–0. Amazingly, it would be the only complete game of his short career. After finishing with a 3–7 record and 5.23 ERA in 22 games, 10 of them starting assignments, Holloman was released and never played in the majors again.

When the Browns moved from St. Louis to Baltimore after the 1953 season, it was the first time a franchise in either league had relocated in 50 years, since the Baltimore Orioles went to New York to become the Highlanders (Yankees) in 1903. St. Louis Browns fans' mourning would have been greater if the team had not lost 20 straight home games at one point in the 1953 season. The Browns may have been hoping the move to Baltimore in 1954 would turn things around for them, but it didn't happen right away. In the team's first season in Baltimore, third baseman Vern Stephens led all Orioles hitters with only eight homers and 46 RBIs.

••••

1954 The Yankees and Orioles set a record after the 1954 season when they completed an 18-player trade. This was the trade that brought perfect-game pitcher Don Larsen to the Yankees.

1959 Oriole Dave Philley set a major league record with nine consecutive pinch-hits.

••••

1961 On May 9, Oriole Jim Gentile hit grand slams in two consecutive innings to lead the O's to a 13–5 victory over the Twins.

••••

1963 For the first time since 1910, no player in the AL played in every one of his team's games. Brooks Robinson came the closest, missing only one game.

••••

1966 When Frank Robinson won the AL MVP Award, he became the first non-rookie in AL history to win the award in his first season in the American League. He would later be joined by Chicago's Dick Allen (1972) and Detroit's Willie Hernandez (1984) as the only three ever to accomplish the feat.

••••

1967 On April 30, Steve Barber and Stu Miller of the Orioles pitched the first combined no-hitter in major league history, but still lost to the Tigers 2–1.

••••

1971 When Baltimore won 101 games in 1971, it became the first team since the 1942–1944 St. Louis Cardinals to win 100+ games in three consecutive seasons.

1974 The Orioles set an American League record when they won five consecutive games by shutouts. They did it again in 1995, when they closed the season with five consecutive shutout wins, beating Toronto and Detroit by a combined 34–0.

••••

1977 When Brooks Robinson played his 23rd consecutive season with the Orioles, he set a new record for playing the most years with the same ballclub.

••••

1970-78 Jim Palmer put together eight 20-win seasons during his career to tie Lefty Grove for second place on the AL's all-time list. Only Walter Johnson (12) has more 20-win seasons in American League history. Palmer was also the first AL pitcher to win three Cy Young Awards (1973, 1975, and 1976).

••••

1980 Pitcher Steve Stone won 25 games for the Orioles (his previous best season had been 15 wins). But midway through the 1981 season, Stone had just four victories when he suffered a career-ending arm injury. His four wins in 1981 represents the lowest total of career wins in history following a 25-win season. He also joined Sandy Koufax as the only pitcher to win a Cy Young Award in his last full season in the majors.

••••

1983 Cal Ripken Jr. became the only player ever to play every inning of every regular season, LCS, and World Series game played by his team.

1987 Cal Ripken Sr. became the first manager in history to have two sons play for him: Cal Jr. and Billy. That same year, Cal Jr.'s consecutive-innings-played streak ended at 8,243.

••••

1991 Cal Ripken Jr. became the first shortstop in American League history to hit .300 with 30 or more homers and 100 or more RBIs.

••••

1992 When the Orioles went 10–1 in their first 11 games at Camden Yards in 1992, it was the best start ever by a team in a new ballpark.

Catcher Chris Hoiles set a new major league record in 1992 for fewest RBIs (40) by a player with 20 or more homers in a season. He partially atoned on August 14, 1998, by becoming the first catcher in major league history to hit two grand slams in the same game when he led the Orioles to a 15–3 rout of the Indians in Cleveland.

••••

1997 The Orioles became just the third team in AL history (and sixth team in major league history) to spend every day of the season in first place.

••••

1998 Cal Ripken Jr.'s incredible consecutive games streak ended at 2,632 on September 20, when he took himself out of the lineup.

Special Achievements

WORLD SERIES RESULTS

Year	Opponent	Result	Games
1944	St. Louis Cardinals	Lost	2–4
1966	L.A. Dodgers	Won	4–0
1969	New York Mets	Lost	1–4
1970	Cincinnati Reds	Won	4–1
1971	Pittsburgh Pirates	Lost	3–4
1979	Pittsburgh Pirates	Lost	3–4
1983	Philadelphia Phillies	Won	4–1

WORLD SERIES MANAGERIAL RECORDS

Manager	Series Record	Games Record
Luke Sewell	0–1	2–4
Hank Bauer	1–0	4–0
Earl Weaver	1–3	11–13
Joe Altobelli	1–0	4–1

ALL-TIME POSTSEASON RECORD

Divisional Playoffs	6–2
League Championship Series	21–16
World Series	21–18

ALL-STAR GAMES AT ST. LOUIS (WHEN AL WAS HOME TEAM)/ BALTIMORE

Year	Date	Winner	Score	Stadium
1948	July 13	American	5–2	Sportsman's Park (St. Louis)
1958	July 8	American	4–3	Memorial Stadium
1993	July 13	American	9–3	Camden Yards

HALL OF FAMERS WHO PLAYED FOR TEAM

	Position	Years	Games with Baltimore/ St. Louis/ Milwaukee
Luis Aparicio	SS	1963–1967	721
Jim Bottomley	1B	1936–1937	205
Jesse Burkett	OF	1902–1904	417
Dizzy Dean	SP	1947	1
Rick Ferrell	C	1929–1933, 1941–1943	703
Goose Goslin	OF	1930–1932	402
Rogers Hornsby	2B	1933–1937	67
Reggie Jackson	OF/DH	1976	134
George Kell	3B/1B	1956–1957	201
Heinie Manush	OF	1928–1930	345
Eddie Murray	1B/DH	1977–1988, 1996	1,884
Satchel Paige	RP/SP	1951–1953	126
Jim Palmer	SP	1965–1984	576
Eddie Plank	SP/RP	1916–1917	57
Robin Roberts	SP	1962–1965	113
Brooks Robinson	3B	1955–1977	2,896
Frank Robinson	OF/1B	1966–1971	827
George Sisler	1B	1915–1922, 1924–1927	1,647
Rube Waddell	SP/RP	1908–1910	84
Bobby Wallace	SS/3B	1903–1916	1,569
Hoyt Wilhelm	RP/SP	1958–1962	185

HALL OF FAMERS WHO MANAGED TEAM

	Years	Games with Baltimore/ St. Louis/ Milwaukee
Jim Bottomley	1937	78
Rogers Hornsby	1933–1937, 1952	647
Frank Robinson	1988–1991	516
George Sisler	1924–1926	462
Bobby Wallace	1911–1912	192
Earl Weaver	1968–1982, 1985	2,541

MVP AWARD WINNERS

Brooks Robinson	3B	1964
Frank Robinson	OF	1966
Boog Powell	1B	1970
Cal Ripken Jr.	SS	1983
Cal Ripken Jr.	SS	1991

CY YOUNG AWARD WINNERS

Pitcher	Year	W–L	SV	ERA
Mike Cuellar (tie)	1969	23–11	0	2.38
Jim Palmer	1973	22–9	1	2.40
Jim Palmer	1975	23–11	1	2.09
Jim Palmer	1976	22–13	0	2.51
Mike Flanagan	1979	23–9	0	3.08
Steve Stone	1980	25–7	0	3.23

Rookie of the Year Award Winners

Roy Sievers	OF	1949
Ron Hansen	SS	1960
Curt Blefary	OF	1965
Al Bumbry	OF	1973
Eddie Murray	1B	1977
Cal Ripken Jr.	SS	1982
Gregg Olson	RP	1989

Gold Glove Winners

Year	Position	Player
1960	3B	Brooks Robinson
1961	3B	Brooks Robinson
1962	3B	Brooks Robinson
1963	3B	Brooks Robinson
1964	3B SS	Brooks Robinson Luis Aparicio
1965	3B	Brooks Robinson
1966	3B SS	Brooks Robinson Luis Aparicio
1967	3B OF	Brooks Robinson Paul Blair
1968	3B	Brooks Robinson
1969	2B 3B SS OF	Davey Johnson Brooks Robinson Mark Belanger Paul Blair
1970	2B 3B OF	Davey Johnson Brooks Robinson Paul Blair
1971	2B 3B SS OF	Davey Johnson Brooks Robinson Mark Belanger Paul Blair
1972	3B OF	Brooks Robinson Paul Blair
1973	2B 3B SS OF	Bobby Grich Brooks Robinson Mark Belanger Paul Blair
1974	2B 3B SS OF	Bobby Grich Brooks Robinson Mark Belanger Paul Blair
1975	2B 3B SS OF	Bobby Grich Brooks Robinson Mark Belanger Paul Blair
1976	SP 2B SS	Jim Palmer Bobby Grich Mark Belanger
1977	SP SS	Jim Palmer Mark Belanger
1978	SP SS	Jim Palmer Mark Belanger
1979	SP	Jim Palmer
1982	1B	Eddie Murray
1983	1B	Eddie Murray
1984	1B	Eddie Murray
1991	SS	Cal Ripken Jr.
1992	SS	Cal Ripken Jr.
1996	SP	Mike Mussina
1997	SP 1B	Mike Mussina Rafael Palmeiro
1998	SP 1B 2B	Mike Mussina Rafael Palmeiro Roberto Alomar
1999	SP	Mike Mussina
2001	SP	Mike Mussina

Triple Crown Winners

Player	Year	Avg	HR	RBI
Frank Robinson	1966	.316	49	122

Fireman of the Year Award Winners

Stu Miller	1963
Lee Smith	1994

World Series MVP

Frank Robinson	1966
Brooks Robinson	1970
Rick Dempsey	1983

League Championship Series MVP

Mike Boddicker	1983

All-Star Game MVP

Brooks Robinson	1966
Frank Robinson	1971
Cal Ripken Jr.	1991
Roberto Alomar	1998
Cal Ripken Jr.	2001
Miguel Tejada	2005

Manager of the Year Award Winners

Frank Robinson	1989
Davey Johnson	1997

Batting Champions

Player	Year	Avg
George Stone	1906	.358
George Sisler	1920	.407
George Sisler	1922	.420
Frank Robinson	1966	.316

Nine-Inning No-Hitters Pitched

Year	Pitcher	Opp.	Score
1912	Earl Hamilton	DET	5–1
1917	Ernie Koob	CWS	1–0
	Bob Groom	CWS	3–0
1953	Bobo Holloman	PHI	6–0
1958	Hoyt Wilhelm	NYY	1–0
1967	Steve Barber/ Stu Miller	DET	1–2
1968	Tom Phoebus	BOS	6–0
1969	Jim Palmer	OAK	8–0
1991	Bob Milacki/ Mike Flanagan/ Mark Williamson/ Gregg Olson	OAK	2–0

20-Game Winners

Year	Pitcher	W–L
1902	Red Donahue Jack Powell	22–11 22–17
1903	Willie Sudhoff	21–15
1919	Allen Sothoron	20–12
1920	Urban Shocker	20–10
1921	Urban Shocker	27–12
1922	Urban Shocker	24–17
1923	Urban Shocker	20–12
1928	General Crowder Sam Gray	21–5 20–12
1930	Lefty Stewart	20–12
1938	Bobo Newsom	20–16
1951	Ned Garver	20–12
1963	Steve Barber	20–13
1968	Dave McNally	22–10
1969	Mike Cuellar Dave McNally	23–11 20–7
1970	Mike Cuellar Dave McNally Jim Palmer	24–8 24–9 20–10
1971	Dave McNally Pat Dobson Jim Palmer Mike Cuellar	21–5 20–8 20–9 20–9
1972	Jim Palmer	21–10
1973	Jim Palmer	22–9
1974	Mike Cuellar	22–10
1975	Jim Palmer Mike Torrez	23–11 20–9
1976	Jim Palmer Wayne Garland	22–13 20–7
1977	Jim Palmer	20–11
1978	Jim Palmer	21–12
1979	Mike Flanagan	23–9
1980	Steve Stone Scott McGregor	25–7 20–8
1984	Mike Boddicker	20–11

Retired Uniform Numbers

Number	Player	Position
4	Earl Weaver	Mgr
5	Brooks Robinson	3B
8	Cal Ripken Jr.	3B/SS
20	Frank Robinson	OF
22	Jim Palmer	SP
33	Eddie Murray	1B/DH

Team Records—Wins & Losses

- Games won in a season: 109 in 1965
- Games lost in a season: 111 in 1939
- Games won in a month: 25 in June 1966
- Games lost in a month: 25 in August 1954
- Consecutive games won: 14 in 1916 and 1973
- Consecutive games lost: 21 in 1988
- Biggest shutout victory: 17–0 over Chicago White Sox on July 27, 1969
- Biggest shutout loss: 18–0 to Detroit, April 29, 1935
- Highest winning percentage: .673 in 1969 (109–53)
- Lowest winning percentage: .279 in 1939 (43–111)

Team Records—Batting

- Highest team batting average: .313 in 1922
- Lowest team batting average: .218 in 1910
- Highest team slugging average: .472 in 1996
- Highest team on-base percentage: .372 in 1922
- Total hits: 1,693 in 1922
- Extra-base hits: 585 in 1996
- Hits in a single game: 26 vs. California Angels on August 28, 1980
- Longest individual hitting streak: 41, George Sisler, 1922
- Most .300 hitters in a single season: 8 in 1922
- Home runs: 257 in 1996
- Home runs in a month: 15, Harlond Clift, August 1938 and Jim Gentile, August 1961
- Home runs in a game: 7 vs. Boston Red Sox on May 17, 1967, and vs. California Angels on August 26, 1985
- Home runs by a rookie: 28, Cal Ripken Jr., 1982

- Home runs by a right-hander: 49, Frank Robinson, 1966
- Home runs by a left-hander: 50, Brady Anderson, 1996
- Home runs by a switch-hitter: 35, Ken Singleton, 1979
- Grand slams: 11 in 1996
- Grand slams (individual; single season): 5, Jim Gentile, 1961
- Grand slams (individual; career): 16, Eddie Murray
- Triples: 106 in 1921
- Doubles: 327 in 1937
- Singles: 1,239 in 1920
- Walks: 775 in 1941
- Runs scored: 949 in 1996
- Runs scored in a game: 23 vs. Toronto, September 28, 2000
- Runs scored in an inning: 12 vs. Tampa Bay on April 11, 2002 (sixth inning)
- Most batters hit by a pitch: 77 in 2001
- Times shut out: 25 in 1904, 1906, and 1910
- Grounded into double plays: 159 in 1986
- Fewest grounded into double plays: 93 in 1944
- Runners left on base: 1,334 in 1941

TEAM RECORDS—BASERUNNING

- Stolen bases: 234 in 1916
- Caught stealing: 189 in 1914

TEAM RECORDS—PITCHING

- Lowest earned run average: 2.15 in 1908
- Complete games: 135 in 1904
- Saves: 59 in 1997
- Strikeouts: 1,139 in 1997
- Shutouts: 21 in 1909 and 1961
- Walks: 801 in 1951
- Hit batsmen: 80 in 2003
- Wild pitches: 70 in 2005
- Consecutive wins (individual): 15, Dave McNally, 1969 (streak actually extended to 17 games over two seasons, 1968–1969)
- Consecutive losses (individual): 10, Jay Tibbs, 1988; Earl Hamilton also lost 12 consecutive games over two seasons in 1916–1917
- Strikeouts in a game: 17, Rube Waddell, September 20, 1908 (10 innings); nine-inning record is 16 by Rube Waddell, July 29, 1908
- Most runs allowed in a game: 29 vs. Boston Red Sox, June 8, 1950

TEAM RECORDS—FIELDING

- Best fielding average: .987 in 1998
- Most errors committed: 393 in 1901
- Fewest errors committed: 81 in 1998
- Most double plays turned: 191 in 1999
- Fewest double plays turned: 106 in 1901

TEAM RECORDS—MISCELLANEOUS

- Number of times league champions: 7
- Number of times finishing last in league: 13
- Largest attendance, single game: 52,395 vs. Milwaukee Brewers, April 4, 1988
- Largest attendance, doubleheader: 51,883 vs. Milwaukee Brewers, October 1, 1982
- Players used in a season: 54 in 1955
- Seasons played: 23 by Brooks Robinson

PRIMARY PITCHING STAFFS

Year	Starter	Starter	Starter	Starter	Starter	Closer	Bullpen	Bullpen	Bullpen
2005	Lopez	Chen	Cabrera	Bedard	Ponson	Ryan	Williams	Kline	Julio
2004	Ponson	Cabrera	Bedard	Lopez	DuBose	Julio	Ryan	Groom	Parrish
2003	Ponson	Johnson	Helling	Lopez	Hentgen	Julio	Ligtenberg	Groom	Ryan
2002	Ponson	Johnson	Erickson	Lopez	Driskill	Julio	Ryan	Groom	Roberts
2001	Ponson	Johnson	Mercedes	Towers	Roberts	Groom	Ryan	Trombley	Kohlmeier
2000	Ponson	Mussina	Mercedes	Rapp	Erickson	Kohlmeier	Groom	Trombley	McElroy
1999	Ponson	Mussina	Johnson	Guzman	Erickson	Timlin	Kamieniecki	Rhodes	Orosco
1998	Ponson	Mussina	Drabek	Guzman	Erickson	Benitez	Orosco	Rhodes	Mills
1997	Key	Mussina	Kamieniecki	Krivda	Erickson	Myers	Orosco	Benitez	Mathews
1996	Wells	Mussina	Coppinger	Mercker	Erickson	Myers	Orosco	Mills	McDowell
1995	Brown	Mussina	Moyer	McDonald	Erickson	Jones	Orosco	Benitez	Lee
1994	Fernandez	Mussina	Moyer	McDonald	Rhodes	Smith	Mills	Eichhorn	Poole
1993	Valenzuela	Mussina	Moyer	McDonald	Sutcliffe	Olson	Frohwirth	Williamson	Poole
1992	Milacki	Mussina	Rhodes	McDonald	Sutcliffe	Olson	Frohwirth	Davis	Flanagan
1991	Milacki	Mesa	Ballard	McDonald	Robinson	Olson	Frohwirth	Williamson	Flanagan
1990	Milacki	Harnisch	Ballard	Johnson	Mitchell	Olson	Price	Williamson	Hickey
1989	Milacki	Harnisch	Ballard	Johnson	Schmidt	Olson	Thurmond	Williamson	Hickey
1988	Bautista	Tibbs	Ballard	Boddicker	Peraza	Niedenfuer	Thurmond	Sisk	Schmidt
1987	Bell	Flanagan	McGregor	Boddicker	Dixon	Niedenfuer	Williamson	O'Connor	Schmidt
1986	Davis	Flanagan	McGregor	Boddicker	Dixon	Aase	Bordi	Havens	Snell
1985	Davis	Martinez	McGregor	Boddicker	Dixon	Aase	Stewart	Martinez	Snell
1984	Davis	Martinez	McGregor	Boddicker	Flanagan	Martinez	Stewart	Underwood	Swaggerty
1983	Davis	Martinez	McGregor	Boddicker	Flanagan	Martinez	Morogiello	Stoddard	Stewart
1982	Palmer	Martinez	McGregor	Stewart	Flanagan	Martinez	Davis	Stoddard	Grimsley
1981	Palmer	Martinez	McGregor	Stone	Flanagan	Martinez	Stewart	Stoddard	Ford
1980	Palmer	Martinez	McGregor	Stone	Flanagan	Stoddard	Stewart	Martinez	Ford
1979	Palmer	Martinez	McGregor	Stone	Flanagan	Stanhouse	Stewart	Martinez	Stoddard
1978	Palmer	Martinez	McGregor	Briles	Flanagan	Stanhouse	Kerrigan	Martinez	Flinn
1977	Palmer	Martinez	May	Grimsley	Flanagan	Martinez	Drago	McGregor	Miller
1976	Palmer	Garland	May	Grimsley	Cuellar	Martinez	Pagan	Flanagan	Miller
1975	Palmer	Torrez	Alexander	Grimsley	Cuellar	Miller	Jackson	Garland	Mitchell
1974	Palmer	McNally	Alexander	Grimsley	Cuellar	Jackson	Reynolds	Garland	Hood
1973	Palmer	McNally	Alexander	Jefferson	Cuellar	Reynolds	Jackson	Watt	Pena
1972	Palmer	McNally	Alexander	Dobson	Cuellar	Jackson	Harrison	Watt	Scott
1971	Palmer	McNally	Jackson	Dobson	Cuellar	Watt	Richert	Dukes	Hall
1970	Palmer	McNally	Phoebus	Hardin	Cuellar	Richert	Watt	Lopez	Hall
1969	Palmer	McNally	Phoebus	Hardin	Cuellar	Watt	Richert	Leonhard	Hall
1968	Leonhard	McNally	Phoebus	Hardin	Brabender	Watt	Richert	Drabowsky	Morris
1967	Richert	McNally	Phoebus	Barber	Dillman	Drabowsky	Watt	Fisher	Miller
1966	Palmer	McNally	Bunker	Barber	Miller	Miller	Drabowsky	Fisher	Watt
1965	Pappas	McNally	Bunker	Barber	Miller	Miller	Hall	Larsen	Palmer
1964	Pappas	McNally	Bunker	Barber	Roberts	Miller	Hall	Vineyard	Haddix
1963	Pappas	McNally	McCormick	Barber	Roberts	Miller	Hall	Stock	Starrette
1962	Pappas	Estrada	Fisher	Barber	Roberts	Wilhelm	Hall	Stock	Hoeft
1961	Pappas	Estrada	Fisher	Barber	Brown	Wilhelm	Hall	Stock	Hoeft
1960	Pappas	Estrada	Fisher	Barber	Brown	Wilhelm	Walker	Jones	Hoeft
1959	Pappas	Wilhelm	O'Dell	Walker	Brown	Loes	Johnson	Portocarrero	Fisher
1958	Pappas	Harshman	O'Dell	Portocarrero	Brown	Zuverink	Loes	Lehman	Johnson
1957	Moore	Johnson	Loes	Wight	Brown	Zuverink	Ceccarelli	Lehman	O'Dell
1956	Moore	Johnson	Palica	Wight	Brown	Zuverink	Ferrarese	Fornieles	Loes
1955	Moore	Wilson	Palica	Wight	Rogovin	Dorish	Zuverink	Schallock	Johnson
1954	Turley	Coleman	Larsen	Pillette	Kretlow	Fox	Chakales	Blyzka	

PRIMARY PITCHING STAFFS (CONT.)

Year	Starter	Starter	Starter	Starter	Starter	Closer	Bullpen	Bullpen	Bullpen
1953	Littlefield	Brecheen	Larsen	Pillette	Cain	Paige	Stuart	Kretlow	Blyzka
1952	Byrne	Garver	Bearden	Pillette	Cain	Paige	Overmire	Madison	Harrist
1951	Byrne	Garver	Widmar	Pillette	McDonald	Mahoney	Suchecki	Paige	
1950	Overmire	Garver	Widmar	Fannin	Starr	Dorish	Marshall	Johnson	
1949	Drews	Garver	Embree	Fannin	Kennedy	Ferrick	Papai	Ostrowski	Starr
1948	Sanford	Garver	Stephens	Fannin	Kennedy	Widmar	Ostrowski	Biscan	
1947	Sanford	Kramer	Kinder	Muncrief	Zoldak	Potter	Moulder	Fannin	
1946	Galehouse	Kramer	Potter	Shirley	Zoldak	Ferens	Kinder	Muncrief	
1945	Jakucki	Kramer	Potter	Shirley	Hollingsworth	Zoldak	West	Muncrief	
1944	Jakucki	Kramer	Potter	Muncrief	Galehouse	Caster	Hollingsworth	Zoldak	Shirley
1943	Sundra	Niggeling	Hollingsworth	Muncrief	Galehouse	Caster	Ostermueller	Fuchs	Potter
1942	Auker	Niggeling	Hollingsworth	Muncrief	Galehouse	Caster	Sundra	Ferens	
1941	Auker	Niggeling	Harris	Muncrief	Galehouse	Caster	Trotter	Kramer	
1940	Auker	Niggeling	Harris	Kennedy	Bildilli	Coffman	Trotter	Lawson	
1939	Kramer	Lawson	Harris	Kennedy	Mills	Gill	Trotter	Whitehead	
1938	Newsom	Hildebrand	Walkup	Van Atta	Mills	Cole	Cox	Linke	
1937	Hogsett	Hildebrand	Walkup	Knott	Bonetti	Trotter	Koupal	Thomas	
1936	Hogsett	Caldwell	Andrews	Knott	Thomas	Van Atta	Liebhardt	Mahaffey	
1935	Cain	Walkup	Andrews	Knott	Thomas	Van Atta	Coffman	Weiland	
1934	Blaeholder	Newsom	Andrews	Hadley	Coffman	Knott	Wells	McAfee	
1933	Blaeholder	Wells	Hebert	Hadley	Coffman	Gray	Stiles	McDonald	
1932	Blaeholder	Stewart	Hebert	Hadley	Gray	Kimsey	Fischer	Cooney	
1931	Blaeholder	Stewart	Coffman	Collins	Gray	Kimsey	Stiles	Hebert	Braxton
1930	Blaeholder	Stewart	Coffman	Collins	Gray	Stiles	Kimsey	Holshouser	
1929	Blaeholder	Stewart	Crowder	Collins	Gray	Ogden	Kimsey	Coffman	
1928	Blaeholder	Stewart	Crowder	Ogden	Gray	Wiltse	Strelecki	Coffman	
1927	Gaston	Stewart	Jones	Vangilder	Wingard	Nevers	Ballou	Crowder	
1926	Gaston	Zachary	Giard	Vangilder	Wingard	Davis	Ballou	Falk	
1925	Gaston	Bush	Giard	Davis	Wingard	Vangilder	Danforth	Stauffer	Falk
1924	Shocker	Danforth	Vangilder	Davis	Wingard	Pruett	Lyons	Kolp	
1923	Shocker	Danforth	Vangilder	Davis	Kolp	Pruett	Root	Wright	
1922	Shocker	Wright	Vangilder	Davis	Kolp	Pruett	Bayne	Danforth	
1921	Shocker	Bayne	Vangilder	Davis	Kolp	Burwell	Palmero	DeBerry	
1920	Shocker	Bayne	Sothoron	Davis	Weilman	Burwell	Vangilder	DeBerry	
1919	Shocker	Gallia	Sothoron	Davenport	Weilman	Koob	Wright	Leifield	
1918	Rogers	Gallia	Sothoron	Davenport	Wright	Houck	Shocker	Leifield	
1917	Groom	Koob	Sothoron	Davenport	Plank	Hamilton	Rogers	Wright	
1916	Groom	Koob	Weilman	Davenport	Plank	Hamilton	Park	McCabe	
1915	Lowdermilk	Koob	Weilman	Hamilton	James	Perryman	Sisler	Hoch	
1914	Baumgardner	Leverenz	Weilman	Hamilton	James	Mitchell	Taylor	Hoch	
1913	Baumgardner	Leverenz	Weilman	Hamilton	Mitchell	Stone	Allison		
1912	Baumgardner	Powell	Allison	Hamilton	Brown	Brown	Mitchell	Adams	
1911	Lake	Powell	Pelty	Hamilton	George	Nelson	Mitchell	Bailey	
1910	Lake	Powell	Pelty	Bailey	Ray	Kinsella	Waddell	Gilligan	
1909	Waddell	Powell	Pelty	Bailey	Grahame	Dineen	Criss	Howell	
1908	Waddell	Powell	Howell	Dineen	Grahame	Bailey	Criss	Pelty	
1907	Pelty	Powell	Howell	Dineen	Glade	Bailey	Morgan	Jacobson	
1906	Pelty	Powell	Howell	Smith	Glade		Jacobson		
1905	Pelty	Sudhoff	Howell	Buchanan	Glade	Morgan	Ables		
1904	Pelty	Sudhoff	Howell	Siever	Glade	Morgan			
1903	Powell	Sudhoff	Donahue	Siever	Wright	Pelty	Evans		
1902	Powell	Sudhoff	Donahue	Harper	Reidy				
1901	Garvin	Sparks	Husting	Hawley	Reidy	Dowling			

PRIMARY STARTING LINEUPS

Year	C	1B	2B	3B	SS	LF	CF	RF	DH
2005	Lopez	Palmeiro	Roberts	Mora	Tejada	Bigbie	Matos	Gibbons	Sosa
2004	Lopez	Palmeiro	Roberts	Mora	Tejada	Bigbie	Matos	Gibbons	Newhan
2003	Fordyce	Conine	Roberts	Batista	Cruz	Bigbie	Matos	Gibbons	Segui
2002	Gil	Conine	Hairston	Batista	Bordick	Mora	Singleton	Gibbons	Cordova
2001	Fordyce	Conine	Hairston	Ripken	Bordick	Anderson	Mora	Richard	Batista
2000	Johnson	Clark	DeShields	Ripken	Bordick	Surhoff	Anderson	Belle	Baines
1999	Johnson	Conine	DeShields	Ripken	Bordick	Surhoff	Anderson	Belle	Baines
1998	Webster	Palmeiro	Alomar	Ripken	Bordick	Surhoff	Anderson	Davis	Baines
1997	Webster	Palmeiro	Alomar	Ripken	Bordick	Surhoff	Anderson	Tarasco	Berroa
1996	Hoiles	Palmeiro	Alomar	Surhoff	Ripken	Hammonds	Anderson	Bonilla	Murray
1995	Hoiles	Palmeiro	Alexander	Manto	Ripken	Anderson	Goodwin	Bass	Baines
1994	Hoiles	Palmeiro	McLemore	Gomez	Ripken	Anderson	Devereaux	Hammonds	Baines
1993	Hoiles	Segui	Reynolds	Hulett	Ripken	Anderson	Devereaux	McLemore	Baines
1992	Hoiles	Milligan	Ripken	Gomez	Ripken	Anderson	Devereaux	Orsulak	Davis
1991	Hoiles	Milligan	Ripken	Gomez	Ripken	Orsulak	Devereaux	Evans	Horn
1990	Tettleton	Milligan	Ripken	Worthington	Ripken	Bradley	Devereaux	Orsulak	Horn
1989	Tettleton	Milligan	Ripken	Worthington	Ripken	Bradley	Devereaux	Orsulak	Sheets
1988	Tettleton	Murray	Ripken	Gonzales	Ripken	Stanicek	Lynn	Orsulak	Sheets
1987	Kennedy	Murray	Ripken	Knight	Ripken	Sheets	Lynn	Lacy	Young
1986	Dempsey	Murray	Bonilla	Rayford	Ripken	Young	Lynn	Lacy	Sheets
1985	Dempsey	Murray	Wiggins	Rayford	Ripken	Young	Lynn	Lacy	Sheets
1984	Dempsey	Murray	Dauer	Gross	Ripken	Roenicke	Shelby	Young	Singleton
1983	Dempsey	Murray	Dauer	Cruz	Ripken	Lowenstein	Shelby	Ford	Singleton
1982	Dempsey	Murray	Dauer	Gulliver	Ripken	Lowenstein	Bumbry	Ford	Singleton
1981	Dempsey	Murray	Dauer	DeCinces	Belanger	Lowenstein	Bumbry	Singleton	Crowley
1980	Dempsey	Murray	Dauer	DeCinces	Belanger	Lowenstein	Bumbry	Singleton	Crowley
1979	Dempsey	Murray	Dauer	DeCinces	Garcia	Roenicke	Bumbry	Singleton	May
1978	Dempsey	Murray	Dauer	DeCinces	Belanger	Kelly	Harlow	Singleton	May
1977	Dempsey	May	Smith	DeCinces	Belanger	Kelly	Bumbry	Singleton	Murray
1976	Duncan	Muser	Grich	DeCinces	Belanger	Bumbry	Blair	Jackson	May
1975	Duncan	May	Grich	Robinson	Belanger	Baylor	Blair	Singleton	Davis
1974	Williams	Powell	Grich	Robinson	Belanger	Baylor	Blair	Coggins	Davis
1973	Williams	Powell	Grich	Robinson	Belanger	Baylor	Blair	Rettenmund	Davis
1972	Oates	Powell	Johnson	Robinson	Belanger	Buford	Blair	Rettenmund	
1971	Hendricks	Powell	Johnson	Robinson	Belanger	Buford	Blair	Robinson	
1970	Hendricks	Powell	Johnson	Robinson	Belanger	Buford	Blair	Robinson	
1969	Hendricks	Powell	Johnson	Robinson	Belanger	Buford	Blair	Robinson	
1968	Etchebarren	Powell	Johnson	Robinson	Belanger	Blefary	Blair	Robinson	
1967	Etchebarren	Powell	Johnson	Robinson	Aparicio	Blefary	Blair	Robinson	
1966	Etchebarren	Powell	Johnson	Robinson	Aparicio	Blefary	Blair	Robinson	
1965	Brown	Powell	Adair	Robinson	Aparicio	Brandt	Blair	Blefary	
1964	Brown	Siebern	Adair	Robinson	Aparicio	Powell	Brandt	Bowens	
1963	Orsino	Gentile	Adair	Robinson	Aparicio	Powell	Brandt	Smith	
1962	Triandos	Gentile	Breeding	Robinson	Adair	Powell	Brandt	Herzog	
1961	Triandos	Gentile	Adair	Robinson	Hansen	Snyder	Brandt	Robinson	
1960	Triandos	Gentile	Breeding	Robinson	Hansen	Woodling	Brandt	Pilarcik	
1959	Triandos	Boyd	Gardner	Robinson	Carrasquel	Nieman	Tasby	Pilarcik	
1958	Triandos	Boyd	Gardner	Robinson	Miranda	Nieman	Busby	Pilarcik	
1957	Triandos	Boyd	Gardner	Kell	Miranda	Nieman	Busby	Pilarcik	
1956	Triandos	Boyd	Gardner	Kell	Miranda	Nieman	Williams	Francona	
1955	Smith	Triandos	Marsh	Causey	Miranda	Dyck	Diering	Philley	
1954	Courtney	Waitkus	Young	Stephens	Hunter	Fridley	Diering	Abrams	
1953	Courtney	Kryhoski	Young	Dyck	Hunter	Lenhardt	Groth	Wertz	

PRIMARY STARTING LINEUPS (CONT.)

Year	C	1B	2B	3B	SS	LF	CF	RF	DH
1952	Courtney	Kryhoski	Young	Dyck	DeMaestri	Zarilla	Rivera	Nieman	
1951	Lollar	Arft	Young	Marsh	Jennings	Coleman	Delsing	Wood	
1950	Lollar	Lenhardt	Friend	Sommers	Upton	Kokos	Sievers	Wood	
1949	Lollar	Graham	Priddy	Dillinger	Pellagrini	Platt	Sievers	Kokos	
1948	Moss	Stevens	Priddy	Dillinger	Pellagrini	Platt	Lehner	Kokos	
1947	Moss	Judnich	Berardino	Dillinger	Stephens	Heath	Lehner	Coleman	
1946	Mancuso	Stevens	Berardino	Christman	Stephens	Heath	Judnich	Laabs	
1945	Mancuso	McQuinn	Gutteridge	Christman	Stephens	Martin	Kreevich	Moore	
1944	Hayworth	McQuinn	Gutteridge	Christman	Stephens	Zarilla	Kreevich	Moore	
1943	Hayes	McQuinn	Gutteridge	Clift	Stephens	Laabs	Byrnes	Chartak	
1942	Ferrell	McQuinn	Gutteridge	Clift	Stephens	McQuillen	Judnich	Laabs	
1941	Ferrell	McQuinn	Heffner	Clift	Berardino	Cullenbine	Judnich	Grace	
1940	Swift	McQuinn	Heffner	Clift	Berardino	Radcliff	Judnich	Cullenbine	
1939	Glenn	McQuinn	Berardino	Clift	Heffner	Gallagher	Laabs	Hoag	
1938	Sullivan	McQuinn	Heffner	Clift	Kress	Mills	Almada	Bell	
1937	Hemsley	Davis	Carey	Clift	Knickerbocker	Vosmik	West	Bell	
1936	Hemsley	Bottomley	Carey	Clift	Lary	Solters	West	Bell	
1935	Hemsley	Burns	Carey	Clift	Lary	Solters	West	Coleman	
1934	Hemsley	Burns	Melillo	Clift	Strange	Pepper	West	Campbell	
1933	Shea	Burns	Melillo	Scharein	Levey	Reynolds	West	Campbell	
1932	Ferrell	Burns	Melillo	Scharein	Levey	Goslin	Schulte	Campbell	
1931	Ferrell	Burns	Melillo	Kress	Levey	Goslin	Schulte	Jenkins	
1930	Ferrell	Blue	Melillo	O'Rourke	Kress	Goslin	Schulte	Gullic	
1929	Schang	Blue	Melillo	O'Rourke	Kress	Manush	Schulte	McGowan	
1928	Schang	Blue	Brannan	O'Rourke	Kress	Manush	Schulte	McNeely	
1927	Schang	Sisler	Melillo	O'Rourke	Gerber	Williams	Miller	Rice	
1926	Schang	Sisler	Melillo	McManus	Gerber	Williams	Jacobson	Rice	
1925	Dixon	Sisler	McManus	Robertson	LaMotte	Williams	Jacobson	Rice	
1924	Severeid	Sisler	McManus	Robertson	Gerber	Williams	Jacobson	Tobin	
1923	Severeid	Schliebner	McManus	Robertson	Gerber	Williams	Jacobson	Tobin	
1922	Severeid	Sisler	McManus	Ellerbe	Gerber	Williams	Jacobson	Tobin	
1921	Severeid	Sisler	McManus	Ellerbe	Gerber	Williams	Jacobson	Tobin	
1920	Severeid	Sisler	Gedeon	Austin	Gerber	Williams	Jacobson	Tobin	
1919	Severeid	Sisler	Gedeon	Austin	Gerber	Tobin	Jacobson	Smith	
1918	Nunamaker	Sisler	Gedeon	Maisel	Austin	Smith	Tobin	Demmitt	
1917	Severeid	Sisler	Pratt	Austin	Lavan	Shotton	Marsans	Jacobson	
1916	Severeid	Sisler	Pratt	Austin	Lavan	Shotton	Marsans	Miller	
1915	Agnew	Leary	Pratt	Austin	Lavan	Shotton	Walker	Williams	
1914	Agnew	Leary	Pratt	Austin	Lavan	Walker	Shotton	Williams	
1913	Agnew	Stovall	Pratt	Austin	Balenti	Johnston	Shotton	Williams	
1912	Stephens	Stovall	Pratt	Austin	Wallace	Hogan	Shotton	Williams	
1911	Clarke	Black	LaPorte	Austin	Wallace	Hogan	Shotton	Meloan	
1910	Stephens	Newnam	Truesdale	Hartzell	Wallace	Stone	Hoffman	Schweitzer	
1909	Criger	Jones	Williams	Ferris	Wallace	Stone	Hoffman	Hartzell	
1908	Spencer	Jones	Williams	Ferris	Wallace	Stone	Jones	Hartzell	
1907	Spencer	Jones	Niles	Yeager	Wallace	Stone	Hemphill	Pickering	
1906	Rickey	Jones	O'Brien	Hartzell	Wallace	Stone	Hemphill	Niles	
1905	Sugden	Jones	Rockenfield	Gleason	Wallace	Stone	Koehler	Frisk	
1904	Sugden	Jones	Padden	Moran	Wallace	Burkett	Heidrick	Hemphill	
1903	Kahoe	Anderson	Friel	Hill	Wallace	Burkett	Heidrick	Hemphill	
1902	Sugden	Anderson	Padden	McCormick	Wallace	Burkett	Heidrick	Hemphill	
1901	Maloney	Anderson	Gilbert	Burke	Conroy	Hogriever	Duffy	Hallman	

Top 10 Batting Leaders, Single Season & Career with Team

Games Played: Career with Team

Player	G	PA
1. Cal Ripken Jr.	3,001	12,883
2. Brooks Robinson	2,896	11,782
3. Mark Belanger	1,962	6,545
4. Eddie Murray	1,884	8,053
5. Boog Powell	1,763	6,912
6. Brady Anderson	1,759	7,464
7. Paul Blair	1,700	6,192
8. George Sisler	1,647	7,269
9. Bobby Wallace	1,569	6,199
10. Ken Singleton	1,446	6,071

At-Bats: Season

Player	AB	Year
1. B.J. Surhoff	673	1999
2. Jack Tobin	671	1921
3. Brooks Robinson	668	1961
4. Cal Ripken Jr.	663	1983
5. Luis Aparicio	659	1966
6. Miguel Tejada	654	2005
7. Mike Devereaux	653	1992
Miguel Tejada	653	2004
9. Cal Ripken Jr.	650	1991
10. George Sisler	649	1925

At-Bats: Career with Team

Player	AB	PA
1. Cal Ripken Jr.	11,551	12,883
2. Brooks Robinson	10,654	11,782
3. Eddie Murray	7,075	8,053
4. George Sisler	6,667	7,269
5. Brady Anderson	6,271	7,464
6. Boog Powell	5,912	6,912
7. Mark Belanger	5,734	6,545
8. Paul Blair	5,606	6,192
9. Bobby Wallace	5,529	6,199
10. Harlond Clift	5,281	6,355

Batting Average: Season

Player	BA	Year
1. George Sisler	.420	1922
2. George Sisler	.407	1920
3. Heinie Manush	.378	1928
4. George Sisler	.371	1921
5. Harry Rice	.359	1925
6. George Stone	.358	1906
7. Ken Williams	.357	1923
8. Heinie Manush	.355	1929
Baby Doll Jacobson	.355	1920
10. George Sisler	.352	1917

Batting Average: Career with Team

Player	BA	PA
1. George Sisler	.344	7,269
2. Ken Williams	.326	4,668
3. Jack Tobin	.318	4,873
4. Baby Doll Jacobson	.317	5,244
5. Bob Dillinger	.309	2,211
Beau Bell	.309	2,256
7. Sam West	.305	3,075
8. George Stone	.301	3,663
Bob Nieman	.301	2,402
Harold Baines	.301	2,415

Total Hits: Season

Player	H	Year
1. George Sisler	257	1920
2. George Sisler	246	1922
3. Heinie Manush	241	1928
4. Jack Tobin	236	1921
5. George Sisler	224	1925
6. Beau Bell	218	1937
7. Baby Doll Jacobson	216	1920
George Sisler	216	1921
9. Beau Bell	212	1936
10. Baby Doll Jacobson	211	1921
Cal Ripken Jr.	211	1983

Total Hits: Career with Team

Player	H	PA
1. Cal Ripken Jr.	3,184	12,883
2. Brooks Robinson	2,848	11,782
3. George Sisler	2,295	7,269
4. Eddie Murray	2,080	8,053
5. Brady Anderson	1,614	7,464
6. Boog Powell	1,574	6,912
7. Baby Doll Jacobson	1,508	5,244
8. Harlond Clift	1,463	6,355
9. Ken Singleton	1,455	6,071
10. Paul Blair	1,426	6,192

Home Runs: Season

Player	HR	Year
1. Brady Anderson	50	1996
2. Frank Robinson	49	1966
3. Jim Gentile	46	1961
4. Rafael Palmeiro	43	1998
5. Rafael Palmeiro	39	1995
Rafael Palmeiro	39	1996
Boog Powell	39	1964
Ken Williams	39	1922
9. Rafael Palmeiro	38	1997
10. Albert Belle	37	1999
Boog Powell	37	1969

Home Runs: Career with Team

Player	HR	PA
1. Cal Ripken Jr.	431	12,883
2. Eddie Murray	343	8,053
3. Boog Powell	303	6,912
4. Brooks Robinson	268	11,782
5. Rafael Palmeiro	223	4,328
6. Brady Anderson	209	7,464
7. Ken Williams	185	4,668
8. Ken Singleton	182	6,071
9. Frank Robinson	179	3,492
10. Harlond Clift	170	6,355

Triples: Season

Player	3B	Year
1. Heinie Manush	20	1928
George Stone	20	1906
3. George Sisler	18	1920
George Sisler	18	1921
George Sisler	18	1922
Jack Tobin	18	1921
7. Baby Doll Jacobson	16	1922
Tilly Walker	16	1914
Gus Williams	16	1913
10. Five tied with . . .	15	—

Triples: Career with Team

Player	3B	PA
1. George Sisler	145	7,269
2. Baby Doll Jacobson	88	5,244

3. Del Pratt	72	3,758
Jack Tobin	72	4,873
5. Ken Williams	70	4,668
6. Brooks Robinson	68	11,782
George Stone	68	3,663
8. Jimmy Austin	67	5,291
9. Bobby Wallace	65	6,199
10. Brady Anderson	64	7,464

Doubles: Season

Player	2B	Year
1. Beau Bell	51	1937
2. Brian Roberts	50	2004
Miguel Tejada	50	2005
4. George Sisler	49	1920
5. Heinie Manush	47	1928
Cal Ripken Jr.	47	1983
Joe Vosmik	47	1937
8. John Anderson	46	1901
Red Kress	46	1931
Cal Ripken Jr.	46	1991

Doubles: Career with Team

Player	2B	PA
1. Cal Ripken Jr.	603	12,883
2. Brooks Robinson	482	11,782
3. Eddie Murray	363	8,053
4. George Sisler	343	7,269
5. Brady Anderson	329	7,464
6. Harlond Clift	294	6,355
7. Paul Blair	269	6,192
Baby Doll Jacobson	269	5,244
9. George McQuinn	254	4,940
10. Boog Powell	243	6,912

Extra-Base Hits: Season

Player	XBH	Year
1. Brady Anderson	92	1996
2. George Sisler	86	1920
3. Cal Ripken Jr.	85	1991
Frank Robinson	85	1966
5. Ken Williams	84	1922
6. Rafael Palmeiro	81	1996
Miguel Tejada	81	2005
8. Heinie Manush	80	1928
Rafael Palmeiro	80	1998
10. Ken Williams	78	1923

Extra-Base Hits: Career with Team

Player	XBH	PA
1. Cal Ripken Jr.	1,078	12,883
2. Brooks Robinson	818	11,782
3. Eddie Murray	731	8,053
4. Brady Anderson	602	7,464
5. George Sisler	581	7,269
6. Boog Powell	557	6,912
7. Harlond Clift	526	6,355
8. Ken Williams	491	4,668
9. Paul Blair	446	6,192
10. Ken Singleton	436	6,071

Total Bases: Season

Player	TB	Year
1. George Sisler	399	1920
2. Brady Anderson	369	1996
3. Cal Ripken Jr.	368	1991
4. Heinie Manush	367	1928
Frank Robinson	367	1966
Ken Williams	367	1922
7. Rafael Palmeiro	350	1998
8. Miguel Tejada	349	2004
9. George Sisler	348	1922
10. Ken Williams	346	1923

Total Bases: Career with Team

Player	TB	PA
1. Cal Ripken Jr.	5,168	12,883
2. Brooks Robinson	4,270	11,782
3. Eddie Murray	3,522	8,053
4. George Sisler	3,207	7,269
5. Boog Powell	2,748	6,912
6. Brady Anderson	2,698	7,464
7. Harlond Clift	2,391	6,355
8. Ken Singleton	2,274	6,071
9. Ken Williams	2,239	4,668
10. Baby Doll Jacobson	2,181	5,244

Runs Batted In: Season

Player	RBI	Year
1. Ken Williams	155	1922
2. Miguel Tejada	150	2004
3. Rafael Palmeiro	142	1996
4. Jim Gentile	141	1961
5. Moose Solters	134	1936
6. Eddie Murray	124	1985
7. Beau Bell	123	1936
8. Baby Doll Jacobson	122	1920
Frank Robinson	122	1966
George Sisler	122	1920

Runs Batted In: Career with Team

Player	RBI	PA
1. Cal Ripken Jr.	1,695	12,883
2. Brooks Robinson	1,357	11,782
3. Eddie Murray	1,224	8,053
4. Boog Powell	1,063	6,912
5. George Sisler	959	7,269
6. Ken Williams	808	4,668
7. Harlond Clift	769	6,355
8. Ken Singleton	766	6,071
9. Brady Anderson	744	7,464
10. Baby Doll Jacobson	704	5,244

Runs Scored: Season

Player	R	Year
1. Harlond Clift	145	1936
2. George Sisler	137	1920
3. George Sisler	134	1922
4. Roberto Alomar	132	1996
Jack Tobin	132	1921
6. Ken Williams	128	1922
7. George Sisler	125	1921
8. Frank Robinson	122	1966
Jack Tobin	122	1922
10. Cal Ripken Jr.	121	1983

Runs Scored: Career with Team

Player	R	PA
1. Cal Ripken Jr.	1,647	12,883
2. Brooks Robinson	1,232	11,782
3. George Sisler	1,091	7,269
4. Eddie Murray	1,084	8,053
5. Brady Anderson	1,044	7,464
6. Harlond Clift	1,013	6,355
7. Boog Powell	796	6,912
8. Al Bumbry	772	5,516
9. Ken Williams	757	4,668
10. Paul Blair	737	6,192

Walks: Season

Player	BB	Year
1. Lu Blue	126	1929
2. Roy Cullenbine	121	1941
3. Harlond Clift	118	1938
Burt Shotton	118	1915
Ken Singleton	118	1975
6. Lyn Lary	117	1936

7. Harlond Clift	115	1936
8. Harlond Clift	113	1941
9. Harlond Clift	111	1939
10. Burt Shotton	110	1916

WALKS: CAREER WITH TEAM

Player	BB	PA
1. Cal Ripken Jr.	1,129	12,883
2. Harlond Clift	986	6,355
3. Brady Anderson	927	7,464
4. Boog Powell	889	6,912
5. Ken Singleton	886	6,071
6. Eddie Murray	884	8,053
7. Brooks Robinson	860	11,782
8. Burt Shotton	595	4,574
9. Mark Belanger	571	6,545
10. Bobby Wallace	526	6,199

STRIKEOUTS: SEASON

Player	SO	Year
1. Mickey Tettleton	160	1990
2. Boog Powell	125	1966
3. Gus Williams	120	1914
4. Lee May	119	1977
5. Ken Singleton	118	1979
6. Bobby Grich	117	1974
Mickey Tettleton	117	1989
8. Mike Devereaux	115	1991
9. Mark Belanger	114	1968
Craig Worthington	114	1989

STRIKEOUTS: CAREER WITH TEAM

Player	SO	PA
1. Cal Ripken Jr.	1,305	12,883
2. Brady Anderson	1,132	7,464
3. Boog Powell	1,102	6,912
4. Brooks Robinson	990	11,782
5. Eddie Murray	969	8,053
6. Ken Singleton	860	6,071
7. Mark Belanger	829	6,545
8. Paul Blair	816	6,192
9. Al Bumbry	700	5,516
10. Harlond Clift	649	6,355

SLUGGING PERCENTAGE: SEASON

Player	SLG	Year
1. Goose Goslin	.652	1930
2. Jim Gentile	.646	1961
3. Brady Anderson	.637	1996
Frank Robinson	.637	1966
5. George Sisler	.632	1920
6. Ken Williams	.627	1922
7. Ken Williams	.623	1923
8. Ken Williams	.613	1925
9. Boog Powell	.606	1964
10. John Lowenstein	.602	1982

SLUGGING PERCENTAGE: CAREER WITH TEAM

Player	SLG	PA
1. Ken Williams	.558	4,668
2. Frank Robinson	.543	3,492
3. Rafael Palmeiro	.520	4,328
4. Jim Gentile	.512	2,286
5. Harold Baines	.502	2,415
6. Eddie Murray	.498	8,053
7. Bob Nieman	.486	2,402
8. George Sisler	.481	7,269
9. Chris Hoiles	.467	3,338
10. Jay Gibbons	.466	2,367

ON-BASE PERCENTAGE: SEASON

Player	OBP	Year
1. George Sisler	.467	1922
2. Roy Cullenbine	.452	1941
3. Harry Rice	.450	1925
4. George Sisler	.449	1920
5. Bob Nieman	.442	1956
6. Ken Williams	.439	1923
7. Ken Singleton	.438	1977
8. Ken Williams	.429	1921
9. Ken Williams	.425	1924
10. Harlond Clift	.424	1936

ON-BASE PERCENTAGE: CAREER WITH TEAM

Player	OBP	PA
1. Ken Williams	.403	4,668
2. Frank Robinson	.401	3,492
3. Harlond Clift	.394	6,355
4. Ken Singleton	.388	6,071
Randy Milligan	.388	2,048
6. Sam West	.386	3,075
7. Don Buford	.385	2,820
8. Bob Nieman	.384	2,402
George Sisler	.384	7,269
10. Merv Rettenmund	.383	2,021

OPS (ON-BASE PERCENTAGE + SLUGGING PERCENTAGE): SEASON

Player	OPS	Year
1. George Sisler	1.082	1920
2. Jim Gentile	1.069	1961
3. Ken Williams	1.062	1923
4. George Sisler	1.061	1922
5. Goose Goslin	1.052	1930
6. Frank Robinson	1.047	1966
7. Ken Williams	1.040	1922
8. Brady Anderson	1.034	1996
9. Harry Rice	1.018	1925
10. John Lowenstein	1.017	1982

OPS (ON-BASE PERCENTAGE + SLUGGING PERCENTAGE): CAREER WITH TEAM

Player	OPS	PA
1. Ken Williams	.961	4,668
2. Frank Robinson	.944	3,492
3. Jim Gentile	.891	2,286
4. Rafael Palmeiro	.886	4,328
5. Harold Baines	.881	2,415
6. Bob Nieman	.869	2,402
7. Eddie Murray	.868	8,053
8. George Sisler	.865	7,269
9. Harlond Clift	.847	6,355
10. Beau Bell	.836	2,256

STOLEN BASES: SEASON

Player	SB	Year
1. Luis Aparicio	57	1964
2. Brady Anderson	53	1992
3. George Sisler	51	1922
4. Armando Marsans	46	1916
5. George Sisler	45	1918
6. Al Bumbry	44	1980
7. Burt Shotton	43	1913
Burt Shotton	43	1915
9. Al Bumbry	42	1976
George Sisler	42	1920

STOLEN BASES: CAREER WITH TEAM

Player	SB	PA
1. George Sisler	351	7,269
2. Brady Anderson	307	7,464

3. Al Bumbry	252	5,516
4. Burt Shotton	247	4,574
5. Jimmy Austin	192	5,291
6. Del Pratt	174	3,758
7. Paul Blair	167	6,192
8. Luis Aparicio	166	3,216
Mark Belanger	166	6,545
10. Ken Williams	144	4,668

Sacrifice Hits: Season

Player	Sac	Year
1. Joe Gedeon	48	1920
2. Joe Gedeon	40	1919
Tom Jones	40	1906
4. Jimmy Austin	35	1915
5. Jimmy Austin	34	1911
Tom Jones	34	1908
7. Wally Gerber	32	1922
Del Pratt	32	1915
9. Tom Jones	31	1907
Hank Severeid	31	1924

Sacrifice Hits: Career with Team

Player	Sac	PA
1. Jimmy Austin	223	5,291
2. Wally Gerber	197	5,151
3. George Sisler	177	7,269
4. Tom Jones	161	3,446
5. Mark Belanger	153	6,545
6. Baby Doll Jacobson	139	5,244
7. Ken Williams	131	4,668
8. Marty McManus	117	3,615
Ski Melillo	117	4,663
Hank Severeid	117	4,290

Hit by Pitch: Season

Player	HBP	Year
1. Brady Anderson	24	1999
2. Brady Anderson	22	1996
3. Bobby Grich	20	1974
Melvin Mora	20	2002
5. Brady Anderson	19	1997
6. Dick Padden	18	1904
7. Brady Anderson	15	1998
8. Melvin Mora	14	2001
Ike Rockenfield	14	1905
10. Don Baylor	13	1973
Don Baylor	13	1975
Jerry Hairston	13	2001
Frank Robinson	13	1969

Hit by Pitch: Career with Team

Player	HBP	PA
1. Brady Anderson	148	7,464
2. Melvin Mora	71	3,090
3. Cal Ripken Jr.	66	12,883
4. Frank Robinson	58	3,492
5. Brooks Robinson	53	1,782
6. Don Baylor	46	1,994
7. Bobby Grich	45	3,344
8. Chris Hoiles	44	3,338
9. Jerry Hairston	43	2,086
10. Mark Belanger	42	6,545

Top 10 Pitching Leaders, Single Season & Career with Team

Games Pitched: Season

Player	GP	Year
1. Tippy Martinez	76	1982
B.J. Ryan	76	2003
B.J. Ryan	76	2004
4. Mike Trombley	75	2000
5. Alan Mills	72	1998
Gregg Olson	72	1991
Todd Williams	72	2005
8. Armando Benitez	71	1997
Armando Benitez	71	1998
Stu Miller	71	1963
Jesse Orosco	71	1997

Games Pitched: Career with Team

Player	GP	IP
1. Jim Palmer	558	3,948.0
2. Tippy Martinez	499	752.3
3. Mike Flanagan	450	2,317.7
4. Dave McNally	412	2,652.7
5. B.J. Ryan	404	379.3
6. Mark Williamson	365	689.7
7. Eddie Watt	363	615.3
8. Scott McGregor	356	2,140.7
9. Alan Mills	346	480.0
10. Dick Hall	342	770.0

Innings Pitched: Season

Player	IP	Year
1. Urban Shocker	348.0	1922
2. Bobo Newsom	329.7	1938
3. Jack Powell	328.3	1902
4. Urban Shocker	326.7	1921
5. Harry Howell	324.3	1908
6. Harry Howell	323.0	1905
Jim Palmer	323.0	1975
8. Jim Palmer	319.0	1977
9. Bump Hadley	316.7	1933
10. Red Donahue	316.3	1902
Harry Howell	316.3	1907

Innings Pitched: Career with Team

Player	IP
1. Jim Palmer	3,948.0
2. Dave McNally	2,652.7
3. Mike Flanagan	2,317.7
4. Jack Powell	2,229.7
5. Scott McGregor	2,140.7
6. Mike Cuellar	2,028.3
7. Mike Mussina	2,009.7
8. Barney Pelty	1,864.3
9. Dennis Martinez	1,775.0
10. Urban Shocker	1,749.7

Batters Faced: Season

Player	BF	Year
1. Bobo Newsom	1,475	1938
2. Urban Shocker	1,441	1922
3. Urban Shocker	1,401	1921
4. Jack Powell	1,391	1902
5. Bump Hadley	1,365	1933
6. Red Donahue	1,330	1902
7. Dolly Gray	1,310	1929
8. Harry Howell	1,297	1908
9. Harry Howell	1,293	1905
10. Harry Howell	1,269	1907
Jim Palmer	1,269	1977
Jack Powell	1,269	1903

Batters Faced: Career with Team

Player	BF	IP
1. Jim Palmer	16,112	3,948.0
2. Dave McNally	10,871	2,652.7
3. Mike Flanagan	9,739	2,317.7
4. Scott McGregor	8,982	2,140.7
5. Mike Cuellar	8,268	2,028.3
6. Mike Mussina	8,201	2,009.7
7. Jack Powell	7,971	2,229.7
8. Dennis Martinez	7,544	1,775.0
9. Urban Shocker	7,261	1,749.7
10. George Blaeholder	7,146	1,631.0

Games Started: Season

Player	GS	Year
1. Mike Cuellar	40	1970
Mike Flanagan	40	1978
Dave McNally	40	1969
Dave McNally	40	1970
Bobo Newsom	40	1938
Jim Palmer	40	1976
7. Mike Cuellar	39	1969
Dave Davenport	39	1917
Ross Grimsley	39	1974
Dennis Martinez	39	1979
Dennis Martinez	39	1982
Jim Palmer	39	1970
Jim Palmer	39	1977
Jack Powell	39	1902

Games Started: Career with Team

Player	GS	IP
1. Jim Palmer	521	3,948.0
2. Dave McNally	384	2,652.7
3. Mike Flanagan	328	2,317.7
4. Scott McGregor	309	2,140.7
5. Mike Mussina	288	2,009.7
6. Mike Cuellar	283	2,028.3
7. Jack Powell	264	2,229.7
8. Dennis Martinez	243	1,775.0
9. Milt Pappas	232	1,632.0
10. George Blaeholder	213	1,631.0
Barney Pelty	213	1,864.3

Complete Games: Season

Player	CG	Year
1. Jack Powell	36	1902
2. Harry Howell	35	1905
3. Red Donahue	33	1902
Jack Powell	33	1903
5. Harry Howell	32	1904
6. Bobo Newsom	31	1938
Barney Pelty	31	1904
8. Fred Glade	30	1904
Harry Howell	30	1906
Urban Shocker	30	1921
Willie Sudhoff	30	1903

Complete Games: Career with Team

Player	CG	IP
1. Jim Palmer	211	3,948.0
2. Jack Powell	210	2,229.7
3. Barney Pelty	174	1,864.3
4. Harry Howell	150	1,580.7
5. Urban Shocker	143	1,749.7
6. Mike Cuellar	133	2,028.3
7. Dave McNally	120	2,652.7
8. Carl Weilman	105	1,521.0
9. Fred Glade	104	1,032.7
10. Mike Flanagan	98	2,317.7

Games Won: Season

Player	W	Year
1. Urban Shocker	27	1921
2. Steve Stone	25	1980
3. Mike Cuellar	24	1970
Dave McNally	24	1970
Urban Shocker	24	1922
6. Mike Cuellar	23	1969
Mike Flanagan	23	1979
Jim Palmer	23	1975
9. Six tied with . . .	22	——

Games Won: Career with Team

Player	W	IP
1. Jim Palmer	268	3,948.0
2. Dave McNally	181	2,652.7
3. Mike Mussina	147	2,009.7
4. Mike Cuellar	143	2,028.3
5. Mike Flanagan	141	2,317.7
6. Scott McGregor	138	2,140.7
7. Urban Shocker	126	1,749.7
8. Jack Powell	117	2,229.7
9. Milt Pappas	110	1,632.0
10. Dennis Martinez	108	1,775.0

Games Lost: Season

Player	L	Year
1. Fred Glade	25	1905
2. Dolly Gray	24	1931
3. Harry Howell	22	1905
4. Harry Howell	21	1904
Don Larsen	21	1954
Barney Pelty	21	1907
Fred Sanford	21	1948
8. Seven tied with . . .	20	——

Games Lost: Career with Team

Player	L	IP
1. Jim Palmer	152	3,948.0
2. Jack Powell	143	2,229.7
3. Mike Flanagan	116	2,317.7
4. Dave McNally	113	2,652.7
Barney Pelty	113	1,864.3
6. George Blaeholder	111	1,631.0
7. Scott McGregor	108	2,140.7
8. Carl Weilman	95	1,521.0
9. Dennis Martinez	93	1,775.0
10. Harry Howell	91	1,580.7
Elam Vangilder	91	1,548.0

Winning Percentage: Season

Player	W%	Year
1. Alvin Crowder	.808	1928
Dave McNally	.808	1971
3. Jim Palmer	.800	1969
4. Wally Bunker	.792	1964
5. Mike Mussina	.783	1992
6. Steve Stone	.781	1980
7. Ray Kolp	.778	1922
8. Bob Muncrief	.765	1945
9. Mike Mussina	.762	1994
10. Mike Cuellar	.750	1970
Mike Flanagan	.750	1983
Jim Palmer	.750	1982

Winning Percentage: Career with Team

Player	W%	IP
1. Mike Mussina	.645	2,009.7
2. Jim Palmer	.638	3,948.0
3. Mike Cuellar	.619	2,028.3
Dick Hall	.619	770.0
5. Dave McNally	.616	2,652.7
6. Urban Shocker	.612	1,749.7

Player		
7. Milt Pappas	.598	1,632.0
8. Storm Davis	.587	944.3
9. Alvin Crowder	.579	661.7
10. Tom Phoebus	.575	807.7

Shutouts: Season

Player	SHO	Year
1. Jim Palmer	10	1975
2. Steve Barber	8	1961
3. Milt Pappas	7	1964
4. Fred Glade	6	1904
Harry Howell	6	1906
Dave McNally	6	1972
Jim Palmer	6	1969
Jim Palmer	6	1973
Jim Palmer	6	1976
Jim Palmer	6	1978

Shutouts: Career with Team

Player	SHO	IP
1. Jim Palmer	53	3,948.0
2. Dave McNally	33	2,652.7
3. Mike Cuellar	30	2,028.3
4. Jack Powell	27	2,229.7
5. Milt Pappas	26	1,632.0
6. Scott McGregor	23	2,140.7
Barney Pelty	23	1,864.3
Urban Shocker	23	1,749.7
9. Steve Barber	19	1,414.7
10. Mike Flanagan	17	2,317.7

ERA: Season

Player	ERA	Year
1. Barney Pelty	1.59	1906
2. Jack Powell	1.77	1906
3. Harry Howell	1.89	1908
Rube Waddell	1.89	1908
5. Harry Howell	1.93	1907
6. Allen Sothoron	1.94	1918
7. Dave McNally	1.95	1968
8. Harry Howell	1.98	1905
9. Jim Palmer	2.07	1972
10. Carl Weilman	2.08	1914

ERA: Career with Team

Player	ERA	IP
1. Harry Howell	2.06	1,580.7
2. Rube Waddell	2.19	539.0
3. Stu Miller	2.37	502.0
4. Hoyt Wilhelm	2.42	616.3
5. Fred Glade	2.52	1,032.7
6. Barney Pelty	2.62	1,864.3
7. Jack Powell	2.63	2,229.7
8. Carl Weilman	2.67	1,521.0
9. Eddie Watt	2.74	615.3
10. Pat Dobson	2.78	550.7

Earned Runs Allowed: Season

Player	ER	Year
1. Bobo Newsom	186	1938
2. Jack Knott	156	1936
3. Dolly Gray	146	1931
4. Milt Gaston	141	1927
Bump Hadley	141	1932
Bill Reidy	141	1901
7. Bump Hadley	138	1933
Vern Kennedy	138	1940
9. Jack Kramer	137	1939
10. George Blaeholder	135	1932

Earned Runs Allowed: Career with Team

Player	ER	IP
1. Jim Palmer	1,253	3,948.0
2. Mike Flanagan	1,001	2,317.7
3. Scott McGregor	949	2,140.7
4. Dave McNally	937	2,652.7
5. George Blaeholder	824	1,631.0
6. Dennis Martinez	820	1,775.0
7. Mike Mussina	789	2,009.7
8. Sidney Ponson	743	1,375.3
9. Elam Vangilder	739	1,548.0
10. Mike Cuellar	716	2,028.3

Strikeouts: Season

Player	K	Year
1. Rube Waddell	232	1908
2. Bobo Newsom	226	1938
3. Mike Mussina	218	1997
4. Mike Mussina	210	2000
5. Mike Mussina	204	1996
6. Dave McNally	202	1968
7. Jim Palmer	199	1970
8. Harry Howell	198	1905
9. Jim Palmer	193	1975
Jim Palmer	193	1977
Tom Phoebus	193	1968

Strikeouts: Career with Team

Player	K	IP
1. Jim Palmer	2,212	3,948.0
2. Mike Mussina	1,535	2,009.7
3. Dave McNally	1,476	2,652.7
4. Mike Flanagan	1,297	2,317.7
5. Mike Cuellar	1,011	2,028.3
6. Milt Pappas	944	1,632.0
7. Steve Barber	918	1,414.7
8. Scott McGregor	904	2,140.7
9. Jack Powell	884	2,229.7
10. Dennis Martinez	858	1,775.0

Strikeouts Per Nine IP: Season

Player	K/9	Year
1. Mike Mussina	8.73	1997
2. Mike Mussina	7.95	2000
3. Tom Phoebus	7.75	1967
4. Mike Mussina	7.63	1998
5. Mike Mussina	7.61	1999
6. Ken Dixon	7.56	1986
7. Mike Mussina	7.55	1996
8. Rube Waddell	7.31	1908
9. Tom Phoebus	7.22	1968
10. Mike Boddicker	7.21	1986

Strikeouts Per Nine IP: Career with Team

Player	K/9	IP
1. Arthur Rhodes	8.37	622.3
2. Stu Miller	7.75	502.0
3. Tippy Martinez	7.00	752.3
4. Mike Mussina	6.87	2,009.7
5. Hoyt Wilhelm	6.69	616.3
6. Rube Waddell	6.50	539.0
7. Tom Phoebus	6.44	807.7
8. Chuck Estrada	6.37	730.0
9. Eddie Watt	6.33	615.3
10. Connie Johnson	6.20	544.0

Hits Allowed: Season

Player	HA	Year
1. Urban Shocker	365	1922
2. Bill Reidy	364	1901
3. Urban Shocker	345	1921
4. Dolly Gray	336	1929
5. Bobo Newsom	334	1938
6. Dolly Gray	323	1931
7. Red Donahue	322	1902
8. Jack Powell	320	1902
9. Bump Hadley	309	1933
10. George Blaeholder	304	1932

Hits Allowed: Career with Team

Player	HA	IP
1. Jim Palmer	3,349	3,948.0
2. Dave McNally	2,400	2,652.7
3. Mike Flanagan	2,326	2,317.7
4. Scott McGregor	2,245	2,140.7
5. Jack Powell	2,083	2,229.7
6. Mike Mussina	1,895	2,009.7
7. George Blaeholder	1,889	1,631.0
8. Dennis Martinez	1,822	1,775.0
9. Mike Cuellar	1,809	2,028.3
10. Urban Shocker	1,758	1,749.7

Hits Allowed per Nine IP: Season

Player	H/9	Year
1. Dave McNally	5.77	1968
2. Bob Turley	6.48	1954
3. Jim Palmer	6.51	1969
4. Barney Pelty	6.53	1906
5. Allen Sothoron	6.55	1918
6. Mike Cuellar	6.60	1969
7. Chuck Estrada	6.75	1961
8. Wally Bunker	6.77	1964
9. Milt Pappas	6.79	1961
10. Jim Palmer	6.83	1973

Hits Allowed per Nine IP: Career with Team

Player	H/9	IP
1. Stu Miller	6.90	502.0
2. Eddie Watt	6.98	615.3
3. Hoyt Wilhelm	7.02	616.3
4. Tom Phoebus	7.41	807.7
5. Chuck Estrada	7.50	730.0
6. Harry Howell	7.54	1,580.7
7. Billy O'Dell	7.56	585.3
8. Dick Hall	7.57	770.0
9. Jim Palmer	7.63	3,948.0
10. Rube Waddell	7.65	539.0

Walks Allowed: Season

Player	BB	Year
1. Bobo Newsom	192	1938
2. Bob Turley	181	1954
3. Bump Hadley	163	1932
4. Dixie Davis	149	1920
Bobo Newsom	149	1934
6. Bump Hadley	141	1933
7. Grover Lowdermilk	133	1915
Mike Torrez	133	1975
9. Chuck Estrada	132	1961
10. Steve Barber	130	1961

Walks Allowed: Career with Team

Player	BB	IP
1. Jim Palmer	1,311	3,948.0
2. Dave McNally	790	2,652.7
3. Mike Flanagan	740	2,317.7
4. Steve Barber	668	1,414.7
5. Dixie Davis	640	1,242.0
6. Elam Vangilder	625	1,548.0
7. Mike Cuellar	601	2,028.3
8. Dennis Martinez	583	1,775.0
9. Milt Pappas	531	1,632.0
10. Barney Pelty	522	1,864.3

Walks Allowed per Nine IP: Season

Player	BB/9	Year
1. Scott McGregor	1.19	1979
2. Ed Siever	1.38	1903
3. Robin Roberts	1.43	1963
4. Urban Shocker	1.47	1922
5. Scott McGregor	1.56	1983
6. Jack Powell	1.58	1909
7. Urban Shocker	1.59	1923
8. Jack Powell	1.65	1908
9. Joe Lake	1.67	1911
10. Jack Powell	1.70	1903

Walks Allowed per Nine IP: Career with Team

Player	BB/9	IP
1. Dick Hall	1.47	770.0
2. Robin Roberts	1.81	761.3
3. Fred Glade	1.92	1,032.7
4. Jack Powell	1.96	2,229.7
5. Hal Brown	1.99	1,030.7
6. Mike Mussina	2.09	2,009.7
7. Urban Shocker	2.10	1,749.7
8. Pat Dobson	2.16	550.7
9. Scott McGregor	2.18	2,140.7
10. Harry Howell	2.22	1,580.7

WHIP (Walks + Hits per Nine IP): Season

Player	WHIP	Year
1. Dave McNally	0.842	1968
2. Barney Pelty	0.951	1906
3. Jack Powell	0.996	1908
4. Mike Cuellar	1.005	1969
5. Fred Glade	1.028	1906
6. Jack Powell	1.029	1906
7. Jim Palmer	1.031	1975
8. Wally Bunker	1.042	1964
9. Harry Howell	1.048	1904
Allen Sothoron	1.048	1918

WHIP (Walks + Hits per Nine IP): Career with Team

Player	WHIP	IP
1. Dick Hall	1.005	770.0
2. Harry Howell	1.085	1,580.7
3. Pat Dobson	1.090	550.7
4. Fred Glade	1.091	1,032.7
5. Hoyt Wilhelm	1.107	616.3
6. Stu Miller	1.120	502.0
7. Billy O'Dell	1.128	585.3
8. Eddie Watt	1.133	615.3
9. Jim Hardin	1.137	643.7
10. Rube Waddell	1.143	539.0

Home Runs Allowed: Season

Player	HRA	Year
1. Scott McGregor	35	1986
Sidney Ponson	35	1999
Robin Roberts	35	1963
4. Mike Cuellar	34	1970
Scott McGregor	34	1985
6. Ken Dixon	33	1986
Bruce Chen	33	2005
8. Eric Bell	32	1987
Ben McDonald	32	1992
David Wells	32	1996

Home Runs Allowed: Career with Team

Player	HRA	IP
1. Jim Palmer	303	3,948.0
2. Scott McGregor	235	2,140.7
3. Dave McNally	222	2,652.7
4. Mike Flanagan	212	2,317.7
5. Mike Mussina	210	2,009.7
6. Dennis Martinez	187	1,775.0
7. Sidney Ponson	180	1,375.3
8. Mike Cuellar	174	2,028.3
9. George Blaeholder	142	1,631.0
Milt Pappas	142	1,632.0

Saves: Season

Player	SV	Year
1. Randy Myers	45	1997
2. Gregg Olson	37	1990
3. Jorge Julio	36	2003
Gregg Olson	36	1992
B.J. Ryan	36	2005
6. Don Aase	34	1986
7. Lee Smith	33	1994
8. Randy Myers	31	1996
Gregg Olson	31	1991
10. Gregg Olson	29	1993

Saves: Career with Team

Player	SV	IP
1. Gregg Olson	160	350.3
2. Tippy Martinez	105	752.3
3. Stu Miller	100	502.0
4. Jorge Julio	83	291.7
5. Randy Myers	76	118.3
6. Eddie Watt	74	615.3
7. Dick Hall	58	770.0
8. Tim Stoddard	57	313.0
9. Don Aase	50	224.3
10. Don Stanhouse	45	174.0

Wild Pitches: Season

Player	WP	Year
1. Milt Pappas	14	1959
2. Ned Garvin	13	1901
Dennis Martinez	13	1984
4. Daniel Cabrera	12	2004
Mike Flanagan	12	1980
Tom Phoebus	12	1967
7. Seven tied with...	11	——

Wild Pitches: Career with Team

Player	WP	IP
1. Jim Palmer	85	3,948.0
2. Mike Flanagan	75	2,317.7
3. Milt Pappas	64	1,632.0
4. Dennis Martinez	56	1,775.0
Dave McNally	56	2,652.7
6. Steve Barber	52	1,414.7
7. Tippy Martinez	49	752.3
8. Barney Pelty	42	1,864.3
Sidney Ponson	42	1,375.3
10. Mike Mussina	39	2,009.7

Hit Batsmen: Season

Player	HB	Year
1. Barney Pelty	20	1904
2. Barney Pelty	19	1906
Barney Pelty	19	1907
4. Harry Howell	17	1908
5. Grover Lowdermilk	16	1915
6. Earl Caldwell	15	1936
Chuck Estrada	15	1960
Chief Hogsett	15	1936
9. Ned Garvin	14	1901
Tully Sparks	14	1901

Hit Batsmen: Career with Team

Player	HB	IP
1. Barney Pelty	103	1864.3
2. Dave McNally	68	2652.7
3. Harry Howell	63	1580.7
4. Scott Erickson	54	1287.7
5. Jack Powell	50	2229.7
6. Earl Hamilton	48	1328.7
7. Willie Sudhoff	45	980.0
8. Dixie Davis	43	1242.0
Fred Glade	43	1032.7
10. Mike Boddicker	39	1273.7
Dennis Martinez	39	1775.0
Elam Vangilder	39	1548.0

Games Finished: Season

Player	GF	Year
1. Gregg Olson	62	1991
2. Jorge Julio	61	2002
B.J. Ryan	61	2005
4. Stu Miller	59	1963
5. Don Aase	58	1986
Gregg Olson	58	1990
7. Randy Myers	57	1997
8. Gregg Olson	56	1992
9. Stu Miller	55	1965
10. Armando Benitez	54	1998

Games Finished: Career with Team

Player	GF	IP
1. Tippy Martinez	298	752.3
2. Gregg Olson	277	350.3
3. Stu Miller	224	502.0
Eddie Watt	224	615.3
5. Jorge Julio	189	291.7
6. Dick Hall	175	770.0
7. Tim Stoddard	162	313.0
8. Sammy Stewart	160	866.0
9. Mark Williamson	142	689.7
10. B.J. Ryan	131	379.3

Significant Orioles/Browns/Brewers

Alomar, Roberto (2B)
(1996–1998)

See Blue Jays bio.

Anderson, Brady (OF)
(1988–2001)

After half a season in Boston, Brady Anderson was traded to the Orioles along with Curt Schilling for Mike Boddicker on July 29, 1988. Anderson patrolled the O's outfield until 2001, although he was only a platoon player his first four years because of his modest batting averages, .231 or lower. He admitted later that he was "one phone call away from going to Japan," when he suddenly turned things around in Baltimore. Anderson was a fan favorite almost from the beginning because of his friendly nature and aggressive style of play, but now he was a major offensive contributor, too. He became a regular in 1992 and his average rose to .271. In 1996 he experienced a one-year power explosion, when he slugged 50 homers—26 more than any other year in his career. What made the year even more amazing was that he played through appendicitis. His production began to slide in 2000, and in 2001 his offense virtually disappeared: He hit just .202 with eight homers. Anderson, a three-time All-Star with Baltimore, was released after the season and signed on with Cleveland, but played just 34 games as a utility outfielder before retiring.

CAREER ORIOLES RECORD:

Games	AB	Hits	Runs
1,759	6,271	1,614	1,044

Avg	HR	RBI	SB
.257	209	744	307

BELANGER, MARK (SS)
(1965–1981)

The Orioles signed Mark Belanger as an amateur free agent in June 1962. After spending most of his first six years of professional baseball in the minors, Belanger made it to the major leagues for good in 1968, replacing Hall of Famer Luis Aparicio. For the next 15 years—14 with Baltimore—Belanger became the poster boy for the gifted-glove/weak-stick shortstop. His .228 career batting average ranks in the bottom 20 or so of all time among players with at least 2,500 at-bats. Belanger won eight Gold Gloves with the O's, forming with Brooks Robinson a virtually impregnable left side of the infield. When Bobby Grich arrived in 1973, the Orioles had one of the best fielding infields in the history of major league baseball, as they all won Gold Gloves from 1973–1975. For some odd reason, Belanger was able to hit well against the toughest pitchers of his time, such as Nolan Ryan and Ron Guidry. After he retired, Belanger joined the Major League Baseball Players Association as a special assistant to Don Fehr, a position he held until his death from lung cancer at the age of 54.

CAREER ORIOLES RECORD:

Games	AB	Hits	Runs
1,962	5,734	1,304	670
Avg	**HR**	**RBI**	**SB**
.227	20	385	166

BLAIR, PAUL (OF)
(1964–1976)

Paul Blair originally signed with the New York Mets as an amateur free agent in 1961, but was claimed by the Orioles in a 1962 expansion draft move. He got an eight-game taste of the big leagues in 1964 before arriving for good in 1965. Blair was a key player during Baltimore's strong years in the late 1960s and early 1970s, earning two trips to the All-Star Game. He won eight Gold Gloves during his time with the O's, and was especially productive in the postseason, making important catches and collecting timely hits.

In May 1970, Blair was hit in the face by a pitch from Ken Tatum and suffered serious facial and eye injuries. When he returned from a six-week stint on the DL, he was extremely timid at the plate and eventually sought the services of a hypnotist to regain his confidence. It seemed to work; in the 1970 World Series, a newly poised Blair went 9-for-19 against the Reds. Blair slumped badly in 1976 and was shipped to the Yankees for Elliott Maddox. He had one so-so year as a part-time player with New York before suffering three consecutive miserable seasons. After just 12 games in 1980, Blair was released by the Yankees as an active player and became a base-running and fielding instructor for the team. He later became a minor league instructor with the Astros and, in 1986, was named the Commissioner of the North American Baseball League. In 1989 he joined Earl Weaver's Gold Coast Suns of the Senior League.

CAREER ORIOLES RECORD:

Games	AB	Hits	Runs
1,700	5,606	1,426	737
Avg	**HR**	**RBI**	**SB**
.254	126	567	167

BUMBRY, AL (OF/DH)
(1972–1984)

The Orioles drafted Al Bumbry in the 11th round of the 1968 amateur draft but had to wait until he was through serving in Vietnam in 1972 before they could employ his speedy services in a late-season call-up. By 1973 Bumbry was on the major league roster, hitting .337 with 11 triples and 23 stolen bases in just 110 games—good enough to earn the AL Rookie of the Year Award. For the next 12 seasons, Bumbry was the O's leadoff hitter. He hit over .300 four times with the O's, though he had little power, never topping nine homers in a season. While not as flashy as some of his teammates, Bumbry was an important part of the team's success throughout the 1970s and early 1980s. After leaving the Orioles via free agency following the 1984 season, Bumbry played one more year with San Diego before retiring to coach with the Red Sox, Orioles, and Indians.

CAREER ORIOLES RECORD:

Games	AB	Hits	Runs
1,428	4,958	1,403	772
Avg	**HR**	**RBI**	**SB**
.283	53	392	252

CLIFT, HARLOND (3B)
(1934–1943)

Harlond Clift might be the best third baseman nobody ever heard of. Playing for the weak St. Louis Browns contributed significantly to his obscurity. Clift was the first third baseman to break the 30-homer barrier when he smacked 34 in 1938. In the nine-year span from 1934 (his rookie year) to 1942, Clift scored more than 100 runs seven times, and the two years he missed the century mark, he scored 90 and 92. Six times he had more than 100 walks in a season; three times he broke up no-hitters; twice he led the AL in fielding. In 1937 he started 50 double plays, a record that stood until Graig Nettles topped it with 54 in 1974. The Detroit Tigers recognized his value and in 1940 offered the Browns $200,000 for Clift and two lesser players, but the Browns refused. By 1943, however, Clift's production had fallen dramatically and he was traded to Washington for three players and $35,000. After suffering a shoulder injury in a fall from a horse in 1944, Clift was essentially done. He hit just .211 in 1945 before calling it a career at age 32.

CAREER BROWNS RECORD:

Games	AB	Hits	Runs
1,443	5,281	1,463	1,013
Avg	**HR**	**RBI**	**SB**
.277	170	769	67

CUELLAR, MIKE (SP)
(1969–1976)

After six seasons in the National League with Cincinnati, St. Louis, and Houston, Cuban-born Mike Cuellar was traded to Baltimore in December 1968 in a deal that sent Curt Blefary to Houston. Over the next seven seasons, Cuellar was one of the main cogs in Baltimore's pitching machine. He made his living with a palm ball and an assortment of breaking pitches of varying arcs. It was said, only half jokingly, that you could catch his fastball barehanded. In his first year with the O's, Cuellar went 23–11 and was a cowinner of the AL Cy Young Award with Denny McLain. Cuellar, a four-time All-Star, would win 20 or more games three more times with Baltimore, helping the O's make it to the postseason five times. His 24 wins in 1970 led the American League. In 1976 Cuellar was 4–13, but he blamed his troubles on Baltimore manager Earl Weaver. Weaver, who noted that Cuellar had been knocked out of 13 straight starts, replied, "I've given him more chances than I gave my first wife." Following the season, the Orioles released their ineffective, disgruntled pitcher. He signed with the Angels as a free agent, but went 0–1 in two games with an ERA of 18.90 and was released. After his playing career, Cuellar became a minor league pitching instructor.

CAREER ORIOLES RECORD:

W	L	W%	ERA	SV
143	88	.619	3.18	1

K	BB	SHO	IP
1,011	601	30	2,028.3

FLANAGAN, MIKE (SP/RP)
(1975–1987, 1991–1992)

The Orioles drafted Mike Flanagan in the seventh round of the June 1973 amateur draft, brought him to the majors in late 1975, and placed him into the starting rotation in 1977. In 1979 the workhorse pitcher won the AL Cy Young Award with a 23–9 record and a 3.08 ERA, leading the O's into the World Series against Pittsburgh. Flanagan was a third-generation baseball player, his grandfather having made it to the majors in 1887, and his father having had a six-year minor league career. From 1977–1984, Flanagan made more starts and pitched more innings than any other pitcher in the American League. His 122 wins during that span were more than anyone else in the league notched with the exception of Ron Guidry.

Flanagan injured his Achilles tendon in a charity basketball game in January 1985 and was never the same again. Though he pitched eight more seasons in the major leagues, he won only 42 games. Flanagan was traded to Toronto on August 31, 1987, and spent the next three-plus seasons with the Blue Jays. He returned to Baltimore for two more years as a middle reliever, pitching mostly in noncritical situations, before retiring after the 1992 season, having spent 15 of his 18 years with the O's. Flanagan currently works as an executive in the O's front office.

CAREER ORIOLES RECORD:

W	L	W%	ERA	SV
141	116	.549	3.89	4

K	BB	SHO	IP
1,297	740	17	2,317.7

JACOBSON, BABY DOLL (OF)
(1915, 1917, 1919–1926)

While not spectacular, Jacobson was a very solid center fielder on one of baseball's best outfields of the era. While George Sisler was clearly the star of the Browns, left fielder Ken Williams, right fielder Jack Tobin, and Jacobson powered the Browns' offense. From 1919 to 1923, all three outfielders hit over .300.

Jacobson acquired his unusual nickname while he was in the minors. After hitting a home run, a band in the grandstand played a popular tune of the day, "Oh, You Baby Doll." In the following day's newspaper, the caption under his photo read, "Baby Doll." The name stuck.

Jacobson's first two years in the majors were less than scintillating. He hit in the low .200s before missing the entire 1918 season due to military service. When he came back in 1919, he was a different player, hitting .323. Jacobson followed that up with .355 in 1920 and .352 in 1921. In 1922 the Browns put together their best team ever, but still finished a game behind the Yankees in the AL race. He was also a fine fielder, holding 13 different fielding records by the time he left the game. Jacobson was traded in mid-1926 and spent his last year and a half with four teams before retiring following the 1927 season.

CAREER BROWNS RECORD:

Games	AB	Hits	Runs
1,243	4,755	1,508	711
Avg	**HR**	**RBI**	**SB**
.317	76	704	81

MARTINEZ, TIPPY (RP)
(1976–1986)

After two-plus seasons with the Yankees, Felix "Tippy" Martinez was traded to the O's early in the 1976 season as part of a 10-player deal. Strictly a reliever his whole career, Martinez pitched in 499 games with Baltimore, more than any other pitcher in Orioles history except Jim Palmer. For more than a decade, Martinez was a durable, dependable pitcher who ate up innings. He managed to accumulate 105 saves along the way, also the second most on the Orioles' all-time list.

CAREER ORIOLES RECORD:

W	L	W%	ERA	SV
52	40	.565	3.46	105
K	**BB**	**SHO**	**IP**	
585	366	0	752.3	

McGREGOR, SCOTT (SP/RP)
(1976–1988)

Minor leaguer Scott McGregor came to the Orioles in the same 10-player deal that brought Tippy Martinez. McGregor spent his entire 13-year career with Baltimore, first as a reliever, then as a starter beginning in 1978. As a starter, McGregor had a winning season every year from 1978 to 1984. McGregor was a durable and steady performer who averaged around 15 wins a year for nine straight years. He had his only 20-win season in 1980 when he captured his 20th victory on the last day of the season. McGregor went just 2–10 in his last two seasons combined and retired following the 1988 campaign at the age of 34.

CAREER ORIOLES RECORD:

W	L	W%	ERA	SV
138	108	.561	3.99	5
K	**BB**	**SHO**	**IP**	
904	518	23	2,140.7	

McNALLY, DAVE (SP)
(1962–1974)

During his prime, Dave McNally was one of the best lefthanders in the game. From 1968 to 1971, McNally won 20 or more games, including an AL record-tying 15 straight to begin the 1969 season. In 1968, his 22–10 record and sparkling 1.95 ERA got lost in the hoopla of Denny McLain's 31–6 season. McNally became the first $100,000 a year pitcher in 1972.

While McNally was instrumental in Baltimore's success in the 1960s and early 1970s, his biggest win came in a courtroom. After spending 13 years with Baltimore, McNally became upset with Baltimore management over a contract battle. He asked for and received a trade, going to the Montreal Expos for Ken Singleton and Mike Torrez following the 1974 season. A shoulder injury suffered in 1975 ended McNally's career at the age of 32. Feeling that the Expos had reneged on several promises made to him, McNally decided to let Marvin Miller, executive director of the Players Association, put his name next to Andy Messersmith's in the test case against professional baseball's reserve clause.

Since McNally and Messersmith had refused to sign 1975 contracts, their teams simply renewed their contracts at their 1974 salaries. Arbitrator Peter Seitz declared both players free agents unbound to their old contracts; they were free to sign with any team. Commissioner Bowie Kuhn fired Seitz and announced his ruling as "destructive to baseball." Messersmith signed a big new contract with Atlanta while McNally retired to his hometown of Billings, Montana, and opened a car dealership, satisfied with the knowledge that his action had changed baseball forever by sweetening the bitter pill players had been forced to swallow for a century.

CAREER ORIOLES RECORD:

W	L	W%	ERA	SV
181	113	.616	3.18	2

K	BB	SHO	IP
1,476	790	33	2,652.7

MURRAY, EDDIE (1B/DH)
(1977–1988, 1996)

The Orioles selected Eddie Murray in the third round of the June 1973 amateur draft. After four years in the minors, Murray made the big league squad with a flash, winning the AL Rookie of the Year Award in 1977 when he hit .283 with 27 homers. His rookie season was no fluke, as Murray hit 20 or more homers in 13 of his first 14 seasons in the majors, the first 12 of which were with the O's. He never posted spectacular numbers, but he was so steady for so many years he actually retired in elite company. For example, he never had a 200-hit season, yet he retired 11th on the all-time list with 3,255 hits.

By the time his career ended, Murray had played in more career games than anyone except Pete Rose, Hank Aaron, Carl Yastrzemski, and Ty Cobb.

Murray, one of the best switch-hitters of all time, said little to his teammates and even less to the press. Murray's desire for solitude was often construed as an attitude problem by some teammates and the media, especially given his penchant for being at odds with management over a variety of issues. During his time in Baltimore, Murray won three Gold Gloves, three Silver Slugger Awards, and was selected to the All-Star Game seven times. After 12 years with the O's, Murray was traded to the Dodgers for three players. He played for six different teams over his last nine years, including the second half of 1996 back in Baltimore. Near the end of his career, Murray eclipsed Hank Aaron's record of most consecutive years with at least 75 RBIs when he posted his 20th in a row. He also joined Aaron and Willie Mays as the only three players to have at least 500 homers and 3,000 base hits (an elite circle later joined by longtime Oriole Rafael Palmeiro). After retiring in 1997, Murray became a coach for the Orioles. In 2003 he was elected to the Hall of Fame.

CAREER ORIOLES RECORD:

Games	AB	Hits	Runs
1,884	7,075	2,080	1,084
Avg	**HR**	**RBI**	**SB**
.294	343	1,224	62

MUSSINA, MIKE (SP)
(1991–2000)

The Orioles first drafted Mike Mussina in the 11th round of the June 1987 amateur draft, but he refused to sign. In 1990 the O's drafted him again, this time in the first round, and he signed. Mussina didn't spend much time in the minors, as he received a call-up in mid-1991. By 1992 he was a regular in the rotation. During his 10 years in Baltimore, Mussina never won 20 games, but he consistently won 16–19 games while losing just 5–9 games every year. His career winning percentage is second among active pitchers, trailing only Pedro Martinez. Mussina's four Gold Gloves with Baltimore attest to his fielding ability and helped him to five All-Star Game appearances in his O's career. Mussina left the O's after the 2000 season to enter the lucrative free-agent market. He signed a huge contract with the rival Yankees that called for salaries of $10–$16 million per year for the first four years. Mussina's performance in five seasons with New York has mirrored that while in Baltimore, reliably notching about 16 wins a year.

CAREER ORIOLES RECORD:

W	L	W%	ERA	SV
147	81	.645	3.53	0
K	**BB**	**SHO**	**IP**	
1,535	467	15	2,009.7	

OLSON, GREGG (RP)
(1988–1993)

Gregg Olson was a first-round pick of the Orioles in the June 1988 amateur draft. He was scheduled to play for the U.S. Olympic team that year, but decided to leave the squad to begin his career with Baltimore, making the big league roster almost immediately. Although Olson was a record-setting starter in college while at Auburn, he was turned into a professional closer right from the beginning. In just five years (1989–1993), he used his devastating curveball to earn 160 saves, a career Orioles record. He won the AL Rookie of the Year Award in 1989 when he posted a 5–2 record with 27 saves and a 1.69 ERA. After suffering elbow problems in late 1993, Olson was released and picked up by Atlanta. Over the next eight seasons Olson would play for eight different teams, including Kansas City twice. He never fully recovered from his arm troubles, though he did put together two decent seasons for the Diamondbacks in 1998 and 1999 where he collected 44 saves. After the 2001 season, his injured arm just couldn't do the job anymore and he retired with 217 career saves.

CAREER ORIOLES RECORD:

W	L	W%	ERA	SV
17	21	.447	2.26	160
K	BB	SHO	IP	
347	158	0	350.3	

PALMEIRO, RAFAEL (1B/DH)
(1994–1998, 2004–2005)

See Rangers bio.

PALMER, JIM (SP)
(1965–1967, 1969–1984)

The Orioles signed Jim Palmer as an amateur free agent in 1963, paying the 17-year-old a $60,000 bonus. He was 11–3 in his first minor league season with a 2.51 ERA. He did pitch a no-hitter as well, but he also walked 130 batters in 129 innings. Nonetheless, he intrigued the O's, who called him up in 1965; that year he fashioned a 5–4 record, mostly in relief. In 1966 he went 15–10 as a starter, and pitched the pennant clincher. Although Palmer outdueled Sandy Koufax in Game 2 of the World Series as the O's swept the Dodgers, he developed a sore arm. The resulting arm problems caused him to pitch only nine major league games in 1967 and none in 1968. He spent nearly two years in the minors trying to regain his form. By 1969 he had worked out his arm trouble and returned to the majors to post a 16–4 record, including, as Palmer put it, "the ugliest no-hitter ever," an 8–0 victory over Oakland that featured six walks and two errors. Palmer then proceeded to run off four straight 20-win years, and eight in nine years.

From 1969 to 1971, the O's swept their opponents in the LCS every year, and Palmer pitched the clincher each year. He won his first Cy Young Award in 1973, then won two more in 1975–1976, becoming the first pitcher ever to win three Cy Young Awards. Palmer went to six All-Star Games and won four Gold Gloves, all during the 1970s. Manager Earl Weaver liked to pitch Palmer during home day games as much as possible because a white house behind the Memorial Stadium fence helped to hide his release point. The youngest pitcher ever to hurl a shutout in the World Series, Palmer also became the first pitcher to win World Series games in three decades (1960s, 1970s, and 1980s). After an 0–3 start with a 9.17 ERA in 1984, Palmer, who never allowed a grand slam in his career, realized his career was over at the age of 38 and he retired. After being elected to the Hall of Fame in 1990, he for some reason felt his career could begin anew at age 44, and he tried to make a comeback, but during spring training he got a big dose of reality and retired for good. Palmer then lent his stardom to television commercials hawking underwear and a money lending company.

CAREER ORIOLES RECORD:

W	L	W%	ERA	SV
268	152	.638	2.86	4

K	BB	SHO	IP
2,212	1,311	53	3,948.0

POWELL, BOOG (1B/OF)
(1961–1974)

John "Boog" Powell, a 6-foot-4-inch 245-pound left-hander, was signed as an amateur free agent before the 1959 season. After a brief call-up in 1961, Powell joined the Orioles in 1962 as an outfielder. Four years later he was switched to first base. Powell, a four-time All-Star, provided the power from the left side as the O's became a dominant team from the mid-1960s to the early 1970s. He helped the team win four pennants and in 1970 he became the first AL first baseman in three decades (since Hank Greenberg, 1940) to win the AL MVP Award after finishing second in 1969 to Harmon Killebrew. On August 15, 1966, he had a three-homer game, all opposite-field shots over Fenway's Green Monster. Earlier that year he had an 11-RBI game. Powell's home run production fell off dramatically as he hit only 23 homers combined in 1973–1974, so he became expendable. The O's sent him to Cleveland for Dave Duncan during spring training 1975. After one good year and one terrible year, the Indians released him and he was picked up by the Dodgers, but after going homerless with just five RBIs in 50 games, the Dodgers released him as well. After leaving baseball, Powell returned to Florida to run a marina. He later became famous in the Miller Lite beer commercials. When Camden Yards opened in 1992, Powell opened Boog's Barbeque stand, a popular fan attraction at the ballpark.

CAREER ORIOLES RECORD:

Games	AB	Hits	Runs
1,763	5,912	1,574	796

Avg	HR	RBI	SB
.266	303	1,063	18

RIPKEN, CAL, JR. (SS/3B) (1981–2001)

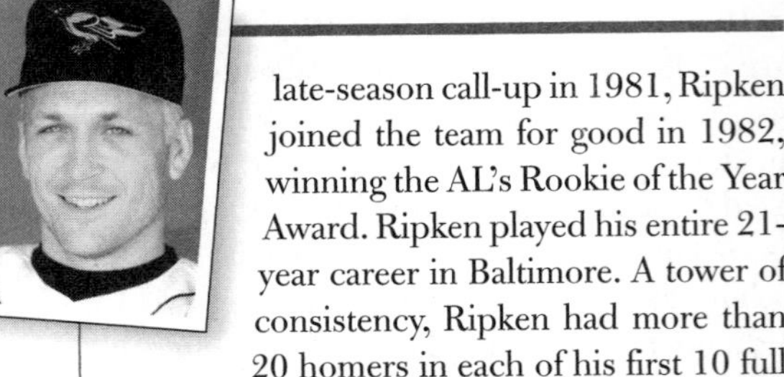

Cal Ripken's name will forever be associated with "the streak," baseball's longest consecutive games played record. For decades it was assumed that no one would ever break Lou Gehrig's 2,130-game streak. Even Gehrig's plaque at Yankee Stadium calls the streak an "unbreakable record." Fortunately for baseball, the timing of Ripken's approach to breaking the record couldn't have been any better. The work stoppage undertaken by the players in 1994 carried over to 1995. Many baseball fans were soured over the labor strife and vowed never to attend another major league game. Some fans actually picketed and boycotted major league baseball stadiums. The 1994 season lost about 50 games; the World Series was cancelled. When the 1995 season finally opened two weeks late, the attendance was down about 25 percent in almost every market. Fans booed the players loudly, no matter the player, no matter the team. When interest in Ripken's streak picked up in the summer of 1995, the fans began to quiet down. Attendance picked up a bit. Ripken's pursuit of Gehrig's record appeared to be the salve on the wound. When he finally broke the record on September 6, the game was stopped and he received a 25-minute standing ovation that was covered in its entirety on television. It proved to be the catharsis baseball needed.

The Orioles drafted Ripken in the second round of the June 1978 amateur draft. After a late-season call-up in 1981, Ripken joined the team for good in 1982, winning the AL's Rookie of the Year Award. Ripken played his entire 21-year career in Baltimore. A tower of consistency, Ripken had more than 20 homers in each of his first 10 full seasons. He played some third base his first two years before moving to shortstop for the next 14 seasons; in 1997 he was moved back to third base for the remainder of his career. Even though the designated hitter was in effect for his whole career, he never played a game as DH until his 20th season in the majors. When his streak ended on September 19, 1998, Ripken had played in 2,632 consecutive games, 502 more than Gehrig. Ripken won two AL MVP Awards in his career (1983 and 1991) and two All-Star Game MVPs (1991 and 2001). He was selected to 19 straight All-Star teams from 1983 to 2001. Ripken also won two Gold Gloves (1991 and 1992) and eight Silver Slugger Awards at shortstop. In 1992 he won both the Roberto Clemente Award and Lou Gehrig Memorial Award. When he becomes eligible, Cal Ripken will be a first-ballot Hall of Famer.

CAREER ORIOLES RECORD:

Games	AB	Hits	Runs
3,001	11,551	3,184	1,647
Avg	**HR**	**RBI**	**SB**
.276	431	1,695	36

ROBINSON, BROOKS (3B)
(1955–1977)

Brooks Robinson was the greatest fielding third baseman in the history of the game. Mike Schmidt and George Brett might have been better hitters, but Robinson was the man when it came to fielding. For 23 years he provided the Baltimore faithful (and baseball fans everywhere) with countless amazing plays at the hot corner. He was known for the way he charged bunts, picked them up barehanded, and fired to first in one smooth motion. When Brooks Robinson made three errors in the first eight games of the 1974 season, pitcher Dave McNally told him, "You've gone from being a human vacuum cleaner to a litterbug." When Robinson retired, he held virtually every career record for fielding by a third baseman, including most games played, highest fielding average, most assists, most putouts, most chances, and most double plays. He won 16 consecutive Gold Gloves, a number matched only by pitcher Jim Kaat.

Robinson was selected to 15 consecutive All-Star teams from 1960 to 1974, winning the game's MVP Award in 1966 when he got three hits (including a triple off Sandy Koufax) and scored the AL's only run in a 2–1 loss. He won the AL MVP Award in 1964 when he hit .317 with 28 homers and 118 RBIs. Robinson received the Lou Gehrig Memorial Award in 1966 and the Roberto Clemente Award in 1972. Robinson won the 1970 World Series MVP Award after hitting .429 with two homers, two doubles, five runs, six RBIs, and a Series-leading nine hits. He made so many fantastic plays in the field that the 1970 Series became known as "the Brooks Robinson Series." Robinson spent the last two years of his career as a backup to Doug DeCinces before retiring following the 1977 season. After his playing days, Robinson spent time as an Orioles coach and member of the team's broadcast crew before teaming up with agent Ron Shapiro to form Shapiro, Robinson & Associates, an agency that represents many of the game's top players. Brooks Robinson was elected to the Hall of Fame in 1983, his first year of eligibility.

CAREER ORIOLES RECORD:

Games	AB	Hits	Runs
2,896	10,654	2,848	1,232
Avg	**HR**	**RBI**	**SB**
.267	268	1,357	28

ROBINSON, FRANK (OF/1B)
(1966–1971)

After coming to the Orioles in a trade with Cincinnati, Robinson, whom Cincinnati Reds GM William DeWitt termed "an old 30," proceeded to win the AL MVP Award and the American League Triple Crown with a .316 average, 49 homers, and 122 RBIs. He also led the O's to a four-game sweep over the Dodgers in the World Series, winning the Series MVP Award as well. Yes, revenge is sweet.

In the six years he was with Baltimore, Frank Robinson led the Orioles to four AL pennants and two World Series championships. Robinson had an awful 1968, hitting .268 with 15 homers, due largely to double vision he was still suffering from after a collision at second base in mid-1967. He also had the mumps in 1968 as well as a muscle tear in his shoulder. Back to normal in 1969, Robinson began holding a "kangaroo court" in the O's clubhouse after each Orioles win. Players and even manager Earl Weaver could be held to account for minor baseball transgressions. Wearing a mop-style wig, Robinson was the judge who passed sentence, always in a humorous way that eased tensions on the team and helped create camaraderie. After his numbers started to slip a bit, Robinson was traded to the Dodgers for four players, following the 1971 season.

In 1975, his next-to-last season as a player, Robinson was named player-manager of the Cleveland Indians, becoming the first African American manager. His last season as a player was 1976, then he turned to managing full time. Cleveland also made him the first African American manager to be fired, after the team got off to a slow start in 1977. He returned to the Orioles organization as a minor league manager for a year and then O's coach for two more. Robinson moved on to manage the Giants for a few years before returning again to Baltimore, this time as manager in 1988. He was Manager of the Year in 1989 after leading the O's to a strong second place finish. He then spent a number of years in various other baseball positions—some with the O's, some with the National League—before returning to manage the Expos for their new owner, Major League Baseball. Robinson moved with the team to Washington when the newly renamed Nationals began play in 2005. *(See Reds bio.)*

CAREER ORIOLES RECORD:

Games	AB	Hits	Runs
827	2,941	882	555
Avg	**HR**	**RBI**	**SB**
.300	179	545	35

SHOCKER, URBAN (SP/RP)
(1918–1924)

One of the great spitball pitchers of his day, Urban Shocker spent seven years with the Browns, sandwiched between two- and four-year stints with the Yankees. His .615 career-winning percentage puts him among baseball's top hurlers of all time. After Miller Huggins traded Shocker to the Browns in January 1918, Shocker became a Yankees nemesis. After winning 20 games in 1920, Shocker led the AL in wins in 1921 with 27. He followed that up by winning 24 and 20 games the next two seasons, making it four straight 20-win years. On September 6, 1924, he pitched two complete-game victories over the White Sox in Chicago, winning both games by the identical score of 6–2. Management always considered Shocker a bit of a difficult player. In 1924 he became involved in a dispute with team officials over the club's policy on taking wives on road trips. He also didn't get along very well with manager George Sisler. In December 1924 he was traded back to the Yankees. The 1928 season began with Shocker in a contract dispute with New York. After pitching one game, he went home to Denver and pitched in a semipro tournament, catching pneumonia in the process. After battling the illness all season long, he died on September 9, 1928, just 38 years old.

CAREER BROWNS RECORD:

W	L	W%	ERA	SV
126	80	.612	3.19	20
K	**BB**	**SHO**	**IP**	
704	409	23	1,749.7	

SINGLETON, KEN (OF/DH)
(1975–1984)

After spending five years with the Mets and Expos, Ken Singleton was traded by Montreal along with Mike Torrez to the Orioles for Dave McNally, Rich Coggins, and minor leaguer Bill Kirkpatrick. It turned out to be one of the most one-sided trades in baseball history. Kirkpatrick never made it to the majors, McNally suffered a career-ending arm injury after just 77 innings, and Coggins was gone from the majors in two years. Torrez won 20 games his first year with the O's and Singleton became a fixture in Baltimore for a decade, playing in three All-Star Games and winning the Roberto Clemente Award in 1982. Singleton was a switch-hitter with power, a rare breed in baseball. In 1981 he collected 10 consecutive hits, the most in the AL in 29 years. Singleton had a solid season in 1983, hitting 18 homers with 84 RBIs as the O's defeated the Phillies in the World Series. Singleton was a productive hitter in the postseason, hitting .333 (19-for-57) in 17 LCS and World Series games. After hitting only .215 with 6 homers and 36 RBIs in 1984, he retired to undertake a broadcasting career with the Expos and Yankees.

CAREER ORIOLES RECORD:

Games	AB	Hits	Runs
1,446	5,115	1,455	684
Avg	**HR**	**RBI**	**SB**
.284	182	766	8

SISLER, GEORGE (1B) (1915–1922, 1924–1927)

George Sisler was the greatest hitter in the history of the St. Louis Browns, twice hitting over .400. His 257 base hits in 1920 stood as the major league record for more than eight decades until it was broken in 2004. Hall of Famer Eddie Collins once said of Sisler, one of baseball's genuinely nice men, "George was a great first baseman and a great hitter, but he was too quiet and clean-living to win headlines." Sisler actually began his career as a college pitcher, once striking out 20 batters in a seven-inning game for a University of Michigan team managed by none other than Branch Rickey. During his college career, Sisler hit .404 and struck out 232 hitters in 153 innings. By the time Sisler's college career ended, Rickey had taken a job with the Browns and convinced St. Louis to sign Sisler. "Gorgeous George" Sisler went directly to the major leagues, splitting his 1915 season between the outfield, first base, and the pitcher's mound. Although Sisler was a very good pitcher, he was moved into the everyday lineup to take advantage of his bat, just like Babe Ruth. By 1918 he had become one of the best first basemen in baseball.

From 1920 to 1922, Sisler hit for a combined average of .400. In 1922 he put together a 41-game hitting streak, hit .420, and won the AL MVP Award. And he only struck out 14 times in 586 at-bats! Sisler was also an accomplished base stealer, leading the AL four times in an era dominated by Ty Cobb. Seven times he led the AL in fielding average and assists. Well on his way to rivaling Ty Cobb in every facet of the game, Sisler came down with a bad case of the flu in January 1923. The illness affected his sinuses, leaving him with an awful case of double vision, and forced him to sit out the entire 1923 season. Although his doctors told him he would never play again, Sisler came back in 1924, though clearly he was not the same player. At the plate, he still saw two baseballs. He worked his way through it, hitting over .300 in six of his last seven seasons in the majors, but hit about 30–50 points lower each season than he had before the illness. His homer, RBI, run, and stolen-base production also dropped dramatically. Bob Shawkey of the Yankees later admitted, "We soon learned something, and this shows how mean it was in those days. When (Sisler) was up at the plate, he could watch you for only so long, and then he'd have to look down to get his eyes focused again. So, we'd keep him waiting up there until he'd have to look down, and then pitch. He was never the same hitter after that."

In 1924 Sisler became the player-manager of the Browns, a position he held for three years, but later regretted taking because of the additional distraction it caused him. Realizing that their former slugger probably was never going to be the same again, the Browns sold Sisler to the Senators in December 1927 for $25,000. He hit so poorly, however, that he only brought $7,500 when sold to the Braves after just 20 games. He rebounded somewhat to post three modestly successful years with the Boston Braves from 1928–1930 before being released. Sisler played in the minor leagues for two years before he was no longer able to see well enough to hit even low minors pitching. Sisler was out of baseball until 1943 when he took a job scouting for the Brooklyn Dodgers. He later managed in the minors before becoming a scout and hitting instructor with the Pirates. George Sisler was elected to the Hall of Fame in 1939.

CAREER BROWNS RECORD:

Games	AB	Hits	Runs
1,647	6,667	2,295	1,091
Avg	**HR**	**RBI**	**SB**
.344	93	959	351

TOBIN, JACK (OF)
(1916, 1918–1925)

Jack Tobin was part of the Browns' potent outfield of 1918–1924, along with Baby Doll Jacobson and Ken Williams. After spending his first two seasons with the St. Louis Terriers of the Federal League, St. Louis native Tobin joined the Browns in 1916 after the Federal League folded. Tobin had 200+ hits in four straight years (1920–1923) as the team's leadoff hitter. A six-time .300 hitter during his nine years with the Browns, Tobin was traded to the Senators in spring training of 1926, who then sold him in midseason to the Red Sox. After one more year in Boston, Tobin retired. He later became a coach and scout for the Browns.

CAREER BROWNS RECORD:

Games	AB	Hits	Runs
1,133	4,404	1,399	680
Avg	**HR**	**RBI**	**SB**
.318	48	438	85

WALLACE, BOBBY (SS)
(1902–1916)

Very few players have managed to stay in the big leagues as long as Bobby Wallace, who enjoyed a 25-year career, spending 15 years with the St. Louis Browns. Wallace was working in a feed store in Pennsylvania and pitching for a semipro team in 1894 when he visited the Pirates and asked for a tryout. He was turned away without a tryout by Pittsburgh manager Connie Mack, who felt that Wallace was too small to make it in the major leagues. Wallace returned home, but in September he received a wire from George Tebeau of the Cleveland Spiders, who was in dire need of a pitcher. Wallace undertook the journey to Cleveland and made the team.

He made his major league debut against Boston on September 15, 1894, and got bombed, allowing 14 hits in just six innings. He defeated the Phillies in his next start, and earned one more win before the season ended to go 2–1. The next year he was in the starting rotation and finished 12–14 for the Spiders. In 1897 he was moved to third base and had the best offensive year of his career, hitting .335, scoring 99 runs, and driving in 112. The owners of the Cleveland club also owned the National League St. Louis franchise. Because they were dissatisfied with Cleveland's attendance, they shipped all their good players (including Wallace) from Cleveland to St. Louis and sent all their weaker players to Cleveland in 1899 in an effort to bolster the better-drawing team of the two.

Because the National League had frozen player salaries at $2,500, Wallace agreed to jump to the new American League in 1901 when he was promised that he would be among the top-paid players in the AL. But after he found out many players were signing for higher salaries, Wallace angrily refused to report to his new AL team and returned to St. Louis, where he hit .324. In 1902 the AL decided to place a team in St. Louis to compete with the established Cardinals. This new team was called the Browns, and they offered

Wallace a $6,500 bonus and a five-year no-trade contract for $32,500, which likely made him the highest paid player in baseball. He was the regular shortstop through 1912, then was a platoon player for four more seasons.

Wallace suffered severe burns in an accident in 1914, which further limited his declining skills as a player. He had tried his hand at managing the Browns in 1911 and part of 1912, but became disenchanted with it and gave it up. In 1915 he quit playing and became an umpire, but before the season was out he returned as a player for a few games. Wallace played just a handful of games over the next three seasons with the Browns and Cardinals before retiring after the 1918 season. He then spent 33 years in the Reds organization as a minor league manager, coach, and scout. Considering he only batted .268 for his career (.258 with the Browns) and played his entire 25-year career in the dead-ball era, Wallace's numbers are fairly impressive, though he never led the league in any offensive category at any time in his career. He accumulated 2,309 hits, 1,057 runs, 1,121 RBIs, and 201 stolen bases. In 1953 Wallace was elected to the Hall of Fame.

CAREER BROWNS RECORD:

Games	AB	Hits	Runs
1,569	5,529	1,424	609
Avg	**HR**	**RBI**	**SB**
.258	8	607	138

WILLIAMS, KEN (OF)
(1918–1927)

Not many realize it, but Ken Williams was one of baseball's best sluggers in his era. He was the first American League player other than Babe Ruth to hit more than 30 homers in a season. In 1922 he had an incredible year, leading the league with 39 homers and 155 RBIs, and becoming the first AL player ever to hit three homers in a game. He also became the first AL player to hit two homers in one inning. Williams had a stretch in late July and early August in which he homered in six consecutive games, setting a major league record that stood for 34 years. He also hit .332 with 11 triples and 37 stolen bases, becoming the first player in major league history to bat .300 with 30 homers and 30 steals in the same season (it wouldn't happen again until Willie Mays accomplished it in 1957). Starting in 1919, Williams hit .300 in 10 of the next 11 seasons. In 1925 Williams finished the season with more RBIs than games played for the second time in his career, a truly rare feat. The only other players to do it twice are Ruth, Gehrig, Greenberg, Simmons, Foxx, and DiMaggio, all Hall of Famers. In the 14 years from 1918 to 1931, Williams and Bob Meusel of the Yankees were the only players to lead the AL in homers besides Ruth.

After slumping to 17 homers and 74 RBIs in both 1926 and 1927, Williams was sold to the Red Sox for $10,000. Williams slumped further in his two seasons in Boston, hitting 11 homers and 88 RBIs combined in 1928–1929. The Red Sox released him and the Yankees tried to sign him for 1930, but he insisted on making the same salary as Babe Ruth, so the Yanks ultimately gave up on him. Williams played two more seasons in the minors before retiring.

CAREER BROWNS RECORD:

Games	AB	Hits	Runs
1,109	4,015	1,308	757
Avg	**HR**	**RBI**	**SB**
.326	185	808	144

Boston Red Sox

Since 1901

1950 Team Ball

1918 The Red Sox win their third World Series in four years. The team will not finish in the first division again until 1934.... **1919** The Red Sox hit 33 homers, and Ruth accounts for 29 of them.... **1939** During spring training, second baseman Bobby Doerr tells rookie Ted Williams, "Wait until you see Jimmie Foxx hit!" to which Williams replies, "Wait till Foxx sees *me* hit."... **1950** The Red Sox become the last club to have a team batting average of .300 when they finish the season at .302, led by AL batting champ Billy Goodman's .354 mark.... **1998–99** The Red Sox make back-to-back postseason appearances for the first time since 1915–1916.... **2004** Curt Schilling becomes the first pitcher in major league history to win World Series starts for three different teams—Boston, Arizona, and Philadelphia.

FRANCHISE HISTORY

The Boston franchise of the American League—and therefore its 86-year World Series drought and dramatic 2004 redemption—almost didn't exist. When AL president Ban Johnson decided to compete on a major league level with the entrenched National League, he first thought of avoiding Boston because of the city's long history of support for its NL team. But, backed by the deep pockets of Cleveland owner Charles Somers—a building contractor and coal baron who actually backed three teams besides his own in the league's initial season, until local buyers could be arranged—Johnson took the plunge. The first owner of the Boston team was Henry Killilea, a Milwaukee attorney, who purchased the team in 1902 and sold it for a quick profit after his team's 1903 World Series triumph. He also made money in several other nontraditional ways, such as charging visiting baseball writers for their World Series seats, and by keeping the entire World Series take for himself. There was some sort of ticket-selling chicanery at Boston during the Series that so angered Ban Johnson that he virtually forced Killilea to sell the team in early 1904.

Killilea sold the team to the owner and publisher of *The Boston Globe* newspaper, Charles H. Taylor, and his son, John Irving Taylor, who ran the team. John Taylor was a spoiled brat of a playboy, whose clubhouse tirades and bizarre trades alienated the players and manager, Jimmy Collins, who finally quit in mid-1906. In spite of his poor handling of the team, Taylor was responsible for bringing many great stars to Boston, including Tris Speaker, Harry Hooper, Smoky Joe Wood, Duffy Lewis, and Bill Carrigan. In order to restore stability to the franchise, Ban Johnson organized the sale of 50 percent of Taylor's stock in the team in 1911 to former outfielder Jim McAleer and Robert McRoy, Johnson's assistant. Although McAleer and McRoy's names appeared on the title, they were clearly a front for Ban Johnson, who then undertook an effort to find a more stable owner—at a profit to himself, if possible.

The 1918 season was shortened due to World War I, ending on September 2, Labor Day. The World Series started on September 5 and the Red Sox ended it in six games on September 11.

Two years later, New Jersey hotel owner Joe Lannin purchased the team. After two decent years, 1913 and 1914, the Red Sox won the pennant and the World Series in both 1915 and 1916 behind the pitching of Babe Ruth, Ernie Shore, and Dutch Leonard. Like Killilea before him, Lannin made a handsome profit, then took the money and ran. He sold the team in December 1916 to Harry Frazee, a Broadway theater producer. Frazee had made a lot of money on his big hit, *No, No, Nanette,* but his fortune usually rested on the success (or failure) of his most recent production. After two successful years in 1917 and 1918, including an amazing sixth AL championship in just 16 years and a fifth World Series title in five tries, Boston's fortunes began to turn sour, primarily because the now financially strapped Frazee was selling off his star players to raise cash for his theater business. He traded Ernie Shore, Dutch Leonard, and Duffy Lewis to the Yankees for $50,000 and three lesser players. Then he sold Carl Mays to the Yankees for $40,000. And on January 9, 1920, Frazee sold Babe Ruth to the Yankees for $125,000 and a $300,000 loan, putting up Fenway Park as collateral. Over the next few years Frazee sold 10 more players to the Yankees. Boston GM Ed

Barrow, who owned a share of the Red Sox, eventually went to New York himself and became the GM of the Yankees.

After totally gutting his team, Frazee finally sold the only thing he had left, the team itself, for $1.5 million to a Midwestern group headed by Robert Quinn. Quinn was a former GM of the St. Louis Browns and was being backed publicly by the money of glassworks manufacturer Palmer Winslow and privately by Ban Johnson, who had orchestrated the deal to rid the league of the woefully inept Harry Frazee. Whatever dream Quinn may have had about fielding a contending team quickly went up in smoke. Winslow died in 1926 and his money supply vanished. Having lost all their good players, the Red Sox finished sixth once, seventh once, and last eight times. Like Frazee, Quinn found himself in the position of needing to sell his star players. But unlike Frazee, Quinn needed the money to keep the team afloat, not to support some outside interest. In 1932, Quinn's last year of ownership, the Red Sox drew an average of just 2,236 paying customers a game as they set the franchise record for most losses in a season with 111. Quinn was hundreds of thousands of dollars in debt and was forced to borrow against his life insurance to meet the team's payroll in the spring of 1933. His only way out was to sell, and he did in February 1933 to Tom Yawkey.

Pitchers Mel Parnell and Ellis Kinder had a combined 48–13 record for the Red Sox in 1949, but the rest of the staff combined for only a 48–45 record.

Yawkey had inherited over $7 million from his mother and foster father (who was also his uncle, and former owner of the Tigers), but the terms of the inheritance prevented him from getting the money until he turned 30. Four days

Spring training 1963: Ted's tutoring turned Yaz into a Hall of Fame–bound hitter.

after his 30th birthday, he bought the Red Sox for $1 million on the advice of longtime friend and former schoolmate Eddie Collins, who also bought a small share of the team and became general manager. As soon as Yawkey bought the team, he said, "I don't intend to mess around with a loser." He was as good as his word. He instructed Collins to quickly buy up any available talent in order to turn the franchise around. Within a year, Collins had secured Joe Cronin, Jimmie Foxx, Lyn Lary, and others. The expensive buying frenzy allowed Boston to finish in fourth place in 1935, its highest finish in 16 years. After finishing sixth and fifth the next two years, Yawkey gave up on trying to buy a contender and focused instead on developing a solid farm system.

One criticism of Yawkey was that he was so well liked by his players and so generous to them that they lacked the "hunger" many felt was necessary to strive for a pennant. Yawkey owned the team until his death in July 1976. Officially he died of pneumonia, but some insiders say he really died from heartache over the new system of free agency, which allowed players to sign with the highest bidder when their contracts expired. At the time of Yawkey's death, Fred Lynn, Rick Burleson, and Carlton Fisk were all engaged in lengthy and contentious holdouts, and all would later leave the Red Sox as free agents. The bitterness of the negotiations hurt Yawkey deeply. After Yawkey died, ownership of the team fell under the control of the Yawkey Trust, which stipulated that the team be sold. Yawkey's wife, Jean, however, engaged in a bitter struggle to take control of the team, and finally prevailed, staving off several attempts to buy the team, including one by Dom and Joe DiMaggio. Jean Yawkey, who used to watch home games in a separate box from her husband's so she wouldn't have to listen to him swear, controlled the team until she died in 1992.

Fisk. Fenway. October 22, 1975. The most famous home run in Red Sox history.

After Jean's death, control of the team fell to General Manager Haywood Sullivan and John Harrington, an executor of Jean's estate and the president of Jean's corporation, JRY, which owned the Yawkey stock. The two men battled for control of the team until 1993, when Sullivan sold his interests in the team to Harrington. In 2002 Harrington sold the team for $730 million to Florida Marlins owner John Henry and former Padres owner Tom Werner. A month later, Henry sold the Marlins to Expos owner Jeffrey Loria for $158.5 million. That same day Loria sold the Expos to Major League Baseball for $120 million and a $38.5 million loan.

On the field, the Red Sox had a lot of success early on, winning six pennants in the team's first 18 years of existence. They went to the World Series five times (and would have gone in 1904 as well if Giants' manager John McGraw hadn't refused to play against the AL champs) and won it all five times. Everything changed, however, after owner Harry Frazee sold virtually all of his star players, most to the

Yankees, including Babe Ruth. Much has been made of the fact that Boston won all those pennants and World Series titles before Ruth's departure, while New York had never won even one pennant. With the outrage of the Ruth sale, many Boston fans came to believe in a magical curse (the Curse of the Bambino) that afflicted the team for nearly nine decades, keeping them from winning another World Series, while the Yankees appeared in 39 and won 26 over that same span. Strange things happened—supposedly—to keep the Sox from winning several AL pennants, including losing the pennant on the final day in 1948, 1949, 1972, and 1978. When the Sox did happen to make it to the World Series four times under the Curse, they lost the Series each time in heartbreaking fashion, always in Game 7 (1946, 1967, 1975, 1986).

Roger Clemens blows one past you.

The Curse, for those who believe in such things, ended when the Red Sox swept the Cardinals in the 2004 World Series after an unprecedented comeback against the Yankees in the ALCS. Another view of Boston's history, however, might suggest reasons less supernatural than a curse. There was incompetence in the large number of poor trades over the decades; shaky finances that "necessitated" selling off stars to raise money for both baseball and non-baseball purposes; stubborn racism, without which the team could have had Willie Mays for only $5,000, and other future stars at even lower prices; and cronyism, whereby the Yankees benefited disproportionately from Red Sox largesse. The cynical among us might even suggest that the Red Sox were nothing more than a farm team for the Yankees for several decades, and whatever ill fate befell them for so very long was deserved, since it came by their own hand. In any event, now that the "Curse" is over, whenever Boston fails, we can assume that the Red Sox ownership will take full responsibility for its actions.

TEAM NAME HISTORY

Official Names

Somersets (1901–1902)
Pilgrims (1903–1906)
Red Sox (1907–current)

Unofficial Names/Nicknames

Crimson Hose, Bosox, Bostons, Boston Americans, Puritans, Plymouth Rocks, Sox

STADIUM HISTORY

Huntington Avenue Grounds	1901–1911
Fenway Park	1912–current

YEARLY RECORD, FINISH, & ATTENDANCE FIGURES

Year	League	Record	DIV/LG Finish	Attendance	Avg/Gm
2005	AL East	95–67	2	2,847,888	35,159
2004	AL East	98–64	2	2,837,294	35,028
2003	AL East	95–67	2	2,724,165	33,632
2002	AL East	93–69	2	2,650,862	32,727
2001	AL East	82–79	2	2,625,333	32,412
2000	AL East	85–77	2	2,585,895	31,925
1999	AL East	94–68	2	2,446,162	30,200
1998	AL East	92–70	2	2,314,704	28,577
1997	AL East	78–84	4	2,226,136	27,483
1996	AL East	85–77	3	2,315,231	28,583
1995	AL East	86–58	1	2,164,410	30,061
1994	AL East	54–61	4	1,775,818	27,747
1993	AL East	80–82	5	2,422,021	29,901
1992	AL East	73–89	7	2,468,574	30,476
1991	AL East	84–78	2	2,562,435	31,635
1990	AL East	88–74	1	2,528,986	31,222
1989	AL East	83–79	3	2,510,012	30,988
1988	AL East	89–73	1	2,464,851	30,430
1987	AL East	78–84	5	2,231,551	27,894
1986	AL East	95–66	1	2,147,641	26,514
1985	AL East	81–81	5	1,786,633	22,057
1984	AL East	86–76	4	1,661,618	20,514
1983	AL East	78–84	6	1,782,285	22,004
1982	AL East	89–73	3	1,950,124	24,076
1981	AL East	59–49	5/2	1,060,379	20,007
1980	AL East	83–77	4	1,956,092	24,149
1979	AL East	91–69	3	2,353,114	29,414
1978	AL East	99–64	2	2,320,643	28,301
1977	AL East	97–64	3	2,074,549	25,932
1976	AL East	83–79	3	1,895,846	23,406
1975	AL East	95–65	1	1,748,587	21,587
1974	AL East	84–78	3	1,556,411	19,215
1973	AL East	89–73	2	1,481,002	18,284
1972	AL East	85–70	2	1,441,718	18,484
1971	AL East	85–77	3	1,678,732	20,984
1970	AL East	87–75	3	1,595,278	19,695
1969	AL East	87–75	3	1,833,246	22,633
1968	AL	86–76	4	1,940,788	23,960
1967	AL	92–70	1	1,727,832	21,331
1966	AL	72–90	9	811,172	10,014
1965	AL	62–100	9	652,201	8,052
1964	AL	72–90	8	883,276	10,905
1963	AL	76–85	7	942,642	11,783
1962	AL	76–84	8	733,080	9,279
1961	AL	76–86	6	850,589	10,373
1960	AL	65–89	7	1,129,866	14,674
1959	AL	75–79	5	984,102	12,781
1958	AL	79–75	3	1,077,047	13,988
1957	AL	82–72	3	1,181,087	15,339
1956	AL	84–70	4	1,137,158	14,579
1955	AL	84–70	4	1,203,200	15,426

YEARLY RECORD, FINISH, & ATTENDANCE FIGURES (CONT.)

Year	League	Record	DIV/LG Finish	Attendance	Avg/Gm
1954	AL	69–85	4	931,127	11,786
1953	AL	84–69	4	1,026,133	13,502
1952	AL	76–78	6	1,115,750	14,490
1951	AL	87–67	3	1,312,282	17,497
1950	AL	94–60	3	1,344,080	17,456
1949	AL	96–58	2	1,596,650	20,736
1948	AL	96–59	2	1,558,798	19,985
1947	AL	83–71	3	1,427,315	17,621
1946	AL	104–50	1	1,416,944	18,166
1945	AL	71–83	7	603,794	7,741
1944	AL	77–77	4	506,975	6,500
1943	AL	68–84	7	358,275	4,653
1942	AL	93–59	2	730,340	9,485
1941	AL	84–70	2	718,497	9,331
1940	AL	82–72	5	716,234	9,066
1939	AL	89–62	2	573,070	7,641
1938	AL	88–61	2	646,459	8,619
1937	AL	80–72	5	559,659	7,563
1936	AL	74–80	6	626,895	8,141
1935	AL	78–75	4	558,568	7,070
1934	AL	76–76	4	610,640	7,930
1933	AL	63–86	7	268,715	3,732
1932	AL	43–111	8	182,150	2,366
1931	AL	62–90	6	350,975	4,387
1930	AL	52–102	8	444,045	5,843
1929	AL	58–96	8	394,620	5,059
1928	AL	57–96	8	396,920	5,364
1927	AL	51–103	8	305,275	3,914
1926	AL	46–107	8	285,155	3,703
1925	AL	47–105	8	267,782	3,570
1924	AL	67–87	7	448,556	5,825
1923	AL	61–91	8	229,688	2,945
1922	AL	61–93	8	259,184	3,550
1921	AL	75–79	5	279,273	3,627
1920	AL	72–81	5	402,445	5,295
1919	AL	66–71	6	417,291	6,323
1918	AL	75–51	1	249,513	3,564
1917	AL	90–62	2	387,856	4,848
1916	AL	91–63	1	496,397	6,364
1915	AL	101–50	1	539,885	7,104
1914	AL	91–62	2	481,359	6,093
1913	AL	79–71	4	437,194	5,829
1912	AL	105–47	1	597,096	7,655
1911	AL	78–75	5	503,961	6,631
1910	AL	81–72	4	584,619	7,308
1909	AL	88–63	3	668,965	8,920
1908	AL	75–79	5	473,048	6,143
1907	AL	59–90	7	436,777	5,600
1906	AL	49–105	8	410,209	5,327
1905	AL	78–74	4	468,828	6,089
1904	AL	95–59	1	623,295	7,695

YEARLY RECORD, FINISH, & ATTENDANCE FIGURES (CONT.)

Year	League	Record	DIV/LG Finish	Attendance	Avg/Gm
1903	AL	91–47	1	379,338	5,419
1902	AL	77–60	3	348,567	4,909
1901	AL	79–57	2	289,448	4,195

MANAGER HISTORY

Manager	Years	W–L	Win %
Jimmy Collins	1901–1906	455–376	.548
Chick Stahl	1906	14–26	.350
George Huff	1907	2–6	.250
Bob Unglaub	1907	9–20	.310
Cy Young	1907	3–3	.500
Deacon McGuire	1907–1908	98–123	.443
Fred Lake	1908–1909	110–80	.579
Patsy Donovan	1910–1911	159–147	.520
Jake Stahl	1912–1913	144–88	621
Bill Carrigan	1913–1916, 1927–1929	489–500	.494
Jack Barry	1917	90–62	.592
Ed Barrow	1918–1920	213–203	.512
Hugh Duffy	1921–1922	136–172	.442
Frank Chance	1923	61–91	.401
Lee Fohl	1924–1926	160–299	.349
Heinie Wagner	1930	52–102	.338
Shano Collins	1931–1932	73–134	.353
Marty McManus	1932–1933	95–153	.383
Bucky Harris	1934	76–76	.500
Joe Cronin	1935–1947	1,071–916	.539
Joe McCarthy	1948–1950	223–145	.606
Steve O'Neill	1950–1951	150–99	.602
Lou Boudreau	1952–1954	229–232	.497
Pinky Higgins	1955–1959, 1960–1962	560–556	.502
Rudy York	1959	0–1	.000
Billy Jurges	1959–1960	59–63	.484
Del Baker	1960	2–5	.286
Johnny Pesky	1963–1964, 1980	147–179	.451
Billy Herman	1964–1966	128–182	.413
Pete Runnels	1966	8–8	.500
Dick Williams	1967–1969	260–217	.545
Eddie Popowski	1969, 1973	6–4	.600
Eddie Kasko	1970–1973	345–295	.539
Darrell Johnson	1974–1976	220–188	.539
Don Zimmer	1976–1980	411–304	.575
Ralph Houk	1981–1984	312–282	.525
John McNamara	1985–1988	297–273	.521
Joe Morgan	1988–1991	301–252	.544
Butch Hobson	1992–1994	207–232	.472
Kevin Kennedy	1995–1996	171–135	.559
Jimy Williams	1997–2001	414–352	.540
Joe Kerrigan	2001	17–26	.395
Grady Little	2002–2003	188–136	.580
Terry Francona	2004–2005	193–131	.596

ALL-TIME WIN-LOSS RECORDS VS. ALL OPPONENTS (SINCE 1901)

Opponent	Record
ALL-TIME	8,358–7,884
Angels	298–257
Astros	3–0
Athletics	1,027–834
Blue Jays	223–171
Braves	13–23
Brewers	213–184
Cardinals	2–4
Cubs	1–2
Devil Rays	88–44
Diamondbacks	0–3
Dodgers	2–4
Giants	1–2
Indians	930–1,002
INTERLEAGUE	77–80
Mariners	187–133
Marlins	11–7
Mets	7–8
Nationals	8–7
Orioles	1,077–902
Padres	4–2
Phillies	13–12
Pirates	4–2
Rangers	297–264
Reds	3–0
Rockies	3–3
Royals	188–197
Tigers	993–934
Twins	929–902
White Sox	934–903
Yankees	899–1,078

October 27, 2004: The Red Sox reach the promised land.

Franchise Highlights, Low Points, and Strange Distinctions

1908 James "King" Brady pitched only one game for Boston—a complete game shutout.

• • • •

1912 Smoky Joe Wood was the youngest pitcher ever to win 30 games when he finished 34–5 at the age of 22.

• • • •

1914 Left-hander Dutch Leonard posted the lowest ERA in the history of the American League, 0.96. He finished 19–5 in 25 starts with seven shutouts.

• • • •

1917 On June 23, Babe Ruth was on the mound for the Red Sox in a game against the Washington Senators. When Ruth walked Ray Morgan, the Senators' leadoff hitter, Ruth became incensed at the home-plate umpire. A vigorous argument ensued and Ruth was tossed out of the game. Ruth was replaced by Ernie Shore. Morgan then tried to steal second and was thrown out. Shore then retired the next 26 batters in order, for the strangest perfect game in major league history.

• • • •

1918 The season was shortened due to World War I, ending on September 2, Labor Day. The World Series started on September 5 and the Red Sox ended it in six games on September 11.

1923 On September 7, Howard Ehmke of the last-place Red Sox pitched a no-hitter to beat the Philadelphia A's, 4–0 in Shibe Park. Four days later, at Yankee Stadium, he pitched a one-hitter in defeating New York, 3–0. The only "hit" was a misplayed grounder that New York's hometown scorer Fred Lieb ruled a hit. Even though the muffed dribbler was the only hit that day, Lieb, under intense lobbying by the Red Sox, refused to change his ruling and Ehmke was denied back-to-back no-hitters.

• • • •

1932 First baseman Dale Alexander of the Red Sox hit .372. In so doing, he became the first batting champion to play for a last-place team.

• • • •

1930s Outfielder Tom Oliver, who played with Boston in the early 1930s, holds the post-1900 record for most career at-bats (1,931) without ever hitting a home run.

• • • •

1938 Outfielder Doc Cramer set an American League record for most at-bats in a season without hitting a home run, 658.

On June 10, Bill Lefebvre of the Red Sox became the first pitcher in American League history to hit a home run in his first major league at-bat, as the Sox lost to Chicago, 15–2, in Fenway Park.

1939–40 The Red Sox were the first team to have all four infielders hit at least 20 homers in back-to-back seasons. The feat wasn't duplicated again until the 2004–2005 Texas Rangers.

• • • •

1941 Lefty Grove had a landmark year, only the second left-hander to win 300 games (and the last until 1963). And on May 12, he became the only pitcher ever to win 20 consecutive home games.

• • • •

1943–45 Despite missing three full years to military service from 1943–1945, Ted Williams hit more home runs during the 1940s than any other player in either league. He also captured two Triple Crowns, four home run crowns, and six runs scored titles during the decade.

• • • •

1939–60 Only two members of the 500-home-run club, Ted Williams and Mel Ott, finished their careers with fewer than 1,000 strikeouts. Williams fanned just 709 times, and never more than 64 times in a season.

• • • •

1948–49 The only manager in history to lose two pennants in a row on the last day of the season was Joe McCarthy of the Red Sox, in 1948 and 1949.

1949 Ted Williams and Vern Stephens collected the most RBIs by a pair of teammates since World War II when they each tallied 159. The following year Stephens again tied for the AL RBI crown with 144.

Pitchers Mel Parnell and Ellis Kinder had a combined 48–13 record for the Red Sox in 1949, but the rest of the staff combined for only a 48–45 record.

• • • •

1950 Utility player Billy Goodman became the only player in major league history to win a batting title without having a regular position. He played 45 games in the outfield, 27 at third base, 21 at first base, five at second base, and one at shortstop. The team set the all-time record for most runs scored at home in a season with 625—more than eight runs a game.

• • • •

1952 First baseman Walt Dropo hit just .265 in 37 games for the Red Sox. Incredibly, he tied the major league record by getting 12 hits in 12 consecutive at-bats. What makes it even more amazing is that Dropo was notoriously slow of foot, stealing only five bases in his entire 13-year career.

• • • •

1953 Ben Flowers became the first relief pitcher ever to appear in eight consecutive games in an eight-day period when he pulled the duty for the Red Sox.

1954 Cleveland second baseman Bobby Avila won the batting championship with a .341 average. Ted Williams hit .345, but had less than the required 400 at-bats (386). He was hurt in his pursuit of the batting title by the 115 walks he received. By today's rules, Williams would have been declared the winner based on his 505 plate appearances (502 required).

• • • •

1957 Ted Williams set an incredible record when he reached base 16 times in 16 consecutive plate appearances.

• • • •

1939–60 Ted Williams was the only player in major league history to hit home runs off a father and son. He homered first off Thornton Lee early in his career, then his son Don Lee near the end of his career.

• • • •

1958–59 Jackie Jensen was the American League RBI champion in 1958 and 1959 without hitting a triple either season.

• • • •

1972 Even though he was a catcher, Carlton Fisk led all major league rookies in triples with nine.

• • • •

1961–83 Carl Yastrzemski played in 23 consecutive seasons beginning in 1961 and collected more than 3,400 hits, but finished over .300 only six times. He is also the only member of the 3,000-hit club who never had 200 hits in a season. His most was 191 in his second year.

1964 Nineteen-year-old Tony Conigliaro hit 24 homers with a .530 slugging average, both records for a teenage player. At 20, he became the youngest player ever to win a league home run crown when he hit 32 for the Sox in 1965.

• • • •

1965 Relief pitcher Arnold Earley appeared in 57 games for the Red Sox without earning a save and figuring in only one decision, a loss.

• • • •

1967 When the Red Sox rose from ninth place in 1966 to first place in 1967, it marked the biggest improvement over the previous year's results by a pennant winner since the National League's 1899 Brooklyn Superbas (now the Dodgers).

• • • •

1975 Rookie Fred Lynn won the American League MVP Award in 1975. Placing third that year was another rookie, Jim Rice, also of the Red Sox.

• • • •

1978 The last major league position player to post a season fielding average below .900 was third baseman Butch Hobson of the Red Sox in 1978, when he finished at .899. He made a whopping 43 errors that season in 133 games. Two years later, he posted a .910 average.

• • • •

1980 Rick Burleson of the Red Sox set a major league record for shortstops that still stands when he participated in 147 double plays on the season.

1983 When Carl Yastrzemski retired in 1983 after his 23rd season with Boston, he tied Oriole Brooks Robinson for the most seasons played with one club.

• • • •

1991 Roger Clemens won the Cy Young Award with just 18 wins, becoming just the second AL pitcher to receive the honor with so few victories.

• • • •

1994 Manager Butch Hobson was fired after the strike-shortened season, when he became the first Red Sox manager in seven decades to finish with three consecutive losing seasons.

• • • •

1998 In his first full season as closer, Tom Gordon set a franchise record with 46 saves, including a major league record 43 straight. He also had a stretch of 28 appearances in which he didn't allow a single run.

• • • •

1999 During the American League season, there were six games pitched in which the starter had 15 or more strikeouts, and Pedro Martinez had all six of them. The next year, he set an all-time record by holding opposing hitters to a .167 average, becoming the first American League pitcher ever to win back-to-back unanimous Cy Young Awards.

On May 3, Creighton Gubanich hit a grand slam for his first major league hit, becoming the fourth player in major league history to do so.

2003 Third baseman Bill Mueller became the first player in major league history to hit grand slams from both sides of the plate in the same game when he performed the trick on July 29 at Texas.

• • • •

2004 When the Red Sox and Yankees played Game 5 of the ALCS in Boston, the game lasted 5 hours and 49 minutes, the longest postseason game—by time—in major league history. In that same series, the Red Sox lost the first three games before winning the next four, the first time that had ever been done in postseason history. When they went on to sweep St. Louis, the Sox became the third consecutive Wild Card team to win the World Series.

Pitcher Derek Lowe finished the 2004 season with a 14–12 record and 5.42 ERA. He was 3–0 with a 1.86 ERA in four postseason games, however, and was the winner in the final game of all three of Boston's postseason series.

The 2004 Red Sox were the first team in major league history to hold a first-inning lead in the first four games of a World Series.

According to history, the Red Sox should have lost the 2004 World Series. Why? Because in four previous World Series that were held in presidential election years in which one of the teams had a candidate from its state, both the team and the candidate won (1920, 1932, 1936, 1972). Therefore…

• • • •

The Boston Red Sox have won more individual batting titles (24) than any other American League team. The Tigers are close with 22, meaning the two teams have accounted for almost half of all batting titles won in American League history.

Special Achievements

World Series Results

Year	Opponent	Result	Games
1903	Pittsburgh Pirates	Won	5–3
1912	New York Giants	Won	4–3
1915	Philadelphia Phillies	Won	4–1
1916	Brooklyn Dodgers	Won	4–1
1918	Chicago Cubs	Won	4–2
1946	St. Louis Cardinals	Lost	3–4
1967	St. Louis Cardinals	Lost	3–4
1975	Cincinnati Reds	Lost	3–4
1986	New York Mets	Lost	3–4
2004	St. Louis Cardinals	Won	4–0

World Series Managerial Records

Manager	Series Record	Games Record
Jimmy Collins	1–0	5–3
Jake Stahl	1–0	4–3
Bill Carrigan	2–0	8–2
Ed Barrow	1–0	4–2
Joe Cronin	0–1	3–4
Dick Williams	0–1	3–4
Darrell Johnson	0–1	3–4
John McNamara	0–1	3–4
Terry Francona	1–0	4–0

All-Time Postseason Record

Divisional Playoffs	10–13
League Championship Series	15–22
World Series	37–26

All-Star Games at Boston

Year	Date	Winner	Score	Stadium
1946	July 9	American	12–0	Fenway Park
1961	July 31	(Tie)	1–1	Fenway Park
1999	July 13	American	4–1	Fenway Park

Hall of Famers Who Played for Team

	Position	Years	Games with Boston
Luis Aparicio	SS	1971–1973	367
Wade Boggs	3B	1982–1992	1,625
Lou Boudreau	SS/3B	1951–1952	86
Jesse Burkett	OF	1905	148
Orlando Cepeda	DH	1973	142
Jack Chesbro	SP	1909	1
Jimmy Collins	3B	1901–1907	741
Joe Cronin	SS	1935–1945	1,134
Bobby Doerr	2B	1937–1944, 1946–1951	1,865
Dennis Eckersley	SP/RP	1978–1984, 1998	241
Rick Ferrell	C	1934–1937	522
Carlton Fisk	C	1969, 1971–1980	1,078
Jimmie Foxx	1B	1936–1942	887
Lefty Grove	SP	1934–1941	217
Harry Hooper	OF	1909–1920	1,647
Waite Hoyt	SP/RP	1919–1920	35
Ferguson Jenkins	SP	1976–1977	58
George Kell	3B	1952–1954	235
Heinie Manush	OF	1936	82
Juan Marichal	SP	1974	11
Herb Pennock	SP/RP	1915–1922	204
Tony Perez	1B/DH	1980–1982	304
Red Ruffing	SP/RP	1924–1930	237
Babe Ruth	OF/SP	1914–1919	391
Tom Seaver	SP	1986	16
Al Simmons	OF	1943	40
Tris Speaker	OF	1907–1915	1,065
Ted Williams	OF	1939–1942, 1946–1960	2,292
Carl Yastrzemski	OF/1B/DH	1961–1983	3,308
Cy Young	SP	1901–1908	334

Hall of Famers Who Managed Team

	Years	Games with Boston
Ed Barrow	1918–1920	416
Lou Boudreau	1952–1954	461
Frank Chance	1923	152
Jimmy Collins	1901–1906	831
Joe Cronin	1935–1947	1,987
Hugh Duffy	1921–1922	308
Bucky Harris	1934	152
Billy Herman	1964–1966	310
Joe McCarthy	1948–1950	368
Cy Young	1907	63

MVP Award Winners

Jimmie Foxx	1B	1938
Ted Williams	OF	1946
Ted Williams	OF	1949
Jackie Jensen	OF	1958
Carl Yastrzemski	OF	1967
Fred Lynn	OF	1975
Jim Rice	OF	1978
Roger Clemens	SP	1986
Mo Vaughn	1B	1995

CY YOUNG AWARD WINNERS

Pitcher	Year	W–L	ERA
Jim Lonborg	1967	22–9	3.16
Roger Clemens	1986	24–4	2.48
Roger Clemens	1987	20–9	2.97
Roger Clemens	1991	18–10	2.62
Pedro Martinez	1999	23–4	2.07
Pedro Martinez	2000	18–6	1.74

ROOKIE OF THE YEAR AWARD WINNERS

Walt Dropo	1B	1950
Don Schwall	SP	1961
Carlton Fisk	C	1972
Fred Lynn	OF	1975
Nomar Garciaparra	SS	1997

GOLD GLOVE WINNERS

Year	Position	Player
1957	3B	Frank Malzone
1958	3B OF	Frank Malzone Jim Piersall
1959	3B OF	Frank Malzone Jackie Jensen
1963	OF	Carl Yastrzemski
1965	OF	Carl Yastrzemski
1967	1B OF	George Scott Carl Yastrzemski
1968	1B OF OF	George Scott Carl Yastrzemski Reggie Smith
1969	OF	Carl Yastrzemski
1971	1B OF	George Scott Carl Yastrzemski
1972	C 2B	Carlton Fisk Doug Griffin
1975	OF	Fred Lynn
1976	OF	Dwight Evans
1977	OF	Carl Yastrzemski
1978	OF OF	Fred Lynn Dwight Evans
1979	SS OF OF	Rick Burleson Dwight Evans Fred Lynn
1980	OF	Fred Lynn
1981	OF	Dwight Evans
1982	OF	Dwight Evans
1983	OF	Dwight Evans
1984	OF	Dwight Evans
1985	OF	Dwight Evans
1990	SP OF	Mike Boddicker Ellis Burks
1991	C	Tony Pena
2005	C	Jason Varitek

TRIPLE CROWN WINNERS

Player	Year	Avg	HR	RBI
Ted Williams	1942	.356	36	114
Ted Williams	1947	.343	32	130
Carl Yastrzemski	1967	.326	44	121

FIREMAN OF THE YEAR AWARD WINNERS

Mike Fornieles	1960
Dick Radatz	1962
Dick Radatz	1964
Bill Campbell	1977
Tom Gordon	1998

WORLD SERIES MVP

Manny Ramirez	2004

LEAGUE CHAMPIONSHIP SERIES MVP

Marty Barrett	1986
David Ortiz	2004

ALL-STAR GAME MVP

Carl Yastrzemski	1970
Roger Clemens	1986
Pedro Martinez	1999

MANAGER OF THE YEAR AWARD WINNERS

John McNamara	1986
Jimy Williams	1999

BATTING CHAMPIONS

Player	Year	Avg
Dale Alexander	1932	.367
Jimmie Foxx	1938	.349
Ted Williams	1941	.406
Ted Williams	1942	.356
Ted Williams	1947	.343
Ted Williams	1948	.369
Billy Goodman	1950	.354
Ted Williams	1957	.388
Ted Williams	1958	.328
Pete Runnels	1960	.320
Pete Runnels	1962	.326
Carl Yastrzemski	1963	.321
Carl Yastrzemski	1967	.326
Carl Yastrzemski	1968	.301
Fred Lynn	1979	.333
Carney Lansford	1981	.336
Wade Boggs	1983	.361
Wade Boggs	1985	.368

Wade Boggs	1986	.357
Wade Boggs	1987	.363
Wade Boggs	1988	.366
Nomar Garciaparra	1999	.357
Nomar Garciaparra	2000	.372
Manny Ramirez	2002	.349
Bill Mueller	2003	.326

NINE-INNING NO-HITTERS PITCHED

Year	Pitcher	Opp.	Score
1904	Cy Young	PHI	3–0 (perfect)
	Jesse Tannehill	CWS	6–0
1905	Bill Dineen	CWS	2–0
1908	Cy Young	NYY	8–0
1911	Joe Wood	STL	5–0
1916	George Foster	NYY	2–0
	Dutch Leonard	STL	4–0
1917	Ernie Shore	WAS	4–0 (perfect)
1918	Dutch Leonard	DET	5–0
1923	Howard Ehmke	PHI	4–0
1956	Mel Parnell	CWS	4–0
1962	Earl Wilson	LAA	2–0
	Bill Monbouquette	CWS	1–0
1965	Dave Morehead	CLE	2–0
2001	Hideo Nomo	BAL	3–0
2002	Derek Lowe	TB	10–0

20-GAME WINNERS

Year	Pitcher	W–L
1901	Cy Young	33–10
1902	Cy Young	32–11
	Bill Dineen	21–21
1903	Cy Young	28–9
	Bill Dineen	21–13
	Tom Hughes	20–7
1904	Cy Young	26–16
	Bill Dineen	23–14
	Jesse Tannehill	21–11
1905	Jesse Tannehill	22–9
1907	Cy Young	21–15
1908	Cy Young	21–11
1911	Joe Wood	23–17
1912	Joe Wood	34–5
	Hugh Bedient	20–9
	Buck O'Brien	20–13
1914	Ray Collins	20–13
1916	Babe Ruth	23–12
1917	Babe Ruth	24–13
	Carl Mays	22–9
1918	Carl Mays	21–13
1921	Sam Jones	23–16
1923	Howard Ehmke	20–17
1935	Wes Ferrell	25–14
	Lefty Grove	20–12
1936	Wes Ferrell	20–15
1942	Tex Hughson	22–6
1945	Dave Ferriss	21–10
1946	Dave Ferriss	25–6
	Tex Hughson	20–11
1949	Mel Parnell	25–7
	Ellis Kinder	23–6
1953	Mel Parnell	21–8
1963	Bill Monbouquette	20–10
1967	Jim Lonborg	22–9
1973	Luis Tiant	20–13
1974	Luis Tiant	22–13
1976	Luis Tiant	21–12
1978	Dennis Eckersley	20–8
1986	Roger Clemens	24–4
1987	Roger Clemens	20–9
1990	Roger Clemens	21–6
1999	Pedro Martinez	23–4
2002	Derek Lowe	21–8
	Pedro Martinez	20–4
2004	Curt Schilling	21–6

RETIRED UNIFORM NUMBERS

Number	Player	Position
1	Bobby Doerr	2B
4	Joe Cronin	SS
8	Carl Yastrzemski	OF
9	Ted Williams	OF
27	Carlton Fisk	C

TEAM RECORDS—WINS & LOSSES

- Games won in a season: 105 in 1912
- Games lost in a season: 111 in 1932
- Games won in a month: 25 in July 1948
- Games lost in a month: 24 (3 times): July 1925; June 1927; July 1928
- Consecutive games won: 15 in 1946
- Consecutive games lost: 20 in 1906
- Biggest shutout victory: 19–0 over Philadelphia A's on April 30, 1950 (first game)
- Biggest shutout loss: 19–0 to Cleveland on August 21, 1920
- Highest winning percentage: .691 in 1912 (105–47)
- Lowest winning percentage: .279 in 1932 (43–111)

TEAM RECORDS—BATTING

- Highest team batting average: .302 in 1950
- Lowest team batting average: .234 in 1905 and 1907
- Highest team slugging average: .491 in 2003

- Highest team on-base percentage: .385 in 1950
- Total hits: 1,684 in 1997
- Extra-base hits: 649 in 2003
- Hits in a single game: 28 vs. St. Louis Browns on June 8, 1950
- Longest individual hitting streak: 34, Dom DiMaggio, 1949
- Most .300 hitters in a single season: 9 in 1950
- Home runs: 238 in 2003
- Home runs in a month: 14, Jackie Jensen, June 1948
- Home runs in a game: 8 vs. Toronto on July 4, 1977
- Home runs by a rookie: 34, Walt Dropo, 1950
- Home runs by a right-hander: 50, Jimmie Foxx, 1938
- Home runs by a left-hander: 47, David Ortiz, 2005
- Home runs by a switch-hitter: 34, Carl Everett, 2000
- Grand slams: 11 in 2005
- Grand slams (individual; single season): 4, Babe Ruth, 1919
- Grand slams (individual; career): 17, Ted Williams
- Triples: 112 in 1903
- Doubles: 373 in 1997 and 2004
- Singles: 1,156 in 1950
- Walks: 835 in 1949
- Runs scored: 1,027 in 1950
- Runs scored in a game: 29 vs. St. Louis Browns, June 8, 1950
- Runs scored in an inning: 17 vs. Detroit on June 18, 1953 (seventh inning)
- Most batters hit by a pitch: 72 in 2002
- Times shut out: 28 in 1906
- Grounded into double plays: 174 in 1990
- Fewest grounded into double plays: 94 in 1942
- Runners left on base: 1,308 in 1989

TEAM RECORDS—BASERUNNING

- Stolen bases: 215 in 1909
- Caught stealing: 111 in 1920

TEAM RECORDS—PITCHING

- Lowest earned run average: 2.12 in 1904
- Complete games: 148 in 1904
- Saves: 53 in 1998
- Strikeouts: 1,259 in 2001
- Shutouts: 26 in 1918
- Walks: 748 in 1950
- Hit batsmen: 93 in 2001
- Wild pitches: 73 in 1968
- Consecutive wins (individual): 16, Joe Wood, 1912
- Consecutive losses (individual): 14, Joe W. Harris, 1906
- Strikeouts in a game (individual): 20, Roger Clemens, April 29, 1986 and September 18, 1996
- Most runs allowed in a game: 27 vs. Cleveland, July 7, 1923 (first game)

TEAM RECORDS—FIELDING

- Best fielding average: .984 in 1988
- Most errors committed: 337 in 1901
- Fewest errors committed: 93 in 1988
- Most double plays turned: 207 in 1949
- Fewest double plays turned: 74 in 1913

TEAM RECORDS—MISCELLANEOUS

- Number of times league champions: 11
- Number of times finishing last in league: 10
- Largest attendance, single game: 36,388 vs. Cleveland, April 22, 1978
- Largest attendance, doubleheader: 47,627 vs. New York Yankees, September 22, 1935
- Players used in a season: 55 in 1996
- Seasons played: 23 by Carl Yastrzemski

PRIMARY PITCHING STAFFS

Year	Starter	Starter	Starter	Starter	Starter	Closer	Bullpen	Bullpen	Bullpen
2005	Wakefield	Arroyo	Clement	Wells	Miller	Foulke	Timlin	Myers	Embree
2004	Lowe	Martinez	Schilling	Wakefield	Arroyo	Foulke	Timlin	Embree	Leskanic
2003	Lowe	Martinez	Burkett	Wakefield	Fossum	Kim	Timlin	Embree	Lyon
2002	Lowe	Martinez	Burkett	Wakefield	Castillo	Urbina	Fossum	Embree	Banks
2001	Nomo	Martinez	Cone	Wakefield	Castillo	Lowe	Beck	Garces	Arrojo
2000	Martinez	Martinez	Fassero	Wakefield	Schourek	Lowe	Cormier	Garces	Pichardo
1999	Portugal	Martinez	Rapp	Saberhagen	Rose	Wakefield	Cormier	Lowe	Guthrie
1998	Wakefield	Martinez	Avery	Saberhagen	Lowe	Gordon	Corsi	Eckersley	Wasdin
1997	Wakefield	Sele	Avery	Gordon	Suppan	Slocumb	Corsi	Henry	Wasdin
1996	Wakefield	Sele	Clemens	Gordon	Eshelman	Slocumb	Stanton	Garces	Hudson
1995	Wakefield	Hanson	Clemens	Smith	Eshelman	Aguilera	Belinda	Cormier	Hudson
1994	Sele	Hesketh	Clemens	Darwin	Nabholz	Ryan	Fossas	Howard	Harris
1993	Sele	Viola	Clemens	Darwin	Dopson	Russell	Fossas	Quantrill	Harris
1992	Hesketh	Viola	Clemens	Gardiner	Dopson	Reardon	Fossas	Darwin	Harris
1991	Hesketh	Harris	Clemens	Gardiner	Bolton	Reardon	Fossas	Lamp	Gray
1990	Boddicker	Harris	Clemens	Kiecker	Bolton	Reardon	Murphy	Lamp	Gray
1989	Boddicker	Dopson	Clemens	Smithson	Gardner	Smith	Murphy	Lamp	Stanley
1988	Hurst	Boyd	Clemens	Smithson	Gardner	Smith	Bolton	Lamp	Stanley
1987	Hurst	Nipper	Clemens	Sellers	Stanley	Gardner	Bolton	Schiraldi	Sambito
1986	Hurst	Nipper	Clemens	Boyd	Seaver	Stanley	Crawford	Lollar	Sambito
1985	Hurst	Nipper	Clemens	Boyd	Ojeda	Crawford	Stanley	Clear	Trujillo
1984	Hurst	Nipper	Clemens	Boyd	Ojeda	Stanley	Crawford	Clear	Johnson
1983	Hurst	Tudor	Eckersley	Brown	Ojeda	Stanley	Aponte	Clear	Johnson
1982	Hurst	Tudor	Eckersley	Torrez	Rainey	Clear	Aponte	Stanley	Burgmeier
1981	Tanana	Tudor	Eckersley	Torrez	Crawford	Clear	Campbell	Stanley	Burgmeier
1980	Renko	Tudor	Eckersley	Torrez	Stanley	Burgmeier	Campbell	Drago	Lockwood
1979	Renko	Rainey	Eckersley	Torrez	Stanley	Drago	Campbell	Burgmeier	Ripley
1978	Tiant	Lee	Eckersley	Torrez	Wright	Stanley	Campbell	Burgmeier	Drago
1977	Tiant	Lee	Jenkins	Cleveland	Wise	Campbell	Stanley	Willoughby	Paxton
1976	Tiant	Pole	Jenkins	Cleveland	Wise	Willoughby	Murphy	House	Jones
1975	Tiant	Lee	Moret	Cleveland	Wise	Drago	Willoughby	Burton	Segui
1974	Tiant	Lee	Moret	Cleveland	Drago	Segui	Veale	Pole	Marichal
1973	Tiant	Lee	Moret	Curtis	Pattin	Bolin	Veale	Pole	Garman
1972	Tiant	Siebert	McGlothen	Curtis	Pattin	Lee	Peters	Newhauser	Tatum
1971	Tiant	Siebert	Culp	Peters	Lonborg	Lyle	Lee	Bolin	Tatum
1970	Nagy	Siebert	Culp	Peters	Brett	Lyle	Romo	Wagner	Koonce
1969	Nagy	Siebert	Culp	Lonborg	Stange	Lyle	Romo	Landis	Jarvis
1968	Ellsworth	Bell	Culp	Lonborg	Santiago	Stange	Waslewski	Landis	Lyle
1967	Stange	Bell	Brandon	Lonborg	Bennett	Wyatt	Lyle	Santiago	Osinski
1966	Stange	Santiago	Brandon	Lonborg	Wilson	McMahon	Wyatt	Stigman	Osinski
1965	Monbouquette	Morehead	Bennett	Lonborg	Wilson	Radatz	Earley	Ritchie	Duliba
1964	Monbouquette	Morehead	Lamabe	Connolly	Wilson	Radatz	Heffner	Spanswick	Charton
1963	Monbouquette	Morehead	Heffner	Conley	Wilson	Radatz	Lamabe	Earley	Wood
1962	Monbouquette	Schwall	Delock	Conley	Wilson	Radatz	Fornieles	Earley	Nichols
1961	Monbouquette	Schwall	Delock	Conley	Stallard	Fornieles	Muffett	Earley	Hillman
1960	Monbouquette	Brewer	Delock	Sullivan	Casale	Fornieles	Muffett	Sturdivant	Borland
1959	Monbouquette	Brewer	Delock	Sullivan	Casale	Fornieles	Kiely	Baumann	Chittum
1958	Sisler	Brewer	Delock	Sullivan	Bowsfield	Kiely	Wall	Fornieles	Byerly
1957	Sisler	Brewer	Nixon	Sullivan	Fornieles	Delock	Susce	Porterfield	Minarcin

PRIMARY PITCHING STAFFS (CONT.)

Year	Starter	Starter	Starter	Starter	Starter	Closer	Bullpen	Bullpen	Bullpen
1956	Parnell	Brewer	Nixon	Sullivan	Porterfield	Delock	Hurd	Sisler	Kiely
1955	Delock	Brewer	Nixon	Sullivan	Susce	Kinder	Hurd	Henry	Kiely
1954	Kiely	Brewer	Nixon	Sullivan	Parnell	Kinder	Brown	Henry	Hudson
1953	McDermott	Brown	Nixon	Hudson	Parnell	Kinder	Flowers	Henry	Delock
1952	McDermott	Trout	Nixon	Hudson	Parnell	Benton	Scarborough	Kinder	Delock
1951	McDermott	Stobbs	Scarborough	Wight	Parnell	Kinder	Nixon	Taylor	Masterson
1950	McDermott	Stobbs	Dobson	Kinder	Parnell	Nixon	Papai	Masterson	
1949	Kramer	Stobbs	Dobson	Kinder	Parnell	Hughson	Johnson	Masterson	
1948	Kramer	Harris	Dobson	Kinder	Parnell	Ferriss	Johnson	Galehouse	
1947	Ferriss	Hughson	Dobson	Galehouse	Johnson	Dorish	Murphy	Klinger	
1946	Ferriss	Hughson	Dobson	Harris	Bagby	Klinger	Johnson	Dreisewerd	Brown
1945	Ferriss	O'Neill	Wilson	Heflin	Hausmann	Barrett	Ryba	Johnson	
1944	Bowman	O'Neill	Hughson	Woods	Terry	Barrett	Hausmann	Ryba	Cecil
1943	Newsome	Judd	Hughson	Dobson	Terry	Brown	Woods	Ryba	Lucier
1942	Newsome	Judd	Hughson	Dobson	Wagner	Brown	Butland	Ryba	Terry
1941	Newsome	Harris	Grove	Dobson	Wagner	Ryba	Wilson	Johnson	Fleming
1940	Bagby	Galehouse	Grove	Ostermueller	Wilson	Heving	Dickman	Hash	
1939	Auker	Galehouse	Grove	Ostermueller	Wilson	Heving	Bagby	Dickman	Rich
1938	Bagby	Marcum	Grove	Ostermueller	Wilson	McKain	Heving	Dickman	Rogers
1937	Newsom	Marcum	Grove	McKain	Wilson	Walberg	Ostermueller	Ferrell	
1936	Ferrell	Marcum	Grove	Ostermueller	Walberg	Wilson	Russell	Henry	
1935	Ferrell	Welch	Grove	Ostermueller	Rhodes	Wilson	Walberg	Hockette	
1934	Ferrell	Welch	Johnson	Ostermueller	Rhodes	Pennock	Walberg	Grove	
1933	Weiland	Brown	Johnson	Pipgras	Rhodes	Welch	Kline	Andrews	
1932	Weiland	Durham	Kline	Andrews	Rhodes	Moore	Michaels	Boerner	
1931	MacFayden	Russell	Gaston	Lisenbee	Moore	Durham	Morris	Kline	
1930	MacFayden	Russell	Gaston	Lisenbee	Durham	Smith	Morris	Bushey	
1929	MacFayden	Russell	Gaston	Ruffing	Morris	Bayne	Carroll	Durham	
1928	MacFayden	Russell	Harriss	Ruffing	Morris	Simmons	Settlemire	Bradley	
1927	Wiltse	Welzer	Harriss	Ruffing	Lundgren	Russell	MacFayden	Wingfield	
1926	Wiltse	Zahniser	Harriss	Ruffing	Wingfield	Russell	Welzer	Heimach	
1925	Ehmke	Zahniser	Quinn	Ruffing	Wingfield	Fuhr	Ross	Neubauer	
1924	Ehmke	Ferguson	Quinn	Fullerton	Piercy	Fuhr	Ross	Murray	
1923	Ehmke	Ferguson	Quinn	Murray	Piercy	Fullerton	O'Doul	Howe	
1922	Collins	Ferguson	Quinn	Pennock	Karr	Fullerton	Russell	Piercy	
1921	Jones	Bush	Myers	Pennock	Russell	Karr	Thormahlen		
1920	Jones	Bush	Harper	Pennock	Hoyt	Karr	Russell	Fortune	
1919	Jones	Mays	Ruth	Pennock	Caldwell	Hoyt	Russell	Dumont	
1918	Jones	Mays	Ruth	Bush	Leonard	Molyneaux			
1917	Shore	Mays	Ruth	Foster	Leonard	Pennock	Bader	Jones	
1916	Shore	Mays	Ruth	Foster	Leonard	Pennock	Gregg	Jones	
1915	Shore	Wood	Ruth	Foster	Leonard	Mays	Collins	Gregg	
1914	Shore	Collins	Bedient	Foster	Leonard	Wood	Coumbe	Johnson	
1913	Wood	Collins	Bedient	Moseley	Leonard	Hall	Foster	O'Brien	
1912	Wood	Collins	Bedient	O'Brien	Hall	Pape	Cicotte		
1911	Wood	Collins	Cicotte	Pape	Karger	Hall	Killilay	Moser	
1910	Wood	Collins	Cicotte	Smith	Karger	Hall	Arellanes	Hunt	
1909	Wood	Arellanes	Cicotte	Chech	Morgan	Steele	Ryan	Schlitzer	

PRIMARY PITCHING STAFFS (CONT.)

Year	Starter	Starter	Starter	Starter	Starter	Closer	Bullpen	Bullpen	Bullpen
1908	Young	Burchell	Cicotte	Winter	Morgan	Steele	Pruiett	Arellanes	
1907	Young	Glaze	Pruiett	Winter	Tannehill	Morgan	Harris	Oberlin	
1906	Young	Dineen	Harris	Winter	Tannehill	Glaze			
1905	Young	Dineen	Gibson	Winter	Tannehill	Barry	Hughes		
1904	Young	Dineen	Gibson	Winter	Tannehill				
1903	Young	Dineen	Gibson	Winter	Hughes	Altrock			
1902	Young	Dineen	Sparks	Winter	Hughes	Prentiss			
1901	Young	Lewis	Mitchell	Winter	Cuppy	Kellum			

PRIMARY STARTING LINEUPS

Year	C	1B	2B	3B	SS	LF	CF	RF	DH
2005	Varitek	Millar	Bellhorn	Mueller	Renteria	Ramirez	Damon	Nixon	Ortiz
2004	Varitek	Millar	Bellhorn	Mueller	Reese	Ramirez	Damon	Kapler	Ortiz
2003	Varitek	Millar	Walker	Mueller	Garciaparra	Ramirez	Damon	Nixon	Ortiz
2002	Varitek	Clark	Sanchez	Hillenbrand	Garciaparra	Ramirez	Damon	Nixon	Baerga
2001	Hatteberg	Daubach	Offerman	Hillenbrand	Lansing	O'Leary	Everett	Nixon	Ramirez
2000	Varitek	Daubach	Offerman	Alexander	Garciaparra	O'Leary	Everett	Nixon	Bichette
1999	Varitek	Stanley	Offerman	Valentin	Garciaparra	O'Leary	Lewis	Nixon	Jefferson
1998	Hatteberg	Vaughn	Benjamin	Valentin	Garciaparra	O'Leary	Lewis	Bragg	Jefferson
1997	Hatteberg	Vaughn	Frye	Naehring	Garciaparra	Cordero	Bragg	O'Leary	Jefferson
1996	Stanley	Vaughn	Frye	Naehring	Valentin	Greenwell	Tinsley	O'Leary	Canseco
1995	Macfarlane	Vaughn	Alicea	Naehring	Valentin	Greenwell	Tinsley	O'Leary	Canseco
1994	Berryhill	Vaughn	Fletcher	Cooper	Valentin	Greenwell	Nixon	Hatcher	Dawson
1993	Pena	Vaughn	Fletcher	Cooper	Valentin	Greenwell	Hatcher	Zupcic	Dawson
1992	Pena	Vaughn	Reed	Boggs	Rivera	Hatcher	Zupcic	Brunansky	Clark
1991	Pena	Quintana	Reed	Boggs	Rivera	Greenwell	Burks	Brunansky	Clark
1990	Pena	Quintana	Reed	Boggs	Rivera	Greenwell	Burks	Brunansky	Evans
1989	Cerone	Esasky	Barrett	Boggs	Rivera	Greenwell	Burks	Evans	Rice
1988	Gedman	Benzinger	Barrett	Boggs	Reed	Greenwell	Burks	Evans	Rice
1987	Sullivan	Evans	Barrett	Boggs	Owen	Rice	Burks	Benzinger	Baylor
1986	Gedman	Buckner	Barrett	Boggs	Romero	Rice	Armas	Evans	Baylor
1985	Gedman	Buckner	Barrett	Boggs	Gutierrez	Rice	Lyons	Evans	Easler
1984	Gedman	Buckner	Barrett	Boggs	Gutierrez	Rice	Armas	Evans	Easler
1983	Allenson	Stapleton	Remy	Boggs	Hoffman	Rice	Armas	Evans	Yastrzemski
1982	Allenson	Stapleton	Remy	Lansford	Hoffman	Rice	Miller	Evans	Yastrzemski
1981	Gedman	Perez	Remy	Lansford	Hoffman	Rice	Miller	Evans	Yastrzemski
1980	Fisk	Perez	Stapleton	Hoffman	Burleson	Rice	Lynn	Evans	Yastrzemski
1979	Allenson	Watson	Remy	Hobson	Burleson	Rice	Lynn	Evans	Yastrzemski
1978	Fisk	Scott	Remy	Hobson	Burleson	Rice	Lynn	Evans	Bailey
1977	Fisk	Scott	Doyle	Hobson	Burleson	Yastrzemski	Lynn	Carbo	Rice
1976	Fisk	Yastrzemski	Doyle	Hobson	Burleson	Rice	Lynn	Evans	Cooper
1975	Fisk	Yastrzemski	Griffin	Petrocelli	Burleson	Rice	Lynn	Evans	Cooper
1974	Montgomery	Yastrzemski	Griffin	Petrocelli	Guerrero	Harper	Beniquez	Evans	Cooper
1973	Fisk	Yastrzemski	Griffin	Petrocelli	Aparicio	Harper	Smith	Evans	Cepeda
1972	Fisk	Cater	Griffin	Petrocelli	Aparicio	Yastrzemski	Harper	Smith	

Primary Starting Lineups (cont.)

Year	C	1B	2B	3B	SS	LF	CF	RF	DH
1971	Josephson	Scott	Griffin	Petrocelli	Aparicio	Yastrzemski	Smith	Lahoud	
1970	Moses	Yastrzemski	Andrews	Scott	Petrocelli	Conigliaro	Smith	Conigliaro	
1969	Gibson	Jones	Andrews	Scott	Petrocelli	Yastrzemski	Smith	Conigliaro	
1968	Gibson	Scott	Andrews	Foy	Petrocelli	Yastrzemski	Smith	Harrelson	
1967	Ryan	Scott	Andrews	Foy	Petrocelli	Yastrzemski	Smith	Conigliaro	
1966	Ryan	Scott	Smith	Foy	Petrocelli	Yastrzemski	Demeter	Conigliaro	
1965	Tillman	Thomas	Mantilla	Malzone	Petrocelli	Yastrzemski	Green	Conigliaro	
1964	Tillman	Stuart	Jones	Malzone	Bressoud	Conigliaro	Yastrzemski	Thomas	
1963	Tillman	Stuart	Schilling	Malzone	Bressoud	Yastrzemski	Geiger	Clinton	
1962	Pagliaroni	Runnels	Schilling	Malzone	Bressoud	Yastrzemski	Geiger	Clinton	
1961	Pagliaroni	Runnels	Schilling	Malzone	Buddin	Yastrzemski	Geiger	Jensen	
1960	Nixon	Wertz	Runnels	Malzone	Buddin	Williams	Tasby	Clinton	
1959	White	Gernert	Runnels	Malzone	Buddin	Williams	Keough	Jensen	
1958	White	Gernert	Runnels	Malzone	Buddin	Williams	Piersall	Jensen	
1957	White	Gernert	Lepcio	Malzone	Klaus	Williams	Piersall	Jensen	
1956	White	Vernon	Goodman	Klaus	Buddin	Williams	Piersall	Jensen	
1955	White	Zauchin	Goodman	Hatton	Klaus	Williams	Piersall	Jensen	
1954	White	Agganis	Lepcio	Hatton	Bolling	Williams	Jensen	Piersall	
1953	White	Gernert	Goodman	Kell	Bolling	Evers	Umphlett	Piersall	
1952	White	Gernert	Goodman	Kell	Lipon	Evers	DiMaggio	Throneberry	
1951	Moss	Dropo	Doerr	Stephens	Pesky	Williams	DiMaggio	Vollmer	
1950	Tebbetts	Dropo	Doerr	Pesky	Stephens	Williams	DiMaggio	Zarilla	
1949	Tebbetts	Goodman	Doerr	Pesky	Stephens	Williams	DiMaggio	Zarilla	
1948	Tebbetts	Goodman	Doerr	Pesky	Stephens	Williams	DiMaggio	Spence	
1947	Tebbetts	Jones	Doerr	Dente	Pesky	Williams	DiMaggio	Mele	
1946	Wagner	York	Doerr	Russell	Pesky	Williams	DiMaggio	Metkovich	
1945	Garbark	Metkovich	Newsome	Tobin	Lake	Johnson	Culberson	Lazor	
1944	Partee	Finney	Doerr	Tabor	Newsome	Johnson	Metkovich	Fox	
1943	Partee	Lupien	Doerr	Tabor	Newsome	Lazor	Metkovich	Fox	
1942	Conroy	Lupien	Doerr	Tabor	Pesky	Williams	DiMaggio	Finney	
1941	Pytlak	Foxx	Doerr	Tabor	Cronin	Williams	DiMaggio	Finney	
1940	Desautels	Foxx	Doerr	Tabor	Cronin	Williams	Cramer	Finney	
1939	Peacock	Foxx	Doerr	Tabor	Cronin	Vosmik	Cramer	Williams	
1938	Desautels	Foxx	Doerr	Higgins	Cronin	Vosmik	Cramer	Chapman	
1937	Desautels	Foxx	McNair	Higgins	Cronin	Mills	Cramer	Chapman	
1936	Ferrell	Foxx	Melillo	Werber	McNair	Manush	Cramer	Almada	
1935	Ferrell	Dahlgren	Melillo	Werber	Cronin	Johnson	Almada	Reynolds	
1934	Ferrell	Morgan	Cissell	Werber	Lary	Johnson	Reynolds	Porter	
1933	Ferrell	Alexander	Hodapp	McManus	Warstler	Jolley	Oliver	Johnson	
1932	Tate	Alexander	Olson	Pickering	Warstler	Jolley	Oliver	Johnson	
1931	Berry	Sweeney	Warstler	Miller	Rhyne	Rothrock	Oliver	Webb	
1930	Berry	Todt	Regan	Miller	Rhyne	Scarritt	Oliver	Webb	
1929	Berry	Todt	Regan	Reeves	Rhyne	Scarritt	Rothrock	Barrett	
1928	Hofmann	Todt	Regan	Myer	Gerber	Williams	Flagstead	Taitt	
1927	Hartley	Todt	Regan	Rogell	Myer	Shaner	Flagstead	Tobin	
1926	Gaston	Todt	Regan	Haney	Rigney	Shaner	Flagstead	Tobin	
1925	Picinich	Todt	Wambsganss	Prothro	Lee	Vache	Flagstead	Boone	
1924	O'Neill	Harris	Wambsganss	Clark	Lee	Veach	Flagstead	Boone	
1923	Picinich	Burns	Fewster	Shanks	Mitchell	Harris	Reichle	Flagstead	
1922	Ruel	Burns	Pratt	Dugan	Mitchell	Menosky	Leibold	Collins	
1921	Ruel	McInnis	Pratt	Foster	Scott	Menosky	Leibold	Collins	

Primary Starting Lineups (cont.)

Year	C	1B	2B	3B	SS	LF	CF	RF	DH
1920	Walters	McInnis	McNally	Foster	Scott	Menosky	Hendryx	Hooper	
1919	Schang	McInnis	Shannon	Vitt	Scott	Ruth	Roth	Hooper	
1918	Agnew	McInnis	Shean	Thomas	Scott	Whiteman	Strunk	Hooper	
1917	Agnew	Hoblitzel	Barry	Gardner	Scott	Lewis	Walker	Hooper	
1916	Thomas	Hoblitzel	Barry	Gardner	Scott	Lewis	Walker	Hooper	
1915	Thomas	Hoblitzel	Wagner	Gardner	Scott	Lewis	Speaker	Hooper	
1914	Carrigan	Hoblitzel	Yerkes	Gardner	Scott	Lewis	Speaker	Hooper	
1913	Carrigan	Engle	Yerkes	Gardner	Wagner	Lewis	Speaker	Hooper	
1912	Carrigan	Stahl	Yerkes	Gardner	Wagner	Lewis	Speaker	Hooper	
1911	Carrigan	Engle	Wagner	Gardner	Yerkes	Lewis	Speaker	Hooper	
1910	Carrigan	Stahl	Gardner	Lord	Wagner	Lewis	Speaker	Hooper	
1909	Carrigan	Stahl	McConnell	Lord	Wagner	Niles	Speaker	Gessler	
1908	Criger	Stahl	McConnell	Lord	Wagner	Thoney	Sullivan	Gessler	
1907	Criger	Unglaub	Ferris	Knight	Wagner	Barrett	Sullivan	Congalton	
1906	Armbruster	Grimshaw	Ferris	Morgan	Parent	Hoey	Stahl	Hayden	
1905	Criger	Grimshaw	Ferris	Collins	Parent	Burkett	Stahl	Selbach	
1904	Criger	LaChance	Ferris	Collins	Parent	Selbach	Stahl	Freeman	
1903	Criger	LaChance	Ferris	Collins	Parent	Dougherty	Stahl	Freeman	
1902	Criger	LaChance	Ferris	Collins	Parent	Dougherty	Stahl	Freeman	
1901	Schreckengost	Freeman	Ferris	Collins	Parent	Dowd	Stahl	Hemphill	

Top 10 Batting Leaders, Single Season & Career with Team

Games Played: Career with Team

Player	G	PA
1. Carl Yastrzemski	3,308	13,991
2. Dwight Evans	2,505	10,240
3. Ted Williams	2,292	9,791
4. Jim Rice	2,089	9,058
5. Bobby Doerr	1,865	8,028
6. Harry Hooper	1,647	7,330
7. Wade Boggs	1,625	7,323
8. Rico Petrocelli	1,553	6,170
9. Dom DiMaggio	1,399	6,478
10. Frank Malzone	1,359	5,702

At-Bats: Season

Player	AB	Year
1. Nomar Garciaparra	684	1997
2. Jim Rice	677	1978
3. Bill Buckner	673	1985
4. Rick Burleson	663	1977
5. Doc Cramer	661	1940
6. Doc Cramer	658	1938
Nomar Garciaparra	658	2003
8. Jim Rice	657	1984
9. Wade Boggs	653	1985
10. Dom DiMaggio	648	1948

At-Bats: Career with Team

Player	AB	PA
1. Carl Yastrzemski	11,988	13,991
2. Dwight Evans	8,726	10,240
3. Jim Rice	8,225	9,058
4. Ted Williams	7,706	9,791
5. Bobby Doerr	7,093	8,028
6. Harry Hooper	6,270	7,330
7. Wade Boggs	6,213	7,323
8. Dom DiMaggio	5,640	6,478
9. Rico Petrocelli	5,390	6,170
10. Frank Malzone	5,273	5,702

Batting Average: Season

Player	BA	Year
1. Ted Williams	.406	1941
2. Ted Williams	.388	1957
3. Tris Speaker	.383	1912
4. Nomar Garciaparra	.372	2000
Dale Alexander	.372	1932
6. Ted Williams	.369	1948
7. Wade Boggs	.368	1985
8. Wade Boggs	.366	1988

9. Tris Speaker	.363	1913
Wade Boggs	.363	1987

Batting Average: Career with Team

Player	BA	PA
1. Ted Williams	.344	9,791
2. Wade Boggs	.338	7,323
3. Tris Speaker	.337	4,551
4. Nomar Garciaparra	.323	4,345
5. Pete Runnels	.320	3,004
Jimmie Foxx	.320	3,934
7. Manny Ramirez	.315	3,130
8. Roy Johnson	.313	2,202
Johnny Pesky	.313	4,760
10. Fred Lynn	.308	3,513

Total Hits: Season

Player	H	Year
1. Wade Boggs	240	1985
2. Tris Speaker	222	1912
3. Wade Boggs	214	1988
4. Jim Rice	213	1978
5. Wade Boggs	210	1983
6. Nomar Garciaparra	209	1997
7. Johnny Pesky	208	1946
8. Wade Boggs	207	1986
Johnny Pesky	207	1947
Mo Vaughn	207	1996

Total Hits: Career with Team

Player	H	PA
1. Carl Yastrzemski	3,419	13,991
2. Ted Williams	2,654	9,791
3. Jim Rice	2,452	9,058
4. Dwight Evans	2,373	10,240
5. Wade Boggs	2,098	7,323
6. Bobby Doerr	2,042	8,028
7. Harry Hooper	1,707	7,330
8. Dom DiMaggio	1,680	6,478
9. Frank Malzone	1,454	5,702
10. Mike Greenwell	1,400	5,166

Home Runs: Season

Player	HR	Year
1. Jimmie Foxx	50	1938
2. David Ortiz	47	2005
3. Jim Rice	46	1978
4. Manny Ramirez	45	2005
5. Mo Vaughn	44	1996
Carl Yastrzemski	44	1967
7. Tony Armas	43	1984
Manny Ramirez	43	2004
Ted Williams	43	1949
10. Dick Stuart	42	1963

Home Runs: Career with Team

Player	HR	PA
1. Ted Williams	521	9,791
2. Carl Yastrzemski	452	13,991
3. Jim Rice	382	9,058
4. Dwight Evans	379	10,240
5. Mo Vaughn	230	4,452
6. Bobby Doerr	223	8,028
7. Jimmie Foxx	222	3,934
8. Rico Petrocelli	210	6,170
9. Manny Ramirez	199	3,130
10. Nomar Garciaparra	178	4,345

Triples: Season

Player	3B	Year
1. Tris Speaker	22	1913
2. Buck Freeman	20	1903
3. Buck Freeman	19	1902
Buck Freeman	19	1904
Larry Gardner	19	1914
Chick Stahl	19	1904
7. Larry Gardner	18	1912
Tris Speaker	18	1914
9. Jimmy Collins	17	1903
Harry Hooper	17	1920
Freddy Parent	17	1903
Russ Scarritt	17	1929

Triples: Career with Team

Player	3B	PA
1. Harry Hooper	130	7,330
2. Tris Speaker	106	4,551
3. Buck Freeman	90	3,385
4. Bobby Doerr	89	8,028
5. Larry Gardner	87	4,511
6. Jim Rice	79	9,058
7. Hobe Ferris	77	3,927
8. Dwight Evans	72	10,240
9. Ted Williams	71	9,791
10. Jimmy Collins	65	3,224

Doubles: Season

Player	2B	Year
1. Earl Webb	67	1931
2. Nomar Garciaparra	56	2002
3. Tris Speaker	53	1912
4. Wade Boggs	51	1989
Joe Cronin	51	1938
Nomar Garciaparra	51	2000
7. Wade Boggs	47	1986
George Burns	47	1923
Fred Lynn	47	1975
David Ortiz	47	2004
John Valentin	47	1997

Doubles: Career with Team

Player	2B	PA
1. Carl Yastrzemski	646	13,991
2. Ted Williams	525	9,791
3. Dwight Evans	474	10,240
4. Wade Boggs	422	7,323
5. Bobby Doerr	381	8,028
6. Jim Rice	373	9,058
7. Dom DiMaggio	308	6,478
8. Nomar Garciaparra	279	4,345
9. Mike Greenwell	275	5,166
10. Joe Cronin	270	4,584

Extra-Base Hits: Season

Player	XBH	Year
1. Jimmie Foxx	92	1938
2. David Ortiz	91	2004
3. David Ortiz	88	2005
4. Manny Ramirez	87	2004
5. Jim Rice	86	1978
Ted Williams	86	1939
7. Nomar Garciaparra	85	1997
Nomar Garciaparra	85	2002
Ted Williams	85	1949
10. Jim Rice	84	1979
Earl Webb	84	1931

Extra-Base Hits: Career with Team

Player	XBH	PA
1. Carl Yastrzemski	1,157	13,991
2. Ted Williams	1,117	9,791
3. Dwight Evans	925	10,240
4. Jim Rice	834	9,058
5. Bobby Doerr	693	8,028
6. Wade Boggs	554	7,323
7. Nomar Garciaparra	507	4,345
8. Rico Petrocelli	469	6,170
9. Dom DiMaggio	452	6,478
10. Jimmie Foxx	448	3,934

Total Bases: Season

Player	TB	Year
1. Jim Rice	406	1978
2. Jimmie Foxx	398	1938
3. Jim Rice	382	1977
4. Mo Vaughn	370	1996
5. Jimmie Foxx	369	1936
Jim Rice	369	1979
7. Ted Williams	368	1949
8. Nomar Garciaparra	365	1997
9. David Ortiz	363	2005
10. Mo Vaughn	360	1998
Carl Yastrzemski	360	1967

Total Bases: Career with Team

Player	TB	PA
1. Carl Yastrzemski	5,539	13,991
2. Ted Williams	4,884	9,791
3. Jim Rice	4,129	9,058
4. Dwight Evans	4,128	10,240
5. Bobby Doerr	3,270	8,028
6. Wade Boggs	2,869	7,323
7. Dom DiMaggio	2,363	6,478
8. Harry Hooper	2,303	7,330
9. Rico Petrocelli	2,263	6,170
10. Nomar Garciaparra	2,194	4,345

Runs Batted In: Season

Player	RBI	Year
1. Jimmie Foxx	175	1938
2. Vern Stephens	159	1949
Ted Williams	159	1949
4. David Ortiz	148	2005
5. Ted Williams	145	1939
6. Walt Dropo	144	1950
Vern Stephens	144	1950
Manny Ramirez	144	2005
9. Jimmie Foxx	143	1936
Mo Vaughn	143	1996

Runs Batted In: Career with Team

Player	RBI	PA
1. Carl Yastrzemski	1,844	13,991
2. Ted Williams	1,839	9,791
3. Jim Rice	1,451	9,058
4. Dwight Evans	1,346	10,240
5. Bobby Doerr	1,247	8,028
6. Jimmie Foxx	788	3,934
7. Rico Petrocelli	773	6,170
8. Mo Vaughn	752	4,452
9. Joe Cronin	737	4,584
10. Jackie Jensen	733	4,518

Runs Scored: Season

Player	R	Year
1. Ted Williams	150	1949
2. Ted Williams	142	1946
3. Ted Williams	141	1942
4. Jimmie Foxx	139	1938
5. Tris Speaker	136	1912
6. Ted Williams	135	1941
7. Ted Williams	134	1940
8. Dom DiMaggio	131	1950
Ted Williams	131	1939
10. Jimmie Foxx	130	1936
Jimmie Foxx	130	1939

Runs Scored: Career with Team

Player	R	PA
1. Carl Yastrzemski	1,816	13,991
2. Ted Williams	1,798	9,791
3. Dwight Evans	1,435	10,240
4. Jim Rice	1,249	9,058
5. Bobby Doerr	1,094	8,028
6. Wade Boggs	1,067	7,323
7. Dom DiMaggio	1,046	6,478
8. Harry Hooper	988	7,330
9. Johnny Pesky	776	4,760
10. Jimmie Foxx	721	3,934

Walks: Season

Player	BB	Year
1. Ted Williams	162	1947
Ted Williams	162	1949
3. Ted Williams	156	1946
4. Ted Williams	147	1941
5. Ted Williams	145	1942
6. Ted Williams	144	1951
7. Ted Williams	136	1954
8. Carl Yastrzemski	128	1970
9. Ted Williams	126	1948
10. Wade Boggs	125	1988

Walks: Career with Team

Player	BB	PA
1. Ted Williams	2,021	9,791
2. Carl Yastrzemski	1,845	13,991
3. Dwight Evans	1,337	10,240
4. Wade Boggs	1,004	7,323
5. Harry Hooper	826	7,330
6. Bobby Doerr	809	8,028
7. Dom DiMaggio	750	6,478
8. Jim Rice	670	9,058
9. Rico Petrocelli	661	6,170
10. Jimmie Foxx	624	3,934

Strikeouts: Season

Player	SO	Year
1. Mark Bellhorn	177	2004
2. Butch Hobson	162	1977
3. Tony Armas	156	1984
4. Mo Vaughn	154	1996
Mo Vaughn	154	1997
6. George Scott	152	1966
7. Mo Vaughn	150	1995
8. Manny Ramirez	147	2001
9. Dick Stuart	144	1963
Mo Vaughn	144	1998

Strikeouts: Career with Team

Player	SO	PA
1. Dwight Evans	1,643	10,240
2. Jim Rice	1,423	9,058
3. Carl Yastrzemski	1,393	13,991
4. Mo Vaughn	954	4,452
5. Rico Petrocelli	926	6,170
6. George Scott	850	4,740
7. Ted Williams	709	9,791
8. Jason Varitek	693	3,624
9. Bobby Doerr	608	8,028
10. Carlton Fisk	588	4,353

Slugging Percentage: Season

Player	SLG	Year
1. Ted Williams	.735	1941
2. Ted Williams	.731	1957
3. Jimmie Foxx	.704	1938
4. Jimmie Foxx	.694	1939
5. Ted Williams	.667	1946
6. Babe Ruth	.657	1919
7. Ted Williams	.650	1949
8. Ted Williams	.648	1942
9. Manny Ramirez	.647	2002
10. Ted Williams	.645	1960

Slugging Percentage: Career with Team

Player	SLG	PA
1. Ted Williams	.634	9,791
2. Manny Ramirez	.608	3,130

3. Jimmie Foxx	.605	3,934
4. Nomar Garciaparra	.553	4,345
5. Mo Vaughn	.542	4,452
6. Fred Lynn	.520	3,513
7. Jim Rice	.502	9,058
8. Vern Stephens	.492	2,872
9. Trot Nixon	.489	3,376
10. Brian Daubach	.488	2,033

On-Base Percentage: Season

Player	OBP	Year
1. Ted Williams	.553	1941
2. Ted Williams	.526	1957
3. Ted Williams	.513	1954
4. Ted Williams	.499	1942
Ted Williams	.499	1947
6. Ted Williams	.497	1946
Ted Williams	.497	1948
8. Ted Williams	.490	1949
9. Ted Williams	.479	1956
10. Wade Boggs	.476	1988

On-Base Percentage: Career with Team

Player	OBP	PA
1. Ted Williams	.482	9,791
2. Jimmie Foxx	.429	3,934
3. Wade Boggs	.428	7,323
4. Tris Speaker	.414	4,551
5. Manny Ramirez	.412	3,130
6. Pete Runnels	.408	3,004
7. Johnny Pesky	.401	4,760
8. Mo Vaughn	.394	4,452
Joe Cronin	.394	4,584
Rick Ferrell	.394	2,098

OPS (On-Base Percentage + Slugging Percentage): Season

Player	OPS	Year
1. Ted Williams	1.287	1941
2. Ted Williams	1.257	1957
3. Jimmie Foxx	1.166	1938
4. Ted Williams	1.164	1946
5. Jimmie Foxx	1.158	1939
6. Ted Williams	1.148	1954
7. Ted Williams	1.147	1942
8. Ted Williams	1.141	1949
9. Ted Williams	1.133	1947
10. Babe Ruth	1.114	1919

OPS (On-Base Percentage + Slugging Percentage): Career with Team

Player	OPS	PA
1. Ted Williams	1.115	9,791
2. Jimmie Foxx	1.034	3,934
3. Manny Ramirez	1.020	3,130
4. Mo Vaughn	.936	4,452
5. Nomar Garciaparra	.923	4,345
6. Fred Lynn	.902	3,513
7. Tris Speaker	.896	4,551
8. Wade Boggs	.890	7,323
9. Joe Cronin	.878	4,584
10. Trot Nixon	.863	2,906

Stolen Bases: Season

Player	SB	Year
1. Tommy Harper	54	1973
2. Tris Speaker	52	1912
3. Tris Speaker	46	1913
4. Otis Nixon	42	1994
Tris Speaker	42	1914
6. Harry Hooper	40	1910
Billy Werber	40	1934
8. Harry Hooper	38	1911
9. Harry Lord	36	1909
10. Patsy Dougherty	35	1903
Tris Speaker	35	1909
Tris Speaker	35	1910

Stolen Bases: Career with Team

Player	SB	PA
1. Harry Hooper	300	7,330
2. Tris Speaker	267	4,551
3. Carl Yastrzemski	168	13,991
4. Heinie Wagner	141	3,714
5. Larry Gardner	134	4,511
6. Freddy Parent	129	4,240
7. Tommy Harper	107	1,783
Billy Werber	107	2,375
9. Chick Stahl	105	3,407
10. Jimmy Collins	102	3,224
Duffy Lewis	102	4,884

Sacrifice Hits: Season

Player	Sac	Year
1. Jack Barry	54	1917
2. Ossie Vitt	47	1919
3. Stuffy McInnis	45	1920
4. Everett Scott	41	1917
5. Larry Gardner	40	1917
6. Bill Wambsganss	37	1924
7. Harry Lord	36	1908
Dave Shean	36	1918
9. Stuffy McInnis	35	1921
Freddy Parent	35	1905

Sacrifice Hits: Career with Team

Player	Sac	PA
1. Duffy Lewis	219	4,884
2. Everett Scott	197	4,266
3. Larry Gardner	182	4,511
4. Harry Hooper	180	7,330
5. Freddy Parent	148	4,240
6. Stuffy McInnis	138	2,234
7. Phil Todt	118	3,558
8. Jack Barry	115	1,312
Bobby Doerr	115	8,028
10. Marty Barrett	102	3,816
Tris Speaker	102	4,551

Hit by Pitch: Season

Player	HBP	Year
1. Don Baylor	35	1986
2. Don Baylor	24	1987
3. Jack Barry	17	1916
Kevin Millar	17	2004
5. Jake Stahl	15	1908
Jake Stahl	15	1909
7. Mike Macfarlane	14	1995
Mo Vaughn	14	1995
Mo Vaughn	14	1996
10. Five tied with . . .	13	—

Hit by Pitch: Career with Team

Player	HBP	PA
1. Mo Vaughn	71	4,452
2. Jim Rice	64	9,058
3. Don Baylor	59	1,096
Carlton Fisk	59	4,353
5. Tris Speaker	55	4,551
6. Harry Hooper	54	7,330
7. Dwight Evans	51	10,240
8. Nomar Garciaparra	46	4,345
Jake Stahl	46	1,890
10. John Valentin	43	4,269

Top 10 Pitching Leaders, Single Season & Career with Team

Games Pitched: Season

Player	GP	Year
1. Mike Timlin	81	2005
2. Greg Harris	80	1993
3. Dick Radatz	79	1964
4. Mike Timlin	76	2004
5. Heathcliff Slocumb	75	1996
6. Derek Lowe	74	1999
Derek Lowe	74	2000
Rob Murphy	74	1989
9. Tom Gordon	73	1998
10. Keith Foulke	72	2004
Mike Timlin	72	2003

Games Pitched: Career with Team

Player	GP	IP
1. Bob Stanley	637	1,707.0
2. Tim Wakefield	420	2,071.7
3. Derek Lowe	384	1,037.0
4. Roger Clemens	383	2,776.0
5. Ellis Kinder	365	1,142.3
6. Cy Young	327	2,728.3
7. Ike Delock	322	1,207.7
8. Bill Lee	321	1,503.3
9. Mel Parnell	289	1,752.7
10. Greg Harris	287	651.0

Innings Pitched: Season

Player	IP	Year
1. Cy Young	384.7	1902
2. Cy Young	380.0	1904
3. Bill Dineen	371.3	1902
Cy Young	371.3	1901
5. Joe Wood	344.0	1912
6. Cy Young	343.3	1907
7. Cy Young	341.7	1903
8. Bill Dineen	335.7	1904
9. Babe Ruth	326.3	1917
10. Babe Ruth	323.7	1916

Innings Pitched: Career with Team

Player	IP
1. Roger Clemens	2,776.0
2. Cy Young	2,728.3
3. Tim Wakefield	2,071.7
4. Luis Tiant	1,774.7
5. Mel Parnell	1,752.7
6. Bob Stanley	1,707.0
7. Bill Monbouquette	1,622.0
8. George Winter	1,599.7
9. Joe Dobson	1,544.0
10. Lefty Grove	1,539.7

Batters Faced: Season

Player	BF	Year
1. Cy Young	1,527	1902
2. Bill Dineen	1,524	1902
3. Cy Young	1,475	1904
4. Cy Young	1,466	1901
5. Wes Ferrell	1,391	1935
6. Howard Ehmke	1,377	1924
7. Joe Wood	1,362	1912
8. Wes Ferrell	1,341	1936
9. Cy Young	1,335	1903
10. Howard Ehmke	1,331	1923

Batters Faced: Career with Team

Player	BF	IP
1. Roger Clemens	11,384	2,776.0
2. Cy Young	10,662	2,728.3
3. Tim Wakefield	8,948	2,071.7
4. Mel Parnell	7,547	1,752.7
5. Luis Tiant	7,289	1,774.7
6. Bob Stanley	7,238	1,707.0
7. Bill Monbouquette	6,810	1,622.0
8. Tom Brewer	6,574	1,509.3
9. Lefty Grove	6,573	1,539.7
10. Joe Dobson	6,526	1,544.0

Games Started: Season

Player	GS	Year
1. Cy Young	43	1902
2. Bill Dineen	42	1902
3. Babe Ruth	41	1916
Cy Young	41	1901
Cy Young	41	1904
6. Howard Ehmke	39	1923
Jim Lonborg	39	1967
8. Wes Ferrell	38	1935
Wes Ferrell	38	1936
Sam Jones	38	1921
Babe Ruth	38	1917
Luis Tiant	38	1974
Luis Tiant	38	1976
Joe Wood	38	1912

Games Started: Career with Team

Player	GS	IP
1. Roger Clemens	382	2,776.0
2. Cy Young	297	2,728.3
3. Tim Wakefield	283	2,071.7
4. Luis Tiant	238	1,774.7
5. Mel Parnell	232	1,752.7
6. Bill Monbouquette	228	1,622.0
7. Tom Brewer	217	1,509.3
Bruce Hurst	217	1,459.0
9. Joe Dobson	202	1,544.0
10. Pedro Martinez	201	1,383.7
Frank Sullivan	201	1,505.3

Complete Games: Season

Player	CG	Year
1. Cy Young	41	1902
2. Cy Young	40	1904
3. Bill Dineen	39	1902
4. Cy Young	38	1901
5. Bill Dineen	37	1904
6. Babe Ruth	35	1917
Joe Wood	35	1912
8. Cy Young	34	1903
9. Cy Young	33	1907
10. Bill Dineen	32	1903

Complete Games: Career with Team

Player	CG	IP
1. Cy Young	275	2,728.3
2. Bill Dineen	156	1,501.0
3. George Winter	141	1,599.7
4. Joe Wood	121	1,418.0
5. Lefty Grove	119	1,539.7
6. Mel Parnell	113	1,752.7
Luis Tiant	113	1,774.7
8. Babe Ruth	105	1,190.3
9. Roger Clemens	100	2,776.0
10. Tex Hughson	99	1,375.7

GAMES WON: SEASON

Player	W	Year
1. Joe Wood	34	1912
2. Cy Young	33	1901
3. Cy Young	32	1902
4. Cy Young	28	1903
5. Cy Young	26	1904
6. Wes Ferrell	25	1935
Dave Ferriss	25	1946
Mel Parnell	25	1949
9. Roger Clemens	24	1986
Babe Ruth	24	1917

GAMES WON: CAREER WITH TEAM

Player	W	IP
1. Roger Clemens	192	2,776.0
Cy Young	192	2,728.3
3. Tim Wakefield	130	2,071.7
4. Mel Parnell	123	1,752.7
5. Luis Tiant	122	1,774.7
6. Pedro Martinez	117	1,383.7
Joe Wood	117	1,418.0
8. Bob Stanley	115	1,707.0
9. Joe Dobson	106	1,544.0
10. Lefty Grove	105	1,539.7

GAMES LOST: SEASON

Player	L	Year
1. Red Ruffing	25	1928
2. Red Ruffing	22	1929
3. Bill Dineen	21	1902
Joe Harris	21	1906
Slim Harriss	21	1927
Cy Young	21	1906
7. Howard Ehmke	20	1925
Milt Gaston	20	1930
Sam Jones	20	1919
Jack Russell	20	1930

GAMES LOST: CAREER WITH TEAM

Player	L	IP
1. Cy Young	112	2,728.3
2. Roger Clemens	111	2,776.0
Tim Wakefield	111	2,071.7
4. Bob Stanley	97	1,707.0
George Winter	97	1,599.7
6. Red Ruffing	96	1,122.3
7. Jack Russell	94	1,215.0
8. Bill Monbouquette	91	1,622.0
9. Bill Dineen	85	1,501.0
10. Tom Brewer	82	1,509.3

WINNING PERCENTAGE: SEASON

Player	W%	Year
1. Bob Stanley	.882	1978
2. Joe Wood	.872	1912
3. Roger Clemens	.857	1986
4. Pedro Martinez	.852	1999
5. Pedro Martinez	.833	2002
6. Roger Moret	.824	1975
7. Dave Ferriss	.806	1946
8. Ellis Kinder	.793	1949
9. Dutch Leonard	.792	1914
10. Lefty Grove	.789	1939

WINNING PERCENTAGE: CAREER WITH TEAM

Player	W%	IP
1. Pedro Martinez	.760	1,383.7
2. Dave Ferriss	.684	880.0
3. Joe Wood	.676	1,418.0
4. Babe Ruth	.659	1,190.3
5. Tex Hughson	.640	1,375.7
6. Ernie Shore	.637	839.0
7. Roger Clemens	.634	2,776.0
8. Cy Young	.632	2,728.3
9. Rube Foster	.630	842.3
10. Lefty Grove	.629	1,539.7

SHUTOUTS: SEASON

Player	SHO	Year
1. Joe Wood	10	1912
Cy Young	10	1904
3. Babe Ruth	9	1916
4. Roger Clemens	8	1988
Carl Mays	8	1918
6. Joe Bush	7	1918
Roger Clemens	7	1987
Dutch Leonard	7	1914
Luis Tiant	7	1974
Cy Young	7	1903

SHUTOUTS: CAREER WITH TEAM

Player	SHO	IP
1. Roger Clemens	38	2,776.0
Cy Young	38	2,728.3
3. Joe Wood	28	1,418.0
4. Luis Tiant	26	1,774.7
5. Dutch Leonard	25	1,361.3
6. Mel Parnell	20	1,752.7
7. Ray Collins	19	1,336.0
Tex Hughson	19	1,375.7
9. Sam Jones	18	1,045.0
10. Joe Dobson	17	1,544.0
Babe Ruth	17	1,190.3

ERA: SEASON

Player	ERA	Year
1. Dutch Leonard	0.96	1914
2. Cy Young	1.26	1908
3. Ray Collins	1.62	1910
Cy Young	1.62	1901
5. Ernie Shore	1.64	1915
6. Joe Wood	1.68	1910
7. Rube Foster	1.70	1914
8. Pedro Martinez	1.74	2000
Carl Mays	1.74	1917
10. Babe Ruth	1.75	1916

ERA: CAREER WITH TEAM

Player	ERA	IP
1. Joe Wood	1.99	1,418.0
2. Cy Young	2.00	2,728.3
3. Ernie Shore	2.12	839.0
4. Dutch Leonard	2.13	1,361.3
5. Babe Ruth	2.19	1,190.3
6. Carl Mays	2.21	1,105.0
7. Rube Foster	2.36	842.3
8. Jesse Tannehill	2.50	885.7
9. Ray Collins	2.51	1,336.0
10. Pedro Martinez	2.52	1,383.7

EARNED RUNS ALLOWED: SEASON

Player	ER	Year
1. Wes Ferrell	140	1936
2. Jack Russell	139	1930
3. Tom Gordon	134	1996
4. Howard Ehmke	133	1923
Jack Russell	133	1931
6. Red Ruffing	132	1929
7. Wes Ferrell	126	1935
Danny MacFayden	126	1930
Mike Torrez	126	1979
10. Red Ruffing	125	1928

EARNED RUNS ALLOWED: CAREER WITH TEAM

Player	ER	IP
1. Tim Wakefield	988	2,071.7
2. Roger Clemens	943	2,776.0

3. Bob Stanley	690	1,707.0
4. Bruce Hurst	686	1,459.0
5. Mel Parnell	682	1,752.7
6. Tom Brewer	671	1,509.3
7. Bill Monbouquette	665	1,622.0
8. Luis Tiant	663	1,774.7
9. Jack Russell	618	1,215.0
10. Joe Dobson	612	1,544.0

Strikeouts: Season

Player	K	Year
1. Pedro Martinez	313	1999
2. Roger Clemens	291	1988
3. Pedro Martinez	284	2000
4. Joe Wood	258	1912
5. Roger Clemens	257	1996
6. Roger Clemens	256	1987
7. Pedro Martinez	251	1998
8. Jim Lonborg	246	1967
9. Roger Clemens	241	1991
10. Pedro Martinez	239	2002

Strikeouts: Career with Team

Player	K	IP
1. Roger Clemens	2,590	2,776.0
2. Pedro Martinez	1,683	1,383.7
3. Tim Wakefield	1,480	2,071.7
4. Cy Young	1,341	2,728.3
5. Luis Tiant	1,075	1,774.7
6. Bruce Hurst	1,043	1,459.0
7. Joe Wood	986	1,418.0
8. Bill Monbouquette	969	1,622.0
9. Frank Sullivan	821	1,505.3
10. Ray Culp	794	1,092.3

Strikeouts Per Nine IP: Season

Player	K/9	Year
1. Pedro Martinez	13.20	1999
2. Pedro Martinez	11.78	2000
3. Pedro Martinez	10.79	2002
4. Hideo Nomo	10.00	2001
5. Pedro Martinez	9.93	2003
6. Roger Clemens	9.92	1988
7. Pedro Martinez	9.67	1998
8. Roger Clemens	9.53	1996
9. Pedro Martinez	9.41	2004
10. Roger Clemens	8.86	1994

Strikeouts Per Nine IP: Career with Team

Player	K/9	IP
1. Pedro Martinez	10.95	1383.7
2. Dick Radatz	10.12	557.3
3. Roger Clemens	8.40	2776.0
4. Dave Morehead	7.12	664.7
5. Aaron Sele	6.92	622.0
6. Greg Harris	6.76	651.0
7. Ray Culp	6.54	1092.3
8. Tim Wakefield	6.43	2071.7
Bruce Hurst	6.43	1459.0
10. Jim Lonborg	6.42	1099.0

Hits Allowed: Season

Player	HA	Year
1. Cy Young	350	1902
2. Bill Dineen	348	1902
3. Wes Ferrell	336	1935
4. Wes Ferrell	330	1936
5. Cy Young	327	1904
6. Howard Ehmke	324	1924
Cy Young	324	1901
8. Bill Lee	320	1974
9. Howard Ehmke	318	1923
Sam Jones	318	1921

Hits Allowed: Career with Team

Player	HA	IP
1. Roger Clemens	2,359	2,776.0
2. Cy Young	2,347	2,728.3
3. Tim Wakefield	1,998	2,071.7
4. Bob Stanley	1,858	1,707.0
5. Mel Parnell	1,715	1,752.7
6. Bill Monbouquette	1,649	1,622.0
7. Luis Tiant	1,630	1,774.7
8. Bill Lee	1,627	1,503.3
9. Lefty Grove	1,587	1,539.7
10. Bruce Hurst	1,569	1,459.0

Hits Allowed Per Nine IP: Season

Player	H/9	Year
1. Pedro Martinez	5.31	2000
2. Dutch Leonard	5.57	1914
3. Roger Clemens	6.34	1986
4. Dutch Leonard	6.38	1915
5. Babe Ruth	6.40	1916
6. Luis Tiant	6.44	1972
7. Pedro Martinez	6.50	2002
8. Roger Clemens	6.54	1994
9. Tim Wakefield	6.67	2002
10. Babe Ruth	6.73	1917

Hits Allowed Per Nine IP: Career with Team

Player	H/9	IP
1. Dick Radatz	6.78	557.3
2. Pedro Martinez	6.79	1,383.7
3. Babe Ruth	7.06	1,190.3
4. Joe Wood	7.09	1,418.0
5. Carl Mays	7.48	1,105.0
6. Dutch Leonard	7.50	1,361.3
7. Mickey McDermott	7.53	773.7
8. Roger Clemens	7.65	2,776.0
9. Cy Young	7.74	2,728.3
10. Rube Foster	7.76	842.3

Walks Allowed: Season

Player	BB	Year
1. Mel Parnell	134	1949
2. Mickey McDermott	124	1950
3. Don Schwall	121	1962
Mike Torrez	121	1979
5. Howard Ehmke	119	1923
Wes Ferrell	119	1936
Bobo Newsom	119	1937
Jack Wilson	119	1937
9. Red Ruffing	118	1929
Babe Ruth	118	1916

Walks Allowed: Career with Team

Player	BB	IP
1. Roger Clemens	856	2,776.0
2. Tim Wakefield	787	2,071.7
3. Mel Parnell	758	1,752.7
4. Tom Brewer	669	1,509.3
5. Joe Dobson	604	1,544.0
6. Jack Wilson	564	1,067.7
7. Willard Nixon	530	1,234.0
8. Ike Delock	514	1,207.7
9. Mickey McDermott	504	773.7
10. Luis Tiant	501	1,774.7

WALKS ALLOWED PER NINE IP: SEASON

Player	BB/9	Year
1. Cy Young	0.69	1904
2. Cy Young	0.78	1906
3. Cy Young	0.84	1905
4. Cy Young	0.90	1901
5. Cy Young	0.97	1903
6. David Wells	1.03	2005
7. Jesse Tannehill	1.05	1904
8. Cy Young	1.11	1908
9. Cy Young	1.24	1902
10. Pedro Martinez	1.33	2000

WALKS ALLOWED PER NINE IP: CAREER WITH TEAM

Player	BB/9	IP
1. Cy Young	0.99	2,728.3
2. Jesse Tannehill	1.56	885.7
3. Ray Collins	1.81	1,336.0
4. Pedro Martinez	2.01	1,383.7
5. Bill Dineen	2.03	1,501.0
6. Dennis Eckersley	2.05	1,371.7
Jack Quinn	2.05	832.7
8. George Winter	2.08	1,599.7
9. Jack Russell	2.18	1,215.0
10. Ernie Shore	2.19	839.0

WHIP (WALKS + HITS PER NINE IP): SEASON

Player	WHIP	Year
1. Pedro Martinez	0.737	2000
2. Cy Young	0.867	1905
3. Dutch Leonard	0.886	1914
4. Cy Young	0.893	1908
5. Pedro Martinez	0.923	2002
Pedro Martinez	0.923	1999
7. Cy Young	0.937	1904
8. Roger Clemens	0.969	1986
Cy Young	0.969	1903
10. Cy Young	0.972	1901

WHIP (WALKS + HITS PER NINE IP): CAREER WITH TEAM

Player	WHIP	IP
1. Cy Young	0.970	2,728.3
2. Pedro Martinez	0.978	1,383.7
3. Joe Wood	1.078	1,418.0
4. Carl Mays	1.093	1,105.0
5. Ernie Shore	1.116	839.0
6. Jesse Tannehill	1.118	885.7
7. Ray Collins	1.134	1,336.0
8. Dutch Leonard	1.136	1,361.3
Dick Radatz	1.136	557.3
10. Bill Dineen	1.139	1,501.0

HOME RUNS ALLOWED: SEASON

Player	HRA	Year
1. Tim Wakefield	38	1996
2. Earl Wilson	37	1964
3. Bruce Hurst	35	1987
Tim Wakefield	35	2005
5. Bill Monbouquette	34	1964
Rick Wise	34	1975
7. Gene Conley	33	1961
8. Oil Can Boyd	32	1986
Bill Monbouquette	32	1965
Luis Tiant	32	1973
John Tudor	32	1983

HOME RUNS ALLOWED: CAREER WITH TEAM

Player	HRA	IP
1. Tim Wakefield	279	2,071.7
2. Roger Clemens	194	2,776.0
3. Bill Monbouquette	180	1,622.0
4. Bruce Hurst	173	1,459.0
5. Luis Tiant	170	1,774.7
6. Dennis Eckersley	167	1,371.7
7. Bill Lee	136	1,503.3
8. Ike Delock	134	1,207.7
9. Oil Can Boyd	126	1,016.7
Tom Brewer	126	1,509.3

SAVES: SEASON

Player	SV	Year
1. Tom Gordon	46	1998
2. Derek Lowe	42	2000
3. Jeff Reardon	40	1991
Ugueth Urbina	40	2002
5. Jeff Russell	33	1993
Bob Stanley	33	1983
7. Keith Foulke	32	2004
8. Bill Campbell	31	1977
Heathcliff Slocumb	31	1996
10. Dick Radatz	29	1964
Lee Smith	29	1988

SAVES: CAREER WITH TEAM

Player	SV	IP
1. Bob Stanley	132	1,707.0
2. Dick Radatz	104	557.3
3. Ellis Kinder	91	1,142.3
4. Jeff Reardon	88	153.0
5. Derek Lowe	85	1,037.0
6. Sparky Lyle	69	331.3
7. Tom Gordon	68	495.3
8. Lee Smith	58	168.7
9. Bill Campbell	51	335.0
10. Ugueth Urbina	49	80.0

WILD PITCHES: SEASON

Player	WP	Year
1. Earl Wilson	21	1963
2. Milt Gaston	17	1929
3. Gary Peters	16	1970
4. Eddie Cicotte	14	1908
5. Matt Clement	13	2005
6. Jim Lonborg	12	1967
Diego Segui	12	1974
Frank Viola	12	1992
9. Nine tied with...	11	—

WILD PITCHES: CAREER WITH TEAM

Player	WP	IP
1. Roger Clemens	72	2,776.0
2. Tim Wakefield	67	2,071.7
3. Earl Wilson	54	1,024.3
4. Tom Brewer	53	1,509.3
5. Jim Lonborg	47	1,099.0
6. Joe Wood	43	1,418.0
7. Mel Parnell	41	1,752.7
8. Ray Culp	39	1,092.3
9. Joe Dobson	37	1,544.0
10. Greg Harris	35	651.0
Cy Young	35	2,728.3

HIT BATSMEN: SEASON

Player	HB	Year
1. Bronson Arroyo	20	2004
Howard Ehmke	20	1923
3. Jim Lonborg	19	1967
4. Tim Wakefield	18	2001
5. Pedro Martinez	16	2004
Tim Wakefield	16	1997
Tim Wakefield	16	2004

Player		
Matt Clement	16	2005
9. Pedro Martinez	15	2002
Aaron Sele	15	1997
Jesse Tannehill	15	1904

Hit Batsmen: Career with Team

Player	HB	IP
1. Tim Wakefield	126	2,071.7
2. Roger Clemens	86	2,776.0
3. Pedro Martinez	77	1,383.7
4. Jim Lonborg	61	1,099.0
Cy Young	61	2,728.3
6. Joe Wood	49	1,418.0
7. Derek Lowe	48	1,037.0
8. Howard Ehmke	46	989.7
9. Carl Mays	44	1,105.0
10. Tom Brewer	43	1,509.3
Jesse Tannehill	43	885.7

Games Finished: Season

Player	GF	Year
1. Tom Gordon	69	1998
2. Dick Radatz	67	1964
3. Derek Lowe	64	2000
4. Keith Foulke	61	2004
5. Bill Campbell	60	1977
Heathcliff Slocumb	60	1996
7. Dick Radatz	58	1963
8. Lee Smith	57	1988
9. Dick Radatz	56	1965
10. Ugueth Urbina	55	2002

Games Finished: Career with Team

Player	GF	IP
1. Bob Stanley	376	1,707.0
2. Dick Radatz	244	557.3
3. Ellis Kinder	200	1,142.3
4. Sparky Lyle	160	331.3
5. Mike Fornieles	158	642.7
6. Mark Clear	154	400.3
Derek Lowe	154	1,037.0
8. Bill Campbell	137	335.0
9. Jeff Reardon	127	153.0
10. Dick Drago	123	547.3

The Green Monster, baseball's most famous "living" architectural oddity.

Significant Red Sox

BOGGS, WADE (3B)
(1982–1992)

The Red Sox drafted Wade Boggs in the seventh round of the June 1976 amateur draft. He toiled in the minors for six seasons, batting over .300 five times, but was slow to be called up to the majors because of his lack of power and inconsistent fielding. When third baseman Carney Lansford was injured in June 1982, Boggs got his chance. For the remainder of the season Boggs hit .349, convincing the Red Sox to trade Lansford to Oakland. Boggs then proceeded to hit over .300 for 10 straight seasons, winning five batting titles in six years. He also had a record seven consecutive 200-hit seasons.

Boggs had a training regimen like few other players, and put great stock in superstition. He ran wind sprints at precisely 7:17 P.M. every evening. He walked the same precise path to his position in the field every game, so by the end of the season his footprints were clearly visible in front of the Red Sox dugout. He always ate chicken for his pregame meal. And he always drew a Hebrew letter in the batter's box before each at-bat. Boggs became embroiled in scandal in 1989 when Margo Adams went public with details of their four-year affair in a palimony suit. Because she requested depositions from a number of Red Sox players, the whole affair caused much dissension in the clubhouse, and Boggs' reputation was tarnished.

After slumping to .259 in 1992, Boggs was deemed expendable, so the eight-time All-Star wasn't offered another contract. He signed on with the Yankees the next season and his performance immediately improved. Boggs hit over .300 for the next four years for New York, before having another off-year and being released. He played his last two seasons with Tampa Bay, where he collected his 3,000th hit on August 7, 1999. The 23rd member of the 3,000-hit club, Boggs was the first to homer for his milestone hit. After the season, he retired and took a job with the Devil Rays' front office. In 2005 Boggs was elected to the Hall of Fame in his first year of eligibility.

CAREER RED SOX RECORD:

Games	AB	Hits	Runs
1,625	6,213	2,098	1,067
Avg	**HR**	**RBI**	**SB**
.338	85	687	16

CLEMENS, ROGER (SP)
(1984–1996)

Roger "the Rocket" Clemens was selected in the first round of the June 1983 amateur draft by the Red Sox and promoted to the majors the following year. He was originally drafted by the Mets in 1981, but chose to stay in college and pitch for the University of Texas, and in 1983 won the championship game of the College World Series. After compiling a combined 16–9 record for the Red Sox in 1984–1985, Clemens exploded onto the scene in 1986 by finishing 24–4 with a 2.48 ERA. He also became the first pitcher ever to strike out 20 batters in a nine-inning game, a feat he would repeat 10 years later. Clemens won a basketful of awards in 1986, including the first of three Cy Young Awards he would win with Boston. He also won the AL MVP Award, the All-Star Game MVP Award, *The Sporting News* Pitcher of the Year Award, and *The Sporting News* Player of the Year Award. After seven great years, Clemens then had four mediocre years in a row from 1993 to 1996, when his combined record was 40–39 and his ERA was nearly 4.00 (compared to six of the previous seven years, when it stayed between 1.93 and 2.97). Feeling he was on the down side of his career, the Red Sox let their five-time All-Star go to free agency, whereupon Clemens signed on with Toronto with something to prove. *(See Blue Jays bio.)*

CAREER RED SOX RECORD:

W	L	W%	ERA	SV
192	111	.634	3.06	0

K	BB	SHO	IP
2,590	856	38	2,776.0

CRONIN, JOE (SS)
(1935–1945)

New Red Sox owner Tom Yawkey ordered GM Eddie Collins to buy up the best talent available, so Joe Cronin was one of Collins' targets. After spending nine years establishing himself as a star shortstop for the Pirates and Senators, player-manager Cronin was acquired by Boston for $250,000. At the time, Cronin played for Washington and was married to the niece of owner Clark Griffith. Griffith kept turning down Collins' offers until the amount got so ridiculous that Cronin told his uncle-in-law he could not afford to turn it down. Before the sale was complete, Griffith arranged for Cronin to get a very lucrative five-year contract as part of the deal. Once in Boston, player-manager Cronin continued to be a strong hitter, but his defensive skills at shortstop were declining. Other players came to resent that he was in the lineup. Cronin also liked to call pitches from the bench, which understandably annoyed his pitchers. Wes Ferrell once stormed out of a game to protest Cronin's managing style. Only Ted Williams seemed to like him.

Cronin was a regular for his first seven seasons in Boston, then played only part-time during his last four. Late in his career, when he was no longer playing regularly, Cronin would occasionally put himself in to pinch-hit, especially when the wind was blowing out. In 1943 he hit five pinch-hit homers, including two grand slams. He also hit pinch-hit home runs in both games of a doubleheader. Cronin was also responsible for negotiating player contracts in his capacity as player-manager. Perhaps his biggest blunder was not signing Willie Mays in 1947. When told repeatedly by Birmingham Black Barons' GM Eddie Glennon about Mays, Cronin refused to sign the 16-year-old Mays, thanks to the Red Sox organization's deeply entrenched racism. The Red Sox were the last major league team to integrate when they signed Pumpsie Green in 1959. Discrimination still reigned off the field; they refused to hire black ushers until threatened by a lawsuit in the 1970s. In 1948 Cronin became the Red Sox GM, then in 1959 the president of the American League, the first former player so honored. In 1970 he fired two umpires for "incompetency" when he learned they were trying to form a union. He retired as AL president in 1974 and was elected to the Hall of Fame in 1956.

CAREER RED SOX RECORD:

Games	AB	Hits	Runs
1,134	3,892	1,168	645

Avg	HR	RBI	SB
.300	119	737	31

DIMAGGIO, DOM (OF)
(1940–1942, 1946–1953)

Dom, the smallest and youngest of the three DiMaggio brothers, was nicknamed "the Little Professor" because of his spectacles and small size, but he was a terrific center fielder with a powerful arm who often covered up for the defensive weaknesses of Ted Williams in right. Because of the way he routinely robbed batters of hits, other players called him "Jesse James without the horse." He played his entire 11-year career in Boston, though, like many players of his era, he missed three years due to World War II. DiMaggio made the All-Star team seven times and five times hit over .300.

In 1949 Dom DiMaggio was threatening his older brother Joe's record 56-game hitting streak. He was at 34 games when the Red Sox played the Yankees. Joe helped end Dom's streak that day, robbing his younger brother of a hit with a fantastic catch. In the 1946 World Series, Dom was instrumental in bringing the Red Sox to the brink of victory. In the eighth inning of Game 7, DiMaggio hit a double to tie the score, 3–3. But he hurt his ankle running out the double, and had to be replaced in center by Leon Culberson, a clearly inferior defensive player with a weaker throwing arm. In the bottom of the eighth, with Enos Slaughter on first, Harry Walker hit a single to center. Slaughter made what came to be called "the mad dash home," when he ran all the way from first on Walker's hit. As Slaughter once told this author, he wouldn't have even tried it had DiMaggio been in center that day.

CAREER RED SOX RECORD:

Games	AB	Hits	Runs
1,399	5,640	1,680	1,046
Avg	**HR**	**RBI**	**SB**
.298	87	618	100

DOERR, BOBBY (2B)
(1937–1944, 1946–1951)

Bobby Doerr, who played his entire 14-year career with Boston, was another of the players Eddie Collins signed when he was ordered by owner Tom Yawkey to buy up the best talent available. Collins had gone on a scouting trip to southern California and signed Doerr and Ted Williams on the same trip. Doerr was a strong second baseman, both offensively and defensively. He led or tied for the lead in fielding six times and knocked in more than 100 runs six times. A nine-time All-Star, Doerr was chosen the 1944 American League MVP when he hit .325 with a .528 slugging average. Doerr, who hit .406 in the 1946 World Series won by the Cardinals, was forced to retire at the age of 33 due to chronic back trouble. He was elected to the Hall of Fame in 1986.

CAREER RED SOX RECORD:

Games	AB	Hits	Runs
1,865	6,213	7,093	1,094
Avg	**HR**	**RBI**	**SB**
.288	223	1,247	54

EVANS, DWIGHT (OF/DH)
(1972–1990)

The Red Sox drafted Dwight Evans in the fifth round of the 1969 amateur draft and gave him his first taste of major league action in 1972. By 1974 he was the regular right fielder for the Sox. Steady, if unspectacular, Evans was always overshadowed by other teammates, including Carl Yastrzemski, Wade Boggs, Jim Rice, and Fred Lynn. Although he was a great defensive player (he won eight Gold Gloves) with a powerful arm that was rarely challenged, he just didn't rise to the offensive level of some of his teammates, at least for the first part of his career. In 1980 Evans was hitting below .200 just before the All-Star break. Hitting coach Walt Hriniak got him to change to one batting stance—just one of the 300 Evans jokingly admitted to having—and the results were almost immediate. Instead of trying to pull everything to left field, he now went with the pitch and, for the first time in his career, he scored more than 75 runs and had more than 70 RBIs. He proceeded to have four more seasons with 109 or more runs and six seasons with at least 97 RBIs. Before the change, Evans managed to hit over .280 only twice in nine seasons; afterwards he hit .280 six times in the next nine years. After 19 seasons in Boston, Evans was released and signed with Baltimore for one final season before retiring.

CAREER RED SOX RECORD:

Games	AB	Hits	Runs
2,505	8,726	2,373	1,435
Avg	**HR**	**RBI**	**SB**
.272	379	1,346	76

FISK, CARLTON (C)
(1969, 1971–1980)

Carlton "Pudge" Fisk, who grew up in New England with hopes of becoming a star player for the Boston Celtics, was selected in the first round of the June 1967 amateur draft by the only baseball team he ever wanted to play for, the Boston Red Sox. After getting the proverbial "cups of coffee" in 1969 and 1971, Fisk became the starting catcher in 1972 and won the American League Rookie of the Year Award in the first unanimous vote in history. He also won the only Gold Glove of his career that same year and played in the first of his 11 All-Star Games.

Very early on, Fisk made a name for himself as a battler. He got into a contentious argument with Bill Singer after claiming the pitcher threw a spitball in the All-Star Game. He got into a fistfight with Thurman Munson and Gene Michael of the Yankees at home plate; tangled with Al Gallagher of the Angels after a collision at home plate; and got into more fisticuffs with Frank Robinson after an argument over a brushback pitch.

In 1974 Fisk was injured in spring training and was given no hope of ever returning to baseball. Instead, he underwent intensive rehabilitation and recovered in time for the 1975 season. However, in his second spring-training game an errant pitch broke his arm, keeping him out until midseason. When he returned, Fisk hit .331 with 52 RBIs in just 79 games and helped the Red Sox to the World Series against the Cincinnati Reds. Down three games to two, Fisk hit what many consider to be the most dramatic home run ever in World Series play to tie the Series at three games apiece—although the Sox ultimately lost the seventh game. In 1977–1978 Fisk caught a combined 309 games, one short of the all-time AL record for back-to-back seasons. Also in 1977 he became just the fifth catcher in major league history to both score and drive in 100 runs in the same season. In 1981, Boston's front office blundered by failing to postmark Fisk's new contract in time, thus allowing their seven-time All-Star catcher to become a free agent. Carlton Fisk then changed his Sox, from Red to White, signing with Chicago. As fate would have it, Chicago opened the 1981 season at Boston and Fisk hit a three-run homer in the eighth inning to win the game, 5–3. *(See White Sox bio.)*

CAREER RED SOX RECORD:

Games	AB	Hits	Runs
1,078	3,860	1,097	627
Avg	**HR**	**RBI**	**SB**
.284	162	568	61

FOXX, JIMMIE (1B)
(1936–1942)

Jimmie Foxx was one of the biggest stars in baseball when cash-strapped Connie Mack of the Philadelphia A's traded the slugger to deep-pocketed Tom Yawkey of Boston in 1936 for two no-name pitchers and $150,000 cash. "Double-X" was an easygoing, well-liked player, both by other players and fans alike. He loved his Scotch—and in quantity—and was forever picking up the tab whenever he went out with his friends. Upon arriving at a bar or restaurant, it was not uncommon for Foxx to announce, "Old Double-X is here! The drinks are on the house!"

Connie Mack had tried to cut Foxx's salary. Yawkey doubled it. Foxx, one of the greatest power hitters in major league history, responded with 41 homers and 143 RBIs in his first Red Sox season, then had 50 homers and a career-high 175 RBIs in 1938 as he captured his third MVP Award. By 1941 Foxx's drinking had caught up with him. His 19 homers, 105 RBIs, and 87 runs were all his lowest totals in 13 years. In early 1942, in declining health and production, the six-time Boston All-Star was waived. He was picked up by the Cubs later in the season, but hit only eight homers total between Boston and Chicago in 100 games. He left baseball at the age of 34, then came back two years later for just 20 at-bats for the Cubs, managing a single hit. The Cubs released him, but he made one more modestly successful comeback attempt in 1945 before retiring. Foxx bounced around between coaching and several failed businesses after retiring as a player. He was elected to the Hall of Fame in 1951 and died in 1967 after choking to death on a piece of meat while dining with his brother. *(See Athletics bio.)*

CAREER RED SOX RECORD:

Games	AB	Hits	Runs
887	3,288	1,051	721
Avg	**HR**	**RBI**	**SB**
.320	222	788	38

GARCIAPARRA, NOMAR (SS) (1996–2004)

The Red Sox chose Nomar Garciaparra, the first freshman ever to make the U.S. Olympic team as a walk-on, in the first round of the 1994 amateur draft and brought him to Boston late in 1996. By 1997 he was the team's starting shortstop. Few players, especially from the shortstop position, have had as much impact on a team at the start of their careers. Nomar (his father's name, Ramon, spelled backwards) became the first rookie in history to bat .300 with 30 homers, 90 RBIs, and 20 steals, when he performed the feat in 1997. He also led the AL in hits, multi-hit games and triples, and finished second in runs. His 98 RBIs were a record for a leadoff hitter. Garciaparra also set a rookie record with a 30-game hitting streak and won the Silver Slugger Award. He was the unanimous selection as Rookie of the Year.

Even though Garciaparra spent two weeks on the disabled list, his 1998 season was even better. He hit 35 homers with 122 RBIs and a .323 average, finishing second in the MVP voting. He became just the fifth player in history to hit at least 30 homers in his first two seasons. In 1999 Garciaparra won the AL batting title, hitting .357. He won it again in 2000, improving to .372. After missing nearly all of 2001 due to injury, he came back in 2002 and 2003 to hit .300 both years with 100+ runs and RBIs each season. In 2004 the Red Sox tried to land superstar Alex Rodriguez in a trade with Texas, but in so doing offended their five-time All-Star. Garciaparra wasn't the same after that, claiming various vague "injuries" were keeping him from playing on a regular basis. At the trading deadline in 2004, the Red Sox dealt their disgruntled shortstop, who had played in only 38 games in the first four months of the season, to the Cubs as part of a complicated four-team trade. After the trade, Garciaparra miraculously recovered, but his performance did not. He missed much of 2005 as well, leading some to speculate that his best days are behind him, his best whines in front of him.

CAREER RED SOX RECORD:

Games	AB	Hits	Runs
966	3,968	1,281	709
Avg	**HR**	**RBI**	**SB**
.323	178	690	84

GREENWELL, MIKE (OF) (1985–1996)

Mike Greenwell was drafted by the Red Sox in the third round of the June 1982 amateur draft. After very limited action in Boston in 1985 and 1986, Greenwell joined the Red Sox to stay in 1987. By 1988 he had beaten out Jim Rice for the left-field job. Greenwell patterned his swing after George Brett—more line-drive hitter than long-ball slugger. In 1988 Greenwell finished second to Jose Canseco of Oakland in the MVP race, but in 2004 he publicly asked to be given the award retroactively, considering Canseco's admitted steroid use in 1988. In 1996 Greenwell drove in all nine runs of a 9–8 Boston victory. After the season, Greenwell refused to ink another contract with the team because of his intense dislike for Boston GM Dan Duquette. He went to Japan, signing a big contract with the Hanshin Tigers, but broke his foot seven games into his Japanese career. Greenwell never played again, either in America or Japan, and was out of baseball at the age of 32.

CAREER RED SOX RECORD:

Games	AB	Hits	Runs
1,269	4,623	1,400	657
Avg	**HR**	**RBI**	**SB**
.303	130	726	80

GROVE, LEFTY (SP/RP)
(1934–1941)

See Athletics bio.

HOOPER, HARRY (O)F
(1909–1920)

Harry Hooper was a full-time surveyor for the Western Pacific Railroad and a part-time player in the outlaw California State League when he was discovered in 1908 by Boston owner John Taylor. Taylor offered Hooper $2,500 to play with the Red Sox, but he balked. When Taylor sweetened the pot with a bit more money and a promise to be one of the surveyors when Boston built their new ballpark (Fenway), Hooper accepted, although he never did get the promised surveyor's gig. Hooper never led the American League in any major offensive category, but he was invaluable to the Red Sox with his .403 on-base average in the leadoff position from 1909–1920. His speed and strong arm made him the best defensive right fielder of his era, averaging more than 20 assists a year with Boston, with a high of 30 in 1910. An excellent base runner and leadoff man, Hooper hit 10 career leadoff homers and stole 375 bases, 300 with Boston, including 11 steals of home. During his career, Hooper got the only hit in three one-hitters by opposing pitchers. He starred on four Red Sox World Series Championship teams (1912, 1915, 1916, 1918).

A strongly religious man, Hooper prayed fervently for a Red Sox win in Game 7 of the 1912 World Series. In that game, with New York ahead, 1–0, the Giants' Larry Doyle smashed a deep drive to right center in Fenway Park. Hooper, with his back to the plate and running at full speed, stuck his bare hand up and caught the ball, then jumped over the fence, still at full speed, and the Boston crowd parted like the Red Sea, allowing him to maintain control of the ball. It was likely the most incredible catch ever made in major league history, especially given the circumstances. Boston won the game and the Series in the 10th inning. In the final game of the 1915 World Series, Hooper hit two home runs as Boston defeated the Phillies, 5–4. In 1918 it was Hooper who convinced the Red Sox manager to let Babe Ruth play some outfield on days he wasn't scheduled to pitch, and the Bambino helped Boston to another pennant.

Just before the 1918 World Series, Ban Johnson and the National Commission informed the players that their share of the gate receipts would be cut that year. On the train after the third game, players from both teams met and decided to challenge the owners. Hooper and Chicago's Leslie Mann were elected to take their grievance to the owners. The owners refused to meet with them before

Game 4. When the owners again refused to meet with them before Game 5, the players refused to take the field unless the Commission agreed to meet with them. The three members of the Commission, who were enjoying excessive libations at a local bar, were forced to go to the ballpark to meet with Hooper and Mann in the umpires' room. The World Series game was delayed while the players argued their case, finally agreeing to play, but only after being promised there would be no retaliation by the Commission. A week before Christmas, all members of the winning Red Sox team received a letter informing them that due to the aborted strike during the World Series, the players would not be getting their emblems (World Series diamond stickpins, the equivalent of today's World Series rings). The players protested, but to no avail. Hooper petitioned every baseball Commissioner through Bowie Kuhn, without success. Finally, in 1993, major league baseball atoned for the 75-year-old miscarriage of justice and awarded the World Series emblems to the players' families.

After the 1918 season, Boston owner Harry Frazee began to sell off his stars in order to raise money for his theater business. Two years later, disgusted with the player sales, Hooper held out for a higher salary. He eventually signed, had a career year, and then was traded to the Chicago White Sox in March of 1921. Charlie Comiskey was desperate for a "clean," popular, big-name player because his team's reputation was being savaged daily in the press since the scandal over the 1919 World Series had broken in September 1920. Hooper had five more decent seasons with the White Sox before retiring after the 1925 season to enter the booming real estate business. He later coached baseball at Princeton and was the postmaster of Capitola, California. Hooper was elected to the Hall of Fame in 1971, three years before his death at the age of 87.

CAREER RED SOX RECORD:

Games	AB	Hits	Runs
1,647	6,270	1,707	988
Avg	**HR**	**RBI**	**SB**
.272	30	497	300

JENSEN, JACKIE (OF)
(1954–1959, 1961)

Jackie Jensen was dubbed "the Golden Boy" after becoming an All-American fullback at the University of California in 1948. He made even more headlines when he married Olympic diving medalist Zoe Ann Olson in 1949; the two were billed as "the world's most famous sweethearts." He initially signed with the Pacific Coast League's Oakland Oaks in 1949 after they paid him $75,000, outbidding several major league teams in the process. He was sold along with Billy Martin the next year to the Yankees for $100,000. Billed as Joe DiMaggio's successor, he had a dismal year in 1950, hitting only .171. After another less-than-stellar year, the Yankees traded Jensen to Washington in May 1952. After two moderately successful years in Washington, Jensen was traded to Boston, although he initially refused to report because of his fear of flying. Jensen, who once said his mother moved every time the rent became due, talked about giving up baseball so he could be home with his family. Boston GM Joe Cronin convinced Jensen to stick it out, and Jensen did—for a $1,000 bonus.

Once in Boston, Jensen became an RBI machine. He knocked in 100+ runs in five of the next six years and won the AL MVP Award in 1958. After the 1959 season, however, Jensen abruptly quit baseball, again citing his fear of flying and being away from his family. A year later, Jensen changed his mind and returned to the Red Sox, but on April 29 he left the team again and sought the services of a nightclub hypnotist to help him overcome his phobia. The hypnotist seemed to help and Jensen returned to the Red Sox, although he had a somewhat poor year at the plate. Frustrated, Jensen retired for good after the season and returned home. Shortly afterwards, the world's most famous sweethearts divorced.

CAREER RED SOX RECORD:

Games	AB	Hits	Runs
1,039	3,857	1,089	597
Avg	**HR**	**RBI**	**SB**
.282	170	733	95

LYNN, FRED (OF)
(1974–1980)

The Red Sox chose Fred Lynn in the second round of the June 1973 amateur draft. He should have gone higher, but there were questions about his attitude, so every team passed on him in the first round. Lynn had actually been drafted by the Yankees in 1970 but chose not to sign, preferring to stay in college at USC where he played center field on three College World Series winners. When he came up in 1975 with fellow rookie Jim Rice, Lynn amazed everyone. He hit .331 with 21 homers, 105 RBIs, 103 runs, 47 doubles, 7 triples, and seemingly made fantastic sprawling catches every other game. For his efforts he became the first player ever to win Rookie of the Year and MVP Awards in the same year (Ichiro repeated the feat in 2001). In a June 18, 1975 game, Lynn hit three homers, a triple, and a single with 10 RBIs, tying the AL record for total bases in a game and missing the single-game RBI record by one. Lynn made the All-Star team all six of his full seasons in Boston, and collected Gold Gloves in four.

Lynn only had one other year (1979) in which he put up numbers similar to his great rookie year. He was dogged by a variety of injuries which, collectively, cost him more than 600 games during his 17-year career. His fragile body and the burden of his great rookie year always made it seem like he wasn't reaching expectations. He longed to return to southern California to be near his home, so with one year left on his contract, the Red Sox traded him to the Angels in a five-player deal that brought Joe Rudi and Frank Tanana to Boston. Lynn played 10 more seasons in the majors with California, Baltimore, Detroit, and San Diego before retiring to the broadcast booth for a time with ESPN.

CAREER RED SOX RECORD:

Games	AB	Hits	Runs
828	3,062	944	523
Avg	**HR**	**RBI**	**SB**
.308	124	521	43

MARTINEZ, PEDRO (SP)
(1998–2004)

After two years with the Dodgers and four more with the Expos, Martinez came to the Red Sox in a trade with Montreal for Carl Pavano and Tony Armas Jr. Known early in his career as Ramon Martinez's younger brother, he has become one of the most dominating pitchers in the history of baseball. After winning the NL Cy Young Award his last season in Montreal, Martinez proceeded to win two more Cy Youngs with Boston in 1999 and 2000. He made the All-Star Game four times with the Red Sox, winning the game's MVP Award in 1999 when he started the game—in Boston that year—by striking out the first four batters of the game (a record) and five of the six he faced. Martinez led the AL in ERA, WHIP, and strikeouts per nine innings four times each. With Boston, Martinez matured. While in the National League, he had earned the reputation as a volatile headhunter. In 1994 alone he was ejected from 12 of his 23 starts for fighting and hitting batters. After attaining an incredible .760 winning percentage in seven years with Boston, Martinez left the Red Sox via free agency after the 2004 season and signed with the New York Mets. *(See Expos bio in the Washington chapter.)*

CAREER RED SOX RECORD:

W	L	W%	ERA	SV
117	37	.760	2.52	0
K	BB	SHO	IP	
1,683	309	8	1,383.7	

PARNELL, MEL (SP/RP)
(1947–1956)

From 1948 to 1953, Mel Parnell was one of the best pitchers in all of baseball. The wily left-hander, who played his entire 10-year career with Boston, was known for his wicked curveball and slider. He won 109 games in the six-year stretch, and compiled a 70–30 career record in Fenway Park, a terrific record for a left-hander. His best year was 1949, when he finished 25–7 with a 2.77 ERA, both league highs, and made the first of his two All-Star Game appearances. After going 21–8 in 1953, Parnell suffered a badly broken arm in 1954 and never regained his form, falling to a combined 12–16 over his final three years before retiring. The one bright spot in his last three years was pitching Boston's first no-hitter in 33 years when he beat the White Sox 4–0 on July 14, 1956.

CAREER RED SOX RECORD:

W	L	W%	ERA	SV
123	75	.621	3.50	10
K	BB	SHO	IP	
732	758	20	1,752.7	

PETROCELLI, RICO (SS/3B)
(1963, 1965–1976)

Rico Petrocelli was signed as an amateur free agent before the 1961 season and made it to Boston to stay in 1965. He was a power-hitting shortstop for a decade, playing on both the 1967 and 1975 World Series teams. Petrocelli was definitely a Fenway hitter, swatting two-thirds of his 210 career homers at home, and batting 40 points higher at home than on the road. Petrocelli had his career year in 1969 when he hit .297 with 40 homers and 97 RBIs, and tied a then record with just 14 errors. He also made the second of his two All-Star appearances. When the Red Sox acquired Luis Aparicio in 1971, Petrocelli was moved to third, where he played for five years. After suffering a leg injury and a beaning in 1975, Petrocelli's production declined. Inner ear problems in 1976 (possibly a result of his beaning) contributed to his decision to retire prematurely at the age of 33. Petrocelli spent several years working for The Jimmy Fund, the team's children's cancer charity. He later joined the Red Sox organization, first as a hitting instructor then later as manager of the team's Triple-A franchise in Pawtucket, where he remained until he retired in 1992 to devote more time to his family.

CAREER RED SOX RECORD:

Games	AB	Hits	Runs
1,553	5,390	1,352	653
Avg	**HR**	**RBI**	**SB**
.251	210	773	10

RAMIREZ, MANNY (OF)
(2001–2005)

When Manny Ramirez joined the Red Sox he signed a contract that currently pays him more than $22 million per season. Over the last five years with the Red Sox, Ramirez has continued to produce big offensive numbers, averaging around .330 with 40 homers and 100+ runs and RBIs per season—and he'll be just 34 when the 2006 season begins. Despite his sometimes temperamental nature, he will long be remembered fondly by Red Sox fans as one of the players most responsible for finally bringing a World Championship back to Boston. Without a doubt, Ramirez, a perennial All-Star and Silver Slugger winner, is well on his way to a Hall of Fame career. *(See Indians bio.)*

CAREER RED SOX RECORD:

Games	AB	Hits	Runs
720	2,656	836	514
Avg	**HR**	**RBI**	**SB**
.315	199	610	6

RICE, JIM (OF/DH)
(1974–1989)

Boston selected Jim Rice in the first round of the June 1971 amateur draft and brought him up late in the 1974 season. Rice was the classic strong, silent type, and his silence was often misunderstood as moodiness. During the late 1970s and early 1980s, Rice was the most feared hitter in all of baseball. In 1978 he won the AL MVP Award, hitting 40 home runs with 139 RBIs, 213 hits, and a .600 slugging average. His 406 total bases were also the most in the AL since Joe DiMaggio's 418 in 1937, and Rice became the last player in the 20th century to have 40 homers and 200 hits in the same season. Rice was incredibly strong, once even breaking a bat on a checked swing that didn't hit the ball. From 1977 to 1979, Rice hit at least 35 homers and collected at least 200 hits each season, the only man in baseball history to accomplish the feat in three consecutive seasons. On the negative side, Rice had an odd penchant for hitting into double plays. He set a major league record in 1984 by hitting into 36 twin killings, and then almost broke his own record the next year by hitting into 35 more. For his career he hit into 315, third on the all-time list. Rice, an eight-time All-Star, led the American League in homers three times and total bases four times. When he retired, ending his 16-year career (all spent with the Red Sox), the team scheduled a "Jim Rice and Bob Stanley Day," but Rice refused to attend because he felt slighted at having to share a day with someone else.

CAREER RED SOX RECORD:

Games	AB	Hits	Runs
2,089	8,225	2,452	1,249
Avg	**HR**	**RBI**	**SB**
.298	382	1,451	58

RUTH, BABE (SP/OF)
(1914–1919)

Babe Ruth emerged from the humblest of beginnings to become the greatest baseball player who ever lived. In 1914, after leaving Baltimore's St. Mary's Industrial School for Boys (where he had been since the age of seven), Ruth immediately joined the minor league Baltimore Orioles. The team's owner, Jack Dunn, had to become Ruth's legal guardian in order for him to leave the school. When Dunn walked to the pitching mound on Ruth's first day with the team, another player yelled, "Look at Dunnie and his new babe." The nickname not only stuck, but it became the most famous nickname in the game, recognized around the world. Ruth had a fine 14–6 record for the Orioles when a cash-strapped Dunn sold Ruth to the Red Sox on July 8, 1914, right after a game in which only 17 fans paid to see the Orioles play. Ruth, pitcher Ernie Shore, and catcher Ben Egan went to the Red Sox for $25,000.

Three days later, Ruth made his major league debut, pitching the Sox to a 4–3 victory over Cleveland. After posting a 2–1 record, Ruth was sent to Providence for seasoning and compiled an 8–3 record in the minors over the balance of the 1914 season before returning to Boston in 1915. From 1915 to 1917, Ruth was the best left-handed pitcher in baseball. He won 18 games in 1915, then 23 in 1916, and 24 in 1917. His ERAs over the three years were 2.44, 1.75, and 2.01. Over those three years, Ruth held opposing batters to the lowest composite average of any pitcher in the league. In 1916 he pitched nine shutouts, and in 1917 he had 35 complete games in 38 starts. In the 1916 World Series, Ruth hooked up with Sherry Smith in one of the greatest pitching duels in Series history. Ruth pitched a six-hitter and won 2–1 in 14 innings, with both pitchers going the distance. In the 1918 World Series, Ruth hurled 29⅔ innings of scoreless ball, a record that stood until Whitey Ford broke it in 1961.

It was during the 1918 season that Harry Hooper first convinced Red Sox manager Ed Barrow to move Ruth to the outfield to take advantage of his powerful bat. Barrow still used Ruth as a starting pitcher 19 times, while playing him in the outfield for 59 games and at first for 13. Even though he only played a total of 95 games, Ruth led the league in homers with 11. In 1919, with the outfield experiment having been judged a success, Ruth pitched in just 17 games while playing 111 in the outfield. He responded to the added playing time by setting a new single-season record for home runs with 29.

Ruth's time in Boston was nearing an end, however. On January 3, 1920, Red Sox owner Harry Frazee sold Babe Ruth for $125,000 cash and a $300,000 loan to the New York Yankees, a team that had never won an American League pennant in its history. *(See Yankees bio.)*

CAREER RED SOX PITCHING RECORD:

W	L	W%	ERA	SV
89	46	.659	2.19	4
K	**BB**	**SHO**	**IP**	
483	425	17	1,190.3	

CAREER RED SOX HITTING RECORD:

Games	AB	Hits	Runs
391	1,110	342	202
Avg	**HR**	**RBI**	**SB**
.308	49	230	13

SPEAKER, TRIS (OF)
(1907–1915)

Tris Speaker worked as a Texas cowboy and telegraph linesman before playing professional baseball for Cleburne of the North Texas League. The next year, now with Houston, Speaker hit .314 and raised the interest of Pittsburgh owner Barney Dreyfuss, who passed on the young outfielder when he discovered Speaker smoked cigarettes. Boston showed some interest and brought him up for seven games in 1907, but Speaker hit only .158 and was released. In 1908 Speaker paid his own way to Marlin, Texas, where the Giants were working out, but John McGraw wouldn't even give Speaker a tryout. Speaker then traveled to Little Rock, Arkansas, where the Red Sox were working out. Boston received him coolly, but did allow him to work out with them. When they broke camp and headed north, the Red Sox gave Speaker to the Little Rock ball club as payment for the use of their facilities with the understanding that they could purchase him later for a nominal price if he made good. After Speaker hit .350 to lead the Southern Association, Boston exercised its $500 option and brought him up to the majors at the end of the 1908 season, when he hit .224 in 31 games.

By 1909, Speaker had won the regular center-field job in Boston and hit over .300 for the next seven seasons. He was a magnificent line-drive hitter who used his great speed to turn singles into doubles and doubles into triples. He still holds the career record for doubles with 792, and is sixth on the all-time list in triples with 222. In the field, Speaker became famous for playing an extremely shallow center field, not far behind second most of the time. Speaker credits Cy Young with helping him become a great defensive outfielder. Young would spend hours hitting fungoes to Speaker every day. Eventually Speaker learned that the ball would go either to his left or right, depending on how the batter swung at the ball. This allowed Speaker to play a very shallow center field since he always got a jump on the ball just before the batter actually hit it. Because he played so shallow, Speaker was able to accumulate 448 assists in his career, still the major league record. When the Red Sox won the pennant in 1912, Speaker won the Chalmers Award and a new Chalmers automobile for being voted the league's MVP.

After the competing Federal League folded following the 1915 season, Boston owner Joe Lannin tried to cut Speaker's salary in half from \$18,000 to \$9,000, but Speaker refused to sign and held out until April, when he was traded to Cleveland for two players and \$50,000 cash. An angry Speaker responded by winning the American League batting title with a .386 average, ending Ty Cobb's long stranglehold as perennial batting champion. *(See Indians bio.)*

CAREER RED SOX RECORD:

Games	AB	Hits	Runs
1,065	3,935	1,327	704
Avg	**HR**	**RBI**	**SB**
.337	39	542	267

STANLEY, BOB (RP/SP)
(1977–1989)

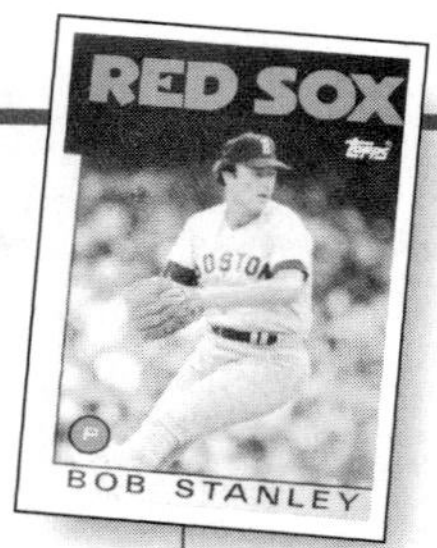

The Red Sox drafted Bob Stanley in the first round of the1974 amateur draft (secondary phase). He had been drafted by the Dodgers the summer before, but refused to sign. Stanley was a durable, reliable team player during his 13-year career, which was all spent with Boston. He would gladly enter a game as a starter, long reliever, short reliever, or closer, and was used extensively in all four capacities by the Red Sox as his 115–97 win-loss record and 132 saves suggests. Stanley's .882 winning percentage in 1978 (15–2) was the 20th century's eighth highest.

Stanley will forever be identified with the 1986 World Series meltdown. The Sox were within one pitch of winning their first World Series since 1918 when Stanley's 2–2 pitch to Mookie Wilson got past catcher Rich Gedman to let in the tying run. Stanley was charged with a wild pitch, but many felt Gedman should have been charged with a passed ball. On the very next pitch, Wilson slapped a ground ball that went between first baseman Bill Buckner's legs, and Ray Knight scored the winning run to knot the Series at three games apiece. The Mets then won Game 7 to extend the Red Sox's World Series drought to 68 years. Stanley retired with 637 appearances, making him far and away the all-time Red Sox leader.

CAREER RED SOX RECORD:

W	L	W%	ERA	SV
115	97	.542	3.64	132
K	**BB**	**SHO**	**IP**	
693	471	7	1,707.0	

TIANT, LUIS (SP/RP)
(1971–1978)

After spending seven years with Cleveland and Minnesota, Luis Tiant joined Boston as a free agent in 1971. His once-promising career, which included a 21–9 record in 1969, had gone into decline because of injury, but this didn't stop the Red Sox from taking a chance on the Cuban pitcher. After a 1–7 record with Boston in 1971, Tiant rebounded in a big way in 1972, finishing 15–6 with a dazzling 1.91 ERA and winning the Comeback Player of the Year Award. Using his signature herky-jerky pirouette pitching motion (in which he completely turned his back to the plate), "El Tiante" won 20 games in 1973 and 22 in 1974. After going 18–14 in the 1975 regular season, Tiant shone as one of the Red Sox stars in the playoffs and World Series. In 1976 Tiant had his last great year, winning 21 games for the Sox. Following a decent 13–8 1978 season, Tiant left Boston via free agency and played four unremarkable years with the Yankees, Pirates, and Angels before retiring. After retirement, Tiant worked for a time with Northeastern University as part of Project Teamwork, a Reebok-sponsored program in which athletes urge students to stay in school.

CAREER RED SOX RECORD:

W	L	W%	ERA	SV
122	81	.601	3.36	3
K	**BB**	**SHO**	**IP**	
1,075	501	26	1,774.7	

VAUGHN, MO (1B/DH)
(1991–1998)

Big Mo Vaughn, the cousin of major leaguer Greg Vaughn, was drafted in the first round of the June 1989 amateur draft by Boston and made it to the big leagues after just two years in the minors. Vaughn was the brash, confident author of many prodigious home runs that flew long and high into the Fenway sky. Extremely popular with the Boston fans and much involved in community events, he not only started the Mo Vaughn Youth Development Program in Dorchester, Massachusetts, but also was involved in its daily activities. Vaughn once promised and delivered a home run for Jason Leader, an 11-year-old stricken with leukemia in 1993. He remained close with Leader for the last year of his life, was one of the boy's pallbearers, and delivered a touching eulogy at his funeral.

Vaughn topped 35 homers and 100 RBIs four times with Boston, but after a long and bitter contract dispute with Boston GM Dan Duquette, left the Red Sox via free agency for the Angels following the 1998 season. After spending two years in California, Vaughn missed the entire 2001 season with a ruptured tendon in his left arm. He came back in 2002 with the Mets, but in 2003 a severely arthritic knee forced him out of action again on May 3. Vaughn subsequently announced his retirement from the game, saying, "I have an injury no doctor can fix."

CAREER RED SOX RECORD:

Games	AB	Hits	Runs
1,046	3,828	1,165	628
Avg	**HR**	**RBI**	**SB**
.304	230	752	28

WILLIAMS, TED (OF)
(1939–1942, 1946–1960)

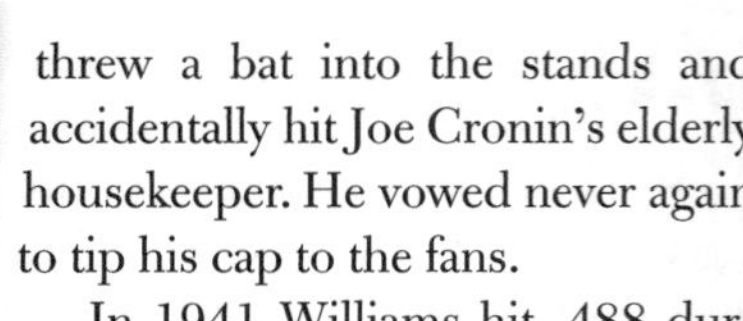

In his autobiography, *My Turn At Bat,* Ted Williams wrote that he had one goal in life: "I want people to say, 'There goes Ted Williams, the greatest hitter who ever lived.'" By the time his career was over, if he wasn't the best hitter who ever lived, he sure was close.

Williams would have become a Yankee in 1936 while still in high school, but his mother, May, refused to sign the contract. She later allowed him to play for the San Diego Padres minor league team as a 17-year-old for $150 a month—money that came in handy for the poor single mother who worked at the Salvation Army. When Williams hit .349 for the Padres in 1937, Boston GM Eddie Collins saw him play late in the season and purchased him from San Diego for $25,000.

Williams was promoted to Minneapolis of the American Association in 1938 where—as a harbinger of things to come—he won the Triple Crown, hitting .366 with 43 homers and 142 RBIs. With two big minor league seasons under his belt, Williams made it to Boston in 1939, where he immediately flaunted his talent, hitting .327 with 31 homers and 145 RBIs. The Boston fans and press fell in love with him, dubbing him "the Splendid Splinter," and he always tipped his cap after hitting a home run or performing some other crowd-pleasing feat. But when Boston finished second four times in five years, the fans and press began to snipe that Williams wasn't able to get the Red Sox over the hump and catch the Yankees. When a disgruntled Williams responded that he'd be happier as a fireman, the war was on. Negative comments and actions escalated between Williams and the press and fans; at various times over the rest of his career, Williams spit at reporters, directed obscene gestures towards the fans, and even threw a bat into the stands and accidentally hit Joe Cronin's elderly housekeeper. He vowed never again to tip his cap to the fans.

In 1941 Williams hit .488 during a 23-game stretch to raise his average to .430 by mid-June. The race for .400 was on, although most fans were more absorbed in Joe DiMaggio's 56-game hitting streak. On the last day of the season, Williams' average stood at .39955, technically giving him a .400 average. Manager Joe Cronin gave Williams the opportunity to sit out the season-ending doubleheader against Philadelphia, but Williams refused. He went 6-for-8 that day, finishing the season at .406, the last time any hitter reached the .400 level for the season. He finished second in the MVP voting to DiMaggio. In 1942 Williams won his first Triple Crown, hitting .356 with 36 homers and 137 RBIs, but finished second in the MVP voting again, this time to New York's Joe Gordon.

With World War II raging in 1943, Williams sought a military deferment because he was his mother's sole source of support. Fans and reporters blasted him for being unpatriotic, and the attention that was drawn to his mother's personal situation further hardened his acrimonious relationship with Boston. Williams gave in to public pressure and enlisted in the Navy Air Corps in May 1943, spending the next 3½ years as a pilot instructor. When he returned in 1946, Williams led the Red Sox into the World Series against the Cardinals, but was a nonfactor due to a fluke injury. While the Cardinals were busy playing the Dodgers in a playoff for the National League title, the Red Sox decided to play a team of American League All Stars in an exhibition game to keep sharp for the upcoming World Series. In that game, a Mickey Haefner pitch struck Williams on the elbow and he played the entire Series in severe pain, hitting just .200 with one RBI in seven games.

Williams won his second Triple Crown in 1947, but once again the press punished him by making Joe DiMaggio the American League MVP by a single vote. One writer left Williams off his ballot entirely. In 1950 Williams lost half a season when he fractured his elbow in the All-Star Game, although he did hit 28 homers with 97 RBIs in just 89 games.

On April 30, 1952, Boston held a Ted Williams Day as a send-off to their star, who was leaving for the Korean War with the Marines. Many felt it would be the last game of the 34-year-old's career, and he treated the fans by homering off Dizzy Trout. Williams flew 39 missions during his Korean tour of duty, once crash landing after taking heavy flak and escaping from his burning fighter jet. Shortly thereafter he contracted pneumonia and was sent back to America and discharged.

When he returned to baseball in August 1953, Williams hit .407 with 13 homers for the remainder of the season. Williams retired in 1955, only to return several months into the season, hitting .356 with 28 homers in just 98 games. In 1957 at the age of 39, Williams again flirted with .400. He finished at .388 and won his fifth batting title. Williams won his sixth, and last, batting title the next year when, at the age of 40, he hit .328. In 1959 Williams hit under .300 for the only time in his career, finishing at a dismal .254. He closed out his career in 1960 hitting .316, including his 521st home run in the last at-bat of the season. As had been the case for the last 20 years, Williams refused to tip his cap or acknowledge the fans.

Williams retired with six batting titles, two MVP Awards (though he should have had at least four), and two Triple Crowns (narrowly missing a third). He led the league in homers and RBIs five times each, and was walked more times than anyone in history except Babe Ruth. By missing the equivalent of six years of playing time due to military service, injury, and his short retirement, Williams lost—conservatively—200 home runs, 1,000 hits, 700 runs, 700 RBIs, and 250 doubles, not to mention several more possible batting titles.

After retiring, Williams spent most of his time fishing (he was named to the Fishing Hall of Fame), but he did help the Red Sox in spring training as a hitting instructor. In 1966 Williams was elected to the Hall of Fame, and in 1969 he took over as manager of the Washington Senators, leading the team to an 86–76 record, a 21-game improvement over 1968. For this he was named Manager of the Year. When the team moved to Texas in 1972, Williams managed one more year and then retired. In the 1990s he came out with his own line of baseball cards and opened his own Ted Williams Museum and Hitters Hall of Fame in Florida. In 1998 he undertook a campaign to get Joe Jackson enshrined in the Baseball Hall of Fame. One final Ted Williams Day was held in Fenway Park in 1991, and to the delight of the fans and press, Williams tipped his cap.

After Williams died in July 2002, his three children became embroiled in a "custody" dispute of sorts. Son John Henry Williams claimed his father wanted to be cryonically preserved, and had his body sent to a facility in Arizona that performed such services. Ted Williams' head was removed and it and his body were placed in separate stainless steel canisters. Williams' daughter by his first marriage, claiming to know her father's final wishes, sought to have her father's body released from the cryonics lab and have it cremated and his ashes spread over his favorite fishing spots in Florida. Meanwhile, the cryonics lab filed a lawsuit against John Henry Williams for the $111,000 portion of their bill that remained unpaid. When John Henry died of leukemia in March 2004, his sister renewed her efforts to have their father thawed out and released from the cryogenics facility, which was still insisting on the payment due. She eventually ended her efforts, agreeing to let her father remain frozen.

CAREER RED SOX RECORD:

Games	AB	Hits	Runs
2,292	7,706	2,654	1,798
Avg	**HR**	**RBI**	**SB**
.344	521	1,839	24

WOOD, JOE (SP/RP)
(1908–1915)

"Smoky" Joe Wood got his nickname from his blazing fastball. In the late 1890s and early 1900s, Wood's father was an attorney who panned for gold in Alaska, and he took his family with him in a covered wagon. Wherever the family moved, Joe would play baseball, his glove always on his hand or at the ready. His first professional baseball job was with the Bloomer Girls, a team of mixed men and women players. After advancing to the American Association's Kansas City Blues, Wood was purchased by Boston in 1908. Wood saw limited action in Boston until 1911, when he won 23 games, including a no-hitter against St. Louis. In 1912 he fashioned one of the best seasons in history by a pitcher. He went 34–5 with a 1.91 ERA and 10 shutouts, including 16 straight wins to tie the record set earlier in the same season by Walter Johnson. On September 5, with 13 straight wins, Wood faced Johnson in a game at Fenway Park. Interest in the head-to-head match was so strong that fans poured into Fenway, even taking over the players' dugouts, forcing the players to move themselves and their equipment just outside the first- and third-base foul lines. Wood defeated Johnson, 1–0, in a game that Harry Hooper described as the most exciting game he ever played in or saw.

When the Red Sox went to the World Series that year, emotions ran high. Wood had to draw the blinds in his cab in New York to keep from being pelted by rocks from Giants fans. When the Series ended, Wood had won three games to lead Boston to victory. That was the last good season Wood would enjoy. In a 1913 game against Detroit, Wood reached down to field a groundball and slipped on the wet grass, breaking his pitching thumb. It was in a cast for weeks, and after it healed it was never the same again. He pitched only on occasion the next three years, and never without pain. He finally quit baseball in 1915, but returned in 1917 and tried his hand as an outfielder for Cleveland. He had modest success for six years—two years as a regular, four years as a part-timer. In 1923 he took the position of baseball coach for Yale University and remained there for 20 years.

CAREER RED SOX RECORD:

W	L	W%	ERA	SV
116	56	.674	1.99	9
K	**BB**	**SHO**	**IP**	
986	412	28	1,418.0	

YASTRZEMSKI, CARL (OF/1B/DH) (1961–1983)

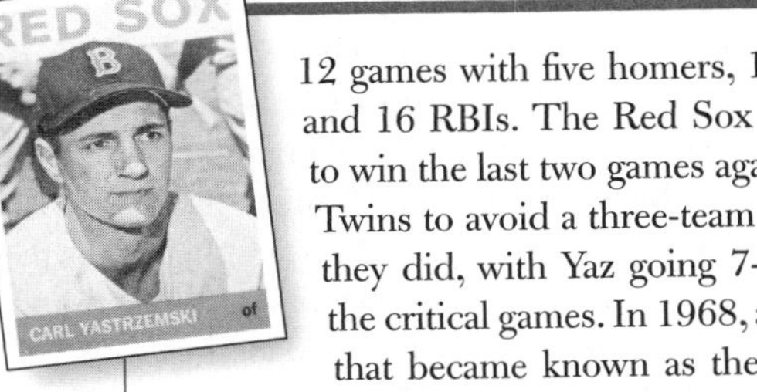

Carl Yastrzemski was signed out of Notre Dame in November 1958 as an amateur free agent. After two years in the minors, "Yaz" had the unenviable task of following Ted Williams as Boston's left fielder. While he struggled a bit, as most rookies do, his numbers weren't all that bad (.266 with 11 homers and 80 RBIs). Yaz benefited greatly from a three-day hitting lesson with Williams, whom the Red Sox located fishing in New Brunswick and flew in for the emergency tutoring session. He improved steadily over the next few years and in 1967 had a career year, hitting .326 with 44 homers and 121 RBIs and winning the American League's Triple Crown. He almost single-handedly drove the Red Sox, whose campaign that year became known as the Impossible Dream, to the 1967 pennant. With four teams in the race until the last week, and three until the last day, Yaz hit .523 over the last 12 games with five homers, 14 runs, and 16 RBIs. The Red Sox needed to win the last two games against the Twins to avoid a three-team tie, and they did, with Yaz going 7-for-8 in the critical games. In 1968, a season that became known as the year of the pitcher, Yaz won the batting crown with the lowest average ever by a champion, .301. Over his 23-year Red Sox career, Yaz won three batting titles, played in 18 All-Star Games, won an MVP Award, joined the super-exclusive 3,000-hit/400-homer club, and was considered to be the best defensive left fielder of his era. Yaz was voted into the Hall of Fame in 1989.

CAREER RED SOX RECORD:

Games	AB	Hits	Runs
3,308	11,988	3,419	1,816
Avg	**HR**	**RBI**	**SB**
.285	452	1,844	168

YOUNG, CY (SP) (1901–1908)

Cy Young, the man whose name is attached to baseball's annual award for pitching excellence, had already won 286 games by the time he arrived in Boston for his 12th major league season. His real name was Denton True Young, but he went by the nickname "Cy" from the time he first got involved in baseball. Some say the name came from his pitches being as fast as a cyclone. Another variation has it that he was observed pitching baseballs against a wooden fence and breaking the fence apart, leaving it as if it had been busted up by a cyclone. Either way, the name stuck.

Young was pitching for Canton in the Tri-State League when Cleveland purchased him for $300 and a suit of clothes for Canton's manager. According to *The Sporting Life* magazine, the first time Young pitched against Cap Anson's powerful Chicago team, Anson—who had heard of the phenom's reputation—and his players teased Young unmercifully about both his physical appearance and his odd clothing. Even the fans laughed loudly at the rookie. After Young had soundly beaten the Chicago nine, the crowd gave him a standing ovation and Anson tried—unsuccessfully—to purchase him on the spot for $1,000. Now it was the Cleveland manager's turn to laugh at Anson.

Young spent nine seasons with the Cleveland Spiders before being traded in unique fashion to the St. Louis Browns (now the Cardinals) in 1899. Brothers Frank and Matthew Robison owned the Spiders but, unhappy with the financial losses of their small-market team, bought the big-market St. Louis team as well. They then traded all their good players (Young included) to their St. Louis team for all of St. Louis's lesser players. After two years in St. Louis, Young got fed up with the Midwest heat and jumped to the new American League's Boston franchise in 1901, when AL president Ban Johnson offered him $3,000—$600 more than his NL contract, which was capped at $2,400 under National League rules.

Young went a combined 93–30 for Boston in his first three years, including two wins in the 1903 World Series against Pittsburgh. In that Series, Young spent time working the ticket booths when he wasn't pitching. Even though baseball was a rough-and-tumble profession in the early days, Cy Young had a reputation as a true gentleman and he was often praised for his sportsmanship. In 1904 Young led Boston to another pennant, but the Giants refused to meet them in the World Series. During that season, Young had a streak of 44 consecutive scoreless innings pitched, including a perfect game on May 5 against the Philadelphia A's. In 1905 he had the first losing season of his career at 18–19, but his ERA was the third lowest of his long career at 1.82. In 1907 the Boston team was officially being called the Red Sox for the first time when their manager, Chick Stahl, committed suicide in spring training. Young was asked to take over the team, but agreed to do so only until a replacement could be found. On June 8, 1908, at the age of 41, Young pitched his third no-hitter when he beat New York, 8–0. On August 13 of that year, the *Boston Post* sponsored a Cy Young Day. More than 20,000 fans jammed the Huntington Avenue Grounds and an estimated 10,000 were turned away. He received various gifts as well as $6,000 cash. Young was sold that offseason and ended his playing days with the Indians and Braves. When opposing teams repeatedly kept bunting against him to get on base, Young retired, complaining that he was too fat to field bunts.

Young retired with 511 career wins, far more than anyone else in history. He was elected to the Hall of Fame in 1937. After losing a fortune in the stock market, Young was forced to board with neighbors. He died in 1955 and the following year baseball named its annual award for best pitcher in his honor. In 1993 Northeastern University erected a statue of him approximately where the pitcher's mound was at the Huntington Avenue Grounds.

CAREER RED SOX RECORD:

W	L	W%	ERA	SV
192	112	.632	2.00	9

K	BB	SHO	IP
1,341	299	38	2,728.3

Chicago Cubs

Since 1876

1928 Team Ball

1876/1880/1885/1906 The top four single-season winning percentages in major league history all belong to the Cubs: .788 (52–14) in 1876; .798 (67–17) in 1880; .777 (87–25) in 1885; and .763 (116–36) in 1906.... **1935** The Cubs win 21-straight games, setting the major league record for a pure winning streak. (The 1916 New York Giants won 26 games in a row, but their streak was interrupted by a 1–1 tie game with Pittsburgh after their twelfth win.)... **1966** The Cubs finish last, setting a major league record for consecutive second-division finishes with 20.... **1969/1977/2001** These are the only three years since World War II in which the Cubs have the best record in the National League at the All-Star break. They don't even make the playoffs in any of those seasons.

FRANCHISE HISTORY

The Chicago Cubs began play in 1876 as one of the National League's charter franchises, though they were first known as the White Stockings. Owner William Hulbert's team had been playing in the dysfunctional National Association in 1875, but the chaos surrounding player defections, incompletely played schedules, and the like made Hulbert think there was a better way—namely, a new league with stricter guidelines and more financially stable owners. During the course of the 1875 season, Hulbert succeeded in getting star pitcher Al Spalding to jump from the powerhouse Boston Red Stockings to his Chicago team. And Spalding, whose pitching record that year was 55–5, did not come alone. He brought three other superstars with him: catcher Deacon White, first baseman Cal McVey, and second baseman Ross Barnes, all of whom were hitting .355 or better. Collectively, they were known at the time as the "Big Four." Because of Hulbert's participation in the defection of the Big Four to Chicago, the White Stockings were facing expulsion from the National Association. Hulbert essentially preempted his fate by spearheading the creation of the National League in time for the 1876 season. When he succeeded in getting some of the National Association's stronger teams to join his new league, the greatly weakened National Association folded. Hulbert's team won the first-ever National League pennant in 1876 and then won three in a row from 1880 to 1882, although Hulbert himself didn't live to see the final pennant; he died unexpectedly just as the 1882 season was beginning.

Not only did Ross Barnes win the National League's first batting title in 1876 with a .429 average, he set a new record for fielding by a second baseman at .910, a terrific number for a barehanded fielder.

After Hulbert's death, minority owner Al Spalding became majority owner and took control of the club along with new minority owner John Walsh, a major Chicago banker. From 1871 to 1876, Spalding compiled an impressive 252–65 record as a pitcher with Boston of the National Association and Chicago of the National League. He won one more game in

The pennant-winning 1906 Cubs.

1877 before retiring as a player at the age of 26 to devote himself full time to his rapidly growing sporting goods business. Spalding's business became so demanding that in 1891 he stepped down from active control of the team and turned it over to James Hart, a former minor league manager, granting him a minority share in the team as well. Hart ran the team's day-to-day operations for a decade, gradually increasing his ownership share until he acquired controlling interest around 1901. During Hart's tenure, Cap Anson, a huge favorite of Chicago fans, left the team in 1897 after his 10-year managing contract expired. Apparently, Anson was upset, claiming that Spalding had reneged on a promise to grant him a controlling interest in the team when Spalding stepped down. However, some sources report that Hart, still a minority owner in 1897, orchestrated Anson's departure because he viewed Anson as a threat to gain control of the team. In any event, Anson and Hart had been engaged in a decade-long feud ever since Anson had refused to chip in for an expensive gift for Hart as a token of appreciation for Hart's work in organizing and coordinating the team's world tour in 1888. In 1905 Hart sold his majority share of the Cubs for $105,000 to Charles Murphy.

Murphy, a former newspaperman in Cincinnati, was the press agent for the New York Giants when he purchased the Cubs from Hart. Murphy, who had little money of his own, was backed by Charles P. Taft, the wealthy half-brother of U.S. President William Howard Taft. Player-manager Frank Chance also purchased a 10 percent share in the team with $10,000 that Murphy had loaned him. Almost from the start, Murphy rubbed the other owners the wrong way. He was abrasive, argumentative, and in general an embarrassment to the league. The team performed well for him, though, winning four pennants and two World Series during his ownership. After the 1912 season, Murphy began to sell off his star players, including Mordecai Brown, Joe Tinker, and Johnny Evers. When the Federal League began operation in 1914, there was spirited bidding for players among the three rival major leagues. Murphy saw this as an opportunity to make some money, so he sold off more players while they were bringing high prices. Because Murphy's actions were detrimental to the league, the other league owners convinced moneyman Taft to buy out Murphy and rid the league of his problematic behavior. Taft gave Murphy just over $500,000 for his controlling interest and Murphy was gone. Once Murphy was out of the picture, Taft turned over the day-to-day operations of the team to Murphy's assistant, William Thompson, until a suitable buyer could be found.

That suitable buyer turned out to be an investment group headed by Charles Weegham, owner of the former Chicago Whales of the Federal League, which folded with that League's demise after the 1915 season. After two years of warring, the three major leagues came to a settlement, allowing Weegham to buy the Cubs and transfer his best players from the Whales to the Cubs. An additional bonus for the National League was that the Cubs got to move into the Whales' former ballpark, an impressive new structure built just two years earlier. Originally called Weegham Park after the team's owner, the stadium was later christened Cubs Park and eventually Wrigley Field, after chewing gum magnate William Wrigley, at the time one of the minority investors. Almost from the outset, Weegham got into financial difficulty and borrowed

Hall-of-Famer Kiki Cuyler

money from Wrigley—using his Cubs stock as collateral—in a failed effort to right his sinking business ship. Even winning the pennant in 1918 failed to rescue Weegham. By 1918 Wrigley had acquired controlling interest in the Cubs and Weegham was forced out.

William Wrigley's father had been a soap manufacturer, and William had worked for him as a soap salesman starting in the 1870s. William would give away chicle (now called gum) as a bonus with a soap purchase, but in 1891 he started his own gum-manufacturing company, eventually becoming a multimillionaire. (A year after he purchased the Cubs, Wrigley bought Catalina Island off the coast of California for $3 million.) One of Wrigley's first actions as new team owner was to hire Bill Veeck Sr. as the team's GM. In 1926 Wrigley's son Phil bought stock in the club and was named to the team's board of directors in 1929, the year the Cubs won their first pennant while under Wrigley's control. When William died in 1932, the year of the Cubs' second pennant for Wrigley, his son Phil inherited his shares and took control of the team in 1934, maintaining it until he died 43 years later in 1977 at the age of 82. During Phil's tenure, the Cubs won three more pennants (1935, 1938, 1945), but none during his last 32 years. Wrigley's heirs held the team for four years until they sold it in 1981 to the Tribune Company, publisher of the *Chicago Tribune* newspaper, and the team's current owner. The Tribune Company was responsible for installing lights for night baseball at Wrigley Field in 1988, making the Cubs the last team by far to do so, 50 years after Cincinnati inaugurated night ball.

The Chicago Cubs have had, essentially, only two owners—the Wrigley family and Tribune—over the last 88 years. Besides stability, the team has had sufficient funds with which to operate. And no one can doubt the loyalty of the team's fan base, drawn primarily from the country's third-largest city. Over the last 23 years, the Cubs have been in the upper half in attendance in the National League 21 times, despite playing in one of the smallest ballparks in the league. Part of the appeal for Cubs fans is the complete Wrigley Field experience, from the unique ivy-covered outfield walls, to the rooftop observers across Waveland Avenue, to the charming rendition of "Take Me Out to the Ball Game" led by the late and hugely-popular, Harry Caray.

Twenty-two-year-old Ernie Banks after breaking the major league record with five grand slams in a season, September 19, 1955.

But this ballpark popularity rarely has been accompanied by success on the field. Since divisional play began in 1969, the Cubs have won their division only three times. The futility stretches much further back: Before 1969, the Cubs had last won the pennant in 1945, and last won a World Series title in 1908. From 1909 through 1945, the Cubs won seven pennants, a very good record indeed, but lost all seven World Series in which they appeared (a very bad record, indeed). The Cubs have made a cult out of failure, to which the sellouts at Wrigley attest. In the team's efforts to escape their habitual destiny, between 1961 and 1965 owner Phil Wrigley decided that he could maximize his team's brain trust by instituting a "College of Coaches," a rotating series of eight coaches who would act as manager for a few weeks at a time. The ignoble experiment failed—naturally. Under the arrangement the Cubs finished seventh twice, eighth twice, and ninth once. The College of Coaches was scrapped after five years.

Some superstitious Cubs fans attribute the long World Series drought to "Da Curse of the Goat." According to legend, a tavern owner who was a rabid Cubs fan brought his pet goat (for which he had even purchased a ticket) to Game 4 of the 1945 World Series against Detroit. The stadium's ushers denied entry to the man and his goat. As the angry saloon owner and his companion left, he shouted that a World Series would never again be played in Wrigley Field. The Cubs lost the game that day to the Tigers, and four days later they lost the Series, dropping three of the four games held in Chicago. The utter frustration over losing that World Series was so all-consuming that an unprecedented hysteria and insanity overcame the entire city of Chicago, which of course blamed it all on "Da Curse of the Goat."

Since 1945 the Cubs have not appeared in the World Series, though they've come tantalizingly close several times. In 1969 they blew a big lead late in the season as the "Miracle Mets" overtook them for the division title and eventually won the pennant. In 1984 the Cubs won their division and took a two-games-to-none lead over the Padres in the best-of-five NLCS, only to lose three straight games in San Diego after taking a lead in every game to see their World Series dreams dashed again. In the 2003 NLCS, the Cubs held a 3-games-to-2 lead over the Marlins and a 3–0 lead in the eighth inning of Game 6 when a Cubs fan reached out and deflected a foul ball that could have been caught for an out and was ultimately (and unfairly) blamed for the Cubs surrendering eight runs immediately afterward in a game the Cubs lost. Chicago then lost the next game and was bounced from the playoffs, so close to the World Series they could taste it. The foul ball deflected by the fan was purchased at auction for nearly $114,000 and then blown up by a Hollywood special effects expert, all in an effort to destroy the curse.

Ironically, in the early days of the National League, Chicago was a dominating team. They shut out their opponents so often that the 19th-century term for being held scoreless was to be "Chicagoed." When listing the stats from the previous year, the annual guides had a category called "Chicagoed Games." Now, when it comes to World Series championships, it's Cubs' fans who have been Chicagoed for, at last count, 97 years.

TEAM NAME HISTORY

Official Names

White Stockings (1876–1889)
Colts (1890–1897)
Orphans (1898–1901)
Cubs (1902–current)

Unofficial Names/Nicknames

Babes, Rainmakers, Zephyrs, Panamas, Recruits, Rough Riders, Cowboys, Broncos, Cubbies

STADIUM HISTORY

23rd Street Grounds	1876–1877
Lakefront Park	1878–1884
Congress Street Park	1885–1891
(Also called West Side Park. Chicago played only half its games in this park in 1891 while playing the other half in Brotherhood Park.)	
Brotherhood Park	1891–1893
West Side Grounds	1893–1915
Cubs Park	1916–1926
(Federal League's Weegham Park renamed)	
Wrigley Field	1927–current
(Cubs Park renamed)	

YEARLY RECORD, FINISH, & ATTENDANCE FIGURES

Year	League	Record	DIV/LG Finish	Attendance	Avg/Gm
2005	NL Cent	79–83	4	3,099,992	38,272
2004	NL Cent	89–73	3	3,170,154	38,660
2003	NL Cent	88–74	1	2,962,630	36,576
2002	NL Cent	67–95	5	2,693,096	33,248
2001	NL Cent	88–74	3	2,779,465	34,314
2000	NL Cent	65–97	6	2,789,511	34,438
1999	NL Cent	67–95	6	2,813,854	34,739
1998	NL Cent	90–73	2	2,623,194	31,990
1997	NL Cent	68–94	5	2,190,308	27,041
1996	NL Cent	76–86	4	2,219,110	27,396
1995	NL Cent	73–71	3	1,918,265	26,643
1994	NL Cent	49–64	5	1,845,208	31,275
1993	NL East	84–78	4	2,653,763	32,363
1992	NL East	78–84	4	2,126,720	26,256
1991	NL East	77–83	4	2,314,250	27,883
1990	NL East	77–85	5	2,243,791	27,701
1989	NL East	93–69	1	2,491,942	30,765
1988	NL East	77–85	4	2,089,034	25,476
1987	NL East	76–85	6	2,035,130	25,439
1986	NL East	70–90	5	1,859,102	23,239
1985	NL East	77–84	4	2,161,534	26,686
1984	NL East	96–65	1	2,107,655	26,346
1983	NL East	71–91	5	1,479,717	18,268
1982	NL East	73–89	5	1,249,278	15,423
1981	NL East	38–65	6/5	565,637	9,752
1980	NL East	64–98	6	1,206,776	14,898
1979	NL East	80–82	5	1,648,587	20,353
1978	NL East	79–83	3	1,525,311	18,601
1977	NL East	81–81	4	1,439,834	17,776
1976	NL East	75–87	4	1,026,217	12,669
1975	NL East	75–87	6	1,034,819	12,776
1974	NL East	66–96	6	1,015,378	12,536
1973	NL East	77–84	5	1,351,705	16,896
1972	NL East	85–70	2	1,299,163	16,872
1971	NL East	83–79	4	1,653,007	20,407
1970	NL East	84–78	2	1,642,705	20,534
1969	NL East	92–70	2	1,674,993	20,427
1968	NL	84–78	3	1,043,409	12,724
1967	NL	87–74	3	977,226	11,634
1966	NL	59–103	10	635,891	7,851
1965	NL	72–90	8	641,361	7,727
1964	NL	76–86	8	751,647	9,280
1963	NL	82–80	7	979,551	12,093
1962	NL	59–103	9	609,802	7,528
1961	NL	64–90	7	673,057	8,629
1960	NL	60–94	7	809,770	10,250
1959	NL	74–80	6	858,255	11,146
1958	NL	72–82	6	979,904	12,726
1957	NL	62–92	8	670,629	8,598
1956	NL	60–94	8	720,118	9,001
1955	NL	72–81	6	875,800	11,374

YEARLY RECORD, FINISH, & ATTENDANCE FIGURES (CONT.)

Year	League	Record	DIV/LG Finish	Attendance	Avg/Gm
1954	NL	64–90	7	748,183	9,717
1953	NL	65–89	7	763,658	9,918
1952	NL	77–77	5	1,024,826	13,309
1951	NL	62–92	8	894,415	11,616
1950	NL	64–89	7	1,165,944	14,948
1949	NL	61–93	8	1,143,139	14,846
1948	NL	64–90	8	1,237,792	15,869
1947	NL	69–85	6	1,364,039	17,266
1946	NL	82–71	3	1,342,970	17,441
1945	NL	98–56	1	1,036,386	13,637
1944	NL	75–79	4	640,110	8,207
1943	NL	74–79	5	508,247	6,777
1942	NL	68–86	6	590,972	7,577
1941	NL	70–84	6	545,159	7,080
1940	NL	75–79	5	534,878	6,946
1939	NL	84–70	4	726,663	9,083
1938	NL	89–63	1	951,640	12,359
1937	NL	93–61	2	895,020	11,475
1936	NL	87–67	2	699,370	9,083
1935	NL	100–54	1	692,604	8,995
1934	NL	86–65	3	707,525	9,189
1933	NL	86–68	3	594,112	7,520
1932	NL	90–64	1	974,688	12,658
1931	NL	84–70	3	1,086,422	14,109
1930	NL	90–64	2	1,463,624	18,527
1929	NL	98–54	1	1,485,166	19,041
1928	NL	91–63	3	1,143,740	14,854
1927	NL	85–68	4	1,159,168	14,861
1926	NL	82–72	4	885,063	11,347
1925	NL	68–86	8	622,610	8,086
1924	NL	81–72	5	716,922	9,191
1923	NL	83–71	4	703,705	9,139
1922	NL	80–74	5	542,283	7,135
1921	NL	64–89	7	410,107	5,396
1920	NL	75–79	6	480,783	6,244
1919	NL	75–65	3	424,430	5,978
1918	NL	84–45	1	337,256	4,558
1917	NL	74–80	5	360,218	4,678
1916	NL	67–86	5	453,685	5,743
1915	NL	73–80	4	217,058	2,819
1914	NL	78–76	4	202,516	2,665
1913	NL	88–65	3	419,000	5,513
1912	NL	91–59	3	514,000	6,590
1911	NL	92–62	2	576,000	6,857
1910	NL	104–50	1	526,152	6,833
1909	NL	104–49	2	633,480	8,227
1908	NL	99–55	1	665,325	8,530
1907	NL	107–45	1	422,550	5,560
1906	NL	116–36	1	654,300	8,282
1905	NL	92–61	3	509,900	6,295
1904	NL	93–60	2	439,100	5,629

YEARLY RECORD, FINISH, & ATTENDANCE FIGURES (CONT.)

Year	League	Record	DIV/LG Finish	Attendance	Avg/Gm
1903	NL	82–56	3	386,205	5,290
1902	NL	68–69	5	263,700	3,767
1901	NL	53–86	6	205,071	2,930
1900	NL	65–75	6	248,577	3,405
1899	NL	75–73	8	352,130	4,633
1898	NL	85–65	4	424,352	5,584
1897	NL	59–73	9	327,160	4,741
1896	NL	71–57	5	317,500	4,811
1895	NL	72–58	4	382,300	5,749
1894	NL	57–75	8	239,000	3,541
1893	NL	56–71	9	223,500	3,492
1892	NL	70–76	7	109,067	1,484
1891	NL	82–53	2	181,431	2,649
1890	NL	84–53	2	102,536	1,475
1889	NL	67–65	3	N/A	N/A
1888	NL	77–58	2	N/A	N/A
1887	NL	71–50	3	N/A	N/A
1886	NL	90–34	1	N/A	N/A
1885	NL	87–25	1	N/A	N/A
1884	NL	62–50	5	N/A	N/A
1883	NL	59–39	2	N/A	N/A
1882	NL	55–29	1	N/A	N/A
1881	NL	56–28	1	N/A	N/A
1880	NL	67–17	1	N/A	N/A
1879	NL	46–33	4	N/A	N/A
1878	NL	30–30	4	N/A	N/A
1877	NL	26–33	5	N/A	N/A
1876	NL	52–14	1	N/A	N/A

MANAGER HISTORY

Manager	Years	W–L	Win %
Al Spalding	1876–1877	78–47	.624
Bob Ferguson	1878	30–30	.500
Silver Flint	1879	5–12	.294
Cap Anson	1879–1897	1,283–932	.579
Tom Burns	1898–1899	160–138	.537
Tom Loftus	1900–1901	118–161	.423
Frank Selee	1902–1905	280–213	.568
Frank Chance	1905–1912	768–389	.664
Johnny Evers	1913, 1921	129–120	.518
Hank O'Day	1914	78–76	.506
Roger Bresnahan	1915	73–80	.477
Joe Tinker	1916	67–86	.438
Fred Mitchell	1917–1920	308–269	.534
Bill Killefer	1921–1925	300–293	.506
Rabbit Maranville	1925	23–30	.434
George Gibson	1925	12–14	.462

MANAGER HISTORY (CONT.)

Manager	Years	W–L	Win %
Joe McCarthy	1926–1930	442–321	.579
Rogers Hornsby	1930–1932	141–116	.549
Charlie Grimm	1932–1938, 1944–1949, 1960	946–782	.547
Gabby Hartnett	1938–1940	203–176	.536
Jimmie Wilson	1941–1944	213–258	.452
Roy Johnson	1944	0–1	.000
Frank Frisch	1949–1951	141–196	.418
Phil Cavarretta	1951–1953	169–213	.442
Stan Hack	1954–1956	196–265	.425
Bob Scheffing	1957–1959	208–254	.450
Lou Boudreau	1960	54–83	.394
*Vedie Himsl	1961	10–21	.323
*Harry Craft	1961	7–9	.438
*Elvin Tappe	1961–1962	46–70	.397
*Lou Klein	1961–1962, 1965	65–82	.442
*Charlie Metro	1962	43–69	.384
Bob Kennedy	1963–1965	182–198	.479
Leo Durocher	1966–1972	535–526	.504
Whitey Lockman	1972–1974	157–162	.492
Jim Marshall	1974–1976	175–218	.445
Herman Franks	1977–1979	238–241	.497
Joe Amalfitano	1979, 1980–1981	66–116	.363
Preston Gomez	1980	38–52	.422
Lee Elia	1982–1983	127–158	.446
Charlie Fox	1983	17–22	.436
Jim Frey	1984–1986	196–182	.519
John Vukovich	1986	1–1	.500
Gene Michael	1986–1987	114–124	.479
Frank Lucchesi	1987	8–17	.320
Don Zimmer	1988–1991	265–258	.507
Joe Altobelli	1991	0–1	.000
Jim Essian	1991	59–63	.484
Jim Lefebvre	1992–1993	162–162	.500
Tom Trebelhorn	1994	49–64	.434
Jim Riggleman	1995–2000	439–516	.460
Don Baylor	2001–2002	122–124	.496
Bruce Kimm	2002	33–45	.423
Dusty Baker	2003–2005	256–230	.527

* Member of the "College of Coaches"

ALL-TIME WIN-LOSS RECORDS VS. ALL OPPONENTS (SINCE 1900)

Opponent	Record
ALL-TIME	8,279–8,127
Angels	2–1
Astros	272–321
Athletics	2–1
Blue Jays	2–4
Braves	1,018–844
Brewers	62–61
Cardinals	1,054–1,020
Devil Rays	2–1
Diamondbacks	26–38
Dodgers	933–932
Giants	900–975
Indians	2–6
INTERLEAGUE	66–64
Mariners	2–1
Marlins	59–56
Mets	328–326
Nationals	249–276
Orioles	2–1
Padres	224–171
Phillies	1,057–945
Pirates	995–1,088
Rangers	1–2
Reds	977–954
Red Sox	2–1
Rockies	61–57
Royals	9–6
Tigers	3–5
Twins	10–5
White Sox	23–25
Yankees	2–4

The 1906 World Series against the cross-town White Sox at West Side Grounds.

Franchise Highlights, Low Points, and Strange Distinctions

1884 Ned Williamson set a new major league record for homers in a season with 27. (His mark would stand for 35 years until Babe Ruth eclipsed it with 29 in 1919.) That year Williamson also became the first player ever to hit three homers in a game. Strangely, he suffered a power outage the next season, hitting only three.

....

1886 Rookie Jocko Flynn went 23–6 for Chicago, then never pitched another game. His only appearance after that season was one game in 1887 as an outfield defensive replacement.

....

1905 On April 26, outfielder Jack McCarthy of the Cubs threw out three runners at home plate in a 2–1 victory over the Pirates, in Pittsburgh.

....

1901–06 From June 20, 1901 to August 9, 1906, pitcher Jack Taylor started 187 games for the Cubs (97 games) and Cardinals (90 games) and completed every one of them.

....

1906 The Cubs, one of the best teams of all time, actually played better on the road (60–15) than at home (56–21) this year. In one stretch they went 50–7, including a 26–3 month of August.

1908 Not only did pitcher Ed Reulbach hurl both games of a September 26 doubleheader against Brooklyn in the heat of the pennant race, but he pitched shutouts in both games, allowing a combined total of eight hits. Reulbach's eyesight was so poor that his catchers helped him out by painting their gloves white.

When Mordecai Brown won Game 1 of the World Series, he became the first pitcher ever to collect a Series win in a relief role.

....

1912 Heinie Zimmerman of the Cubs became the first third baseman in major league history to win a batting title when he hit .372. He also won the Triple Crown that year with 14 homers and 103 RBIs. Or so he thought. Years later, when baseball historians examined the box scores of the day, they discovered that Zimmerman had erroneously been given credit for four RBIs that weren't his. The true RBI champion that year was actually Honus Wagner with 102, but baseball officials have refused to change the record, feeling that they are carved in stone. Many reference books, however, now recognize Wagner as the real RBI champion for 1912.

1918 Rookie shortstop Charlie Hollocher hit .316 for the Cubs and led the National League with 202 total bases. While he did have several other decent seasons, Hollocher was continually sidelined with mental troubles, to the point where he left baseball in 1924 at the age of 28. After returning home to Missouri, Hollocher continued to battle his inner demons until he committed suicide in 1940.

• • • •

1922 Cubs first baseman Oscar Grimes set a still-standing major league record when he collected at least one RBI in 17 consecutive games during the season.

• • • •

1935 The Cubs' 18-year-old first baseman Phil Cavarretta had a terrific rookie season, setting all-time records by a teenage major leaguer for hits (162), runs (85), RBIs (82), doubles (28), triples (12), and total bases (238).

• • • •

1955 Sam Jones's no-hitter against the Pirates was not without its drama, especially in the ninth inning. After walking the bases full, Jones ended the game by striking out the side.

• • • •

1954 Ernie Banks was a talented, all-around player for the Cubs. In 1954 he set a record by playing in 424 consecutive games from the start of a career. In 1955 he set a record by hitting six grand slams in one season. And in 1959 he set two new National League records for shortstops in a season, the first for his 143 RBIs, the second for his .985 fielding average.

1968 When Ernie Banks played his 1,000th game at first base in 1968, he became just the third player in major league history to play 1,000 games at two different positions. Banks had started his career at shortstop, playing 1,125 games there before moving to first base in 1962.

• • • •

1967 Ken Holtzman got off to a terrific start, going 9–0 in 12 starts, when his season was suddenly ended by a military call-up.

• • • •

1972 When Milt Pappas won his 200th career victory in 1972 as a member of the Cubs, he became the first pitcher in history to reach the milestone without having a 20-win season. On September 2 of that year, he lost a perfect game against San Diego with two outs in the ninth when he walked a batter on a 3–2 pitch. He finished with an 8–0 no-hit victory.

• • • •

1986 Greg Maddux of the Cubs and Mike Maddux of the Phillies became the first rookie brothers ever to square off against each other as starting pitchers when they met in Philadelphia on September 29. The Cubs won, 8–3.

• • • •

1991 The Cubs finished below .500, the 17th time in 19 years they were below the water level. No wonder. Their bullpen blew 27 of their 67 save opportunities. Had they maintained their leads in those games, the Cubs would have been 104–56, far and away the best team in the majors.

1994 The Cubs lost their first 12 home games, the worst home start in the National League during the 20th century. Outfielder Tuffy Rhodes did his part to try and get the Cubs off on the right foot when he set a new major league Opening Day record by hitting home runs in his first three trips to the plate, but Chicago still dropped its opener to the Mets, 12–8.

• • • •

1993–96 The Cubs went three years without starting a left-handed pitcher between September 29, 1993, and the end of the 1996 season.

• • • •

1997 The Cubs set a new National League record when they started the season 0–14. In their previous 121 years, their worst start had been 0–7.

• • • •

1998 On May 6, Kerry Wood, in just his fifth major league start, struck out 20 Houston Astros in a 2–0 win at Wrigley Field.

• • • •

1999 When Sammy Sosa hit his 60th homer of the season against the Brewers on September 18, he became the first player in major league history to hit 60 homers in back-to-back seasons.

Sammy Sosa, among the friendliest to ever roam The Friendly Confines of Wrigley Field.

2001 The Cubs pitching staff set the major league record for strikeouts in a season with 1,344, eclipsing the old record of 1,245 set by the Braves in 1996.

Sammy Sosa's 425 total bases were the most in Cubs' history, surpassing Hack Wilson's 1930 record of 423. Sosa's 306 combined runs scored and RBIs was the most in the majors since Ted Williams' 309 in 1949.

Special Achievements

World Series Results

Year	Opponent	Result	Games
1906	Chicago White Sox	Lost	2–4
1907	Detroit Tigers	Won	4–0
1908	Detroit Tigers	Won	4–1
1910	Philadelphia A's	Lost	1–4
1918	Boston Red Sox	Lost	2–4
1929	Philadelphia A's	Lost	1–4
1932	New York Yankees	Lost	0–4
1935	Detroit Tigers	Lost	2–4
1938	New York Yankees	Lost	0–4
1945	Detroit Tigers	Lost	3–4

World Series Managerial Records

Manager	Series Record	Games Record
Pat Moran	2–2	11–9
Fred Mitchell	0–1	2–4
Joe McCarthy	0–1	1–4
Charlie Grimm	0–3	5–12
Gabby Hartnett	0–1	0–4

All-Time Postseason Record

Divisional Playoffs	3–5
League Championship Series	6–11
World Series	19–33

All-Star Games at Chicago (When NL Was Home Team)

Year	Date	Winner	Score	Stadium
1947	July 8	American	2–1	Wrigley Field
1962	July 30	American	9–4	Wrigley Field
1990	July 10	American	2–0	Wrigley Field

Hall of Famers Who Played for Team

	Position	Years	Games with Chicago
Grover Alexander	SP	1918–1926	242
Cap Anson	1B/3B	1876–1897	2,276
Richie Ashburn	OF	1960–1961	260
Ernie Banks	1B/SS	1953–1971	2,528
Roger Bresnahan	C	1900, 1913–1915	249
Lou Brock	OF	1961–1964	327
Mordecai Brown	SP/RP	1904–1912, 1916	357
Frank Chance	1B/C	1898–1912	1,274
John Clarkson	SP	1884–1887	211
Kiki Cuyler	OF	1928–1935	949
Dizzy Dean	SP/RP	1938–1941	43

Hall of Famers Who Played for Team (cont.)

	Position	Years	Games with Chicago
Hugh Duffy	OF	1888–1889	207
Dennis Eckersley	SP	1984–1986	83
Johnny Evers	2B	1902–1913	1,409
Jimmie Foxx	1B	1942, 1944	85
Clark Griffith	SP	1893–1900	284
Burleigh Grimes	SP/RP	1932–1933	47
Gabby Hartnett	C	1922–1940	1,926
Billy Herman	2B	1931–1941	1,344
Rogers Hornsby	2B/3B	1929–1932	317
Monte Irvin	OF	1956	111
Fergie Jenkins	SP/RP	1966–1973, 1982–1983	402
George Kelly	1B	1930	39
King Kelly	OF/C	1880–1886	681
Ralph Kiner	OF	1953–1954	264
Chuck Klein	OF	1934–1936	263
Tony Lazzeri	SS	1938	54
Fred Lindstrom	OF/3B	1935	90
Rabbit Maranville	SS	1925	75
Robin Roberts	SP/RP	1966	11
Ryne Sandberg	2B/3B	1981–1994, 1996–1997	2,151
Al Spalding	SP	1876–1878	127
Joe Tinker	SS	1902–1912, 1916	1,537
Rube Waddell	SP	1901	30
Hoyt Wilhelm	RP	1970	3
Billy Williams	OF	1959–1974	2,213
Hack Wilson	OF	1926–1931	850

Hall of Famers Who Managed Team

	Years	Games with Chicago
Cap Anson	1879–1897	2,215
Lou Boudreau	1960	137
Roger Bresnahan	1915	153
Frank Chance	1905–1912	1,157
Leo Durocher	1966–1972	1,061
Johnny Evers	1913, 1921	249
Frankie Frisch	1949–1951	337
Gabby Hartnett	1938–1940	379
Rogers Hornsby	1930–1932	257
Rabbit Maranville	1925	53
Joe McCarthy	1926–1930	763
Frank Selee	1902–1905	493
Al Spalding	1876–1877	125
Joe Tinker	1916	153

MVP AWARD WINNERS

Gabby Hartnett	C	1935
Phil Cavarretta	1B	1945
Hank Sauer	OF	1952
Ernie Banks	SS	1958
Ernie Banks	SS	1959
Ryne Sandberg	2B	1984
Andre Dawson	OF	1987
Sammy Sosa	OF	1998

CY YOUNG AWARD WINNERS

Pitcher	Year	W–L	SV	ERA
Ferguson Jenkins	1971	24–13	0	2.77
Bruce Sutter	1979	6–6	37	2.23
Rick Sutcliffe	1984	16–1	0	2.69 (w/Chicago)
(2 teams)	——	4–5	0	5.15 (w/Cleveland)
Greg Maddux	1992	20–11	0	2.18

ROOKIE OF THE YEAR AWARD WINNERS

Billy Williams	OF	1961
Ken Hubbs	2B	1962
Jerome Walton	OF	1989
Kerry Wood	SP	1998

GOLD GLOVE WINNERS

Year	Position	Player
1960	SS	Ernie Banks
1962	2B	Ken Hubbs
1964	3B	Ron Santo
1965	3B	Ron Santo
1966	3B	Ron Santo
1967	C 3B	Randy Hundley Ron Santo
1968	2B 3B	Glenn Beckert Ron Santo
1969	SS	Don Kessinger
1970	SS	Don Kessinger
1983	2B	Ryne Sandberg
1984	2B OF	Ryne Sandberg Bob Dernier
1985	2B	Ryne Sandberg
1986	C 2B	Jody Davis Ryne Sandberg
1987	2B OF	Ryne Sandberg Andre Dawson
1988	2B OF	Ryne Sandberg Andre Dawson
1989	2B	Ryne Sandberg
1990	SP 2B	Greg Maddux Ryne Sandberg
1991	SP 2B	Greg Maddux Ryne Sandberg
1992	SP 1B	Greg Maddux Mark Grace
1993	1B	Mark Grace
1995	1B	Mark Grace
1996	1B	Mark Grace
2004	SP	Greg Maddux
2005	SP 1B	Greg Maddux Derrek Lee

TRIPLE CROWN WINNERS

Player	Year	Avg	HR	RBI
Heinie Zimmerman	1912	.372	14	98

FIREMAN OF THE YEAR AWARD WINNERS

Lindy McDaniel	1963
Ted Abernathy	1965
Phil Regan	1968
Bruce Sutter	1979
Lee Smith	1983 (tie)
Randy Myers	1993
Randy Myers	1995

WORLD SERIES MVP

None

LEAGUE CHAMPIONSHIP SERIES MVP

None

ALL-STAR GAME MVP

Bill Madlock	1975 (tie)

MANAGER OF THE YEAR AWARD WINNERS

Jim Frey	1984
Don Zimmer	1989

BATTING CHAMPIONS

Player	Year	Avg
Ross Barnes	1876	.429
George Gore	1880	.360
Cap Anson	1881	.399
King Kelly	1884	.354
King Kelly	1886	.388
Cap Anson	1888	.344
Heinie Zimmerman	1912	.372
Phil Cavarretta	1945	.355
Billy Williams	1972	.333
Bill Madlock	1975	.354
Bill Madlock	1976	.339
Bill Buckner	1980	.324
Derrek Lee	2005	.335

Nine-Inning No-Hitters Pitched

Year	Pitcher	Opp.	Score
1880	Larry Corcoran	BOS	6–0
1882	Larry Corcoran	WOR	5–0
1884	Larry Corcoran	PRO	6–0
1885	John Clarkson	PRO	4–0
1898	Walter Thornton	BRK	2–0
1915	Jim Lavender	NYG	2–0
1955	Sam Jones	PIT	4–0
1960	Don Cardwell	STL	4–0
1969	Ken Holtzman	ATL	3–0
1971	Ken Holtzman	CIN	1–0
1972	Burt Hooton	PHI	4–0
	Milt Pappas	SD	8–0

20-Game Winners

Year	Pitcher	W–L
1876	Al Spalding	47–13
1878	Terry Larkin	29–26
1879	Terry Larkin	30–23
1880	Larry Corcoran	43–14
	Fred Goldsmith	22–3
1881	Larry Corcoran	31–14
	Fred Goldsmith	25–13
1882	Fred Goldsmith	28–16
	Larry Corcoran	27–13
1883	Larry Corcoran	31–21
	Fred Goldsmith	28–18
1884	Larry Corcoran	35–23
1885	John Clarkson	53–16
	Jim McCormick	21–7 (20–4 w/Chicago, 1–3 w/Providence)
1886	John Clarkson	36–17
	Jim McCormick	31–11
	John Flynn	23–6
1887	John Clarkson	38–21
1888	Gus Krock	25–14
1890	Bill Hutchinson	42–25
	Pat Luby	20–9
1891	Bill Hutchinson	44–19
1892	Bill Hutchinson	36–36
	Ad Gumbert	22–19
1894	Clark Griffith	21–14
1895	Clark Griffith	26–14
	William Terry	21–14
1896	Clark Griffith	23–11
1897	Clark Griffith	21–18
1898	Clark Griffith	24–10
	Jim Callahan	20–10
1899	Clark Griffith	22–14
	Jim Callahan	21–12
1902	Jack Taylor	23–11
1903	Jack Taylor	21–14
	Jake Weimer	21–9
1904	Jake Weimer	20–14
1906	Mordecai Brown	26–6
	Jack Pfiester	20–8
1907	Orval Overall	23–7
	Mordecai Brown	20–6
1908	Mordecai Brown	29–9
	Ed Reulbach	24–7
1909	Mordecai Brown	27–9
	Orval Overall	20–11
1910	Mordecai Brown	25–13
	Leonard Cole	20–4
1911	Mordecai Brown	21–11
1912	Larry Cheney	26–10
1913	Larry Cheney	21–14
1914	Hippo Vaughn	21–13
	Larry Cheney	20–18
1915	Hippo Vaughn	20–12
1917	Hippo Vaughn	23–13
1918	Hippo Vaughn	22–10
1919	Hippo Vaughn	21–14
1920	Grover Alexander	27–14
1923	Grover Alexander	22–12
1927	Charlie Root	26–15
1929	Pat Malone	22–10
1930	Pat Malone	20–9
1932	Lon Warneke	22–6
1933	Guy Bush	20–12
1934	Lon Warneke	22–10
1935	Bill Lee	20–6
	Lon Warneke	20–13
1938	Bill Lee	22–9
1940	Claude Passeau	20–13
1945	Hank Wyse	22–10
1963	Dick Ellsworth	22–10
1964	Larry Jackson	24–11
1967	Ferguson Jenkins	20–13
1968	Ferguson Jenkins	20–15
1969	Ferguson Jenkins	21–15
	Bill Hands	20–14
1970	Ferguson Jenkins	22–16
1971	Ferguson Jenkins	24–13
1972	Ferguson Jenkins	20–12
1977	Rick Reuschel	20–10
1992	Greg Maddux	20–11
2001	Jon Lieber	20–6

Retired Uniform Numbers

Number	Player	Position
10	Ron Santo	3B
14	Ernie Banks	SS/1B
23	Ryne Sandberg	2B
26	Billy Williams	OF

Team Records—Wins & Losses

- Games won in a season: 116 in 1906
- Games lost in a season: 103 in 1962 and 1966

- Games won in a month: 26 (3 times), in August 1906, July 1935, and July 1945
- Games lost in a month: 24 in July 1957 and August 1999
- Consecutive games won: 21 in 1880 and 1935
- Consecutive games lost: 14 in 1997
- Biggest shutout victory: 20–0 over Washington on May 28, 1886
- Biggest shutout loss: 22–0 to Pittsburgh on September 16, 1975
- Highest winning percentage: .798 in 1880 (67–17)
- Lowest winning percentage: .364 in 1962 and 1966 (59–103)

TEAM RECORDS—BATTING

- Highest team batting average: .333 in 1887
- Lowest team batting average: .235 in 1892
- Highest team slugging average: .481 in 1930
- Highest team on-base percentage: .388 in 1887
- Total hits: 1,722 in 1930
- Extra-base hits: 572 in 1904
- Hits in a game: 32 vs. Buffalo on July 3, 1883 and vs. Louisville on June 29, 1897
- Longest individual hitting streak: 42, Bill Dahlen, 1894
- Most .300 hitters in a single season: 8 in 1921
- Home runs: 235 in 2004
- Home runs in a month: 20, Sammy Sosa, June 1998
- Home runs in a game: 7 (three times) vs. New York Mets on June 11, 1967 (second game); vs. San Diego on August 19, 1970; and vs. San Diego on May 17, 1977
- Home runs by a rookie: 25, Billy Williams, 1961
- Home runs by a right-hander: 66, Sammy Sosa, 1998
- Home runs by a left-hander: 42, Billy Williams, 1970
- Home runs by a switch-hitter: 27, Mark Bellhorn, 2002
- Grand slams: 9 in 1929
- Grand slams (individual; single season): 5, Ernie Banks, 1955
- Grand slams (individual; career): 12, Ernie Banks
- Triples: 101 in 1911
- Doubles: 340 in 1931
- Singles: 1,230 in 1887
- Walks: 650 in 1975
- Runs scored: 1,041 in 1894
- Runs scored in a game: 36 vs. Louisville, June 29, 1897
- Runs scored in an inning: 18 vs. Detroit Wolverines on September 6, 1883 (seventh inning)
- Most batters hit by a pitch: 66 in 2001
- Times shut out: 22 in 1915 and 1968
- Grounded into double plays: 161 in 1933
- Fewest grounded into double plays: 87 in 1991
- Runners left on base: 1,262 in 1975

TEAM RECORDS—BASERUNNING

- Stolen bases: 382 in 1887
- Caught stealing: 149 in 1924

TEAM RECORDS—PITCHING

- Lowest earned run average: 1.73 in 1907
- Complete games: 147 in 1889
- Saves: 56 in 1993 and 1998
- Strikeouts: 1,404 in 2001
- Shutouts: 32 in 1907 and 1909
- Walks: 658 in 2000
- Hit batsmen: 82 in 1898 and 1899
- Wild pitches: 86 in 1887
- Consecutive wins (individual): 17, John Luby, 1890
- Consecutive losses (individual): 13, Dutch McCall, 1948
- Strikeouts in a game (individual): 20, Kerry Wood, May 6, 1998
- Most runs allowed in a game: 25 vs. Boston Beaneaters, September 10, 1894

TEAM RECORDS—FIELDING

- Best fielding average: .986 in 2004
- Most errors committed: 595 in 1884
- Fewest errors committed: 86 in 2004
- Most double plays turned: 176 in 1928
- Fewest double plays turned: 33 in 1876

TEAM RECORDS—MISCELLANEOUS

- Number of times league champions: 16
- Number of times finishing last in league: 11
- Largest attendance, single game: 51,556 vs. Brooklyn, June 27, 1930
- Largest attendance, doubleheader: 46,965 vs. Pittsburgh, May 31, 1948
- Players used in a season: 51 in 2000
- Seasons played: 22 by Cap Anson

PRIMARY PITCHING STAFFS

Year	Starter	Starter	Starter	Starter	Starter	Closer	Bullpen	Bullpen	Bullpen
2005	Maddux	Zambrano	Prior	Rusch	Williams	Dempster	Wuertz	Ohman	Novoa
2004	Maddux	Zambrano	Prior	Clement	Wood	Hawkins	Farnsworth	Mercker	Remlinger
2003	Estes	Zambrano	Prior	Clement	Wood	Borowski	Farnsworth	Guthrie	Remlinger
2002	Lieber	Zambrano	Prior	Clement	Wood	Alfonseca	Borowski	Fassero	Cruz
2001	Lieber	Bere	Tapani	Tavarez	Wood	Gordon	Farnsworth	Van Poppel	Fassero
2000	Lieber	Downs	Tapani	Quevedo	Wood	Aguilera	Heredia	Van Poppel	Worrell
1999	Lieber	Trachsel	Tapani	Farnsworth	Mulholland	Adams	Heredia	Sanders	Myers
1998	Clark	Trachsel	Tapani	Wood	Gonzalez	Beck	Mulholland	Adams	Pisciotta
1997	Foster	Trachsel	Mulholland	Castillo	Gonzalez	Adams	Patterson	Bottenfield	Tatis
1996	Navarro	Trachsel	Bullinger	Castillo	Telemaco	Wendell	Patterson	Bottenfield	Adams
1995	Navarro	Trachsel	Bullinger	Castillo	Foster	Myers	Perez	Wendell	Walker
1994	Banks	Trachsel	Young	Morgan	Foster	Myers	Bautista	Plesac	Crim
1993	Hibbard	Guzman	Harkey	Morgan	Castillo	Myers	Bautista	Plesac	Scanlan
1992	Maddux	Jackson	Boskie	Morgan	Castillo	Scanlan	McElroy	Assenmacher	Robinson
1991	Maddux	Bielecki	Boskie	Sutcliffe	Castillo	Smith	McElroy	Assenmacher	Lancaster
1990	Maddux	Bielecki	Boskie	Harkey	Wilson	Williams	Long	Assenmacher	Lancaster
1989	Maddux	Bielecki	Sutcliffe	Sanderson	Kilgus	Williams	Schiraldi	Pico	Wilson
1988	Maddux	Moyer	Sutcliffe	Schiraldi	Pico	Gossage	DiPino	Lancaster	Perry
1987	Maddux	Moyer	Sutcliffe	Sanderson	Lancaster	Smith	DiPino	Lynch	Noles
1986	Eckersley	Moyer	Sutcliffe	Sanderson	Trout	Smith	Fontenot	Gumpert	Baller
1985	Eckersley	Fontenot	Sutcliffe	Sanderson	Trout	Smith	Brusstar	Frazier	Sorensen
1984	Eckersley	Ruthven	Sutcliffe	Sanderson	Trout	Smith	Brusstar	Frazier	Stoddard
1983	Rainey	Ruthven	Jenkins	Noles	Trout	Smith	Brusstar	Campbell	Proly
1982	Bird	Martz	Jenkins	Noles	Ripley	Smith	Hernandez	Campbell	Tidrow
1981	Bird	Martz	Krukow	Reuschel	Kravec	Tidrow	Capilla	Smith	Eastwick
1980	Lamp	McGlothen	Krukow	Reuschel	Capilla	Sutter	Hernandez	Caudill	Tidrow
1979	Lamp	McGlothen	Krukow	Reuschel	Holtzman	Sutter	Hernandez	Moore	Tildrow
1978	Lamp	Burris	Krukow	Reuschel	Roberts	Sutter	McGlothen	Hernandez	Moore
1977	Bonham	Burris	Krukow	Reuschel	Renko	Sutter	Hernandez	Moore	Reuschel
1976	Bonham	Burris	Stone	Reuschel	Renko	Sutter	Reuschel	Knowles	Garman
1975	Bonham	Burris	Stone	Reuschel	Zahn	Knowles	Zamora	Frailing	Dettore
1974	Bonham	Hooton	Stone	Reuschel	Frailing	Zamora	LaRoche	Todd	Burris
1973	Bonham	Hooton	Jenkins	Reuschel	Pappas	Locker	LaRoche	Aker	Burris
1972	Hands	Hooton	Jenkins	Reuschel	Pappas	Aker	McGinn	Phoebus	Hamilton
1971	Hands	Holtzman	Jenkins	Pizarro	Pappas	Regan	Tompkins	Bonham	Newman
1970	Hands	Holtzman	Jenkins	Decker	Pappas	Regan	Colborn	Rodriguez	Gura
1969	Hands	Holtzman	Jenkins	Selma		Regan	Abernathy	Aguirre	Nye
1968	Hands	Holtzman	Jenkins	Niekro	Nye	Regan	Stoneman	Hartenstein	Lamabe
1967	Culp	Simmons	Jenkins	Niekro	Nye	Hartenstein	Stoneman	Koonce	Hands
1966	Ellsworth	Holtzman	Jenkins	Hands	Broglio	Hendley	Abernathy	Koonce	Hoeft

PRIMARY PITCHING STAFFS (CONT.)

Year	Starter	Starter	Starter	Starter	Starter	Closer	Bullpen	Bullpen	Bullpen
1965	Ellsworth	Jackson	Buhl	Koonce	Faul	Abernathy	Humphreys	McDaniel	Hoeft
1964	Ellsworth	Jackson	Buhl	Burdette	Broglio	McDaniel	Elston	Schurr	Shantz
1963	Ellsworth	Jackson	Buhl	Hobbie	Toth	McDaniel	Elston	Brewer	Koonce
1962	Ellsworth	Koonce	Buhl	Hobbie	Cardwell	Elston	Anderson	Schultz	Gerard
1961	Ellsworth	Curtis	Anderson	Hobbie	Cardwell	Elston	Brewer	Schultz	Drott
1960	Ellsworth	Drott	Anderson	Hobbie	Cardwell	Elston	Schaffernoth	Drabowsky	Morehead
1959	Hillman	Drabowsky	Anderson	Hobbie	Ceccarelli	Elston	Singleton	Buzhardt	Henry
1958	Drott	Drabowsky	Phillips	Hobbie	Briggs	Elston	Henry	Hillman	Nichols
1957	Drott	Drabowsky	Rush	Elston	Hillman	Lown	Littlefield	Poholsky	Brosnan
1956	Jones	Hacker	Rush	Kaiser	Davis	Lown	Valentinetti	Brosnan	Hughes
1955	Jones	Hacker	Rush	Minner	Davis	Jeffcoat	Perkowski	Hillman	Pollet
1954	Klippstein	Hacker	Rush	Minner	Pollet	Jeffcoat	Davis	Tremel	Brosnan
1953	Klippstein	Hacker	Rush	Minner	Pollet	Leonard	Lown	Simpson	Church
1952	Klippstein	Hacker	Rush	Minner	Lown	Leonard	Ramsdell	Schultz	Kelly
1951	Hiller	McLish	Rush	Minner	Lown	Kelly	Leonard	Klippstein	
1950	Hiller	Schmitz	Rush	Minner	Dubiel	Leonard	Klippstein	Vander Meer	Lade
1949	Leonard	Schmitz	Rush	Lade	Dubiel	Chipman	Muncrief	Adkins	
1948	Meyer	Schmitz	McCall	Hamner	Borowy	Chipman	Dobernic	Rush	
1947	Lade	Schmitz	Erickson	Wyse	Borowy	Chipman	Kush	Meers	
1946	Passeau	Schmitz	Erickson	Wyse	Borowy	Chipman	Kush	Bithorn	
1945	Passeau	Derringer	Prim	Wyse	Borowy	Chipman	Vandenberg	Erickson	
1944	Passeau	Derringer	Chipman	Wyse	Fleming	Lynn	Vandenberg	Erickson	
1943	Passeau	Derringer	Bithorn	Wyse	Hanyzewski	Prim	Burrows	Warneke	
1942	Passeau	Lee	Bithorn	Olsen	Fleming	Pressnell	Schmitz	Mooty	
1941	Passeau	Lee	French	Olsen	Root	Pressnell	Erickson	Mooty	
1940	Passeau	Lee	French	Olsen	Mooty	Raffensberger	Root	Page	
1939	Passeau	Lee	French	Page	Root	Russell	Whitehill	Lillard	
1938	Bryant	Lee	French	Carleton	Root	Russell	Logan	Dean	
1937	Parmelee	Lee	French	Carleton	Root	Bryant	Shoun	Davis	
1936	Warneke	Lee	French	Carleton	Davis	Bryant	Henshaw	Root	
1935	Warneke	Lee	French	Carleton	Henshaw	Kowalik	Casey	Root	
1934	Warneke	Lee	Bush	Malone	Weaver	Tinning	Joiner	Root	
1933	Warneke	Root	Bush	Malone	Tinning	Nelson	Henshaw	Grimes	
1932	Warneke	Root	Bush	Malone	Grimes	May	Smith	Tinning	
1931	Smith	Root	Bush	Malone	Sweetland	May	Teachout	Baecht	
1930	Blake	Root	Bush	Malone	Teachout	Nelson	Osborn	Shealy	
1929	Blake	Root	Bush	Malone	Nehf	Cvengros	Carlson	Jonnard	
1928	Blake	Root	Bush	Malone	Nehf	Jones	Carlson	Holley	
1927	Blake	Root	Bush	Carlson	Osborn	Jones	Brillheart	Roy	
1926	Blake	Root	Bush	Kaufmann	Jones	Osborn	Piercy	Milstead	
1925	Blake	Alexander	Bush	Kaufmann	Cooper	Keen	Jones	Jacobs	
1924	Aldridge	Alexander	Keen	Kaufmann	Jacobs	Wheeler	Blake	Bush	
1923	Aldridge	Alexander	Keen	Kaufmann	Osborne	Dumovich	Fussell	Cheeves	
1922	Aldridge	Alexander	Jones	Kaufmann	Cheeves	Osborne	Stueland	Freeman	
1921	Martin	Alexander	Freeman	Vaughn	Cheeves	York	Jones	Ponder	
1920	Martin	Alexander	Tyler	Vaughn	Hendrix	Carter	Bailey	Gaw	
1919	Martin	Alexander	Douglas	Vaughn	Hendrix	Carter	Bailey	Tyler	
1918	Tyler	Walker	Douglas	Vaughn	Hendrix	Carter	Martin	Weaver	
1917	Demaree	Carter	Douglas	Vaughn	Hendrix	Prendergast	Aldridge	Seaton	
1916	Lavender	McConnell	Packard	Vaughn	Hendrix	Prendergast	Brown	Seaton	
1915	Lavender	Humphries	Pearce	Vaughn	Cheney	Zabel	Standridge	Adams	
1914	Lavender	Humphries	Pearce	Vaughn	Cheney	Zabel	Hageman	Smith	

PRIMARY PITCHING STAFFS (CONT.)

Year	Starter	Starter	Starter	Starter	Starter	Closer	Bullpen	Bullpen	Bullpen
1913	Lavender	Humphries	Pearce	Smith	Cheney	Richie	Overall	Stack	
1912	Lavender	Richie	Reulbach	Leifield	Cheney	Smith	Brown	Moroney	
1911	Brown	Richie	Reulbach	Cole	McIntire	Smith	Richter	Toney	
1910	Brown	Overall	Reulbach	Cole	McIntire	Richie	Pfiester	Pfeffer	
1909	Brown	Overall	Reulbach	Pfiester	Kroh	Higginbotham	Hagerman		
1908	Brown	Overall	Reulbach	Pfiester	Fraser	Lundgren			
1907	Brown	Overall	Reulbach	Pfiester	Lundgren	Fraser	Taylor		
1906	Brown	Taylor	Reulbach	Pfiester	Lundgren	Overall	Beebe	Wicker	
1905	Brown	Weimer	Reulbach	Wicker	Briggs	Lundgren	Pfeffer		
1904	Brown	Weimer	Lundgren	Wicker	Briggs	Corridon			
1903	Taylor	Weimer	Lundgren	Wicker	Menefee	Currie			
1902	Taylor	Williams	Lundgren	Rhoads	Menefee	St.Vrain			
1901	Taylor	Hughes	Waddell	Eason	Menefee				
1900	Taylor	Callahan	Griffith	Garvin	Menefee	Cunningham	Killen		
1899	Taylor	Callahan	Griffith	Garvin	Phyle				
1898	Thornton	Callahan	Griffith	Woods	Kilroy	Isbell			
1897	Thornton	Callahan	Griffith	Friend	Briggs	Denzer			
1896	Terry	Parker	Griffith	Friend	Briggs				
1895	Terry	Parker	Griffith	Hutchison		Thornton			
1894	Terry	McGill	Griffith	Hutchison	Stratton	Abbey			
1893	Mauck	McGill	Clausen	Hutchison	Abbey	McGinnis	Donnelly		
1892	Gumbert	Luby		Hutchison					
1891	Gumbert	Luby	Vickery	Hutchison	Stein				
1890	Sullivan	Luby	Coughlin	Hutchison	Stein				
1889	Dwyer	Tener	Gumbert	Hutchison	Krock				
1888	Baldwin	Tener	Van Haltren	Borchers	Krock	Ryan	Gumbert		
1887	Baldwin	Clarkson	Van Haltren			Ryan			
1886	McCormick	Clarkson	Flynn						
1885	McCormick	Clarkson	Kennedy	Corcoran					
1884	Goldsmith	Clarkson	Brown	Corcoran					
1883	Goldsmith			Corcoran					
1882	Goldsmith			Corcoran					
1881	Goldsmith			Corcoran					
1880	Goldsmith	Poorman	Guth	Corcoran					
1879	Larkin	Hankinson							
1878	Larkin	Reis							
1877	Bradley	McVey	Reis		Spalding				
1876	Spalding	McVey							

PRIMARY STARTING LINEUPS

Year	C	1B	2B	3B	SS	LF	CF	RF	DH
2005	Barrett	Lee	Walker	Ramirez	Perez	Hollandsworth	Patterson	Burnitz	
2004	Barrett	Lee	Walker	Ramirez	Martinez	Alou	Patterson	Sosa	
2003	Miller	Karros	Grudzielanek	Ramirez	Gonzalez	Alou	Patterson	Sosa	
2002	Girardi	McGriff	Bellhorn	Mueller	Gonzalez	Alou	Patterson	Sosa	
2001	Girardi	Stairs	Young	Coomer	Gutierrez	White	Matthews	Sosa	
2000	Girardi	Grace	Young	Greene	Gutierrez	Rodriguez	Buford	Sosa	
1999	Santiago	Grace	Morandini	Gaetti	Hernandez	Rodriguez	Johnson	Sosa	
1998	Servais	Grace	Morandini	Hernandez	Blauser	Rodriguez	Johnson	Sosa	
1997	Servais	Grace	Sandberg	Orie	Dunston	Glanville	McRae	Sosa	
1996	Servais	Grace	Sandberg	Gomez	Sanchez	Gonzalez	McRae	Sosa	
1995	Servais	Grace	Sanchez	Zeile	Dunston	Gonzalez	McRae	Sosa	
1994	Wilkins	Grace	Sandberg	Buechele	Dunston	May	Rhodes	Sosa	
1993	Wilkins	Grace	Sandberg	Buechele	Sanchez	May	Wilson	Sosa	
1992	Girardi	Grace	Sandberg	Buechele	Sanchez	May	Dascenzo	Dawson	
1991	Wilkins	Grace	Sandberg	Salazar	Dunston	Bell	Walton	Dawson	
1990	Girardi	Grace	Sandberg	Salazar	Dunston	Dascenzo	Walton	Dawson	
1989	Berryhill	Grace	Sandberg	Law	Dunston	Smith	Walton	Dawson	
1988	Berryhill	Grace	Sandberg	Law	Dunston	Palmeiro	Martinez	Dawson	
1987	Davis	Durham	Sandberg	Moreland	Dunston	Mumphrey	Martinez	Dawson	
1986	Davis	Durham	Sandberg	Cey	Dunston	Matthews	Dernier	Moreland	
1985	Davis	Durham	Sandberg	Cey	Dunston	Matthews	Dernier	Moreland	
1984	Davis	Durham	Sandberg	Cey	Bowa	Matthews	Dernier	Moreland	
1983	Davis	Buckner	Sandberg	Cey	Bowa	Durham	Hall	Moreland	
1982	Davis	Buckner	Wills	Sandberg	Bowa	Henderson	Woods	Durham	
1981	Davis	Buckner	Tyson	Reitz	DeJesus	Henderson	Morales	Durham	
1980	Blackwell	Buckner	Tyson	Randle	DeJesus	Kingman	Martin	Vail	
1979	Foote	Buckner	Sizemore	Ontiveros	DeJesus	Kingman	Martin	Thompson	
1978	Rader	Buckner	Trillo	Ontiveros	DeJesus	Kingman	Gross	Murcer	
1977	Mitterwald	Buckner	Trillo	Ontiveros	DeJesus	Cardenal	Morales	Murcer	
1976	Swisher	LaCock	Trillo	Madlock	Kelleher	Cardenal	Monday	Morales	
1975	Swisher	Thornton	Trillo	Madlock	Kessinger	Cardenal	Monday	Morales	
1974	Swisher	Thornton	Harris	Madlock	Kessinger	Morales	Monday	Cardenal	
1973	Hundley	Hickman	Beckert	Santo	Kessinger	Williams	Monday	Cardenal	
1972	Hundley	Hickman	Beckert	Santo	Kessinger	Williams	Monday	Cardenal	
1971	Cannizzaro	Pepitone	Beckert	Santo	Kessinger	Williams	Davis	Callison	
1970	Hundley	Hickman	Beckert	Santo	Kessinger	Williams	James	Callison	
1969	Hundley	Banks	Beckert	Santo	Kessinger	Williams	Young	Hickman	
1968	Hundley	Banks	Beckert	Santo	Kessinger	Williams	Phillips	Johnson	
1967	Hundley	Banks	Beckert	Santo	Kessinger	Williams	Phillips	Savage	
1966	Hundley	Banks	Beckert	Santo	Kessinger	Browne	Phillips	Williams	
1965	Roznovsky	Banks	Beckert	Santo	Kessinger	Stewart	Landrum	Williams	
1964	Bertell	Banks	Amalfitano	Santo	Rodgers	Williams	Cowan	Gabrielson	
1963	Bertell	Banks	Hubbs	Santo	Rodgers	Williams	Burton	Brock	
1962	Bertell	Banks	Hubbs	Santo	Rodgers	Williams	Brock	Altman	
1961	Bertell	Bouchee	Zimmer	Santo	Banks	Williams	Heist	Altman	
1960	Thacker	Bouchee	Kindall	Santo	Banks	Thomas	Ashburn	Will	
1959	Taylor	Long	Taylor	Dark	Banks	Moryn	Altman	Walls	
1958	Taylor	Long	Taylor	Dark	Banks	Moryn	Thomson	Walls	
1957	Neeman	Long	Morgan	Adams	Banks	Walls	Speake	Moryn	
1956	Landrith	Fondy	Baker	Hoak	Banks	Irvin	Whisenant	Moryn	
1955	Chiti	Fondy	Baker	Jackson	Banks	Sauer	Miksis	King	
1954	Garagiola	Fondy	Baker	Jackson	Banks	Kiner	Talbot	Sauer	

PRIMARY STARTING LINEUPS (CONT.)

Year	C	1B	2B	3B	SS	LF	CF	RF	DH
1953	McCullough	Fondy	Miksis	Jackson	Smalley	Kiner	Jeffcoat	Sauer	
1952	Atwell	Fondy	Miksis	Jackson	Smalley	Sauer	Jeffcoat	Hermanski	
1951	Burgess	Connors	Miksis	Jackson	Smalley	Sauer	Baumholtz	Hermanski	
1950	Owen	Ward	Terwilliger	Serena	Smalley	Sauer	Pafko	Jeffcoat	
1949	Owen	Reich	Verban	Gustine	Smalley	Sauer	Pafko	Baumholtz	
1948	Scheffing	Waitkus	Schenz	Pafko	Smalley	Lowrey	Jeffcoat	Nicholson	
1947	Scheffing	Waitkus	Johnson	Lowrey	Merullo	Cavarretta	Pafko	Nicholson	
1946	McCullough	Waitkus	Johnson	Hack	Jurges	Rickert	Pafko	Nicholson	
1945	Livingston	Cavarretta	Johnson	Hack	Merullo	Lowrey	Pafko	Nicholson	
1944	Williams	Cavarretta	Johnson	Hack	Merullo	Dallessandro	Pafko	Nicholson	
1943	McCullough	Cavarretta	Stanky	Hack	Merullo	Novikoff	Lowrey	Nicholson	
1942	McCullough	Foxx	Stringer	Hack	Merullo	Novikoff	Cavarretta	Nicholson	
1941	McCullough	Dahlgren	Stringer	Hack	Sturgeon	Dallessandro	Cavarretta	Nicholson	
1940	Todd	Cavarretta	Herman	Hack	Mattick	Dallessandro	Gleeson	Nicholson	
1939	Hartnett	Russell	Herman	Hack	Bartell	Galan	Leiber	Gleeson	
1938	Hartnett	Collins	Herman	Hack	Jurges	Galan	Reynolds	Demaree	
1937	Hartnett	Collins	Herman	Hack	Jurges	Galan	Marty	Demaree	
1936	Hartnett	Cavarretta	Herman	Hack	Jurges	Allen	Galan	Demaree	
1935	Hartnett	Cavarretta	Herman	Hack	Jurges	Galan	Demaree	Klein	
1934	Hartnett	Grimm	Herman	Hack	Jurges	Klein	Cuyler	Herman	
1933	Hartnett	Grimm	Herman	English	Jurges	Stephenson	Demaree	Herman	
1932	Hartnett	Grimm	Herman	English	Jurges	Stephenson	Moore	Cuyler	
1931	Hartnett	Grimm	Hornsby	Bell	English	Stephenson	Wilson	Cuyler	
1930	Hartnett	Grimm	Blair	English	Beck	Stephenson	Wilson	Cuyler	
1929	Taylor	Grimm	Hornsby	McMillan	English	Stephenson	Wilson	Cuyler	
1928	Hartnett	Grimm	Maguire	Beck	English	Stephenson	Wilson	Cuyler	
1927	Hartnett	Grimm	Beck	Adams	English	Stephenson	Wilson	Webb	
1926	Hartnett	Grimm	Adams	Freigau	Cooney	Stephenson	Wilson	Heathcote	
1925	Hartnett	Grimm	Adams	Freigau	Maranville	Jahn	Brooks	Heathcote	
1924	Hartnett	Cotter	Grantham	Friberg	Adams	Grigsby	Statz	Heathcote	
1923	O'Farrell	Grimes	Grantham	Friberg	Adams	Miller	Statz	Heathcote	
1922	O'Farrell	Grimes	Terry	Krug	Hollocher	Miller	Statz	Friberg	
1921	O'Farrell	Grimes	Terry	Deal	Hollocher	Barber	Maisel	Flack	
1920	O'Farrell	Merkle	Terry	Deal	Hollocher	Robertson	Paskert	Flack	
1919	Killefer	Merkle	Pick	Deal	Hollocher	Mann	Paskert	Flack	
1918	Killefer	Merkle	Zeider	Deal	Hollocher	Mann	Paskert	Flack	
1917	Wilson	Merkle	Doyle	Deal	Wortman	Mann	Williams	Wolter	
1916	Archer	Saier	Knabe	Zimmerman	Wortman	Mann	Williams	Flack	
1915	Archer	Saier	Zimmerman	Phelan	Fisher	Schulte	Williams	Good	
1914	Bresnahan	Saier	Sweeney	Zimmerman	Corriden	Schulte	Leach	Good	
1913	Archer	Saier	Evers	Zimmerman	Bridwell	Mitchell	Leach	Schulte	
1912	Archer	Saier	Evers	Zimmerman	Tinker	Sheckard	Leach	Schulte	
1911	Archer	Saier	Zimmerman	Doyle	Tinker	Sheckard	Hofman	Schulte	
1910	Kling	Chance	Evers	Steinfeldt	Tinker	Sheckard	Hofman	Schulte	
1909	Archer	Chance	Evers	Steinfeldt	Tinker	Sheckard	Hofman	Schulte	
1908	Kling	Chance	Evers	Steinfeldt	Tinker	Sheckard	Slagle	Schulte	
1907	Kling	Chance	Evers	Steinfeldt	Tinker	Sheckard	Slagle	Schulte	
1906	Kling	Chance	Evers	Steinfeldt	Tinker	Sheckard	Slagle	Schulte	
1905	Kling	Chance	Evers	Casey	Tinker	Schulte	Slagle	Maloney	
1904	Kling	Chance	Evers	Casey	Tinker	Slagle	McCarthy	Jones	
1903	Kling	Chance	Evers	Casey	Tinker	Slagle	Jones	Harley	
1902	Kling	Chance	Lowe	Schaefer	Tinker	Slagle	Dobbs	Congalton	

PRIMARY STARTING LINEUPS (CONT.)

Year	C	1B	2B	3B	SS	LF	CF	RF	DH
1901	Kling	Doyle	Childs	Raymer	McCormick	Hartsel	Green	Chance	
1900	Donahue	Ganzel	Childs	Bradley	McCormick	McCarthy	Mertes	Ryan	
1899	Donahue	Everitt	McCormick	Wolverton	DeMontreville	Ryan	Lange	Green	
1898	Donahue	Everitt	Connor	McCormick	Dahlen	Ryan	Lange	Mertes	
1897	Kittridge	Anson	Connor	Everitt	Dahlen	Decker	Lange	Ryan	
1896	Kittridge	Anson	Pfeffer	Everitt	Dahlen	Decker	Lange	Ryan	
1895	Donahue	Anson	Stewart	Everitt	Dahlen	Wilmot	Lange	Ryan	
1894	Schriver	Anson	Parrott	Irwin	Dahlen	Wilmot	Lange	Ryan	
1893	Kittridge	Anson	Lange	Parrott	Dahlen	Wilmot	Ryan	Dungan	
1892	Schriver	Anson	Canavan	Parrott	Dahlen	Wilmot	Ryan	Dungan	
1891	Kittridge	Anson	Pfeffer	Dahlen	Cooney	Wilmot	Ryan	Carroll	
1890	Kittridge	Anson	Glenalvin	Burns	Cooney	Carroll	Wilmot	Andrews	
1889	Farrell	Anson	Pfeffer	Burns	Williamson	Van Haltren	Ryan	Duffy	
1888	Daly	Anson	Pfeffer	Burns	Williamson	Sullivan	Ryan	Duffy	
1887	Daly	Anson	Pfeffer	Burns	Williamson	Sullivan	Ryan	Pettit	
1886	Flint	Anson	Pfeffer	Burns	Williamson	Dalrymple	Gore	Kelly	
1885	Flint	Anson	Pfeffer	Williamson	Burns	Dalrymple	Gore	Kelly	
1884	Flint	Anson	Pfeffer	Williamson	Burns	Dalrymple	Gore	Kelly	
1883	Flint	Anson	Pfeffer	Williamson	Burns	Dalrymple	Gore	Kelly	
1882	Flint	Anson	Burns	Williamson	Kelly	Dalrymple	Gore	Nicol	
1881	Flint	Anson	Quest	Williamson	Burns	Dalrymple	Gore	Kelly	
1880	Flint	Anson	Quest	Williamson	Burns	Dalrymple	Gore	Kelly	
1879	Flint	Anson	Quest	Williamson	Peters	Dalrymple	Gore	Shaffer	
1878	Harbidge	Start	McClellan	Hankinson	Ferguson	Anson	Remsen	Cassidy	
1877	McVey	Spalding	Barnes	Anson	Peters	Glenn	Eggler	Hallinan	
1876	White	McVey	Barnes	Anson	Peters	Glenn	Hines	Bielaski	

Top 10 Batting Leaders, Single Season & Career with Team

GAMES PLAYED: CAREER WITH TEAM

Player	G	PA
1. Ernie Banks	2,528	10,395
2. Cap Anson	2,276	10,112
3. Billy Williams	2,213	9,504
4. Ryne Sandberg	2,151	9,276
5. Ron Santo	2,126	8,979
6. Phil Cavarretta	1,953	7,509
7. Stan Hack	1,938	8,506
8. Gabby Hartnett	1,926	7,132
9. Mark Grace	1,910	8,234
10. Sammy Sosa	1,811	7,898

AT-BATS: SEASON

Player	AB	Year
1. Billy Herman	666	1935
2. Don Kessinger	664	1969
3. Ken Hubbs	661	1962
4. Bill Buckner	657	1982
5. Glenn Beckert	656	1966
Billy Herman	656	1932
7. Don Kessinger	655	1968
Jigger Statz	655	1923
9. Billy Williams	648	1966
10. Sparky Adams	647	1927

AT-BATS: CAREER WITH TEAM

Player	AB	PA
1. Ernie Banks	9,421	10,395
2. Cap Anson	9,101	10,112
3. Billy Williams	8,479	9,504
4. Ryne Sandberg	8,379	9,276
5. Ron Santo	7,768	8,979
6. Stan Hack	7,278	8,506
7. Mark Grace	7,156	8,234
8. Sammy Sosa	6,990	7,898
9. Jimmy Ryan	6,757	7,542
10. Phil Cavarretta	6,592	7,509

BATTING AVERAGE: SEASON

Player	BA	Year
1. Bill Lange	.389	1895
2. King Kelly	.388	1886
3. Rogers Hornsby	.380	1929
4. Heinie Zimmerman	.372	1912
5. Cap Anson	.371	1886
6. Riggs Stephenson	.367	1930
7. Riggs Stephenson	.362	1929

8. Jimmy Ryan	.361	1894
9. Kiki Cuyler	.360	1929
10. Bill Everitt	.358	1895

Batting Average: Career with Team

Player	BA	PA
1. Riggs Stephenson	.336	3,964
2. Bill Lange	.330	3,609
3. Cap Anson	.329	10,112
4. Kiki Cuyler	.325	4,195
5. Bill Everitt	.323	2,987
6. Hack Wilson	.322	3,719
7. King Kelly	.316	3,072
8. George Gore	.315	3,306
9. Frank Demaree	.309	2,922
Billy Herman	.309	6,166

Total Hits: Season

Player	H	Year
1. Rogers Hornsby	229	1929
2. Kiki Cuyler	228	1930
3. Billy Herman	227	1935
4. Woody English	214	1930
5. Frank Demaree	212	1936
6. Billy Herman	211	1936
7. Jigger Statz	209	1923
8. Hack Wilson	208	1930
9. Heinie Zimmerman	207	1912
10. Billy Herman	206	1932

Total Hits: Career with Team

Player	H	PA
1. Cap Anson	2,995	10,112
2. Ernie Banks	2,583	10,395
3. Billy Williams	2,510	9,504
4. Ryne Sandberg	2,385	9,276
5. Mark Grace	2,201	8,234
6. Stan Hack	2,193	8,506
7. Ron Santo	2,171	8,979
8. Jimmy Ryan	2,073	7,542
9. Sammy Sosa	1,985	7,898
10. Phil Cavarretta	1,927	7,509

Home Runs: Season

Player	HR	Year
1. Sammy Sosa	66	1998
2. Sammy Sosa	64	2001
3. Sammy Sosa	63	1999
4. Hack Wilson	56	1930
5. Sammy Sosa	50	2000
6. Andre Dawson	49	1987
Sammy Sosa	49	2002
8. Dave Kingman	48	1979
9. Ernie Banks	47	1958
10. Derrek Lee	46	2005

Home Runs: Career with Team

Player	HR	PA
1. Sammy Sosa	545	7,898
2. Ernie Banks	512	10,395
3. Billy Williams	392	9,504
4. Ron Santo	337	8,979
5. Ryne Sandberg	282	9,276
6. Gabby Hartnett	231	7,132
7. Bill Nicholson	205	5,614
8. Hank Sauer	198	3,566
9. Hack Wilson	190	3,719
10. Andre Dawson	174	3,520

Triples: Season

Player	3B	Year
1. Vic Saier	21	1913
Frank Schulte	21	1911
3. Bill Dahlen	19	1892
Bill Dahlen	19	1896
Ryne Sandberg	19	1984
6. Billy Herman	18	1939
7. Kiki Cuyler	17	1930
Woody English	17	1930
Jimmy Ryan	17	1897
Heinie Zimmerman	17	1911

Triples: Career with Team

Player	3B	PA
1. Jimmy Ryan	142	7,542
2. Cap Anson	124	10,112
3. Frank Schulte	117	6,602
4. Bill Dahlen	106	4,506
5. Phil Cavarretta	99	7,509
6. Joe Tinker	93	6,146
7. Ernie Banks	90	10,395
8. Billy Williams	87	9,504
9. Stan Hack	81	8,506
10. Bill Lange	80	3,609
Ned Williamson	80	4,522
Heinie Zimmerman	80	3,981

Doubles: Season

Player	2B	Year
1. Billy Herman	57	1935
Billy Herman	57	1936
3. Mark Grace	51	1995
4. Kiki Cuyler	50	1930
Derrek Lee	50	2005
6. Riggs Stephenson	49	1932
Ned Williamson	49	1883
8. Rogers Hornsby	47	1929
9. Riggs Stephenson	46	1927
10. Ray Grimes	45	1922
Walt Wilmot	45	1894

Doubles: Career with Team

Player	2B	PA
1. Cap Anson	528	10,112
2. Mark Grace	456	8,234
3. Ernie Banks	407	10,395
4. Ryne Sandberg	403	9,276
5. Billy Williams	402	9,504
6. Gabby Hartnett	391	7,132
7. Stan Hack	363	8,506
8. Jimmy Ryan	362	7,542
9. Ron Santo	353	8,979
10. Billy Herman	346	6,166

Extra-Base Hits: Season

Player	XBH	Year
1. Sammy Sosa	103	2001
2. Derrek Lee	99	2005
3. Hack Wilson	97	1930
4. Rogers Hornsby	94	1929
5. Sammy Sosa	89	1999
Sammy Sosa	89	2000
7. Sammy Sosa	86	1998
8. Ernie Banks	83	1957
9. Ernie Banks	82	1955
10. Ernie Banks	81	1958

Extra-Base Hits: Career with Team

Player	XBH	PA
1. Ernie Banks	1,009	10,395
2. Billy Williams	881	9,504
3. Sammy Sosa	873	7,898
4. Ryne Sandberg	761	9,276
5. Ron Santo	756	8,979
6. Cap Anson	749	10,112
7. Gabby Hartnett	686	7,132
8. Mark Grace	647	8,234
9. Jimmy Ryan	603	7,542
10. Phil Cavarretta	532	7,509

Total Bases: Season

Player	TB	Year
1. Sammy Sosa	425	2001
2. Hack Wilson	423	1930
3. Sammy Sosa	416	1998
4. Rogers Hornsby	409	1929
5. Sammy Sosa	397	1999
6. Derrek Lee	393	2005
7. Sammy Sosa	383	2000
8. Ernie Banks	379	1958
9. Billy Williams	373	1970
10. Billy Williams	356	1965

Total Bases: Career with Team

Player	TB	PA
1. Ernie Banks	4,706	10,395
2. Billy Williams	4,262	9,504
3. Cap Anson	4,062	10,112
4. Sammy Sosa	3,980	7,898
5. Ryne Sandberg	3,786	9,276
6. Ron Santo	3,667	8,979
7. Mark Grace	3,187	8,234
8. Gabby Hartnett	3,079	7,132
9. Jimmy Ryan	3,016	7,542
10. Stan Hack	2,889	8,506

Runs Batted In: Season

Player	RBI	Year
1. Hack Wilson	191	1930
2. Sammy Sosa	160	2001
3. Hack Wilson	159	1929
4. Sammy Sosa	158	1998
5. Rogers Hornsby	149	1929
6. Cap Anson	147	1886
7. Ernie Banks	143	1959
8. Sammy Sosa	141	1999
9. Sammy Sosa	138	2000
10. Andre Dawson	137	1987

Runs Batted In: Career with Team

Player	RBI	PA
1. Cap Anson	1,879	10,112
2. Ernie Banks	1,636	10,395
3. Sammy Sosa	1,414	7,898
4. Billy Williams	1,353	9,504
5. Ron Santo	1,290	8,979
6. Gabby Hartnett	1,153	7,132
7. Ryne Sandberg	1,061	9,276
8. Mark Grace	1,004	8,234
9. Jimmy Ryan	914	7,542
10. Phil Cavarretta	896	7,509

Runs Scored: Season

Player	R	Year
1. Rogers Hornsby	156	1929
2. Kiki Cuyler	155	1930
King Kelly	155	1886
4. Woody English	152	1930
5. George Gore	150	1886
6. Bill Dahlen	149	1894
7. Sammy Sosa	146	2001
Hack Wilson	146	1930
9. Hugh Duffy	144	1889
10. Jimmy Ryan	140	1889

Runs Scored: Career with Team

Player	R	PA
1. Cap Anson	1,719	10,112
2. Jimmy Ryan	1,409	7,542
3. Ryne Sandberg	1,316	9,276
4. Billy Williams	1,306	9,504
5. Ernie Banks	1,305	10,395
6. Sammy Sosa	1,245	7,898
7. Stan Hack	1,239	8,506
8. Ron Santo	1,109	8,979
9. Mark Grace	1,057	8,234
10. Phil Cavarretta	968	7,509

Walks: Season

Player	BB	Year
1. Jimmy Sheckard	147	1911
2. Jimmy Sheckard	122	1912
3. Richie Ashburn	116	1960
Sammy Sosa	116	2001
5. Cap Anson	113	1890
6. Johnny Evers	108	1910
7. Hack Wilson	105	1930
8. Gary Matthews	103	1984
Sammy Sosa	103	2002
10. George Gore	102	1886

Walks: Career with Team

Player	BB	PA
1. Stan Hack	1,092	8,506
2. Ron Santo	1,071	8,979
3. Cap Anson	952	10,112
4. Mark Grace	946	8,234
5. Billy Williams	911	9,504
6. Sammy Sosa	798	7,898
7. Phil Cavarretta	794	7,509
8. Ernie Banks	763	10,395
9. Ryne Sandberg	761	9,276
10. Bill Nicholson	696	5,614

Strikeouts: Season

Player	SO	Year
1. Sammy Sosa	174	1997
2. Sammy Sosa	171	1998
Sammy Sosa	171	1999
4. Corey Patterson	168	2004
Sammy Sosa	168	2000
6. Sammy Sosa	153	2001
7. Mark Bellhorn	144	2002
Sammy Sosa	144	2002
9. Byron Browne	143	1966
Sammy Sosa	143	2003

Strikeouts: Career with Team

Player	SO	PA
1. Sammy Sosa	1,815	7,898
2. Ron Santo	1,271	8,979
3. Ryne Sandberg	1,259	9,276
4. Ernie Banks	1,236	10,395
5. Billy Williams	934	9,504
6. Shawon Dunston	770	4,842
7. Bill Nicholson	684	5,614
8. Gabby Hartnett	683	7,132
9. Jody Davis	647	3,688
10. Don Kessinger	629	7,065

Slugging Percentage: Season

Player	SLG	Year
1. Sammy Sosa	.737	2001
2. Hack Wilson	.723	1930
3. Rogers Hornsby	.679	1929
4. Derrek Lee	.662	2005
5. Sammy Sosa	.647	1998
6. Sammy Sosa	.635	1999
7. Sammy Sosa	.634	2000
8. Gabby Hartnett	.630	1930
9. Hack Wilson	.618	1929
10. Ernie Banks	.614	1958

Slugging Percentage: Career with Team

Player	SLG	PA
1. Hack Wilson	.590	3,719
2. Sammy Sosa	.569	7,898

3. Hank Sauer	.512	3,566
4. Andre Dawson	.507	3,520
5. Billy Williams	.503	9,504
6. Ernie Banks	.500	10,395
7. Gabby Hartnett	.490	7,132
8. Kiki Cuyler	.485	4,195
9. Leon Durham	.484	3,659
10. Ron Santo	.472	8,979

On-Base Percentage: Season

Player	OBP	Year
1. King Kelly	.483	1886
2. Rogers Hornsby	.459	1929
3. Bill Lange	.456	1895
4. Hack Wilson	.454	1930
5. Frank Chance	.450	1905
6. Phil Cavarretta	.449	1945
7. Riggs Stephenson	.445	1929
8. Bill Dahlen	.444	1894
9. Cap Anson	.443	1890
10. Ray Grimes	.442	1922

On-Base Percentage: Career with Team

Player	OBP	PA
1. Hack Wilson	.412	3,719
2. Riggs Stephenson	.408	3,964
3. Bill Lange	.401	3,609
4. Cap Anson	.395	10,112
5. Stan Hack	.394	8,506
Frank Chance	.394	5,066
7. Kiki Cuyler	.391	4,195
8. Mark Grace	.386	8,234
George Gore	.386	3,306
10. Bill Dahlen	.384	4,506

OPS (On-Base Percentage + Slugging Percentage): Season

Player	OPS	Year
1. Hack Wilson	1.177	1930
2. Sammy Sosa	1.174	2001
3. Rogers Hornsby	1.139	1929
4. Derrek Lee	1.080	2005
5. Hack Wilson	1.044	1929
6. Sammy Sosa	1.040	2000
7. Gabby Hartnett	1.034	1930
8. Bill Lange	1.032	1895
9. Sammy Sosa	1.024	1998
10. King Kelly	1.018	1886

OPS (On-Base Percentage + Slugging Percentage): Career with Team

Player	OPS	PA
1. Hack Wilson	1.002	3,719
2. Sammy Sosa	.928	7,898
3. Riggs Stephenson	.877	3,964
4. Kiki Cuyler	.876	4,195
5. Billy Williams	.867	9,504
6. Hank Sauer	.860	3,566
Gabby Hartnett	.860	7,132
8. Bill Lange	.859	3,609
9. Leon Durham	.846	3,659
10. Cap Anson	.841	10,112

Stolen Bases: Season

Player	SB	Year
1. Bill Lange	84	1896
2. Walt Wilmot	76	1890
3. Walt Wilmot	74	1894
4. Bill Lange	73	1897
5. Frank Chance	67	1903
Bill Lange	67	1895
7. Bill Lange	65	1894
8. Fred Pfeffer	64	1888
9. Bill Dahlen	60	1892
Jimmy Ryan	60	1888

Stolen Bases: Career with Team

Player	SB	PA
1. Frank Chance	400	5,066
2. Bill Lange	399	3,609
3. Jimmy Ryan	369	7,542
4. Ryne Sandberg	344	9,276
5. Joe Tinker	304	6,146
6. Johnny Evers	291	5,634
7. Walt Wilmot	290	3,191
8. Bill Dahlen	285	4,506
9. Fred Pfeffer	263	4,628
10. Cap Anson	247	10,112

Sacrifice Hits: Season

Player	Sac	Year
1. Jimmy Sheckard	46	1909
2. Bob Fisher	42	1915
3. Jimmy Sheckard	40	1906
4. Max Flack	39	1916
Zeb Terry	39	1922
6. Charlie Hollocher	37	1922
Freddie Maguire	37	1928
8. Joe Tinker	36	1906
9. Jimmy Sheckard	35	1907
10. Charlie Deal	34	1920
Zeb Terry	34	1921
Joe Tinker	34	1912

Sacrifice Hits: Career with Team

Player	Sac	PA
1. Frank Schulte	263	6,602
2. Joe Tinker	246	6,146
3. Jimmy Sheckard	198	4,385
4. Johnny Evers	184	5,634
5. Solly Hofman	154	3,536
6. Charlie Hollocher	151	3,390
7. Charlie Grimm	144	5,465
Harry Steinfeldt	144	2,996
9. Billy Herman	140	6,166
10. Charlie Deal	126	2,373

Hit by Pitch: Season

Player	HBP	Year
1. Bill Dahlen	23	1898
2. Frank Chance	17	1905
3. Frank Chance	16	1904
4. Cliff Carroll	15	1891
Frank Chance	15	1900
6. Scott Servais	14	1996
Harry Steinfeldt	14	1906
8. Frank Chance	13	1907
9. Frank Chance	12	1906
Jerry Hairston	12	2005
Brian McRae	12	1996
Adolfo Phillips	12	1966

Hit by Pitch: Career with Team

Player	HBP	PA
1. Frank Chance	137	5,066
2. Ernie Banks	70	10,395
3. Bill Dahlen	68	4,506
4. Jimmy Ryan	64	7,542
5. Andy Pafko	48	3,995
6. Frank Schulte	47	6,602
7. Kiki Cuyler	44	4,195
Sammy Sosa	44	7,898
9. Bill Nicholson	43	5,614
Harry Steinfeldt	43	2,996

Top 10 Pitching Leaders, Single Season & Career with Team

GAMES PITCHED: SEASON

Player	GP	Year
1. Ted Abernathy	84	1965
Dick Tidrow	84	1980
3. Bill Campbell	82	1983
Jeff Fassero	82	2001
5. Rod Beck	81	1998
6. Bob Patterson	79	1996
7. Kyle Farnsworth	77	2003
LaTroy Hawkins	77	2004
9. Kyle Farnsworth	76	2001
Bob Patterson	76	1997
Mitch Williams	76	1989

GAMES PITCHED: CAREER WITH TEAM

Player	GP	IP
1. Charley Root	605	3,137.3
2. Lee Smith	458	681.3
3. Don Elston	449	754.7
4. Guy Bush	428	2,201.7
5. Fergie Jenkins	401	2,673.7
6. Bill Hutchison	367	3,021.0
7. Bill Lee	364	2,271.3
8. Rick Reuschel	358	2,290.0
9. Mordecai Brown	346	2,329.0
10. Kyle Farnsworth	343	478.7

INNINGS PITCHED: SEASON

Player	IP	Year
1. John Clarkson	623.0	1885
2. Bill Hutchison	622.0	1892
3. Bill Hutchison	603.0	1890
4. Bill Hutchison	561.0	1891
5. Larry Corcoran	536.3	1880
6. Al Spalding	528.7	1876
7. John Clarkson	523.0	1887
8. Larry Corcoran	516.7	1884
9. Terry Larkin	513.3	1879
10. Terry Larkin	506.0	1878

INNINGS PITCHED: CAREER WITH TEAM

Player	IP
1. Charley Root	3,137.3
2. Bill Hutchison	3,021.0
3. Fergie Jenkins	2,673.7
4. Larry Corcoran	2,338.3
5. Mordecai Brown	2,329.0
6. Rick Reuschel	2,290.0
7. Bill Lee	2,271.3
8. Hippo Vaughn	2,216.3
9. Guy Bush	2,201.7
10. Clark Griffith	2,188.7

BATTERS FACED: SEASON

Player	BF	Year
1. John Clarkson	2,487	1885
2. Al Spalding	2,219	1876
3. John Clarkson	2,183	1887
4. Larry Corcoran	2,180	1884
5. Terry Larkin	2,176	1879
6. Larry Corcoran	2,133	1880
7. Terry Larkin	2,105	1878
8. Larry Corcoran	2,041	1883
9. John Clarkson	1,914	1886
10. George Bradley	1,719	1877

BATTERS FACED: CAREER WITH TEAM

Player	BF	IP
1. Charley Root	13,266	3,137.3
2. Fergie Jenkins	10,898	2,673.7
3. Larry Corcoran	9,740	2,338.3
4. Rick Reuschel	9,679	2,290.0
5. Bill Lee	9,632	2,271.3
6. Guy Bush	9,506	2,201.7
7. Mordecai Brown	9,135	2,329.0
8. Hippo Vaughn	9,097	2,216.3
9. Bob Rush	9,058	2,132.7
10. Claude Passeau	8,063	1,914.7

GAMES STARTED: SEASON

Player	GS	Year
1. John Clarkson	70	1885
Bill Hutchison	70	1892
3. Bill Hutchison	66	1890
4. Larry Corcoran	60	1880
Al Spalding	60	1876
6. John Clarkson	59	1887
Larry Corcoran	59	1884
8. Bill Hutchison	58	1891
Terry Larkin	58	1879
10. Terry Larkin	56	1878

GAMES STARTED: CAREER WITH TEAM

Player	GS	IP
1. Fergie Jenkins	347	2,673.7
2. Rick Reuschel	343	2,290.0
3. Bill Hutchison	339	3,021.0
Charley Root	339	3,137.3
5. Bill Lee	296	2,271.3
6. Bob Rush	292	2,132.7
7. Greg Maddux	276	1,879.7
8. Hippo Vaughn	270	2,216.3
9. Larry Corcoran	262	2,338.3
10. Guy Bush	252	2,201.7
Clark Griffith	252	2,188.7

COMPLETE GAMES: SEASON

Player	CG	Year
1. John Clarkson	68	1885
2. Bill Hutchison	67	1892
3. Bill Hutchison	65	1890
4. Larry Corcoran	57	1880
Larry Corcoran	57	1884
Terry Larkin	57	1879
7. John Clarkson	56	1887
Bill Hutchison	56	1891
Terry Larkin	56	1878
10. Al Spalding	53	1876

COMPLETE GAMES: CAREER WITH TEAM

Player	CG	IP
1. Bill Hutchison	317	3,021.0
2. Larry Corcoran	252	2,338.3
3. Clark Griffith	240	2,188.7
4. Mordecai Brown	206	2,329.0
5. Jack Taylor	188	1,801.0
6. John Clarkson	186	1,730.7
7. Charley Root	177	3,137.3
Hippo Vaughn	177	2,216.3
9. Fred Goldsmith	164	1,516.7
10. Grover Alexander	159	1,884.3

Games Won: Season

Player	W	Year
1. John Clarkson	53	1885
2. Al Spalding	47	1876
3. Bill Hutchison	44	1891
4. Larry Corcoran	43	1880
5. Bill Hutchison	42	1890
6. John Clarkson	38	1887
7. John Clarkson	36	1886
Bill Hutchison	36	1892
9. Larry Corcoran	35	1884
10. Larry Corcoran	34	1883

Games Won: Career with Team

Player	W	IP
1. Charley Root	201	3,137.3
2. Mordecai Brown	188	2,329.0
3. Bill Hutchison	181	3,021.0
4. Larry Corcoran	175	2,338.3
5. Fergie Jenkins	167	2,673.7
6. Guy Bush	152	2,201.7
Clark Griffith	152	2,188.7
8. Hippo Vaughn	151	2,216.3
9. Bill Lee	139	2,271.3
10. John Clarkson	137	1,730.7

Games Lost: Season

Player	L	Year
1. Bill Hutchison	36	1892
2. Terry Larkin	26	1878
3. Bill Hutchison	25	1890
4. Bill Hutchison	24	1893
5. George Bradley	23	1877
Larry Corcoran	23	1884
Tom Hughes	23	1901
Terry Larkin	23	1879
9. Bill Bonham	22	1974
Dick Ellsworth	22	1966

Games Lost: Career with Team

Player	L	IP
1. Bill Hutchison	158	3,021.0
2. Charley Root	156	3,137.3
3. Bob Rush	140	2,132.7
4. Fergie Jenkins	132	2,673.7
5. Rick Reuschel	127	2,290.0
6. Bill Lee	123	2,271.3
7. Dick Ellsworth	110	1,613.3
8. Hippo Vaughn	105	2,216.3
9. Guy Bush	101	2,201.7
Greg Maddux	101	1,879.7

Winning Percentage: Season

Player	W%	Year
1. Rick Sutcliffe	.941	1984
2. Fred Goldsmith	.875	1880
3. King Cole	.833	1910
Jim McCormick	.833	1885
5. Ed Reulbach	.826	1906
6. Mordecai Brown	.812	1906
7. Ed Reulbach	.810	1907
8. Bert Humphries	.800	1913
9. Al Spalding	.797	1876
10. Jocko Flynn	.793	1886

Winning Percentage: Career with Team

Player	W%	IP
1. John Clarkson	.706	1,730.7
2. Mordecai Brown	.686	2,329.0
3. Ed Reulbach	.677	1,864.7
4. Larry Corcoran	.673	2,338.3
5. Orval Overall	.667	1,135.0
6. Bob Wicker	.646	726.3
7. Jack Pfiester	.636	1,028.3
8. Jake Weimer	.630	839.3
9. Fred Goldsmith	.629	1,516.7
10. Carl Lundgren	.623	1,322.0

Shutouts: Season

Player	SHO	Year
1. John Clarkson	10	1885
2. Grover Alexander	9	1919
Mordecai Brown	9	1906
Mordecai Brown	9	1908
Bill Lee	9	1938
Orval Overall	9	1909
7. Mordecai Brown	8	1909
Orval Overall	8	1907
Al Spalding	8	1876
Hippo Vaughn	8	1918

Shutouts: Career with Team

Player	SHO	IP
1. Mordecai Brown	48	2,329.0
2. Hippo Vaughn	35	2,216.3
3. Ed Reulbach	31	1,864.7
4. Fergie Jenkins	29	2,673.7
5. Orval Overall	28	1,135.0
6. Bill Lee	25	2,271.3
7. Grover Alexander	24	1,884.3
8. Larry Corcoran	22	2,338.3
Claude Passeau	22	1,914.7

10. Larry French	21	1,486.0
Bill Hutchison	21	3,021.0
Charley Root	21	3,137.3

ERA: Season

Player	ERA	Year
1. Mordecai Brown	1.04	1906
2. Jack Pfiester	1.15	1907
3. Carl Lundgren	1.17	1907
4. Mordecai Brown	1.31	1909
5. Jack Taylor	1.33	1902
6. Mordecai Brown	1.39	1907
7. Ed Reulbach	1.42	1905
Orval Overall	1.42	1909
9. Mordecai Brown	1.47	1908
10. Jack Pfiester	1.51	1906

ERA: Career with Team

Player	ERA	IP
1. Al Spalding	1.78	539.7
2. Mordecai Brown	1.80	2,329.0
3. Jack Pfiester	1.85	1,028.3
4. Orval Overall	1.91	1,135.0
5. Jake Weimer	2.14	839.3
6. Ed Reulbach	2.24	1,864.7
7. Larry Corcoran	2.26	2,338.3
8. Phil Douglas	2.29	636.7
9. Hippo Vaughn	2.33	2,216.3
10. Terry Larkin	2.34	1,019.3

Earned Runs Allowed: Season

Player	ER	Year
1. Bill Hutchison	191	1892
2. Bill Hutchison	187	1894
3. Bill Hutchison	184	1893
4. Bill Hutchison	181	1890
5. John Clarkson	179	1887
6. Bill Hutchison	175	1891
7. Adonis Terry	166	1895
8. Guy Bush	155	1930
Willie McGill	155	1893
10. Clark Griffith	154	1895

Earned Runs Allowed: Career with Team

Player	ER	IP
1. Charley Root	1,236	3,137.3
2. Bill Hutchison	1,196	3,021.0
3. Fergie Jenkins	952	2,673.7
4. Guy Bush	933	2,201.7

5. Rick Reuschel	891	2,290.0
6. Bill Lee	885	2,271.3
7. Bob Rush	878	2,132.7
8. Clark Griffith	826	2,188.7
9. Greg Maddux	737	1,879.7
10. Dick Ellsworth	663	1,613.3

Strikeouts: Season

Player	K	Year
1. Bill Hutchison	314	1892
2. John Clarkson	313	1886
3. John Clarkson	308	1885
4. Bill Hutchison	289	1890
5. Fergie Jenkins	274	1970
6. Fergie Jenkins	273	1969
7. Larry Corcoran	272	1884
8. Larry Corcoran	268	1880
9. Kerry Wood	266	2003
10. Fergie Jenkins	263	1971

Strikeouts: Career with Team

Player	K	IP
1. Fergie Jenkins	2038	2673.7
2. Charley Root	1432	3137.3
3. Rick Reuschel	1367	2290.0
4. Kerry Wood	1286	1109.0
5. Bill Hutchison	1224	3021.0
Greg Maddux	1224	1879.7
7. Hippo Vaughn	1138	2216.3
8. Larry Corcoran	1086	2338.3
9. Bob Rush	1076	2132.7
10. Mordecai Brown	1043	2329.0

Strikeouts Per Nine IP: Season

Player	K/9	Year
1. Kerry Wood	12.58	1998
2. Kerry Wood	11.35	2003
3. Kerry Wood	11.20	2001
4. Mark Prior	10.43	2003
5. Mark Prior	10.15	2005
6. Matt Clement	9.45	2004
7. Matt Clement	9.44	2002
8. Kerry Wood	9.14	2002
9. Dick Selma	8.59	1969
10. Sam Jones	8.40	1956

Strikeouts Per Nine IP: Career with Team

Player	K/9	IP
1. Mark Prior	10.55	613.3
2. Kerry Wood	10.44	1,109.0
3. Matt Clement	8.82	587.7
4. Lee Smith	8.51	681.3
5. Carlos Zambrano	7.73	763.0
6. Fergie Jenkins	6.86	2,673.7
7. Jon Lieber	6.67	827.7
8. Steve Trachsel	6.51	1,146.3
9. Rick Sutcliffe	6.46	1,267.3
10. Bill Bonham	6.33	1,152.3

Hits Allowed: Season

Player	HA	Year
1. Bill Hutchison	571	1892
2. Al Spalding	542	1876
3. Terry Larkin	514	1879
4. John Clarkson	513	1887
5. Terry Larkin	511	1878
6. Bill Hutchison	508	1891
7. Bill Hutchison	505	1890
8. John Clarkson	497	1885
9. Larry Corcoran	483	1883
10. Larry Corcoran	473	1884

Hits Allowed: Career with Team

Player	HA	IP
1. Charley Root	3,184	3,137.3
2. Bill Hutchison	3,054	3,021.0
3. Clark Griffith	2,445	2,188.7
4. Fergie Jenkins	2,402	2,673.7
5. Rick Reuschel	2,365	2,290.0
6. Guy Bush	2,354	2,201.7
7. Bill Lee	2,317	2,271.3
8. Larry Corcoran	2,084	2,338.3
9. Bob Rush	2,043	2,132.7
10. Hippo Vaughn	1,971	2,216.3

Hits Allowed Per Nine IP: Season

Player	H/9	Year
1. Ed Reulbach	5.33	1906
2. Carl Lundgren	5.65	1907
3. Mordecai Brown	6.17	1908
4. Jack Pfiester	6.21	1906
5. Kerry Wood	6.32	1998
6. Ed Reulbach	6.42	1905
7. Mordecai Brown	6.43	1906
8. Orval Overall	6.44	1909
9. Mordecai Brown	6.46	1909
10. Kerry Wood	6.48	2003

Hits Allowed Per Nine IP: Career with Team

Player	H/9	IP
1. Orval Overall	6.86	1,135.0
2. Kerry Wood	6.95	1,109.0
3. Ed Reulbach	7.04	1,864.7
4. Jack Pfiester	7.13	1,028.3
5. Mordecai Brown	7.26	2,329.0
6. Jake Weimer	7.31	839.3
7. Matt Clement	7.44	587.7
8. Carlos Zambrano	7.51	763.0
9. Larry Cheney	7.63	1,061.0
10. Carl Lundgren	7.69	1,322.0

Walks Allowed: Season

Player	BB	Year
1. Bill Hutchison	199	1890
2. Bill Hutchison	190	1892
3. Sam Jones	185	1955
4. Willie McGill	181	1893
5. Bill Hutchison	178	1891
6. Bill Hutchison	156	1893
7. Larry Cheney	140	1914
Bill Hutchison	140	1894
9. Danny Friend	139	1896
10. Adonis Terry	131	1895

Walks Allowed: Career with Team

Player	BB	IP
1. Bill Hutchison	1,109	3,021.0
2. Charley Root	871	3,137.3
3. Guy Bush	734	2,201.7
4. Bob Rush	725	2,132.7
5. Bill Lee	704	2,271.3
6. Sheriff Blake	661	1,455.3
7. Ed Reulbach	650	1,864.7
8. Rick Reuschel	640	2,290.0
9. Hippo Vaughn	621	2,216.3
10. Fergie Jenkins	600	2,673.7

Walks Allowed Per Nine IP: Season

Player	BB/9	Year
1. Al Spalding	0.44	1876
2. Terry Larkin	0.53	1879
3. Terry Larkin	0.55	1878

4. Fred Goldsmith	0.77	1880
5. Fred Goldsmith	0.84	1882
6. Grover Alexander	0.89	1923
George Bradley	0.89	1877
8. Fred Goldsmith	0.92	1883
9. Dennis Eckersley	1.01	1985
10. Fergie Jenkins	1.02	1971

Walks Allowed Per Nine IP: Career with Team

Player	BB/9	IP
1. Al Spalding	0.43	539.7
2. Terry Larkin	0.54	1,019.3
3. Fred Goldsmith	1.00	1,516.7
4. Grover Alexander	1.28	1,884.3
5. Bert Humphries	1.44	523.7
6. John Clarkson	1.56	1,730.7
7. Dennis Eckersley	1.66	530.7
Jon Lieber	1.66	827.7
9. Mordecai Brown	1.72	2,329.0
Phil Douglas	1.72	636.7

WHIP (Walks + Hits Per Nine IP): Season

Player	WHIP	Year
1. Mordecai Brown	0.842	1908
2. Mordecai Brown	0.873	1909
3. Grover Alexander	0.928	1919
4. Mordecai Brown	0.934	1906
5. Larry Corcoran	0.938	1880
6. Jack Pfiester	0.941	1906
7. Mordecai Brown	0.944	1907
8. Warren Hacker	0.946	1952
9. John Clarkson	0.953	1885
10. Ed Reulbach	0.963	1905

WHIP (Walks + Hits Per Nine IP): Career with Team

Player	WHIP	IP
1. Mordecai Brown	0.998	2,329.0
2. John Clarkson	1.053	1,730.7
3. Jack Pfiester	1.059	1,028.3
4. Terry Larkin	1.065	1,019.3
5. Phil Douglas	1.077	636.7
6. Orval Overall	1.078	1,135.0
7. Al Spalding	1.084	539.7
8. Larry Corcoran	1.089	2,338.3
9. Fergie Jenkins	1.123	2,673.7
10. Ed Reulbach	1.131	1,864.7

Home Runs Allowed: Season

Player	HRA	Year
1. Warren Hacker	38	1955
2. Jon Lieber	36	2000
3. Larry Corcoran	35	1884
Warren Hacker	35	1953
Fergie Jenkins	35	1973
Greg Maddux	35	2004
Kevin Tapani	35	2000
8. Dick Ellsworth	34	1964
9. Kevin Foster	32	1995
Fergie Jenkins	32	1972
Steve Trachsel	32	1997
Steve Trachsel	32	1999

Home Runs Allowed: Career with Team

Player	HRA	IP
1. Fergie Jenkins	271	2,673.7
2. Charley Root	183	3,137.3
3. Steve Trachsel	169	1,146.3
4. Dick Ellsworth	156	1,613.3
Warren Hacker	156	1,091.7
6. Bob Rush	153	2,132.7
7. Ken Holtzman	147	1,447.0
8. Greg Maddux	146	1,879.7
9. Rick Reuschel	140	2,290.0
10. Bill Hands	132	1,564.0

Saves: Season

Player	SV	Year
1. Randy Myers	53	1993
2. Rod Beck	51	1998
3. Randy Myers	38	1995
4. Bruce Sutter	37	1979
5. Lee Smith	36	1987
Mitch Williams	36	1989
7. Joe Borowski	33	2003
Ryan Dempster	33	2005
Lee Smith	33	1984
Lee Smith	33	1985

Saves: Career with Team

Player	SV	IP
1. Lee Smith	180	681.3
2. Bruce Sutter	133	493.3
3. Randy Myers	112	171.3
4. Don Elston	63	754.7
5. Phil Regan	60	392.0
6. Rod Beck	58	110.3
7. Mitch Williams	52	148.0
8. Joe Borowski	44	198.0
9. Charley Root	40	3,137.3
10. Ted Abernathy	39	258.3
Mordecai Brown	39	2,329.0
Lindy McDaniel	39	311.7

Wild Pitches: Season

Player	WP	Year
1. Mark Baldwin	41	1887
2. George Bradley	39	1877
3. Terry Larkin	37	1878
4. Jocko Flynn	28	1886
5. Larry Corcoran	27	1881
Larry Corcoran	27	1884
Bill Hutchison	27	1890
8. Larry Cheney	26	1914
9. John Clarkson	25	1887
Bill Hutchison	25	1891

Wild Pitches: Career with Team

Player	WP	IP
1. Bill Hutchison	120	3,021.0
2. Larry Corcoran	111	2,338.3
3. Larry Cheney	71	1,061.0
4. Rick Reuschel	66	2,290.0
5. John Clarkson	63	1,730.7
6. Rick Sutcliffe	60	1,267.3
7. Mark Baldwin	59	585.0
8. Ken Holtzman	57	1,447.0
Terry Larkin	57	1,019.3
10. Bill Bonham	54	1,152.3
Dick Ellsworth	54	1,613.3
Fred Goldsmith	54	1,516.7

Hit Batsmen: Season

Player	HB	Year
1. Nixey Callahan	24	1899
2. Nixey Callahan	22	1900
Jack Taylor	22	1899
4. Kerry Wood	21	2003
5. Clark Griffith	20	1898
Carlos Zambrano	20	2004
7. Ned Garvin	18	1900
Ed Reulbach	18	1905
Walter Thornton	18	1898
10. Mark Baldwin	17	1887
Danny Friend	17	1897
Clark Griffith	17	1897
Tom Hughes	17	1901

Hit Batsmen: Career with Team

Player	HB	IP
1. Ed Reulbach	85	1,864.7
2. Kerry Wood	80	1,109.0
3. Charley Root	73	3,137.3
4. Clark Griffith	67	2,188.7
5. Nixey Callahan	64	1,043.7
6. Hippo Vaughn	63	2,216.3
7. Jack Taylor	61	1,801.0
8. Greg Maddux	60	1,879.7
9. Rick Reuschel	59	2,290.0
10. Jimmy Lavender	53	1,078.0

Games Finished: Season

Player	GF	Year
1. Rod Beck	70	1998
2. Randy Myers	69	1993
3. Ted Abernathy	62	1965
4. Mitch Williams	61	1989
5. Phil Regan	60	1968
6. Joe Borowski	59	2003
Lee Smith	59	1984
Lee Smith	59	1986
9. Lee Smith	57	1985
10. Lee Smith	56	1983
Bruce Sutter	56	1979

Games Finished: Career with Team

Player	GF	IP
1. Lee Smith	342	681.3
2. Don Elston	240	754.7
3. Bruce Sutter	222	493.3
4. Phil Regan	181	392.0
5. Charley Root	170	3,137.3
6. Randy Myers	150	171.3
7. Turk Lown	127	661.7
8. Terry Adams	121	330.7
9. Dick Tidrow	120	397.0
10. Lindy McDaniel	114	311.7

The 1938 infield: first baseman Rip Collins, second baseman Billy Herman, shortstop Bill Jurges, and third baseman Stan Hack.

Significant Cubs

ALEXANDER, GROVER CLEVELAND ("PETE") (SP) (1918–1926)

See Phillies bio.

ANSON, CAP (1B/3B) (1876–1897)

Adrian "Cap" Anson, baseball's first superstar, had a 27-year career that included 22 seasons with Chicago's National League franchise. He batted over .300 in 24 of those years and was baseball's first member of the 3,000-hit club. He won two batting titles, eight RBI crowns, five fielding titles, and was the first player to hit three homers in a game and five homers in two consecutive games. Born in a log cabin in Marshalltown, Iowa, Anson began his career with the Forest Citys club of Rockford, Illinois, in the National Association. When William Hulbert organized his Chicago White Stockings team, Anson, like so many in that era, jumped to the new league for a pay increase from $66 a month to $2,000 for the season. Anson signed a multiyear contract that he soon tried to escape. It seems Anson had met and married a Philadelphia woman who had no intention of living in the "wild west," but Hulbert would have none of it. To show his displeasure, Anson played one game wearing formal trousers and a Prince Albert coat. Hulbert overlooked Anson's insubordinate display and the star first baseman soon warmed up to the idea of living in Chicago. By 1879 Anson had become the team's captain (hence his nickname, "Cap").

Anson was a great innovator of baseball strategy, employing the hit-and-run, signals, the platoon system, and pitching rotations. Anson, a big man at six feet, 230 pounds, was a strict disciplinarian who enforced his team rules, even if he had to do it with his fists. No one could argue with his success, as he won five pennants in seven years from 1880 to 1886. But Anson was a racist who had a significant impact on the game's long history of segregation. In an 1883 game in Toledo, Ohio, Anson's White Stockings were set to take the field when he noticed a black player, Moses Fleetwood Walker, in the opposition's lineup and threatened to take his team off the field if Walker played. The Toledo team threatened to withhold Chicago's take of the gate receipts and Anson backed down. Five years later, Anson's team was getting set to play Newark when he noticed they, too, had a black player—ace pitcher George Washington Stovey—scheduled to play that day. Again Anson refused to play, and this time the opposition backed down. The New York Giants were on the verge of signing Stovey, but after they received word of Anson's actions, they decided they didn't need the potential hassle with one of the game's most influential figures and dropped their plans to acquire Stovey. After the incident, the color barrier held firm until Jackie Robinson's arrival in the majors 59 years later.

Anson, who had 10 games with five or more hits to his credit, was a remarkable line-drive hitter who sprayed the ball to all fields. He virtually never swung at the first pitch and often waited until he had two strikes before he swung the bat. In 1885 Anson hit .423 as his White Stockings beat the American Association's St. Louis Browns in the World Series, three games to one. Both clubs repeated as league champions in 1886, so new White Stockings owner Al Spalding and Cap Anson challenged Browns owner Chris Von der Ahe to a best-of-seven "winner take all" championship series. Von der Ahe agreed and St. Louis won the Series, four games to two, taking home the entire $14,000 in gate receipts.

In the spring of 1886, Anson took his team to Hot Springs, Arkansas, to "sweat out all the beer and booze swilled all winter long" by his players. That same year Harry Wright took his Philadelphia team to Charleston, South Carolina. Together they are credited with originating the idea of spring training. Anson signed a 10-year contract in 1888, but he won no more championships, and in 1897 he was let go. The move so outraged Chicago fans that they began calling the team "the Orphans" instead of the White Stockings, since for 22 years they had known only Anson as the team leader. Anson moved on to manage the Giants, but that lasted less than a month. In 1900 Anson participated in the genesis of another major league, a new American Association to replace the one that had gone belly up after the 1891 season. But when the National League threatened a war, and other financial problems developed, Anson, the new league's president, suddenly and arbitrarily scrapped the whole undertaking. In 1905 he was elected Chicago City Clerk, but his office came under official investigation and he was defeated in the 1907 election. Anson turned to managing a semipro team and touring the vaudeville circuit with his daughters, but he ultimately failed at these enterprises and had to declare bankruptcy. When the National League tried to come to his financial aid, he refused. When the job of baseball commissioner was first being discussed in the press, Anson had visions of winning the position, but the job went to Judge Kenesaw Mountain Landis. Anson ran a golf course for his remaining years, and when he died in 1922, the National League paid for his funeral. Cap Anson, who collected 3,418 lifetime hits, was elected to the Hall of Fame in 1939.

CAREER CUBS RECORD:

Games	AB	Hits	Runs
2,276	9,101	2,995	1,719
Avg	**HR**	**RBI**	**SB**
.329	97	1,879	247

BANKS, ERNIE (1B/SS) (1953–1971)

"Mr. Cub" was discovered playing for the Kansas City Monarchs of the old Negro Leagues and signed as an amateur free agent in 1953. A two-time National League MVP (1958 and 1959) and 11-time All-Star, Ernie Banks played his entire 19-year career with the Cubs, but never made it to the postseason. A durable player, he led the league six times in games played. Banks, always smiling and in good spirits, was an unusual player in his day: a shortstop with power, and lots of it. The always-positive Banks, who retired with 512 homers and 1,636 RBIs, is best remembered for his famous line, "It's a great day for a ball game. Let's play two." Banks was a tough, focused hitter. In 1957 he was knocked down by only four pitchers—Don Drysdale, Bob Friend, Jack Sanford, and Bob Purkey—and each time he got up, dusted himself off, and hit a home run on the very next pitch. Banks was such a potent offensive force at one time that St. Louis owner August Busch offered Cubs owner P. K. Wrigley $500,000 for the shortstop.

With his fielding abilities beginning to slip by the early 1960s, Banks was moved to first base. By the mid-1960s, Banks had become a liability to the team, but manager Leo Durocher, aware of Banks's tremendous popularity in Chicago, didn't dare take him out of the lineup. Banks eventually read the tea leaves and retired after the 1971 season. In a fan vote, the infectiously friendly Banks was voted the "Greatest Cub of All Time." In 1977 he was elected to the Hall of Fame. After leaving baseball, Banks became involved first in banking in the Chicago area, then later moved to Los Angeles, where he undertook a career placing products in movies. Later he became an executive with a moving company.

CAREER CUBS RECORD:

Games	AB	Hits	Runs
2,528	9,421	2,583	1,305
Avg	**HR**	**RBI**	**SB**
.274	512	1,636	50

BROWN, MORDECAI (SP/RP)
(1904–1912, 1916)

Mordecai "Three Finger" Brown was one of the best pitchers in the history of the game. He got his nickname as the result of two boyhood accidents on the family's Indiana farm. When he was seven years old, Brown lost his index finger after sticking it too far into a corn grinder. Then, with his hand still in a cast, he fell while chasing a hog and broke two more of his fingers. When they healed, the fingers were bent and twisted in an unnatural way. This hand deformity allowed him to put unusual pressure on a baseball that caused it to drop straight down, as if it had been rolled off a table.

From 1906 to 1911, Brown won 20 or more games, four times winning 25 or more. Six times in his career he had an ERA below 2.00, and he finished with a career ERA of 2.06, third best in major league history, trailing only Ed Walsh (1.82) and Addie Joss (1.89). From 1906 to 1910, the Cubs won four pennants in five years, and Brown was instrumental in all of them. In 1906, when the Cubs won 116 games, Brown was 26–6 with nine shutouts and a 1.04 ERA, the second lowest ERA in the 20th century. In 1908 the Cubs and Giants finished the season in a tie and had to play a one-game sudden death playoff to see who would go to the World Series. (The Giants should have won the pennant outright that year, but Giants first baseman Fred Merkle had made a baserunning error in an earlier game between the two teams that cost New York a certain win that was later ruled a tie game by the league office. The baserunning gaffe came to be known as Merkle's Boner because it ultimately cost the Giants the pennant.) In the one-game tiebreaker, Christy Mathewson was on the mound for the Giants against Jack "the Giant Killer" Pfiester of the Cubs. Pfiester, who had a history of beating the Giants, gave up three hits and two walks to the first five batters, allowing two runs. With the bases loaded and no outs, Mordecai Brown just walked to the mound without saying a word to Chicago manager Frank Chance, and took the ball from Pfiester. Without even warming up, Brown stopped the Giants cold, shutting them out for the remainder of the game, and the Cubs rallied for a 4–2 win, Brown's 29th of the season and ninth straight win against Mathewson. Brown then won two games in the World Series as the Cubs beat the Tigers in five games.

The Cubs often used Brown in relief, and from 1908 to 1911 he led the league in saves each year while posting 102 wins as a starter in the same four-year stretch. After six consecutive years of 20+ wins, Brown developed arm trouble in 1912 that limited him to a 5–6 record. He was released after the season and spent the next four years playing for five teams, including a second short stint with the Cubs in 1916 before calling it quits. After his major league career was over, Brown played and managed in the minors for four years before leaving baseball for good. He then ran a gas station in Indiana for 25 years and died in 1948, one year before he was elected to the Hall of Fame.

CAREER CUBS RECORD:

W	L	W%	ERA	SV
188	86	.686	1.80	39
K	**BB**	**SHO**	**IP**	
1,043	445	48	2,329.0	

CHANCE, FRANK (1B/C)
(1898–1912)

A career .296 hitter, Frank Chance had uncommon speed for a first baseman, stealing 401 bases during his career. He became the Cubs' regular first baseman in 1903 and took over the player-manager duties in mid-1905. In 1906 he led the Cubs to a 116–36 record (the most wins ever in the National League and tied for the most ever with the 2001 Seattle Mariners), though the crosstown rival White Sox surprised the heavily favored Cubs in the World Series with a six-game upset. In his eight seasons as manager, Chance led the Cubs to four pennants and two World Series titles. As a hitter, he batted over .300 four times and twice led the league in stolen bases.

Chance's last season as a regular player was 1908, when his health began to decline. Notorious for crowding the plate, Chance had received many beanings during his career. By 1909 he was suffering from blinding headaches and loss of hearing, so he played less and less over the remaining six years of his career. By 1912 Chance was engaged in an ongoing feud with owner Charles Murphy over the team's lack of spending on quality players, and Chance was let go at the end of the season. After undergoing offseason surgery on the blood clots that were the suspected cause of his headaches, Chance signed on as manager of the Yankees but was fired after two poor finishes. Nine years later, in 1923, Chance returned to manage the Red Sox for a year, but was fired after a last-place finish. He was hired as the new manager of the White Sox, but fell ill before taking the job and died during the 1924 season. Chance was elected to the Hall of Fame in 1946 with teammates Joe Tinker and Johnny Evers. The trio's fielding genius was immortalized in F.P. Adams' poem, "Baseball's Sad Lexicon," a brief verse that first appeared in the *New York Globe.*

CAREER CUBS RECORD:

Games	AB	Hits	Runs
1,274	4,273	1,268	794
Avg	**HR**	**RBI**	**SB**
.297	20	590	400

CLARKSON, JOHN (SP)
(1884–1887)

John Clarkson played only four years of his 12-year career with Chicago, but he won 137 games for them, 127 coming in just three seasons. During his career, Clarkson had five consecutive 30-win seasons, including a career-best 53 wins for Chicago in 1885, the second-highest victory total in major league history, trailing only Charles Radbourn's 59 wins in 1884. That year he also completed 68 games, had a 1.85 ERA, and tossed a no-hitter against future Hall of Famer Radbourn's Providence team, 4–0.

Clarkson, who had two brothers in the majors (Arthur and Walter), had a sense of humor. While on the mound during a game in which the skies became very dark, Clarkson sought to have the game called on account of darkness. When the umpire refused, Clarkson was miffed, but he had a plan. He had one of the other players bring him a lemon from the dugout and on a subsequent pitch, he tossed the lemon instead of the baseball. When the umpire called it a strike, the catcher turned and showed the lemon to the ump, who promptly called the game.

After the 1887 season, Clarkson's fourth in Chicago, the pitcher demanded to be sold to Boston so he could be closer to home. The team agreed to his demand and sold him to the Red Stockings in 1888 for $10,000, equaling the $10,000 record amount paid for King Kelly a year earlier. After four-plus fine seasons with Boston (149–82) and two-plus mediocre seasons with Cleveland (41–37), Clarkson retired at the age of 32 with a dead arm, the result of overuse, a common fate suffered by many 19th- and early 20th-century pitchers. Three times he had pitched over 500 innings in a season, and twice over 600. He died at 47 from pneumonia and in 1963 he was elected to the Hall of Fame.

CAREER CUBS RECORD:

W	L	W%	ERA	SV
137	57	.706	2.39	0

K	BB	SHO	IP
960	300	15	1,730.7

CORCORAN, LARRY (SP)
(1880–1885)

From 1880 to 1884, Larry Corcoran was one of the best pitchers in baseball, winning 170 games for Chicago. He won over 30 games in four of those five years, including a career-high 43 in his rookie season, the most ever by a first-year player. (Al Spalding had 47 wins and George Bradley 45 in their first National League seasons, but both had prior major league experience in the National Association during the 1870s.) Corcoran reeled off 13 straight wins in 1880 and threw a no-hitter against Boston on August 19, winning 6–0. An excellent fielder, Corcoran often played shortstop or in the outfield when he wasn't pitching. On September 20, 1882, he became the first major league pitcher to throw two no-hitters when he beat Worcester, 5–0. On June 27, 1884, Corcoran threw his third no-hitter, this time beating Providence 6–0.

Corcoran and catcher Silver Flint were among the first batteries to use signs. Corcoran would park his tobacco chaw on one side of his mouth if he intended on throwing a fastball, and on the other side of his mouth if he were going to throw a curveball. In 1885 he started the season 5–2, but strained his shoulder so badly he was unable to pitch and he was released. The Giants picked him up late in the season, but he was able to pitch only three games. He tried coming back twice for Washington and Indianapolis, both National League teams, in 1886 and 1887, but managed to pitch only two games for each team, compiling an 0–3 record before giving up on his dead arm for good. He tried his hand at umpiring in 1890, but died in 1891 of Bright's disease at the age of 32.

CAREER CUBS RECORD:

W	L	W%	ERA	SV
175	85	.673	2.26	2

K	BB	SHO	IP
1,086	462	22	2,338.3

CUYLER, KIKI (OF)
(1928–1935)

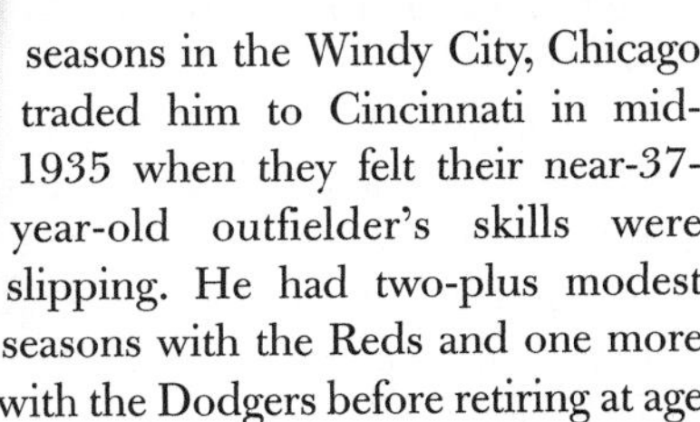

After establishing himself as an emerging star with the Pirates, Cuyler came to the Cubs after falling into disfavor with Pittsburgh's manager and owner. With the Cubs, Cuyler became a full-fledged star, hitting over .300 five times and leading the National League in steals three straight years (1928–1930). Cuyler helped the Cubs to the 1929 World Series, batting .360 during the regular season and .300 in the Fall Classic, though the Cubbies lost to the A's. Though Cuyler was a steady producer for the Cubs during his seven-plus seasons in the Windy City, Chicago traded him to Cincinnati in mid-1935 when they felt their near-37-year-old outfielder's skills were slipping. He had two-plus modest seasons with the Reds and one more with the Dodgers before retiring at age 40. Cuyler was elected to the Hall of Fame in 1968. *(See Pirates bio.)*

CAREER CUBS RECORD:

Games	AB	Hits	Runs
949	3,687	1,199	665

Avg	HR	RBI	SB
.325	79	602	161

EVERS, JOHNNY (2B)
(1902–1913)

Johnny Evers, known more for his fielding than his hitting, spent the first 12 years of his 18-year career with the Cubs. Evers was disliked by many of those who knew him, especially players, managers, umpires, and reporters. Though they played side by side, Evers and shortstop Joe Tinker didn't speak to each other for many years after a disagreement over a cab fare. He was particularly caustic towards umpires, resulting in many ejections and suspensions. Chicago owner Charles Murphy once offered to buy Evers a new suit if he could go even two weeks without getting thrown out of a game. Evers managed to collect the prize, then was thrown out of the very next game. In 1909

Evers, who often went to sleep at night reading baseball's rulebook, got into a major argument with umpire Bill Klem. The two of them agreed to let the league president settle the matter in his office. "I'll bet you five bucks you don't show up," said Evers. Klem accepted the bet but, as Evers predicted, did not show up for the meeting in the league's office. Klem didn't pay up, and after that, whenever Evers played in a game umpired by Klem, Evers would loudly boast about the five bucks Klem owed him and draw a large number five in the dirt in front of home plate with his bat every time he came to the plate. Finally, on a train between major league cities, the two men met and Klem paid Evers the $5, but he made Evers write him a receipt. After he got his receipt, Klem tore it into pieces in front of Evers.

In the famous "Merkle Boner" game of 1908, it was Evers who brought it to the attention of the umpires that Merkle hadn't actually touched second base on the force play and, with a ball he had rounded up, touched the base to make the force out. Evers endured an especially bad year off the field in 1910. He was the driver in an automobile accident that killed his best friend; he lost his life's savings in a bad business venture; his daughter died; he caught pneumonia; and he suffered a nervous breakdown. After playing very little in 1911, he returned in 1912 to have the best season of his career, hitting .341. He became the Cubs' player-manager in 1913 and led the team to a third-place finish before being traded to the Braves in 1914. That year he helped the "Miracle Braves" win a surprise pennant and an unexpected World Series victory over the heavily favored Philadelphia A's. He won the NL MVP Award for his efforts. That was the last good year for Evers. He played five more seasons as a part-time player for several teams before retiring to operate his own sporting goods store. In 1938 he appeared on a radio show, unaware that Joe Tinker was scheduled to be on the same show. When the two saw each other, they fell into each other's arms and began to sob, speaking to each other for the first time in nearly 30 years. Evers was elected to the Hall of Fame in 1946, the same year as Tinker and first baseman Frank Chance.

CAREER CUBS RECORD:

Games	AB	Hits	Runs
1,409	4,858	1,340	742
Avg	**HR**	**RBI**	**SB**
.276	9	448	291

GRACE, MARK (1B)
(1988–2000)

The Chicago Cubs drafted Mark Grace in the 24th round of the June 1985 amateur draft and brought him up to the majors in 1988, when he immediately became the team's starting first baseman. A true gentleman and fan favorite, Grace was a fine fielder who won four Gold Gloves. In 1990 he set a new National League record with 180 assists. He was also an accomplished hitter, hitting over .300 nine times in his 13 seasons with the Cubs. During the 1990s, Grace led all major league players with 1,754 hits and 364 doubles. The three-time All-Star left Chicago via free agency following the 2000 season and played three years with the Arizona Diamondbacks before retiring after the 2003 campaign, which saw his skills rapidly diminish.

CAREER CUBS RECORD:

Games	AB	Hits	Runs
1,910	7,156	2,201	1,057
Avg	**HR**	**RBI**	**SB**
.308	148	1,004	67

GRIFFITH, CLARK (SP)
(1893–1900)

During his 64-year major league career, Clark Griffith won 237 games as a major league pitcher, then 1,491 games as a manager, before becoming an influential owner. After spending the 1891 season with Boston and St. Louis in the American Association, Griffith moved to the Pacific Coast League (which in those days was every bit as good as the major leagues), where he put together a 30–18 record with Oakland. While there, Griffith helped organize a player strike when they weren't getting paid on time. He came to Chicago for four games at the end of 1893 and by 1894 was in the starting rotation, where he won 21 games, the first of six straight 20-win seasons with the Colts (now Cubs). Griffith's best pitch was his screwball, which he claimed to have invented. He also liked the scuffball, a pitch made possible by scraping the ball on one's spikes—entirely legal in those days. Famed Chicago sportswriter Hugh Fullerton (who got much of his fame when the Black Sox scandal hit in late 1920) once called Griffith the smartest pitcher in baseball. It was said of Griffith that he could, from the dugout or stands, accurately call 97 percent of the pitches that would be thrown.

When the American League was formed in 1901, Griffith, at American League president Ban Johnson's urging, jumped to the crosstown rival White Sox. As their player-manager, he became the staff ace, winning 24 games and leading the team to the first-ever American League pennant. After two seasons with the White Sox, Griffith moved to New York, again at Ban Johnson's request, to take over the New York Highlanders (now Yankees). He stayed with New York until mid-1908, when he left the team after a series of long, ongoing battles with the team's owners. By this time he was doing more managing than playing. From 1909 to 1911 he managed the Cincinnati Reds, then returned to the AL in 1912 as manager of the Washington Senators. He bought the team in 1920, and in 1960, the franchise moved to Minnesota, where it became the Twins. His son Calvin sold the Twins in 1984, after more than six decades of family ownership.

CAREER CUBS RECORD:

W	L	W%	ERA	SV
152	96	.613	3.40	1

K	BB	SHO	IP
573	517	9	2,188.7

HACK, STAN (3B)
(1932–1947)

Stan Hack played 16 seasons in the major leagues, all with the Cubs. It was once said of Hack that he was so popular, he had more friends than Leo Durocher had enemies. Hack was Chicago's leadoff hitter for more than a decade, and he was especially good at drawing walks, receiving nearly 1,100 of them during his career. He rarely struck out, and from 1936 to 1941, he scored more than 100 runs each year. A durable player who rarely missed more than a handful of games a year, Hack led the league in steals twice (and came in second three other times) and hits twice. Hack was an excellent fielder, leading the league in assists, chances per game, putouts, fielding average, and double plays on numerous occasions during his career. Hack, a five-time All-Star, retired after the 1943 season following a number of disagreements with manager Jimmie Wilson. When Wilson was fired in mid-1944, Hack returned and played four more seasons with the Cubs. In 1945 he played 54 straight errorless games at third base, hit .323, and scored 110 runs as the Cubs won their last pennant to date.

After ending his playing career a second time in 1947, Hack spent half a dozen years as a minor league manager before being named manager of the Cubs in 1954. As manager, Hack began the odd habit of starting each game as the team's third-base coach, then, after the first inning, returning to the dugout for the remainder of the game. After three years as Chicago's manager, Hack was fired and spent the next decade or so as a major league coach and minor league manager.

CAREER CUBS RECORD:

Games	AB	Hits	Runs
1,938	7,278	2,193	1,239
Avg	**HR**	**RBI**	**SB**
.301	57	642	165

HARTNETT, GABBY (C)
(1922–1940)

Charles Hartnett was dubbed "Gabby" in his rookie year by sarcastic sportswriters, frustrated that they couldn't get the young catcher to talk about anything. (Maybe he wouldn't open up because some of them called him by his other nickname, "Old Tomato Face," which he'd earned because of his ruddy complexion.) Hartnett played 19 of his 20 years with the Cubs, becoming the first catcher to reach the 200-homer and 1,000-RBI plateaus. He won six fielding titles during his career, including four straight from 1934–1937, tied for best in National League history. Hartnett also holds the NL record for double plays by a catcher. Six times during his career he topped .300, including 1935, when he won the National League MVP Award with a .344 average. In 1937 he fashioned a 26-game hitting streak on his way to a .354 average. Hartnett was named the starting catcher for the National League in the first five All-Star Games.

The Cubs won four NL pennants during his tenure (1929, 1932, 1935, 1938), but never a World Series. In 1938 he took over as player-manager midway through the season and brought the Cubs back from the doldrums to a first-place finish over the Pirates, a comeback highlighted by a three-game sweep of Pittsburgh in the next-to-last series of the season to finish just two games in front of the Bucs. Hartnett's game-winning homer in the last inning of the second game became known as "the home run in the gloamin'" because of the dark, foggy conditions under which he hit it. After three years as Chicago's player-manager, Hartnett was released in 1940. He played one final year as a player-coach for the Giants before retiring. After five years as a minor league manager, Hartnett returned to the majors for a couple years as a scout and coach with the A's, but left baseball for good in 1966 after repeated run-ins with Kansas City manager Alvin Dark. In 1955 he was elected to the Hall of Fame.

CAREER CUBS RECORD:

Games	AB	Hits	Runs
1,926	6,282	1,867	847
Avg	**HR**	**RBI**	**SB**
.297	231	1,153	28

HERMAN, BILLY (2B)
(1931–1941)

Second baseman Billy Herman was an intelligent player who helped the Cubs win three pennants during his 10-plus seasons with the team. He hit over .300 seven times with the Cubs (nine times overall), and led the league in doubles, triples, and hits once each. Herman was an excellent fielder, too, leading the NL in fielding average three times, double plays four times, and putouts and games played seven times each. Herman excelled in All-Star Game play, hitting .433 in his 10 All-Star appearances, a National League record.

In 1941 the Cubs had a new manager, Jimmie Wilson, who was somewhat paranoid that if he didn't live up to expectations, the Cubs front office might replace him as manager with Herman. Wilson convinced the Cubs to trade Herman to the Dodgers, ostensibly to make room for rookie second baseman Lou Stringer, whom Wilson touted. So, on May 6, 1941, the Cubs traded Herman to the Dodgers for two players and $65,000 cash. GM Larry MacPhail, still hardly believing his good fortune in getting Herman, bragged to the press, "I've just bought the pennant." Herman indeed helped the Dodgers to their first pennant in 21 years, though he tore a rib cage muscle in the Series and missed most of it as the Yankees took the Dodgers in five games. After spending three-plus seasons with the Dodgers, Herman was sent to the Braves after a heated argument over a $30 hotel bill for damages he claimed were not his. In 1947 he moved on to Pittsburgh as their player-manager for a year before leaving the major leagues. Herman came back later to coach for the Dodgers and Braves before taking the job as Red Sox manager in 1965 and 1966, guiding Boston to two consecutive ninth-place finishes. In 1975 he was elected to the Hall of Fame.

CAREER CUBS RECORD:

Games	AB	Hits	Runs
1,344	5,532	1,710	875
Avg	**HR**	**RBI**	**SB**
.309	37	577	53

HUTCHISON, BILL (SP)
(1889–1895)

The son of a famous minister, Bill Hutchison played briefly for the Kansas City Cowboys of the Union Association—a one-year major league—before playing semipro ball for several years. Disenchanted, he left baseball to open businesses in the lumber and railroad industries. After his business ventures failed, he returned to baseball and eventually became its highest-paid player. "Wild Bill" Hutchison joined the Chicago team in 1889, compiling a 16–17 record. He drew a lot of attention in 1890 when he won 42 games for Cap Anson's team. Reporters and other players were amazed to discover that he actually worked out during the offseason, something that endeared him to Anson. After winning 44 games in 1891 and 36 more in 1892, Hutchison was on top of the world. From 1890 to 1892, Hutchison averaged 41 wins and 595 innings, leading the league in wins, games started, complete games, and innings pitched. But in 1893 the pitcher's box was moved back

10 feet in an effort to help the offense. While some pitchers adjusted nicely, others did not. Hutchison was one of those who did not, and his performance plummeted. His ERA doubled over the next three seasons and he had a losing record each year. Frustrated, he quit baseball after the 1895 season and returned to the railroad business. In 1897 he made a brief but failed comeback attempt with St. Louis before retiring for good.

CAREER CUBS RECORD:

W	L	W%	ERA	SV
181	158	.534	3.56	4
K	**BB**	**SHO**	**IP**	
1,224	1,109	21	3,021.0	

JENKINS, FERGUSON (SP/RP)
(1966–1973, 1982–1983)

After little more than a season with the Philadelphia Phillies, Ferguson Jenkins was traded to the Cubs along with John Herrnstein and Adolfo Phillips for Larry Jackson and Bob Buhl on April 21, 1966. Over the remainder of the season, Jenkins started 12 games and relieved in 49, but in 1967 the Cubs, in a brilliant move, made Jenkins a full-time starter. He won 20 or more games for six straight years, becoming one of the best pitchers in baseball from 1967 to 1972, and causing much gnashing of teeth in Philadelphia. Jenkins was often overlooked and always overshadowed by other National League pitchers of the era—Sandy Koufax, Juan Marichal, Bob Gibson, and Tom Seaver, among others. Jenkins recognition was also affected by the fact that in 19 major league seasons, he never once pitched in the World Series. In spite of his 20-victory seasons, Jenkins was somewhat of a tough-luck pitcher, losing 13 1–0 games and 45 games by shutouts during his career, both numbers among the top six of all time. In 1968 alone, he lost five 1–0 games, yet still went 20–15. With just a smidgeon of offense, he could have been 25–10 that year.

During Jenkins' six-year run of 20-win seasons, he averaged 306 innings pitched per year, a healthy number in the modern era. He also finished about three out of every four games he started, a phenomenal number for his time. In 1971 the three-time All-Star won his only Cy Young Award, going 24–13 with a 2.77 ERA. He also hit six homers to help his own cause. One intangible often overlooked when considering Jenkins' career is that he pitched half his games during the day in cozy Wrigley Field, an environment that gives hitters the upper hand. After falling to 14–16 with a career-high (up to then) ERA of 3.89 in 1973, the Cubs felt their 30-year-old ace had seen his best days and traded him to Texas for Vic Harris and Bill Madlock. The Cubs, as it happened, had made a mistake. *(See Rangers bio.)*

CAREER CUBS RECORD:

W	L	W%	ERA	SV
167	132	.559	3.20	6
K	**BB**	**SHO**	**IP**	
2,038	600	29	2,673.7	

KELLY, KING (OF/C)
(1880–1886)

Simply put, Michael Joseph "King" Kelly was a stud, but a current-day baseball fan might not realize it without a close examination of Kelly's stats. A hard-drinking player who always dressed immaculately when he went out in public, Kelly had a keen eye for the ladies and rarely slept in his own bed. For Kelly, life was baseball during the day and parties at night. He played many different positions during his career, though mostly outfield and catcher. After two seasons in Cincinnati, Kelly signed with Cap Anson's White Stockings in 1880.

From 1880 to 1886, Kelly helped Anson win five pennants in seven years. He was an incredible run-producing machine. In 1884, for example, he scored 120 runs and knocked in 95—in a season that was only 112 games long. In 1885 he scored 125 runs, again in a 112-game season. In 1886 he scored 155 runs in a 124-game season (and he played in just 118 games). If you prorate these numbers over a 162-game season, he would fall somewhere between 180–200 runs scored each year. Consider, too, his base-stealing prowess. Stolen bases weren't accurately recorded until 1886, when he had 53, a year when Kelly had crested the hill of his productive years and was on the down side of his career. Still, he followed this up with 84, 56, 68, and 51 steals in his next four seasons. It would be very interesting to know what kind of numbers he put up from 1878 to 1885 during his prime. Kelly was such a prolific base stealer the fans would yell, "Slide, Kelly, slide!" The chant was even turned into a popular song in its day.

After hitting .388 in 1886, King Kelly, one of baseball's first true superstars, was sold to Boston for $10,000 (a record amount at the time), a move that stunned and angered Chicago fans. No player of Kelly's stature had ever been sold before. In 1887 the angry Chicago fans orchestrated a boycott of White Stockings games, turning out in large numbers only when Kelly and his Boston Beaneaters were in town. In 1890 the players revolted, forming their own Players' League. Kelly was offered huge money to stay in Boston, but he sided with the players and jumped to the new league. He managed the Boston franchise to the PL pennant and hit .326, playing catcher and shortstop. But Kelly's body began to quickly deteriorate, the years of drinking taking their toll. After playing poorly for four different teams in the next three years, Kelly retired at age 35. He opened a saloon in New York, which failed, then undertook a vaudeville act, reciting Ernest Thayer's "Casey at the Bat." While on his way to Boston in 1894 for an appearance at the Palace Theater, Kelly took ill with pneumonia. As he was being carried into the hospital, the attendants slipped and dumped Kelly on the floor. "That's my last slide," he told them prophetically. A few days later he was dead at the age of 36. King Kelly was elected to the Hall of Fame in 1945.

CAREER CUBS RECORD:

Games	AB	Hits	Runs
681	2,843	899	728
Avg	**HR**	**RBI**	**SB**
.316	33	480	53

LANGE, BILL (OF)
(1893–1899)

Outfielder Bill Lange was one of the best players of the 19th century and, had his career not ended unexpectedly after just seven seasons, he likely would have gone down as one of the best players of all time. A.H. Spink, publisher of *The Sporting News,* later called Lange the equal of Ty Cobb. There were many legendary stories about Lange, including one in which he supposedly ran right through an outfield fence and caught a fly ball on the other side for an out. He was one of the fastest players of his day, stealing 399 bases during his seven-year career, all of which was spent playing for Cap Anson in Chicago. Lange was one of Chicago's players known as "the Dawn Patrol," a group of players who routinely stayed out all night enjoying Chicago's nightlife. The late-night lifestyle apparently did not affect Lange's performance. In 1895 he batted .389 with 98 RBIs, 120 runs, and 67 stolen bases in just 123 games. Lange hit over .300 in all but his rookie season, scoring 689 runs and knocking in 589 more in his seven seasons, truly prodigious totals for the 19th century.

At the age of 28, Lange abruptly left baseball. He had fallen in love with a young woman whose father was a wealthy San Francisco real estate tycoon. Her father declared that he would never allow his daughter to marry a ballplayer, so Lange gave up the game. Over the next few years he received a number of lucrative offers to return, but he rejected them all, pursuing a career in real estate and insurance instead. Later, freed by divorce to return to baseball, Lange became a scout for Cincinnati and the coach of Stanford University. Lange's nephew, George Lange Kelly, eventually became a Hall of Famer.

CAREER CUBS RECORD:

Games	AB	Hits	Runs
811	3,195	1,055	689
Avg	**HR**	**RBI**	**SB**
.330	39	578	399

REULBACH, ED (SP/RP)
(1905–1913)

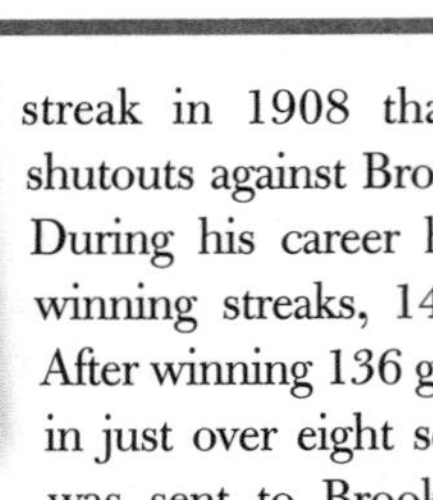

"Big Ed" Reulbach joined the Cubs in 1905 after playing semipro ball while studying electrical engineering and premed courses at Notre Dame and the University of Vermont. He posted a fine 18–14 record with a 1.42 ERA in his rookie season of 1905, and then got even better. From 1906 to 1908, the Cubs won three consecutive NL pennants, and Reulbach led the National League in winning percentage all three years, going 19–4, 17–4, and 24–7. He had a 44-inning scoreless streak in 1908 that included two shutouts against Brooklyn in one day. During his career he had two long winning streaks, 14 and 12 games. After winning 136 games for Chicago in just over eight seasons, Reulbach was sent to Brooklyn in 1913. In 1914 he fell to 11–18 and was released. He signed with the Federal League's Newark Pepper, going 21–10 in his last good season. When the Federal League folded following the 1915 season, Reulbach hooked up with the

Braves for two years, but won only seven games combined in 1916 and 1917 and retired. During his life, Reulbach strove to improve players' rights. He helped form the Base Ball Players' Fraternity and was its first secretary. He spent time in the shipyards during World War I, then, after the war, he undertook various business ventures in manufacturing, construction, and insurance. He died on July 17, 1961, the same day as Ty Cobb.

CAREER CUBS RECORD:

W	L	W%	ERA	SV
136	65	.677	2.24	9

K	BB	SHO	IP
799	650	31	1,864.7

ROOT, CHARLEY (SP/RP) (1926–1941)

After a dismal 1923 season in which he went 0–4 for the St. Louis Browns, Charley Root spent the next couple of years in the minors tuning up his game before returning WITH the Cubs in 1926. He fared much better the second time around, going 18–17 with a 2.82 ERA. The next year he had his only 20-win season, finishing 26–15 in 48 starts. But from 1928 to 1933, Root won between 14–19 games each year, and in his career, won over 200 games for the Cubs in 16 seasons.

In spite of that, Root will be remembered more for one pitch than any of his wins. In Game 3 of the 1932 World Series between the Cubs and Yankees in Wrigley Field, Root was on the mound facing Babe Ruth in an especially contentious game. The Chicago fans were throwing lemons at the Bambino; Ruth was cursing at the Cubs players and they at him. Ruth and his Yankee teammates were upset at the Cubs' treatment of Mark Koenig, a player who had started the season with the Yankees but had been traded to the Cubs in midseason and had been instrumental in helping them win the National League pennant. The Yankees' anger stemmed from the fact that the Cubs voted to give Koenig only a half-share of the World Series purse. As Ruth stepped to the plate, he was cursing the Cubs for being cheapskates. In turn, the Cubs players and fans were screaming at Ruth so loudly that hardly anyone could hear. Ruth, who had already homered in his first trip to the plate that day, was being pelted with lemons and other produce. After Root threw a strike with his first pitch, Ruth held up one finger, indicating strike one. After a second strike, Ruth held up two fingers, indicating strike two. Before the next pitch, Ruth pointed his bat to dead center field, indicating where he would hit the next pitch. On Root's next delivery, Ruth, as he predicted, hit a home run to deep center field, exactly where he had pointed. Root vehemently denies that Ruth "called his shot," stating if Ruth had done so, Root would have knocked him down with the next pitch instead of delivering it. In any event, the called shot has become a part of baseball lore, and contemporaneous accounts by many journalists confirm that Ruth indeed called the home run. After retiring in 1941, Root spent the next 16 years playing in the minors, and coaching in both the minor and major leagues. In 1969 he was named in a fan poll as the Cubs' all-time right-handed pitcher.

CAREER CUBS RECORD:

W	L	W%	ERA	SV
201	156	.563	3.55	40

K	BB	SHO	IP
1,432	871	21	3,137.3

RYAN, JIMMY (OF)
(1885–1889, 1891–1900)

Outfielder Jimmy Ryan, who spent 15 of his 18 seasons with the Cubs, was one of baseball's better offensive threats in the 19th century, hitting over .300 12 times. A fleet-footed power hitter in the dead-ball era, Ryan five times finished in the league's top five in homers, leading the league in 1888. Ryan also strung together 17 consecutive seasons with 100 or more hits. More than 100 years after he left the game, Ryan still ranks 58th all time with 419 stolen bases. After leaving baseball, Ryan stayed in Chicago, where he became first a clerk in the assessor's office and later a deputy sheriff.

CAREER CUBS RECORD:

Games	AB	Hits	Runs
1,660	6,757	2,073	1,409
Avg	**HR**	**RBI**	**SB**
.307	99	914	369

SANDBERG, RYNE (2B/3B)
(1982–1994, 1996–1997)

Ryne Sandberg, selected as *Parade* magazine's starting All-America high school quarterback and recruited heavily by both Nebraska and Oklahoma, abandoned the gridiron for the baseball diamond. Sandberg, selected by the Phillies in the 20th round of the June 1978 amateur draft, was projected to be a third baseman. When he came up to Philadelphia in 1981, he was, of course, stuck behind Mike Schmidt, and got only six at-bats in 13 games. Figuring Sandberg had no reasonable chance of playing for them, the Phillies sent him to Chicago along with shortstop Larry Bowa for shortstop Ivan DeJesus. Sandberg played third for the Cubs in 1982, finishing with a respectable .271 average and a better-than-respectable 32 steals and 103 runs. When the Cubs signed Ron Cey for the 1983 season, Sandberg was again faced with playing behind an established third-base star. Sandberg was moved to second and began compiling a record string of nine consecutive Gold Gloves at the keystone. In 1984 he had his best season, hitting .314 with 32 steals, 114 runs scored, 19 triples and homers, and 36 doubles. For his efforts, Sandberg was chosen as the National League's MVP. He had a stretch of four years where he didn't make one throwing error, including a record 123-game errorless streak.

Sandberg was an offensive force as well, collecting 25 or more homers six times in his career, including a league-leading 40 in 1990, becoming the first second baseman to lead the league in home runs since Rogers Hornsby in 1925. He scored over 100 runs seven times and batted over .300 five times. Sandberg, who appeared in 10 consecutive All-Star Games, also had speed, stealing 20 or more bases nine times. Due to personal problems and a disappointing start to the 1994 season, Sandberg retired. After sitting out the remainder of 1994 and all of 1995, Sandberg returned to the Cubs in 1996 and had a decent season, hitting 25 homers with 92 RBIs, although his .244 batting average concerned him. After struggling through the 1997 season, Sandberg, a winner of seven Silver Slugger Awards, put away his bat and glove for good. In 2005 he was enshrined in the Baseball Hall of Fame in Cooperstown.

CAREER CUBS RECORD:

Games	AB	Hits	Runs
2,151	8,379	2,385	1,316
Avg	**HR**	**RBI**	**SB**
.285	282	1,061	344

SANTO, RON (3B)
(1960–1973)

Because of his fielding ability, Ron Santo has often been referred to as the National League's Brooks Robinson. A winner of five Gold Gloves, Santo set a major league record by leading his league in total chances nine times. He shares the NL record for most years leading the league in assists with seven, and in double plays with six. Santo played his entire career with diabetes, a condition he kept hidden from all but a few individuals. He once said that the reason he played so hard all the time was because he knew that his career could suddenly end at any minute.

Santo was such a good player in high school that he was recruited by all 16 major league teams. Even though Cleveland offered him an $80,000 bonus, he signed with Chicago for $20,000 because he felt he had a better shot at getting to the major leagues sooner with the Cubs. Santo came up to the majors for good in 1961, but didn't enjoy his first few years because of the team's College of Coaches concept, in which numerous Cubs coaches would take turns managing the team throughout the season. "Every two weeks we had a new manager," complained Santo. "One day they want you to steal bases, the next day they want you to swing for home runs." The strategy was finally abandoned after five futile seasons.

Santo, a nine-time All-Star, was a consistent offensive performer, hitting 30 or more homers each year from 1964 to 1967, and 20 or more on seven other occasions. He was also durable, missing only about two games a year from 1961 to 1970. After 14 years with the Cubs, Santo spent his last year with the White Sox, much of it in conflict with Dick Allen, a player whom Santo felt gave less than his full effort. Though he had a year left on his contract, Santo retired at the end of 1974. After initially losing a lot of money in a Chicago pizzeria, Santo recouped it in the crude-oil business, real estate investments, and several fast food franchises. He also did quite well as one-third owner in a chain of truck stops before joining the Cubs broadcast team in 1990. Over the last decade or so, Santo has suffered increasing disabilities, mostly due to his diabetes, including loss of vision, amputation of both legs, numerous heart attacks, and bladder cancer. (He died and was revived on the operating table during one of his 20 operations.) He has been very active for many years on behalf of the Juvenile Diabetes Research Foundation. Ron Santo is one of the best players—if not *the* best—not yet enshrined in the Hall of Fame. Justice would be served if Santo gets elected while he's still alive to enjoy it.

CAREER CUBS RECORD:

Games	AB	Hits	Runs
2,126	7,768	2,171	1,109
Avg	**HR**	**RBI**	**SB**
.279	337	1,290	35

SMITH, LEE (RP)
(1980–1987)

The Chicago Cubs drafted Lee Smith in the second round of the June 1975 amateur draft. After five years in the minors, he arrived in Chicago and became a middle reliever. After 1979 Cy Young winner Bruce Sutter left the Cubs as a free agent in 1981, Smith saw some work as closer in 1982, and then became the team's full-time stopper in 1983. A seven-time All-Star, Smith became the Cubs' all-time leader in saves with 180 before being traded to the Red Sox following the 1987 season. Smith recorded 30 or more saves nine times in his career, including 33 in 1984 when he helped the Cubs win the NL East Division, the Cubs' first title of any kind since 1945. Despite his 6'6" size, Smith was a terrific fielder. He set a major league record by not making an error from 1982 to 1992. In the 10 years Smith spent in the majors after leaving Chicago, he played for seven different teams, but all told he finished his career with 478 saves, tops in major league history. *(See Cardinals bio.)*

CAREER CUBS RECORD:

W	L	W%	ERA	SV
40	51	.440	2.92	180
K	BB	SHO	IP	
644	264	0	681.3	

SOSA, SAMMY (OF)
(1992–2004)

After three years with the Rangers and White Sox, Sosa came to the Cubs along with Ken Patterson in a trade with the Pale Hose for George Bell just before the 1992 season opened. Sosa's first four years in the major leagues gave no hint of his later power; 15 round trippers in 1990 was his high-water mark. When Sosa hit 33 homers in 1993, he established himself as a threat. When he hit 36–40 each year from 1995 to 1997, he established himself as a consistent threat. In 1998 Sosa became a force, as he and Mark McGwire engaged in the best home run race since Mantle and Maris in 1961. Sosa and McGwire matched each other all season long, bash for bash. By the time September rolled around, it was a foregone conclusion that both sluggers would break Roger Maris's record of 61 homers in a season. It was just a matter of how wide the margin would be. Sosa finished the season with 66 homers, second to McGwire's 70. Fans were charmed by the ever-smiling Sosa, whose enthusiasm for the race transcended baseball and drew in millions of new observers to watch the race unfold, night after night, in ballparks around America. While McGwire won the race, Sosa won the hearts—and votes—of baseball's writers, as they made him the overwhelming choice for National League MVP in 1998.

The next year Sosa again finished second to McGwire in the home run race, 65 to 63, making the pair the only men in history to hit more than 60 homers in a season twice. In 2001 Sosa became the only player to do it three times when he hit 64 homers, but once again he was the runner-up, this time to Barry Bonds' 73 dingers. A seven-time All-Star and six-time Silver Slugger Award winner, Sosa put together nine consecutive years with more than 100 RBIs. Following several years of declining production, whispers (and later accusations) about steroid use, and an ugly season-ending confrontation in which he was accused of leaving Wrigley Field on the last day of the 2004 season before the game was over, Sosa was traded to Baltimore for three players. In 2005 he had an absolutely horrible season, finishing with a .221 average and just 14 homers, leaving him just 12 home runs short of 600 for his career, and throwing his future into question.

CAREER CUBS RECORD:

Games	AB	Hits	Runs
1,811	6,990	1,985	1,245
Avg	**HR**	**RBI**	**SB**
.284	545	1,414	181

TINKER, JOE (SS)
(1902–1912, 1916)

The Cubs' Joe Tinker was the shortstop made famous in Franklin P. Adams' poem, "Baseball's Sad Lexicon," with its refrain, "Tinker to Evers to Chance." While the poem extolled the crisp, deadly precision of the double-play combo, it wasn't always the case with Tinker, who made 141 errors in his first two seasons with Chicago in 1902–1903. To his credit, however, he worked very hard on his fielding skills before the 1904 season and became a stellar fielder, leading the National League in fielding percentage four times. The tight infield defense played by the trio helped propel the Cubs to four pennants in five years from 1906 to 1910. While Tinker was only a fair hitter at best, he was exceptional at the hit-and-run, getting on base, and stealing bases once he got on. While many fans are aware of the Tinker-to-Evers-to-Chance connection, most are not aware of the fact that for most of the years they played together, Tinker and second baseman Johnny Evers never spoke a word to each other—thanks to a petty argument over a cab ride.

Tinker's best year with Chicago was 1912, his 11th season with the Cubs, when he finished fourth in the NL MVP voting after setting career highs in hits, runs, and RBIs, and near-career highs in doubles and batting average. Yet after the season, he was sold to Cincinnati, where he hit .317, the only .300 year of his career. In 1914 he jumped to the new Federal League as the player-manager of the Chicago franchise (called the Chi-Feds in 1914, the Whales in 1915). When the Federal League folded after two years, Whales owner Charles Weegham gained control of the Cubs and merged the two teams, keeping the best players of both, and made Tinker the manager for one year.

After the 1916 season, Tinker managed the Columbus team of the American Association. While there, Tinker pulled a stunt that eventually led to the outlawing of the spitball in the major leagues. Since Columbus's batters couldn't hit the spitball, which was legal at the time, he sent one of his pitchers into the game with a large file and had his pitcher very openly hack away at the ball before every pitch. Tinker's actions caused so much controversy that the spitball was outlawed in the American Association at season's end, and shortly thereafter in the major leagues. After bouncing around various minor league managing jobs, Tinker spent a short time as a scout for the Cubs. He had invested virtually all of his money in Florida real estate, but lost it when the stock market collapsed in 1929. In 1930 he opened a billiards parlor and, when Prohibition was repealed, the first bar in Orlando, Florida. Tinker was elected to the Hall of Fame in 1946 with his double-play partners, Evers and first baseman Frank Chance.

CAREER CUBS RECORD:

Games	AB	Hits	Runs
1,537	5,547	1,436	670
Avg	**HR**	**RBI**	**SB**
.259	28	670	304

VAUGHN, HIPPO (SP/RP)
(1913–1921)

After a 27–32 record for the Yankees and Senators from 1908–1912, James "Hippo" Vaughn was traded to the Kansas City club of the American Association. Late in the 1913 season he was traded to the Cubs, who felt he had improved his skills enough to pitch again on the major league level. Their assessment was correct, as Vaughn, whose nickname came from his large size (6'4", nearly 300 pounds at the end of his career) became a 20-game winner in five of his first six full seasons in Chicago.

On May 2, 1917, Vaughn and Fred Toney of the Cincinnati Reds hooked up in one of the greatest pitching duels ever in Chicago's Cubs Park. For nine innings, both hurlers pitched a no-hitter, something never done before or since. The Reds eventually won, 1–0, on two hits in the 10th. In June of that year, Vaughn won both ends of a doubleheader against the Pirates, and in August he stole home, capping his unusual year. In 1918 Vaughn won the National League's pitching Triple Crown with 22 wins, 148 strikeouts, and a 1.74 ERA. He pitched three complete games in that year's World Series against the Red Sox, giving up just three runs, though he lost two of the games. Babe Ruth beat him in Game 1, 1–0, and Carl Mays beat him in Game 3, 2–1. Vaughn won Game 5 against Sam Jones, 3–0, but Boston prevailed in six games. After winning 143 games in seven full seasons with the Cubs (1914–1920), including 10 1–0 games, Vaughn suddenly lost his ability to pitch. In 1921 he went 3–11 with a 6.01 ERA after always posting ERAs in the 1.74–2.89 range, and was released at the age of 33, never to pitch again.

CAREER CUBS RECORD:

W	L	W%	ERA	SV
151	105	.590	2.33	4
K	**BB**	**SHO**	**IP**	
1,138	621	35	2,216.3	

WILLIAMS, BILLY (OF)
(1959–1974)

The Cubs signed Billy Williams as an amateur free agent in 1956 after discovering him playing for the Mobile Black Bears semipro team. He got no bonus, although the scout did award Williams' father a cigar. While in the minors, Williams had the good fortune of being tutored by Rogers Hornsby, a three-time .400 hitter. After brief stints with the team in 1959 and 1960, Williams became the team's starting left fielder in 1961 and put together a long and productive—if unspectacular—career with the Cubs. He was a model of consistency for 13 years, missing only about 30 games during that time. He was almost always around 30 homers, 35 doubles, 100 runs, 100 RBIs, and a .290 average. Williams was the 1961 NL Rookie of the Year and a six-time All-Star. His one batting title came in 1972 when he hit .333. From September 1963 through September 1970, Williams played in 1,117 consecutive games, a new National League record that stood until broken by San Diego's Steve Garvey in 1983. In 1968 he hit five consecutive homers, three in one game and two in the next. When the Cubs collapsed near the end of the 1969 season and lost the division to the Mets after holding a large lead most of the year, Billy Williams was the only Cub who didn't succumb to the general malaise, hitting over .300 in the final month. In 1972 Williams went 8-for-8 in a doubleheader. After 16 seasons with the Cubs, Williams was traded to the A's and spent his last two years in baseball as Oakland's designated hitter. In 1987 he was elected to the Hall of Fame.

CAREER CUBS RECORD:

Games	AB	Hits	Runs
2,213	8,479	2,510	1,306
Avg	**HR**	**RBI**	**SB**
.296	392	1,353	86

WILSON, HACK (OF)
(1926–1931)

After three seasons with the New York Giants, the hard-drinking, brawling Lewis "Hack" Wilson was optioned to Toledo. When the Giants failed to renew their option (a clerical error, said Giants manager John McGraw), the Cubs drafted the young slugger away from New York's control.

With Chicago, Wilson blossomed. Wilson had an odd physical appearance. He was just 5'6" tall, but weighed nearly 200 pounds. He had massive, muscular arms and shoulders, but a big belly. He wore size 6 shoes. (Think of a cross between Danny DeVito and Arnold Schwarzenegger.) Despite his odd build, Wilson was a decent outfielder, though he is best remembered more for his famous miscues than exceptional plays. In the 1929 World Series he lost two fly balls in the sun in the same inning. Another time, Wilson fell asleep (think hangover) in right field while his team made a pitching change.

The pitcher, leaving the mound in disgust, threw the ball over Wilson's head and it bounced off the tin-plated right-field wall. Startled from his slumber, Wilson, who thought he had slept into the next at-bat, played the carom perfectly off the wall and fired a strike to second base. Players and fans alike howled with laughter. Wilson moved through life like it was a never-ending party, and only Cubs manager Joe McCarthy seemed to make any moral progress with him, though it wore him out trying. McCarthy once tried to demonstrate the evils of alcohol to Wilson. "If I drop a worm into a glass of water, it swims around. If I drop a worm into a glass of whiskey, the worm dies. What does that prove?" Said Wilson, "If you drink whiskey, you'll never get worms."

Wilson, who got his nickname from his strong resemblance to George Hackenschmidt—a famous wrestler and strong man of the era—once thought of turning professional boxer during baseball's offseason, but Commissioner Landis vetoed the plan. Wilson had KO'd several players already in his career and Landis didn't want him to get any formal training as a boxer. Wilson had five great years with the Cubs, all under the watchful eye of Joe McCarthy, who knew how to coax the most out of his temperamental little outfielder. Wilson had an extraordinary 1930 season, hitting 56 homers (the NL record until Sosa and McGwire both topped it in 1998) with 191 RBIs (still the major league record), 146 runs, and a .356 average.

After the 1930 season, Joe McCarthy left to manage the Yankees and was replaced by Rogers Hornsby, who had virtually no interpersonal skills. In 1931, Hornsby was relentless in his criticism of Wilson, and the outfielder responded with a .261 average, 13 homers, and 61 RBIs. He was dealt to the Cardinals after the season, who in turn traded him to Brooklyn before he had even played for St. Louis. After three very mortal seasons with the Dodgers and Phillies, he was released. He tried making a comeback in the minors, but alcoholism had eroded his skills so badly that he had become a joke. Wilson then took one menial job after another to support himself. He eventually appeared on radio, commenting on the evils of alcohol, presenting himself as a prime example. Wilson died in 1948 at the age of 48. After a long lobbying campaign, his supporters succeeded in getting him elected to the Hall of Fame in 1979.

CAREER CUBS RECORD:

Games	AB	Hits	Runs
850	3,154	1,017	652
Avg	**HR**	**RBI**	**SB**
.322	190	769	34

Chicago White Sox

Since 1901

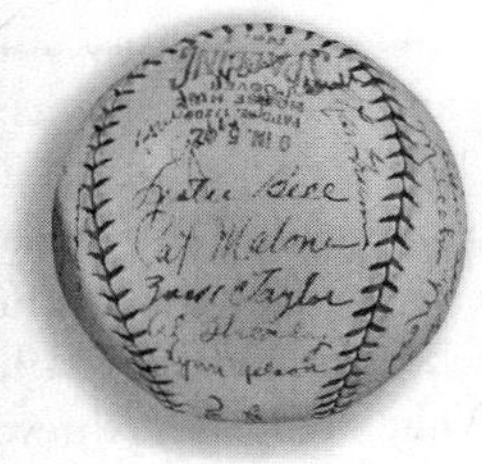

1936 Team Ball

1908 Knuckleballer Ed Walsh is the last pitcher in major league history to win 40 games in a season, and he does it with little run support. The Sox are so weak offensively that Walsh ties for the team lead in homers with one.... **1920** The White Sox pitching staff becomes the first ever to feature four 20-game winners (a feat that has been repeated only once since). Two of the pitchers, Lefty Williams and Ed Cicotte, are under investigation for the alleged game-fixing of the 1919 World Series.... **1950** The White Sox finish last in the majors in stolen bases with a paltry 19, but by the next year new manager Paul Richards transforms them into the "Go-Go White Sox," who lead the majors in 1951 with 93 steals. The team goes on to lead the American League in steals for 11 consecutive seasons.... **2005** The team sets a new major league record in 2005 by holding a lead in every one of their first 37 games of the season.

FRANCHISE HISTORY

The American League's Chicago franchise began play in 1900 when owner Charles Comiskey relocated his St. Paul team of the Western League to the Windy City. The franchise became a major league team in 1901, when the newly named American League received major league status. The original team name was the White Stockings, chosen by Comiskey as a slap in the face to the crosstown Chicago National League franchise, which had just changed its name from the White Stockings to the Cubs the year before. In 1902, the name was shortened to White Sox, supposedly to assist the editorial writers and typesetters of the day. The name has remained White Sox ever since.

The first owner of the White Sox was Charles Comiskey, the son of a longtime Chicago alderman who represented the Irish ghettos of the near West Side. Although his father wanted him to be a plumber, Charles rebelled and spent his time playing semipro baseball on Chicago's sandlots. Comiskey became the first baseman and player-manager of the St. Louis Browns of the American Association and is credited with being the first of the early-era first basemen to play off the bag, rather than keeping one foot on it. When Ban Johnson took over the fledgling Western League, Comiskey purchased the Sioux City franchise, eventually shifting it to St. Paul and then Chicago. During Comiskey's 31 years at the helm, the White Sox won four American League pennants: 1901, 1906, 1917, and 1919.

In 1951 Chico Carrasquel of the White Sox became the first Latin player to play in the All-Star Game.

It was Comiskey's own pettiness and greed that ultimately led to the most infamous affair in baseball history: the Black Sox scandal of 1919, in which a number of White Sox players threw that year's World Series against the Reds in exchange for cash from gamblers. The whole sordid affair exposed Comiskey for the incredible tightwad that he was, but in spite of his contributions to the debacle, Comiskey was elected to the Hall of Fame as an executive in 1939, eight years after his death.

When Charles Comiskey died in 1931, his invalid son Lou, who weighed nearly 400 pounds, took over the team and ran it until his own death in 1939. Lou Comiskey is credited with starting what ultimately became an extensive White Sox farm system. After Lou Comiskey died, the family's interest in the team was put into a trust controlled by the First National Bank, which acted on behalf of Lou's widow, Grace Comiskey, and her two children, Dorothy and Chuck. The bank tried to sell the

Judge Kenesaw Mountain Landis (rear left) questions White Sox players in 1921 about "Black Sox" scandal.

lub before the 1940 season, but Grace imme-iately took steps to block the sale. After a year-ɔng battle, the bank withdrew as trustee and ransferred the estate to Grace, who remained ı control of the club until she died in 1956. he had made prior arrangements to transfer 4 percent of the club to Dorothy and 46 per-ent to Chuck. Chuck Comiskey was relentless ı his pursuit of control of the team and even-ually wore down his sister until she decided to ell out. Though Dorothy wished to sell her ıterest to her brother, his lowball offer and onstant legal maneuvering against her pushed er to sell to Bill Veeck in 1959 for $2.7 million.

Bill Veeck headed an investment group ıat included former Detroit slugger Hank ;reenberg and was backed by Arthur and John ıllyn, heirs to a large investment company and ıe sons of the man who helped Veeck buy ıe Indians and Browns earlier in his life. :harlie Finley was initially a member of the roup, but after Veeck discovered that Finley ad made a second, secret deal with the Vrigley family in case Veeck's deal fell through, 'eeck gave him the boot. In the group's first ear of ownership, the White Sox won their rst American League pennant in 40 years. Chuck Comiskey's refusal to sell Veeck his 46 percent caused Veeck to incur extra taxes to the tune of $1 million. Due to ill health, Veeck was forced to sell in 1961. He and Greenberg sold their interests to brothers Arthur and John Allyn. (Arthur ıllyn would later open the Allyn Museum of :ntomology in Sarasota, Florida, to house and lisplay his collection of nearly one million ›utterflies.)

Willie Kamm of the White Sox n 1928 became he first third ɔaseman in major eague history to ıandle more than !00 consecutive :hances without naking an error.

The Allyns bought controlling interest in he club through their company, Artnell. Once gain, the stubborn Chuck Comiskey refused to sell his 46 percent share, although he did sell an option-to-buy to the group that ultimately purchased the Milwaukee Braves. The Milwaukee group eventually bought Chuck Comiskey's interest on the erroneous promise from an anonymous source that they would be able to buy out the Allyns. The Milwaukee group proceeded to buy the Braves, selling their recently acquired minority interest in the White Sox to the Allyns, finally eliminating the disagreeable Chuck Comiskey from the picture. In 1969 Arthur Allyn sold his share of the club to his brother John. In 1975 John Allyn sold a majority interest in the team for $10 million to Bill Veeck, who undertook ownership of the club for a second time. He again brought in Hank Greenberg as a minority owner. The Allyns also retained a minority share.

Go-Go White Sox Luis Aparicio stopped cold at home by the Indians' Russ Nixon in 1959.

The White Sox franchise was in terrible shape when Veeck took over in 1975. In order to revive the team, Veeck made six deals involving 22 players in 48 hours. The bizarre trading bazaar didn't work, as the White Sox and all of their minor league teams finished in last place in 1976. The ballpark was in awful condition. To make matters worse, Veeck had little capital to work with. Due to mounting financial problems, Veeck was forced to sell the team a second time in 1981. It initially appeared that Edward DeBartolo would buy it, but major league baseball executives vetoed the sale due to DeBartolo's racetrack interests and the fact that he lived in

Ohio instead of Illinois. DeBartolo bought the NFL's San Francisco 49ers instead.

Veeck sold the White Sox to Eddie Einhorn and Jerry Reinsdorf, who had been friends since their law school days at Northwestern. Reinsdorf, who already had sports franchise experience as the owner of the Chicago Bulls, made his money in real estate development, selling his company to American Express for $50 million. Einhorn, meanwhile, was a one-time television executive who had a background as a syndicator of sporting events, and he sold his company, Sportsvision, a cable outlet that aired major Chicago sporting events, for $5 million. A quarter of a century later, the two men still own the White Sox, and Reinsdorf has become a power player in major league baseball. During their tenure, the Sox built a new stadium and became more competitive through their capable oversight and sound investment of players, both free agent and system grown. Their capable stewardship culminated with a World Series title in 2005, the team's first since 1917, and its first World Series appearance since 1959. And they won it in impressive fashion, going 11–1 in the postseason, including a four-game sweep of the Houston Astros, who were making their first appearance in the World Series.

TEAM NAME HISTORY

Official Names

White Stockings (1901)
White Sox (1902–current)

Unofficial Names/Nicknames

Pale Hose, ChiSox, Hitless Wonders (1906), Black Sox (1917–1921), Go-Go Sox (1950s era)

STADIUM HISTORY

South Side Park	1901–June 27, 1910
White Sox Park	July 1, 1910–1912
Comiskey Park (White Sox Park renamed)	1913–1990
New Comiskey Park	1991–2002
U.S. Cellular Field (New Comiskey Park renamed)	2003–current

After an 88-year drought, the White Sox taste World Series victory again with a 2005 dunking of the Houston Astros.

YEARLY RECORD, FINISH, & ATTENDANCE FIGURES

Year	League	Record	DIV/LG Finish	Attendance	Avg/Gm
2005	AL Cent	99–63	1	2,342,833	28,924
2004	AL Cent	83–79	2	1,930,537	23,834
2003	AL Cent	86–76	2	1,939,524	23,945
2002	AL Cent	81–81	2	1,676,911	20,703
2001	AL Cent	83–79	3	1,766,172	21,805
2000	AL Cent	95–67	1	1,947,799	24,047
1999	AL Cent	75–86	2	1,338,851	16,529
1998	AL Cent	80–82	2	1,391,146	16,965
1997	AL Cent	80–81	2	1,864,782	23,022
1996	AL Cent	85–77	2	1,676,403	20,696
1995	AL Cent	68–76	3	1,609,773	22,358
1994	AL Cent	67–46	1	1,697,398	32,026
1993	AL West	94–68	1	2,581,091	31,865
1992	AL West	86–76	3	2,681,156	32,697
1991	AL West	87–75	2	2,934,154	36,224
1990	AL West	94–68	2	2,002,357	25,029
1989	AL West	69–92	7	1,045,651	13,071
1988	AL West	71–90	5	1,115,749	13,775
1987	AL West	77–85	5	1,208,060	14,914
1986	AL West	72–90	5	1,424,313	17,584
1985	AL West	85–77	3	1,669,888	20,616
1984	AL West	74–88	6	2,136,988	26,383
1983	AL West	99–63	1	2,132,821	26,331
1982	AL West	87–75	3	1,567,787	19,597
1981	AL West	54–52	3/6	946,651	19,319
1980	AL West	70–90	5	1,200,365	14,819
1979	AL West	73–87	5	1,280,702	16,211
1978	AL West	71–90	5	1,491,100	18,639
1977	AL West	90–72	3	1,657,135	20,458
1976	AL West	64–97	6	914,945	11,437
1975	AL West	75–86	5	750,802	9,269
1974	AL West	80–80	4	1,149,596	14,019
1973	AL West	77–85	5	1,302,527	16,081
1972	AL West	87–67	2	1,177,318	15,094
1971	AL West	79–83	3	833,891	10,295
1970	AL West	56–106	6	495,355	5,897
1969	AL West	68–94	5	589,546	7,278
1968	AL	67–95	9	803,775	9,923
1967	AL	89–73	4	985,634	12,020
1966	AL	83–79	4	990,016	12,222
1965	AL	95–67	2	1,130,519	13,957
1964	AL	98–64	2	1,250,053	15,433
1963	AL	94–68	2	1,158,848	14,132
1962	AL	85–77	5	1,131,562	13,970
1961	AL	86–76	4	1,146,019	14,148
1960	AL	87–67	3	1,644,460	21,357
1959	AL	94–60	1	1,423,144	18,245
1958	AL	82–72	2	797,451	10,357
1957	AL	90–64	2	1,135,668	14,749
1956	AL	85–69	3	1,000,090	12,988
1955	AL	91–63	3	1,175,684	15,269

YEARLY RECORD, FINISH, & ATTENDANCE FIGURES (CONT.)

Year	League	Record	DIV/LG Finish	Attendance	Avg/Gm
1954	AL	94–60	3	1,231,629	15,790
1953	AL	89–65	3	1,191,353	15,274
1952	AL	81–73	3	1,231,675	15,591
1951	AL	81–73	4	1,328,234	17,029
1950	AL	60–94	6	781,330	9,890
1949	AL	63–91	6	937,151	12,171
1948	AL	51–101	8	777,844	10,235
1947	AL	70–84	6	876,948	11,693
1946	AL	74–80	5	983,403	12,448
1945	AL	71–78	6	657,981	8,892
1944	AL	71–83	7	563,539	7,319
1943	AL	82–72	4	508,962	6,697
1942	AL	66–82	6	425,734	6,082
1941	AL	77–77	3	677,077	8,571
1940	AL	82–72	4	660,336	8,466
1939	AL	85–69	4	594,104	7,716
1938	AL	65–83	6	338,278	4,634
1937	AL	86–68	3	589,245	7,653
1936	AL	81–70	3	440,810	5,877
1935	AL	74–78	5	470,281	6,108
1934	AL	53–99	8	236,559	3,154
1933	AL	67–83	6	397,789	5,166
1932	AL	49–102	7	233,198	3,029
1931	AL	56–97	8	403,550	5,241
1930	AL	62–92	7	406,123	5,207
1929	AL	59–93	7	426,795	5,616
1928	AL	72–82	5	494,152	6,335
1927	AL	70–83	5	614,423	8,192
1926	AL	81–72	5	710,339	8,992
1925	AL	79–75	5	832,231	10,808
1924	AL	66–87	8	606,658	7,879
1923	AL	69–85	7	573,778	7,650
1922	AL	77–77	5	602,860	7,829
1921	AL	62–92	7	543,650	7,060
1920	AL	96–58	2	833,492	10,825
1919	AL	88–52	1	627,186	8,960
1918	AL	57–67	6	195,081	3,484
1917	AL	100–54	1	684,521	8,665
1916	AL	89–65	2	679,923	8,830
1915	AL	93–61	3	539,461	6,829
1914	AL	70–84	7	469,290	5,794
1913	AL	78–74	5	644,501	8,370
1912	AL	78–76	4	602,241	7,721
1911	AL	77–74	4	583,208	7,477
1910	AL	68–85	6	552,084	6,988
1909	AL	78–74	4	478,400	5,906
1908	AL	88–64	3	636,096	8,155
1907	AL	87–64	3	666,307	8,434
1906	AL	93–58	1	585,202	7,408
1905	AL	92–60	2	687,419	8,383
1904	AL	89–65	3	557,123	7,143

YEARLY RECORD, FINISH, & ATTENDANCE FIGURES (CONT.)

Year	League	Record	DIV/LG Finish	Attendance	Avg/Gm
1903	AL	60–77	7	286,183	4,088
1902	AL	74–60	4	337,898	4,693
1901	AL	83–53	1	354,350	4,991

MANAGER HISTORY

Manager	Years	W–L	Win %
Clark Griffith	1901–1902	157–113	.581
Nixey Callahan	1903–1904, 1912–1914	309–329	.484
Fielder Jones	1904–1908	426–293	.592
Billy Sullivan	1909	78–74	.513
Hugh Duffy	1910–1911	145–159	.477
Pants Rowland	1915–1918	339–247	.578
Kid Gleason	1919–1923	392–364	.519
Johnny Evers	1924	66–87	.431
Ed Walsh	1924	1–2	.333
Eddie Collins	1925–1926	160–147	.521
Ray Schalk	1927–1928	102–125	.449
Lena Blackburne	1928–1929	99–123	.427
Donie Bush	1930–1931	118–189	.384
Lew Fonseca	1932–1934	120–196	.380
Jimmie Dykes	1934–1946	899–940	.489
Ted Lyons	1946–1948	185–245	.430
Jack Onslow	1949–1950	71–113	.386
Red Corriden	1950	52–72	.419
Paul Richards	1951–1954, 1976	406–362	.529
Marty Marion	1954–1956	179–138	.565
Al Lopez	1957–1965, 1968–1969	840–650	.540
Eddie Stanky	1966–1968	206–197	.511
Don Gutteridge	1969–1970	109–172	.388
Chuck Tanner	1970–1975	401–414	.492
Bob Lemon	1977–1978	124–112	.525
Larry Doby	1978	37–50	.425
Don Kessinger	1979	46–60	.434
Tony LaRussa	1979–1986	522–510	.506
Jim Fregosi	1986–1988	193–226	.461
Jeff Torborg	1989–1991	250–235	.515
Gene Lamont	1992–1995	258–210	.551
Terry Bevington	1995–1997	222–214	.509
Jerry Manuel	1998–2003	500–471	.515
Ozzie Guillen	2004–2005	182–141	.563

ALL-TIME WIN-LOSS RECORDS VS. ALL OPPONENTS (SINCE 1901)

Opponent	Record
ALL-TIME	8,210–8,020
Angels	315–318
Astros	7–5
Athletics	996–938
Blue Jays	147–157
Braves	2–4
Brewers	197–173
Cardinals	5–10
Cubs	25–23
Devil Rays	37–26
Diamondbacks	2–4
Dodgers	5–1
Giants	1–2
Indians	979–940
INTERLEAGUE	86–71
Mariners	181–163
Marlins	1–2
Mets	2–1
Nationals	2–4
Orioles	973–845
Padres	4–2
Phillies	4–2
Pirates	6–5
Rangers	331–273
Reds	9–2
Red Sox	903–934
Rockies	3–0
Royals	281–254
Tigers	944–970
Twins	1,036–938
Yankees	812–1,024

Bill Veeck's Disco Demolition night in 1979 demolished more turf than LPs.

Franchise Highlights, Low Points, and Strange Distinctions

1901 On April 24, playing at the Chicago Cricket club, the White Sox won the first game in AL history when they defeated Cleveland, 6–2. By the time the season ended, the Sox had won the first AL pennant.

• • • •

1902 Shortstop George Davis of the White Sox became the first switch-hitter in history to collect 2,000 hits.

• • • •

1904 Doc White became the first pitcher in major league history to hurl six shutouts in one calendar month when he performed the feat for the Pale Hose in September.

• • • •

1906 The White Sox set an American League record with 19 straight wins. When they began their streak, the Sox were in fourth place, nine games behind; when they completed their streak they were in first by a half-game.

• • • •

1908 Knuckleballer Ed Walsh became the last pitcher in major league history to win 40 games in a season, truly remarkable considering his team's pathetic lack of run support. How bad was it? So bad that Walsh tied for the team lead in homers that year with ...one! His 40 wins that year were 44.5% of the team's 88 victories, an AL record. Walsh also set another AL record by pitching 139 more innings than any other pitcher in the league. He also won 16 more games than his closest competitor.

1912 When it comes to RBIs in a season, who was the least productive player in major league history? Easily second baseman Morrie Rath of the White Sox in 1912. In 157 games (591 at-bats), he knocked in only 19 runs.

• • • •

1917 The only World Series championship team to lose two no-hitters during a championship season was the 1917 White Sox.

• • • •

1917–19 When Ed Cicotte led the AL in wins in 1917 and 1919, the White Sox won the pennant. When he led the league in losses in 1918, the Sox finished in sixth place.

• • • •

1920 Under the cloud of an investigation into alleged game-fixing during the 1919 World Series, the White Sox pitching staff became the first ever to feature four 20-game winners (a feat that has been repeated only once). Red Faber led the way with 23 wins. He was followed by Lefty Williams with 22 and Ed Cicotte and Dickie Kerr with 21 each. The following year Cicotte and Williams were gone, banished by the Black Sox scandal. Faber and Kerr combined for 44 wins, but the team tumbled to seventh place, finishing with only 62 wins.

1922 On April 30, rookie Charlie Robertson of the White Sox—with only a couple weeks of major league experience under his belt—pitched the last perfect game in the majors for 34 years when he defeated the Tigers 2–0 in Detroit. Robertson pitched in the majors for eight years and had a losing record all eight years, finishing with a .380 winning percentage and a 49–80 record.

• • • •

1924 Sloppy Thurston won 20 games for the last-place White Sox. He also led the AL with 28 complete games.

• • • •

1926 Ted Lyons no-hit the Boston Red Sox, 6–0, on August 21, in just one hour and seven minutes.

• • • •

1928 Willie Kamm of the White Sox became the first third baseman in major league history to handle more than 200 consecutive chances without making an error.

• • • •

1933 Sox pitcher Ted Lyons won 260 games in 21 major league seasons, but never once struck out 100 batters in a season. His high was only 74 in 1933.

• • • •

1936 Chicago's Luke Appling set a 20th-century record for shortstops when he batted .388 to win the AL batting title.

Luke Appling was famous for his ability to foul off pitches, virtually at will. During pregame batting practice he once asked a White Sox official for two baseballs to give to a couple of admiring fans but was refused because, said the official, the balls cost $2.75 each. When Appling stepped to the plate for his first at-bat that day, he proceeded to foul off 10 consecutive pitches into the stands. He stepped out of the batter's box, glared at the official in his box seat, then yelled at him, "That's $27.50 and I'm not done yet!"

• • • •

1938 First baseman Merv Connors received a late-season call-up with the White Sox. After hitting .355 with six homers, four doubles, and 13 RBIs in just 24 games—including the first-ever three-homer game in Comiskey Park—the 24-year-old Connors was released and never played in the majors again.

• • • •

1941 Chicago outfielder Taffy Wright set an American League record when he collected at least one RBI in 13 straight games.

The 1941 White Sox pitching staff recorded 106 complete games, the last time any major league team topped the 100 mark.

• • • •

1942 Pitcher Ted Lyons took the mound 20 times and got 20 decisions, going 14–6. Furthermore, every one of his appearances was a complete game.

• • • •

1943 Outfielder Guy Cartwright set a new AL rookie record when he hit safely in 26 straight games.

1948 On July 18, Pat Seerey hit four homers in one game for the White Sox. Six days later he became the first player in major league history to strike out seven times in a doubleheader.

••••

1951 Chico Carrasquel of the White Sox became the first Latin player to play in the All-Star Game.

••••

1956 In an incredible display of RBI production, Ron Northey of the White Sox stepped to the plate just 48 times, yet he knocked in 23 runs. Projected over a 600-at-bat season, Northey would have had 287 RBIs on the season.

••••

1956–57 Relief pitcher Dixie Howell of the White Sox hit five homers in just 44 at-bats.

••••

1958 Nellie Fox set a new major league record when he played in 98 consecutive games without striking out.

••••

1960 The White Sox became the first team to put their names on their uniform backs when owner Bill Veeck ordered the change. Veeck also unveiled the major leagues' first exploding scoreboard that year.

1963 When Sox outfielder Dave Nicholson struck out 175 times, he broke the major league record by a whopping 33. The next year he struck out 126 more times, giving him a two-year total of 301 strikeouts in just 743 at-bats.

••••

1965 White Sox catcher J.C. Martin committed a modern-era record of 33 passed balls. He could be forgiven somewhat, though, because he had to catch two knuckleballers, Hoyt Wilhelm and Eddie Fisher.

••••

1971 When the season began, the White Sox were the only team of the 16 in existence since 1901 never to have had a home run champion. Bill Melton ended that 70-year drought when he led the AL that year with 33, just one more than Reggie Jackson and Norm Cash. In 1972, fellow White Sox slugger Dick Allen led the American League in homers with 37, giving Chicago back-to-back home run champions.

••••

1972 The first American League MVP Award winner to wear glasses was Chicago's Dick Allen.

••••

1973 Wilbur Wood became the last American League pitcher to both win and lose 20 games in a season when he finished 24–20 for Chicago. In the five years from 1971–1975, Wood started 223 games, a 20th-century record for a five-year period. During his career, Wood won 20 games four times, but never a Cy Young, one of three pitchers—along with Dave Stewart and Luis Tiant—who can make that claim.

1974 It took only 74 years, but the White Sox led the American League in home runs (135) for the first time ever.

....

1976 On September 12, 54-year-old Minnie Minoso of the White Sox became the oldest player in history to get a hit in a major league game when he singled in a 5–1 win over the Angels.

....

1986 Tom Seaver of the White Sox pitched his 16th consecutive Opening Day starting assignment, a major league record.

....

1990 When Bobby Thigpen collected 57 saves, he smashed the existing major league record by 11 saves. He also collected either a win or a save in 61 of the 77 games he appeared in that year.

....

1991 The White Sox opened their new Comiskey Park, built right next door to the old one, amid much fanfare and celebration. Only trouble was, the visiting Detroit Tigers spoiled the party by drubbing the White Sox, 16–0.

In his first major league game, White Sox pitcher Wilson Alvarez was rocked so hard he didn't even make it out of the first inning. In his second start, on August 11, 1991, he threw a no-hitter against the Orioles.

....

1993 On June 22, Carlton Fisk set a major league record by catching his 2,226th career game. The White Sox released him less than a week later.

1994 When Lance Johnson led the American League with 14 triples, the White Sox outfielder became the first player in major league history to lead his league in triples four consecutive seasons.

....

1995 First baseman Frank Thomas became the first player in major league history to hit .300 with at least 20 homers, 100 RBIs, 100 runs, and 100 walks in five consecutive seasons.

....

1997 The White Sox ended their major league record streak for consecutive seasons without a batting champion at 54 when Frank Thomas took the crown with a .347 average. The last White Sox player to win the batting title was Luke Appling in 1943.

After signing a $20 million free agent contract, Jaime Navarro was expected to be the White Sox ace in 1997. Instead he was a flop, finishing 9–14 with 5.79 ERA. Navarro led the AL in hits allowed, runs allowed, opposing batting average, and wild pitches.

....

1999 Second baseman Ray Durham became the first White Sox player ever to score 100 runs and steal 30 bases in three consecutive seasons.

....

2001 Magglio Ordoñez became the first player in American League history to hit .300 with at least 30 homers, 100 RBIs, 40 doubles, and 25 steals in the same season.

Special Achievements

WORLD SERIES RESULTS

Year	Opponent	Result	Games
1906	Chicago Cubs	Won	4–2
1917	New York Giants	Won	4–2
1919	Cincinnati Reds	Lost	3–5
1959	L.A. Dodgers	Lost	2–4
2005	Houston Astros	Won	4–0

WORLD SERIES MANAGERIAL RECORDS

Manager	Series Record	Games Record
Fielder Jones	1–0	4–2
Pants Rowland	1–0	4–2
Kid Gleason	0–1	3–5
Al Lopez	0–1	2–4
Ozzie Guillen	1–0	4–0

ALL-TIME POSTSEASON RECORD

Divisional Playoffs	3–3
League Championship Series	7–8
World Series	17–13

ALL-STAR GAMES AT CHICAGO (WHEN AL WAS HOME TEAM)

Year	Date	Winner	Score	Stadium
1933	July 6	American	4–2	Comiskey Park
1950	July 11	National	4–3	Comiskey Park
1983	July 6	American	13–3	Comiskey Park
2003	July 15	American	7–6	U.S. Cellular Field

HALL OF FAMERS WHO PLAYED FOR TEAM

	Position	Years	Games with Chicago
Luis Aparicio	SS	1956–1962, 1968–1970	1,513
Luke Appling	SS	1930–1943, 1945–1950	2,422
Chief Bender	RP	1925	1
Steve Carlton	SP	1986	10
Eddie Collins	2B	1915–1926	1,670
George Davis	SS/2B	1902, 1904–1909	856
Larry Doby	OF	1956–1957, 1959	280
Johnny Evers	2B	1922	1
Red Faber	SP/RP	1914–1933	670
Carlton Fisk	C	1981–1993	1,421
Nellie Fox	2B	1950–1963	2,115
Clark Griffith	SP	1901–1902	70
Harry Hooper	OF	1921–1925	662
George Kell	3B/1B	1954–1956	220
Ted Lyons	SP/RP	1923–1942, 1946	705
Edd Roush	OF	1913	9
Red Ruffing	SP	1947	14
Ray Schalk	C	1912–1928	1,757
Tom Seaver	SP	1984–1986	81
Al Simmons	OF	1933–1935	412
Ed Walsh	SP/RP	1904–1916	455
Hoyt Wilhelm	RP	1963–1968	361
Early Wynn	SP	1958–1962	157

HALL OF FAMERS WHO MANAGED TEAM

	Years	Games with Chicago
Eddie Collins	1924–1926	307
Larry Doby	1978	87
Hugh Duffy	1910–1911	304
Johnny Evers	1924	153
Clark Griffith	1901–1902	270
Bob Lemon	1977–1978	236
Al Lopez	1957–1965, 1968–1969	1,490
Ted Lyons	1946–1948	430
Ray Schalk	1927–1928	227
Ed Walsh	1924	3

MVP AWARD WINNERS

Nellie Fox	2B	1959
Dick Allen	1B	1972
Frank Thomas	1B	1993
Frank Thomas	1B	1994

CY YOUNG AWARD WINNERS

Pitcher	Year	W–L	ERA
Early Wynn	1959	22–10	3.17
LaMarr Hoyt	1983	24–10	3.66
Jack McDowell	1993	22–10	3.37

ROOKIE OF THE YEAR AWARD WINNERS

Luis Aparicio	SS	1956
Gary Peters	SP	1963
Tommie Agee	OF	1966
Ron Kittle	OF	1983
Ozzie Guillen	SS	1985

Gold Glove Winners

Year	Position	Player
1957	C	Sherm Lollar
	2B	Nellie Fox
	OF	Minnie Minoso
1958	C	Sherm Lollar
	SS	Luis Aparicio
1959	C	Sherm Lollar
	2B	Nellie Fox
	SS	Luis Aparicio
1960	2B	Nellie Fox
	SS	Luis Aparicio
	OF	Minnie Minoso
	OF	Jim Landis
1961	SS	Luis Aparicio
	OF	Jim Landis
1962	SS	Luis Aparicio
	OF	Jim Landis
1963	OF	Jim Landis
1964	OF	Jim Landis
1966	OF	Tommie Agee
1968	SS	Luis Aparicio
1970	SS	Luis Aparicio
	OF	Ken Berry
1974	SP	Jim Kaat
1975	SP	Jim Kaat
1977	1B	Jim Spencer
1981	1B	Mike Squires
1990	SS	Ozzie Guillen
1991	3B	Robin Ventura
1992	3B	Robin Ventura
1993	3B	Robin Ventura
1996	3B	Robin Ventura
1998	3B	Robin Ventura

Triple Crown Winners

None

Fireman of the Year Award Winners

Eddie Fisher	1965
Wilbur Wood	1968
Terry Forster	1974
Goose Gossage	1975
Bobby Thigpen	1990

World Series MVP

Jermaine Dye	2005

League Championship Series MVP

Paul Konerko	2005

All-Star Game MVP

None

Manager of the Year Award Winners

Tony LaRussa	1983
Jeff Torborg	1990
Gene Lamont	1993
Jerry Manuel	2000
Ozzie Guillen	2005

Batting Champions

Player	Year	Avg
Luke Appling	1936	.388
Luke Appling	1943	.328
Frank Thomas	1997	.347

Nine-Inning No-Hitters Pitched

Year	Pitcher	Opp.	Score
1902	Nixey Callahan	DET	3–0
1905	Frank Smith	DET	15–0
1908	Frank Smith	PHI	1–0
1911	Ed Walsh	BOS	5–0
1914	Joe Benz	CLE	6–1
1917	Ed Cicotte	STL	11–0
1922	Charlie Robertson	DET	2–0 (perfect)
1926	Ted Lyons	BOS	6–0
1935	Vern Kennedy	CLE	5–0
1937	Bill Dietrich	STL	8–0
1957	Bob Keegan	WAS	6–0
1967	Joe Horlen	DET	6–0
1976	Blue Moon Odom/ Francisco Barrios	OAK	2–1
1986	Joe Cowley	CAL	7–1
1991	Wilson Alvarez	BAL	7–0

20-Game Winners

Year	Pitcher	W–L
1901	Clark Griffith	24–7
	Roy Patterson	20–15
1904	Frank Owen	21–15
1905	Nick Altrock	23–12
	Frank Owen	21–13
1906	Frank Owen	22–13
	Nick Altrock	20–13
1907	Guy White	27–13
	Ed Walsh	24–18
	Frank Smith	23–10
1908	Ed Walsh	40–15
1909	Frank Smith	25–17
1911	Ed Walsh	27–18
1912	Ed Walsh	27–17
1913	Reb Russell	22–16
	Jim Scott	20–21
1915	Jim Scott	24–11
	Urban Faber	24–14
1917	Ed Cicotte	28–12

1919	Ed Cicotte Lefty Williams	29–7 23–11
1920	Red Faber Lefty Williams Dickie Kerr Ed Cicotte	23–13 22–14 21–9 21–10
1921	Red Faber	25–15
1922	Red Faber	21–17
1924	Sloppy Thurston	20–14
1925	Ted Lyons	21–11
1927	Ted Lyons	22–14
1930	Ted Lyons	22–15
1936	Vern Kennedy	21–9
1941	Thornton Lee	22–11
1956	Billy Pierce	20–9
1957	Billy Pierce	20–12
1959	Early Wynn	22–10
1962	Ray Herbert	20–9
1964	Gary Peters	20–8
1971	Wilbur Wood	22–13
1972	Wilbur Wood Stan Bahnsen	24–17 21–16
1973	Wilbur Wood	24–20
1974	Jim Kaat Wilbur Wood	21–13 20–19
1975	Jim Kaat	20–14
1983	LaMarr Hoyt Rich Dotson	24–10 22–7
1992	Jack McDowell	20–10
1993	Jack McDowell	22–10
2003	Esteban Loaiza	21–9

RETIRED UNIFORM NUMBERS

Number	Player	Position
2	Nellie Fox	2B
3	Harold Baines	OF
4	Luke Appling	SS
9	Minnie Minoso	OF
11	Luis Aparicio	SS
16	Ted Lyons	SP
19	Billy Pierce	SP
72	Carlton Fisk	C

TEAM RECORDS—WINS & LOSSES

- Games won in a season: 100 in 1917
- Games lost in a season: 106 in 1970
- Games won in a month: 23 in September 1905
- Games lost in a month: 24 in June 1934 and August 1968
- Consecutive games won: 19 in 1906
- Consecutive games lost: 13 in 1924
- Biggest shutout victory: 17–0 over Washington Senators on September 19, 1925 (second game) and vs. Cleveland on July 5, 1987
- Biggest shutout loss: 19–0 to Anaheim Angels, May 10, 2002
- Highest winning percentage: .649 in 1917 (100–54)
- Lowest winning percentage: .325 in 1932 (49–102)

TEAM RECORDS—BATTING

- Highest team batting average: .295 in 1920
- Lowest team batting average: .212 in 1910
- Highest team slugging average: .470 in 2000
- Highest team on-base percentage: .373 in 1936
- Total hits: 1,615 in 2000
- Extra-base hits: 574 in 2000
- Most hits in a game: 29 vs. Kansas City Athletics on April 23, 1955
- Longest individual hitting streak: 28, Carlos Lee, 2004
- Most .300 hitters in a single season: 8 in 1924
- Home runs: 242 in 2004
- Home runs in a month: 16, Albert Belle, July 1998
- Home runs in a game: 7 vs. Kansas City Athletics on April 23, 1955
- Home runs by a rookie: 35, Ron Kittle, 1983
- Home runs by a right-hander: 49, Albert Belle, 1998
- Home runs by a left-hander: 34, Robin Ventura, 1996
- Home runs by a switch-hitter: 28, Jose Valentin, 2001 and 2003
- Grand slams: 8 in 1996 and 2002
- Grand slams (individual; single season): 4, Albert Belle, 1997
- Grand slams (individual; career): 10, Robin Ventura
- Triples: 102 in 1915
- Doubles: 325 in 2000
- Singles: 1,199 in 1936
- Walks: 702 in 1949
- Runs scored: 978 in 2000
- Runs scored in a game: 29 vs. Kansas City Athletics, April 23, 1955
- Runs scored in an inning: 13 vs. Washington Senators on September 26, 1943 (first game, fourth inning)
- Most batters hit by a pitch: 79 in 2005
- Most times shut out: 24 in 1910

- Grounded into double plays: 156 in 1950 and 1974
- Fewest grounded into double plays: 94 in 1966
- Runners left on base: 1,279 in 1936

TEAM RECORDS—BASERUNNING

- Stolen bases: 275 in 1901
- Caught stealing: 119 in 1923

TEAM RECORDS—PITCHING

- Lowest earned run average: 1.99 in 1905
- Complete games: 134 in 1904
- Saves: 68 in 1990
- Strikeouts: 1,056 in 2003
- Shutouts: 32 in 1906
- Walks: 734 in 1950
- Hit batsmen: 88 in 2001
- Wild pitches: 71 in 1997
- Consecutive wins (individual): 13, LaMarr Hoyt, 1983
- Consecutive losses (individual): 14, Howard Judson, 1949
- Strikeouts in a game: 16, by Jack Harshman, July 25, 1954 (first game)
- Runs allowed in a game: 22 vs. New York Yankees, July 26, 1931 (second game)

TEAM RECORDS—FIELDING

- Best fielding average: .984 in 2002, 2003, and 2004
- Most errors committed: 358 in 1901
- Fewest errors committed: 93 in 2003
- Most double plays turned: 190 in 2000
- Fewest double plays turned: 94 in 1915

TEAM RECORDS—MISCELLANEOUS

- Number of times league champions: 6
- Number of times finishing last in league: 6
- Largest attendance, single game: 53,940 vs. New York Yankees, June 8, 1951
- Largest attendance, doubleheader: 55,555 vs. Minnesota, May 20, 1973
- Players used in a season: 50 in 1932
- Seasons played: 21 by Ted Lyons

Pitcher Eddie Cicotte chats with manager Clarence "Pants" Rowland when the White Sox were still White.

PRIMARY PITCHING STAFFS

Year	Starter	Starter	Starter	Starter	Starter	Closer	Bullpen	Bullpen	Bullpen
2005	Garcia	Buehrle	Contreras	Garland	Hernandez	Hermanson	Cotts	Politte	Marte
2004	Buehrle	Garland	Loaiza	Schoeneweis	Garcia	Takatsu	Marte	Cotts	Politte
2003	Buehrle	Garland	Loaiza	Colon	Wright	Gordon	Marte	Koch	Wunsch
2002	Buehrle	Garland	Ritchie	Glover	Wright	Osuna	Marte	Foulke	Wunsch
2001	Buehrle	Garland	Biddle	Wells	Wells	Foulke	Howry	Glover	Lowe
2000	Parque	Sirotka	Baldwin	Wells	Eldred	Foulke	Howry	Wunsch	Simas
1999	Parque	Sirotka	Baldwin	Navarro	Snyder	Howry	Foulke	Lowe	Simas
1998	Parque	Sirotka	Baldwin	Navarro	Eyre	Simas	Foulke	Castillo	Howry
1997	Drabek	Alvarez	Baldwin	Navarro	Darwin	Hernandez	Castillo	Karchner	McElroy
1996	Fernandez	Alvarez	Baldwin	Tapani	Magrane	Hernandez	Simas	Karchner	Thomas
1995	Fernandez	Alvarez	Bere	Abbott	Keyser	Hernandez	McCaskill	Radinsky	DeLeon
1994	Fernandez	Alvarez	Bere	McDowell	Sanderson	Hernandez	Assenmacher	McCaskill	DeLeon
1993	Fernandez	Alvarez	Bere	McDowell	McCaskill	Hernandez	Radinsky	Schwarz	Pall
1992	Fernandez	Hibbard	Hough	McDowell	McCaskill	Thigpen	Radinsky	Hernandez	Leach
1991	Fernandez	Hibbard	Hough	McDowell	Garcia	Thigpen	Radinsky	Pall	Perez
1990	Fernandez	Hibbard	Perez	McDowell	King	Thigpen	Radinsky	Pall	Jones
1989	Rosenberg	Hibbard	Perez	Reuss	King	Thigpen	Hillegas	Pall	Patterson
1988	McDowell	LaPoint	Perez	Reuss	Long	Thigpen	Horton	Davis	Rosenberg
1987	Bannister	LaPoint	Dotson	DeLeon	Long	Thigpen	Searage	Winn	James
1986	Bannister	Cowley	Dotson	Davis	Allen	James	Nelson	Schmidt	Dawley
1985	Bannister	Burns	Seaver	Nelson	Lollar	James	Agosto	Spillner	Gleaton
1984	Bannister	Burns	Seaver	Hoyt	Dotson	Reed	Agosto	Spillner	Barojas
1983	Bannister	Burns	Koosman	Hoyt	Dotson	Lamp	Agosto	Tidrow	Barojas
1982	Lamp	Burns	Trout	Hoyt	Dotson	Barojas	Hickey	Koosman	Escarrega
1981	Lamp	Burns	Trout	Baumgarten	Dotson	Farmer	Hickey	McGlothen	Hoyt
1980	Kravec	Burns	Trout	Baumgarten	Dotson	Farmer	Proly	Hoyt	Wortham
1979	Kravec	Wortham	Trout	Baumgarten	Barrios	Farmer	Proly	Scarbery	Howard
1978	Kravec	Wortham	Stone	Wood	Barrios	LaGrow	Willoughby	Schueler	Hinton
1977	Kravec	Knapp	Stone	Wood	Barrios	LaGrow	Hamilton	Johnson	Kirkwood
1976	Johnson	Gossage	Brett	Forster	Barrios	Hamilton	Vuckovich	Carroll	Jefferson
1975	Wood	Kaat	Osteen	Jefferson	Bahnsen	Gossage	Hamilton	Upshaw	Osborn
1974	Wood	Kaat	Johnson	Kucek	Bahnsen	Forster	Pitlock	Gossage	Acosta
1973	Wood	Stone	Fisher	Forster	Bahnsen	Acosta	Johnson	Gossage	Frailing
1972	Wood	Bradley	Lemonds		Bahnsen	Forster	Kealey	Gossage	Romo
1971	Wood	Bradley	John	Horlen	Johnson	Kealey	Forster	Eddy	Romo
1970	Janeski	Miller	John	Horlen	Johnson	Wood	Murphy	Crider	Weaver
1969	Peters	Wynne	John	Horlen	Edmondson	Wood	Osinski	Carlos	Bell
1968	Peters	Fisher	John	Horlen	Carlos	Wood	Wilhelm	Locker	Priddy
1967	Peters	Howard	John	Horlen	O'Toole	Locker	Wilhelm	McMahon	Wood
1966	Peters	Howard	John	Horlen	Buzhardt	Locker	Wilhelm	Higgins	Lamabe
1965	Peters	Howard	John	Horlen	Buzhardt	Fisher	Wilhelm	Locker	Pizarro
1964	Peters	Pizarro	Herbert	Horlen	Buzhardt	Wilhelm	Fisher	Mossi	Baumann
1963	Peters	Pizarro	Herbert	Horlen	Buzhardt	Wilhelm	DeBusschere	Brosnan	Fisher
1962	Wynn	Pizarro	Herbert	Horlen	Buzhardt	Lown	Fisher	Zanni	Baumann
1961	Pierce	Pizarro	Herbert	McLish	Baumann	Lown	Kemmerer	Hacker	Larsen
1960	Pierce	Wynn	Shaw	Score	Baumann	Staley	Kemmerer	Lown	Donovan
1959	Pierce	Wynn	Shaw	Donovan	Latman	Lown	Staley	Arias	Moore
1958	Pierce	Wynn	Wilson	Donovan	Moore	Lown	Staley	Shaw	Qualters
1957	Pierce	Harshman	Wilson	Donovan	Keegan	LaPalme	Staley	Howell	Fischer
1956	Pierce	Harshman	Wilson	Donovan	Keegan	LaPalme	Howell	Kinder	
1955	Pierce	Harshman	Trucks	Donovan	Johnson	Howell	Consuegra	Martin	Fornieles
1954	Pierce	Harshman	Trucks	Keegan	Consuegra	Johnson	Dorish	Martin	Fornieles
1953	Pierce	Rogovin	Trucks	Fornieles	Dobson	Dorish	Consuegra	Bearden	Aloma

PRIMARY PITCHING STAFFS (CONT.)

Year	Starter	Starter	Starter	Starter	Starter	Closer	Bullpen	Bullpen	Bullpen
1952	Pierce	Rogovin	Grissom	Stobbs	Dobson	Dorish	Kennedy	Brown	Aloma
1951	Pierce	Rogovin	Holcombe	Kretlow	Dobson	Gumpert	Dorish	Judson	
1950	Pierce	Wight	Scarborough	Cain	Gumpert	Aloma	Haefner	Judson	
1949	Pierce	Wight	Kuzava	Haefner	Gumpert	Surkont	Pieretti	Judson	
1948	Haynes	Wight	Gettel	Pieretti	Papish	Judson	Moulder	Grove	Caldwell
1947	Haynes	Lopat	Grove	Gillespie	Papish	Caldwell	Maltzberger	Harrist	Gebrian
1946	Haynes	Lopat	Grove	Smith	Papish	Caldwell	Hollingsworth	Hamner	Maltzberger
1945	Lee	Lopat	Grove	Humphries	Dietrich	Johnson	Caldwell	Papish	
1944	Lee	Lopat	Grove	Humphries	Dietrich	Maltzberger	Haynes	Ross	Wade
1943	Smith	Ross	Grove	Humphries	Dietrich	Maltzberger	Haynes	Lee	Wade
1942	Smith	Ross	Lyons	Humphries	Dietrich	Haynes	Grove	Lee	Wade
1941	Smith	Lee	Lyons	Rigney	Dietrich	Hallett	Humphries	Ross	
1940	Smith	Lee	Lyons	Rigney	Knott	Brown	Appleton	Dietrich	
1939	Smith	Lee	Lyons	Rigney	Knott	Brown	Marcum	Dietrich	Frazier
1938	Whitehead	Lee	Lyons	Stratton	Knott	Rigney	Gabler	Boyles	
1937	Whitehead	Lee	Lyons	Stratton	Kennedy	Brown	Rigney	Dietrich	Cain
1936	Whitehead	Cain	Lyons	Stratton	Kennedy	Brown	Chelini	Evans	
1935	Whitehead	Tietje	Lyons	Jones	Kennedy	Wyatt	Phelps	Fischer	
1934	Earnshaw	Tietje	Lyons	Jones	Gaston	Wyatt	Gallivan	Heving	
1933	Durham	Gregory	Lyons	Jones	Gaston	Heving	Faber	Kimsey	Miller
1932	Frazier	Caraway	Lyons	Jones	Gaston	Faber	Chamberlain	Gallivan	Gregory
1931	Frazier	Caraway	Lyons	Thomas	Faber	Moore	McKain	Braxton	
1930	Henry	Caraway	Lyons	Thomas	Faber	Walsh	McKain	Braxton	
1929	Walsh	Adkins	Lyons	Thomas	Faber	Dugan	McKain	Weiland	
1928	Blankenship	Adkins	Lyons	Thomas	Faber	Connally	Cox	Walsh	
1927	Blankenship	Connally	Lyons	Thomas	Faber	Cole	Jacobs	Barnabe	
1926	Blankenship	Edwards	Lyons	Thomas	Faber	Connally	Thurston	Steengrafe	
1925	Blankenship	Thurston	Lyons	Robertson	Faber	Connally	Cvengros	Kerr	Edwards
1924	Cvengros	Thurston	Lyons	Robertson	Faber	Connally	Blankenship	Leverett	McWeeny
1923	Cvengros	Leverett	Blankenship	Robertson	Faber	Thurston	Mack	Lyons	
1922	Schupp	Leverett	Blankenship	Robertson	Faber	Hodge	Courtney	Davenport	
1921	Kerr	Wilkinson	Mulrenan	Hodge	Faber	McWeeny	Russell	Davenport	
1920	Kerr	Wilkinson	Williams	Cicotte	Faber	Payne			
1919	Kerr	Lowdermilk	Williams	Cicotte	Faber	Danforth	Shellenback	Mayer	
1918	Shellenback	Benz	Williams	Cicotte	Russell	Danforth	Faber	Quinn	
1917	Faber	Scott	Williams	Cicotte	Russell	Danforth	Benz		
1916	Faber	Scott	Williams	Cicotte	Russell	Benz	Danforth	Wolfgang	
1915	Faber	Scott	Benz	Cicotte	Russell			Wolfgang	
1914	Faber	Scott	Benz	Cicotte	Russell	Lathrop	Jasper	Wolfgang	
1913	Walsh	Scott	Benz	Cicotte	Russell	White	Smith	Lange	
1912	Walsh	Lange	Benz	Cicotte	White	Peters	Mogridge	Scott	
1911	Walsh	Lange	Scott	Young	White	Olmstead	Baker	Hovlik	
1910	Walsh	Olmstead	Scott	Young	White	Lange	Smith		
1909	Walsh	Smith	Scott	Burns	White	Suter	Fiene	Olmstead	
1908	Walsh	Smith	Owen	Altrock	White	Manuel			
1907	Walsh	Smith	Patterson	Altrock	White	Owen	Fiene		
1906	Walsh	Owen	Patterson	Altrock	White	Smith	Fiene		
1905	Walsh	Owen	Smith	Altrock	White	Patterson			
1904	Patterson	Owen	Smith	Altrock	White	Walsh			
1903	Patterson	Owen	Flaherty	Altrock	White	Dunkle			
1902	Patterson	Callahan	Piatt	Griffith	Garvin				
1901	Patterson	Callahan	Katoll	Griffith	Skopec	Harvey	Piatt		

PRIMARY STARTING LINEUPS

Year	C	1B	2B	3B	SS	LF	CF	RF	DH
2005	Pierzynski	Konerko	Iguchi	Crede	Uribe	Podsednik	Rowand	Dye	Everett
2004	Davis	Konerko	Harris	Crede	Valentin	Lee	Rowand	Borchard	Thomas
2003	Olivo	Konerko	Jimenez	Crede	Valentin	Lee	Everett	Ordonez	Thomas
2002	Johnson	Konerko	Durham	Valentin	Clayton	Lee	Lofton	Ordonez	Thomas
2001	Alomar	Konerko	Durham	Perry	Clayton	Lee	Singleton	Ordonez	Canseco
2000	Johnson	Konerko	Durham	Perry	Valentin	Lee	Singleton	Ordonez	Thomas
1999	Fordyce	Konerko	Durham	Norton	Caruso	Lee	Singleton	Ordonez	Thomas
1998	Kreuter	Cordero	Durham	Ventura	Caruso	Belle	Cameron	Ordonez	Thomas
1997	Fabregas	Thomas	Durham	Snopek	Guillen	Belle	Cameron	Martinez	Baines
1996	Karkovice	Thomas	Durham	Ventura	Guillen	Phillips	Lewis	Tartabull	Baines
1995	Karkovice	Thomas	Durham	Ventura	Guillen	Raines	Johnson	Devereaux	Kruk
1994	Karkovice	Thomas	Cora	Ventura	Guillen	Raines	Johnson	Jackson	Franco
1993	Karkovice	Thomas	Cora	Ventura	Guillen	Raines	Johnson	Burks	Bell
1992	Karkovice	Thomas	Sax	Ventura	Grebeck	Raines	Johnson	Pasqua	Bell
1991	Fisk	Pasqua	Fletcher	Ventura	Guillen	Raines	Johnson	Sosa	Thomas
1990	Fisk	Martinez	Fletcher	Ventura	Guillen	Calderon	Johnson	Sosa	Pasqua
1989	Fisk	Walker	Lyons	Martinez	Guillen	Boston	Gallagher	Calderon	Baines
1988	Fisk	Walker	Manrique	Lyons	Guillen	Pasqua	Gallagher	Calderon	Baines
1987	Fisk	Walker	Manrique	Hulett	Guillen	Redus	Williams	Calderon	Baines
1986	Fisk	Walker	Cruz	Hulett	Guillen	Bonilla	Cangelosi	Baines	Kittle
1985	Fisk	Walker	Cruz	Hulett	Guillen	Law	Boston	Baines	Kittle
1984	Fisk	Walker	Cruz	Law	Fletcher	Kittle	Law	Baines	Luzinski
1983	Fisk	Squires	Cruz	Law	Dybzinski	Kittle	Law	Baines	Luzinski
1982	Fisk	Squires	Bernazard	Rodriguez	Almon	Kemp	Law	Baines	Luzinski
1981	Fisk	Squires	Bernazard	Morrison	Almon	LeFlore	Lemon	Baines	Luzinski
1980	Kimm	Squires	Morrison	Bell	Cruz	Molinaro	Lemon	Baines	Johnson
1979	May	Squires	Bannister	Bell	Pryor	Garr	Lemon	Washington	Orta
1978	Nahorodny	Johnson	Orta	Soderholm	Kessinger	Garr	Lemon	Washington	Blomberg
1977	Essian	Spencer	Orta	Soderholm	Bannister	Garr	Lemon	Zisk	Gamble
1976	Downing	Spencer	Brohamer	Bell	Dent	Orta	Lemon	Garr	Kelly
1975	Downing	May	Orta	Melton	Dent	Nyman	Henderson	Kelly	Johnson
1974	Herrmann	Allen	Orta	Melton	Dent	May	Henderson	Sharp	Kelly
1973	Herrmann	Muser	Orta	Melton	Leon	Hairston	Sharp	Kelly	May
1972	Herrmann	Allen	Andrews	Spiezio	Morales	May	Johnstone	Kelly	
1971	Herrmann	May	Andrews	Melton	Alvarado	Reichardt	Johnstone	Williams	
1970	Herrmann	Hopkins	Knoop	O'Brien	Aparicio	May	Berry	Melton	
1969	Herrmann	Hopkins	Knoop	Melton	Aparicio	May	Berry	Williams	
1968	Josephson	McCraw	Alomar	Ward	Aparicio	Davis	Berry	Bradford	
1967	Martin	McCraw	Causey	Buford	Hansen	Ward	Agee	Berry	
1966	Romano	McCraw	Weis	Buford	Adair	Berry	Agee	Robinson	
1965	Martin	Skowron	Buford	Ward	Hansen	Cater	Berry	Robinson	
1964	Martin	McCraw	Weis	Ward	Hansen	Nicholson	Landis	Robinson	
1963	Martin	McCraw	Fox	Ward	Hansen	Nicholson	Landis	Robinson	
1962	Carreon	Cunningham	Fox	Smith	Aparicio	Robinson	Landis	Hershberger	
1961	Lollar	Sievers	Fox	Smith	Aparicio	Minoso	Landis	Robinson	
1960	Lollar	Sievers	Fox	Freese	Aparicio	Minoso	Landis	Smith	
1959	Lollar	Torgeson	Fox	Phillips	Aparicio	Smith	Landis	McAnany	
1958	Lollar	Torgeson	Fox	Goodman	Aparicio	Smith	Landis	Mueller	
1957	Lollar	Torgeson	Fox	Phillips	Aparicio	Minoso	Doby	Rivera	
1956	Lollar	Dropo	Fox	Hatfield	Aparicio	Minoso	Doby	Rivera	
1955	Lollar	Dropo	Fox	Kell	Carrasquel	Minoso	Busby	Rivera	
1954	Lollar	Fain	Fox	Michaels	Carrasquel	Minoso	Groth	Rivera	
1953	Lollar	Fain	Fox	Elliott	Carrasquel	Minoso	Rivera	Mele	

PRIMARY STARTING LINEUPS (CONT.)

Year	C	1B	2B	3B	SS	LF	CF	RF	DH
1952	Lollar	Robinson	Fox	Rodriguez	Carrasquel	Minoso	Rivera	Mele	
1951	Masi	Robinson	Fox	Dillinger	Carrasquel	Lenhardt	Busby	Zarilla	
1950	Masi	Robinson	Fox	Majeski	Carrasquel	Zernial	McCormick	Philley	
1949	Wheeler	Kress	Michaels	Baker	Appling	Zernial	Metkovich	Philley	
1948	Robinson	Lupien	Kolloway	Appling	Michaels	Seerey	Philley	Wright	
1947	Tresh	York	Kolloway	Baker	Appling	Hodgin	Philley	Kennedy	
1946	Tresh	Trosky	Kolloway	Lodigiani	Appling	Kennedy	Tucker	Wright	
1945	Tresh	Farrell	Schalk	Cuccinello	Michaels	Dickshot	Hockett	Moses	
1944	Tresh	Trosky	Schalk	Hodgin	Webb	Carnett	Tucker	Moses	
1943	Tresh	Kuhel	Kolloway	Hodgin	Appling	Curtright	Tucker	Moses	
1942	Tresh	Kuhel	Kolloway	Kennedy	Appling	Wright	Hoag	Moses	
1941	Tresh	Kuhel	Knickerbocker	Lodigiani	Appling	Hoag	Kreevich	Wright	
1940	Tresh	Kuhel	Webb	Kennedy	Appling	Solters	Kreevich	Wright	
1939	Tresh	Kuhel	Bejma	McNair	Appling	Walker	Kreevich	Rosenthal	
1938	Sewell	Kuhel	Hayes	Owen	Appling	Radcliff	Kreevich	Steinbacher	
1937	Sewell	Bonura	Hayes	Piet	Appling	Radcliff	Kreevich	Walker	
1936	Sewell	Bonura	Hayes	Dykes	Appling	Radcliff	Rosenthal	Haas	
1935	Sewell	Bonura	Hayes	Dykes	Appling	Radcliff	Simmons	Washington	
1934	Madjeski	Bonura	Hayes	Dykes	Appling	Simmons	Haas	Swanson	
1933	Grube	Kress	Hayes	Dykes	Appling	Simmons	Haas	Swanson	
1932	Grube	Blue	Hayes	Selph	Appling	Fothergill	Funk	Seeds	
1931	Tate	Blue	Kerr	Sullivan	Cissell	Fonseca	Watwood	Reynolds	
1930	Tate	Watwood	Cissell	Kamm	Mulleavy	Harris	Barnes	Jolley	
1929	Berg	Shires	Kerr	Kamm	Cissell	Metzler	Hoffman	Reynolds	
1928	Crouse	Clancy	Hunnefield	Kamm	Cissell	Falk	Mostil	Reynolds	
1927	McCurdy	Clancy	Ward	Kamm	Hunnefield	Falk	Metzler	Barrett	
1926	Schalk	Sheely	Collins	Kamm	Hunnefield	Falk	Mostil	Barrett	
1925	Schalk	Sheely	Collins	Kamm	Davis	Falk	Mostil	Hooper	
1924	Crouse	Sheely	Collins	Kamm	Barrett	Falk	Mostil	Hooper	
1923	Schalk	Sheely	Collins	Kamm	McClellan	Falk	Mostil	Hooper	
1922	Schalk	Sheely	Collins	Mulligan	Johnson	Falk	Mostil	Hooper	
1921	Schalk	Sheely	Collins	Mulligan	Johnson	Falk	Mostil	Hooper	
1920	Schalk	Collins	Collins	Weaver	Risberg	Jackson	Felsch	Leibold	
1919	Schalk	Gandil	Collins	Weaver	Risberg	Jackson	Felsch	Leibold	
1918	Schalk	Gandil	Collins	McMullin	Weaver	Leibold	Felsch	Murphy	
1917	Schalk	Gandil	Collins	Weaver	Risberg	Jackson	Felsch	Leibold	
1916	Schalk	Fournier	Collins	Weaver	Terry	Jackson	Felsch	Collins	
1915	Schalk	Fournier	Collins	Blackburne	Weaver	Roth	Felsch	Murphy	
1914	Schalk	Fournier	Blackburne	Breton	Weaver	Demmitt	Bodie	Collins	
1913	Schalk	Chase	Rath	Lord	Weaver	Chappell	Bodie	Collins	
1912	Kuhn	Zeider	Rath	Lord	Weaver	Callahan	Bodie	Collins	
1911	Sullivan	Collins	McConnell	Lord	Tannehill	Callahan	Bodie	McIntyre	
1910	Payne	Gandil	Zeider	Purtell	Blackburne	Dougherty	Parent	Meloan	
1909	Sullivan	Isbell	Atz	Tannehill	Parent	Dougherty	Cole	Hahn	
1908	Sullivan	Donahue	Davis	Tannehill	Parent	Dougherty	Jones	Hahn	
1907	Sullivan	Donahue	Isbell	Rohe	Davis	Dougherty	Jones	Hahn	
1906	Sullivan	Donahue	Isbell	Tannehill	Davis	Dougherty	Jones	O'Neill	
1905	Sullivan	Donahue	Dundon	Tannehill	Davis	Holmes	Jones	Green	
1904	Sullivan	Donahue	Dundon	Tannehill	Davis	Callahan	Jones	Green	
1903	McFarland	Isbell	Magoon	Callahan	Tannehill	Holmes	Jones	Green	
1902	Sullivan	Isbell	Daly	Strang	Davis	Mertes	Jones	Green	
1901	Sullivan	Isbell	Mertes	Hartman	Shugart	McFarland	Hoy	Jones	

Top 10 Batting Leaders, Single Season & Career with Team

Games Played: Career with Team

Player	G	PA
1. Luke Appling	2,422	10,243
2. Nellie Fox	2,115	9,491
3. Frank Thomas	1,959	8,602
4. Ray Schalk	1,757	6,215
5. Ozzie Guillen	1,743	6,451
6. Harold Baines	1,670	6,797
Eddie Collins	1,670	7,405
8. Luis Aparicio	1,513	6,438
9. Carlton Fisk	1,421	5,500
10. Minnie Minoso	1,373	5,914

At-Bats: Season

Player	AB	Year
1. Nellie Fox	649	1956
2. Nellie Fox	648	1952
3. Harold Baines	640	1985
4. Nellie Fox	636	1955
Jorge Orta	636	1976
6. Ray Durham	635	1998
7. Albert Belle	634	1997
Ray Durham	634	1997
9. Nellie Fox	631	1954
10. Tommie Agee	629	1966
Buck Weaver	629	1920

At-Bats: Career with Team

Player	AB	PA
1. Luke Appling	8,856	10,243
2. Nellie Fox	8,486	9,491
3. Frank Thomas	6,956	8,602
4. Harold Baines	6,149	6,797
5. Ozzie Guillen	6,067	6,451
6. Eddie Collins	6,065	7,405
7. Luis Aparicio	5,856	6,438
8. Ray Schalk	5,304	6,215
9. Minnie Minoso	5,011	5,914
10. Carlton Fisk	4,896	5,500

Batting Average: Season

Player	BA	Year
1. Luke Appling	.388	1936
2. Joe Jackson	.382	1920
3. Eddie Collins	.372	1920
4. Eddie Collins	.360	1923
5. Carl Reynolds	.359	1930
6. Frank Thomas	.353	1994
7. Bibb Falk	.352	1924
8. Joe Jackson	.351	1919
9. Frank Thomas	.349	1996
Eddie Collins	.349	1924

Batting Average: Career with Team

Player	BA	PA
1. Joe Jackson	.340	2,797
2. Eddie Collins	.331	7,405
3. Carl Reynolds	.322	2,024
4. Zeke Bonura	.317	2,375
5. Bibb Falk	.315	4,379
6. Taffy Wright	.312	2,981
7. Luke Appling	.310	10,243
Rip Radcliff	.310	3,027
9. Frank Thomas	.307	8,602
Magglio Ordoñez	.307	4,212

Total Hits: Season

Player	H	Year
1. Eddie Collins	224	1920
2. Joe Jackson	218	1920
3. Buck Weaver	208	1920
4. Rip Radcliff	207	1936
5. Luke Appling	204	1936
6. Joe Jackson	202	1916
Carl Reynolds	202	1930
8. Nellie Fox	201	1954
9. Albert Belle	200	1998
Al Simmons	200	1933

Total Hits: Career with Team

Player	H	PA
1. Luke Appling	2,749	10,243
2. Nellie Fox	2,470	9,491
3. Frank Thomas	2,136	8,602
4. Eddie Collins	2,007	7,405
5. Harold Baines	1,773	6,797
6. Ozzie Guillen	1,608	6,451
7. Luis Aparicio	1,576	6,438
8. Minnie Minoso	1,523	5,914
9. Ray Schalk	1,345	6,215
10. Buck Weaver	1,308	5,292

Home Runs: Season

Player	HR	Year
1. Albert Belle	49	1998
2. Frank Thomas	43	2000
3. Frank Thomas	42	2003
4. Paul Konerko	41	2004
Frank Thomas	41	1993
6. Frank Thomas	40	1995
Frank Thomas	40	1996
Paul Konerko	40	2005
9. Magglio Ordoñez	38	2002
Frank Thomas	38	1994

Home Runs: Career with Team

Player	HR	PA
1. Frank Thomas	448	8,602
2. Harold Baines	221	6,797
3. Carlton Fisk	214	5,500
4. Paul Konerko	203	4,232
5. Magglio Ordoñez	187	4,212
6. Robin Ventura	171	5,310
7. Bill Melton	154	4,011
8. Carlos Lee	152	3,646
9. Ron Kittle	140	2,433
10. Jose Valentin	136	2,750

Triples: Season

Player	3B	Year
1. Joe Jackson	21	1916
2. Joe Jackson	20	1920
3. Jack Fournier	18	1915
Harry Lord	18	1911
Minnie Minoso	18	1954
Carl Reynolds	18	1930
7. Eddie Collins	17	1916
Shano Collins	17	1915
Joe Jackson	17	1917
Sam Mertes	17	1901

Triples: Career with Team

Player	3B	PA
1. Shano Collins	104	5,307
Nellie Fox	104	9,491
3. Luke Appling	102	10,243
Eddie Collins	102	7,405
5. Johnny Mostil	82	4,096
6. Joe Jackson	79	2,797
Minnie Minoso	79	5,914
8. Lance Johnson	77	3,820
9. Buck Weaver	69	5,292
10. Ozzie Guillen	68	6,451

Doubles: Season

Player	2B	Year
1. Albert Belle	48	1998
2. Magglio Ordoñez	47	2002
3. Magglio Ordoñez	46	2003
Frank Thomas	46	1992
5. Albert Belle	45	1997
Floyd Robinson	45	1962
7. Ivan Calderon	44	1990
Chet Lemon	44	1979
Frank Thomas	44	2000
10. Bibb Falk	43	1926
Earl Sheely	43	1925

Doubles: Career with Team

Player	2B	PA
1. Frank Thomas	447	8,602
2. Luke Appling	440	10,243
3. Nellie Fox	335	9,491
4. Harold Baines	320	6,797
5. Eddie Collins	266	7,405
6. Minnie Minoso	260	5,914
7. Ray Durham	249	5,095
8. Bibb Falk	245	4,379
9. Willie Kamm	243	4,842
10. Ozzie Guillen	240	6,451
Magglio Ordoñez	240	4,212

Extra-Base Hits: Season

Player	XBH	Year
1. Albert Belle	99	1998
2. Frank Thomas	87	2000
3. Magglio Ordoñez	86	2002
4. Magglio Ordoñez	78	2003
5. Frank Thomas	77	1993
Frank Thomas	77	2003
7. Albert Belle	76	1997
8. Joe Jackson	74	1920
9. Frank Thomas	73	1994
10. Ray Durham	72	2001
Magglio Ordoñez	72	2001
Frank Thomas	72	1992

Extra-Base Hits: Career with Team

Player	XBH	PA
1. Frank Thomas	906	8,602
2. Luke Appling	587	10,243
3. Harold Baines	585	6,797
4. Nellie Fox	474	9,491
Minnie Minoso	474	5,914
6. Carlton Fisk	442	5,500
Magglio Ordoñez	442	4,212
8. Ray Durham	408	5,095
9. Robin Ventura	402	5,310
10. Paul Konerko	400	4,232

Total Bases: Season

Player	TB	Year
1. Albert Belle	399	1998
2. Frank Thomas	364	2000
3. Magglio Ordoñez	352	2002
4. Joe Jackson	336	1920
5. Frank Thomas	333	1993
6. Magglio Ordoñez	331	2003
7. Frank Thomas	330	1996
8. Carl Reynolds	329	1930
9. Frank Thomas	324	1997
10. Magglio Ordoñez	321	2000

Total Bases: Career with Team

Player	TB	PA
1. Frank Thomas	3,949	8,602
2. Luke Appling	3,528	10,243
3. Nellie Fox	3,118	9,491
4. Harold Baines	2,844	6,797
5. Eddie Collins	2,570	7,405
6. Minnie Minoso	2,346	5,914
7. Carlton Fisk	2,143	5,500
8. Ozzie Guillen	2,056	6,451
9. Luis Aparicio	2,036	6,438
10. Robin Ventura	2,000	5,310

Runs Batted In: Season

Player	RBI	Year
1. Albert Belle	152	1998
2. Frank Thomas	143	2000
3. Zeke Bonura	138	1936
4. Magglio Ordoñez	135	2002
5. Frank Thomas	134	1996
6. Luke Appling	128	1936
Frank Thomas	128	1993
8. Magglio Ordoñez	126	2000
9. Frank Thomas	125	1997
10. Joe Jackson	121	1920

Runs Batted In: Career with Team

Player	RBI	PA
1. Frank Thomas	1,465	8,602
2. Luke Appling	1,116	10,243
3. Harold Baines	981	6,797
4. Minnie Minoso	808	5,914
5. Eddie Collins	804	7,405
6. Carlton Fisk	762	5,500
7. Robin Ventura	741	5,310
8. Nellie Fox	740	9,491
9. Magglio Ordoñez	703	4,212
10. Paul Konerko	663	4,232

Runs Scored: Season

Player	R	Year
1. Johnny Mostil	135	1925
2. Ray Durham	126	1998
3. Ray Durham	121	2000
4. Zeke Bonura	120	1936
Fielder Jones	120	1901
Johnny Mostil	120	1926
Rip Radcliff	120	1936
8. Lu Blue	119	1931
Minnie Minoso	119	1954
Tony Phillips	119	1996

Runs Scored: Career with Team

Player	R	PA
1. Frank Thomas	1,327	8,602
2. Luke Appling	1,319	10,243
3. Nellie Fox	1,187	9,491
4. Eddie Collins	1,065	7,405
5. Minnie Minoso	893	5,914
6. Luis Aparicio	791	6,438
7. Harold Baines	786	6,797
8. Ray Durham	784	5,095
9. Ozzie Guillen	693	6,451
Fielder Jones	693	5,077

Walks: Season

Player	BB	Year
1. Frank Thomas	138	1991
2. Frank Thomas	136	1995
3. Lu Blue	127	1931
4. Tony Phillips	125	1996
5. Luke Appling	122	1935
Frank Thomas	122	1992
7. Luke Appling	121	1949
8. Eddie Collins	119	1915
9. Frank Thomas	112	1993
Frank Thomas	112	2000

Walks: Career with Team

Player	BB	PA
1. Frank Thomas	1,466	8,602
2. Luke Appling	1,302	10,243
3. Eddie Collins	965	7,405
4. Robin Ventura	668	5,310
5. Nellie Fox	658	9,491
Minnie Minoso	658	5,914

7. Ray Schalk	638	6,215
8. Willie Kamm	569	4,842
9. Harold Baines	565	6,797
10. Fielder Jones	550	5,077

Strikeouts: Season

Player	SO	Year
1. Dave Nicholson	175	1963
2. Ron Kittle	150	1983
Sammy Sosa	150	1990
4. Jose Valentin	139	2004
5. Ron Kittle	137	1984
6. Tony Phillips	132	1996
7. Tommie Agee	129	1967
8. Danny Tartabull	128	1996
9. Tommie Agee	127	1966
10. Dick Allen	126	1972
Ron Karkovice	126	1993
Dave Nicholson	126	1964

Strikeouts: Career with Team

Player	SO	PA
1. Frank Thomas	1,165	8,602
2. Harold Baines	918	6,797
3. Carlton Fisk	798	5,500
4. Ray Durham	758	5,095
5. Ron Karkovice	749	2,948
6. Robin Ventura	659	5,310
7. Jim Landis	608	4,183
8. Ron Kittle	606	2,433
9. Bill Melton	595	4,011
10. Jose Valentin	572	2,750

Slugging Percentage: Season

Player	SLG	Year
1. Frank Thomas	.729	1994
2. Albert Belle	.655	1998
3. Frank Thomas	.626	1996
4. Frank Thomas	.625	2000
5. Frank Thomas	.611	1997
6. Frank Thomas	.607	1993
7. Frank Thomas	.606	1995
8. Dick Allen	.603	1972
9. Magglio Ordoñez	.597	2002
10. Joe Jackson	.589	1920

Slugging Percentage: Career with Team

Player	SLG	PA
1. Frank Thomas	.568	8,602
2. Magglio Ordoñez	.525	4,212
3. Zeke Bonura	.518	2,375
4. Carl Reynolds	.499	2,024
Joe Jackson	.499	2,797
6. Paul Konerko	.498	4,232
7. Carlos Lee	.488	3,646
8. Jose Valentin	.483	2,750
9. Ron Kittle	.470	2,433
10. Minnie Minoso	.468	5,914

On-Base Percentage: Season

Player	OBP	Year
1. Frank Thomas	.487	1994
2. Luke Appling	.474	1936
3. Eddie Collins	.461	1925
4. Eddie Collins	.460	1915
5. Frank Thomas	.459	1996
6. Frank Thomas	.456	1997
7. Eddie Collins	.455	1923
8. Frank Thomas	.454	1995
9. Frank Thomas	.453	1991
10. Joe Jackson	.444	1920

On-Base Percentage: Career with Team

Player	OBP	PA
1. Frank Thomas	.427	8,602
2. Eddie Collins	.426	7,405
3. Joe Jackson	.407	2,797
4. Luke Appling	.399	10,243
5. Minnie Minoso	.397	5,914
6. Zeke Bonura	.396	2,375
7. Earl Sheely	.391	4,092
8. Johnny Mostil	.386	4,096
9. Harry Hooper	.383	2,914
10. Taffy Wright	.381	2,981

OPS (On-Base Percentage + Slugging Percentage): Season

Player	OPS	Year
1. Frank Thomas	1.217	1994
2. Frank Thomas	1.085	1996
3. Frank Thomas	1.067	1997
4. Frank Thomas	1.061	2000
Frank Thomas	1.061	1995
6. Albert Belle	1.055	1998
7. Joe Jackson	1.033	1920
Frank Thomas	1.033	1993
9. Dick Allen	1.023	1972
10. Frank Thomas	1.006	1991

OPS (On-Base Percentage + Slugging Percentage): Career with Team

Player	OPS	PA
1. Frank Thomas	.996	8,478
2. Zeke Bonura	.914	2,375
3. Joe Jackson	.906	2,797
4. Magglio Ordoñez	.889	4,212
5. Minnie Minoso	.865	5,914
6. Carl Reynolds	.858	2,024
7. Paul Konerko	.851	4,232
8. Eddie Collins	.849	7,405
9. Carlos Lee	.828	3,646
10. Harry Hooper	.819	2,914

Stolen Bases: Season

Player	SB	Year
1. Rudy Law	77	1983
2. Scott Podsednik	59	2005
3. Luis Aparicio	56	1959
Wally Moses	56	1943
5. Luis Aparicio	53	1961
Eddie Collins	53	1917
7. Frank Isbell	52	1901
Gary Redus	52	1987
9. Luis Aparicio	51	1960
Don Buford	51	1966
Tim Raines	51	1991

Stolen Bases: Career with Team

Player	SB	PA
1. Eddie Collins	368	7,405
2. Luis Aparicio	318	6,438
3. Frank Isbell	250	4,483
4. Lance Johnson	226	3,820
5. Ray Durham	219	5,095
6. Fielder Jones	206	5,077
7. Shano Collins	192	5,307
8. Luke Appling	179	10,243
9. Ray Schalk	177	6,215
10. Johnny Mostil	176	4,096

Sacrifice Hits: Season

Player	Sac	Year
1. Buck Weaver	44	1916
2. Buck Weaver	42	1915
3. Eddie Collins	40	1919
Shano Collins	40	1915
George Davis	40	1905
Ike Davis	40	1925

Player	Sac	Year
7. Eddie Collins	39	1916
Eddie Collins	39	1923
9. Willie Kamm	37	1925
10. Jiggs Donahue	36	1906
Fielder Jones	36	1904
Harvey McClellan	36	1923

Sacrifice Hits: Career with Team

Player	Sac	PA
1. Eddie Collins	341	7,405
2. Buck Weaver	242	5,292
3. Ray Schalk	214	6,215
4. Fielder Jones	206	5,077
5. Shano Collins	199	5,307
6. Frank Isbell	196	4,483
7. Willie Kamm	190	4,842
8. Nellie Fox	177	9,491
9. Bibb Falk	163	4,379
10. Earl Sheely	156	4,092

Hit by Pitch: Season

Player	HBP	Year
1. Minnie Minoso	23	1956
2. Minnie Minoso	21	1957
Aaron Rowand	21	2005
4. Carlton Fisk	17	1985
Nellie Fox	17	1955
Minnie Minoso	17	1953
7. Dave Altizer	16	1909
Nellie Fox	16	1957
Sherm Lollar	16	1956
Minnie Minoso	16	1954
Minnie Minoso	16	1961

Hit by Pitch: Career with Team

Player	HBP	PA
1. Minnie Minoso	145	5,914
2. Nellie Fox	125	9,491
3. Sherm Lollar	101	4,922
4. Carlton Fisk	84	5,500
5. Frank Thomas	71	8,602
6. Johnny Mostil	70	4,096
7. Chet Lemon	64	3,197
8. Ray Schalk	59	6,215
9. Buck Weaver	58	5,292
10. Jim Landis	53	4,183

Top 10 Pitching Leaders, Single Season & Career with Team

Games Pitched: Season

Player	GP	Year
1. Wilbur Wood	88	1968
2. Kelly Wunsch	83	2000
3. Eddie Fisher	82	1965
4. Bob Locker	77	1967
Bobby Thigpen	77	1990
Wilbur Wood	77	1970
7. Wilbur Wood	76	1969
8. Damaso Marte	74	2004
9. Scott Radinsky	73	1993
Hoyt Wilhelm	73	1964

Games Pitched: Career with Team

Player	GP	IP
1. Red Faber	669	4,086.7
2. Ted Lyons	594	4,161.0
3. Wilbur Wood	578	2,524.3
4. Billy Pierce	456	2,931.0
5. Ed Walsh	426	2,946.3
6. Bobby Thigpen	424	541.7
7. Hoyt Wilhelm	361	675.7
8. Doc White	360	2,498.3
9. Eddie Cicotte	353	2,322.3
10. Keith Foulke	346	446.0

Innings Pitched: Season

Player	IP	Year
1. Ed Walsh	464.0	1908
2. Ed Walsh	422.3	1907
3. Ed Walsh	393.0	1912
4. Wilbur Wood	376.7	1972
5. Ed Walsh	369.7	1910
6. Ed Walsh	368.7	1911
7. Frank Smith	365.0	1909
8. Wilbur Wood	359.3	1973
9. Red Faber	352.0	1922
10. Eddie Cicotte	346.7	1917

Innings Pitched: Career with Team

Player	IP
1. Ted Lyons	4,161.0
2. Red Faber	4,086.7
3. Ed Walsh	2,946.3
4. Billy Pierce	2,931.0
5. Wilbur Wood	2,524.3
6. Doc White	2,498.3
7. Eddie Cicotte	2,322.3
8. Joe Horlen	1,918.0
9. Jim Scott	1,892.0
10. Thornton Lee	1,888.0

Batters Faced: Season

Player	BF	Year
1. Ed Walsh	1,799	1908
2. Ed Walsh	1,663	1907
3. Ed Walsh	1,564	1912
4. Wilbur Wood	1,531	1973
5. Wilbur Wood	1,490	1972
6. Ed Walsh	1,480	1911
7. Red Faber	1,464	1922
8. Frank Smith	1,427	1909
9. Ed Walsh	1,386	1910
10. Dickie Kerr	1,360	1921

Batters Faced: Career with Team

Player	BF	IP
1. Ted Lyons	17,846	4,161.0
2. Red Faber	17,360	4,086.7
3. Billy Pierce	12,278	2,931.0
4. Ed Walsh	11,631	2,946.3
5. Wilbur Wood	10,472	2,524.3
6. Eddie Cicotte	9,036	2,322.3
7. Doc White	8,160	2,498.3
8. Thornton Lee	8,007	1,888.0
9. Joe Horlen	7,895	1,918.0
10. Jim Scott	7,468	1,892.0

Games Started: Season

Player	GS	Year
1. Ed Walsh	49	1908
Wilbur Wood	49	1972
3. Wilbur Wood	48	1973
4. Ed Walsh	46	1907
5. Wilbur Wood	43	1975
6. Stan Bahnsen	42	1973
Wilbur Wood	42	1971

Wilbur Wood	42	1974
9. Stan Bahnsen	41	1972
Jim Kaat	41	1975
Ed Walsh	41	1912

GAMES STARTED: CAREER WITH TEAM

Player	GS	IP
1. Ted Lyons	484	4,161.0
2. Red Faber	483	4,086.7
3. Billy Pierce	390	2,931.0
4. Ed Walsh	312	2,946.3
5. Doc White	301	2,498.3
6. Wilbur Wood	286	2,524.3
7. Joe Horlen	284	1,918.0
8. Eddie Cicotte	258	2,322.3
9. Richard Dotson	250	1,606.0
10. Thornton Lee	232	1,888.0

COMPLETE GAMES: SEASON

Player	CG	Year
1. Ed Walsh	42	1908
2. Frank Smith	37	1909
Ed Walsh	37	1907
4. Frank Owen	34	1904
5. Ed Walsh	33	1910
Ed Walsh	33	1911
7. Red Faber	32	1921
Frank Owen	32	1905
Ed Walsh	32	1912
10. Nick Altrock	31	1904
Nick Altrock	31	1905
Red Faber	31	1922

COMPLETE GAMES: CAREER WITH TEAM

Player	CG	IP
1. Ted Lyons	356	4,161.0
2. Red Faber	273	4,086.7
3. Ed Walsh	249	2,946.3
4. Doc White	206	2,498.3
5. Eddie Cicotte	183	2,322.3
Billy Pierce	183	2,931.0
7. Frank Smith	156	1,717.3
8. Thornton Lee	142	1,888.0
9. Jim Scott	123	1,892.0
10. Roy Patterson	119	1,365.0

GAMES WON: SEASON

Player	W	Year
1. Ed Walsh	40	1908
2. Eddie Cicotte	29	1919
3. Eddie Cicotte	28	1917
4. Ed Walsh	27	1911
Ed Walsh	27	1912
Doc White	27	1907
7. Red Faber	25	1921
Frank Smith	25	1909
9. Seven tied with...	24	——

GAMES WON: CAREER WITH TEAM

Player	W	IP
1. Ted Lyons	260	4,161.0
2. Red Faber	254	4,086.7
3. Ed Walsh	195	2,946.3
4. Billy Pierce	186	2,931.0
5. Wilbur Wood	163	2,524.3
6. Doc White	159	2,498.3
7. Eddie Cicotte	156	2,322.3
8. Joe Horlen	113	1,918.0
9. Frank Smith	108	1,717.3
10. Jim Scott	107	1,892.0

GAMES LOST: SEASON

Player	L	Year
1. Patsy Flaherty	25	1903
2. Pat Caraway	24	1931
3. Stan Bahnsen	21	1973
Ted Lyons	21	1933
5. Ted Lyons	20	1929
Jim Scott	20	1913
Eddie Smith	20	1942
Ed Walsh	20	1910
Bill Wight	20	1948
Roy Wilkinson	20	1921
Wilbur Wood	20	1973
Wilbur Wood	20	1975

GAMES LOST: CAREER WITH TEAM

Player	L	IP
1. Ted Lyons	230	4,161.0
2. Red Faber	213	4,086.7
3. Billy Pierce	152	2,931.0
4. Wilbur Wood	148	2,524.3
5. Ed Walsh	125	2,946.3
6. Doc White	123	2,498.3
7. Joe Horlen	113	1,918.0
Jim Scott	113	1,892.0
9. Thornton Lee	104	1,888.0
10. Eddie Cicotte	102	2,322.3

WINNING PERCENTAGE: SEASON

Player	W%	Year
1. Sandy Consuegra	.842	1954
2. Eddie Cicotte	.806	1919
3. Clark Griffith	.774	1901
4. Earl Caldwell	.765	1946
5. Richard Dotson	.759	1983
6. Eric King	.750	1990
Reb Russell	.750	1917
Bob Shaw	.750	1959
Monty Stratton	.750	1937
Doc White	.750	1906

WINNING PERCENTAGE: CAREER WITH TEAM

Player	W%	IP
1. Lefty Williams	.648	1,156.0
2. Mark Buehrle	.616	1,224.0
3. Juan Pizarro	.615	1,037.3
4. Jack McDowell	.611	1,343.7
5. Ed Walsh	.609	2,946.3
Dickie Kerr	.609	811.3
7. Eddie Cicotte	.605	2,322.3
8. La Marr Hoyt	.602	942.0
9. Ray Herbert	.600	710.7
10. Dick Donovan	.594	1,148.7

SHUTOUTS: SEASON

Player	SHO	Year
1. Ed Walsh	11	1908
2. Ed Walsh	10	1906
3. Reb Russell	8	1913
Ed Walsh	8	1909
Wilbur Wood	8	1972
6. Eddie Cicotte	7	1917
Ray Herbert	7	1963
Frank Owen	7	1906
Billy Pierce	7	1953
Jim Scott	7	1915
Frank Smith	7	1909
Ed Walsh	7	1910
Doc White	7	1904
Doc White	7	1906
Wilbur Wood	7	1971

SHUTOUTS: CAREER WITH TEAM

Player	SHO	IP
1. Ed Walsh	57	2,946.3
2. Doc White	42	2,498.3
3. Billy Pierce	35	2,931.0
4. Red Faber	29	4,086.7
5. Eddie Cicotte	28	2,322.3
6. Ted Lyons	27	4,161.0
7. Jim Scott	26	1,892.0
8. Frank Smith	25	1,717.3
9. Reb Russell	24	1,291.7
Wilbur Wood	24	2,524.3

ERA: Season

Player	ERA	Year
1. Ed Walsh	1.27	1910
2. Ed Walsh	1.41	1909
3. Ed Walsh	1.42	1908
4. Doc White	1.52	1906
5. Eddie Cicotte	1.53	1917
6. Eddie Cicotte	1.58	1913
7. Ed Walsh	1.60	1907
8. Doc White	1.72	1909
9. Doc White	1.76	1905
10. Doc White	1.78	1904

ERA: Career with Team

Player	ERA	IP
1. Ed Walsh	1.81	2,946.3
2. Hoyt Wilhelm	1.92	675.7
3. Frank Smith	2.18	1,717.3
4. Eddie Cicotte	2.25	2,322.3
5. Jim Scott	2.30	1,892.0
Doc White	2.30	2,498.3
7. Reb Russell	2.33	1,291.7
8. Nick Altrock	2.40	1,340.0
9. Joe Benz	2.43	1,359.7
10. Frank Owen	2.48	1,312.3

Earned Runs Allowed: Season

Player	ER	Year
1. Dickie Kerr	162	1921
2. Pat Caraway	152	1931
3. Vern Kennedy	141	1936
4. Wilbur Wood	138	1973
5. Jaime Navarro	135	1997
6. Ted Blankenship	133	1927
Wilbur Wood	133	1975
8. Lefty Williams	130	1920
9. Tommy Thomas	129	1931
10. Wilbur Wood	128	1974

Earned Runs Allowed: Career with Team

Player	ER	IP
1. Ted Lyons	1,696	4,161.0
2. Red Faber	1,430	4,086.7
3. Charley Root	1,236	3,137.3
4. Billy Pierce	1,038	2,931.0
5. Wilbur Wood	891	2,524.3
6. Richard Dotson	718	1,606.0
7. Thornton Lee	699	1,888.0
8. Bill Dietrich	675	1,437.7
9. Joe Horlen	663	1,918.0
10. Tommy Thomas	653	1,557.3
Doc White	638	2,498.3

Strikeouts: Season

Player	K	Year
1. Ed Walsh	269	1908
2. Ed Walsh	258	1910
3. Ed Walsh	255	1911
4. Ed Walsh	254	1912
5. Gary Peters	215	1967
6. Wilbur Wood	210	1971
7. Tom Bradley	209	1972
8. Esteban Loaiza	207	2003
9. Tom Bradley	206	1971
Ed Walsh	206	1907

Strikeouts: Career with Team

Player	K	IP
1. Billy Pierce	1,796	2,931.0
2. Ed Walsh	1,732	2,946.3
3. Red Faber	1,471	4,086.7
4. Wilbur Wood	1,332	2,524.3
5. Gary Peters	1,098	1,560.0
6. Ted Lyons	1,073	4,161.0
7. Doc White	1,067	2,498.3
8. Joe Horlen	1,007	1,918.0
9. Eddie Cicotte	961	2,322.3
10. Alex Fernandez	951	1,346.3

Strikeouts Per Nine IP: Season

Player	K/9	Year
1. Juan Pizarro	8.69	1961
2. Floyd Bannister	8.46	1985
3. Esteban Loaiza	8.23	2003
4. Floyd Bannister	7.99	1983
5. Bart Johnson	7.74	1971
6. Juan Pizarro	7.66	1962
7. Wilson Alvarez	7.50	1996
8. Gary Peters	7.44	1967
9. Melido Perez	7.36	1990
10. Joe Cowley	7.32	1986

Strikeouts Per Nine IP: Career with Team

Player	K/9	IP
1. Jason Bere	7.50	551.0
2. Melido Perez	7.17	713.0
3. Terry Forster	7.13	605.0
4. Hoyt Wilhelm	6.94	675.7
5. Juan Pizarro	6.88	1,037.3
6. Tom Bradley	6.84	545.7
7. Floyd Bannister	6.57	1,040.0
8. Wilson Alvarez	6.51	1,064.0
9. Rich Gossage	6.45	584.7
10. Alex Fernandez	6.36	1,346.3

Hits Allowed: Season

Player	HA	Year
1. Wilbur Wood	381	1973
2. Dickie Kerr	357	1921
3. Roy Patterson	345	1901
4. Ed Walsh	343	1908
5. Ed Walsh	341	1907
6. Patsy Flaherty	338	1903
7. Red Faber	334	1922
8. Red Faber	332	1920
Ed Walsh	332	1912
10. Ted Lyons	331	1930

Hits Allowed: Career with Team

Player	HA	IP
1. Ted Lyons	4,489	4,161.0
2. Red Faber	4,106	4,086.7
3. Billy Pierce	2,643	2,931.0
4. Wilbur Wood	2,422	2,524.3
5. Ed Walsh	2,324	2,946.3
6. Doc White	2,225	2,498.3
7. Eddie Cicotte	2,050	2,322.3
8. Thornton Lee	1,851	1,888.0
9. Joe Horlen	1,755	1,918.0
10. Tommy Thomas	1,625	1,557.3

Hits Allowed Per Nine IP: Season

Player	H/9	Year
1. Ed Walsh	5.89	1910
2. Joe Horlen	6.07	1964
3. Eddie Cicotte	6.39	1917
4. Eddie Fisher	6.42	1965
5. Frank Smith	6.44	1908
6. Gary Peters	6.47	1967
7. Ed Walsh	6.49	1909
8. Joe Horlen	6.56	1967
9. Doc White	6.57	1906
10. Frank Smith	6.63	1905

Hits Allowed Per Nine IP: Career with Team

Player	H/9	IP
1. Hoyt Wilhelm	6.19	675.7
2. Ed Walsh	7.10	2,946.3
3. Frank Smith	7.12	1,717.3
4. Jack Harshman	7.67	734.3

5. Jim Scott	7.73	1,892.0
6. Gary Peters	7.74	1,560.0
7. Juan Pizarro	7.83	1,037.3
8. Reb Russell	7.86	1,291.7
9. Eddie Cicotte	7.94	2,322.3
10. Early Wynn	7.97	1,010.7

Walks Allowed: Season

Player	BB	Year
1. Vern Kennedy	147	1936
2. Billy Pierce	137	1950
3. Bill Wight	135	1948
4. Vic Frazier	127	1931
5. Vern Kennedy	124	1937
6. Wilson Alvarez	122	1993
7. Early Wynn	119	1959
8. Stan Bahnsen	117	1973
9. Eddie Smith	114	1941
10. Billy Pierce	112	1949
Early Wynn	112	1960

Walks Allowed: Career with Team

Player	BB	IP
1. Red Faber	1,213	4,086.7
2. Ted Lyons	1,121	4,161.0
3. Billy Pierce	1,052	2,931.0
4. Wilbur Wood	671	2,524.3
5. Richard Dotson	637	1,606.0
6. Thornton Lee	633	1,888.0
7. Jim Scott	609	1,892.0
8. Ed Walsh	608	2,946.3
9. Bill Dietrich	561	1,437.7
10. Eddie Smith	545	1,228.7

Walks Allowed per Nine IP: Season

Player	BB/9	Year
1. La Marr Hoyt	1.07	1983
2. Ed Walsh	1.09	1908
3. Doc White	1.18	1907
4. Ted Lyons	1.30	1942
5. Nick Altrock	1.31	1907
Roy Patterson	1.31	1904
Nick Altrock	1.31	1906
8. Eddie Cicotte	1.35	1918
9. Ted Lyons	1.36	1939
10. Ray Herbert	1.40	1963

Walks Allowed per Nine IP: Career with Team

Player	BB/9	IP
1. Nick Altrock	1.49	1,340.0
2. Roy Patterson	1.80	1,365.0
3. La Marr Hoyt	1.82	942.0
4. Frank Owen	1.84	1,312.3
5. Ed Walsh	1.86	2,946.3
Reb Russell	1.86	1,291.7
7. Doc White	1.95	2,498.3
8. Sloppy Thurston	2.01	800.0
9. Ray Herbert	2.05	710.7
10. Mark Buehrle	2.06	1,224.0

WHIP (Walk + Hits per IP): Season

Player	WHIP	Year
1. Ed Walsh	.820	1910
2. Ed Walsh	.860	1908
3. Doc White	.903	1906
4. Eddie Cicotte	.912	1917
5. Joe Horlen	.935	1964
6. Ed Walsh	.938	1909
7. Reb Russell	.942	1916
8. Frank Smith	.953	1909
Joe Horlen	.953	1967
10. Frank Smith	.961	1908

WHIP (Walks + Hits per Nine IP): Career with Team

Player	WHIP	IP
1. Hoyt Wilhelm	0.935	675.7
2. Ed Walsh	0.995	2,946.3
3. Frank Smith	1.080	1,717.3
Reb Russell	1.080	1,291.7
5. Nick Altrock	1.083	1,340.0
6. Frank Owen	1.103	1,312.3
7. Doc White	1.108	2,498.3
8. Eddie Cicotte	1.112	2,322.3
9. Joe Benz	1.147	1,359.7
10. Gerry Staley	1.148	541.7

Home Runs Allowed: Season

Player	HRA	Year
1. Floyd Bannister	38	1987
2. James Baldwin	34	1999
James Baldwin	34	2000
Alex Fernandez	34	1996
Jon Garland	34	2004
Kevin Tapani	34	1996
7. Mark Buehrle	33	2004
Billy Pierce	33	1958
9. Dan Wright	32	2002
10. La Marr Hoyt	31	1984

Home Runs Allowed: Career with Team

Player	HRA	IP
1. Billy Pierce	241	2,931.0
2. Ted Lyons	223	4,161.0
3. Wilbur Wood	193	2,524.3
4. Richard Dotson	156	1,606.0
5. James Baldwin	150	1,015.7
6. Alex Fernandez	148	1,346.3
7. Joe Horlen	142	1,918.0
8. Jon Garland	137	1,009.0
9. Floyd Bannister	134	1,040.0
10. Mark Buehrle	129	1,224.0

Saves: Season

Player	SV	Year
1. Bobby Thigpen	57	1990
2. Keith Foulke	42	2001
3. Roberto Hernandez	38	1993
Roberto Hernandez	38	1996
5. Keith Foulke	34	2000
Bobby Thigpen	34	1988
Bobby Thigpen	34	1989
Dustin Hermanson	34	2005
9. Roberto Hernandez	32	1995
Bob James	32	1985

Saves: Career with Team

Player	SV	IP
1. Bobby Thigpen	201	541.7
2. Roberto Hernandez	161	404.7
3. Keith Foulke	100	446.0
4. Hoyt Wilhelm	98	675.7
5. Terry Forster	75	605.0
6. Wilbur Wood	57	2,524.3
7. Bob James	56	222.3
8. Ed Farmer	54	233.7
9. Clint Brown	53	381.0
10. Bobby Howry	49	322.3

Wild Pitches: Season

Player	WP	Year
1. Jose Contreras	20	2005
Freddy Garcia	20	2005
3. Jaime Navarro	18	1998
4. Tommy John	17	1970

5. Tommy John	15	1969
Gary Peters	15	1964
7. James Baldwin	14	1997
Joe Horlen	14	1966
Jaime Navarro	14	1997
Ed Walsh	14	1907
Kip Wells	14	2001
Rich Wortham	14	1979

Wild Pitches: Career with Team

Player	WP	IP
1. Ed Walsh	83	2,946.3
2. Tommy John	67	1,493.3
3. Joe Horlen	64	1,918.0
Gary Peters	64	1,560.0
5. Wilbur Wood	63	2,524.3
6. Frank Smith	56	1,717.3
7. Ted Lyons	55	4,161.0
8. Red Faber	52	4,086.7
9. James Baldwin	51	1,015.7
10. Doc White	48	2,498.3

Hit Batsmen: Season

Player	HB	Year
1. Clark Griffith	16	1902
Jim Scott	16	1909
3. Patsy Flaherty	14	1903
Joe Horlen	14	1968
Ken Kravec	14	1979
Doc White	14	1903
7. Mike Cvengros	13	1923
8. Eight tied with...	12	—

Hit Batsmen: Career with Team

Player	HB	IP
1. Red Faber	103	4,086.7
2. Doc White	92	2,498.3
3. Wilbur Wood	57	2,524.3
4. Jim Scott	53	1,892.0
Ed Walsh	53	2,946.3
6. Joe Horlen	49	1,918.0
7. Gary Peters	46	1,560.0
8. Lefty Williams	45	1,156.0
9. Tommy John	41	1,493.3
Roy Patterson	41	1,365.0

Games Finished: Season

Player	GF	Year
1. Bobby Thigpen	73	1990
2. Keith Foulke	69	2001
3. Roberto Hernandez	67	1993
4. Wilbur Wood	62	1970
5. Roberto Hernandez	61	1996
6. Eddie Fisher	60	1965
Bob James	60	1985
8. Bobby Thigpen	59	1988
9. Keith Foulke	58	2000
Bobby Thigpen	58	1991

Games Finished: Career with Team

Player	GF	IP
1. Bobby Thigpen	348	541.7
2. Roberto Hernandez	299	404.7
3. Hoyt Wilhelm	239	675.7
4. Keith Foulke	216	446.0
5. Clint Brown	177	381.0
6. Wilbur Wood	174	2,524.3
7. Terry Forster	158	605.0
8. Gerry Staley	146	541.7
9. Bobby Howry	138	322.3
10. Eddie Fisher	137	762.0
Bob Locker	137	423.3

Significant White Sox

APARICIO, LUIS (SS) (1956–1962, 1968–1970)

The White Sox signed Aparicio as an amateur free agent before the 1954 season. By 1956 the speedy, slick-fielding shortstop was in the majors. Starting with his rookie season, Aparicio led the AL in stolen bases for nine straight years, the first seven of which were with the White Sox. Manager Paul Richards liked to say about Aparicio, who won the American League's Rookie of the Year Award in 1956, that he "ran like a scalded dog." A 10-time All-Star and the winner of nine Gold Gloves, Aparicio was the highest octane gas in the "Go-Go" White Sox, who won the 1959 AL pennant—their first since the scandalous 1919 World Series season—but lost to the Dodgers in the World Series in six games. After suffering through an off year in 1962, Aparicio was traded to Baltimore as part of a six-player deal that brought Hoyt Wilhelm to Chicago. After five decent seasons with the Orioles, Aparicio was traded back to Chicago in a deal that included Don Buford. He spent three more years with Chicago in his second stint before being traded to Boston for the final three years of his career. Retiring after 18 seasons, Aparicio returned to his native Venezuela and opened an insurance agency. He was also a baseball commentator in his native country. In 1984 Aparicio became the first Venezuelan to be elected to the Hall of Fame.

CAREER WHITE SOX RECORD:

Games	AB	Hits	Runs
1,513	5,856	1,576	791
Avg	**HR**	**RBI**	**SB**
269	43	464	318

APPLING, LUKE (SS) (1930–1943, 1945–1950)

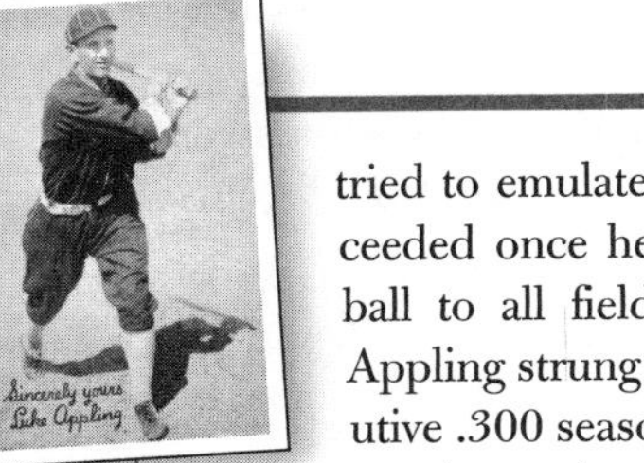

A seven-time All-Star, Luke Appling played every one of his 20 major league seasons with the White Sox, but because he played during the 40-year pennant drought experienced by the White Sox between 1919 and 1959, he was one of the few Hall of Famers who never played in a World Series. After Appling starred in the Southern Association, his contract was purchased at the end of the 1930 season. He performed poorly during his first two years as he tried to emulate Babe Ruth, but succeeded once he started to spray the ball to all fields. Starting in 1933, Appling strung together nine consecutive .300 seasons.

A notorious complainer, Appling blamed his less-than-stellar fielding on the uneven infield surface at Comiskey Park. He seemed to suffer constantly from some sort of pain, and he always made sure his teammates knew about it. If it wasn't a sore back, it was shin splints. If not a sore shoulder, then pinkeye. His nickname, "Old Aches and Pains," stuck with him throughout his career. An excellent leadoff hitter, Appling was a master at coaxing walks out of opposition pitchers. Three times he passed the 100 mark for walks in a season. In 1936, when Appling won the batting title with a .388 average, the first time an AL shortstop had won the crown, he was a close runner-up to Lou Gehrig for the AL MVP Award. He won a second batting title in 1943. Of all his abilities, Appling was most famous for being able to foul off pitches until he got one he liked. He once fouled off 14 pitches before swatting a triple. Appling missed nearly two years of playing time due to military service in World War II, but when he returned in late 1945, he hit .368 for the remainder of the season. After the war, from the ages of 39 to 42, Appling hit over .300 each year, giving him 16 .300 seasons out of 20. After his playing career, Appling managed in the minors for many years, winning the Minor League Manager of the Year Award in 1952. At the age of 75 he appeared in the Cracker Jack All-Star Game in Washington, D.C., and hit a home run off Warren Spahn. Appling was elected to the Hall of Fame in 1964.

CAREER WHITE SOX RECORD:

Games	AB	Hits	Runs
2,422	8,856	2,749	1,319
Avg	**HR**	**RBI**	**SB**
.310	45	1,116	179

BAINES, HAROLD (OF/DH)
(1980–1989, 1996–1997, 2000–2001)

The White Sox selected Harold Baines with the first pick of the first round in the June 1977 amateur draft when he was just 18 years old. A pure hitter, Baines played the outfield when he first came up, but eventually switched to being a full-time DH. During his career, Baines accumulated 2,866 hits in 22 seasons. Had he not lost well over 100 games to several players' strikes during his career, he likely would have made it to 3,000 hits and been assured entry into the Hall of Fame. Because he spent so much of his career at DH, and because he bounced around with so many teams during his career, Baines didn't attract much media attention. It will be a close call whether or not he makes it into Cooperstown.

CAREER WHITE SOX RECORD:

Games	AB	Hits	Runs
1,670	6,149	1,773	786
Avg	**HR**	**RBI**	**SB**
.288	221	981	32

CICOTTE, EDDIE (SP/RP)
(1912–1920) • *Member of the Black Sox*

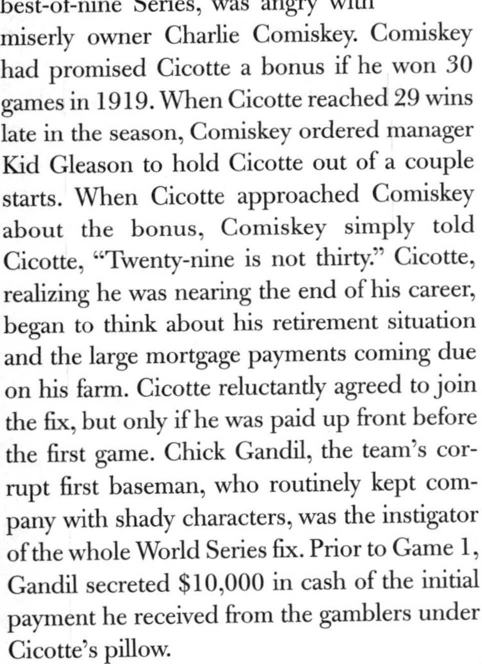

Eddie Cicotte was the main cog that the gamblers and conspirators needed in order to succeed with their planned fix of the 1919 World Series. Cicotte, the ace of the White Sox staff and likely to pitch three or four of the games in the best-of-nine Series, was angry with miserly owner Charlie Comiskey. Comiskey had promised Cicotte a bonus if he won 30 games in 1919. When Cicotte reached 29 wins late in the season, Comiskey ordered manager Kid Gleason to hold Cicotte out of a couple starts. When Cicotte approached Comiskey about the bonus, Comiskey simply told Cicotte, "Twenty-nine is not thirty." Cicotte, realizing he was nearing the end of his career, began to think about his retirement situation and the large mortgage payments coming due on his farm. Cicotte reluctantly agreed to join the fix, but only if he was paid up front before the first game. Chick Gandil, the team's corrupt first baseman, who routinely kept company with shady characters, was the instigator of the whole World Series fix. Prior to Game 1, Gandil secreted $10,000 in cash of the initial payment he received from the gamblers under Cicotte's pillow.

Cicotte was ordered to hit the first batter of the game as a sign the fix was on, which he dutifully did. Cicotte made noticeable miscues in throwing away Game 1 of the Series. In Game 4 he tried to be less obvious, but didn't get much help from his coconspirators, as the game remained scoreless into the fifth inning. He finally took matters into his own hands and made several key errors that cost the Sox a 2–0 game. After Game 4, the gamblers refused to pay the players any more money, instead threatening them with exposure if they failed to continue to throw the games. An angry Cicotte then retaliated by pitching a brilliant Game 7 victory, 4–1, setting the stage for a possible comeback. The Series didn't get that far, however, as Lefty Williams caved in to the gamblers' threats on his and his wife's lives. After the scandal broke the following year, Cicotte seemed the most affected of the bunch. He admitted his guilt in front of the grand jury, but his confession had mysteriously disappeared from the Cook County Courthouse. After being acquitted at trial, then banished for life the next day by Commissioner Kenesaw Mountain Landis, Cicotte took an assumed name and worked for the Ford Motor Company for many years. Four years before his death he again admitted his guilt, this time to a reporter. "I admit I did wrong, but I've paid for it. I've tried to make up for it by living as clean a life as I could. Nobody can hurt me anymore."

CAREER WHITE SOX RECORD:

W	L	W%	ERA	SV
156	102	.605	2.25	21

K	BB	SHO	IP
961	533	28	2,322.3

COLLINS, EDDIE (2B)
(1915–1926)

After nine years with the Philadelphia A's, Eddie Collins was sold to the White Sox following his 1914 MVP season when Connie Mack needed to raise some cash. Collins was an intelligent and dedicated player who required from his teammates everything that he himself was willing to give. As the highest-paid player on the White Sox, Collins was the object of the jealousy felt by some members of the team, who were seething over the cheapness of owner Charles Comiskey. Collins was the leader of one clique of players on the team, while the remaining White Sox flocked to Chick Gandil. Typically, the two groups would not talk to each other off the field. Such was the breeding ground for the 1919 World Series scandal. During the Black Sox Series, Collins, unlike many other "clean" Sox who chose to remain quiet, reported his suspicions to Comiskey and manager Kid Gleason. When the scandal broke the following year and the eight suspected players were indicted, Collins and his clique had a celebratory dinner out on the town, relieved that the world at last knew that he and his group had nothing to do with the ugly rumors that had been circulating for a year. In 1925 Collins became player-manager of the Sox, a position he held for two years. In 1927 he returned to the A's as a part-time player and pinch-hitter for the final four years of his career. After his playing career ended, Collins served as a Red Sox executive for 20 years until his death in 1951. He was elected to the Hall of Fame in 1939. *(See Athletics bio.)*

CAREER WHITE SOX RECORD:

Games	AB	Hits	Runs
1,670	6,065	2,007	1,065
Avg	**HR**	**RBI**	**SB**
.331	31	804	368

FABER, RED (SP/RP)
(1914–1933)

Spitballer Red Faber spent his entire 20-year career with the White Sox. On August 18, 1910, Faber pitched the first perfect game in minor league history and was purchased the following day by the Pittsburgh Pirates. While in the minors, Faber injured his arm trying to throw the curveball and the Pirates released him. Out of necessity, Faber learned how to throw the spitball. Following a 20-win season in the minors in 1913, Faber was brought up to the big leagues in 1914. After the 1914 season, the Giants and White Sox scheduled an around-the-world baseball tour. Charles Comiskey invited his rookie pitcher to go with them as far as Seattle. Once in Seattle, however, several Giants, including Christy Mathewson, decided not to make the globe-trotting trip. Short a pitcher, John McGraw took Comiskey up on his offer to use Faber on the Giants squad for the exhibition. Faber did so well pitching against his White Sox teammates on the world tour that he won a job in the rotation the next year, going 24–14.

Comiskey was so impressed with his young pitcher that he named a moose at his Wisconsin hunting preserve after him. The moose escaped from his pen and scared a couple of farm boys, one of whom was carrying a rifle. After the boys killed the moose, the local paper ran the story with the headline, "Red Faber Killed in Self-Defense."

When the Giants and White Sox faced each other in the 1917 World Series, Faber lost Game 4, but won Games 2, 5, and 6. An injured ankle in 1919 forced Faber to miss the entire Black Sox World Series. "If Red had been able to pitch," catcher Ray Schalk later mused, "I'm sure there would have been no Black Sox scandal." Starting in 1920, Faber won 20 or more games three straight years, leading the league in many categories in 1921 and 1922. Red Faber pitched a dozen more years on a lousy White Sox team before retiring, and was elected to the Hall of Fame in 1964.

CAREER WHITE SOX RECORD:

W	L	W%	ERA	SV
254	213	.544	3.15	28
K	BB	SHO	IP	
1,471	1,213	29	4,086.7	

FELSCH, HAPPY (OF)

(1915–1920) • *Member of the Black Sox*

Happy Felsch was an easygoing player who was having a great season in 1919. Other than batting average, many of his stats were similar to Joe Jackson's that year. In 1917 he had helped lead the White Sox to the World Series title over the New York Giants after posting a fine season. And in 1920, he posted one of the best seasons ever by a White Sox player when he hit a career-high .338 with 69 extra-base hits, 115 RBIs, and 300 total bases, truly great numbers in the dead-ball era. Unfortunately, Felsch was an integral part of the Black Sox scandal. At his grand jury hearing, Felsch admitted, "I am going to hell, I guess. The beans are all spilled and I think that I am through with baseball. I got my $5,000, and I guess the others got theirs, too." After being banned for life in 1921, Felsch sued White Sox owner Charles Comiskey for back pay and won. Comiskey had withheld the World Series share of the eight Black Sox pending the investigation and trial.

CAREER WHITE SOX RECORD:

Games	AB	Hits	Runs
749	2,812	825	385
Avg	HR	RBI	SB
.293	38	446	88

FISK, CARLTON (C)
(1981–1993)

After coming to the White Sox in 1981, Fisk changed his uniform number from 27 to 72 because, as he put it, "It was a turning point in my life." Although the distances to the Comiskey Park fences were less appealing than those in Fenway Park, and even though he was in his mid-30s, Fisk picked up right where he left off, matching his usual Boston numbers. In fact, all three of the Silver Slugger Awards Fisk won in his career came while with the White Sox. He also added four more All-Star appearances to the seven he accumulated in Boston. In 1985, at the age of 37, Fisk had his career year, hitting 37 homers with 107 RBIs. He slugged 33 of his homers as a catcher, setting a new league record. In 1987 Fisk became the oldest catcher ever to hit 20 homers. In 1988 he broke Rick Ferrell's AL record for games played at catcher with 1,807, celebrating the game with five hits while Ferrell watched from the stands. In 1989 Fisk broke Yogi Berra's career record for home runs by a catcher when he slugged number 307, fittingly, against the Yankees in Yankee Stadium. In 1990 he set both the new major league mark for homers by a catcher in a career and the White Sox's record for career homers, although he has since been passed in both. In 1991 Fisk became the oldest player (43) to get a hit in All-Star Game history. He also hit 70 homers after the age of 40, another major league record. On June 22, 1993, he caught his 2,226th major league game, another record. Carlton Fisk was elected to the Hall of Fame in 2000. *(See Red Sox bio.)*

CAREER WHITE SOX RECORD:

Games	AB	Hits	Runs
1,421	4,896	1,259	649
Avg	**HR**	**RBI**	**SB**
.257	214	762	67

FOX, NELLIE (2B)
(1950–1963)

After three seasons of little playing time with the Philadelphia A's, Nellie Fox, one of the best defensive second basemen ever to play the game, was traded to the White Sox for Joe Tipton right after the 1949 season. Almost immediately Fox stepped into the starting job. Fox hit over .300 six times during his career and led the league in hits four times. At one point, Fox played 798 consecutive games at second base, a record. Only two second basemen have played more games, and only Bill Mazeroski has turned more double plays. Fox, a 12-time All-Star with Chicago, holds the AL records for most years leading the league in total chances (8) and putouts (10). He won three Gold Gloves along the way. At the plate, Fox rarely struck out. Only Joe Sewell and Lloyd Waner had better strikeout-to-at-bat ratios. In 1959 Fox won the AL MVP Award, though he didn't lead the league in a single offensive category. Two of Fox's fellow "Go-Go" Sox—Luis Aparicio and Early Wynn—finished second and third in the MVP voting. Nellie Fox was elected to the Hall of Fame in 1997.

CAREER WHITE SOX RECORD:

Games	AB	Hits	Runs
2,115	8,486	2,470	1,187
Avg	**HR**	**RBI**	**SB**
.291	35	740	73

GANDIL, CHICK (1B)
(1910, 1917–1919) • *Member of the Black Sox*

GANDIL. CHICAGO AMER.

Arnold "Chick" Gandil was born in Minnesota, but he ran away from his chaotic home at the age of 17, and wound up in Arizona, playing baseball in the rough mining towns along the Mexican border. He bounced back and forth between the minors and majors for several years, unable to stick mostly because he was a strong fielder but a weak hitter. Gandil's real weakness, however, was money. After a brief stint with the White Sox, then four years with the Senators and another with the Indians, Gandil returned to the White Sox in 1917 for a second tour, an established major leaguer with petty underworld connections. Having experienced the hoopla and hype around the team's first trip to the World Series in 1917, Gandil became a man on a mission in the 1919 World Series, and he wasn't about to let the opportunity pass without making his big score.

Gandil approached some gambling friends and let them know the Series could be bought for a price. It was he who recruited the other coconspirators. Gandil, Swede Risberg, and Buck Weaver were in a clique of their own, united in their fury at skinflint owner Charles Comiskey and resentful of the other faction that included the more educated and dedicated players on the White Sox, such as Eddie Collins and Ray Schalk.

The term "Black Sox" was actually coined in 1917 when Chicago players, in protest, refused to wash their uniforms because Comiskey docked their paychecks to cover the laundry fee. Soon the players' uniforms turned black from dirt. Comiskey, publicly embarrassed over the matter, was shamed into picking up the cleaning bill. After the Sox won the 1917 World Series, Comiskey again withheld the laundry fee, this time from their World Series paychecks.

Gandil used several players' outrage to persuade a number of them to join him in throwing the World Series for money. The gamblers, however, didn't come up with all the promised money, only about $100,000. Cicotte and Williams received a portion of what was promised, but Gandil appears to have kept the lion's share. When the rumors of a fix began to fly after the 1919 Series, American League president Ban Johnson began his own investigation. He began with Chick Gandil, but Gandil made himself scarce—in fact, he did not return for the 1920 season, as the other players did. He finally showed up for the trial like the others and, after the not-guilty verdicts were announced, was banished for life by Commissioner Landis. Gandil returned to California and became a plumber.

CAREER WHITE SOX RECORD:

Games	AB	Hits	Runs
455	1,708	451	177
Avg	**HR**	**RBI**	**SB**
.264	3	193	47

GUILLEN, OZZIE (SS)
(1985–1997)

After four years in San Diego's minor league system, the Padres traded Guillen to the White Sox after the 1984 season. Guillen became the Opening Day shortstop in 1985, having never played a game in Chicago's minor league system. Another in a long line of fine fielding shortstops from Venezuela, Guillen was named the American League Rookie of the Year in 1985 after hitting .273 and committing a franchise record-low 12 errors at shortstop. A three-time All-Star with Chicago, Guillen left the White Sox via free agency following the 1997 season, after spending 13 years with the Sox, but was able only to become a part-time player for three different teams over the next three years, his last in the majors. In 2004 the fiery Guillen became the manager of the White Sox, a position he called his "dream job." In 2005 he led the Sox to a World Series title over Houston.

CAREER WHITE SOX RECORD:

Games	AB	Hits	Runs
1,743	6,067	1,608	693
Avg	**HR**	**RBI**	**SB**
.265	24	565	163

HORLEN, JOE (SP/RP)
(1961–1971)

The White Sox signed Joe Horlen to a $50,000 bonus after watching him help Oklahoma State win the 1959 NCAA championship. He made it up to Chicago as a late-season call-up in 1961, and then joined the starting rotation in 1962. From 1964 to 1968, Horlen posted ERAs from 1.88–2.88, yet he barely had a winning record due to the light support he received from his hitters. On September 10, 1967, Horlen pitched a no-hitter against Detroit. Released by the White Sox during spring training 1972, Horlen signed with Oakland two weeks later. Despite decent numbers with the A's that year, he was released following the season and no other team picked him up, though he was only 34 years old. Since he was the player representative for both the White Sox and A's during a time of contentious labor negotiations, some felt it was his union involvement that led to his unemployability. After his playing career, Horlen became the golf coach at the University of Texas, and later a minor league coach.

CAREER WHITE SOX RECORD:

W	L	W%	ERA	SV
113	113	.500	3.11	3
K	**BB**	**SHO**	**IP**	
1,007	534	18	1,918.0	

JACKSON, "SHOELESS" JOE (OF)
(1915–1920) • *Member of the Black Sox*

After coming to Chicago from Cleveland, Jackson discovered that the White Sox team was fractured into two main factions, who rarely spoke off the field. One clique consisted of better-educated players such as Eddie Collins, Ray Schalk, Red Faber, and Dickie Kerr, while the other circle included the courser, less sophisticated players such as Swede Risberg, Chick Gandil, Hap Felsch, and Lefty Williams. Jackson's own illiteracy and the fact that he was a Southerner like Williams, his roommate, assured his membership in the second group.

When World War I arrived, players who were classified 1-A were expected to either join the military or take up draft-exempt employment. Jackson chose to go to work for the Bethlehem Steel shipyards, where he could continue to play ball for the company team. This choice brought Jackson a lot of criticism, including a rebuke from Charles Comiskey, who called Jackson "a slacker." Comiskey said, "There is no room on my club for players who wish to evade the army draft by entering the employ of shipbuilders." But finances, not a lack of courage, motivated Jackson. At the time, he provided the sole support to his parents and several siblings and their families in South Carolina, and had purchased a poolroom, a farm, and a butcher shop for various relatives in order to provide them their livings. Once the war ended, Comiskey was more than happy to have Jackson back on his team.

When the White Sox lost the 1919 World Series to the Reds, rumors began to fly that there had been a fix. For a year, AL president Ban Johnson conducted an investigation into the matter, motivated more by his hatred of Charles Comiskey than ethical concerns. When the story broke in late September 1920, Jackson and seven other White Sox players were implicated along with a number of gamblers, as well as several players from other teams. Most accounts make mention—correctly—that Jackson confessed to his part in the fix. Here's what they fail to mention: that while some of the "Black Sox" had obviously played badly in the Series, Jackson had not; that his 12 hits were the most on either team; that he led both teams with a .375 batting average; that his five runs and six RBIs led the Sox; that Jackson committed no errors and threw a runner out at home plate. Contemporary news accounts and other biographies mention that Jackson received $5,000 from Lefty Williams. What they often fail to mention is that when Jackson refused the money, Williams tossed it on the floor of Jackson's hotel room. Or that Jackson twice went to Comiskey's office to give him the $5,000 and tell him what had occurred, but that Comiskey refused to meet with him.

Contemporary accounts also fail to mention that Comiskey's attorney, Alfred Austrian, met privately with Jackson in the courthouse prior to his grand jury testimony and told him to admit his part. When Jackson told him he had no part to admit, Austrian reminded him that the investigation wasn't about going after the ballplayers, but about ridding the gamblers from baseball's doorstep. He also told Jackson he had better rethink his upcoming testimony or else the angry gamblers would seek violent retribution against him and his family with guns. Comiskey, Austrian reassured him, would take care of his ballplayers. After three hours, much of it spent with Austrian pouring moonshine whiskey down Jackson's throat, Jackson at last agreed to admit to playing a part in the fix. Then, just prior to his grand jury testimony, the unsophisticated, uneducated, *illiterate* Jackson signed a waiver of immunity shoved in front of him by the Harvard Law School–educated Austrian. If such tactics were discovered to have been used in this day and age, the attorney involved would likely go to prison. When he did give his grand jury testimony, many of the details were vague—as if they were being related by someone who'd heard the allegations, not by someone who'd participated in the deeds. Few accounts bother to mention that, when he was sober, Jackson later recanted his confession.

All of the other implicated players and all the gamblers confirmed that Jackson was never present at any of the meetings between the players and the gamblers. Even Lefty Williams, Jackson's roommate and best friend on the team, admitted later that he had brought up Jackson's name as one of the players they had in the fold just to give their group more credibility and clout with the gamblers, who at that time were still reluctant to give the group any money because they didn't feel they had enough of a core group of players to pull off the fix. Jackson's name did the trick, though he had no knowledge of the plot. Sadly, Jackson also fell victim to the rampant yellow journalism of the time. One oft-repeated *Chicago Herald and Examiner* article concerns a young boy who supposedly grabbed Jackson's arm as he left the courthouse following his grand jury testimony and pleaded, "Say it ain't so, Joe. Say it ain't so." Supposedly Jackson admitted that it was. It never happened. When one reads Jackson's actual grand jury testimony and then the newspaper accounts of it, the number of inconsistencies is astounding.

When the trial concluded, the players were found innocent of any wrongdoing. Commissioner Landis, however, banned the eight players from baseball for life. Jackson's legal wrangling continued for several years, much of it focusing on a dispute with Comiskey over the salary for the remaining two years of Jackson's contract. They eventually settled out of court. Jackson continued to play baseball in various outlaw leagues for the next 15 years, making far more money than he had while with the White Sox. He and his wife, Katie, operated several very successful businesses, including a liquor store and a dry cleaners. In 1942 Jackson gave a lengthy interview to *The Sporting News* and reiterated his innocence. In 1951 the South Carolina legislature passed a measure seeking Jackson's reinstatement to baseball. "Fact and fancy have been so confused," the resolution read, "that today it is still not known what actually took place (in the Series). Thirty-two years is too long for any man to be penalized for an act . . . (when there was) strong evidence that he was no party to the conspiracy." Commissioner Happy Chandler refused to consider it. In 1998 the South Carolina Senate passed a unanimous resolution asking major league baseball to exonerate Jackson with the hope that he would one day be admitted to the Hall of Fame. Commissioner A. Bartlett Giamatti turned down the request. On December 5, 1951, a week before a scheduled appearance on *The Ed Sullivan Show,* Jackson suffered a massive heart attack and died. As of this writing, Joe Jackson, whose .356 lifetime batting average is third best all time, is still not in the Hall of Fame.

CAREER WHITE SOX RECORD:

Games	AB	Hits	Runs
648	2,439	829	396
Avg	**HR**	**RBI**	**SB**
.340	30	426	64

LYONS, TED (SP/RP)
(1923–1942, 1946)

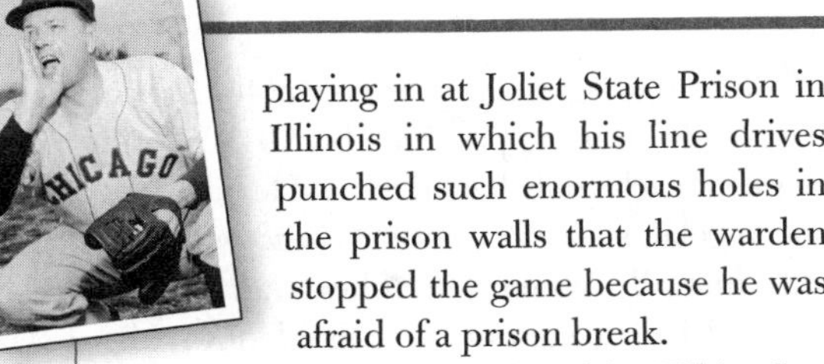

After helping Baylor University win the Southwest Conference championship in 1923, law school student Ted Lyons had occasion to pitch in a publicity stunt against White Sox catcher Ray Schalk while the team was in Waco, Texas, home of Baylor. After the exhibition, Schalk told manager Kid Gleason to immediately sign Lyons to a contract, which he did. Lyons took his signing bonus, bought a new Model T Ford, and joined the White Sox on the road in St. Louis, never spending an inning in the minor leagues. Lyons had great control, once pitching 42 consecutive innings without issuing a walk. Consequently, the games he pitched tended to finish quickly. He once won a complete game in just one hour and 18 minutes. In September 1925, Lyons lost a perfect game with two out in the ninth when Washington's Bobby Veach hit a single. The next year he won a 6–0 no-hitter over the Red Sox. On May 24, 1929, Lyons pitched all 21 innings of a 6–5 loss to Detroit, the third longest outing by a pitcher in AL history.

Lyons, a .364 lifetime hitter (11th all time among pitchers), was a friendly fellow who liked to tell tall tales, especially about his prowess as a hitter. He liked to say that he could hit the hot dog out of a fan's hands without splattering the mustard. On another occasion, he told of an exhibition game he was playing in at Joliet State Prison in Illinois in which his line drives punched such enormous holes in the prison walls that the warden stopped the game because he was afraid of a prison break.

Lyons was beloved by White Sox fans, and management took advantage of it in an unusual way. From 1939 to 1942, the White Sox started him at home only on Sunday, typically the best day of the week to draw fans. It also gave him at least six days of rest between starts. During these four years of Sunday-only assignments, Lyons compiled a 52–30 record with 72 complete games. During his career, Lyons started 484 games and completed 356 of them. Only two players in history—Phil Niekro and Gaylord Perry—have played more seasons without appearing in a World Series. For twenty years after his retirement as an active player, Lyons held various coaching, scouting, and managing jobs for the White Sox, Tigers, and Dodgers. In 1966 he left baseball to help his sister manage the family rice plantation. Lyons, who spent his entire 21-year playing career with the Sox, was elected to the Hall of Fame in 1955.

CAREER WHITE SOX RECORD:

W	L	W%	ERA	SV
260	230	.531	3.67	23

K	BB	SHO	IP
1,073	1,121	27	4,161.0

McMullin, Fred (3B)
(1916–1920) • *Member of the Black Sox*

Of the eight Black Sox, McMullin had the least impact on the 1919 World Series since he only batted twice. He had been the regular shortstop until August when he was injured. When McMullin was healthy again, Risberg continued to hold down the shortstop job for the remainder of the regular season and the World Series. McMullin wasn't even going to be included in the plot because of his insignificant role on the team, but he overheard Risberg and Gandil discussing the plot and demanded to be let in. The other two agreed, fearing McMullin would expose the plot. After banishment from baseball, McMullin entered, ironically, law enforcement, joining the Los Angeles bureau of the U.S. Marshal's Office.

CAREER WHITE SOX RECORD:

Games	AB	Hits	Runs
303	913	234	120
Avg	**HR**	**RBI**	**SB**
.256	1	70	30

Minoso, Minnie (OF)
(1951–1957, 1960–1961, 1964, 1976, 1980)

Born in Cuba, Saturnino Orestes Armas "Minnie" Minoso worked in the sugar fields and, while still a teenager, organized a plantation baseball team. In 1946 he signed with the black ball club, the New York Cubans. The Indians saw him and signed him to a contract in 1948. Minoso played a handful of games with Cleveland in 1949 before being sent back down to the minors. In 1951 he was traded to the White Sox and his career took off. He hit .326 in his rookie season and led the AL in triples and stolen bases, but was runner-up to the Yankees' Gil McDougald in the AL Rookie of the Year voting even though he beat McDougald in 15 of 16 offensive categories. Minoso, a seven-time All-Star and three-time Gold Glove winner, had a gift for getting hit by pitches. He retired as the all-time leader in that department with 189. After hitting .310 with 103 RBIs in 1957, Minoso was traded back to Cleveland in a deal that sent Early Wynn to Chicago. Minoso was devastated; Chicago was his home. When the White Sox won the World Series in 1959, owner Bill Veeck awarded a championship ring to Minoso even though he wasn't on the team. He soon would be, however, as Veeck traded for him in time for the 1960 season. Minoso was so happy to be back in Chicago that he led the AL in hits and finished second in RBIs to Roger Maris.

After spending 1962 with the Cardinals and 1963 with the Senators, Minoso returned to Chicago before—supposedly—retiring in 1964. In September 1976, Veeck brought Minoso back in one of his usual publicity stunts. Minoso played three games and collected a hit, becoming a four-decade player. In September 1980, Veeck brought Minoso back to play in two games. Though he didn't get a hit, Minoso became baseball's second five-decade player, joining Nick Altrock. In June 1993, Minoso played in a game for the St. Paul Saints to become the first six-decade professional ballplayer. Later that year, Veeck announced that the 70-year-old Minoso would play a game for the White Sox as well, but

Commissioner Bud Selig put an end to Veeck's sideshow and prohibited the promotion.

CAREER WHITE SOX RECORD:

Games	AB	Hits	Runs
1,373	5,011	1,523	893
Avg	**HR**	**RBI**	**SB**
.304	135	808	171

ORDOÑEZ, MAGGLIO (OF)
(1997–2004)

The White Sox signed Magglio Ordoñez as a 17-year-old amateur free agent out of Venezuela on May 18, 1991. Although it took him a little over six years to make it to the major leagues, Ordoñez has proved to be one of the best, most consistent, all-around players the game has seen in the last decade. He hits for average as well as power, and has some speed, although a serious leg injury in 2004 appears to have curtailed his stolen-base attempts. When healthy, Ordoñez, a four-time All-Star and six-time .300 hitter, routinely puts up a .300+ average with 30 homers, 100+ runs, and 100+ RBIs. Following the 2004 season, Ordoñez left Chicago via free agency for Detroit. Although he was injured at the start of the season and missed considerable time, when he came back in the middle of the year he seemed to be his old productive self, raising the hopes of Tigers fans for 2006.

CAREER WHITE SOX RECORD:

Games	AB	Hits	Runs
1,001	3,807	1,167	624
Avg	**HR**	**RBI**	**SB**
.307	187	703	82

PIERCE, BILLY (SP/RP)
(1949–1961)

After two years in Detroit, Billy Pierce was traded to the White Sox following the 1948 season for Aaron Robinson. Detroit later tried to cancel the deal, but Chicago refused. Pierce blossomed into a fine pitcher in Chicago, making it to the All-Star Game seven times; he started the Summer Classic three times, allowing just one run total. Pierce was an incomplete pitcher, or so thought Ted Williams. The Boston slugger once told Chicago GM Frank Lane that Pierce would be a much more effective pitcher if he came up with a slider. A few months later, Boston came to Chicago for a series. When Williams got up in the ninth inning with two on and two out, and the game on the line, Pierce induced Williams to pop up on his new pitch—a slider. Pierce won 20 games in both 1956 and 1957, including a near-perfect game that was erased with two out in the ninth when Senators pinch-hitter Ed Fitzgerald hit a double. Following the 1961 season, Pierce was traded to San Francisco, ending his 13-year stint in Chicago. After three years with the Giants, Pierce retired and joined Continental Envelope's sales team.

CAREER WHITE SOX RECORD:

W	L	W%	ERA	SV
186	152	.550	3.19	19
K	**BB**	**SHO**	**IP**	
1,796	1,052	35	2,931.0	

RISBERG, SWEDE (SS)

(1917–1920) • *Member of the Black Sox*

Shortstop Charles "Swede" Risberg was one of the main conspirators in the plot to throw the 1919 World Series for money. Not only did he make numerous obvious errors of commission and omission, but Risberg threatened physical violence to anyone who spoke to the authorities investigating the scandal. Risberg, it was later learned, wired a friend (St. Louis Browns second baseman Joe Gedeon) about the plot. White Sox manager Kid Gleason, having heard the rumors of game fixing, became suspicious of Risberg when he saw him and Ed Cicotte in the Hotel Sinton lobby laughing uncharacteristically after one of the losses. After being kicked out of baseball, Risberg and several other Black Sox tried to undertake a three-state barnstorming tour, but it had to be cancelled when Commissioner Landis threatened to ban for life anyone in organized baseball who played with or against the disgraced players. Going to Plan B, the Black Sox players decided to play a regular exhibition game every Sunday in Chicago. This time the Chicago City Council stepped in and threatened to revoke the ballpark's license if they allowed the weekly event to take place. A decade after the scandal, Risberg announced that other members of the White Sox had participated in a separate game-fixing incident in 1917. This time, it was White Sox players bribing Detroit Tigers players to throw four games their way so Chicago could win the pennant. The accusations were never substantiated. After banishment from baseball, Risberg took up dairy farming in Minnesota and later ran a tavern in California, near the Oregon border.

CAREER WHITE SOX RECORD:

Games	AB	Hits	Runs
476	1,619	394	196
Avg	**HR**	**RBI**	**SB**
.243	6	175	52

SCHALK, RAY (C)

(1912–1928)

Ray Schalk was very small for a catcher, and he looked young for his age. His size and appearance led to many taunts from opposing players, such as, "Hey, Raymond, you got your diapers on?" and "Hey, sonny, where's your mama?" One time Schalk arrived at the ballpark only to be turned away by the policeman guarding the players' entrance. "No kids allowed! Now move along!" When Schalk put up a considerable argument, the policeman finally grabbed him by the collar and dragged him into the locker room where his teammates were dressing for practice. When the cop asked the other players if Schalk was indeed a player, they all denied they had ever seen him before.

During his career, Schalk caught a record four no-hitters, including Charlie Robertson's perfect game. Schalk played defense like a madman, seemingly covering the whole field. Four times in his career he made the putout at second base when the shortstop, second baseman, and center fielder all converged on a pop fly, only to have it fall in for a hit. When the runner tried for second, he was surprised to find Schalk waiting there for him with the ball. He was the first catcher to make putouts at all four bases. When the fix was put on in the 1919 World Series, Schalk was one of the first to suspect something was rotten, and he told manager Kid Gleason of his concerns. In 1927 Schalk became the player-manager of the White Sox. On July 4, 1928, he walked into Comiskey's office and resigned the managerial portion of his job. He told Comiskey that he'd take a pay cut from $25,000 to $15,000 to only catch again. Comiskey offered him $6,000. At first, Schalk threatened to sue, but he eventually dropped the matter. After finishing his 18-year playing career, 17 with Chicago, Schalk coached for the White Sox for two years before managing in the minors for 10 more. He later opened a bowling alley in Chicago. In 1955 Schalk was named to the Hall of Fame.

CAREER WHITE SOX RECORD:

Games	AB	Hits	Runs
1,757	5,304	1,345	579
Avg	**HR**	**RBI**	**SB**
.254	11	594	177

THIGPEN, BOBBY (RP)
(1986–1993)

The White Sox selected Thigpen in the fourth round of the June 1985 amateur draft and brought him up to Chicago the following year. Thigpen was groomed to be a reliever, never once starting a game in nine major league seasons. Thigpen became one of the top closers in baseball when he collected 34 saves for the Sox in both 1988 and 1989. In 1990 he was almost unhittable, collecting a major league record 57 saves. He returned to Earth in 1991 with 30 saves, but he quickly went downhill from there. After just 22 saves in 1992, and an alarming increase in his ERA, Thigpen fell off the charts the next two years, collecting only two saves total. Mysteriously, Thigpen lost his touch. While he officially retired at 30, for all practical purposes his career was over at 28. In his brief time with the White Sox, he did manage to become the team's all-time leader in saves with 201.

CAREER WHITE SOX RECORD:

W	L	W%	ERA	SV
28	33	.459	3.26	201
K	**BB**	**SHO**	**IP**	
362	224	0	541.7	

THOMAS, FRANK (1B/DH)
(1990–2004)

Nicknamed "The Big Hurt," Frank Thomas came up to the White Sox in 1990 after just a year in the minors. He had been a first-round pick in the June 1989 amateur draft. Thomas burst onto the major league scene, putting up overall numbers not seen since the days of Ted Williams. In 1991, his first full season, Thomas hit .318 with 32 homers and walked 138 times. Thomas won the AL MVP Award in both 1993 and 1994. For a decade, Thomas was posting numbers in the range of .330, with 30+ homers, 100+ runs, and 100+ RBIs. Injuries in 2001 and 2004 began to take their toll on Thomas, and his average began to slide. A 2004 foot injury carried over to 2005 and was so serious that some have speculated that Thomas' career may be over, especially given his age (37 at the start of the 2006 season).

CAREER WHITE SOX RECORD:

Games	AB	Hits	Runs
1,925	6,851	2,113	1,308
Avg	**HR**	**RBI**	**SB**
.308	436	1,439	32

VENTURA, ROBIN (3B)
(1989–1998)

Robin Ventura was one of the best college players ever. After three years at Oklahoma State, Ventura was voted the College Player of the Decade (1980s) by *Baseball America* and was also the magazine's choice for third baseman on the All-Time College All-Star Team. In 1988 he helped the United States win a gold medal at the Olympics in Seoul. After just one year in Double-A ball, Ventura, a first-round pick in the June 1988 amateur draft, received a late-season call-up to Chicago in 1989, and by 1990 was the starting third baseman. Although he struggled somewhat in his first year, by 1991 he had it figured out; for most of the next decade he averaged around 20–25 homers with 90+ runs and RBIs. He was also a stellar defensive third baseman, picking up five Gold Gloves. On September 4, 1995, Ventura became just the eighth player in history to hit two grand slams in one game. In 1999, after signing as a free agent with the New York Mets, Ventura became the first major leaguer ever to hit grand slams in both ends of a doubleheader. After 10 years with the White Sox, three with the Mets, and three more with the Yankees and Dodgers, Ventura, his skills fading fast, retired after the 2004 season.

CAREER WHITE SOX RECORD:

Games	AB	Hits	Runs
1,254	4,542	1,244	658
Avg	**HR**	**RBI**	**SB**
.274	171	741	15

WALSH, ED (SP/RP)
(1904–1916)

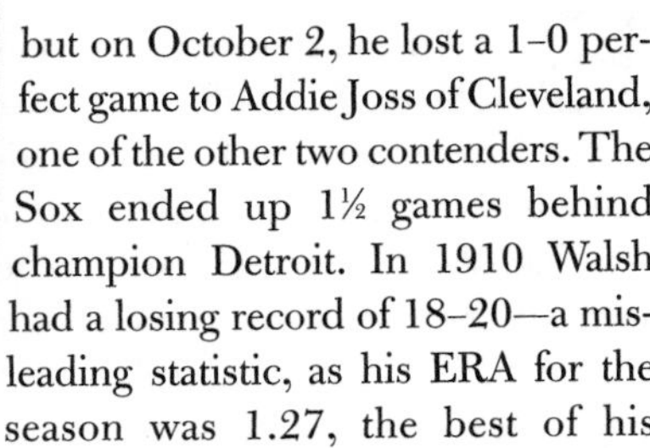

Although big Ed Walsh spent 14 years in the majors, 13 with Chicago, his impressive career statistics were largely compiled in just seven years, 1906–1912. Like many ballplayers of the day, Walsh spent time in the coal mines while playing for a local semipro team. After being a spot starter in 1904 and 1905, Walsh joined the Chicago rotation in 1906, finishing 17–13 and helping the team to the World Series. Owner Charles Comiskey was so overjoyed at his team's pennant, that he threw an extra $15,000 bonus into the World Series money for the players to divide. Then the notoriously tight Comiskey decided to count the bonus against the players' 1907 salaries.

Walsh got even better in 1907, winning 24 games, his sudden improvement coming from mastering the spitball. In 1908 Walsh had a season that could almost be called superhuman. He started 49 games, relieved in 17 more, and collected 40 wins and 6 saves. Within his 464 innings pitched (the 20th-century record), Walsh tossed 42 complete games and 11 shutouts, all the while maintaining a 1.42 ERA. Down the stretch in the heat of a three-team pennant race, Walsh pitched seven of the team's last nine games. He nearly pulled it off, but on October 2, he lost a 1–0 perfect game to Addie Joss of Cleveland, one of the other two contenders. The Sox ended up 1½ games behind champion Detroit. In 1910 Walsh had a losing record of 18–20—a misleading statistic, as his ERA for the season was 1.27, the best of his career. However, the White Sox had compiled a truly anemic .211 team batting average, and were even worse in the field, committing 314 errors. On August 27, 1911, Walsh threw a no-hitter, defeating Boston, 5–0. Following the 1912 season, Walsh pitched almost daily in a series of exhibition games, ruining his arm in the process. Over his remaining five years, Walsh's inning count fell to 98, 45, 27, 3, and 18. Once again, another great pitcher had been ruined by overuse. After his playing days were over, Walsh spent time as a minor league manager, college coach, and umpire. Walsh's career ERA of 1.82 is the lowest of any pitcher with more than 1,000 innings pitched. Walsh was elected to the Hall of Fame in 1946.

CAREER WHITE SOX RECORD:

W	L	W%	ERA	SV
195	125	.609	1.81	34

K	BB	SHO	IP
1,732	608	57	2,946.3

WEAVER, BUCK (SS/3B)
(1912–1920) • *Member of the Black Sox*

Buck Weaver did not take part in the World Series fix, nor did he accept any money, but he apparently knew it was taking place. For this he was banished along with the other seven. Weaver had a great Series, hitting .324, with four doubles, a triple, and six singles, and fielding 27 chances without an error. Weaver, considered one of the premier third basemen in the league, played in, almost daring the batter to bunt against him. Even Ty Cobb refused to bunt against Weaver. In 1920, his last year before banishment, Weaver hit a career-high .331.

When the Black Sox trial took place, Weaver requested separate proceedings, but was denied. In court he sat apart from the other players, trying to distance himself. Before Judge Hugo Friend gave the jury their instructions, he told them there was so little evidence against Weaver that he would not let stand a guilty verdict against him. New York Giants manager John McGraw watched the trial with interest, wanting to sign Weaver the moment his name was cleared. When the not-guilty verdicts were read in court, Weaver and Swede Risberg danced around the courtroom. Their joy was short-lived. The next day Commissioner Landis banned all eight players for life. On numerous occasions over the years, Weaver applied for reinstatement from Landis, as well as his successors, Happy Chandler and Ford Frick. They all turned him down. After banishment, Weaver became a pharmacist in Chicago and, like most of the other Black Sox, played on a succession of outlaw semipro teams.

CAREER WHITE SOX RECORD:

Games	AB	Hits	Runs
1,254	4,809	1,308	623
Avg	**HR**	**RBI**	**SB**
.272	21	420	172

WHITE, DOC (SP/RP)
(1903–1913)

Guy "Doc" White was an actual doctor, maintaining a dentistry practice in Washington, D.C., from 1902 to 1906. He was also an accomplished singer and businessman. While pitching for Georgetown University, White drew notice from the baseball world when he once struck out the first nine Holy Cross batters to face him. He went directly from the college campus to the big leagues in Philadelphia, then jumped to Chicago two years later during the war between the leagues. In 1906 White pitched five consecutive shutouts, the major league record until Don Drysdale broke it in 1968—and White accomplished his feat in the midst of a September pennant race. After leading the "Hitless Wonders" White Sox to the Series, Doc White pitched the clincher in Game 6 to give the title to Chicago. In 1907 his 27 victories led the American League and he had a streak of 65 consecutive innings without allowing a walk. White had four seasons in which his ERA was below 2.00, including three in a row from 1904 to

1906. After his playing career ended in 1913, White spent seven years in the minors as a manager and team executive. Later he became a longtime college teacher and coach. When Drysdale broke White's record in 1968, the 89-year-old White sent Drysdale a congratulatory telegram on the day of the sixth shutout. A few months later he died.

CAREER WHITE SOX RECORD:

W	L	W%	ERA	SV
159	123	.564	2.30	4

K	BB	SHO	IP
1,067	542	42	2,498.3

WILLIAMS, LEFTY (SP/RP)

(1916–1920) • *Member of the Black Sox*

Chick Gandil and Swede Risberg knew they needed another pitcher besides Ed Cicotte on their side in order to have a chance of throwing the Series. Their choice of Claude "Lefty" Williams was curious since he was a young and talented pitcher, had just come off a 23–11 season, with his whole future in front of him. Gandil and Risberg had to have been great salesmen. After Cicotte's Game 1 loss, Williams, who had excellent control, pitched his usual solid game for three innings. Then he walked three batters in the fourth inning, something he had never done. (During the season he walked only 58 batters in nearly 300 innings.) White Sox catcher Ray Schalk, livid with Williams because he felt the pitcher was crossing him up on his pitches and locations, shared his suspicions with manager Kid Gleason. Some fanciful articles and movies of the scandal have depicted an angry Schalk pummeling Williams on the way to the clubhouse after the Game 2 loss, but both Williams and Schalk said it never happened. After Cicotte lost Game 4, Williams lost Game 5, though more due to miserable outfield play than compromised pitching.

Dickie Kerr got his second win in Game 6 while Cicotte, angry over the gamblers not paying what they promised, won Game 7 of the nine-game Series. Williams went in Game 8 under the watchful eyes of Gleason and Schalk. Unbeknownst to the two, Williams and his wife had been threatened the night before in their hotel. Either Williams got knocked out in the first, or one or both of them would wind up dead. Williams did as instructed. He threw only moderate-speed fastballs, allowing four runs in the first before Gleason yanked him. The Sox couldn't overcome Williams' treason and lost the Series, five games to three. The offseason swirled with rumors, but 1920 began as usual. Williams won 22 games in 1920 before the scandal broke in late September. Though acquitted at trial of trying to defraud the public, Williams and the seven other implicated Black Sox were banned for life by Commissioner Landis. After his banishment, Williams ran a poolroom in Chicago for years while playing in several outlaw leagues. He later moved to California and opened a plant nursery.

CAREER WHITE SOX RECORD:

W	L	W%	ERA	SV
81	44	.648	3.09	4

K	BB	SHO	IP
506	341	10	1,156.0

WOOD, WILBUR (SP/RP)
(1967–1978)

After five years with the Red Sox and Pirates, Wilbur Wood joined the White Sox when Pittsburgh traded him to Chicago for Juan Pizarro. The knuckleballer then spent the last 12 years of his 17-year career with the White Sox. From 1971 to 1974, he won more than 20 games each year, topping out with 24 wins twice. He made the All-Star team three times during that span as well. Because the knuckleball put little strain on his arm, Wood was able to start more games than the average pitcher. In 1971 when he won 22 games, 14 of the wins came on just two day's rest. In 1972 Wood started 49 games, two short of Jack Chesbro's 20th-century record set in 1904. His 376⅔ innings were the most pitched since Grover Cleveland Alexander's 387 in 1917.

In 1973 Wood won both ends of a doubleheader on May 28 and lost both ends of a doubleheader on July 20. In May 1976 a line drive off the bat of the Tigers' Ron LeFlore hit Wood in the kneecap and knocked him out for the rest of the season. Wood was never the same after that. He only won 17 more games in two years, with an ERA much higher than normal, and he retired. After leaving baseball, Wood opened a fish store in Boston.

CAREER WHITE SOX RECORD:

W	L	W%	ERA	SV
163	148	.524	3.18	57

K	BB	SHO	IP
1,332	671	24	2,524.3

Cincinnati Reds

Since 1882

1935 Team Ball

1892 On June 2, Benjamin Harrison becomes the first U.S. president to attend a major league baseball game while in office when he watches the Washington Senators lose to the visiting Cincinnati Reds, 7–4....**1917** On May 2, the Cincinnati Reds' Fred Toney and the Chicago Cubs' Hippo Vaughn pitch the only double no-hitter in major league history, won by the Reds, 1–0, on a 10th-inning hit....**1935** Cincinnati wins the first night game in major league history, beating the Phillies, 2–1, on May 24 in Crosley Field....**1968** Pete Rose wins the batting title with a .335 average, marking the first time in National League history that a switch-hitter wears the batting crown....**1975** The Boston-Cincinnati World Series is the first to feature two teams without a 20-game winner. Rick Wise leads the Red Sox with 19 wins, while three Reds (Jack Billingham, Gary Nolan, and Don Gullett) have 15 wins each.

FRANCHISE HISTORY

The current Cincinnati Reds franchise began play in the American Association in 1882 and moved to the National League in 1890. A *different* Cincinnati Reds franchise had begun play in the National League in 1876, but disbanded after the 1877 season due to financial problems. It was resurrected under new ownership before the 1878 season but by 1880 was again suffering financial strain. Cincinnati Reds owner W.H. Kennett tried to help his bottom line by selling whiskey during the games and leasing the park out for Sunday games to other local teams, two things prohibited under National League bylaws, and he was told to cease and desist or face expulsion. Kennett refused to sign a pledge banning Sunday baseball and whiskey sales and Cincinnati was booted out of the National League, replaced by the Detroit Wolverines for the 1881 season. A Cincinnati reporter noted in his column that "while the league is in the missionary field . . . they should turn their attention to Chicago and prohibit the admission to the Lake Front Grounds of the great number of prostitutes who patronize the game up there." The Cincinnati club went bankrupt following the 1880 season and the players scattered where they could.

Because most major league players didn't use gloves for the first 15–20 years of professional baseball, fielding averages were much lower than we are accustomed to today. The fielding averages gradually rose, and in 1896, when all their players finally began wearing gloves, the Reds became the first team to break the .950 fielding percentage barrier.

After the original Cincinnati team was kicked out of the National League in 1880, Cincinnati sportswriter O.P. Caylor joined with the Spink family of St. Louis to create a new major league, the American Association. Colonel Harris, the receiver of the bankrupt team, persuaded local clothier Aaron Stern to purchase principal interest in the club in 1881, and in 1882 the team joined the newly formed league, playing games on Sundays, selling whiskey, and charging just 25¢ admission compared to the National League's 50¢. Stern put together a strong team and won the American Association pennant in the league's first year of operation. It would be the team's only pennant during their eight-year stay in the league.

During the 1882 and 1883 seasons, the Reds played their home games at Bank Street Grounds. Just before the 1884 season, the team learned that the Cincinnati franchise of the new Union Association would also be playing their home games at Bank Street Grounds, so the Reds players ransacked the ballpark just before the Union Association team was about to occupy it, then built a new park on the site where Crosley Field eventually stood. By 1889 owner Stern was fed up with the American Association's leadership and tried to force a change during the 1889 winter meetings but a deadlock resulted. Consequently, Cincinnati and Brooklyn left the American Association and joined the National League in time for the 1890 season.

Just when things were looking better for Stern, *another* new major league, the Players' League, formed and began play in 1890. So confusion continued as teams were raided for personnel, and players jumped back and forth from team to team and league to league. When all the wrangling was over, Stern had been forced out and the Cincinnati franchise belonged to John Brush, former owner of the Indianapolis team. Brush retained ownership of the team until 1902, when he sold it to August "Garry" Hermann for $125,000. In a parlay move similar to what would be employed in 2002 between the Expos, Red Sox and Marlins, Brush, one of baseball's most influential owners of the 1890s,

The 1888 Cincinnati Red Stockings.

In stark contrast to 1886, when Cincinnati shortstop Frank Fennelly committed 117 errors himself, the entire 1958 Cincinnati team made only 100 errors, setting a new major league record.

took the money and bought the New York Giants, something everyone approved of because it got rid of despised New York owner Andrew Freedman.

Hermann was the principal owner of the Reds from 1902 to 1927. From 1903 to 1920, he was also chairman of baseball's version of the Supreme Court, the National Commission, a three-member body that governed baseball until the commissioner's position was created in 1920. Hermann also was in charge of Cincinnati Waterworks and served as Grand Exalted Ruler of All the Elks in America. There were several prominent minority owners during Hermann's tenure, including Cincinnati mayor George Cox, and Max and Julius Fleischmann, sons of Charles Fleischmann (of Fleischmann's Margarine and Fleischmann's Yeast fame). Julius Fleischmann later became the youngest mayor ever in Cincinnati's history. Hermann began to encounter various health problems in the last few years of his ownership, including blindness, and he turned over the affairs of the team to C.J. McDiarmod, who sold the club in 1930. Ty Cobb had offered $275,000 for the team in 1928, but his offer was rejected. Wrote Cobb in his diary in 1946, "If I had bought the Cincinnati club in 1930 at $300,000, I would have lost my shirt. Team drew under 500,000 for 10 years. Horseshit town today." The man who did buy the team in 1930 for $300,000 was Sidney Weil, a man who made his fortune in a Ford automobile dealership and a chain of garages. When the stock market crashed, Weil lost the team to bankruptcy in 1933. He later became a millionaire again in the life insurance business.

After Weil went into bankruptcy, his bank repossessed the team and employed baseball executive Larry MacPhail to run the team. MacPhail approached local businessman Powell Crosley about buying the team for $450,000 and saving it for the city of Cincinnati. After considerable effort on MacPhail's part, Crosley, whose company

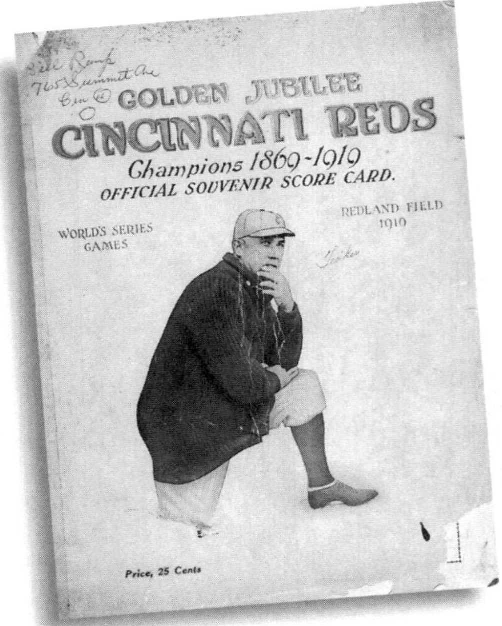

Rare program for the ill-fated World Series.

manufactured radios, appliances, and automobile bodies, finally agreed to buy the team. Crosley also owned the Crosley Broadcasting Company, which included station WLW, the leading Cincinnati station. The station was so powerful (500,000 watts) that it could be heard in Australia. After World War II the power was reduced to 50,000 watts, the maximum now available under federal law. Crosley owned the team until his death in 1961, whereupon his brother ran the team for two more years before selling out in 1963 to a group headed by Bill DeWitt. DeWitt owned the team for just a few years, selling in early 1967, primarily because of his dissatisfaction over leasing arrangements at Crosley Field involving the NFL. He sold the team for $7 million to an ownership group headed by Francis Dale, publisher of the *Cincinnati Enquirer* newspaper. The ownership group incorporated under the name 617, Inc., the street address of the *Enquirer*. By 1973 Louis Nippert, one of the 12 owners who had purchased minority shares in the team in 1967, had taken control of 51 percent of the team. By 1980 he owned 90 percent. In 1981 a new group took control, headed by Cincinnati financier brothers James and William Williams, minority shareholders in the Francis Dale group. Other limited partners were Lloyd Miller, Morley Baldwin, Carl Kroch, and Marge Schott.

Schott, owner of two car dealerships, a large amount of General Motors stock, and a dozen or so other businesses, gained control in 1985 by acquiring 40 percent of the team. Raised in a convent, Schott came from a strict German family. Her father had made his fortune in plywood and veneer. Schott's tenure was riddled with controversy, both behind the scenes (in 1991 several of her partners sued her over nonpayment of funds) and in public (she was suspended on two separate occasions for racist remarks). She became embattled with the city over various demands and threatened to move the team to another city if they weren't met. Schott exasperated virtually everyone she came in contact with—her limited partners, her players, other owners, and baseball commissioners. Baseball heaved a huge sigh of relief when she sold out in 1999 to a group of her limited partners headed by Carl Lindner, owner of Great American Insurance Co., for $67 million. Several of the limited partners put their combined 51 percent share of the team up for sale in 2005 and a tentative deal was struck to sell the team to a group of Cincinnati area businessmen headed by Robert Castellini, chairman of a Cincinnati-based produce company, but the sale was still pending the approval of Major League Baseball at the end of 2005.

The Cincinnati team has always been known officially as the Reds, Red Stockings, or Redlegs. The original National League franchise was known as the Red Stockings from 1876 to 1880, as was the American Association franchise from 1882 to 1889. When the team switched to the National League in 1890, it changed its official name to the Reds, but was known unofficially as the Kellys for two years. Because of the anti-Communist fervor toward the end of World War II, the team felt itself "Better Dead Than Reds" and changed its official name to the Redlegs in 1944–1945. From 1946 to 1953 the name reverted to the Reds, and then in 1954 went back to the Redlegs again, no doubt for fear of being called before Senator Joe McCarthy's House Un-American Activities Committee. Cincinnati sportswriter Tom Swope said of the name changes, "We were known as the Reds before the Communists. Let them change their name." The team changed its name one final time in 1961—back to the Reds.

TEAM NAME HISTORY

Official Names

Red Stockings (1882–1889)
Reds (1890–1943)
Redlegs (1944–1945)
Reds (1946–1953)
Redlegs (1954–1960)
Reds (1961–current)

Unofficial Names/Nicknames

Kellys, Big Red Machine

STADIUM HISTORY

Bank Street Grounds	1882–1883
Cincinnati Base Ball Grounds	1884–1889
Western Avenue Grounds (Cincinnati Base Ball Grounds renamed)	1890–1891
League Park (Western Avenue Grounds renamed)	1892–1901
Palace of the Fans (League Park rebuilt and renamed)	1902–1911
Redland Field (Palace of the Fans improved and renamed)	1912–1933
Crosley Field (Redland Field renamed)	1934–June 24, 1970
Riverfront Stadium	June 30, 1970–1996
Cinergy Field (Riverfront Stadium renamed)	1997–2002
Great American Ball Park	2003–current

The 1919 World Series at Redland Field, later known as Crosley Field.

YEARLY RECORD, FINISH, & ATTENDANCE FIGURES

Year	League	Record	DIV/LG Finish	Attendance	Avg/Gm
2005	NL Cent	73–89	5	1,943,067	23,696
2004	NL Cent	76–86	4	2,287,250	28,238
2003	NL Cent	69–93	5	2,355,259	29,077
2002	NL Cent	78–84	3	1,855,787	22,911
2001	NL Cent	66–96	5	1,879,757	23,207
2000	NL Cent	85–77	2	2,577,371	31,431
1999	NL Cent	96–67	2	2,061,222	25,137
1998	NL Cent	77–85	4	1,793,649	22,144
1997	NL Cent	76–86	3	1,785,788	22,047
1996	NL Cent	81–81	3	1,861,428	22,981
1995	NL Cent	85–59	1	1,837,649	25,523
1994	NL Cent	66–48	1	1,897,681	31,628
1993	NL West	73–89	5	2,453,232	30,287
1992	NL West	90–72	2	2,315,946	28,592
1991	NL West	74–88	5	2,372,377	29,289
1990	NL West	91–71	1	2,400,892	29,641
1989	NL West	75–87	5	1,979,320	24,436
1988	NL West	87–74	2	2,072,528	25,907
1987	NL West	84–78	2	2,185,205	26,978
1986	NL West	86–76	2	1,692,432	20,894
1985	NL West	89–72	2	1,834,619	22,650
1984	NL West	70–92	5	1,275,887	15,752
1983	NL West	74–88	6	1,190,419	14,697
1982	NL West	61–101	6	1,326,528	16,377
1981	NL West	66–42	2/2	1,093,730	20,254
1980	NL West	89–73	3	2,022,450	24,664
1979	NL West	90–71	1	2,356,933	29,462
1978	NL West	92–69	2	2,532,497	31,656
1977	NL West	88–74	2	2,519,670	31,107
1976	NL West	102–60	1	2,629,708	32,466
1975	NL West	108–54	1	2,315,603	28,588
1974	NL West	98–64	2	2,164,307	26,394
1973	NL West	99–63	1	2,017,601	24,909
1972	NL West	95–59	1	1,611,459	21,203
1971	NL West	79–83	5	1,501,122	18,532
1970	NL West	102–60	1	1,803,568	22,266
1969	NL West	89–73	3	987,991	12,197
1968	NL	83–79	4	733,354	8,943
1967	NL	87–75	4	958,300	11,831
1966	NL	76–84	7	742,958	9,405
1965	NL	89–73	4	1,047,824	12,936
1964	NL	92–70	3	862,466	10,518
1963	NL	86–76	5	858,805	10,603
1962	NL	98–64	3	982,095	12,125
1961	NL	93–61	1	1,117,603	14,514
1960	NL	67–87	6	663,486	8,617
1959	NL	74–80	5	801,298	10,406
1958	NL	76–78	4	788,582	10,241
1957	NL	80–74	4	1,070,850	13,907
1956	NL	91–63	3	1,125,928	14,622
1955	NL	75–79	5	693,662	9,009

YEARLY RECORD, FINISH, & ATTENDANCE FIGURES (CONT.)

Year	League	Record	DIV/LG Finish	Attendance	Avg/Gm
1954	NL	74–80	5	704,167	9,145
1953	NL	68–86	6	548,086	7,027
1952	NL	69–85	6	604,197	7,847
1951	NL	68–86	6	588,268	7,640
1950	NL	66–87	6	538,794	7,089
1949	NL	62–92	7	707,782	9,074
1948	NL	64–89	7	823,386	10,693
1947	NL	73–81	5	899,975	11,688
1946	NL	67–87	6	715,751	9,295
1945	NL	61–93	7	290,070	3,767
1944	NL	89–65	3	409,567	5,251
1943	NL	87–67	2	379,122	4,861
1942	NL	76–76	4	427,031	5,546
1941	NL	88–66	3	643,513	8,146
1940	NL	100–53	1	850,180	11,041
1939	NL	97–57	1	981,443	12,117
1938	NL	82–68	4	706,756	9,179
1937	NL	56–98	8	411,221	5,140
1936	NL	74–80	5	466,345	6,136
1935	NL	68–85	6	448,247	5,898
1934	NL	52–99	8	206,773	2,651
1933	NL	58–94	8	218,281	2,763
1932	NL	60–94	8	356,950	4,636
1931	NL	58–96	8	263,316	3,420
1930	NL	59–95	7	386,727	5,022
1929	NL	66–88	7	295,040	3,783
1928	NL	78–74	5	490,490	6,288
1927	NL	75–78	5	442,164	5,527
1926	NL	87–67	2	672,987	8,740
1925	NL	80–73	3	464,920	6,117
1924	NL	83–70	4	473,707	6,233
1923	NL	91–63	2	575,063	7,373
1922	NL	86–68	2	493,754	6,250
1921	NL	70–83	6	311,227	4,095
1920	NL	82–71	3	568,107	7,378
1919	NL	96–44	1	532,501	7,607
1918	NL	68–60	3	163,009	2,296
1917	NL	78–76	4	269,056	3,363
1916	NL	60–93	8	255,846	3,366
1915	NL	71–83	7	218,878	2,771
1914	NL	60–94	8	100,791	1,309
1913	NL	64–89	7	258,000	3,308
1912	NL	75–78	4	344,000	4,468
1911	NL	70–83	6	300,000	3,659
1910	NL	75–79	5	380,622	4,943
1909	NL	77–76	4	424,643	5,308
1908	NL	73–81	5	399,200	5,184
1907	NL	66–87	6	317,500	3,920
1906	NL	64–87	6	330,056	4,231
1905	NL	79–74	5	313,927	3,974
1904	NL	88–65	3	391,915	4,961

YEARLY RECORD, FINISH, & ATTENDANCE FIGURES (CONT.)

Year	League	Record	DIV/LG Finish	Attendance	Avg/Gm
1903	NL	74–65	4	351,680	4,627
1902	NL	70–70	4	217,300	3,104
1901	NL	52–87	8	205,728	2,857
1900	NL	62–77	7	170,000	2,361
1899	NL	83–67	6	259,536	3,327
1898	NL	92–60	3	336,378	4,285
1897	NL	76–56	4	336,800	5,027
1896	NL	77–50	3	373,000	5,828
1895	NL	66–64	8	281,000	4,258
1894	NL	55–75	10	158,000	2,394
1893	NL	65–63	6	194,250	2,966
1892	NL	82–68	5	196,473	2,535
1891	NL	56–81	7	97,500	1,413
1890	NL	77–55	4	131,980	1,970
1889	AA	76–63	4	N/A	N/A
1888	AA	80–54	4	N/A	N/A
1887	AA	81–54	2	N/A	N/A
1886	AA	65–73	5	N/A	N/A
1885	AA	63–49	2	N/A	N/A
1884	AA	68–41	5	N/A	N/A
1883	AA	61–37	3	N/A	N/A
1882	AA	55–25	1	N/A	N/A

MANAGER HISTORY

Manager	Years	W–L	Win %
Pop Snyder	1882–1883, 1884	140–76	.648
Will White	1884	44–27	.620
Oliver Caylor	1885–1886	128–122	.512
Gus Schmelz	1887–1889	237–171	.581
Tom Loftus	1890–1891	133–136	.494
Charles Comiskey	1892–1894	202–206	.495
Buck Ewing	1895–1899	394–297	.570
Bob Allen	1900	62–77	.446
Biddy McPhee	1901–1902	79–124	.389
Frank Bancroft	1902	9–7	.563
Joe Kelley	1902–1905	275–230	.545
Ned Hanlon	1906–1907	130–174	.428
John Ganzel	1908	73–81	.474
Clark Griffith	1909–1911	222–238	.483
Hank O'Day	1912	75–78	.490
Joe Tinker	1913	64–89	.418
Buck Herzog	1914–1916	165–226	.422
Christy Mathewson	1916–1918	164–176	.482
Heinie Groh	1918	7–3	.700
Pat Moran	1919–1923	425–329	.564
Jack Hendricks	1924–1929	469–450	.510
Dan Howley	1930–1932	177–285	.383
Donie Bush	1933	58–94	.382
Bob O'Farrell	1934	30–60	.333

MANAGER HISTORY (CONT.)

Manager	Years	W–L	Win %
Chuck Dressen	1934–1937	214–282	.431
Bobby Wallace	1937	5–20	.200
Bill McKechnie	1938–1946	744–631	.541
Hank Gowdy	1946	3–1	.750
Johnny Neun	1947–1948	117–137	.461
Bucky Walters	1948–1949	81–123	.397
Luke Sewell	1950–1952	174–234	.426
Earle Brucker	1952	3–2	.600
Rogers Hornsby	1952–1953	91–106	.462
Buster Mills	1953	4–4	.500
Birdie Tebbetts	1954–1958	372–357	.510
Jimmie Dykes	1958	24–17	.585
Mayo Smith	1959	35–45	.438
Fred Hutchinson	1959–1964	443–372	.544
Dick Sisler	1964–1965	121–94	.563
Don Heffner	1966	37–46	.446
Dave Bristol	1966–1969	298–265	.529
Sparky Anderson	1970–1978	863–586	.596
John McNamara	1979–1982	279–244	.533
Russ Nixon	1982–1983	101–131	.435
Vern Rapp	1984	51–70	.421
Pete Rose	1984–1989	412–373	.525
Tommy Helms	1988, 1989	28–36	.438
Lou Piniella	1990–1992	255–231	.525
Tony Perez	1993	20–24	.455
Davey Johnson	1993–1995	204–172	.543
Ray Knight	1996–1997	124–137	.475
Jack McKeon	1997–2000	291–259	.529
Bob Boone	2001–2003	190–238	.444
Dave Miley	2003–2005	125–164	.433
Jerry Narron	2005	46–46	.500

ALL-TIME WIN-LOSS RECORDS VS. ALL OPPONENTS (SINCE 1900)

Opponent	W–L
ALL TIME	8,242–8,169
Angels	1–2
Astros	381–351
Athletics	0–6
Blue Jays	1–2
Braves	1,057–953
Brewers	60–63
Cardinals	908–1,027
Cubs	954–977
Devil Rays	6–0
Diamondbacks	28–30
Dodgers	992–1,015
Giants	899–1,108
Indians	16–23
INTERLEAGUE	55–69
Mariners	0–3
Marlins	63–51
Mets	286–235
Nationals	214–179
Orioles	2–1
Padres	301–239
Phillies	1,036–826
Pirates	945–992
Rangers	4–2
Red Sox	0–3
Rockies	63–54
Royals	5–3
Tigers	6–6
Twins	7–8
White Sox	2–9
Yankees	2–1

Franchise Highlights, Low Points, and Strange Distinctions

1886 When Cincinnati shortstop Frank Fennelly committed 117 errors, he was the first player in history to break the 100-error mark.

• • • •

1889 Rookie pitcher Jesse Duryea won 32 games and was second in the league with a 2.56 ERA. But he would win only 27 more games in his career, which spanned four seasons with the Reds, Cardinals, and Senators.

• • • •

1896 Because most major league players didn't use gloves for the first 15–20 years of professional baseball, fielding averages were much lower than we are accustomed to today. The fielding averages gradually rose, and in 1896, when all their players finally began wearing gloves, the Reds became first team to break the .950 fielding percentage barrier.

• • • •

1898 Ted Breitenstein of Cincinnati and Jim Hughes of Baltimore both pitched no-hitters on April 22, the first time in major league history that two no-hitters were pitched on the same day.

• • • •

1899 When the pathetic Cleveland Spiders came to Cincinnati for their season finale, they didn't even bother to bring any of their regular pitchers with them, so they drafted Cincinnati cigar store clerk Eddie Kolb out of the stands to pitch for them. He lost, of course, but he did pitch a complete game. He allowed 18 hits, five walks, and hit one batter. The Reds scored 19 runs, but in Kolb's defense, only nine were earned, making his game/season/career ERA 10.12. He also went 1-for-4 at the plate, hitting a single and scoring a run.

• • • •

1901 Noodles Hahn won 22 games for the last-place Reds, who finished at 52–87. He was the last left-handed 20-game winner for a last-place team until Steve Carlton accomplished the same feat in 1972. Hahn also recorded 41 complete games in 1901, a record for a 20th-century left-hander.

On June 9, 1901, Cincinnati pitchers allowed the most hits ever in a nine-inning National League game when the Giants knocked them around for 31 hits.

• • • •

1903 Cincinnati shortstop Tommy Corcoran made a record 14 assists in a 4–2 win at St. Louis on August 7.

• • • •

1905 The Triple Crown is baseball's most elusive honor. In fact, no one has won it since Carl Yastrzemski in 1967. Cincinnati outfielder Cy Seymour came close in 1905, when he led the National League with a .377 average, 121 RBIs, and also led in hits, total bases, doubles, triples, and slugging average. Unfortunately, he finished with eight home runs, one behind league leader and teammate Fred Odwell, who had nine. Incidentally, Odwell never hit another homer in the majors after 1905.

1920 Cincinnati participated in the last tripleheader in major league history when they took two out of three from the Pirates on October 2.

• • • •

1921 Eppa Rixey allowed only one home run in 301 innings, a National League record since the end of the dead-ball era.

• • • •

1923 Led by three 20-game winners (Dolf Luque, Pete Donohue, and Eppa Rixey), the Cincinnati staff posted an ERA that was nearly a half run better than any other team in the majors.

• • • •

1924 It was a tragic year for the Reds. Manager Pat Moran died during spring training and first baseman Jake Daubert died following surgery on October 9.

• • • •

1930 After playing 15 years for the Detroit Tigers, outfielder Harry Heilmann came to Cincinnati and homered against every National League team. That gave him the distinction of becoming the first player to hit a home run in every major league park in use during his career.

• • • •

1933 The last-place Cincinnati Reds set a National League record when their pitching staff issued just 257 walks all season.

1934 Several Cincinnati teammates flew to a game in Chicago during the season, thus becoming the first teammates to travel together by air.

• • • •

1938 When Johnny Vander Meer pitched his back-to-back no-hitters, it was the only season between 1917 and 1944 that the National League featured two no-nos in the same season.

• • • •

1939 Bucky Walters and Paul Derringer combined for 52 wins, the best 1–2 tandem in the National League during the 1930s.

• • • •

1940 Cincinnati first baseman Frank McCormick tied a National League record when he led the league in hits for the third straight season.

The Reds won a major league record 41 one-run games.

• • • •

1946 Forgetting how they did it in 1940, the Reds lost a major league record 41 one-run games, the same number they won six years earlier.

• • • •

1948 Catcher Ray Lamanno had 93 hits, but only 105 total bases. His .273 slugging average was only 31 points higher than his .242 batting average.

1949 Reds shortstop Virgil Stallcup, a notorious free swinger, walked just nine times in 575 at-bats.

• • • •

1954 Though he amassed big home-run totals, Ted Kluszewski very seldom struck out. In 1954, when he clouted 49 homers to lead the league, he struck out only 35 times.

• • • •

1956 After finishing in the second division for 11 straight years, the Reds exploded into contention when rookie Frank Robinson sparked the team. Though they finished third, just two games back of the pennant-winning Dodgers, the Reds served notice that they had arrived, particularly in the power department. Cincinnati tied the existing major league record held by the New York Giants by hitting 221 home runs on the season, led by Robinson's 38, Wally Post's 36, and Ted Kluszewski's 35. Gus Bell hit 29 and Ed Bailey 28 as the Reds came oh, so close, to having the first team in history with five 30-homer men.

• • • •

1957 The fans chose the eight starting position players in the All-Star teams by ballot. In order to help the local boys, a Cincinnati newspaper printed All-Star ballots and urged their readers to vote for the Reds players and stuff the ballot boxes. The readers happily obliged, and the Reds won all the 1957 National League starting jobs except one. An infuriated Commissioner Ford Frick later kicked Wally Post and Gus Bell off the team and replaced them with Hank Aaron and Willie Mays. He also took the vote away from the fans and gave it to the players, coaches, and managers. It wasn't returned to the fans until 1970.

1958 In stark contrast to 1886, when Cincinnati shortstop Frank Fennelly committed 117 errors himself, the entire Cincinnati team made only 100 errors, setting a new major league record.

• • • •

1960 The Reds set a 20th-century record for the lowest winning percentage (.435) by a team that would win the pennant the following year. That record was broken by the 1990 Atlanta Braves (.401).

• • • •

1961 After averaging just over three wins a year in seven seasons with the Braves, Joey Jay came to the Reds in a trade before the 1961 season and surprised everyone by winning 21 games and helping the Reds to their first pennant since 1940. He followed it up with another 21-victory season in 1962 and then faded into obscurity, winning an average of just eight games a year for the next four years before leaving baseball.

• • • •

1962 Cincinnati pitchers got no respect in the 1960s when it came to Cy Young balloting. Even though Joey Jay led the league in wins in 1961 with 21, he failed to get a single first-place Cy Young vote. In 1962 when he won 21 again, Jay didn't get any votes. Teammate Bob Purkey finished 23–5 with a major league leading .821 winning percentage that same year, but got only one first-place vote. In 1963 Jim Maloney finished 23–7 with 265 strikeouts but didn't get a single first-place vote. And in 1965 Sammy Ellis went 22–10 and failed to get even one first-place vote.

1968 Longtime Reds outfielder Vada Pinson, who played his last year with Cincinnati in 1968, is one of only three players with 2,750 or more career hits who is eligible for the Hall of Fame, but not enshrined. Harold Baines and Andre Dawson are the others. Fellow Red Pete Rose is currently ineligible.

• • • •

1975 The nickname "Big Red Machine" was an appropriate one in 1975. That season the Reds outscored every other team in the league by at least 105 runs. In 1976, the Reds scored 857 runs, 232 more than any other team in their division.

• • • •

1976 The Reds won their second straight World Series title despite leaving a National League–record 1,328 men on base during the season.

Dan Driessen became the first designated hitter in National League history when he came to bat as the team's DH in the 1976 World Series, the first year the two leagues agreed to use it in American League parks during World Series play.

• • • •

1978 Second baseman Joe Morgan put together a 91-game errorless streak that ended in 1978.

• • • •

1981 The Reds had the best record in baseball, but because of the player strike, a split-season format was implemented. The Reds ended up finishing second in their division in both halves and failed to make the postseason.

1984 Pete Rose set a record when he had his 22nd consecutive season with 100 or more hits.

• • • •

1987 Eric Davis set a record for the most combined home runs and steals by a member of the 30–30 club with 87. He had 37 homers and 50 steals.

• • • •

1990 The Reds, with a 9–0 start, became the first team in National League history to reside in first place from start to finish in a 162-game season. They also swept the A's in the World Series. The only time the Reds trailed in their pursuit of the World Series championship was after the first game of the NLCS when the Pirates beat them, 4–3, to take a 1–0 lead in the series. The Reds took the next three in a row and won the series, four games to two.

In the 1990 World Series, Billy Hatcher got seven hits in his first seven at-bats and hit .750 (9-for-12) for the Series, a record.

• • • •

1991 Barry Larkin tied a major league record in 1991 when he hit five home runs in two consecutive games, two against San Diego on June 27 and three against Houston on June 28.

• • • •

1992 For the first time in major league history, two teammates each recorded at least 25 saves in the same season when Norm Charlton collected 26 saves and Rob Dibble 25.

Utility player Bip Roberts tied a National League record in September when he became the first player since 1943 to get 10 consecutive hits.

....

1995 Ron Gant hit four extra-inning, game-winning home runs, tying Willie Mays' record.

....

1996 Hal Morris finished the season with a 29-game hitting streak, the highest in the majors that year and second-highest in franchise history behind Pete Rose's 44-game streak in 1978.

....

1997 Bret Boone set two major league fielding records, the first for fielding percentage by a second baseman playing at least 100 games (.997), and the second for playing the most games by a second baseman with two or fewer errors (136).

On Labor Day, Pete Rose Jr. made his major league debut for Cincinnati in front of his hometown fans. He received numerous standing ovations as he went 1-for-3 with a walk, even hustling to first like his dad had done 34 years before in a tribute to his father. Watching his debut in the front row (with special permission from major league baseball) were two suspended figures, Pete Rose Sr. and team owner Marge Schott. Unfortunately for the younger Rose, that was as good as it got. He collected just two singles in 14 at-bats during the season for a .143 batting average and never played in the major leagues again.

1998 On September 27, for the first time in major league history, two sets of brothers played on the same team in the same game. Boone brothers Bret (second base) and Aaron (third base), and Larkin brothers Barry (shortstop) and Stephen (first base), all played for the Reds in their 4–1 win over the Pirates in the team's season-ending game.

....

1999 The Reds set a National League record on September 4, at Philadelphia when they hit nine homers in one game, a 22–3 romp. They established another record because the homers were hit by eight different players. The next day the Reds hit five more homers for a two-game total of 14, still another major league record.

....

2000 The Cincinnati Reds became only the second team in history to play an entire season without being shut out. That same team became the first team ever to reach 3 million in road attendance.

....

2001 Reds pitcher Jose Rijo, after six seasons of inactivity, became the first player to appear in a major league game after receiving a Hall of Fame vote since outfielder Minnie Minoso received six votes in 1969 and played for the White Sox in 1976.

....

The Cincinnati Reds are the only one of the eight NL franchises that has been in existence since 1892 that has never had a 30-game winner.

Special Achievements

WORLD SERIES RESULTS

Year	Opponent	Result	Games
1919	Chicago White Sox	Won	5–3
1939	New York Yankees	Lost	0–4
1940	Detroit Tigers	Won	4–3
1961	New York Yankees	Lost	1–4
1970	Baltimore Orioles	Lost	1–4
1972	Oakland A's	Lost	3–4
1975	Boston Red Sox	Won	4–3
1976	New York Yankees	Won	4–0
1990	Oakland A's	Won	4–0

WORLD SERIES MANAGERIAL RECORDS

Manager	Series Record	Games Record
Pat Moran	1–0	5–3
Bill McKechnie	1–1	4–7
Fred Hutchinson	0–1	1–4
Sparky Anderson	2–2	12–11
Lou Piniella	1–0	4–0

ALL-TIME POSTSEASON RECORD

Divisional Playoffs	3–4
League Championship Series	18–10
World Series	26–25

ALL-STAR GAMES AT CINCINNATI

Year	Date	Winner	Score	Stadium
1938	July 6	National	4–1	Crosley Field
1953	July 14	National	5–1	Crosley Field
1970	July 14	National	5–4	Riverfront Stadium
1988	July 12	American	2–1	Riverfront Stadium

HALL OF FAMERS WHO PLAYED FOR TEAM

	Position	Years	Games with Cincinnati
Jake Beckley	1B	1897–1903	879
Johnny Bench	C	1967–1983	2,158
Jim Bottomley	1B	1933–1935	394
Mordecai Brown	RP/SP	1913	39
Charles Comiskey	1B	1892–1894	266
Sam Crawford	OF	1899–1902	403
Kiki Cuyler	OF	1935–1937	323
Leo Durocher	SS	1930–1933	399
Buck Ewing	1B	1895–1897	175
Clark Griffith	SP	1909	1
Chick Hafey	OF	1932–1937	471
Jesse Haines	RP	1918	1
Harry Heilmann	OF/1B	1930, 1932	157
Miller Huggins	2B	1904–1909	783
Joe Kelley	OF/1B	1902–1906	487
George Kelly	1B	1927–1930	375
Ernie Lombardi	C	1932–1941	1,203
Rube Marquard	SP	1921	39
Christy Mathewson	SP	1916	1
Bill McKechnie	3B/2B/SS	1916–1917	85
Bid McPhee	2B	1882–1899	2,135
Joe Morgan	2B	1972–1979	1,154
Tony Perez	1B/3B	1964–1976, 1984–1986	1,948
Charles Radbourn	SP	1891	29
Eppa Rixey	SP	1921–1933	440
Frank Robinson	OF/1B	1956–1965	1,502
Edd Roush	OF	1916–1926, 1931	1,399
Amos Rusie	SP	1901	3
Tom Seaver	SP	1977–1982	160
Al Simmons	OF	1939	9
Joe Tinker	SS	1913	110
Dazzy Vance	RP/SP	1934	6
Lloyd Waner	OF	1941	55

HALL OF FAMERS WHO MANAGED TEAM

	Years	Games with Cincinnati
Sparky Anderson	1970–1978	1,449
Ned Hanlon	1906–1907	304
Bill McKechnie	1938–1946	1,375

MVP AWARD WINNERS

Ernie Lombardi	C	1938
Bucky Walters	SP	1939
Frank McCormick	1B	1940
Frank Robinson	OF	1961
Johnny Bench	C	1970
Johnny Bench	C	1972
Pete Rose	OF	1973
Joe Morgan	2B	1975
Joe Morgan	2B	1976
George Foster	OF	1977
Barry Larkin	SS	1995

CY YOUNG AWARD WINNERS

None

ROOKIE OF THE YEAR AWARD WINNERS

Frank Robinson	OF	1956
Pete Rose	2B	1963
Tommy Helms	3B	1966
Johnny Bench	C	1968
Pat Zachry	SP	1976 (tie)
Chris Sabo	3B	1988
Scott Williamson	RP	1999

GOLD GLOVE WINNERS

Year	Position	Player
1957	SS	Roy McMillan
1958	SP SS OF	Harvey Haddix Roy McMillan Frank Robinson
1959	SS	Roy McMillan
1961	OF	Vada Pinson
1963	C	Johnny Edwards
1964	C	Johnny Edwards
1965	SS	Leo Cardenas
1968	C	Johnny Bench
1969	C OF	Johnny Bench Pete Rose
1970	C 2B OF	Johnny Bench Tommy Helms Pete Rose
1971	C 2B	Johnny Bench Tommy Helms
1972	C	Johnny Bench
1973	C 2B	Johnny Bench Joe Morgan
1974	C 2B SS OF	Johnny Bench Joe Morgan Dave Concepcion Cesar Geronimo
1975	C 2B SS OF	Johnny Bench Joe Morgan Dave Concepcion Cesar Geronimo
1976	C 2B SS OF	Johnny Bench Joe Morgan Dave Concepcion Cesar Geronimo
1977	C 2B SS OF	Johnny Bench Joe Morgan Dave Concepcion Cesar Geronimo
1979	SS	Dave Concepcion
1987	OF	Eric Davis
1988	OF	Eric Davis
1989	OF	Eric Davis
1994	SS	Barry Larkin
1995	SS	Barry Larkin
1996	SS	Barry Larkin
1998	2B	Brett Boone
1999	2B	Pokey Reese
2000	2B	Pokey Reese

TRIPLE CROWN WINNERS

None

FIREMAN OF THE YEAR AWARD WINNERS

Ted Abernathy	1967
Wayne Granger	1969
Wayne Granger	1970
Clay Carroll	1972
Rawly Eastwick	1976
Tom Hume	1980 (tie)
John Franco	1988
Jeff Shaw	1997

WORLD SERIES MVP

Pete Rose	1975
Johnny Bench	1976
Jose Rijo	1990

LEAGUE CHAMPIONSHIP SERIES MVP

Rob Dibble	1990 (tie)
Randy Myers	1990 (tie)

ALL-STAR GAME MVP

Tony Perez	1967
Joe Morgan	1972
George Foster	1976
Ken Griffey Sr.	1980
Dave Concepcion	1982

MANAGER OF THE YEAR AWARD WINNERS

Jack McKeon	1999

BATTING CHAMPIONS

Player	Year	Avg
Cy Seymour	1905	.377
Hal Chase	1916	.339
Edd Roush	1917	.341
Edd Roush	1919	.321
Bubbles Hargrave	1926	.353
Ernie Lombardi	1938	.342
Pete Rose	1968	.335
Pete Rose	1969	.348
Pete Rose	1973	.338

NINE-INNING NO-HITTERS PITCHED

Year	Pitcher	Opp.	Score
1892	Bumpus Jones	PIT	7–1
1898	Ted Breitenstein	PIT	11–0
1900	Noodles Hahn	PHI	4–0
1917	Fred Toney	CHC	1–0 (10 inn.)

1919	Hod Eller	STL	6–0
1938	Johnny Vander Meer	BOS	3–0
	Johnny Vander Meer	BRK	6–0
1944	Clyde Shoun	BOS	1–0
1947	Ewell Blackwell	BOS	6–0
1965	Jim Maloney	CHC	1–0 (10 inn.)
1968	George Culver	PHI	6–1
1969	Jim Maloney	HOU	10–0
1978	Tom Seaver	STL	4–0
1988	Tom Browning	LA	1–0 (perfect)

20-Game Winners

Year	Pitcher	W–L
1882	Will White	40–12
1883	Will White	43–22
1884	Will White	34–18
1885	Larry McKeon	20–13
1886	Tony Mullane	33–17
1887	Elmer Smith	34–18
	Tony Mullane	31–17
1888	Lee Viau	27–14
	Tony Mullane	26–16
	Elmer Smith	22–17
1889	Jesse Duryea	32–19
	Lee Viau	22–20
1890	Billy Rhines	28–17
1891	Tony Mullane	23–26
1892	Tony Mullane	21–13
1896	Frank Dwyer	24–11
1897	Ted Breitenstein	23–12
	Billy Rhines	21–15
1898	Pink Hawley	27–11
	Ted Breitenstein	20–14
1899	Noodles Hahn	23–8
1901	Noodles Hahn	22–19
1902	Noodles Hahn	23–12
1903	Noodles Hahn	22–12
1904	Jack Harper	23–9
1905	Bob Ewing	20–11
1906	Jake Weimer	20–14
1910	George Suggs	20–12
1917	Fred Toney	24–16
	Pete Schneider	20–19
1919	Slim Sallee	21–7
1922	Eppa Rixey	25–13
1923	Adolfo Luque	27–8
	Pete Donohue	21–15
	Eppa Rixey	20–15
1924	Carl Mays	20–9
1925	Eppa Rixey	21–11
	Pete Donohue	21–14
1926	Pete Donohue	20–14
1935	Paul Derringer	22–13
1938	Paul Derringer	21–14
1939	Bucky Walters	27–11
	Paul Derringer	25–7
1940	Bucky Walters	22–10
	Paul Derringer	20–12
1943	Elmer Riddle	21–11
1944	Bucky Walters	23–8
1947	Ewell Blackwell	22–8
1961	Joey Jay	21–10
1962	Bob Purkey	23–5
	Joey Jay	21–14
1963	Jim Maloney	23–7
1965	Sammy Ellis	22–10
	Jim Maloney	20–9
1970	Jim Merritt	20–12
1985	Tom Browning	20–9
1988	Danny Jackson	23–8

Retired Uniform Numbers

Number	Player	Position
1	Fred Hutchinson	Mgr
5	Johnny Bench	C
8	Joe Morgan	2B
10	Sparky Anderson	Mgr
18	Ted Kluszewski	OF
20	Frank Robinson	OF
24	Tony Perez	1B

Team Records—Wins & Losses

- Games won in a season: 108 in 1975
- Games lost in a season: 101 in 1982
- Games won in a month: 24 in August 1918 and July 1973
- Games lost in a month: 26 in September 1914
- Consecutive games won: 14 in 1899
- Consecutive games lost: 19 in 1914
- Biggest shutout victory: 18–0 over Los Angeles Dodgers on August 8, 1965
- Biggest shutout loss: 18–0, three times: to Philadelphia on August 10, 1930 (first game); to Philadelphia on July 14, 1934 (first game); to St. Louis on June 10, 1944
- Highest winning percentage: .686 in 1919 (96–44)
- Lowest winning percentage: .344 in 1934 (52–99)

Team Records—Batting

- Highest batting average: .296 in 1922
- Lowest batting average: .227 in 1968
- Slugging average: .451 in 1999
- On-base percentage: .368 in 1894
- Total hits: 1,599 in 1976
- Extra-base hits: 572 in 2005
- Hits in a game: 32 vs. Louisville on June 18, 1893

- Longest batting streak: 44, Pete Rose, 1978
- Most .300 hitters: 8 in 1926
- Home runs: 222 in 2005
- Home runs in a month: 14, Frank Robinson, August 1962 and Greg Vaughn, September 1999
- Home runs in a game: 9 vs. Philadelphia, September 4, 1999
- Home runs by a rookie: 38, Frank Robinson, 1956
- Home runs by a right-hander: 52, George Foster, 1977
- Home runs by a left-hander: 49, Ted Kluszewski, 1949
- Home runs by a switch-hitter: 23, Felipe Lopez, 2005
- Grand slams: 9 in 2002
- Grand slams (individual): 3, by five different players
- Grand slams in a career: 11, Johnny Bench
- Triples: 120 in 1926
- Doubles: 312 in 1999
- Singles: 1,191 in 1922
- Walks: 693 in 1974
- Runs scored: 865 in 1999
- Runs scored in a game: 30 vs. Louisville on June 18, 1893
- Runs scored in an inning: 14 vs. Louisville on June 18, 1893 (first) and Houston on August 3, 1989 (first)
- Most batters hit by a pitch: 81 in 2004
- Times shut out: 24 in 1908

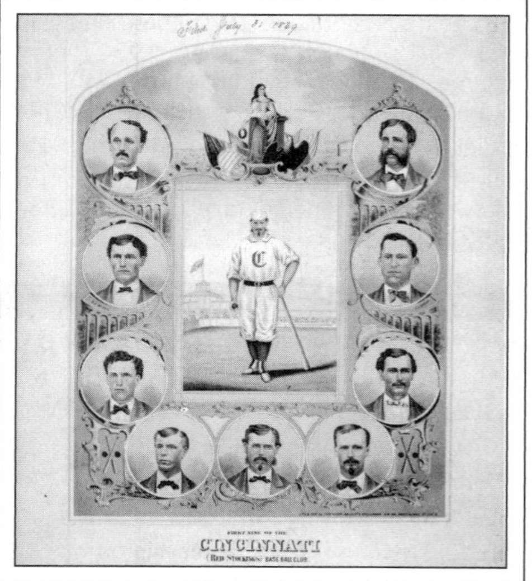

- Grounded into double plays: 161 in 1933
- Fewest grounded into double plays: 85 in 1991
- Runners left on base: 1,328 in 1976

TEAM RECORDS—BASERUNNING

- Stolen bases: 310 in 1910
- Caught stealing: 1236 in 1922

TEAM RECORDS—PITCHING

- Earned run average: 1.65 in 1882
- Complete games: 142 in 1904
- Saves: 60 in 1970 and 1972
- Strikeouts: 1,159 in 1997
- Shutouts: 23 in 1919
- Walks: 659 in 2000
- Hit batsmen: 80 in 2005
- Wild pitches: 96 in 2000
- Consecutive wins, pitcher: 16, Ewell Blackwell, 1947
- Consecutive losses, pitcher: 12, by 3 pitchers: Henry Thielman, 1902; Pete Schneider, 1914; Si Johnson, 1933
- Strikeouts in a game: 18, Jim Maloney, June 14, 1965 (11 innings); 9 innings, 16 by 3 pitchers: Noodles Hahn, May 22, 1901; Jim Maloney, May 1, 1963; Ron Villone, September 29, 2000
- Runs allowed in a game: 26 by Philadelphia, July 26, 1892

TEAM RECORDS—FIELDING

- Fielding average: .985 in 1995
- Errors committed: 314 in 1914
- Fewest errors committed: 95 in 1977
- Most double plays turned: 194 (3 times): 1928, 1931, and 1954
- Fewest double plays turned: 108 in 1989

TEAM RECORDS—MISCELLANEOUS

- Number of times league champions: 9
- Number of times finishing last in league: 11
- Largest attendance, single game: 55,596 vs. Milwaukee, April 3, 2000
- Largest attendance, doubleheader: 53,328 vs. Pittsburgh, July 9, 1976
- Players used in a season: 57 in 2003
- Seasons played: 19 (3 players): Dave Concepcion, Barry Larkin, and Pete Rose

Primary Pitching Staffs

Year	Starter	Starter	Starter	Starter	Starter	Closer	Bullpen	Bullpen	Bullpen
2005	Milton	Harang	Ortiz	Claussen	Hudson	Weathers	Mercker	Belisle	Coffey
2004	Wilson	Harang	Acevedo	Lidle	Claussen	Graves	Riedling	Norton	Jones
2003	Wilson	Harang	Graves	Dempster	Haynes	Williamson	Riedling	Heredia	Reitsma
2002	Dessens	Reitsma	Hamilton	Dempster	Haynes	Graves	Sullivan	Williamson	White
2001	Dessens	Reitsma	Davis	Acevedo	Fernandez	Graves	Sullivan	Mercado	Brower
2000	Parris	Bell	Villone	Harnisch	Neagle	Graves	Sullivan	Reyes	Williamson
1999	Parris	Tomko	Villone	Harnisch	Neagle	Graves	Sullivan	Reyes	Williamson
1998	Parris	Tomko	Remlinger	Harnisch	Winchester	Shaw	Sullivan	White	Graves
1997	Morgan	Tomko	Burba	Mercker	Smiley	Shaw	Sullivan	Belinda	Remlinger
1996	Portugal	Jarvis	Burba	Salkeld	Smiley	Brantley	Shaw	Carrasco	Ruffin
1995	Portugal	Schourek	Rijo	Pugh	Smiley	Brantley	Hernandez	Carrasco	McElroy
1994	Hanson	Schourek	Rijo	Roper	Smiley	Brantley	Ruffin	Carrasco	McElroy
1993	Pugh	Belcher	Rijo	Browning	Smiley	Dibble	Reardon	Ayala	Spradlin
1992	Swindell	Belcher	Rijo	Browning	Hammond	Charlton	Dibble	Henry	Ruskin
1991	Armstrong	Scudder	Rijo	Browning	Hammond	Dibble	Power	Myers	Charlton
1990	Armstrong	Jackson	Rijo	Browning	Charlton	Myers	Dibble	Layana	Mahler
1989	Mahler	Jackson	Rijo	Browning	Scudder	Franco	Dibble	Charlton	Birtsas
1988	Robinson	Jackson	Rijo	Browning	Soto	Franco	Dibble	Murphy	Williams
1987	Robinson	Power	Gullickson	Browning	Hoffman	Franco	Landrum	Murphy	Williams
1986	Denny	Welsh	Gullickson	Browning	Soto	Franco	Robinson	Murphy	Power
1985	Tibbs	McGaffigan	Stuper	Browning	Soto	Power	Robinson	Franco	Hume
1984	Tibbs	Russell	Price	Pastore	Soto	Power	Owchinko	Franco	Hume
1983	Berenyi	Puleo	Price	Pastore	Soto	Scherrer	Hayes	Power	Hume
1982	Berenyi	Seaver	Shirley	Pastore	Soto	Hume	Price	Kern	Leibrandt
1981	Berenyi	Seaver	LaCoss	Pastore	Soto	Hume	Price	Moskau	Bair
1980	Leibrandt	Seaver	LaCoss	Pastore	Moskau	Hume	Soto	Tomlin	Bair
1979	Norman	Seaver	LaCoss	Bonham	Moskau	Hume	Borbon	Tomlin	Bair
1978	Norman	Seaver	Hume	Bonham	Moskau	Bair	Borbon	Tomlin	Sarmiento
1977	Norman	Seaver	Billingham	Capilla	Moskau	Borbon	Murray	Eastwick	Sarmiento
1976	Norman	Nolan	Billingham	Zachry	Alcala	Eastwick	Borbon	McEnaney	Gullett
1975	Norman	Nolan	Billingham	Gullett	Darcy	Eastwick	Borbon	McEnaney	Carroll
1974	Norman	Kirby	Billingham	Gullett	Carroll	Borbon	Hall	McEnaney	Carroll
1973	Norman	Grimsley	Billingham	Gullett	McGlothlin	Borbon	Hall	Sprague	Carroll
1972	Nolan	Grimsley	Billingham	Simpson	McGlothlin	Carroll	Hall	Sprague	Borbon
1971	Nolan	Grimsley	Gullett	Simpson	McGlothlin	Carroll	Granger	Gibbon	Merritt
1970	Nolan	Merritt	Cloninger	Simpson	McGlothlin	Granger	Carroll	Gullett	Washburn
1969	Nolan	Merritt	Cloninger	Maloney	Arrigo	Granger	Carroll	Ramos	Fisher
1968	Nolan	Culver	Cloninger	Maloney	Arrigo	Carroll	Abernathy	Lee	Kelso
1967	Nolan	Pappas	Ellis	Maloney	Queen	Abernathy	Nottebart	Arrigo	McCool
1966	O'Toole	Pappas	Ellis	Maloney	Nuxhall	McCool	Nottebart	Davidson	Baldschun
1965	O'Toole	Jay	Ellis	Maloney	Tsitouris	McCool	Craig	Nuxhall	Arrigo
1964	O'Toole	Jay	Purkey	Maloney	Tsitouris	Ellis	McCool	Nuxhall	Henry
1963	O'Toole	Jay	Purkey	Maloney	Nuxhall	Worthington	Henry	Zanni	Tsitouris
1962	O'Toole	Jay	Purkey	Maloney	Drabowsky	Brosnan	Klippstein	Henry	Sisler
1961	O'Toole	Jay	Purkey	Hunt	Johnson	Brosnan	Maloney	Henry	Jones
1960	O'Toole	Hook	Purkey	McLish	Newcombe	Henry	Brosnan	Nuxhall	Grim
1959	O'Toole	Hook	Purkey	Nuxhall	Newcombe	Lawrence	Pena	Acker	Schmidt
1958	Haddix	Lawrence	Purkey	Nuxhall	Newcombe	Jeffcoat	Kellner	Acker	Schmidt
1957	Jeffcoat	Lawrence	Klippstein	Nuxhall	Gross	Freeman	Sanchez	Acker	Fowler
1956	Jeffcoat	Lawrence	Klippstein	Nuxhall	Fowler	Freeman	Black	Acker	Gross
1955	Staley	Collum	Klippstein	Nuxhall	Fowler	Freeman	Black	Minarcin	Podbielan
1954	Valentine	Podbielan	Baczewski	Nuxhall	Fowler	Smith	Judson	Collum	Perkowski

PRIMARY PITCHING STAFFS (CONT.)

Year	Starter	Starter	Starter	Starter	Starter	Closer	Bullpen	Bullpen	Bullpen
1953	Raffensberger	Podbielan	Baczewski	Nuxhall	Perkowski	Smith	Collum	King	Kelly
1952	Raffensberger	Wehmeier	Church	Blackwell	Perkowski	Smith	Nuxhall	Hiller	Podbielan
1951	Raffensberger	Wehmeier	Ramsdell	Blackwell	Fox	Smith	Byerly	Perkowski	Erautt
1950	Raffensberger	Wehmeier	Ramsdell	Blackwell	Fox	Smith	Hetki	Erautt	Perkowski
1949	Raffensberger	Wehmeier	Vander Meer	Lively	Fox	Erautt	Peterson	Blackwell	Gumbert
1948	Raffensberger	Wehmeier	Vander Meer	Blackwell	Fox	Gumbert	Cress	Peterson	Blackburn
1947	Walters	Lively	Vander Meer	Blackwell	Peterson	Gumbert	Hetki	Erautt	Raffensberger
1946	Walters	Beggs	Vander Meer	Blackwell	Heusser	Hetki	Gumbert	Shoun	
1945	Walters	Bowman	Kennedy	Fox	Heusser	Lisenbee	Modak	Dasso	
1944	Walters	Shoun	de la Cruz	Gumbert	Heusser	Carter	Konstanty	Malloy	
1943	Walters	Vander Meer	Starr	Riddle	Heusser	Shoun	Beggs	Stone	Malloy
1942	Walters	Vander Meer	Starr	Riddle	Derringer	Beggs	Shoun	Thompson	
1941	Walters	Vander Meer	Thompson	Riddle	Derringer	Beggs	Moore	Turner	
1940	Walters	Turner	Thompson	Moore	Derringer	Beggs	Shoffner	Hutchings	Riddle
1939	Walters	Grissom	Vander Meer	Moore	Derringer	Thompson	Johnson	Davis	
1938	Walters	Davis	Vander Meer	Weaver	Derringer	Cascarella	Schott	Moore	
1937	Grissom	Davis	Hollingsworth	Schott	Derringer	Vander Meer	Mooty	Hallahan	
1936	Hallahan	Davis	Hollingsworth	Schott	Derringer	Brennan	Stine	Frey	Hilcher
1935	Johnson	Freitas	Hollingsworth	Schott	Derringer	Brennan	Frey	Herrmann	
1934	Johnson	Freitas	Frey	Stout	Derringer	Brennan	Kolp	Kleinhans	
1933	Johnson	Lucas	Benton	Kolp	Derringer	Frey	Stout	Rixey	
1932	Johnson	Lucas	Benton	Kolp	Carroll	Frey	Ogden	Rixey	
1931	Johnson	Lucas	Benton	Frey	Rixey	Kolp	Ogden	Carroll	
1930	Kolp	Lucas	Benton	Frey	Rixey	Johnson	May	Campbell	
1929	Donohue	Lucas	May	Luque	Rixey	Kolp	Ash	Ehrhardt	
1928	Donohue	Lucas	Kolp	Luque	Rixey	Appleton	May	Edwards	
1927	Donohue	Lucas	May	Luque	Rixey	Kolp	Nehf	Mays	
1926	Donohue	Mays	May	Luque	Rixey	Lucas	Nehf	Meeker	
1925	Donohue	Benton	May	Luque	Rixey	Biemiller	Brady	Mays	
1924	Donohue	Mays	Sheehan	Luque	Rixey	May	Benton	Dibut	
1923	Donohue	Benton	Couch	Luque	Rixey	Keck	Harris	McQuaid	
1922	Donohue	Keck	Couch	Luque	Rixey	Gillespie	Markle	Schnell	
1921	Donohue	Marquard	Brenton	Luque	Rixey	Coumbe	Napier	Eller	
1920	Ruether	Ring	Fisher	Luque	Eller	Sallee	Napier	Bressler	
1919	Ruether	Ring	Fisher	Sallee	Eller	Luque	Mitchell	Bressler	
1918	Schneider	Ring	Toney	Bressler	Eller	Luque	Regan	Smith	
1917	Schneider	Regan	Toney	Mitchell	Eller	Ring	Knetzer	Ruether	
1916	Schneider	Schulz	Toney	Mitchell	Knetzer	Moseley	Dale	McKenry	
1915	Schneider	Dale	Toney	Benton	Lear	Ames	Douglas	McKenry	
1914	Schneider	Ames	Yingling	Benton	Douglas	Lear	Rowan	Davenport	
1913	Johnson	Ames	Suggs	Benton	Packard	Brown	Harter	Fromme	Herbert
1912	Fromme	Humphries	Suggs	Benton	Keefe	Smith	Davis	Gaspar	
1911	Fromme	Gaspar	Suggs	Smith	Keefe	McQuillan	Humphries	Compton	
1910	Rowan	Gaspar	Suggs	Beebe	Burns	Benton	Fromme	Coveleski	
1909	Rowan	Gaspar	Fromme	Ewing	Campbell	Dubuc	Spade	Karger	
1908	Spade	Coakley	Weimer	Ewing	Campbell	Dubuc	Rowan	Volz	
1907	Hitt	Coakley	Weimer	Ewing	Mason	Smith	Hall		
1906	Fraser	Wicker	Weimer	Ewing	Overall	Chech	Hall	Essick	
1905	Chech	Harper	Walker	Ewing	Overall	Hahn	Vowinkel		
1904	Hahn	Harper	Walker	Ewing	Kellum	Sutthoff	Elliott		
1903	Hahn	Harper	Sutthoff	Ewing	Poole	Phillips			

PRIMARY PITCHING STAFFS (CONT.)

Year	Starter	Starter	Starter	Starter	Starter	Closer	Bullpen	Bullpen	Bullpen
1902	Hahn	Phillips	Thielman	Ewing	Poole	Currie			
1901	Hahn	Phillips	Newton	Stimmel		Sutthoff	McFadden	Guese	
1900	Hahn	Phillips	Newton	Scott	Breitenstein				
1899	Hahn	Phillips	Hawley	Taylor	Breitenstein	Frisk	Dammann		
1898	Hill	Dwyer	Hawley	Dammann	Breitenstein				
1897	Rhines	Dwyer	Ehret	Dammann	Breitenstein	Brown	Peitz		
1896	Rhines	Dwyer	Ehret	F. Foreman	Fisher	B. Foreman	Inks		
1895	Rhines	Dwyer	Parrott	F. Foreman	Phillips	Bailey			
1894	Chamberlain	Dwyer	Parrott	Fisher	Whitrock	Cross	Fournier	Tannehill	
1893	Chamberlain	Dwyer	Parrott	Sullivan	King	Mullane	Jones	Darby	
1892	Chamberlain	Dwyer	Mullane	Sullivan	Rhines	Duryea	McGill	Daub	
1891	Radbourn	Crane	Mullane	Duryea	Rhines	Stephens			
1890	Foreman	Viau	Mullane	Duryea	Rhines	Dolan			
1889	Smith	Viau	Mullane	Duryea		Petty			
1888	Smith	Viau	Mullane	Weyhing		Serad	Corkhill		
1887	Smith	Serad	Mullane	McGinnis	Corkhill	Shea	Watson		
1886	Smith	Pechiney	Mullane	McKeon	Murphy	Richmond	White	Irwin	
1885	White	Pechiney	Mountjoy	McKeon	Shallix	Corkhill	Peoples	Baldwin	McCaffery
1884	White	Mountjoy	Shallix			Deagle	Corkhill		
1883	White	Deagle	McCormick		Mountjoy	Sommer			
1882	White		McCormick		Wheeler				

PRIMARY STARTING LINEUPS

Year	C	1B	2B	3B	SS	LF	CF	RF
2005	LaRue	Casey	Aurilia	Randa	Lopez	Dunn	Griffey	Kearns
2004	LaRue	Casey	Jimenez	Castro	Larkin	Dunn	Griffey	Kearns
2003	LaRue	Casey	Jimenez	Boone	Larkin	Dunn	Taylor	Guillen
2002	LaRue	Casey	Walker	Boone	Larkin	Dunn	Taylor	Kearns
2001	LaRue	Casey	Walker	Boone	Reese	Young	Griffey	Ochoa
2000	Santiago	Casey	Reese	Boone	Larkin	Young	Griffey	Bichette
1999	Taubensee	Casey	Reese	Boone	Larkin	Vaughn	Cameron	Tucker
1998	Taubensee	Casey	Boone	Greene	Larkin	Young	Sanders	Nunnally
1997	Oliver	Morris	Boone	Greene	Reese	Stynes	Sanders	Sanders
1996	Oliver	Morris	Boone	Greene	Larkin	Owens	Davis	Sanders
1995	Santiago	Morris	Boone	Branson	Larkin	Gant	Lewis	Sanders
1994	Dorsett	Morris	Boone	Fernandez	Larkin	Mitchell	Kelly	Sanders
1993	Oliver	Morris	Samuel	Sabo	Larkin	Mitchell	Kelly	Sanders
1992	Oliver	Morris	Doran	Sabo	Larkin	Roberts	Martinez	O'Neill
1991	Oliver	Morris	Doran	Sabo	Larkin	Hatcher	Davis	O'Neill
1990	Oliver	Benzinger	Duncan	Sabo	Larkin	Hatcher	Davis	O'Neill
1989	Reed	Benzinger	Oester	Sabo	Larkin	Griffey	Davis	O'Neill
1988	Diaz	Esasky	Treadway	Sabo	Larkin	Daniels	Davis	O'Neill
1987	Diaz	Esasky	Oester	Bell	Larkin	Daniels	Davis	Parker
1986	Diaz	Esasky	Oester	Bell	Stillwell	Davis	Milner	Parker
1985	Van Gorder	Rose	Oester	Bell	Concepcion	Redus	Milner	Parker

PRIMARY STARTING LINEUPS (CONT.)

Year	C	1B	2B	3B	SS	LF	CF	RF
1984	Gulden	Driessen	Oester	Esasky	Concepcion	Redus	Milner	Parker
1983	Bilardello	Driessen	Oester	Esasky	Concepcion	Redus	Milner	Householder
1982	Trevino	Driessen	Oester	Bench	Concepcion	Milner	Cedeno	Householder
1981	Nolan	Driessen	Oester	Knight	Concepcion	Foster	Griffey	Collins
1980	Bench	Driessen	Kennedy	Knight	Concepcion	Foster	Collins	Griffey
1979	Bench	Driessen	Morgan	Knight	Concepcion	Foster	Geronimo	Griffey
1978	Bench	Driessen	Morgan	Rose	Concepcion	Foster	Geronimo	Griffey
1977	Bench	Driessen	Morgan	Rose	Concepcion	Foster	Geronimo	Griffey
1976	Bench	Perez	Morgan	Rose	Concepcion	Foster	Geronimo	Griffey
1975	Bench	Perez	Morgan	Rose	Concepcion	Foster	Geronimo	Griffey
1974	Bench	Perez	Morgan	Driessen	Concepcion	Rose	Geronimo	Foster
1973	Bench	Perez	Morgan	Menke	Concepcion	Rose	Geronimo	Kosco
1972	Bench	Perez	Morgan	Menke	Concepcion	Rose	Tolan	Geronimo
1971	Bench	May	Helms	Perez	Concepcion	Carbo	Foster	Rose
1970	Bench	May	Helms	Perez	Concepcion	Carbo	Tolan	Rose
1969	Bench	May	Helms	Perez	Woodward	Johnson	Tolan	Rose
1968	Bench	May	Helms	Perez	Cardenas	Johnson	Pinson	Rose
1967	Edwards	May	Helms	Perez	Cardenas	Rose	Pinson	Harper
1966	Edwards	Perez	Rose	Helms	Cardenas	Johnson	Pinson	Harper
1965	Edwards	Perez	Rose	Johnson	Cardenas	Harper	Pinson	Robinson
1964	Edwards	Johnson	Rose	Boros	Cardenas	Harper	Pinson	Robinson
1963	Edwards	Coleman	Rose	Freese	Cardenas	Robinson	Pinson	Harper
1962	Edwards	Coleman	Blasingame	Kasko	Cardenas	Post	Pinson	Robinson
1961	Zimmerman	Coleman	Blasingame	Freese	Kasko	Bell	Pinson	Robinson
1960	Bailey	Robinson	Martin	Kasko	McMillan	Post	Pinson	Bell
1959	Bailey	Robinson	Temple	Jones	Kasko	Lynch	Pinson	Bell
1958	Bailey	Crowe	Temple	Hoak	McMillan	Robinson	Bell	Lynch
1957	Bailey	Crowe	Temple	Hoak	McMillan	Robinson	Bell	Post
1956	Bailey	Kluszewski	Temple	Jablonski	McMillan	Robinson	Bell	Post
1955	Burgess	Kluszewski	Temple	Bridges	McMillan	Palys	Bell	Post
1954	Seminick	Kluszewski	Temple	Adams	McMillan	Greengrass	Bell	Post
1953	Seminick	Kluszewski	Bridges	Adams	McMillan	Greengrass	Bell	Marshall
1952	Seminick	Kluszewski	Hatton	Adams	McMillan	Adcock	Borkowski	Marshall
1951	Howell	Kluszewski	Ryan	Hatton	Stallcup	Adcock	Usher	Wyrostek
1950	Howell	Kluszewski	Ryan	Hatton	Stallcup	Adcock	Merriman	Wyrostek
1949	Cooper	Kluszewski	Bloodworth	Hatton	Stallcup	Lowrey	Merriman	Litwhiler
1948	Lamanno	Kluszewski	Adams	Hatton	Stallcup	Sauer	Wyrostek	Litwhiler
1947	Lamanno	Young	Zientara	Hatton	Miller	Galan	Haas	Baumholtz
1946	Mueller	Haas	Adams	Hatton	Miller	Lukon	Clay	Libke
1945	Lakeman	McCormick	Williams	Mesner	Miller	Tipton	Clay	Libke
1944	Mueller	McCormick	Williams	Mesner	Miller	Tipton	Clay	Walker
1943	Mueller	McCormick	Frey	Mesner	Miller	Tipton	Walker	Marshall
1942	Lamanno	McCormick	Frey	Haas	Joost	Tipton	Walker	Marshall
1941	Lombardi	McCormick	Frey	Werber	Joost	McCormick	Craft	Gleeson
1940	Lombardi	McCormick	Frey	Werber	Myers	Arnovich	Craft	Goodman
1939	Lombardi	McCormick	Frey	Werber	Myers	Berger	Craft	Goodman
1938	Lombardi	McCormick	Frey	Riggs	Myers	Berger	Craft	Goodman
1937	Lombardi	Jordan	Kampouris	Riggs	Myers	Weintraub	Cuyler	Goodman
1936	Lombardi	Scarsella	Kampouris	Riggs	Myers	Herman	Cuyler	Goodman
1935	Lombardi	Bottomley	Kampouris	Riggs	Myers	Herman	Byrd	Goodman
1934	Lombardi	Bottomley	Piet	Koenig	Slade	Pool	Hafey	Comorosky
1933	Lombardi	Bottomley	Morrissey	Adams	Bluege	Moore	Hafey	Rice

PRIMARY STARTING LINEUPS (CONT.)

Year	C	1B	2B	3B	SS	LF	CF	RF
1932	Lombardi	Hendrick	Grantham	Gilbert	Durocher	Roettger	Douthit	Herman
1931	Sukeforth	Hendrick	Cuccinello	Stripp	Durocher	Cullop	Douthit	Crabtree
1930	Sukeforth	Stripp	Ford	Cuccinello	Durocher	Walker	Swanson	Heilmann
1929	Gooch	Kelly	Critz	Dressen	Ford	Swanson	Allen	Walker
1928	Picinich	Kelly	Critz	Dressen	Ford	Purdy	Allen	Walker
1927	Hargrave	Pipp	Critz	Dressen	Ford	Bressler	Allen	Walker
1926	Hargrave	Pipp	Critz	Dressen	Emmer	Bressler	Roush	Walker
1925	Hargrave	Holke	Critz	Pinelli	Caveney	Zitzmann	Roush	Walker
1924	Hargrave	Daubert	Critz	Pinelli	Caveney	Duncan	Roush	Walker
1923	Hargrave	Daubert	Bohne	Pinelli	Caveney	Duncan	Roush	Burns
1922	Hargrave	Daubert	Bohne	Pinelli	Caveney	Duncan	Burns	Harper
1921	Wingo	Daubert	Bohne	Groh	Kopf	Duncan	Roush	Bressler
1920	Wingo	Daubert	Rath	Groh	Kopf	Duncan	Roush	Neale
1919	Wingo	Daubert	Rath	Groh	Kopf	Magee	Roush	Neale
1918	Wingo	Chase	Magee	Groh	Blackburne	Neale	Roush	Griffith
1917	Wingo	Chase	Shean	Groh	Kopf	Neale	Roush	Griffith
1916	Wingo	Chase	Louden	Groh	Herzog	Neale	Roush	Griffith
1915	Wingo	Mollwitz	Rodgers	Groh	Herzog	Killefer	Leach	Griffith
1914	Clarke	Hoblitzel	Groh	Niehoff	Herzog	Twombly	Bates	Moran
1913	Clarke	Hoblitzel	Groh	Dodge	Tinker	Bescher	Devore	Bates
1912	McLean	Hoblitzel	Egan	Phelan	Esmond	Bescher	Marsans	Mitchell
1911	McLean	Hoblitzel	Egan	Grant	Downey	Bescher	Bates	Mitchell
1910	McLean	Hoblitzel	Egan	Lobert	McMillan	Bescher	Paskert	Mitchell
1909	McLean	Hoblitzel	Egan	Lobert	Downey	Bescher	Oakes	Mitchell
1908	Schlei	Ganzel	Huggins	Lobert	Hulswitt	Paskert	Kane	Mitchell
1907	McLean	Ganzel	Huggins	Mowrey	Lobert	Odwell	Kruger	Mitchell
1906	Schlei	Deal	Huggins	Delahanty	Corcoran	Kelley	Seymour	Jude
1905	Schlei	Barry	Huggins	Steinfeldt	Corcoran	Kelley	Seymour	Odwell
1904	Schlei	Kelley	Huggins	Steinfeldt	Corcoran	Odwell	Seymour	Dolan
1903	Peitz	Beckley	Daly	Steinfeldt	Corcoran	Donlin	Seymour	Dolan
1902	Bergen	Beckley	Peitz	Steinfeldt	Corcoran	Dobbs	Hoy	Crawford
1901	Bergen	Beckley	Steinfeldt	Irwin	Magoon	Harley	Dobbs	Crawford
1900	Peitz	Beckley	Quinn	Steinfeldt	Corcoran	Crawford	Barrett	McBride
1899	Peitz	Beckley	McPhee	Irwin	Corcoran	Selbach	McBride	Miller
1898	Peitz	Beckley	McPhee	Irwin	Corcoran	Smith	McBride	Miller
1897	Peitz	Beckley	McPhee	Irwin	Ritchey	Burke	Hoy	Miller
1896	Peitz	Ewing	McPhee	Irwin	Smith	Burke	Hoy	Miller
1895	Vaughn	Ewing	McPhee	Latham	Smith	Hoy	Hogriever	Miller
1894	Murphy	Comiskey	McPhee	Latham	Smith	Holliday	Hoy	Canavan
1893	Vaughn	Comiskey	McPhee	Latham	Smith	Canavan	Holliday	Ward
1892	Murphy	Comiskey	McPhee	Latham	Smith	O'Neill	Holliday	Wood
1891	Harrington	Reilly	McPhee	Latham	Smith	Browning	Holliday	Marr
1890	Harrington	Reilly	McPhee	Latham	Beard	Knight	Holliday	Marr
1889	Keenan	Reilly	McPhee	Carpenter	Beard	Tebeau	Holliday	Nicol
1888	Keenan	Reilly	McPhee	Carpenter	Fennelly	Tebeau	Corkhill	Nicol
1887	Baldwin	Reilly	McPhee	Carpenter	Fennelly	Tebeau	Corkhill	Nicol
1886	Baldwin	Reilly	McPhee	Carpenter	Fennelly	Jones	Lewis	Corkhill
1885	Snyder	Reilly	McPhee	Carpenter	Fennelly	Jones	Clinton	Corkhill
1884	Snyder	Reilly	McPhee	Carpenter	Peoples	Jones	West	Corkhill
1883	Snyder	Reilly	McPhee	Carpenter	Fulmer	Sommer	Jones	Corkhill
1882	Snyder	Stearns	McPhee	Carpenter	Fulmer	Sommer	Macullar	Wheeler

Top 10 Batting Leaders, Single Season & Career with Team

GAMES PLAYED: CAREER WITH TEAM

Player	G	PA
1. Pete Rose	2,722	12,325
2. Dave Concepcion	2,488	9,640
3. Barry Larkin	2,180	9,057
4. Johnny Bench	2,158	8,669
5. Bid McPhee	2,135	9,409
6. Tony Perez	1,948	7,630
7. Vada Pinson	1,565	6,850
8. Frank Robinson	1,502	6,409
9. Dan Driessen	1,480	5,487
10. Edd Roush	1,399	5,965

AT-BATS: SEASON

Player	AB	Year
1. Pete Rose	680	1973
2. Pete Rose	670	1965
3. Vada Pinson	669	1965
4. Pete Rose	665	1976
5. Pete Rose	662	1975
6. Dain Clay	656	1945
7. Pete Rose	655	1977
Pete Rose	655	1978
9. Pete Rose	654	1966
10. Woody Williams	653	1944

AT-BATS: CAREER WITH TEAM

Player	AB	PA
1. Pete Rose	10,934	12,325
2. Dave Concepcion	8,723	9,640
3. Bid McPhee	8,291	9,409
4. Barry Larkin	7,937	9,057
5. Johnny Bench	7,658	8,669
6. Tony Perez	6,846	7,630
7. Vada Pinson	6,335	6,850
8. Frank Robinson	5,527	6,409
9. Edd Roush	5,384	5,965
10. Ted Kluszewski	4,961	5,404

BATTING AVERAGE: SEASON

Player	BA	Year
1. Cy Seymour	.377	1905
2. Bug Holliday	.372	1894
3. Bubbles Hargrave	.353	1926
4. Edd Roush	.352	1921
5. Edd Roush	.351	1923
Mike Donlin	.351	1903
7. Cuckoo Christensen	.350	1926
8. Edd Roush	.348	1924
Pete Rose	.348	1969
10. Rube Bressler	.347	1924

BATTING AVERAGE: CAREER WITH TEAM

Player	BA	PA
1. Cy Seymour	.332	2,420
2. Edd Roush	.331	5,965
3. Jake Beckley	.325	3,824
4. Bubbles Hargrave	.314	2,671
5. Rube Bressler	.311	2,543
Ernie Lombardi	.311	4,286
Bug Holliday	.311	4,036
8. Dusty Miller	.308	2,644
9. Pete Rose	.307	12,325
Pat Duncan	.307	3,002

TOTAL HITS: SEASON

Player	H	Year
1. Pete Rose	230	1973
2. Cy Seymour	219	1905
3. Pete Rose	218	1969
4. Pete Rose	215	1976
5. Pete Rose	210	1968
Pete Rose	210	1975
7. Frank McCormick	209	1938
Frank McCormick	209	1939
Pete Rose	209	1965
10. Vada Pinson	208	1961
Frank Robinson	208	1962

TOTAL HITS: CAREER WITH TEAM

Player	H	PA
1. Pete Rose	3,358	12,325
2. Barry Larkin	2,340	9,057
3. Dave Concepcion	2,326	9,640
4. Bid McPhee	2,250	9,409
5. Johnny Bench	2,048	8,669
6. Tony Perez	1,934	7,630
7. Vada Pinson	1,881	6,850
8. Edd Roush	1,784	5,965
9. Frank Robinson	1,673	6,409
10. Ted Kluszewski	1,499	5,404

HOME RUNS: SEASON

Player	HR	Year
1. George Foster	52	1977
2. Ted Kluszewski	49	1954
3. Ted Kluszewski	47	1955
4. Adam Dunn	46	2004
5. Johnny Bench	45	1970
Greg Vaughn	45	1999
7. Johnny Bench	40	1972
George Foster	40	1978
Ken Griffey	40	2000
Ted Kluszewski	40	1953
Tony Perez	40	1970
Wally Post	40	1955
Adam Dunn	40	2005

HOME RUNS: CAREER WITH TEAM

Player	HR	PA
1. Johnny Bench	389	8,669
2. Frank Robinson	324	6,409
3. Tony Perez	287	7,630
4. Ted Kluszewski	251	5,404
5. George Foster	244	5,010
6. Eric Davis	203	3,819
7. Barry Larkin	198	9,057
8. Vada Pinson	186	6,850
9. Wally Post	172	3,313
10. Gus Bell	160	5,111

TRIPLES: SEASON

Player	3B	Year
1. John Reilly	26	1890
2. Sam Crawford	22	1902
Jake Daubert	22	1922
Bid McPhee	22	1890
Mike Mitchell	22	1911
6. Edd Roush	21	1924
Cy Seymour	21	1905
8. Curt Walker	20	1926
9. Babe Herman	19	1932
Bid McPhee	19	1887
John Reilly	19	1884

TRIPLES: CAREER WITH TEAM

Player	3B	PA
1. Bid McPhee	188	9,409
2. Edd Roush	152	5,965
3. John Reilly	135	4,660
4. Pete Rose	115	12,325
5. Vada Pinson	96	6,850
6. Curt Walker	94	3,942
7. Mike Mitchell	88	3,550
8. Ival Goodman	79	4,020
9. Jake Daubert	78	3,523
10. Jake Beckley	77	3,824

DOUBLES: SEASON

Player	2B	Year
1. Frank Robinson	51	1962
Pete Rose	51	1978
3. Dmitri Young	48	1998
4. Vada Pinson	47	1959
Pete Rose	47	1975
6. George Kelly	45	1929
Pete Rose	45	1974
8. Sean Casey	44	2004
Pat Duncan	44	1922
Frank McCormick	44	1940

DOUBLES: CAREER WITH TEAM

Player	2B	PA
1. Pete Rose	601	12,325
2. Barry Larkin	441	9,057
3. Dave Concepcion	389	9,640
4. Johnny Bench	381	8,669
5. Vada Pinson	342	6,850
6. Tony Perez	339	7,630
7. Frank Robinson	318	6,409
8. Bid McPhee	303	9,409
9. Frank McCormick	285	5,202
10. Edd Roush	260	5,965

EXTRA-BASE HITS: SEASON

Player	XBH	Year
1. Frank Robinson	92	1962
2. George Foster	85	1977
3. Johnny Bench	84	1970
4. Adam Dunn	80	2004
Ted Kluszewski	80	1954
Dave Parker	80	1985
7. Adam Dunn	77	2005
8. Vada Pinson	76	1959
Wally Post	76	1955
Frank Robinson	76	1961

EXTRA-BASE HITS: CAREER WITH TEAM

Player	XBH	PA
1. Pete Rose	868	12,325
2. Johnny Bench	794	8,669
3. Barry Larkin	715	9,057
4. Frank Robinson	692	6,409
5. Tony Perez	682	7,630
6. Vada Pinson	624	6,850
7. Bid McPhee	544	9,409
8. Dave Concepcion	538	9,640
9. Ted Kluszewski	518	5,404
10. George Foster	488	5,010

TOTAL BASES: SEASON

Player	TB	Year
1. George Foster	388	1977
2. Frank Robinson	380	1962
3. Ted Kluszewski	368	1954
4. Ted Kluszewski	358	1955
5. Johnny Bench	355	1970
6. Dave Parker	350	1985
7. Tony Perez	346	1970
8. Wally Post	345	1955
9. Vada Pinson	335	1963
10. Frank Robinson	333	1961

TOTAL BASES: CAREER WITH TEAM

Player	TB	PA
1. Pete Rose	4,645	12,325
2. Johnny Bench	3,644	8,669
3. Barry Larkin	3,527	9,057
4. Tony Perez	3,246	7,630
5. Dave Concepcion	3,114	9,640
6. Bid McPhee	3,088	9,409
7. Frank Robinson	3,063	6,409
8. Vada Pinson	2,973	6,850
9. Ted Kluszewski	2,542	5,404
10. Edd Roush	2,489	5,965

RUNS BATTED IN: SEASON

Player	RBI	Year
1. George Foster	149	1977
2. Johnny Bench	148	1970
3. Ted Kluszewski	141	1954
4. Frank Robinson	136	1962
5. Deron Johnson	130	1965
6. Johnny Bench	129	1974
Tony Perez	129	1970
8. Frank McCormick	128	1939
9. Frank McCormick	127	1940
10. Johnny Bench	125	1972
Dave Parker	125	1985
Frank Robinson	125	1959

RUNS BATTED IN: CAREER WITH TEAM

Player	RBI	PA
1. Johnny Bench	1,376	8,669
2. Tony Perez	1,192	7,630
3. Bid McPhee	1,067	9,409
4. Pete Rose	1,036	12,325
5. Frank Robinson	1,009	6,409
6. Barry Larkin	960	9,057
7. Dave Concepcion	950	9,640
8. Ted Kluszewski	886	5,404
9. George Foster	861	5,010
10. Vada Pinson	814	6,850

RUNS SCORED: SEASON

Player	R	Year
1. Bid McPhee	139	1886
2. Bid McPhee	137	1887
3. Frank Robinson	134	1962
4. Frank Fennelly	133	1887
5. Vada Pinson	131	1959
6. Pete Rose	130	1976
7. Arlie Latham	129	1894
8. Tommy Harper	126	1965
9. Bid McPhee	125	1890
10. George Foster	124	1977

RUNS SCORED: CAREER WITH TEAM

Player	R	PA
1. Pete Rose	1,741	12,325
2. Bid McPhee	1,678	9,409
3. Barry Larkin	1,329	9,057
4. Johnny Bench	1,091	8,669
5. Frank Robinson	1,043	6,409
6. Dave Concepcion	993	9,640
7. Vada Pinson	978	6,850
8. Tony Perez	936	7,630
9. John Reilly	877	4,660
10. Joe Morgan	816	4,973

WALKS: SEASON

Player	BB	Year
1. Joe Morgan	132	1975
2. Adam Dunn	128	2002

3. Joe Morgan	120	1974
4. Joe Morgan	117	1977
5. Joe Morgan	115	1972
6. Joe Morgan	114	1976
Adam Dunn	114	2005
8. Joe Morgan	111	1973
9. Adam Dunn	108	2004
10. Pete Rose	106	1974

Walks: Career with Team

Player	BB	PA
1. Pete Rose	1,210	12,325
2. Bid McPhee	981	9,409
3. Barry Larkin	939	9,057
4. Johnny Bench	891	8,669
5. Joe Morgan	881	4,973
6. Dave Concepcion	736	9,640
7. Frank Robinson	698	6,409
8. Dan Driessen	678	5,487
9. Tony Perez	671	7,630
10. Heinie Groh	513	5,159

Strikeouts: Season

Player	SO	Year
1. Adam Dunn	195	2004
2. Adam Dunn	170	2002
3. Adam Dunn	168	2005
4. Mike Cameron	145	1999
5. Lee May	142	1969
6. George Foster	138	1978
7. Reggie Sanders	137	1998
Greg Vaughn	137	1999
9. Lee May	135	1971
10. Eric Davis	134	1987
Tony Perez	134	1970

Strikeouts: Career with Team

Player	SO	PA
1. Tony Perez	1,306	7,630
2. Johnny Bench	1,278	8,669
3. Dave Concepcion	1,186	9,640
4. Pete Rose	972	12,325
5. George Foster	882	5,010
6. Eric Davis	874	3,819
7. Vada Pinson	831	6,850
8. Barry Larkin	817	9,057
9. Frank Robinson	789	6,409
10. Reggie Sanders	777	3,292

Slugging Percentage: Season

Player	SLG	Year
1. Ted Kluszewski	.642	1954
2. George Foster	.631	1977
3. Frank Robinson	.624	1962
4. Kal Daniels	.617	1987
5. Frank Robinson	.611	1961
6. Frank Robinson	.595	1960
7. Eric Davis	.593	1987
8. Tony Perez	.589	1970
9. Johnny Bench	.587	1970
10. Alex Ochoa	.586	2000

Slugging Percentage: Career with Team

Player	SLG	PA
1. Frank Robinson	.554	6,409
2. George Foster	.514	5,010
3. Ted Kluszewski	.512	5,404
Adam Dunn	.512	2,112
5. Eric Davis	.510	3,819
6. Wally Post	.498	3,313
7. Lee May	.490	3,069
8. Dmitri Young	.488	2,178
9. Reggie Sanders	.476	3,292
Johnny Bench	.476	8,669

On-Base Percentage: Season

Player	OBP	Year
1. Joe Morgan	.466	1975
2. Bernie Carbo	.454	1970
3. Augie Galan	.449	1947
4. Joe Morgan	.444	1976
5. Cy Seymour	.429	1905
Kal Daniels	.429	1987
7. Pete Rose	.428	1969
8. Joe Morgan	.427	1974
9. Cuckoo Christensen	.426	1926
10. Elmer Smith	.425	1898

On-Base Percentage: Career with Team

Player	OBP	PA
1. Joe Morgan	.415	4,973
2. Dummy Hoy	.390	2,560
3. Frank Robinson	.389	6,409
4. Adam Dunn	.382	2,112
5. Pete Rose	.379	12,325
Rube Bressler	.379	2,543
7. Heinie Groh	.378	5,159
Curt Walker	.378	3,942
Cy Seymour	.378	2,420
10. Edd Roush	.377	5,965

OPS (On-Base Percentage + Slugging Percentage): Season

Player	OPS	Year
1. Ted Kluszewski	1.049	1954
2. Kal Daniels	1.046	1987
3. Frank Robinson	1.045	1962
4. Joe Morgan	1.020	1976
5. Frank Robinson	1.015	1961
6. George Foster	1.013	1977
7. Bernie Carbo	1.004	1970
8. Frank Robinson	1.002	1960
9. Harry Heilmann	.993	1930
10. Eric Davis	.991	1987

OPS (On-Base Percentage + Slugging Percentage): Career with Team

Player	OPS	PA
1. Frank Robinson	.943	6,409
2. Adam Dunn	.893	2,112
3. Joe Morgan	.885	4,973
4. Eric Davis	.877	3,819
5. George Foster	.870	5,010
6. Ted Kluszewski	.869	5,404
7. Dmitri Young	.842	2,178
8. Cy Seymour	.841	2,420
9. Sean Casey	.840	3,891
10. Edd Roush	.839	5,965

Stolen Bases: Season

Player	SB	Year
1. Hugh Nicol	138	1887
2. Hugh Nicol	103	1888
3. Bid McPhee	95	1887
4. Arlie Latham	87	1891
5. John Reilly	82	1888
6. Bob Bescher	81	1911
7. Eric Davis	80	1986
Hugh Nicol	80	1889
9. Dave Collins	79	1980
10. Dusty Miller	76	1896

STOLEN BASES: CAREER WITH TEAM

Player	SB	PA
1. Bid McPhee	568	9,409
2. Joe Morgan	406	4,973
3. Barry Larkin	379	9,057
4. Hugh Nicol	345	1,926
5. Arlie Latham	337	3,203
6. Dave Concepcion	321	9,640
7. Bob Bescher	320	3,299
8. Eric Davis	270	3,819
9. Bug Holliday	248	4,036
10. John Reilly	245	4,660

SACRIFICE HITS: SEASON

Player	Sac	Year
1. Jake Daubert	39	1919
2. Babe Pinelli	34	1925
3. Jake Daubert	33	1921
Dick Egan	33	1910
Dummy Hoy	33	1896
Babe Pinelli	33	1924
Edd Roush	33	1918
8. Hans Lobert	32	1908
9. Jake Daubert	31	1922
Heinie Groh	31	1915
Roy McMillan	31	1954
Greasy Neale	31	1919

SACRIFICE HITS: CAREER WITH TEAM

Player	Sac	PA
1. Edd Roush	186	5,965
2. Jake Daubert	155	3,523
3. Heinie Groh	146	5,159
4. Dick Hoblitzel	137	3,577
5. Curt Walker	136	3,942
6. Dick Egan	131	2,641
7. Babe Pinelli	122	2,544
8. Hughie Critz	120	3,428
9. Pat Duncan	113	3,002
10. Tommy Corcoran	111	5,157

HIT BY PITCH: SEASON

Player	HBP	Year
1. Jason LaRue	24	2004
2. Jason LaRue	20	2003
Frank Robinson	20	1956
4. Red Killefer	19	1915
5. Frank Fennelly	18	1886
John Reilly	18	1888
John Reilly	18	1889
Frank Robinson	18	1965
9. Ival Goodman	15	1938
John Reilly	15	1887
Bobby Tolan	15	1969

HIT BY PITCH: CAREER WITH TEAM

Player	HBP	PA
1. Frank Robinson	118	6,409
2. John Reilly	94	4,660
3. Bid McPhee	87	9,409
4. Pete Rose	86	12,325
5. Jason LaRue	85	2,314
6. Heinie Groh	61	5,159
7. Barry Larkin	55	9,057
8. Jake Beckley	50	3,824
Sean Casey	50	4,478
10. Dummy Hoy	47	2,560

Top 10 Pitching Leaders, Single Season & Career with Team

GAMES PITCHED: SEASON

Player	GP	Year
1. Wayne Granger	90	1969
2. Rob Murphy	87	1987
3. Frank Williams	85	1987
4. Stan Belinda	84	1997
5. Pedro Borbon	80	1973
6. Scott Sullivan	79	1999
Scott Sullivan	79	2000
Scott Sullivan	79	2001
9. Ted Abernathy	78	1968
Tom Hume	78	1980
Ted Power	78	1984
Jeff Shaw	78	1996
Jeff Shaw	78	1997
Kent Mercker	78	2005

GAMES PITCHED: CAREER WITH TEAM

Player	GP	IP
1. Pedro Borbon	531	920.7
2. Scott Sullivan	494	662.7
3. Clay Carroll	486	856.0
4. Joe Nuxhall	484	2,169.3
5. Danny Graves	465	733.0
6. Tom Hume	457	921.0
7. Eppa Rixey	440	2,890.7
8. Dolf Luque	395	2,668.7
9. Paul Derringer	393	2,615.3
John Franco	393	528.0

INNINGS PITCHED: SEASON

Player	IP	Year
1. Will White	577.0	1883
2. Tony Mullane	529.7	1886
3. Will White	480.0	1882
4. Will White	456.0	1884
5. Elmer Smith	447.3	1887
6. Tony Mullane	426.3	1891
7. Tony Mullane	416.3	1887
8. Elton Chamberlain	406.3	1892
9. Billy Rhines	401.3	1890
10. Jesse Duryea	401.0	1889

INNINGS PITCHED: CAREER WITH TEAM

Player	IP
1. Eppa Rixey	2,890.7
2. Dolf Luque	2,668.7
3. Paul Derringer	2,615.3
4. Tony Mullane	2,599.0
5. Bucky Walters	2,355.7
6. Joe Nuxhall	2,169.3
7. Johnny Vander Meer	2,028.0
8. Bob Ewing	2,020.3
9. Pete Donohue	1,996.3
10. Noodles Hahn	1,987.3

BATTERS FACED: SEASON

Player	BF	Year
1. Will White	2,320	1883
2. Tony Mullane	2,258	1886
3. Will White	1,986	1884
4. Will White	1,900	1882
5. Elmer Smith	1,872	1887

6. Tony Mullane	1,763	1887
7. Jesse Duryea	1,731	1889
8. Lee Viau	1,612	1889
9. Noodles Hahn	1,550	1901
10. Tony Mullane	1,504	1888

BATTERS FACED: CAREER WITH TEAM

Player	BF	IP
1. Eppa Rixey	12,127	2,890.7
2. Dolf Luque	11,099	2,668.7
3. Paul Derringer	10,947	2,615.3
4. Bucky Walters	9,796	2,355.7
5. Joe Nuxhall	9,204	2,169.3
6. Johnny Vander Meer	8,679	2,028.0
7. Pete Donohue	8,517	1,996.3
8. Tom Browning	8,017	1,911.0
9. Jim Maloney	7,598	1,818.7
10. Will White	7,571	1,832.3

GAMES STARTED: SEASON

Player	GS	Year
1. Will White	64	1883
2. Tony Mullane	56	1886
3. Will White	54	1882
4. Elmer Smith	52	1887
Will White	52	1884
6. Elton Chamberlain	49	1892
7. Jesse Duryea	48	1889
Tony Mullane	48	1887
9. Tony Mullane	47	1891
10. Billy Rhines	45	1890

GAMES STARTED: CAREER WITH TEAM

Player	GS	IP
1. Eppa Rixey	356	2,890.7
2. Paul Derringer	322	2,615.3
3. Dolf Luque	319	2,668.7
4. Tom Browning	298	1,911.0
5. Bucky Walters	296	2,355.7
6. Tony Mullane	285	2,599.0
7. Johnny Vander Meer	278	2,028.0
8. Joe Nuxhall	274	2,169.3
9. Jim Maloney	258	1,818.7
10. Pete Donohue	256	1,996.3

COMPLETE GAMES: SEASON

Player	CG	Year
1. Will White	64	1883
2. Tony Mullane	55	1886
3. Will White	52	1882
Will White	52	1884
5. Elmer Smith	49	1887
6. Tony Mullane	47	1887
7. Billy Rhines	45	1890
8. Elton Chamberlain	43	1892
9. Tony Mullane	42	1891
Lee Viau	42	1888

COMPLETE GAMES: CAREER WITH TEAM

Player	CG	IP
1. Tony Mullane	264	2,599.0
2. Noodles Hahn	209	1,987.3
3. Will White	204	1,832.3
4. Bucky Walters	195	2,355.7
5. Paul Derringer	189	2,615.3
6. Frank Dwyer	187	1,983.7
7. Bob Ewing	184	2,020.3
8. Dolf Luque	183	2,668.7
9. Eppa Rixey	180	2,890.7
10. Red Lucas	158	1,768.7

GAMES WON: SEASON

Player	W	Year
1. Will White	43	1883
2. Will White	40	1882
3. Elmer Smith	34	1887
Will White	34	1884
5. Tony Mullane	33	1886
6. Jesse Duryea	32	1889
7. Tony Mullane	31	1887
8. Billy Rhines	28	1890
9. Pink Hawley	27	1898
Dolf Luque	27	1923
Lee Viau	27	1888
Bucky Walters	27	1939

GAMES WON: CAREER WITH TEAM

Player	W	IP
1. Eppa Rixey	179	2,890.7
2. Tony Mullane	163	2,599.0
3. Paul Derringer	161	2,615.3
4. Bucky Walters	160	2,355.7
5. Dolf Luque	154	2,668.7
6. Will White	136	1,832.3
7. Jim Maloney	134	1,818.7
8. Frank Dwyer	132	1,983.7
9. Joe Nuxhall	130	2,169.3
10. Pete Donohue	127	1,996.3
Noodles Hahn	127	1,987.3

GAMES LOST: SEASON

Player	L	Year
1. Tony Mullane	27	1886
2. Tony Mullane	26	1891
3. Paul Derringer	25	1933
4. Billy Rhines	24	1891
5. Red Ames	23	1914
Elton Chamberlain	23	1892
Dolf Luque	23	1922
Orval Overall	23	1905
9. Frank Dwyer	22	1894
Si Johnson	22	1934
Will White	22	1883

GAMES LOST: CAREER WITH TEAM

Player	L	IP
1. Dolf Luque	152	2,668.7
2. Paul Derringer	150	2,615.3
3. Eppa Rixey	148	2,890.7
4. Tony Mullane	124	2,599.0
5. Johnny Vander Meer	116	2,028.0
6. Pete Donohue	110	1,996.3
7. Joe Nuxhall	109	2,169.3
8. Bucky Walters	107	2,355.7
9. Bob Ewing	103	2,020.3
10. Frank Dwyer	101	1,983.7

WINNING PERCENTAGE: SEASON

Player	W%	Year
1. Tom Seaver	.875	1981
2. Elmer Riddle	.826	1941
3. Tom Seaver	.824	1977
Wayne Simpson	.824	1970
5. Bob Purkey	.821	1962
6. Don Gullett	.789	1975
7. Tom Browning	.783	1988
8. Paul Derringer	.781	1939
9. Dolf Luque	.771	1923
10. Will White	.769	1882

WINNING PERCENTAGE: CAREER WITH TEAM

Player	W%	IP
1. Don Gullett	.674	1,187.0
2. Will White	.663	1,832.3
3. Pedro Borbon	.653	920.7

4. Jim Maloney	.623	1,818.7
Clay Carroll	.623	856.0
6. Gary Nolan	.621	1,656.3
7. Tom Seaver	.620	1,085.7
8. Jose Rijo	.614	1,478.0
9. Elmer Riddle	.605	757.7
10. Hod Eller	.600	863.0

SHUTOUTS: SEASON

Player	SHO	Year
1. Will White	8	1882
2. Jack Billingham	7	1973
Hod Eller	7	1919
Fred Toney	7	1917
Will White	7	1884
6. 14 tied with . . .	6	—

SHUTOUTS: CAREER WITH TEAM

Player	SHO	IP
1. Bucky Walters	32	2,355.7
2. Jim Maloney	30	1,818.7
3. Johnny Vander Meer	29	2,028.0
4. Ken Raffensberger	25	1,490.0
5. Paul Derringer	24	2,615.3
Noodles Hahn	24	1,987.3
Dolf Luque	24	2,668.7
8. Eppa Rixey	23	2,890.7
Will White	23	1,832.3
10. Joe Nuxhall	20	2,169.3

ERA: SEASON

Player	ERA	Year
1. Harry McCormick	1.52	1882
2. Will White	1.54	1882
3. Fred Toney	1.58	1915
4. Bob Ewing	1.73	1907
5. Noodles Hahn	1.77	1902
6. Dutch Ruether	1.82	1919
7. Andy Coakley	1.86	1908
8. Art Fromme	1.90	1909
9. Dolf Luque	1.93	1923
10. Billy Rhines	1.95	1890

ERA: CAREER WITH TEAM

Player	ERA	IP
1. Andy Coakley	2.11	507.7
2. Fred Toney	2.18	999.0
3. Dutch Ruether	2.26	554.0
4. Jake Weimer	2.31	630.3
5. Bob Ewing	2.37	2,020.3
6. John Franco	2.49	528.0
7. Will White	2.51	1,832.3
8. Noodles Hahn	2.52	1,987.3
9. Joe Beggs	2.56	569.0
10. Hod Eller	2.62	863.0

EARNED RUNS ALLOWED: SEASON

Player	ER	Year
1. Tony Mullane	218	1886
2. Frank Dwyer	196	1894
3. Tom Parrott	192	1894
4. Will White	168	1884
5. Tom Parrott	160	1895
6. Lee Viau	157	1889
7. Elton Chamberlain	153	1892
Tony Mullane	153	1891
9. George Pechiney	152	1886
10. Tony Mullane	150	1887

EARNED RUNS ALLOWED: CAREER WITH TEAM

Player	ER	IP
1. Eppa Rixey	1,068	2,890.7
2. Paul Derringer	975	2,615.3
3. Dolf Luque	917	2,668.7
4. Joe Nuxhall	916	2,169.3
5. Tony Mullane	911	2,599.0
6. Frank Dwyer	833	1,983.7
7. Tom Browning	832	1,911.0
8. Pete Donohue	827	1,996.3
9. Johnny Vander Meer	768	2,028.0
10. Bucky Walters	766	2,355.7

STRIKEOUTS: SEASON

Player	K	Year
1. Mario Soto	274	1982
2. Jim Maloney	265	1963
3. Tony Mullane	250	1886
4. Jim Maloney	244	1965
5. Mario Soto	242	1983
6. Noodles Hahn	239	1901
7. Jose Rijo	227	1993
8. Tom Seaver	226	1978
9. Jim Maloney	216	1966
10. Jim Maloney	214	1964
Mario Soto	214	1985

STRIKEOUTS: CAREER WITH TEAM

Player	K	IP
1. Jim Maloney	1,592	1,818.7
2. Mario Soto	1,449	1,730.3
3. Joe Nuxhall	1,289	2,169.3
4. Jose Rijo	1,251	1,478.0
Johnny Vander Meer	1,251	2,028.0
6. Paul Derringer	1,062	2,615.3
7. Gary Nolan	1,035	1,656.3
8. Jim O'Toole	1,002	1,561.0
9. Tom Browning	997	1,911.0
10. Tony Mullane	993	2,599.0

STRIKEOUTS PER NINE IP: SEASON

Player	K/9	Year
1. Mario Soto	9.57	1982
2. Jim Maloney	9.53	1963
3. Jose Rijo	8.93	1994
4. Jim Maloney	8.92	1964
5. Jose Rijo	8.89	1988
6. Jim Maloney	8.65	1966
7. Mario Soto	8.61	1980
8. Jim Maloney	8.60	1965
9. Gary Nolan	8.18	1967
10. Johnny Vander Meer	8.03	1941

STRIKEOUTS PER NINE IP: CAREER WITH TEAM

Player	K/9	IP
1. Jim Maloney	7.88	1,818.7
2. Scott Sullivan	7.66	662.7
3. Jose Rijo	7.62	1,478.0
4. Norm Charlton	7.54	503.7
Mario Soto	7.54	1,730.3
6. Bruce Berenyi	7.13	613.3
7. Brett Tomko	6.88	508.7
8. John Smiley	6.51	775.3
9. Sammy Ellis	6.32	810.7
10. John Franco	6.26	528.0

HITS ALLOWED: SEASON

Player	HA	Year
1. Tony Mullane	501	1886
2. Will White	479	1884
3. Will White	473	1883
4. Frank Dwyer	471	1894
5. Tony Mullane	414	1887

6. Will White	411	1882
7. Tom Parrott	402	1894
8. Elmer Smith	400	1887
9. Elton Chamberlain	391	1892
10. Tony Mullane	390	1891

Hits Allowed: Career with Team

Player	HA	IP
1. Eppa Rixey	3,115	2,890.7
2. Paul Derringer	2,755	2,615.3
3. Dolf Luque	2,619	2,668.7
4. Tony Mullane	2,391	2,599.0
5. Frank Dwyer	2,350	1,983.7
6. Pete Donohue	2,263	1,996.3
7. Joe Nuxhall	2,168	2,169.3
8. Bucky Walters	2,142	2,355.7
9. Tom Browning	1,918	1,911.0
10. Noodles Hahn	1,878	1,987.3

Hits Allowed Per Nine IP: Season

Player	H/9	Year
1. Mario Soto	5.96	1980
2. Art Fromme	6.28	1909
3. Wayne Simpson	6.39	1970
4. Fred Toney	6.47	1915
5. Tom Seaver	6.49	1981
6. Tom Seaver	6.53	1977
7. Jim Maloney	6.58	1963
8. Jim Maloney	6.66	1965
9. Jose Rijo	6.67	1988
10. Tony Mullane	6.77	1892

Hits Allowed Per Nine IP: Career with Team

Player	H/9	IP
1. Mario Soto	7.26	1,730.3
2. Jim Maloney	7.34	1,818.7
3. Tom Seaver	7.63	1,085.7
4. Jake Weimer	7.68	630.3
Johnny Vander Meer	7.68	2,028.0
6. Fred Toney	7.70	999.0
7. Don Gullett	7.75	1,187.0
8. Norm Charlton	7.77	503.7
9. Art Fromme	7.79	888.7
Ray Starr	7.79	528.0

Walks Allowed: Season

Player	BB	Year
1. Tony Mullane	187	1891
2. Elton Chamberlain	170	1892
3. Tony Mullane	166	1886
4. Johnny Vander Meer	162	1943
5. Orval Overall	147	1905
6. Lee Viau	136	1889
7. Herm Wehmeier	135	1950
8. George Pechiney	133	1886
9. Jesse Duryea	127	1889
Tony Mullane	127	1892

Walks Allowed: Career with Team

Player	BB	IP
1. Johnny Vander Meer	1,072	2,028.0
2. Tony Mullane	926	2,599.0
3. Bucky Walters	806	2,355.7
4. Jim Maloney	786	1,818.7
5. Dolf Luque	756	2,668.7
6. Joe Nuxhall	706	2,169.3
7. Mario Soto	657	1,730.3
8. Eppa Rixey	603	2,890.7
9. Herm Wehmeier	591	1,087.0
10. Ewell Blackwell	532	1,281.3

Walks Allowed Per Nine IP: Season

Player	BB/9	Year
1. Red Lucas	0.74	1933
2. Slim Sallee	0.79	1919
3. Gary Nolan	1.02	1976
4. Paul Derringer	1.05	1939
5. Noodles Hahn	1.06	1904
6. Don Newcombe	1.09	1959
7. Red Lucas	1.17	1932
8. Pete Donohue	1.23	1926
9. Gary Nolan	1.24	1975
10. Eppa Rixey	1.29	1922

Walks Allowed Per Nine IP: Career with Team

Player	BB/9	IP
1. Red Lucas	1.55	1,768.7
2. Will White	1.59	1,832.3
3. Paul Derringer	1.69	2,615.3
4. Noodles Hahn	1.70	1,987.3
5. Carl Mays	1.71	703.3
6. Pete Donohue	1.75	1,996.3
7. Ken Raffensberger	1.84	1,490.0
8. Eppa Rixey	1.88	2,890.7
9. George Suggs	1.91	1,028.7
10. Bob Purkey	1.97	1,588.0

WHIP (Walks + Hits Per Nine IP): Season

Player	WHIP	Year
1. Tom Seaver	0.956	1977
2. Noodles Hahn	0.984	1904
3. Harry McCormick	0.997	1882
4. Will White	1.000	1883
5. Will White	1.004	1882
6. Gary Nolan	1.006	1972
7. Ray Fisher	1.027	1919
8. Bob Ewing	1.035	1908
9. Fred Toney	1.046	1915
10. Mel Queen	1.058	1967

WHIP (Walks + Hits Per Nine IP): Career with Team

Player	WHIP	IP
1. Will White	1.096	1,832.3
2. Fred Toney	1.115	999.0
3. Noodles Hahn	1.134	1,987.3
4. Gary Nolan	1.138	1,656.3
5. Bob Ewing	1.160	2,020.3
6. Tom Seaver	1.177	1,085.7
7. Hod Eller	1.181	863.0
8. Mario Soto	1.186	1,730.3
9. Jose Rijo	1.187	1,478.0
10. Jake Weimer	1.190	630.3

Home Runs Allowed: Season

Player	HRA	Year
1. Eric Milton	40	2005
2. Tom Browning	36	1988
3. Sammy Ellis	35	1966
4. Ken Raffensberger	34	1950
Ramon Ortiz	34	2005
6. Bill Gullickson	33	1987
Jim Merritt	33	1969
8. Rob Bell	32	2000
Tom Browning	32	1991
Elmer Dessens	32	2001

HOME RUNS ALLOWED: CAREER WITH TEAM

Player	HRA	IP
1. Tom Browning	234	1,911.0
2. Joe Nuxhall	197	2,169.3
3. Mario Soto	172	1,730.3
4. Bob Purkey	156	1,588.0
Ken Raffensberger	156	1,490.0
6. Gary Nolan	141	1,656.3
7. Jim Maloney	135	1,818.7
8. Herm Wehmeier	132	1,087.0
9. Fred Norman	127	1,315.0
10. Joey Jay	116	1,102.7

SAVES: SEASON

Player	SV	Year
1. Jeff Brantley	44	1996
2. Jeff Shaw	42	1997
3. Danny Graves	41	2004
4. John Franco	39	1988
5. Clay Carroll	37	1972
6. Wayne Granger	35	1970
7. John Franco	32	1987
John Franco	32	1989
Danny Graves	32	2001
Danny Graves	32	2002

SAVES: CAREER WITH TEAM

Player	SV	IP
1. Danny Graves	182	733.0
2. John Franco	148	528.0
3. Clay Carroll	119	856.0
4. Jeff Brantley	88	218.3
Rob Dibble	88	450.7
Tom Hume	88	921.0
7. Pedro Borbon	76	920.7
8. Wayne Granger	73	329.3
9. Jeff Shaw	69	249.0
10. Bill Henry	64	267.3

WILD PITCHES: SEASON

Player	WP	Year
1. Tony Mullane	51	1886
2. Will White	25	1885
3. Tony Mullane	21	1889
Scott Williamson	21	2000
5. Jesse Duryea	20	1889
6. Jim Maloney	19	1963
Jim Maloney	19	1965
8. Bill Mountjoy	18	1884
Tony Mullane	18	1891
Orval Overall	18	1905
Billy Rhines	18	1891
Tony Mullane	18	1886
Tom Walker	18	1904

WILD PITCHES: CAREER WITH TEAM

Player	WP	IP
1. Tony Mullane	126	2,599.0
2. Jim Maloney	121	1,818.7
3. Billy Rhines	55	1,557.0
4. Scott Williamson	51	322.3
5. Jesse Duryea	50	820.0
6. Jack Billingham	46	1,270.0
7. Rube Benton	45	1,504.7
Fred Norman	45	1,315.0
Bucky Walters	45	2,355.7
10. Elton Chamberlain	42	825.0
Bob Ewing	42	2,020.3

HIT BATSMEN: SEASON

Player	HB	Year
1. Will White	35	1884
2. Tony Mullane	32	1887
3. Will White	27	1885
4. Gus Shallix	26	1884
5. Jake Weimer	23	1907
6. Pink Hawley	22	1898
7. Pink Hawley	20	1899
8. Henry Thielman	19	1902
9. Rube Benton	18	1912

HIT BATSMEN: CAREER WITH TEAM

Player	HB	IP
1. Will White	68	1,832.3
2. Rube Benton	66	1,504.7
Joe Nuxhall	66	2,169.3
4. Bill Phillips	56	1,213.7
5. Scott Sullivan	52	662.7
6. Tony Mullane	50	2,599.0
7. Noodles Hahn	49	1,987.3
Pete Schneider	49	1,245.0
9. Bob Ewing	48	2,020.3
Bob Purkey	48	1,588.0

GAMES FINISHED: SEASON

Player	GF	Year
1. Tom Hume	62	1980
Jeff Shaw	62	1997
3. Ted Abernathy	61	1967
Jeff Brantley	61	1996
John Franco	61	1988
6. John Franco	60	1987
7. Rawly Eastwick	59	1976
Wayne Granger	59	1970
Danny Graves	59	2004
Randy Myers	59	1990

GAMES FINISHED: CAREER WITH TEAM

Player	GF	IP
1. Danny Graves	337	733.0
2. John Franco	286	528.0
3. Clay Carroll	282	856.0
4. Pedro Borbon	255	920.7
Tom Hume	255	921.0
6. Rob Dibble	196	450.7
7. Frank Smith	161	456.7
8. Ted Power	158	719.7
9. Wayne Granger	155	329.3
10. Jeff Brantley	154	218.3

Significant Reds

BECKLEY, JAKE (1B)
(1897–1903)

After 10 years with the Pirates and Giants, Beckley was traded to Cincinnati in 1897. The big first baseman finished in the top 10 of many offensive categories during his 20 years in the major leagues, but he never led the league in anything in an individual season. His strength was longevity. In the 130 years of major league baseball, no player at any position has more total chances in the field than Beckley's 25,000. His 23,696 putouts are also first all-time. On September 26, 1897, Beckley hit three home runs in a game, something no other National Leaguer would do until 1922. On May 16, 1898, he hit three triples in a game. During Beckley's seven years in Cincinnati, he hit over .300 in six. Beckley was elected to the Hall of Fame in 1971.

CAREER REDS RECORD:

Games	AB	Hits	Runs
879	3,465	1,125	592
Avg	**HR**	**RBI**	**SB**
.325	26	570	114

BELL, GUS (OF)
(1953–1961)

Gus Bell had three good years in Pittsburgh but was traded to the Reds after the 1952 season following a long-simmering dispute with General Manager Branch Rickey. He wanted to take his family with him to spring training (including his young son Buddy, who would later become a major leaguer himself), but management refused, insisting that he ride alone and by train. Upon being traded to Cincinnati, Bell made the All-Star team four times in nine seasons with the Reds, cracking 100 RBIs four times. He was remarkably steady. From 1953 to 1957, Bell hit between .292 and .308 every year. After the 1961 season, Bell was selected by the Mets in the expansion draft and, on April 11, 1962, got the first hit in New York Mets history.

CAREER REDS RECORD:

Games	AB	Hits	Runs
1,235	4,667	1,343	634
Avg	**HR**	**RBI**	**SB**
.288	160	711	24

BENCH, JOHNNY (C)
(1967–1983)

The dominant catcher in the National League for 15 years, Johnny Bench is considered by many baseball observers to be the best catcher in history. Selected in the second round of the June 1965 amateur draft (the Reds took Bernie Carbo with their first pick), Bench tore up the minors for two seasons before becoming the Reds' regular catcher at the age of 19. In 1968 Bench came out of the gate hitting and throwing in spectacular fashion and became the first catcher in history to win the Rookie of the Year Award, setting a record for most games caught by a rookie (154). With a powerful and accurate throwing arm unrivaled during his era, Bench won 10 consecutive Gold Gloves from 1968 to 1977. He was selected to 13 consecutive All-Star Games, 14 overall. A two-time MVP, Bench was the main cog in the Big Red Machine days of the 1970s, when the Reds won six division titles, four NL pennants, and two World Series. In his first MVP season (1970), Bench set a record for most home runs by July 31 with 36, a record broken by Mark McGwire in 1998 when he smacked 45 by the same date.

Bench preferred to be a quiet star, letting his play speak for itself. Just before the 1976 World Series with the Yankees, when Reds Manager Sparky Anderson was asked about Thurman Munson, he replied, "I don't want to embarrass any other catcher by comparing him with Johnny Bench." Anderson's remark set off a firestorm in the press and infuriated Munson, who hit .529 in the Series. Bench, however, hit .533 with two homers and 6 RBIs and won the MVP Award as the Reds swept the Yankees. Near the end of his career, Bench requested a change of position due to the physical toll that catching was taking on him. He had already played some third base to spell his aching knees. The team granted his request and he closed out his career spending more time at first and the outfield than he did at catcher. Bench, who spent his entire 17-year career with Cincinnati, held many records at the time of his retirement, both offensive and defensive. In 1989 he was elected to the Baseball Hall of Fame.

CAREER REDS RECORD:

Games	AB	Hits	Runs
2,158	7,658	2,048	1,091
Avg	**HR**	**RBI**	**SB**
.267	389	1,376	68

BROWNING, TOM (SP)
(1984–1994)

The Cincinnati Reds chose Tom Browning with the ninth pick in the June 1982 amateur draft. In 1985 Browning became the first rookie to win 20 games since Bob Grim of the Yankees when he finished 20–9 in 1954. Since he only had an average fastball, Browning baffled hitters with a variety of off-speed pitches, including two different screwballs. On September 16, 1988, Browning pitched the first perfect game in the National League in 23 years when he blanked the Dodgers. While the perfect game is his main claim to fame, Browning will forever be remembered for a zany moment that occurred in Chicago during the 1993 season. Television cameras captured Browning sitting on top of a residential building across the street from Wrigley Field—in uniform—watching the Cubs-Reds game with Cubs fans. After leading the NL in games started four times in five years, a series of major injuries curtailed his playing time over his final several seasons in Cincinnati. Browning left the Reds via free agency after the 1994 season and signed with Kansas City, but he pitched in only two games in 1995, allowing nine earned runs in 10 innings, before retiring.

CAREER REDS RECORD:

W	L	W%	ERA	SV
123	88	.583	3.92	0
K	BB	SHO	IP	
997	506	12	1,911.0	

CARROLL, CLAY (RP)
(1968–1975)

Clay Carroll was traded to the Reds from the Braves on June 11, 1968, as part of a six-player deal that sent Milt Pappas to Atlanta. A two-time All-Star with Cincinnati, Carroll was a fireballer who was at his best in the postseason, and he got plenty of opportunity for postseason play with Cincinnati's Big Red Machine. In 22 career postseason games with Cincinnati, Carroll posted a 4–2 record with 2 saves and a 1.39 ERA. In 1972 he led the NL with a record 37 saves. Carroll was the winner of Game 7 of the 1975 World Series against Boston, and then was traded to the White Sox two months later.

CAREER REDS RECORD:

W	L	W%	ERA	SV
71	43	.623	2.73	119
K	BB	SHO	IP	
460	307	0	856.0	

CONCEPCION, DAVE (SS)
(1970–1988)

The Reds signed Venezuelan Dave Concepcion as an amateur free agent on September 12, 1967. Once he arrived in the majors in 1970, Concepcion remained with the team for the next 19 years, playing his entire career in Cincinnati. At first he shared the shortstop position with Woody Woodward, but Concepcion won the job permanently in 1974 and remained a fixture in the infield until the late 1980s when Barry Larkin replaced him. Concepcion was a great fielder (he won five Gold Gloves) and a good RBI man who could hit for average and steal bases. Pee Wee Reese and Tim McCarver both considered Concepcion one of the best shortstops of all time.

When the Big Red Machine rolled over National League opponents in the 1970s, Concepcion played a major part. In 1978 Concepcion became the first Cincinnati shortstop to hit .300 since Joe Tinker in 1913. A nine-time All-Star, Concepcion was named the 1982 All-Star Game MVP as his two-run homer helped the NL to its 11th straight Summer Classic win. When he retired after the 1988 season (just 44 games short of Larry Bowa's NL record for games played by a shortstop), Concepcion trailed only Pete Rose on the Reds' all-time list in games, hits, at-bats, and doubles. He trailed only Joe Morgan in stolen bases.

CAREER REDS RECORD:

Games	AB	Hits	Runs
2,488	8,723	2,326	993

Avg	HR	RBI	SB
.267	101	950	321

DAVIS, ERIC (OF)
(1984–1991, 1996)

The Cincinnati Reds made Eric Davis their eighth choice in the June 1980 amateur draft. While unspectacular in stints in 1984 and 1985, Davis showed promise and in 1986 he exploded onto the National League scene when he hit 27 homers and stole 80 bases. Dubbed "Eric the Red" by Cincinnati fans, Davis, a two-time All-Star and three-time Gold Glove winner, had a rare combination of power and speed. In 1987 he hit 37 homers, stole 50 bases, and made many breathtaking catches in center field. He also set a league record by hitting three grand slams in the month of May. Davis had an extraordinary body, lithe and muscular with almost no body fat. But his body suffered from constant injuries because of his all-out style of play, forcing him to miss many games in his career.

While helping the Reds to the World Series title in 1990 with a home run in his first at-bat, he also finished the Series in the hospital after suffering a lacerated kidney when he dove for a ball in Game 4. After a disappointing 1991 season in which he played in only 89 games, Davis was traded to his hometown Dodgers along with Kip Gross for Tim Belcher and John Wetteland on November 27, 1991. Following three disappointing years with Los Angeles and Detroit, Davis sat out the 1995 season while he recovered from a badly herniated disc. When he came back in 1996, Davis signed a contract with Cincinnati and had a fine year, hitting .287 with 26 homers and 23 stolen bases, winning the Comeback Player of the Year Award. He left via free agency after one year, however, and then bounced around with Baltimore, St. Louis, and the Giants for five more years, all the while battling colon cancer.

CAREER REDS RECORD:

Games	AB	Hits	Runs
985	3,272	886	635
Avg	**HR**	**RBI**	**SB**
.271	203	615	270

DERRINGER, PAUL (SP)
(1933–1942)

After falling into disfavor with St. Louis GM Branch Rickey, Paul Derringer was traded to the Reds early in the 1933 season as part of a six-player deal that sent Leo Durocher to the Cardinals. After an 0–2 start for St. Louis, Derringer went 7–25 for Cincinnati, finishing 7–27 for the year, only two losses off Vic Willis's all-time season mark. While Derringer was discouraged, Cincinnati's Larry MacPhail was not, since he recognized that Derringer had actually pitched much better than his record indicated. MacPhail gave Derringer a $1,500 raise and sent him out to the mound in 1934. Derringer responded with a 15–21 record, then went 22–13 in 1935 as he was selected to the first of his six All-Star Game appearances.

On one occasion, MacPhail fined Derringer $250 for not sliding into second base and lectured him for an hour. Derringer finally exploded and threw an inkwell at MacPhail, missing his head by inches. When MacPhail screamed that he could have been killed, Derringer yelled right back that he had intended to kill him. MacPhail promptly got out his checkbook and gave Derringer a check for $750. "What's this for?" Derringer asked. "That's a bonus for missing me," replied MacPhail. When the first night game in major league history was played in Cincinnati, MacPhail gave Derringer the honor of starting the game and he responded with a 2–1 win. From 1938 to 1940 Derringer won 20 or more games each year, teaming with Bucky Walters to lead the Reds to NL pennants in 1939 and 1940. In the 1940 World Series, Derringer won two games, including the decisive Game 7, 2–1, giving the Reds the title over Detroit. Following the 1942 season, Derringer was sold to the Cubs, where he pitched three more years before retiring.

CAREER REDS RECORD:

W	L	W%	ERA	SV
161	150	.518	3.36	17
K	**BB**	**SHO**	**IP**	
1,062	491	24	2,615.3	

DRIESSEN, DAN (1B/3B)
(1973–1984)

The Reds signed Dan Driessen as an amateur free agent on August 29, 1969. Driessen had a long and productive, if unspectacular career for Cincinnati, playing nearly 1,500 games, much of it during the Big Red Machine days. Driessen, an especially good fielder and base stealer for a first baseman, was typically overshadowed by the many other stars on the team such as Rose, Bench, Morgan, Perez, Concepcion, and Foster. In mid-1984 he was traded to Montreal where he wandered the league with the Expos, Giants, Astros, and Cardinals before retiring in 1987.

CAREER REDS RECORD:

Games	AB	Hits	Runs
1,480	4,717	1,277	661

Avg	HR	RBI	SB
.271	133	670	152

DWYER, FRANK (SP)
(1892–1899)

Frank Dwyer came to Cincinnati from St. Louis early in the 1892 season after posting a 2–8 record for the Cardinals. He promptly turned things around, going 19–10 for the Reds and finishing with 21 wins. After the pitching mounds were moved back in 1893 from 50 feet to 60 feet 6 inches, Dwyer still had a respectable 18–15 record while many pitchers were taking a beating getting used to the new distance. Dwyer won at least 16 games a year for his first seven years in Cincinnati, including a career-best 24–11 record in 1896. After starting the 1899 season 0–5 in his first five starts, Dwyer retired as a player and became a National League umpire. He later umpired in the American League, was a coach and scout, and managed the Detroit Tigers to a seventh-place finish in 1902. He eventually became the New York State Boxing Commissioner for several years before establishing a successful business in the coal industry.

CAREER REDS RECORD:

W	L	W%	ERA	SV
132	101	.567	3.78	5

K	BB	SHO	IP
322	489	10	1,983.7

EWING, BOB (SP)
(1902–1909)

Bob Ewing, a spitball-tossing workhorse for the Reds during the first decade of the 20th century, averaged over 300 innings per year from 1905–1908. His best season was 1905, when he went 20–11, although in 1907 he had a sparkling 1.73 ERA despite a losing record of 17–19. On January 20, 1910, Ewing was traded along with Ad Brennan to the Philadelphia Phillies for Harry Coveleski and Frank Corridon.

CAREER REDS RECORD:

W	L	W%	ERA	SV
108	103	.512	2.37	4

K	BB	SHO	IP
884	513	15	2,020.3

FOSTER, GEORGE (OF)
(1971–1981)

After playing in just 54 games for San Francisco over three years, George Foster was traded to the Reds on May 29, 1971, for Frank Duffy and Vern Geishert. It took four more years before Foster finally blossomed, but when he did, he put together a four-year stretch, including the best single season ever by a Cincinnati player, that has few equivalents in National League history. One of the main cogs of Cincinnati's Big Red Machine of the 1970s, Foster was arguably the best power hitter in baseball in the late 1970s. He began his ascent in 1976, winning the MVP Award in the All-Star Game and being named the NL Player of the Year by the *Sporting News* for leading the Reds to the NL title and seven straight postseason wins, including a sweep of the Yankees in the World Series. In 1977 Foster hit .320 with 52 homers, 149 RBIs, 124 runs, and won the NL's MVP Award. In so doing, Foster was the only major leaguer to hit 50 homers in a season during the 1970s. Of his 52 homers that year, 31 came on the road, setting a new major league record. Foster tied a major league record when he won his league's RBI crown three consecutive years from 1976 to 1978.

During his time in Cincinnati, the brooding Foster was openly criticized by several of his teammates for not being a team player. Said Pete Rose, "I never once saw him get his uniform dirty. He doesn't dive for balls and will never go to the wall if it means crashing into it." After several more solid seasons, the Reds traded their five-time All-Star to the New York Mets before the 1982 season for three players, whereupon Foster signed the richest contract in baseball history, $10 million for five years. His performance declined dramatically, however, and some said he quit trying after signing for the big money. After hitting only .227 with 13 homers midway through the fifth year of his Mets contract, Foster was traded to the White Sox. He claimed racism at the time, but with the White Sox his performance declined even more (1 homer in 15 games) and he was released after playing in only 15 games, his brilliant career at an end.

CAREER REDS RECORD:

Games	AB	Hits	Runs
1,253	4,454	1,276	680

Avg	HR	RBI	SB
.286	244	861	46

FRANCO, JOHN (RP)
(1984–1989)

While still in the Dodgers' minor league system, John Franco was traded to the Reds for Rafael Landestoy on May 9, 1983. Franco was promoted to the big leagues in 1984 and played the first six years of his 20-plus-year major league career with the Reds. In 1985 Franco had an 11-game winning streak out of the bullpen and finished 12–3 on the season. In 1988 Franco recorded 39 saves, breaking Clay Carroll's Cincinnati single-season and career-saves records. From 1986–1989, Franco was the main closer in the Reds' bullpen, collecting 148 saves and three of his four career All-Star nominations. In December 1989 Franco was traded to the Mets in a four-player deal that brought Randy Myers to Cincinnati. *(See Mets bio.)*

CAREER REDS RECORD:

W	L	W%	ERA	SV
42	30	.583	2.49	148

K	BB	SHO	IP
367	210	0	528.0

GRAVES, DANNY (RP)
(1997–2005)

Danny Graves was traded to the Cincinnati Reds in July 1997 as part of a six-player deal that sent John Smiley to the Indians. A middle reliever, Graves became the Reds' closer in 1999, eventually becoming the team's all-time leader in saves. In 2003 he was converted to a starter for a year, but a 4–15 record with a 5.33 ERA put an end to that experiment. In 2005 he was released by Cincinnati after making derogatory statements and gestures towards Cincinnati fans during a period of frustration over blown saves by both him and other Cincinnati pitchers. He was eventually picked up by the Mets and became a middle reliever for New York.

CAREER REDS RECORD:

W	L	W%	ERA	SV
38	42	.475	3.85	172

K	BB	SHO	IP
380	227	1	714.7

GRIFFEY, KEN, JR. (OF)
(2000–2005)

See Mariners bio.

GRIFFEY, KEN, SR. (OF/1B) (1973–1981, 1988–1990)

Ken Griffey Sr. was drafted by the Cincinnati Reds in the 29th round of the June 1969 amateur draft. After playing partial seasons in Cincinnati in 1973 and 1974, he made the team for good in 1975 as a regular outfielder when Pete Rose was moved to third base. On playing with the star-studded Big Red Machine, Griffey once said, "I just did my job and kept my mouth shut." Griffey hit over .300 in five of his seven seasons as a Reds regular, even competing for the batting titles in 1976 and 1977, losing the 1976 title on the last day of the season to Bill Madlock, .339 to .336. Griffey was a three-time All-Star with the Reds and won the game's MVP Award in 1980. (In 1992 Ken Griffey Jr. would also win the award, making them the first father-son combo in history to be All-Star Game MVPs.) Griffey collected 75 at-bats in postseason play for the Reds and, though he only hit for a .240 average, many of his hits produced important runs for the Reds. After the 1981 season Griffey was traded to the Yankees for Brian Ryder and Freddie Toliver.

After seven years with the Yankees and Braves, Griffey returned to Cincinnati for a second tour in 1988. In 1990, with his career clearly in decline, he was given his release so he could sign with the Seattle Mariners and join his son as the first father-son combo to play for the same team at the same time. Playing side by side with his son in the Seattle outfield sparked a resurgence in Griffey's performance. The two Griffeys singled back-to-back in their first at-bats, then later homered back-to-back. Griffey won the first Player of the Week Award of his career in September 1990, had a 12-game hitting streak, and hit .377 for Seattle in 1990. After 30 games in 1991, Griffey suffered a career-ending neck injury.

CAREER REDS RECORD:

Games	AB	Hits	Runs
1,224	4,206	1,275	709
Avg	**HR**	**RBI**	**SB**
.303	71	466	156

GROH, HEINIE (3B/2B) (1913–1921)

After playing in just 31 games for the Giants in 1912 and 1913, Heinie Groh was traded to the Reds on May 22, 1913 in a five-player deal. Groh had nine productive seasons for Cincinnati, using his famous bottle bat to become a deft bunter, helping him to attain a .290–.330 average in eight of his nine seasons as a Red. He was also one of the league's top defensive third basemen, leading the National League in fielding five times and double plays four times. Groh had one of the best seasons of his career in 1919 when he helped Cincinnati set an all-time team record for winning percentage in a season (.686) and to victory over the Chicago White Sox in the famous scandal-ridden Series. After a bitter holdout in 1921, Groh agreed to return to the team with the understanding that he would be traded after the season. The Reds shipped him back to the Giants for two players and a whopping

$150,000 in cash. He played five more seasons with New York followed by one at Pittsburgh before retiring.

CAREER REDS RECORD:

Games	AB	Hits	Runs
1,211	4,439	1,323	663

Avg	HR	RBI	SB
.298	17	408	158

HAHN, NOODLES (SP)
(1899–1905)

After two impressive seasons pitching for Detroit of the Western League, Frank "Noodles" Hahn was promoted to the Cincinnati Reds in 1899 and posted a terrific 23–8 record in his rookie year. Noodles got his nickname from his oft-declared love of his mother's noodle soup. Hahn fell to 16–20 in 1900, but he did pitch a 4–0 no-hitter against the Phillies. In 1901 he completed 41 of 42 starts, finishing 22–19 for the last-place Reds, making him the only left-hander until Steve Carlton seven decades later to win 20 games for a last-place team. He also led the league in strikeouts for the third consecutive year. He won 23 games in 1902 and 22 more in 1903. In 1904 he developed arm trouble due to overwork and finished 16–18. Hahn's injury turned out to be worse than first thought and he was able to pitch in only 19 more games over the next two seasons, the last for the New York Highlanders. With his arm perhaps used up from 210 complete games in 229 starts, Hahn's career was over at the age of 27. After his retirement, Hahn worked as a federal meat inspector in the Cincinnati area for more than 30 years. He also was a volunteer assistant coach for the Reds for many years, assisting with batting practice.

CAREER REDS RECORD:

W	L	W%	ERA	SV
127	92	.580	2.52	0

K	BB	SHO	IP
900	375	24	1,987.3

KLUSZEWSKI, TED (1B)
(1947–1957)

Big Ted Kluszewski became a major league ballplayer almost by accident. Because of World War II and restricted travel, the major league teams held their spring training camps in the North throughout and just after the war. In the spring of 1946, the Reds used the Indiana University campus. The Cincinnati groundskeeper was sent ahead to prepare the Indiana baseball field. Kluszewski, an All-American end on the Indiana football team, volunteered to help. When the Reds arrived for batting practice, they let "Big Klu" take some swings and he hit balls much farther than anyone on the team. He signed as an amateur free agent before the 1946 season, made the major league roster in 1947, and became a regular in 1948.

Kluszewski's arms were so big that the flannel uniforms of the day proved too restrictive, causing his arms to bind up in the sleeves when he swung. So, to remedy the situation, Big Klu simply used scissors to cut off the uniform's sleeves, leaving him with his trademark bare-armed look. From 1953 to 1956, Kluszewski averaged 43 homers and

116 RBIs, and was selected to all four of his All-Star appearances. He also hit over .300 seven times. Kluszewski finished second to Willie Mays in the 1954 MVP Award balloting after slugging 49 homers and 141 RBIs. In 1955 he set a major league record by scoring at least one run in 17 straight games.

Big Klu was also an adept fielder, leading National League first basemen in fielding five straight years beginning in 1951, a major league record. Leo Durocher once contended that Gil Hodges was the strongest man in baseball. When asked about Kluszewski, Durocher responded, "Kluszewski isn't human." Easily on his way to his fourth consecutive year of 40+ homers, and already over 100 RBIs, Kluszewski suffered a slipped disc in a clubhouse fight late in 1956 that altered his performance forever more. Unable to swing like he used to, Big Klu hit only six homers for the Reds in 1957 and was traded to Pittsburgh. It was no better there, however, as he hit just six more in a year and a half with the Pirates before they traded him to the White Sox. In a season and a half with Chicago, Kluszewski hit just another six homers before the White Sox left him unprotected in the 1961 expansion draft. Picked by the Angels, Kluszewski posted a modest comeback in 1961, hitting 15 homers for the Angels before retiring and becoming a hitting coach with Cincinnati.

CAREER REDS RECORD:

Games	AB	Hits	Runs
1,339	4,961	1,499	745
Avg	**HR**	**RBI**	**SB**
.302	251	886	20

LARKIN, BARRY (SS)
(1986–2004)

A Cincinnati native, Larkin was always coveted by the Reds. Cincinnati selected him in the second round of the 1982 amateur draft out of high school, but Larkin chose instead to attend the University of Michigan, where he would become the first-ever two-time Big 10 MVP. After playing on the U.S. Olympic team in 1984, he was again chosen by the Reds, this time in the first round of the 1984 amateur draft. During his two years in the minors, Larkin won the American Association MVP Award for the Denver Zephyrs in 1986 and was called up later that same year.

Larkin was a good hitter, compiling a .295 career average with nearly 200 homers, both solid numbers for a middle infielder. He also had speed, stealing 379 bases in his career. Almost as important, though, was his place as team leader. Larkin even went to the trouble of learning Spanish so he could communicate with his Hispanic teammates. Larkin, the 1995 National League MVP, was selected to 12 All-Star Games, won three Gold Gloves, nine Silver Slugger Awards, and became the first shortstop in history to hit 30 homers and steal 30 bases in the same season (1996). Larkin hit .338 in 17 career postseason games and .353 in the 1990 World Series sweep of the heavily favored Oakland A's. After playing his entire 19-year career with his hometown team, Larkin slipped awkwardly into retirement following the 2004 season.

CAREER REDS RECORD:

Games	AB	Hits	Runs
2,180	7,937	2,340	1,329
Avg	**HR**	**RBI**	**SB**
.295	198	960	379

LOMBARDI, ERNIE (C)
(1932–1941)

Nicknamed "Schnozz" for his large nose, Ernie Lombardi hit .377, .366, and .370 in three minor league seasons before the Dodgers picked up his contract. After hitting a solid .297 for Brooklyn in 1931, Lombardi was traded to Cincinnati as part of a six-player deal just before the 1932 season opened. He immediately won the catcher's job and became one of baseball's top catchers during the 1930s and 1940s. In his decade as Cincinnati's catcher, Lombardi hit over .300 seven times, including .342 in 1938 to earn the NL MVP Award, and became only the second catcher ever to lead a major league in batting average. He also caught both of Johnny Vander Meer's no-hitters that year. Lombardi was a notoriously slow runner. Infielders would routinely play him on the outfield grass, knowing they had time to throw him out on almost any grounder they could field. Numerous times during his career, he singled to the outfield only to be thrown out at first. Lombardi once said, "Pee Wee Reese was in the league three years before I realized he wasn't an outfielder."

A strong man who used the heaviest bat in the league, Lombardi was also known for his wicked line drives. He once lined a ball so hard back at Larry French that he broke three of the pitcher's fingers. On May 8, 1935, Lombardi hit four doubles in four consecutive innings off four different pitchers. Lombardi had long feuded publicly with Cincinnati GM Warren Giles over salary. After Lombardi hit only .264 in 1941, his worst season with Cincinnati, Giles sold his five-time All-Star catcher to the Boston Braves, announcing publicly that Lombardi was clearly on the down side of his career. Lombardi proved Giles wrong—and publicly pointed it out—by hitting .330 and winning his second batting title. After one season in Boston, Lombardi was traded to the New York Giants, where he played five more years before retiring, batting over .300 in two of those.

After his retirement, Lombardi spent seven years as a press box attendant in San Francisco and many years working in a gas station. The outspoken Lombardi became embittered over his failure to reach Cooperstown, claiming there was a conspiracy inside baseball to keep him out. He was right. Warren Giles, an influential member of the Hall of Fame, successfully lobbied to keep Lombardi out of the Hall for many years. Lombardi was eventually elected to the Hall of Fame by the Veteran's Committee, eight years after his death.

CAREER REDS RECORD:

Games	AB	Hits	Runs
1,203	3,980	1,238	420
Avg	**HR**	**RBI**	**SB**
.311	120	682	5

LUQUE, DOLF (SP/RP)
(1918–1929)

Adolfo Luque, "The Pride of Havana," was one of the best players ever to come out of Cuba, spending 12 of his 20 years in the majors with the Reds. Luque used his devastating curveball to pitch five scoreless innings in the infamous 1919 World Series. In 1923 he had his career year, going 27–8 with six shutouts and a 1.93 ERA. Teammates Pete Donohue and Eppa Rixey joined him that year as 20-game winners. In 1925 Luque finished 16–18 despite leading the league in ERA at 2.63. After a poor 5–16 season in 1929, Luque was traded to Brooklyn just before the start of the 1930 campaign.

CAREER REDS RECORD:

W	L	W%	ERA	SV
154	152	.503	3.09	10
K	BB	SHO	IP	
970	756	24	2,668.7	

MALONEY, JIM (SP)
(1960–1970)

The Reds signed Jim Maloney as an amateur free agent on April 1, 1959, and by 1960 he was pitching in the majors. With a 100-mph fastball, Maloney pitched many memorable games during his 11-year career in Cincinnati. On May 21, 1963, Maloney struck out eight consecutive Braves, including Eddie Mathews and Hank Aaron, to tie the record. He also pitched three no-hitters and five one-hitters. The first no-hitter, however, never made it into the record books. On June 14, 1965, Maloney no-hit the Mets at Crosley field for 10 innings but lost 1–0 in the 11th on a Johnny Lewis home run. Two months later Maloney no-hit the Cubs, winning1–0 in a 10-inning affair in which he struck out 12 batters and walked 10. His next official no-hitter came on April 30, 1969, when he beat the Astros 10–0, striking out 13. The next day, as it happened, Don Wilson of the Astros returned the favor by no-hitting the Reds. Maloney won 20 games twice, 1963 and 1965, and appeared in one All-Star Game. Maloney's career ended prematurely due to injuries to his shoulder and Achilles tendon. After going 0–1 with an 11.34 ERA in 1970, his last year in Cincinnati, Maloney was traded to the Angels. After struggling in 13 appearances, nine of them in relief, he retired.

CAREER REDS RECORD:

W	L	W%	ERA	SV
134	81	.623	3.16	4
K	BB	SHO	IP	
1,592	786	30	1,818.7	

MCCORMICK, FRANK (1B)
(1934, 1937–1945)

Frank McCormick failed in a tryout with the Giants in 1932, but got a tryout with the Reds after a letter-writing campaign to Reds GM Larry MacPhail. He had to borrow $50 from an uncle to make the trip to Cincinnati's tryout camp in West Virginia. He was signed by the Reds and sent to the minors where he bounced around until making the majors for good in 1938. In his first three full seasons, McCormick led the National League in hits each year. He led the Reds to the World Series in 1939 and 1940 with RBI totals of 128 and 127 respectively, winning the NL's MVP Award in 1940. McCormick was an early iron man, once playing in 652 consecutive games, an NL record for first basemen. After hitting over .300 seven times during his 10-year Cincinnati career, the Reds sold their eight-time All-Star first baseman to Philadelphia following the 1945 season. In 1948 he retired and spent his later years as a minor league manager, scout, and coach for the Reds, before joining the team's broadcast crew in 1958.

CAREER REDS RECORD:

Games	AB	Hits	Runs
1,228	4,787	1,439	631
Avg	**HR**	**RBI**	**SB**
.301	110	800	23

McPHEE, BID (2B)
(1882–1899)

John "Bid" McPhee, the finest second baseman in baseball during the 19th century, played his entire 18-year career with Cincinnati, first with the city's American Association franchise from 1882 to 1889, and then with the National League franchise from 1890 to 1899. McPhee wasn't like many other players of his day. He was quiet, polite, decent, didn't drink or carouse, and always went home to his wife and children after the game. On the field he played bare-handed, continuing to do so long after most other players donned gloves. To toughen them up for the season, he would soak his hands in brine each spring. Offensively, McPhee scored over 100 runs 10 times in his career and led the league in homers in 1886 with eight, seven of them inside-the-park jobs. In an 1890 game against future Hall of Famer Amos Rusie, McPhee hit three triples.

During his era, most second basemen played either on or close to the bag. McPhee, a stellar player on defense, helped start the trend of moving off the bag, toward first. He led the league in putouts eight times, assists six times, double plays 11 times, and fielding percentage eight times, which are all remarkable considering he did it without benefit of a glove until 1896, the first year he joined in on the new "craze." Once he started wearing a glove, his fielding got even better. His .978 fielding percentage in 1896 was a record that stood for 23 years. In 1897 McPhee suffered a nasty ankle injury that limited his playing time and appeared to end his career. So well loved was McPhee that a group of Cincinnati fans and sportswriters organized a benefit and raised $3,500 for their star. He recovered, however, and played two more years before retiring. After his retirement as a player, he returned to manage the Reds in 1901, but resigned midway through the 1902 season upon hearing rumors that he was going to be fired. He later became a West Coast scout for the Reds. McPhee was elected to the Hall of Fame in 2000.

CAREER REDS RECORD:

Games	AB	Hits	Runs
2,135	8,291	2,250	1,678
Avg	**HR**	**RBI**	**SB**
.271	53	1,067	568

MORGAN, JOE (2B)
(1972–1979)

Joe Morgan's major league career lasted 22 years, but he will be remembered most for his eight seasons as the sparkplug of Cincinnati's Big Red Machine. On a team loaded with All-Stars, many consider Joe Morgan to have been the best player on the team. After nine seasons in Houston, Joe Morgan was traded to Cincinnati because Astros Manager Harry Walker felt Morgan was a "troublemaker."

Morgan made the NL All-Star team all eight years he was with the Reds, winning the game's MVP Award in 1972. In 1975 and 1976, Morgan became the only second baseman in major league history to win back-to-back MVP Awards as he led the Reds to back-to-back World Series titles over the Red Sox and Yankees. In doing so, the Reds became the first NL team to repeat as World Series champs since the 1921–1922 New York Giants. Morgan was a terrific base stealer who could drive pitchers crazy when on base. Once, during Game 5 of the 1975 World Series, Morgan drew 16 pick-off throws at first before an exasperated and distracted Red Sox pitcher allowed a single to Johnny Bench and a three-run homer to Tony Perez. Morgan was also a great fielder, winning five consecutive Gold Gloves from 1973–1977. In 1977 he set a record for second basemen by committing only five errors in 715 total chances.

After Morgan fell off badly offensively in 1978 and 1979, the Reds decided not to pursue his services again. Morgan spent the next five years playing for the Astros, Giants, Phillies, and A's before retiring to become a longtime color commentator for ESPN's *Baseball Tonight* game crew. *(See Astros bio.)*

CAREER REDS RECORD:

Games	AB	Hits	Runs
1,154	4,008	1,155	816
Avg	**HR**	**RBI**	**SB**
.288	152	612	406

MULLANE, TONY (SP)
(1886–1893)

The Irish-born Tony Mullane was a showman, on and off the field, stylishly dressed and handsome, and very popular with the ladies. Were he as popular with baseball owners and league officials, he might have won 300 games in his career and a Hall of Fame plaque to boot. Instead, he preferred to fight and connive his way through his baseball career. Mullane played with four major league teams in four years from 1881–1884 (Detroit, Louisville, St. Louis, and Toledo). After being suspended for the entire 1885 season, Mullane landed in Cincinnati where he would remain, surprisingly, for eight seasons. Before coming to Cincinnati, Mullane had repeatedly, at various times, jumped contracts, held out, signed with two teams at the same time, and refused to pitch. One of his convoluted off-the-field contract hassles even ended up in court, but the judge threw it out on the grounds that baseball was a sport and beneath the dignity of the court.

Mullane was as colorful on the field as he was persnickety off the field. Although three other major league pitchers have been documented to have pitched with both hands (each doing it only once), Mullane was the only true ambidextrous pitcher in the game's history. In 1881 Detroit offered him a tryout but he refused to show up until he had a contract. Once Mullane was signed, the Wolverines were surprised to discover that he was pitching with his left hand, and not his right. Mullane had injured his right arm and was unable to pitch, thus he wanted the contract inked before he showed up for the tryout. Stuck with the deal, Detroit let him pitch in five games and Mullane compiled a 1–4 record. Detroit sent him packing after one year, of course, but he regained the use of his right arm before the next season and signed with Louisville and won 30 games. He jumped to St. Louis the next year and won 35 games.

In 1884, now a prized pitcher, Mullane signed with two teams in two different major leagues (setting off the court battle), but ultimately pitched for Toledo and won 36 games. The Union Association and the Toledo team of the American Association both folded after the 1884 season, so Mullane was sold back to St. Louis, but he signed with Cincinnati (setting off another legal battle) for $5,000, including a $2,000 advance. In a weird series of events, St. Louis owner Chris Von der Ahe brought Mullane before the American Association's board of governors, citing Mullane with violating baseball law. The board agreed, forced Mullane to return half of the advance, suspended him for a year, but allowed him to remain Cincinnati property. After sitting out the 1885 season, Mullane joined the Reds in 1886 and won 33 games. He followed that up by winning 31 games in 1887.

Even when most players started wearing gloves, Mullane remained a bare-handed pitcher, holding the ball in both hands on the mound so the batter couldn't tell which hand he would be using to deliver the pitch. Being ambidextrous, Mullane would usually throw right-handed, but when a runner got on first, he would switch to pitching left-handed so he could both hold the runner closer to the bag and have a better pickoff move. Mullane loved to intimidate batters, hitting so many of them that almost single-handedly he was responsible for the creation of the rule that awarded batters first base when hit by a pitch.

In mid-1892, Mullane had the tables turned on him when Cincinnati suddenly cut his salary from $4,200 to $3,500. When handed the new contract, he protested, but he was told that his contract wasn't worth the paper it was written on. He left the team and held out for the rest of the season. By January 1893, Mullane was desperate, so he signed a new contract, this one for $2,100. In mid-1893 Cincinnati traded their problematic pitcher to Baltimore. After splitting the 1894 season between Baltimore and Cleveland, Mullane's label as a troublemaker effectively ended his major league career. He did pitch for three more years in the Western League (which would become the American League in 1900 and a major league in 1901) before retiring. After retiring as a player, Mullane spent a short time as an umpire, then became a Chicago policeman who rose to the rank of detective.

CAREER REDS RECORD:

W	L	W%	ERA	SV
163	124	.568	3.15	9
K	BB	SHO	IP	
993	926	15	2,599.0	

PEREZ, TONY (1B/3B)
(1964–1976, 1984–1986)

Cuban-born Tony Perez spent 23 years in the major leagues, the first 13 and the last three with Cincinnati. A seven-time All-Star with the Reds, Perez was one of the big RBI men for the Big Red Machine team of the 1970s. While he never led the league in any offensive category during his long career, Perez quietly provided consistent run production. From 1967 to 1976, he hit at least 18 homers and had at least 90 RBIs each year. In 1967 he was named the All-Star Game MVP after hitting a 15th-inning homer to win the game. His three home runs in the 1975 World Series helped propel the Reds to the title. Perez was a fine fielder who played more than 750 games at third base early in his Reds career before moving to first base. After the 1976 season he was traded to Montreal, where he played for three years. Following three more years with the Red Sox and one with Philadelphia, Perez returned to Cincinnati for his second stint. For three years he was a pinch-hitter and role player. On October 4, 1986, Perez hit the 379th and last homer of his career, tying him with Orlando Cepeda for most home runs by a Latin player. Perez retired as a player in 1986 at the age of 44 and became a Reds coach. In 1993 he was named manager of the team, but lasted only 44 games before he was fired. Perez was elected to the Hall of Fame in 2000.

CAREER REDS RECORD:

Games	AB	Hits	Runs
1,948	6,846	1,934	936
Avg	**HR**	**RBI**	**SB**
.283	287	1,192	39

PINSON, VADA (OF)
(1958–1968)

Before the 1956 season, the Cincinnati Reds signed Vada Pinson as an amateur free agent out of Oakland's McClymonds High School, the same school that had produced Frank Robinson and Curt Flood a few years before. After two marvelous years in the minors, Pinson received a late-season call-up in 1958, then joined the team as a regular in 1959. In his rookie season of 1959, Pinson hit .316 with 20 home runs, 47 doubles, scored 131 runs, stole 21 bases, and had 205 hits. Yet he lost the Rookie of the Year Award to the Giants' Willie McCovey, who played in only 52 games and compiled clearly inferior numbers. Pinson proved his rookie season was no fluke, averaging over his first five full seasons 197 hits, 108 runs, 37 doubles, 20 homers, 88 RBIs, 26 stolen bases, and a .310 batting average. During that span he won a Gold Glove and was named to the All-Star team twice. Although a true star, Pinson was often overshadowed by Frank Robinson, Pete Rose, and Tony Perez. By 1968, however, Pinson's performance was in decline. After never having been on the disabled list in 10 years, Pinson was suddenly hampered by recurring hamstring pulls. He was traded to St. Louis after the 1968 season for Bobby Tolan and Wayne Granger and his career spiraled downward on four more teams over seven years before he retired in 1975.

CAREER REDS RECORD:

Games	AB	Hits	Runs
1,565	6,335	1,881	978
Avg	**HR**	**RBI**	**SB**
.297	186	814	221

RIXEY, EPPA (SP)
(1921–1933)

After pitching eight years for the Phillies, Eppa Rixey was traded to Cincinnati following the 1920 season for Greasy Neale and Jimmy Ring. The 6'5" Rixey would pitch 13 more years in Cincinnati, and his 21 total years in the National League were a record for a left-handed pitcher until surpassed by Steve Carlton. Rixey, who never played a game in the minors, also held the career win record for a lefty with 266 until Warren Spahn passed him. After posting only two winning records in his first eight seasons in Philadelphia, Rixey turned it around in Cincinnati. After winning 19 games in 1921, Rixey won 25 games in 1922 to lead the National League. After two more 20-win seasons in 1923 and 1925, Rixey went into a slow, steady decline over the next eight years. Once after a particularly tough outing, Rixey was cited for speeding on his way home from the ballpark. When Rixey appeared in court, the judge fined him $10 then suspended the fine, explaining afterwards, "It seemed to me that Mr. Rixey deserved some consideration because he was probably preoccupied with worry over having been knocked out of the box yesterday afternoon, and wasn't really himself when he was driving last night." Rixey ended his career in 1933 with a 266–251 record. He was elected to the Hall of Fame in 1963 with the lowest career-winning percentage (.515) of any starting pitcher in Cooperstown. He holds the distinction to this day.

CAREER REDS RECORD:

W	L	W%	ERA	SV
179	148	.547	3.33	8

K	BB	SHO	IP
660	603	23	2,890.7

ROBINSON, FRANK (OF/1B)
(1956–1965)

The Cincinnati Reds signed Frank Robinson as an amateur free agent before the 1953 season. After two years in the minors, Robinson burst onto the major league scene like few before him. He won the Rookie of the Year Award in 1956 when he slugged 38 homers with 122 runs scored, 83 RBIs, and a .290 average. His 38 homers tied the National League rookie record. Robinson's numbers improved during his tenure with Cincinnati. Over his 10-year stretch with the Reds, Robinson, the team's undisputed leader, averaged .303 with 32 homers, 101 RBIs, 104 runs, and 16 steals. He was also a six-time All-Star and a Gold Glove winner.

Robinson, who was seen—accurately—as an angry civil rights activist, oftentimes saw things, racially speaking, in black and white. In 1959, when major league baseball utilized two All-Star Games, Robinson seethed as he sat on the bench during the first game. In the second game, Robinson responded with three hits, including a homer. A few days later he slid hard into the Braves' Eddie Mathews in a play at third base, initiating one of the most memorable brawls in baseball history, and the first between black and white stars. Booed intensely after that, Robinson began carrying a gun in self-defense after receiving death threats. He was later arrested for brandishing it at a short-order cook who had refused to serve him.

In 1961 Robinson won the NL MVP Award as the Reds won their first pennant in 21 years. After the 1965 season, Cincinnati GM William DeWitt traded Robinson to Baltimore for Milt Pappas, Jack Baldschun, and Joe Simpson. The trade caused an immediate uproar in Cincinnati, where it was clearly the most unpopular trade in team history. DeWitt called Robinson "an old 30" in an attempt to justify his unpopular move. Attendance, offense, and morale all dropped sharply and didn't rebound until Johnny Bench arrived three years later to provide the needed spark to assuage the public relations disaster brought on by DeWitt. In Robinson's first season in Baltimore, all he did was win the American League MVP Award, *The Sporting News* Player of the Year Award, the World Series MVP Award, and the Triple Crown, baseball's rarest accomplishment. And William DeWitt was fired. *(See Orioles bio.)*

CAREER REDS RECORD:

Games	AB	Hits	Runs
1,502	5,527	1,673	1,043
Avg	**HR**	**RBI**	**SB**
.303	324	1,009	161

ROSE, PETE (OF/3B/2B) (1963–1978, 1984–1986)

Born and raised in Cincinnati, Pete Rose was signed by the Reds as an amateur free agent on July 8, 1960. He became the team's starting second baseman in 1963, winning the NL Rookie of the Year Award and earning a reputation early on as an arrogant, hard-nosed player who had an all-consuming passion for playing baseball. He would even run to first base after receiving a walk. On April 23, 1964, Rose reached first on an error and scored on another error to make Houston Astros rookie Ken Johnson the only pitcher to lose a complete game no-hitter. Whitey Ford tagged him with the nickname "Charlie Hustle," but initially Rose resented it.

During his career, Rose would play more than 500 games at five different positions, always to allow another player to make the starting lineup at their strong position. Rose led the National League in many offensive categories over his 24-year career, 19 of which were with the Reds. He made the All-Star Game 13 times with the Reds, won two Gold Gloves, and three batting titles, including 1969 when he bunted for a base hit in his last at-bat of the season to edge out Roberto Clemente. He won the NL MVP Award in 1973 and the World Series MVP Award in 1975. In 1978 Rose captured the attention of the baseball world when he chased Joe DiMaggio's 56-game hitting streak. His streak ended at 44 games, the longest in National League history. That same season Rose became the youngest player in history to collect 3,000 base hits. After the season, Rose left Cincinnati via free agency and played five seasons in Philadelphia and two-thirds of a season in Montreal before returning to Cincinnati to close out his career with two-plus seasons as player-manager. On September 11, 1985, Rose broke Ty Cobb's record for career hits when he collected number 4,192. Fireworks erupted, the Goodyear blimp flashed the news, and a red Corvette with license plate "PR4192" drove onto the field during the seven-minute standing ovation.

In 1988 Rose received one of the longest suspensions in baseball history—30 days—for on-the-field conduct when he got into a shoving match with umpire Dave Pallone. But the real trouble was just around the corner. Rumors of Rose's gambling problems surfaced in the spring of 1989. He was accused of violating major league baseball's rule against wagering on any contest in which a person has a duty to perform. At first Rose tried to laugh off the matter, but it wouldn't go away. When John Dowd completed his official 225-page report on May 9, Baseball Commissioner A. Bartlett Giamatti stressed that it was highly confidential, but its contents eventually made their way into the papers. Evidence showed that Rose had wagered at least $852,000 on 390 games, including 52 involving the Reds. The explosive report led to charges and countercharges, lawsuits and countersuits, but when the dust settled, Rose agreed to conditions that put him on baseball's permanently ineligible list. Just a week after the highly charged matter was settled, Giamatti, clearly affected by the ordeal, died of a heart attack.

Rose's troubles did not end there, however. He was charged with income tax evasion and pleaded guilty to felony counts that resulted in two concurrent five-month sentences with no possibility of parole. While in prison, Rose worked in the machine shop for 11¢ per day. After his release, he spent three months in a halfway house, followed by 1,000 hours of community service. Public attention now shifted to whether or not he was eligible for election to the Hall of Fame, even though he was ineligible to participate in any active capacity in major league baseball. While the argument raged, the Hall of Fame acted unilaterally and adopted a rule that said, "Any player on Baseball's ineligible list shall not be an eligible candidate." That ended the argument. In July 1999, the Pete Rose Museum opened in Cooperstown, just a block from the Hall of Fame. That same year he was voted onto baseball's All-Century Team. Rose has applied for reinstatement, something the Giamatti accord allows, but has been denied by Commissioner Bud Selig.

CAREER REDS RECORD:

Games	AB	Hits	Runs
2,722	10,934	3,358	1,741
Avg	**HR**	**RBI**	**SB**
.307	152	1,036	146

ROUSH, EDD (OF)
(1916–1926, 1931)

After playing his first four years in the majors for four different teams, Edd Roush was traded to Cincinnati from the New York Giants in a five-player deal that also brought Christy Mathewson and Bill McKechnie to the Reds. All three players the Reds received eventually made it to the Hall of Fame and, shortly after the trade, Giants Manager John McGraw realized the error of his ways and tried to reacquire Roush, who personally loathed McGraw and his controlling tactics. Over the next 10 full seasons in Cincinnati, Roush became the best (and highest paid) center fielder in baseball and never hit less than .323. He was the most feared hitter in the dead-ball era. Roush used one of the heaviest bats in the majors, 46–48 ounces, with an extremely thick handle. This allowed him to get good wood on inside pitches and drive outside pitches with authority. He won batting titles in 1917 and 1919, and just missed in 1918. In the 1919 World Series against the

Black Sox, Roush scored six runs and drove in seven. He always bristled when someone would talk about how the Sox threw the Series. He felt strongly that the Reds were the better team anyway and would have won the Series even if it had been on the level. In 1920 and 1924, Roush put together 27-game hitting streaks.

It took McGraw a decade to get Roush back, but he finally managed to make the Cincinnati Reds an offer they couldn't refuse. Roush, however, failed to report, even when the Giants repeatedly kept upping their offer. Finally, an exasperated McGraw met with Roush in person. "What's the matter, don't you want to play for me?" McGraw asked. "Hell, no!" answered Roush. He finally accepted a $70,000 offer for three years after McGraw promised not to direct any of his tirades against Roush. Three years later, the Giants tried to cut his salary by $7,500. Roush refused to report for the entire 1930 season. Exasperated once again, McGraw finally released Roush and he signed a one-year contract with Cincinnati. After the 1931 season, Roush retired and traveled extensively, doing whatever he pleased since he had saved his money and invested wisely. Edd Roush was elected to the Hall of Fame in 1962.

CAREER REDS RECORD:

Games	AB	Hits	Runs
1,399	5,384	1,784	815
Avg	**HR**	**RBI**	**SB**
.331	47	763	199

VANDER MEER, JOHNNY (SP)
(1937–1943, 1946–1949)

Johnny Vander Meer had bounced around in the minors with the Braves, Dodgers, and Giants before being purchased by Cincinnati late in the 1936 season. He made his major league debut in 1937 for the Reds. Vander Meer was a wild left-hander with a blazing fastball who often walked as many as he struck out. In fact, in five of his 13 major league seasons he did just that. It was this tendency toward wildness combined with a scorching fastball that helped Vander Meer accomplish one of baseball's most incredible pitching feats—back-to-back no-hitters, something no other pitcher in major league history has been able to duplicate. His first no-hitter came on June 11, 1938, against Boston, and he was dominating from the start. Only five Boston hitters managed to hit fly-ball outs. His second no-hitter came four days later in Brooklyn, the first night game ever in Ebbets Field, in front of 40,000 fans. Leading 6–0 in the ninth, Vander Meer's control left him and he walked the bases full with one out. After a ground-out force at home, Leo Durocher stepped to the plate. After fouling off a pitch, Durocher hit the next one into the upper deck, just foul, for strike two. Durocher took the next pitch for a ball, but Vander Meer, his catcher Ernie Lombardi, and, later, even home-plate umpire Bill Stewart all agreed the pitch was strike three and should have ended the game right there. As it was, Durocher then smacked a sinking line drive to the outfield that center fielder Harry Craft nabbed to end the game.

JOHNNY VANDER MEER

In the game before his double no-hitters, Vander Meer had pitched six hitless innings before allowing one hit in the ninth inning. In the game just after his two no-hitters, with Cy

Young in the stands, Vander Meer didn't allow a hit until the fourth inning. His 21 consecutive hitless innings set a National League record and remains second to Cy Young's major league record 24 consecutive innings. Had he not given up the hit in the ninth inning of the preceding game, Vander Meer would have tallied 28 consecutive hitless innings. Vander Meer always accepted his wildness, saying, "As far as I was concerned, I was out there to pitch eleven innings, because my nine was the equivalent of someone else's eleven." It is probably fitting, given Vander Meer's mix of raw ability and wildness that he ended his Reds career as a .500 pitcher, 116–116. He was a four-time All-Star for the Reds who led the league in strikeouts three consecutive years (1941–1943). After his major league career was over, Vander Meer played for a time in the minors, even managing another no-hitter for Tulsa in the Texas League. The manager of the opposing team that day was Harry Craft, the man whose catch off Durocher's line drive had preserved his second no-hitter.

CAREER REDS RECORD:

W	L	W%	ERA	SV
116	116	.500	3.41	1

K	BB	SHO	IP
1,251	1,072	29	2,028.0

WALTERS, BUCKY (SP)
(1938–1948)

Bucky Walters began his career first as a pitcher, failed miserably, then became an infielder, failed to impress, and then went back to pitching and became a phenomenal success. Walters was just 38–53 for the Phillies when he was traded to Cincinnati for two players and $50,000 cash, mostly because the habitually broke owner of the Phillies, Gerry Nugent, needed the money to pay operating expenses. Almost immediately Walters' fortunes turned around as he went 11–6 for the Reds in the second half of 1938. In 1939 Walters took the baseball world by storm, posting an incredible 27–11 record with a 2.29 ERA and leading the Reds into the World Series against the Yankees. He followed it up with a 22–10 record and 2.48 ERA in 1940, and then won two games in the World Series as the Reds defeated the Tigers for their first World Series title since 1919. He had one more great year, 1944, when he went 23–8. From 1939 to 1944 he was the best pitcher in baseball. His 121 victories during that span were 20 more than his closest rival, Mort Cooper. Of Walters' 198 career wins, an incredible 42 were shutouts. In seven of his 10 years in Cincinnati, Walters had an ERA below 3.00. After 1944, however, Walters won only 28 more games in four years and was released in 1948.

CAREER REDS RECORD:

W	L	W%	ERA	SV
160	107	.599	2.93	4

K	BB	SHO	IP
879	806	32	2,355.7

WHITE, WILL (SP)
(1882–1886)

Will White and his brother Deacon were second only to George and Harry Wright in terms of baseball stature during the 19th century. White spent eight of his 10 major league seasons in Cincinnati, three with the National League franchise that was kicked out of the league after the 1880 season and five with the American Association franchise that later moved to the National League in 1890. With Cincinnati's original NL franchise, White won 30 games in 1878 and 43 games in 1879. Will White was an exceptional right-handed pitcher and the first player to wear glasses on the field. In his first three seasons in the American Association, White posted win totals of 40, 43, and 34. After going just 1–2 in 1886, White retired at the age of 31 and became a successful Buffalo businessman.

CAREER REDS RECORD:

W	L	W%	ERA	SV
136	69	.663	2.51	0

K	BB	SHO	IP
467	323	23	1,832.3

Cleveland Indians

Since 1901

1949 Team Ball

1905 Napoleon Lajoie suffers blood poisoning when dye from his socks infects a spike wound. As a result, players everywhere begin wearing white "sanitary" socks with colored stirrups over them.... **1934–1946** Cleveland is the only 20th-century team to have two home ballparks at the same time: League Park for Monday through Saturday, Municipal Stadium for Sundays and holidays.... **1963** On July 31, the Indians become the first American League team in history to hit four consecutive home runs.... **1975** Frank Robinson becomes the first black manager in major league baseball.... **1997** Cleveland hits 220 home runs, setting a new team record and becoming the first team in American League history to hit 200 or more homers in three straight seasons.

FRANCHISE HISTORY

Cleveland was a charter member of the American League when it changed its name from the Western League in 1900; the team assumed major league status along with AL itself in 1901. The original owners were Charles Somers, a coal magnate, and Jack Kilfoyl, a Cleveland-area clothier. Somers' deep pockets not only allowed him to fund his Cleveland team, but, at the behest of AL president Ban Johnson, four other teams in the fledgling league as well. Kilfoyl remained part-owner until 1908, when ill health forced him to sell his share. It was reported that Kilfoyl suffered from extreme stress brought on by the poor play and financial woes of his team. By 1916, Somers' businesses were suffering and the coal baron/baseball owner found himself $2 million in debt, so he was forced to relinquish his team to the American League.

Cleveland's Terry Turner broke the season-best fielding average record for shortstops with a .973 mark in 1910. In 1911 he was moved to third base and set the new record for that position as well, at .970.

Jim Dunn, a Chicago railroad contractor, bought the team in 1916 for $500,000, aided by $100,000 loans from both Ban Johnson and Charles Comiskey. The team's fortunes rose during Dunn's tenure, with the Indians even winning the World Series in 1920. When Dunn died in 1922, his widow took control of the team until 1927, when she sold out for $1 million to a group of investors headed by financier Alva Bradley. Bradley initially spent heavily on new players, which improved the team, but the stock market crash of 1929 forced her to stop spending so freely. On June 21, 1946, Bradley's business associates forced her to sell the team. Bill Veeck Jr., an ex-marine who had recovered from his war wounds, bought the team for $1.6 million, with entertainer Bob Hope chipping in for a small share of the team. Veeck owned the team for only three years, but succeeded in winning the AL pennant and World Series in 1948, as the Indians smashed previous attendance records. Following the 1949 season, Veeck sold the team for $2.2 million to an investment group headed by insurance executive Ellis Ryan.

In the four years of Ryan's stewardship, the Indians fielded a competitive team, but couldn't overtake the Yankees. Ryan tried to get the Indians to play all their games at night except on Sunday, but was only partly successful. A dispute arose among the syndicate's owners and, in 1953, Ryan was forced out of the top spot and replaced by Myron Wilson. Wilson controlled the syndicate for 10 years until long-time baseball figure Gabe Paul put together his own syndicate and purchased the Indians in 1963. Paul held the majority stake in the team with a 21 percent share. After just three years, the Paul syndicate sold the team for $8.3 million to Vern Stouffer.

Larry Doby, here with manager Lou Boudreau in 1947, integrated the American League.

"Rapid Robert" Feller pauses for photographers in October 1948.

Vern Stouffer's family had opened their first restaurant in 1924. They also owned a butter-manufacturing business that evolved into a frozen-food empire. The restaurant concept developed into a chain of lunch counters. Stouffer bought the Indians right after selling his company in a stock transaction deal to Litton Industries. Rather than money, Stouffer took Litton Industries stock. During the six years Stouffer owned the team, his Litton stock dropped drastically and he was forced to sell the team in 1972. Stouffer sold the Indians to an investment group headed by Cleveland attorney Nick Mileti, who also owned the Cleveland Cavaliers of the NBA and the Cleveland Barons of the American Hockey League. In 1975 Mileti sold controlling interest in the team to Ted Bonda of the IBC Corporation, but retained a minority interest. Bonda, who also was one of the founding members of APCOA, the largest parking-lot company in the United States, held the team for two years until he sold out to an investment group headed by Steve O'Neill in 1977. The O'Neill syndicate owned the team until 1986, when it sold out to brothers Richard and David Jacobs. The Jacobs brothers owned 43 shopping malls, six hotels, and a number of office buildings. In 1994, with an estimated wealth of nearly $300 million, David Jacobs paid $13 million for the right to have Cleveland's new baseball stadium named after his family, although he has no ownership interest in the stadium. In 2000 the Indians were sold to Larry Dolan for $320 million, an all-time record for a major league baseball team, eclipsing the $311 million paid for the Dodgers just two years earlier.

On the field, the Indians have won five pennants in their history: 1920, 1948, 1954, 1995, and 1997. Their only two World Series titles came in 1920 and 1948. They have finished a heartbreaking second place 13 times, six of those times to the powerful Yankees teams of the 1950s. Starting in 1960, the Indians embarked on a remarkably long journey of mediocrity, failing to finish within 10 games of first for more than 30 years.

The Indians weren't always known as the Indians. As was the case with many teams with roots dating back to 1900 and before, Cleveland was known by a variety of unofficial names, official names, and even several names at the same time. For example, while the 1901

1920s programs

In 1975, Frank Robinson was the majors' first African-American manager to be hired—and, in 1977, the first to be fired.

team was commonly referred to as the Blues, its official name was the Bluebirds. The players, being manly men, didn't like to be called Bluebirds, and barely tolerated its abbreviated form, although an earlier Cleveland National League franchise had gone by the name Blues. So they took matters into their own hands and called themselves the Broncos in 1902 and part of 1903. The name didn't stick. As was common during that era, local newspapers and fans reserved the right to refer to the team by their favorite names; sometimes a team was referred to by two or three different names in the same season, even if only one of them was the official name. So, to put an end to the confusion, a Cleveland newspaper conducted a write-in campaign in 1903 to choose an official name for the team. That winning name was Naps, in honor of the new team captain. (To further add to the confusion, some of today's record and reference books list the Naps name as beginning in 1903, when Napoleon Lajoie became captain of the team, while other books list the date as 1905 when Lajoie became manager of the team.) From mid-1910 to 1911 the team was known—in some circles—as the Molly McGuires, after new manager Deacon McGuire, and in other circles as the Naps, a carryover of the popularity of Napoleon Lajoie, who resigned as manager in mid-1910 but remained as team captain through 1914.

Cleveland's Terry Turner broke the season-low fielding average record for shortstops with a .973 mark in 1910. In 1911 he was moved to third base and set the new record for that position as well.

TEAM NAME HISTORY

Official Names

Bluebirds (Blues; 1901–1902)
Naps (1903–1914)
Indians (1915–current)

Unofficial Names/Nicknames

Broncos (1902 and part of 1903),
Molly McGuires (mid-1910 to 1911),
the Tribe, Cleveland Americans

STADIUM HISTORY

League Park	1901–1915
Dunn Field (League Park renamed)	1916–1927
League Park (Dunn Field renamed)	1928–July 30, 1932
Municipal Stadium (also known as Lakefront Stadium when it opened)	July 31, 1932–1933
League Park (Monday–Saturday games only)	1934–1946
Municipal Stadium (Sundays and holidays only)	1934–1946
Municipal Stadium	1947–1993
Jacobs Field	1994–current

YEARLY RECORD, FINISH, & ATTENDANCE FIGURES

Year	League	Record	DIV/LG Finish	Attendance	Avg/Gm
2005	AL Cent	93–69	2	2,013,763	24,861
2004	AL Cent	80–82	3	1,814,401	22,400
2003	AL Cent	68–94	4	1,730,002	21,358
2002	AL Cent	74–88	3	2,616,940	32,308
2001	AL Cent	91–71	1	3,175,523	39,694
2000	AL Cent	90–72	2	3,456,278	42,670
1999	AL Cent	97–65	1	3,468,456	42,820
1998	AL Cent	89–73	1	3,467,299	42,806
1997	AL Cent	86–75	1	3,404,750	42,034
1996	AL Cent	99–62	1	3,318,174	41,477
1995	AL Cent	100–44	1	2,842,745	39,483
1994	AL Cent	66–47	2	1,995,174	39,121
1993	AL East	76–86	6	2,177,908	26,888
1992	AL East	76–86	5	1,224,094	15,112
1991	AL East	57–105	7	1,051,863	12,828
1990	AL East	77–85	4	1,225,240	15,126
1989	AL East	73–89	6	1,285,542	15,871
1988	AL East	78–84	6	1,411,610	17,427
1987	AL East	61–101	7	1,077,898	13,307
1986	AL East	84–78	5	1,471,805	18,170
1985	AL East	60–102	7	655,181	8,089
1984	AL East	75–87	6	734,079	9,063
1983	AL East	70–92	7	768,941	9,493
1982	AL East	78–84	7	1,044,021	12,889
1981	AL East	52–51	6/5	661,395	12,248
1980	AL East	79–81	6	1,033,827	13,086
1979	AL East	81–80	6	1,011,644	12,489
1978	AL East	69–90	6	800,584	10,264
1977	AL East	71–90	5	900,365	11,116
1976	AL East	81–78	4	948,776	12,010
1975	AL East	79–80	4	977,039	12,213
1974	AL East	77–85	4	1,114,262	13,756
1973	AL East	71–91	6	615,107	7,594
1972	AL East	72–84	5	626,354	8,134
1971	AL East	60–102	6	591,361	7,301
1970	AL East	76–86	5	729,752	9,009
1969	AL East	62–99	6	619,970	7,654
1968	AL	86–75	3	857,994	10,593
1967	AL	75–87	8	662,980	8,185
1966	AL	81–81	5	903,359	11,153
1965	AL	87–75	5	934,786	11,400
1964	AL	79–83	7	653,293	7,967
1963	AL	79–83	6	562,507	6,945
1962	AL	80–82	6	716,076	8,840
1961	AL	78–83	5	725,547	8,957
1960	AL	76–78	4	950,985	12,350
1959	AL	89–65	2	1,497,976	19,454
1958	AL	77–76	4	663,805	8,734
1957	AL	76–77	6	722,256	9,380
1956	AL	88–66	2	865,467	11,240
1955	AL	93–61	2	1,221,780	15,867
1954	AL	111–43	1	1,335,472	17,344

YEARLY RECORD, FINISH, & ATTENDANCE FIGURES (CONT.)

Year	League	Record	DIV/LG Finish	Attendance	Avg/Gm
1953	AL	92–62	2	1,069,176	13,707
1952	AL	93–61	2	1,444,607	18,761
1951	AL	93–61	2	1,704,984	22,143
1950	AL	92–62	4	1,727,464	22,435
1949	AL	89–65	3	2,233,771	29,010
1948	AL	97–58	1	2,620,627	33,172
1947	AL	80–74	4	1,521,978	19,513
1946	AL	68–86	6	1,057,289	13,731
1945	AL	73–72	5	558,182	7,249
1944	AL	72–82	6	475,272	6,093
1943	AL	82–71	3	438,894	5,700
1942	AL	75–79	4	459,447	5,743
1941	AL	75–79	5	745,948	9,688
1940	AL	89–65	2	902,576	11,007
1939	AL	87–67	3	563,926	7,324
1938	AL	86–66	3	652,006	8,579
1937	AL	83–71	4	564,849	7,242
1936	AL	80–74	5	500,391	6,178
1935	AL	82–71	3	397,615	5,164
1934	AL	85–69	3	391,338	5,017
1933	AL	75–76	4	387,936	5,038
1932	AL	87–65	4	468,953	6,090
1931	AL	78–76	4	483,027	6,356
1930	AL	81–73	4	528,657	6,866
1929	AL	81–71	3	536,210	7,055
1928	AL	62–92	7	375,907	4,882
1927	AL	66–87	6	373,138	4,846
1926	AL	88–66	2	627,426	7,843
1925	AL	70–84	6	419,005	5,442
1924	AL	67–86	6	481,905	6,425
1923	AL	82–71	3	558,856	7,165
1922	AL	78–76	4	528,145	6,602
1921	AL	94–60	2	748,705	9,723
1920	AL	98–56	1	912,832	11,703
1919	AL	84–55	2	538,135	7,799
1918	AL	73–54	2	295,515	4,766
1917	AL	88–66	3	477,298	6,119
1916	AL	77–77	6	492,106	6,309
1915	AL	57–95	7	159,285	2,069
1914	AL	51–102	8	185,997	2,354
1913	AL	86–66	3	541,000	6,762
1912	AL	75–78	5	336,844	4,375
1911	AL	80–73	3	406,296	5,277
1910	AL	71–81	5	293,456	3,668
1909	AL	71–82	6	354,627	4,606
1908	AL	90–64	2	422,262	5,414
1907	AL	85–67	4	382,046	4,659
1906	AL	89–64	3	325,733	4,123
1905	AL	76–78	5	316,306	4,108
1904	AL	86–65	4	264,749	3,394
1903	AL	77–63	3	311,280	4,206
1902	AL	69–67	5	275,395	4,237
1901	AL	54–82	7	131,380	1,904

MANAGER HISTORY

Manager	Years	W–L	Win %
Jimmy McAleer	1901	55–82	.401
Bill Armour	1902–1904	232–195	.543
Nap Lajoie	1905–1909	377–309	.550
Deacon McGuire	1909–1911	91–117	.438
George Stovall	1911	74–62	.536
Harry Davis	1912	54–71	.432
Joe Birmingham	1912–1915	170–191	.471
Lee Fohl	1915–1919	327–310	.513
Tris Speaker	1919–1926	617–520	.543
Jack McCallister	1927	66–87	.431
Roger Peckinpaugh	1928–1933, 1941	490–481	.505
Walter Johnson	1933–1935	179–168	.516
Steve O'Neill	1935–1937	199–168	.542
Oscar Vitt	1938–1940	262–198	.570
Lou Boudreau	1942–1950	728–649	.529
Al Lopez	1951–1956	570–354	.617
Kerby Farrell	1957	76–77	.497
Bobby Bragan	1958	31–36	.463
Joe Gordon	1958–1960	184–151	.549
Jimmie Dykes	1960–1961	103–115	.472
Mel McGaha	1962	78–82	.488
Birdie Tebbetts	1963–1966	278–259	.518
George Strickland	1964, 1966	48–63	.432
Joe Adcock	1967	75–87	.463
Alvin Dark	1968–1971	266–321	.453
Johnny Lipon	1971	18–41	.305
Ken Aspromonte	1972–1974	220–260	.458
Frank Robinson	1975–1977	186–189	.496
Jeff Torborg	1977–1979	157–201	.439
Dave Garcia	1979–1982	247–244	.503
Mike Ferraro	1983	40–60	.400
Pat Corrales	1983–1987	280–355	.441
Doc Edwards	1987–1989	173–207	.455
John Hart	1989	8–11	.421
John McNamara	1990–1991	102–137	.427
Mike Hargrove	1991–1999	721–591	.550
Charlie Manuel	2000–2002	220–190	.537
Joel Skinner	2002	35–41	.461
Eric Wedge	2003–2005	241–245	.496

ALL-TIME WIN-LOSS RECORDS VS. ALL OPPONENTS

Opponent	Record
ALL-TIME	8,301–7,944
Angels	264–282
Astros	7–8
Athletics	989–858
Blue Jays	159–169
Braves	2–1
Brewers	201–199
Cardinals	8–3
Cubs	6–2
Devil Rays	41–23
Diamondbacks	5–4
Dodgers	0–3
Giants	3–0
INTERLEAGUE	85–72
Mariners	175–133
Marlins	1–5
Mets	1–2
Nationals	1–2
Orioles	1,088–822
Padres	4–2
Phillies	1–2
Pirates	8–10
Rangers	274–293
Reds	23–16
Red Sox	1,002–930
Rockies	7–5
Royals	232–233
Tigers	980–1,002
Twins	1,025–889
White Sox	940–979
Yankees	854–1,067

The Tribe takes the field during the 1948 World Series.

Franchise Highlights, Low Points, and Strange Distinctions

1901 On April 28, rookie pitcher Bock Baker made his major league debut with Cleveland against the White Sox in Chicago. He pitched a complete game, allowing 23 hits (all singles) in a 13–1 loss. He never pitched for Cleveland again.

• • • •

1903 Cleveland shortstop John Gochnauer must have been looking over his shoulder after the season he put together. Not only did he hit just .185, but he also committed 98 errors, a 20th-century record.

• • • •

1908 Sometimes the most significant trades in baseball are those that aren't made. In the spring of 1908, the Indians were training in Macon, Georgia, while the Tigers practiced in Augusta, Georgia. Cleveland owner Charlie Somers received a call one night from Detroit manager Hughie Jennings, who offered to trade Ty Cobb straight up for outfielder Elmer Flick. Aware of Cobb's penchant for fighting and creating team disharmony, Somers refused. It soon proved to be a disastrous mistake as Flick became ill and missed most of the 1908 season and never played regularly again. Cobb, on the other hand, went on to play 20 more years, and the rest, as they say, is history.

• • • •

1910 Cleveland's Terry Turner broke the season-low fielding average record for shortstops with a .973 mark. In 1911 he was moved to third base and set the new record for that position as well, at .970.

1911–12 Despite hitting .356 for his career (third all time), and .375 while with Cleveland, Joe Jackson never won a major league batting title. In 1911, as a rookie, Jackson hit .408, but lost out to Ty Cobb, who hit .420 that year. Also, when he hit .395 in 1912, he set a record for the highest combined batting average for a player's first two years (.402), the only player ever to crack the .400 barrier for his first two seasons.

• • • •

1911–13 Cleveland rookie Vean Gregg was a 20-game winner in each of his first three major league seasons from 1911 to 1913, compiling win totals of 23, 20, and 20. Cleveland must have known something, because after they traded him in midseason 1914, he only won 20 more games over five years with four different teams.

• • • •

1916 Indian Marty Kavanagh hit the first pinch-hit grand slam in American League history on September 24, when his smash rolled through a hole in the fence and the outfielder couldn't retrieve the ball.

• • • •

1918 Because of schedule inequities created by the war-shortened season, Cleveland played 11 more road games than Boston did, and lost the pennant to the Red Sox by just $1^1/_2$ games.

1919 Rookie George Uhle won a 20-inning shutout. Ten years later he pitched a 19-inning complete game.

• • • •

1920 In the 1920 World Series, Cleveland second baseman Bill Wambsganss made the only unassisted triple play in postseason history.

In that same Series, first baseman Doc Johnston of Cleveland faced pitcher Jimmy Johnston of Brooklyn, the first time two brothers ever played against each other in a World Series.

Jim Bagby Sr. won 31 games for Cleveland in 1920 at the age of 31, but won only 21 over the rest of his career, which lasted three more years.

Third baseman Larry Gardner of the 1920 Indians attempted 23 steals on the season, and was nailed 20 times for a pathetic 130 success rate.

• • • •

1923 Senators pitcher Cy Warmoth won just seven games and recorded only 45 strikeouts, but somehow he managed to fan Joe Sewell twice in one game. Sewell struck out only 12 times all year in 553 at-bats. (Two years later, he'd set a record that still stands by striking out just four times in 608 at-bats.) Only one other time in Sewell's 14-year career did he happen to strike out twice in the same game.

In 1923 George Uhle collected 52 hits, a season record for pitchers. Two years earlier he had a six-RBI game.

1926 On August 28, Dutch Levsen of the Indians became the last pitcher to win two complete games in one day.

• • • •

1929 The Indians joined the Yankees in becoming the first teams to put numbers on their uniform shirts and keep them on.

• • • •

1929–30 Rookie pitcher Wes Ferrell won more than 20 games in each of his first four seasons with the Tribe from 1929 to 1932. After posting win totals of 21, 25, 22, and 23 to start his career, Ferrell slumped to 11–12 in 1933 and was promptly traded to the Red Sox. After going 14–5 in his first year with Boston, Ferrell won 25 and 20 games the next two years. Incidentally, in 1931 Ferrell hit nine home runs as a pitcher, still a season record for pitchers.

• • • •

1932 In an 18–17 extra-inning loss to the Philadelphia A's on July 10, Cleveland shortstop Johnny Burnett set a major league record by getting nine hits in the game.

• • • •

1934 Mel Harder became the first 20-game winner in American League history to wear glasses while he accomplished the feat.

• • • •

1937 In 1937 Johnny Allen won his first 15 starts of the season before losing—on the last day of the season.

1939 Cleveland won the first night game ever played in American League history, defeating the A's at Philadelphia's Shibe Park 8–3 in 10 innings on May 16.

• • • •

1940 Bob Feller pitched the only Opening Day no-hitter in history when he shut down the Chicago White Sox, 1–0, on April 16, 1940, in Chicago.

• • • •

1941 Jeff Heath became the first player in AL history to collect 20 doubles, 20 triples, and 20 homers in the same season.

• • • •

1948 Lou Boudreau became the first shortstop in American League history to hit over .350 and drive in more than 100 runs in the same season.

Rookie Satchel Paige, who was somewhere between 42 and 50 years old—no one knew for sure—pitched a shutout against the White Sox in his first major league start in 1948. It also marked the first major league shutout by a black pitcher. That October, Paige became the first black player to pitch in the World Series.

In 1948 Joe Early, a night watchman and Indians fan, wrote a letter to owner Bill Veeck complaining about all the special days the Indians had to honor various players for various reasons. After all, he surmised, the players hardly needed either the attention or the prizes. He suggested a day for the average fan. Veeck agreed, and promptly created "Joe Early Night." To honor Early, the Indians owner presented the night watchman with an outhouse, a backfiring Model T, some weird animals, a Ford convertible, and lots more. Veeck's promotions—traditional and otherwise—helped Cleveland draw more than 2.6 million fans in 1948, shattering every existing attendance record.

The 1948 Indians won the team Triple Crown, leading the league in batting average, earned run average, and fielding average, the last team to do so until the 2001 Seattle Mariners.

• • • •

1950 The Cleveland Indians finished with a 92–62 record, an excellent .597 winning percentage. Unfortunately, it was only good for fourth place in that year's strong American League. Over in the National, the Philadelphia Phillies won the pennant that year with a 91–63 mark, one game worse than the Indians!

• • • •

1951 On July 1, Bob Feller became the first 20th-century pitcher to toss three career no-hitters.

• • • •

1952 The Indians are the only team ever to have three 20-game winners plus the home run and RBI champions and still fail to win the pennant. Bob Lemon, Mike Garcia, and Early Wynn finished 1–2–3 in the American League in innings pitched.

• • • •

1953 In 1953 Al Rosen hit .336 with 43 homers and 145 RBIs. He lost the Triple Crown when he grounded out in his final at-bat of the season.

1954 First baseman Luke Easter retired with the distinction of being the only player in major league history to have hit 25 or more homers in three consecutive seasons, yet fail to reach 100 homers in his career. In 1979 Easter was shot and killed by two payroll robbers outside a Cleveland bank.

• • • •

1955 After being sidelined with polio for much of the season, Vic Wertz came back to have two straight 100+ RBI seasons.

Cleveland rookie Herb Score set a rookie record in 1955 when he struck out 245 batters, and another when he averaged 9.7 strikeouts per nine innings pitched.

• • • •

1965 Indians shortstop Dick Howser had just 6 RBIs in 107 games played and 307 at-bats.

• • • •

1965–69 Indians outfielder Richie Scheinblum, who played in Cleveland from 1965–1969, once said, "The only good thing about playing in Cleveland is you don't have to make road trips there."

• • • •

1970 After leading Cleveland with 27 homers and 93 RBIs in 1969, first baseman Tony Horton hit a wall. In a game on May 24 against the Yankees, Horton hit three homers, but, when he failed to hit a fourth and the Tribe lost 8–7 in extra innings, he became depressed over his inability to slug the needed fourth homer. Then, on June 24 in a doubleheader against the Yankees, Horton watched as Bobby Murcer hit four consecutive home runs. In that same doubleheader, Yankee pitcher Steve Hamilton twice struck out Horton on his "folly floater" pitch—a blooper—and Horton was so embarrassed that he literally crawled back to the dugout amid a thunderous chorus of boos. Finally, on August 28, Horton, extremely despondent over his batting slump, played his last game. After the season he was hospitalized for depression, unable to handle the fans' booing, and, at just 25 years of age, he left baseball forever.

• • • •

1975 Frank Robinson became the first black manager in major league history when he took the reins of the Indians, while still an active player. As player-manager, Robinson homered on Opening Day.

• • • •

1981 Cleveland's Len Barker pitched a perfect game against the Blue Jays on May 15, as the Indians defeated Toronto, 3–0.

• • • •

1984 Rick Sutcliffe became the only Cy Young winner to have begun the season with another team. After starting the season 4–5 with Cleveland, he finished the year with the Chicago Cubs, going 16–1 in the National League.

• • • •

1987 Three pitchers tied for the club lead in wins for the Indians: Tom Candiotti, Scott Bailes, and Phil Niekro. They each recorded just seven wins, a 20th-century record for fewest wins by a staff leader.

1992 When Kenny Lofton led the league with 66 stolen bases, it marked the first year since 1956 that a rookie had led the American League in steals.

• • • •

1993 On April 8, second baseman Carlos Baerga became the first player in major league history to hit home runs from both sides of the plate in the same inning, as the Tribe blasted the Yankees, 15–5.

• • • •

1995 Jose Mesa's 46 saves were not only more than any other closer in baseball that year—they were more than any other team that year.

Cleveland's 30-game margin of victory in the AL Central in 1995 over the Kansas City Royals set the all-time record for divisional play.

• • • •

1996 The Indians led the AL in batting average and ERA for the second straight year, becoming the first team since the 1957–1958 Yankees to do so. The back-to-back batting titles were the first time the Indians had accomplished the feat since 1905–1906. Finally, the Indians had the best record in baseball in both 1995 and 1996, the first time in the team's history they had done so.

• • • •

1999 When Manny Ramirez knocked in 165 runs, he became the first major leaguer to top the 160 RBI mark since Jimmie Foxx's 175 in 1938.

On May 5, 1999, the Indians trailed Tampa Bay, 10–2, and wound up winning the game by nine runs (20–11), the greatest turnaround in major league history. (This incredible comeback margin has since been tied by the Yankees in 2005, also against Tampa Bay and also by a final score of 20–11!)

• • • •

2000 On September 25, the Indians—who were engaged in an extremely tight battle with the Seattle Mariners for the AL Wild Card spot—played host to the Chicago White Sox and Minnesota Twins in a day-night doubleheader, the first time since 1951 that a team had played two full games against two different opponents in the same day. The Indians had to squeeze the White Sox in on the same day as their regularly scheduled game with Minnesota due to an earlier season rainout.

• • • •

1996–2001 In a stretch that spanned from 1996 to 2001, the Indians recorded 455 consecutive sellouts, the most in major league history.

• • • •

2005 Through 2005, American League pitchers have hit seven homers in interleague play since it began in 1997, and four were by Cleveland pitchers.

Special Achievements

World Series Results

Year	Opponent	Result	Games
1920	Brooklyn Dodgers	Won	5–2
1948	Boston Braves	Won	4–2
1954	New York Giants	Lost	0–4
1995	Atlanta Braves	Lost	2–4
1997	Florida Marlins	Lost	3–4

World Series Managerial Records

Manager	Record	Series Game Record
Tris Speaker	1–0	5–2
Lou Boudreau	1–0	4–2
Al Lopez	0–1	0–4
Mike Hargrove	0–2	5–8

All-Time Postseason Record

Divisional Playoffs	14–12
League Championship Series	10–8
World Series	14–16

All-Star Games at Cleveland

Year	Date	Winner	Score	Stadium
1935	July 8	American	4–1	Municipal Stadium
1954	July 13	American	11–9	Municipal Stadium
1963	July 9	National	5–3	Municipal Stadium
1981	Aug 9	National	5–4	Municipal Stadium
1997	July 8	American	3–1	Jacobs Field

Hall of Famers Who Played for Team

	Position	Years	Games with Cleveland
Earl Averill	OF	1929–1939	1,509
Lou Boudreau	SS	1938–1950	1,560
Steve Carlton	SP/RP	1987	23
Stan Coveleski	SP	1916–1924	361
Larry Doby	OF	1947–1955, 1958	1,235
Dennis Eckersley	SP/RP	1975–1977	103
Bob Feller	SP	1936–1941, 1945–1956	570
Elmer Flick	OF	1902–1910	935
Addie Joss	SP	1902–1910	296
Ralph Kiner	OF	1955	113
Nap Lajoie	2B	1902–1914	1,614
Bob Lemon	SP/RP	1941–1942, 1946–1958	615
Al Lopez	C	1947	61
Eddie Murray	DH/1B	1994–1996	309
Hal Newhouser	RP	1954–1955	28
Phil Niekro	SP	1986–1987	56
Satchel Paige	RP/SP	1948–1949	52
Gaylord Perry	SP	1972–1975	134
Sam Rice	OF	1934	97
Frank Robinson	DH	1974–1976	100
Joe Sewell	SS/3B	1920–1930	1,513
Tris Speaker	OF	1916–1926	1,519
Hoyt Wilhelm	RP	1957–1958	32
Dave Winfield	DH	1995	46
Early Wynn	SP	1949–1957, 1963	368
Cy Young	SP	1909–1911	63

Hall of Famers Who Managed Team

	Years	Games with Cleveland
Lou Boudreau	1942–1950	1,377
Walter Johnson	1933–1935	347
Nap Lajoie	1905–1909	686
Al Lopez	1951–1956	924
Frank Robinson	1975–1977	375
Tris Speaker	1919–1926	1,137

MVP Award Winners

Lou Boudreau	SS	1948
Al Rosen	3B	1953

Cy Young Award Winners

Pitcher	Year	W–L	SV	ERA
Gaylord Perry	1972	24–16	1	1.92

Rookie of the Year Award Winners

Herb Score	SP	1955
Chris Chambliss	1B	1971
Joe Charboneau	OF	1980
Sandy Alomar Jr.	C	1990

Gold Glove Winners

Year	Position	Player
1958	1B	Vic Power
1959	1B OF	Vic Power Minnie Minoso
1960	1B	Vic Power
1961	1B OF	Vic Power Jim Piersall
1964	OF	Vic Davalillo

1970	C	Ray Fosse
1971	C	Ray Fosse
1976	OF	Rick Manning
1990	C	Sandy Alomar Jr.
1993	OF	Kenny Lofton
1994	SS OF	Omar Vizquel Kenny Lofton
1995	SS OF	Omar Vizquel Kenny Lofton
1996	SS OF	Omar Vizquel Kenny Lofton
1997	3B SS	Matt Williams Omar Vizquel
1998	SS	Omar Vizquel
1999	2B SS	Roberto Alomar Omar Vizquel
2000	2B 3B SS	Roberto Alomar Travis Fryman Omar Vizquel
2001	2B SS	Roberto Alomar Omar Vizquel

Triple Crown Winners

None

Fireman of the Year Award Winners

Jose Mesa	1995

World Series MVP

None

League Championship Series MVP

Orel Hershiser	1995
Marquis Grissom	1997

All-Star Game MVP

Sandy Alomar Jr.	1997

Manager of the Year Award Winners

None

Batting Champions

Player	Year	Avg
Napoleon Lajoie	1903	.344
Napoleon Lajoie	1904	.376
Elmer Flick	1905	.306
Tris Speaker	1914	.386
Lew Fonseca	1929	.369
Lou Boudreau	1944	.327
Bobby Avila	1954	.341

Nine-Inning No-Hitters Pitched

Year	Pitcher	Opp.	Score
1908	Robert Rhoads Addie Joss	BOS CWS	2–1 1–0 (perfect)
1910	Addie Joss	CWS	1–0
1919	Ray Caldwell	NYY	3–0
1931	Wes Ferrell	STL	9–0
1940	Bob Feller	CWS	1–0
1946	Bob Feller	NYY	1–0
1947	Don Black	PHI	3–0
1948	Bob Lemon	DET	2–0
1951	Bob Feller	DET	2–1
1966	Sonny Siebert	WAS	2–0
1974	Dick Bosman	OAK	4–0
1977	Dennis Eckersley	CAL	1–0
1981	Len Barker	TOR	3–0 (perfect)

20-Game Winners

Year	Pitcher	W–L
1903	Earl Moore	20–8
1904	William Bernhard	23–13
1905	Addie Joss	20–11
1906	Robert Rhodes Addie Joss Otto Hess	22–10 21–9 20–17
1907	Addie Joss	27–10
1908	Addie Joss	24–11
1911	Vean Gregg	23–7
1912	Vean Gregg	20–13
1913	Fred Falkenberg Vean Gregg	23–10 20–13
1917	Jim Bagby	23–13
1918	Stan Coveleski	22–13
1919	Stan Coveleski	23–17
1920	Jim Bagby Stan Coveleski Ray Caldwell	31–12 24–14 20–10
1921	Stan Coveleski	23–13
1922	George Uhle	22–16
1923	George Uhle	26–16
1924	Joe Shaute	20–17
1926	George Uhle	27–11
1929	Wes Ferrell	21–10
1930	Wes Ferrell	25–13
1931	Wes Ferrell	22–12
1932	Wes Ferrell	23–13
1934	Mel Harder	20–12
1935	Mel Harder	22–11
1936	Johnny Allen	20–10
1939	Bob Feller	24–9
1940	Bob Feller	27–11

1941	Bob Feller	25–12
1946	Bob Feller	26–15
1947	Bob Feller	20–11
1948	Gene Bearden Bob Lemon	20–7 20–14
1949	Bob Lemon	22–10
1950	Bob Lemon	23–11
1951	Bob Feller Mike Garcia Early Wynn	22–8 20–13 20–13
1952	Early Wynn Mike Garcia Bob Lemon	23–12 22–11 22–11
1953	Bob Lemon	21–15
1954	Bob Lemon Early Wynn	23–7 23–11
1956	Herb Score Early Wynn Bob Lemon	20–9 20–9 20–14
1962	Dick Donovan	20–10
1968	Luis Tiant	21–9
1970	Sam McDowell	20–12
1972	Gaylord Perry	24–16
1974	Gaylord Perry	21–13

RETIRED UNIFORM NUMBERS

Number	Player	Position
3	Earl Averill	OF
5	Lou Boudreau	SS
14	Larry Doby	OF
18	Mel Harder	SP
19	Bob Feller	SP
21	Bob Lemon	SP

TEAM RECORDS—WINS & LOSSES

- Games won in a season: 111 in 1954
- Games lost in a season: 105 in 1991
- Games won in a month: 26 in August 1954
- Games lost in a month: 24 in July 1914
- Consecutive games won: 13 in 1942 and 1951
- Consecutive games lost: 12 in 1931
- Biggest shutout victory: 22–0 over New York Yankees on August 31, 2004
- Biggest shutout loss: 21–0 to Detroit on September 15, 1901
- Highest winning percentage: .721 in 1954 (111–43)
- Lowest winning percentage: .333 in 1914 (51–102)

TEAM RECORDS—BATTING

- Highest team batting average: .308 in 1921
- Lowest team batting average: .234 in 1968 and 1972
- Highest team slugging average: .484 in 1994
- Highest team on-base percentage: .383 in 1921
- Total hits: 1,715 in 1936
- Extra-base hits: 576 in 1996
- Hits in a game: 29 vs. St. Louis Browns on August 12, 1948 (second game) and Boston on June 20, 1980
- Longest individual hitting streak: 31, Napoleon Lajoie, 1906
- Most .300 hitters in a single season: 9 in 1921
- Home runs: 221 in 2000
- Home runs in a month: 17, Albert Belle, September 1995
- Home runs in a game: 8 vs. Milwaukee on April 25, 1997 and Seattle on July 16, 2004
- Home runs by a rookie: 37, Al Rosen, 1950
- Home runs by a right-hander: 50, Albert Belle, 1995
- Home runs by a left-hander: 52, Jim Thome, 2002
- Home runs by a switch-hitter: 24, Roberto Alomar, 1999
- Grand slams: 12 in 1999
- Grand slams (individual; single season): 4, Al Rosen, 1951
- Grand slams (individual; career): 13, Manny Ramirez
- Triples: 95 in 1920
- Doubles: 358 in 1930
- Singles: 1,218 in 1925
- Walks: 743 in 1999
- Runs scored: 1,009 in 1999
- Runs scored in a game: 27 vs. Boston Red Sox, July 7, 1923
- Runs scored in an inning: 14 vs. Philadelphia A's on June 18, 1950, second game (first inning)
- Most batters hit by a pitch: 78 in 2004
- Times shut out: 24 in 1914
- Grounded into double plays: 165 in 1980
- Fewest grounded into double plays: 94 in 1941
- Runners left on base: 1,260 in 2000

TEAM RECORDS—BASERUNNING

- Stolen bases: 210 in 1917
- Caught stealing: 92 in 1920

TEAM RECORDS—PITCHING

- Lowest earned run average: 2.02 in 1908
- Complete games: 141 in 1904
- Saves: 51 in 2005
- Strikeouts: 1,218 in 2001
- Shutouts: 27 in 1906
- Walks: 770 in 1971
- Hit batsmen: 73 in 1901
- Wild pitches: 87 in 1973
- Consecutive wins (individual): 15, Johnny Allen, 1937 and Gaylord Perry, 1974; over two seasons: 17, Johnny Allen, 1936–1937
- Consecutive losses (individual): 13, Guy Morton, 1914
- Strikeouts in a game (individual): 19, Luis Tiant, July 3, 1968 (10 innings); 18, Bob Feller, October 2, 1938 (1st game)
- Runs allowed in a game: 24 vs. Boston Red Sox, August 21, 1986

TEAM RECORDS—FIELDING

- Best fielding average: .988 in 2000
- Most errors committed: 329 in 1901
- Fewest errors committed: 72 in 2000
- Most double plays turned: 197 in 1953
- Fewest double plays turned: 77 in 1915

TEAM RECORDS—MISCELLANEOUS

- Number of times league champions: 5
- Number of times finishing last in league: 6
- Largest attendance, single game: 78,382 vs. Chicago White Sox, August 20, 1948
- Largest attendance, doubleheader: 84,587 vs. New York Yankees, September 12, 1954
- Players used in a season: 59 in 2002
- Seasons played: 20 by Mel Harder

PRIMARY PITCHING STAFFS

Year	Starter	Starter	Starter	Starter	Starter	Closer	Bullpen	Bullpen	Bullpen
2005	Westbrook	Lee	Sabathia	Elarton	Millwood	Wickman	Howry	Sauerbeck	Riske
2004	Lee	Sabathia	Westbrook	Elarton	Davis	Wickman	Riske	Betancourt	White
2003	Anderson	Sabathia	Westbrook	Traber	Davis	Baez	Riske	Mulholland	Boyd
2002	Baez	Sabathia	Drese	Finley	Colon	Wickman	Riske	Wohlers	Rincon
2001	Burba	Sabathia	Nagy	Finley	Colon	Wickman	Rodriguez	Shuey	Rincon
2000	Burba	Bere	Woodard	Finley	Colon	Karsay	Reed	Shuey	Speier
1999	Burba	Nagy	Wright	Gooden	Colon	Jackson	Reed	Shuey	Rincon
1998	Burba	Nagy	Wright	Gooden	Colon	Jackson	Assenmacher	Shuey	Mesa
1997	Hershiser	Nagy	Wright	Ogea	Colon	Mesa	Assenmacher	Jackson	Plunk
1996	Hershiser	Nagy	McDowell	Ogea	Martinez	Mesa	Assenmacher	Tavarez	Plunk
1995	Hershiser	Nagy	Clark	Ogea	Martinez	Mesa	Assenmacher	Tavarez	Plunk
1994	Morris	Nagy	Clark	Grimsley	Martinez	Mesa	Lilliquist	Plunk	Farr
1993	Mesa	Kramer	Clark	Mutis	Bielecki	Plunk	Hernandez	Lilliquist	Dipoto
1992	Nagy	Cook	Armstrong	Scudder	Otto	Olin	Power	Lilliquist	Plunk
1991	Nagy	Swindell	King	Nichols	Candiotti	Olin	Hillegas	Orosco	Jones
1990	Black	Swindell	Farrell	Valdez	Candiotti	Jones	Olin	Orosco	Guante
1989	Black	Swindell	Farrell	Yett	Candiotti	Jones	Bailes	Orosco	Atherton
1988	Bailes	Swindell	Farrell	Yett	Candiotti	Jones	Gordon	Havens	Dedmon
1987	Bailes	Swindell	Schrom	Niekro	Candiotti	Jones	Vande Berg	Yett	Stewart
1986	Schulze	Heaton	Schrom	Niekro	Candiotti	Camacho	Bailes	Yett	Oelkers
1985	Schulze	Heaton	Blyleven	Ruhle	Wardle	Waddell	Thompson	Easterly	Reed
1984	Comer	Heaton	Blyleven	Farr	Sutcliffe	Camacho	Jeffcoat	Easterly	Waddell
1983	Sorensen	Heaton	Blyleven	Barker	Sutcliffe	Spillner	Anderson	Eichelberger	Easterly
1982	Sorensen	Denny	Waits	Barker	Sutcliffe	Spillner	Glynn	Whitson	Brennan
1981	Blyleven	Denny	Waits	Barker	Garland	Spillner	Monge	Stanton	Lacey
1980	Spillner	Denny	Waits	Barker	Garland	Monge	Cruz	Owchinko	Stanton
1979	Wise	Paxton	Waits	Barker	Wilkins	Monge	Cruz	Spillner	Garland
1978	Wise	Paxton	Waits	Clyde	Hood	Kern	Monge	Spillner	Kinney

PRIMARY PITCHING STAFFS (CONT.)

Year	Starter	Starter	Starter	Starter	Starter	Closer	Bullpen	Bullpen	Bullpen
1977	Garland	Eckersley	Bibby	Fitzmorris	Dobson	Kern	Monge	Hood	Waits
1976	Brown	Eckersley	Bibby	Waits	Dobson	LaRoche	Kern	Buskey	Thomas
1975	Peterson	Eckersley	Hood	Harrison	Raich	LaRoche	Brown	Buskey	Bibby
1974	Peterson	Perry	Perry	Bosman	Kline	Buskey	Wilcox	Hilgendorf	Beene
1973	Tidrow	Perry	Wilcox	Bosman	Strom	Hilgendorf	Johnson	Timmermann	Lamb
1972	Tidrow	Perry	Wilcox	Dunning	Colbert	Mingori	Hennigan	Riddleberger	Farmer
1971	McDowell	Foster	Lamb	Dunning	Hargan	Hennigan	Farmer	Mingori	Colbert
1970	McDowell	Hand	Chance	Dunning	Hargan	Higgins	Lasher	Hennigan	Austin
1969	McDowell	Tiant	Ellsworth	Williams	Hargan	Pizarro	Paul	Law	Pina
1968	McDowell	Tiant	Siebert	Williams	Hargan	Romo	Fisher	Paul	Kurtz
1967	McDowell	Tiant	Siebert	O'Donoghue	Hargan	Pena	Culver	Allen	Bailey
1966	McDowell	Tiant	Siebert	Bell	Hargan	Radatz	O'Donoghue	Allen	Kelley
1965	McDowell	Tiant	Siebert	Terry	Kralick	Bell	McMahon	Stange	Weaver
1964	McDowell	Tiant	Donovan	Ramos	Kralick	McMahon	Bell	Abernathy	Siebert
1963	Grant	Latman	Donovan	Ramos	Kralick	Abernathy	Bell	Allen	Walker
1962	Grant	Latman	Donovan	Ramos	Perry	Bell	Funk	Allen	Dailey
1961	Grant	Latman	Bell	Hawkins	Perry	Funk	Locke	Allen	Stigman
1960	Grant	Latman	Bell	Stigman	Perry	Klippstein	Locke	Newcombe	Briggs
1959	Grant	McLish	Bell	Score	Perry	Locke	Garcia	Ferrarese	Cicotte
1958	Grant	McLish	Bell	Narleski	Ferrarese	Mossi	Woodeshick	Tomanek	Wilhelm
1957	Wynn	Garcia	Mossi	Narleski	Lemon	McLish	Daley	Tomanek	Pitula
1956	Wynn	Garcia	Score	Aguirre	Lemon	Mossi	Houtteman	Narleski	McLish
1955	Wynn	Garcia	Score	Houtteman	Lemon	Narleski	Mossi	Feller	Santiago
1954	Wynn	Garcia	Feller	Houtteman	Lemon	Narleski	Mossi	Newhouser	Hooper
1953	Wynn	Garcia	Feller	Houtteman	Lemon	Hooper	Hoskins	Wight	Brissie
1952	Wynn	Garcia	Feller	Gromek	Lemon	Harris	Jones	Brissie	Rozek
1951	Wynn	Garcia	Feller	Chakales	Lemon	Brissie	Gromek	Zuverink	Rozek
1950	Wynn	Garcia	Feller	Gromek	Lemon	Benton	Zoldak	Pieretti	Flores
1949	Wynn	Garcia	Feller	Bearden	Lemon	Benton	Paige	Zoldak	Gromek
1948	Zoldak	Black	Feller	Bearden	Lemon	Christopher	Paige	Klieman	Gromek
1947	Embree	Black	Feller	Gettel	Harder	Klieman	Lemon	Stephens	Gromek
1946	Embree	Reynolds	Feller	Gromek	Harder	Lemon	Krakauskas	Center	Berry
1945	Bagby	Reynolds	Smith	Gromek	Klieman	Center	Henry	Salveson	
1944	Harder	Reynolds	Smith	Gromek	Klieman	Heving	Poat	Calvert	Bagby
1943	Harder	Reynolds	Smith	Bagby	Kennedy	Heving	Naymick	Salveson	Center
1942	Harder	Dean	Smith	Bagby	Milnar	Ferrick	Eisenstat	Kennedy	Heving
1941	Harder	Feller	Smith	Bagby	Milnar	Brown	Eisenstat	Heving	
1940	Harder	Feller	Smith	Allen	Milnar	Dobson	Eisenstat	Humphries	
1939	Harder	Feller	Hudlin	Allen	Milnar	Dobson	Eisenstat	Broaca	
1938	Harder	Feller	Hudlin	Allen	Whitehill	Humphries	Galehouse	Milnar	Zuber
1937	Harder	Galehouse	Hudlin	Allen	Whitehill	Heving	Brown	Wyatt	
1936	Harder	Hildebrand	Blaeholder	Allen	Brown	Lee	Galehouse	Hudlin	
1935	Harder	Hildebrand	Hudlin	Pearson	Lee	Brown	Winegarner	Stewart	
1934	Harder	Hildebrand	Hudlin	Pearson	Brown	Lee	Winegarner	Bean	
1933	Harder	Hildebrand	Hudlin	Ferrell	Brown	Connally	Pearson	Bean	
1932	Harder	Hildebrand	Hudlin	Ferrell	Brown	Connally	Pearson	Russell	
1931	Harder	Connally	Hudlin	Ferrell	Brown	Appleton	Lawson	Thomas	
1930	Harder	Shoffner	Hudlin	Ferrell	Brown	Appleton	Miller	Bean	
1929	Miller	Shaute	Hudlin	Ferrell	Miljus	Holloway	Zinn	Grant	
1928	Miller	Shaute	Hudlin	Uhle	Grant	Bayne	Harder	Levsen	
1927	Miller	Shaute	Hudlin	Uhle	Buckeye	Grant	Karr	Levsen	
1926	Levsen	Shaute	Smith	Uhle	Buckeye	Miller	Karr	Benge	

PRIMARY PITCHING STAFFS (CONT.)

Year	Starter	Starter	Starter	Starter	Starter	Closer	Bullpen	Bullpen	Bullpen
1925	Karr	Miller	Smith	Uhle	Buckeye	Speece	Shaute	Cole	
1924	Shaute	Coveleski	Smith	Uhle	Edwards	Metivier	Roy	Clark	
1923	Shaute	Coveleski	Smith	Uhle	Edwards	Metivier	Morton	Boone	
1922	Morton	Coveleski	Mails	Uhle	Bagby	Lindsey	Edwards	Keefe	
1921	Sothoron	Coveleski	Mails	Uhle	Bagby	Caldwell	Morton	Odenwald	
1920	Caldwell	Coveleski	Mails	Morton	Bagby	Uhle	Niehaus	Myers	
1919	Myers	Coveleski	Uhle	Morton	Bagby	Phillips	Enzmann	Jasper	
1918	Coumbe	Coveleski	Enzmann	Morton	Bagby	Groom	McQuillan		
1917	Coumbe	Coveleski	Klepfer	Morton	Bagby	Gould	Lambeth	Boehling	
1916	Coumbe	Coveleski	Klepfer	Morton	Bagby	Gould	Lambeth	Beebe	
1915	Coumbe	Mitchell	Hagerman	Morton	Walker	Jones	Harstad	Collamore	
1914	Steen	Mitchell	Hagerman	Morton	Blanding	Bowman	Gregg	Collamore	
1913	Falkenberg	Mitchell	Gregg	Kahler	Blanding	Cullop	Steen	James	
1912	Steen	Mitchell	Gregg	Kahler	Blanding	Baskette	George	Krapp	
1911	Krapp	Mitchell	Gregg	Kahler	Blanding	Falkenberg	West	Harkness	
1910	Falkenberg	Mitchell	Young	Harkness	Koestner	Link	Fanwell	Berger	
1909	Falkenberg	Berger	Young	Joss	Rhoads	Sitton	Liebhardt	Upp	
1908	Liebhardt	Berger	Chech	Joss	Rhoads	Thielman	Ryan	Falkenberg	
1907	Liebhardt	Thielman	Hess	Joss	Rhoads	Clarkson	Berger	Bernhard	
1906	Bernhard	Townsend	Hess	Joss	Rhoads	Eells	Moore	Liebhardt	
1905	Bernhard	Moore	Hess	Joss	Rhoads	West	Halla		
1904	Bernhard	Moore	Donahue	Joss	Rhoads	Hess	Hickey		
1903	Bernhard	Moore	Donahue	Joss	Wright	Dorner	Killian	Stovall	
1902	Bernhard	Moore	Streit	Joss	Wright	Lundbom	Hess		
1901	Dowling	Moore	Hart	Scott	Bracken	Hoffer	McNeal	Cristall	

PRIMARY STARTING LINEUPS

Year	C	1B	2B	3B	SS	LF	CF	RF	DH
2005	Martinez	Broussard	Belliard	Boone	Peralta	Crisp	Sizemore	Blake	Hafner
2004	Martinez	Broussard	Belliard	Blake	Vizquel	Lawton	Crisp	Gerut	Hafner
2003	Bard	Broussard	Phillips	Blake	Peralta	Lawton	Bradley	Gerut	Burks
2002	Diaz	Thome	Gutierrez	Fryman	Vizquel	Magruder	Bradley	Lawton	Burks
2001	Diaz	Thome	Alomar	Fryman	Vizquel	Cordova	Lofton	Gonzalez	Burks
2000	Alomar	Thome	Alomar	Fryman	Vizquel	Sexson	Lofton	Ramirez	Branyan
1999	Diaz	Thome	Alomar	Fryman	Vizquel	Justice	Lofton	Ramirez	Baines
1998	Alomar	Thome	Bell	Fryman	Vizquel	Giles	Lofton	Ramirez	Justice
1997	Alomar	Thome	Fernandez	Williams	Vizquel	Giles	Grissom	Ramirez	Justice
1996	Alomar	Franco	Baerga	Thome	Vizquel	Belle	Lofton	Ramirez	Murray
1995	Pena	Sorrento	Baerga	Thome	Vizquel	Belle	Lofton	Ramirez	Murray
1994	Alomar	Sorrento	Baerga	Thome	Vizquel	Belle	Lofton	Ramirez	Murray
1993	Ortiz	Sorrento	Baerga	Espinoza	Fermin	Belle	Lofton	Kirby	Jefferson
1992	Alomar	Sorrento	Baerga	Jacoby	Lewis	Howard	Lofton	Whiten	Belle
1991	Skinner	Jacoby	Lewis	Baerga	Fermin	Belle	Cole	Whiten	James
1990	Alomar	Hernandez	Browne	Jacoby	Fermin	Maldonado	Webster	Snyder	James
1989	Allanson	O'Brien	Browne	Jacoby	Fermin	McDowell	Carter	Snyder	Clark
1988	Allanson	Upshaw	Franco	Jacoby	Bell	Hall	Carter	Snyder	Kittle
1987	Bando	Carter	Bernazard	Jacoby	Franco	Hall	Butler	Snyder	Tabler
1986	Allanson	Tabler	Bernazard	Jacoby	Franco	Hall	Butler	Carter	Thornton
1985	Willard	Tabler	Bernazard	Jacoby	Franco	Carter	Butler	Vukovich	Thornton

PRIMARY STARTING LINEUPS (CONT.)

Year	C	1B	2B	3B	SS	LF	CF	RF	DH
1984	Willard	Hargrove	Bernazard	Jacoby	Franco	Hall	Butler	Vukovich	Thornton
1983	Hassey	Hargrove	Trillo	Harrah	Franco	Tabler	Thomas	Vukovich	Thornton
1982	Hassey	Hargrove	Perconte	Harrah	Fischlin	Dilone	Manning	Hayes	Thornton
1981	Hassey	Hargrove	Kuiper	Harrah	Veryzer	Dilone	Manning	Orta	Thornton
1980	Hassey	Hargrove	Brohamer	Harrah	Veryzer	Dilone	Manning	Orta	Charboneau
1979	Alexander	Thornton	Kuiper	Harrah	Veryzer	Hargrove	Manning	Bonds	Johnson
1978	Alexander	Thornton	Kuiper	Bell	Veryzer	Grubb	Manning	Dade	Carbo
1977	Kendall	Thornton	Kuiper	Bell	Duffy	Bochte	Norris	Dade	Carty
1976	Ashby	Powell	Kuiper	Bell	Duffy	Hendrick	Manning	Spikes	Carty
1975	Ashby	Powell	Kuiper	Bell	Duffy	Gamble	Hendrick	Spikes	Carty
1974	Duncan	Ellis	Brohamer	Bell	Duffy	Lowenstein	Hendrick	Spikes	Gamble
1973	Duncan	Chambliss	Brohamer	Bell	Duffy	Spikes	Hendrick	Torres	Gamble
1972	Fosse	Chambliss	Brohamer	Nettles	Duffy	Johnson	Unser	Bell	
1971	Fosse	Chambliss	Leon	Nettles	Heidemann	Uhlaender	Pinson	Foster	
1970	Fosse	Horton	Leon	Nettles	Heidemann	Foster	Uhlaender	Pinson	
1969	Sims	Horton	Fuller	Alvis	Brown	Baker	Cardenal	Harrelson	
1968	Azcue	Horton	Fuller	Alvis	Brown	Maye	Cardenal	Davalillo	
1967	Azcue	Horton	Fuller	Alvis	Brown	Wagner	Davalillo	Hinton	
1966	Azcue	Whitfield	Gonzalez	Alvis	Brown	Wagner	Davalillo	Colavito	
1965	Azcue	Whitfield	Gonzalez	Alvis	Brown	Wagner	Davalillo	Colavito	
1964	Romano	Chance	Brown	Alvis	Howser	Wagner	Davalillo	Francona	
1963	Azcue	Whitfield	Held	Alvis	Brown	Francona	Davalillo	Luplow	
1962	Romano	Francona	Kindall	Phillips	Held	Essegian	Cline	Kirkland	
1961	Romano	Power	Temple	Phillips	Held	Francona	Piersall	Kirkland	
1960	Romano	Power	Aspromonte	Phillips	Held	Francona	Piersall	Kuenn	
1959	Nixon	Power	Martin	Strickland	Held	Minoso	Piersall	Colavito	
1958	Nixon	Vernon	Avila	Harrell	Hunter	Minoso	Doby	Colavito	
1957	Hegan	Wertz	Avila	Smith	Carrasquel	Woodling	Maris	Colavito	
1956	Hegan	Wertz	Avila	Rosen	Carrasquel	Woodling	Busby	Colavito	
1955	Hegan	Wertz	Avila	Rosen	Strickland	Kiner	Doby	Smith	
1954	Hegan	Glynn	Avila	Rosen	Strickland	Smith	Doby	Philley	
1953	Hegan	Glynn	Avila	Rosen	Strickland	Mitchell	Doby	Simpson	
1952	Hegan	Easter	Avila	Rosen	Boone	Mitchell	Doby	Simpson	
1951	Hegan	Easter	Avila	Rosen	Boone	Mitchell	Doby	Kennedy	
1950	Hegan	Easter	Gordon	Rosen	Boone	Mitchell	Doby	Kennedy	
1949	Hegan	Vernon	Gordon	Keltner	Boudreau	Mitchell	Doby	Kennedy	
1948	Hegan	Robinson	Gordon	Keltner	Boudreau	Mitchell	Doby	Kennedy	
1947	Hegan	Robinson	Gordon	Keltner	Boudreau	Mitchell	Metkovich	Peck	
1946	Hegan	Fleming	Meyer	Keltner	Boudreau	Case	Mackiewicz	Edwards	
1945	Hayes	Rocco	Meyer	Ross	Boudreau	Heath	Mackiewicz	Seerey	
1944	Rosar	Rocco	Mack	Keltner	Boudreau	Seerey	Hoag	Cullenbine	
1943	Rosar	Rocco	Mack	Keltner	Boudreau	Heath	Hockett	Cullenbine	
1942	Denning	Fleming	Mack	Keltner	Boudreau	Heath	Weatherly	Hockett	
1941	Hemsley	Trosky	Mack	Keltner	Boudreau	Walker	Weatherly	Heath	
1940	Hemsley	Trosky	Mack	Keltner	Boudreau	Heath	Weatherly	Bell	
1939	Hemsley	Trosky	Hale	Keltner	Webb	Heath	Chapman	Campbell	
1938	Pytlak	Trosky	Hale	Keltner	Lary	Heath	Averill	Campbell	
1937	Pytlak	Trosky	Kroner	Hale	Lary	Solters	Averill	Campbell	
1936	Sullivan	Trosky	Hughes	Hale	Knickerbocker	Vosmik	Averill	Weatherly	
1935	Phillips	Trosky	Berger	Hale	Knickerbocker	Vosmik	Averill	Campbell	
1934	Pytlak	Trosky	Hale	Kamm	Knickerbocker	Vosmik	Averill	Rice	
1933	Spencer	Boss	Hale	Kamm	Knickerbocker	Vosmik	Averill	Porter	

PRIMARY STARTING LINEUPS (CONT.)

Year	C	1B	2B	3B	SS	LF	CF	RF	DH
1932	Sewell	Morgan	Cissell	Kamm	Burnett	Vosmik	Averill	Porter	
1931	Sewell	Morgan	Hodapp	Kamm	Montague	Vosmik	Averill	Porter	
1930	Sewell	Morgan	Hodapp	Sewell	Goldman	Jamieson	Averill	Porter	
1929	Sewell	Fonseca	Hodapp	Sewell	Tavener	Jamieson	Averill	Morgan	
1928	Sewell	Fonseca	Lind	Hodapp	Sewell	Jamieson	Langford	Summa	
1927	Sewell	Burns	Fonseca	Lutzke	Sewell	Jamieson	Eichrodt	Summa	
1926	Sewell	Burns	Spurgeon	Lutzke	Sewell	Jamieson	Speaker	Summa	
1925	Myatt	Burns	Fewster	Lutzke	Sewell	Jamieson	Speaker	McNulty	
1924	Myatt	Burns	Fewster	Lutzke	Sewell	Jamieson	Speaker	Summa	
1923	O'Neill	Brower	Wambsganss	Lutzke	Sewell	Jamieson	Speaker	Summa	
1922	O'Neill	McInnis	Wambsganss	Gardner	Sewell	Jamieson	Speaker	Wood	
1921	O'Neill	Johnston	Wambsganss	Gardner	Sewell	Jamieson	Speaker	Smith	
1920	O'Neill	Johnston	Wambsganss	Gardner	Chapman	Jamieson	Speaker	Smith	
1919	O'Neill	Johnston	Wambsganss	Gardner	Chapman	Graney	Speaker	Smith	
1918	O'Neill	Johnston	Wambsganss	Evans	Chapman	Wood	Speaker	Roth	
1917	O'Neill	Harris	Wambsganss	Evans	Chapman	Graney	Speaker	Roth	
1916	O'Neill	Gandil	Howard	Turner	Wambsganss	Graney	Speaker	Roth	
1915	O'Neill	Kirke	Wambsganss	Barbare	Chapman	Graney	Leibold	Smith	
1914	O'Neill	Johnston	Lajoie	Turner	Chapman	Graney	Leibold	Jackson	
1913	O'Neill	Johnston	Lajoie	Olson	Chapman	Graney	Leibold	Jackson	
1912	O'Neill	Griggs	Lajoie	Turner	Peckinpaugh	Graney	Birmingham	Jackson	
1911	Fisher	Stovall	Ball	Turner	Olson	Graney	Birmingham	Jackson	
1910	Easterly	Stovall	Lajoie	Bradley	Turner	Graney	Birmingham	Niles	
1909	Easterly	Stovall	Lajoie	Bradley	Ball	Hinchman	Birmingham	Good	
1908	Clarke	Stovall	Lajoie	Bradley	Hinchman	Clarke	Birmingham	Turner	
1907	Clarke	Stovall	Lajoie	Bradley	Turner	Hinchman	Birmingham	Flick	
1906	Bemis	Rossman	Lajoie	Bradley	Turner	Jackson	Flick	Congalton	
1905	Buelow	Carr	Lajoie	Bradley	Turner	Jackson	Bay	Flick	
1904	Bemis	Hickman	Lajoie	Bradley	Turner	Lush	Bay	Flick	
1903	Bemis	Hickman	Lajoie	Bradley	Gochnauer	McCarthy	Bay	Flick	
1902	Bemis	Hickman	Lajoie	Bradley	Gochnauer	McCarthy	Bay	Flick	
1901	Wood	LaChance	Beck	Bradley	Scheibeck	McCarthy	Pickering	O'Brien	

Top 10 Batting Leaders, Single Season & Career with Team

GAMES PLAYED: CAREER WITH TEAM

Player	G	PA
1. Terry Turner	1,619	6,515
2. Nap Lajoie	1,614	6,695
3. Lou Boudreau	1,560	6,707
4. Jim Hegan	1,526	4,982
5. Tris Speaker	1,519	6,628
6. Ken Keltner	1,513	6,280
Joe Sewell	1,513	6,576
8. Earl Averill	1,509	6,708
9. Charlie Jamieson	1,483	6,343
10. Omar Vizquel	1,478	6,542

AT-BATS: SEASON

Player	AB	Year
1. Joe Carter	663	1986
2. Kenny Lofton	662	1996
3. Julio Franco	658	1984
4. Carlos Baerga	657	1992
5. Mickey Rocco	653	1944
6. Joe Carter	651	1989
7. Carl Lind	650	1928
8. Charlie Jamieson	644	1923
Lyn Lary	644	1937
10. Leon Wagner	641	1964

AT-BATS: CAREER WITH TEAM

Player	AB	PA
1. Nap Lajoie	6,034	6,695
2. Earl Averill	5,909	6,708
3. Terry Turner	5,787	6,515
4. Lou Boudreau	5,754	6,707
5. Omar Vizquel	5,708	6,542
6. Ken Keltner	5,655	6,280
7. Joe Sewell	5,621	6,576
8. Charlie Jamieson	5,551	6,343
9. Tris Speaker	5,546	6,628
10. Kenny Lofton	4,872	5,570

Batting Average: Season

Player	BA	Year
1. Joe Jackson	.408	1911
2. Joe Jackson	.395	1912
3. Tris Speaker	.389	1925
4. Tris Speaker	.388	1920
5. Tris Speaker	.386	1916
6. Nap Lajoie	.384	1910
7. Tris Speaker	.380	1923
8. Charlie Hickman	.378	1902
Tris Speaker	.378	1922
Earl Averill	.378	1936

Batting Average: Career with Team

Player	BA	PA
1. Joe Jackson	.374	2,852
2. Tris Speaker	.354	6,628
3. Nap Lajoie	.339	6,695
4. George Burns	.327	2,883
5. Ed Morgan	.323	2,640
Roberto Alomar	.323	2,068
7. Earl Averill	.322	6,708
8. Joe Sewell	.320	6,576
9. Johnny Hodapp	.318	2,416
10. Charlie Jamieson	.316	6,343

Total Hits: Season

Player	H	Year
1. Joe Jackson	233	1911
2. Earl Averill	232	1936
3. Nap Lajoie	227	1910
4. Joe Jackson	226	1912
5. Johnny Hodapp	225	1930
6. Charlie Jamieson	222	1923
7. Tris Speaker	218	1923
8. George Burns	216	1926
Hal Trosky	216	1936
Joe Vosmik	216	1935

Total Hits: Career with Team

Player	H	PA
1. Nap Lajoie	2,046	6,695
2. Tris Speaker	1,965	6,628
3. Earl Averill	1,903	6,708
4. Joe Sewell	1,800	6,576
5. Charlie Jamieson	1,753	6,343
6. Lou Boudreau	1,706	6,707
7. Omar Vizquel	1,616	6,542
8. Ken Keltner	1,561	6,280
9. Terry Turner	1,472	6,515
10. Kenny Lofton	1,463	5,570

Home Runs: Season

Player	HR	Year
1. Jim Thome	52	2002
2. Albert Belle	50	1995
3. Jim Thome	49	2001
4. Albert Belle	48	1996
5. Manny Ramirez	45	1998
6. Manny Ramirez	44	1999
7. Al Rosen	43	1953
8. Rocky Colavito	42	1959
Hal Trosky	42	1936
10. Rocky Colavito	41	1958

Home Runs: Career with Team

Player	HR	PA
1. Jim Thome	334	5,723
2. Albert Belle	242	3,922
3. Manny Ramirez	236	4,095
4. Earl Averill	226	6,708
5. Hal Trosky	216	4,853
6. Larry Doby	215	5,082
7. Andre Thornton	214	5,095
8. Al Rosen	192	4,374
9. Rocky Colavito	190	3,700
10. Ken Keltner	163	6,280

Triples: Season

Player	3B	Year
1. Joe Jackson	26	1912
2. Dale Mitchell	23	1949
3. Bill Bradley	22	1903
Elmer Flick	22	1906
5. Jeff Heath	20	1941
Joe Vosmik	20	1935
7. Joe Jackson	19	1911
8. Elmer Flick	18	1905
Elmer Flick	18	1907
Jeff Heath	18	1938

Triples: Career with Team

Player	3B	PA
1. Earl Averill	121	6,708
2. Tris Speaker	108	6,628
3. Elmer Flick	106	4,020
4. Joe Jackson	89	2,852
5. Jeff Heath	83	3,875
6. Ray Chapman	81	4,590
7. Jack Graney	79	5,576
8. Nap Lajoie	78	6,695
9. Terry Turner	77	6,515
10. Bill Bradley	74	5,193
Charlie Jamieson	74	6,343

Doubles: Season

Player	2B	Year
1. George Burns	64	1926
2. Tris Speaker	59	1923
3. Albert Belle	52	1995
Tris Speaker	52	1921
Tris Speaker	52	1926
6. George Burns	51	1927
Johnny Hodapp	51	1930
Nap Lajoie	51	1910
9. Odell Hale	50	1936
Tris Speaker	50	1920

Doubles: Career with Team

Player	2B	PA
1. Tris Speaker	486	6,628
2. Nap Lajoie	424	6,695
3. Earl Averill	377	6,708
4. Joe Sewell	375	6,576
5. Lou Boudreau	367	6,707
6. Ken Keltner	306	6,280
7. Charlie Jamieson	296	6,343
8. Omar Vizquel	288	6,542
9. Hal Trosky	287	4,853
10. Jim Thome	259	5,723

Extra-Base Hits: Season

Player	XBH	Year
1. Albert Belle	103	1995
2. Hal Trosky	96	1936
3. Albert Belle	89	1996
Hal Trosky	89	1934
5. Tris Speaker	87	1923
6. Earl Averill	85	1934
7. Ed Morgan	84	1930
8. Earl Averill	83	1932
9. Earl Averill	82	1936
Manny Ramirez	82	1998

Extra-Base Hits: Career with Team

Player	XBH	PA
1. Earl Averill	724	6,708
2. Tris Speaker	667	6,628
3. Jim Thome	613	5,723
4. Hal Trosky	556	4,853
5. Ken Keltner	538	6,280
6. Nap Lajoie	536	6,695
7. Lou Boudreau	495	6,707
8. Manny Ramirez	484	4,095
9. Albert Belle	481	3,922
10. Joe Sewell	468	6,576

TOTAL BASES: SEASON

Player	TB	Year
1. Hal Trosky	405	1936
2. Earl Averill	385	1936
3. Albert Belle	377	1995
4. Albert Belle	375	1996
5. Hal Trosky	374	1934
6. Al Rosen	367	1953
7. Earl Averill	361	1931
8. Earl Averill	359	1932
9. Ed Morgan	351	1930
10. Tris Speaker	350	1923

TOTAL BASES: CAREER WITH TEAM

Player	TB	PA
1. Earl Averill	3,200	6,708
2. Tris Speaker	2,886	6,628
3. Nap Lajoie	2,728	6,695
4. Jim Thome	2,633	5,723
5. Ken Keltner	2,494	6,280
6. Hal Trosky	2,406	4,853
7. Lou Boudreau	2,392	6,707
8. Joe Sewell	2,391	6,576
9. Charlie Jamieson	2,251	6,343
10. Omar Vizquel	2,162	6,542

RUNS BATTED IN: SEASON

Player	RBI	Year
1. Manny Ramirez	165	1999
2. Hal Trosky	162	1936
3. Albert Belle	148	1996
4. Manny Ramirez	145	1998
Al Rosen	145	1953
6. Earl Averill	143	1931
7. Hal Trosky	142	1934
8. Juan Gonzalez	140	2001
9. Ed Morgan	136	1930
10. Tris Speaker	130	1923

RUNS BATTED IN: CAREER WITH TEAM

Player	RBI	PA
1. Earl Averill	1,084	6,708
2. Jim Thome	927	5,723
3. Nap Lajoie	919	6,695
4. Hal Trosky	911	4,853
5. Tris Speaker	884	6,628
6. Joe Sewell	869	6,576
7. Ken Keltner	850	6,280
8. Manny Ramirez	804	4,095
9. Larry Doby	776	5,082
10. Albert Belle	751	3,922

RUNS SCORED: SEASON

Player	R	Year
1. Earl Averill	140	1931
2. Roberto Alomar	138	1999
3. Tris Speaker	137	1920
4. Earl Averill	136	1936
5. Tris Speaker	133	1923
6. Kenny Lofton	132	1996
7. Manny Ramirez	131	1999
8. Charlie Jamieson	130	1923
9. Earl Averill	128	1934
10. Odell Hale	126	1936
Joe Jackson	126	1911

RUNS SCORED: CAREER WITH TEAM

Player	R	PA
1. Earl Averill	1,154	6,708
2. Tris Speaker	1,079	6,628
3. Kenny Lofton	951	5,570
4. Charlie Jamieson	942	6,343
5. Jim Thome	917	5,723
6. Omar Vizquel	906	6,542
7. Nap Lajoie	865	6,695
8. Joe Sewell	857	6,576
9. Lou Boudreau	823	6,707
10. Larry Doby	808	5,082

WALKS: SEASON

Player	BB	Year
1. Jim Thome	127	1999
2. Jim Thome	123	1996
3. Jim Thome	122	2002
4. Jim Thome	120	1997
5. Jim Thome	118	2000
6. Mike Hargrove	111	1980
Jim Thome	111	2001
8. Andre Thornton	109	1982
9. Les Fleming	106	1942
10. Jack Graney	105	1919

WALKS: CAREER WITH TEAM

Player	BB	PA
1. Jim Thome	997	5,723
2. Tris Speaker	857	6,628
3. Lou Boudreau	766	6,707
4. Earl Averill	725	6,708
5. Jack Graney	712	5,576
6. Larry Doby	703	5,082
7. Andre Thornton	685	5,095
8. Joe Sewell	654	6,576
9. Charlie Jamieson	627	6,343
10. Omar Vizquel	612	6,542

STRIKEOUTS: SEASON

Player	SO	Year
1. Jim Thome	185	2001
2. Jim Thome	171	1999
Jim Thome	171	2000
4. Cory Snyder	166	1987
5. Jim Thome	146	1997
6. Jim Thome	141	1996
Jim Thome	141	1998
8. Casey Blake	139	2004
Jim Thome	139	2002
10. Brook Jacoby	137	1986

STRIKEOUTS: CAREER WITH TEAM

Player	SO	PA
1. Jim Thome	1,377	5,723
2. Larry Doby	805	5,082
3. Manny Ramirez	780	4,095
4. Brook Jacoby	738	4,804
5. Andre Thornton	683	5,095
6. Jim Hegan	664	4,982
7. Max Alvis	642	3,864
Cory Snyder	642	2,592
9. Woodie Held	629	3,226
Kenny Lofton	629	5,570

SLUGGING PERCENTAGE: SEASON

Player	SLG	Year
1. Albert Belle	.714	1994
2. Manny Ramirez	.697	2000
3. Albert Belle	.690	1995
4. Jim Thome	.677	2002
5. Manny Ramirez	.663	1999
6. Hal Trosky	.644	1936
7. Earl Averill	.627	1936
8. Jim Thome	.624	2001
9. Albert Belle	.623	1996
10. Rocky Colavito	.620	1958

SLUGGING PERCENTAGE: CAREER WITH TEAM

Player	SLG	PA
1. Manny Ramirez	.592	4,095
2. Albert Belle	.580	3,922
3. Jim Thome	.567	5,723
4. Hal Trosky	.551	4,853
5. Joe Jackson	.542	2,852
Earl Averill	.542	6,708
7. David Justice	.526	2,025
8. Tris Speaker	.520	6,628
9. Roberto Alomar	.515	2,068
10. Jeff Heath	.506	3,875

On-Base Percentage: Season

Player	OBP	Year
1. Tris Speaker	.483	1920
2. Tris Speaker	.479	1925
3. Tris Speaker	.474	1922
4. Tris Speaker	.470	1916
5. Tris Speaker	.469	1923
6. Joe Jackson	.468	1911
7. Joe Jackson	.460	1913
8. Joe Jackson	.458	1912
9. Manny Ramirez	.457	2000
10. Joe Sewell	.456	1923

On-Base Percentage: Career with Team

Player	OBP	PA
1. Tris Speaker	.444	6,628
2. Joe Jackson	.441	2,852
3. Jim Thome	.414	5,723
4. Manny Ramirez	.407	4,095
5. Ed Morgan	.405	2,640
Roberto Alomar	.405	2,068
7. Earl Averill	.399	6,708
8. Joe Sewell	.398	6,576
9. Mike Hargrove	.396	3,538
10. David Justice	.392	2,025

OPS (On-Base Percentage + Slugging Percentage): Season

Player	OPS	Year
1. Manny Ramirez	1.154	2000
2. Albert Belle	1.152	1994
3. Jim Thome	1.122	2002
4. Manny Ramirez	1.105	1999
5. Albert Belle	1.091	1995
6. Tris Speaker	1.080	1922
7. Tris Speaker	1.079	1923
8. Earl Averill	1.065	1936
9. Jim Thome	1.062	1996
10. Joe Jackson	1.058	1911

OPS (On-Base Percentage + Slugging Percentage): Career with Team

Player	OPS	PA
1. Manny Ramirez	.998	4,095
2. Joe Jackson	.983	2,852
3. Jim Thome	.982	5,723
4. Tris Speaker	.965	6,628
5. Albert Belle	.949	3,922
6. Earl Averill	.941	6,708
7. Hal Trosky	.930	4,853
8. Roberto Alomar	.920	2,068
9. David Justice	.918	2,025
10. Ed Morgan	.898	2,640

Stolen Bases: Season

Player	SB	Year
1. Kenny Lofton	75	1996
2. Kenny Lofton	70	1993
3. Kenny Lofton	66	1992
4. Miguel Dilone	61	1980
5. Kenny Lofton	60	1994
6. Kenny Lofton	54	1995
Kenny Lofton	54	1998
8. Brett Butler	52	1984
Ray Chapman	52	1917
10. Braggo Roth	51	1917

Stolen Bases: Career with Team

Player	SB	PA
1. Kenny Lofton	450	5,570
2. Omar Vizquel	279	6,542
3. Terry Turner	254	6,515
4. Nap Lajoie	240	6,695
5. Ray Chapman	233	4,590
6. Elmer Flick	207	4,020
7. Harry Bay	165	2,765
8. Brett Butler	164	2,676
9. Bill Bradley	157	5,193
10. Tris Speaker	151	6,628

Sacrifice Hits: Season

Player	Sac	Year
1. Ray Chapman	67	1917
2. Bill Bradley	60	1908
3. Ray Chapman	50	1919
4. Bill Bradley	46	1907
5. Ray Chapman	45	1913
6. Bill Wambsganss	43	1921
7. Bill Wambsganss	42	1922
8. Ray Chapman	41	1920
Joe Sewell	41	1929
10. Ray Chapman	40	1916
Bill Wambsganss	40	1920

Sacrifice Hits: Career with Team

Player	Sac	PA
1. Ray Chapman	334	4,590
2. Terry Turner	264	6,515
Bill Wambsganss	264	4,872
4. Bill Bradley	238	5,193
5. Joe Sewell	234	6,576
6. Tris Speaker	183	6,628
7. Nap Lajoie	174	6,695
8. Lou Boudreau	159	6,707
9. Charlie Jamieson	134	6,343
George Stovall	134	3,842

Hit by Pitch: Season

Player	HBP	Year
1. Travis Hafner	17	2004
Minnie Minoso	17	1959
3. Einar Diaz	16	2001
4. Bill Bradley	15	1905
George Burns	15	1924
Bill Hinchman	15	1907
Nap Lajoie	15	1913
Minnie Minoso	15	1958
Al Smith	15	1955
10. Carlos Baerga	13	1992
Bill Bradley	13	1908
Manny Ramirez	13	1999

Hit by Pitch: Career with Team

Player	HBP	PA
1. Nap Lajoie	79	6,695
2. Joe Sewell	67	6,576
3. Bill Bradley	65	5,193
4. Elmer Flick	47	4,020
5. Carlos Baerga	45	3,973
6. George Burns	43	2,883
7. Tris Speaker	42	6,628
Jim Thome	42	5,723
9. Bill Wambsganss	41	4,872
10. Jack Graney	40	5,576
Woodie Held	40	3,226

Top 10 Pitching Leaders, Single Season & Career with Team

Games Pitched: Season

Player	GP	Year
1. Bobby Howry	79	2005
2. Sid Monge	76	1979
3. Paul Assenmacher	75	1997
4. Danys Baez	73	2003
5. Mike Jackson	72	1999
Steve Karsay	72	2000
Steve Olin	72	1992
David Riske	72	2004
Paul Shuey	72	1999
10. Mike Jackson	71	1997
Derek Lilliquist	71	1992

Games Pitched: Career with Team

Player	GP	IP
1. Mel Harder	582	3,426.3
2. Bob Feller	570	3,827.0
3. Willis Hudlin	475	2,557.7
4. Bob Lemon	460	2,850.0
5. Gary Bell	419	1,550.3
6. Mike Garcia	397	2,138.0
7. Eric Plunk	373	462.0
8. Paul Shuey	361	404.7
9. Stan Coveleski	360	2,502.3
10. George Uhle	357	2,200.3

Innings Pitched: Season

Player	IP	Year
1. Bob Feller	371.3	1946
2. George Uhle	357.7	1923
3. Gaylord Perry	344.0	1973
4. Bob Feller	343.0	1941
5. Gaylord Perry	342.7	1972
6. Jim Bagby	339.7	1920
7. Addie Joss	338.7	1907
8. Otto Hess	333.7	1906
9. Addie Joss	325.0	1908
10. Gaylord Perry	322.3	1974

Innings Pitched: Career with Team

Player	IP
1. Bob Feller	3,827.0
2. Mel Harder	3,426.3
3. Bob Lemon	2,850.0
4. Willis Hudlin	2,557.7
5. Stan Coveleski	2,502.3
6. Addie Joss	2,327.0
7. Early Wynn	2,286.7
8. George Uhle	2,200.3
9. Mike Garcia	2,138.0
10. Sam McDowell	2,109.7

Batters Faced: Season

Player	BF	Year
1. George Uhle	1,548	1923
2. Bob Feller	1,512	1946
3. Bob Feller	1,466	1941
4. Gaylord Perry	1,410	1973
5. George Uhle	1,367	1926
6. Jim Bagby	1,364	1920
7. Stan Coveleski	1,360	1921
8. Gaylord Perry	1,345	1972
9. Bill Bernhard	1,343	1904
10. Addie Joss	1,332	1907

Batters Faced: Career with Team

Player	BF	IP
1. Bob Feller	16,180	3,827.0
2. Mel Harder	14,862	3,426.3
3. Bob Lemon	12,099	2,850.0
4. Willis Hudlin	11,283	2,557.7
5. Stan Coveleski	10,284	2,502.3
6. George Uhle	9,694	2,200.3
7. Early Wynn	9,611	2,286.7
8. Addie Joss	9,209	2,327.0
9. Mike Garcia	9,058	2,138.0
10. Sam McDowell	8,889	2,109.7

Games Started: Season

Player	GS	Year
1. George Uhle	44	1923
2. Bob Feller	42	1946
3. Gaylord Perry	41	1973
4. Stan Coveleski	40	1921
Bob Feller	40	1941
Gaylord Perry	40	1972
Dick Tidrow	40	1973
George Uhle	40	1922
9. Sam McDowell	39	1970
10. Six tied with . . .	38	——

Games Started: Career with Team

Player	GS	IP
1. Bob Feller	484	3,827.0
2. Mel Harder	433	3,426.3
3. Bob Lemon	350	2,850.0
4. Willis Hudlin	320	2,557.7
5. Stan Coveleski	305	2,502.3
6. Charles Nagy	297	1,942.3
7. Early Wynn	296	2,286.7
8. Sam McDowell	295	2,109.7
9. Mike Garcia	281	2,138.0
10. George Uhle	267	2,200.3

Complete Games: Season

Player	CG	Year
1. Bob Feller	36	1946
2. Bill Bernhard	35	1904
3. Addie Joss	34	1907
4. Otto Hess	33	1906
5. George Uhle	32	1926
6. Bob Feller	31	1940
Addie Joss	31	1903
Addie Joss	31	1905
Bob Rhoads	31	1906
10. Jim Bagby	30	1920
Red Donahue	30	1904
Cy Young	30	1909

Complete Games: Career with Team

Player	CG	IP
1. Bob Feller	279	3,827.0
2. Addie Joss	234	2,327.0
3. Stan Coveleski	194	2,502.3
4. Bob Lemon	188	2,850.0
5. Mel Harder	181	3,426.3
6. George Uhle	166	2,200.3
7. Willis Hudlin	154	2,557.7
8. Early Wynn	144	2,286.7
9. Earl Moore	137	1,337.7
10. Jim Bagby	131	1,735.7

Games Won: Season

Player	W	Year
1. Jim Bagby	31	1920
2. Bob Feller	27	1940
Addie Joss	27	1907
George Uhle	27	1926
5. Bob Feller	26	1946
George Uhle	26	1923
7. Bob Feller	25	1941
Wes Ferrell	25	1930
9. Stan Coveleski	24	1919

Stan Coveleski	24	1920
Bob Feller	24	1939
Addie Joss	24	1908
Gaylord Perry	24	1972

GAMES WON: CAREER WITH TEAM

Player	W	IP
1. Bob Feller	266	3,827.0
2. Mel Harder	223	3,426.3
3. Bob Lemon	207	2,850.0
4. Stan Coveleski	172	2,502.3
5. Early Wynn	164	2,286.7
6. Addie Joss	160	2,327.0
7. Willis Hudlin	157	2,557.7
8. George Uhle	147	2,200.3
9. Mike Garcia	142	2,138.0
10. Charles Nagy	129	1,942.3

GAMES LOST: SEASON

Player	L	Year
1. Pete Dowling	22	1901
2. Luis Tiant	20	1969
3. Wayne Garland	19	1977
George Kahler	19	1912
Al Milnar	19	1941
Gaylord Perry	19	1973
Rick Wise	19	1978
8. Tom Candiotti	18	1987
9. 12 tied with ...	17	——

GAMES LOST: CAREER WITH TEAM

Player	L	IP
1. Mel Harder	186	3,426.3
2. Bob Feller	162	3,827.0
3. Willis Hudlin	151	2,557.7
4. Bob Lemon	128	2,850.0
5. Stan Coveleski	123	2,502.3
6. George Uhle	119	2,200.3
7. Sam McDowell	109	2,109.7
8. Charles Nagy	103	1,942.3
9. Early Wynn	102	2,286.7
10. Addie Joss	97	2,327.0

WINNING PERCENTAGE: SEASON

Player	W%	Year
1. Johnny Allen	.938	1937
2. Bob Feller	.812	1954
3. Bartolo Colon	.783	1999
Cliff Lee	.783	2005
5. Ed Klepfer	.778	1917
6. Bill Bernhard	.773	1902
Charles Nagy	.773	1996
C.C. Sabathia	.773	2001
9. Vean Gregg	.767	1911
Bob Lemon	.767	1954

WINNING PERCENTAGE: CAREER WITH TEAM

Player	W%	IP
1. Vean Gregg	.667	898.3
2. Johnny Allen	.663	929.7
3. Bartolo Colon	.625	1,029.7
4. Addie Joss	.623	2,327.0
5. Wes Ferrell	.622	1,321.3
Bob Feller	.622	3,827.0
7. Dave Burba	.620	799.7
8. Bob Lemon	.618	2,850.0
9. Early Wynn	.617	2,286.7
10. C.C. Sabathia	.605	972.7

SHUTOUTS: SEASON

Player	SHO	Year
1. Bob Feller	10	1946
Bob Lemon	10	1948
3. Stan Coveleski	9	1917
Addie Joss	9	1906
Addie Joss	9	1908
Luis Tiant	9	1968
7. Jim Bagby	8	1917
8. Otto Hess	7	1906
Gaylord Perry	7	1973
Bob Rhoads	7	1906

SHUTOUTS: CAREER WITH TEAM

Player	SHO	IP
1. Addie Joss	45	2,327.0
2. Bob Feller	44	3,827.0
3. Stan Coveleski	31	2,502.3
Bob Lemon	31	2,850.0
5. Mike Garcia	27	2,138.0
6. Mel Harder	25	3,426.3
7. Early Wynn	24	2,286.7
8. Sam McDowell	22	2,109.7
9. Luis Tiant	21	1,200.0
10. Guy Morton	19	1,629.7
Bob Rhoads	19	1,444.7

ERA: SEASON

Player	ERA	Year
1. Addie Joss	1.16	1908
2. Addie Joss	1.59	1904
3. Luis Tiant	1.60	1968
4. Addie Joss	1.71	1909
5. Addie Joss	1.72	1906
6. Charlie Chech	1.74	1908
Earl Moore	1.74	1903
8. Bob Rhoads	1.77	1908
9. Bob Rhoads	1.80	1906
Vean Gregg	1.80	1911

ERA: CAREER WITH TEAM

Player	ERA	IP
1. Addie Joss	1.89	2,327.0
2. Glenn Liebhardt	2.17	612.7
3. Vean Gregg	2.31	898.3
4. Bob Rhoads	2.39	1,444.7
5. Bill Bernhard	2.45	1,175.0
6. Cy Young	2.50	504.7
Otto Hess	2.50	842.7
8. Earl Moore	2.58	1,337.7
9. Heinie Berger	2.60	599.0
10. Red Donahue	2.66	551.3

EARNED RUNS ALLOWED: SEASON

Player	ER	Year
1. George Uhle	150	1923
2. Dick Tidrow	135	1973
3. Willis Hudlin	130	1931
George Uhle	130	1922
5. Mel Harder	129	1936
Gaylord Perry	129	1973
7. Monte Pearson	128	1934
Sherry Smith	128	1925
9. Bob Feller	126	1938
Early Wynn	126	1957

EARNED RUNS ALLOWED: CAREER WITH TEAM

Player	ER	IP
1. Mel Harder	1,447	3,426.3
2. Bob Feller	1,384	3,827.0
3. Willis Hudlin	1,233	2,557.7
4. Bob Lemon	1,024	2,850.0
5. Charles Nagy	974	1,942.3
6. George Uhle	959	2,200.3
7. Early Wynn	824	2,286.7
8. Stan Coveleski	779	2,502.3
9. Mike Garcia	770	2,138.0
10. Sam McDowell	702	2,109.7

STRIKEOUTS: SEASON

Player	K	Year
1. Bob Feller	348	1946
2. Sam McDowell	325	1965
3. Sam McDowell	304	1970
4. Sam McDowell	283	1968
5. Sam McDowell	279	1969
6. Luis Tiant	264	1968
7. Herb Score	263	1956

8. Bob Feller	261	1940
9. Bob Feller	260	1941
10. Bob Feller	246	1939

STRIKEOUTS: CAREER WITH TEAM

Player	K	IP
1. Bob Feller	2,581	3,827.0
2. Sam McDowell	2,159	2,109.7
3. Bob Lemon	1,277	2,850.0
Early Wynn	1,277	2,286.7
5. Charles Nagy	1,235	1,942.3
6. Mel Harder	1,160	3,426.3
7. Gary Bell	1,104	1,550.3
8. Mike Garcia	1,095	2,138.0
9. Luis Tiant	1,041	1,200.0
10. Addie Joss	920	2,327.0

STRIKEOUTS PER NINE IP: SEASON

Player	K/9	Year
1. Sam McDowell	10.71	1965
2. Sam McDowell	10.42	1966
3. Bartolo Colon	10.15	2000
4. Herb Score	9.70	1955
5. Herb Score	9.49	1956
6. Sam McDowell	9.47	1968
7. Luis Tiant	9.22	1967
8. Luis Tiant	9.20	1968
9. Sam McDowell	9.19	1964
10. Sonny Siebert	9.11	1965

STRIKEOUTS PER NINE IP: CAREER WITH TEAM

Player	K/9	IP
1. Herb Score	9.35	714.3
2. Sam McDowell	9.21	2,109.7
3. Luis Tiant	7.81	1,200.0
4. Dennis Eckersley	7.72	633.3
5. Bartolo Colon	7.63	1,029.7
6. Sonny Siebert	7.14	991.0
7. Dave Burba	7.08	799.7
8. C.C. Sabathia	7.04	972.7
9. Len Barker	6.75	932.3
10. Greg Swindell	6.53	1,071.7

HITS ALLOWED: SEASON

Player	HA	Year
1. George Uhle	378	1923
2. Stan Coveleski	341	1921
3. Jim Bagby	338	1920
4. George Uhle	328	1922
5. Bill Bernhard	323	1904
6. Joe Shaute	317	1924
7. Gaylord Perry	315	1973
8. Mel Harder	313	1935
Willis Hudlin	313	1931
10. Earl Moore	304	1902

HITS ALLOWED: CAREER WITH TEAM

Player	HA	IP
1. Mel Harder	3,706	3,426.3
2. Bob Feller	3,271	3,827.0
3. Willis Hudlin	2,930	2,557.7
4. Bob Lemon	2,559	2,850.0
5. Stan Coveleski	2,450	2,502.3
6. George Uhle	2,442	2,200.3
7. Charles Nagy	2,173	1,942.3
8. Mike Garcia	2,102	2,138.0
9. Early Wynn	2,037	2,286.7
10. Addie Joss	1,888	2,327.0

HITS ALLOWED PER NINE IP: SEASON

Player	H/9	Year
1. Luis Tiant	5.30	1968
2. Herb Score	5.85	1956
3. Sam McDowell	5.87	1965
4. Sam McDowell	6.02	1966
5. Sam McDowell	6.06	1968
6. Stan Coveleski	6.09	1917
7. Herb Score	6.26	1955
8. Vean Gregg	6.33	1911
Sonny Siebert	6.33	1968
10. Allie Reynolds	6.34	1943

HITS ALLOWED PER NINE IP: CAREER WITH TEAM

Player	H/9	IP
1. Herb Score	6.17	714.3
2. Sam McDowell	6.84	2,109.7
3. Sonny Siebert	6.95	991.0
4. Luis Tiant	7.04	1,200.0
5. Addie Joss	7.30	2,327.0
6. Gaylord Perry	7.31	1,130.7
7. Dennis Eckersley	7.33	633.3
8. Ray Narleski	7.54	597.7
9. Heinie Berger	7.57	599.0
10. Vean Gregg	7.61	898.3

WALKS ALLOWED: SEASON

Player	BB	Year
1. Bob Feller	208	1938
2. Bob Feller	194	1941
3. Herb Score	154	1955
4. Bob Feller	153	1946
Sam McDowell	153	1971
6. Bob Lemon	146	1950
7. Bob Feller	142	1939
8. Gene Krapp	138	1911
9. Bob Lemon	137	1949
10. Sam McDowell	132	1965
Early Wynn	132	1952

WALKS ALLOWED: CAREER WITH TEAM

Player	BB	IP
1. Bob Feller	1,764	3,827.0
2. Bob Lemon	1,251	2,850.0
3. Mel Harder	1,118	3,426.3
4. Sam McDowell	1,072	2,109.7
5. Early Wynn	877	2,286.7
6. Willis Hudlin	832	2,557.7
7. George Uhle	709	2,200.3
8. Mike Garcia	696	2,138.0
9. Gary Bell	670	1,550.3
10. Stan Coveleski	616	2,502.3

WALKS ALLOWED PER NINE IP: SEASON

Player	BB/9	Year
1. Addie Joss	0.83	1908
2. Bill Bernhard	1.14	1903
3. Addie Joss	1.15	1909
4. Greg Swindell	1.17	1991
Addie Joss	1.17	1903
6. Dick Donovan	1.22	1963
7. Ralph Terry	1.25	1965
8. Addie Joss	1.37	1906
9. Addie Joss	1.40	1904
10. Bill Bernhard	1.41	1902

WALKS ALLOWED PER NINE IP: CAREER WITH TEAM

Player	BB/9	IP
1. Red Donahue	1.40	551.3
2. Addie Joss	1.41	2,327.0
3. Bill Bernhard	1.55	1,175.0
Dick Donovan	1.55	637.7
5. Cy Young	1.77	504.7
6. Sherry Smith	1.85	850.7
7. Greg Swindell	1.97	1,071.7
8. Clint Brown	2.09	1,104.7
9. Jim Bagby	2.20	1,735.7
10. Stan Coveleski	2.22	2,502.3

WHIP (WALKS + HITS PER NINE IP): SEASON

Player	WHIP	Year
1. Addie Joss	.806	1908
2. Luis Tiant	.871	1968
3. Addie Joss	.933	1906

4. Bill Bernhard	.935	1902
5. Addie Joss	.944	1909
6. Addie Joss	.948	1903
7. Gaylord Perry	.978	1972
8. Sonny Siebert	.981	1965
9. Addie Joss	.983	1907
10. Addie Joss	.988	1904

WHIP (Walks + Hits Per Nine IP): Career with Team

Player	WHIP	IP
1. Addie Joss	0.968	2,327.0
2. Sonny Siebert	1.090	991.0
3. Gaylord Perry	1.104	1,130.7
4. Bill Bernhard	1.126	1,175.0
5. Cy Young	1.127	504.7
6. Heinie Berger	1.135	599.0
7. Luis Tiant	1.143	1,200.0
8. Red Donahue	1.163	551.3
9. Dennis Eckersley	1.165	633.3
10. Otto Hess	1.184	842.7

Home Runs Allowed: Season

Player	HRA	Year
1. Luis Tiant	37	1969
2. Jim Perry	35	1960
3. Charles Nagy	34	1998
Gaylord Perry	34	1973
Ken Schrom	34	1986
6. Gary Bell	32	1961
Mudcat Grant	32	1961
Early Wynn	32	1957
Scott Elarton	32	2005
10. Dennis Eckersley	31	1977
Dick Tidrow	31	1973

Home Runs Allowed: Career with Team

Player	HRA	IP
1. Bob Feller	224	3,827.0
2. Charles Nagy	217	1,942.3
3. Bob Lemon	181	2,850.0
Early Wynn	181	2,286.7
5. Gary Bell	167	1,550.3
6. Mudcat Grant	166	1,214.7
7. Mel Harder	161	3,426.3
8. Sam McDowell	138	2,109.7
9. Luis Tiant	126	1,200.0
10. Mike Garcia	119	2,138.0

Saves: Season

Player	SV	Year
1. Jose Mesa	46	1995
2. Bob Wickman	45	2005
3. Doug Jones	43	1990
4. Mike Jackson	40	1998
5. Mike Jackson	39	1999
Jose Mesa	39	1996
7. Doug Jones	37	1988
8. Doug Jones	32	1989
Bob Wickman	32	2001
10. Steve Olin	29	1992

Saves: Career with Team

Player	SV	IP
1. Doug Jones	129	452.3
2. Bob Wickman	124	220.3
3. Jose Mesa	104	647.3
4. Mike Jackson	94	207.7
5. Ray Narleski	53	597.7
6. Steve Olin	48	273.0
7. Jim Kern	46	423.3
Sid Monge	46	407.0
9. Gary Bell	45	1,550.3
10. Ernie Camacho	44	179.7

Wild Pitches: Season

Player	WP	Year
1. Otto Hess	18	1905
Sam McDowell	18	1967
3. Sam McDowell	17	1965
Sam McDowell	17	1970
Gaylord Perry	17	1973
6. Monte Pearson	15	1934
7. Len Barker	14	1980
Bob Feller	14	1939
Gene Krapp	14	1911
Sam McDowell	14	1969
Bob Rhoads	14	1907
Herb Score	14	1959

Wild Pitches: Career with Team

Player	WP	IP
1. Sam McDowell	114	2,109.7
2. Bob Feller	75	3,827.0
3. Bob Lemon	63	2,850.0
4. Tom Candiotti	53	1,201.7
5. Gary Bell	50	1,550.3
6. Earl Moore	49	1,337.7
7. Len Barker	45	932.3
Willie Mitchell	45	1,301.3
Charles Nagy	45	1,942.3
10. Steve Hargan	44	1,053.3

Hit Batsmen: Season

Player	HB	Year
1. Otto Hess	24	1906
2. Earl Moore	18	1905
3. Pete Dowling	17	1901
4. Otto Hess	15	1907
Willie Mitchell	15	1910
6. Vean Gregg	14	1913
Bob Rhoads	14	1907
8. Addie Joss	13	1902
George Kahler	13	1911
Willie Mitchell	13	1911
George Uhle	13	1922
George Uhle	13	1924
George Uhle	13	1926

Hit Batsmen: Career with Team

Player	HB	IP
1. George Uhle	95	2,200.3
2. Bob Feller	60	3,827.0
Addie Joss	60	2,327.0
4. Mel Harder	59	3,426.3
5. Bob Lemon	57	2,850.0
6. Willie Mitchell	56	1,301.3
7. Otto Hess	54	842.7
8. Sam McDowell	53	2,109.7
9. Earl Moore	51	1,337.7
Charles Nagy	51	1,942.3

Games Finished: Season

Player	GF	Year
1. Mike Jackson	65	1999
2. Doug Jones	64	1990
3. Steve Olin	62	1992
4. Jose Mesa	60	1996
5. Mike Jackson	57	1998
Jose Mesa	57	1995
7. Bob Wickman	56	2001
8. Bob Wickman	55	2005
9. Dan Spillner	54	1982
10. Doug Jones	53	1989
Sid Monge	53	1979

Games Finished: Career with Team

Player	GF	IP
1. Doug Jones	234	452.3
2. Jose Mesa	195	647.3
3. Bob Wickman	186	220.3
4. Mike Jackson	160	207.7
5. Dan Spillner	157	782.7
6. Sid Monge	152	407.0
7. Gary Bell	144	1,550.3
8. Eric Plunk	140	462.0
9. Paul Shuey	127	404.7
10. Jim Kern	125	423.3

Significant Indians

AVERILL, EARL SR. (OF)
(1929–1939)

After tearing up the Pacific Coast League for three years, Averill got his big league chance in 1929 after being purchased by the Indians from the San Francisco Seals for $50,000. In Averill's first major league at-bat, he homered off Detroit's Earl Whitehill to become the first American Leaguer ever to homer in his first plate appearance. He had a great rookie year in 1929, hitting .332 with 19 homers and 96 RBIs (he promised his teammates he would do better the next year). Near the end of the 1930 season, it was obvious Averill was going to hit for a higher average and have more RBIs, but a teammate reminded him he was four homers short of his rookie year's performance. "Well, I'd better step on it," Averill replied. He went out that day and hit four homers in a doubleheader—and just missed a fifth when the ball curved foul just in front of the foul pole. He fulfilled his promise of beating his 1929 numbers by hitting another a few days later. Averill, easily the most popular of the Indians players, played in 673 straight games, fourth most in history at the time. Averill was the AL's first All-Star center fielder when the game was inaugurated in 1933, and was the only American League outfielder named to the first six All-Star Games.

In 1937, Averill suddenly found himself temporarily paralyzed from the waist down. He was diagnosed with a congenital spinal problem that forced him to alter his swing, and his power numbers and production dropped dramatically. By 1939, when it became obvious he wasn't the same player, the Indians traded him to Detroit, incensing the fans. After struggling for the next two years, Averill realized he could no longer perform at a major league level and retired. In 1975, he was elected to the Hall of Fame. His son, Earl Jr., followed him to the majors, lasting seven years.

CAREER INDIANS RECORD:

Games	AB	Hits	Runs
1,509	5,909	1,903	1,154
Avg	**HR**	**RBI**	**SB**
.322	226	1,084	66

BELLE, ALBERT (OF/DH)
(1989–1996)

The Cleveland Indians drafted Albert "Joey" Belle in the second round of the June 1989 amateur draft and brought him to the majors that same year, although he did miss most of the 1990 season while undergoing alcohol rehabilitation. Belle was a severe malcontent, liked by very few other players and even fewer fans. Belle had awesome potential, but he let himself get in his own way. In 1991 he became enraged by a fan's comment, so he hurled a baseball at full force and hit the fan, who was standing less than 20 feet away, directly in the chest, receiving a seven-game suspension. He was also suspended for throwing a baseball at a photographer. On another occasion, Belle chased a female reporter out of the clubhouse. When he deigned to speak to the media, it was often an angry, profanity-laced statement. In 1995 Belle became the first player ever to hit 50 homers and 50 doubles in the same season as he helped the Indians reach the postseason for the first time in more than four decades. His stats were clearly superior to Mo Vaughn's, but Vaughn was named the league's MVP by the voters, who were members of the media Belle constantly did battle with.

Following the 1996 season, Belle signed the richest contract in baseball history when the White Sox inked him to an $11 million-per-year contract. After just two years, he exercised an option in his contract that allowed him to leave via free agency and signed with Baltimore. In his first season with the Orioles, Belle hit 37 homers with 117 RBIs, his eighth consecutive season with at least 30 homers and 100 RBIs, tying him with Babe Ruth for the third longest such streak. In 2000, however, Belle began to suffer from a degenerative hip condition that eventually forced him to retire after the season.

CAREER INDIANS RECORD:

Games	AB	Hits	Runs
913	3,441	1,014	592
Avg	**HR**	**RBI**	**SB**
.295	242	751	61

BOUDREAU, LOU (SS)
(1938–1950)

Lou Boudreau was a star basketball and baseball player at the University of Illinois when, as a junior, he accepted money from Cleveland GM Cy Slapnicka with the understanding that he would play baseball for the Indians when he was out of college. When Boudreau's jealous stepfather complained to the Big 10, Boudreau was ruled ineligible for collegiate sports and he left for Cleveland immediately. A natural third baseman, Boudreau was moved to shortstop because Cleveland already had Ken Keltner at the hot corner.

In 1940, Boudreau's first full season in the majors, the young shortstop hit .295 with 101 RBIs, 46 doubles and 10 triples, and was named to the first of his eight All-Star teams. At 24, and after just two full seasons in the majors, Boudreau applied for the vacant manager's job by letter. After a two-hour interview he was awarded the job of player-manager, becoming the youngest manager ever to manage a team from the start of the season. On July 14, 1946, Boudreau hit four doubles and a homer in the first game of a doubleheader, becoming the first AL player ever to have five extra-base hits in one game (which the Indians nonetheless lost to the Red Sox). In the second game of the doubleheader, to counteract Ted Williams' great power, Boudreau initiated the "Williams shift," in which he placed six fielders on the first-base side of the diamond. Although the Williams shift had been used sparingly five years before by White Sox manager Jimmy Dykes, Boudreau was the first to implement it on a regular basis. He also was responsible for moving Bob Lemon from the outfield to full-time pitcher.

After the 1947 season, rumors began to circulate that owner Bill Veeck was about to trade Boudreau to St. Louis for Vern Stephens. Outraged Cleveland fans protested the intended trade by flooding Veeck's office with thousands of letters. The *Cleveland News* ran a front-page ballot seeking fans' votes. The more than 100,000 responses ran 10–1 in favor of keeping Boudreau. Veeck relented, and wisely. In 1948 Cleveland and Boston finished the regular season tied for first, and played the first-ever AL playoff game. The Indians won, 8–3, as Boudreau hit two singles and two homers, and went on to the World Series, where Boudreau hit four doubles as Cleveland defeated the Boston Braves. Boudreau won the AL MVP Award for his excellent 1948 season, in which he established career highs in homers, runs, RBIs, average, and walks. After being released by the Indians following the 1950 season, the eight-time All-Star signed on with the Red Sox and played just 86 games over two years before retiring. He then managed the Red Sox and A's for five years before retiring to the broadcast booth where he remained for more than 30 years. In 1970 Boudreau was elected to the Hall of Fame.

CAREER INDIANS RECORD:

Games	AB	Hits	Runs
1,560	5,754	1,903	1,706
Avg	**HR**	**RBI**	**SB**
.296	63	740	50

CHAPMAN, RAY (SS)
(1912–1920)

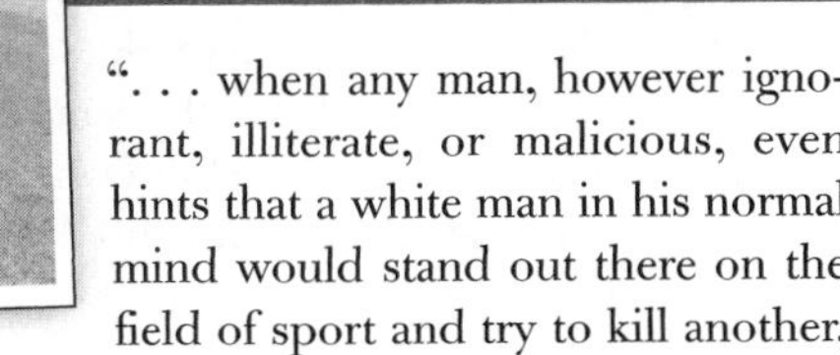

Ray Chapman was one of the best shortstops in the game when, on August 17, 1920, he became the first and only player ever to be killed as a direct result of an injury suffered in a game on the field. The Indians were engaged in a tight three-team race for the pennant with the Yankees and White Sox. Cleveland was playing in New York that day and Carl Mays, a headhunting pitcher who was known to scuff baseballs, was on the mound for the Yanks. When Mays delivered the pitch to Chapman, it was barely outside the strike zone. Problem was, Chapman had a habit of leaning over the plate. The ball hit Chapman in the head with such force that it actually bounced back to Mays, who threw it to first baseman Wally Pipp for what he thought was the inning's first out. Pipp then proceeded to toss the ball around the infield like normal. It was only then that everyone realized something was wrong with Chapman. He was on the ground, unable to speak. There were calls for a doctor, and the Yankee team physician applied ice. After several minutes, Chapman was able to stand. He walked across the field toward the clubhouse, but collapsed near second base. He was taken to the hospital, where he died 12 hours later.

After Chapman's death, the blame game began. Mays quainly defended himself, saying, ". . . when any man, however ignorant, illiterate, or malicious, even hints that a white man in his normal mind would stand out there on the field of sport and try to kill another, the man making the assertion is inhuman, uncivilized, bestial." Some blamed the umpires for not tossing out scuffed or dirty baseballs. The umpires blamed the owners and Ban Johnson, citing a league bulletin that directed umpires to keep balls in play as long as possible after owners complained umpires were tossing out too many balls. After Chapman's death, both leagues began to toss out many more baseballs than before. The National League used 22,095 baseballs in 1919; by 1924 they had used 54,030, all because of the Chapman incident. The surprise is that no moves were made to implement mandatory batting helmets for more than 30 years.

After Chapman's departure from his last game, he was replaced by rookie Joe Sewell, who would eventually make it to the Hall of Fame. Baseball analyst Bill James opined that Chapman, had he lived, eventually would have made it to Cooperstown himself.

CAREER INDIANS RECORD:

Games	AB	Hits	Runs
1,051	3,785	1,053	671
Avg	**HR**	**RBI**	**SB**
.278	17	364	233

COLAVITO, ROCKY (OF)
(1955–1959, 1965–1967)

The good-looking, homer-hitting Rocky Colavito was the most popular player in Cleveland Indians history, as a fan vote in 1976 bore out. To begin with, Colavito was a clean-living player who always made time for his fans, often lingering for hours after a game to sign autographs. He had the strongest arm of any outfielder in baseball with the possible exception of Roberto Clemente, and he liked to show it off. Just for fun he would stand at home plate and fire the ball over the center-field fence. His longest throw in a ball-throwing contest was measured at 436 feet, just short of Don Grate's all-time record of 443 feet. He was no slouch at the plate, either. In a game on June 10, 1959, Colavito hit four homers in four trips to the plate. That season he finished with 42 homers and became the first Indian ever with two 40-homer seasons.

Just before the 1960 season began, however, Colavito, the defending home run champion, was traded to Detroit for defending batting champion Harvey Kuenn. Hundreds of fans, many of them teenage girls, picketed Cleveland Stadium as a sign of their anger. Cleveland GM Frank Lane poured fuel on the fire when he responded to the criticism by saying, "What's all the fuss about? All I did was trade hamburger for steak." The trade went through, and in 1961 Colavito hit 45 homers with 140 RBIs, prompting Detroit GM Bill DeWitt to quip, "I like hamburger." But Colavito didn't like Detroit, and many in Detroit didn't like him. When fans in the right-field stands wouldn't stop razzing him, Colavito threw a ball over the Briggs Stadium roof. He was engaged in a running battle with *Detroit News* writer Joe Falls, who chronicled Colavito's "RNBIs"—runs not batted in. Falls, an official scorer in Detroit, once credited Colavito with an error on a disputed play and Colavito responded by trying to attack him. After four years in Detroit and another in Kansas City, Colavito returned to Cleveland in 1965. Slumping badly in 1967, Colavito was traded to the White Sox in midseason. After one final year split between the Dodgers and Yankees in 1968, Colavito was released and he retired.

CAREER INDIANS RECORD:

Games	AB	Hits	Runs
913	3,185	851	464
Avg	**HR**	**RBI**	**SB**
.267	190	574	9

COVELESKI, STAN (SP/RP)
(1916–1924)

At the age of 12, Stan Coveleski was working the coal mines in Pennsylvania, 72 hours a week for a nickel an hour. His only form of amusement was to tie strings onto tin cans and hang them from the branches of a tree and then throw rocks at them. This, according to Coveleski, is how he attained the accuracy for which he was famous in his baseball career. After a brief trial with the A's in 1912, Coveleski—who threw a three-hitter in his major league debut with Philadelphia, but couldn't crack the vaunted A's rotation—was sent to the minors. In 1916 he came to the majors with Cleveland and was immediately impressive. From 1918 to 1921, he won at least 22 games each year, dominating hitters with an excellent spitball. (His older brother Harry pitched for Detroit, but refused to pitch against his younger brother Stan, fearing that whoever lost would be accused of laying down for the other.) Coveleski had a marvelous 1920 season as he helped the Indians win their first-ever World Series title. He won three games in the Series, all five-hit complete games. Coveleski's control was so legendary that he actually went the first seven innings of a 1920 game *without a single pitch being called for a ball.* After the 1924 season, when he posted a 15–16 record and an ERA of 4.04, the best of his career seemed behind him, and Coveleski was traded to the Senators, where he responded with a surprising 20–5 record and 2.84 ERA. But over the next three years he combined for only 21 wins for Washington and the Yankees and retired in 1928. Coveleski was named to the Hall of Fame in 1969.

CAREER INDIANS RECORD:

W	L	W%	ERA	SV
172	123	.583	2.80	20

K	BB	SHO	IP
856	616	31	2,502.3

DOBY, LARRY (OF)
(1947–1955, 1958)

When baseball's color barrier was broken in 1947 by the arrival of Jackie Robinson, it eased the way for Larry Doby, a six-year veteran of the Negro Leagues, to become the second black player in the majors and the first in the American League. Doby, who played his first major league game on July 5, 1947, endured the same flagrant racism that Robinson did. However, as Doby said, "You didn't hear much about what I was going through because the media didn't want to repeat the same story." Doby, a seven-time All-Star with Cleveland, averaged over 25 homers a year in his eight full seasons with the Tribe. In 1948, his first full year, Doby helped Cleveland to the World Series title by hitting .301 during the season and .318 in the Series, winning Game 4 with a 400-foot homer off Johnny Sain. After he retired, Doby played in Japan for a year, then went into private business in New Jersey for 10 years. He returned as a coach for the Expos, Indians, and later as manager of the White Sox for part of one season. Larry Doby was elected to the Hall of Fame in 1998.

CAREER INDIANS RECORD:

Games	AB	Hits	Runs
1,235	4,315	1,234	808

Avg	HR	RBI	SB
.286	215	776	44

FELLER, BOB (SP/RP)
(1936–1941, 1945–1956)

"Rapid Robert" Feller grew up knowing he would be a major league ballplayer. When he was a youth growing up in rural Van Meter, Iowa, his father carved out a real Field of Dreams in a corner of his cornfield—a little ballpark that even had an outfield fence and a small grandstand behind first base. They formed their own area team and competed against other teams from the community on weekends. Feller was a phenom from the start. With a fastball clocked at 99 mph, the 17-year-old Feller made his major league debut in July 1936 in an exhibition against the St. Louis Cardinals. After striking out eight Cardinals in three innings, Feller's fame spread. He made his first start in August and struck out 15 St. Louis Browns in a 4–1 victory. In September he struck out 17 Philadelphia A's to tie the major league mark and set a new American League record. Then he went home to finish high school.

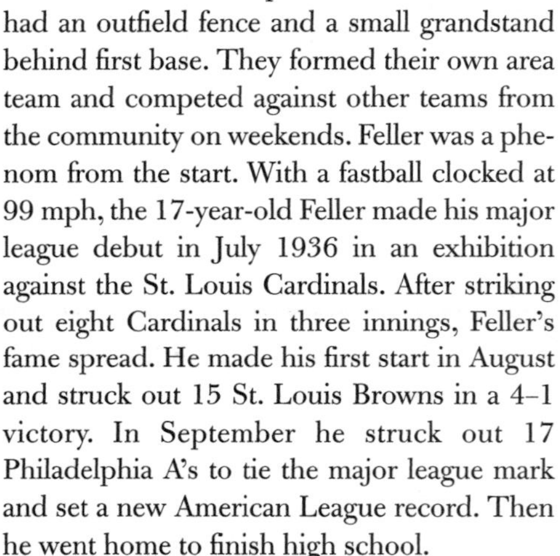

In 1937 at the age of 18, Feller went 9–7 in half a season. In 1938 he was selected to the first of his eight All-Star appearances. On the last day of the season, Feller struck out 18 Tigers to set a new major league record. On April 16, 1940, Feller pitched the only Opening Day no-hitter in major league history when he beat the White Sox, 1–0. Feller won 25 games in 1941 despite missing a month of the season. The day after Pearl Harbor was bombed, Feller enlisted in the Navy and served on the battleship *Alabama,* winning five campaign ribbons and eight battle stars.

Freshly returned from the war, on April 30, 1946, Feller pitched his second no-hitter, defeating the Yankees 1–0. He finished the season with 26 wins (including 10 shutouts) while pitching for the sixth-place Indians. By 1947 Feller was making an estimated $150,000 a year in salary and endorsements, an enormous sum at the time. On July 1, 1951, he threw his third no-hitter, this time against Detroit. Feller's career began to wind down in the mid-1950s. In 1954 he went 13–3 as a spot starter for the pennant-winning Indians, but didn't pitch in the World Series as the Giants swept Cleveland four straight.

After retiring in 1956, Feller entered the insurance business and became an unofficial spokesman for baseball, never fearing to speak his mind. When Feller was elected to the Hall of Fame in 1962, his plaque listed his career as spanning "1936 to 1941" and "1945 to 1956." Miffed about the excluded war years, Feller asked Commissioner Peter Ueberroth to have the plaque changed. Ueberroth told Feller that such a change would be inconvenient. "Well," said Feller, "it was inconvenient to get shot at." In 1996 the Society for American Baseball Research honored Feller as the first recipient of SABR's Hero of Baseball Award. In his mid-80s, Feller still throws almost daily to keep in shape, and is a regular autograph signer at baseball card shows around the country. He is such a prolific autographer that baseball card show regulars joke that an unsigned Bob Feller baseball is worth more than a signed one. What it really means, however, is that for seven decades Bob Feller has been—and continues to be—immensely popular with baseball fans, and deservedly so.

CAREER INDIANS RECORD:

W	L	W%	ERA	SV
266	162	.621	3.25	21
K	**BB**	**SHO**	**IP**	
2,581	1,764	44	3,827.0	

GARCIA, MIKE (SP/RP)
(1948–1959)

Mike Garcia was an integral part of the great Cleveland pitching staffs of the late 1940s to mid-1950s. After going 14–5 in his rookie season of 1949 with a league-leading 2.36 ERA, Garcia plodded through an 11–11 sophomore season before becoming a 20-game winner in back-to-back seasons in 1951 and 1952. He was 19–8 with a 2.64 ERA in 1954 when he joined Bob Feller, Bob Lemon, and Early Wynn in leading the Indians to a romp of the American League with 111 victories and a .721 winning percentage. However, Cleveland was swept by the Giants in the World Series and it would be Garcia's last good season. Over the next five years with Cleveland, Garcia would win only 38 more games. The Indians released him after the 1959 season and he signed on with the White Sox, but didn't win a game for them and was released in late May. He joined the Senators in 1961, but failed to win a game with them either, and retired after the season and opened a dry-cleaning business in the Cleveland area. After becoming disabled with diabetes and kidney failure in the 1970s, Garcia had to sell his business to pay for his frequent dialysis treatments and medical bills. Just a month before he died in January 1986, his former Indians teammates organized a benefit to help their stricken comrade.

CAREER INDIANS RECORD:

W	L	W%	ERA	SV
142	96	.597	3.24	21

K	BB	SHO	IP
1,095	696	27	2,138.0

HARDER, MEL (SP/RP)
(1928–1947)

While never considered to be a dominant pitcher, Harder was good enough to stick around for 20 years, all with Cleveland. Only Walter Johnson with the Senators and Ted Lyons with the White Sox pitched more years with one club than Harder. Only Bob Feller won more games with Cleveland. In 1932, the year cavernous Cleveland Municipal Stadium opened, Harder lost a 1–0 duel to the Philadelphia A's and Lefty Grove in front of 76,979 fans. Harder led the American League in ERA in 1933 at 2.95, but pitching for such a weak-hitting team left his record at only 15–17. Harder was the winner of the 1934 All-Star Game, although most fans only remember Carl Hubbell's feat of striking out five of the game's best hitters in a row. Harder is the only pitcher to have pitched more than 10 innings in All-Star Game competition without giving up a run.

In 1940 the soft-spoken Harder triggered one of baseball's weirder episodes. After getting shelled by the Red Sox, Harder approached the dugout. Cleveland manager Ossie Vitt, who had a reputation for mean-spiritedness and was disliked by the players, sarcastically said to Harder, "It's about time you won one, with all the money you're making." Harder led a group of players to meet with Cleveland owner Alva Bradley to complain about Vitt's managing style. Bradley sided with Vitt and, when word leaked out of their meeting, the press branded the players "the Cleveland Crybabies." Baby bottles were thrown at them on the field; diapers were hung from the top of the dugout. Eventually the dissension settled and Cleveland came within one game of winning the pennant. For most of the next seven years, Harder was a spot starter. He retired after the 1947 season, having played 20 years without making it to the World Series. Only five players in major league history have played more seasons than Harder without making it to the World Series. After retiring, he became one of the first coaches in baseball history exclusively devoted to pitching, spending 16 years with the Indians. He later coached for the Mets, Cubs, Reds, and Royals.

CAREER INDIANS RECORD:

W	L	W%	ERA	SV
223	186	.545	3.80	23

K	BB	SHO	IP
1,160	1,118	25	3,426.3

JACKSON, JOE (OF)
(1910–1915)

Joe Jackson is considered by many baseball historians to have been the greatest natural hitter the game has ever seen. Babe Ruth so admired Jackson's hitting ability that he copied Jackson's batting stance. Jackson, known more famously as "Shoeless Joe," was an illiterate mill worker from South Carolina who first displayed his tremendous baseball talent in Southern mill league games. He received his nickname—which he despised—from a fan of an opposing mill league team. When a pair of new spikes made his feet sore, Jackson took them off for one inning in the field and one at-bat, during which he hit a triple. When he slid safely into third, the fan yelled at him, "You shoeless bastard!" The nickname followed him everywhere.

Jackson's abilities on the field had made him famous throughout the South and he eventually signed with the Greenville team. Advised of Jackson's abilities, Philadelphia's Connie Mack signed him sight unseen to a contract. Jackson, socially unsophisticated and terrified of playing "up North in one of them big cities," jumped the train before it got to Philadelphia and returned home to Greenville. An irritated Mack sent a trusted aide to fetch him. He succeeded in getting Jackson back to Philadelphia, but only for one game before he fled Philadelphia again. A third attempt lasted only four more games before Jackson, by now being teased unmercifully by his college-educated Athletics teammates, disappeared again. When Jackson didn't show up for the next day's game, Mack sent out a search party that eventually located the missing outfielder in a Philadelphia burlesque house. Mack decided to let Jackson stay in the South for the remainder of 1908.

In 1909, Mack chose to bring Jackson along slowly, letting him play the season at Augusta, so he could be near his Southern roots. Jackson led the South Atlantic League in hitting and Mack brought him back up to Philadelphia at the end of 1909. Once again, Jackson failed to get along with his teammates and he fled to South Carolina. Mack was furious. Despite Jackson's obvious ability, the exasperated Mack traded Jackson to Cleveland for Bris Lord. Mack would later say that he was quite aware of Jackson's potential, but he actually traded Jackson more as a favor to Cleveland owner Charlie Somers for all his financial help to the A's in the league's early days. In 1910, Somers, having learned from Mack's mistakes, allowed Jackson to play in the South, this time at New Orleans. Jackson won the Southern Association batting title and then reported to Cleveland in September. He hit .387 in 20 games for the Indians and matured to the point where he could handle being "up North in one of them big cities." It helped that he had married his hometown sweetheart, Katie (she was 15 at the time), and was now responsible for a wife.

In 1911, with Katie in the stands at every home game, Jackson hit .408 in his first full season in the majors, though he lost the batting title to Ty Cobb, who hit .420. Jackson loved Cleveland, which didn't seem as overwhelming as Philadelphia. The fans adored him, and he often walked the streets in the evenings, arm-in-arm with Katie, stopping to talk with anyone. Jackson had some of the best years of his career in Cleveland, hitting .395 and .373 in 1912 and 1913, respectively. In 1914 he slumped a bit to .338, and in 1915 he was hitting just .327 in midseason when Somers, now nearly $2 million in debt, sold Jackson to the Chicago White Sox for $31,500 and three players. Jackson, distressed about going to Chicago, was soothed by Katie, who told him that sometimes change offered new opportunities. She had no idea how much change lay ahead. *(See White Sox bio.)*

CAREER INDIANS RECORD:

Games	AB	Hits	Runs
674	2,502	937	474.
Avg	**HR**	**RBI**	**SB**
.375	24	353	138

JONES, DOUG (SP/RP)
(1986–1991, 1998)

Jones was 29 by the time he joined Cleveland in 1986, having played his entire career in the minors except for four games with Milwaukee in 1982. He lasted until he was 43, collecting over 300 saves with seven different teams. His 129 saves for Cleveland is still the team record, although Bob Wickman is poised to pass him early in 2006 after pulling within five saves of Jones by the end of 2005. Jones played in five All-Star Games, three while with the Indians.

CAREER INDIANS RECORD:

W	L	W%	ERA	SV
27	34	.443	3.06	129
K	**BB**	**SHO**	**IP**	
367	104	0	452.3	

JOSS, ADDIE (SP)
(1902–1910)

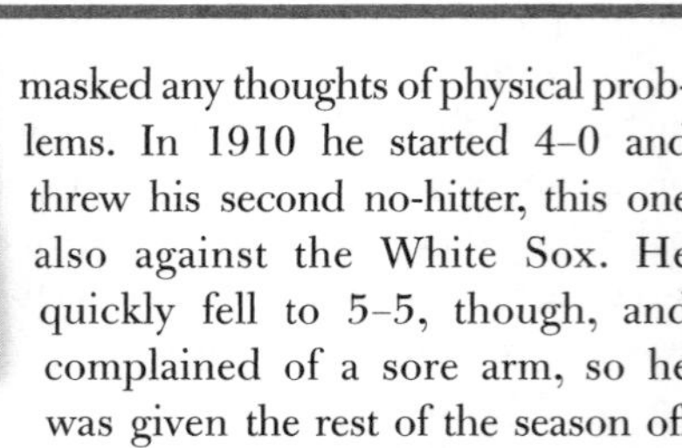

Addie Joss was one of the best-liked players in baseball history. After his death, many of the American League's top players came together to play an All-Star Game and donate the proceeds to his family. Joss, who played only nine years in the majors, all with Cleveland, was a control specialist who averaged just 1.43 walks per nine innings pitched, the third best mark in history. In his major league debut, Joss pitched a disputed one-hitter against the St. Louis Browns on April 26, 1902. (The umpire ruled that one of the Browns' line drives was trapped, although the fielder and witnesses say the ball never touched the ground.) Joss was a 20-game winner each year from 1905–1908, including a league leading 27 wins in 1907. Five times in his career he had ERAs of 1.83 or below. On October 2, 1908, Joss squared off against Ed Walsh of the White Sox (a 40-game winner that year) in one of the greatest pitching duels in history. The two teams were among three (Detroit was the other) that stood just a game apart in the standings with but a few games to go in the season. With a pennant on the line, Walsh pitched a four-hitter, allowing only one unearned run. But Joss pitched a perfect game—one of the most clutch performances in major league history. Cleveland, however, ended up a half-game behind eventual winner Detroit.

Joss was strangely ill for much of his career. He missed a month in 1903 with a high fever. In 1904 he suffered from malaria. In 1905 he missed time with back trouble. By 1909 he was noticeably slipping, and he ended the season with a 14–13 record, although his 1.71 ERA masked any thoughts of physical problems. In 1910 he started 4–0 and threw his second no-hitter, this one also against the White Sox. He quickly fell to 5–5, though, and complained of a sore arm, so he was given the rest of the season off and sent home. The following spring Joss seemed ready to make a comeback, although his teammates noticed that he had lost a lot of weight over the winter. During an exhibition game, Joss fell unconscious on the bench. He dismissed it as no big deal, but by the time the team arrived in Cincinnati, Joss was very ill. He was diagnosed with pleurisy and sent home. Two days after the season started, Joss died of tubercular meningitis at the age of 31. Former ballplayer Billy Sunday presided over the funeral, which drew a huge throng and forced the cancellation of Cleveland's opener in Detroit. In his brief time in the majors, Joss threw 46 shutouts. He completed 234 of his 260 starts, amazing even in that era. In more than 2,300 innings, Joss allowed only 19 home runs. Ty Cobb batted just .071 against him in 28 at-bats. Joss allowed fewer baserunners per nine innings pitched than any pitcher in major league history. Addie Joss, whose career lasted only nine years, was elected to the Hall of Fame in 1978 by the Veterans Committee, which waived their requirement that a player must have played in at least parts of ten major league seasons to be considered for enshrinement.

CAREER INDIANS RECORD:

W	L	W%	ERA	SV
160	97	.623	1.89	5

K	BB	SHO	IP
920	364	45	2,327.0

KELTNER, KEN (3B)
(1937–1944, 1946–1949)

Keltner played in the majors for 13 seasons, 12 of them with the Indians. In his 10 full seasons in Cleveland, Keltner led American League third basemen in fielding three times, assists four times, and double plays five times. He was a seven-time All-Star with a knack for driving in clutch runs. Keltner had a career year in 1948, when he helped the Indians win their first World Series championship in 28 years. He hammered 31 homers with 119 RBIs as he hit .297. In the one-game playoff with Boston, made necessary because the two teams ended in a dead tie, Keltner hit a towering three-run homer to give Cleveland a lead they wouldn't relinquish. Injuries forced him to retire prematurely at the age of 33.

Ken Keltner was the best third baseman of his time. His shining moment came on July 17, 1941. The Cleveland Indians played host to the Yankees in front of nearly 70,000 fans. The huge crowd turned out to see if New York's Joe DiMaggio would extend his 56-game hitting streak, or if the Cleveland nine would stop him cold. In the top of the first inning, DiMaggio hit a bullet down the third-base line. Keltner, playing deep, lunged for the ball, caught it backhanded as his momentum carried him into foul territory, turned and fired a perfect bullet to first base, just nipping DiMaggio. After receiving a walk in the fourth, DiMaggio came to the plate in the seventh. In a virtual replay of the first inning, DiMaggio again drove the ball down the third-base line. Again, Keltner made an incredible backhand grab and threw out the Yankee Clipper at first. When DiMaggio bounced into a double play in the eighth, Keltner forever became known as the man who stopped DiMaggio's streak.

CAREER INDIANS RECORD:

Games	AB	Hits	Runs
1,513	5,655	1,561	735
Avg	**HR**	**RBI**	**SB**
.276	163	850	39

LAJOIE, NAPOLEON (2B/1B)
(1902–1914)

Napoleon Lajoie was one of the game's biggest stars in the early days. A graceful, well-liked second baseman, Lajoie spent 13 of his 21-year major league career with the Indians. After playing his first five years with the Philadelphia Phillies in the National League with its $2,400 salary cap, Lajoie jumped to the new American League's Philadelphia franchise, the A's. The American League was under no such salary cap, and that helped to lure many of the NL's established stars to the AL. Connie Mack offered Lajoie $24,000 for four years, more than double his Phillies salary. After Lajoie signed his new AL contract, the Phillies owner offered him $25,000 for just two years, but Lajoie rebuffed him. Lajoie hit .426 in his first season with the A's, the highest single-season average in the 20th century, and the fourth highest ever, and he became the new league's biggest star. In addition to average, Lajoie led the league in homers, runs, doubles, hits, and RBIs, becoming the first official winner of a Triple Crown (though historians have awarded Triple Crowns after the fact to two 19th-century qualifiers).

The Phillies filed a lawsuit in 1901 to keep Lajoie from leaving the National League team. The case was finally heard in February 1902 before the Pennsylvania Supreme Court, making Lajoie, in effect, the first player to challenge baseball's reserve clause, which bound a player to a single team for life. The judges ruled in favor of the Phillies, declaring that Lajoie was prohibited from playing for any team other than the Phillies for the length of the contract, which, because of the reserve clause, essentially meant life. The court decision threw organized baseball into a shambles. The two warring leagues now had no hope of an early peace agreement. When the 1902 season started, the A's defied the court order and put Lajoie in at second base for Opening Day. But in the ninth inning, Connie Mack received a telegram informing him of an injunction that ordered Lajoie not to play. For the next two months, Lajoie sat idle while lawyers and baseball officials argued the case. When a sharp attorney mentioned that, since the case was heard in the Pennsylvania Supreme Court, it could only be enforced in Pennsylvania, the American League officials came up with a plan. They would transfer Lajoie's contract to the Cleveland Blues, an Ohio franchise suffering from low attendance and financial woes. Although Connie Mack hated to lose Lajoie, he also knew it was the only way he'd get anything out of the deal. He also agreed to the deal in order to help Cleveland's owner, Charlie Somers, the man whose deep pockets had helped start the American League by financially backing at least five of the league's teams, including Mack's A's. Lajoie was an immediate hit in Cleveland, with 10,000 fans turning out to see his June 4th debut. His play on the field sparked renewed interest in the team and made it financially viable for Somers, who gave up thoughts of moving the franchise to Pittsburgh or Cincinnati.

During spring training in 1903, a Cleveland newspaper ran a contest to choose a new team name. The official name Bluebirds (usually shortened to Blues) didn't sit well with many of the players, who had chosen their own name, the Broncos, the year before. Broncos never stuck, and the winning name in the fan contest was Naps—short for Napoleon, in honor of the team's new captain. Late in the 1904 season, manager Bill Armour resigned and Lajoie took his place, becoming a player-manager, a position he held for five years. By mid-1909, Lajoie had had enough of managing. He always felt it was a distraction that hurt his own playing.

In 1910 Lajoie battled Ty Cobb for the batting title. The winner was to receive a new Chalmers "30" automobile. The race was so close and exciting that fans and sportswriters began to call it "the automobile race." Cobb was universally hated, Lajoie universally liked. When it came down to the wire, Cobb felt he had the race won, so he sat out the two games. In Lajoie's final two games, a doubleheader against St. Louis, he smacked a triple in his first at-bat against the Browns. St. Louis manager Jack O'Connor "recommended" to his rookie third baseman that he play very, very deep at third so as not to be injured by Lajoie's wicked line drives. When Lajoie saw the defensive positioning, he bunted for six straight singles in front of the rookie third baseman. On another at-bat, a runner was forced out on the base paths, but rather than receive a fielder's choice, Lajoie received credit for a sacrifice. And on his final at-bat, the shortstop threw wildly to first, but rather than being safe on an error, the official scorer ruled that Lajoie would have been safe anyway, and awarded him a hit. Despite the collusion, Cobb won the batting title anyway—by the razor-thin margin of .0007. After the doubleheader, the St. Louis owner fired manager O'Connor. The whole scandal resulted in a new policy for the awarding of automobiles and other prizes to players competing for individual titles. More than seven decades later, Paul MacFarlane of *The Sporting News* discovered that Cobb had erroneously been given credit for two extra hits when one of his games had been counted twice. When Commissioner

Bowie Kuhn was presented with the evidence, he declined to change the existing record.

Although he clearly wasn't the hitter he used to be, batting only .258 in 1914, Lajoie collected his 3,000th hit that year, joining Honus Wagner as the second 20th-century player to achieve the milestone. In 1915, with his career in decline, and after continual run-ins with Joe Birmingham, the new Cleveland manager, Lajoie was sold to the A's before the 1915 season. The Phillies didn't even feel it was worth pursuing their earlier claim on his services. Lajoie hit .280 and .246 for the A's in his last two years in the majors before retiring. In 1917 he became the player-manager of the Toronto Maple Leafs and hit .380 to lead the league. In 1918 he was managing the Indianapolis team in the American Association when World War I forced the closure of the league, and Lajoie left baseball for good. Lajoie was elected to the Hall of Fame in 1937.

CAREER INDIANS RECORD:

Games	AB	Hits	Runs
1,614	6,034	2,046	865
Avg	**HR**	**RBI**	**SB**
.339	34	919	240

LEMON, BOB (SP/RP) (1946–1958)

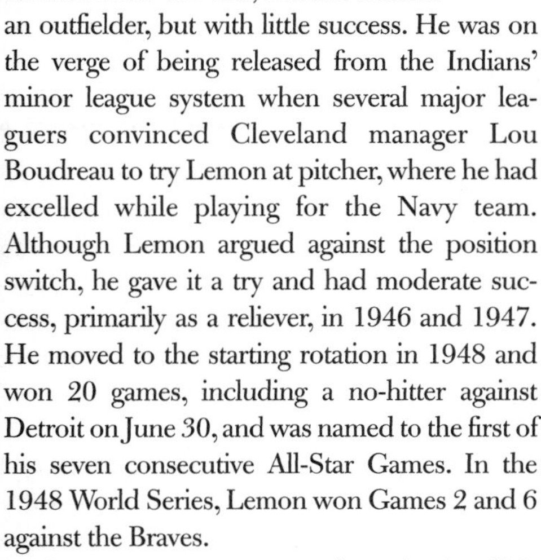

Bob Lemon signed on with the Indians as an amateur free agent before the 1938 season opened. With the outbreak of World War II, Lemon left the minors to join the Navy, where he pitched for a service team in Hawaii. After the war, Lemon became an outfielder, but with little success. He was on the verge of being released from the Indians' minor league system when several major leaguers convinced Cleveland manager Lou Boudreau to try Lemon at pitcher, where he had excelled while playing for the Navy team. Although Lemon argued against the position switch, he gave it a try and had moderate success, primarily as a reliever, in 1946 and 1947. He moved to the starting rotation in 1948 and won 20 games, including a no-hitter against Detroit on June 30, and was named to the first of his seven consecutive All-Star Games. In the 1948 World Series, Lemon won Games 2 and 6 against the Braves.

Lemon was a 20-game winner in six of his first seven seasons as a starter. In the nine years from 1948 to 1956, workhorse Lemon led the American League in wins three times, complete games five times, and innings pitched four times. As a hitter, Lemon finished his career with 37 home runs, one behind Wes Ferrell on the career list for pitchers. Lemon was an easygoing guy whose career and life were summed up in a declaration he followed faithfully: "I had my bad days on the field, but I didn't take them home with me. I left them in a bar along the way." After a leg injury forced him to retire as a player, Lemon became a scout for the Indians, Royals, and Yankees before managing in the minors. He later managed the Royals, White Sox, and Yankees. After he replaced Billy Martin in midseason 1978, Lemon's low-key style of managing brought together the dissension-ridden Yankees, rallying them from fourth place in their division to a World Series championship. For the last 20 years of his life, Lemon remained a scout and adviser to New York Yankees owner George Steinbrenner. Lemon was elected to the Hall of Fame in 1976, and died in 2000.

CAREER INDIANS RECORD:

W	L	W%	ERA	SV
207	128	.618	3.23	22
K	**BB**	**SHO**	**IP**	
1,277	1,251	31	2,850.0	

LOFTON, KENNY (OF)
(1992–1996, 1998–2001)

Kenny Lofton was the point guard on Arizona's Final Four basketball team in 1988 and was expecting to play in the NBA, but instead he fell in love with baseball. He didn't play baseball in college until late in his junior year, when he made the Arizona team as a walk-on. Though he hardly played in college, the Houston Astros drafted him in the 17th round of the June 1988 amateur draft. After playing only 20 games with Houston in 1991, Lofton was traded to Cleveland, where he became a star with the emerging Indians.

Lofton became the team's leadoff hitter and center fielder. An excellent base stealer, Lofton led the American League in steals five straight years from 1992 to 1996, averaging 65 stolen bases a year. He also won four consecutive Gold Gloves from 1993 to 1996 and hit well over .300 in each of those years. On March 25, 1997, Lofton was traded to Atlanta along with Alan Embree for Marquis Grissom and Dave Justice. After just a year in Atlanta, Lofton became a free agent and signed on with Cleveland for a second tour of duty. His next four years with Cleveland were decent, but no match for his first five years. Lofton's batting average in his second stint was in the .270s and his stolen bases averaged 31. After the 2001 season, Lofton left Cleveland a second time, this time as a free agent. Over the next four years, Lofton bounced around with six teams, finishing 2005 as a part-time player with the Phillies.

CAREER INDIANS RECORD:

Games	AB	Hits	Runs
1,224	4,872	1,463	951
Avg	**HR**	**RBI**	**SB**
.300	87	503	450

MCDOWELL, SAM (SP/RP)
(1961–1971)

"Sudden Sam" McDowell was so dominating for six years in the 1960s that he earned the nickname, "the American League Sandy Koufax." Signed by the Indians as a 17-year-old right out of high school for a $75,000 bonus, McDowell was in the Cleveland rotation by age 19. With his immense talent at such a young age, McDowell felt the pressure of competing on the major league level and soon turned to alcohol to cope. He became an alcoholic at a very young age and constantly argued with umpires and teammates. Former pitcher Dick Radatz recalled, "We thought he was just stupid. Turns out he was never sober." Once McDowell got a handle on his alcoholism by seeking treatment and admitting he was—according to *Baseball: The Biographical Encyclopedia*— ". . . the biggest, most hopeless, and most violent drunk in baseball," he began to counsel other major leaguers with similar problems.

When he could harness his talent, McDowell was dominating. In 1965 he led the league with a 2.18 ERA and 325 strikeouts, winning 17 games for a weak Indians team. In 1966 he pitched back-to-back one-hitters. In 1968 McDowell struck out 283 batters to lead an Indians staff that struck out 1,157 batters while giving up only 1,087 hits, the only time in major league history that a pitching staff has recorded more strikeouts in a season than hits allowed. In 1970 McDowell was named *The Sporting News* Pitcher of the Year when he had his only 20-win season and struck out 304 batters.

When he asked for a salary raise to $100,000, Cleveland GM/manager Alvin Dark balked. Together they worked out an incentive-laden contract that could have netted McDowell as much as $92,000, but Commissioner Bowie Kuhn voided the 1971 deal because baseball at the time prohibited performance bonuses. Kuhn also fined the Indians $5,000 for the mistake. McDowell was so angry at Kuhn's action that he left the team and demanded to be declared a free agent. Cleveland suspended him. McDowell returned to the team a few days later, but sulked about the situation the entire year. He went 13–17 in 1971 with his lowest strikeout total in seven years. By the end of the season, McDowell and the Indians were both ready to sever their relationship. In November, Cleveland traded McDowell to San Francisco for Gaylord Perry. While Perry won 24 games for Cleveland in 1972, the brooding McDowell would win only 19 more games over the next four years for the Giants, Yankees, and Pirates before calling it quits.

CAREER INDIANS RECORD:

W	L	W%	ERA	SV
122	109	.528	2.99	11
K	BB	SHO	IP	
2,159	1,072	22	2,109.7	

RAMIREZ, MANNY (OF)
(1993–2000)

Manny Ramirez was selected in the first round of the June 1991 amateur draft. After seeing some major league action in 1993 and 1994, Ramirez joined the team for good in 1995 and quickly established himself as one of the best sluggers in the game. In the decade since, he has made his mark as one of the greatest sluggers of all time. Although Ramirez has earned a reputation for childish behavior, the numbers he puts up year after year are clearly the work of a talented grownup. In his first full season, the strike-shortened 1995, he hit .308 with 31 homers and 107 RBIs—and those numbers remain very nearly career lows in each category! While he approached Ruthian numbers at times in the regular season, his performances with Cleveland in the postseason often petered out. He was picked off first base in various playoff games, ending potential rallies. He committed key mental and physical errors that cost Cleveland dearly. He seemed so distracted at times on the field that the Indians sought the services of a psychologist in 1998 to help him improve his focus.

The results were amazing. Ramirez responded by hitting 45 homers with 145 RBIs. The next year he slugged 44 homers with 165 RBIs, breaking Hal Trosky's 63-year-old club RBI record. In 2000, his final year with Cleveland, he hit .351, his highest average yet, although his power numbers dipped just a bit to 38 homers and 122 RBIs. In December 2000, Ramirez, one of the most feared hitters in the game today, left Cleveland via free agency and signed a huge deal with the Red Sox. *(See Red Sox bio.)*

CAREER INDIANS RECORD:

Games	AB	Hits	Runs
967	3,470	1,086	665
Avg	HR	RBI	SB
.313	236	804	28

SEWELL, JOE (SS/3B) (1920–1930)

Joe Sewell's dad was an Alabama country doctor who encouraged all three of his sons to attend the University of Alabama, which they did. All three made it to the major leagues after playing on an Alabama team that sent an amazing total of seven players to the majors. Luke was a catcher in the American League for 20 years while Tommy had one at-bat with the Cubs in 1927. Upon leaving Alabama, Joe Sewell signed with the New Orleans Pelicans of the Southern Association. After just 92 games in New Orleans, Sewell was called up to Cleveland. The Indians' beloved shortstop, Ray Chapman, had been killed by a pitch from Carl Mays and Chapman's replacement, Harry Lunte, had become injured after just two weeks. As a rookie operating under the dual pressures of a tight pennant race and replacing a fan favorite in Chapman, Sewell had a remarkable September. He hit .329 with 12 RBIs and 14 runs in his 22-game run to help the Indians capture their first-ever AL pennant and World Series title. His performance locked up the shortstop spot, a position he held for the next eight years.

No batter in major league history was harder to strike out than Joe Sewell, who fanned only once every 63 at-bats. (His closest competitor is Lloyd Waner of the Pirates, at once every 45 at-bats.) Sewell claimed he could see the ball leave his bat. When others scoffed at his claim, he answered by saying that players see the ball all the time before they hit it, so why was it so hard to believe they can see it *after* they hit it? Sewell had a 460-consecutive-game streak ended when he was spiked on play at second base. After missing just one game, he began another streak of 1,103 consecutive games before the flu knocked him out of the lineup. His second streak was a major league record at the time. In 1929 he was moved to third base for two years before being released.

He played the next three years as the Yankees' third baseman before retiring. While with the Yankees, Sewell played in the 1932 World Series. When asked about Ruth's alleged called shot, Sewell said, "Yes, sir. I was there. I saw it. I don't care what anybody says. He did it. He probably couldn't have done it again for a thousand years, but he did it that time." After retiring as a player, Sewell coached for the Yankees for two years, then scouted for Cleveland and the Mets for 12 more. Following six years of coaching the University of Alabama team, Sewell opened a hardware store. In 1977 he was inducted in the Baseball Hall of Fame.

CAREER INDIANS RECORD:

Games	AB	Hits	Runs
1,513	5,621	1,800	857
Avg	**HR**	**RBI**	**SB**
.320	30	869	71

SPEAKER, TRIS (OF)
(1916–1926)

After Speaker joined Cleveland in 1916 over a salary dispute with Boston owner Joe Lannin, he promptly won the American League batting title with a .386 average. He also led the league with 211 hits, 41 doubles, a .470 on-base percentage, and a .502 slugging average. In nine of his 10 seasons in Cleveland, Speaker hit over .300. The only year he missed was 1919, his first year as player-manager. In 1920 Speaker rallied his team after the death of shortstop Ray Chapman. He used a platoon system for half his team and cajoled every win possible from his pitching staff as the Indians squeaked out their first pennant—by two games over the scandal-ridden White Sox and three games over the Yankees. He also led the team with a .388 average and 107 RBIs. In the 1920 World Series against Brooklyn that produced the first Series grand slam, the first home run by a pitcher, and first (and only) unassisted triple play, Speaker's Indians defeated the Robins (now Dodgers), five games to two in the best-of-nine Series. In 1923 Speaker hit .380 with 130 RBIs, and in 1925 he hit a career-high .389.

After the 1926 season, Dutch Leonard, a disgruntled former player, accused Speaker and Ty Cobb of game-fixing and gambling on a game back in 1919. *(See Ty Cobb bio, Tigers.)* Commissioner Landis cleared Speaker and Cobb, but the Cleveland player-manager resigned and retired after 11 seasons with the Indians. Before the next season, however, Speaker came out of retirement and played two more years, one each with the Senators and A's. After retiring for good, Speaker managed in the minors for two years, then became a broadcaster in Kansas City. After World War II he coached for Cleveland, tutoring Larry Doby to stardom. In 1937 Speaker was elected to the Hall of Fame. *(See Red Sox bio.)*

CAREER INDIANS RECORD:

Games	AB	Hits	Runs
1,519	5,546	1,965	1,079
Avg	**HR**	**RBI**	**SB**
.354	73	884	151

THOME, JIM (1B/3B/DH)
(1991–2002)

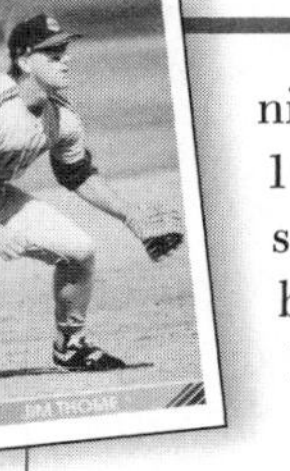

The Indians drafted Jim Thome out of junior college in the 13th round of the June 1989 draft. Originally a third baseman for his first six years in Cleveland, Thome was moved to first base in 1997 and has remained there since. Thome and his home run bat were instrumental in helping Cleveland to five consecutive postseasons from 1995 to 1999, and six of seven overall. A steady run producer, Thome averaged around 40+ homers and 100+ runs and RBIs in the nine years from 1996–2004. In 1999, Thome drove in 108 runs and scored 101 to help the Indians become the first team since the 1950 Boston Red Sox to score more than 1,000 runs in a season.

Thome has been very productive in postseason play, hitting 17 homers with 36 RBIs and 32 runs in 55 games. After the 2002 season, Thome, a three-time All-Star with the Indians, left Cleveland via free agency and signed with Philadelphia. In 2005, he returned to the American League and was traded to the White Sox in a deal that sent Aaron Rowand to Philadelphia.

CAREER INDIANS RECORD:

Games	AB	Hits	Runs
1,377	4,640	1,332	917
Avg	**HR**	**RBI**	**SB**
.287	334	927	18

THORNTON, ANDRE (DH/1B) (1977–1979, 1981–1987)

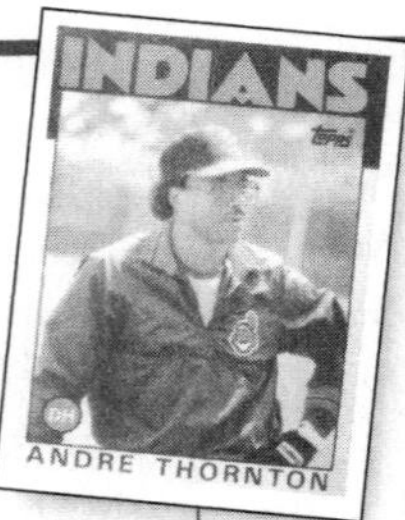

After four years with the Cubs and Expos, Thornton was traded to the Indians following the 1976 season for Jackie Brown, one of the more lopsided trades in Cleveland history. Thornton was a quiet man of devout Christian beliefs who also happened to lead the Indians in home runs seven times in his 11 years with the Tribe. Thornton was only the second Indian ever—Al Rosen was the first in 1950—to record 100 RBIs and 100 walks in the same season. Thornton stands second on Cleveland's all-time home run list, and had he not missed nearly two years of playing time due to injuries (including all of 1980), he easily would have become Cleveland's all-time leader, since he retired just 12 homers behind Earl Averill.

CAREER INDIANS RECORD:

Games	AB	Hits	Runs
1,225	4,313	1,095	650
Avg	**HR**	**RBI**	**SB**
.254	214	749	39

TROSKY, HAL (1B) (1933–1941)

Born and raised an Iowa farm boy, Trosky began his career in the minors playing for the Cedar Rapids, Dubuque, Quincy, and Burlington teams of the Mississippi Valley League. He also played for Toledo of the American Association. Wherever he played, he hit at least .300 and was an excellent fielding first baseman. After a late-season call-up to Cleveland in 1933, Trosky joined the Indians for good in 1934 and won the first-base job in spring training. Trosky's rookie season in 1934 was one of the best ever recorded. He hit .330 with 35 homers and 142 RBIs and played in all 154 games. Mark McGwire and Al Rosen are the only two rookies in American League history to hit more homers, and Ted Williams and Walt Dropo are the only two AL rookies to record more RBIs. After a mild sophomore slump to .271 with 26 homers and 113 RBIs, Trosky set career highs across the board in 1936 with a .343 average, 42 homers, and 162 RBIs, compiling a 28-game hitting streak along the way. He also joined an elite group by recording 40 homers and 200 hits in the same season. Over the next three years Trosky averaged .323 with 25 homers, 100 runs, and 114 RBIs.

Then, in 1940, trouble set in. Trosky became known as one of the "Cleveland

Crybabies." *(See Mel Harder bio, earlier in this chapter.)* The whole affair seemed to affect his play. While he did hit .295 with 25 homers, 93 RBIs and 84 runs, all of those numbers were either career lows or close to it. In 1941 Trosky, suffering from severe migraine headaches, played in little more than half of Cleveland's games and after the season he announced his retirement from the game. Just 28 years old, Trosky finished his Indians career just 10 homers behind Earl Averill on Cleveland's career list and returned to farm the rich Iowa soil. Three years later, in 1944, he decided to try a comeback and signed with the White Sox. After hitting just .241 with 10 homers in 135 games, Trosky retired again. Two years later he again tried a comeback, but hit only .254 with just two homers and 31 RBIs in 88 games. He retired a third time, this time for good, and later became a scout for the White Sox.

CAREER INDIANS RECORD:

Games	AB	Hits	Runs
1,124	4,365	1,365	758
Avg	**HR**	**RBI**	**SB**
.313	216	911	21

VIZQUEL, OMAR (SS)
(1994–2004)

Venezuelan Omar Vizquel was a light-hitting, bottom-of-the-order shortstop for the Seattle Mariners for five years before he was traded to Cleveland for Felix Fermin and Reggie Jefferson following the 1993 season. Once in Cleveland, Vizquel discovered that defensive whizzes were allowed to produce offensively, too, and he became a base-stealing threat who doubled his previous totals in runs and doubles, and raised his average by 40–50 points. And, after averaging less than eight steals a year for Seattle, he suddenly began to swipe 35–40 bases for Cleveland each year. Vizquel had won his first Gold Glove in 1993, his last year in Seattle. Beginning in 1994 Vizquel, a three-time All-Star, won eight consecutive Gold Gloves in Cleveland. After the 2004 season—his 11th in Cleveland—Vizquel left via free agency and signed with the Giants.

CAREER INDIANS RECORD:

Games	AB	Hits	Runs
1,478	5,708	1,616	906
Avg	**HR**	**RBI**	**SB**
.283	60	584	279

WYNN, EARLY (SP/RP)
(1949–1957, 1963)

After spending eight seasons pitching for the lowly Senators, Early Wynn was traded to the Indians along with Mickey Vernon for three players after the 1948 season. Mickey Mantle, Ted Williams, and other great hitters of the era considered Wynn the meanest pitcher in baseball. Wynn liked to use inside fastballs to establish his control of the plate, which for him consisted of the plate and one foot on either side of it. He once asked fellow fishing enthusiast Ted Williams to accompany him on a fishing trip to the Florida Everglades, but Williams refused, telling Wynn, "No hitter would ever go into the Everglades with you. His body might never be found." Wynn was a very good hitting pitcher, compiling 17 homers and 173 RBIs over his career.

Once Wynn arrived in Cleveland, he credited Mel Harder with making him a consistent winner. In 1950 he was 18–8 and led the league in ERA at 3.20. In 1951 he was one of three Indians pitchers to win 20 games, joining Bob Feller and Mike Garcia, as the Indians lost a close pennant race to the Yankees. In 1952 Wynn won 23 games, but again the Indians lost a close pennant race to the Yanks. After another second-place finish to New York in 1953, the Indians turned it on in 1954 and routed the league with 111 wins, 23 of them belonging to Wynn. His last 20-win season with Cleveland came in 1956. During the season, Wynn was hit in the face by a line drive off the bat of Jose Valdivielso. Wynn didn't come out of the game right away, but when he did later, it turned out he had lost seven teeth and needed 16 stitches to close the gash. Wynn endured a tough year in 1957, going 14–17 and posting his highest ERA in a decade.

After the 1957 season, Wynn was traded to the White Sox in a four-player deal that brought Minnie Minoso to Cleveland. After five seasons in Chicago, including a 22-win season in 1959, Wynn was released in 1962 by the White Sox with 299 career wins. In mid-1963 the Indians picked him up and let him pitch a few games in order to get his 300th career win, which he did on July 13 against Kansas City. Some felt Wynn backed into his 300th win by pitching only five innings and hanging on for the victory, but Wynn, who pitched in four different decades, didn't see it that way, considering all the games he lost early in his career. He cited the paltry support he'd gotten for many years, enduring 45 losses in which his team was shut out. Worth noting is the fact that Wynn had only 83 victories by the time he was 30, yet won 217 more after turning 30. After retiring as a player, Wynn became a pitching coach with the Indians and Twins, and later managed in Minnesota's farm system. He then became a broadcaster for the Blue Jays and White Sox. Wynn was inducted into the Hall of Fame in 1972.

CAREER INDIANS RECORD:

W	L	W%	ERA	SV
164	102	.617	3.24	10

K	BB	SHO	IP
1,277	877	24	2,286.7

Colorado Rockies

Since 1993

1993 The Rockies sweep a four-game series against the Dodgers in Los Angeles on August 9–12. It is the first time an expansion team has ever swept a four-game series from an established team in the latter's home park. The same season, Andres Galarraga becomes the first expansion player to win the batting crown, with a .370 average.... **1995** The Rockies make the playoffs in only their third season of existence—the fastest team in major league history to do so.... **1996** The Rockies become the first team to have at least 200 homers and 200 stolen bases in the same season, as well as the first team to have four players with at least 30 homers *twice*.... **1999** Rockies pitchers allow 1,028 runs, the first time since 1930 that a National League team has allowed more than 1,000 runs.

FRANCHISE HISTORY

The Colorado Rockies began play in 1993, the same year as the Florida Marlins. A consortium of minority investors came together to raise the necessary expansion fee of $95 million. Principal among the numerous owners were John Antonucci, owner of a wholesale beverage business and a chain of Midwestern drug- and grocery stores, and Jerry McMorris, a man who made his fortune in the trucking business. The Coors Brewing Company and the Denver Newspaper Agency also had significant stakes in the new team. In 2003, limited partner Charles K. Monfort took over as team chairman and CEO, replacing McMorris, who had held the position since 1992.

The Rockies set an Opening Day attendance record in 1993 when they attracted 80,277 fans to their April 9th game in Mile High Stadium. The team repaid them by establishing a new National League record for wins by an expansion team, with 67. In 1995 the Rockies finished in second place in the NL West, one game behind the Dodgers. This earned them the distinction of being the first Wild Card winner in the National League under the league's new playoff format. By reaching the playoffs in only their third year of existence, the Rockies achieved the feat faster than any previous expansion team.

The Rockies proved a popular franchise, drawing 4,483,350 fans in the team's first season, a major league record. Over the next eight seasons, the Rockies drew more than 3 million fans each year. They rewarded their fans with winning records in four of their first eight years, and an exciting brand of offensive baseball enhanced by the Mile High City's thin air. However, because the offense is so abundant in Colorado, many top free-agent pitchers have refused to sign with the Rockies, fearing the inflated stats will hinder better contracts down the road.

TEAM NAME HISTORY

Official Names
Rockies

Unofficial Names/Nicknames
Rocks

STADIUM HISTORY

Mile High Stadium	1993–1994
Coors Field	1995–current

The Rockies take their traditional end-of-season walk around Coor's Field—this one led by manager Don Baylor on September 27, 1998.

YEARLY RECORD, FINISH, & ATTENDANCE FIGURES

Year	League	Record	DIV/LG Finish	Attendance	Avg/Gm
2005	NL West	67–95	5	1,914,389	23,634
2004	NL West	68–94	4	2,338,069	28,865
2003	NL West	74–88	4	2,334,085	28,816
2002	NL West	73–89	4	2,737,838	33,800
2001	NL West	73–89	5	3,166,821	39,097
2000	NL West	82–80	4	3,295,129	40,681
1999	NL West	72–90	5	3,481,065	42,976
1998	NL West	77–85	4	3,792,683	46,823
1997	NL West	83–79	3	3,888,453	48,006
1996	NL West	83–79	3	3,891,014	48,037
1995	NL West	77–67	2	3,390,037	47,084
1994	NL West	53–64	3	3,281,511	57,570
1993	NL West	67–95	6	4,483,350	55,350

MANAGER HISTORY

Manager	Years	W–L	Win %
Don Baylor	1993–1998	440–469	.484
Jim Leyland	1999	72–90	.444
Buddy Bell	2000–2002	161–185	.465
Clint Hurdle	2002–2005	276–350	.441

ALL-TIME WIN-LOSS RECORDS VS. ALL OPPONENTS

ALL-TIME	949–1,094
Angels	4–12
Astros	55–58
Athletics	7–9
Blue Jays	0–3
Braves	41–75
Brewers	30–29
Cardinals	62–58
Cubs	57–61
Devil Rays	3–3
Diamondbacks	59–73
Dodgers	85–109
Giants	79–114
Indians	5–7
INTERLEAGUE	55–75
Mariners	7–12
Marlins	59–59
Mets	52–58
Nationals	58–50
Orioles	3–3
Padres	97–96
Phillies	49–57
Pirates	57–59
Rangers	8–8
Reds	54–63
Red Sox	3–3
Royals	4–2
Tigers	9–3
Twins	1–2
White Sox	0–3
Yankees	1–5

Franchise Highlights, Low Points, and Strange Distinctions

1993 Several Rockies set individual major league expansion records: Andres Galarraga and Charlie Hayes with 98 RBIs each; Hayes with 175 hits and 45 doubles; and Dante Bichette with 93 runs.

••••

1995 The Rockies became the second team in history to have four players with 30 or more homers in a season (despite a shortened season due to labor strife). They were Dante Bichette (40), Larry Walker (36), Vinny Castilla (32), and Andres Galarraga (31).

In 1995, John Vander Wal set a major league single-season record with 28 pinch hits.

••••

1996 When the season was over, outfielder Ellis Burks had done something only one other player in history (Hank Aaron) had done: hit 40 homers, steal 30 bases, and collect 200 hits in the same season.

••••

1997 The Rockies became the first team in major league history to hit more than 200 homers (239) and turn 200 double plays (202) in the same season.

••••

1999 Larry Walker won his second consecutive batting title. He also became the first National Leaguer since Stan Musial in 1948 to lead the league in batting average, slugging percentage, and on-base percentage—the so-called "percentage Triple Crown." The next year, fellow Rockies teammate Todd Helton performed the same amazing feat.

Colorado ended the 1999 season in the National League West's cellar, their first-ever last-place finish. This was, amazingly, the expansion team's seventh season.

Larry Walker hit an incredible .461 for the 1999 season during home games at Coors Field.

When Colorado scored in every inning of a 13–6 win over the Cubs at Wrigley Field on May 5, 1999, it marked the first time in 35 years that a major league team had accomplished the feat.

••••

2000 As if we needed any more evidence for the trials and tribulations of pitching in Coors Field: In 2000 starting pitcher Brian Bohanon had a National League-best road ERA of 2.789, just nipping Cy Young winner Randy Johnson, who finished with a road ERA of 2.793. But thanks to the thin mountain air in Colorado, Bohanon's overall ERA for the year was 4.68.

••••

2001 On August 23, 2001, rookie Jason Jennings had one of the most memorable major league debuts in history. He pitched a complete game, five-hit shutout at New York and also hit a home run in the 10–0 gem.

Third baseman Jeff Cirillo ended the 2001 season with an 85-game errorless streak that shattered the old National League record.

Special Achievements

WORLD SERIES RESULTS

None

WORLD SERIES MANAGERIAL RECORDS

None

ALL-TIME POST-SEASON RECORD

Divisional Playoffs	1–3
League Championship Series	0–0
World Series	0–0

ALL-STAR GAMES AT COLORADO

Year	Date	Winner	Score	Stadium
1998	July 7	American	13–8	Coors Field

HALL OF FAMERS WHO PLAYED FOR TEAM

None

HALL OF FAMERS WHO MANAGED TEAM

None

MVP AWARD WINNERS

Larry Walker	OF	1997

CY YOUNG AWARD WINNERS

None

ROOKIE OF THE YEAR AWARD WINNERS

Jason Jennings	SP	2002

GOLD GLOVE WINNERS

Year	Position	Player
1997	OF	Larry Walker
1998	OF	Larry Walker
1999	OF	Larry Walker
2000	SS	Neifi Perez
2001	1B OF	Todd Helton Larry Walker
2002	1B OF	Todd Helton Larry Walker
2004	1B	Todd Helton

TRIPLE CROWN WINNERS

None

FIREMAN OF THE YEAR AWARD WINNERS

None

WORLD SERIES MVP

None

LEAGUE CHAMPIONSHIP SERIES MVP

None

ALL-STAR GAME MVP

None

MANAGER OF THE YEAR AWARD WINNERS

Don Baylor	1995

BATTING CHAMPIONS

Player	Year	Avg
Andres Galarraga	1993	.370
Larry Walker	1998	.363
Larry Walker	1999	.379
Todd Helton	2000	.372
Larry Walker	2001	.350

NINE-INNING NO-HITTERS PITCHED

None

20-GAME WINNERS

None

RETIRED UNIFORM NUMBERS

None

TEAM RECORDS—WINS & LOSSES

- Games won in a season: 83 in 1996 and 1997
- Games lost in a season: 95 in 1993 and 2005
- Games won in a month: 19 in May 2002
- Games lost in a month: 22 in July 2000
- Consecutive games won: 9 in 1997
- Consecutive games lost: 13 in 1993
- Biggest shutout victory: 11–0 over Florida (August 6, 1996) and San Diego (September 13, 2000)

- Biggest shutout loss: 17–0 to Florida on Sept. 17, 1995
- Highest winning percentage: .535 in 1995 (77–67)
- Lowest winning percentage: .414 in 1993 and 2005 (67–95)

TEAM RECORDS—BATTING

- Highest team batting average: .294 in 2000
- Lowest team batting average: .267 in 2003 and 2005
- Highest team slugging average: .483 in 2001
- Highest on-base percentage: .362 in 2000
- Total hits: 1,664 in 2000
- Extra-base hits: 598 in 2001
- Hits in a game: 24 vs. Montreal on May 3, 2000, and Pittsburgh on August 3, 2003
- Longest individual hitting streak: 23, Dante Bichette, 1995
- Most .300 hitters in a single season: 5 in 1996
- Home runs: 239 in 1997
- Home runs in a month: 12, accomplished four times (Dante Bichette, August 1995; Andres Galarraga, August 1996; and Vinny Castilla twice, June 1996 and July 1998)
- Home runs in a game: 7 vs. Montreal on April 5, 1997
- Home runs by a rookie: 25, Todd Helton, 1998
- Home runs by a right-hander: 47, Andres Galarraga, 1996
- Home runs by a left-hander: 49, Larry Walker, 1997, and Todd Helton, 2001
- Home runs by a switch-hitter: 13, Greg Norton, 2001
- Grand slams: 5 in four different seasons
- Grand slams (individual; single season): 2, accomplished by many players
- Grand slams (individual; career): 6, Andres Galarraga and Dante Bichette
- Triples: 61 in 2001
- Doubles: 333 in 1998
- Singles: 1,130 in 2000
- Walks: 619 in 2003
- Runs scored: 968 in 2000
- Runs scored in a game: 20 (twice) vs. Arizona on September 23, 2003 and vs. San Diego on September 20, 2005
- Runs scored in an inning: 11 vs. San Diego on July 12, 1996 (seventh inning)
- Most batters hit by a pitch: 82 in 1996
- Times shut out: 13 in 1993
- Grounded into double plays: 148 in 1998
- Fewest grounded into double plays: 116 in 2001
- Runners left on base: 1,244 in 2005

TEAM RECORDS—BASERUNNING

- Stolen bases: 201 in 1996
- Caught stealing: 90 in 1993

TEAM RECORDS—PITCHING

- Lowest earned run average: 4.97 in 1995
- Complete games: 12 in 1999
- Saves: 43 in 1995 and 2002
- Strikeouts: 1,058 in 2001
- Shutouts: 8 in 2001 and 2002
- Walks: 737 in 1999
- Hit batsmen: 84 in 2003 and 2005
- Wild pitches: 82 in 1993
- Consecutive wins (individual): 9, Julian Tavarez, 2000
- Consecutive losses (individual): 8, Greg Harris, 1994, and Darryl Kile, 1998
- Strikeouts in a game (individual): 14, Darryl Kile, August 20, 1998
- Runs allowed in a game: 26 vs. Chicago Cubs, August 18, 1995

TEAM RECORDS—FIELDING

- Best fielding average: .986 in 2004
- Most errors committed: 167 in 1993
- Fewest errors committed: 89 in 2004
- Most double plays turned: 202 in 1997
- Fewest double plays turned: 149 in 1993

TEAM RECORDS—MISCELLANEOUS

- Number of times league champions: 0
- Number of times finishing last in league: 1
- Largest attendance, single game: 80,227 vs. Montreal, April 9, 1993
- Largest attendance, doubleheader: 60,613 vs. New York, August 21, 1993
- Players used in a season: 54 in 2005
- Seasons played: 10, Larry Walker

Primary Pitching Staffs

Year	Starter	Starter	Starter	Starter	Starter	Closer	Bullpen	Bullpen	Bullpen
2005	Francis	Wright	Kim	Jennings	Kennedy	Fuentes	Cortes	Carvajal	DeJean
2004	Estes	Jennings	Kennedy	Cook	Wright	Chacon	Harikkala	Lopez	Reed
2003	Oliver	Jennings	Chacon	Cook	Stark	Jimenez	Fuentes	Lopez	Speier
2002	Hampton	Jennings	Chacon	Neagle	Thomson	Jimenez	Jones	Mercker	Speier
2001	Hampton	Astacio	Chacon	Neagle	Bohanon	Jimenez	Myers	White	Davis
2000	Yoshii	Astacio	Arrojo	Jarvis	Bohanon	Jimenez	Myers	White	DeJean
1999	Kile	Astacio	Jones	Wright	Bohanon	Veres	Leskanic	Dipoto	DeJean
1998	Kile	Astacio	Jones	Wright	Thomson	Dipoto	Leskanic	McElroy	Veres
1997	Bailey	Ritz	Castillo	Wright	Thomson	Dipoto	Leskanic	Munoz	Reed
1996	Reynoso	Ritz	Thompson	Wright	Freeman	Ruffin	Leskanic	Holmes	Reed
1995	Reynoso	Ritz	Swift	Rekar	Freeman	Holmes	Leskanic	Munoz	Reed
1994	Nied	Ritz	Harris	Painter	Freeman	Ruffin	Blair	Munoz	Reed
1993	Nied	Reynoso	Blair	Henry	Bottenfield	Holmes	Wayne	Ruffin	Reed

Primary Starting Lineups

Year	C	1B	2B	3B	SS	LF	CF	RF
2005	Ardoin	Helton	Gonzalez	Atkins	Barmes	Holliday	Sullivan	Hawpe
2004	Johnson	Helton	Miles	Castilla	Clayton	Holliday	Wilson	Burnitz
2003	Johnson	Helton	Belliard	Stynes	Uribe	Payton	Wilson	Walker
2002	Bennett	Helton	Butler	Zeile	Uribe	Hollandsworth	Pierre	Walker
2001	Petrick	Helton	Walker	Cirillo	Perez	Gant	Pierre	Walker
2000	Mayne	Helton	Lansing	Cirillo	Perez	Shumpert	Goodwin	Hammonds
1999	Blanco	Helton	Abbott	Castilla	Perez	Bichette	Hamilton	Walker
1998	Manwaring	Helton	Lansing	Castilla	Perez	Bichette	Burks	Walker
1997	Manwaring	Galarraga	Young	Castilla	Weiss	Bichette	McCracken	Walker
1996	Reed	Galarraga	Young	Castilla	Weiss	Burks	McCracken	Bichette
1995	Girardi	Galarraga	Bates	Castilla	Weiss	Bichette	Kingery	Walker
1994	Girardi	Galarraga	Liriano	Hayes	Weiss	Johnson	Kingery	Bichette
1993	Girardi	Galarraga	Young	Hayes	Castilla	Clark	Cole	Bichette

Coors Field

Top 10 Batting Leaders, Single Season & Career with Team

Games Played: Career with Team

Player	G	PA
1. Todd Helton	1,279	5,424
2. Larry Walker	1,170	4,795
3. Vinny Castilla	1,083	4,429
4. Dante Bichette	1,018	4,351
5. Andres Galarraga	679	2,924
6. Neifi Perez	668	2,936
7. Eric Young	613	2,450
8. Walt Weiss	523	2,115
9. Ellis Burks	520	2,053
10. John Vander Wal	465	641

At-Bats: Season

Player	AB	Year
1. Neifi Perez	690	1999
2. Dante Bichette	662	1998
3. Neifi Perez	651	2000
4. Neifi Perez	647	1998
5. Vinny Castilla	645	1998
6. Dante Bichette	633	1996
7. Vinny Castilla	629	1996
8. Andres Galarraga	626	1996
9. Juan Pierre	617	2001
10. Vinny Castilla	615	1999

At-Bats: Career with Team

Player	AB	PA
1. Todd Helton	4,560	5,424
2. Vinny Castilla	4,078	4,429
3. Larry Walker	4,076	4,795
4. Dante Bichette	4,050	4,351
5. Neifi Perez	2,728	2,936
6. Andres Galarraga	2,667	2,924
7. Eric Young	2,120	2,450
8. Ellis Burks	1,821	2,053
9. Walt Weiss	1,760	2,115
10. Juan Pierre	1,409	1,542

Batting Average: Season

Player	BA	Year
1. Larry Walker	.379	1999
2. Todd Helton	.372	2000
3. Andres Galarraga	.370	1993
4. Larry Walker	.366	1997
5. Larry Walker	.363	1998
6. Todd Helton	.358	2003
7. Larry Walker	.350	2001
8. Mike Kingery	.349	1994
9. Todd Helton	.347	2004
John Vander Wal	.347	1995

Batting Average: Career with Team

Player	BA	PA
1. Todd Helton	.337	5,424
2. Larry Walker	.334	4,795
3. Andres Galarraga	.316	2,924
Dante Bichette	.316	4,351
5. Juan Pierre	.308	1,542
6. Ellis Burks	.306	2,053
7. Eric Young	.295	2,450
Vinny Castilla	.295	4,429
9. Neifi Perez	.282	2,936
10. Walt Weiss	.266	2,115

Total Hits: Season

Player	H	Year
1. Dante Bichette	219	1998
2. Todd Helton	216	2000
3. Ellis Burks	211	1996
4. Todd Helton	209	2003
5. Larry Walker	208	1997
6. Vinny Castilla	206	1998
7. Juan Pierre	202	2001
8. Dante Bichette	198	1996
9. Dante Bichette	197	1995
Todd Helton	197	2001

Total Hits: Career with Team

Player	H	PA
1. Todd Helton	1,535	5,424
2. Larry Walker	1,361	4,795
3. Dante Bichette	1,278	4,351
4. Vinny Castilla	1,202	4,429
5. Andres Galarraga	843	2,924
6. Neifi Perez	769	2,936
7. Eric Young	626	2,450
8. Ellis Burks	558	2,053
9. Walt Weiss	469	2,115
10. Juan Pierre	434	1,542

Home Runs: Season

Player	HR	Year
1. Todd Helton	49	2001
Larry Walker	49	1997
3. Andres Galarraga	47	1996
4. Vinny Castilla	46	1998
5. Todd Helton	42	2000
6. Andres Galarraga	41	1997
7. Dante Bichette	40	1995
Ellis Burks	40	1996
Vinny Castilla	40	1996
Vinny Castilla	40	1997

Home Runs: Career with Team

Player	HR	PA
1. Todd Helton	271	5,424
2. Larry Walker	258	4,795
3. Vinny Castilla	238	4,429
4. Dante Bichette	201	4,351
5. Andres Galarraga	172	2,924
6. Ellis Burks	115	2,053
7. Preston Wilson	57	1,179
8. Neifi Perez	43	2,936
9. Jeromy Burnitz	37	606
10. Jay Payton	36	839
Jeff Reed	36	1,121

Triples: Season

Player	3B	Year
1. Neifi Perez	11	1999
Neifi Perez	11	2000
Juan Pierre	11	2001
Juan Uribe	11	2001
5. Neifi Perez	10	1997
6. Neifi Perez	9	1998
Eric Young	9	1995
8. Ellis Burks	8	1996
Tom Goodwin	8	2000
Mike Kingery	8	1994
Neifi Perez	8	2001
Eric Young	8	1993

Triples: Career with Team

Player	3B	PA
1. Neifi Perez	49	2,936
2. Larry Walker	44	4,795
3. Eric Young	28	2,450
4. Ellis Burks	24	2,053
Todd Helton	24	5,424
6. Juan Uribe	21	1,244
7. Vinny Castilla	20	4,429
8. Dante Bichette	18	4,351

9. Juan Pierre	16	1,542
Terry Shumpert	16	1,165

DOUBLES: SEASON

Player	2B	Year
1. Todd Helton	59	2000
2. Todd Helton	54	2001
3. Jeff Cirillo	53	2000
4. Todd Helton	49	2003
Todd Helton	49	2004
6. Dante Bichette	48	1998
7. Larry Walker	46	1997
Larry Walker	46	1998
9. Ellis Burks	45	1996
Charlie Hayes	45	1993
Todd Helton	45	2005

DOUBLES: CAREER WITH TEAM

Player	2B	PA
1. Todd Helton	373	5,424
2. Larry Walker	297	4,795
3. Dante Bichette	270	4,351
4. Vinny Castilla	208	4,429
5. Andres Galarraga	155	2,924
6. Neifi Perez	125	2,936
7. Ellis Burks	104	2,053
8. Eric Young	102	2,450
9. Jeff Cirillo	79	1,270
10. Walt Weiss	71	2,115

EXTRA-BASE HITS: SEASON

Player	XBH	Year
1. Todd Helton	105	2001
2. Todd Helton	103	2000
3. Larry Walker	99	1997
4. Ellis Burks	93	1996
5. Andres Galarraga	89	1996
6. Todd Helton	87	2003
7. Todd Helton	83	2004
8. Vinny Castilla	81	2004
9. Dante Bichette	80	1995
Preston Wilson	80	2003

EXTRA-BASE HITS: CAREER WITH TEAM

Player	XBH	PA
1. Todd Helton	668	5,424
2. Larry Walker	599	4,795
3. Dante Bichette	489	4,351
4. Vinny Castilla	466	4,429
5. Andres Galarraga	340	2,924
6. Ellis Burks	243	2,053
7. Neifi Perez	217	2,936
8. Eric Young	160	2,450
9. Preston Wilson	128	1,179
10. Jeff Cirillo	113	1,270

TOTAL BASES: SEASON

Player	TB	Year
1. Larry Walker	409	1997
2. Todd Helton	405	2000
3. Todd Helton	402	2001
4. Ellis Burks	392	1996
5. Vinny Castilla	380	1998
6. Andres Galarraga	376	1996
7. Todd Helton	367	2003
8. Dante Bichette	359	1995
9. Andres Galarraga	351	1997
10. Vinny Castilla	345	1996

TOTAL BASES: CAREER WITH TEAM

Player	TB	PA
1. Todd Helton	2,769	5,424
2. Larry Walker	2,520	4,795
3. Dante Bichette	2,187	4,351
4. Vinny Castilla	2,164	4,429
5. Andres Galarraga	1,540	2,924
6. Neifi Perez	1,121	2,936
7. Ellis Burks	1,055	2,053
8. Eric Young	874	2,450
9. Walt Weiss	610	2,115
10. Jeff Cirillo	535	1,270

RUNS BATTED IN: SEASON

Player	RBI	Year
1. Andres Galarraga	150	1996
2. Todd Helton	147	2000
3. Todd Helton	146	2001
4. Vinny Castilla	144	1998
5. Dante Bichette	141	1996
Preston Wilson	141	2003
7. Andres Galarraga	140	1997
8. Dante Bichette	133	1999
9. Vinny Castilla	131	2004
10. Larry Walker	130	1997

RUNS BATTED IN: CAREER WITH TEAM

Player	RBI	PA
1. Todd Helton	915	5,424
2. Larry Walker	848	4,795
3. Dante Bichette	826	4,351
4. Vinny Castilla	741	4,429
5. Andres Galarraga	579	2,924
6. Ellis Burks	337	2,053
7. Neifi Perez	281	2,936
8. Eric Young	227	2,450
9. Preston Wilson	217	1,179
10. Jeff Cirillo	198	1,270

RUNS SCORED: SEASON

Player	R	Year
1. Larry Walker	143	1997
2. Ellis Burks	142	1996
3. Todd Helton	138	2000
4. Todd Helton	135	2003
5. Todd Helton	132	2001
6. Andres Galarraga	120	1997
7. Andres Galarraga	119	1996
8. Todd Helton	115	2004
9. Dante Bichette	114	1996
Todd Helton	114	1999

RUNS SCORED: CAREER WITH TEAM

Player	R	PA
1. Todd Helton	924	5,424
2. Larry Walker	892	4,795
3. Dante Bichette	665	4,351
4. Vinny Castilla	609	4,429
5. Andres Galarraga	476	2,924
6. Neifi Perez	395	2,936
7. Eric Young	378	2,450
8. Ellis Burks	361	2,053
9. Walt Weiss	264	2,115
10. Juan Pierre	224	1,542

WALKS: SEASON

Player	BB	Year
1. Todd Helton	127	2004
2. Todd Helton	111	2003
3. Todd Helton	106	2005
4. Todd Helton	103	2000
5. Todd Helton	99	2002
6. Todd Helton	98	2001
Larry Walker	98	2003
Walt Weiss	98	1995
9. Larry Walker	82	2001
10. Walt Weiss	80	1996

WALKS: CAREER WITH TEAM

Player	BB	PA
1. Todd Helton	773	5,424
2. Larry Walker	584	4,795
3. Walt Weiss	300	2,115

4. Vinny Castilla	273	4,429
5. Eric Young	254	2,450
6. Dante Bichette	226	4,351
7. Ellis Burks	202	2,053
8. Andres Galarraga	169	2,924
9. Neifi Perez	133	2,936
10. Jeff Reed	132	1,121

Strikeouts: Season

Player	SO	Year
1. Andres Galarraga	157	1996
2. Andres Galarraga	146	1995
3. Andres Galarraga	141	1997
4. Preston Wilson	139	2003
5. Royce Clayton	125	2004
6. Jeromy Burnitz	124	2004
7. Juan Uribe	120	2002
8. Ellis Burks	114	1996
9. Vinny Castilla	113	2004
10. Vinny Castilla	108	1997

Strikeouts: Career with Team

Player	SO	PA
1. Larry Walker	659	4,795
2. Vinny Castilla	628	4,429
3. Todd Helton	622	5,424
4. Dante Bichette	620	4,351
5. Andres Galarraga	610	2,924
6. Ellis Burks	380	2,053
7. Neifi Perez	287	2,936
8. Preston Wilson	265	1,179
9. Walt Weiss	249	2,115
10. Juan Uribe	235	1,244

Slugging Percentage: Season

Player	SLG	Year
1. Larry Walker	.720	1997
2. Larry Walker	.710	1999
3. Todd Helton	.698	2000
4. Todd Helton	.685	2001
5. Larry Walker	.662	2001
6. Ellis Burks	.639	1996
7. Larry Walker	.630	1998
8. Todd Helton	.629	2003
9. Dante Bichette	.620	1995
Todd Helton	.620	2004

Slugging Percentage: Career with Team

Player	SLG	PA
1. Larry Walker	.618	4,795
2. Todd Helton	.607	5,424
3. Ellis Burks	.579	2,053
4. Andres Galarraga	.577	2,924
5. Dante Bichette	.540	4,351
6. Vinny Castilla	.531	4,429
7. Eric Young	.412	2,450
8. Neifi Perez	.411	2,936
9. Juan Pierre	.371	1,542
10. Walt Weiss	.347	2,115

On-Base Percentage: Season

Player	OBP	Year
1. Todd Helton	.469	2004
2. Todd Helton	.463	2000
3. Larry Walker	.458	1999
Todd Helton	.458	2003
5. Larry Walker	.452	1997
6. Larry Walker	.449	2001
7. Larry Walker	.445	1998
Todd Helton	.445	2005
9. John Vander Wal	.432	1995
Todd Helton	.432	2001

On-Base Percentage: Career with Team

Player	OBP	PA
1. Todd Helton	.433	5,424
2. Larry Walker	.426	4,795
3. Ellis Burks	.378	2,053
Eric Young	.378	2,450
5. Walt Weiss	.375	2,115
6. Andres Galarraga	.367	2,924
7. Juan Pierre	.356	1,542
8. Dante Bichette	.352	4,351
9. Vinny Castilla	.341	4,429
10. Neifi Perez	.313	2,936

OPS (On-Base Percentage + Slugging Percentage): Season

Player	OPS	Year
1. Larry Walker	1.172	1997
2. Larry Walker	1.168	1999
3. Todd Helton	1.162	2000
4. Todd Helton	1.116	2001
5. Larry Walker	1.111	2001
6. Todd Helton	1.088	2004
Todd Helton	1.088	2003
8. Larry Walker	1.075	1998
9. Ellis Burks	1.047	1996
10. John Vander Wal	1.026	1995

OPS (On-Base Percentage + Slugging Percentage): Career with Team

Player	OPS	PA
1. Larry Walker	1.044	4,795
2. Todd Helton	1.040	5,424
3. Ellis Burks	.957	2,053
4. Andres Galarraga	.944	2,924
5. Dante Bichette	.892	4,351
6. Vinny Castilla	.871	4,429
7. Eric Young	.790	2,450
8. Juan Pierre	.727	1,542
9. Neifi Perez	.724	2,936
10. Walt Weiss	.722	2,115

Stolen Bases: Season

Player	SB	Year
1. Eric Young	53	1996
2. Juan Pierre	47	2002
3. Juan Pierre	46	2001
4. Eric Young	42	1993
5. Tom Goodwin	39	2000
6. Eric Young	35	1995
7. Larry Walker	33	1997
8. Ellis Burks	32	1996
Eric Young	32	1997
10. Dante Bichette	31	1996

Stolen Bases: Career with Team

Player	SB	PA
1. Eric Young	180	2,450
2. Larry Walker	126	4,795
3. Dante Bichette	105	4,351
4. Juan Pierre	100	1,542
5. Andres Galarraga	55	2,924
6. Ellis Burks	52	2,053
7. Quinton McCracken	45	705
8. Walt Weiss	42	2,115
9. Terry Shumpert	40	1,165
10. Tom Goodwin	39	377

Sacrifice Hits: Season

Player	Sac	Year
1. Royce Clayton	24	2004
2. Neifi Perez	22	1998
3. Juan Pierre	14	2001
Walt Weiss	14	1996
5. Joe Girardi	12	1993
Joe Girardi	12	1995

Quinton McCracken	12	1996
Masato Yoshii	12	2000
9. Pedro Astacio	11	1998
Brian Bohanon	11	2000
Kevin Ritz	11	1995
Kevin Ritz	11	1996

SACRIFICE HITS: CAREER WITH TEAM

Player	Sac	PA
1. Neifi Perez	48	2,936
2. Pedro Astacio	31	319
Walt Weiss	31	2,115
4. Joe Girardi	30	1,217
Jamey Wright	30	276
6. Kevin Ritz	29	215
7. Juan Pierre	26	1,542
8. Royce Clayton	24	652
John Thomson	24	214
10. Eric Young	22	2,450

HIT BY PITCH: SEASON

Player	HBP	Year
1. Eric Young	21	1996
2. Andres Galarraga	17	1996
Andres Galarraga	17	1997
4. Larry Walker	14	1995
Larry Walker	14	1997
Larry Walker	14	2001
7. Andres Galarraga	13	1995
8. Larry Walker	12	1999
9. Larry Walker	11	2003
10. Jerald Clark	10	1993
Juan Pierre	10	2001

HIT BY PITCH: CAREER WITH TEAM

Player	HBP	PA
1. Larry Walker	98	4,795
2. Andres Galarraga	61	2,924
3. Todd Helton	40	5,424
4. Eric Young	37	2,450
5. Vinny Castilla	32	4,429
6. Dante Bichette	27	4,351
7. Juan Pierre	20	1,542
8. Terry Shumpert	15	1,165
9. Ellis Burks	13	2,053
Walt Weiss	13	2,115
Matt Holliday	13	965

Top 10 Pitching Leaders, Single Season & Career with Team

GAMES PITCHED: SEASON

Player	GP	Year
1. Todd Jones	79	2002
2. Chuck McElroy	78	1998
Mike Myers	78	2000
Brian Fuentes	78	2005
5. Curt Leskanic	76	1995
6. Brian Fuentes	75	2003
Javier Lopez	75	2003
8. Jerry Dipoto	74	1997
Jose Jimenez	74	2002
10. Mike Myers	73	2001
Dave Veres	73	1999

GAMES PITCHED: CAREER WITH TEAM

Player	GP	IP
1. Steve Reed	461	499.0
2. Curt Leskanic	356	470.0
3. Mike Munoz	300	239.0
4. Jose Jimenez	265	300.7
5. Darren Holmes	263	328.0
6. Mike DeJean	262	293.0
7. Bruce Ruffin	246	321.0
8. Brian Fuentes	231	221.0
9. Jerry Dipoto	222	267.3
10. Justin Speier	177	191.7

INNINGS PITCHED: SEASON

Player	IP	Year
1. Pedro Astacio	232.0	1999
2. Darryl Kile	230.3	1998
3. Kevin Ritz	213.0	1996
4. Pedro Astacio	209.3	1998
5. Jamey Wright	206.3	1998
6. Mike Hampton	203.0	2001
7. Shawn Estes	202.0	2004
8. Jason Jennings	201.0	2004
9. Brian Bohanon	197.3	1999
10. Pedro Astacio	196.3	2000

INNINGS PITCHED: CAREER WITH TEAM

Player	IP
1. Pedro Astacio	827.3
2. Jamey Wright	791.7
3. Jason Jennings	729.0
4. John Thomson	611.0
5. Kevin Ritz	576.3
6. Shawn Chacon	552.3
7. Armando Reynoso	503.0
8. Steve Reed	499.0
9. Brian Bohanon	471.3
10. Curt Leskanic	470.0

BATTERS FACED: SEASON

Player	BF	Year
1. Darryl Kile	1,020	1998
2. Pedro Astacio	1,008	1999
3. Kevin Ritz	966	1996
4. Pedro Astacio	938	1998
5. Jason Jennings	925	2004
6. Jamey Wright	919	1998
7. Shawn Estes	904	2004
Mike Hampton	904	2001
9. Brian Bohanon	903	1999
10. Darryl Kile	888	1999

BATTERS FACED: CAREER WITH TEAM

Player	BF	IP
1. Pedro Astacio	3,646	827.3
2. Jamey Wright	3,589	791.7
3. Jason Jennings	3,278	729.0
4. John Thomson	2,642	611.0
5. Kevin Ritz	2,576	576.3
6. Shawn Chacon	2,482	552.3
7. Armando Reynoso	2,207	503.0
8. Brian Bohanon	2,131	471.3
9. Steve Reed	2,092	499.0
10. Curt Leskanic	2,060	470.0

GAMES STARTED: SEASON

Player	GS	Year
1. Darryl Kile	35	1998
Kevin Ritz	35	1996
3. Pedro Astacio	34	1998
Pedro Astacio	34	1999
Shawn Estes	34	2004
Jamey Wright	34	1998

7. Brian Bohanon	33	1999
Jason Jennings	33	2004
Jeff Francis	33	2005
10. Six tied with . . .	32	——

GAMES STARTED: CAREER WITH TEAM

Player	GS	IP
1. Jamey Wright	132	791.7
2. Pedro Astacio	129	827.3
3. Jason Jennings	124	729.0
4. John Thomson	101	611.0
5. Kevin Ritz	98	576.3
6. Armando Reynoso	87	503.0
7. Shawn Chacon	83	552.3
8. Brian Bohanon	78	471.3
9. Darryl Kile	67	421.0
10. Denny Neagle	65	370.3

COMPLETE GAMES: SEASON

Player	CG	Year
1. Pedro Astacio	7	1999
2. Roger Bailey	5	1997
3. Pedro Astacio	4	2001
Darryl Kile	4	1998
Armando Reynoso	4	1993
6. Pedro Astacio	3	2000
Brian Bohanon	3	1999
Mark Thompson	3	1996
9. Seven tied with . . .	2	——

COMPLETE GAMES: CAREER WITH TEAM

Player	CG	IP
1. Pedro Astacio	14	827.3
2. John Thomson	6	611.0
3. Roger Bailey	5	356.0
Brian Bohanon	5	471.3
Darryl Kile	5	421.0
Armando Reynoso	5	503.0
7. Aaron Cook	4	339.7
8. David Nied	3	218.7
Kevin Ritz	3	576.3
Mark Thompson	3	282.7
Jason Jennings	3	729.0

GAMES WON: SEASON

Player	W	Year
1. Pedro Astacio	17	1999
Kevin Ritz	17	1996
3. Jason Jennings	16	2002
4. Shawn Estes	15	2004
5. Mike Hampton	14	2001
Jeff Francis	14	2005
7. Pedro Astacio	13	1998
Darryl Kile	13	1998
Darren Oliver	13	2003
10. Pedro Astacio	12	2000
Brian Bohanon	12	1999
Brian Bohanon	12	2000
Jason Jennings	12	2003
Armando Reynoso	12	1993

GAMES WON: CAREER WITH TEAM

Player	W	IP
1. Pedro Astacio	53	827.3
2. Jason Jennings	49	729.0
3. Kevin Ritz	39	576.3
4. Jamey Wright	35	791.7
5. Steve Reed	33	499.0
6. Curt Leskanic	31	470.0
7. Armando Reynoso	30	503.0
8. Brian Bohanon	29	471.3
9. John Thomson	27	611.0
10. Shawn Chacon	24	552.3

GAMES LOST: SEASON

Player	L	Year
1. Darryl Kile	17	1998
2. Jamey Wright	16	2005
3. Mike Hampton	15	2002
Masato Yoshii	15	2000
5. Pedro Astacio	14	1998
Jamey Wright	14	1998
7. Pedro Astacio	13	2001
Mike Hampton	13	2001
Jason Jennings	13	2003
Darryl Kile	13	1999

GAMES LOST: CAREER WITH TEAM

Player	L	IP
1. Jamey Wright	52	791.7
2. Pedro Astacio	48	827.3
3. Shawn Chacon	45	552.3
4. Jason Jennings	43	729.0
John Thomson	43	611.0
6. Kevin Ritz	38	576.3
7. Armando Reynoso	31	503.0
8. Brian Bohanon	30	471.3
Darryl Kile	30	421.0
10. Steve Reed	29	499.0

WINNING PERCENTAGE: SEASON

Player	W%	Year
1. Julian Tavarez	.688	2000
2. Jason Jennings	.667	2002
3. Shawn Estes	.652	2004
4. Pedro Astacio	.607	1999
Kevin Ritz	.607	1996
6. Shawn Chacon	.579	2003
7. Pedro Astacio	.571	2000
8. Joe Kennedy	.562	2004
David Nied	.562	1994
10. Brian Bohanon	.545	2000

WINNING PERCENTAGE: CAREER WITH TEAM

Player	W%	IP
1. Darren Holmes	.639	328.0
2. Curt Leskanic	.608	470.0
3. Aaron Cook	.594	339.7
4. Jason Jennings	.533	729.0
5. Steve Reed	.532	499.0
6. Marvin Freeman	.526	337.0
7. Pedro Astacio	.525	827.3
8. Kevin Ritz	.506	576.3
9. Armando Reynoso	.492	503.0
Brian Bohanon	.492	471.3

SHUTOUTS: SEASON

Player	SHO	Year
1. Roger Bailey	2	1997
2. Pedro Astacio	1	2001
Brian Bohanon	1	1999
Brian Bohanon	1	2000
Mark Brownson	1	1998
Mike Hampton	1	2001
Jason Jennings	1	2001
Darryl Kile	1	1998
David Nied	1	1994
Mark Thompson	1	1996
John Thomson	1	1997
John Thomson	1	2001
Sun-Woo Kim	1	2005

SHUTOUTS: CAREER WITH TEAM

Player	SHO	IP
1. Roger Bailey	2	356.0
Brian Bohanon	2	471.3
John Thomson	2	611.0
4. Pedro Astacio	1	827.3
Mark Brownson	1	43.0
Mike Hampton	1	381.7
Jason Jennings	1	607.0
Darryl Kile	1	421.0
David Nied	1	218.7
Mark Thompson	1	282.7
Sun-Woo Kim	1	53.3

ERA: Season

Player	ERA	Year
1. Joe Kennedy	3.66	2004
2. Armando Reynoso	4.00	1993
3. Kevin Ritz	4.21	1995
4. Roger Bailey	4.29	1997
5. Jason Jennings	4.52	2002
6. Brian Bohanon	4.68	2000
7. John Thomson	4.71	1997
8. Armando Reynoso	4.96	1996
9. Darren Oliver	5.04	2003
Pedro Astacio	5.04	1999

ERA: Career with Team

Player	ERA	IP
1. Steve Reed	3.63	499.0
2. Bruce Ruffin	3.84	321.0
3. Jose Jimenez	4.13	300.7
4. Darren Holmes	4.42	328.0
5. Armando Reynoso	4.65	503.0
6. Aaron Cook	4.80	339.7
7. Roger Bailey	4.90	356.0
8. Marvin Freeman	4.91	337.0
9. Curt Leskanic	4.92	470.0
10. John Thomson	5.01	611.0

Earned Runs Allowed: Season

Player	ER	Year
1. Pedro Astacio	145	1998
2. Darryl Kile	140	1999
3. Brian Bohanon	136	1999
4. Darryl Kile	133	1998
5. Shawn Estes	131	2004
6. Pedro Astacio	130	1999
Jamey Wright	130	1998
8. Kevin Ritz	125	1996
9. Jason Jennings	123	2004
10. Mike Hampton	122	2001
Mike Hampton	122	2002

Earned Runs Allowed: Career with Team

Player	ER	IP
1. Pedro Astacio	499	827.3
2. Jamey Wright	475	791.7
3. Jason Jennings	407	729.0
4. John Thomson	340	611.0
5. Kevin Ritz	333	576.3
6. Shawn Chacon	319	552.3
7. Brian Bohanon	305	471.3
8. Darryl Kile	273	421.0
9. Armando Reynoso	260	503.0
10. Curt Leskanic	257	470.0

Strikeouts: Season

Player	K	Year
1. Pedro Astacio	210	1999
2. Pedro Astacio	193	2000
3. Pedro Astacio	170	1998
4. Darryl Kile	158	1998
5. Denny Neagle	139	2001
6. Shawn Chacon	134	2001
7. Jason Jennings	133	2004
8. Jeff Francis	128	2005
9. Jason Jennings	127	2002
10. Bruce Ruffin	126	1993

Strikeouts: Career with Team

Player	K	IP
1. Pedro Astacio	749	827.3
2. Jason Jennings	480	729.0
3. Curt Leskanic	415	470.0
4. John Thomson	390	611.0
5. Shawn Chacon	385	552.3
6. Jamey Wright	381	791.7
7. Steve Reed	352	499.0
8. Kevin Ritz	337	576.3
9. Bruce Ruffin	319	321.0
10. Darren Holmes	297	328.0

Strikeouts Per Nine IP: Season

Player	K/9	Year
1. Pedro Astacio	8.85	2000
2. Pedro Astacio	8.15	1999
3. Denny Neagle	7.33	2001
4. Pedro Astacio	7.31	1998
5. Joe Kennedy	6.49	2004
6. Jeff Francis	6.27	2005
7. Kevin Ritz	6.23	1995
8. Darryl Kile	6.17	1998
Jason Jennings	6.17	2002
10. Denny Neagle	6.08	2002

Strikeouts Per Nine IP: Career with Team

Player	K/9	IP
1. Bruce Ruffin	8.94	321.0
2. Pedro Astacio	8.15	827.3
Darren Holmes	8.15	328.0
4. Curt Leskanic	7.95	470.0
5. Denny Neagle	6.59	370.3
6. Steve Reed	6.35	370.3
7. Shawn Chacon	6.27	552.3
8. Jason Jennings	5.93	729.0
9. Darryl Kile	5.86	421.0
10. John Thomson	5.74	611.0

Hits Allowed: Season

Player	HA	Year
1. Pedro Astacio	258	1999
2. Darryl Kile	257	1998
3. Pedro Astacio	245	1998
4. Jason Jennings	241	2004
5. Brian Bohanon	236	1999
Mike Hampton	236	2001
Kevin Ritz	236	1996
8. Jamey Wright	235	1998
9. Mike Hampton	228	2002
Jeff Francis	228	2005

Hits Allowed: Career with Team

Player	HA	IP
1. Jamey Wright	931	791.7
2. Pedro Astacio	920	827.3
3. Jason Jennings	826	729.0
4. John Thomson	672	611.0
5. Kevin Ritz	654	576.3
6. Armando Reynoso	571	503.0
7. Brian Bohanon	544	471.3
8. Shawn Chacon	543	552.3
9. Darryl Kile	482	421.0
10. Curt Leskanic	472	470.0

Hits Allowed Per Nine IP: Season

Player	H/9	Year
1. Kevin Ritz	8.88	1995
2. Joe Kennedy	9.04	2004
3. Brian Bohanon	9.20	2000
4. Denny Neagle	9.31	2002
5. Jason Jennings	9.76	2002
6. Armando Reynoso	9.81	1993
7. Roger Bailey	9.90	1997
8. Shawn Estes	9.94	2004
9. Pedro Astacio	9.95	2000
10. Kevin Ritz	9.97	1996

Hits Allowed Per Nine IP: Career with Team

Player	H/9	IP
1. Bruce Ruffin	8.38	321.0
2. Steve Reed	8.40	499.0
3. Shawn Chacon	8.85	552.3
4. Curt Leskanic	9.04	470.0
5. Darren Holmes	9.36	328.0

6. John Thomson	9.90	611.0
7. Roger Bailey	9.91	356.0
8. Denny Neagle	9.94	370.3
Jose Jimenez	9.94	300.7
10. Pedro Astacio	10.01	827.3

Walks Allowed: Season

Player	BB	Year
1. Darryl Kile	109	1999
2. Shawn Estes	105	2004
Kevin Ritz	105	1996
4. Jason Jennings	101	2004
5. Darryl Kile	96	1998
6. Jamey Wright	95	1998
7. Brian Bohanon	92	1999
8. Mike Hampton	91	2002
9. Jason Jennings	88	2003
10. Shawn Chacon	87	2001

Walks Allowed: Career with Team

Player	BB	IP
1. Jamey Wright	387	791.7
2. Jason Jennings	340	729.0
3. Shawn Chacon	293	552.3
4. Pedro Astacio	290	827.3
5. Kevin Ritz	253	576.3
6. Curt Leskanic	221	470.0
7. Brian Bohanon	218	471.3
8. Darryl Kile	205	421.0
9. John Thomson	188	611.0
10. Mike Hampton	176	381.7

Walks Allowed Per Nine IP: Season

Player	BB/9	Year
1. Armando Reynoso	2.61	1996
2. John Thomson	2.76	1997
3. Masato Yoshii	2.85	2000
4. Pedro Astacio	2.91	1999
5. Armando Reynoso	3.00	1993
6. Darren Oliver	3.04	2003
7. Denny Neagle	3.16	2001
8. Pedro Astacio	3.18	1998
9. Roger Bailey	3.30	1997
10. Kevin Ritz	3.38	1995

Walks Allowed Per Nine IP: Career with Team

Player	BB/9	IP
1. John Thomson	2.77	611.0
2. Jose Jimenez	2.78	300.7
3. Steve Reed	2.99	499.0
4. Armando Reynoso	3.04	503.0
5. Pedro Astacio	3.15	827.3
6. Marvin Freeman	3.23	337.0
7. Denny Neagle	3.28	370.3
8. Aaron Cook	3.31	339.7
9. Darren Holmes	3.73	328.0
10. Kevin Ritz	3.95	576.3

WHIP (Walks + Hits Per Nine IP): Season

Player	WHIP	Year
1. Kevin Ritz	1.362	1995
2. Joe Kennedy	1.417	2004
3. Denny Neagle	1.418	2002
4. Armando Reynoso	1.423	1993
5. Pedro Astacio	1.435	1999
6. Armando Reynoso	1.447	1996
7. Darren Oliver	1.453	2003
8. Jason Jennings	1.462	2002
9. Roger Bailey	1.466	1997
10. John Thomson	1.467	1997

WHIP (Walks + Hits Per Nine IP): Career with Team

Player	WHIP	IP
1. John Thomson	1.408	611.0
2. Jose Jimenez	1.414	300.7
3. Bruce Ruffin	1.445	321.0
4. Darren Holmes	1.454	328.0
5. Pedro Astacio	1.463	827.3
6. Armando Reynoso	1.473	503.0
7. Marvin Freeman	1.504	337.0
8. Shawn Chacon	1.514	552.3
9. Kevin Ritz	1.574	576.3
10. Aaron Cook	1.587	339.7

Home Runs Allowed: Season

Player	HRA	Year
1. Pedro Astacio	39	1998
2. Pedro Astacio	38	1999
3. Darryl Kile	33	1999
4. Pedro Astacio	32	2000
Masato Yoshii	32	2000
6. Mike Hampton	31	2001
7. Brian Bohanon	30	1999
Shawn Estes	30	2004
9. Denny Neagle	29	2001
10. Darryl Kile	28	1998

Home Runs Allowed: Career with Team

Player	HRA	IP
1. Pedro Astacio	139	827.3
2. Jamey Wright	91	791.7
3. Jason Jennings	86	729.0
4. John Thomson	83	611.0
5. Shawn Chacon	82	552.3
6. Brian Bohanon	74	471.3
7. Denny Neagle	67	370.3
Steve Reed	67	499.0
9. Armando Reynoso	66	503.0
10. Kevin Ritz	62	576.3

Saves: Season

Player	SV	Year
1. Jose Jimenez	41	2002
2. Shawn Chacon	35	2004
3. Dave Veres	31	1999
Brian Fuentes	31	2005
5. Darren Holmes	25	1993
6. Jose Jimenez	24	2000
Bruce Ruffin	24	1996
8. Jose Jimenez	20	2003
9. Jerry Dipoto	19	1998
10. Jose Jimenez	17	2001

Saves: Career with Team

Player	SV	IP
1. Jose Jimenez	102	300.7
2. Bruce Ruffin	60	321.0
3. Darren Holmes	46	328.0
4. Dave Veres	39	153.3
5. Jerry Dipoto	36	267.3
6. Shawn Chacon	35	552.3
Brian Fuentes	35	221.0
8. Curt Leskanic	20	470.0
9. Steve Reed	15	499.0
10. Justin Speier	10	191.7

Wild Pitches: Season

Player	WP	Year
1. Marvin Freeman	13	1996
Darryl Kile	13	1999
3. Darryl Kile	12	1998
4. Jeff Parrett	11	1993
Byung-Hyun Kim	11	2005
6. Aaron Cook	10	2003
Jason Jennings	10	2002

Kevin Ritz	10	1996
Bruce Ruffin	10	1996
10. Shawn Chacon	9	2004
Mike Hampton	9	2002
Gary Wayne	9	1993

WILD PITCHES: CAREER WITH TEAM

Player	WP	IP
1. Curt Leskanic	34	470.0
2. Jason Jennings	32	729.0
3. Kevin Ritz	30	576.3
4. Shawn Chacon	26	552.3
Bruce Ruffin	26	321.0
6. Darryl Kile	25	421.0
7. Marvin Freeman	22	337.0
8. Jamey Wright	21	791.7
9. Pedro Astacio	19	827.3
Aaron Cook	19	339.7

HIT BATSMEN: SEASON

Player	HB	Year
1. Pedro Astacio	17	1998
2. Pedro Astacio	15	2000
Jamey Wright	15	2005
4. Brian Bohanon	14	1999
Byung-Hyun Kim	14	2005
6. Roger Bailey	13	1997
Mark Thompson	13	1996
8. Rolando Arrojo	12	2000
Shawn Chacon	12	2003
Kevin Ritz	12	1996

HIT BATSMEN: CAREER WITH TEAM

Player	HB	IP
1. Pedro Astacio	58	827.3
2. Jamey Wright	54	791.7
3. Shawn Chacon	42	552.3
4. Steve Reed	36	499.0
5. Armando Reynoso	29	503.0
6. Brian Bohanon	27	471.3
7. Jason Jennings	26	729.0
8. Kevin Ritz	24	576.3
Mark Thompson	24	282.7
10. Brian Fuentes	23	221.0

GAMES FINISHED: SEASON

Player	GF	Year
1. Jose Jimenez	69	2002
2. Dave Veres	63	1999
3. Shawn Chacon	60	2004
4. Bruce Ruffin	56	1996
5. Jose Jimenez	55	2000
Brian Fuentes	55	2005
7. Jerry Dipoto	51	1998
Darren Holmes	51	1993
9. Jose Jimenez	49	2001
10. Jose Jimenez	40	2003

GAMES FINISHED: CAREER WITH TEAM

Player	GF	IP
1. Jose Jimenez	213	300.7
2. Bruce Ruffin	137	321.0
3. Darren Holmes	129	328.0
4. Curt Leskanic	110	470.0
Steve Reed	110	499.0
6. Jerry Dipoto	109	267.3
7. Brian Fuentes	99	221.0
8. Dave Veres	89	153.3
9. Mike Munoz	70	239.0
10. Mike DeJean	63	293.0

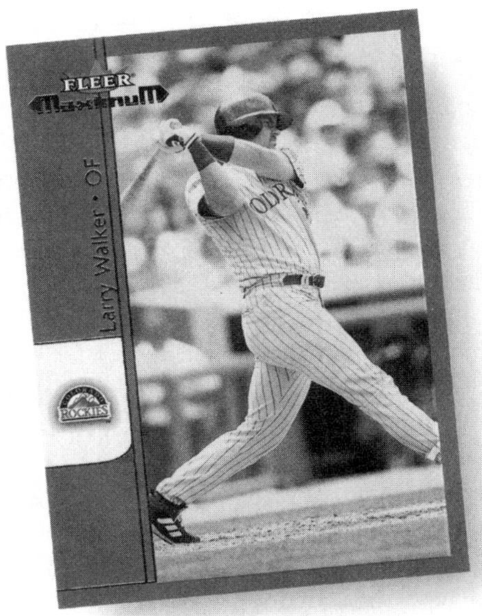

Larry Walker

Significant Rockies

BICHETTE, DANTE (OF)
(1993–1999)

Dante Bichette was one of the biggest beneficiaries of hitter-friendly Mile High Stadium and Coors Field. His career really took off in 1993, once he was traded from the Milwaukee Brewers to the Rockies. A mediocre player at best with the Angels and Brewers, Bichette quickly became a fan favorite in Colorado, hitting over .300 in six of his seven years with the Rockies and just missing his other year (.298). His best season was 1995, when he won a Silver Slugger Award and was runner-up to Barry Larkin of the Reds for the National League MVP. A four-time All-Star with Colorado, Bichette still ranks in the top five of almost every individual hitting category in Rockies history. Bichette was traded to the Reds after the 1999 season and discovered what every Colorado player discovers when they play for another team—their production tails off. After playing two more years for three different teams, Bichette retired following the 2001 season.

CAREER ROCKIES RECORD:

Games	AB	Hits	Runs
1,018	4,050	1,278	665
Avg	**HR**	**RBI**	**SB**
.316	201	826	105

CASTILLA, VINNY (3B)
(1993–1999, 2004)

Vinny Castilla was 25 years old when he was selected in the expansion draft from Atlanta after playing in only 21 games for the Braves over the previous two years. That was a stroke of luck for Castilla, as it allowed him to become one of the National League's most prominent third basemen rather than remaining in Atlanta to battle it out with Chipper Jones. In the five seasons from 1995 to 1999, Castilla hit nearly 200 homers to pace a powerful Colorado attack. A two-time All-Star and three-time Silver Slugger Award winner, Castilla remains among the top five all-time Rockies in nearly every hitting category. Castilla was traded to Tampa Bay after the 1999 season. He played for three different teams in four years, hitting just 65 homers during that span. In 2004, he returned to the Rockies, where he found his thin-air power stroke again, clubbing 35 homers. In 2005, he left again, this time via free agency, for Washington, a team for whom he would hit just 12 homers.

CAREER ROCKIES RECORD:

Games	AB	Hits	Runs
1,083	4,078	1,202	609
Avg	**HR**	**RBI**	**SB**
.295	238	741	22

GALARRAGA, ANDRES (1B)
(1993–1997)

Galarraga was already a star—albeit a fading one—with the Expos and Cardinals when he came to the expansion Rockies in 1993 as a free agent. His career was rejuvenated. In his first season in Colorado he won the National League batting title with a .370 average. In 1996 he led the league in homers (47) and RBIs (150). During his five-year stint in Colorado, "the Big Cat" was named to the All-Star team twice, won a Silver Slugger Award, and averaged more than 34 homers and 115 RBIs a season. After leaving Colorado following the 1997 season, Galarraga hung around until he was 43 years old, playing for five different teams (and two stints with the Giants) over his last six years, although he missed all of 1999 as he underwent treatment for lymphatic cancer. He retired after the 2004 season.

CAREER ROCKIES RECORD:

Games	AB	Hits	Runs
679	2,667	843	476
Avg	**HR**	**RBI**	**SB**
.316	172	579	55

HELTON, TODD (1B)
(1997–2005)

Todd Helton, selected in the first round of the June 1995 amateur draft, has emerged as the greatest player in Colorado Rockies history. A perennial National League All-Star with four Silver Slugger Awards under his belt, Helton has also established himself as one of the top players in all of baseball with almost unmatched consistency year after year. The left-handed slugger played mostly outfield in his first year with the Rockies (1997), but with the departure of Andres Galarraga after the season, Helton moved to first and has been there ever since, winning three Gold Glove Awards in the process. With a rare mix of power and average, Helton's hitting has given rise to speculation of a .400 season or possibly a Triple Crown. Helton was still over the .400 mark as late as August 21 of the 2000 season and won two of the three legs of the Triple Crown that year, hitting an NL-best .372 and knocking in a league-leading 147 runs to go with his 42 homers. If Helton stays healthy (and with Colorado), he has a legitimate shot at 500 homers, 3,000 hits, 2,000 RBIs, and a career average far above .300, all first-ballot Hall of Fame numbers. Helton will, however, have to avoid whatever plagued him in 2005 as he had the worst season of his big-league career, setting career lows (or near lows) in homers, average, hits, runs, slugging average, and total bases. If he bounces back to his norm, he will once again be a one-man wrecking crew, especially now that he has some talented young players around him.

CAREER ROCKIES RECORD:

Games	AB	Hits	Runs
1,279	4,560	1,535	924
Avg	**HR**	**RBI**	**SB**
.337	271	915	33

JIMENEZ, JOSE (RP)
(2000–2003)

The hitter-friendly confines of Coors Field can make life very difficult for pitchers. The lone bright spot in the team's pitching history was Jimenez, who arrived from St. Louis prior to the 2000 season as part of a seven-player deal that sent Darryl Kile to the Cardinals. From 2000 to 2003, the reliever managed to record 102 saves with an ERA of 4.13—not that good under most circumstances, but an admirable figure at Coors Field. After leaving Colorado for the green grass of free agency, Jimenez suffered through a horrible 2004 season with Cleveland (1–7, 8.42 ERA) before dropping out of the majors.

CAREER ROCKIES RECORD:

W	L	W%	ERA	SV
15	23	.395	4.13	102
K	BB	SHO	IP	
173	93	0	300.7	

WALKER, LARRY (OF)
(1995–2004)

With numbers almost identical to Todd Helton's, Larry Walker was for 10 years a potent force in his own right in Colorado. Like Andres Galarraga two years before him, Walker was an emerging star with the Montreal Expos before coming to the Rockies, signing a free-agent contract in April 1995. And, like Galarraga's, his career really took off in the shadow of the Rocky Mountains. During one five-year stretch, Walker was one of the most feared hitters in the game, compiling averages of .366, .363, .379, .309, and .350, with 37 or more homers in three of those seasons. He won three batting titles (1998, 1999, 2001), five Gold Gloves, two Silver Slugger Awards, and the league's MVP Award in 1997. With his career seemingly on the decline, the five-time All-Star (four with Colorado) was traded to St. Louis in mid-2004. After two decent, yet unspectacular seasons with the Cardinals, the continually injured Walker might have played the last games of his career in 2005.

CAREER ROCKIES RECORD:

Games	AB	Hits	Runs
1,170	4,076	1,361	892
Avg	HR	RBI	SB
.334	258	848	126

Detroit Tigers

Since 1901

1916 Team Ball

1907 The Tigers win the American League pennant, although six of their regular players fail to hit a home run all year, and the team finishes with just 11 total homers....**1937** Second baseman Charlie Gehringer becomes the oldest player to win a batting title, hitting .371 at age 34....**1955** Al Kaline becomes the youngest batting champion in history at the age of 20, hitting .340 to lead the American League....**1984** The Tigers start the season 26–4, then 35–5, both records the best starts by a major league team in the 20th century....**1997** Of the 19 teams in major league history that have lost 109 games in a season (as the Tigers do in 1996), none of them improves as much the following season as the Tigers, who finish 79–83.

FRANCHISE HISTORY

The Detroit Tigers began play in 1901 as one of the original American League franchises. (The Tigers were members of the Western League when president Ban Johnson renamed it the American League in 1899 as part of his overall scheme to compete with the National League. The National Association of Professional Baseball Leagues didn't recognize the AL as a major league until 1901.) Johnson's plan was to move the unsuccessful Detroit franchise to New York to compete with the National League's Giants, but due to constant bickering and resistance from Detroit's owners, Johnson had to abandon the idea. So Detroit played its first-ever game in the American League on April 25, 1901, when more than 10,000 fans jammed into 6,000-seat Bennett Park. It was a barnburner. Trailing Milwaukee 13–4 in the bottom of the ninth, the Tigers scored 10 runs to win 14–13, one of the greatest single-game comebacks in major league history.

Insurance magnate Sam Angus bought the Tigers in 1902 at the urging of Ban Johnson, and appointed employee Frank Navin as the team's bookkeeper. Angus consistently lost money on his investment and eventually told Navin to find a buyer for the team. Navin arranged a deal with lumber tycoon William Clyman Yawkey, the richest man in Michigan, but Yawkey died in the middle of the deal. Yawkey left $10 million to his son, William Hoover Yawkey, who eventually was persuaded by Navin to complete the $50,000 deal his father had started. Yawkey, who would die 15 years later at the age of 43 (supposedly in Ty Cobb's arms in Georgia), left his $40 million estate to his foster son, Thomas Austin Yawkey, who would eventually become the longtime owner of the Red Sox. When Yawkey purchased the Tigers, he allowed Navin to buy a $5,000 share in the team. After collecting more than $50,000 as his World Series share in 1909, Navin was able to buy out Yawkey and took control of the team.

During the decade of the 1910s, Ty Cobb led the majors with a .387 batting average, 33 points higher than his closest competitor, Shoeless Joe Jackson at .354.

Navin, whose income came solely from the team, was tightfisted. He was also highly respected in the inner circles of baseball. On occasion Commissioner Kenesaw Mountain Landis is reputed to have called Navin as many as 20 times a day for his advice. In 1920 Navin sold a 25 percent share of the team to Walter O. Briggs for $250,000. Tire manufacturer John Kelsey, another 25 percent shareholder, died later in the 1920s and Briggs bought out his interest as well, giving both Navin and him 50 percent stakes in the team. While an equal owner, Briggs never interfered in the club's operation, leaving all the decisions to Navin. In 1935, just one month after seeing his beloved Tigers win their first World Series, Navin died in a horseback rid-

Frank Navin

ing accident, although he may have had a heart attack while riding. By prior arrangement, Briggs paid $1 million to Navin's heirs for their interest in the team.

Ty Cobb, holder of almost 100 American and Major League records, including perhaps, Most Hated Player.

Briggs, who made his fortune as owner of an auto-body manufacturing plant, was an extremely prejudiced man who refused to sign any black players after the color barrier was broken by Jackie Robinson. No black player joined the team until after his death in 1952. Upon Briggs' death, his son, Walter O. (Spike) Briggs Jr., became president of the team, but, in a bizarre series of events, the probate court ruled that the baseball team was not a prudent investment for the minor heirs of the estate and it was ordered sold. For several years Spike Briggs was unable—or, more likely, not entirely willing—to sell the team. Briggs tried to buy the team from his sisters, who rebuffed his $3.5 million offer. Finally, in 1956, the trustees of the estate announced a sealed bid sale of the team. The winning bid of $5.5 million was placed by an investment group led by local radio magnate John Fetzer. His partners were Fred Knorr, one of his executives, and Kenyon Brown. Fetzer bought out Brown, who wanted out, in 1959. Knorr died in a bathtub accident and Fetzer bought his interest from the estate in 1961.

Fetzer remained sole owner until 1983, when, at the age of 82, he sold the team for $53 million to Tom Monaghan, the 46-year-old owner of Domino's Pizza. In 1984, his first season as owner, Monaghan's Tigers cruised to the American League pennant, winning it by 15 games, and romping in the ALCS and World Series. When his pizza empire ran into financial trouble in 1991, Monaghan put the team up for sale. Although one of the interested buyers was Ford Motor Company heir Edsel Ford II, Monaghan eventually sold the team in 1992 for $85 million to Michael Illitch, owner of the Little Caesars pizza chain and the NHL's Detroit Red Wings. Illitch had once been signed by the Tigers for $5,000, at the urging of Tiger great Charlie Gehringer, and played for the Detroit Smokies, where he met his future wife. Together they opened their first pizza parlor in 1959. In the early 1990s, they owned over 4,000 stores. Illitch, who still owns the team today, is estimated to be worth more than $1 billion.

On the field, the team has always been known as the Tigers. During Ty Cobb's tenure as manager, the papers liked to refer to the team as the "Tygers." The first strong Tigers team came during Ty Cobb's early days as a player, when Detroit won three consecutive American League pennants from 1907 to 1909, but lost the World Series each year. In 1915, Detroit became the first AL team to win

The boy who would grow up to be Denny McLain, the only 30-game winner since 1934.

100 games but not win the pennant, when the Red Sox nipped them by a game. The Tigers languished for two decades until 1934, when they had four 100-RBI men and reached the Fall Classic again. Once again, they lost the Series. The Tigers repeated as AL champs in 1935 and finally won their first World Series, defeating the Cubs. The team remained competitive for the next few years and won the pennant again in 1940, but lost the Series to Cincinnati. In 1945 the Tigers won the AL pennant by a mere game over Washington, then defeated the Cubs again in the World Series. It took more than two decades for the Tigers to win another pennant, this one in 1968, behind Denny McLain's magical 31–6 season. The Tigers defeated the Cardinals in an exciting World Series, but it was Mickey Lolich who led the way with three victories. The next pennant came in 1984 when Detroit ran away with the title, starting the year 35–5 and never looking back. The Tigers crushed the Royals in the ALCS and the Padres in the World Series.

It's been a long dry spell ever since, as the Tigers have accumulated one of the worst records in baseball over the last decade or so. In 1996 the Tigers lost a franchise-record 109 games, then nearly matched it in 2002 when they lost 106. The next year Detroit lost an American League-record 119 games, and had they not won five of their last six games of the season, they would have broken the 1962 Mets' record for most losses in a season (120).

From 1901–1999, the Tigers played in essentially the same ballpark, albeit with some modifications and name changes. Bennett Park was used by various 19th-century major league clubs before it became the Tigers' home in 1901 for all but Sunday games, which were played in Burns Park. In 2000 the Tigers opened Comerica Park.

TEAM NAME HISTORY

Official Names

Tigers (1901–current)

Unofficial Names/Nicknames

Bengals, Tygers, Detroits, Detroit Americans

STADIUM HISTORY

Bennett Park (Monday–Saturday games)	1901–1911
Burns Park (Sunday games only)	1901–1909
Navin Field (Bennett Park torn down, Navin Field constructed in the same place with a reorientation of the playing field)	1912–1937
Briggs Stadium (Navin Field renamed)	1938–1960
Tiger Stadium (Briggs Stadium renamed)	1961–1999
Comerica Park	2000–current

YEARLY RECORD, FINISH, & ATTENDANCE FIGURES

Year	League	Record	DIV/LG Finish	Attendance	Avg/Gm
2005	AL Cent	71–91	4	2,024,431	24,993
2004	AL Cent	72–90	4	1,917,004	23,667
2003	AL Cent	43–119	5	1,368,245	16,892
2002	AL Cent	55–106	5	1,503,623	18,795
2001	AL Cent	66–96	4	1,921,305	23,720
2000	AL Cent	79–83	3	2,438,617	30,106
1999	AL Cent	69–92	3	2,026,441	25,018
1998	AL Cent	65–97	5	1,409,391	17,400
1997	AL East	79–83	3	1,365,157	16,854
1996	AL East	53–109	5	1,168,610	14,427
1995	AL East	60–84	4	1,180,979	16,402
1994	AL East	53–62	5	1,184,783	20,427
1993	AL East	85–77	4	1,971,421	24,339
1992	AL East	75–87	6	1,423,963	17,800
1991	AL East	84–78	2	1,641,661	20,267
1990	AL East	79–83	3	1,495,785	18,466
1989	AL East	59–103	7	1,543,656	19,057
1988	AL East	88–74	2	2,081,162	25,693
1987	AL East	98–64	1	2,061,830	25,455
1986	AL East	87–75	3	1,899,437	23,450
1985	AL East	84–77	3	2,286,609	28,230
1984	AL East	104–58	1	2,704,794	32,985
1983	AL East	92–70	2	1,829,636	22,588
1982	AL East	83–79	4	1,636,058	20,198
1981	AL East	60–49	4/2	1,149,144	20,894
1980	AL East	84–78	5	1,785,293	21,772
1979	AL East	85–76	5	1,630,929	20,387
1978	AL East	86–76	5	1,714,893	21,172
1977	AL East	74–88	4	1,359,856	16,788
1976	AL East	74–87	5	1,467,020	18,338
1975	AL East	57–102	6	1,058,836	13,235
1974	AL East	72–90	6	1,243,080	15,347
1973	AL East	85–77	3	1,724,146	21,286
1972	AL East	86–70	1	1,892,386	24,261
1971	AL East	91–71	2	1,591,073	19,643
1970	AL East	79–83	4	1,501,293	18,534
1969	AL East	90–72	2	1,577,481	19,475
1968	AL	103–59	1	2,031,847	25,085
1967	AL	91–71	2	1,447,143	17,648
1966	AL	88–74	3	1,124,293	13,880
1965	AL	89–73	4	1,029,645	12,712
1964	AL	85–77	4	816,139	9,953
1963	AL	79–83	5	821,952	10,148
1962	AL	85–76	4	1,207,881	14,730
1961	AL	101–61	2	1,600,710	19,521
1960	AL	71–83	6	1,167,669	15,165
1959	AL	76–78	4	1,221,221	15,860
1958	AL	77–77	5	1,098,924	14,272
1957	AL	78–76	4	1,272,346	16,524
1956	AL	82–72	5	1,051,182	13,477
1955	AL	79–75	5	1,181,838	15,349

YEARLY RECORD, FINISH, & ATTENDANCE FIGURES (CONT.)

Year	League	Record	DIV/LG Finish	Attendance	Avg/Gm
1954	AL	68–86	5	1,079,847	14,024
1953	AL	60–94	6	884,658	11,198
1952	AL	50–104	8	1,026,846	13,336
1951	AL	73–81	5	1,132,641	14,710
1950	AL	95–59	2	1,951,474	24,092
1949	AL	87–67	4	1,821,204	23,349
1948	AL	78–76	5	1,743,035	22,637
1947	AL	85–69	2	1,398,093	17,476
1946	AL	92–62	2	1,722,590	21,805
1945	AL	88–65	1	1,280,341	16,847
1944	AL	88–66	2	923,176	11,836
1943	AL	78–76	5	606,287	7,773
1942	AL	73–81	5	580,087	7,534
1941	AL	75–79	4	684,915	8,895
1940	AL	90–64	1	1,112,693	14,085
1939	AL	81–73	5	836,279	10,722
1938	AL	84–70	4	799,557	10,121
1937	AL	89–65	2	1,072,276	13,926
1936	AL	83–71	2	875,948	11,376
1935	AL	93–58	1	1,034,929	13,100
1934	AL	101–53	1	919,161	11,490
1933	AL	75–79	5	320,972	4,115
1932	AL	76–75	5	397,157	5,092
1931	AL	61–93	7	434,056	5,637
1930	AL	75–79	5	649,450	8,326
1929	AL	70–84	6	869,318	11,290
1928	AL	68–86	6	474,323	6,160
1927	AL	82–71	4	773,716	9,919
1926	AL	79–75	6	711,914	8,789
1925	AL	81–73	4	820,766	10,659
1924	AL	86–68	3	1,015,136	13,015
1923	AL	83–71	2	911,377	11,836
1922	AL	79–75	3	861,206	11,184
1921	AL	71–82	6	661,527	8,591
1920	AL	61–93	7	579,650	7,431
1919	AL	80–60	4	643,805	9,197
1918	AL	55–71	7	203,719	3,512
1917	AL	78–75	4	457,289	6,017
1916	AL	87–67	3	616,772	8,010
1915	AL	100–54	2	476,105	6,183
1914	AL	80–73	4	416,225	5,336
1913	AL	66–87	6	398,502	5,243
1912	AL	69–84	6	402,870	5,301
1911	AL	89–65	2	484,988	6,381
1910	AL	86–68	3	391,288	5,017
1909	AL	98–54	1	490,490	6,288
1908	AL	90–63	1	436,199	5,592
1907	AL	92–58	1	297,079	3,760
1906	AL	71–78	6	174,043	2,231
1905	AL	79–74	3	193,384	2,545
1904	AL	62–90	7	177,796	2,251

YEARLY RECORD, FINISH, & ATTENDANCE FIGURES (CONT.)

Year	League	Record	DIV/LG Finish	Attendance	Avg/Gm
1903	AL	65–71	5	224,523	3,454
1902	AL	52–83	7	189,469	2,828
1901	AL	74–61	3	259,430	3,706

MANAGER HISTORY

Manager	Years	W–L	Win %
George Stallings	1901	74–61	.548
Frank Dwyer	1902	52–83	.385
Ed Barrow	1903–1904	97–117	.453
Bobby Lowe	1904	30–44	.405
Bill Armour	1905–1906	150–152	.497
Hugh Jennings	1907–1920	1,131–972	.538
Ty Cobb	1921–1926	479–444	.519
George Moriarty	1927–1928	150–157	.489
Bucky Harris	1929–1933,		
	1955–1956	516–557	.481
Del Baker	1933,		
	1937–1942	399–339	.541
Mickey Cochrane	1934–1938	366–266	.579
Steve O'Neill	1943–1948	509–414	.551
Red Rolfe	1949–1952	278–256	.521
Fred Hutchinson	1952–1954	155–235	.397
Jack Tighe	1957–1958	99–104	.488
Bill Norman	1958–1959	58–64	.475
Jimmie Dykes	1959–1960	118–115	.506
Joe Gordon	1960	26–31	.456
Bob Scheffing	1961–1963	210–173	.548
Chuck Dressen	1963–1965,		
	1966	221–189	.539
Bob Swift	1965, 1966	56–43	.566
Frank Skaff	1966	40–39	.506
Mayo Smith	1967–1970	363–285	.560
Billy Martin	1971–1973	248–204	.549
Joe Schultz	1973	14–14	.500
Ralph Houk	1974–1978	363–443	.450
Les Moss	1979	27–26	.509
Sparky Anderson	1979–1995	1,331–1,248	.516
Buddy Bell	1996–1998	184–277	.399
Larry Parrish	1998–1999	82–104	.441
Phil Garner	2000–2002	145–185	.439
Luis Pujols	2002	55–100	.355
Alan Trammell	2003–2005	186–300	.383
Jim Leyland	(Took over beginning in 2006)		

ALL-TIME WIN-LOSS RECORDS VS. ALL OPPONENTS

Opponent	Record
ALL-TIME	8,221–8,050
Angels	288–259
Astros	2–7
Athletics	956–876
Blue Jays	154–184
Braves	5–4
Brewers	215–194
Cardinals	8–6
Cubs	5–3
Devil Rays	29–31
Diamondbacks	7–11
Dodgers	1–5
Giants	2–4
Indians	1,002–980
INTERLEAGUE	71–86
Mariners	166–142
Marlins	4–5
Mets	3–3
Nationals	2–4
Orioles	1,009–918
Padres	5–1
Phillies	4–5
Pirates	8–7
Rangers	312–265
Reds	6–6
Red Sox	934–993
Rockies	3–9
Royals	218–244
Twins	995–921
White Sox	970–944
Yankees	908–1,019

Sparky Anderson, the winningest manager in Tiger history.

Franchise Highlights, Low Points, and Strange Distinctions

1901 The Tigers committed 12 errors in their game against the White Sox on May 1, to set an American League record that has never been broken. The White Sox tied it, however, two years later in a game against the Tigers.

• • • •

1904 In 1904 Bobby Lowe of the Tigers hit .207, the lowest batting average ever by a second baseman with at least 500 at-bats. Ten years earlier Lowe became the first player in history to hit four home runs in a game.

• • • •

1907 Pitcher George Mullin finished the season with a 20–20 record for the Tigers. He's the only 20th-century pitcher to lose 20 games while pitching for a pennant winner.

• • • •

1914 Catcher Oscar Stanage set a record for the fewest runs scored (16) in a season by a player with at least 400 at-bats.

• • • •

1915 In 1915 Detroit's three regular outfielders—Bobby Veach, Sam Crawford, and Ty Cobb—finished 1–2–3 in the American League in RBIs.

1921 In spite of setting the American League record for batting average by a team for a season when they hit .316, the Tigers finished in sixth place in the eight-team American League.

• • • •

1925 Tigers outfielder Al Wingo established a unique record, his only season as a regular, when he hit .370 for the season. It remains as the highest batting average ever by a player who only played one year as a regular.

• • • •

1926 Detroit's trio of outfielders was also tough to match offensively. Bob Fothergill and Harry Heilmann each hit .367 for the season. But center fielder Heinie Manush beat them both, hitting .378. (The next-best Tigers regular was first baseman Lu Blue, who hit .287.) Going into the final day of the 1926 season, Manush trailed Babe Ruth and his two fellow outfielders in the batting race, but he went 6-for-9 in a doubleheader to overtake all three.

• • • •

1932 Ray Hayworth became the first catcher ever to play 100 consecutive errorless games.

1934 Detroit pitcher Schoolboy Rowe tied the American League record for consecutive wins with 16.

Lou Gehrig of the Yankees won the American League's Triple Crown in 1934, hitting .363 with 49 homers and 165 RBIs. Amazingly, he didn't win the league's MVP Award. Tigers player-manager Mickey Cochrane copped the prize by hitting—ahem—.320 with 2 homers and 76 RBIs and leading his team to their first pennant since 1909.

• • • •

1935 Tigers owner Frank Navin died shortly after seeing his team win their first-ever World Series title in 1935.

• • • •

1940 Tiger Floyd Giebell had only won two games in his brief two-year major league career when he was called upon to pitch one of the last games of the season for Detroit. To add to the drama, Detroit was in Cleveland to face the Indians, who were only two games behind them with three to go. If Detroit won, they would clinch the pennant. If the Tigers lost, they would be just one game ahead of the Indians with two to go in Cleveland. On the mound for Cleveland was 26-game winner Bob Feller. In spite of all the pressure and his larger-than-life mound opponent, Giebell pitched a masterful 2–0 shutout to clinch the pennant for the Tigers—and they needed it, too, because Cleveland did come back to win the next two games, giving the Tigers a one-game margin of victory in the pennant race.

The Tigers became the last team to fail to win a pennant with two 25-game winners on their pitching staff. Hal Newhouser was 29–9 with a 2.22 ERA and Dizzy Trout 27–14 with a 2.12 ERA for the 88–66 second-place Tigers. Their combined 56 wins established a record for two teammates after the dead-ball era.

Newhouser was last pitcher to win 25 or more games in back-to-back seasons—1944 and 1945 (he won 29 and 25 games respectively). He then followed that up by winning 26 games in 1946, giving him three consecutive 25-win seasons. After winning the AL MVP Awards in 1944 and 1945, he finished a close second to Ted Williams in 1946 when he finished 26–9 with a 1.94 ERA and 275 strikeouts. His strikeout total was the highest by a left-hander since 1905.

• • • •

1945 Hank Greenberg returned from military service in July 1945, and slugged a grand slam on the season's final day to help defeat the St. Louis Browns, 6–3, and clinch the AL pennant for the Tigers.

• • • •

1946 In Greenberg's last season in Detroit, he hit 44 homers with a .277 batting average, the first time ever a player had hit over 40 homers while hitting under .280.

• • • •

1947 Detroit's Roy Cullenbine set an American League record for first basemen when he walked 137 times. The amazing thing about his record is that he collected just 104 hits while batting only .224 on the season! His walks total set another record: the most walks received by a player in his final season.

1949 In 1949 Detroit third baseman George Kell kept Ted Williams from winning his third Triple Crown, but barely. Williams won the homer title with 43, and had 159 RBIs to tie Red Sox teammate Vern Stephens in that category, which would have allowed him to win the Triple Crown provided he won the batting title. Williams and Kell both finished with .343 averages, but Kell's average was .00016 higher than Williams', denying the Red Sox slugger his third Triple Crown.

••••

1949–50 Before Wade Boggs, the only 20th-century third baseman to hit .340 or better in back-to-back years was Kell, when he hit .343/.340 in 1949/1950.

••••

1952 The last pitcher to serve as a player-manager was Fred Hutchinson when he pulled the double duty for the Tigers.

••••

1961 When the American League expanded by two teams for the 1961 season, batting averages rose across the league, thanks to the 20 or so extra pitchers that would have been toiling in the minors if not for expansion. Mickey Mantle's average went from .275 in 1960 to .317 in 1961, and Al Kaline's from .278 to .324. No batter fared better than the Tigers' Norm Cash, however, who went from .286 to .361, with 41 homers and 132 RBIs. He also won the batting championship. All three numbers were career highs for Cash by a wide margin. In 1962 Cash's average fell to .243, the largest drop in history by a defending batting titlist.

••••

1963 The first black American League player to homer in his first at-bat was Gates Brown of the Tigers when he debuted with a four-bagger on June 19.

••••

1968 Although Mickey Stanley won a Gold Glove as an American League outfielder, in the 1968 World Series he played all seven games at shortstop.

••••

1971 Mickey Lolich (25–14) became the last pitcher to win 25 or more games in a season and not receive the Cy Young Award, as Vida Blue of Oakland copped the prize with a 24–8 record. In addition, Lolich's 48 starts and 376 innings were the most by any pitcher since the dead-ball era.

••••

1972 Outfielder Al Kaline recorded 242 consecutive errorless games, an American League record (since broken), a streak which ended in 1972.

••••

1973–74 Reliever John Hiller had incredible back-to-back seasons in 1973 and 1974. In 1973 he set a new major league record in saves with 38, since broken many times, and in 1974 he compiled an amazing record of 31 decisions as a relief pitcher when he went 17–14.

1974 When Detroit brought Ron LeFlore up to the majors, it made more than a few people in baseball uncomfortable. LeFlore, a convicted armed robber from the Detroit ghetto who spent time in prison, was shunned by most other players. In 1976, LeFlore's second full season, he led the Tigers in hitting with a .316 average. His 30-game hitting streak in 1976 was the longest in the American League during the 1970s. In 1978 he led the American League in stolen bases. During his nine years in the majors, LeFlore averaged 50 thefts—legal ones—a year.

• • • •

1975 Gates Brown was the first American League player to reach 100 career pinch-hits, retiring after the 1975 season with 108.

Detroit's 19-game losing streak in 1975 was the longest in the American League since 1943, when the Philadelphia Athletics lost 20 straight.

• • • •

1964–76 From 1964 to 1976, Mickey Lolich never started fewer than 30 games a year and four times he started more than 40.

• • • •

1979 Starting pitcher Pat Underwood of the Tigers had an especially memorable major league debut when, on May 31, he defeated his brother Tom, of the Blue Jays, 1–0.

1983 When he failed to finish even one of his 33 starts, Milt Wilcox set an American League record for most starts in a season without recording a complete game. What makes the record even more amazing is that on April 23 of that year, Wilcox lost a perfect game with two out in the ninth, and still failed to finish the game.

• • • •

1984 In a rare accomplishment, reliever Willie Hernandez won both the AL Cy Young and MVP Awards. Hernandez earned a save in all 32 of his opportunities—a record.

• • • •

1985 When Darrel Evans hit 40 homers for the Tigers, he became the first player ever to hit 40 homers in both leagues. In 1987 he set a record for home runs by a player over age 40 when he hit 34 round-trippers for Detroit.

• • • •

1987 Second baseman Lou Whitaker and shortstop Alan Trammell became the first keystone partners in major league history to play together on a regular basis for the same team for 10 consecutive years. When the 1995 season ended, Whitaker and Trammell had played in 1,918 games together, eclipsing the American League record for teammates (1,914) set by Kansas City's George Brett and Frank White.

1989 Just five short years after their 1984 World Series season, the Tigers lost 103 games, a franchise record (since broken).

• • • •

1991 Valuable utility player Tony Phillips became the first player in major league history to play at least 10 games at five different positions in one season when he played second, third, short, the outfield, and DH.

• • • •

1992 When Cecil Fielder collected 124 RBIs for Detroit he joined Babe Ruth as the only players in history to lead the major leagues in RBIs for three straight seasons.

• • • •

1993 Third baseman Travis Fryman hit for the cycle on July 28. Incredibly, it was the first time a Tiger had hit for the cycle since Hoot Evers in 1950, a span of 43 years.

• • • •

1996 The pitiful 1996 Tigers lost a franchise record 109 games (since broken). The team had one stretch from mid-April to early June when they went a dismal 5–39. The pitching staff had a 6.38 ERA—worst in American League history. Other dubious records: most home runs allowed in major league history at 241; and most strikeouts in a season by their hitters, with 1,268. They also ended the season by losing their last 17 straight home games.

Todd Jones

1990–99 The Tigers went the entire decade of the 1990s without having even one Gold Glove winner.

• • • •

2000 Reliever Todd Jones set a franchise record with 42 saves. Along the way he recorded one staggering stretch in which he allowed only two runs in 31 appearances.

• • • •

2001 From August 1–5, the Tigers scored exactly one run in each game, tying the major league record. For the month, the Tigers scored one run in 11 different games.

Special Achievements

World Series Results

Year	Opponent	Result	Games
1907	Chicago Cubs	Lost	0–4
1908	Chicago Cubs	Lost	1–4
1909	Pittsburgh Pirates	Lost	3–4
1934	St. Louis Cardinals	Lost	3–4
1935	Chicago Cubs	Won	4–2
1940	Cincinnati Reds	Lost	3–4
1945	Chicago Cubs	Won	4–3
1968	St. Louis Cardinals	Won	4–3
1984	San Diego Padres	Won	4–1

World Series Managerial Records

Manager	Series Record	Games Record
Hugh Jennings	0–3	4–12
Mickey Cochrane	1–1	7–6
Del Baker	0–1	3–4
Steve O'Neill	1–0	4–3
Mayo Smith	1–0	4–3
Sparky Anderson	1–0	4–1

All-Time Postseason Record

Divisional Playoffs	0–0
League Championship Series	6–7
World Series	26–29

All-Star Games at Detroit

Year	Date	Winner	Score	Stadium
1941	July 8	American	7–5	Briggs Stadium
1951	July 10	National	8–3	Briggs Stadium
1971	July 13	American	6–4	Tiger Stadium
2005	July 12	American	7–5	Comerica Park

Hall of Famers Who Played for Team

	Position	Years	Games with Detroit
Earl Averill	OF	1939–1940	151
Jim Bunning	SP	1955–1963	311
Ty Cobb	OF	1905–1926	2,806
Mickey Cochrane	C	1934–1937	315
Sam Crawford	OF	1903–1917	2,114
Larry Doby	OF	1959	18
Charlie Gehringer	2B	1924–1942	2,323
Goose Goslin	OF	1934–1937	524
Hank Greenberg	1B/OF	1930, 1933–1941, 1945–1946	1,269
Bucky Harris	2B	1929, 1931	11
Harry Heilmann	OF/1B	1914, 1916–1930	1,991
Waite Hoyt	SP	1930–1931	42
Hughie Jennings	1B/2B/SS	1907, 1909, 1918	5
Al Kaline	OF/DH/1B	1953–1974	2,834
George Kell	3B	1946–1952	826
Heinie Manush	OF	1923–1927	615
Eddie Mathews	3B/1B	1967–1968	67
Hal Newhouser	SP/RP	1939–1953	464
Al Simmons	OF	1936	143
Sam Thompson	OF	1906	8

Hall of Famers Who Managed Team

	Years	Games with Detroit
Sparky Anderson	1979–1995	2,579
Ed Barrow	1903–1904	214
Ty Cobb	1921–1926	923
Mickey Cochrane	1934–1938	632
Bucky Harris	1929–1933, 1955–1956	1,073
Hughie Jennings	1907–1920	2,103

MVP Award Winners

Mickey Cochrane	C	1934
Hank Greenberg	1B	1935
Charlie Gehringer	2B	1937
Hank Greenberg	OF	1940
Hal Newhouser	SP	1944
Hal Newhouser	SP	1945
Denny McLain	SP	1968
Willie Hernandez	RP	1984

Cy Young Award Winners

Pitcher	Year	W–L	SV	ERA
Denny McLain	1968	31–6	0	1.96
Denny McLain (tie)	1969	24–9	0	2.80
Willie Hernandez	1984	9–3	32	1.92

Rookie of the Year Award Winners

Harvey Kuenn	SS	1953
Mark Fidrych	SP	1976
Lou Whitaker	2B	1978

GOLD GLOVE WINNERS

Year	Position	Player
1957	OF	Al Kaline
1958	2B OF	Frank Bolling Al Kaline
1959	OF	Al Kaline
1961	SP OF	Frank Lary Al Kaline
1962	OF	Al Kaline
1963	OF	Al Kaline
1964	OF	Al Kaline
1965	C OF	Bill Freehan Al Kaline
1966	C OF	Bill Freehan Al Kaline
1967	C OF	Bill Freehan Al Kaline
1968	C OF	Bill Freehan Mickey Stanley
1969	C OF	Bill Freehan Mickey Stanley
1970	OF	Mickey Stanley
1972	SS	Ed Brinkman
1973	OF	Mickey Stanley
1976	3B	Aurelio Rodriguez
1980	SS	Alan Trammell
1981	SS	Alan Trammell
1983	C 2B SS	Lance Parrish Lou Whitaker Alan Trammell
1984	C 2B SS	Lance Parrish Lou Whitaker Alan Trammell
1985	C 2B	Lance Parrish Lou Whitaker
1988	OF	Gary Pettis
1989	OF	Gary Pettis
2004	C	Ivan Rodriguez

TRIPLE CROWN WINNERS

Player	Year	Avg	HR	RBI
Ty Cobb	1909	.377	9	115

FIREMAN OF THE YEAR AWARD WINNERS

John Hiller	1973
Todd Jones	2000

WORLD SERIES MVP

Mickey Lolich	1968
Alan Trammell	1984

LEAGUE CHAMPIONSHIP SERIES MVP

Kirk Gibson	1984

ALL-STAR GAME MVP

None

MANAGER OF THE YEAR AWARD WINNERS

Sparky Anderson	1984
Sparky Anderson	1987

BATTING CHAMPIONS

Player	Year	Avg
Ty Cobb	1907	.350
Ty Cobb	1908	.324
Ty Cobb	1909	.377
Ty Cobb	1910	.385
Ty Cobb	1911	.420
Ty Cobb	1912	.410
Ty Cobb	1913	.390
Ty Cobb	1914	.368
Ty Cobb	1915	.369
Ty Cobb	1917	.383
Ty Cobb	1918	.382
Ty Cobb	1919	.384
Harry Heilmann	1921	.394
Harry Heilmann	1923	.403
Harry Heilmann	1925	.393
Heinie Manush	1926	.378
Harry Heilmann	1927	.398
Charlie Gehringer	1937	.371
George Kell	1949	.343
Al Kaline	1955	.340
Harvey Kuenn	1959	.353
Norm Cash	1961	.361

NINE-INNING NO-HITTERS PITCHED

Year	Pitcher	Opp.	Score
1912	George Mullin	STL	7–0
1952	Virgil Trucks Virgil Trucks	WAS NYY	1–0 1–0
1958	Jim Bunning	BOS	3–0
1984	Jack Morris	CWS	4–0

20-GAME WINNERS

Year	Pitcher	W–L
1901	Roscoe Miller	23–13
1905	Ed Killian George Mullin	23–14 21–21
1906	George Mullin	21–18
1907	Bill Donovan Ed Killian George Mullin	25–4 25–13 20–20
1908	Ed Summers	24–12
1909	George Mullin Edgar Willett	29–9 21–10
1910	George Mullin	21–12

1914	Harry Coveleski	22–12
1915	George Dauss Harry Coveleski	24–13 22–13
1916	Harry Coveleski	21–11
1919	George Dauss	21–9
1923	George Dauss	21–13
1934	Schoolboy Rowe Tommy Bridges	24–8 22–11
1935	Tommy Bridges	21–10
1936	Tommy Bridges	23–11
1940	Bobo Newsom	21–5
1943	Dizzy Trout	20–12
1944	Hal Newhouser Dizzy Trout	29–9 27–14
1945	Hal Newhouser	25–9
1946	Hal Newhouser	26–9
1948	Hal Newhouser	21–12
1956	Frank Lary Billy Hoeft	21–13 20–14
1957	Jim Bunning	20–8
1961	Frank Lary	23–9
1966	Denny McLain	20–14
1967	Earl Wilson	22–11
1968	Denny McLain	31–6
1969	Denny McLain	24–9
1971	Mickey Lolich Joe Coleman	25–14 20–9
1972	Mickey Lolich	22–14
1973	Joe Coleman	23–15
1983	Jack Morris	20–13
1986	Jack Morris	21–8
1991	Bill Gullickson	20–9

RETIRED UNIFORM NUMBERS

Number	Player	Position
2	Charlie Gehringer	2B
5	Hank Greenberg	1B/OF
6	Al Kaline	OF
16	Hal Newhouser	SP
23	Willie Horton	OF/DH

TEAM RECORDS—WINS & LOSSES

- Games won in a season: 104 in 1984
- Games lost in a season: 119 in 2003
- Games won in a month: 23, 4 times: July 1908; August 1915; August 1934; August 1935
- Games lost in a month: 24 in June 1975
- Consecutive games won: 14 in 1909 and 1934
- Consecutive games lost: 19 in 1975
- Biggest shutout victory: 21–0 over Cleveland on September 15, 1901
- Biggest shutout loss: 16–0 to St. Louis Browns on September 9, 1922
- Highest winning percentage: .656 in 1934 (101–53)
- Lowest winning percentage: .265 in 2003 (43–119)

TEAM RECORDS—BATTING

- Highest team batting average: .316 in 1921
- Lowest team batting average: .231 in 1904
- Highest team slugging average: .454 in 1994
- Highest team on-base percentage: .385 in 1921
- Total hits: 1,724 in 1921
- Extra-base hits: 546 in 1929
- Hits in a game: 27 vs. New York Yankees on September 29, 1928 and Kansas City Royals on May 27, 2004
- Longest individual hitting streak: 40, Ty Cobb, 1911
- Most .300 hitters in a single season: 8 in 1922, 1924, and 1934
- Home runs: 225 in 1987
- Home runs in a month: 18, Rudy York, August 1937
- Home runs in a game: 8 vs. Toronto on June 20, 2000
- Home runs by a rookie: 35, Rudy York, 1937
- Home runs by a right-hander: 58, Hank Greenberg, 1938
- Home runs by a left-hander: 41, Norm Cash, 1961
- Home runs by a switch-hitter: 34, Tony Clark, 1998
- Grand slams: 10 in 1938
- Grand slams (individual; single season): 4, Rudy York, 1938 and Jim Northrup, 1968
- Grand slams (individual; career): 10, Rudy York, Hank Greenberg, and Cecil Fielder
- Triples: 102 in 1913
- Doubles: 349 in 1934
- Singles: 1,298 in 1921
- Walks: 765 in 1993
- Runs scored: 958 in 1934
- Runs scored in a game: 21, (4 times): vs. Cleveland, September 15, 1901; vs. Philadelphia A's, July 17, 1908; vs. St. Louis Browns, July 25, 1920; and vs. Chicago White Sox, July 1, 1936

- Runs scored in an inning: 13 vs. New York Yankees on September 22, 1936 (sixth inning) and vs. Texas on August 8, 2001 (ninth)
- Most batters hit by a pitch: 82 in 1999
- Times shut out: 22 in 1904
- Grounded into double plays: 164 in 1949
- Fewest grounded into double plays: 81 in 1985
- Runners left on base: 1,312 in 1993

TEAM RECORDS—BASERUNNING

- Stolen bases: 281 in 1909
- Caught stealing: 92 in 1921

TEAM RECORDS—PITCHING

- Lowest earned run average: 2.26 in 1909
- Complete games: 143 in 1904
- Saves: 51 in 1984
- Strikeouts: 1,115 in 1968
- Shutouts: 20 in 1917, 1944, and 1969
- Walks: 784 in 1996
- Hit batsmen: 84 in 1922
- Wild pitches: 82 in 1996
- Consecutive wins (individual): 16, Schoolboy Rowe, 1934
- Consecutive losses (individual): 10, Mickey Lolich, 1967; Mike Moore, 1995
- Strikeouts in a game (individual): 16, Mickey Lolich, May 23, 1969; Mickey Lolich, June 9, 1969
- Runs allowed in a game: 26 vs. Kansas City Royals, September 9, 2004

TEAM RECORDS—FIELDING

- Best fielding average: .985 in 1997
- Most errors committed: 425 in 1901
- Fewest errors committed: 92 in 1997
- Most double plays turned: 194 in 1950 and 2003
- Fewest double plays turned: 94 in 1912 and 1917

TEAM RECORDS—MISCELLANEOUS

- Number of times league champions: 9
- Number of times finishing last in league: 6
- Largest attendance, single game: 57,888 vs. Cleveland, September 26, 1948
- Largest attendance, doubleheader: 58,369 vs. New York Yankees, July 20, 1947
- Players used in a season: 57 in 2002
- Seasons played: 22 by Ty Cobb and Al Kaline

PRIMARY PITCHING STAFFS

Year	Starter	Starter	Starter	Starter	Starter	Closer	Bullpen	Bullpen	Bullpen
2005	Maroth	Johnson	Robertson	Bonderman	Douglass	Urbina	Walker	German	Spurling
2004	Maroth	Johnson	Bonderman	Robertson	Knotts	Urbina	Walker	Yan	Levine
2003	Maroth	Cornejo	Bonderman	Bernero	Knotts	Walker	Spurling	German	
2002	Maroth	Redman	Sparks	Weaver	Lima	Acevedo	Paniagua	Farnsworth	Walker
2001	Holt	Mlicki	Sparks	Weaver	Lima	Anderson	Patterson	Nitkowski	Jones
2000	Nomo	Mlicki	Moehler	Weaver	Blair	Jones	Anderson	Nitkowski	Patterson
1999	Thompson	Mlicki	Moehler	Weaver	Blair	Jones	Brocail	Nitkowski	Kida
1998	Thompson	Greisinger	Moehler	Castillo	Powell	Jones	Brocail	Runyan	Bochtler
1997	Thompson	Blair	Moehler	Olivares	Lira	Jones	Brocail	Myers	Miceli
1996	Thompson	Williams	Gohr	Olivares	Lira	Olson	Lewis	Myers	Lima
1995	Bergman	Moore	Wells	Lima	Lira	Henneman	Boever	Bohanon	Doherty
1994	Belcher	Moore	Wells	Gullickson	Doherty	Henneman	Boever	Groom	Gardiner
1993	Leiter	Moore	Wells	Gullickson	Doherty	Henneman	MacDonald	Bolton	Krueger
1992	Leiter	Tanana	King	Gullickson	Terrell	Henneman	Munoz	Knudsen	Doherty
1991	Leiter	Tanana	Aldred	Gullickson	Terrell	Henneman	Gibson	Gleaton	Cerutti
1990	Morris	Tanana	Robinson	Petry	Searcy	Henneman	Gibson	Gleaton	Nunez
1989	Morris	Tanana	Robinson	Alexander	Gibson	Hernandez	Henneman	Williams	Nunez
1988	Morris	Tanana	Robinson	Alexander	Terrell	Henneman	Hernandez	Gibson	King
1987	Morris	Tanana	Robinson	Petry	Terrell	King	Hernandez	Henneman	Thurmond
1986	Morris	Tanana	King	Petry	Terrell	Hernandez	O'Neal	Campbell	Thurmond
1985	Morris	Tanana	Berenguer	Petry	Terrell	Hernandez	O'Neal	Lopez	Scherrer
1984	Morris	Wilcox	Berenguer	Petry	Rozema	Hernandez	Bair	Lopez	Monge
1983	Morris	Wilcox	Berenguer	Petry	Rozema	Lopez	Bair	Bailey	Gumpert
1982	Morris	Wilcox	Ujdur	Petry	Pashnick	Tobik	Sosa	Underwood	Saucier
1981	Morris	Wilcox	Schatzeder	Petry	Rozema	Saucier	Cappuzzello	Tobik	Lopez
1980	Morris	Wilcox	Schatzeder	Petry	Rozema	Lopez	Underwood	Tobik	Weaver
1979	Morris	Wilcox	Billingham	Underwood	Rozema	Lopez	Hiller	Tobik	Baker
1978	Slaton	Wilcox	Billingham	Young	Rozema	Hiller	Morris	Foucault	Sykes
1977	Arroyo	Wilcox	Roberts	Sykes	Rozema	Foucault	Hiller	Crawford	Grilli
1976	Ruhle	Fidrych	Roberts	Bare	Coleman	Hiller	Laxton	Crawford	Grilli
1975	Ruhle	Lolich	LaGrow	Bare	Coleman	Hiller	Walker	Lemanczyk	Reynolds
1974	Fryman	Lolich	LaGrow	Walker	Coleman	Hiller	Ray	Lemanczyk	Slayback
1973	Fryman	Lolich	Perry	Strahler	Coleman	Hiller	Scherman	Farmer	Miller
1972	Fryman	Lolich	Timmermann	Slayback	Coleman	Seelbach	Scherman	Zachary	Hiller
1971	Cain	Lolich	Niekro	Chance	Coleman	Scherman	Timmermann	Denehy	Kilkenny
1970	Cain	Lolich	Niekro	Kilkenny	Wilson	Timmermann	Scherman	Hiller	Patterson
1969	McLain	Lolich	Sparma	Kilkenny	Wilson	McMahon	Dobson	Hiller	Lasher
1968	McLain	Lolich	Sparma	Hiller	Wilson	Patterson	Dobson	Warden	Lasher
1967	McLain	Lolich	Sparma	Podres	Wilson	Gladding	Marshall	Wickersham	Aguirre
1966	McLain	Lolich	Monbouquette	Wickersham	Wilson	Sherry	Pena	Gladding	Podres
1965	McLain	Lolich	Aguirre	Wickersham	Sparma	Fox	Pena	Gladding	Sherry
1964	McLain	Lolich	Aguirre	Wickersham	Regan	Sherry	Rakow	Gladding	Fox
1963	Bunning	Lolich	Aguirre	Mossi	Regan	Fox	Anderson	Faul	Sturdivant
1962	Bunning	Foytack	Aguirre	Mossi	Regan	Fox	Nischwitz	Kline	Jones
1961	Bunning	Foytack	Lary	Mossi	Regan	Fox	Aguirre	Fischer	Bruce
1960	Bunning	Bruce	Lary	Mossi	Burnside	Aguirre	Sisler	Foytack	Morgan
1959	Bunning	Foytack	Lary	Mossi	Narleski	Morgan	Sisler	Burnside	Schultz
1958	Bunning	Foytack	Lary	Hoeft	Moford	Aguirre	Morgan	Susce	
1957	Bunning	Foytack	Lary	Hoeft	Maas	Sleater	Byrd	Aber	
1956	Trucks	Foytack	Lary	Hoeft	Gromek	Aber	Masterson	Maas	Bunning
1955	Garver	Maas	Lary	Hoeft	Gromek	Aber	Birrer	Foytack	

PRIMARY PITCHING STAFFS (CONT.)

Year	Starter	Starter	Starter	Starter	Starter	Closer	Bullpen	Bullpen	Bullpen
1954	Garver	Zuverink	Aber	Hoeft	Gromek	Herbert	Marlowe	Miller	
1953	Garver	Gray	Branca	Hoeft	Gromek	Herbert	Madison	Marlowe	Erickson
1952	Trucks	Gray	Houtteman	Wight	Newhouser	White	Hoeft	Stuart	
1951	Trucks	Gray	Trout	Cain	Hutchinson	White	Bearden	Stuart	
1950	Houtteman	Gray	Trout	Newhouser	Hutchinson	White	Calvert	Stuart	
1949	Houtteman	Gray	Trucks	Newhouser	Hutchinson	Trout	Grissom	Kretlow	
1948	Houtteman	Trout	Trucks	Newhouser	Hutchinson	Overmire	Benton	White	
1947	Overmire	Trout	Trucks	Newhouser	Hutchinson	Benton	Gorsica	Houtteman	White
1946	Benton	Trout	Trucks	Newhouser	Hutchinson	Gorsica	Caster	Overmire	
1945	Benton	Trout	Overmire	Newhouser	Mueller	Wilson	Caster	Eaton	
1944	Gentry	Trout	Overmire	Newhouser	Gorsica	Beck	Mooty	Orrell	
1943	Trucks	Trout	White	Newhouser	Bridges	Gorsica	Overmire	Henshaw	
1942	Benton	Trout	White	Newhouser	Bridges	Gorsica	Trucks	Henshaw	
1941	Newsom	Trout	Gorsica	Newhouser	Bridges	Benton	Rowe	Thomas	Giebell
1940	Newsom	Rowe	Gorsica	Newhouser	Bridges	Benton	Trout	McKain	Seats
1939	Newsom	Rowe	Trout	Benton	Bridges	Thomas	McKain	Coffman	
1938	Kennedy	Auker	Gill	Lawson	Bridges	Eisenstat	Wade	Coffman	
1937	Wade	Auker	Poffenberger	Lawson	Bridges	Gill	Russell	Coffman	
1936	Wade	Auker	Rowe	Sorrell	Bridges	Lawson	Sullivan	Phillips	
1935	Crowder	Auker	Rowe	Sullivan	Bridges	Hogsett	Sorrell	Hatter	
1934	Marberry	Auker	Rowe	Sorrell	Bridges	Hogsett	Hamlin	Fischer	
1933	Marberry	Fischer	Rowe	Sorrell	Bridges	Hogsett	Herring	Frazier	Auker
1932	Whitehill	Wyatt	Hogsett	Sorrell	Bridges	Uhle	Marrow	Goldstein	
1931	Whitehill	Uhle	Herring	Sorrell	Bridges	Sullivan	Hogsett	Hoyt	
1930	Whitehill	Uhle	Hoyt	Sorrell	Hogsett	Sullivan	Herring	Wyatt	
1929	Whitehill	Uhle	Carroll	Sorrell	Graham	Prudhomme	Yde	Stoner	
1928	Whitehill	Gibson	Carroll	Sorrell	Billings	Smith	Vangilder	Stoner	
1927	Whitehill	Gibson	Collins	Stoner	Holloway	Smith	Carroll	Hankins	
1926	Whitehill	Gibson	Wells	Stoner	Johns	Dauss	Smith	Holloway	Collins
1925	Whitehill	Dauss	Collins	Stoner	Leonard	Doyle	Wells	Holloway	Cole
1924	Whitehill	Wells	Collins	Stoner	Holloway	Dauss	Johnson	Pillette	Cole
1923	Dauss	Pillette	Collins	Johnson	Holloway	Francis	Olsen	Cole	
1922	Dauss	Pillette	Ehmke	Oldham	Olsen	Johnson	Stoner	Cole	
1921	Dauss	Leonard	Ehmke	Oldham	Cole	Middleton	Holling	Sutherland	Parks
1920	Dauss	Leonard	Ehmke	Oldham	Ayers	Okrie	Alten	Glaiser	
1919	Dauss	Leonard	Ehmke	Boland	Love	Ayers	Cunningham	Kallio	
1918	Dauss	Kallio	James	Boland	Cunningham	Jones	Erickson	Bailey	
1917	Dauss	Ehmke	James	Boland	Mitchell	Jones	Cunningham	Coveleski	
1916	Dauss	Coveleski	James	Dubuc	Mitchell	Boland	Cunningham	Erickson	
1915	Dauss	Coveleski	James	Dubuc	Boland	Steen	Cavet	Oldham	
1914	Dauss	Coveleski	Cavet	Dubuc	Main	Reynolds	Hall	Boehler	
1913	Dauss	Willett	Hall	Dubuc	Lake	House	Zamloch	Comstock	
1912	Mullin	Willett	Works	Dubuc	Lake	Covington	Burns		
1911	Mullin	Willett	Lafitte	Summers	Donovan	Covington	Works	Lively	
1910	Mullin	Willett	Stroud	Summers	Donovan	Pernoll	Works	Browning	
1909	Mullin	Willett	Killian	Summers	Donovan	Speer	Works	Suggs	
1908	Mullin	Willett	Killian	Summers	Donovan	Siever	Winter	Suggs	
1907	Mullin	Siever	Killian	Eubank	Donovan	Willett			
1906	Mullin	Siever	Killian	Donahue	Donovan	Eubank			
1905	Mullin	Kitson	Killian	Wiggs	Donovan	Disch	Ford		

PRIMARY PITCHING STAFFS (CONT.)

Year	Starter	Starter	Starter	Starter	Starter	Closer	Bullpen	Bullpen	Bullpen
1904	Mullin	Kitson	Killian	Stovall	Donovan	Jaeger			
1903	Mullin	Kitson	Kisinger	Deering	Donovan	Eason	Skopec		
1902	Mullin	Mercer	Siever	Miller	Yeager	McCarthy			
1901	Cronin	Frisk	Siever	Miller	Yeager	Owen			

PRIMARY STARTING LINEUPS

Year	C	1B	2B	3B	SS	LF	CF	RF	DH
2005	Rodriguez	Shelton	Polanco	Inge	Guillen	White	Logan	Monroe	Young
2004	Rodriguez	Peña	Infante	Munson	Guillen	White	Sanchez	Higginson	Young
2003	Inge	Peña	Morris	Munson	Santiago	Monroe	Sanchez	Higginson	Young
2002	Inge	Peña	Easley	Truby	Halter	Higginson	Magee	Fick	Simon
2001	Inge	Clark	Easley	Macias	Cruz	Higginson	Cedeno	Encarnacion	Palmer
2000	Ausmus	Clark	Easley	Palmer	Cruz	Higginson	Encarnacion	Gonzalez	Polonia
1999	Ausmus	Clark	Easley	Palmer	Cruz	Encarnacion	Kapler	Higginson	Polonia
1998	Bako	Clark	Easley	Randa	Cruz	Gonzalez	Hunter	Higginson	Berroa
1997	Casanova	Clark	Easley	Fryman	Cruz	Higginson	Hunter	Nieves	Hamelin
1996	Ausmus	Clark	Lewis	Fryman	Cedeno	Higginson	Bartee	Nieves	Williams
1995	Flaherty	Fielder	Fletcher	Fryman	Gomez	Cuyler	Curtis	Bautista	Gibson
1994	Kreuter	Fielder	Whitaker	Fryman	Trammell	Phillips	Davis	Felix	Gibson
1993	Kreuter	Fielder	Whitaker	Livingstone	Fryman	Phillips	Cuyler	Deer	Gibson
1992	Tettleton	Fielder	Whitaker	Livingstone	Fryman	Gladden	Cuyler	Deer	Phillips
1991	Tettleton	Fielder	Whitaker	Fryman	Trammell	Moseby	Cuyler	Deer	Incaviglia
1990	Heath	Fielder	Whitaker	Phillips	Trammell	Ward	Moseby	Lemon	Bergman
1989	Heath	Bergman	Whitaker	Schu	Trammell	Lynn	Pettis	Lemon	Moreland
1988	Nokes	Knight	Whitaker	Brookens	Trammell	Sheridan	Pettis	Lemon	Evans
1987	Nokes	Evans	Whitaker	Brookens	Trammell	Gibson	Lemon	Sheridan	Madlock
1986	Parrish	Evans	Whitaker	Coles	Trammell	Herndon	Lemon	Gibson	Grubb
1985	Parrish	Evans	Whitaker	Brookens	Trammell	Herndon	Lemon	Gibson	Grubb
1984	Parrish	Bergman	Whitaker	Johnson	Trammell	Herndon	Lemon	Gibson	Evans
1983	Parrish	Cabell	Whitaker	Brookens	Trammell	Herndon	Lemon	Wilson	Gibson
1982	Parrish	Cabell	Whitaker	Brookens	Trammell	Herndon	Wilson	Lemon	Ivie
1981	Parrish	Hebner	Whitaker	Brookens	Trammell	Kemp	Cowens	Jones	Wockenfuss
1980	Parrish	Hebner	Whitaker	Brookens	Trammell	Kemp	Peters	Cowens	Summers
1979	Parrish	Thompson	Whitaker	Rodriguez	Trammell	Kemp	LeFlore	Morales	Staub
1978	May	Thompson	Whitaker	Rodriguez	Trammell	Kemp	LeFlore	Corcoran	Staub
1977	May	Thompson	Fuentes	Rodriguez	Veryzer	Kemp	LeFlore	Oglivie	Staub
1976	Freehan	Thompson	Garcia	Rodriguez	Veryzer	Johnson	LeFlore	Staub	Horton
1975	Freehan	Pierce	Sutherland	Rodriguez	Veryzer	Oglivie	LeFlore	Roberts	Horton
1974	Moses	Freehan	Sutherland	Rodriguez	Brinkman	Horton	Stanley	Northrup	Kaline
1973	Freehan	Cash	McAuliffe	Rodriguez	Brinkman	Horton	Stanley	Northrup	Brown
1972	Freehan	Cash	McAuliffe	Rodriguez	Brinkman	Horton	Stanley	Kaline	
1971	Freehan	Cash	McAuliffe	Rodriguez	Brinkman	Horton	Stanley	Kaline	
1970	Freehan	Cash	McAuliffe	Wert	Gutierrez	Horton	Stanley	Kaline	
1969	Freehan	Cash	McAuliffe	Wert	Tresh	Horton	Stanley	Kaline	
1968	Freehan	Cash	McAuliffe	Wert	Oyler	Horton	Stanley	Northrup	
1967	Freehan	Cash	McAuliffe	Wert	Oyler	Horton	Stanley	Kaline	
1966	Freehan	Cash	Lumpe	Wert	McAuliffe	Horton	Kaline	Northrup	
1965	Freehan	Cash	Lumpe	Wert	McAuliffe	Horton	Kaline	Northrup	
1964	Freehan	Cash	Lumpe	Wert	McAuliffe	Brown	Bruton	Kaline	
1963	Triandos	Cash	Wood	Phillips	McAuliffe	Colavito	Bruton	Kaline	
1962	Brown	Cash	Wood	Boros	Fernandez	Colavito	Bruton	Kaline	

PRIMARY STARTING LINEUPS (CONT.)

Year	C	1B	2B	3B	SS	LF	CF	RF	DH
1961	Brown	Cash	Wood	Boros	Fernandez	Colavito	Bruton	Kaline	
1960	Berberet	Cash	Bolling	Yost	Fernandez	Maxwell	Kaline	Colavito	
1959	Berberet	Harris	Bolling	Yost	Bridges	Maxwell	Kaline	Kuenn	
1958	Wilson	Harris	Bolling	Bertoia	Martin	Maxwell	Kuenn	Kaline	
1957	House	Boone	Bolling	Bertoia	Kuenn	Maxwell	Tuttle	Kaline	
1956	House	Torgeson	Bolling	Boone	Kuenn	Maxwell	Tuttle	Kaline	
1955	House	Torgeson	Hatfield	Boone	Kuenn	Delsing	Tuttle	Kaline	
1954	House	Dropo	Bolling	Boone	Kuenn	Delsing	Tuttle	Kaline	
1953	Batts	Dropo	Pesky	Boone	Kuenn	Nieman	Delsing	Lund	
1952	Ginsberg	Dropo	Priddy	Hatfield	Berry	Mullin	Groth	Wertz	
1951	Ginsberg	Kryhoski	Priddy	Kell	Lipon	Mullin	Groth	Wertz	
1950	Robinson	Kolloway	Priddy	Kell	Lipon	Evers	Groth	Wertz	
1949	Robinson	Campbell	Berry	Kell	Lipon	Evers	Groth	Wertz	
1948	Swift	Vico	Mayo	Kell	Lipon	Wakefield	Evers	Mullin	
1947	Swift	Cullenbine	Mayo	Kell	Lake	Wakefield	Evers	Mullin	
1946	Tebbetts	Greenberg	Bloodworth	Kell	Lake	Wakefield	Evers	Mullin	
1945	Swift	York	Mayo	Maier	Webb	Outlaw	Cramer	Cullenbine	
1944	Richards	York	Mayo	Higgins	Hoover	Wakefield	Cramer	Hostetler	
1943	Richards	York	Bloodworth	Higgins	Hoover	Wakefield	Cramer	Harris	
1942	Tebbetts	York	Bloodworth	Higgins	Hitchcock	McCosky	Cramer	Harris	
1941	Tebbetts	York	Gehringer	Higgins	Croucher	Radcliff	McCosky	Campbell	
1940	Tebbetts	York	Gehringer	Higgins	Bartell	Greenberg	McCosky	Fox	
1939	Tebbetts	Greenberg	Gehringer	Higgins	Croucher	Averill	McCosky	Fox	
1938	York	Greenberg	Gehringer	Ross	Rogell	Walker	Morgan	Fox	
1937	York	Greenberg	Gehringer	Owen	Rogell	Walker	White	Fox	
1936	Hayworth	Burns	Gehringer	Owen	Rogell	Goslin	Simmons	Walker	
1935	Cochrane	Greenberg	Gehringer	Owen	Rogell	Goslin	White	Fox	
1934	Cochrane	Greenberg	Gehringer	Owen	Rogell	Goslin	White	Fox	
1933	Hayworth	Greenberg	Gehringer	Owen	Rogell	Walker	Fox	Stone	
1932	Hayworth	Davis	Gehringer	Schuble	Rogell	Stone	Walker	Webb	
1931	Hayworth	Alexander	Gehringer	McManus	Rogell	Stone	Walker	Johnson	
1930	Hayworth	Alexander	Gehringer	McManus	Koenig	Stone	Funk	Johnson	
1929	Phillips	Alexander	Gehringer	McManus	Schuble	Johnson	Rice	Heilmann	
1928	Hargrave	Sweeney	Gehringer	McManus	Tavener	Fothergill	Rice	Heilmann	
1927	Woodall	Blue	Gehringer	Warner	Tavener	Fothergill	Manush	Heilmann	
1926	Manion	Blue	Gehringer	Warner	Tavener	Fothergill	Manush	Heilmann	
1925	Bassler	Blue	O'Rourke	Haney	Tavener	Wingo	Cobb	Heilmann	
1924	Bassler	Blue	Pratt	Jones	Rigney	Manush	Cobb	Heilmann	
1923	Bassler	Blue	Haney	Jones	Rigney	Manush	Cobb	Heilmann	
1922	Bassler	Blue	Cutshaw	Jones	Rigney	Veach	Cobb	Heilmann	
1921	Bassler	Blue	Young	Jones	Bush	Veach	Cobb	Heilmann	
1920	Stanage	Heilmann	Young	Pinelli	Bush	Veach	Cobb	Flagstead	
1919	Ainsmith	Heilmann	Young	Jones	Bush	Veach	Cobb	Flagstead	
1918	Yelle	Heilmann	Young	Vitt	Bush	Veach	Cobb	Harper	
1917	Stanage	Burns	Young	Vitt	Bush	Veach	Cobb	Heilmann	
1916	Stanage	Burns	Young	Vitt	Bush	Veach	Cobb	Crawford	
1915	Stanage	Burns	Young	Vitt	Bush	Veach	Cobb	Crawford	
1914	Stanage	Burns	Kavanagh	Moriarty	Bush	Veach	Cobb	Crawford	
1913	Stanage	Gainer	Vitt	Moriarty	Bush	Veach	Cobb	Crawford	
1912	Stanage	Moriarty	Louden	Deal	Bush	Jones	Cobb	Crawford	
1911	Stanage	Delahanty	O'Leary	Moriarty	Bush	Jones	Cobb	Crawford	
1910	Stanage	Jones	Delahanty	Moriarty	Bush	Jones	Cobb	Crawford	

PRIMARY STARTING LINEUPS (CONT.)

Year	C	1B	2B	3B	SS	LF	CF	RF	DH
1909	Schmidt	Rossman	Schaefer	Moriarty	Bush	McIntyre	Crawford	Cobb	
1908	Schmidt	Rossman	Downs	Coughlin	Schaefer	McIntyre	Crawford	Cobb	
1907	Schmidt	Rossman	Downs	Coughlin	O'Leary	Jones	Crawford	Cobb	
1906	Schmidt	Lindsay	Schaefer	Coughlin	O'Leary	McIntyre	Jones	Crawford	
1905	Drill	Lindsay	Schaefer	Coughlin	O'Leary	McIntyre	Cooley	Crawford	
1904	Drill	Carr	Lowe	Gremminger	O'Leary	McIntyre	Barrett	Crawford	
1903	McGuire	Carr	Smith	Yeager	McAllister	Lush	Barrett	Crawford	
1902	McGuire	Dillon	Gleason	Casey	Elberfeld	Harley	Barrett	Holmes	
1901	Buelow	Dillon	Gleason	Casey	Elberfeld	Nance	Barrett	Holmes	

Top 10 Batting Leaders, Single Season & Career with Team

GAMES PLAYED: CAREER WITH TEAM

Player	G	PA
1. Al Kaline	2,834	11,597
2. Ty Cobb	2,806	12,105
3. Lou Whitaker	2,390	9,967
4. Charlie Gehringer	2,323	10,237
5. Alan Trammell	2,293	9,375
6. Sam Crawford	2,114	8,869
7. Norm Cash	2,018	7,772
8. Harry Heilmann	1,991	8,390
9. Donie Bush	1,872	8,451
10. Bill Freehan	1,774	6,899

AT-BATS: SEASON

Player	AB	Year
1. Harvey Kuenn	679	1953
2. Ron LeFlore	666	1978
3. Jake Wood	663	1961
4. Travis Fryman	659	1992
5. Brian Hunter	658	1997
6. Harvey Kuenn	656	1954
7. Ron LeFlore	652	1977
8. Lou Whitaker	643	1983
9. Rusty Staub	642	1978
10. Charlie Gehringer	641	1936
George Kell	641	1950

AT-BATS: CAREER WITH TEAM

Player	AB	PA
1. Ty Cobb	10,591	12,105
2. Al Kaline	10,116	11,597
3. Charlie Gehringer	8,860	10,237
4. Lou Whitaker	8,570	9,967
5. Alan Trammell	8,288	9,375
6. Sam Crawford	7,984	8,869
7. Harry Heilmann	7,297	8,390
8. Donie Bush	6,970	8,451
9. Norm Cash	6,593	7,772
10. Bill Freehan	6,073	6,899

BATTING AVERAGE: SEASON

Player	BA	Year
1. Ty Cobb	.420	1911
2. Ty Cobb	.409	1912
3. Harry Heilmann	.403	1923
4. Ty Cobb	.401	1922
5. Harry Heilmann	.398	1927
6. Harry Heilmann	.394	1921
7. Harry Heilmann	.393	1925
8. Ty Cobb	.390	1913
9. Ty Cobb	.389	1921
10. Ty Cobb	.384	1919

BATTING AVERAGE: CAREER WITH TEAM

Player	BA	PA
1. Ty Cobb	.368	12,105
2. Harry Heilmann	.342	8,390
3. Bob Fothergill	.337	2,693
4. George Kell	.325	3,734
5. Heinie Manush	.321	2,377
6. Charlie Gehringer	.320	10,237
7. Hank Greenberg	.319	5,586
8. Gee Walker	.317	3,241
9. Harvey Kuenn	.314	4,750
10. Barney McCosky	.312	2,706

TOTAL HITS: SEASON

Player	H	Year
1. Ty Cobb	248	1911
2. Harry Heilmann	237	1921
3. Charlie Gehringer	227	1936
4. Ty Cobb	226	1912
5. Ty Cobb	225	1917
Harry Heilmann	225	1925
7. George Kell	218	1950
8. Sam Crawford	217	1911
9. Ty Cobb	216	1909
10. Dale Alexander	215	1929
Charlie Gehringer	215	1929

TOTAL HITS: CAREER WITH TEAM

Player	H	PA
1. Ty Cobb	3900	12,105
2. Al Kaline	3007	11,597
3. Charlie Gehringer	2839	10,237
4. Harry Heilmann	2499	8,390
5. Sam Crawford	2466	8,869
6. Lou Whitaker	2369	9,967
7. Alan Trammell	2365	9,375
8. Bobby Veach	1859	6,782
9. Norm Cash	1793	7,772
10. Donie Bush	1745	8,451

HOME RUNS: SEASON

Player	HR	Year
1. Hank Greenberg	58	1938
2. Cecil Fielder	51	1990
3. Rocky Colavito	45	1961
4. Cecil Fielder	44	1991
Hank Greenberg	44	1946
6. Norm Cash	41	1961
Hank Greenberg	41	1940
8. Darrell Evans	40	1985
Hank Greenberg	40	1937
10. Norm Cash	39	1962

HOME RUNS: CAREER WITH TEAM

Player	HR	PA
1. Al Kaline	399	11,597
2. Norm Cash	373	7,772
3. Hank Greenberg	306	5,586
4. Willie Horton	262	5,978
5. Cecil Fielder	245	4,252
6. Lou Whitaker	244	9,967
7. Rudy York	239	5,350
8. Lance Parrish	212	4,674
9. Bill Freehan	200	6,899
10. Kirk Gibson	195	4,773

TRIPLES: SEASON

Player	3B	Year
1. Sam Crawford	26	1914
2. Sam Crawford	25	1903
3. Ty Cobb	24	1911
Ty Cobb	24	1917
5. Ty Cobb	23	1912
Sam Crawford	23	1913
7. Sam Crawford	21	1912
8. Ty Cobb	20	1908
9. Sam Crawford	19	1910
Sam Crawford	19	1915
Charlie Gehringer	19	1929
Roy Johnson	19	1931
Barney McCosky	19	1940

TRIPLES: CAREER WITH TEAM

Player	3B	PA
1. Ty Cobb	284	12,105
2. Sam Crawford	249	8,869
3. Charlie Gehringer	146	10,237
4. Harry Heilmann	145	8,390
5. Bobby Veach	136	6,782
6. Al Kaline	75	11,597
7. Donie Bush	73	8,451
8. Dick McAuliffe	70	6,829
9. Hank Greenberg	69	5,586
10. Lu Blue	66	4,124

DOUBLES: SEASON

Player	2B	Year
1. Hank Greenberg	63	1934
2. Charlie Gehringer	60	1936
3. George Kell	56	1950
4. Gee Walker	55	1936
5. Charlie Gehringer	50	1934
Hank Greenberg	50	1940
Harry Heilmann	50	1927
8. Hank Greenberg	49	1937
9. Dale Alexander	47	1931
Ty Cobb	47	1911
Charlie Gehringer	47	1930

DOUBLES: CAREER WITH TEAM

Player	2B	PA
1. Ty Cobb	665	12,105
2. Charlie Gehringer	574	10,237
3. Al Kaline	498	11,597
4. Harry Heilmann	497	8,390
5. Lou Whitaker	420	9,967
6. Alan Trammell	412	9,375
7. Sam Crawford	402	8,869
8. Hank Greenberg	366	5,586
9. Bobby Veach	345	6,782
10. Bobby Higginson	270	5,633

EXTRA-BASE HITS: SEASON

Player	XBH	Year
1. Hank Greenberg	103	1937
2. Hank Greenberg	99	1940
3. Hank Greenberg	98	1935
4. Hank Greenberg	96	1934
5. Charlie Gehringer	87	1936
6. Hank Greenberg	85	1938
Rudy York	85	1940
8. Dale Alexander	83	1929
9. Hank Greenberg	82	1939
10. Ty Cobb	79	1911

EXTRA-BASE HITS: CAREER WITH TEAM

Player	XBH	PA
1. Ty Cobb	1,060	12,105
2. Al Kaline	972	11,597
3. Charlie Gehringer	904	10,237
4. Harry Heilmann	806	8,390
5. Hank Greenberg	741	5,586
6. Lou Whitaker	729	9,967
7. Sam Crawford	721	8,869
8. Norm Cash	654	7,772
9. Alan Trammell	652	9,375
10. Bobby Veach	540	6,782

TOTAL BASES: SEASON

Player	TB	Year
1. Hank Greenberg	397	1937
2. Hank Greenberg	389	1935
3. Hank Greenberg	384	1940
4. Hank Greenberg	380	1938
5. Ty Cobb	367	1911
6. Harry Heilmann	365	1921
7. Dale Alexander	363	1929
8. Charlie Gehringer	356	1936
Hank Greenberg	356	1934
10. Norm Cash	354	1961

TOTAL BASES: CAREER WITH TEAM

Player	TB	PA
1. Ty Cobb	5,466	12,105
2. Al Kaline	4,852	11,597
3. Charlie Gehringer	4,257	10,237
4. Harry Heilmann	3,778	8,390
5. Lou Whitaker	3,651	9,967
6. Sam Crawford	3,576	8,869
7. Alan Trammell	3,442	9,375
8. Norm Cash	3,233	7,772
9. Hank Greenberg	2,950	5,586
10. Bobby Veach	2,653	6,782

RUNS BATTED IN: SEASON

Player	RBI	Year
1. Hank Greenberg	183	1937
2. Hank Greenberg	170	1935
3. Hank Greenberg	150	1940
4. Hank Greenberg	146	1938
5. Rocky Colavito	140	1961
6. Hank Greenberg	139	1934
Harry Heilmann	139	1921
8. Dale Alexander	137	1929
9. Dale Alexander	135	1930
10. Harry Heilmann	134	1925
Rudy York	134	1940

Runs Batted In: Career with Team

Player	RBI	PA
1. Ty Cobb	1,804	12,105
2. Al Kaline	1,583	11,597
3. Harry Heilmann	1,442	8,390
4. Charlie Gehringer	1,427	10,237
5. Sam Crawford	1,264	8,869
6. Hank Greenberg	1,202	5,586
7. Norm Cash	1,087	7,772
8. Lou Whitaker	1,084	9,967
9. Bobby Veach	1,042	6,782
10. Alan Trammell	1,003	9,375

Runs Scored: Season

Player	R	Year
1. Ty Cobb	147	1911
2. Ty Cobb	144	1915
Charlie Gehringer	144	1930
Charlie Gehringer	144	1936
Hank Greenberg	144	1938
6. Hank Greenberg	137	1937
7. Charlie Gehringer	134	1934
8. Charlie Gehringer	133	1937
Charlie Gehringer	133	1938
10. Lu Blue	131	1922
Charlie Gehringer	131	1929

Runs Scored: Career with Team

Player	R	PA
1. Ty Cobb	2,088	12,105
2. Charlie Gehringer	1,774	10,237
3. Al Kaline	1,622	11,597
4. Lou Whitaker	1,386	9,967
5. Donie Bush	1,242	8,451
6. Alan Trammell	1,231	9,375
7. Harry Heilmann	1,209	8,390
8. Sam Crawford	1,115	8,869
9. Norm Cash	1,028	7,772
10. Hank Greenberg	980	5,586

Walks: Season

Player	BB	Year
1. Roy Cullenbine	137	1947
2. Eddie Yost	135	1959
3. Tony Phillips	132	1993
4. Eddie Yost	125	1960
5. Norm Cash	124	1961
6. Mickey Tettleton	122	1992
7. Eddie Lake	120	1947
8. Hank Greenberg	119	1938
9. Donie Bush	118	1915
Ty Cobb	118	1915

Walks: Career with Team

Player	BB	PA
1. Al Kaline	1,277	11,597
2. Lou Whitaker	1,197	9,967
3. Charlie Gehringer	1,186	10,237
4. Ty Cobb	1,148	12,105
5. Donie Bush	1,125	8,451
6. Norm Cash	1,025	7,772
7. Alan Trammell	850	9,375
8. Dick McAuliffe	842	6,829
9. Harry Heilmann	792	8,390
10. Hank Greenberg	748	5,586

Strikeouts: Season

Player	SO	Year
1. Cecil Fielder	182	1990
2. Rob Deer	175	1991
3. Melvin Nieves	158	1996
4. Melvin Nieves	157	1997
5. Dean Palmer	153	1999
6. Cecil Fielder	151	1991
Cecil Fielder	151	1992
8. Travis Fryman	149	1991
9. Dean Palmer	146	2000
Carlos Peña	146	2004

Strikeouts: Career with Team

Player	SO	PA
1. Lou Whitaker	1,099	9,967
2. Norm Cash	1,081	7,772
3. Al Kaline	1,020	11,597
4. Willie Horton	945	5,978
5. Dick McAuliffe	932	6,829
6. Travis Fryman	931	4,792
7. Kirk Gibson	930	4,773
8. Cecil Fielder	926	4,252
9. Alan Trammell	874	9,375
10. Lance Parrish	847	4,674

Slugging Percentage: Season

Player	SLG	Year
1. Hank Greenberg	.683	1938
2. Hank Greenberg	.670	1940
3. Hank Greenberg	.668	1937
4. Norm Cash	.662	1961
5. Rudy York	.651	1937
6. Harry Heilmann	.632	1923
7. Hank Greenberg	.628	1935
8. Hank Greenberg	.622	1939
9. Ty Cobb	.621	1911
10. Harry Heilmann	.616	1927

Slugging Percentage: Career with Team

Player	SLG	PA
1. Hank Greenberg	.616	5,586
2. Harry Heilmann	.518	8,390
3. Ty Cobb	.516	12,105
4. Rudy York	.503	5,350
5. Tony Clark	.502	3,212
6. Rocky Colavito	.501	2,723
7. Cecil Fielder	.498	4,252
8. Norm Cash	.490	7,772
9. Ray Boone	.482	2,856
. Bob Fothergill	.482	2,693

On-Base Percentage: Season

Player	OBP	Year
1. Norm Cash	.487	1961
2. Ty Cobb	.486	1915
3. Harry Heilmann	.481	1923
4. Roy Cullenbine	.477	1946
5. Harry Heilmann	.475	1927
6. Ty Cobb	.468	1925
7. Ty Cobb	.467	1913
Ty Cobb	.467	1911
9. Ty Cobb	.462	1922
10. Charlie Gehringer	.458	1937

On-Base Percentage: Career with Team

Player	OBP	PA
1. Ty Cobb	.434	12,105
2. Johnny Bassler	.420	2,763
3. Hank Greenberg	.412	5,586
4. Harry Heilmann	.410	8,390

Player		
5. Charlie Gehringer	.404	10,237
6. Lu Blue	.403	4,124
7. Dick Wakefield	.396	2,499
8. Tony Phillips	.395	3,320
9. George Kell	.391	3,734
10. Topper Rigney	.389	2,005

OPS (On-Base Percentage + Slugging Percentage): Season

Player	OPS	Year
1. Norm Cash	1.148	1961
2. Hank Greenberg	1.122	1938
3. Harry Heilmann	1.113	1923
4. Hank Greenberg	1.105	1937
5. Hank Greenberg	1.103	1940
6. Harry Heilmann	1.091	1927
7. Ty Cobb	1.088	1911
8. Ty Cobb	1.066	1925
9. Harry Heilmann	1.051	1921
10. Ty Cobb	1.048	1921

OPS (On-Base Percentage + Slugging Percentage): Career with Team

Player	OPS	PA
1. Hank Greenberg	1.028	5,586
2. Ty Cobb	.950	12,105
3. Harry Heilmann	.927	8,390
4. Charlie Gehringer	.884	10,237
5. Rudy York	.873	5,350
6. Mickey Tettleton	.867	2,343
7. Rocky Colavito	.865	2,723
Norm Cash	.865	7,772
9. Bob Fothergill	.861	2,693
10. Tony Clark	.857	3,212

Stolen Bases: Season

Player	SB	Year
1. Ty Cobb	96	1915
2. Ty Cobb	83	1911
3. Ron LeFlore	78	1979
4. Ty Cobb	76	1909
5. Brian Hunter	74	1997
6. Ty Cobb	68	1916
Ron LeFlore	68	1978
8. Ty Cobb	65	1910
9. Ty Cobb	61	1912
10. Ron LeFlore	58	1976

Stolen Bases: Career with Team

Player	SB	PA
1. Ty Cobb	865	12,105
2. Donie Bush	400	8,451
3. Sam Crawford	317	8,869
4. Ron LeFlore	294	3,559
5. Alan Trammell	236	9,375
6. Kirk Gibson	194	4,773
7. George Moriarty	190	3,000
8. Bobby Veach	189	6,782
9. Charlie Gehringer	181	10,237
10. Lou Whitaker	143	9,967

Sacrifice Hits: Season

Player	Sac	Year
1. Donie Bush	52	1909
2. Donie Bush	48	1920
3. Ralph Young	46	1919
4. Germany Schaefer	43	1908
5. Ossie Vitt	42	1915
6. Donie Bush	40	1921
7. Topper Rigney	37	1922
8. Bill Coughlin	36	1906
Bobby Veach	36	1922
10. Lu Blue	34	1925
Billy Lush	34	1903

Sacrifice Hits: Career with Team

Player	Sac	PA
1. Donie Bush	327	8,451
2. Ty Cobb	281	12,105
3. Harry Heilmann	262	8,390
4. Bobby Veach	238	6,782
5. Sam Crawford	223	8,869
6. Ossie Vitt	173	3,269
Ralph Young	173	3,780
8. Bob Jones	160	3,366
9. Charlie Gehringer	141	10,237
10. Charley O'Leary	138	3,135

Hit by Pitch: Season

Player	HBP	Year
1. Bill Freehan	24	1968
2. Bill Freehan	20	1967
Chet Lemon	20	1983
4. Damion Easley	19	1999
5. Heinie Manush	17	1923
6. Damion Easley	16	1997
Damion Easley	16	1998
Heinie Manush	16	1924
9. Chet Lemon	15	1982
10. Brad Ausmus	14	1999

Hit by Pitch: Career with Team

Player	HBP	PA
1. Bill Freehan	114	6,899
2. Damion Easley	87	3,512
Chet Lemon	87	4,675
4. Norm Cash	85	7,772
Ty Cobb	85	12,105
6. Al Kaline	55	11,597
7. Bobby Veach	53	6,782
8. Charlie Gehringer	50	10,237
9. Willie Horton	49	5,978
10. Heinie Manush	45	2,377

Top 10 Pitching Leaders, Single Season & Career with Team

Games Pitched: Season

Player	GP	Year
1. Mike Myers	88	1997
Sean Runyan	88	1998
3. Mike Myers	83	1996
4. Willie Hernandez	80	1984
5. Jamie Walker	78	2003
6. Willie Hernandez	74	1985
7. Richie Lewis	72	1996
8. Aurelio Lopez	71	1984
Dan Miceli	71	1997
10. Doug Brocail	70	1999
Jamie Walker	70	2004

Games Pitched: Career with Team

Player	GP	IP
1. John Hiller	545	1,242.0
2. Hooks Dauss	538	3,390.7
3. Mickey Lolich	508	3,361.7
4. Dizzy Trout	493	2,591.7
5. Mike Henneman	491	669.7
6. Hal Newhouser	460	2,944.0
7. George Mullin	435	3,394.0
8. Jack Morris	430	3,042.7
9. Tommy Bridges	424	2,826.3
10. Willie Hernandez	358	483.7

Innings Pitched: Season

Player	IP	Year
1. George Mullin	382.3	1904
2. Mickey Lolich	376.0	1971
3. George Mullin	357.3	1907
4. Dizzy Trout	352.3	1944
5. George Mullin	347.7	1905
6. Denny McLain	336.0	1968
7. Roscoe Miller	332.0	1901
8. Ed Killian	331.7	1904
9. George Mullin	330.0	1906
10. Mickey Lolich	327.3	1972

Innings Pitched: Career with Team

Player	IP
1. George Mullin	3,394.0
2. Hooks Dauss	3,390.7
3. Mickey Lolich	3,361.7
4. Jack Morris	3,042.7
5. Hal Newhouser	2,944.0
6. Tommy Bridges	2,826.3
7. Dizzy Trout	2,591.7
8. Earl Whitehill	2,171.3
9. Bill Donovan	2,137.3
10. Frank Lary	2,008.7

Batters Faced: Season

Player	BF	Year
1. George Mullin	1,597	1904
2. Mickey Lolich	1,538	1971
3. George Mullin	1,493	1907
4. George Mullin	1,473	1905
5. Dizzy Trout	1,421	1944
6. George Mullin	1,408	1906
7. Ed Killian	1,364	1904
8. Hooks Dauss	1,340	1923
9. Mickey Lolich	1,321	1972
10. Denny McLain	1,304	1969

Batters Faced: Career with Team

Player	BF	IP
1. Hooks Dauss	14,203	3,390.7
2. Mickey Lolich	13,980	3,361.7
3. George Mullin	12,959	3,394.0
4. Jack Morris	12,745	3,042.7
5. Hal Newhouser	12,449	2,944.0
6. Tommy Bridges	12,165	2,826.3
7. Dizzy Trout	11,019	2,591.7
8. Earl Whitehill	9,557	2,171.3
9. Bill Donovan	8,862	2,137.3
10. Frank Lary	8,472	2,008.7

Games Started: Season

Player	GS	Year
1. Mickey Lolich	45	1971
2. George Mullin	44	1904
3. Mickey Lolich	42	1973
George Mullin	42	1907
5. Joe Coleman	41	1974
Mickey Lolich	41	1972
Mickey Lolich	41	1974
Denny McLain	41	1968
Denny McLain	41	1969
George Mullin	41	1905

Games Started: Career with Team

Player	GS	IP
1. Mickey Lolich	459	3,361.7
2. Jack Morris	408	3,042.7
3. George Mullin	395	3,394.0
4. Hooks Dauss	388	3,390.7
5. Hal Newhouser	373	2,944.0
6. Tommy Bridges	362	2,826.3
7. Dizzy Trout	305	2,591.7
8. Earl Whitehill	287	2,171.3
9. Frank Lary	274	2,008.7
Dan Petry	274	1,843.0

Complete Games: Season

Player	CG	Year
1. George Mullin	42	1904
2. Roscoe Miller	35	1901
George Mullin	35	1905
George Mullin	35	1906
George Mullin	35	1907
6. Bill Donovan	34	1903
7. Ed Killian	33	1905
Dizzy Trout	33	1944
9. Ed Killian	32	1904
10. George Mullin	31	1903

Complete Games: Career with Team

Player	CG	IP
1. George Mullin	336	3,394.0
2. Hooks Dauss	245	3,390.7
3. Bill Donovan	213	2,137.3
4. Hal Newhouser	212	2,944.0
5. Tommy Bridges	200	2,826.3
6. Mickey Lolich	190	3,361.7
7. Dizzy Trout	156	2,591.7
8. Jack Morris	154	3,042.7
9. Earl Whitehill	147	2,171.3
10. Ed Killian	142	1,536.7

Games Won: Season

Player	W	Year
1. Denny McLain	31	1968
2. George Mullin	29	1909

Hal Newhouser	29	1944
4. Dizzy Trout	27	1944
5. Hal Newhouser	26	1946
6. Bill Donovan	25	1907
Ed Killian	25	1907
Mickey Lolich	25	1971
Hal Newhouser	25	1945
10. Hooks Dauss	24	1915
Denny McLain	24	1969
Schoolboy Rowe	24	1934
Ed Summers	24	1908

Games Won: Career with Team

Player	W	IP
1. Hooks Dauss	222	3,390.7
2. George Mullin	209	3,394.0
3. Mickey Lolich	207	3,361.7
4. Hal Newhouser	200	2,944.0
5. Jack Morris	198	3,042.7
6. Tommy Bridges	194	2,826.3
7. Dizzy Trout	161	2,591.7
8. Bill Donovan	141	2,137.3
9. Earl Whitehill	133	2,171.3
10. Frank Lary	123	2,008.7

Games Lost: Season

Player	L	Year
1. George Mullin	23	1904
2. Hooks Dauss	21	1920
Mickey Lolich	21	1974
Mike Maroth	21	2003
George Mullin	21	1905
6. Art Houtteman	20	1952
Ed Killian	20	1904
George Mullin	20	1907
Bobo Newsom	20	1941
10. Jeremy Bonderman	19	2003
Lerrin LaGrow	19	1974
Mickey Lolich	19	1970
Herman Pillette	19	1923
Virgil Trucks	19	1952

Games Lost: Career with Team

Player	L	IP
1. Hooks Dauss	182	3,390.7
2. George Mullin	179	3,394.0
3. Mickey Lolich	175	3,361.7
4. Dizzy Trout	153	2,591.7
5. Jack Morris	150	3,042.7
6. Hal Newhouser	148	2,944.0
7. Tommy Bridges	138	2,826.3
8. Earl Whitehill	119	2,171.3
9. Frank Lary	110	2,008.7
10. Vic Sorrell	101	1,671.7

Winning Percentage: Season

Player	W%	Year
1. Bill Donovan	.862	1907
2. Schoolboy Rowe	.842	1940
3. Denny McLain	.838	1968
4. Bobo Newsom	.808	1940
5. George Mullin	.784	1909
6. Ken Holloway	.765	1925
7. Hal Newhouser	.763	1944
8. Firpo Marberry	.750	1934
Schoolboy Rowe	.750	1934
10. Hal Newhouser	.743	1946

Winning Percentage: Career with Team

Player	W%	IP
1. Denny McLain	.654	1,593.0
2. Aurelio Lopez	.639	713.0
3. Schoolboy Rowe	.629	1,445.0
4. Mike Henneman	.626	669.7
5. Harry Coveleski	.616	1,023.3
6. Ed Summers	.602	999.0
7. Elden Auker	.597	1,083.7
8. Bill Donovan	.595	2,137.3
9. Bobo Newsom	.588	760.3
10. Earl Wilson	.587	962.3

Shutouts: Season

Player	SHO	Year
1. Denny McLain	9	1969
2. Ed Killian	8	1905
Hal Newhouser	8	1945
4. Billy Hoeft	7	1955
George Mullin	7	1904
Dizzy Trout	7	1944
7. 11 tied with ...	6	——

Shutouts: Career with Team

Player	SHO	IP
1. Mickey Lolich	39	3,361.7
2. George Mullin	34	3,394.0
3. Tommy Bridges	33	2,826.3
Hal Newhouser	33	2,944.0
5. Bill Donovan	29	2,137.3
6. Dizzy Trout	28	2,591.7
7. Denny McLain	26	1,593.0
8. Jack Morris	24	3,042.7
9. Hooks Dauss	22	3,390.7
10. Frank Lary	20	2,008.7
Virgil Trucks	20	1,800.7

ERA: Season

Player	ERA	Year
1. Ed Summers	1.64	1908
2. Ed Killian	1.71	1909
3. Ed Killian	1.78	1907
4. Hal Newhouser	1.81	1945
5. Ed Siever	1.91	1902
6. Hal Newhouser	1.94	1946
7. Denny McLain	1.96	1968
8. Harry Coveleski	1.97	1916
9. Al Benton	2.02	1945
10. Bill Donovan	2.08	1908

ERA: Career with Team

Player	ERA	IP
1. Harry Coveleski	2.34	1,023.3
2. Ed Killian	2.38	1,536.7
3. Ed Summers	2.42	999.0
4. Bill Donovan	2.49	2,137.3
5. Ed Siever	2.61	1,036.0
6. George Mullin	2.76	3,394.0
7. John Hiller	2.83	1,242.0
8. Ed Willett	2.89	1,545.7
9. Bill James	3.01	548.0
10. Frank Kitson	3.02	683.0

Earned Runs Allowed: Season

Player	ER	Year
1. Mickey Lolich	142	1974
2. Joe Coleman	137	1974
3. Howard Ehmke	131	1922
Mickey Lolich	131	1973
5. Vic Sorrell	130	1929
6. Bobo Newsom	128	1941
7. Hooks Dauss	127	1923
Roxie Lawson	127	1937
9. Earl Whitehill	126	1929
10. Jack Morris	125	1990

Earned Runs Allowed: Career with Team

Player	ER	IP
1. Mickey Lolich	1,289	3,361.7
2. Jack Morris	1,262	3,042.7
3. Hooks Dauss	1,245	3,390.7
4. Tommy Bridges	1,122	2,826.3

Player	K	IP
5. George Mullin	1,042	3,394.0
6. Earl Whitehill	1,004	2,171.3
7. Hal Newhouser	1,003	2,944.0
8. Dizzy Trout	922	2,591.7
9. Vic Sorrell	823	1,671.7
10. Dan Petry	787	1,843.0

Strikeouts: Season

Player	K	Year
1. Mickey Lolich	308	1971
2. Denny McLain	280	1968
3. Hal Newhouser	275	1946
4. Mickey Lolich	271	1969
5. Mickey Lolich	250	1972
6. Joe Coleman	236	1971
7. Jack Morris	232	1983
8. Mickey Lolich	230	1970
9. Mickey Lolich	226	1965
10. Jack Morris	223	1986

Strikeouts: Career with Team

Player	K	IP
1. Mickey Lolich	2,679	3,361.7
2. Jack Morris	1,980	3,042.7
3. Hal Newhouser	1,770	2,944.0
4. Tommy Bridges	1,674	2,826.3
5. Jim Bunning	1,406	1,867.3
6. George Mullin	1,380	3,394.0
7. Hooks Dauss	1,201	3,390.7
8. Dizzy Trout	1,199	2,591.7
9. Denny McLain	1,150	1,593.0
10. Bill Donovan	1,079	2,137.3

Strikeouts Per Nine IP: Season

Player	K/9	Year
1. Mickey Lolich	8.69	1969
2. Hideo Nomo	8.57	2000
3. Hal Newhouser	8.46	1946
4. Mickey Lolich	8.35	1965
5. Jeremy Bonderman	8.22	2004
6. Mickey Lolich	8.06	1968
7. Denny McLain	7.84	1965
8. Les Cain	7.77	1970
9. Mickey Lolich	7.68	1967
10. Mickey Lolich	7.64	1966

Strikeouts Per Nine IP: Career with Team

Player	K/9	IP
1. John Hiller	7.51	1,242.0
2. Mickey Lolich	7.17	3,361.7
3. Jeremy Bonderman	7.08	535.0
4. Jim Bunning	6.78	1,867.3
5. Earl Wilson	6.63	962.3
6. Aurelio Lopez	6.55	713.0
7. Denny McLain	6.50	1,593.0
8. Mike Henneman	6.45	669.7
9. Joe Coleman	6.39	1,407.7
10. Joe Sparma	6.07	835.3

Hits Allowed: Season

Player	HA	Year
1. George Mullin	346	1907
2. George Mullin	345	1904
3. Roscoe Miller	339	1901
4. Mickey Lolich	336	1971
5. Ed Siever	334	1901
6. Hooks Dauss	331	1923
7. Mickey Lolich	315	1973
George Mullin	315	1906
9. Dizzy Trout	314	1944
10. Mickey Lolich	310	1974

Hits Allowed: Career with Team

Player	HA	IP
1. Hooks Dauss	3,407	3,390.7
2. George Mullin	3,206	3,394.0
3. Mickey Lolich	3,093	3,361.7
4. Jack Morris	2,767	3,042.7
5. Tommy Bridges	2,675	2,826.3
6. Hal Newhouser	2,639	2,944.0
7. Dizzy Trout	2,504	2,591.7
8. Earl Whitehill	2,329	2,171.3
9. Frank Lary	1,975	2,008.7
10. Bill Donovan	1,862	2,137.3

Hits Allowed Per Nine IP: Season

Player	H/9	Year
1. Jeff Robinson	6.33	1988
2. Denny McLain	6.46	1968
3. Hal Newhouser	6.61	1946
4. Hal Newhouser	6.71	1942
5. Hank Aguirre	6.75	1962
6. Virgil Trucks	6.84	1949
7. Mickey Lolich	6.86	1969
Hal Newhouser	6.86	1945
9. Joe Coleman	6.94	1972
Earl Wilson	6.94	1966

Hits Allowed Per Nine IP: Career with Team

Player	H/9	IP
1. Denny McLain	7.46	1,593.0
2. John Hiller	7.54	1,242.0
3. Aurelio Lopez	7.69	713.0
4. Bernie Boland	7.75	1,035.0
5. Earl Wilson	7.76	962.3
6. Harry Coveleski	7.80	1,023.3
7. Bill Donovan	7.84	2,137.3
8. Hank Aguirre	7.87	1,179.0
9. Joe Sparma	7.97	835.3
10. Jean Dubuc	8.06	1,145.0

Walks Allowed: Season

Player	BB	Year
1. Joe Coleman	158	1974
2. Paul Foytack	142	1956
3. George Mullin	138	1905
4. Hal Newhouser	137	1941
5. George Mullin	131	1904
6. Howard Ehmke	124	1920
Virgil Trucks	124	1949
8. Mickey Lolich	122	1969
9. Tommy Bridges	119	1932
10. Bobo Newsom	118	1941
Earl Whitehill	118	1931

Walks Allowed: Career with Team

Player	BB	IP
1. Hal Newhouser	1,227	2,944.0
2. Tommy Bridges	1,192	2,826.3
3. George Mullin	1,106	3,394.0
4. Jack Morris	1,086	3,042.7
5. Hooks Dauss	1,067	3,390.7
6. Mickey Lolich	1,014	3,361.7
7. Dizzy Trout	978	2,591.7
8. Earl Whitehill	831	2,171.3
9. Dan Petry	744	1,843.0
10. Virgil Trucks	732	1,800.7

WALKS ALLOWED PER NINE IP: SEASON

Player	BB/9	Year
1. Fred Hutchinson	1.29	1951
2. Frank Kitson	1.33	1903
3. Dave Rozema	1.40	1977
4. Ed Siever	1.53	1902
5. Ed Summers	1.64	1908
6. Ed Summers	1.66	1909
7. Denny McLain	1.69	1968
8. Ed Siever	1.70	1907
9. Frank Kitson	1.71	1904
10. Jack Cronin	1.72	1901

WALKS ALLOWED PER NINE IP: CAREER WITH TEAM

Player	BB/9	IP
1. Don Mossi	1.75	929.7
Frank Kitson	1.75	683.0
3. Ed Siever	1.80	1,036.0
4. Ed Summers	1.99	999.0
5. Bill Gullickson	2.03	722.7
6. Dave Rozema	2.08	1,007.3
7. Steve Gromek	2.36	724.0
Mike Maroth	2.36	748.0
9. Harry Coveleski	2.37	1,023.3
10. John Doherty	2.38	515.0

WHIP (WALKS + HITS PER NINE IP): SEASON

Player	WHIP	Year
1. Denny McLain	0.905	1968
2. Earl Wilson	1.004	1966
3. Ed Summers	1.047	1909
4. Hank Aguirre	1.051	1962
Ed Siever	1.051	1902
Harry Coveleski	1.051	1916
7. Hal Newhouser	1.069	1946
8. Jim Bunning	1.070	1957
9. Denny McLain	1.071	1965
10. Ed Willett	1.076	1909

WHIP (WALKS + HITS PER NINE IP): CAREER WITH TEAM

Player	WHIP	IP
1. Denny McLain	1.112	1,593.0
2. Harry Coveleski	1.131	1,023.3
3. Ed Summers	1.152	999.0
4. Earl Wilson	1.170	962.3
5. Don Mossi	1.174	929.7
6. Bill Donovan	1.192	2,137.3
7. Hank Aguirre	1.208	1,179.0
Jim Bunning	1.208	1,867.3
9. Ed Killian	1.218	1,536.7
10. Mickey Lolich	1.222	3,361.7

HOME RUNS ALLOWED: SEASON

Player	HRA	Year
1. Denny McLain	42	1966
2. Jack Morris	40	1986
3. Jack Morris	39	1987
4. Jim Bunning	38	1963
Mickey Lolich	38	1974
6. Jim Bunning	37	1959
Jack Morris	37	1982
Dan Petry	37	1983
9. Mickey Lolich	36	1971
10. Bill Gullickson	35	1992
Mickey Lolich	35	1973
Denny McLain	35	1967
Mike Moore	35	1993

HOME RUNS ALLOWED: CAREER WITH TEAM

Player	HRA	IP
1. Mickey Lolich	329	3,361.7
2. Jack Morris	321	3,042.7
3. Jim Bunning	223	1,867.3
4. Denny McLain	195	1,593.0
5. Dan Petry	187	1,843.0
6. Frank Tanana	182	1,551.3
7. Tommy Bridges	181	2,826.3
8. Frank Lary	180	2,008.7
9. Paul Foytack	165	1,425.3
10. Milt Wilcox	143	1,495.3

SAVES: SEASON

Player	SV	Year
1. Todd Jones	42	2000
2. John Hiller	38	1973
3. Willie Hernandez	32	1984
4. Willie Hernandez	31	1985
Todd Jones	31	1997
6. Todd Jones	30	1999
7. Juan Acevedo	28	2002
Todd Jones	28	1998
9. Tom Timmermann	27	1970
10. Mike Henneman	24	1992
Mike Henneman	24	1993
Willie Hernandez	24	1986

SAVES: CAREER WITH TEAM

Player	SV	IP
1. Mike Henneman	154	669.7
2. Todd Jones	142	312.3
3. John Hiller	125	1,242.0
4. Willie Hernandez	120	483.7
5. Aurelio Lopez	85	713.0
6. Terry Fox	55	344.3
7. Al Benton	45	1,218.7
8. Hooks Dauss	40	3,390.7
9. Larry Sherry	37	250.3
10. Fred Scherman	34	342.3
Dizzy Trout	34	2,591.7

WILD PITCHES: SEASON

Player	WP	Year
1. Jack Morris	24	1987
2. Jack Morris	18	1983
3. Jason Johnson	17	2005
4. Jean Dubuc	16	1912
Jack Morris	16	1990
Hideo Nomo	16	2000
Jeff Robinson	16	1990
8. Joe Coleman	15	1975
Jack Morris	15	1985
10. Richie Lewis	14	1996
Mickey Lolich	14	1969
Mickey Lolich	14	1970
Jack Morris	14	1984

WILD PITCHES: CAREER WITH TEAM

Player	WP	IP
1. Jack Morris	155	3,042.7
2. Mickey Lolich	109	3,361.7
3. George Mullin	80	3,394.0
4. Dan Petry	68	1,843.0
5. Hal Newhouser	64	2,944.0
6. Tommy Bridges	59	2,826.3
7. Joe Coleman	56	1,407.7
8. Ed Willett	54	1,545.7
9. Hooks Dauss	48	3,390.7
Frank Tanana	48	1,551.3

HIT BATSMEN: SEASON

Player	HB	Year
1. Howard Ehmke	23	1922
2. Harry Coveleski	20	1915
Ed Summers	20	1908
4. Frank Lary	19	1960

5. Hooks Dauss	18	1914
6. Ed Killian	17	1904
Jeff Weaver	17	1999
Ed Willett	17	1910
Ed Willett	17	1912
10. Hooks Dauss	16	1916
Jesse Stovall	16	1904

Hit Batsmen: Career with Team

Player	HB	IP
1. Hooks Dauss	121	3,390.7
2. George Mullin	116	3,394.0
3. Ed Willett	93	1,545.7
4. Mickey Lolich	91	3,361.7
5. Frank Lary	90	2,008.7
6. Jim Bunning	73	1,867.3
7. Ed Killian	68	1,536.7
8. Bill Donovan	65	2,137.3
Earl Whitehill	65	2,171.3
10. Howard Ehmke	60	1,236.3

Games Finished: Season

Player	GF	Year
1. Willie Hernandez	68	1984
2. Willie Hernandez	64	1985
3. Todd Jones	62	1999
4. John Hiller	60	1973
Todd Jones	60	2000
6. Aurelio Lopez	59	1980
7. Mike Henneman	53	1990
Mike Henneman	53	1992
Willie Hernandez	53	1986
Todd Jones	53	1998

Games Finished: Career with Team

Player	GF	IP
1. Mike Henneman	369	669.7
2. John Hiller	363	1,242.0
3. Willie Hernandez	279	483.7
4. Todd Jones	254	312.3
5. Aurelio Lopez	245	713.0
6. Chief Hogsett	130	738.3
7. Terry Fox	128	344.3
8. Dizzy Trout	126	2,591.7
9. Hooks Dauss	121	3,390.7
10. Hal White	116	820.3

Significant Tigers

BRIDGES, TOMMY (SP)
(1930–1943, 1945–1946)

Tommy Bridges was one of the American League's better pitchers in the mid- to late 1930s. A six-time All-Star (and the winning pitcher of the 1939 game), Bridges played his entire 16-year major league career with Detroit. Known for having the best curveball in the game, Bridges was a 20-game winner for three straight years (1934–1936), including an AL-leading 23 wins in 1936. On August 5, 1932, Bridges came within one out of pitching a perfect game against the Senators, who were managed by Walter Johnson. With the score 13–0 and two out in the bottom of the ninth, pitcher Bobby Burke was due up, but Johnson sent up Dave Harris, a gifted pinch-hitter who led the league with 14 pinch-hits that year. Some observers at the time felt that Johnson (being a bit of a poor sport) sent up Harris to pinch-hit because Bridges was about to achieve the perfect game that had always eluded Johnson himself. Sure enough, Harris got a clean single to left to spoil the perfect game. Bridges played in four World Series with Detroit, compiling a 4–1 record in seven World Series games. After the 1943 season, Bridges was drafted into the armed forces at the age of 37. When he returned at the tail end of the 1945 season, his major league career was effectively over. He pitched in just a few games in 1945 and 1946 before being released by the Tigers. Remarkably, he proceeded to pitch quite effectively in the minors for about five more years.

CAREER TIGERS RECORD:

W	L	W%	ERA	SV
194	138	.584	3.57	10

K	BB	SHO	IP
1,674	1,192	33	2,826.3

BUNNING, JIM (SP)
(1955–1963)

JIM BUNNING, Detroit Tigers

Jim Bunning was signed as an amateur free agent by the Detroit Tigers before the 1950 season. After pitching in the minors for five years, Bunning was called up to Detroit in 1955 and pitched briefly for the Tigers that year and in 1956, compiling an 8–6 record. During the winter before the 1957 season, Bunning developed a good slider to complement his superb fastball, and he was ready to become a great pitcher. In his first full season, Bunning went 20–8 with a 2.69 ERA, leading the American League in wins, and was named to the All-Star team for the first of seven times. On July 20, 1958, Bunning pitched his first no-hitter, defeating the Red Sox at Fenway Park, 3–0. Bunning won 118 games with Detroit before being traded to Philadelphia after the 1963 season. He would later become the first pitcher in modern times to win more than 100 games in each league, as he won 106 National League games for the Phillies, Pirates, and Dodgers. Bunning also became the first pitcher to record more than 1,000 strikeouts in each league, record no-hitters in each league (his NL no-hitter was a perfect game against the Mets in 1964), and pitch for both leagues in the All-Star Game, being scored upon only once in eight appearances. After he retired, Bunning became a player agent and investment broker for a while, and then entered politics. He first served in the Kentucky state legislature, then, in 1986, was elected to Congress. After losing a bid for governor, Bunning, who was elected to the Baseball Hall of Fame in 1996, was elected in 1998 to the U.S. Senate, where he still serves today.

CAREER TIGERS RECORD:

W	L	W%	ERA	SV
118	87	.576	3.45	12
K	**BB**	**SHO**	**IP**	
1,406	564	16	1,867.3	

BUSH, DONIE (SS)
(1908–1921)

For 14 years, Little Donie Bush played shortstop and batted lead off for the Tigers. His skill was getting on base any way he could—so Hall of Famers Ty Cobb, Sam Crawford, and Harry Heilmann could get him home. Four times Bush scored more than 100 runs, and four more times over 90. Three times he surpassed 100 walks in a season. Bush was also a skilled base runner, stealing 400 bases during his Tigers career. Though his career was long and respectable, Bush is mostly remembered for his stints as manager of the Senators, Pirates, White Sox, and Reds. Bush spent 65 years in organized baseball as a player, manager, scout, and owner. A lifelong bachelor, Bush died at the age of 84, still working with the White Sox.

CAREER TIGERS RECORD:

Games	AB	Hits	Runs
1,872	6,970	1,745	1,242
Avg	**HR**	**RBI**	**SB**
.250	9	427	400

CASH, NORM (1B)
(1960–1974)

Norm Cash was traded to the Tigers by the Cleveland Indians for Steve Demeter just before the 1960 season opened. It turned out to be one of the most lopsided trades in major league history. Demeter got just five more at-bats in his career after the trade. Cash didn't actually play for Cleveland; the Indians had acquired him in December from the White Sox in a seven-player deal that sent Minnie Minoso back to Chicago. Cash's first two years were spent playing part time for the White Sox in 1958 and 1959. Once he arrived in Detroit, Cash became the regular first baseman, a position he held with the team for the next 15 years.

Cash put together one of the best seasons in baseball history, but almost no one noticed because he did it in 1961, the year Roger Maris and Mickey Mantle were engaged in their pursuit of Babe Ruth's single-season home run record, a chase Maris ultimately won with his 61 homers. That year Cash hit .361 to lead the league by 37 points over teammate Al Kaline, with an on-base percentage of .488, a figure only about a dozen players in major league history have topped. Cash also had a slugging average of .662, 41 homers, a league-leading 193 hits, 132 RBIs, 119 runs scored, and 124 walks. For all this he ended up fourth in the AL MVP voting behind Maris, Mantle, and Jim Gentile. Many years later Cash would admit (and demonstrate for a *Sports Illustrated* article) that he used a corked bat in 1961. In 1962 Cash's average fell to .243, the largest drop by a batting champion from one season to the next.

Cash was a durable player—he had also been drafted by the NFL Chicago Bears—who never went on the DL in his career. He also had a strong sense of humor. On July 15, 1973, as he strode to the plate to face Nolan Ryan with two outs in the ninth of Ryan's second no-hitter, Cash carried a table leg with him instead of a bat. Cash twice won the AL Comeback Player of the Year Award, in 1965 and 1971. Cash hit 20 or more homers 11 times, and five times hit over 30. He was an adept fielder who led the AL numerous times in various fielding categories. Cash was the Tigers' hitting star of the 1968 World Series, batting .385 with a homer, five RBIs and five runs. He hit more balls (four) over the right field roof in Tigers Stadium than anyone else in history. After he retired, Cash briefly played professional soft-ball and then became a member of the Detroit Tigers broadcast team for several years. In 1986, at the age of 51, Cash slipped on a boat, hit his head, and drowned.

CAREER TIGERS RECORD:

Games	AB	Hits	Runs
2,018	6,593	1,793	1,028
Avg	**HR**	**RBI**	**SB**
.272	373	1,087	42

COBB, TY (OF)
(1905–1926)

Ty Cobb was the greatest player in the history of the Detroit Tigers, and possibly all of baseball. When the Hall of Fame held its inaugural election, the hated Ty Cobb received more votes than any other player, including the beloved Babe Ruth and Honus Wagner. Misnamed "the Georgia Peach," Cobb was anything but sweet. He was egotistical, rude, quick-tempered, vindictive, racist, and a bully who would fight at the drop of a hat. Cobb is credited with winning 12 batting titles during his long career, although there is some dispute regarding the 1910 crown. He won the Triple Crown in 1909 at the age of 22, and the AL MVP Award in 1911.

When he retired after the 1928 season, Cobb held nearly 100 major league and American League records, including: lifetime batting average, .366; stolen bases, 892; hits, 4,189; runs, 2,246; and RBIs, 1,937. Cobb hit over .400 three times; 14 times he had at least five hits in a game; and seven times he had batting streaks of 20 or more games. He was driven with an insatiable need to win; when Cobb left home at the age of 17 to play pro ball, his father's last words to him were, "Don't come home a failure." The next year his father was shot and killed by his mother (some say accidentally, some say not). Many hypothesize that the loss of his father, to whom Cobb desperately wanted to prove himself, was the driving force behind Cobb's fierce and lifelong determination to excel on the field.

Cobb stories are legendary, and some are even true. As to sharpening his spikes in plain sight of opposing players, he did that as a psychological ploy. While he wasn't opposed to spiking an opponent who got in his way, Cobb did try to use a fadeaway hook slide whenever possible. As to the famous story of his taunting of Pittsburgh's Honus Wagner in the 1909 World Series, for which Wagner supposedly reciprocated by bashing Cobb in the mouth on a steal attempt, most agree it never happened and Cobb, citing his lifelong respect for Wagner, denies that it did. One true story: In 1925 a reporter asked Cobb just before a game about Babe Ruth and the art of the home run. Cobb, always disdainful of both Ruth and the home run as a winning strategy, told the reporter that hitting home runs was no big deal. To prove his point, he batted that day with his hands together, instead of spread several inches apart as usual, and proceeded to hit three home runs, a double, and a single to set an AL record (since broken) for total bases in a game. To prove it was no fluke, the next day he used the same batting style to club two more homers for a total of five in two games.

Cobb often found himself at the center of controversy, both on the field and off. In 1912, enraged at a heckler in New York, he jumped into the stands and beat the man unconscious. American League President Ban Johnson suspended Cobb indefinitely. Two games later his Tigers teammates refused to take the field unless Cobb was reinstated. Tigers owner Frank Navin, caught in the middle, was told he would face a $5,000 fine if he didn't field a team against the Athletics. When the players held true to their word, Navin and manager Hughie Jennings went into the stands and recruited a team of coaches and ex-college players to face the A's that day. The A's prevailed, 24–2, making a mockery of the whole affair. Johnson then threatened the striking players with lifetime expulsion from baseball if they didn't play the next game. Cobb thanked his teammates for their support and told them to end their strike, which they did. Cobb's suspension was then reduced to 10 days, with a $50 fine.

Another time, Cobb was called out twice in the same game by two different umpires. He challenged the second umpire, Billy Evans, to a fight after the game and Evans accepted. Cobb, in front of a group of players and other onlookers that included his son, Ty Jr., gave the umpire a sound thrashing, splitting open Evans' eyebrow and cheek. Cobb was banging Evans' head into the ground when a large groundskeeper intervened. After tending his wounds, Evans showered, dressed, and went to the Tigers' locker room, whereupon he and Ty Cobb shook hands.

Cobb became embroiled in perhaps the greatest controversy of his career in 1926. On November 2, he abruptly announced his retirement. A month later, Tris Speaker, another big star of the day (and Hall of Famer), resigned as well. It eventually came out that American League President Ban Johnson had forced both players to resign after rumors arose that Cobb and Speaker had been caught up in a game-throwing scandal. Former pitcher Dutch Leonard had written a letter to Commissioner Kenesaw Mountain Landis, alleging that seven years earlier, in 1919, he, Smoky Joe Wood, Cobb, and Speaker had gotten together and planned to throw a game to Detroit, allowing the Tigers to finish in third place and collect some World Series money (fourth place received no prize money). According to Leonard, he, Wood, and Cobb bet on the game to make some extra money since the outcome was a foregone conclusion. With both baseball and the public still reeling from the scandal over the 1919 Black Sox World Series, baseball couldn't afford another scandal. By retiring, Cobb and Speaker were no longer under the authority of major league baseball and couldn't be forced to cooperate with Commissioner Landis. When Landis asked Leonard to come to his office to testify, the ex-pitcher refused to leave the state of California. Landis then held a closed-door meeting with Cobb and Speaker, declared the two players innocent of any allegations, and reinstated them. Although the particulars of that closed-door meeting have never fully come to light, conventional wisdom suggests that Landis knew Cobb and Speaker were guilty, but he also knew that baseball could ill afford another scandal involving two of its biggest stars, so he publicly exonerated the pair and then had them quietly shuffle off to new teams the next year—Speaker to the Senators and Cobb to the A's. Cobb played his last two seasons for Connie Mack in Philadelphia, hitting .357 at the age of 40 and .323 at 41.

Cobb was already a millionaire by the time he quit playing baseball. He had shrewdly invested in Coca-Cola, General Motors, real estate, cotton, and automobiles. In an effort to clean up his image in his later years, Cobb turned philanthropist, endowing a hometown medical center with $100,000 and starting an educational fund, among other things. When Cobb died in 1961, he was still so despised at the age of 74 that only three people connected to major league baseball—past or present—attended his funeral.

CAREER TIGERS RECORD:

Games	AB	Hits	Runs
2,806	10,591	3,900	2,088
Avg	**HR**	**RBI**	**SB**
.368	111	1,804	865

CRAWFORD, SAM (OF/1B)
(1903–1917)

Sam Crawford was one of the best all-around players of the dead-ball era, although he was often overshadowed by teammate Ty Cobb. Nicknamed "Wahoo Sam" after his hometown of Wahoo, Nebraska, Crawford was a live power hitter in a dead-ball era. He could hit home runs and triples, almost at will. Crawford's 309 career triples are still the major league record. A former barber, Crawford played four seasons with Cincinnati before jumping to the rival American League in 1903 for more money. Problem was, Crawford signed contracts with both teams. Following a bitter battle between the two teams for his services, Crawford was awarded to Detroit, the team for which he would play the next 15 years. Crawford was a natural right fielder with a powerful arm, but usually played center because left fielder Matty McIntyre and right fielder Ty Cobb hated each other.

Crawford was the perfect complement to Ty Cobb, batting cleanup to Cobb's third. With the American League's most potent 1–2 punch, Detroit went to the World Series three straight years from 1907–1909, but lost all three times due to poor pitching and, surprisingly, poor hitting from Cobb and Crawford. Crawford's power was legendary for the dead-ball era. Cleveland owner Ernest Barnard even built a 40-foot right field wall at League Park especially to counter Crawford's home-run prowess. Having led the National League in homers in 1901 and the American League in homers in 1908, Crawford was the only player to lead both leagues in home runs until Mark McGwire joined him in 1998. After retiring as a player in 1917, Crawford umpired in the Pacific Coast League for four years. In 1957, with a strong lobbying effort by Ty Cobb, Crawford was elected to the Hall of Fame.

CAREER TIGERS RECORD:

Games	AB	Hits	Runs
2,114	7,984	2,466	1,115
Avg	**HR**	**RBI**	**SB**
.309	70	1,264	317

DAUSS, HOOKS (SP/RP)
(1912–1926)

George "Hooks" Dauss is Detroit's career leader in pitching victories. His nickname was derived from his fantastic curveball. Dauss, a three-time 20-game winner, played for the Tigers in between their World Series teams of the late 1900s and the mid-1930s. Dauss holds the distinction of being the winning pitcher in the most lopsided victory ever over New York in Yankee Stadium, 19–1, on June 17, 1925. Dauss, who played his entire 15-year career with Detroit, had only three losing seasons while playing for a mostly second-division team.

CAREER TIGERS RECORD:

W	L	W%	ERA	SV
222	182	.550	3.30	40
K	**BB**	**SHO**	**IP**	
1,201	1,067	22	3,390.7	

DONOVAN, BILL (SP)
(1903–1912, 1918)

"Wild Bill" Donovan was one of the best pitchers in the National League with Brooklyn before he jumped to the Detroit Tigers in 1903 after five years in the senior circuit. While he was one of the best pitchers in the league, he walked a lot of batters—hence his nickname. In 1907 Donovan went 25–4 to help the Tigers reach the World Series for the first of three straight years. That year, teammates Ed Killian (25) and George Mullin (20) gave Detroit three 20-game winners. The Tigers were disappointing in the three World Series, however, losing them all. Donovan was winless in two starts in 1907, then lost the deciding games in both 1908 and 1909. After retiring as a player, Donovan spent four years managing the Yankees and Phillies. He then became a very successful minor league manager in the Eastern League. On his way to the winter meetings in 1923, Donovan was killed in a train wreck while sleeping in a lower berth. In the upper berth was George Weiss, who survived and later became a Hall of Famer for his executive career with the Yankees.

CAREER TIGERS RECORD:

W	L	W%	ERA	SV
141	96	.595	2.49	3
K	**BB**	**SHO**	**IP**	
1,079	685	29	2,137.3	

FIELDER, CECIL (1B/DH)
(1990–1996)

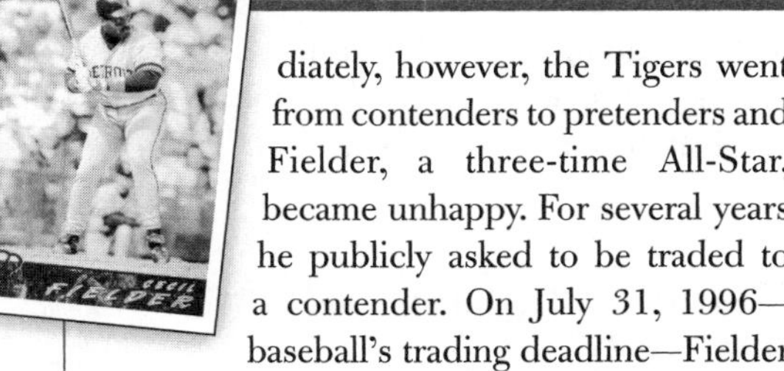

Cecil "Big Daddy" Fielder was the premier home run hitter in the major leagues in the early 1990s. After playing four years in Toronto and failing to establish himself, Fielder left for Japan and signed on with the Hanshin Tigers. After hitting 38 homers for Hanshin in 1989, Fielder returned to the United States as a free agent and signed on with another Tigers team, Detroit. He immediately exploded onto the American baseball scene by hitting some of the longest home runs seen in years. He finished the season with 51 homers (the most in the AL since Maris and Mantle in 1961) and 132 RBIs, the first of three straight RBI crowns. For this performance he finished a close second to Rickey Henderson in the MVP Award balloting.

Fielder again led the American League in 1991 with 44 homers and 133 RBIs. And, once again, he was runner-up in the MVP balloting, this time to Cal Ripken in another close vote. For this he was rewarded with the richest contract in baseball history to that point, $32 million for five years. Almost immediately, however, the Tigers went from contenders to pretenders and Fielder, a three-time All-Star, became unhappy. For several years he publicly asked to be traded to a contender. On July 31, 1996—baseball's trading deadline—Fielder was shipped to the Yankees for Ruben Sierra. Fielder hit 13 homers during New York's stretch run, and hit .391 in the World Series to help the Yankees win their first championship since 1978. After slumping badly on the field in 1997, and becoming entangled in messy off-the-field activities, Fielder was traded to the Angels and then the Indians in 1998, before finally being released by Cleveland before the season ended. At the age of 35, Fielder was out of baseball for good, but in 2005 his son, super-prospect Prince Fielder, broke into the big leagues with Milwaukee.

CAREER TIGERS RECORD:

Games	AB	Hits	Runs
982	3,674	947	558
Avg	**HR**	**RBI**	**SB**
.258	245	758	2

FREEHAN, BILL (C/1B)
(1961, 1963–1976)

An 11-time All-Star and five-time Gold Glover, Bill Freehan was one of the best catchers in baseball during the 1960s and early 1970s. He received a $100,000 bonus in 1961 from the Tigers, but had a deal with his father that prevented him from getting any of the money until he earned his college degree, which he eventually completed by attending the University of Michigan during the off-season. Freehan was the consummate team player who handled a talented pitching staff that included Denny McLain and Mickey Lolich. He authored a controversial book, *Behind the Mask,* which detailed the events of the 1968 season, when the Tigers won the World Series. In his book, Freehan relates that Tigers manager Mayo Smith allowed Denny McLain to enjoy special privileges. Smith was later fired and McLain traded. When he retired, Freehan held the major league career records for most chances, most putouts, and highest fielding average by a catcher. After his playing days, Freehan became the baseball coach at the University of Michigan.

CAREER TIGERS RECORD:

Games	AB	Hits	Runs
1,774	6,073	1,591	706
Avg	**HR**	**RBI**	**SB**
.262	200	758	24

GEHRINGER, CHARLIE (2B) (1924–1942)

Nicknamed "the Mechanical Man" because of the quiet, methodical way he went about his job, Gehringer played his entire 19-year career with the Tigers after being signed by manager Ty Cobb in 1924 following an extended tryout. As Gehringer later recalled Cobb's weeklong test of the young second baseman, "I didn't get a bonus, but I did get a lot of tips on the stock market." A slick-fielding second baseman, Gehringer led the league in fielding seven times. Gehringer also had seven seasons in which he collected at least 200 hits and seven in which he had 100 RBIs. His best year was 1937 when he hit .371 and won the AL MVP Award. In an embarrassing moment that typified his quiet approach to the game, Gehringer once grounded out for the second out of the inning, but thought it was the third out. He rounded first and jogged to his position at second, then absent-mindedly stood next to St. Louis's second baseman, Oscar Mellilo, pounding his glove. Mellilo told Gehringer, "Thanks all the same, Charlie, but I don't need any help."

Gehringer left the team in 1942 at the age of 39 to join the Navy, rising to the rank of lieutenant commander. After the war, Gehringer started an auto-parts business. In 1949 Gehringer was elected to the Hall of Fame, and in 1951 he became the Tigers' GM and vice president, remaining GM until 1953 and vice president until 1959.

CAREER TIGERS RECORD:

Games	AB	Hits	Runs
2,323	8,860	2,839	1,774
Avg	**HR**	**RBI**	**SB**
.320	184	1,427	181

GREENBERG, HANK (1B/OF) (1930, 1933–1941, 1945–1946)

Hank Greenberg was the classic home run hitter—big, strong, and powerful. In his younger days, he was clumsy; his fear of looking foolish on the field drove him to practice long and hard to become successful. The Yankees first offered him a contract, but Greenberg declined because New York had 26-year-old Lou Gehrig on first and Greenberg felt he wouldn't get much playing time. He turned down Washington's offer for the same reason—the Senators having Joe Judge on first. Detroit was a different matter.

By 1933 Greenberg was in the majors for good. He hit .301 that year, the first of eight consecutive .300 seasons. In 1934 he smacked 63 doubles to go along with a .339 average, 26 homers, and 139 RBIs to help the Tigers reach the World Series for the first time since 1909. In 1935 Greenberg won his first MVP Award as he hit 36 homers with 170 RBIs. After missing almost the whole 1936 season due to injury, Greenberg returned in 1937 to hit .337 with 40 homers and 183 RBIs, the third-highest total ever and just one short of Lou Gehrig's AL record. In 1938 Greenberg, who by now had become the biggest Jewish star in baseball history, gave chase to Babe Ruth's single-season home run record of 60, but he fell just short at 58, failing to homer in the last five games of the season.

Greenberg moved to the outfield in 1940 to allow the Tigers to play Rudy York at first and he responded to his new role by winning his second MVP Award. Just after the season started in 1941, Greenberg was inducted into the Army. He was discharged on December 5, 1941. Two days later Pearl Harbor was attacked and Greenberg immediately reenlisted, spending the next three-plus years on active duty, mostly in China and India. On his return, Greenberg played another season and a half with Detroit before leaving for Pittsburgh, where he became baseball's first $100,000 player. It would be 11 years before Stan Musial would become the next.

Greenberg retired in 1947 after one year with the Pirates and became the farm-system director for Bill Veeck's Cleveland team. In 1950 he became Cleveland's GM and built the great 1954 Indians team. Greenberg then moved on to the Chicago White Sox and helped build their 1959 pennant-winning team. He retired in 1963 to become a successful investment banker. During his career, Greenberg missed so much time due to injury, military service, and early retirement that he played the equivalent of only nine-plus seasons. Greenberg was elected to the Hall of Fame in 1956, and died in 1986.

CAREER TIGERS RECORD:

Games	AB	Hits	Runs
1,269	4,791	1,528	980
Avg	**HR**	**RBI**	**SB**
.319	306	1,202	58

HEILMANN, HARRY (OF)
(1914, 1916–1929)

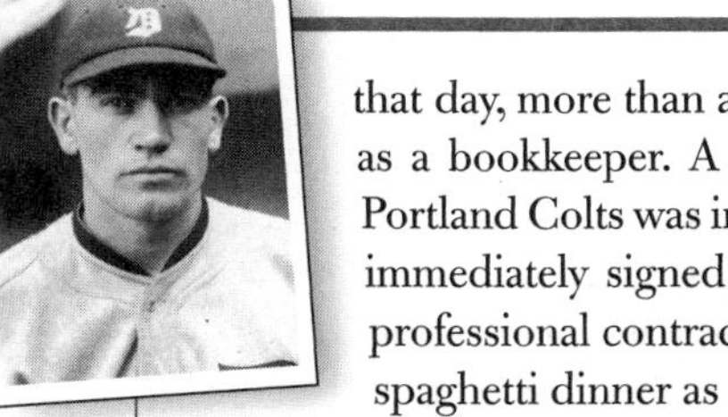

In 1913, when Harry Heilmann was just 19, he was working as a bookkeeper in San Francisco one Saturday when he left the office for lunch, but forgot his coat. Returning to get his coat, Heilmann ran into a friend who told him that the baseball team he managed was without their third baseman due to illness. The friend offered Heilmann $10 to play in the next day's game. Heilmann agreed and hit a game-winning double in the 11th inning. The fans were so appreciative of his hit that they showered him with coins and bills. Heilmann collected $150 that day, more than a month's salary as a bookkeeper. A scout from the Portland Colts was in the stands and immediately signed Heilmann to a professional contract, throwing in a spaghetti dinner as a bonus.

Heilmann was a slow, awkward runner who made more than his share of errors when in the field but, oh, how he could hit. He was a decent player in his first six years in Detroit, but his numbers exploded in 1921 when new manager Ty Cobb took him aside and started tutoring him in the art of hitting. Cobb did such a good job of teaching

Heilmann that the young outfielder actually won the AL batting title that year, edging out Cobb himself, .394 to .389. Heilmann would win three more batting titles (1923, 1925, 1927) with the Tigers, including two on the last day of the season. With Cobb's tutelage, Heilmann had four seasons over .390, including a .403 average in 1923. After the 1929 season, Heilmann was purchased by Cincinnati and had one good year for the Reds, but missed the entire 1931 season due to arthritic wrists. He attempted a comeback in 1932, but after 15 unproductive games he called it a career. Among 20th-century right-handed hitters, Heilmann's .342 career batting average is second all-time to Rogers Hornsby.

In 1926, disgruntled pitcher Dutch Leonard wrote to Heilmann and told him of the two letters he had written to American League President Ban Johnson detailing the throwing of a game and a wagering scandal involving Ty Cobb, Tris Speaker, Smoky Joe Wood, and himself. After Heilmann showed the letter to Detroit owner Frank Navin, the story became public and Commissioner Landis was forced to confront another potentially explosive allegation of scandal, just a few short years removed from the Black Sox scandal. *(See Ty Cobb bio.)*

A big loser in the 1929 stock market crash, Heilmann became the voice of the Tigers in 1933 for WXYZ radio, a job he held for 17 years. The 1951 All-Star Game was played in Detroit and Heilmann was first choice to be the radio announcer, but he was gravely ill from lung cancer. Ty Cobb led an effort for a special election to get Heilmann inducted into the Hall of Fame so that he could present Heilmann with his plaque at the All-Star Game. Thinking he had succeeded, Cobb told Heilmann of his election to the Hall, and Heilmann died the day before the All-Star Game, believing he had made it. Heilmann, however, had not been named in a special election, and it wasn't until the regular election of 1952 that Heilmann finally received his posthumous place in Cooperstown.

CAREER TIGERS RECORD:

Games	AB	Hits	Runs
1,991	7,297	2,499	1,209
Avg	**HR**	**RBI**	**SB**
.342	164	1,442	111

HENNEMAN, MIKE (RP)
(1987–1995)

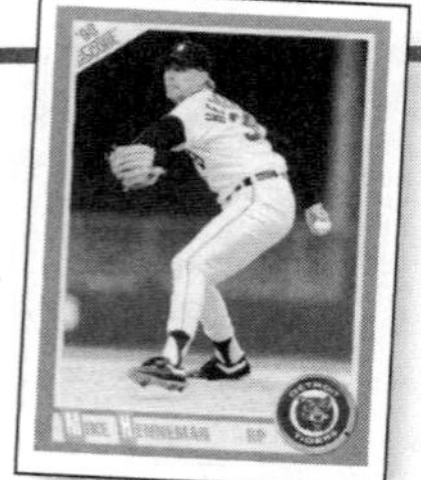

The Tigers selected Mike Henneman in the fourth round of the June 1984 amateur draft. He had actually been drafted the two previous years by Toronto and then Philadelphia, but refused to sign either year. After spending three years in the minors, Henneman made it to the majors in 1987 and fashioned an 11–3 record in his rookie season. Over the next nine years, Henneman didn't have any spectacular seasons, but did perform steadily enough to become the Tigers' all-time leader in saves with 154. In mid-1995, Henneman was traded to Houston for Phil Nevin. After the 1995 campaign, Henneman signed a free-agent contract with Texas and played the 1996 season with the Rangers before a bloated ERA brought on by injuries forced his early retirement at the age of 34.

CAREER TIGERS RECORD:

W	L	W%	ERA	SV
57	34	.626	3.05	154
K	**BB**	**SHO**	**IP**	
480	250	0	669.7	

HERNANDEZ, WILLIE (RP)
(1984–1989)

After seven seasons with the Cubs and Phillies, Guillermo "Willie" Hernandez was traded to the Tigers during spring training in 1984. It was a huge pickup for the Tigers, as Hernandez converted all 32 of his save opportunities that year—to go along with a 9–3 record and a 1.92 ERA—as he helped Detroit romp to the American League title, 15 games in front of any other team in the league. The Tigers swept Kansas City in the ALCS and dispatched the Padres in five games in the World Series. Hernandez won both the AL Cy Young Award and AL MVP Award for his efforts. Hernandez never had another year that came close to the one he put up in 1984, but he did pitch six seasons with Detroit, long enough to reach the top five in many of Detroit's career-relief pitching categories. He retired after the 1989 season.

CAREER TIGERS RECORD:

W	L	W%	ERA	SV
36	31	.537	2.98	120
K	**BB**	**SHO**	**IP**	
384	138	0	483.7	

HILLER, JOHN (RP/SP)
(1965–1970, 1972–1980)

John Hiller was a steady bullpen performer for the Tigers for six seasons before suffering a massive stroke in 1971 that nearly killed him. He survived, but nearly everyone figured his career was over, including the Tigers, who released him. Hiller came back in 1972 to become the Tigers' batting-practice pitcher. By July of that year he looked so good that Detroit returned him to their active roster. In 1973 Hiller recorded 38 saves to establish a new major league record. He won the Fireman of the Year Award and was named the Comeback Player of the Year in the American League. After 15 seasons with Detroit, Hiller retired after the 1980 season as the Tigers' all-time leader in saves and entered the insurance business in Minnesota.

CAREER TIGERS RECORD:

W	L	W%	ERA	SV
87	76	.534	2.83	125
K	**BB**	**SHO**	**IP**	
1,036	535	6	1,242.0	

HORTON, WILLIE (OF/DH)
(1963–1977)

Raised in inner-city Detroit, Willie Horton was signed as an amateur free agent by the Tigers on August 7, 1961. From 1965 to 1974, Horton was the regular left fielder for Detroit. He constantly battled weight problems, but still hit prodigious home runs and furious line drives. Horton was one of the most popular Detroit players of his era, if not all time. When the city was being torn apart and burned in the 1967 riots, Horton climbed on top of a truck and pleaded with his fellow African Americans to stop their violence and looting. A four-time All-Star, Horton hit .304 in the 1968 World Series to help Detroit win the championship. Horton was also a very superstitious player, using one batting helmet his entire career. He simply repainted it whenever he went from one team to the next. After playing in only one game in his 15th season, Horton, whose home run and RBI production had dropped dramatically, was traded in 1977 to the Rangers. Over the next four seasons, Horton would bounce around with five different American League teams before retiring after the 1980 season. He later played in the Pacific Coast League and in Mexico before becoming first a minor league batting instructor for the Tigers, then later a coach for the Yankees and White Sox.

CAREER TIGERS RECORD:

Games	AB	Hits	Runs
1,515	5,405	1,490	671
Avg	**HR**	**RBI**	**SB**
.276	262	886	14

KALINE, AL (OF/DH/1B)
(1953–1974)

Al Kaline was Mr. Tiger, and not just because he played more games with the Tigers than any other player. He didn't have the power of Mickey Mantle or the speed of Willie Mays, but Detroit fans adored him just as much as New York's fans adored his counterparts. Kaline came directly out of high school in the summer of 1953 and joined the big league team. For 22 years Kaline toiled in Detroit, becoming the most beloved Tiger of all time. The blue-collar fans of Detroit loved the way Kaline gave it his all every time out. In 1955, at the age of 20, Kaline became the youngest batting champion ever, surpassing Ty Cobb's record. On April 17 of that year, Kaline hit three home runs in one game, two in the same inning. While not spectacular, Kaline put up solid numbers for many years; his typical season was about 20 homers and 85 RBIs with a .300 average. Although continually dogged by injuries (he missed an average of 10–15 games a year), Kaline was a 15-time All-Star who won 10 Gold Gloves during his long career. In the 1968 World Series, Kaline hit .379 with two homers and eight RBIs to help the Tigers defeat the Cardinals in seven games. As his career wound down, he was moved to first base, then DH. Many Tigers fans were upset with the move, even though it insured the aging Kaline a place in the lineup. On September 24, 1974, Kaline collected his 3,000th hit when he doubled off Baltimore's Dave McNally. He retired at the end of the season with 3,007 career hits, and was elected to the Hall of Fame in 1980, one of only 23 players up to that time to be elected in his first year of eligibility. After he retired, Kaline became a member of the Detroit Tigers broadcasting crew.

CAREER TIGERS RECORD:

Games	AB	Hits	Runs
2,834	10,116	3,007	1,622
Avg	**HR**	**RBI**	**SB**
.297	399	1,583	137

KELL, GEORGE (3B)
(1946–1952)

George Kell, easily the best player to emerge during the player-shortage years of World War II, played four seasons for the Philadelphia A's before being traded to the Tigers in mid-1946. Kell was one of the best all-around third basemen ever to play the game. Seven times he led American League third sackers in fielding, and nine times (including eight consecutive) he batted over .300. In 1949 Kell won his only batting title, edging out Ted Williams, .342911 to .342756 and striking out only 13 times all season, a major league record for a batting champion. (Kell's batting title kept Williams from winning his third Triple Crown.) Kell also was the first third baseman to win a batting title since Heinie Zimmerman in 1912, and would be the last until Bill Madlock in 1975. Even though Kell was having solid seasons for Detroit, year after year, the Tigers traded him to the Red Sox in a nine-player deal in mid-1952. He played five more seasons for the Red Sox, White Sox, and Orioles to round out his 15-year career, retiring in 1957. In his last season in Baltimore, he tutored rookie third baseman Brooks Robinson. Kell was elected to the Hall of Fame, ironically, on the same day in 1983 as his protégé, Robinson. When Mel Ott died in a November 1958 automobile crash, Kell took his spot on the Tigers broadcast team and remained a Detroit play-by-play announcer for more than 30 years.

CAREER TIGERS RECORD:

Games	AB	Hits	Runs
826	3,303	1,075	503
Avg	**HR**	**RBI**	**SB**
.325	25	414	34

KUENN, HARVEY (SS/OF)
(1952–1959)

The Tigers signed Harvey Kuenn as an amateur free agent before the 1952 season and he played just 63 games in the minors before coming up to Detroit late in the season. In 1953 Kuenn—sbig for a shortstop at 6'3" and nearly 200 pounds—won the AL Rookie of the Year Award when he posted a .308 average with 209 hits and set a major league rookie record with 679 at-bats. Kuenn would hit over .300 in six of his seven seasons with the Tigers. In 1958 Kuenn was moved to the outfield. The next year he won the AL batting title with a .353 average. Detroit then shocked the baseball world by trading their seven-time

All-Star to Cleveland for Rocky Colavito, the reigning home-run champion. The year Kuenn spent in Cleveland was the least productive of his career up to that point, and it didn't help that Indians fans booed him constantly, blaming him for the loss of the popular Colavito. After the season, Kuenn was traded to the National League where he played his last six years for the Giants, Cubs, and Phillies and acquired the distinction of making the last outs in two of Sandy Koufax's no-hitters. Kuenn retired after the 1966 season and suffered through numerous medical problems, including a heart bypass, removal of his colon, and a leg amputation. He became a coach with the Brewers in 1971, and then the manager in 1982. He led his team of Brewers sluggers—affectionately called "Harvey's Wallbangers"—to the 1982 World Series, where they lost to the Cardinals in seven games.

CAREER TIGERS RECORD:

Games	AB	Hits	Runs
1,049	4,372	1,372	620
Avg	**HR**	**RBI**	**SB**
.314	53	423	51

LOLICH, MICKEY (SP)
(1963–1975)

The Detroit Tigers signed left-hander Mickey Lolich as an amateur free agent on June 30, 1958. While pitching for the Denver Bears in the minors, Lolich was struck in the eye by a line drive on Opening Day of the 1962 season and temporarily blinded. Afraid of being hit again, he quit, only to return later in the season. He made the major league team in 1963 as a spot starter and reliever. Lolich was born a right-hander, but when a motorcycle accident in his youth injured his left shoulder, the doctor ordered him to throw a baseball left-handed in order to build up his left arm's strength, and he discovered a new talent.

In 1964 Lolich began a streak of 12 straight years for the Tigers in which he started at least 30 games each year. He won at least 14 games a year for 11 straight years, including 25 wins in 1971 and 22 in 1972. When the Tigers squared off against the Cardinals in the 1968 World Series, it was billed as a Gibson-McLain duel, since Gibson had gone 22–9 with an unbelievable 1.12 ERA on the season and McLain had gone 31–6 with a 1.96 ERA. Lolich stole the spotlight, however, winning three games in the Series, including Game 7 against Gibson, 4–1, on two days' rest.

Considerably heavier than most major league players, Lolich often joked about his weight, once saying, "I guess you could say I'm the redemption of the fat man. A guy will be watching me on TV and see that I don't look in any better shape than he is. 'Hey, Maude!' he'll holler. 'Get a load of this guy, and he's a 20-game winner.'" Lolich was traded to the Mets for Rusty Staub after the 1975 season. After going 8–13 for New York in 1976, Lolich sat out the 1977 season in order to become a free agent. He then signed with San Diego, but was just 2–3 in his two seasons with the Padres before calling it quits. After retiring, Lolich opened a pastry shop in Michigan and has been a baker ever since.

CAREER TIGERS RECORD:

W	L	W%	ERA	SV
207	175	.542	3.45	10
K	**BB**	**SHO**	**IP**	
2,679	1,014	39	3,361.7	

McAuliffe, Dick (2B/SS/3B) (1960–1973)

Detroit signed Dick McAuliffe as an amateur free agent before the 1957 season. Known for his wide-open batting stance and Mel Ott-style leg kick, McAuliffe played for the Tigers briefly in 1960 and then joined the team for good in 1961. For his first several years, McAuliffe bounced between second, third, and short, but ended up playing most of his career at second and short. He was a rarity in his day, a middle infielder with power, three times topping 20 homers. Although his career average was under .250, McAuliffe usually batted leadoff. In 1968 he led the AL in runs scored and went through the entire season without grounding into a double play. McAuliffe was the catalyst of the Tigers' victory over St. Louis in 1968, scoring five runs and driving in three. In 1969 he led off two consecutive games with homers, something only 10 other American Leaguers had ever accomplished. After spending the first 14 years of his 16-year career with Detroit, McAuliffe was traded to Boston for Ben Oglivie following the 1973 season. Two years later he retired and opened a coin-operated laundry business in Connecticut.

CAREER TIGERS RECORD:

Games	AB	Hits	Runs
1,656	5,898	1,471	856
Avg	**HR**	**RBI**	**SB**
.249	192	672	61

McLain, Denny (SP) (1963–1970)

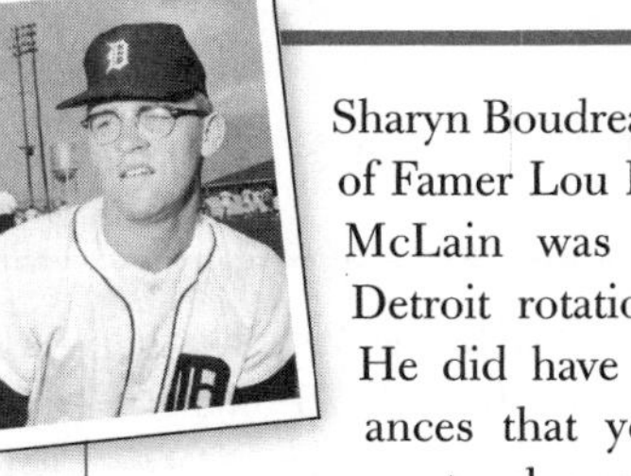

By the time Tigers pitcher Denny McLain was 25 years old in 1969, he had won 114 games against only 57 losses, been a 20-game winner three times, become baseball's only 30-game winner in 35 years, won two Cy Young Awards and an AL MVP Award, been a three-time All-Star, been named *The Sporting News* Pitcher of the Year twice, and helped Detroit win the World Series in 1968. He was well on his way to what should have been a Hall of Fame career. Three years later, he was out of baseball, the victim of arm injuries, a gambling problem, and his own inability to deal with fame.

McLain had been claimed off waivers at the age of 19 while still in the White Sox's minor league system early in 1963, and came up to Detroit later that same year. After pitching in a few games, McLain eloped with Sharyn Boudreau, daughter of Hall of Famer Lou Boudreau. By 1965 McLain was a regular in the Detroit rotation, finishing 16–6. He did have four relief appearances that year, including one spectacular appearance in which he struck out 14 Red Sox hitters in 6⅔ innings, including an AL-tying seven consecutive batters. After winning 20 games in 1966 and 17 more in 1967, McLain became a favorite of Detroit fans and a darling of the media, which loved to quote the brash young pitcher. He relished the attention and the fame, but was ill-suited to handle it. He drank a case of Pepsi a day and bragged that his pitching success was due to his offseason bowling. He appeared on *The Ed Sullivan Show, The Smothers Brothers Comedy Hour,* the *Today* show, and many other programs—and was featured in many magazines, including *Time* and *Life.* By the All-Star break, McLain was 16–2. On September 14, he beat Oakland to become the first 30-game winner in 34 years. McLain had another stellar year in 1969, going 24–9.

But McLain's fast living finally caught up to him. Before the 1970 season began, an article appeared in *Sports Illustrated* that linked McLain to gamblers. Commissioner Bowie Kuhn suspended McLain for half a season and McLain was eventually forced into bankruptcy. Back with the team for just one week, McLain was suspended for a week by the Tigers for dumping a bucket of water on a sportswriter, then suspended *again* for carrying a gun. McLain wound up his miserable half-year with a 3–5 record and was traded to Washington in a deal to which Senators manager Ted Williams strongly objected. McLain and Williams hated each other, and it showed in McLain's performance. He finished the season 10–22 and was experiencing arm trouble from a long history of cortisone shots. In 1972 McLain was dumped on Oakland, which in turn dumped him on Atlanta. His combined record for the two teams was 4–7, with a 6.37 ERA.

He never pitched in the majors again. After leaving the game, McLain got into television and radio work in Detroit and ran nightclubs before falling into bankruptcy a second time. His house burned to the ground in 1978, and in 1985 he went to prison for 2½ years before his 25-year sentence for extortion, racketeering, and drug possession was overturned. In 1996 he went to prison a second time, this time for stealing $3 million from the pension fund of his meat-packing company. In October 2003, McLain was paroled, expressing a desire to spend time with his family.

CAREER TIGERS RECORD:

W	L	W%	ERA	SV
117	62	.654	3.13	1

K	BB	SHO	IP
1,150	450	26	1,593.0

MORRIS, JACK (SP)
(1977–1990)

Jack Morris was taken by the Tigers in the fifth round of the June 1976 amateur draft. He pitched briefly for the Tigers in 1977 and became a regular in the rotation by 1979, winning 17 games, the first of 10 straight years he led the Tigers in wins. During the decade of the 1980s, Morris was the winningest pitcher in the majors, collecting 172 victories, including a no-hitter against the White Sox in 1984, the same year he led the Tigers to their World Series title. After 14 years in Detroit, Morris left the Tigers via free agency and signed with Minnesota for one year, leading the Twins to a World Series victory over Atlanta in 1991. Morris then spent two years with Toronto (making the World Series again in 1992) and a final year with Cleveland in 1994 before retiring after the strike-shortened season.

CAREER TIGERS RECORD:

W	L	W%	ERA	SV
198	150	.569	3.73	0

K	BB	SHO	IP
1,980	1,086	24	3,042.7

MULLIN, GEORGE (SP)
(1902–1913)

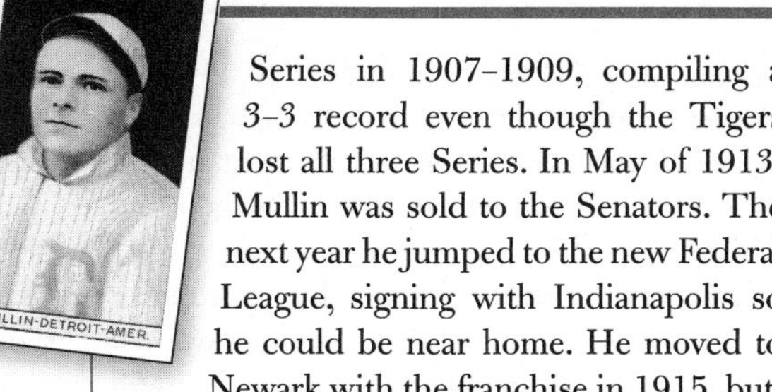
MULLIN-DETROIT-AMER.

George Mullin joined the Tigers in 1902 when the upstart junior circuit was in its second year. He had signed contracts with both the Tigers and the NL's Brooklyn team, so he chose Detroit since it was closer to his home in Indiana. Mullin was a powerfully built fastball pitcher, one of the best pitchers in Detroit Tigers history. From 1903 to 1906, Mullin pitched more than 300 innings each year. Five times he was a 20-game winner; in 1909 he finished 29–8 with a 2.22 ERA. On July 4, 1912, his 32nd birthday, Mullin presented himself with a no-hitter against the St. Louis Browns. Mullin pitched in three consecutive World Series in 1907–1909, compiling a 3–3 record even though the Tigers lost all three Series. In May of 1913, Mullin was sold to the Senators. The next year he jumped to the new Federal League, signing with Indianapolis so he could be near home. He moved to Newark with the franchise in 1915, but, homesick for Indiana, he returned after just five games with the team, never to play major league baseball again.

CAREER TIGERS RECORD:

W	L	W%	ERA	SV
209	179	.539	2.76	6
K	**BB**	**SHO**	**IP**	
1,380	1,106	34	3,394.0	

NEWHOUSER, HAL (SP)
(1939–1953)

The Tigers signed Hal Newhouser as an amateur free agent before the 1939 season and he appeared in one game for Detroit late in the year. By 1940 he was a regular in the Detroit rotation. Newhouser was allowed a medical deferment in World War II because of a heart condition. In his first four years in Detroit, Newhouser was a disappointing 34–51. Once he learned to throw a slider, however, his fortunes changed. Over the next five years he went 118–46, including 25 shutouts. He became the only pitcher ever to win back-to-back MVP Awards when he turned the trick in 1944 and 1945. In 1945 he led the Tigers to a World Series victory over the Chicago Cubs, winning two of his three starts, including the deciding Game 7. A seven-time All-Star, Newhouser led the league in wins four times, posting win totals of 29, 25, 26, and 21. He is often discounted as a great pitcher because he pitched during the talent-thin World War II years, but a close inspection of his record indicates otherwise. He won 26 games in 1946, a year when all the stars were back for the whole year. After a sore shoulder resulted in several mediocre years, the Tigers released Newhouser in July 1953. He pitched sparingly in relief for the 1954 pennant-winning Indians, and then one game in 1955 before hanging up his spikes. He dabbled in coaching and scouting before finally settling in as a banker. In 1992 he was elected to the Hall of Fame.

CAREER TIGERS RECORD:

W	L	W%	ERA	SV
200	148	.575	3.07	19
K	**BB**	**SHO**	**IP**	
1,770	1,227	33	2,944.0	

PARRISH, LANCE (C/DH)
(1977–1986)

Lance Parrish was drafted in the first round of the June 1974 amateur draft by the Tigers. He played in a dozen games in 1977 before making the team for good in 1978. Parrish was a hard-working player whose determination helped him win three Gold Gloves and five Silver Slugger Awards; he made the All-Star team six times while with Detroit. In the 1982 All-Star Game in Montreal, Parrish excited the fans by throwing out three of four runners trying to steal—Steve Sax, Al Oliver, and Ozzie Smith. Only Tony Peña was called safe, and the call was so close that AL manager Billy Martin flew out of the dugout and argued hard. Once, while Carlton Fisk was still playing, Orioles-great Brooks Robinson called Parrish the best catcher in the American League. Parrish had good power, too, and in 1982 he broke Yogi Berra's record for homers in a season by a catcher by hitting 32, a record broken by Fisk the very next year. Parrish left Detroit via free agency after the 1986 season, his 10th with the Tigers, and signed with Philadelphia. He played for six different teams in the next nine years, retiring in 1995 after 19 years with the third-highest home run total by a catcher, trailing only Carlton Fisk and Johnny Bench. He later became a coach for the Tigers.

CAREER TIGERS RECORD:

Games	AB	Hits	Runs
1,146	4,273	1,123	577
Avg	**HR**	**RBI**	**SB**
.263	212	700	22

TRAMMELL, ALAN (SS)
(1977–1996)

The Tigers chose Alan Trammell with their second pick in the June 1976 amateur draft and, after coming up in 1977, he played the next 20 years in Detroit, more seasons than any other Tiger except Ty Cobb and Al Kaline. On September 9, 1977, Trammell made his major league debut at shortstop for the Tigers. At second base that game was Lou Whitaker, also making his major league debut. They would play together for 1,918 games. Trammell was a steady shortstop who could hold his own at the bat with the likes of Cal Ripken and Robin Yount. He was one of the driving forces behind the Tigers' rout of the American League in 1984, and the World Series against San Diego as well, in which Trammell hit .450 with two homers, six RBIs, and five runs to earn World Series MVP honors. Trammell hit .300 or better in seven of his 20 seasons. Although injuries slowed him down in the second half of his career, he retired in the top 10 of many Tigers career batting categories. Upon his retirement, Trammell's .977 fielding average was higher than that of any shortstop in the Hall of Fame. Trammell spent several years in the Tigers' front office and then as the team's hitting instructor before joining the Padres as a coach. In 2003 he returned to become the team's manager, but was let go after his third losing season in 2005.

CAREER TIGERS RECORD:

Games	AB	Hits	Runs
2,293	8,288	2,365	1,231
Avg	**HR**	**RBI**	**SB**
.285	185	1,003	236

TROUT, DIZZY (SP)
(1939–1952)

Paul "Dizzy" Trout pitched the first 13½ years of his 15-year career for Detroit, forming a potent lefty-righty combo with Hal Newhouser. He was given his nickname by a local paper while he was in the minors for performing zany stunts. His reasoning was that if he could draw extra customers to the game and furnish good copy for the newspapers, he could make more money for himself come contract time. When he arrived at spring training by motorcycle in 1938, still a minor leaguer, he circled the field several times before dismounting and reporting to manager Mickey Cochrane. "That's very nice, Dizzy," Cochrane said. "Now you can keep on going to Toledo." Trout arrived in Detroit in 1939, but posted losing records his first four years. He finally had a breakout year in 1943, when he went 20–12 with five shutouts. He followed it up in 1944 with a 27–14 record, seven shutouts, and a 2.12 league-leading ERA. In 1945 Trout won 18 games; incredibly, in September he pitched six games in nine days to help the Tigers win the AL pennant.

Trout, a two-time All-Star, once struck out Ted Williams with two on and two out to win a game, 2–1. After the game, Trout asked Williams to autograph the ball. Williams glared at Trout, but obliged, tossing the ball at him after signing it. The next week, Trout faced Williams in almost the exact same circumstance, two on and two out, with the Tigers leading 2–1. This time Williams hit a mammoth home run to win the game. As he was circling the bases, Williams yelled to Trout, "I'll sign that son of a bitch, too, if you can find it." Trout's career began to slide after the 1946 season. Some say it was because he hurt his back when he bet someone he could lift a 365-pound barrel. After playing his last season and a half with Boston and Baltimore, Trout retired in 1952 and became a colorful broadcaster in Detroit. In 1959, he joined the Bill Veeck's White Sox as club spokesman.

CAREER TIGERS RECORD:

W	L	W%	ERA	SV
161	153	.513	3.20	34

K	BB	SHO	IP
1,199	978	28	2,591.7

VEACH, BOBBY (OF)
(1912–1923)

Bobby Veach was a fine outfielder who just seemed to get better as he got older. The problem was, Veach was always overshadowed by Ty Cobb, Sam Crawford, and Harry Heilmann. Veach drove in more than 100 runs six times, leading the league three times. He also led the league once in hits, once in triples, and twice in doubles, no small feat considering the prowess of his teammates. On September 17, 1920, Veach got six hits and hit for the cycle in a 14–13, 12-inning win over Boston. After playing 12 years with Detroit, Veach finished his career playing with the Red Sox, Yankees, and Senators. He achieved a bit of notoriety in 1925 when he was called upon to pinch-hit for Babe Ruth during one of the Bambino's famous squabbles with manager Miller Huggins.

CAREER TIGERS RECORD:

Games	AB	Hits	Runs
1,604	5.979	1,859	859

Avg	HR	RBI	SB
.311	59	1,042	189

WHITAKER, LOU (2B)
(1977–1995)

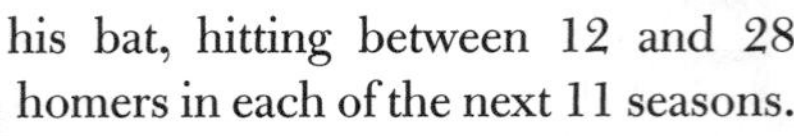

The Tigers drafted Lou Whitaker in the fifth round of the June 1975 amateur draft. Whitaker played more games at second base (2,308) than fellow Tiger Hall of Famer Charlie Gehringer (2,206). Along with Joe Morgan, Whitaker became the only second baseman to log at least 2,000 games, 2,000 hits, and 200 homers in a career. He is best remembered, though, for the years he spent as keystone partner with shortstop Alan Trammell, playing a record 1,918 games together. He and Trammell debuted in the same game in September 1977, but it was Whitaker who shone brighter early in their careers, winning the 1978 Rookie of the Year Award. "Sweet Lou" Whitaker appeared in five consecutive All-Star Games from 1983–1987 and won three consecutive Gold Gloves from 1983 to 1985. He also won four Silver Slugger Awards as the best-hitting second baseman in the American League. After hitting only 12 homers in his first five years, Whitaker suddenly discovered some boom in his bat, hitting between 12 and 28 homers in each of the next 11 seasons.

In 1983 Whitaker and Trammell, batting 1–2 in the order, hit a combined .319, becoming the first AL double-play combo to hit over .300 in 34 years. Whitaker dominated in the 1984 World Series, when the Tigers dismantled the Padres in five games. He led all players with six runs scored and 18 assists, and played flawlessly in the field. In 1986 Whitaker's 20 homers allowed helped the Tigers sport an "all-20 homer infield." Joining him were catcher Lance Parrish (22), first baseman Darrell Evans (29), third baseman Darnell Coles (20), and shortstop Alan Trammell (21). After 19 big-league seasons, all with Detroit, Whitaker retired at the age of 38 after the 1995 season, one year before Trammell ended his career.

CAREER TIGERS RECORD:

Games	AB	Hits	Runs
2,390	8,570	2,369	1,386
Avg	**HR**	**RBI**	**SB**
.276	244	1,084	143

YORK, RUDY (1B/C)
(1934, 1937–1945)

York was a man without a position for many years. Although he was a decent fielder, even setting several American League records along the way, York was a first baseman/catcher who was trapped behind future Hall of Famers Hank Greenberg at first and Mickey Cochrane behind the plate. Sportswriters did like to poke fun at the half-Cherokee York. One writer said of York, "He's part Indian and part first baseman," and Red Smith quipped, "No matter where York was stationed in the field, he always played the same position—at bat."

After York won MVP Awards in the Texas League in 1935 and the American Association in 1936, the Tigers knew they had to get him into the lineup somehow. When Cochrane was severely beaned in May 1937, York got his chance, although he still didn't play regularly.

Then, on August 4, after the Tigers had lost six straight, York was put into the lineup as the everyday catcher. He homered that day, then again and again, all month long, until he had 16 blasts through August 30th. Needing one more to tie Babe Ruth's record of 17 in one month, York hit two against the Senators on August 31st to establish a new record. He also had a whopping 49 RBIs for the month, breaking Lou Gehrig's mark of 48. York finished his rookie year with 35 homers and 103 RBIs in just 375 at-bats. Knowing that York belonged at first base, the Tigers gave Hank Greenberg a $10,000 bonus in 1940 to move to the outfield. With their new lineup, Detroit went on to win the AL pennant, but lost the World Series to Cincinnati in seven games. After two subpar years in 1944 and 1945, York was traded to the Red Sox, where he had one decent year before bouncing briefly from Boston to the White Sox to the Phillies. York retired in midseason 1948 after failing to hit a homer for Philadelphia in 31 games. After leaving baseball, he became a coach for the Red Sox for a few years, but eventually became a firefighter in Georgia.

CAREER TIGERS RECORD:

Games	AB	Hits	Runs
1,268	4,677	1,317	738
Avg	**HR**	**RBI**	**SB**
.282	239	936	34

The Tigers and the Cubs tangled in the 1907 World Series.

Florida Marlins

Since 1993

1993 Marlins third baseman Gary Sheffield is the first player in major league history to represent a first-year expansion team as an All-Star Game starter.... **1997** In the first year of interleague play, Florida goes 12–3, sharing with Montreal the best record in the majors against teams of the other league.... **1998** The Marlins post the worst record ever by a defending World Series champion when they end the season 54–108. The previous worst record for a defending champion is the 1991 Cincinnati Reds, who went 74–88.... **2003** The Marlins win their second World Series title in 2003, once again entering the postseason as a Wild Card. They are still the only National League Wild Card team to win the World Series.

FRANCHISE HISTORY

The National League expanded from 12 to 14 teams in 1993, adding the Florida Marlins (in Miami) and the Colorado Rockies. Owner H. Wayne Huizenga was awarded the Florida franchise in June 1991 for a $95 million franchise fee after fierce competition from other Florida interests in Orlando and St. Petersburg. Huizenga built his fortune in the garbage business; he began in 1962 with a one-truck garbage route and eventually transformed the operation into the nation's largest waste-collection company by 1971. In 1987, he bought the Blockbuster Video chain, expanding in just five years from 19 to 3,000 stores. By the time the Marlins took the field in 1993, Huizenga's personal fortune was estimated to be worth more than $600 million. Huizenga chose the team's nickname because he loved sportfishing, and considered the marlin "a fierce fighter and adversary that tests your mettle." The name also had regional roots, as the minor league teams in Miami (1956–1970 and 1982–1988) were named the Marlins.

In 1999, outfielder Jeff Conine became the first player in major league history to play in all 162 games of an expansion team's first season.

As a first-year expansion team, Florida gave a good account of itself. The Marlins managed to avoid the NL East cellar in their first season, finishing five games ahead of the New York Mets. In 1997, due in large part to heavy spending on free agents, the Marlins became the youngest team ever to win the World Series, taking the title in just their fifth year in existence. (In 2001, Arizona eclipsed this record when it won the World Series in its fourth year.) Almost immediately after the Series, however, Huizenga stunned the team's fans when he announced that many of the high-priced players would be traded during the offseason. The cost-cutting move actually turned into a fire sale. Huizenga had long wanted a baseball team, preparing for it years in advance by purchasing Joe Robbie Stadium purely on the speculative chance of getting a major league franchise, but once he got his team he was rudely introduced to negative cash flow. After the salary dump, the Marlins fell from 92 wins to 54 the very next year. Huizenga was so soured on the whole red-ink experience that just over a year later (1999) he sold the team.

Series MVP Livan Hernandez faces Cleveland in Game 5 of the 1997 World Series. The Marlins won in 7.

The Marlins improved both their winning percentage and place in the standings in each of their first five seasons.

Huizenga sold the Marlins to south Florida commodities trader John Henry for $150 million after an earlier bid by Marlins team president Don Smiley fell through. Three years later, Henry turned around and sold the team to Montreal Expos owner Jeffrey Loria for $158.5 million in a three-way deal that allowed Henry and former Padres owner Tom Werner to buy the Boston Red Sox for $730 million from the Jean R. Yawkey Trust. Loria then sold the Expos to Major League Baseball. Along the way, the Marlins surprised the baseball world again by winning their second World Series title, this time in 2003 against the heavily favored New York Yankees. But once again, lack of fan support led to heavy losses for the new Marlins owner. Loria then conducted a fire sale of his own after the 2005 season, sending stars Josh Beckett, Mike Lowell, and Guillermo Mota to Boston and Carlos Delgado to the Mets, shedding half the team's salary in two quick deals. A.J. Burnett was allowed to leave for the free-agent market without a bid. Star center fielder Juan Pierre was traded to the Cubs. Damion Easley went to Arizona; Todd Jones went to Detroit; closer Antonio Alfonseca wasn't offered a contract for 2006; speedy second baseman Luis Castillo unpacked his bags in Minnesota. And the dealing will likely continue, leaving South Florida's fans with a pile of prospects, and a pile of losses in 2006 as the Marlins owner heads for deep water. On top of all the other grim news, the Marlins are threatening to leave Miami unless they get a new stadium deal in the works very soon.

TEAM NAME HISTORY

Official Names

Marlins (1993–current)

Unofficial Names/Nicknames

Fish

STADIUM HISTORY

Joe Robbie Stadium	1993–August 25, 1996
Pro Player Stadium	August 26, 1996–January 8, 2005
(Joe Robbie Stadium renamed)	
Dolphins Stadium	January 9, 2005–current
(Pro Player Stadium renamed)	

The Marlins' home has had three names since the team started playing here in 1993: Dolphins Stadium, Joe Robbie Stadium, and Pro Player Stadium

Yearly Record, Finish, & Attendance Figures

Year	League	Record	DIV/LG Finish	Attendance	Avg/Gm
2004	NL East	83–79	3	1,723,105	21,539
2003	NL East	91–71	2	1,303,215	16,089
2002	NL East	79–83	4	813,118	10,038
2001	NL East	76–86	4	1,261,226	15,765
2000	NL East	79–82	3	1,218,326	15,041
1999	NL East	64–98	5	1,369,421	17,118
1998	NL East	54–108	5	1,730,384	21,363
1997	NL East	92–70	2	2,364,387	29,190
1996	NL East	80–82	3	1,746,767	21,565
1995	NL East	67–76	4	1,700,466	23,950
1994	NL East	51–64	5	1,937,467	32,838
1993	NL East	64–98	6	3,064,847	37,838

Manager History

Manager	Years	W–L	Win %
Rene Lachemann	1993–1996	221–285	.437
Cookie Rojas	1996	1–0	1.000
John Boles	1996, 1999–2001	205–241	.460
Jim Leyland	1997–1998	146–178	.451
Tony Perez	2001	54–60	.474
Jeff Torborg	2002–2003	95–105	.475
Jack McKeon	2003–2005	241–207	.538
Joe Girardi	(Took over beginning in 2006)		

All-Time Win-Loss Records vs. All Opponents

Opponent	Record
ALL-TIME	963–1,076
Angels	2–4
Astros	49–61
Athletics	2–1
Blue Jays	11–4
Braves	83–110
Brewers	30–29
Cardinals	47–62
Cubs	56–59
Devil Rays	28–15
Diamondbacks	24–34
Dodgers	52–60
Giants	41–67
Indians	5–1
INTERLEAGUE	87–63
Mariners	1–2
Mets	92–100
Nationals	100–91
Orioles	11–4
Padres	51–53
Phillies	92–102
Pirates	49–63
Rangers	4–5
Reds	51–63
Red Sox	7–11
Rockies	59–59
Royals	2–1
Tigers	5–4
Twins	1–2
White Sox	2–1
Yankees	6–8

Franchise Highlights, Low Points, and Strange Distinctions

1993 On July 28, Anthony Young of the Mets ended his personal 27-game losing streak when he defeated the Marlins, 5–4, in New York.

• • • •

1994 On July 10, the Marlins paid first-round draft choice Josh Booty a $1.6 million signing bonus, a record for a draft pick at that time. Booty managed to get 26 at-bats with Florida, collecting just six singles and a double to go along with his .840 fielding average (four errors in 21 chances).

• • • •

1996 Ace pitcher Kevin Brown compiled a 17–11 record. Incredibly, the Marlins scored a total of only 11 runs in his 11 losses.

Until the Braves called up Andruw Jones during the 1996 season, the Marlins had the three youngest players in the major leagues on their roster: Felix Heredia (21), Luis Castillo (20), and Edgar Renteria (20).

• • • •

1997 Manager Jim Leyland took the Marlins to the World Series in his first year as the team's manager.

1997 On April 2, the Marlins and Gary Sheffield agreed to the largest total contract package ($72 million) ever awarded to a baseball player up to that time.

• • • •

1997 Catcher Charles Johnson set a major league record in 1997 by handling 973 fielding chances in 123 games without making an error. The American League record for consecutive errorless chances belongs to the Yankees' Joe Girardi, now the manager of the Marlins.

• • • •

2001 Of Florida's 86 losses in 2001, a whopping 24 of them came during their opponents' last at-bat.

On May 12, 2001, A.J. Burnett pitched a 3–0 no-hitter over the San Diego Padres. In the process, he walked nine Padres, a major league record for walks given up in a no-hitter.

• • • •

2005 On August 31, Jeremy Hermida became the first player in major league history to hit a pinch-hit grand slam in his first major league at-bat, though the Marlins lost to St. Louis, 10–5.

Special Achievements

World Series Results

Year	Opponent	Result	Games
1997	Cleveland	Won	4–3
2003	NY Yankees	Won	4–2

World Series Managerial Records

Manager	Series Record	Games Record
Jim Leyland	1–0	4–3
Jack McKeon	1–0	4–2

All-Time Postseason Record

Divisional Playoffs	6–1
League Championship Series	8–5
World Series	8–5

All-Star Games at Florida

None

Hall of Famers Who Played for Team

None

Hall of Famers Who Managed Team

	Position	Years	Games with Florida
Tony Perez	Mgr	2001	114

MVP Award Winners

None

Cy Young Award Winners

None

Rookie of the Year Award Winners

Dontrelle Willis	SP	2003

Gold Glove Winners

Year	Position	Player
1995	C	Charles Johnson
1996	C	Charles Johnson
1997	C	Charles Johnson
1998	C	Charles Johnson
2003	1B 2B	Derrek Lee Luis Castillo
2004	2B	Luis Castillo
2005	2B 3B	Luis Castillo Mike Lowell

Triple Crown Winners

None

Fireman of the Year Award Winners

None

World Series MVP

Livan Hernandez	1997
Josh Beckett	2003

League Championship Series MVP

Livan Hernandez	1997
Ivan Rodriguez	2003

All-Star Game MVP

None

Manager of the Year Award Winners

Jack McKeon	2003

Batting Champions

None

Nine-Inning No-Hitters Pitched

Year	Pitcher	Opp.	Score
1996	Al Leiter	COL	11–0
1997	Kevin Brown	SF	9–0
2001	A.J. Burnett	SD	3–0

20-Game Winners

Year	Pitcher	W–L
2005	Dontrelle Willis	22–10

Retired Uniform Numbers

Number	Player	Position
5	Carl Barger	Executive

Team Records—Wins & Losses

- Games won in a season: 92 in 1997
- Games lost in a season: 108 in 1998
- Games won in a month: 19 in August 1997
- Games lost in a month: 20, four times (May of 1995 and 1998, and August of 1998 and 2001)
- Consecutive games won: 9 in 1996

- Consecutive games lost: 11 in 1998
- Biggest shutout victory: 17–0 over Colorado on September 17, 1995
- Biggest shutout loss: 18–0 to Atlanta on October 3, 1999
- Highest winning percentage: .568 in 1997 (92–70)
- Lowest winning percentage: .333 in 1998 (54–108)

TEAM RECORDS—BATTING

- Highest team batting average: .272 in 2005
- Lowest team batting average: .248 in 1993 and 1998
- Highest team slugging average: .423 in 2001
- Highest team on-base percentage: .346 in 1997
- Total hits: 1,499 in 2005
- Extra-base hits: 521 in 2001
- Hits in a game: 25 vs. Atlanta on July 1, 2003
- Longest individual hitting streak: 35, Luis Castillo, 2002
- Most .300 hitters in a single season: 4 in 2005
- Home runs: 166 in 2001
- Home runs in a month: 11, Gary Sheffield, April 1996
- Home runs in a game: 4, accomplished many times
- Home runs by a rookie: 26, Preston Wilson, 1999
- Home runs by a right-hander: 42, Gary Sheffield, 1996
- Home runs by a left-hander: 33, Carlos Delgado, 2005
- Home runs by a switch-hitter: 20, Orestes Destrade, 1993
- Grand slams: 9 in 1997
- Grand slams (individual; single season): 3, Bobby Bonilla, 1997
- Grand slams (individual; career): 4, Derrek Lee
- Triples: 44 in 1999 and 2003
- Doubles: 325 in 2001
- Singles: 1,034 in 1993
- Walks: 686 in 1997
- Runs scored: 751 in 2003
- Runs scored in a game: 20 vs. Atlanta on July 1, 2003
- Runs scored in an inning: 8, accomplished many times
- Most batters hit by a pitch: 67 in 2001 and 2005
- Times shut out: 14 in 1993 and 1996
- Grounded into double plays: 144 in 2005
- Fewest grounded into double plays: 100 in 2000
- Runners left on base: 1,248 in 1997

TEAM RECORDS—BASERUNNING

- Stolen bases: 177 in 2002
- Caught stealing: 74 in 2003

TEAM RECORDS—PITCHING

- Lowest earned run average: 3.83 in 1997
- Complete games: 14 in 2005
- Saves: 53 in 2004
- Strikeouts: 1,188 in 1997
- Shutouts: 15 in 2005
- Walks: 715 in 1998
- Hit batsmen: 70 in 2001
- Wild pitches: 85 in 1993
- Consecutive wins (individual): 9, Pat Rapp in 1995 and Livan Hernandez in 1997
- Consecutive losses (individual): 8, Reid Cornelius in 2000 and Brad Penny in 2001
- Strikeouts in a game: 14, A.J. Burnett, August 29, 2004
- Runs allowed in a game: 25 by Boston, June 27, 2003

TEAM RECORDS—FIELDING

- Best fielding average: .987 in 2003
- Most errors committed: 129 in 1998
- Fewest errors committed: 78 in 2003
- Most double plays turned: 187 in 1996
- Fewest double plays turned: 130 in 1993

TEAM RECORDS—MISCELLANEOUS

- Number of times league champions: 2
- Number of times finishing last in league: 2
- Largest attendance, single game: 57,405 vs. Atlanta, April 5, 2005
- Largest attendance, doubleheader: 37,007 vs. Philadelphia, Sept. 27, 1998
- Players used in a season: 49 in 1998
- Seasons played: 10, Luis Castillo

PRIMARY PITCHING STAFFS

Year	Starter	Starter	Starter	Starter	Starter	Closer	Bullpen	Bullpen	Bullpen
2005	Willis	Burnett	Beckett	Moehler	Leiter	Jones	Mota	Mecir	Alfonseca
2004	Willis	Pavano	Beckett	Penny	Burnett	Benitez	Perisho	Howard	Bump
2003	Willis	Pavano	Beckett	Penny	Redman	Looper	Almanza	Spooneybarger	Tejera
2002	Burnett	Tavarez	Beckett	Penny	Dempster	Nunez	Almanza	Tejera	Looper
2001	Burnett	Clement	Smith	Penny	Dempster	Alfonseca	Bones	Darensbourg	Looper
2000	Sanchez	Cornelius	Smith	Penny	Dempster	Alfonseca	Almanza	Darensbourg	Looper
1999	Meadows	Springer	Fernandez	Hernandez	Dempster	Alfonseca	Edmondson	Sanchez	Looper
1998	Meadows	Sanchez	Larkin	Hernandez	Ojala	Mantei	Edmondson	Darensbourg	Alfonseca
1997	Brown	Fernandez	Leiter	Saunders	Rapp	Nen	Powell	Heredia	Cook
1996	Brown	Burkett	Leiter	Hammond	Rapp	Nen	Powell	Mathews	Perez
1995	Witt	Burkett	Weathers	Hammond	Rapp	Nen	Veres	Mathews	Perez
1994	Hough	Gardner	Weathers	Hammond	Rapp	Nen	Lewis	Perez	Mutis
1993	Hough	Armstrong	Bowen	Hammond	Rapp	Harvey	Lewis	Klink	Turner

PRIMARY STARTING LINEUPS

Year	C	1B	2B	3B	SS	LF	CF	RF
2005	Lo Duca	Delgado	Castillo	Lowell	Gonzalez	Cabrera	Pierre	Encarnacion
2004	Redmond	Choi	Castillo	Lowell	Gonzalez	Conine	Pierre	Cabrera
2003	Rodriguez	Lee	Castillo	Lowell	Gonzalez	Hollandsworth	Pierre	Encarnacion
2002	Johnson	Lee	Castillo	Lowell	Fox	Millar	Wilson	Encarnacion
2001	Johnson	Lee	Castillo	Lowell	Gonzalez	Floyd	Wilson	Owens
2000	Redmond	Lee	Castillo	Lowell	Gonzalez	Floyd	Wilson	Kotsay
1999	Redmond	Millar	Castillo	Lowell	Gonzalez	Aven	Wilson	Kotsay
1998	Zaun	Lee	Counsell	Zeile	Renteria	Floyd	Dunwoody	Kotsay
1997	Johnson	Conine	Castillo	Bonilla	Renteria	Alou	White	Sheffield
1996	Johnson	Colbrunn	Veras	Pendleton	Renteria	Conine	White	Sheffield
1995	Johnson	Colbrunn	Veras	Pendleton	Abbott	Conine	Carr	Sheffield
1994	Santiago	Colbrunn	Barberie	Browne	Abbott	Conine	Carr	Sheffield
1993	Santiago	Destrade	Barberie	Sheffield	Weiss	Conine	Carr	Whitmore

Top 10 Batting Leaders, Single Season & Career with Team

GAMES PLAYED: CAREER WITH TEAM

Player	G	PA
1. Luis Castillo	1,128	4,966
2. Jeff Conine	1,014	3,914
3. Mike Lowell	981	4,003
4. Alex Gonzalez	896	3,488
5. Derrek Lee	844	3,251
6. Cliff Floyd	637	2,569
7. Preston Wilson	588	2,350
8. Charles Johnson	587	2,208
9. Gary Sheffield	558	2,358
10. Kevin Millar	500	1,699

AT-BATS: SEASON

Player	AB	Year
1. Juan Pierre	678	2004
2. Juan Pierre	668	2003
3. Juan Pierre	656	2005
4. Edgar Renteria	617	1997
5. Miguel Cabrera	613	2005
6. Luis Castillo	606	2002
7. Preston Wilson	605	2000
8. Miguel Cabrera	603	2004
9. Juan Encarnacion	601	2003
10. Mike Lowell	598	2004

AT-BATS: CAREER WITH TEAM

Player	AB	PA
1. Luis Castillo	4,347	4,966
2. Mike Lowell	3,554	4,003
3. Jeff Conine	3,471	3,914
4. Alex Gonzalez	3,221	3,488
5. Derrek Lee	2,830	3,251
6. Cliff Floyd	2,247	2,569
7. Preston Wilson	2,096	2,350
8. Juan Pierre	2,002	2,212
9. Charles Johnson	1,936	2,208
10. Gary Sheffield	1,870	2,358

Batting Average: Season

Player	BA	Year
1. Luis Castillo	.334	2000
2. Juan Pierre	.326	2004
3. Miguel Cabrera	.323	2005
4. Jeff Conine	.319	1994
5. Cliff Floyd	.317	2001
6. Luis Castillo	.314	2003
Gary Sheffield	.314	1996
Kevin Millar	.314	2001
9. Edgar Renteria	.309	1996
10. Kevin Millar	.306	2002

Batting Average: Career with Team

Player	BA	PA
1. Juan Pierre	.303	2,212
2. Cliff Floyd	.294	2,569
3. Luis Castillo	.293	4,966
4. Jeff Conine	.290	3,914
5. Gary Sheffield	.288	2,358
6. Mike Lowell	.272	4,003
7. Derrek Lee	.264	3,251
8. Preston Wilson	.262	2,350
9. Alex Gonzalez	.245	3,488
10. Charles Johnson	.241	2,208

Total Hits: Season

Player	H	Year
1. Juan Pierre	221	2004
2. Juan Pierre	204	2003
3. Miguel Cabrera	198	2005
4. Luis Castillo	187	2003
5. Luis Castillo	185	2002
6. Juan Pierre	181	2005
7. Luis Castillo	180	2000
8. Miguel Cabrera	177	2004
9. Cliff Floyd	176	2001
10. Jeff Conine	175	1996
Mike Lowell	175	2004

Total Hits: Career with Team

Player	H	PA
1. Luis Castillo	1,273	4,966
2. Jeff Conine	1,005	3,914
3. Mike Lowell	965	4,003
4. Alex Gonzalez	788	3,488
5. Derrek Lee	746	3,251
6. Cliff Floyd	661	2,569
7. Juan Pierre	606	2,212
8. Preston Wilson	549	2,350
9. Gary Sheffield	538	2,358
10. Charles Johnson	467	2,208

Home Runs: Season

Player	HR	Year
1. Gary Sheffield	42	1996
2. Miguel Cabrera	33	2004
Miguel Cabrera	33	2005
Carlos Delgado	33	2005
5. Mike Lowell	32	2003
6. Cliff Floyd	31	2001
Derrek Lee	31	2003
Preston Wilson	31	2000
9. Derrek Lee	28	2000
10. Derrek Lee	27	2002
Mike Lowell	27	2004
Gary Sheffield	27	1994

Home Runs: Career with Team

Player	HR	PA
1. Mike Lowell	143	4,003
2. Derrek Lee	129	3,251
3. Gary Sheffield	122	2,358
4. Jeff Conine	120	3,914
5. Cliff Floyd	110	2,569
6. Preston Wilson	104	2,350
7. Alex Gonzalez	81	3,488
8. Miguel Cabrera	78	1,716
9. Charles Johnson	75	2,208
10. Kevin Millar	59	1,699

Triples: Season

Player	3B	Year
1. Juan Pierre	13	2005
2. Juan Pierre	12	2004
3. Luis Castillo	10	2001
4. Mark Kotsay	9	1999
5. Alex Gonzalez	8	1999
6. Kurt Abbott	7	1995
Kurt Abbott	7	1996
Luis Castillo	7	2004
Todd Dunwoody	7	1998
Mark Kotsay	7	1998
Derrek Lee	7	2002
Juan Pierre	7	2003
Quilvio Veras	7	1995

Triples: Career with Team

Player	3B	PA
1. Luis Castillo	42	4,966
2. Alex Gonzalez	23	3,010
3. Mark Kotsay	22	1,793
4. Kurt Abbott	19	1,461
Juan Pierre	19	1,494
6. Derrek Lee	18	3,251
7. Jeff Conine	17	3,914
8. Todd Dunwoody	12	720
Kevin Millar	12	1,699
10. Preston Wilson	11	2,350

Doubles: Season

Player	2B	Year
1. Cliff Floyd	45	1998
2. Cliff Floyd	44	2001
Mike Lowell	44	2002
Mike Lowell	44	2004
5. Miguel Cabrera	43	2005
6. Carlos Delgado	41	2005
Kevin Millar	41	2002
8. Bobby Bonilla	39	1997
Kevin Millar	39	2001
10. Mike Lowell	38	2000

Doubles: Career with Team

Player	2B	PA
1. Mike Lowell	241	4,003
2. Alex Gonzalez	183	3,488
3. Jeff Conine	180	3,914
4. Cliff Floyd	167	2,569
5. Derrek Lee	159	3,251
6. Luis Castillo	130	4,966
7. Charles Johnson	111	2,208
Kevin Millar	111	1,699
9. Preston Wilson	108	2,350
10. Gary Sheffield	98	2,358

Extra-Base Hits: Season

Player	XBH	Year
1. Cliff Floyd	79	2001
2. Miguel Cabrera	78	2005
3. Carlos Delgado	77	2005
4. Gary Sheffield	76	1996
5. Mike Lowell	72	2004
6. Cliff Floyd	70	1998
7. Derrek Lee	69	2002
Preston Wilson	69	2000
9. Mike Lowell	68	2002
10. Miguel Cabrera	65	2004

Extra-Base Hits: Career with Team

Player	XBH	PA
1. Mike Lowell	387	4,003
2. Jeff Conine	317	3,914
3. Derrek Lee	306	3,251
4. Alex Gonzalez	287	3,488
5. Cliff Floyd	286	2,569
6. Gary Sheffield	227	2,358
7. Preston Wilson	223	2,350

8. Luis Castillo	192	4,966
9. Charles Johnson	189	2,208
10. Kevin Millar	182	1,699

TOTAL BASES: SEASON

Player	TB	Year
1. Miguel Cabrera	344	2005
2. Gary Sheffield	324	1996
3. Cliff Floyd	321	2001
4. Miguel Cabrera	309	2004
5. Carlos Delgado	303	2005
6. Mike Lowell	302	2004
7. Preston Wilson	294	2000
8. Jeff Conine	289	1996
9. Derrek Lee	287	2002
10. Cliff Floyd	283	1998

TOTAL BASES: CAREER WITH TEAM

Player	TB	PA
1. Mike Lowell	1,641	4,003
2. Jeff Conine	1,579	3,914
3. Luis Castillo	1,547	4,966
4. Derrek Lee	1,328	3,251
5. Alex Gonzalez	1,260	3,488
6. Cliff Floyd	1,176	2,569
7. Gary Sheffield	1,016	2,358
8. Preston Wilson	991	2,350
9. Charles Johnson	809	2,208
10. Miguel Cabrera	800	1,716

RUNS BATTED IN: SEASON

Player	RBI	Year
1. Preston Wilson	121	2000
2. Gary Sheffield	120	1996
3. Miguel Cabrera	116	2005
4. Moises Alou	115	1997
Carlos Delgado	115	2005
6. Miguel Cabrera	112	2004
7. Jeff Conine	105	1995
Mike Lowell	105	2003
9. Cliff Floyd	103	2001
10. Mike Lowell	100	2001

RUNS BATTED IN: CAREER WITH TEAM

Player	RBI	PA
1. Mike Lowell	578	4,003
2. Jeff Conine	553	3,914
3. Derrek Lee	417	3,251
4. Cliff Floyd	409	2,569
5. Gary Sheffield	380	2,358
6. Alex Gonzalez	375	3,488
7. Preston Wilson	329	2,350
8. Miguel Cabrera	290	1,716
9. Charles Johnson	277	2,208
10. Luis Castillo	271	4,966

RUNS SCORED: SEASON

Player	R	Year
1. Cliff Floyd	123	2001
2. Gary Sheffield	118	1996
3. Miguel Cabrera	106	2005
4. Miguel Cabrera	101	2004
Luis Castillo	101	2000
6. Juan Pierre	100	2003
Juan Pierre	100	2004
8. Luis Castillo	99	2003
9. Juan Pierre	96	2005
10. Derrek Lee	95	2002

RUNS SCORED: CAREER WITH TEAM

Player	R	PA
1. Luis Castillo	675	4,966
2. Mike Lowell	477	4,003
3. Jeff Conine	447	3,914
4. Derrek Lee	422	3,251
5. Cliff Floyd	392	2,569
6. Gary Sheffield	365	2,358
7. Alex Gonzalez	363	3,488
8. Preston Wilson	315	2,350
9. Juan Pierre	296	2,212
10. Miguel Cabrera	246	1,716

WALKS: SEASON

Player	BB	Year
1. Gary Sheffield	142	1996
2. Gary Sheffield	121	1997
3. Derrek Lee	98	2002
4. Derrek Lee	88	2003
5. Quilvio Veras	80	1995
6. Walt Weiss	79	1993
7. Luis Castillo	78	2000
8. Luis Castillo	75	2004
9. Bobby Bonilla	73	1997
10. Carlos Delgado	72	2005

WALKS: CAREER WITH TEAM

Player	BB	PA
1. Luis Castillo	533	4,966
2. Gary Sheffield	424	2,358
3. Jeff Conine	376	3,914
4. Derrek Lee	363	3,251
5. Mike Lowell	354	4,003
6. Cliff Floyd	268	2,569
7. Charles Johnson	232	2,208
8. Preston Wilson	199	2,350
9. Alex Gonzalez	170	3,488
10. Miguel Cabrera	157	1,716

STRIKEOUTS: SEASON

Player	SO	Year
1. Preston Wilson	187	2000
2. Derrek Lee	164	2002
3. Preston Wilson	156	1999
4. Miguel Cabrera	148	2004
5. Preston Wilson	140	2002
6. Jeff Conine	135	1993
7. Charles Johnson	133	2001
8. Derrek Lee	131	2003
9. Orestes Destrade	130	1993
10. Alex Gonzalez	126	2004
Derrek Lee	126	2001

STRIKEOUTS: CAREER WITH TEAM

Player	SO	PA
1. Derrek Lee	734	3,251
2. Jeff Conine	677	3,914
3. Alex Gonzalez	672	3,488
4. Luis Castillo	629	4,966
5. Preston Wilson	603	2,350
6. Mike Lowell	528	4,003
7. Charles Johnson	499	2,208
8. Cliff Floyd	443	2,569
9. Kurt Abbott	375	1,461
10. Miguel Cabrera	357	1,716

SLUGGING PERCENTAGE: SEASON

Player	SLG	Year
1. Gary Sheffield	.624	1996
2. Carlos Delgado	.582	2005
3. Cliff Floyd	.578	2001
4. Miguel Cabrera	.561	2005
5. Kevin Millar	.557	2001
6. Mike Lowell	.530	2003
7. Cliff Floyd	.529	2000
8. Jeff Conine	.525	1994
9. Jeff Conine	.520	1995
10. Miguel Cabrera	.512	2004

Slugging Percentage: Career with Team

Player	SLG	PA
1. Gary Sheffield	.543	2,358
2. Cliff Floyd	.523	2,569
3. Preston Wilson	.473	2,350
4. Derrek Lee	.469	3,251
5. Mike Lowell	.462	4,003
6. Jeff Conine	.455	3,914
7. Charles Johnson	.418	2,208
8. Alex Gonzalez	.391	3,488
9. Juan Pierre	.378	2,212
10. Luis Castillo	.356	4,966

On-Base Percentage: Season

Player	OBP	Year
1. Gary Sheffield	.465	1996
2. Gary Sheffield	.424	1997
3. Luis Castillo	.418	2000
4. Carlos Delgado	.399	2005
5. Jerry Browne	.392	1994
6. Luis Castillo	.391	2005
7. Cliff Floyd	.390	2001
8. Miguel Cabrera	.385	2005
9. Luis Castillo	.384	1999
Quilvio Veras	.384	1995

On-Base Percentage: Career with Team

Player	OBP	PA
1. Gary Sheffield	.426	2,358
2. Cliff Floyd	.374	2,569
3. Luis Castillo	.370	4,966
4. Jeff Conine	.358	3,914
5. Juan Pierre	.354	2,212
6. Derrek Lee	.353	3,251
7. Mike Lowell	.339	4,003
8. Preston Wilson	.333	2,350
9. Charles Johnson	.324	2,208
10. Alex Gonzalez	.291	3,488

OPS (On-Base Percentage + Slugging Percentage): Season

Player	OPS	Year
1. Gary Sheffield	1.090	1996
2. Carlos Delgado	.981	2005
3. Cliff Floyd	.968	2001
4. Miguel Cabrera	.947	2005
5. Kevin Millar	.931	2001
6. Cliff Floyd	.906	2000
7. Jeff Conine	.899	1995
8. Jeff Conine	.898	1994
9. Derrek Lee	.888	2003
10. Mike Lowell	.881	2003

OPS (On-Base Percentage + Slugging Percentage): Career with Team

Player	OPS	PA
1. Gary Sheffield	.970	2,358
2. Cliff Floyd	.898	2,569
3. Derrek Lee	.822	3,251
4. Jeff Conine	.813	3,914
5. Preston Wilson	.806	2,350
6. Mike Lowell	.801	4,003
7. Charles Johnson	.742	2,208
8. Juan Pierre	.732	2,212
9. Luis Castillo	.726	4,966
10. Alex Gonzalez	.682	3,488

Stolen Bases: Season

Player	SB	Year
1. Juan Pierre	65	2003
2. Luis Castillo	62	2000
3. Chuck Carr	58	1993
4. Juan Pierre	57	2005
5. Quilvio Veras	56	1995
6. Luis Castillo	50	1999
7. Luis Castillo	48	2002
8. Juan Pierre	45	2004
9. Edgar Renteria	41	1998
10. Preston Wilson	36	2000

Stolen Bases: Career with Team

Player	SB	PA
1. Luis Castillo	281	4,966
2. Juan Pierre	167	2,212
3. Chuck Carr	115	1,446
4. Cliff Floyd	90	2,569
5. Edgar Renteria	89	1,742
6. Preston Wilson	87	2,350
7. Gary Sheffield	74	2,358
8. Quilvio Veras	64	846
9. Derrek Lee	51	3,251
10. Andy Fox	41	905

Sacrifice Hits: Season

Player	Sac	Year
1. Edgar Renteria	19	1997
2. Luis Castillo	18	2005
3. Ryan Dempster	16	2001
4. Luis Castillo	15	2003
Juan Pierre	15	2003
Juan Pierre	15	2004
7. Juan Pierre	10	2005
8. Seven tied with...	9	——

Sacrifice Hits: Career with Team

Player	Sac	PA
1. Luis Castillo	65	4,966
2. Juan Pierre	40	2,212
3. A.J. Burnett	33	300
4. Edgar Renteria	30	1,742
5. Ryan Dempster	26	264
6. Josh Beckett	25	223
7. Alex Gonzalez	24	3,488
8. Chuck Carr	20	1,446
9. Pat Rapp	19	241
10. Mike Redmond	18	1,504

Hit by Pitch: Season

Player	HBP	Year
1. Carlos Delgado	17	2005
2. Gary Sheffield	15	1997
3. Greg Colbrunn	14	1996
4. Alex Gonzalez	13	2003
5. Alex Gonzalez	12	1999
6. Cliff Floyd	10	2001
Andy Fox	10	2002
Alex Gonzalez	10	2001
Derrek Lee	10	1998
Derrek Lee	10	2003
Mike Lowell	10	2001
Gary Sheffield	10	1996

Hit by Pitch: Career with Team

Player	HBP	PA
1. Alex Gonzalez	51	3,488
2. Gary Sheffield	43	2,358
3. Mike Lowell	39	4,003
4. Mike Redmond	38	1,504
5. Derrek Lee	37	3,251
6. Preston Wilson	33	2,350
7. Cliff Floyd	32	2,569
8. Kevin Millar	25	1,699
9. Greg Colbrunn	22	1,283
Juan Pierre	22	2,212

Top 10 Pitching Leaders, Single Season & Career with Team

Games Pitched: Season

Player	GP	Year
1. Braden Looper	78	2002
2. Vladimir Nuñez	77	2002
3. Robb Nen	75	1996
4. Braden Looper	74	2003
Jay Powell	74	1997
6. Antonio Alfonseca	73	1999
Braden Looper	73	2000
Robb Nen	73	1997
9. Braden Looper	72	1999
10. Braden Looper	71	2001

Games Pitched: Career with Team

Player	GP	IP
1. Braden Looper	368	388.0
2. Antonio Alfonseca	307	333.0
3. Vic Darensbourg	271	264.7
4. Robb Nen	269	314.0
5. Armando Almanza	235	199.0
6. Jay Powell	183	195.7
7. Vladimir Nuñez	177	343.3
Yorkis Perez	177	135.0
9. Jesus Sanchez	142	494.0
10. Terry Mathews	138	180.7

Innings Pitched: Season

Player	IP	Year
1. Kevin Brown	237.3	1997
2. Dontrelle Willis	236.3	2005
3. Livan Hernandez	234.3	1998
4. Kevin Brown	233.0	1996
5. Ryan Dempster	226.3	2000
6. Carl Pavano	222.3	2004
7. Alex Fernandez	220.7	1997
8. Al Leiter	215.3	1996
9. Ryan Dempster	211.3	2001
10. A.J. Burnett	209.0	2005

Innings Pitched: Career with Team

Player	IP
1. A.J. Burnett	853.7
2. Brad Penny	781.7
3. Ryan Dempster	759.7
4. Pat Rapp	665.7
5. Josh Beckett	609.0
6. Dontrelle Willis	594.0
7. Chris Hammond	520.0
8. Jesus Sanchez	494.0
9. Carl Pavano	485.0
10. Kevin Brown	470.3

Batters Faced: Season

Player	BF	Year
1. Livan Hernandez	1,040	1998
2. Kevin Brown	976	1997
3. Ryan Dempster	974	2000
4. Dontrelle Willis	960	2005
5. Ryan Dempster	954	2001
6. Carl Pavano	909	2004
7. Kevin Brown	906	1996
8. Alex Fernandez	904	1997
9. Al Leiter	896	1996
10. Jack Armstrong	879	1993

Batters Faced: Career with Team

Player	BF	IP
1. A.J. Burnett	3,592	853.7
2. Ryan Dempster	3,387	759.7
3. Brad Penny	3,292	781.7
4. Pat Rapp	2,924	665.7
5. Josh Beckett	2,537	609.0
6. Dontrelle Willis	2,476	594.0
7. Chris Hammond	2,256	520.0
8. Jesus Sanchez	2,206	494.0
9. Livan Hernandez	2,070	469.7
10. Carl Pavano	2,024	485.0

Games Started: Season

Player	GS	Year
1. Ryan Dempster	34	2001
Charlie Hough	34	1993
Dontrelle Willis	34	2005
4. Jack Armstrong	33	1993
Kevin Brown	33	1997
Ryan Dempster	33	2000
Livan Hernandez	33	1998
Al Leiter	33	1996
9. Eight tied with . . .	32	—

Games Started: Career with Team

Player	GS	IP
1. A.J. Burnett	131	853.7
2. Brad Penny	130	781.7
3. Ryan Dempster	121	759.7
4. Pat Rapp	115	665.7
5. Josh Beckett	103	609.0
6. Dontrelle Willis	93	594.0
7. Chris Hammond	81	520.0
8. Jesus Sanchez	80	494.0
9. Al Leiter	76	446.7
10. Carl Pavano	71	485.0

Complete Games: Season

Player	CG	Year
1. Livan Hernandez	9	1998
2. A.J. Burnett	7	2002
Dontrelle Willis	7	2005
4. Kevin Brown	6	1997
5. Kevin Brown	5	1996
Alex Fernandez	5	1997
7. John Burkett	4	1995
A.J. Burnett	4	2005
9. Five tied with . . .	3	—

Complete Games: Career with Team

Player	CG	IP
1. A.J. Burnett	14	853.7
2. Kevin Brown	11	470.3
Livan Hernandez	11	469.7
Dontrelle Willis	11	594.0
5. Ryan Dempster	7	759.7
Pat Rapp	7	665.7
7. Alex Fernandez	6	414.0
8. John Burkett	5	342.3
Chris Hammond	5	520.0
10. Carl Pavano	4	485.0

Games Won: Season

Player	W	Year
1. Dontrelle Willis	22	2005
2. Carl Pavano	18	2004
3. Kevin Brown	17	1996
Alex Fernandez	17	1997
5. Kevin Brown	16	1997
Al Leiter	16	1996
7. Ryan Dempster	15	2001

Josh Beckett	15	2005
9. Six tied with . . .	14	——

GAMES WON: CAREER WITH TEAM

Player	W	IP
1. A.J. Burnett	49	853.7
2. Brad Penny	48	781.7
3. Dontrelle Willis	46	594.0
4. Ryan Dempster	42	759.7
5. Josh Beckett	41	609.0
6. Pat Rapp	37	665.7
7. Kevin Brown	33	470.3
Carl Pavano	33	485.0
9. Al Leiter	30	446.7
10. Chris Hammond	29	520.0

GAMES LOST: SEASON

Player	L	Year
1. Jack Armstrong	17	1993
2. Charlie Hough	16	1993
Pat Rapp	16	1996
Dennis Springer	16	1999
5. Brian Meadows	15	1999
6. John Burkett	14	1995
7. Brian Meadows	13	1998
Carl Pavano	13	2003
9. 12 tied with . . .	12	——

GAMES LOST: CAREER WITH TEAM

Player	L	IP
1. A.J. Burnett	50	853.7
2. Ryan Dempster	43	759.7
Pat Rapp	43	665.7
4. Brad Penny	42	781.7
5. Josh Beckett	34	609.0
6. Chris Hammond	32	520.0
Jesus Sanchez	32	494.0
8. Al Leiter	28	446.7
Brian Meadows	28	352.7
10. Vladimir Nuñez	27	343.3
Dontrelle Willis	27	594.0

WINNING PERCENTAGE: SEASON

Player	W%	Year
1. Dontrelle Willis	.700	2003
2. Carl Pavano	.692	2004
3. Dontrelle Willis	.688	2005
4. Kevin Brown	.667	1997
Pat Rapp	.667	1995
6. Josh Beckett	.652	2005
7. Mark Redman	.609	2003
8. Kevin Brown	.607	1996
9. Alex Fernandez	.586	1997
10. Ryan Dempster	.583	2000
Brad Penny	.583	2003

WINNING PERCENTAGE: CAREER WITH TEAM

Player	W%	IP
1. Kevin Brown	.635	470.3
2. Dontrelle Willis	.630	594.0
3. Carl Pavano	.589	485.0
4. Josh Beckett	.547	609.0
5. Alex Fernandez	.538	414.0
6. Brad Penny	.533	781.7
7. Al Leiter	.517	446.7
8. Livan Hernandez	.500	469.7
9. A.J. Burnett	.495	853.7
10. Ryan Dempster	.494	759.7

SHUTOUTS: SEASON

Player	SHO	Year
1. A.J. Burnett	5	2002
Dontrelle Willis	5	2005
3. Kevin Brown	3	1996
4. Kevin Brown	2	1997
Chris Hammond	2	1995
Carl Pavano	2	2004
Pat Rapp	2	1995
Jesus Sanchez	2	2000
Dennis Springer	2	1999
Dontrelle Willis	2	2003
A.J. Burnett	2	2005

SHUTOUTS: CAREER WITH TEAM

Player	SHO	IP
1. A.J. Burnett	8	853.7
2. Dontrelle Willis	7	594.0
3. Kevin Brown	5	470.3
4. Pat Rapp	4	665.7
5. Chris Hammond	3	520.0
6. Ryan Dempster	2	759.7
Carl Pavano	2	485.0
Brad Penny	2	781.7
Jesus Sanchez	2	494.0
Dennis Springer	2	196.3
Josh Beckett	2	609.0

ERA: SEASON

Player	ERA	Year
1. Kevin Brown	1.89	1996
2. Dontrelle Willis	2.63	2005
3. Kevin Brown	2.69	1997
4. Al Leiter	2.93	1996
5. Carl Pavano	3.00	2004
6. A.J. Burnett	3.30	2002
7. Josh Beckett	3.38	2005
8. Pat Rapp	3.44	1995
A.J. Burnett	3.44	2005
10. Mark Redman	3.59	2003

ERA: CAREER WITH TEAM

Player	ERA	IP
1. Kevin Brown	2.30	470.3
2. Dontrelle Willis	3.27	594.0
3. Josh Beckett	3.46	609.0
4. Alex Fernandez	3.59	414.0
5. Carl Pavano	3.64	485.0
6. A.J. Burnett	3.73	853.7
7. Brad Penny	4.04	781.7
8. Al Leiter	4.07	446.7
9. Pat Rapp	4.18	665.7
10. Livan Hernandez	4.39	469.7

EARNED RUNS ALLOWED: SEASON

Player	ER	Year
1. Livan Hernandez	123	1998
2. Ryan Dempster	116	2001
3. Brian Meadows	111	1999
4. Jesus Sanchez	108	2000
5. Dennis Springer	106	1999
6. Brian Meadows	101	1998
7. Chris Hammond	99	1993
8. Jack Armstrong	98	1993
9. Charlie Hough	97	1993
10. Carl Pavano	96	2003

EARNED RUNS ALLOWED: CAREER WITH TEAM

Player	ER	IP
1. Ryan Dempster	392	759.7
2. A.J. Burnett	354	853.7
3. Brad Penny	351	781.7
4. Pat Rapp	309	665.7
5. Jesus Sanchez	278	494.0
6. Chris Hammond	261	520.0
7. Josh Beckett	234	609.0
8. Livan Hernandez	229	469.7
9. Dontrelle Willis	216	594.0
10. Brian Meadows	212	352.7

STRIKEOUTS: SEASON

Player	K	Year
1. Ryan Dempster	209	2000
2. Kevin Brown	205	1997
3. A.J. Burnett	203	2002
4. Al Leiter	200	1996
5. A.J. Burnett	198	2005
6. Alex Fernandez	183	1997
7. Ryan Dempster	171	2001
8. Dontrelle Willis	170	2005

9. Josh Beckett	166	2005
10. Livan Hernandez	162	1998

Strikeouts: Career with Team

Player	K	IP
1. A.J. Burnett	753	853.7
2. Ryan Dempster	628	759.7
3. Josh Beckett	607	609.0
4. Brad Penny	570	781.7
5. Dontrelle Willis	451	594.0
6. Al Leiter	384	446.7
Pat Rapp	384	665.7
8. Jesus Sanchez	368	494.0
9. Kevin Brown	364	470.3
10. Livan Hernandez	333	469.7

Strikeouts Per Nine IP: Season

Player	K/9	Year
1. A.J. Burnett	8.94	2002
2. A.J. Burnett	8.53	2005
3. Al Leiter	8.36	1996
Josh Beckett	8.36	2005
5. Ryan Dempster	8.31	2000
6. Kevin Brown	7.77	1997
7. Alex Fernandez	7.46	1997
8. Ryan Dempster	7.28	2001
9. Mark Redman	7.13	2003
Jesus Sanchez	7.13	1998

Strikeouts Per Nine IP: Career with Team

Player	K/9	IP
1. Josh Beckett	8.97	609.0
2. A.J. Burnett	7.94	853.7
3. Al Leiter	7.74	446.7
4. Ryan Dempster	7.44	759.7
5. Kevin Brown	6.97	470.3
6. Dontrelle Willis	6.83	594.0
7. Jesus Sanchez	6.70	494.0
8. Brad Penny	6.56	781.7
9. Alex Fernandez	6.54	414.0
10. Livan Hernandez	6.38	469.7

Hits Allowed: Season

Player	HA	Year
1. Livan Hernandez	265	1998
2. Dennis Springer	231	1999
3. Brian Meadows	222	1998
4. Ryan Dempster	218	2001
5. Kevin Brown	214	1997
Brian Meadows	214	1999
7. Dontrelle Willis	213	2005
8. Carl Pavano	212	2004
9. Jack Armstrong	210	1993
Ryan Dempster	210	2000
Dontrelle Willis	210	2004

Hits Allowed: Career with Team

Player	HA	IP
1. Ryan Dempster	772	759.7
2. Brad Penny	770	781.7
3. A.J. Burnett	719	853.7
4. Pat Rapp	696	665.7
5. Dontrelle Willis	571	594.0
6. Chris Hammond	567	520.0
7. Josh Beckett	529	609.0
8. Jesus Sanchez	520	494.0
9. Livan Hernandez	510	469.7
10. Carl Pavano	492	485.0

Hits Allowed Per Nine IP: Season

Player	H/9	Year
1. Al Leiter	6.39	1996
2. A.J. Burnett	6.74	2002
3. Kevin Brown	7.22	1996
4. A.J. Burnett	7.53	2001
5. Josh Beckett	7.71	2005
6. Alex Fernandez	7.87	1997
7. A.J. Burnett	7.92	2005
8. Brad Penny	8.03	2001
9. Dontrelle Willis	8.11	2005
10. Kevin Brown	8.12	1997

Hits Allowed Per Nine IP: Career with Team

Player	H/9	IP
1. Al Leiter	7.54	446.7
2. A.J. Burnett	7.58	853.7
3. Kevin Brown	7.67	470.3
4. Josh Beckett	7.82	609.0
5. Alex Fernandez	8.41	414.0
6. Dontrelle Willis	8.65	594.0
7. Brad Penny	8.87	781.7
8. Carl Pavano	9.13	485.0
9. Ryan Dempster	9.15	759.7
10. Pat Rapp	9.41	665.7

Walks Allowed: Season

Player	BB	Year
1. Al Leiter	119	1996
2. Ryan Dempster	112	2001
3. Livan Hernandez	104	1998
4. Ryan Dempster	97	2000
5. Ryan Dempster	93	1999
6. Al Leiter	91	1997
Pat Rapp	91	1996
Jesus Sanchez	91	1998
9. A.J. Burnett	90	2002
10. Ryan Bowen	87	1993

Walks Allowed: Career with Team

Player	BB	IP
1. Ryan Dempster	395	759.7
2. A.J. Burnett	377	853.7
3. Pat Rapp	326	665.7
4. Al Leiter	270	446.7
5. Brad Penny	259	781.7
6. Jesus Sanchez	258	494.0
7. Josh Beckett	223	609.0
8. Livan Hernandez	199	469.7
9. Dontrelle Willis	174	594.0
10. Chris Hammond	171	520.0

Walks Allowed Per Nine IP: Season

Player	BB/9	Year
1. Kevin Brown	1.27	1996
2. Carl Pavano	1.98	2004
3. Dontrelle Willis	2.09	2005
4. Carl Pavano	2.19	2003
5. Brad Penny	2.37	2001
Brian Meadows	2.37	1998
7. Kevin Brown	2.50	1997
8. Brad Penny	2.57	2003
9. John Burkett	2.72	1995
10. Dontrelle Willis	2.79	2004

Walks Allowed Per Nine IP: Career with Team

Player	BB/9	IP
1. Kevin Brown	1.89	470.3
2. Carl Pavano	2.08	485.0
3. Dontrelle Willis	2.64	594.0
4. Alex Fernandez	2.74	414.0
5. Chris Hammond	2.96	520.0
6. Brad Penny	2.98	781.7
7. Josh Beckett	3.30	609.0
8. Livan Hernandez	3.81	469.7
9. A.J. Burnett	3.97	853.7
10. Pat Rapp	4.41	665.7

WHIP (Walks + Hits Per Nine IP): Season

Player	WHIP	Year
1. Kevin Brown	0.944	1996
2. Dontrelle Willis	1.134	2005
3. Brad Penny	1.156	2001
4. Carl Pavano	1.174	2004

5. Kevin Brown	1.180	1997
6. Josh Beckett	1.181	2005
7. Alex Fernandez	1.187	1997
8. A.J. Burnett	1.189	2002
9. Mark Redman	1.222	2003
10. A.J. Burnett	1.258	2005

WHIP (Walks + Hits Per Nine IP): Career with Team

Player	WHIP	IP
1. Kevin Brown	1.063	470.3
2. Josh Beckett	1.235	609.0
3. Alex Fernandez	1.239	414.0
4. Carl Pavano	1.245	485.0
5. Dontrelle Willis	1.254	594.0
6. A.J. Burnett	1.284	853.7
7. Brad Penny	1.316	781.7
8. Chris Hammond	1.419	520.0
9. Al Leiter	1.442	446.7
10. Livan Hernandez	1.510	469.7

Home Runs Allowed: Season

Player	HRA	Year
1. Livan Hernandez	37	1998
2. Jesus Sanchez	32	2000
3. Brian Meadows	31	1999
4. Ryan Dempster	30	2000
5. Jack Armstrong	29	1993
6. Alex Fernandez	25	1997
7. Dennis Springer	23	1999
8. John Burkett	22	1995
9. Ryan Dempster	21	1999
Ryan Dempster	21	2001
Brad Penny	21	2003

Home Runs Allowed: Career with Team

Player	HRA	IP
1. Ryan Dempster	90	759.7
2. Brad Penny	77	781.7
3. Jesus Sanchez	73	494.0
4. A.J. Burnett	66	853.7
5. Livan Hernandez	59	469.7
6. Chris Hammond	57	520.0
7. Josh Beckett	55	609.0
8. Pat Rapp	53	665.7
9. Brian Meadows	51	352.7
10. Vladimir Nuñez	45	343.3

Saves: Season

Player	SV	Year
1. Armando Benitez	47	2004
2. Antonio Alfonseca	45	2000
Bryan Harvey	45	1993
4. Todd Jones	40	2005
5. Robb Nen	35	1996
Robb Nen	35	1997
7. Antonio Alfonseca	28	2001
Braden Looper	28	2003
9. Robb Nen	23	1995
10. Antonio Alfonseca	21	1999

Saves: Career with Team

Player	SV	IP
1. Robb Nen	108	314.0
2. Antonio Alfonseca	102	333.0
3. Bryan Harvey	51	79.3
4. Armando Benitez	47	69.7
5. Braden Looper	46	388.0
6. Todd Jones	40	73.0
7. Vladimir Nuñez	20	343.3
8. Matt Mantei	19	122.7
9. Jeremy Hernandez	9	30.3
10. Terry Mathews	7	180.7
Jay Powell	7	195.7

Wild Pitches: Season

Player	WP	Year
1. Matt Clement	15	2001
2. A.J. Burnett	14	2002
3. Pat Rapp	13	1996
4. A.J. Burnett	12	2005
5. Charlie Hough	11	1993
6. Ryan Bowen	10	1993
Chris Hammond	10	1993
Richie Lewis	10	1994
9. Alex Fernandez	9	1997
Charlie Hough	9	1994
Richie Lewis	9	1993

Wild Pitches: Career with Team

Player	WP	IP
1. A.J. Burnett	44	853.7
2. Pat Rapp	36	665.7
3. Josh Beckett	22	609.0
Ryan Dempster	22	759.7
5. Charlie Hough	20	318.0
Richie Lewis	20	167.3
7. Robb Nen	18	314.0
Brad Penny	18	781.7
Dave Weathers	18	359.0
10. Chris Hammond	17	520.0
Jesus Sanchez	17	494.0

Hit Batsmen: Season

Player	HB	Year
1. Kevin Brown	16	1996
2. Matt Clement	15	2001
Julian Tavarez	15	2002
4. Kevin Brown	14	1997
5. Al Leiter	12	1997
6. Al Leiter	11	1996
Carl Pavano	11	2004
8. Ryan Dempster	10	2001
Charlie Hough	10	1994
10. A.J. Burnett	9	2002
Ryan Dempster	9	1998
Chris Hammond	9	1995

Hit Batsmen: Career with Team

Player	HB	IP
1. Ryan Dempster	37	759.7
2. A.J. Burnett	31	853.7
3. Kevin Brown	30	470.3
4. Al Leiter	29	446.7
5. Pat Rapp	22	665.7
6. Carl Pavano	21	485.0
7. Brad Penny	19	781.7
Dontrelle Willis	19	594.0
9. Charlie Hough	18	318.0
10. Josh Beckett	17	609.0

Games Finished: Season

Player	GF	Year
1. Robb Nen	66	1996
2. Robb Nen	65	1997
3. Braden Looper	64	2003
4. Antonio Alfonseca	62	2000
5. Armando Benitez	59	2004
6. Todd Jones	55	2005
7. Bryan Harvey	54	1993
Robb Nen	54	1995
9. Antonio Alfonseca	52	2001
10. Antonio Alfonseca	49	1999

Games Finished: Career with Team

Player	GF	IP
1. Robb Nen	215	314.0
2. Antonio Alfonseca	193	333.0
3. Braden Looper	170	388.0
4. Jay Powell	66	195.7
5. Vic Darensbourg	64	264.7
Bryan Harvey	64	79.3
Vladimir Nuñez	64	343.3
8. Armando Benitez	59	69.7
Matt Mantei	59	122.7
10. Todd Jones	55	73.0

Significant Marlins

CASTILLO, LUIS (2B)
(1996–2005)

Luis Castillo has played more games in a Marlins uniform than any other player in the team's history, which is remarkable considering the Marlins signed him as a free-agent amateur in 1992. As a speedy second baseman, he grew to become both an offensive and defensive star, perennially hitting over .300, ranking among the National League leaders in stolen bases, and winning Gold Gloves for his infield play. There may be trouble on the horizon, however, as Castillo's stolen-base totals have declined sharply in recent years. He used to be counted on to steal 50 bases a year, but over the last three years combined he's stolen only 52 total. Also, he has turned into a pure singles hitter, rapping out only 12 doubles in each of the last two seasons, and 11 triples combined—poor numbers indeed for a speedster. Castillo was traded to the Twins after the 2005 season in the latest round of Florida salary dumping.

CAREER MARLINS RECORD:

Games	AB	Hits	Runs
1,128	4,347	1,273	675
Avg	**HR**	**RBI**	**SB**
.293	20	271	281

CONINE, JEFF (OF/1B)
(1993–1997, 2003–2005)

After being selected by the Marlins in the 1992 expansion draft from the Kansas City Royals, Jeff Conine became one of Florida's biggest stars in the early years of the team. He was selected to the All-Star team twice (1994 and 1995) and was the MVP of the 1995 All-Star Game. He held many of Florida's all-time hitting records until Mike Lowell came along to surpass him. After spending six years in the American League, Conine returned to Florida for a second stint in 2003, and still ranks among the top five of most Florida all-time hitting categories.

CAREER MARLINS RECORD:

Games	AB	Hits	Runs
1,014	3,471	1,005	447
Avg	**HR**	**RBI**	**SB**
.290	120	553	15

LEE, DERREK (1B)
(1998–2003)

Picked in the first round of the 1993 amateur draft by San Diego, Derrek Lee was traded in December 1997 to the Marlins for star pitcher Kevin Brown. Over the next six seasons, Lee proved to be a steady, productive player. Before leaving for the Cubs via free agency after the 2003 campaign, Lee accumulated stats that put him in the top five of most Marlins hitting categories. He won a Gold Glove in 2003. With Chicago, Lee became a genuine star, setting career highs across the board in 2004, then breaking them all in 2005 when he made a run at the Triple Crown, finishing with a .335 batting average (to win the crown), 46 homers, and 107 RBIs.

CAREER MARLINS RECORD:

Games	AB	Hits	Runs
844	2,830	746	422
Avg	**HR**	**RBI**	**SB**
.264	129	417	51

LOWELL, MIKE (3B)
(1999–2005)

After playing in only eight games for the New York Yankees, Mike Lowell was sent to the Florida Marlins on February 1, 1999 in what turned out to be a vastly one-sided trade for several players who never made it on the big league level. Lowell has become one of the National League's top hitters, even winning the Silver Slugger Award for third basemen in 2003. In 2002 he appeared in the first of his three All-Star Games, and has become the Marlins' all-time leader in many hitting categories, including home runs, doubles, RBIs, total bases, extra-base hits, and sacrifice flies. In 2005, however, Lowell experienced a mysterious power outage that affected his whole game. By the time the season ended, Lowell had put together the worst year—by far—of his career. He hit only eight homers after averaging nearly 25 a season over the previous five years. His RBI production was half of his normal total, and his batting average was 40 points below his career average. With a huge salary scheduled for the next two years, Lowell was sent to Boston after the season in another of Florida's famous fire sales.

CAREER MARLINS RECORD:

Games	AB	Hits	Runs
981	3,554	965	477
Avg	**HR**	**RBI**	**SB**
.272	143	578	21

NEN, ROBB (RP)
(1993–1997)

As is the case with most expansion teams, pitching stars are few and far between. One of Florida's bright spots for five seasons was its closer, Robb Nen, who was acquired in a trade from Texas in the middle of the 1993 season for pitcher Cris Carpenter. From 1993–1997, the first five years of the franchise, Nen saved 108 games and won 20 more. He also averaged more than a strikeout per inning during his tenure with the Marlins. *(See Giants bio.)*

CAREER MARLINS RECORD:

W	L	W%	ERA	SV
20	16	.556	3.41	108
K	BB	SHO	IP	
328	121	0	314.0	

WILLIS, DONTRELLE (SP)
(2003–2005)

The Chicago Cubs drafted Dontrelle Willis in the eighth round of the June 2000 amateur draft and traded him to the Marlins on March 27, 2002 as part of a six-player deal that sent Matt Clement and Antonio Alfonseca to Chicago. Willis arrived in the majors in 2003 and promptly went 14–6 in 27 starts to win the National League Rookie of the Year Award. Willis, whose delivery includes a high leg kick and a jerky motion, slumped to 10–11 with a 4.02 ERA in 2004, but he bounced back big in 2005 as he nearly won the Cy Young Award after posting a 22–10 record with a 2.63 ERA. The two-time All-Star left-hander has become a fan favorite, especially among the kids, as the "D-Train" plays the game with a refreshing, childlike zeal and a smile on his face. Since he's going to be one of the stars *not* sold off in the latest Marlins salary dump, it remains to be seen if he'll keep his smile, given his supporting cast beginning in 2006.

CAREER MARLINS RECORD:

W	L	W%	ERA	SV
46	27	.630	3.27	0
K	BB	SHO	IP	
451	174	7	594.0	

Houston Astros

Since 1962

1984 Team Ball

1971 The Astros play a National League record 75 one-run games, losing 43 of them.... **1981** One day after Nolan Ryan fires his fifth career no-hitter, a 5–0 gem over the Dodgers on September 26, Astros pitcher Don Sutton two-hits the Dodgers. The combined two hits sets a record for the fewest hits allowed another team in consecutive games.... **1987** When Ryan wins the National League's strikeout crown in 1987, he becomes only the third pitcher in history to lead both leagues in strikeouts (Rube Waddell and Jim Bunning are the others).... **1992** When Steve Finley, Jeff Bagwell, and Craig Biggio each play in all 162 games of the team's schedule, they become the first trio of teammates in the majors to do so in 18 years, since Larry Bowa, Dave Cash, and Mike Schmidt of Philadelphia did it in 1974.

FRANCHISE HISTORY

The Houston Astros, known as the Houston Colt .45s for their first three seasons, began play in 1962 as part of a two-team expansion by the National League, which also created the New York Mets. The National League revealed its plans in a formal announcement late in the 1960 season. Because of intense rivalry, the American League then hastily put together a two-team expansion plan of its own, and surprised the baseball world when they announced that their two new teams, the Los Angeles Angels and the replacement Washington Senators, would debut in 1961, a full year ahead of the National League's new franchises.

Surprisingly, the first time the Astros occupied the cellar at season's end was in 1968, the team's seventh year in existence, when they finished last with a 72–90 record, one game behind the Mets.

The idea of a major league team in Houston had been around since the mid-1950s, when former St. Louis Cardinals shortstop Marty Marion put together a group of investors who paid $100,000 for the Houston minor league club at the time, hoping that eventually they would be considered the leading contenders for a possible Houston expansion team. Their plans fell through, though, and they sold out to the investment group that eventually did land the major league franchise. The group had announced plans to join the Continental League and put a team in Houston, but Major League Baseball pre-empted the group's plans by awarding a franchise to them, and another to the most financially sound group in the proposed Continental League, the one behind a New York franchise.

The ill-fated Cesar Cedeño.

The first Houston owners were R. E. "Bob" Smith, an oil magnate, and Roy Hofheinz, a man who wasn't shy about voicing his Texas-size ideas on how a major league ballclub should be run. Because of the constant feuding, Hofheinz eventually bought out Smith, taking control of 86 percent of the team. He had always moved quickly: At age 19, he had passed the Texas bar; at 22, he was elected to the Texas state legislature; and by the time he was 24, he was a judge. Active in Texas politics his whole life, Hofheinz was by turns Lyndon Johnson's campaign manager, the mayor of Houston, and the owner of the Ringling Bros. and Barnum & Bailey circus. His penchant for large-scale showmanship finally proved to be his downfall. By 1970, the combination of the new Astrodome's construction costs, and the debt he had incurred in building a series of nearby hotels and an entertainment complex, left the Astros $30 million in arrears. Hofheinz then suffered a stroke, leaving the front office a mess. By late 1970, he was bankrupt. Various creditors, including Ford Motor Credit Corporation

Craig Biggio. Next stop: Cooperstown.

and General Electric Credit Corporation, took control in 1970. By 1975, Ford and GE had bought out the other creditors and were the two controlling partners of the club. In 1978, Ford acquired sole control of the Astros.

The following year, Ford sold the Astros, an adjacent convention center, and the Astrodome lease for $19 million to a group of 25 investors headed by New Yorker John McMullen. McMullen, a former minority owner of the Yankees and owner of the New Jersey Devils of the NHL, was a marine architect and had made his fortune as a designer of ships. In the first year or so, the investors squabbled among themselves, but McMullen maintained control and eventually sold the team to Drayton McLane for $116 million in 1992. McLane had made his fortune in the grocery business, building his family's small grocery distributorship into a huge grocery chain. He had then sold the chain to Sam Walton of Wal-Mart for $300 million in 1990, becoming a vice-chairman of Wal-Mart in the process. As of 2005, he still owns the team.

The team changed its nickname from the Colt .45s to the Astros in 1965, when it moved from tiny Colts Stadium into the Astrodome, the first indoor (and air-conditioned) baseball stadium, which was constructed in order to keep out the Texas sun and various nasty insects. The team had wanted to keep its name, but the Colt gun manufacturing company refused to allow its name to be plastered all over the novelties and gimmicky marketing items that Hofheinz was famous for. And so the team was named after Houston's connection to the NASA space program. Houston fans often refer to their team simply as the 'Stros. (Because the natural grass used for the field kept dying inside

> On May 4, 1969, the Astros reeled off seven double plays in a 3–1 win against the San Francisco Giants, setting the National League record.

the Astrodome, the team began using plastic "grass," which came to be called "Astroturf.") The Astros played their last game in the Astrodome in 1999; in 2000 they moved into their new ballpark, Enron Field (after the Enron scandal, the name was hastily changed to Astros Field and then Minute Maid Park).

On the field, it took 11 years for the Astros to finish above .500. Their 1972 record of 84–69 was good enough for second place in the NL West. Houston won its first division title in 1980 in exciting fashion. Leading the Dodgers by three games with three to go, the Astros invaded Dodger Stadium for the season's final series. The Dodgers won all three games in squeakers, 3–2, 2–1, and 4–3, forcing a one-game playoff in Los Angeles to determine the division winner. Houston won the game 7–1 behind its ace, Joe Niekro, and advanced to the LCS against the Phillies. But Philadelphia ended the Astros' World Series dreams by knocking them out, three games to two.

> From their inception in 1962 through the entire 1979 season, the Astros did not lose a single player to free agency.

Houston won the second half of the 1981 split-season format, but lost to the Dodgers in the mini-divisional series. Five years later, in 1986, the Astros romped to the division title and played the New York Mets in one of the wildest and most memorable matchups in LCS history. The Mets won the series, four games to two, with three of the wins coming in the last inning, two of them after trailing by two and three runs going into the ninth inning. One game went 12 innings, another 16, and four of the games were decided by one run. How fitting that this particular LCS preceded the equally wild 1986 World Series of Mookie Wilson-Bill Buckner fame.

The Astros won their second division title in 1997, this time in the National League Central division, under rookie manager and former Astros pitcher Larry Dierker, whom the team had brought out of the broadcast booth. It marked only the sixth time in history that a rookie manager had guided a team to a first-place finish. The Astros, after three straight second-place finishes from 1994 to 1996, became one of the better teams in the National League in the late 1990s under Dierker, winning their division four out of five years from 1997 to 2001. However, they were beaten in the first round of the playoffs each time, three times by Atlanta. In 2004 the Astros finally got over the hump and won their first Division Series, three games to two over the Braves, but lost a gut-wrenching seven-game LCS to the Cardinals. Houston finally made it to their first Fall Classic in 2005 by returning the favor to the Cardinals, defeating them 4–2 in the NLCS. However, a four-game sweep by the White Sox stunned the Astros and gave them the dubious distinction of being the first team ever to be swept in their first World Series appearance.

TEAM NAME HISTORY

Official Names

Colt .45s (1962–1964)
Astros (1965–current)

Unofficial Names/Nicknames

'Stros

STADIUM HISTORY

Colt Stadium	1962–1964
The Astrodome	1965–1999
Enron Field	2000–2001
Astros Field	2002 (partial season)
(Enron Field renamed)	
Minute Maid Park	mid-2002 to current
(Astros Field renamed)	

YEARLY RECORD, FINISH, & ATTENDANCE FIGURES

Year	League	Record	DIV/LG Finish	Attendance	Avg/Gm
2005	NL Cent	89–73	2	2,804,760	34,627
2004	NL Cent	92–70	2	3,087,872	38,122
2003	NL Cent	87–75	2	2,454,241	30,299
2002	NL Cent	84–78	2	2,517,357	31,078
2001	NL Cent	93–69	1	2,904,277	35,855
2000	NL Cent	72–90	4	3,056,139	37,730
1999	NL Cent	97–65	1	2,706,017	33,000
1998	NL Cent	102–60	1	2,458,451	30,351
1997	NL Cent	84–78	1	2,046,781	25,269
1996	NL Cent	82–80	2	1,975,888	24,394
1995	NL Cent	76–68	2	1,363,801	18,942
1994	NL Cent	66–49	2	1,561,136	26,460
1993	NL West	85–77	3	2,084,618	25,736
1992	NL West	81–81	4	1,211,412	14,956
1991	NL West	65–97	6	1,196,152	14,767
1990	NL West	75–87	5	1,310,927	16,184
1989	NL West	86–76	3	1,834,908	22,377
1988	NL West	82–80	5	1,933,505	23,870
1987	NL West	76–86	3	1,909,902	23,579
1986	NL West	96–66	1	1,734,276	21,411
1985	NL West	83–79	4	1,184,314	14,621
1984	NL West	80–82	2	1,229,862	15,183
1983	NL West	85–77	3	1,351,962	16,487
1982	NL West	77–85	5	1,558,555	19,241
1981	NL West	61–49	3/1	1,321,282	25,907
1980	NL West	93–70	1	2,278,217	28,126
1979	NL West	89–73	2	1,900,312	23,461
1978	NL West	74–88	5	1,126,145	13,903
1977	NL West	81–81	3	1,109,560	13,698
1976	NL West	80–82	3	886,146	10,807
1975	NL West	64–97	6	858,002	10,593
1974	NL West	81–81	4	1,090,728	13,466
1973	NL West	82–80	4	1,394,004	17,210
1972	NL West	84–69	2	1,469,247	19,081
1971	NL West	79–83	4	1,261,589	15,575
1970	NL West	79–83	4	1,253,444	15,475
1969	NL West	81–81	5	1,442,995	17,815
1968	NL	72–90	10	1,312,887	16,208
1967	NL	69–93	9	1,348,303	16,646
1966	NL	72–90	8	1,872,108	23,112
1965	NL	65–97	9	2,151,470	26,561
1964	NL	66–96	9	725,773	8,960
1963	NL	66–96	9	719,502	8,883
1962	NL	64–96	8	924,456	11,274

MANAGER HISTORY

Manager	Years	W–L	Win %
Harry Craft	1962–1964	191–280	.406
Lum Harris	1964–1965	70–105	.400
Grady Hatton	1966–1968	164–221	.426
Harry Walker	1968–1972	355–353	.501
Leo Durocher	1972–1973	98–95	.508
Salty Parker	1972	1–0	1.000
Preston Gomez	1973–1975	128–161	.443
Bill Virdon	1975–1982	544–522	.510
Bob Lillis	1982–1985	276–261	.514
Hal Lanier	1986–1988	254–232	.523
Art Howe	1989–1993	392–418	.484
Terry Collins	1994–1996	224–197	.532
Larry Dierker	1997–2001	448–362	.553
Jimy Williams	2002–2004	215–197	.522
Phil Garner	2004–2005	137–99	.581

ALL-TIME WIN-LOSS RECORDS VS. ALL OPPONENTS

ALL-TIME	3,497–3,503
Angels	2–1
Athletics	0–3
Blue Jays	3–0
Braves	304–353
Brewers	78–45
Cardinals	278–315
Cubs	321–272
Devil Rays	3–0
Diamondbacks	25–30
Dodgers	297–363
Giants	324–343
Indians	8–7
INTERLEAGUE	71–60
Mariners	3–3
Marlins	61–49
Mets	288–233
Nationals	222–173
Orioles	3–3
Padres	285–257
Phillies	254–266
Pirates	280–308
Rangers	16–14
Reds	351–381
Red Sox	0–3
Rockies	58–55
Royals	13–5
Tigers	7–2
Twins	6–8
White Sox	5–7
Yankees	1–2

The Astrodome

Franchise Highlights, Low Points, and Strange Distinctions

1962 After being awarded the Houston franchise, team owners set about securing a ballpark, since no suitable facility existed. They got approval for their new domed stadium, originally to be called the Harris County Domed Stadium, but building plans were delayed. Short on time, the team built a temporary facility, Colt Stadium, in just five months at a cost of just $800,000. It was completed the day before the season opened in 1962. The temporary ballpark, built to hold 32,000 fans, had rainbow-colored seats. Three years later, the Astrodome opened in 1965 at a cost of $19 million. An additional $12 million was spent acquiring and developing the land and building a parking facility. The new air-conditioning system cost another $4.5 million.

The Astrodome teemed with glitches in its first year. First, there was the glare problem. The day before a five-game exhibition series to inaugurate the stadium, the Astros were conducting a team workout when it was discovered that the sun shining through the 4,600 Lucite panels on the Dome's roof caused such a glare that outfielders were blinded when tracking fly balls. Luckily, the two day-games of the exhibition series enjoyed cloudy skies. The day before their first regular-season game, the Astros hired a team of painters to spray paint the panels with an off-white color to shield the fielders' eyes. The plan worked, but it took 700 gallons of paint at a cost of $20,000. Five weeks later, a "touch-up" required another 125 gallons at an additional cost of $4,000.

Then there was the "wind current" controversy. After an April 27–28 series with the Mets, several New York reporters and players complained that when the Astros were batting, the air conditioners blew the wind toward the outfield seats, but when the Mets were batting, the wind blew toward the batters. Commissioner Frick immediately sent a Chicago engineer to investigate the matter. He reported that there was no way to control the air inside the Astrodome and the controversy came to an end.

In May came the scoreboard controversy. Houston's fabulous new 474-foot-long exploding scoreboard was unlike anything else in the majors, and at times seemed to have too many opinions of its own. On May 19, umpire John Kibler called Houston's Joe Morgan out on a close play at the plate in the bottom of the 13th inning against Los Angeles. The Dodgers went on to win the game in the 14th inning, 4–2. Two nights later, when Kibler ejected Houston's third baseman Ken Aspromonte, a message blazed across the scoreboard, "Kibler Did It Again." Umpire crew chief Frank Secory protested to league president Warren Giles, charging that the scoreboard message was an attempt to incite the fans. Giles agreed and promptly chastised the operator of the scoreboard, Houston's public relations director Bill Giles, who happened to be his own son.

In spite of the snafus, the season was a financial success for the Astros. Their attendance nearly tripled from the year before. In addition, the team sold more than 400,000 tickets for their guided tour of the Astrodome at $1 a head.

The way the Astros played—at least initially—in their radical new indoor ballpark caused many observers to wonder if there was some sort of extra, unusual home-field advantage. The Astros won their first nine games in the Astrodome after starting the season 3–6 on the road, and looked like world-beaters. However, these "Astronauts" came back to Earth soon thereafter, compiling a 27–45 record in their remaining home games.

• • • •

1965 The specially grown grass used in the Astrodome in 1965 kept dying, so owner Roy Hofheinz installed artificial grass in the infield before the 1966 season. The artificial grass, known as "Astroturf," came in strips and was zippered together. Because the players quickly accepted the new surface, Hofheinz replaced the outfield grass as well in July. Another 1966 Hofheinz innovation was a portable pitching mound. Due to other events taking place inside the Astrodome, the pitching mound constantly had to be removed and replaced, a tedious chore for the grounds crew. Hofheinz created the portable pitching mound by placing the mound on top of a large steel tray, which was transported by a large tricycle device.

• • • •

1968 One of baseball's most remarkable pitching duels was played in the Astrodome on April 15, between the Astros and the Mets, with the Astros winning 1–0 in 24 innings.

1969 The Astros got off to a horrible start, standing at 4–20 on April 30th. In their final April game, they were no-hit by Cincinnati's Jim Maloney, 10–0. Collectively embarrassed, they resolved to have a better May. On May 1, a grim-faced Don Wilson took the mound and returned the favor by no-hitting the Reds, 4–0. It was just the second time in history that teams traded no-hitters in consecutive games. The win seemed to inspire the Astros, as they proceeded to put together a 20–6 record in the month of May, turning their potentially disastrous season around. By September 10, the team had pulled within two games of first place in the NL West before fading.

• • • •

1979 The Astros finished 89–73, just 1½ games behind division winner Cincinnati, a remarkable feat considering they had one of the most anemic hitting performances in baseball history. The Astros hit only 49 homers all season, just one more than the Cubs' Dave Kingman's total that year. Denny Walling led all Houston batters in homers in the 81 home games with ... three. George Foster of the Reds hit four in his team's visits to the Astrodome. After July 6, only two Astros regulars hit a home run at home with anyone on base. But the Astros stayed close with pitching. Astros pitchers set a record of sorts, when for the first time in history, one team had four different National League Pitchers of the Month. Ken Forsch won the honor in April, Joe Niekro in May, Joaquin Andujar in June, and J.R. Richard in September.

1981 Houston pitchers were again masters of the mound. The individual ERAs of the Astros starters were nothing short of spectacular. Nolan Ryan led the way (and the league) at 1.69. Bob Knepper followed with a 2.18 mark. Don Sutton finished at 2.60, Joe Niekro at 2.82, and Vern Ruhle rounded out the sub-3.00 crew with a 2.91 average.

• • • •

1983 The Astros began the season 0–9. Coupled with a 3–16 spring training record, the team began the year 3–25, and was called "the worst team in baseball," in the Houston press. The panicky press was eventually put at ease, as the Astros finished the season 85–77, good for third place in the NL West, just six games behind the division-winning Dodgers.

• • • •

1984 A year the Padres won the National League title and Houston finished below .500 and 12 games behind the Padres, the Astros were a bit frustrated. Why? Compare the following season-ending numbers: Both Houston and San Diego had winning records against eight clubs, and losing records against three clubs. Houston hit .264, San Diego .259. Houston scored 693 runs, San Diego 686. Houston's team ERA was 3.32, San Diego's 3.48. In fielding, Houston committed 133 errors, San Diego 138. Houston turned 160 double plays to San Diego's 144.

Why the stark difference in where the teams ended up? Because Houston lost many close games and 12 of 18 meetings with San Diego, and that alone made for a 12-game swing in the standings.

1986 Houston first baseman Glenn Davis won four games for the Astros in the 1986 season with homers in Houston's last at-bat.

• • • •

1988 When third baseman Buddy Bell hit his 200th career homer on September 11, against the Giants, he and his father, Gus, became the first father-son duo in major league history with 200 career homers apiece.

• • • •

1989 From May 26 to June 11, the Astros were 16–1. Incredibly, 11 of those 16 wins were by one run. The hot streak moved the team from fifth to first place in their division.

Talk about a Jekyll-and-Hyde performance: Second baseman Bill Doran hit .280 with seven homers and 46 RBIs before the All-Star break. After the break he mysteriously hit .131 with no homers and 9 RBIs. He knocked in only three runs after July 29. And, just as mysteriously, Doran came back in 1990 to hit a career-best .300.

• • • •

1990 The Astros had a horrible road streak. From June 1 through July 7, the team was 1–20 away from the Astrodome. Overall they were 26–55 on the road for the season.

1992 Because the Republican National Convention took over the Astrodome for a protracted period, the Astros were forced to undertake a brutal 26-game road trip, which they finished 12–14.

Doug Jones performed a truly rare feat as Houston's closer in 1992: He led the team in both saves (36) and wins (11).

••••

1993 On July 10, pitcher Mark Portugal's record stood at 6–4. He then reeled off 12 straight victories to finish the season 18–4.

When the Astros went 2–11 against the Colorado Rockies, it was the worst record by an established team against an expansion team in major league history.

••••

1994 Relief pitcher John Hudek began the season in the minors, but by July the 27-year-old rookie had made the All-Star Game. Finishing with 16 saves, Hudek became only the fifth player in major league history to start a season in the minors, yet make the All-Star team in the same season. His glory was short lived, however. In 1999, after an 0–2 record and an 8.44 ERA, Hudek was released and out of baseball, having compiled just a 10–15 record and 13 more saves in his six-year career.

••••

1996 Houston batters were hit by pitches 84 times, more than any other National League team in the 20th century up to that time.

Outfielder Derek Bell had 113 RBIs, but none, strangely, in Houston's 13 games against division rival St. Louis.

••••

1997 Second baseman Craig Biggio became the first player in major league history not to ground into a double play in a 162-game season.

Closer Billy Wagner averaged 14.4 strikeouts per nine innings pitched, the most ever in major league history by a pitcher who pitched at least 50 innings in a season. He then topped that in 1998 with a 14.6 average, and beat it again in 1999 by averaging 14.9.

Third baseman Bill Spiers reached base safely in 13 consecutive plate appearances, one short of Pedro Guerrero's National League record of 14 in 1985, set with the Dodgers.

••••

2000 Home-run records were smashed in 2000, Houston's first season in Enron Field, with its cozy left- and right-field fences. As a team, the Astros slugged 249, a new National League record, eclipsing the old record of 239 set by the Colorado Rockies in 1997. Both Jeff Bagwell (47) and Richard Hidalgo (44) broke Bagwell's old franchise record of 43 homers in a season. On the pitching side, Jose Lima gave up 48 homers, smashing the old club record of 34 in a season, which had also belonged to him.

Special Achievements

WORLD SERIES RESULTS

Year	Opponent	Result	Games
2005	Chicago White Sox	Lost	0–4

WORLD SERIES MANAGERIAL RECORDS

Manager	Series Record	Games Record
Phil Garner	0–1	0–4

ALL-TIME POSTSEASON RECORD

Divisional Playoffs	10–18
League Championship Series	11–13
World Series	0–4

ALL-STAR GAMES AT HOUSTON

Year	Date	Winner	Score	Stadium
1968	July 9	National	1–0	Astrodome
1986	July 15	American	3–2	Astrodome
2004	July 13	American	9–4	Minute Maid Park

HALL OF FAMERS WHO PLAYED FOR TEAM

	Position	Years	Games with Houston
Nellie Fox	2B	1964–65	154
Eddie Mathews	1B/3B	1967	101
Joe Morgan	2B	1963–71, 1980	1.032
Robin Roberts	SP	1965–66	23
Nolan Ryan	SP	1980–1988	282
Don Sutton	SP	1981–1982	50

HALL OF FAMERS WHO MANAGED TEAM

	Years	Games with Houston
Leo Durocher	1972–73	193

MVP AWARD WINNERS

Jeff Bagwell	1B	1994

CY YOUNG AWARD WINNERS

Pitcher	Year	W–L	ERA
Mike Scott	1986	18–10	2.22
Roger Clemens	2004	18–4	2.98

ROOKIE OF THE YEAR AWARD WINNERS

Jeff Bagwell	1B	1991

GOLD GLOVE WINNERS

Year	Position	Player
1970	3B	Doug Rader
1971	3B	Doug Rader
1972	3B	Doug Rader
	OF	Cesar Cedeño
1973	3B	Doug Rader
	SS	Roger Metzger
	OF	Cesar Cedeño
1974	3B	Doug Rader
	OF	Cesar Cedeño
1975	OF	Cesar Cedeño
1976	OF	Cesar Cedeño
1994	1B	Jeff Bagwell
	2B	Craig Biggio
1995	2B	Craig Biggio
1996	2B	Craig Biggio
1997	2B	Craig Biggio
2001	C	Brad Ausmus
2002	C	Brad Ausmus

TRIPLE CROWN WINNERS

None

FIREMAN OF THE YEAR AWARD WINNERS

Doug Jones	1992

WORLD SERIES MVP

None

LEAGUE CHAMPIONSHIP SERIES MVP

Mike Scott	1986
Roy Oswalt	2005

ALL-STAR GAME MVP

None

MANAGER OF THE YEAR AWARD WINNERS

Hal Lanier	1986
Larry Dierker	1998

BATTING CHAMPIONS

None

NINE-INNING NO-HITTERS PITCHED

Year	Pitcher	Opp.	Score
1963	Don Nottebart	PHI	4–1
1964	Ken Johnson	CIN	0–1
1967	Don Wilson	ATL	2–0
1969	Don Wilson	CIN	4–0
1976	Larry Dierker	MON	6–0
1979	Ken Forsch	ATL	6–0
1981	Nolan Ryan	LA	5–0
1986	Mike Scott	SF	2–0
1993	Darryl Kile	NYM	7–1
2003	(Six pitchers combined)	NYY	8–0

20-GAME WINNERS

Year	Pitcher	W–L
1969	Larry Dierker	20–13
1976	J.R. Richard	20–15
1979	Joe Niekro	21–11
1980	Joe Niekro	20–12
1989	Mike Scott	20–10
1999	Mike Hampton	22–4
	Jose Lima	21–10
2004	Roy Oswalt	20–10
2005	Roy Oswalt	20–12

RETIRED UNIFORM NUMBERS

Number	Player	Position
25	Jose Cruz	OF
27	Jim Wynn	OF
32	Jim Umbricht	RP
33	Mike Scott	SP
34	Nolan Ryan	SP
40	Don Wilson	SP

TEAM RECORDS—WINS & LOSSES

- Games won in a season: 102 in 1998
- Games lost in a season: 97 in 1965, 1975, and 1991
- Games won in a month: 22 in August 1998 and July 2005
- Games lost in a month: 24 in July 1962
- Consecutive games won: 12 in 1999 and 2004
- Consecutive games lost: 11 in 1995
- Biggest shutout victory: 15–0 over Montreal on April 26, 1998
- Biggest shutout loss: 16–0 (twice) to Philadelphia on September 10, 1963 and to Atlanta on May 8, 2005
- Highest winning percentage: .630 in 1998 (102–60)
- Lowest winning percentage: .398 in 1975 (64–97)

TEAM RECORDS—BATTING

- Highest team batting average: .280 in 1998
- Lowest team batting average: .220 in 1963
- Highest team slugging average: .477 in 2000
- Highest team on-base percentage: .361 in 2000
- Total hits: 1,578 in 1998
- Extra-base hits: 574 in 2000
- Hits in a game: 25 vs. Atlanta on May 30, 1976 (second game); vs. Cincinnati, July 2, 1976 (first game, 14 innings)
- Longest individual hitting streak: 25, Jeff Kent, 2004
- Most .300 hitters in a single season: 4, 1998
- Home runs: 249 in 2000
- Home runs in a month: 13, Jeff Bagwell, June 1994
- Home runs in a game: 7 vs. Chicago Cubs on September 9, 2000
- Home runs by a rookie: 21, Lance Berkman, 2000
- Home runs by a right-hander: 47, Jeff Bagwell, 2000
- Home runs by a left-hander: 23, Franklin Stubbs, 1990
- Home runs by a switch-hitter: 42, Lance Berkman, 2002
- Grand slams: 7 in 2001
- Grand slams (individual; single season): 2, by many players
- Grand slams (individual; career): 6, Bob Aspromonte
- Triples: 67 in 1980 and 1984
- Doubles: 326 in 1998
- Singles: 1,097 in 1984
- Walks: 728 in 1999
- Runs scored: 938 in 2000
- Runs scored in a game: 19 vs. Chicago Cubs on June 25, 1995 and vs. Pittsburgh on May 11, 1999
- Runs scored in an inning: 12 vs. Philadelphia on May 31, 1975 (eighth inning) and vs. Chicago Cubs on May 12, 1997 (seventh inning)
- Most batters hit by a pitch: 100, 1997
- Times shut out: 23 in 1963

- Grounded into double plays: 154 in 2000
- Fewest grounded into double plays: 76 in 1983
- Runners left on base: 1,252 in 1999

TEAM RECORDS—BASERUNNING

- Stolen bases: 198 in 1988
- Caught stealing: 95 in 1979 and 1983

TEAM RECORDS—PITCHING

- Lowest earned run average: 2.66 in 1981
- Complete games: 55 in 1979
- Saves: 51 in 1986
- Strikeouts: 1,228 in 2001
- Shutouts: 19 in 1979, 1981, and 1986
- Walks: 679 in 1975
- Hit batsmen: 74 in 2003
- Wild pitches: 91 in 1970
- Consecutive wins (individual): 12, Mark Portugal, 1993; Wade Miller, 2002
- Consecutive losses (individual): 13, Jose Lima in 2000
- Strikeouts in a game (individual): 18, Don Wilson, July 14, 1968 (second game)
- Runs allowed in a game: 22 vs. Chicago Cubs, June 3, 1987

TEAM RECORDS—FIELDING

- Best fielding average: .986 in 2002
- Most errors committed: 174 in 1966
- Fewest errors committed: 83 in 2002
- Most double plays turned: 175 in 1999
- Fewest double plays turned: 100 in 1963

TEAM RECORDS—MISCELLANEOUS

- Number of times league champions: 1
- Number of times finishing last in league: 3
- Largest attendance, single game: 54,037 vs. Cincinnati, September 28, 1999
- Largest attendance, doubleheader: 45,115 vs. Atlanta, August 4, 1979
- Players used in a season: 48 in 1965
- Seasons played: 18, Craig Biggio

PRIMARY PITCHING STAFFS

Year	Starter	Starter	Starter	Starter	Starter	Closer	Bullpen	Bullpen	Bullpen
2005	Oswalt	Pettitte	Clemens	Backe	Rodriguez	Lidge	Qualls	Wheeler	Springer
2004	Oswalt	Clemens	Munro	Redding	Pettitte	Lidge	Miceli	Gallo	Harville
2003	Oswalt	Miller	Robertson	Redding	Villone	Wagner	Lidge	Dotel	Stone
2002	Oswalt	Miller	Hernandez	Saarloos	Mlicki	Wagner	Borbon	Dotel	Stone
2001	Oswalt	Miller	Reynolds	Elarton	Mlicki	Wagner	Jackson	Dotel	Cruz
2000	Lima	Holt	Reynolds	Elarton	Dotel	Wagner	Slusarski	Valdes	Cabrera
1999	Lima	Holt	Reynolds	Hampton	Bergman	Wagner	Powell	Williams	Miller
1998	Lima	Schourek	Reynolds	Hampton	Bergman	Wagner	Henry	Magnante	Nitkowski
1997	Kile	Holt	Reynolds	Hampton	Garcia	Wagner	Martin	Springer	Lima
1996	Kile	Drabek	Reynolds	Hampton	Wall	Jones	Hernandez	Morman	Wagner
1995	Kile	Drabek	Reynolds	Hampton	Swindell	Jones	Dougherty	Hartgraves	Veres
1994	Kile	Drabek	Reynolds	Harnisch	Swindell	Hudek	Jones	Hampton	Edens
1993	Kile	Drabek	Portugal	Harnisch	Swindell	Jones	Hernandez	Osuna	Williams
1992	Kile	Henry	Jones	Harnisch	Williams	Jones	Hernandez	Osuna	Boever
1991	Kile	Deshaies	Jones	Harnisch	Portugal	Osuna	Schilling	Henry	Corsi
1990	Scott	Deshaies	Gullickson	Darwin	Portugal	Smith	Schatzeder	Andersen	Agosto
1989	Scott	Deshaies	Clancy	Knepper	Rhoden	Smith	Agosto	Andersen	Darwin
1988	Scott	Deshaies	Ryan	Knepper	Darwin	Smith	Agosto	Andersen	Andujar
1987	Scott	Deshaies	Ryan	Knepper	Darwin	Smith	Meads	Andersen	Childress
1986	Scott	Deshaies	Ryan	Knepper	Darwin	Smith	Kerfeld	Andersen	Lopez
1985	Scott	Niekro	Ryan	Knepper	Mathis	Smith	DiPino	Dawley	Calhoun
1984	Scott	Niekro	Ryan	Knepper	LaCoss	DiPino	Smith	Dawley	Ruhle
1983	Scott	Niekro	Ryan	Knepper	LaCoss	DiPino	Smith	Dawley	Ruhle
1982	Sutton	Niekro	Ryan	Knepper	Ruhle	Smith	LaCorte	LaCoss	Moffitt
1981	Sutton	Niekro	Ryan	Knepper	Ruhle	Sambito	LaCorte	Smith	Sprowl

PRIMARY PITCHING STAFFS (CONT.)

Year	Starter	Starter	Starter	Starter	Starter	Closer	Bullpen	Bullpen	Bullpen
1980	Forsch	Niekro	Ryan	Richard	Ruhle	Sambito	LaCorte	Smith	Andujar
1979	Forsch	Niekro	Andujar	Richard	Williams	Sambito	Niemann	Roberge	Dixon
1978	Lemongello	Niekro	Dixon	Richard	Bannister	Sambito	Forsch	Andujar	Williams
1977	Lemongello	Niekro	Andujar	Richard	Bannister	Forsch	McLaughlin	Sambito	Pentz
1976	Dierker	Niekro	Andujar	Richard	Cosgrove	Forsch	Sambito	Griffin	Pentz
1975	Dierker	Konieczny	Roberts	Richard	Griffin	Granger	Crawford	Niekro	
1974	Dierker	Wilson	Roberts	Osteen	Griffin	Forsch	Scherman	Cosgrove	Johnson
1973	Reuss	Wilson	Roberts	Forsch	Griffin	York	Crawford	Ray	Upshaw
1972	Reuss	Wilson	Roberts	Forsch	Dierker	Gladding	Culver	Ray	Griffin
1971	Billingham	Wilson	Blasingame	Forsch	Dierker	Gladding	Culver	Ray	Lemaster
1970	Billingham	Wilson	Lemaster	Griffin	Dierker	Gladding	Dilauro	Ray	Cook
1969	Ray	Wilson	Lemaster	Griffin	Dierker	Gladding	Billingham	Womack	Guinn
1968	Giusti	Wilson	Lemaster	Cuellar	Dierker	Shea	Dukes	Ray	Coombs
1967	Giusti	Wilson	Belinsky	Cuellar	Dierker	Sherry	Schneider	Sembera	Latman
1966	Giusti	Bruce	Farrell	Cuellar	Dierker	Raymond	Owens	Taylor	Latman
1965	Giusti	Bruce	Farrell	Nottebart	Dierker	Owens	Woodeshick	Raymond	Taylor
1964	Johnson	Bruce	Farrell	Nottebart	Brown	Woodeshick	Raymond	Owens	Jones
1963	Johnson	Bruce	Farrell	Nottebart	Brown	Woodeshick	McMahon	Umbricht	Drott
1962	Johnson	Bruce	Farrell	Woodeshick	Golden	McMahon	Tiefenauer	Kemmerer	Umbricht

PRIMARY STARTING LINEUPS

Year	C	1B	2B	3B	SS	LF	CF	RF
2005	Ausmus	Berkman	Biggio	Ensberg	Everett	Burke	Taveras	Lane
2004	Ausmus	Bagwell	Kent	Ensberg	Everett	Biggio	Beltran	Berkman
2003	Ausmus	Bagwell	Kent	Ensberg	Everett	Berkman	Biggio	Hidalgo
2002	Ausmus	Bagwell	Biggio	Blum	Lugo	Ward	Berkman	Hidalgo
2001	Ausmus	Bagwell	Biggio	Castilla	Lugo	Berkman	Hidalgo	Alou
2000	Meluskey	Bagwell	Biggio	Truby	Bogar	Ward	Hidalgo	Alou
1999	Eusebio	Bagwell	Biggio	Caminiti	Bogar	Hidalgo	Everett	Bell
1998	Ausmus	Bagwell	Biggio	Spiers	Gutierrez	Alou	Everett	Bell
1997	Ausmus	Bagwell	Biggio	Berry	Bogar	Gonzalez	Carr	Bell
1996	Wilkins	Bagwell	Biggio	Berry	Miller	Mouton	Hunter	Bell
1995	Eusebio	Bagwell	Biggio	Magadan	Miller	Gonzalez	Hunter	Bell
1994	Servais	Bagwell	Biggio	Caminiti	Cedeño	Gonzalez	Finley	Mouton
1993	Taubensee	Bagwell	Biggio	Caminiti	Cedeño	Gonzalez	Finley	Anthony
1992	Taubensee	Bagwell	Biggio	Caminiti	Cedeño	Gonzalez	Finley	Anthony
1991	Biggio	Bagwell	Candaele	Caminiti	Yelding	Gonzalez	Finley	Rhodes
1990	Biggio	Davis	Doran	Caminiti	Ramirez	Stubbs	Yelding	Wilson
1989	Biggio	Davis	Doran	Caminiti	Ramirez	Hatcher	Young	Puhl
1988	Trevino	Davis	Doran	Bell	Ramirez	Hatcher	Young	Bass
1987	Ashby	Davis	Doran	Walling	Reynolds	Cruz	Hatcher	Bass
1986	Ashby	Davis	Doran	Walling	Thon	Cruz	Hatcher	Bass
1985	Bailey	Davis	Doran	Garner	Reynolds	Cruz	Bass	Mumphrey
1984	Bailey	Cabell	Doran	Garner	Reynolds	Cruz	Mumphrey	Puhl
1983	Ashby	Knight	Doran	Garner	Thon	Cruz	Moreno	Puhl
1982	Ashby	Knight	Garner	Howe	Thon	Cruz	Scott	Puhl
1981	Ashby	Cedeno	Pittman	Howe	Reynolds	Cruz	Scott	Puhl
1980	Ashby	Howe	Morgan	Cabell	Reynolds	Cruz	Cedeno	Puhl
1979	Ashby	Cedeno	Landestoy	Cabell	Reynolds	Cruz	Puhl	Leonard

PRIMARY STARTING LINEUPS (CONT.)

Year	C	1B	2B	3B	SS	LF	CF	RF
1978	Pujols	Watson	Howe	Cabell	Sexton	Walling	Puhl	Cruz
1977	Ferguson	Watson	Howe	Cabell	Metzger	Puhl	Cedeno	Cruz
1976	Herrmann	Watson	Andrews	Cabell	Metzger	Cruz	Cedeno	Gross
1975	May	Watson	Andrews	Rader	Metzger	Howard	Cedeno	Cruz
1974	May	May	Helms	Rader	Metzger	Watson	Cedeno	Gross
1973	Jutze	May	Helms	Rader	Metzger	Watson	Cedeno	Wynn
1972	Edwards	May	Helms	Rader	Metzger	Watson	Cedeno	Wynn
1971	Edwards	Menke	Morgan	Rader	Metzger	Watson	Cedeno	Wynn
1970	Edwards	Watson	Morgan	Rader	Menke	Davis	Wynn	Alou
1969	Edwards	Blefary	Morgan	Rader	Menke	Alou	Wynn	Miller
1968	Bateman	Staub	Menke	Rader	Torres	Watson	Wynn	Miller
1967	Bateman	Mathews	Morgan	Aspromonte	Jackson	Davis	Wynn	Staub
1966	Bateman	Harrison	Morgan	Aspromonte	Jackson	Maye	Wynn	Staub
1965	Brand	Bond	Morgan	Aspromonte	Lillis	Maye	Wynn	Staub
1964	Grote	Bond	Fox	Aspromonte	Kasko	Spangler	White	Gaines
1963	Bateman	Staub	Fazio	Aspromonte	Lillis	Spangler	Goss	Warwick
1962	Smith	Larker	Amalfitano	Aspromonte	Lillis	Spangler	Warwick	Mejias

Top 10 Batting Leaders, Single Season & Career with Team

GAMES PLAYED: CAREER WITH TEAM

Player	G	PA
1. Craig Biggio	2,564	11,341
2. Jeff Bagwell	2,150	9,431
3. Jose Cruz	1,870	7,448
4. Terry Puhl	1,516	5,458
5. Cesar Cedeño	1,512	6,389
6. Jimmy Wynn	1,426	6,013
7. Bob Watson	1,381	5,496
8. Doug Rader	1,178	4,724
9. Craig Reynolds	1,170	3,721
10. Bill Doran	1,165	4,922

AT-BATS: SEASON

Player	AB	Year
1. Enos Cabell	660	1978
2. Craig Biggio	646	1998
3. Roger Metzger	641	1972
4. Craig Biggio	639	1999
5. Craig Biggio	633	2004
6. Derek Bell	630	1998
7. Craig Biggio	628	2003
8. Derek Bell	627	1996
9. Enos Cabell	625	1977
Bill Doran	625	1987

AT-BATS: CAREER WITH TEAM

Player	AB	PA
1. Craig Biggio	9,811	11,341
2. Jeff Bagwell	7,797	9,431
3. Jose Cruz	6,629	7,448
4. Cesar Cedeño	5,732	6,389
5. Jimmy Wynn	5,063	6,013
6. Bob Watson	4,883	5,496
7. Terry Puhl	4,837	5,458
8. Bill Doran	4,264	4,922
9. Doug Rader	4,232	4,724
10. Enos Cabell	4,005	4,240

BATTING AVERAGE: SEASON

Player	BA	Year
1. Jeff Bagwell	.367	1994
2. Moises Alou	.355	2000
3. Derek Bell	.334	1995
4. Rusty Staub	.333	1967
5. Moises Alou	.331	2001
Lance Berkman	.331	2001
7. Carl Everett	.325	1999
Craig Biggio	.325	1998
9. Bob Watson	.324	1975
10. Cesar Cedeño	.320	1972

BATTING AVERAGE: CAREER WITH TEAM

Player	BA	PA
1. Lance Berkman	.302	3,813
2. Jeff Bagwell	.297	9,431
Bob Watson	.297	5,496
4. Jose Cruz	.292	7,448
5. Cesar Cedeño	.289	6,389
6. Craig Biggio	.285	11,341
7. Derek Bell	.284	2,993
8. Enos Cabell	.281	4,240
Terry Puhl	.281	5,458
Steve Finley	.281	2,344

TOTAL HITS: SEASON

Player	H	Year
1. Craig Biggio	210	1998
2. Derek Bell	198	1998
3. Enos Cabell	195	1978
4. Lance Berkman	191	2001
Craig Biggio	191	1997
6. Jose Cruz	189	1983
7. Craig Biggio	188	1999
8. Jose Cruz	187	1984
9. Jose Cruz	185	1980
Greg Gross	185	1974

TOTAL HITS: CAREER WITH TEAM

Player	H	PA
1. Craig Biggio	2,795	11,341
2. Jeff Bagwell	2,314	9,431
3. Jose Cruz	1,937	7,448
4. Cesar Cedeño	1,659	6,389
5. Bob Watson	1,448	5,496
6. Terry Puhl	1,357	5,458
7. Jimmy Wynn	1,291	6,013
8. Bill Doran	1,139	4,922
9. Enos Cabell	1,124	4,240
10. Doug Rader	1,060	4,724

HOME RUNS: SEASON

Player	HR	Year
1. Jeff Bagwell	47	2000
2. Richard Hidalgo	44	2000
3. Jeff Bagwell	43	1997
4. Jeff Bagwell	42	1999
Lance Berkman	42	2002
6. Jeff Bagwell	39	1994
Jeff Bagwell	39	2001
Jeff Bagwell	39	2003
9. Moises Alou	38	1998
10. Jimmy Wynn	37	1967

HOME RUNS: CAREER WITH TEAM

Player	HR	PA
1. Jeff Bagwell	449	9,431
2. Craig Biggio	260	11,341
3. Jimmy Wynn	223	6,013
4. Lance Berkman	180	3,813
5. Glenn Davis	166	3,425
6. Cesar Cedeño	163	6,389
7. Bob Watson	139	5,496
8. Jose Cruz	138	7,448
9. Richard Hidalgo	134	3,230
10. Doug Rader	128	4,724

TRIPLES: SEASON

Player	3B	Year
1. Roger Metzger	14	1973
2. Jose Cruz	13	1984
Steve Finley	13	1992
Steve Finley	13	1993
5. Joe Morgan	12	1965
Craig Reynolds	12	1981
7. Bill Doran	11	1984
Roger Metzger	11	1971
Omar Moreno	11	1983
Joe Morgan	11	1967
Joe Morgan	11	1971
Craig Reynolds	11	1984

TRIPLES: CAREER WITH TEAM

Player	3B	PA
1. Jose Cruz	80	7,448
2. Joe Morgan	63	4,482
3. Roger Metzger	62	4,100
4. Terry Puhl	56	5,458
5. Cesar Cedeño	55	6,389
Craig Reynolds	55	3,721
7. Craig Biggio	52	11,341
8. Enos Cabell	45	4,240
9. Steve Finley	41	2,344
10. Bill Doran	35	4,922

DOUBLES: SEASON

Player	2B	Year
1. Craig Biggio	56	1999
2. Lance Berkman	55	2001
3. Craig Biggio	51	1998
4. Jeff Bagwell	48	1996
5. Craig Biggio	47	2004
6. Craig Biggio	44	1994
Craig Biggio	44	2003
Rusty Staub	44	1967
9. Jeff Bagwell	43	2001
Richard Hidalgo	43	2003

DOUBLES: CAREER WITH TEAM

Player	2B	PA
1. Craig Biggio	604	11,341
2. Jeff Bagwell	488	9,431
3. Cesar Cedeño	343	6,389
4. Jose Cruz	335	7,448
5. Bob Watson	241	5,496
6. Lance Berkman	229	3,813
7. Jimmy Wynn	228	6,013
8. Terry Puhl	226	5,458
9. Ken Caminiti	204	4,370
10. Doug Rader	197	4,724

EXTRA-BASE HITS: SEASON

Player	XBH	Year
1. Lance Berkman	94	2001
2. Richard Hidalgo	89	2000
3. Jeff Bagwell	86	2001
4. Jeff Bagwell	85	1997
Jeff Bagwell	85	2000
6. Jeff Bagwell	81	1996
7. Lance Berkman	79	2002
8. Moises Alou	77	1998
Jeff Bagwell	77	1999
10. Richard Hidalgo	75	2003

EXTRA-BASE HITS: CAREER WITH TEAM

Player	XBH	PA
1. Jeff Bagwell	969	9,431
2. Craig Biggio	916	11,341
3. Cesar Cedeño	561	6,389
4. Jose Cruz	553	7,448
5. Jimmy Wynn	483	6,013
6. Lance Berkman	427	3,813
7. Bob Watson	410	5,496
8. Doug Rader	355	4,724
9. Terry Puhl	344	5,458
10. Richard Hidalgo	343	3,230

TOTAL BASES: SEASON

Player	TB	Year
1. Jeff Bagwell	363	2000
2. Lance Berkman	358	2001
3. Richard Hidalgo	355	2000
4. Jeff Bagwell	341	2001
5. Moises Alou	340	1998
6. Jeff Bagwell	335	1997
7. Lance Berkman	334	2002
8. Jeff Bagwell	332	1999
9. Craig Biggio	325	1998
10. Jeff Bagwell	324	1996

TOTAL BASES: CAREER WITH TEAM

Player	TB	PA
1. Craig Biggio	4,283	11,341
2. Jeff Bagwell	4,213	9,431
3. Jose Cruz	2,846	7,448
4. Cesar Cedeño	2,601	6,389
5. Jimmy Wynn	2,252	6,013
6. Bob Watson	2,166	5,496
7. Terry Puhl	1,881	5,458
8. Lance Berkman	1,756	3,813
9. Doug Rader	1,701	4,724
10. Bill Doran	1,596	4,922

RUNS BATTED IN: SEASON

Player	RBI	Year
1. Jeff Bagwell	135	1997
2. Jeff Bagwell	132	2000
3. Jeff Bagwell	130	2001
4. Lance Berkman	128	2002
5. Jeff Bagwell	126	1999
Lance Berkman	126	2001
7. Moises Alou	124	1998
8. Richard Hidalgo	122	2000
9. Jeff Bagwell	120	1996
10. Jeff Bagwell	116	1994

RUNS BATTED IN: CAREER WITH TEAM

Player	RBI	PA
1. Jeff Bagwell	1,529	9,431
2. Craig Biggio	1,063	11,341
3. Jose Cruz	942	7,448
4. Bob Watson	782	5,496
5. Cesar Cedeño	778	6,389
6. Jimmy Wynn	719	6,013
7. Lance Berkman	617	3,813
8. Doug Rader	600	4,724
9. Ken Caminiti	546	4,370
10. Glenn Davis	518	3,425

RUNS SCORED: SEASON

Player	R	Year
1. Jeff Bagwell	152	2000
2. Craig Biggio	146	1997
3. Jeff Bagwell	143	1999
4. Jeff Bagwell	126	2001
5. Jeff Bagwell	124	1998
6. Craig Biggio	123	1995
Craig Biggio	123	1998
Craig Biggio	123	1999
9. Craig Biggio	118	2001
Richard Hidalgo	118	2000

RUNS SCORED: CAREER WITH TEAM

Player	R	PA
1. Craig Biggio	1,697	11,341
2. Jeff Bagwell	1,517	9,431
3. Cesar Cedeño	890	6,389
4. Jose Cruz	871	7,448
5. Jimmy Wynn	829	6,013
6. Terry Puhl	676	5,458
7. Bob Watson	640	5,496
8. Bill Doran	611	4,922
9. Joe Morgan	597	4,482
10. Lance Berkman	592	3,813

WALKS: SEASON

Player	BB	Year
1. Jeff Bagwell	149	1999
2. Jimmy Wynn	148	1969
3. Jeff Bagwell	135	1996
4. Jeff Bagwell	127	1997
Lance Berkman	127	2004
6. Joe Morgan	110	1969
7. Jeff Bagwell	109	1998
8. Jeff Bagwell	107	2000
Lance Berkman	107	2002
Lance Berkman	107	2003

WALKS: CAREER WITH TEAM

Player	BB	PA
1. Jeff Bagwell	1,401	9,431
2. Craig Biggio	1,097	11,341
3. Jimmy Wynn	847	6,013
4. Jose Cruz	730	7,448
5. Joe Morgan	678	4,482
6. Lance Berkman	592	3,813
7. Bill Doran	585	4,922
8. Cesar Cedeño	534	6,389
9. Bob Watson	508	5,496
10. Terry Puhl	502	5,458

STRIKEOUTS: SEASON

Player	SO	Year
1. Lee May	145	1972
2. Jimmy Wynn	142	1969
3. Jimmy Wynn	137	1967
4. Jeff Bagwell	135	2001
5. Jeff Bagwell	131	2004
Doug Rader	131	1974
Jimmy Wynn	131	1968
8. Jeff Bagwell	130	2002
9. Derek Bell	129	1999
10. Howie Goss	128	1963

STRIKEOUTS: CAREER WITH TEAM

Player	SO	PA
1. Jeff Bagwell	1,558	9,431
2. Craig Biggio	1,557	11,341
3. Jimmy Wynn	1,088	6,013
4. Doug Rader	848	4,724
5. Jose Cruz	841	7,448
6. Cesar Cedeño	735	6,389
7. Ken Caminiti	659	4,370
8. Bob Watson	635	5,496
9. Lance Berkman	614	3,813
10. Richard Hidalgo	587	3,230

SLUGGING PERCENTAGE: SEASON

Player	SLG	Year
1. Jeff Bagwell	.750	1994
2. Richard Hidalgo	.636	2000
3. Moises Alou	.623	2000
4. Lance Berkman	.620	2001
5. Jeff Bagwell	.615	2000
6. Jeff Bagwell	.592	1997
7. Jeff Bagwell	.591	1999
8. Moises Alou	.582	1998
9. Lance Berkman	.578	2002
10. Richard Hidalgo	.572	2003

SLUGGING PERCENTAGE: CAREER WITH TEAM

Player	SLG	PA
1. Lance Berkman	.557	3,813
2. Jeff Bagwell	.540	9,431
3. Richard Hidalgo	.501	3,230
4. Glenn Davis	.483	3,425
5. Cesar Cedeño	.454	6,389
6. Jimmy Wynn	.445	6,013
7. Bob Watson	.444	5,496
8. Craig Biggio	.437	11,341
9. Derek Bell	.430	2,993
10. Jose Cruz	.429	7,448

ON-BASE PERCENTAGE: SEASON

Player	OBP	Year
1. Jeff Bagwell	.454	1999
2. Jeff Bagwell	.451	1994
Jeff Bagwell	.451	1996
4. Lance Berkman	.450	2004
5. Bill Spiers	.438	1997
6. Jimmy Wynn	.436	1969
7. Lance Berkman	.430	2001
8. Dave Magadan	.428	1995
9. Jeff Bagwell	.425	1997
10. Jeff Bagwell	.424	2000

ON-BASE PERCENTAGE: CAREER WITH TEAM

Player	OBP	PA
1. Lance Berkman	.416	3,813
2. Jeff Bagwell	.408	9,431
3. Joe Morgan	.374	4,482
4. Craig Biggio	.370	11,341
5. Bob Watson	.364	5,496
6. Jimmy Wynn	.362	6,013
7. Jose Cruz	.359	7,448
8. Richard Hidalgo	.356	3,230
9. Denis Menke	.355	2,524
Bill Doran	.355	4,922

OPS (ON-BASE PERCENTAGE + SLUGGING PERCENTAGE): SEASON

Player	OPS	Year
1. Jeff Bagwell	1.201	1994
2. Lance Berkman	1.051	2001
3. Jeff Bagwell	1.045	1999
4. Jeff Bagwell	1.039	2000
Moises Alou	1.039	2000

6. Richard Hidalgo	1.028	2000
7. Jeff Bagwell	1.021	1996
8. Jeff Bagwell	1.017	1997
9. Lance Berkman	1.016	2004
10. Lance Berkman	.982	2002

OPS (On-Base Percentage + Slugging Percentage): Career with Team

Player	OPS	PA
1. Lance Berkman	.973	3,813
2. Jeff Bagwell	.948	9,431
3. Richard Hidalgo	.857	3,230
4. Glenn Davis	.819	3,425
5. Bob Watson	.808	5,496
6. Craig Biggio	.807	11,341
7. Jimmy Wynn	.806	6,013
8. Cesar Cedeño	.805	6,389
9. Jose Cruz	.789	7,448
10. Derek Bell	.771	2,993

Stolen Bases: Season

Player	SB	Year
1. Gerald Young	65	1988
2. Eric Yelding	64	1990
3. Cesar Cedeño	61	1977
4. Cesar Cedeño	58	1976
5. Cesar Cedeño	57	1974
6. Cesar Cedeño	56	1973
7. Cesar Cedeño	55	1972
8. Billy Hatcher	53	1987
9. Craig Biggio	50	1998
Cesar Cedeño	50	1975

Stolen Bases: Career with Team

Player	SB	PA
1. Cesar Cedeño	487	6,389
2. Craig Biggio	407	11,341
3. Jose Cruz	288	7,448
4. Joe Morgan	219	4,482
5. Terry Puhl	217	5,458
6. Jeff Bagwell	202	9,431
7. Enos Cabell	191	4,240
Bill Doran	191	4,922
9. Jimmy Wynn	180	6,013
10. Gerald Young	153	2,016

Sacrifice Hits: Season

Player	Sac	Year
1. Craig Reynolds	34	1979
2. Sonny Jackson	27	1966
3. Adam Everett	22	2004
4. Roger Metzger	21	1974
5. Nellie Fox	20	1964
6. Joe Niekro	18	1980
Craig Reynolds	18	1981
8. Shane Reynolds	17	1999
9. Steve Finley	16	1992
Craig Reynolds	16	1984

Sacrifice Hits: Career with Team

Player	Sac	PA
1. Joe Niekro	100	816
2. Craig Reynolds	98	3,721
3. Craig Biggio	89	11,341
4. Shane Reynolds	87	595
5. Roger Metzger	77	4,100
6. Larry Dierker	68	866
7. Bob Knepper	58	627
8. Terry Puhl	57	5,458
Mike Scott	57	622
10. Nolan Ryan	55	679

Hit by Pitch: Season

Player	HBP	Year
1. Craig Biggio	34	1997
2. Craig Biggio	28	2001
3. Craig Biggio	27	1996
Craig Biggio	27	2003
5. Craig Biggio	23	1998
6. Craig Biggio	22	1995
7. Richard Hidalgo	21	2000
8. Craig Biggio	17	2002
Craig Biggio	17	2005
10. Jeff Bagwell	16	1997
Craig Biggio	16	2000
Richard Hidalgo	16	2001

Hit by Pitch: Career with Team

Player	HBP	PA
1. Craig Biggio	273	11,341
2. Jeff Bagwell	128	9,431
3. Richard Hidalgo	58	3,230
4. Glenn Davis	47	3,425
5. Cesar Cedeño	45	6,389
6. Bob Watson	42	5,496
7. Lance Berkman	41	3,813
8. Derek Bell	36	2,993
9. Doug Rader	33	4,724
10. Luis Gonzalez	31	2,890

Top 10 Pitching Leaders, Single Season & Career with Team

Games Pitched: Season

Player	GP	Year
1. Octavio Dotel	83	2002
2. Juan Agosto	82	1990
3. Joe Boever	81	1992
4. Doug Jones	80	1992
Brad Lidge	80	2004
6. Brad Lidge	78	2003
Ricky Stone	78	2002
Billy Wagner	78	2003
9. Xavier Hernandez	77	1992
Chad Qualls	77	2005

Games Pitched: Career with Team

Player	GP	IP
1. Dave Smith	563	762.0
2. Billy Wagner	464	504.3
3. Ken Forsch	421	1,493.7
4. Joe Niekro	397	2,270.0
5. Joe Sambito	353	536.0
6. Larry Dierker	345	2,294.3
7. Octavio Dotel	302	449.0
8. Bob Knepper	284	1,738.0
9. Nolan Ryan	282	1,854.7
10. Jim Ray	280	565.3

Innings Pitched: Season

Player	IP	Year
1. Larry Dierker	305.3	1969
2. J.R. Richard	292.3	1979
3. J.R. Richard	291.0	1976
4. Jerry Reuss	279.3	1973
5. J.R. Richard	275.3	1978
Mike Scott	275.3	1986
7. Joe Niekro	270.0	1982
8. Larry Dierker	269.7	1970
9. Don Wilson	268.0	1971
10. J.R. Richard	267.0	1977

Innings Pitched: Career with Team

Player	IP
1. Larry Dierker	2,294.3
2. Joe Niekro	2,270.0
3. Nolan Ryan	1,854.7
4. Don Wilson	1,748.3
5. Bob Knepper	1,738.0
6. Mike Scott	1,704.0
7. Shane Reynolds	1,622.3
8. J.R. Richard	1,606.0
9. Ken Forsch	1,493.7
10. Darryl Kile	1,200.0

Batters Faced: Season

Player	BF	Year
1. J.R. Richard	1,218	1976
2. Larry Dierker	1,207	1969
3. Jerry Reuss	1,198	1973
4. J.R. Richard	1,175	1979
5. J.R. Richard	1,139	1978
6. Larry Dierker	1,132	1970
7. Joe Niekro	1,113	1983
8. Joe Niekro	1,096	1980
9. Joe Niekro	1,095	1979
10. J.R. Richard	1,092	1977

Batters Faced: Career with Team

Player	BF	IP
1. Larry Dierker	9,492	2,294.3
2. Joe Niekro	9,490	2,270.0
3. Nolan Ryan	7,716	1,854.7
4. Bob Knepper	7,315	1,738.0
5. Don Wilson	7,305	1,748.3
6. Mike Scott	6,989	1,704.0
7. Shane Reynolds	6,865	1,622.3
8. J.R. Richard	6,674	1,606.0
9. Ken Forsch	6,213	1,493.7
10. Darryl Kile	5,241	1,200.0

Games Started: Season

Player	GS	Year
1. Jerry Reuss	40	1973
2. J.R. Richard	39	1976
3. Bob Knepper	38	1986
Joe Niekro	38	1979
Joe Niekro	38	1983
Joe Niekro	38	1984
J.R. Richard	38	1979
8. Larry Dierker	37	1969
Bob Knepper	37	1985
Denny Lemaster	37	1969
Mike Scott	37	1986

Games Started: Career with Team

Player	GS	IP
1. Larry Dierker	320	2,294.3
2. Joe Niekro	301	2,270.0
3. Nolan Ryan	282	1,854.7
4. Bob Knepper	267	1,738.0
5. Mike Scott	259	1,704.0
6. Shane Reynolds	248	1,622.3
7. Don Wilson	245	1,748.3
8. J.R. Richard	221	1,606.0
9. Darryl Kile	182	1,200.0
10. Jim Deshaies	178	1,102.0

Complete Games: Season

Player	CG	Year
1. Larry Dierker	20	1969
2. J.R. Richard	19	1979
3. Don Wilson	18	1971
4. Larry Dierker	17	1970
5. Mike Cuellar	16	1967
Joe Niekro	16	1982
J.R. Richard	16	1978
8. Larry Dierker	14	1975
J.R. Richard	14	1976
10. J.R. Richard	13	1977
Don Wilson	13	1969
Don Wilson	13	1972

Complete Games: Career with Team

Player	CG	IP
1. Larry Dierker	106	2,294.3
2. Joe Niekro	82	2,270.0
3. Don Wilson	78	1,748.3
4. J.R. Richard	76	1,606.0
5. Mike Scott	42	1,704.0
6. Turk Farrell	41	1,015.0
Bob Knepper	41	1,738.0
8. Mike Cuellar	38	700.3
Nolan Ryan	38	1,854.7
10. Ken Forsch	36	1,493.7

Games Won: Season

Player	W	Year
1. Mike Hampton	22	1999
2. Jose Lima	21	1999
Joe Niekro	21	1979
4. Larry Dierker	20	1969
Joe Niekro	20	1980
Roy Oswalt	20	2004
J.R. Richard	20	1976
Mike Scott	20	1989
Roy Oswalt	20	2005
10. Darryl Kile	19	1997
Roy Oswalt	19	2002
Shane Reynolds	19	1998

Games Won: Career with Team

Player	W	IP
1. Joe Niekro	144	2,270.0
2. Larry Dierker	137	2,294.3
3. Mike Scott	110	1,704.0
4. J.R. Richard	107	1,606.0
5. Nolan Ryan	106	1,854.7
6. Don Wilson	104	1,748.3
7. Shane Reynolds	103	1,622.3
8. Bob Knepper	93	1,738.0
9. Roy Oswalt	83	980.7
10. Ken Forsch	78	1,493.7

Games Lost: Season

Player	L	Year
1. Turk Farrell	20	1962
2. Bob Bruce	18	1965
Doug Drabek	18	1993
4. Ken Johnson	17	1963
Bob Knepper	17	1987
Denny Lemaster	17	1969
7. 10 tied with...	16	——

Games Lost: Career with Team

Player	L	IP
1. Larry Dierker	117	2,294.3
2. Joe Niekro	116	2,270.0
3. Bob Knepper	100	1,738.0
4. Nolan Ryan	94	1,854.7
5. Don Wilson	92	1,748.3
6. Shane Reynolds	86	1,622.3
7. Ken Forsch	81	1,493.7
Mike Scott	81	1,704.0
9. J.R. Richard	71	1,606.0
10. Darryl Kile	65	1,200.0

Winning Percentage: Season

Player	W%	Year
1. Mike Hampton	.846	1999
2. Roy Oswalt	.824	2001
3. Roger Clemens	.818	2004
Mark Portugal	.818	1993

5. Wade Miller	.789	2002
6. Vern Ruhle	.750	1980
7. Bob Knepper	.737	1988
8. Darryl Kile	.731	1997
9. Scott Elarton	.708	2000
10. Jim Deshaies	.706	1986

Winning Percentage: Career with Team

Player	W%	IP
1. Roy Oswalt	.680	980.7
2. Mark Portugal	.634	782.3
3. Mike Hampton	.633	1,026.0
4. J.R. Richard	.601	1,606.0
5. Wade Miller	.598	768.0
6. Pete Harnisch	.577	736.0
7. Mike Scott	.576	1,704.0
8. Danny Darwin	.573	769.0
9. Joe Niekro	.554	2,270.0
10. Shane Reynolds	.545	1,622.3

Shutouts: Season

Player	SHO	Year
1. Dave Roberts	6	1973
2. Larry Dierker	5	1972
Bob Knepper	5	1981
Bob Knepper	5	1986
Joe Niekro	5	1979
Joe Niekro	5	1982
Mike Scott	5	1986
Mike Scott	5	1988
9. 11 tied with...	4	—

Shutouts: Career with Team

Player	SHO	IP
1. Larry Dierker	25	2,294.3
2. Joe Niekro	21	2,270.0
Mike Scott	21	1,704.0
4. Don Wilson	20	1,748.3
5. J.R. Richard	19	1,606.0
6. Bob Knepper	18	1,738.0
7. Nolan Ryan	13	1,854.7
8. Dave Roberts	11	843.7
9. Ken Forsch	9	1,493.7
Tom Griffin	9	863.3

ERA: Season

Player	ERA	Year
1. Roger Clemens	1.87	2005
2. Danny Darwin	2.21	1990
3. Mike Cuellar	2.22	1966
Mike Scott	2.22	1986
5. Larry Dierker	2.33	1969
6. Andy Pettitte	2.39	2005
7. Don Wilson	2.45	1971
8. Joe Niekro	2.47	1982
9. Ken Forsch	2.53	1971
10. Darryl Kile	2.57	1997

ERA: Career with Team

Player	ERA	IP
1. Joe Sambito	2.42	536.0
2. Dave Smith	2.53	762.0
Billy Wagner	2.53	504.3
4. Mike Cuellar	2.74	700.3
5. Roy Oswalt	3.07	980.7
6. Nolan Ryan	3.13	1,854.7
7. Don Wilson	3.15	1,748.3
J.R. Richard	3.15	1,606.0
9. Ken Forsch	3.18	1,493.7
10. Danny Darwin	3.21	769.0

Earned Runs Allowed: Season

Player	ER	Year
1. Jose Lima	145	2000
2. Chris Holt	123	2000
3. Larry Dierker	116	1970
Jerry Reuss	116	1973
5. Bob Knepper	104	1987
6. Larry Dierker	103	1975
Scott Elarton	103	2000
Dave Giusti	103	1967
9. Darryl Kile	102	1996
Joe Niekro	102	1983

Earned Runs Allowed: Career with Team

Player	ER	IP
1. Larry Dierker	837	2,294.3
2. Joe Niekro	811	2,270.0
3. Shane Reynolds	712	1,622.3
4. Bob Knepper	706	1,738.0
5. Nolan Ryan	645	1,854.7
6. Mike Scott	625	1,704.0
7. Don Wilson	611	1,748.3
8. J.R. Richard	562	1,606.0
9. Ken Forsch	528	1,493.7
10. Darryl Kile	505	1,200.0

Strikeouts: Season

Player	K	Year
1. J.R. Richard	313	1979
2. Mike Scott	306	1986
3. J.R. Richard	303	1978
4. Nolan Ryan	270	1987
5. Nolan Ryan	245	1982
6. Don Wilson	235	1969
7. Mike Scott	233	1987
8. Larry Dierker	232	1969
9. Nolan Ryan	228	1988
10. Darryl Kile	219	1996

Strikeouts: Career with Team

Player	K	IP
1. Nolan Ryan	1,866	1,854.7
2. J.R. Richard	1,493	1,606.0
3. Larry Dierker	1,487	2,294.3
4. Mike Scott	1,318	1,704.0
5. Shane Reynolds	1,309	1,622.3
6. Don Wilson	1,283	1,748.3
7. Joe Niekro	1,178	2,270.0
8. Darryl Kile	973	1,200.0
9. Bob Knepper	946	1,738.0
10. Roy Oswalt	850	980.7

Strikeouts Per Nine IP: Season

Player	K/9	Year
1. Nolan Ryan	11.48	1987
2. Mike Scott	10.00	1986
3. J.R. Richard	9.90	1978
4. Nolan Ryan	9.81	1986
5. Nolan Ryan	9.65	1984
6. J.R. Richard	9.64	1979
7. Tom Griffin	9.56	1969
8. Don Wilson	9.40	1969
9. Nolan Ryan	9.33	1988
10. Roger Clemens	9.15	2004

Strikeouts Per Nine IP: Career with Team

Player	K/9	IP
1. Billy Wagner	12.38	504.3
2. Nolan Ryan	9.05	1,854.7
3. J.R. Richard	8.37	1,606.0
4. Roy Oswalt	7.80	980.7
5. Wade Miller	7.72	768.0
6. Darryl Kile	7.30	1,200.0
7. Shane Reynolds	7.26	1,622.3
8. Mike Cuellar	7.16	700.3
9. Pete Harnisch	7.13	736.0
10. Joe Sambito	7.07	536.0

Hits Allowed: Season

Player	HA	Year
1. Jerry Reuss	271	1973
2. Joe Niekro	268	1980

3. Dave Roberts	264	1973
4. Larry Dierker	263	1970
5. Shane Reynolds	257	1998
6. Jose Lima	256	1999
7. Bob Knepper	253	1985
8. Jose Lima	251	2000
9. Shane Reynolds	250	1999
10. Chris Holt	247	2000

HITS ALLOWED: CAREER WITH TEAM

Player	HA	IP
1. Larry Dierker	2,090	2,294.3
2. Joe Niekro	2,052	2,270.0
3. Bob Knepper	1,748	1,738.0
4. Shane Reynolds	1,738	1,622.3
5. Don Wilson	1,479	1,748.3
6. Mike Scott	1,444	1,704.0
7. Nolan Ryan	1,441	1,854.7
8. Ken Forsch	1,439	1,493.7
9. J.R. Richard	1,227	1,606.0
10. Darryl Kile	1,128	1,200.0

HITS ALLOWED PER NINE IP: SEASON

Player	H/9	Year
1. Mike Scott	5.95	1986
2. Nolan Ryan	6.02	1986
3. Nolan Ryan	6.14	1983
4. J.R. Richard	6.28	1978
5. Roger Clemens	6.43	2005
6. Nolan Ryan	6.55	1987
Don Wilson	6.55	1971
8. Mike Scott	6.67	1988
9. J.R. Richard	6.77	1979
10. J.R. Richard	6.84	1976

HITS ALLOWED PER NINE IP: CAREER WITH TEAM

Player	H/9	IP
1. Billy Wagner	5.94	504.3
2. J.R. Richard	6.88	1,606.0
3. Nolan Ryan	6.99	1,854.7
4. Joe Sambito	7.40	536.0
5. Pete Harnisch	7.61	736.0
Don Wilson	7.61	1,748.3
7. Mike Scott	7.63	1,704.0
Dave Smith	7.63	762.0
9. Jim Ray	7.83	565.3
10. Jim Deshaies	7.84	1,102.0

WALKS ALLOWED: SEASON

Player	BB	Year
1. J.R. Richard	151	1976
2. J.R. Richard	141	1978
3. J.R. Richard	138	1975
4. Jerry Reuss	117	1973
5. Nolan Ryan	109	1982
6. Joe Niekro	107	1979
7. J.R. Richard	104	1977
8. Mike Hampton	101	1999
Joe Niekro	101	1983
Nolan Ryan	101	1983

WALKS ALLOWED: CAREER WITH TEAM

Player	BB	IP
1. Joe Niekro	818	2,270.0
2. Nolan Ryan	796	1,854.7
3. J.R. Richard	770	1,606.0
4. Larry Dierker	695	2,294.3
5. Don Wilson	640	1,748.3
6. Darryl Kile	562	1,200.0
7. Bob Knepper	521	1,738.0
8. Mike Scott	505	1,704.0
9. Tom Griffin	441	863.3
10. Ken Forsch	428	1,493.7

WALKS ALLOWED PER NINE IP: SEASON

Player	BB/9	Year
1. Jose Lima	1.23	1998
2. Shane Reynolds	1.44	1999
3. Bob Bruce	1.47	1964
4. Bob Bruce	1.49	1965
5. Turk Farrell	1.51	1965
6. Turk Farrell	1.56	1963
7. Jose Lima	1.61	1999
8. Shane Reynolds	1.66	1996
Ken Forsch	1.66	1980
Andy Pettitte	1.66	2005

WALKS ALLOWED PER NINE IP: CAREER WITH TEAM

Player	BB/9	IP
1. Turk Farrell	1.88	1,015.0
2. Ken Johnson	1.97	690.7
Jose Lima	1.97	804.0
4. Shane Reynolds	1.99	1,622.3
Vern Ruhle	1.99	749.7
6. Greg Swindell	2.03	514.7
7. Roy Oswalt	2.06	980.7
8. Don Nottebart	2.32	508.0
9. Mike Cuellar	2.33	700.3
10. Danny Darwin	2.35	769.0

WHIP (WALKS + HITS PER NINE IP): SEASON

Player	WHIP	Year
1. Mike Scott	0.923	1986
2. Turk Farrell	0.969	1963
3. Mike Scott	0.983	1988
4. Roger Clemens	1.008	2005
5. Larry Dierker	1.022	1969
Don Wilson	1.022	1971
7. Danny Darwin	1.027	1990
8. Andy Pettitte	1.030	2005
9. Mike Scott	1.057	1989
10. Joe Niekro	1.067	1982

WHIP (WALKS + HITS PER NINE IP): CAREER WITH TEAM

Player	WHIP	IP
1. Billy Wagner	1.039	504.3
2. Joe Sambito	1.112	536.0
3. Turk Farrell	1.142	1,015.0
4. Mike Scott	1.144	1,704.0
5. Mike Cuellar	1.162	700.3
6. Danny Darwin	1.164	769.0
7. Ken Johnson	1.174	690.7
8. Roy Oswalt	1.181	980.7
9. Dave Smith	1.189	762.0
10. Pete Harnisch	1.205	736.0

HOME RUNS ALLOWED: SEASON

Player	HRA	Year
1. Jose Lima	48	2000
2. Jose Lima	34	1998
3. Larry Dierker	31	1970
Wade Miller	31	2001
5. Jose Lima	30	1999
6. Scott Elarton	29	2000
7. Mike Scott	27	1990
8. Octavio Dotel	26	2000
Scott Elarton	26	2001
Bob Knepper	26	1984
Bob Knepper	26	1987

HOME RUNS ALLOWED: CAREER WITH TEAM

Player	HRA	IP
1. Larry Dierker	177	2,294.3
2. Shane Reynolds	171	1,622.3
3. Bob Knepper	148	1,738.0
4. Mike Scott	144	1,704.0
5. Joe Niekro	139	2,270.0
6. Jose Lima	133	804.0
7. Don Wilson	119	1,748.3
8. Jim Deshaies	113	1,102.0
9. Nolan Ryan	111	1,854.7
10. Ken Forsch	96	1,493.7

SAVES: SEASON

Player	SV	Year
1. Billy Wagner	44	2003
2. Brad Lidge	42	2005
3. Billy Wagner	39	1999
Billy Wagner	39	2001
5. Doug Jones	36	1992
6. Billy Wagner	35	2002
7. Dave Smith	33	1986
8. Billy Wagner	30	1998
9. Fred Gladding	29	1969
Brad Lidge	29	2004

SAVES: CAREER WITH TEAM

Player	SV	IP
1. Billy Wagner	225	504.3
2. Dave Smith	199	762.0
3. Fred Gladding	76	264.0
4. Joe Sambito	72	536.0
Brad Lidge	72	259.0
6. Doug Jones	62	197.0
7. Ken Forsch	50	1,493.7
8. Frank DiPino	43	291.3
9. Octavio Dotel	42	449.0
10. Todd Jones	39	267.0

WILD PITCHES: SEASON

Player	WP	Year
1. Joe Niekro	21	1985
2. Larry Dierker	20	1968
J.R. Richard	20	1975
4. Joe Niekro	19	1979
Joe Niekro	19	1982
J.R. Richard	19	1979
7. Nolan Ryan	18	1982
8. Bo Belinsky	16	1967
J.R. Richard	16	1978
Nolan Ryan	16	1981
Don Wilson	16	1969

WILD PITCHES: CAREER WITH TEAM

Player	WP	IP
1. Joe Niekro	128	2,270.0
2. Nolan Ryan	104	1,854.7
3. Larry Dierker	102	2,294.3
4. J.R. Richard	92	1,606.0
5. Don Wilson	77	1,748.3
6. Darryl Kile	58	1,200.0
7. Dave Giusti	56	913.3
8. Tom Griffin	55	863.3
9. Shane Reynolds	38	1,622.3
10. Ken Forsch	36	1,493.7
Bob Knepper	36	1,738.0

HIT BATSMEN: SEASON

Player	HB	Year
1. Jack Billingham	16	1971
Darryl Kile	16	1996
3. Darryl Kile	15	1993
4. Wade Blasingame	13	1971
5. Bob Bruce	12	1962
Darryl Kile	12	1995
7. Roy Oswalt	11	2004
8. Jack Billingham	10	1970
Darryl Kile	10	1997
Wade Miller	10	2003
Peter Munro	10	2004
Jerry Reuss	10	1972

HIT BATSMEN: CAREER WITH TEAM

Player	HB	IP
1. Darryl Kile	72	1,200.0
2. Larry Dierker	48	2,294.3
3. Don Wilson	47	1,748.3
4. Nolan Ryan	44	1,854.7
5. Joe Niekro	41	2,270.0
6. Bob Bruce	40	907.0
7. Roy Oswalt	35	980.7
8. Shane Reynolds	33	1,622.3
9. Jack Billingham	31	498.7
10. Mike Scott	30	1,704.0

GAMES FINISHED: SEASON

Player	GF	Year
1. Doug Jones	70	1992
2. Billy Wagner	67	2003
3. Brad Lidge	65	2005
4. Billy Wagner	61	2002
5. Doug Jones	60	1993
6. Billy Wagner	58	2001
7. Billy Wagner	55	1999
8. Joe Sambito	51	1979
Dave Smith	51	1986
10. Billy Wagner	50	1998

GAMES FINISHED: CAREER WITH TEAM

Player	GF	IP
1. Dave Smith	400	762.0
2. Billy Wagner	379	504.3
3. Joe Sambito	229	536.0
4. Ken Forsch	171	1,493.7
5. Fred Gladding	163	264.0
6. Doug Jones	130	197.0
7. Brad Lidge	120	259.0
8. Frank DiPino	119	291.3
9. Frank LaCorte	117	281.7
10. Octavio Dotel	109	449.0

Significant Astros

BAGWELL, JEFF (1B)
(1991–2005)

In what turned out to be one of the worst deals in Red Sox history, Boston traded Jeff Bagwell to Houston in 1990 for pitcher Larry Andersen on the August 31 trading deadline to bolster its pitching staff for the pennant drive. (Andersen pitched in only 15 games for the Red Sox before moving on to free agency.) Meanwhile, Bagwell promptly became the National League Rookie of the Year in 1991. He then won the NL MVP Award in 1994 after posting incredible numbers for the strike-shortened season. In only 110 games, Bagwell hit .368 with 39 home runs and 116 RBIs. He scored 104 runs and finished with a .750 slugging average. The big first baseman finished in the top 10 in the MVP race five more times. He won a Gold Glove in 1994, three Silver Slugger Awards (1994, 1997, 1999), and made the All-Star team four times. Bagwell missed most of the 2005 season due to injury, coming back in the last month of the season in time for the playoffs and Worlds Series, the first for him and the Astros. If he regains his health, he should have a couple more decent years left in him. When he finally retires, Bagwell stands an excellent chance of becoming the first Astros player to be elected to the Hall of Fame, unless Craig Biggio hangs it up sooner.

CAREER ASTROS RECORD:

Games	AB	Hits	Runs
2,150	7,797	2,314	1,517
Avg	**HR**	**RBI**	**SB**
.297	449	1,529	202

BERKMAN, LANCE (OF)
(1999–2005)

The Houston Astros drafted Lance Berkman in the first round of the June 1997 amateur draft with the 16th pick. He has quickly become one of the National League's brightest young stars. After making the team in a late-season call-up in 1999, Berkman arrived for good in 2000. In his first five full seasons, he made the All-Star team three times (2001, 2002, 2004) and placed in the top seven in the MVP balloting each of those years. A switch-hitter who hits for both average and power, Berkman has averaged 30+ homers, 100+ RBIs, and 100+ runs in all but one of his full seasons with the Astros.

CAREER ASTROS RECORD:

Games	AB	Hits	Runs
907	3,151	951	592
Avg	**HR**	**RBI**	**SB**
.302	180	617	44

BIGGIO, CRAIG (C/2B/OF)
(1988–2005)

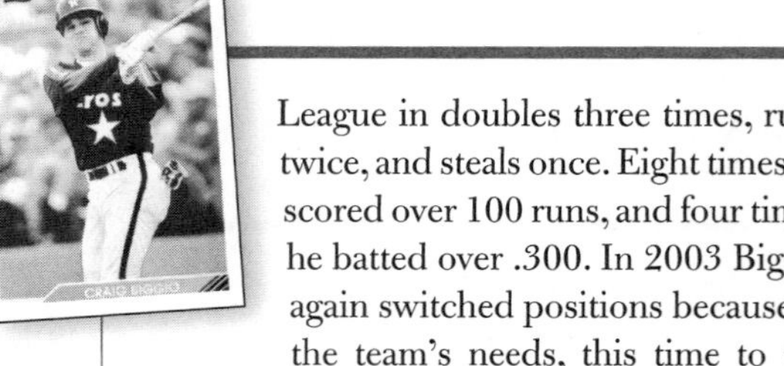

Drafted in the first round of the June 1987 amateur draft, Craig Biggio moved quickly through the minors and joined the big leagues in mid-1988 as a catcher. Fast for a catcher, he averaged 22 stolen bases in his first three full years from 1989 to 1991, a total that only two catchers in history had achieved just one time each. In 1992, in order to protect him from injuries and keep his bat in the lineup, the Astros moved Biggio to second base, a position where he would win four Gold Gloves. A seven-time All-Star, Biggio also won five Silver Slugger Awards, one as catcher and four as a second baseman.

In the late 1990s, the Astros lineup became a potent, run-producing machine. Biggio and several teammates whose last names began with "B" (Bagwell, Berkman, Bell) became known as the Killer Bs. In 1998 Biggio joined Hall of Famer Tris Speaker as the only players to collect 50 doubles and 50 steals in the same season. A durable player who consistently finished in the league's top 10 in games played and at-bats, Biggio also led the National League in doubles three times, runs twice, and steals once. Eight times he scored over 100 runs, and four times he batted over .300. In 2003 Biggio again switched positions because of the team's needs, this time to the outfield. He set the all-time major league record for number of times being hit by a pitch in 2005, eclipsing Don Baylor's long-held record. A consummate team player, he refused to enter the free-agent market several times in his career, opting to remain in Houston for less money; he will likely end his career as a lifelong Astro. After signing another contract for the 2006 season, Biggio appears a lock for Hall of Fame election someday. He has already stolen 400 bases and driven in 1,000 runs, and is nearing 3,000 hits, 300 homers, and 1,700 runs scored.

CAREER ASTROS RECORD:

Games	AB	Hits	Runs
2,564	9,811	2,795	1,697
Avg	**HR**	**RBI**	**SB**
.285	260	1,063	407

CEDEÑO, CESAR (OF)
(1970–1981)

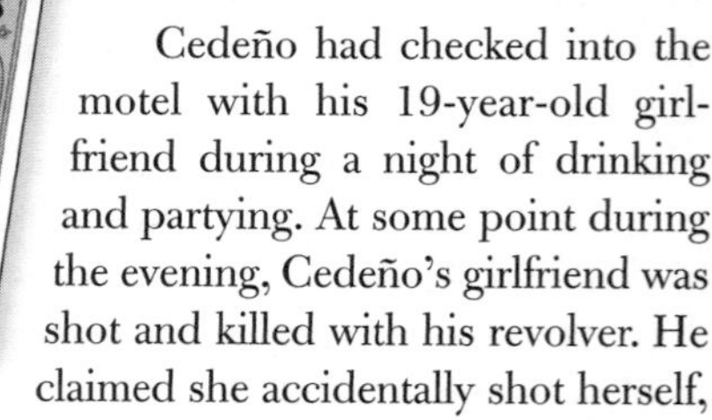

Houston signed Cesar Cedeño out of the Dominican Republic at the age of 16 as an amateur free agent in 1967. Heralded by many as the next Willie Mays, Roberto Clemente, or Hank Aaron, Cedeño lived up to the hype in his first two full seasons, 1972 and 1973. Then, on December 11, 1973, Cedeño's life—and career—took a dramatic turn in a Santo Domingo motel.

Cedeño had checked into the motel with his 19-year-old girlfriend during a night of drinking and partying. At some point during the evening, Cedeño's girlfriend was shot and killed with his revolver. He claimed she accidentally shot herself, but was charged with voluntary manslaughter. While he sat in jail, a forensic test revealed gunpowder residue on his girlfriend's right hand, indicating that she had, indeed, pulled the trigger. The charge was reduced to involuntary manslaughter, and Cedeño faced a potential three-year prison sentence. Instead, he paid a 100-peso fine and was released. On the field, however, he was never the same. He was hounded for many years by hecklers taunting him with "Killer!" In 1981, his last year in Houston, Cedeño charged into the stands in Atlanta and attacked an abusive fan, which resulted in a $5,000 fine and an offseason trade to Cincinnati.

During his 12 years in Houston, Cedeño won five Gold Gloves and was selected to the All-Star team four times. Although he never won the stolen-base title, Cedeño finished in the top four six times, stealing 50 or more bases each time. With his career clearly waning, he played five more seasons with the Reds, Cardinals, and Dodgers before calling it quits.

CAREER ASTROS RECORD:

Games	AB	Hits	Runs
1,512	5,732	1,659	890
Avg	**HR**	**RBI**	**SB**
.289	163	778	487

CLEMENS, ROGER (SP)
(2004–2005)

See Red Sox and Blue Jays bios.

CRUZ, JOSE (OF)
(1975–1987)

After playing five years for the St. Louis Cardinals, outfielder Jose Cruz was purchased by the Astros on October 24, 1974. He quickly became a fan favorite in Houston, six times hitting over .300 and leading the Astros in RBIs seven times. A two-time All-Star, Cruz won Silver Slugger Awards in 1983 and 1984, and finished his Houston career as the Astros' all-time leader in games played, at-bats, hits, triples, and RBIs. Cruz left Houston after the 1987 season and signed as a free agent with the Yankees, playing part of the year before retiring. He is the father of major leaguer Jose Cruz Jr., and the brother of former major leaguers Hector and Tommy.

CAREER ASTROS RECORD:

Games	AB	Hits	Runs
1,870	6,629	1,937	871
Avg	**HR**	**RBI**	**SB**
.292	138	942	288

DIERKER, LARRY (SP)
(1964–1976)

On September 22, 1964, pitcher Larry Dierker celebrated his 18th birthday by striking out Willie Mays in the first inning of his major league debut. Highly sought by no fewer than 18 major league teams, Dierker had signed with Houston as a 17-year-old just before the 1964 season began; he was the youngest player in the majors that year. He went on to become Houston's first 20-game winner (1969) and holder of nearly every Astros pitching record by the time he retired. After four near misses, the two-time All-Star finally achieved a no-hitter on July 9, 1976, when he beat the Expos.

After 13 seasons in Houston, Dierker was traded to St. Louis on November 23, 1976. He pitched in only 11 games for the Cardinals before retiring in 1977, whereupon he joined the Astros' front office. In 1979 he moved to the team's broadcast booth, where he remained for 18 years. He was then given the opportunity to manage the team in 1997 and, despite the howls of critics, promptly led the Astros to their first division title in 11 years, then repeated it in 1998, winning the NL's Manager of the Year Award in the process. By the time he won his third consecutive division title in 1999, his critics had long since been silenced. He added a fourth division title in 2001, making it four in five years, before returning to the broadcast booth.

CAREER ASTROS RECORD:

W	L	W%	ERA	SV
137	117	.539	3.28	1

K	BB	SHO	IP
1,487	695	25	2,294.3

MORGAN, JOE (2B)
(1963–1971, 1980)

After getting passed over in baseball's annual free-agent draft in 1962, largely due to his small stature, Joe Morgan signed with the Houston Colt .45s as an amateur free agent on November 1, 1962 and joined the team in 1963. After playing just a few games with Houston in both 1963 and 1964, Morgan finally made the team as a regular in 1965. Under Hall of Famer Nellie Fox's tutelage, the young second baseman developed his signature arm flap while waiting at the plate for the pitch—a timing mechanism and reminder to keep his shoulder up. A two-time All-Star with Houston, Morgan was traded on November 29, 1971, as part of an eight-player deal. He landed in Cincinnati, where his career skyrocketed. *(See Reds bio.)*

CAREER ASTROS RECORD:

Games	AB	Hits	Runs
1,032	3,729	972	597

Avg	HR	RBI	SB
.261	72	327	219

NIEKRO, JOE (SP)
(1975–1985)

After bouncing among four teams over eight years and compiling a record of 58–63, Joe Niekro was purchased from the Atlanta Braves by the Astros on April 6, 1975. He stayed put for the next 11 years, becoming Houston's all-time winningest pitcher with 144 wins, a record that still stands today. Joe had a decent fastball and curve, but his transformation occurred just before he joined Houston. During his stint in Atlanta, his brother, Hall of Fame knuckleball pitcher Phil, taught him how to throw the knuckler, which dramatically changed his effectiveness. Niekro was a relief pitcher his first two years before becoming a starter. In 1979 he led the National League in victories with 21 and shutouts with five. He made the All-Star team and was runner-up to Bruce Sutter for the Cy Young Award. Niekro was a 20-game winner again in 1980, leading the Astros to their first division title. In Game 3 of the LCS, he pitched 10 scoreless innings of a game won by Houston 1–0 in 11 innings. In 1981, the Astros made the playoffs again, and he pitched another stellar game, this time eight scoreless innings in another 11-inning, 1–0 game. After three more fine seasons with Houston, Niekro was traded to the Yankees near the end of the 1985 campaign, spending the last three-plus seasons of his career with New York and Minnesota. In all, Niekro spent 11 of his 22 major league seasons with the Astros. In the rarefied category of most pitching wins by two brothers, he and brother Phil won nine more games than Gaylord and Jim Perry, 538 to 529.

CAREER ASTROS RECORD:

W	L	W%	ERA	SV
144	116	.554	3.22	9
K	BB	SHO	IP	
1,178	818	21	2,270.0	

OSWALT, ROY (SP)
(2001–2005)

After only five years, Roy Oswalt has become a force to be reckoned with in the National League. Considering that he wasn't drafted until the 23rd round of the June 1996 free-agent draft, Houston management should consider itself lucky that he became a member of the Astros at all. Oswalt has maintained an incredible winning percentage and strikeout-to-walk ratio in each of his five years in the league. In 2001, 2002, and 2004 he finished in the top five of the NL's Cy Young Award balloting. He finished first in the NL in winning percentage in 2001 (.824), first in wins in 2004 (20), and made his first All-Star Game appearance in 2005. Oswalt's gritty performance, winning 20 games for the second straight year in 2005, helped the Astros win the Wild Card spot and make it to their first-ever World Series.

CAREER ASTROS RECORD:

W	L	W%	ERA	SV
83	39	.680	3.07	0
K	BB	SHO	IP	
850	225	4	980.7	

PUHL, TERRY (OF)
(1977–1990)

The Astros signed Canadian-born Terry Puhl as a free-agent amateur on September 19, 1973. Puhl finally made it to the majors in mid-1977, and after becoming a regular in 1978, he batted .289 with 32 stolen bases, and made it to the All-Star Game as Houston's only representative that season. While never spectacular, Puhl was a solid all-around player. He excelled defensively, retiring as the major league record holder among outfielders in fielding percentage at .9932. In 15 major league seasons, Puhl committed only 18 errors. After 14 seasons with the Astros, Puhl was granted free agency after the 1990 season, but only collected 18 at-bats with Kansas City before retiring after the 1991 season.

CAREER ASTROS RECORD:

Games	AB	Hits	Runs
1,516	4,837	1,357	676
Avg	**HR**	**RBI**	**SB**
.281	62	432	217

REYNOLDS, SHANE (SP)
(1992–2002)

Shane Reynolds was drafted by the Astros in the third round of the June 1989 amateur draft. He pitched in a few games in the 1992 and 1993 seasons before making the club for good in 1994. Reynolds was a steady, if unspectacular player who won 103 games during his 11-year Astros career, using a nasty split-finger fastball as his out pitch. His lone All-Star appearance was in 2000. Reynolds was released by Houston just before the start of the 2003 season and was picked up by Atlanta.

CAREER ASTROS RECORD:

W	L	W%	ERA	SV
103	86	.545	3.95	0
K	**BB**	**SHO**	**IP**	
1,309	358	7	1,622.3	

RICHARD, J.R. (SP)
(1971–1980)

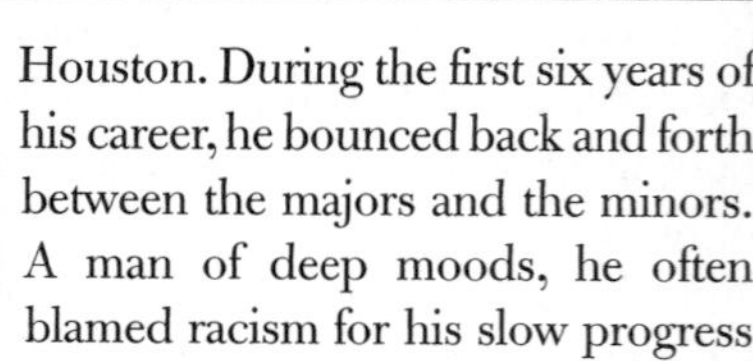

The Houston Astros used the second overall pick to select the 6'8" tall James Rodney Richard in the June 1969 amateur draft. Richard had excelled at three sports in high school—football, basketball, and baseball—and had received more than 200 scholarship offers, but opted for the $100,000 bonus offered by Houston. During the first six years of his career, he bounced back and forth between the majors and the minors. A man of deep moods, he often blamed racism for his slow progress through the Astros system; the Astros, on the other hand, attributed his slow development to his wildness and poor fielding.

The evidence is with the Astros, because even after making the team for good in 1975, Richard led the National League in walks three times and had two seasons in which his fielding averages were .853 and .902, abysmal to say the least. But when he was on his game, he was terrific. With a 100-mph fastball and a 94-mph slider, both of them made more intimidating by his wildness, Richard was truly feared by National League batters. Even teammate Bob Watson once said of J.R., "I've never taken batting practice against him and I never will. I have a family to think about." Richard reached the upper echelon of pitching in 1978 and 1979 when he struck out more than 300 batters each year, becoming the first National League right-hander to do so.

In 1980, his lone All-Star year, J.R. Richard was almost unhittable, holding a 10–4 record and a 1.89 ERA at the All-Star break, when trouble hit. He had been complaining about a "dead arm" for most of the season, but some of his critics discounted him as lazy, gutless, jealous of Nolan Ryan's contract, or suffering from drug abuse. In a July 14 start, a wobbly Richard appeared dazed and had trouble seeing his catcher's signs. He was diagnosed as having a blocked artery leading to his right arm, but doctors felt it wasn't threatening. After spending two weeks on the disabled list, Richard returned to duty. But while playing catch on the sidelines with one of his teammates, Richard collapsed. It was discovered that he had a blood clot in his brain that had caused a stroke. As his wife Carolyn put it at the time, "It took death, or nearly death, to get an apology. They should have believed him." The entire left side of Richard's body was paralyzed. Surgery and therapy eventually allowed him to regain the use of his arm and leg, but the facial paralysis had left his speech impaired. He tried a comeback in the minor leagues, but it was a dismal failure. He then went through two bad marriages and lost all his money in a series of poor investments, ultimately joining the ranks of the homeless. Richard was found living under a bridge in 1994 and was taken in by a local church, where he became a minister and turned his life around, establishing baseball programs for kids in the Houston area.

CAREER ASTROS RECORD:

W	L	W%	ERA	SV
107	71	.601	3.15	0

K	BB	SHO	IP
1,493	770	19	1,606.0

RYAN, NOLAN (SP)
(1980–1988)

Hall of Famer Nolan Ryan spent more seasons with the Astros (nine) than with any of the other teams he played with in his 27-year major league career. He came to the Astros through free agency after playing five years with the Mets and eight with the Angels. His brand-new $4.5 million dollar four-year contract made him baseball's first $1 million-a-year player. On September 26, 1981, Ryan pitched a record fifth no-hitter as he defeated the Dodgers. Then on April 27, 1983, he broke Walter Johnson's career record for strikeouts. In 1987, "the Ryan Express" had one of the most inexplicable years ever recorded by a pitcher: He struck out 270 batters in 211 innings, becoming the only pitcher to record 2,000 strikeouts in each league, and his ERA was 2.76, yet his win-loss record stood at 8–16. As a result, he became the first pitcher in history to lead the league in strikeouts and ERA, but not win the Cy Young Award.

Although he is the reigning all-time strikeout king, led the National League in ERA for two of his Houston years, and twice led in strikeouts, he never won a Cy Young. After the 1988 season, the Astros offered him a contract with a 20 percent cut in salary, so the two-time Astro All-Star left via free agency, this time landing with Houston's cross-state rivals, the Texas Rangers, where he would play five more years before retiring. *(See Angels and Rangers bios.)*

CAREER ASTROS RECORD:

W	L	W%	ERA	SV
106	94	.530	3.13	0
K	BB	SHO	IP	
1,866	796	13	1,854.7	

SCOTT, MIKE (SP)
(1983–1991)

Mike Scott was, at best, a mediocre pitcher barely hanging onto a major league job when the New York Mets gave up on him and traded him to the Astros on December 10, 1982, for outfielder Danny Heep. With the Mets, Scott had compiled a dismal 14–27 record and an ERA around 5.00; he was only a little better in his first two seasons with Houston, going 15–17 with a 4.25 ERA. Then third baseman Enos Cabell suggested that he try the split-finger fastball like the one used with success by Bruce Sutter. Cabell had spent two years in Detroit, where he observed Tiger pitching coach Roger Craig's tutelage of Jack Morris, whom Craig had turned into a 20-game winner almost overnight. Scott contacted Craig, who was in between jobs at the time and agreed to work with Scott over the winter before the 1985 season.

The turnaround was staggering. In 1985 Scott posted an 18–8 record and 3.29 ERA. He had 137 strikeouts, a modest total, but it was nearly twice as many as he had posted before. In 1986, Scott was phenomenal, going 18–10 with a 2.22 ERA and 306 strikeouts, both totals leading the league. On September 25, he pitched a no-hitter against the Giants to clinch the pennant. In the NLCS against the Mets, he dominated—winning both of his games, giving up a total of one run, and striking out 19 batters in 18 innings. Fortunately for the Mets, they won the series in six games, the last two in extra innings, because in a seventh and deciding game they would have faced Scott.

Even though the Astros lost the series, Scott was voted the NLCS MVP. The following month he was awarded the Cy Young. Scott was so unhittable and his turnaround so sudden that opposing hitters began to complain that he must be doctoring the baseball. However, no evidence was ever found. Scott led the National League with 20 wins in 1989, the only year of his career he would cross that threshold, and finished second to reliever Mark Davis of the Padres in Cy Young balloting. After suffering through two final seasons plagued by arm troubles, Scott, a three-time NL All-Star, retired after the 1991 season.

CAREER ASTROS RECORD:

W	L	W%	ERA	SV
110	81	.576	3.30	0
K	BB	SHO	IP	
1,318	505	21	1,704.0	

SMITH, DAVE (RP)
(1980–1990)

Dave Smith became an Astro when he was selected in the eighth round of the June 1976 amateur draft. After making the big-league roster in 1980, he played 11 of his 13 major league seasons with Houston, retiring as the franchise leader in saves and appearances. Although Smith, a two-time All-Star, had a long and successful career with Houston, he will forever be remembered for blowing his only two save opportunities in the 1986 NLCS against the Mets: the first in Game 3 and the second in Game 6, the series' final game.

CAREER ASTROS RECORD:

W	L	W%	ERA	SV
53	47	.530	2.53	199

K	BB	SHO	IP
529	260	0	762.0

WAGNER, BILLY (RP)
(1995–2003)

Drafted by the Astros in the first round of the June 1993 amateur draft, Wagner used a blazing fastball to become Houston's career leader in saves, surpassing Dave Smith. With the exception of one injury-plagued year (2000), Wagner's ERA has always been in the 1.00s and 2.00s. He averaged more than 12 strikeouts per nine innings pitched for his Astros career before he was traded to the Phillies on November 3, 2003 for three players, ending the three-time All-Star's nine-year career with Houston.

CAREER ASTROS RECORD:

W	L	W%	ERA	SV
26	29	.473	2.53	225

K	BB	SHO	IP
694	191	0	504.3

WATSON, BOB (OF/1B)
(1966–1979)

Eighteen-year-old Bob Watson signed with the Astros on January 31, 1965 as an amateur free agent. After playing in a handful of games with Houston in 1966 and 1967, he made the team as a role player in 1968 and a regular in 1971. Watson, a two-time All-Star who hit over .300 four times for the Astros, was the right fielder of the early 1970s outfield that included Jimmy Wynn and Cesar Cedeño. After Lee May was traded to Baltimore, Watson took over as the team's first baseman, playing for the next 4½ seasons until he was traded to Boston on June 13, 1979. During the 1976 season, Major League Baseball was actively promoting the upcoming one-millionth run in baseball history with much fanfare. Watson scored that run. He is also the only player in history to have hit for the cycle in both leagues, the first time with Houston, the second with Boston. After his playing career ended, Watson became the first

African American general manager of a major league team when Houston hired him after the 1993 season. He left in 1995 to take the same position with the Yankees.

CAREER ASTROS RECORD:

Games	AB	Hits	Runs
1,381	4,883	1,448	640
Avg	**HR**	**RBI**	**SB**
.297	139	782	21

WILSON, DON (SP)
(1966–1974)

Hard-throwing Don Wilson was signed by the Colt .45s as an amateur free agent prior to the 1964 season and played his entire nine-year major league career with Houston. Wilson was labeled as a troublemaker, probably unfairly, by two Astros managers, Leo Durocher and Harry Walker. He was a winning pitcher on a losing club during that span, and is one of only a handful of pitchers to have tossed more than one no-hitter in his career. The first came on June 18, 1967, against Atlanta, and the second came two years later against Cincinnati. He had a shot for a third, but manager Preston Gomez, in a controversial move, took Wilson out of a September 4, 1974 game against the Reds after eight no-hit innings. He had another remarkable game on July 14, 1968 against Cincinnati when he tied the then-major league record held by Bob Feller and Sandy Koufax by striking out 18 batters in a game. Wilson, who had a history of being troubled, committed suicide by carbon monoxide poisoning four months later, at the age of 29. The tragedy cut short a career that could have been spectacular.

CAREER ASTROS RECORD:

W	L	W%	ERA	SV
104	92	.531	3.15	2
K	**BB**	**SHO**	**IP**	
1.283	640	20	1,748.3	

WYNN, JIMMY (OF)
(1963–1973)

Outfielder Jimmy Wynn was selected by the Colt .45s from the Cincinnati Reds as part of the National League's 1962 expansion draft. Small in stature but with an explosive bat, he earned the nickname "the Toy Cannon." The best year of his career came in 1967 when he slugged 37 homers and had 107 RBIs while scoring 102 runs. This led to his one selection (as an Astro) to the NL All-Star team. After spending the first 11 years of his 15-year major league career with Houston, Wynn was traded to the Dodgers for pitcher Claude Osteen after the 1973 season. With his skills rapidly declining, Wynn played for four different teams over the next four years before retiring at the age of 35.

CAREER ASTROS RECORD:

Games	AB	Hits	Runs
1,426	5,063	1,291	829
Avg	**HR**	**RBI**	**SB**
.255	223	719	180

Kansas City Royals

Since 1969

1976 Team Ball

1977 The Royals win 102 games, making them the first expansion team in history to lead the major leagues in victories.... **1984** The Detroit Tigers so dominate their 1984 playoff sweep of Kansas City that the Royals never once hold a lead in any game of the series.... **1990** George Brett becomes the first player in history to win batting titles in three decades when he hits .329 in 1990 (his other two titles came in 1980 and 1976).... **1996** The Royals finish last in their division, after going 27 seasons without finishing in the cellar—quite a feat considering that Kansas City is the least populated market in the major leagues.

FRANCHISE HISTORY

The Kansas City Royals (the nickname was chosen in a fan vote) began play in 1969 after being awarded a franchise in 1968. Not coincidentally, Congress was threatening Major League Baseball with a revocation of its antitrust exemption—the legislation having been led by Missouri Senator Stuart Symington after Missouri lost the Kansas City A's to Oakland following the 1967 season. The Royals joined the Seattle Pilots as the 11th and 12th teams in the American League, while the National League expanded to 12 teams as well with the additions of San Diego and Montreal. Both leagues then split into two six-team divisions. The American League owners had actually approved the move of the Kansas City A's to Oakland in the fall of 1967 with the understanding that two new teams would be added to the league in Seattle and Kansas City no later than 1971.

The Royals franchise was awarded to Kansas City pharmaceutical magnate Ewing Kauffman, who had made his fortune by turning Marion Laboratories, a company he founded in 1950, into a health care giant. Kauffman, however, had to be persuaded to buy the team since he had little interest in baseball. He only bought the team as a civic venture after intense lobbying by local community leaders. He sold 19,000 shares of his company's stock to purchase the team. (In 1989 he sold his share of the company for $675 million.)

When the Royals finished fourth in their inaugural 1969 season with a first-year record of 69–93, they were surprisingly adept at winning one-run games, taking 31 of 59.

George Brett in 1983.

Kauffman become ill in the early 1980s, and, wanting to make sure the team remained in Kansas City after his death, entered into an agreement with Avron Fogelman, a Memphis real estate businessman, that would give Fogelman a stake in the club and transfer majority ownership of the team to him by 1991. Fogelman, however, ran into financial difficulty and, despite a large loan from Kauffman, the deal fell through. When Kauffman became terminally ill, a five-member board was chosen to run the team after his death until a buyer could be found who would keep the team in Kansas City. David Glass, the president of Wal-Mart, was elected CEO of the Royals after Kauffman's death on August 1, 1993. The IRS eventually approved an ownership structure that designated the team as a city-held charity called the Greater Kansas City Community Foundation and Affiliated Trust, and gave the city until 2001 to find a buyer. In 1995 former Royals player George Brett led an investment group that reportedly included radio talk show host Rush Limbaugh (himself a former Royals front-office employee) in a $100 million bid to buy the team, but again the deal fell through. In 1998 New York attor-

Bret Saberhagen hugs George Brett after his five-hitter gives Kansas City a World Series victory over St. Louis.

ney Miles Prentice announced an agreement to purchase the team for $75 million, but that deal fell through as well. Finally, with time running out, Glass purchased the team himself in 2000 for $96 million. On the field, the Royals had a respectable first season, going 69–93 and finishing fourth in the new six-team division format. Just two years later, in 1971, the team finished second with a very respectable 85–76 record. The Royals made a few astute trades, but by and large they developed their players from within their own minor league system. In 1976 the team won its first divisional title, finishing three games ahead of the Oakland A's, but lost a heartbreaking fifth and deciding game in the ALCS to the Yankees when Chris Chambliss hit a home run in the bottom of the ninth. In 1977 the Royals finished with the best record in all of baseball, winning 102 games. But once again, they met the Yankees in the playoffs and lost the deciding fifth game in the ninth inning, this time 5–3, with New York scoring three runs in their last at-bat. Proving that bad things always happen in threes, the Royals met the Yankees yet again in 1978, this time losing in four games after leading late in each of the last two games. Kansas City made amends in 1980, when they romped to the division title and then swept the Yankees in the playoffs. The team was led by third baseman George Brett, who made a valiant run at .400, finally ending the season at .390. However, in their first World Series appearance the Royals lost to the Phillies, four games to two. The Royals won their division again in 1981 and 1984, but were swept in the playoffs both years, by the A's and Tigers respectively, continuing their postseason frustration.

Then came 1985. First, the team nosed out the Angels by one game for the AL West division title. Next they defeated the Blue Jays in an exciting seven-game playoff for the AL championship. Finally, they won an exciting seven-game World Series from their cross-state rivals, the St. Louis Cardinals, with the help of a very controversial umpiring call. Trailing 1–0 going into the bottom of the ninth of Game 6, the Royals received two gifts, one from the first-base umpire who erroneously called a Royals batter safe, and the second from Cardinals' first baseman Jack Clark, who muffed a foul pop-up after which Steve Balboni got a hit to keep the rally going. The resulting 2–1 win in Game 6 kept the Royals alive, and in Game 7 they blew out the discouraged Cards, 11–0, to win the franchise's first World Series title. Royals fans still savor that victory today, because it marked the last time their team would make it to the playoffs for more than 20 years (and counting).

TEAM NAME HISTORY

Official Names

Royals

Unofficial Names/Nicknames

None

STADIUM HISTORY

Municipal Stadium	1969–1972
Royals Stadium	1973–1993
Kauffman Stadium	1994–current

(Royals Stadium renamed, mid-1993)

YEARLY RECORD, FINISH, & ATTENDANCE FIGURES

Year	League	Record	DIV/LG Finish	Attendance	Avg/Gm
2005	AL Cent	56–106	5	1,371,181	16,928
2004	AL Cent	58–104	5	1,661,478	20,768
2003	AL Cent	83–79	3	1,779,895	22,249
2002	AL Cent	62–100	4	1,323,036	16,334
2001	AL Cent	65–97	5	1,536,371	18,968
2000	AL Cent	77–85	4	1,564,847	19,319
1999	AL Cent	64–97	4	1,506,068	18,826
1998	AL Cent	72–89	3	1,494,875	18,686
1997	AL Cent	67–94	5	1,517,638	18,970
1996	AL Cent	75–86	5	1,435,997	17,950
1995	AL Cent	70–74	2	1,233,530	17,132
1994	AL Cent	64–51	3	1,400,494	23,737
1993	AL West	84–78	3	1,934,578	23,884
1992	AL West	72–90	5	1,867,689	23,058
1991	AL West	82–80	6	2,161,537	26,686
1990	AL West	75–86	6	2,244,956	27,716
1989	AL West	92–70	2	2,477,700	30,589
1988	AL West	84–77	3	2,350,181	29,377
1987	AL West	83–79	2	2,392,471	29,537
1986	AL West	76–86	3	2,320,794	28,652
1985	AL West	91–71	1	2,162,717	26,375
1984	AL West	84–78	1	1,810,018	22,346
1983	AL West	79–83	2	1,963,875	23,950
1982	AL West	90–72	2	2,284,464	28,203
1981	AL West	50–53	5/1	1,279,403	27,221
1980	AL West	97–65	1	2,288,714	28,256
1979	AL West	85–77	2	2,261,845	27,924
1978	AL West	92–70	1	2,255,493	27,846
1977	AL West	102–60	1	1,852,603	22,872
1976	AL West	90–72	1	1,680,265	20,744
1975	AL West	91–71	2	1,151,836	14,220
1974	AL West	77–85	5	1,173,292	14,485
1973	AL West	88–74	2	1,345,341	16,609
1972	AL West	76–78	4	707,656	9,190
1971	AL West	85–76	2	910,784	11,244
1970	AL West	65–97	4	693,047	8,773
1969	AL West	69–93	4	902,414	11,005

MANAGER HISTORY

Manager	Years	W–L	Win %
Joe Gordon	1969	69–93	.426
Charlie Metro	1970	19–33	.365
Bob Lemon	1970–1972	207–218	.487
Jack McKeon	1973–1975	215–205	.512
Whitey Herzog	1975–1979	410–304	.574
Jim Frey	1980–1981	127–105	.547
Dick Howser	1981–1986	404–365	.525
Mike Ferraro	1986	36–38	.486
Billy Gardner	1987	62–64	.492
John Wathan	1987–1991	287–270	.515
Bob Schaefer	1991	1–0	1.000
Hal McRae	1991–1994	286–277	.508
Bob Boone	1995–1997	181–206	.468
Tony Muser	1997–2002	317–431	.424
John Mizerock	2002	5–8	.385
Tony Peña	2002–2005	198–285	.410
Bob Schaefer	2005	5–12	.294
Buddy Bell	2005	43–69	.384

ALL-TIME WIN-LOSS RECORDS VS. ALL OPPONENTS

Opponent	W–L
ALL-TIME	2,872–2,982
Angels	243–239
Astros	5–13
Athletics	218–267
Blue Jays	155–155
Braves	2–1
Brewers	198–162
Cardinals	14–19
Cubs	6–9
Devil Rays	33–34
Diamondbacks	4–4
Dodgers	4–2
Giants	4–2
Indians	233–232
INTERLEAGUE	66–91
Mariners	182–164
Marlins	1–2
Mets	3–3
Nationals	1–5
Orioles	174–221
Padres	2–4
Phillies	1–2
Pirates	9–8
Rangers	244–218
Reds	3–5
Red Sox	197–188
Rockies	2–4
Tigers	244–218
Twins	267–282
White Sox	254–281
Yankees	164–231

Franchise Highlights, Low Points, and Strange Distinctions

1972 In an exceptional display of hitting finesse for a fourth-year expansion team, the young Royals had four hitters among the AL's top 10: Lou Piniella was the runner-up to Rod Carew for the batting title at .312; Richie Scheinblum finished sixth in the batting race at .300; young slugger John Mayberry finished seventh, batting .298, and Amos Otis came in ninth with a .293 average.

....

1976–77 When the Royals won their first division title in 1976, they nearly blew the nine-game lead they held on August 28, finishing with a 12–22 record over their last 34 games, including a 1–7 record in their last eight games. But when they won their second division title in 1977, they won it going away, at one point winning 16 games in a row, the most in the majors in 24 years. They also won 24 of 25 in one stretch, finishing with the best record in baseball (102–60). The only game that kept the Royals from attaining a 25-game winning streak from August 31 to September 25 was a 4–1 loss at home to Seattle on September 16.

....

1979 Darrell Porter became only the second catcher in American League history to collect more than 100 runs, RBIs, and walks in a season. Hall of Famer Mickey Cochrane was the other, accomplishing the feat for the Philadelphia A's in 1932.

1980 The Royals' incredible season was fueled by two batters, Willie Wilson and George Brett. Wilson became the first player to accumulate more than 700 at-bats in a season (705), stole 79 bases, led the majors in runs scored with 133 and in hits with 230, stroking more than 100 from each side of the plate. George Brett, whose run at .400 fell short when he finished the season hitting .390, had 118 RBIs in just 117 games, the first player to have more RBIs than games played since Walt Dropo had 144 RBIs in 136 games for the Boston Red Sox in 1950.

Catcher Jamie Quirk and pitcher Dan Quisenberry became the first "Q" battery in major league history when they appeared together in an April 13, 1980 game against the Tigers.

....

1982 John Wathan's 36 stolen bases set a major league record for catchers.

Willie Wilson won the American League batting title in 1982, but he had to sweat it out, partially because he took the less-than-admirable path of choosing to sit out the season's last game in order to protect his lead over Milwaukee's Robin Yount. Yount, meanwhile, collected three hits in his last game in a valiant effort to catch Wilson, but came up one point shy, .331 to Wilson's .332.

Dennis Leonard's six-year run of being the winningest right-handed pitcher in the major leagues ended in 1982 due to a severe injury. When Buddy Bell of the Rangers smashed a line drive back at the Kansas City ace's head, Leonard put up his hand to protect his face. The ball shattered two of his fingers and he missed nearly three months.

1983 Kansas City's 1983 season epitomized frustration. From a plethora of injuries to key players, to a federal drug investigation that eventually netted four players short prison sentences, the Royals just seemed cursed. When George Brett's famous "Pine Tar Incident" took place on July 24, Kansas City was just a game out of first. After the Pine Tar game, Brett hit just .254 the rest of the way and the Royals ended up 20 games behind the first-place White Sox.

• • • •

1984 Dan Quisenberry's 44 saves marked the first time in major league history that a reliever recorded at least 40 saves in consecutive seasons.

• • • •

1987 When Kevin Seitzer collected 207 hits, he became just the 13th major leaguer in history to get 200 hits in his rookie season. Batting .323, he also had 15 homers, 83 RBIs, and 100 runs while shattering virtually every Royals rookie record. Seitzer finished second to Oakland's Mark McGwire in the American League Rookie of the Year voting. When he hit .304 for the 1988 season, Seitzer became the first Royals player ever to hit .300 in his first two seasons.

• • • •

1989 After collecting 44 saves and winning the National League's Cy Young Award for San Diego, Mark Davis signed a big free-agent contract with Kansas City before the 1990 season. For Kansas City, however, he was awful. He ended the 1990 season with a 2–7 record, 5.11 ERA, and six saves, only one of which came after May 11.

1995 The Royals were on the short end of the largest discrepancy in major league history between first and second place teams when the Royals finished second to Cleveland, 30 games out, in the American League Central Division.

• • • •

1998 The Royals performed quite oddly in 1998. They had the worst home record in the majors at 29–51, yet they had one of the best road records at 43–38.

• • • •

1999 Several players had remarkable hitting performances in 1999. First, Carlos Beltran became the first major league rookie to reach 100 RBIs and 100 runs in his first season. Mike Sweeney tied the American League record by collecting at least one RBI in 13 straight games. And Mark Quinn became the fourth player in major league history to hit two home runs in his first game, accomplishing the feat in an 8–6 loss to Anaheim on September 14.

Sadly, Kansas City's bullpen in 1999 actually blew more saves (30) than it recorded (29).

• • • •

2000 In April, the Royals won six straight games in their last at-bat.

• • • •

2001 Impatient outfielder Mark Quinn had an incredible stretch of 241 consecutive plate appearances without receiving an unintentional walk. In 473 plate appearances that season, he walked only 12 times.

1991, 2005 Bob Schaefer compiled both the best and worst winning percentages in the team's history during his two managerial stints for the Royals. He was 1–0 in 1991 (1.000), and 5–12 in 2005 (.294).

Only twice in American League history have players hit three homers in a game on Opening Day, and the Royals allowed both of them. Toronto's George Bell hit three against Kansas City on April 4, 1988, and Detroit's Dmitri Young did the same on April 4, 2005.

2004 When the Kansas City Royals lost 104 games, it established a new franchise record for futility, and marked only the second time since the team's inception in 1969 that they broke the 100 mark in losses. Fans didn't have to wait long for their fortunes to change, because in 2005 they got worse—the Royals lost 106 games to break their own year-old record.

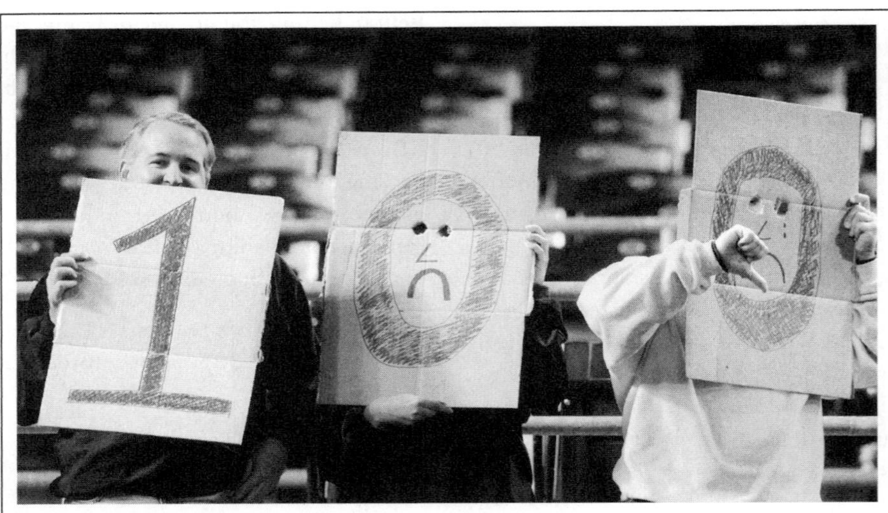

Royals fans celebrate the team's 100th loss of the 2004 season. They went on to lose 104.

Special Achievements

WORLD SERIES RESULTS

Year	Opponent	Result	Games
1980	Philadelphia	Lost	4–2
1985	St. Louis	Won	4–3

WORLD SERIES MANAGERIAL RECORDS

Manager	Series Record	Games Record
Jim Frey	0–1	2–4
Dick Howser	1–0	4–3

ALL-TIME POSTSEASON RECORD

Divisional Playoffs	0–0
League Championship Series	12–15
World Series	6–7

ALL-STAR GAMES AT ROYALS STADIUM

Year	Date	Winner	Score
1973	July 24	National	7–1

HALL OF FAMERS WHO PLAYED FOR TEAM

	Position	Years	Games with Kansas City
George Brett	3B	1973–1993	2,707
Orlando Cepeda	DH	1974	33
Harmon Killebrew	DH	1975	106
Gaylord Perry	SP	1983	14

HALL OF FAMERS WHO MANAGED TEAM

	Years	Games with Kansas City
Bob Lemon	1970–1972	425

MVP AWARD WINNERS

George Brett	3B	1980

CY YOUNG AWARD WINNERS

Pitcher	Year	W–L	ERA
Bret Saberhagen	1985	20–6	2.87
Bret Saberhagen	1989	23–6	2.16
David Cone	1994	16–5	2.94

ROOKIE OF THE YEAR AWARD WINNERS

Lou Piniella	OF	1969
Bob Hamelin	DH	1994
Carlos Beltran	OF	1999
Angel Berroa	SS	2003

GOLD GLOVE WINNERS

Year	Position	Player
1971	OF	Amos Otis
1973	OF	Amos Otis
1974	OF	Amos Otis
1977	2B	Frank White
	OF	Al Cowens
1978	2B	Frank White
1979	2B	Frank White
1980	2B	Frank White
	OF	Willie Wilson
1981	2B	Frank White
1982	2B	Frank White
1985	3B	George Brett
1986	2B	Frank White
1987	2B	Frank White
1989	SP	Bret Saberhagen
	C	Bob Boone
2000	OF	Jermaine Dye

TRIPLE CROWN WINNERS

None

FIREMAN OF THE YEAR AWARD WINNERS

Dan Quisenberry	1980
Dan Quisenberry	1982
Dan Quisenberry	1983
Dan Quisenberry	1984
Dan Quisenberry	1985
Jeff Montgomery	1993

WORLD SERIES MVP

Bret Saberhagen	1985

LEAGUE CHAMPIONSHIP SERIES MVP

Frank White	1980
George Brett	1985

ALL-STAR GAME MVP

Bo Jackson	1989

MANAGER OF THE YEAR AWARD WINNERS

Tony Peña	2003

Batting Champions

Year	Player	Avg
1976	George Brett	.333
1980	George Brett	.390
1982	Willie Wilson	.332
1990	George Brett	.329

Nine-Inning No-Hitters Pitched

Year	Pitcher	Opp.	Score
1973	Steve Busby	DET	3–0
1974	Steve Busby	MIL	2–0
1977	Jim Colborn	TEX	6–0
1991	Bret Saberhagen	CWS	7–0

20-Game Winners

Year	Pitcher	W–L
1973	Paul Splittorff	20–11
1974	Steve Busby	22–14
1977	Dennis Leonard	20–12
1978	Dennis Leonard	21–17
1980	Dennis Leonard	20–11
1985	Bret Saberhagen	20–6
1988	Mark Gubicza	20–8
1989	Bret Saberhagen	23–6

Retired Uniform Numbers

Number	Player	Position
5	George Brett	3B
10	Dick Howser	Mgr
20	Frank White	2B

Team Records—Wins & Losses

- Games won in a season: 102 in 1977
- Games lost in a season: 106 in 2005
- Games won in a month: 25 in September 1977
- Games lost in a month: 21 in August 1999 and August 2005
- Consecutive games won: 16 in 1977
- Consecutive games lost: 19 in 2005
- Biggest shutout victory: 16–0 over Oakland on June 25, 1984
- Biggest shutout loss: 17–0 to Detroit on July 19, 1991
- Highest winning percentage: .630 in 1977 (102–60)
- Lowest winning percentage: .346 in 2005 (56–106)

Team Records—Batting

- Highest team batting average: .288 in 2000
- Lowest team batting average: .240 in 1969
- Highest team slugging average: .436 in 1977
- Highest team on-base percentage: .348 in 1999 and 2000
- Total hits: 1,644 in 2000
- Extra-base hits: 522 in 1977
- Hits in a game: 26 vs. Detroit on September 9, 2004 (first game)
- Longest individual hitting streak: 30, George Brett, 1980
- Most .300 hitters in a single season: 4 in 2000
- Home runs: 168 in 1987
- Home runs in a month: 12, John Mayberry, July 1975 and Chili Davis, August 1997
- Home runs in a game: 6 vs. Detroit on July 14, 1991
- Home runs by a rookie: 24, Bob Hamelin, 1994
- Home runs by a right-hander: 36, Steve Balboni, 1985
- Home runs by a left-hander: 34, John Mayberry, 1975
- Home runs by a switch-hitter: 30, Chili Davis, 1997
- Grand slams: 7 in 1991
- Grand slams (individual; single season): 3, Danny Tartabull, 1988
- Grand slams (individual; career): 6, Frank White
- Triples: 79 in 1979
- Doubles: 316 in 1990
- Singles: 1,193 in 1980
- Walks: 644 in 1973
- Runs scored: 879 in 2000
- Runs scored in a game: 26 vs. Detroit on September 9, 2004
- Runs scored in an inning: 12 vs. Minnesota on June 17, 2003 (sixth inning)
- Most batters hit by a pitch: 76 in 2004
- Times shut out: 18 in 1971 and 1989
- Grounded into double plays: 156 in 1999
- Fewest grounded into double plays: 95 in 1978
- Runners left on base: 1,209 in 1980

TEAM RECORDS—BASERUNNING

- Stolen bases: 218 in 1976
- Caught stealing: 106 in 1976

TEAM RECORDS—PITCHING

- Lowest earned run average: 3.21 in 1976
- Complete games: 54 in 1974
- Saves: 50 in 1984
- Strikeouts: 1,006 in 1990
- Shutouts: 16 in 1972
- Walks: 694 in 2000
- Hit batsmen: 74 in 2005
- Wild pitches: 77 in 2000
- Consecutive wins (individual): 11, Rich Gale in 1980
- Consecutive losses (individual): 9, Jeff Suppan in 2002, and Brian Anderson in 2004
- Strikeouts in a game (individual): 14, Mark Gubicza, August 27, 1988
- Runs allowed in a game: 22 vs. Boston, April 12, 1994

TEAM RECORDS—FIELDING

- Best fielding average: .985 in 1997
- Most errors committed: 167 in 1973
- Fewest errors committed: 91 in 1997
- Most double plays turned: 204 in 2001
- Fewest double plays turned: 114 in 1969

TEAM RECORDS—MISCELLANEOUS

- Number of times league champions: 2
- Number of times finishing last in league: 2
- Largest attendance, single game: 41,860 vs. New York Yankees, July 26, 1980
- Largest attendance, doubleheader: 42,039 vs. Milwaukee, August 8, 1983
- Players used in a season: 58 in 2004
- Seasons played: 21, George Brett

PRIMARY PITCHING STAFFS

Year	Starter	Starter	Starter	Starter	Starter	Closer	Bullpen	Bullpen	Bullpen
2005	Greinke	Lima	Hernandez	Carrasco	Howell	MacDougal	Sisco	Burgos	Affeldt
2004	May	Anderson	Greinke	Gobble	Wood	Affeldt	Cerda	Sullivan	Field
2003	May	George	Affeldt	Hernandez	Snyder	MacDougal	Grimsley	Carrasco	Wilson
2002	May	Byrd	Suppan	Asencio	Sedlacek	Hernandez	Grimsley	Mullen	Bailey
2001	Durbin	Byrd	Suppan	Reichert	Wilson	Hernandez	Grimsley	Henry	Bailey
2000	Durbin	Suzuki	Suppan	Reichert	Stein	Bottalico	Spradlin	Santiago	Witasick
1999	Rosado	Witasick	Suppan	Appier	Stein	Montgomery	Service	Whisenant	Morman
1998	Rosado	Belcher	Rapp	Rusch	Pichardo	Montgomery	Service	Whisenant	Pittsley
1997	Rosado	Belcher	Appier	Rusch	Pittsley	Montgomery	Walker	Pichardo	Olson
1996	Haney	Belcher	Appier	Gubicza	Linton	Montgomery	Jacome	Pichardo	Magnante
1995	Haney	Gordon	Appier	Gubicza	Jacome	Montgomery	Meacham	Pichardo	Brewer
1994	Cone	Gordon	Appier	Gubicza	Milacki	Montgomery	Belinda	Pichardo	Brewer
1993	Cone	Pichardo	Appier	Haney	Gardner	Montgomery	Gubicza	Gordon	Brewer
1992	Reed	Pichardo	Appier	Gubicza	Aquino	Montgomery	Meacham	Gordon	Magnante
1991	Boddicker	Saberhagen	Appier	Gubicza	Aquino	Montgomery	Davis	Gordon	Magnante
1990	Gordon	Saberhagen	Appier	Gubicza	Davis	Montgomery	Farr	Davis	Crawford
1989	Gordon	Saberhagen	Leibrandt	Gubicza	Aquino	Farr	Montgomery	Leach	Crawford
1988	Bannister	Saberhagen	Leibrandt	Gubicza	Power	Farr	Montgomery	Gleaton	Garber
1987	Jackson	Saberhagen	Leibrandt	Gubicza	Black	Quisenberry	Farr	Gleaton	Davis
1986	Jackson	Saberhagen	Leibrandt	Gubicza	Leonard	Quisenberry	Farr	Black	Bankhead
1985	Jackson	Saberhagen	Leibrandt	Gubicza	Black	Quisenberry	Beckwith	Jones	LaCoss
1984	Gura	Saberhagen	Leibrandt	Gubicza	Black	Quisenberry	Beckwith	Jones	Huismann
1983	Gura	Splittorff	Renko	Blue	Black	Quisenberry	Armstrong	Hood	Creel
1982	Gura	Splittorff	Leonard	Blue	Frost	Quisenberry	Armstrong	Hood	Black
1981	Gura	Splittorff	Leonard	Gale	Jones	Quisenberry	Martin	Brett	Wright
1980	Gura	Splittorff	Leonard	Gale	Martin	Quisenberry	Pattin	Christenson	Eastwick

PRIMARY PITCHING STAFFS (CONT.)

Year	Starter	Starter	Starter	Starter	Starter	Closer	Bullpen	Bullpen	Bullpen
1979	Gura	Splittorff	Leonard	Gale	Busby	Hrabosky	Quisenberry	Pattin	Mingori
1978	Gura	Splittorff	Leonard	Gale	Hassler	Hrabosky	Pattin	Bird	Mingori
1977	Colborn	Splittorff	Leonard	Pattin	Hassler	Bird	Gura	Littell	Mingori
1976	Fitzmorris	Splittorff	Leonard	Pattin	Bird	Littell	Gura	Hall	Mingori
1975	Fitzmorris	Splittorff	Leonard	Busby	Briles	Bird	Pattin	McDaniel	Mingori
1974	Fitzmorris	Splittorff	Dal Canton	Busby	Briles	Bird	Hoerner	McDaniel	Mingori
1973	Fitzmorris	Splittorff	Drago	Busby	Wright	Bird	Hoerner	Dal Canton	Garber
1972	Nelson	Splittorff	Drago	Dal Canton	Hedlund	Burgmeier	Abernathy	Fitzmorris	Angelini
1971	Fitzmorris	Splittorff	Drago	Dal Canton	Hedlund	Abernathy	Burgmeier	York	Wright
1970	Rooker	Johnson	Drago	Morehead	Butler	Abernathy	Burgmeier	Fitzmorris	Wright
1969	Rooker	Bunker	Drago	Nelson	Butler	Drabowsky	Wickersham	Burgmeier	Hedlund

PRIMARY STARTING LINEUPS

Year	C	1B	2B	3B	SS	LF	CF	RF	DH
2005	Buck	Stairs	Gotay	Teahen	Berroa	Long	DeJesus	Brown	Sweeney
2004	Buck	Harvey	Graffanino	Randa	Berroa	Brown	DeJesus	Stairs	Sweeney
2003	Mayne	Harvey	Relaford	Randa	Berroa	Ibanez	Beltran	Guiel	Sweeney
2002	Mayne	Sweeney	Febles	Randa	Perez	Knoblauch	Beltran	Tucker	Ibanez
2001	Ortiz	Sweeney	Febles	Randa	Sanchez	Brown	Beltran	Dye	Ibanez
2000	Zaun	Sweeney	Febles	Randa	Sanchez	Quinn	Beltran	Dye	Damon
1999	Kreuter	Sutton	Febles	Randa	Sanchez	Damon	Beltran	Dye	Sweeney
1998	Sweeney	King	Offerman	Palmer	Lopez	Conine	Damon	Dye	Pendleton
1997	Macfarlane	King	Offerman	Paquette	Bell	Roberts	Goodwin	Dye	Davis
1996	Macfarlane	Offerman	Lockhart	Randa	Howard	Goodwin	Damon	Tucker	Vitiello
1995	Mayne	Joyner	Lockhart	Gaetti	Gagne	Coleman	Goodwin	Nunnally	Hamelin
1994	Macfarlane	Joyner	Lind	Gaetti	Gagne	Coleman	McRae	Jose	Hamelin
1993	Macfarlane	Joyner	Lind	Gaetti	Gagne	McReynolds	McRae	Jose	Brett
1992	Macfarlane	Joyner	Miller	Jefferies	Howard	McReynolds	McRae	Eisenreich	Brett
1991	Mayne	Benzinger	Shumpert	Pecota	Stillwell	Gibson	McRae	Tartabull	Brett
1990	Macfarlane	Brett	White	Seitzer	Stillwell	Wilson	Jackson	Eisenreich	Perry
1989	Boone	Brett	White	Seitzer	Stillwell	Jackson	Wilson	Tartabull	Tabler
1988	Quirk	Brett	White	Seitzer	Stillwell	Jackson	Wilson	Tartabull	Buckner
1987	Quirk	Brett	White	Seitzer	Salazar	Jackson	Wilson	Tartabull	Balboni
1986	Sundberg	Balboni	White	Brett	Salazar	Smith	Wilson	Motley	Orta
1985	Sundberg	Balboni	White	Brett	Concepcion	Smith	Wilson	Motley	McRae
1984	Slaught	Balboni	White	Pryor	Concepcion	Motley	Wilson	Sheridan	McRae
1983	Wathan	Aikens	White	Brett	Washington	Roberts	Wilson	Sheridan	McRae
1982	Wathan	Aikens	White	Brett	Washington	Wilson	Otis	Martin	McRae
1981	Wathan	Aikens	White	Brett	Washington	Wilson	Otis	Geronimo	McRae
1980	Porter	Aikens	White	Brett	Washington	Wilson	Otis	Hurdle	McRae
1979	Porter	LaCock	White	Brett	Patek	Wilson	Otis	Cowens	McRae
1978	Porter	LaCock	White	Brett	Patek	Wilson	Otis	Cowens	McRae
1977	Porter	Mayberry	White	Brett	Patek	Zdeb	Otis	Cowens	McRae
1976	Martinez	Mayberry	White	Brett	Patek	Wohlford	Otis	Cowens	McRae
1975	Martinez	Mayberry	Rojas	Brett	Patek	McRae	Otis	Wohlford	Killebrew
1974	Healy	Mayberry	Rojas	Brett	Patek	Wohlford	Otis	Pinson	McRae
1973	Healy	Mayberry	Rojas	Schaal	Patek	Piniella	Otis	Kirkpatrick	McRae
1972	Kirkpatrick	Mayberry	Rojas	Schaal	Patek	Piniella	Otis	Scheinblum	
1971	May	Hopkins	Rojas	Schaal	Patek	Piniella	Otis	Keough	
1970	Kirkpatrick	Oliver	Rojas	Schaal	Hernandez	Piniella	Otis	Kelly	
1969	Rodriguez	Fiore	Adair	Foy	Hernandez	Piniella	Oliver	Kelly	

Top 10 Batting Leaders, Single Season & Career with Team

GAMES PLAYED: CAREER WITH TEAM

Player	G	PA
1. George Brett	2,707	11,624
2. Frank White	2,324	8,467
3. Amos Otis	1,891	7,969
4. Hal McRae	1,837	7,361
5. Willie Wilson	1,787	7,302
6. Freddie Patek	1,245	4,867
7. Mike Sweeney	1,148	4,737
8. Joe Randa	1,019	4,158
9. John Mayberry	897	3,752
10. Mike Macfarlane	890	3,150

AT-BATS: SEASON

Player	AB	Year
1. Willie Wilson	705	1980
2. Carlos Beltran	663	1999
3. Johnny Damon	655	2000
4. George Brett	645	1976
George Brett	645	1979
6. Johnny Damon	642	1998
7. Hal McRae	641	1977
Kevin Seitzer	641	1987
9. Carlos Beltran	637	2002
10. George Brett	634	1975

AT-BATS: CAREER WITH TEAM

Player	AB	PA
1. George Brett	10,349	11,624
2. Frank White	7,859	8,467
3. Amos Otis	7,050	7,969
4. Willie Wilson	6,799	7,302
5. Hal McRae	6,568	7,361
6. Freddie Patek	4,305	4,867
7. Mike Sweeney	4,187	4,737
8. Joe Randa	3,764	4,158
9. Carlos Beltran	3,134	3,512
10. John Mayberry	3,131	3,752

BATTING AVERAGE: SEASON

Player	BA	Year
1. George Brett	.390	1980
2. Mike Sweeney	.340	2002
3. George Brett	.335	1985
4. George Brett	.333	1976
Mike Sweeney	.333	2000
6. Hal McRae	.332	1976
Willie Wilson	.332	1982
8. George Brett	.329	1990
George Brett	.329	1979
10. Johnny Damon	.327	2000

BATTING AVERAGE: CAREER WITH TEAM

Player	BA	PA
1. George Brett	.305	11,624
2. Mike Sweeney	.304	4,737
3. Kevin Seitzer	.294	3,163
4. Wally Joyner	.293	2,173
Hal McRae	.293	7,361
6. Johnny Damon	.292	3,407
7. Danny Tartabull	.290	2,684
8. Willie Wilson	.289	7,302
9. Joe Randa	.288	4,158
10. Carlos Beltran	.287	3,512

TOTAL HITS: SEASON

Player	H	Year
1. Willie Wilson	230	1980
2. George Brett	215	1976
3. Johnny Damon	214	2000
4. George Brett	212	1979
5. Kevin Seitzer	207	1987
6. Mike Sweeney	206	2000
7. Joe Randa	197	1999
8. George Brett	195	1975
9. Carlos Beltran	194	1999
Willie Wilson	194	1982

TOTAL HITS: CAREER WITH TEAM

Player	H	PA
1. George Brett	3,154	11,624
2. Frank White	2,006	8,467
3. Amos Otis	1,977	7,969
4. Willie Wilson	1,968	7,302
5. Hal McRae	1,924	7,361
6. Mike Sweeney	1,273	4,737
7. Joe Randa	1,084	4,158
8. Freddie Patek	1,036	4,867
9. Carlos Beltran	899	3,512
10. Johnny Damon	894	3,407

HOME RUNS: SEASON

Player	HR	Year
1. Steve Balboni	36	1985
2. Gary Gaetti	35	1995
3. John Mayberry	34	1975
Dean Palmer	34	1998
Danny Tartabull	34	1987
6. Jermaine Dye	33	2000
7. Bo Jackson	32	1989
8. Danny Tartabull	31	1991
9. George Brett	30	1985
Chili Davis	30	1997

HOME RUNS: CAREER WITH TEAM

Player	HR	PA
1. George Brett	317	11,624
2. Amos Otis	193	7,969
3. Mike Sweeney	182	4,787
4. Hal McRae	169	7,361
5. Frank White	160	8,467
6. John Mayberry	143	3,752
7. Danny Tartabull	124	2,684
8. Carlos Beltran	123	3,512
9. Steve Balboni	119	2,201
10. Bo Jackson	109	2,010

TRIPLES: SEASON

Player	3B	Year
1. Willie Wilson	21	1985
2. George Brett	20	1979
3. Willie Wilson	15	1980
Willie Wilson	15	1982
Willie Wilson	15	1987
6. George Brett	14	1976
Al Cowens	14	1977
8. George Brett	13	1975
George Brett	13	1977
Jose Offerman	13	1998
Willie Wilson	13	1979

TRIPLES: CAREER WITH TEAM

Player	3B	PA
1. George Brett	137	11,624
2. Willie Wilson	133	7,302
3. Amos Otis	65	7,969
4. Hal McRae	63	7,361
5. Frank White	58	8,467
6. Johnny Damon	47	3,407
7. Carlos Beltran	45	3,512
8. Al Cowens	44	3,042
9. Freddie Patek	41	4,867
10. Brian McRae	32	2,627

Doubles: Season

Player	2B	Year
1. Hal McRae	54	1977
2. Hal McRae	46	1982
Mike Sweeney	46	2001
4. George Brett	45	1978
George Brett	45	1990
Frank White	45	1982
7. Carlos Beltran	44	2002
Jermaine Dye	44	1999
Mike Sweeney	44	1999
10. George Brett	42	1979
George Brett	42	1988
Johnny Damon	42	2000

Doubles: Career with Team

Player	2B	PA
1. George Brett	665	11,624
2. Hal McRae	449	7,361
3. Frank White	407	8,467
4. Amos Otis	365	7,969
5. Mike Sweeney	267	4,737
6. Willie Wilson	241	7,302
7. Joe Randa	223	4,158
8. Freddie Patek	182	4,867
9. Mike Macfarlane	174	3,150
10. Carlos Beltran	156	3,512
Johnny Damon	156	3,407

Extra-Base Hits: Season

Player	XBH	Year
1. Hal McRae	86	1977
2. George Brett	85	1979
3. Hal McRae	81	1982
4. Carlos Beltran	80	2002
5. Jermaine Dye	79	1999
6. Jermaine Dye	76	2000
7. Mike Sweeney	75	2001
8. George Brett	73	1985
John Mayberry	73	1975
10. George Brett	69	1988
Al Cowens	69	1977
Danny Tartabull	69	1991

Extra-Base Hits: Career with Team

Player	XBH	PA
1. George Brett	1,119	11,624
2. Hal McRae	681	7,361
3. Frank White	625	8,467
4. Amos Otis	623	7,969
5. Mike Sweeney	453	4,737
6. Willie Wilson	414	7,302
7. Joe Randa	332	4,158
8. Carlos Beltran	324	3,512
9. Mike Macfarlane	293	3,150
10. John Mayberry	292	3,752

Total Bases: Season

Player	TB	Year
1. George Brett	363	1979
2. Jermaine Dye	337	2000
3. Hal McRae	332	1982
4. Hal McRae	330	1977
5. Johnny Damon	324	2000
6. Mike Sweeney	323	2000
7. George Brett	322	1985
8. Jermaine Dye	320	1999
9. Carlos Beltran	319	2002
10. Al Cowens	318	1977

Total Bases: Career with Team

Player	TB	PA
1. George Brett	5,044	11,624
2. Amos Otis	3,051	7,969
3. Frank White	3,009	8,467
4. Hal McRae	3,006	7,361
5. Willie Wilson	2,595	7,302
6. Mike Sweeney	2,094	4,737
7. Joe Randa	1,611	4,158
8. Carlos Beltran	1,514	3,512
9. John Mayberry	1,404	3,752
10. Freddie Patek	1,384	4,867

Runs Batted In: Season

Player	RBI	Year
1. Mike Sweeney	144	2000
2. Hal McRae	133	1982
3. Jermaine Dye	119	1999
Dean Palmer	119	1998
5. George Brett	118	1980
Jermaine Dye	118	2000
7. George Brett	112	1985
Al Cowens	112	1977
Jeff King	112	1997
Darrell Porter	112	1979

Runs Batted In: Career with Team

Player	RBI	PA
1. George Brett	1,595	11,624
2. Hal McRae	1,012	7,361
3. Amos Otis	992	7,969
4. Frank White	886	8,467
5. Mike Sweeney	766	4,737
6. John Mayberry	552	3,752
7. Joe Randa	533	4,158
8. Carlos Beltran	516	3,512
9. Willie Wilson	509	7,302
10. Danny Tartabull	425	2,684

Runs Scored: Season

Player	R	Year
1. Johnny Damon	136	2000
2. Willie Wilson	133	1980
3. George Brett	119	1979
4. Carlos Beltran	114	2002
5. Willie Wilson	113	1979
6. Carlos Beltran	112	1999
7. George Brett	108	1985
8. Jermaine Dye	107	2000
9. Carlos Beltran	106	2001
10. George Brett	105	1977
Kevin Seitzer	105	1987
Mike Sweeney	105	2000

Runs Scored: Career with Team

Player	R	PA
1. George Brett	1,583	11,624
2. Amos Otis	1,074	7,969
3. Willie Wilson	1,060	7,302
4. Frank White	912	8,467
5. Hal McRae	873	7,361
6. Mike Sweeney	651	4,737
7. Freddie Patek	571	4,867
8. Carlos Beltran	546	3,512
9. Johnny Damon	504	3,407
10. Joe Randa	489	4,158

Walks: Season

Player	BB	Year
1. John Mayberry	122	1973
2. Darrell Porter	121	1979
3. John Mayberry	119	1975
4. George Brett	103	1985
Paul Schaal	103	1971
6. Kevin Seitzer	102	1989
7. Jeff King	89	1997
Jose Offerman	89	1998
9. Chili Davis	85	1997
10. Mike Fiore	84	1969

Walks: Career with Team

Player	BB	PA
1. George Brett	1,096	11,624
2. Amos Otis	739	7,969
3. Hal McRae	616	7,361
4. John Mayberry	561	3,752

Player		
5. Mike Sweeney	439	4,737
6. Freddie Patek	413	4,867
7. Frank White	412	8,467
8. Kevin Seitzer	369	3,163
9. Willie Wilson	360	7,302
10. Danny Tartabull	325	2,684

Strikeouts: Season

Player	SO	Year
1. Bo Jackson	172	1989
2. Steve Balboni	166	1985
3. Bo Jackson	158	1987
4. Steve Balboni	146	1986
Bo Jackson	146	1988
6. Steve Balboni	139	1984
7. Jerry Martin	138	1982
8. Danny Tartabull	136	1987
9. Carlos Beltran	135	2002
10. Dean Palmer	134	1998

Strikeouts: Career with Team

Player	SO	PA
1. Frank White	1,035	8,467
2. Willie Wilson	990	7,302
3. Amos Otis	953	7,969
4. George Brett	908	11,624
5. Hal McRae	697	7,361
6. Bo Jackson	638	2,010
7. Danny Tartabull	592	2,684
8. Freddie Patek	586	4,867
9. Carlos Beltran	584	3,512
10. Steve Balboni	568	2,201

Slugging Percentage: Season

Player	SLG	Year
1. George Brett	.664	1980
2. Bob Hamelin	.599	1994
3. Danny Tartabull	.593	1991
4. George Brett	.585	1985
5. George Brett	.563	1979
Mike Sweeney	.563	2002
7. George Brett	.562	1983
8. Jermaine Dye	.561	2000
9. John Mayberry	.547	1975
10. Mike Sweeney	.542	2001

Slugging Percentage: Career with Team

Player	SLG	PA
1. Danny Tartabull	.518	2,684
2. Mike Sweeney	.500	4,737
3. George Brett	.487	11,624
4. Carlos Beltran	.483	3,512
5. Bo Jackson	.480	2,010
6. Jermaine Dye	.477	2,275
7. Willie Aikens	.469	2,019
8. Steve Balboni	.459	2,201
9. Hal McRae	.458	7,361
10. John Mayberry	.448	3,752

On-Base Percentage: Season

Player	OBP	Year
1. George Brett	.454	1980
2. George Brett	.436	1985
3. Darrell Porter	.421	1979
4. Mike Fiore	.420	1969
5. John Mayberry	.417	1973
Mike Sweeney	.417	2002
7. John Mayberry	.416	1975
8. Mike Sweeney	.407	2000
Hal McRae	.407	1976
10. Jose Offerman	.403	1998

On-Base Percentage: Career with Team

Player	OBP	PA
1. Kevin Seitzer	.380	3,163
2. Danny Tartabull	.376	2,684
3. Darrell Porter	.375	2,262
4. John Mayberry	.374	3,752
Mike Sweeney	.374	4,737
6. Wally Joyner	.371	2,173
7. George Brett	.369	11,624
8. Willie Aikens	.362	2,019
9. Paul Schaal	.360	2,340
10. Hal McRae	.356	7,361

OPS (On-Base Percentage + Slugging Percentage): Season

Player	OPS	Year
1. George Brett	1.118	1980
2. George Brett	1.022	1985
3. Danny Tartabull	.990	1991
4. Bob Hamelin	.987	1994
5. Mike Sweeney	.979	2002
6. John Mayberry	.963	1975
7. Jermaine Dye	.951	2000
8. George Brett	.947	1983
9. George Brett	.939	1979
10. Danny Tartabull	.931	1987

OPS (On-Base Percentage + Slugging Percentage): Career with Team

Player	OPS	PA
1. Danny Tartabull	.894	2,684
2. Mike Sweeney	.874	4,737
3. George Brett	.857	11,624
4. Carlos Beltran	.835	3,512
5. Willie Aikens	.830	2,019
6. John Mayberry	.822	3,752
7. Jermaine Dye	.820	2,275
8. Hal McRae	.814	7,361
9. Darrell Porter	.809	2,262
10. Wally Joyner	.805	2,173

Stolen Bases: Season

Player	SB	Year
1. Willie Wilson	83	1979
2. Willie Wilson	79	1980
3. Tom Goodwin	66	1996
4. Willie Wilson	59	1983
Willie Wilson	59	1987
6. Freddie Patek	53	1977
7. Amos Otis	52	1971
8. Freddie Patek	51	1976
9. Vince Coleman	50	1994
Tom Goodwin	50	1995

Stolen Bases: Career with Team

Player	SB	PA
1. Willie Wilson	612	7,302
2. Amos Otis	340	7,969
3. Freddie Patek	336	4,867
4. George Brett	201	11,624
5. Frank White	178	8,467
6. Carlos Beltran	164	3,512
7. Johnny Damon	156	3,407
8. Tom Goodwin	150	1,526
9. U.L. Washington	120	2,746
10. Hal McRae	105	7,361
John Wathan	105	2,764

Sacrifice Hits: Season

Player	Sac	Year
1. Tom Goodwin	21	1996
2. Frank White	18	1976
3. David Howard	17	1996
4. Tom Goodwin	14	1995
Brian McRae	14	1993

6. Angel Berroa	13	2003
Carlos Febles	13	2000
Jose Lind	13	1993
Freddie Patek	13	1976
Freddie Patek	13	1977
Willie Wilson	13	1979

SACRIFICE HITS: CAREER WITH TEAM

Player	Sac	PA
1. Frank White	101	8,467
2. Freddie Patek	89	4,867
3. Willie Wilson	59	7,302
4. Amos Otis	49	7,969
5. David Howard	48	1,586
6. Tom Goodwin	46	1,526
7. U.L. Washington	38	2,746
8. Carlos Febles	36	1,892
9. Brian McRae	33	2,627
10. Johnny Damon	32	3,407
Dick Drago	32	327

HIT BY PITCH: SEASON

Player	HBP	Year
1. Angel Berroa	18	2003
Mike Macfarlane	18	1994
3. Sal Fasano	16	1998
Mike Macfarlane	16	1993
5. Mike Macfarlane	15	1992
Mike Sweeney	15	2000
7. Keith Miller	14	1992
Angel Berroa	14	2005
9. Aaron Guiel	13	2003
Hal McRae	13	1977

HIT BY PITCH: CAREER WITH TEAM

Player	HBP	PA
1. Mike Macfarlane	78	3,150
2. Hal McRae	74	7,361
3. Mike Sweeney	57	4,737
4. Willie Wilson	54	7,302
5. Angel Berroa	45	1,980
6. Joe Randa	38	4,158
7. George Brett	33	11,624
8. Carlos Febles	32	1,892
Amos Otis	32	7,969
10. Frank White	30	8,467

Top 10 Pitching Leaders, Single Season & Career with Team

GAMES PITCHED: SEASON

Player	GP	Year
1. Dan Quisenberry	84	1985
2. Jason Grimsley	76	2003
3. Dan Quisenberry	75	1980
4. Jason Grimsley	73	2001
Jeff Montgomery	73	1990
Scott Service	73	1998
7. Dan Quisenberry	72	1982
Dan Quisenberry	72	1984
9. Jason Grimsley	70	2002
Matt Whisenant	70	1998

GAMES PITCHED: CAREER WITH TEAM

Player	GP	IP
1. Jeff Montgomery	686	849.3
2. Dan Quisenberry	573	920.3
3. Paul Splittorff	429	2,554.7
4. Mark Gubicza	382	2,218.7
5. Dennis Leonard	312	2,187.0
6. Larry Gura	310	1,701.3
7. Doug Bird	292	714.7
8. Steve Farr	289	511.0
9. Kevin Appier	287	1,843.7
10. Hipolito Pichardo	281	669.7

INNINGS PITCHED: SEASON

Player	IP	Year
1. Dennis Leonard	294.7	1978
2. Dennis Leonard	292.7	1977
3. Steve Busby	292.3	1974
4. Larry Gura	283.3	1980
5. Dennis Leonard	280.3	1980
6. Mark Gubicza	269.7	1988
7. Bret Saberhagen	262.3	1989
8. Paul Splittorff	262.0	1973
Paul Splittorff	262.0	1978
10. Bret Saberhagen	260.7	1988

INNINGS PITCHED: CAREER WITH TEAM

Player	IP
1. Paul Splittorff	2,554.7
2. Mark Gubicza	2,218.7
3. Dennis Leonard	2,187.0
4. Kevin Appier	1,843.7
5. Larry Gura	1,701.3
6. Bret Saberhagen	1,660.3
7. Charlie Leibrandt	1,257.0
8. Tom Gordon	1,149.7
9. Dick Drago	1,134.0
10. Al Fitzmorris	1,098.0

BATTERS FACED: SEASON

Player	BF	Year
1. Steve Busby	1,220	1974
2. Dennis Leonard	1,218	1978
3. Dennis Leonard	1,186	1977
4. Larry Gura	1,175	1980
5. Dennis Leonard	1,172	1980
6. Paul Splittorff	1,119	1973
7. Mark Gubicza	1,111	1988
8. Bret Saberhagen	1,089	1988
9. Dennis Leonard	1,072	1976
10. Paul Splittorff	1,069	1978

BATTERS FACED: CAREER WITH TEAM

Player	BF	IP
1. Paul Splittorff	10,824	2,554.7
2. Mark Gubicza	9,457	2,218.7
3. Dennis Leonard	9,149	2,187.0
4. Kevin Appier	7,688	1,843.7
5. Larry Gura	7,108	1,701.3
6. Bret Saberhagen	6,725	1,660.3

7. Charlie Leibrandt	5,308	1,257.0
8. Tom Gordon	4,971	1,149.7
9. Dick Drago	4,738	1,134.0
10. Al Fitzmorris	4,591	1,098.0

Games Started: Season

Player	GS	Year
1. Dennis Leonard	40	1978
2. Steve Busby	38	1974
Dennis Leonard	38	1980
Paul Splittorff	38	1973
Paul Splittorff	38	1978
6. Steve Busby	37	1973
Larry Gura	37	1982
Dennis Leonard	37	1977
Paul Splittorff	37	1977
10. Mark Gubicza	36	1989
Larry Gura	36	1980
Paul Splittorff	36	1974

Games Started: Career with Team

Player	GS	IP
1. Paul Splittorff	392	2,554.7
2. Mark Gubicza	327	2,218.7
3. Dennis Leonard	302	2,187.0
4. Kevin Appier	275	1,843.7
5. Bret Saberhagen	226	1,660.3
6. Larry Gura	219	1,701.3
7. Charlie Leibrandt	187	1,257.0
8. Dick Drago	160	1,134.0
9. Steve Busby	150	1,060.7
10. Tom Gordon	144	1,149.7

Complete Games: Season

Player	CG	Year
1. Dennis Leonard	21	1977
2. Steve Busby	20	1974
Dennis Leonard	20	1978
4. Steve Busby	18	1975
5. Larry Gura	16	1980
Dennis Leonard	16	1976
7. Dick Drago	15	1971
Bret Saberhagen	15	1987
9. Paul Splittorff	13	1978
10. Larry Gura	12	1981
Dennis Leonard	12	1979
Bret Saberhagen	12	1989
Paul Splittorff	12	1972
Paul Splittorff	12	1973

Complete Games: Career with Team

Player	CG	IP
1. Dennis Leonard	103	2,187.0
2. Paul Splittorff	88	2,554.7
3. Bret Saberhagen	64	1,660.3
4. Larry Gura	61	1,701.3
5. Steve Busby	53	1,060.7
Dick Drago	53	1,134.0
7. Mark Gubicza	42	2,218.7
8. Al Fitzmorris	35	1,098.0
9. Charlie Leibrandt	34	1,257.0
10. Kevin Appier	32	1,843.7

Games Won: Season

Player	W	Year
1. Bret Saberhagen	23	1989
2. Steve Busby	22	1974
3. Dennis Leonard	21	1978
4. Mark Gubicza	20	1988
Dennis Leonard	20	1977
Dennis Leonard	20	1980
Bret Saberhagen	20	1985
Paul Splittorff	20	1973
9. Paul Splittorff	19	1978
10. Kevin Appier	18	1993
Steve Busby	18	1975
Jim Colborn	18	1977
Larry Gura	18	1980
Larry Gura	18	1982
Bret Saberhagen	18	1987

Games Won: Career with Team

Player	W	IP
1. Paul Splittorff	166	2,554.7
2. Dennis Leonard	144	2,187.0
3. Mark Gubicza	132	2,218.7
4. Kevin Appier	115	1,843.7
5. Larry Gura	111	1,701.3
6. Bret Saberhagen	110	1,660.3
7. Tom Gordon	79	1,149.7
8. Charlie Leibrandt	76	1,257.0
9. Steve Busby	70	1,060.7
Al Fitzmorris	70	1,098.0

Games Lost: Season

Player	L	Year
1. Darrell May	19	2004
Paul Splittorff	19	1974
3. Mark Gubicza	18	1987
Larry Gura	18	1983
Danny Jackson	18	1987
6. Dick Drago	17	1972
Dennis Leonard	17	1978
Paul Splittorff	17	1979
Zack Greinke	17	2005
10. Chad Durbin	16	2001
Jim Rooker	16	1969
Bret Saberhagen	16	1988
Jeff Suppan	16	2002
Jose Lima	16	2005

Games Lost: Career with Team

Player	L	IP
1. Paul Splittorff	143	2,554.7
2. Mark Gubicza	135	2,218.7
3. Dennis Leonard	106	2,187.0
4. Kevin Appier	92	1,843.7
5. Larry Gura	78	1,701.3
Bret Saberhagen	78	1,660.3
7. Tom Gordon	71	1,149.7
8. Dick Drago	70	1,134.0
9. Charlie Leibrandt	61	1,257.0
10. Bud Black	57	977.7

Winning Percentage: Season

Player	W%	Year
1. Larry Gura	.800	1978
2. Bret Saberhagen	.793	1989
3. Bret Saberhagen	.769	1985
4. David Cone	.762	1994
5. Paul Splittorff	.727	1977
6. Mark Gubicza	.714	1988
7. Kevin Appier	.692	1993
8. Al Fitzmorris	.684	1974
9. Dennis Leonard	.682	1975
10. Tom Gordon	.667	1993
Mark Gubicza	.667	1986

Winning Percentage: Career with Team

Player	W%	IP
1. Al Fitzmorris	.593	1,098.0
2. Larry Gura	.587	1,701.3
3. Bret Saberhagen	.585	1,660.3
4. Doug Bird	.576	714.7
Dennis Leonard	.576	2,187.0
6. Steve Busby	.565	1,060.7
7. Rich Gale	.560	666.3
8. Kevin Appier	.556	1,843.7
9. Charlie Leibrandt	.555	1,257.0
10. Paul Splittorff	.537	2,554.7

SHUTOUTS: SEASON

Player	SHO	Year
1. Roger Nelson	6	1972
2. Dennis Leonard	5	1977
Dennis Leonard	5	1979
4. Bill Butler	4	1969
Dick Drago	4	1971
Al Fitzmorris	4	1974
Mark Gubicza	4	1988
Larry Gura	4	1980
Dennis Leonard	4	1978
Bret Saberhagen	4	1987
Bret Saberhagen	4	1989

SHUTOUTS: CAREER WITH TEAM

Player	SHO	IP
1. Dennis Leonard	23	2,187.0
2. Paul Splittorff	17	2,554.7
3. Mark Gubicza	16	2,218.7
4. Larry Gura	14	1,701.3
Bret Saberhagen	14	1,660.3
6. Al Fitzmorris	11	1,098.0
7. Kevin Appier	10	1,843.7
Dick Drago	10	1,134.0
Charlie Leibrandt	10	1,257.0
10. Steve Busby	7	1,060.7
Roger Nelson	7	418.3
Jim Rooker	7	488.0

ERA: SEASON

Player	ERA	Year
1. Roger Nelson	2.08	1972
2. Bret Saberhagen	2.16	1989
3. Kevin Appier	2.46	1992
4. Kevin Appier	2.56	1993
5. Charlie Leibrandt	2.69	1985
6. Mark Gubicza	2.70	1988
7. Mike Hedlund	2.71	1971
8. Larry Gura	2.72	1981
Larry Gura	2.72	1978
10. Kevin Appier	2.76	1990

ERA: CAREER WITH TEAM

Player	ERA	IP
1. Dan Quisenberry	2.55	920.3
2. Steve Farr	3.05	511.0
3. Jeff Montgomery	3.20	849.3
4. Bret Saberhagen	3.21	1,660.3
5. Al Fitzmorris	3.46	1,098.0
6. Marty Pattin	3.48	825.7
7. Kevin Appier	3.49	1,843.7
8. Dick Drago	3.52	1,134.0
9. Doug Bird	3.56	714.7
10. Charlie Leibrandt	3.60	1,257.0

EARNED RUNS ALLOWED: SEASON

Player	ER	Year
1. Jose Lima	131	2005
2. Jeff Suppan	123	2002
3. Tim Belcher	119	1997
Chris Haney	119	1996
Jeff Suppan	119	2000
6. Dennis Leonard	118	1980
Zack Greinke	118	2005
8. Larry Gura	116	1979
Darrell May	116	2004
Paul Splittorff	116	1973

EARNED RUNS ALLOWED: CAREER WITH TEAM

Player	ER	IP
1. Paul Splittorff	1,082	2,554.7
2. Mark Gubicza	965	2,218.7
3. Dennis Leonard	898	2,187.0
4. Kevin Appier	714	1,843.7
5. Larry Gura	704	1,701.3
6. Bret Saberhagen	593	1,660.3
7. Tom Gordon	514	1,149.7
8. Charlie Leibrandt	503	1,257.0
9. Jeff Suppan	454	864.7
10. Dick Drago	444	1,134.0

STRIKEOUTS: SEASON

Player	K	Year
1. Dennis Leonard	244	1977
2. Kevin Appier	207	1996
3. Bob Johnson	206	1970
4. Steve Busby	198	1974
5. Kevin Appier	196	1997
6. Bret Saberhagen	193	1989
7. David Cone	191	1993
8. Kevin Appier	186	1993
9. Kevin Appier	185	1995
10. Mark Gubicza	183	1988
Dennis Leonard	183	1978

STRIKEOUTS: CAREER WITH TEAM

Player	K	IP
1. Kevin Appier	1,458	1,843.7
2. Mark Gubicza	1,366	2,218.7
3. Dennis Leonard	1,323	2,187.0
4. Bret Saberhagen	1,093	1,660.3
5. Paul Splittorff	1,057	2,554.7
6. Tom Gordon	999	1,149.7
7. Jeff Montgomery	720	849.3
8. Steve Busby	659	1,060.7
9. Larry Gura	633	1,701.3
10. Charlie Leibrandt	618	1,257.0

STRIKEOUTS PER NINE IP: SEASON

Player	K/9	Year
1. Kevin Appier	8.82	1996
2. Bob Johnson	8.66	1970
3. Tom Gordon	8.45	1989
4. Kevin Appier	8.27	1995
5. Tom Gordon	8.06	1990
6. Dennis Leonard	7.50	1977
7. Kevin Appier	7.49	1997
8. Bill Butler	7.25	1969
9. Kevin Appier	7.01	1993
10. Jose Rosado	6.96	1998

STRIKEOUTS PER NINE IP: CAREER WITH TEAM

Player	K/9	IP
1. Tom Gordon	7.82	1,149.7
2. Jeff Montgomery	7.63	849.3
3. Steve Farr	7.56	511.0
4. Kevin Appier	7.12	1,843.7
5. Jose Rosado	6.05	720.3
6. Bret Saberhagen	5.92	1,660.3
7. Doug Bird	5.84	714.7
8. Darrell May	5.63	527.3
9. Steve Busby	5.59	1,060.7
10. Mark Gubicza	5.54	2,218.7

HITS ALLOWED: SEASON

Player	HA	Year
1. Steve Busby	284	1974
2. Dennis Leonard	283	1978
3. Paul Splittorff	279	1973

4. Larry Gura	272	1980
5. Dennis Leonard	271	1980
Bret Saberhagen	271	1988
7. Chris Haney	267	1996
8. Tim Belcher	262	1996
9. Dick Drago	252	1973
Mark Gubicza	252	1989
Paul Splittorff	252	1974

HITS ALLOWED: CAREER WITH TEAM

Player	HA	IP
1. Paul Splittorff	2,644	2,554.7
2. Mark Gubicza	2,226	2,218.7
3. Dennis Leonard	2,137	2,187.0
4. Kevin Appier	1,671	1,843.7
5. Larry Gura	1,628	1,701.3
6. Bret Saberhagen	1,551	1,660.3
7. Charlie Leibrandt	1,294	1,257.0
8. Dick Drago	1,162	1,134.0
9. Al Fitzmorris	1,075	1,098.0
10. Tom Gordon	1,040	1,149.7

HITS ALLOWED PER NINE IP: SEASON

Player	H/9	Year
1. Roger Nelson	6.23	1972
2. Tom Gordon	6.74	1989
3. David Cone	6.82	1994
4. Kevin Appier	6.90	1993
5. Bruce Dal Canton	6.93	1974
6. Bret Saberhagen	7.17	1989
7. Kevin Appier	7.21	1992
8. Larry Gura	7.26	1981
David Cone	7.26	1993
10. Kevin Appier	7.29	1995

HITS ALLOWED PER NINE IP: CAREER WITH TEAM

Player	H/9	IP
1. Jeff Montgomery	8.05	849.3
2. Tom Gordon	8.14	1,149.7
3. Kevin Appier	8.16	1,843.7
4. Steve Farr	8.26	511.0
5. Bret Saberhagen	8.41	1,660.3
6. Steve Busby	8.51	1,060.7
7. Larry Gura	8.61	1,701.3
8. Bud Black	8.67	977.7
9. Rich Gale	8.70	666.3
10. Marty Pattin	8.73	825.7

WALKS ALLOWED: SEASON

Player	BB	Year
1. Mark Gubicza	120	1987
2. David Cone	114	1993
3. Danny Jackson	109	1987
4. Pat Rapp	107	1998
5. Steve Busby	105	1973
6. Jim Rooker	102	1970
7. Rich Gale	100	1978
8. Rich Gale	99	1979
Tom Gordon	99	1990
10. Mac Suzuki	94	2000

WALKS ALLOWED: CAREER WITH TEAM

Player	BB	IP
1. Mark Gubicza	783	2,218.7
2. Paul Splittorff	780	2,554.7
3. Kevin Appier	634	1,843.7
4. Dennis Leonard	622	2,187.0
5. Tom Gordon	587	1,149.7
6. Larry Gura	503	1,701.3
7. Steve Busby	433	1,060.7
8. Al Fitzmorris	359	1,098.0
Charlie Leibrandt	359	1,257.0
10. Bret Saberhagen	331	1,660.3

WALKS ALLOWED PER NINE IP: SEASON

Player	BB/9	Year
1. Doug Bird	1.41	1976
2. Bret Saberhagen	1.45	1985
3. Bret Saberhagen	1.48	1989
4. Paul Byrd	1.50	2002
5. Roger Nelson	1.61	1972
6. Dick Drago	1.72	1971
7. Larry Gura	1.83	1981
Dennis Leonard	1.83	1981
9. Bret Saberhagen	1.86	1987
10. Paul Splittorff	1.90	1980

WALKS ALLOWED PER NINE IP: CAREER WITH TEAM

Player	BB/9	IP
1. Dan Quisenberry	1.36	920.3
2. Bret Saberhagen	1.79	1,660.3
3. Marty Pattin	2.37	825.7
Doug Bird	2.37	714.7
5. Dick Drago	2.46	1,134.0
6. Dennis Leonard	2.56	2,187.0
7. Charlie Leibrandt	2.57	1,257.0
8. Bud Black	2.66	977.7
Larry Gura	2.66	1,701.3
10. Darrell May	2.70	527.3

WHIP (WALKS + HITS PER NINE IP): SEASON

Player	WHIP	Year
1. Roger Nelson	0.871	1972
2. Bret Saberhagen	0.961	1989
3. Larry Gura	1.010	1981
4. Bret Saberhagen	1.058	1985
5. Bret Saberhagen	1.070	1991
6. David Cone	1.072	1994
7. Larry Gura	1.096	1978
8. Kevin Appier	1.106	1993
9. Dennis Leonard	1.110	1977
10. Doug Bird	1.123	1976

WHIP (WALKS + HITS PER NINE IP): CAREER WITH TEAM

Player	WHIP	IP
1. Bret Saberhagen	1.134	1,660.3
2. Dan Quisenberry	1.150	920.3
3. Jeff Montgomery	1.233	849.3
Marty Pattin	1.233	825.7
5. Doug Bird	1.245	714.7
6. Kevin Appier	1.250	1,843.7
7. Larry Gura	1.253	1,701.3
8. Bud Black	1.259	977.7
9. Dennis Leonard	1.262	2,187.0
10. Dick Drago	1.298	1,134.0

HOME RUNS ALLOWED: SEASON

Player	HRA	Year
1. Darrell May	38	2004
2. Tim Belcher	37	1998
3. Paul Byrd	36	2002
Jeff Suppan	36	2000
5. Brian Anderson	33	2004

Dennis Leonard	33	1979
7. Jeff Suppan	32	2002
8. Tim Belcher	31	1997
Larry Gura	31	1982
Darrell May	31	2003
Jose Lima	31	2005

HOME RUNS ALLOWED: CAREER WITH TEAM

Player	HRA	IP
1. Dennis Leonard	202	2,187.0
2. Paul Splittorff	192	2,554.7
3. Larry Gura	166	1,701.3
4. Mark Gubicza	153	2,218.7
5. Kevin Appier	138	1,843.7
6. Bret Saberhagen	126	1,660.3
7. Jeff Suppan	123	864.7
8. Charlie Leibrandt	102	1,257.0
9. Bud Black	100	977.7
10. Darrell May	97	527.3

SAVES: SEASON

Player	SV	Year
1. Jeff Montgomery	45	1993
Dan Quisenberry	45	1983
3. Dan Quisenberry	44	1984
4. Jeff Montgomery	39	1992
5. Dan Quisenberry	37	1985
6. Jeff Montgomery	36	1998
7. Dan Quisenberry	35	1982
8. Jeff Montgomery	33	1991
Dan Quisenberry	33	1980
10. Jeff Montgomery	31	1995

SAVES: CAREER WITH TEAM

Player	SV	IP
1. Jeff Montgomery	304	849.3
2. Dan Quisenberry	238	920.3
3. Doug Bird	58	714.7
4. Roberto Hernandez	54	119.7
5. Steve Farr	49	511.0
Mike MacDougal	49	170.0
7. Ted Abernathy	40	195.0
8. Al Hrabosky	31	140.0
9. Tom Burgmeier	28	276.0
Mark Littell	28	271.0

WILD PITCHES: SEASON

Player	WP	Year
1. Dan Reichert	18	2000
2. Tom Gordon	17	1993
3. Bruce Dal Canton	16	1974
4. Al Fitzmorris	15	1971
Mark Gubicza	15	1986
6. Kevin Appier	14	1997
David Cone	14	1993
Mark Gubicza	14	1987
Dennis Leonard	14	1977
Pat Rapp	14	1998

WILD PITCHES: CAREER WITH TEAM

Player	WP	IP
1. Mark Gubicza	107	2,218.7
2. Dennis Leonard	73	2,187.0
3. Kevin Appier	72	1,843.7
4. Tom Gordon	71	1,149.7
5. Al Fitzmorris	56	1,098.0
6. Bret Saberhagen	41	1,660.3
Paul Splittorff	41	2,554.7
8. Charlie Leibrandt	39	1,257.0
9. Dan Reichert	34	379.0
10. Jeff Montgomery	32	849.3
Mac Suzuki	32	333.7

HIT BATSMEN: SEASON

Player	HB	Year
1. Mike Boddicker	13	1991
Jim Colborn	13	1977
Zack Greinke	13	2005
4. Jeff Suppan	12	2001
5. Chad Durbin	11	2001
Bob Johnson	11	1970
Dennis Leonard	11	1976
8. David Cone	10	1993
Pat Rapp	10	1998
10. Seven tied with ...	9	——

HIT BATSMEN: CAREER WITH TEAM

Player	HB	IP
1. Mark Gubicza	58	2,218.7
2. Dennis Leonard	52	2,187.0
3. Larry Gura	40	1,701.3
4. Kevin Appier	39	1,843.7
5. Paul Splittorff	34	2,554.7
6. Dick Drago	31	1,134.0
7. Bud Black	29	977.7
Jeff Suppan	29	864.7
9. Hipolito Pichardo	27	669.7
Bret Saberhagen	27	1,660.3

GAMES FINISHED: SEASON

Player	GF	Year
1. Dan Quisenberry	76	1985
2. Dan Quisenberry	68	1980
Dan Quisenberry	68	1982
4. Dan Quisenberry	67	1984
5. Jeff Montgomery	63	1993
6. Jeff Montgomery	62	1992
Dan Quisenberry	62	1983
8. Mike MacDougal	61	2003
9. Jeff Montgomery	59	1990
10. Roberto Hernandez	55	2001
Jeff Montgomery	55	1991

GAMES FINISHED: CAREER WITH TEAM

Player	GF	IP
1. Jeff Montgomery	543	849.3
2. Dan Quisenberry	503	920.3
3. Doug Bird	171	714.7
4. Steve Farr	166	511.0
5. Mike MacDougal	123	170.0
6. Steve Mingori	115	439.0
7. Ted Abernathy	102	195.0
8. Tom Burgmeier	98	276.0
9. Roberto Hernandez	97	119.7
10. Hipolito Pichardo	93	669.7

Significant Royals

APPIER, KEVIN (SP)
(1989–1999, 2003–2004)

Kevin Appier, a gritty, tough-luck starting pitcher, was drafted by the Kansas City Royals as the ninth pick of the first round of the June 1987 amateur draft. After being called up to the big leagues in 1989, Appier spent the next 11 seasons as a mainstay of the Kansas City rotation, although his win total was hampered by a team that offered him little run support. Royals hitters scored either one or zero runs in 35 of Appier's first 80 career losses with the team. In that same stretch he also had 73 no-decisions, often leaving a low-scoring game in a tie. Frustrated with so many years of bad luck, Appier formally asked to be traded in 1997, though he had just completed the first year of a new long-term contract. His plans were thwarted, however, when he injured himself in a fall at his home during the offseason, and he missed most of the 1998 season. When he returned to the field, he wasn't the same pitcher. Before, his ERA was between 2.46 and 3.89; after he returned, his ERA was typically 4.50–5.40. On the trading deadline in 1999, he finally got his long-sought trade, going to the Oakland A's for Jeff D'Amico, Brad Rigby, and Blake Stein. The next four years were spent playing for the A's, Mets, and Angels, then one last two-game stint with Kansas City in 2004 before he retired. Appier was selected to the All-Star team in 1995 and led the league in ERA in 1993 at 2.56.

CAREER ROYALS RECORD:

W	L	W%	ERA	SV
115	92	.556	3.49	0

K	BB	SHO	IP
1,458	634	10	1,843.7

BELTRAN, CARLOS (OF)
(1998–2004)

The Puerto Rican-born Beltran was drafted by Kansas City in the second round of the June 1995 amateur draft. After playing in a handful of games late in 1998, Beltran became a regular in the Kansas City outfield in 1999, performing so spectacularly that he won the American League Rookie of the Year Award in a runaway vote, capturing 26 of 28 first-place votes. Almost immediately, however, the young star proved difficult to get along with, both for management and teammates. After hitting over .300 in three of his last four seasons with the Royals, Beltran, on the verge of greatness but with a salary onerous to the Royals, was traded to Houston in mid-2004. His one All-Star appearance with Kansas City actually occurred *after* he was traded to the Astros.

CAREER ROYALS RECORD:

Games	AB	Hits	Runs
795	3,134	899	546

Avg	HR	RBI	SB
.287	123	516	164

BRETT, GEORGE (3B/DH/1B) (1973–1993)

George Brett, easily the greatest player ever to play for the Royals, was drafted in the second round of the June 1971 amateur draft. He was one of those rare players who played a long and remarkable career for just one team, 21 years to be exact. Along the way the third baseman collected a Gold Glove in 1985, three Silver Slugger Awards (1980, 1985, 1988), the Lou Gehrig Memorial Award (1986), the Hutch Award (1980), the American League MVP Award (1980), and was selected to the All-Star team 12 times, including 11 consecutive times, from 1976 to 1986. He was runner-up for the MVP Award in 1976 and 1985, and third in 1979. He won three batting titles, all in different decades (1976, 1980, and 1990), the first player in history to do so. Brett led the AL in hits three times (1975, 1976, 1979), doubles twice, and triples three times.

Simply put, George Brett was one of the best hitters in the game for two decades. Eleven times he hit over .300 in a season. In 1976 he had six consecutive three-hit games. In 1979 Brett became only the sixth player in major league history to hit 20 or more doubles, triples, and homers in one season. Brett's .390 batting average in 1980 was the highest average for a third baseman in the 20th century. Despite missing 40 games that season due to two injuries, Brett still had a 30-game hitting streak and knocked in 118 runs in only 117 games, one of the rare times a player actually had more RBIs than games played. He also had fewer strikeouts (22) than home runs (24)—a rare feat as well, and one that hadn't been achieved in the previous 24 years.

Without question, the most memorable event of Brett's career occurred on July 24, 1983 in Yankee Stadium. With the Royals down 4–3 in the top of the ninth, Brett hit a two-run homer off closer Rich Gossage. Yankees manager Billy Martin protested that Brett had used an illegal bat, since the pine tar on the handle exceeded the 18-inch limitation set forth in major league rules. Home-plate umpire Tim McClelland agreed and called Brett out, nullifying his home run. The usually mild-mannered Brett, already happily celebrating in the dugout, went berserk. He exploded out of the dugout and charged McClelland, face red, eyes bulging. It took two players and another umpire to restrain Brett. After a Royals protest, AL president Lee MacPhail ordered the home run reinstated and the game to be replayed from that point on. The Royals prevailed in spite of a Yankees lawsuit to prevent it. Twenty-five days later the game was resumed and, despite other Billy Martin trickery, the Royals won the game. The whole affair has become known in baseball lore as "the Pine Tar Incident." George Brett, with 3,154 hits under his belt, called it a career after the 1993 season and, in his first year of eligibility, was elected to the Hall of Fame in 1999.

CAREER ROYALS RECORD:

Games	AB	Hits	Runs
2,707	10,349	3,154	1,583
Avg	**HR**	**RBI**	**SB**
.305	317	1,595	201

GUBICZA, MARK (SP)
(1984–1996)

Mark Gubicza was selected by the Royals in the second round of the June 1981 amateur draft and joined the major league roster in 1984. For thirteen years Gubicza toiled in the Kansas City rotation, making the All-Star team twice (1988 and 1989). His best year was 1988 when he won 20 games, pitched four shutouts, posted a 2.70 ERA, and finished third in the Cy Young voting. He twice led the American League in starts (1989 and 1995). After the 1996 season, the Royals traded Gubicza to the Angels for DH Chili Davis. Gubicza pitched in only two games for the Angels before injuries forced him to retire. He finished his career as Kansas City's all-time leader in strikeouts with 1,366.

CAREER ROYALS RECORD:

W	L	W%	ERA	SV
132	135	.494	3.91	2

K	BB	SHO	IP
1,366	783	16	1,366.0

GURA, LARRY (SP/RP)
(1976–1985)

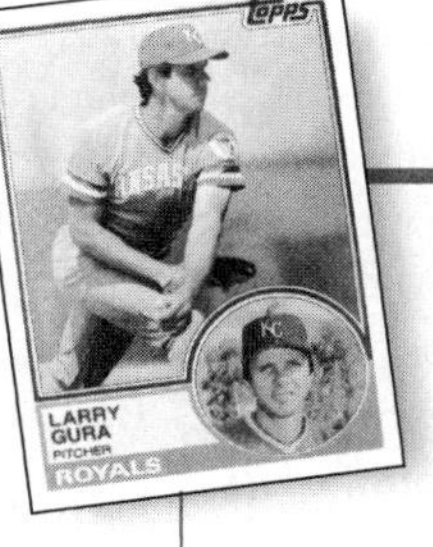

Larry Gura came to the Royals in a trade with the Yankees for Fran Healy in May 1976. For the next 10 seasons he toiled for Kansas City—as a reliever his first two years, then as a starter for the next eight. He twice won 18 games (1980 and 1982), and was selected to the All-Star team in 1980. He was a fitness enthusiast before it became commonplace among major leaguers. In 1985, his last season in the majors, with his career winding down, he was released by the Royals and picked up as a free agent by the Cubs, the team he began his major league career with in 1970.

CAREER ROYALS RECORD:

W	L	W%	ERA	SV
111	78	.587	3.72	12

K	BB	SHO	IP
633	503	14	1,701.3

LEONARD, DENNIS (SP)
(1974–1983, 1985–1986)

Dennis Leonard was drafted by the Kansas City Royals in the second round of the June 1972 amateur draft, and by 1974 had made the big-league roster. In the seven years from 1975 through 1981, Leonard won more games (120) in the major leagues than any other right-handed pitcher. During the strike-shortened season of 1981, he was the only pitcher in the majors to compile more than 200 innings. A severe knee injury ended his 1982 season in midyear and limited him to just 12 appearances over the next three years, 10 in 1983 and just two in 1985. He missed the entire 1984 campaign due to the injury. He rejoined the rotation in 1986, compiling an 8–13 record in 33 appearances, but he wasn't the same pitcher as before. He retired before the 1987 season began as the franchise's career leader in complete games, strikeouts, and shutouts. Leonard was a 20-game winner three times in his career (1977, 1978, 1980), and led the AL in games started three times as well (1978, 1980, 1981).

CAREER ROYALS RECORD:

W	L	W%	ERA	SV
144	106	.576	3.70	1

K	BB	SHO	IP
1,323	622	23	2,187.0

McRae, Hal (DH/OF)
(1973–1987)

Hal McRae was traded from the Cincinnati Reds along with Wayne Simpson for Roger Nelson and Richie Scheinblum in November 1972. McRae spent the next 15 seasons as Kansas City's primary DH, although he did play a fair number of games in the outfield. In 1974 McRae tied the major league record for extra-base hits in a doubleheader with six. McRae was involved in a bit of controversy in 1976 when he was fighting it out with George Brett for the AL batting title. Brett won the title on the last day of the season, .333 to .332, when Steve Brye, the Twins left fielder, played deep on Brett's last at-bat of the season and allowed an easy fly ball to drop for an inside-the-park homer. McRae accused Brye of racism. Others claimed it was in retaliation for McRae's aggressive style of play, a style he had learned from four years with Pete Rose in Cincinnati. (Many opposing players considered McRae a dirty player, not an aggressive player, particularly when it came to breaking up double plays at second base.) A three-time All-Star, McRae batted over .300 seven times in his career. McRae retired as a player after the 1987 season and was inducted into the Kansas City Royals Hall of Fame in 1989. In 1991 he replaced John Wathan as manager of the Royals and managed the team for nearly four years before he was replaced by Bob Boone after the 1994 season.

CAREER ROYALS RECORD:

Games	AB	Hits	Runs
1,837	6,568	1,924	873

Avg	HR	RBI	SB
.293	169	1,012	105

Montgomery, Jeff (RP)
(1988–1999)

Jeff Montgomery came to the Royals in February 1988 in a trade with Cincinnati for Van Snider. In twelve seasons with Kansas City, Montgomery never started a game, instead taking over the closer role from Dan Quisenberry. Over those 12 seasons Montgomery saved 304 games, including 45 in 1993, his career year when he was named the AL Rolaids Relief Award winner. He appeared in three All-Star games during his career before retiring after the 1999 season.

CAREER ROYALS RECORD:

W	L	W%	ERA	SV
44	50	.468	3.20	304

K	BB	SHO	IP
720	287	0	849.3

OTIS, AMOS (OF)
(1970–1983)

The Royals acquired Amos Otis along with pitcher Bob Johnson in what turned out to be a terribly lopsided trade with the Mets for Joe Foy in December 1969. Otis immediately joined the starting team for the Royals in 1970 and remained a fixture in the outfield for more than a decade. He was the first Royals player ever selected to play in the All-Star Game, an honor he received five times. In 1971 Otis stole five bases in one game against Milwaukee, ending the season with 52 steals. Besides possessing power and speed, Otis collected three Gold Gloves for his outfield play. Four times in his career he placed in the top 10 of the AL MVP voting. In the 1980 World Series, Otis hit .478 with three homers in a losing cause. He was released by the Royals after the 1983 season over a contract dispute and signed with Pittsburgh, but played just 40 games for the Pirates before retiring. In 1986 Otis and Steve Busby were the first two players inducted into the Kansas City Royals Hall of Fame.

CAREER ROYALS RECORD:

Games	AB	Hits	Runs
1,891	7,050	1,977	1,074
Avg	**HR**	**RBI**	**SB**
.280	193	992	340

PATEK, FRED (SS)
(1971–1979)

At just 5'5" and less than 150 pounds, Freddie Patek was the smallest player in the majors at the time, but was a valuable contributor during his nine seasons in Kansas City. Patek arrived in Kansas City as part of a six-player trade with Pittsburgh in December 1970 after playing three seasons with the Pirates. Patek became the starting shortstop for the Royals as soon as he arrived. Although he was a light hitter—batting just .241 in his Royals career—he was a solid defensive shortstop and speedy baserunner. He collected 336 steals in his Royals career, finishing in the league's top 10 his first eight seasons. In 1977 Patek led the league with 53 steals. From 1971 to 1973 he led AL shortstops in double plays. Although his career batting average was low, he excelled when the Royals made the playoffs. In both the 1976 and 1977 American League Championship Series, Patek hit .389, driving in a combined nine runs with five doubles and a triple. A three-time All-Star with Kansas City, he left after the 1979 season via free agency, signing with the Angels for the last two years of his career.

CAREER ROYALS RECORD:

Games	AB	Hits	Runs
1,245	4,305	1,036	571
Avg	**HR**	**RBI**	**SB**
.241	28	382	336

QUISENBERRY, DAN (RP)
(1979–1988)

Signed by the Royals as an amateur free agent in 1975, Dan Quisenberry was, from 1980 to 1985, the best closer in the American League. Five times (1980, 1982–1985) he won the American League Rolaids Relief Pitcher of the Year Award, leading the league in saves in each of those years. Quisenberry finished either second or third in the Cy Young voting from 1982 to 1985, and finished third in the league in the 1984 MVP race. He was a member of the American League All-Star team from 1982 to 1984. With an unorthodox submariner pitching style, "Quiz" didn't possess a blazing fastball or wicked breaking pitch, but relied on a sinker to induce harmless ground balls. Quisenberry had incredible control, walking only 139 batters in more than 900 innings during his Royals career. After being released by the Royals during the 1988 season, Quisenberry signed with the Cardinals for the remainder of 1988 and 1989, then spent 1990 with San Francisco before retiring. Quisenberry died in 1998 from a brain tumor at the age of 45.

CAREER ROYALS RECORD:

W	L	W%	ERA	SV
51	44	.537	2.55	238

K	BB	SHO	IP
321	139	0	920.3

SABERHAGEN, BRET (SP)
(1984–1991)

Drafted by the Royals in the 19th round of the June 1982 amateur draft at the age of 18, Bret Saberhagen became a member of the Kansas City rotation when he was just 20 years old. By the time he was 21, Saberhagen had defeated the St. Louis Cardinals in Game 7 of the 1985 World Series, snagging the World Series MVP Award in the process. A few weeks later he won the AL's Cy Young Award for his 20–6 season. He won his second Cy Young in 1989 after posting a 23–6 record with a 2.16 ERA. Saberhagen also, oddly enough, won two Comeback Player of the Year Awards, the first with Kansas City in 1987. After falling to 7–12 in 1986 after his terrific 1985 season, he came back with an 18–10 record in 1987. This strange pattern of good year-bad year continued for much of Saberhagen's career, even after he was traded from Kansas City following the 1991 season to the New York Mets. Saberhagen was named to the AL All-Star team twice (1987 and 1990), and won the AL Babe Ruth Award in 1985.

CAREER ROYALS RECORD:

W	L	W%	ERA	SV
110	78	.585	3.21	1

K	BB	SHO	IP
1,093	331	14	1,660.3

SPLITTORFF, PAUL (SP)
(1970–1984)

The Royals made Paul Splittorff their 25th-round selection in the June 1968 amateur draft and he played his entire 15-year major league career with the team. Splittorff was a reliable and successful starter who remains among Kansas City's all-time leaders in most pitching categories. His best season was 1973, when he went 20–11.

CAREER ROYALS RECORD:

W	L	W%	ERA	SV
166	143	.537	3.81	1

K	BB	SHO	IP
1,057	780	17	2,554.7

SWEENEY, MIKE (1B/DH)
(1995–2005)

Mike Sweeney was drafted by the Royals in the 10th round of the June 1991 amateur draft; he made the big league team as a late-season call-up in 1995. After three seasons of part-time play, Sweeney became a regular in 1999, splitting his time between first base and DH, although a series of nagging injuries has, from time to time, limited both his playing time and awesome potential. During his 11-year career, all of which has been spent with Kansas City, Sweeney has been named to the American League All-Star team five times, and in 2002 he was the runner-up in the race for batting champion, hitting .340 to winner Manny Ramirez's .349. Sweeney is starting to creep up in the Royals' all-time lists in a number of categories. He'll be just 32 in 2006, so if he can eliminate his recent injury troubles, within a few years he will rank high among Kansas City's all-time career leaders.

CAREER ROYALS RECORD:

Games	AB	Hits	Runs
1,148	4,187	1,273	651

Avg	HR	RBI	SB
.304	182	766	48

WHITE, FRANK (2B)
(1973–1990)

Like a number of other Royals stars of his era, Frank White played his entire career with Kansas City. Signed in July 1970 out of the Kansas City Royals Baseball Academy as an amateur free agent, White made the major league roster in 1973 and anchored the second-base bag for the Royals for most of the 1970s and all of the 1980s, finishing his 18-year career in 1990. An adequate hitter (.255 career average), White was known for his defensive skill. He won eight Gold Gloves, including six in a row from 1977 to 1982. White had one stretch of 62 consecutive errorless games in 1977. He made the All-Star team five times and won the 1980 ALCS MVP Award for his .545 batting average in Kansas City's three-game sweep of the Yankees. Although not known as a hitter,

White did hit 10 or more homers 13 times in his career, earning the AL's Silver Slugger Award for second basemen in 1986. After his retirement he became a coach, first for Boston and later for the Royals.

CAREER ROYALS RECORD:

Games	AB	Hits	Runs
2,324	7,859	2,006	912
Avg	**HR**	**RBI**	**SB**
.255	160	886	178

WILSON, WILLIE (OF)
(1976–1990)

Willie Wilson was a first-round selection in the June 1974 amateur draft and played the first 15 of his 19 major league seasons with the Royals. He was one of the fastest men ever to play in the majors, stealing more than 600 bases in his Kansas City career. He hit 13 career inside-the-park homers. Only Roberto Clemente hit more career triples between World War II and the end of the 20th century. Wilson was a free swinger who didn't walk as much as a leadoff hitter typically does. He set a major league record in 1980 with 705 at-bats while knocking out 230 hits, the second highest total in the American League since 1936. Wilson set another record in 1980, however, that he wishes he hadn't: He struck out 12 times in the six games of the 1980 World Series against Philadelphia. The two-time All-Star won the American League batting title in 1982 with a .332 average. He also won two Silver Slugger Awards, the first in 1980 and the second in 1982, and a Gold Glove in 1980. With his talents diminishing, Wilson left Kansas City via free agency after the 1990 season and spent his last four seasons with the A's and Cubs. Wilson received one dark blemish to his otherwise brilliant career in 1983 when he, along with several other Royals players, admitted to attempting to purchase cocaine, resulting in a short prison sentence.

CAREER ROYALS RECORD:

Games	AB	Hits	Runs
1,787	6,799	1,968	1,060
Avg	**HR**	**RBI**	**SB**
.289	40	509	612

Los Angeles Angels of Anaheim

Since 1961

2002 Team Ball

1964 Led by Cy Young winner Dean Chance, who finishes at 20–9 with a 1.65 ERA and an absolutely incredible 11 shutouts, the Angels pitch 28 shutouts in 1964, tops in the major leagues since 1909.... **1971** The Angels field by far the best starting rotation in baseball, with Nolan Ryan, Clyde Wright, Rudy May, and Andy Messersmith all ending the season with sub-3.00 ERAs.... **1975** The Angels steal 220 bases, the most in the majors since Pittsburgh stole 200 in 1918. But lack of offense—they hit just 55 homers—and porous defense consign them to the cellar.... **1991** Mark Langston (19–8), Jim Abbott (18–11), and Chuck Finley (18–9) become the first trio of left-handed teammates in major league history to win 18 or more games each in the same season.... **2000** The Angels become the first American League team in history with four players who hit at least 30 home runs in the same season. Troy Glaus (47), Mo Vaughn (36), Garret Anderson (35), and Tim Salmon (34) help smash the team home run record by 44 round-trippers.

FRANCHISE HISTORY

The Angels were born in a highly political climate. In the fall of 1960, a week after the National League had voted to expand to 10 teams for the 1962 season, the American League hurriedly voted to expand to 10 teams for the 1961 season. In retaliation for the National League having placed a team in New York City, in direct competition with the Yankees, the American League owners voted to place a team in Los Angeles, despite the fact it would be alone on the West Coast, in order to compete with the Dodgers. This Los Angeles team was called the Angels, after the Pacific Coast League's popular Los Angeles entry. The minor league Angels, who had played their games in Wrigley Field (named after Chicago Cubs owner William Wrigley, who also owned the minor league Angels) had moved to Spokane, Wash., after the 1957 season when the National League's Dodgers relocated from Brooklyn to Los Angeles. The other American League expansion team to begin play in 1961 was the second Washington Senators team, which was approved to replace the original Senators team that had relocated to Minnesota and became the Twins.

The major league Angels franchise was awarded on December 6, 1960, to Gene Autry, Bob Richards, and their associates. Autry, a famous early movie star who was loved by many Americans as a singing cowboy, owned the Golden West Broadcasting Corporation, whose Los Angeles-based flagship station, KMPC, had just lost the broadcast rights to Dodgers games. On December 14, the new Angels team was stocked with players from major league baseball's first-ever expansion draft. The Angels played their first home game on April 26, 1961. Ty Cobb threw out the first pitch.

Alex Johnson is the only Angel ever to win a batting title, accomplishing the feat on the final day of the 1970 season when he went 2-for-3, edging out Boston's Carl Yastrzemski, .3289 to .3286.

The Angels originally intended to play their home games in the Los Angeles Coliseum, but Commissioner Ford Frick decided that the abbreviated left-field fence in the Coliseum would be inappropriate for major league baseball. So the team played their first season in Wrigley Field, the old Pacific Coast League stadium. From 1962 through 1965, they shared Dodger Stadium with the Dodgers (although the

Early movie star Gene Autry owned the Angels for more than 35 years before selling to Disney.

Angels referred to it as Chavez Ravine when they played there). In 1966, longtime Yankees owner Del Webb helped the Angels move to Anaheim in return for the contract to build the new ballpark. That park was named Anaheim Stadium, sometimes called "the Big A" in honor of the stadium's 230-foot high A-shaped scoreboard. In 1994 that scoreboard came crashing down into the bleachers during an earthquake (luckily, it was a January earthquake). The Angels still play in the same place today, but the stadium has undergone several name changes.

In 1983 Gene Autry bought out his partners and became sole owner of the team. In the early 1980s, he married a much younger woman, Jackie, who ran the club into the mid-1990s, after Autry grew too old for the task. After a proposed sale to former baseball commissioner Peter Ueberroth fell through in 1994, the Autrys sold a 25 percent interest to the Disney Company in 1995 for $30 million with an option to purchase the remaining 75 percent upon Autry's death. It took nearly a year for the deal to be finalized, though, because Disney had to reach a settlement and understanding with the city of Anaheim on a renovation of Anaheim Stadium. The two entities also had to renegotiate an acceptable new lease arrangement. In 2003, citing heavy losses, the Disney Company sold the team to current owner Arturo Moreno, owner of a large advertising company and a big Angels fan, for $184 million.

Nolan Ryan tied one of Sandy Koufax's strikeout records on July 4, 1977.

While the team has always been known as the Angels, its "first" name has changed several times. The franchise was originally known as the Los Angeles Angels. In 1965 the name was changed in midseason to the California Angels. When Disney took control, it changed the name to the Anaheim Angels, starting with the 1997 season. In 2004, current owner Arturo Moreno approved a name change back to the Los Angeles Angels in an effort to attract more advertising dollars. After the city of Anaheim filed a lawsuit over the name change (the stadium lease required the city's name "Anaheim" to be included in the team name), Moreno changed the name again to its current name: the Los Angeles Angels of Anaheim. Sometimes the team is referred to by its nickname, the Halos, in reference to the halo that appears above the "A" on the team logo.

On the field, the Angels surprised many in 1961 by finishing with a respectable 70–91 record, good for eighth place in the 10-team league. The Angels' success in 1961 was likely connected to the major league record number of homers that were hit in Wrigley Field that year, 248. The Angels had five players with at least 20 homers. In 1962 (with apologies to Mets fans), the Angels truly were amazing. In just their second year in existence, the Angels finished in third place, just five games behind second-place Minnesota and 10 games behind the champion Yankees. In 1967 the team was in the pennant race until mid-September before fading. It wasn't until 1979 that the Angels won their first division championship, finishing three games ahead of Kansas City. The Angels' Don Baylor was the American League MVP. They were dispatched by the Orioles, however, three games to one in the ALCS.

Jim Abbott had the best ERA on the team in 1992—2.77—yet lost more games than any other Angels pitcher—15.

The Angels won their second division title in 1982 behind newly-acquired free agent Reggie Jackson's league-leading 39 homers. In the ALCS, however, the Angels lost a heart-breaking series to the Milwaukee Brewers, three games to two, after winning the first two games. Four years later, in 1986, the Angels won the AL West again. This time they would face the Red Sox in the ALCS. Up three games to one on the Sox, with a three-run lead in the ninth, Angels relievers couldn't hold the lead. One strike away from advancing to the World Series against the Mets, Donnie Moore gave up a two-run homer to Boston's Dave Henderson. The Red Sox then won in extra innings and blew the Angels away in Games 6 and 7. Forever distraught over what happened, Donnie Moore later committed suicide.

In 1995, after leading the AL West by 11 games in August, the Angels experienced a serious meltdown. In the last five weeks of the season, the Angels had two nine-game losing streaks while the Seattle Mariners went 17–5 in their final 22 games. The two teams ended up in a dead tie on the last day of the season and had to play a one-game playoff in Seattle for the division championship. Seattle won, 5–1, helping the Angels complete one of the most incredible collapses in major league baseball history.

Four decades of frustration finally came to an end in 2002. Although the Angels won 99 games, the most in the history of the franchise, they only earned the Wild Card spot because Oakland won 103 games to finish first. The Angels easily handled the Yankees in the Division Series, winning three games to one, and just as easily dispatched the Twins in the ALCS, four games to one. The Angels won the World Series against the San Francisco Giants in seven games after trailing three games to two, coming from behind in all four of their wins, winning three of them by one run.

TEAM NAME HISTORY

Official Names

Los Angeles Angels (1961 to mid-1965)
California Angels (mid-1965 to 1996)
Anaheim Angels (1997–2004)
Los Angeles Angels of Anaheim (2005–current)

Unofficial Names/Nicknames

Halos

STADIUM HISTORY

Wrigley Field (L.A.)	1961
Chavez Ravine (Dodger Stadium, actually, but so named for Angels games)	1962–1965
Anaheim Stadium	1966–1996
Edison International Field (Anaheim Stadium renamed)	1997–2003
Angels Stadium of Anaheim (Edison International Field renamed)	2004–current

---

Yearly Record, Finish, & Attendance Figures

Year	League	Record	DIV/LG Finish	Attendance	Avg/Gm
2005	AL West	95–67	1	3,404,686	42,033
2004	AL West	92–70	1	3,375,677	41,675
2003	AL West	77–85	3	3,061,094	37,330
2002	AL West	99–63	2	2,305,547	28,464
2001	AL West	75–87	3	2,000,919	24,703
2000	AL West	82–80	3	2,066,982	25,518
1999	AL West	70–92	4	2,253,123	27,816
1998	AL West	85–77	2	2,519,280	31,102
1997	AL West	84–78	2	1,767,330	21,553
1996	AL West	70–91	4	1,820,521	22,476
1995	AL West	78–67	2	1,748,680	24,287
1994	AL West	47–68	4	1,512,622	24,010
1993	AL West	71–91	5	2,057,460	25,401
1992	AL West	72–90	6	2,065,444	25,499
1991	AL West	81–81	7	2,416,236	29,830
1990	AL West	80–82	4	2,555,688	31,552
1989	AL West	91–71	3	2,647,291	32,683
1988	AL West	75–87	4	2,340,925	28,900
1987	AL West	75–87	7	2,696,299	33,288
1986	AL West	92–70	1	2,655,872	32,389
1985	AL West	90–72	2	2,567,427	32,499
1984	AL West	81–81	2	2,402,997	29,667
1983	AL West	70–92	5	2,555,016	31,543
1982	AL West	93–69	1	2,807,360	34,659
1981	AL West	51–59	4/7	1,441,545	26,695
1980	AL West	65–95	6	2,297,327	28,362
1979	AL West	88–74	1	2,523,575	31,155
1978	AL West	87–75	3	1,755,386	21,671
1977	AL West	74–88	5	1,432,633	17,687
1976	AL West	76–86	5	1,006,774	12,429
1975	AL West	72–89	6	1,058,163	13,064
1974	AL West	68–94	6	917,269	11,324
1973	AL West	79–83	4	1,058,206	13,064
1972	AL West	75–80	5	744,190	9,302
1971	AL West	76–86	4	926,373	11,437
1970	AL West	86–76	3	1,077,741	13,305
1969	AL West	71–91	3	758,388	9,363
1968	AL	67–95	8	1,025,956	12,666
1967	AL	84–77	5	1,317,713	15,876
1966	AL	80–82	6	1,400,321	17,288
1965	AL	75–87	7	566,727	7,084
1964	AL	82–80	5	760,439	9,388
1963	AL	70–91	9	821,015	10,136
1962	AL	86–76	3	1,144,063	14,124
1961	AL	70–91	8	603,510	7,360

Manager History

Manager	Years	W–L	Win %
Bill Rigney	1961–1969	625–70	.469
Lefty Phillips	1969–1971	222–225	.497
Del Rice	1972	75–80	.484
Bobby Winkles	1973–1974	109–127	.462
Whitey Herzog	1974	2–2	.500
Dick Williams	1974–1976	147–194	.431
Norm Sherry	1976–1977	76–71	.517
Dave Garcia	1977–1978	60–66	.476
Jim Fregosi	1978–1981	237–249	.488
Gene Mauch	1981–1982, 1985–1987	379–332	.533
John McNamara	1983–1984,1996	161–191	.457
Cookie Rojas	1988	75–79	.487
Moose Stubing	1988	0–8	.000
Doug Rader	1989–1991	232–216	.518
Buck Rodgers	1991–1994	140–172	.449
John Wathan	1992	39–50	.438
Marcel Lachemann	1994–1996	161–170	.486
Joe Maddon	1996, 1999	27–24	.529
Terry Collins	1997–1999	220–237	.481
Mike Scioscia	2000–current	520–452	.535

All-Time Win-Loss Records vs. All Opponents

ALL-TIME	3,505–3,653
Astros	1–2
Athletics	320–372
Blue Jays	154–163
Braves	2–1
Brewers	180–168
Cardinals	1–2
Cubs	1–2
Devil Rays	50–28
Diamondbacks	5–7
Dodgers	28–22
Giants	5–11
Indians	282–264
INTERLEAGUE	83–75
Mariners	211–190
Marlins	4–2
Mets	3–3
Nationals	3–3
Orioles	248–317
Padres	7–9
Phillies	2–1
Pirates	3–3
Rangers	343–323
Reds	2–1
Red Sox	257–298
Rockies	12–4
Royals	239–243
Tigers	259–288
Twins	318–303
White Sox	318–315
Yankees	247–307

Franchise Highlights, Low Points, and Strange Distinctions

1962 The Angels were surprisingly competitive, just their second year of existence. On July 4 the Angels swept a doubleheader in Washington to take over first place in the 10-team American League. They were still in the race into September and finished the season in third place, just 10 games behind the Yankees and five behind runner-up Minnesota. For this surprising showing, Fred Haney was voted Executive of the Year in the American League, and Bill Rigney was voted Manager of the Year.

••••

1964 When the Angels recorded 28 shutouts, the best in the majors since 1909, Cy Young winner Dean Chance was responsible for 11 of them. Six of those were 1–0 victories, a major league record. If Chance had received decent run support in his losses, he would have won 25 or more games. He lost one 1–0 game, three 2–1 games, two 3–2 games, one game in relief, and games of 3–0, 4–2, and 6–1. Against the pennant-winning Yankees, Chance was especially tough. In 50 innings against New York, Chance gave up only one run, a homer by Mickey Mantle.

The Angels lost two of their pitchers during the 1964 season to bad tempers. Bo Belinsky, 9–8 at the time, was suspended for the season on August 14 when he assaulted 64-year-old *Los Angeles Times* sportswriter Braven Dyer. Then Bob Lee, one of the top relievers in the majors (6–5, 17 saves, 1.51 ERA at the time), missed the remainder of the season when he broke his hand after slugging a heckler in Boston on September 11.

1965 Pitcher Fred Newman was especially snakebitten by a lack of run support in 1965. Although he had a sparkling 2.93 ERA, his 14–16 record wasn't nearly as good as it could have been. In a stretch of nine consecutive winless starts late in the season, the Angels scored a combined total of 12 runs for Newman.

••••

1967 The Angels made a remarkable turnaround during the season. After being pummeled in front of the home fans by the Orioles in a doubleheader on June 6, 16–4 and 11–1, the Angels had a soul-searching team meeting. Angels' ownership gave Manager Bill Rigney a strong vote of confidence and the team responded by going 34–12 in their next 46 games, moving from 12 games under .500 to just 1 1/2 games out of first on August 12. They remained in the pennant race until late September.

••••

1973 How good was Nolan Ryan's season? He won 21 games, the last seven in a row, all complete games, and had 26 complete games for the season. He hurled two no-hitters. He set the single-season record for strikeouts with 383, and showed uncommon courage and strength in the process. The record-breaking game came on September 28 against Minnesota. Needing 16 strikeouts to break Sandy Koufax's record, Ryan tore a thigh muscle on his 15th strikeout in the eighth inning. Unable to push off the mound because of the injury, Ryan lost the use of his fastball. The game went into extra innings, but Ryan failed to record a strikeout in the ninth or 10th. In the 11th, with the winning run on second, Ryan somehow managed to summon the strength to fire three consecutive fastballs past Rich Reese for the record.

• • • •

1974 The Angels had a dismal showing, but it wasn't Ryan's fault. Three times during the season he struck out 19 batters in a game. He finished with a 22–16 record, but the Angels only scored 22 runs for him during his 16 losses. He struck out 367 batters, third highest total in history. He set or tied strikeout records for one (19), two consecutive (32), and three consecutive (47) games. Ryan became the first pitcher in modern history to strike out 300 batters in three consecutive seasons.

• • • •

1976 Nolan Ryan (17–18 with 327 strikeouts and a 3.36 ERA) finished the season in incredible fashion. From September 5 on, Ryan was 6–1 with two two-hitters and four three-hitters with three shutouts. To illustrate why he had such a hard time accumulating big win totals over the years, consider the game scores of his six victories to end the season: 3–2, 3–2, 2–1, 1–0, 1–0, and 3–0. He virtually had to pitch as well as he did every time out in order to earn his modest win-loss record of 138–121 while with the Angels.

• • • •

1978 After hitting .323 and .336 in his two previous seasons with the Minnesota Twins, Outfielder Lyman Bostock signed a big free-agent contract with the Angels before the 1978 season. After batting only .147 in April with no home runs, he refused to accept his first month's pay. When owner Gene Autry insisted that he take his money, Bostock gave it all away to charity. Less than five months later Bostock was dead, the unintended victim of a jealous estranged husband, murdered by a shotgun blast as he was riding in a car with his uncle in Gary, Indiana. The killer, Leonard Smith, was eventually found not guilty by reason of insanity and spent a total of just 21 months in custody, part of it in jail awaiting trial, the rest in Logansport State Hospital following his acquittal.

• • • •

1980 After winning the AL West in 1979, the team was expecting great things in 1980. But the Angels, mainly due to poor pitching and many injuries, fell to sixth place with a 65–95 record. At one point during the 1980 season, the floundering Angels were hit so hard by injuries that the total salaries of the players on the disabled list exceeded the entire payrolls of Seattle, Chicago, and Toronto.

• • • •

1983 The injury curse returned in 1983, the year after the team won the division title with their best record ever (93–69). The '83 Angels went 70–92, suffering so many key injuries that Bob Boone, the team's catcher, played the most games at 142.

• • • •

1984 Mike Witt pitched the 13th perfect game in major league history on the last day of the season, a nail-biting 1–0 gem over the Rangers in Texas. Only four Rangers succeeded in getting the ball out of the infield.

1985 The two-day players' strike likely cost the Angels, who ended the season one game behind Kansas City, a division title. The strike cancelled the Angels' two-game set against weak Seattle, and the makeup games were shifted to Seattle as part of two back-to-back doubleheaders, which the teams split.

••••

1986 The Angels suffered one of the most bitterly disappointing pennant losses in baseball history. Leading the AL East champion Boston Red Sox three games to one in the ALCS, and up by a score of 5–2 with one out in the ninth inning of Game 5, reliever Donnie Moore gave up a two-run homer to former Angel Don Baylor. Still leading, 5–4, with two outs and two strikes on batter Dave Henderson, Moore surrendered another two-run homer. The Angels scored a run in the bottom of the ninth to tie the game, but Boston prevailed in 11 innings. When the series shifted to Boston, the Red Sox trounced the demoralized Angels, 10–4 and 8–1 in Games 6 and 7 to advance to the World Series. Manager Gene Mauch again failed to win his first pennant after 25 years of trying.

••••

1987 Aging Bob Boone caught his 1,919th career game on September 16, breaking Al Lopez's 40-year-old major league record. He finished the season with 1,935 games caught and his fifth Gold Glove.

1990 In the first 94 games of the season, Manager Doug Rader used 93 different starting lineups.

After pitcher Mark Langston signed a lucrative $16 million five-year contract prior to the 1990 season, he promptly went out and compiled a 10–17 record, making him the losingest Angel pitcher in 16 years.

••••

1991 One of the biggest disappointments of the season was the team's inability to find a fifth starter. Through the end of August, the various fifth starters used by the Angels had compiled a 1–16 record.

••••

1992 Jim Abbott had the best ERA on the team in 1992—2.77—yet lost more games than any other Angels pitcher—15.

••••

1997 Although the Angels improved by winning 14 more games than they did in 1996 and ended up in second place, their major league-leading 27 blown saves prevented them from doing even better.

••••

1999 On September 11, interim manager Joe Maddon, having inherited a disheartened team full of acrimony, decided to give almost all his regular players the day off. The team, full of replacements, was no-hit 7–0 by Minnesota's Eric Milton, who had entered the game with a 6–11 record.

2000 After hitting just .253 in 1999, Darin Erstad had a breakthrough season in 2000. He led the majors with 240 hits, batted .355, and set an all-time record for leadoff hitters by collecting 100 RBIs. Erstad also hit 25 homers, stole 28 bases, and won a Gold Glove.

• • • •

2001 The Angels were in the Wild Card race until a memorably terrible September, when they went 2–19 in their last 21 games. The DH problem was a big part of it; the Angels used 15 different players at DH, who hit only .212 with 8 homers and 56 RBIs.

2005 Through the 2005 season, the Angels were the only current American League team—and one of only two in the majors—which has never won or lost 100 games in a season. They've never lost more than the 95 they lost in 1980. On the winning side, when the Angels won it all in 2002, they won 99 regular season games for their franchise record. Only Colorado in the National League can say the same thing.

Series MVP Troy Glaus and manager Mike Scioscia—and the mouse—celebrate their World Series victory over San Francisco in 2002.

Special Achievements

WORLD SERIES RESULTS

Year	Opponent	Result	Games
2002	San Francisco	Won	4–3

WORLD SERIES MANAGERIAL RECORDS

Manager	Series Record	Games Record
Mike Scioscia	1–0	4–3

ALL-TIME POSTSEASON RECORD

Divisional Playoffs	6–6
League Championship Series	11–15
World Series	4–3

ALL-STAR GAMES AT LOS ANGELES/ANAHEIM

Year	Date	Winner	Score	Stadium
1967	July 11	National	2–1	Anaheim Stadium
1989	July 11	American	5–3	Anaheim Stadium

HALL OF FAMERS WHO PLAYED FOR TEAM

	Position	Years	Games with Angels
Rod Carew	1B	1979–1985	834
Reggie Jackson	DH/OF	1982–1986	687
Eddie Murray	DH	1997	46
Frank Robinson	DH	1973–1974	276
Nolan Ryan	SP	1972–1979	291
Don Sutton	SP	1985–1987	74
Hoyt Wilhelm	RP	1969	44
Dave Winfield	OF	1990–1991	262

HALL OF FAMERS WHO MANAGED TEAM

None

MVP AWARD WINNERS

Don Baylor	OF	1979
Vladimir Guerrero	OF	2004

CY YOUNG AWARD WINNERS

Pitcher	Year	W–L	ERA
Dean Chance	1964	20–9	1.65
Bartolo Colon	2005	21–8	3.48

ROOKIE OF THE YEAR AWARD WINNERS

Tim Salmon	OF	1993

GOLD GLOVE WINNERS

Year	Position	Player
1964	1B	Vic Power
1966	2B	Bobby Knoop
1967	2B SS	Bobby Knoop Jim Fregosi
1968	2B	Bobby Knoop
1970	1B	Jim Spencer
1972	OF	Ken Berry
1978	OF	Rick Miller
1982	C	Bob Boone
1985	OF	Gary Pettis
1986	C OF	Bob Boone Gary Pettis
1987	C	Bob Boone
1988	C OF	Bob Boone Devon White
1989	OF	Devon White
1991	SP	Mark Langston
1992	SP	Mark Langston
1993	SP	Mark Langston
1994	SP	Mark Langston
1995	SP 1B	Mark Langston J.T. Snow
1996	1B	J.T. Snow
1997	OF	Jim Edmonds
1998	OF	Jim Edmonds
2000	OF	Darin Erstad
2002	C OF	Bengie Molina Darin Erstad
2003	C	Bengie Molina
2004	1B	Darin Erstad

TRIPLE CROWN WINNERS

None

FIREMAN OF THE YEAR AWARD WINNERS

Minnie Rojas	1967
Bryan Harvey	1991 (tie)

WORLD SERIES MVP

Troy Glaus	2002

LEAGUE CHAMPIONSHIP SERIES MVP

Fred Lynn	1982
Adam Kennedy	2002

ALL-STAR GAME MVP

Fred Lynn	1983
Garret Anderson	2003

MANAGER OF THE YEAR AWARD WINNERS

Mike Scioscia	2002

BATTING CHAMPIONS

1970	Alex Johnson	.329

NINE-INNING NO-HITTERS PITCHED

Year	Pitcher	Opp.	Score
1962	Bo Belinsky	BAL	2–0
1970	Clyde Wright	OAK	4–0
1973	Nolan Ryan Nolan Ryan	KC DET	3–0 6–0
1974	Nolan Ryan	MIN	4–0
1975	Nolan Ryan	BAL	1–0
1984	Mike Witt	TEX	1–0 (perfect)
1990	Mark Langston & Mike Witt	SEA	1–0

20-GAME WINNERS

Year	Pitcher	W–L
1964	Dean Chance	20–9
1970	Clyde Wright	22–12
1971	Andy Messersmith	20–13
1973	Nolan Ryan Bill Singer	21–16 20–14
1974	Nolan Ryan	22–16
2005	Bartolo Colon	21–8

RETIRED UNIFORM NUMBERS

Number	Player	Position
11	Jim Fregosi	SS/Mgr
26	Gene Autry	Owner
29	Rod Carew	1B/2B
30	Nolan Ryan	SP
50	Jimmie Reese	Coach

TEAM RECORDS—WINS & LOSSES

- Games won in a season: 99 in 2002
- Games lost in a season: 95 in 1968 and 1980
- Games won in a month: 22 in June 1998
- Games lost in a month: 22, three times, in June 1961, May 1964, and August 1968
- Consecutive games won: 11 in 1964
- Consecutive games lost: 12 in 1988
- Biggest shutout victory: 19–0 over Chicago White Sox on May 10, 2003
- Biggest shutout loss: 14–0 to Seattle on August 7, 1987
- Highest winning percentage: .611 in 2002 (99–63)
- Lowest winning percentage: .406 in 1980 (65–95)

TEAM RECORDS—BATTING

- Highest team batting average: .282 in 2002 and 2004
- Lowest team batting average: .227 in 1968
- Highest team slugging average: .472 in 2000
- Highest team on-base percentage: .352 in 2000
- Total hits: 1,603 in 2002 and 2004
- Extra-base hits: 579 in 2000
- Hits in a game: 26 vs. Toronto on August 25, 1979 and vs. Boston on June 20, 1980
- Longest individual hitting streak: 28, Garret Anderson, 1998
- Most .300 hitters in a single season: 2, accomplished eight times
- Home runs: 236 in 2000
- Home runs in a month (individual): 13, Tim Salmon, June 1996, and Mo Vaughn, May 2000
- Home runs in a game: 7 vs. Montreal on June 4, 2003
- Home runs by a rookie: 31, Tim Salmon, 1993
- Home runs by a right-hander: 47, Troy Glaus, 2000
- Home runs by a left-hander: 39, Reggie Jackson, 1982
- Home runs by a switch-hitter: 28, Chili Davis, 1996
- Grand slams: 8 in 1979 and 1983
- Grand slams (individual; single season): 3, Joe Rudi (twice), 1978 and 1979; David Eckstein, 2002
- Grand slams (individual; career): 7, Joe Rudi
- Triples: 54 in 1966
- Doubles: 333 in 2002
- Singles: 1,132 in 2004
- Walks: 681 in 1961
- Runs scored: 866 in 1979
- Runs scored in a game: 24 vs. Toronto on August 25, 1979

- Runs scored in an inning: 13 vs. Texas on September 14, 1978 (ninth inning) and Chicago White Sox on May 12, 1997 (seventh inning)
- Most batters hit by a pitch: 77 in 2001
- Times shut out: 23 in 1971
- Grounded into double plays: 148 in 1966
- Fewest grounded into double plays: 98 in 1975
- Runners left on base: 1,209 in 1966

Team Records—Baserunning

- Stolen bases: 220 in 1975
- Caught stealing: 108 in 1975

Team Records—Pitching

- Lowest earned run average: 2.91 in 1964
- Complete games: 72 in 1973
- Saves: 54 in 2002 and 2005
- Strikeouts: 1,126 in 2005
- Shutouts: 28 in 1964
- Walks: 713 in 1961
- Hit batsmen: 84 in 1996
- Wild pitches: 80 in 1966
- Consecutive wins (individual): 12, Jarrod Washburn in 2002
- Consecutive losses (individual): 11, Andy Hassler in 1975 and Jim Abbott in 1996
- Strikeouts in a game: 19, Nolan Ryan (four times): August 12, 1974; June 14, 1974 (13 innings); August 20, 1974 (11 innings); and June 8, 1977 (11 innings)
- Runs allowed in a game: 21 vs. Seattle, September 30, 2000

Team Records—Fielding

- Best fielding average: .986 in 2002
- Most errors committed: 192 in 1961
- Fewest errors committed: 87 in 2002 and 2005
- Most double plays turned: 202 in 1985
- Fewest double plays turned: 126 in 2004

Team Records—Miscellaneous

- Number of times league champions: 1
- Number of times finishing last in league: 2
- Largest attendance, single game: 63,132 vs. Kansas City, July 4, 1983
- Largest attendance, doubleheader: 43,461 vs. Chicago White Sox, August 5, 1988
- Players used in a season: 52 in 1996
- Seasons played: 14, Chuck Finley

Primary Pitching Staffs

Year	Starter	Starter	Starter	Starter	Starter	Closer	Bullpen	Bullpen	Bullpen
2005	Colon	Lackey	Byrd	Washburn	Santana	Rodriguez	Shields	Donnelly	Yan
2004	Colon	Escobar	Lackey	Washburn	Sele	Percival	Rodriguez	Shields	Gregg
2003	Ortiz	Appier	Lackey	Washburn	Sele	Percival	Rodriguez	Donnelly	Weber
2002	Ortiz	Appier	Lackey	Washburn	Sele	Percival	Schoeneweis	Levine	Weber
2001	Ortiz	Schoeneweis	Rapp	Washburn	Valdez	Percival	Holtz	Levine	Weber
2000	Ortiz	Schoeneweis	Bottenfield	Hill	Cooper	Percival	Holtz	Hasegawa	Petkovsek
1999	Finley	Sparks	Belcher	Hill	Olivares	Percival	Magnante	Hasegawa	Petkovsek
1998	Finley	Sparks	Dickson	Hill	Olivares	Percival	DeLucia	Hasegawa	Holtz
1997	Finley	Watson	Dickson	Hill	Springer	Percival	Harris	James	Holtz
1996	Finley	Boskie	Abbott	Grimsley	Langston	Percival	McElroy	James	Holtz
1995	Finley	Boskie	Abbott	Anderson	Langston	Smith	Patterson	James	Percival
1994	Finley	Leftwich	Magrane	Anderson	Langston	Grahe	Patterson	Leiter	Butcher
1993	Finley	Leftwich	Sanderson	Farrell	Langston	Frey	Nelson	Patterson	Grahe
1992	Finley	Abbott	Valera	Blyleven	Langston	Grahe	Crim	Frey	Eichhorn
1991	Finley	Abbott	McCaskill	Lewis	Langston	Harvey	Bailes	Robinson	Eichhorn
1990	Finley	Abbott	McCaskill	Blyleven	Langston	Harvey	Bailes	Fraser	Eichhorn
1989	Finley	Abbott	McCaskill	Blyleven	Witt	Harvey	Minton	Fraser	McClure
1988	Finley	Fraser	McCaskill	Petry	Witt	Harvey	Minton	Cliburn	Corbett
1987	Sutton	Fraser	Candelaria	Reuss	Witt	Buice	Minton	Lucas	Finley
1986	Sutton	McCaskill	Candelaria	Romanick	Witt	Moore	Corbett	Lucas	Forster
1985	Slaton	McCaskill	Candelaria	Romanick	Witt	Moore	Corbett	Cliburn	Clements
1984	Slaton	John	Zahn	Romanick	Witt	Sanchez	Corbett	Kaufman	Aase

PRIMARY PITCHING STAFFS (CONT.)

Year	Starter	Starter	Starter	Starter	Starter	Closer	Bullpen	Bullpen	Bullpen
1983	Forsch	John	Zahn	Kison	Witt	Sanchez	Hassler	Curtis	Steirer
1982	Forsch	Renko	Zahn	Kison	Witt	Corbett	Hassler	Sanchez	Goltz
1981	Forsch	Renko	Zahn	Frost	Witt	Aase	Hassler	Sanchez	Jefferson
1980	Tanana	Martinez	Aase	Frost	Knapp	Hassler	Clear	LaRoche	Montague
1979	Ryan	Barr	Aase	Frost	Knapp	Clear	Barlow	LaRoche	Tanana
1978	Ryan	Tanana	Aase	Hartzell	Knapp	LaRoche	Miller	Brett	Griffin
1977	Ryan	Tanana	Simpson	Hartzell	Brett	LaRoche	Miller	Barlow	Ross
1976	Ryan	Tanana	Ross	Hartzell	Kirkwood	Drago	Scott	Monge	Verhoeven
1975	Ryan	Tanana	Figueroa	Singer	Hassler	Kirkwood	Scott	Lange	Brewer
1974	Ryan	Tanana	Lange	Singer	Hassler	Lockwood	Figueroa	Sells	Selma
1973	Ryan	Wright	May	Singer	Hand	Sells	Barber	Lange	Monteagudo
1972	Ryan	Wright	May	Messersmith	Clark	Fisher	Barber	Allen	Queen
1971	Murphy	Wright	May	Messersmith	Clark	Allen	LaRoche	Fisher	Queen
1970	Murphy	Wright	May	Messersmith	Bradley	Tatum	LaRoche	Fisher	Doyle
1969	Murphy	McGlothlin	May	Messersmith	Brunet	Tatum	Wilhelm	Fisher	Wright
1968	Murphy	McGlothlin	Ellis	Clark	Brunet	Rojas	Burgmeier	Pattin	Wright
1967	Wright	McGlothlin	Hamilton	Clark	Brunet	Rojas	Kelso	Cimino	Coates
1966	Chance	Lopez	Wright	Newman	Brunet	Lee	Burdette	Sanford	Rojas
1965	Chance	Lopez	May	Newman	Brunet	Lee	Gatewood	Sukla	Latman
1964	Chance	Belinsky	McBride	Newman	Latman	Lee	Duliba	Osinski	Lee
1963	Chance	Belinsky	McBride	Lee	Osinski	Navarro	Fowler	Spring	Nelson
1962	Chance	Belinsky	McBride	Grba	Bowsfield	Morgan	Fowler	Spring	Duren
1961	Moeller	Duren	McBride	Grba	Bowsfield	Fowler	Morgan	Donohue	James

PRIMARY STARTING LINEUPS

Year	C	1B	2B	3B	SS	LF	CF	RF	DH
2005	Molina	Erstad	Kennedy	McPherson	Cabrera	Anderson	Finley	Guerrero	Davanon
2004	Molina	Erstad	Kennedy	Figgins	Eckstein	Guillen	Anderson	Guerrero	Glaus
2003	Molina	Spiezio	Kennedy	Glaus	Eckstein	Anderson	Erstad	Davanon	Salmon
2002	Molina	Spiezio	Kennedy	Glaus	Eckstein	Anderson	Erstad	Salmon	Fullmer
2001	Molina	Spiezio	Kennedy	Glaus	Eckstein	Anderson	Erstad	Salmon	Palmeiro
2000	Molina	Vaughn	Kennedy	Glaus	Gil	Erstad	Anderson	Salmon	Spiezio
1999	Walbeck	Erstad	Velarde	Glaus	DiSarcina	Palmeiro	Anderson	Salmon	Vaughn
1998	Walbeck	Fielder	Baughman	Hollins	DiSarcina	Erstad	Edmonds	Anderson	Salmon
1997	Kreuter	Erstad	Alicea	Hollins	DiSarcina	Anderson	Edmonds	Salmon	Murray
1996	Fabregas	Snow	Velarde	Arias	DiSarcina	Anderson	Edmonds	Salmon	Davis
1995	Fabregas	Snow	Easley	Phillips	DiSarcina	Anderson	Edmonds	Salmon	Davis
1994	Turner	Snow	Reynolds	Owen	DiSarcina	Edmonds	Curtis	Salmon	Davis
1993	Myers	Snow	Lovullo	Gonzales	DiSarcina	Polonia	Curtis	Salmon	Davis
1992	Fitzgerald	Stevens	Sojo	Gaetti	DiSarcina	Polonia	Felix	Hayes	Brooks
1991	Parrish	Joyner	Sojo	Gaetti	Schofield	Polonia	Felix	Winfield	Parker
1990	Parrish	Joyner	Ray	Howell	Schofield	Polonia	White	Winfield	Downing
1989	Parrish	Joyner	Ray	Howell	Schofield	Davis	White	Washington	Downing
1988	Boone	Joyner	Ray	Howell	Schofield	Armas	White	Davis	Downing
1987	Boone	Joyner	McLemore	DeCinces	Schofield	Howell	Pettis	White	Downing
1986	Boone	Joyner	Wilfong	DeCinces	Schofield	Downing	Pettis	Jones	Jackson
1985	Boone	Carew	Grich	DeCinces	Schofield	Downing	Pettis	Jackson	Jones
1984	Boone	Carew	Wilfong	DeCinces	Schofield	Downing	Pettis	Lynn	Jackson
1983	Boone	Carew	Grich	DeCinces	Foli	Downing	Lynn	Valentine	Jackson
1982	Boone	Carew	Grich	DeCinces	Foli	Downing	Lynn	Jackson	Baylor

Primary Starting Lineups (cont.)

Year	C	1B	2B	3B	SS	LF	CF	RF	DH
1981	Ott	Carew	Grich	Hobson	Burleson	Downing	Lynn	Ford	Baylor
1980	Donohue	Carew	Grich	Lansford	Patek	Rudi	Miller	Harlow	Thompson
1979	Downing	Carew	Grich	Lansford	Campaneris	Baylor	Miller	Ford	Aikens
1978	Downing	Fairly	Grich	Lansford	Chalk	Rudi	Miller	Bostock	Baylor
1977	Humphrey	Solaita	Remy	Chalk	Mulliniks	Rudi	Flores	Bonds	Baylor
1976	Etchebarren	Solaita	Remy	Jackson	Chalk	Bochte	Torres	Bonds	Davis
1975	Rodriguez	Bochte	Remy	Chalk	Miley	Collins	Rivers	Stanton	Harper
1974	Rodriguez	Doherty	Doyle	Schaal	Chalk	Lahoud	Rivers	Stanton	Robinson
1973	Torborg	Epstein	Alomar	Gallagher	Meoli	Pinson	Berry	Stanton	Robinson
1972	Kusnyer	Oliver	Alomar	McMullen	Cardenas	Pinson	Berry	Stanton	
1971	Stephenson	Spencer	Alomar	McMullen	Fregosi	Gonzalez	Berry	Repoz	
1970	Azcue	Spencer	Alomar	McMullen	Fregosi	Johnson	Johnstone	Repoz	
1969	Azcue	Spencer	Alomar	Rodriguez	Fregosi	Reichardt	Johnstone	Voss	
1968	Rodgers	Mincher	Knoop	Rodriguez	Fregosi	Reichardt	Repoz	Morton	
1967	Rodgers	Mincher	Knoop	Schaal	Fregosi	Reichardt	Cardenal	Hall	
1966	Rodgers	Siebern	Knoop	Schaal	Fregosi	Reichardt	Cardenal	Kirkpatrick	
1965	Rodgers	Power	Knoop	Schaal	Fregosi	Smith	Cardenal	Pearson	
1964	Rodgers	Adcock	Knoop	Torres	Fregosi	Kirkpatrick	Perry	Clinton	
1963	Rodgers	Thomas	Moran	Torres	Fregosi	Wagner	Pearson	Thomas	
1962	Rodgers	Thomas	Moran	Torres	Koppe	Wagner	Pearson	Thomas	
1961	Averill	Bilko	Aspromonte	Yost	Koppe	Wagner	Hunt	Pearson	

Top 10 Batting Leaders, Single Season & Career with Team

Games Played: Career with Team

Player	G	PA
1. Brian Downing	1,661	6,912
2. Garret Anderson	1,619	6,849
3. Tim Salmon	1,596	6,795
4. Jim Fregosi	1,429	5,944
5. Darin Erstad	1,280	5,673
6. Bobby Grich	1,222	4,876
7. Gary DiSarcina	1,086	4,032
Dick Schofield	1,086	3,918
9. Bob Boone	968	3,391
10. Chili Davis	950	4,031

At-Bats: Season

Player	AB	Year
1. Sandy Alomar	689	1971
2. Darin Erstad	676	2000
3. Sandy Alomar	672	1970
Garret Anderson	672	2001
5. Billy Moran	659	1962
6. Carney Lansford	654	1979
7. Garret Anderson	647	2000
8. Chone Figgins	642	2005
9. Devon White	639	1987
10. Garret Anderson	638	2002
Garret Anderson	638	2003

At-Bats: Career with Team

Player	AB	PA
1. Garret Anderson	6,472	6,849
2. Brian Downing	5,854	6,912
3. Tim Salmon	5,723	6,795
4. Jim Fregosi	5,244	5,944
5. Darin Erstad	5,163	5,673
6. Bobby Grich	4,100	4,876
7. Gary DiSarcina	3,744	4,032
8. Chili Davis	3,491	4,031
9. Dick Schofield	3,434	3,918
10. Wally Joyner	3,356	3,774

Batting Average: Season

Player	BA	Year
1. Darin Erstad	.355	2000
2. Rod Carew	.339	1983
3. Vladimir Guerrero	.337	2004
4. Juan Beniquez	.336	1984
Luis Polonia	.336	1990
6. Rod Carew	.331	1980
7. Tim Salmon	.330	1995
8. Alex Johnson	.329	1970
9. Brian Downing	.326	1979
10. Garret Anderson	.321	1995

Batting Average: Career with Team

Player	BA	PA
1. Rod Carew	.314	3,570
2. Garret Anderson	.298	6,849
3. Luis Polonia	.294	2,347
4. Jim Edmonds	.290	2,951
5. Darin Erstad	.287	5,673
6. Wally Joyner	.286	3,774
7. Tim Salmon	.283	6,795
8. Adam Kennedy	.282	3,185
9. Chili Davis	.279	4,031
10. David Eckstein	.278	2,520

TOTAL HITS: SEASON

Player	H	Year
1. Darin Erstad	240	2000
2. Vladimir Guerrero	206	2004
3. Alex Johnson	202	1970
4. Garret Anderson	201	2003
5. Garret Anderson	195	2002
6. Garret Anderson	194	2001
7. Garret Anderson	189	1997
8. Garret Anderson	188	1999
Carney Lansford	188	1979
10. Don Baylor	186	1979
Billy Moran	186	1962
Chone Figgins	186	2005

TOTAL HITS: CAREER WITH TEAM

Player	H	PA
1. Garret Anderson	1,929	6,849
2. Tim Salmon	1,618	6,795
3. Brian Downing	1,588	6,912
4. Darin Erstad	1,484	5,673
5. Jim Fregosi	1,408	5,944
6. Bobby Grich	1,103	4,876
7. Chili Davis	973	4,031
8. Rod Carew	968	3,570
9. Gary DiSarcina	966	4,032
10. Wally Joyner	961	3,774

HOME RUNS: SEASON

Player	HR	Year
1. Troy Glaus	47	2000
2. Troy Glaus	41	2001
3. Vladimir Guerrero	39	2004
Reggie Jackson	39	1982
5. Bobby Bonds	37	1977
Leon Wagner	37	1962
7. Don Baylor	36	1979
Mo Vaughn	36	2000
9. Garret Anderson	35	2000
10. Don Baylor	34	1978
Wally Joyner	34	1987
Tim Salmon	34	1995
Tim Salmon	34	2000

HOME RUNS: CAREER WITH TEAM

Player	HR	PA
1. Tim Salmon	290	6,795
2. Garret Anderson	224	6,849
3. Brian Downing	222	6,912
4. Troy Glaus	182	3,479
5. Chili Davis	156	4,031
6. Bobby Grich	154	4,876
7. Don Baylor	141	3,536
8. Doug DeCinces	130	3,268
9. Reggie Jackson	123	2,721
10. Jim Edmonds	121	2,951

TRIPLES: SEASON

Player	3B	Year
1. Chone Figgins	17	2004
2. Jim Fregosi	13	1968
Mickey Rivers	13	1975
Devon White	13	1989
5. Jim Fregosi	12	1963
6. Adam Kennedy	11	2000
Bobby Knoop	11	1966
Mickey Rivers	11	1974
9. Jerry Remy	10	1977
Chone Figgins	10	2005

TRIPLES: CAREER WITH TEAM

Player	3B	PA
1. Jim Fregosi	70	5,944
2. Mickey Rivers	32	1,833
3. Chone Figgins	31	1,640
4. Garret Anderson	29	6,849
Darin Erstad	29	5,673
6. Luis Polonia	27	2,347
Dick Schofield	27	3,918
8. Adam Kennedy	26	3,185
9. Bobby Knoop	25	2,886
10. Devon White	24	2,429

DOUBLES: SEASON

Player	2B	Year
1. Garret Anderson	56	2002
2. Garret Anderson	49	2003
3. Doug DeCinces	42	1982
Jim Edmonds	42	1998
Johnny Ray	42	1988
6. Garret Anderson	41	1998
7. Garret Anderson	40	2000
8. Garret Anderson	39	2001
Gary DiSarcina	39	1998
Darin Erstad	39	1998
Darin Erstad	39	2000
Vladimir Guerrero	39	2004

DOUBLES: CAREER WITH TEAM

Player	2B	PA
1. Garret Anderson	403	6,849
2. Tim Salmon	331	6,795
3. Brian Downing	282	6,912
4. Darin Erstad	271	5,673
5. Jim Fregosi	219	5,944
6. Gary DiSarcina	186	4,032
7. Bobby Grich	183	4,876
8. Wally Joyner	175	3,774
9. Chili Davis	167	4,031
10. Troy Glaus	165	3,479

EXTRA-BASE HITS: SEASON

Player	XBH	Year
1. Garret Anderson	88	2002
2. Troy Glaus	85	2000
3. Garret Anderson	82	2003
4. Troy Glaus	81	2001
5. Vladimir Guerrero	80	2004
6. Garret Anderson	78	2000
7. Doug DeCinces	77	1982
8. Don Baylor	72	1979
Tim Salmon	72	2000
10. Tim Salmon	71	1995

EXTRA-BASE HITS: CAREER WITH TEAM

Player	XBH	PA
1. Garret Anderson	656	6,849
2. Tim Salmon	643	6,795
3. Brian Downing	526	6,912
4. Darin Erstad	414	5,673
5. Jim Fregosi	404	5,944
6. Bobby Grich	357	4,876
7. Troy Glaus	354	3,479
8. Chili Davis	329	4,031
9. Wally Joyner	304	3,774
10. Doug DeCinces	294	3,268
Jim Edmonds	294	2,951

TOTAL BASES: SEASON

Player	TB	Year
1. Darin Erstad	366	2000
Vladimir Guerrero	366	2004
3. Garret Anderson	345	2003
4. Garret Anderson	344	2002
5. Troy Glaus	340	2000
6. Garret Anderson	336	2000
7. Don Baylor	333	1979
8. Garret Anderson	321	2001
9. Tim Salmon	319	1995
10. Doug DeCinces	315	1982

TOTAL BASES: CAREER WITH TEAM

Player	TB	PA
1. Garret Anderson	3,062	6,849
2. Tim Salmon	2,863	6,795
3. Brian Downing	2,580	6,912
4. Darin Erstad	2,155	5,673
5. Jim Fregosi	2,112	5,944

6. Bobby Grich	1,788	4,876
7. Chili Davis	1,620	4,031
8. Wally Joyner	1,511	3,774
9. Troy Glaus	1,473	3,479
10. Don Baylor	1,390	3,536

Runs Batted In: Season

Player	RBI	Year
1. Don Baylor	139	1979
2. Tim Salmon	129	1997
3. Vladimir Guerrero	126	2004
4. Garret Anderson	123	2001
Garret Anderson	123	2002
6. Garret Anderson	117	2000
Wally Joyner	117	1987
Mo Vaughn	117	2000
9. Garret Anderson	116	2003
10. Bobby Bonds	115	1977

Runs Batted In: Career with Team

Player	RBI	PA
1. Garret Anderson	1,043	6,849
2. Tim Salmon	989	6,795
3. Brian Downing	846	6,912
4. Darin Erstad	620	5,673
5. Chili Davis	618	4,031
6. Bobby Grich	557	4,876
7. Jim Fregosi	546	5,944
8. Wally Joyner	532	3,774
9. Don Baylor	523	3,536
10. Troy Glaus	515	3,479

Runs Scored: Season

Player	R	Year
1. Vladimir Guerrero	124	2004
2. Darin Erstad	121	2000
3. Don Baylor	120	1979
Jim Edmonds	120	1995
Troy Glaus	120	2000
6. Tony Phillips	119	1995
7. Jim Edmonds	115	1998
Albie Pearson	115	1962
9. Carney Lansford	114	1979
10. Chone Figgins	113	2005

Runs Scored: Career with Team

Player	R	PA
1. Tim Salmon	956	6,795
2. Brian Downing	889	6,912
3. Garret Anderson	828	6,849
4. Darin Erstad	810	5,673
5. Jim Fregosi	691	5,944

6. Bobby Grich	601	4,876
7. Troy Glaus	523	3,479
8. Chili Davis	520	4,031
9. Don Baylor	481	3,536
10. Rod Carew	474	3,570

Walks: Season

Player	BB	Year
1. Tony Phillips	113	1995
2. Troy Glaus	112	2000
3. Troy Glaus	107	2001
4. Brian Downing	106	1987
5. Tim Salmon	104	2000
6. Albie Pearson	96	1961
Tim Salmon	96	2001
8. Albie Pearson	95	1962
Tim Salmon	95	1997
10. Jim Fregosi	93	1969
Tim Salmon	93	1996

Walks: Career with Team

Player	BB	PA
1. Tim Salmon	941	6,795
2. Brian Downing	866	6,912
3. Bobby Grich	630	4,876
4. Jim Fregosi	558	5,944
5. Chili Davis	493	4,031
6. Troy Glaus	470	3,479
7. Darin Erstad	413	5,673
8. Rod Carew	405	3,570
9. Albie Pearson	369	2,666
10. Reggie Jackson	362	2,721

Strikeouts: Season

Player	SO	Year
1. Mo Vaughn	181	2000
2. Troy Glaus	163	2000
3. Troy Glaus	158	2001
4. Reggie Jackson	156	1982
5. Troy Glaus	144	2002
Bobby Knoop	144	1966
7. Troy Glaus	143	1999
8. Tim Salmon	142	1997
9. Bobby Bonds	141	1977
Reggie Jackson	141	1984

Strikeouts: Career with Team

Player	SO	PA
1. Tim Salmon	1,316	6,795
2. Garret Anderson	891	6,849
3. Jim Fregosi	835	5,944
4. Troy Glaus	784	3,479
5. Darin Erstad	778	5,673

6. Brian Downing	759	6,912
7. Bobby Grich	758	4,876
8. Chili Davis	713	4,031
9. Reggie Jackson	690	2,721
10. Bobby Knoop	634	2,886

Slugging Percentage: Season

Player	SLG	Year
1. Troy Glaus	.604	2000
2. Vladimir Guerrero	.598	2004
3. Tim Salmon	.594	1995
4. Jim Edmonds	.571	1996
5. Vladimir Guerrero	.565	2005
6. Chili Davis	.561	1994
7. Doug DeCinces	.548	1982
8. Steve Bilko	.544	1961
9. Bobby Grich	.543	1981
10. Darin Erstad	.541	2000
Garret Anderson	.541	2003

Slugging Percentage: Career with Team

Player	SLG	PA
1. Tim Salmon	.500	6,795
2. Jim Edmonds	.498	2,951
3. Troy Glaus	.497	3,479
4. Garret Anderson	.473	6,849
5. Chili Davis	.464	4,031
6. Doug DeCinces	.463	3,268
7. Wally Joyner	.450	3,774
8. Don Baylor	.448	3,536
9. Scott Spiezio	.446	2,000
10. Brian Downing	.441	6,912

On-Base Percentage: Season

Player	OBP	Year
1. Jason Thompson	.439	1980
2. Tim Salmon	.429	1995
Chili Davis	.429	1995
4. Albie Pearson	.420	1961
5. Rod Carew	.419	1979
6. Brian Downing	.418	1979
7. Bobby Grich	.414	1983
8. Chili Davis	.410	1994
Tim Salmon	.410	1998
10. Darin Erstad	.409	2000

On-Base Percentage: Career with Team

Player	OBP	PA
1. Rod Carew	.393	3,570
2. Tim Salmon	.386	6,795

Player	OBP	PA
3. Albie Pearson	.379	2,666
4. Brian Downing	.372	6,912
5. Bobby Grich	.370	4,876
6. Chili Davis	.365	4,031
7. Jim Edmonds	.359	2,951
8. Troy Glaus	.357	3,479
9. Wally Joyner	.350	3,774
10. David Eckstein	.347	2,520

OPS (On-Base Percentage + Slugging Percentage): Season

Player	OPS	Year
1. Tim Salmon	1.024	1995
2. Troy Glaus	1.008	2000
3. Vladimir Guerrero	.989	2004
4. Chili Davis	.971	1994
5. Jason Thompson	.965	1980
6. Vladimir Guerrero	.959	2005
7. Darin Erstad	.951	2000
8. Jim Edmonds	.946	1996
9. Tim Salmon	.945	2000
10. Tim Salmon	.943	1998
Chili Davis	.943	1995

OPS (On-Base Percentage + Slugging Percentage): Career with Team

Player	OPS	PA
1. Tim Salmon	.886	6,795
2. Jim Edmonds	.856	2,951
3. Troy Glaus	.854	3,479
4. Chili Davis	.829	4,031
5. Brian Downing	.813	6,912
6. Bobby Grich	.806	4,876
7. Wally Joyner	.801	3,774
8. Garret Anderson	.800	6,849
9. Doug DeCinces	.798	3,268
10. Scott Spiezio	.787	2,000

Stolen Bases: Season

Player	SB	Year
1. Mickey Rivers	70	1975
2. Chone Figgins	62	2005
3. Gary Pettis	56	1985
4. Luis Polonia	55	1993
5. Luis Polonia	51	1992
6. Gary Pettis	50	1986
7. Chad Curtis	48	1993
Gary Pettis	48	1984
Luis Polonia	48	1991
10. Devon White	44	1989

Stolen Bases: Career with Team

Player	SB	PA
1. Gary Pettis	186	2,156
2. Luis Polonia	174	2,347
3. Darin Erstad	169	5,673
4. Sandy Alomar	139	3,314
5. Mickey Rivers	126	1,833
6. Devon White	123	2,429
7. Chad Curtis	116	1,684
8. Chone Figgins	111	1,640
9. Jerry Remy	110	1,845
10. Adam Kennedy	107	3,185

Sacrifice Hits: Season

Player	Sac	Year
1. Tim Foli	26	1982
2. Bob Boone	23	1982
3. Bobby Grich	19	1978
Jerry Remy	19	1977
Luis Sojo	19	1991
6. Juan Beniquez	16	1982
Bob Boone	16	1985
Rod Carew	16	1982
Gary DiSarcina	16	1996
David Eckstein	16	2001

Sacrifice Hits: Career with Team

Player	Sac	PA
1. Bob Boone	90	3,391
2. Dick Schofield	89	3,918
3. Bobby Grich	78	4,876
4. Gary DiSarcina	77	4,032
5. Jim Fregosi	74	5,944
6. Rod Carew	60	3,570
7. David Eckstein	54	2,520
8. Dave Chalk	52	2,825
9. Jerry Remy	44	1,845
10. Sandy Alomar	40	3,314

Hit by Pitch: Season

Player	HBP	Year
1. David Eckstein	27	2002
2. David Eckstein	21	2001
3. Don Baylor	18	1978
Rick Reichardt	18	1968
5. Brian Downing	17	1986
Brian Downing	17	1987
7. David Eckstein	15	2003
Brad Fullmer	15	2002
Jose Guillen	15	2004
10. Brian Downing	14	1988
Mo Vaughn	14	2000

Hit by Pitch: Career with Team

Player	HBP	PA
1. Brian Downing	105	6,912
2. David Eckstein	76	2,520
3. Don Baylor	66	3,536
4. Tim Salmon	64	6,795
5. Adam Kennedy	50	3,185
6. Rick Reichardt	47	2,193
7. Bobby Grich	41	4,876
8. Dick Schofield	39	3,918
9. Gary DiSarcina	36	4,032
10. Darin Erstad	33	5,673

Top 10 Pitching Leaders, Single Season & Career with Team

Games Pitched: Season

Player	GP	Year
1. Scot Shields	78	2005
2. Minnie Rojas	72	1967
3. Mark Eichhorn	70	1991
4. Mike James	69	1996
Bill Kelso	69	1967
Bob Lee	69	1965
Francisco Rodriguez	69	2004
8. Eddie Fisher	67	1970
Bryan Harvey	67	1991
Troy Percival	67	1998

Games Pitched: Career with Team

Player	GP	IP
1. Troy Percival	579	586.7
2. Chuck Finley	436	2,675.0
3. Mike Witt	314	1,965.3

Player	BF	IP
4. Dave LaRoche	304	512.3
5. Mike Holtz	301	203.3
6. Nolan Ryan	291	2,181.3
7. Shig. Hasegawa	287	442.3
8. Clyde Wright	266	1,403.3
9. Andy Hassler	259	659.3
10. Bryan Harvey	250	307.7

Innings Pitched: Season

Player	IP	Year
1. Nolan Ryan	332.7	1974
2. Nolan Ryan	326.0	1973
3. Bill Singer	315.7	1973
4. Nolan Ryan	299.0	1977
5. Frank Tanana	288.3	1976
6. Nolan Ryan	284.3	1976
7. Nolan Ryan	284.0	1972
8. Dean Chance	278.3	1964
9. Andy Messersmith	276.7	1971
Clyde Wright	276.7	1971

Innings Pitched: Career with Team

Player	IP
1. Chuck Finley	2,675.0
2. Nolan Ryan	2,181.3
3. Mike Witt	1,965.3
4. Frank Tanana	1,615.3
5. Mark Langston	1,445.3
6. Clyde Wright	1,403.3
7. Dean Chance	1,236.7
8. Kirk McCaskill	1,221.0
9. Jarrod Washburn	1,153.3
10. Rudy May	1,138.7

Batters Faced: Season

Player	BF	Year
1. Nolan Ryan	1,392	1974
2. Nolan Ryan	1,355	1973
3. Bill Singer	1,348	1973
4. Nolan Ryan	1,272	1977
5. Nolan Ryan	1,196	1976
6. Andy Messersmith	1,170	1971
7. Nolan Ryan	1,154	1972
8. Frank Tanana	1,142	1976
9. Frank Tanana	1,127	1974
10. Clyde Wright	1,107	1971

Batters Faced: Career with Team

Player	BF	IP
1. Chuck Finley	11,398	2,675.0
2. Nolan Ryan	9,178	2,181.3
3. Mike Witt	8,312	1,965.3
4. Frank Tanana	6,645	1,615.3
5. Mark Langston	6,042	1,445.3
6. Clyde Wright	5,833	1,403.3
7. Kirk McCaskill	5,153	1,221.0
8. Dean Chance	5,120	1,236.7
9. Jarrod Washburn	4,842	1,153.3
10. Rudy May	4,761	1,138.7

Games Started: Season

Player	GS	Year
1. Nolan Ryan	41	1974
2. Bill Singer	40	1973
3. Nolan Ryan	39	1972
Nolan Ryan	39	1973
Nolan Ryan	39	1976
Clyde Wright	39	1970
7. Andy Messersmith	38	1971
Tom Murphy	38	1970
9. George Brunet	37	1967
Dean Chance	37	1966
Nolan Ryan	37	1977
Clyde Wright	37	1971

Games Started: Career with Team

Player	GS	IP
1. Chuck Finley	379	2,675.0
2. Nolan Ryan	288	2,181.3
3. Mike Witt	272	1,965.3
4. Frank Tanana	218	1,615.3
5. Mark Langston	210	1,445.3
6. Kirk McCaskill	189	1,221.0
Clyde Wright	189	1,403.3
8. Jarrod Washburn	183	1,153.3
9. Rudy May	170	1,138.7
10. Dean Chance	168	1,236.7

Complete Games: Season

Player	CG	Year
1. Nolan Ryan	26	1973
Nolan Ryan	26	1974
3. Frank Tanana	23	1976
4. Nolan Ryan	22	1977
5. Nolan Ryan	21	1976
6. Nolan Ryan	20	1972
Frank Tanana	20	1977
8. Bill Singer	19	1973
9. Nolan Ryan	17	1979
10. Ed Figueroa	16	1975
Frank Tanana	16	1975

Complete Games: Career with Team

Player	CG	IP
1. Nolan Ryan	156	2,181.3
2. Frank Tanana	92	1,615.3
3. Mike Witt	70	1,965.3
4. Chuck Finley	57	2,675.0
5. Clyde Wright	51	1,403.3
6. Dean Chance	48	1,236.7
7. Andy Messersmith	42	972.3
Geoff Zahn	42	830.0
9. Rudy May	35	1,138.7
Bill Singer	35	603.3

Games Won: Season

Player	W	Year
1. Nolan Ryan	22	1974
Clyde Wright	22	1970
3. Nolan Ryan	21	1973
Bartolo Colon	21	2005
5. Dean Chance	20	1964
Andy Messersmith	20	1971
Bill Singer	20	1973
8. Mark Langston	19	1991
Nolan Ryan	19	1972
Nolan Ryan	19	1977
Frank Tanana	19	1976

Games Won: Career with Team

Player	W	IP
1. Chuck Finley	165	2,675.0
2. Nolan Ryan	138	2,181.3
3. Mike Witt	109	1,965.3
4. Frank Tanana	102	1,615.3
5. Mark Langston	88	1,445.3
6. Clyde Wright	87	1,403.3
7. Kirk McCaskill	78	1,221.0
8. Jarrod Washburn	75	1,153.3
9. Dean Chance	74	1,236.7
10. Andy Messersmith	59	972.3
Ramon Ortiz	59	893.7

Games Lost: Season

Player	L	Year
1. George Brunet	19	1967
Kirk McCaskill	19	1991
Frank Tanana	19	1974
Clyde Wright	19	1973
5. Jim Abbott	18	1996
Dean Chance	18	1963
Nolan Ryan	18	1976

8. George Brunet	17	1968
Dean Chance	17	1966
Mark Langston	17	1990
Rudy May	17	1973
Tom Murphy	17	1971
Clyde Wright	17	1971

Games Lost: Career with Team

Player	L	IP
1. Chuck Finley	140	2,675.0
2. Nolan Ryan	121	2,181.3
3. Mike Witt	107	1,965.3
4. Clyde Wright	85	1,403.3
5. Frank Tanana	78	1,615.3
6. Rudy May	76	1,138.7
7. Jim Abbott	74	1,073.7
Mark Langston	74	1,445.3
Kirk McCaskill	74	1,221.0
10. George Brunet	69	1,047.3

Winning Percentage: Season

Player	W%	Year
1. Bert Blyleven	.773	1989
2. Jarrod Washburn	.750	2002
3. John Lackey	.737	2005
4. Bartolo Colon	.724	2005
5. Mark Langston	.704	1991
6. Geoff Zahn	.692	1982
7. Dean Chance	.690	1964
8. Mark Clear	.688	1979
Bruce Kison	.688	1983
Ken McBride	.688	1962

Winning Percentage: Career with Team

Player	W%	IP
1. Jarrod Washburn	.568	1,153.3
2. Frank Tanana	.567	1,615.3
3. Andy Messersmith	.557	972.3
4. Geoff Zahn	.553	830.0
John Lackey	.553	719.7
6. Ramon Ortiz	.546	893.7
7. Mark Langston	.543	1,445.3
8. Chuck Finley	.541	2,675.0
9. Nolan Ryan	.533	2,181.3
10. Dean Chance	.529	1,236.7

Shutouts: Season

Player	SHO	Year
1. Dean Chance	11	1964
2. Nolan Ryan	9	1972
3. Nolan Ryan	7	1976
Frank Tanana	7	1977
5. Jim McGlothlin	6	1967
6. Bert Blyleven	5	1989
George Brunet	5	1968
Nolan Ryan	5	1975
Nolan Ryan	5	1979
Frank Tanana	5	1975
Geoff Zahn	5	1984

Shutouts: Career with Team

Player	SHO	IP
1. Nolan Ryan	40	2,181.3
2. Frank Tanana	24	1,615.3
3. Dean Chance	21	1,236.7
4. George Brunet	14	1,047.3
Chuck Finley	14	2,675.0
6. Geoff Zahn	13	830.0
7. Rudy May	12	1,138.7
8. Kirk McCaskill	11	1,221.0
Andy Messersmith	11	972.3
10. Mike Witt	10	1,965.3

ERA: Season

Player	ERA	Year
1. Dean Chance	1.65	1964
2. Nolan Ryan	2.28	1972
3. Chuck Finley	2.40	1990
4. Frank Tanana	2.43	1976
5. Andy Messersmith	2.52	1969
6. Frank Tanana	2.54	1977
7. George Brunet	2.56	1965
8. Chuck Finley	2.57	1989
9. Rickey Clark	2.59	1967
10. Andy Hassler	2.61	1974

ERA: Career with Team

Player	ERA	IP
1. Andy Messersmith	2.78	972.3
2. Dean Chance	2.83	1,236.7
3. Troy Percival	2.99	586.7
4. Nolan Ryan	3.07	2,181.3
5. Frank Tanana	3.08	1,615.3
6. George Brunet	3.13	1,047.3
7. Paul Hartzell	3.27	512.3
8. Clyde Wright	3.28	1,403.3
9. Jim McGlothlin	3.37	692.3
10. Fred Newman	3.41	610.0

Earned Runs Allowed: Season

Player	ER	Year
1. Jim Abbott	118	1996
2. Willie Fraser	117	1988
3. Bartolo Colon	116	2004
Scott Schoeneweis	116	2001
5. Mike Witt	115	1988
6. Tommy John	113	1983
Bill Singer	113	1973
8. Shawn Boskie	112	1996
Dennis Springer	112	1997
10. Mike Witt	111	1989

Earned Runs Allowed: Career with Team

Player	ER	IP
1. Chuck Finley	1,107	2,675.0
2. Mike Witt	820	1,965.3
3. Nolan Ryan	743	2,181.3
4. Mark Langston	637	1,445.3
5. Frank Tanana	553	1,615.3
6. Kirk McCaskill	524	1,221.0
7. Clyde Wright	512	1,403.3
8. Jarrod Washburn	504	1,153.3
9. Jim Abbott	485	1,073.7
10. Rudy May	464	1,138.7

Strikeouts: Season

Player	K	Year
1. Nolan Ryan	383	1973
2. Nolan Ryan	367	1974
3. Nolan Ryan	341	1977
4. Nolan Ryan	329	1972
5. Nolan Ryan	327	1976
6. Frank Tanana	269	1975
7. Frank Tanana	261	1976
8. Nolan Ryan	260	1978
9. Bill Singer	241	1973
10. Nolan Ryan	223	1979

Strikeouts: Career with Team

Player	K	IP
1. Nolan Ryan	2,416	2,181.3
2. Chuck Finley	2,151	2,675.0
3. Mike Witt	1,283	1,965.3
4. Frank Tanana	1,233	1,615.3
5. Mark Langston	1,112	1,445.3
6. Dean Chance	857	1,236.7
7. Rudy May	844	1,138.7
8. Andy Messersmith	768	972.3
9. Kirk McCaskill	714	1,221.0
10. Jarrod Washburn	699	1,153.3

Strikeouts Per Nine IP: Season

Player	K/9	Year
1. Nolan Ryan	10.57	1973
2. Nolan Ryan	10.43	1972
3. Nolan Ryan	10.35	1976
4. Nolan Ryan	10.26	1977
5. Nolan Ryan	9.97	1978
6. Nolan Ryan	9.93	1974
7. Frank Tanana	9.41	1975
8. Nolan Ryan	9.01	1979
9. Chuck Finley	8.65	1995
10. John Lackey	8.57	2005

Strikeouts Per Nine IP: Career with Team

Player	K/9	IP
1. Troy Percival	10.43	586.7
2. Nolan Ryan	9.97	2,181.3
3. Chuck Finley	7.24	2,675.0
4. Andy Messersmith	7.11	972.3
5. John Lackey	7.04	719.7
6. Mark Langston	6.92	1,445.3
7. Frank Tanana	6.87	1,615.3
8. Dave LaRoche	6.78	512.3
9. Rudy May	6.67	1,138.7
10. Dean Chance	6.24	1,236.7

Hits Allowed: Season

Player	HA	Year
1. Tommy John	287	1983
2. Bill Singer	280	1973
3. Clyde Wright	273	1973
4. Mike Witt	263	1988
5. Frank Tanana	262	1974
6. Mike Witt	252	1987
Mike Witt	252	1989
8. Jim Abbott	246	1990
9. Chuck Finley	243	1993
10. Chuck Finley	241	1996

Hits Allowed: Career with Team

Player	HA	IP
1. Chuck Finley	2,544	2,675.0
2. Mike Witt	1,932	1,965.3
3. Nolan Ryan	1,520	2,181.3
4. Frank Tanana	1,461	1,615.3
5. Mark Langston	1,341	1,445.3
6. Clyde Wright	1,310	1,403.3
7. Kirk McCaskill	1,191	1,221.0
8. Jim Abbott	1,130	1,073.7
9. Jarrod Washburn	1,122	1,153.3
10. Dean Chance	1,054	1,236.7

Hits Allowed Per Nine IP: Season

Player	H/9	Year
1. Nolan Ryan	5.26	1972
2. Nolan Ryan	5.96	1977
3. Nolan Ryan	5.98	1974
4. Andy Messersmith	6.08	1969
5. Nolan Ryan	6.11	1976
6. Dean Chance	6.27	1964
7. Nolan Ryan	6.57	1973
8. Frank Tanana	6.62	1976
9. Andy Messersmith	6.63	1972
10. Andy Messersmith	6.66	1970

Hits Allowed Per Nine IP: Career with Team

Player	H/9	IP
1. Troy Percival	6.03	586.7
2. Nolan Ryan	6.27	2,181.3
3. Andy Messersmith	6.53	972.3
4. George Brunet	7.41	1,047.3
5. Dean Chance	7.67	1,236.7
Rudy May	7.67	1,138.7
7. Ken McBride	7.97	780.3
8. Dave LaRoche	8.12	512.3
9. Frank Tanana	8.14	1,615.3
10. Bill Singer	8.25	603.3

Walks Allowed: Season

Player	BB	Year
1. Nolan Ryan	204	1977
2. Nolan Ryan	202	1974
3. Nolan Ryan	183	1976
4. Nolan Ryan	162	1973
5. Nolan Ryan	157	1972
6. Nolan Ryan	148	1978
7. Nolan Ryan	132	1975
8. Bill Singer	130	1973
9. Bo Belinsky	122	1962
10. Andy Messersmith	121	1971

Walks Allowed: Career with Team

Player	BB	IP
1. Nolan Ryan	1,302	2,181.3
2. Chuck Finley	1,118	2,675.0
3. Mike Witt	656	1,965.3
4. Mark Langston	551	1,445.3
5. Rudy May	484	1,138.7
6. Dean Chance	462	1,236.7
7. Clyde Wright	449	1,403.3
8. Kirk McCaskill	448	1,221.0
9. Frank Tanana	422	1,615.3
10. Andy Messersmith	402	972.3

Walks Allowed Per Nine IP: Season

Player	BB/9	Year
1. Paul Byrd	1.23	2005
2. Bert Blyleven	1.64	1989
3. Bartolo Colon	1.74	2005
4. Paul Hartzell	1.81	1977
5. Fred Newman	1.85	1964
6. Tommy John	1.88	1983
7. Don Sutton	1.93	1987
8. Mike Witt	1.96	1989
9. Frank Tanana	1.99	1980
10. Don Sutton	2.13	1986

Walks Allowed Per Nine IP: Career with Team

Player	BB/9	IP
1. Bert Blyleven	1.74	508.0
2. Paul Hartzell	2.14	512.3
3. Ken Forsch	2.24	633.7
4. Fred Newman	2.27	610.0
5. Frank Tanana	2.35	1,615.3
6. Geoff Zahn	2.40	830.0
7. Jim McGlothlin	2.60	692.3
8. Jarrod Washburn	2.72	1,153.3
9. Ron Romanick	2.83	531.0
10. John Lackey	2.88	719.7

WHIP (Walks + Hits Per Nine IP): Season

Player	WHIP	Year
1. Frank Tanana	0.988	1976
2. Dean Chance	1.006	1964
3. George Brunet	1.056	1968
4. Andy Messersmith	1.076	1969
5. Mike Witt	1.082	1986
6. Frank Tanana	1.086	1977

7. Frank Tanana	1.104	1975
8. George Brunet	1.107	1965
9. Fred Newman	1.109	1965
10. Clyde Wright	1.110	1971

WHIP (Walks + Hits Per Nine IP): Career with Team

Player	WHIP	IP
1. Troy Percival	1.101	586.7
2. Andy Messersmith	1.140	972.3
3. Frank Tanana	1.166	1,615.3
4. George Brunet	1.202	1,047.3
5. Jim McGlothlin	1.206	692.3
6. Fred Newman	1.218	610.0
7. Dean Chance	1.226	1,236.7
8. Ken Forsch	1.247	633.7
9. Bert Blyleven	1.252	508.0
10. Clyde Wright	1.253	1,403.3

Home Runs Allowed: Season

Player	HRA	Year
1. Shawn Boskie	40	1996
Ramon Ortiz	40	2002
3. Bartolo Colon	38	2004
Don Sutton	38	1987
5. Allen Watson	37	1997
6. Jarrod Washburn	34	2003
Mike Witt	34	1987
8. Willie Fraser	33	1988
9. Jason Dickson	32	1997
Tom Murphy	32	1970
Dennis Springer	32	1997

Home Runs Allowed: Career with Team

Player	HRA	IP
1. Chuck Finley	254	2,675.0
2. Mike Witt	167	1,965.3
3. Jarrod Washburn	150	1,153.3
4. Frank Tanana	146	1,615.3
5. Mark Langston	145	1,445.3
6. Ramon Ortiz	136	893.7
7. Nolan Ryan	115	2,181.3
8. Clyde Wright	114	1,403.3
9. Kirk McCaskill	109	1,221.0
10. Rudy May	96	1,138.7

Saves: Season

Player	SV	Year
1. Bryan Harvey	46	1991
2. Francisco Rodriguez	45	2005
3. Troy Percival	42	1998
4. Troy Percival	40	2002
5. Troy Percival	39	2001
6. Lee Smith	37	1995
7. Troy Percival	36	1996
8. Troy Percival	33	2003
Troy Percival	33	2004
10. Troy Percival	32	2000

Saves: Career with Team

Player	SV	IP
1. Troy Percival	316	586.7
2. Bryan Harvey	126	307.7
3. Dave LaRoche	65	512.3
4. Donnie Moore	61	235.3
5. Francisco Rodriguez	59	243.0
6. Bob Lee	58	370.0
7. Joe Grahe	45	311.0
8. Minnie Rojas	43	261.0
9. Ken Tatum	39	175.0
10. Lee Smith	37	60.3

Wild Pitches: Season

Player	WP	Year
1. Nolan Ryan	21	1977
2. Nolan Ryan	18	1972
John Lackey	18	2005
4. Chuck Finley	17	1996
Tom Murphy	17	1971
6. Andy Messersmith	16	1969
Tom Murphy	16	1969
8. Chuck Finley	15	1999
Nolan Ryan	15	1973
10. Seven tied with . . .	13	—

Wild Pitches: Career with Team

Player	WP	IP
1. Chuck Finley	117	2,675.0
2. Nolan Ryan	102	2,181.3
3. Mike Witt	65	1,965.3
4. Kirk McCaskill	48	1,221.0
5. John Lackey	47	719.7
6. Mark Langston	45	1,445.3
7. Tom Murphy	44	795.3
8. Frank Tanana	41	1,615.3
9. Rickey Clark	36	431.7
Clyde Wright	36	1,403.3
10. Andy Hassler	35	659.3

Hit Batsmen: Season

Player	HB	Year
1. Tom Murphy	21	1969
2. Ken McBride	16	1964
3. Ken McBride	14	1963
Scott Schoeneweis	14	2001
5. Bo Belinsky	13	1962
Shawn Boskie	13	1996
Jason Grimsley	13	1996
8. Ramon Ortiz	12	2001
Ramon Ortiz	12	2003
Aaron Sele	12	2003
Frank Tanana	12	1977

Hit Batsmen: Career with Team

Player	HB	IP
1. Chuck Finley	71	2,675.0
2. Nolan Ryan	56	2,181.3
3. Frank Tanana	55	1,615.3
4. Ken McBride	48	780.3
Mike Witt	48	1,965.3
6. Tom Murphy	42	795.3
7. Jarrod Washburn	38	1,153.3
8. Ramon Ortiz	37	893.7
9. Dean Chance	34	1,236.7
10. John Lackey	33	719.7

Games Finished: Season

Player	GF	Year
1. Bryan Harvey	63	1991
2. Troy Percival	60	1998
3. Francisco Rodriguez	58	2005
4. Donnie Moore	57	1985
5. Minnie Rojas	53	1967
6. Troy Percival	52	1996
7. Lee Smith	51	1995
8. Bob Lee	50	1965
Troy Percival	50	1999
Troy Percival	50	2001
Troy Percival	50	2002

Games Finished: Career with Team

Player	GF	IP
1. Troy Percival	466	586.7
2. Bryan Harvey	214	307.7
3. Dave LaRoche	170	512.3
4. Donnie Moore	133	235.3
5. Bob Lee	128	370.0
6. Luis Sanchez	127	369.7
7. Francisco Rodriguez	114	243.0
8. Eddie Fisher	113	427.3
9. Shigetoshi Hasegawa	99	442.3
10. Doug Corbett	98	284.0
Andy Hassler	98	659.3

Significant Angels

Anderson, Garret (OF)
(1994–2005)

The Angels selected Garret Anderson in the fourth round of the June 1990 amateur draft. Anderson received a brief call-up in 1994, then made the team for good in 1995. He has been a model of consistency for the last 11 seasons, always around the .300 mark in average, 600+ at-bats, 20–30 homers, 100 RBIs, 80–90 runs, and 40+ doubles. Anderson quietly goes about his job day in and day out, and he's missed very little time due to injury. He's a four-time All-Star who was voted the MVP of the 2003 All-Star Game. He's won two Silver Slugger Awards and routinely finishes in the top 10 in the American League in at-bats, total bases, hits, and doubles. Given his age and ability, if he stays healthy and plays for the next six years, he could make the 3,000-hit club, which would earn him a deserved spot in Cooperstown.

CAREER ANGELS RECORD:

Games	AB	Hits	Runs
1,619	6,472	1,929	828
Avg	**HR**	**RBI**	**SB**
.298	224	1,043	69

Baylor, Don (DH/OF)
(1977–1982)

After playing six years with Baltimore and one with Oakland, Don Baylor signed with the Angels as a free agent before the 1977 season. With the Angels he established himself as the best designated hitter in the game, occasionally playing a game at first or in the outfield. In 1979 he led the major leagues with 120 runs and 139 RBIs and won the American League's MVP Award; that was also the only year he made the All-Star team. An adept base stealer, Baylor took pride in his ability to break up double plays. He also wasn't afraid to crowd the plate; his major league record of being hit by pitches 267 times was broken by Craig Biggio in 2005. Baylor had an off year in 1981, probably due to his role as a member of the MLB Players Association executive board and the contentious strike that year. He came back with a solid year in 1982 and, when the Angels met the Brewers in the playoffs, led all batters with 10 RBIs in the five-game series. Baylor left the Angels via free agency after the 1982 season, accumulating six more seasons with the Yankees, Red Sox, Twins, and A's with decent, yet declining, numbers before retiring following the 1988 season.

CAREER ANGELS RECORD:

Games	AB	Hits	Runs
824	3,105	813	481
Avg	**HR**	**RBI**	**SB**
.262	141	523	89

BOONE, BOB (C)
(1982–1988)

After 10 seasons with the Phillies, Boone (son of major leaguer Ray Boone and father of infielders Bret and Aaron) was purchased outright from Philadelphia in December 1981. Over the next seven seasons he caught nearly 1,000 games for the Angels, providing a steady influence for the team's many young pitchers and winning four Gold Gloves in the process. Never more than a mediocre hitter, Boone was recognized as a great student of the game with superb knowledge of virtually every hitter and pitcher in the league. In 1982, his first year with the Angels, Boone nailed 63 out of 109 runners attempting to steal. In 1986, Boone, at age 38, became the oldest non-pitcher to win a Gold Glove. On September 16, 1987, Boone broke Al Lopez's longstanding record for career games caught. In 1988, his final season with the Angels, Boone hit a career-high .295. As a result of ownership collusion, he was allowed to exercise the "new look" free agency and, at the age of 41, signed with Kansas City. He played two years for the Royals before retiring.

CAREER ANGELS RECORD:

Games	AB	Hits	Runs
968	3,033	742	286
Avg	**HR**	**RBI**	**SB**
.245	39	318	11

CAREW, ROD (1B)
(1979–1985)

In terms of batting average, Rod Carew was the best hitter of his era. By the time he came to the Angels in a 1979 trade with the Twins for four players, Carew already had a streak of 10 consecutive .300 seasons. He added five more to make it 15 straight before the streak was snapped in 1984 when he hit .295 for the Angels. Of his seven seasons with the Angels, Carew made the All-Star team six times. And while he wasn't quite the hitter he was during his 12 seasons in Minnesota, Carew did manage to hit over .300 five times with the Angels. Because Carew left the Twins in a bitter salary dispute, it was a bit of sweet irony that he collected career-hit number 3,000 against Minnesota on August 4, 1985. After the 1985 season, the Angels chose not to resign him, nor would any other team, primarily because his defensive skills had deteriorated, so he retired. Carew was a first-ballot selection to the Hall of Fame in 1991. He later became a hitting coach with the Angels. *(See Twins bio.)*

CAREER ANGELS RECORD:

Games	AB	Hits	Runs
834	3,080	968	474
Avg	**HR**	**RBI**	**SB**
.314	18	282	82

CHANCE, DEAN (SP)
(1961–1966)

Dean Chance was chosen by the Angels from the Orioles as part of the 1960 American League expansion draft. After pitching just a few games for the Angels in 1961, Chance made the big league squad for good in 1962. In 1964 he went 20–9 with a 1.65 ERA and 11 shutouts on his way to capturing the Cy Young Award in an era when there was only one award for both leagues. Six of his shutouts were 1–0 wins. In another game, on June 6, he pitched 14 shutout innings against the Yankees, only to see the Angels lose 2–0 after he came out of the game. Always scheming to get himself traded to a strong team, Chance sometimes made up stories about being considered in potential trades for some of the game's biggest stars. He finally got his wish in December 1966, when he was traded to the Twins for Jimmie Hall, Don Mincher, and Pete Cimino. After winning 36 games for Minnesota in the next two years, Chance was plagued by injuries thereafter and managed to win only 18 more games over the next three years with the Twins, Indians, Mets, and Tigers before dropping out of baseball for good in mid-1971 at the age of 30.

CAREER ANGELS RECORD:

W	L	W%	ERA	SV
74	66	.529	2.83	16

K	BB	SHO	IP
857	462	21	1,236.7

DAVIS, CHILI (DH/OF)
(1988–1990, 1993–1996)

Outfielder Chili Davis played seven seasons in San Francisco before declaring free agency and signing with the Angels in 1988. While he did set a then-career high in RBIs that year with 93, he also shattered the Angels' team record for errors in a season by an outfielder with 19. Chili, whose nickname came from a bad haircut (a friend teased him about having had a chili bowl put on his head before the haircut), was born for the DH position. After two years in the Angels outfield, Davis switched to DH and remained there for the next nine years. He played three years for the Angels before declaring free agency again, this time signing with the Twins for two years, after which he returned to the Angels for a second stint, this one lasting four years. Upon his return to the Angels, Davis established a new career high in RBIs with 112 in 1993. He was having the best year of his career (.311, 26 homers, 84 RBIs) in 1994 when play was stopped by the players' strike in early August. Following the 1996 season, he was traded to the Royals and spent one season there and two more with the Yankees before retiring after a 19-year career.

CAREER ANGELS RECORD:

Games	AB	Hits	Runs
950	3,491	973	520

Avg	HR	RBI	SB
.279	156	618	28

DOWNING, BRIAN (DH/OF/C)
(1978–1990)

Brian Downing played five years with the White Sox before being traded to the Angels in December 1977 in a six-player deal that brought Bobby Bonds to Chicago. The tough, hustling Downing continued at the catcher position for his first three years with the Angels, but a bad ankle injury ended his days behind the plate. After missing most of the 1980 season due to the injury, Downing returned in 1981, this time to his new position in the outfield. He adapted well to the outfield—so well, in fact, that he set a new AL record for consecutive errorless chances with 330 (a mark that has since been broken). Downing usually batted either leadoff or cleanup for the Angels. He was an unusual leadoff hitter in that he had very little speed (only 27 stolen bases in 13 years with the Angels), but he was patient at the plate, walking or being hit by a pitch nearly 1,000 times in his Angels career.

When Angels owner Gene Autry announced his all-Angels team for their 25th-anniversary celebration, Downing was chosen as the left fielder. His one All-Star Game appearance occurred in 1979. After 13 years with the Angels, Downing left via free agency and played two final years with the Rangers. Upon leaving the Angels, Downing was the club's all-time leader in homers, RBIs, runs scored, extra-base hits, total bases, hits, doubles, and games played, and still ranks highly in most categories, although Tim Salmon and Garret Anderson have begun to pass him in many.

CAREER ANGELS RECORD:

Games	AB	Hits	Runs
1,661	5,854	1,588	889
Avg	**HR**	**RBI**	**SB**
.271	222	846	27

EDMONDS, JIM (OF)
(1993–1999)

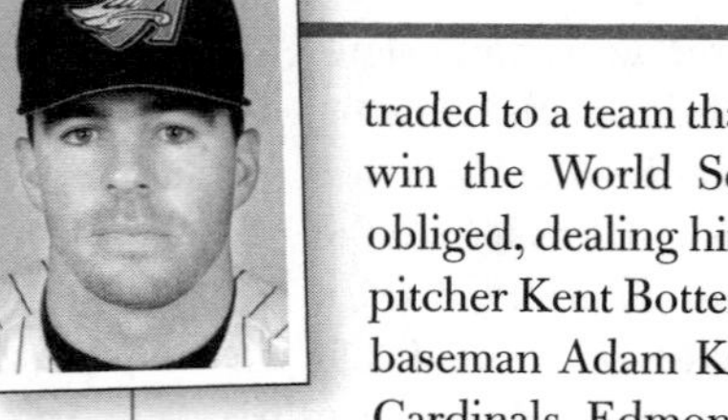

Jim Edmonds was drafted by the Angels in the seventh round of the June 1988 amateur draft. It took him five years to get to the majors, but he has seemingly gotten better every year since. A steady offensive force, Edmonds typically can be counted on for 25–35 homers, 90 runs and RBIs, and a .290 average. But his career has been truly distinguished by his spectacular defensive play in center field. His highlight reel teems with fantastic leaping and diving catches in center. During his seven-year stint with the Angels, Edmonds won two Gold Gloves and had one All-Star Game appearance. Just before the 2000 season began, Edmonds asked to be traded to a team that had a chance to win the World Series; the Angels obliged, dealing him to St. Louis for pitcher Kent Bottenfield and second baseman Adam Kennedy. With the Cardinals, Edmonds has continued to impress with his spectacular defense and steady offensive production. Ironically, though, the Angels won a World Series two years later, while the Cardinals have yet to win a championship since the Edmonds trade.

CAREER ANGELS RECORD:

Games	AB	Hits	Runs
709	2,644	768	464
Avg	**HR**	**RBI**	**SB**
.290	121	408	26

ERSTAD, DARIN (OF/1B)
(1996–2005)

The Angels selected Darin Erstad as the first overall pick of the June 1995 amateur draft. He had been selected three years earlier by the Mets, but chose not to sign with them at the time. Erstad has become the current "Mr. Angel." For 10 years he has hustled his way into the hearts of Angels fans, playing whichever position the team needed him to. He has played full seasons in both the outfield and at first base, and has had several years when he split time almost equally between the two. Erstad, a two-time All-Star, so proficient at both that he has won Gold Gloves both as an outfielder and as a first baseman; he is the only player in major league history to do so. Erstad has performed especially well in the postseason, hitting .370 with 3 homers, 16 runs, 9 RBIs, and 3 stolen bases in 19 games. His career year up to this point was 2000 when he hit .355 with 25 homers, 100 RBIs, 121 runs, 28 steals, and 240 hits. If Erstad stays healthy and plays a full career, like Garret Anderson he could become a member of the 3,000-hit club.

CAREER ANGELS RECORD:

Games	AB	Hits	Runs
1,280	5,163	1,484	810
Avg	**HR**	**RBI**	**SB**
.287	114	620	169

FINLEY, CHUCK (SP)
(1986–1999)

Chuck Finley was originally drafted by the Angels in the June 1984 amateur draft, but chose not to sign with the team. The following year, when he was again drafted by the Angels, he did sign. Finley only played in the minors a short time before making the major league roster as a reliever in 1986 and 1987. In 1988 he was converted to a starter and remained a fixture in the Angels' rotation for the next 12 years. Although he never did win 20 games in a season, he was very consistent, chalking up 15 or more victories six times. By the time Finley left the Angels, he had overtaken Nolan Ryan as the Angels' all-time leader in wins, games, starts, and innings pitched. After playing 14 seasons in an Angels uniform, Finley left via free agency and played three more years with the Indians and Cardinals before retiring after the 2002 season.

CAREER ANGELS RECORD:

W	L	W%	ERA	SV
165	140	.541	3.72	0
K	**BB**	**SHO**	**IP**	
2,151	1,118	14	2,675.0	

FREGOSI, JIM (SS)
(1961–1971)

The Angels dipped into the minor league system of the Boston Red Sox to select Jim Fregosi in the 1960 American League expansion draft. He appeared with the Angels briefly in 1961, then made the team for good in 1962. Over the next decade, Fregosi, a fan favorite, became the expansion team's brightest star. Considered the best power-hitting shortstop in the American League at the time, Fregosi made the All-Star team six times and won a Gold Glove in 1967. He is one of only a few players to have hit for the cycle twice, the first time in 1964, the second in 1968. During a horrible 1971 season, it was discovered that Fregosi had a tumor in his foot. Uncertain about Fregosi's ability to come back from the surgery, the Angels traded their star shortstop to the New York Mets for four young but unproven players, one of whom was Nolan Ryan. Fregosi never did regain his earlier form, but did manage to hang around the majors for seven more seasons, with the Mets, Rangers, and Pirates. While still playing, with the Pirates in 1978, Fregosi was offered the managerial job with the Angels and accepted, thus ending his playing career. In 1979, his first full season as manager, he led the Angels to the playoffs for the first time in the team's history. In 1981 he was replaced by Gene Mauch.

CAREER ANGELS RECORD:

Games	AB	Hits	Runs
1,429	5,244	1,408	691
Avg	**HR**	**RBI**	**SB**
.268	115	546	71

GLAUS, TROY (3B)
(1998–2004)

Troy Glaus was first drafted by the San Diego Padres in the second round of the June 1994 amateur draft, but did not sign with the team. Three years later he was selected by the Angels as the third pick of the first round in the June 1997 amateur draft. By 1998 the young slugging third baseman was in the majors. In 1999 Glaus became the starting third baseman and hit 29 home runs, a sign of things to come. In 2000 he led the American League with 47 homers, won the first of two Silver Slugger Awards, and was selected for his first of three All-Star Game appearances. After clouting 41 more homers in 2001, Glaus led the Angels to the World Series title in 2002, copping the World Series MVP Award in the process. Due to injuries, Glaus missed more than half of all Angels games over the next two years. Because of his uncertain health issues and traditionally modest batting average (he only hit over .251 once during his seven seasons with the Angels), the team chose not to resign Glaus after the 2004 season and the slugger joined the Arizona Diamondbacks as a free agent.

CAREER ANGELS RECORD:

Games	AB	Hits	Runs
827	2,962	748	523
Avg	**HR**	**RBI**	**SB**
.253	182	515	49

Grich, Bobby (2B)
(1977–1986)

Bobby Grich spent the last 10 years of his stellar career with the Angels after playing his first seven years with the Orioles. As a boy growing up in southern California, Grich had always dreamed of playing for the Angels. His hero was Jim Fregosi. When the players were given the opportunity to enter free agency, Grich was one of the first to jump into the market, and he was one of the most sought-after players. He had just come off four straight Gold Glove years with Baltimore, and was known as the best fielding second baseman in the majors—and a guy who also had some pop in his bat. Determined to play for the Angels, Grich signed a five-year contract.

But before he ever played a game for the Angels, he injured his back during the offseason lifting an air conditioner. By July 1977, Grich's season was over and he had to have surgery for a herniated disc. He came back in 1978, but he clearly wasn't the same, offensively or defensively, and he had the worst year of his career. Worried that his career might be over, he gave it one more shot in 1979 and had the best year of his career, slugging 30 homers and 30 doubles with 101 RBIs and a .294 average, while leading the Angels to the playoffs for the first time in team history. In the strike-shortened 1981 season, Grich hit .304 and led the American League with 22 homers. In Grich's last season, 1986, he was at bat in the bottom of the ninth of Game 5 of the ALCS with two out and the bases loaded. A hit would have sent the Angels to the World Series against the Mets and made him the greatest hero in Angels history. Instead, he hit a soft, broken-bat liner back to the pitcher for the third out. When the Red Sox routed the Angels in Games 6 and 7, Grich's season and career were over. He retired with a career .984 fielding percentage, the highest for a second baseman in major league history at the time.

CAREER ANGELS RECORD:

Games	AB	Hits	Runs
1,222	4,100	1,103	601
Avg	**HR**	**RBI**	**SB**
.269	154	557	27

Guerrero, Vladimir (OF)
(2004–2005)

See Expos bio in the Washington chapter.

HARVEY, BRYAN (RP)
(1987–1992)

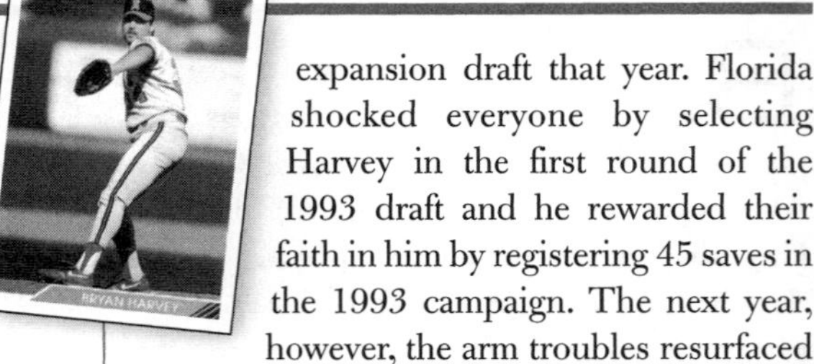

Until Troy Percival came along, Bryan Harvey was the best closer in Angels history. Harvey was signed as an amateur free agent in August 1984 and made the majors in 1987. His 46 saves in 1991 led the American League and helped him win the AL Rolaids Relief Award and a spot on the 1991 AL All-Star team. Harvey's 126 career saves with the Angels still ranks him second all time, trailing only Percival's 316. Elbow problems reduced his save total to 13 the next year and the Angels felt his career was in decline, so they left him unprotected in the expansion draft that year. Florida shocked everyone by selecting Harvey in the first round of the 1993 draft and he rewarded their faith in him by registering 45 saves in the 1993 campaign. The next year, however, the arm troubles resurfaced and he pitched only briefly in 1994 and 1995 before retiring.

CAREER ANGELS RECORD:

W	L	W%	ERA	SV
16	20	.444	2.49	126
K	BB	SHO	IP	
365	126	0	307.7	

JACKSON, REGGIE (DH/OF)
(1982–1986)

Tired of the constant battles with Billy Martin and George Steinbrenner, Jackson played out his contract in 1981 and entered the free-agent market. Steinbrenner didn't mind, since he felt Jackson, after 15 years in the majors, was washed up. Jackson signed on with the Angels in January 1982, and, in his first season with the Angels, surprised many by leading the American League in homers with 39 and helping the Angels to a division title. For this he was rewarded with only the second Silver Slugger Award of his career. Jackson was voted onto the AL All-Star team three times while an Angel, but his last four years with the team could be considered nothing more than modestly decent. After his five-year contract ran out, Jackson signed on for one final year—his 21st—with the team where it had all begun, the A's, before retiring. *(See A's and Yankees bios.)*

CAREER ANGELS RECORD:

Games	AB	Hits	Runs
687	2,331	557	331
Avg	HR	RBI	SB
.239	123	374	14

LANGSTON, MARK (SP)
(1990–1997)

After playing more than five years with the Seattle Mariners and four months with the Montreal Expos, Langston signed on with the Angels as a highly coveted free agent in December 1989. In his first game as an Angel, Langston combined with Mike Witt to no-hit Langston's former team, the Mariners. A series of injuries seemed to plague Langston off and on during his time with the Angels, and, strangely, it fell into a pattern of alternating between odd and even years. He pitched well in odd-numbered years, poorly in even-numbered. His first year with the Angels was disappointing, and he finished the year with a 10–17 record and a 4.40 ERA. Langston did turn it around in 1991, coming in at 19–8 with a 3.00 ERA. But in 1992 he slipped back to a 13–14 record. Once again, though, he turned it around the following year, improving to 16–11 with a 3.20 ERA in 1993. In 1994 the pattern continued as Langston fell to 7–8 with a 4.68 ERA. He rebounded in 1995 with a 15–7 record, but in 1996 he won only six games and compiled a 4.82 ERA. The good-year/bad-year cycle ended in 1997 when he had another bad season, posting a 2–4 record with a 5.85 ERA, the worst of his career up to that point. Convinced his career was over, the Angels didn't pursue him when his contract expired at the end of the 1997 season. Langston played two more years, one each with San Diego and Cleveland, with even worse results before retiring. During his time with the Angels, Langston won five Gold Gloves and made three All-Star Game appearances.

CAREER ANGELS RECORD:

W	L	W%	ERA	SV
88	74	.543	3.97	0
K	**BB**	**SHO**	**IP**	
1,112	551	5	1,445.3	

PERCIVAL, TROY (RP)
(1995–2004)

Troy Percival was drafted by the Angels in the sixth round of the June 1990 amateur draft. He joined the team in 1995 and pitched in 62 games, mostly as a set-up man for one of the best closers in history, Lee Smith. Manager Marcel Lachemann saw Percival's potential and made him the new closer in 1996, eventually trading Smith to Cincinnati early in the season. Over the next nine years, Percival collected 316 saves to become far and away the all-time saves leader in Angels history. Remarkably consistent, Percival was among the league leaders in saves and games finished virtually every year. In the Angels' World Series year of 2002, Percival appeared in nine postseason games and registered seven saves. He was named to the All-Star team four times. After playing out his contract in 2004, Percival left via free agency and signed with Detroit, but an injury in 2005 left his career in question.

CAREER ANGELS RECORD:

W	L	W%	ERA	SV
29	38	.433	2.99	316
K	**BB**	**SHO**	**IP**	
680	253	0	586.7	

RYAN, NOLAN (SP)
(1972–1979)

At the age of 24, Nolan Ryan already had five major league seasons under his belt with the Mets—four with losing records. In his two previous seasons, Ryan had walked 213 batters in just 284 innings. He had a lifetime 29–38 record. The Mets needed a shortstop, and the Angels needed pitching, so when the Mets traded four unproven players, including Ryan, to the Angels for star shortstop Jim Fregosi, the Mets felt they had made a good deal. Ryan almost quit baseball before the 1972 season began. He was struggling in spring training and the labor strife was genuinely upsetting to Ryan. He later stated that if the players' strike had gone on one more week, he would have quit and returned home to Alvin, Texas, never to play again. Fortunately for the Angels and baseball (and baseball fans everywhere!), the 1972 strike ended quickly.

Almost immediately Ryan gave the Mets reason to regret the trade. In his first season with the offensively impotent Angels, Ryan won 19 games, sported a 2.28 ERA, and struck out 329 batters, nearly 200 more than in his best season with New York (137). During his eight-year career with the Angels, Ryan led the league in strikeouts seven times, five times passing the 300 mark. In his second year with the Angels, Ryan struck out 383 batters, still the major league record. He also pitched two no-hitters in 1973, another in 1974 (on the last day of the season), and a fourth and final one with the Angels in 1975, tying him with Sandy Koufax for most no-hitters pitched all time. The Angels finished in the cellar in 1974, but Ryan was 22–16, the only 20-win season of his career. It was also only the fifth time in AL history that a pitcher had won 20 games for a last-place team. On August 20, 1974, Ryan's fastball was timed at 100.9 mph by a sophisticated measuring device. The feat landed him a spot in the *Guinness Book of World Records.* Ryan made the All-Star team five times as an Angel. After the 1979 season, Ryan left for the free-agent market, partly because he wanted to play near his home in Texas and partly because he had come to intensely dislike Angels GM Buzzie Bavasi. Before the 1980 season, Ryan signed a four-year $4.5 million deal with Houston, making him the first player in baseball history to make at least $1 million per year. *(See Astros and Rangers bios.)*

CAREER ANGELS RECORD:

W	L	W%	ERA	SV
138	121	.533	3.07	1

K	BB	SHO	IP
2,416	1,302	40	2,181.3

Salmon, Tim (OF)
(1992–2004)

Tim Salmon was originally drafted by the Atlanta Braves in the 18th round of the 1986 amateur draft, but decided not to sign with them. Three years later the Angels selected Salmon in the third round of the 1989 amateur draft. In a minor league game in 1990, Salmon was hit in the face by a pitch and required plastic surgery to repair the damage. After a late-season call-up in 1992, Salmon joined the team full-time in 1993 and won the American League's Rookie of the Year Award with a .283 average, 31 homers, and 95 RBIs, numbers that are remarkably consistent with his usual yearly output when he is healthy. At the end of the 2004 season, Salmon ranked at or near the top of most Angels career batting categories. He suffered a serious injury before the 2005 season began and his future career was still in doubt at the end of the year, a season in which he didn't play a game. On the last day possible, Salmon filed for free agency, but it seems likely that his career is over after suffering debilitating knee and shoulder injuries.

CAREER ANGELS RECORD:

Games	AB	Hits	Runs
1,596	5,723	1,618	956
Avg	**HR**	**RBI**	**SB**
.283	290	989	48

Tanana, Frank (SP)
(1973–1980)

The Angels drafted Frank Tanana in the first round of the June 1971 amateur draft and brought him to the majors for a few games in 1973. By 1974 he had earned a spot in the starting rotation and compiled a 14–19 record with a 3.12 ERA. In 1975 Tanana recorded 269 strikeouts to lead the American League, the only year in the eight-year stretch from 1972–1979 that teammate Nolan Ryan didn't lead the league. Tanana lowered his ERA that year to 2.62. In 1976 he set a career high in wins with 19 and again lowered his ERA, this time to 2.43. He also had 261 strikeouts and 23 complete games. Tanana had two more good years with the Angels in 1977 and 1978, winning 15 and 18 games, but his strikeout totals dipped drastically to 205 and 137. He faltered in 1979 and 1980, winning only 18 games combined, and striking out only about four or five batters per nine innings pitched. After three years of watching his performance slide, the Angels traded Tanana and Joe Rudi to Boston for Fred Lynn and Steve Renko. By the time he left the Angels, Tanana ranked second all time to Nolan Ryan on the Angels' career lists for wins, starts, complete games, strikeouts, innings, and shutouts. Tanana's seven-year Angels career was over, but he discovered how to pitch with finesse instead of speed, enabling him to extend his career 14 more seasons with five different teams.

CAREER ANGELS RECORD:

W	L	W%	ERA	SV
102	78	.567	3.08	0
K	**BB**	**SHO**	**IP**	
1,233	422	24	1,615.3	

WITT, MIKE (SP)
(1981–1990)

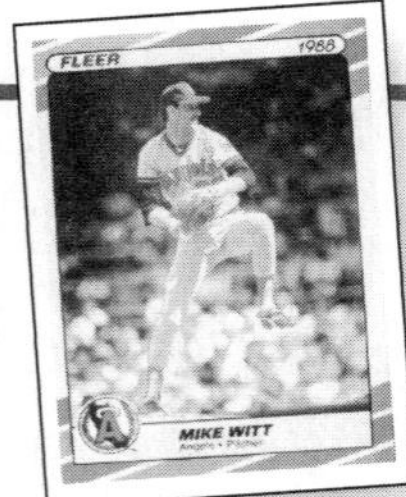

The Angels drafted Mike Witt in the fourth round of the June 1978 amateur draft and brought him to the majors in 1981. During the mid-1980s he was the ace of the Angels staff, averaging just over 15 wins a year from 1984 through 1988. His biggest claim to fame occurred on September 30, 1984, when he pitched only the 13th perfect game in major league history. It was a 1–0 gem over Charlie Hough and the Texas Rangers in Texas. Witt, a two-time All-Star, was instrumental in leading the Angels to the playoffs in 1986. He had the best season of his career, going 18–10 with 208 strikeouts and a 2.84 ERA, finishing third in the Cy Young voting. He had one complete game victory over Boston in the ALCS and would have been the winner in Game 5 had the Angels' bullpen done their job in the ninth. Witt recorded losing seasons from 1987–1989; his wins fell and his ERA rose. He was traded to the Yankees in May 1990 for Dave Winfield, but in his second start of 1991 he blew out his elbow and pitched in only nine more games in his career over the next three years before hanging it up.

CAREER ANGELS RECORD:

W	L	W%	ERA	SV
109	107	.505	3.76	6
K	**BB**	**SHO**	**IP**	
1,283	656	10	1,965.3	

WRIGHT, CLYDE (SP)
(1966–1973)

The Angels selected Wright in the sixth round of the June 1965 amateur draft. Since the Angels were a fifth-year expansion team and badly in need of pitching, Wright was rushed to the majors the following season. As a spot starter and middle reliever, Wright had a combined record of 19–18 from 1966–1968. His record fell to a dismal 1–8 in 1969 and the Angels waived him. No other team picked him up, so Wright went to winter ball to work on his pitching. While there, he discovered and mastered the screwball. When the Angels gave him a tryout in 1970, he was so impressive with his new pitch that he was immediately placed in the starting rotation. He won 22 games with a 2.83 ERA and was voted the AL Comeback Player of the Year. Wright pitched in the All-Star Game and threw a no-hitter against the A's on July 3. Over the next two years, Wright's screwball got him 34 more wins. But as quickly as success had come, it left him. In 1973 he finished 11–19, recording just 65 strikeouts in 257 innings. The Angels gave up on him and traded him to Milwaukee after the season in a nine-player deal. After a 9–20 year in Milwaukee, Wright played one more year for the Rangers, winning four games, before calling it quits.

CAREER ANGELS RECORD:

W	L	W%	ERA	SV
87	85	.506	3.28	3
K	**BB**	**SHO**	**IP**	
571	449	9	1,403.3	

Los Angeles Dodgers

Since 1884

1948 Team Ball

1899 Brooklyn inaugurates Ladies' Day and attendance soars from 122,000 the previous year to an all-time high of nearly 270,000.... **1951** Bobby Thomson of the Giants hits his famous "Shot Heard 'Round the World" homer in a one-game playoff to decide the 1951 National League champion. It marks the third time in six years that the Dodgers have lost the pennant on the last day of the season.... **1963** Sandy Koufax becomes the first-ever unanimous choice for the Cy Young Award—then follows it up with two more unanimous selections in 1965 and 1966.... **1992** Dodgers finish with the worst record in the National League (63–99) for the first time since 1905. Their 99 losses are the most by the franchise since the 1908 club lost 101 games.

FRANCHISE HISTORY

Most baseball fans know that the National League's Los Angeles Dodgers originated in Brooklyn, but not that the team was originally in the American Association (AA) and transferred to the National League intact. The team was formed in 1883 after *New York Herald* city editor George Taylor got the idea and approached real estate investor Charles H. Byrne for financial backing. Byrne was agreeable, but he brought in Joseph J. Doyle and Ferdinand H. Abel, owners of a gambling hall, as additional investors. In 1883 the citizens of Brooklyn were forced to weave their way through a maze of trolleys on the Brooklyn side of the Brooklyn Bridge, and it was in their honor that the team took its first name of Trolley-Dodgers. The Trolley-Dodgers played in the Interstate League in 1883 while Byrne was getting all his affairs in order to join the American Association the following year. The club's bookkeeper that year was Charles Ebbets, a future owner. The team stumbled its way through the league until 1889, when the Trolley-Dodgers won their first pennant. As soon as Byrne saw that the American Association was on thin financial ice, and with the new Players' League looming on the horizon, he moved his team to the stronger National League in time for the 1890 season.

The 1890 financial bloodbath involving the three major circuits—National League, Players' League, and American Association—affected all the teams adversely. The Players' League folded after one season and many of the players were shuffled around among teams of the two remaining major leagues. After the 1891 season, the two leagues came to a settlement whereby the AA shut down and the NL

In 1912 outfielder Casey Stengel of the Dodgers became the first player in history to get four hits in his major league debut.

Duke Snider homers in the first game of the 1952 World Series against the Yankees.

absorbed some of the better franchises. Baseball would know 10 years of relative peace—but not necessarily prosperity— until the American League formed in 1900. Under the settlement of 1890, Players' League owners Wendell Goodwin and George Chauncey were given just under 50 percent interest in the Brooklyn team (now called the Bridegrooms after a number of players all got married the same year). Byrne, Abel, and Doyle continued to own controlling stock. Goodwin, Chauncey, and Abel all eventually sold their interests to Byrne and Doyle. When Byrne died in January 1898, Abel took control of the team, then later traded some of his stock to Ned Hanlon and Harry Von der Horst, owners of the Baltimore club, for stock in their team until he eventually owned 40 percent of both teams, a practice that was common in those days. Hanlon and Von der Horst accumulated 50 percent interest in both teams while bookkeeper Charles Ebbets held 10 percent in both teams. Hanlon and Von der Horst then proceeded to move the best Baltimore players to their Brooklyn club because Brooklyn was the larger market. Hanlon, who was president of the Brooklyn club that won the 1899 National League pennant, was the manager of the 1899 Baltimore club, which finished fourth. Brooklyn repeated as NL champs in 1900.

In 1902 many owners in both the National and American Leagues were suffering great financial losses due to their player salary war and split market share in five of the eight cities. Abel and Von der Horst both wanted out and sold their shares to Ebbets. A power struggle developed between Ebbets and Hanlon, with Hanlon ultimately taking court action to block Ebbets' moves. Ebbets eventually borrowed money from Henry Medicus to buy out Hanlon in 1905. He got into cash flow problems in 1913 during construction of Ebbets Field, the team's new ballpark, so he sold half his shares to his close friends, brothers Steve and Edward McKeever, for $500,000. The McKeevers had become rich delivering quarried rock for the New York Central's railroad line to Buffalo. As part of the deal, Medicus was bought out and two corporations were created, one that owned the team (now called the Robins in honor of their manager, Wilbert Robinson), and one that owned the ballpark and the land beneath it. The team achieved some success in their new stadium, winning the NL pennant in both 1916 and 1920, though they lost the World Series each year, something that would become a habit for decades to come.

Charles Ebbets died of heart problems in 1925 and, a week later, Ed McKeever died of pneumonia (supposedly after catching a severe cold at Ebbets' funeral), leaving only Steve McKeever to run things. McKeever then gave team manager Wilbert Robinson an additional role as the club's new president, but soon the two were feuding, largely over Brooklyn's poor showing in the standings. After four years of rancor between Robinson and McKeever, the two corporations' boards of directors were split in their loyalties to the two men. National League president John Heydler stepped in and appointed another director, attorney Walter Carter, to help mediate matters. Two years later, in 1931, Robinson resigned under pressure after 18 years as Brooklyn's manager. The team then dumped the name Robins and returned to using the Dodgers, the name they've kept ever since.

The years of infighting had taken a toll on the Dodgers, and by the mid-

Casey Stengel, outfielder

1930s the club was deeply in debt to the Brooklyn Trust Company. George Barnewall, who sat on the boards of both the club and Brooklyn Trust, took control of the team, but he was more interested in the financial well-being of Brooklyn Trust than he was in the Dodgers, so for a period of time he rubber-stamped all waiver deals that brought the team $6,000 or more. The resulting chaos and near-bankruptcy of the Dodgers in 1938 caused the National League to again step in. The National League and the Dodger board of directors agreed to let Baseball executive Larry MacPhail take over the team with unlimited powers in an attempt to straighten things out. Two months later Steve McKeever died and his 25 percent interest passed to his daughter, Dearie Mulvey. In 1939 MacPhail brought Leo Durocher on board to be the team's new manager and Branch Rickey Jr. to be the director of the farm system.

After developing a consistent contender, MacPhail left after five years to join the Army in 1943. Branch Rickey Sr., a classmate of MacPhail's at the University of Michigan's law school, succeeded MacPhail as GM. Later in 1943 Rickey, Brooklyn Trust Company attorney Walter O'Malley, and front man Andrew Schmitz purchased the 25 percent interest in the team that had originally been owned by Ed McKeever, but was now controlled by Brooklyn Trust. O'Malley had become wealthy publishing a handbook for building subcontractors. Schmitz was acting for John Smith, owner of Pfizer Pharmaceutical. A year later the three men purchased the 50 percent interest held by the heirs of Charles Ebbets, giving them each a 25 percent stake in the club. In 1950 Walter O'Malley was voted in as team president when Rickey's contract expired. O'Malley and Rickey had been at odds for several years and O'Malley wanted Rickey out. Rickey offered to sell his shares to O'Malley for $1 million, but O'Malley countered with $320,000, the price the three of them had paid in 1943. Rickey balked and found an outside buyer, real estate magnate William Zeckendorf, who was willing to pay the $1 million. Because the three men had included a clause that gave any of them right of first refusal if a bona fide offer was made, O'Malley exercised the option and paid the $1 million to Rickey plus another $50,000 to Zeckendorf as required by the agreement. O'Malley was so angry over having to pay the additional $50,000 that he had the cancelled check framed and put on the wall of his office.

Sandy Koufax, the youngest player (36) ever to make the Hall of Fame.

From the mid-1940s until the mid-1950s, Brooklyn was the most profitable franchise in the National League, although attendance declined steadily during the period to just 45 percent of capacity by 1956. O'Malley saw the potential of a lucrative southern California market and began investigating a move west. He had tried to get officials to build a new, possibly domed stadium in Brooklyn, to no avail. He sold Ebbets Field after the 1956 season for $4 million and the Montreal minor league park for $1 million to help finance the move to Los Angeles. In early 1957 a group of California politicians, eager to have major league baseball on the West Coast, visited O'Malley in

Brooklyn and offered to build him a new ballpark if he moved to Los Angeles. Once he made up his mind to move, O'Malley bought the minor league franchise of the Cubs that was located in Los Angeles and the ballpark they played in, also called Wrigley Field and designed similarly to the Chicago ballpark. On October 8, 1957, O'Malley announced the team's move to Los Angeles.

Upon arriving in Los Angeles, the Dodgers played their home games at the Los Angeles Memorial Coliseum for four years until Dodger Stadium opened. The team drew nearly 79,000 paying customers to their first game in Los Angeles, a new major league record. While O'Malley had gotten the Brooklyn officials to promise him only 12 acres for a new ballpark, the Los Angeles officials gave him 300 acres of land around Dodger Stadium. Over the years, O'Malley bought the outstanding shares of all the other minority owners, including John Smith's widow (25 percent) after her death, and Ed McKeever's heirs, in 1975, after the death of Dearie Mulvey, making him the sole owner. When Walter O'Malley died in 1979, his shares were split equally between his son Peter and his sister, Teresa Seidler. In 1998 the O'Malleys sold out to the Fox Group, an affiliate of Rupert Murdoch's for $311 million. The sale included the team, the stadium, the 300 acres surrounding the stadium, the spring training facilities in Vero Beach, Florida, and the training facilities in the Dominican Republic. In 2004 the team was sold again, this time for $430 million to real estate developer Frank McCourt, whose tenure has so far received very mixed reviews.

On the field, the Dodgers have been the most successful major league team outside of the Yankees, winning 22 pennants since their American Association inception in 1884. However, the Dodgers have only won six World Series titles, and the resulting frustration and heartbreak among the team's fans is legendary, especially regarding all their losses to the Yankees in the '40s, '50s, and '70s. The franchise has had the worst record in the National League only twice in 122 seasons (1905 and 1992). Another trademark of the franchise is stability, the 1930s notwithstanding. The Dodgers have had fewer managers and general managers—by far—than any team in baseball history, as they developed more of a family approach to running their operation. During the 1970s, the Dodgers had an infield that stayed together for eight years, a major league record. Even their main television announcer, Vin Scully, the best announcer in baseball, just completed his 56th consecutive year with the team in 2005. All of this has translated into a large, loyal fan base that has traditionally made the Dodgers one of the best draws in major league baseball, and one of the most successful franchises in history. Other teams would do well to copy the Dodger "blue"-print.

TEAM NAME HISTORY

Official Names

Trolley-Dodgers (1884–1888)
Bridegrooms (1889–1898)
Superbas (1899–1910)
Dodgers (1911–1913)
Robins (1914–1931)
Dodgers (1932–current)

Unofficial Names/Nicknames

Brooklyns; Grooms; Atlantics; the Flock; Nationals; Ward's Wonders; Foutz's Fillies; Dem Bums

STADIUM HISTORY

Washington Park	1884–April 16, 1891
Eastern Park	April 27, 1891–1897
Washington Park (II)	1898–1912
Ebbets Field	1913–1957
Roosevelt Stadium	1956–1957
(Jersey City, N.J., 15 games total over two years)	
L.A. Memorial Coliseum	1958–1961
Dodger Stadium	1962–current

YEARLY RECORD, FINISH, & ATTENDANCE FIGURES

Year	League	Record	DIV/LG Finish	Attendance	Avg/Gm
2005	NL West	71–91	4	3,603,646	44,489
2004	NL West	93–69	1	3,488,283	43,065
2003	NL West	85–77	2	3,138,626	38,748
2002	NL West	92–70	3	3,131,255	38,657
2001	NL West	86–76	3	3,017,143	37,249
2000	NL West	86–76	2	2,880,242	35,559
1999	NL West	77–85	3	3,095,346	38,214
1998	NL West	83–79	3	3,089,222	38,139
1997	NL West	88–74	2	3,319,504	40,982
1996	NL West	90–72	2	3,188,454	39,364
1995	NL West	78–66	1	2,766,251	38,420
1994	NL West	58–56	1	2,279,355	41,443
1993	NL West	81–81	4	3,170,393	39,141
1992	NL West	63–99	6	2,473,266	30,534
1991	NL West	93–69	2	3,348,170	41,335
1990	NL West	86–76	2	3,002,396	37,067
1989	NL West	77–83	4	2,944,653	36,354
1988	NL West	94–67	1	2,980,262	36,793
1987	NL West	73–89	4	2,797,409	34,536
1986	NL West	73–89	5	3,023,208	37,324
1985	NL West	95–67	1	3,264,593	40,304
1984	NL West	79–83	4	3,134,824	38,702
1983	NL West	91–71	1	3,510,313	43,879
1982	NL West	88–74	2	3,608,881	44,554
1981	NL West	63–47	1/4	2,381,292	42,523
1980	NL West	92–71	2	3,249,287	39,625
1979	NL West	79–83	3	2,860,954	35,320
1978	NL West	95–67	1	3,347,845	41,331
1977	NL West	98–64	1	2,955,087	36,483
1976	NL West	92–70	2	2,386,301	29,461
1975	NL West	88–74	2	2,539,349	31,350
1974	NL West	102–60	1	2,632,474	32,500
1973	NL West	95–66	2	2,136,192	26,373
1972	NL West	85–70	3	1,860,858	24,811
1971	NL West	89–73	2	2,064,594	25,489
1970	NL West	87–74	2	1,697,142	20,952
1969	NL West	85–77	4	1,784,527	22,031
1968	NL	76–86	8	1,581,093	19,520
1967	NL	73–89	8	1,664,362	20,548
1966	NL	95–67	1	2,617,029	32,309
1965	NL	97–65	1	2,553,577	31,526
1964	NL	80–82	7	2,228,751	27,515
1963	NL	99–63	1	2,538,602	31,341
1962	NL	102–63	2	2,755,184	33,195
1961	NL	89–65	2	1,804,250	23,432
1960	NL	82–72	4	2,253,887	29,271
1959	NL	88–68	1	2,071,045	26,552
1958	NL	71–83	7	1,845,556	23,968
1957	NL	84–70	3	1,028,258	13,354
1956	NL	93–61	1	1,213,562	15,761
1955	NL	98–55	1	1,033,589	13,423

Yearly Record, Finish, & Attendance Figures (cont.)

Year	League	Record	DIV/LG Finish	Attendance	Avg/Gm
1954	NL	92–62	2	1,020,531	13,254
1953	NL	105–49	1	1,163,419	14,916
1952	NL	96–57	1	1,088,704	13,609
1951	NL	97–60	2	1,282,628	16,444
1950	NL	89–65	2	1,185,896	15,204
1949	NL	97–57	1	1,633,747	20,945
1948	NL	84–70	3	1,398,967	17,935
1947	NL	94–60	1	1,807,526	23,173
1946	NL	96–60	2	1,796,824	22,745
1945	NL	87–67	3	1,059,220	13,580
1944	NL	63–91	7	605,905	7,869
1943	NL	81–72	3	661,739	8,594
1942	NL	104–50	2	1,037,765	13,136
1941	NL	100–54	1	1,214,910	15,379
1940	NL	88–65	2	975,978	12,049
1939	NL	84–69	3	955,668	12,252
1938	NL	69–80	7	663,087	8,961
1937	NL	62–91	6	482,481	6,348
1936	NL	67–87	7	489,618	6,198
1935	NL	70–83	5	470,517	6,111
1934	NL	71–81	6	434,188	5,639
1933	NL	65–88	6	526,815	6,585
1932	NL	81–73	3	681,827	8,741
1931	NL	79–73	4	753,133	9,910
1930	NL	86–68	4	1,097,329	14,251
1929	NL	70–83	6	731,886	9,505
1928	NL	77–76	6	664,863	8,635
1927	NL	65–88	6	637,230	8,611
1926	NL	71–82	6	650,819	8,563
1925	NL	68–85	7	659,435	8,564
1924	NL	92–62	2	818,883	10,635
1923	NL	76–78	6	564,666	7,239
1922	NL	76–78	6	498,865	6,396
1921	NL	77–75	5	613,245	7,862
1920	NL	93–61	1	808,722	10,368
1919	NL	69–71	5	360,721	5,153
1918	NL	57–69	5	83,831	1,552
1917	NL	70–81	7	221,619	2,841
1916	NL	94–60	1	447,747	5,740
1915	NL	80–72	3	297,766	3,818
1914	NL	75–79	5	122,671	1,553
1913	NL	65–84	6	347,000	4,506
1912	NL	58–95	7	243,000	3,197
1911	NL	64–86	7	269,000	3,635
1910	NL	64–90	6	279,321	3,492
1909	NL	55–98	6	321,300	4,067
1908	NL	53–101	7	275,600	3,579
1907	NL	65–83	5	312,500	4,058
1906	NL	66–86	5	277,400	3,650
1905	NL	48–104	8	227,924	2,960
1904	NL	56–97	6	214,600	2,824

YEARLY RECORD, FINISH, & ATTENDANCE FIGURES (CONT.)

Year	League	Record	DIV/LG Finish	Attendance	Avg/Gm
1903	NL	70–66	5	224,670	3,078
1902	NL	75–63	2	199,868	2,897
1901	NL	79–57	3	198,200	2,915
1900	NL	82–54	1	183,000	2,577
1899	NL	101–47	1	269,641	3,595
1898	NL	54–91	10	122,514	1,644
1897	NL	61–71	7	220,831	3,248
1896	NL	58–73	10	201,000	3,023
1895	NL	71–60	5	230,000	3,459
1894	NL	70–61	5	214,000	3,194
1893	NL	65–63	7	235,000	3,615
1892	NL	95–59	3	183,727	2,326
1891	NL	61–76	6	181,477	2,649
1890	NL	86–43	1	121,412	1,882
1889	AA	93–44	1	N/A	N/A
1888	AA	88–52	2	N/A	N/A
1887	AA	60–74	6	N/A	N/A
1886	AA	76–61	3	N/A	N/A
1885	AA	53–59	5	N/A	N/A
1884	AA	40–64	9	N/A	N/A

MANAGER HISTORY

Manager	Years	W–L	Win %
George Taylor	1884	40–64	.385
Charlie Hackett	1885	15–22	.405
Charlie Byrne	1885–1887	174–172	.503
Bill McGunnigle	1888–1890	268–138	.660
Monte Ward	1891–1892	156–135	.536
Dave Foutz	1893–1896	264–257	.507
Billy Barnie	1897–1898	76–91	.455
Ned Hanlon	1899–1905	511–488	.512
Patsy Donovan	1906–1908	184–270	.405
Harry Lumley	1909	55–98	.359
Bill Dahlen	1910–1913	251–355	.414
Wilbert Robinson	1914–1931	1,375–1,341	.506
Max Carey	1932–1933	146–161	.476
Casey Stengel	1934–1936	208–251	.453
Burleigh Grimes	1937–1938	131–171	.434
Leo Durocher	1939–1946,1948	738–565	.566
Clyde Sukeforth	1947	2–0	1.000
Burt Shotton	1947,1948–1950	326–215	.603
Chuck Dressen	1951–1953	298–166	.642
Walter Alston	1954–1976	2,040–1,613	.558
Tommy Lasorda	1976–1996	1,599–1,439	.526
Bill Russell	1996–1998	173–149	.537
Glenn Hoffman	1998	47–41	.534
Davey Johnson	1999–2000	163–162	.502
Jim Tracy	2001–2005	427–383	.527

ALL-TIME WIN-LOSS RECORDS VS. ALL OPPONENTS

Opponent	Record
ALL-TIME	8,574–7,820
Angels	22–28
Astros	363–297
Athletics	7–9
Blue Jays	3–3
Braves	1,090–907
Brewers	37–18
Cardinals	925–939
Cubs	932–933
Devil Rays	2–1
Diamondbacks	69–63
Giants	1,033–1,059
Indians	3–0
INTERLEAGUE	75–71
Mariners	8–8
Marlins	60–52
Mets	289–232
Nationals	229–171
Orioles	5–1
Padres	323–294
Phillies	1,046–816
Pirates	979–891
Rangers	9–7
Reds	1,015–992
Red Sox	4–2
Rockies	109–85
Royals	2–4
Tigers	5–1
Twins	2–1
White Sox	1–5
Yankees	2–1

Jackie Robinson, Sal Maglie, and Carl Furillo in 1956.

Franchise Highlights, Low Points, and Strange Distinctions

1901 The first major league player to hit grand slams in consecutive games was Brooklyn's Jimmy Sheckard.

••••

1903 Rookie pitcher Henry Schmidt of Brooklyn went 22–13 with 29 complete games, five shutouts, and two saves, then never pitched or played in another major league game in his life.

••••

1909 Catcher Bill Bergen of the Brooklyn Superbas hit just .139, the lowest average ever by a regular player. He had only 48 hits in 346 at-bats with one double, one triple, and one homer.

••••

1911 After losing 23 straight decisions in 1910–1911, Boston Braves pitcher Cliff Curtis finally ended his dry spell with a win over Brooklyn.

••••

1919 In an amazing show of National League non-production, Brooklyn Robins outfielder Hy Myers led the league with just 73 RBIs.

••••

1920 On May 1, Brooklyn played an epic 26-inning game against Boston that ended in a 1–1 tie. Pitchers Joe Oeschger of the Braves and Leon Cadore of the Robins both pitched the entire way.

1924 Following the American League's lead, the National League began handing out MVP Awards. The first one went to pitcher Dazzy Vance of Brooklyn, who went 28–6 with a 2.16 ERA and posted 30 complete games.

••••

1925 Second baseman Milt Stock of the Robins got four hits in a 6–3 win over the Giants on July 3, his fourth four-hit game in four days.

••••

1929 Outfielder Johnny Frederick of Brooklyn hit 52 doubles, still the major league record for rookies. In 1932 he had nine pinch-hits on the season, and six of them were homers, also still a major league record.

••••

1935 Al Cuccinello (Giants) and Tony Cuccinello (Dodgers) became the first brothers on opposing teams to homer in the same National League game when they performed the feat on July 5.

••••

1942 The Dodgers tied the major league record for wins in a season (104) by a second-place team when the Cardinals edged them out by two games.

1945 The youngest player to hit a home run in the major leagues during the 20th century was Tommy Brown of the Dodgers. On August 20, the 17-year-old accounted for the only run in an 11–1 loss to the Pirates.

• • • •

1946 Pete Reiser set a new National League record by stealing home seven times in one season.

• • • •

1950 First baseman Gil Hodges joined an elite group when he hit four home runs in one game on August 31, leading the Dodgers to a 19–3 thrashing of the Boston Braves.

• • • •

1953 The Dodgers tied the major league record for most players (six) with 100 or more runs scored in a season. Duke Snider led the way with 132, followed by Jim Gilliam (125), Jackie Robinson (109), Pee Wee Reese (108), Roy Campanella (103), and Gil Hodges (101). The team also slugged home runs in a record 24 consecutive games.

1954 Karl Spooner pitched only two games for the Dodgers, and they were both complete-game shutouts.

• • • •

1956 Outfielder Dale Mitchell spent 10-plus seasons with the Indians before being traded to Brooklyn in midseason. In over 4,000 regular and postseason at-bats, Mitchell struck out only 120 times. So, when the Dodgers were down to their last out in Don Larsen's perfect World Series game in 1956, Dale Mitchell—an American Leaguer for more than a decade who had faced Larsen many times before—seemed Brooklyn's best chance to put the ball in play and spoil Larsen's bid. But Mitchell struck out—on a called third strike.

• • • •

1957 Outfielder Duke Snider of the Dodgers hit 40 home runs, but had only 92 RBIs, becoming the first player in major league history to collect fewer than 100 RBIs in a 40-homer season.

• • • •

1958 When Pee Wee Reese retired, he opined on his career: "If I had my career to play over, one thing I'd do differently is swing more. Those 1,200 walks I got, nobody remembers them."

1959 Sandy Koufax became the first 20th-century National League pitcher to strike out 18 batters in a game when he shut down the San Francisco Giants, 5–2, on August 31.

Manager Walter Alston became the only skipper in major league history to lead the same franchise to World Series titles in two different cities when he led the Los Angeles Dodgers to a victory over the White Sox. Four years earlier he had piloted the Dodgers to a World Series win over the Yankees while the team was still in Brooklyn.

The Los Angeles Dodgers set an all-time major league attendance record for a single game when, on May 7, they attracted 93,103 fans into the L.A. Coliseum for an exhibition game against the Yankees to honor and benefit Roy Campanella.

• • • •

1963 The only Los Angeles Dodger to win a batting title was Tommy Davis, and he did it twice: 1962 and 1963.

The first team to ever have back-to-back MVP and Cy Young Award winners were the Dodgers of 1962–1963. In 1962 Don Drysdale won the Cy Young and Maury Wills the MVP, while in 1963 Sandy Koufax won both the Cy Young *and* MVP Awards.

• • • •

1968 Don Drysdale's amazing feat of pitching 58⅔ consecutive scoreless innings—including six straight shutouts—generally obscures the fact that his record at the end of the year (14–12) was less than stellar.

1974–81 In 1973 Steve Garvey was moved from third to first base, opening the way for rookie prospect Ron Cey. From 1974 to 1981, the Dodgers had an infield that remained intact, a major league record. Along with Garvey and Cey, the Dodgers had Davey Lopes at second and Bill Russell at shortstop. During that eight-year stretch, the Dodgers won four National League pennants and one World Series.

• • • •

1974 The mechanical pitching machines used in major league batting practices are nicknamed "Iron Mike." Though they didn't get the moniker from pitcher Mike Marshall, they certainly could have. In 1974 Marshall appeared in 106 games for the Dodgers, a major league record which also helped him earn the league's Cy Young Award. In 1972 Marshall had become the first pitcher in history to appear in all five games of a five-game World Series.

• • • •

1977 The Los Angeles Dodgers became the first team in history to have four 30-homer players. Steve Garvey paced the quartet with 33, followed by Reggie Smith (32), Ron Cey (30), and Dusty Baker (30). The feat was not accomplished again until 1995, when the Rockies did it for the first of four times in five years. In addition, the Dodgers performed it again in 1997 and were later joined by the Braves (1998), Angels (2000), Blue Jays (2000), and Cubs (2004).

1978 The Dodgers attracted 3,347,845 paying customers, becoming the first team to crack the 3 million mark in attendance.

• • • •

1982 Second baseman Steve Sax won the National League Rookie of the Year Award, becoming the fourth consecutive Dodger to snag the prize. He was preceded by three pitchers, Rick Sutcliffe (1979), Steve Howe (1980), and Fernando Valenzuela (1981). Incredibly, the Dodgers would break their own record when they had five consecutive Rookies of the Year from 1992 to 1996 (Eric Karros, Mike Piazza, Raul Mondesi, Hideo Nomo, and Todd Hollandsworth).

• • • •

1988 When Orel Hershiser pitched 59 consecutive scoreless innings, he bested the record set by fellow Dodger Don Drysdale in 1968 by a mere one-third of an inning.

• • • •

1991 The Dodgers were held hitless for the first nine innings of a game twice in three days, the first team since the 1917 Chicago White Sox to suffer the fate. On July 26, Mark Gardner of the Expos held the Dodgers hitless before losing, 1–0, to a three-hit Dodger rally in the bottom of the 10th. On July 28, the Dodgers lost to the Expos, 2–0, as Dennis Martinez pitched a perfect game.

• • • •

1993 When Eric Karros hit 23 homers, he became the first Dodger ever to hit at least 20 homers in his first two seasons.

1993–96 The Dodgers played 582 games (two seasons were shortened by player strikes). Incredibly, all 582 were started by right-handed pitchers.

• • • •

1998 Of the Dodgers' Opening Day lineup, outfielder Trenidad Hubbard was the only member who was not traded or lost for the season due to injury.

• • • •

1999 Pitcher Kevin Brown of the Dodgers became baseball's first $100 million player when he signed a seven-year, $105 million contract prior to the season.

• • • •

2000 Infielder Dave Hansen set a new major league record for pinch-hit home runs in a season with seven.

• • • •

2002–04 Eric Gagne pitched exactly 82.3 innings in three consecutive years.

• • • •

2005 On August 27, Dodger Jeff Kent became the major league career leader in home runs by a second baseman when he smacked a homer against his former team, the Astros, in an 8–3 win. He finished the season with 331 career homers.

In one July game, the Dodgers started four players whose first name was Jason, including the entire outfield. Catcher Jason Phillips joined an outfield of Jason Repko, Jason Grabowski, and Jayson Werth.

Special Achievements

World Series Results

Year	Opponent	Result	Games
1916	Boston Red Sox	Lost	1–4
1920	Cleveland Indians	Lost	2–5
1941	New York Yankees	Lost	1–4
1947	New York Yankees	Lost	3–4
1949	New York Yankees	Lost	1–4
1952	New York Yankees	Lost	3–4
1953	New York Yankees	Lost	2–4
1955	New York Yankees	Won	4–3
1956	New York Yankees	Lost	3–4
1959	Chicago White Sox	Won	4–2
1963	New York Yankees	Won	4–0
1965	Minnesota Twins	Won	4–3
1966	Baltimore Orioles	Lost	0–4
1974	Oakland A's	Lost	1–4
1977	New York Yankees	Lost	2–4
1978	New York Yankees	Lost	2–4
1981	New York Yankees	Won	4–2
1988	Oakland A's	Won	4–1

World Series Managerial Records

Manager	Series Record	Games Record
Wilbert Robinson	0–2	3–9
Leo Durocher	0–1	1–4
Burt Shotton	0–2	4–8
Chuck Dressen	0–2	5–8
Walter Alston	4–3	20–20
Tommy Lasorda	2–2	12–11

All-Time Postseason Record

Divisional Playoffs	4–11
League Championship Series	19–15
World Series	45–60

All-Star Games at Brooklyn & Los Angeles (when NL was home team)

Year	Date	Winner	Score	Stadium
1949	July 12	American	11–7	Ebbets Field
1959	August 3	American	5–3	L.A. Memorial Coliseum
1980	July 8	National	4–2	Dodger Stadium

Hall of Famers Who Played for Team

	Position	Years	Games with Dodgers
Dave Bancroft	SS	1928–1929	253
Dan Brouthers	1B	1892–1893	229
Jim Bunning	SP	1969	9
Roy Campanella	C	1948–1957	1,215
Max Carey	OF	1926–1929	298
Gary Carter	C/1B	1991	101
Don Drysdale	SP	1956–1969	547
Leo Durocher	SS	1938–1941, 1943, 1945	345
Burleigh Grimes	SP	1918–1926	328
Billy Herman	2B/3B	1941–1943, 1946	488
Waite Hoyt	SP/RP	1932, 1937–1938	41
Hughie Jennings	1B	1899–1900, 1903	188
Willie Keeler	OF	1893, 1899–1902	566
Joe Kelley	OF/1B	1899–1901	384
George Kelly	1B	1932	64
Sandy Koufax	SP/RP	1955–1966	397
Tommy Lasorda	RP	1954–1955	8
Tony Lazzeri	2B	1939	14
Freddy Lindstrom	OF	1936	26
Ernie Lombardi	C	1931	73
Al Lopez	C	1928, 1930–1935	762
Heinie Manush	OF	1937–1938	149
Rabbit Maranville	SS/2B	1926	78
Juan Marichal	SP	1975	2
Rube Marquard	SP/RP	1915–1920	149
Tommy McCarthy	OF	1896	104
Joe McGinnity	SP/RP	1900	46
Joe Medwick	OF	1940–1943, 1946	470
Eddie Murray	1B	1989–1991, 1997	477
Pee Wee Reese	SS	1940–1942, 1946–1958	2,166
Frank Robinson	OF	1972	103
Jackie Robinson	2B/3B/1B/OF	1947–1956	1,382

Duke Snider	OF	1947–1962	1,923
Casey Stengel	OF	1912–1917	676
Don Sutton	SP	1966–1980, 1988	561
Dazzy Vance	SP	1922–1932, 1935	378
Arky Vaughan	3B/SS/OF	1942–1943, 1947–1948	406
Lloyd Waner	PH/OF	1944	15
Paul Waner	OF	1941, 1943–1944	176
John Ward	2B/SS	1891–1892	253
Zack Wheat	OF	1909–1926	2,322
Hoyt Wilhelm	RP	1971–1972	25
Hack Wilson	OF	1932–1934	319

Hall of Famers Who Managed Team

Manager	Years	Games with Brooklyn/ Los Angeles
Walter Alston	1954–1976	3,658
Max Carey	1932–1933	311
Leo Durocher	1939–1946, 1948	1,318
Burleigh Grimes	1937–1938	306
Ned Hanlon	1899–1905	1,018
Tommy Lasorda	1976–1996	3,041
Wilbert Robinson	1914–1931	2,736
Casey Stengel	1934–1936	463
John Ward	1891–1892	295

MVP Award Winners

Dolph Camilli	1B	1941
Jackie Robinson	2B	1949
Roy Campanella	C	1951
Roy Campanella	C	1953
Roy Campanella	C	1955
Don Newcombe	SP	1956
Maury Wills	SS	1962
Sandy Koufax	SP	1963
Steve Garvey	1B	1974
Kirk Gibson	OF	1988

Cy Young Award Winners

Pitcher	Year	W–L	SV	ERA
Don Newcombe	1956	27–7	0	3.49
Don Drysdale	1962	25–9	1	2.83
Sandy Koufax	1963	25–5	0	1.88
Sandy Koufax	1965	26–8	2	2.04
Sandy Koufax	1966	27–9	0	1.73
Mike Marshall	1974	15–12	21	2.42
Fernando Valenzuela	1981	13–7	0	2.48
Orel Hershiser	1988	23–8	1	2.26
Eric Gagne	2003	2–3	55	1.20

Rookie of the Year Award Winners

Jackie Robinson	1B	1947
Don Newcombe	SP	1949
Joe Black	RP	1952
Jim Gilliam	2B	1953
Frank Howard	OF	1960
Jim Lefebvre	2B	1965
Ted Sizemore	2B	1969
Rick Sutcliffe	SP	1979
Steve Howe	RP	1980
Fernando Valenzuela	SP	1981
Steve Sax	2B	1982
Eric Karros	1B	1992
Mike Piazza	C	1993
Raul Mondesi	OF	1994
Hideo Nomo	SP	1995
Todd Hollandsworth	OF	1996

Gold Glove Winners

Year	Position	Player
1957	1B	Gil Hodges
1958	1B	Gil Hodges
1959	1B 2B	Gil Hodges Charlie Neal
1960	OF	Wally Moon
1961	C SS	Johnny Roseboro Maury Wills
1962	SS	Maury Wills
1966	C	Johnny Roseboro
1967	1B	Wes Parker
1968	1B	Wes Parker
1969	1B	Wes Parker
1970	1B	Wes Parker
1971	1B OF	Wes Parker Willie Davis
1972	1B OF	Wes Parker Willie Davis
1973	OF	Willie Davis
1974	SP 1B	Andy Messersmith Steve Garvey
1975	SP 1B	Andy Messersmith Steve Garvey
1976	1B	Steve Garvey
1977	1B	Steve Garvey
1978	2B	Davey Lopes
1981	OF	Dusty Baker
1986	SP	Fernando Valenzuela
1988	SP	Orel Hershiser
1995	OF	Raul Mondesi
1997	OF	Raul Mondesi
1998	C	Charles Johnson
2004	SS	Cesar Izturis

Triple Crown Winners

None

Fireman of the Year Award Winners

Phil Regan	1966
Mike Marshall	1974
Eric Gagne	2003
Eric Gagne	2004

World Series MVP

Johnny Podres	1955
Larry Sherry	1959
Sandy Koufax	1963
Sandy Koufax	1965
Ron Cey	1981 (tie)
Pedro Guerrero	1981 (tie)
Steve Yeager	1981 (tie)
Orel Hershiser	1988

League Championship Series MVP

Dusty Baker	1977
Steve Garvey	1978
Burt Hooton	1981
Orel Hershiser	1988

All-Star Game MVP

Maury Wills	1962 (Game 1)
Steve Garvey	1974
Don Sutton	1977
Steve Garvey	1978
Mike Piazza	1996

Manager of the Year Award Winners

Tommy Lasorda	1983
Tommy Lasorda	1988

Batting Champions

Year	Player	Avg
1892	Dan Brouthers	.335
1913	Jake Daubert	.350
1914	Jake Daubert	.329
1918	Zack Wheat	.335
1932	Lefty O'Doul	.368
1941	Pete Reiser	.343
1944	Dixie Walker	.357
1949	Jackie Robinson	.342
1953	Carl Furillo	.344
1962	Tommy Davis	.346
1963	Tommy Davis	.326

Nine-Inning No-Hitters Pitched

Year	Pitcher	Opp.	Score
1891	Thomas Lovett	NYG	4–0
1906	Malcolm Eason	STL	2–0
1908	Nap Rucker	BOS	6–0
1925	Dazzy Vance	PHI	10–1
1940	Tex Carleton	CIN	3–0
1946	Edward Head	BOS	5–0
1948	Rex Barney	NYG	2–0
1952	Carl Erskine	CHI	5–0
1956	Carl Erskine	NYG	3–0
	Sal Maglie	PHI	5–0
1962	Sandy Koufax	NYM	5–0
1963	Sandy Koufax	SF	8–0
1964	Sandy Koufax	PHI	3–0
1965	Sandy Koufax	CHI	1–0 (perfect)
1970	Bill Singer	PHI	5–0
1980	Jerry Reuss	SF	8–0
1990	Fernando Valenzuela	STL	6–0
1992	Kevin Gross	SF	2–0
1995	Ramon Martinez	FLA	7–0
1996	Hideo Nomo	COL	9–0

20-Game Winners

Year	Pitcher	W–L
1885	Henry Porter	33–21
1886	Henry Porter	27–19
1888	Bob Caruthers	29–15
	Mickey Hughes	25–13
1889	Bob Caruthers	40–11
	Adonis Terry	22–15
1890	Tom Lovett	30–11
	Adonis Terry	26–16
	Bob Caruthers	23–11
1891	Tom Lovett	23–19
1892	George Haddock	29–13
	Ed Stein	27–16
1893	Brickyard Kennedy	25–20
1894	Ed Stein	26–14
	Brickyard Kennedy	24–20
1899	Jay Hughes	28–6
	Jack Dunn	23–13
	Brickyard Kennedy	22–9
1900	Joe McGinnity	28–8
	Brickyard Kennedy	20–13
1901	William Donovan	25–15
1903	Henry Schmidt	22–13
1911	Nap Rucker	22–18
1914	Jeff Pfeffer	23–12
1916	Jeff Pfeffer	25–11
1920	Burleigh Grimes	23–11
1921	Burleigh Grimes	22–13
1922	Walter Reuther	21–12
1923	Burleigh Grimes	21–18
1924	Dazzy Vance	28–6
	Burleigh Grimes	22–13

1925	Dazzy Vance	22–9
1928	Dazzy Vance	22–10
1932	Watty Clark	20–12
1939	Luke Hamlin	20–13
1941	Kirby Higbe Whit Wyatt	22–9 22–10
1947	Ralph Branca	21–12
1951	Preacher Roe Don Newcombe	22–3 20–9
1953	Carl Erskine	20–6
1955	Don Newcombe	20–5
1956	Don Newcombe	27–7
1962	Don Drysdale	25–9
1963	Sandy Koufax	25–5
1965	Sandy Koufax Don Drysdale	26–8 23–12
1966	Sandy Koufax	27–9
1969	Claude Osteen Bill Singer	20–15 20–12
1971	Al Downing	20–9
1972	Claude Osteen	20–11
1974	Andy Messersmith	20–6
1976	Don Sutton	21–10
1977	Tommy John	20–7
1986	Fernando Valenzuela	21–11
1988	Orel Hershiser	23–8
1990	Ramon Martinez	20–6

Retired Uniform Numbers

Number	Player	Position
1	Pee Wee Reese	SS
2	Tommy Lasorda	Mgr
4	Duke Snider	OF
19	Jim Gilliam	2B/3B/OF
20	Don Sutton	SP
24	Walter Alston	Mgr
32	Sandy Koufax	SP
39	Roy Campanella	C
42	Jackie Robinson	2B
53	Don Drysdale	SP

Team Records—Wins & Losses

- Games won in a season: 105 in 1953
- Games lost in a season: 104 in 1905
- Games won in a month: 25 in July 1947 and August 1953
- Games lost in a month: 27 in September 1908
- Consecutive games won: 15 in 1924
- Consecutive games lost: 16 in 1944
- Biggest shutout victory: 19–0 over San Diego on June 28, 1969
- Biggest shutout loss: 18–0 to Cincinnati on August 8, 1965
- Highest winning percentage: .682 in 1899 (101–47) and 1953 (105–49)
- Lowest winning percentage: .316 in 1905 (48–104)

Team Records—Batting

- Highest team batting average: .313 in 1894
- Lowest team batting average: .213 in 1908
- Highest team slugging average: .474 in 1953
- Highest team on-base percentage: .378 in 1894
- Total hits: 1,654 in 1930
- Extra-base hits: 541 in 1953
- Hits in a game: 28 vs. Pittsburgh on June 23, 1930
- Longest individual hitting streak: 31, Willie Davis, 1969
- Most .300 hitters in a single season: 6 (six times): 1900, 1922, 1925, 1930, 1943, 1953
- Home runs: 211 in 2000
- Home runs in a month: 15, Duke Snider, August 1953 and Pedro Guerrero, June 1985
- Home runs in a game: 8, vs. Milwaukee Brewers on May 23, 2002
- Home runs by a rookie: 35, Mike Piazza, 1993
- Home runs by a right-hander: 48, Adrian Beltre, 2004
- Home runs by a left-hander: 49, Shawn Green, 2001
- Home runs by a switch-hitter: 32, Reggie Smith, 1977
- Grand slams: 9 in 2000
- Grand slams (individual; single season): 3, Kal Daniels, 1990; Mike Piazza, 1998; Adrian Beltre, 2004
- Grand slams (individual; career): 13, Gil Hodges
- Triples: 130 in 1894
- Doubles: 303 in 1930
- Singles: 1,223 in 1925
- Walks: 732 in 1947
- Runs scored: 1,021 in 1894
- Runs scored in a game: 25 vs. Pittsburgh on May 20, 1896 and Cincinnati on September 23, 1901
- Runs scored in an inning: 15 vs. Cincinnati on May 21, 1952 (first inning)
- Most batters hit by a pitch: 125 in 1899
- Times shut out: 26 in 1907

- Grounded into double plays: 151 in 1952
- Fewest grounded into double plays: 79 in 1965
- Runners left on base: 1,278 in 1947

TEAM RECORDS—BASERUNNING

- Stolen bases: 409 in 1887
- Caught stealing: 126 in 1915

TEAM RECORDS—PITCHING

- Lowest earned run average: 2.12 in 1916
- Complete games: 138 in 1886 and 1888
- Saves: 58 in 2003
- Strikeouts: 1,289 in 2003
- Shutouts: 24 in 1963 and 1988
- Walks: 671 in 1946
- Hit batsmen: 75 in 2000
- Wild pitches: 80 in 1885
- Consecutive wins (individual): 15, Dazzy Vance, 1924 and Phil Regan (over two seasons), 1966–1967
- Consecutive losses (individual): 14, Jim Pastorius, 1908
- Strikeouts in a game: 18, Sandy Koufax (twice): August 31, 1959 and April 24, 1962; Ramon Martinez, June 4, 1990
- Runs allowed in a game: 28 by Chicago White Stockings, August 25, 1891

TEAM RECORDS—FIELDING

- Best fielding average: .993 in 1952
- Most errors committed: 610 in 1886
- Fewest errors committed: 73 in 2004
- Most double plays turned: 198 in 1958
- Fewest double plays turned: 56 in 1885

TEAM RECORDS—MISCELLANEOUS

- Number of times league champions: 22
- Number of times finishing last in league: 2
- Largest attendance, single game: 78,672 vs. San Francisco, April 18, 1958
- Largest attendance, doubleheader: 72,140 vs. Cincinnati, August 16, 1961
- Players used in a season: 53 in 1944 and 1998
- Seasons played: 18 by Zack Wheat and Bill Russell

PRIMARY PITCHING STAFFS

Year	Starter	Starter	Starter	Starter	Starter	Closer	Bullpen	Bullpen	Bullpen
2005	Lowe	Weaver	Penny	Houlton	Perez	Brazoban	Sanchez	Carrara	Schmoll
2004	Ishii	Weaver	Lima	Nomo	Perez	Gagne	Sanchez	Dreifort	Mota
2003	Ishii	Brown	Alvarez	Nomo	Perez	Gagne	Quantrill	Martin	Mota
2002	Ishii	Ashby	Daal	Nomo	Perez	Gagne	Quantrill	Carrara	Orosco
2001	Park	Gagne	Prokopec	Adams	Brown	Shaw	Herges	Carrara	Orosco
2000	Park	Gagne	Dreifort	Perez	Brown	Shaw	Herges	Adams	Fetters
1999	Park	Valdez	Dreifort	Perez	Brown	Shaw	Borbon	Masaoka	Mills
1998	Park	Valdez	Dreifort	Mlicki	Martinez	Shaw	Radinsky	Osuna	Guthrie
1997	Park	Valdez	Nomo	Astacio	Martinez	Worrell	Radinsky	Hall	Guthrie
1996	Candiotti	Valdez	Nomo	Astacio	Martinez	Worrell	Radinsky	Osuna	Guthrie
1995	Candiotti	Valdez	Nomo	Astacio	Martinez	Worrell	Seanez	Cummings	Osuna
1994	Candiotti	Gross	Hershiser	Astacio	Martinez	Worrell	Gott	McDowell	Dreifort
1993	Candiotti	Gross	Hershiser	Astacio	Martinez	Gott	Martinez	McDowell	Daal
1992	Candiotti	Gross	Hershiser	Ojeda	Martinez	McDowell	Gott	Candelaria	Wilson
1991	Belcher	Morgan	Hershiser	Ojeda	Martinez	Howell	Gott	Candelaria	Crews
1990	Belcher	Morgan	Valenzuela	Neidlinger	Martinez	Howell	Gott	Crews	Aase
1989	Belcher	Morgan	Valenzuela	Hershiser	Leary	Howell	Pena	Crews	Searage
1988	Belcher	Sutton	Valenzuela	Hershiser	Leary	Howell	Pena	Orosco	Holton
1987	Welch	Honeycutt	Valenzuela	Hershiser	Leary	Young	Pena	Howell	Holton
1986	Welch	Honeycutt	Valenzuela	Hershiser	Reuss	Howell	Vande Berg	Niedenfuer	Powell
1985	Welch	Honeycutt	Valenzuela	Hershiser	Reuss	Niedenfuer	Howell	Diaz	Castillo

Primary Pitching Staffs (cont.)

Year	Starter	Starter	Starter	Starter	Starter	Closer	Bullpen	Bullpen	Bullpen
1984	Welch	Honeycutt	Valenzuela	Hershiser	Pena	Niedenfuer	Zachry	Diaz	Hooton
1983	Welch	Reuss	Valenzuela	Hooton	Pena	Howe	Niedenfuer	Beckwith	Stewart
1982	Welch	Reuss	Valenzuela	Hooton	Stewart	Howe	Niedenfuer	Forster	Pena
1981	Welch	Reuss	Valenzuela	Hooton	Goltz	Howe	Castillo	Forster	Stewart
1980	Welch	Reuss	Sutton	Hooton	Goltz	Howe	Beckwith	Sutcliffe	Castillo
1979	Sutcliffe	Reuss	Sutton	Hooton	Hough	Castillo	Patterson	LaGrow	Brett
1978	John	Rau	Sutton	Hooton	Rhoden	Forster	Hough	Rautzhan	Welch
1977	John	Rau	Sutton	Hooton	Rhoden	Hough	Garman	Rautzhan	Sosa
1976	John	Rau	Sutton	Hooton	Rhoden	Hough	Wall	Marshall	Sosa
1975	Messersmith	Rau	Sutton	Hooton	Rhoden	Marshall	Hough	Downing	Brewer
1974	Messersmith	Rau	Sutton	John	Downing	Marshall	Hough	Zahn	Brewer
1973	Messersmith	Osteen	Sutton	John	Downing	Brewer	Hough	Richert	Rau
1972	Singer	Osteen	Sutton	John	Downing	Brewer	Mikkelsen	Richert	Strahler
1971	Singer	Osteen	Sutton	Alexander	Downing	Brewer	Mikkelsen	Moeller	Pena
1970	Foster	Osteen	Sutton	Moeller	Vance	Brewer	Mikkelsen	Lamb	Norman
1969	Foster	Osteen	Sutton	Singer	Drysdale	Brewer	Mikkelsen	McBean	Moeller
1968	Kekich	Osteen	Sutton	Singer	Drysdale	Brewer	Billingham	Grant	Purdin
1967	Brewer	Osteen	Sutton	Singer	Drysdale	Perranoski	Regan	Miller	Egan
1966	Koufax	Osteen	Sutton	Moeller	Drysdale	Regan	Perranoski	Miller	Brewer
1965	Koufax	Osteen	Podres	Willhite	Drysdale	Perranoski	Reed	Miller	Brewer
1964	Koufax	Ortega	Moeller	Miller	Drysdale	Perranoski	Reed	Miller	Brewer
1963	Koufax	Podres	Miller	Richert	Drysdale	Perranoski	Sherry	Roebuck	Calmus
1962	Koufax	Podres	Williams	Moeller	Drysdale	Perranoski	Sherry	Roebuck	Ortega
1961	Koufax	Podres	Williams	Craig	Drysdale	Sherry	Perranoski	Farrell	Golden
1960	Koufax	Podres	Williams	Craig	Drysdale	Roebuck	Palmquist	McDevitt	Sherry
1959	Koufax	Podres	McDevitt	Craig	Drysdale	Labine	Klippstein	Williams	Fowler
1958	Koufax	Podres	McDevitt	Williams	Drysdale	Labine	Klippstein	Roebuck	Kipp
1957	Newcombe	Podres	McDevitt	Maglie	Drysdale	Labine	Koufax	Roebuck	Craig
1956	Newcombe	Craig	Erskine	Maglie	Drysdale	Labine	Bessent	Roebuck	Lehman
1955	Newcombe	Podres	Erskine	Loes	Spooner	Roebuck	Bessent	Labine	Hughes
1954	Newcombe	Podres	Erskine	Loes	Meyer	Hughes	Palica	Labine	Milliken
1953	Roe	Podres	Erskine	Loes	Meyer	Hughes	Black	Labine	Milliken
1952	Roe	Wade	Erskine	Loes	Van Cuyk	Black	Rutherford	Labine	King
1951	Roe	Newcombe	Erskine	Branca	Palica	King	Podbielan	Haugstad	Schmitz
1950	Roe	Newcombe	Erskine	Branca	Palica	Podbielan	Bankhead	Hatten	
1949	Roe	Newcombe	Hatten	Branca	Barney	Palica	Banta	Minner	Erskine
1948	Roe	Taylor	Hatten	Branca	Barney	Behrman	Ramsdell	Minner	Palica
1947	Lombardi	Taylor	Hatten	Branca	Gregg	Casey	Behrman	King	Barney
1946	Lombardi	Higbe	Hatten	Melton	Gregg	Behrman	Casey	Herring	
1945	Lombardi	Davis	Seats	Branca	Gregg	Buker	King	Herring	
1944	Melton	Davis	McLish	Chapman	Gregg	Webber	Warren	Branca	
1943	Melton	Davis	Higbe	Wyatt	Head	Webber	Macon	Newsom	Allen
1942	Allen	Davis	Higbe	Wyatt	Head	Casey	Macon	French	Webber
1941	Hamlin	Davis	Higbe	Wyatt	Casey	Brown	Wicker	Kimball	
1940	Hamlin	Davis	Fitzsimmons	Wyatt	Carleton	Casey	Tamulis	Pressnell	
1939	Hamlin	Casey	Fitzsimmons	Pressnell	Tamulis	Hutchinson	Evans	Wyatt	
1938	Hamlin	Mungo	Fitzsimmons	Pressnell	Tamulis	Posedel	Frankhouse	Butcher	
1937	Hamlin	Mungo	Frankhouse	Butcher	Hoyt	Henshaw	Jeffcoat	Lindsey	
1936	Brandt	Mungo	Frankhouse	Butcher	Clark	Baker	Jeffcoat	Earnshaw	
1935	Babich	Mungo	Earnshaw	Zachary	Clark	Leonard	Benge	Munns	Vance
1934	Babich	Mungo	Benge	Zachary	Leonard	Carroll	Munns	Beck	
1933	Beck	Mungo	Benge	Carroll	Thurston	Shaute	Ryan	Clark	

PRIMARY PITCHING STAFFS (CONT.)

Year	Starter	Starter	Starter	Starter	Starter	Closer	Bullpen	Bullpen	Bullpen
1932	Clark	Mungo	Vance	Heimach	Thurston	Quinn	Shaute	Phelps	Moore
1931	Clark	Phelps	Vance	Shaute	Thurston	Quinn	Heimach	Day	Moore
1930	Clark	Phelps	Vance	Luque	Elliott	Moss	Thurston	Dudley	
1929	Clark	McWeeny	Vance	Dudley	Moss	Morrison	Moore	Ballou	Koupal
1928	Clark	McWeeny	Vance	Petty	Elliott	Ehrhardt	Doak	Moss	
1927	Doak	McWeeny	Vance	Petty	Elliott	Ehrhardt	Clark	Plitt	
1926	Grimes	McWeeny	Vance	Petty	Barnes	Ehrhardt	McGraw	Boehler	
1925	Grimes	Ehrhardt	Vance	Petty	Osborne	Hubbell	Oeschger	Brown	
1924	Grimes	Ruether	Vance	Doak	Osborne	Decatur	Henry	Ehrhardt	
1923	Grimes	Ruether	Vance	Dickerman	Henry	Decatur	Smith	Schreiber	
1922	Grimes	Ruether	Vance	Cadore	Shriver	Decatur	Mamaux	Smith	
1921	Grimes	Ruether	Mitchell	Cadore	Smith	Miljus	Mamaux	Schupp	
1920	Grimes	Pfeffer	Marquard	Cadore	Mamaux	Smith	Mitchell	Mohart	
1919	Grimes	Pfeffer	Smith	Cadore	Mamaux	Cheney	Mitchell	Marquard	
1918	Grimes	Marquard	Cheney	Coombs	Robertson	Griner	Smith		
1917	Pfeffer	Marquard	Cheney	Cadore	Smith	Coombs	Dell		
1916	Pfeffer	Marquard	Cheney	Coombs	Smith	Appleton	Dell	Mails	
1915	Pfeffer	Dell	Rucker	Coombs	Smith	Appleton	Douglas	Cadore	
1914	Pfeffer	Reulbach	Ragan	Allen	Aitchison	Schmutz	Rucker	Brown	
1913	Rucker	Curtis	Ragan	Allen	Yingling	Stack	Wagner	Reulbach	
1912	Rucker	Stack	Ragan	Knetzer	Yingling	Kent	Allen	Curtis	
1911	Rucker	Barger	Schardt	Knetzer	Scanlan	Ragan	Bell	Burk	
1910	Rucker	Barger	Bell	Knetzer	Scanlan	Dessau	Wilhelm	Miller	
1909	Rucker	McIntire	Bell	Wilhelm	Scanlan	Hunter	Pastorius	Dent	
1908	Rucker	McIntire	Bell	Wilhelm	Pastorius	Holmes			
1907	Rucker	McIntire	Bell	Stricklett	Pastorius	Scanlan	Henley		
1906	Scanlan	McIntire	Eason	Stricklett	Pastorius				
1905	Scanlan	McIntire	Eason	Stricklett	Jones	Mitchell	Doscher		
1904	Scanlan	Cronin	Poole	Garvin	Jones	Mitchell	Reisling	Reidy	
1903	Schmidt	Reidy	Evans	Garvin	Jones				
1902	Donovan	Kitson	Evans	Hughes	Newton				
1901	Donovan	Kitson	McJames	Hughes	Newton	Kennedy	McCann		
1900	McGinnity	Kitson	Kennedy	Howell	Nops	Dunn	Weyhing		
1899	Hughes	Dunn	Kennedy	McJames		Yeager			
1898	Yeager	Dunn	Kennedy	Miller	McKenna				
1897	Payne	Dunn	Kennedy	Daub	Fisher	McMahon			
1896	Payne	Abbey	Kennedy	Daub	Harper	Stein			
1895	Stein	Gumbert	Kennedy	Daub	Lucid	Abbey			
1894	Stein	Gastright	Kennedy	Daub	Lucid	Underwood			
1893	Stein	Haddock	Kennedy	Daub	Sharrott	Lovett	Foutz		
1892	Stein	Haddock	Kennedy	Hart	Foutz	Inks			
1891	Lovett	Caruthers	Hemming	Terry	Inks	Foutz			
1890	Lovett	Caruthers	Hughes	Terry					
1889	Lovett	Caruthers	Hughes	Terry		Foutz			
1888	Foutz	Caruthers	Hughes	Terry	Mays				
1887	Porter	Harkins	Toole	Terry	Henderson				
1886	Porter	Harkins	Toole	Terry	Henderson				
1885	Porter	Harkins		Terry					
1884	Kimber	Conway		Terry					

Primary Starting Lineups

Year	C	1B	2B	3B	SS	LF	CF	RF
2005	Phillips	Choi	Kent	Robles	Izturis	Werth	Bradley	Cruz
2004	Lo Duca	Green	Cora	Beltre	Izturis	Werth	Bradley	Encarnacion
2003	Lo Duca	McGriff	Cora	Beltre	Izturis	Burnitz	Roberts	Green
2002	Lo Duca	Karros	Grudzielanek	Beltre	Izturis	Jordan	Roberts	Green
2001	Lo Duca	Karros	Grudzielanek	Beltre	Cora	Sheffield	Grissom	Green
2000	Hundley	Karros	Grudzielanek	Beltre	Cora	Sheffield	Hollandsworth	Green
1999	Hundley	Karros	Young	Beltre	Grudzielanek	Sheffield	White	Mondesi
1998	Johnson	Karros	Young	Beltre	Vizcaino	Hollandsworth	Mondesi	Sheffield
1997	Piazza	Karros	Guerrero	Zeile	Gagne	Hollandsworth	Cedeño	Mondesi
1996	Piazza	Karros	DeShields	Blowers	Gagne	Hollandsworth	Cedeño	Mondesi
1995	Piazza	Karros	DeShields	Wallach	Offerman	Ashley	Butler	Mondesi
1994	Piazza	Karros	DeShields	Wallach	Offerman	Rodriguez	Butler	Mondesi
1993	Piazza	Karros	Reed	Wallach	Offerman	Davis	Butler	Snyder
1992	Scioscia	Karros	Harris	Hansen	Offerman	Davis	Butler	Webster
1991	Scioscia	Murray	Samuel	Harris	Griffin	Daniels	Butler	Strawberry
1990	Scioscia	Murray	Samuel	Sharperson	Griffin	Daniels	Javier	Brooks
1989	Scioscia	Murray	Randolph	Hamilton	Griffin	Gibson	Shelby	Marshall
1988	Scioscia	Stubbs	Sax	Hamilton	Griffin	Gibson	Shelby	Marshall
1987	Scioscia	Stubbs	Sax	Hatcher	Duncan	Guerrero	Shelby	Marshall
1986	Scioscia	Brock	Sax	Madlock	Duncan	Stubbs	Williams	Marshall
1985	Scioscia	Brock	Sax	Anderson	Duncan	Guerrero	Landreaux	Marshall
1984	Scioscia	Brock	Sax	Rivera	Anderson	Marshall	Landreaux	Maldonado
1983	Yeager	Brock	Sax	Guerrero	Russell	Baker	Landreaux	Marshall
1982	Scioscia	Garvey	Sax	Cey	Russell	Baker	Landreaux	Guerrero
1981	Scioscia	Garvey	Lopes	Cey	Russell	Baker	Landreaux	Guerrero
1980	Yeager	Garvey	Lopes	Cey	Russell	Baker	Law	Smith
1979	Yeager	Garvey	Lopes	Cey	Russell	Baker	Thomas	Smith
1978	Yeager	Garvey	Lopes	Cey	Russell	Baker	North	Smith
1977	Yeager	Garvey	Lopes	Cey	Russell	Baker	Monday	Smith
1976	Yeager	Garvey	Lopes	Cey	Russell	Buckner	Baker	Smith
1975	Yeager	Garvey	Lopes	Cey	Russell	Buckner	Wynn	Crawford
1974	Yeager	Garvey	Lopes	Cey	Russell	Buckner	Wynn	Crawford
1973	Ferguson	Buckner	Lopes	Cey	Russell	Mota	Davis	Crawford
1972	Cannizzaro	Parker	Lacy	Garvey	Russell	Mota	Davis	Robinson
1971	Sims	Parker	Lefebvre	Garvey	Wills	Crawford	Davis	Buckner
1970	Haller	Parker	Sizemore	Grabarkewitz	Wills	Mota	Davis	Crawford
1969	Haller	Parker	Sizemore	Sudakis	Wills	Mota	Davis	Kosco
1968	Haller	Parker	Popovich	Bailey	Versalles	Gabrielson	Davis	Fairly
1967	Roseboro	Parker	Hunt	Lefebvre	Michael	Johnson	Davis	Fairly
1966	Roseboro	Parker	Lefebvre	Kennedy	Wills	Johnson	Davis	Fairly
1965	Roseboro	Parker	Lefebvre	Kennedy	Wills	Johnson	Davis	Fairly
1964	Roseboro	Fairly	Oliver	Gilliam	Wills	Davis	Davis	Howard
1963	Roseboro	Fairly	Gilliam	McMullen	Wills	Davis	Davis	Howard
1962	Roseboro	Fairly	Gilliam	Spencer	Wills	Davis	Davis	Howard
1961	Roseboro	Hodges	Neal	Gilliam	Wills	Moon	Davis	Fairly
1960	Roseboro	Larker	Neal	Gilliam	Wills	Moon	Demeter	Howard
1959	Roseboro	Hodges	Neal	Gilliam	Zimmer	Moon	Demeter	Snider
1958	Roseboro	Hodges	Neal	Gray	Zimmer	Gilliam	Snider	Furillo
1957	Campanella	Hodges	Gilliam	Reese	Neal	Cimoli	Snider	Furillo
1956	Campanella	Hodges	Gilliam	Jackson	Reese	Amoros	Snider	Furillo
1955	Campanella	Hodges	Gilliam	Robinson	Reese	Amoros	Snider	Furillo
1954	Campanella	Hodges	Gilliam	Hoak	Reese	Robinson	Snider	Furillo

PRIMARY STARTING LINEUPS (CONT.)

Year	C	1B	2B	3B	SS	LF	CF	RF
1953	Campanella	Hodges	Gilliam	Cox	Reese	Robinson	Snider	Furillo
1952	Campanella	Hodges	Robinson	Cox	Reese	Pafko	Snider	Furillo
1951	Campanella	Hodges	Robinson	Cox	Reese	Pafko	Snider	Furillo
1950	Campanella	Hodges	Robinson	Cox	Reese	Hermanski	Snider	Furillo
1949	Campanella	Hodges	Robinson	Cox	Reese	Hermanski	Snider	Furillo
1948	Campanella	Hodges	Robinson	Cox	Reese	Shuba	Furillo	Hermanski
1947	Edwards	Robinson	Stanky	Jorgensen	Reese	Hermanski	Furillo	Walker
1946	Edwards	Stevens	Stanky	Lavagetto	Reese	Reiser	Furillo	Walker
1945	Sandlock	Galan	Stanky	Bordagaray	Basinski	Olmo	Rosen	Walker
1944	Owen	Schultz	Stanky	Bordagaray	Bragan	Galan	Rosen	Walker
1943	Owen	Camilli	Herman	Bordagaray	Vaughan	Medwick	Galan	Walker
1942	Owen	Camilli	Herman	Vaughan	Reese	Medwick	Reiser	Walker
1941	Owen	Camilli	Herman	Lavagetto	Reese	Medwick	Reiser	Walker
1940	Phelps	Camilli	Coscarart	Lavagetto	Reese	Medwick	Walker	Vosmik
1939	Phelps	Camilli	Coscarart	Lavagetto	Durocher	Koy	Walker	Moore
1938	Phelps	Camilli	Hudson	Lavagetto	Durocher	Hassett	Koy	Rosen
1937	Phelps	Hassett	Lavagetto	Stripp	English	Winsett	Cooney	Manush
1936	Berres	Hassett	Jordan	Stripp	Frey	Watkins	Cooney	Wilson
1935	Lopez	Leslie	Cuccinello	Stripp	Frey	Taylor	Koenecke	Boyle
1934	Lopez	Leslie	Cuccinello	Stripp	Frey	Taylor	Koenecke	Boyle
1933	Lopez	Leslie	Cuccinello	Stripp	Jordan	Wilson	Taylor	Frederick
1932	Lopez	Kelly	Cuccinello	Stripp	Wright	O'Doul	Taylor	Wilson
1931	Lopez	Bissonette	Finn	Gilbert	Slade	O'Doul	Frederick	Herman
1930	Lopez	Bissonette	Finn	Gilbert	Wright	Bressler	Frederick	Herman
1929	Picinich	Bissonette	Moore	Gilbert	Bancroft	Bressler	Frederick	Herman
1928	DeBerry	Bissonette	Flowers	Hendrick	Bancroft	Bressler	Carey	Herman
1927	DeBerry	Herman	Partridge	Barrett	Butler	Felix	Statz	Carey
1926	O'Neil	Herman	Fewster	Marriott	Butler	Wheat	Felix	Cox
1925	Taylor	Fournier	Stock	Johnston	Mitchell	Wheat	Brown	Cox
1924	Taylor	Fournier	High	Stock	Mitchell	Wheat	Brown	Griffith
1923	Taylor	Fournier	Johnston	High	Berg	Wheat	Neis	Griffith
1922	DeBerry	Schmandt	Olson	High	Johnston	Wheat	Myers	Griffith
1921	Miller	Schmandt	Kilduff	Johnston	Olson	Wheat	Myers	Griffith
1920	Miller	Konetchy	Kilduff	Johnston	Olson	Wheat	Myers	Griffith
1919	Krueger	Konetchy	Johnston	Malone	Olson	Wheat	Myers	Griffith
1918	Miller	Daubert	Doolan	O'Mara	Olson	Wheat	Myers	Johnston
1917	Miller	Daubert	Cutshaw	Mowrey	Olson	Wheat	Hickman	Stengel
1916	Meyers	Daubert	Cutshaw	Mowrey	Olson	Wheat	Myers	Stengel
1915	Miller	Daubert	Cutshaw	Getz	O'Mara	Wheat	Myers	Stengel
1914	McCarty	Daubert	Cutshaw	Smith	Egan	Wheat	Dalton	Stengel
1913	Miller	Daubert	Cutshaw	Smith	Fisher	Wheat	Stengel	Moran
1912	Miller	Daubert	Cutshaw	Smith	Tooley	Wheat	Moran	Northen
1911	Bergen	Daubert	Hummel	Zimmerman	Tooley	Wheat	Davidson	Coulson
1910	Bergen	Daubert	Hummel	Lennox	Smith	Wheat	Davidson	Dalton
1909	Bergen	Jordan	Alperman	Lennox	McMillan	Clement	Burch	Lumley
1908	Bergen	Jordan	Pattee	Sheehan	Lewis	Hummel	Maloney	Lumley
1907	Ritter	Jordan	Alperman	Casey	Lewis	Batch	Maloney	Lumley
1906	Bergen	Jordan	Alperman	Casey	Lewis	McCarthy	Maloney	Lumley
1905	Ritter	Gessler	Malay	Batch	Lewis	Sheckard	Dobbs	Lumley
1904	Bergen	Dillon	Jordan	McCormick	Babb	Sheckard	Dobbs	Lumley
1903	Ritter	Doyle	Flood	Strang	Dahlen	Sheckard	Dobbs	McCredie
1902	Hearne	McCreery	Flood	Irwin	Dahlen	Sheckard	Dolan	Keeler

Primary Starting Lineups (cont.)

Year	C	1B	2B	3B	SS	LF	CF	RF
1901	McGuire	Kelley	Daly	Irwin	Dahlen	Sheckard	McCreery	Keeler
1900	Farrell	Jennings	Daly	Cross	Dahlen	Kelley	Jones	Keeler
1899	Farrell	McGann	Daly	Casey	Dahlen	Kelley	Jones	Keeler
1898	Ryan	LaChance	Hallman	Shindle	Magoon	Sheckard	Griffin	Jones
1897	Grim	LaChance	Shoch	Shindle	Smith	Anderson	Griffin	Jones
1896	Grim	LaChance	Daly	Shindle	Corcoran	McCarthy	Griffin	Jones
1895	Grim	LaChance	Daly	Shindle	Corcoran	Anderson	Griffin	Treadway
1894	Kinslow	Foutz	Daly	Shindle	Corcoran	Treadway	Griffin	Burns
1893	Kinslow	Brouthers	Daly	Shoch	Corcoran	Foutz	Griffin	Burns
1892	Daily	Brouthers	Ward	Joyce	Corcoran	O'Brien	Griffin	Burns
1891	Kinslow	Foutz	Collins	Pinkney	Ward	O'Brien	Griffin	Burns
1890	Daly	Foutz	Collins	Pinkney	Smith	O'Brien	Corkhill	Burns
1889	Clark	Foutz	Collins	Pinkney	Smith	O'Brien	Corkhill	Burns
1888	Bushong	Orr	Burdock	Pinkney	Smith	O'Brien	Radford	Foutz
1887	Peoples	Phillips	McClellan	Pinkney	Smith	Greer	McTamany	Swartwood
1886	Peoples	Phillips	McClellan	Pinkney	Smith	Burch	McTamany	Swartwood
1885	Hayes	Phillips	Pinkney	McClellan	Smith	McTamany	Hotaling	Cassidy
1884	Corcoran	Householder	Greenwood	Warner	Geer	Benners	Remsen	Cassidy

Top 10 Batting Leaders, Single Season & Career with Team

Games Played: Career with Team

Player	G	PA
1. Zack Wheat	2,322	9,720
2. Bill Russell	2,181	8,020
3. Pee Wee Reese	2,166	9,470
4. Gil Hodges	2,006	7,937
5. Jim Gilliam	1,956	8,321
6. Willie Davis	1,952	8,035
7. Duke Snider	1,923	7,633
8. Carl Furillo	1,806	7,022
9. Steve Garvey	1,727	7,027
10. Eric Karros	1,601	6,624

At-Bats: Season

Player	AB	Year
1. Maury Wills	695	1962
2. Cesar Izturis	670	2004
3. Carl Furillo	667	1951
4. Tommy Davis	665	1962
5. Steve Garvey	659	1975
6. Steve Garvey	658	1980
7. Ivy Olson	652	1921
8. Maury Wills	650	1965
9. Steve Garvey	648	1979
10. Steve Garvey	646	1977

At-Bats: Career with Team

Player	AB	PA
1. Zack Wheat	8,859	9,720
2. Pee Wee Reese	8,058	9,470
3. Willie Davis	7,495	8,035
4. Bill Russell	7,318	8,020
5. Jim Gilliam	7,119	8,321
6. Gil Hodges	6,881	7,937
7. Duke Snider	6,640	7,633
8. Steve Garvey	6,543	7,027
9. Carl Furillo	6,378	7,022
10. Maury Wills	6,156	6,744

Batting Average: Season

Player	BA	Year
1. Babe Herman	.393	1930
2. Babe Herman	.381	1929
3. Willie Keeler	.379	1899
4. Zack Wheat	.375	1924
5. Lefty O'Doul	.368	1932
6. Babe Phelps	.367	1936
7. Willie Keeler	.362	1900
Mike Piazza	.362	1997
9. Zack Wheat	.359	1925
10. Mike Griffin	.358	1894

Batting Average: Career with Team

Player	BA	PA
1. Willie Keeler	.352	2,594
2. Babe Herman	.339	3,598
3. Jack Fournier	.337	2,176
4. Mike Piazza	.331	3,017
5. Zack Wheat	.317	9,720
6. Manny Mota	.315	2,187
7. Fielder Jones	.313	2,807
8. Gary Sheffield	.312	2,276
9. Jackie Robinson	.311	5,802
Dixie Walker	.311	5,092

Total Hits: Season

Player	H	Year
1. Babe Herman	241	1930
2. Tommy Davis	230	1962
3. Zack Wheat	221	1925
4. Lefty O'Doul	219	1932
5. Babe Herman	217	1929
6. Willie Keeler	216	1899
7. Zack Wheat	212	1924
8. Steve Garvey	210	1975
Steve Sax	210	1986
10. Maury Wills	208	1962

TOTAL HITS: CAREER WITH TEAM

Player	H	PA
1. Zack Wheat	2,804	9,720
2. Pee Wee Reese	2,170	9,470
3. Willie Davis	2,091	8,035
4. Duke Snider	1,995	7,633
5. Steve Garvey	1,968	7,027
6. Bill Russell	1,926	8,020
7. Carl Furillo	1,910	7,022
8. Jim Gilliam	1,889	8,321
9. Gil Hodges	1,884	7,937
10. Maury Wills	1,732	6,744

HOME RUNS: SEASON

Player	HR	Year
1. Shawn Green	49	2001
2. Adrian Beltre	48	2004
3. Gary Sheffield	43	2000
Duke Snider	43	1956
5. Shawn Green	42	2002
Gil Hodges	42	1954
Duke Snider	42	1953
Duke Snider	42	1955
9. Roy Campanella	41	1953
10. Gil Hodges	40	1951
Mike Piazza	40	1997
Duke Snider	40	1954
Duke Snider	40	1957

HOME RUNS: CAREER WITH TEAM

Player	HR	PA
1. Duke Snider	389	7,633
2. Gil Hodges	361	7,937
3. Eric Karros	270	6,624
4. Roy Campanella	242	4,816
5. Ron Cey	228	6,108
6. Steve Garvey	211	7,027
7. Carl Furillo	192	7,022
8. Mike Piazza	177	3,017
9. Pedro Guerrero	171	4,089
10. Raul Mondesi	163	3,765

TRIPLES: SEASON

Player	3B	Year
1. George Treadway	26	1894
2. Hy Myers	22	1920
3. Dan Brouthers	20	1892
Tommy Corcoran	20	1894
5. Jimmy Sheckard	19	1901
6. Oyster Burns	18	1892
Harry Lumley	18	1904
8. John Anderson	17	1896
Jim Gilliam	17	1953
Joe Kelley	17	1900
Pete Reiser	17	1941

TRIPLES: CAREER WITH TEAM

Player	3B	PA
1. Zack Wheat	171	9,720
2. Willie Davis	110	8,035
3. Hy Myers	97	4,822
4. Jake Daubert	87	5,219
5. Oyster Burns	85	3,552
6. John Hummel	82	4,303
Duke Snider	82	7,633
8. Pee Wee Reese	80	9,470
9. Tom Daly	76	4,619
Jimmy Sheckard	76	3,771

DOUBLES: SEASON

Player	2B	Year
1. Johnny Frederick	52	1929
2. Shawn Green	49	2003
3. Babe Herman	48	1930
4. Wes Parker	47	1970
5. Johnny Frederick	44	1930
Shawn Green	44	2000
7. Augie Galan	43	1944
Babe Herman	43	1931
Steve Sax	43	1986
10. Babe Herman	42	1929
Raul Mondesi	42	1997
Dixie Walker	42	1945
Zack Wheat	42	1925

DOUBLES: CAREER WITH TEAM

Player	2B	PA
1. Zack Wheat	464	9,720
2. Duke Snider	343	7,633
3. Steve Garvey	333	7,027
4. Pee Wee Reese	330	9,470
5. Carl Furillo	324	7,022
6. Willie Davis	321	8,035
7. Jim Gilliam	304	8,321
8. Eric Karros	302	6,624
9. Gil Hodges	294	7,937
10. Bill Russell	293	8,020

EXTRA-BASE HITS: SEASON

Player	XBH	Year
1. Babe Herman	94	1930
2. Duke Snider	89	1954
3. Shawn Green	84	2001
Duke Snider	84	1953
5. Johnny Frederick	82	1929
Duke Snider	82	1955
7. Adrian Beltre	80	2004
8. Duke Snider	78	1956
9. Babe Herman	77	1931
Raul Mondesi	77	1997

EXTRA-BASE HITS: CAREER WITH TEAM

Player	XBH	PA
1. Duke Snider	814	7,633
2. Zack Wheat	766	9,720
3. Gil Hodges	703	7,937
4. Willie Davis	585	8,035
5. Eric Karros	582	6,624
6. Steve Garvey	579	7,027
7. Carl Furillo	572	7,022
8. Pee Wee Reese	536	9,470
9. Ron Cey	469	6,108
10. Jackie Robinson	464	5,802

TOTAL BASES: SEASON

Player	TB	Year
1. Babe Herman	416	1930
2. Duke Snider	378	1954
3. Adrian Beltre	376	2004
4. Shawn Green	370	2001
Duke Snider	370	1953
6. Tommy Davis	356	1962
7. Mike Piazza	355	1997
8. Babe Herman	348	1929
9. Duke Snider	343	1950
10. Johnny Frederick	342	1929

TOTAL BASES: CAREER WITH TEAM

Player	TB	PA
1. Zack Wheat	4,003	9,720
2. Duke Snider	3,669	7,633
3. Gil Hodges	3,357	7,937
4. Willie Davis	3,094	8,035
5. Pee Wee Reese	3,038	9,470
6. Steve Garvey	3,004	7,027
7. Carl Furillo	2,922	7,022
8. Eric Karros	2,740	6,624
9. Jim Gilliam	2,530	8,321
10. Bill Russell	2,471	8,020

RUNS BATTED IN: SEASON

Player	RBI	Year
1. Tommy Davis	153	1962
2. Roy Campanella	142	1953
3. Duke Snider	136	1955

4. Jack Fournier	130	1925
Babe Herman	130	1930
Gil Hodges	130	1954
Duke Snider	130	1954
8. Oyster Burns	128	1890
9. Duke Snider	126	1953
Glenn Wright	126	1930

RUNS BATTED IN: CAREER WITH TEAM

Player	RBI	PA
1. Duke Snider	1,271	7,633
2. Gil Hodges	1,254	7,937
3. Zack Wheat	1,210	9,720
4. Carl Furillo	1,058	7,022
5. Steve Garvey	992	7,027
6. Eric Karros	976	6,624
7. Pee Wee Reese	885	9,470
8. Roy Campanella	856	4,816
9. Willie Davis	849	8,035
10. Ron Cey	842	6,108

RUNS SCORED: SEASON

Player	R	Year
1. Hub Collins	148	1890
2. Darby O'Brien	146	1889
3. Babe Herman	143	1930
4. Mike Griffin	140	1895
Willie Keeler	140	1899
6. Hub Collins	139	1889
7. Mike Griffin	136	1897
8. Tom Daly	135	1894
9. Fielder Jones	134	1897
George Pinkney	134	1888

RUNS SCORED: CAREER WITH TEAM

Player	R	PA
1. Pee Wee Reese	1,338	9,470
2. Zack Wheat	1,255	9,720
3. Duke Snider	1,199	7,633
4. Jim Gilliam	1,163	8,321
5. Gil Hodges	1,088	7,937
6. Willie Davis	1,004	8,035
7. Jackie Robinson	947	5,802
8. Carl Furillo	895	7,022
9. Mike Griffin	881	4,450
10. Maury Wills	876	6,744

WALKS: SEASON

Player	BB	Year
1. Eddie Stanky	148	1945
2. Eddie Stanky	137	1946
3. Dolph Camilli	119	1938
4. Pee Wee Reese	116	1949
5. Augie Galan	114	1945
6. Dolph Camilli	110	1939
Jimmy Wynn	110	1975
8. Brett Butler	108	1991
Jimmy Wynn	108	1974
10. Gil Hodges	107	1952

WALKS: CAREER WITH TEAM

Player	BB	PA
1. Pee Wee Reese	1,210	9,470
2. Jim Gilliam	1,036	8,321
3. Gil Hodges	925	7,937
4. Duke Snider	893	7,633
5. Ron Cey	765	6,108
6. Jackie Robinson	740	5,802
7. Zack Wheat	632	9,720
8. Davey Lopes	603	5,308
9. Dolph Camilli	584	3,605
10. Mike Scioscia	567	5,056

STRIKEOUTS: SEASON

Player	SO	Year
1. Billy Grabarkewitz	149	1970
2. Cory Snyder	147	1993
3. Mike Marshall	137	1985
4. Raul Mondesi	134	1999
5. Juan Samuel	133	1991
6. John Shelby	128	1988
7. Mike Marshall	127	1983
8. Juan Samuel	126	1990
9. Darryl Strawberry	125	1991
10. Delino DeShields	124	1996

STRIKEOUTS: CAREER WITH TEAM

Player	SO	PA
1. Duke Snider	1,123	7,633
2. Gil Hodges	1,108	7,937
3. Eric Karros	1,105	6,624
4. Pee Wee Reese	890	9,470
5. Ron Cey	838	6,108
6. Willie Davis	815	8,035
7. Steve Garvey	751	7,027
8. Mike Marshall	724	3,546
9. Steve Yeager	703	3,869
10. Bill Russell	667	8,020

SLUGGING PERCENTAGE: SEASON

Player	SLG	Year
1. Babe Herman	.678	1930
2. Duke Snider	.647	1954
3. Gary Sheffield	.643	2000
4. Mike Piazza	.638	1997
5. Adrian Beltre	.629	2004
6. Duke Snider	.628	1955
7. Duke Snider	.627	1953
8. Babe Herman	.612	1929
9. Roy Campanella	.611	1953
10. Mike Piazza	.606	1995

SLUGGING PERCENTAGE: CAREER WITH TEAM

Player	SLG	PA
1. Gary Sheffield	.573	2,276
2. Mike Piazza	.572	3,017
3. Babe Herman	.557	3,598
4. Duke Snider	.553	7,633
5. Jack Fournier	.552	2,176
6. Reggie Smith	.528	2,055
7. Pedro Guerrero	.512	4,089
8. Shawn Green	.510	3,462
9. Raul Mondesi	.504	3,765
10. Roy Campanella	.500	4,816

ON-BASE PERCENTAGE: SEASON

Player	OBP	Year
1. Mike Griffin	.467	1894
2. Babe Herman	.455	1930
3. Jack Fournier	.446	1925
4. Mike Griffin	.444	1895
5. Jackie Robinson	.440	1952
6. Gary Sheffield	.438	2000
7. Babe Herman	.436	1929
Eddie Stanky	.436	1946
Tom Daly	.436	1894
10. Wally Moon	.434	1961

ON-BASE PERCENTAGE: CAREER WITH TEAM

Player	OBP	PA
1. Gary Sheffield	.424	2,276
2. Jack Fournier	.421	2,176
3. Augie Galan	.416	2,567
4. Jackie Robinson	.409	5,802
5. Eddie Stanky	.405	2,362
6. Mike Griffin	.399	4,450
7. Babe Herman	.396	3,598
8. Mike Piazza	.394	3,017
9. Dolph Camilli	.392	3,605
Brett Butler	.392	3,342

OPS (ON-BASE PERCENTAGE + SLUGGING PERCENTAGE): SEASON

Player	OPS	Year
1. Babe Herman	1.132	1930
2. Gary Sheffield	1.081	2000

3. Duke Snider	1.071	1954
4. Mike Piazza	1.070	1997
5. Babe Herman	1.048	1929
6. Duke Snider	1.046	1953
Duke Snider	1.046	1955
8. Adrian Beltre	1.017	2004
9. Jack Fournier	1.015	1925
10. Mike Piazza	1.006	1995

OPS (On-Base Percentage + Slugging Percentage): Career with Team

Player	OPS	PA
1. Gary Sheffield	.998	2,276
2. Jack Fournier	.973	2,176
3. Mike Piazza	.966	3,017
4. Babe Herman	.953	3,598
5. Duke Snider	.936	7,633
6. Reggie Smith	.915	2,055
7. Pedro Guerrero	.893	4,089
8. Dolph Camilli	.889	3,605
9. Jackie Robinson	.883	5,802
10. Shawn Green	.876	3,462

Stolen Bases: Season

Player	SB	Year
1. Maury Wills	104	1962
2. Maury Wills	94	1965
3. Darby O'Brien	91	1889
4. John Ward	88	1892
5. Hub Collins	85	1890
6. Davey Lopes	77	1975
7. Bill McClellan	70	1887
8. Jimmy Sheckard	67	1903
9. Jim McTamany	66	1887
10. Hub Collins	65	1889
Mike Griffin	65	1891

Stolen Bases: Career with Team

Player	SB	PA
1. Maury Wills	490	6,744
2. Davey Lopes	418	5,308
3. Willie Davis	335	8,035
4. Tom Daly	298	4,619
5. Steve Sax	290	4,745
6. George Pinkney	280	4,203
7. Darby O'Brien	272	2,562
8. Mike Griffin	264	4,450
9. Dave Foutz	241	3,599
10. Pee Wee Reese	232	9,470

Sacrifice Hits: Season

Player	Sac	Year
1. Jake Daubert	39	1915
2. Jake Daubert	35	1916
3. Jake Daubert	33	1914
Hy Myers	33	1920
5. Doc Casey	32	1907
6. Jake Daubert	31	1910
John Hummel	31	1909
Mike Mowrey	31	1916
9. George Cutshaw	29	1916
10. Jimmy Johnston	28	1920
Jackie Robinson	28	1947

Sacrifice Hits: Career with Team

Player	Sac	PA
1. Jake Daubert	237	5,219
2. Hy Myers	173	4,822
3. Pee Wee Reese	157	9,470
4. Zack Wheat	156	9,720
5. Jimmy Johnston	142	5,373
6. Bill Russell	132	8,020
7. Don Sutton	127	1,423
8. George Cutshaw	121	3,482
9. John Hummel	113	4,303
Ivy Olson	113	4,530

Hit by Pitch: Season

Player	HBP	Year
1. Hughie Jennings	20	1900
2. Dan McGann	19	1899
3. Alex Cora	18	2004
4. Hughie Jennings	17	1899
5. Dan Brouthers	16	1892
Lou Johnson	16	1965
Mike Kinkade	16	2003
Darby O'Brien	16	1889
9. Bill Dahlen	15	1899
10. Whitey Alperman	14	1906
Doc Gessler	14	1905
Lou Johnson	14	1966
Jackie Robinson	14	1952

Hit by Pitch: Career with Team

Player	HBP	PA
1. Zack Wheat	73	9,720
2. Jackie Robinson	72	5,802
3. Mike Griffin	54	4,450
4. Alex Cora	52	2,203
5. Tom Daly	47	4,619
Carl Furillo	47	7,022
7. Jimmy Sheckard	45	3,771
8. Ron Cey	43	6,108
George Pinkney	43	4,203
10. Willie Davis	41	8,035

Top 10 Pitching Leaders, Single Season & Career with Team

Games Pitched: Season

Player	GP	Year
1. Mike Marshall	106	1974
2. Paul Quantrill	89	2003
3. Paul Quantrill	86	2002
4. Tom Martin	80	2003
5. Duaner Sanchez	79	2005
6. Eric Gagne	77	2002
Eric Gagne	77	2003
Charlie Hough	77	1976
Jeff Shaw	77	2001
10. Guillermo Mota	76	2003

Games Pitched: Career with Team

Player	GP	IP
1. Don Sutton	550	3,816.3
2. Don Drysdale	518	3,432.0
3. Jim Brewer	474	822.3
4. Ron Perranoski	457	766.7
5. Clem Labine	425	933.3
6. Charlie Hough	401	799.7
7. Sandy Koufax	397	2,324.3
8. Brickyard Kennedy	381	2,857.0
9. Dazzy Vance	378	2,757.7
10. Johnny Podres	366	2,029.3

Innings Pitched: Season

Player	IP	Year
1. Henry Porter	481.7	1885
2. Adonis Terry	476.0	1884

3. Bob Caruthers	445.0	1889
4. Henry Porter	424.0	1886
5. Bob Caruthers	391.7	1888
6. Brickyard Kennedy	382.7	1893
7. George Haddock	381.3	1892
8. Ed Stein	377.3	1892
9. Oscar Jones	377.0	1904
10. Tom Lovett	372.0	1890

Innings Pitched: Career with Team

Player	IP
1. Don Sutton	3,816.3
2. Don Drysdale	3,432.0
3. Brickyard Kennedy	2,857.0
4. Dazzy Vance	2,757.7
5. Burleigh Grimes	2,426.0
6. Claude Osteen	2,396.7
7. Adonis Terry	2,376.3
8. Nap Rucker	2,375.3
9. Fernando Valenzuela	2,348.7
10. Sandy Koufax	2,324.3

Batters Faced: Season

Player	BF	Year
1. Adonis Terry	2,046	1884
2. Henry Porter	2,035	1885
3. Henry Porter	1,864	1886
4. Bob Caruthers	1,827	1889
5. Oscar Jones	1,593	1904
6. Bob Caruthers	1,575	1888
7. Sam Kimber	1,559	1884
8. Bill Donovan	1,529	1901
9. Henry Porter	1,504	1887
10. Joe McGinnity	1,498	1900

Batters Faced: Career with Team

Player	BF	IP
1. Don Sutton	15,567	3,816.3
2. Don Drysdale	14,097	3,432.0
3. Dazzy Vance	11,452	2,757.7
4. Burleigh Grimes	10,409	2,426.0
5. Fernando Valenzuela	9,857	2,348.7
6. Claude Osteen	9,855	2,396.7
7. Nap Rucker	9,625	2,375.3
8. Sandy Koufax	9,497	2,324.3
9. Orel Hershiser	9,070	2,180.7
10. Johnny Podres	8,574	2,029.3

Games Started: Season

Player	GS	Year
1. Adonis Terry	55	1884
2. Henry Porter	54	1885
3. Bob Caruthers	50	1889
4. Henry Porter	48	1886
5. George Haddock	44	1892
Brickyard Kennedy	44	1893
Adonis Terry	44	1890
8. Bob Caruthers	43	1888
Tom Lovett	43	1891
10. Don Drysdale	42	1963
Don Drysdale	42	1965
Ed Stein	42	1892

Games Started: Career with Team

Player	GS	IP
1. Don Sutton	533	3,816.3
2. Don Drysdale	465	3,432.0
3. Claude Osteen	335	2,396.7
4. Brickyard Kennedy	332	2,857.0
5. Dazzy Vance	326	2,757.7
6. Fernando Valenzuela	320	2,348.7
7. Sandy Koufax	314	2,324.3
8. Johnny Podres	310	2,029.3
9. Orel Hershiser	309	2,180.7
10. Burleigh Grimes	287	2,426.0

Complete Games: Season

Player	CG	Year
1. Adonis Terry	54	1884
2. Henry Porter	53	1885
3. Henry Porter	48	1886
4. Bob Caruthers	46	1889
5. Bob Caruthers	42	1888
6. Sam Kimber	41	1884
7. Mickey Hughes	40	1888
Brickyard Kennedy	40	1893
9. George Haddock	39	1892
Tom Lovett	39	1890
Tom Lovett	39	1891

Complete Games: Career with Team

Player	CG	IP
1. Brickyard Kennedy	279	2,857.0
2. Adonis Terry	255	2,376.3
3. Dazzy Vance	212	2,757.7
4. Burleigh Grimes	205	2,426.0

5. Nap Rucker	186	2,375.3
6. Don Drysdale	167	3,432.0
7. Jeff Pfeffer	157	1,748.3
8. Don Sutton	156	3,816.3
9. Bob Caruthers	147	1,433.7
10. Henry Porter	139	1,245.3

Games Won: Season

Player	W	Year
1. Bob Caruthers	40	1889
2. Henry Porter	33	1885
3. Tom Lovett	30	1890
4. Bob Caruthers	29	1888
George Haddock	29	1892
6. Jay Hughes	28	1899
Joe McGinnity	28	1900
Dazzy Vance	28	1924
9. Sandy Koufax	27	1966
Don Newcombe	27	1956
Henry Porter	27	1886
Ed Stein	27	1892

Games Won: Career with Team

Player	W	IP
1. Don Sutton	233	3,816.3
2. Don Drysdale	209	3,432.0
3. Dazzy Vance	190	2,757.7
4. Brickyard Kennedy	177	2,857.0
5. Sandy Koufax	165	2,324.3
6. Burleigh Grimes	158	2,426.0
7. Claude Osteen	147	2,396.7
8. Fernando Valenzuela	141	2,348.7
9. Johnny Podres	136	2,029.3
10. Orel Hershiser	135	2,180.7

Games Lost: Season

Player	L	Year
1. Adonis Terry	35	1884
2. George Bell	27	1910
3. Oscar Jones	25	1904
Harry McIntire	25	1905
5. Henry Porter	24	1887
6. Jack Cronin	23	1904
7. Brickyard Kennedy	22	1898
Kaiser Wilhelm	22	1908
Joe Yeager	22	1898
10. Five tied with . . .	21	—

Games Lost: Career with Team

Player	L	IP
1. Don Sutton	181	3,816.3
2. Don Drysdale	166	3,432.0
3. Brickyard Kennedy	149	2,857.0

Player		
4. Adonis Terry	139	2,376.3
5. Nap Rucker	134	2,375.3
6. Dazzy Vance	131	2,757.7
7. Claude Osteen	126	2,396.7
8. Burleigh Grimes	121	2,426.0
9. Fernanado Valenzuela	116	2,348.7
10. Orel Hershiser	107	2,180.7

Winning Percentage: Season

Player	W%	Year
1. Fred Fitzsimmons	.889	1940
2. Preacher Roe	.880	1951
3. Orel Hershiser	.864	1985
4. Ron Perranoski	.842	1963
5. Sandy Koufax	.833	1963
6. Jay Hughes	.824	1899
Dazzy Vance	.824	1924
8. Tommy John	.812	1974
9. Don Newcombe	.800	1955
10. Don Newcombe	.794	1956

Winning Percentage: Career with Team

Player	W%	IP
1. Preacher Roe	.715	1,277.3
2. Bob Caruthers	.683	1,433.7
3. Tommy John	.674	1,198.0
Jay Hughes	.674	796.3
5. Billy Loes	.658	639.7
6. Sandy Koufax	.655	2,324.3
7. Don Newcombe	.651	1,662.7
8. Kirby Higbe	.648	931.0
9. Kevin Brown	.644	872.7
10. Whit Wyatt	.640	1,072.3

Shutouts: Season

Player	SHO	Year
1. Sandy Koufax	11	1963
2. Don Sutton	9	1972
3. Tim Belcher	8	1989
Don Drysdale	8	1968
Orel Hershiser	8	1988
Sandy Koufax	8	1965
Fernando Valenzuela	8	1981
8. Bob Caruthers	7	1889
Don Drysdale	7	1965
Burleigh Grimes	7	1918
Sandy Koufax	7	1964
Andy Messersmith	7	1975
Claude Osteen	7	1969
Whit Wyatt	7	1941

Shutouts: Career with Team

Player	SHO	IP
1. Don Sutton	52	3,816.3
2. Don Drysdale	49	3,432.0
3. Sandy Koufax	40	2,324.3
4. Nap Rucker	38	2,375.3
5. Claude Osteen	34	2,396.7
6. Fernando Valenzuela	29	2,348.7
Dazzy Vance	29	2,757.7
8. Jeff Pfeffer	25	1,748.3
9. Orel Hershiser	24	2,180.7
10. Johnny Podres	23	2,029.3
Bob Welch	23	1,820.7

ERA: Season

Player	ERA	Year
1. Rube Marquard	1.58	1916
2. Ned Garvin	1.68	1904
3. Sandy Koufax	1.73	1966
4. Sandy Koufax	1.74	1964
5. Kaiser Wilhelm	1.87	1908
6. Sandy Koufax	1.88	1963
7. Jeff Pfeffer	1.92	1916
Larry Cheney	1.92	1916
9. Jeff Pfeffer	1.97	1914
10. Orel Hershiser	2.03	1985

ERA: Career with Team

Player	ERA	IP
1. Jeff Pfeffer	2.31	1,748.3
2. Nap Rucker	2.42	2,375.3
3. Larry Cheney	2.45	730.0
4. Ron Perranoski	2.56	766.7
5. Rube Marquard	2.58	950.0
6. Jim Brewer	2.62	822.3
Kaiser Wilhelm	2.62	563.3
8. Andy Messersmith	2.67	926.0
9. Sandy Koufax	2.76	2,324.3
10. Elmer Stricklett	2.78	758.7

Earned Runs Allowed: Season

Player	ER	Year
1. Brickyard Kennedy	197	1894
2. Adonis Terry	188	1884
3. Ed Stein	180	1894
4. Henry Porter	161	1886
5. Brickyard Kennedy	159	1895
Henry Porter	159	1887
7. Brickyard Kennedy	158	1893
8. Bob Caruthers	155	1889
9. Sam Kimber	153	1884
10. Dan Daub	152	1894

Earned Runs Allowed: Career with Team

Player	ER	IP
1. Don Sutton	1,311	3,816.3
2. Brickyard Kennedy	1,264	2,857.0
3. Don Drysdale	1,124	3,432.0
4. Dazzy Vance	972	2,757.7
5. Burleigh Grimes	934	2,426.0
6. Adonis Terry	903	2,376.3
7. Fernando Valenzuela	864	2,348.7
8. Johnny Podres	826	2,029.3
9. Claude Osteen	822	2,396.7
10. Carl Erskine	763	1,718.7

Strikeouts: Season

Player	K	Year
1. Sandy Koufax	382	1965
2. Sandy Koufax	317	1966
3. Sandy Koufax	306	1963
4. Sandy Koufax	269	1961
5. Dazzy Vance	262	1924
6. Don Drysdale	251	1963
7. Bill Singer	247	1969
8. Don Drysdale	246	1960
9. Don Drysdale	242	1959
Fernando Valenzuela	242	1986

Strikeouts: Career with Team

Player	K	IP
1. Don Sutton	2,696	3,816.3
2. Don Drysdale	2,486	3,432.0
3. Sandy Koufax	2,396	2,324.3
4. Dazzy Vance	1,918	2,757.7
5. Fernando Valenzuela	1,759	2,348.7
6. Orel Hershiser	1,456	2,180.7
7. Johnny Podres	1,331	2,029.3
8. Ramon Martinez	1,314	1,731.7
9. Bob Welch	1,292	1,820.7
10. Nap Rucker	1,217	2,375.3

Strikeouts Per Nine IP: Season

Player	K/9	Year
1. Hideo Nomo	11.10	1995
2. Sandy Koufax	10.55	1962

3. Sandy Koufax	10.24	1965
4. Sandy Koufax	10.13	1960
5. Hideo Nomo	10.11	1997
6. Sandy Koufax	9.47	1961
7. Hideo Nomo	9.22	1996
8. Sandy Koufax	9.00	1964
9. Sandy Koufax	8.86	1963
10. Sandy Koufax	8.83	1966

Strikeouts Per Nine IP: Career with Team

Player	K/9	IP
1. Eric Gagne	10.37	543.3
2. Sandy Koufax	9.28	2,324.3
3. Hideo Nomo	8.87	1,217.3
4. Chan Ho Park	8.35	1,183.7
5. Darren Dreifort	8.27	872.7
6. Kevin Brown	8.09	872.7
7. Jim Brewer	7.35	822.3
8. Tim Belcher	7.07	806.0
9. Bill Singer	6.98	1,274.3
10. Kevin Gross	6.97	680.0

Hits Allowed: Season

Player	HA	Year
1. Adonis Terry	486	1884
2. Brickyard Kennedy	445	1894
3. Bob Caruthers	444	1889
4. Henry Porter	439	1886
5. Henry Porter	427	1885
6. Henry Porter	416	1887
7. Ed Stein	388	1894
8. Oscar Jones	387	1904
9. Brickyard Kennedy	376	1893
10. Brickyard Kennedy	370	1897

Hits Allowed: Career with Team

Player	HA	IP
1. Don Sutton	3,291	3,816.3
2. Brickyard Kennedy	3,102	2,857.0
3. Don Drysdale	3,084	3,432.0
4. Dazzy Vance	2,579	2,757.7
5. Burleigh Grimes	2,547	2,426.0
6. Claude Osteen	2,350	2,396.7
7. Adonis Terry	2,292	2,376.3
8. Fernando Valenzuela	2,099	2,348.7
9. Nap Rucker	2,089	2,375.3
10. Johnny Podres	2,009	2,029.3

Hits Allowed Per Nine IP: Season

Player	H/9	Year
1. Sandy Koufax	5.79	1965
2. Hideo Nomo	5.83	1995
3. Don Sutton	6.14	1972
4. Sandy Koufax	6.19	1963
5. Sandy Koufax	6.22	1964
6. Larry Cheney	6.33	1916
7. Sandy Koufax	6.54	1962
8. Fernando Valenzuela	6.55	1981
9. Adonis Terry	6.69	1888
10. Sandy Koufax	6.72	1966

Hits Allowed Per Nine IP: Career with Team

Player	H/9	IP
1. Sandy Koufax	6.79	2,324.3
2. Jim Brewer	6.90	822.3
3. Eric Gagne	7.01	543.3
4. Andy Messersmith	7.02	926.0
5. Rex Barney	7.14	597.7
6. Charlie Hough	7.21	799.7
7. Larry Cheney	7.41	730.0
8. Hideo Nomo	7.56	1,217.3
9. Tim Belcher	7.59	806.0
10. Kevin Brown	7.60	872.7

Walks Allowed: Season

Player	BB	Year
1. Ed Stein	170	1894
2. Brickyard Kennedy	168	1893
3. George Haddock	163	1892
4. Bill Donovan	152	1901
5. Ed Stein	150	1892
6. Brickyard Kennedy	149	1894
Brickyard Kennedy	149	1897
8. Tom Lovett	141	1890
9. Hal Gregg	137	1944
10. Adonis Terry	133	1890

Walks Allowed: Career with Team

Player	BB	IP
1. Brickyard Kennedy	1,128	2,857.0
2. Don Sutton	996	3,816.3
3. Fernando Valenzuela	915	2,348.7
4. Don Drysdale	855	3,432.0
5. Sandy Koufax	817	2,324.3
6. Dazzy Vance	764	2,757.7
7. Burleigh Grimes	744	2,426.0
8. Adonis Terry	734	2,376.3
9. Ramon Martinez	704	1,731.7
10. Nap Rucker	701	2,375.3

Walks Allowed Per Nine IP: Season

Player	BB/9	Year
1. Watty Clark	1.22	1935
Bob Caruthers	1.22	1888
3. Adonis Terry	1.36	1884
4. Leon Cadore	1.40	1919
5. Don Newcombe	1.46	1955
6. Don Drysdale	1.48	1966
7. Don Newcombe	1.49	1957
8. Fred Heimach	1.50	1932
9. Sherry Smith	1.51	1919
10. Odalis Perez	1.54	2002

Walks Allowed Per Nine IP: Career with Team

Player	BB/9	IP
1. Curt Davis	1.77	1,007.3
2. Watty Clark	1.92	1,659.0
3. Frank Kitson	1.94	793.7
4. Rube Marquard	1.96	950.0
5. Odalis Perez	1.97	712.7
6. Sherry Smith	1.98	1,197.3
7. Leon Cadore	2.04	1,251.0
8. Jerry Reuss	2.13	1,407.7
Claude Osteen	2.13	2,396.7
10. Jeff Pfeffer	2.14	1,748.3

WHIP (Walks + Hits Per Nine IP): Season

Player	WHIP	Year
1. Sandy Koufax	0.855	1965
2. Sandy Koufax	0.875	1963
3. Don Sutton	0.913	1972
4. Sandy Koufax	0.928	1964
5. Don Drysdale	0.965	1964
6. Don Sutton	0.983	1973
7. Sandy Koufax	0.985	1966
8. Don Newcombe	0.989	1956
Don Sutton	0.989	1980
10. Odalis Perez	0.990	2002

WHIP (Walks + Hits Per Nine IP): Career with Team

Player	WHIP	IP
1. Kevin Brown	1.100	872.7
2. Andy Messersmith	1.105	926.0
3. Sandy Koufax	1.106	2,324.3
4. Eric Gagne	1.113	543.3
5. Don Sutton	1.123	3,816.3
6. Rube Marquard	1.127	950.0
7. Jim Brewer	1.128	822.3
8. Jeff Pfeffer	1.134	1,748.3
9. Whit Wyatt	1.141	1,072.3
10. Don Drysdale	1.148	3,432.0

Home Runs Allowed: Season

Player	HRA	Year
1. Don Sutton	38	1970
2. Don Newcombe	35	1955
Jeff Weaver	35	2005
4. Preacher Roe	34	1950
5. Jose Lima	33	2004
Don Newcombe	33	1956
7. Ismael Valdez	32	1999
8. Darren Dreifort	31	2000
Carl Erskine	31	1954
Chan Ho Park	31	1999

Home Runs Allowed: Career with Team

Player	HRA	IP
1. Don Sutton	309	3,816.3
2. Don Drysdale	280	3,432.0
3. Johnny Podres	211	2,029.3
4. Sandy Koufax	204	2,324.3
5. Carl Erskine	199	1,718.7
6. Don Newcombe	189	1,662.7
7. Claude Osteen	160	2,396.7
8. Preacher Roe	157	1,277.3
9. Fernando Valenzuela	152	2,348.7
10. Ramon Martinez	148	1,731.7

Saves: Season

Player	SV	Year
1. Eric Gagne	55	2003
2. Eric Gagne	52	2002
3. Eric Gagne	45	2004
4. Todd Worrell	44	1996
5. Jeff Shaw	43	2001
6. Todd Worrell	35	1997
7. Jeff Shaw	34	1999
8. Todd Worrell	32	1995
9. Jay Howell	28	1989
10. Jeff Shaw	27	2000

Saves: Career with Team

Player	SV	IP
1. Eric Gagne	160	543.3
2. Jeff Shaw	129	235.3
3. Todd Worrell	127	268.0
4. Jim Brewer	125	822.3
5. Ron Perranoski	101	766.7
6. Jay Howell	85	308.3
7. Clem Labine	83	933.3
8. Tom Niedenfuer	64	440.3
9. Charlie Hough	60	799.7
10. Steve Howe	59	328.7

Wild Pitches: Season

Player	WP	Year
1. John Harkins	39	1885
2. Adonis Terry	32	1886
3. Adonis Terry	27	1890
4. John Harkins	26	1886
Henry Porter	26	1885
6. Adonis Terry	25	1889
7. Bob Caruthers	22	1889
8. George Haddock	21	1892
Brickyard Kennedy	21	1894
Tom Lovett	21	1891

Wild Pitches: Career with Team

Player	WP	IP
1. Adonis Terry	107	2,376.3
2. Fernando Valenzuela	94	2,348.7
3. Sandy Koufax	87	2,324.3
4. Don Sutton	86	3,816.3
5. Brickyard Kennedy	83	2,857.0
6. Don Drysdale	82	3,432.0
7. Orel Hershiser	78	2,180.7
8. Ed Stein	69	1,394.3
9. John Harkins	65	784.3
10. Hideo Nomo	64	1,217.3

Hit Batsmen: Season

Player	HB	Year
1. Joe McGinnity	41	1900
2. Harry McIntire	21	1909
Henry Schmidt	21	1903
4. Don Drysdale	20	1961
Harry McIntire	20	1905
Harry McIntire	20	1908
Chan Ho Park	20	2001
8. Nap Rucker	19	1908
9. Don Drysdale	18	1959
Jack Dunn	18	1899
Jeff Weaver	18	2005

Hit Batsmen: Career with Team

Player	HB	IP
1. Don Drysdale	154	3,432.0
2. Harry McIntire	82	1,300.3
3. Jeff Pfeffer	79	1,748.3
4. Nap Rucker	73	2,375.3
5. Chan Ho Park	70	1,183.7
Dazzy Vance	70	2,757.7
7. Orel Hershiser	65	2,180.7
8. Don Sutton	62	3,816.3
9. Ramon Martinez	53	1,731.7
10. Burleigh Grimes	52	2,426.0

Games Finished: Season

Player	GF	Year
1. Mike Marshall	83	1974
2. Eric Gagne	68	2002
3. Eric Gagne	67	2003
Todd Worrell	67	1996
5. Jeff Shaw	66	2001
6. Eric Gagne	59	2004
7. Jeff Shaw	56	1999
8. Charlie Hough	55	1976
Todd Worrell	55	1997
10. Charlie Hough	53	1977
Todd Worrell	53	1995

Games Finished: Career with Team

Player	GF	IP
1. Jim Brewer	302	822.3
2. Ron Perranoski	273	766.7
3. Clem Labine	242	933.3
4. Todd Worrell	224	268.0
5. Charlie Hough	222	799.7
6. Eric Gagne	210	543.3
7. Jeff Shaw	207	235.3
8. Jay Howell	175	308.3
9. Tom Niedenfuer	169	440.3
10. Hugh Casey	159	867.7

Significant Dodgers

Campanella, Roy (C)
(1948–1957)

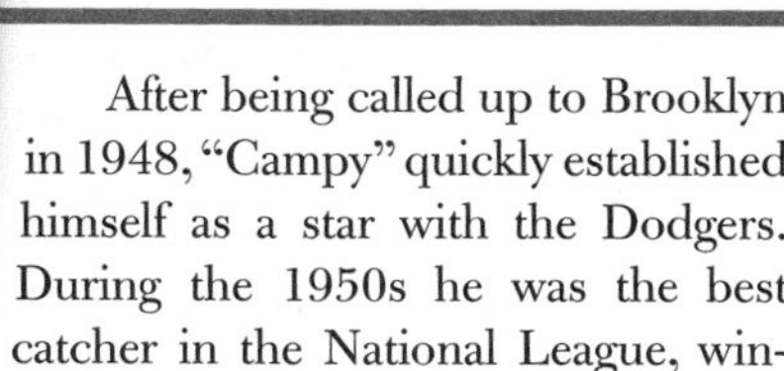

Roy Campanella became the starting catcher for the Negro National League's Baltimore Elite Giants at the age of 16 in 1938. He was so durable that he once caught four games in a single day (a doubleheader in Cincinnati in the afternoon and a doubleheader in Youngstown that evening). As he once put it, "In the Negro Leagues, if you didn't play, you didn't get paid." Campanella also spent several years in the Mexican League after a salary dispute with Baltimore's owner. In the fall of 1945 he was a member of a barnstorming team that played a group of major leaguers in some exhibition games and so impressed Dodgers coach Charlie Dressen that he asked Campanella to meet with Brooklyn's Branch Rickey. He signed with the Dodgers, taking a pay cut from his $3,000 Negro League salary to $1,100. He was originally scheduled to play in the 3-I League, but they refused all black players in 1946 so he ended up with Nashua of the New England League. When Rickey later asked Campanella to go to St. Paul to facilitate the integrating of the American Association, Campanella refused, telling Rickey that he was a ballplayer, not a pioneer. When Rickey offered to raise his salary to a whopping $6,500, Campanella decided he had some pioneering spirit in his body after all.

After being called up to Brooklyn in 1948, "Campy" quickly established himself as a star with the Dodgers. During the 1950s he was the best catcher in the National League, winning the MVP Award three times (1951, 1953, 1955) as he helped the Dodgers win five pennants between 1949–1956. As the 1950s wound down, Campanella's long catching career was taking its toll on him and he started preparing for a life outside of baseball, opening a liquor store in Harlem. On January 28, 1958, the eight-time All-Star had finished his store's book work and was headed home when his car slid on the icy highway, hit a telephone pole, and flipped over. Nearly killed, Campanella was left paralyzed in both arms and legs. On May 7, 1959, the Dodgers held a benefit exhibition game with the Yankees in L.A. Memorial Coliseum. More than 93,000 fans turned out to honor their fallen star. Campanella was inducted into the Hall of Fame in 1969, and died in 1993.

CAREER DODGERS RECORD:

Games	AB	Hits	Runs
1,215	4,205	1,161	627
Avg	**HR**	**RBI**	**SB**
.276	242	856	25

CARUTHERS, BOB (SP)
(1888–1891)

Bob Caruthers' lifetime winning percentage of .688 (219–99) is one of the best in baseball history, and four times he posted percentages of .755 or higher. He also was a decent hitter, with a lifetime average of .282, and played a lot of outfield when he wasn't pitching. From 1885 to 1890, he pitched on five pennant winners, including two with Brooklyn (1889, 1890), and twice won 40 games in a season. After winning 106 games in four years for St. Louis, Caruthers was sold to Brooklyn for $8,250 by Browns owner Chris Von der Ahe. Von der Ahe blamed his team's loss in the 1887 World Series on Caruthers, who went 4–4 in the 15-game Series (which St. Louis lost, 10 games to five, to the Detroit Wolverines). Brooklyn was so happy to get Caruthers that they made him the highest-paid player in the American Association, inking a $5,000 one-year deal. Caruthers paid immediate dividends, winning 29 games in 1888 and 40 in 1889 as he led the Bridegrooms to the American Association title. In 1890 he won 23 as he helped Brooklyn win the National League title after Brooklyn switched leagues. When the pitching distance was increased to 60'6" in 1893, Caruthers decided not to pitch any longer, opting to play outfield instead for his last year in the majors. After retiring as an active player, Caruthers, who had been a substitute umpire during his playing days, became an American League umpire until his death in 1911 at the age of 47.

CAREER DODGERS RECORD:

W	L	W%	ERA	SV
110	51	.683	2.92	2
K	BB	SHO	IP	
391	351	14	1,433.7	

CEY, RON (3B)
(1971–1982)

Nicknamed "the Penguin" because of his oddly shaped physique and the manner in which he ran, Ron Cey was drafted by the Dodgers in the third round of the June 1968 amateur draft (secondary phase). After two short stints in Los Angeles in 1971 and 1972, Cey became the Dodgers' starting third baseman on Opening Day 1973 and became part of a Dodger infield that remained intact for eight years, helping Los Angeles win four pennants during that time (1974, 1977, 1978, and 1981). Cey was a consistent performer, both in the field and at the plate. He won two NL fielding titles (even with Mike Schmidt in the league) and hit between 22–30 homers in 10 of 11 years, missing only in the strike-shortened 1981 season. In 1981 Cey, a six-time All-Star, was co-MVP of the World Series as the Dodgers defeated the Yankees. Following the 1982 season, the Dodgers, in order to trim salary, practically gave Cey away to the Cubs for Dan Cataline and Vance Lovelace. Cey retired after four years in Chicago and one more in Oakland, fifth all time in home runs among third basemen with 316.

CAREER DODGERS RECORD:

Games	AB	Hits	Runs
1,481	5,216	1,378	715
Avg	HR	RBI	SB
.264	228	842	20

DAVIS, WILLIE (OF)
(1960–1973)

The Dodgers signed Willie Davis as an amateur free agent in June 1958 and in 1960 brought him to the major leagues. He spent the first 14 seasons of his 18-year major league career with the team. The Dodgers of the 1960s were designed around pitching, speed, and defense, and Davis fit the mold perfectly. He won three Gold Gloves patrolling the L.A. outfield, helping the Dodgers to pennants in 1963, 1965, and 1966. Considered the fastest man in baseball at one time, Davis collected 335 career steals to give the Dodgers a double dose of speed along with Maury Wills. In 1969 Davis had a 31-game hitting streak, the longest in the league since Tommy Holmes hit in 37 straight in 1945. By 1971 Davis had become a member of a Buddhist sect, which led to fervent chanting before every game. It wasn't a coincidence that from 1973 to 1976 he played for five different teams, as numerous teammates felt uneasy around the chanting Davis. The speedy outfielder eventually went to Japan in 1977, feeling that both his play and Buddhist religion would be received better in Asia. He was wrong, as the Japanese players were even more spooked by his chanting than their American counterparts—many felt they were at a Buddhist funeral every day instead of the ballpark, according to Chunichi manager Wally Yonamine. After two years in Japan, Davis returned to the U.S. and signed with California, but played only sparingly with the Angels before retiring at season's end.

CAREER DODGERS RECORD:

Games	AB	Hits	Runs
1,952	7,495	2,091	1,004
Avg	**HR**	**RBI**	**SB**
.279	154	849	335

DRYSDALE, DON (SP)
(1956–1969)

The Brooklyn Dodgers signed the hulking Don Drysdale as an amateur free agent right out of high school in 1954 and brought him up to the majors two years later. For the next 14 years he was probably the most intimidating pitcher in baseball. He regularly hit batters as part of his pitching strategy, and after doing so would stare the hitter down, daring him to respond in any way. He led the league in hit batsmen each year from 1958–1961 and retired as the National League's all-time leader with 154 plunks. Drysdale's personal philosophy was that if a Dodger batter was hit, he'd hit two on the opposing team. Drysdale was as durable as he was mean, averaging 315 innings per year from 1962 to 1965. In 1962 he won 25 games with a 2.83 ERA and took home the Cy Young Award. Drysdale was a good hitter, too, clubbing 29 career home runs. In 1965 he hit .300 with seven homers, making him the sole .300 hitter for the Dodgers that year and placing him third on the team in homers, trailing only Lou Johnson and Jim Lefebvre, both of whom hit 12 that year. After the Dodgers won the 1965 World Series, Drysdale and teammate Sandy Koufax—one of the best 1–2 pitching punches in baseball history—engaged in a joint holdout in an effort to win big three-year contracts. They each wanted $500,000 for three years, but the club held firm in its policy of only issuing one-year contracts. During the tense holdout, the two pitchers signed a movie deal and appeared with actor David Janssen in the easily forgotten film *Warning Shot*. Koufax also inked a book deal with Viking Press that paid him a $110,000 advance for his autobiography. Just before the season began, the two pitchers caved, Koufax signing for $130,000 and Drysdale for $105,000.

In 1968, Drysdale's last full year in the majors, the eight-time All-Star broke Carl Hubbell's NL consecutive scoreless innings streak of 46 set in 1933 and Walter Johnson's major league record of 56 innings by amassing 56⅔ scoreless innings of his own. Along the way he pitched six consecutive shutouts. In 1969 he tore his rotator cuff and his career was over at the age of 32, as the surgical procedure we have today did not exist in 1969. After his playing career, Drysdale was a successful announcer for many years until 1993, when he was found dead of a heart attack in his hotel room in Montreal while there to announce a game. Drysdale, who was elected to the Baseball Hall of Fame in 1984, saw his wife, Ann Meyers Drysdale, a former basketball star with UCLA, elected to the Basketball Hall of Fame just a few months before he died.

CAREER DODGERS RECORD:

W	L	W%	ERA	SV
209	166	.557	2.95	6

K	BB	SHO	IP
2,486	855	49	3,432.0

FURILLO, CARL (OF)
(1946–1960)

While playing for Reading in the International League, Furillo so impressed the Dodgers that they offered to buy his contract on the spot, but the Reading owner wouldn't sell unless the Dodgers agreed to buy the entire Reading franchise—and Brooklyn did, just to get the right fielder known as the "Reading Rifle" for his powerful throwing arm. Although Furillo played with the "Boys of Summer" Dodgers, he wasn't really part of the gang, largely because of his lack of education. His other nickname was "Rock," a reference to the consistency of his brain. Furillo had six solid seasons in a row after joining the team before mysteriously slumping to .247 in 1952. After discovering that his problem was cataracts, he underwent an operation to correct the problem and came back in 1953 with the best year of his career, batting .344. An outstanding defensive outfielder, Furillo once used his powerful arm to throw out Mel Queen of the Pirates at first base by a step after Queen had seemingly singled to right field. The Dodgers released the injured Furillo in mid-1960 and the outfielder sought to have his medical bills paid for by the team, but they refused. Furillo won $21,000 in a lawsuit he brought against the team, but was dismayed later to discover that he had been blackballed because of his suit. He never got an offer to play or coach, not even in the minor leagues. Essentially, Furillo sued himself out of baseball.

CAREER DODGERS RECORD:

Games	AB	Hits	Runs
1,806	6,378	1,910	895

Avg	HR	RBI	SB
.299	192	1,058	48

GAGNE, ERIC (RP)
(1999–2005)

Los Angeles signed Eric Gagne as an amateur free agent in July 1995 and brought him up in 1999 when they needed another starting pitcher. Gagne was a starter for his first three years in L.A. before the team made him their closer in 2002—and what a closer he's been. Gagne put together three consecutive unbelievable years from 2002 to 2004, collecting 52, 55, and 45 saves respectively, establishing himself as the top closer in baseball with better numbers for that period than Mariano Rivera. The three-time All-Star was so dominant in 2003 (55 saves and zero blown chances, 1.20 ERA) that he won the league's Cy Young Award. From August 2002 to July 2004, Gagne had a streak of 84 consecutive saves without blowing one, beating Tom Gordon's record of 54 set in 1998–1999 with the Red Sox. He has the highest strikeout-to-innings pitched ratio of any closer in history. Early in 2005, however, Gagne suffered serious arm trouble and was shelved for the season. By season's end it was still unclear if the surgery he had during the season would allow him to return in 2006 or not.

CAREER DODGERS RECORD:

W	L	W%	ERA	SV
25	21	.543	3.28	160

K	BB	SHO	IP
626	182	0	543.3

GARVEY, STEVE (1B/3B)
(1969–1982)

The Minnesota Twins first drafted Steve Garvey in 1966, but he chose not to sign. Two years later the Dodgers selected him in the first round of the June 1968 amateur draft (secondary phase) and a year later he was playing in the majors. First baseman Garvey was the anchor of a solid infield (including Davey Lopes, Bill Russell, and Ron Cey) that played together for eight years (longer than any infield in major league history) and brought four pennants home to L.A. Garvey always believed he was born to be a Dodger. When he was a boy, his father drove the Dodgers team bus in Florida during spring training, and Garvey occasionally rode along.

After beginning his career as a third baseman, the error-prone Garvey was moved to first to give third-base prospect Ron Cey a shot. Ironically, Garvey went on to win four Gold Gloves at first, and establish several fielding records. His .996 career fielding average is still the major league record. In the seven years from 1974 to 1980, Garvey had 200+ hits and a .300+ average six times, and 100+ RBIs five times. In 1974 he became the first player ever to start an All-Star Game after being a write-in choice, and to top if off, he won the game's MVP Award. He followed it up by winning the league's MVP Award for the 1974 season. Named to eight consecutive All-Star Teams, Garvey again won the game's MVP Award in 1978. From 1975 to 1983, Garvey played in an NL record 1,207 consecutive games, a streak ended by a broken thumb. After the 1982 season, Garvey left L.A. for San Diego as a free agent and led the Padres to their first-ever World Series berth in 1984. Garvey retired in 1987 after a 19-year major league career. In 2000 he received $3 million in court-ordered salary compensation as a result of collusion among major league baseball owners to keep player salaries down.

CAREER DODGERS RECORD:

Games	AB	Hits	Runs
1,727	6,543	1,968	852
Avg	**HR**	**RBI**	**SB**
.301	211	992	77

GILLIAM, JIM (2B/3B/OF) (1953–1966)

Jim Gilliam dropped out of high school to play professional baseball for the Nashville Black Vols of the Negro Southern League just after World War II. Shortly thereafter he joined the Baltimore Elite Giants and performed so well that he made the Negro National League East All-Star team three straight years from 1948 to 1950. The Dodgers signed him in 1951 and, after two great seasons in the International League, brought him up to Brooklyn in 1953 to replace Jackie Robinson at second base. After leading the league in triples and setting a new rookie record with 100 walks, Gilliam was named the NL Rookie of the Year.

For the next 14 years Gilliam was a fixture in the Dodger lineup. Manager Walter Alston said of Gilliam, "He didn't hit with power, he had no arm, and he couldn't run, but he did all the little things to win ball games. He never griped or complained. He was one of the most unselfish players I ever knew." Gilliam was a player-coach from 1964–1966, averaging just over 300 at-bats a season. In 1965 he joined first baseman Wes Parker, second baseman Jim Lefebvre, and shortstop Maury Wills to form the first all switch-hitting infield. Considered by many to be the logical choice as the first black manager in baseball history, Gilliam was passed over and had no regrets. "I don't care about being a pioneer, just so I don't get left out." Just before the start of the 1978 World Series, Gilliam died of a brain hemorrhage. He was buried with his uniform in his casket.

CAREER DODGERS RECORD:

Games	AB	Hits	Runs
1,956	7,119	1,889	1,163
Avg	**HR**	**RBI**	**SB**
.265	65	558	203

GRIMES, BURLEIGH (SP) (1918–1926)

When Burleigh Grimes was 16 years old, his father gave him $25, shoved him out the door, and told him to go out into the world and make something of himself. He took up ballplaying for several semipro teams and eventually made his way to the majors in 1916 with the Pirates. After two years in Pittsburgh, Grimes was traded to Brooklyn as part of a five-player deal that sent Casey Stengel to the Pirates. Grimes, a spitball pitcher, had five 20-win seasons in his 19-year career, four with Brooklyn. Following the beaning death of Ray Chapman in 1920, Major League Baseball banned the practice of defacing baseballs or applying illegal substances to them. Grimes was one of 17 major league pitchers who were allowed to continue to throw the spitball after its ban, and is commonly regarded as the last legal spitballer in the majors. After two straight losing seasons in 1925–1926, Grimes was traded to the Giants, where he went 19–8. The following year he was traded back to Pittsburgh, where he sparkled, winning 25 games. Over his last six seasons, Grimes was traded six more times before finally retiring after the 1934 season at the age of 41. After his playing days, he spent many years coaching, scouting, and managing, mostly in the minors, but he did skipper the Dodgers in 1937 and 1938 as Casey Stengel's replacement. Grimes was elected to the Hall of Fame in 1964.

CAREER DODGERS RECORD:

W	L	W%	ERA	SV
158	121	.566	3.46	5
K	BB	SHO	IP	
952	744	20	2,426.0	

HERMAN, BABE (OF/1B) (1926–1931, 1945)

After spending several years in the minor leagues with the Red Sox and Tigers organizations, Babe Herman was traded to Brooklyn and arrived in the majors with the Robins in 1926. Although a notoriously poor fielder, Herman was a solid hitter with speed, maintaining a career average of .324 and routinely finishing in the league's top 10 in steals, doubles, triples, and home runs. Herman, prone to bizarre behavior, was the leader of Brooklyn's "Daffiness Boys," the equivalent to St. Louis's "Gas House Gang," and easily its most quotable member. Once, when his banker told him that someone was passing bad checks in his name, Herman told the banker, "Hit him some fly balls, and if he catches any, he ain't me." On another occasion, a reporter asked him why he always held out every spring. "I don't do it for the money," replied Herman. "The longer I stay away from training camp, the less chance I have of being hit by a fly ball." When an encyclopedia salesman tried to sell Herman a set of books, stating, "It will help your children get their education," Herman replied, "Nothing doing. My kids can walk to school." In spite of his adventures in the field, Herman's prowess at the plate left no doubt. He once collected nine consecutive hits, and three times hit for the cycle, a feat no other player has exceeded and only Bob Meusel and John Reilly have equaled. After spending his first six years with Brooklyn, Herman was traded five times over the next five years, before retiring in 1937. After an eight-year hiatus, Herman came out of retirement in 1945 to play one last season with the Dodgers before retiring for good.

CAREER DODGERS RECORD:

Games	AB	Hits	Runs
888	3,221	1,093	540
Avg	HR	RBI	SB
.339	112	594	69

HERSHISER, OREL (SP/RP)
(1983–1994, 2000)

Nicknamed "the Bulldog" because of the tenacious way he went after hitters, Orel Hershiser spent 13 years of his 18-year career bleeding Dodger blue. Los Angeles drafted Hershiser in the 17th round of the June 1979 amateur draft and brought him to the majors in 1983. The Dodgers made him a reliever at first and then converted him to starter in the middle of his second season. He had his career year in 1988, going 23–8 with a 2.26 ERA as he led the Dodgers to the World Series title. Hershiser ended the regular season by pitching 59 consecutive scoreless innings, breaking the record held by Don Drysdale. In that year's postseason he was 3–0 with a 1.05 ERA and two shutouts in 42.7 innings. That season Hershiser won the NL's Babe Ruth Award, the Major League Player of the Year Award, *The Sporting News* Pitcher of the Year Award, the NLCS MVP Award, the World Series MVP Award, a Gold Glove, and the NL Cy Young. Unconfirmed reports claim he had to purchase a new pickup truck to haul the seven trophies home. Hershiser had only one winning season from 1990 to 1994 and injuries were taking their toll, so the Dodgers released him. Hershiser signed as a free agent with Cleveland in 1995 and won 45 games as a starter with the Indians over three years. After one more year each with the Giants and Mets, Hershiser returned to the Dodgers for a final campaign in 2000 before calling it quits. Following his playing career, Hershiser became the pitching coach for the Texas Rangers.

CAREER DODGERS RECORD:

W	L	W%	ERA	SV
135	107	.558	3.12	5

K	BB	SHO	IP
1,456	667	24	2,180.7

HODGES, GIL (1B)
(1943, 1947–1961)

After a one-game appearance with Brooklyn in 1943, Gil Hodges joined the Marines and fought in the Pacific theater, where he saw action at Okinawa, before returning to baseball in 1946. Originally a catcher, Hodges was moved to first base when Roy Campanella arrived in Brooklyn in 1948, and the powerful first baseman became a mainstay in the Brooklyn lineup for nearly two decades. Hodges was such a graceful fielder that he was often compared to a ballet dancer, winning the first-ever Gold Glove awarded to a first baseman in the National League. Hodges appeared in seven consecutive All-Star Games from 1949 to 1955, and drove in 100+ runs in each of those years. For a decade he routinely placed in the top 10 in the National League in homers, RBIs, and slugging percentage. On August 31, 1950, Hodges became the sixth player in major league history to clout four homers in one game when he went 5-for-5 with 9 RBIs against the Phillies. In 1952 he encountered a sudden slump at the end of the season, going hitless in his last nine games of the regular season followed by an 0–26 World Series. Dodger fans were so worried about the protracted slump that they sent him letters, rosaries, good-luck charms, and prayers in an effort to right their first baseman's bat. He began the 1953 season right where he left off, collecting just 14 hits in his first 75 at-bats. After studying films of himself, Hodges discovered that he was bailing out of the box on nearly every pitch. Once he corrected the flaw, Hodges went on a tear, finishing the season with new career highs in batting average (.302) and RBIs (122) before hitting .364 in the World Series to redeem the previous year's fiasco.

In 1955 he helped the Dodgers end their World Series frustrations by leading Brooklyn to the championship over the Yankees—their first World Series title after losing seven straight Series. After 16 years with the Dodgers, Hodges was left unprotected in the expansion draft and the New York Mets picked him up. After playing briefly with the Mets in 1962–1963, Hodges retired as a player and became the manager of the Washington Senators after they asked the Mets to release him for the job. During his tenure in Washington, Hodges once talked a drunken, disconsolate Ryne Duren off a bridge where the pitcher was threatening to commit suicide. After five seasons of managing the expansion Senators to an increasing victory total each year, manager Hodges was traded to the Mets for pitcher Bill Denehy and $100,000. The Mets felt Hodges, with his drill sergeant approach, was the man who could lead them out of their doldrums, and they were right. In 1968, Hodges' first year, he led the Mets to 73 wins, seven more than they had ever achieved before. In 1969 he implemented a series of platoons on the team in order to achieve maximum results from all his players. The team responded with 100 wins and a World Series upset of the heavily favored Orioles. Hodges squeezed a winning record out of his team during the next two years as well, and was looking forward to a fine 1972 season when the players went on strike during spring training. Playing one last round of golf in Florida before heading north to prepare for the season, Hodges suffered a massive heart attack and died at the age of 47.

CAREER DODGERS RECORD:

Games	AB	Hits	Runs
2,006	6,881	1,884	1,088
Avg	**HR**	**RBI**	**SB**
.274	361	1,254	63

Dodgers fans snack before a 1920 World Series game.

KARROS, ERIC (1B)
(1991–2002)

First baseman Eric Karros became one of the Dodgers' most productive players ever, but his career began inauspiciously. Playing in the Venezuelan winter league while still in the minors, Karros was batting so poorly (.113) that the fans pelted him with bottle caps. After only 14 at-bats with Los Angeles in 1991, Karros arrived for good in 1992, winning the National League's Rookie of the Year Award with 20 homers and 88 RBIs. In 1993 he became the first Dodger ever to hit 20 or more homers in his first two seasons in the big leagues, a feat matched the following year by Mike Piazza. From 1995 to 2000, Karros passed the 100+ RBI mark in all but one season. A steady producer, Karros hit 20–34 homers in the nine years from 1992 to 2000, missing only in 1994 due to the season-ending players' strike. After a dozen years in Los Angeles, Karros was traded to the Cubs following the 2002 season, where he played for just one year before leaving via free agency for Oakland. During mid-2004 he was released by the A's after hitting just .194, his career over.

CAREER DODGERS RECORD:

Games	AB	Hits	Runs
1,601	6,002	1,608	752
Avg	**HR**	**RBI**	**SB**
.268	270	976	57

KENNEDY, BRICKYARD (SP/RP)
(1892–1901)

William "Brickyard" Kennedy was an integral member of the Brooklyn pitching staff during the 1890s, averaging nearly 325 innings pitched per year from 1893 to 1900. He was strong, once pitching both games of a doubleheader against Louisville, winning 3–0 and 6–2, allowing only eight hits combined. He received his nickname from his hometown of Bellaire, Ohio, location of a giant brick manufacturer. A four-time 20-game winner, Kennedy was illiterate and, like Shoeless Joe Jackson a few years later, would order in restaurants what other players ordered. After falling to 3–5 in 1901, Kennedy was released and picked up by the Giants, for whom he went 1–4 in 1902. The Giants sold him to Pittsburgh before the 1903 season, just in time for the first modern World Series. Kennedy rebounded a bit for the Pirates, finishing 9–6 in 15 starts. In the World Series he pitched one game, facing off against Cy Young in Game 5, losing 11–2. It was the last game of his career.

CAREER DODGERS RECORD:

W	L	W%	ERA	SV
177	149	.543	3.98	9
K	**BB**	**SHO**	**IP**	
749	1,128	11	2,857.0	

KOUFAX, SANDY (SP/RP) (1955–1966)

Born Sanford Braun, Koufax assumed his stepfather's name when he was two years old. He grew up playing basketball in the Jewish neighborhoods of Brooklyn with playmates Buddy Hackett and talk show host Larry King. Koufax remembers continually ramming his elbows into the steel support posts that held up the backboards, something he speculates caused the severe arthritis in his pitching elbow years later. Koufax went to the University of Cincinnati on a basketball scholarship, intending to become an architect. His basketball coach was also the school's baseball coach, and when Koufax found out the baseball team was going to make a spring trip to New Orleans, Koufax volunteered to play baseball just so he could come along. After striking out 51 batters in 32 innings, Koufax caught the attention of major league scouts. The Dodgers signed Koufax, giving him a $14,000 bonus and putting him on their roster, dropping pitcher Tommy Lasorda to make room.

In the first half of his career, Koufax went 36–40, but showed Jekyll-and-Hyde brilliance that drove team officials mad. In his first start, for example, he walked eight batters in 4.7 innings. In his second start, Koufax struck out 14 batters in a two-hit shutout performance. On August 31, 1959 he tied Bob Feller's record with 18 strikeouts in a game. Combined with the 13 strikeouts in his previous game, Koufax set a new two-game record of 31. When he struck out 10 in his next game, his 41 became a new three-game record. In 1960 he held hitters to the lowest batting average in the league, but his 8–13 record got him so frustrated he nearly quit baseball to sell lighting fixtures. He thought playing for a new team might do him good, but when he asked management to trade him, they refused.

During the offseason, Koufax worked on his delivery, changing his grip, his angle, his arm motion, and more. The results were stunning. In 1961 Koufax used his rising fastball and sharp curveball to record the best year of his career by far, up to that point, going 18–13 with 269 strikeouts and earning the first of his six straight All-Star honors. In the five years from 1962 to 1966, Koufax won 111 games and lost only 34, winning the ERA crown every year and leading the Dodgers to three pennants and two World Series titles. He also pitched four no-hitters during that span, including a perfect game against the Cubs in 1965. Three times he won pitching's Triple Crown (1963, 1965, 1966), and in 1963 he became the first National League pitcher ever to collect 300 strikeouts in a season. That season he became the first pitcher ever to be a unanimous selection for the Cy Young Award, and he followed it up with two more unanimous selections in 1965 and 1966.

In World Series play, Koufax compiled a 4–3 record in seven starts, but his ERA was 0.95, an indication of how punchless the Dodger offense truly was in the 1960s. In 1964 Koufax was 19–5 with 1.74 ERA on August 16, when he injured his elbow diving back into second base; it was the same elbow he had banged up for years on the basketball courts of Brooklyn. He didn't play again that year, and the Dodgers faded from the pennant race. He went 26–8 in 1965, though the elbow bothered him constantly and he had to take cortisone injections in order to pitch. In 1966, at the age of 30,

Koufax went 27–9 with a 1.73 ERA, both career bests, but his elbow continued to plague him. In November of that year, at the pinnacle of his career and not wanting to risk a crippling arm injury, Koufax announced his retirement, telling the press, "When I'm done playing baseball, I want to be able to comb my hair." After his playing days, Koufax became an announcer, and to this day still instructs Dodger rookies during spring training. When he was inducted into the Hall of Fame in 1972 at the age of 36, he was the youngest player ever so honored, and just the fifth player in history to be chosen in his first year of eligibility.

CAREER DODGERS RECORD:

W	L	W%	ERA	SV
165	87	.655	2.76	9

K	BB	SHO	IP
2,396	817	40	2,324.3

NEWCOMBE, DON (SP)
(1949–1951, 1954–1958)

Don Newcombe was just 19 and in his second year with the Newark Eagles of the Negro National League in October 1945 when he pitched an exhibition game at Ebbets Field. A Dodger official, impressed by what he saw, signed Newcombe to a contract the next day. In 1946 Newcombe, Jackie Robinson, and Roy Campanella played together for the Montreal Royals, a Dodger farm team. During the 1949 season, Newcombe was promoted to Brooklyn and went 17–8, winning the NL Rookie of the Year Award and the first of four All-Star Game selections. Newcombe had a habit of losing focus, sometimes seeming not to care. Jackie Robinson became so angered at Newcombe's lackadaisical approach that he would occasionally scream at the pitcher, telling him to take off his uniform and go home. After winning 19 games in 1950 and 20 in 1951, Newcombe spent 1952, 1953, and the first part of 1954 in the military during the Korean War. In 1955 he went 20–5, despite missing time when manager Walter Alston suspended him for refusing to pitch batting practice. He returned only after apologizing to the team and pitching in relief for a while. In 1956 he had his best year, going 27–7 and winning both the NL Cy Young and MVP Awards, making him the only player in history to have won all three major awards (MVP, Rookie of the Year, and Cy Young) at some point in his career. Newcombe was one of the best hitting pitchers in the history of the game, retiring with a .271 average. In 1955 he set the NL record for homers in a season by a pitcher with seven.

After falling to 11–12 in 1957, and getting off to an 0–6 start with a 7.86 ERA in 1958, Newcombe, troubled by alcoholism, was traded to Cincinnati; two years later he was sold to Cleveland. After compiling a 26–30 record over his last three years, Newcombe was released, his major league career over. He attempted a comeback in Japan in 1962, but his heavy drinking caused problems for him there, too, and he was soon back in America. Newcombe's drinking blighted his personal life as well, implicated in the failure of his first marriage, a bad car accident in which he nearly killed himself and his second wife, and the near drowning of his son in a swimming pool. Finally, after his second wife took their children away, Newcombe swore he would never drink again, and he didn't. He eventually became a substance-abuse counselor, working with young players in the Dodgers organization.

CAREER DODGERS RECORD:

W	L	W%	ERA	SV
123	66	.651	3.51	4

K	BB	SHO	IP
913	413	22	1,662.7

Osteen, Claude (SP)
(1965–1973)

After seven seasons with the Reds and Senators, Claude Osteen was traded to the Dodgers along with $100,000 in December 1964 as part of a seven-player deal that sent Frank Howard to Washington. In 1965 he joined a rotation that included Sandy Koufax, Don Drysdale, and Johnny Podres. Over the next nine years, Osteen averaged more than 16 wins a year. Even though he was often the fourth or fifth starter on a team that included the aforementioned three, plus Tommy John, Andy Messersmith and Don Sutton, Osteen held his own, and sometimes even outperformed the others. In the 1965 and 1966 World Series, he compiled a sterling ERA of 0.86. In 1967 he earned the first of his three All-Star Game appearances, and in 1969 he became a 20-game winner for the first of two times in his career. After a 16–11 season in 1973, Osteen was traded to the Astros for Jimmy Wynn, and in mid-1974 was sent to the Cardinals. St. Louis released him on the eve of the 1975 season and he signed as a free agent with the White Sox. He went 7–16 with a 4.36 ERA and only 63 strikeouts in 37 starts for Chicago in 1975, a mere shadow of his former self. Chicago released him after the season and his career was over. Following his retirement as a player, Osteen spent time as a coach for the Cardinals, Phillies, Rangers, and Dodgers.

CAREER DODGERS RECORD:

W	L	W%	ERA	SV
147	126	.538	3.09	0

K	BB	SHO	IP
1,162	568	34	2,396.7

Piazza, Mike (C)
(1992–1998)

By the end of the 2005 season, Mike Piazza had established himself as one of the best-hitting catchers in the history of the game. But at the start of his career, no one imagined he would achieve greatness. Piazza was only drafted as a favor to his father, a close friend of Tommy Lasorda's, and then not until the 62nd round of the June 1988 amateur draft. After the draft, Piazza wasn't offered a contract, so Lasorda, as a further favor to Piazza's father, arranged a private tryout. Following the tryout, Lasorda announced that Piazza would be converted from pitcher to catcher, given a contract, and sent to the Dominican Republic to learn his new position. After playing in half a dozen minor leagues plus the Mexican League, Piazza finally arrived in Los Angeles in 1992 as a late-season call-up. He hit .232 with one home run in 21 games, hardly a sign of what was to come.

In 1993 Piazza exploded onto the baseball scene when he hit .318 with 35 homers and 112 RBIs and won the Rookie of the Year Award in a unanimous vote. He only got better over his next four years in L.A., hitting between .319–.362, slugging 24–40 homers (even with two strike-shortened years), and driving in between 92–124 runs each year. Piazza won the 1996 All-Star Game MVP Award in Philadelphia's Veteran's Stadium, where he had worked as a batboy in his youth. Twice a runner-up for the NL MVP Award in 1996 and 1997, Piazza became embroiled in a salary dispute with the Dodgers. Early in the 1998 season, he was traded to Florida, and a week later he was sent to the Mets. During his career, Piazza has been selected to the All-Star Game 12 times and won 10 Silver Slugger Awards as the best hitting catcher in the National League. *(See Mets bio.)*

CAREER DODGERS RECORD:

Games	AB	Hits	Runs
726	2,707	896	443
Avg	**HR**	**RBI**	**SB**
.331	177	563	10

PODRES, JOHNNY (SP)
(1953–1955, 1957–1966)

Johnny Podres, a lifelong Dodgers fan, was signed by Brooklyn as an amateur free agent in 1951, and by 1953 he was in the major leagues. In more than 12 seasons with the Dodgers, Podres never won more than 18 games in any one season, but he provided the stability the Dodgers needed at the back end of their rotation. He went 9–4 in his rookie season (1953) and got his first taste of World Series action that October when Mickey Mantle took him deep for a grand slam, handing him the only World Series defeat of his career. Two years later he won two games as the Dodgers ended seven years of World Series frustration at the hands of the Yankees, and in the process he was voted the MVP of the 1955 Fall Classic, the only World Series the Dodgers would win while in Brooklyn. Podres was 1–0 in both the 1959 and 1963 World Series as the Dodgers won both. After being hit by a pitch in 1964, Podres suffered from bone chips in his elbow and only played in two games. Following a 7–6 season in 1965, the three-time Dodger All-Star was sold early in 1966 to Detroit, where he went just 4–5 and 3–1 the next two years. After missing the entire 1968 season, he attempted a comeback in 1969 with the expansion San Diego Padres, but after going 5–6 he hung up his spikes for good in midseason. Upon retirement as an active player, Podres spent more than three decades as a pitching coach with the Padres, Red Sox, Twins, and Phillies.

CAREER DODGERS RECORD:

W	L	W%	ERA	SV
136	104	.567	3.66	6
K	**BB**	**SHO**	**IP**	
1,331	670	23	2,029.3	

REESE, PEE WEE (SS)
(1940–1942, 1946–1958)

Harold "Pee Wee" Reese played his entire 16-year career with the Dodgers (it would have been 19 years had he not lost three years to military service in World War II). He led the league in a major offensive category only twice (runs scored in 1949 and stolen bases in 1952), but Reese gave the Dodgers leadership, defense, and the ability to do the little things needed to win: advance a runner, execute the hit and run, bunt, steal a critical base, or drive the ball hard to the outfield. Reese, whose nickname came from his marble-shooting prowess as a kid, helped the Dodgers win seven pennants in those 16 years. Originally in the Red Sox organization, he was targeted by Boston owner Tom Yawkey as the replacement for player-manager Joe Cronin. Yawkey sent Cronin on a scouting trip to assess his highly prized minor league shortstop, but when Cronin returned he convinced Yawkey that Reese was overrated and should be traded. After Yawkey begrudgingly traded Reese to the Dodgers, contemporaries of Cronin's allege that Cronin wanted Reese traded because he felt his own position as Boston's shortstop was threatened.

After a slow start in his first two years, Reese finally blossomed in 1942, winning his first of 10 consecutive spots on the National League All-Star team. After playing on a Navy team with Phil Rizzuto from 1943 to 1945, Reese returned to Brooklyn in 1946 and became the clear inspirational leader of the Dodgers. His finest moment came in 1947, when Jackie Robinson took the field in a game in Cincinnati. The fans were booing Robinson loudly, yelling racist threats, and throwing debris onto the field, when Reese walked over to him and put his arm around Robinson's shoulder near second base in a show of support. That gesture quieted the ugly display from the fans and broke the ice with many of the other Brooklyn and opposing players. Shortly after the Dodgers moved to Los Angeles, Reese retired as a player and became a coach for one year before joining Dizzy Dean in the broadcast booth for a number of years. He later returned to Louisville and took an executive position with bat maker Hillerich & Bradsby. Reese was elected to the Hall of Fame in 1984.

CAREER DODGERS RECORD:

Games	AB	Hits	Runs
2,166	8,058	2,170	1,338
Avg	**HR**	**RBI**	**SB**
.269	126	885	232

ROBINSON, JACKIE (2B/3B/1B/OF) (1947–1956)

Jackie Robinson's courage and willingness to be subjected to insult, abuse, pressure, scrutiny, and threats led directly to the integration of baseball and gave others the courage to claim their civil rights in other areas of daily life. Dodgers GM Branch Rickey envisioned a time when blacks would play in the major leagues and he concocted a scheme to see his plan implemented. The first stage of his plan was to create the United States Baseball League, a six-team African American confederation that would include the Brooklyn Brown Dodgers. This would enable Rickey to openly scout black players, both home and away, without arousing suspicion. Next, Rickey had to choose the appropriate black player to test the waters. Jackie Robinson, who played for the Negro League's Kansas City Monarchs, was a good player, but by no means the best black player available. The established stars, by and large, were older and past their prime, and Rickey knew he needed someone who was younger and tougher. Rickey also wanted a player with good moral values, since he felt sure a hostile media would have a field day with a player's peccadilloes. Robinson seemed to fill the bill on both counts: He appeared to have a conservative lifestyle, his military record proved his courage, and he was an educated officer to boot.

Rickey invited him in for a tryout. Robinson, who thought he was trying out for the Brooklyn Brown Dodgers, passed the baseball tryout with flying colors, so Rickey invited him into his office. When Rickey revealed his ultimate plan to Robinson, the ballplayer said he could handle the pressure. As a further test, Rickey hurled ugly racial insults and threats at Robinson, telling him if he couldn't handle what he was giving him in the office, he'd never be able to handle it on the field. Robinson assured Rickey that when the situation called for it, he could "turn the other cheek."

After signing Robinson, Rickey sent him to Montreal, leaving everyone under the impression he had signed Robinson for his Brown Dodgers. The Dodgers were in Havana for spring training in 1947 when a rumored player revolt came to light. Some of the white Dodger players, led by Dixie Walker, circulated a petition that stated their opposition to playing with a black player. When manager Leo Durocher caught wind of it, he woke the team up in the middle of the night and held a heated team meeting to discuss the matter. When Rickey arrived the next day, the team held another meeting and the mutiny was quieted. When Robinson took the field for his first regular-season game on April 15, 1947, in Ebbets Field, nearly 27,000 fans—most of them black—packed the ballpark to watch Robinson go hitless as the Dodgers beat the Braves, 5–3.

In His Big League Debut
JACKIE SCORES WINNING RUN
Robbie's Bunt Turns Tide
WASHINGTON
Big Day for Dodgers
Jackie Romps Home From Second Base As 26,000 Cheer

In May, National League president Ford Frick addressed a threatened player boycott in St. Louis, threatening any striking player with expulsion from the league. "I don't care if it wrecks the National League for five years," said Frick. "This is the United States of America and one citizen has as much right to play as another. The National League will go down the line with Robinson, whatever the consequences." Frick's strong stance squelched the planned strike. Once the ice was broken and the rebellious forces calmed, Robinson proceeded to shine on the field, winning the NL Rookie of the Year Award at the somewhat advanced age of 28. In 1949 he won the league's MVP Award after hitting .342 to win the batting title. During his career, Robinson, a six-time All-Star, stole home an incredible 19 times.

Robinson's career ended amid controversy in 1956. In a *Look* magazine article (for which he was paid $50,000), Robinson announced his intention to retire. This, however, was news to the Dodgers, who quickly traded him to the New York Giants. When the Giants offered Robinson $60,000 to continue playing, he took their offer under consideration. The Dodgers cried foul, claiming that Robinson had used the article to coerce a higher salary. In order to prove the Dodgers wrong, the stubborn Robinson retired. Following his baseball career, Robinson took executive positions with a bank and a coffee company. After becoming increasingly ill from diabetes, Robinson died of a heart attack in 1972. He was elected to the Hall of Fame in 1962 and, in 1997, baseball commissioner Bud Selig ordered his number 42 be retired by all major league teams.

CAREER DODGERS RECORD:

Games	AB	Hits	Runs
1,382	4,877	1,518	947
Avg	**HR**	**RBI**	**SB**
.311	137	734	197

RUCKER, NAP (SP/RP)
(1907–1916)

George "Nap" Rucker was probably the best left-hander in the Dodgers organization until the arrival of Sandy Koufax. During his minor league days, Rucker played with second baseman Grantland Rice, who wasn't a very good ballplayer but eventually became one of the leading sportswriters of all time. One of Rucker's roommates in Augusta was Ty Cobb, who was even then a borderline psycho. Rucker and Cobb had an arrangement that called for Cobb to come home first after a game and bathe. Rucker would arrive later. Once, when Rucker got knocked out of a game early, he came home first. When Cobb arrived after the game, he found Rucker in the tub. Furious, Cobb tried to strangle Rucker, who eventually fought him off. "Are you crazy?!" shouted Rucker. "You don't understand," said Cobb. "I've got to be first, ALL the time!" Rucker pitched a no-hitter against the Braves on September 5, 1908, the only three base runners coming on errors. Rucker's only 20-win season came in 1911 when he finished 22–18. The next year he lost 20, going 18–21. After retiring as a player, Rucker became a farmer, using his 1916 World Series player share to purchase the land. He later entered local politics, winning election as mayor of Roswell, Georgia.

CAREER DODGERS RECORD:

W	L	W%	ERA	SV
134	134	.500	2.42	14
K	**BB**	**SHO**	**IP**	
1,217	701	38	2,375.3	

RUSSELL, BILL (SS/OF)
(1969–1986)

Los Angeles drafted Bill Russell in the ninth round of the June 1966 amateur draft and he remained in a Dodger uniform for more than three decades as player, coach, and manager. Russell was pressed from the mold of an earlier Dodger shortstop, Pee Wee Reese. Like Reese, Russell was a leader on the field who excelled at the little things, such as bunting, advancing the runner by hitting behind him, and keeping opposing runners from advancing. He was a capable and durable shortstop who played more games in a Los Angeles uniform than any other player, and second most by a Dodger all time, trailing only Zack Wheat, who played while the team was in Brooklyn. Russell was part of a Dodger infield that played together for eight seasons. When the other members moved on, it was Russell who remained the longest.

In 1980 Russell's career took a turn when he was hit by a pitch that shattered one of his fingers. Never able to throw the same again, Russell became only a part-time player for most of his remaining six seasons in the majors. After retiring as a player in 1986, Russell spent five years as a Dodger coach, five more as a minor league manager, and then became the Dodgers manager in 1996. After two-plus seasons he was fired, and eventually returned to managing in the minors.

CAREER DODGERS RECORD:

Games	AB	Hits	Runs
2,181	7,318	1,926	796
Avg	**HR**	**RBI**	**SB**
.263	46	627	167

SNIDER, DUKE (OF)
(1947–1962)

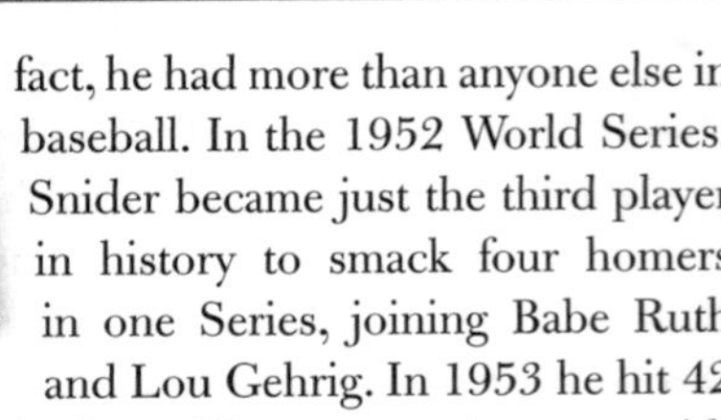

The Brooklyn Dodgers signed Edwin "Duke" Snider as an amateur free agent in 1943 at the age of 16 and brought him to the majors in 1947 after Snider spent two years in the military during World War II. His father gave him his nickname at the age of five because of his tendency toward arrogance and his habit of pouting and brooding if he didn't get his way. As an adult, Snider's superiority complex manifested itself in different ways; he would become enraged when he struck out or if his hotel accommodations were not up to his standards. As a young player, Snider felt many of the training exercises were beneath him and would often throw a fit if he was expected to perform them. When he went too far with his pouting one day in 1947, Dodger GM Branch Rickey told him to remove his uniform and go home. Snider apologized, but Rickey sent him to the minors anyway to teach him a lesson. Snider eventually worked his way back to the majors in 1948, but he was striking out too often and Rickey arranged to have Hall of Famer George Sisler work with him on the strike zone. Sisler's strategy involved having Snider stand in the batter's box with a bat, but not hit any of the pitches thrown to him—only to call out whether they were strikes or balls. The plan worked and Snider developed such a good eye at the plate that he walked almost 1,000 times in his career.

Snider eventually developed into a solid player for the Dodgers, giving all three New York teams a star in center field; the Yankees had Mantle, the Giants had Mays, and the Dodgers had Snider. During the 1950s, when the three center fielders were all at the peak of their careers, Snider had more homers (326) and RBIs (1,031) than Mantle or Mays—in fact, he had more than anyone else in baseball. In the 1952 World Series, Snider became just the third player in history to smack four homers in one Series, joining Babe Ruth and Lou Gehrig. In 1953 he hit 42 homers, the first of five consecutive years with 40+ home runs. Snider was mired in a slump in 1955 when the Brooklyn fans began to boo him. He went on a tirade, calling Brooklyn's fans the lousiest in all of baseball. The quote, of course, made the papers, and the "Duke" had to apologize again. The next year *Collier's* magazine ran an article about Snider titled, "I Play Baseball for Money, Not for Fun," which only exacerbated his relationship with the fans and his teammates.

By 1960, Snider's skills began to diminish, and injuries came more frequently. In 1963 the Mets purchased the seven-time All-Star from the Dodgers—now in Los Angeles—hoping that nostalgic fans would pay to see him again in New York. Snider, who was the only Met selected for the 1963 All-Star Game, also helped the team's young hitters. San Francisco purchased Snider from the Mets in 1964 for the same reason the Mets had, hoping to boost attendance among its new fan base, and Snider played his final year as . . . horror of horrors! . . . a Giant. After his playing career ended, Snider spent many years as a major league scout and minor league manager for a number of teams, then joined the Dodgers broadcast booth. Snider was elected to the Hall of Fame in 1980.

CAREER DODGERS RECORD:

Games	AB	Hits	Runs
1,923	6,640	1,995	1,199
Avg	**HR**	**RBI**	**SB**
.300	389	1,271	99

SUTTON, DON (SP)
(1966–1980, 1988)

The Dodgers signed Don Sutton as an amateur free agent in September 1964 and brought him to the major leagues in 1966, when he joined the starting rotation right out of spring training. (The Dodgers gave Sutton a long look that spring since both Sandy Koufax and Don Drysdale were engaged in a lengthy holdout at the time.) Sutton struck out 209 batters in 1966, the most by a National League rookie since Grover Alexander's 227 in 1911. Over the next 23 years, Sutton would win 10 or more games 21 times, although he is the only 300-game winner in history to record only one 20-victory season. He pitched over 200 innings in all but one of his first 21 seasons, missing only in 1981 because of the players' strike. Eight times in his career, Sutton posted an ERA below 3.00, and he finished with 3,574 strikeouts, good for seventh place all time through 2005. He was not only a good strikeout pitcher, but had good control, as his 16 top-10 finishes in strikeout-to-walk ratio attests. Sutton won two awards of significance during his career, the Lou Gehrig Memorial Award in 1976 and the 1977 All-Star Game MVP Award.

Sutton was constantly suspected of doctoring the ball. When asked if he used any foreign substances on the ball, he replied, "No. Vaseline is made right here in the U.S.A." Longtime pitching coach Ray Miller once said that Sutton so perfected the art of defiantly doctoring a baseball that he someday expected to see Sutton walk to the mound with a file, chisel, screwdriver, and glue dangling from a utility belt, ready to throw a ball to the plate with bolts attached to it.

Sutton left Los Angeles after the 1980 season as a free agent, landing in Houston for nearly two years before being traded to Milwaukee on the trading deadline in 1982. He helped Milwaukee win their only pennant as he defeated Jim Palmer for the pennant clincher on the last day of the season. After two-plus years with the Brewers, Sutton finished his career with four years split between the A's, Angels, and a second stint with the Dodgers. He won his 300th career game in 1986 as a member of the Angels. Following the 1988 season, Sutton retired as a player and went to work in the broadcast booth, and in 1998 he was named to the Hall of Fame.

CAREER DODGERS RECORD:

W	L	W%	ERA	SV
233	181	.563	3.09	5
K	BB	SHO	IP	
2,696	996	52	3,816.3	

VALENZUELA, FERNANDO (SP)
(1980–1990)

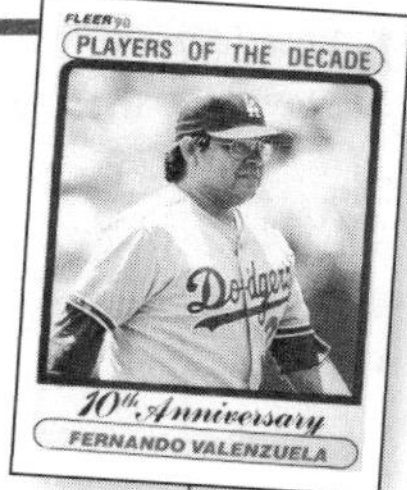

Like Mark "the Bird" Fidrych, Fernando Valenzuela got off to such a hot start as a rookie that he became a media sensation—in his case, sparking an outbreak of "Fernandomania." After making the team in September 1980, Valenzuela pitched 10 scoreless outings in relief to close the year. On Opening Day 1981, Valenzuela, thrust into the lineup as the starting pitcher due to an injury to Jerry Reuss, shut out the Astros. He reeled off eight straight wins in eight starts, including five shutouts and 36 straight scoreless innings, as he compiled an unbelievable 0.50 ERA. Fans and the media alike, especially the Hispanic population of southern California, went nuts over the pudgy Mexican who rolled his eyes skyward with every pitch as he delivered his killer screwball. Even though the season was cut short by about 50 games, Valenzuela tied the all-time record for shutouts in a season by a rookie with eight, set in 1913 by Ewell Russell of the White Sox. Valenzuela won both the NL Rookie of the Year Award and the Cy Young Award. From that great start in 1981, Valenzuela made 255 consecutive starts without missing a turn in the rotation.

Following the 1982 season, Valenzuela became the first player ever to be awarded a $1 million salary in arbitration. Despite his odd physique, Valenzuela was also a good hitter and fielder, winning two Silver Slugger Awards and one Gold Glove. Valenzuela's career took a turn for the worse in 1988, when he suffered an arm injury from which he never fully recovered. Though he pitched nine more seasons, the six-time All-Star won only a combined 60 games and lost 71 over that span, with a greatly inflated ERA. He did have one moment of glory in 1989, when he no-hit St. Louis in Dodger Stadium the same night that Dave Stewart of the A's tossed a no-hitter against Toronto, marking the first time since 1898 that two separate no-hitters were pitched on the same day in the major leagues. Valenzuela's last hurrah came on August 16, 1996, when, as a member of the Padres, he pitched the first major league game ever played in Mexico, defeating the New York Mets in Monterrey. After being traded to the Cardinals in 1997, Valenzuela got off to a 2–12 start and was released by St. Louis. Since 2003, he has been a commentator for the Dodgers' Spanish-language radio broadcasts.

CAREER DODGERS RECORD:

W	L	W%	ERA	SV
141	116	.549	3.31	2

K	BB	SHO	IP
1,759	915	29	2,348.7

VANCE, DAZZY (SP)
(1922–1932, 1935)

Except for two very brief stints with the Pirates and Yankees in 1915 and 1918, Clarence "Dazzy" Vance spent more than a decade in the minor leagues before finally making it big in 1922 at the age of 31 with the Dodgers. During his childhood, Vance had a neighbor who owned a rifle that fascinated Dazzy. Whenever the neighbor brought it out, Vance would say, "Ain't it a dazzy?" He used the term so often it became his nickname. As a 31-year-old rookie with Brooklyn, Vance went 18–12 and led the National League in strikeouts and shutouts. After winning 18 again in 1923, Vance put together the best season of his career in 1924, when he finished 28–6 with a 2.16 ERA, leading the league in wins, ERA, strikeouts, and complete games. He won 15 straight games at one point and earned the NL's MVP Award in a surprising vote over Rogers Hornsby, who hit .424, the highest batting average of the 20th century. After signing a new three-year contract worth $47,500 per year (an astronomical sum in 1925), Vance, now the highest-paid pitcher in the league, again led the NL in wins, going 22–9. He had two spectacular single games: On July 20th he struck out 17 Cardinals, and on September 13th he pitched a no-hitter against the Phillies.

Vance had long arms and legs and used a high leg kick and a sweatshirt with a tattered right sleeve to distract the hitter. He was also an intelligent pitcher who was always thinking.

Once, when a runner on third tried to steal home on him, Vance—instead of pitching home—threw the ball and plunked the runner in the side. According to the rules, the runner had to return to third base, and the run didn't score. In 1928 Vance won 22 games and led the league for the seventh consecutive year in strikeouts with 200. After he went 12–11 in 1932, the Dodgers traded the 41-year-old Vance to St. Louis. He lasted three more years as a reliever with the Cardinals, Reds, and Dodgers again before retiring at the age of 44 to manage his extensive real estate holdings in Florida. Vance, who collected all 197 of his career wins after the age of 31, was elected to the Hall of Fame in 1955.

CAREER DODGERS RECORD:

W	L	W%	ERA	SV
190	131	.592	3.17	7
K	**BB**	**SHO**	**IP**	
1,918	764	29	2,757.7	

WHEAT, ZACK (OF)
(1909–1926)

Zachary Davis Wheat was playing semipro ball in Kansas when he signed his first professional contract, joining Shreveport of the Texas League. After less than two years in the minors, Wheat arrived in Brooklyn for good near the end of the 1909 season, becoming the team's starting left fielder for the next 18 years. Wheat, once described as "165 pounds of scrap iron, rawhide, and guts," hit over .300 in 14 of those seasons, and was a defensive standout. He compiled four hitting streaks of at least 20 games, the longest being 29. A 1917 *Baseball Magazine* article said of him, "Tris Speaker may be the greatest outfielder in the world, but Zack Wheat is the easiest, most graceful of all outfielders." In the early 1920s, when Babe Ruth was clouting his mammoth homers for the Yankees and Frankie Frisch was leading the Giants to four consecutive NL pennants, a New York newspaper asked its readers to select the city's most popular baseball player. The winner was Zack Wheat, a fact that didn't surprise Wheat's teammate Casey Stengel, who later said that Wheat was the only great ballplayer who was never booed.

Wheat helped Brooklyn win pennants in 1916 and 1920, though they lost the Series each time. In 1918 he won the National League batting title with a .335 average. After 18 seasons in Brooklyn, the Robins released Wheat in 1926 and Connie Mack picked him up, whereupon he hit .324 for the 1927 A's in one last major league campaign. Following his playing career, Wheat joined the Kansas City, Missouri, police department, where he served until 1936, when a car accident forced him to leave the force. He then operated a fishing resort for a number of years. Wheat was elected to the Hall of Fame in 1959 and died in 1972.

CAREER DODGERS RECORD:

Games	AB	Hits	Runs
2,322	8,859	2,804	1,255
Avg	**HR**	**RBI**	**SB**
.317	131	1,210	203

WILLS, MAURY (SS)
(1959–1966, 1969–1972)

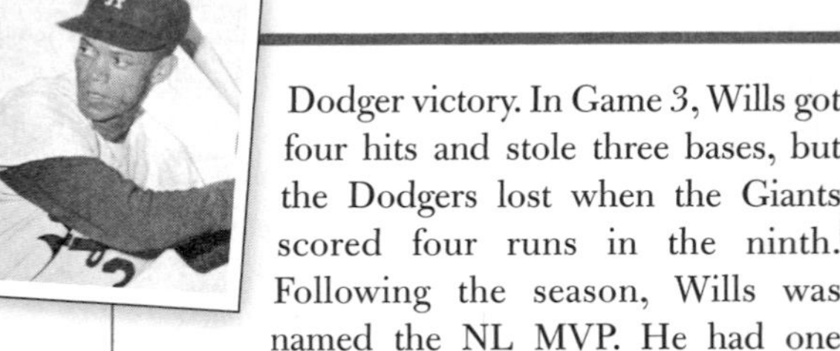

It took Maury Wills a long time to make his mark in the major leagues. After Brooklyn signed him as an amateur free agent before the 1951 season, Wills spent eight years in the minors playing all nine positions before finally getting his first chance in "the show." Originally a right-handed hitter, Wills became an impact player only after learning to switch-hit. As a left-hander, Wills had the added advantage of being closer to first base, thereby increasing his on-base percentage. And once on base, Wills became an offensive weapon the likes of which had not been seen in baseball since the days of Ty Cobb. He stole 50 bases in 1960, the most in the National League since Max Carey swiped 51 in 1923. In 1962 he destroyed Ty Cobb's 1915 single-season record of 96 by stealing 104 (the rest of the Dodgers combined to steal 94 bases that year). Wills was caught only 13 times in 1962, compared to Cobb, who was nailed 38 times in 1915.

Wills's base-stealing ability had such a demoralizing effect on opposing teams during the 1962 season that the rival Giants decided to take action. The Giants and Dodgers had ended the season tied for first with identical 101–61 records. A best-of-three playoff was scheduled to determine the league winner, with Game 1 scheduled for San Francisco. Wills, who liked the ground around first base to be very hard (the way the Dodger groundskeepers kept it) so he could get good traction, was horrified to discover that in San Francisco the groundskeepers had turned the dirt around first base into a veritable swamp. After losing Game 1, the Series shifted to Los Angeles for the remainder of the playoff. Wills stole a base and scored a run in the Game 2 Dodger victory. In Game 3, Wills got four hits and stole three bases, but the Dodgers lost when the Giants scored four runs in the ninth. Following the season, Wills was named the NL MVP. He had one more big year, 1965, in which he stole 94 bases.

After stealing 38 in 1966, Wills was traded to Pittsburgh, where he stayed for two years until Montreal selected him in the 1968 expansion draft. Two months later the Expos traded him back to the Dodgers, where he played until he retired in 1972. Following his playing career, Wills stayed in baseball as a broadcaster, minor league coach, and manager. In 1980 he became the second black manager in the majors when he took over the reins of the Seattle Mariners. However, his career with the Mariners was a mess. He never established team discipline and often didn't seem focused himself. Wills once submitted a lineup card that listed two players at the same position. His career ended ignominiously early in the 1981 season, when Oakland manager Billy Martin noticed something amiss about the batters' boxes in the Kingdome. When the home-plate umpire measured them, the boxes were a foot too long, an illegality Wills had ordered so that the Seattle hitters could get a foot closer to the hard-breaking curveballs of the Oakland pitchers. Wills was ejected, fined $500, suspended for two games, and ultimately fired over the incident; he was soon out of baseball.

CAREER DODGERS RECORD:

Games	AB	Hits	Runs
1,593	6,156	1,732	876
Avg	**HR**	**RBI**	**SB**
.281	17	374	490

Milwaukee Brewers

Since 1969

1982 Team Ball

1969 Gene Brabender wins 13 games for the Seattle Pilots to become the winningest pitcher in expansion team history, breaking the record of 12 set by the Angels' Ken McBride and the Senators' Bennie Daniels, both in 1961.... **1987** Paul Molitor hits safely in 39 straight games, the seventh longest streak in major league history. Despite missing 44 games, he finishes the season with a remarkable 114 runs scored, 41 doubles, and 45 stolen bases.... **1993** On April 14, catcher Dave Nilsson combines with pitcher Graeme Lloyd to become the first Australian battery in major league history.... **1998** In Milwaukee's first season in the National League, its pitching staff sets an NL record and ties the major league record with just two complete games all season, both by Jeff Juden, who is traded in midseason.

FRANCHISE HISTORY

The Milwaukee Brewers began play in 1969 as the Seattle Pilots, one of two American League expansion teams that year (along with the Kansas City Royals). Although Seattle had been viewed as a plum city for expansion, the new franchise couldn't quite get off the ground. After a single lackluster season playing in inadequate Sick's Stadium, the team filed for bankruptcy, and just four days before the start of the 1970 season, was sold and moved to Milwaukee, a proven baseball town which had lost the Braves to Atlanta after the 1965 season.

The buyer, Bud Selig, was a lifelong baseball fan who earnestly sought to bring baseball back to Milwaukee after the Braves left. Selig, who had made his small fortune selling Ford automobiles, sat on the board of directors of the Green Bay Packers. By the time he was 29 years old, Selig was the largest shareholder of the Brewers with about 25 percent. His control of the team continued into the mid-1990s, when he voluntarily stepped aside to take over the job of acting Commissioner after the ouster of Fay Vincent. Selig's daughter eventually took over the day-to-day affairs of the team so Selig could concentrate on his new position. In January of 2004, Selig and his family put the team up for sale and received an offer from Daniel Gilbert, chairman of Quicken Loans, but in September, Selig announced an agreement to sell the Brewers to Mark L. Attanasio, an investment officer with Trust Company of the West (TCW). The sale to Attanasio was approved in early 2005, ending 35 years of Selig ownership.

Don Mincher, of the short-lived, low-flying Seattle Pilots.

When the Brewers hitters set a major league record for strikeouts in a season with 1,399 in 2001, they actually had more whiffs than hits (1,378).

On the field, the poor play that had begun in Seattle continued. Playing in County Stadium, the Braves' old ballpark, the Brewers exceeded 69 victories only twice in their first nine seasons. Then, out of nowhere, they won 93 games in 1978, a 26-game improvement from the year before, and finished third in the division. In 1979 the Brewers improved again, winning 95 games and finishing with the second-best record in the American League. Unfortunately, Milwaukee now shared a division with Baltimore, which won 102 games and the AL East division title. Had the Brewers still been in the AL West (they shifted to the East before the 1972 season), they would have won their division and been in the playoffs for the first time in their history. That distinction had to wait until 1981, when the "Brew Crew," led by pitcher Pete Vukovich's league-leading 14 wins, won the second-half title in the strike-shortened, split-season format used by the major leagues for that one year. The Brewers lost the Division Series to the Yankees, three games to two.

The Brewers had their best season in franchise history in 1982, when they won 95 games and the East Division title in a terrific finish. Milwaukee went to Baltimore for four games on the season's final weekend with a three-game lead over the Orioles, needing only one win to clinch the title. The Orioles, however, took the first three games in resounding fashion (8–3, 7–1, and 11–3), leaving the two teams in a dead tie with one game to go. Future Hall of Famers Jim Palmer of the Orioles and Don Sutton of the Brewers, whom the team had just picked up from the Astros on August 30 as insurance, squared off to settle the matter. Robin Yount homered off Baltimore's ace in the first inning, and then again in the third, setting the tone for the Brewers' 10–2 rout. In the ALCS against the Angels, Milwaukee trailed two games to none in the five-game series, but stormed back to win three straight, becoming the first playoff team in history to do so. The Brewers led the Cardinals, three games to two in the 1982 World Series, before St. Louis came back to win the last two games at home to take the Series, four games to three. The Brewers have yet to make another playoff appearance.

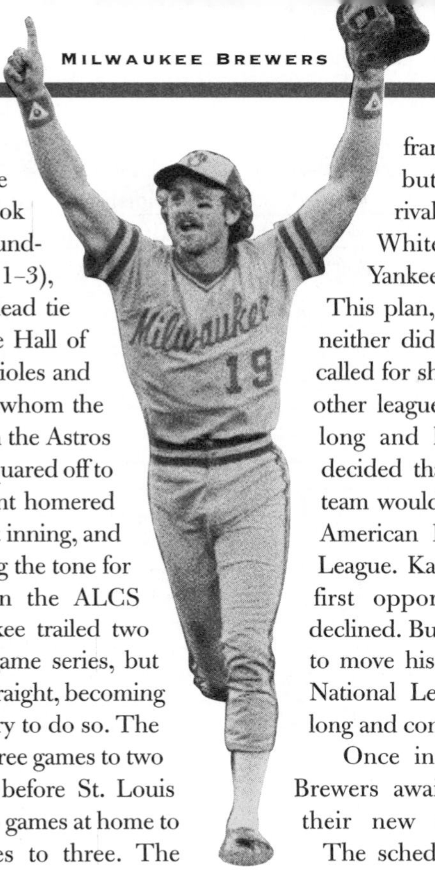

Robin Yount celebrating the Brewers' American League championship in 1982

The franchise not only changed cities (in 1970) and divisions (in 1972 and again in 1994, when they moved to the American League Central), but also leagues in 1998—the first time such a shift had happened in the 20th century. The decision to move Milwaukee to the National League's Central Division ended months of bickering among major league baseball's owners. With the addition of Arizona to the National and Tampa Bay to the American, the major leagues now had 30 teams. If the leagues remained equal, with 15 teams each, one team in each league would have to sit idle each day of the season, and likely for two or three games at a stretch while everyone else played their traditional series. To rectify the matter, the two leagues each would have to have an even number of teams—16 in one, 14 in the other. The owners discussed various options, including one scheme that would require 14 different franchises to switch leagues, but permitting regional rivals such as the Cubs and White Sox, and Mets and Yankees, to share a division. This plan, however, didn't fly, and neither did a similar proposal that called for shifting seven teams to the other league. Eventually, after many long and bitter meetings, it was decided that only one Midwestern team would need to move from the American League to the National League. Kansas City was given the first opportunity to switch, but declined. Bud Selig then volunteered to move his Milwaukee team to the National League, thereby ending a long and contentious battle.

Once in their new league, the Brewers awaited the completion of their new stadium, Miller Park. The scheduled 2000 opening was delayed due to a tragic accident that occurred during stadium construction when a large crane fell over, killing three ironworkers and causing much damage. Miller Park finally opened in 2001, a year later than originally scheduled.

TEAM NAME HISTORY

Official Names

Pilots (1969, while in Seattle)
Brewers (1970–current)

Unofficial Names/Nicknames

Brew Crew, Harvey's Wallbangers (1982–83)

STADIUM HISTORY

Sick's Stadium (Seattle)	1969
County Stadium	1970–2000
Miller Park	2001–current

YEARLY RECORD, FINISH, & ATTENDANCE FIGURES

Year	League	Record	DIV/LG Finish	Attendance	Avg/Gm
2005	NL Cent	81–81	3	2,211,023	27,297
2004	NL Cent	67–94	6	2,062,382	25,462
2003	NL Cent	68–94	6	1,700,354	20,992
2002	NL Cent	56–106	6	1,969,153	24,311
2001	NL Cent	68–94	4	2,811,041	34,704
2000	NL Cent	73–89	3	1,573,621	19,427
1999	NL Cent	74–87	5	1,701,796	21,272
1998	NL Cent	74–88	5	1,811,593	22,365
1997	AL Cent	78–83	3	1,444,027	18,050
1996	AL Cent	80–82	3	1,327,155	16,385
1995	AL Cent	65–79	4	1,087,560	15,105
1994	AL Cent	53–62	5	1,268,399	22,650
1993	AL East	69–93	7	1,688,080	20,840
1992	AL East	92–70	2	1,857,351	22,930
1991	AL East	83–79	4	1,478,729	18,484
1990	AL East	74–88	6	1,752,900	21,641
1989	AL East	81–81	4	1,970,735	24,330
1988	AL East	87–75	4	1,923,238	23,744
1987	AL East	91–71	3	1,909,244	23,571
1986	AL East	77–84	6	1,265,041	15,813
1985	AL East	71–90	6	1,360,265	17,003
1984	AL East	67–94	7	1,608,509	19,858
1983	AL East	87–75	5	2,397,131	29,594
1982	AL East	95–67	1	1,978,896	24,133
1981	AL East	62–47	3/1	874,292	17,843
1980	AL East	86–76	3	1,857,408	22,651
1979	AL East	95–66	2	1,918,343	23,683
1978	AL East	93–69	3	1,601,406	19,770
1977	AL East	67–95	6	1,114,938	13,765
1976	AL East	66–95	6	1,012,164	12,496
1975	AL East	68–94	5	1,213,357	14,980
1974	AL East	76–86	5	955,741	11,799
1973	AL East	74–88	5	1,092,158	13,483
1972	AL East	65–91	6	600,440	7,601
1971	AL West	69–92	6	731,531	8,921
1970	AL West	65–97	4	933,690	11,527
1969	AL West	64–98	6	677,944	8,268

MANAGER HISTORY

Manager	Years	W–L	Win %
Joe Schultz	1969	64–98	.395
Dave Bristol	1970–1972	144–209	.408
Del Crandall	1972–1975	271–338	.445
Alex Grammas	1976–1977	133–190	.418
George Bamberger	1978–1980, 1985–1986	377–351	.518
Buck Rodgers	1980–1982	124–102	.549
Harvey Kuenn	1982–1983	160–118	.576

Manager History (cont.)

Manager	Years	W–L	Win %
Rene Lachemann	1984	67–94	.416
Tom Trebelhorn	1986–1991	422–397	.515
Phil Garner	1992–1999	563–617	.477
Jim Lefebvre	1999	22–27	.449
Davey Lopes	2000–2002	144–195	.425
Jerry Royster	2002	53–94	.361
Ned Yost	2003–2005	216–267	.447

All-Time Win-Loss Records vs. All Opponents

ALL-TIME	2,761–3,100
Angels	169–182
Astros	47–79
Athletics	159–189
Blue Jays	155–115
Braves	18–37
Cardinals	45–74
Cubs	61–62
Devil Rays	1–2
Diamondbacks	27–30
Dodgers	18–37
Giants	24–37
Indians	199–201
INTERLEAGUE	58–66
Mariners	117–113
Marlins	29–30
Mets	20–38
Nationals	30–29
Orioles	162–227
Padres	24–33
Phillies	23–35
Pirates	58–67
Rangers	181–152
Reds	63–63
Red Sox	184–213
Rockies	29–30
Royals	169–203
Tigers	194–215
Twins	197–202
White Sox	173–197
Yankees	182–208

Dan Plesac

Franchise Highlights, Low Points, and Strange Distinctions

1970 The Brewers' franchise shift from Seattle came only four days before the season. Milwaukee fans were so excited about the return of major league baseball that 37,237 people poured into County Stadium for Opening Day against the Angels. One particularly exuberant fan, Milt Mason, dubbed "Bernie Brewer" by the locals, vowed to climb to the top of the scoreboard on July 6 and stay there until 40,000 people attended a game. After nearly six weeks, he got his wish on Bat Day (August 16), when a crowd of 44,387 showed up.

• • • •

1971 In a remarkable turn of pitching fortunes, the Milwaukee staff hurled 23 shutouts, just a year after collecting only two. And the team needed every shutout it could muster because the hitters compiled a measly .229 batting average, lowest in the majors. This led to a whopping 60 one-run games, 35 of which Milwaukee lost.

• • • •

1972 The Brewers moved from the West Division to the East Division for the season. On the one hand, it was a timely move, since Milwaukee failed to win even one season series against the West Division all year. On the other hand, it didn't matter much because the Brewers ended up in last place in the East, the team's third last-place finish in its first four years in the league.

1976 All-time home run leader Hank Aaron, got an infield hit in his final at-bat of Milwaukee's final game of the season—the very last at-bat of his career. When manager Alex Grammas pulled him from the game, giving fans a chance to cheer him one last time, the moody Aaron was miffed. Why? He wanted to score one more run, since he was tied at 2,174 with . . . Babe Ruth.

• • • •

1977 The Brewers were perennially bad in the 1970s and morale was low. In 1977, uninspired player Mike Hegan said of his manager, "Alex Grammas is a nice guy, but as manager he makes a good third-base coach." Hegan was released a few days later and Grammas was fired at the end of the season.

• • • •

1982 The Brewers won their only pennant, thanks to their hitting skills. After a sluggish 23–24 start, owner Bud Selig fired manager Buck Rodgers and replaced him with Harvey Kuenn. Kuenn told his players to just have fun. They did, going 72–43 the rest of the way and earning the nickname "Harvey's Wallbangers." Robin Yount, Cecil Cooper, and Paul Molitor finished 1–2–3 in the American League in hits. Cooper, Gorman Thomas, and Ben Oglivie each hit more than 30 homers, and the Brewers as a team smashed 216 round-trippers while scoring a prodigious 891 runs.

After 48 years of services, County Stadium bites the dust in 2001.

1987 The Brewers embarked on one of the great roller-coaster rides in baseball history. They began the season with 13 straight wins, establishing a new American League record and tying the major league record set by Atlanta in 1982. They stayed hot through April and stood at 20–3 on May 2. Then, inexplicably, they lost 12 straight games, won two, then lost six more in a row. The 2–18 stretch put them at 22–21 on May 29. They were actually below .500 at the All-Star break, going 42–43. However, they won 49 of their last 77 games and finished the season at 91–71, good for third place.

• • • •

1992 The Brewers record for consecutive pitching wins is 10, held jointly by Chris Bosio and Cal Eldred, who both set the record in 1992.

1995 Although the Brewers hit only 128 homers in 1995, 10 of them were grand slams, tying the all-time record for slams in a season.

• • • •

1996 On April 2, Milwaukee set an Opening Day record by lacing 22 hits in a 15–9 victory over the Angels.

• • • •

2004 Milwaukee's record after the All-Star break was 22–53, a winning percentage of only .293, the worst in major league history for a team with a winning record (45–41) before the All-Star break.

Special Achievements

World Series Results

Year	Opponent	Result	Games
1982	St. Louis	Lost	4–3

World Series Managerial Records

Manager	Series Record	Games Record
Harvey Kuenn	0–1	3–4

All-Time Postseason Record

Divisional Playoffs	2–3
League Championship Series	3–2
World Series	3–4

All-Star Games at Milwaukee

Year	Date	Winner	Score	Stadium
1975	July 15	National	6–3	County Stadium
2002	July 9	(Tie)	7–7	Miller Park

Hall of Famers Who Played for Team

	Position	Years	Games with Milwaukee
Hank Aaron	DH	1975–1976	222
Rollie Fingers	RP	1981–1982, 1984–1985	177
Paul Molitor	3B/DH/ 2B/OF	1978–1992	1,856
Don Sutton	SP	1982–1984	71
Robin Yount	SS/OF/ DH	1974–1993	2,856

Hall of Famers Who Managed Team

None

MVP Award Winners

Rollie Fingers	RP	1981
Robin Yount	SS	1982
Robin Yount	OF	1989

Cy Young Award Winners

Pitcher	Year	W–L	SV	ERA
Rollie Fingers	1981	6–3	28	1.04
Pete Vuckovich	1982	18–6	0	3.34

Rookie of the Year Award Winners

Pat Listach	SS	1992

Gold Glove Winners

Year	Position	Player
1972	1B	George Scott
1973	1B	George Scott
1974	1B	George Scott
1975	1B	George Scott
1976	1B	George Scott
1979	1B OF	Cecil Cooper Sixto Lezcano
1980	1B	Cecil Cooper
1982	SS	Robin Yount

Triple Crown Winners

None

Fireman of the Year Award Winners

Ken Sanders	1971
Rollie Fingers	1981

World Series MVP

None

League Championship Series MVP

None

All-Star Game MVP

None

Manager of the Year Award Winners

None

Batting Champions

None

Nine-Inning No-Hitters Pitched

Year	Pitcher	Opp.	Score
1987	Juan Nieves	BAL	7–0

20-Game Winners

Year	Pitcher	W–L
1973	Jim Colborn	20–12
1978	Mike Caldwell	22–9
1986	Teddy Higuera	20–11

RETIRED UNIFORM NUMBERS

Number	Player	Position
4	Paul Molitor	DH/3B
19	Robin Yount	SS/OF
34	Rollie Fingers	RP
44	Hank Aaron	OF

TEAM RECORDS—WINS & LOSSES

- Games won in a season: 95 in 1979 and 1982
- Games lost in a season: 106 in 2002
- Games won in a month: 21 in June 1978
- Games lost in a month: 23 in August 1977
- Consecutive games won: 13 in 1987
- Consecutive games lost: 14 in 1994
- Biggest shutout victory: 18–0 over Boston on April 16, 1990
- Biggest shutout loss: 17–0 to Cincinnati on August 7, 1998
- Highest winning percentage: .590 in 1979 (95–66)
- Lowest winning percentage: .346 in 2002 (56–106)

TEAM RECORDS—BATTING

- Highest team batting average: .280 in 1979
- Lowest team batting average: .229 in 1971
- Highest team slugging average: .455 in 1982
- Highest on-base team percentage: .353 in 1996 and 1999
- Total hits: 1,599 in 1982
- Extra-base hits: 537 in 1980
- Hits in a game: 31 vs. Toronto on August 28, 1992
- Longest individual hitting streak: 39, Paul Molitor, 1987
- Most .300 hitters in a single season: 3, accomplished five times: 1979, 1980, 1982, 1983, 1986
- Home runs: 216 in 1982
- Home runs in a month: 12, Gorman Thomas, August 1979; Greg Vaughn, June 1996; Jeromy Burnitz, June 1999
- Home runs in a game: 7 vs. Cleveland on April 29, 1980
- Home runs by a rookie: 17, Danny Walton, 1970; Greg Vaughn, 1990
- Home runs by a right-hander: 45, Gorman Thomas, 1979; Richie Sexson, 2001; Richie Sexson, 2003
- Home runs by a left-hander: 41, Ben Oglivie, 1980
- Home runs by a switch-hitter: 25, Dale Sveum, 1987
- Grand slams: 10 in 1995
- Grand slams (individual; season): 3, John Jaha, 1995; Devon White, 2001; John Vander Wal, 2003
- Grand slams (individual; career): 5, Cecil Cooper; John Jaha; Jeromy Burnitz
- Triples: 57 in 1983
- Doubles: 327 in 2005
- Singles: 1,107 in 1991
- Walks: 658 in 1999
- Runs scored: 894 in 1996
- Runs scored in a game: 22 vs. Toronto on August 28, 1992
- Runs scored in an inning: 13 vs. Angels on July 8, 1990 (fifth)
- Most batters hit by a pitch: 73 in 2005
- Times shut out: 20 in 1972
- Grounded into double plays: 158 in 2003
- Fewest grounded into double plays: 94 in 1978
- Runners left on base: 1,276 in 1999

TEAM RECORDS—BASERUNNING

- Stolen bases: 256 in 1992
- Caught stealing: 115 in 1992

TEAM RECORDS—PITCHING

- Lowest earned run average: 3.38 in 1971
- Complete games: 62 in 1978
- Saves: 51 in 1988
- Strikeouts: 1,173 in 2005
- Shutouts: 23 in 1971
- Walks: 728 in 2000
- Hit batsmen: 72 in 2001
- Wild pitches: 66 in 2005
- Consecutive wins (individual): 10, Chris Bosio, 1992; Cal Eldred, 1992
- Consecutive losses (individual): 10, Danny Darwin in 1985
- Strikeouts in a game (individual): 18, Ben Sheets, May 16, 2004
- Runs allowed in a game: 20 vs. Boston, September 6, 1975, and vs. Chicago White Sox, May 15, 1996

TEAM RECORDS—FIELDING

- Best fielding average: .986 in 1992
- Most errors committed: 180 in 1975
- Fewest errors committed: 89 in 1992
- Most double plays turned: 192 in 1998
- Fewest double plays turned: 132 in 2004

TEAM RECORDS—MISCELLANEOUS

- Number of times league champions: 1
- Number of times finishing last in league: 2
- Largest attendance, single game: 56,354 vs. Cincinnati, September 28, 2000
- Largest attendance, doubleheader: 54,630 vs. Detroit, July 6, 1979
- Players used in a season: 49 in 2002
- Seasons played: 20, Robin Yount

PRIMARY PITCHING STAFFS

Year	Starter	Starter	Starter	Starter	Starter	Closer	Bullpen	Bullpen	Bullpen
2005	Davis	Capuano	Santos	Sheets	Ohka	Turnbow	Wise	Santana	Bottalico
2004	Sheets	Davis	Santos	Obermueller	Capuano	Kolb	Vizcaino	Bennett	Adams
2003	Sheets	Franklin	Kinney	Obermueller	Rusch	Kolb	Vizcaino	DeJean	Estrella
2002	Sheets	Quevedo	Wright	Neugebauer	Rusch	DeJean	Vizcaino	King	del. Santos
2001	Sheets	Haynes	Wright	Levrault	Rigdon	Leskanic	DeJean	King	Fox
2000	D'Amico	Haynes	Wright	Snyder	Bere	Wickman	Leskanic	Weathers	del. Santos
1999	Karl	Woodard	Nomo	Pulsipher	Abbott	Wickman	Myers	Weathers	Plunk
1998	Karl	Woodard	Juden	Eldred	Woodall	Wickman	Myers	Reyes	Fox
1997	Karl	Mercedes	D'Amico	Eldred	McDonald	Jones	Wickman	Fetters	Villone
1996	Karl	Bones	D'Amico	Eldred	McDonald	Fetters	Lloyd	Miranda	Garcia
1995	Karl	Bones	Sparks	Givens	Scanlan	Fetters	Lloyd	Wegman	Rightnowar
1994	Eldred	Bones	Wegman	Higuera	Scanlan	Fetters	Lloyd	Orosco	Navarro
1993	Eldred	Bones	Wegman	Navarro	Miranda	Henry	Lloyd	Orosco	Fetters
1992	Eldred	Bones	Wegman	Navarro	Bosio	Henry	Austin	Orosco	Fetters
1991	August	Brown	Wegman	Navarro	Bosio	Henry	Crim	Lee	Machado
1990	Higuera	Knudson	Robinson	Navarro	Bosio	Plesac	Crim	Mirabella	Edens
1989	Higuera	August	Filer	Navarro	Bosio	Plesac	Crim	Fossas	Knudson
1988	Higuera	August	Wegman	Birkbeck	Bosio	Plesac	Crim	Mirabella	Jones
1987	Higuera	Nieves	Wegman	Barker	Bosio	Plesac	Crim	Clear	Aldrich
1986	Higuera	Nieves	Wegman	Leary	Darwin	Clear	Plesac	Clutterbuck	Johnson
1985	Higuera	Burris	Haas	Vuckovich	Darwin	Fingers	Gibson	McClure	Searage
1984	Sutton	Cocanower	Haas	Caldwell	McClure	Fingers	Ladd	Tellmann	Waits
1983	Sutton	Porter	Haas	Caldwell	McClure	Ladd	Slaton	Tellmann	Augustine
1982	Lerch	Vuckovich	Haas	Caldwell	McClure	Fingers	Slaton	Bernard	Easterly
1981	Lerch	Vuckovich	Haas	Caldwell	Slaton	Fingers	Cleveland	Augustine	Easterly
1980	Sorensen	Travers	Haas	Caldwell	Cleveland	McClure	Castro	Augustine	Flinn
1979	Sorensen	Travers	Haas	Caldwell	Slaton	Castro	McClure	Augustine	Galasso
1978	Sorensen	Travers	Augustine	Caldwell	Replogle	McClure	Castro	Rodriguez	Stein
1977	Sorensen	Travers	Augustine	Haas	Slaton	Castro	McClure	Rodriguez	Hinds
1976	Colborn	Travers	Augustine	Rodriguez	Slaton	Frisella	Castro	Sadecki	Broberg
1975	Colborn	Travers	Broberg	Champion	Slaton	Murphy	Rodriguez	Austin	Hausman
1974	Colborn	Wright	Kobel	Champion	Slaton	Murphy	Rodriguez	Travers	Sprague
1973	Colborn	Bell	Parsons	Lockwood	Slaton	Linzy	Rodriguez	Short	Champion
1972	Lonborg	Brett	Parsons	Lockwood	Ryerson	Sanders	Linzy	Colborn	Stephenson
1971	Pattin	Slaton	Parsons	Lockwood	Krausse	Sanders	Morris	Lopez	Hannan
1970	Pattin	Brabender	Bolin	Lockwood	Krausse	Sanders	Gelnar	Baldwin	Locker
1969	Pattin	Brabender	Talbot	Barber	Marshall	Segui	Bouton	O'Donoghue	Locker

PRIMARY STARTING LINEUPS

Year	C	1B	2B	3B	SS	LF	CF	RF	DH
2005	Miller	Overbay	Weeks	Branyan	Hardy	Lee	Clark	Jenkins	Fielder
2004	Moeller	Overbay	Spivey	Helms	Counsell	Jenkins	Podsednik	Clark	Liefer
2003	Perez	Sexson	Young	Helms	Clayton	Jenkins	Podsednik	Vander Wal	Kieschnick
2002	Bako	Sexson	Young	Houston	Hernandez	Jenkins	Sanchez	Ochoa	Harris
2001	Blanco	Sexson	Belliard	Houston	Hernandez	Jenkins	White	Burnitz	Loretta
2000	Blanco	Sexson	Belliard	Hernandez	Loretta	Jenkins	Grissom	Burnitz	Sweeney
1999	Nilsson	Loretta	Belliard	Cirillo	Valentin	Jenkins	Grissom	Burnitz	Becker
1998	Matheny	Loretta	Vina	Cirillo	Valentin	Jenkins	Grissom	Burnitz	Jaha
1997	Matheny	Nilsson	Vina	Cirillo	Valentin	Voigt	Williams	Burnitz	Franco
1996	Matheny	Jaha	Vina	Cirillo	Valentin	Vaughn	Listach	Mieske	Seitzer
1995	Oliver	Jaha	Vina	Cirillo	Valentin	Hulse	Hamilton	Mieske	Vaughn
1994	Nilsson	Jaha	Reed	Seitzer	Valentin	Vaughn	Diaz	Mieske	Harper
1993	Nilsson	Jaha	Spiers	Surhoff	Listach	Vaughn	Yount	Brunansky	Reimer
1992	Surhoff	Stubbs	Fletcher	Seitzer	Listach	Vaughn	Yount	Bichette	Molitor
1991	Surhoff	Stubbs	Randolph	Gantner	Spiers	Vaughn	Yount	Bichette	Molitor
1990	Surhoff	Brock	Gantner	Sheffield	Spiers	Vaughn	Yount	Deer	Parker
1989	Surhoff	Brock	Gantner	Molitor	Spiers	Braggs	Yount	Deer	Meyer
1988	Surhoff	Brock	Gantner	Molitor	Sveum	Leonard	Yount	Deer	Meyer
1987	Surhoff	Brock	Castillo	Riles	Sveum	Deer	Yount	Braggs	Cooper
1986	Moore	Cooper	Gantner	Molitor	Riles	Braggs	Yount	Deer	Oglivie
1985	Moore	Cooper	Gantner	Molitor	Riles	Yount	Manning	Householder	Simmons
1984	Sundberg	Cooper	Gantner	Romero	Yount	Oglivie	Manning	James	Simmons
1983	Simmons	Cooper	Gantner	Molitor	Yount	Oglivie	Manning	Moore	Howell
1982	Simmons	Cooper	Gantner	Molitor	Yount	Oglivie	Thomas	Moore	Howell
1981	Simmons	Cooper	Gantner	Money	Yount	Oglivie	Thomas	Brouhard	Hisle
1980	Moore	Cooper	Molitor	Gantner	Yount	Oglivie	Thomas	Lezcano	Davis
1979	Moore	Cooper	Molitor	Bando	Yount	Oglivie	Thomas	Lezcano	Davis
1978	Moore	Cooper	Molitor	Bando	Yount	Hisle	Thomas	Lezcano	Davis
1977	Moore	Cooper	Money	Bando	Yount	Wohlford	Joshua	Lezcano	Quirk
1976	Porter	Scott	Johnson	Money	Yount	Thomas	Joshua	Lezcano	Aaron
1975	Porter	Scott	Garcia	Money	Yount	Mitchell	Thomas	Lezcano	Aaron
1974	Porter	Scott	Garcia	Money	Yount	Briggs	Coluccio	May	Mitchell
1973	Porter	Scott	Garcia	Money	Johnson	Briggs	May	Coluccio	Brown
1972	Rodriguez	Scott	Theobald	Ferraro	Auerbach	Briggs	May	Lahoud	
1971	Rodriguez	Briggs	Theobald	Matchick	Auerbach	Harper	May	Voss	
1970	Roof	Hegan	Kubiak	Harper	Pena	Walton	May	Burda	
1969	McNertney	Mincher	Donaldson	Harper	Oyler	Davis	Comer	Hegan	

Top 10 Batting Leaders, Single Season & Career with Team

Games Played: Career with Team

Player	G	PA
1. Robin Yount	2,856	12,249
2. Paul Molitor	1,856	8,438
3. Jim Gantner	1,801	6,782
4. Cecil Cooper	1,490	6,492
5. Charlie Moore	1,283	4,357
6. Don Money	1,196	4,901
7. Ben Oglivie	1,149	4,658
8. B.J. Surhoff	1,102	4,304
Gorman Thomas	1,102	4,133
10. Geoff Jenkins	955	3,913

At-Bats: Season

Player	AB	Year
1. Paul Molitor	666	1982
2. Paul Molitor	665	1991
3. Cecil Cooper	661	1983
4. Cecil Cooper	654	1982
5. Cecil Cooper	643	1977
6. Scott Podsednik	640	2004
7. Robin Yount	638	1976
8. Fernando Viña	637	1998
9. Robin Yount	635	1982
Robin Yount	635	1987

At-Bats: Career with Team

Player	AB	PA
1. Robin Yount	11,008	12,249
2. Paul Molitor	7,520	8,438
3. Jim Gantner	6,189	6,782
4. Cecil Cooper	6,019	6,492
5. Don Money	4,330	4,901
6. Ben Oglivie	4,136	4,658
7. Charlie Moore	3,926	4,357
8. B.J. Surhoff	3,884	4,304
9. Gorman Thomas	3,544	4,133
10. Geoff Jenkins	3,503	3,913

Batting Average: Season

Player	BA	Year
1. Paul Molitor	.353	1987
2. Cecil Cooper	.352	1980
3. Dave Nilsson	.331	1996
Robin Yount	.331	1982
5. Willie Randolph	.327	1991
6. Jeff Cirillo	.326	1999
7. Jeff Cirillo	.325	1996
Paul Molitor	.325	1991
9. Paul Molitor	.322	1979
10. Sixto Lezcano	.321	1979

Batting Average: Career with Team

Player	BA	PA
1. Jeff Cirillo	.306	3,437
2. Paul Molitor	.303	8,438
3. Cecil Cooper	.302	6,492
4. Kevin Seitzer	.300	2,292
5. Darryl Hamilton	.290	2,451
6. Mark Loretta	.289	2,943
7. Fernando Viña	.286	2,187
8. Robin Yount	.285	12,249
9. Dave Nilsson	.284	3,153
10. George Scott	.283	3,320

Total Hits: Season

Player	H	Year
1. Cecil Cooper	219	1980
2. Paul Molitor	216	1991
3. Robin Yount	210	1982
4. Cecil Cooper	205	1982
5. Cecil Cooper	203	1983
6. Paul Molitor	201	1982
7. Jeff Cirillo	198	1999
Fernando Viña	198	1998
Robin Yount	198	1987
10. Paul Molitor	195	1992
Robin Yount	195	1989

Total Hits: Career with Team

Player	H	PA
1. Robin Yount	3,142	12,249
2. Paul Molitor	2,281	8,438
3. Cecil Cooper	1,815	6,492
4. Jim Gantner	1,696	6,782
5. Don Money	1,168	4,901
6. Ben Oglivie	1,144	4,658
7. B.J. Surhoff	1,064	4,304
8. Charlie Moore	1,029	4,357
9. Geoff Jenkins	983	3,913
10. Jeff Cirillo	916	3,437

Home Runs: Season

Player	HR	Year
1. Richie Sexson	45	2001
Richie Sexson	45	2003
Gorman Thomas	45	1979
4. Ben Oglivie	41	1980
5. Gorman Thomas	39	1982
6. Jeromy Burnitz	38	1998
Gorman Thomas	38	1980
8. George Scott	36	1975
9. Jeromy Burnitz	34	2001
Larry Hisle	34	1978
John Jaha	34	1996
Geoff Jenkins	34	2000
Ben Oglivie	34	1982

Home Runs: Career with Team

Player	HR	PA
1. Robin Yount	251	12,249
2. Gorman Thomas	208	4,133
3. Cecil Cooper	201	6,492
4. Ben Oglivie	176	4,658
5. Geoff Jenkins	174	3,913
6. Greg Vaughn	169	3,727
7. Jeromy Burnitz	165	3,269
8. Paul Molitor	160	8,438
9. Rob Deer	137	2,710
10. Don Money	134	4,901

Triples: Season

Player	3B	Year
1. Paul Molitor	16	1979
2. Paul Molitor	13	1991
3. Robin Yount	12	1982
4. Robin Yount	11	1988
5. Fernando Viña	10	1996
Robin Yount	10	1980
Robin Yount	10	1983
8. Ron Belliard	9	2000
Robin Yount	9	1978
Robin Yount	9	1987
Robin Yount	9	1989

Triples: Career with Team

Player	3B	PA
1. Robin Yount	126	12,249
2. Paul Molitor	86	8,438
3. Charlie Moore	42	4,357
4. Jim Gantner	38	6,782

Player		
5. Cecil Cooper	33	6,492
6. Fernando Viña	26	2,187
7. B.J. Surhoff	24	4,304
8. Sixto Lezcano	22	3,132
9. Darryl Hamilton	21	2,451
Ben Oglivie	21	4,658

DOUBLES: SEASON

Player	2B	Year
1. Lyle Overbay	53	2004
2. Robin Yount	49	1980
3. Jeff Cirillo	46	1996
Jeff Cirillo	46	1997
Robin Yount	46	1982
6. Cecil Cooper	44	1979
7. Geoff Jenkins	43	1999
8. Robin Yount	42	1983
Geoff Jenkins	42	2005
10. Paul Molitor	41	1987
Carlos Lee	41	2005

DOUBLES: CAREER WITH TEAM

Player	2B	PA
1. Robin Yount	583	12,249
2. Paul Molitor	405	8,438
3. Cecil Cooper	345	6,492
4. Jim Gantner	262	6,782
5. Geoff Jenkins	237	3,913
6. Don Money	215	4,901
7. Jeff Cirillo	201	3,437
8. Ben Oglivie	194	4,658
B.J. Surhoff	194	4,304
10. Charlie Moore	177	4,357

EXTRA-BASE HITS: SEASON

Player	XBH	Year
1. Robin Yount	87	1982
2. Robin Yount	82	1980
3. Richie Sexson	75	2003
4. Geoff Jenkins	74	2000
Gorman Thomas	74	1979
6. Cecil Cooper	73	1982
Carlos Lee	73	2005
8. Jeromy Burnitz	72	1997
Richie Sexson	72	2001
10. Jeromy Burnitz	70	2001
Cecil Cooper	70	1983
Tommy Harper	70	1970
Lyle Overbay	70	2004

EXTRA-BASE HITS: CAREER WITH TEAM

Player	XBH	PA
1. Robin Yount	960	12,249
2. Paul Molitor	651	8,438
3. Cecil Cooper	579	6,492
4. Geoff Jenkins	430	3,913
5. Gorman Thomas	392	4,133
6. Ben Oglivie	391	4,658
7. Don Money	369	4,901
8. Jim Gantner	347	6,782
9. Jeromy Burnitz	345	3,269
10. Greg Vaughn	340	3,727

TOTAL BASES: SEASON

Player	TB	Year
1. Robin Yount	367	1982
2. Cecil Cooper	345	1982
3. Cecil Cooper	336	1983
4. Cecil Cooper	335	1980
5. Ben Oglivie	333	1980
6. Richie Sexson	332	2003
7. Richie Sexson	327	2001
8. Paul Molitor	325	1991
9. George Scott	318	1975
10. Robin Yount	317	1980

TOTAL BASES: CAREER WITH TEAM

Player	TB	PA
1. Robin Yount	4,730	12,249
2. Paul Molitor	3,338	8,438
3. Cecil Cooper	2,829	6,492
4. Jim Gantner	2,175	6,782
5. Ben Oglivie	1,908	4,658
6. Don Money	1,825	4,901
7. Geoff Jenkins	1,780	3,913
8. Gorman Thomas	1,635	4,133
9. Greg Vaughn	1,490	3,727
10. B.J. Surhoff	1,477	4,304

RUNS BATTED IN: SEASON

Player	RBI	Year
1. Cecil Cooper	126	1983
2. Jeromy Burnitz	125	1998
Richie Sexson	125	2001
4. Richie Sexson	124	2003
5. Gorman Thomas	123	1979
6. Cecil Cooper	122	1980
7. Cecil Cooper	121	1982
8. John Jaha	118	1996
Ben Oglivie	118	1980
10. Larry Hisle	115	1978

RUNS BATTED IN: CAREER WITH TEAM

Player	RBI	PA
1. Robin Yount	1,406	12,249
2. Cecil Cooper	944	6,492
3. Paul Molitor	790	8,438
4. Ben Oglivie	685	4,658
5. Gorman Thomas	605	4,133
6. Geoff Jenkins	570	3,913
7. Jim Gantner	568	6,782
8. Greg Vaughn	566	3,727
9. Don Money	529	4,901
10. Jeromy Burnitz	525	3,269

RUNS SCORED: SEASON

Player	R	Year
1. Paul Molitor	136	1982
2. Paul Molitor	133	1991
3. Robin Yount	129	1982
4. Robin Yount	121	1980
5. Paul Molitor	115	1988
6. Paul Molitor	114	1987
7. John Jaha	108	1996
8. Cecil Cooper	106	1983
9. Robin Yount	105	1984
10. Jeromy Burnitz	104	2001
Cecil Cooper	104	1982
Tommy Harper	104	1970

RUNS SCORED: CAREER WITH TEAM

Player	R	PA
1. Robin Yount	1,632	12,249
2. Paul Molitor	1,275	8,438
3. Cecil Cooper	821	6,492
4. Jim Gantner	726	6,782
5. Don Money	596	4,901
6. Ben Oglivie	567	4,658
7. Geoff Jenkins	554	3,913
8. Greg Vaughn	528	3,727
9. Gorman Thomas	524	4,133
10. Jeff Cirillo	473	3,437

WALKS: SEASON

Player	BB	Year
1. Jeromy Burnitz	99	2000
2. Richie Sexson	98	2003
Gorman Thomas	98	1979
4. Tommy Harper	95	1969
5. Jeromy Burnitz	91	1999
6. Darrell Porter	89	1975
Greg Vaughn	89	1993
8. Johnny Briggs	87	1973
9. Rob Deer	86	1987
10. John Jaha	85	1996

WALKS: CAREER WITH TEAM

Player	BB	PA
1. Robin Yount	966	12,249
2. Paul Molitor	755	8,438

3. Gorman Thomas	501	4,133
4. Don Money	440	4,901
5. Ben Oglivie	432	4,658
6. Jeromy Burnitz	423	3,269
7. Greg Vaughn	421	3,727
8. Jim Gantner	383	6,782
9. Cecil Cooper	367	6,492
10. Jeff Cirillo	353	3,437

Strikeouts: Season

Player	SO	Year
1. Jose Hernandez	188	2002
2. Rob Deer	186	1987
3. Jose Hernandez	185	2001
4. Rob Deer	179	1986
5. Richie Sexson	178	2001
6. Gorman Thomas	175	1979
7. Gorman Thomas	170	1980
8. Jeromy Burnitz	158	1998
Rob Deer	158	1989
10. Rob Deer	153	1988

Strikeouts: Career with Team

Player	SO	PA
1. Robin Yount	1,350	12,249
2. Gorman Thomas	1,033	4,133
3. Paul Molitor	882	8,438
4. Geoff Jenkins	873	3,913
5. Rob Deer	823	2,710
6. Greg Vaughn	761	3,727
7. Cecil Cooper	721	6,492
8. Jeromy Burnitz	680	3,269
9. Jose Valentin	585	2,768
10. Don Money	539	4,901

Slugging Percentage: Season

Player	SLG	Year
1. Geoff Jenkins	.588	2000
2. Robin Yount	.578	1982
3. Sixto Lezcano	.573	1979
4. Greg Vaughn	.571	1996
5. Paul Molitor	.566	1987
6. Geoff Jenkins	.564	1999
7. Ben Oglivie	.562	1980
8. Jeromy Burnitz	.561	1999
9. Dave Nilsson	.554	1999
10. Jeromy Burnitz	.553	1997

Slugging Percentage: Career with Team

Player	SLG	PA
1. Richie Sexson	.536	2,288
2. Jeromy Burnitz	.508	3,269
Geoff Jenkins	.508	3,913
4. Cecil Cooper	.470	6,492
5. John Jaha	.463	2,530
6. Gorman Thomas	.461	4,133
Ben Oglivie	.461	4,658
Dave Nilsson	.461	3,153
9. Greg Vaughn	.459	3,727
10. George Scott	.456	3,320

On-Base Percentage: Season

Player	OBP	Year
1. Paul Molitor	.438	1987
2. Willie Randolph	.424	1991
3. Sixto Lezcano	.414	1979
4. Dave Nilsson	.407	1996
5. Kevin Seitzer	.406	1996
6. Alex Ochoa	.404	1999
7. Ted Savage	.402	1970
Jeff Cirillo	.402	1998
Jeromy Burnitz	.402	1999
10. Jeff Cirillo	.401	1999

On-Base Percentage: Career with Team

Player	OBP	PA
1. Jeff Cirillo	.384	3,437
2. Kevin Seitzer	.376	2,292
3. Paul Molitor	.367	8,438
4. Richie Sexson	.366	2,288
5. Jeromy Burnitz	.362	3,269
6. John Jaha	.361	2,530
7. Johnny Briggs	.358	2,237
8. Dave Nilsson	.356	3,153
9. Mark Loretta	.355	2,943
10. Sixto Lezcano	.354	3,132

OPS (On-Base Percentage + Slugging Percentage): Season

Player	OPS	Year
1. Paul Molitor	1.003	1987
2. Sixto Lezcano	.987	1979
3. Jeromy Burnitz	.963	1999
4. Robin Yount	.957	1982
5. Dave Nilsson	.954	1999
6. Greg Vaughn	.948	1996
Geoff Jenkins	.948	2000
8. John Jaha	.941	1996
9. Geoff Jenkins	.935	1999
10. Jeromy Burnitz	.934	1997

OPS (On-Base Percentage + Slugging Percentage): Career with Team

Player	OPS	PA
1. Richie Sexson	.902	2,288
2. Jeromy Burnitz	.870	3,269
3. Geoff Jenkins	.857	3,913
4. Jeff Cirillo	.835	3,437
5. John Jaha	.824	2,530
6. Dave Nilsson	.817	3,153
7. Paul Molitor	.811	8,438
8. Cecil Cooper	.809	6,492
9. Ben Oglivie	.806	4,658
10. Sixto Lezcano	.805	3,132

Stolen Bases: Season

Player	SB	Year
1. Tommy Harper	73	1969
2. Scott Podsednik	70	2004
3. Pat Listach	54	1992
4. Paul Molitor	45	1987
5. Scott Podsednik	43	2003
6. Darryl Hamilton	41	1992
Paul Molitor	41	1982
Paul Molitor	41	1983
Paul Molitor	41	1988
10. Tommy Harper	38	1970

Stolen Bases: Career with Team

Player	SB	PA
1. Paul Molitor	412	8,438
2. Robin Yount	271	12,249
3. Jim Gantner	137	6,782
4. Tommy Harper	136	1,985
5. Scott Podsednik	113	1,340
6. Pat Listach	112	1,840
7. Darryl Hamilton	109	2,451
8. Mike Felder	108	1,266
9. B.J. Surhoff	102	4,304
10. Jose Valentin	78	2,768

Sacrifice Hits: Season

Player	Sac	Year
1. Ron Theobald	19	1971
2. Jim Gantner	18	1988
3. Juan Castillo	14	1987
Don Money	14	1978
Charlie Moore	14	1983
Glendon Rusch	14	2002
7. Ted Kubiak	13	1970

B.J. Surhoff	13	1991
Robin Yount	13	1978
10. Six tied with . . .	12	——

Sacrifice Hits: Career with Team

Player	Sac	PA
1. Jim Gantner	106	6,782
2. Robin Yount	104	12,249
3. Don Money	70	4,901
4. Paul Molitor	68	8,438
5. Charlie Moore	67	4,357
6. B.J. Surhoff	52	4,304
7. Mark Loretta	42	2,943
8. Gorman Thomas	36	4,133
9. Tim Johnson	33	1,220
Bill Spiers	33	1,867
Devon White	12	2001

Hit by Pitch: Season

Player	HBP	Year
1. Fernando Viña	25	1998
2. Geoff Jenkins	19	2005
3. Brady Clark	18	2005
4. Keith Ginter	17	2003
5. Jeromy Burnitz	16	1999
6. Geoff Jenkins	15	2000
7. Jeromy Burnitz	14	2000
Jeff Cirillo	14	1997
9. Fernando Viña	13	1996
10. Geoff Jenkins	12	2004

Hit by Pitch: Career with Team

Player	HBP	PA
1. Geoff Jenkins	75	3,913
2. Fernando Viña	58	2,187
3. Jim Gantner	52	6,782
4. Robin Yount	48	12,249
5. Jeromy Burnitz	46	3,269
6. Jeff Cirillo	40	3,437
7. John Jaha	38	2,530
8. Brady Clark	36	1,447
9. Paul Molitor	34	8,438
10. Mark Loretta	33	2,943

Top 10 Pitching Leaders, Single Season & Career with Team

Games Pitched: Season

Player	GP	Year
1. Ken Sanders	83	1971
2. Ray King	82	2001
3. Chuck Crim	76	1989
Ray King	76	2002
Luis Vizcaino	76	2002
6. Mike DeJean	75	2001
Doug Jones	75	1997
Luis Vizcaino	75	2003
9. Bob Wickman	74	1997
10. Curt Leskanic	73	2000
Luis Vizcaino	73	2004

Games Pitched: Career with Team

Player	GP	IP
1. Dan Plesac	365	524.3
2. Jim Slaton	364	2,025.3
3. Bob McClure	352	842.0
4. Chuck Crim	332	529.7
5. Mike Fetters	289	334.3
6. Jerry Augustine	279	944.0
7. Bob Wickman	272	315.0
8. Bill Wegman	262	1,482.7
9. Bill Castro	253	411.0
10. Moose Haas	245	1,542.0

Innings Pitched: Season

Player	IP	Year
1. Jim Colborn	314.3	1973
2. Mike Caldwell	293.3	1978
3. Jim Slaton	292.7	1976
4. Lary Sorensen	280.7	1978
5. Jim Slaton	276.3	1973
6. Marty Pattin	264.7	1971
7. Teddy Higuera	261.7	1987
Bill Wegman	261.7	1992
9. Mike Caldwell	258.0	1982
Cal Eldred	258.0	1993

Innings Pitched: Career with Team

Player	IP
1. Jim Slaton	2,025.3
2. Mike Caldwell	1,604.7
3. Moose Haas	1,542.0
4. Bill Wegman	1,482.7
5. Teddy Higuera	1,380.0
6. Chris Bosio	1,190.0
7. Jim Colborn	1,118.0
8. Cal Eldred	1,078.7
9. Bill Travers	1,068.3
10. Jaime Navarro	1,061.7

Batters Faced: Season

Player	BF	Year
1. Jim Colborn	1,287	1973
2. Jim Slaton	1,235	1976
3. Mike Caldwell	1,176	1978
4. Jim Slaton	1,170	1973
5. Lary Sorensen	1,150	1978
6. Cal Eldred	1,087	1993
7. Teddy Higuera	1,084	1987
8. Bill Wegman	1,079	1992
9. Jim Slaton	1,072	1974
10. Mike Caldwell	1,064	1982

Batters Faced: Career with Team

Player	BF	IP
1. Jim Slaton	8,668	2,025.3
2. Mike Caldwell	6,688	1,604.7
3. Moose Haas	6,457	1,542.0
4. Bill Wegman	6,254	1,482.7
5. Teddy Higuera	5,752	1,380.0
6. Chris Bosio	4,957	1,190.0
7. Cal Eldred	4,669	1,078.7
8. Jim Colborn	4,649	1,118.0
9. Jaime Navarro	4,601	1,061.7
10. Bill Travers	4,590	1,068.3

Games Started: Season

Player	GS	Year
1. Jim Slaton	38	1973
Jim Slaton	38	1976
3. Jim Colborn	36	1973
Cal Eldred	36	1993
Marty Pattin	36	1971
Lary Sorensen	36	1978
7. Eight tied with . . .	35	——

Games Started: Career with Team

Player	GS	IP
1. Jim Slaton	268	2,025.3
2. Moose Haas	231	1,542.0

3. Mike Caldwell	217	1,604.7
4. Bill Wegman	216	1,482.7
5. Teddy Higuera	205	1,380.0
6. Cal Eldred	169	1,078.7
7. Chris Bosio	163	1,190.0
8. Bill Travers	157	1,068.3
9. Jaime Navarro	156	1,061.7
10. Ben Sheets	149	982.3

Complete Games: Season

Player	CG	Year
1. Mike Caldwell	23	1978
2. Jim Colborn	22	1973
3. Lary Sorensen	17	1978
4. Mike Caldwell	16	1979
Lary Sorensen	16	1979
6. Teddy Higuera	15	1986
Bill Travers	15	1976
Clyde Wright	15	1974
9. Moose Haas	14	1980
Teddy Higuera	14	1987

Complete Games: Career with Team

Player	CG	IP
1. Mike Caldwell	81	1,604.7
2. Jim Slaton	69	2,025.3
3. Moose Haas	55	1,542.0
4. Jim Colborn	51	1,118.0
5. Teddy Higuera	50	1,380.0
Lary Sorensen	50	854.0
7. Bill Travers	46	1,068.3
8. Bill Wegman	33	1,482.7
9. Chris Bosio	32	1,190.0
10. Jerry Augustine	27	944.0

Games Won: Season

Player	W	Year
1. Mike Caldwell	22	1978
2. Jim Colborn	20	1973
Teddy Higuera	20	1986
4. Teddy Higuera	18	1987
Lary Sorensen	18	1978
Pete Vuckovich	18	1982
Chris Capuano	18	2005
8. Mike Caldwell	17	1982
Jaime Navarro	17	1992
10. Chris Bosio	16	1992
Mike Caldwell	16	1979
Cal Eldred	16	1993
Moose Haas	16	1980
Teddy Higuera	16	1988

Games Won: Career with Team

Player	W	IP
1. Jim Slaton	117	2,025.3
2. Mike Caldwell	102	1,604.7
3. Teddy Higuera	94	1,380.0
4. Moose Haas	91	1,542.0
5. Bill Wegman	81	1,482.7
6. Chris Bosio	67	1,190.0
7. Bill Travers	65	1,068.3
8. Cal Eldred	64	1,078.7
9. Jaime Navarro	62	1,061.7
10. Jim Colborn	57	1,118.0

Games Lost: Season

Player	L	Year
1. Clyde Wright	20	1974
2. Jerry Augustine	18	1977
Danny Darwin	18	1985
Lew Krausse	18	1970
Jim Slaton	18	1975
6. Jimmy Haynes	17	2001
Bill Parsons	17	1971
8. Pete Broberg	16	1975
Jaime Cocanower	16	1984
Cal Eldred	16	1993
Glendon Rusch	16	2002
Ben Sheets	16	2002
Jim Slaton	16	1974
Bill Travers	16	1976

Games Lost: Career with Team

Player	L	IP
1. Jim Slaton	121	2,025.3
2. Bill Wegman	90	1,482.7
3. Mike Caldwell	80	1,604.7
4. Moose Haas	79	1,542.0
5. Bill Travers	67	1,068.3
6. Cal Eldred	65	1,078.7
7. Teddy Higuera	64	1,380.0
Jaime Navarro	64	1,061.7
9. Chris Bosio	62	1,190.0
Ben Sheets	62	982.3

Winning Percentage: Season

Player	W%	Year
1. Moose Haas	.812	1983
2. Pete Vuckovich	.778	1981
3. Pete Vuckovich	.750	1982
4. Chris Bosio	.727	1992
Mike Caldwell	.727	1979
6. Mike Caldwell	.710	1978
7. Ron Robinson	.706	1990
8. Jim Slaton	.700	1983
9. Bill Wegman	.682	1991
10. Diego Segui	.667	1969
Bill Travers	.667	1980

Winning Percentage: Career with Team

Player	W%	IP
1. Teddy Higuera	.595	1,380.0
2. Mike Caldwell	.560	1,604.7
3. Moose Haas	.535	1,542.0
4. Lary Sorensen	.531	854.0
5. Chris Bosio	.519	1,190.0
6. Bob McClure	.511	842.0
7. Cal Eldred	.496	1,078.7
8. Scott Karl	.495	914.7
9. Bill Travers	.492	1,068.3
Jaime Navarro	.492	1,061.7

Shutouts: Season

Player	SHO	Year
1. Mike Caldwell	6	1978
2. Marty Pattin	5	1971
3. Mike Caldwell	4	1979
Jim Colborn	4	1973
Teddy Higuera	4	1986
Bill Parsons	4	1971
Jim Slaton	4	1971
8. 13 tied with . . .	3	——

Shutouts: Career with Team

Player	SHO	IP
1. Jim Slaton	19	2,025.3
2. Mike Caldwell	18	1,604.7
3. Teddy Higuera	12	1,380.0
4. Bill Travers	10	1,068.3
5. Chris Bosio	8	1,190.0
Moose Haas	8	1,542.0
7. Jim Colborn	7	1,118.0
Lary Sorensen	7	854.0
9. Jerry Augustine	6	944.0
Jaime Navarro	6	1,061.7
Bill Parsons	6	518.3
Marty Pattin	6	656.7

ERA: Season

Player	ERA	Year
1. Mike Caldwell	2.36	1978
2. Teddy Higuera	2.45	1988
3. Jeff D'Amico	2.66	2000
4. Ben Sheets	2.70	2004
5. Teddy Higuera	2.79	1986

6. Bill Travers	2.81	1976
7. Jim Lonborg	2.83	1972
8. Bill Wegman	2.84	1991
9. Lew Krausse	2.94	1971
10. Chris Bosio	2.95	1989

ERA: Career with Team

Player	ERA	IP
1. Dan Plesac	3.21	524.3
2. Chuck Crim	3.47	529.7
3. Teddy Higuera	3.61	1,380.0
4. Jim Colborn	3.65	1,118.0
5. Lary Sorensen	3.72	854.0
6. Mike Caldwell	3.74	1,604.7
7. Skip Lockwood	3.75	729.3
8. Chris Bosio	3.76	1,190.0
9. Eduardo Rodriguez	3.78	659.7
10. Marty Pattin	3.82	656.7

Earned Runs Allowed: Season

Player	ER	Year
1. Jaime Navarro	127	1993
2. Wayne Franklin	119	2003
3. Jimmy Haynes	118	2000
4. Mike Caldwell	115	1983
Cal Eldred	115	1993
6. Lew Krausse	114	1970
Jim Slaton	114	1973
Clyde Wright	114	1974
9. Bill Wegman	113	1986
10. Five tied with . . .	112	——

Earned Runs Allowed: Career with Team

Player	ER	IP
1. Jim Slaton	869	2,025.3
2. Moose Haas	690	1,542.0
3. Bill Wegman	685	1,482.7
4. Mike Caldwell	667	1,604.7
5. Teddy Higuera	554	1,380.0
6. Cal Eldred	541	1,078.7
7. Jaime Navarro	524	1,061.7
8. Chris Bosio	497	1,190.0
9. Bill Travers	474	1,068.3
10. Scott Karl	464	914.7

Strikeouts: Season

Player	K	Year
1. Ben Sheets	264	2004
2. Teddy Higuera	240	1987
3. Doug Davis	208	2005
4. Teddy Higuera	207	1986
5. Teddy Higuera	192	1988
6. Cal Eldred	180	1993
7. Chris Capuano	176	2005
8. Chris Bosio	173	1989
9. Ben Sheets	170	2002
10. Marty Pattin	169	1971

Strikeouts: Career with Team

Player	K	IP
1. Teddy Higuera	1,081	1,380.0
2. Jim Slaton	929	2,025.3
3. Ben Sheets	826	982.3
4. Moose Haas	800	1,542.0
5. Chris Bosio	749	1,190.0
6. Bill Wegman	696	1,482.7
7. Cal Eldred	686	1,078.7
8. Mike Caldwell	540	1,604.7
9. Jaime Navarro	531	1,061.7
10. Bob McClure	497	842.0

Strikeouts Per Nine IP: Season

Player	K/9	Year
1. Ben Sheets	10.03	2004
2. Doug Davis	8.41	2005
3. Teddy Higuera	8.25	1987
4. Hideo Nomo	8.22	1999
5. Chris Bosio	7.94	1987
6. Teddy Higuera	7.60	1988
7. Teddy Higuera	7.50	1986
Juan Nieves	7.50	1987
9. Steve Woodard	7.33	1998
10. Chris Capuano	7.23	2005

Strikeouts Per Nine IP: Career with Team

Player	K/9	IP
1. Dan Plesac	7.69	524.3
2. Ben Sheets	7.57	982.3
3. Teddy Higuera	7.05	1,380.0
4. Marty Pattin	6.25	656.7
5. Cal Eldred	5.72	1,078.7
6. Chris Bosio	5.66	1,190.0
7. Eduardo Rodriguez	5.51	659.7
8. Bob McClure	5.31	842.0
9. Skip Lockwood	5.07	729.3
10. Bill Parsons	4.86	518.3

Hits Allowed: Season

Player	HA	Year
1. Jim Colborn	297	1973
2. Jim Slaton	287	1976
3. Lary Sorensen	277	1978
4. Mike Caldwell	269	1982
Mike Caldwell	269	1983
6. Jim Slaton	266	1973
7. Clyde Wright	264	1974
8. Mike Caldwell	258	1978
9. Jim Slaton	255	1974
10. Jaime Navarro	254	1993

Hits Allowed: Career with Team

Player	HA	IP
1. Jim Slaton	2,054	2,025.3
2. Mike Caldwell	1,708	1,604.7
3. Moose Haas	1,602	1,542.0
4. Bill Wegman	1,567	1,482.7
5. Teddy Higuera	1,262	1,380.0
6. Chris Bosio	1,184	1,190.0
7. Jaime Navarro	1,159	1,061.7
8. Jim Colborn	1,109	1,118.0
9. Bill Travers	1,067	1,068.3
10. Cal Eldred	1,057	1,078.7

Hits Allowed Per Nine IP: Season

Player	H/9	Year
1. Teddy Higuera	6.65	1988
2. Ben Sheets	7.63	2004
3. Marty Pattin	7.65	1971
4. Skip Lockwood	7.84	1972
5. Marty Pattin	7.87	1970
6. Teddy Higuera	7.88	1985
7. Bill Travers	7.91	1976
8. Mike Caldwell	7.92	1978
Doug Davis	7.92	2005
10. Jeff D'Amico	7.93	2000

Hits Allowed Per Nine IP: Career with Team

Player	H/9	IP
1. Dan Plesac	7.90	524.3
2. Marty Pattin	8.15	656.7
3. Bill Parsons	8.20	518.3
4. Eduardo Rodriguez	8.21	659.7
5. Teddy Higuera	8.23	1,380.0
6. Skip Lockwood	8.64	729.3
7. Cal Eldred	8.82	1,078.7

8. Bob McClure	8.93	842.0
Jim Colborn	8.93	1,118.0
10. Chris Bosio	8.95	1,190.0

Walks Allowed: Season

Player	BB	Year
1. Pete Broberg	106	1975
2. Gene Brabender	103	1969
3. Jim Slaton	102	1974
Pete Vuckovich	102	1982
5. Jimmy Haynes	100	2000
Juan Nieves	100	1987
7. Jim Slaton	99	1973
8. Jamey Wright	98	2001
9. Bill Travers	95	1976
10. Wayne Franklin	94	2003
Jim Slaton	94	1976

Walks Allowed: Career with Team

Player	BB	IP
1. Jim Slaton	760	2,025.3
2. Cal Eldred	448	1,078.7
3. Teddy Higuera	443	1,380.0
4. Moose Haas	408	1,542.0
5. Bill Travers	392	1,068.3
6. Bob McClure	363	842.0
7. Mike Caldwell	353	1,604.7
8. Bill Wegman	352	1,482.7
9. Jerry Augustine	340	944.0
10. Jaime Navarro	336	1,061.7

Walks Allowed Per Nine IP: Season

Player	BB/9	Year
1. Ben Sheets	1.22	2004
2. Mike Caldwell	1.49	1979
3. Lary Sorensen	1.60	1978
4. Lary Sorensen	1.61	1979
5. Mike Caldwell	1.66	1978
6. Chris Bosio	1.71	1992
7. Steve Woodard	1.75	1999
Ben Sheets	1.75	2003
9. Steve Woodard	1.79	1998
10. Moose Haas	1.82	1982

Walks Allowed Per Nine IP: Career with Team

Player	BB/9	IP
1. Lary Sorensen	1.82	854.0
2. Mike Caldwell	1.98	1,604.7
3. Ben Sheets	2.00	982.3
4. Bill Wegman	2.14	1,482.7
5. Chris Bosio	2.19	1,190.0
6. Moose Haas	2.38	1,542.0
7. Jim Colborn	2.49	1,118.0
8. Chuck Crim	2.57	529.7
9. Jaime Navarro	2.85	1,061.7
10. Teddy Higuera	2.89	1,380.0

WHIP (Walks + Hits Per Nine IP): Season

Player	WHIP	Year
1. Ben Sheets	0.983	2004
2. Teddy Higuera	0.999	1988
3. Mike Caldwell	1.064	1978
4. Bill Wegman	1.117	1991
5. Marty Pattin	1.126	1971
6. Chris Bosio	1.154	1992
7. Chris Bosio	1.163	1989
8. Jeff D'Amico	1.164	2000
9. Lary Sorensen	1.165	1978
10. Bill Wegman	1.169	1992

WHIP (Walks + Hits Per Nine IP): Career with Team

Player	WHIP	IP
1. Ben Sheets	1.218	982.3
2. Dan Plesac	1.232	524.3
3. Marty Pattin	1.234	656.7
4. Teddy Higuera	1.236	1,380.0
5. Chris Bosio	1.238	1,190.0
6. Jim Colborn	1.268	1,118.0
7. Lary Sorensen	1.275	854.0
8. Mike Caldwell	1.284	1,604.7
9. Bill Wegman	1.294	1,482.7
10. Moose Haas	1.304	1,542.0

Home Runs Allowed: Season

Player	HRA	Year
1. Wayne Franklin	36	2003
2. Mike Caldwell	35	1983
3. Danny Darwin	34	1985
4. Lew Krausse	33	1970
Bill Travers	33	1979
6. Cal Eldred	32	1993
Bill Wegman	32	1986
8. Cal Eldred	31	1997
Bill Wegman	31	1987
Chris Capuano	31	2005

Home Runs Allowed: Career with Team

Player	HRA	IP
1. Jim Slaton	192	2,025.3
2. Bill Wegman	187	1,482.7
3. Mike Caldwell	161	1,604.7
4. Moose Haas	151	1,542.0
5. Cal Eldred	137	1,078.7
6. Teddy Higuera	131	1,380.0
7. Bill Travers	128	1,068.3
8. Ricky Bones	126	883.0
9. Ben Sheets	117	982.3
10. Chris Bosio	107	1,190.0

Saves: Season

Player	SV	Year
1. Danny Kolb	39	2004
Derrick Turnbow	39	2005
3. Bob Wickman	37	1999
4. Doug Jones	36	1997
5. Dan Plesac	33	1989
6. Mike Fetters	32	1996
7. Ken Sanders	31	1971
8. Dan Plesac	30	1988
9. Rollie Fingers	29	1982
Doug Henry	29	1992

Saves: Career with Team

Player	SV	IP
1. Dan Plesac	133	524.3
2. Rollie Fingers	97	259.0
3. Mike Fetters	79	334.3
Bob Wickman	79	315.0
5. Doug Henry	61	187.3
Ken Sanders	61	321.0
7. Danny Kolb	60	98.7
8. Doug Jones	49	168.7
9. Mike DeJean	47	224.0
10. Bill Castro	44	411.0

Wild Pitches: Season

Player	WP	Year
1. Chris Bosio	14	1987
Jim Slaton	14	1974
3. Jaime Cocanower	13	1984
Jaime Cocanower	13	1985
5. Jim Slaton	12	1975
6. Jaime Navarro	11	1993
Jim Slaton	11	1973
Jim Slaton	11	1976

Bill Travers	11	1977
10. Six tied with . . .	10	—

WILD PITCHES: CAREER WITH TEAM

Player	WP	IP
1. Jim Slaton	71	2,025.3
2. Chris Bosio	41	1,190.0
3. Moose Haas	40	1,542.0
Jaime Navarro	40	1,061.7
Bill Travers	40	1,068.3
6. Mike Caldwell	37	1,604.7
7. Ben Sheets	34	982.3
Jaime Cocanower	32	365.7
9. Cal Eldred	28	1,078.7
10. Ben Sheets	27	825.7

HIT BATSMEN: SEASON

Player	HB	Year
1. Jamey Wright	20	2001
2. Jamey Wright	18	2000
3. Pete Broberg	16	1975
4. Gene Brabender	13	1969
5. Chris Capuano	12	2005
6. Scott Karl	11	1996
Jim Lonborg	11	1972
Jaime Navarro	11	1993
Jim Slaton	11	1977
Bill Travers	11	1975
Jamey Wright	11	2002

HIT BATSMEN: CAREER WITH TEAM

Player	HB	IP
1. Jamey Wright	49	473.7
2. Bill Travers	42	1,068.3
3. Bill Wegman	40	1,482.7
4. Cal Eldred	35	1,078.7
5. Ricky Bones	33	883.0
Jim Slaton	33	2,025.3
7. Jaime Navarro	32	1,061.7
8. Scott Karl	30	914.7
9. Ben Sheets	27	982.3
10. Bob McClure	26	842.0

GAMES FINISHED: SEASON

Player	GF	Year
1. Ken Sanders	77	1971
2. Doug Jones	73	1997
3. Tom Murphy	66	1974
4. Bob Wickman	63	1999
5. Derrick Turnbow	62	2005
6. Mike DeJean	60	2002
7. Curt Leskanic	58	2001
8. Doug Henry	56	1992
9. Mike Fetters	55	1996
10. Mark Clear	52	1986
Dan Plesac	52	1990

GAMES FINISHED: CAREER WITH TEAM

Player	GF	IP
1. Dan Plesac	269	524.3
2. Bill Castro	179	411.0
3. Bob Wickman	174	315.0
4. Mike Fetters	165	334.3
5. Ken Sanders	158	321.0
6. Rollie Fingers	153	259.0
7. Doug Henry	129	187.3
Bob McClure	129	842.0
9. Chuck Crim	128	529.7
10. Mike DeJean	119	224.0

Bob Uecker—Brewer radio announcer, baseball personality, and former mediocre major league catcher.

Significant Brewers

CALDWELL, MIKE (SP)
(1977–1984)

Left-hander Mike Caldwell, who showed one year of promise in 1974 before being beset by injuries, bounced around among four National League teams before coming to Milwaukee on June 15, 1977, in a trade with Cincinnati for a couple of minor leaguers. He would spend the last 7½ years of his career with the Brewers. Under the tutelage of manager George Bamberger, who as pitching coach had been instrumental in Baltimore's success, Caldwell put together a terrific 1978 season, going 22–9 with an astounding 23 complete games and a 2.36 ERA. He was runner-up to Ron Guidry in the AL Cy Young Award voting. Caldwell, who was voted Comeback Player of the Year, threw three shutouts against the defending world-champion Yankees. He followed this with a 16–6 record in 1979, including eight consecutive victories, setting a Brewers team record. After helping Milwaukee to its only pennant in 1982 with 17 wins, Caldwell won two games in the World Series against the Cardinals. The first was a three-hit shutout in Game 1; the second was a 15-hitter in Game 5. Following more arm trouble in 1984, "Iron Mike" retired as Milwaukee's career leader in complete games with 81.

CAREER BREWERS RECORD:

W	L	W%	ERA	SV
102	80	.560	3.74	2
K	BB	SHO	IP	
540	353	18	1,604.7	

COOPER, CECIL (1B)
(1977–1987)

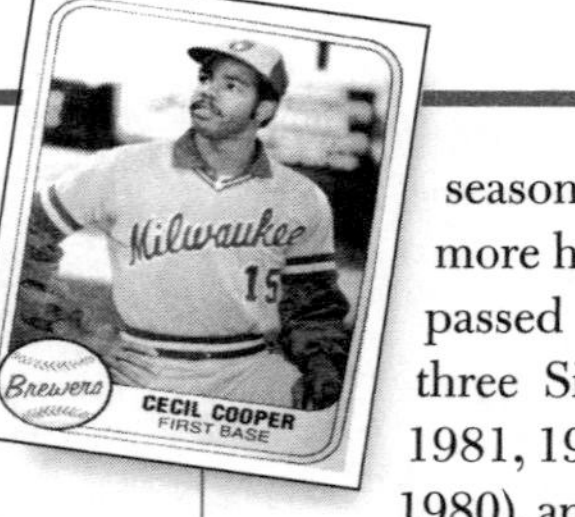

After spending six seasons with the Red Sox, Cecil Cooper arrived in Milwaukee in December 1976 in a trade from Boston for Bernie Carbo and George Scott. Never really appreciated in Boston, Cooper blossomed in Milwaukee, hitting over .300 his first seven years as a Brewer, eventually becoming a five-time All-Star. He never won a batting title, though, because he played in the era of Rod Carew and George Brett. When Cooper hit a career-high .352 in 1980, Brett hit a career-high .390. For the Brewers, Cooper was Mr. Steady. Five times in his 11 seasons as a Brewer, he hit 20 or more homers, and four times he surpassed 100 RBIs. Cooper also won three Silver Slugger Awards (1980, 1981, 1982), two Gold Gloves (1979, 1980), and the 1983 Roberto Clemente Award, before retiring after the 1987 season.

CAREER BREWERS RECORD:

Games	AB	Hits	Runs
1,490	6,019	1,815	821
Avg	HR	RBI	SB
.302	201	944	77

FINGERS, ROLLIE (RP)
(1981–1982, 1984–1985)

Hall of Famer Rollie Fingers, more famous for his years in Oakland, played the last four years of his 17-year major league career with Milwaukee. San Diego sent him to the Brewers, who were desperate for any kind of relief help, as part of an 11-player deal. Although the best part of his career was behind him, he won his only Cy Young Award in 1981, during his first season with Milwaukee, compiling 28 saves and a sparkling 1.04 ERA in the strike-shortened year. That same year, he won the American League's MVP Award and the AL Rolaids Relief Award. Fingers made two of his seven All-Star Game appearances with the Brewers. He retired after the 1985 season due to recurring arm troubles and subpar performances. *(See A's and Padres bios.)*

CAREER BREWERS RECORD:

W	L	W%	ERA	SV
13	17	.433	2.54	97
K	BB	SHO	IP	
196	65	0	259.0	

GANTNER, JIM (2B)
(1976–1992)

The Milwaukee Brewers selected Jim Gantner in the 12th round of the 1974 amateur draft. When he made the major league roster in 1976, it was the first season of his 17-year career, all spent with Milwaukee. Originally a third baseman, Gantner made the switch to full-time second base in 1981 and became the team's regular at that position for the next 13 years. He teamed with Robin Yount to lead the American League in double plays in 1981 and 1982. While not a spectacular player, Gantner did serve the team well for many years. His performance in the 1982 World Series (.333 BA, 5 runs, 4 doubles, 1 triple, and 4 RBIs) was one of the reasons Milwaukee nearly won the Series. A severe injury in 1989 required reconstructive knee surgery, almost ending his career. With his skills diminishing due to the injury and age, Gantner retired after the 1992 season, one of Milwaukee's most popular players of all time.

CAREER BREWERS RECORD:

Games	AB	Hits	Runs
1,801	6,189	1,696	726
Avg	HR	RBI	SB
.274	47	568	137

HAAS, MOOSE (SP)
(1976–1985)

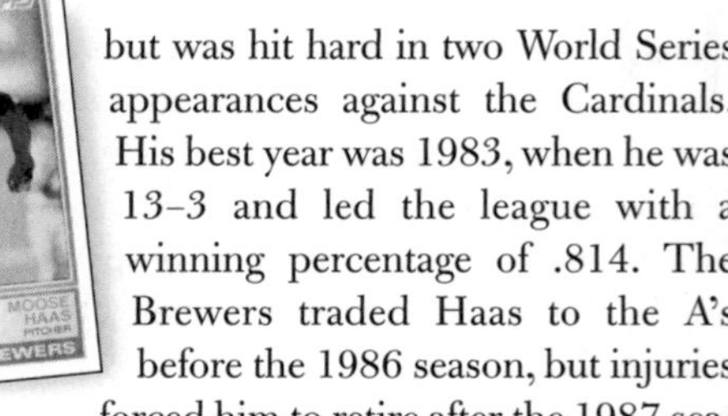

Pitcher Bryan "Moose" Haas was drafted in the second round of the 1974 amateur draft by the Brewers, the same draft that produced infielder Jim Gantner; like Gantner, he made the transition to the big league squad in 1976. Haas was a finesse pitcher who used pinpoint control to win 91 games for the Brewers during his 10 years with the team. He saw a lot of postseason action in the 1981 and 1982 playoff years. In 1981 he lost both of his starts against the Yankees in the Division Series. In 1982 he defeated the Yankees in Game 4 of the LCS, but was hit hard in two World Series appearances against the Cardinals. His best year was 1983, when he was 13–3 and led the league with a winning percentage of .814. The Brewers traded Haas to the A's before the 1986 season, but injuries forced him to retire after the 1987 season at the age of 31.

CAREER BREWERS RECORD:

W	L	W%	ERA	SV
91	79	.535	4.03	2

K	BB	SHO	IP
800	408	8	1,542.0

HIGUERA, TEDDY (SP)
(1985–1991, 1993–1994)

After they saw phenom pitcher Teddy Higuera leading the Mexican League in wins, complete games, innings pitched, and strikeouts in 1983, the Brewers purchased his contract from the Ciudad Juarez team, adding him to the roster in 1985. Higuera would play his entire nine-year major league career with Milwaukee. His 5–8 record was the best ever for a Brewers' rookie pitcher, and he finished second in the AL Rookie of the Year balloting. He followed this up with a 20–11 record in 1986, finishing as runner-up to Roger Clemens in the AL Cy Young voting. He also became the first-ever Mexican-born 20-game winner in major league history, beating Fernando Valenzuela by mere days. His 240 strikeouts in 1987 surpassed that of every Milwaukee pitcher before him, breaking the 1965 record of 211 set by Tony Cloninger. One arm injury after another took its toll on Higuera after the 1988 season, however, eventually causing him to miss the entire 1992 campaign. After six frustrating years of injury problems, Higuera called it quits after the 1994 season, ending a once-promising career.

CAREER BREWERS RECORD:

W	L	W%	ERA	SV
94	64	.595	3.61	0

K	BB	SHO	IP
1,081	443	12	1,380.0

MOLITOR, PAUL (2B/3B/OF/DH) (1978–1992)

Paul Molitor was claimed by the Brewers in the first round of the 1977 amateur draft, the third pick overall. He had actually been drafted three years earlier by the Cardinals in the 28th round, but did not want to play baseball at the time. Molitor joined the team in 1978 and spent 15 summers in a Brewers uniform. He began as a second baseman but switched to the outfield, then third, then first, and finally DH. The eventual switch to DH was an effort to keep him healthy and his bat in the lineup, since he was quite often sidelined by injury. In fact, he missed nearly 500 games during his 21-year career, and was on the disabled list 10 times from 1980 to 1990 alone. On the plus side, Molitor was named to the All-Star team five times, won two Silver Slugger Awards, finished in the top 10 in batting eight times, and received votes in the AL MVP balloting six times—all during his 15-year stint with Milwaukee. In 1982, he became the first player to get five hits in a World Series game. Five years later, he put together a 39-game hitting streak, the fourth-longest in the American League at the time. Molitor opted for free agency after the 1992 season, signing with the Toronto Blue Jays. In 2004, he became the second Brewers player elected to the Hall of Fame, joining longtime teammate Robin Yount.

CAREER BREWERS RECORD:

Games	AB	Hits	Runs
1,856	7,520	2,281	1,275
Avg	**HR**	**RBI**	**SB**
.303	160	790	412

MONEY, DON (3B/2B/DH) (1973–1983)

After spending five seasons playing for the Philadelphia Phillies, third baseman Don Money was traded to the Milwaukee Brewers along with John Vukovich and Bill Champion for Jim Lonborg, Ken Brett, Ken Sanders, and Earl Stephenson in order to make room for young Mike Schmidt. Nicknamed "Brooks," Money was a great fielder in his own right, often compared to Brooks Robinson. In 1974 he set major league records for fewest errors by a third baseman (5) and highest fielding percentage (.989). He also set a major league record that year with 88 consecutive errorless games and 261 consecutive errorless chances. He had a combination of power and speed, often batting leadoff for the Brewers. Money was a selfless player, happily playing other positions as needed, including first, second, short, the outfield, and DH. On June 24, 1977, he tied the major league record for assists in a nine-inning game by a second baseman with 12. In 1983, Money ended his 16-year major league career, the last 11 seasons spent with Milwaukee, and went to Japan to play for the Kintetsu Buffaloes.

CAREER BREWERS RECORD:

Games	AB	Hits	Runs
1,196	4,330	1,168	596
Avg	**HR**	**RBI**	**SB**
.270	134	529	66

MOORE, CHARLIE (C/OF)
(1973–1986)

Light-hitting catcher Charlie Moore was selected by the Milwaukee Brewers in the fifth round of the June 1971 amateur draft. After playing a few games for the big league team in 1973, he arrived for good in 1974. Moore was a popular platoon player for much of his career, backing up Darrell Porter for three years and later Ted Simmons. For two years he was a regular outfielder, but his light offensive production eventually landed him back in a platoon role. When the Brewers made the playoffs in 1982, however, Moore raised his play, batting a team-high .462 in the LCS against the Angels and a .346 (9 for 26) against the Cardinals in the World Series. He left the team for free agency after 14 years, following the 1986 season, and played one final year with Toronto before retiring.

CAREER BREWERS RECORD:

Games	AB	Hits	Runs
1,283	3,926	1,029	441
Avg	**HR**	**RBI**	**SB**
.262	35	401	51

OGLIVIE, BEN (OF)
(1978–1986)

Panamanian-born Ben Oglivie came to the Brewers in December 1977 in a trade with Detroit for pitchers Jim Slaton and Rich Folkers, after spending his first seven seasons mostly as a platoon player with the Red Sox and Tigers. Once he became a regular in Milwaukee, Oglivie's career took off. He had the first .300 season of his career in 1978, finishing at .303. In 1979 he set a personal high with 29 homers. Then, in 1980, the three-time All-Star had his career year, batting .304 with 41 home runs and 118 RBIs, capturing his only Silver Slugger Award in the process. In the 1982 ALCS, Oglivie hit a crucial home run in Game 5, helping Milwaukee become the first team in playoff history to come back from a two-games-to-none deficit to win a league pennant. He also hit a homer in Game 7 of the World Series to keep the game close, but the Cardinals prevailed. After the 1986 season, Oglivie went to Japan and played two seasons for the Kintetsu Buffaloes before retiring.

CAREER BREWERS RECORD:

Games	AB	Hits	Runs
1,149	4,136	1,144	567
Avg	**HR**	**RBI**	**SB**
.277	176	685	44

PLESAC, DAN (RP)
(1986–1992)

Milwaukee drafted Dan Plesac in the first round of the June 1983 amateur draft. He had been drafted three years earlier by the St. Louis Cardinals in the second round, but declined to sign with them. Plesac made it to the majors in 1986 as a reliever, even though he had been used exclusively as a starter in the minors. He used a blazing fastball, a sharp-breaking slider, and remarkable control to fashion a 10–7 record with 14 saves and a 2.97 ERA in his rookie season. Over the next four seasons, he saved 110 games for

Milwaukee and made the All-Star team three times. But arm trouble set in and he was never the same again. He left Milwaukee for free agency after the 1992 season, his seventh with the team, and played 11 more years for five different teams, garnering only 25 more saves.

CAREER BREWERS RECORD:

W	L	W%	ERA	SV
29	37	.439	3.21	133
K	BB	SHO	IP	
448	186	0	524.3	

SLATON, JIM (SP)
(1971–1977, 1979–1983)

Right-handed pitcher Jim Slaton was drafted in the 15th round of the 1969 amateur draft by the Seattle Pilots. He was a workhorse for the Brewers during the 1970s, pitching 200 or more innings for six straight years from 1972 to 1977, although he had a losing record each year. He was Milwaukee's lone representative on the 1977 American League All-Star team, but was traded to Detroit for Ben Oglivie after the season. After just one season with the Tigers (actually the best year of his career, at 17–11), however, Slaton opted for free agency and re-signed with the Brewers for five more seasons. He began as a starter (best season in 1979, going 15–9), but converted to relief pitcher by 1982 due to a rotator cuff injury. He set a Milwaukee record in 1983, going 14–6 with all 14 wins in relief. After the season, he was traded to the Angels for Bobby Clark and played three more years for the Angels and Tigers before retiring.

CAREER BREWERS RECORD:

W	L	W%	ERA	SV
117	121	.492	3.86	11
K	BB	SHO	IP	
929	760	19	2,025.3	

THOMAS, GORMAN (OF/DH)
(1973–1976, 1978–1983, 1986)

Gorman Thomas was the first player selected by the Seattle Pilots in the June 1969 amateur draft. After making the major league squad in Milwaukee in 1973, he quickly became a fan favorite because of his hustling style of play. He swung hard, ran hard, crashed into fences hard, and made no apologies—hence the nickname "Stormin' Gorman." Thomas spent a combined 10 of his 13 major league seasons in Milwaukee, and was selected once (1981) for the All-Star team. He led the American League in both homers and strikeouts in 1979, smashing 45 of the former and 175 of the latter. In Milwaukee's pennant-winning season of 1982, he hit 39 homers to tie for the league lead, but struck out 143 times. His lifetime batting average was only .225, one of the lowest in major league history for players with more than 2,500 at-bats. He struck out 1,339 times in 4,677 at-bats—a ratio of once every 3.5 at-bats—also one of the worst ratios in major league history. He did, however, homer once every 17.5 at-bats, beating the ratios of Joe DiMaggio, Mel Ott, Ernie Banks, Johnny Mize, Duke Snider, and Reggie Jackson, all Hall of Famers.

CAREER BREWERS RECORD:

Games	AB	Hits	Runs
1,102	3,544	815	524
Avg	HR	RBI	SB
.230	208	605	38

YOUNT, ROBIN (SS/OF)
(1974–1993)

The Milwaukee Brewers selected Robin Yount, at the age of 18, as the third overall pick of the first round in the June 1973 amateur draft. He left Taft High School in Woodland Hills, California, and played just a few months in the minors before making the Milwaukee roster in 1974, still just 18 years old, the youngest player in the major leagues. In 1978, at the age of 22, Yount left the team during spring training to consider another career. A talented golfer, he considered joining the PGA tour as a professional, but his father eventually counseled him to return to baseball. With renewed vigor, he set new career highs in batting average, RBIs, triples, and homers.

In 1980 he made his first of three appearances on the American League All-Star team and won his first of three Silver Slugger Awards for a season in which he amassed 317 total bases, the third-highest total ever by a shortstop, and 23 homers, the same total he had for his first four seasons combined. By 1982, he had one of the greatest seasons ever by a shortstop: 210 hits, 46 doubles, 12 triples, 29 homers, 367 total bases, a .331 batting average, 114 RBIs, 129 runs scored, a .578 slugging average, plus leading all AL shortstops in assists (earning his only Gold Glove in the process). To add to the drama, Baltimore and Milwaukee were tied for the division lead with one game to go. Yount homered twice off future Hall of Famer Jim Palmer to win the game and the AL East division title for the Brewers. For this he was rewarded with his first MVP Award. Yount hit .414 in the 1982 World Series, but the Brewers lost to the Cardinals, four games to three.

In 1983, Yount received more All-Star votes than any other player, but it would be his third and last appearance in the Summer Classic. Chronic shoulder problems caused his offensive numbers to drop and eventually forced him out of the infield and into the outfield. After two shoulder surgeries in less than a year, Yount rebounded offensively, hitting over .300 for the next four years. In 1989 he won his second MVP Award, this time as an outfielder, becoming only the third player in major league history (joining Hank Greenberg and Stan Musial) to win MVP Awards at two different positions. In 1986, he became the first player in American League history to have led both the outfield and the infield in fielding average for a season. In September 1992, Yount became the 17th player in major league history (and third youngest) to rack up 3,000 hits. Only Ty Cobb and Hank Aaron were younger when they passed that benchmark. Following the 1993 season, Yount's 20th in Milwaukee, Yount retired at the age of 38, announcing to the public that he could no longer dedicate himself fully to the offseason training required to maintain his baseball abilities. In 1999, the first year of his eligibility, Robin Yount was elected to the Baseball Hall of Fame.

CAREER BREWERS RECORD:

Games	AB	Hits	Runs
2,856	11,008	3,142	1,632
Avg	**HR**	**RBI**	**SB**
.285	251	1,406	271

Minnesota Twins

Since 1901

1965 Team Ball

1907 An Idaho supporter of Walter Johnson writes a letter to the Washington Senators touting the young pitcher, saying, "He knows where he's throwing because if he didn't, there would be dead bodies all over the place."...**1919** Walter Johnson pitches a record fifth Opening Day shutout in 1919 when he blanks the Philadelphia A's 1–0 in 13 innings....**1945** The Senators hit only one home run all season at roomy Griffith Stadium, their home park—and even that is an inside-the-park job by first baseman Joe Kuhel....**1963** The Twins set a record for the most home runs hit by a non-pennant-winning team with 225.... **1987** The Twins set a major league record for the lowest winning percentage by a World Series champion when they finish 85–77 (.525).

FRANCHISE HISTORY

After several failed attempts to establish a viable franchise in Washington, D.C., the National League abandoned the city following the 1899 season. But Ban Johnson, president of the Western League, had a grand design to create a major rival to the National League. As part of that plan, he renamed his organization as the American League in 1900, and orchestrated the shift of its Kansas City team to Washington in 1900, quickly filling the void created by the National League's departure. In 1901 the American League was declared a major league and the Washington team, named the Senators like the two NL franchises before it, became a charter member of Ban Johnson's new creation.

The first owner of the American League Senators was—at least publicly—Detroit hotel owner Fred Postal. He actually owned only 49 percent of the team; AL President Ban Johnson owned 51 percent and secretly controlled the club. The former Kansas City owner, Tom Manning, quietly sold his interests to the two men and became the team's manager. In 1903 Ban Johnson announced that the American League had bought out Fred Postal for $15,000 and would be controlling the team. Early in 1904, the team was sold to an investment group headed by *Washington Star* newspaper owner Thomas C. Noyes. There were two other major investors, attorney Wilton J. Lambert and former sportswriter William Dwyer. The team officially changed its name in 1905 to the Washington Nationals, but the fans and the press refused to acknowledge it and continued to call their team the Senators. Much team-sponsored ephemera such as programs, tickets, postcards, and the like continued to be printed bearing the Senators name, not the Nationals. The name was officially changed back to the Senators in 1956, but no one noticed since no one had ever really stopped calling them the Senators.

In 1912, future Hall of Famer Clark Griffith entered the picture. Griffith, who won 240 games in his pitching career, could be described as a "company man." He was still managing the Cincinnati Reds in 1909 when Ban Johnson asked him to take over the reins of the Senators in 1912. Griffith agreed, and was

Goose Goslin (left), who would have played for free.

Team owner Calvin Griffith, former Senators' batboy.

allowed to buy a 10 percent interest in the team for $27,000. Over the years, Griffith bought up more and more Senators stock from the other investors until he controlled 52 percent interest in the team. William Richardson, an exporter from Philadelphia, controlled 40 percent, and a number of smaller investors the remaining 8 percent. Griffith controlled the team until his death in 1955.

After Griffith's death, control of the team passed to his nephew Calvin Griffith, whom Clark had adopted along with Calvin's sister Thelma in 1922. While growing up, Calvin served as batboy for the Senators and, as a young man, he managed in the minor leagues. Although Calvin ran the club, he and Thelma each owned 26 percent of the team. The two siblings had inherited a team that had rarely been competitive in the American League. For Clark Griffith, the team had not been a tycoon's plaything, but his sole livelihood. His consequent penny-pinching inevitably resulted in underperforming teams. Poor attendance persuaded the new owners to relocate to Minnesota.

Word first leaked out at the 1958 All-Star Game that the Senators were working on a deal to move to Minnesota and its new ballpark, Metropolitan Stadium. Despite Congressional threats to reexamine baseball's antitrust exemption, plans for the move continued, with a target date of 1961. A compromise was worked out when the American League agreed to expand by two teams, one of which would become a new Washington Senators team. When the old Senators team departed for Minnesota on October 26, 1960, the new one took the field in the nation's capital.

When a Minneapolis reporter asked Calvin Griffith in 1961 why he had chosen to relocate to Minnesota, Griffith replied with racist aplomb, "You only have 15,000 blacks here. You've got good, hard-working people here. Blacks don't go to ballgames." Nicknamed for the twin cities of Minneapolis and St. Paul, the Twins would be the only game in town. The nearest competing baseball markets would be a few hundred miles away in Kansas City, St. Louis, Chicago, and Milwaukee, not in Griffith's backyard (in Washington, the team had to compete with the Orioles for fans). Calvin Griffith controlled the club until September 1984, when he sold his share of the team for $43 million in the wake of a hostile takeover attempt by Tampa businessman Frank Morsani.

Morsani succeeded in purchasing a 42 percent interest in the club in April 1984 and was pressuring Griffith to sell his share to him as well. When he announced his intention of moving the team to Florida once he got control, Commissioner Bowie Kuhn stepped in. Kuhn convinced Morsani that a hostile takeover of a major league team wouldn't be in anyone's long-term interests. He also persuaded Morsani to sell his newly acquired 42 percent stake in the team to Minneapolis banker Carl Pohlad "at cost" for "future considerations," which Morsani interpreted as first chance to purchase one of baseball's existing or next expansion teams. Morsani then unsuccessfully tried to buy and relocate the Oakland A's and

In 1910, President William Taft began the tradition of the U.S. presidents throwing out the first ball at Washington's home games.

Texas Rangers.

When the Rockies and Marlins were awarded to others in 1992, an angry Morsani immediately filed suit against Major League Baseball. After 11 years of procedural wrangling, the case was finally scheduled to go to trial in the fall of 2003 when an out-of-court settlement was reached, terms of which were ordered kept confidential.

Carl Pohlad was a godsend to Major League Baseball, which needed a local connection like him to keep the team in Minnesota. Unlike Clark and Calvin Griffith, Pohlad had another source of income. A decorated World War II hero, Pohlad turned a small finance company into a conglomerate of 40 banks with more than $40 billion in assets. Pohlad, estimated to be worth around $500 million at the time he purchased the Twins, also made parts of his fortune in the soft drink bottling business and through corporate takeovers. Pohlad, who still owns the team today, also owned a share in the Minnesota Vikings. By the mid-1990s, his fortune had grown to $1 billion, assuring financial stability for the small-market Twins.

On the field, the franchise almost always performed poorly while in Washington, with the exception of 1924, 1925, and 1933, when the team won its only three AL pennants, and its only World Series (1924). The team was often the butt of jokes, none more enduring than the one popularized by a sportswriter in 1909: "Washington: first in war, first in peace, and last in the American League." During the Vietnam War, the slogan changed to: "Last in war, last in peace, and still last in the American League." Author John Steinbeck was once asked which team was his favorite. He replied, "I almost went to the Senators, but there is a federal law which forbids them to win." In the 1950s Broadway musical (and later movie) *Damn Yankees,* the devil turns a frustrated lifelong Senators fan into a superhuman ballplayer in order to knock off the team's nemesis.

In Minnesota, the franchise enjoyed more success, winning the pennant in 1965, its fifth year in its new home. It was also a contender for a number of years in the late 1960s and 1970s, but didn't win its next pennant until 1987, when the Twins also won the franchise's second World Series. The Twins won another thrilling Series in 1991 after finishing last in their division the previous year. They took seven games to beat the Braves, a team, ironically, that had also finished last in their division in 1990.

TEAM NAME HISTORY

Official Names

Senators (1901–1904)
Nationals (1905–1955)
Senators (1956–1960)
Twins (1961–current)

Unofficial Names/Nicknames

While in Washington: Washingtons, Washington Americans, Nats, Senators (1905–1955)
While in Minnesota: Twinkies

STADIUM HISTORY

In Washington, D.C.

American League Park	1901–1902
Washington Park	1903–1910
(American League Park renamed; also known as National Park and Boundary Field)	
Griffith Stadium	1911–1960
(Washington Park renamed)	

In Minnesota

Metropolitan Stadium	1961–1981
The Metrodome	1982–current

YEARLY RECORD, FINISH, & ATTENDANCE FIGURES

Year	League	Record	DIV/LG Finish	Attendance	Avg/Gm
2005	AL Cent	83–79	3	2,034,243	25,114
2004	AL Cent	92–70	1	1,911,490	23,599
2003	AL Cent	90–72	1	1,946,011	24,025
2002	AL Cent	94–67	1	1,924,473	23,759
2001	AL Cent	85–77	2	1,782,929	22,011
2000	AL Cent	69–93	5	1,000,760	12,355
1999	AL Cent	63–97	5	1,202,829	14,850
1998	AL Cent	70–92	4	1,165,976	14,395
1997	AL Cent	68–94	4	1,411,064	17,421
1996	AL Cent	78–84	4	1,437,352	17,529
1995	AL Cent	56–88	5	1,057,667	14,690
1994	AL Cent	53–60	4	1,398,565	23,704
1993	AL West	71–91	6	2,048,673	25,292
1992	AL West	90–72	2	2,482,428	30,647
1991	AL West	95–67	1	2,293,842	28,319
1990	AL West	74–88	7	1,751,584	21,624
1989	AL West	80–82	5	2,277,438	28,117
1988	AL West	91–71	2	3,030,672	37,416
1987	AL West	85–77	1	2,081,976	25,703
1986	AL West	71–91	6	1,255,453	15,499
1985	AL West	77–85	4	1,651,814	19,664
1984	AL West	81–81	3	1,598,692	19,737
1983	AL West	70–92	6	858,939	10,604
1982	AL West	60–102	7	921,186	11,373
1981	AL West	41–68	7/4	469,090	7,690
1980	AL West	77–84	3	769,206	9,615
1979	AL West	82–80	4	1,070,521	13,216
1978	AL West	73–89	4	787,878	9,727
1977	AL West	84–77	4	1,162,727	14,534
1976	AL West	85–77	3	715,394	8,832
1975	AL West	76–83	4	737,156	8,990
1974	AL West	82–80	3	662,401	8,078
1973	AL West	81–81	3	907,499	11,204
1972	AL West	77–77	3	797,901	10,782
1971	AL West	74–86	5	940,858	11,910
1970	AL West	98–64	1	1,261,887	15,579
1969	AL West	97–65	1	1,349,328	16,658
1968	AL	79–83	7	1,143,257	14,114
1967	AL	91–71	2	1,483,547	18,315
1966	AL	89–73	2	1,259,374	15,548
1965	AL	102–60	1	1,463,258	18,065
1964	AL	79–83	6	1,207,514	14,726
1963	AL	91–70	3	1,406,652	17,366
1962	AL	91–71	2	1,433,116	17,477
1961	AL	70–90	7	1,256,723	15,515
1960	AL	73–81	5	743,404	9,655
1959	AL	63–91	8	615,372	7,992
1958	AL	61–93	8	475,288	6,093
1957	AL	55–99	8	457,079	5,936
1956	AL	59–95	7	431,647	5,606
1955	AL	53–101	8	425,238	5,523

YEARLY RECORD, FINISH, & ATTENDANCE FIGURES (CONT.)

Year	League	Record	DIV/LG Finish	Attendance	Avg/Gm
1954	AL	66–88	6	503,542	6,456
1953	AL	76–76	5	595,594	7,941
1952	AL	78–76	5	699,457	8,967
1951	AL	62–92	7	695,167	9,147
1950	AL	67–87	5	699,697	8,970
1949	AL	50–104	8	770,745	10,010
1948	AL	56–97	7	795,254	10,196
1947	AL	64–90	7	850,758	11,049
1946	AL	76–78	4	1,027,216	13,516
1945	AL	87–67	2	652,660	8,367
1944	AL	64–90	8	525,235	6,821
1943	AL	84–69	2	574,694	7,562
1942	AL	62–89	7	403,493	5,240
1941	AL	70–84	6	415,663	5,329
1940	AL	64–90	7	381,241	4,951
1939	AL	65–87	6	339,257	4,406
1938	AL	75–76	5	522,694	6,701
1937	AL	73–80	6	397,799	4,972
1936	AL	82–71	4	379,525	4,929
1935	AL	67–86	6	255,011	3,312
1934	AL	66–86	7	330,074	4,343
1933	AL	99–53	1	437,533	5,757
1932	AL	93–61	3	371,396	4,823
1931	AL	92–62	3	492,657	6,236
1930	AL	94–60	2	614,474	7,980
1929	AL	71–81	5	355,506	4,558
1928	AL	75–79	4	378,501	4,731
1927	AL	85–69	3	528,976	6,696
1926	AL	81–69	4	551,580	7,454
1925	AL	96–55	1	817,199	10,753
1924	AL	92–62	1	584,310	7,396
1923	AL	75–78	4	357,406	4,524
1922	AL	69–85	6	458,552	5,804
1921	AL	80–73	4	456,069	6,001
1920	AL	68–84	6	359,260	4,727
1919	AL	56–84	7	234,096	3,251
1918	AL	72–56	3	182,122	2,461
1917	AL	74–79	5	89,682	1,121
1916	AL	76–77	7	177,265	2,188
1915	AL	85–68	4	167,332	2,092
1914	AL	81–73	3	243,888	3,167
1913	AL	90–64	2	325,831	4,177
1912	AL	91–61	2	350,663	4,496
1911	AL	64–90	7	244,884	3,180
1910	AL	66–85	7	254,591	3,306
1909	AL	42–110	8	205,199	2,665
1908	AL	67–85	7	264,252	3,388
1907	AL	49–102	8	221,929	2,959
1906	AL	55–95	7	129,903	1,732
1905	AL	64–87	7	252,027	3,273
1904	AL	38–113	8	131,744	1,689

YEARLY RECORD, FINISH, & ATTENDANCE FIGURES (CONT.)

Year	League	Record	DIV/LG Finish	Attendance	Avg/Gm
1903	AL	43–94	8	128,878	1,815
1902	AL	61–75	6	188,158	2,767
1901	AL	61–72	6	161,661	2,377

MANAGER HISTORY

Manager	Years	W–L	Win %
Jimmy Manning	1901	61–72	.459
Tom Loftus	1902–1903	104–169	.381
Patsy Donovan	1904	38–113	.252
Jake Stahl	1905–1906	119–182	.395
Joe Cantillon	1907–1909	158–297	.347
Jimmy McAleer	1910–1911	130–175	.426
Clark Griffith	1912–1920	693–646	.518
George McBride	1921	80–73	.523
Clyde Milan	1922	69–85	.448
Donie Bush	1923	75–78	.490
Bucky Harris	1924–1928,		
	1935–1942		
	1950–1954	1,336–1,416	.485
Walter Johnson	1929–1932	350–264	.570
Joe Cronin	1933–1934	165–139	.543
Ossie Bluege	1943–1947	375–394	.488
Joe Kuhel	1948–1949	106–201	.345
Chuck Dressen	1955–1957	116–212	.354
Cookie Lavagetto	1957–1961	271–384	.414
Sam Mele	1961–1967	524–436	.546
Cal Ermer	1967–1968	145–129	.529
Billy Martin	1969	97–65	.599
Bill Rigney	1970–1972	208–184	.531
Frank Quilici	1972–1975	280–287	.494
Gene Mauch	1976–1980	378–394	.490
Johnny Goryl	1980–1981	34–38	.472
Billy Gardner	1981–1985	268–353	.432
Ray Miller	1985–1986	109–130	.456
Tom Kelly	1986–2001	1,140–1,244	.478
Ron Gardenhire	2002–2005	359–288	.555

ALL-TIME WIN-LOSS RECORDS VS. ALL OPPONENTS (SINCE 1901)

Opponent	Record
ALL-TIME	7,788–8,448
Angels	303–318
Astros	8–6
Athletics	960–953
Blue Jays	138–159
Braves	1–2
Brewers	202–197
Cardinals	6–9
Cubs	5–10
Devil Rays	38–28
Diamondbacks	5–4
Dodgers	1–2
Giants	3–3
Indians	889–1,025
INTERLEAGUE	79–77
Mariners	164–179
Marlins	2–1
Mets	4–2
Nationals	3–0
Orioles	910–931
Padres	3–3
Phillies	3–3
Pirates	8–7
Rangers	324–291
Reds	8–7
Red Sox	902–929
Rockies	2–1
Royals	282–267
Tigers	921–995
White Sox	938–1,036
Yankees	755–1,080

Harmon Killebrew hits one of his 573 major league homers.

Franchise Highlights, Low Points, and Strange Distinctions

1901 Irv Waldron batted .311 for the Senators and led the American League in at-bats with 598 in his only season in the big leagues.

....

1902 Washington outfielder Ed Delahanty became the first player to win batting titles in both the National and American Leagues when he hit .376 for the Senators. He had won the NL batting title in 1899 with a .410 average for the Philadelphia Phillies.

....

1904 Shortstop Joe Cassidy of the Senators set a rookie record when he hit 19 triples.

....

1906 The first American League pitcher to hit a grand slam was Cy Falkenberg of the Senators.

....

1909 Walter Johnson of Washington set a record when he was on the losing end of 10 shutout games, five times by the White Sox.

....

1913 If only Washington pitchers Walter Johnson and Joe Boehling had had more support from the other pitchers on the team, when the Senators finished in second place, just 6½ games behind the Philadelphia A's. Johnson and Boehling were a combined 53–14 while the rest of the staff finished a combined 37–50.

1915 On July 19, the Senators stole eight bases off Cleveland catcher Steve O'Neill—in the first inning!

....

1919 Walter Johnson pitched a record fifth Opening Day shutout when he defeated the Philadelphia A's 1–0 in 13 innings.

....

1925 Walter Johnson was no slouch at the plate. In 1925 he hit .433, the single-season major league record for pitchers with at least 75 at-bats. He went 42-for-97 with two homers, 20 RBIs, and 12 runs.

....

1941 It was the year Ted Williams hit .406 and Joe DiMaggio put together his 56-game hitting streak. But it was a Senator, Cecil Travis, who led the American League in hits with 218.

....

1950 It took nearly half a century before Washington's cavernous Griffith Stadium saw a player hit three homers in a game. Joe DiMaggio accomplished the feat on September 10, as the Yanks belted the Senators, 8–1.

....

1953 On April 17, Mickey Mantle hit the longest measured home run in history, a 565-foot blast in Griffith Stadium as the Yankees beat the Senators, 7–3, in the season's second game.

1956 Former pitcher Ed Rommel became the first umpire to wear glasses in a game when he called the game between the Senators and Yankees on April 26.

....

1960 When first baseman Mickey Vernon retired in 1960, his career batting average was .286, the lowest ever by a two-time batting champion.

....

1962–63 Jim Kaat won 14 consecutive games.

....

1963 The Twins set a record for the most home runs hit by a non-pennant-winning team with their 225 round-trippers.

....

1964 When Tony Oliva won the AL batting title, he became the first rookie since Pete Browning in 1882 to win a major league batting crown.

Outfielder Harmon Killebrew had only one assist in 157 games, the all-time low for an outfielder with at least 150 games played in the field.

....

1969 Rod Carew tied Pete Reiser's major league record when he stole home seven times in one season.

1970 Gaylord Perry tied Bob Gibson with the most victories in the NL while brother Jim Perry of the Twins tied two other pitchers for the most victories in the AL, marking the first time two brothers had led their respective leagues in wins.

....

1972 When Rod Carew won the batting title, he compiled only 203 total bases, the lowest total ever by a batting champion. That same year, NL batting champ Billy Williams had 348 total bases. Carew was also the first batting champion since Zach Wheat in 1918 to go homerless on the season.

....

1977 Rod Carew became the first player ever to receive 4 million All-Star votes.

....

1979 Reliever Mike Marshall set a new AL record for appearances in a season with 90, a record that still stands. Five years earlier Marshall set the NL record with 106 for the Dodgers, a record that also still stands.

....

1981 On September 20, Gary Gaetti, Kent Hrbek, and Tim Laudner all hit solo home runs in their first major league game, a 4–3 loss at Texas.

....

1990 Kirby Puckett became baseball's first $3 million-a-year player.

1991 When the Twins won the World Series over the Braves, four games to three, it marked only the second time in history a World Series champion had failed to win at least one game on the road. The only other team with the distinction was . . . the 1987 Twins!

When the Twins visited Texas on May 28, they were in sixth place in the AL West with a 20–24 record. The Rangers were riding high with a 14-game winning streak. Twins pitcher Scott Erickson boldly predicted to the Texas media he would end the Rangers' streak that night, and did, 3–0, to start the Twins on a 22–2 streak that eventually led them to their World Series title.

• • • •

1993 Kevin Tapani (12–15) became the first Twins pitcher since Camilo Pascual (15–16) in 1961 to lead the team in wins while posting a losing record.

• • • •

1994 When Kent Hrbek retired in 1994, he had more career indoor homers (166) than any player in major league history.

• • • •

1995 The Twins got only two wins from left-handed starters, both by Rich Robertson in September. That same year Minnesota set a team record by playing 19 rookies at some point during the season.

1996 Lending credence to the old adage that some people get better, not older, Paul Molitor collected his 3,000th hit as a 40-year-old member of the Twins. Nothing unusual about that. However, Molitor recorded 225 hits, 41 doubles, and 113 RBIs that season—his 19th in the big leagues—all career highs. He also hit .341, the second-best average of his career.

• • • •

2001 Corey Koskie became the first AL third baseman in history to record at least 25 homers, 25 steals, and 100 RBIs in the same season.

The 2001 Twins were 55–32 (.632) before the All-Star break and 30–45 (.400) after the break, the second biggest collapse from the first half of a season to the second in major league history.

• • • •

2004 Johan Santana became the first Venezuelan ever to win 20 games in a season when he finished 20–6.

Twins catcher Pat Borders and pitcher Terry Mulholland became the first over-40 battery mates in the major leagues since catcher Clyde Sukeforth and pitcher Curt Davis of the 1945 Dodgers.

• • • •

2005 Pitcher Jesse Crain set a new AL record for consecutive wins in relief to start a career with 11.

Special Achievements

WORLD SERIES RESULTS

Year	Opponent	Result	Games
1924	New York Giants	Won	4–3
1925	Pittsburgh Pirates	Lost	3–4
1933	New York Giants	Lost	1–4
1965	L.A. Dodgers	Lost	4–3
1987	St. Louis Cardinals	Won	4–3
1991	Atlanta Braves	Won	4–3

WORLD SERIES MANAGERIAL RECORDS

Manager	Series Record	Games Record
Bucky Harris	1–1	7–7
Joe Cronin	0–1	1–4
Sam Mele	0–1	3–4
Tom Kelly	2–0	8–6

ALL-TIME POSTSEASON RECORD

Divisional Playoffs	5–8
League Championship Series	9–12
World Series	19–21

ALL-STAR GAMES AT WASHINGTON/MINNESOTA

Year	Date	Winner	Score	Stadium
1937	July 7	American	8–3	Griffith Stadium (Washington, D.C.)
1956	July 10	National	7–3	Griffith Stadium (Washington, D.C.)
1965	July 13	National	6–5	Metropolitan Stadium
1985	July 16	National	6–1	The Metrodome

HALL OF FAMERS WHO PLAYED FOR TEAM

	Position	Years	Games with Washington/ Minnesota
Rod Carew	2B/1B	1967–1978	1,635
Steve Carlton	SP/RP	1987–1988	13
Stan Coveleski	SP	1925–1927	73
Joe Cronin	SS	1928–1934	940
Ed Delahanty	OF	1902–1903	165
Rick Ferrell	C	1937–1941, 1944–1945, 1947	659
Lefty Gomez	SP	1943	1
Goose Goslin	OF	1921–1930, 1933, 1938	1,361
Clark Griffith	RP	1912–1914	3
Bucky Harris	2B	1919–1928	1,252
Walter Johnson	SP/RP	1907–1927	933
Harmon Killebrew	1B/3B/ OF	1954–1974	2,329
Heinie Manush	OF	1930–1935	792
Paul Molitor	DH/1B	1996–1998	422
Kirby Puckett	OF	1984–1995	1,783
Sam Rice	OF	1915–1933	2,307
Al Simmons	OF	1937–1938	228
George Sisler	1B/OF	1928	20
Tris Speaker	OF/1B	1927	141
Dave Winfield	DH/OF	1993–1994	220
Early Wynn	SP/RP	1939, 1941–1944, 1946–1948	271

HALL OF FAMERS WHO MANAGED TEAM

	Years	Games with Washington/ Minnesota
Joe Cronin	1933–1934	304
Clark Griffith	1912–1920	1,339
Bucky Harris	1924–1928, 1935–1942, 1950–1954	2,752
Walter Johnson	1929–1932	614

MVP AWARD WINNERS

Zoilo Versalles	SS	1965
Harmon Killebrew	1B/3B	1969
Rod Carew	1B	1977

CY YOUNG AWARD WINNERS

Pitcher	Year	W–L	SV ERA
Jim Perry	1970	24–12	3.04
Frank Viola	1988	24–7	2.64
Johan Santana	2004	20–6	2.61

ROOKIE OF THE YEAR AWARD WINNERS

Albie Pearson	OF	1958
Bob Allison	OF	1959
Tony Oliva	OF	1964
Rod Carew	2B	1967
John Castino	3B	1979 (tie)

Chuck Knoblauch	2B	1991
Marty Cordova	OF	1995

GOLD GLOVE WINNERS

Year	Position	Player
1960	C	Earl Battey
1961	C	Earl Battey
1962	SP C 1B	Jim Kaat Earl Battey Vic Power
1963	SP 1B SS	Jim Kaat Vic Power Zoilo Versalles
1964	SP	Jim Kaat
1965	SP SS	Jim Kaat Zoilo Versalles
1966	SP OF	Jim Kaat Tony Oliva
1967	SP	Jim Kaat
1968	SP	Jim Kaat
1969	SP	Jim Kaat
1970	SP	Jim Kaat
1971	SP	Jim Kaat
1972	SP	Jim Kaat
1973	SP	Jim Kaat
1986	3B OF	Gary Gaetti Kirby Puckett
1987	3B OF	Gary Gaetti Kirby Puckett
1988	3B OF	Gary Gaetti Kirby Puckett
1989	3B OF	Gary Gaetti Kirby Puckett
1991	OF	Kirby Puckett
1992	OF	Kirby Puckett
1997	2B	Chuck Knoblauch
2001	1B OF	Doug Mientkiewicz Torii Hunter
2002	OF	Torii Hunter
2003	OF	Torii Hunter
2004	OF	Torii Hunter
2005	OF	Torii Hunter

TRIPLE CROWN WINNERS

None

FIREMAN OF THE YEAR AWARD WINNERS

Ron Perranowski	1969
Ron Perranowski	1970
Bill Campbell	1976
Mike Marshall	1979 (tie)
Jeff Reardon	1987 (tie)

WORLD SERIES MVP

Frank Viola	1987
Jack Morris	1991

LEAGUE CHAMPIONSHIP SERIES MVP

Gary Gaetti	1987
Kirby Puckett	1991

ALL-STAR GAME MVP

Kirby Puckett	1993

MANAGER OF THE YEAR AWARD WINNERS

Tom Kelly	1991

BATTING CHAMPIONS

Year	Player	Avg
1902	Ed Delahanty	.376
1928	Goose Goslin	.379
1935	Buddy Myer	.349
1946	Mickey Vernon	.353
1953	Mickey Vernon	.337
1964	Tony Oliva	.323
1965	Tony Oliva	.321
1969	Rod Carew	.332
1971	Tony Oliva	.337
1972	Rod Carew	.318
1973	Rod Carew	.350
1974	Rod Carew	.364
1975	Rod Carew	.359
1977	Rod Carew	.388
1978	Rod Carew	.333
1989	Kirby Pucket	.339

NINE-INNING NO-HITTERS PITCHED

Year	Pitcher	Opp.	Score
1920	Walter Johnson	BOS	1–0
1931	Bobby Burke	BOS	5–0
1962	Jack Kralick	KC	1–0
1967	Dean Chance	CLE	2–1
1994	Scott Erickson	MIL	6–0
1999	Eric Milton	ANA	7–0

20-GAME WINNERS

Year	Pitcher	W–L
1910	Walter Johnson	25–17
1911	Walter Johnson	25–13
1912	Walter Johnson Bob Groom	33–12 24–13
1913	Walter Johnson	36–7
1914	Walter Johnson	28–18
1915	Walter Johnson	27–13
1916	Walter Johnson	25–20
1917	Walter Johnson	23–16
1918	Walter Johnson	23–13
1919	Walter Johnson	20–14

1924	Walter Johnson	23–7
1925	Stan Coveleski Walter Johnson	20–5 20–7
1932	General Crowder Monte Weaver	26–13 22–10
1933	General Crowder Earl Whitehill	24–15 22–8
1939	Dutch Leonard	20–8
1945	Roger Wolff	20–10
1953	Bob Porterfield	22–10
1962	Camilo Pascual	20–11
1963	Camilo Pascual	21–9
1965	Mudcat Grant	21–7
1966	Jim Kaat	25–13
1967	Dean Chance	20–14
1969	Jim Perry Dave Boswell	20–6 20–12
1970	Jim Perry	24–12
1973	Bert Blyleven	20–17
1977	Dave Goltz	20–11
1979	Jerry Koosman	20–13
1988	Frank Viola	24–7
1991	Scott Erickson	20–8
1997	Brad Radke	20–10
2004	Johan Santana	20–6

Retired Uniform Numbers

Number	Player	Position
3	Harmon Killebrew	3B/1B
6	Tony Oliva	OF
14	Kent Hrbek	1B
29	Rod Carew	2B/1B
34	Kirby Puckett	OF

Team Records—Wins & Losses

- Games won in a season: 102 in 1965
- Games lost in a season: 113 in 1904
- Games won in a month: 24 in August 1945
- Games lost in a month: 29 in July 1909
- Consecutive games won: 17 in 1912
- Consecutive games lost: 18 in 1948 and 1959
- Biggest shutout victory: 16–0 over Boston on May 25, 1990
- Biggest shutout loss: 17–0 (four times): to New York Yankees, April 24, 1909; to New York Yankees, July 6, 1920; to Chicago White Sox, September 19, 1925 (second game); to California Angels, April 23, 1980
- Highest winning percentage: .651 in 1933 (99–53)
- Lowest winning percentage: .252 in 1904 (38–113)

Team Records—Batting

- Highest team batting average: .303 in 1925
- Lowest team batting average: .223 in 1909
- Highest team slugging average: .437 in 2002
- Highest team on-base percentage: .372 in 1925
- Total hits: 1,633 in 1966
- Extra-base hits: 551 in 2002
- Hits in a game: 25 vs. Boston June 20, 1980 and Cleveland on June 4, 2002
- Longest individual hitting streak: 33, Heinie Manush, 1933
- Most .300 hitters in a single season: 9 in 1925
- Home runs: 225 in 1963
- Home runs in a month: 15, Harmon Killebrew, May 1959
- Home runs in a game: 8 vs. Washington Senators on August 29, 1963 (first game)
- Home runs by a rookie: 33, Jimmie Hall, 1963
- Home runs by a right-hander: 49, Harmon Killebrew, 1964 and 1969
- Home runs by a left-hander: 34, Kent Hrbek, 1987
- Home runs by a switch-hitter: 29, Chili Davis, 1991
- Grand slams: 8 in 1938 and 1961
- Grand slams (individual; single season): 3, Bob Allison, 1961; Rod Carew, 1976; Kent Hrbek, 1985; Kirby Puckett, 1992
- Grand slams (individual; career): 10, Harmon Killebrew
- Triples: 100 in 1932
- Doubles: 348 in 2002
- Singles: 1,209 in 1935
- Walks: 690 in 1956
- Runs scored: 892 in 1930
- Runs scored in a game: 24 vs. Detroit, April 24, 1996
- Runs scored in an inning: 12 vs. St. Louis Browns on July 10, 1926 (eighth inning) and vs. Chicago White Sox on May 12, 1997 (seventh inning)
- Most batters hit by a pitch: 80 in 1911
- Times shut out: 29 in 1909
- Grounded into double plays: 172 in 1996
- Fewest grounded into double plays: 93 in 1965
- Runners left on base: 1,305 in 1935

TEAM RECORDS—BASERUNNING

- Stolen bases: 291 in 1913
- Caught stealing: 75 in 1976

TEAM RECORDS—PITCHING

- Lowest earned run average: 2.14 in 1918
- Complete games: 137 in 1904
- Saves: 58 in 1970
- Strikeouts: 1,123 in 2004
- Shutouts: 25 in 1914
- Walks: 779 in 1949
- Hit batsmen: 69 in 1913
- Wild pitches: 73 in 1964
- Consecutive wins (individual): 16, Walter Johnson, 1912; (2 seasons): 17, Johan Santana, 2004 (13) and 2005 (4)
- Consecutive losses (individual): 15, Bob Groom, 1909
- Strikeouts in a game (individual): 15 (five times): Camilo Pascual, April 18, 1960; Camilo Pascual, July 19, 1961 (first game); Joe Decker, June 26, 1973; Jerry Koosman, June 23, 1980; Bert Blyleven, August 1, 1986
- Runs allowed in a game: 24 vs. Boston Red Sox, September 27, 1940

TEAM RECORDS—FIELDING

- Best fielding average: .987 in 2002
- Most errors committed: 325 in 1901
- Fewest errors committed: 74 in 2002
- Most double plays turned: 203 in 1979
- Fewest double plays turned: 93 in 1912

TEAM RECORDS—MISCELLANEOUS

- Number of times league champions: 6
- Number of times finishing last in league: 14
- Largest attendance, single game: 53,106 vs. Kansas City Royals, September 27, 1987
- Largest attendance, doubleheader: 51,017 vs. Oakland A's, July 28, 1990
- Players used in a season: 46 in 1995
- Seasons played: 21 by Walter Johnson

PRIMARY PITCHING STAFFS

Year	Starter	Starter	Starter	Starter	Starter	Closer	Bullpen	Bullpen	Bullpen
2005	Santana	Radke	Lohse	Silva	Mays	Nathan	Rincon	Crain	Romero
2004	Radke	Lohse	Santana	Silva	Mulholland	Nathan	Rincon	Romero	Fultz
2003	Radke	Lohse	Rogers	Reed	Mays	Guardado	Rincon	Romero	Hawkins
2002	Radke	Lohse	Milton	Reed	Mays	Guardado	Jackson	Romero	Hawkins
2001	Radke	Lohse	Milton	Reed	Mays	Hawkins	Guardado	Wells	Carrasco
2000	Radke	Redman	Milton	Bergman	Mays	Hawkins	Guardado	Wells	Miller
1999	Radke	Hawkins	Milton	Lincoln	Mays	Trombley	Guardado	Wells	Miller
1998	Radke	Hawkins	Milton	Tewksbury	Morgan	Aguilera	Guardado	Trombley	Carrasco
1997	Radke	Hawkins	Robertson	Tewksbury	Rodriguez	Aguilera	Guardado	Trombley	Swindell
1996	Radke	Aguilera	Robertson	Aldred	Rodriguez	Stevens	Guardado	Hansell	Naulty
1995	Radke	Tapani	Trombley	Erickson	Rodriguez	Aguilera	Guardado	Stevens	Mahomes
1994	Deshaies	Tapani	Mahomes	Erickson	Pulido	Aguilera	Guthrie	Willis	Casian
1993	Deshaies	Tapani	Banks	Erickson	Guardado	Aguilera	Hartley	Willis	Casian
1992	Smiley	Tapani	Krueger	Erickson	Mahomes	Aguilera	Guthrie	Willis	Edens
1991	Morris	Tapani	Anderson	Erickson	West	Aguilera	Guthrie	Bedrosian	Leach
1990	Smith	Tapani	Anderson	Guthrie	West	Aguilera	Berenguer	Wayne	Leach
1989	Smith	Rawley	Anderson	Viola	Dyer	Reardon	Berenguer	Wayne	Gonzalez
1988	Blyleven	Lea	Anderson	Viola	Toliver	Reardon	Berenguer	Atherton	Portugal
1987	Blyleven	Straker	Smithson	Viola	Niekro	Reardon	Berenguer	Atherton	Frazier
1986	Blyleven	Heaton	Smithson	Viola	Portugal	Atherton	Davis	Pastore	Jackson
1985	Blyleven	Butcher	Smithson	Viola	Schrom	Davis	Filson	Eufemia	Lysander
1984	Hodge	Butcher	Smithson	Viola	Schrom	Davis	Filson	Whitehouse	Lysander

PRIMARY PITCHING STAFFS (CONT.)

Year	Starter	Starter	Starter	Starter	Starter	Closer	Bullpen	Bullpen	Bullpen
1983	Williams	Castillo	Havens	Viola	Schrom	Davis	O'Connor	Whitehouse	Lysander
1982	Williams	Castillo	Havens	Viola	O'Connor	Davis	Felton	Little	Redfern
1981	Williams	Redfern	Arroyo	Erickson	Koosman	Corbett	Verhoeven	Cooper	O'Connor
1980	Zahn	Redfern	Jackson	Erickson	Koosman	Corbett	Verhoeven	Kinnunen	Arroyo
1979	Zahn	Goltz	Hartzell	Erickson	Koosman	Marshall	Redfern	Bacsik	Jackson
1978	Zahn	Goltz	Serum	Erickson	Jackson	Marshall	Thayer	Johnson	Scarce
1977	Zahn	Goltz	Thormodsgard	Redfern	Schueler	Johnson	Burgmeier	Johnson	Holly
1976	Singer	Goltz	Hughes	Redfern	Bane	Campbell	Burgmeier	Luebber	Albury
1975	Blyleven	Goltz	Hughes	Albury	Corbin	Burgmeier	Campbell	Butler	Johnson
1974	Blyleven	Goltz	Decker	Albury	Corbin	Campbell	Burgmeier	Butler	Hands
1973	Blyleven	Kaat	Decker	Woodson	Hands	Corbin	Goltz	Campbell	Sanders
1972	Blyleven	Kaat	Perry	Woodson	Corbin	Granger	LaRoche	Strickland	Norton
1971	Blyleven	Kaat	Perry	Luebber	Corbin	Hall	Williams	Perranoski	Haydel
1970	Blyleven	Kaat	Perry	Zepp	Tiant	Perranoski	Williams	Hall	Woodson
1969	Boswell	Kaat	Perry	Hall	Chance	Perranoski	Miller	Worthington	Woodson
1968	Boswell	Kaat	Perry	Merritt	Chance	Worthington	Miller	Perranoski	Roland
1967	Boswell	Kaat	Grant	Merritt	Chance	Worthington	Kline	Perry	Roland
1966	Boswell	Kaat	Grant	Perry	Pascual	Worthington	Cimino	Merritt	Klippstein
1965	Boswell	Kaat	Grant	Perry	Pascual	Worthington	Pleis	Stigman	Klippstein
1964	Stigman	Kaat	Grant	Roland	Pascual	Worthington	Pleis	Perry	Arrigo
1963	Stigman	Kaat	Perry	Stange	Pascual	Dailey	Pleis	Roggenburk	Moore
1962	Stigman	Kaat	Kralick	Bonikowski	Pascual	Moore	Stange	Maranda	Sullivan
1961	Ramos	Kaat	Kralick	Lee	Pascual	Moore	Pleis	Stobbs	McDevitt
1960	Ramos	Woodeshick	Kralick	Lee	Pascual	Moore	Clevenger	Hernandez	Stobbs
1959	Ramos	Fischer	Kemmerer	Griggs	Pascual	Clevenger	Woodeshick	Stobbs	Hyde
1958	Ramos	Valentinetti	Kemmerer	Griggs	Pascual	Hyde	Clevenger	Romonosky	Stobbs
1957	Ramos	Stobbs	Kemmerer	Abernathy	Pascual	Clevenger	Hernandez	Byerly	Hyde
1956	Ramos	Stobbs	Stone	Wiesler	Pascual	Chakales	Grob	Griggs	
1955	Porterfield	Stobbs	Stone	Schmitz	McDermott	Ramos	Pascual	Abernathy	
1954	Porterfield	Stobbs	Stone	Schmitz	McDermott	Stewart	Pascual	Shea	
1953	Porterfield	Stobbs	Shea	Marrero	Masterson	Dixon	Sima	Schmitz	
1952	Porterfield	Moreno	Shea	Marrero	Masterson	Consuegra	Johnson	Ferrick	
1951	Porterfield	Moreno	Johnson	Marrero	Hudson	Consuegra	Harris	Haynes	
1950	Kuzava	Consuegra	Haynes	Marrero	Hudson	Harris	Singleton	Pearce	Sima
1949	Scarborough	Calvert	Harris	Weik	Hudson	Welteroth	Haynes	Hittle	
1948	Scarborough	Wynn	Masterson	Haefner	Hudson	Ferrick	Welteroth	Thompson	Candini
1947	Scarborough	Wynn	Masterson	Haefner	Hudson	Ferrick	Cary	Pieretti	Candini
1946	Scarborough	Leonard	Newsom	Haefner	Wolff	Hudson	Pieretti	Masterson	
1945	Pieretti	Leonard	Niggeling	Haefner	Wolff	Carrasquel	Ullrich	Holborow	
1944	Wynn	Leonard	Niggeling	Haefner	Wolff	Carrasquel	Candini	Lefebvre	
1943	Wynn	Leonard	Candini	Haefner	Carrasquel	Mertz	Scarborough	Pyle	
1942	Wynn	Hudson	Newsom	Masterson	Carrasquel	Zuber	Scarborough	Trotter	
1941	Leonard	Hudson	Chase	Sundra	Kennedy	Zuber	Carrasquel	Masterson	
1940	Leonard	Hudson	Chase	Masterson	Krakauskas	Monteagudo	Carrasquel	Haynes	
1939	Leonard	Haynes	Chase	Carrasquel	Krakauskas	Appleton	Masterson	Kelley	DeShong
1938	Leonard	Ferrell	Chase	Weaver	Kelley	Appleton	Hogsett	DeShong	
1937	DeShong	Ferrell	Appleton	Weaver	Fischer	Linke	Cohen	Chase	
1936	DeShong	Newsom	Appleton	Whitehill	Cascarella	Weaver	Cohen	Russell	
1935	Hadley	Newsom	Linke	Whitehill	Burke	Pettit	Coppola	Russell	
1934	Weaver	Stewart	Thomas	Whitehill	Burke	Russell	McColl	Crowder	Prim
1933	Weaver	Stewart	Thomas	Whitehill	Crowder	Russell	McAfee	Burke	Chapman
1932	Weaver	Brown	Thomas	Marberry	Crowder	Coffman	Burke	Ragland	

PRIMARY PITCHING STAFFS (CONT.)

Year	Starter	Starter	Starter	Starter	Starter	Closer	Bullpen	Bullpen	Bullpen
1931	Jones	Brown	Fischer	Marberry	Crowder	Hadley	Tauscher	Burke	
1930	Jones	Brown	Hadley	Marberry	Crowder	Liska	Burke	Braxton	
1929	Jones	Braxton	Hadley	Marberry	Burke	Liska	Brown	Thomas	
1928	Jones	Braxton	Hadley	Gaston	Zachary	Marberry	Brown	Burke	
1927	Lisenbee	Thurston	Hadley	Johnson	Zachary	Braxton	Marberry	Crowder	Burke
1926	Coveleski	Ruether	Crowder	Johnson	Murray	Marberry	Morrell	Ogden	Ferguson
1925	Coveleski	Ruether	Zachary	Johnson	Mogridge	Marberry	Russell	Ogden	Gregg
1924	Ogden	Marberry	Zachary	Johnson	Mogridge	Russell	Zahniser	Martina	Speece
1923	Zahniser	Warmoth	Zachary	Johnson	Mogridge	Russell	Hollingsworth	Brillheart	Marberry
1922	Francis	Erickson	Zachary	Johnson	Mogridge	Phillips	Brillheart	Gleason	
1921	Courtney	Erickson	Zachary	Johnson	Mogridge	Acosta	Schacht	Shaw	
1920	Courtney	Erickson	Zachary	Johnson	Shaw	Acosta	Schacht	Snyder	
1919	Harper	Erickson	Zachary	Johnson	Shaw	Gill	Craft	Thompson	
1918	Harper	Ayers	Matteson	Johnson	Shaw	Hovlik			
1917	Harper	Gallia	Dumont	Johnson	Shaw	Ayers	Craft		
1916	Harper	Gallia	Boehling	Johnson	Ayers	Shaw	Dumont	Thomas	
1915	Shaw	Gallia	Boehling	Johnson	Ayers	Harper	Hopper	Engel	
1914	Shaw	Engel	Boehling	Johnson	Ayers	Harper	Bentley		
1913	Groom	Engel	Boehling	Johnson	Hughes	Gallia	Mullin		
1912	Groom	Engel	Cashion	Johnson	Hughes	Vaughn	Pelty	Walker	
1911	Groom	Walker	Gray	Johnson	Hughes	Otey	Becker	Cashion	
1910	Groom	Walker	Gray	Johnson	Reisling	Otey	Oberlin	Moyer	
1909	Groom	Smith	Gray	Johnson	Hughes	Witherup	Oberlin	Reisling	
1908	Burns	Smith	Keeley	Johnson	Hughes	Cates	Falkenberg	Tannehill	
1907	Patten	Smith	Falkenberg	Graham	Hughes	Gehring	Johnson	Oberlin	
1906	Patten	Smith	Falkenberg	Kitson	Hughes	Sudhoff			
1905	Patten	Townsend	Wolfe	Jacobson	Hughes	Falkenberg	Adams		
1904	Patten	Townsend	Wolfe	Jacobson	Hughes	Dunkle	Orth		
1903	Patten	Orth	Wilson	Lee	Dunkle	Townsend			
1902	Patten	Orth	Carrick	Lee	Townsend				
1901	Patten	Mercer	Carrick	Lee	Gear				

PRIMARY STARTING LINEUPS

Year	C	1B	2B	3B	SS	LF	CF	RF	DH
2005	Mauer	Morneau	Punto	Cuddyer	Castro	Stewart	Hunter	Jones	LeCroy
2004	Blanco	Mientkiewicz	Rivas	Koskie	Guzman	Ford	Hunter	Jones	Offerman
2003	Pierzynski	Mientkiewicz	Rivas	Koskie	Guzman	Jones	Hunter	Mohr	LeCroy
2002	Pierzynski	Mientkiewicz	Rivas	Koskie	Guzman	Jones	Hunter	Mohr	Ortiz
2001	Pierzynski	Mientkiewicz	Rivas	Koskie	Guzman	Jones	Hunter	Lawton	Ortiz
2000	LeCroy	Coomer	Canizaro	Koskie	Guzman	Jones	Hunter	Lawton	Ortiz
1999	Steinbach	Mientkiewicz	Walker	Koskie	Guzman	Allen	Hunter	Lawton	Cordova
1998	Steinbach	Ortiz	Walker	Gates	Meares	Cordova	Nixon	Lawton	Molitor
1997	Steinbach	Stahoviak	Knoblauch	Coomer	Meares	Cordova	Becker	Lawton	Molitor
1996	Myers	Stahoviak	Knoblauch	Hollins	Meares	Cordova	Becker	Lawton	Molitor
1995	Walbeck	Stahoviak	Knoblauch	Leius	Meares	Cordova	Becker	Puckett	Munoz
1994	Walbeck	Hrbek	Knoblauch	Leius	Meares	Mack	Cole	Puckett	Winfield
1993	Harper	Hrbek	Knoblauch	Pagliarulo	Meares	Munoz	Puckett	Larkin	Winfield
1992	Harper	Hrbek	Knoblauch	Leius	Gagne	Mack	Puckett	Munoz	Davis
1991	Harper	Hrbek	Knoblauch	Pagliarulo	Gagne	Gladden	Puckett	Mack	Davis
1990	Harper	Hrbek	Newman	Gaetti	Gagne	Gladden	Puckett	Moses	Larkin

PRIMARY STARTING LINEUPS (CONT.)

Year	C	1B	2B	3B	SS	LF	CF	RF	DH
1989	Harper	Hrbek	Backman	Gaetti	Gagne	Gladden	Puckett	Bush	Dwyer
1988	Laudner	Hrbek	Lombardozzi	Gaetti	Gagne	Gladden	Puckett	Bush	Larkin
1987	Laudner	Hrbek	Lombardozzi	Gaetti	Gagne	Gladden	Puckett	Brunansky	Smalley
1986	Salas	Hrbek	Lombardozzi	Gaetti	Gagne	Bush	Puckett	Brunansky	Smalley
1985	Salas	Hrbek	Teufel	Gaetti	Gagne	Hatcher	Puckett	Brunansky	Smalley
1984	Engle	Hrbek	Teufel	Gaetti	Jimenez	Hatcher	Puckett	Brunansky	Bush
1983	Engle	Hrbek	Castino	Gaetti	Washington	Ward	Brown	Brunansky	Bush
1982	Laudner	Hrbek	Castino	Gaetti	Washington	Ward	Mitchell	Brunansky	Johnson
1981	Butera	Goodwin	Wilfong	Castino	Smalley	Ward	Hatcher	Engle	Adams
1980	Wynegar	Jackson	Wilfong	Castino	Smalley	Sofield	Landreaux	Powell	Morales
1979	Wynegar	Jackson	Wilfong	Castino	Smalley	Rivera	Landreaux	Powell	Morales
1978	Wynegar	Carew	Randall	Cubbage	Smalley	Norwood	Ford	Powell	Adams
1977	Wynegar	Carew	Randall	Cubbage	Smalley	Hisle	Bostock	Ford	Kusick
1976	Wynegar	Carew	Randall	Cubbage	Smalley	Hisle	Bostock	Ford	Kusick
1975	Borgmann	Kusick	Carew	Soderholm	Thompson	Braun	Ford	Bostock	Oliva
1974	Borgmann	Kusick	Carew	Soderholm	Thompson	Braun	Brye	Darwin	Oliva
1973	Mitterwald	Lis	Carew	Braun	Thompson	Holt	Hisle	Darwin	Oliva
1972	Mitterwald	Killebrew	Carew	Soderholm	Thompson	Brye	Darwin	Tovar	
1971	Mitterwald	Reese	Carew	Braun	Cardenas	Tovar	Holt	Oliva	
1970	Mitterwald	Reese	Thompson	Killebrew	Cardenas	Holt	Tovar	Oliva	
1969	Roseboro	Reese	Carew	Killebrew	Cardenas	Allison	Uhlaender	Oliva	
1968	Roseboro	Reese	Carew	Tovar	Hernandez	Allison	Uhlaender	Oliva	
1967	Zimmerman	Killebrew	Carew	Rollins	Versalles	Allison	Uhlaender	Oliva	
1966	Battey	Mincher	Allen	Killebrew	Versalles	Hall	Uhlaender	Oliva	
1965	Battey	Mincher	Kindall	Rollins	Versalles	Allison	Hall	Oliva	
1964	Battey	Allison	Allen	Rollins	Versalles	Killebrew	Hall	Oliva	
1963	Battey	Power	Allen	Rollins	Versalles	Killebrew	Green	Allison	
1962	Battey	Power	Allen	Rollins	Versalles	Killebrew	Green	Allison	
1961	Battey	Killebrew	Martin	Tuttle	Versalles	Lemon	Green	Allison	
1960	Battey	Becquer	Gardner	Bertoia	Valdivielso	Lemon	Green	Allison	
1959	Naragon	Sievers	Bertoia	Killebrew	Consolo	Lemon	Allison	Throneberry	
1958	Courtney	Zauchin	Aspromonte	Yost	Bridges	Sievers	Pearson	Lemon	
1957	Berberet	Runnels	Plews	Yost	Bridges	Sievers	Usher	Lemon	
1956	Courtney	Runnels	Plews	Yost	Valdivielso	Sievers	Herzog	Lemon	
1955	Fitz Gerald	Vernon	Runnels	Yost	Valdivielso	Sievers	Umphlett	Paula	
1954	Fitz Gerald	Vernon	Terwilliger	Yost	Runnels	Sievers	Busby	Umphlett	
1953	Fitz Gerald	Vernon	Terwilliger	Yost	Runnels	Vollmer	Busby	Jensen	
1952	Grasso	Vernon	Baker	Yost	Runnels	Coan	Busby	Jensen	
1951	Guerra	Vernon	Michaels	Yost	Runnels	Coan	Noren	Mele	
1950	Evans	Vernon	Michaels	Yost	Dente	Coan	Noren	Mele	
1949	Evans	Robinson	Kozar	Yost	Dente	Stewart	Vollmer	Lewis	
1948	Early	Vernon	Kozar	Yost	Christman	Coan	Gillenwater	Stewart	
1947	Evans	Vernon	Priddy	Yost	Christman	Grace	Spence	Lewis	
1946	Evans	Vernon	Priddy	Hitchcock	Travis	Grace	Spence	Lewis	
1945	Ferrell	Kuhel	Myatt	Clift	Torres	Case	Binks	Lewis	
1944	Ferrell	Kuhel	Myatt	Torres	Sullivan	Case	Spence	Ortiz	
1943	Early	Vernon	Priddy	Clary	Sullivan	Johnson	Spence	Case	
1942	Early	Vernon	Clary	Estalella	Sullivan	Case	Spence	Campbell	
1941	Early	Vernon	Bloodworth	Archie	Travis	Case	Cramer	Lewis	
1940	Ferrell	Bonura	Bloodworth	Travis	Pofahl	Walker	Case	Lewis	
1939	Ferrell	Vernon	Bloodworth	Lewis	Travis	Estalella	Case	Wright	
1938	Ferrell	Bonura	Myer	Lewis	Travis	Simmons	West	Case	

PRIMARY STARTING LINEUPS (CONT.)

Year	C	1B	2B	3B	SS	LF	CF	RF	DH
1937	Ferrell	Kuhel	Myer	Lewis	Travis	Simmons	Almada	Stone	
1936	Bolton	Kuhel	Bluege	Lewis	Travis	Stone	Chapman	Reynolds	
1935	Bolton	Kuhel	Myer	Travis	Bluege	Manush	Powell	Stone	
1934	Phillips	Kuhel	Myer	Travis	Cronin	Manush	Schulte	Stone	
1933	Sewell	Kuhel	Myer	Bluege	Cronin	Manush	Schulte	Goslin	
1932	Spencer	Kuhel	Myer	Bluege	Cronin	Manush	West	Reynolds	
1931	Spencer	Kuhel	Myer	Bluege	Cronin	Manush	West	Rice	
1930	Spencer	Judge	Myer	Bluege	Cronin	Manush	West	Rice	
1929	Tate	Judge	Myer	Hayes	Cronin	Goslin	West	Rice	
1928	Ruel	Judge	Harris	Bluege	Reeves	Goslin	Barnes	Rice	
1927	Ruel	Judge	Harris	Bluege	Reeves	Goslin	Speaker	Rice	
1926	Ruel	Judge	Harris	Bluege	Myer	Goslin	Jeanes	Rice	
1925	Ruel	Judge	Harris	Bluege	Peckinpaugh	Goslin	McNeely	Rice	
1924	Ruel	Judge	Harris	Bluege	Peckinpaugh	Goslin	Leibold	Rice	
1923	Ruel	Judge	Harris	Bluege	Peckinpaugh	Goslin	Leibold	Rice	
1922	Gharrity	Judge	Harris	LaMotte	Peckinpaugh	Goslin	Rice	Brower	
1921	Gharrity	Judge	Harris	Shanks	O'Rourke	Miller	Rice	Milan	
1920	Gharrity	Judge	Harris	Ellerbe	O'Neill	Milan	Rice	Roth	
1919	Picinich	Judge	Janvrin	Foster	Shanks	Menosky	Milan	Rice	
1918	Ainsmith	Judge	Morgan	Foster	Lavan	Shotton	Milan	Schulte	
1917	Ainsmith	Judge	Morgan	Foster	Shanks	Menosky	Milan	Rice	
1916	Henry	Judge	Morgan	Foster	McBride	Shanks	Milan	Rice	
1915	Henry	Gandil	Morgan	Foster	McBride	Shanks	Milan	Moeller	
1914	Henry	Gandil	Morgan	Foster	McBride	Shanks	Milan	Moeller	
1913	Henry	Gandil	Morgan	Foster	McBride	Shanks	Milan	Moeller	
1912	Henry	Gandil	Morgan	Foster	McBride	Shanks	Milan	Moeller	
1911	Street	Schaefer	Cunningham	Conroy	McBride	Walker	Milan	Gessler	
1910	Street	Unglaub	Killefer	Elberfeld	McBride	Lelivelt	Milan	Gessler	
1909	Street	Donahue	Delahanty	Conroy	McBride	Browne	Milan	Clymer	
1908	Street	Freeman	Delahanty	Shipke	McBride	Ganley	Milan	Clymer	
1907	Warner	Anderson	Delahanty	Shipke	Altizer	Clymer	Jones	Ganley	
1906	Wakefield	Stahl	Schlafly	Cross	Altizer	Anderson	Jones	Hickman	
1905	Heydon	Stahl	Hickman	Hill	Cassidy	Huelsman	Jones	Anderson	
1904	Kittridge	Stahl	McCormick	Hill	Cassidy	Huelsman	O'Neill	Donovan	
1903	Kittridge	Clarke	McCormick	Coughlin	Moran	Selbach	Ryan	Lee	
1902	Clarke	Carey	Doyle	Coughlin	Ely	Delahanty	Ryan	Lee	
1901	Clarke	Grady	Farrell	Coughlin	Clingman	Foster	Waldron	Dungan	

Top 10 Batting Leaders, Single Season & Career with Team

Games Played: Career with Team

Player	G	PA
1. Harmon Killebrew	2,329	9,462
2. Sam Rice	2,307	9,879
3. Joe Judge	2,084	8,906
4. Clyde Milan	1,982	8,312
5. Ossie Bluege	1,867	7,452
6. Mickey Vernon	1,805	7,769
7. Kirby Puckett	1,783	7,831
8. Kent Hrbek	1,747	7,137
9. Eddie Yost	1,690	7,461
10. Tony Oliva	1,676	6,879

At-Bats: Season

Player	AB	Year
1. Kirby Puckett	691	1985
2. Kirby Puckett	680	1986
3. Tony Oliva	672	1964
4. Buddy Lewis	668	1937
5. Zoilo Versalles	666	1965
6. Doc Cramer	660	1941
Paul Molitor	660	1996
8. Zoilo Versalles	659	1964
9. Heinie Manush	658	1933
10. Kirby Puckett	657	1988
Cesar Tovar	657	1971

At-Bats: Career with Team

Player	AB	PA
1. Sam Rice	8,934	9,879
2. Harmon Killebrew	7,835	9,462
3. Joe Judge	7,663	8,906
4. Clyde Milan	7,359	8,312
5. Kirby Puckett	7,244	7,831
6. Mickey Vernon	6,930	7,769
7. Ossie Bluege	6,440	7,452
8. Tony Oliva	6,301	6,879
9. Rod Carew	6,235	6,980
10. Kent Hrbek	6,192	7,137

Batting Average: Season

Player	BA	Year
1. Rod Carew	.388	1977
2. Goose Goslin	.379	1928
3. Ed Delahanty	.376	1902
4. Rod Carew	.364	1974
5. Rod Carew	.359	1975
Cecil Travis	.359	1941
7. Kirby Puckett	.356	1988
8. Goose Goslin	.354	1926
9. Mickey Vernon	.353	1946
10. Rod Carew	.350	1973

Batting Average: Career with Team

Player	BA	PA
1. Rod Carew	.334	6,980
2. Heinie Manush	.328	3,564
3. Sam Rice	.323	9,879
Goose Goslin	.323	5,810
5. Kirby Puckett	.318	7,831
6. John Stone	.317	2,334
7. Cecil Travis	.314	5,414
8. Shane Mack	.309	2,434
9. Brian Harper	.306	2,691
10. Joe Cronin	.304	4,138

Total Hits: Season

Player	H	Year
1. Rod Carew	239	1977
2. Kirby Puckett	234	1988
3. Sam Rice	227	1925
4. Paul Molitor	225	1996
5. Kirby Puckett	223	1986
6. Heinie Manush	221	1933
7. Rod Carew	218	1974
Cecil Travis	218	1941
9. Tony Oliva	217	1964
10. Sam Rice	216	1924
Sam Rice	216	1926

Total Hits: Career with Team

Player	H	PA
1. Sam Rice	2,889	9,879
2. Kirby Puckett	2,304	7,831
3. Joe Judge	2,291	8,906
4. Clyde Milan	2,100	8,312
5. Rod Carew	2,085	6,980
6. Harmon Killebrew	2,024	9,462
7. Mickey Vernon	1,993	7,769
8. Tony Oliva	1,917	6,879
9. Buddy Myer	1,828	7,028
10. Ossie Bluege	1,751	7,452

Home Runs: Season

Player	HR	Year
1. Harmon Killebrew	49	1964
Harmon Killebrew	49	1969
3. Harmon Killebrew	48	1962
4. Harmon Killebrew	46	1961
5. Harmon Killebrew	45	1963
6. Harmon Killebrew	44	1967
7. Harmon Killebrew	42	1959
Roy Sievers	42	1957
9. Harmon Killebrew	41	1970
10. Harmon Killebrew	39	1966
Roy Sievers	39	1958

Home Runs: Career with Team

Player	HR	PA
1. Harmon Killebrew	559	9,462
2. Kent Hrbek	293	7,137
3. Bob Allison	256	5,921
4. Tony Oliva	220	6,879
5. Kirby Puckett	207	7,831
6. Gary Gaetti	201	5,459
7. Roy Sievers	180	3,574
8. Tom Brunansky	163	3,760
9. Jim Lemon	159	3,624
10. Torii Hunter	133	3,633

Triples: Season

Player	3B	Year
1. Goose Goslin	20	1925
Cristian Guzman	20	2000
3. Joe Cassidy	19	1904
Cecil Travis	19	1941
5. Joe Cronin	18	1932
Goose Goslin	18	1923
Sam Rice	18	1923
Howie Shanks	18	1921
John Stone	18	1935
10. Goose Goslin	17	1924
Heinie Manush	17	1933

Triples: Career with Team

Player	3B	PA
1. Sam Rice	183	9,879
2. Joe Judge	157	8,906
3. Goose Goslin	125	5,810
4. Buddy Myer	113	7,028

5. Mickey Vernon	108	7,769
6. Clyde Milan	105	8,312
7. Buddy Lewis	93	5,937
8. Rod Carew	90	6,980
9. Howie Shanks	87	5,508
10. Cecil Travis	78	5,414

Doubles: Season

Player	2B	Year
1. Mickey Vernon	51	1946
2. Stan Spence	50	1946
3. Marty Cordova	46	1996
4. Joe Cronin	45	1933
Chuck Knoblauch	45	1994
Kirby Puckett	45	1989
Zoilo Versalles	45	1965
8. Joe Cronin	44	1931
Matt Lawton	44	2000
10. Six tied with . . .	43	—

Doubles: Career with Team

Player	2B	PA
1. Sam Rice	479	9,879
2. Joe Judge	421	8,906
3. Kirby Puckett	414	7,831
4. Mickey Vernon	391	7,769
5. Tony Oliva	329	6,879
6. Kent Hrbek	312	7,137
7. Rod Carew	305	6,980
Buddy Myer	305	7,028
9. Goose Goslin	289	5,810
10. Eddie Yost	282	7,461

Extra-Base Hits: Season

Player	XBH	Year
1. Tony Oliva	84	1964
2. Stan Spence	76	1946
Zoilo Versalles	76	1965
4. Kirby Puckett	74	1986
5. Harmon Killebrew	73	1961
6. Goose Goslin	72	1925
7. Harmon Killebrew	71	1969
Kirby Puckett	71	1988
9. Torii Hunter	70	2002
Harmon Killebrew	70	1962
Roy Sievers	70	1957

Extra-Base Hits: Career with Team

Player	XBH	PA
1. Harmon Killebrew	860	9,462
2. Sam Rice	695	9,879
3. Kirby Puckett	678	7,831
4. Joe Judge	649	8,906
5. Kent Hrbek	623	7,137
6. Mickey Vernon	620	7,769
7. Tony Oliva	597	6,879
8. Goose Goslin	541	5,810
9. Bob Allison	525	5,921
10. Gary Gaetti	478	5,459

Total Bases: Season

Player	TB	Year
1. Tony Oliva	374	1964
2. Kirby Puckett	365	1986
3. Kirby Puckett	358	1988
4. Rod Carew	351	1977
5. Kirby Puckett	333	1987
6. Roy Sievers	331	1957
7. Goose Goslin	329	1925
8. Harmon Killebrew	328	1961
9. Heinie Manush	325	1932
10. Harmon Killebrew	324	1969

Total Bases: Career with Team

Player	TB	PA
1. Harmon Killebrew	4,026	9,462
2. Sam Rice	3,833	9,879
3. Kirby Puckett	3,453	7,831
4. Joe Judge	3,239	8,906
5. Tony Oliva	3,002	6,879
6. Kent Hrbek	2,976	7,137
7. Mickey Vernon	2,963	7,769
8. Rod Carew	2,792	6,980
9. Clyde Milan	2,601	8,312
10. Goose Goslin	2,579	5,810

Runs Batted In: Season

Player	RBI	Year
1. Harmon Killebrew	140	1969
2. Goose Goslin	129	1924
3. Joe Cronin	126	1930
Joe Cronin	126	1931
Harmon Killebrew	126	1962
6. Harmon Killebrew	122	1961
7. Kirby Puckett	121	1988
8. Goose Goslin	120	1927
9. Larry Hisle	119	1977
Harmon Killebrew	119	1971

Runs Batted In: Career with Team

Player	RBI	PA
1. Harmon Killebrew	1,540	9,462
2. Kent Hrbek	1,086	7,137
3. Kirby Puckett	1,085	7,831
4. Sam Rice	1,045	9,879
5. Mickey Vernon	1,026	7,769
6. Joe Judge	1,001	8,906
7. Tony Oliva	947	6,879
8. Goose Goslin	931	5,810
9. Ossie Bluege	848	7,452
10. Bob Allison	796	5,921

Runs Scored: Season

Player	R	Year
1. Chuck Knoblauch	140	1996
2. Rod Carew	128	1977
3. Joe Cronin	127	1930
4. Zoilo Versalles	126	1965
5. Buddy Lewis	122	1938
6. Heinie Manush	121	1932
Sam Rice	121	1930
8. Buddy Myer	120	1932
Cesar Tovar	120	1970
10. Kirby Puckett	119	1986
Sam Rice	119	1929

Runs Scored: Career with Team

Player	R	PA
1. Sam Rice	1,466	9,879
2. Harmon Killebrew	1,258	9,462
3. Joe Judge	1,154	8,906
4. Kirby Puckett	1,071	7,831
5. Buddy Myer	1,037	7,028
6. Clyde Milan	1,004	8,312
7. Eddie Yost	971	7,461
8. Mickey Vernon	956	7,769
9. Rod Carew	950	6,980
10. Kent Hrbek	903	7,137

Walks: Season

Player	BB	Year
1. Eddie Yost	151	1956
2. Harmon Killebrew	145	1969
3. Eddie Yost	141	1950
4. Harmon Killebrew	131	1967
Eddie Yost	131	1954

6. Eddie Yost	129	1952
7. Harmon Killebrew	128	1970
8. Eddie Yost	126	1951
9. Eddie Yost	123	1953
10. Harmon Killebrew	114	1971

Walks: Career with Team

Player	BB	PA
1. Harmon Killebrew	1,505	9,462
2. Eddie Yost	1,274	7,461
3. Joe Judge	943	8,906
4. Buddy Myer	864	7,028
5. Kent Hrbek	838	7,137
6. Bob Allison	795	5,921
7. Mickey Vernon	735	7,769
8. Ossie Bluege	723	7,452
9. Clyde Milan	685	8,312
10. Sam Rice	680	9,879

Strikeouts: Season

Player	SO	Year
1. Bobby Darwin	145	1972
2. Harmon Killebrew	142	1962
3. Jim Lemon	138	1956
4. Bobby Darwin	137	1973
5. Harmon Killebrew	135	1964
6. Rich Becker	130	1997
7. Jacque Jones	129	2002
8. Larry Hisle	128	1973
9. Bobby Darwin	127	1974
Corey Koskie	127	2002

Strikeouts: Career with Team

Player	SO	PA
1. Harmon Killebrew	1,629	9,462
2. Bob Allison	1,033	5,921
3. Kirby Puckett	965	7,831
4. Gary Gaetti	877	5,459
5. Kent Hrbek	798	7,137
6. Jacque Jones	737	3,783
7. Rod Carew	716	6,980
8. Jim Lemon	710	3,624
9. Eddie Yost	705	7,461
10. Greg Gagne	676	3,695

Slugging Percentage: Season

Player	SLG	Year
1. Goose Goslin	.614	1928
2. Harmon Killebrew	.606	1961
3. Ed Delahanty	.590	1902
4. Harmon Killebrew	.584	1969
5. Roy Sievers	.579	1957
6. Joe Harris	.573	1925
7. Rod Carew	.570	1977
8. Harmon Killebrew	.558	1967
9. Tony Oliva	.557	1964
10. Harmon Killebrew	.555	1963

Slugging Percentage: Career with Team

Player	SLG	PA
1. Harmon Killebrew	.514	9,462
2. Goose Goslin	.502	5,810
3. Roy Sievers	.500	3,574
4. Jimmie Hall	.481	2,104
Kent Hrbek	.481	7,137
6. Shane Mack	.479	2,434
7. Heinie Manush	.478	3,564
8. Kirby Puckett	.477	7,831
9. Tony Oliva	.476	6,879
John Stone	.476	2,334

On-Base Percentage: Season

Player	OBP	Year
1. Buddy Myer	.454	1938
2. Ed Delahanty	.453	1902
3. Rod Carew	.449	1977
4. Chuck Knoblauch	.448	1996
5. Goose Goslin	.442	1928
6. Eddie Yost	.440	1950
Buddy Myer	.440	1935
8. Rod Carew	.433	1974
9. Joe Harris	.430	1925
10. Harmon Killebrew	.427	1969

On-Base Percentage: Career with Team

Player	OBP	PA
1. Rod Carew	.393	6,980
Buddy Myer	.393	7,028
3. John Stone	.392	2,334
4. Chuck Knoblauch	.391	4,571
5. Eddie Yost	.389	7,461
6. Joe Cronin	.387	4,138
7. Goose Goslin	.386	5,810
8. Muddy Ruel	.382	3,405
9. Matt Lawton	.379	3,150
Joe Judge	.379	8,906

OPS (On-Base Percentage + Slugging Percentage): Season

Player	OPS	Year
1. Goose Goslin	1.056	1928
2. Ed Delahanty	1.043	1902
3. Rod Carew	1.019	1977
4. Harmon Killebrew	1.012	1961
5. Harmon Killebrew	1.011	1969
6. Joe Harris	1.003	1925
7. Goose Goslin	.967	1926
Roy Sievers	.967	1957
9. Harmon Killebrew	.965	1967
Chuck Knoblauch	.965	1996

OPS (On-Base Percentage + Slugging Percentage): Career with Team

Player	OPS	PA
1. Harmon Killebrew	.892	9,462
2. Goose Goslin	.888	5,810
3. John Stone	.867	2,334
4. Roy Sievers	.859	3,574
5. Shane Mack	.854	2,434
6. Heinie Manush	.849	3,564
7. Kent Hrbek	.848	7,137
8. Joe Cronin	.842	4,138
9. Rod Carew	.841	6,980
10. Kirby Puckett	.837	7,831

Stolen Bases: Season

Player	SB	Year
1. Clyde Milan	88	1912
2. Clyde Milan	75	1913
3. Sam Rice	63	1920
4. Chuck Knoblauch	62	1997
Danny Moeller	62	1913
6. George Case	61	1943
7. Clyde Milan	58	1911
8. George Case	51	1939
9. Rod Carew	49	1976
George Case	49	1944

Stolen Bases: Career with Team

Player	SB	PA
1. Clyde Milan	495	8,312
2. Sam Rice	346	9,879
3. George Case	321	4,987
4. Chuck Knoblauch	276	4,571
5. Rod Carew	271	6,980
6. Joe Judge	210	8,906
7. Cesar Tovar	186	4,595
8. Howie Shanks	177	5,508
9. Eddie Foster	166	4,891
Bucky Harris	166	5,533

Sacrifice Hits: Season

Player	Sac	Year
1. Bob Ganley	52	1908
2. Bucky Harris	46	1924
3. Bucky Harris	41	1925
4. Roger Peckinpaugh	40	1923
5. Chick Gandil	38	1914
6. Hunter Hill	36	1905
7. Howie Shanks	32	1919
8. Bucky Harris	30	1927
Howie Shanks	30	1914
10. Red Killefer	29	1910
Muddy Ruel	29	1924

Sacrifice Hits: Career with Team

Player	Sac	PA
1. Joe Judge	249	8,906
2. Bucky Harris	248	5,533
3. Howie Shanks	230	5,508
4. Ossie Bluege	218	7,452
5. Sam Rice	211	9,879
6. George McBride	209	5,481
7. Clyde Milan	188	8,312
8. Goose Goslin	140	5,810
9. Roger Peckinpaugh	108	2,560
10. Buddy Myer	106	7,028

Hit by Pitch: Season

Player	HBP	Year
1. Kid Elberfeld	25	1911
2. Bucky Harris	21	1920
3. Doc Gessler	20	1911
4. Chuck Knoblauch	19	1996
5. Bucky Harris	18	1921
6. Chuck Knoblauch	17	1997
Jake Stahl	17	1905
Cesar Tovar	17	1968
9. Doc Gessler	16	1910
Red Killefer	16	1910
Pat Meares	16	1997
Lew Ford	16	2005

Hit by Pitch: Career with Team

Player	HBP	PA
1. Bucky Harris	99	5,533
2. Clyde Milan	80	8,312
3. Eddie Yost	76	7,461
4. Chuck Knoblauch	74	4,571
5. Ossie Bluege	71	7,452
6. Cesar Tovar	68	4,595
7. Tony Oliva	59	6,879
8. George McBride	58	5,481
9. Kirby Puckett	56	7,831
10. Sam Rice	54	9,879

Top 10 Pitching Leaders, Single Season & Career with Team

Games Pitched: Season

Player	GP	Year
1. Mike Marshall	90	1979
2. Eddie Guardado	83	1996
3. J.C. Romero	81	2002
4. Eddie Guardado	79	1998
5. Bill Campbell	78	1976
6. Juan Rincon	77	2004
Mike Trombley	77	1998
8. Bob Wells	76	1999
Bob Wells	76	2000
10. Ron Perranoski	75	1969
Mike Trombley	75	1999
Jesse Crain	75	2005
Juan Rincon	75	2005

Games Pitched: Career with Team

Player	GP	IP
1. Walter Johnson	802	5,914.7
2. Eddie Guardado	639	697.7
3. Rick Aguilera	490	694.0
4. Jim Kaat	484	3,014.3
5. Firpo Marberry	470	1,654.0
6. Camilo Pascual	432	2,465.0
7. Jim Perry	376	1,883.3
8. LaTroy Hawkins	366	819.0
9. Mike Trombley	365	645.7
10. Brad Radke	350	2,288.7

Innings Pitched: Season

Player	IP	Year
1. Walter Johnson	371.7	1914
2. Walter Johnson	370.0	1910
3. Walter Johnson	369.7	1916
4. Walter Johnson	369.0	1912
5. Case Patten	357.7	1904
6. Walter Johnson	346.0	1913
7. Walter Johnson	336.7	1915
8. Alvin Crowder	327.0	1932
9. Walter Johnson	326.0	1917
Walter Johnson	326.0	1918

Innings Pitched: Career with Team

Player	IP
1. Walter Johnson	5,914.7
2. Jim Kaat	3,014.3
3. Bert Blyleven	2,566.7
4. Camilo Pascual	2,465.0
5. Brad Radke	2,288.7
6. Case Patten	2,059.3
7. Dutch Leonard	1,899.3
8. Jim Perry	1,883.3
9. Sid Hudson	1,819.3
10. Tom Hughes	1,776.0

Batters Faced: Season

Player	BF	Year
1. Case Patten	1,507	1904
2. Walter Johnson	1,449	1916
3. Bill Carrick	1,448	1901
4. Walter Johnson	1,438	1914

5. Walter Johnson	1,426	1912
6. Walter Johnson	1,402	1910
7. Al Orth	1,388	1902
8. Alvin Crowder	1,356	1932
9. Case Patten	1,342	1902
10. Walter Johnson	1,335	1911

BATTERS FACED: CAREER WITH TEAM

Player	BF	IP
1. Walter Johnson	23,749	5,914.7
2. Jim Kaat	12,642	3,014.3
3. Bert Blyleven	10,542	2,566.7
4. Camilo Pascual	10,471	2,465.0
5. Brad Radke	9,555	2,288.7
6. Sid Hudson	8,030	1,819.3
7. Dutch Leonard	7,956	1,899.3
8. Jim Perry	7,791	1,883.3
9. Frank Viola	7,450	1,772.7
10. Firpo Marberry	7,004	1,654.0

GAMES STARTED: SEASON

Player	GS	Year
1. Walter Johnson	42	1910
Jim Kaat	42	1965
3. Jim Kaat	41	1966
4. Bert Blyleven	40	1973
Bob Groom	40	1912
Walter Johnson	40	1914
Jim Perry	40	1970
8. Dean Chance	39	1967
Dean Chance	39	1968
Alvin Crowder	39	1932
Dave Goltz	39	1977
Mudcat Grant	39	1965
Walter Johnson	39	1915
Case Patten	39	1904
Jim Perry	39	1971

GAMES STARTED: CAREER WITH TEAM

Player	GS	IP
1. Walter Johnson	666	5,914.7
2. Jim Kaat	433	3,014.3
3. Brad Radke	349	2,288.7
4. Bert Blyleven	345	2,566.7
5. Camilo Pascual	331	2,465.0
6. Frank Viola	259	1,772.7
7. Dutch Leonard	251	1,899.3
8. Jim Perry	249	1,883.3
9. Sid Hudson	239	1,819.3
10. Case Patten	237	2,059.3

COMPLETE GAMES: SEASON

Player	CG	Year
1. Walter Johnson	38	1910
2. Case Patten	37	1904
3. Walter Johnson	36	1911
Walter Johnson	36	1916
Al Orth	36	1902
6. Walter Johnson	35	1915
7. Bill Carrick	34	1901
Walter Johnson	34	1912
9. Walter Johnson	33	1914
Case Patten	33	1902

COMPLETE GAMES: CAREER WITH TEAM

Player	CG	IP
1. Walter Johnson	531	5,914.7
2. Case Patten	206	2,059.3
3. Bert Blyleven	141	2,566.7
4. Tom Hughes	139	1,776.0
5. Jim Kaat	133	3,014.3
6. Dutch Leonard	130	1,899.3
7. Camilo Pascual	119	2,465.0
8. Sid Hudson	112	1,819.3
9. Bob Groom	104	1,353.3
10. Jim Shaw	96	1,600.3

GAMES WON: SEASON

Player	W	Year
1. Walter Johnson	36	1913
2. Walter Johnson	33	1912
3. Walter Johnson	28	1914
4. Walter Johnson	27	1915
5. Alvin Crowder	26	1932
6. Walter Johnson	25	1910
Walter Johnson	25	1911
Walter Johnson	25	1916
Jim Kaat	25	1966
10. Alvin Crowder	24	1933
Bob Groom	24	1912
Jim Perry	24	1970
Frank Viola	24	1988

GAMES WON: CAREER WITH TEAM

Player	W	IP
1. Walter Johnson	417	5,914.7
2. Jim Kaat	190	3,014.3
3. Bert Blyleven	149	2,566.7
4. Camilo Pascual	145	2,465.0
5. Brad Radke	136	2,288.7
6. Jim Perry	128	1,883.3
7. Dutch Leonard	118	1,899.3
8. Firpo Marberry	117	1,654.0
9. Frank Viola	112	1,772.7
10. Case Patten	105	2,059.3

GAMES LOST: SEASON

Player	L	Year
1. Bob Groom	26	1909
Happy Townsend	26	1904
3. Walter Johnson	25	1909
4. Beany Jacobson	23	1904
Case Patten	23	1904
6. Bill Carrick	22	1901
Al Orth	22	1903
Case Patten	22	1903
Case Patten	22	1905
10. Harry Harper	21	1919

GAMES LOST: CAREER WITH TEAM

Player	L	IP
1. Walter Johnson	279	5,914.7
2. Jim Kaat	159	3,014.3
3. Camilo Pascual	141	2,465.0
4. Bert Blyleven	138	2,566.7
5. Sid Hudson	130	1,819.3
Brad Radke	130	2,288.7
7. Case Patten	127	2,059.3
8. Tom Hughes	125	1,776.0
9. Pedro Ramos	112	1,544.3
10. Tom Zachary	103	1,589.0

WINNING PERCENTAGE: SEASON

Player	W%	Year
1. Walter Johnson	.837	1913
2. Stan Coveleski	.800	1925
Firpo Marberry	.800	1931
4. Frank Viola	.774	1988
5. Bill Campbell	.773	1976
6. Jim Perry	.769	1969
Johan Santana	.769	2004
8. Walter Johnson	.767	1924
9. Mudcat Grant	.750	1965
Firpo Marberry	.750	1930

WINNING PERCENTAGE: CAREER WITH TEAM

Player	W%	IP
1. Johan Santana	.702	856.0
2. Firpo Marberry	.622	1,654.0

3. Sam Jones	.602	709.7
4. Walter Johnson	.599	5,914.7
5. Earl Whitehill	.598	996.7
6. Mudcat Grant	.588	780.7
7. Jim Perry	.587	1,883.3
Alvin Crowder	.587	1,331.0
9. Monte Weaver	.583	1,031.7
10. Joe Boehling	.571	805.3

SHUTOUTS: SEASON

Player	SHO	Year
1. Walter Johnson	11	1913
2. Bert Blyleven	9	1973
Walter Johnson	9	1914
Bob Porterfield	9	1953
5. Walter Johnson	8	1910
Walter Johnson	8	1917
Walter Johnson	8	1918
Camilo Pascual	8	1961
9. Walter Johnson	7	1912
Walter Johnson	7	1915
Walter Johnson	7	1919
Case Patten	7	1906

SHUTOUTS: CAREER WITH TEAM

Player	SHO	IP
1. Walter Johnson	110	5,914.7
2. Camilo Pascual	31	2,465.0
3. Bert Blyleven	29	2,566.7
4. Jim Kaat	23	3,014.3
Dutch Leonard	23	1,899.3
6. Bob Porterfield	19	1,041.7
7. Tom Hughes	17	1,776.0
Case Patten	17	2,059.3
Jim Perry	17	1,883.3
Jim Shaw	17	1,600.3

ERA: SEASON

Player	ERA	Year
1. Walter Johnson	1.14	1913
2. Walter Johnson	1.27	1918
3. Walter Johnson	1.36	1910
4. Walter Johnson	1.39	1912
5. Walter Johnson	1.49	1919
6. Walter Johnson	1.55	1915
7. Walter Johnson	1.65	1908
8. Bill Burns	1.69	1908
9. Walter Johnson	1.72	1914
10. Walter Johnson	1.90	1911

ERA: CAREER WITH TEAM

Player	ERA	IP
1. Walter Johnson	2.17	5,914.7
2. Doc Ayers	2.64	1,122.3
3. Dean Chance	2.67	664.0
4. Cy Falkenberg	2.69	690.3
5. Harry Harper	2.75	1,037.0
6. Charlie Smith	2.76	823.7
7. Bert Gallia	2.83	855.0
8. Joe Boehling	2.86	805.3
9. Stan Coveleski	2.98	500.7
10. Tom Hughes	3.02	1,776.0

EARNED RUNS ALLOWED: SEASON

Player	ER	Year
1. Jimmie DeShong	144	1937
2. Al Orth	143	1902
3. Bill Carrick	139	1902
4. Bobo Newsom	137	1936
5. Bill Carrick	135	1901
Al Orth	135	1903
Case Patten	135	1902
8. Earl Whitehill	133	1935
9. Alvin Crowder	132	1933
10. LaTroy Hawkins	129	1999

EARNED RUNS ALLOWED: CAREER WITH TEAM

Player	ER	IP
1. Walter Johnson	1,424	5,914.7
2. Jim Kaat	1,118	3,014.3
3. Brad Radke	1,072	2,288.7
4. Camilo Pascual	1,002	2,465.0
5. Bert Blyleven	934	2,566.7
6. Sid Hudson	886	1,819.3
7. Case Patten	765	2,059.3
8. Frank Viola	760	1,772.7
9. Pedro Ramos	719	1,544.3
10. Dutch Leonard	690	1,899.3

STRIKEOUTS: SEASON

Player	K	Year
1. Walter Johnson	313	1910
2. Walter Johnson	303	1912
3. Johan Santana	265	2004
4. Bert Blyleven	258	1973
5. Bert Blyleven	249	1974
6. Walter Johnson	243	1913
7. Johan Santana	238	2005
8. Dean Chance	234	1968
9. Bert Blyleven	233	1975
10. Bert Blyleven	228	1972
Walter Johnson	228	1916

STRIKEOUTS: CAREER WITH TEAM

Player	K	IP
1. Walter Johnson	3,509	5,914.7
2. Bert Blyleven	2,035	2,566.7
3. Camilo Pascual	1,885	2,465.0
4. Jim Kaat	1,851	3,014.3
5. Brad Radke	1,384	2,288.7
6. Frank Viola	1,214	1,772.7
7. Jim Perry	1,025	1,883.3
8. Johan Santana	901	856.0
9. Dave Goltz	887	1,638.0
10. Tom Hughes	884	1,776.0

STRIKEOUTS PER NINE IP: SEASON

Player	K/9	Year
1. Johan Santana	10.46	2004
2. Johan Santana	9.25	2005
3. Dave Boswell	9.19	1966
4. Dave Boswell	8.25	1967
5. Bert Blyleven	7.98	1974
6. Camilo Pascual	7.88	1961
7. Camilo Pascual	7.73	1956
8. Walter Johnson	7.61	1910
Bert Blyleven	7.61	1975
10. Dick Stigman	7.53	1964

STRIKEOUTS PER NINE IP: CAREER WITH TEAM

Player	K/9	IP
1. Johan Santana	9.47	856.0
2. Eddie Guardado	7.80	697.7
3. Rick Aguilera	7.60	694.0
4. Dick Stigman	7.52	643.7
5. Dave Boswell	7.51	1,036.3
6. Mike Trombley	7.36	645.7
7. Bert Blyleven	7.14	2,566.7
8. Jim Merritt	6.91	686.7
9. Camilo Pascual	6.88	2,465.0
10. Dean Chance	6.83	664.0

HITS ALLOWED: SEASON

Player	HA	Year
1. Bill Carrick	367	1901
Al Orth	367	1902
Case Patten	367	1904

4. Bill Carrick	344	1902
5. Case Patten	331	1902
6. Watty Lee	328	1901
Dutch Leonard	328	1940
8. Al Orth	326	1903
9. Alvin Crowder	319	1932
Happy Townsend	319	1904

Hits Allowed: Career with Team

Player	HA	IP
1. Walter Johnson	4,913	5,914.7
2. Jim Kaat	2,982	3,014.3
3. Brad Radke	2,446	2,288.7
4. Bert Blyleven	2,369	2,566.7
5. Camilo Pascual	2,283	2,465.0
6. Case Patten	2,146	2,059.3
7. Sid Hudson	1,992	1,819.3
8. Dutch Leonard	1,951	1,899.3
9. Tom Zachary	1,822	1,589.0
10. Frank Viola	1,775	1,772.7

Hits Allowed per Nine IP: Season

Player	H/9	Year
1. Walter Johnson	6.03	1913
2. Johan Santana	6.16	2004
3. Walter Johnson	6.32	1912
4. Walter Johnson	6.37	1910
5. Dave Boswell	6.38	1966
6. Dave Boswell	6.55	1967
7. Walter Johnson	6.65	1918
8. Harry Harper	6.71	1918
9. Joe Engel	6.78	1913
10. Walter Johnson	6.81	1908

Hits Allowed per Nine IP: Career with Team

Player	H/9	IP
1. Dave Boswell	7.15	1,036.3
2. Johan Santana	7.35	856.0
3. Dean Chance	7.37	664.0
4. Walter Johnson	7.48	5,914.7
5. Harry Harper	7.61	1,037.0
6. Jim Merritt	7.64	686.7
7. Dick Stigman	7.70	643.7
8. Dick Woodson	7.83	561.0
9. Cy Falkenberg	7.99	690.3
10. Jim Shaw	8.13	1,600.3

Walks Allowed: Season

Player	BB	Year
1. Bobo Newsom	146	1936
2. Ken Chase	143	1940
3. Jim Shaw	137	1914
4. Eric Erickson	128	1920
5. Jim Hughes	127	1975
6. Jimmie DeShong	124	1937
7. Jim Shaw	123	1917
8. Walt Masterson	122	1948
9. Joe Boehling	119	1915
10. Rich Robertson	116	1996

Walks Allowed: Career with Team

Player	BB	IP
1. Walter Johnson	1,363	5,914.7
2. Camilo Pascual	909	2,465.0
3. Jim Kaat	729	3,014.3
4. Sid Hudson	720	1,819.3
5. Walt Masterson	694	1,347.0
6. Jim Shaw	688	1,600.3
7. Bert Blyleven	674	2,566.7
8. Bump Hadley	572	1,299.0
9. Firpo Marberry	568	1,654.0
10. Tom Hughes	567	1,776.0

Walks Allowed per Nine IP: Season

Player	BB/9	Year
1. Carlos Silva	0.43	2005
2. Bill Burns	0.98	1908
3. Walter Johnson	0.99	1913
4. Brad Radke	1.03	2005
5. Brad Radke	1.04	2001
6. Brad Radke	1.07	2004
7. Al Orth	1.11	1902
8. Jim Merritt	1.19	1967
Brad Radke	1.19	2003
10. Dale Gear	1.21	1901

Walks Allowed per Nine IP: Career with Team

Player	BB/9	IP
1. Al Orth	1.55	677.3
2. Brad Radke	1.62	2,288.7
3. Jim Merritt	1.77	686.7
4. Watty Lee	1.79	526.7
5. Mudcat Grant	1.88	780.7
6. Dutch Leonard	1.91	1,899.3
7. Kevin Tapani	1.96	1,171.3
8. Walter Johnson	2.07	5,914.7
9. Garland Braxton	2.11	583.0
10. John Butcher	2.15	502.7

WHIP (Walks + Hits per Nine IP): Season

Player	WHIP	Year
1. Walter Johnson	.780	1913
2. Walter Johnson	.908	1912
3. Walter Johnson	.914	1910
4. Johan Santana	.921	2004
5. Bill Burns	.927	1908
6. Walter Johnson	.933	1915
7. Walter Johnson	.954	1918
8. Walter Johnson	.964	1908
9. Walter Johnson	.969	1917
10. Walter Johnson	.971	1914
Johan Santana	.971	2005

WHIP (Walks + Hits per Nine IP): Career with Team

Player	WHIP	IP
1. Jim Merritt	1.046	686.7
2. Walter Johnson	1.061	5,914.7
3. Dean Chance	1.069	664.0
4. Johan Santana	1.126	856.0
5. Rick Aguilera	1.182	694.0
6. Doc Ayers	1.185	1,122.3
7. Bert Blyleven	1.186	2,566.7
8. Jim Perry	1.196	1,883.3
9. Garland Braxton	1.199	583.0
10. Mudcat Grant	1.212	780.7

Home Runs Allowed: Season

Player	HRA	Year
1. Bert Blyleven	50	1986
2. Bert Blyleven	46	1987
3. Pedro Ramos	43	1957
4. Brad Radke	40	1996
5. Jim Perry	39	1971
Pedro Ramos	39	1961
7. Pedro Ramos	38	1958
8. Frank Viola	37	1986
9. Eric Milton	35	2000
Eric Milton	35	2001
Mike Smithson	35	1984

HOME RUNS ALLOWED: CAREER WITH TEAM

Player	HRA	IP
1. Brad Radke	302	2,288.7
2. Jim Kaat	279	3,014.3
3. Bert Blyleven	243	2,566.7
4. Camilo Pascual	214	2,465.0
5. Frank Viola	213	1,772.7
6. Pedro Ramos	209	1,544.3
7. Jim Perry	166	1,883.3
8. Eric Milton	149	987.3
9. Chuck Stobbs	128	1,238.3
10. Joe Mays	127	946.3

SAVES: SEASON

Player	SV	Year
1. Eddie Guardado	45	2002
2. Joe Nathan	44	2004
3. Joe Nathan	43	2005
4. Rick Aguilera	42	1991
Jeff Reardon	42	1988
6. Rick Aguilera	41	1992
Eddie Guardado	41	2003
8. Rick Aguilera	38	1998
9. Rick Aguilera	34	1993
Ron Perranoski	34	1970

SAVES: CAREER WITH TEAM

Player	SV	IP
1. Rick Aguilera	254	694.0
2. Eddie Guardado	116	697.7
3. Ron Davis	108	381.3
4. Jeff Reardon	104	226.3
5. Firpo Marberry	96	1,654.0
6. Al Worthington	88	473.3
7. Joe Nathan	87	142.3
8. Ron Perranoski	76	360.3
9. Mike Marshall	54	274.0
10. Bill Campbell	51	460.7

WILD PITCHES: SEASON

Player	WP	Year
1. Walter Johnson	21	1910
2. Happy Townsend	19	1904
3. Walter Johnson	17	1911
4. Dave Goltz	15	1976
Jack Morris	15	1991
Johan Santana	15	2002
Mike Smithson	15	1986
8. Hector Carrasco	14	2000
Cy Falkenberg	14	1906
Walter Johnson	14	1914

WILD PITCHES: CAREER WITH TEAM

Player	WP	IP
1. Walter Johnson	155	5,914.7
2. Jim Kaat	106	3,014.3
3. Camilo Pascual	69	2,465.0
4. Jim Shaw	58	1,600.3
5. Bert Blyleven	56	2,566.7
6. Dutch Leonard	55	1,899.3
7. Dave Goltz	54	1,638.0
8. Harry Harper	51	1,037.0
Tom Hughes	51	1,776.0
10. LaTroy Hawkins	50	819.0

HIT BATSMEN: SEASON

Player	HB	Year
1. Bill Carrick	20	1901
Walter Johnson	20	1923
Case Patten	20	1904
4. Walter Johnson	19	1915
5. Jim Kaat	18	1962
Case Patten	18	1901
7. Bert Blyleven	16	1988
Walter Johnson	16	1912
9. Walter Johnson	15	1909
Mike Smithson	15	1985
Happy Townsend	15	1905

HIT BATSMEN: CAREER WITH TEAM

Player	HB	IP
1. Walter Johnson	203	5,914.7
2. Jim Kaat	96	3,014.3
3. Bert Blyleven	80	2,566.7
4. Case Patten	75	2,059.3
5. Tom Hughes	68	1,776.0
6. Brad Radke	61	2,288.7
7. Jim Perry	50	1,883.3
8. Camilo Pascual	47	2,465.0
Happy Townsend	47	901.3
10. Pedro Ramos	46	1,544.3
Mike Smithson	46	816.0

GAMES FINISHED: SEASON

Player	GF	Year
1. Mike Marshall	84	1979
2. Bill Campbell	68	1976
3. Rick Aguilera	64	1998
4. Doug Corbett	63	1980
Joe Nathan	63	2004
6. Eddie Guardado	62	2002
7. Rick Aguilera	61	1992
Rick Aguilera	61	1993
Ron Davis	61	1983
Jeff Reardon	61	1989

GAMES FINISHED: CAREER WITH TEAM

Player	GF	IP
1. Rick Aguilera	434	694.0
2. Eddie Guardado	258	697.7
3. Firpo Marberry	250	1,654.0
4. Ron Davis	248	381.3
5. Al Worthington	213	473.3
6. Jeff Reardon	177	226.3
7. Bill Campbell	171	460.7
8. Ron Perranoski	167	360.3
9. Mike Marshall	147	274.0
10. Mike Trombley	132	645.7

Significant Senators/Twins

AGUILERA, RICK (RP)
(1989–1999)

After five years with the Mets, Aguilera was traded to the Twins on July 31, 1989, along with four other pitchers for Frank Viola, the reigning American League Cy Young Award winner. Aguilera finished the year as a starter for Minnesota, but moved to the bullpen in 1990, saving 32 games for the last-place Twins. In 1991, he earned 42 saves in helping Minnesota go from last place to first place in one year. In the 1991 ALCS and World Series, Aguilera allowed only one run in seven appearances as the Twins defeated the Blue Jays and Braves. A three-time All-Star, Aguilera finished his 11-year Twins career in 1999 as the all-time leader in saves. After a season and a half with the Cubs, Aguilera retired following the 2000 campaign.

CAREER TWINS RECORD:

W	L	W%	ERA	SV
40	47	.460	3.50	254

K	BB	SHO	IP
586	179	0	694.0

ALLISON, BOB (OF/1B)
(1958–1970)

The Washington Senators signed Bob Allison as an amateur free agent before the 1955 season. After a brief late-season call-up in 1958, Allison began his Senators career with a bang in 1959, hitting 30 homers and winning Rookie of the Year honors. With Harmon Killebrew debuting in the same season, the lowly Senators experienced unaccustomed power. A fierce competitor with a strong throwing arm, Allison hit 20 or more homers eight times during his 13-year career, all spent with the Twins franchise. On May 17, 1963, he hit three homers in one game, and on July 18 of the same year he teamed with roommate Killebrew to become the first teammates in history to hit grand slams in the same inning. After leaving baseball, Allison, a three-time All-Star, became a general manager for Coca-Cola in the Minneapolis area and died in 1995 after contracting Lou Gehrig's disease.

CAREER SENATORS/TWINS RECORD:

Games	AB	Hits	Runs
1,541	5,032	1,281	811

Avg	HR	RBI	SB
.255	256	796	84

BLUEGE, OSSIE (3B/SS/2B) (1922–1939)

Ossie Bluege not only spent his entire 18-year playing career with the Senators, but spent the next 33 years working for the team in one capacity or another—a total of 51 years in the same organization. An excellent fielder at three different infield positions, Bluege was a scrappy hitter who could steal a base when needed or drive in a clutch run. Bluege had been an accountant before his Senators career and he kept up his accounting business after becoming a ballplayer. When owner Clark Griffith ordered him to give up his offseason profession, fearing Bluege would damage his eyesight, Bluege refused. He developed an impressive client list that included many of D.C.'s finer hotels. Bluege played with Washington during their three pennant years of 1924, 1925, and 1932, though he hit just .200 in 60 World Series at-bats. After his playing career ended, Bluege spent three years as a coach for the Senators, then five more as the manager. From 1948 to 1956, Bluege was the director of Washington's farm system. His last job with the Senators/Twins was as team controller from 1958–1972.

CAREER SENATORS RECORD:

Games	AB	Hits	Runs
1,867	6,440	1,751	883
Avg	**HR**	**RBI**	**SB**
.272	43	848	140

BLYLEVEN, BERT (SP) (1970–1976, 1985–1988)

Minnesota drafted the Dutch-born Blyleven in the third round of the June 1969 amateur draft. When Luis Tiant became injured early in the 1970 season, Blyleven, just 19 and the youngest player in the majors at the time, was called up to Minnesota. In his first start, he gave up a homer to Lee May, then shut Washington out the rest of the way in a 2–1 win. In a game against the Angels later that season, Blyleven would strike out the first six batters to face him, tying the major league record. Although Blyleven gave up a lot of homers in his career (seventh most on the all-time list when he retired), he was feared for his wicked curveball, a pitch—according to Dave Winfield—that could turn a hitter's legs to jelly. After a rough start in 1976, the Twins figured Blyleven would never live up to his potential and traded him to the Texas Rangers where he responded with two consecutive 10-inning, 1–0 shutouts, the first a one-hitter. He threw a no-hitter later that year. After nine years with the Rangers, Pirates, and Indians, Blyleven returned to Minnesota in a 1985 trade with Cleveland. In 1986 he allowed a major league–record 50 home runs, but also won 17 games and led the majors in innings pitched with 271.7. Blyleven won 15 games in the Twins' World Series championship year of 1987, as well as two games in the ALCS and one more in the World Series. After the 1988 season Blyleven was traded to the Angels, where he pitched the last three years of his 22-year career. Blyleven has been a baseball announcer since he retired.

CAREER TWINS RECORD:

W	L	W%	ERA	SV
149	138	.519	3.28	0
K	**BB**	**SHO**	**IP**	
2,035	674	29	2,566.7	

CAREW, ROD (2B/1B)
(1967–1978)

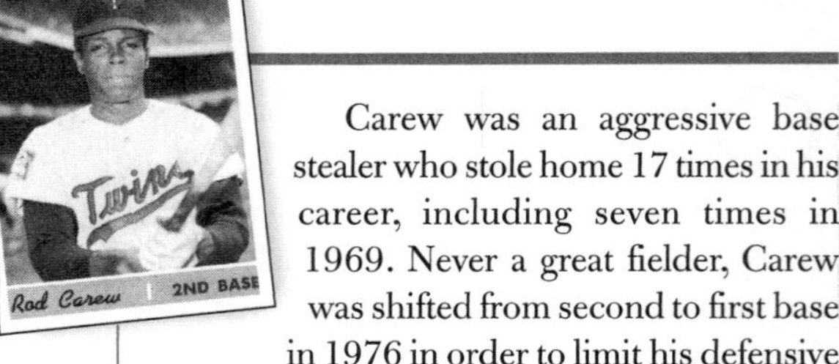

Rod Carew was born in 1945 in a Coloreds Only car on a train in the Panama Canal Zone. The doctor who delivered him, Rodney Kline, left the Whites Only car to make the delivery. Carew's grateful mother named her son after him. After immigrating to America at the age of 16, Carew was discovered playing on the sandlots of New York City and signed by the Twins. After spending six years in the minors, Carew made it to the big leagues in 1967. He was honored as the AL Rookie of the Year for his 150 hits and .292 average. He followed up his rookie year with a .273 average in 1968, then reeled off 10 straight .300 seasons, including five years over .350. White Sox infielder Alan Bannister once said of Carew, "He's the only guy I know who can go 4-for-3." Gaylord Perry complained about Carew, "All I throw him is greaseball, greaseball, greaseball, and he still hits them. I guess he can see the ball so well he can pick out the dry side."

Carew was an aggressive base stealer who stole home 17 times in his career, including seven times in 1969. Never a great fielder, Carew was shifted from second to first base in 1976 in order to limit his defensive liabilities. In 1977 Carew won the AL MVP Award when he made a strong run at .400. He finished at .388, the highest average in the majors since Ted Williams hit for the same average in 1950. After hitting .333 in 1978, his 12th and final season in Minnesota, Carew became angered at the penny-pinching ways of the Twins and demanded a trade. A deal was worked out for him to go to San Francisco, but he vetoed it because he wanted to stay in the American League. Another deal was then worked out which sent him to the Angels for four players. *(See Angels bio.)*

CAREER TWINS RECORD:

Games	AB	Hits	Runs
1,635	6,235	2,085	950
Avg	**HR**	**RBI**	**SB**
.334	74	733	271

CASE, GEORGE (OF)
(1937–1945, 1947)

George Case was without a doubt the fastest man in baseball in the four decades from 1920 to 1960. In an era when base stealing wasn't a widely used strategy, Case led the AL in steals for five straight years (1939–1943) and six times in an eight-year stretch, finishing second the other two years. In the first 90 years of baseball history, Case was the hardest man to double up, hitting into a double play only once every 94 at-bats; he still ranks in the top five all time. In his best season, 1943, he stole 61 bases. In a pregame exhibition in Griffith Stadium, Case circled the bases in 13.5 seconds, breaking the established record of 13.8 set by Hans Lobert. In another exhibition he lost a close race to Jesse Owens. After injuries curtailed his career at the age of 31, Case, a four-time All-Star, became a minor league manager in the Yankees' system. He later became a roving batting instructor, first for the Yankees and then the Mariners.

CAREER SENATORS RECORD:

Games	AB	Hits	Runs
1,108	4,532	1,306	739
Avg	**HR**	**RBI**	**SB**
.288	20	355	321

GOSLIN, GOOSE (OF)
(1921–1930, 1933, 1938)

Some say Leon Goslin got his nickname from the way he flapped his arms when running down fly balls in the outfield, but others say it was because of his long neck and big nose. Either way, Goslin was one of the best hitters of his era. He was playing in an industrial league when umpire Bill McGowan told him he was good enough to play professionally and that he should give it a try. Goslin took the advice and was signed by a Class C team, where he was discovered by Senators owner Clark Griffith. After a late-season call-up in 1921, Goslin joined the Senators for good in 1922.

He was an exuberant player who admitted that he would have played for free if he'd had to. Upon joining the Senators, Goslin asked Griffith to use his influence to bring umpire McGowan to the majors, which he did; McGowan was elected to the Hall of Fame in 1992. In 1922, Goslin's first full season, he hit .324, the first of seven consecutive .300 seasons. Like Babe Ruth, Goslin swung so hard he sometimes ended up on the ground after missing a pitch. Goslin starred in the 1924 and 1925 World Series, hitting three home runs in each Series, collecting 11 RBIs in 1924 and eight in 1925. On the last day of the 1928 season, Goslin and Heinie Manush of the Browns were in a dead tie for the batting title, and the Browns and Senators were squaring off. Goslin got hits in his first two trips to the plate and knew he'd win the batting title if he didn't bat again, but one of his teammates goaded him into staying in the game. In his next at-bat, Goslin quickly got two strikes on him and saw his batting title fading away, so he came up with an idea. He knew if he got himself thrown out of the game, whichever batter replaced him would get the credit for the at-bat, good or bad. So Goslin began to argue with the home-plate umpire, at one point even standing on the ump's shoes. The umpire knew what Goslin was trying to do and refused to toss him out of the game. When Goslin stepped back in the box, he promptly singled to win the batting title.

Goslin created a stir in the early 1930s when he began using a zebra-striped bat in order to confuse the opposition. AL president William Harridge eventually ruled the bat illegal. In mid-1930, Goslin was traded to the Browns, where he spent 2½ seasons before returning to Washington, where he reminded Clark Griffith that Washington had never won a pennant without him in the lineup. While he did have a bit of an off year in 1933, hitting .297, Goslin did lead the Senators to another AL pennant, though they lost to the Giants in five games in the World Series. After the season, he was traded to Detroit, where he hit around .300 each year with 100 runs and 100 RBIs, leading the Tigers to back-to-back World Series appearances. Detroit released him after the 1937 season and he signed on with Washington for a third time in 1938, though he played just 38 games before retiring. After leaving the major leagues, Goslin became a player-manager in the minor leagues for a time before opening a boat and fishing-tackle business. In 1968 he was elected to the Hall of Fame.

CAREER SENATORS RECORD:

Games	AB	Hits	Runs
1,361	5,140	1,659	854
Avg	**HR**	**RBI**	**SB**
.323	127	931	116

HARRIS, BUCKY (2B)
(1919–1928)

Stanley "Bucky" Harris quit school to work in the Pennsylvania coal mines at the age of 13. He played baseball for several amateur teams near his hometown of Pittston, Pennsylvania, when he was discovered by Tigers manager Hughie Jennings, who was also from Pittston. After Harris got a taste of big league action in 1919, the Senators brought him up for good in 1920 and made him the starting second baseman. Harris was a remarkably consistent performer from year to year. In 1924, just before the season began, Clark Griffith fired manager Donie Bush and surprised virtually everyone by hiring the 27-year-old Harris as the new Washington player-manager. Naturally, many of the older players resented the choice, but Harris disarmed them by asking for their help in learning how to be a good manager.

In his first year as "the Boy Manager," the Senators won the AL pennant, earning the right to play John McGraw's New York Giants in the World Series. With the Series tied at three games each, Harris employed a clever tactic in Game 7. He started righthander Warren Ogden, who pitched to two batters before Harris replaced him with lefthander George Mogridge. The switch forced McGraw to take out slugger Bill Terry, a first baseman whom McGraw had been platooning. When the game went into extra innings, Harris was able to bring in a rested Walter Johnson to shut down the Giants until Washington was able to score the winning run in the 12th. Harris guided the Senators to the World Series again in 1925, though they lost to the Pirates in seven games. When Harris's playing career was finished for all practical purposes after the 1928 season, he was traded to Detroit, where he immediately became the new manager. In 29 years of managing, Harris compiled a 2,157–2,218 record, mostly with poor teams. Only Connie Mack lost more career games as a manager (3,948) than Harris. He later served as a scout for the Senators and White Sox, remaining in baseball for 57 years. Harris was elected to the Hall of Fame in 1975 as a manager. He died in 1977.

CAREER SENATORS RECORD:

Games	AB	Hits	Runs
1,252	4,717	1,295	718
Avg	**HR**	**RBI**	**SB**
.275	9	506	166

HRBEK, KENT (1B)
(1981–1994)

Kent Hrbek was a local baseball hero when he was drafted by the Twins in the 17th round of the June 1978 amateur draft. The move was more of a tribute to a hometown boy than anything else, but he retired in 1994, having played the second-most games in Twins history. In between, Hrbek helped the Twins win two World Series, in 1987 and 1991. He never won a Gold Glove, although he did lead the AL in fielding twice. Hrbek also appeared in only one All-Star Game, in his rookie season of 1982, when he was the runner-up to Cal Ripken Jr., for the American League Rookie of the Year Award. After six consistently solid seasons, Hrbek was angered over being left off the 1987 All-Star team and vowed never, if selected, to play in one (he was never again selected as an All-Star). While Hrbek's numbers were solid throughout his career, he tended to stumble in postseason play. His postseason batting average of .154 is the lowest on record for a player with at least 75 postseason at-bats. Persistent shoulder problems spelled an end to his 14-year career, which was all spent with Minnesota, after the 1994 season. In 1998 Hrbek was asked by future Minnesota governor Jesse Ventura to be his running mate, but Hrbek declined, stating that holding the lieutenant governor's position would take too much time away from his preferred pursuits: hunting, fishing, and bowling.

CAREER TWINS RECORD:

Games	AB	Hits	Runs
1,252	4,717	1,295	718
Avg	**HR**	**RBI**	**SB**
.275	9	506	166

JOHNSON, WALTER (SP/RP)
(1907–1927)

Walter "Big Train" Johnson, who played his entire 21-year major league career with the Senators, was one of the most dominating pitchers in the history of baseball. He got his nickname from the sound of his fastball, which other players said sounded like a train coming down the tracks. There are countless anecdotes about Johnson and his fastball. Ping Bodie once said, "You can't hit what you can't see." Another player said the only way to hit a Johnson fastball was to start swinging on strike two—then maybe you stood a chance of connecting on the next pitch. On another occasion, Cleveland shortstop Ray Chapman, badly overpowered on the first two pitches, simply gave up and walked back to the dugout, not wishing to put off the inevitable. When the third pitch blasted into the catcher's mitt for strike three, the catcher turned around and asked umpire Billy Evans if it had been a fastball or curve ball, Evans replied, "I never saw it. I had to close my eyes." Later Evans would say, "I knew the ballplayers couldn't second guess me if they were closing their eyes, too."

From 1910 to 1919, Johnson won at least 20 games every year, including back-to-back 30-win seasons in 1912–1913. Johnson's 416 wins stand second only to Cy Young, and had he not played for the lowly Senators he could have won many, many more games. Of his 279 career losses, 65 were shutouts, and 26 of those were 1–0 jobs. Johnson relied almost exclusively on his fastball, and even then he refused to pitch inside on hitters because he was afraid he might kill someone. Johnson led the AL in strikeouts 12 times. Twice in his career he struck out the side on nine pitches after loading the bases (once against Detroit's Ty Cobb, Sam Crawford, and Bobby Veach, the other time facing Cleveland's Tris Speaker, Chick Gandil, and Elmer Smith).

In 1907 Johnson lost his major league debut to Detroit, 3–2. After the game, Ty Cobb tried to convince the Tigers' front office to purchase Johnson, even if it cost $25,000 to get him. They refused. In 1908 he shut out the New York Highlanders three times in four days, the first on a four-hitter, the second on a three-hitter, and the last on a two-hitter. In 1912 he won 16 straight games, still the American League record, although several pitchers have since tied his record. Johnson's best season was 1913 when he won 36 games with a 1.09 ERA, 11 shutouts, and five one-hitters. He had three winning streaks of 10, 11, and 14 games as he won his first AL MVP Award. He also set the American League record for consecutive scoreless innings with 56.7. When the rival Federal League formed in 1914, Johnson signed with the Chicago Whales after receiving a threatening letter from Washington president Harry Minor. Only a personal appeal from Washington manager Clark Griffith convinced Johnson to stay with the Senators.

Surprisingly, Johnson only threw one no-hitter in his career, a 1–0 gem in 1920 that would have been a perfect game if not for an error by Bucky Harris. When Washington won its only World Series title in 1924, Johnson was the winning pitcher in Game 7, pitching four innings of stellar relief. He also won his second MVP Award. After retiring following the 1927 season, Johnson managed in the minors for a year before taking over the helm of the Senators from 1929 to 1932. He then managed the Indians from 1933 to August 1935, when he left the team following a dispute over disciplining a player. In 1936 he was one of the first players elected to the Hall of Fame. In 1938 he was elected to the Rockville, Maryland, County Board of Governors. Johnson was a broadcaster for the Senators in 1939 before making a losing run for Congress in 1940. In 1946 he died in Washington, D.C., after suffering a stroke.

CAREER SENATORS RECORD:

W	L	W%	ERA	SV
417	279	.599	2.17	34

K	BB	SHO	IP
3,509	1,363	110	5,914.7

JUDGE, JOE (1B)
(1915–1932)

Slick-fielding first baseman Joe Judge spent the first 18 seasons of his 20-year career with the Senators. Primarily a singles hitter, Judge batted over .300 nine times, and is one of only a score of players to have hit three triples in one game. Judge led the AL in fielding five times, and, when he retired following the 1934 season, he held the AL career record for games played, putouts, double plays, and total chances. Judge was part of one of baseball's greatest defensive infields ever when he teamed with second baseman Bucky Harris, shortstop Roger Peckinpaugh, and third baseman Ossie Bluege. Judge was an important part of Washington's two pennant-winning teams in

1924 and 1925, and hit .385 (going 10-for-26) in the World Series, as the Senators won the championship. After retiring as a player, Judge coached baseball at Georgetown University.

CAREER SENATORS RECORD:

Games	AB	Hits	Runs
2,084	7,663	2,291	1,154

Avg	HR	RBI	SB
.299	71	1,001	210

KAAT, JIM (SP/RP)
(1959–1973)

The Washington Senators signed Jim Kaat as an amateur free agent in June 1957. By 1961 he was a regular in the Twins' starting rotation, a position he held until late 1973 when he was traded to the White Sox. Kaat had a 25-year career, longer than any other pitcher in history at the time he retired. In addition to his pitching ability, his hitting and fielding skills contributed to his longevity. He had 16 homers in his career and 134 sacrifice hits, a major league record. As for fielding, Kaat won 14 consecutive Gold Gloves, second only to Brooks Robinson's 16. Considered by most baseball historians as the best fielding pitcher of all time, Kaat also had a very quick move to the plate that kept runners from getting a big lead.

Kaat was the last member of the original Senators team to play in the majors. In 1966 he won 25 games for Minnesota, but was denied a Cy Young when Sandy Koufax swept the voting (in a year when there was still only one Cy Young awarded for the two leagues combined). After 15 years with the Senators/Twins, Kaat played 10 more seasons with the White Sox, Phillies, Yankees, and Cardinals before retiring. He coached for the Reds for one year before undertaking a long career as one of baseball's most intelligent broadcasters.

CAREER SENATORS/TWINS RECORD:

W	L	W%	ERA	SV
190	159	.544	3.34	6

K	BB	SHO	IP
1,851	729	23	3,014.3

KILLEBREW, HARMON (1B/3B/OF)
(1954–1974)

Harmon Killebrew was tearing up a semipro league in Idaho when U.S. Senator Herman Welker of Idaho saw him play. He conveyed news of the young phenom to Washington owner Clark Griffith, who then dispatched scout Ossie Bluege. Bluege watched Killebrew play four games. The young slugger smacked four homers, three triples, and four singles, convincing Bluege to tell Griffith, "The sky's the limit." The Senators signed Killebrew to a three-year deal in 1954 when Boston failed to match Washington's offer. (Killebrew had verbally agreed to sign with Boston if they matched Washington's offer, but they declined.) Killebrew's strength was part genetic, part work-related. His grandfather was said to have been the strongest man in the Union Army during the Civil War. His father was a collegiate fullback and professional wrestler. As a young boy, Killebrew helped out on the family farm, often carrying 10-gallon buckets of milk.

Killebrew, a .256 career hitter terribly vulnerable to the strikeout (and too pleasant a man to ever argue with an umpire), was a one-dimensional player in the majors: He hit for power. Eight times in his career he hit more than 40 homers, six times leading the American League. He drove in 100+ runs nine times, three times leading the league. Killebrew was named to the All-Star team 11 times at three different positions (first, third, and the outfield). On July 18, 1962, Killebrew and teammate Bob Allison each hit grand slams in the same inning in a game against the Indians. Later in the same game, Killebrew hit another grand slam. Killebrew won the AL MVP Award in 1969 after hitting 49 homers with 140 RBIs. After 21 years with the Senators/Twins, Killebrew was released and signed on with Kansas City as their DH for one season before retiring. Killebrew's career home run ratio ranks him among baseball's elite sluggers, as he trails only Babe Ruth, Ralph Kiner, and Mark McGwire among retired players. Killebrew joined the Minnesota broadcast crew for three years before returning to Idaho to open an insurance and securities firm. In 1984 he was elected to the Hall of Fame.

CAREER SENATORS/TWINS RECORD:

Games	AB	Hits	Runs
2,329	7,835	2,024	1,258
Avg	**HR**	**RBI**	**SB**
.256	559	1,540	18

MANUSH, HEINIE (OF)
(1930–1935)

Heinie Manush had already been a star with the Tigers and Browns for 7½ seasons when he was traded in a blockbuster deal to the Senators in mid-1930 for Goose Goslin. When he first came up with Detroit, Manush tried to be a home run hitter like Babe Ruth, but Detroit manager Ty Cobb convinced him to hit more line drives. It worked. Manush was consistently among the league leaders in hits, doubles, and triples, and hit over .300 11 times, including five of his six seasons with Washington. In 1933 he was the runner up in the batting race to Jimmie Foxx, accumulating a 33-game hitting streak at one point and leading the league with 221 hits and 17 triples.

In the 1933 World Series, Manush had the distinction of being only the second player ever ejected from a World Series game. After disagreeing with an inning-ending ground-out call made by umpire Charlie Moran, Manush took hold of Moran's bow tie with both hands and stretched it out as far as the tie's elastic band would allow, then let it snap back. Manush was ejected from the game, but refused to go. He took his place in the field in the next inning, but Moran wouldn't let the game proceed until Manush left the field, which he did only after considerable urging by his teammates. After the incident, Commissioner Landis ruled that a player could no longer be ejected from a World Series game without his personal approval, a ruling which remained in effect as long as Landis was in office.

After the 1935 season, Manush was traded to the Red Sox. He spent his last four years in baseball playing for the Red Sox, Dodgers, and Pirates before retiring to coach minor league baseball for six years. After that he became a scout and coach for the Red Sox and Senators. In 1964 he was elected to the Hall of Fame.

CAREER SENATORS RECORD:

Games	AB	Hits	Runs
792	3,290	1,078	576
Avg	**HR**	**RBI**	**SB**
.328	47	491	29

MILAN, CLYDE (OF)
(1907–1922)

Clyde Milan was signed on the same scouting trip as Walter Johnson. The two friendly and easygoing players roomed together on the road for 15 seasons until Milan became Washington's player-manager for one year in 1922. Many consider Milan to have been the best center fielder in franchise history. Nicknamed "Deerfoot" because of his speed, Milan broke Ty Cobb's grip on the stolen-base title in 1912 when he stole 88 bases. He led the league again the next year with 75. Milan had very little power, hitting only 17 homers in 16 seasons, but he did hit over .300 four times and over .290 three other times, significant performances in the dead-ball era. After he retired, Milan coached in the minors for many years before becoming a coach with the Senators in 1937. In 1953 he died of a heart attack while hitting fungoes in the intense heat of spring training.

CAREER SENATORS RECORD:

Games	AB	Hits	Runs
1,982	7,359	2,100	1,004
Avg	**HR**	**RBI**	**SB**
.285	17	617	495

MYER, BUDDY (2B/SS)
(1925–1927, 1929–1941)

Buddy Myer spent more than 15 seasons of his 17-year major league career with the Senators. After hitting .336 with New Orleans, Myer's contract was purchased by the Senators for $25,000. A career .303 hitter, Myer led the American League in batting in 1935 with a .349 average. He went into the final day of the season trailing Cleveland outfielder Joe Vosmik, who tried to protect his lead by sitting out the last day. Myer collected several hits to nip Vosmik, .3495 to .3489. In 1926 Myer replaced Roger Peckinpaugh at shortstop, but Washington owner Clark Griffith became disenchanted with Myer's less-than-adequate fielding ability and traded him to Boston early in the 1927 season for Topper Rigney. Rigney played only 45 more games while Myer flourished, hitting .288 for the remainder of the season and .313 with 60 drag-bunt hits in 1928, while leading the league in steals. Griffith had trader's remorse almost immediately and tried to get Myer back, but it took him two years and five players before Boston would agree. Griffith once called his trade of Myer "the dumbest deal I ever made." In Myer's 13 additional seasons in Washington, he hit over .300 seven times and over .290 three more times.

CAREER SENATORS RECORD:

Games	AB	Hits	Runs
1,643	6,033	1,828	1,037
Avg	**HR**	**RBI**	**SB**
.303	35	759	117

OLIVA, TONY (OF/DH) (1962–1976)

Pedro Oliva y Lopez was born in Cuba in 1940. To escape Castro's regime, Pedro used his brother Tony's passport. Once in the United States, he got a three-day trial with the Twins. Since he spoke no English and was using his brother's passport, Pedro forever after went by his brother's name. After the Twins signed Oliva to a minor league contract, he had three very good years in the minors from 1961 to 1963, hitting .410, .350, and .304. In two short major league trials in 1962 and 1963, Oliva hit .444 and .429. When the Twins brought him up for good in 1964, he was expected to be the team's utility outfielder. Instead, Oliva won the everyday right-field job and hit .323 with 32 homers, 43 doubles, 109 runs, and 94 RBIs, racking up a rookie record 374 total bases. He also led the league in hits with 217, tying the major league rookie record and claiming the batting title. His monster season earned him the Rookie of the Year Award. Oliva suffered no sophomore jinx in 1965 as he won his second straight batting title with a .321 average, making him the first player ever to win batting titles in his first two years in the majors. In 1966 he led the AL in hits for the third consecutive year, hitting .307 and winning a Gold Glove. In his first eight seasons, Oliva finished in the top three in the AL batting race seven times. He was selected to the All-Star team in his first eight major league seasons, breaking Joe DiMaggio's record of six.

But Oliva had an Achilles' heel—and it was his knees. They were so painful for many years that roommate Rod Carew was often forced to leave their hotel room in the middle of the night to find ice to put on Oliva's knees. The Twins knew that Oliva was living on borrowed time as far as his knees were concerned. When he severely injured a knee while diving for a Joe Rudi fly ball in July 1971, it spelled the beginning of the end. Hitting .375 at the time, Oliva literally limped to a third batting title, finishing at .337. He would never lead the league in any offensive category again.

Limited to just 10 games in 1972, Oliva's career received a boost in 1973 with the advent of the DH. Oliva once recounted an amusing story to this author about his first game at DH. It was Opening Day 1973, and the Twins were in Oakland. It was the first game in which either team made use of the new DH. Greg Kusick had been the Twins' DH at the start of the game, but manager Frank Quilici sent Oliva in to pinch-hit for him late in the game. Oliva promptly hit the first home run ever by a DH. After returning to the dugout, Oliva received congratulations from his teammates and then left for the locker room. While he was showering, a teammate ran into the shower and yelled for him to get dressed and get back to the field. Oliva had wrongly assumed his role was pinch-hitter, when in fact, he had replaced the previous DH in the lineup. Rod Carew had walked and now it was Oliva's turn to bat. Oliva hurriedly dressed, still soaking wet, ran to the dugout, grabbed the first bat he saw, and strode to the plate. After all that, Oliva was walked on four pitches.

Oliva played DH in every single one of the 406 games he played from 1973 to the end of his career in 1976, when he was a shadow of his former self. He hit a near-career low .291 in 1973, and then declined each year after that to a dismal .211 in 1976 before calling it quits at the age of 35. After retiring, Oliva spent time as the Twins batting coach and is credited with making the critical difference in Kirby Puckett's career. He also served as a minor league hitting instructor and manager in the Mexican League.

CAREER TWINS RECORD:

Games	AB	Hits	Runs
1,676	6,301	1,917	870
Avg	**HR**	**RBI**	**SB**
.304	220	947	86

PASCUAL, CAMILO (SP/RP) (1954–1966)

Cuban-born Camilo Pascual joined the Washington Senators' farm system in 1952 and made it to the big leagues in 1954. Because the Senators were terrible at the time, Pascual was just 28–66 in his first five years with the team, but nonetheless he was often a dominating pitcher with a devastating curveball considered the equal of Sandy Koufax's. Pascual's fortunes began to change in 1959, when he went 17–10 and was selected to the first of his five All-Star Games. After going 15–16 in his first season in Minnesota, Pascual put together back-to-back 20-win seasons in 1962–1963. He led the AL in strikeouts three straight years from 1961–1963, and twice led in shutouts and complete games. After a 15-win season in 1964, Pascual began to suffer chronic arm problems, and won just 17 games over the next two seasons. Following the 1966 season he was traded to the replacement Senators team, where he went 25–22, but without the same ability to dominate. From 1969–1971, limited to spot starting because of his arm trouble, he won only four more games for four different teams before retiring after the 1971 season.

CAREER SENATORS/TWINS RECORD:

W	L	W%	ERA	SV
145	141	.507	3.66	10
K	**BB**	**SHO**	**IP**	
1,885	909	31	2,465.0	

PERRY, JIM (SP/RP) (1963–1972)

After four-plus years in Cleveland, Jim Perry was traded to Minnesota early in the 1963 season for Jack Kralick. For six seasons Perry alternated between the bullpen and spot starting, usually only when an injury or doubleheader necessitated it. In 1965 the Twins placed him on waivers, but he went unclaimed, so Minnesota kept him and he won seven straight games to help Minnesota to the AL title. In 1969 manager Billy Martin made Perry the team's number one starter and he responded with a surprising 20–6 record. In 1970 he won 24 games and the AL Cy Young Award while his brother Gaylord won 23 games for the San Francisco Giants in the National League. That year they became the first brothers ever to face each other in the All-Star Game. Together the Perrys had more career strikeouts and shutouts than any brother combination in major league history, and the second-most wins next to Phil and Joe Niekro. Just before the 1973 season began, Perry was traded to Detroit, where he played for just a year. After two more years with Cleveland and Oakland, Perry retired.

CAREER TWINS RECORD:

W	L	W%	ERA	SV
128	90	.587	3.15	5
K	**BB**	**SHO**	**IP**	
1,025	541	17	1,883.3	

PUCKETT, KIRBY (OF)
(1984–1995)

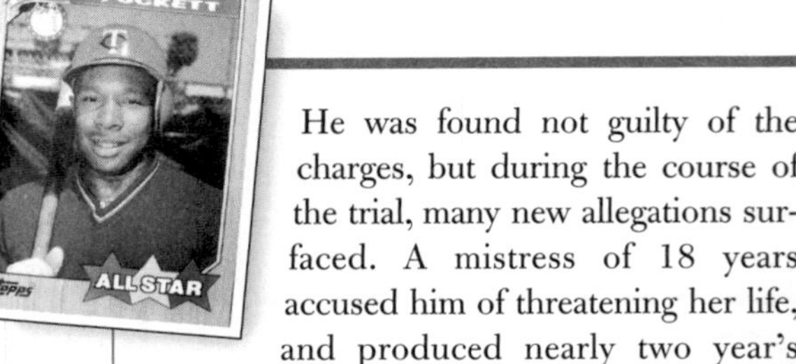

Kirby Puckett was drafted by the Twins in the first round of the 1982 amateur draft and made it to the major leagues as a full-time player in 1984. Over the next 12 years he was one of the most popular Twins ever. Always jovial and smiling, he became a favorite of fans across the country as well. Puckett was heavily involved in numerous charities, and in 1993 won the Branch Rickey Award for his community involvement. Puckett's accomplishments on the field are many. He appeared in 10 straight All-Star Games, winning the MVP honors in 1993. He won six Gold Gloves and six Silver Slugger Awards. Puckett almost always finished near the top in the AL batting race, winning it in 1989 with a .339 average. He led the AL in hits three straight years from 1987 to 1989, joining only Ty Cobb and Tony Oliva in performing the feat. He hit over .300 in eight of his 12 major league seasons.

Puckett's career ended abruptly. On September 28, 1995, Puckett was hit in the face by a Dennis Martinez pitch. It was the last time Puckett would play in a game. The following spring, Puckett awoke one morning with blurred vision in his right eye. Diagnosed with glaucoma that had caused irreversible damage to his right eye, Puckett was forced to retire when several laser surgeries failed to correct the problem. In 2001 he was elected to the Hall of Fame.

But Puckett's secret life off the field was about to explode onto the front pages. He was arrested for criminal sexual assault and false imprisonment for allegedly forcing a woman into a restaurant restroom and fondling her. He was found not guilty of the charges, but during the course of the trial, many new allegations surfaced. A mistress of 18 years accused him of threatening her life, and produced nearly two year's worth of taped phone conversations to back that and other claims. His wife filed for divorce and accused him of threatening her life. Her police complaint also alleges that Puckett once locked her in the basement, and on another occasion used a power saw to cut through the door of a room where she had locked herself. A private investigator hired by Puckett's wife turned up evidence he was having affairs with more than just one mistress. Further, both his wife and mistress claimed that Puckett actually loathed the charity events that he was involved with, doing it only for the acclaim and not the cause. It also came out that a former female Twins employee had filed a sexual harassment lawsuit against both Puckett and the Twins, but a financial settlement reached just before the Hall of Fame induction ceremonies were to take place kept it out of public view. Kirby Puckett, once declared "Baseball's Best Role Model" by a *Baseball America* reader poll in 1993, established one final mark when he went from fan icon to public pariah in record time.

If Puckett's was a tormented soul, it was put to rest on March 6, 2006, when the former Twin great died from a stroke at age 45.

CAREER TWINS RECORD:

Games	AB	Hits	Runs
1,783	7,244	2,304	1,071
Avg	**HR**	**RBI**	**SB**
.318	207	1,085	134

RADKE, BRAD (SP)
(1995–2005)

The Twins drafted Brad Radke in the eighth round of the June 1991 amateur draft. In 1995 he made it to the big league ballclub and joined the starting rotation, a position he has held for the last 11 years, averaging about 32 starts per year over that span. Radke's ERA has traditionally been a bit high (over 4.00), but he's been a remarkably dependable workhorse, eating many innings and missing only a short time in 2002 due to injury. Over time he has crept into the top ten of many of Minnesota's all-time pitching categories. Radke's best season so far was 1997, when he went 20–10; he's had no other season with more than 15 wins.

CAREER TWINS RECORD:

W	L	W%	ERA	SV
127	118	.518	4.23	0
K	**BB**	**SHO**	**IP**	
1,267	390	9	2,088.0	

RICE, SAM (OF)
(1915–1933)

Edgar Charles Rice was one of the most prolific singles hitters in baseball history. Of his 2,987 career hits, nearly 2,300 were singles. Rice was a 22-year-old husband and father living in Illinois in 1912 when a tornado ripped through the family home and killed his wife, two children, and both parents. Shocked and depressed, he wandered the country, taking odd jobs where he could and when he needed to. He eventually joined the Navy and played baseball for the base's team. In 1914, while still in the Navy, Rice pitched a game for Petersburg of the Virginia League. The team's owner was impressed with Rice and bought his release from the Navy. In 1915 the owner sent Rice to the Washington Senators as payment for a debt. Washington Senators owner Clark Griffith soon moved Rice from the pitcher's mound to the outfield. At a press release to announce his team's latest acquisition, Griffith was asked what Rice's first name was. Griffith didn't know, so he just said, "Sam." Forever after, Edgar Rice was known as Sam Rice.

Rice was amazingly consistent during his 20-year career, 19 seasons of which he spent with Washington. He hit over .300 15 times. In the other five years he hit .293–.299. An able base stealer, Rice led the league in 1920 with 63. Rice's lasting claim to fame is a catch he made in the 1925 World Series against Pittsburgh. Rice was playing right field in Game 3 when the Pirates' Earl Smith hit a drive to deep-right-center field. Rice took off on a dead run towards the temporary bleachers that had been set up in the outfield of Griffith Stadium to accommodate the overflow crowd. He arrived at the ball and the bleachers at the same time. Rice stuck up his glove and disappeared into the crowd. A full ten seconds later he walked out of the crowd, ball in hand. The umpire ruled it a catch and the Pirates went nuts, appealing the call to Commissioner Landis, who was in attendance. When asked by Landis if he had caught the ball, Rice replied, "The umpire said I did." The play stood, but the Pirates protested, even going so far as to demand notarized affidavits from everyone in the right-field bleacher section. More than 1,600 signed affidavits were turned in, some claiming the ball was caught, some claiming it was not. The Pirates eventually prevailed in seven games to put the matter to rest, at least temporarily.

Rice was one of the toughest men in baseball history to strike out, fanning only once every 34 at-bats, eighth-best all time. Of his 34 career homers, 21 were inside-the-park jobs. During his career Rice had three long-hitting streaks: 28, 29, and 31 games. He also participated in all three of the Senators' World Series, collecting 19 hits in 63 at-bats (all singles). Few players have ever hit over .300 when in their forties, but Rice did it a major league record three times.

The World Series catch incident followed Rice the rest of his life. After he was elected to the Hall of Fame in 1963, he sent a letter to the Hall of Fame with the instructions that the letter could not be opened until after his death. When Rice died in 1974, the letter was opened. In it, Rice had written, "At no time did I lose possession of the ball."

CAREER SENATORS RECORD:

Games	AB	Hits	Runs
2,307	8,934	2,889	1,466
Avg	**HR**	**RBI**	**SB**
.323	33	1,045	346

VERNON, MICKEY (OF/1B) (1939–1943, 1946–1948, 1950–1955)

James "Mickey" Vernon signed on with Washington as an amateur free agent in 1937 and made it to the big leagues in 1939. He was a dependable, solid player who didn't seek the limelight. During his career he set a number of fielding records and played more games at first base than any player in the 20th century. He was, however, strangely inconsistent in his batting average. Baseball historian Bill James even described Vernon as ". . . the most inconsistent player ever to play the game." He won two batting titles with averages of .353 and .337. He also had six seasons in which he batted .250 or below. Vernon was enjoying one of his great years in 1953 as he fought for the batting title with Cleveland's Al Rosen. Going into the last day of the season, Rosen was hitting .333 and Vernon .336. Rosen went 3-for-5 to raise his average to .336. After going 2-for-4 to raise his average to .337, just one point ahead of Rosen, it looked as if Vernon would get one more at-bat in the last inning, so his teammates took it upon themselves to make sure Vernon didn't step to the plate again. When Mickey Grasso hit a two-out double in the eighth, he "wandered" off the bag and got picked off. In the ninth, Kite Thomas led off with a single but was cut down when he tried to "leisurely" stretch it into a double. The next batter, Eddie Yost, known for his incredible batting eye, struck out on a pitch over his head. Pete Runnels, the only batter left in front of Vernon, struck out on an "excuse me" half-swing to end the game and assure Vernon his batting title. Vernon spent 15 of his 20 big league seasons in Washington. After he retired, Vernon spent many years as a minor league manager, coach, batting instructor, and scout. When the second Washington Senators team began play in 1961, Vernon became the manager and ran the club for two-plus seasons before being fired.

CAREER SENATORS RECORD:

Games	AB	Hits	Runs
1,805	6,930	1,993	956
Avg	**HR**	**RBI**	**SB**
.288	121	1,026	125

New York Mets

Since 1962

1969 Team Ball

1962 The Mets play an incredible 28 doubleheaders plus two day-night affairs, getting swept 17 times, splitting 10, and sweeping three. The 17 double losses breaks the old record of 16 set by Pittsburgh in 1953....**1973** The Mets' 82–79 regular-season record is the worst ever by a World Series champion (they are the only team over .500 in the National League's East Division), and it takes a 20–8 September to get there....**1977** Joe Torre becomes the first native New Yorker to manage a major league New York team in the 20th century when the Mets name him as their new manager on May 31....**1999** The Mets set an all-time major league record by committing only 68 errors all season. Adrian Beltre of the Dodgers and Ed Sprague of the Pirates each have 29 errors themselves.

FRANCHISE HISTORY

After New York fans lost both the Giants and Dodgers to California following the 1957 season, baseball fans lobbied loud and hard to attract another team to the Big Apple, making overtures to the National League's Pirates, Reds, and Phillies. However, the inside track belonged to New York attorney Frank Shea, formerly on the board of directors for the New York Giants. When the National League moved too slowly, he worked behind the scenes with Branch Rickey to form a third major league—the Continental League. He called for locating new franchises in cities already occupied by major league teams, including New York. When their plans became public in 1960, the National League short-circuited them by quickly announcing an expansion plan for 1962 that would include franchises in New York and Houston, which would be awarded to Continental League owners. As a result, the New York Mets were born.

The name was chosen in a fan poll, after newspaper reporters narrowed the choices to the Continentals, Skyliners, Jets, Meadowlarks, Burros, Skyscrapers, Rebels, Avengers, and Metropolitans. Owner Joan Payson preferred the Meadowlarks, but gave in to the fans' choice. In 1962, the team began play in the National League to the cheer of "Let's go Mets!"

Payson was a former Giants fan who made a conscious effort to hire people who would help invoke the past and get fans to reminisce about the "good old days." They even played their home games in the same stadium the Giants had abandoned, the historic Polo Grounds, even though workers were still planting grass and painting the outfield fence on the day of the first game. She hired Casey Stengel and George Weiss, both recently let go by the Yankees, to give the team instant credibility.

A miracle: the 1969 Mets—including (l. to r.) Jerry Koosman, Jerry Grote, and Ed Kranepool—beat Baltimore in the World Series.

Payson also signed numerous former New York stars or local favorites. Gil Hodges (who would later become a Mets manager), Don Zimmer, Gus Bell, Roger Craig, Clem Labine, Richie Ashburn, Frank Thomas, Gene Woodling, Duke Snider, Jimmy Piersall, Roy McMillan, Yogi Berra, Warren Spahn, Joe Pignatano, and local high school star Ed Kranepool all played for the Mets in the team's first few years. Although the ragtag bunch of players didn't win many games in the early years, the tactic was a great promotional success. Like the fans of the former Brooklyn Dodgers, Mets fans fell in love with their team almost as much for their faults as for their virtues. As an expression of their enthusiasm, they began to bring posters and banners to the ballpark, some made out of bed sheets. At first, ballpark security quickly removed the banners under the direction of George Weiss, whose Yankee sensibilities were stunned by this undignified behavior. However, under pressure from the press, Weiss relented, and eventually the practice of displaying banners at the ballpark became encouraged. The Mets even initiated Major League Baseball's first-ever Banner Day.

On April 22, 1970,Tom Seaver became the first pitcher in history to strike out 19 batters in a day game, and he did it in style, striking out the last 10 Padres in a row.

Perhaps it was an omen of things to come, but the Mets' first-ever game against the Cardinals was rained out in St. Louis. When the inaugural game did take place the next day, April 11, Met third baseman Charlie Neal fielded a grounder on the first play of the game and threw the ball into right field. Then the Cardinals scored their first run on a balk by Roger Craig. The Mets lost 11–4. Their first home game was on Friday the 13th; they lost. In fact, they lost their first nine games of the season en route to a dismal 40–120 record, the worst in modern baseball history. Manager Casey Stengel, who knew early on how awful his young team was going to be, made full use of his comic nature. He clownishly provided the press with colorful quotes and stories to distract the press and public from his team's execrable performance on the field. When the Mets moved into their new ballpark, Shea Stadium, in 1964, they actually attracted more paying fans than the pennant-bound Yankees. Over the next decade or so, they would outdraw the Yankees by double, sometimes more.

Joan Payson owned the team until her death in 1975, at which point control shifted to her husband, Charles, who took little interest in it. After five years, he sold the majority interest to Nelson Doubleday Jr., of Doubleday Publishing, for $21.3 million—a record amount at the time, with the purchase being financed through the publishing company. Doubleday is a direct descendant of Abner Doubleday, the supposed inventor of baseball. Real estate mogul Fred Wilpon, who purchased the remaining 10 percent, also owned a 10 percent interest in the New York Islanders hockey team and had once been a teammate of Sandy Koufax's at Brooklyn's Lafayette High School (he was the pitcher, while Koufax played first base). In 1986, Doubleday

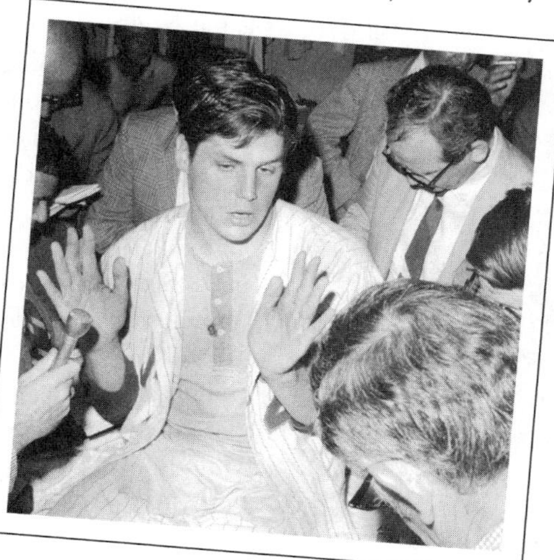

Tom Seaver discusses his one-hitter against the Cubs on July 9, 1969.

sold his publishing company for $500 million. He and Wilpon then bought out the company's interest and became equal partners, each owning 50 percent. In August 2002, Doubleday divested his interest, and Wilpon owns the team to this day.

> The Mets tied the all-time worst record by an established team in an expansion year when they finished the 1993 season with a 59–103 record.

On the field, the Mets were simply horrible their first seven years, finishing either last or next to last every year. Then, in 1969, a miracle occurred. Backed by a talented young pitching staff, Manager Gil Hodges used a platoon system for five of his eight position players to lead the "Miracle Mets" to the World Series title. They surprisingly swept the Braves in the first-ever NLCS, then dispatched the heavily favored Orioles in five games in the World Series. They returned to the World Series in 1973, despite barely playing .500 ball during the regular season. However, they failed to recapture the magic of 1969, losing to Oakland. In 1986, the Mets again used a strong pitching staff led by Doc Gooden to romp to the East Division title, winning 108 games, including a thrilling six-game NLCS over the Astros (the clinching game was a 16-inning affair that some consider the greatest single game ever played). They then came from behind to defeat the Red Sox in one of the most memorable World Series of all time, taking advantage of the infamous Bill Buckner error on Mookie Wilson's ground ball. They made it to the World Series again in 2000, but were unceremoniously dispatched by the powerful Yankees in five games.

Nineteen-year-old Rookie of the Year Dwight Gooden

TEAM NAME HISTORY

Official Names

Mets (1962–current)

Unofficial Names/Nicknames

The Amazin's

STADIUM HISTORY

Polo Grounds	1962–1963
Shea Stadium	1964–current

YEARLY RECORD, FINISH, & ATTENDANCE FIGURES

Year	League	Record	DIV/LG Finish	Attendance	Avg/Gm
2005	NL East	83–79	3	2,829,929	34,937
2004	NL East	71–91	4	2,318,951	28,629
2003	NL East	66–95	5	2,140,599	26,757
2002	NL East	75–86	5	2,804,838	34,628
2001	NL East	82–80	3	2,658,330	32,819
2000	NL East	94–68	2	2,820,530	34,821
1999	NL East	97–66	2	2,725,668	33,650
1998	NL East	88–74	2	2,287,948	28,246
1997	NL East	88–74	3	1,766,174	21,805
1996	NL East	71–91	4	1,588,323	19,609
1995	NL East	69–75	2	1,273,183	17,683
1994	NL East	55–58	3	1,151,471	21,726
1993	NL East	59–103	7	1,873,183	23,126
1992	NL East	72–90	5	1,779,534	21,970
1991	NL East	77–84	5	2,284,484	27,860
1990	NL East	91–71	2	2,732,745	33,738
1989	NL East	87–75	2	2,918,710	36,033
1988	NL East	100–60	1	3,055,445	38,193
1987	NL East	92–70	2	3,034,129	37,458
1986	NL East	108–54	1	2,767,601	34,168
1985	NL East	98–64	2	2,761,601	34,094
1984	NL East	90–72	2	1,842,695	22,749
1983	NL East	68–94	6	1,112,774	13,570
1982	NL East	65–97	6	1,323,036	16,334
1981	NL East	41–62	5/4	704,244	13,543
1980	NL East	67–95	5	1,192,073	14,537
1979	NL East	63–99	6	788,905	9,621
1978	NL East	66–96	6	1,007,328	12,592
1977	NL East	64–98	6	1,066,825	13,504
1976	NL East	86–76	3	1,468,754	17,912
1975	NL East	82–80	3	1,730,566	21,365
1974	NL East	71–91	5	1,722,209	21,262
1973	NL East	82–79	1	1,912,390	23,610
1972	NL East	83–73	3	2,134,185	27,361
1971	NL East	83–79	3	2,266,680	27,984
1970	NL East	83–79	3	2,697,479	32,896
1969	NL East	100–62	1	2,175,373	26,529
1968	NL	73–89	9	1,781,657	21,728
1967	NL	61–101	10	1,565,492	20,070
1966	NL	66–95	9	1,932,693	23,860
1965	NL	50–112	10	1,768,389	21,566
1964	NL	53–109	10	1,732,597	21,129
1963	NL	51–111	10	1,080,108	13,335
1962	NL	40–120	10	922,530	11,532

MANAGER HISTORY

Manager	Years	W–L	Win %
Casey Stengel	1962–1965	175–404	.302
Wes Westrum	1965–1967	142–237	.375
Salty Parker	1967	4–7	.364
Gil Hodges	1968–1971	339–309	.523
Yogi Berra	1972–1975	292–296	.497
Roy McMillan	1975	26–27	.491
Joe Frazier	1976–1977	101–106	.488
Joe Torre	1977–1981	286–420	.405
George Bamberger	1982–1983	81–127	.389
Frank Howard	1983	52–64	.448
Davey Johnson	1984–1990	595–417	.588
Bud Harrelson	1990–1991	145–129	.529
Mike Cubbage	1991	3–4	.429
Jeff Torborg	1992–1993	85–115	.425
Dallas Green	1993–1996	229–283	.447
Bobby Valentine	1996–2002	536–467	.534
Art Howe	2002–2004	137–185	.425
Willie Randolph	2005	83–79	.512

ALL-TIME WIN-LOSS RECORDS VS. ALL OPPONENTS

Opponent	W–L
ALL-TIME	3,311–3,677
Angels	3–3
Astros	233–288
Athletics	1–2
Blue Jays	12–3
Braves	271–328
Brewers	38–20
Cardinals	307–350
Cubs	326–328
Devil Rays	7–5
Diamondbacks	31–29
Dodgers	232–289
Giants	237–288
Indians	4–2
INTERLEAGUE	77–74
Mariners	1–5
Marlins	100–92
Nationals	310–306
Orioles	11–5
Padres	200–203
Phillies	347–399
Pirates	309–345
Rangers	2–1
Reds	235–286
Red Sox	8–7
Rockies	58–52
Royals	3–3
Tigers	3–3
Twins	2–1
White Sox	1–2
Yankees	19–29

Franchise Highlights, Low Points, and Strange Distinctions

1962–70 The Mets got off to a rough start in their inaugural year of 1962, losing their first nine games, which tied the National League record at the time for most consecutive losses to open a season. Curiously, when they ended their 0–9 start with a 9–1 victory over the Pirates, it was the first loss of the year for Pittsburgh, which had tied the existing National League record of ten consecutive wins to open a season.

The 1963 Mets fared little better than the 1962 team. They, too, began the season with a long losing streak, this time eight straight. While the second-year team did win 11 more games than the 1962 squad, they were still last in hitting, pitching, and fielding, and were shut out 30 times, just three short of the major league record of 33 set by the 1908 Cardinals.

The Mets got off to a horrible start in 1964 as well, going 3–16 to start the campaign. They again lost more than 100 games, and in so doing became the first New York team in history to lose more than 100 games in three consecutive seasons. And for the third year in a row, the Mets had a 20-game loser on their pitching staff. This time it was Tracy Stallard, who finished at 10–20. In 1963, it was Roger Craig, who suffered through a 5–22 season, losing 18 straight at one point. And in 1962, there were two 20-game losers—Roger Craig at 10–24 and Alvin Jackson at 8–20. Fan attendance, on the other hand, was fantastic. The Mets attracted more than 1.7 million paying customers, the second-highest total in the major leagues.

The 1965 Mets continued their dismal tradition, losing at least 100 games (112) and having at least one 20-game loser on the pitching staff (actually, they had two: Jack Fisher at 8–24 and Alvin Jackson at 8–20). Both streaks would end in 1966, when the Mets would lose 95 games and their losingest pitcher would have only 14 losses.

The Mets returned to their old ways in 1967, losing 101 games. They were shut out 26 times, 11 more than any other NL team, and lost their opening game for the sixth straight year. However, they did manage to end two impressive losing streaks. First, on July 4, they snagged an 8–7 victory over Giant ace Juan Marichal, a pitcher who had been 19–0 against them. Then, on August 14, they defeated Larry Jackson of the Phillies 8–3, who had been 18–0 against them. Oddly enough, the winning pitcher both times was Jack Fisher, whose 9–18 record was the worst on the team.

After a 1967 season in which new manager Gil Hodges shuttled 54 different players in and out of the New York lineup, Hodges used only 34 during the 1968 campaign. Behind surprising youngsters Tom Seaver and Jerry Koosman, the Mets won a team-record 73 games while losing 89.

In 1969, the Mets lost their season opener for the eighth straight year, this time to the expansion Montreal Expos. But by the time the season was over, they were being called the Miracle Mets after winning their division flag and the World Series title. It was the first time in history that a team had won the World Series after finishing as low as ninth the preceding year.

It took nine years, but the Mets finally won a season-opening game. They defeated the Pirates 5–3 on April 7, 1970, after 13 innings.

• • • •

1962–2005 Since the New York Mets first took the field, there have been 59 no-hitters pitched in the National League, but none by a Met. Former Mets who left New York and then threw no-hitters for another team include: Tom Seaver, Mike Scott, Dwight Gooden, David Cone, Hideo Nomo, A.J. Burnett, and Nolan Ryan (seven times). Pitchers who threw no-hitters before they joined the Mets but not afterwards include: John Candelaria, Bret Saberhagen, Kenny Rogers, and Al Leiter.

• • • •

1962 The New York Mets played their home games in the historic Polo Grounds, home of the departed Giants, when they began their first year in 1962. Their new ballpark, Shea Stadium, took its name from William A. Shea, a New York attorney who was instrumental in getting a National League franchise back in the Big Apple after the Giants left for San Francisco.

New York fans were happy to see National League baseball return to the city, with 922,530 paying to see the Mets play their inaugural home season. This turnout marked the highest attendance ever in the National League by a last-place team, and the second highest in Major League Baseball by a last-place team, trailing only the 1,026,846 who for some reason paid to witness the dismal 1952 Detroit Tigers' season.

1964 Two extraordinary events took place in Shea Stadium in 1964. The first occurred on May 31 when the Mets and the Giants played a marathon doubleheader. The first game went the regulation nine innings, with the Giants winning 5–3. San Francisco then swept the doubleheader by winning the second game 8–6 in 23 innings. The first pitch of the opening game was made at 1:08 p.m., and the final out of the second game was recorded at 11:25 P.M. The combined actual playing time of nine hours, 52 minutes was a record. The two teams used 22 dozen baseballs in the twin bill, which was attended by 57,037 people, 15,000 of whom remained until the end.

The second event was a perfect game pitched by Jim Bunning of Philadelphia as the Phillies topped the Mets, 6–0. It was the first regular-season perfect game pitched in the majors in more than 42 years. Bunning, the father of seven, pitched the game on June 21—Father's Day.

When Shea Stadium opened in April 1964, newspaper copy had to be submitted via runners to the nearby World's Fair press center, because the usual telephone and telegraph communications networks hadn't been set up yet.

• • • •

1975 Tom Seaver set a major league record when he struck out more than 200 batters in a season for the eighth straight year. He would make it nine in a row the next year before his streak ended in 1977, when he fell just short with 196 strikeouts.

1976 After a secret deal to trade Tom Seaver to the Dodgers became public late in spring training, fan furor forced the Mets to reconsider. As a result, they awarded Seaver the biggest contract given to a pitcher up to that time: $225,000 a year for three years. The deal also included many performance incentives, one of the first contracts of this kind.

....

1977 The Mets' season was one of their most miserable. Besides sliding back into last place for the first time in 10 years, the team's management incurred the wrath of fans at the trade deadline when they traded away their top two stars, Tom Seaver and Dave Kingman. The resulting drop in attendance, down 1.6 million from just seven years earlier, was the largest drop in major league baseball history.

....

1978 The Mets finished the season with the worst record in the National League and a continued drop in attendance. Catcher John Stearns provided the only bright spot, stealing 25 bases—breaking a National League record for catchers that had stood for nearly 80 years.

....

1979 Things were so bad that the team couldn't even draw 30,000 fans to a game. The best they drew for a non-promotional game was the 20,619 who showed up to watch Tom Seaver shut out his former teammates, 8–0. The team's 63–99 record was made possible by an egregious 6–32 home record after the All-Star break.

The Strawberry that stirred the Mets' drink in the 1980s.

1980 The Mets had the fewest homers in the majors, clubbing only 61. And they got no homers from their catchers all season.

....

1982 The acquisition of high-priced slugger George Foster gave the Mets hope that their poor finishes were at an end. But the former power cog in Cincinnati's Big Red Machine had one of his worst seasons in years. He hit only 13 homers with 70 RBIs and left a whopping 47 runners on third base with fewer than two out. Foster's inability to produce in the clutch contributed mightily to the Mets' 5–24 record in August.

The Mets finished with the worst record in the National League again in 1983. It's hard to find a bright spot: Rusty Staub tied the major league record for consecutive pinch-hits with eight, and Darryl Strawberry was voted the National League's Rookie of the Year.

1984–86 Several young pitchers sparked the Mets to a turnaround in 1984, most notably Dwight Gooden. The 19-year-old set a new rookie record for strikeouts in a season with 276, breaking Herb Score's longstanding record of 245. The rookie sensation had back-to-back 16-strikeout performances in September (one of them in only eight innings), and the 32 strikeouts set a new two-game National League record. Gooden also had 15 games in which he struck out at least 10 batters.

The resurgent Mets, who finished just three games behind the division-winning Cardinals, continued to climb in the standings in 1985. For that, they have to thank first baseman Keith Hernandez, who had 24 game winners out of his 91 RBIs, a new major league record. In addition, 20-year-old Dwight Gooden avoided a sophomore slump. He followed his impressive 1984 Rookie of the Year season with a Cy Young season, going 24–4 with a 1.53 ERA and 268 strikeouts, winning pitching's Triple Crown. He also won 14 straight games at one point and had a 31-inning scoreless streak.

During the team's 1986 spring training season, Manager Davey Johnson was quoted as saying, "We don't just want to win. We want to dominate." And dominate they did. After romping to 108 wins in the regular season, the Mets won the NLCS and the World Series to cap a dominant season. Their 21½ game margin over second-place Philadelphia in the NL East was the second-biggest winning margin in major league history, behind Pittsburgh's 27½ game margin over Brooklyn in 1902.

1988 Davey Johnson, helped by pitcher David Cone, who finished 20–3 in his first full major league season, became the first manager in National League history to record at least 90 wins in his first five seasons at the helm, when the Mets finished at 100–60.

• • • •

1990 Although the Mets didn't win the pennant, it wasn't the pitching staff's fault. Four Mets were among the NL's top five in strikeouts: David Cone, 233; Dwight Gooden, 223; Frank Viola, 182; and Sid Fernandez, 181. Ramon Martinez of the Dodgers was the only non-Met to crack the top five in strikeouts, finishing with 223.

• • • •

1996 Todd Hundley's 41 home runs not only set a new major league record for catchers, but it was also the most by any New York player since Roger Maris hit 61 for the Yankees in 1961.

• • • •

1999 Third baseman Robin Ventura became the first player in major league history to hit grand slams in both games of a doubleheader on May 20, against the Milwaukee Brewers.

• • • •

2001 When Lenny Harris collected his 21st and last pinch-hit of the season, it was the 151st of his career, breaking Manny Mota's long-held record of 150 career pinch-hits.

Special Achievements

World Series Results

Year	Opponent	Result	Games
1969	Baltimore	Won	4–1
1973	Oakland	Lost	4–3
1986	Boston	Won	4–3
2000	New York	Lost	4–1

World Series Managerial Records

Manager	Series Record	Games Record
Gil Hodges	1–0	4–1
Yogi Berra	0–1	3–4
Davey Johnson	1–0	4–3
Bobby Valentine	0–1	1–4

All-Time Postseason Record

Divisional Playoffs	6–2
League Championship Series	19–13
World Series	12–12

All-Star Games at New York

Year	Date	Winner	Score	Stadium
1964	July 7	National	7–4	Shea Stadium

Hall of Famers Who Played for Team

	Position	Years	Games with New York
Richie Ashburn	OF	1962	135
Yogi Berra	C Mgr	1965 1972–75	4 588
Gary Carter	C	1985–89	600
Willie Mays	OF/1B	1972–73	135
Eddie Murray	1B	1992–93	310
Nolan Ryan	SP	1966, 1968–71	105
Tom Seaver	SP	1966–77, 1983	401
Duke Snider	OF	1963	129
Warren Spahn	SP	1965	20
Casey Stengel	Mgr	1962–65	579

Hall of Famers Who Managed Team

None

MVP Award Winners

None

Cy Young Award Winners

Pitcher	Year	W–L	ERA
Tom Seaver	1969	25–7	2.21
Tom Seaver	1973	19–10	2.08
Tom Seaver	1975	22–9	2.38
Dwight Gooden	1985	24–4	1.53

Rookie of the Year Award Winners

Tom Seaver	SP	1967
John Matlack	SP	1972
Darryl Strawberry	OF	1983
Dwight Gooden	SP	1984

Gold Glove Winners

Year	Position	Player
1970	OF	Tommie Agee
1971	SS	Bud Harrelson
1980	2B	Doug Flynn
1983	1B	Keith Hernandez
1984	1B	Keith Hernandez
1985	1B	Keith Hernandez
1986	1B	Keith Hernandez
1987	1B	Keith Hernandez
1988	1B	Keith Hernandez
1989	SP	Ron Darling
1997	SS	Rey Ordoñez
1998	SS	Rey Ordoñez
1999	3B SS	Robin Ventura Rey Ordoñez

Triple Crown Winners

None

Fireman of the Year Award Winners

John Franco	1990
John Franco	1994
Armando Benitez	2001 (tie)

World Series MVP

Donn Clendenon	1969
Ray Knight	1986

League Championship Series MVP

Mike Hampton	2000

All-Star Game MVP

Jon Matlack	1975

Manager of the Year Award Winners

None

Batting Champions

None

Nine-Inning No-Hitters Pitched

None

20-Game Winners

Year	Pitcher	W–L
1969	Tom Seaver	25–7
1971	Tom Seaver	20–10
1972	Tom Seaver	21–12
1975	Tom Seaver	22–9
1976	Jerry Koosman	21–10
1985	Dwight Gooden	24–4
1988	David Cone	20–3
1990	Frank Viola	20–12

Retired Uniform Numbers

Number	Player	Position
14	Gil Hodges	Mgr
37	Casey Stengel	Mgr
41	Tom Seaver	SP

Team Records—Wins & Losses

- Games won in a season: 108 in 1986
- Games lost in a season: 120 in 1962
- Games won in a month: 23 in September 1969
- Games lost in a month: 26 in August 1962
- Consecutive games won: 11, four times: 1969, 1972, 1986, 1990
- Consecutive games lost: 17 in 1962
- Biggest shutout victory: 14–0 over Chicago Cubs on July 29, 1965 (first game) and Cincinnati on April 19, 1998
- Biggest shutout loss: 16–0 to Atlanta on July 2, 1999
- Highest winning percentage: .667 in 1986 (108–54)
- Lowest winning percentage: .250 in 1962 (40–120)

Team Records—Batting

- Highest team batting average: .279 in 1999
- Lowest team batting average: .219 in 1963
- Highest team slugging average: .434 in 1987 and 1999
- Highest team on-base percentage: .363 in 1999
- Total hits: 1,553 in 1999
- Extra-base hits: 513 in 1987
- Hits in a game: 28 vs. Atlanta on July 4, 1985 (19 innings); 23 twice in 9-inning games
- Longest individual hitting streak: 24, Hubie Brooks, 1984 and Mike Piazza, 1999
- Most .300 hitters in a single season: 5 in 1999
- Home runs: 198 in 2000
- Home runs in a month: 13, Dave Kingman, July 1975 and Gary Carter, September 1985
- Home runs in a game: 7 vs. Philadelphia on April 19, 2005
- Home runs by a rookie: 26, Darryl Strawberry, 1983
- Home runs by a right-hander: 40, Mike Piazza, 1999
- Home runs by a left-hander: 39, Darryl Strawberry, twice: 1987 and 1988
- Home runs by a switch-hitter: 41, Todd Hundley, 1996
- Grand slams: 8 in 1999 and 2000
- Grand slams (individual; single season): 3, Danny Tartabull, 1976; Robin Ventura, 1999; Mike Piazza, 2000
- Grand slams (individual; career): 6, Mike Piazza
- Triples: 47 in 1978 and 1996
- Doubles: 297 in 1999
- Singles: 1,087 in 1980
- Walks: 717 in 1999
- Runs scored: 853 in 1999
- Runs scored in a game: 23 vs. Chicago Cubs on August 16, 1987
- Runs scored in an inning: 10 vs. Cincinnati on June 12, 1979 (sixth inning) and vs. Atlanta on June 30, 2000 (eighth inning)
- Most batters hit by a pitch: 65 in 2001
- Times shut out: 30 in 1963
- Grounded into double plays: 149 in 1999
- Fewest grounded into double plays: 87 in 1989
- Runners left on base: 1,267 in 1999

Team Records—Baserunning

- Stolen bases: 159 in 1987
- Caught stealing: 99 in 1980

Team Records—Pitching

- Lowest earned run average: 2.72 in 1968
- Complete games: 53 in 1976
- Saves: 51 in 1987

- Strikeouts: 1,217 in 1990
- Shutouts: 28 in 1969
- Walks: 617 in 1999
- Hit batsmen: 68 in 1998
- Wild pitches: 76 in 1966
- Consecutive wins (individual): 14, Dwight Gooden in 1985
- Consecutive losses (individual): 18, Roger Craig in 1963 (27 by Anthony Young over two seasons, 1992–1993)
- Strikeouts in a game (individual): 19, Tom Seaver, April 22, 1970; David Cone, October 6, 1991
- Runs allowed in a game: 26 by Philadelphia, June 11, 1985

TEAM RECORDS—FIELDING

- Best fielding average: .989 in 1999
- Most errors committed: 210 in 1962 and 1963
- Fewest errors committed: 68 in 1999
- Most double plays turned: 171 in 1966 and 1983
- Fewest double plays turned: 107 in 1990

TEAM RECORDS—MISCELLANEOUS

- Number of times league champions: 4
- Number of times finishing last in league: 9
- Largest attendance, single game: 56,738 vs. Los Angeles Dodgers, June 23, 1968
- Largest attendance, doubleheader: 57,175 vs. Los Angeles Dodgers, June 13, 1965
- Players used in a season: 54 in 1967
- Seasons played: 18, Ed Kranepool

PRIMARY PITCHING STAFFS

Year	Starter	Starter	Starter	Starter	Starter	Closer	Bullpen	Bullpen	Bullpen
2005	Glavine	Martinez	Benson	Zambrano	Ishii	Looper	Hernandez	Heilman	Bell
2004	Trachsel	Glavine	Leiter	Seo	Ginter	Looper	Stanton	Bottalico	Franco
2003	Trachsel	Glavine	Leiter	Seo	Heilman	Benitez	Stanton	Weathers	Franco
2002	Trachsel	Astacio	Leiter	Estes	D'Amico	Benitez	Strickland	Weathers	Guthrie
2001	Trachsel	Appier	Leiter	Rusch	Reed	Benitez	Franco	White	Wendell
2000	Hampton	Jones	Leiter	Rusch	Reed	Benitez	Franco	Cook	Wendell
1999	Hershiser	Yoshii	Leiter	Dotel	Reed	Benitez	Franco	Cook	Wendell
1998	Jones	Yoshii	Leiter	Nomo	Reed	Franco	Rojas	Cook	Wendell
1997	Jones	Mlicki	Clark	Reynoso	Reed	Franco	McMichael	Lidle	Kashiwada
1996	Jones	Harnisch	Clark	Isringhausen	Wilson	Franco	Henry	Dipoto	Mlicki
1995	Jones	Harnisch	Mlicki	Pulsipher	Saberhagen	Franco	Henry	Dipoto	Minor
1994	Jones	Smith	Remlinger	Jacome	Saberhagen	Franco	Mason	Manzanillo	Linton
1993	Tanana	Gooden	Hillman	Fernandez	Saberhagen	Franco	Innis	Maddux	Schourek
1992	Cone	Gooden	Schourek	Fernandez	Saberhagen	Franco	Innis	Young	Whitehurst
1991	Cone	Gooden	Viola	Whitehurst	Darling	Franco	Innis	Peña	Simons
1990	Cone	Gooden	Viola	Fernandez	Darling	Franco	Ojeda	Peña	Whitehurst
1989	Cone	Gooden	Ojeda	Fernandez	Darling	Myers	Aase	Aguilera	Innis
1988	Cone	Gooden	Ojeda	Fernandez	Darling	Myers	McDowell	Leach	Walter
1987	Mitchell	Gooden	Aguilera	Fernandez	Darling	McDowell	Orosco	Sisk	Myers
1986	Ojeda	Gooden	Aguilera	Fernandez	Darling	McDowell	Orosco	Sisk	Niemann
1985	Lynch	Gooden	Aguilera	Fernandez	Darling	McDowell	Orosco	Sisk	Gorman
1984	Terrell	Gooden	Berenyi	Fernandez	Darling	Orosco	Gaff	Sisk	Lynch
1983	Terrell	Torrez	Seaver	Lynch	Swan	Orosco	Diaz	Sisk	Holman
1982	Puleo	Falcone	Scott	Jones	Swan	Allen	Orosco	Lynch	Zachry
1981	Zachry	Harris	Scott	Jones	Lynch	Allen	Falcone	Searage	Miller
1980	Zachry	Burris	Bomback	Falcone	Swan	Allen	Reardon	Hausman	Glynn
1979	Kobel	Ellis	Hausman	Falcone	Swan	Lockwood	Murray	Allen	Glynn
1978	Espinosa	Koosman	Bruhert	Zachry	Swan	Lockwood	Murray	Kobel	Bernard
1977	Espinosa	Koosman	Matlack	Zachry	Swan	Lockwood	Apodaca	Myrick	Baldwin
1976	Seaver	Koosman	Matlack	Lolich	Swan	Lockwood	Apodaca	Myrick	Sanders

PRIMARY PITCHING STAFFS (CONT.)

Year	Starter	Starter	Starter	Starter	Starter	Closer	Bullpen	Bullpen	Bullpen
1975	Seaver	Koosman	Matlack	Tate	Webb	Apodaca	Baldwin	Hall	Sanders
1974	Seaver	Koosman	Matlack	Parker	Stone	Miller	McGraw	Apodaca	Sadecki
1973	Seaver	Koosman	Matlack	McAndrew	Stone	McGraw	Parker	Sadecki	Hennigan
1972	Seaver	Koosman	Matlack	McAndrew	Gentry	McGraw	Frisella	Sadecki	Taylor
1971	Seaver	Koosman	Ryan	Sadecki	Gentry	Frisella	McGraw	Taylor	Williams
1970	Seaver	Koosman	Ryan	McAndrew	Gentry	Taylor	McGraw	Frisella	Sadecki
1969	Seaver	Koosman	Cardwell	McAndrew	Gentry	Taylor	McGraw	Koonce	Ryan
1968	Seaver	Koosman	Cardwell	Selma	Ryan	Taylor	Short	Koonce	Jackson
1967	Seaver	Fisher	Cardwell	Shaw	Hendley	Taylor	Shaw	Selma	Reniff
1966	Ribant	Fisher	Gardner	Shaw	Friend	Hamilton	Hepler	Sutherland	Selma
1965	Jackson	Fisher	Spahn	Cisco	Kroll	Bearnarth	McGraw	Richardson	Parsons
1964	Jackson	Fisher	Stallard	Cisco	Lary	Bearnarth	Wakefield	Hunter	Locke
1963	Jackson	Craig	Stallard	Willey	Hook	Bearnarth	Cisco	Mackenzie	Rowe
1962	Jackson	Craig	Miller	Anderson	Hook	Moorhead	Daviault	Mackenzie	Hunter

PRIMARY STARTING LINEUPS

Year	C	1B	2B	3B	SS	LF	CF	RF
2005	Piazza	Mientkiewicz	Cairo	Wright	Reyes	Floyd	Beltran	Diaz
2004	Phillips	Piazza	Garcia	Wright	Matsui	Floyd	Cameron	Hidalgo
2003	Wilson	Phillips	Alomar	Wigginton	Reyes	Floyd	Duncan	Cedeño
2002	Piazza	Vaughn	Alomar	Alfonzo	Ordoñez	Cedeño	Perez	Burnitz
2001	Piazza	Zeile	Alfonzo	Ventura	Ordoñez	Agbayani	Payton	Perez
2000	Piazza	Zeile	Alfonzo	Ventura	Bordick	Agbayani	Payton	Bell
1999	Piazza	Olerud	Alfonzo	Ventura	Ordoñez	Henderson	McRae	Cedeño
1998	Piazza	Olerud	Baerga	Alfonzo	Ordoñez	Gilkey	McRae	Huskey
1997	Hundley	Olerud	Baerga	Alfonzo	Ordoñez	Gilkey	Everett	Ochoa
1996	Hundley	Huskey	Vizcaino	Kent	Ordoñez	Gilkey	Johnson	Ochoa
1995	Hundley	Brogna	Kent	Alfonzo	Vizcaino	Orsulak	Butler	Everett
1994	Hundley	Segui	Kent	Bonilla	Vizcaino	McReynolds	Thompson	Orsulak
1993	Hundley	Murray	Kent	Johnson	Bogar	Coleman	Thompson	Bonilla
1992	Hundley	Murray	Randolph	Magadan	Schofield	Boston	Johnson	Bonilla
1991	Cerone	Magadan	Jefferies	Johnson	Elster	McReynolds	Boston	Brooks
1990	Sasser	Magadan	Jefferies	Johnson	Elster	McReynolds	Boston	Strawberry
1989	Lyons	Magadan	Jefferies	Johnson	Elster	McReynolds	Samuel	Strawberry
1988	Carter	Hernandez	Backman	Johnson	Elster	McReynolds	Dykstra	Strawberry
1987	Carter	Hernandez	Teufel	Johnson	Santana	McReynolds	Dykstra	Strawberry
1986	Carter	Hernandez	Backman	Knight	Santana	Wilson	Dykstra	Strawberry
1985	Carter	Hernandez	Backman	Johnson	Santana	Foster	Wilson	Strawberry
1984	Fitzgerald	Hernandez	Backman	Brooks	Oquendo	Foster	Wilson	Strawberry
1983	Hodges	Hernandez	Giles	Brooks	Oquendo	Foster	Wilson	Strawberry
1982	Stearns	Kingman	Backman	Brooks	Gardenhire	Foster	Wilson	Valentine
1981	Stearns	Kingman	Flynn	Brooks	Taveras	Mazzilli	Wilson	Valentine
1980	Trevino	Mazzilli	Flynn	Maddox	Taveras	Henderson	Morales	Youngblood
1979	Stearns	Montanez	Flynn	Hebner	Taveras	Henderson	Mazzilli	Youngblood
1978	Stearns	Montanez	Flynn	Randle	Foli	Henderson	Mazzilli	Maddox
1977	Stearns	Milner	Millan	Randle	Harrelson	Henderson	Mazzilli	Vail
1976	Grote	Kranepool	Millan	Staiger	Harrelson	Milner	Unser	Kingman
1975	Grote	Kranepool	Millan	Garrett	Phillips	Kingman	Unser	Staub
1974	Grote	Milner	Millan	Garrett	Harrelson	Jones	Hahn	Staub
1973	Grote	Milner	Millan	Garrett	Harrelson	Jones	Hahn	Staub

Primary Starting Lineups (cont.)

Year	C	1B	2B	3B	SS	LF	CF	RF
1972	Dyer	Kranepool	Boswell	Fregosi	Harrelson	Milner	Agee	Staub
1971	Grote	Kranepool	Boswell	Aspromonte	Harrelson	Jones	Agee	Singleton
1970	Grote	Clendenon	Boswell	Foy	Harrelson	Jones	Agee	Swoboda
1969	Grote	Kranepool	Boswell	Garrett	Harrelson	Jones	Agee	Swoboda
1968	Grote	Kranepool	Linz	Charles	Harrelson	Jones	Agee	Swoboda
1967	Grote	Kranepool	Buchek	Charles	Harrelson	Davis	Jones	Swoboda
1966	Grote	Kranepool	Hunt	Boyer	Bressoud	Swoboda	Jones	Luplow
1965	Cannizzaro	Kranepool	Hiller	Smith	McMillan	Swoboda	Cowan	Lewis
1964	Gonder	Kranepool	Hunt	Smith	McMillan	Altman	Hickman	Christopher
1963	Coleman	Harkness	Hunt	Neal	Moran	Thomas	Hickman	Snider
1962	Cannizzaro	Throneberry	Neal	Mantilla	Chacon	Thomas	Hickman	Christopher

Top 10 Batting Leaders, Single Season & Career with Team

Games Played: Career with Team

Player	G	PA
1. Ed Kranepool	1,853	5,997
2. Bud Harrelson	1,322	5,083
3. Jerry Grote	1,235	4,335
4. Cleon Jones	1,201	4,683
5. Howard Johnson	1,154	4,591
6. Mookie Wilson	1,116	4,307
7. Darryl Strawberry	1,109	4,549
8. Edgardo Alfonzo	1,086	4,449
9. Lee Mazzilli	979	3,496
10. Mike Piazza	972	3,941

At-Bats: Season

Player	AB	Year
1. Jose Reyes	696	2005
2. Lance Johnson	682	1996
3. Felix Millan	676	1975
4. Mookie Wilson	639	1982
5. Felix Millan	638	1973
Mookie Wilson	638	1983
7. Tommie Agee	636	1970
8. Frank Taveras	635	1979
9. Edgardo Alfonzo	628	1999
10. Eddie Murray	610	1993

At-Bats: Career with Team

Player	AB	PA
1. Ed Kranepool	5,436	5,997
2. Bud Harrelson	4,390	5,083
3. Cleon Jones	4,223	4,683
4. Mookie Wilson	4,027	4,307
5. Howard Johnson	3,968	4,591
6. Darryl Strawberry	3,903	4,549
7. Edgardo Alfonzo	3,897	4,449
8. Jerry Grote	3,881	4,335
9. Mike Piazza	3,478	3,941
10. Keith Hernandez	3,164	3,684

Batting Average: Season

Player	BA	Year
1. John Olerud	.354	1998
2. Mike Piazza	.348	1998
3. Cleon Jones	.340	1969
4. Lance Johnson	.333	1996
5. Dave Magadan	.328	1990
6. Mike Piazza	.324	2000
Edgardo Alfonzo	.324	2000
8. Ed Kranepool	.323	1975
9. Wally Backman	.320	1986
10. Cleon Jones	.319	1971

Batting Average: Career with Team

Player	BA	PA
1. John Olerud	.315	2,018
2. Keith Hernandez	.297	3,684
3. Mike Piazza	.296	3,941
4. Dave Magadan	.292	2,483
Edgardo Alfonzo	.292	4,449
6. Steve Henderson	.287	2,029
7. Wally Backman	.283	2,704
8. Cleon Jones	.281	4,683
9. Felix Millan	.278	2,954
10. Mookie Wilson	.276	4,307

Total Hits: Season

Player	H	Year
1. Lance Johnson	227	1996
2. John Olerud	197	1998
3. Edgardo Alfonzo	191	1999
Felix Millan	191	1975
5. Jose Reyes	190	2005
6. Felix Millan	185	1973
7. Keith Hernandez	183	1985
8. Tommie Agee	182	1970
9. Bernard Gilkey	181	1996
Lee Mazzilli	181	1979

Total Hits: Career with Team

Player	H	PA
1. Ed Kranepool	1,418	5,997
2. Cleon Jones	1,188	4,683
3. Edgardo Alfonzo	1,136	4,449
4. Mookie Wilson	1,112	4,307
5. Bud Harrelson	1,029	5,083
6. Mike Piazza	1,028	3,941
7. Darryl Strawberry	1,025	4,549
8. Howard Johnson	997	4,591
9. Jerry Grote	994	4,335
10. Keith Hernandez	939	3,684

Home Runs: Season

Player	HR	Year
1. Todd Hundley	41	1996
2. Mike Piazza	40	1999
3. Darryl Strawberry	39	1987
Darryl Strawberry	39	1988
5. Howard Johnson	38	1991
Mike Piazza	38	2000
7. Dave Kingman	37	1976
Dave Kingman	37	1982
Darryl Strawberry	37	1990
10. Howard Johnson	36	1987
Howard Johnson	36	1989
Dave Kingman	36	1975
Mike Piazza	36	2001

Home Runs: Career with Team

Player	HR	PA
1. Darryl Strawberry	252	4,549
2. Mike Piazza	220	3,941
3. Howard Johnson	192	4,591
4. Dave Kingman	154	2,573
5. Todd Hundley	124	2,904
6. Kevin McReynolds	122	3,218
7. Edgardo Alfonzo	120	4,449
8. Ed Kranepool	118	5,997
9. George Foster	99	2,610
10. Bobby Bonilla	95	2,040

Triples: Season

Player	3B	Year
1. Lance Johnson	21	1996
2. Jose Reyes	17	2005
3. Mookie Wilson	10	1984
4. Steve Henderson	9	1978
Charlie Neal	9	1962
Frank Taveras	9	1979
Mookie Wilson	9	1982
8. 12 tied with . . .	8	—

Triples: Career with Team

Player	3B	PA
1. Mookie Wilson	62	4,307
2. Bud Harrelson	45	5,083
3. Cleon Jones	33	4,683
4. Steve Henderson	31	2,029
5. Darryl Strawberry	30	4,549
6. Lance Johnson	27	1,023
7. Doug Flynn	26	2,269
8. Ed Kranepool	25	5,997
9. Jose Reyes	23	1,254
10. Lee Mazzilli	22	3,496

Doubles: Season

Player	2B	Year
1. Bernard Gilkey	44	1996
2. David Wright	42	2005
3. Edgardo Alfonzo	41	1999
Howard Johnson	41	1989
5. Edgardo Alfonzo	40	2000
Gregg Jefferies	40	1990
7. John Olerud	39	1999
8. Robin Ventura	38	1999
9. Lenny Dykstra	37	1987
Howard Johnson	37	1990
Felix Millan	37	1975
Eddie Murray	37	1992
Joel Youngblood	37	1979

Doubles: Career with Team

Player	2B	PA
1. Ed Kranepool	225	5,997
2. Howard Johnson	214	4,591
3. Edgardo Alfonzo	212	4,449
4. Mike Piazza	193	3,941
5. Darryl Strawberry	187	4,549
6. Cleon Jones	182	4,683
7. Mookie Wilson	170	4,307
8. Keith Hernandez	159	3,684
9. Kevin McReynolds	153	3,218
10. John Stearns	152	3,080

Extra-Base Hits: Season

Player	XBH	Year
1. Howard Johnson	80	1989
2. Bernard Gilkey	77	1996
3. Howard Johnson	76	1991
Darryl Strawberry	76	1987
5. Todd Hundley	74	1996
6. Robin Ventura	70	1999
David Wright	70	2005
8. Edgardo Alfonzo	69	1999
Darryl Strawberry	69	1988
10. Edgardo Alfonzo	67	2000

Extra-Base Hits: Career with Team

Player	XBH	PA
1. Darryl Strawberry	469	4,549
2. Howard Johnson	424	4,591
3. Mike Piazza	415	3,941
4. Ed Kranepool	368	5,997
5. Edgardo Alfonzo	346	4,449
6. Cleon Jones	308	4,683
7. Mookie Wilson	292	4,307
8. Kevin McReynolds	289	3,218
9. Keith Hernandez	249	3,684
Todd Hundley	249	2,904

Total Bases: Season

Player	TB	Year
1. Lance Johnson	327	1996
2. Bernard Gilkey	321	1996
3. Howard Johnson	319	1989
4. Edgardo Alfonzo	315	1999
5. Robin Ventura	311	1999
6. Darryl Strawberry	310	1987
7. John Olerud	307	1998
Mike Piazza	307	1999
9. Howard Johnson	302	1991
10. David Wright	301	2005

Total Bases: Career with Team

Player	TB	PA
1. Ed Kranepool	2,047	5,997
2. Darryl Strawberry	2,028	4,549
3. Mike Piazza	1,885	3,941
4. Howard Johnson	1,823	4,591
5. Edgardo Alfonzo	1,736	4,449
6. Cleon Jones	1,715	4,683
7. Mookie Wilson	1,586	4,307
8. Keith Hernandez	1,358	3,684

Player	R	PA
9. Kevin McReynolds	1,338	3,218
10. Jerry Grote	1,278	4,335

Runs Batted In: Season

Player	RBI	Year
1. Mike Piazza	124	1999
2. Robin Ventura	120	1999
3. Bernard Gilkey	117	1996
Howard Johnson	117	1991
5. Mike Piazza	113	2000
6. Todd Hundley	112	1996
7. Edgardo Alfonzo	108	1999
Darryl Strawberry	108	1990
9. Gary Carter	105	1986
Rusty Staub	105	1975

Runs Batted In: Career with Team

Player	RBI	PA
1. Darryl Strawberry	733	4,549
2. Mike Piazza	655	3,941
3. Howard Johnson	629	4,591
4. Ed Kranepool	614	5,997
5. Edgardo Alfonzo	538	4,449
6. Cleon Jones	521	4,683
7. Keith Hernandez	468	3,684
8. Kevin McReynolds	456	3,218
9. Rusty Staub	399	2,965
10. Todd Hundley	397	2,904

Runs Scored: Season

Player	R	Year
1. Edgardo Alfonzo	123	1999
2. Lance Johnson	117	1996
3. Edgardo Alfonzo	109	2000
4. Bernard Gilkey	108	1996
Howard Johnson	108	1991
Darryl Strawberry	108	1987
7. Tommie Agee	107	1970
John Olerud	107	1999
9. Howard Johnson	104	1989
10. Darryl Strawberry	101	1988

Runs Scored: Career with Team

Player	R	PA
1. Darryl Strawberry	662	4,549
2. Howard Johnson	627	4,591
3. Edgardo Alfonzo	614	4,449
4. Mookie Wilson	592	4,307
5. Cleon Jones	563	4,683
6. Ed Kranepool	536	5,997
7. Mike Piazza	532	3,941
8. Bud Harrelson	490	5,083
9. Keith Hernandez	455	3,684
10. Kevin McReynolds	405	3,218

Walks: Season

Player	BB	Year
1. John Olerud	125	1999
2. Keith Hernandez	97	1984
Darryl Strawberry	97	1987
4. John Olerud	96	1998
5. Edgardo Alfonzo	95	2000
Bud Harrelson	95	1970
7. Keith Hernandez	94	1986
8. Lee Mazzilli	93	1979
9. Wayne Garrett	89	1974
10. Robin Ventura	88	2001

Walks: Career with Team

Player	BB	PA
1. Darryl Strawberry	580	4,549
2. Bud Harrelson	573	5,083
3. Howard Johnson	556	4,591
4. Wayne Garrett	482	3,361
5. Keith Hernandez	471	3,684
6. Edgardo Alfonzo	458	4,449
7. Ed Kranepool	454	5,997
8. Lee Mazzilli	438	3,496
9. Mike Piazza	424	3,941
10. Jerry Grote	363	4,335

Strikeouts: Season

Player	SO	Year
1. Tommie Agee	156	1970
Dave Kingman	156	1982
3. Dave Kingman	153	1975
4. Todd Hundley	146	1996
5. Mo Vaughn	145	2002
6. Mike Cameron	143	2004
7. Darryl Strawberry	141	1986
8. Tommie Agee	137	1969
9. Jeromy Burnitz	135	2002
Dave Kingman	135	1976

Strikeouts: Career with Team

Player	SO	PA
1. Darryl Strawberry	960	4,549
2. Howard Johnson	827	4,591
3. Cleon Jones	697	4,683
4. Mookie Wilson	692	4,307
5. Dave Kingman	672	2,573
6. Todd Hundley	624	2,904
7. Bud Harrelson	595	5,083
8. Ed Kranepool	581	5,997
9. Tommie Agee	572	2,687
10. Ron Swoboda	549	2,485

Slugging Percentage: Season

Player	SLG	Year
1. Mike Piazza	.614	2000
2. Mike Piazza	.607	1998
3. Darryl Strawberry	.583	1987
4. Mike Piazza	.575	1999
5. Mike Piazza	.573	2001
6. Bernard Gilkey	.562	1996
7. Howard Johnson	.559	1989
8. Darryl Strawberry	.557	1985
9. John Olerud	.551	1998
10. Todd Hundley	.550	1996

Slugging Percentage: Career with Team

Player	SLG	PA
1. Mike Piazza	.542	3,941
2. Darryl Strawberry	.520	4,549
3. John Olerud	.501	2,018
4. Bobby Bonilla	.495	2,040
5. Kevin McReynolds	.460	3,218
6. Howard Johnson	.459	4,591
7. Dave Kingman	.453	2,573
8. Edgardo Alfonzo	.445	4,449
9. Todd Hundley	.438	2,904
10. Keith Hernandez	.429	3,684

On-Base Percentage: Season

Player	OBP	Year
1. John Olerud	.447	1998
2. John Olerud	.427	1999
3. Edgardo Alfonzo	.425	2000
4. Richie Ashburn	.424	1962
5. Rickey Henderson	.423	1999
6. Cleon Jones	.422	1969
7. Dave Magadan	.417	1990
Mike Piazza	.417	1998
9. Keith Hernandez	.413	1986
10. Keith Hernandez	.409	1984

On-Base Percentage: Career with Team

Player	OBP	PA
1. John Olerud	.425	2,018
2. Dave Magadan	.391	2,483
3. Keith Hernandez	.387	3,684
4. Mike Piazza	.373	3,941
5. Edgardo Alfonzo	.367	4,449
6. Steve Henderson	.360	2,029
7. Darryl Strawberry	.359	4,549
8. Rusty Staub	.358	2,965
9. Lee Mazzilli	.357	3,496
10. Bobby Bonilla	.356	2,040

OPS (On-Base Percentage + Slugging Percentage): Season

Player	OPS	Year
1. Mike Piazza	1.024	1998
2. Mike Piazza	1.012	2000
3. John Olerud	.998	1998
4. Darryl Strawberry	.981	1987
5. Edgardo Alfonzo	.967	2000
6. Mike Piazza	.957	2001
7. Bernard Gilkey	.955	1996
8. Darryl Strawberry	.947	1985
9. Todd Hundley	.943	1997
10. Mike Piazza	.936	1999

OPS (On-Base Percentage + Slugging Percentage): Career with Team

Player	OPS	PA
1. John Olerud	.926	2,018
2. Mike Piazza	.915	3,941
3. Darryl Strawberry	.878	4,549
4. Bobby Bonilla	.851	2,040
5. Keith Hernandez	.816	3,684
6. Edgardo Alfonzo	.812	4,449
7. Howard Johnson	.801	4,591
8. Kevin McReynolds	.790	3,218
9. Steve Henderson	.783	2,029
10. Rusty Staub	.778	2,965

Stolen Bases: Season

Player	SB	Year
1. Roger Cedeño	66	1999
2. Jose Reyes	60	2005
3. Mookie Wilson	58	1982
4. Mookie Wilson	54	1983
5. Lance Johnson	50	1996
6. Mookie Wilson	46	1984
7. Frank Taveras	42	1979
8. Howard Johnson	41	1989
Lee Mazzilli	41	1980
10. Vince Coleman	38	1993

Stolen Bases: Career with Team

Player	SB	PA
1. Mookie Wilson	281	4,307
2. Howard Johnson	202	4,591
3. Darryl Strawberry	191	4,549
4. Lee Mazzilli	152	3,496
5. Lenny Dykstra	116	1,908
6. Bud Harrelson	115	5,083
7. Wally Backman	106	2,704
8. Roger Cedeño	105	1,614
9. Vince Coleman	99	978
10. Tommie Agee	92	2,687
Jose Reyes	92	1,254

Sacrifice Hits: Season

Player	Sac	Year
1. Felix Millan	24	1974
2. Bobby Jones	18	1995
Felix Millan	18	1973
4. Felix Millan	17	1975
5. Roy McMillan	16	1965
6. Jerry Koosman	15	1973
Rey Ordoñez	15	1998
8. Wally Backman	14	1985
Wally Backman	14	1986
Dwight Gooden	14	1990
Rey Ordoñez	14	1997
Rick Reed	14	2000

Sacrifice Hits: Career with Team

Player	Sac	PA
1. Dwight Gooden	85	837
Jerry Koosman	85	926
3. Bud Harrelson	77	5,083
Tom Seaver	77	1,139
5. Felix Millan	68	2,954
6. Ron Darling	64	600
Sid Fernandez	64	577
Rey Ordoñez	64	3,216
9. Bobby Jones	61	426
10. Wally Backman	60	2,704

Hit by Pitch: Season

Player	HBP	Year
1. Ron Hunt	13	1963
John Olerud	13	1997
3. Felix Millan	12	1975
Fernando Viña	12	1994
5. Cliff Floyd	11	2004
Cliff Floyd	11	2005
Ron Hunt	11	1964
Ron Hunt	11	1966
John Olerud	11	1999
10. Eight tied with. . .	10	—

Hit by Pitch: Career with Team

Player	HBP	PA
1. Ron Hunt	41	1,887
2. Cleon Jones	39	4,683
3. Felix Millan	36	2,954
4. Edgardo Alfonzo	29	4,449
5. Jeff Kent	28	1,992
John Olerud	28	2,018
7. Darryl Strawberry	26	4,549
8. John Stearns	25	3,080
Cliff Floyd	25	1,508
10. Todd Hundley	22	2,904

Top 10 Pitching Leaders, Single Season & Career with Team

Games Pitched: Season

Player	GP	Year
1. Mike Stanton	83	2004
2. Turk Wendell	80	1999
3. Armando Benitez	77	1999
Dave Weathers	77	2003
Turk Wendell	77	2000
6. Armando Benitez	76	2000
Jeff Innis	76	1992
8. Roger McDowell	75	1986
9. Armando Benitez	73	2001
Dennis Cook	73	1998
Greg McMichael	73	1997

Games Pitched: Career with Team

Player	GP	IP
1. John Franco	695	702.7
2. Tom Seaver	401	3,045.3
3. Jerry Koosman	376	2,544.7
4. Jesse Orosco	372	595.7
5. Tug McGraw	361	792.7
6. Armando Benitez	333	347.0
7. Dwight Gooden	305	2,169.7
8. Jeff Innis	288	360.0
9. Turk Wendell	285	312.7
10. Roger McDowell	280	468.3

Innings Pitched: Season

Player	IP	Year
1. Tom Seaver	290.7	1970
2. Tom Seaver	290.0	1973
3. Tom Seaver	286.3	1971
4. Tom Seaver	280.3	1975
5. Tom Seaver	277.7	1968
6. Dwight Gooden	276.7	1985
7. Tom Seaver	273.3	1969
8. Tom Seaver	271.0	1976
9. Jon Matlack	265.3	1974
10. Jerry Koosman	265.0	1974

Innings Pitched: Career with Team

Player	IP
1. Tom Seaver	3,045.3
2. Jerry Koosman	2,544.7
3. Dwight Gooden	2,169.7
4. Ron Darling	1,620.0
5. Sid Fernandez	1,584.7
6. Jon Matlack	1,448.0
7. Al Leiter	1,360.0
8. Craig Swan	1,230.7
9. Bobby Jones	1,215.7
10. David Cone	1,209.3

Batters Faced: Season

Player	BF	Year
1. Tom Seaver	1,173	1970
2. Tom Seaver	1,147	1973
3. Jerry Koosman	1,118	1974
4. Tom Seaver	1,115	1975
5. Tom Seaver	1,103	1971
6. Tom Seaver	1,089	1969
7. Tom Seaver	1,088	1968
8. Tom Seaver	1,079	1976
9. Jon Matlack	1,076	1974
10. Jerry Koosman	1,071	1973

Batters Faced: Career with Team

Player	BF	IP
1. Tom Seaver	12,191	3,045.3
2. Jerry Koosman	10,517	2,544.7
3. Dwight Gooden	8,898	2,169.7
4. Ron Darling	6,807	1,620.0
5. Sid Fernandez	6,456	1,584.7
6. Jon Matlack	5,953	1,448.0
7. Al Leiter	5,774	1,360.0
8. Bobby Jones	5,154	1,215.7
9. Craig Swan	5,140	1,230.7
10. David Cone	5,008	1,209.3

Games Started: Season

Player	GS	Year
1. Jack Fisher	36	1965
Tom Seaver	36	1970
Tom Seaver	36	1973
Tom Seaver	36	1975
5. 13 tied with ...	35	—

Games Started: Career with Team

Player	GS	IP
1. Tom Seaver	395	3,045.3
2. Jerry Koosman	346	2,544.7
3. Dwight Gooden	303	2,169.7
4. Sid Fernandez	250	1,584.7
5. Ron Darling	241	1,620.0
6. Al Leiter	213	1,360.0
7. Jon Matlack	199	1,448.0
8. Bobby Jones	190	1,215.7
9. Craig Swan	184	1,230.7
10. David Cone	169	1,209.3

Complete Games: Season

Player	CG	Year
1. Tom Seaver	21	1971
2. Tom Seaver	19	1970
3. Tom Seaver	18	1967
Tom Seaver	18	1969
Tom Seaver	18	1973
6. Jerry Koosman	17	1968
Jerry Koosman	17	1976
8. Dwight Gooden	16	1985
Jerry Koosman	16	1969
Jon Matlack	16	1976

Complete Games: Career with Team

Player	CG	IP
1. Tom Seaver	171	3,045.3
2. Jerry Koosman	108	2,544.7
3. Dwight Gooden	67	2,169.7
4. Jon Matlack	65	1,448.0
5. Al Jackson	41	980.7
6. Jack Fisher	35	931.7
7. David Cone	34	1,209.3
8. Roger Craig	27	469.3
9. Ron Darling	25	1,620.0
Craig Swan	25	1,230.7

Games Won: Season

Player	W	Year
1. Tom Seaver	25	1969
2. Dwight Gooden	24	1985
3. Tom Seaver	22	1975
4. Jerry Koosman	21	1976
Tom Seaver	21	1972

6. David Cone	20	1988
Tom Seaver	20	1971
Frank Viola	20	1990
9. Dwight Gooden	19	1990
Jerry Koosman	19	1968
Tom Seaver	19	1973

Games Won: Career with Team

Player	W	IP
1. Tom Seaver	198	3,045.3
2. Dwight Gooden	157	2,169.7
3. Jerry Koosman	140	2,544.7
4. Ron Darling	99	1,620.0
5. Sid Fernandez	98	1,584.7
6. Al Leiter	95	1,360.0
7. Jon Matlack	82	1,448.0
8. David Cone	81	1,209.3
9. Bobby Jones	74	1,215.7
10. Rick Reed	59	888.7
Craig Swan	59	1,230.7

Games Lost: Season

Player	L	Year
1. Roger Craig	24	1962
Jack Fisher	24	1965
3. Roger Craig	22	1963
4. Al Jackson	20	1962
Al Jackson	20	1965
Jerry Koosman	20	1977
Tracy Stallard	20	1964
8. Galen Cisco	19	1964
Jay Hook	19	1962
10. Jack Fisher	18	1967

Games Lost: Career with Team

Player	L	IP
1. Jerry Koosman	137	2,544.7
2. Tom Seaver	124	3,045.3
3. Dwight Gooden	85	2,169.7
4. Jon Matlack	81	1,448.0
5. Al Jackson	80	980.7
6. Sid Fernandez	78	1,584.7
7. Jack Fisher	73	931.7
8. Craig Swan	71	1,230.7
9. Ron Darling	70	1,620.0
10. Al Leiter	67	1,360.0

Winning Percentage: Season

Player	W%	Year
1. David Cone	.870	1988
2. Dwight Gooden	.857	1985
3. Bob Ojeda	.783	1986
4. Tom Seaver	.781	1969
5. Bret Saberhagen	.778	1994
6. Dwight Gooden	.739	1986
Al Leiter	.739	1998
8. Sid Fernandez	.737	1989
9. Dwight Gooden	.731	1990
10. Ron Darling	.727	1985
Sid Fernandez	.727	1986

Winning Percentage: Career with Team

Player	W%	IP
1. Dwight Gooden	.649	2,169.7
2. Rick Reed	.621	888.7
3. Tom Seaver	.615	3,045.3
4. David Cone	.614	1,209.3
5. Al Leiter	.586	1,360.0
Ron Darling	.586	1,620.0
7. Bobby Jones	.569	1,215.7
8. Bob Ojeda	.560	764.0
9. Sid Fernandez	.557	1,584.7
10. Steve Trachsel	.515	754.7

Shutouts: Season

Player	SHO	Year
1. Dwight Gooden	8	1985
2. Jerry Koosman	7	1968
Jon Matlack	7	1974
4. Jerry Koosman	6	1969
Jon Matlack	6	1976
6. David Cone	5	1992
Bob Ojeda	5	1988
Tom Seaver	5	1968
Tom Seaver	5	1969
Tom Seaver	5	1974
Tom Seaver	5	1975
Tom Seaver	5	1976

Shutouts: Career with Team

Player	SHO	IP
1. Tom Seaver	44	3,045.3
2. Jerry Koosman	26	2,544.7
Jon Matlack	26	1,448.0
4. Dwight Gooden	23	2,169.7
5. David Cone	15	1,209.3
6. Ron Darling	10	1,620.0
Al Jackson	10	980.7
8. Sid Fernandez	9	1,584.7
Bob Ojeda	9	764.0
10. Gary Gentry	8	789.3

ERA: Season

Player	ERA	Year
1. Dwight Gooden	1.53	1985
2. Tom Seaver	1.76	1971
3. Tom Seaver	2.08	1973
Jerry Koosman	2.08	1968
5. Tom Seaver	2.20	1968
6. Tom Seaver	2.21	1969
7. David Cone	2.22	1988
8. Jerry Koosman	2.28	1969
9. Jon Matlack	2.32	1972
10. Tom Seaver	2.38	1975

ERA: Career with Team

Player	ERA	IP
1. Tom Seaver	2.57	3,045.3
2. Jesse Orosco	2.73	595.7
3. Jon Matlack	3.03	1,448.0
4. Jerry Koosman	3.09	2,544.7
5. Dwight Gooden	3.10	2,169.7
John Franco	3.10	702.7
7. Bob Ojeda	3.12	764.0
8. David Cone	3.13	1,209.3
9. Sid Fernandez	3.14	1,584.7
10. Bret Saberhagen	3.16	524.3

Earned Runs Allowed: Season

Player	ER	Year
1. Roger Craig	117	1962
2. Jack Fisher	115	1967
Jay Hook	115	1962
4. Al Jackson	113	1962
5. Jack Fisher	111	1965
6. Mike Torrez	108	1983
7. Nino Espinosa	107	1978
Jack Fisher	107	1964
9. Pedro Astacio	102	2002
Frank Viola	102	1991

Earned Runs Allowed: Career with Team

Player	ER	IP
1. Jerry Koosman	875	2,544.7
2. Tom Seaver	870	3,045.3
3. Dwight Gooden	747	2,169.7
4. Ron Darling	630	1,620.0
5. Bobby Jones	558	1,215.7
6. Sid Fernandez	553	1,584.7

Player	K	IP
7. Al Leiter	517	1,360.0
8. Craig Swan	508	1,230.7
9. Jon Matlack	488	1,448.0
10. Al Jackson	464	980.7

Strikeouts: Season

Player	K	Year
1. Tom Seaver	289	1971
2. Tom Seaver	283	1970
3. Dwight Gooden	276	1984
4. Dwight Gooden	268	1985
5. Tom Seaver	251	1973
6. Tom Seaver	249	1972
7. Tom Seaver	243	1975
8. David Cone	241	1991
9. Tom Seaver	235	1976
10. David Cone	233	1990

Strikeouts: Career with Team

Player	K	IP
1. Tom Seaver	2,541	3,045.3
2. Dwight Gooden	1,875	2,169.7
3. Jerry Koosman	1,799	2,544.7
4. Sid Fernandez	1,449	1,584.7
5. David Cone	1,172	1,209.3
6. Ron Darling	1,148	1,620.0
7. Al Leiter	1,106	1,360.0
8. Jon Matlack	1,023	1,448.0
9. Bobby Jones	714	1,215.7
10. Craig Swan	671	1,230.7

Strikeouts Per Nine IP: Season

Player	K/9	Year
1. Dwight Gooden	11.39	1984
2. David Cone	9.91	1990
3. David Cone	9.79	1992
4. Sid Fernandez	9.51	1985
5. David Cone	9.32	1991
6. Sid Fernandez	9.10	1988
7. Tom Seaver	9.08	1971
Sid Fernandez	9.08	1990
9. Sid Fernandez	8.81	1986
10. Tom Seaver	8.76	1970

Strikeouts Per Nine IP: Career with Team

Player	K/9	IP
1. David Cone	8.72	1,209.3
2. Nolan Ryan	8.70	510.0
3. Sid Fernandez	8.23	1,584.7
4. Dwight Gooden	7.78	2,169.7
5. Jesse Orosco	7.65	595.7
6. John Franco	7.58	702.7
7. Tom Seaver	7.51	3,045.3
8. Al Leiter	7.32	1,360.0
9. Dave Mlicki	7.22	501.3
10. Tug McGraw	7.02	792.7

Hits Allowed: Season

Player	HA	Year
1. Roger Craig	261	1962
2. Frank Viola	259	1991
3. Jerry Koosman	258	1974
4. Jack Fisher	256	1964
5. Jack Fisher	252	1965
6. Jack Fisher	251	1967
7. Roger Craig	249	1963
8. Al Jackson	244	1962
9. Dwight Gooden	242	1988
10. Craig Swan	241	1979

Hits Allowed: Career with Team

Player	HA	IP
1. Tom Seaver	2,431	3,045.3
2. Jerry Koosman	2,281	2,544.7
3. Dwight Gooden	1,898	2,169.7
4. Ron Darling	1,473	1,620.0
5. Jon Matlack	1,312	1,448.0
6. Bobby Jones	1,255	1,215.7
7. Al Leiter	1,222	1,360.0
8. Craig Swan	1,191	1,230.7
9. Sid Fernandez	1,167	1,584.7
10. Al Jackson	1,033	980.7

Hits Allowed Per Nine IP: Season

Player	H/9	Year
1. Sid Fernandez	5.71	1985
2. Sid Fernandez	6.11	1988
3. Dwight Gooden	6.44	1985
Sid Fernandez	6.44	1989
5. Sid Fernandez	6.52	1990
6. Pedro Martinez	6.59	2005
7. Tom Seaver	6.60	1971
8. Dwight Gooden	6.65	1984
Tom Seaver	6.65	1969
10. Sid Fernandez	6.79	1992

Hits Allowed Per Nine IP: Career with Team

Player	H/9	IP
1. Nolan Ryan	6.51	510.0
2. Sid Fernandez	6.63	1,584.7
3. Tom Seaver	7.18	3,045.3
4. Jesse Orosco	7.25	595.7
5. David Cone	7.52	1,209.3
6. Gary Gentry	7.61	789.3
7. Tug McGraw	7.78	792.7
8. Dwight Gooden	7.87	2,169.7
9. Jerry Koosman	8.07	2,544.7
10. Al Leiter	8.09	1,360.0

Walks Allowed: Season

Player	BB	Year
1. Nolan Ryan	116	1971
2. Ron Darling	114	1985
3. Mike Torrez	113	1983
4. Ron Darling	104	1984
5. Mike Hampton	99	2000
Jon Matlack	99	1973
7. Jerry Koosman	98	1975
8. Al Leiter	97	2004
Nolan Ryan	97	1970
10. Ron Darling	96	1987

Walks Allowed: Career with Team

Player	BB	IP
1. Tom Seaver	847	3,045.3
2. Jerry Koosman	820	2,544.7
3. Dwight Gooden	651	2,169.7
4. Ron Darling	614	1,620.0
5. Sid Fernandez	596	1,584.7
6. Al Leiter	546	1,360.0
7. David Cone	431	1,209.3
8. Jon Matlack	419	1,448.0
9. Craig Swan	368	1,230.7
10. Bobby Jones	353	1,215.7

Walks Allowed Per Nine IP: Season

Player	BB/9	Year
1. Bret Saberhagen	0.66	1994
2. Rick Reed	1.23	1998
3. Ed Lynch	1.27	1985
4. Rick Reed	1.34	1997
5. Tom Seaver	1.56	1968

Player		
6. Bob Ojeda	1.56	1988
7. Rick Reed	1.66	2000
8. Jim McAndrew	1.86	1970
9. Dennis Ribant	1.91	1966
10. Tom Seaver	1.92	1971

Walks Allowed Per Nine IP: Career with Team

Player	BB/9	IP
1. Bret Saberhagen	1.32	524.3
2. Rick Reed	1.60	888.7
3. Ed Lynch	1.95	730.3
4. Frank Viola	2.24	566.3
5. Jack Fisher	2.34	931.7
6. Jim McAndrew	2.47	729.7
7. Tom Seaver	2.50	3,045.3
8. Bob Ojeda	2.51	764.0
9. Jon Matlack	2.60	1,448.0
10. Bobby Jones	2.61	1,215.7

WHIP (Walks + Hits Per Nine IP): Season

Player	WHIP	Year
1. Tom Seaver	0.946	1971
2. Pedro Martinez	0.949	2005
3. Dwight Gooden	0.965	1985
4. Tom Seaver	0.976	1973
5. Tom Seaver	0.980	1968
Bob Ojeda	1.004	1988
7. Bret Saberhagen	1.026	1994
8. Tom Seaver	1.039	1969
9. Rick Reed	1.042	1997
10. Sid Fernandez	1.053	1988

WHIP (Walks + Hits Per Nine IP): Career with Team

Player	WHIP	IP
1. Tom Seaver	1.076	3,045.3
2. Bret Saberhagen	1.079	524.3
3. Sid Fernandez	1.113	1,584.7
4. Rick Reed	1.155	888.7
5. Dwight Gooden	1.175	2,169.7
6. Bob Ojeda	1.182	764.0
7. Jim McAndrew	1.184	729.7
8. David Cone	1.192	1,209.3
9. Jon Matlack	1.195	1,448.0
10. Jesse Orosco	1.209	595.7

Home Runs Allowed: Season

Player	HRA	Year
1. Roger Craig	35	1962
2. Pedro Astacio	32	2002
3. Jay Hook	31	1962
4. Pete Harnisch	30	1996
Rick Reed	30	1998
6. Roger Craig	28	1963
Rick Reed	28	2000
Steve Trachsel	28	2001
9. Jack Fisher	26	1966
Bobby Jones	26	1996
Frank Tanana	26	1993
Steve Trachsel	26	2003

Home Runs Allowed: Career with Team

Player	HRA	IP
1. Tom Seaver	212	3,045.3
2. Jerry Koosman	187	2,544.7
3. Ron Darling	155	1,620.0
4. Sid Fernandez	138	1,584.7
5. Bobby Jones	137	1,215.7
6. Dwight Gooden	123	2,169.7
7. Al Leiter	118	1,360.0
8. Rick Reed	116	888.7
9. Craig Swan	112	1,230.7
10. Steve Trachsel	101	791.7

Saves: Season

Player	SV	Year
1. Armando Benitez	43	2001
2. Armando Benitez	41	2000
3. John Franco	38	1998
4. John Franco	36	1997
5. Armando Benitez	33	2002
John Franco	33	1990
7. Jesse Orosco	31	1984
8. John Franco	30	1991
John Franco	30	1994
10. John Franco	29	1995
Braden Looper	29	2004

Saves: Career with Team

Player	SV	IP
1. John Franco	276	702.7
2. Armando Benitez	160	347.0
3. Jesse Orosco	107	595.7
4. Tug McGraw	86	792.7
5. Roger McDowell	84	468.3
6. Neil Allen	69	381.7
7. Skip Lockwood	65	379.7
8. Braden Looper	57	142.7
9. Randy Myers	56	240.0
10. Ron Taylor	49	361.0

Wild Pitches: Season

Player	WP	Year
1. Jack Hamilton	18	1966
2. David Cone	17	1991
3. David Cone	14	1989
Jason Isringhausen	14	1996
5. Jon Matlack	13	1976
6. Kevin Appier	12	2001
Ron Darling	12	1989
Jack Fisher	12	1966
Bob Miller	12	1962
Tom Seaver	12	1976
Tracy Stallard	12	1964

Wild Pitches: Career with Team

Player	WP	IP
1. Tom Seaver	81	3,045.3
2. Jerry Koosman	66	2,544.7
3. Ron Darling	63	1,620.0
4. David Cone	62	1,209.3
5. Dwight Gooden	47	2,169.7
6. Tug McGraw	44	792.7
7. Jon Matlack	42	1,448.0
8. John Franco	39	702.7
9. Jim McAndrew	34	729.7
10. Pete Falcone	31	607.7

Hit Batsmen: Season

Player	HB	Year
1. Pedro Astacio	16	2002
2. Kevin Appier	15	2001
Nolan Ryan	15	1971
Victor Zambrano	15	2005
5. Al Jackson	12	1963
6. Orel Hershiser	11	1999
Al Leiter	11	1998
Al Leiter	11	2000
Al Leiter	11	2004
10. Don Cardwell	10	1968
Jack Fisher	10	1964
Paul Wilson	10	1996

HIT BATSMEN: CAREER WITH TEAM

Player	HB	IP
1. Al Leiter	63	1,360.0
2. Tom Seaver	52	3,045.3
3. Jerry Koosman	49	2,544.7
4. Dwight Gooden	41	2,169.7
5. Ron Darling	36	1,620.0
Sid Fernandez	36	1,584.7
7. Bobby Jones	33	1,215.7
8. Al Jackson	32	980.7
9. David Cone	28	1,209.3
10. Jack Fisher	26	931.7
Gary Gentry	26	789.3

GAMES FINISHED: SEASON

Player	GF	Year
1. Armando Benitez	68	2000
2. Armando Benitez	64	2001
3. Braden Looper	60	2004
4. John Franco	54	1998
Braden Looper	54	2005
6. John Franco	53	1997
7. Armando Benitez	52	2002
Roger McDowell	52	1986
Jesse Orosco	52	1984
10. Skip Lockwood	50	1977

GAMES FINISHED: CAREER WITH TEAM

Player	GF	IP
1. John Franco	484	702.7
2. Armando Benitez	266	347.0
3. Jesse Orosco	246	595.7
4. Tug McGraw	228	792.7
5. Roger McDowell	189	468.3
6. Ron Taylor	184	361.0
7. Skip Lockwood	164	379.7
8. Neil Allen	160	381.7
9. Doug Sisk	128	412.3
10. Jeff Innis	126	360.0

Kevin Elster and the Mets toast their victory over the Red Sox in the 1986 World Series.

Significant Mets

AGEE, TOMMIE (OF)
(1968–1972)

Tommie Agee came to the Mets on December 15, 1967, along with Al Weis in a trade with the White Sox for Tommy Davis, Jack Fisher, Billy Wynne, and Buddy Booker. During 1968 spring training, Agee, who had won the AL Rookie of the Year Award just two years before, was hit in the head by a Bob Gibson fastball and couldn't get a hit to save his life. He went 0-for-34 in April, one of the worst streaks in Mets history, finishing the season at .217 with a paltry 17 RBIs. A year later, however, he made a complete 180, helping the Mets accomplish their "miracle" season. He hit 26 homers and won a Gold Glove while leading the team to the World Series title. He is probably best remembered for two circus catches during Game 3, which saved a combined five runs. After slumping badly in batting average and steals in 1972, Agee was traded to the Astros for Rich Chiles and Buddy Harris.

CAREER METS RECORD:

Games	AB	Hits	Runs
661	2,416	632	344

Avg	HR	RBI	SB
.262	82	265	92

CONE, DAVID (SP)
(1987–1992, 2003)

After spending six seasons in Kansas City's minor league organization, David Cone was traded to the Mets for three fairly insignificant players in one of the greatest trades in Mets history. After an injury limited his appearances in his first season in New York, Cone joined the rotation in 1988 and put together five solid seasons. He led the National League in strikeouts in 1990 and 1991 and finished in the top four the other three years. In four of the five seasons, he struck out more than 200 batters. When he went 20–3 in 1988, it was the fewest losses in a season by a 20-game winner in the National League since Preacher Roe went 22–3 in 1951. On October 6, 1991, Cone tied the National League record with 19 strikeouts in a game as he beat the Phillies 7–0 on a three-hitter. A two-time All-Star with the Mets, Cone was going to enter free agency at season's end in 1992, but was traded to Toronto for Jeff Kent and Ryan Thompson on August 27. Although he lost the NL strikeout crown that year by a mere one, his combined strikeout totals between New York and Toronto made him the major league leader for the third straight year. After spending the next 11 years with four teams, Cone returned to the Mets for five uninspired appearances in 2003 before retiring.

CAREER METS RECORD:

W	L	W%	ERA	SV
81	51	.614	3.13	1

K	BB	SHO	IP
1,172	431	15	1,209.3

DARLING, RON (SP)
(1983–1991)

Ron Darling was drafted by the Texas Rangers in the first round of the June 1981 amateur draft and traded to the Mets for Lee Mazzilli the following year while still in the minors. In 1983 he made it to the majors and spent his first nine major league seasons with the Mets. Darling started at least 32 games for the Mets in each of the six years from 1984 to 1989, teaming with the likes of Dwight Gooden, Sid Fernandez, and Bob Ojeda to form the best starting rotation in the National League during a period of strong Mets teams. With one All-Star appearance and one Gold Glove under his belt, Darling still ranks fourth on the all-time Mets' victory list.

CAREER METS RECORD:

W	L	W%	ERA	SV
99	70	.586	3.50	0

K	BB	SHO	IP
1,148	614	10	1,620.0

FERNANDEZ, SID (SP)
(1984–1993)

After having a cup of coffee with the Dodgers in 1983, Fernandez was traded to the Mets along with Ross Jones for Carlos Diaz and Bob Bailor. For the next ten years, he was a mainstay in the Mets' rotation, making the first of two All-Star appearances in 1986 (he was the first native Hawaiian to do so). Fernandez was one of the best in the league in terms of hits allowed per nine innings pitched, leading the National League three times and finishing in the top four three more times. He also finished in the top five in strikeouts six times. After the 1993 season, Fernandez entered the free-agent market and signed with Baltimore.

CAREER METS RECORD:

W	L	W%	ERA	SV
98	78	.557	3.14	1

K	BB	SHO	IP
1,449	596	9	1,584.7

FRANCO, JOHN (RP)
(1990–2001, 2003–2004)

Like several other great New York Mets relievers—Tug McGraw, Jesse Orosco, and Randy Myers—John Franco was a left-hander. He came to the Mets in a big December 1989 trade with Cincinnati for ace closer Myers and Kip Gross and spent his next 14 seasons throwing for the Mets, eventually becoming the team's captain. Along the way he established the major league record for saves by a left-hander with 424 (276 with the Mets). In 1990 and 1994 he led the league in saves, and finished in the top five three other times. His only All-Star Game appearance as a Met came in 1990. Franco left the Mets after the 2004 season and played briefly with the Astros in 2005 before retiring in midseason.

CAREER METS RECORD:

W	L	W%	ERA	SV
48	56	.462	3.10	276

K	BB	SHO	IP
592	276	0	702.7

GOODEN, DWIGHT (SP)
(1984–1994)

The Mets selected 17-year-old Dwight Gooden in the first round of the June 1982 amateur draft as the fifth overall pick. He spent the 1983 season with Lynchburg in the Class A Carolina League, leading the league in wins and ERA and striking out 300 batters in just 191 innings. By the time the 1984 season began, Gooden had become a starter in the New York rotation. A virtual unknown only a few months earlier, Gooden stormed onto the scene with a blazing fastball and sharp breaking curveball. At the age of 19, he won the National League Rookie of the Year Award with a 17–9 record and a 2.60 ERA with 276 strikeouts in 218 innings. Gooden not only became the youngest player to win the award, but also became the youngest player to play in the All-Star Game. Not only did he shatter the rookie record for strikeouts in a season (breaking Herb Score's 29-year-old record), he was the first teenager to lead the major leagues in strikeouts. He also set another major league record with 43 strikeouts over three consecutive games. Only Chicago's Rick Sutcliffe finished ahead of him in the 1984 Cy Young balloting.

Gooden followed his incredible rookie season with an even better year in 1985, winning 24 games while losing only four, and compiled a 1.53 ERA with 268 strikeouts. During one stretch he won 14 consecutive games, becoming the youngest player ever to win a Cy Young Award. Fans dubbed Gooden "Doctor K" and began to hang "K" signs—at both home and away games—whenever he struck out a batter. In 1986 "Doc" Gooden, a four-time All-Star with the Mets, became the first pitcher to strike out at least 200 batters in his first three seasons. He was a good hitter, too, slugging eight homers, 15 doubles, and five triples among the 145 hits of his career, collecting 67 RBIs in the process. He won the Silver Slugger Award as the National League's best-hitting pitcher in 1992.

But trouble started in 1987, when, at the age of 22, Gooden admitted to a drug problem. (This admission was preceded by an off-season incident in his hometown of Tampa in which he and his nephew, future major leaguer Gary Sheffield, suffered beatings at the hands of the local police.) Gooden didn't pitch until June, but still finished with a fine 15–7 record. For the rest of his career, however, Gooden battled injuries and drug problems. He struck out more than 200 batters just one more time in the next 13 seasons, and was never again a 20-game winner.

Gooden had winning records in each of his first eight years and was the third-youngest pitcher in modern times to win 100 games, but floundered thereafter. Over his last six seasons, he averaged fewer than seven wins per year, and had a losing record in four of his last eight. After recording 19 shutouts in his first five seasons, he threw only five more over his next 11 years. Gooden also had a disappointing record in postseason play, going 0–4 in 12 games, including nine starts. Twice he was the losing pitcher in the All-Star Game. After missing most of 1994, Gooden was granted free agency, but sat out the entire 1995 season. He returned to baseball in 1996 when he signed with the Yankees (even throwing a no-hitter that season) and then bounced around with four teams, but in his remaining five years he was but a shadow of his former self.

CAREER METS RECORD:

W	L	W%	ERA	SV
157	85	.649	3.10	1
K	BB	SHO	IP	
1,875	651	23	2,169.7	

GROTE, JERRY (C)
(1966–1977)

Jerry Grote came to the Mets just after the 1965 season in a trade with Houston for Tom Parsons. Never much of a hitter (he only averaged three homers, 26 runs, and 30 RBIs during his Mets career), Grote survived 16 major league seasons (12 with the Mets) almost solely on his defense and signal-calling abilities. Lou Brock once said that Grote was the toughest catcher for him to steal against. Grote caught every inning behind the plate during the 1969 and 1973 LCS and World Series, setting three World Series fielding records in 1973. Much of the credit for the development of pitchers Tom Seaver, Jerry Koosman, Nolan Ryan, and Jon Matlack belongs to Grote. He was traded to the Dodgers for a couple of minor leaguers at the trading deadline in 1977.

CAREER METS RECORD:

Games	AB	Hits	Runs
1,235	3,881	994	314
Avg	**HR**	**RBI**	**SB**
.256	35	357	14

HARRELSON, BUD (SS)
(1965–1977)

Signed by the Mets in 1963 as an amateur free agent, Bud Harrelson was the classic example of an "all-field, no-hit" player. He got a taste of the big leagues in 1965 and 1966 before coming to New York for good in 1967. Late in the 1966 season, Harrelson made a name for himself when he stole home twice in less than a week, in the process dealing death blows to the pennant hopes of the Giants and Pirates. In 1970 he tied the since-broken National League record of 54 consecutive games without an error. During the Mets' "miracle" season of 1969, Harrelson was one of only three Mets (along with Cleon Jones and Tommie Agee) who played regularly, the other five positions being filled by platoon players.

Harrelson's biggest claim to fame, however, is his famous on-field fight with Pete Rose during the 1973 NLCS. Harrelson was covering second when Rose slid hard into him. The two players exchanged words, then blows, before both benches emptied. When Rose later took his position in left field, the New York fans bombarded him with whatever was on hand. It was so intense that Reds manager Sparky Anderson pulled his team off the field. Hostilities continued through the remainder of the NLCS until the Mets finally knocked the Reds out.

Harrelson still ranks an all-time second in Mets history in games played, at-bats, and triples. He was named to the All-Star Game twice (1970 and 1971) and won one Gold Glove (1971). After the 1977 season, his 13-year Mets career came to an end when he was traded to Philadelphia for Fred Andrews; there he played three more seasons before retiring from the majors. He later returned to the Mets organization as a coach and minor league manager, working up to manager of the Mets in 1990. After posting a 145–129 record in just over a year and a half, he was fired with a week to go in the 1991 season.

CAREER METS RECORD:

Games	AB	Hits	Runs
1,322	4,390	1,029	490
Avg	**HR**	**RBI**	**SB**
.234	6	242	115

JOHNSON, HOWARD (3B/SS/OF)
(1985–1993)

Howard Johnson, known as "HoJo" during his New York years, came to the Mets following the 1984 season in a trade with the Tigers for Walt Terrell. Johnson became a regular in 1987 when he took over the third-base job left vacant when the Mets allowed 1986 World Series MVP Ray Knight to leave. Johnson was a switch-hitter who possessed both power and speed. He made the "30-30" club three times during his career (1987, 1989, and 1991), hitting more than 30 homers and stealing more than 30 bases in the same season. In 1987, he joined Darryl Strawberry to become the first "30-30" teammates in baseball history, and his 36 homers set a National League record for switch-hitters. However, a series of injuries began to take its toll, and a switch to the outfield didn't help. By 1992, his power was gone, and by 1993, his speed had left as well. He was granted free agency and signed on with Colorado for 1994, but played sparingly. After a brief stint with the Cubs in 1995, Johnson retired at the age of 34.

CAREER METS RECORD:

Games	AB	Hits	Runs
1,154	3,968	997	627
Avg	**HR**	**RBI**	**SB**
.251	192	629	202

JONES, CLEON (OF)
(1963, 1965–1975)

Cleon Jones was signed as an amateur free agent before the 1963 season. After joining the team permanently in 1966, Jones became the regular left fielder. He had his career year in 1969, the Mets' "miracle" World Championship season, when he hit .340 and made his lone All-Star Game appearance. But it wasn't so much his bat as an incident in the field that sparked the Mets to believe they could be champions. On July 30, locked in a pennant race, the Mets were playing the Astros. Suddenly, Manager Gil Hodges called time and walked out to Jones in left field. After a brief argument, he turned and walked back to the dugout, with Jones about 10 paces behind him. Upset at his lack of hustle, Hodges had decided to remove Jones in front of everyone, embarrassing him in public. Every Met knew then that Hodges demanded 100 percent effort from all players, even the team's biggest star, and this turned the team around. On July 18, 1975, Jones was again the center of controversy. Manager Yogi Berra had inserted him as a defensive replacement, but he refused to enter the game because he was angry over his lack of playing time. When Berra demanded that the team suspend him, management delayed for eight days before finally disciplining Jones. Shortly afterwards, with emotions still running high after the front office confrontation over the Jones incident, Berra was fired. The Mets released Jones after the season and he signed on with the White Sox, where he played only 12 games before retiring.

CAREER METS RECORD:

Games	AB	Hits	Runs
1,201	4,223	1,188	563
Avg	**HR**	**RBI**	**SB**
.281	93	521	91

KOOSMAN, JERRY (SP)
(1967–1978)

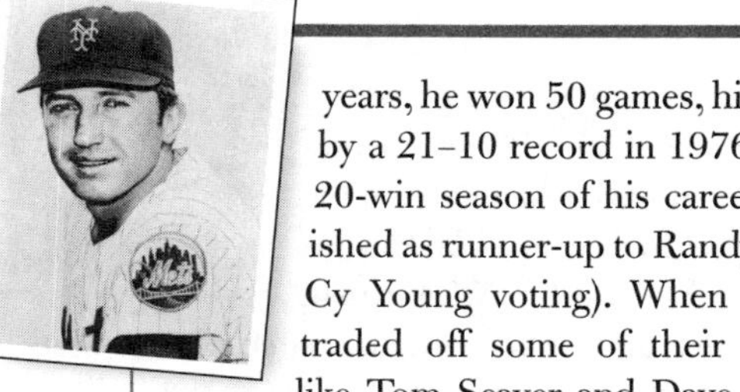

Discovered while pitching for the U.S. Army team, Jerry Koosman was signed as an amateur free agent by the Mets on August 27, 1964. After leading the International League in strikeouts in 1967, Koosman joined the Mets in 1968 and became the team's left-handed ace, winning 19 games (including an NL-record seven shutouts). He was selected the National League Rookie Pitcher of the Year and was runner-up to Johnny Bench in the Rookie of the Year balloting. In 1969, he won 17 games and teamed with Tom Seaver to lead the Mets to the World Series title over Baltimore, collecting two of New York's four wins. He also played in the second of his two All-Star Games. Koosman was hampered by injuries from 1970–1972, but was back in form by 1973 and helped lead the Mets to another National League title. He earned a win in both the NLCS and the World Series, making his postseason record 4–0. Over the next three years, he won 50 games, highlighted by a 21–10 record in 1976, the first 20-win season of his career (he finished as runner-up to Randy Jones in Cy Young voting). When the Mets traded off some of their big stars like Tom Seaver and Dave Kingman in 1977, its fortunes declined along with Koosman's record (8–20). After a horrible 1978 season during which he finished at 3–15 (although his ERA was a respectable 3.75), the Mets figured the left-hander's 12-year career was basically over and traded him to the Minnesota Twins for reliever Jesse Orosco and a minor leaguer. Koosman proved the Mets wrong, however, rebounding with a 20–13 record in 1979 and spending six more years in the majors.

CAREER METS RECORD:

W	L	W%	ERA	SV
140	137	.505	3.09	5
K	**BB**	**SHO**	**IP**	
1,799	820	26	2,544.7	

KRANEPOOL, ED (1B)
(1962–1979)

Each franchise has one player who is most identifiable to its fans, and for the Mets, if it's not Tom Seaver, it's Ed Kranepool. An original Met, Kranepool played his entire 18-year career with the team. He was signed as a 17-year-old amateur free agent in June 1962 and made the team before the end of the year, while still just 17. Kranepool was a modest hitter at best, but excelled as a pinch-hitter later in his career, setting a National League record in 1974 by hitting .486 in that role. During the five years from 1974 to 1978, he hit .396 as a pinch-hitter. When he retired after the 1979 season, he was the all-time leader for the Mets in eight offensive categories, and as of 2005, still holds five of those records (games played, at-bats, hits, doubles, and total bases).

CAREER METS RECORD:

Games	AB	Hits	Runs
1,853	5,436	1,418	536
Avg	**HR**	**RBI**	**SB**
.261	118	614	15

LEITER, AL (SP)
(1998–2004)

Al Leiter had already played in the majors for 11 years when he was traded to the Mets before the 1998 season by the Florida Marlins with Ralph Milliard for A.J. Burnett, Jesus Sanchez, and Robert Stratto. Leiter, who grew up a Mets fan, immediately posted the best season of his career—before or since—by winning 17 games and posting a 2.47 ERA. He signed a large contract and promptly gave $1 million to charity. In 1999 he was awarded the Branch Rickey Award for outstanding community service. He won the Roberto Clemente Award in 2000 as well, the same year as his only All-Star Game appearance as a Met. When the Mets found themselves in a tie with Cincinnati at the end of the 1999 regular season, Manager Bobby Valentine chose Leiter to pitch the one-game playoff in Cincinnati to see which team would win the Wild Card berth. Leiter responded with a two-hit shutout. During his seven years with the Mets, Leiter had a winning record every year but 2001, in which he finished 11–11. After the 2004 season, the Mets decided not to pick up Leiter's option and he entered the free-agent market, signing on again with the Marlins, who then traded him in midseason 2005 to the Yankees.

CAREER METS RECORD:

W	L	W%	ERA	SV
95	67	.586	3.42	0

K	BB	SHO	IP
1,106	546	7	1,360.0

MCGRAW, TUG (SP/RP)
(1965–1967, 1969–1974)

Frank McGraw, nicknamed "Tug" by his mother because of the way he tugged on her when she breast-fed him as a baby, was signed by the Mets as an amateur free agent on June 12, 1964. By the following year, the zany McGraw was on the major league roster of the struggling team. During his first three years, he bounced between relieving and starting, but by 1969, he was strictly a reliever. In 1965 he won two games, one of which was against Sandy Koufax, the first time the team had ever defeated the Dodger ace. For several years he was up and down between New York and the minors, only mildly effective with the Mets. While in the minors, however, he eventually developed a screwball and finally became a better pitcher. By 1969, he was a major part of the Mets' relief staff and an integral part of their march to the championship.

A free spirit, McGraw was a favorite of sportswriters because of his entertaining quotes. When asked whether he preferred Astroturf to grass, he replied, "I don't know. I never smoked Astroturf." During the 1973 pennant race, when no team seemed able to take charge, team chairman M. Donald Grant visited the players in the dugout prior to a game and told them that if they believed they could win, they would. McGraw went nuts, jumping around the clubhouse, grabbing his teammates and slapping them on the back, yelling, "He's right! He's right! Just believe! You gotta believe!" He kept repeating the phrase, over and over, until eventually it became the team's mantra. With McGraw winning four games and saving 11 during September 1973, New York went from last place on August 30 to win the tight divisional race. The Mets then beat the heavily favored Cincinnati Reds in the NLCS before losing to the A's in the World Series.

After one final season in New York, McGraw was traded to rival Philadelphia in December 1974. He pitched ten seasons for the Phillies before retiring. In February 2004, McGraw, father of country music star Tim McGraw, died in his son's home in Nashville at the age of 59 after a year-long battle with brain cancer.

CAREER METS RECORD:

W	L	W%	ERA	SV
47	55	.461	3.17	86
K	**BB**	**SHO**	**IP**	
618	350	1	792.7	

PIAZZA, MIKE (C/1B) (1998–2005)

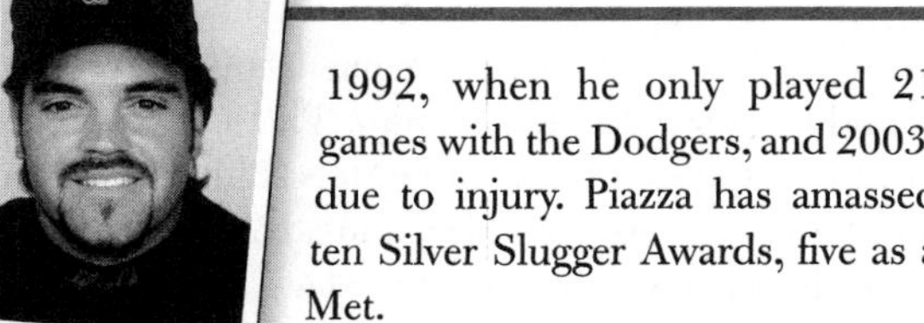

After more than six seasons with the Dodgers and five *games* with the Marlins, Mike Piazza became a Met when Florida traded him to New York on May 22, 1998, for Preston Wilson, Ed Yarnall, and Geoff Goetz. After a mixed reception in New York in 1998 that sometimes bordered on hostile, Piazza put together a remarkable season in 1999 to lead the Mets to the playoffs. He hit .303, smacked 40 homers, knocked in 124, and scored 100 runs. Hampered by a thumb injury and a slight concussion, Piazza's playing time was limited in the Division Series against Arizona and the NLCS against Atlanta. Although he hit only .182 in the postseason, he did have 10 RBIs as he delivered in the clutch. In 2000 Piazza again led the Mets to the playoffs, this time hitting .324 with 38 homers and 113 RBIs. In the three postseason series, he hit .302 with 4 homers and 8 RBIs, though the Mets lost to the Yankees in the World Series. He has been selected to the All-Star Game seven times as a Met, 12 overall. The only two years of his 14-year career that he missed were 1992, when he only played 21 games with the Dodgers, and 2003, due to injury. Piazza has amassed ten Silver Slugger Awards, five as a Met.

In recent years there had been much talk of switching the defensively suspect Piazza to first base in order to prolong his career, and in 2004 he actually played more games at first than catcher, but by 2005 the experiment seemed to be over and he returned to playing catcher most of the time. By the close of the 2005 campaign, Piazza, who holds the major league record for career home runs by a catcher, was closing in on a number of Mets all-time records in spite of his relatively short tenure with the team. A certain first-ballot Hall of Famer, Piazza will undoubtedly enter Cooperstown wearing a Mets hat.

CAREER METS RECORD:

Games	AB	Hits	Runs
972	3,478	1,028	532
Avg	**HR**	**RBI**	**SB**
.296	220	655	7

SEAVER, TOM (SP)
(1967–1977, 1983)

Tom Seaver was nicknamed "the Franchise" for good reason: During his 11 years with the team (1967–1977), he accounted for 25 percent of all the Mets' wins. Seaver arrived in New York in unusual fashion. While playing baseball at USC in 1966, he signed a contract with the Atlanta Braves. However, Baseball commissioner William Eckert voided the contract because USC's playing schedule had already begun when it was signed. Eckert decided that any club having an interest in Seaver and willing to pay him what the Braves initially offered would be allowed to bid on him. The names of three interested teams—the Mets, Phillies, and Indians—were then placed in a hat. New York, the team Seaver wanted to play for, won the drawing, so Seaver became a Met.

In 1967, after posting a 16–13 record for the dismal Mets, he won the National League Rookie of the Year Award. In 1969, he went 25–7 with a 2.21 ERA and led the Mets to the World Series title. On July 9 of that year, he lost a perfect game with one out in the ninth when Jimmy Qualls of the Cubs hit a clean single to left. On April 22, 1970, Seaver struck out 19 Padres (including the last 10 in a row to end the game) in a nine-inning game, tying Steve Carlton's record. His 19–10 record led the Mets to the World Series again in 1973, and he won his second Cy Young Award, becoming the first pitcher to capture the honor without winning at least 20 games. In 1975, his 22–9 record earned him a third Cy Young trophy. Seaver posted a solid winning record every year from 1967 to 1977, except 1974, when he finished 11–11, the only year that he did not make the National League All-Star team.

Despite Seaver's desire to play for New York, and despite his obvious value to the team, trouble surfaced. He was engaged in an ongoing feud with Mets general manager M. Donald Grant and Grant didn't hesitate to use his influence in the New York press to publicly humiliate him. Seaver eventually demanded a trade and Grant was only too happy to oblige his star pitcher. On June 15, 1977, in what became known as "the Midnight Massacre," Grant traded Seaver to Cincinnati for four players (Pat Zachry, Doug Flynn, Steve Henderson, and Dan Norman) and sent another disgruntled star, Dave Kingman, to San Diego. In an emotional post-trade press conference, Seaver broke down and was unable to continue. Mets fans were very unhappy over the loss of "Tom Terrific," their favorite Mets player.

After playing nearly six years with the Reds, Seaver returned to New York in a trade for Charlie Puleo, Lloyd McClendon, and Jason Felice. While the fans welcomed him back enthusiastically, the management was cool. Seaver posted his only losing record ever as a Met, finishing 9–14, but that was due mostly to the weak Mets offense. He left New York against his will before the 1984 season when he was left unprotected by the Mets, and the White Sox selected him in the compensation draft for losing free-agent pitcher Dennis Lamp to the Blue Jays. Seaver, very upset, threatened to retire rather than pitch for the White Sox. However, he gave in, and fashioned two fine seasons in the Windy City, winning 31 games in 1984 and 1985. After starting the 1986 season with Chicago, he was traded to Boston and finished his career with the Red Sox. Ironically, Seaver was sitting in the visitor's dugout when the Mets won the 1986 World Series in Shea Stadium. The Mets retired his uniform number 41 in 1992, the same year he was elected to the Hall of Fame in his first year of eligibility. Seaver's 98.84 percent vote is still the highest margin ever earned by a Hall of Fame inductee.

CAREER METS RECORD:

W	L	W%	ERA	SV
198	124	.615	2.57	1
K	BB	SHO	IP	
2,541	847	44	3,045.3	

STRAWBERRY, DARRYL (OF) (1983–1990)

After starring at Crenshaw High School in Los Angeles, Darryl Strawberry was chosen by the Mets as the first overall pick of the June 1980 amateur draft. After quickly working his way through New York's farm system, Strawberry joined the Mets in 1983 with seemingly unlimited potential. He lived up to that potential for the first part of his career, winning the National League's Rookie of the Year Award in 1983 after slugging 26 homers and stealing 19 bases. The 26 homers would be the fewest homers in a season for Strawberry for his first nine seasons in the majors, eight of which were with the Mets. He also had speed, averaging 30 steals a year from 1984 to 1988. Strawberry made the All-Star team seven consecutive years with the Mets, missing only his rookie year. He won Silver Slugger Awards in 1988 and 1990.

Strawberry's slide from fame to shame began in 1988 when he angered many Mets fans by publicly confessing his desire to play in Los Angeles with his longtime friend Eric Davis, who at the time was still in Cincinnati. In 1989 Strawberry got into a fight with teammate Keith Hernandez during a photo shoot. In 1990 he sat out several crucial games, claiming a sore back, during a stretch run when the Mets had a chance to catch the Pirates. Throughout his Mets career, Strawberry's desire to be the team's leader was undermined by his often moody temperament and by immature behavior that alienated him from many teammates. He was so disliked by some that, after a 1988 interview, several teammates criticized him to the media. Even during spring training, pitchers would throw at his head. On numerous occasions, he charged the mound, instigating brawls. In 1989, Shea Stadium security had to intercept him and Juan Samuel on their way to a postgame confrontation with three Cincinnati pitchers.

Strawberry's occasional mental lapses and lack of concentration contributed to the perception that he was "dogging it." After a series of nagging injuries that cut into his playing time, and with a personal life that was in as much turmoil as his professional life, Strawberry was not pursued by the Mets when his contract expired after the 1990 season. He signed a big five-year deal with the Dodgers, but only had one productive season with Los Angeles. The remaining eight years of his career were marked by injuries, drug problems, an IRS indictment, colon cancer, and arrests for solicitation and drug violations. The best that can be said about Darryl Strawberry is that he had enormous promise, although he never fully delivered, despite setting many Mets career records.

CAREER METS RECORD:

Games	AB	Hits	Runs
1,109	3,903	1,025	662
Avg	HR	RBI	SB
.263	252	733	191

Casey at the desk.

New York Yankees

Since 1901

2001 Team Ball

1920 New York becomes the first team ever to have more home runs than stolen bases.... **1934** Burleigh Grimes records the last victory by a pitcher legally allowed to throw the spitball when he picks up a win in relief.... **1956** Mickey Mantle wins the American League batting title with a .353 average, becoming the first switch-hitter to do so since Baltimore's Tommy Tucker in 1889.... **1968** The Yankees record the lowest batting average since the dead-ball era, hitting just .214.... **1977** Sparky Lyle becomes the first relief pitcher to win the American League Cy Young Award.... **2004** The Yankees set a major league record in 2004 by notching 61 come-from-behind victories during the season.

FRANCHISE HISTORY

The New York Yankees franchise, unquestionably the most storied and decorated in baseball history, started out in Baltimore. When the National League's Baltimore franchise folded in 1899, the city was left without a major league team for the 1900 season. Ban Johnson, who was cultivating his scheme to create a rival major league, seized the opportunity to place a new American League franchise in Baltimore for the 1901 season. The new team was backed by investment money from a group that included Harry Goldman, John McGraw, Wilbert Robinson, and Sydney Frank, who held the most stock in the team. Robinson and McGraw each accepted stock in lieu of part of their salaries as manager and coach. They both hit over .300 in limited action during the 1901 season (McGraw was suspended in midseason for fighting with umpires), and Joe McGinnity won 26 games as the staff ace. In 1902 McGraw was suspended again by Ban Johnson—this time indefinitely—for continual problems with the umpires.

While under suspension, McGraw worked a deal to move to the New York Giants. Since the Orioles owed McGraw $7,000 at the time he moved to New York, he agreed to give up the money in exchange for the right to take some of the Baltimore players with him to New York. Several of the players were also sent to Cincinnati to shore up that struggling franchise. With a decimated roster, Baltimore could not field a team for its July 17 game against St. Louis. Ban Johnson then stocked the team with players from several of the other teams and appointed Wilbert Robinson manager. Baltimore's 50–88 record that year was fairly

Fritz Maisel of the Yankees set an American League record for third basemen in 1914 when he stole 74 bases.

DiMaggio's first hit as a Yankee in 1938, while pretelephoto-lens photographers snap it.

respectable, considering everything that happened. After the season, Johnson paid off Baltimore's owners and revoked the team's franchise. The American League then funded Baltimore's operations until Johnson, partly seeking to get into the New York market, and partly to get revenge on John McGraw, moved the team to New York in time for the 1903 season.

With little time to spare, New York's new owners quickly raised the money to build Hilltop Park, the first home of the newly relocated franchise. The team was known first as the Highlanders. Some say the name referred to the high ground upon which the new ballpark was constructed, and some say it was a nod to the team's first president, a coal merchant and figurehead owner named Joseph Gordon, who shared a name with a famous British regiment of the time, known as Gordon's Highlanders. The initial owners of the Highlanders were Frank Farrell and Big Bill Devery, who paid the American League $18,000 for the team. Ban Johnson recruited these two corrupt New York figures because of their strong connections to the powerful Tammany Hall political machine (Johnson probably figured that a little muscle might come in handy in the event of a battle with a rival baseball league). Farrell owned a large poolroom that was essentially a front for his bookmaking operations. Big Bill Devery was a real estate investor and a police captain (some sources say police chief) who operated out of the nearby 19th Precinct station and was the target of numerous fraud and corruption investigations. Further, Farrell had connections to the Fleischmanns (of margarine fame), who owned the Cincinnati Reds, had a plant in New York, and, as chance would have it, loved horse racing as much as Farrell. In 1907 Gordon was relieved of his figurehead duties and Farrell and Devery openly took over the team. By 1914 the team was suffering financially and the two owners were feuding, so they sold the team to Colonel Jacob Ruppert and Captain Tillinghast Huston in January 1915 for $460,000.

Barnstorming comrades, Ruth and Gehrig, 1927.

Ruppert owned a brewery and Huston was a civil engineer as well as an actual captain in the military. The two had attempted to buy the Giants earlier, but failed. They also had an opportunity to buy the Cubs, but opted for the New York team, which by now was officially called the Yankees, since many of the fans were Irish and objected to the Scottish nickname. Although the Yankees name wasn't officially adopted until 1913, it had been in widespread use almost since the team's inception, particularly by the press, who detested the length of the Highlanders' name. In 1918 Ruppert and Huston began feuding over who should manage the Yankees; Huston preferred Wilbert Robinson and Ruppert preferred Miller Huggins. Since Huston was serving in Europe during World War I, the feud had to be conducted long distance via telegrams. The bickering escalated and eventually encompassed other matters. The feud continued for five years, ending on May 23, 1923, when Ruppert bought out Huston for $1.5 million. Huston attempted to buy the Dodgers in the early 1930s, but failed,

> The first black player to win the American League MVP Award was Elston Howard of the Yankees in 1963.

Mantle wins the Triple Crown in 1956 and wears one of them while Stengel pontificates.

By most people's accounts at the time, George Steinbrenner was a despicable man. He lied to many people about a variety of things, routinely broke promises, and treated his limited partners so badly that they eventually took him to court. Among players, commissioners, and other owners, Steinbrenner

and was never involved in baseball again. Ruppert, meanwhile, controlled the Yankees until his death in 1939. Then his estate ran it until near the end of World War II, when it was sold to help Ruppert's three nieces pay estate taxes.

Using baseball man Larry MacPhail as a front man, Phoenix land developer and building contractor Del Webb, and Dan Topping, who owned a tin-plating manufacturing business, bought the Yankees in 1945 for $2.8 million. The deal included the stadium and several of the Yankees' minor league teams. Topping and Webb allowed MacPhail to purchase about 10 percent of the team, although they had to loan him the money. After two years, MacPhail sold his interest back to Webb and Topping for a tidy $1 million profit. Topping and Webb sold the team in 1964 to CBS for $11.2 million. CBS in turn sold controlling interest in the Yankees in 1972 to an investment group headed by shipping magnate George Steinbrenner for $10 million.

When David Cone won 20 games in 1998, he set a record for the longest time between 20-win seasons—10 years.

was almost universally disliked from the beginning. Shortly after he bought the club, Steinbrenner was suspended for a year when he was convicted of illegal campaign contributions to Richard Nixon's 1972 presidential campaign.

In 1990 Steinbrenner was forced to resign as managing general partner because of his involvement in an effort to discredit outfielder Dave Winfield. Steinbrenner was found to have paid $40,000 to known gambler Howard Spira to dig up dirt on Winfield, a player with whom Steinbrenner had been feuding for years. When Yankee fans learned of Steinbrenner's suspension during a game, they gave the news a standing ovation. He continued to own his 55 percent controlling interest in the team, but could not be involved in the day-to-day affairs of running the team. Commissioner Fay Vincent imposed a three-year ban on Steinbrenner, but relented after only two years. During Steinbrenner's banishment, several of the limited partners brought lawsuits against him for a variety of reasons and

Steinbrenner became embattled with them. During this time, Vincent told Steinbrenner that he would not consider reinstatement until all the suits were settled. Steinbrenner, who still owns the team to this day, settled the suits in short order.

On the field, the Yankees have had unrivaled success. They failed to win a pennant during their first 21 years, but once Babe Ruth arrived in 1920, the franchise flourished. During the Ruth era (1920–1934), the Yankees won seven pennants and four World Series and finished second five times. Attendance doubled and tripled over previous highs as fans clamored to watch the "Sultan of Swat" knock his homers out of the ballpark. The tremendous upsurge in attendance allowed the team's owners to build an impressive new ballpark, Yankee Stadium. Ruth and Lou Gehrig gave the Yankees a 1–2 punch that has never been equaled in baseball history. After Ruth departed, the Yankees kept on winning, taking seven more pennants and six more Series in eight years, from 1936 to 1943. After a brief three-year hiatus, the Yankees went on a tear from 1947 to1964, winning 15 pennants and 10 World Series in 18 years. New stars Yogi Berra, Mickey Mantle, Whitey Ford, Roger Maris, Phil Rizzuto, and others led the next dynasty.

From 1965 to 1975 the Yankees entered a downturn, failing even to make the playoffs in the new divisional format. In 1974 and 1975, the Yankees shared Shea Stadium with the crosstown Mets while Yankee Stadium underwent a near-complete renovation. The Yankees returned to the Bronx and to prominence in 1976, winning four more pennants and two more World Series championships over the next six years behind Thurman Munson, Reggie Jackson, Ron Guidry, Willie Randolph, Graig Nettles and others. The Yankees then went through another drought from 1982 to 1994, when they failed to make the playoffs even once. Since 1995, however, the Yankees have made the playoffs every year, winning six pennants and four more World Series titles. Through 2005, the Yankees have won 39 pennants and 26 World Series titles, far and away the most by any team in either league.

TEAM NAME HISTORY

Official Names

Orioles (1901–1902, while in Baltimore)
Highlanders, (1903–1912)
Yankees, (1913–current)

Unofficial Names/Nicknames:

Invaders, Cliffmen, Hilltoppers, Burglars, Hill Dwellers, Porch Climbers, Yanks, New York Americans, Bronx Bombers, Pinstripers

STADIUM HISTORY

Oriole Park	1901–1902 (Baltimore)
Hilltop Park	1903–1912
Polo Grounds	1913–1922
Yankee Stadium	1923–1973
Shea Stadium	1974–1975
Yankee Stadium	1976–current

Yogi Berra. Don Larsen. October 8, 1956. The most famous hug in baseball history.

YEARLY RECORD, FINISH, & ATTENDANCE FIGURES

Year	League	Record	DIV/LG Finish	Attendance	Avg/Gm
2005	AL East	95–67	1	4,090,696	50,502
2004	AL East	101–61	1	3,775,292	46,609
2003	AL East	101–61	1	3,465,600	42,263
2002	AL East	103–58	1	3,465,807	43,323
2001	AL East	95–65	1	3,264,907	40,811
2000	AL East	87–74	1	3,055,435	38,193
1999	AL East	98–64	1	3,292,736	40,651
1998	AL East	114–48	1	2,955,193	36,484
1997	AL East	96–66	2	2,580,325	32,254
1996	AL East	92–70	1	2,250,877	28,136
1995	AL East	79–65	2	1,705,263	23,360
1994	AL East	70–43	1	1,675,556	29,396
1993	AL East	88–74	2	2,416,942	29,839
1992	AL East	76–86	4	1,748,737	21,589
1991	AL East	71–91	5	1,863,733	23,009
1990	AL East	67–95	7	2,006,436	24,771
1989	AL East	74–87	5	2,170,485	26,796
1988	AL East	85–76	5	2,633,701	32,921
1987	AL East	89–73	4	2,427,672	29,971
1986	AL East	90–72	2	2,268,030	28,350
1985	AL East	97–64	2	2,214,587	27,682
1984	AL East	87–75	3	1,821,815	22,492
1983	AL East	91–71	3	2,257,976	27,876
1982	AL East	79–83	5	2,041,219	25,200
1981	AL East	59–48	1/6	1,614,353	31,654
1980	AL East	103–59	1	2,627,417	32,437
1979	AL East	89–71	4	2,537,765	31,330
1978	AL East	100–63	1	2,335,871	28,838
1977	AL East	100–62	1	2,103,092	25,964
1976	AL East	97–62	1	2,012,434	25,155
1975	AL East	83–77	3	1,288,048	16,513
1974	AL East	89–73	2	1,273,075	15,717
1973	AL East	80–82	4	1,262,103	15,582
1972	AL East	79–76	4	966,328	12,550
1971	AL East	82–80	4	1,070,771	13,219
1970	AL East	93–69	2	1,136,879	14,036
1969	AL East	80–81	5	1,067,996	13,350
1968	AL	83–79	5	1,185,666	14,459
1967	AL	72–90	9	1,259,514	15,360
1966	AL	70–89	10	1,124,648	13,715
1965	AL	77–85	6	1,213,552	14,621
1964	AL	99–63	1	1,305,638	16,119
1963	AL	104–57	1	1,308,920	16,362
1962	AL	96–66	1	1,493,574	18,670
1961	AL	109–53	1	1,747,725	21,577
1960	AL	97–57	1	1,627,349	21,134
1959	AL	79–75	3	1,552,030	20,156
1958	AL	92–62	1	1,428,438	18,313
1957	AL	98–56	1	1,497,134	19,443
1956	AL	97–57	1	1,491,784	19,374
1955	AL	96–58	1	1,490,138	19,352

YEARLY RECORD, FINISH, & ATTENDANCE FIGURES (CONT.)

Year	League	Record	DIV/LG Finish	Attendance	Avg/Gm
1954	AL	103–51	2	1,475,171	18,912
1953	AL	99–52	1	1,537,811	19,972
1952	AL	95–59	1	1,629,665	21,164
1951	AL	98–56	1	1,950,107	25,001
1950	AL	98–56	1	2,081,380	27,031
1949	AL	97–57	1	2,283,676	29,278
1948	AL	94–60	3	2,373,901	30,830
1947	AL	97–57	1	2,178,937	28,298
1946	AL	87–67	3	2,265,512	29,422
1945	AL	81–71	4	881,845	11,603
1944	AL	83–71	3	789,995	10,128
1943	AL	98–56	1	618,330	8,030
1942	AL	103–51	1	922,011	11,974
1941	AL	101–53	1	964,722	12,368
1940	AL	88–66	3	988,975	13,013
1939	AL	106–45	1	859,785	11,166
1938	AL	99–53	1	970,916	12,290
1937	AL	102–52	1	998,148	12,635
1936	AL	102–51	1	976,913	12,687
1935	AL	89–60	2	657,508	8,885
1934	AL	94–60	2	854,682	11,100
1933	AL	91–59	2	728,014	9,707
1932	AL	107–47	1	962,320	12,498
1931	AL	94–59	2	912,437	11,850
1930	AL	86–68	3	1,169,230	15,385
1929	AL	88–66	2	960,148	12,469
1928	AL	101–53	1	1,072,132	13,924
1927	AL	110–44	1	1,164,015	15,117
1926	AL	91–63	1	1,027,675	13,702
1925	AL	69–85	7	697,267	8,826
1924	AL	89–63	2	1,053,533	13,507
1923	AL	98–54	1	1,007,066	13,251
1922	AL	94–60	1	1,026,134	13,326
1921	AL	98–55	1	1,230,696	15,778
1920	AL	95–59	3	1,289,422	16,746
1919	AL	80–59	3	619,164	8,482
1918	AL	60–63	4	282,047	4,210
1917	AL	71–82	6	330,294	4,404
1916	AL	80–74	4	469,211	5,939
1915	AL	69–83	5	256,035	3,122
1914	AL	70–84	6	359,477	4,609
1913	AL	57–94	7	357,551	4,767
1912	AL	50–102	8	242,194	3,187
1911	AL	76–76	6	302,444	3,928
1910	AL	88–63	2	355,857	4,622
1909	AL	74–77	5	501,000	6,506
1908	AL	51–103	8	305,500	3,968
1907	AL	70–78	5	350,020	4,667
1906	AL	90–61	2	434,700	5,720
1905	AL	71–78	6	309,100	4,121
1904	AL	92–59	2	438,919	5,852

YEARLY RECORD, FINISH, & ATTENDANCE FIGURES (CONT.)

Year	League	Record	DIV/LG Finish	Attendance	Avg/Gm
1903	AL	72–62	4	211,808	3,161
1902	AL	50–88	8	174,606	2,728
1901	AL	68–65	5	141,952	2,151

MANAGER HISTORY

Manager	Years	W–L	Win %
John McGraw	1901–1902	94–96	.495
Wilbert Robinson	1902	24–57	.296
Clark Griffith	1903–1908	419–370	.531
Kid Elberfeld	1908	27–71	.276
George Stallings	1909–1910	152–136	.528
Hal Chase	1910–1911	86–80	.518
Harry Wolverton	1912	50–102	.329
Frank Chance	1913–1914	117–168	.411
Roger Peckinpaugh	1914	10–10	.500
Bill Donovan	1915–1917	220–239	.479
Miller Huggins	1918–1929	1,067–719	.597
Art Fletcher	1929	6–5	.545
Bob Shawkey	1930	86–68	.558
Joe McCarthy	1931–1946	1,460–867	.627
Bill Dickey	1946	57–48	.543
Johnny Neun	1946	8–6	.571
Bucky Harris	1947–1948	191–117	.620
Casey Stengel	1949–1960	1,149–696	.623
Ralph Houk	1961–1963, 1966–1973	944–806	.539
Yogi Berra	1964, 1984–1985	192–148	.565
Johnny Keane	1965–1966	81–101	.445
Bill Virdon	1974–1975	142–124	.534
Billy Martin	1975–1978, 1979, 1983, 1985, 1988	556–385	.591
Bob Lemon	1978–1979, 1981–1982	99–73	.576
Dick Howser	1978, 1980	103–60	.632
Gene Michael	1981, 1982	92–76	.548
Clyde King	1982	29–33	.460
Lou Piniella	1986–1987, 1988	224–193	.537
Dallas Green	1989	56–65	.463
Bucky Dent	1989–1990	36–53	.404
Stump Merrill	1990–1991	120–155	.436
Buck Showalter	1992–1995	313–268	.539
Joe Torre	1996–2005	982–634	.608

ALL-TIME WIN-LOSS RECORDS VS. ALL OPPONENTS (SINCE 1901)

Opponent	Record
ALL-TIME	9,192–7,029
Angels	307–247
Astros	2–1
Athletics	1,095–745
Blue Jays	218–174
Braves	8–8
Brewers	208–182
Cardinals	4–2
Cubs	4–2
Devil Rays	88–42
Diamondbacks	4–2
Dodgers	1–2
Giants	2–1
Indians	1,067–854
INTERLEAGUE	93–63
Mariners	176–143
Marlins	8–6
Mets	29–19
Nationals	9–6
Orioles	1,177–810
Padres	4–2
Phillies	8–7
Pirates	3–0
Rangers	332–233
Reds	1–2
Red Sox	1,078–899
Rockies	5–1
Royals	231–164
Tigers	1,015–908
Twins	1,080–755
White Sox	1,024–812

The Yankees dispatch the Mets in five in 2000.

Franchise Highlights, Low Points, and Strange Distinctions

1912 The first sibling battery occurred when Homer Thompson caught his brother Tommy Thompson. It was the only major league game ever played by Homer.

....

1914 Fritz Maisel of the Yankees set an American League record for third basemen when he stole 74 bases.

....

1921 This was a banner year for Babe Ruth. He hit his 137th career homer, breaking Roger Connor's record of 136. He also set numerous other season records, including most RBIs (171), most home runs (59), most runs scored (177), and most total bases (457).

....

1923 In August, pitcher Carl Mays beat the Philadelphia A's for the 23rd consecutive time.

When the Yankees won their first-ever World Series title, defense played a big part. They were the first team ever to average less than one error per game.

....

1925 It's been oft reported that Lou Gehrig began his 2,130 consecutive games played streak after taking over for first baseman Wally Pipp, who came down with a headache in a 1925 game, but that's not the case. Gehrig actually began his streak the day before when he pinch-hit for shortstop Pee Wee Wanniger. And when Pipp came out of the game the next day, it was not Gehrig who replaced him, but rather Fred Merkle. Gehrig actually replaced Merkle when the heat got to him

....

1927 The Yankees beat the St. Louis Browns 21 times during the season, an AL record for victories against one team in one season. The only Browns victory was a 6–2 game on September 11, the last meeting between the two teams for the year.

....

1930 Babe Ruth became the first player in history to strike out 1,000 times in a career.

....

1931 Lou Gehrig set the American League record for RBIs in a season with 184. A record three grand slams in four days helped. Gehrig finished with 23 grand slams in his career, a major league record. With Gehrig's heroics, it's no wonder that the Yankees had six players who scored at least 100 runs that year, also a record.

Lou Gehrig became the first 20th-century major leaguer to belt four homers in one game when he led the Yanks to a 20–13 win over the Philadelphia A's at Shibe Park on June 3, 1932.

When Lou Gehrig knocked in 114 runs in 1938, it was his 13th consecutive season with at least 100 RBIs, a major league record.

• • • •

1933 On April 25, pitcher Russ Van Atta of the Yankees made his major league debut. Not only did he blank the Senators, 16–0, but he also collected four hits.

• • • •

1935 The longest pitching stint in All-Star Game history took place when Lefty Gomez of the Yankees pitched six innings in helping the AL to a 4–1 win.

• • • •

1936 When Bill Dickey hit .362, it became—and remains—the all-time record batting average in a season for a catcher.

The Yankees became the first team ever to have five 100-RBI men. Lou Gehrig led the way with 152. He was followed by Joe DiMaggio (125), Tony Lazzeri (109), and Bill Dickey and George Selkirk (107 each). The quintet helped the Yanks win the race by an AL record 19½ games over the Tigers.

Lou Gehrig's 14 home runs against Cleveland is still the record for most homers by a player against one team in one season.

• • • •

1941 The New York Yankees clinched the pennant in just 136 games, a record for an AL champion.

1942 The Yankees set the record for double plays in a game with seven on August 14, in an 11–2 win over the A's.

• • • •

1944 After hitting just .219 in 1943, second baseman Snuffy Stirnweiss apparently found his batting eye when he hit .319—100 points higher—and led the American League with 205 hits. In 1945 he won the AL batting crown with a .309 average. Interestingly, of the American League's top five batters in 1945—the last war year—Stirnweiss was the only one who ever again played a full season in the major leagues. When he retired in 1952 with a .268 batting average, he set the all-time record for lowest career batting average by a batting champion.

• • • •

1947 Surprisingly, the first World Series pinch-hit home run wasn't hit until 1947. Yogi Berra had the honor.

• • • •

1949 The first $100,000-a-year player was Joe DiMaggio.

• • • •

1950 Pitcher Vic Raschi of the Yankees set a major league record when he retired 32 batters in a row.

• • • •

1951 Allie Reynolds became the first American League pitcher ever to hurl two no-hitters in the same season when he accomplished the feat.

The first major league catcher to wear glasses in a game was Clint Courtney of the Yankees on September 29.

• • • •

1954 Bob Grim of the Yankees became the first pitcher in history to win 20 games in a season while pitching fewer than 200 innings.

• • • •

1956 Don Larsen of the Yankees pitched the only perfect game in World Series history when he blanked the Dodgers, 2–0, in Game 5.

• • • •

1961 Mickey Mantle may have lost the exciting battle with Roger Maris in pursuit of Babe Ruth's home run record, but he did set a new major league record for homers in a season by a switch-hitter with 54.

• • • •

1962 The first pitcher ever to win a 1–0 Game 7 of a World Series was Ralph Terry of the Yankees.

1963 The first black player to win the American League MVP Award was Elston Howard of the Yankees.

• • • •

1966 The Yankees finished in the cellar for the first time since 1912.

• • • •

1969 "During my 18 years, I came to bat almost 10,000 times. I struck out about 1,700 times and walked about 1,800 times. You figure a ballplayer will average about 500 at-bats per season. That means I played seven years in the major leagues without ever hitting the ball."—Mickey Mantle

• • • •

1973 On April 6, Ron Blomberg of the Yankees became the first designated hitter in major league history.

In spring training, Yankee pitchers Mike Kekich and Fritz Peterson publicly announced that they had swapped wives—permanently. While Fritz Peterson and Susan Kekich eventually got married in 1974, Mike Kekich and Marilyn Peterson soon split.

1975 The last major league pitcher to have as many as 30 complete games in a season was Catfish Hunter.

• • • •

1982 Prior to the 1982 season, the Yankees traded Willie McGee to the Cardinals for pitcher Bob Sykes. While Sykes never pitched another inning in the major leagues, McGee went on to win two batting titles.

• • • •

1987 Yankee first baseman Don Mattingly tied Dale Long's 31-year-old record when he homered in eight consecutive games. He also broke Ernie Banks' record of five grand slams in a season when he hit six.

• • • •

1990 Yankee pitcher Andy Hawkins threw a no-hitter against the White Sox on July 1, but lost the game, 4–0.

• • • •

1994 When Buck Showalter guided the Yankees to the best record in the American League, he became the first manager to last three consecutive years since George Steinbrenner took control of the team in 1973.

• • • •

1996 When Yankee third baseman Wade Boggs appeared in his 12th consecutive All-Star Game, he became only the fourth player to do so, joining Brooks Robinson, Yogi Berra, and Cal Ripken Jr.

• • • •

1998 When the Yankees won 114 games in the regular season, they set a new major league record by holding a lead at some point in 48 consecutive games.

When David Cone won 20 games in 1998, he set a record for the longest time between 20-win seasons—10 years.

• • • •

2001 The Yankees hosted the first-ever World Series game played in November—a 3–2 Game 5 win over Arizona—on November 1. On the flip side, when the Yankees lost Games 6 and 7 of the 2001 Series, they became the all-time leader in November World Series losses (2).

• • • •

2005 On March 31, the North Dakota state senate voted 45–0 to approve a resolution asking Major League Baseball to reinstate native Roger Maris' 61 home runs in 1961 as the official major league record due to suspected steroid use by Barry Bonds, Mark McGwire, and Sammy Sosa.

New York's $199.77 million payroll was more than five other teams combined. (Tampa Bay, $29.9 million; Kansas City, $36.9 million; Pittsburgh, $38.1 million; Milwaukee, $40.2 million; Cleveland, $41.8 million.)

Four times in major league history a team has managed to collect three sacrifice flies in an inning, and the Yankees have been involved in three of them. Basically, to make three sacrifice flies in an inning, somewhere along the line an outfielder has to drop a fly ball for an error while a runner advances a base. The Mets made three sacrifice flies against the Yankees on June 27. The Yankees made three sacrifice flies themselves twice in 2000, and the White Sox did it in 1962.

Pitcher Randy Johnson has been one of the most dominating pitchers in the last 15 years. He has only lost to one team three times in a row—the Tampa Bay Devil Rays!

Special Achievements

World Series Results

Year	Opponent	Result	Games
1921	New York Giants	Lost	3–5
1922	New York Giants	Lost	0–4
1923	New York Giants	Won	4–2
1926	St. Louis Cardinals	Lost	3–4
1927	Pittsburgh Pirates	Won	4–0
1928	St. Louis Cardinals	Won	4–0
1932	Chicago Cubs	Won	4–0
1936	New York Giants	Won	4–2
1937	New York Giants	Won	4–1
1938	Chicago Cubs	Won	4–0
1939	Cincinnati Reds	Won	4–0
1941	Brooklyn Dodgers	Won	4–1
1942	St. Louis Cardinals	Lost	1–4
1943	St. Louis Cardinals	Won	4–1
1947	Brooklyn Dodgers	Won	4–3
1949	Brooklyn Dodgers	Won	4–1
1950	Philadelphia Phillies	Won	4–0
1951	New York Giants	Won	4–2
1952	Brooklyn Dodgers	Won	4–3
1953	Brooklyn Dodgers	Won	4–2
1955	Brooklyn Dodgers	Lost	3–4
1956	Brooklyn Dodgers	Won	4–3
1957	Milwaukee Braves	Lost	3–4
1958	Milwaukee Braves	Won	4–3
1960	Pittsburgh Pirates	Lost	3–4
1961	Cincinnati Reds	Won	4–1
1962	S.F. Giants	Won	4–3
1963	L.A. Dodgers	Lost	0–4
1964	St. Louis Cardinals	Lost	3–4
1976	Cincinnati	Lost	0–4
1977	L.A. Dodgers	Won	4–2
1978	L.A. Dodgers	Won	4–2
1981	L.A. Dodgers	Lost	2–4
1996	Atlanta Braves	Won	4–2
1998	San Diego Padres	Won	4–0
1999	Atlanta Braves	Won	4–0
2000	New York Mets	Won	4–1
2001	Arizona D'backs	Lost	3–4
2003	Florida Marlins	Lost	2–4

World Series Managerial Records

Manager	Series Record	Games Record
Miller Huggins	3–3	18–15
Joe McCarthy	7–1	29–9
Bucky Harris	1–0	4–3
Casey Stengel	7–3	37–26
Ralph Houk	2–1	8–8
Yogi Berra	0–1	3–4
Billy Martin	1–1	4–6
Bob Lemon	1–1	6–6
Joe Torre	4–2	21–11

All-Time Postseason Record

Divisional Playoffs	25–19
League Championship Series	39–22
World Series	130–88

All-Star Games at New York

Year	Date	Winner	Score	Stadium
1939	July 11	American	3–1	Yankee Stadium
1960	July 13	National	6–0	Yankee Stadium
1977	July 19	National	7–5	Yankee Stadium

Hall of Famers Who Played for Team

	Position	Years	Games with New York/ Baltimore
Frank Baker	3B	1916–1919, 1921–1922	676
Yogi Berra	C/OF	1946–1963	2,116
Wade Boggs	3B	1993–1997	601
Frank Chance	1B	1913–1914	13
Jack Chesbro	SP	1903–1909	270
Earle Combs	OF	1924–1935	1,455
Stan Coveleski	SP/RP	1928	12
Bill Dickey	C	1928–1943, 1946	1,789
Joe DiMaggio	OF	1936–1942, 1946–1951	1,736
Leo Durocher	SS/2B	1925, 1928–1929	210
Whitey Ford	SP/RP	1950, 1953–1967	500
Lou Gehrig	1B	1923–1939	2,164
Lefty Gomez	SP/RP	1930–1942,	367
Clark Griffith	RP/SP	1903–1907	89
Burleigh Grimes	RP	1934	10
Waite Hoyt	SP/RP	1921–1930	365
Catfish Hunter	SP	1975–1979	137
Reggie Jackson	OF/DH	1977–1981	653
Willie Keeler	OF	1903–1909	873
Tony Lazzeri	2B/3B	1926–1937	1,659
Mickey Mantle	OF/1B	1951–1968	2,401
Bill McKechnie	2B	1913	45
Johnny Mize	1B	1949–1953	375
Phil Niekro	SP	1984–1985	65
Herb Pennock	SP/RP	1923–1933	346
Gaylord Perry	SP/RP	1980	10
Phil Rizzuto	SS	1941–1942, 1946–1956	1,661
Red Ruffing	SP	1930–1942, 1945–1946	631

Babe Ruth	OF	1920–1934	2,084
Joe Sewell	3B	1931–1933	390
Enos Slaughter	OF	1954–1959	350
Dazzy Vance	RP/SP	1915, 1918	10
Paul Waner	PH	1944–1945	10
Dave Winfield	OF	1981–88, 1990	1,172

HALL OF FAMERS WHO MANAGED TEAM

	Years	Games with New York/ Baltimore
Yogi Berra	1964, 1984–1985	340
Frank Chance	1913–1914	285
Bill Dickey	1946	105
Clark Griffith	1903–1908	789
Bucky Harris	1947–1948	308
Miller Huggins	1918–1929	1,786
Bob Lemon	1978–1979, 1981–1982	172
Joe McCarthy	1931–1946	2,327
Casey Stengel	1949–1960	1,845

MVP AWARD WINNERS

Lou Gehrig	1B	1936
Joe DiMaggio	OF	1939
Joe DiMaggio	OF	1941
Joe Gordon	2B	1942
Spud Chandler	SP	1943
Joe DiMaggio	OF	1947
Phil Rizzuto	SS	1950
Yogi Berra	C	1951
Yogi Berra	C	1954
Yogi Berra	C	1955
Mickey Mantle	OF	1956
Mickey Mantle	OF	1957
Roger Maris	OF	1960
Roger Maris	OF	1961
Mickey Mantle	OF	1962
Elston Howard	C	1963
Thurman Munson	C	1976
Don Mattingly	1B	1985
Alex Rodriguez	3B	2005

CY YOUNG AWARD WINNERS

Pitcher	Year	W–L	SV	ERA
Bob Turley	1958	21–7	1	2.97
Whitey Ford	1961	25–4	0	3.21
Sparky Lyle	1977	13–5	26	2.17
Ron Guidry	1978	25–3	0	1.74
Roger Clemens	2001	20–3	0	3.51

ROOKIE OF THE YEAR AWARD WINNERS

Gil McDougald	3B	1951
Bob Grim	SP/RP	1954
Tony Kubek	SS/OF	1957
Tom Tresh	SS/OF	1962
Stan Bahnsen	SP	1968
Thurman Munson	C	1970
Dave Righetti	SP	1981
Derek Jeter	SS	1996

GOLD GLOVE WINNERS

Year	Position	Player
1957	SP	Bobby Shantz
1958	SP OF	Bobby Shantz Norm Siebern
1959	SP	Bobby Shantz
1960	SP OF	Bobby Shantz Roger Maris
1961	2B	Bobby Richardson
1962	2B OF	Bobby Richardson Mickey Mantle
1963	C 2B	Elston Howard Bobby Richardson
1964	C 2B	Elston Howard Bobby Richardson
1965	1B 2B OF	Joe Pepitone Bobby Richardson Tom Tresh
1966	1B	Joe Pepitone
1969	1B	Joe Pepitone
1972	OF	Bobby Murcer
1973	C	Thurman Munson
1974	C	Thurman Munson
1975	C	Thurman Munson
1977	3B	Graig Nettles
1978	1B 3B	Chris Chambliss Graig Nettles
1982	SP OF	Ron Guidry Dave Winfield
1983	SP OF	Ron Guidry Dave Winfield
1984	SP OF	Ron Guidry Dave Winfield
1985	SP 1B OF	Ron Guidry Don Mattingly Dave Winfield
1986	SP 1B	Ron Guidry Don Mattingly
1987	1B OF	Don Mattingly Dave Winfield
1988	1B	Don Mattingly
1989	1B	Don Mattingly
1991	1B	Don Mattingly
1992	1B	Don Mattingly
1993	1B	Don Mattingly

1994	1B 3B	Don Mattingly Wade Boggs
1995	3B	Wade Boggs
1997	OF	Bernie Williams
1998	OF	Bernie Williams
1999	3B OF	Scott Brosius Bernie Williams
2000	OF	Bernie Williams
2004	SS	Derek Jeter
2005	SS	Derek Jeter

Triple Crown Winners

Player	Year	Avg	HR	RBI
Lou Gehrig	1934	.363	49	165
Mickey Mantle	1956	.353	52	130

Fireman of the Year Award Winners

Luis Arroyo	1961
Sparky Lyle	1972
Goose Gossage	1978
Dave Righetti	1986
Dave Righetti	1987 (tie)
John Wetteland	1996
Mariano Rivera	1997
Mariano Rivera	1999
Mariano Rivera	2001
Mariano Rivera	2004

World Series MVP

Joe Page	1949
Jerry Coleman	1950
Phil Rizzuto	1951
Johnny Mize	1952
Billy Martin	1953
Don Larsen	1956
Bob Turley	1958
Bobby Richardson	1960
Whitey Ford	1961
Ralph Terry	1962
Reggie Jackson	1977
Bucky Dent	1978
John Wetteland	1996
Scott Brosius	1998
Mariano Rivera	1999
Derek Jeter	2000

League Championship Series MVP

Graig Nettles	1981
Bernie Williams	1996
David Wells	1998
Orlando Hernandez	1999
David Justice	2000
Andy Pettitte	2001
Mariano Rivera	2003

All-Star Game MVP

Derek Jeter	2000

Manager of the Year Award Winners

Buck Showalter	1994
Joe Torre	1996 (tie)
Joe Torre	1998

Batting Champions

Year	Player	Avg
1924	Babe Ruth	.378
1934	Lou Gehrig	.363
1939	Joe DiMaggio	.381
1940	Joe DiMaggio	.352
1945	Snuffy Stirnweiss	.309
1956	Mickey Mantle	.353
1984	Don Mattingly	.343
1994	Paul O'Neill	.359
1998	Bernie Williams	.339

Nine-Inning No-Hitters Pitched

Year	Pitcher	Opp.	Score
1917	George Mogridge	BOS	2–1
1923	Sam Jones	PHI	2–0
1938	Monte Pearson	CLE	13–0
1951	Allie Reynolds Allie Reynolds	CLE BOS	1–0 8–0
1956	Don Larsen	BRK	2–0 (perfect, World Series)
1983	Dave Righetti	BOS	4–0
1990	Andy Hawkins	CWS	0–4
1993	Jim Abbott	CLE	4–0
1996	Dwight Gooden	SEA	2–0
1998	David Wells	MIN	4–0 (perfect)
1999	David Cone	MON	6–0 (perfect)

20-Game Winners

Year	Pitcher	W–L
1901	Joe McGinnity	26–20
1903	Jack Chesbro	21–15
1904	Jack Chesbro Jack Powell	41–12 23–19
1906	Albert Orth Jack Chesbro	27–17 23–17
1910	Russell Ford	26–6
1911	Russell Ford	22–11
1916	Bob Shawkey	24–14
1919	Bob Shawkey	20–11
1920	Carl Mays Bob Shawkey	26–11 20–13

1921	Carl Mays	27–9
1922	Joe Bush Bob Shawkey	26–7 20–12
1923	Sam Jones	21–8
1924	Herb Pennock	21–9
1926	Herb Pennock	23–11
1927	Waite Hoyt	22–7
1928	George Pipgras Waite Hoyt	24–13 23–7
1931	Lefty Gomez	21–9
1932	Lefty Gomez	24–7
1934	Lefty Gomez	26–5
1936	Red Ruffing	20–12
1937	Lefty Gomez Red Ruffing	21–11 20–7
1938	Red Ruffing	21–7
1939	Red Ruffing	21–7
1942	Ernie Bonham	21–5
1943	Spud Chandler	20–4
1946	Spud Chandler	20–8
1949	Vic Raschi	21–10
1950	Vic Raschi	21–8
1951	Eddie Lopat Vic Raschi	21–9 21–10
1952	Allie Reynolds	20–8
1954	Bob Grim	20–6
1958	Bob Turley	21–7
1961	Whitey Ford	25–4
1962	Ralph Terry	23–12
1963	Whitey Ford Jim Bouton	24–7 21–7
1965	Mel Stottlemyre	20–9
1968	Mel Stottlemyre	21–12
1969	Mel Stottlemyre	20–14
1970	Fritz Peterson	20–11
1975	Catfish Hunter	23–14
1978	Ron Guidry Ed Figueroa	25–3 20–9
1979	Tommy John	21–9
1980	Tommy John	22–9
1983	Ron Guidry	21–9
1985	Ron Guidry	22–6
1996	Andy Pettitte	21–8
1998	David Cone	20–7
2001	Roger Clemens	20–3
2003	Andy Pettitte	21–8

RETIRED UNIFORM NUMBERS

Number	Player	Position
1	Billy Martin	2B/Mgr
3	Babe Ruth	OF
4	Lou Gehrig	1B
5	Joe DiMaggio	OF
7	Mickey Mantle	OF
8	Bill Dickey Yogi Berra	C C
9	Roger Maris	OF
10	Phil Rizzuto	SS
15	Thurman Munson	C
16	Whitey Ford	SP
23	Don Mattingly	1B
32	Elston Howard	C
37	Casey Stengel	Mgr
44	Reggie Jackson	OF

TEAM RECORDS—WINS & LOSSES

- Games won in a season: 114 in 1998
- Games lost in a season: 103 in 1908
- Games won in a month: 28 in August 1938
- Games lost in a month: 24 in July 1908
- Consecutive games won: 19 in 1947
- Consecutive games lost: 13 in 1913
- Biggest shutout victory: 21–0 over Philadelphia A's on August 13, 1939 (second game)
- Biggest shutout loss: 22–0 to Cleveland, August 31, 2004
- Highest winning percentage: .714 in 1927 (110–44)
- Lowest winning percentage: .329 in 1912 (50–102)

TEAM RECORDS—BATTING

- Highest team batting average: .309 in 1930
- Lowest team batting average: .214 in 1968
- Highest team slugging average: .489 in 1927
- Highest team on-base percentage: .384 in 1930
- Total hits: 1,683 in 1930
- Extra-base hits: 580 in 1936
- Hits in a game: 30 vs. Boston Red Sox on September 28, 1923
- Longest individual hitting streak: 56, Joe DiMaggio, 1941
- Most .300 hitters in a single season: 9 in 1930
- Home runs: 242 in 2004
- Home runs in a month: 17, Babe Ruth, September 1927
- Home runs in a game: 8 vs. Philadelphia A's on June 28, 1939 (first game)
- Home runs by a rookie: 29, Joe DiMaggio, 1936
- Home runs by a right-hander: 48, Alex Rodriguez, 2005

- Home runs by a left-hander: 61, Roger Maris, 1961
- Home runs by a switch-hitter: 54, Mickey Mantle, 1961
- Grand slams: 10 in 1987
- Grand slams (individual; season): 6, Don Mattingly, 1987
- Grand slams (individual; career): 23, Lou Gehrig
- Triples: 110 in 1930
- Doubles: 325 in 1997
- Singles: 1,157 in 1931
- Walks: 766 in 1932
- Runs scored: 1,067 in 1931
- Runs scored in a game: 25 vs. Philadelphia A's, May 24, 1936
- Runs scored in an inning: 14 vs. Washington Senators on July 6, 1920 (fifth inning)
- Most batters hit by a pitch: 81 in 2003
- Times shut out: 27 in 1914
- Grounded into double plays: 157 in 2004
- Fewest grounded into double plays: 91 in 1963
- Runners left on base: 1,276 in 1997

Team Records—Baserunning

- Stolen bases: 289 in 1910
- Caught stealing: 82 in 1920

Team Records—Pitching

- Lowest earned run average: 2.57 in 1904
- Complete games: 123 in 1904
- Saves: 59 in 2004
- Strikeouts: 1,266 in 2001
- Shutouts: 24 1951
- Walks: 812 in 1949
- Hit batsmen: 84 in 2005
- Wild pitches: 83 in 1990
- Consecutive wins (individual): 16, Roger Clemens, 2001
- Consecutive losses (individual): 11, George Mogridge, 1916
- Strikeouts in a game (individual): 18, Ron Guidry, June 17, 1978
- Runs allowed in a game: 24 vs. Cleveland, July 29, 1928

Team Records—Fielding

- Best fielding average: .986 in 1995
- Most errors committed: 401 in 1901
- Fewest errors committed: 91 in 1996
- Most double plays turned: 214 in 1956
- Fewest double plays turned: 76 in 1901

Team Records—Miscellaneous

- Number of times league champions: 39
- Number of times finishing last in league: 6
- Largest attendance, single game: 73,205 vs. Philadelphia A's, April 19, 1931
- Largest attendance, doubleheader: 81,841 vs. Boston Red Sox, May 30, 1938
- Players used in a season: 51 in 2005
- Seasons played: 18 by Yogi Berra and Mickey Mantle

PRIMARY PITCHING STAFFS

Year	Starter	Starter	Starter	Starter	Starter	Closer	Bullpen	Bullpen	Bullpen
2005	Johnson	Mussina	Wang	Pavano	Brown	Rivera	Gordon	Sturtze	Rodriguez
2004	Vazquez	Mussina	Lieber	Brown	Contreras	Rivera	Quantrill	Gordon	Heredia
2003	Pettitte	Mussina	Clemens	Wells	Weaver	Rivera	Hammond	Osuna	Hitchcock
2002	Pettitte	Mussina	Clemens	Wells	Hernandez	Rivera	Stanton	Karsay	Mendoza
2001	Pettitte	Mussina	Clemens	Lilly	Hernandez	Rivera	Stanton	Choate	Mendoza
2000	Pettitte	Cone	Clemens	Neagle	Hernandez	Rivera	Stanton	Nelson	Grimsley
1999	Pettitte	Cone	Clemens	Irabu	Hernandez	Rivera	Stanton	Mendoza	Grimsley
1998	Pettitte	Cone	Wells	Irabu	Hernandez	Rivera	Stanton	Lloyd	Nelson
1997	Pettitte	Cone	Wells	Rogers	Gooden	Rivera	Stanton	Lloyd	Nelson
1996	Pettitte	Cone	Key	Rogers	Gooden	Wetteland	Rivera	Wickman	Nelson
1995	Pettitte	Cone	McDowell	Hitchcock	Kamieniecki	Wetteland	MacDonald	Wickman	Howe
1994	Key	Abbott	Perez	Mulholland	Kamieniecki	Howe	Hernandez	Wickman	Gibson
1993	Key	Abbott	Perez	Wickman	Kamieniecki	Farr	Howe	Monteleone	Munoz
1992	Sanderson	Leary	Perez	Cadaret	Kamieniecki	Farr	Habyan	Monteleone	Burke
1991	Sanderson	Leary	Johnson	Taylor	Perez	Farr	Guetterman	Cadaret	Habyan
1990	Cary	Leary	LaPoint	Hawkins	Witt	Righetti	Guetterman	Cadaret	Robinson
1989	Parker	Cadaret	LaPoint	Hawkins	Terrell	Righetti	Guetterman	Mohorcic	McCullers
1988	John	Rhoden	Dotson	Candelaria	Leiter	Righetti	Guante	Allen	Shields
1987	John	Rhoden	Rasmussen	Guidry	Hudson	Righetti	Guante	Stoddard	Clements
1986	Niekro	Drabek	Rasmussen	Guidry	Tewksbury	Righetti	Fisher	Shirley	Scurry
1985	Niekro	Whitson	Rasmussen	Guidry	Cowley	Righetti	Fisher	Shirley	Bordi
1984	Niekro	Fontenot	Rasmussen	Guidry	Montefusco	Righetti	Armstrong	Shirley	Howell
1983	Rawley	Fontenot	Righetti	Guidry	Shirley	Gossage	Howell	Frazier	Murray
1982	Rawley	John	Righetti	Guidry	Morgan	Gossage	May	Frazier	LaRoche
1981	May	John	Righetti	Guidry	Reuschel	Gossage	Davis	Bird	LaRoche
1980	May	John	Underwood	Guidry	Tiant	Gossage	Davis	Bird	Figueroa
1979	Hunter	John	Figueroa	Guidry	Tiant	Gossage	Davis	Kaat	Clay
1978	Hunter	Tidrow	Figueroa	Guidry	Beattie	Gossage	Lyle	Eastwick	Clay
1977	Hunter	Torrez	Figueroa	Guidry	Gullett	Lyle	Tidrow	Holtzman	Clay
1976	Hunter	Ellis	Figueroa	Holtzman	Alexander	Lyle	Tidrow	Jackson	Martinez
1975	Hunter	Medich	May	Dobson	Gura	Martinez	Tidrow	Lyle	Pagan
1974	Tidrow	Medich	May	Dobson	Stottlemyre	Lyle	Upshaw	Wallace	Pagan
1973	Peterson	Medich	McDowell	Dobson	Stottlemyre	Lyle	McDaniel	Beene	Kline
1972	Peterson	Kline	Kekich	Gardner	Stottlemyre	Lyle	McDaniel	Beene	Roland
1971	Peterson	Kline	Kekich	Bahnsen	Stottlemyre	McDaniel	Aker	Waslewski	
1970	Peterson	Kline	Kekich	Bahnsen	Stottlemyre	McDaniel	Klimkowski	Aker	Hamilton
1969	Peterson	Burbach	Downing	Bahnsen	Stottlemyre	Aker	McDaniel	Kekich	Hamilton
1968	Peterson	Barber	Downing	Bahnsen	Stottlemyre	Hamilton	Womack	Verbanic	Talbot
1967	Peterson	Barber	Downing	Talbot	Stottlemyre	Womack	Monbouquette	Tillotson	Hamilton
1966	Peterson	Bouton	Downing	Talbot	Stottlemyre	Ramos	Hamilton	Reniff	Womack
1965	Ford	Bouton	Downing	Stafford	Stottlemyre	Ramos	Hamilton	Reniff	Mikkelsen
1964	Ford	Bouton	Downing	Terry	Stottlemyre	Mikkelsen	Hamilton	Reniff	Stafford
1963	Ford	Bouton	Downing	Terry	Williams	Reniff	Hamilton	Bridges	Stafford
1962	Ford	Bouton	Stafford	Terry	Sheldon	Bridges	Coates	Daley	Arroyo
1961	Ford	Daley	Stafford	Terry	Sheldon	Arroyo	Coates	Reniff	Clevenger
1960	Ford	Ditmar	Turley	Terry	Coates	Shantz	Duren	Maas	Arroyo
1959	Ford	Ditmar	Turley	Maas	Larsen	Duren	Coates	Shantz	Terry
1958	Ford	Kucks	Turley	Maas	Larsen	Duren	Ditmar	Shantz	Trucks
1957	Sturdivant	Kucks	Turley	Shantz	Larsen	Grim	Ditmar	Byrne	Ford
1956	Sturdivant	Kucks	Turley	Ford	Larsen	Morgan	Coleman	Byrne	Grim
1955	Byrne	Kucks	Turley	Ford	Larsen	Konstanty	Morgan	Sturdivant	Grim
1954	Lopat	Byrd	Grim	Ford	Reynolds	Sain	Morgan	Gorman	Kuzava

PRIMARY PITCHING STAFFS (CONT.)

Year	Starter	Starter	Starter	Starter	Starter	Closer	Bullpen	Bullpen	Bullpen
1953	Lopat	Raschi	Sain	Ford	McDonald	Reynolds	Scarborough	Gorman	Kuzava
1952	Lopat	Raschi	Sain	Reynolds	Miller	Hogue	McDonald	Kuzava	
1951	Lopat	Raschi	Morgan	Reynolds	Shea	Ostrowski	Kramer	Kuzava	
1950	Lopat	Raschi	Byrne	Reynolds	Sanford	Page	Ostrowski	Ferrick	Ford
1949	Lopat	Raschi	Byrne	Reynolds	Sanford	Page	Marshall	Shea	Buxton
1948	Lopat	Raschi	Shea	Reynolds	Porterfield	Page	Byrne	Hiller	Embree
1947	Bevens	Chandler	Shea	Reynolds	Newsom	Page	Drews	Gumpert	Johnson
1946	Bevens	Chandler	Page	Bonham	Gumpert	Murphy	Gettel	Marshall	Wight
1945	Bevens	Dubiel	Borowy	Bonham	Gettel	Turner	Holcombe	Zuber	Page
1944	Donald	Dubiel	Borowy	Bonham	Page	Turner	Johnson	Zuber	Roser
1943	Donald	Chandler	Borowy	Bonham	Wensloff	Murphy	Russo	Zuber	Turner
1942	Donald	Chandler	Borowy	Bonham	Ruffing	Murphy	Breuer	Lindell	Gomez
1941	Donald	Chandler	Russo	Gomez	Ruffing	Murphy	Breuer	Branch	Bonham
1940	Breuer	Chandler	Russo	Pearson	Ruffing	Murphy	Sundra	Hadley	Donald
1939	Gomez	Donald	Hadley	Pearson	Ruffing	Murphy	Sundra	Hildebrand	Russo
1938	Gomez	Chandler	Hadley	Pearson	Ruffing	Murphy	Sundra	Andrews	Beggs
1937	Gomez	Chandler	Hadley	Pearson	Ruffing	Murphy	Malone	Makosky	Wicker
1936	Gomez	Broaca	Hadley	Pearson	Ruffing	Malone	Murphy	Brown	Kleinhans
1935	Gomez	Broaca	Allen	Tamulis	Ruffing	Murphy	Malone	DeShong	
1934	Gomez	Broaca	Murphy	DeShong	Ruffing	Van Atta	MacFayden	Allen	
1933	Gomez	Allen	Van Atta	Brennan	Ruffing	Moore	Pennock	MacFayden	Brown
1932	Gomez	Allen	Pipgras	Pennock	Ruffing	Wells	MacFayden	Brown	
1931	Gomez	Johnson	Pipgras	Pennock	Ruffing	Wells	Rhodes	Weaver	
1930	Sherid	Wells	Pipgras	Pennock	Ruffing	Johnson	McEvoy	Holloway	
1929	Sherid	Wells	Pipgras	Pennock	Hoyt	Moore	Johnson	Heimach	Zachary
1928	Johnson	Shealy	Pipgras	Pennock	Hoyt	Moore	Heimach	Campbell	
1927	Shocker	Ruether	Pipgras	Pennock	Hoyt	Moore	Thomas	Shawkey	Giard
1926	Shocker	Jones	Thomas	Pennock	Hoyt	Braxton	Shawkey	Beall	
1925	Shocker	Jones	Shawkey	Pennock	Hoyt	Johnson	Ferguson	Beall	
1924	Bush	Jones	Shawkey	Pennock	Hoyt	Gaston	Mamaux	Pipgras	
1923	Bush	Jones	Shawkey	Pennock	Hoyt	Mays	Pipgras		
1922	Bush	Jones	Shawkey	Mays	Hoyt	Murray	O'Doul		
1921	Collins	Quinn	Shawkey	Mays	Hoyt	Ferguson	Piercy	Sheehan	
1920	Collins	Quinn	Shawkey	Mays	Mogridge	Thormahlen	McGraw	Shore	
1919	Thormahlen	Quinn	Shawkey	Mays	Mogridge	Russell	Nelson	Shore	
1918	Love	Caldwell	Russell	Finneran	Mogridge	Thormahlen	Keating	Robinson	
1917	Shawkey	Caldwell	Cullop	Fisher	Mogridge	Love	Shocker	Russell	
1916	Shawkey	Caldwell	Cullop	Fisher	Mogridge	Russell	Love	Shocker	Keating
1915	Warhop	Caldwell	Brown	Fisher	McHale	Pieh	Shawkey	Keating	
1914	Warhop	Caldwell	Keating	Fisher	McHale	Pieh	Cole	Brown	
1913	Ford	Schulz	Keating	Fisher	McConnell	Caldwell	Warhop	Clark	
1912	Ford	Caldwell	Warhop	Fisher	McConnell	Quinn	Vaughn	Davis	
1911	Ford	Caldwell	Warhop	Fisher	Vaughn	Quinn	Brockett		
1910	Ford	Quinn	Warhop	Hughes	Vaughn	Fisher	Manning	Frill	
1909	Lake	Manning	Warhop	Hughes	Brockett	Quinn	Doyle	Wilson	
1908	Lake	Manning	Chesbro	Hogg	Orth	Newton	Doyle	Wilson	
1907	Doyle	Newton	Chesbro	Hogg	Orth	Keefe	Kitson	Moore	
1906	Clarkson	Newton	Chesbro	Hogg	Orth	Griffith	Leroy	Doyle	
1905	Powell	Puttmann	Chesbro	Hogg	Orth	Griffith	Newton	Clarkson	
1904	Powell	Hughes	Chesbro	Griffith	Orth	Puttmann	Wolfe	Clarkson	
1903	Tannehill	Wolfe	Chesbro	Griffith	Howell	Deering			
1902	McGinnity	Wiltse	Shields	Butler	Howell	Katoll	Hughes	Cronin	
1901	McGinnity	Nops	Foreman	Dunn	Howell		Schmit		

PRIMARY STARTING LINEUPS

Year	C	1B	2B	3B	SS	LF	CF	RF	DH
2005	Posada	Martinez	Cano	Rodriguez	Jeter	Matsui	B. Williams	Sheffield	Giambi
2004	Posada	Clark	Cairo	Rodriguez	Jeter	Matsui	B. Williams	Sheffield	Sierra
2003	Posada	Giambi	Soriano	Ventura	Jeter	Matsui	B. Williams	Mondesi	Johnson
2002	Posada	Giambi	Soriano	Ventura	Jeter	White	B. Williams	Mondesi	Johnson
2001	Posada	Martinez	Soriano	Brosius	Jeter	Knoblauch	B. Williams	O'Neill	Justice
2000	Posada	Martinez	Knoblauch	Brosius	Jeter	Ledee	B. Williams	O'Neill	Spencer
1999	Posada	Martinez	Knoblauch	Brosius	Jeter	Curtis	B. Williams	O'Neill	Davis
1998	Posada	Martinez	Knoblauch	Brosius	Jeter	Curtis	B. Williams	O'Neill	Strawberry
1997	Girardi	Martinez	Sojo	Hayes	Jeter	Raines	B. Williams	O'Neill	Fielder
1996	Girardi	Martinez	Duncan	Boggs	Jeter	G. Williams	B. Williams	O'Neill	Sierra
1995	Stanley	Mattingly	Kelly	Boggs	Fernandez	G. Williams	B. Williams	O'Neill	Sierra
1994	Stanley	Mattingly	Kelly	Boggs	Gallego	Polonia	B. Williams	O'Neill	Tartabull
1993	Stanley	Mattingly	Kelly	Boggs	Owen	James	B. Williams	O'Neill	Tartabull
1992	Nokes	Mattingly	Kelly	Hayes	Stankiewicz	Hall	Kelly	Tartabull	Maas
1991	Nokes	Mattingly	Sax	Kelly	Espinoza	Meulens	B. Williams	Barfield	Maas
1990	Geren	Mattingly	Sax	Velarde	Espinoza	Azocar	Kelly	Barfield	Balboni
1989	Slaught	Mattingly	Sax	Pagliarulo	Espinoza	Henderson	Kelly	Barfield	Balboni
1988	Slaught	Mattingly	Randolph	Pagliarulo	Santana	Henderson	Washington	Winfield	Clark
1987	Cerone	Mattingly	Randolph	Pagliarulo	Tolleson	Ward	Washington	Winfield	Kittle
1986	Wynegar	Mattingly	Randolph	Pagliarulo	Tolleson	Pasqua	Henderson	Winfield	Easler
1985	Wynegar	Mattingly	Randolph	Pagliarulo	Meacham	Griffey	Henderson	Winfield	Baylor
1984	Wynegar	Mattingly	Randolph	Harrah	Meacham	Kemp	Moreno	Winfield	Baylor
1983	Wynegar	Griffey	Randolph	Nettles	Smalley	Winfield	Mumphrey	Kemp	Baylor
1982	Cerone	Mayberry	Randolph	Nettles	Smalley	Winfield	Mumphrey	Griffey	Gamble
1981	Cerone	Watson	Randolph	Nettles	Dent	Winfield	Mumphrey	Jackson	Gamble
1980	Cerone	Watson	Randolph	Nettles	Dent	Piniella	Jones	Jackson	Soderholm
1979	Munson	Chambliss	Randolph	Nettles	Dent	Piniella	Rivers	Jackson	Spencer
1978	Munson	Chambliss	Randolph	Nettles	Dent	Piniella	Rivers	Jackson	Johnson
1977	Munson	Chambliss	Randolph	Nettles	Dent	White	Rivers	Jackson	May
1976	Munson	Chambliss	Randolph	Nettles	Stanley	White	Rivers	Gamble	May
1975	Munson	Chambliss	Alomar	Nettles	Mason	White	Maddox	Bonds	Herrmann
1974	Munson	Chambliss	Alomar	Nettles	Mason	Piniella	Maddox	Murcer	Blomberg
1973	Munson	Alou	Clarke	Nettles	Michael	White	Murcer	Alou	Hart
1972	Munson	Blomberg	Clarke	Sanchez	Michael	White	Murcer	Callison	
1971	Munson	Cater	Clarke	Kenney	Michael	White	Murcer	Blomberg	
1970	Munson	Cater	Clarke	Kenney	Michael	White	Murcer	Blefary	
1969	Gibbs	Pepitone	Clarke	Kenney	Michael	White	Woods	Murcer	
1968	Gibbs	Mantle	Clarke	Cox	Tresh	White	Pepitone	Kosco	
1967	Gibbs	Mantle	Clarke	Smith	Amaro	Tresh	Pepitone	Whitaker	
1966	Howard	Pepitone	Richardson	Boyer	Clarke	White	Mantle	Maris	
1965	Howard	Pepitone	Richardson	Boyer	Kubek	Mantle	Tresh	Lopez	
1964	Howard	Pepitone	Richardson	Boyer	Kubek	Tresh	Mantle	Maris	
1963	Howard	Pepitone	Richardson	Boyer	Kubek	Lopez	Tresh	Maris	
1962	Howard	Skowron	Richardson	Boyer	Tresh	Lopez	Mantle	Maris	
1961	Howard	Skowron	Richardson	Boyer	Kubek	Berra	Mantle	Maris	
1960	Howard	Skowron	Richardson	Boyer	Kubek	Lopez	Mantle	Maris	
1959	Berra	Skowron	Richardson	Lopez	Kubek	Siebern	Mantle	Bauer	
1958	Berra	Skowron	McDougald	Carey	Kubek	Siebern	Mantle	Bauer	
1957	Berra	Skowron	Richardson	Carey	McDougald	Howard	Mantle	Bauer	
1956	Berra	Skowron	Martin	Carey	McDougald	Howard	Mantle	Bauer	
1955	Berra	Skowron	McDougald	Carey	Hunter	Noren	Mantle	Bauer	
1954	Berra	Collins	McDougald	Carey	Rizzuto	Woodling	Mantle	Bauer	

PRIMARY STARTING LINEUPS (CONT.)

Year	C	1B	2B	3B	SS	LF	CF	RF	DH
1953	Berra	Collins	Martin	McDougald	Rizzuto	Woodling	Mantle	Bauer	
1952	Berra	Collins	Martin	McDougald	Rizzuto	Woodling	Mantle	Bauer	
1951	Berra	Collins	Coleman	Brown	Rizzuto	Woodling	DiMaggio	Mantle	
1950	Berra	Collins	Coleman	Johnson	Rizzuto	Woodling	DiMaggio	Bauer	
1949	Berra	Kryhoski	Coleman	Brown	Rizzuto	Woodling	DiMaggio	Henrich	
1948	Niarhos	McQuinn	Stirnweiss	Johnson	Rizzuto	Lindell	DiMaggio	Henrich	
1947	Robinson	McQuinn	Stirnweiss	Johnson	Rizzuto	Lindell	DiMaggio	Henrich	
1946	Robinson	Etten	Gordon	Stirnweiss	Rizzuto	Keller	DiMaggio	Henrich	
1945	Garbark	Etten	Stirnweiss	Grimes	Crosetti	Martin	Stainback	Metheny	
1944	Garbark	Etten	Stirnweiss	Grimes	Milosevich	Martin	Lindell	Metheny	
1943	Dickey	Etten	Gordon	Johnson	Crosetti	Keller	Weatherly	Metheny	
1942	Dickey	Hassett	Gordon	Crosetti	Rizzuto	Keller	DiMaggio	Henrich	
1941	Dickey	Sturm	Gordon	Rolfe	Rizzuto	Keller	DiMaggio	Henrich	
1940	Dickey	Dahlgren	Gordon	Rolfe	Crosetti	Selkirk	DiMaggio	Keller	
1939	Dickey	Dahlgren	Gordon	Rolfe	Crosetti	Selkirk	DiMaggio	Keller	
1938	Dickey	Gehrig	Gordon	Rolfe	Crosetti	Selkirk	DiMaggio	Henrich	
1937	Dickey	Gehrig	Lazzeri	Rolfe	Crosetti	Powell	DiMaggio	Hoag	
1936	Dickey	Gehrig	Lazzeri	Rolfe	Crosetti	DiMaggio	Powell	Selkirk	
1935	Dickey	Gehrig	Lazzeri	Rolfe	Crosetti	Hill	Chapman	Selkirk	
1934	Dickey	Gehrig	Lazzeri	Saltzgaver	Crosetti	Selkirk	Chapman	Ruth	
1933	Dickey	Gehrig	Lazzeri	Sewell	Crosetti	Lary	Combs	Ruth	
1932	Dickey	Gehrig	Lazzeri	Sewell	Crosetti	Hoag	Combs	Ruth	
1931	Dickey	Gehrig	Lazzeri	Sewell	Lary	Chapman	Combs	Ruth	
1930	Dickey	Gehrig	Lazzeri	Chapman	Lary	Combs	Rice	Ruth	
1929	Dickey	Gehrig	Lazzeri	Robertson	Durocher	Meusel	Combs	Ruth	
1928	Grabowski	Gehrig	Lazzeri	Dugan	Koenig	Meusel	Combs	Ruth	
1927	Collins	Gehrig	Lazzeri	Dugan	Koenig	Meusel	Combs	Ruth	
1926	Collins	Gehrig	Lazzeri	Dugan	Koenig	Ruth	Combs	Paschal	
1925	Bengough	Gehrig	Ward	Dugan	Wanninger	Meusel	Combs	Ruth	
1924	Schang	Pipp	Ward	Dugan	Scott	Meusel	Witt	Ruth	
1923	Schang	Pipp	Ward	Dugan	Scott	Meusel	Witt	Ruth	
1922	Schang	Pipp	Ward	Dugan	Scott	Ruth	Witt	Meusel	
1921	Schang	Pipp	Ward	Baker	Peckinpaugh	Ruth	Miller	Meusel	
1920	Ruel	Pipp	Pratt	Ward	Peckinpaugh	Lewis	Bodie	Ruth	
1919	Ruel	Pipp	Pratt	Baker	Peckinpaugh	Lewis	Bodie	Vick	
1918	Hannah	Pipp	Pratt	Baker	Peckinpaugh	Bodie	Miller	Gilhooley	
1917	Nunamaker	Pipp	Maisel	Baker	Peckinpaugh	High	Miller	Hendryx	
1916	Nunamaker	Pipp	Gedeon	Baker	Peckinpaugh	High	Magee	Gilhooley	
1915	Nunamaker	Pipp	Boone	Maisel	Peckinpaugh	Hartzell	High	Cook	
1914	Sweeney	Mullen	Boone	Maisel	Peckinpaugh	Hartzell	Cree	Cook	
1913	Sweeney	Knight	Hartzell	Midkiff	Peckinpaugh	Cree	Wolter	Daniels	
1912	Sweeney	Chase	Simmons	Hartzell	Martin	Daniels	Lelivelt	Zinn	
1911	Blair	Chase	Gardner	Hartzell	Knight	Cree	Daniels	Wolter	
1910	Sweeney	Chase	LaPorte	Austin	Knight	Daniels	Cree	Wolter	
1909	Kleinow	Chase	LaPorte	Austin	Knight	Engle	Demmitt	Keeler	
1908	Kleinow	Chase	Niles	Conroy	Ball	Stahl	Hemphill	Keeler	
1907	Kleinow	Chase	Williams	Moriarty	Elberfeld	Conroy	Hoffman	Keeler	
1906	Kleinow	Chase	Williams	LaPorte	Elberfeld	Delahanty	Hoffman	Keeler	
1905	Kleinow	Chase	Williams	Yeager	Elberfeld	Dougherty	Fultz	Keeler	
1904	McGuire	Ganzel	Williams	Conroy	Elberfeld	Dougherty	Fultz	Keeler	
1903	Beville	Ganzel	Williams	Conroy	Elberfeld	Davis	Fultz	Keeler	

PRIMARY STARTING LINEUPS (CONT.)

Year	C	1B	2B	3B	SS	LF	CF	RF	DH
1902	Robinson	McGann	Williams	Bresnahan	Gilbert	Selbach	McFarland	Seymour	
1901	Bresnahan	Hart	Williams	McGraw	Keister	Donlin	Brodie	Seymour	

Top 10 Batting Leaders, Single Season & Career with Team

GAMES PLAYED: CAREER WITH TEAM

Player	G	PA
1. Mickey Mantle	2401	9,909
2. Lou Gehrig	2164	9,660
3. Yogi Berra	2116	8,355
4. Babe Ruth	2084	9,198
5. Bernie Williams	1945	8,591
6. Roy White	1881	7,735
7. Bill Dickey	1789	7,060
8. Don Mattingly	1785	7,721
9. Joe DiMaggio	1736	7,671
10. Willie Randolph	1694	7,465

AT-BATS: SEASON

Player	AB	Year
1. Alfonso Soriano	696	2002
2. Bobby Richardson	692	1962
3. Horace Clarke	686	1970
4. Alfonso Soriano	682	2003
5. Bobby Richardson	679	1964
6. Don Mattingly	677	1986
7. Bobby Richardson	664	1965
8. Bobby Richardson	662	1961
9. Frankie Crosetti	656	1939
10. Derek Jeter	654	1997
Derek Jeter	654	2005

AT-BATS: CAREER WITH TEAM

Player	AB	PA
1. Mickey Mantle	8,102	9,909
2. Lou Gehrig	8,001	9,660
3. Yogi Berra	7,546	8,355
4. Bernie Williams	7,449	8,591
5. Babe Ruth	7,217	9,198
6. Don Mattingly	7,003	7,721
7. Joe DiMaggio	6,821	7,671
8. Roy White	6,650	7,735
9. Willie Randolph	6,303	7,465
10. Bill Dickey	6,300	7,060

BATTING AVERAGE: SEASON

Player	BA	Year
1. Babe Ruth	.393	1923
2. Joe DiMaggio	.381	1939
3. Lou Gehrig	.379	1930
4. Babe Ruth	.378	1924
Babe Ruth	.378	1921
6. Babe Ruth	.376	1920
7. Lou Gehrig	.374	1928
8. Lou Gehrig	.373	1927
Babe Ruth	.373	1931
10. Babe Ruth	.372	1926

BATTING AVERAGE: CAREER WITH TEAM

Player	BA	PA
1. Babe Ruth	.349	9,198
2. Lou Gehrig	.340	9,660
3. Earle Combs	.325	6,507
Joe DiMaggio	.325	7,671
5. Derek Jeter	.314	6,996
6. Wade Boggs	.313	2,600
Bill Dickey	.313	7,060
8. Bob Meusel	.311	5,544
9. Don Mattingly	.307	7,721
10. Ben Chapman	.305	4,014

TOTAL HITS: SEASON

Player	H	Year
1. Don Mattingly	238	1986
2. Earle Combs	231	1927
3. Lou Gehrig	220	1930
4. Derek Jeter	219	1999
5. Lou Gehrig	218	1927
6. Joe DiMaggio	215	1937
7. Red Rolfe	213	1939
8. Lou Gehrig	211	1931
Don Mattingly	211	1985
10. Lou Gehrig	210	1928
Lou Gehrig	210	1934

TOTAL HITS: CAREER WITH TEAM

Player	H	PA
1. Lou Gehrig	2721	9,660
2. Babe Ruth	2518	9,198
3. Mickey Mantle	2415	9,909
4. Bernie Williams	2218	8,591
5. Joe DiMaggio	2214	7,671
6. Don Mattingly	2153	7,721
7. Yogi Berra	2148	8,355
8. Bill Dickey	1969	7,060
9. Derek Jeter	1936	6,996
10. Earle Combs	1866	6,507

HOME RUNS: SEASON

Player	HR	Year
1. Roger Maris	61	1961
2. Babe Ruth	60	1927
3. Babe Ruth	59	1921
4. Mickey Mantle	54	1961
Babe Ruth	54	1920
Babe Ruth	54	1928
7. Mickey Mantle	52	1956
8. Lou Gehrig	49	1934
Lou Gehrig	49	1936
Babe Ruth	49	1930

HOME RUNS: CAREER WITH TEAM

Player	HR	PA
1. Babe Ruth	659	9,198
2. Mickey Mantle	536	9,909
3. Lou Gehrig	493	9,660
4. Joe DiMaggio	361	7,671
5. Yogi Berra	358	8,355

6. Bernie Williams	275	8,591
7. Graig Nettles	250	6,247
8. Don Mattingly	222	7,721
9. Dave Winfield	205	5,021
10. Roger Maris	203	3,475

TRIPLES: SEASON

Player	3B	Year
1. Earle Combs	23	1927
2. Earle Combs	22	1930
Birdie Cree	22	1911
Snuffy Stirnweiss	22	1945
5. Earle Combs	21	1928
Bill Keister	21	1901
Jimmy Williams	21	1901
Jimmy Williams	21	1902
9. Lou Gehrig	20	1926
10. Wally Pipp	19	1924

TRIPLES: CAREER WITH TEAM

Player	3B	PA
1. Lou Gehrig	163	9,660
2. Earle Combs	154	6,507
3. Joe DiMaggio	131	7,671
4. Wally Pipp	121	6,341
5. Tony Lazzeri	115	7,058
6. Babe Ruth	106	9,198
7. Bob Meusel	87	5,544
Jimmy Williams	87	3,934
9. Tommy Henrich	73	5,409
10. Bill Dickey	72	7,060
Mickey Mantle	72	9,909

DOUBLES: SEASON

Player	2B	Year
1. Don Mattingly	53	1986
2. Lou Gehrig	52	1927
3. Alfonso Soriano	51	2002
4. Don Mattingly	48	1985
5. Lou Gehrig	47	1926
Lou Gehrig	47	1928
Bob Meusel	47	1927
8. Red Rolfe	46	1939
9. Bob Meusel	45	1928
Babe Ruth	45	1923
Hideki Matsui	45	2005

DOUBLES: CAREER WITH TEAM

Player	2B	PA
1. Lou Gehrig	534	9,660
2. Don Mattingly	442	7,721
3. Babe Ruth	424	9,198
4. Bernie Williams	420	8,591
5. Joe DiMaggio	389	7,671
6. Mickey Mantle	344	9,909
7. Bill Dickey	343	7,060
8. Bob Meusel	338	5,544
9. Tony Lazzeri	327	7,058
10. Yogi Berra	321	8,355

EXTRA-BASE HITS: SEASON

Player	XBH	Year
1. Babe Ruth	119	1921
2. Lou Gehrig	117	1927
3. Lou Gehrig	100	1930
4. Babe Ruth	99	1920
Babe Ruth	99	1923
6. Babe Ruth	97	1927
7. Joe DiMaggio	96	1937
8. Lou Gehrig	95	1934
9. Lou Gehrig	93	1936
10. Lou Gehrig	92	1931
Babe Ruth	92	1924
Alfonso Soriano	92	2002

EXTRA-BASE HITS: CAREER WITH TEAM

Player	XBH	PA
1. Lou Gehrig	1,190	9,660
2. Babe Ruth	1,189	9,198
3. Mickey Mantle	952	9,909
4. Joe DiMaggio	881	7,671
5. Bernie Williams	750	8,591
6. Yogi Berra	728	8,355
7. Don Mattingly	684	7,721
8. Bill Dickey	617	7,060
9. Tony Lazzeri	611	7,058
10. Bob Meusel	571	5,544

TOTAL BASES: SEASON

Player	TB	Year
1. Babe Ruth	457	1921
2. Lou Gehrig	447	1927
3. Lou Gehrig	419	1930
4. Joe DiMaggio	418	1937
5. Babe Ruth	417	1927
6. Lou Gehrig	410	1931
7. Lou Gehrig	409	1934
8. Lou Gehrig	403	1936
9. Babe Ruth	399	1923
10. Babe Ruth	391	1924

TOTAL BASES: CAREER WITH TEAM

Player	TB	PA
1. Babe Ruth	5,131	9,198
2. Lou Gehrig	5,060	9,660
3. Mickey Mantle	4,511	9,909
4. Joe DiMaggio	3,948	7,671
5. Yogi Berra	3,641	8,355
6. Bernie Williams	3,573	8,591
7. Don Mattingly	3,301	7,721
8. Bill Dickey	3,062	7,060
9. Tony Lazzeri	2,848	7,058
10. Derek Jeter	2,845	6,996

RUNS BATTED IN: SEASON

Player	RBI	Year
1. Lou Gehrig	184	1931
2. Lou Gehrig	175	1927
3. Lou Gehrig	174	1930
4. Babe Ruth	171	1921
5. Joe DiMaggio	167	1937
6. Lou Gehrig	165	1934
7. Babe Ruth	164	1927
8. Babe Ruth	163	1931
9. Lou Gehrig	159	1937
10. Joe DiMaggio	155	1948

RUNS BATTED IN: CAREER WITH TEAM

Player	RBI	PA
1. Lou Gehrig	1,995	9,660
2. Babe Ruth	1,971	9,198
3. Joe DiMaggio	1,537	7,671
4. Mickey Mantle	1,509	9,909
5. Yogi Berra	1,430	8,355
6. Bill Dickey	1,209	7,060
7. Bernie Williams	1,196	8,591
8. Tony Lazzeri	1,154	7,058
9. Don Mattingly	1,099	7,721
10. Bob Meusel	1,005	5,544

RUNS SCORED: SEASON

Player	R	Year
1. Babe Ruth	177	1921
2. Lou Gehrig	167	1936
3. Lou Gehrig	163	1931
Babe Ruth	163	1928
5. Babe Ruth	158	1920
Babe Ruth	158	1927
7. Joe DiMaggio	151	1937

Babe Ruth	151	1923
9. Babe Ruth	150	1930
10. Lou Gehrig	149	1927
Babe Ruth	149	1931

Runs Scored: Career with Team

Player	R	PA
1. Babe Ruth	1,959	9,198
2. Lou Gehrig	1,888	9,660
3. Mickey Mantle	1,677	9,909
4. Joe DiMaggio	1,390	7,671
5. Bernie Williams	1,301	8,591
6. Earle Combs	1,186	6,507
7. Yogi Berra	1,174	8,355
8. Derek Jeter	1,159	6,996
9. Willie Randolph	1,027	7,465
10. Don Mattingly	1,007	7,721

Walks: Season

Player	BB	Year
1. Babe Ruth	170	1923
2. Babe Ruth	150	1920
3. Mickey Mantle	146	1957
4. Babe Ruth	145	1921
5. Babe Ruth	144	1926
6. Babe Ruth	142	1924
7. Babe Ruth	137	1927
Babe Ruth	137	1928
9. Babe Ruth	136	1930
10. Lou Gehrig	132	1935

Walks: Career with Team

Player	BB	PA
1. Babe Ruth	1,852	9,198
2. Mickey Mantle	1,733	9,909
3. Lou Gehrig	1,508	9,660
4. Bernie Williams	1,036	8,591
5. Willie Randolph	1,005	7,465
6. Roy White	934	7,735
7. Tony Lazzeri	830	7,058
8. Frankie Crosetti	792	7,273
9. Joe DiMaggio	790	7,671
10. Charlie Keller	760	4,466

Strikeouts: Season

Player	SO	Year
1. Alfonso Soriano	157	2002
2. Danny Tartabull	156	1993
3. Jorge Posada	151	2000
4. Jesse Barfield	150	1990
5. Roberto Kelly	148	1990
6. Jorge Posada	143	2002
7. Jack Clark	141	1988
8. Jason Giambi	140	2003
9. Alex Rodriguez	139	2005
10. Bobby Bonds	137	1975

Strikeouts: Career with Team

Player	SO	PA
1. Mickey Mantle	1,710	9,909
2. Bernie Williams	1,159	8,591
3. Babe Ruth	1,122	9,198
4. Derek Jeter	1,089	6,996
5. Jorge Posada	850	3,999
6. Tony Lazzeri	821	7,058
7. Frankie Crosetti	799	7,273
8. Lou Gehrig	790	9,660
9. Graig Nettles	739	6,247
10. Elston Howard	717	5,485

Slugging Percentage: Season

Player	SLG	Year
1. Babe Ruth	.847	1920
2. Babe Ruth	.846	1921
3. Babe Ruth	.772	1927
4. Lou Gehrig	.765	1927
5. Babe Ruth	.764	1923
6. Babe Ruth	.739	1924
7. Babe Ruth	.737	1926
8. Babe Ruth	.732	1930
9. Lou Gehrig	.721	1930
10. Babe Ruth	.709	1928

Slugging Percentage: Career with Team

Player	SLG	PA
1. Babe Ruth	.711	9,198
2. Lou Gehrig	.632	9,660
3. Joe DiMaggio	.579	7,671
4. Mickey Mantle	.557	9,909
5. Jason Giambi	.529	2,246
6. Reggie Jackson	.526	2,707
7. Charlie Keller	.518	4,466
8. Roger Maris	.515	3,475
9. Alfonso Soriano	.502	2,150
10. Bob Meusel	.500	5,544

On-Base Percentage: Season

Player	OBP	Year
1. Babe Ruth	.545	1923
2. Babe Ruth	.532	1920
3. Babe Ruth	.516	1926
4. Babe Ruth	.513	1924
5. Babe Ruth	.512	1921
Mickey Mantle	.512	1957
7. Babe Ruth	.495	1931
8. Babe Ruth	.493	1930
9. Babe Ruth	.489	1932
10. Mickey Mantle	.486	1962

On-Base Percentage: Career with Team

Player	OBP	PA
1. Babe Ruth	.484	9,198
2. Lou Gehrig	.447	9,660
3. Mickey Mantle	.421	9,909
4. Jason Giambi	.416	2,246
5. Charlie Keller	.410	4,466
6. George Selkirk	.400	3,322
7. Joe DiMaggio	.398	7,671
8. Earle Combs	.397	6,507
9. Wade Boggs	.396	2,600
10. Rickey Henderson	.395	2,735

OPS (On-Base Percentage + Slugging Percentage): Season

Player	OPS	Year
1. Babe Ruth	1.379	1920
2. Babe Ruth	1.359	1921
3. Babe Ruth	1.309	1923
4. Babe Ruth	1.258	1927
5. Babe Ruth	1.253	1926
6. Babe Ruth	1.252	1924
7. Lou Gehrig	1.240	1927
8. Babe Ruth	1.225	1930
9. Babe Ruth	1.195	1931
10. Lou Gehrig	1.194	1930

OPS (On-Base Percentage + Slugging Percentage): Career with Team

Player	OPS	PA
1. Babe Ruth	1.195	9,198
2. Lou Gehrig	1.080	9,660
3. Mickey Mantle	.977	9,909
Joe DiMaggio	.977	7,671
5. Jason Giambi	.945	2,246
6. Charlie Keller	.928	4,466

7. Reggie Jackson	.897	2,707
8. George Selkirk	.883	3,322
9. Bernie Williams	.875	8,045
10. Tommy Henrich	.873	5,409

Stolen Bases: Season

Player	SB	Year
1. Rickey Henderson	93	1988
2. Rickey Henderson	87	1986
3. Rickey Henderson	80	1985
4. Fritz Maisel	74	1914
5. Ben Chapman	61	1931
6. Snuffy Stirnweiss	55	1944
7. Fritz Maisel	51	1915
8. Birdie Cree	48	1911
9. Dave Fultz	44	1905
10. Mickey Rivers	43	1976
Steve Sax	43	1989
Steve Sax	43	1990
Alfonso Soriano	43	2001

Stolen Bases: Career with Team

Player	SB	PA
1. Rickey Henderson	326	2,735
2. Willie Randolph	251	7,465
3. Hal Chase	248	4,466
4. Roy White	233	7,735
5. Derek Jeter	215	6,996
6. Ben Chapman	184	4,014
Wid Conroy	184	3,300
8. Fritz Maisel	183	2,095
9. Mickey Mantle	153	9,909
10. Horace Clarke	151	5,143
Roberto Kelly	151	2,527

Sacrifice Hits: Season

Player	Sac	Year
1. Willie Keeler	42	1905
2. Willie Keeler	35	1906
3. Willie Keeler	33	1909
Roger Peckinpaugh	33	1915
Roger Peckinpaugh	33	1921
Wally Pipp	33	1921
7. Aaron Ward	32	1922
8. Jimmy Austin	30	1909
Wally Pipp	30	1919
10. Aaron Ward	29	1921

Sacrifice Hits: Career with Team

Player	Sac	PA
1. Wally Pipp	226	6,341
2. Willie Keeler	211	3,792
3. Phil Rizzuto	193	6,711
4. Roger Peckinpaugh	190	5,269
5. Hal Chase	145	4,466
6. Bob Meusel	143	5,544
7. Aaron Ward	128	3,565
8. Tony Lazzeri	115	7,058
9. Joe Dugan	107	3,328
10. Lou Gehrig	106	9,660

Hit by Pitch: Season

Player	HBP	Year
1. Don Baylor	24	1985
2. Don Baylor	23	1984
3. Jason Giambi	21	2003
Chuck Knoblauch	21	1999
5. Jason Giambi	19	2005
6. Bert Daniels	18	1911
Bert Daniels	18	1912
Bert Daniels	18	1913
Chuck Knoblauch	18	1998
10. Bert Daniels	16	1910
Kid Elberfeld	16	1905
Alex Rodriguez	16	2005

Hit by Pitch: Career with Team

Player	HBP	PA
1. Frankie Crosetti	114	7,273
2. Derek Jeter	103	6,996
3. Kid Elberfeld	81	2,743
4. Bert Daniels	70	1,938
5. Jason Giambi	63	2,246
6. Chuck Knoblauch	61	2,478
7. Don Baylor	60	1,719
8. Yogi Berra	52	8,355
9. Phil Rizzuto	49	6,711
10. Willie Keeler	48	3,792

Top 10 Pitching Leaders, Single Season & Career with Team

Games Pitched: Season

Player	GP	Year
1. Paul Quantrill	86	2004
2. Tom Gordon	80	2004
3. Mike Stanton	79	2002
Tom Gordon	79	2005
5. Steve Karsay	78	2002
6. Jeff Nelson	77	1997
7. Mike Stanton	76	2001
8. Dave Righetti	74	1985
Dave Righetti	74	1986
Mariano Rivera	74	2004

Games Pitched: Career with Team

Player	GP	IP
1. Mariano Rivera	657	806.7
2. Dave Righetti	522	1,136.7
3. Whitey Ford	498	3,170.3
4. Mike Stanton	428	434.3
5. Red Ruffing	426	3,168.7
6. Sparky Lyle	420	745.7
7. Bob Shawkey	415	2,488.7
8. Johnny Murphy	383	990.3
9. Ron Guidry	368	2,392.0
10. Lefty Gomez	367	2,498.3

Innings Pitched: Season

Player	IP	Year
1. Jack Chesbro	454.7	1904
2. Jack Powell	390.3	1904
3. Joe McGinnity	382.0	1901
4. Al Orth	338.7	1906
5. Carl Mays	336.7	1921
6. Catfish Hunter	328.0	1975
7. Jack Chesbro	325.0	1906
8. Jack Chesbro	324.7	1903
9. Carl Mays	312.0	1920
10. Al Orth	305.3	1905

Innings Pitched: Career with Team

Player	IP
1. Whitey Ford	3,170.3
2. Red Ruffing	3,168.7
3. Mel Stottlemyre	2,661.3
4. Lefty Gomez	2,498.3
5. Bob Shawkey	2,488.7
6. Ron Guidry	2,392.0
7. Waite Hoyt	2,272.3
8. Herb Pennock	2,203.3
9. Jack Chesbro	1,952.0
10. Fritz Peterson	1,857.3

Batters Faced: Season

Player	BF	Year
1. Jack Chesbro	1,778	1904
2. Joe McGinnity	1,685	1901
3. Jack Powell	1,572	1904
4. Al Orth	1,412	1906
5. Carl Mays	1,400	1921
6. Jack Chesbro	1,363	1906
7. Jack Chesbro	1,354	1903
8. George Pipgras	1,352	1928
9. Harry Howell	1,302	1901
10. Carl Mays	1,301	1920

Batters Faced: Career with Team

Player	BF	IP
1. Red Ruffing	13,353	3,168.7
2. Whitey Ford	13,036	3,170.3
3. Mel Stottlemyre	10,972	2,661.3
4. Lefty Gomez	10,706	2,498.3
5. Bob Shawkey	10,241	2,488.7
6. Ron Guidry	9,794	2,392.0
7. Waite Hoyt	9,719	2,272.3
8. Herb Pennock	9,402	2,203.3
9. Jack Chesbro	8,026	1,952.0
10. Andy Pettitte	7,670	1,792.7

Games Started: Season

Player	GS	Year
1. Jack Chesbro	51	1904
2. Jack Powell	45	1904
3. Joe McGinnity	43	1901
4. Jack Chesbro	42	1906
5. Pat Dobson	39	1974
Whitey Ford	39	1961
Catfish Hunter	39	1975
Al Orth	39	1906
Mel Stottlemyre	39	1969
Ralph Terry	39	1962

Games Started: Career with Team

Player	GS	IP
1. Whitey Ford	438	3,170.3
2. Red Ruffing	391	3,168.7
3. Mel Stottlemyre	356	2,661.3
4. Ron Guidry	323	2,392.0
5. Lefty Gomez	319	2,498.3
6. Waite Hoyt	276	2,272.3
Andy Pettitte	276	1,792.7
8. Bob Shawkey	275	2,488.7
9. Herb Pennock	268	2,203.3
10. Fritz Peterson	265	1,857.3

Complete Games: Season

Player	CG	Year
1. Jack Chesbro	48	1904
2. Joe McGinnity	39	1901
3. Jack Powell	38	1904
4. Al Orth	36	1906
5. Jack Chesbro	33	1903
6. Harry Howell	32	1901
7. Ray Caldwell	31	1915
8. Russ Ford	30	1912
Catfish Hunter	30	1975
Carl Mays	30	1921

Complete Games: Career with Team

Player	CG	IP
1. Red Ruffing	261	3,168.7
2. Lefty Gomez	173	2,498.3
3. Jack Chesbro	168	1,952.0
4. Herb Pennock	164	2,203.3
Bob Shawkey	164	2,488.7
6. Whitey Ford	156	3,170.3
Waite Hoyt	156	2,272.3
8. Mel Stottlemyre	152	2,661.3
9. Ray Caldwell	150	1,718.3
10. Spud Chandler	109	1,485.0

Games Won: Season

Player	W	Year
1. Jack Chesbro	41	1904
2. Carl Mays	27	1921
Al Orth	27	1906
4. Joe Bush	26	1922
Russ Ford	26	1910
Lefty Gomez	26	1934
Carl Mays	26	1920
Joe McGinnity	26	1901
9. Whitey Ford	25	1961
Ron Guidry	25	1978

Games Won: Career with Team

Player	W	IP
1. Whitey Ford	236	3,170.3
2. Red Ruffing	231	3,168.7
3. Lefty Gomez	189	2,498.3
4. Ron Guidry	170	2,392.0
5. Bob Shawkey	168	2,488.7
6. Mel Stottlemyre	164	2,661.3
7. Herb Pennock	162	2,203.3
8. Waite Hoyt	157	2,272.3
9. Andy Pettitte	149	1,792.7
10. Allie Reynolds	131	1,700.0

Games Lost: Season

Player	L	Year
1. Joe Lake	22	1908
2. Russ Ford	21	1912
Harry Howell	21	1901
Sam Jones	21	1925
Al Orth	21	1907
6. Jack Chesbro	20	1908
Joe McGinnity	20	1901
Mel Stottlemyre	20	1966
9. Tim Leary	19	1990
Jack Powell	19	1904
Jack Warhop	19	1912

Games Lost: Career with Team

Player	L	IP
1. Mel Stottlemyre	139	2,661.3
2. Bob Shawkey	131	2,488.7
3. Red Ruffing	124	3,168.7
4. Whitey Ford	106	3,170.3
Fritz Peterson	106	1,857.3
6. Lefty Gomez	101	2,498.3
7. Ray Caldwell	99	1,718.3
8. Waite Hoyt	98	2,272.3
9. Jack Chesbro	93	1,952.0
Jack Warhop	93	1,412.7

Winning Percentage: Season

Player	W%	Year
1. Ron Guidry	.893	1978
2. Ron Davis	.875	1979
3. Roger Clemens	.870	2001
4. Whitey Ford	.862	1961
5. Ralph Terry	.842	1961
6. Lefty Gomez	.839	1934
7. Spud Chandler	.833	1943
8. David Wells	.818	1998
9. Jim Coates	.812	1960
Atley Donald	.812	1939
Russ Ford	.812	1910

Winning Percentage: Career with Team

Player	W%	IP
1. Spud Chandler	.717	1,485.0
2. David Wells	.708	851.7
3. Vic Raschi	.706	1,537.0
4. Monte Pearson	.700	825.7
5. Whitey Ford	.690	3,170.3
6. Allie Reynolds	.686	1,700.0
7. Roger Clemens	.681	1,004.0
8. Carl Mays	.669	1,090.0
9. Atley Donald	.663	932.3
10. Ed Lopat	.657	1,497.3

Shutouts: Season

Player	SHO	Year
1. Ron Guidry	9	1978
2. Russ Ford	8	1910
Whitey Ford	8	1964
4. Whitey Ford	7	1958
Catfish Hunter	7	1975
Allie Reynolds	7	1951
Mel Stottlemyre	7	1971
Mel Stottlemyre	7	1972
9. 12 tied with . . .	6	——

Shutouts: Career with Team

Player	SHO	IP
1. Whitey Ford	45	3,170.3
2. Red Ruffing	40	3,168.7
Mel Stottlemyre	40	2,661.3
4. Lefty Gomez	28	2,498.3
5. Allie Reynolds	27	1,700.0
6. Spud Chandler	26	1,485.0
Ron Guidry	26	2,392.0
Bob Shawkey	26	2,488.7
9. Vic Raschi	24	1,537.0
10. Bob Turley	21	1,269.0

ERA: Season

Player	ERA	Year
1. Spud Chandler	1.64	1943
2. Russ Ford	1.65	1910
3. Ron Guidry	1.74	1978
4. Jack Chesbro	1.82	1904
5. Hippo Vaughn	1.83	1910
6. Joe Lake	1.88	1909
7. Ray Caldwell	1.94	1914
8. Whitey Ford	2.01	1958
9. Nick Cullop	2.05	1916
Stan Bahnsen	2.05	1968

ERA: Career with Team

Player	ERA	IP
1. Rich Gossage	2.14	533.0
2. Mariano Rivera	2.33	806.7
3. Sparky Lyle	2.41	745.7
4. Russ Ford	2.54	1,112.7
5. Jack Chesbro	2.58	1,952.0
6. Al Orth	2.72	1,172.7
7. Tiny Bonham	2.73	1,176.7
George Mogridge	2.73	965.7
9. Hank Borowy	2.74	780.7
10. Whitey Ford	2.75	3,170.3

Earned Runs Allowed: Season

Player	ER	Year
1. Joe McGinnity	151	1901
2. Sam Jones	127	1925
3. Lefty Gomez	124	1932
4. Harry Howell	120	1901
5. David Cone	119	2000
6. Catfish Hunter	117	1976
7. Red Ruffing	116	1931
Red Ruffing	116	1936
9. Russ Ford	115	1912
10. Carl Mays	114	1921
Vic Raschi	114	1950

Earned Runs Allowed: Career with Team

Player	ER	IP
1. Red Ruffing	1,222	3,168.7
2. Whitey Ford	967	3,170.3
3. Lefty Gomez	927	2,498.3
4. Waite Hoyt	879	2,272.3
5. Mel Stottlemyre	878	2,661.3
6. Ron Guidry	874	2,392.0
7. Herb Pennock	867	2,203.3
8. Bob Shawkey	862	2,488.7
9. Andy Pettitte	785	1,792.7
10. Fritz Peterson	640	1,857.3

Strikeouts: Season

Player	K	Year
1. Ron Guidry	248	1978
2. Jack Chesbro	239	1904
3. David Cone	222	1997
4. Melido Perez	218	1992
5. Al Downing	217	1964
6. Mike Mussina	214	2001
7. Roger Clemens	213	2001
8. Randy Johnson	211	2005
9. Bob Turley	210	1955
10. David Cone	209	1998
Russ Ford	209	1910
Whitey Ford	209	1961

Strikeouts: Career with Team

Player	K	IP
1. Whitey Ford	1,956	3,170.3
2. Ron Guidry	1,778	2,392.0
3. Red Ruffing	1,526	3,168.7
4. Lefty Gomez	1,468	2,498.3
5. Andy Pettitte	1,275	1,792.7
6. Mel Stottlemyre	1,257	2,661.3
7. Bob Shawkey	1,163	2,488.7
8. Al Downing	1,028	1,235.3
9. Allie Reynolds	967	1,700.0
10. Roger Clemens	946	1,004.0

Strikeouts per Nine IP: Season

Player	K/9	Year
1. David Cone	10.25	1997
2. Roger Clemens	9.60	2002
3. David Cone	9.06	1998
4. Al Downing	8.76	1963
5. Roger Clemens	8.70	2001
6. Mike Mussina	8.42	2001
Randy Johnson	8.42	2005
8. Roger Clemens	8.28	2000
9. David Cone	8.24	1999
10. Mike Mussina	8.18	2003

Strikeouts Per Nine IP: Career with Team

Player	K/9	IP
1. David Cone	8.67	922.0
2. Rich Gossage	8.65	533.0
3. Roger Clemens	8.48	1,004.0
4. Mariano Rivera	8.12	806.7
5. Mike Mussina	7.76	1,003.3
6. Al Downing	7.49	1,235.3
7. Dave Righetti	7.44	1,136.7
8. Melido Perez	7.40	631.3
9. Orlando Hernandez	7.22	876.3
10. Ron Guidry	6.69	2,392.0

Hits Allowed: Season

Player	HA	Year
1. Joe McGinnity	412	1901
2. Jack Powell	340	1904
3. Jack Chesbro	338	1904
4. Harry Howell	333	1901
5. Carl Mays	332	1921
6. Russ Ford	317	1912
Al Orth	317	1906
8. Jack Chesbro	314	1906
George Pipgras	314	1928
10. Carl Mays	310	1920

Hits Allowed: Career with Team

Player	HA	IP
1. Red Ruffing	2,995	3,168.7
2. Whitey Ford	2,766	3,170.3
3. Herb Pennock	2,471	2,203.3
4. Mel Stottlemyre	2,435	2,661.3
5. Waite Hoyt	2,405	2,272.3
6. Bob Shawkey	2,304	2,488.7
7. Lefty Gomez	2,286	2,498.3
8. Ron Guidry	2,198	2,392.0
9. Andy Pettitte	1,901	1,792.7
10. Fritz Peterson	1,796	1,857.3

Hits Allowed Per Nine IP: Season

Player	H/9	Year
1. Tommy Byrne	5.74	1949
2. Russ Ford	5.83	1910
3. Al Downing	5.84	1963
4. Bob Turley	6.12	1957
5. Bob Turley	6.13	1955
6. Ron Guidry	6.15	1978
7. Spec Shea	6.40	1947
8. Ray Caldwell	6.46	1914
9. Bob Turley	6.53	1958
10. Bob Shawkey	6.64	1916

Hits Allowed Per Nine IP: Career with Team

Player	H/9	IP
1. Rich Gossage	6.59	533.0
2. Mariano Rivera	7.03	806.7
3. Tommy Byrne	7.24	993.7
4. Bob Turley	7.27	1,269.0
5. Al Downing	7.39	1,235.3
6. Don Larsen	7.54	655.3
7. Rudy May	7.65	841.7
8. Tom Sturdivant	7.71	524.3
9. Whitey Ford	7.85	3,170.3
10. Hank Borowy	7.87	780.7

Walks Allowed: Season

Player	BB	Year
1. Tommy Byrne	179	1949
2. Bob Turley	177	1955
3. Tommy Byrne	160	1950
4. Vic Raschi	138	1949
Allie Reynolds	138	1950
6. Monte Pearson	135	1936
7. Bob Turley	128	1958
8. Allie Reynolds	123	1947
Allie Reynolds	123	1949
10. Lefty Gomez	122	1936

Walks Allowed: Career with Team

Player	BB	IP
1. Lefty Gomez	1,090	2,498.3
2. Whitey Ford	1,086	3,170.3
3. Red Ruffing	1,066	3,168.7
4. Bob Shawkey	855	2,488.7
5. Allie Reynolds	819	1,700.0
6. Mel Stottlemyre	809	2,661.3
7. Tommy Byrne	763	993.7
8. Bob Turley	761	1,269.0
9. Ron Guidry	633	2,392.0
10. Waite Hoyt	631	2,272.3

Walks Allowed Per Nine IP: Season

Player	BB/9	Year
1. David Wells	0.85	2003
2. Jon Lieber	0.92	2004
3. Tiny Bonham	0.96	1942
4. Tiny Bonham	1.10	1945
5. David Wells	1.22	1998
6. Fritz Peterson	1.23	1968
7. Scott Sanderson	1.25	1991
8. Jesse Tannehill	1.28	1903
9. Ralph Terry	1.31	1963
10. Fritz Peterson	1.38	1971

Walks Allowed Per Nine IP: Career with Team

Player	BB/9	IP
1. David Wells	1.47	851.7
2. Tiny Bonham	1.58	1,176.7
3. Fritz Peterson	1.61	1,857.3
4. Al Orth	1.77	1,172.7
5. Herb Pennock	1.92	2,203.3
6. Steve Kline	1.93	659.0
7. Mike Mussina	1.95	1,003.3
8. Ramiro Mendoza	1.98	698.7
9. Jack Chesbro	2.00	1,952.0
10. Ralph Terry	2.03	1,198.0

WHIP (Walks + Hits Per Nine IP): Season

Player	WHIP	Year
1. Russ Ford	0.881	1910
2. Jack Chesbro	0.937	1904
3. Ron Guidry	0.946	1978
4. Ray Caldwell	0.958	1914
5. Tiny Bonham	0.987	1942
6. Spud Chandler	0.992	1943
7. Fritz Peterson	0.996	1969
8. Catfish Hunter	1.009	1975
9. Fritz Peterson	1.017	1968
10. Art Ditmar	1.030	1959

WHIP (Walks + Hits Per Nine IP): Career with Team

Player	WHIP	IP
1. Mariano Rivera	1.048	806.7
2. Rich Gossage	1.079	533.0
3. Tiny Bonham	1.117	1,176.7

Jack Chesbro	1.117	1,952.0
5. Al Orth	1.131	1,172.7
6. Fritz Peterson	1.146	1,857.3
7. Steve Kline	1.150	659.0
8. Ralph Terry	1.151	1,198.0
9. Mike Mussina	1.153	823.7
10. Catfish Hunter	1.154	993.0

Home Runs Allowed: Season

Player	HRA	Year
1. Ralph Terry	40	1962
2. Orlando Hernandez	34	2000
3. Javier Vazquez	33	2004
4. Jim Bouton	32	1964
Randy Johnson	32	2005
6. Dennis Rasmussen	31	1987
7. Joe Cowley	29	1985
Catfish Hunter	29	1977
Phil Niekro	29	1985
Ralph Terry	29	1963
David Wells	29	1998

Home Runs Allowed: Career with Team

Player	HRA	IP
1. Whitey Ford	228	3,170.3
2. Ron Guidry	226	2,392.0
3. Red Ruffing	200	3,168.7
4. Mel Stottlemyre	171	2,661.3
5. Andy Pettitte	143	1,792.7
6. Fritz Peterson	139	1,857.3
7. Lefty Gomez	138	2,498.3
8. Ralph Terry	133	1,198.0
9. Bob Turley	118	1,269.0
10. Ed Lopat	116	1,497.3

Saves: Season

Player	SV	Year
1. Mariano Rivera	53	2004
2. Mariano Rivera	50	2001
3. Dave Righetti	46	1986
4. Mariano Rivera	45	1999
5. Mariano Rivera	43	1997
John Wetteland	43	1996
Mariano Rivera	43	2005
8. Mariano Rivera	40	2003
9. Dave Righetti	36	1990
Mariano Rivera	36	1998
Mariano Rivera	36	2000

Saves: Career with Team

Player	SV	IP
1. Mariano Rivera	379	806.7
2. Dave Righetti	224	1,136.7
3. Rich Gossage	151	533.0
4. Sparky Lyle	141	745.7
5. Johnny Murphy	104	990.3
6. Steve Farr	78	169.0
7. Joe Page	76	780.3
8. John Wetteland	74	125.0
9. Lindy McDaniel	58	544.7
10. Luis Arroyo	43	199.3
Ryne Duren	43	206.3

Wild Pitches: Season

Player	WP	Year
1. Tim Leary	23	1990
2. Jason Grimsley	16	2000
3. Greg Cadaret	14	1990
Roger Clemens	14	2001
Roger Clemens	14	2002
David Cone	14	1997
Al Downing	14	1964
Bill Hogg	14	1905
9. Melido Perez	13	1992
10. Joe Bush	12	1923
Jack Powell	12	1904
Javier Vazquez	12	2004

Wild Pitches: Career with Team

Player	WP	IP
1. Whitey Ford	75	3,170.3
2. Mel Stottlemyre	57	2,661.3
3. Ron Guidry	56	2,392.0
4. David Cone	47	922.0
5. Tommy John	46	1,367.0
Allie Reynolds	46	1,700.0
7. Roger Clemens	43	1,004.0
8. Jack Chesbro	42	1,952.0
9. Al Downing	40	1,235.3
Tim Leary	40	425.7
Andy Pettitte	40	1,792.7

Hit Batsmen: Season

Player	HB	Year
1. Jack Warhop	26	1909
2. Joe McGinnity	21	1901
3. Rube Manning	18	1908
Jack Warhop	18	1910
5. Tommy Byrne	17	1950
6. Jack Warhop	16	1912
7. David Cone	15	1998
Jack Warhop	15	1911
9. Jack Chesbro	14	1908
10. Tommy Byrne	13	1949
Ray Caldwell	13	1911
Bill Hogg	13	1905
Jerry Nops	13	1901

Hit Batsmen: Career with Team

Player	HB	IP
1. Jack Warhop	114	1,412.7
2. Tommy Byrne	62	993.7
3. Jack Chesbro	55	1,952.0
4. Ray Caldwell	53	1,718.3
5. Mel Stottlemyre	44	2,661.3
Bob Turley	44	1,269.0
7. David Cone	42	922.0
Bob Shawkey	42	2,488.7
9. Allie Reynolds	40	1,700.0
10. Orlando Hernandez	38	876.3

Games Finished: Season

Player	GF	Year
1. Mariano Rivera	69	2004
2. Dave Righetti	68	1986
3. Mariano Rivera	67	2005
4. Mariano Rivera	66	2001
5. Mariano Rivera	63	1999
6. Mariano Rivera	61	2000
7. Sparky Lyle	60	1977
Dave Righetti	60	1985
9. Sparky Lyle	59	1974
10. Rich Gossage	58	1980
Sparky Lyle	58	1976
John Wetteland	58	1996

Games Finished: Career with Team

Player	GF	IP
1. Mariano Rivera	541	806.7
2. Dave Righetti	379	1,136.7
3. Sparky Lyle	348	745.7
4. Johnny Murphy	277	990.3
5. Rich Gossage	272	533.0
6. Lindy McDaniel	186	544.7
7. Joe Page	178	780.3
8. Steve Hamilton	140	486.0
9. Hal Reniff	132	428.3
10. Steve Farr	127	169.0

Significant Yankees

BERRA, YOGI (C/OF)
(1946–1963)

Lawrence "Yogi" Berra was signed as an amateur free agent in 1943 and sent to the Piedmont League. Before the next season, however, at age 18, he enlisted in the Navy. After returning from the war, Berra joined the Newark Bears in 1946 and received a late-season call-up in September. By 1947 he made the Yankees, but split his time between the outfield and platooning behind the plate. In 1949 Berra became the team's regular catcher. Manager Casey Stengel said Berra was so important to the Yankees that he wouldn't trade him for Ted Williams.

Berra was a wild swinger at the plate, but in spite of it he didn't strike out very often—in 1950, for example, only 12 times in 597 at-bats. As a catcher, one of Berra's trademarks was to jabber away at the hitter while he stood in the batter's box in an effort to distract him. Another was his tendency to spout guileless, goofy wisdom in sayings that can only be described as "Yogi-isms." He uttered his most famous Yogi-ism—"It ain't over 'til it's over"—in the 1973 pennant race while managing the Mets, who charged from last to first in the final month of the season. Then there's: "When you come to a fork in the road, take it"; "Ninety percent of this game is half mental"; "You can observe a lot just by watching"; "Nobody goes there anymore, it's too crowded"; "It's deja vu all over again"; and "It gets late early out there."

Humor aside, Yogi Berra was a no-nonsense player on the field. He was selected to 15 consecutive All-Star Games from 1948 to 1962. He won three AL MVP Awards (1951, 1954, 1955) and was runner-up twice more (1953, 1956). Berra played on 14 pennant-winning teams and with 10 World Series champions. He set the World Series record for most career hits, with 71. In 1958 he played the entire season without having even one passed ball.

After retiring in 1963, Berra became the Yankee manager in 1964. He led his team to the AL pennant, but after a loss to the Cardinals in the World Series he was fired, supposedly for losing control of his players. The New York Mets, in an opportunistic public relations move, scooped up Berra and made him a coach under Casey Stengel. He became manager in 1971 when Gil Hodges died, and in 1973 he led the "You Gotta Believe!" Mets to the World Series against the A's. After being fired in 1975, Berra returned to the Yankees in 1976 as a coach. In 1984 he became manager again, but lasted only a bit more than a season before Steinbrenner fired him. Berra then spent about six years coaching with the Astros before retiring. In 1972 Berra was inducted into the Hall of Fame.

CAREER YANKEES RECORD:

Games	AB	Hits	Runs
2,116	7,546	2,148	1,174
Avg	**HR**	**RBI**	**SB**
.285	358	1,430	30

CLEMENS, ROGER (SP)
(1999–2003)

See Red Sox and Blue Jays bios.

COMBS, EARLE (OF)
(1924–1935)

Outfielder Earle Combs' career lasted only 12 years, but it was long enough for him to win election to the Hall of Fame. After batting .344 with Louisville, the Yankees bought his contract for $50,000 and two players and promoted him to the big leagues. Combs was very adept at getting on base via the walk, and once there he was a real threat to steal a base, but Yankee manager Miller Huggins told Combs on his arrival in New York that once he got on base, he was to "hold his position." Huggins told Combs that with Ruth, Gehrig, and Meusel to follow him in the batting order, he didn't want to take the bat out of his sluggers' hands. Consequently, even though Combs had stolen a lot of bases in the minors, he never stole more than 16 while in the majors. Combs, considered the best leadoff man in the American League in his day, scored 100+ runs in eight of his 12 seasons and finished with a career .325 batting average. Three times he led the league in triples, ending his career with 154. Sportswriter Fred Lieb once wrote that Combs was probably a more popular player in New York than either Ruth or Gehrig. After retiring as a player, Combs coached for the Yankees and several other teams for two decades before spending his last years on his Kentucky farm. He was named to the Hall of Fame in 1970.

CAREER YANKEES RECORD:

Games	AB	Hits	Runs
1,455	5,746	1,866	1,186
Avg	**HR**	**RBI**	**SB**
.325	58	632	96

DICKEY, BILL (C)
(1928–1943, 1946)

An 11-time All-Star, Bill Dickey spent his entire 17-year career with the Yankees. Considered one of the best catchers of all time, Dickey was an important reason the Yankees won eight pennants and seven World Series titles during his tenure. A model of longevity, Dickey was the first player ever to catch 100 or more games in 13 seasons. On July 6, 1939, he hit three homers in one game. He caught 125 games in the 1931 season without having a passed ball. Like many other players of the era, Dickey missed two years due to World War II. Upon returning to the team in 1946, he replaced Joe McCarthy as manager, but didn't last the season. Dickey later became a scout and coach for the Yankees and discovered Mickey Mantle. He also tutored Yogi Berra, molding him into another great Yankee catcher. Bill Dickey was elected to the Hall of Fame in 1954, and he died in 1993.

CAREER YANKEES RECORD:

Games	AB	Hits	Runs
1,789	6,300	1,969	930
Avg	**HR**	**RBI**	**SB**
.313	202	1,209	36

DIMAGGIO, JOE (OF)
(1936–1942, 1946–1951)

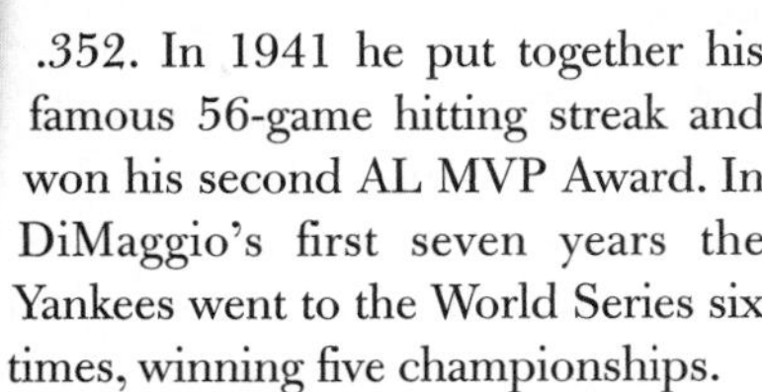

"Graceful" and "classy" are two adjectives that seemed to follow Joe DiMaggio around. After he joined his older brother Vince on the San Francisco Seals team, Joe proceeded to tear up the Pacific Coast League in 1933, hitting .340 with 28 homers and 169 RBIs. He also hit safely in 61 straight games, a portent of things to come. Major league scouts were hot to sign DiMaggio, but when he broke his knee getting out of a cab in 1934, the phone calls stopped. Prior to the 1935 season, the Yankees offered the Seals $25,000 and five minor leaguers. The Seals accepted on the condition they could keep "Joltin' Joe" through the 1935 campaign. New York agreed, and must have felt like they'd gotten quite a bargain when DiMaggio hit .398 and led the PCL in RBIs and outfield assists. In 1936 DiMaggio debuted in the major leagues, hitting .323 with 29 homers, 15 triples, 125 RBIs, and 132 runs. He also gunned down 22 base runners to lead the AL in assists. In the next two years he had 21 and 20 assists before AL runners finally got smart.

From 1936 to 1942, DiMaggio, now dubbed "the Yankee Clipper," hit over .300 every year, three times surpassing .350. He also had over 100 RBIs in each of those years, topping out at 167 in 1937. He won back-to-back batting titles in 1939 and 1940, hitting .381 (and earning his first MVP Award) and .352. In 1941 he put together his famous 56-game hitting streak and won his second AL MVP Award. In DiMaggio's first seven years the Yankees went to the World Series six times, winning five championships.

After hitting "only" .305 in 1942, DiMaggio left baseball and entered the military during World War II. The three years away from baseball, on top of many injuries, affected DiMaggio; his numbers after the war were good, but mortal. In 1950 DiMaggio became the first player ever to hit three homers at the cavernous Griffith Stadium in Washington. The 1951 season was a struggle for DiMaggio. He hit only .263 in 116 games and decided to retire. When the Yankees offered him $100,000 just to play in New York's 1952 home games, he declined, not wanting to embarrass himself.

In 1954 he had a short-lived marriage to Marilyn Monroe, and in the 1970s became a television spokesman for Mr. Coffee. In the 1980s and 1990s he became a popular autograph figure at baseball card shows, commanding $250,000 per two-day appearance. DiMaggio, who died in 1999, was elected to the Hall of Fame in 1955.

CAREER YANKEES RECORD:

Games	AB	Hits	Runs
1,736	6,821	2,214	1,390
Avg	**HR**	**RBI**	**SB**
.325	361	1,537	30

FORD, WHITEY (SP/RP)
(1950, 1953–1967)

The Yankees signed Edward "Whitey" Ford as an amateur free agent in 1947. After a taste of major league action in 1950, Ford missed the next two years to military service. But the Yankees had glimpsed the young left-hander's greatness. He was 9–1 during the 1950 regular season and pitched an 8⅔ innings shutout in his only World Series appearance. Upon returning from the military, Ford added 13 consecutive winning seasons to his fine rookie start. His .690 career winning percentage was the best of any 20th-century pitcher. In World Series play he was dominant. Ford had a stretch of 32 consecutive scoreless Series innings, breaking Babe Ruth's mark of 29⅔ innings. He also holds the World Series records for wins (10), strikeouts (94), and innings pitched (146). Ford won his only Cy Young in 1961, when he went 25–4.

Elston Howard nicknamed Ford "the Chairman of the Board" for the way he controlled the game and directed the players around him when he pitched. Ford was accused of doctoring the baseball late in his career, and he was circumspect in his defense: "I didn't cheat when I won the 25 games in 1961. I don't want anyone to get any ideas and take my Cy Young Award away. And I didn't cheat in 1963 when I won 24 games. Well, maybe just a little. I didn't begin cheating until late in my career, when I needed it to survive." One of his ways of doctoring the baseball was to use a tiny rasp hidden in his wedding ring to nick the ball. It worked until rival manager Alvin Dark collected a basket of baseballs Ford had used and noticed that they were all scuffed in exactly the same way. When Dark protested, umpire Hank Soar made Ford remove his ring when he pitched.

Ford was a notorious carousing buddy of Mickey Mantle; he once said that rooming with Mickey took five years off his life. Ford was elected to the Hall of Fame in 1974.

CAREER YANKEES RECORD:

W	L	W%	ERA	SV
236	106	.690	2.75	10
K	**BB**	**SHO**	**IP**	
1,956	1,086	45	3,170.3	

GEHRIG, LOU (1B)
(1923–1939)

Lou Gehrig was a true American hero, not only because of his baseball greatness, but because of his dignified handling of the tragic blow fate dealt him off the field. Gehrig's decency and clean living made him an oddity in a time when most ballplayers where known for their carousing and rough edges. After playing just a handful of games in both 1923 and 1924, Gehrig became a regular in 1925 and stayed in the lineup for 2,130 consecutive games, eventually earning the nickname "Iron Horse" for his streak. A career .340 hitter, Gehrig reached 400 total bases in a season five times, something Babe Ruth did only twice, Chuck Klein did three times, and only a dozen or so other players have ever done once. Gehrig was an incredible RBI man. In his 13 full seasons with the Yankees, he averaged 147 RBIs per year. In the four decades after Gehrig's last full year, only six players in the majors would even reach 147 RBIs in a season. What makes this even more amazing is that Gehrig batted behind Babe Ruth and Joe DiMaggio, two players who were incredibly good themselves at clearing the bases before Gehrig stepped to the plate.

Little-known among Gehrig's accomplishments is that he stole home 15 times during his career. He also holds the major league record for career grand slams with 23 (although Manny Ramirez of the Red Sox is closing in on him as of 2005). In 34 World Series games, Gehrig hit .361 with 10 homers and 35 RBIs. In 1926 Gehrig began a string of 12 consecutive years in which he hit over .300. In 1927 Gehrig led the "Murderer's Row" Yankees to 110 wins, a 19-game margin over the second-place A's, and a World Series sweep of the Pirates. His .373 average, 47 homers, 52 doubles, and 175 RBIs earned him the first of his two AL MVP Awards, the second coming in 1936. On June 3, 1932, Gehrig became the first American League player to hit four homers in one game. In 1934 he won the AL Triple Crown, hitting .363 with 49 homers and 165 RBIs. Over the years, a rivalry developed between the quiet, clean-living Gehrig and Babe Ruth, who lacked both those traits. The rivalry became a feud in 1934 when Gehrig's wife apparently said something about the way Ruth's daughter was dressed one day. Ruth didn't speak to Gehrig again.

In 1938 Gehrig's average dipped to .295, and almost all his other numbers were down as well. Balls that would have been homers in his heyday were now just long fly-outs. Something was clearly wrong. He was diagnosed with a gallbladder problem. During a golf outing, teammate Wes Ferrell noticed that Gehrig wore tennis shoes instead of golf shoes and was sliding his feet on the ground. In 1939 Gehrig played in the first eight games of the season, collecting just four singles in 28 at-bats. When he had trouble getting to first to take a throw after a comebacker to the pitcher, Gehrig knew he was embarrassing himself and took himself out of the lineup. The next day he took the lineup card to the umpire and the public address announcer told the crowd, "Ladies and gentlemen, Lou Gehrig's consecutive streak of 2,130 games played has ended."

Soon thereafter doctors at the Mayo Clinic diagnosed Gehrig as having amyotrophic lateral sclerosis, which has been known ever since as Lou Gehrig's disease. He would never play again. On July 4, 1939, the Yankees held a Lou Gehrig Day to honor their captain. On that day, Gehrig gave his famous speech that concluded, ". . . Today I consider myself the luckiest man on the face of the Earth." Babe Ruth hugged him and spoke to him for the first time in five years. In December 1939, Cooperstown waived its requirement that a player be retired for five years before induction and named him to the Hall of Fame. On June 2, 1941, Lou Gehrig died at the age of 38.

CAREER YANKEES RECORD:

Games	AB	Hits	Runs
2,164	8,001	2,721	1,888
Avg	**HR**	**RBI**	**SB**
.340	493	1,995	102

GOMEZ, LEFTY (SP/RP)
(1930–1942)

One of the best pitchers in Yankee history, Vernon "Lefty" Gomez pitched the first 13 years of his 14-year career with New York. A four-time 20-game winner, Gomez made seven All-Star appearances, starting the game four times and winning it three times, including the first-ever All-Star Game, on July 6, 1933. He also collected the first All-Star Game RBI when he singled in a run.

Gomez hated pitching to Jimmie Foxx, almost to the point of a phobia. Gomez was the one who claimed Foxx was so strong he had muscles in his hair. "Jimmie Foxx wasn't scouted," he claimed. "He was trapped." When facing Foxx during one game, Gomez shook off every one of catcher Bill Dickey's signs. An exasperated Dickey finally went to the mound and asked Gomez what he wanted to pitch to Foxx. "Nothing," said Gomez. "Let's just stall around and maybe he'll get mad and go away." Foxx hit the very next pitch for a home run.

Despite an earnest desire to be a good hitter, Gomez was simply awful at the plate. On one at-bat, Gomez went through all the motions many hitters do—he tugged his belt, he adjusted his cap, and he hit his cleats with his bat to knock the mud from his spikes. Trouble was, he hit himself so hard in the foot that he smashed his ankle and spent the next three days in the hospital.

After winning just 24 games for the Yankees over his last three years, Gomez was sold to the Braves in January 1943, who subsequently released him without pitching him in a game. He signed as a free agent with Washington but was released after one poor appearance. Gomez was elected to the Hall of Fame in 1972 and died in 1989.

CAREER YANKEES RECORD:

W	L	W%	ERA	SV
189	101	.652	3.34	9

K	BB	SHO	IP
1,468	1,090	28	2,498.3

GUIDRY, RON (SP)
(1975–1988)

"Louisiana Lightning" was an appropriate nickname for Ron Guidry, at least for the 1978 season, when he seemingly captured lightning in a bottle with one of the best years by any pitcher in major league history. Guidry's 25–3 record in 1978 almost single-handedly held the team together while the Yankees completed one of the greatest team comebacks in history to force a one-game playoff with the Red Sox at season's end. Guidry's win in the playoff game allowed New York to advance to the World Series, where they would win their second consecutive championship.

But things hadn't started so gloriously for Guidry. His major league debut in 1975 was so bad he sat in the bullpen—unused—for 46 days. While in the bullpen, he learned his devastating slider from Sparky Lyle. By 1977 he had perfected his slider and joined the starting lineup, going 16–7 with a 2.82 ERA. After his incredible 1978 Cy Young season, Guidry would twice more be a 20-game winner. He would also win five Gold Gloves and make four appearances in the All-Star Game. From 1977 to 1985 Guidry won 154 games, more than any other pitcher in the majors during that span. He was on top of the world in 1985 when he posted another fine season, going 22–6, but he blew his arm out in 1986 and won only 16 more games over three years before retiring.

CAREER YANKEES RECORD:

W	L	W%	ERA	SV
170	91	.651	3.29	4

K	BB	SHO	IP
1,778	633	26	2,392.0

HOYT, WAITE (SP/RP)
(1921–1930)

Although Waite Hoyt spent only nine of his 21 years in the major leagues with New York, he earned about 70 percent of his career wins with the Yankees. From 1921 to 1928, Hoyt won 145 games during the regular season and six more in World Series play.

Hoyt used to pitch batting practice for the Giants at the Polo Grounds when he was 15 years old. Eventually the long subway ride to and from the ballpark without pay got old, and Hoyt asked for compensation. John McGraw gave him a contract—which Hoyt's father signed—and promptly paid him $5. Hoyt was happy.

Hoyt played in the Giants' minor league system for a time before being called up to the majors at 18. He pitched just one inning for McGraw's team before being traded to the Red Sox. After a 10–12 record in Boston over two years, Hoyt was traded in 1921 to the Yankees, where he quickly became an established member of the rotation, winning 19 games. In the World Series that year, Hoyt pitched 27 innings without allowing an earned run. On the Yankees, Hoyt rejoined former teammate and roommate Babe Ruth, someone Hoyt had always held in high regard. During the 1920s, when Hoyt wasn't pitching for the Yankees, he danced and sang in a vaudeville act. He was also a mortician, which earned the nickname "the Merry Mortician."

Hoyt was traded to Detroit in mid-1930 after becoming involved in a nasty dispute with Yankees manager Bob Shawkey over how to pitch to Al Simmons. Over the remaining nine years of his career, Hoyt pitched for five different teams, including two stints with the Dodgers, but never again attained the success he had with the Yankees. After his playing career, Hoyt became a very successful broadcaster, both on early television shows and later with the Cincinnati Reds radio team, a position he held for 25 years. Hoyt was elected to the Hall of Fame in 1969, and he died in 1984.

CAREER YANKEES RECORD:

W	L	W%	ERA	SV
157	98	.616	3.48	28

K	BB	SHO	IP
713	631	15	2,272.3

HUNTER, CATFISH (SP)
(1975–1979)

See A's bio.

JACKSON, REGGIE (OF/DH) (1977–1981)

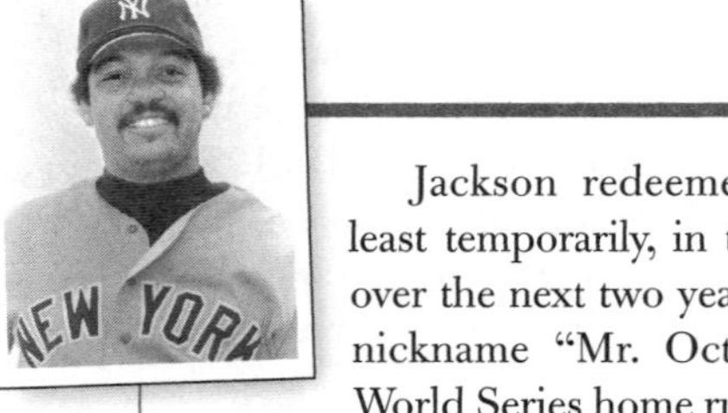

After signing his huge new contract with the Yankees before the 1977 season, Reggie Jackson bragged to the media that someone would name a candy bar after him, and they did. It was said that you could tell if you were eating a Reggie Bar even in the dark because once you unwrapped it, it would tell you how good it was. Before Jackson even played a game with New York, he became the center of controversy when he was quoted in a magazine interview as saying, "I am the straw that stirs the drink." Numerous Yankee players, especially team captain Thurman Munson, took exception to the remark. Manager Billy Martin took particular dislike to Jackson. During a 1977 game, Martin took Jackson out of the field in the middle of an inning when Jackson muffed a fly ball. When Jackson returned to the dugout, Martin challenged Jackson to a fight in front of a national television audience and the two had to be restrained from going after one another.

Jackson redeemed himself, at least temporarily, in the postseason over the next two years, earning the nickname "Mr. October" for his World Series home runs. In Game 6 of the 1977 World Series he homered in three straight at-bats on three straight pitches. Coupled with a four-pitch walk earlier in the game and a home run in his last at-bat in Game 5, Jackson had hit homers on four consecutive swings. On his first swing of the 1978 season, Jackson extended the streak to five homers on five swings. Thousands of fans who had received Reggie Bars as an Opening Day promotion threw them on the field in approval, marking the first time a baseball game was delayed by chocolate. After a dismal 1981 season in which Jackson hit .237 with 15 homers, Yankees owner George Steinbrenner felt Jackson was washed up and didn't attempt to sign him. Jackson signed with the Angels and had one good year before experiencing four less-than-stellar years. After one final year back in Oakland, Reggie retired after 21 big league seasons. In 1993 he was elected to the Hall of Fame, choosing to enter the Hall with a Yankee hat, even though he spent only five years with the team. For many years, he has served as a special advisor to the Yankees. *(See also A's and Angels bios.)*

CAREER YANKEES RECORD:

Games	AB	Hits	Runs
653	2,349	661	380
Avg	**HR**	**RBI**	**SB**
.281	144	461	41

JETER, DEREK (SS)
(1995–2005)

The New York Yankees selected Derek Jeter in the first round of the June 1992 amateur draft. After a late-season call-up in 1995, Jeter won the team's starting shortstop position in 1996 and has been the model of consistency ever since. He won the American League Rookie of the Year Award that year when he helped the Yankees win the AL pennant and the World Series title. In 2000 Jeter became the first player ever to win both the All-Star Game MVP Award and the World Series MVP Award. For the past decade, Jeter has been among the elite shortstops in the game. Although not a power hitter like Alex Rodriguez, Nomar Garciaparra, or Miguel Tejada, Jeter has still averaged 15 homers per year with 100+ runs scored and about 20 steals. He has also averaged over .300 in more than 110 postseason games. Jeter, a six-time All-Star and the Yankees' captain, is now among the game's highest-paid players, making nearly $20 million per season.

CAREER YANKEES RECORD:

Games	AB	Hits	Runs
1,525	6,167	1,936	1,159

Avg	HR	RBI	SB
.314	169	763	215

LAZZERI, TONY (2B/3B)
(1926–1937)

Tony Lazzeri was an intelligent second baseman who possessed both a fine glove and a powerful bat. In 1925 Lazzeri had one of the greatest minor league seasons in history when, playing for the Salt Lake City Bees of the Pacific Coast League, he hit .355 with 60 homers and 222 RBIs. Sufficiently impressed, the Yankees gave Salt Lake $55,000 and five players for Lazzeri.

In 1926, his rookie year, Lazzeri hit 18 homers, 14 triples, 28 doubles, and had 114 RBIs to help the Yankees win the AL pennant and rebound from a seventh-place finish the preceding year. A team leader to whom other players often looked for advice and moral support, Lazzeri was part of the Murderer's Row Yankees of 1927, hitting .309 with 18 homers and 102 RBIs. On May 24, 1936, Lazzeri became the first hitter in major league history to hit two grand slams in one game, setting an AL record of 11 RBIs in the process.

After his production slipped over his last several years, Lazzeri was released following the 1937 season. He spent his last two years playing minimal roles for the Cubs, Dodgers, and Giants before retiring. Over the next several years he managed a number of minor league teams. An epileptic, Lazzeri died at the age of 42 from a fall down a stairway in his home, apparently the result of a seizure. He was elected to the Hall of Fame in 1991.

CAREER YANKEES RECORD:

Games	AB	Hits	Runs
1,659	6,094	1,784	952

Avg	HR	RBI	SB
.293	169	1,154	147

MANTLE, MICKEY (OF/1B) (1951–1968)

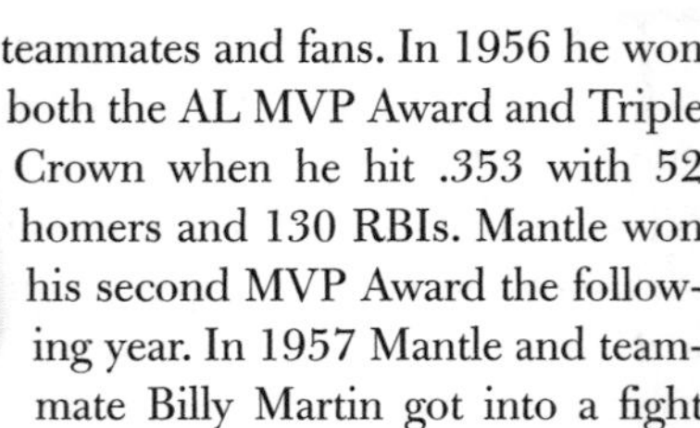

The Yankees signed Mickey Mantle as an amateur free agent before the 1949 season. Originally a shortstop, Mantle hit well in the minors but struggled when called up to New York in 1951. After being sent down to New York's farm club in Kansas City, Mantle's slump continued. Discouraged, he called his father one day and told him, "I don't think I can play baseball any more." Mantle's dad showed up in Kansas City the next day and, upon entering his son's room, began to pack Mantle's things into his suitcase. When Mickey asked his father what he was doing, he told his son, "Packing. You're going home to work with me in the zinc mines, that's what we'll do. You can go back down in the mines with me." That was enough to shock Mickey out of both his poor attitude and his batting slump. He improved at the plate immediately, hitting .361 with 11 homers and 50 RBIs in his 40-game stay in Kansas City.

Back in New York, Mantle turned it around, raising his average to a respectable .267 by season's end. In Game 2 of the 1951 World Series, Mantle tripped over an exposed drainpipe in Yankee Stadium's outfield, tore up his knee, and missed the rest of the Series. The next day, Mantle's father, a spectator in the stands, took seriously ill. He died the next summer of Hodgkin's disease. Mickey figured the disease that had claimed both his grandfather and his father would spell his own early doom. Later in Mantle's life he would say that the reason he partied so hard was because he didn't expect to live long—and that if he had known, he would have taken better care of himself.

During the 1950s, the "Commerce Comet" became one of the best switch-hitters in history and baseball's biggest star. He was the most beloved member of the Yankees, both by teammates and fans. In 1956 he won both the AL MVP Award and Triple Crown when he hit .353 with 52 homers and 130 RBIs. Mantle won his second MVP Award the following year. In 1957 Mantle and teammate Billy Martin got into a fight at New York's Copacabana nightclub. Shortly thereafter, Martin was traded to Kansas City in an effort to protect Mantle from further trouble. In the 1957 World Series, Mantle suffered a shoulder injury when Milwaukee second baseman Red Schoendienst fell on him in a play at the bag. The injury would affect Mantle for years, and hasten his retirement from the game.

In 1961 Mantle and Roger Maris engaged in a duel to break Babe Ruth's single-season home run record. Mantle, who was clearly the favorite of the media, his teammates, and fans, fell out of the race when he suffered a bizarre injury. He had caught a severe cold that he couldn't shake and, upon the recommendation of team announcer Mel Allen, received medical aid from a New York physician. The doctor, who was wearing a bloodstained smock, injected Mantle with an unknown substance that instantly caused him to become dizzy and feverish. The area of the injection became infected and required further medical treatment, resulting in lost games for "the Mick."

Mantle won his third MVP Award in 1962, though his numbers were starting to decline. In 1964 he had his last hurrah when he hit .333 with three homers, two doubles, and eight runs and RBIs in the 1964 World Series. Over the last four or five years of his career, Mantle had trouble throwing and batting from the left side, haunted by the old injury from the 1957 World Series. Mantle, a 16-time All-Star, retired during spring training in 1969 and was elected to the Hall of Fame in 1974.

After his career was over, Mantle became involved in a number of business ventures, including a Manhattan restaurant. He was an NBC announcer for a short time on the *Saturday Game of the Week.* Mantle joined Willie Mays as spokesman for Bally's Park Place Casino in Atlantic City, a move that got them both banned from baseball by Commissioner Bowie Kuhn. Both were reinstated in 1985. He became a popular autograph guest at baseball card shows, almost always requiring the show promoter to bring in another of the lesser-known Yankees of his era as well, such as Johnny Blanchard, Moose Skowron, Hank Bauer, and others in an effort to take care of his teammates. After spending time in the Betty Ford Center in California in 1993, Mantle emerged as a television spokesman for clean living. He warned children about drug and alcohol abuse. In 1994 Mantle received a successful liver transplant, but it was during the transplant operation that doctors discovered an inoperable cancer. On August 13, 1995, Mantle died at the age of 63, having outlived his father by many years.

CAREER YANKEES RECORD:

Games	AB	Hits	Runs
2,401	8,102	2,415	1,677
Avg	**HR**	**RBI**	**SB**
.298	536	1,509	153

MARIS, ROGER (OF)
(1960–1966)

After spending three seasons with the Indians and A's, Roger Maris was traded to New York in December 1959 as part of a seven-player deal that sent Don Larsen to the A's. Maris's impact was immediate. He led the American League in RBIs (112), extra-base hits (64), slugging (.581), and was second in homers (39), runs (98), and total bases (290). He won a Gold Glove to boot. For his efforts he was named the American League MVP. In spite of his great season, however, Maris wasn't totally embraced by his teammates or the fans. Much of the problem resided with Maris. During his minor league and early major league career he had been a difficult player to manage. On more than one occasion he refused assignments, issued ultimatums, and was just generally stubborn.

When he arrived in New York City, the boy from Fargo, North Dakota, was truly out of place. Such was the setting in 1961, when Maris launched his assault on Babe Ruth's supposedly unbreakable home run record. While Maris faced an uphill battle in catching Ruth, he faced an impossible battle on a number of other fronts. The man whose record he was chasing was a god to most Yankees and baseball fans everywhere, and the teammate who was matching him homer for homer almost the entire season, Mickey Mantle, was also an idol. Mantle was clearly the fans' choice to break the record, and they let Maris know it. Maris, who had zero charisma with the press, suffered constant verbal abuse during the games, and sometimes even physical abuse when fans threw objects at him on the field. He and his wife received threatening phone calls, some in the middle of the night, and he received death threats in the mail.

Once it became a possibility that either Mantle or Maris might break Ruth's record, Commissioner Ford Frick announced that it would have to be accomplished in 154 games or less, or else it would go into the record books as a separate category since the 1961 season contained eight more games than Ruth's 1927 season. All of these facts caused Maris to withdraw from the fans, his teammates, the media, and even his family. About the only thing Maris had going for him in pursuit of the record was the fact that he batted ahead of Mantle in the lineup. Consequently, despite hitting 61 homers, Maris didn't receive even one intentional walk the entire 1961 season. What pitcher would walk Maris to get to the switch-hitting Mantle? As he closed in on the record, Maris lost clumps of hair due to stress. He finally broke the hallowed record on the last day of the season—in a stadium that wasn't even sold out. His 61 homers and 142 RBIs earned him his second straight AL MVP Award.

Maris had his last good year with the Yankees in 1962, when he hit 33 homers with 100 RBIs. Over the next four years, Maris suffered a series of injuries that greatly reduced both his performance and his playing time. Traded to St. Louis after the 1966 season, Maris, happy to be out of New York, became a part-time player, but did see action in two more World Series with the Cardinals and was a positive role model for younger Cardinals. After Maris retired, grateful Cardinals owner August Busch set Maris up with a lucrative beer distributorship. In December 1985, Maris died of lymphatic cancer at the age of 51. His home run record stood for 37 years, until 1998, when both Sammy Sosa (66) and Mark McGwire (70) broke it amid wildly adoring and enthusiastic fans from every city in America, including New York.

CAREER YANKEES RECORD:

Games	AB	Hits	Runs
850	3,007	797	520
Avg	**HR**	**RBI**	**SB**
.265	203	548	7

MATTINGLY, DON (1B)
(1982–1995)

That Don Mattingly lasted until the 19th round of the June 1979 amateur draft is unbelievable in retrospect. In a 1986 *New York Times* poll of major league players, Don Mattingly was voted overwhelmingly as the best player in the major leagues. Known in New York as "Donnie Baseball" or "the Hit Man," Mattingly was one of the most popular players ever to play for the Yankees.

After a late-season call-up in 1982, Mattingly joined the club for good in 1983. In 1984, his first full season in New York, Mattingly won the AL batting title with a .343 average and led the league with 207 hits and 44 doubles. He also won the first of his nine Gold Gloves. In 1985 Mattingly won the AL MVP Award with a .324 average, 35 homers, 145 RBIs, and 86 extra-base hits. On July 18, 1987, he homered in his eighth consecutive game, tying Dale Long's 31-year-old record (a mark that would later be equaled by Ken Griffey Jr.). That same season he would hit six grand slams, a new major league record. When he suffered a back injury in 1990, Mattingly lost much of his power and his production plummeted for the remainder of his career. Although his last year was 1995, Mattingly didn't officially retire until January 1997. A six-time All-Star, Mattingly had sat out the entire 1996 season hoping that his back would recover; it never did, so he called it quits. The Yankees retired his number 23 later that year. In the 2004 season, Mattingly, the team's former captain, became the Yankees' hitting coach.

CAREER YANKEES RECORD:

Games	AB	Hits	Runs
1,785	7,003	2,153	1,007
Avg	**HR**	**RBI**	**SB**
.307	222	1,099	14

MEUSEL, BOB (OF)
(1920–1929)

Outfielder Bob Meusel, the younger brother of major leaguer "Irish" Meusel, was a member of the Murderer's Row Yankees, but he was typically overshadowed by Ruth, Gehrig, Lazzeri, and Combs. He did, however, manage to lead the American League in homers and RBIs in 1925, when Ruth missed nearly 60 games due to what was called euphemistically at the time "the Bellyache Heard 'Round the World." Five times during Meusel's career he hit 40+ doubles and 100+ RBIs. He is one of only two major leaguers (Babe Herman is the other) to hit for the cycle three times in his career.

On September 5, 1921, Meusel tied the major league record with four outfield assists in one game. In 1921 the Yankees won their first pennant, aided by Meusel's 24 homers and 135 RBIs, and met the Giants in the World Series. Brother "Irish" led the Giants to the title in an eight-game Series. The Giants beat the Yankees again in the 1922 Series. In 1923, Bob Meusel got a measure of revenge when he racked up 8 RBIs to help the Yanks finally best his brother's Giants in the Series. On May 16, 1927, he stole second, third, and home in the same game. After nine solid seasons, including seven .300 campaigns, Meusel's performance fell dramatically in 1929, his 10th and final season in New York. He was waived after the season and picked up by Cincinnati. He had a fairly good year with the Reds, but retired after the 1930 season at the age of 33. He died in 1977.

CAREER YANKEES RECORD:

Games	AB	Hits	Runs
1,294	5,032	1,565	764
Avg	**HR**	**RBI**	**SB**
.311	146	1,005	133

MUNSON, THURMAN (C)
(1969–1979)

Thurman Munson was selected by the Yankees in the first round of the June 1968 amateur draft and made it to New York at the end of the next season. In 1970, as the team's full-time catcher, he hit .302 and won the AL Rookie of the Year Award. Munson was a terribly insecure man who spent his entire career trying to get the respect he felt he was owed. He was particularly jealous of both Carlton Fisk and Johnny Bench. Once, when the Yankees daily press notes listed the AL leaders in assists by position, Fisk was listed first with 27 and Munson second with 25. A furious Munson went on a tirade wanting to know why his own team's media people would "show him up." In that day's ball game, Munson intentionally dropped three third strikes so that he could throw to first and take over the AL lead in assists.

A five-time .300 hitter and seven-time All-Star, Munson in 1975 became the first captain of the Yankees since Lou Gehrig in 1939. In 1974 Munson strained his right forearm and it affected his throws. He committed 22 errors, many of them when his throws sailed wide to the right. When members of the media tried to question him about it, he became angry and refused to speak with them.

In 1976 Munson easily won the AL MVP Award, but became incensed when an informal team poll conducted by one of the Yankees beat writers cited Mickey Rivers as the team MVP. In the World Series that year, the Yankees were swept aside by the Big Red Machine in four straight. Munson hit .529 for the Series, but all his hits were singles and he didn't drive in a run. Johnny Bench, on the other hand, hit .533 with two homers and six RBIs. During a postseason interview, Reds manager Sparky Anderson was asked to compare Munson with Bench, unaware that Munson had just walked into the room and was standing behind him. Said Anderson, "Don't ever embarrass a man by comparing him to Johnny Bench." Ouch! When George Steinbrenner signed Reggie Jackson for the 1977 season, Jackson gave an interview to *Sport* magazine—before he ever joined the team—in which he stated, "I'm the straw that stirs the drink. It all comes back to me. Maybe I should say me and Munson. But he really doesn't enter into it. He can only stir it bad." Double ouch! In addition to Jackson's slam, Steinbrenner paid Jackson $3 million, more than Munson was making, thereby breaking his promise to Munson that he would always be the highest-paid Yankee. Thereafter, Munson refused to talk to the media.

Despite their constant bickering, Munson and Jackson helped New York to back-to-back World Series titles over the Dodgers in 1977 and 1978, but by 1979 Munson's skills were declining. Come August 1 he had only three homers and 39 RBIs. His knees and shoulders gave him constant pain and he was seriously talking about retirement. On August 2, 1979, Munson was piloting his private plane when he crash-landed 1,000 feet short of the Akron-Canton airport runway. His two passengers, who were wearing their seat belts, survived and escaped before the plane was engulfed in flames. Munson, who was not wearing his shoulder harness, died on impact. His locker in the Yankee Stadium clubhouse remains empty to this day.

CAREER YANKEES RECORD:

Games	AB	Hits	Runs
1,423	5,344	1,558	696
Avg	**HR**	**RBI**	**SB**
.292	113	701	48

PENNOCK, HERB (SP/RP)
(1923–1933)

After averaging fewer than eight wins a year in 10 seasons with the A's and Red Sox, Pennock was traded from Boston to New York and immediately turned his career into high gear. From 1923 to 1928, Pennock averaged nearly 20 wins a year for the Murderer's Row Yankees. Manager Miller Huggins said that Pennock was the best lefthander in the history of the game. Said Huggins, "If you were to cut that bird's head open, the weakness of every batter in the league would fall out." Pennock won 241 games in his career and went 5–0 with a 1.95 ERA in World Series play relying on a notorious variety of junk pitches. An opponent once said of a Pennock fastball, "Even if he hits you in the head, he won't knock your hat off."

Somewhat of an oddball, Pennock liked to host foxhunts in his hometown of Kennett Square, Pennsylvania. In 1928 he came down with a sore arm and tried an unusual method to cure it. He used "bee therapy," in which he let a horde of bees sting his arm repeatedly. After his arm painfully swelled up without the hoped for cure, Pennock told reporters, "All I can say is that nature intended self-respecting bees to spend their time getting honey out of flowers and not go drilling into a pitcher's arm."

The Yankees released him after 11 years, whereupon Pennock signed with the Red Sox and pitched one more year of decent relief before retiring. Once his playing days were over, Pennock worked in the Red Sox farm systems for a number of years before becoming GM of the Phillies. He died in 1948, the same year he was elected to the Hall of Fame.

CAREER YANKEES RECORD:

W	L	W%	ERA	SV
162	90	.643	3.54	20
K	**BB**	**SHO**	**IP**	
700	471	19	2,203.3	

REYNOLDS, ALLIE (SP/RP)
(1947–1954)

Allie Reynolds spent five years in Cleveland before being traded to the Yankees for Joe Gordon. Reynolds was a 51–47 pitcher for Cleveland. Once in New York, Reynolds received some sound advice from 40-year-old pitcher Spud Chandler. "Don't just throw the ball," said Chandler. "Think about what you're doing. Change speeds. Set hitters up. Think, think, *think.*" The pep talk turned Reynolds around. Nicknamed "Superchief" because he was one-quarter Creek Indian, Reynolds won 19 games in his first year with the Yankees, and averaged between 16–20 wins for his first six years. During his eight years in New York, the Yankees went to the World Series six times and Reynolds won at least one game in each of the Fall Classics, finishing with a 7–2 mark and four saves in World Series play. In 1951 Reynolds joined Cincinnati's Johnny Vander Meer as the only pitchers to throw two no-hitters in the same season. The following year he went 20–8 with six saves and a league-best 2.06 ERA. He also led the league in strikeouts and shutouts. The next season, however, he injured his back when the Yankee team bus was in an accident and he was never the same again. Although he went 26–11 in 1953–1954, his injury forced him to retire prematurely. After his playing career was over, Reynolds, a five-time Yankee All-Star, became the baseball coach at Oklahoma State. He died in 1994.

CAREER YANKEES RECORD:

W	L	W%	ERA	SV
131	60	.686	3.30	41
K	**BB**	**SHO**	**IP**	
967	819	27	1,700.0	

RIGHETTI, DAVE (RP/SP)
(1979, 1981–1990)

While still a minor leaguer in the Rangers system, Dave Righetti was part of a 10-player trade that landed him in New York and sent Sparky Lyle to Texas. Righetti was a starter in his first four seasons in New York, compiling a modest 33–23 record. He won the AL Rookie of the Year Award in 1981 with an 8–4 record and 2.05 ERA. On July 4, 1983, he pitched the first no-hitter for the Yankees since Don Larsen's perfect game in the 1956 World Series. In 1984 Yogi Berra made him the team's closer after the Yankees lost Goose Gossage to free agency; "Rags" promptly recorded 31 saves, good for fourth in the American League. In 1986 Righetti was selected to his first of two All-Star Games while on his way to what was then an American League-record 46 saves. By the end of the 1990 season, Righetti had compiled 224 career saves, easily outdistancing Gossage and Lyle on the Yankees' all-time saves list. He wanted to move closer to home, so he opted for free agency and signed with the Giants. After one decent year with the Giants and two very bad ones, Righetti finished his career playing for the A's, Blue Jays, and White Sox in 1994–1995. After his playing days, Righetti joined the Giants as a roving instructor and then pitching coach.

CAREER YANKEES RECORD:

W	L	W%	ERA	SV
74	61	.548	3.11	224
K	**BB**	**SHO**	**IP**	
940	473	2	1,136.7	

RIVERA, MARIANO (RP)
(1995–2005)

The Yankees signed Panamanian-born Mariano Rivera as an amateur free agent in February 1990. Over the last nine years, Rivera, who always seems calm on the mound, has been the best reliever in baseball, and will go down as one of the very best in history. By the end of the 2005 season, his save total had reached 379, all with the Yankees. Rivera has, at times, been absolutely invincible; in 1999 he didn't allow an earned run over the last three months of the season. Given his age, and barring injury, Rivera should someday easily become baseball's all-time saves leader. As great as he's been in the regular season, "Mo" has been even tougher in the postseason. Through 2005, he has posted an 8–1 record with an 0.75 ERA and 32 saves in 70 postseason appearances covering 108.7 innings.

CAREER YANKEES RECORD:

W	L	W%	ERA	SV
54	35	.607	2.33	379
K	**BB**	**SHO**	**IP**	
728	215	0	806.7	

RIZZUTO, PHIL (SS)
(1941–1942, 1946–1956)

Phil "Scooter" Rizzuto was an excellent fielding shortstop who was often compared with his counterpart on the Dodgers, Pee Wee Reese, who played in almost the identical time span. Although they hit for about the same average, Reese collected around 600 more hits, 90 more homers, 300 more RBIs, and 460 more runs, which is why Reese was elected to the Hall of Fame 10 years before Rizzuto. Rizzuto's value lay more in his glove and his leadership, which were less quantifiable assets. Ted Williams once said that five-time All-Star Phil Rizzuto made the difference between the pennant races of the Yankees and Red Sox of the '40s and '50s. Yankee pitcher Vic Raschi once said, "My best pitch is anything the batter grounds, lines, or pops up in the direction of Rizzuto." One of the best defensive shortstops of his era, Rizzuto played 21 consecutive World Series games without an error. When World War II broke out, Rizzuto entered the military and found himself on the same Navy team as Pee Wee Reese. Their manager happened to be Yankee great Bill Dickey, who moved Rizzuto to third and left Reese at short.

When Rizzuto returned to the majors in 1946 after the war, he received a severe beaning from Nels Potter of the Browns and suffered from dizzy spells the rest of his career. Nonetheless, Rizzuto had his career year in 1950, when he hit .324 with 200 hits, scored 125 runs, won the AL MVP Award, and helped the Yanks sweep the Phillies in the World Series. From 1953 to 1956 Rizzuto's career wound down. After the 1956 season, Rizzuto was released and he joined the Yankees' broadcast team, where he remained for decades. His trademark phrase was, "Holy cow!" In 1977 Rizzuto's voice provided the background dialogue for rock star Meatloaf's song "Paradise by the Dashboard Light." Rizzuto was finally elected to the Hall of Fame in 1994.

CAREER YANKEES RECORD:

Games	AB	Hits	Runs
1,661	5,816	1,588	877
Avg	**HR**	**RBI**	**SB**
.273	38	563	149

RUFFING, RED (SP)
(1930–1942, 1945–1946)

After compiling a woeful 39–93 record in six-plus years with pitifully weak Boston, Charles "Red" Ruffing was traded to the Yankees for $50,000 cash and a player on May 6, 1930. Ruffing turned it around immediately with the powerful Yankees, winning 15 games over the remainder of the season. With one exception, over the next dozen seasons Ruffing won 14–21 games each year, and from 1936–1939 he won 20 or more each season. He was so solid and consistent that Bill Dickey called Ruffing, a six-time All-Star, the best pitcher he ever caught. When Ruffing, a right-hander, followed through, he had to land on the side of his left foot because he lost four toes in an Illinois coal mine accident when he was a teenager.

Ruffing had the honor of pitching the opening game of the World Series five times, and in 10 Series starts he compiled a 7–2 record with eight complete games and a 2.63 ERA. In 1939 Ruffing was a 20-game winner and .300 hitter, one of only a few pitchers who've ever accomplished the feat in the same year. In 1943, when Ruffing was 38 years old, he was drafted into the military—with a severely damaged left foot, a wife, two children, and as the sole supporter of his family and mother-in-law. After losing two years to the war, Ruffing returned at the end of the 1945 season and pitched well, going 7–3 with a 2.89 ERA. After going a combined 8–6 over the next two years in limited action with the Yankees and White Sox, the 42-year-old retired. A career .269 hitter, Ruffing drove in more runs than any pitcher in major league history (273). He also hit 36 homers, 98 doubles, and 13 triples. In 1962 he became the pitching coach of the Mets, and in 1967 he was elected to the Hall of Fame.

CAREER YANKEES RECORD:

W	L	W%	ERA	SV
231	124	.651	3.47	8

K	BB	SHO	IP
1,526	1,066	40	3,168.7

RUTH, BABE (OF)
(1920–1934)

When George Herman "Babe" Ruth arrived in New York amid much fanfare, he immediately rocked the baseball world. The Yankees had never won a pennant before Ruth arrived. Though they didn't win one in 1920, the Yankees were engaged in a terrific pennant race with the Indians and the White Sox, finishing in third, just three games out. Ruth hit .376, scored 158 runs, drove in 137, and clubbed 54 homers, annihilating the major league home run record, which he had set himself the year before with 29. More important—certainly from the standpoint of the club's owners—attendance soared. The Yankees had set an attendance record in 1919, the year before Ruth arrived, with 619,000 fans. In Ruth's first year almost 1.3 million fans flocked to see the new slugger. Ruth also attracted large crowds at all the other parks in the league. From a business standpoint, the "Bambino" more than earned his huge salary. Within a few years, other players started reaping the benefits of Ruth's power display as salaries increased almost across the board.

After Ray Chapman's death in 1920, baseball's owners decided that scuffed, dirty balls had to be removed from play and replaced with brand-new white baseballs. As did all hitters, Ruth benefited from the new rule, hammering 59 homers in 1921, again breaking the home run record. This time the Yankees won their first pennant and made it to their first World Series. Though the Yankees lost in eight games to the Giants, they established themselves as a force to be reckoned with for years to come. From 1920 to 1932, with one exception, the Yankees drew between 912,000 and 1.3 million fans. The one year in that stretch when they drew only 697,000 fans was 1925, the year Ruth missed the first 60 games of the year because he was laid up in the hospital. His "bellyache" was truly costly for New York's owners. Almost as important to baseball, Ruth succeeded in bringing back many of the American League fans who had soured over the Black Sox scandal that filled the newspapers in late 1920 and all through 1921.

After the 1921 season, Ruth decided to capitalize on his fame and scheduled a post-season barnstorming tour with a number of other major league players. Commissioner Kenesaw Mountain Landis, who was trying to establish the World Series as the game's premier postseason event, warned the players against undertaking the tour. Most of the players opted out of the tour, but Ruth and teammate Bob Meusel were defiant. Landis suspended both for the first six weeks of the 1922 season. Once he returned in 1922, Ruth was in a combative mood, and he took it out on the umpires and other players. He was suspended three different times during the season, but still hit 35 homers. In 1923 the Yankees opened Yankee Stadium, leaving the Polo Grounds behind forever. Sportswriter Fred Lieb dubbed the new park "The House That Ruth Built." On Opening Day, more than 74,000 fans showed up to watch Ruth hit a three-run homer to win the game.

In 1925 Ruth arrived at training camp in terrible shape. After collapsing several times on the train ride north, he was hospitalized and operated on for what was called an intestinal abscess. He remained in the hospital for seven weeks. When Ruth returned for his first game on June 1, manager Miller Huggins suspended him for carousing and fined him $5,000, a tenth of his annual salary. He also told Ruth he'd have to apologize to the team before he could be reinstated. Ruth refused at first, and tried to have Huggins fired, but management backed Huggins. The team suffered greatly due to the discord, finishing in seventh place. Ruth eventually capitulated and vowed to come back in 1926 in better shape than ever, and he did, hitting .372 with 47 homers and leading the Yankees to another pennant, though they lost the Series in seven games to the Cardinals when Ruth was thrown out trying to steal second base with two out and Bob Meusel at the plate in the bottom of the ninth at Yankee Stadium.

In 1927 Ruth set another home run record, this time with 60 bombs as the famed "Murderer's Row" Yankees won the AL race by 19 games and swept the Pirates in four straight in the Series. Ruth now had a rival on the Yankees, first baseman Lou Gehrig. For the seven years from 1927 to 1933, Ruth and Gehrig embarked on an unprecedented two-man tear, averaging a combined 84 homers and 303 RBIs each year during the span. The Yankees won pennants again in 1928 and 1932, both years sweeping their opponents in the World Series. In 1930 a reporter pointed out to Ruth that he made $5,000 more than President Hoover. Ruth replied, "So what? I had a better year than he did."

Babe Ruth getting home the hard way.

Before the 1932 World Series against the Cubs, Ruth was a star. But after the Series, he was a legend. In batting practice before Game 3 at Wrigley Field, Ruth and the Cubs players were trading profane insults by the basketful. As Ruth knocked ball after ball over the fence, he yelled at the Cubs bench, "I'd play for half my salary to hit in this dump all year." When he came to bat in the fifth inning, Cubs fans rained debris down on Ruth, including lemons, tomatoes, and grapefruit. Ruth, who had already hit a three-run homer in the first inning of the 4–4 game, took Charlie Root's first pitch for strike one, then held up one finger to indicate he had only one strike on him. After watching strike two go by, Ruth repeated his hand gesture, holding up two fingers. Then he held up his bat and pointed it to center field, holding it in place for a few moments, telling Cubs catcher Gabby Hartnett, "It only takes one to hit it." Ruth then slugged the next pitch into the center-field stands, exactly where he had pointed his bat. The "called shot" forever became a part of baseball lore, whether he actually called it or not. In the contemporary reporting of the account, there was no doubt that he called the home run. *The Spalding Guide,* baseball's official record book, mentions that he clearly called his home run. What is rarely reported, however, is what took place just after the called shot. When Ruth crossed the plate after his homer, he was met by Lou Gehrig. Ruth, who was feuding with Gehrig at the time, smugly said to Gehrig, "Okay, let's see you hit one of those." Gehrig replied, "Okay." When Gehrig stepped to the plate, he promptly hit a home run as well, essentially calling his shot, too—just not in such flamboyant fashion as Ruth had done.

As Ruth's career wound down, his skills began to suffer dramatically. He truly wanted to manage the Yankees, and the Yankee management tried to oblige him by asking him to manage their Newark team in order to gain some experience, but Ruth refused. The Tigers were considering making Ruth their manager, but Ruth failed to show up for his meeting with Tigers owner Frank Navin. Ruth slid to a .288 average and 22 homers in 1934 and the Yankees released him after the season. He signed on with the Boston Braves with the promise that someday he'd be the manager, but they never fulfilled their promise, using Ruth only to spark their pathetic attendance. On May 25, 1935, Ruth hit three mammoth home runs against the Pirates in cavernous Forbes Field, the last leaving the park entirely as it sailed over the right-field roof. After playing in just a few more games, Ruth retired. For the next decade, the Babe awaited the call to manage a big league ballclub, but it never came. He spent a short time as a coach for the Dodgers, but when the team's managerial post opened up, Leo Durocher got the job and Ruth was let go.

Ruth contracted throat cancer in 1946 and it claimed his life in 1948. His body was laid in state at Yankee Stadium and tens of thousands of mourners paid their last respects to the Sultan of Swat. At the time of his death, Ruth held 56 major league batting records and 10 more AL records. His lifetime total of 714 home runs stood until 1974 when it was broken by Hank Aaron, who needed almost 3,000 more at-bats to do it. Babe Ruth, the greatest baseball player ever, was elected to the Hall of Fame in 1936 as one of the original inductees. *(See Red Sox bio.)*

CAREER YANKEES RECORD:

Games	AB	Hits	Runs
2,084	7,217	2,518	1,959
Avg	**HR**	**RBI**	**SB**
.349	659	1,971	110

SHAWKEY, BOB (SP/RP)
(1915–1927)

Connie Mack, in one of his many efforts to raise money to meet expenses, sold third-year pitcher Bob Shawkey to the Yankees for $18,000 on June 28, 1915. For the next 12½ years, Shawkey toiled for the Yankees, four times collecting at least 20 victories in a season. In 1916, his first full year in New York, Shawkey won 24 games with a 2.21 ERA. After missing almost all of 1918 after enlisting in the Navy, Shawkey returned in 1919 to go 20–11 with a league-leading 2.45 ERA. During one stretch, he won 11 consecutive games. After winning 110 games in the six years from 1919 to 1924, Shawkey slumped to 6–14 in 1925 when the Yankees as a team melted down. He hurt his foot badly in 1926, finishing 8–7, then won only two games in 1927 before retiring. In 1929 he took a job as the pitching coach for the Yankees and did such a good job that Miller Huggins recommended him as a possible successor for the managerial post. When Huggins died on September 29, 1929, Shawkey got the job, but held it only one year, guiding the Yanks to an 86–68 record before being fired. He died in 1980.

CAREER YANKEES RECORD:

W	L	W%	ERA	SV
168	131	.562	3.12	26
K	**BB**	**SHO**	**IP**	
1,163	855	26	2,488.7	

STOTTLEMYRE, MEL (SP)
(1964–1974)

Mel Stottlemyre pitched his entire 11-year career with the Yankees, but unfortunately for him, it was at a time when the Yankees were stuck in a protracted down cycle. Still, he managed to win 20 or more games three times in his short career. Stottlemyre was a five-time All-Star who pitched more than 250 innings in nine straight seasons. In 1965 he was 20–9, the following year 12–20, thereby earning a rare and dubious distinction of winning 20 games one year and then losing 20 the next. In 1974 he tore his rotator cuff and never pitched again. After his playing career, Stottlemyre took the Seattle pitching coach job in 1977. In 1984 he took the same job for the Mets, developing Dwight Gooden into a star pitcher. After the 1993 season he left the Mets and moved on to the Astros for two years. In 1996 he returned to the Yankees as their pitching coach, a position he left following the 2005 season.

CAREER YANKEES RECORD:

W	L	W%	ERA	SV
164	139	.541	2.97	1
K	**BB**	**SHO**	**IP**	
1,257	809	40	2,661.3	

WHITE, ROY (OF)
(1965–1979)

In July 1961 the Yankees signed Roy White as an amateur free agent and he got his first brief taste of big league experience with the parent team in late 1965. White was one of those players who didn't stand out, but did all the little things that make a player successful. Overshadowed by many bigger stars such as Mantle, Maris, Munson, Jackson, and others, the fleet-footed switch-hitter quietly went about his job day in and day out, avoiding the limelight and the controversy that so often enveloped the Bronx Zoo. White never hit .300 in any of his 14 full seasons, never reached 100 RBIs, only once topped 20 homers, and only twice collected 100 runs. Yet because of his long, steady career, White's name is sprinkled among the leaders of many of New York's all-time hitting categories. After hitting just .215 in 1979, his last year in the majors, White went to Japan and played three years for the Tokyo Giants, becoming one of the most popular American players ever.

CAREER YANKEES RECORD:

Games	AB	Hits	Runs
1,881	6,650	1,803	964
Avg	HR	RBI	SB
.271	160	758	233

WILLIAMS, BERNIE (OF)
(1991–2005)

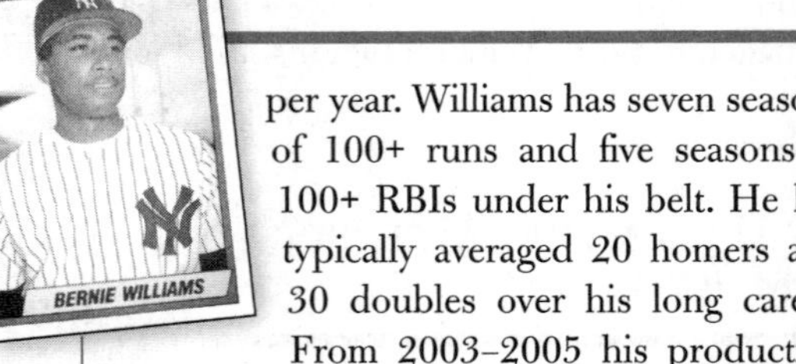

Signed as an amateur free agent in September 1985, Bernie Williams spent all or most of seven seasons in the minors before becoming a fixture in New York's center field for the next 13 years. He is a talented switch-hitter who quietly goes about his job. Williams, who owns four Gold Gloves, has made five trips to the All-Star Game. In 1998 he won the AL batting title with a .339 average, a most fortuitous bit of timing on his part since it was his contract year. For a while it looked like he would be moving on to the Red Sox as a free agent, but at the last minute, he struck a deal with the Yankees and signed a new seven-year deal that paid him more than $12 million per year. Williams has seven seasons of 100+ runs and five seasons of 100+ RBIs under his belt. He has typically averaged 20 homers and 30 doubles over his long career. From 2003–2005 his production began to slide, hitting a low point in 2005, leading most observers to conclude that Williams would not return to the Yankees in 2006.

CAREER YANKEES RECORD:

Games	AB	Hits	Runs
1,804	6,964	2,097	1,248
Avg	HR	RBI	SB
.301	263	1,132	144

WINFIELD, DAVE (OF)
(1981–1988; 1990)

See Padres bio.

Oakland Athletics

Since 1901

1973 Team Ball

1904 Eddie Plank wins 26 games and Rube Waddell wins 25, marking the only time in the 20th century that two left-handed pitchers on the same team win 25 games or more in the same year.... **1927** The A's have a major league record seven future Hall of Famers on their active roster: Ty Cobb, Al Simmons, Mickey Cochrane, Eddie Collins, Zack Wheat, Jimmie Foxx, and Lefty Grove.... **1964** Kansas City's Johnny Wyatt becomes the first 20th-century pitcher to appear in at least half of his team's games in a season (pitching in 81 of the A's 162 games, to be precise).... **1972–74** The A's become the only franchise other than the Yankees to win three consecutive World Series.... **1986–1988** The Oakland A's produce three consecutive Rookies of the Year: Jose Canseco in 1986, Mark McGwire in 1987, and Walt Weiss in 1988.

FRANCHISE HISTORY

When Ban Johnson's Western League renamed itself the American League in 1900, Connie Mack's Milwaukee club was a member. When the new entity was granted major league status in 1901, the Philadelphia franchise was awarded to Connie Mack and Benjamin Shibe, and the two men shifted their Milwaukee franchise to Philadelphia. They chose the name "Athletics" because for more than 40 years, there had always been an amateur or professional team of note going by that name within the city, and they reclaimed it. John McGraw, bristling over the number of former National League players who had jumped to the new league, called the A's "a bunch of white elephants," a remark that generated a lot of publicity. Making the most of it, Mack adopted the elephant as the A's mascot.

Mack, a longtime baseball player and official, owned 25 percent of the team while Shibe, a sporting goods manufacturer, held most of the remaining stock. Mack was also the team's manager for half a century, from 1901 to 1950. Shibe bought into the team only because he had been promised an exclusive contract to provide all the baseballs for the new league. The two owners worked a deal with two Philadelphia newspaper owners, giving them each large holdings of stock in the team in exchange for favorable press. (Newspaper ownership of teams—such as the Cubs and the Rockies—continues to this day, although it raises questions about the possibility of biased coverage of team affairs.) Frank Hough, owner of the *Philadelphia Inquirer,* soon sold his 25 percent to Mack. Shibe held his stock until his death in 1922, which came as a result of lingering injuries suffered during a 1920 automobile accident.

The A's were a very successful team early in the league's history, winning six pennants

Left to right, Home Run Baker; Jack McInnis; Eddie Murphy; and Jack Barry, circa 1912.

and three World Series between 1902 and 1914. Trouble arose, however, when the new Federal League formed in 1914. Mack's team had produced many stars, but a number of them were lured away to the Federal League, whose owners dangled huge salaries to attract AL and NL players. In addition, the existence of the new Federal League affected attendance, forcing Mack to sell off his remaining stars in order to meet expenses. After four first-place finishes in five years from 1910 to 1914, the A's finished in last place for seven straight years starting in 1915.

Over time, the astute Mack was able to rebuild the A's into another powerhouse team by the late 1920s. From 1929 to 1931, the A's won three straight pennants and two World Series. But history repeated itself. Due to declining attendance and huge losses suffered during the Depression, Mack, whose sole source of income was his baseball franchise, was again forced to sell off his stars to make ends meet.

Economics more than anything played a hand in keeping the A's down for decades. Unlike many of the other owners who regarded their teams as expensive toys, Mack didn't have the extra money to pay the big stars to stay competitive with the league's powerful teams. This time the downturn lasted much longer. From 1934 to 1968, the A's finished in the first division only twice, in 1948 and 1952, climbing to fourth place each year. Even after selling off all his stars, Mack had to borrow $400,000 from Red Sox owner Tom Yawkey to get through the Depression. Mack continued to run the team with the help of family members until he retired in 1950 at the age of 87. In 1954 the Mack family sold the team to Arnold Johnson, who moved the team to Kansas City. Mack died two years later at the age of 93.

Arnold Johnson was a Kansas City businessman who made his fortune in real estate,

Connie Mack, reliving his playing days.

the vending business, and various manufacturing enterprises. He paid the Mack family $3.5 million for the A's and held it until his sudden and unexpected death in 1960. At a probate sale in December 1960, Charlie O. Finley, who had been trying to purchase a major league team for six years, purchased 52 percent of the A's for just under $2 million. Baseball owners approved the sale to Finley on the condition that he keep the team in Kansas City for at least five years. He kept the team there until 1967, when he moved it to Oakland.

The 1957 Kansas City A's were the first team in history that did not have a single pitcher who pitched enough innings to qualify for the ERA title.

The one thing the A's seemed to be good at during their 13 dismal seasons in Kansas City was feeding good players to the Yankees and taking retreads in return. The most famous of these trades sent Roger Maris to New York in December 1959. (Maris promptly won the AL MVP Award twice and broke Babe Ruth's single-season home run record in 1961.) There were other connections between the two clubs as well. Yankee owner Del Webb, a construction contractor, received the contract to expand Kansas City's Municipal Stadium, home of the Kansas City A's. Dan Topping, a minority owner of the Yankees, sat on the Board of Directors of Arnold Johnson's corporation.

Charlie Finley received permission to relocate his A's from Kansas City to Oakland in time for the 1968 season. He had succeeded in purchasing 100 percent of the A's, which he held throughout the 1970s as his team evolved from a laughingstock to a powerhouse, winning three straight AL pennants and World Series titles from 1972 to 1974. Finley's tenure was a contentious one, with his players and with the other owners. He unveiled garish gold-and-green uniforms. He also tried to convince baseball's other owners to adopt fluorescent yellow baseballs (since they were scientifically proven to be easier to see than white baseballs) and colored bases. After selling off, trading, or losing its biggest stars to free agency in the mid-1970s, the Oakland A's tumbled, becoming one of the worst teams in the league during the late 1970s.

Finley grew weary of his team and tried to sell it to oil magnate Marvin Davis, who wanted to move the team to Denver, but the deal fell through when A's couldn't get out of their stadium lease. In 1908 Finley finally sold the team to Walter A. Haas Jr., owner of the Levi Strauss Co. for $12.7 million. Walter Haas was the great-great-grandnephew of Levi Strauss. During Haas' ownership, the A's were revitalized, thanks largely to the efforts of brilliant GM Sandy Alderson. From 1988 to 1990, the A's won three straight AL pennants and one World Series before slipping in the standings for the next decade. In 1994 Walter Haas' son Wally, who ran the team, announced that the A's were for sale for $85 million. A few weeks before Walter Haas died of prostate cancer at age 79, the sale of the team was completed to local real estate developers Steve Schott and Ken Hofmann for the $85 million asking price.

Catfish Hunter

Schott and Hofmann saw their A's become competitive again in the early 2000s. But despite making the postseason each year from 2000 to 2003, each year brought an early exit from the playoffs. On March 30, 2005, Schott and Hofmann sold the A's to an investment group headed by Los Angeles hotel developer Lewis Wolff for $180 million. John Fisher, son of Gap Inc. founder Don Fisher, is a minority partner.

TEAM NAME HISTORY

Official Names

Athletics (1901–current)

Unofficial Names/Nicknames

White Elephants, A's, Mackmen, Philadelphia Americans

STADIUM HISTORY

In Philadelphia

Columbia Park	1901–1908
Shibe Park	1909–1952
Connie Mack Stadium (Shibe Park renamed)	1953–1954

In Kansas City

Municipal Stadium	1955–1967

In Oakland

Oakland-Alameda County Stadium	1968–2003
Network Associates Coliseum (Oakland-Alameda County Stadium renamed)	2004–current

YEARLY RECORD, FINISH, & ATTENDANCE FIGURES

Year	League	Record	DIV/LG Finish	Attendance	Avg/Gm
2005	AL West	88–74	2	2,109,118	26,038
2004	AL West	91–71	2	2,201,516	27,179
2003	AL West	96–66	1	2,216,596	27,365
2002	AL West	103–59	1	2,169,811	26,788
2001	AL West	102–60	2	2,133,277	26,337
2000	AL West	91–70	1	1,603,744	19,799
1999	AL West	87–75	2	1,434,610	17,711
1998	AL West	74–88	4	1,232,343	15,214
1997	AL West	65–97	4	1,264,218	15,608
1996	AL West	78–84	3	1,148,380	14,178
1995	AL West	67–77	4	1,174,310	16,310
1994	AL West	51–63	2	1,242,692	22,191
1993	AL West	68–94	7	2,035,025	25,124
1992	AL West	96–66	1	2,494,160	30,792
1991	AL West	84–78	4	2,713,493	33,500
1990	AL West	103–59	1	2,900,217	35,805
1989	AL West	99–63	1	2,667,225	32,929
1988	AL West	104–58	1	2,287,335	28,239
1987	AL West	81–81	3	1,678,921	20,727
1986	AL West	76–86	4	1,314,646	15,839
1985	AL West	77–85	5	1,334,599	16,894
1984	AL West	77–85	4	1,353,281	16,707
1983	AL West	74–88	4	1,294,941	15,987
1982	AL West	68–94	5	1,735,489	21,426
1981	AL West	64–45	1/2	1,304,052	23,287
1980	AL West	83–79	2	842,259	10,398
1979	AL West	54–108	7	306,763	3,787
1978	AL West	69–93	6	526,999	6,587
1977	AL West	63–98	7	495,599	6,119
1976	AL West	87–74	2	780,593	9,637
1975	AL West	98–64	1	1,075,518	13,278
1974	AL West	90–72	1	845,693	10,441
1973	AL West	94–68	1	1,000,763	12,355
1972	AL West	93–62	1	921,323	11,965
1971	AL West	101–60	1	914,993	11,296
1970	AL West	89–73	2	778,355	9,609
1969	AL West	88–74	2	778,232	9,608
1968	AL	82–80	6	837,466	10,090
1967	AL	62–99	10	726,639	8,971
1966	AL	74–86	7	773,929	9,555
1965	AL	59–103	10	528,344	6,523
1964	AL	57–105	10	642,478	7,932
1963	AL	73–89	8	762,364	9,412
1962	AL	72–90	9	635,675	7,848
1961	AL	61–100	10	683,817	8,548
1960	AL	58–96	8	774,944	9,935
1959	AL	66–88	7	963,683	12,515
1958	AL	73–81	7	925,090	11,860
1957	AL	59–94	7	901,067	11,702
1956	AL	52–102	8	1,015,154	13,184
1955	AL	63–91	6	1,393,054	18,330

YEARLY RECORD, FINISH, & ATTENDANCE FIGURES (CONT.)

Year	League	Record	DIV/LG Finish	Attendance	Avg/Gm
1954	AL	51–103	8	304,666	3,957
1953	AL	59–95	7	362,113	4,642
1952	AL	79–75	4	627,100	8,040
1951	AL	70–84	6	465,469	5,892
1950	AL	52–102	8	309,805	4,023
1949	AL	81–73	5	816,514	10,604
1948	AL	84–70	4	945,076	12,274
1947	AL	78–76	5	911,566	11,687
1946	AL	49–105	8	621,793	7,972
1945	AL	52–98	8	462,631	6,008
1944	AL	72–82	5	505,322	6,649
1943	AL	49–105	8	376,735	4,769
1942	AL	55–99	8	423,487	5,572
1941	AL	64–90	8	528,894	6,869
1940	AL	54–100	8	432,145	6,087
1939	AL	55–97	7	395,022	5,198
1938	AL	53–99	8	385,357	5,070
1937	AL	54–97	7	430,738	5,452
1936	AL	53–100	8	285,173	3,704
1935	AL	58–91	8	233,173	3,239
1934	AL	68–82	5	305,847	4,024
1933	AL	79–72	3	297,138	3,910
1932	AL	94–60	2	405,500	5,266
1931	AL	107–45	1	627,464	8,366
1930	AL	102–52	1	721,663	9,496
1929	AL	104–46	1	839,176	11,340
1928	AL	98–55	2	689,756	8,958
1927	AL	91–63	2	605,529	7,864
1926	AL	83–67	3	714,508	10,063
1925	AL	88–64	2	869,703	11,295
1924	AL	71–81	5	531,992	7,093
1923	AL	69–83	6	534,122	7,122
1922	AL	65–89	7	425,356	5,453
1921	AL	53–100	8	344,430	4,473
1920	AL	48–106	8	287,888	3,739
1919	AL	36–104	8	225,209	3,217
1918	AL	52–76	8	177,926	2,617
1917	AL	55–98	8	221,432	2,914
1916	AL	36–117	8	184,471	2,427
1915	AL	43–109	8	146,223	1,976
1914	AL	99–53	1	346,641	4,444
1913	AL	96–57	1	571,896	7,525
1912	AL	90–62	3	517,653	6,723
1911	AL	101–50	1	605,749	8,077
1910	AL	102–48	1	588,905	7,550
1909	AL	95–58	2	674,915	8,880
1908	AL	68–85	6	455,062	5,834
1907	AL	88–57	2	625,581	8,570
1906	AL	78–67	4	489,129	6,700
1905	AL	92–56	1	554,576	7,494
1904	AL	81–70	5	512,294	6,485

YEARLY RECORD, FINISH, & ATTENDANCE FIGURES (CONT.)

Year	League	Record	DIV/LG Finish	Attendance	Avg/Gm
1903	AL	75–60	2	422,473	6,306
1902	AL	83–53	1	420,078	5,754
1901	AL	74–62	4	206,329	3,126

MANAGER HISTORY

Manager	Years	W–L	Win %
Connie Mack	1901–1950	3,582–3,814	.484
Jimmie Dykes	1951–1953	208–254	.450
Eddie Joost	1954	51–103	.331
Lou Boudreau	1955–1957	151–260	.367
Harry Craft	1957–1959	162–196	.453
Bob Elliott	1960	58–96	.377
Joe Gordon	1961	26–33	.441
Hank Bauer	1961–1962,		
	1969	187–226	453
Eddie Lopat	1963–1964	90–124	.421
Mel McGaha	1964–1965	45–91	.331
Haywood Sullivan	1965	54–82	. 397
Alvin Dark	1966–1967,	.519	
	1974–1975	314–291	.519
Luke Appling	1967	10–30	.250
Bob Kennedy	1968	82–80	.506
John McNamara	1969–1970	97–78	.554
Dick Williams	1971–1973	288–190	.603
Chuck Tanner	1976	87–74	.540
Jack McKeon	1977, 1978	71–105	.403
Bobby Winkles	1977–1978	61–86	.415
Jim Marshall	1979	54–108	.333
Billy Martin	1980–1982	215–218	.497
Steve Boros	1983–1984	94–112	.456
Jackie Moore	1984–1986	163–190	.462
Tony LaRussa	1986–1995	798–673	.542
Art Howe	1996–2002	600–533	.530
Ken Macha	2003–2005	275–211	.566

ALL-TIME WIN-LOSS RECORDS VS. ALL OPPONENTS

Opponent	Record
ALL-TIME	7,870–8,343
Angels	372–320
Astros	3–0
Blue Jays	172–143
Braves	3–3
Brewers	189–159
Cardinals	0–3
Cubs	1–2
Devil Rays	53–22
Diamondbacks	9–3
Dodgers	9–7
Giants	26–24
Indians	858–989
INTERLEAGUE	95–63
Mariners	233–162
Marlins	1–2
Mets	2–1
Nationals	3–3
Orioles	950–907
Padres	11–5
Phillies	3–3
Pirates	6–0
Rangers	338–326
Reds	6–0
Red Sox	834–1,027
Rockies	9–7
Royals	267–218
Tigers	876–956
Twins	953–960
White Sox	938–996
Yankees	745–1,095

"Home Run" Baker hit only 48 of them in his six-year career during the dead-ball era.

Franchise Highlights, Low Points, and Strange Distinctions

1901 Napoleon Lajoie of the A's set the 20th-century record for batting average in a season by hitting .426. He also won the Triple Crown. He was so intimidating that year that on May 23, he became the first player in history to be intentionally walked with the bases loaded when the White Sox gave him a free RBI in an 11–9 Chicago victory.

••••

1904 A's shortstop Monte Cross hit .189 in 503 at-bats, the lowest average in major league history by a player with 500 or more at-bats.

First baseman Harry Davis of the Philadelphia A's was the first player ever to lead his league in home runs four consecutive years. He accomplished the feat from 1904 to 1907.

••••

1910 When Earl Mack played one game for Connie Mack's A's, it marked the first time in major league history that a son played on a team managed by his father.

••••

1912 Twice in an 11-day period (September 11 and 22), second baseman Eddie Collins of the A's stole a major league record six bases in a single game.

1914 Chief Bender led the American League in winning percentage at .850 (17–3). Seeking the big money offered by the upstart Federal League in 1915, Bender jumped to the rival organization. When he finished with a 4–16 record, his .200 winning percentage was the lowest in the new league.

••••

1915 The A's suffered the biggest fall from first place one season to the next when they finished in last place at 43–109 after winning the American League pennant the year before with a 99–53 record, a whopping 56-game drop.

••••

1917 First baseman George Burns of the Tigers hit .226 and was released from the team. The A's picked him up and he hit .352 in 1918, second in the American League to Ty Cobb's .382.

••••

1918 As hard as it is to win 20 games for a last-place team, consider how much tougher Scott Perry had it when he won 20 for the last-place A's. Due to the "Work or Fight" order in place during World War I, the major league season was halted on Labor Day. Perry finished 20–19 with a 1.98 ERA for the 52–76 A's. Almost as stunning is how quickly his career turned sour. In 1919 he went 4–17, followed by 11–25 in 1920, and in 1921—his last in baseball—Perry went 3–6.

1910–20 The Philadelphia A's were so bad in the last half of the 1910s that they finished in last place a record seven straight seasons. Shibe Park was a veritable graveyard for pitchers. After going 0–5 in his rookie season of 1915, Jack Nabors had the worst season by any pitcher in history in 1916, finishing 1–20 (including 19 straight losses), even though his ERA was a respectable 3.47. Nabors got so frustrated with his team's lack of run support that in the ninth inning of a tie game he intentionally threw a wild pitch just to lose and get the game over with rather than drawing out the foregone conclusion.

• • • •

1924–34 Few rookies have ever had 100 RBIs in a season. Fewer still have had 100+ RBIs in their first two seasons. And—until Albert Pujols of the Cardinals posted his fifth straight 100+ RBI season in 2005—no player other than Al Simmons of the A's had ever done it more than two consecutive years from the start of a career. Pujols will have to go a ways to catch him, though, as Simmons collected 100+ RBIs in his first 11 seasons (1924–1934), the first nine of which were with the A's. Simmons also became the first American League player to get 200 hits in five consecutive seasons (1929–1933).

• • • •

1927 When Ty Cobb hit his first home run for his new team, the Philadelphia A's, he became the first player in major league history to homer before the age of 20 and after the age of 40. The only other player to accomplish the feat is Rusty Staub.

1929 Even though he hit only .232, second baseman Max Bishop of the A's somehow managed to lead the major leagues in walks that year with 128.

• • • •

1932–33 The first player ever to win back-to-back MVP Awards was Jimmie Foxx of the Philadelphia A's in 1932–1933.

• • • •

1933 Winning a Triple Crown is one of the rarest accomplishments in baseball, having happened only 16 times. Imagine, then, the odds of what happened in 1933. Not only was there a Triple Crown winner in both leagues, but the winners both played for Philadelphia teams. The Phillies' Chuck Klein won the National League Triple Crown with a .368 average, 28 homers, and 120 RBIs. Jimmie Foxx of the Philadelphia A's won the American League Triple Crown with a .356 average, 48 homers, and 163 RBIs.

• • • •

1965 The oldest player ever to appear in a major league game was Kansas City's Satchel Paige who was either 58 or 65 at the time—depending on the source—when he pitched three scoreless innings against Boston in a 5–2 loss to the Red Sox on September 25.

• • • •

1968 It's easy to see why baseball executives made some adjustments after 1968's "Season of the Pitcher." The Oakland A's led the American League in hitting with a paltry .240 average, the lowest ever by a league leader. The Yankees finished last in 1968 with a .214 average.

1971 When Oakland's Vida Blue struck out 301 batters, his first full season in baseball, he became the first pitcher in major league history to strike out at least 300 batters and not lead the league. Mickey Lolich of the Tigers nipped him with 308.

• • • •

1972 Proving he was a money player, Oakland's Gene Tenace hit home runs in his first two World Series plate appearances.

On September 19, the A's used eight different second basemen in an 8–7, 15-inning loss to the White Sox. It was the most players ever used at one position other than pitcher in a single major league game.

• • • •

1979 In the A's first 25 years in Oakland, the team turned five triple plays. Third baseman Wayne Gross was involved in four of those, three in 1979 alone.

• • • •

1982 Not only did Rickey Henderson of the A's break the record for stolen bases in a season with 130, but he also set the new mark for most times caught in a season, 42.

• • • •

1988 Outfielder Jose Canseco became the first player in baseball history to hit at least 40 homers and steal at least 40 bases in the same season when he accomplished the feat in 1988. Barry Bonds and Alex Rodriguez have since joined him in the 40–40 club.

• • • •

1991 Dennis Eckersley of Oakland became the first pitcher in major league history with both 150 career saves and 150 career wins.

When Eckersley recorded 36 saves in 1993, he became the first reliever in history to have 30 or more saves in six consecutive seasons. His streak would end in 1994, however, when he compiled only 19 saves, due to the protracted season-ending players strike.

• • • •

1998 When Rickey Henderson led the American League with 66 stolen bases, he became the oldest player ever (39) to lead either league in steals.

• • • •

2000 The A's set a major league record with 14 grand slams on the season, two more than Atlanta hit in 1997.

• • • •

2001 The A's were the first team in history to have both a shortstop (Miguel Tejada, 31) and third baseman (Eric Chavez, 32) hit at least 30 homers in the same season. That year's club also was the first team in major league history to win 100 games after being 10 games below .500 during the season. They also had the second-best record ever after the All-Star break, 58–17 (.773). Only the 1974 Indians at 55–16 (.775) were better. Despite their sparkling record, the A's had to settle for the Wild Card because they were in the same division as the Seattle Mariners, who set an all-time record with 116 wins.

• • • •

2004 Shortstop Bobby Crosby's .239 batting average was the lowest ever for a Rookie of the Year Award winner (other than a pitcher).

Special Achievements

WORLD SERIES RESULTS

Year	Opponent	Result	Games
1905	New York Giants	Lost	1–4
1910	Chicago Cubs	Won	4–1
1911	New York Giants	Won	4–2
1913	New York Giants	Won	4–1
1914	Boston Braves	Lost	0–4
1929	Chicago Cubs	Won	4–1
1930	St. Louis Cardinals	Won	4–2
1931	St. Louis Cardinals	Lost	3–4
1972	Cincinnati Reds	Won	4–3
1973	New York Mets	Won	4–3
1974	L.A. Dodgers	Won	4–1
1988	L.A. Dodgers	Lost	1–4
1989	S.F. Giants	Won	4–0
1990	Cincinnati Reds	Lost	0–4

WORLD SERIES MANAGERIAL RECORDS

Manager	Series Record	Games Record
Connie Mack	5–3	24–19
Dick Williams	2–0	8–6
Alvin Dark	1–0	4–1
Tony LaRussa	1–2	5–8

ALL-TIME POSTSEASON RECORD

Divisional Playoffs	8–12
League Championship Series	23–19
World Series	41–34

ALL-STAR GAMES AT PHILADELPHIA (WHEN AL WAS HOME TEAM)/KANSAS CITY/OAKLAND

Year	Date	Winner	Score	Stadium
1943	July 13	American	5–3	Shibe Park
1960	July 11	National	5–3	Municipal Stadium
1987	July 14	National	2–0	Oakland-Alameda County Coliseum

HALL OF FAMERS WHO PLAYED FOR TEAM

	Position	Years	Games with Philadelphia/ Kansas City/ Oakland
Frank Baker	3B	1908–1914	899
Chief Bender	SP/RP	1903–1914	432
Orlando Cepeda	PH	1972	3
Ty Cobb	OF	1927–1928	229
Mickey Cochrane	C	1925–1933	1,167
Eddie Collins	2B	1906–1914, 1927–1930	1,156
Jimmy Collins	3B	1907–1908	214
Stan Coveleski	RP/SP	1912	5
Dennis Eckersley	RP	1987–1995	525
Rollie Fingers	RP	1968–1976	503
Elmer Flick	OF	1902	11
Nellie Fox	2B	1947–1949	98
Jimmie Foxx	1B/3B	1925–1935	1,256
Lefty Grove	SP/RP	1925–1933	402
Waite Hoyt	SP	1931	16
Catfish Hunter	SP	1965–1974	378
Reggie Jackson	OF/DH	1967–1975, 1987	1,346
George Kell	3B	1943–1946	313
Nap Lajoie	2B	1901–1902, 1915–1916	374
Tommy Lasorda	RP/SP	1956	19
Willie McCovey	DH	1976	11
Joe Morgan	2B	1984	116
Satchel Paige	SP	1965	1
Herb Pennock	RP/SP	1912–1915	70
Eddie Plank	SP/RP	1901–1914	531
Al Simmons	OF	1924–1932, 1940–1941, 1944	1,290
Enos Slaughter	OF	1955–1956	199
Tris Speaker	OF	1928	64
Don Sutton	SP	1985	29
Rube Waddell	SP/RP	1902–1907	252
Zack Wheat	OF	1927	88
Billy Williams	DH	1975–1976	275

HALL OF FAMERS WHO MANAGED TEAM

	Years	Games with Philadelphia/ Kansas City/ Oakland
Luke Appling	1967	40
Lou Boudreau	1955–1957	411
Connie Mack	1901–1950	7,396

MVP AWARD WINNERS

Lefty Grove	SP	1931
Jimmie Foxx	1B	1932
Jimmie Foxx	1B	1933
Bobby Shantz	SP	1952
Vida Blue	SP	1971
Reggie Jackson	OF	1973
Jose Canseco	OF	1988
Rickey Henderson	OF	1990
Dennis Eckersley	RP	1992
Jason Giambi	1B	2000
Miguel Tejada	SS	2002

CY YOUNG AWARD WINNERS

Pitcher	Year	W–L	SV	ERA
Vida Blue	1971	24–8	0	1.82
Catfish Hunter	1974	25–12	0	2.49
Bob Welch	1990	27–6	0	2.95
Dennis Eckersley	1992	7–1	51	1.91
Barry Zito	2002	23–5	0	2.75

ROOKIE OF THE YEAR AWARD WINNERS

Harry Byrd	SP	1952
Jose Canseco	OF	1986
Mark McGwire	1B	1987
Walt Weiss	SS	1988
Ben Grieve	OF	1998
Bobby Crosby	SS	2004
Huston Street	RP	2005

GOLD GLOVE WINNERS

Year	Position	Player
1974	OF	Joe Rudi
1975	OF	Joe Rudi
1976	OF	Joe Rudi
1980	SP OF	Mike Norris Dwayne Murphy
1981	SP OF OF	Mike Norris Dwayne Murphy Rickey Henderson
1982	OF	Dwayne Murphy
1983	OF	Dwayne Murphy
1984	OF	Dwayne Murphy
1985	SS OF	Alfredo Griffin Dwayne Murphy
1990	1B	Mark McGwire
2001	3B	Eric Chavez
2002	3B	Eric Chavez
2003	3B	Eric Chavez
2004	3B	Eric Chavez
2005	3B	Eric Chavez

TRIPLE CROWN WINNERS

Player	Year	Avg	HR	RBI
Napoleon Lajoie	1901	.422	14	125
Jimmie Foxx	1933	.356	48	163

FIREMAN OF THE YEAR AWARD WINNERS

Jack Aker	1966
Dennis Eckersley	1988
Dennis Eckersley	1991
Dennis Eckersley	1992
Billy Koch	2002
Keith Foulke	2003

WORLD SERIES MVP

Gene Tenace	1972
Reggie Jackson	1973
Rollie Fingers	1974
Dave Stewart	1989

LEAGUE CHAMPIONSHIP SERIES MVP

Dennis Eckersley	1988
Rickey Henderson	1989
Dave Stewart	1990

ALL-STAR GAME MVP

Terry Steinbach	1988

MANAGER OF THE YEAR AWARD WINNERS

Tony LaRussa	1988
Tony LaRussa	1992

BATTING CHAMPIONS

Year	Player	Avg
1901	Napoleon Lajoie	.426
1930	Al Simmons	.381
1931	Al Simmons	.390
1933	Jimmie Foxx	.356
1951	Ferris Fain	.344
1952	Ferris Fain	.327

Nine-Inning No-Hitters Pitched

Year	Pitcher	Opp.	Score
1905	Weldon Henley	STL	6–0
1910	Chief Bender	CLE	4–0
1916	Joe Bush	CLE	5–0
1945	Dick Fowler	STL	1–0
1947	Bill McCahan	WAS	3–0
1968	Catfish Hunter	MIN	4–0 (perfect)
1970	Vida Blue	MIN	6–0
1975	Vida Blue/ Glenn/Abbott/ Paul Lindblad Rollie Fingers	CAL	5–0
1983	Mike Warren	CWS	3–0
1990	Dave Stewart	TOR	5–0

20-Game Winners

Year	Pitcher	W–L
1901	Chick Fraser	22–16
1902	Rube Waddell Eddie Plank	24–7 20–15
1903	Eddie Plank Rube Waddell	23–16 21–16
1904	Eddie Plank Rube Waddell	26–17 25–19
1905	Rube Waddell Eddie Plank	27–10 24–12
1907	Eddie Plank Jimmy Dygert	24–16 21–8
1910	Jack Coombs Chief Bender	31–9 23–5
1911	Jack Coombs Eddie Plank	28–12 23–8
1912	Eddie Plank Jack Coombs	26–6 21–10
1913	Chief Bender	21–10
1918	Scott Perry	20–19
1922	Eddie Rommel	27–13
1925	Eddie Rommel	21–10
1927	Lefty Grove	20–13
1928	Lefty Grove	24–8
1929	George Earnshaw Lefty Grove	24–8 20–6
1930	Lefty Grove George Earnshaw	28–5 22–13
1931	Lefty Grove George Earnshaw Rube Walberg	31–4 21–7 20–12
1932	Lefty Grove	25–10
1933	Lefty Grove	24–8
1949	Alex Kellner	20–12
1952	Bobby Shantz	24–7
1971	Vida Blue Catfish Hunter	24–8 21–11
1972	Catfish Hunter	21–7
1973	Catfish Hunter Ken Holtzman Vida Blue	21–5 21–13 20–9
1974	Catfish Hunter	25–12
1975	Vida Blue	22–11
1980	Mike Norris	22–9
1987	Dave Stewart	20–13
1988	Dave Stewart	21–12
1989	Dave Stewart	21–9
1990	Bob Welch Dave Stewart	27–6 22–11
2000	Tim Hudson	20–6
2001	Mark Mulder	21–8
2002	Barry Zito	23–5

Retired Uniform Numbers

Number	Player	Position
9	Reggie Jackson	OF
27	Catfish Hunter	SP
34	Rollie Fingers	RP
43	Dennis Eckersley	RP

Team Records—Wins & Losses

- Games won in a season: 107 in 1931
- Games lost in a season: 117 in 1916
- Games won in a month: 26 in July 1931
- Games lost in a month: 28 in July 1916
- Consecutive games won: 20 in 2002
- Consecutive games lost: 20 in 1916 and 1943
- Biggest shutout victory: 16–0 (three times vs. White Sox): July 25, 1928 (first game); August 29, 1937 (first game); and May 23, 1959. Also vs. San Francisco, June 26, 2005
- Biggest shutout loss: 21–0 to New York Yankees, August 13, 1939
- Highest winning percentage: .704 in 1931 (107–45)
- Lowest winning percentage: .235 in 1916 (36–117)

Team Records—Batting

- Highest team batting average: .307 in 1925
- Lowest team batting average: .223 in 1908
- Highest team slugging average: .458 in 2000
- Highest team on-base percentage: .372 in 1927
- Total hits: 1,659 in 1925
- Extra-base hits: 555 in 2001
- Hits in a game: 29 vs. Boston Red Sox on May 1, 1929; vs. Texas on July 1, 1979 (15 innings)

- Longest individual hitting streak: 29, Bill Lamar, 1925
- Most .300 hitters in a single season: 11 in 1927
- Home runs: 243 in 1996
- Home runs in a month: 15, Bob Johnson, June 1934 and Mark McGwire, May 1987
- Home runs in a game: 8 vs. California Angels on June 27, 1996
- Home runs by a rookie: 49, Mark McGwire, 1987
- Home runs by a right-hander: 58, Jimmie Foxx, 1932
- Home runs by a left-hander: 47, Reggie Jackson, 1969
- Home runs by a switch-hitter: 23, Ruben Sierra, 1994
- Grand slams: 14 in 2000
- Grand slams (individual; season): 4, Jason Giambi, 2000
- Grand slams (individual; career): 9 (three players): Jimmie Foxx, Sam Chapman, Mark McGwire
- Triples: 108 in 1912
- Doubles: 336 in 2004
- Singles: 1,206 in 1925
- Walks: 783 in 1949
- Runs scored: 981 in 1932
- Runs scored in a game: 24 vs. Detroit, May 18, 1912 and vs. Boston Red Sox, May 1, 1929
- Runs scored in an inning: 13 (four times): vs. Cleveland on June 15, 1925 (eighth inning); vs. Chicago White Sox on April 21, 1956 (second inning); vs. California Angels on July 5, 1996 (first inning); and vs. Chicago White Sox on May 12, 1997 (seventh)
- Most batters hit by a pitch: 88 in 2001
- Times shut out: 24 in 1943
- Grounded into double plays: 170 in 1950
- Fewest grounded into double plays: 79 in 1967
- Runners left on base: 1,274 in 2004

TEAM RECORDS—BASERUNNING

- Stolen bases: 341 in 1976
- Caught stealing: 188 in 1914

TEAM RECORDS—PITCHING

- Lowest earned run average: 1.79 in 1910
- Complete games: 136 in 1904
- Saves: 64 in 1988 and 1990
- Strikeouts: 1,117 in 2001
- Shutouts: 28 in 1909
- Walks: 827 in 1915
- Hit batsmen: 81 in 1911
- Wild pitches: 72 in 1979
- Consecutive wins (individual): 16, Lefty Grove, 1931
- Consecutive losses (individual): 19, Jack Nabors, 1916
- Strikeouts in a game (individual): 18, Jack Coombs (twice): September 1, 1906 (24 innings) and August 4, 1910 (16 innings); 16, Jose Rijo, April 19, 1986 (nine innings)
- Runs allowed in a game: 29 vs. Chicago White Sox, April 23, 1955

TEAM RECORDS—FIELDING

- Best fielding average: .986 in 1990, 2004, and 2005
- Most errors committed: 338 in 1915
- Fewest errors committed: 87 in 1990
- Most double plays turned: 217 in 1949
- Fewest double plays turned: 64 in 1905

TEAM RECORDS—MISCELLANEOUS

- Number of times league champions: 15
- Number of times finishing last in league: 26
- Largest attendance, single game: 55,601 vs. Anaheim Angels, July 5, 2003
- Largest attendance, doubleheader: 48,592 vs. New York Yankees, May 3, 1981
- Players used in a season: 56 in 1915
- Seasons played: 16 by Harry Davis

PRIMARY PITCHING STAFFS

Year	Starter	Starter	Starter	Starter	Starter	Closer	Bullpen	Bullpen	Bullpen
2005	Zito	Haren	Blanton	Saarloos	Harden	Street	Rincon	Duchscherer	Calero
2004	Zito	Mulder	Redman	Harden	Hudson	Dotel	Bradford	Rincon	Mecir
2003	Zito	Mulder	Lilly	Halama	Hudson	Foulke	Bradford	Rincon	Mecir
2002	Zito	Mulder	Lidle	Harang	Hudson	Koch	Bradford	Venafro	Mecir
2001	Zito	Mulder	Lidle	Heredia	Hudson	Isringhausen	Tam	Magnante	Mecir
2000	Appier	Mulder	Olivares	Heredia	Hudson	Isringhausen	Tam	Magnante	Jones
1999	Haynes	Oquist	Rogers	Heredia	Hudson	Taylor	Groom	Worrell	Jones
1998	Haynes	Oquist	Rogers	Candiotti	Stein	Taylor	Groom	Mathews	Mohler
1997	Karsay	Oquist	Prieto	Telgheder	Rigby	Taylor	Groom	Small	Mohler
1996	Wengert	Johns	Prieto	Wasdin	Wojciechowski	Taylor	Groom	Corsi	Mohler
1995	Stottlemyre	Ontiveros	Darling	Stewart	Van Poppel	Eckersley	Honeycutt	Acre	Reyes
1994	Witt	Ontiveros	Darling	Reyes	Van Poppel	Eckersley	Taylor	Acre	Briscoe
1993	Witt	Welch	Darling	Downs	Van Poppel	Eckersley	Nunez	Honeycutt	Mohler
1992	Moore	Welch	Darling	Stewart	Slusarski	Eckersley	Parrett	Honeycutt	Horsman
1991	Moore	Welch	Hawkins	Stewart	Slusarski	Eckersley	Klink	Chitren	Nelson
1990	Moore	Welch	Sanderson	Stewart	Young	Eckersley	Honeycutt	Burns	Nelson
1989	Moore	Welch	Davis	Stewart	Young	Eckersley	Honeycutt	Burns	Nelson
1988	Burns	Welch	Davis	Stewart	Young	Eckersley	Honeycutt	Cadaret	Nelson
1987	Ontiveros	Rijo	Andujar	Stewart	Young	Eckersley	Leiper	Lamp	Nelson
1986	Codiroli	Rijo	Andujar	Stewart	Young	Howell	Mooneyham	Ontiveros	Leiper
1985	Codiroli	Sutton	Birtsas	Krueger	John	Howell	Atherton	Ontiveros	McCatty
1984	McCatty	Burris	Sorensen	Krueger	Young	Caudill	Atherton	Conroy	Codiroli
1983	McCatty	Codiroli	Conroy	Krueger	Norris	Beard	Underwood	Burgmeier	Baker
1982	McCatty	Keough	Langford	Kingman	Norris	Beard	Underwood	Owchinko	Hanna
1981	McCatty	Keough	Langford	Kingman	Norris	McLaughlin	Owchinko	Jones	Underwood
1980	McCatty	Keough	Langford	Kingman	Norris	Lacey	Hamilton	Beard	Jones
1979	McCatty	Keough	Langford	Kingman	Norris	Heaverlo	Hamilton	Todd	Lacey
1978	Johnson	Keough	Langford	Broberg	Renko	Sosa	Heaverlo	Wirth	Lacey
1977	Blue	Medich	Langford	Norris	Coleman	Bair	Torrealba	Giusti	Lacey
1976	Blue	Torrez	Mitchell	Norris	Bosman	Fingers	Lindblad	Todd	Bahnsen
1975	Blue	Holtzman	Bahnsen	Abbott	Bosman	Fingers	Lindblad	Todd	Siebert
1974	Blue	Holtzman	Hunter	Abbott	Hamilton	Fingers	Lindblad	Knowles	Odom
1973	Blue	Holtzman	Hunter	Odom	Hamilton	Fingers	Lindblad	Knowles	Pina
1972	Blue	Holtzman	Hunter	Odom	Hamilton	Fingers	Locker	Knowles	Horlen
1971	Blue	Dobson	Hunter	Odom	Segui	Fingers	Locker	Knowles	Roland
1970	Fingers	Dobson	Hunter	Odom	Segui	Grant	Lachemann	Lindblad	Locker
1969	Nash	Dobson	Hunter	Odom	Krausse	Fingers	Lachemann	Lindblad	Roland
1968	Nash	Dobson	Hunter	Odom	Krausse	Aker	Segui	Lindblad	Sprague
1967	Nash	Dobson	Hunter	Odom	Krausse	Aker	Segui	Lindblad	Pierce
1966	Nash	Dobson	Hunter	Odom	Krausse	Aker	Sanders	Lindblad	Stock
1965	Talbot	O'Donoghue	Hunter	Sheldon	Segui	Wyatt	Dickson	Mossi	Stock
1964	Pena	O'Donoghue	Drabowsky	Bowsfield	Segui	Wyatt	Santiago	Sanders	Stock
1963	Pena	Wickersham	Drabowsky	Rakow	Segui	Wyatt	Fischer	Bowsfield	Willis
1962	Pfister	Walker	Fischer	Rakow	Segui	Wyatt	McDevitt	Wickersham	Bass
1961	Archer	Walker	Shaw	Bass	Nuxhall	Kunkel	Rakow	Staley	
1960	Daley	Herbert	Hall	Kucks	Larsen	Kutyna	Johnson	Garver	
1959	Daley	Herbert	Garver	Kucks	Coleman	Grim	Dickson	Sturdivant	
1958	Terry	Herbert	Garver	Urban	Grim	Gorman	Tomanek	Dickson	Daley
1957	Terry	Kellner	Garver	Urban	Portocarrero	Morgan	Trucks	Burnette	Gorman
1956	Ditmar	Kellner	Kretlow	Herriage	Burnette	Shantz	Crimian	Harrington	Gorman
1955	Ditmar	Kellner	Portocarrero	Raschi	Shantz	Gorman	Ceccarelli	Harrington	Boyer
1954	Fricano	Kellner	Portocarrero	Trice	Gray	Burtschy	Dixon	Sima	

PRIMARY PITCHING STAFFS (CONT.)

Year	Starter	Starter	Starter	Starter	Starter	Closer	Bullpen	Bullpen	Bullpen
1953	Fricano	Kellner	Byrd	Bishop	Shantz	Martin	Scheib	Fanovich	Coleman
1952	Scheib	Kellner	Byrd	Hooper	Shantz	Kucab	Wright	Fowler	
1951	Fowler	Kellner	Zoldak	Hooper	Shantz	Scheib	Kucab	Martin	Coleman
1950	Brissie	Kellner	Wyse	Hooper	Shantz	Scheib	Fowler	Coleman	
1949	Brissie	Kellner	Coleman	Fowler	Scheib	Harris	Shantz	McCahan	
1948	Brissie	Marchildon	Coleman	Fowler	Scheib	Harris	Savage	McCahan	
1947	Flores	Marchildon	Coleman	Fowler	McCahan	Christopher	Scheib	Savage	Dietrich
1946	Flores	Marchildon	Knerr	Fowler	Savage	Harris	Christopher	Fagan	
1945	Flores	Newsom	Knerr	Christopher	Black	Berry	Gassaway	Gerkin	
1944	Flores	Newsom	Hamlin	Christopher	Black	Berry	Harris	Scheib	Wheaton
1943	Flores	Harris	Wolff	Arntzen	Black	Christopher	Fagan	Ciola	
1942	Marchildon	Harris	Wolff	Christopher	Fowler	Besse	Knott	Harris	
1941	Marchildon	Knott	McCrabb	Beckmann	Babich	Ferrick	Harris	Hadley	Dean
1940	Potter	Caster	Ross	Dean	Babich	Heusser	Beckmann	Vaughan	
1939	Potter	Caster	Ross	Nelson	Beckmann	Dean	Joyce	Pippen	Parmelee
1938	Potter	Caster	Ross	Nelson	Thomas	Smith	Williams	Smith	
1937	Kelley	Caster	Ross	Smith	Thomas	Turbeville	Nelson	Fink	
1936	Kelley	Rhodes	Ross	Fink	Lisenbee	Gumpert	Dietrich	Flythe	
1935	Marcum	Blaeholder	Wilshere	Mahaffey	Dietrich	Benton	Caster	Turbeville	
1934	Marcum	Cain	Cascarella	Benton	Dietrich	Mahaffey	Kline	Flohr	
1933	Grove	Cain	Mahaffey	Walberg	Earnshaw	Peterson	Coombs	Freitas	
1932	Grove	Freitas	Mahaffey	Walberg	Earnshaw	Krausse	Rommel	Cain	
1931	Grove	Hoyt	Mahaffey	Walberg	Earnshaw	McDonald	Rommel	Shores	
1930	Grove	Shores	Mahaffey	Walberg	Earnshaw	Quinn	Perkins	Rommel	
1929	Grove	Shores	Quinn	Walberg	Earnshaw	Yerkes	Rommel	Orwoll	
1928	Grove	Ehmke	Quinn	Walberg	Earnshaw	Bush	Rommel	Orwoll	
1927	Grove	Ehmke	Quinn	Walberg	Rommel	Pate	Gray	Johnson	Willis
1926	Grove	Ehmke	Quinn	Walberg	Rommel	Pate	Gray	Heimach	Willis
1925	Grove	Harriss	Gray	Walberg	Rommel	Baumgartner	Quinn	Stokes	
1924	Heimach	Burns	Gray	Baumgartner	Rommel	Harriss	Meeker	Hasty	
1923	Heimach	Hasty	Harriss	Naylor	Rommel	Walberg	Ogden		
1922	Heimach	Hasty	Harriss	Naylor	Rommel	Eckert	Sullivan	Yarrison	
1921	Moore	Hasty	Harriss	Naylor	Rommel	Keefe	Freeman	Perry	
1920	Moore	Perry	Harriss	Naylor	Keefe	Rommel	Hasty	Bigbee	
1919	Johnson	Perry	Kinney	Naylor	Rogers	Seibold	Noyes	Geary	
1918	Gregg	Perry	Watson	Myers	Adams	Johnson	Pierson	Geary	
1917	Bush	Johnson	Noyes	Myers	Schauer	Seibold	Falkenberg	Anderson	
1916	Bush	Johnson	Nabors	Myers	Sheehan	Williams	Crowell	Wyckoff	
1915	Bush	Wyckoff	Bressler	Shawkey	Sheehan	Davis	Knowlson	Pennock	
1914	Bush	Wyckoff	Bender	Shawkey	Plank	Bressler	Brown	Pennock	
1913	Bush	Brown	Bender	Houck	Plank	Shawkey	Wyckoff	Pennock	
1912	Coombs	Brown	Bender	Houck	Plank	Morgan	Crabb	Pennock	
1911	Coombs	Morgan	Bender	Krause	Plank	Danforth	Martin	Russell	
1910	Coombs	Morgan	Bender	Krause	Plank	Dygert	Atkins		
1909	Coombs	Morgan	Bender	Krause	Plank	Dygert	Vickers		
1908	Coombs	Vickers	Dygert	Schlitzer	Plank	Bender	Carter		
1907	Coombs	Waddell	Dygert	Bender	Plank	Bartley	Vickers		
1906	Coombs	Waddell	Dygert	Bender	Plank	Coakley			
1905	Coakley	Waddell	Henley	Bender	Plank	Dygert			
1904	Coakley	Waddell	Henley	Bender	Plank	Fairbank	Applegate		
1903	Waddell	Henley	Bender	Plank	Coakley	Fairbank			
1902	Husting	Waddell	Wiltse	Mitchell	Plank	Wilson			
1901	Fraser	Bernhard	Wiltse	Piatt	Plank	Milligan			

PRIMARY STARTING LINEUPS

Year	C	1B	2B	3B	SS	LF	CF	RF	DH
2005	Kendall	Johnson	Ellis	Chavez	Crosby	Kielty	Kotsay	Swisher	Hatteberg
2004	Miller	Hatteberg	Scutaro	Chavez	Crosby	Byrnes	Kotsay	Dye	Durazo
2003	Hernandez	Hatteberg	Ellis	Chavez	Tejada	Long	Singleton	Dye	Durazo
2002	Hernandez	Hatteberg	Ellis	Chavez	Tejada	Justice	Long	Dye	Durham
2001	Hernandez	Giambi	Menechino	Chavez	Tejada	Long	Damon	Dye	Giambi
2000	Hernandez	Giambi	Velarde	Chavez	Tejada	Grieve	Long	Stairs	Jaha
1999	Macfarlane	Giambi	Phillips	Chavez	Tejada	Grieve	Christenson	Stairs	Jaha
1998	Hinch	Giambi	Spiezio	Blowers	Tejada	R. Henderson	Christenson	Grieve	Stairs
1997	Mayne	McGwire	Spiezio	Brosius	Bournigal	Giambi	Mashore	Stairs	Canseco
1996	Steinbach	McGwire	Bournigal	Brosius	Bordick	Plantier	Young	Herrera	Berroa
1995	Steinbach	McGwire	Gates	Paquette	Bordick	R. Henderson	Javier	Sierra	Berroa
1994	Steinbach	Neel	Gates	Brosius	Bordick	R. Henderson	Javier	Sierra	Berroa
1993	Steinbach	Aldrete	Gates	Paquette	Bordick	R. Henderson	D. Henderson	Sierra	Neel
1992	Steinbach	McGwire	Bordick	Lansford	Weiss	R. Henderson	Wilson	Canseco	Baines
1991	Steinbach	McGwire	Gallego	Riles	Bordick	R. Henderson	D. Henderson	Canseco	Baines
1990	Steinbach	McGwire	Randolph	Lansford	Weiss	R. Henderson	D. Henderson	Canseco	Baines
1989	Steinbach	McGwire	Phillips	Lansford	Gallego	R. Henderson	D. Henderson	Javier	Parker
1988	Hassey	McGwire	Hubbard	Lansford	Weiss	Polonia	D. Henderson	Canseco	Baylor
1987	Steinbach	McGwire	Phillips	Lansford	Griffin	Canseco	Murphy	Davis	Jackson
1986	Tettleton	Bochte	Phillips	Lansford	Griffin	Canseco	Murphy	Davis	Kingman
1985	Heath	Bochte	Hill	Lansford	Griffin	Collins	Murphy	Davis	Kingman
1984	Heath	Bochte	Morgan	Lansford	Phillips	R. Henderson	Murphy	Davis	Kingman
1983	Kearney	Gross	Lopes	Lansford	Phillips	R. Henderson	Murphy	Davis	Burroughs
1982	Heath	Meyer	Lopes	Gross	Stanley	R. Henderson	Murphy	Armas	Burroughs
1981	Heath	Spencer	Babitt	Gross	Picciolo	R. Henderson	Murphy	Armas	Johnson
1980	Essian	Revering	McKay	Gross	Guerrero	R. Henderson	Murphy	Armas	Page
1979	Newman	Revering	Edwards	Gross	Picciolo	R. Henderson	Murphy	Murray	Page
1978	Essian	Revering	Edwards	Gross	Guerrero	Page	Wallis	Armas	Alexander
1977	Newman	Allen	Perez	Gross	Picciolo	Page	Armas	Tyrone	Sanguillen
1976	Haney	Tenace	Garner	Bando	Campaneris	Rudi	North	Washington	Williams
1975	Tenace	Rudi	Garner	Bando	Campaneris	Washington	North	Jackson	Williams
1974	Haney	Tenace	Green	Bando	Campaneris	Rudi	North	Jackson	Alou
1973	Fosse	Tenace	Green	Bando	Campaneris	Rudi	North	Jackson	Johnson
1972	Duncan	Epstein	Cullen	Bando	Campaneris	Rudi	Jackson	Mangual	
1971	Duncan	Epstein	Green	Bando	Campaneris	Rudi	Monday	Jackson	
1970	Fernandez	Mincher	Green	Bando	Campaneris	Alou	Monday	Jackson	
1969	Roof	Cater	Green	Bando	Campaneris	Reynolds	Monday	Jackson	
1968	Duncan	Cater	Donaldson	Bando	Campaneris	Hershberger	Monday	Jackson	
1967	Roof	Webster	Donaldson	Green	Campaneris	Cater	Monday	Hershberger	
1966	Roof	Harrelson	Green	Charles	Campaneris	Stahl	Nossek	Hershberger	
1965	Bryan	Harrelson	Green	Charles	Campaneris	Reynolds	Landis	Hershberger	
1964	Edwards	Gentile	Green	Charles	Causey	Jimenez	Mathews	Colavito	
1963	Edwards	Siebern	Lumpe	Charles	Causey	Essegian	Del Greco	Cimoli	
1962	Sullivan	Siebern	Lumpe	Charles	Howser	Jimenez	Del Greco	Cimoli	
1961	Sullivan	Siebern	Lumpe	Causey	Howser	Posada	Del Greco	Rivera	
1960	Daley	Throneberry	Lumpe	Carey	Hamlin	Siebern	Tuttle	Bauer	
1959	House	Hadley	Terwilliger	Williams	DeMaestri	Cerv	Tuttle	Maris	
1958	Chiti	Power	Lopez	Smith	DeMaestri	Cerv	Tuttle	Maris	
1957	Smith	Power	Hunter	Lopez	DeMaestri	Zernial	Held	Skizas	
1956	Thompson	Power	Finigan	Lopez	DeMaestri	Zernial	Pilarcik	Simpson	
1955	Astroth	Power	Finigan	Lopez	DeMaestri	Zernial	Simpson	Slaughter	
1954	Astroth	Limmer	Jacobs	Finigan	DeMaestri	Zernial	Wilson	Renna	

PRIMARY STARTING LINEUPS (CONT.)

Year	C	1B	2B	3B	SS	LF	CF	RF	DH
1953	Astroth	Robinson	Michaels	Babe	DeMaestri	Zernial	McGhee	Philley	
1952	Astroth	Fain	Kell	Hitchcock	Joost	Zernial	Philley	Valo	
1951	Tipton	Fain	Suder	Majeski	Joost	Zernial	Philley	Valo	
1950	Guerra	Fain	Hitchcock	Dillinger	Joost	Lehner	Chapman	Valo	
1949	Guerra	Fain	Suder	Majeski	Joost	Valo	Chapman	Moses	
1948	Rosar	Fain	Suder	Majeski	Joost	McCosky	Chapman	Valo	
1947	Rosar	Fain	Suder	Majeski	Joost	McCosky	Chapman	Valo	
1946	Rosar	McQuinn	Handley	Majeski	Suder	Chapman	McCosky	Valo	
1945	Rosar	Siebert	Hall	Kell	Busch	Metro	Estalella	Peck	
1944	Hayes	McGhee	Hall	Kell	Busch	Garrison	Estalella	White	
1943	Wagner	Siebert	Suder	Mayo	Hall	Estalella	White	Valo	
1942	Wagner	Siebert	Knickerbocker	Blair	Suder	Johnson	Kreevich	Valo	
1941	Hayes	Siebert	McCoy	Suder	Brancato	Johnson	Chapman	Moses	
1940	Hayes	Siebert	McCoy	Rubeling	Brancato	Johnson	Chapman	Moses	
1939	Hayes	Siebert	Gantenbein	Lodigiani	Newsome	Johnson	Chapman	Moses	
1938	Hayes	Finney	Lodigiani	Werber	Ambler	Chapman	Johnson	Moses	
1937	Brucker	Dean	Peters	Werber	Newsome	Johnson	Hill	Moses	
1936	Hayes	Finney	Warstler	Higgins	Newsome	Johnson	Moses	Puccinelli	
1935	Richards	Foxx	Warstler	Higgins	McNair	Johnson	Cramer	Moses	
1934	Berry	Foxx	Warstler	Higgins	McNair	Johnson	Cramer	Coleman	
1933	Cochrane	Foxx	Bishop	Higgins	Williams	Johnson	Cramer	Coleman	
1932	Cochrane	Foxx	Bishop	Dykes	McNair	Simmons	Haas	Miller	
1931	Cochrane	Foxx	Bishop	Dykes	Williams	Simmons	Haas	Miller	
1930	Cochrane	Foxx	Bishop	Dykes	Boley	Simmons	Haas	Miller	
1929	Cochrane	Foxx	Bishop	Hale	Boley	Simmons	Haas	Miller	
1928	Cochrane	Hauser	Bishop	Hale	Boley	Simmons	Haas	Cobb	
1927	Cochrane	Dykes	Bishop	Hale	Boley	Lamar	Simmons	French	
1926	Cochrane	Poole	Bishop	Dykes	Galloway	Lamar	Simmons	French	
1925	Cochrane	Poole	Bishop	Hale	Galloway	Lamar	Simmons	Miller	
1924	Perkins	Hauser	Bishop	Riconda	Galloway	Lamar	Simmons	Miller	
1923	Perkins	Hauser	Dykes	Hale	Galloway	Miller	Matthews	Welch	
1922	Perkins	Hauser	Young	Dykes	Galloway	Walker	Miller	Welch	
1921	Perkins	Walker	Dykes	Dugan	Galloway	Walker	Welch	Witt	
1920	Perkins	Griffin	Dykes	Thomas	Galloway	Walker	Welch	Witt	
1919	Perkins	Burns	Witt	Thomas	Dugan	Kopp	Walker	Roth	
1918	McAvoy	Burns	Dykes	Gardner	Dugan	Kopp	Walker	Jamieson	
1917	Schang	McInnis	Grover	Bates	Witt	Bodie	Strunk	Jamieson	
1916	Meyer	McInnis	Lajoie	Pick	Witt	Schang	Strunk	Walsh	
1915	Lapp	McInnis	Lajoie	Schang	Kopf	Oldring	Strunk	Murphy	
1914	Schang	McInnis	Collins	Baker	Barry	Oldring	Strunk	Murphy	
1913	Lapp	McInnis	Collins	Baker	Barry	Oldring	Strunk	Murphy	
1912	Lapp	McInnis	Collins	Baker	Barry	Strunk	Oldring	Lord	
1911	Thomas	McInnis	Collins	Baker	Barry	Lord	Oldring	Murphy	
1910	Lapp	Davis	Collins	Baker	Barry	Hartsel	Oldring	Murphy	
1909	Thomas	Davis	Collins	Baker	Barry	Hartsel	Ganley	Murphy	
1908	Schreckengost	Davis	Collins	Collins	Nicholls	Hartsel	Oldring	Murphy	
1907	Schreckengost	Davis	Murphy	Collins	Nicholls	Hartsel	Oldring	Seybold	
1906	Schreckengost	Davis	Murphy	Knight	M. Cross	Hartsel	Lord	Seybold	
1905	Schreckengost	Davis	Murphy	L. Cross	Knight	Hartsel	Hoffman	Seybold	
1904	Schreckengost	Davis	Murphy	L. Cross	M. Cross	Hartsel	Pickering	Seybold	
1903	Schreckengost	Davis	Murphy	L. Cross	M. Cross	Hartsel	Pickering	Seybold	
1902	Schreckengost	Davis	Murphy	L. Cross	M. Cross	Hartsel	Fultz	Seybold	
1901	Powers	Davis	Lajoie	Cross	Dolan	McIntyre	Fultz	Seybold	

Top 10 Batting Leaders, Single Season & Career with Team

Games Played: Career with Team

Player	G	PA
1. Bert Campaneris	1,795	7,895
2. Rickey Henderson	1,704	7,481
3. Jimmie Dykes	1,702	6,990
4. Sal Bando	1,468	6,086
5. Bob Johnson	1,459	6,323
6. Pete Suder	1,421	5,473
7. Harry Davis	1,413	5,945
8. Danny Murphy	1,412	5,676
9. Bing Miller	1,361	5,256
Elmer Valo	1,361	5,229

At-Bats: Season

Player	AB	Year
1. Al Simmons	670	1932
2. Miguel Tejada	662	2002
3. Doc Cramer	661	1933
4. Al Simmons	654	1925
5. Lou Finney	653	1936
6. Doc Cramer	649	1934
Wally Moses	649	1937
8. Doc Cramer	644	1935
Johnny Damon	644	2001
10. Bert Campaneris	642	1968

At-Bats: Career with Team

Player	AB	PA
1. Bert Campaneris	7,180	7,895
2. Rickey Henderson	6,140	7,481
3. Jimmie Dykes	6,023	6,990
4. Bob Johnson	5,428	6,323
5. Harry Davis	5,367	5,945
6. Sal Bando	5,145	6,086
7. Danny Murphy	5,138	5,676
8. Al Simmons	5,130	5,586
9. Pete Suder	5,085	5,473
10. Bing Miller	4,762	5,256

Batting Average: Season

Player	BA	Year
1. Nap Lajoie	.426	1901
2. Al Simmons	.392	1927
3. Al Simmons	.390	1931
4. Al Simmons	.387	1925
5. Al Simmons	.381	1930
6. Eddie Collins	.365	1911
Al Simmons	.365	1929
8. Jimmie Foxx	.364	1932
Elmer Valo	.364	1955
10. Mickey Cochrane	.357	1930

Batting Average: Career with Team

Player	BA	PA
1. Al Simmons	.356	5,586
2. Jimmie Foxx	.339	5,239
3. Eddie Collins	.337	4,632
4. Mickey Cochrane	.321	4,856
Frank Baker	.321	3,840
6. Stuffy McInnis	.313	4,215
7. Bing Miller	.311	5,256
8. Doc Cramer	.308	2,862
Jason Giambi	.308	4,083
10. Wally Moses	.307	4,841

Total Hits: Season

Player	H	Year
1. Al Simmons	253	1925
2. Nap Lajoie	232	1901
3. Al Simmons	216	1932
4. Doc Cramer	214	1935
5. Jimmie Foxx	213	1932
6. Al Simmons	212	1929
7. Al Simmons	211	1930
8. Wally Moses	208	1937
9. Jimmie Foxx	204	1933
Miguel Tejada	204	2002

Total Hits: Career with Team

Player	H	PA
1. Bert Campaneris	1,882	7,895
2. Al Simmons	1,827	5,586
3. Rickey Henderson	1,768	7,481
4. Jimmie Dykes	1,705	6,990
5. Bob Johnson	1,617	6,323
6. Harry Davis	1,500	5,945
7. Jimmie Foxx	1,492	5,239
8. Danny Murphy	1,489	5,676
9. Bing Miller	1,480	5,256
10. Mickey Cochrane	1,317	4,856
Carney Lansford	1,317	5,046

Home Runs: Season

Player	HR	Year
1. Jimmie Foxx	58	1932
2. Mark McGwire	52	1996
3. Mark McGwire	49	1987
4. Jimmie Foxx	48	1933
5. Reggie Jackson	47	1969
6. Jose Canseco	44	1991
Jimmie Foxx	44	1934
8. Jason Giambi	43	2000
9. Jose Canseco	42	1988
Mark McGwire	42	1992
Gus Zernial	42	1953

Home Runs: Career with Team

Player	HR	PA
1. Mark McGwire	363	5,409
2. Jimmie Foxx	302	5,239
3. Reggie Jackson	269	5,430
4. Jose Canseco	254	4,531
5. Bob Johnson	252	6,323
6. Al Simmons	209	5,586
7. Sal Bando	192	6,086
8. Gus Zernial	191	3,471
9. Eric Chavez	190	4,201
10. Jason Giambi	187	4,083

Triples: Season

Player	3B	Year
1. Frank Baker	21	1912
2. Frank Baker	19	1909
3. Danny Murphy	18	1910
4. Danny Murphy	17	1904
5. Bing Miller	16	1929
Al Simmons	16	1930
Amos Strunk	16	1915
8. Frank Baker	15	1910
Gino Cimoli	15	1962
Eddie Collins	15	1910
Whitey Witt	15	1916

Triples: Career with Team

Player	3B	PA
1. Danny Murphy	102	5,676
2. Al Simmons	98	5,586
3. Frank Baker	88	3,840
4. Eddie Collins	85	4,632
5. Harry Davis	82	5,945
6. Jimmie Foxx	79	5,239
7. Rube Oldring	75	4,890
8. Topsy Hartsel	74	4,905
Bing Miller	74	5,256
10. Jimmie Dykes	73	6,990

Doubles: Season

Player	2B	Year
1. Al Simmons	53	1926
2. Nap Lajoie	48	1901
Wally Moses	48	1937
4. Harry Davis	47	1905
Jason Giambi	47	2001
Eric McNair	47	1932
7. Socks Seybold	45	1903
8. Bob Johnson	44	1933
9. Eric Chavez	43	2001
Harry Davis	43	1902
Ferris Fain	43	1952
Bing Miller	43	1931
Al Simmons	43	1925

Doubles: Career with Team

Player	2B	PA
1. Jimmie Dykes	365	6,990
2. Al Simmons	348	5,586
3. Harry Davis	319	5,945
4. Bob Johnson	307	6,323
5. Bing Miller	292	5,256
6. Rickey Henderson	289	7,481
7. Danny Murphy	279	5,676
8. Wally Moses	274	4,841
9. Bert Campaneris	270	7,895
10. Jimmie Foxx	257	5,239

Extra-Base Hits: Season

Player	XBH	Year
1. Jimmie Foxx	100	1932
2. Jimmie Foxx	94	1933
3. Al Simmons	93	1930
4. Jason Giambi	87	2001
5. Reggie Jackson	86	1969
Wally Moses	86	1937
7. Al Simmons	84	1929
8. Jimmie Foxx	83	1930
9. Al Simmons	82	1926
10. Mark McGwire	81	1987

Extra-Base Hits: Career with Team

Player	XBH	PA
1. Al Simmons	655	5,586
2. Jimmie Foxx	638	5,239
3. Bob Johnson	631	6,323
4. Mark McGwire	563	5,409
5. Reggie Jackson	530	5,430
6. Jimmie Dykes	524	6,990
7. Rickey Henderson	497	7,481
8. Harry Davis	470	5,945
9. Bing Miller	460	5,256
10. Jose Canseco	448	4,531

Total Bases: Season

Player	TB	Year
1. Jimmie Foxx	438	1932
2. Jimmie Foxx	403	1933
3. Al Simmons	392	1925
Al Simmons	392	1930
5. Al Simmons	373	1929
6. Al Simmons	367	1932
7. Jimmie Foxx	358	1930
8. Wally Moses	357	1937
9. Jimmie Foxx	352	1934
10. Nap Lajoie	350	1901

Total Bases: Career with Team

Player	TB	PA
1. Al Simmons	2,998	5,586
2. Bob Johnson	2,824	6,323
3. Jimmie Foxx	2,813	5,239
4. Rickey Henderson	2,640	7,481
5. Bert Campaneris	2,502	7,895
6. Jimmie Dykes	2,474	6,990
7. Mark McGwire	2,451	5,409
8. Reggie Jackson	2,323	5,430
9. Bing Miller	2,202	5,256
10. Harry Davis	2,190	5,945

Runs Batted In: Season

Player	RBI	Year
1. Jimmie Foxx	169	1932
2. Al Simmons	165	1930
3. Jimmie Foxx	163	1933
4. Al Simmons	157	1929
5. Jimmie Foxx	156	1930
6. Al Simmons	151	1932
7. Jason Giambi	137	2000
8. Miguel Tejada	131	2002
9. Frank Baker	130	1912
Jimmie Foxx	130	1934

Runs Batted In: Career with Team

Player	RBI	PA
1. Al Simmons	1,178	5,586
2. Jimmie Foxx	1,075	5,239
3. Bob Johnson	1,040	6,323
4. Mark McGwire	941	5,409
5. Sal Bando	796	6,086
6. Jose Canseco	793	4,531
7. Reggie Jackson	776	5,430
8. Jimmie Dykes	764	6,990
9. Bing Miller	762	5,256
10. Harry Davis	761	5,945

Runs Scored: Season

Player	R	Year
1. Al Simmons	152	1930
2. Jimmie Foxx	151	1932
3. Nap Lajoie	145	1901
4. Al Simmons	144	1932
5. Eddie Collins	137	1912
6. Eddie Joost	128	1949
7. Jimmie Foxx	127	1930
8. Eddie Collins	125	1913
Jimmie Foxx	125	1933
10. Jimmie Foxx	123	1929
Reggie Jackson	123	1969

Runs Scored: Career with Team

Player	R	PA
1. Rickey Henderson	1,270	7,481
2. Bob Johnson	997	6,323
3. Bert Campaneris	983	7,895
4. Jimmie Foxx	975	5,239
5. Al Simmons	969	5,586
6. Max Bishop	882	5,273

Player	BB	PA
7. Jimmie Dykes	881	6,990
8. Mickey Cochrane	823	4,856
9. Harry Davis	811	5,945
10. Mark McGwire	773	5,409

Walks: Season

Player	BB	Year
1. Eddie Joost	149	1949
2. Jason Giambi	137	2000
3. Ferris Fain	136	1949
4. Ferris Fain	133	1950
5. Jason Giambi	129	2001
6. Max Bishop	128	1929
Max Bishop	128	1930
8. Eddie Joost	122	1952
9. Topsy Hartsel	121	1905
10. Eddie Joost	119	1948
Elmer Valo	119	1949

Walks: Career with Team

Player	BB	PA
1. Rickey Henderson	1,227	7,481
2. Max Bishop	1,043	5,273
3. Bob Johnson	853	6,323
4. Mark McGwire	847	5,409
5. Elmer Valo	820	5,229
6. Sal Bando	792	6,086
7. Jimmie Foxx	781	5,239
8. Eddie Joost	768	4,210
9. Topsy Hartsel	733	4,905
10. Dwayne Murphy	694	4,886

Strikeouts: Season

Player	SO	Year
1. Jose Canseco	175	1986
2. Reggie Jackson	171	1968
3. Reggie Jackson	161	1971
4. Jose Canseco	158	1990
5. Jose Canseco	157	1987
6. Jose Canseco	152	1991
7. Nelson Mathews	143	1964
Rick Monday	143	1968
9. Reggie Jackson	142	1969
10. Bobby Crosby	141	2004

Strikeouts: Career with Team

Player	SO	PA
1. Reggie Jackson	1,226	5,430
2. Jose Canseco	1,096	4,531
3. Mark McGwire	1,043	5,409
4. Bert Campaneris	933	7,895
5. Rickey Henderson	915	7,481
6. Dwayne Murphy	883	4,886
7. Dick Green	785	4,462
8. Jimmie Dykes	706	6,990
9. Sal Bando	702	6,086
10. Eric Chavez	690	4,201

Slugging Percentage: Season

Player	SLG	Year
1. Jimmie Foxx	.749	1932
2. Mark McGwire	.731	1996
3. Al Simmons	.708	1930
4. Jimmie Foxx	.703	1933
5. Mark McGwire	.685	1995
6. Jason Giambi	.660	2001
7. Jimmie Foxx	.653	1934
8. Jason Giambi	.647	2000
9. Al Simmons	.645	1927
10. Nap Lajoie	.643	1901

Slugging Percentage: Career with Team

Player	SLG	PA
1. Jimmie Foxx	.640	5,239
2. Al Simmons	.584	5,586
3. Mark McGwire	.551	5,409
4. Jason Giambi	.545	4,083
5. Bob Johnson	.520	6,323
6. Matt Stairs	.509	2,346
7. Jose Canseco	.507	4,531
8. Eric Chavez	.496	4,201
Reggie Jackson	.496	5,430
10. Mickey Cochrane	.490	4,856

On-Base Percentage: Season

Player	OBP	Year
1. Jason Giambi	.477	2001
2. Jason Giambi	.476	2000
3. Jimmie Foxx	.469	1932
4. Mark McGwire	.467	1996
5. Jimmie Foxx	.463	1929
Nap Lajoie	.463	1901
7. Jimmie Foxx	.461	1935
8. Elmer Valo	.460	1955
9. Mickey Cochrane	.459	1933
10. Eddie Collins	.452	1914

On-Base Percentage: Career with Team

Player	OBP	PA
1. Jimmie Foxx	.440	5,239
2. Ferris Fain	.426	3,700
3. Eddie Collins	.423	4,632
Max Bishop	.423	5,273
5. Jason Giambi	.412	4,083
Mickey Cochrane	.412	4,856
7. Rickey Henderson	.409	7,481
8. Elmer Valo	.403	5,229
9. Al Simmons	.398	5,586
10. Bob Johnson	.395	6,323

OPS (On-Base Percentage + Slugging Percentage): Season

Player	OPS	Year
1. Jimmie Foxx	1.218	1932
2. Mark McGwire	1.198	1996
3. Jimmie Foxx	1.153	1933
4. Jason Giambi	1.137	2001
5. Al Simmons	1.130	1930
6. Mark McGwire	1.125	1995
7. Jason Giambi	1.123	2000
8. Nap Lajoie	1.106	1901
9. Jimmie Foxx	1.102	1934
10. Jimmie Foxx	1.096	1935

OPS (On-Base Percentage + Slugging Percentage): Career with Team

Player	OPS	PA
1. Jimmie Foxx	1.079	5,239
2. Al Simmons	.983	5,586
3. Jason Giambi	.957	4,083
4. Mark McGwire	.931	5,409
5. Bob Johnson	.915	6,323
6. Mickey Cochrane	.902	4,856
7. Matt Stairs	.871	2,346
8. Eddie Collins	.860	4,632
9. Eric Chavez	.856	3,507
10. Jose Canseco	.851	4,531

STOLEN BASES: SEASON

Player	SB	Year
1. Rickey Henderson	130	1982
2. Rickey Henderson	108	1983
3. Rickey Henderson	100	1980
4. Eddie Collins	81	1910
5. Billy North	75	1976
6. Eddie Collins	67	1909
7. Rickey Henderson	66	1984
Rickey Henderson	66	1998
9. Rickey Henderson	65	1990
10. Eddie Collins	63	1912

STOLEN BASES: CAREER WITH TEAM

Player	SB	PA
1. Rickey Henderson	867	7,481
2. Bert Campaneris	566	7,895
3. Eddie Collins	376	4,632
4. Billy North	232	2,859
5. Harry Davis	223	5,945
6. Topsy Hartsel	196	4,905
7. Rube Oldring	187	4,890
8. Danny Murphy	185	5,676
9. Frank Baker	172	3,840
10. Carney Lansford	146	5,046

SACRIFICE HITS: SEASON

Player	Sac	Year
1. Roy Grover	43	1917
2. Mule Haas	40	1929
3. Bob Ganley	36	1909
4. Dave Fultz	35	1902
5. Frank Baker	34	1909
Danny Murphy	34	1909
Simon Nicholls	34	1907
8. Mule Haas	33	1930
9. Jack Barry	31	1914
Simon Nicholls	31	1908

SACRIFICE HITS: CAREER WITH TEAM

Player	Sac	PA
1. Jimmie Dykes	188	6,990
2. Danny Murphy	183	5,676
3. Eddie Collins	171	4,632
4. Jack Barry	169	3,590
5. Stuffy McInnis	163	4,215
Amos Strunk	163	4,037
7. Rube Oldring	151	4,890
8. Bing Miller	145	5,256
9. Mule Haas	130	2,861
10. Mickey Cochrane	127	4,856
Chick Galloway	127	3,827

HIT BY PITCH: SEASON

Player	HBP	Year
1. Don Baylor	20	1976
Jason Kendall	20	2005
3. Frank Menechino	19	2001
4. Eddie Collins	15	1911
Jimmie Dykes	15	1921
Olmedo Saenz	15	1999
7. Wally Schang	14	1915
8. Bobby Del Greco	13	1962
Jason Giambi	13	2001
Nap Lajoie	13	1901
Olmedo Saenz	13	2001
Miguel Tejada	13	2001

HIT BY PITCH: CAREER WITH TEAM

Player	HBP	PA
1. Jimmie Dykes	93	6,990
2. Sal Bando	62	6,086
Reggie Jackson	62	5,430
4. Bing Miller	58	5,256
5. Bert Campaneris	55	7,895
Rickey Henderson	55	7,481
7. Miguel Tejada	54	3,967
8. Carney Lansford	53	5,046
9. Mark McGwire	52	5,409
Wally Schang	52	1,939

Top 10 Pitching Leaders, Single Season & Career with Team

GAMES PITCHED: SEASON

Player	GP	Year
1. Billy Koch	84	2002
2. John Wyatt	81	1964
3. Buddy Groom	78	1997
4. Rollie Fingers	76	1974
Buddy Groom	76	1999
6. Chad Bradford	75	2002
Rollie Fingers	75	1975
Buddy Groom	75	1998
9. Bob Lacey	74	1978
10. Seven tied with...	72	—

GAMES PITCHED: CAREER WITH TEAM

Player	GP	IP
1. Dennis Eckersley	525	637.0
2. Eddie Plank	524	3,860.7
3. Rollie Fingers	502	1,016.0
4. Eddie Rommel	500	2,556.3
5. Paul Lindblad	479	873.7
6. Rube Walberg	412	2,186.7
7. Lefty Grove	402	2,401.0
8. Rick Honeycutt	387	406.3
9. Chief Bender	385	2,602.0
10. Catfish Hunter	363	2,456.3

INNINGS PITCHED: SEASON

Player	IP	Year
1. Rube Waddell	383.0	1904
2. Eddie Plank	357.3	1904
3. Jack Coombs	353.0	1910
4. Eddie Plank	346.7	1905
5. Eddie Plank	343.7	1907
6. Jack Coombs	336.7	1911
7. Eddie Plank	336.0	1903
8. Scott Perry	332.3	1918
9. Chick Fraser	331.0	1901
10. Rube Waddell	328.7	1905

INNINGS PITCHED: CAREER WITH TEAM

Player	IP
1. Eddie Plank	3,860.7
2. Chief Bender	2,602.0
3. Eddie Rommel	2,556.3
4. Catfish Hunter	2,456.3
5. Lefty Grove	2,401.0
6. Rube Walberg	2,186.7
7. Vida Blue	1,945.7
8. Rube Waddell	1,869.3
9. Alex Kellner	1,730.3
10. Dave Stewart	1,717.3

BATTERS FACED: SEASON

Player	BF	Year
1. Rube Waddell	1,548	1904
2. Chick Fraser	1,484	1901
3. Eddie Plank	1,464	1904
4. Jack Coombs	1,422	1911
5. Eddie Plank	1,391	1905
6. Eddie Plank	1,390	1907
7. Jack Coombs	1,388	1910
8. Eddie Plank	1,378	1903
9. Scott Perry	1,342	1918
10. Elmer Myers	1,310	1916

BATTERS FACED: CAREER WITH TEAM

Player	BF	IP
1. Eddie Plank	15,711	3,860.7
2. Eddie Rommel	10,873	2,556.3
3. Lefty Grove	10,060	2,401.0
4. Catfish Hunter	9,983	2,456.3
5. Rube Walberg	9,516	2,186.7
6. Chief Bender	8,436	2,602.0
7. Vida Blue	7,935	1,945.7
8. Rube Waddell	7,542	1,869.3
9. Alex Kellner	7,538	1,730.3
10. Dave Stewart	7,305	1,717.3

GAMES STARTED: SEASON

Player	GS	Year
1. Rube Waddell	46	1904
2. Eddie Plank	43	1904
3. Catfish Hunter	41	1974
Eddie Plank	41	1905
5. Vida Blue	40	1974
George Caster	40	1938
Jack Coombs	40	1911
Chuck Dobson	40	1970
Ken Holtzman	40	1973
Catfish Hunter	40	1970
Eddie Plank	40	1903
Eddie Plank	40	1907

GAMES STARTED: CAREER WITH TEAM

Player	GS	IP
1. Eddie Plank	458	3,860.7
2. Catfish Hunter	340	2,456.3
3. Chief Bender	288	2,602.0
4. Lefty Grove	267	2,401.0
Rube Walberg	267	2,186.7
6. Vida Blue	262	1,945.7
7. Eddie Rommel	249	2,556.3
8. Dave Stewart	245	1,717.3
9. Alex Kellner	239	1,730.3
10. Blue Moon Odom	214	1,414.7

COMPLETE GAMES: SEASON

Player	CG	Year
1. Rube Waddell	39	1904
2. Eddie Plank	37	1904
3. Jack Coombs	35	1910
Chick Fraser	35	1901
Eddie Plank	35	1905
6. Rube Waddell	34	1903
7. Eddie Plank	33	1903
Eddie Plank	33	1907
9. Weldon Henley	31	1904
Elmer Myers	31	1916
Eddie Plank	31	1902

COMPLETE GAMES: CAREER WITH TEAM

Player	CG	IP
1. Eddie Plank	362	3,860.7
2. Chief Bender	228	2,602.0
3. Lefty Grove	179	2,401.0
4. Rube Waddell	168	1,869.3
5. Eddie Rommel	147	2,556.3
6. Jack Coombs	135	1,629.7
7. Rube Walberg	126	2,186.7
8. Catfish Hunter	116	2,456.3
9. Vida Blue	105	1,945.7
10. Alex Kellner	95	1,730.3

GAMES WON: SEASON

Player	W	Year
1. Jack Coombs	31	1910
Lefty Grove	31	1931
3. Jack Coombs	28	1911
Lefty Grove	28	1930
5. Eddie Rommel	27	1922
Rube Waddell	27	1905
Bob Welch	27	1990
8. Eddie Plank	26	1904
Eddie Plank	26	1912
10. Lefty Grove	25	1932
Catfish Hunter	25	1974
Rube Waddell	25	1904

GAMES WON: CAREER WITH TEAM

Player	W	IP
1. Eddie Plank	284	3,860.7
2. Lefty Grove	195	2,401.0
3. Chief Bender	193	2,602.0
4. Eddie Rommel	171	2,556.3
5. Catfish Hunter	161	2,456.3
6. Rube Walberg	134	2,186.7
7. Rube Waddell	131	1,869.3
8. Vida Blue	124	1,945.7
9. Dave Stewart	119	1,717.3
10. Jack Coombs	115	1,629.7

GAMES LOST: SEASON

Player	L	Year
1. Scott Perry	25	1920
2. Joe Bush	24	1916
3. Elmer Myers	23	1916
Rollie Naylor	23	1920
Eddie Rommel	23	1921
6. Art Ditmar	22	1956
Weldon Wyckoff	22	1915
8. Lum Harris	21	1943
Harry Kelley	21	1937
10. Nine tied with . . .	20	—

GAMES LOST: CAREER WITH TEAM

Player	L	IP
1. Eddie Plank	162	3,860.7
2. Eddie Rommel	119	2,556.3
3. Rube Walberg	114	2,186.7
4. Catfish Hunter	113	2,456.3
5. Alex Kellner	108	1,730.3
6. Rick Langford	105	1,468.0
7. Chief Bender	102	2,602.0
8. Slim Harriss	93	1,291.3
9. Vida Blue	86	1,945.7
10. Rollie Naylor	83	1,011.0

WINNING PERCENTAGE: SEASON

Player	W%	Year
1. Lefty Grove	.886	1931
2. Chief Bender	.850	1914
3. Lefty Grove	.848	1930
4. Chief Bender	.821	1910
Barry Zito	.821	2002
6. Bob Welch	.818	1990
7. Eddie Plank	.812	1912
8. Catfish Hunter	.808	1973

Player	W%	Year
9. Roy Mahaffey	.789	1931
10. Jack Coombs	.775	1910

WINNING PERCENTAGE: CAREER WITH TEAM

Player	W%	IP
1. Lefty Grove	.712	2,401.0
2. Tim Hudson	.702	1,240.7
3. Mark Mulder	.659	1,003.0
4. Chief Bender	.654	2,602.0
5. Eddie Plank	.637	3,860.7
6. Jack Coombs	.632	1,629.7
7. George Earnshaw	.628	1,353.7
8. Barry Zito	.619	1,209.3
9. Bob Welch	.615	1,271.3
Rube Waddell	.615	1,869.3

SHUTOUTS: SEASON

Player	SHO	Year
1. Jack Coombs	13	1910
2. Vida Blue	8	1971
Joe Bush	8	1916
Eddie Plank	8	1907
Rube Waddell	8	1904
Rube Waddell	8	1906
7. Chief Bender	7	1914
Harry Krause	7	1909
Eddie Plank	7	1904
Eddie Plank	7	1913
Rube Waddell	7	1905
Rube Waddell	7	1907

SHUTOUTS: CAREER WITH TEAM

Player	SHO	IP
1. Eddie Plank	59	3,860.7
2. Rube Waddell	37	1,869.3
3. Chief Bender	36	2,602.0
4. Catfish Hunter	31	2,456.3
5. Vida Blue	28	1,945.7
Jack Coombs	28	1,629.7
7. Lefty Grove	20	2,401.0
8. Eddie Rommel	18	2,556.3
9. Jimmy Dygert	16	986.0
10. Joe Bush	15	1,115.3
Rube Walberg	15	2,186.7

ERA: SEASON

Player	ERA	Year
1. Jack Coombs	1.30	1910
2. Harry Krause	1.39	1909
3. Rube Waddell	1.48	1905
4. Cy Morgan	1.55	1910
5. Chief Bender	1.58	1910
6. Rube Waddell	1.62	1904
7. Cy Morgan	1.65	1909
8. Chief Bender	1.66	1909
9. Eddie Plank	1.76	1909
10. Vida Blue	1.82	1971

ERA: CAREER WITH TEAM

Player	ERA	IP
1. Rube Waddell	1.97	1,869.3
2. Cy Morgan	2.15	862.7
3. Chief Bender	2.32	2,602.0
4. Eddie Plank	2.39	3,860.7
5. Harry Krause	2.42	520.7
6. Andy Coakley	2.51	530.7
7. Jack Coombs	2.60	1,629.7
8. Jimmy Dygert	2.65	986.0
9. Dennis Eckersley	2.74	637.0
10. Lefty Grove	2.88	2,401.0

EARNED RUNS ALLOWED: SEASON

Player	ER	Year
1. George Earnshaw	146	1930
2. Harry Byrd	145	1953
3. Nels Potter	144	1939
4. Rube Walberg	143	1932
5. Chick Fraser	140	1901
6. Gordon Rhodes	138	1936
7. Alex Kellner	137	1950
8. George Caster	136	1938
9. Matt Keough	133	1982
10. Jack Coombs	132	1911

EARNED RUNS ALLOWED: CAREER WITH TEAM

Player	ER	IP
1. Eddie Plank	1,025	3,860.7
2. Eddie Rommel	1,006	2,556.3
3. Rube Walberg	999	2,186.7
4. Alex Kellner	872	1,730.3
5. Catfish Hunter	853	2,456.3
6. Lefty Grove	768	2,401.0
7. Dave Stewart	712	1,717.3
8. Chief Bender	670	2,602.0
9. Rick Langford	648	1,468.0
10. Vida Blue	638	1,945.7

STRIKEOUTS: SEASON

Player	K	Year
1. Rube Waddell	349	1904
2. Rube Waddell	302	1903
3. Vida Blue	301	1971
4. Rube Waddell	287	1905
5. Rube Waddell	232	1907
6. Jack Coombs	224	1910
7. Eddie Plank	210	1905
Rube Waddell	210	1902
9. Lefty Grove	209	1930
10. Dave Stewart	205	1987
Todd Stottlemyre	205	1995
Barry Zito	205	2001

STRIKEOUTS: CAREER WITH TEAM

Player	K	IP
1. Eddie Plank	1,985	3,860.7
2. Rube Waddell	1,576	1,869.3
3. Chief Bender	1,536	2,602.0
4. Lefty Grove	1,523	2,401.0
5. Catfish Hunter	1,520	2,456.3
6. Vida Blue	1,315	1,945.7
7. Dave Stewart	1,152	1,717.3
8. Barry Zito	945	1,209.3
9. Rube Walberg	907	2,186.7
10. Tim Hudson	899	1,240.7

STRIKEOUTS PER NINE IP: SEASON

Player	K/9	Year
1. Todd Stottlemyre	8.80	1995
2. Vida Blue	8.68	1971
3. Barry Zito	8.61	2001
4. Rube Waddell	8.39	1903
5. Rube Waddell	8.20	1904
6. Jose Rijo	8.18	1986
7. Rich Harden	7.92	2004
8. Rube Waddell	7.86	1905
9. Orlando Peña	7.55	1964
10. Jim Nash	7.53	1967

STRIKEOUTS PER NINE IP: CAREER WITH TEAM

Player	K/9	IP
1. Dennis Eckersley	9.30	637.0
2. Rube Waddell	7.59	1,869.3
3. Barry Zito	7.03	1,209.3
4. Rollie Fingers	6.94	1,016.0

5. Jim Nash	6.85	693.3
6. Tim Hudson	6.52	1,240.7
7. Orlando Peña	6.29	561.3
8. Vida Blue	6.08	1,945.7
9. Diego Segui	6.05	1,147.7
10. Dave Stewart	6.04	1,717.3

Hits Allowed: Season

Player	HA	Year
1. Jack Coombs	360	1911
2. Chick Fraser	344	1901
3. Bill Bernhard	328	1901
4. Eddie Plank	319	1902
5. Eddie Plank	317	1903
6. Eddie Rommel	312	1921
7. Eddie Plank	311	1904
8. George Caster	310	1938
Scott Perry	310	1920
10. Rube Waddell	307	1904

Hits Allowed: Career with Team

Player	HA	IP
1. Eddie Plank	3,438	3,860.7
2. Eddie Rommel	2,729	2,556.3
3. Rube Walberg	2,280	2,186.7
4. Lefty Grove	2,262	2,401.0
5. Chief Bender	2,225	2,602.0
6. Catfish Hunter	2,079	2,456.3
7. Alex Kellner	1,820	1,730.3
8. Vida Blue	1,650	1,945.7
9. Dave Stewart	1,608	1,717.3
10. Rick Langford	1,543	1,468.0

Hits Allowed Per Nine IP: Season

Player	H/9	Year
1. Cy Morgan	5.98	1909
2. Vida Blue	6.03	1971
3. Catfish Hunter	6.09	1972
4. Jack Coombs	6.32	1910
5. Rube Waddell	6.33	1905
6. Harry Krause	6.38	1909
7. Chief Bender	6.55	1910
8. Cy Morgan	6.63	1910
9. Steve McCatty	6.79	1981
10. Mike Norris	6.81	1980

Hits Allowed Per Nine IP: Career with Team

Player	H/9	IP
1. Cy Morgan	6.86	862.7
2. Rube Waddell	7.18	1,869.3
3. Dennis Eckersley	7.28	637.0
Jimmy Dygert	7.28	986.0
5. Harry Krause	7.52	520.7
6. Barry Zito	7.57	1,209.3
7. Catfish Hunter	7.62	2,456.3
Rollie Fingers	7.62	1,016.0
9. Vida Blue	7.63	1,945.7
10. Jack Coombs	7.66	1,629.7

Walks Allowed: Season

Player	BB	Year
1. Elmer Myers	168	1916
2. Weldon Wyckoff	165	1915
3. Phil Marchildon	141	1947
4. Phil Marchildon	140	1942
5. George Earnshaw	139	1930
6. Sugar Cain	137	1933
7. Chick Fraser	132	1901
8. Lefty Grove	131	1925
Phil Marchildon	131	1948
10. Joe Bush	130	1916

Walks Allowed: Career with Team

Player	BB	IP
1. Eddie Plank	913	3,860.7
2. Rube Walberg	853	2,186.7
3. Lefty Grove	740	2,401.0
4. Blue Moon Odom	732	1,414.7
5. Eddie Rommel	724	2,556.3
6. Alex Kellner	717	1,730.3
7. Catfish Hunter	687	2,456.3
8. Phil Marchildon	682	1,213.0
9. Dave Stewart	655	1,717.3
10. Vida Blue	617	1,945.7

Walks Allowed Per Nine IP: Season

Player	BB/9	Year
1. Catfish Hunter	1.30	1974
2. Lum Harris	1.34	1944
3. Eddie Rommel	1.35	1928
4. Chief Bender	1.40	1907
5. Jack Quinn	1.45	1928
6. Gil Heredia	1.53	1999
7. Chief Bender	1.62	1909
8. Jack Quinn	1.65	1927
9. Chief Bender	1.69	1910
Eddie Plank	1.69	1908

Walks Allowed Per Nine IP: Career with Team

Player	BB/9	IP
1. Dennis Eckersley	1.30	637.0
2. Jack Quinn	1.79	926.7
3. Chief Bender	2.12	2,602.0
4. Eddie Plank	2.13	3,860.7
5. Gil Heredia	2.15	551.3
6. Ken Holtzman	2.30	1,084.3
7. Rube Waddell	2.38	1,869.3
8. Rick Langford	2.46	1,468.0
9. Harry Krause	2.49	520.7
10. Catfish Hunter	2.52	2,456.3

WHIP (Walks + Hits Per Nine IP): Season

Player	WHIP	Year
1. Catfish Hunter	.914	1972
2. Chief Bender	.916	1910
3. Harry Krause	.939	1909
4. Vida Blue	.952	1971
5. Chief Bender	.964	1909
6. Cy Morgan	.975	1909
7. Rube Waddell	.977	1905
8. Catfish Hunter	.986	1974
9. Chief Bender	.998	1907
10. Eddie Plank	1.014	1908

WHIP (Walks + Hits Per Nine IP): Career with Team

Player	WHIP	IP
1. Dennis Eckersley	0.953	637.0
2. Rube Waddell	1.062	1,869.3
3. Chief Bender	1.091	2,602.0
4. Harry Krause	1.112	520.7
5. Catfish Hunter	1.126	2,456.3
6. Eddie Plank	1.127	3,860.7
7. Rollie Fingers	1.135	1,016.0
8. Vida Blue	1.165	1,945.7
9. Jim Nash	1.170	693.3
10. Cy Morgan	1.171	862.7

Home Runs Allowed: Season

Player	HRA	Year
1. Orlando Peña	40	1964
2. Catfish Hunter	39	1973
3. Matt Keough	38	1982
Curt Young	38	1987

5. Catfish Hunter	34	1969
6. Rick Langford	33	1982
7. Chuck Dobson	32	1970
Catfish Hunter	32	1970
9. Ed Rakow	31	1962
10. Tom Candiotti	30	1998
Art Ditmar	30	1956
Diego Segui	30	1964

Home Runs Allowed: Career with Team

Player	HRA	IP
1. Catfish Hunter	261	2,456.3
2. Alex Kellner	167	1,730.3
3. Rick Langford	158	1,468.0
4. Dave Stewart	152	1,717.3
5. Curt Young	145	1,039.3
6. Vida Blue	139	1,945.7
7. Eddie Rommel	138	2,556.3
8. Rube Walberg	134	2,186.7
Bob Welch	134	1,271.3
10. Steve McCatty	124	1,188.3

Saves: Season

Player	SV	Year
1. Dennis Eckersley	51	1992
2. Dennis Eckersley	48	1990
3. Dennis Eckersley	45	1988
4. Billy Koch	44	2002
5. Dennis Eckersley	43	1991
Keith Foulke	43	2003
7. Bill Caudill	36	1984
Dennis Eckersley	36	1993
9. Jason Isringhausen	34	2001
10. Dennis Eckersley	33	1989
Jason Isringhausen	33	2000
Billy Taylor	33	1998

Saves: Career with Team

Player	SV	IP
1. Dennis Eckersley	320	637.0
2. Rollie Fingers	136	1,016.0
3. Billy Taylor	100	295.7
4. Jason Isringhausen	75	165.7
5. John Wyatt	73	473.0
6. Jay Howell	61	195.7
7. Jack Aker	58	343.3
8. Lefty Grove	51	2,401.0
9. Billy Koch	44	93.7
10. Keith Foulke	43	86.7

Wild Pitches: Season

Player	WP	Year
1. Mike Moore	22	1992
2. Mike Moore	17	1989
Blue Moon Odom	17	1968
4. Storm Davis	16	1988
Stu Flythe	16	1936
Rick Langford	16	1979
7. Vida Blue	15	1973
Joe Bush	15	1916
Blake Stein	15	1998
10. Eight tied with . . .	14	—

Wild Pitches: Career with Team

Player	WP	IP
1. Blue Moon Odom	87	1,414.7
2. Eddie Plank	80	3,860.7
3. Dave Stewart	78	1,717.3
4. Mike Moore	66	874.0
5. Chief Bender	61	2,602.0
6. Vida Blue	57	1,945.7
7. Matt Keough	55	1,060.3
8. Mike Norris	53	1,124.3
9. Alex Kellner	52	1,730.3
Rube Waddell	52	1,869.3

Hit Batsmen: Season

Player	HB	Year
1. Chick Fraser	32	1901
2. Chief Bender	25	1903
3. Eddie Plank	24	1905
4. Eddie Plank	23	1903
5. Cy Morgan	21	1911
6. Weldon Henley	19	1904
Eddie Plank	19	1904
8. Jimmy Dygert	18	1907
Cy Morgan	18	1910
Eddie Plank	18	1902

Hit Batsmen: Career with Team

Player	HB	IP
1. Eddie Plank	185	3,860.7
2. Chief Bender	78	2,602.0
3. Rube Waddell	69	1,869.3
4. Jack Coombs	60	1,629.7
Cy Morgan	60	862.7
6. Jimmy Dygert	52	986.0
Barry Zito	52	1,209.3
8. Tim Hudson	47	1,240.7
9. Mike Norris	45	1,124.3
10. Dave Stewart	42	1,717.3
Bob Welch	42	1,271.3

Games Finished: Season

Player	GF	Year
1. Billy Koch	79	2002
2. Keith Foulke	67	2003
3. Dennis Eckersley	65	1992
4. Bill Caudill	62	1984
Rollie Fingers	62	1976
6. Dennis Eckersley	61	1990
7. Rollie Fingers	60	1974
8. Dennis Eckersley	59	1991
Rollie Fingers	59	1975
10. Jay Howell	58	1985
Billy Taylor	58	1998

Games Finished: Career with Team

Player	GF	IP
1. Dennis Eckersley	456	637.0
2. Rollie Fingers	338	1,016.0
3. John Wyatt	206	473.0
4. Eddie Rommel	182	2,556.3
Billy Taylor	182	295.7
6. Paul Lindblad	165	873.7
7. Jack Aker	142	343.3
8. Jason Isringhausen	129	165.7
9. Carl Scheib	124	1,066.0
10. Jay Howell	118	195.7

Significant A's

BAKER, FRANK (3B)
(1908–1914)

Frank "Home Run" Baker got his nickname not from his number of homers or the length of his clouts, but from the timeliness of the blasts he did hit. Using a huge 52-ounce bat, Baker hit a grand slam on Opening Day of 1909, his first full season in the majors. From 1911 to 1914, he led the American League in homers, hitting 11, 10, 12, and 9. (These are puny numbers by today's standards, for sure, but in the dead-ball era, major league baseball was using a mush ball that was very, very difficult to hit over the fence. Consequently, most hitters choked up and sprayed the ball to all fields. When the dead-ball era officially ended in 1920 with the introduction of a harder, more tightly wound ball, home run totals skyrocketed.) In 1911, Baker was part of the famous "$100,000 infield," not because of what the infielders actually cost owner Connie Mack, but because Mack said he wouldn't take even that amount to part with them.

In the 1911 World Series against the Giants, Baker hit two home runs in two days, thus earning his nickname. After Baker retired, he was asked how many homers he would have hit with the new, livelier ball, and he answered "At least 50. After all," he pointed out, "when I hit 12 in 1913, I hit 38 off the right-field fence in Shibe Park alone." After the A's lost a disappointing Series to the Braves in 1914, Connie Mack decided it was time to cut expenses, so he sold off some of his star players. He kept Baker, but when Mack refused to give Baker a raise, the third baseman sat out the entire 1915 season in protest. In 1916 Mack sold Baker's contract to the Yankees for $35,000, and Baker spent his final six years with New York, four as a full-time player and two as a part-timer, with a year off in between to care for his first wife, who became ill and died. In six World Series, Baker hit .363 with 18 RBIs and three home runs. After retiring, Baker managed and later bought the Easton, Maryland, minor league team. He also raised horses on his Maryland farm until his death in 1963. In 1955 he was elected to the Hall of Fame.

CAREER A'S RECORD:

Games	AB	Hits	Runs
899	3,436	1,103	573
Avg	**HR**	**RBI**	**SB**
.321	48	612	172

BENDER, CHIEF (SP/RP)
(1903–1914)

Charles Albert Bender, better known as "Chief," was one-quarter Chippewa Indian. When white people would tease him or allude to his Indian heritage, he would good-naturedly call the whites "foreigners," his way of deflecting the racism of the day. Connie Mack was the only person who didn't refer to him as Chief, opting instead to call him by his middle name, Albert. He never made a big deal of it, but Bender didn't like "Chief" and he always signed his name "Charles Bender."

While playing for a semipro club, Bender had occasion to pitch against the Cubs in an exhibition game. He defeated them so soundly that he impressed a scout for the A's who was sitting in the stands, and soon Bender was signed to a contract. Bender joined the A's in 1903 and posted a 17–14 record in his rookie year. Connie Mack felt Bender didn't quite have the stamina to pitch every three or four days, so he gave him extra time off between starts and made liberal use of him as a reliever, saving him for many "must-win" games. In the 1905 World Series, Bender won the only game for the A's, a four-hit shutout in Game 2. In that Series, all five games were shutouts, three by the Giants' Christy Mathewson. Bender developed and mastered a pitch that was halfway between a fastball and a curveball—later known as a slider—and used it with devastating results. He was such a good sign stealer that Mack often used him as the third-base coach. Ty Cobb called Bender the most intelligent pitcher he ever faced. Mack was engaged in serious cost-cutting in 1915 and, when the Federal League came calling for both Bender and Eddie Plank, Mack gave them both their release rather than make them decide their future based on loyalty. Bender got a large bonus and salary, but he went just 4–16 for the Baltimore Terrapins in the second and final year of the new league. He later called it the biggest mistake of his life. After retiring as a player, Bender spent time as a minor league manager and a major league coach and scout. In 1953 he was elected to the Hall of Fame; he died a year later.

CAREER A'S RECORD:

W	L	W%	ERA	SV
193	102	.654	2.32	28

K	BB	SHO	IP
1,536	614	36	2,602.0

BLUE, VIDA (SP)
(1969–1977)

Vida Blue was such a talented high school football star that in 1967 he received scholarship offers from at least 25 major colleges. Although he signed a letter of intent with the University of Houston, Charlie Finley came calling with a $25,000 bonus, and suddenly baseball looked a lot better. Blue had brief call-ups to the A's in 1969 and 1970, even tossing a no-hitter against the Twins on September 21, 1970, in one of his six games that season. Blue came up for good in 1971 and immediately established himself as the best pitcher in baseball, finishing 24–8 with eight shutouts and a 1.82 ERA and winning both the Cy Young and the AL MVP Award. After making only $14,750 in that stellar season, Blue wanted more money in 1972 and asked for $115,000. When Finley countered with an offer of $45,000, Blue staged a holdout. The whole affair got widespread play in the media until even President Richard Nixon commented that Finley should pay Blue what he was asking!

In May, he eventually settled for $50,000 and $13,000 in additional bonuses. When Blue went 6–10 after returning from his holdout, he absorbed a lot of criticism. The next year he rebounded with a 20–9 record and helped the A's make it to their second straight World Series, although he did nothing to help them win it. After the 1977 season, Finley tried to sell off a number of his stars, including Blue, for cash, but Commissioner Bowie Kuhn vetoed deals to the Yankees ($1.5 million cash) and Reds ($1.75 million cash). Finley finally was able to trade Blue to the Giants for seven players and $390,000 cash. When Blue started the All-Star Game for the National League in 1978, he became the first pitcher ever to start for both leagues.

After four seasons in San Francisco, Blue fell out of favor with the team and was traded to Kansas City. In 1983 Blue and several other Royals became ensnared in a government sting operation that was investigating the use, sale, and distribution of cocaine. In a plea bargain, Blue pleaded guilty to attempting to purchase cocaine and received a one-year prison sentence. After missing the 1984 season, Blue spent two more years with the Giants before trying to rejoin the A's, but after failing a urine test, he retired.

CAREER A'S RECORD:

W	L	W%	ERA	SV
124	86	.590	2.95	2

K	BB	SHO	IP
1,315	617	28	1,945.7

CAMPANERIS, BERT (SS)
(1964–1976)

Signed as an amateur free agent in April 1961, Campaneris joined the A's in 1964 and became the team's regular shortstop for more than a dozen years. In his first game he hit a homer on the first pitch he saw, then added another dinger later in the game. He led the league in stolen bases his first four years and six of his first eight. On September 8, 1965, Campaneris became the first player in major league history to play all nine positions in one game. In the 1972 ALCS against Billy Martin's Detroit Tigers, Campaneris was tearing it up, so Martin ordered his pitcher, Lerrin LaGrow, to throw at Campaneris's legs. LaGrow hit him above the left ankle and Campaneris responded by throwing his bat at the pitcher, missing his head by inches. The resulting melee became one of baseball's more famous brawls. After 13 years with the A's, the five-time All-Star shortstop left Oakland via free agency. Of his last six years with the Rangers, Angels, and Yankees, five were spent in a greatly diminished role as a platoon player.

CAREER A'S RECORD:

Games	AB	Hits	Runs
1,795	7,180	1,882	983

Avg	HR	RBI	SB
.262	70	529	566

CANSECO, JOSE (OF/DH)
(1985–1992, 1997)

Jose Canseco, along with Mark McGwire, formed the "Bash Brothers" of Oakland, a potent one-two home run punch. Drafted in the 15th round of the June 1982 amateur draft, Canseco received a September call-up in 1985 before joining the team for good in 1986. After stroking 33 homers and 117 RBIs in 1986, Canseco was named AL Rookie of the Year. In 1988 he won the AL MVP Award after becoming baseball's first "40–40" man, hitting 42 homers and stealing 40 bases.

Canseco, one of the most feared sluggers of his time, was loaded with talent, but he was loaded with immaturity as well. Among his news-making exploits were a speeding ticket, an intentional car crash with his first wife, an arrest on weapons charges, a 900-number phone line for his fans, and a reported fling with Madonna. After eight years with the A's, Canseco, a five-time All-Star, was traded to the Rangers and just seemed to drift after that, playing for seven different teams in his last nine years. After he retired from baseball, Canseco wrote a tell-all book about steroids in baseball, admitting his own use and implicating many other players. The ensuing firestorm resulted in televised Congressional hearings into the matter in 2005. Canseco became so disenchanted with baseball that he auctioned off all of his baseball awards and personal memorabilia.

CAREER A'S RECORD:

Games	AB	Hits	Runs
1,058	3,970	1,048	662
Avg	**HR**	**RBI**	**SB**
.264	254	793	135

COCHRANE, MICKEY (C)
(1925–1933)

Gordon "Mickey" Cochrane was tearing up the Pacific Coast League in 1924 when Connie Mack came to sign him. Unfortunately, the Portland owner wanted $50,000 for his prized hitter. Mack was discouraged, but when he found out the whole team was available for $200,000, he bought it and sold off all the other players, making a nice profit on the deal. Mickey Cochrane turned into not just one of the best-hitting catchers in major league history, but also one of the best handlers of pitchers. Once, when he felt a pitcher wasn't putting forth enough effort, Cochrane charged the mound, spun his pitcher around, and then kicked him in the butt. Lefty Grove had his 16-game winning streak with Cochrane behind the plate, and so did Schoolboy Rowe for Detroit in 1934. Cochrane's .320 lifetime batting average is tops among catchers. He had an incredible batting eye, striking out only 217 times in 5,169 career at-bats. That's *once every 24 games.*

From 1925 to 1935, he appeared in five World Series (three with the A's and two with the Tigers). In the 1929 Series, feelings were running especially hot between the A's and Cubs. The profanity going back and forth between the two clubs' dugouts was so vile that Commissioner Kenesaw Mountain Landis told both teams in the middle of the Series that any player who swore during the remainder of the Series would receive a substantial fine. Before the last game, won by Cochrane's A's, he yelled to the Cubs, "Hurry up, sweethearts. Tea will be served at four o'clock." Everyone near the field, including Landis, heard Cochrane. At the post-Series clubhouse celebration, Landis joined in and congratulated everyone except Cochrane, whom he ignored. Just before leaving, Landis turned to Cochrane and said, "Hello, sweetheart. I came by for tea."

The A's were so successful in the late '20s and early '30s that many of the team's stars commanded escalating salaries, leaving Connie Mack with no choice but to once again sell off his high-priced talent, just as he had done nearly 20 years before. In 1934 he traded Cochrane to the Tigers for Johnny Pasek and $100,000 cash. Cochrane became the Tigers' player-manager and immediately led the Tigers to the AL pennant, though they lost the Series to the Cardinals. In 1935 Cochrane got the Tigers over the hump, leading them to their first-ever World Series in six games over the Cubs.

Early in 1937 Cochrane homered off Bump Hadley of the Yankees. The next time up, Hadley hit Cochrane in the head. The beanball fractured his skull in three places. After laying unconscious for 10 days, Cochrane finally came around, but he never played again. The medical bills and lost income took their toll on Cochrane. Ty Cobb reportedly sent him money on a regular basis to help with his financial situation. When Cobb died, Cochrane was one of only three players who attended his funeral. After his playing career, Cochrane spent many years as a coach and scout with the A's, Yankees, and Tigers, eventually becoming vice-president of the Tigers. Cochrane was elected to the Hall of Fame in 1947; he died in 1962.

CAREER A'S RECORD:

Games	AB	Hits	Runs
1,167	4,097	1,317	823
Avg	**HR**	**RBI**	**SB**
.321	108	680	50

COLLINS, EDDIE (2B)
(1906–1914, 1927–1930)

Eddie Collins was one of the best second basemen in the history of the game. After seeing limited action in 1906 and 1907, Collins became the A's regular second sacker in 1908. After a year of adjustment in 1908, in which he hit .273, Collins hit .324 or higher in his next six seasons with the A's. Collins was a base-stealing, run-scoring machine from 1909 to 1914, leading the A's to four World Series, three of which they won. Had it not been for Ty Cobb monopolizing newspaper coverage of the day, Collins would have received much more recognition. He led the league in steals four times, including a high of 81 in 1910. Three times he was the runner-up in the batting race. Defensively, Collins won eight fielding crowns. He had more games played, putouts, assists, and total chances than any second baseman in history. After the 1914 World Series, Connie Mack sold his superstar second baseman to the Chicago White Sox. *(See White Sox bio.)*

CAREER A'S RECORD:

Games	AB	Hits	Runs
1,156	3,884	1,308	756
Avg	**HR**	**RBI**	**SB**
.337	16	496	376

COOMBS, JACK (SP)
(1906–1914)

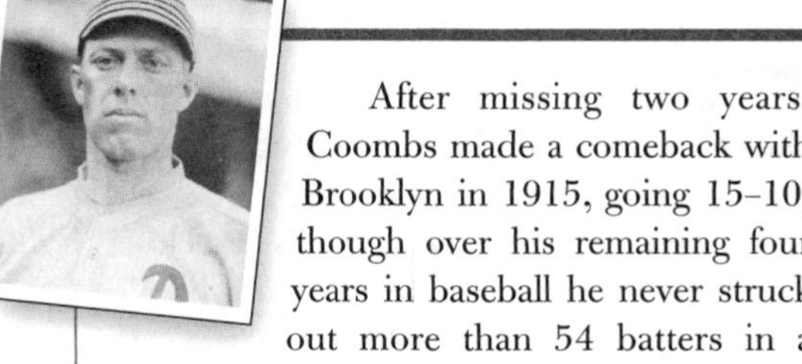

Connie Mack discovered Jack Coombs pitching in Maine for Colby College. He gave him the nickname "Colby Jack" and a $2,400 contract to pitch for the A's. On September 24, 1906, rookie Coombs hooked up in a pitcher's duel with fellow rookie Joe Harris of Boston. Coombs won, 4–1, as both pitchers went the distance in the 24-inning marathon. Coombs was a good hitter as well, and Connie Mack occasionally used him as an outfielder.

In 1910, Coombs had a dream season. He won 31 games during the regular season, including 13 shutouts. In the World Series that year, he won three games against the Cubs and batted .385. He followed this up with 28 wins in 1911 and 21 in 1912. During spring training 1913, however, Coombs was stricken with typhoid fever, which settled in his spine and nearly killed him.

After missing two years, Coombs made a comeback with Brooklyn in 1915, going 15–10, though over his remaining four years in baseball he never struck out more than 54 batters in a season—compared to striking out around 200 batters in both 1910 and 1911. His production declined in each of his remaining years, until he left baseball in 1920. Coombs coached baseball at Williams College, Princeton, and Duke University; authored a highly regarded instructional book on baseball; and ran a traveling baseball clinic. He died in 1957.

CAREER A'S RECORD:

W	L	W%	ERA	SV
115	67	.632	2.60	8

K	BB	SHO	IP
870	606	28	1,629.7

DAVIS, HARRY (1B)
(1901–1911, 1913–1917)

After an undistinguished five-year career in the National League, Harry Davis left baseball in 1900 and took a job with the railroad. But Connie Mack, who was building his new Philadelphia franchise in the American League, remembered the slugging first baseman from the days the two of them played together in Pittsburgh and recruited him. From 1904 to 1907, Davis led the American League in home runs, the first player ever to lead the category for four consecutive years. Only Frank Baker, Babe Ruth, and Ralph Kiner have equaled or exceeded the feat. Davis once hit a three-run homer when the pitcher was trying to intentionally walk him by reaching across the plate and serving the ball into the bleachers for a 4–3 victory over the Highlanders. From 1912 to 1917, his career trailed off and he never played in more than seven games in a season. Upon retiring from baseball, Davis, a skilled trapshooter, undertook a national tour with former A's pitchers Eddie Plank and Chief Bender to promote the sport. He died in his birthplace of Philadelphia in 1947.

CAREER A'S RECORD:

Games	AB	Hits	Runs
1,413	5,367	1,500	811

Avg	HR	RBI	SB
.279	69	761	223

ECKERSLEY, DENNIS (RP)
(1987–1995)

Dennis Eckersley was a man of two careers. The first was as a starter, in 12 years spent with the Indians, Red Sox, and Cubs. The second was as baseball's best closer for 12 more years, spent mostly with the A's. When Eckersley came to the A's in 1987, he had a 151–128 record as a starter, but manager Tony LaRussa converted "Eck" into a closer. Before he retired after 24 years in baseball, Eckersley compiled nearly 400 career saves, only three of which came in his first 12 years in the big leagues. His 1992 season ranks as one of the best all-time by a reliever. With a great fastball and a wicked slider, both of which he consistently threw for strikes, Eckersley had a 7–1 record with 51 saves and a 1.91 ERA. He became the first reliever in history to have four 40-save seasons. For his efforts he was rewarded with the Reliever of the Year Award, the Cy Young, and the AL MVP. After leaving baseball, Eckersley, a six-time All-Star, joined the A's broadcast team. In 2004 he was elected to the Hall of Fame.

CAREER A'S RECORD:

W	L	W%	ERA	SV
41	31	.569	2.74	320

K	BB	SHO	IP
658	92	0	637.0

FINGERS, ROLLIE (RP)
(1968–1976)

When the Oakland A's dynasty of the early 1970s needed relief, Rollie Fingers was their man. For the first nine seasons of his 17-year career, Fingers, who sported a flamboyant handlebar mustache, fashioned himself into baseball's premier closer, helping the A's to five division titles, three pennants, and three World Series titles. Fingers won the 1974 World Series MVP Award for his one win and two saves. On June 15, 1976, Charlie Finley sold Fingers to Boston for $1 million, but Commissioner Bowie Kuhn voided the deal. A few months later, Fingers left Oakland via free agency and signed with San Diego. He did so well in his first two years with the Padres that a San Diego broadcaster said of him, "Fingers has 35 saves, a better record than John the Baptist." Following the 1980 season, Fingers was traded to Milwaukee. *(See Brewers and Padres bios.)*

CAREER A'S RECORD:

W	L	W%	ERA	SV
67	61	.523	2.91	136

K	BB	SHO	IP
784	293	2	1,016.0

FOXX, JIMMIE (1B)
(1925–1935)

Jimmie Foxx, also known as "the Beast" and "Old Double-X," was the true successor to Babe Ruth as baseball's greatest slugger. When Foxx retired, he was second only to Ruth on the all-time home run list, and remained there until Willie Mays passed him in 1966. During the 1930s, Foxx hit 415 homers, more than anyone in baseball. He accomplished one of baseball's rarest feats by winning the AL Triple Crown in 1933, racking up 48 homers, 163 RBIs, and a .356 average. He also won three MVP Awards in his career. "He is the easiest boy on the team to handle," said Connie Mack, who favored him. "He does whatever I ask, plays any position, and never complains." Foxx was so strong that some players even accused him of having muscles in his hair. He once crushed a home run off New York's Lefty Gomez into the upper reaches of the upper deck in Yankee Stadium. After the game, when Gomez went to inspect where the ball had landed, he discovered a shattered seat. In 1932 and 1933, Foxx compiled over 400 total bases each year. Twice he hit over 50 homers in a season, and four times he passed the 150-RBI mark. In what would be an oft-repeated story in Philadelphia, Connie Mack eventually could not afford all his stars and was forced to sell some of them to make ends meet. After the 1935 season, Mack traded Foxx to Boston in a four-player deal that also netted Mack $150,000. *(See Red Sox bio.)*

CAREER A'S RECORD:

Games	AB	Hits	Runs
1,256	4,397	1,492	975
Avg	**HR**	**RBI**	**SB**
.339	302	1,075	48

GROVE, LEFTY (SP/RP)
(1925–1933)

Robert "Lefty" Grove, son of a Maryland coal miner and a descendant of Betsy Ross, was playing minor league ball in Martinsburg, West Virginia, when Jack Dunn of the independent Baltimore Orioles expressed interest. The owner of the Martinsburg team told Dunn that he could have Grove for the price of a badly needed new fence for the ballpark ($3,500). Grove later joked that he was the only player ever traded for a fence. He played for Dunn's unaffiliated Orioles team for five years, and didn't mind because the pay was so good—better than what many players were getting in the major leagues. Plus, Orioles players got a cut of the profits from every exhibition game they played. The Giants offered Dunn $75,000 for Grove, but he wouldn't sell. When Connie Mack offered $100,600, Dunn accepted. (The extra $600 was just to make sure the price paid was a record.)

After getting his feet wet with a 23–25 record in his first two years, Grove suddenly realized his potential. He reeled off seven straight 20-win seasons, including a combined 103–23 record in the four years from 1928 to 1931. In 1931 he won the AL MVP Award. During his career, Grove fashioned a league-leading winning percentage four times, a major league record. He led the AL in strikeouts in his first seven years. No wonder baseball historian Bill James calls Lefty Grove the best pitcher in baseball history. Grove was a fierce competitor with a fiery temper. His opponents hated standing in the batter's box when he was angry. His teammates didn't want to be around him when got into dark moods, and he often tore up the dugout and clubhouse after a loss. First baseman Tony Lupien, who admitted to being scared to death of Grove, once observed a young boy approach Grove for an autograph. Grove, who was carrying a rolled-up copy of a newspaper, ". . . hit that kid across the puss with that paper, and the kid went flying," said Lupien. When Grove's 16-game winning streak ended in 1931 due to an error by rookie substitute outfielder Jimmy Moore, Grove went into a tirade against Al Simmons, the regular outfielder who normally would have been playing if not for an injury. Grove never forgave Simmons for missing the game.

After nine years with the A's, Grove was traded to the Red Sox in another of Connie Mack's many moves to raise cash (Grove brought in $125,000). Almost immediately, Grove hurt his arm during the offseason and considered retiring. He did pitch again, but he wasn't the same. In eight years with Boston, Grove won 105 games, an average of just 13 wins per year, after averaging nearly 25 wins a year in the previous seven years with Philadelphia. When he retired following the 1941 season, Grove had exactly 300 wins, and his .680 winning percentage is the highest of all 300-game winners. After his playing career was over, Grove coached Little League baseball and owned and managed three bowling alleys in Ohio. He was elected to the Hall of Fame in 1947 and died 1975.

CAREER A'S RECORD:

W	L	W%	ERA	SV
195	79	.712	2.88	51
K	**BB**	**SHO**	**IP**	
1,523	740	20	2,401.0	

HENDERSON, RICKEY (OF)
(1979–1984, 1989–1995, 1998)

Rickey Henderson was the best leadoff hitter in baseball history, and he didn't mind telling you that. He could get on base with a hit or a walk, and many times his walks and singles turned into doubles or triples due to his base-stealing ability. He also had power, hitting more leadoff homers than any player in history. In his first full year in the majors, Henderson stole 100 bases. Two years later he set the all-time single-season record with 130 steals, then followed it up with 108 the next year. In 1990 Henderson won the AL MVP Award when he hit .325 with 28 homers, 119 runs, and 65 steals. A 10-time All-Star, Henderson never lacked confidence, only modesty. In 1991, when he set the career mark for stolen bases, he drew catcalls by announcing to the crowd, "Today, I am the greatest of all time." (In a game later that night, Nolan Ryan pitched his seventh no-hitter, all but wiping Rickey Henderson off the front page of most sports sections the next morning.) By the time Henderson retired after 25 seasons in the major leagues, he had played for nine teams. He won 12 stolen-base titles, all with Oakland, including one in 1998 at the age of 40. As of 2005, he was still playing organized baseball in the minors and hoping for another shot at the big leagues.

CAREER A'S RECORD:

Games	AB	Hits	Runs
1,704	6,140	1,768	1,270
Avg	**HR**	**RBI**	**SB**
.288	167	648	867

HUNTER, CATFISH (SP)
(1965–1974)

The Kansas City Athletics signed Jim Hunter as an amateur free agent in June 1964, and by 1965 he was on the major league roster, never spending a day in the minors. A's owner Charlie Finley, in an attempt to make the team more colorful, invented the nickname "Catfish" for his prized pitcher. Hunter was eased into the rotation, going 8–8 in 20 starts, but by 1966 he was an All-Star. On May 8, 1968, against the Twins, Hunter pitched the AL's first regular-season perfect game in 46 years. From 1971–1973, Hunter won 21 games each year as the A's built their first Oakland mini-dynasty. In 1974 he won 25 games and the AL Cy Young Award. During the Athletics' three World Series title years of 1972–1974, Hunter went 3–1 in ALCS games and 4–1 in World Series games. His World Series ERA improved each year, from 2.81 to 2.02 to 1.17. By the end of the 1974 season, Hunter was the hottest pitching commodity in baseball.

A six-time All-Star with the A's, Hunter was also about to become a free agent because of a Charlie Finley screwup. Hunter's contract called for Finley to put half of his $100,000 annual salary into a deferred compensation life-insurance fund. Because Finley failed to do so, Hunter felt that Finley violated part of the contract, rendering the whole contract null and void, including the reserve clause. On December 13, 1974, an arbitrator ruled in Hunter's favor, making the pitcher a free agent. An unprecedented bidding war commenced. Over a 13-day period, officials from 15 teams—including six owners—flew to rural North Carolina to talk terms with Hunter's agent. Hunter eventually agreed to a five-year deal with the Yankees, telling them that once his contract was up, he would be retiring. Hunter won 23 games in his first year in pinstripes, then helped the Yanks to pennants in 1976, 1977, and 1978. He was limited to half-time duty in 1977 due to a variety of ailments, and during spring training of 1978, Hunter was diagnosed with diabetes. For 1978 and 1979, Hunter again pitched only half-time. Some claimed it was arm trouble, but Hunter denied it. When his five-year contract expired, Hunter was as good as his word and retired to his North Carolina farm, turning down several very lucrative offers to stay in New York. When Hunter was elected to the Hall of Fame in 1987, he chose to enter the Hall without a team designation on his cap. After retirement, Hunter's health slowly deteriorated. In 1998 he was diagnosed with Lou Gehrig's disease, and a year later he died.

CAREER A'S RECORD:

W	L	W%	ERA	SV
161	113	.588	3.13	1

K	BB	SHO	IP
1,520	687	31	2,456.3

JACKSON, REGGIE (OF)
(1967–1975, 1987)

After making the 1966 College All-America Team, Jackson was drafted in the first round of the amateur draft by the Kansas City Athletics and signed for an $85,000 bonus. After a late-season call-up in 1967, Jackson became a full-time outfielder in 1968. In 1969 Jackson burst onto the national baseball scene when he challenged Roger Maris's single-season home run record. Through the end of August, Jackson, who by now was being referred to in the press simply as "Reggie," had 45 homers. With all eyes on Reggie and the season's final month, Reggie proved to be no Mr. September, hitting only two more homers the rest of the way. Still, he achieved the national acclaim he sought. In the 1971 All-Star Game, Jackson's second of 14 career appearances, he hit a home run off the light tower on the roof of Tiger Stadium that had folks talking for years. In 1973 he won the AL MVP Award as he led the brash, battling A's to their second World Series championship. A third straight title would follow in 1974, as Jackson and the A's both established themselves as baseball powers. Just before the 1976 season opened, the A's traded Jackson to the O's, knowing full well that Reggie was going to enter the free-agent market after the season anyway. Jackson did become a free agent after one year in Baltimore, signing with the defending AL champion Yankees and rejoining his former teammate Catfish Hunter. *(See Yankees and Angels bios.)*

CAREER A'S RECORD:

Games	AB	Hits	Runs
1,346	5,686	1,228	756
Avg	**HR**	**RBI**	**SB**
.262	269	776	145

JOHNSON, BOB (OF)
(1933–1942)

Although Bob Johnson spent 10 years playing for poor Philadelphia A's teams, he had a remarkably solid, consistent career. In his first nine years with the A's, he hit at least 20 homers every year. He also had 100+ RBIs in seven straight years, with totals in the 90s the other two seasons. Sometimes it seemed like Johnson was the only serious offensive threat the team had. On June 12, 1938, he drove in all eight runs of a win over the St. Louis Browns. Feeling underpaid following the 1942 season, he demanded a trade. Owner Connie Mack obliged him during spring training 1943, sending the five-time All-Star to Washington for a player and, as per usual in a Connie Mack deal, cash thrown in. After having the worst season of his career, Johnson was sold to the Red Sox, where he had two more decent years before retiring.

CAREER A'S RECORD:

Games	AB	Hits	Runs
1,459	5,428	1,617	997
Avg	**HR**	**RBI**	**SB**
.298	252	1,040	78

McGWIRE, MARK (1B)
(1986–1997)

Mark McGwire was voted the 1984 College Player of the Year after setting a Pac-10 Conference record with 32 homers. He also played for the 1984 U.S. Olympic team. Drafted in the first round of the June 1984 amateur draft, McGwire received a late-season call-up to the A's in 1986, then took the major league baseball by storm in 1987, slamming 49 home runs in his rookie season. He won the AL Rookie of the Year Award—naturally—and played in the first of his dozen All-Star Games. From 1988 to 1990, the A's made it to the World Series each year, largely on the back of their big slugging first baseman. Over the course of the next 12 years, the lumberjack-size McGwire established himself as one of the greatest home run hitters in baseball history, but he had a problem. Well, two, actually. His feet and his back. Injuries to both hampered him throughout his career. McGwire missed more than 250 games with Oakland because of painful heel and back problems. In 1995 "Big Mac" had just 317 at-bats, but he actually hit more home runs than singles (39 to 35), compiling the most home runs ever in so few at-bats. When McGwire hit 52 homers in 1996, he became the first to pass the 50 mark in less than 600 plate appearances. On the trading deadline in 1997, a season in which McGwire and Ken Griffey Jr. were chasing Roger Maris's single-season home run record, McGwire was sent to St. Louis, where he rejoined former A's manager Tony LaRussa. *(See Cardinals bio.)*

CAREER A'S RECORD:

Games	AB	Hits	Runs
1,329	4,448	1,157	773
Avg	**HR**	**RBI**	**SB**
.260	363	941	8

PLANK, EDDIE (SP)
(1901–1914)

Eddie Plank worked as a tour guide at the Gettysburg battlefield while attending Gettysburg College and playing for the school's baseball team. Gettysburg's coach, former major league pitcher Frank Foreman, contacted Connie Mack about his school's star pitcher. Mack liked what he saw and signed Plank to a contract, taking him directly to Philadelphia without a stop in the minors. In 1902 Plank won 20 games to help the A's to their first pennant. He would have eight 20-win seasons before he was through. A major part of Plank's pitching strategy, aside from the quality of his pitches, was to drive the batters crazy. In slow, deliberative fashion, Plank would stand on the mound, rub up the baseball, kick the dirt off his spikes, adjust his belt, reposition his hat, get a sign from the catcher, shake him off, step off the rubber, tinker with his glove, step back on the rubber, then finally throw a pitch. Before the next pitch he would do it all again, sometimes unbuttoning his shirt and rebuttoning it, rubbing his hand through his hair, and asking for a new ball. His endless rituals infuriated batters and also meant that when Plank pitched, it would be a very long game indeed. The umpires routinely had to order him to pitch. Many fans actually stayed away from games he pitched because they might miss the last train home.

Plank helped the A's to five World Series berths, but once in the Fall Classic, he was often the victim of bad luck, bad run support, or both. Although Plank posted a 1.38 career ERA in World Series play, his record was 2–5. Plank watched as many AL and NL stars jumped to the new Federal League in 1914 for big salaries. In 1915, although Plank was still a talented pitcher, Connie Mack released him along with Chief Bender so they could pursue the big money as well. Plank won 21 games for the St. Louis Terriers in 1915, then watched as the Federal League folded around him. Plank stayed in St. Louis and pitched two years for the Browns, compiling a 21–21 record before hanging up his glove in 1917 at the age of 41. At the time of his retirement, Plank was the all-time winningest left-hander in major league history with 327 wins. He held the record until it was surpassed by Warren Spahn in 1961. Upon leaving baseball, Plank returned to Gettysburg, where he farmed and opened an automobile dealership. Plank, who died suddenly of a heart attack at the age of 50 in 1926, was named to the Hall of Fame in 1946.

CAREER A'S RECORD:

W	L	W%	ERA	SV
284	162	.637	2.39	16

K	BB	SHO	IP
1,985	913	59	3,860.7

ROMMEL, EDDIE (RP/SP)
(1920–1932)

During World War I, minor league pitcher Eddie Rommel was working as a steamfitter's helper when he suffered a terrible scalding of his hand. After his hand had healed somewhat, Rommel began experimenting with a knuckleball. When he made it to the major leagues in 1920 with the Philadelphia A's, Rommel used the pitch effectively. Because he had great control of the knuckler, and because batters found swinging at it hard to resist, Rommel's games tended to be quick. One lasted only 55 minutes. In 1922 Rommel compiled an amazing 27–13 record for the seventh-place A's. When Rommel completed his 13-year career, all with the A's, he served as an American League umpire for more than 20 years.

CAREER A'S RECORD:

W	L	W%	ERA	SV
171	119	.590	3.54	29

K	BB	SHO	IP
599	724	18	2,556.3

SIMMONS, AL (OF)
(1924–1932, 1940–1941, 1944)

Aloys Syzmanski rechristened himself Al Simmons after seeing the name in a newspaper ad for a hardware store. Simmons was one of the most fiercely driven hitters the game has ever seen, ranking with Ty Cobb and Rogers Hornsby in terms of dedication to his craft. "I hate pitchers," Simmons once said. "Those guys are trying to take the meat and potatoes right off my plate, and the bread and butter right out of my mouth." Former Yankee outfielder Tommy Henrich called Simmons the most vicious hitter he ever saw. His nickname was "Bucketfoot Al," given to him because of the way he "stepped into the bucket" (bailed out) with his left foot when the pitch came in. While coaches and other players tried to correct his batting stance, Connie Mack told them all to leave Simmons alone and let him bat any way he wanted to.

In Simmons' rookie year of 1924, he hit .308 with 102 RBIs, the first of 11 consecutive 100+ RBI seasons to start his career, far and away the major league record. (Albert Pujols of St. Louis is second with five consecutive seasons through 2005.) In his second season, Simmons laced 253 hits, the fifth most ever, and hit .387. By the late 1920s, Jimmie Foxx had joined Simmons on the A's and the pair rivaled the one-two punch of New York's Babe Ruth and Lou Gehrig. In 1927 Simmons suffered a groin injury that limited him to 106 games, but he still collected 108 RBIs. He missed time again in 1928 due to illness, but still had 107 RBIs in 119 games. During the A's three pennant-winning years of 1929 to 1931, Simmons was a one-man wrecking crew. He hit .365, .381, and .390, winning batting titles in '30 and '31. He also averaged 30+ homers, 150 RBIs, and 134 runs per season.

Simmons, who was as talented in the field as he was at the plate, held out for a higher salary before the 1931 season. Just before the season started, Connie Mack announced to the media that Simmons would not be in the team's lineup come Opening Day. When the Philadelphia owner took a cab to the ballpark a few days later and tried to pay for the ride, the cabbie told him, "If you can't afford Al Simmons, you can't afford me, either." Mack signed Simmons to a three-year contract a few hours later and Simmons was in the lineup again. On the first pitch he saw that day, Simmons hit a home run. After the 1932 season, Mack sold Simmons, Jimmy Dykes, and Mule Haas to the White Sox for $150,000 in his never-ending crusade to raise operating capital. After spending nine years with the A's, Simmons spent the next 11 years with seven different teams, including two more stints with the A's, before retiring after just four games of the 1944 season. Following his playing career, Simmons coached for the A's and Indians. He was elected to the Hall of Fame in 1953 and died in 1956.

CAREER A'S RECORD:

Games	AB	Hits	Runs
1,290	5,130	1,827	969
Avg	**HR**	**RBI**	**SB**
.356	209	1,178	65

STEWART, DAVE (SP)
(1986–1992, 1995)

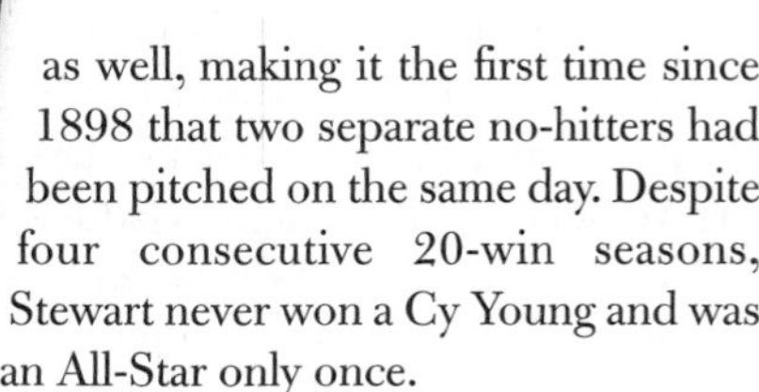

Dave Stewart had enjoyed limited success with the Dodgers, Rangers, and Phillies, compiling a 30–35 record over seven years before he was traded to the Oakland A's in mid-1986. In 1987 his real talent came out of the closet. He won 20 games and followed that up with 20-win seasons the next three years, helping the A's to three straight World Series appearances. In 1990 he tossed a no-hitter against the Blue Jays. On that same night, Fernando Valenzuela of the Dodgers pitched a no-hitter as well, making it the first time since 1898 that two separate no-hitters had been pitched on the same day. Despite four consecutive 20-win seasons, Stewart never won a Cy Young and was an All-Star only once.

Stewart shined especially bright in the playoffs, compiling an 8–0 record with a 2.03 ERA in 10 ALCS starts. Strangely, he struggled in World Series play, going 2–4 in eight starts. After Stewart's final 20-win season in 1990, he turned back into a pumpkin. His ERA rose mysteriously after 1990, and he went 45–44 for the rest of his career, never winning more than 12 games in a season again. After his playing career ended in 1995, Stewart took various front office jobs with the A's, Padres, and Blue Jays. He also spent time as the pitching coach for San Diego.

CAREER A'S RECORD:

W	L	W%	ERA	SV
119	78	.604	3.73	0
K	**BB**	**SHO**	**IP**	
1,152	655	9	1,717.3	

WADDELL, RUBE (SP/RP)
(1902–1907)

When it comes to zany players, Jose Canseco wasn't even in the same league as George "Rube" Waddell. Nor was anyone else. When Waddell was 18 and playing for a semipro team, he signed his first contract, a $500 deal with Louisville of the National League. But after two games in 1897, Waddell left the team when manager Fred Clarke fined him $50 for excessive drinking. He went to Detroit, played nine games, then left to play in Canada. He surfaced in 1899 with the Columbus team of the Western League, where he won 27 games. Louisville decided to give him another chance and brought him back. He went 7–2 and was a big draw, partly because of his pitching and partly because of his antics. After the season he moved to Florida and became an alligator wrestler.

When Louisville owner Barney Dreyfuss got word that his Louisville team was going to be folded after the next season, he bought into the Pirates and "traded" all of his stars, including Waddell, to Pittsburgh. Waddell had an 8–13 record in July of 1900 when he skipped out on the Pirates and ended up in Milwaukee playing for Connie Mack's Western League (soon to be American League) team. Mack wouldn't give Waddell a regular paycheck like the other players because he would squander it in a matter of hours. Instead, Mack gave Waddell $10 or so every once in a while—always in $1 bills—to protect Waddell from himself. Mack knew how to get the most from Waddell. Once, his team was scheduled to play a doubleheader, but the first game went 17 innings and Waddell pitched the whole game. When Mack and the other manager agreed to play only a five-inning contest in the second game, Mack told Waddell he'd give him three days off if he'd pitch the second game. Waddell did, pitching a shutout.

When it appeared that Waddell had straightened himself out, the Pirates demanded he return to Pittsburgh. So, against his will, Waddell returned to the Pirates in 1901. When he gave up 12 runs in seven innings over two starts, allowing 10 hits and nine walks, it appeared to the Pittsburgh brass that Waddell was throwing a tantrum. Clarke told Dreyfuss, "Sell him, release him, drop him off the Monongahela Bridge; do anything with him you like, so long as you get him off my ball team." Dreyfuss agreed, and sold Waddell to the Chicago Orphans (Cubs). Waddell won 14 games with a 2.81 ERA for Chicago, but they couldn't handle his antics, either, and suspended him for the last month of the season. He then joined a group of barnstorming players on a trip to the West Coast. Once there, Waddell decided to stay. But Connie Mack had purchased his contract from Chicago and had to send two Pinkerton agents to California to fetch him back to Philadelphia to play for Mack's new American League team, the A's. As with Pittsburgh,

Waddell pouted in his first game or two, but Mack stuck with him. He eventually won 10 games in a row and finished 24–7 in 1902. Waddell pitched for the A's from 1902 to 1907, leading the American League in strikeouts all six years. Along with Eddie Plank and Chief Bender, the three formed one of the most potent rotations in the game's history.

Consider some of Waddell's antics: He routinely chased after fire engines on foot, even rushing into burning buildings to rescue others, and he sometimes did this on days and at times he was scheduled to pitch. He was the left end on a rugby team; he toured the nation with a play called *The Stain of Guilt;* he courted, married, and separated from May Wynne Skinner of Lynn, Mass. (the second of four wives he would marry while in Philadelphia); he saved a woman from drowning; he accidentally shot a friend through the hand; and he was bitten by a lion. And that was just 1903.

In 1905 the A's faced the Giants in the World Series, but Waddell, the team's ace with a 27–10 record, wasn't available. He had missed the last month of the season after suffering an arm injury in a fight with a teammate after ridiculing him about his new straw hat. The A's lost in five games. After six years, even Connie Mack ran out of patience with Waddell and sold him to the St. Louis Browns for just $5,000. In his first appearance against his former teammates, Waddell struck out 16 batters, a new major league record. After finishing his first season in St. Louis with a 19–14 record, the Browns management, worried about what offseason trouble their new pitcher might get himself into, hired him as a hunter for the entire offseason. Waddell managed to stay out of trouble until the spring and the St. Louis front office was always well stocked with duck and venison. Eventually, St. Louis also grew weary of Waddell's escapades and released him early in the 1910 season.

He pitched for several minor league teams before settling in Minnesota and playing for the Minneapolis Millers, the best minor league team of the era. Waddell became good friends with the team's owner, Joe Cantillon, even staying with his family after the 1912 season. That winter a dike broke near the Cantillon home and Waddell helped by stacking sandbags. He spent hours standing armpit-deep in the icy cold water. He took ill from the incident and never recovered. After Waddell pitched poorly in 1913, Cantillon saw to it that his friend entered a tuberculosis sanitarium in San Antonio, but on April 1, 1914, Waddell died in the facility. In 1946 he was elected to the Hall of Fame.

CAREER A'S RECORD:

W	L	W%	ERA	SV
131	82	.615	1.97	0
K	BB	SHO	IP	
1,576	495	37	1,869.3	

Lefty Grove, all smiles here, was a mad man on the mound and, says Bill James, the best pitcher ever.

Philadelphia Phillies

Since 1883

1980 Team Ball

1896 The Phillies field both the last regular left-handed catcher (Jack Clements) and the last regular left-handed shortstop (Billy Hulen) in major league history.... **1930** Phillies set a 20th-century club record when they hit .315 for the season, but the team nonetheless finishes in last place, thanks to a pitching staff with a 6.71 staff ERA, the worst in the 20th century.... **1961** The Phillies set a 20th-century record with 23 straight losses, but yield the spotlight of failure the following year to the expansion Mets, who manage to lose 120 games.... **1978** The Phillies lose the NLCS for the third year in a row while, in the American League, Kansas City loses the ALCS for the third year in a row. Two years later, the kindred spirits meet in the World Series and Philadelphia comes away with the only World Series title in its 123-year history.

FRANCHISE HISTORY

The National League granted the Philadelphia Phillies a franchise in 1883. The league had had a franchise in Philadelphia in its charter season of 1876, known as the Athletics, but after one season the team folded due to financial difficulties. Lack of money prevented the team from completing its schedule, and making its western swing to Chicago, St. Louis, Cincinnati, and Louisville. The owner blamed it on fierce competition for the public's discretionary dollars from the 1876 Centennial Exposition that was taking place in Philadelphia at the same time that summer, but gambling problems may have been the unspoken reason.

Jack Clements hit .394 for the 1895 Phillies, to this day the highest average ever by a major league catcher.

The rival American Association had placed a team in Philadelphia in 1882, also called the Athletics (seven prominent professional Philadelphia teams of that era went by the nickname Athletics), and it was quite successful. The National League, itching to get back into the Philadelphia market, shut down its troublesome, small-market Worcester Ruby Legs franchise following the 1882 season and granted a new franchise to partners Alfred J. Reach, a sporting goods manufacturer, and John Rogers, a politically connected Philadelphia attorney. Most sources cite that the Worcester franchise was moved to Philadelphia after the 1882 season, but this hardly seems the case since no players from Worcester ended up with the Phillies in 1883, and there were certainly some players worth having, such as John Clarkson (an eventual major Hall of Famer), Lee Richmond (of perfect-game fame), and stars Harry Stovey and Doc Bushong. An inspection of the player movements reveals that the Worcester players were scattered to the wind, all landing with different teams.

Baker Bowl's cozy right field fence turned Cy Williams into the most prolific home run hitter in National League history during the 20s.

Alfred Reach unimaginatively called his new team the "Philadelphias," which was eventually shortened to "Phillies." Most sources cite the original team name as the Quakers, but that seems to have been more of a nickname. (Even in *Sporting News* publications in the 1950s and 1960s, the name Quakers is frequently used even though the team was clearly officially known as the Phillies.) Reach was also in business with Benjamin Shibe, a manufacturer of whips and other leather items, eventually to include baseball gloves. The new owners built a ballpark for their team, Huntingdon Grounds, which was the envy of every major league team of the era. After a fire destroyed the facility in 1894, its steel-and-concrete replacement was again the jewel of the baseball world. The state-of-the-art ballpark was costly and the owners tended to cut corners, typically at players' expense. At least the owners allowed their players to earn extra money by manning the turnstiles as ticket takers if they weren't scheduled to start that day. Reach and Rogers controlled the team together until 1899, when Reach, wanting to concentrate on his sporting-goods business and tired of the increasing arguments with Rogers over the direction of the team, sold his interest to Rogers. Rogers owned the team until 1903 when he, too, had had enough. The final straw for Rogers was having to deal with the avalanche of lawsuits that resulted from a bleachers

collapse in 1903 that killed 12 fans who were among 500 or so who rushed to a back wall to watch either a fight or a fire (sources give conflicting versions) across the street from the ballpark.

Rogers sold the team to an investment group headed by James Potter, a Philadelphia socialite whose only qualification as team owner (or anything else, for that matter) seemed to be that he had a lot of money. He knew very little about baseball, since he traveled in circles that were more accustomed to squash and indoor tennis. Potter's group paid $200,000 for the team in 1903 and held it until 1909, when they sold it for $350,000 to another investment group, this one headed by newspaperman Horace Fogel. The largest investor in the group was Charles P. Taft, a minority owner of the Cubs and brother of U.S. President William Howard Taft (who later would become the first president to throw out the honorary first pitch). Fogel, who had no money of his own, was clearly a front man for the majority owner of the Cubs, Charles Murphy. Two years later Fogel conducted a campaign alleging that former members of the New York Giants had fixed the pennant race in favor of the Giants by throwing games for money. He also alleged that National League president Thomas Lynch and the umpires were in on the fix. Fogel wrote numerous letters, articles, and telegrams asserting his allegations, causing an uproar in baseball's inner circles. Cubs owner Charles Murphy encouraged Fogel's efforts, but when Fogel also implicated Murphy, the league decided to end the matter and barred only Fogel from baseball, leaving his claims unsupported. Fogel returned to the newspaper business, where he remained until he died in 1928.

The whole embarrassing Fogel affair in 1911 took its toll on the investment group and they sold out in November of that year to William F. Baker, a former New York City

Grover Cleveland Alexander and manager Red Dooin confer in 1912.

police official. Baker, a renowned penny-pincher, controlled the club until his death in 1930. He was so stingy that up until 1925, the grass on the playing field was trimmed by a flock of sheep that lived with one ram under the stands. When the ram tried to butt Phillies secretary Bill Shetsline, the days of the sheep were numbered, finally necessitating the purchase of a lawn mower. Baker was not very good about keeping his ballpark, now called Baker Bowl, up to snuff, either. Fans were routinely pelted with rust when Chuck Klein bounced home runs and foul balls off the park's girders. On one occasion, Klein hit a ball right through the outfield fence, leaving a rusty hole in its wake. On May 14, 1927, a whole section of the right-field stands collapsed, sending thousands of fans tumbling on top of those below. Incredibly, the only person who died was from the resulting stampede of the patrons onto the field. A final example of Baker's frugality comes from a cynical sportswriter of the 1920s who was reporting about an ongoing remodeling project taking place at the Baker Bowl: "National League players will be pleased to learn that the visiting dressing room at Baker Bowl is being completely refurbished for next season—brand-new nails are being installed on which to hang their clothes."

Robin Roberts delivers during the 1950 World Series.

In 1925, Gerry Nugent, a leather goods and shoe dealer, married Mae Mallen, Baker's long-time club secretary, and a year later became the team's business manager. When Baker died, he left half of his estate to Mallen and the other half to his wife. With Mrs. Baker's approval, Nugent then took control of the team. When Mrs. Baker died two years later, she also left a large amount of team stock to Mae Mallen Nugent, thereby giving total control of the team to the couple. The Nugents held the team until 1943, when the team was put into receivership and the National League took control and put the Phillies up for sale. Bill Veeck Jr. tried to buy the team, but Commissioner Kenesaw Mountain Landis squashed the deal when he found out that Veeck had proposed stocking the team with black players since so many of the white stars were gone fighting in World War II.

The Phillies were sold, instead, in early 1943 to an investment group headed by William D. Cox, president of a lumber brokerage. He was a 36-year-old graduate of Yale and an avid stamp collector. Cox hired Bucky Harris to be the team's manager, but in mid-1943 he abruptly fired him. Almost immediately, Harris told the press that Cox had been betting on the Phillies. The players were so upset over losing Harris that they refused to play until a personal appeal by Harris changed their minds. When word of the alleged betting reached Commissioner Landis, he called Cox into his office to investigate the matter. Cox first told Landis that the bets were made by his business associates, but eventually admitted that he himself had placed several dozen small bets in the $25–$100 range. A furious Landis forced Cox to sell his stock in the team and barred him from any further involvement in organized baseball.

Cox's share of the team was purchased for $400,000 by Robert M. Carpenter Sr., the CEO of DuPont. He then turned the club over to his son, Robert Jr., who controlled the team for the next 38 years. The Carpenters had previously owned the minor league Wilmington

Blue Rocks. In 1944 Robert Jr. became the first major league owner ever to be drafted into the military. Before leaving for military duty, Robert Jr. hired Herb Pennock to be the team's general manager. Pennock had begun to build a decent team when he died suddenly of a brain hemorrhage during the January 1948 winter meetings. The Carpenter family owned the Phillies until 1981 when they sold out to an investment group headed by Bill Giles, son of former National League president Warren Giles, for just over $30 million. Giles put very little of his own money into the syndicate, but was given 10 percent of the stock for putting the deal together. He eventually acquired about 20 percent of the stock while the remaining investors controlled the other 80 percent. Over the years numerous limited partners have come and gone, at times controlling more stock than Giles, but Giles still has his hand in the day-to-day operations of the club.

On the field, it would probably be fair to say the Phillies have been, for the most part, if not a disaster, then at least a flop—five pennants and just one World Series title in their 123-year existence in one of the largest markets in the country. The expansion Diamondbacks have one championship flag in just eight seasons, while the Marlins have racked up two titles in 13 years of existence. In 1964, the Phillies managed to engineer one of the great collapses in baseball history, blowing a 10-game lead with just two weeks to go and losing the pennant to the Cardinals. The Phillies also hold the major league record for most consecutive losing seasons—16—an embarrassment that won't be erased until 2009, in the likely event that the pathetic Pittsburgh Pirates supplant Philadelphia's dubious achievement by posting their own 17th straight losing season.

Hallelujah: Tug McGraw celebrates the Phillies' 1980 World Series victory, the only one in team history.

TEAM NAME HISTORY

Official Names

Phillies, 1883–1942
(originally the Philadelphias, eventually shortened to Phillies)
Jays, 1943–1944
Phillies, 1945–current

Unofficial Names/Nicknames

Quakers, Red Quakers, Phils

STADIUM HISTORY

Recreation Park	1883–1886
Baker Bowl	1887–1926; 1928–June 30, 1938
(also known as Huntingdon Grounds)	
Shibe Park	1927; July 4, 1938–1952
Connie Mack Stadium (Shibe Park renamed)	1953–1970
Veteran's Stadium	1971–2003
Citizens Bank Park	2004–current

YEARLY RECORD, FINISH, & ATTENDANCE FIGURES

Year	League	Record	DIV/LG Finish	Attendance	Avg/Gm
2005	NL East	88–74	2	2,665,304	32,905
2004	NL East	86–76	2	3,250,092	40,125
2003	NL East	86–76	3	2,259,948	27,901
2002	NL East	80–81	3	1,618,467	20,231
2001	NL East	86–76	2	1,782,054	22,001
2000	NL East	65–97	5	1,612,769	19,911
1999	NL East	77–85	3	1,825,337	22,535
1998	NL East	75–87	3	1,715,722	21,182
1997	NL East	68–94	5	1,490,638	18,403
1996	NL East	67–95	5	1,801,677	22,243
1995	NL East	69–75	3	2,043,598	28,383
1994	NL East	54–61	4	2,290,971	38,183
1993	NL East	97–65	1	3,137,674	38,737
1992	NL East	70–92	6	1,927,448	23,796
1991	NL East	78–84	3	2,050,012	24,699
1990	NL East	77–85	4	1,992,484	24,599
1989	NL East	67–95	6	1,861,985	22,987
1988	NL East	65–96	6	1,990,041	24,568
1987	NL East	80–82	5	2,100,110	25,927
1986	NL East	86–75	2	1,933,335	24,167
1985	NL East	75–87	5	1,830,350	22,597
1984	NL East	81–81	4	2,062,693	25,465
1983	NL East	90–72	1	2,128,339	25,955
1982	NL East	89–73	2	2,376,394	29,338
1981	NL East	59–48	1/3	1,638,752	29,795
1980	NL East	91–71	1	2,651,650	32,736
1979	NL East	84–78	4	2,775,011	34,259
1978	NL East	90–72	1	2,583,389	31,505
1977	NL East	101–61	1	2,700,070	33,334
1976	NL East	101–61	1	2,480,150	30,619
1975	NL East	86–76	2	1,909,233	23,571
1974	NL East	80–82	3	1,808,648	22,329
1973	NL East	71–91	6	1,475,934	18,221
1972	NL East	59–97	6	1,343,329	17,004
1971	NL East	67–95	6	1,511,223	18,657
1970	NL East	73–88	5	708,247	8,853
1969	NL East	63–99	5	519,414	6,413
1968	NL	76–86	7	664,546	8,204
1967	NL	82–80	5	828,888	10,361
1966	NL	87–75	4	1,108,201	13,681
1965	NL	85–76	6	1,166,376	14,580
1964	NL	92–70	2	1,425,891	17,604
1963	NL	87–75	4	907,141	11,199
1962	NL	81–80	7	762,034	9,525
1961	NL	47–107	8	590,039	7,565
1960	NL	59–95	8	862,205	11,197
1959	NL	64–90	8	802,815	10,292
1958	NL	69–85	8	931,110	12,092
1957	NL	77–77	5	1,146,230	14,695
1956	NL	71–83	5	934,798	12,140
1955	NL	77–77	4	922,886	11,986

YEARLY RECORD, FINISH, & ATTENDANCE FIGURES (CONT.)

Year	League	Record	DIV/LG Finish	Attendance	Avg/Gm
1954	NL	75–79	4	738,991	9,474
1953	NL	83–71	4	853,644	10,944
1952	NL	87–67	4	755,417	9,940
1951	NL	73–81	5	937,658	12,177
1950	NL	91–63	1	1,217,035	15,603
1949	NL	81–73	3	819,698	10,645
1948	NL	66–88	6	767,429	10,098
1947	NL	62–92	8	907,332	11,784
1946	NL	69–85	5	1,045,247	13,401
1945	NL	46–108	8	285,057	3,702
1944	NL	61–92	8	369,586	4,678
1943	NL	64–90	7	466,975	5,987
1942	NL	42–109	8	230,183	3,111
1941	NL	43–111	8	231,401	3,045
1940	NL	50–103	8	207,177	2,622
1939	NL	45–106	8	277,973	3,756
1938	NL	45–105	8	166,111	2,215
1937	NL	61–92	7	212,790	2,876
1936	NL	54–100	8	249,219	3,195
1935	NL	64–89	7	205,470	2,601
1934	NL	56–93	7	169,885	2,393
1933	NL	60–92	7	156,421	2,173
1932	NL	78–76	4	268,914	3,492
1931	NL	66–88	6	284,849	3,748
1930	NL	52–102	8	299,007	3,883
1929	NL	71–82	5	281,200	3,700
1928	NL	43–109	8	182,168	2,429
1927	NL	51–103	8	305,420	3,916
1926	NL	58–93	8	240,600	3,166
1925	NL	68–85	6	304,905	3,960
1924	NL	55–96	7	299,818	3,945
1923	NL	50–104	8	228,168	3,042
1922	NL	57–96	7	232,471	3,019
1921	NL	51–103	8	273,961	3,605
1920	NL	62–91	8	330,998	4,299
1919	NL	47–90	8	240,424	3,386
1918	NL	55–68	6	122,266	2,145
1917	NL	87–65	2	354,428	4,664
1916	NL	91–62	2	515,365	6,524
1915	NL	90–62	1	449,898	5,920
1914	NL	74–80	6	138,474	1,775
1913	NL	88–63	2	470,000	6,026
1912	NL	73–79	5	250,000	3,333
1911	NL	79–73	4	416,000	5,474
1910	NL	78–75	4	296,597	3,803
1909	NL	74–79	5	303,177	3,937
1908	NL	83–71	4	420,660	5,393
1907	NL	83–64	3	341,216	4,550
1906	NL	71–82	4	294,680	3,827
1905	NL	83–69	4	317,932	4,183
1904	NL	52–100	8	140,771	1,928

YEARLY RECORD, FINISH, & ATTENDANCE FIGURES (CONT.)

Year	League	Record	DIV/LG Finish	Attendance	Avg/Gm
1903	NL	49–86	7	151,729	2,487
1902	NL	56–81	7	112,066	1,624
1901	NL	83–57	2	234,937	3,405
1900	NL	75–63	3	301,913	4,282
1899	NL	94–58	3	388,933	5,051
1898	NL	78–71	6	265,414	3,539
1897	NL	55–77	10	290,027	4,329
1896	NL	62–68	8	357,025	5,493
1895	NL	78–53	3	474,971	7,142
1894	NL	71–57	4	352,773	5,469
1893	NL	72–57	4	293,019	4,406
1892	NL	87–66	4	193,731	2,500
1891	NL	68–69	4	217,282	3,149
1890	NL	78–54	3	148,366	2,231
1889	NL	63–64	4	N/A	N/A
1888	NL	69–61	3	N/A	N/A
1887	NL	75–48	2	N/A	N/A
1886	NL	71–43	4	N/A	N/A
1885	NL	56–54	3	N/A	N/A
1884	NL	39–73	6	N/A	N/A
1883	NL	17–81	8	N/A	N/A

MANAGER HISTORY

Manager	Years	W–L	Win %
Bob Ferguson	1883	4–13	.235
Blondie Purcell	1883	13–68	.160
Harry Wright	1884–1893	636–566	.529
Jack Clements	1890	13–6	.684
Al Reach	1890	4–7	.364
Bob Allen	1890	25–10	.714
Albert Irwin	1894–1895	149–110	.575
Billy Nash	1896	62–68	.477
George Stallings	1897–1898	74–104	.416
Bill Shettsline	1898–1902	367–303	.548
Chief Zimmer	1903	49–86	.363
Hugh Duffy	1904–1906	206–251	.451
Bill Murray	1907–1909	240–214	.449
Red Dooin	1910–1914	392–370	.514
Pat Moran	1915–1918	323–257	.557
Jack Coombs	1919	18–44	.290
Gavvy Cravath	1919–1920	91–137	.399
Bill Donovan	1921	25–62	.287
Kaiser Wilhelm	1921–1922	83–137	.377
Art Fletcher	1923–1926	231–378	.379
Stuffy McInnis	1927	51–103	.331
Burt Shotton	1928–1933	370–549	.403
Jimmy Wilson	1934–1938	280–477	.369

MANAGER HISTORY (CONT.)

Manager	Years	W–L	Win %
Hans Lobert	1938, 1942	42–111	.275
Doc Prothro	1939–1941	138–320	.301
Bucky Harris	1943	38–52	.413
Fred Fitzsimmons	1943–1945	105–181	.367
Ben Chapman	1945–1948	196–276	.415
Dusty Cooke	1948	6–6	.500
Eddie Sawyer	1948–1952, 1958–1960	390–423	.480
Steve O'Neill	1952–1954	182–140	.565
Terry Moore	1954	35–42	.455
Mayo Smith	1955–1958	264–282	.484
Andy Cohen	1960	1–0	1.000
Gene Mauch	1960–1968	646–684	.486
George Myatt	1968, 1969	20–35	.364
Bob Skinner	1968–1969	92–123	.428
Frank Lucchesi	1970–1972	166–233	.416
Paul Owens	1972, 1983–1984	161–158	.505
Danny Ozark	1973–1979	594–510	.538
Dallas Green	1979–1981	169–130	.565
Pat Corrales	1982–1983	132–115	.534
John Felske	1985–1987	190–194	.495
Lee Elia	1987–1988	111–142	.439
John Vukovich	1988	5–4	.556
Nick Leyva	1989–1991	148–189	.439
Jim Fregosi	1991–1996	431–463	.482
Terry Francona	1997–2000	285–363	.440
Larry Bowa	2001–2004	337–308	.522
Gary Varsho	2004	1–1	.500
Charlie Manuel	2005	88–74	.54

ALL-TIME WIN-LOSS RECORDS VS. ALL OPPONENTS

Opponent	W–L	Opponent	W–L
ALL-TIME	7,546–8,825	Marlins	102–92
Angels	1–2	Mets	399–347
Astros	266–254	Nationals	315–299
Athletics	3–3	Orioles	20–19
Blue Jays	8–7	Padres	215–182
Braves	932–1,009	Pirates	906–1,094
Brewers	35–23	Rangers	3–0
Cardinals	866–1,137	Reds	826–1,036
Cubs	945–1,057	Red Sox	12–13
Devil Rays	4–8	Rockies	57–49
Diamondbacks	27–33	Royals	2–1
Dodgers	816–1,046	Tigers	5–4
Giants	766–1,089	Twins	3–3
Indians	2–1	White Sox	2–4
INTERLEAGUE	73–78	Yankees	7–8
Mariners	1–5		

Franchise Highlights, Low Points, and Strange Distinctions

1894 When Billy Hamilton hit .404 for the Phillies, it was only the fourth highest average on the team. Tuck Turner hit .416, and Sam Thompson and Ed Delahanty both hit .407. As a team, the Phils finished with a .349 batting average, but they ended up in fourth place, 18 games out, because their porous pitching staff posted a 5.63 ERA on the season.

• • • •

1896 When Philadelphia and Washington hooked up for a July 4 doubleheader, they set off some fireworks of their own, collecting 73 hits between them—still a major league record for hits by both teams in a doubleheader.

• • • •

1898 On April 21, Phillies pitcher Bill Duggleby became the first player ever to hit a grand slam in his first major league at-bat.

• • • •

1900–09 From 1900 to 1909, center fielder Roy Thomas of the Phils collected 100 or more walks six times. During that same time, no other National League player could manage to amass that total more than once.

• • • •

1904 Chick Fraser lost 24 games for the Phillies. He then lost 21 for Brooklyn in 1905 and 20 for Cincinnati in 1906, giving him the dubious distinction of losing 20 or more games three years in a row for three different teams.

1911 Rookie pitcher Grover Alexander of the Phillies set a 20th-century record when he won 28 games in his first major league season.

• • • •

1919 The Philadelphia Phillies had 14 pitchers of record, and all 14 of them posted a losing record! They had seven pitchers who won at least five games, but no pitcher who won more than eight games.

• • • •

1925 After a long career with the Giants and Reds, outfielder George Burns played the final year of his 15-year career with the Phillies. When he stole home for the 27th time in his career that year, he established the National League career record for steals of home plate.

• • • •

1927 When Philadelphia outfielder Cy Williams hit 30 homers, he had 98 RBIs, making him the first 30-homer player to fail to collect at least 100 RBIs. His home run output that year was more than half of the team's total of 57. Also, during his long career he had just 41 pinch-hits, but 11 of them were homers.

• • • •

1929 The Phillies had four 200-hit men (Lefty O'Doul, 254; Chuck Klein, 219; Pinky Whitney, 207; and Fresco Thompson, 202), the only team in major league history to achieve the feat. Still, the team finished in just fifth place.

1932 Eight players in major league history have collected more than 100 extra-base hits in a season, but only Chuck Klein of the Phillies (1930 and 1932) has done it more than once.

• • • •

1933 Just how did the Phillies reward Chuck Klein for his 1933 Triple Crown season, a year in which he collected 200+ hits for the fifth straight season? On November 21 of that year they traded him to the Cubs for three players and $65,000, making him the only player ever to be traded after a Triple Crown season. With the Cubs the next season, Klein slipped to career lows in all three Triple Crown categories (.301, 20 HR, 80 RBIs).

• • • •

1938 On April 19, Ernie Koy of the Dodgers and Heinie Mueller of the Phillies each homered in their first major league at-bat in the same game.

• • • •

1941 The first major league player to be drafted for America's expected involvement in World War II was Hugh Mulcahy of the Phillies, on March 8.

Although Philadelphia rookie second baseman Danny Murtaugh played in just 85 games in 1941, he led the NL in stolen bases with 18. He did this despite hitting just .219, the lowest batting average in the 20th century by a stolen-base champion.

• • • •

1942 The first full-time player at any position to field a perfect 1.000 for a season was outfielder Danny Litwhiler of the Phils.

1947 When Philadelphia outfielder Harry "the Hat" Walker won the NL batting title with a .363 average, he joined brother Dixie Walker (Dodgers, 1944) as the first brothers to win batting titles.

• • • •

1948 When the Phillies finished the season with a 66–88 record, it was their 16th straight losing season, still the major league record. They would break their string of futile seasons in 1949 by finishing with a record of 81–73. The Phillies won just one NL pennant in their first 67 years of existence (1915) and had only one first-division finish between 1917 and 1949.

• • • •

1958 When Richie Ashburn of the Phillies won the batting title, he became just the second player in NL history from a last place team to do so.

The previous year, Ashburn achieved a quirkier kind of notoriety. He injured a fan with a foul ball, and as the fan was being taken out of the stadium for medical treatment, Ashburn hit him again with another foul ball.

After his playing career was over, he offered his opinion on why the 1950 Whiz Kids never won another pennant: "We were all white."

• • • •

1959 Philadelphia's Gene Freese had seven pinch-hits, but five of them were homers.

1971 On June 23, pitcher Rick Wise of the Phillies more than earned his pay. Not only did he toss a no-hitter against the Cincinnati Reds, but he belted two homers as well.

• • • •

1972 Steve Carlton went 27–10 with the last-place Phillies; in 1983, when he went 15–16, Philadelphia won the NL pennant. More 1972 Carlton: his 27 wins tied the 20th-century NL record for wins by a left-hander, set by Sandy Koufax in 1966. He also set a major league record for most consecutive wins (15) by a pitcher on a last-place team. While Carlton was 27–10 that season, the rest of the staff was 32–87.

• • • •

1979 Outfielder Del Unser of the Phillies hit home runs in three consecutive pinch-hit appearances.

• • • •

1981 In the strike-shortened season, Pete Rose of the Phillies led the majors in hits with 140, becoming the only 40-year-old player ever to top both leagues in hits in one season.

• • • •

1984 Mike Schmidt became the first major leaguer in history to end up in a tie for both his league's home-run (36) and RBI (106) crowns in the same season. In 1986 he set a major league record by leading his league in homers for the eighth time.

1992 Phillies second baseman Mickey Morandini turned the ninth unassisted triple play in major league history on September 20, at Pittsburgh in a 3–2, 13-inning loss to the Pirates.

Left-hander Terry Mulholland picked off a major league record 16 runners.

Darren Daulton became the first left-handed-hitting catcher in major league history to win an RBI title when he knocked in 109.

• • • •

1998 Curt Schilling became only the fifth pitcher in major league history to record back-to-back seasons with at least 300 strikeouts. In 1997 his 319 strikeouts had set the NL record for right-handers.

• • • •

1999 Rico Brogna became the first Philadelphia first baseman in team history to collect 100 RBIs in consecutive seasons (104 in 1998 and 102 in 1999).

• • • •

2001 It took 119 years, but the Phillies finally had their first-ever 30–30 man. Bobby Abreu turned the trick when he hit 31 homers and stole 36 bases.

Special Achievements

World Series Results

Year	Opponent	Result	Games
1915	Boston Red Sox	Lost	1–4
1950	New York Yankees	Lost	0–4
1980	Kansas City Royals	Won	4–2
1983	Baltimore Orioles	Lost	1–4
1993	Toronto Blue Jays	Lost	2–4

World Series Managerial Records

Manager	Series Record	Games Record
Pat Moran	0–1	1–4
Eddie Sawyer	0–1	0–4
Dallas Green	1–0	4–2
Paul Owens	0–1	1–4
Jim Fregosi	0–1	2–4

All-Time Postseason Record

Divisional Playoffs	2–3
League Championship Series	12–14
World Series	8–18

All-Star Games at Philadelphia (when NL was home team at Shibe Park)

Year	Date	Winner	Score	Stadium
1952	July 8	National	3–2	Shibe Park
1976	July 13	National	7–1	Veterans Stadium
1996	July 9	National	6–0	Veterans Stadium

Hall of Fameers Who Played for Team

	Position	Years	Games with Philadelphia
Grover Alexander	SP/RP	1911–1917	345
Sparky Anderson	2B	1959	152
Richie Ashburn	OF	1948–1959	1,794
Dave Bancroft	SS	1915–1920	681
Chief Bender	RP/SP	1916–1917	48
Dan Brouthers	1B	1896	57
Jim Bunning	SP	1964–1967, 1970–1971	229
Steve Carlton	SP	1972–1986	501
Roger Connor	1B	1892	155
Ed Delahanty	OF/1B	1888–1889, 1891–1901	1,555
Hugh Duffy	OF	1904–1906	34
Johnny Evers	2B/3B	1917	56
Elmer Flick	OF	1898–1901	537
Jimmie Foxx	1B/3B/RP	1945	89
Billy Hamilton	OF	1890–1895	729
Fergie Jenkins	RP	1965–1966	8
Hughie Jennings	1B	1901–1902	160
Tim Keefe	SP	1891–1893	72
Chuck Klein	OF	1928–1933, 1936–1944	1,405
Nap Lajoie	2B/1B	1896–1900	492
Tommy McCarthy	OF/2B	1886–1887	26
Joe Morgan	2B	1983	123
Kid Nichols	SP	1905–1906	21
Tony Perez	1B	1983	91
Eppa Rixey	SP/RP	1912–1920	254
Robin Roberts	SP	1948–1961	541
Ryne Sandberg	SS	1981	13
Mike Schmidt	3B/1B	1972–1989	2,404
Casey Stengel	OF	1920–1921	153
Sam Thompson	OF	1889–1898	1,031
Lloyd Waner	OF	1942	101
Hack Wilson	OF	1934	7

Hall of Fameers Who Managed Team

	Years	Games with Philadelphia
Hugh Duffy	1904–1906	457
Bucky Harris	1943	90
Harry Wright	1884–1893	1,202

MVP Award Winners

Chuck Klein	OF	1932
Jim Konstanty	RP	1950
Mike Schmidt	3B	1980
Mike Schmidt	3B	1981
Mike Schmidt	3B	1986

Cy Young Award Winners

Pitcher	Year	W–L	SV	ERA
Steve Carlton	1972	27–10	0	1.97
Steve Carlton	1977	23–10	0	2.64
Steve Carlton	1980	24–9	0	2.34
Steve Carlton	1982	23–11	0	3.10
John Denny	1983	19–6	0	2.37
Steve Bedrosian	1987	5–3	40	2.83

Rookie of the Year Award Winners

Jack Sanford	SP	1957
Dick Allen	3B	1964
Scott Rolen	3B	1997
Ryan Howard	1B	2005

GOLD GLOVE WINNERS

Year	Position	Player
1963	SS	Bobby Wine
1964	SP	Bobby Shantz
	SS	Ruben Amaro
1966	1B	Bill White
1972	SS	Larry Bowa
1975	OF	Garry Maddox
1976	SP	Jim Kaat
	3B	Mike Schmidt
	OF	Garry Maddox
1977	SP	Jim Kaat
	3B	Mike Schmidt
	OF	Garry Maddox
1978	C	Bob Boone
	3	Mike Schmidt
	SS	Larry Bowa
	OF	Garry Maddox
1979	C	Bob Boone
	2B	Manny Trillo
	3B	Mike Schmidt
	OF	Garry Maddox
1980	3B	Mike Schmidt
	OF	Garry Maddox
1981	SP	Steve Carlton
	2B	Manny Trillo
	3B	Mike Schmidt
	OF	Garry Maddox
1982	2B	Manny Trillo
	3B	Mike Schmidt
	OF	Garry Maddox
1983	3B	Mike Schmidt
1984	3B	Mike Schmidt
1986	3B	Mike Schmidt
1998	3B	Scott Rolen
1999	C	Mike Lieberthal
2000	3B	Scott Rolen
2001	3B	Scott Rolen
2005	OF	Bobby Abreu

TRIPLE CROWN WINNERS

Player	Year	Avg	HR	RBI
Chuck Klein	1933	.368	28	120

FIREMAN OF THE YEAR AWARD WINNERS

Al Holland	1983 (tie)
Steve Bedrosian	1987

WORLD SERIES MVP

Mike Schmidt	1980

LEAGUE CHAMPIONSHIP SERIES MVP

Manny Trillo	1980
Gary Matthews	1983
Curt Schilling	1993

ALL-STAR GAME MVP

Johnny Callison	1964

MANAGER OF THE YEAR AWARD WINNERS

Larry Bowa	2001

BATTING CHAMPIONS

Year	Player	Avg
1891	Billy Hamilton	.340
1899	Ed Delahanty	.410
1910	Sherry Magee	.331
1929	Lefty O'Doul	.398
1933	Chuck Klein	.368
1947	Harry Walker	.363
1955	Richie Ashburn	.338
1958	Richie Ashburn	.350

NINE-INNING NO-HITTERS PITCHED

Year	Pitcher	Opp.	Score
1885	Charles Ferguson	PRO	1–0
1898	Red Donahue	BOS	5–0
1903	Charles Fraser	CHI	10–0
1906	John Lush	BRK	6–0
1964	Jim Bunning	NYM	6–0 (perfect)
1971	Rick Wise	CIN	4–0
1990	Terry Mulholland	SF	6–0
1991	Tommy Greene	MON	2–0
2003	Kevin Millwood	SF	1–0

20-GAME WINNERS

Year	Pitcher	W–L
1884	Charles Ferguson	21–25
1885	Charles Ferguson	26–20
	Ed Daily	26–23
1886	Charles Ferguson	30–9
	Dan Casey	24–18
1887	Dan Casey	28–13
	Charles Ferguson	22–10
	Charlie Buffinton	21–17
1888	Charlie Buffinton	28–17
1889	Charlie Buffinton	28–16
1890	Kid Gleason	38–17
	Tom Vickery	24–22
1891	Kid Gleason	24–22
	Charles Esper	20–15
1892	Gus Weyhing	32–21

1893	Gus Weyhing	23–16
1894	Jack Taylor	23–13
1895	Jack Taylor Kid Carsey	26–14 24–16
1896	Jack Taylor	20–21
1898	Wiley Piatt	24–14
1899	Wiley Piatt Red Donahue Charles Fraser	23–15 21–8 21–12
1901	Al Orth Red Donahue	20–12 21–13
1905	Togie Pittinger	23–14
1907	Tully Sparks	22–8
1908	George McQuillan	23–17
1910	Earl Moore	22–15
1911	Grover Alexander	28–13
1913	Tom Seaton Grover Alexander	27–12 22–8
1914	Grover Alexander Erskine Mayer	27–15 21–19
1915	Grover Alexander Erskine Mayer	31–10 21–15
1916	Grover Alexander Eppa Rixey	33–12 22–10
1917	Grover Alexander	30–13
1950	Robin Roberts	20–11
1951	Robin Roberts	21–15
1952	Robin Roberts	28–7
1953	Robin Roberts	23–16
1954	Robin Roberts	23–15
1955	Robin Roberts	23–14
1966	Chris Short	20–10
1972	Steve Carlton	27–10
1976	Steve Carlton	20–7
1977	Steve Carlton	23–10
1980	Steve Carlton	24–9
1982	Steve Carlton	23–11

RETIRED UNIFORM NUMBERS

Number	Player	Position
1	Richie Ashburn	OF
14	Jim Bunning	SP
20	Mike Schmidt	3B
32	Steve Carlton	SP
36	Robin Roberts	SP

TEAM RECORDS–WINS & LOSSES

- Games won in a season: 101 in 1976 and 1977
- Games lost in a season: 111 in 1941
- Games won in a month: 22 (six times): September 1916; July 1950; July 1952; May 1976; August 1977; September 1983
- Games lost in a month: 27 in September 1939
- Consecutive games won: 16 in 1887, 1890, and 1892
- Consecutive games lost: 23 in 1961
- Biggest shutout victory: 24–0 over Indianapolis on June 28, 1887
- Biggest shutout loss: 28–0 to Providence, August 21, 1883
- Highest winning percentage: .623 in 1886 (71–43), 1976 (101–61), and 1977 (101–61)
- Lowest winning percentage: .173 in 1883 (17–81)

TEAM RECORDS—BATTING

- Highest team batting average: .343 in 1894
- Lowest team batting average: .225 in 1888
- Highest team slugging average: .467 in 1929
- Highest team on-base percentage: .414 in 1894
- Total hits: 1,783 in 1930
- Extra-base hits: 541 in 2004
- Hits in a game: 36 vs. Louisville on August 17, 1894
- Longest individual hitting streak: 36, Billy Hamilton, 1894, and Jimmy Rollins, 2005
- Most .300 hitters in a single season: 10 in 1925
- Home runs: 215 in 2004
- Home runs in a month: 15, Cy Williams, May 1923, and Jim Thome, June 2004
- Home runs in a game: 7 vs. New York Mets on September 8, 1998
- Home runs by a rookie: 30, Willie Montanez, 1971
- Home runs by a right-hander: 48, Mike Schmidt, 1980
- Home runs by a left-hander: 47, Jim Thome, 2003
- Home runs by a switch-hitter: 27, Dave Hollins, 1992
- Grand slams: 8 in 1993 and 2005
- Grand slams (individual; season): 4, Vince DiMaggio, 1945
- Grand slams (individual; career): 7, Mike Schmidt
- Triples: 148 in 1894
- Doubles: 345 in 1930
- Singles: 1,338 in 1894
- Walks: 665 in 1993
- Runs scored: 944 in 1930

- Runs scored in a game: 29 vs. Louisville, August 17, 1894
- Runs scored in an inning: 13 vs. Cincinnati on April 13, 2003 (fourth inning)
- Most batters hit by a pitch: 58 in 2004
- Times shut out: 23 in 1908 and 1909
- Grounded into double plays: 144 in 1950
- Fewest grounded into double plays: 91 in 1935 and 1973
- Runners left on base: 1,281 in 1993

TEAM RECORDS—BASERUNNING

- Stolen bases: 355 in 1887
- Caught stealing: 83 in 1920

TEAM RECORDS—PITCHING

- Lowest earned run average: 2.18 in 1915
- Complete games: 131 in 1904
- Saves: 48 in 1987
- Strikeouts: 1,209 in 1997
- Shutouts: 24 in 1916
- Walks: 682 in 1974
- Hit batsmen: 77 in 2003
- Wild pitches: 91 in 1989
- Consecutive wins (individual): 15, Steve Carlton, 1972
- Consecutive losses (individual): 12, Russ Miller, 1928; Hugh Mulcahy, 1940; Ken Reynolds, 1972
- Strikeouts in a game (individual): 18, Chris Short, October 2, 1965 (second game, 18 innings); 9 innings: 17, Art Mahaffey, April 23, 1961 (second game)
- Runs allowed in a game: 29 vs. Boston Braves, June 20, 1883 and vs. New York Giants, June 15, 1887

TEAM RECORDS—FIELDING

- Best fielding average: .987 in 2004
- Most errors committed: 639 in 1883
- Fewest errors committed: 81 in 2004
- Most double plays turned: 179 in 1961 and 1973
- Fewest double plays turned: 46 in 1886

TEAM RECORDS—MISCELLANEOUS

- Number of times league champions: 5
- Number of times finishing last in league: 27
- Largest attendance, single game: 63,816 vs. Cincinnati, July 3, 1984
- Largest attendance, doubleheader: 63,346 vs. Pittsburgh, August 10, 1979
- Players used in a season: 54 in 1996
- Seasons played: 18 by Mike Schmidt

PRIMARY PITCHING STAFFS

Year	Starter	Starter	Starter	Starter	Starter	Closer	Bullpen	Bullpen	Bullpen
2005	Lieber	Myers	Lidle	Padilla	Wolf	Wagner	Madson	Fultz	Cormier
2004	Milton	Myers	Millwood	Wolf	Padilla	Wagner	Hernandez	Worrell	Cormier
2003	Duckworth	Myers	Millwood	Wolf	Padilla	Mesa	Cormier	Adams	Silva
2002	Duckworth	Adams	Person	Wolf	Padilla	Mesa	Cormier	Santiago	Silva
2001	Daal	Coggin	Person	Wolf	Chen	Mesa	Bottalico	Santiago	Cormier
2000	Schilling	Ashby	Person	Wolf	Byrd	Brantley	Gomes	Brock	Vosberg
1999	Schilling	Ogea	Person	Wolf	Byrd	Gomes	Montgomery	Telemaco	Poole
1998	Schilling	Green	Portugal	Beech	Loewer	Leiter	Gomes	Spradlin	Perez
1997	Schilling	Green	Leiter	Beech	Stephenson	Bottalico	Gomes	Spradlin	Harris
1996	Schilling	Williams	Mulholland	Mimbs	Hunter	Bottalico	Borland	Ryan	Springer
1995	Schilling	Quantrill	Green	Mimbs	Fernandez	Slocumb	Bottalico	Williams	Borland
1994	Schilling	Jackson	West	Boskie	Munoz	Jones	Borland	Andersen	Slocumb
1993	Schilling	Jackson	Greene	Rivera	Mulholland	Williams	West	Andersen	Mason
1992	Schilling	Abbott	Greene	Rivera	Mulholland	Williams	Hartley	Jones	Ritchie
1991	DeJesus	Cox	Greene	Ruffin	Mulholland	Williams	Boever	McDowell	Ritchie
1990	DeJesus	Combs	Howell	Ruffin	Mulholland	McDowell	Akerfelds	Carman	Parrett
1989	Carman	McWilliams	Howell	Ruffin	Mulholland	McDowell	Frohwirth	Harris	Parrett
1988	Carman	Gross	Rawley	Ruffin	Palmer	Bedrosian	Tekulve	Harris	Maddux

PRIMARY PITCHING STAFFS (CONT.)

Year	Starter	Starter	Starter	Starter	Starter	Closer	Bullpen	Bullpen	Bullpen
1987	Carman	Gross	Rawley	Ruffin	Jackson	Bedrosian	Tekulve	Ritchie	Calhoun
1986	Hudson	Gross	Rawley	Ruffin	Maddux	Bedrosian	Tekulve	Carman	Hume
1985	Hudson	Gross	Rawley	Denny	Koosman	Tekulve	Andersen	Carman	Rucker
1984	Hudson	Carlton	Rawley	Denny	Koosman	Holland	Andersen	Campbell	Gross
1983	Hudson	Carlton	Bystrom	Denny	Gross	Holland	Hernandez	Reed	McGraw
1982	Krukow	Carlton	Bystrom	Christenson	Ruthven	Reed	Monge	Farmer	McGraw
1981	Espinosa	Carlton	Davis	Christenson	Ruthven	McGraw	Lyle	Reed	Proly
1980	Walk	Carlton	Lerch	Christenson	Ruthven	McGraw	Noles	Reed	Saucier
1979	Espinosa	Carlton	Lerch	Christenson	Ruthven	McGraw	Eastwick	Reed	Bird
1978	Kaat	Carlton	Lerch	Christenson	Lonborg	Reed	Eastwick	Brusstar	McGraw
1977	Kaat	Carlton	Lerch	Christenson	Lonborg	Garber	Reed	Brusstar	McGraw
1976	Kaat	Carlton	Underwood	Christenson	Lonborg	Reed	Garber	Schueler	McGraw
1975	Twitchell	Carlton	Underwood	Christenson	Lonborg	McGraw	Garber	Hilgendorf	Schueler
1974	Twitchell	Carlton	Ruthven	Schueler	Lonborg	Watt	Garber	Scarce	Hernaiz
1973	Twitchell	Carlton	Ruthven	Brett	Lonborg	Scarce	Wilson	Lersch	Brandon
1972	Twitchell	Carlton	Reynolds	Champion	Fryman	Selma	Lersch	Brandon	
1971	Wise	Lersch	Reynolds	Short	Fryman	Hoerner	Wilson	Champion	Brandon
1970	Wise	Bunning	Jackson	Short	Fryman	Selma	Hoerner	Lersch	Palmer
1969	Wise	Johnson	Jackson	Champion	Fryman	Wilson	Boozer	Farrell	Raffo
1968	Wise	Short	Jackson	James	Fryman	Farrell	Boozer	Wagner	Jackson
1967	Wise	Short	Jackson	Bunning	Ellsworth	Farrell	Boozer	Hall	Jackson
1966	Wise	Short	Jackson	Bunning	Buhl	Knowles	Fox	Culp	Herbert
1965	Culp	Short	Herbert	Bunning	Belinsky	Wagner	Baldschun	Mahaffey	Roebuck
1964	Culp	Short	Bennett	Bunning	Mahaffey	Baldschun	Wise	Roebuck	Green
1963	Culp	Short	Bennett	McLish	Mahaffey	Baldschun	Klippstein	Duren	Green
1962	Hamilton	Owens	Bennett	McLish	Mahaffey	Baldschun	Short	Smith	Green
1961	Buzhardt	Owens	Roberts	Sullivan	Mahaffey	Baldschun	Ferrarese	Green	
1960	Buzhardt	Owens	Roberts	Conley	Mahaffey	Farrell	Short	Robinson	Green
1959	Cardwell	Owens	Roberts	Conley	Semproch	Farrell	Meyer	Robinson	Phillips
1958	Cardwell	Simmons	Roberts	Sanford	Semproch	Farrell	Morehead	Hearn	Meyer
1957	Cardwell	Simmons	Roberts	Sanford	Haddix	Farrell	Morehead	Hearn	Miller
1956	Rogovin	Simmons	Roberts	Miller	Haddix	Miller	Meyer	Negray	
1955	Rogovin	Simmons	Roberts	Wehmeier	Dickson	Meyer	Mrozinski	Kipper	Miller
1954	Miller	Simmons	Roberts	Wehmeier	Dickson	Ridzik	Konstanty	Mrozinski	
1953	Miller	Simmons	Roberts	Drews	Konstanty	Ridzik	Hansen	Kipper	
1952	Meyer	Simmons	Roberts	Drews	Fox	Konstanty	Heintzelman	Hansen	Ridzik
1951	Meyer	Church	Roberts	Johnson	Thompson	Konstanty	Heintzelman	Hansen	Miller
1950	Meyer	Church	Roberts	Simmons	Miller	Konstanty	Heintzelman	Donnelly	Candini
1949	Meyer	Heintzelman	Roberts	Simmons	Borowy	Konstanty	Trinkle	Donnelly	Rowe
1948	Leonard	Rowe	Roberts	Simmons	Donnelly	Dubiel	Heusser	Nahem	
1947	Leonard	Rowe	Heintzelman	Judd	Hughes	Donnelly	Jurisich	Schanz	
1946	Raffensberger	Rowe	Schanz	Judd	Hughes	Karl	Mauney	Mulligan	
1945	Barrett	Sproull	Schanz	Mauney	Lee	Karl	Judd	Kraus	Coffman
1944	Barrett	Raffensberger	Schanz	Gerheauser	Lee	Karl	Covington	Shuman	
1943	Barrett	Kraus	Rowe	Gerheauser	Johnson	Kimball	Dietz	Fuchs	
1942	Hughes	Melton	Podgajny	Hoerst	Johnson	Nahem	Pearson	Beck	
1941	Hughes	Blanton	Podgajny	Grissom	Johnson	Pearson	Hoerst	Melton	Beck
1940	Higbe	Mulcahy	Pearson	Beck	Johnson	Smoll	Brown	Johnson	
1939	Higbe	Mulcahy	Butcher	Beck	Johnson	Pearson	Kerksieck	Harrell	
1938	Passeau	Mulcahy	Hollingsworth	LaMaster	Walters	Sivess	Smith	Johnson	
1937	Passeau	Mulcahy	Johnson	LaMaster	Walters	Jorgens	Kelleher	Burkart	
1936	Passeau	Bowman	Jorgens	Davis	Walters	Johnson	Kowalik	Moore	Sivess
1935	Johnson	Bowman	Jorgens	Davis	Walters	Bivin	Pezzullo	Prim	

PRIMARY PITCHING STAFFS (CONT.)

Year	Starter	Starter	Starter	Starter	Starter	Closer	Bullpen	Bullpen	Bullpen
1934	Collins	Moore	Hansen	Davis	Moore	Johnson	Grabowski	Darrow	
1933	Holley	Elliott	Hansen	Rhem	Moore	Collins	Liska	Pearce	Berly
1932	Holley	Elliott	Hansen	Benge	Collins	Rhem	Elliott	Berly	
1931	Dudley	Elliott	Bolen	Benge	Collins	Watt	Fallenstein	Schesler	
1930	Sweetland	Willoughby	Collard	Benge	Collins	Elliott	Smythe	Hansen	
1929	Sweetland	Willoughby	Roy	Benge	Koupal	Elliott	Collins	McGraw	
1928	Sweetland	Willoughby	Ring	Benge	Ferguson	Walsh	Miller	McGraw	
1927	Sweetland	Pruett	Scott	Ulrich	Ferguson	Willoughby	Decatur	Mitchell	
1926	Carlson	Dean	Mitchell	Ulrich	Willoughby	Pierce	Knight	Baecht	
1925	Carlson	Ring	Mitchell	Decatur	Knight	Pierce	Betts	Couch	
1924	Carlson	Ring	Mitchell	Glazner	Hubbell	Oeschger	Betts	Couch	
1923	Weinert	Ring	Mitchell	Glazner	Behan	Head	Hubbell	Winters	
1922	Weinert	Ring	Meadows	Hubbell	Smith	Singleton	Pinto	Winters	
1921	Winters	Ring	Meadows	Hubbell	Smith	Betts	Baumgartner	Sedgwick	
1920	Rixey	Causey	Meadows	Hubbell	Smith	Betts	Gallia	Enzmann	
1919	Rixey	Hogg	Meadows	Packard	Smith	Jacobs	Woodward	Cheney	
1918	Prendergast	Hogg	Oeschger	Jacobs	Mayer	Watson	Davis	Main	
1917	Alexander	Rixey	Oeschger	Lavender	Mayer	Bender	Fittery		
1916	Alexander	Rixey	Demaree	Bender	Mayer	McQuillan	Oeschger	Chalmers	
1915	Alexander	Rixey	Demaree	Chalmers	Mayer	McQuillan	Baumgartner	Tincup	
1914	Alexander	Rixey	Marshall	Tincup	Mayer	Oeschger	Baumgartner	Matteson	
1913	Alexander	Rixey	Seaton	Brennan	Mayer	Chalmers	Marshall	Moore	
1912	Alexander	Rixey	Seaton	Brennan	Moore	Chalmers	Shultz	Finneran	
1911	Alexander	Chalmers	Burns	Stack	Moore	Rowan	Humphries	Beebe	
1910	Ewing	Moren	McQuillan	Stack	Moore	Schettler	Brennan	Foxen	
1909	Corridon	Moren	McQuillan	Coveleski	Moore	Sparks	Richie	Foxen	
1908	Corridon	Moren	McQuillan	Sparks	Foxen	Coveleski	Richie		
1907	Corridon	Moren	Brown	Sparks	Pittinger	Lush	Richie	McQuillan	
1906	Lush	Duggleby	Richie	Sparks	Pittinger	McCloskey	Roy	Kane	
1905	Corridon	Duggleby	Nichols	Sparks	Pittinger	Sutthoff	Caldwell		
1904	Fraser	Duggleby	Sutthoff	Sparks	Mitchell	McPherson	Corridon	Brackenridge	
1903	Fraser	Duggleby	McFetridge	Sparks	Mitchell	Burchell			
1902	Fraser	Duggleby	White	Iburg	Magee	Vorhees	Felix		
1901	Orth	Duggleby	White	Donahue	Townsend				
1900	Orth	Bernhard	Fraser	Donahue	Piatt	Dunn			
1899	Orth	Bernhard	Fraser	Donahue	Piatt	Fifield	Magee	Wheeler	
1898	Orth	Fifield	Wheeler	Donahue	Piatt	Dunkle	Duggleby	Murphy	
1897	Orth	Fifield	Wheeler	Taylor	Dunkle				
1896	Orth	Carsey	Keener	Taylor	McGill	Gumbert			
1895	Orth	Carsey	Lucid	Taylor	McGill	Smith	Beam	Lampe	
1894	Weyhing	Carsey	Harper	Taylor	Haddock	Callahan			
1893	Weyhing	Carsey	Keefe	Taylor	Vickery	Sharrott			
1892	Weyhing	Carsey	Keefe	Esper	Knell				
1891	Gleason	Thornton	Keefe	Esper	Kling	Cassian	Schultze		
1890	Gleason	Vickery	Smith	Esper		Day	Anderson		
1889	Gleason	Buffinton	Sanders	Casey					
1888	Gleason	Buffinton	Sanders	Casey					
1887	Ferguson	Buffinton	Devlin	Casey		Maul	Daily		
1886	Ferguson	Daily	Titcomb	Casey	Strike				
1885	Ferguson	Daily	Vinton	Nolan					
1884	Ferguson	Coleman	Vinton	McElroy	Knight				
1883	Hagan	Coleman	Purcell	Neagle					

PRIMARY STARTING LINEUPS

Year	C	1B	2B	3B	SS	LF	CF	RF
2005	Lieberthal	Howard	Utley	Bell	Rollins	Burrell	Lofton	Abreu
2004	Lieberthal	Thome	Polanco	Bell	Rollins	Burrell	Byrd	Abreu
2003	Lieberthal	Thome	Polanco	Bell	Rollins	Burrell	Byrd	Abreu
2002	Lieberthal	Lee	Anderson	Rolen	Rollins	Burrell	Glanville	Abreu
2001	Estrada	Lee	Anderson	Rolen	Rollins	Burrell	Glanville	Abreu
2000	Lieberthal	Burrell	Morandini	Rolen	Relaford	Gant	Glanville	Abreu
1999	Lieberthal	Brogna	Anderson	Rolen	Arias	Gant	Glanville	Abreu
1998	Lieberthal	Brogna	Lewis	Rolen	Relaford	Jefferies	Glanville	Abreu
1997	Lieberthal	Brogna	Morandini	Rolen	Stocker	Jefferies	Cummings	Daulton
1996	Santiago	Jefferies	Morandini	Zeile	Stocker	Incaviglia	Otero	Eisenreich
1995	Daulton	Hollins	Morandini	Hayes	Stocker	Jefferies	Van Slyke	Eisenreich
1994	Daulton	Kruk	Morandini	Hollins	Stocker	Thompson	Dykstra	Eisenreich
1993	Daulton	Kruk	Morandini	Hollins	Stocker	Thompson	Dykstra	Eisenreich
1992	Daulton	Kruk	Morandini	Hollins	Bell	Duncan	Dykstra	Amaro
1991	Daulton	Kruk	Morandini	Hayes	Thon	Chamberlain	Dykstra	Murphy
1990	Daulton	Jordan	Herr	Hayes	Thon	Kruk	Dykstra	Hayes
1989	Daulton	Jordan	Herr	Hayes	Thon	Kruk	Dykstra	Hayes
1988	Parrish	Hayes	Samuel	Schmidt	Jeltz	Bradley	Thompson	James
1987	Parrish	Hayes	Samuel	Schmidt	Jeltz	James	Thompson	Wilson
1986	Russell	Hayes	Samuel	Schmidt	Jeltz	Redus	Thompson	Wilson
1985	Virgil	Schmidt	Samuel	Schu	Jeltz	Stone	Hayes	Wilson
1984	Virgil	Matuszek	Samuel	Schmidt	DeJesus	Wilson	Hayes	Lezcano
1983	Diaz	Rose	Morgan	Schmidt	DeJesus	Matthews	Maddox	Hayes
1982	Diaz	Rose	Trillo	Schmidt	DeJesus	Matthews	Maddox	Vukovich
1981	Boone	Rose	Trillo	Schmidt	Bowa	Matthews	Maddox	McBride
1980	Boone	Rose	Trillo	Schmidt	Bowa	Luzinski	Maddox	McBride
1979	Boone	Rose	Trillo	Schmidt	Bowa	Luzinski	Maddox	McBride
1978	Boone	Hebner	Sizemore	Schmidt	Bowa	Luzinski	Maddox	McBride
1977	Boone	Hebner	Sizemore	Schmidt	Bowa	Luzinski	Maddox	Johnstone
1976	Boone	Allen	Cash	Schmidt	Bowa	Luzinski	Maddox	Johnstone
1975	Boone	Allen	Cash	Schmidt	Bowa	Luzinski	Maddox	Johnstone
1974	Boone	Montanez	Cash	Schmidt	Bowa	Luzinski	Unser	Anderson
1973	Boone	Montanez	Doyle	Schmidt	Bowa	Luzinski	Unser	Robinson
1972	Bateman	Hutton	Doyle	Money	Bowa	Luzinski	Montanez	Freed
1971	McCarver	Johnson	Doyle	Vukovich	Bowa	Gamble	Montanez	Freed
1970	Ryan	Johnson	Doyle	Money	Bowa	Briggs	Hisle	Browne
1969	Ryan	Allen	Rojas	Taylor	Money	Briggs	Hisle	Callison
1968	Ryan	White	Rojas	Taylor	Pena	Allen	Gonzalez	Callison
1967	Dalrymple	White	Rojas	Allen	Wine	Gonzalez	Lock	Callison
1966	Dalrymple	White	Rojas	Allen	Groat	Gonzalez	Briggs	Callison
1965	Dalrymple	Stuart	Taylor	Allen	Wine	Johnson	Briggs	Callison
1964	Dalrymple	Herrnstein	Taylor	Allen	Wine	Covington	Gonzalez	Callison
1963	Dalrymple	Sievers	Taylor	Hoak	Wine	Covington	Gonzalez	Callison
1962	Dalrymple	Sievers	Taylor	Demeter	Wine	Savage	Gonzalez	Callison
1961	Dalrymple	Herrera	Taylor	Smith	Amaro	Callison	Gonzalez	Walters
1960	Coker	Herrera	Taylor	Dark	Amaro	Smith	Del Greco	Walters
1959	Sawatski	Bouchee	Anderson	Freese	Koppe	Anderson	Ashburn	Post
1958	Lopata	Bouchee	Hemus	Jones	Fernandez	Anderson	Ashburn	Post
1957	Lopata	Bouchee	Hamner	Jones	Fernandez	Anderson	Ashburn	Repulski
1956	Lopata	Blaylock	Kazanski	Jones	Hamner	Ennis	Ashburn	Valo
1955	Seminick	Blaylock	Morgan	Jones	Smalley	Ennis	Ashburn	Greengrass
1954	Burgess	Torgeson	Hamner	Jones	Morgan	Ennis	Ashburn	Wyrostek

PRIMARY STARTING LINEUPS (CONT.)

Year	C	1B	2B	3B	SS	LF	CF	RF
1953	Burgess	Torgeson	Hamner	Jones	Kazanski	Ennis	Ashburn	Wyrostek
1952	Burgess	Waitkus	Ryan	Jones	Hamner	Ennis	Ashburn	Wyrostek
1951	Seminick	Waitkus	Caballero	Jones	Hamner	Sisler	Ashburn	Ennis
1950	Seminick	Waitkus	Goliat	Jones	Hamner	Sisler	Ashburn	Ennis
1949	Seminick	Sisler	Miller	Jones	Hamner	Ennis	Ashburn	Nicholson
1948	Seminick	Sisler	Hamner	Caballero	Miller	Blatnik	Ashburn	Ennis
1947	Seminick	Schultz	Verban	Handley	Newsome	Ennis	Walker	Wyrostek
1946	Seminick	McCormick	Verban	Tabor	Newsome	Ennis	Wyrostek	Northey
1945	Mancuso	Wasdell	Daniels	Antonelli	Mott	Triplett	DiMaggio	Powell
1944	Finley	Lupien	Mullen	Stewart	Hamrick	Wasdell	Adams	Northey
1943	Livingston	Wasdell	Murtaugh	May	Stewart	Triplett	Adams	Northey
1942	Warren	Etten	Glossop	May	Bragan	Litwhiler	Waner	Northey
1941	Warren	Etten	Murtaugh	May	Bragan	Litwhiler	Marty	Benjamin
1940	Warren	Mahan	Schulte	May	Bragan	Rizzo	Marty	Klein
1939	Davis	Suhr	Hughes	May	Scharein	Arnovich	Martin	Scott
1938	Atwood	Weintraub	Mueller	Whitney	Young	Arnovich	Martin	Klein
1937	Atwood	Camilli	Young	Whitney	Scharein	Arnovich	Martin	Klein
1936	Grace	Camilli	Gomez	Whitney	Norris	Moore	Chiozza	Klein
1935	Todd	Camilli	Chiozza	Vergez	Haslin	Watkins	Allen	Moore
1934	Todd	Camilli	Chiozza	Walters	Bartell	Allen	Davis	Moore
1933	Davis	Hurst	Warner	McLeod	Bartell	Schulmerich	Fullis	Klein
1932	Davis	Hurst	Mallon	Whitney	Bartell	Lee	Davis	Klein
1931	Davis	Hurst	Mallon	Whitney	Bartell	Klein	Brickell	Arlett
1930	Davis	Hurst	Thompson	Whitney	Thevenow	O'Doul	Sothern	Klein
1929	Lerian	Hurst	Thompson	Whitney	Thevenow	O'Doul	Sothern	Klein
1928	Lerian	Hurst	Thompson	Whitney	Sand	Leach	Sothern	Klein
1927	Wilson	Wrightstone	Thompson	Friberg	Sand	Spalding	Leach	Williams
1926	Wilson	Bentley	Friberg	Huber	Sand	Harper	Nixon	Williams
1925	Wilson	Hawks	Friberg	Huber	Sand	Burns	Leach	Williams
1924	Henline	Holke	Ford	Wrightstone	Sand	Mokan	Williams	Harper
1923	Henline	Holke	Tierney	Wrightstone	Sand	Mokan	Williams	Walker
1922	Henline	Leslie	Parkinson	Rapp	Fletcher	Lee	Williams	Walker
1921	Bruggy	Konetchy	Smith	Wrightstone	Parkinson	King	Williams	LeBourveau
1920	Wheat	Paulette	Rawlings	Miller	Fletcher	Meusel	Williams	Stengel
1919	Adams	Luderus	Paulette	Blackburne	Bancroft	Meusel	Williams	Cravath
1918	Adams	Luderus	McGaffigan	Stock	Bancroft	Meusel	Williams	Cravath
1917	Killefer	Luderus	Niehoff	Stock	Bancroft	Whitted	Paskert	Cravath
1916	Killefer	Luderus	Niehoff	Stock	Bancroft	Whitted	Paskert	Cravath
1915	Killefer	Luderus	Niehoff	Byrne	Bancroft	Becker	Paskert	Cravath
1914	Killefer	Luderus	Byrne	Lobert	Martin	Becker	Paskert	Cravath
1913	Killefer	Luderus	Knabe	Lobert	Doolan	Magee	Paskert	Cravath
1912	Killefer	Luderus	Knabe	Lobert	Doolan	Magee	Paskert	Cravath
1911	Dooin	Luderus	Knabe	Lobert	Doolan	Magee	Paskert	Titus
1910	Dooin	Bransfield	Knabe	Grant	Doolan	Magee	Bates	Titus
1909	Dooin	Bransfield	Knabe	Grant	Doolan	Magee	Bates	Titus
1908	Dooin	Bransfield	Knabe	Grant	Doolan	Magee	Osborn	Titus
1907	Dooin	Bransfield	Knabe	Courtney	Doolan	Magee	Thomas	Titus
1906	Dooin	Bransfield	Gleason	Courtney	Doolan	Magee	Thomas	Titus
1905	Dooin	Bransfield	Gleason	Courtney	Doolan	Magee	Thomas	Titus
1904	Dooin	Doyle	Gleason	Wolverton	Hulswitt	Titus	Thomas	Magee
1903	Roth	Douglass	Gleason	Wolverton	Hulswitt	Barry	Thomas	Keister
1902	Dooin	Jennings	Childs	Hallman	Hulswitt	Browne	Thomas	Barry

PRIMARY STARTING LINEUPS (CONT.)

Year	C	1B	2B	3B	SS	LF	CF	RF
1901	McFarland	Jennings	Hallman	Wolverton	Cross	Delahanty	Thomas	Flick
1900	McFarland	Delahanty	Lajoie	Wolverton	Cross	Slagle	Thomas	Flick
1899	McFarland	Cooley	Lajoie	Lauder	Cross	Delahanty	Thomas	Flick
1898	McFarland	Douglass	Lajoie	Lauder	Cross	Delahanty	Cooley	Flick
1897	Boyle	Lajoie	Cross	Nash	Gillen	Delahanty	Cooley	Dowd
1896	Grady	Brouthers	Hallman	Nash	Hulen	Delahanty	Cooley	Thompson
1895	Clements	Boyle	Hallman	Cross	Sullivan	Delahanty	Hamilton	Thompson
1894	Clements	Boyle	Hallman	Cross	Sullivan	Delahanty	Hamilton	Thompson
1893	Clements	Boyle	Hallman	Reilly	Allen	Delahanty	Hamilton	Thompson
1892	Clements	Connor	Hallman	Reilly	Allen	Hamilton	Delahanty	Thompson
1891	Clements	Brown	Myers	Shindle	Allen	Hamilton	Delahanty	Thompson
1890	Clements	McCauley	Myers	Mayer	Allen	Hamilton	Burke	Thompson
1889	Clements	Farrar	Myers	Mulvey	Hallman	Wood	Fogarty	Thompson
1888	Clements	Farrar	Bastian	Mulvey	Irwin	Wood	Andrews	Fogarty
1887	Clements	Farrar	McLaughlin	Mulvey	Irwin	Wood	Andrews	Fogarty
1886	McGuire	Farrar	Bastian	Mulvey	Irwin	Wood	Andrews	Fogarty
1885	Clements	Farrar	Myers	Mulvey	Bastian	Andrews	Fogarty	Manning
1884	Crowley	Farrar	Andrews	Mulvey	McClellan	Purcell	Fogarty	Manning
1883	Gross	Farrar	Ferguson	Purcell	McClellan	Doyle	Lewis	Manning

Top 10 Batting Leaders, Single Season & Career with Team

GAMES PLAYED: CAREER WITH TEAM

Player	G	PA
1. Mike Schmidt	2,404	10,062
2. Richie Ashburn	1,794	8,223
3. Larry Bowa	1,739	7,353
4. Tony Taylor	1,669	6,424
5. Del Ennis	1,630	6,937
6. Ed Delahanty	1,555	7,130
7. Sherry Magee	1,521	6,314
8. Willie Jones	1,520	6,237
9. Granny Hamner	1,501	6,222
10. Cy Williams	1,463	5,783

AT-BATS: SEASON

Player	AB	Year
1. Juan Samuel	701	1984
2. Dave Cash	699	1975
3. Dave Cash	687	1974
4. Doug Glanville	678	1998
5. Jimmy Rollins	677	2005
6. Larry Bowa	669	1974
7. Dave Cash	666	1976
8. Juan Samuel	663	1985
9. Richie Ashburn	662	1949
Granny Hamner	662	1949

AT-BATS: CAREER WITH TEAM

Player	AB	PA
1. Mike Schmidt	8,352	10,062
2. Richie Ashburn	7,122	8,223
3. Larry Bowa	6,815	7,353
4. Ed Delahanty	6,359	7,130
5. Del Ennis	6,327	6,937
6. Tony Taylor	5,799	6,424
7. Granny Hamner	5,772	6,222
8. Sherry Magee	5,505	6,314
9. Willie Jones	5,419	6,237
10. Johnny Callison	5,306	5,930

BATTING AVERAGE: SEASON

Player	BA	Year
1. Ed Delahanty	.410	1899
2. Ed Delahanty	.407	1894
3. Billy Hamilton	.404	1894
Ed Delahanty	.404	1895
5. Lefty O'Doul	.398	1929
6. Ed Delahanty	.397	1896
7. Sam Thompson	.392	1895
8. Billy Hamilton	.389	1895
9. Chuck Klein	.386	1930
Lave Cross	.386	1894

BATTING AVERAGE: CAREER WITH TEAM

Player	BA	PA
1. Billy Hamilton	.361	3,606
2. Ed Delahanty	.348	7,130
3. Nap Lajoie	.345	2,204
4. Elmer Flick	.338	2,346
5. Sam Thompson	.333	4,812
6. Chuck Klein	.326	5,770
7. Spud Davis	.321	2,711
8. Freddy Leach	.312	2,178
9. Richie Ashburn	.311	8,223
10. John Kruk	.309	3,001

TOTAL HITS: SEASON

Player	H	Year
1. Lefty O'Doul	254	1929
2. Chuck Klein	250	1930
3. Ed Delahanty	238	1899

4. Chuck Klein	226	1932
5. Chuck Klein	223	1933
6. Sam Thompson	222	1893
7. Richie Ashburn	221	1951
8. Billy Hamilton	220	1894
9. Ed Delahanty	219	1893
Chuck Klein	219	1929

TOTAL HITS: CAREER WITH TEAM

Player	H	PA
1. Mike Schmidt	2,234	10,062
2. Richie Ashburn	2,217	8,223
3. Ed Delahanty	2,213	7,130
4. Del Ennis	1,812	6,937
5. Larry Bowa	1,798	7,353
6. Chuck Klein	1,705	5,770
7. Sherry Magee	1,647	6,314
8. Cy Williams	1,553	5,783
9. Granny Hamner	1,518	6,222
10. Tony Taylor	1,511	6,424

HOME RUNS: SEASON

Player	HR	Year
1. Mike Schmidt	48	1980
2. Jim Thome	47	2003
3. Mike Schmidt	45	1979
4. Chuck Klein	43	1929
5. Jim Thome	42	2004
6. Cy Williams	41	1923
7. Dick Allen	40	1966
Chuck Klein	40	1930
Mike Schmidt	40	1983
10. Greg Luzinski	39	1977

HOME RUNS: CAREER WITH TEAM

Player	HR	PA
1. Mike Schmidt	548	10,062
2. Del Ennis	259	6,937
3. Chuck Klein	243	5,770
4. Greg Luzinski	223	5,317
5. Cy Williams	217	5,783
6. Dick Allen	204	4,510
7. Bobby Abreu	187	5,447
8. Johnny Callison	185	5,930
9. Willie Jones	180	6,237
10. Pat Burrell	159	3,578

TRIPLES: SEASON

Player	3B	Year
1. Sam Thompson	27	1894
2. Nap Lajoie	23	1897
3. Ed Delahanty	21	1892
Sam Thompson	21	1895
5. Juan Samuel	19	1984
George Wood	19	1887
7. Ed Delahanty	18	1893
Ed Delahanty	18	1894
9. Ed Delahanty	17	1896
Elmer Flick	17	1901
Jim Fogarty	17	1889
Sherry Magee	17	1905
Sherry Magee	17	1910

TRIPLES: CAREER WITH TEAM

Player	3B	PA
1. Ed Delahanty	157	7,130
2. Sherry Magee	127	6,314
3. Sam Thompson	106	4,812
4. Richie Ashburn	97	8,223
5. Johnny Callison	84	5,930
6. Larry Bowa	81	7,353
7. Gavvy Cravath	72	4,241
8. Juan Samuel	71	3,780
9. Del Ennis	65	6,937
10. Dick Allen	64	4,510
Chuck Klein	64	5,770
John Titus	64	5,086

DOUBLES: SEASON

Player	2B	Year
1. Chuck Klein	59	1930
2. Ed Delahanty	55	1899
3. Bobby Abreu	50	2002
Chuck Klein	50	1932
5. Ed Delahanty	49	1895
6. Bobby Abreu	48	2001
Dick Bartell	48	1932
8. Bobby Abreu	47	2004
9. Ethan Allen	46	1935
Von Hayes	46	1986

DOUBLES: CAREER WITH TEAM

Player	2B	PA
1. Ed Delahanty	442	7,130
2. Mike Schmidt	408	10,062
3. Sherry Magee	337	6,314
4. Chuck Klein	336	5,770
5. Bobby Abreu	323	5,447
6. Del Ennis	310	6,937
7. Richie Ashburn	287	8,223
8. Sam Thompson	272	4,812
9. Granny Hamner	271	6,222
10. Johnny Callison	265	5,930

EXTRA-BASE HITS: SEASON

Player	XBH	Year
1. Chuck Klein	107	1930
2. Chuck Klein	103	1932
3. Chuck Klein	94	1929
4. Sam Thompson	84	1895
5. Bobby Abreu	83	2001
6. Mike Schmidt	81	1980
7. Dick Allen	80	1964
Scott Rolen	80	1998
Juan Samuel	80	1987
Jim Thome	80	2003

EXTRA-BASE HITS: CAREER WITH TEAM

Player	XBH	PA
1. Mike Schmidt	1,015	10,062
2. Ed Delahanty	686	7,130
3. Chuck Klein	643	5,770
4. Del Ennis	634	6,937
5. Bobby Abreu	550	5,447
6. Sherry Magee	539	6,314
7. Johnny Callison	534	5,930
8. Cy Williams	503	5,783
9. Greg Luzinski	497	5,317
10. Sam Thompson	473	4,812

TOTAL BASES: SEASON

Player	TB	Year
1. Chuck Klein	445	1930
2. Chuck Klein	420	1932
3. Chuck Klein	405	1929
4. Lefty O'Doul	397	1929
5. Chuck Klein	365	1933
6. Dick Allen	352	1964
Sam Thompson	352	1895
8. Ed Delahanty	347	1893
Chuck Klein	347	1931
10. Mike Schmidt	342	1980

TOTAL BASES: CAREER WITH TEAM

Player	TB	PA
1. Mike Schmidt	4,404	10,062
2. Ed Delahanty	3,230	7,130
3. Del Ennis	3,029	6,937
4. Chuck Klein	2,898	5,770
5. Richie Ashburn	2,764	8,223
6. Cy Williams	2,539	5,783
7. Sherry Magee	2,463	6,314

Player		
8. Johnny Callison	2,426	5,930
9. Bobby Abreu	2,344	5,447
10. Greg Luzinski	2,263	5,317

Runs Batted In: Season

Player	RBI	Year
1. Chuck Klein	170	1930
2. Sam Thompson	165	1895
3. Ed Delahanty	146	1893
4. Chuck Klein	145	1929
5. Don Hurst	143	1932
6. Sam Thompson	141	1894
7. Ed Delahanty	137	1899
Chuck Klein	137	1932
9. Ed Delahanty	131	1894
Jim Thome	131	2003

Runs Batted In: Career with Team

Player	RBI	PA
1. Mike Schmidt	1,595	10,062
2. Ed Delahanty	1,286	7,130
3. Del Ennis	1,124	6,937
4. Chuck Klein	983	5,770
5. Sam Thompson	957	4,812
6. Sherry Magee	886	6,314
7. Greg Luzinski	811	5,317
8. Cy Williams	795	5,783
9. Willie Jones	753	6,237
10. Bobby Abreu	749	5,447

Runs Scored: Season

Player	R	Year
1. Billy Hamilton	192	1894
2. Billy Hamilton	166	1895
3. Chuck Klein	158	1930
4. Chuck Klein	152	1932
Lefty O'Doul	152	1929
6. Ed Delahanty	149	1895
7. Ed Delahanty	147	1894
8. Ed Delahanty	145	1893
9. Lenny Dykstra	143	1993
10. Billy Hamilton	141	1891

Runs Scored: Career with Team

Player	R	PA
1. Mike Schmidt	1,506	10,062
2. Ed Delahanty	1,367	7,130
3. Richie Ashburn	1,114	8,223
4. Chuck Klein	963	5,770
5. Sam Thompson	924	4,812
6. Roy Thomas	923	5,788
7. Sherry Magee	898	6,314
8. Del Ennis	891	6,937
9. Billy Hamilton	874	3,606
10. Bobby Abreu	830	5,447

Walks: Season

Player	BB	Year
1. Lenny Dykstra	129	1993
2. Mike Schmidt	128	1983
3. Bobby Abreu	127	2004
4. Billy Hamilton	126	1894
5. Richie Ashburn	125	1954
6. Von Hayes	121	1987
7. Mike Schmidt	120	1979
8. Darren Daulton	117	1993
Bobby Abreu	117	2005
10. Dolph Camilli	116	1936
Roger Connor	116	1892

Walks: Career with Team

Player	BB	PA
1. Mike Schmidt	1,507	10,062
2. Richie Ashburn	946	8,223
Roy Thomas	946	5,788
4. Bobby Abreu	856	5,447
5. Willie Jones	693	6,237
6. Ed Delahanty	643	7,130
7. Von Hayes	619	4,988
8. Darren Daulton	607	4,185
9. Greg Luzinski	572	5,317
10. Billy Hamilton	551	3,606
Cy Williams	551	5,783

Strikeouts: Season

Player	SO	Year
1. Jim Thome	182	2003
2. Mike Schmidt	180	1975
3. Juan Samuel	168	1984
4. Pat Burrell	162	2001
Juan Samuel	162	1987
6. Dick Allen	161	1968
7. Pat Burrell	160	2005
8. Pat Burrell	153	2002
9. Larry Hisle	152	1969
10. Greg Luzinski	151	1975
Juan Samuel	151	1988

Strikeouts: Career with Team

Player	SO	PA
1. Mike Schmidt	1,883	10,062
2. Greg Luzinski	1,098	5,317
3. Dick Allen	1,023	4,510
4. Bobby Abreu	992	5,447
5. Pat Burrell	886	3,578
6. Johnny Callison	854	5,930
7. Juan Samuel	825	3,780
8. Tony Taylor	818	6,424
9. Scott Rolen	714	3,643
10. Darren Daulton	709	4,185

Slugging Percentage: Season

Player	SLG	Year
1. Chuck Klein	.687	1930
2. Chuck Klein	.657	1929
3. Sam Thompson	.654	1895
4. Chuck Klein	.646	1932
5. Mike Schmidt	.644	1981
6. Dick Allen	.632	1966
7. Ed Delahanty	.631	1896
8. Mike Schmidt	.624	1980
9. Lefty O'Doul	.622	1929
10. Ed Delahanty	.617	1895

Slugging Percentage: Career with Team

Player	SLG	PA
1. Chuck Klein	.553	5,770
2. Dick Allen	.530	4,510
3. Mike Schmidt	.527	10,062
4. Nap Lajoie	.520	2,204
5. Bobby Abreu	.519	5,447
6. Dolph Camilli	.510	2,322
7. Ed Delahanty	.508	7,130
8. Sam Thompson	.507	4,812
9. Scott Rolen	.504	3,643
10. Cy Williams	.500	5,783

On-Base Percentage: Season

Player	OBP	Year
1. Billy Hamilton	.523	1894
2. Ed Delahanty	.500	1895
3. Billy Hamilton	.490	1895
4. Ed Delahanty	.478	1894
5. Ed Delahanty	.472	1896
6. Lefty O'Doul	.465	1929
7. Ed Delahanty	.464	1899
8. Roy Thomas	.457	1899
9. Roy Thomas	.453	1903
Lefty O'Doul	.453	1930

On-Base Percentage: Career with Team

Player	OBP	PA
1. Billy Hamilton	.468	3,606
2. Roy Thomas	.421	5,788
3. Elmer Flick	.419	2,346
4. Bobby Abreu	.415	5,447
Ed Delahanty	.415	7,130
6. John Kruk	.400	3,001
7. Dolph Camilli	.395	2,322
8. Richie Ashburn	.394	8,223
9. Lenny Dykstra	.388	3,374
Sam Thompson	.388	4,812

OPS (On-Base Percentage + Slugging Percentage): Season

Player	OPS	Year
1. Chuck Klein	1.123	1930
2. Ed Delahanty	1.117	1895
3. Ed Delahanty	1.103	1896
4. Lefty O'Doul	1.087	1929
5. Sam Thompson	1.085	1895
6. Mike Schmidt	1.080	1981
7. Chuck Klein	1.065	1929
8. Ed Delahanty	1.063	1894
9. Lefty O'Doul	1.057	1930
10. Billy Hamilton	1.050	1894

OPS (On-Base Percentage + Slugging Percentage): Career with Team

Player	OPS	PA
1. Chuck Klein	.935	5,770
2. Bobby Abreu	.933	5,447
3. Billy Hamilton	.928	3,606
4. Ed Delahanty	.923	7,130
5. Mike Schmidt	.908	10,062
6. Elmer Flick	.907	2,346
7. Dolph Camilli	.905	2,322
8. Dick Allen	.902	4,510
9. Sam Thompson	.895	4,812
10. Nap Lajoie	.894	2,204

Stolen Bases: Season

Player	SB	Year
1. Billy Hamilton	111	1891
2. Jim Fogarty	102	1887
Billy Hamilton	102	1890
4. Jim Fogarty	99	1889
5. Billy Hamilton	98	1894
6. Billy Hamilton	97	1895
7. Juan Samuel	72	1984
8. Ed Delahanty	58	1898
Jim Fogarty	58	1888
10. Ed Andrews	57	1887
Billy Hamilton	57	1892

Stolen Bases: Career with Team

Player	SB	PA
1. Billy Hamilton	508	3,606
2. Ed Delahanty	411	7,130
3. Sherry Magee	387	6,314
4. Jim Fogarty	289	2,849
5. Larry Bowa	288	7,353
6. Juan Samuel	249	3,780
7. Bobby Abreu	234	5,447
8. Roy Thomas	228	5,788
9. Von Hayes	202	4,988
10. Richie Ashburn	199	8,223

Sacrifice Hits: Season

Player	Sac	Year
1. Kid Gleason	43	1905
2. Otto Knabe	42	1908
3. Otto Knabe	41	1913
4. Otto Knabe	40	1907
5. Hans Lobert	38	1911
6. Dick Bartell	37	1933
Otto Knabe	37	1910
8. Dick Bartell	35	1932
Kid Gleason	35	1904
10. Eddie Grant	34	1910

Sacrifice Hits: Career with Team

Player	Sac	PA
1. Otto Knabe	216	4,057
2. Sherry Magee	185	6,314
3. Mickey Doolan	148	5,014
4. Roy Thomas	147	5,788
5. Kid Gleason	139	3,191
6. Dode Paskert	128	4,019
7. Larry Bowa	127	7,353
8. John Titus	126	5,086
9. Pinky Whitney	117	4,772
10. Dick Bartell	111	2,704

Hit by Pitch: Season

Player	HBP	Year
1. Dave Hollins	19	1992
2. Roy Thomas	17	1899
3. Phil Bradley	16	1988
Elmer Flick	16	1900
John Titus	16	1909
6. Elmer Flick	15	1898
Roy Thomas	15	1900
8. Ed Bouchee	14	1957
Mike Lieberthal	14	2002
John Titus	14	1908

Hit by Pitch: Career with Team

Player	HBP	PA
1. Ed Delahanty	80	7,130
2. Mike Schmidt	79	10,062
3. Sherry Magee	78	6,314
John Titus	78	5,086
5. Mike Lieberthal	71	3,940
6. Roy Thomas	66	5,788
7. Greg Luzinski	61	5,317
8. Tony Taylor	60	6,424
9. Cy Williams	55	5,783
10. Scott Rolen	54	3,643

Top 10 Pitching Leaders, Single Season & Career with Team

Games Pitched: Season

Player	GP	Year
1. Kent Tekulve	90	1987
2. Rheal Cormier	84	2004
3. Ryan Madson	78	2005
4. Tim Worrell	77	2004
5. Jerry Spradlin	76	1997
David West	76	1993
7. Billy Wagner	75	2005
8. Jim Konstanty	74	1950
Jose Mesa	74	2002
10. Wayne Gomes	73	1999
Dick Selma	73	1970
Kent Tekulve	73	1986

Games Pitched: Career with Team

Player	GP	IP
1. Robin Roberts	529	3,739.3
2. Steve Carlton	499	3,697.3
3. Tug McGraw	463	722.0
4. Chris Short	459	2,253.0
5. Ron Reed	458	809.3
6. Turk Farrell	359	601.0
7. Grover Alexander	338	2,513.7
8. Jack Baldschun	333	543.3
9. Ricky Bottalico	330	370.0
10. Curt Simmons	325	1,939.7

Innings Pitched: Season

Player	IP	Year
1. John Coleman	538.3	1883
2. Kid Gleason	506.0	1890
3. Gus Weyhing	469.7	1892
4. Ed Daily	440.0	1885
5. Kid Gleason	418.0	1891
6. Charlie Ferguson	416.7	1884
7. Charlie Ferguson	405.0	1885
8. Charlie Buffinton	400.3	1888
9. Charlie Ferguson	395.7	1886
10. Dan Casey	390.3	1887

Innings Pitched: Career with Team

Player	IP
1. Robin Roberts	3,739.3
2. Steve Carlton	3,697.3
3. Grover Alexander	2,513.7
4. Chris Short	2,253.0
5. Curt Simmons	1,939.7
6. Tully Sparks	1,698.0
7. Bill Duggleby	1,683.7
8. Curt Schilling	1,659.3
9. Eppa Rixey	1,604.0
10. Jim Bunning	1,520.7

Batters Faced: Season

Player	BF	Year
1. John Coleman	2,546	1883
2. Charlie Ferguson	1,844	1884
3. Ed Daily	1,797	1885
4. Charlie Buffinton	1,661	1889
5. Dan Casey	1,660	1887
6. Charlie Ferguson	1,657	1885
7. Charlie Buffinton	1,586	1888
8. Charlie Ferguson	1,582	1886
9. Dan Casey	1,566	1886
10. Ben Sanders	1,539	1889

Batters Faced: Career with Team

Player	BF	IP
1. Robin Roberts	15,294	3,739.3
2. Steve Carlton	15,229	3,697.3
3. Grover Alexander	10,031	2,513.7
4. Chris Short	9,465	2,253.0
5. Curt Simmons	8,229	1,939.7
6. Tully Sparks	6,797	1,698.0
7. Curt Schilling	6,749	1,659.3
8. Eppa Rixey	6,627	1,604.0
9. Jimmy Ring	6,531	1,458.0
10. Charlie Ferguson	6,310	1,514.7

Games Started: Season

Player	GS	Year
1. John Coleman	61	1883
2. Kid Gleason	55	1890
3. Ed Daily	50	1885
4. Gus Weyhing	49	1892
5. Charlie Ferguson	47	1884
6. Charlie Buffinton	46	1888
Tom Vickery	46	1890
8. Grover Alexander	45	1916
Dan Casey	45	1887
Charlie Ferguson	45	1885
Charlie Ferguson	45	1886

Games Started: Career with Team

Player	GS	IP
1. Steve Carlton	499	3,697.3
2. Robin Roberts	472	3,739.3
3. Chris Short	301	2,253.0
4. Grover Alexander	280	2,513.7
5. Curt Simmons	263	1,939.7
6. Curt Schilling	226	1,659.3
7. Larry Christenson	220	1,402.7
8. Jim Bunning	208	1,520.7
9. Dick Ruthven	198	1,262.7
Tully Sparks	198	1,698.0

Complete Games: Season

Player	CG	Year
1. John Coleman	59	1883
2. Kid Gleason	54	1890
3. Ed Daily	49	1885
4. Charlie Ferguson	46	1884
Gus Weyhing	46	1892
6. Charlie Ferguson	45	1885
7. Charlie Buffinton	43	1888
Dan Casey	43	1887
Charlie Ferguson	43	1886
10. Tom Vickery	41	1890

Complete Games: Career with Team

Player	CG	IP
1. Robin Roberts	272	3,739.3
2. Grover Alexander	219	2,513.7
3. Steve Carlton	185	3,697.3
4. Charlie Ferguson	165	1,514.7
5. Bill Duggleby	156	1,683.7
6. Tully Sparks	150	1,698.0

Jack Taylor	150	1,505.3
8. Al Orth	149	1,504.7
9. Kid Carsey	141	1,470.7
10. Chick Fraser	133	1,270.0

GAMES WON: SEASON

Player	W	Year
1. Kid Gleason	38	1890
2. Grover Alexander	33	1916
3. Gus Weyhing	32	1892
4. Grover Alexander	31	1915
5. Grover Alexander	30	1917
Charlie Ferguson	30	1886
7. Grover Alexander	28	1911
Charlie Buffinton	28	1888
Charlie Buffinton	28	1889
Dan Casey	28	1887
Robin Roberts	28	1952

GAMES WON: CAREER WITH TEAM

Player	W	IP
1. Steve Carlton	241	3,697.3
2. Robin Roberts	234	3,739.3
3. Grover Alexander	190	2,513.7
4. Chris Short	132	2,253.0
5. Curt Simmons	115	1,939.7
6. Curt Schilling	101	1,659.3
7. Al Orth	100	1,504.7
8. Charlie Ferguson	99	1,514.7
9. Jack Taylor	96	1,505.3
10. Tully Sparks	95	1,698.0

GAMES LOST: SEASON

Player	L	Year
1. John Coleman	48	1883
2. Charlie Ferguson	25	1884
3. Chick Fraser	24	1904
4. Ed Daily	23	1885
5. Kid Gleason	22	1891
Hugh Mulcahy	22	1940
Eppa Rixey	22	1920
Robin Roberts	22	1957
Tom Vickery	22	1890
10. Five tied with . . .	21	—

GAMES LOST: CAREER WITH TEAM

Player	L	IP
1. Robin Roberts	199	3,739.3
2. Steve Carlton	161	3,697.3
3. Chris Short	127	2,253.0

4. Curt Simmons	110	1,939.7
5. Eppa Rixey	103	1,604.0
6. Bill Duggleby	99	1,683.7
7. Jimmy Ring	98	1,458.0
8. Tully Sparks	95	1,698.0
9. Grover Alexander	91	2,513.7
10. Hugh Mulcahy	89	1,155.0

WINNING PERCENTAGE: SEASON

Player	W%	Year
1. Al Orth	.824	1899
2. Tommy Greene	.800	1993
Robin Roberts	.800	1952
4. Charlie Ferguson	.769	1886
5. Steve Carlton	.765	1981
6. Larry Christenson	.760	1977
John Denny	.760	1983
8. Grover Alexander	.756	1915
9. Steve Carlton	.741	1976
10. Grover Alexander	.733	1913
Grover Alexander	.733	1916
Tully Sparks	.733	1907

WINNING PERCENTAGE: CAREER WITH TEAM

Player	W%	IP
1. Grover Alexander	.676	2,513.7
2. Charlie Ferguson	.607	1,514.7
3. Charlie Buffinton	.606	1,112.7
4. Red Donahue	.600	1,098.7
Ron Reed	.600	809.3
Steve Carlton	.600	3,697.3
7. Wiley Piatt	.589	771.7
8. Al Orth	.581	1,504.7
9. Ray Culp	.573	653.3
Gus Weyhing	.573	1,090.3

SHUTOUTS: SEASON

Player	SHO	Year
1. Grover Alexander	16	1916
2. Grover Alexander	12	1915
3. Grover Alexander	9	1913
4. Grover Alexander	8	1917
Steve Carlton	8	1972
Ben Sanders	8	1888
7. Grover Alexander	7	1911
Jim Bunning	7	1965
George McQuillan	7	1908
10. 11 tied with . . .	6	—

SHUTOUTS: CAREER WITH TEAM

Player	SHO	IP
1. Grover Alexander	61	2,513.7
2. Steve Carlton	39	3,697.3
3. Robin Roberts	35	3,739.3
4. Chris Short	24	2,253.0
5. Jim Bunning	23	1,520.7
6. Curt Simmons	18	1,939.7
Tully Sparks	18	1,698.0
8. George McQuillan	17	926.3
Earl Moore	17	1,151.3
10. Bill Duggleby	16	1,683.7

ERA: SEASON

Player	ERA	Year
1. Grover Alexander	1.22	1915
2. George McQuillan	1.53	1908
3. Grover Alexander	1.55	1916
4. Grover Alexander	1.83	1917
5. Eppa Rixey	1.85	1916
6. Ben Sanders	1.90	1888
7. Charlie Buffinton	1.91	1888
8. Steve Carlton	1.97	1972
9. Charlie Ferguson	1.98	1886
10. Tully Sparks	2.00	1907

ERA: CAREER WITH TEAM

Player	ERA	IP
1. George McQuillan	1.79	926.3
2. Lew Richie	2.06	525.3
3. Grover Alexander	2.18	2,513.7
4. Tully Sparks	2.48	1,698.0
5. Frank Corridon	2.61	959.7
6. Earl Moore	2.63	1,151.3
7. Charlie Ferguson	2.67	1,514.7
8. Ed Daily	2.77	699.3
9. Erskine Mayer	2.81	1,191.7
10. Doc White	2.82	542.7

EARNED RUNS ALLOWED: SEASON

Player	ER	Year
1. John Coleman	291	1883
2. Jack Taylor	191	1896
3. Kid Carsey	187	1895
4. Gus Weyhing	182	1893
5. Gus Weyhing	172	1894

6. Kid Carsey	171	1894
7. Kid Carsey	170	1893
8. Jack Taylor	167	1895
9. Charlie Ferguson	164	1884
10. Kid Gleason	163	1891

Earned Runs Allowed: Career with Team

Player	ER	IP
1. Robin Roberts	1,437	3,739.3
2. Steve Carlton	1,270	3,697.3
3. Chris Short	845	2,253.0
4. Curt Simmons	789	1,939.7
5. Kid Carsey	771	1,470.7
6. Jack Taylor	726	1,505.3
7. Jimmy Ring	723	1,458.0
8. Phil Collins	642	1,236.7
9. Curt Schilling	617	1,659.3
10. Grover Alexander	610	2,513.7

Strikeouts: Season

Player	K	Year
1. Curt Schilling	319	1997
2. Steve Carlton	310	1972
3. Curt Schilling	300	1998
4. Steve Carlton	286	1980
Steve Carlton	286	1982
6. Steve Carlton	275	1983
7. Jim Bunning	268	1965
8. Jim Bunning	253	1967
9. Jim Bunning	252	1966
10. Grover Alexander	241	1915

Strikeouts: Career with Team

Player	K	IP
1. Steve Carlton	3,031	3,697.3
2. Robin Roberts	1,871	3,739.3
3. Chris Short	1,585	2,253.0
4. Curt Schilling	1,554	1,659.3
5. Grover Alexander	1,409	2,513.7
6. Jim Bunning	1,197	1,520.7
7. Curt Simmons	1,052	1,939.7
8. Randy Wolf	866	1,038.3
9. Larry Christenson	781	1,402.7
10. Charlie Ferguson	728	1,514.7

Strikeouts Per Nine IP: Season

Player	K/9	Year
1. Curt Schilling	11.29	1997
2. Curt Schilling	10.05	1998
3. Brandon Duckworth	9.22	2002
4. Curt Schilling	8.93	1996
5. Steve Carlton	8.73	1983
6. Steve Carlton	8.71	1982
7. Brett Myers	8.69	2005
8. Robert Person	8.52	2000
9. Steve Carlton	8.48	1981
10. Steve Carlton	8.47	1980

Strikeouts Per Nine IP: Career with Team

Player	K/9	IP
1. Curt Schilling	8.43	1,659.3
2. Robert Person	7.94	606.3
3. Randy Wolf	7.46	1,118.3
4. Steve Carlton	7.38	3,697.3
5. Jim Bunning	7.08	1,520.7
6. Wayne Twitchell	7.04	733.0
7. Ray Culp	6.97	653.3
8. Jack Baldschun	6.96	543.3
9. Grant Jackson	6.89	563.3
10. Brett Myers	6.87	656.3

Hits Allowed: Season

Player	HA	Year
1. John Coleman	772	1883
2. Kid Gleason	479	1890
3. Kid Carsey	460	1895
4. Jack Taylor	459	1896
5. Charlie Ferguson	443	1884
6. Kid Gleason	431	1891
7. Gus Weyhing	411	1892
8. Ben Sanders	406	1889
9. Tom Vickery	405	1890
10. Jack Taylor	403	1895

Hits Allowed: Career with Team

Player	HA	IP
1. Robin Roberts	3,661	3,739.3
2. Steve Carlton	3,224	3,697.3
3. Grover Alexander	2,141	2,513.7
4. Chris Short	2,129	2,253.0
5. Curt Simmons	1,865	1,939.7
6. Kid Carsey	1,812	1,470.7
7. Jack Taylor	1,802	1,505.3
8. Bill Duggleby	1,791	1,683.7
9. Al Orth	1,687	1,504.7
10. Jimmy Ring	1,661	1,458.0

Hits Allowed Per Nine IP: Season

Player	H/9	Year
1. Grover Alexander	6.05	1915
2. Ray Culp	6.55	1963
3. Curt Schilling	6.56	1992
4. George McQuillan	6.58	1908
5. Steve Carlton	6.68	1972
6. Ken Howell	6.84	1989
7. Wayne Twitchell	6.93	1973
Tully Sparks	6.93	1906
9. Grover Alexander	6.99	1911
10. Chris Short	7.10	1964

Hits Allowed Per Nine IP: Career with Team

Player	H/9	IP
1. George McQuillan	6.93	926.3
2. Lew Richie	7.25	525.3
3. Grover Alexander	7.67	2,513.7
4. Earl Moore	7.72	1,151.3
5. Ron Reed	7.81	809.3
6. Curt Schilling	7.83	1,659.3
7. Steve Carlton	7.85	3,697.3
8. Tug McGraw	7.89	722.0
9. Robert Person	7.90	606.3
10. Frank Corridon	7.92	959.7

Walks Allowed: Season

Player	BB	Year
1. Tom Vickery	184	1890
2. Gus Weyhing	168	1892
3. Kid Gleason	167	1890
4. Kid Gleason	165	1891
5. Earl Moore	164	1911
6. Gus Weyhing	145	1893
7. Steve Carlton	136	1974
Tom Seaton	136	1913
9. Grover Alexander	129	1911
10. Jose DeJesus	128	1991

Walks Allowed: Career with Team

Player	BB	IP
1. Steve Carlton	1,252	3,697.3
2. Chris Short	762	2,253.0
3. Robin Roberts	718	3,739.3
Curt Simmons	718	1,939.7
5. Jimmy Ring	636	1,458.0
6. Grover Alexander	561	2,513.7
7. Kid Carsey	536	1,470.7
8. Earl Moore	518	1,151.3
9. Kid Gleason	482	1,328.7
10. Hugh Mulcahy	480	1,155.0

Walks Allowed Per Nine IP: Season

Player	BB/9	Year
1. John Coleman	0.80	1883
2. Al Orth	1.02	1901
3. Ben Sanders	1.08	1888
4. Grover Alexander	1.16	1916
5. Robin Roberts	1.21	1956
6. Robin Roberts	1.22	1959
7. Robin Roberts	1.23	1952
8. Jim Kaat	1.27	1976
9. Robin Roberts	1.29	1960
10. Bill Duggleby	1.30	1901

Walks Allowed Per Nine IP: Career with Team

Player	BB/9	IP
1. John Coleman	0.91	692.7
2. Syl Johnson	1.56	792.0
3. Charlie Ferguson	1.72	1,514.7
4. Robin Roberts	1.73	3,739.3
Schoolboy Rowe	1.73	744.0
6. Jim Kaat	1.83	536.7
7. Ken Raffensberger	1.84	528.0
8. Ben Sanders	1.86	625.0
9. Al Orth	1.88	1,504.7
10. Terry Mulholland	1.93	1,070.3

WHIP (Walks + Hits Per Nine IP): Season

Player	WHIP	Year
1. Grover Alexander	0.842	1915
2. Charlie Buffinton	0.957	1888
3. Grover Alexander	0.959	1916
4. Tully Sparks	0.966	1906
5. Charlie Ferguson	0.976	1886
6. George McQuillan	0.984	1908
7. Curt Schilling	0.990	1992
8. Ben Sanders	0.992	1888
9. Steve Carlton	0.993	1972
10. Al Orth	1.001	1901

WHIP (Walks + Hits Per Nine IP): Career with Team

Player	WHIP	IP
1. George McQuillan	1.020	926.3
2. Grover Alexander	1.075	2,513.7
3. Jim Bunning	1.111	1,520.7
4. Charlie Ferguson	1.117	1,514.7
5. Curt Schilling	1.120	1,659.3
6. Tully Sparks	1.133	1,698.0
7. Ron Reed	1.150	809.3
8. Ed Daily	1.154	699.3
9. Lew Richie	1.155	525.3
10. Robin Roberts	1.171	3,739.3

Home Runs Allowed: Season

Player	HRA	Year
1. Robin Roberts	46	1956
2. Eric Milton	43	2004
3. Robin Roberts	41	1955
4. Robin Roberts	40	1957
5. Art Mahaffey	36	1962
Chad Ogea	36	1999
7. Robin Roberts	35	1954
8. Paul Byrd	34	1999
Don Carman	34	1987
Robert Person	34	2001
Robin Roberts	34	1959

Home Runs Allowed: Career with Team

Player	HRA	IP
1. Robin Roberts	402	3,739.3
2. Steve Carlton	286	3,697.3
3. Chris Short	178	2,253.0
4. Curt Schilling	162	1,659.3
5. Randy Wolf	144	1,118.3
6. Curt Simmons	135	1,939.7
7. Jim Bunning	120	1,520.7
8. Phil Collins	119	1,236.7
9. Art Mahaffey	118	964.0
10. Jim Lonborg	111	1,142.3

Saves: Season

Player	SV	Year
1. Jose Mesa	45	2002
2. Mitch Williams	43	1993
3. Jose Mesa	42	2001
4. Steve Bedrosian	40	1987
5. Billy Wagner	38	2005
6. Ricky Bottalico	34	1996
Ricky Bottalico	34	1997
8. Heathcliff Slocumb	32	1995
9. Mitch Williams	30	1991
10. Steve Bedrosian	29	1986
Al Holland	29	1984
Mitch Williams	29	1992

Saves: Career with Team

Player	SV	IP
1. Jose Mesa	111	203.0
2. Steve Bedrosian	103	287.3
3. Mitch Williams	102	231.3
4. Tug McGraw	94	722.0
5. Ron Reed	90	809.3
6. Ricky Bottalico	78	370.0
7. Turk Farrell	65	601.0
8. Jack Baldschun	59	543.3
Billy Wagner	59	125.3
10. Al Holland	55	194.0

Wild Pitches: Season

Player	WP	Year
1. Jim McElroy	46	1884
2. Ed Daily	40	1885
3. Charlie Ferguson	33	1884
4. Charlie Buffinton	25	1887
Dan Casey	25	1886
6. Tom Vickery	23	1890
7. Art Hagan	22	1883
Jack Hamilton	22	1962
9. Ken Howell	21	1989
10. Bill Vinton	20	1884

Wild Pitches: Career with Team

Player	WP	IP
1. Steve Carlton	120	3,697.3
2. Chris Short	71	2,253.0
3. Charlie Ferguson	64	1,514.7

4. Jimmy Ring	63	1,458.0
5. Ed Daily	60	699.3
6. Eppa Rixey	58	1,604.0
7. Dan Casey	57	1,197.7
8. Charlie Buffinton	55	1,112.7
9. Kid Carsey	54	1,470.7
10. Kid Gleason	53	1,328.7

HIT BATSMEN: SEASON

Player	HB	Year
1. Jack Taylor	28	1897
2. Wiley Piatt	24	1899
3. Chick Fraser	22	1899
4. Jim Bunning	19	1966
Fred Mitchell	19	1903
Wiley Piatt	19	1898
7. Jack Fifield	18	1898
8. Paul Byrd	17	1999
9. Six tied with...	16	——

HIT BATSMEN: CAREER WITH TEAM

Player	HB	IP
1. Bill Duggleby	82	1,683.7
2. Chick Fraser	75	1,270.0
3. Jim Bunning	72	1,520.7
4. Wiley Piatt	59	771.7
Chris Short	59	2,253.0
6. Grover Alexander	54	2,513.7
7. Tully Sparks	52	1,698.0
8. Vicente Padilla	50	741.3
9. Erskine Mayer	48	1,191.7
10. Randy Wolf	47	1,118.3

GAMES FINISHED: SEASON

Player	GF	Year
1. Billy Wagner	70	2005
2. Jose Mesa	64	2002
3. Jim Konstanty	62	1950
4. Ricky Bottalico	61	1997
Al Holland	61	1984
6. Roger McDowell	60	1990
Mitch Williams	60	1991
8. Jose Mesa	59	2001
9. Wayne Gomes	58	1999
10. Mitch Williams	57	1993

GAMES FINISHED: CAREER WITH TEAM

Player	GF	IP
1. Tug McGraw	313	722.0
2. Ron Reed	255	809.3
3. Turk Farrell	244	601.0
4. Jack Baldschun	214	543.3
5. Jim Konstanty	203	675.3
6. Ricky Bottalico	192	370.0
7. Steve Bedrosian	188	287.3
8. Mitch Williams	173	231.3
9. Jose Mesa	170	203.0
10. Gene Garber	154	392.7

Until 1938, the Phillies called the quaint and cozy Baker Bowl home.

Significant Phillies

ABREU, BOBBY (OF)
(1998–2005)

After two years with the Houston Astros, the Venezuelan Bobby Abreu was selected by the Tampa Bay Devil Rays in the 1997 expansion draft and traded away the same day to Philadelphia for Kevin Stocker. With Philadelphia, Abreu almost immediately became a star in the National League and has been a consistent performer for the last seven years. Virtually every year, Abreu scores 100 runs, knocks in 100 more, and hits .300 with 40+ doubles and 20–30 steals, making him one of the most valuable players in the game today. He is finally starting to get the recognition he deserves, having made the All-Star team in 2004 and 2005.

CAREER PHILLIES RECORD:

Games	AB	Hits	Runs
1,093	3,930	1,212	726
Avg	**HR**	**RBI**	**SB**
.308	163	647	203

ALEXANDER, GROVER CLEVELAND ("PETE") (SP/RP)
(1911–1917, 1930)

Not only was Grover Cleveland Alexander named after a U.S. president, but he was also played by a future chief executive (Ronald Reagan) in the 1952 movie *The Winning Team*. One of the greatest pitchers in the history of the game, Alexander (who was also known as "Old Pete," and is sometimes listed as "Pete Alexander" in record books) suffered from epileptic seizures later in life that may have been induced by a childhood baseball injury: Trying to break up a double play, Alexander was hit squarely in the head with the throw by the shortstop and lay unconscious in a hospital bed for two days.

Alexander's rookie season in 1911 was like no other pitcher's, before or since. He was 28–13 with 31 complete games, seven shutouts, and a 2.57 ERA. Four of Alexander's shutouts were in consecutive games, including a 12-inning, 1–0 win over Cy Young. After three more fine seasons in which he won 19, 22, and 27 games, Alexander turned it up still another notch from 1915 to 1917, amassing 31, 33, and 30 victories and winning pitching's Triple Crown (leading the league in wins, strikeouts, and ERA in the same year) all three seasons. In 1915 he led the Phillies to their first-ever NL pennant. In 1915 he began a stretch of six straight years in which his ERA was under 2.00. What makes his record truly remarkable is that he accomplished these incredible seasons while playing in tiny Baker Bowl with its 272-foot right-field fence.

Sensing they were about to lose Alexander to military service in World War I—they were right—the Phillies unexpectedly sold him along with catcher Bill Killefer to the Cubs for $60,000 after Alexander's 30–13 season in 1917. While serving in France in an artillery unit, Alexander suffered from shell shock, loss of hearing, and increasing seizures. Alexander's heavy drinking began to be a real problem after the war. He pitched 12 years with the Cubs and Cardinals, attaining the 20-win mark only three more times before returning to the Phillies for one more brief stint in 1930. His last claim to fame was an incident in Game 7 of the 1926 World Series while with St. Louis. With the Cards leading, 3–2, in the bottom of the seventh at Yankee Stadium, starting pitcher Jesse Haines developed a blister on his pitching hand and had to come out of the game. Cardinal manager Rogers Hornsby called on Alexander to relieve Haines. Unfortunately, having drunk heavily after winning Game 6 the day before, Alexander was passed out in the bullpen. He was revived and came in to face slugger Tony Lazzeri with two outs and the bases loaded. Lazzeri smoked an Alexander pitch into the bleachers, but it was foul, missing a grand slam by a foot. Alexander then struck out the Yankee second baseman and held New York scoreless over the final two innings, saving the Cardinals' first-ever World Series championship. After his 20-year major league career ended, Alexander spent eight years barnstorming with the House of David team. During Alexander's last years, his alcoholism worsened and he barely got by a day at a time. In 1938 he was elected to the Hall of Fame.

CAREER PHILLIES RECORD:

W	L	W%	ERA	SV
190	91	.676	2.18	15

K	BB	SHO	IP
1,409	561	61	2,513.7

ALLEN, DICK (3B/1B) (1963–1969, 1975–1976)

The Phillies signed Dick Allen as an amateur free agent in 1960 for a $60,000 bonus. When he was sent to Arkansas to begin his minor league career, protest parades greeted him, for he was the first black player in the newly desegregated Little Rock squad. After a brief late-season call-up in 1963, Allen arrived for good in 1964, winning the NL Rookie of the Year Award after hitting 29 homers with 91 RBIs, 125 runs scored, and a .318 average.

Although Allen had seven very good years in Philadelphia, he eventually wore out his welcome after antagonizing fans, managers, other players, and local writers. He was suspended numerous times for showing up late for games and practices, missing team flights, getting drunk, fighting, and failing to hustle. After hurting his hand when he put it through a car's headlight, Allen was moved from third to first. His ongoing battle with the Philadelphia media—they called him "schizophrenic" and "a con man with muscles"—eventually led him to say, "I'll play third, first, left, wherever. Anywhere except Philadelphia."

Growing weary of Allen's bad-boy antics, the Phillies traded him to the Cardinals after the 1969 season. They, too, got rid of Allen after just one season, shipping him to the Dodgers. A year later he was in Chicago, where he won the AL MVP with the White Sox, but 1972 was to be his last great year. His last five years with the White Sox, Phillies, and A's were tainted by constant controversy. After leaving baseball, Allen continued to reap the benefits of a misspent life: His uninsured house burnt to the ground, and his wife received the rights to his baseball pension in a divorce settlement. The only thing he apparently didn't lose was the chip he carried around on his shoulder his whole life.

CAREER PHILLIES RECORD:

Games	AB	Hits	Runs
1,070	3,935	1,143	697

Avg	HR	RBI	SB
.290	204	655	86

ASHBURN, RICHIE (OF)
(1948–1959)

The Phillies signed Richie Ashburn as an amateur free agent in 1945 and brought him up to the majors in 1948. He impressed immediately, hitting .333 with 32 steals, reeling off a 23-game hitting streak, and playing stellar defense in center field. Ashburn was also the only rookie selected to the 1948 All-Star Game. In 1950 he led Philadelphia's "Whiz Kids" to their first pennant in 35 years. He only got to play initially because of an injury to Harry "the Hat" Walker, the NL's defending batting champ, who was hurt in spring training. Walker never got his job back. Ashburn hit over .300 nine times, led the NL in times getting on base five times, and won two batting titles himself (1955 and 1958). Over the course of a full season, he would catch about 50 more balls in center than Willie Mays, a true indication of Ashburn's speed. Baseball historian Bill James ranks Ashburn as the best defensive outfielder ever to play the game. After 12 years with the Phillies, Ashburn spent his last three years with the Cubs and Mets. Following his retirement in 1962, Ashburn joined the Phillies broadcast booth and remained there until his death 35 years later. He was enshrined in the Hall of Fame in 1995.

CAREER PHILLIES RECORD:

Games	AB	Hits	Runs
1,794	7,122	2,217	1,114
Avg	**HR**	**RBI**	**SB**
.311	22	499	199

BOWA, LARRY (SS)
(1970–1981)

Larry Bowa was signed as an amateur free agent in 1965. After four years in the minors, the Phillies brought him up to the big leagues. He was an excellent fielding shortstop, setting several NL records and winning six fielding titles, a record until Ozzie Smith eclipsed it. A five-time All-Star, Bowa won two Gold Gloves. In 1980 he played a big part in Philadelphia's World Series win over the Royals, hitting .375 and committing all three of the team's steals. He also participated in a Series-record seven double plays. After a dozen years in Philly, Bowa was traded to the Cubs, where he teamed with Ryne Sandberg as the NL's best double-play combination. Following his playing career, Bowa managed the Padres in 1987–1988 before returning to Philadelphia to manage his old team from 2001 to 2004.

CAREER PHILLIES RECORD:

Games	AB	Hits	Runs
1,739	6,815	1,798	816
Avg	**HR**	**RBI**	**SB**
.264	13	421	288

BUNNING, JIM (SP)
(1964–1967, 1970–1971)

See Tigers bio.

CALLISON, JOHNNY (OF)
(1960–1969)

After two years with the White Sox, Johnny Callison was traded to the Phillies following the 1959 season. During his decade in Philadelphia, Callison was never a spectacular player, but he was solid, both on defense and at the plate. He tied a National League record when he led all outfielders in assists for four straight years (1962–1965). In 1968 he played the entire season without making an error. Callison, a three-time All-Star who once hit three homers in a game, led the NL in triples twice and doubles once. In the 1964 All-Star Game at Shea Stadium, Callison hit a three-run homer in the bottom of the ninth to give the NL a 7–4 victory over the AL. His clutch hit earned him the MVP Award, the first time it had been awarded in All-Star Game history. After his retirement, Callison made a living selling cars in Pennsylvania.

CAREER PHILLIES RECORD:

Games	AB	Hits	Runs
1,432	5,306	1,438	774
Avg	**HR**	**RBI**	**SB**
.271	185	666	60

CARLTON, STEVE (SP)
(1972–1986)

Steve Carlton spent seven years with the Cardinals before St. Louis traded him to Philadelphia during spring training in 1972. The trade was precipitated by Carlton's second contract dispute and holdout in three years. After going 17–11 in 1969, he held out during the entire spring of 1970 in an effort to get more money, then fell flat on his face with a 10–19 record. In 1971 Carlton went 20–9, then held out again in spring training 1972. Carlton demanded a $60,000 salary; the Cardinals offered $55,000. Neither side would budge. Tired of bickering with their troublesome pitcher, the Cardinals traded him to Philadelphia on February 25, 1972, for pitcher Rick Wise.

Carlton proceeded to put together a 27–10 record for the last-place Phillies, including a 15-game winning streak. By earning 27 of the team's 59 victories, he set a record by accounting for 45.8 percent of his team's win total. Carlton, whose 30 complete games were the highest total since the 1940s, was the unanimous choice for the NL Cy Young Award. Carlton also carried the revenge factor with him, compiling a 38–14 record against St. Louis over the rest of his career.

Carlton, who refused to talk to the media for most of his career, would post five more 20-win seasons with the Phillies and win three more Cy Youngs as he helped to end a quarter century of frustration by leading Philadelphia to six division titles, two NL pennants, and a World Series title during his tenure. Carlton's workout routine bordered on the bizarre; he made use of a variety of martial arts forms, the sessions sometimes lasting two hours. He also engaged in a pregame meditation routine in the trainer's room, where he visualized the "fertile lanes" on the inside and outside of the plate. On September 24, 1983, Carlton won his 300th game—against the Cardinals. After a 1–8 record in 1985 and a 4–8 start to the 1986 season, he was given his release in

June of that year. Over the next year-plus, Carlton bounced around with four different teams before retiring as baseball's all-time left-handed strikeout king, and second on the all-time win list for lefties, behind only Warren Spahn. Carlton was elected to the Hall of Fame in 1994, his first year of eligibility, by the same writers with whom he refused to talk for almost his whole career.

CAREER PHILLIES RECORD:

W	L	W%	ERA	SV
241	161	.600	3.09	0

K	BB	SHO	IP
3,031	1,252	39	3,697.3

CRAVATH, GAVVY (OF)
(1912–1920)

After two unproductive years spent with three different major league teams, Gavvy Cravath spent a couple years in the minors improving his game. Once he looked promising, the Phillies bought his contract and brought him up to Philadelphia in 1912 at the age of 31, his first full season in the majors. Over the next eight years Cravath became the leading home run hitter during baseball's dead-ball era. At a time when it was rare for a hitter to reach double figures in homers, Cravath did so seven times, leading the AL six times. Sometimes called "Cactus" because of his abrasive personality, Cravath helped the Phillies win their first-ever AL pennant in 1915 with 24 homers and 115 RBIs, both league-leading figures. Cravath spent his last two seasons (1919–1920) as the team's player-manager.

CAREER PHILLIES RECORD:

Games	AB	Hits	Runs
1,103	3,618	1,054	525

Avg	HR	RBI	SB
.291	117	676	80

DELAHANTY, ED (OF/1B)
(1888–1889, 1891–1901)

One of the best hitters in major league history, Delahanty spent 13 seasons of his 16-year major league career with the Phillies, hitting over .400 three times and leading the league in slugging and doubles five times, extra-base hits four times, RBIs three times, and homers twice. He is also the only player to win batting titles in both leagues. Delahanty, who had four younger brothers who also played in the majors, hit four homers in a game against the Cubs on July 13, 1896, all inside-the-park jobs. He had two 6-for-6 games in his career, one in the Players' League and one with the Phillies. Delahanty was part of the greatest outfield ever assembled when he teamed up with "Sliding Billy" Hamilton and Sam Thompson. In 1894, they all hit over .400 and were eventually enshrined in Cooperstown. Only Ty Cobb and Rogers Hornsby have matched Delahanty's three .400 seasons. In the early 1900s, Delahanty was among the many players in the National League—which had a $2,500 salary cap—who jumped to the upstart American League, which had no maximum.

Unfortunately, Delahanty will likely be remembered more for his strange death than his superb career. On July 2, 1903, Delahanty, the defending AL batting champion, was in the midst of a drinking binge on a train while traveling on a road trip with the team. The drunken Delahanty got into an argument with some passengers and pulled a razor, causing a nasty disturbance. The conductor tried unsuccessfully to quiet Delahanty, and finally kicked him off the train at Niagara Falls, Ontario. Under Canadian law, Delahanty should have been placed in the custody of a constable, but he wasn't, probably because the conductor was trying to keep his train running on schedule. When the train left the station to cross the bridge into the United States, Delahanty pushed his way past a guard and followed on foot, crossing the trestle in the dark—or at least attempting to. The bridge tender warned Delahanty that the draw was open, but Delahanty kept going. A week later his battered body was found in the Niagara River, 20 miles below the falls. While it might be assumed he died in a drunken fall from the trestle in the dark, Delahanty's money and jewelry were missing, causing some to speculate that he was robbed and pushed to his death. Ed Delahanty was elected to the Hall of Fame in 1945.

CAREER PHILLIES RECORD:

Games	AB	Hits	Runs
1,555	6,359	2,213	1,367
Avg	**HR**	**RBI**	**SB**
.348	87	1,286	411

ENNIS, DEL (OF)
(1946–1956)

Del Ennis, signed as an amateur free agent by the Philadelphia Blue Jays in 1943, captured the first-ever *Sporting News* Rookie of the Year Award in 1946, one year before the Baseball Writers Association of America began handing out their annual award. For over a decade Ennis was one of the top RBI men in the league, seven times topping the 100 mark. He had his career year in 1950, hitting 31 homers and 126 RBIs, leading the Phillies to their first pennant in 35 years. Always a fan favorite, Ennis, a three-time All-Star, was chosen as a member of the Phillies' Centennial Team in 1983.

CAREER PHILLIES RECORD:

Games	AB	Hits	Runs
1,630	6,327	1,812	891
Avg	**HR**	**RBI**	**SB**
.286	259	1,124	44

FERGUSON, CHARLIE (SP)
(1884–1887)

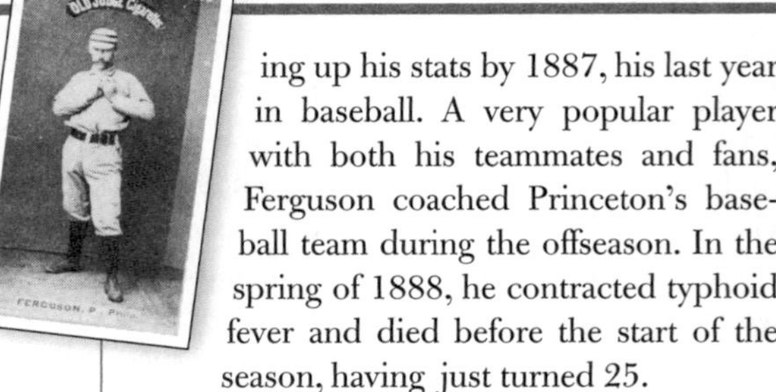

Charlie Ferguson was one of baseball's brightest stars in the 1880s and very well could have become one of the game's best players ever if he hadn't suffered a tragic early death. Like Babe Ruth, Ferguson was a top pitcher and solid hitter. By the time he was just 24, Ferguson won 99 games with a 2.67 ERA in his four big league seasons with the Phillies. When he didn't pitch, Ferguson would often play the outfield or second base, because of his fine hitting and fielding abilities. In two of his four years, Ferguson hit over .300, and was really ratcheting up his stats by 1887, his last year in baseball. A very popular player with both his teammates and fans, Ferguson coached Princeton's baseball team during the offseason. In the spring of 1888, he contracted typhoid fever and died before the start of the season, having just turned 25.

CAREER PHILLIES RECORD:

W	L	W%	ERA	SV
99	64	.607	2.67	4
K	**BB**	**SHO**	**IP**	
728	290	13	1,514.7	

HAMILTON, BILLY (OF)
(1890–1895)

"Sliding Billy" Hamilton was the most prolific run-scorer ever to play major league baseball. By the time he retired, Hamilton had scored an average of 1.06 runs for every game he played in his career, a record that still stands today. In 1894 he scored an incredible 192 runs, also still a record. That same season he hit .404 and put together a 46-game hitting streak. His .523 on-base percentage that year is still the sixth best of all time. The fact that he was also one of baseball's best base-stealers ever helped him in his run-scoring onslaught. He won five base-stealing titles on his way to 912 career steals, ranking him third all time behind Rickey Henderson and Lou Brock. After six seasons in Philadelphia, Hamilton was traded in 1895 to the Boston Beaneaters (now the Atlanta Braves), where he played six more years before retiring. Hamilton, a two-time batting champion, hit over .300 in 12 of his 14 big league seasons. After his retirement from the major leagues, Hamilton spent many years playing and managing in the minors. He died in 1940 and was elected to the Hall of Fame in 1961.

CAREER PHILLIES RECORD:

Games	AB	Hits	Runs
729	2,993	1,079	874
Avg	**HR**	**RBI**	**SB**
.361	23	367	508

KLEIN, CHUCK (OF)
(1928–1933, 1936–1944)

Chuck Klein was a strong man, having worked in a steel mill tossing 200-pound white-hot ingots into blast furnaces during eight-hour shifts without a lunch break. On his own time he played semipro baseball. After advancing to Fort Wayne of the Central League in 1928, Klein hit .331 with 26 homers in just 88 games and was about to be promoted to the parent St. Louis Cardinals when Commissioner Kenesaw Mountain Landis discovered that—contrary to baseball rules—the Cardinals owned a second team, Dayton, in the Central League. As punishment, Landis ordered the Cardinals to sell off Fort Wayne and all of its players. The Phillies outbid the Yankees and got Klein for $7,500. He would spend 14 seasons of his 17-year major league career in three remarkably different stints with the Phillies, separated by short periods with the Cubs and Pirates.

In Klein's first, six-year stay in Philadelphia, he was the best hitter in the National League, bar none. He averaged 36 homers, 139 RBIs, and a .359 average while leading the NL in homers four times. He also led the NL in doubles, hits, and RBIs twice each. In 1929, his first full year in the majors, Klein won the home run title with 43, although he had a little help from his teammates. With one game to go in the season, Klein was leading the Giants' Mel Ott by a single home run and the two teams were playing each other. Philadelphia's pitchers walked Ott five straight times, including once with the bases loaded. In 1930 Klein not only amassed a .386 batting average with 59 doubles, 158 runs, and 170 RBIs, but he also set the modern major league record for outfielders with an almost unbelievable 44 assists. Klein won the NL MVP Award in 1932 and the Triple Crown in 1933.

With a degree of foresight that might raise eyebrows among the cynics, the Phillies traded Klein to the Cubs for three players and $65,000 cash immediately after his Triple Crown season. Klein's average promptly fell by 60 points and his home run and RBI production fell by almost half. Two years later the Cubs sent Klein back to the Phillies with $50,000 for two marginal players. Although his numbers picked up a bit, clearly the magic was gone from Klein's bat. He did have one bit of glory in his second tour when, on July 10, 1936, in a game against the Pirates at cavernous Forbes Field, he became the first NL player in modern history to hit four homers in a game. Three years later he was sent to Pittsburgh for half a season, then returned again to Philadelphia for five more years, but he was just a part-time role player and player-manager by then. After leaving baseball, Klein opened a tavern in Philadelphia, but apparently he was his own best customer—he suffered from severe alcoholism to point of malnutrition. Eventually his drinking damaged his nervous system and left one leg paralyzed. He died in 1958 of a brain hemorrhage. It took an intense and prolonged lobbying effort on the part of his supporters, but Klein was inducted into the Hall of Fame in 1980.

CAREER PHILLIES RECORD:

Games	AB	Hits	Runs
1,405	5,238	1,705	963
Avg	**HR**	**RBI**	**SB**
.326	243	983	71

LUZINSKI, GREG (OF)
(1970–1980)

The Phillies selected Greg "the Bull" Luzinski with the first pick of the June 1968 amateur draft and brought him to the majors in limited duty at the age of 19 in 1970. By 1972 he had become a regular outfielder. From 1975 to 1979, Luzinski was selected to the National League All-Star Team, largely because of his home run hitting. Four times in his career he hit over .300 and four times he surpassed the 100-RBI plateau. He was prone to the strikeout, though, eventually retiring with one of the worst strikeout ratios in major league history. Luzinski and Mike Schmidt led the offense for the Phillies when they won three straight NL East titles from 1976 to 1978, only to be eliminated in the playoffs each year. The Phillies did win the World Series in 1980, but Luzinski went hitless in the Series after having the worst year of his career, hitting only .228 with 19 homers. The Phils traded him to the White Sox following the Series and he put in four modestly successful campaigns before calling it quits at the age of 33 in 1984. He did have a few bright moments with Chicago. In 1983 he led the Sox to the AL West title with 32 homers, including three prodigious blasts that sailed over the roof and out of Comiskey Park. In 1984 he became the eighth American League player to hit grand slams in consecutive games and enjoyed a stretch of 10 consecutive games with at least one RBI.

CAREER PHILLIES RECORD:

Games	AB	Hits	Runs
1,289	4,630	1,299	618
Avg	**HR**	**RBI**	**SB**
.281	223	811	29

MAGEE, SHERRY (OF)
(1904–1914)

For more than a decade during the dead-ball era, Sherry Magee was one of the best players in baseball. He was an excellent defensive player who led the league in hitting once and RBIs four times. Five times he hit over .300 and had more than 40 steals, and he routinely hit 30–40 doubles. In 1911 Magee was suspended for five weeks for knocking umpire Bill Finneran unconscious during an argument over a called third strike. Magee was an intelligent player who anticipated being named player-manager after the 1914 season. When he wasn't, he demanded—and got—a trade to the Boston Braves, who had just won the NL pennant. Ironically, in 1915, while Magee was with Boston, Philadelphia won its first-ever NL pennant. After retiring, Magee spent a year as an umpire before he died of pneumonia in 1929.

CAREER PHILLIES RECORD:

Games	AB	Hits	Runs
1,521	5,505	1,647	898
Avg	**HR**	**RBI**	**SB**
.299	75	886	387

ROBERTS, ROBIN (SP/RP)
(1948–1961)

The Phillies signed Robin Roberts as an amateur free agent in 1948 and brought him up in the middle of the year. After a 15–15 season in 1949, Roberts moved into baseball's elite circle of pitchers in 1950, when he won 20 games and helped the "Whiz Kids" Phillies, packed with excellent young players, to their first NL pennant in 35 years. He was the first 20-game winner for Philadelphia in 33 years. But Roberts was just warming up. He would win more than 20 games for the next five years as well, including a 28–7 record in 1952. From 1950 to 1955, Roberts pitched more than 300 innings per season. He just missed extending his string in 1956, when he pitched 297.3.

But he was becoming another victim in a long line of pitchers who were incredibly overused during their careers; his impressive run of six straight 20-win seasons was followed by a mediocre record of 126–143 over his remaining 11 seasons. The Phillies' stretch drive in 1950 is a good example of the team's abuse of Roberts' arm. Philadelphia had a 7½ game lead with 11 days to go in the season. Remarkably, they blew their large lead, with Roberts pitching three times in the last five days in an effort to clinch the pennant for the Phils, which they did on the season's last day. After 14 years with the Phillies, Roberts spent his last five with Baltimore, Houston, and the Cubs before retiring in 1966. Following his playing days, Roberts spent a time as coach of the University of South Florida before taking a minor league instructor job with Philadelphia. Roberts was elected to the Hall of Fame in 1976.

CAREER PHILLIES RECORD:

W	L	W%	ERA	SV
234	199	.540	3.46	24
K	BB	SHO	IP	
1,871	718	35	3,739.3	

SCHILLING, CURT (SP)
(1992–2000)

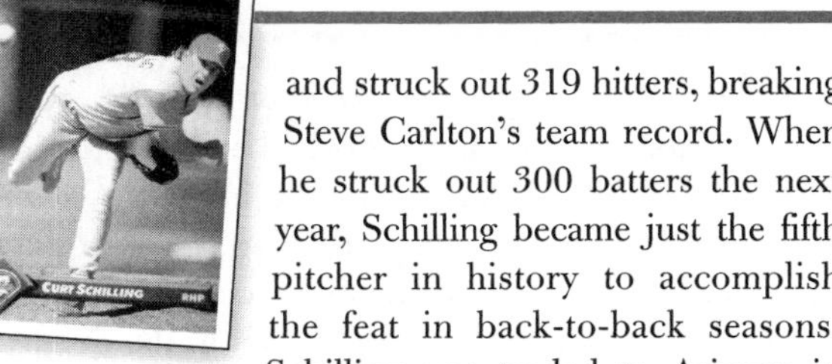

After four years with the Orioles and Astros, Curt Schilling was traded to the Phillies for pitcher Jason Grimsley just as the 1992 season was beginning. Strictly a reliever in the three years preceding the trade, Schilling was converted to a starter immediately upon arriving in Philadelphia. During his nine years with the Phillies, Schilling had five seasons in which he won 14–17 games, and four seasons when—because of a variety of injuries—he won fewer than 10. Schilling had his best year in Philadelphia in 1997, when he won 17 games and struck out 319 hitters, breaking Steve Carlton's team record. When he struck out 300 batters the next year, Schilling became just the fifth pitcher in history to accomplish the feat in back-to-back seasons. Schilling was traded to Arizona in mid-2000, and finally developed into a true ace in 2001. *(See Diamondbacks bio.)*

CAREER PHILLIES RECORD:

W	L	W%	ERA	SV
101	78	.564	3.35	2
K	BB	SHO	IP	
1,554	415	14	1,659.3	

SCHMIDT, MIKE (3B)
(1972–1989)

Mike Schmidt is Mr. Phillie, at least according to a 1983 vote of Philadelphia fans. Schmidt was drafted by the Phillies in the 2nd round of the June 1971 amateur draft and brought up for a late-season call-up the next year. By 1973 he was the starting third baseman, but hit only .196, lowest in the National League among regulars. He turned it around in 1974, though, as he raised his batting average to .282 and doubled his home run output from 18 to 36, the first of 13 seasons in which he would smack at least 30 homers. Schmidt would hit 35 or more 11 times, a mark surpassed only by Babe Ruth. He would lead the NL in homers a record eight times; only Ruth led his league more often. Schmidt and Ralph Kiner are the only two batters to have hit four consecutive homers twice in their careers. On one of those occasions, April 17, 1976, Schmidt's fourth homer of the day helped the Phillies defeat the Cubs 18–16 in Wrigley Field after Philadelphia at one point trailed 13–2.

Schmidt spent his entire 18-year career in Philadelphia, knocking in 100+ runs nine times. He was also an excellent fielder, winning 10 Gold Gloves, more than any third baseman except Brooks Robinson. When the Phillies won their only World Series title in 1980 by defeating the Royals in six games, Schmidt led the way with a .381 average, two homers, six runs, and seven RBIs as he captured the Series MVP Award. A three-time NL MVP and 12-time All-Star, Schmidt holds the record for career homers by a third baseman. In 1995 he was voted into the Hall of Fame, receiving 444 of the 460 votes cast, in his first year of eligibility.

CAREER PHILLIES RECORD:

Games	AB	Hits	Runs
2,404	8,352	2,234	1,506
Avg	**HR**	**RBI**	**SB**
.267	548	1,595	174

SHORT, CHRIS (SP/RP)
(1959–1972)

The Phillies signed Chris Short as an amateur free agent in 1957 and brought him up to the show for just a taste in 1959 before bringing him up for good the next season. Short was an innings eater for much of his career, but he did have a good stretch in the mid-1960s in which he won 17–20 games in four years out of five. His success came almost overnight, after he developed a vicious curveball to go with his fastball and slider. A back injury in 1969 ended his effectiveness and he struggled over the next few years trying to work through it, but the pain eventually became too much; the 14-year Phillie retired after one season with the Brewers in 1973. After his playing days he became an insurance agent in Delaware. He suffered a brain aneurysm in 1988 and died after spending three years in a coma.

CAREER PHILLIES RECORD:

W	L	W%	ERA	SV
132	127	.510	3.38	16
K	**BB**	**SHO**	**IP**	
1,585	762	24	2,253.0	

THOMPSON, SAM (OF)
(1889–1898)

After four years with the Detroit Wolverines, "Big Sam" Thompson was purchased outright by the Philadelphia Phillies just after the 1888 season. At 6' 2" and 200+ pounds, Thompson was not only physically larger than almost every other player, but he was a hitter before his time, cut in the mold of Babe Ruth. He liked to hit home runs before home runs were fashionable. Thompson was even criticized in *The Spalding Guide* for being one of the hitters who tried to appease the goundlings (fans) by using brute strength and no brains in an effort to hit "stupid" home runs instead of "intelligent" singles. What the media might not have noticed is that Sam Thompson was hitting plenty of singles . . . and doubles . . . and triples to go along with his home runs. He also was the leading RBI man of the day, eight times eclipsing the 100 mark, and twice posting more than 165 RBIs in a season—incredible numbers for the 19th century, with its shorter schedule and comatose ball.

After leaving Detroit as one of its most popular players ever, Thompson won the home run crown in his first season with the Phillies by slugging 20, an astounding number for that era. His best year was 1895, when he hit .392 with 211 hits, 131 runs, 45 doubles, 21 triples, 165 RBIs, and a league-leading 18 homers. He retired in 1898 after 10 seasons with the Phils and returned to Detroit, but came back for a brief period in 1906 with the Tigers at age 46 when the team lost a number of players to injuries late in the year. In his career, Thompson averaged 0.923 RBIs per game played, the most of any player in history with at least 10 years of playing time, ranking him just ahead of Lou Gehrig (0.922) and Hank Greenberg (0.915). Thompson became involved in local politics and real estate investments after his baseball career and was elected to the Hall of Fame in 1974.

CAREER PHILLIES RECORD:

Games	AB	Hits	Runs
1,031	4,413	1,469	924
Avg	**HR**	**RBI**	**SB**
.333	95	957	189

WILLIAMS, CY (OF)
(1918–1930)

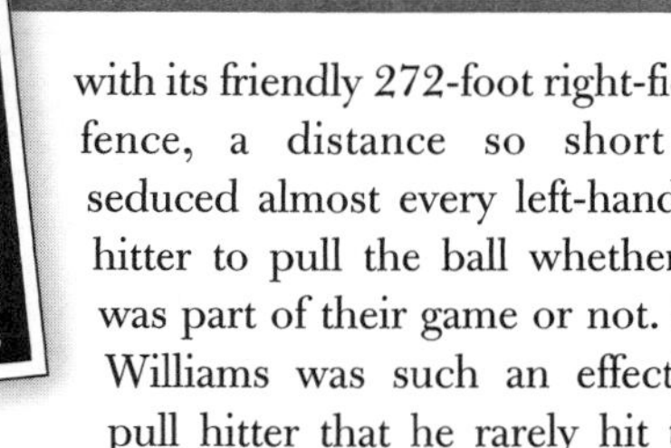

Many baseball fans have heard of the "Williams Shift," in which opposing managers moved all the players towards right—including putting the shortstop on the right side of the infield—in an effort to stymie the great Ted Williams. But many people don't know that there was an earlier version of the Williams Shift employed throughout the 1920s, particularly in Baker Bowl, Philadelphia's home park, with its friendly 272-foot right-field fence, a distance so short it seduced almost every left-handed hitter to pull the ball whether it was part of their game or not. Cy Williams was such an effective pull hitter that he rarely hit the ball to the left side of the field. He led the league in homers four times, compiling a healthy .470 slugging average. He started his career with the Cubs, who were so impressed with him after a college exhibition game that they signed him and brought him directly to the majors. Williams was a six-time .300 hitter, but unfortunately for him, the Phillies never finished above seventh place during his years as a regular player. When he retired following the 1930 season, Williams had 251 homers, the most by any left-hander in National League history. Williams became a successful architect in Wisconsin after his playing career.

CAREER PHILLIES RECORD:

Games	AB	Hits	Runs
1,463	5,077	1,553	825
Avg	**HR**	**RBI**	**SB**
.305	217	795	77

Mike Schmidt ties Mickey Mantle with his 536th home run at Shea Stadium in 1988.

Pittsburgh Pirates

Since 1882

1963 Team Ball

1883 Ed Swartwood wins the American Association batting title with a .356 average, becoming the first in a long line of Pittsburgh batting champions.... **1903** The Pirates pitching staff hurls 57 consecutive shutout innings, setting a record that has yet to be broken.... **1921** On August 5, the Pirates become the first team ever to broadcast a game over the radio when Harold Arlen of KDKA calls the game.... **1971** The Pirates usher in baseball's Polyester Age when they become the first team to wear form-fitting double knit uniforms.... **1983** When Bill Madlock wins the National League batting title, it's the 24th time a Pirate has won the crown, more than any other team in the league. Although Madlock's title was the Pirates' last, the team still holds the record (St. Louis is closing in with 22 batting titles through 2005).

FRANCHISE HISTORY

The origin of the Pittsburgh Pirates must be traced through two other rival major leagues. From 1882 to 1886, the Pittsburgh Alleghenys, owned by Horace Phillips, were members of the American Association. After steadily improving in the American Association, the team was invited to join the National League in 1887, and Phillips accepted, keeping the Alleghenys name. Dennis McKnight became the principal owner after the league switch. For its first three years in the National League, Pittsburgh was reasonably competitive, posting winning percentages between .444 and .493. In 1890, however, Pittsburgh suffered tremendously when many of its stars jumped to the new Players' League; the team finished 23–113. After battling the new league for a year, McKnight had had enough and technically dissolved the team, then joined forces with the owners of the disbanded Players' League franchise and formed a new entity known as the Pittsburgh Athletic Company. This company, controlled by J. Palmer O'Neill, became the new owner of the Pittsburgh National League franchise, which thereafter was known as the Pittsburgh Pirates. It also allowed the new owners to legally recover the services of many of the players originally lost to the Pittsburgh franchise of the Players' League. O'Neill sold the team in 1894 to William Kerr of Arbuckle Coffee, who in turn held it until 1900, whereupon he sold a half-interest to former Louisville owner Barney Dreyfuss when the National League contracted from 12 teams to eight.

Honus Wagner, the greatest shortstop of them all.

Tommy Leach hit four triples in the first modern World Series in 1903 against Boston. More than a century later, that record still stands.

Dreyfuss began hearing rumors during the 1899 season that when the National League contracted at the end of the season, his Louisville team would be among those eliminated. So, in a shrewd preemptive move, Dreyfuss quietly made a deal with William Kerr to purchase a 50 percent interest in the Pittsburgh club. Then, after the season, he arranged a lopsided trade of 12 of his players—including all of his stars—to Pittsburgh, for four players and $25,000 cash. The players who went to Pittsburgh included Fred Clarke, Tommy Leach, Deacon Phillippe, Rube Waddell, Honus Wagner, Chief Zimmer, and six others. Dreyfuss also brought along his team secretary, Harry Pulliam, who would later become the president of the National League.

Kerr became involved in a nasty dispute with Pulliam, who was loyal to Dreyfuss. Dreyfuss offered to buy Kerr out, and did, after coming up with Kerr's $75,000 asking price. Dreyfuss was the sole owner for more than three decades until he

They were fam-i-ly: Willie Stargell's World Championship Pirates, 1979.

died of pneumonia in 1932, following complications from a prostate operation. Following his death, Dreyfuss's son-in-law, Bill Benswanger, took over the day-to-day operation of the team while Dreyfuss's wife retained control of the team's stock. When she died, Benswanger became the team's owner and held it until selling out during the 1946 season.

> In the decade of the 1900s, the Pirates' .636 winning percentage was the best in either league.

John W. Galbreath, a realtor from Columbus, Ohio, was the leader of the ownership group that purchased the Pirates from Benswanger. Others in the group included Indianapolis banker Frank McKinney, Pittsburgh attorney Thomas Johnson, and entertainer Bing Crosby. Galbreath brought Branch Rickey on board as general manager in 1952 in a failed attempt to bring respectability to a team that perennially had one of the worst records in baseball. In 1955 Galbreath replaced Rickey with Joe Brown, son of movie comedian Joe E. Brown, and he is credited with ushering in the franchise's success in the 1960s and 1970s, when the Pirates won all three World Series they played in.

After the glory days of 1979, the Pirates lost their luster and began to slide downhill, ceding the local limelight to the NFL Steelers. Several Pirates became ensnared in an embarrassing baseball-wide drug scandal. Attendance in the small-market city, never big even in the World Series years, began to drop dramatically. In 1984 and 1985, annual attendance reached only around 700,000. The Pirates finished last in the NL East for three straight years (1984–1986). After 40 years of owning the Pirates, the Galbreath family announced in 1985 that they would have to move the Pirates to another city in order to survive. A community-wide effort was undertaken in an attempt to keep the Pirates in Pittsburgh. Nine corporations and four individuals stepped up to the plate and paid $2 million each to keep the team in Pittsburgh. The group formed a legal entity called Pittsburgh Associates and purchased the team in 1986. Pittsburgh Associates included, among others: Alcoa, Westinghouse, the Mellon Bank, Pittsburgh Plate Glass, U.S. Steel, and Carnegie-Mellon University. The city of Pittsburgh gave the group a $20 million loan and a $34 million line of credit, but by the mid-1990s, the team was $60 million in debt and anticipated losing another $20 million in the upcoming 1995 season.

In 2005, the Pirates had their 13th consecutive losing season, a team record. The previous longest streak had been the nine years from 1949 to 1957.

An investment group, led by Sacramento newspaper heir Kevin McClatchy, bought the Pirates in September 1995 for $85 million. His lease required him to keep the team in Pittsburgh, but it did give him an out if a new stadium wasn't built or under construction by 2000. That requirement was fulfilled with the creation of PNC Park, the Pirates' new stadium, which opened in 2001. Other investors included quarterback Dan Marino, who had played football at the University of Pittsburgh before leading the NFL's Dolphins; Chip Ganassi, who owned an Indy-car team with Joe Montana; real estate developer Dick Means; scrap-metal dealer Bill Snyder; and Fred Anderson, part owner of the NBA's Sacramento Kings. McClatchy still owns the team today.

Beautiful on the field and off: Roberto Clemente, homeing here in 1971 World Series.

As with virtually all major league teams that played in the 19th and early 20th centuries, the Pittsburgh franchise was known by a variety of unofficial nicknames before settling on its current name. At various times the team was known as: the Pittsburghs, the Potato Bugs (because of their outlandish striped uniforms), the Zulus, the Smoked Italians, the Innocents, the Alleghenys, and the Stogies (after Pittsburgh's smokestacks). Originally and officially known as the Alleghenys from 1882 to 1890, the team came by its current moniker in 1891 when then-owner, J. Palmer O'Neill, made a name for himself by raiding American Association teams and former Players' League teams for ballplayers. O'Neill's snaring of second baseman Lou Bierbauer of the Philadelphia Athletics gave rise to much public outcry. The press and many in baseball began referring to the team as "O'Neill's Pirates." The name stuck and was later made official.

On the field, the Pirates first became a force in 1900 when the team was stocked with ex-Louisville players, most notably Honus Wagner. The Pirates won three straight National League pennants from 1901 to 1903, and in 1903 they played in the first modern World Series, which they lost to the Boston Pilgrims (now the Red Sox). In 1909 the Pirates won their fourth NL pennant and defeated Ty Cobb's Detroit Tigers in the World Series, playing their home games in Pittsburgh's brand-new concrete-and-steel stadium, Forbes Field (one of baseball's first two stadiums). After Honus Wagner retired,

the team went into a decline until the mid-1920s, when the Pirates again reloaded with many star players. Pittsburgh defeated Walter Johnson and his Washington Senators in the 1925 World Series in seven games. Down three games to one, the Pirates became the first team ever to come back from such a deficit and win the Series. Two years later, however, the Pirates lost in four straight to the "Murderer's Row" Yankees. Although the Pirates were swept, two of the losses were by one run, and the final game was decided by a wild pitch in the ninth inning. From 1929 to 1938, the Pirates achieved four second-place finishes, but no titles. For the following two decades the Pirates resided mostly in the second division. They finished last five times and next to last five times.

The 33-year title drought ended in 1960, when the upstart Pirates stunned the baseball world by defeating the heavily favored New York Yankees in seven games in an exciting World Series. In their three losses, the Pirates were drubbed 16–3, 10–0, and 12–0. Their four wins came by the scores of 6–4, 3–2, 5–2, and 10–9, with Bill Mazeroski's bottom-of-the-ninth homer in Game 7 breaking a 9–9 tie. Mickey Mantle was said to have cried for hours after the loss. The Pirates remained competitive for the next decade and moved into Three Rivers Stadium in 1970. They reached the World Series again in 1971, this time beating Baltimore in seven games as Roberto Clemente put on a spectacular hitting show. The Pirates remained strong throughout most of the 1970s, winning six division titles. In 1979 the Pirates and Orioles once again squared off in the Fall Classic, the Pirates winning again in seven games with Willie Stargell now in the role of offensive hero. This time, though, the Pirates fell behind three games to one and had to rally back, just as they had in 1925. In so doing, the Pirates became—and still are—the only team to twice come back from three-games-to-one deficits to win the World Series.

After bringing the championship to Pittsburgh in 1979, the Pirates stumbled for the next decade. Then, with young star Barry Bonds starting to reach his potential, the Pirates won three straight division titles from 1990 to 1992, but lost in the NLCS each time. Ever since Bonds left Pittsburgh to sign with San Francisco as a free agent following the 1992 season, the Pirates have endured the utter futility of 13-straight losing seasons. And counting.

TEAM NAME HISTORY

Official Names

Alleghenys (1882–1890)
Pirates (1891–current)

Unofficial Names/Nicknames

Potato Bugs, Zulus, Smoked Italians, Stogies, Innocents, Bucs, Buccaneers, Buccos, Corsairs, Pittsburgh Nationals

STADIUM HISTORY

Exposition Park	1882–1884
Recreation Park	1885–1890
Exposition Park	1891–June 21, 1909
Forbes Field	June 30, 1909–June 28, 1970
Three Rivers Stadium	July 16, 1970–2000
PNC Park	2001–current

YEARLY RECORD, FINISH, & ATTENDANCE FIGURES

Year	League	Record	DIV/LG Finish	Attendance	Avg/Gm
2005	NL Cent	67–95	6	1,817.245	22,435
2004	NL Cent	72–89	5	1,580,031	19,750
2003	NL Cent	75–87	4	1,636,751	20,207
2002	NL Cent	72–89	4	1,784,988	22,312
2001	NL Cent	62–100	6	2,464,870	30,430
2000	NL Cent	69–93	5	1,748,908	21,591
1999	NL Cent	78–83	3	1,638,023	20,223
1998	NL Cent	69–93	6	1,560,950	19,271
1997	NL Cent	79–83	2	1,657,022	20,457
1996	NL Cent	73–89	5	1,332,150	16,652
1995	NL Cent	58–86	5	905,517	12,577
1994	NL Cent	53–61	3	1,222,520	20,041
1993	NL East	75–87	5	1,650,593	20,378
1992	NL East	96–66	1	1,829,395	22,585
1991	NL East	98–64	1	2,065,302	24,587
1990	NL East	95–67	1	2,049,908	25,308
1989	NL East	74–88	5	1,374,141	16,965
1988	NL East	85–75	2	1,866,713	23,046
1987	NL East	80–82	4	1,161,193	14,336
1986	NL East	64–98	6	1,000,917	12,357
1985	NL East	57–104	6	735,900	9,199
1984	NL East	75–87	6	773,500	9,549
1983	NL East	84–78	2	1,225,916	15,135
1982	NL East	84–78	4	1,024,106	12,643
1981	NL East	46–56	4/6	541,789	10,623
1980	NL East	83–79	3	1,646,757	20,330
1979	NL East	98–64	1	1,435,454	17,722
1978	NL East	88–73	2	964,106	11,903
1977	NL East	96–66	2	1,237,349	15,276
1976	NL East	92–70	2	1,025,945	12,666
1975	NL East	92–69	1	1,270,018	15,875
1974	NL East	88–74	1	1,110,552	13,711
1973	NL East	80–82	3	1,319,913	16,295
1972	NL East	96–59	1	1,427,460	18,301
1971	NL East	97–65	1	1,501,132	18,764
1970	NL East	89–73	1	1,341,947	16,365
1969	NL East	88–74	3	769,369	9,498
1968	NL	80–82	6	693,485	8,562
1967	NL	81–81	6	907,012	11,198
1966	NL	92–70	3	1,196,618	14,773
1965	NL	90–72	3	909,279	11,089
1964	NL	80–82	6	759,496	9,376
1963	NL	74–88	8	783,648	9,675
1962	NL	93–68	4	1,090,648	13,465
1961	NL	75–79	6	1,199,128	15,573
1960	NL	95–59	1	1,705,828	21,870
1959	NL	78–76	4	1,359,917	17,661
1958	NL	84–70	2	1,311,988	17,039
1957	NL	62–92	7	850,732	11,048
1956	NL	66–88	7	949,878	12,178
1955	NL	60–94	8	469,397	6,259

YEARLY RECORD, FINISH, & ATTENDANCE FIGURES (CONT.)

Year	League	Record	DIV/LG Finish	Attendance	Avg/Gm
1954	NL	53–101	8	475,494	6,175
1953	NL	50–104	8	572,757	7,438
1952	NL	42–112	8	686,673	8,918
1951	NL	64–90	7	980,590	12,572
1950	NL	57–96	8	1,166,267	15,146
1949	NL	71–83	6	1,449,435	18,824
1948	NL	83–71	4	1,517,021	18,963
1947	NL	62–92	7	1,283,531	16,247
1946	NL	63–91	7	749,962	9,615
1945	NL	82–72	4	604,694	7,654
1944	NL	90–63	2	604,278	7,460
1943	NL	80–74	4	498,740	6,394
1942	NL	66–81	5	448,897	5,830
1941	NL	81–73	4	482,241	6,183
1940	NL	78–76	4	507,934	6,772
1939	NL	68–85	6	376,734	4,893
1938	NL	86–64	2	641,033	8,218
1937	NL	86–68	3	459,679	5,893
1936	NL	84–70	4	372,524	4,902
1935	NL	86–67	4	352,885	4,583
1934	NL	74–76	5	322,622	4,136
1933	NL	87–67	2	288,747	3,750
1932	NL	86–68	2	287,262	3,780
1931	NL	75–79	5	260,392	3,338
1930	NL	80–74	5	357,795	4,647
1929	NL	88–65	2	491,377	6,465
1928	NL	85–67	4	495,070	6,429
1927	NL	94–60	1	869,720	11,009
1926	NL	84–69	3	798,542	10,108
1925	NL	95–58	1	804,354	10,446
1924	NL	90–63	3	736,883	9,570
1923	NL	87–67	3	611,082	7,936
1922	NL	85–69	4	523,675	6,714
1921	NL	90–63	2	701,567	9,231
1920	NL	79–75	4	429,037	5,500
1919	NL	71–68	4	276,810	3,954
1918	NL	65–60	4	213,610	3,009
1917	NL	51–103	8	192,807	2,441
1916	NL	65–89	6	289,132	3,707
1915	NL	73–81	5	225,743	2,858
1914	NL	69–85	7	139,620	1,813
1913	NL	78–71	4	296,000	3,747
1912	NL	93–58	2	384,000	5,120
1911	NL	85–69	3	432,000	5,538
1910	NL	86–67	3	436,586	5,745
1909	NL	110–42	1	534,950	6,858
1908	NL	98–56	2	382,444	4,967
1907	NL	91–63	2	319,506	4,149
1906	NL	93–60	3	394,877	5,128
1905	NL	96–57	2	369,124	4,732
1904	NL	87–66	4	340,615	4,367

YEARLY RECORD, FINISH, & ATTENDANCE FIGURES (CONT.)

Year	League	Record	DIV/LG Finish	Attendance	Avg/Gm
1903	NL	91–49	1	326,855	4,669
1902	NL	103–36	1	243,826	3,434
1901	NL	90–49	1	251,955	3,652
1900	NL	79–60	2	264,000	3,771
1899	NL	76–73	7	251,834	3,271
1898	NL	72–76	8	150,900	1,986
1897	NL	60–71	8	165,950	2,459
1896	NL	66–63	6	197,000	3,008
1895	NL	71–61	7	188,000	2,806
1894	NL	65–65	7	159,000	2,409
1893	NL	81–48	2	184,000	2,809
1892	NL	80–73	6	177,205	2,287
1891	NL	55–80	8	128,000	1,869
1890	NL	23–113	8	16,064	233
1889	NL	61–71	5	N/A	N/A
1888	NL	66–68	6	N/A	N/A
1887	NL	55–69	6	N/A	N/A
1886	AA	80–57	2	N/A	N/A
1885	AA	56–55	3	N/A	N/A
1884	AA	30–78	11	N/A	N/A
1883	AA	31–67	7	N/A	N/A
1882	AA	39–39	4	N/A	N/A

MANAGER HISTORY

Manager	Years	W–L	Win %
Al Pratt	1882–1883	51–59	.464
Ormond Butler	1883	17–36	.321
Joe Battin	1883, 1884	8–18	.308
Denny McKnight	1884	4–8	.333
Bob Ferguson	1884	11–31	.262
George Creamer	1884	0–8	.000
Horace Phillips	1884–1889	294–316	.482
Fred Dunlap	1889	7–10	.412
Ned Hanlon	1889, 1891	57–65	.467
Guy Hecker	1890	23–113	.169
Bill McGunnigle	1891	24–33	.421
Tom Burns	1892	27–32	.458
Al Buckenberger	1892–1894	187–144	.565
Connie Mack	1894–1896	149–134	.527
Patsy Donovan	1897, 1899	129–129	.500
Bill Watkins	1898–1899	79–91	.465
Fred Clarke	1900–1915	1,422–969	.595
Jimmy Callahan	1916–1917	85–129	.397
Honus Wagner	1917	1–4	.200
Hugo Bezdek	1917–1919	166–187	.470
George Gibson	1920–1922, 1932–1934	401–330	.549
Bill McKechnie	1922–1926	409–293	.583

MANAGER HISTORY (CONT.)

Manager	Years	W–L	Win %
Donie Bush	1927–1929	246–178	.580
Jewel Ens	1929–1931	176–167	.513
Pie Traynor	1934–1939	457–406	.530
Frank Frisch	1940–1946	539–528	.505
Spud Davis	1946	1–2	.333
Billy Herman	1947	61–92	.399
Bill Burwell	1947	1–0	1.000
Billy Meyer	1948–1952	317–452	.411
Fred Haney	1953–1955	163–299	.353
Bobby Bragan	1956–1957	102–155	.397
Danny Murtaugh	1957–1964, 1967, 1970–1971, 1973–1976	1,115–950	.540
Harry Walker	1965–1967	224–184	.549
Larry Shepard	1968–1969	164–155	.514
Alex Grammas	1969	4–1	.800
Bill Virdon	1972–1973	163–128	.560
Chuck Tanner	1977–1985	711–685	.509
Jim Leyland	1986–1996	851–863	.496
Gene Lamont	1997–2000	295–352	.456
Lloyd McClendon	2001–2005	336–447	.429
Pete Mackanin	2005	12–14	.462

ALL-TIME WIN-LOSS RECORDS VS. ALL OPPONENTS (SINCE 1901)

Opponent	W–L
ALL-TIME	8,422–7,969
Angels	3–3
Astros	308–280
Athletics	0–6
Blue Jays	0–3
Braves	1,003–854
Brewers	67–58
Cardinals	1,070–1,004
Cubs	1,088–995
Devil Rays	4–2
Diamondbacks	22–34
Dodgers	891–979
Giants	864–1,004
Indians	10–8
INTERLEAGUE	49–72
Mariners	0–3
Marlins	63–49
Mets	345–309
Nationals	281–254
Orioles	2–1
Padres	227–171
Phillies	1,094–906
Rangers	0–6
Reds	992–945
Red Sox	2–4
Rockies	59–57
Royals	8–9
Tigers	7–8
Twins	7–8
White Sox	5–6
Yankees	0–3

Franchise Highlights, Low Points, and Strange Distinctions

1885–92 Hall of Famer Pud Galvin, who pitched all or part of eight of his 14 seasons with the Pirates, set a 19th-century record of 361 victories without once being the league leader in wins, strikeouts, or ERA.

• • • •

1891 Despite having future Hall of Famer Pud Galvin, as well as Silver King and Mark Baldwin—the two top pitchers in the Players' League—Pittsburgh finished last in the National League in 1891.

• • • •

1892 In baseball's early days, forfeited games weren't as unusual as they are today, with an average of three or four a year in the first 25 years of baseball history. During the season there were six forfeited games, and the Pirates were involved in four of them, all at home.

It had been raining all day in Pittsburgh on May 10, so at 4:10 P.M., New York Giant manager Pat Powers took his team and left the park. Unfortunately, umpire Jack McQuaid, who had not yet called the game, ordered it to begin half an hour later and awarded the Pirates a forfeit when he realized the opposition had left the premises.

On August 16, in a game against Washington, with the score tied in the bottom of the 10th, 2–2, Pirates batter Doggie Miller was hit by a pitch and awarded first base. When Washington protested, claiming Miller had tried to get hit, the umpire disagreed and ordered play to continue. Washington simply refused, so umpire Charles Mitchell awarded the game to Pittsburgh.

On September 22, with the host Pirates leading 9–2 in the middle of the fourth of a game played in a constant drizzle, Chicago, hoping for a rainout, began using delaying tactics until umpire John Gaffney awarded the Pirates a forfeit due to Chicago's excessive stalling.

And finally, on October 11, the Pirates and Cleveland played to a tie. The next day, according to the rules of the time, Pittsburgh asked for and was granted the right to replay the game. Unfortunately, Cleveland had left Pittsburgh the night before to play a scheduled benefit, and the game was forfeited to Pittsburgh.

• • • •

1896 When southpaw Frank Killen went 30–18, it marked the last time a left-hander won at least 30 games in the National League.

• • • •

1899 On May 3, the Pirates achieved one of the most bizarre temporary victories in baseball history. With visiting Louisville leading 6–1 in the bottom of the 9th, the Pirates scored three runs to close the gap. Then, with two men on base, Jack McCarthy hit a ball down the right-field line that appeared foul, but was ruled fair by the umpire. The ball then took a crazy bounce to the right, towards a small boy standing near the dressing-room door. As the ball approached, the boy opened the door and entered, the ball following him through the door. The boy shut the door behind him. By the time right fielder Charlie Dexter retrieved the ball, three runs had scored and the Pirates had seemingly won, 7–6.

Louisville claimed fan interference, but both umpires disagreed, awarding the game to Pittsburgh. Louisville filed a protest and the game was later declared to be a no-decision.

....

1900 When the National League contracted from 12 teams to eight, the Pirates made out like bandits, absorbing Honus Wagner, Fred Clarke, Rube Waddell, Tommy Leach, Deacon Phillippe, and several others from the disbanded Louisville team.

....

1902 Pirate third baseman Tommy Leach led the National League in homers with six, the fewest by any 20th-century home run champ.

The Pirates savaged the rest of the National League, finishing 27½ games ahead, the biggest margin ever. The Pirates were particularly tough at home, going 56–15, the best home record ever in the National League.

....

1903 Jimmy Sebring hit the first home run in World Series history when he connected off Boston's Cy Young in Game 1 of the 1903 Series.

In a record that will undoubtedly never be beaten, because of late-season injuries to two Pirate pitchers, Deacon Phillippe threw five complete games in one World Series. Phillippe won his first three starts, giving the Pirates a 3–1 advantage over Boston. He was the loser, however, in Games 7 and 8, when Boston rallied to take the best-of-nine Series, five games to three.

1909 George Gibson became the first catcher in history to catch at least 150 games in a season.

In 1909 Babe Adams became the first rookie pitcher to start the opening game of a World Series. He responded by pitching three complete-game victories.

The first all concrete-and-steel stadium to open in the National League was Forbes Field. Shibe Park, home of the AL's Philadelphia A's, was the first such stadium in the American League, opening a couple months before Forbes Field.

....

1914 On June 9, Honus Wagner became the second player ever to reach 3,000 hits, joining Cap Anson in the exclusive club, although some record books do not recognize Anson's hits during his time in the National Association (1871–1875) as major league hits. If those hits are taken away, Wagner was the first to reach 3,000 hits.

....

1920 On October 2, Pittsburgh and Cincinnati played the last tripleheader in major league history. The Reds won the first two games, 13–4 and 7–3, while the Pirates took the last game, 6–0. Umpire Peter Harrison was behind the plate for all three games.

....

1922 Reb Russell, a former 20-game winner but now serving as a utility outfielder for the Pirates, played in just 60 games, but accumulated an incredible 75 RBIs with his .368 average.

Speedy Max Carey set a stolen-base percentage record in 1922 with 51 steals in 53 attempts, a .962 success mark.

....

1923 First baseman Charlie Grimm set a National League record by getting a hit in 23 consecutive games to start a season.

....

1924 Wilbur Cooper completed 26 of his 38 starts, giving him at least 25 complete games for the seventh straight season. In so doing, he became the last pitcher in major league history to record 25 or more complete games as many as five years in a row.

....

1925 Since 1900, no National League player has hit as many triples in a season as Kiki Cuyler's 26. Joe Jackson (with Cleveland in 1912) and Sam Crawford (with Detroit in 1914) also had 26 in the American League.

The 1925 Pirates were the first team to come back and win the World Series after trailing three games to one. When they did it again in 1979, they became the only team in history to do it twice. No other National League team has done it even once. Three teams in the American League have come back from 3-to-1 deficits to win the World Series: the Yankees in 1958, the Tigers in 1968, and the Royals in 1985.

1927 The Waner brothers, Paul and Lloyd, set numerous records while playing side by side in the Pirates' outfield. Older brother Paul—in only his second year in the majors—led the National League in batting with a .380 average. Lloyd, a rookie, chimed in with .355, making their combined average .367, the highest for any pair of brothers in major league history. It was also the first time ever that a pair of brothers ended up 1–2 on their team in batting. In addition, Lloyd's 223 hits and 198 singles were both rookie records. Lloyd also scored a 20th-century rookie-record 133 runs, a record which also still stands. Then again, he drove in a mere 27 runs that year.

....

1929 Probably the most incredible aspect of Pie Traynor's awesome season (in which he hit .356 with 108 RBIs) was the fact that he only struck out seven times in 540 at-bats.

....

1931 For the first time in National League history, there were no 20-game winners. Pittsburgh's Heinie Meine finished with 19, tying the Cardinals' Wild Bill Hallahan and the Phillies' Jumbo Jim Elliott for the top spot.

....

1935 On May 25, finishing out his career with the Boston Braves, an aging, overweight Babe Ruth hit three mammoth home runs at Forbes Field, including the first ever hit completely out of the stadium, for career home runs 712, 713, and 714. A few days later he retired.

Catcher Aubrey Epps played only one game in the major leagues, a September 29, 1935, affair in which he went 3-for-4 with 3 RBIs against Cincinnati on the last day of the season.

• • • •

1936 On July 10, slugger Chuck Klein of the Phillies smacked four homers out of Forbes Field—without doubt the toughest park in the National League in which to hit a home run.

In 1936 outfielder Woody Jensen set the all-time record for at-bats in a 154-game season when he collected 696 for the Pirates.

• • • •

1937 First baseman Gus Suhr's National League record 822 consecutive games played streak ended. It still ranks today in the top 10 streaks of all time.

• • • •

1942 When Paul Waner collected his 3,000th hit, he became the last player to join the exclusive club until 1957.

• • • •

1946 Ralph Kiner became the first rookie to lead the National League in homers when he socked just 23. But by the time he led the National League in home runs with 37 in 1952, it was his seventh straight league home run title, the most in baseball history. Closest to him are Babe Ruth (6), Frank Baker (4), Mark McGwire (4), and Harry Davis (4).

1955 It was one of the more unusual innings in the annals of baseball. The Pirates were being no-hit by the Cubs' Sam Jones when they loaded the bases on three walks in the ninth. They couldn't make him pay, though, as Jones struck out the next three Pirate hitters he faced.

• • • •

1956 Dale Long set a major league record when he homered in eight consecutive games. The record has since been tied by Don Mattingly and Ken Griffey Jr.

• • • •

1957 The Pirates had the distinction of being the last visiting team to play in both Ebbets Field and the Polo Grounds before the Dodgers and Giants moved to the West Coast following the season.

• • • •

1959 One of the most incredible pitching performances ever to occur on a major league field took place on May 26, in Milwaukee. Pirate pitcher Harvey Haddix pitched twelve perfect innings against the Braves, but was locked in a scoreless duel with Lew Burdette. When Haddix struck out Burdette to end the ninth, he received a standing ovation from the Braves' fans, who similarly cheered him after the 10th, 11th, and 12th innings. Amazingly the Pirates collected 12 hits, but failed to score. They even had three singles in the third, but one runner was thrown out trying to advance from first to third on a single.

In the decisive 13th inning, Felix Mantilla hit a ground ball to Pirate third baseman Don Hoak. Hoak threw low to first base and the ball hit first baseman Rocky Nelson in the foot, with Mantilla reaching on the error. Eddie Mathews sacrificed Mantilla to second. Hank Aaron was then intentionally walked to set up the double-play possibility. Joe Adcock, who had struck out twice and grounded out twice in his first four plate appearances, then hit a drive that barely cleared the right-center-field fence for what at least some thought was a home run. Mantilla scored from second base, but Aaron, thinking the ball had stayed in the ballpark, decided after touching second base that Mantilla's run had ended the game and headed across the pitcher's mound toward the Milwaukee dugout on the first-base side. Meanwhile, Adcock, running with his head down, continued on toward third base. Braves Manager Fred Haney and the Milwaukee coaches promptly sought to get Aaron and Adcock to retrace their steps. Aaron, who hadn't yet touched third, went back to second base and then, with Adcock following him, they ran to third base and home plate. However, the umpires, who were still on the field, ruled Adcock's hit a double, but both Mantilla and Aaron were credited with runs, making the score 2–0. The next day, however, National League President Warren Giles announced that only Mantilla's run would count and the game would go into the record books as a 1–0 contest. He ruled that Adcock, although hitting the ball out of the park, would be credited with only a double because of the baserunning mistake, and the game ended when Mantilla crossed the plate.

Haddix had better luck the next year. In the 1960 World Series, Harvey Haddix got the win in Game 5, 5–2, as a starter, then another win in relief in Game 7, one of the most exciting World Series games ever played, when the Pirates beat the Yanks, 10–9, on Bill Mazeroski's home run in the bottom of the ninth.

Roy Face set a major league record in 1959 when he won his first 17 straight games, all out of the bullpen. Combined with the last five straight he won in 1958, Face had a two-year total of 22 consecutive wins.

• • • •

1962 Although it pales by today's standards, Roy Face set a new National League saves record with 28.

• • • •

1960–67 Bill Mazeroski led all National League second basemen in double plays a record eight consecutive seasons, from 1960 to 1967.

• • • •

1966–69 From 1966 to 1969, outfielder Matty Alou hit over .330, making him the last National Leaguer to hit for such an average four consecutive seasons until Tony Gwynn accomplished the feat five consecutive years from 1993 to 1997. Roberto Clemente came close when he did it three years in a row (1969 to 1971), but fell to .312 in 1972, the last year he played before his tragic death.

• • • •

1969 Willie Stargell became the first player ever to hit a home run completely out of Dodger Stadium when he did so on August 5.

When Roy Face retired in 1969, he was the major league record holder for saves (193), wins in relief (96), appearances (821), and most appearances for one team (802 with the Pirates).

1971 The first night game in World Series history took place on October 13, in Pittsburgh, when the Pirates defeated the Orioles 4–3 in Game 4.

• • • •

1974 Richie Zisk had an incredible 10-game span in which he collected 21 RBIs.

• • • •

1975 The Pirates thrashed the Cubs 22–0 in a game at Wrigley Field on September 16. It was the worst shutout one team has inflicted on another in the majors since 1901.

• • • •

1979 Pirates hurler John Candelaria set a record when he led the team in victories with 14, the lowest total ever by the wins leader on a world-champion team.

First sackers Willie Stargell of the Pirates and Keith Hernandez of the Cardinals finished in an exact tie for the 1979 National League MVP Award, the first time in history the balloting had ended thus. Stargell was 39 at the time, making him the oldest player ever to have won the MVP Award.

• • • •

1984 Some say that pitching and defense are the secret to winning, but you couldn't prove it by the Pirates. They had the best ERA in the National League at 3.11 and allowed the fewest runs in the major leagues, 567, but still ended up in last place in the NL East.

1985 Tough-luck pitcher Jose DeLeon established a 20th-century National League record in 1985 when he attained the lowest winning percentage ever by a pitcher with at least 20 decisions. He finished 2–19 for a .095 mark.

When they lost 104 games in 1985, it marked the first time since 1954 the team had lost 100 games.

• • • •

1986 The Pirates again had the worst record in the majors when they finished 64–98. They owed a lot of it to the eventual World Series champion Mets, who beat them 17 out of 18 in the season series.

• • • •

1990 Barry Bonds became the first player in major league history to hit at least .300 with 30 homers, 100 RBIs, and 50 stolen bases when he accomplished the feat. He also became the first Pirate to hit 30 homers and steal 30 bases in a season.

• • • •

1991 Barry Bonds and Bobby Bonilla became the first Pirate teammates ever to record back-to-back seasons with 100 or more RBIs. This performance helped the Pirates to a 46–32 road record, best in the majors.

• • • •

1992 When the Pirates finished the season at 96–66, it was their third winning season in the three years of the 1990s. Amazingly, they were the only National League team to post winning records in all three of those years.

1993 Shortstop Jay Bell had a breakthrough season. Not only did he set career highs in hits, runs, steals, batting average, walks, and triples, he played such good defense that he won the Gold Glove, ending Ozzie Smith's 13-year reign as the NL's best shortstop.

• • • •

1994 Although the Pirates were tied for last in the league in homers, they broke a team record set in 1966 by hitting home runs in 13 consecutive games.

• • • •

1995 When Jeff King hit two home runs in the second inning of an August 8 game against San Francisco, he became the first Pirate to hit two homers in one inning since Jake Stenzel did it in 1894.

• • • •

1996 Rookie Jason Kendall was hit by 15 pitches, a team record, and the most ever by a National League catcher.

• • • •

1997 When Tony Womack stole 32 consecutive bases, it broke Max Carey's franchise record set back in 1922.

On July 12, 1997, Francisco Cordova and Ricardo Rincon combined on a 10-inning no-hitter against the Houston Astros, the first combined extra-inning no-hitter in major league history. The victory pulled the Pirates into a tie with Houston atop the NL Central standings, although Houston would eventually win the division.

• • • •

1999 Kevin Young became only the second Pirate player in history to record consecutive seasons with 40 or more doubles. Despite all the great hitters and batting champions in Pirates history, the only other Pirate to accomplish the feat was Paul Waner, who did it three years in a row from 1927 to 1929. Even the great Honus Wagner, who led the NL in doubles seven times, didn't have 40 in back-to-back seasons as a Pirate. Wagner did hit 40-plus, in 1899 and 1900, but in 1899 he was playing for Louisville.

In 1999, for the first time, the Pirates had four players with at least 20 homers in the same season. Brian Giles led the way with 39. Kevin Young (26), Al Martin (24), and Ed Sprague (22) joined him in setting the record.

• • • •

2000 Brian Giles became the first Pirate in history to hit at least .300 with 30 homers and 100 RBIs in back-to-back seasons.

Special Achievements

World Series Results

Year	Opponent	Result	Games
1903	Boston Red Sox	Lost	3–5
1909	Detroit Tigers	Won	4–3
1925	Washington Senators	Won	4–3
1927	New York Yankees	Lost	3–4
1960	New York Yankees	Won	4–3
1971	Baltimore Orioles	Won	4–3
1979	Baltimore Orioles	Won	4–3

World Series Managerial Records

Manager	Series Record	Games Record
Fred Clarke	1–1	7–8
Bill McKechnie	1–0	4–3
Donie Bush	0–1	3–4
Danny Murtaugh	2–0	8–6
Chuck Tanner	1–0	4–3

All-Time Postseason Record

Divisional Playoffs	0–0
League Championship Series	17–25
World Series	26–24

All-Star Games at Pittsburgh

Year	Date	Winner	Score	Stadium
1944	July 11	National	7–1	Forbes Field
1959	July 7	National	5–4	Forbes Field
1974	July 23	National	7–2	Three Rivers Stadium
1994	July 12	National	8–7	Three Rivers Stadium

Hall of Famers Who Played for Team

	Position	Years	Games with Pittsburgh
Jake Beckley	1B	1888–1889, 1891–1896	928
Jim Bunning	SP	1968–1969	52
Max Carey	OF	1910–1926	2,178
Jack Chesbro	SP	1899–1902	122
Fred Clarke	OF	1900–1911, 1913–1915	1,479
Roberto Clemente	OF	1955–1972	2,433
Joe Cronin	2B/SS	1926–1927	50
Kiki Cuyler	OF	1921–1927	525
Pud Galvin	SP	1887–1889, 1891–1892	246
Hank Greenberg	1B	1947	125
Burleigh Grimes	SP	1916–1917, 1928–1929, 1934	137
Ned Hanlon	OF	1889, 1891	235
Billy Herman	2B	1947	15
Waite Hoyt	RP/SP	1933–1937	156
Joe Kelley	OF	1892	56
George Kelly	OF	1917	8
Ralph Kiner	OF	1946–1953	1,095
Chuck Klein	OF	1939	85
Freddy Lindstrom	OF	1933–1934	235
Al Lopez	C	1940–1946	656
Connie Mack	C/1B	1891–1896	325
Heinie Manush	OF	1938–1939	25
Rabbit Maranville	SS/2B	1921–1924	601
Bill Mazeroski	2B	1956–1972	2,163
Willie Stargell	OF/1B	1962–1982	2,360
Casey Stengel	OF	1918–1919	128
Pie Traynor	3B	1920–1937	1,941
Dazzy Vance	SP	1915	1
Arky Vaughan	SS	1932–1941	1,411
Rube Waddell	SP	1900–1901	32
Honus Wagner	SS/OF/1B/3B	1900–1907	2,433
Lloyd Waner	OF	1927–1941, 1944–1945	1,803
Paul Waner	OF	1926–1940	2,154
Vic Willis	SP	1906–1909	160

Hall of Famers Who Managed Team

	Years	Games with Pittsburgh
Fred Clarke	1900–1915	2,427
Frankie Frisch	1940–1946	1,085
Ned Hanlon	1889, 1891	124
Billy Herman	1947	155
Connie Mack	1894–1896	289
Bill McKechnie	1922–1926	707
Pie Traynor	1934–1939	868
Honus Wagner	1917	5

MVP Award Winners

Dick Groat	SS	1960
Roberto Clemente	OF	1966
Dave Parker	OF	1978
Willie Stargell	1B	1979 (tie)
Barry Bonds	OF	1990
Barry Bonds	OF	1992

CY YOUNG AWARD WINNERS

Pitcher	Year	W–L	ERA
Vernon Law	1960	20–9	3.08
Doug Drabek	1990	22–6	2.76

ROOKIE OF THE YEAR AWARD WINNERS

Jason Bay	OF	2004

GOLD GLOVE WINNERS

Year	Position	Player
1958	2B	Bill Mazeroski
1959	SP	Harvey Haddix
1960	SP 2B	Harvey Haddix Bill Mazeroski
1961	SP 2B	Bobby Shantz Bill Mazeroski
	OF	Roberto Clemente
1962	OF OF	Roberto Clemente Bill Virdon
1963	2B OF	Bill Mazeroski Roberto Clemente
1964	2B OF	Bill Mazeroski Roberto Clemente
1965	2B OF	Bill Mazeroski Roberto Clemente
1966	2B SS OF	Bill Mazeroski Gene Alley Roberto Clemente
1967	2B SS	Bill Mazeroski Gene Alley
	OF	Roberto Clemente
1968	OF	Roberto Clemente
1969	OF	Roberto Clemente
1970	OF	Roberto Clemente
1971	OF	Roberto Clemente
1972	OF	Roberto Clemente
1977	OF	Dave Parker
1978	OF	Dave Parker
1979	OF	Dave Parker
1983	C	Tony Peña
1984	C	Tony Peña
1985	SP C	Rick Reuschel Tony Peña
1987	C	Mike LaValliere
1988	OF	Andy Van Slyke
1989	OF	Andy Van Slyke
1990	OF OF	Andy Van Slyke Barry Bonds
1991	OF OF	Andy Van Slyke Barry Bonds
1992	2B OF OF	Jose Lind Andy Van Slyke Barry Bonds
1993	SS	Jay Bell

TRIPLE CROWN WINNERS

None

FIREMAN OF THE YEAR AWARD WINNERS

Roy Face	1962
Al McBean	1964
Dave Giusti	1971

WORLD SERIES MVP

Roberto Clemente	1971
Willie Stargell	1979

LEAGUE CHAMPIONSHIP SERIES MVP

Willie Stargell	1979

ALL-STAR GAME MVP

Dave Parker	1979

MANAGER OF THE YEAR AWARD WINNERS

Jim Leyland	1990
Jim Leyland	1992

BATTING CHAMPIONS

Year	Player	Avg
1900	Honus Wagner	.381
1902	Clarence Beaumont	.357
1903	Honus Wagner	.355
1904	Honus Wagner	.349
1906	Honus Wagner	.339
1907	Honus Wagner	.350
1908	Honus Wagner	.354
1909	Honus Wagner	.339
1911	Honus Wagner	.334
1927	Paul Waner	.380
1934	Paul Waner	.362
1935	Arky Vaughan	.385
1936	Paul Waner	.373
1940	Debs Garms	.355
1960	Dick Groat	.325
1961	Roberto Clemente	.351
1964	Roberto Clemente	.339
1965	Roberto Clemente	.329
1966	Matty Alou	.342
1967	Roberto Clemente	.357
1977	Dave Parker	.338
1978	Dave Parker	.334
1981	Bill Madlock	.341
1983	Bill Madlock	.323

NINE-INNING NO-HITTERS PITCHED

Year	Pitcher	Opp.	Score
1907	Nick Maddox	BRK	2–1
1951	Cliff Chambers	BOS	3–0
1959	Harvey Haddix (12-inning perfect game, lost in 13th)	MIL	0–1
1969	Bob Moose	NYM	4–0
1970	Dock Ellis	SD	2–0
1976	John Candelaria	LAD	2–0
1997	Francisco Cordova/ Ricardo Rincon	HOU	3–0

20-GAME WINNERS

Year	Pitcher	W–L
1882	Harry Salisbury	20–18
1885	Ed Morris	39–24
1886	Ed Morris	41–20
	Pud Galvin	29–21
1887	Pud Galvin	28–21
1888	Ed Morris	29–23
	Pud Galvin	23–25
1889	Pud Galvin	23–16
	Harry Staley	21–26
1891	Mark Baldwin	22–28
1892	Mark Baldwin	26–27
1893	Frank Killen	36–14
1895	Pink Hawley	31–22
1896	Frank Killen	30–18
	Pink Hawley	22–21
1898	Jesse Tannehill	25–13
1899	Jesse Tannehill	24–14
	Sam Leever	21–23
1900	Jesse Tannehill	20–6
	Deacon Phillippe	20–13
1901	Deacon Phillippe	22–12
	Jack Chesbro	21–10
1902	Jack Chesbro	28–6
	Jesse Tannehill	20–6
	Deacon Phillippe	20–9
1903	Sam Leever	25–7
	Deacon Phillippe	25–9
1905	Sam Leever	20–5
	Deacon Phillippe	20–13
1906	Vic Willis	23–13
	Sam Leever	22–7
1907	Vic Willis	21–11
	Al Leifield	20–16
1908	Nick Maddox	23–8
	Vic Willis	23–11
1909	Howard Camnitz	25–6
	Vic Willis	22–11
1911	Babe Adams	22–12
	Howard Camnitz	20–15
1912	Claude Hendrix	24–9
	Howard Camnitz	22–12
1913	Babe Adams	21–10
1915	Al Mamaux	21–8
1916	Al Mamaux	21–15
1920	Wilbur Cooper	24–15
1921	Wilbur Cooper	22–14
1922	Wilbur Cooper	23–14
1923	John Morrison	25–13
1924	Wilbur Cooper	20–14
1926	Remy Kremer	20–6
	Lee Meadows	20–9
1927	Carmen Hill	22–11
1928	Burleigh Grimes	25–14
1930	Remy Kremer	20–12
1943	Rip Sewell	21–9
1944	Rip Sewell	21–12
1951	Murry Dickson	20–16
1958	Bob Friend	22–14
1960	Vernon Law	20–9
1977	John Candelaria	20–5
1990	Doug Drabek	22–6
1991	John Smiley	20–8

RETIRED UNIFORM NUMBERS

Number	Player	Position
1	Billy Meyer	Mgr
4	Ralph Kiner	OF
8	Willie Stargell	1B
9	Bill Mazeroski	2B
20	Pie Traynor	3B
21	Roberto Clemente	OF
33	Honus Wagner	SS
40	Danny Murtaugh	Mgr

TEAM RECORDS—WINS & LOSSES

- Games won in a season: 110 in 1909
- Games lost in a season: 113 in 1890
- Games won in a month: 25, three times: September 1901, September 1908, and July 1932
- Games lost in a month: 24 in September 1916
- Consecutive games won: 16 in 1909
- Consecutive games lost: 23 in 1890
- Biggest shutout victory: 22–0 over Chicago Cubs on September 16, 1975
- Biggest shutout loss: 18–0 to Philadelphia Phillies on July 11, 1910
- Highest winning percentage: .741 in 1902 (103–36)
- Lowest winning percentage: .169 in 1890 (23–113)

TEAM RECORDS—BATTING

- Highest team batting average: .309 in 1928
- Lowest team batting average: .231 in 1952

- Highest team slugging average: .449 in 1930
- Highest team on-base percentage: .379 in 1894
- Total hits: 1,698 in 1922
- Extra-base hits: 519 in 2000
- Hits in a game: 27 vs. Philadelphia Phillies on August 8, 1922 (first game)
- Longest individual hitting streak: 27, Jimmy Williams, 1899
- Most .300 hitters in a single season: 9 in 1928
- Home runs: 171 in 1999
- Home runs in a month: 16, Ralph Kiner, September 1949
- Home runs in a game: 7 (three times): vs. Boston Braves, June 8, 1894; vs. St. Louis, August 16, 1947; vs. St. Louis, August 20, 2003
- Home runs by a rookie: 26, Jason Bay, 2004
- Home runs by a right-hander: 54, Ralph Kiner, 1949
- Home runs by a left-hander: 48, Willie Stargell, 1971
- Home runs by a switch-hitter: 32, Bobby Bonilla, 1990
- Grand slams: 7 in 1978 and 1996
- Grand slams (individual; season): 4, Ralph Kiner, 1949
- Grand slams (individual; career): 11, Ralph Kiner and Willie Stargell
- Triples: 129 in 1912
- Doubles: 320 in 2000
- Singles: 1,297 in 1922
- Walks: 620 in 1991
- Runs scored: 912 in 1925
- Runs scored in a game: 27 vs. Boston Braves on June 6, 1894
- Runs scored in an inning: 12 vs. St. Louis on April 22, 1892 (first inning) and vs. Boston Braves on June 6, 1894 (third inning)
- Most batters hit by a pitch: 95 in 2004 and 2005
- Times shut out: 27 in 1916
- Grounded into double plays: 142 in 1950
- Fewest grounded into double plays: 95 in 1978
- Runners left on base: 1,241 in 1936

TEAM RECORDS—BASERUNNING

- Stolen bases: 264 in 1907
- Caught stealing: 120 in 1977

TEAM RECORDS—PITCHING

- Lowest earned run average: 2.07 in 1909
- Complete games: 133 in 1904
- Saves: 52 in 1979
- Strikeouts: 1,124 in 1969
- Shutouts: 26 in 1906
- Walks: 711 in 2000
- Hit batsmen: 80 in 2001
- Wild pitches: 67 in 2000
- Consecutive wins (individual): 17, Roy Face, 1959; over two seasons: 22, Roy Face, 1958–1959
- Consecutive losses (individual): 13, Burleigh Grimes, 1917
- Strikeouts in a game (individual): 16, Bob Veale, June 1, 1965
- Runs allowed in a game: 28 vs. Boston Braves, August 27, 1887

TEAM RECORDS—FIELDING

- Best fielding average: .984 in 1992
- Most errors committed: 291 in 1904
- Fewest errors committed: 101 in 1992
- Most double plays turned: 215 in 1966
- Fewest double plays turned: 94 in 1935

TEAM RECORDS—MISCELLANEOUS

- Number of times league champions: 9
- Number of times finishing last in league: 12
- Largest attendance, single game: 55,351 vs. Chicago Cubs, October 1, 2000
- Largest attendance, doubleheader: 49,886 vs. New York Mets, July 27, 1972
- Players used in a season: 49 in 1987 and 2001
- Seasons played: 21 by Willie Stargell

PRIMARY PITCHING STAFFS

Year	Starter	Starter	Starter	Starter	Starter	Closer	Bullpen	Bullpen	Bullpen
2005	Wells	Redman	Fogg	Williams	Perez	Mesa	Torres	White	Meadows
2004	Wells	Vogelsong	Fogg	Benson	Perez	Mesa	Torres	Grabow	Meadows
2003	Wells	D'Amico	Fogg	Benson	Suppan	Williams	Beimel	Tavarez	Boehringer
2002	Wells	Anderson	Fogg	Benson	Meadows	Williams	Sauerbeck	Lincoln	Boehringer
2001	Ritchie	Anderson	Williams	Beimel	Schmidt	Williams	Sauerbeck	Manzanillo	Olivares
2000	Ritchie	Anderson	Benson	Silva	Cordova	Williams	Sauerbeck	Wilkins	Christiansen
1999	Ritchie	Schmidt	Benson	Schourek	Cordova	Williams	Sauerbeck	Wilkins	Clontz
1998	Lieber	Schmidt	Peters	Silva	Cordova	Loiselle	Rincon	Christiansen	Dessens
1997	Lieber	Schmidt	Loaiza	Cooke	Cordova	Loiselle	Rincon	Wilkins	Sodowsky
1996	Lieber	Neagle	Darwin	Smith	Wagner	Cordova	Plesac	Wilkins	Miceli
1995	Loaiza	Neagle	Ericks	Parris	Wagner	Miceli	Plesac	Christiansen	McCurry
1994	Smith	Neagle	Cooke	Lieber	Wagner	Pena	Manzanillo	Dewey	White
1993	Walk	Wakefield	Cooke	Tomlin	Wagner	Belinda	Minor	Neagle	Johnston
1992	Walk	Drabek	Smith	Tomlin	Jackson	Belinda	Mason	Neagle	Patterson
1991	Walk	Drabek	Smith	Tomlin	Smiley	Landrum	Belinda	Kipper	Patterson
1990	Walk	Drabek	Heaton	Terrell	Smiley	Landrum	Belinda	Ruskin	Patterson
1989	Walk	Drabek	Heaton	Robinson	Smiley	Landrum	Kipper	Bair	Kramer
1988	Walk	Drabek	Dunne	Fisher	Smiley	Gott	Kipper	Robinson	Jones
1987	Reuschel	Drabek	Dunne	Fisher	Kipper	Gott	Smiley	Robinson	Walk
1986	Reuschel	Rhoden	Bielecki	McWilliams	Kipper	Robinson	Clements	Guante	Winn
1985	Reuschel	Rhoden	DeLeon	McWilliams	Tunnell	Candelaria	Robinson	Guante	Holland
1984	Tudor	Rhoden	DeLeon	McWilliams	Candelaria	Tekulve	Robinson	Guante	Scurry
1983	Tunnell	Rhoden	DeLeon	McWilliams	Candelaria	Tekulve	Sarmiento	Guante	Scurry
1982	Robinson	Rhoden	Sarmiento	McWilliams	Candelaria	Tekulve	Romo	Niemann	Scurry
1981	Solomon	Rhoden	Bibby	Perez	Tiant	Romo	Tekulve	Jackson	Scurry
1980	Candelaria	Rhoden	Bibby	Blyleven	Robinson	Tekulve	Romo	Jackson	Solomon
1979	Candelaria	Kison	Rooker	Blyleven	Robinson	Tekulve	Romo	Jackson	Bibby
1978	Candelaria	Bibby	Rooker	Blyleven	Robinson	Tekulve	Whitson	Jackson	Kison
1977	Candelaria	Reuss	Rooker	Kison	Jones	Gossage	Tekulve	Jackson	Demery
1976	Candelaria	Reuss	Rooker	Kison	Medich	Moose	Tekulve	Giusti	Hernandez
1975	Candelaria	Reuss	Rooker	Kison	Ellis	Giusti	Tekulve	Demery	Hernandez
1974	Brett	Reuss	Rooker	Kison	Ellis	Giusti	Morlan	Demery	Hernandez
1973	Briles	Moose	Rooker	Blass	Ellis	Giusti	Johnson	Walker	Hernandez
1972	Briles	Moose	Kison	Blass	Ellis	Giusti	Johnson	Miller	Hernandez
1971	Johnson	Moose	Walker	Blass	Ellis	Giusti	Grant	Veale	Briles
1970	Veale	Moose	Walker	Blass	Ellis	Giusti	Dal Canton	Gibbon	Pena
1969	Veale	Moose	Bunning	Blass	Ellis	Hartenstein	Dal Canton	Gibbon	Walker
1968	Veale	Moose	Bunning	Blass	McBean	Face	Kline	Sisk	Walker
1967	Veale	Sisk	Ribant	Blass	Fryman	Face	McBean	Pizarro	Mikkelsen
1966	Veale	Sisk	Law	Blass	Fryman	Face	McBean	O'Dell	Mikkelsen
1965	Veale	Friend	Law	Cardwell	Gibbon	McBean	Schwall	Carpin	Sisk
1964	Veale	Friend	Law	Blass	Gibbon	McBean	Face	Bork	Sisk
1963	Cardwell	Friend	Schwall	Francis	Gibbon	Face	McBean	Haddix	Sisk
1962	McBean	Friend	Law	Francis	Haddix	Face	Olivo	Sturdivant	Lamabe
1961	Gibbon	Friend	Mizell	Francis	Haddix	Face	Labine	Shantz	McBean
1960	Gibbon	Friend	Mizell	Law	Haddix	Face	Green	Umbricht	Giel
1959	Kline	Friend	Daniels	Law	Haddix	Face	Blackburn	Gross	Smith
1958	Kline	Friend	Raydon	Law	Witt	Face	Blackburn	Gross	Porterfield
1957	Kline	Friend	Purkey	Law	Arroyo	Face	King	Swanson	Smith
1956	Kline	Friend	Munger	Law	Hall	Face	King	Waters	Pollet
1955	Kline	Friend	Surkont	Law	Littlefield	King	Face	Donoso	
1954	Thies	Friend	Surkont	Law	Littlefield	Hetki	Purkey	LaPalme	O'Donnell

PRIMARY PITCHING STAFFS (CONT.)

Year	Starter	Starter	Starter	Starter	Starter	Closer	Bullpen	Bullpen	Bullpen
1953	Dickson	Friend	LaPalme	Lindell	Hall	Hetki	Face	Bowman	
1952	Dickson	Friend	Pollet	Hogue	Kline	Main	Wilks	LaPalme	
1951	Dickson	Friend	Pollet	Queen	Law	Wilks	Werle	Walsh	LaPalme
1950	Dickson	Chambers	Werle	Queen	MacDonald	Lombardi	Walsh	Law	
1949	Dickson	Chambers	Werle	Chesnes	Bonham	Lombardi	Casey	Sewell	
1948	Riddle	Ostermueller	Lombardi	Chesnes	Bonham	Higbe	Singleton	Queen	Gregg
1947	Higbe	Ostermueller	Roe	Sewell	Bonham	Singleton	Bagby	Strincevich	
1946	Heintzelman	Ostermueller	Strincevich	Sewell	Bahr	Gerheauser	Hallett	Gables	
1945	Roe	Butcher	Strincevich	Sewell	Gables	Rescigno	Gerheauser	Cuccurullo	Ostermueller
1944	Roe	Butcher	Strincevich	Sewell	Ostermueller	Rescigno	Cuccurullo	Starr	
1943	Klinger	Butcher	Hebert	Sewell	Gornicki	Rescigno	Brandt	Gee	
1942	Klinger	Butcher	Heintzelman	Sewell	Hamlin	Dietz	Wilkie	Lanning	
1941	Klinger	Butcher	Heintzelman	Sewell	Lanning	Dietz	Wilkie	Bowman	
1940	Klinger	Butcher	Bowman	Sewell	Brown	Lanahan	Heintzelman	Lanning	
1939	Klinger	Butcher	Bowman	Tobin	Brown	Sewell	Heintzelman	Swift	
1938	Klinger	Bauers	Blanton	Tobin	Brandt	Brown	Bowman	Swift	
1937	Lucas	Bauers	Blanton	Bowman	Brandt	Brown	Weaver	Tobin	Swift
1936	Lucas	Swift	Blanton	Weaver	Birkofer	Brown	Hoyt	Bush	
1935	Lucas	Swift	Blanton	Weaver	Bush	Hoyt	Brown	Birkofer	
1934	Lucas	Swift	French	Birkofer	Hoyt	Chagnon	Meine	Smith	
1933	Meine	Swift	French	Swetonic	Smith	Chagnon	Hoyt	Harris	
1932	Meine	Swift	French	Swetonic	Harris	Chagnon	Spencer	Brame	
1931	Meine	Kremer	French	Brame	Spencer	Osborn	Wood	Swetonic	
1930	Meine	Kremer	French	Brame	Spencer	Chagnon	Petty	Swetonic	
1929	Grimes	Kremer	French	Brame	Petty	Hill	Meine	Swetonic	
1928	Grimes	Kremer	Hill	Brame	Fussell	Dawson	Miljus	Tauscher	
1927	Meadows	Kremer	Hill	Aldridge	Dawson	Cvengros	Miljus	Morrison	
1926	Meadows	Kremer	Yde	Aldridge	Songer	Bush	Adams	Morrison	
1925	Meadows	Kremer	Yde	Aldridge	Morrison	Sheehan	Adams	Oldham	
1924	Meadows	Kremer	Yde	Cooper	Morrison	Stone	Adams	Pfeffer	
1923	Meadows	Adams	Hamilton	Cooper	Morrison	Bagby	Kunz	Steineder	
1922	Glazner	Adams	Carlson	Cooper	Morrison	Hamilton	Yellowhorse	Hollingsworth	
1921	Glazner	Adams	Hamilton	Cooper	Morrison	Zinn	Yellowhorse	Carlson	
1920	Carlson	Adams	Hamilton	Cooper	Ponder	Wisner	Meador	Blake	
1919	Carlson	Adams	Hamilton	Cooper	Miller	Mayer	Ponder	Evans	
1918	Sanders	Mayer	Harmon	Cooper	Miller	Comstock	Steele	Jacobs	
1917	Jacobs	Steele	Grimes	Cooper	Miller	Carlson	Mamaux	Evans	
1916	Mamaux	Kantlehner	Harmon	Cooper	Miller	Jacobs	Adams	Evans	
1915	Mamaux	Adams	Harmon	Cooper	McQuillan	Kantlehner	Conzelman	Hill	
1914	O'Toole	Adams	Harmon	Cooper	McQuillan	Kantlehner	Conzelman	Mamaux	
1913	O'Toole	Adams	Hendrix	Robinson	Camnitz	Cooper	McQuillan		
1912	O'Toole	Adams	Hendrix	Robinson	Camnitz	Cole	Ferry	Warner	
1911	Leifield	Adams	Hendrix	Steele	Camnitz	Gardner	Ferry	Nagle	
1910	Leifield	Adams	White	Powell	Camnitz	Phillippe	Leever	Maddox	
1909	Leifield	Willis	Maddox	Phillippe	Camnitz	Adams	Leever	Brandom	
1908	Leifield	Willis	Maddox	Leever	Camnitz	Young	Young		
1907	Leifield	Willis	Phillippe	Leever	Camnitz	Duggleby	Lynch	Maddox	
1906	Leifield	Willis	Phillippe	Leever	Lynch	Hillebrand	Karger	McFarland	
1905	Case	Flaherty	Phillippe	Leever	Lynch	Hillebrand	Robitaille	Leifield	
1904	Case	Flaherty	Phillippe	Leever	Lynch	Miller	Robitaille	Camnitz	
1903	Doheny	Kennedy	Phillippe	Leever	Wilhelm	Veil	Falkenberg		
1902	Doheny	Chesbro	Phillippe	Leever	Tannehill				

PRIMARY PITCHING STAFFS (CONT.)

Year	Starter	Starter	Starter	Starter	Starter	Closer	Bullpen	Bullpen	Bullpen
1901	Poole	Chesbro	Phillippe	Leever	Tannehill	Doheny	Wiltse		
1900	Waddell	Chesbro	Phillippe	Leever	Tannehill				
1899	Hoffer	Chesbro	Sparks	Leever	Tannehill	Gray	Rhines	Gardner	
1898	Rhines	Killen	Gardner	Hart	Tannehill	Hastings			
1897	Hawley	Killen	Gardner	Hughey	Tannehill	Hastings			
1896	Hawley	Killen	Hastings	Hughey	Foreman				
1895	Hawley	Killen	Hart	Gardner	Foreman	Moran	Colcolough		
1894	Ehret	Killen	Gumbert	Colcolough	Menefee	Nicol			
1893	Ehret	Killen	Gumbert	Terry		Gastright	Colcolough		
1892	Ehret	Baldwin	Smith	Terry	Galvin	Gumbert			
1891	King	Baldwin	Staley		Galvin	Maul			
1890	Baker	Anderson	Hecker	Sowders	Gumbert	Schmit	Phillips	Bowman	
1889	Staley	Galvin	Morris	Sowders		Maul			
1888	Staley	Galvin	Morris						
1887	McCormick	Galvin	Morris						
1886	Handiboe	Galvin	Morris	Hofford					
1885	Meegan	Galvin	Morris	O'Day					
1884	Sullivan	Neagle	Fox						
1883	Driscoll	Neagle	Barr	Taylor	Nolan				
1882	Driscoll	Salisbury	Arundel						

PRIMARY STARTING LINEUPS

Year	C	1B	2B	3B	SS	LF	CF	RF
2005	Cota	Ward	Castillo	Sanchez	Wilson	Bay	Redman	Lawton
2004	Kendall	Ward	Castillo	Stynes	Wilson	Bay	Redman	Wilson
2003	Kendall	Simon	Reboulet	Ramirez	Wilson	Giles	Lofton	Sanders
2002	Kendall	Young	Reese	Ramirez	Wilson	Giles	Brown	Mackowiak
2001	Kendall	Young	Meares	Ramirez	Wilson	Giles	Brown	Vander Wal
2000	Kendall	Young	Morris	Ramirez	Meares	Cordero	Giles	Vander Wal
1999	Kendall	Young	Morris	Sprague	Benjamin	Martin	Giles	Brown
1998	Kendall	Young	Womack	Ramirez	Collier	Martin	Allensworth	Guillen
1997	Kendall	Young	Womack	Randa	Polcovich	Martin	Allensworth	Guillen
1996	Kendall	Johnson	Garcia	Hayes	Bell	Martin	Kingery	Merced
1995	Parent	Johnson	Garcia	King	Bell	Martin	Brumfield	Merced
1994	Slaught	Hunter	Garcia	King	Bell	Martin	Van Slyke	Merced
1993	Slaught	Young	Garcia	King	Bell	Martin	Van Slyke	Merced
1992	LaValliere	Merced	Lind	Buechele	Bell	Bonds	Van Slyke	Espy
1991	LaValliere	Merced	Lind	Wehner	Bell	Bonds	Van Slyke	Bonilla
1990	LaValliere	Bream	Lind	King	Bell	Bonds	Van Slyke	Bonilla
1989	Ortiz	Redus	Lind	Bonilla	Bell	Bonds	Van Slyke	Wilson
1988	LaValliere	Bream	Lind	Bonilla	Belliard	Bonds	Van Slyke	Reynolds
1987	LaValliere	Bream	Ray	Bonilla	Pedrique	Bonds	Van Slyke	Reynolds
1986	Peña	Bream	Ray	Morrison	Belliard	Reynolds	Bonds	Orsulak
1985	Peña	Thompson	Ray	Madlock	Khalifa	Kemp	Wynne	Hendrick
1984	Peña	Thompson	Ray	Madlock	Berra	Mazzilli	Wynne	Frobel
1983	Peña	Thompson	Ray	Madlock	Berra	Easler	Wynne	Parker
1982	Peña	Thompson	Ray	Madlock	Berra	Easler	Moreno	Lacy
1981	Peña	Thompson	Garner	Madlock	Foli	Easler	Moreno	Parker
1980	Ott	Milner	Garner	Madlock	Foli	Easler	Moreno	Parker
1979	Ott	Stargell	Stennett	Madlock	Foli	Robinson	Moreno	Parker

PRIMARY STARTING LINEUPS (CONT.)

Year	C	1B	2B	3B	SS	LF	CF	RF
1978	Ott	Stargell	Garner	Berra	Taveras	Robinson	Moreno	Parker
1977	Dyer	Robinson	Stennett	Garner	Taveras	Oliver	Moreno	Parker
1976	Sanguillen	Stargell	Stennett	Hebner	Taveras	Zisk	Oliver	Parker
1975	Sanguillen	Stargell	Stennett	Hebner	Taveras	Zisk	Oliver	Parker
1974	Sanguillen	Robertson	Stennett	Hebner	Taveras	Stargell	Oliver	Zisk
1973	Sanguillen	Robertson	Cash	Hebner	Maxvill	Stargell	Oliver	Zisk
1972	Sanguillen	Stargell	Cash	Hebner	Alley	Davalillo	Oliver	Clemente
1971	Sanguillen	Robertson	Cash	Hebner	Alley	Stargell	Oliver	Clemente
1970	Sanguillen	Robertson	Mazeroski	Hebner	Alley	Stargell	Alou	Clemente
1969	Sanguillen	Oliver	Mazeroski	Hebner	Patek	Stargell	Alou	Clemente
1968	May	Clendenon	Mazeroski	Wills	Alley	Stargell	Alou	Clemente
1967	May	Clendenon	Mazeroski	Wills	Alley	Stargell	Alou	Clemente
1966	Pagliaroni	Clendenon	Mazeroski	Bailey	Alley	Stargell	Alou	Clemente
1965	Pagliaroni	Clendenon	Mazeroski	Bailey	Alley	Stargell	Virdon	Clemente
1964	Pagliaroni	Clendenon	Mazeroski	Bailey	Schofield	Lynch	Virdon	Clemente
1963	Pagliaroni	Clendenon	Mazeroski	Bailey	Schofield	Lynch	Virdon	Clemente
1962	Burgess	Stuart	Mazeroski	Hoak	Groat	Skinner	Virdon	Clemente
1961	Burgess	Stuart	Mazeroski	Hoak	Groat	Skinner	Virdon	Clemente
1960	Burgess	Stuart	Mazeroski	Hoak	Groat	Skinner	Virdon	Clemente
1959	Burgess	Stuart	Mazeroski	Hoak	Groat	Skinner	Virdon	Clemente
1958	Foiles	Kluszewski	Mazeroski	Thomas	Groat	Skinner	Virdon	Clemente
1957	Foiles	Fondy	Mazeroski	Freese	Groat	Skinner	Virdon	Clemente
1956	Shepard	Long	Mazeroski	Thomas	Groat	Walls	Virdon	Clemente
1955	Shepard	Long	O'Brien	Freese	Groat	Thomas	O'Brien	Clemente
1954	Atwell	Skinner	Roberts	Cole	Allie	Lynch	Thomas	Gordon
1953	Sandlock	Ward	O'Brien	O'Connell	O'Brien	Rice	Thomas	Abrams
1952	Garagiola	Bartirome	Merson	Castiglione	Groat	Kiner	Del Greco	Bell
1951	McCullough	Phillips	Murtaugh	Castiglione	Strickland	Kiner	Metkovich	Bell
1950	McCullough	Hopp	Murtaugh	Fernandez	Rojek	Kiner	Westlake	Bell
1949	McCullough	Hopp	Basgall	Castiglione	Rojek	Kiner	Saffell	Westlake
1948	Fitz Gerald	Stevens	Murtaugh	Gustine	Rojek	Kiner	Hopp	Walker
1947	Howell	Greenberg	Bloodworth	Gustine	Cox	Kiner	Russell	Westlake
1946	Lopez	Fletcher	Gustine	Handley	Cox	Van Robays	Kiner	Elliott
1945	Lopez	Dahlgren	Coscarart	Elliott	Gustine	Russell	Gionfriddo	O'Brien
1944	Lopez	Dahlgren	Coscarart	Elliott	Gustine	Russell	DiMaggio	Barrett
1943	Lopez	Fletcher	Coscarart	Elliott	Gustine	Russell	DiMaggio	Barrett
1942	Lopez	Fletcher	Gustine	Elliott	Coscarart	Van Robays	DiMaggio	Barrett
1941	Lopez	Fletcher	Gustine	Handley	Vaughan	Van Robays	DiMaggio	Elliott
1940	Davis	Fletcher	Gustine	Handley	Vaughan	Van Robays	DiMaggio	Elliott
1939	Mueller	Fletcher	Young	Handley	Vaughan	Rizzo	Waner	Waner
1938	Todd	Suhr	Young	Handley	Vaughan	Rizzo	Waner	Waner
1937	Todd	Suhr	Handley	Brubaker	Vaughan	Jensen	Waner	Waner
1936	Padden	Suhr	Young	Brubaker	Vaughan	Jensen	Waner	Waner
1935	Padden	Suhr	Young	Thevenow	Vaughan	Jensen	Waner	Waner
1934	Grace	Suhr	Lavagetto	Traynor	Vaughan	Lindstrom	Waner	Waner
1933	Grace	Suhr	Piet	Traynor	Vaughan	Waner	Lindstrom	Waner
1932	Grace	Suhr	Piet	Traynor	Vaughan	Barbee	Waner	Waner
1931	Phillips	Grantham	Piet	Traynor	Thevenow	Comorosky	Waner	Waner
1930	Hemsley	Suhr	Grantham	Traynor	Bartell	Comorosky	Waner	Waner
1929	Hargreaves	Sheely	Grantham	Traynor	Bartell	Comorosky	Waner	Waner
1928	Hargreaves	Grantham	Adams	Traynor	Wright	Barnhart	Waner	Waner
1927	Gooch	Harris	Grantham	Traynor	Wright	Barnhart	Waner	Waner

PRIMARY STARTING LINEUPS (CONT.)

Year	C	1B	2B	3B	SS	LF	CF	RF
1926	Smith	Grantham	Rhyne	Traynor	Wright	Barnhart	Carey	Waner
1925	Smith	Grantham	Moore	Traynor	Wright	Barnhart	Carey	Cuyler
1924	Gooch	Grimm	Maranville	Traynor	Wright	Cuyler	Carey	Barnhart
1923	Schmidt	Grimm	Rawlings	Traynor	Maranville	Bigbee	Carey	Barnhart
1922	Gooch	Grimm	Tierney	Traynor	Maranville	Bigbee	Carey	Russell
1921	Schmidt	Grimm	Cutshaw	Barnhart	Maranville	Bigbee	Carey	Whitted
1920	Schmidt	Grimm	Cutshaw	Whitted	Caton	Bigbee	Carey	Southworth
1919	Schmidt	Mollwitz	Cutshaw	Barbare	Terry	Southworth	Bigbee	Stengel
1918	Schmidt	Mollwitz	Cutshaw	McKechnie	Caton	Bigbee	Carey	Southworth
1917	Fischer	Wagner	Pitler	Boeckel	Ward	Bigbee	Carey	King
1916	Schmidt	Johnston	Farmer	Baird	Wagner	Costello	Carey	Hinchman
1915	Gibson	Johnston	Viox	Baird	Wagner	Carey	Collins	Hinchman
1914	Gibson	Konetchy	Viox	Mowrey	Wagner	Carey	Kelly	Mitchell
1913	Simon	Miller	Viox	Byrne	Wagner	Carey	Mitchell	Wilson
1912	Gibson	Miller	McCarthy	Byrne	Wagner	Carey	Wilson	Donlin
1911	Gibson	Hunter	Miller	Byrne	Wagner	Clarke	Leach	Wilson
1910	Gibson	Flynn	Miller	Byrne	Wagner	Clarke	Leach	Wilson
1909	Gibson	Abstein	Miller	Barbeau	Wagner	Clarke	Leach	Wilson
1908	Gibson	Swacina	Abbaticchio	Leach	Wagner	Clarke	Thomas	Wilson
1907	Gibson	Nealon	Abbaticchio	Storke	Wagner	Clarke	Leach	Anderson
1906	Gibson	Nealon	Ritchey	Sheehan	Wagner	Clarke	Beaumont	Ganley
1905	Peitz	Howard	Ritchey	Brain	Wagner	Clarke	Beaumont	Clymer
1904	Phelps	Bransfield	Ritchey	Leach	Wagner	Clarke	Beaumont	Sebring
1903	Phelps	Bransfield	Ritchey	Leach	Wagner	Clarke	Beaumont	Sebring
1902	Smith	Bransfield	Ritchey	Leach	Conroy	Clarke	Beaumont	Davis
1901	Zimmer	Bransfield	Ritchey	Leach	Ely	Clarke	Beaumont	Davis
1900	Zimmer	Cooley	Ritchey	Williams	Ely	Clarke	Beaumont	Wagner
1899	Bowerman	Clark	O'Brien	Williams	Ely	McCarthy	Beaumont	Donovan
1898	Schriver	Clark	Padden	Gray	Ely	McCarthy	O'Brien	Donovan
1897	Sugden	Davis	Padden	Hoffmeister	Ely	Smith	Brodie	Donovan
1896	Sugden	Beckley	Padden	Lyons	Ely	Smith	Stenzel	Donovan
1895	Merritt	Beckley	Bierbauer	Clingman	Cross	Smith	Stenzel	Donovan
1894	Mack	Beckley	Bierbauer	Lyons	Glasscock	Smith	Stenzel	Donovan
1893	Miller	Beckley	Bierbauer	Lyons	Glasscock	Smith	Van Haltren	Donovan
1892	Mack	Beckley	Bierbauer	Farrell	Shugart	Smith	Kelley	Donovan
1891	Mack	Beckley	Bierbauer	Reilly	Shugart	Browning	Hanlon	Carroll
1890	Decker	Hecker	LaRoque	Miller	Sales	Kelty	Sunday	Berger
1889	Miller	Beckley	Dunlap	Kuehne	Rowe	Fields	Hanlon	Sunday
1888	Miller	Beckley	Dunlap	Kuehne	Smith	Dalrymple	Sunday	Coleman
1887	Miller	Barkley	Smith	Whitney	Kuehne	Dalrymple	Brown	Coleman
1886	Carroll	Schomberg	Barkley	Whitney	Smith	Glenn	Mann	Brown
1885	Carroll	Field	Smith	Kuehne	Whitney	Eden	Mann	Brown
1884	Colgan	Knowles	Creamer	Battin	White	Miller	Taylor	Swartwood
1883	Hayes	Swartwood	Creamer	Battin	Mack	Mansell	Neagle	Dickerson
1882	Taylor	Lane	Strief	Battin	Peters	Mansell	Morton	Swartwood

Top 10 Batting Leaders, Single Season & Career with Team

Games Played: Career with Team

Player	G	PA
1. Roberto Clemente	2,433	10,212
Honus Wagner	2,433	10,220
3. Willie Stargell	2,360	9,026
4. Max Carey	2,178	9,654
5. Bill Mazeroski	2,163	8,379
6. Paul Waner	2,154	9,532
7. Pie Traynor	1,941	8,293
8. Lloyd Waner	1,803	7,776
9. Tommy Leach	1,574	6,646
10. Fred Clarke	1,479	6,368

At-Bats: Season

Player	AB	Year
1. Matty Alou	698	1969
2. Woody Jensen	696	1936
3. Omar Moreno	695	1979
4. Lloyd Waner	681	1931
5. Dick Groat	678	1962
6. Matty Alou	677	1970
7. Omar Moreno	676	1980
8. Rennie Stennett	673	1974
9. Rabbit Maranville	672	1922
10. Bill Virdon	663	1962

At-Bats: Career with Team

Player	AB	PA
1. Roberto Clemente	9,454	10,212
2. Honus Wagner	9,034	10,220
3. Paul Waner	8,429	9,532
4. Max Carey	8,406	9,654
5. Willie Stargell	7,927	9,026
6. Bill Mazeroski	7,755	8,379
7. Pie Traynor	7,559	8,293
8. Lloyd Waner	7,256	7,776
9. Tommy Leach	5,910	6,646
10. Fred Clarke	5,472	6,368

Batting Average: Season

Player	BA	Year
1. Arky Vaughan	.385	1935
2. Honus Wagner	.381	1900
3. Paul Waner	.380	1927
4. Jake Stenzel	.374	1895
5. Paul Waner	.373	1936
6. Paul Waner	.370	1928
7. Paul Waner	.368	1930
8. Pie Traynor	.366	1930
9. Honus Wagner	.363	1905
10. Paul Waner	.362	1934

Batting Average: Career with Team

Player	BA	PA
1. Paul Waner	.340	9,532
2. Kiki Cuyler	.336	2,288
3. Honus Wagner	.328	10,220
4. Matty Alou	.327	3,224
5. Elmer Smith	.324	3,425
Arky Vaughan	.324	6,181
7. Ginger Beaumont	.321	4,452
8. Pie Traynor	.320	8,293
9. Lloyd Waner	.319	7,776
10. Roberto Clemente	.317	10,212

Total Hits: Season

Player	H	Year
1. Paul Waner	237	1927
2. Lloyd Waner	234	1929
3. Matty Alou	231	1969
4. Lloyd Waner	223	1927
Paul Waner	223	1928
6. Lloyd Waner	221	1928
7. Kiki Cuyler	220	1925
8. Paul Waner	219	1937
Jimmy Williams	219	1899
10. Paul Waner	218	1936

Total Hits: Career with Team

Player	H	PA
1. Roberto Clemente	3,000	10,212
2. Honus Wagner	2,967	10,220
3. Paul Waner	2,868	9,532
4. Max Carey	2,416	9,654
Pie Traynor	2,416	8,293
6. Lloyd Waner	2,317	7,776
7. Willie Stargell	2,232	9,026
8. Bill Mazeroski	2,016	8,379
9. Arky Vaughan	1,709	6,181
10. Fred Clarke	1,638	6,368

Home Runs: Season

Player	HR	Year
1. Ralph Kiner	54	1949
2. Ralph Kiner	51	1947
3. Willie Stargell	48	1971
4. Ralph Kiner	47	1950
5. Willie Stargell	44	1973
6. Ralph Kiner	42	1951
7. Ralph Kiner	40	1948
8. Brian Giles	39	1999
9. Brian Giles	38	2002
10. Brian Giles	37	2001
Ralph Kiner	37	1952

Home Runs: Career with Team

Player	HR	PA
1. Willie Stargell	475	9,026
2. Ralph Kiner	301	4,732
3. Roberto Clemente	240	10,212
4. Barry Bonds	176	4,255
5. Dave Parker	166	5,267
6. Brian Giles	165	3,114
7. Frank Thomas	163	3,838
8. Bill Mazeroski	138	8,379
9. Kevin Young	136	4,208
10. Al Oliver	135	5,424

Triples: Season

Player	3B	Year
1. Chief Wilson	36	1912
2. Harry Davis	28	1897
3. Jimmy Williams	27	1899
4. Kiki Cuyler	26	1925
5. Adam Comorosky	23	1930
Elmer Smith	23	1893
7. Jake Beckley	22	1890
Tommy Leach	22	1902
Joe Visner	22	1890
Honus Wagner	22	1900
Paul Waner	22	1926

Triples: Career with Team

Player	3B	PA
1. Honus Wagner	232	10,220
2. Paul Waner	187	9,532
3. Roberto Clemente	166	10,212

4. Pie Traynor	164	8,293
5. Fred Clarke	156	6,368
6. Max Carey	148	9,654
7. Tommy Leach	139	6,646
8. Jake Beckley	134	4,737
9. Arky Vaughan	116	6,181
10. Lloyd Waner	114	7,776

DOUBLES: SEASON

Player	2B	Year
1. Paul Waner	62	1932
2. Paul Waner	53	1936
3. Paul Waner	50	1928
4. Adam Comorosky	47	1930
5. Dave Parker	45	1979
Andy Van Slyke	45	1992
Honus Wagner	45	1900
8. Bobby Bonilla	44	1991
Dave Parker	44	1977
Honus Wagner	44	1904
Jason Bay	44	2005

DOUBLES: CAREER WITH TEAM

Player	2B	PA
1. Paul Waner	558	9,532
2. Honus Wagner	551	10,220
3. Roberto Clemente	440	10,212
4. Willie Stargell	423	9,026
5. Max Carey	375	9,654
6. Pie Traynor	371	8,293
7. Dave Parker	296	5,267
8. Bill Mazeroski	294	8,379
9. Arky Vaughan	291	6,181
10. Al Oliver	276	5,424
Gus Suhr	276	5,725

EXTRA-BASE HITS: SEASON

Player	XBH	Year
1. Willie Stargell	90	1973
2. Kiki Cuyler	87	1925
3. Adam Comorosky	82	1930
Jason Bay	82	2005
5. Brian Giles	81	2001
6. Brian Giles	80	2002
Paul Waner	80	1932
8. Brian Giles	79	2000
Ralph Kiner	79	1951
10. Bobby Bonilla	78	1990
Ralph Kiner	78	1947
Ralph Kiner	78	1949

EXTRA-BASE HITS: CAREER WITH TEAM

Player	XBH	PA
1. Willie Stargell	953	9,026
2. Honus Wagner	865	10,220
3. Paul Waner	854	9,532
4. Roberto Clemente	846	10,212
5. Pie Traynor	593	8,293
6. Max Carey	590	9,654
7. Dave Parker	524	5,267
8. Bill Mazeroski	494	8,379
9. Arky Vaughan	491	6,181
10. Ralph Kiner	486	4,732

TOTAL BASES: SEASON

Player	TB	Year
1. Kiki Cuyler	369	1925
2. Ralph Kiner	361	1947
Ralph Kiner	361	1949
4. Roberto Clemente	342	1966
Paul Waner	342	1927
6. Brian Giles	340	2001
Dave Parker	340	1978
8. Dave Parker	338	1977
9. Willie Stargell	337	1973
10. Jason Bay	335	2005

TOTAL BASES: CAREER WITH TEAM

Player	TB	PA
1. Roberto Clemente	4,492	10,212
2. Honus Wagner	4,228	10,220
3. Willie Stargell	4,190	9,026
4. Paul Waner	4,127	9,532
5. Pie Traynor	3,289	8,293
6. Max Carey	3,288	9,654
7. Lloyd Waner	2,895	7,776
8. Bill Mazeroski	2,848	8,379
9. Arky Vaughan	2,484	6,181
10. Dave Parker	2,397	5,267

RUNS BATTED IN: SEASON

Player	RBI	Year
1. Paul Waner	131	1927
2. Ralph Kiner	127	1947
Ralph Kiner	127	1949
4. Honus Wagner	126	1901
5. Willie Stargell	125	1971
6. Pie Traynor	124	1928
7. Brian Giles	123	2000
Ralph Kiner	123	1948
9. Jake Stenzel	121	1894
Glenn Wright	121	1925

RUNS BATTED IN: CAREER WITH TEAM

Player	RBI	PA
1. Willie Stargell	1,540	9,026
2. Honus Wagner	1,475	10,220
3. Roberto Clemente	1,305	10,212
4. Pie Traynor	1,273	8,293
5. Paul Waner	1,177	9,532
6. Bill Mazeroski	853	8,379
7. Ralph Kiner	801	4,732
8. Gus Suhr	789	5,725
9. Jake Beckley	781	4,737
10. Arky Vaughan	764	6,181

RUNS SCORED: SEASON

Player	R	Year
1. Jake Stenzel	148	1894
2. Patsy Donovan	145	1894
3. Kiki Cuyler	144	1925
4. Paul Waner	142	1928
5. Max Carey	140	1922
6. Ginger Beaumont	137	1903
7. Lloyd Waner	134	1929
8. Lloyd Waner	133	1927
9. Paul Waner	131	1929
10. George Van Haltren	129	1893

RUNS SCORED: CAREER WITH TEAM

Player	R	PA
1. Honus Wagner	1,521	10,220
2. Paul Waner	1,493	9,532
3. Roberto Clemente	1,416	10,212
4. Max Carey	1,414	9,654
5. Willie Stargell	1,195	9,026
6. Pie Traynor	1,183	8,293
7. Lloyd Waner	1,151	7,776
8. Fred Clarke	1,015	6,368
9. Tommy Leach	1,009	6,646
10. Arky Vaughan	936	6,181

WALKS: SEASON

Player	BB	Year
1. Ralph Kiner	137	1951
2. Brian Giles	135	2002

Player		
3. Barry Bonds	127	1992
4. Ralph Kiner	122	1950
5. Elbie Fletcher	119	1940
6. Elbie Fletcher	118	1941
Arky Vaughan	118	1936
8. Ralph Kiner	117	1949
9. Brian Giles	114	2000
10. Ralph Kiner	112	1948

WALKS: CAREER WITH TEAM

Player	BB	PA
1. Willie Stargell	937	9,026
2. Max Carey	918	9,654
3. Paul Waner	909	9,532
4. Honus Wagner	877	10,220
5. Ralph Kiner	795	4,732
6. Arky Vaughan	778	6,181
7. Gus Suhr	679	5,725
8. Fred Clarke	630	6,368
9. Elbie Fletcher	625	3,820
10. Roberto Clemente	621	10,212

STRIKEOUTS: SEASON

Player	SO	Year
1. Craig Wilson	169	2004
2. Donn Clendenon	163	1968
3. Willie Stargell	154	1971
4. Donn Clendenon	142	1966
Jason Bay	142	2005
6. Donn Clendenon	136	1963
7. Jason Bay	129	2004
Willie Stargell	129	1972
Willie Stargell	129	1973
10. Donn Clendenon	128	1965
Jason Thompson	128	1983

STRIKEOUTS: CAREER WITH TEAM

Player	SO	PA
1. Willie Stargell	1,936	9,026
2. Roberto Clemente	1,230	10,212
3. Kevin Young	850	4,208
4. Donn Clendenon	840	3,865
5. Jay Bell	780	4,787
6. Dave Parker	777	5,267
7. Andy Van Slyke	733	4,432
8. Bill Mazeroski	706	8,379
9. Al Martin	684	3,583
10. Max Carey	646	9,654

SLUGGING PERCENTAGE: SEASON

Player	SLG	Year
1. Ralph Kiner	.658	1949
2. Willie Stargell	.646	1973
3. Ralph Kiner	.639	1947
4. Willie Stargell	.628	1971
5. Ralph Kiner	.627	1951
6. Barry Bonds	.624	1992
7. Brian Giles	.622	2002
8. Brian Giles	.614	1999
9. Arky Vaughan	.607	1935
10. Kiki Cuyler	.598	1925

SLUGGING PERCENTAGE: CAREER WITH TEAM

Player	SLG	PA
1. Brian Giles	.592	3,114
2. Ralph Kiner	.567	4,732
3. Willie Stargell	.529	9,026
4. Kiki Cuyler	.513	2,288
5. Dick Stuart	.512	2,213
6. Barry Bonds	.503	4,255
7. Dave Parker	.494	5,267
8. George Grantham	.491	3,765
9. Paul Waner	.490	9,532
10. Wally Westlake	.484	2,225

ON-BASE PERCENTAGE: SEASON

Player	OBP	Year
1. Arky Vaughan	.491	1935
2. Barry Bonds	.456	1992
3. Elmer Smith	.454	1896
George Grantham	.454	1929
5. Arky Vaughan	.453	1936
6. Ralph Kiner	.452	1951
7. Brian Giles	.450	2002
8. Jake Stenzel	.447	1895
9. Paul Waner	.446	1928
Paul Waner	.446	1936

ON-BASE PERCENTAGE: CAREER WITH TEAM

Player	OBP	PA
1. Brian Giles	.426	3,114
2. Arky Vaughan	.415	6,181
Elmer Smith	.415	3,425
4. George Grantham	.410	3,765
5. Paul Waner	.407	9,532
6. Ralph Kiner	.405	4,732
7. Elbie Fletcher	.403	3,820
8. Kiki Cuyler	.399	2,288
9. Honus Wagner	.394	10,220
10. Jason Kendall	.387	5,282

OPS (ON-BASE PERCENTAGE + SLUGGING PERCENTAGE): SEASON

Player	OPS	Year
1. Arky Vaughan	1.098	1935
2. Ralph Kiner	1.089	1949
3. Barry Bonds	1.080	1992
4. Ralph Kiner	1.079	1951
5. Brian Giles	1.072	2002
6. Ralph Kiner	1.055	1947
7. Willie Stargell	1.038	1973
8. Brian Giles	1.032	1999
9. Willie Stargell	1.026	1971
Brian Giles	1.026	2000

OPS (ON-BASE PERCENTAGE + SLUGGING PERCENTAGE): CAREER WITH TEAM

Player	OPS	PA
1. Brian Giles	1.018	3,114
2. Ralph Kiner	.971	4,732
3. Kiki Cuyler	.912	2,288
4. George Grantham	.901	3,765
5. Paul Waner	.896	9,532
6. Willie Stargell	.889	9,026
7. Arky Vaughan	.887	6,181
8. Barry Bonds	.883	4,255
9. Elmer Smith	.881	3,425
10. Honus Wagner	.862	10,220

STOLEN BASES: SEASON

Player	SB	Year
1. Omar Moreno	96	1980
2. Omar Moreno	77	1979
3. Omar Moreno	71	1978
Billy Sunday	71	1888
5. Frank Taveras	70	1977
6. Ned Hanlon	65	1890
7. Max Carey	63	1916
8. Max Carey	61	1913
Jake Stenzel	61	1894
Honus Wagner	61	1907

Stolen Bases: Career with Team

Player	SB	PA
1. Max Carey	688	9,654
2. Honus Wagner	639	10,220
3. Omar Moreno	412	3,978
4. Patsy Donovan	312	4,512
5. Tommy Leach	271	6,646
6. Fred Clarke	261	6,368
7. Barry Bonds	251	4,255
8. Doggie Miller	209	4,262
9. Frank Taveras	206	2,718
10. Ginger Beaumont	200	4,452

Sacrifice Hits: Season

Player	Sac	Year
1. Pie Traynor	42	1928
2. Jay Bell	39	1990
3. Max Carey	37	1912
George Cutshaw	37	1920
5. Bob Ganley	35	1906
Pie Traynor	35	1927
7. Doc Johnston	34	1915
8. Adam Comorosky	33	1930
9. Jay Bell	30	1991
Max Carey	30	1921
Fritz Mollwitz	30	1918

Sacrifice Hits: Career with Team

Player	Sac	PA
1. Max Carey	257	9,654
2. Pie Traynor	231	8,293
3. Honus Wagner	202	10,220
4. Fred Clarke	196	6,368
Tommy Leach	196	6,646
6. Paul Waner	158	9,532
7. Jay Bell	128	4,787
8. Dots Miller	127	2,962
9. Ginger Beaumont	119	4,452
10. Claude Ritchey	118	4,003

Hit by Pitch: Season

Player	HBP	Year
1. Jason Kendall	31	1997
Jason Kendall	31	1998
3. Craig Wilson	30	2004
4. Jason Kendall	25	2003
5. Jake Beckley	21	1895
Craig Wilson	21	2002
7. Jake Beckley	20	1893
Jason Kendall	20	2001
9. Jake Beckley	19	1894
Jason Kendall	19	2004
Dick Padden	19	1898

Hit by Pitch: Career with Team

Player	HBP	PA
1. Jason Kendall	177	5,282
2. Honus Wagner	107	10,220
3. Jake Beckley	106	4,737
4. Craig Wilson	81	1,847
5. Willie Stargell	78	9,026
6. Max Carey	73	9,654
7. Fred Clarke	70	6,368
8. Kevin Young	62	4,208
9. Al Oliver	61	5,424
10. Fred Carroll	50	3,290

Top 10 Pitching Leaders, Single Season & Career with Team

Games Pitched: Season

Player	GP	Year
1. Kent Tekulve	94	1979
2. Kent Tekulve	91	1978
3. Kent Tekulve	85	1982
4. Enrique Romo	84	1979
Salomon Torres	84	2004
6. Scott Sauerbeck	78	2002
Kent Tekulve	78	1980
Salomon Torres	78	2005
9. Rod Scurry	76	1982
Kent Tekulve	76	1983

Games Pitched: Career with Team

Player	GP	IP
1. Roy Face	802	1,314.7
2. Kent Tekulve	722	1,017.0
3. Bob Friend	568	3,480.3
4. Vern Law	483	2,672.0
5. Babe Adams	481	2,991.3
6. Wilbur Cooper	469	3,199.0
7. Dave Giusti	410	618.0
8. Sam Leever	388	2,660.7
9. Rip Sewell	385	2,108.7
10. Al McBean	376	1,016.0

Innings Pitched: Season

Player	IP	Year
1. Ed Morris	581.0	1885
2. Ed Morris	555.3	1886
3. Frank Mountain	503.0	1883
4. Ed Morris	480.0	1888
5. Pink Hawley	444.3	1895
6. Fleury Sullivan	441.0	1884
7. Pud Galvin	440.7	1887
8. Mark Baldwin	440.3	1892
9. Mark Baldwin	437.7	1891
10. Pud Galvin	437.3	1888

Innings Pitched: Career with Team

Player	IP
1. Bob Friend	3,480.3
2. Wilbur Cooper	3,199.0
3. Babe Adams	2,991.3
4. Ed Morris	2,678.0
5. Vern Law	2,672.0
6. Sam Leever	2,660.7
7. Pud Galvin	2,301.7
8. Deacon Phillippe	2,286.0
9. Rip Sewell	2,108.7
10. Ray Kremer	1,954.7

Batters Faced: Season

Player	BF	Year
1. Ed Morris	2,321	1885
2. Ed Morris	2,252	1886
3. Frank Mountain	2,177	1883
4. Ed Morris	2,002	1888
5. Fleury Sullivan	1,967	1884
6. Pud Galvin	1,897	1887
7. Pud Galvin	1,820	1886
8. Pud Galvin	1,809	1888
9. Harry Staley	1,791	1889
10. Ed Morris	1,703	1884

Batters Faced: Career with Team

Player	BF	IP
1. Bob Friend	14,644	3,480.3
2. Wilbur Cooper	13,123	3,199.0
3. Babe Adams	11,926	2,991.3
4. Vern Law	11,231	2,672.0
5. Ed Morris	11,120	2,678.0
6. Pud Galvin	9,928	2,301.7
7. Rip Sewell	9,042	2,108.7
8. Ray Kremer	8,330	1,954.7
9. Deacon Phillippe	8,016	2,286.0
10. Bob Veale	7,924	1,868.7

Games Started: Season

Player	GS	Year
1. Ed Morris	63	1885
Ed Morris	63	1886
3. Frank Mountain	59	1883
4. Ed Morris	55	1888
5. Mark Baldwin	53	1892
6. Ed Morris	52	1884
7. Fleury Sullivan	51	1884
8. Mark Baldwin	50	1891
Pud Galvin	50	1886
Pud Galvin	50	1888
Pink Hawley	50	1895
Frank Killen	50	1896

Games Started: Career with Team

Player	GS	IP
1. Bob Friend	477	3,480.3
2. Wilbur Cooper	371	3,199.0
3. Vern Law	364	2,672.0
4. Babe Adams	354	2,991.3
5. Ed Morris	307	2,678.0
6. Sam Leever	299	2,660.7
7. John Candelaria	271	1,873.0
8. Pud Galvin	267	2,301.7
9. Bob Veale	255	1,868.7
10. Deacon Phillippe	250	2,286.0

Complete Games: Season

Player	CG	Year
1. Ed Morris	63	1885
Ed Morris	63	1886
3. Frank Mountain	57	1883
4. Ed Morris	54	1888
5. Fleury Sullivan	51	1884
6. Pud Galvin	49	1886
Pud Galvin	49	1888
8. Mark Baldwin	48	1891
9. Pud Galvin	47	1887
Ed Morris	47	1884

Complete Games: Career with Team

Player	CG	IP
1. Ed Morris	297	2,678.0
2. Wilbur Cooper	263	3,199.0
3. Pud Galvin	248	2,301.7
4. Sam Leever	241	2,660.7
5. Deacon Phillippe	209	2,286.0
6. Babe Adams	206	2,991.3
7. Frank Killen	163	1,661.3
8. Bob Friend	161	3,480.3
9. Jesse Tannehill	148	1,499.0
10. Rip Sewell	137	2,108.7

Games Won: Season

Player	W	Year
1. Ed Morris	41	1886
2. Ed Morris	39	1885
3. Frank Killen	36	1893
4. Ed Morris	34	1884
5. Pink Hawley	31	1895
6. Frank Killen	30	1896
7. Pud Galvin	29	1886
Ed Morris	29	1888
9. Jack Chesbro	28	1902
Pud Galvin	28	1887

Games Won: Career with Team

Player	W	IP
1. Wilbur Cooper	202	3,199.0
2. Babe Adams	194	2,991.3
Sam Leever	194	2,660.7
4. Bob Friend	191	3,480.3
5. Ed Morris	171	2,678.0
6. Deacon Phillippe	168	2,286.0
7. Vern Law	162	2,672.0
8. Ray Kremer	143	1,954.7
Rip Sewell	143	2,108.7
10. Pud Galvin	137	2,301.7

Games Lost: Season

Player	L	Year
1. Fleury Sullivan	35	1884
2. Frank Mountain	33	1883
3. Silver King	29	1891
4. Mark Baldwin	28	1891
5. Mark Baldwin	27	1892
6. Jack Neagle	26	1884
Harry Staley	26	1889
8. Pud Galvin	25	1888
Harry Staley	25	1890
10. Ed Morris	24	1885

Games Lost: Career with Team

Player	L	IP
1. Bob Friend	218	3,480.3
2. Wilbur Cooper	159	3,199.0
3. Vern Law	147	2,672.0
4. Babe Adams	139	2,991.3
5. Pud Galvin	123	2,301.7
6. Ed Morris	122	2,678.0
7. Sam Leever	100	2,660.7
8. Rip Sewell	97	2,108.7
9. Roy Face	93	1,314.7
10. Deacon Phillippe	92	2,286.0

Winning Percentage: Season

Player	W%	Year
1. Roy Face	.947	1959
2. Deacon Phillippe	.875	1910
3. Emil Yde	.842	1924
4. Jack Chesbro	.824	1902
Bob Moose	.824	1969
6. Al McBean	.812	1963
Rip Sewell	.812	1948
8. Howie Camnitz	.806	1909
9. John Candelaria	.800	1977
Ed Doheny	.800	1902
Sam Leever	.800	1905

Winning Percentage: Career with Team

Player	W%	IP
1. Jesse Tannehill	.667	1,499.0
2. Sam Leever	.660	2,660.7
3. Vic Willis	.659	1,209.0
4. Jack Chesbro	.648	938.7
5. Deacon Phillippe	.646	2,286.0
6. Lee Meadows	.629	1,248.3
7. Ray Kremer	.627	1,954.7
Dave Giusti	.627	618.0
9. Jim Bibby	.610	654.7
10. Carmen Hill	.603	735.3

Shutouts: Season

Player	SHO	Year
1. Ed Morris	12	1886
2. Babe Adams	8	1920
Jack Chesbro	8	1902
Lefty Leifield	8	1906
Al Mamaux	8	1915
6. Steve Blass	7	1968
Wilbur Cooper	7	1917
Sam Leever	7	1903
Ed Morris	7	1885
Bob Veale	7	1965
Vic Willis	7	1908

Shutouts: Career with Team

Player	SHO	IP
1. Babe Adams	44	2,991.3
2. Sam Leever	39	2,660.7
3. Bob Friend	35	3,480.3
4. Wilbur Cooper	33	3,199.0
5. Lefty Leifield	29	1,578.0
Ed Morris	29	2,678.0
7. Vern Law	28	2,672.0
8. Deacon Phillippe	25	2,286.0
9. Vic Willis	23	1,209.0
10. Rip Sewell	20	2,108.7
Bob Veale	20	1,868.7

ERA: Season

Player	ERA	Year
1. Denny Driscoll	1.21	1882
2. Howie Camnitz	1.56	1908
3. Howie Camnitz	1.62	1909
4. Sam Leever	1.66	1907
5. Vic Willis	1.73	1906
6. Lefty Leifield	1.87	1906
Wilbur Cooper	1.87	1916
8. Jesse Tannehill	1.95	1902
9. Babe Adams	1.98	1919
10. Al Mamaux	2.04	1915

ERA: Career with Team

Player	ERA	IP
1. Vic Willis	2.08	1,209.0
2. Nick Maddox	2.29	605.3
3. Lefty Leifield	2.38	1,578.0
4. Sam Leever	2.47	2,660.7
5. Deacon Phillippe	2.50	2,286.0
6. Bob Harmon	2.60	769.7
7. Al Mamaux	2.61	713.3
8. Howie Camnitz	2.63	1,754.3
9. Kent Tekulve	2.68	1,017.0
10. Claude Hendrix	2.71	648.3

Earned Runs Allowed: Season

Player	ER	Year
1. Fleury Sullivan	206	1884
2. Frank Mountain	201	1883
3. Red Ehret	198	1894
4. Ad Gumbert	180	1894
5. Mark Baldwin	170	1892
6. Frank Killen	168	1893
7. Frank Killen	167	1897
8. Pink Hawley	166	1897
9. Frank Killen	164	1896
Harry Staley	164	1889

Earned Runs Allowed: Career with Team

Player	ER	IP
1. Bob Friend	1,372	3,480.3
2. Vern Law	1,118	2,672.0
3. Wilbur Cooper	974	3,199.0
4. Babe Adams	911	2,991.3
5. Ed Morris	838	2,678.0
6. Pud Galvin	824	2,301.7
7. Ray Kremer	816	1,954.7
8. Rip Sewell	804	2,108.7
9. Frank Killen	733	1,661.3
10. Sam Leever	731	2,660.7

Strikeouts: Season

Player	K	Year
1. Ed Morris	326	1886
2. Ed Morris	302	1884
3. Ed Morris	298	1885
4. Bob Veale	276	1965
5. Bob Veale	250	1964
6. Oliver Perez	239	2004
7. Bob Veale	229	1966
8. Bob Veale	213	1969
9. Larry McWilliams	199	1983
10. Mark Baldwin	197	1891

Strikeouts: Career with Team

Player	K	IP
1. Bob Friend	1,682	3,480.3
2. Bob Veale	1,652	1,868.7
3. Ed Morris	1,217	2,678.0
4. Wilbur Cooper	1,191	3,199.0
5. John Candelaria	1,159	1,873.0
6. Vern Law	1,092	2,672.0
7. Babe Adams	1,036	2,991.3
8. Steve Blass	896	1,597.3
9. Dock Ellis	869	1,430.0
10. Deacon Phillippe	861	2,286.0

Strikeouts per Nine IP: Season

Player	K/9	Year
1. Oliver Perez	10.97	2004
2. Bob Veale	9.34	1965
3. Bob Moose	8.74	1969
4. Bob Veale	8.49	1969
5. Jose DeLeon	8.24	1985
6. Bob Veale	8.05	1964
7. Bob Veale	7.94	1967
8. Bob Veale	7.93	1970
9. Bob Veale	7.68	1966
10. Jon Lieber	7.65	1997

Strikeouts per Nine IP: Career with Team

Player	K/9	IP
1. Bob Veale	7.96	1,868.7
2. Denny Neagle	7.14	697.0
3. Paul Wagner	6.96	536.7
4. Bert Blyleven	6.73	697.7
5. Jason Schmidt	6.71	799.7
6. Jon Lieber	6.70	682.7
7. Kip Wells	6.65	716.0
8. Francisco Cordova	6.41	753.7
9. Kris Benson	6.36	782.0
10. Luke Walker	6.22	732.7

Hits Allowed: Season

Player	HA	Year
1. Frank Mountain	546	1883
2. Fleury Sullivan	496	1884
3. Pud Galvin	490	1887
4. Frank Killen	476	1896
5. Ed Morris	470	1888
6. Ed Morris	459	1885
7. Pud Galvin	457	1886
8. Ed Morris	455	1886
9. Pink Hawley	449	1895
10. Mark Baldwin	447	1892

HITS ALLOWED: CAREER WITH TEAM

Player	HA	IP
1. Bob Friend	3,610	3,480.3
2. Wilbur Cooper	3,074	3,199.0
3. Vern Law	2,833	2,672.0
4. Babe Adams	2,832	2,991.3
5. Pud Galvin	2,517	2,301.7
6. Ed Morris	2,468	2,678.0
7. Sam Leever	2,449	2,660.7
8. Deacon Phillippe	2,187	2,286.0
9. Ray Kremer	2,108	1,954.7
10. Rip Sewell	2,082	2,108.7

HITS ALLOWED PER NINE IP: SEASON

Player	H/9	Year
1. Al Mamaux	6.51	1915
2. Howie Camnitz	6.58	1909
3. Oliver Perez	6.66	2004
4. Howie Camnitz	6.75	1907
5. Bob Veale	6.86	1968
6. Jose DeLeon	6.88	1984
7. Wilbur Cooper	6.91	1916
Lefty Leifield	6.91	1908
9. Howie Camnitz	6.92	1908
10. Adonis Terry	6.94	1892

HITS ALLOWED PER NINE IP: CAREER WITH TEAM

Player	H/9	IP
1. Nick Maddox	7.24	605.3
2. Al Mamaux	7.33	713.3
3. Vic Willis	7.53	1,209.0
4. Claude Hendrix	7.73	648.3
5. Howie Camnitz	7.84	1,754.3
6. Bob Veale	7.85	1,868.7
7. Frank Miller	7.88	769.0
8. Kent Tekulve	7.96	1,017.0
9. Lefty Leifield	8.00	1,578.0
10. Doug Drabek	8.10	1,362.7

WALKS ALLOWED: SEASON

Player	BB	Year
1. Mark Baldwin	227	1891
2. Mark Baldwin	194	1892
3. Marty O'Toole	159	1912
4. Pink Hawley	157	1896
5. Silver King	144	1891
6. Frank Killen	140	1893
7. Al Mamaux	136	1916
8. Bill Hart	135	1895
9. Red Ehret	128	1894
10. Bob Veale	124	1964

WALKS ALLOWED: CAREER WITH TEAM

Player	BB	IP
1. Bob Friend	869	3,480.3
2. Bob Veale	839	1,868.7
3. Wilbur Cooper	762	3,199.0
4. Rip Sewell	740	2,108.7
5. Steve Blass	597	1,597.3
Vern Law	597	2,672.0
7. Sam Leever	587	2,660.7
8. Howie Camnitz	532	1,754.3
9. Frank Killen	519	1,661.3
10. Ed Morris	498	2,678.0

WALKS ALLOWED PER NINE IP: SEASON

Player	BB/9	Year
1. Denny Driscoll	0.54	1882
2. Babe Adams	0.62	1920
3. Babe Adams	0.79	1919
Babe Adams	0.79	1922
5. Deacon Phillippe	0.86	1902
6. Deacon Phillippe	0.90	1903
7. Jesse Tannehill	0.97	1902
8. Harry Salisbury	0.99	1882
9. Denny Driscoll	1.04	1883
10. Ed Morris	1.07	1884

WALKS ALLOWED PER NINE IP: CAREER WITH TEAM

Player	BB/9	IP
1. Denny Driscoll	.85	537.3
2. Deacon Phillippe	1.18	2,286.0
3. Babe Adams	1.29	2,991.3
4. Jesse Tannehill	1.45	1,499.0
5. Zane Smith	1.57	768.3
6. Pud Galvin	1.64	2,301.7
7. Ed Morris	1.67	2,678.0
8. Waite Hoyt	1.68	616.3
Red Lucas	1.68	684.3
10. Bill Swift	1.79	1,555.0

WHIP (WALKS + HITS PER NINE IP): SEASON

Player	WHIP	Year
1. Denny Driscoll	0.866	1882
2. Babe Adams	0.896	1919
3. Ed Morris	0.898	1884
4. Ed Morris	0.964	1885
5. Howie Camnitz	0.972	1909
6. Babe Adams	0.981	1920
7. Jesse Tannehill	0.987	1902
8. Vern Law	0.998	1965
9. Babe Adams	1.006	1911
Hank Robinson	1.006	1912

WHIP (WALKS + HITS PER IP): CAREER WITH TEAM

Player	WHIP	IP
1. Vic Willis	1.082	1,209.0
2. Nick Maddox	1.085	605.3
3. Deacon Phillippe	1.087	2,286.0
4. Babe Adams	1.090	2,991.3
5. Ed Morris	1.108	2,678.0
6. Frank Miller	1.109	769.0
7. Sam Leever	1.141	2,660.7
8. Doug Drabek	1.148	1,362.7
9. Bob Harmon	1.152	769.7
10. Nelson Briles	1.174	550.3

HOME RUNS ALLOWED: SEASON

Player	HRA	Year
1. Murry Dickson	32	1951
2. John Candelaria	29	1977
Ray Kremer	29	1930
4. Josh Fogg	28	2002
Bob Friend	28	1957
Ron Kline	28	1957
7. Murry Dickson	27	1953
Brian Fisher	27	1987
Josh Fogg	27	2005
10. Murry Dickson	26	1952
Harvey Haddix	26	1959
Ron Kline	26	1956
Todd Ritchie	26	2000
Don Robinson	26	1982

HOME RUNS ALLOWED: CAREER WITH TEAM

Player	HRA	IP
1. Bob Friend	273	3,480.3
2. Vern Law	268	2,672.0
3. John Candelaria	172	1,873.0
4. Roy Face	130	1,314.7
5. Steve Blass	128	1,597.3
6. Ron Kline	124	1,251.3
7. Murry Dickson	122	1,216.3

Ray Kremer	122	1,954.7
9. Rip Sewell	114	2,108.7
10. Doug Drabek	112	1,362.7

SAVES: SEASON

Player	SV	Year
1. Mike Williams	46	2002
2. Jose Mesa	43	2004
3. Jim Gott	34	1988
4. Kent Tekulve	31	1978
Kent Tekulve	31	1979
6. Dave Giusti	30	1971
7. Rich Loiselle	29	1997
8. Roy Face	28	1962
9. Jose Mesa	27	2005
10. Dave Giusti	26	1970
Rich Gossage	26	1977
Bill Landrum	26	1989

SAVES: CAREER WITH TEAM

Player	SV	IP
1. Roy Face	188	1,314.7
2. Kent Tekulve	158	1,017.0
3. Mike Williams	140	321.7
4. Dave Giusti	133	618.0
5. Jose Mesa	70	126.0
6. Stan Belinda	61	260.7
7. Al McBean	59	1,016.0
8. Bill Landrum	56	229.0
9. Jim Gott	50	140.3
10. Rich Loiselle	49	224.0

WILD PITCHES: SEASON

Player	WP	Year
1. Harry Staley	30	1889
2. Ed Morris	28	1886
3. Ed Morris	25	1885
4. Mark Baldwin	24	1891
5. Kirtley Baker	22	1890
Silver King	22	1891
7. Harry Staley	18	1890
Bob Veale	18	1964
9. Mark Baldwin	17	1892
Pink Hawley	17	1896
Don Robinson	17	1982
Bob Veale	17	1965

WILD PITCHES: CAREER WITH TEAM

Player	WP	IP
1. Bob Veale	90	1,868.7
2. Ed Morris	84	2,678.0
3. Pud Galvin	67	2,301.7
4. Bob Walk	66	1,303.0
5. Harry Staley	63	1,086.7
6. Don Robinson	61	1,203.0
7. Steve Blass	56	1,597.3
8. Rick Rhoden	51	1,448.0
9. Bob Friend	50	3,480.3
10. Bruce Kison	47	1,266.3

HIT BATSMEN: SEASON

Player	HB	Year
1. Pink Hawley	27	1897
2. Jack Chesbro	21	1902
3. Fleury Sullivan	20	1884
4. Ed Doheny	19	1903
5. Jack Neagle	18	1884
6. Kirtley Baker	17	1890
Jesse Tannehill	17	1900
8. Don Cardwell	16	1963
Lefty Leifield	16	1911
10. Charlie Case	15	1905
Wilbur Cooper	15	1919
Ed Doheny	15	1902
Mike Lynch	15	1904
Nick Maddox	15	1909

HIT BATSMEN: CAREER WITH TEAM

Player	HB	IP
1. Wilbur Cooper	93	3,199.0
2. Sam Leever	90	2,660.7
3. Lefty Leifield	76	1,578.0
4. Jesse Tannehill	70	1,499.0
5. Ed Morris	60	2,678.0
6. Jack Chesbro	58	938.7
7. Pud Galvin	57	2,301.7
8. Howie Camnitz	55	1,754.3
9. Deacon Phillippe	53	2,286.0
10. Bruce Kison	49	1,266.3

GAMES FINISHED: SEASON

Player	GF	Year
1. Kent Tekulve	67	1979
2. Jose Mesa	65	2004
Kent Tekulve	65	1978
4. Kent Tekulve	64	1982
5. Mike Williams	63	2000
6. Roy Face	61	1960
7. Dave Giusti	60	1973
8. Jim Gott	59	1988
Mike Williams	59	2002
10. Rich Loiselle	58	1997

GAMES FINISHED: CAREER WITH TEAM

Player	GF	IP
1. Roy Face	547	1,314.7
2. Kent Tekulve	470	1,017.0
3. Dave Giusti	306	618.0
4. Mike Williams	252	321.7
5. Al McBean	167	1,016.0
6. Ramon Hernandez	146	347.7
7. Don Robinson	140	1,203.0
8. Stan Belinda	135	260.7
9. Rich Loiselle	129	224.0
10. Mace Brown	128	852.7

Significant Pirates

ADAMS, BABE (SP)
(1907, 1909–1916, 1918–1926)

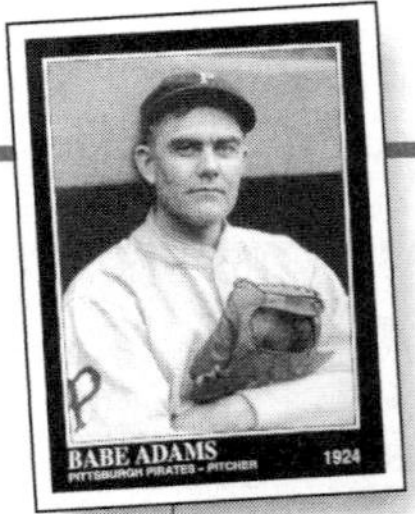

The Pirates purchased Babe Adams from the Cardinals in September 1906 after he had appeared in only one game for St. Louis all year. Pittsburgh brought Adams up for a few games in 1907, then for good in 1909 in time to join the powerhouse Pirates in their championship run. During the 1909 season, Adams, who possessed a blazing fastball and incredible control, was a spot starter and reliever. He had a 12–3 record with a sterling 1.11 ERA by season's end. Before the World Series against the Tigers, National League President John Heydler suggested to Pittsburgh Manager Fred Clarke that he consider starting Adams in the first game, instead of staff ace and 25-game winner Howie Camnitz, because Detroit had had trouble all year against pitchers with exceptional fastballs. Clarke took Heydler's advice and started his rookie in Game 1. After a shaky first inning, Adams settled down and won, 4–1. He then won Game 5 and Game 7, pitching an 8–0 shutout in the clincher. In each win, Adams pitched a complete-game six-hitter. He became an overnight sensation and went on to have two 20-win seasons in 1911 and 1913. On May 17, 1914, Adams lost a 21-inning duel with Rube Marquard and didn't walk a batter, still a major league record for most innings pitched in a game without issuing a walk. Adams' control was so good that by the time he retired after 18 seasons in a Pirate uniform, he had averaged only 1.29 walks per nine innings pitched. He also led the league five times in WHIP.

In 1926, the defending World Series Champion Pirates were experiencing a team meltdown, with future Hall of Famer Max Carey mired in a horrible slump. Fred Clarke, now the team vice president, often sat on the bench in full uniform. He suggested to Manager Bill McKechnie that he bench Carey, even if he had to put the batboy in. When asked what they thought of the situation, Adams and several other players supported McKechnie's decision to leave Carey in the game. Carey called a team meeting and a player revolt ensued, although a majority of the players voted that Clarke should be allowed to sit on the bench. Still, Clarke retaliated for the mutiny by demanding that the outspoken players be disciplined. Pittsburgh management lashed out at everyone involved. Team morale sank. Carey was suspended and then traded to Brooklyn. Adams and Carson Bigbee were unconditionally released. McKechnie was fired at season's end, and Clarke soon thereafter. National League President Heydler eventually exonerated Adams and the others on insubordination charges, but maintained the team's right to let them go. Adams never played in the major leagues again. He died in 1968.

CAREER PIRATES RECORD:

W	L	W%	ERA	SV
194	139	.583	2.74	15

K	BB	SHO	IP
1,036	428	44	2,991.3

BECKLEY, JAKE (1B)
(1888–1889, 1891–1896)

Jake Beckley was purchased from the St. Louis Whites in midseason 1888, and finished the year with Pittsburgh. A big man for his time, the 5'10" 200-pound first baseman hit so well he gave Cap Anson a run for the batting title, ultimately losing out .344 to .343. Beckley hit over .300 six times in his eight-year Pittsburgh career. Like many other major leaguers in 1890, Beckley jumped to the Players' League, joining its Pittsburgh club for its one season in operation before returning to the National League's Pittsburgh club in 1891. On July 25, 1896, Beckley was traded to the New York Giants for Harry Davis and $1,000 cash. He played 11½ more years with New York, Cincinnati, and St. Louis before retiring. He was elected to the Hall of Fame in 1971.

CAREER PIRATES RECORD:

Games	AB	Hits	Runs
928	3,795	1,137	699
Avg	**HR**	**RBI**	**SB**
.300	43	661	138

BONDS, BARRY (OF)
(1986–1992)

Barry Bonds may or may not eventually break Hank Aaron's all-time home run mark, and he'll eventually go into the Hall of Fame as a Giant, but he started his amazing career in Pittsburgh in 1986. Bonds came to the majors with a bona fide baseball pedigree: Major leaguer Bobby Bonds was his father; his mother was Reggie Jackson's cousin; his godfather was Willie Mays. Bonds was originally drafted by the San Francisco Giants in the June 1982 amateur draft, but chose not to sign when the Giants offered him only $70,000, five grand less than he wanted. He went to Arizona State instead and played for three years. The Pirates then chose him as the sixth pick overall in the June 1985 amateur draft (after San Francisco had passed over Bonds, taking Will Clark with the second pick).

By early 1986, Bonds was playing for the Pirates. He wasn't all that productive in his first few years, however, and he ruffled more than a few feathers with his moodiness. With a four-year average around .250 and no more than 59 RBIs in any of his first four years, Bonds was shopped around, but the Pirates found no takers. As fortune would have it, Bonds had a breakout year in 1990, hitting .301 with 33 homers, 114 RBIs, 104 runs, and 52 steals as he led the Pirates to the NL East title. He won his first Gold Glove and the NL MVP Award. Bonds had similarly productive years in 1991 and 1992 (when he won his second MVP Award); in each of those seasons the Pirates won nearly 100 games and the NL East championship, but were beaten in the NLCS. In the fall of 1992, with three tremendous seasons under his belt, Bonds entered the free-agent market and returned to his hometown of San Francisco, signing a seven-year deal with the Giants worth $43 million. *(See Giants bio.)*

CAREER PIRATES RECORD:

Games	AB	Hits	Runs
1,010	3,584	984	672
Avg	**HR**	**RBI**	**SB**
.275	176	556	251

CAREY, MAX (OF) (1910–1926)

Maximilian Carnarius had just completed six years of seminary school in 1909 and was about to embark on a career as a minister when he attended a Central League game in Terre Haute, Indiana. After the game, Carnarius told the manager of the South Bend Greens that he could play better than the Greens shortstop. Carnarius was given a tryout and made the team. To protect his amateur status, he played under the name Max Carey. The next fall he enrolled in Concordia Seminary in St. Louis. When he returned to his team, he discovered a better shortstop had taken his place, so he switched to the outfield. After he hit .293, the Pirates bought his contract and brought him to Pittsburgh in 1911.

For the next 12 years or so, Carey was the best outfielder in the National League. His great speed was perfectly suited for running down fly balls in spacious Forbes Field. He led the National League in putouts nine times, and trails only Willie Mays and Tris Speaker in career outfield putouts. Five times he led the NL in double plays and four times in assists. As a hitter, Carey led the league in steals 10 times and finished second three times. In six seasons he swiped more than 50 bases. (In 1922, he stole 51 bases and was caught only twice.) When he retired, his 738 career steals stood at the top of the National League's all-time list until Lou Brock surpassed him. Carey was about a .260–.270 hitter for most of his career until he played in an exhibition game against Detroit in 1924. After studying Cobb's stance and grip, which were similar to Honus Wagner's, Carey adopted them both. Suddenly, after 15 years in the majors, at the age of 35, he hit a blistering .343 with a career high in doubles (39). The new stance and grip allowed him to raise his career average to .284 by the time he retired. In the 1925 World Series against Washington, Carey hit .458 and scored six runs. Afflicted with sinus trouble in 1926, Carey got off to a slow start and was having a bad year when Fred Clarke, now a Pirate executive, suggested to Manager McKechnie that Carey be benched, even in favor of the batboy. This set off a chain of events that led to Carey's suspension. *(See Babe Adams bio, above.)* After Carey's suspension was overturned by NL President Heydler, the Pirates put Carey on waivers and he was picked up by Brooklyn. After three-plus years with the Dodgers, Carey retired. Eighty years later, Carey is still the Pirates' all-time leader in stolen bases with 688. He was elected to the Hall of Fame in 1961 and died in 1976.

CAREER PIRATES RECORD:

Games	AB	Hits	Runs
2,178	8,406	2,416	1,414
Avg	**HR**	**RBI**	**SB**
.287	67	719	688

CLARKE, FRED (OF) (1900–1911, 1913, 1915); MGR (1900–1915)

Outfielder Fred Clarke had been playing and starring for the Louisville Colonels for six years, and managing the team for three, when the National League decided to contract from 12 teams to eight. As part of the deal, Louisville owner Barney Dreyfuss was made half-owner of the Pittsburgh Pirates and was allowed to bring his best players with him. This nucleus of incredibly talented players included Rube Waddell, Honus Wagner, Deacon Phillippe, Tommy Leach, and Fred Clarke as player-manager. With this influx of star power, Pittsburgh competed with Brooklyn for the pennant, but finished a close second. Under Clarke, the Pirates then went on to win NL pennants in 1901, 1902, and 1903. Clarke was especially talented at grooming his pitching staff; during his 19-year managing tenure, his pitchers accumulated 25 seasons of 20 or more wins. Only fellow Hall of Famer Al Lopez, who produced 16 such pitchers in 17 seasons with Cleveland and the White Sox, approaches Clarke's record. As a hitter, Clarke batted over .300 six times with the Pirates and 11 times overall. Ten times he scored over 95 runs, five with the Pirates. He had nearly 2,700 hits when he retired. He was elected to the Hall of Fame as a player in 1945, though his Pittsburgh managerial career (1,422–969, for a winning percentage of .595) was equally impressive. He died in 1960.

CAREER PIRATES RECORD:

Games	AB	Hits	Runs
1,479	5,472	1,638	1,015

Avg	HR	RBI	SB
.299	33	622	261

PIRATES MANAGERIAL RECORD:

Wins	Losses	W%
1,422	969	.595

CLEMENTE, ROBERTO (OF)
(1955–1972)

Roberto Clemente will always hold a special place in the hearts of Pirates fans for both his stellar playing career and his sterling character. The Brooklyn Dodgers originally signed the Puerto Rican-born Clemente in 1952 for $10,000. Shortly thereafter, he received offers of two and three times that amount, but he was contractually bound. The Dodgers kept trying to hide Clemente from the Giants, keeping him buried in the minors. Once he hit three triples in a game, only to be benched in the next. When he struck out two or three times in a game, he was immediately penciled in for the next day's lineup. On another occasion he came up with the bases loaded in the first inning and was pulled for a pinch-hitter. The moves frustrated Clemente, who didn't understand the Dodgers' bizarre strategy.

After Clemente returned to Puerto Rico following his exasperating first season, his car was rammed by a drunk driver and he suffered injuries to three spinal discs that would hamper him for the rest of his life. The last-place Pirates drafted Clemente away from the Dodgers on November 22, 1954, in the Rule V Draft. (Rule V stated that a minor leaguer could be claimed by any team if he wasn't brought up to the majors within a certain amount of time.) Clemente had a great arm, and in his first two seasons he threw out a combined 38 runners on the base paths. He also hit .311 in 1956. In 1960 Clemente hit .314, leading the Pirates to the NL title and a World Series championship over the Yankees. He felt slighted at placing only eighth in the MVP voting, especially after hitting safely in all seven games of the World Series for a .310 Series average.

In 1961, in an effort to curb himself from swinging at so many wild pitches, Clemente changed to a heavier bat. He immediately won his first batting title, hitting .351. In the first of the two All-Star Games played in 1961, Clemente tripled off Whitey Ford for the NL's first hit, scored the game's first run, knocked in the second run with a sacrifice fly, and singled home the game winner in the bottom of the

10th. From then on, Clemente wore his 1961 All-Star Game ring, not his 1960 World Series ring. In the 13 years from 1960 to 1972, he would hit over .300 12 times, falling short only in an injury-plagued 1968 season, when he hit .291. Clemente was a very aggressive player, and frequently injured; the press often called him a hypochondriac as they covered his shoulder, his backaches, flu attacks, a nervous stomach, infected tonsils, diarrhea spasms, headaches, and bone chips in his throwing arm. He even contracted malaria in 1965. In spite of his ailments, Clemente won batting titles again in 1964 and 1965 and made some legendary throws from the outfield. Once, with the bases loaded, the batter hit a seeming single to right and the runner on third jogged home, only to be nailed for a force-out by Clemente's powerful throw!

In 1966, when he won the National League's MVP Award, Clemente felt the injustice of 1960 had been corrected and he became a true team leader. When teammate Matty Alou arrived in Pittsburgh, he was struggling at the plate. Manager Harry Walker, a hitting expert, couldn't convince Alou to slow down by switching to a heavier bat, but Clemente got through to him; Alou raised his average more than 100 points and won the 1966 batting title. Clemente won a fourth batting title in 1967, hitting .357. When the Pirates began a youth movement in 1969, bringing in Richie Hebner, Manny Sanguillen, and Al Oliver, Clemente's role as a mentor was enhanced. He led by example, hitting .345, .352, and .341 in 1969–1971. When Three Rivers Stadium was unveiled, a ceremony was held to honor Clemente—a contingent of Puerto Ricans delivered a scroll signed by 300,000 fellow islanders to wish him well.

Perhaps Clemente's greatest season came in 1971 when he led the young Bucs into the playoffs. After dispatching the Giants in the NLCS, the Pirates were heavy underdogs to the pitching-rich Orioles, whose staff included Jim Palmer, Dave McNally, and Mike Cuellar. There was some bad blood between Cuellar and Clemente since Cuellar had haughtily dismissed Clemente's attempt to help him during an offseason winter league game. The Orioles team as a whole seemed to share Cuellar's arrogance, especially since Baltimore had won its last 11 regular-season games and swept Oakland in the ALCS. Matters only got worse in the press as the Orioles took the first two games of the Series, extending their winning streak to 16 straight games. But the Pirates won Game 3 when Clemente, hustling on an easy grounder to Cuellar, forced the pitcher to make a bad throw. Cuellar, visibly rattled as Clemente danced off first base, subsequently walked Willie Stargell before Bob Robertson won the game with a three-run homer. The Pirates took Games 4 and 5, the Orioles Game 6. Cuellar started Game 7 for Baltimore and had a perfect game going with two out in the fourth when Clemente stepped to the plate, jumped on the first pitch, and sent it over the left-field wall. The Pirates won 2–1 and Clemente was named the Series MVP. For a second time, Clemente had gotten a hit in all seven games of the World Series.

In an injury-riddled 1972 season, Clemente still managed to hit .312. He collected his 3000th hit on a double off Jon Matlack in the last game of the season. In late December of that year, a devastating earthquake struck

Nicaragua, killing more than 6,000 and leaving tens of thousands homeless. Clemente took it upon himself to raise money and needed supplies for the survivors. Upon hearing that some or all of his intended relief supplies were not reaching the right people, Clemente decided to fly to Nicaragua to check things out for himself. Shortly after takeoff, the plane crashed into the ocean, killing all aboard. The 12-time All-Star and 12-time Gold Glove winner was dead at the age of 38. Major league baseball had just instituted a new award in 1971 for the player who best exemplified baseball on and off the field; it was renamed the Roberto Clemente Award in 1973. The Hall of Fame waived the required five-year waiting period from a player's last game and inducted him into Cooperstown in 1973, just as it had done for Lou Gehrig. A statue of Clemente was unveiled outside Three Rivers Stadium during the 1994 All-Star Game in Pittsburgh.

CAREER PIRATES RECORD:

Games	AB	Hits	Runs
2,433	9,454	3,000	1,416
Avg	**HR**	**RBI**	**SB**
.317	240	1,305	83

COOPER, WILBUR (SP)
(1912–1924)

Pitcher Wilbur Cooper signed with the Pirates in 1912 and played the first 13 years of his 15-year career in Pittsburgh. Cooper won 20 or more games four times in his career, leading the National League in 1921 with 22 wins (his career best was 24 in 1920). Cooper was a fast worker, skilled at picking off runners, especially at third base. He worked so well with his catching staff that often they wouldn't even use signals. After the 1924 season, Cooper was traded to the Cubs and played two more uneventful years for the Cubs and the Tigers before retiring. His 202 wins as a Pirate is still the team record. He died in 1973.

CAREER PIRATES RECORD:

W	L	W%	ERA	SV
202	159	.560	2.74	14
K	**BB**	**SHO**	**IP**	
1,191	762	33	3,199.0	

CUYLER, KIKI (OF)
(1921–1927)

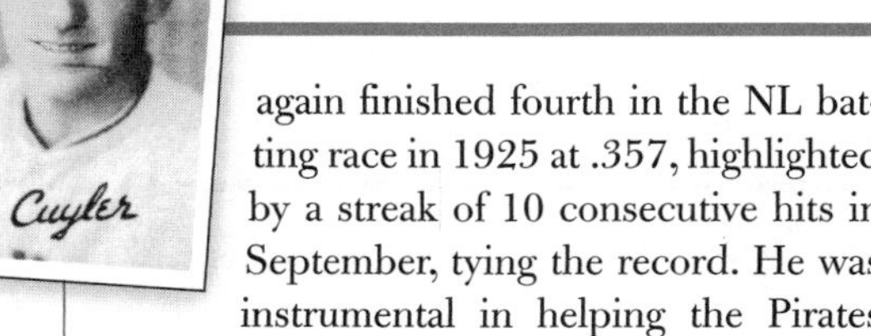

After being named the Southern Association's Most Valuable Player in 1923, Hazen "Kiki" Cuyler was called up to the Pirates at season's end, and, by 1924, had become a regular in the Pittsburgh outfield. Cuyler finished fourth in the NL batting race in 1924 with a .354 average. He was fourth in triples with 16 and second in steals with 32, behind teammate Max Carey. Cuyler again finished fourth in the NL batting race in 1925 at .357, highlighted by a streak of 10 consecutive hits in September, tying the record. He was instrumental in helping the Pirates win the 1925 World Series against the Senators.

When Paul Waner arrived in 1926, followed the next year by his younger brother Lloyd (who promptly hit .355 as a rookie), it appeared as if the Pirates were in the early stages of a true dynasty. But discord was growing. Cuyler disappeared after a heated squabble with new Pirates manager Donie Bush, who moved Cuyler from his usual #3 slot in the batting order to #2. Cuyler felt his skills were better suited for the three-hole, where he could drive in more runs. He offered to bat anywhere in the lineup but #2, but his pleas fell on deaf ears. Cuyler responded by having a bad year (for him), hitting .309. Halfway through the '27 season, he was tagged out on the base paths while attempting to break up a double play by standing up to block the fielder instead of sliding. Bush benched Cuyler for the remaining 70 games of the season, and even held him out during the 1927 World Series drubbing at the hands of the Yankees. Siding with his manager, owner Barney Dreyfuss traded Cuyler to the Cubs after the World Series. Cuyler achieved genuine stardom during eight years with the Cubs, before spending the last four years of his career with Cincinnati and Brooklyn. Cuyler died in 1950 and was elected to the Hall of Fame in 1968. *(See Cubs bio.)*

CAREER PIRATES RECORD:

Games	AB	Hits	Runs
525	2,025	680	415
Avg	**HR**	**RBI**	**SB**
.336	38	312	130

DONOVAN, PATSY (OF)
(1892–1899)

Donovan was a fine base runner who hit over .300 during six of his eight seasons patrolling the outfield. Three times he stole more than 40 bases in a season. He was also the player-manager for the Pirates in 1897 and 1899. However, his biggest claim to fame occurred after his playing and managing career ended; he was personally acquainted with one of the Xaverian brothers who coached a teenager named Babe Ruth at a Baltimore orphanage. Thanks to this connection, Ruth was brought to the attention of the Boston Red Sox.

CAREER PIRATES RECORD:

Games	AB	Hits	Runs
979	4,175	1,283	839
Avg	**HR**	**RBI**	**SB**
.307	13	424	312

FACE, ROY (RP)
(1953, 1955–1968)

One of baseball's smallest pitchers, Roy Face had a big-time forkball (called the split-fingered fastball today). Acquired from the Dodgers in the 1952 Rule V Draft (the same process that would be used two years later to spirit Roberto Clemente away from the Dodgers), he came up to the Pirates immediately in 1953. During his first two seasons, Face was a spot starter and reliever, but for the rest of his career he was strictly a reliever, usually the closer. After winning his last five decisions in 1958, Face had one of baseball's most memorable pitching seasons ever in 1959 when he won his first 17 decisions, giving him

22 straight wins over two seasons. He finished the 1959 season 18–1, setting new records for winning percentage and relief wins in a year. Face, a three-time All-Star with the Pirates, recorded three saves in the 1960 World Series victory over the Yankees. During his career, he led the National League in saves three times and finished in the top five 10 different seasons. After 15 seasons in Pittsburgh, Face was purchased by the Tigers near the end of the 1968 season, but pitched just one inning for Detroit before being released. He played one final year for the Montreal Expos before retiring after the 1969 season.

CAREER PIRATES RECORD:

W	L	W%	ERA	SV
100	93	.518	3.46	188

K	BB	SHO	IP
842	346	0	1,314.7

FRIEND, BOB (SP)
(1951–1965)

The Pirates signed Bob Friend as an amateur free agent before the 1949 season. After being called up in 1951, Friend remained with the team for 15 years. He was a workhorse pitcher who always gave his manager a lot of steady, if unspectacular, innings. His below .500 career win-loss record reflects the lousy Pirate teams of the early and mid-1950s. From 1955 through 1965, Friend pitched at least 200 innings each year, twice leading the league. In 1956 he led the National League with 314 innings, and in 1957 he led with 277. In 1955 he earned the dubious but significant distinction of being the only pitcher in major league history to lead his league in ERA while playing for a last-place team. In 1958, however, things turned around for Friend as the Pirates improved. He led the league with 22 victories, and in 1960 he was 18–12 for the World Series champions. Following the 1965 season, the Pirates traded their three-time All-Star pitcher to the Yankees, where he spent half a season before being traded to the Mets, where he completed the season and his career in 1966. After his career, Friend became involved in Pittsburgh-area business and politics, serving for years in elected office in Allegheny County.

CAREER PIRATES RECORD:

W	L	W%	ERA	SV
191	218	.467	3.55	10

K	BB	SHO	IP
1,682	869	35	3,480.3

GALVIN, PUD (SP)
(1885–1889, 1891–1892)

Pittsburgh, an American Association team in 1885, purchased Jim "Pud" Galvin from the National League's Buffalo Bisons on July 13 in an effort to bolster its pitching staff. The eight-year veteran had already posted season win totals of 46, 46, 37, 28, and 28 during his career and Pittsburgh was hoping for more of the same. What they got, however, was a pitcher on the down side of his career. Over the seven seasons he played with Pittsburgh, Galvin had only three winning seasons and won "just" 125 games, an average of about 18 a year, a far cry from his earlier days. On July 21, 1892, Galvin faced

Tim Keefe in the last battle of 300-game winners until Don Sutton and Phil Niekro hooked up in 1986. Galvin had 11 children, and often joked about forming his own baseball team and calling it the "Galvanized Nine." He died, penniless, in a Pittsburgh rooming house in 1902 at the age of 45. Fan contributions paid for his funeral. In 1965 Galvin was elected to the Hall of Fame and, almost miraculously, two of his children were still alive and attended the ceremonies in Cooperstown.

CAREER PIRATES RECORD:

W	L	W%	ERA	SV
125	110	.532	3.10	0
K	BB	SHO	IP	
434	370	16	2,084.7	

GROAT, DICK (SS)
(1952, 1955–1962)

As an All-American basketball player at Duke University in the early 1950s, Groat set an NCAA single-season scoring record of 831 points (a total that has since been surpassed). He was also a baseball All-American at shortstop, coveted by many major league teams. Since he had been born and raised just a few miles from Forbes Field and grown up a Pirates fan, there was never any doubt which team he would play for if he got the chance. After playing just over half a season with the Pirates in 1952, Groat left baseball to play professional basketball for a year with the Fort Wayne Pistons, then spent two years in the Army at Fort Belvoir, Virginia, where he led the base's baseball and basketball teams to the worldwide Army championships—the first time in history a single Army base won both titles the same year. During his two years in the Army, Groat averaged 35 points a game in basketball and hit .362 and .377 on the baseball diamond.

Groat returned to the Pirates in 1955 when his Army tour was up and teamed up with Bill Mazeroski at second base to form one of the most formidable double-play combinations in baseball. Groat hit .315 in 1957 and .300 in 1958. Prior to the 1960 season, rumors were flying that Groat was going to be traded for Roger Maris, but Pirates Manager Danny Murtaugh vetoed the deal. Groat responded by hitting a National League-leading .325 for his beloved Pirates and winning the National League's MVP Award, the first Pirate to do so since 1927. He also won the Lou Gehrig Memorial Award that same year. Though he had a fractured wrist during the World Series against the Yankees, Groat was instrumental in helping the Bucs bring home the title, hitting a key RBI single in the five-run eighth inning of Game 7.

After having his third All-Star year in 1962, Groat was unexpectedly traded to the Cardinals for pitcher Don Cardwell in an effort to bolster the Pirate pitching staff. The trade not only stunned Pirates fans, but Groat as well. No Pirate was identified with more than local hero Dick Groat and he had aspirations of becoming a coach and manager for the Pirates after he retired. Groat played five more years for St. Louis, Philadelphia, and San Francisco before retiring after the 1967 season. Even though he continued to live in the Pittsburgh area, running a golf course and announcing Duquesne University basketball games, he refused to have any formal contact with the Pirates until 1990, when his ailing wife requested he take part in a 30-year reunion of the 1960 World Series champion team.

CAREER PIRATES RECORD:

Games	AB	Hits	Runs
1,258	4,950	1,435	554
Avg	HR	RBI	SB
.290	30	454	6

KENDALL, JASON (C)
(1996–2004)

Jason Kendall was drafted by the Pirates in the first round of the June 1992 amateur draft. After his 1996 call-up, he was Pittsburgh's regular catcher on Opening Day; he then proceeded to hit .300 and become the first Pirate rookie ever to make the All-Star team. Kendall's hitting numbers improved in almost every category each of his first three years. While playing in approximately the same number of games each season, his homer totals went from 3 to 8 to 12; his RBIs from 42 to 49 to 75; his runs scored from 54 to 71 to 95; his stolen bases from 5 to 18 to 26 (which set a new National League record for a catcher); and his batting average from .300 to .294 to .327. In 1999, his fourth season in the majors, Kendall was on his way to easily surpassing every one of his previous personal bests when, on July 4, he fractured his leg in horrific fashion as he crossed the first-base bag. The videotape, which was replayed for weeks on television, made viewers physically ill. Kendall bounced back in 2000, setting new career highs in runs scored, triples, hits, homers, plate appearances, and walks. He also hit .320. After hitting over .300 in six of his nine seasons with the Pirates, the speedy catcher was sent to Oakland for pitchers Arthur Rhodes and Mark Redman by the cost-conscious Pittsburgh owners.

CAREER PIRATES RECORD:

Games	AB	Hits	Runs
1,252	4,606	1,409	706
Avg	**HR**	**RBI**	**SB**
.306	67	471	140

KINER, RALPH (OF)
(1946–1953)

The Pirates signed Ralph Kiner as an amateur free agent just before the 1941 season. After playing a couple of minor league seasons, Kiner enlisted in the Navy during World War II, and devoted two years to military service. Kiner arrived in Pittsburgh in 1946 and became the team's left fielder, hitting 23 homers in gigantic Forbes Field to tie the team record and win the NL crown.

In 1947 the Pirates acquired slugger Hank Greenberg, the 1946 American League home run champion, giving the team a powerful 1–2 home run punch. To take advantage of the two right-handed sluggers' power, the Pirates reconfigured Forbes Field by placing a double-wide bullpen in left field, effectively reducing the distance down the left-field line from 365 feet to 335, and the distance in the left-center power alley from 406 to 355. Kiner's home run totals flourished. Although he only had three homers by Memorial Day in 1947, Kiner hit 48 more over the final four months of the season to finish his second year with 51, again winning the NL home run crown. During one four-game stretch in September, Kiner set a record by hitting eight home runs.

When Bing Crosby bought into the Pirates in 1946, Kiner gained access to the Hollywood scene, even dating Elizabeth Taylor and Esther Williams. His homers brought fans back to the stadium. Even though the Pirates were perennial losers, attendance soared in Pittsburgh. Fans would stay in the park watching hopeless causes just to watch Kiner's last at-bat. Kiner won the NL home run title again in 1948 by hitting 40 blasts. In 1949 he clouted 16 homers in September to finish at 54, two short of Hack Wilson's all-time National League record. He also became the first NL player in history to hit 50 or more homers twice. Kiner hit 47 homers in 1950 to win the NL home run crown for the fifth straight year; his 101 homers in two consecutive years set another record. In 1951 and 1952, he again led the NL in homers, giving him seven straight home run titles from the start of his career, something neither Babe Ruth nor Hank Aaron ever accomplished.

Ralph Kiner had a lot of fans, but Pirates General Manager Branch Rickey was not one of them. After Kiner won his seventh straight home run crown, Rickey tried to cut Kiner's salary by 25 percent. In a famous statement, Rickey said to Kiner, a six-time All-Star, "We finished last with you, we can finish last without you." On June 4, 1953, Rickey traded Kiner to the Cubs as part of a 10-player deal. Kiner, who was beginning to be plagued by recurring back problems, hit 35 homers in Chicago, finishing fifth in the league, the first time in his career he didn't win the title. He only played $2^1/_2$ seasons with the Cubs and then Indians after the trade before retiring at the age of 33. In 1962 he joined the lowly New York Mets as part of their broadcast crew and has been an announcer for the team for the last 44 years.

CAREER PIRATES RECORD:

Games	AB	Hits	Runs
1,095	3,713	1,097	754
Avg	**HR**	**RBI**	**SB**
.280	301	801	19

KREMER, RAY (SP)
(1924–1933)

The Pirates bought Ray Kremer from the Oakland minor league club late in the 1923 season while actually scouting another player. The hard-drinking Kremer looked much older than his 30 years when he arrived in Pittsburgh, causing management to reprimand the scout for signing a 50-year-old pitcher (to which the scout replied, "I don't care if he's 60—he's still a good pitcher.") When Kremer broke into the big leagues in 1924, he finished with a fine 18–10 record. In his first seven years in Pittsburgh, Kremer won between 15 and 20 games each year. Twice (1926 and 1927) he led the National League in ERA, and twice (1926 and 1930) he led in wins. Kremer was the winning pitcher in both Game 6 and Game 7 of the 1925 World Series against Washington. Known for his drinking binges, he once wrecked a Pullman car on a road trip and threw all of his teammates' shoes out the window. Kremer pitched his entire 10-year career with the Pirates and only had one losing year, 1931, when he finished 11–15. He retired in 1933 after compiling a 10.35 ERA in just seven games.

CAREER PIRATES RECORD:

W	L	W%	ERA	SV
143	85	.627	3.76	10
K	**BB**	**SHO**	**IP**	
516	483	14	1,954.7	

LAW, VERNON (SP)
(1950–1951, 1954–1967)

Vern Law was signed as an amateur free agent in 1948 when Idaho Senator Herman Welker recommended him to Pirates Vice President Bing Crosby. He arrived in Pittsburgh in 1950 and played his entire 16-year career with the Pirates, missing only 1952 and 1953 because of Korean War military service. Like his stablemate Bob Friend, Law was a workhorse of a pitcher who ate up a lot of innings in unspectacular fashion for the Pirates for many years. He suddenly blossomed in 1959, going 18–9 with a 2.98 ERA for the improving Pirates. In 1960 he improved to 20–9, leading the Pirates to the World Series. He not only won two games in the Series, but snagged the NL Cy Young Award as well. Law had only one other notable year in 1965, when he finished 17–9 with a sparkling 2.15 ERA. Vern and his wife VaNita had six children: Veldon, Veryl, Vaughn, Varlin, VaLynda, and Vance, who became a major leaguer himself in 1980 with the Pirates.

CAREER PIRATES RECORD:

W	L	W%	ERA	SV
162	147	.524	3.77	13
K	**BB**	**SHO**	**IP**	
1,092	597	28	2,672.0	

LEEVER, SAM (SP)
(1898–1910)

Pitcher Sam Leever signed with the Pirates in 1898 and played his entire 13-year career with the team, suffering only one losing season during his career in 1899, when he finished 21–23—although he did lead the league in innings pitched that year with 379. He was a 20-game winner three more times, with a career-best 25–7 record and 2.08 ERA in 1903, the year he led the Pirates to the World Series against Boston. During one stretch in 1903, Pirates pitchers hurled six consecutive shutouts (Leever had two of them), setting a major league record that still stands. Before the Series, however, Leever injured his arm skeet shooting, another sport at which he was a champion performer. He was ineffective in his two starts against Boston, losing both as he allowed 13 hits and two walks in just 10 innings. He rebounded in 1905 and 1906, going 20–5 and 22–7, respectively. Over the next four seasons, Leever began to be used more in relief than as a starter. In Pittsburgh's next championship season, 1909, he was 8–1, but did not appear in the World Series against Detroit. After the 1910 season, Leever retired with a .660 winning percentage, which ranks him third in 20th-century National League history, and tenth all time.

CAREER PIRATES RECORD:

W	L	W%	ERA	SV
194	100	.660	2.47	13
K	**BB**	**SHO**	**IP**	
847	587	39	2,660.7	

MAZEROSKI, BILL (2B)
(1956–1972)

Bill Mazeroski was signed as an amateur free agent before the 1954 season, at the age of 17. After two and a half years in the minors, he was called up to Pittsburgh in July 1957 and remained there for the next 17 seasons. A decent hitter, "Maz" made his name in the majors with consistently excellent defense. His nickname was "No Touch," because he never seemed to touch the ball when he turned the double play, but only seemed to redirect the ball to first. He earned such a reputation for his defense that when he went to the first of his seven All-Star Games and took infield practice, all the other players stopped what they were doing to watch him field and throw. It was the ultimate tribute, as when opposing players used to stop their practice to watch Ted Williams hit. Mazeroski, who won eight Gold Gloves during his career, holds more defensive records than any other player in major league history.

Author Bill James concluded that Mazeroski was the most impressive defensive player in history. In the book *Baseball Ratings,* author Charles Faber awards points for various categories of statistics and takes into account certain variables. Faber's analysis determines that Mazeroski was the best defensive player at any position in any era of baseball history. Ironically, despite all the accolades for his defense, Mazeroski will always be most remembered for one trip to the plate during the 1960 World Series. With the Series tied at three games apiece, and Game 7 tied, 9–9, in the bottom of the ninth, Mazeroski hit a fastball from New York's Ralph Terry over the left-field wall to give Pittsburgh the World Series title against the heavily favored Yankees. It was the first World Series ever to end in such dramatic fashion, and it is said that Mickey Mantle literally cried for hours after the game. Casey Stengel was fired. And Bill Mazeroski went down in history. In 1972, with injuries taking their toll, Mazeroski retired at the age of 35 after playing just 34 games in his final year. In 2001, Mazeroski finally received his long-overdue selection to the Baseball Hall of Fame in Cooperstown.

CAREER PIRATES RECORD:

Games	AB	Hits	Runs
2,163	7,755	2,016	769
Avg	**HR**	**RBI**	**SB**
.260	138	853	27

MORRIS, ED (SP)
(1885–1889)

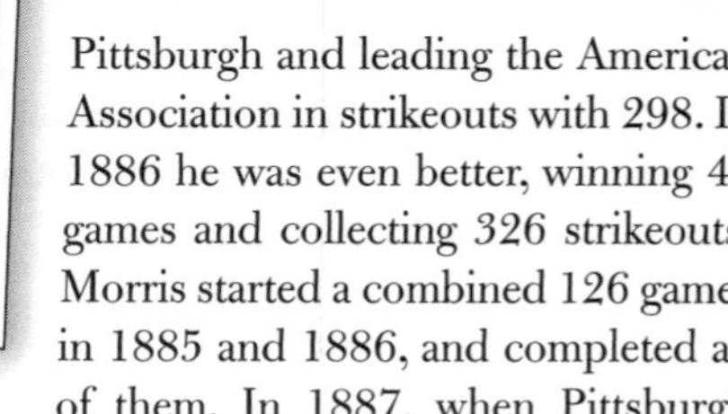

Ed "Cannonball" Morris was purchased by Pittsburgh after his Columbus Buckeyes franchise in the American Association folded up shop following the 1884 season. Morris had won 34 games for Columbus in his rookie season, using an explosive leaping delivery. In 1885 he continued to impress, winning 39 games for Pittsburgh and leading the American Association in strikeouts with 298. In 1886 he was even better, winning 41 games and collecting 326 strikeouts. Morris started a combined 126 games in 1885 and 1886, and completed all of them. In 1887, when Pittsburgh switched major leagues by jumping from the American Association to the National League,

Morris fell on hard times, finishing 14–22. Overwork had caused arm trouble and a new major league rule now prevented his leaping delivery. After a year of perfecting a new delivery, Morris bounced back in 1888 to win 29 games. He also threw 54 complete games in 1888. The excessive innings, however, destroyed his arm. In 1889 Morris was only able to start 21 games, finishing 6–13. Morris jumped to the new Players' League in 1890, but managed only an 8–7 record and retired at the age of 27 with worsening arm troubles.

CAREER PIRATES RECORD:

W	L	W%	ERA	SV
129	102	.558	2.81	1
K	BB	SHO	IP	
890	412	25	2,104.0	

OLIVER, AL (OF)
(1968–1977)

Al Oliver signed with the Pirates as an amateur free agent in June 1964. After five years in the minors he was called up to Pittsburgh to play first base. After a year or so, he was moved to the outfield, primarily because he was such a poor fielder at first. Oliver was noted for his line drives, routinely hitting the ball harder than most other players. Pirate announcer Bob Prince liked to say, "Oliver is hitting .280, but it's a hard .280." Oliver was at the core of a new batch of young Pirates who arrived in the late 1960s—Manny Sanguillen and Richie Hebner were also rookies who came up in 1969—joining veterans like Willie Stargell, Roberto Clemente, and Bob Robertson. Soon the Pirates became known as "the Lumber Company." Oliver helped the Pirates win five division titles. He spent the first ten years of his career in Pittsburgh, topping .300 four times, and making the All-Star team three times. In December 1977, Oliver was involved in a four-team deal that sent him to Texas.

CAREER PIRATES RECORD:

Games	AB	Hits	Runs
1,302	5,026	1,490	689
Avg	HR	RBI	SB
.296	135	717	54

PARKER, DAVE (OF)
(1973–1983)

The Pittsburgh Pirates drafted Parker in the 14th round of the June 1970 amateur draft. Despite his size and power numbers in high school, Parker went low in the draft for two reasons: a knee injury suffered while playing football during his senior year and his reputation for being loud and disruptive. The Pirates brought Parker up to the majors in 1973, mainly to fill the void created by Roberto Clemente's death a few months earlier. He excelled in the field and at the plate. Parker could steal bases, throw runners out at home, and hit the ball out of the park. During the last half of the 1970s, Parker was considered the best player in all of baseball. When his stats overshadowed Clemente's at the same stage of their careers, the local papers built Parker up to be a savior. He won three straight Gold Gloves from 1977 to 1979, won back-to-back batting titles in 1977 and 1978, and appeared in four All-Star Games in the five years from 1977 to 1981, copping the All-Star Game MVP Award in 1979. He won the National League MVP in 1978 for a courageous season that almost single-handedly brought the Pirates back from a 12-game deficit to a half-game out from August 12 to September 5. After breaking his jaw in a collision at the plate in July, Parker returned, wearing a football facemask connected to his batting helmet. He finished with 30 homers, 117 RBIs, and a .334 average.

Parker then became baseball's highest-paid player, making $900,000 per year. In 1979 he hit .310 for his fifth straight .300+ season, and he led Pittsburgh's "We Are Family" team to a World Series title over the Orioles in seven games. Starting in 1980, Parker's numbers began to fall. His old knee injury acted up. His weight ballooned. And he started using cocaine. Not only did the Pittsburgh fans and press turn on him—so much for "Family"—but they also became vicious. During the 1982 ceremony honoring Willie Stargell's career, a fan threw a battery that just missed Parker's head. When his contract expired following the 1983 season, no one in Pittsburgh seemed to care that the Pirates made no attempt to resign him. In December 1983 Parker signed as a free agent with Cincinnati and played the next four years with the Reds before he was traded to Oakland.

CAREER PIRATES RECORD:

Games	AB	Hits	Runs
1,301	4,848	1,479	728
Avg	**HR**	**RBI**	**SB**
.305	166	758	123

PHILLIPPE, DEACON (SP)
(1900–1911)

Charles "Deacon" Phillippe was a control specialist who spent his rookie season in 1899 with the National League's Louisville Colonels, where he compiled a 21–17 record. When the National League contracted in 1900 and did away with the Louisville team, Phillippe was one of the players owner Barney Dreyfuss was allowed to take with him as the new part-owner of the Pittsburgh team. Phillippe then played the remaining 12 years of his career with Pittsburgh, becoming an integral part of the powerhouse Pirates of the first decade of the 20th century.

Phillippe won 20 or more games in five of his first six seasons in Pittsburgh, helping to assuage the loss of Jack Chesbro and Jesse Tannehill, who had jumped to the rival American League. When the two leagues made a tentative peace in 1903, Dreyfuss challenged Boston, the American League champion, to a best-of-nine World Series against his champion Pirates. The Pirates were loaded with great pitching in 1903, but by the time the Series arrived, several of Pittsburgh's pitchers were laid up with injuries. Once the World Series began, it looked as if Deacon Phillippe might be able to pull off the pitching duties all by himself. He beat Cy Young in Game 1, 7–3. With just one day's rest, Phillippe came back in Game 3 and pitched a four-hitter to lead the Pirates to victory again. A travel day and a rainout gave Phillippe two days' rest, so he came back in Game 4 and won again, 5–4. No other Pirate pitcher could win, however, and the series was eventually tied at three games apiece. Dreyfuss wanted to give Phillippe another day of rest, so he canceled Game 7, claiming it was too cold to play. After three full days off, Phillippe came back in Game 7, but lost, 7–3. With the Series on the line, the teams moved to Boston for Game 8. Another travel day and another rainout gave Phillippe an extra day's rest before he took to the mound again. He pitched his fifth complete game of the Series (a record that will likely never be broken), but lost 3–0.

Not surprisingly, he was bothered by arm trouble for the rest of his career; over the next eight seasons, Phillippe won 20 games only once more. When he retired after the 1911 season, his career ratio of 1.25 walks per nine innings pitched was destined to become the best of any 20th-century pitcher. He died in 1952. In 1969, Phillippe was voted as the best right-handed pitcher in Pittsburgh's history.

CAREER PIRATES RECORD:

W	L	W%	ERA	SV
168	92	.646	2.50	11

K	BB	SHO	IP
861	299	25	2,286.0

SANGUILLEN, MANNY (C)
(1967, 1969–1976, 1978–1980)

The Pirates signed ever-smiling Panamanian Manny Sanguillen as an amateur free agent on October 2, 1964. He arrived in Pittsburgh in 1969 with fellow rookies Al Oliver and Richie Hebner; together they formed the nucleus of the powerful Pirates teams of the 1970s. A free-swinging catcher who bounced around behind the plate like a cat, Sanguillen, who rarely saw a pitch he didn't like, walked only 223 times in 13 major league seasons, 12 of which were spent with Pittsburgh. His best friend in the world was Roberto Clemente; Sanguillen was devastated when the great right fielder died in the December 31, 1972 plane crash. Sanguillen was the only Pirate who did not attend Clemente's funeral, choosing instead to dive the waters where Clemente's plane had crashed in a futile effort to find his friend. In 1973 Sanguillen was moved to right field to take over for Clemente, but the experiment failed badly. After a couple months, he returned to catching and the Pirates brought up Dave Parker to play right field.

Although he helped them to five division championships, Pittsburgh traded their three-time All-Star catcher to Oakland following the 1976 season for manager Chuck Tanner in a rare player-for-manager trade. Sanguillen stayed in Oakland for only one season, however, as the A's traded him back to Pittsburgh just before the 1978 season began. Sanguillen played three more seasons in Pittsburgh before retiring after the 1980 campaign.

CAREER PIRATES RECORD:

Games	AB	Hits	Runs
1,296	4,491	1,343	524

Avg	HR	RBI	SB
.299	59	527	33

SEWELL, RIP (SP)
(1938–1949)

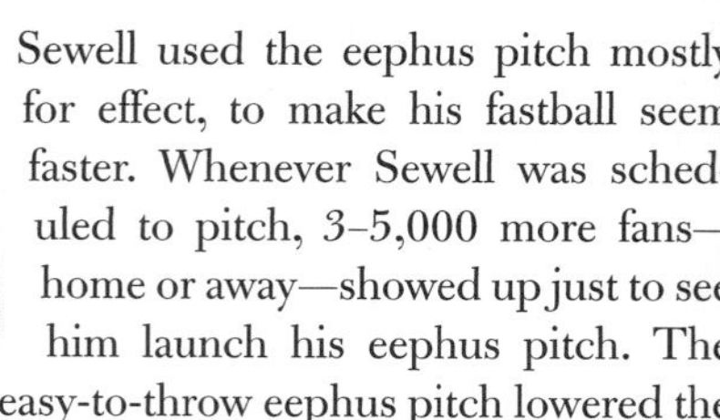
TRUETT "Rip" SEWELL

Truett "Rip" Sewell had pitched in only five games as a rookie for Detroit when he got into a fistfight with superstar teammate Hank Greenberg. Demoted to the minors, Sewell languished there for seven years before the Pirates claimed him in 1938 and brought him to Pittsburgh almost immediately. He won 10 games in 1939, 16 in 1940, and 14 in 1941. While hunting in the fall of 1941, a fellow hunter mistook Sewell for game and accidentally shot him at close range with a shotgun. The pellets tore holes in his foot as big as marbles. Sewell's injury required him to learn a new way to walk as well as pitch. His new delivery led to the development of a new "blooper" pitch. The blooper was thrown in an arc, about 25 feet high, and dropped over (or onto) the plate. The first time Sewell used it in an exhibition game, he struck out Tigers bonus baby Dick Wakefield and the crowd loved it. When members of the press asked him what he called his new pitch, fellow Pirate Maurice Van Robays suggested the name "eephus," adding somewhat enigmatically, "Eephus ain't nothin', and that's a nothin' pitch." The name stuck.

The eephus pitch made its regular-season debut in dramatic fashion. The Pirates were leading Chicago, 1–0, in the ninth inning. The bases were loaded, there were two outs, and the count was full on Cubs hitter Dom Dallessandro. When Sewell arced the ball 25 feet into the air and it dropped over the plate for strike three, ending the game, Dallessandro stood like a statue at the plate while the crowd went crazy. Dallessandro eventually pointed the bat at Sewell and told him, "If this was a rifle, I'd shoot you right between the eyes."

Sewell used the eephus pitch mostly for effect, to make his fastball seem faster. Whenever Sewell was scheduled to pitch, 3–5,000 more fans—home or away—showed up just to see him launch his eephus pitch. The easy-to-throw eephus pitch lowered the stress on Sewell's arm, allowing him to pitch many more complete games. In 1943 Sewell pitched 25 complete games and notched 21 wins to lead the National League. He won 21 again in 1944, and earned a spot on the All-Star team for four consecutive years from 1943 to 1946.

In the pregame warmups at the 1946 All-Star Game, Ted Williams watched as Sewell practiced his eephus pitch. Williams asked Sewell, "You're not going to throw that pitch to me, are you?" Sewell assured Williams he would. When Williams came to bat in the bottom of the eighth inning with the American League already ahead, 8–0, Williams just shook his head at Sewell, letting him know that he didn't want any blooper pitches thrown to him. Sewell responded by announcing loudly that the eephus was on its way. Williams fouled it off for a strike, watched another one for a ball, then took a surprise fastball for a strike. On the next pitch, an eephus, Ted Williams jumped ahead in the batter's box and crushed the eephus for a home run, the only homer ever hit off Sewell's blooper pitch. Sewell retired after the 1949 season with a fine .596 winning percentage, due largely to a nothin' pitch. He died in 1989.

CAREER PIRATES RECORD:

W	L	W%	ERA	SV
143	97	.596	3.43	15
K	BB	SHO	IP	
634	740	20	2,108.7	

STARGELL, WILLIE (OF/1B) (1962–1982)

The Pirates signed Willie Stargell as an amateur free agent on August 7, 1958. After a late-season call-up in 1962, Stargell joined the team for good in 1963 and played his entire 21-year career with Pittsburgh. Initially an outfielder, Stargell eventually moved to first base. In the batter's box, Stargell twirled his bat before each pitch like he was winding up a spring, read to uncoil and explode. Often there was an explosion. Stargell launched the only two home runs that ever completely flew out of Dodger Stadium. Of the 18 balls that cleared the 86-foot-high right-field stands in Forbes Field, Stargell hit seven. For 13 straight seasons from 1964 to 1976, Stargell hit at least 20 homers. It undoubtedly would have been 16 straight seasons, but in 1977 he suffered an elbow injury while breaking up an on-field fight and missed almost 100 games, finishing with 13 homers.

Stargell was always described as a player with class and decency. He tried to make playing ball fun. Once, when he tried to steal second, but was still 30 feet from second base when the second baseman caught the catcher's throw, he simply stopped in the basepath and tried to call timeout.

When Roberto Clemente died in 1972, Stargell reluctantly became the team's leader, but eventually came to relish the role. A very popular player in Pittsburgh, Stargell used his fame to open a chain of fried chicken restaurants in the Pittsburgh area. As a promotion, his restaurants would give away free chicken dinners to anyone waiting in line whenever he hit a home run. In 1978 Stargell was voted Comeback Player of the Year when he hit .295 with 28 homers and 97 RBIs and led the Pirates to within 1½ games of winning the division. In 1979 it all came together. "Pops" Stargell led the "We Are Family" Pirates to a division title, the NL championship, and the World Series crown. In the 1979 World Series, he racked up three homers, four doubles, and seven RBIs to go with his .400 average and Series-record 25 total bases. He handed out Stargell Stars to teammates for exceptional performances or spirited play. The gold stars adorned the Pirates' black retro hats. For his remarkable season, Stargell was named the NL co-MVP, the NLCS MVP, and the World Series MVP (and he gave away a lot of chicken dinners). After the 1982 season, Stargell retired as the Pirates' career leader in homers, RBIs, and eight other categories. In 1988, his first year of eligibility, Stargell was elected to the Baseball Hall of Fame. He died in 2001 at the age of 61.

CAREER PIRATES RECORD:

Games	AB	Hits	Runs
2,360	7,927	2,232	1,195
Avg	**HR**	**RBI**	**SB**
.282	475	1,540	17

TANNEHILL, JESSE (SP)
(1897–1902)

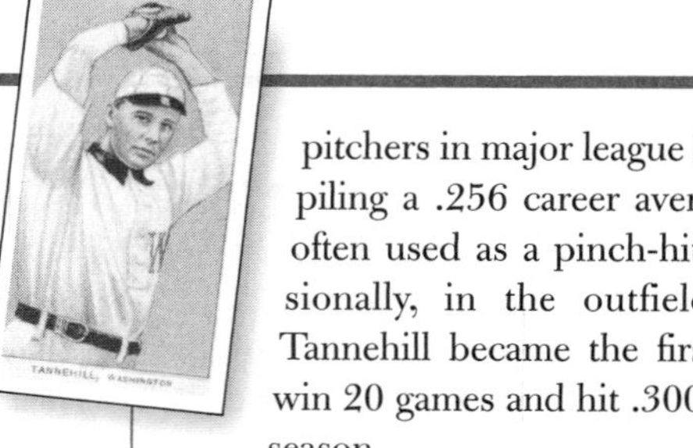

Jesse Tannehill signed with the Pirates in 1897 after playing just a few games with Cincinnati three years earlier. During his six years in Pittsburgh, Tannehill was a 20-game winner four times, with his best year coming in 1898 when he was 25–13. He also had a sub-3.00 ERA in five of his six Pirate seasons, including a 1.95 ERA in 1902, his last year with Pittsburgh before jumping to the New York Highlanders (later the Yankees). Tannehill was also one of the best-hitting pitchers in major league history, compiling a .256 career average. He was often used as a pinch-hitter or, occasionally, in the outfield. In 1900 Tannehill became the first pitcher to win 20 games and hit .300 in the same season.

CAREER PIRATES RECORD:

W	L	W%	ERA	SV
116	58	.667	2.73	5

K	BB	SHO	IP
462	242	17	1,499.0

TEKULVE, KENT (RP)
(1974–1985)

Kent Tekulve signed with the Pirates as an amateur free agent on July 16, 1969. After five years in the minors, the tall and very thin Tekulve was finally called up to the big leagues. Tekulve, who used a sidearm delivery that intimidated right-handed batters, never started a game during his entire 16-year career, the first 11+ seasons of which were spent with the Pirates. Tekulve led the majors in appearances three times while with the Pirates, and when he retired he held the major league record in appearances with 1,050 games, a record that was later topped by Jesse Orosco. During the 1979 World Series, Tekulve appeared in five games and recorded the final out of Game 7 to finish off the Orioles. Early in the 1985 season he was traded to rival Philadelphia for Al Holland and a minor leaguer.

CAREER PIRATES RECORD:

W	L	W%	ERA	SV
70	61	.534	2.68	158

K	BB	SHO	IP
552	367	0	1,017.0

TRAYNOR, PIE (3B)
(1920–1935, 1937)

Harold "Pie" Traynor, nicknamed for his preferred dessert, was purchased by the Pirates from the Portsmouth minor league team in 1920 and helped usher in a second wave of strong Pittsburgh clubs for owner Barney Dreyfuss. After two years of seasoning in Pittsburgh's minor league system, Traynor made it to the bigs for good in 1922. Considered one of the nicest, most polite men ever to wear a baseball uniform, Traynor would often stop and talk to passersby in the street about baseball in general and the Pirates in particular. John McGraw called Traynor the greatest team player of his time. Although Traynor was not a fast runner, he was usually near the top of the league in doubles and triples, thanks to gap-hitting in sprawling Forbes Field. He didn't walk much—during his 17-year Pirates career, he walked more than 50 times only twice—but he didn't strike out much, either.

Traynor was a legendary fielder at third base, often the subject of wire-service stories about his robbery of potential doubles down the third-base line. Traynor led the NL in putouts seven times, assists three times, and holds the NL career record for putouts. In 1925 he helped lead the Pirates to victory in the World Series against the legendary Walter Johnson and the Senators. For the Series he hit .346 and led all fielders with 24 assists. In the 1927 Series against Babe Ruth and the Yankees, Traynor hit a single to break up Herb Pennock's no-hit bid in the eighth inning of Game 3.

At the end of his career, the All-Star Game was inaugurated and Traynor was the NL's third baseman in both 1933 and 1934. Late in the 1934 season, he suffered a serious arm injury in a collision at the plate and his career was virtually over; he played in only 62 more games. Traynor became the Pirates' player-manager in 1934 and piloted the team for six seasons before being fired. He then became a part-time scout and instructor for the Pirates and remained a scout for the team until he died in 1972. In 1948 he was named to the Hall of Fame. When Major League Baseball announced its all-time team in 1969 to celebrate professional baseball's 100th anniversary, Pie Traynor was the chosen as third baseman—a just dessert.

CAREER PIRATES RECORD:

Games	AB	Hits	Runs
1,941	7,559	2,416	1,183
Avg	**HR**	**RBI**	**SB**
.320	58	1,273	158

VAUGHAN, ARKY (SS) (1932–1941)

Floyd "Arky" Vaughn (his nickname came from his Arkansas birthplace) was signed as an amateur free agent by the Pirates in late 1930 after a Pittsburgh scout spotted the high school phenom. After an excellent 1931 season in the minors, Vaughn was brought up to the Pirates in 1932 and installed as the new shortstop. Vaughn hit .318, the first of ten consecutive .300 seasons. He led the NL three times in triples and walks, and over the course of his first decade in baseball (1932–1941), he hit more triples than any other player in either league. Over that same decade he maintained the fifth-highest batting average, setting a career high in 1935 with .385. Vaughn is one of only a handful of players who hit for the cycle twice. After the 1941 season, Vaughn, who didn't get along with new manager Frankie Frisch at all, was traded to the Brooklyn Dodgers for four players. Vaughn came to dislike Leo Durocher passionately, and eventually sat out several seasons while Durocher was manager, returning only after Durocher had left the team. At the age of 40, Arky Vaughn drowned in a fishing boat accident trying to save a companion who couldn't swim. Vaughn was elected to the Hall of Fame in 1985.

CAREER PIRATES RECORD:

Games	AB	Hits	Runs
1,411	5,268	1,709	936
Avg	**HR**	**RBI**	**SB**
.324	84	764	86

WAGNER, HONUS (SS/OF/1B/3B) (1900–1917)

Simply put, Johannes "Honus" Wagner was the greatest shortstop who ever played the game. He was signed at the age of 18, almost by accident. A Pittsburgh scout had been sent to watch Honus's older brother, Al, near the Pennsylvania coal mines where they both worked. The scout observed Honus flinging rocks across the Monongahela River and signed him on the spot. Wagner spent four years in the minors before being called up to the National League's Louisville Colonels in 1897, where he hit .338 in his first major league season. After three excellent seasons in Louisville, Wagner went to Pittsburgh with several other Louisville stars when the National League contracted from 12 teams to eight for the 1900 season. Wagner spent the next 17 years as a Pirate, dominating the National League and playing every position except catcher (although most of his time was spent at shortstop). Wagner, good-natured and modest, was the National League's answer to Ty Cobb, who was mean and full of himself.

If baseball had selected an all-time team in 1910, Wagner would have been the shortstop. When Major League Baseball did pick an all-time team in 1969, Wagner was the shortstop. And if a new all-time team were chosen tomorrow, Wagner would still be the shortstop. Why? Because no other player has ever combined both the offensive and defensive skills at shortstop like Honus Wagner. "The Flying Dutchman" hit over .300 in 16 different seasons and won eight batting titles. He led the league in total bases six times, doubles seven times, triples three times, RBIs five times, stolen bases five times, and slugging average six times. Three times he stole second, third, and home in an inning. In 1908 Wagner missed winning the Triple Crown by two home runs. In 1909 he led the Pirates to a World Series championship over Ty Cobb's Detroit Tigers, hitting .333 with six steals, including one of home. A favorite but unsubstantiated story about Wagner concerned Game 1 of the World Series. The venomous Cobb, it was told, was on first base and shouted to Wagner his intention to steal, "Hey, krauthead, I'm coming on the next pitch!" Cobb did, and Wagner's message-laden tag on Cobb's mouth left him with three stitches and his eternal respect.

With Ty Cobb

Wagner didn't care much about money, never making more than $10,000 in a year. Ban Johnson tried to lure him to the American League, but he refused. Washington owner Clark Griffith offered him a huge sum to jump to the American League, but he turned it down. Ty Cobb and Nap Lajoie once offered Wagner $1,000 a week to go on a barnstorming tour with them, but he passed. Wagner was humble, friendly, and forthright, a man the fans and common folk could identify with. He was so hugely popular by his third year in the National League that couples were naming their children after him and fans were holding "Wagner Days." Pittsburgh eventually had several "Wagner Days" of their own, and the entire league held "Wagner Days" in 1917, his last year as a player. In 1909, a tobacco company put out a set of baseball cards including one of Wagner. Not wanting to encourage youngsters to smoke, Wagner sent the check back and requested that his image be pulled from the set (inadvertently helping to create the most valuable baseball card ever, a copy of which once fetched more than $1 million).

After Wagner retired, he continued to play semipro ball for another seven years. He also opened a sporting goods store in Pittsburgh on Forbes Avenue in downtown Pittsburgh that retains his name to this day. In 1933, 16 years after his retirement, the Pirates held another "Wagner Day." The 800-car parade through Pittsburgh lasted two hours. Wagner served as a Pittsburgh coach from 1933 to 1951. In 1936 he was one of the original inductees into the Baseball Hall of Fame. He died in 1955.

CAREER PIRATES RECORD:

Games	AB	Hits	Runs
2,433	9,034	2,967	1,521
Avg	**HR**	**RBI**	**SB**
.328	82	1,475	639

WANER, LLOYD (OF)
(1927–1941, 1944–1945)

Lloyd was the smaller and younger brother of fellow Pirates outfielder Paul Waner. Together they formed the best-hitting sibling combo in baseball history. Lloyd played 15 full seasons and parts of two others with the Pirates during his 18-year career, hitting over .300 during 11 of his Pittsburgh years. Lloyd was a good contact hitter with an exceptional batting eye. His ratio of just one strikeout per 44.9 at-bats is second all-time in major league history. When Lloyd arrived in Pittsburgh in 1927, he was hoping to win a reserve outfield role, but because regular Clyde Barnhart reported to camp grossly overweight and was unable to shed enough pounds before the regular season, Lloyd joined his brother Paul in the starting outfield. He got off to such a hot start that Barnhart was never able to win his job back. Lloyd's 223 hits (198 of which were singles) in 1927 were a rookie record. Together, he and his brother Paul combined for 460 hits and 247 runs in 1927.

A Brooklyn newspaper reporter overheard a local fan talking about the two brothers in total Brooklynese: "Every time I look up there's that little poyson on thoid and that big poyson on foist." The quote generated two of the oddest nicknames in baseball history. Forever after, the Waners were dubbed Little Poison and Big Poison in the press.

By 1941 Lloyd had become a part-time player and he was traded to the Braves just after the season started, and, a month later, he was traded again to the Reds. After bouncing around for a few more years, including a second brief tour with Pittsburgh, Lloyd Waner retired after the 1945 season. In 1967, Lloyd "Little Poison" Waner joined his big brother in Cooperstown. He died in 1982.

CAREER PIRATES RECORD:

Games	AB	Hits	Runs
1,803	7,256	2,317	1,151
Avg	**HR**	**RBI**	**SB**
.319	27	577	65

WANER, PAUL (OF)
(1926–1940)

Paul Waner played in the big leagues for 20 years, the first 15 with the Pirates. In eight of those years he collected more than 200 hits. Only Ty Cobb and Pete Rose ever managed more 200-hit seasons. Paul Waner made a concerted effort to hit down the lines or in the gaps to maximize his extra-base hits. After hitting .336 with 22 triples as a rookie in 1926,

Paul led the National League in batting in 1927 with a .380 average, winning the first of three batting championships. He finished in the top five in the National League nine times during his Pirates career. Once he rapped six hits in one game—using six different bats!

Casey Stengel called Paul Waner the best right fielder he ever saw because he could slide without breaking the whiskey bottle on his hip. One writer wrote about the notoriously hard-drinking, hard-partying Waner, "Paul Waner hits doubles and triples during games, and drinks them after games." He thought nothing of playing while drunk or, worse, hung over. Younger brother Lloyd once said, "Paul thinks you play better when you're relaxed, and drinking was a good way to relax." In 1938 Pirates Manager Pie Traynor felt it was time to sober up his right fielder, so Paul quit drinking. When his average plummeted to .240, Traynor took Waner out to get him drunk. Waner responded by raising his average to .280 by the end of the year, the only season in his first 14 years that he finished below .300.

In 1927 Paul's younger brother, Lloyd, joined him in the Pirates' outfield and together they tore up the National League. From June 3–19, Paul had at least one extra-base hit (12 doubles, 4 triples, 4 homers) in 14 consecutive games, still a major league record. Although the Yankees swept the Pirates in the 1927 World Series, the two brothers outhit Babe Ruth and Lou Gehrig by 10 points, .367 to .357. With their newfound fame, the Waner brothers embarked on an offseason vaudeville tour, earning $2,000 a week telling baseball jokes and playing a saxophone and violin along with the orchestra—at times even playing the same notes. They were so popular an act that they had to turn down an extended tour in order to prepare for the next season. During the next decade, the Pirates fell from prominence, but Paul Waner continued to produce. The Pirates released the 37-year-old outfielder after the 1940 season and he bounced around for five more years as a part-time player for the Dodgers, Braves, and Yankees before calling it quits. Paul "Big Poison" Waner was inducted into the Hall of Fame in 1952. He died in 1965.

CAREER PIRATES RECORD:

Games	AB	Hits	Runs
2,154	8,429	2,868	1,493
Avg	**HR**	**RBI**	**SB**
.340	109	1,177	100

WILLIS, VIC (SP)
(1906–1909)

WILLIS, PITTSBURG

Curveball specialist Vic Willis had played for the Boston Braves for eight seasons before he was traded to Pittsburgh in December 1905 for three players. He had fallen out of favor in Boston after registering 25 losses in 1904 and a modern-era record 29 losses in 1905 after being a 20-game winner in four of his first five seasons in Boston. The trade to Pittsburgh gave him new life and he became a 20-game winner again, posting four consecutive 20-win seasons for the Pirates. In the 1909 World Series against Detroit, Willis made two appearances, losing Game 6 as the starter. After the 1909 season, Willis was sold to the St. Louis Cardinals where he pitched one more year, going 9–12 before retiring. He died in 1947, and was elected to the Hall of Fame in 1995 by the Veterans Committee.

CAREER PIRATES RECORD:

W	L	W%	ERA	SV
89	46	.659	2.08	3
K	**BB**	**SHO**	**IP**	
423	297	23	1,209.0	

St. Louis Cardinals

Since 1882

1968 Team Ball

1911 Helen Britton becomes the first woman to own a major league team when she takes over the Cardinals.... **1926** After 26 years with both a National and American League team, the city of St. Louis wins its first 20th-century league championship.... **1944** The Cardinals win their third pennant in a row, becoming the last National League team to do so. They also become the last NL team to top 100 wins for three straight years until the Braves equal their feat in 1997–1999.... **1968** Bob Gibson's 13 shutouts are the most by any pitcher in the majors since Grover Alexander's 16 in 1916—and his 1.12 ERA is still the record since the end of the dead-ball era in 1920.... **2004** When the Red Sox sweep the Cardinals in four straight in the World Series, it is the first time in the Cardinals' last eight World Series appearances ('46, '64, '67, '68, '82, '85, and '87) that the Series didn't go the full seven games.

FRANCHISE HISTORY

The convoluted history of the St. Louis Cardinals franchise can be traced back to 1882, when the team played in the American Association as the Brown Stockings. St. Louis, like Philadelphia, had a long tradition of professional teams that played in various leagues over the years. In 1875, for example, there were two different St. Louis teams in the National Association: the Red Stockings (who played only briefly) and, later in the year, the Brown Stockings. When the chaotic National Association folded after its five-year run in 1875, the Brown Stockings moved to the National League and became one of its charter members when the league began play in 1876.

When the St. Louis Cardinals vacated Robison Field in 1920, it marked the last use of an all-wooden ballpark in the major leagues.

After the Louisville team folded in 1877 amid a gambling scandal, the owner of the Brown Stockings, John R. Lucas, absorbed some of the Louisville players into his St. Louis team. Lucas was then accused of having knowledge of the gambling scandal, so he voluntarily withdrew his team from the National League following the 1877 season and returned his franchise rights to the league.

Lucas kept his team together, but they played as an independent team for the next four years. In 1880 Lucas sold a majority interest in the team to Christopher Von der Ahe, and a minority interest to newspaperman Al Spink. Von der Ahe owned a saloon and boarding house next to the ballpark and put beer concessions inside the park. When the American Association—a new major league—was formed in 1882, Von der Ahe's Brown Stockings joined the league as a charter member. In 1883 the team shortened its name from the Brown Stockings to the Browns and Charles Comiskey came on board as the team's new player-manager. From 1885 to 1888, the Browns won four consecutive American

The Gas House Gang

Association championships, and in each of those years, they played a "World Series" match against the champions of the National League. Though the games at the time were billed as the World Series, they were really more of a series of exhibition games than what we now think of as the World Series. The 1885 Series between the Browns and the Chicago White Stockings, for example, ended with each team winning three games with one tie game, though some accounts give the Browns a controversial win in the Series. In 1886 the Browns defeated the White Stockings, four games to two. In 1887 the Detroit Wolverines defeated the Browns 10 games to five in a 15-game series that was played in a number of cities around the league so that all fans could have a chance to witness the World Series. In 1888 the New York Giants defeated the Browns in a 10-game Series, six games to four.

Dizzied Dizzy Dean is carried from field after encounter with a baseball in the 1934 World Series against Detroit.

Since 1948, no player has topped the 429 total bases achieved by the Cardinals' Stan Musial that season.

Von der Ahe's St. Louis Browns were not without local competition during the 1880s. In 1884 a third major league, the Union Association, began play. The St. Louis franchise was called the Maroons. The owner was millionaire (by inheritance only) Henry Lucas, the nephew of John Lucas. Adolphus Busch of brewery fame was a minority owner (his grandson, August Busch, would buy the Cardinals nearly seven decades later). When the Union Association folded after one year, the champion Maroons (91–16) were absorbed, intact, into the National League as competitors to the Browns for the St. Louis market. This move by the National League would have been in violation of the National Agreement, which had reserved the St. Louis market for the American Association, but a compromise was reached between the three leagues, and no doubt some cash was sent Von der Ahe's way as part of the overall settlement. The National League's St. Louis Maroons lasted just two years (1885–1886) before disbanding, clearly unable to compete for fans with the powerful St. Louis Browns.

In 1890 the upstart Players' League was formed as an act of defiance. Even though there was no St. Louis franchise in the new league, the overall financial health of all three leagues again suffered. The economic impact of the three-league war in 1890 was devastating—the Players' League folded and the American Association was left in poor financial health. Following the 1891 season, during which the financial bloodletting continued, the two remaining leagues reached a settlement in which the American Association would fold up shop and the National League would absorb four of its strongest teams—including the Browns—in time for the 1892 season, thereby making the National League a 12-team league.

Chris Von der Ahe had been living large while his pennant-winning Browns were romping through the American Association in front of large crowds, but the excesses of the 1880s gave way to the stresses of the 1890s. The Browns played poorly in the 1890s and

Bob Gibson did it all: pitch, run, hit, make batters mad.

revenues fell sharply, prompting Von der Ahe to rent out his ballpark for other events such as races, circuses, and amusement parks. When his mistress began spreading gossip about him in the newspapers in 1895, Von der Ahe's wife divorced him and his son sued him over a property dispute, which got him thrown into a Pennsylvania jail. Because of the added financial strain in his personal life, Von der Ahe sold off some of his star players in order to raise cash to pay his debts. Naturally, he could ill afford to replace the stars he sold, and the team plummeted in the standings. By 1898 Von der Ahe was so far in debt that he was jailed again. This time the National League stepped in to protect its interests, revoking the team's charter for Von der Ahe's failure to pay his minor league players. Now the league could control whom the new owner would be. The team was literally auctioned off from the courthouse steps, bringing $35,000 for Von der Ahe's creditors.

The new owners were brothers Frank and Stanley Robison, Midwest tractor magnates, who also owned the National League's Cleveland Spiders. The Robison brothers had tried to sell their weak Cleveland franchise to Detroit investors, but the National League vetoed the sale because it didn't want to move a team to a smaller market. The Robisons then bought the Browns, changed the team's name to the Perfectos in 1899 and then the Cardinals (because of the color of their socks) in 1900, and proceeded to transfer their best Cleveland players, including Cy Young and Jesse Burkett, to St. Louis. The Spiders were so bad (they finished 20–134!) and drew so few fans (averaging only about 50 paid customers at home games!) that the team began playing its home games on the road or at neutral sites. Because the team played exclusively on the road after June, and finished the season with a 4–70 record in its last 74 games, the National League shut the team down after the season. Frank died in 1905, leaving his share of the team to his daughter, Helene Schuyler Britton. When Stanley died in 1911 from blood poisoning, Helene inherited the rest of the stock and named her husband, Parsons Britton, as club president, even though she controlled the purse strings. In those days, after all, it wasn't proper for a woman to own a baseball team, but in 1916 Helene, who had become an activist in the suffragette movement, openly announced that she was the real owner of the team and took the title of club president from her figurehead husband.

Helene Britton sold the club in 1917 for $375,000 to James C. Jones, an attorney who headed an investment syndicate that sold shares of stock in the club. Among the larger investors were Sam Breadon, an automobile manufacturer and dealership owner, and singer Al Jolson. The syndicate hired Branch Rickey, a savvy baseball man, as the team's general manager. When the syndicate put the team's stock up for public sale in 1917, Breadon originally purchased 80 shares for $2,000. Over the next five years he gradually bought more and more stock until, in 1922, a 1,048-share purchase from James C. Jones put him at the magic 51 percent. He then declared himself the new team president. Breadon, who was from a poor background in New York and had worked his way up from bank clerk to automobile industry magnate, owned the team for 25 years, finally selling out in 1947, because of failing health. Before he did so, however, he "traded" many of his talented players to the Boston Braves for lesser players and a lot of cash. Sarcastic St. Louis fans dubbed the 1948 team "the Cape Cod Cardinals" in reference to the large number of former Boston players on the team.

On May 24, 1994, the Cardinals set a major league record by stranding 16 base runners in a 4-0 loss to the Phillies.

Before Breadon sold the Cardinals, he was faced a dilemma. He had set aside $5 million in cash to build a new ballpark; according to IRS law at the time, he was required to do so within five years or declare the money as income and pay the taxes on it. Fred Saigh was a tax-law specialist who wanted to buy the team and knew of Breadon's tax situation. Saigh convinced Breadon that if he sold the team to him, he wouldn't have to pay the taxes on the $5 million stash. In order to put Breadon at ease, Saigh brought another investor on board, Bob Hannegan, who had been a U.S. senator from Missouri, the Postmaster General, and, more important, the director of the IRS. Hannegan's assurances put Breadon at ease and the nifty little deal between the newfound best buddies was consummated in late 1947 for just over $4 million. In 1948 Hannegan sold his $10,000 share in the team to Saigh for $1 million, a tidy little profit in any era.

But Saigh's ship was about to sink, thanks apparently to someone's loose lips. Unfortunately for the conniving Saigh, both Hannegan and Breadon died on him in 1949, leaving Saigh holding the bag. Not the tax genius he thought he was, Saigh spent 15 months behind bars for income tax fraud. Once Saigh's protracted tax troubles became public, baseball commissioner Ford Frick forced him to sell the team in 1953.

The new owner was August Busch, owner of the Anheuser-Busch brewery. Although ownership of St. Louis baseball teams had been in the Busch family before, Busch bought the Cardinals primarily to keep them in St. Louis and away from aggressive bidders from Milwaukee and Houston. Busch paid $3.75 million for the team and remained its owner until his death in 1990. His heirs continued to run the team for several more years, but they were uninterested in baseball and put the team up for sale in 1995 with a $200 million asking price. The team ultimately sold for $150 million in 1996 to an investment group headed by William DeWitt Jr. and Frederick Hauser, the current owners. DeWitt's father, William DeWitt Sr., had owned the St. Louis Browns from 1936 to

Mark McGuire admiring handiwork.

1945 and the Cincinnati Reds from 1961 to 1966. DeWitt, who made his fortune as the owner of an investment firm, owned various other sports franchises, all for short periods, in the NFL, ABA, and WHA, and once made a failed bid to purchase the Cincinnati Reds. In 1989 Dewitt helped a longtime friend in the oil and gas business, George W. Bush, purchase the Texas Rangers.

On the field, the Cardinals have been one of the more successful baseball franchises. After the four consecutive American Association pennants from 1885 to 1888, St. Louis suffered through a long dry spell, not winning another pennant until 1926, when they won the first of five more pennants in a nine-year stretch. In three of those years (1926, 1931, and 1934), the Cardinals won the World Series.

When Albert Pujols won the 2001 NL Rookie of the Year Award, he played at least 30 games at four different positions—first, third, left, and right.

During the mid-1930s, the Cardinals had a bunch of wacky players whose antics both on and off the field gave rise to the nickname the Gas House Gang in 1935, although it has been applied retroactively to the 1934 team. There are conflicting versions of how exactly the moniker came about. One version has it that Leo Durocher, in talking with a sportswriter, commented that the Cardinals wouldn't be allowed to play in the American League because they would be perceived as "... just a bunch of gas house players." The other version has it that the Cardinals were unable to get their uniforms cleaned between series on a road trip and were forced to play in uniforms caked with mud from the previous rainy series; a sportswriter who witnessed the game wrote that the Cardinals were "... a bunch of dirty kids on the tracks who looked like a gas house gang."

St. Louis won four pennants and three World Series championships from 1942 to 1946, the first years of Stan Musial's career, though they would be the last pennants he would take part in during his 17-year career. The next hot streak for St. Louis came in the 1960s, when they won three pennants and two more World Series behind Lou Brock's base-stealing and Bob Gibson's pitching.

The Cardinals were shut out in the 1970s, but in the 1980s they won three more pennants and another World Series. The streaky Cardinals were almost shut out during the 1990s, winning a lone divisional title in 1996. Since 2000, however, the Cards have made the playoffs five times, although they have won only one pennant (2004) and no World Series. The current team has a dedicated owner, one of the best GM-manager tandem in baseball, a new ballpark opening in 2006, and one of the strongest fan bases in baseball.

TEAM NAME HISTORY

Official Names

Brown Stockings (1882)
Browns (1883–1898)
Perfectos (1899)
Cardinals (1900–curent)

Unofficial Names/Nicknames

Redbirds, Cards, Gas House Gang

STADIUM HISTORY

Sportsman's Park	1882–1892
Sportsman's Park (II)	1893–1898
Robison Field	1899–June 6, 1920
(Sportsman's Park II renamed, also known as League Park)	
Sportsman's Park (IV)	July 1, 1920–1952
Busch Stadium	1953–May 8, 1966
(Sportsman's Park IV renamed)	
Busch Memorial Stadium	May 12, 1966–2005
Busch Stadium	Scheduled to open in April 2006

YEARLY RECORD, FINISH, & ATTENDANCE FIGURES

Year	League	Record	DIV/LG Finish	Attendance	Avg/Gm
2005	NL Cent	100–62	1	3,538,988	43,691
2004	NL Cent	105–57	1	3,048,427	37,635
2003	NL Cent	85–77	3	2,910,386	35,931
2002	NL Cent	97–65	1	3,011,756	37,182
2001	NL Cent	93–69	2	3,109,578	37,922
2000	NL Cent	95–67	1	3,336,493	41,191
1999	NL Cent	75–86	4	3,225,334	40,317
1998	NL Cent	83–79	3	3,195,691	38,972
1997	NL Cent	73–89	4	2,634,014	32,519
1996	NL Cent	88–74	1	2,654,718	32,774
1995	NL Cent	62–81	4	1,756,727	24,399
1994	NL Cent	53–61	3	1,866,544	33,331
1993	NL East	87–75	3	2,844,977	35,123
1992	NL East	83–79	3	2,418,483	29,858
1991	NL East	84–78	2	2,448,699	29,151
1990	NL East	70–92	6	2,573,225	31,768
1989	NL East	86–76	3	3,080,980	37,120
1988	NL East	76–86	5	2,892,799	35,714
1987	NL East	95–67	1	3,072,122	37,927
1986	NL East	79–82	3	2,471,974	30,518
1985	NL East	101–61	1	2,637,563	32,563
1984	NL East	84–78	3	2,037,448	25,154
1983	NL East	79–83	4	2,317,914	28,616
1982	NL East	92–70	1	2,111,906	26,073
1981	NL East	59–43	2/2	1,010,247	19,061
1980	NL East	74–88	4	1,385,147	17,101
1979	NL East	86–76	3	1,627,256	19,845
1978	NL East	69–93	5	1,278,215	15,780
1977	NL East	83–79	3	1,659,287	19,991
1976	NL East	72–90	5	1,207,079	14,902
1975	NL East	82–80	4	1,695,270	20,674
1974	NL East	86–75	2	1,838,413	22,696
1973	NL East	81–81	2	1,574,046	19,433
1972	NL East	75–81	4	1,196,894	15,544
1971	NL East	90–72	2	1,604,671	19,569
1970	NL East	76–86	4	1,629,736	20,120
1969	NL East	87–75	4	1,682,783	21,035
1968	NL	97–65	1	2,011,167	24,829
1967	NL	101–60	1	2,090,145	25,804
1966	NL	83–79	6	1,712,980	21,148
1965	NL	80–81	7	1,241,201	15,323
1964	NL	93–69	1	1,143,294	14,115
1963	NL	93–69	2	1,170,546	14,451
1962	NL	84–78	6	953,895	11,776
1961	NL	80–74	5	855,305	10,965
1960	NL	86–68	3	1,096,632	14,242
1959	NL	71–83	7	929,953	12,077
1958	NL	72–82	5	1,063,730	13,815
1957	NL	87–67	2	1,183,575	15,371
1956	NL	76–78	4	1,029,773	13,202
1955	NL	68–86	7	849,130	11,028

YEARLY RECORD, FINISH, & ATTENDANCE FIGURES (CONT.)

Year	League	Record	DIV/LG Finish	Attendance	Avg/Gm
1954	NL	72–82	6	1,039,698	13,503
1953	NL	83–71	3	880,242	11,285
1952	NL	88–66	3	913,113	11,859
1951	NL	81–73	3	1,013,429	12,828
1950	NL	78–75	5	1,093,411	14,387
1949	NL	96–58	2	1,430,676	18,110
1948	NL	85–69	2	1,111,440	14,434
1947	NL	89–65	2	1,247,913	16,207
1946	NL	98–58	1	1,061,807	13,613
1945	NL	95–59	2	594,630	7,623
1944	NL	105–49	1	461,968	6,000
1943	NL	105–49	1	517,135	6,384
1942	NL	106–48	1	553,552	7,097
1941	NL	97–56	2	633,645	8,021
1940	NL	84–69	3	324,078	4,209
1939	NL	92–61	2	400,245	5,066
1938	NL	71–80	6	291,418	3,598
1937	NL	81–73	4	430,811	5,385
1936	NL	87–67	2	448,078	5,819
1935	NL	96–58	2	506,084	6,573
1934	NL	95–58	1	325,056	4,222
1933	NL	82–71	5	256,171	3,327
1932	NL	72–82	6	279,219	3,534
1931	NL	101–53	1	608,535	7,802
1930	NL	92–62	1	508,501	6,604
1929	NL	78–74	4	399,887	5,193
1928	NL	95–59	1	761,574	9,891
1927	NL	92–61	2	749,340	9,367
1926	NL	89–65	1	668,428	8,461
1925	NL	77–76	4	404,959	5,328
1924	NL	65–89	6	272,885	3,544
1923	NL	79–74	5	338,551	4,340
1922	NL	85–69	3	536,998	6,974
1921	NL	87–66	3	384,773	4,933
1920	NL	75–79	5	326,836	4,300
1919	NL	54–83	7	167,059	2,421
1918	NL	51–78	8	110,599	1,515
1917	NL	82–70	3	288,491	3,699
1916	NL	60–93	7	224,308	2,951
1915	NL	72–81	6	252,666	3,119
1914	NL	81–72	3	256,099	3,242
1913	NL	51–99	8	203,531	2,750
1912	NL	63–90	6	241,759	3,140
1911	NL	75–74	5	447,768	5,668
1910	NL	63–90	7	355,668	4,680
1909	NL	54–98	7	299,982	3,947
1908	NL	49–105	8	205,129	2,664
1907	NL	52–101	8	185,377	2,347
1906	NL	52–98	7	283,770	3,685
1905	NL	58–96	6	292,800	3,803
1904	NL	75–79	5	386,750	5,089

Yearly Record, Finish, & Attendance Figures (cont.)

Year	League	Record	DIV/LG Finish	Attendance	Avg/Gm
1903	NL	43–94	8	226,538	3,283
1902	NL	56–78	6	226,417	3,235
1901	NL	76–64	4	379,988	5,278
1900	NL	65–75	5	270,000	3,803
1899	NL	84–67	5	373,909	4,825
1898	NL	39–111	12	151,700	1,970
1897	NL	29–102	12	136,400	2,067
1896	NL	40–90	11	184,000	2,809
1895	NL	39–92	11	170,000	2,519
1894	NL	56–76	9	155,000	2,331
1893	NL	57–75	10	195,000	2,889
1892	NL	56–94	11	192,442	2,483
1891	AA	86–52	2	N/A	N/A
1890	AA	78–58	3	N/A	N/A
1889	AA	90–45	2	N/A	N/A
1888	AA	92–43	1	N/A	N/A
1887	AA	95–40	1	N/A	N/A
1886	AA	93–46	1	N/A	N/A
1885	AA	79–33	1	N/A	N/A
1884	AA	67–40	4	N/A	N/A
1883	AA	65–33	2	N/A	N/A
1882	AA	37–43	5	N/A	N/A

Manager History

Manager	Years	W–L	Win %
Ned Cuthbert	1882	37–43	.463
Ted Sullivan	1883	53–26	.671
Charlie Comiskey	1883, 1884–1889, 1891	561–273	.673
Tommy McCarthy	1890	15–12	.556
John Kerins	1890	9–8	.529
Chief Roseman	1890	7–8	.467
Count Campau	1890	27–14	.659
Joe Gerhardt	1890	20–16	.556
Jack Glasscock	1892	1–3	.250
John Stricker	1892	6–17	.261
John Crooks	1892	27–33	.450
George Gore	1892	6–9	.400
Bob Caruthers	1892	16–32	.333
Bill Watkins	1893	57–75	.431
George Miller	1894	56–76	.424
Al Buckenberger	1895	16–34	.320
Chris Von Der Ahe	1895, 1896, 1897	3–14	.176
Joe Quinn	1895	11–28	.282
Lew Phelan	1895	11–30	.268

MANAGER HISTORY (CONT.)

Manager	Years	W–L	Win %
Harry Diddlebock	1896	7–10	.412
Arlie Latham	1896	0–3	.000
Roger Connor	1896	8–37	.178
Tom Dowd	1896–1897	31–60	.341
Hugh Nicol	1897	8–32	.200
Bill Hallman	1897	13–36	.265
Tim Hurst	1898	39–111	.260
Patsy Tebeau	1899–1900	126–117	.519
Patsy Donovan	1901–1903	175–236	.426
Kid Nichols	1904–1905	80–88	.476
Jimmy Burke	1905	34–56	.378
Stanley Robison	1905	19–31	.380
John McCloskey	1906–1908	153–304	.335
Roger Bresnahan	1909–1912	255–352	.420
Miller Huggins	1913–1917	346–415	.455
Jack Hendricks	1918	51–78	.395
Branch Rickey	1919–1925	458–485	.486
Rogers Hornsby	1925–1926	153–116	.569
Bob O'Farrell	1927	92–61	.601
Bill McKechnie	1928–1929	129–88	.594
Billy Southworth	1929, 1940–1945	620–346	.642
Gabby Street	1929, 1930–1933	312–242	.563
Frank Frisch	1933–1938	458–354	.564
Mike Gonzalez	1938, 1940	9–13	.409
Ray Blades	1939–1940	106–85	.555
Eddie Dyer	1946–1950	446–325	.578
Marty Marion	1951	81–73	.526
Eddie Stanky	1952–1955	260–238	.522
Harry Walker	1955	51–67	.432
Fred Hutchinson	1956–1958	232–220	.513
Stan Hack	1958	3–7	.300
Solly Hemus	1959–1961	190–192	.497
Johnny Keane	1961–1964	317–249	.560
Red Schoendienst	1965–1976, 1980, 1990	1,041–955	.522
Vern Rapp	1977–1978	89–90	.497
Ken Boyer	1978–1980	166–190	.466
Whitey Herzog	1980, 1981–1990	822–728	.530
Joe Torre	1990–1995	351–354	.498
Mike Jorgensen	1995	42–54	.438
Tony LaRussa	1996–2005	894–725	.552

All-Time Win-Loss Records vs. All Opponents

Opponent	Record	Opponent	Record
ALL-TIME	8,501–7,894	Mets	350–307
Angels	2–1	Nationals	271–264
Astros	315–278	Orioles	2–1
Athletics	3–0	Padres	234–163
Blue Jays	4–2	Phillies	1,137–866
Braves	1,003–863	Pirates	1,004–1,070
Brewers	74–48	Rangers	2–1
Cubs	1,020–1,054	Reds	1,027–908
Devil Rays	3–0	Red Sox	4–2
Diamondbacks	36–21	Rockies	58–62
Dodgers	939–925	Royals	19–14
Giants	898–964	Tigers	6–8
Indians	3–8	Twins	9–6
INTERLEAGUE	73–57	White Sox	10–5
Mariners	4–2	Yankees	2–4
Marlins	62–47		

The wizardly Ozzie Smith

Franchise Highlights, Low Points, and Strange Distinctions

1902 Brothers Jack and Mike O'Neill comprised the first sibling battery in the National League.

• • • •

1905 Cardinals' owner Stanley Robison was so disgusted with the results of his team's first two managers of the season that he took over the reins himself, though his own 19–31 record was no better than theirs.

• • • •

1908 When Bobby Byrne of the Cardinals collected just 14 RBIs, it marked the all-time low by a third baseman with 400 or more at-bats.

• • • •

1909 On July 3, the Cardinals committed a major league record 17 errors in a doubleheader loss to Cincinnati.

• • • •

1914 St. Louis second baseman Miller Huggins stole 32 bases, but he was caught stealing 36 times, a National League record that still stands for times caught in a season.

• • • •

1922 The first major league infielder to wear glasses was Specs Toporcer of the Cardinals, who hit .324 as the Redbirds' regular shortstop.

1928 Center fielder Taylor Douthit of the Cardinals seemingly came out of nowhere to obliterate the record for putouts in a season. His speed and instincts enabled him to run down 123 more balls than any other outfielder in the majors that season. His total of 547 putouts has never been seriously challenged.

• • • •

1930 Outfielder George Watkins of the Cardinals hit .373, still the National League record for rookies.

• • • •

1931 Outfielder Chick Hafey of the Cardinals was the first batting champion who wore glasses. When he won the NL batting title with a .349 average, it was also the closest batting race in history. Statisticians had to calculate the averages of Hafey, teammate Jim Bottomley, and the Giants' Bill Terry to the ten-thousandths of a point before they could determine the winner.

Cardinals pitcher Dizzy Dean was the last of a breed, in more ways than one. In 1931, while playing for Houston in the minor leagues, Dean hit a solo home run to give his team the early lead. Later in the game, when Dizzy ran into trouble on the mound and manager Joe Schultz took him out of the game, Dean stomped out to the scoreboard in center field and removed the "1" that represented his earlier homer, stating that if he couldn't keep pitching, Houston couldn't have his run. On a more serious note, Dean was the last National League pitcher to win at least 30 games in a season when he went 30–7 in 1934. In 1936 he became the last major league pitcher to lead his league in both complete games (28) and saves (11) in the same season.

1934 On September 21, Dizzy Dean shut out the Dodgers on a two-hitter in the first game of a doubleheader. In the second game, his brother Paul threw a no-hitter against Brooklyn. Said Dizzy later in the clubhouse, "If Paul woulda told me he was going to do that, I'd of pitched one, too."

Daffy and Dizzy Dean share some sibling secrets in spring training, 1935.

1936 Eddie Morgan of the Cardinals became the first player ever to hit a pinch-hit home run in his first major league at-bat when he turned the trick on April 14.

• • • •

1937 When St. Louis's Joe Medwick hit for the Triple Crown, it marked the last time the feat was accomplished in the National League. There have been five Triple Crowns achieved in the American League since 1937 (Ted Williams in 1942 and 1947, Mickey Mantle in 1956, Frank Robinson in 1966, and Carl Yastrzemski in 1967).

• • • •

1936–41 First baseman Johnny Mize, who spent six of his 15 major league seasons with St. Louis (1936–1941), is the only major league player in history to hit three homers in a game six times.

• • • •

1949 The St. Louis Cardinals set the all-time low for stolen bases in a season by a National League team with just 17. Second baseman Red Schoendienst had almost half the team's total, with eight.

• • • •

1950 On April 18, the Cardinals played host to the first-ever Opening Day night game in major league history, defeating the Pittsburgh Pirates, 4–2.

1954 Stan Musial hit a record five home runs in a doubleheader on May 2; Cardinal rookie outfielder Rip Repulski set a major league record in 1954 when he collected at least two hits in 10 consecutive games; and second baseman Red Schoendienst hit safely in 28 straight games in 1954, the record by a switch-hitter until Pete Rose broke it in 1978 with his 44-game streak.

• • • •

1963 Through the 2005 season, only one player ranks among the top 25 all-time in singles, doubles, triples, and homers: Stan Musial, who retired after the 1963 season.

• • • •

1964 On September 13, the Cardinals scored in every inning of a 15–2 win over the Cubs in Wrigley Field, only the second time the feat had been done in the 20th century. The New York Giants accomplished it first on June 1, 1923, in a 22–8 win at Philadelphia.

• • • •

1966 Cardinal pitcher Larry Jaster pitched five consecutive shutouts against the defending National League champion Dodgers—in his only five appearances against them all year.

• • • •

1967 Lou Brock set a new World Series record with seven stolen bases against the Red Sox. In 1968 he tied his own record by swiping seven more against the Tigers. Brock's 14 career World Series steals is still the National League record and is tied with Eddie Collins' for the major league record (though Collins did it in 34 games, as compared to 14 Series games for Brock).

1970 Shortstop Dal Maxvill set a major league record for the fewest hits in a season (80) by a player who played in at least 152 games in a season. Among the hits used to compile his anemic .201 batting average were 73 singles, five doubles, and two triples.

••••

1979 Shortstop Garry Templeton became the first switch-hitter in major league history to collect at least 100 hits from both sides of the plate.

••••

1982 Light hitting, however, didn't hurt the World Series champion Cardinals, who finished a major league last in homers that year with 67. Sixteen years later, another Cardinal—Mark McGwire—hit 70 home runs all by himself.

••••

1985 Cardinal John Tudor threw 10 shutouts, one short of the modern-era record for left-handers set by Sandy Koufax in 1963.

Vince Coleman established a new rookie record in 1985 for stolen bases in a season with 110.

••••

1986 Todd Worrell set a major league record for saves by a rookie with 36.

••••

1991 Todd Zeile led St. Louis in homers with only 11, the lowest total to lead the Cardinals since 1920 when Austin McHenry led the team with 10.

1992 Pitcher Bob Tewksbury finished the season with a 0.77 walks-per-nine-innings ratio, the lowest in the major leagues since 1933, when Red Lucas of the Reds had a 0.74 ratio.

••••

1993 On September 7, outfielder Mark Whiten of St. Louis accomplished something no other major league player in history ever had—he hit four homers and had 12 RBIs in the same game.

••••

1994 On July 18, the Cardinals tied a National League record when they lost a game after leading by 11 runs. Leading Houston 11–0 after three innings in the Astrodome, the Cardinals allowed 15 runs and lost 15–12.

••••

1996 The Cardinals ended the season on an extremely sour note. After leading Atlanta in the NLCS, three games to one, St. Louis was outscored 32–1 in the final three games. The Braves scored victories of 14–0, 3–1, and 15–0 to end the Cardinals' season and advance to the World Series. It was also the first time the Cardinals had ever lost a pre-World Series playoff series, having won their first five.

••••

1997 In the first-ever regular season game played in Hawaii, the Cardinals defeated the San Diego Padres 1–0 on April 19, in the first game of a doubleheader. The Cardinals completed the sweep in the nightcap, 2–1. The Padres won the next day, 8–2, to avoid the series sweep.

1998 Relief pitcher Lance Painter of the Cardinals had a perfect season in every sense. In 65 games, his fielding average was 1.000 (18 total chances with no errors), his batting average was 1.000 (1-for-1), and his winning percentage was 1.000 (4–0).

• • • •

1999 On April 23, Fernando Tatis of St. Louis became the first player in major league history to hit two grand slams in one inning when he accomplished the feat in a 12–5 win over the Dodgers in Los Angeles. Almost as incredibly, he hit both grand slams off the same pitcher, Chan Ho Park.

When Mark McGwire hit 65 home runs in 1999, it was his fourth straight season with at least 50 homers, a major league record. He also reached 500 career homers faster than anyone in history.

• • • •

2004 On October 27, in Game 4 of the World Series, pitcher Jason Marquis of the Cardinals faced Jason Varitek of the Red Sox. It was the first time ever that two former Little League World Series players faced each other in the major league World Series. Marquis helped his Staten Island, New York, team to a third-place finish in 1991, while Varitek helped his Altamonte Springs, Florida, team to a second-place finish in 1984.

2005 When first baseman Albert Pujols slugged 41 homers for St. Louis in 2005, he became the first player in history to hit 30 or more home runs in his first five major league seasons. He also became just the fourth player ever to record 100+ RBIs in his first five years, joining Al Simmons (first 11 years), Ted Williams (8), and Joe DiMaggio (7).

On April 27, 2005, second baseman Mark Grudzielanek became the player with the longest last name (12 letters) to hit for the cycle. The previous record holder was Carl Yastrzemski (11 letters).

On August 25, 2005, Cardinals manager Tony LaRussa recorded win number 2,195 in his illustrious career, moving him into third place all-time in managerial victories, trailing only Hall of Famers Connie Mack (3,731) and John McGraw (2,763).

The Cardinals set a new franchise attendance record in 2005 by drawing 3,538,988 fans. That was the last year the team played in Busch Memorial Stadium.

Special Achievements

World Series Results

Year	Opponent	Result	Games
1926	New York Yankees	Won	4–3
1928	New York Yankees	Lost	0–4
1930	Philadelphia A's	Lost	2–4
1931	Philadelphia A's	Won	4–3
1934	Detroit Tigers	Won	4–3
1942	New York Yankees	Won	4–1
1943	New York Yankees	Lost	1–4
1944	St. Louis Browns	Won	4–2
1946	Boston Red Sox	Won	4–3
1964	New York Yankees	Won	4–3
1967	Boston Red Sox	Won	4–3
1968	Detroit Tigers	Lost	3–4
1982	Milwaukee Brewers	Won	4–3
1985	Kansas City Royals	Lost	3–4
1987	Minnesota Twins	Lost	3–4
2004	Boston Red Sox	Lost	0–4

World Series Managerial Records

Manager	Series Record	Games Record
Rogers Hornsby	1–0	4–3
Bill McKechnie	0–1	0–4
Gabby Street	1–1	6–7
Frank Frisch	1–0	4–3
Billy Southworth	2–1	9–7
Eddie Dyer	1–0	4–3
Johnny Keane	1–0	4–3
Red Schoendienst	1–1	7–7
Whitey Herzog	1–2	10–11
Tony LaRussa	0–1	0–4

All-Time Postseason Record

Divisional Playoffs	17–4
League Championship Series	22–24
World Series	48–52

All-Star Games at St. Louis (when NL was home team)

Year	Date	Winner	Score	Stadium
1940	July 9	National	4–0	Sportsman's Park
1957	July 9	American	6–5	Busch Stadium
1966	July 12	National	2–1	Busch Memorial Stadium

Hall of Famers Who Played for Team

	Position	Years	Games with St. Louis
Grover Alexander	SP/RP	1926–1929	116
Walter Alston	1B	1936	1
Jake Beckley	1B	1904–1907	395
Jim Bottomley	1B	1922–1932	1,392
Roger Bresnahan	C	1909–1912	289
Lou Brock	OF	1964–1979	2,289
Mordecai Brown	SP	1903	26
Jesse Burkett	OF	1899–1901	424
Steve Carlton	SP	1965–1971	192
Orlando Cepeda	1B	1966–1968	431
Charles Comiskey	1B	1882–1889, 1891	1,036
Roger Connor	1B	1894–1897	350
Dizzy Dean	SP/RP	1930, 1932–1937	281
Leo Durocher	SS	1933–1937	683
Dennis Eckersley	RP	1996–1997	120
Dave Foutz	SP	1884–1887	171
Frankie Frisch	2B/3B	1927–1937	1,311
Pud Galvin	SP	1892	12
Bob Gibson	SP	1959–1975	596
Burleigh Grimes	SP	1930–1931, 1933–1934	60
Chick Hafey	OF	1924–1931	812
Jesse Haines	SP/RP	1920–1937	559
Rogers Hornsby	2B/SS/3B	1915–1926, 1933	1,580
Miller Huggins	2B	1910–1916	803
Silver King	SP	1887–1889	167
Rabbit Maranville	SS	1927–1928	121
John McGraw	3B	1900	99
Joe Medwick	OF	1932–1940, 1947–1948	1,216
Johnny Mize	1B	1936–1941	854
Stan Musial	OF/1B	1941–1944, 1946–1963	3,026
Kid Nichols	SP	1904–1905	44
Wilbert Robinson	C	1900	60
Red Schoendienst	2B	1945–1956, 1961–1963	1,795
Enos Slaughter	OF	1938–1942, 1946–1953	1,820
Ozzie Smith	SS	1982–1996	1,990
Dazzy Vance	RP/SP	1933–1934	47
Bobby Wallace	SS/3B	1899–1901, 1917–1918	451
Hoyt Wilhelm	RP	1957	40
Vic Willis	SP/RP	1910	33
Cy Young	SP	1899–1900	85

HALL OF FAMERS WHO MANAGED TEAM

	Years	Games with St. Louis
Roger Bresnahan	1909–1912	618
Roger Connor	1896	46
Frankie Frisch	1933–1938	822
Rogers Hornsby	1925–1926	271
Miller Huggins	1913–1917	774
Bill McKechnie	1928–1929	217
Kid Nichols	1904–1905	169
Red Schoendienst	1965–1976, 1980, 1990	1,999

MVP AWARD WINNERS

Frank Frisch	2B	1931
Dizzy Dean	SP	1934
Joe Medwick	OF	1937
Mort Cooper	SP	1942
Stan Musial	OF	1943
Marty Marion	SS	1944
Stan Musial	1B	1946
Stan Musial	OF	1948
Ken Boyer	3B	1964
Orlando Cepeda	1B	1967
Bob Gibson	SP	1968
Joe Torre	3B	1971
Keith Hernandez	1B	1979 (tie)
Willie McGee	OF	1985
Albert Pujols	1B	2005

CY YOUNG AWARD WINNERS

Pitcher	Year	W–L	ERA
Bob Gibson	1968	22–9	1.12
Bob Gibson	1970	23–7	3.12
Chris Carpenter	2005	21–5	2.83

ROOKIE OF THE YEAR AWARD WINNERS

Wally Moon	OF	1954
Bill Virdon	OF	1955
Bake McBride	OF	1974
Vince Coleman	OF	1985
Todd Worrell	RP	1986
Albert Pujols	OF/3B/1B	2001

GOLD GLOVE WINNERS

Year	Position	Player
1958	3B	Ken Boyer
1959	3B	Ken Boyer
1960	1B 3B	Bill White Ken Boyer
1961	1B 3B	Bill White Ken Boyer
1962	RP 1B	Bobby Shantz Bill White
1963	RP 1B 3B OF	Bobby Shantz Bill White Ken Boyer Curt Flood
1964	1B OF	Bill White Curt Flood
1965	SP 1B OF	Bob Gibson Bill White Curt Flood
1966	SP OF	Bob Gibson Curt Flood
1967	SP OF	Bob Gibson Curt Flood
1968	SP SS OF	Bob Gibson Dal Maxvill Curt Flood
1969	SP OF	Bob Gibson Curt Flood
1970	SP	Bob Gibson
1971	SP	Bob Gibson
1972	SP	Bob Gibson
1973	SP	Bob Gibson
1975	3B	Ken Reitz
1978	1B	Keith Hernandez
1979	1B	Keith Hernandez
1980	1B	Keith Hernandez
1981	1B	Keith Hernandez
1982	1B SS	Keith Hernandez Ozzie Smith
1983	SS OF	Ozzie Smith Willie McGee
1984	SP SS	Joaquin Andujar Ozzie Smith
1985	SS OF	Ozzie Smith Willie McGee
1986	SS OF	Ozzie Smith Willie McGee
1987	3B SS	Terry Pendleton Ozzie Smith
1988	SS	Ozzie Smith
1989	3B SS	Terry Pendleton Ozzie Smith
1990	SS	Ozzie Smith
1991	C SS	Tom Pagnozzi Ozzie Smith
1992	C SS	Tom Pagnozzi Ozzie Smith
1994	C	Tom Pagnozzi
2000	C OF	Mike Matheny Jim Edmonds
2001	2B	Fernando Viña
	OF	Jim Edmonds
2002	2B 3B SS OF	Fernando Viña Scott Rolen Edgar Renteria Jim Edmonds

2003	C	Mike Matheny
	3B	Scott Rolen
	SS	Edgar Renteria
	OF	Jim Edmonds
2004	C	Mike Matheny
	3B	Scott Rolen
	OF	Jim Edmonds
2005	OF	Jim Edmonds

Triple Crown Winners

Player	Year	Avg	HR	RBI
Rogers Hornsby	1922	.401	42	152
Rogers Hornsby	1925	.403	39	143
Joe Medwick	1937	.374	31	154

Fireman of the Year Award Winners

Lindy McDaniel	1960
Al Hrabosky	1975
Bruce Sutter	1981
Bruce Sutter	1982
Bruce Sutter	1984
Todd Worrell	1986
Lee Smith	1991
Lee Smith	1992 (tie)

World Series MVP

Bob Gibson	1964
Bob Gibson	1967
Darrell Porter	1982

League Championship Series MVP

Darrell Porter	1982
Ozzie Smith	1985
Albert Pujols	2004

All-Star Game MVP

None

Manager of the Year Award Winners

Whitey Herzog	1985
Tony LaRussa	2002

Batting Champions

Year	Player	Avg
1901	Jesse Burkett	.376
1920	Rogers Hornsby	.370
1921	Rogers Hornsby	.397
1922	Rogers Hornsby	.401
1923	Rogers Hornsby	.384
1924	Rogers Hornsby	.424
1925	Rogers Hornsby	.403
1931	Chick Hafey	.349
1937	Joe Medwick	.374
1939	Johnny Mize	.349
1943	Stan Musial	.357
1946	Stan Musial	.365
1948	Stan Musial	.376
1950	Stan Musial	.346
1951	Stan Musial	.355
1952	Stan Musial	.336
1957	Stan Musial	.351
1971	Joe Torre	.363
1979	Keith Hernandez	.344
1985	Willie McGee	.353
1990	Willie McGee	.335
2003	Albert Pujols	.359

Nine-Inning No-Hitters Pitched

Year	Pitcher	Opp.	Score
1924	Jesse Haines	BOS	5–0
1934	Paul Dean	BRK	3–0
1941	Lon Warneke	CIN	2–0
1968	Ray Washburn	SF	2–0
1971	Bob Gibson	PIT	11–0
1978	Bob Forsch	PHI	5–0
1983	Bob Forsch	MON	3–0
1999	Jose Jimenez	ARZ	1–0
2001	Bud Smith	SD	4–0

20-Game Winners

Year	Pitcher	W–L
1882	Jumbo McGinnis	25–18
1883	Tony Mullane	35–15
	Jumbo McGinnis	28–16
1884	Jumbo McGinnis	24–16
1885	Bob Caruthers	40–13
	Dave Foutz	33–14
1886	Dave Foutz	41–16
	Bob Caruthers	30–14
1887	Silver King	32–12
	Bob Caruthers	29–9
	Dave Foutz	25–12
1888	Silver King	45–21
	Nat Hudson	25–10
1889	Silver King	35–16
	Elton Chamberlain	32–15
1890	Jack Stivetts	27–21
	Toad Ramsey	24–17
1891	Jack Stivetts	27–21
1892	Kid Gleason	20–24
1893	Kid Gleason	21–22
1894	Ted Breitenstein	27–23
1899	Cy Young	26–16
	Jack Powell	23–19
1901	Jack Harper	23–13
1904	Kid Nichols	21–13
	Jack Taylor	20–19

1911	Bob Harmon	23–16
1920	Bill Doak	20–12
1923	Jesse Haines	20–13
1926	Flint Rhem	20–7
1927	Jesse Haines Grover Alexander	24–10 21–10
1928	Bill Sherdel Jesse Haines	21–10 20–8
1933	Dizzy Dean	20–18
1934	Dizzy Dean	30–7
1935	Dizzy Dean	28–12
1936	Dizzy Dean	24–13
1939	Curt Davis	22–16
1942	Mort Cooper Johnny Beazley	22–7 21–6
1943	Mort Cooper	21–8
1944	Mort Cooper	22–7
1945	Red Barrett	21–9
1946	Howie Pollet	21–10
1948	Harry Brecheen	20–7
1949	Howie Pollet	20–9
1953	Harvey Haddix	20–9
1960	Ernie Broglio	21–9
1964	Ray Sadecki	20–11
1965	Bob Gibson	20–12
1966	Bob Gibson	21–12
1968	Bob Gibson	22–9
1969	Bob Gibson	20–13
1970	Bob Gibson	23–7
1971	Steve Carlton	20–9
1977	Bob Forsch	20–7
1984	Joaquin Andujar	20–14
1985	Joaquin Andujar John Tudor	21–12 21–8
2000	Darryl Kile	20–9
2001	Matt Morris	22–8
2005	Chris Carpenter	21–5

Retired Uniform Numbers

Number	Player	Position
1	Ozzie Smith	SS
2	Red Schoendienst	2B
6	Stan Musial	OF/1B
9	Enos Slaughter	OF
14	Ken Boyer	3B
17	Dizzy Dean	SP
20	Lou Brock	OF
45	Bob Gibson	SP
85	August Busch Jr.	Owner

Team Records—Wins & Losses

- Games won in a season: 106 in 1942
- Games lost in a season: 111 in 1898
- Games won in a month: 26 in July 1944
- Games lost in a month: 27 in September 1908
- Consecutive games won: 14 in 1935
- Consecutive games lost: 18 in 1897
- Biggest shutout victory: 18–0 over Cincinnati on June 10, 1944
- Biggest shutout loss: 19–0 to Pittsburgh on August 3, 1961
- Highest winning percentage: .688 in 1942 (106–48)
- Lowest winning percentage: .221 in 1897 (29–102)

Team Records—Batting

- Highest team batting average: .314 in 1930
- Lowest team batting average: .223 in 1908
- Highest team slugging average: .471 in 1930
- Highest team on-base percentage: .372 in 1930
- Total hits: 1,732 in 1930
- Extra-base hits: 570 in 2003
- Hits in a game: 30 vs. New York Giants on June 1, 1895
- Longest individual hitting streak: 33, Rogers Hornsby, 1922
- Most .300 hitters in a single season: 11 in 1930
- Home runs: 235 in 2000
- Home runs in a month: 16, Mark McGwire (twice), May 1998 and July 1999
- Home runs in a game: 7, vs. Brooklyn on May 7, 1940 and vs. Chicago Cubs on July 12, 1996
- Home runs by a rookie: 37, Albert Pujols, 2001
- Home runs by a right-hander: 70, Mark McGwire, 1998
- Home runs by a left-hander: 43, Johnny Mize, 1940
- Home runs by a switch-hitter: 35, Rip Collins, 1934

- Grand slams: 12 in 2000
- Grand slams (individual; season): 3, Jim Bottomley, 1925; Keith Hernandez, 1977; Fernando Tatis, 1999
- Grand slams (individual; career): 9, Stan Musial
- Triples: 96 in 1920
- Doubles: 373 in 1939
- Singles: 1,223 in 1920
- Walks: 676 in 1998
- Runs scored: 1,004 in 1930
- Runs scored in a game: 28 vs. Philadelphia Phillies on July 6, 1929 (second game)
- Runs scored in an inning: 12 vs. Philadelphia Phillies on September 16, 1926, first game (third inning)
- Most batters hit by a pitch: 84 in 2000
- Times shut out: 33 in 1908
- Grounded into double plays: 166 in 1958
- Fewest grounded into double plays: 75 in 1945
- Runners left on base: 1,251 in 1939

TEAM RECORDS—BASERUNNING

- Stolen bases: 581 in 1887
- Caught stealing: 118 in 1992

TEAM RECORDS—PITCHING

- Lowest earned run average: 2.09 in 1888
- Complete games: 146 in 1904
- Saves: 57 in 2004
- Strikeouts: 1,130 in 1997
- Shutouts: 30 in 1968
- Walks: 667 in 1999
- Hit batsmen: 86 in 1898
- Wild pitches: 66 in 1970
- Consecutive wins (individual): 15, Bob Gibson, 1968
- Consecutive losses (individual): 12, Bill Hart, 1897
- Strikeouts in a game (individual): 19, Steve Carlton, September 15, 1969
- Runs allowed in a game: 28 vs. Boston Beaneaters, September 3, 1896

TEAM RECORDS—FIELDING

- Best fielding average: .987 in 2003
- Most errors committed: 494 in 1886
- Fewest errors committed: 77 in 2003
- Most double plays turned: 196 in 2005
- Fewest double plays turned: 41 in 1882

TEAM RECORDS—MISCELLANEOUS

- Number of times league champions: 20
- Number of times finishing last in league: 8
- Largest attendance, single game: 53,415 vs. Chicago Cubs, July 30, 1994
- Largest attendance, doubleheader: 52,657 vs. Atlanta, July 22, 1994
- Players used in a season: 51 in 1997
- Seasons played: 22 by Stan Musial

PRIMARY PITCHING STAFFS

Year	Starter	Starter	Starter	Starter	Starter	Closer	Bullpen	Bullpen	Bullpen
2005	Carpenter	Mulder	Marquis	Suppan	Morris	Isringhausen	King	Tavarez	Reyes
2004	Carpenter	Williams	Marquis	Suppan	Morris	Isringhausen	King	Tavarez	Kline
2003	Tomko	Williams	Stephenson	Simontacchi	Morris	Isringhausen	Eldred	Fassero	Kline
2002	Benes	Williams	Kile	Simontacchi	Morris	Isringhausen	Veres	Crudale	Kline
2001	Benes	Hermanson	Kile	Smith	Morris	Veres	Timlin	Stechschulte	Kline
2000	Benes	Hentgen	Kile	Stephenson	Ankiel	Veres	James	Slocumb	Morris
1999	Bottenfield	Oliver	Jimenez	Mercker	Acevedo	Bottalico	Aybar	Croushore	Painter
1998	Bottenfield	Stottlemyre	Morris	Mercker	Osborne	Acevedo	Frascatore	Brantley	Painter
1997	Benes	Stottlemyre	Morris	Benes	Osborne	Eckersley	Frascatore	Petkovsek	Fossas
1996	Benes	Stottlemyre	Morgan	Benes	Osborne	Eckersley	Mathews	Honeycutt	Fossas
1995	Petkovsek	Watson	Jackson	Hill	Osborne	Henke	Parrett	Fossas	DeLucia
1994	Tewksbury	Watson	Palacios	Sutcliffe	Olivares	Perez	Rodriguez	Habyan	Murphy
1993	Tewksbury	Arocha	Osborne	Cormier	Magrane	Smith	Perez	Olivares	Murphy
1992	Tewksbury	Olivares	Osborne	Cormier	Clark	Smith	Perez	Carpenter	McClure
1991	Tewksbury	Olivares	Smith	Hill	DeLeon	Smith	Agosto	Carpenter	Terry
1990	Tewksbury	Magrane	Smith	Tudor	DeLeon	Smith	DiPino	Niedenfuer	Dayley
1989	Hill	Magrane	Terry	Power	DeLeon	Worrell	DiPino	Quisenberry	Dayley
1988	Tudor	Magrane	McWilliams	Cox	DeLeon	Worrell	Terry	Dayley	Peters
1987	Tudor	Magrane	Mathews	Cox	Forsch	Worrell	Horton	Dayley	Dawley
1986	Tudor	Conroy	Mathews	Cox	Forsch	Worrell	Horton	Dayley	Perry
1985	Tudor	Andujar	Kepshire	Cox	Forsch	Lahti	Horton	Campbell	Dayley
1984	LaPoint	Andujar	Kepshire	Cox	Horton	Sutter	Lahti	Allen	Rucker
1983	LaPoint	Andujar	Forsch	Stuper	Allen	Sutter	Lahti	Von Ohlen	Rucker
1982	LaPoint	Andujar	Forsch	Stuper	Mura	Sutter	Lahti	Bair	Kaat
1981	Sorensen	Martinez	Forsch	Martin	Shirley	Sutter	Littell	Otten	Kaat
1980	Vuckovich	Martinez	Forsch	Sykes	Kaat	Littlefield	Hood	Otten	Urrea
1979	Vuckovich	Martinez	Forsch	Denny	Fulgham	Littell	Knowles	McEnaney	Schultz
1978	Vuckovich	Martinez	Forsch	Denny	Falcone	Littell	Urrea	Lopez	Schultz
1977	Rasmussen	Underwood	Forsch	Denny	Falcone	Hrabosky	Metzger	Eastwick	Carroll
1976	Rasmussen	McGlothen	Forsch	Denny	Falcone	Hrabosky	Wallace	Greif	Curtis
1975	Reed	McGlothen	Forsch	Denny	Curtis	Hrabosky	Garman	Gibson	Terlecky
1974	Gibson	McGlothen	Foster	Siebert	Curtis	Hrabosky	Garman	Folkers	Pena
1973	Gibson	Wise	Foster	Cleveland	Murphy	Segui	Hrabosky	Folkers	Pena
1972	Gibson	Wise	Santorini	Cleveland	Spinks	Segui	Drabowsky	Cloninger	Grzenda
1971	Gibson	Carlton	Reuss	Cleveland	Zachary	Drabowsky	Linzy	Shaw	Taylor
1970	Gibson	Carlton	Reuss	Torrez	Briles	Taylor	Linzy	Hilgendorf	Campisi
1969	Gibson	Carlton	Washburn	Torrez	Briles	Hoerner	Grant	Taylor	Willis
1968	Gibson	Carlton	Washburn	Jaster	Briles	Hoerner	Granger	Hughes	Willis
1967	Gibson	Carlton	Washburn	Jaster	Hughes	Hoerner	Briles	Jackson	Willis
1966	Gibson	Jackson	Washburn	Jaster	Briles	Hoerner	Woodeshick	Dennis	Stallard
1965	Gibson	Simmons	Sadecki	Stallard	Purkey	Woodeshick	Briles	Dennis	Schultz
1964	Gibson	Simmons	Sadecki	Craig	Broglio	Schultz	Taylor	Humphreys	Cuellar
1963	Gibson	Simmons	Sadecki	Burdette	Broglio	Taylor	Shantz	Bauta	Schultz
1962	Gibson	Simmons	Jackson	Washburn	Broglio	McDaniel	Shantz	Ferrarese	Duliba
1961	Gibson	Simmons	Jackson	Sadecki	Broglio	McDaniel	Miller	Anderson	Cicotte
1960	Kline	Simmons	Jackson	Sadecki	Broglio	McDaniel	Duliba	Gibson	Bridges
1959	Mizell	Blaylock	Jackson	Miller	Broglio	McDaniel	Brosnan	Stone	Bridges
1958	Mizell	Jones	Jackson	McDaniel	Mabe	Brosnan	Paine	Muffett	Wight
1957	Mizell	Jones	Jackson	McDaniel	Wehmeier	Wilhelm	Merritt	Muffett	Schmidt
1956	Mizell	Poholsky	Dickson	Schmidt	Wehmeier	Jackson	McDaniel	Konstanty	Collum
1955	Haddix	Poholsky	Jackson	Schmidt	Arroyo	LaPalme	Lawrence	Wright	
1954	Haddix	Poholsky	Raschi	Staley	Lawrence	Brazle	Presko	Deal	Lint

PRIMARY PITCHING STAFFS (CONT.)

Year	Starter	Starter	Starter	Starter	Starter	Closer	Bullpen	Bullpen	Bullpen
1953	Haddix	Mizell	Presko	Staley	Miller	Brazle	White	Chambers	Clark
1952	Boyer	Mizell	Presko	Staley	Brecheen	Brazle	Yuhas	Chambers	Werle
1951	Poholsky	Lanier	Chambers	Staley	Brecheen	Brazle	Munger	Bokelmann	Boyer
1950	Pollet	Lanier	Munger	Staley	Brecheen	Brazle	Martin	Wilks	Boyer
1949	Pollet	Brazle	Munger	Staley	Brecheen	Wilks	Martin	Reeder	Hearn
1948	Pollet	Brazle	Munger	Dickson	Brecheen	Wilks	Staley	Burkhart	Hearn
1947	Pollet	Hearn	Munger	Dickson	Brecheen	Brazle	Burkhart	Wilks	
1946	Pollet	Beazley	Brazle	Dickson	Brecheen	Barrett	Burkhart	Wilks	
1945	Barrett	Donnelly	Burkhart	Wilks	Brecheen	Byerly	Dockins	Jurisich	
1944	Cooper	Lanier	Jurisich	Wilks	Brecheen	Schmidt	Donnelly	Munger	
1943	Cooper	Lanier	Gumbert	Krist	Pollet	Dickson	Brecheen	Munger	
1942	Cooper	Lanier	Gumbert	Beazley	White	Dickson	Krist	Pollet	
1941	Cooper	Lanier	Gumbert	Warneke	White	Crouch	Hutchinson	Krist	Shoun
1940	Cooper	McGee	Shoun	Warneke	Bowman	Lanier	Russell	Doyle	
1939	Cooper	McGee	Davis	Warneke	Weiland	Shoun	Bowman	Sunkel	Dean
1938	Henshaw	McGee	Davis	Warneke	Weiland	Shoun	Macon	Harrell	
1937	Dean	Johnson	Harrell	Warneke	Weiland	Ryba	Winford	Haines	
1936	Dean	Parmelee	Winford	Dean	Walker	Heusser	Earnshaw	Haines	
1935	Dean	Hallahan	Haines	Dean	Walker	Heusser	Collins	Harrell	
1934	Dean	Hallahan	Carleton	Dean	Walker	Haines	Mooney	Vance	
1933	Dean	Hallahan	Carleton	Vance	Walker	Haines	Mooney	Johnson	
1932	Dean	Hallahan	Carleton	Derringer	Johnson	Haines	Stout	Lindsey	
1931	Grimes	Hallahan	Rhem	Derringer	Johnson	Lindsey	Haines	Kaufmann	Stout
1930	Grimes	Hallahan	Rhem	Haines	Johnson	Bell	Lindsey	Grabowski	Haid
1929	Sherdel	Mitchell	Alexander	Haines	Johnson	Frankhouse	Hallahan	Haid	
1928	Sherdel	Mitchell	Alexander	Haines	Rhem	Johnson	Reinhart	Haid	
1927	Sherdel	McGraw	Alexander	Haines	Rhem	Bell	Reinhart	Keen	
1926	Sherdel	Keen	Alexander	Haines	Rhem	Bell	Reinhart	Johnson	
1925	Sherdel	Sothoron	Dickerman	Haines	Rhem	Dyer	Reinhart	Mails	
1924	Stuart	Sothoron	Dickerman	Haines	Dyer	Sherdel	Bell	Pfeffer	
1923	Toney	Sherdel	Doak	Haines	Pfeffer	Stuart	North	Barfoot	
1922	Pertica	Sherdel	Doak	Haines	Pfeffer	Walker	North	Barfoot	
1921	Pertica	Walker	Doak	Haines	Pfeffer	North	Sherdel	Bailey	Riviere
1920	Schupp	Goodwin	Doak	Haines	Jacobs	Sherdel	North	May	Kircher
1919	May	Goodwin	Doak	Tuero	Meadows	Sherdel	Ames	Jacobs	
1918	Ames	Packard	Doak	Sherdel	Meadows	May	Tuero	Horstmann	
1917	Ames	Watson	Doak	Goodwin	Meadows	May	Packard	Horstmann	
1916	Ames	Watson	Doak	Steele	Meadows	Williams	Jasper	Sallee	
1915	Sallee	Griner	Doak	Robinson	Meadows	Perdue	Niehaus	Ames	
1914	Sallee	Griner	Doak	Perritt	Perdue	Robinson	Steele	Hageman	
1913	Sallee	Griner	Doak	Perritt	Harmon	Geyer	Steele	Burk	
1912	Sallee	Steele	Geyer	Willis	Harmon	Woodburn	Dale	Griner	
1911	Sallee	Steele	Geyer	Golden	Harmon	Woodburn	Lowdermilk	Lowdermilk	
1910	Sallee	Lush	Willis	Corridon	Harmon	Backman	Rieger	Steele	
1909	Sallee	Lush	Beebe	Backman	Harmon	Melter	Higgins	Raleigh	
1908	Raymond	Lush	Beebe	Karger	Fromme	Sallee	Higginbotham	McGlynn	
1907	McGlynn	Lush	Beebe	Karger	Fromme	Brown	Raymond		
1906	Brown	Taylor	Beebe	Karger	Druhot	Thompson	Egan	Hoelskoetter	
1905	Brown	Taylor	Thielman	McFarland	Egan	Kellum	Nichols		
1904	Nichols	Taylor	O'Neill	McFarland	Corbett	Dunleavy			
1903	Brown	Currie	O'Neill	McFarland	Rhoads	Dunleavy	Murphy	Sanders	
1902	Yerkes	Currie	O'Neill	Murphy	Wicker	Pearson	Popp	Dunham	

PRIMARY PITCHING STAFFS (CONT.)

Year	Starter	Starter	Starter	Starter	Starter	Closer	Bullpen	Bullpen	Bullpen
1901	Harper	Powell	Sudhoff	Murphy	Jones				
1900	Young	Powell	Sudhoff	Hughey	Jones	Weyhing			
1899	Young	Powell	Sudhoff	Cuppy	Jones	McBride			
1898	Taylor	Hughey	Sudhoff	Carsey	Esper	Daniels	Gillpatrick		
1897	Donahue	Hart	Sudhoff	Carsey	Esper	Coleman	Kissinger	Lucid	
1896	Donahue	Hart	Breitenstein	Kissinger		Parrott			
1895	Ehret	Staley	Breitenstein	Kissinger	McDougal	Clarkson			
1894	Hawley	Clarkson	Breitenstein	Gleason					
1893	Hawley	Clarkson	Breitenstein	Gleason					
1892	Hawley	Getzein	Breitenstein	Gleason	Galvin	Caruthers	Hawke	Dwyer	
1891	Stivetts	McGill	Griffith	Rettger	Neale	Easton	Burrell	Breitenstein	
1890	Stivetts	Ramsey	Hart	Whitrock	Neale				
1889	Stivetts	King	Chamberlain	Devlin		Hudson			
1888	Hudson	King	Chamberlain	Devlin	Knouff				
1887	Hudson	King	Caruthers	Foutz	Knouff				
1886	Hudson	McGinnis	Caruthers	Foutz					
1885	McGinnis	Caruthers	Foutz						
1884	Davis	McGinnis	Caruthers	Foutz	O'Neill				
1883	Mullane	McGinnis	Hodnett						
1882	Schappert	McGinnis	Dorr						

PRIMARY STARTING LINEUPS

Year	C	1B	2B	3B	SS	LF	CF	RF
2005	Molina	Pujols	Grudzielanek	Nunez	Eckstein	Sanders	Edmonds	Walker
2004	Matheny	Pujols	Womack	Rolen	Renteria	Lankford	Edmonds	Sanders
2003	Matheny	Martinez	Hart	Rolen	Renteria	Pujols	Edmonds	Perez
2002	Matheny	Martinez	Vina	Polanco	Renteria	Pujols	Edmonds	Drew
2001	Matheny	McGwire	Vina	Polanco	Renteria	Lankford	Edmonds	Drew
2000	Matheny	McGwire	Vina	Tatis	Renteria	Lankford	Edmonds	Drew
1999	Marrero	McGwire	McEwing	Tatis	Renteria	Lankford	Drew	Davis
1998	Marrero	McGwire	DeShields	Gaetti	Clayton	Gant	Lankford	Jordan
1997	Difelice	Young	DeShields	Gaetti	Clayton	Gant	Lankford	Mabry
1996	Pagnozzi	Mabry	Alicea	Gaetti	Clayton	Gant	Lankford	Jordan
1995	Sheaffer	Mabry	Oquendo	Cooper	Cromer	Gilkey	Lankford	Jordan
1994	Pagnozzi	Jefferies	Pena	Zeile	Smith	Gilkey	Lankford	Whiten
1993	Pagnozzi	Jefferies	Alicea	Zeile	Smith	Gilkey	Lankford	Whiten
1992	Pagnozzi	Galarraga	Alicea	Zeile	Smith	Gilkey	Lankford	Jose
1991	Pagnozzi	Guerrero	Oquendo	Zeile	Smith	Gilkey	Lankford	Jose
1990	Zeile	Guerrero	Oquendo	Pendleton	Smith	Coleman	McGee	Thompson
1989	Pena	Guerrero	Oquendo	Pendleton	Smith	Coleman	Thompson	Brunansky
1988	Pena	Horner	Alicea	Pendleton	Smith	Coleman	McGee	Brunansky
1987	Pena	Clark	Herr	Pendleton	Smith	Coleman	McGee	Morris
1986	LaValliere	Clark	Herr	Pendleton	Smith	Coleman	McGee	Van Slyke
1985	Nieto	Clark	Herr	Pendleton	Smith	Coleman	McGee	Van Slyke
1984	Porter	Green	Herr	Pendleton	Smith	Smith	McGee	Hendrick
1983	Porter	Hendrick	Herr	Oberkfell	Smith	Smith	McGee	Green
1982	Porter	Hernandez	Herr	Oberkfell	Smith	Smith	McGee	Hendrick
1981	Porter	Hernandez	Herr	Oberkfell	Templeton	Iorg	Scott	Hendrick

PRIMARY STARTING LINEUPS (CONT.)

Year	C	1B	2B	3B	SS	LF	CF	RF
1980	Simmons	Hernandez	Oberkfell	Reitz	Templeton	Bonds	Scott	Hendrick
1979	Simmons	Hernandez	Oberkfell	Reitz	Templeton	Brock	Scott	Hendrick
1978	Simmons	Hernandez	Tyson	Reitz	Templeton	Brock	Hendrick	Morales
1977	Simmons	Hernandez	Tyson	Reitz	Templeton	Brock	Scott	Cruz
1976	Simmons	Hernandez	Tyson	Cruz	Kessinger	Brock	Mumphrey	Crawford
1975	Simmons	Smith	Sizemore	Reitz	Tyson	Brock	McBride	Davis
1974	Simmons	Torre	Sizemore	Reitz	Tyson	Brock	McBride	Smith
1973	Simmons	Torre	Sizemore	Reitz	Tyson	Brock	Cruz	Carbo
1972	Simmons	Alou	Sizemore	Torre	Maxvill	Brock	Cruz	Carbo
1971	Simmons	Hague	Sizemore	Torre	Maxvill	Brock	Cruz	Cardenal
1970	Torre	Hague	Javier	Shannon	Maxvill	Brock	Cardenal	Lee
1969	McCarver	Torre	Javier	Shannon	Maxvill	Brock	Flood	Pinson
1968	McCarver	Cepeda	Javier	Shannon	Maxvill	Brock	Flood	Maris
1967	McCarver	Cepeda	Javier	Shannon	Maxvill	Brock	Flood	Maris
1966	McCarver	Cepeda	Javier	Smith	Maxvill	Brock	Flood	Shannon
1965	McCarver	White	Javier	Boyer	Groat	Brock	Flood	Shannon
1964	McCarver	White	Javier	Boyer	Groat	Brock	Flood	Shannon
1963	McCarver	White	Javier	Boyer	Groat	Musial	Flood	Altman
1962	Oliver	White	Javier	Boyer	Gotay	Musial	Flood	James
1961	Schaffer	White	Javier	Boyer	Grammas	Musial	Flood	Cunningham
1960	Smith	White	Javier	Boyer	Spencer	Musial	Flood	Cunningham
1959	Smith	Musial	Blasingame	Boyer	Grammas	White	Flood	Cunningham
1958	Smith	Musial	Blasingame	Boyer	Kasko	Ennis	Flood	Green
1957	Smith	Musial	Blasingame	Kasko	Dark	Moon	Boyer	Cunningham
1956	Smith	Musial	Blasingame	Boyer	Dark	Repulski	Del Greco	Moon
1955	Sarni	Musial	Schoendienst	Boyer	Grammas	Repulski	Virdon	Elliott
1954	Sarni	Cunningham	Schoendienst	Jablonski	Grammas	Repulski	Moon	Musial
1953	Rice	Bilko	Schoendienst	Jablonski	Hemus	Musial	Repulski	Slaughter
1952	Rice	Sisler	Schoendienst	Johnson	Hemus	Rice	Musial	Slaughter
1951	Rice	Jones	Schoendienst	Johnson	Hemus	Musial	Lowrey	Slaughter
1950	Rice	Nelson	Schoendienst	Glaviano	Marion	Musial	Diering	Slaughter
1949	Rice	Jones	Schoendienst	Kazak	Marion	Slaughter	Diering	Musial
1948	Rice	Jones	Schoendienst	Lang	Marion	Slaughter	Moore	Musial
1947	Rice	Musial	Schoendienst	Kurowski	Marion	Slaughter	Moore	Northey
1946	Garagiola	Musial	Schoendienst	Kurowski	Marion	Dusak	Walker	Slaughter
1945	O'Dea	Sanders	Verban	Kurowski	Marion	Schoendienst	Adams	Hopp
1944	Cooper	Sanders	Verban	Kurowski	Marion	Litwhiler	Hopp	Musial
1943	Cooper	Sanders	Klein	Kurowski	Marion	Litwhiler	Walker	Musial
1942	Cooper	Hopp	Crespi	Kurowski	Marion	Musial	Moore	Slaughter
1941	Mancuso	Mize	Crespi	Brown	Marion	Padgett	Moore	Slaughter
1940	Owen	Mize	Orengo	Martin	Marion	Koy	Moore	Slaughter
1939	Owen	Mize	Martin	Gutteridge	Brown	Medwick	Moore	Slaughter
1938	Owen	Mize	Martin	Gutteridge	Myers	Medwick	Moore	Slaughter
1937	Ogrodowski	Mize	Brown	Gutteridge	Durocher	Medwick	Moore	Padgett
1936	Davis	Mize	Martin	Gelbert	Durocher	Medwick	Moore	Martin
1935	DeLancey	Collins	Frisch	Martin	Durocher	Medwick	Moore	Rothrock
1934	Davis	Collins	Frisch	Martin	Durocher	Medwick	Orsatti	Rothrock
1933	Wilson	Collins	Frisch	Martin	Durocher	Medwick	Orsatti	Watkins
1932	Mancuso	Collins	Reese	Flowers	Gelbert	Puccinelli	Martin	Watkins
1931	Wilson	Bottomley	Frisch	Adams	Gelbert	Hafey	Martin	Watkins
1930	Wilson	Bottomley	Frisch	Adams	Gelbert	Hafey	Douthit	Watkins
1929	Wilson	Bottomley	Frisch	High	Gelbert	Hafey	Douthit	Orsatti

PRIMARY STARTING LINEUPS (CONT.)

Year	C	1B	2B	3B	SS	LF	CF	RF
1928	Wilson	Bottomley	Frisch	Holm	Maranville	Hafey	Douthit	Harper
1927	Snyder	Bottomley	Frisch	Bell	Schuble	Hafey	Douthit	Southworth
1926	O'Farrell	Bottomley	Hornsby	Bell	Thevenow	Blades	Douthit	Southworth
1925	O'Farrell	Bottomley	Hornsby	Bell	Toporcer	Blades	Mueller	Hafey
1924	Gonzalez	Bottomley	Hornsby	Freigau	Cooney	Blades	Holm	Smith
1923	Ainsmith	Bottomley	Hornsby	Stock	Freigau	Blades	Myers	Flack
1922	Ainsmith	Fournier	Hornsby	Stock	Toporcer	McHenry	Smith	Flack
1921	Clemons	Fournier	Hornsby	Stock	Lavan	McHenry	Mann	Smith
1920	Clemons	Fournier	Hornsby	Stock	Lavan	McHenry	Heathcote	Schultz
1919	Clemons	Miller	Stock	Hornsby	Lavan	McHenry	Heathcote	Smith
1918	Gonzalez	Paulette	Fisher	Baird	Hornsby	McHenry	Heathcote	Anderson
1917	Snyder	Paulette	Miller	Baird	Hornsby	Bescher	Cruise	Long
1916	Gonzalez	Miller	Betzel	Hornsby	Corhan	Bescher	Smith	Long
1915	Snyder	Miller	Huggins	Betzel	Butler	Bescher	Wilson	Long
1914	Snyder	Miller	Huggins	Beck	Butler	Dolan	Magee	Wilson
1913	Wingo	Konetchy	Huggins	Mowrey	O'Leary	Magee	Oakes	Evans
1912	Wingo	Konetchy	Huggins	Mowrey	Hauser	Magee	Oakes	Evans
1911	Bliss	Konetchy	Huggins	Mowrey	Hauser	Ellis	Oakes	Evans
1910	Phelps	Konetchy	Huggins	Mowrey	Hauser	Ellis	Oakes	Evans
1909	Phelps	Konetchy	Charles	Byrne	Hulswitt	Ellis	Shaw	Evans
1908	Ludwig	Konetchy	Gilbert	Byrne	O'Rourke	Delahanty	Murray	Barry
1907	Marshall	Konetchy	Bennett	Byrne	Holly	Murray	Barnett	Barry
1906	Grady	Beckley	Bennett	Arndt	McBride	Shannon	Burch	Barry
1905	Grady	Beckley	Arndt	Burke	McBride	Shannon	Smoot	Dunleavy
1904	Grady	Beckley	Farrell	Burke	Shay	Barclay	Smoot	Shannon
1903	O'Neill	Hackett	Farrell	Burke	Brain	Barclay	Smoot	Donovan
1902	Ryan	Brashear	Farrell	Hartman	Krueger	Barclay	Smoot	Donovan
1901	Ryan	McGann	Padden	Krueger	Wallace	Burkett	Heidrick	Donovan
1900	Criger	McGann	Keister	McGraw	Wallace	Burkett	Heidrick	Donovan
1899	Criger	Tebeau	Childs	Cross	Wallace	Burkett	Blake	Heidrick
1898	Clements	Decker	Crooks	Cross	Smith	Harley	Stenzel	Dowd
1897	Douglass	Grady	Hallman	Hartman	Cross	Lally	Harley	Turner
1896	McFarland	Connor	Dowd	Myers	Cross	Sullivan	Parrott	Turner
1895	Peitz	Connor	Quinn	Miller	Ely	Cooley	Brown	Dowd
1894	Peitz	Connor	Quinn	Miller	Ely	Frank	Shugart	Dowd
1893	Peitz	Werden	Quinn	Crooks	Glasscock	Dowd	Brodie	Bannon
1892	Buckley	Werden	Crooks	Pinkney	Glasscock	Carroll	Brodie	Caruthers
1891	Boyle	Comiskey	Eagan	Lyons	Fuller	O'Neill	Hoy	McCarthy
1890	Munyan	Cartwright	Higgins	Davis	Fuller	Gettinger	Duffee	McCarthy
1889	Boyle	Comiskey	Robinson	Latham	Fuller	O'Neill	Duffee	McCarthy
1888	Boyle	Comiskey	Robinson	Latham	White	O'Neill	Lyons	McCarthy
1887	Boyle	Comiskey	Robinson	Latham	Gleason	O'Neill	Welch	Caruthers
1886	Bushong	Comiskey	Robinson	Latham	Gleason	O'Neill	Welch	Nicol
1885	Bushong	Comiskey	Barkley	Latham	Gleason	O'Neill	Welch	Nicol
1884	Deasley	Comiskey	Quest	Latham	Gleason	O'Neill	Lewis	Nicol
1883	Deasley	Comiskey	Strief	Latham	Gleason	Mansell	Lewis	Nicol
1882	Sullivan	Comiskey	Smiley	Gleason	Gleason	Cuthbert	Walker	Seward

Top 10 Batting Leaders, Single Season & Career with Team

Games Played: Career with Team

Player	G	PA
1. Stan Musial	3,026	12,712
2. Lou Brock	2,289	9,927
3. Ozzie Smith	1,990	8,242
4. Enos Slaughter	1,820	7,710
5. Red Schoendienst	1,795	7,446
6. Curt Flood	1,738	6,914
7. Ken Boyer	1,667	7,046
8. Willie McGee	1,661	6,100
9. Rogers Hornsby	1,580	6,714
Ray Lankford	1,580	6,289

At-Bats: Season

Player	AB	Year
1. Lou Brock	689	1967
2. Curt Flood	679	1964
3. Garry Templeton	672	1979
4. Lou Brock	664	1970
Taylor Douthit	664	1930
6. Curt Flood	662	1963
7. Lou Brock	660	1968
8. Red Schoendienst	659	1947
9. Bill White	658	1963
10. Lou Brock	655	1969

At-Bats: Career with Team

Player	AB	PA
1. Stan Musial	10,972	12,712
2. Lou Brock	9,125	9,927
3. Ozzie Smith	7,160	8,242
4. Red Schoendienst	6,841	7,446
5. Enos Slaughter	6,775	7,710
6. Ken Boyer	6,334	7,046
7. Curt Flood	6,318	6,914
8. Rogers Hornsby	5,881	6,714
9. Willie McGee	5,734	6,100
10. Ted Simmons	5,725	6,450

Batting Average: Season

Player	BA	Year
1. Tip O'Neill	.435	1887
2. Rogers Hornsby	.424	1924
3. Rogers Hornsby	.403	1925
4. Rogers Hornsby	.401	1922
5. Rogers Hornsby	.397	1921
6. Jesse Burkett	.396	1899
7. Rogers Hornsby	.384	1923
8. Stan Musial	.376	1948
Jesse Burkett	.376	1901
10. Joe Medwick	.374	1937

Batting Average: Career with Team

Player	BA	PA
1. Rogers Hornsby	.359	6,714
2. Tip O'Neill	.343	3,519
3. Johnny Mize	.336	3,582
4. Joe Medwick	.335	5,056
5. Albert Pujols	.332	3,428
6. Stan Musial	.331	12,712
7. Chick Hafey	.326	3,277
8. Jim Bottomley	.325	6,008
9. Patsy Donovan	.314	2,131
10. Frankie Frisch	.312	5,653

Total Hits: Season

Player	H	Year
1. Rogers Hornsby	250	1922
2. Joe Medwick	237	1937
3. Rogers Hornsby	235	1921
4. Stan Musial	230	1948
Joe Torre	230	1971
6. Stan Musial	228	1946
7. Jim Bottomley	227	1925
Rogers Hornsby	227	1924
9. Jesse Burkett	226	1901
10. Tip O'Neill	225	1887

Total Hits: Career with Team

Player	H	PA
1. Stan Musial	3,630	12,712
2. Lou Brock	2,713	9,927
3. Rogers Hornsby	2,110	6,714
4. Enos Slaughter	2,064	7,710
5. Red Schoendienst	1,980	7,446
6. Ozzie Smith	1,944	8,242
7. Ken Boyer	1,855	7,046
8. Curt Flood	1,853	6,914
9. Jim Bottomley	1,727	6,008
10. Ted Simmons	1,704	6,450

Home Runs: Season

Player	HR	Year
1. Mark McGwire	70	1998
2. Mark McGwire	65	1999
3. Albert Pujols	46	2004
4. Johnny Mize	43	1940
Albert Pujols	43	2003
6. Jim Edmonds	42	2000
Jim Edmonds	42	2004
Rogers Hornsby	42	1922
9. Albert Pujols	41	2005
10. Jim Edmonds	39	2003
Rogers Hornsby	39	1925
Stan Musial	39	1948

Home Runs: Career with Team

Player	HR	PA
1. Stan Musial	475	12,712
2. Ken Boyer	255	7,046
3. Ray Lankford	228	6,289
4. Mark McGwire	220	2,251
5. Jim Edmonds	210	3,537
6. Albert Pujols	201	3,428
7. Rogers Hornsby	193	6,714
8. Jim Bottomley	181	6,008
9. Ted Simmons	172	6,450
10. Johnny Mize	158	3,582

Triples: Season

Player	3B	Year
1. Perry Werden	29	1893
2. Roger Connor	25	1894
Tom Long	25	1915
4. Jim Bottomley	20	1928
Duff Cooley	20	1895
Rogers Hornsby	20	1920
Stan Musial	20	1943
Stan Musial	20	1946
9. Tip O'Neill	19	1887
Garry Templeton	19	1979

Triples: Career with Team

Player	3B	PA
1. Stan Musial	177	12,712
2. Rogers Hornsby	143	6,714
3. Enos Slaughter	135	7,710

4. Lou Brock	121	9,927
5. Jim Bottomley	119	6,008
6. Ed Konetchy	94	4,152
7. Willie McGee	83	6,100
8. Joe Medwick	81	5,056
9. Pepper Martin	75	4,521
10. Tip O'Neill	70	3,519

DOUBLES: SEASON

Player	2B	Year
1. Joe Medwick	64	1936
2. Joe Medwick	56	1937
3. Stan Musial	53	1953
4. Tip O'Neill	52	1887
Enos Slaughter	52	1939
6. Stan Musial	51	1944
Albert Pujols	51	2003
Albert Pujols	51	2004
9. Stan Musial	50	1946
10. Scott Rolen	49	2003

DOUBLES: CAREER WITH TEAM

Player	2B	PA
1. Stan Musial	725	12,712
2. Lou Brock	434	9,927
3. Joe Medwick	377	5,056
4. Rogers Hornsby	367	6,714
5. Enos Slaughter	366	7,710
6. Red Schoendienst	352	7,446
7. Jim Bottomley	344	6,008
8. Ray Lankford	339	6,289
9. Ozzie Smith	338	8,242
10. Ted Simmons	332	6,450

EXTRA-BASE HITS: SEASON

Player	XBH	Year
1. Stan Musial	103	1948
2. Rogers Hornsby	102	1922
3. Albert Pujols	99	2004
4. Joe Medwick	97	1937
5. Joe Medwick	95	1936
Albert Pujols	95	2003
7. Jim Bottomley	93	1928
8. Stan Musial	92	1953
9. Mark McGwire	91	1998
10. Rogers Hornsby	90	1925
Stan Musial	90	1949

EXTRA-BASE HITS: CAREER WITH TEAM

Player	XBH	PA
1. Stan Musial	1,377	12,712
2. Rogers Hornsby	703	6,714
3. Lou Brock	684	9,927
4. Enos Slaughter	647	7,710
5. Jim Bottomley	644	6,008
6. Ray Lankford	619	6,289
7. Joe Medwick	610	5,056
8. Ken Boyer	585	7,046
9. Ted Simmons	541	6,450
10. Red Schoendienst	482	7,446

TOTAL BASES: SEASON

Player	TB	Year
1. Rogers Hornsby	450	1922
2. Stan Musial	429	1948
3. Joe Medwick	406	1937
4. Albert Pujols	394	2003
5. Albert Pujols	389	2004
6. Mark McGwire	383	1998
7. Stan Musial	382	1949
8. Rogers Hornsby	381	1925
9. Rogers Hornsby	378	1921
10. Rogers Hornsby	373	1924

TOTAL BASES: CAREER WITH TEAM

Player	TB	PA
1. Stan Musial	6,134	12,712
2. Lou Brock	3,776	9,927
3. Rogers Hornsby	3,342	6,714
4. Enos Slaughter	3,138	7,710
5. Ken Boyer	3,011	7,046
6. Jim Bottomley	2,852	6,008
7. Red Schoendienst	2,657	7,446
8. Ted Simmons	2,626	6,450
9. Ray Lankford	2,606	6,289
10. Joe Medwick	2,585	5,056

RUNS BATTED IN: SEASON

Player	RBI	Year
1. Joe Medwick	154	1937
2. Rogers Hornsby	152	1922
3. Mark McGwire	147	1998
Mark McGwire	147	1999
5. Rogers Hornsby	143	1925
6. Joe Medwick	138	1936
7. Jim Bottomley	137	1929
Johnny Mize	137	1940
Joe Torre	137	1971
10. Jim Bottomley	136	1928

RUNS BATTED IN: CAREER WITH TEAM

Player	RBI	PA
1. Stan Musial	1,951	12,712
2. Enos Slaughter	1,148	7,710
3. Jim Bottomley	1,105	6,008
4. Rogers Hornsby	1,072	6,714
5. Ken Boyer	1,001	7,046
6. Ted Simmons	929	6,450
7. Joe Medwick	923	5,056
8. Ray Lankford	829	6,289
9. Lou Brock	814	9,927
10. Frankie Frisch	720	5,653

RUNS SCORED: SEASON

Player	R	Year
1. Tip O'Neill	167	1887
2. Arlie Latham	163	1887
3. Arlie Latham	152	1886
4. Jesse Burkett	142	1901
5. Rogers Hornsby	141	1922
6. Charlie Comiskey	139	1887
7. Tommy McCarthy	137	1890
Albert Pujols	137	2003
9. Dummy Hoy	136	1891
Tommy McCarthy	136	1889

RUNS SCORED: CAREER WITH TEAM

Player	R	PA
1. Stan Musial	1,949	12,712
2. Lou Brock	1,427	9,927
3. Rogers Hornsby	1,089	6,714
4. Enos Slaughter	1,071	7,710
5. Red Schoendienst	1,025	7,446
6. Ozzie Smith	991	8,242
7. Ken Boyer	988	7,046
8. Ray Lankford	928	6,289
9. Jim Bottomley	921	6,008
10. Curt Flood	845	6,914

WALKS: SEASON

Player	BB	Year
1. Mark McGwire	162	1998
2. Jack Clark	136	1987
Jack Crooks	136	1892

4. Mark McGwire	133	1999
5. Jack Crooks	121	1893
6. Dummy Hoy	119	1891
7. Yank Robinson	118	1889
8. Miller Huggins	116	1910
Yank Robinson	116	1888
10. Stan Musial	107	1949

Walks: Career with Team

Player	BB	PA
1. Stan Musial	1,599	12,712
2. Ozzie Smith	876	8,242
3. Enos Slaughter	838	7,710
4. Ray Lankford	780	6,289
5. Lou Brock	681	9,927
6. Rogers Hornsby	660	6,714
7. Ken Boyer	631	7,046
8. Ted Simmons	624	6,450
9. Keith Hernandez	585	4,724
10. Miller Huggins	572	3,427

Strikeouts: Season

Player	SO	Year
1. Jim Edmonds	167	2000
2. Ron Gant	162	1997
3. Mark McGwire	155	1998
4. Ray Lankford	151	1998
5. Jim Edmonds	150	2004
6. Ray Lankford	148	2000
7. Ray Lankford	147	1992
8. Mark McGwire	141	1999
9. Jack Clark	139	1987
Jim Edmonds	139	2005

Strikeouts: Career with Team

Player	SO	PA
1. Lou Brock	1,469	9,927
2. Ray Lankford	1,449	6,289
3. Willie McGee	926	6,100
4. Ken Boyer	859	7,046
5. Jim Edmonds	853	3,537
6. Julian Javier	801	6,079
7. Stan Musial	696	12,712
8. Vince Coleman	628	3,906
9. Curt Flood	606	6,914
10. Bill White	601	4,617

Slugging Percentage: Season

Player	SLG	Year
1. Rogers Hornsby	.756	1925
2. Mark McGwire	.752	1998
3. Rogers Hornsby	.722	1922
4. Stan Musial	.702	1948
5. Mark McGwire	.697	1999
6. Rogers Hornsby	.696	1924
7. Tip O'Neill	.691	1887
8. Albert Pujols	.667	2003
9. Albert Pujols	.657	2004
10. Chick Hafey	.652	1930

Slugging Percentage: Career with Team

Player	SLG	PA
1. Mark McGwire	.683	2,251
2. Albert Pujols	.621	3,428
3. Johnny Mize	.600	3,582
4. Jim Edmonds	.584	3,537
5. Rogers Hornsby	.568	6,714
Chick Hafey	.568	3,277
7. Stan Musial	.559	12,712
8. Joe Medwick	.545	5,056
9. Jim Bottomley	.537	6,008
10. Ripper Collins	.517	3,077

On-Base Percentage: Season

Player	OBP	Year
1. Rogers Hornsby	.507	1924
2. Tip O'Neill	.490	1887
3. Rogers Hornsby	.489	1925
4. Mark McGwire	.470	1998
5. Jesse Burkett	.463	1899
6. Jack Clark	.459	1987
Rogers Hornsby	.459	1922
Rogers Hornsby	.459	1923
9. Rogers Hornsby	.458	1921
10. Joe Cunningham	.453	1959

On-Base Percentage: Career with Team

Player	OBP	PA
1. Mark McGwire	.427	2,251
Rogers Hornsby	.427	6,714
3. Johnny Mize	.419	3,582
4. Stan Musial	.417	12,712
5. Albert Pujols	.416	3,428
6. Joe Cunningham	.413	2,622
7. Tip O'Neill	.406	3,519
Jim Edmonds	.406	3,537
9. Miller Huggins	.402	3,427
10. Ray Blades	.395	2,846

OPS (On-Base Percentage + Slugging Percentage): Season

Player	OPS	Year
1. Rogers Hornsby	1.245	1925
2. Mark McGwire	1.222	1998
3. Rogers Hornsby	1.203	1924
4. Rogers Hornsby	1.181	1922
5. Tip O'Neill	1.180	1887
6. Stan Musial	1.152	1948
7. Mark McGwire	1.120	1999
8. Albert Pujols	1.106	2003
9. Rogers Hornsby	1.097	1921
10. Rogers Hornsby	1.086	1923

OPS (On-Base Percentage + Slugging Percentage): Career with Team

Player	OPS	PA
1. Mark McGwire	1.111	2,251
2. Albert Pujols	1.037	3,428
3. Johnny Mize	1.018	3,582
4. Rogers Hornsby	.995	6,714
5. Jim Edmonds	.989	3,537
6. Stan Musial	.976	12,712
7. Chick Hafey	.948	3,277
8. Jim Bottomley	.924	6,008
9. Joe Medwick	.917	5,056
10. Tip O'Neill	.895	3,519

Stolen Bases: Season

Player	SB	Year
1. Arlie Latham	129	1887
2. Lou Brock	118	1974
3. Charlie Comiskey	117	1887
4. Vince Coleman	110	1985
5. Vince Coleman	109	1987
Arlie Latham	109	1888
7. Vince Coleman	107	1986
8. Tommy McCarthy	93	1888
9. Curt Welch	89	1887
10. Tommy McCarthy	83	1890

Stolen Bases: Career with Team

Player	SB	PA
1. Lou Brock	888	9,927
2. Vince Coleman	549	3,906
3. Ozzie Smith	433	8,242
4. Arlie Latham	369	3,971
5. Charlie Comiskey	336	4,554
6. Willie McGee	301	6,100
7. Tommy McCarthy	270	2,471
8. Ray Lankford	250	6,289
9. Yank Robinson	221	2,584
10. Jack Smith	203	4,147

Sacrifice Hits: Season

Player	Sac	Year
1. Taylor Douthit	37	1926
2. Milt Stock	36	1921
Harry Walker	36	1943
4. Lee Magee	35	1914
5. Les Bell	31	1926
Doc Lavan	31	1920
7. Spike Shannon	29	1904
8. Arnold Hauser	28	1911
Marty Marion	28	1941
Milt Stock	28	1920

Sacrifice Hits: Career with Team

Player	Sac	PA
1. Jim Bottomley	154	6,008
2. Marty Marion	147	5,924
3. Rogers Hornsby	135	6,714
4. Ozzie Smith	131	8,242
Milt Stock	131	3,256
6. Frankie Frisch	128	5,653
7. Ed Konetchy	119	4,152
8. Bob Forsch	108	1,003
Jack Smith	108	4,147
10. Taylor Douthit	107	3,844

Hit by Pitch: Season

Player	HBP	Year
1. Steve Evans	31	1910
2. Chief Roseman	29	1890
3. Fernando Vina	28	2000
4. Dan McGann	24	1900
5. Dan McGann	23	1901
John McGraw	23	1900
7. Dick Harley	22	1898
Fernando Viña	22	2001
9. Solly Hemus	20	1952
10. Steve Evans	19	1911

Hit by Pitch: Career with Team

Player	HBP	PA
1. Steve Evans	87	2,673
2. Fernando Viña	79	2,221
3. Yank Robinson	57	2,584
4. Stan Musial	53	12,712
5. Curt Flood	52	6,914
6. Ray Blades	47	2,846
Dan McGann	47	976
8. Solly Hemus	45	2,494
Ed Konetchy	45	4,152
10. Albert Pujols	44	3,428

Top 10 Pitching Leaders, Single Season & Career with Team

Games Pitched: Season

Player	GP	Year
1. Steve Kline	89	2001
2. Ray King	86	2004
3. Steve Kline	78	2003
4. Ray King	77	2005
Mike Perez	77	1992
Julian Tavarez	77	2004
7. Todd Worrell	75	1987
8. Jason Isringhausen	74	2004
Julian Tavarez	74	2005
Todd Worrell	74	1986

Games Pitched: Career with Team

Player	GP	IP
1. Jesse Haines	554	3,203.7
2. Bob Gibson	528	3,884.3
3. Bill Sherdel	465	2,450.7
4. Bob Forsch	455	2,658.7
5. Al Brazle	441	1,376.7
6. Bill Doak	376	2,387.0
7. Todd Worrell	348	425.7
8. Lindy McDaniel	336	884.7
9. Larry Jackson	330	1,672.3
10. Al Hrabosky	329	451.3

Innings Pitched: Season

Player	IP	Year
1. Silver King	585.7	1888
2. Dave Foutz	504.0	1886
3. Bob Caruthers	482.3	1885
4. Tony Mullane	460.7	1883
5. Silver King	458.0	1889
6. Ted Breitenstein	447.3	1894
7. Jack Stivetts	440.0	1891
8. Ted Breitenstein	429.7	1895
9. Elton Chamberlain	421.7	1889
10. Jack Stivetts	419.3	1890

Innings Pitched: Career with Team

Player	IP
1. Bob Gibson	3,884.3
2. Jesse Haines	3,203.7
3. Bob Forsch	2,658.7
4. Bill Sherdel	2,450.7
5. Bill Doak	2,387.0
6. Ted Breitenstein	1,925.3
7. Slim Sallee	1,905.3
8. Harry Brecheen	1,790.3
9. Dizzy Dean	1,737.3
10. Larry Jackson	1,672.3

Batters Faced: Season

Player	BF	Year
1. Silver King	2,294	1888
2. Dave Foutz	2,091	1886
3. Bob Caruthers	1,948	1885
4. Silver King	1,920	1889
5. Tony Mullane	1,841	1883

6. Elton Chamberlain	1,818	1889
7. Jack Stivetts	1,782	1890
8. Jack Stivetts	1,701	1891
9. Silver King	1,666	1887
10. Dave Foutz	1,659	1885

Batters Faced: Career with Team

Player	BF	IP
1. Bob Gibson	16,068	3,884.3
2. Jesse Haines	13,624	3,203.7
3. Bob Forsch	11,088	2,658.7
4. Bill Sherdel	10,473	2,450.7
5. Bill Doak	9,908	2,387.0
6. Slim Sallee	7,811	1,905.3
7. Harry Brecheen	7,327	1,790.3
8. Dizzy Dean	7,212	1,737.3
9. Larry Jackson	7,056	,672.3
10. Bill Hallahan	6,313	1,453.3

Games Started: Season

Player	GS	Year
1. Silver King	65	1888
2. Dave Foutz	57	1886
3. Jack Stivetts	56	1891
4. Bob Caruthers	53	1885
5. Elton Chamberlain	52	1889
Silver King	52	1889
7. Ted Breitenstein	50	1894
Ted Breitenstein	50	1895
9. Tony Mullane	49	1883
10. Jack Taylor	47	1898

Games Started: Career with Team

Player	GS	IP
1. Bob Gibson	482	3,884.3
2. Bob Forsch	401	2,658.7
3. Jesse Haines	388	3,203.7
4. Bill Doak	319	2,387.0
5. Bill Sherdel	242	2,450.7
6. Harry Brecheen	224	1,790.3
7. Ted Breitenstein	221	1,925.3
8. Slim Sallee	215	1,905.3
9. Larry Jackson	209	1,672.3
10. Matt Morris	206	1,377.3

Complete Games: Season

Player	CG	Year
1. Silver King	64	1888
2. Dave Foutz	55	1886
3. Bob Caruthers	53	1885
4. Tony Mullane	49	1883
5. Ted Breitenstein	46	1894
Ted Breitenstein	46	1895
Dave Foutz	46	1885
Silver King	46	1889
9. Elton Chamberlain	45	1889
10. Kid Gleason	43	1892
Silver King	43	1887
Jumbo McGinnis	43	1882

Complete Games: Career with Team

Player	CG	IP
1. Bob Gibson	255	3,884.3
2. Jesse Haines	208	3,203.7
3. Ted Breitenstein	197	1,925.3
4. Dave Foutz	156	1,457.7
5. Silver King	153	1,433.7
6. Bob Caruthers	151	1,395.0
7. Jumbo McGinnis	145	1,325.0
8. Bill Doak	144	2,387.0
Bill Sherdel	144	2,450.7
10. Dizzy Dean	141	1,737.3

Games Won: Season

Player	W	Year
1. Silver King	45	1888
2. Dave Foutz	41	1886
3. Bob Caruthers	40	1885
4. Tony Mullane	35	1883
5. Elton Chamberlain	34	1889
Silver King	34	1889
7. Dave Foutz	33	1885
Jack Stivetts	33	1891
9. Silver King	32	1887
10. Bob Caruthers	30	1886
Dizzy Dean	30	1934

Games Won: Career with Team

Player	W	IP
1. Bob Gibson	251	3,884.3
2. Jesse Haines	210	3,203.7
3. Bob Forsch	163	2,658.7
4. Bill Sherdel	153	2,450.7
5. Bill Doak	144	2,387.0
6. Dizzy Dean	134	1,737.3
7. Harry Brecheen	128	1,790.3
8. Dave Foutz	114	1,457.7
9. Silver King	111	1,433.7
10. Bob Caruthers	108	1,395.0

Games Lost: Season

Player	L	Year
1. Red Donahue	35	1897
2. Ted Breitenstein	30	1895
3. Bill Hart	29	1896
Jack Taylor	29	1898
5. Bill Hart	27	1897
Pink Hawley	27	1894
Willie Sudhoff	27	1898
8. Ted Breitenstein	26	1896
9. Stoney McGlynn	25	1907
Bugs Raymond	25	1908

Games Lost: Career with Team

Player	L	IP
1. Bob Gibson	174	3,884.3
2. Jesse Haines	158	3,203.7
3. Bill Doak	136	2,387.0
4. Bill Sherdel	131	2,450.7
5. Bob Forsch	127	2,658.7
6. Ted Breitenstein	125	1,925.3
7. Slim Sallee	107	1,905.3
8. Larry Jackson	86	1,672.3
9. Bob Harmon	81	1,284.3
10. Harry Brecheen	79	1,790.3

Winning Percentage: Season

Player	W%	Year
1. Al Hrabosky	.812	1975
Howie Krist	.812	1942
3. Dizzy Dean	.811	1934
4. Ted Wilks	.810	1944
5. Chris Carpenter	.808	2005
6. Harry Brecheen	.789	1945
7. Johnny Beazley	.778	1942
8. Bob Gibson	.767	1970
9. Jesse Haines	.765	1926
10. Bob Caruthers	.763	1887

Winning Percentage: Career with Team

Player	W%	IP
1. John Tudor	.705	881.7
2. Dave Foutz	.704	1,457.7

Player	Pct.	IP
3. Bob Caruthers	.692	1,395.0
4. Silver King	.689	1,433.7
5. Mort Cooper	.677	1,480.3
6. Dizzy Dean	.641	1,737.3
7. Lon Warneke	.629	1,157.7
8. Matt Morris	.620	1,377.3
9. Harry Brecheen	.618	1,790.3
Grover Alexander	.618	792.0

Shutouts: Season

Player	SHO	Year
1. Bob Gibson	13	1968
2. Dave Foutz	11	1886
3. Mort Cooper	10	1942
John Tudor	10	1985
5. Harry Brecheen	7	1948
Mort Cooper	7	1944
Dizzy Dean	7	1934
Bill Doak	7	1914
9. 10 tied with . . .	6	——

Shutouts: Career with Team

Player	SHO	IP
1. Bob Gibson	56	3,884.3
2. Bill Doak	30	2,387.0
3. Mort Cooper	28	1,480.3
4. Harry Brecheen	25	1,790.3
5. Jesse Haines	24	3,203.7
6. Dizzy Dean	23	1,737.3
7. Max Lanier	20	1,454.7
Howie Pollet	20	1,401.7
9. Bob Forsch	19	2,658.7
10. Ernie Broglio	18	1,124.0
Jumbo McGinnis	18	1,325.0

ERA: Season

Player	ERA	Year
1. Bob Gibson	1.12	1968
2. Silver King	1.64	1888
3. Bill Doak	1.72	1914
4. Mort Cooper	1.78	1942
5. Max Lanier	1.90	1943
6. John Tudor	1.93	1985
7. Kid Nichols	2.02	1904
8. Bugs Raymond	2.03	1908
9. Ed Karger	2.04	1907
10. Bob Caruthers	2.07	1885

ERA: Career with Team

Player	ERA	IP
1. Ed Karger	2.46	647.0
2. John Tudor	2.52	881.7
3. Slim Sallee	2.67	1,905.3
Jack Taylor	2.67	816.0
Dave Foutz	2.67	1,457.7
6. Silver King	2.71	1,433.7
7. Jumbo McGinnis	2.73	1,325.0
Mike O'Neill	2.73	694.3
9. Johnny Lush	2.74	841.3
Red Ames	2.74	827.0

Earned Runs Allowed: Season

Player	ER	Year
1. Ted Breitenstein	238	1894
2. Red Donahue	237	1897
3. Pink Hawley	214	1894
4. Ted Breitenstein	212	1895
5. Bill Hart	205	1897
6. Kid Gleason	195	1893
7. Bill Hart	191	1896
8. Red Donahue	172	1896
Jack Taylor	172	1898
10. Ted Breitenstein	169	1896

Earned Runs Allowed: Career with Team

Player	ER	IP
1. Jesse Haines	1,297	3,203.7
2. Bob Gibson	1,258	3,884.3
3. Bob Forsch	1,085	2,658.7
4. Bill Sherdel	992	2,450.7
5. Ted Breitenstein	919	1,925.3
6. Bill Doak	776	2,387.0
7. Larry Jackson	682	1,672.3
8. Bill Hallahan	617	1,453.3
9. Harry Brecheen	578	1,790.3
10. Dizzy Dean	577	1,737.3

Strikeouts: Season

Player	K	Year
1. Jack Stivetts	289	1890
2. Dave Foutz	283	1886
3. Bob Gibson	274	1970
4. Bob Gibson	270	1965
5. Bob Gibson	269	1969
6. Bob Gibson	268	1968
7. Jack Stivetts	259	1891
8. Silver King	258	1888
9. Toad Ramsey	257	1890
10. Bob Gibson	245	1964

Strikeouts: Career with Team

Player	K	IP
1. Bob Gibson	3,117	3,884.3
2. Dizzy Dean	1,095	1,737.3
3. Bob Forsch	1,079	2,658.7
4. Matt Morris	986	1,377.3
5. Jesse Haines	979	3,203.7
6. Steve Carlton	951	1,265.0
7. Bill Doak	938	2,387.0
8. Larry Jackson	899	1,672.3
9. Harry Brecheen	857	1,790.3
10. Vinegar Bend Mizell	789	1,218.7

Strikeouts Per Nine IP: Season

Player	K/9	Year
1. Rick Ankiel	9.98	2000
2. Andy Benes	8.90	1997
3. Bob Gibson	8.39	1970
4. Jose DeLeon	8.31	1988
5. Bob Gibson	8.13	1965
6. Sam Jones	8.10	1958
7. Jose DeLeon	8.08	1990
8. Bob Gibson	8.01	1962
9. Steve Carlton	8.00	1969
10. Todd Stottlemyre	7.96	1997

Strikeouts Per Nine IP: Career with Team

Player	K/9	IP
1. Todd Stottlemyre	7.97	565.7
2. Jose DeLeon	7.48	917.7
3. Bob Gibson	7.22	3,884.3
4. Andy Benes	7.11	777.7
5. Darryl Kile	6.96	544.3
6. Steve Carlton	6.77	1,265.0
7. Matt Morris	6.44	1,377.3
8. Woody Williams	6.30	588.7
9. Harvey Haddix	6.23	786.3
10. Ernie Broglio	5.98	1,124.0

Hits Allowed: Season

Player	HA	Year
1. Ted Breitenstein	497	1894
2. Red Donahue	484	1897
3. Pink Hawley	481	1894
4. Jack Taylor	465	1898

5. Silver King	462	1889
6. Ted Breitenstein	458	1895
7. Silver King	437	1888
8. Kid Gleason	436	1893
9. Jack Powell	433	1899
10. Bob Caruthers	430	1885

HITS ALLOWED: CAREER WITH TEAM

Player	HA	IP
1. Jesse Haines	3,455	3,203.7
2. Bob Gibson	3,279	3,884.3
3. Bill Sherdel	2,721	2,450.7
4. Bob Forsch	2,602	2,658.7
5. Bill Doak	2,285	2,387.0
6. Ted Breitenstein	2,009	1,925.3
7. Slim Sallee	1,831	1,905.3
8. Larry Jackson	1,689	1,672.3
9. Dizzy Dean	1,684	1,737.3
10. Harry Brecheen	1,609	1,790.3

HITS ALLOWED PER NINE IP: SEASON

Player	H/9	Year
1. Bob Gibson	5.85	1968
2. Jose DeLeon	6.36	1989
3. Bugs Raymond	6.55	1908
4. Dick Hughes	6.64	1967
5. Mort Cooper	6.69	1942
6. Bob Gibson	6.70	1962
7. Silver King	6.72	1888
8. Bob Gibson	6.74	1966
9. Bill Doak	6.79	1914
10. Ernie Broglio	6.84	1960

HITS ALLOWED PER NINE IP: CAREER WITH TEAM

Player	H/9	IP
1. Fred Beebe	7.29	861.0
2. Bob Gibson	7.60	3,884.3
3. Jose DeLeon	7.63	917.7
4. Elton Chamberlain	7.66	568.7
5. John Tudor	7.73	881.7
6. Ernie Broglio	7.78	1,124.0
Jack Stivetts	7.78	1,051.0
8. Todd Stottlemyre	7.83	565.7
9. Mort Cooper	7.95	1,480.3
10. Dave Foutz	8.06	1,457.7

WALKS ALLOWED: SEASON

Player	BB	Year
1. Jack Stivetts	232	1891
2. Ted Breitenstein	191	1894
3. Kid Gleason	187	1893
4. Bob Harmon	181	1911
5. Jack Stivetts	179	1890
6. Ted Breitenstein	178	1895
7. Elton Chamberlain	165	1889
8. Ted Breitenstein	156	1893
9. Kid Gleason	151	1892
10. Pink Hawley	149	1894

WALKS ALLOWED: CAREER WITH TEAM

Player	BB	IP
1. Bob Gibson	1,336	3,884.3
2. Jesse Haines	870	3,203.7
3. Ted Breitenstein	839	1,925.3
4. Bob Forsch	780	2,658.7
5. Bill Doak	740	2,387.0
6. Bill Hallahan	648	1,453.3
7. Bill Sherdel	595	2,450.7
8. Bob Harmon	594	1,284.3
9. Vinegar Bend Mizell	568	1,218.7
10. Max Lanier	524	1,454.7

WALKS ALLOWED PER NINE IP: SEASON

Player	BB/9	Year
1. Bob Tewksbury	0.77	1992
2. Bob Tewksbury	0.84	1993
3. Jumbo McGinnis	0.89	1884
4. Cy Young	1.01	1900
5. Bob Caruthers	1.06	1885
6. Cy Young	1.07	1899
7. Silver King	1.17	1888
8. Jumbo McGinnis	1.23	1882
9. Grover Alexander	1.28	1927
10. Jack Powell	1.33	1901

WALKS ALLOWED PER NINE IP: CAREER WITH TEAM

Player	BB/9	IP
1. Cy Young	1.04	690.7
2. Bob Tewksbury	1.16	968.7
3. Jumbo McGinnis	1.38	1,325.0
4. Grover Alexander	1.39	792.0
5. Bob Caruthers	1.59	1,395.0
6. Jack Powell	1.91	999.0
7. Paul Dean	1.94	669.0
8. Silver King	1.95	1,433.7
9. John Tudor	1.99	881.7
10. Nat Hudson	2.02	694.3

WHIP (WALKS + HITS PER NINE IP): SEASON

Player	WHIP	Year
1. Bob Gibson	0.853	1968
2. Silver King	0.876	1888
3. John Tudor	0.938	1985
4. Dick Hughes	0.954	1967
5. Tony Mullane	0.968	1883
6. Dave Foutz	0.982	1884
7. Mort Cooper	0.987	1942
8. Kid Nichols	1.003	1904
9. Bob Caruthers	1.010	1885
10. Bob Tewksbury	1.017	1992

WHIP (WALKS + HITS PER NINE IP): CAREER WITH TEAM

Player	WHIP	IP
1. John Tudor	1.080	881.7
2. Bob Caruthers	1.095	1,395.0
3. Jumbo McGinnis	1.098	1,325.0
4. Silver King	1.123	1,433.7
5. Cy Young	1.137	690.7
6. Dave Foutz	1.144	1,457.7
7. Jack Taylor	1.159	816.0
8. Ed Karger	1.168	647.0
9. Grover Alexander	1.174	792.0
10. Harry Brecheen	1.181	1,790.3

HOME RUNS ALLOWED: SEASON

Player	HRA	Year
1. Murry Dickson	39	1948
2. Matt Morris	35	2004
Brett Tomko	35	2003
4. Bob Gibson	34	1965
Dustin Hermanson	34	2001
6. Darryl Kile	33	2000
7. Lon Warneke	32	1937

8. Gerry Staley	31	1953
Garrett Stephenson	31	2000
10. Andy Benes	30	2000
Andy Benes	30	2001
Garrett Stephenson	30	2003
Todd Stottlemyre	30	1996

Home Runs Allowed: Career with Team

Player	HRA	IP
1. Bob Gibson	257	3,884.3
2. Bob Forsch	204	2,658.7
3. Jesse Haines	165	3,203.7
4. Larry Jackson	152	1,672.3
5. Matt Morris	129	1,377.3
6. Bill Sherdel	126	2,450.7
7. Ray Sadecki	125	1,103.7
8. Gerry Staley	115	1,274.7
9. Harry Brecheen	110	1,790.3
Ernie Broglio	110	1,124.0

Saves: Season

Player	SV	Year
1. Jason Isringhausen	47	2004
Lee Smith	47	1991
3. Bruce Sutter	45	1984
4. Lee Smith	43	1992
Lee Smith	43	1993
6. Jason Isringhausen	39	2005
7. Dennis Eckersley	36	1997
Tom Henke	36	1995
Bruce Sutter	36	1982
Todd Worrell	36	1986

Saves: Career with Team

Player	SV	IP
1. Lee Smith	160	266.7
2. Jason Isringhausen	140	241.7
3. Todd Worrell	129	425.7
4. Bruce Sutter	127	396.7
5. Dennis Eckersley	66	113.0
6. Lindy McDaniel	64	884.7
7. Al Brazle	60	1,376.7
Joe Hoerner	60	244.0
9. Al Hrabosky	59	451.3
10. Dave Veres	48	224.0

Wild Pitches: Season

Player	WP	Year
1. Jack Stivetts	33	1890
2. Toad Ramsey	31	1890
3. Silver King	29	1889
4. Dave Foutz	26	1886
5. Jack Stivetts	25	1891
6. Dave Foutz	22	1885
7. Bob Caruthers	21	1885
Pink Hawley	21	1894
9. Billy Hart	20	1890
10. Jack Harper	19	1901

Wild Pitches: Career with Team

Player	WP	IP
1. Bob Gibson	108	3,884.3
2. Bob Forsch	88	2,658.7
3. Jack Stivetts	74	1,051.0
4. Bill Hallahan	56	1,453.3
5. Jesse Haines	55	3,203.7
6. Steve Carlton	52	1,265.0
7. Lindy McDaniel	51	884.7
8. Joe Magrane	50	921.0
9. Dave Foutz	48	1,457.7
10. Ray Sadecki	47	1,103.7

Hit Batsmen: Season

Player	HB	Year
1. Willie Sudhoff	27	1898
2. Jack Taylor	25	1898
3. Red Donahue	22	1897
4. Bob Caruthers	19	1885
Cowboy Jones	19	1900
6. Dave Foutz	18	1885
Willie Sudhoff	18	1901
8. Bill Hart	17	1897
Silver King	17	1887
Gerry Staley	17	1953

Hit Batsmen: Career with Team

Player	HB	IP
1. Bob Gibson	102	3,884.3
2. Willie Sudhoff	72	1,000.3
3. Jesse Haines	57	3,203.7
4. Bill Doak	54	2,387.0
5. Bill Sherdel	51	2,450.7
6. Matt Morris	49	1,377.3
Gerry Staley	49	1,274.7
8. Dave Foutz	47	1,457.7
9. Bob Caruthers	45	1,395.0
10. Bob Forsch	42	2,658.7

Games Finished: Season

Player	GF	Year
1. Jason Isringhausen	66	2004
2. Bruce Sutter	63	1984
3. Lee Smith	61	1991
Dave Veres	61	2000
5. Todd Worrell	60	1986
6. Bruce Sutter	58	1982
7. Lee Smith	55	1992
8. Todd Worrell	54	1987
Todd Worrell	54	1988
10. Dennis Eckersley	53	1996

Games Finished: Career with Team

Player	GF	IP
1. Todd Worrell	232	425.7
2. Lee Smith	209	266.7
3. Bruce Sutter	203	396.7
4. Jason Isringhausen	200	241.7
5. Lindy McDaniel	188	884.7
6. Al Hrabosky	182	451.3
7. Al Brazle	178	1,376.7
8. Bill Sherdel	152	2,450.7
9. Joe Hoerner	137	244.0
10. Ken Dayley	136	374.0

Significant Cardinals

Bottomley, Jim (1B)
(1922–1932)

Jim Bottomley worked as a blacksmith's apprentice while playing semipro ball in Illinois. When he caught the eye of a St. Louis scout with a two-homer, three-triple game, he was signed and sent to Syracuse in 1922. After a late-season call-up to St. Louis that year, he joined the team for good in 1923, hitting .371 in his first full season. Hitting .300 would become a habit for Bottomley, as he reached the mark in nine of his 11 seasons in St. Louis, barely missing two other years with averages of .299 and .296. In 1924 Bottomley, a prolific run producer, began a streak of six straight seasons with at least 110 RBIs. In 1928 he accomplished the rare feat of leading the league in both homers (31) and triples (20). He also led the league with 136 RBIs and 362 total bases on his way to the NL MVP Award. He barely lost the batting title to teammate Chick Hafey, .3489 to .3482, which would have given him the Triple Crown.

Bottomley was traded to Cincinnati after the 1932 season, just before the famed "Gas House Gang" got a full head of steam. After three years with the Reds and two more with the Browns, Bottomley retired after the 1937 season. After one season as the manager of the Syracuse Chiefs, Bottomley left baseball for two decades. He returned as a scout for the Cubs in 1957, then took over as manager of the Pulaski Cubs before dying of a heart attack in 1959. He was elected to the Hall of Fame in 1974.

CAREER CARDINALS RECORD:

Games	AB	Hits	Runs
1,392	5,314	1,727	921
Avg	HR	RBI	SB
.325	181	1,105	50

Boyer, Ken (3B)
(1955–1965)

The St. Louis Cardinals signed Ken Boyer as an amateur free agent before the 1949 season, and after three years in the minors and three more in the Army, they brought him up to the majors in 1955. The Redbirds were grooming him to be a pitcher, but his .455 batting average in the minors changed all that. After trying various positions, the Cardinals finally put him at third base, a position where he would win five Gold Gloves. A seven-time All-Star with St. Louis, Boyer was consistent, as evidenced by a seven-year streak with at least 23 homers and 90 RBIs. In 1956 he hit .306, the first of five .300 seasons in a six-year stretch, and in 1959 he had a 29-game hitting streak. In 1964 Boyer won the NL MVP Award as he helped the Cardinals come back from seventh place to overtake the Phillies in one of baseball's all-time great comebacks. The next year, however, back problems took their toll on Boyer and after the season he was traded to the Mets. He spent his last four years playing with the Mets, White Sox, and Dodgers before retiring early in the 1969 season. Boyer spent the next dozen years bouncing around among various coaching and managing jobs in both the minors and majors—including two-plus seasons as the Cardinals' manager—before dying from inoperable lung cancer in 1982, at the age of 51.

CAREER CARDINALS RECORD:

Games	AB	Hits	Runs
1,667	6,334	1,855	988
Avg	**HR**	**RBI**	**SB**
.293	255	1,001	97

BROCK, LOU (OF)
(1964–1979)

Lou Brock's love of baseball began in a most unusual way. When he was 10 years old, Brock got in trouble for hitting a teacher with a spitball in a playground game. Given the assignment of writing a report on five baseball players (Stan Musial, Roy Campanella, Joe DiMaggio, Don Newcombe, and Jackie Robinson), Brock was amazed to discover that major league players received meal money in addition to their salaries. This made an impression on Brock, who knew real poverty and hunger. Even while in college at Southern University, Brock felt the pangs of hunger. During one baseball practice session with the school's team, Brock collapsed. School officials discovered that Brock was so poor that he fed himself by dropping by friends' homes during mealtimes. Brock initially was to sign with the Cardinals, but when he arrived in St. Louis from his home in Louisiana to sign with the scout, Brock learned the scout was in Seattle, and no one else would give him the time of day. Brock got back on a bus to Chicago; after a tryout, the Cubs signed him for a $30,000 bonus. He would not go hungry again.

After three-plus seasons with the Cubs, Lou Brock was traded to the Cardinals in mid-1964 for pitcher Ernie Broglio, a former 20-game winner, arousing the anger of many in St. Louis. During Brock's time in Chicago he had established himself as a .260 hitter with little power who swiped about 20 bases a year. Brock underwent an almost immediate transformation thanks to Cardinal manager Johnny Keane, who told Brock he wasn't capitalizing on his speed. Keane gave Brock the green light to steal at will. For the final four months of the 1964 season, Brock hit .348 and helped the seventh-place Cardinals emerge from the pack and overtake the Phillies in dramatic fashion, erasing a 10-game Philadelphia lead in the last two weeks of the season.

Starting in 1965, Brock turned the stolen base into an offensive weapon that hadn't been seen in major league baseball since the days of Ty Cobb. From 1965 to 1973, Brock stole between 51 and 74 bases each year, helping turn the Cardinals into a perennial contender. In 1974 he smashed Maury Wills's single-season record of 104 stolen bases by swiping 118. In 1977 Brock eclipsed Ty Cobb's career stolen-base record when he stole his 893rd base. Finishing his career in 1979 with 938 steals, Brock became the 14th player in major league history to join the 3,000-hit club, ending with 3,023. In tribute to Brock, the National League trophy given to each year's stolen base king is named the Lou Brock Award. Brock was inducted into the Hall of Fame in 1985.

CAREER CARDINALS RECORD:

Games	AB	Hits	Runs
2,289	9,125	2,713	1,427
Avg	**HR**	**RBI**	**SB**
.297	129	814	888

Comiskey, Charles (1B) (1882–1889, 1891)

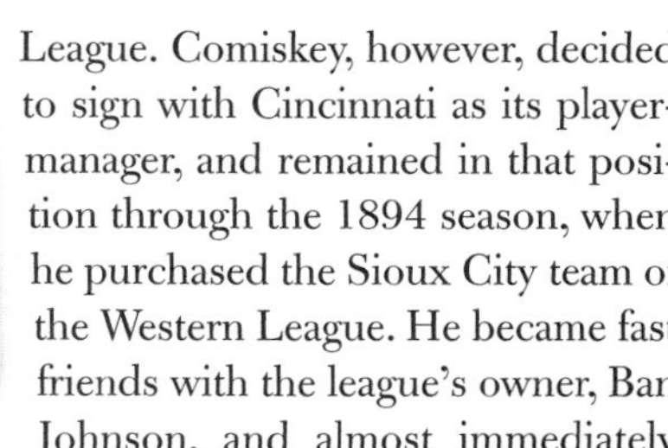

While playing with the Dubuque Rabbits, pitcher Charles Comiskey received a letter from Al Spink, secretary of the American Association's St. Louis Browns, informing him that owner Chris Von der Ahe was seeking quality players, and was paying between $90 and $125 per month. "Make your terms as low as possible so I can clinch one of the jobs for you," wrote Spink. Comiskey wrote back that he'd take the $90 pay, figuring he would stand a better chance of making the team if he was willing to take less. He did make the team, but after a month Von der Ahe raised his salary to $150. Almost immediately upon arriving in St. Louis, however, Comiskey hurt his pitching arm and convinced the manager to shift him to first base.

The move not only proved to be a good one for St. Louis, but also had lasting impact on the game itself. Before Comiskey, first basemen typically played either with one foot on the bag, or within a step of the bag. Comiskey ranged well off of first, cutting off balls in the hole that normally went for hits. He also forced the pitchers to rethink how they played their position because they now had to cover first on balls fielded by Comiskey in the hole. This in turn led to other infielders playing off the other two bases, dramatically altering the defensive strategy used in baseball for the previous 35 years.

Comiskey became the team's player-manager in 1883, and from 1885 to1888 he led the Browns to four consecutive American Association pennants. Comiskey, like many other major league players, jumped to the Players' League in 1890, but returned to St. Louis in 1891 when the upstart league folded. After a final year in the American Association, that league folded, too, and the St. Louis Browns were absorbed into the National League. Comiskey, however, decided to sign with Cincinnati as its player-manager, and remained in that position through the 1894 season, when he purchased the Sioux City team of the Western League. He became fast friends with the league's owner, Ban Johnson, and almost immediately moved his team to St. Paul. Together, Johnson and Comiskey came up with the idea of creating a new major league to rival the entrenched National League. By 1900 the Western League had been renamed the American League and Comiskey was awarded the Chicago franchise, calling his team the White Stockings. A year later the American League became a major league and Charles Comiskey was one of its prominent founding members.

Comiskey's legacy as baseball's biggest tightwad reached its apotheosis in the sordid Black Sox affair that exploded onto the national scene in late 1920. The Black Sox tag had first been applied in 1917 after the players refused to wash their uniforms since Comiskey charged the players to wash them, a hardship no other team imposed. The players rebelled and their unwashed uniforms turned black with dirt. Embarrassed by the entirely justified newspaper coverage of his miserliness, Comiskey eventually gave in, then later deducted the laundry fees from the players' 1917 World Series shares. In addition, he had promised his players a bonus if they won the pennant, but reneged, giving them a case of cheap champagne instead. While all other teams paid their players $4 a day in meal money, Comiskey paid $3. All of the White Sox players except Eddie Collins were grossly underpaid, and this more than anything led to the game-fixing scandal during the 1919 World Series in which a number of White Sox players threw games to the Reds in exchange for money. While the White Sox had won four pennants and two World Series in the team's first 19 years of existence, and were regular contenders, after the scandal broke in September 1920, Comiskey's team never again got out of the second division during his lifetime. Comiskey died in 1931, still devastated over the Black Sox scandal he had engendered. In 1939 he was elected to the Hall of Fame, an honor richly deserved—despite the scandal—because of his career as a player, innovator, manager, owner, and industry magnate.

CAREER CARDINALS RECORD:

Games	AB	Hits	Runs
1,036	4,389	1,198	816
Avg	**HR**	**RBI**	**SB**
.273	26	694	336

DEAN, DIZZY (SP/RP)
(1930, 1932–1937)

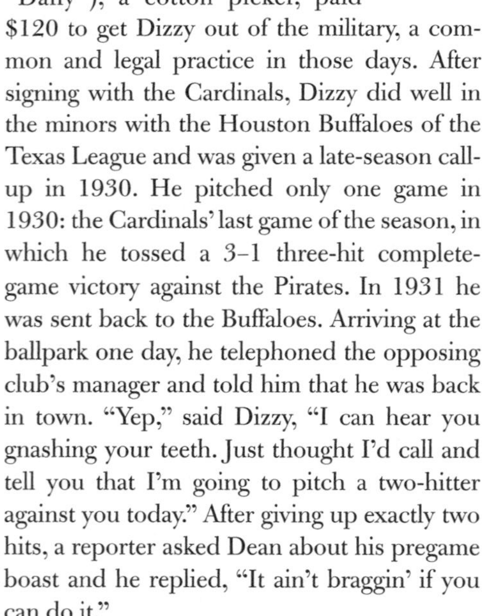

Jay "Dizzy" Dean dropped out of school in fourth grade and enlisted in the Army when he was 16, playing ball for the base team. His brother Paul (aka "Daffy"), a cotton picker, paid $120 to get Dizzy out of the military, a common and legal practice in those days. After signing with the Cardinals, Dizzy did well in the minors with the Houston Buffaloes of the Texas League and was given a late-season call-up in 1930. He pitched only one game in 1930: the Cardinals' last game of the season, in which he tossed a 3–1 three-hit complete-game victory against the Pirates. In 1931 he was sent back to the Buffaloes. Arriving at the ballpark one day, he telephoned the opposing club's manager and told him that he was back in town. "Yep," said Dizzy, "I can hear you gnashing your teeth. Just thought I'd call and tell you that I'm going to pitch a two-hitter against you today." After giving up exactly two hits, a reporter asked Dean about his pregame boast and he replied, "It ain't braggin' if you can do it."

After winning 26 games with a 1.57 ERA for the Buffaloes in 1931, Dean was called up to St. Louis in 1932, where he went 18–15 in 33 starts and 13 relief appearances, leading the NL in innings, strikeouts, and shutouts. In 1933 he won 20 games, including a July 30 game against the Cubs in which he became the first major leaguer ever to strike out 17 batters in a nine-inning game.

Dean earned his nickname because reporters loved talking with the comical pitcher, but often found his interviews, which were laced with tall tales, too "dizzying" to keep up with. When he first came up to the big leagues, he gave different names, birthdates, hometowns, and other biographical information to different reporters. When they confronted him with his inconsistencies, he replied, "I was helpin' you fellas out. Them ain't lies; them's scoops." In January 1934, Dizzy boldly predicted that the Cardinals would win the National League pennant; that he would win 20–25 games; and his brother Paul would chip in with 18–20. The Redbirds did win the pennant and Paul won 19 games. Dizzy was off, however, in his own predicted win total. Instead of the estimated 20–25 wins, he won 30, becoming the last National League pitcher to reach that level. And the brothers might have won more had they not been suspended for two games each after missing an exhibition game over a salary dispute. Before the 1934 World Series, Dizzy predicted that he and his brother would each win two games against the Tigers in bringing the championship home to St. Louis, and that's exactly what happened. Dizzy won Games 1 and 7, and Paul won Games 3 and 6.

Dizzy was used as a pinch-runner in Game 4. While running to second, he was nailed in the head by a throw from infielder Billy Rogell. The ball hit him so hard it caromed 100 feet into the outfield. Dean was carried off the field and taken to the hospital. When the reporters caught up with him, Dizzy—in classic Dizzy style—told them, "The doctors X-rayed my head and found nothing."

After being selected for the 1937 All-Star Game, Dizzy wanted to spend the three-day break fishing, but his wife insisted that he play, saying he owed it to the fans. In the third inning, Earl Averill hit a line drive that struck Dean in the foot. When told it was fractured, Dean argued, "Fractured, hell! The damned thing's broken!" Several weeks later, Dizzy was pitching again, but with an oversized shoe and wooden splints. Because he couldn't put any weight on his injured foot, Dean changed his pitching style to compensate. This change in style caused him to put more pressure on his arm, and, while throwing a pitch that day, Dean heard a loud crack in his shoulder and his whole arm went numb, including his fingers. He was never the same again. After the season he was traded to the Cubs for three players and $185,000. "Geez," said Dean later. "I wonder what I'd a brought if I'd had a good arm."

Dean pitched in only 44 games over the next five years with the Cubs and Browns before retiring to the broadcast booth and becoming a spokesman for Falstaff beer. When several members of the St. Louis Board of Education heard Dean's frequent disregard for correct grammar—particularly his use of the word "ain't"—they demanded he be taken off the air. Dean refused to change, arguing, "There is a lot of people in the United States who say 'isn't,' and they ain't eatin'." Although Dizzy's career technically lasted 12 years, it was, for all practical purposes, only six years long due to his injury. Dizzy Dean was elected to the Hall of Fame in 1953. He died in 1974.

CAREER CARDINALS RECORD:

W	L	W%	ERA	SV
134	75	.641	2.99	30

K	BB	SHO	IP
1,095	407	23	1,737.3

Doak, Bill (SP/RP)
(1913–1924, 1929)

Bill Doak was a good spitball pitcher on a bad team. For the first 25 years of the 20th century, the Cardinals were an also-ran team, never winning a pennant. Despite that, Doak twice won 20 games for St. Louis, posting a 20–6 record with a league-leading 1.72 ERA in 1914. On September 18, 1917, Doak won both games of a doubleheader against the Dodgers, 2–0 and 12–4.

Doak's main claim to fame, however, was not his playing ability, but rather his invention of a baseball glove that was so superior to any other in use that he earned royalties off its sale for more than three decades. When Doak first began playing baseball, fielders' gloves were, essentially, small leather pillows held in the palm of one's hand. They were so hard to break in that it often took players several years to make a glove comfortable. Many players simply cut the palm out of the "glove" to form a pocket. Doak's idea was to insert a series of leather strips between the thumb and index finger to form a webbed pocket, whereas the two fingers had been connected simply with one slab of leather. Instead of just protecting the hand, his glove now allowed players to clasp or "snag" the ball. Doak approached the Rawlings Sporting Goods Company with drawings of his ideas. Eventually almost everyone who played baseball used a Doak Glove by Rawlings. When the spitball was made illegal in 1920, Doak was one of 17 players grandfathered in who were allowed to continue using the pitch until they retired, which Doak did in 1929.

CAREER CARDINALS RECORD:

W	L	W%	ERA	SV
144	136	.514	2.93	13

K	BB	SHO	IP
938	740	30	2,387.0

EDMONDS, JIM (OF)
(2000–2005)

See Angels bio.

FLOOD, CURT (OF)
(1958–1969)

After two very brief stints with the Cincinnati Reds in 1956 and 1957, Curt Flood was traded to the Cardinals for three players prior to the 1958 campaign. He got his break with St. Louis and posted 12 solid seasons with the Cardinals, winning seven consecutive Gold Gloves and making it to the All-Star Game three times. Many felt he was the best center fielder in the game. But, like Bill Doak before him, Flood will be remembered more for what he did off the field than between the white lines.

Immediately after the 1969 season, Flood was traded to Philadelphia as part of a seven-player deal. Flood, who disliked the city of Philadelphia's treatment of black players in general and the team's overall approach in particular, announced he would retire rather than report to the Phillies. Once the initial shock at having been traded settled, Flood consulted an attorney who convinced him that he could possibly win a lawsuit against Major League Baseball and its reserve clause, which bound a player to a club for life.

Flood then discussed the possibility of a suit with Marvin Miller, executive director of the Major League Baseball Players Association. Miller warned Flood to consider the matter carefully, advising that such a suit would probably end his career and cost him hundreds of thousands of dollars. Flood decided to proceed and the Players Association voted unanimously to pay Flood's legal fees and expenses. Flood wrote a letter to Commissioner Bowie Kuhn, expressing his views on being treated like property, and asked Kuhn to let all teams know that he was available as a free agent for the 1970 season. Kuhn denied Flood's request, of course, and the matter wound up in U.S. District Court in New York in January 1970. Flood received the support of Jackie Robinson and Hank Greenberg, who both testified for him in court, but not one active major leaguer would testify on Flood's behalf, nor did any show up to provide moral support. Flood sat out the 1970 season so as not to prejudice his case; he went to Europe instead and painted pictures.

In August the court ruled against Flood, citing that baseball was a sport, not interstate commerce. After a federal appeals court upheld the ruling, the U.S. Supreme Court decided to hear the matter. On June 12, 1972, the High Court ruled against Flood, 5–3, with Justice Lewis Powell abstaining because he held stock in Anheuser-Busch, the owner of the Cardinals. In the majority's written opinion, however, the Court warned Baseball that its antitrust exemption was an "aberration" and an "anomaly." Flood's case had exposed the weakness in Baseball's century-old position on the reserve clause and led the way for modification of the reserve rules—all of which set the stage for arbitrator Peter Seitz's 1976 ruling. Every ballplayer who signs a multimillion-dollar contract to this day should thank Curt Flood for the trail he blazed at great sacrifice to himself.

While the suit was making its way through the court system, Bob Short of the Senators offered Flood a contract to play for him. Flood accepted, but only after getting Major League Baseball to sign an agreement that the deal would have no impact whatsoever on his suit. Flood's performance with Washington was poor, however, and after just 13 games he retired, never to play again. After leaving baseball, Flood again went to Europe to paint. He later returned to America and became the broadcast voice of his hometown Oakland A's in 1978, continued his painting, and headed the Oakland Little League Association. In 1989 he became the commissioner of the short-lived Senior League, and in 1997 he passed away after a battle with throat cancer.

CAREER CARDINALS RECORD:

Games	AB	Hits	Runs
1,738	6,318	1,853	845
Avg	HR	RBI	SB
.293	84	633	88

Forsch, Bob (SP/RP)
(1974–1988)

The Cardinals selected Bob Forsch in the 26th round of the June 1968 amateur draft and brought him up to the majors in 1974, where he quickly established himself as a dependable starter. Bob, the younger brother of major league pitcher Ken Forsch, played the first 15 years of his 16-year career in St. Louis, starting more than 30 games each year for nine straight years, except for the strike-shortened season of 1981. Forsch pitched two no-hitters during his long career with the Redbirds, and won two Silver Slugger Awards as the best-hitting pitcher in the National League. Although he ranks third on the Cardinals' all-time victory list with 163, and third in innings pitched with 2,658.7, he had only one 20-win season, in 1977, when he finished 20–7. Forsch was traded to the Astros near the end of the 1988 season and played one more year with them before retiring.

CAREER CARDINALS RECORD:

W	L	W%	ERA	SV
163	127	.562	3.67	3
K	BB	SHO	IP	
1,079	780	19	2,658.7	

FOUTZ, DAVE (SP/OF)
(1884–1887)

In the early 1880s Dave Foutz was a Colorado gold prospector who played for a local team that went belly up in early 1884. Bitten by the baseball bug, Foutz left the riverbeds of the Rockies and ventured eastward, settling in St. Louis. After a successful tryout with the Browns, Foutz quickly became an integral part of a St. Louis team that would establish a mini-dynasty in the American Association during the 1880s before the franchise moved to the National League in 1892.

Foutz, who missed part of the 1884 season after contracting malaria, played the outfield when he didn't pitch, compiling nearly 800 runs and RBIs during his career, strong numbers for a 19th-century player. Following the season, he reportedly lost a large amount of money betting on the presidential election between Grover Cleveland and James Blaine. In 1885 Foutz went 33–14 as the Browns won the first of four consecutive pennants. In 1886 he led the league with 41 wins, 11 shutouts, and a 2.11 ERA. He completed 55 of his 57 starts, racking up 504 innings. Things took a turn for the worse well into the 1887 season, however, when he suffered a broken thumb from a line drive, and for the rest of his career could no longer control his curveball. After the 1887 season, St. Louis sold Foutz to Brooklyn, where he won only 33 more games in the next seven years, although he did play more in the field. In 1889 he had 113 RBIs while playing first for the Brooklyn Bridegrooms (now the Dodgers) and won a gold medal from the league as the circuit's best player. From 1893 to 1896 he was Brooklyn's player-manager, although the team never finished higher than fifth place during his tenure.

CAREER CARDINALS PITCHING RECORD:

W	L	W%	ERA	SV
114	48	.704	2.67	1
K	BB	SHO	IP	
619	362	16	1,457.7	

CAREER CARDINALS HITTING RECORD:

Games	AB	Hits	Runs
302	1,194	353	204
Avg	HR	RBI	SB
.296	7	201	38

FRISCH, FRANKIE (2B/3B)
(1927–1937)

In one of the biggest trades of the era, the Giants and Cardinals swapped star second basemen following the 1926 season. The Cardinals sent Rogers Hornsby, the greatest right-handed hitter ever, to New York for Frankie Frisch. "The Fordham Flash" became expendable for the Giants when manager John McGraw felt threatened by the up-and-coming second baseman, who had begun to show managerial aspirations. Hornsby became expendable when his average fell 80 points from his previous five-year average and, as happened everywhere he went, his nasty disposition wore out his welcome. Naturally, St. Louis fans were quite upset over losing Hornsby and many took it out on Frisch when the 1927 season got underway by booing him intensely. Frisch quickly turned the boos into cheers, however, by performing like the demon-possessed player he had been for New York. The switch-hitting Frisch set near-career-highs across the board in virtually every offensive category, including a league-leading 48 stolen bases. He helped the Cardinals win pennants in 1928 and 1931, which especially pleased Frisch because St. Louis beat out a team managed by Hornsby and another managed by McGraw. Frisch won the National League's MVP Award in 1931 for his sterling play and team leadership.

In 1933 Frisch became the player-manager of the Cardinals, a wild team—on and off the field—that became known as "the Gas House Gang" because of their aggressive play and never-ending horseplay. Frisch's arguments with umpires are legendary. On one occasion, he wanted a game called on account of rain, so he approached the home-plate umpire under an umbrella—which, of course, got him ejected. On another occasion in the midst of an argument with umpire Bill Klem, Frisch fell to the ground, motionless. "Frisch," said Klem, "if you ain't dead, you're out of the game." Frisch led the Redbirds to the 1934 pennant and World Series title, the only championship of his 16-year managerial career. After his playing and managing career, Frisch spent time in the broadcast booth for the Braves and the Giants. Frisch, who played in baseball's first three All-Star Games, was elected to the Hall of Fame in 1947. He died in 1973. *(See Giants bio.)*

CAREER CARDINALS RECORD:

Games	AB	Hits	Runs
1,311	5,059	1,577	831
Avg	**HR**	**RBI**	**SB**
.312	51	720	195

Gibson, Bob (SP)
(1959–1975)

Bob Gibson was a star basketball player in high school and had planned to attend the University of Indiana, but changed his mind when the school told him they had already filled their "quota" of black students. He went to Creighton University instead and became good enough to play with the Harlem Globetrotters for several years during the off-season before concentrating solely on his major league baseball career. The St. Louis Cardinals signed Bob Gibson as an amateur free agent prior to the 1957 season and brought him up for a 13-game taste of the big leagues in 1959. By 1961 he was entrenched in the Cardinals' starting rotation, where he would remain for 15 years.

On the baseball field, Gibson—considered by far the meanest pitcher during his era—could do it all: pitch, hit, and field. A five-time 20-game winner, Gibson struck out 200 or more batters nine times. In 1968 he had the best season of any pitcher since the introduction of the lively ball in 1920 when he went 22–9, including 15 straight wins, with a 1.12 ERA. Only Dutch Leonard (0.96 in 1914) and Mordecai Brown (1.04 in 1906) posted lower ERAs for a season in the 20th century. That same year Gibson, an eight-time All-Star, had a scoreless streak of 47.7 innings snapped with his own wild pitch, after which he ran off another 17.3 scoreless innings. In one 95-inning stretch, he allowed only two earned runs. He was also a fine fielder, winning nine consecutive Gold Gloves from 1965 to 1973. As a hitter, Gibson was a genuine threat, hitting .206 for his career with 24 home runs, 44 doubles, and 144 RBIs.

As good as he was during the regular season, Gibson took his game to another level in World Series play. In 1967 he went 3–0 against

Boston with three complete games and a 1.00 ERA. In Game 1 of the 1968 Series, Gibson set a record by striking out 17 Tigers. For his career, he was 7–2 with a 1.89 ERA and 92 strikeouts in 81 innings of World Series competition. He also won the World Series MVP Awards in 1964 and 1967. In 1981 Gibson, who won Cy Young Awards in 1968 and 1970, became only the 11th player ever to be inducted into the Hall of Fame in his first year of eligibility.

CAREER CARDINALS RECORD:

W	L	W%	ERA	SV
251	174	.591	2.91	6

K	BB	SHO	IP
3,117	1,336	56	3,884.3

HAFEY, CHICK (OF)
(1924–1931)

Charles "Chick" Hafey was a very good ballplayer who likely would have been great if not for his poor eyesight and lingering sinus problems. As it was, Hafey played in the big leagues for 13 seasons, the first eight for the Cardinals, and hit over .300 nine times during his career. His eyesight was not only poor, but it varied from day to day, requiring the speedy outfielder to keep three different pairs of glasses on hand. His throwing arm was so strong that when Willie Mays arrived in the National League, Hall of Famers Ernie Lombardi and Paul Waner described him as "another Chick Hafey." In 1928 Hafey collected eight consecutive hits during a season in which he hit .337 with 27 homers, scored 101 runs, and drove in 111. On July 28 of that year he had six extra-base hits in a doubleheader, setting a major league record. In 1929 he hit .338 with 29 homers, 101 runs, and 125 RBIs, and had a streak of 10 consecutive hits. On July 6 he hit two grand slams in the same game.

In 1930 Hafey continued his string of great seasons with unusual feats when he hit .336 with 26 homers, 108 runs, and 107 RBIs. On May 17 of that year he had five RBIs in one inning, and on August 21 he hit for the cycle. In the 1930 World Series, Hafey set a record with five doubles. In 1931 he won the NL batting title with a .349 average in the closest batting race in major league history.

Over the winter Hafey and Cardinals management argued over a new contract, and when they couldn't come to terms Hafey was traded to Cincinnati on the eve of the 1932 season. The Reds met Hafey's contract demands, but he missed half the season after undergoing two sinus operations and suffering from an extended bout of the flu. He missed most of 1935 and all of 1936 when his sinus trouble flared up. During his five years in Cincinnati, Hafey's production dropped dramatically and he retired following the 1937 season to raise sheep and cattle. He continued to suffer from poor health for more than three decades. He was elected to the Hall of Fame in 1971, two years before his death.

CAREER CARDINALS RECORD:

Games	AB	Hits	Runs
812	2,953	963	542

Avg	HR	RBI	SB
.326	127	618	56

HAINES, JESSE (SP/RP)
(1920–1937)

After pitching one game with Cincinnati in 1918, Jesse Haines spent the next 18 years of his career with the St. Louis Cardinals, retiring as the team's career leader in wins (he's still second on the list, trailing only Bob Gibson). A three-time 20-game winner, Haines pitched in St. Louis's first four World Series, compiling a 3–1 record with a 1.67 ERA. Haines' specialty pitch was a hard knuckler, which broke straight down at the plate. He used it effectively in a no-hitter against the Boston Braves on July 17, 1924, though that season was his worst in the majors, as he posted an 8–19 record with a 4.41 ERA. The Cardinals used Haines as a mop-up man and spot starter over his last seven seasons before he retired in 1937. In 1970, Cooperstown came calling, eight years before he died.

CAREER CARDINALS RECORD:

W	L	W%	ERA	SV
210	158	.571	3.64	10

K	BB	SHO	IP
979	870	24	3,203.7

HORNSBY, ROGERS (2B/SS/3B)
(1915–1926, 1933)

After a mildly successful 1915 season in the minors, Rogers Hornsby was purchased by the Cardinals for $500 in midseason and brought to St. Louis near the end of the year, hitting only .246. In 1916 Cardinal coach Bob Connery convinced Hornsby he would be a better hitter if he stood straight up rather than crouching at the plate, and put his hands at the end of the bat instead of choking up, thereby taking full advantage of his size and strength. The results were almost immediate, as Hornsby hit .313 and used a perfectly level swing that gave a glimpse of the power that was to come later in his career.

Over his 23-year career, Hornsby would hit over .300 19 times, including three seasons in which he hit over .400. From 1920 to 1925, he hit for a combined average of .397, the highest average ever maintained for such a long period, and won the batting title each year. Hornsby won the Triple Crown in both 1922 and 1925, and took home MVP honors in 1925 and 1929. (If the NL had handed out an MVP Award in 1922, he surely would have won it in '22 with his 450 total bases, 42 homers, 14 triples, 46 doubles, and .401 average.) In 1924 Hornsby hit .424, the highest average by any player during the 20th century, which helped him attain the highest lifetime batting average by a right-hander (.359) in major league history and second highest average overall, trailing only Ty Cobb (.366). He was also made the Cardinals' player-manager early in the 1925 season and led the team to the World Series title in 1926. When Branch Rickey was fired as manager, Hornsby bought out Rickey's stock in the team for $45,000, an action that would later lead to a sticky wicket for the National League.

Hornsby was a fanatic when it came to staying in shape. He was a believer in red meat, often eating a blood-red steak three times a day. He never smoked or drank, and refused to read books or newspapers or go to the movies, viewing them as activities that would damage his keen eyesight. His only enjoyment outside of baseball was horse racing, and he was a heavy bettor. In 1927 a betting partner of Hornsby's filed suit against him, claiming that the ballplayer had borrowed nearly $100,000 from him and lost it on the ponies. Court testimony revealed that Hornsby had wagered $327,995 at various racetracks during the previous two years alone. When Commissioner Kenesaw Mountain Landis called Hornsby into his office to chastise him for his gambling habit, Hornsby didn't mince words, rebuking Landis over the commissioner's investing of organized baseball's money in the stock market, which resulted in huge losses. "At least I'm not gambling other people's money away," he tweaked the commissioner.

He was as tough to live with as he was talented. Contemporary accounts indicate that Hornsby was nastier, ruder, and meaner than even Ty Cobb, and Hornsby spared no one his vitriol. Teammates, opponents, managers, owners, reporters, fans, even Commissioner Landis all felt the sting of Hornsby's barbed tongue with equal bitterness. After the 1926 season, Hornsby was up for a new contract. Even though his average had fallen from .403 in 1925 to .317 in 1926, and his homers from 39 to 11, and all his other numbers had declined significantly as well, Hornsby demanded a substantial raise to $50,000, and he wanted a five-year contract. St. Louis owner Sam Breadon seemed more than fair when he countered with a five-year, $40,000 per year deal (especially given Hornsby's huge drop in production), or a one-year deal at Hornsby's requested $50,000. The stubborn Hornsby refused and Breadon traded him to the Giants for Frankie Frisch.

St. Louis fans were outraged at the trade. Hornsby was the biggest star in the National League, having hit over .400 in three of the previous five seasons, and had just managed the Cardinals to the World Series championship. The mayor of St. Louis and the city's Chamber of Commerce filed official protests with the Cardinals while fans talked openly about boycotting the Redbirds in 1927. But a more practical problem arose, namely Hornsby's stock in the team. When Hornsby and the Cardinals parted ways, St. Louis owner Breadon offered Hornsby the same $45 a share that Hornsby had paid Rickey for the 1,000 shares of team stock. True to his nature, Hornsby refused, insisting on $100 a share. When the two men couldn't reach an agreement, Commissioner Landis intervened, ruling that no one could play for one team while owning stock in another. Hornsby then hired a law firm to investigate his options. When the dust settled, Hornsby received the $100,000 he wanted, plus $12,000 in attorney's fees. All the National League owners had to kick in to buy out Hornsby.

Hornsby rebounded to have a great year with the New York Giants, hitting .361, but after just one season, he had alienated himself from virtually everyone in New York, and the Giants traded him to the Braves before the 1928 season. Hornsby had an even better year with Boston in 1928, hitting .387 and reaching the same level of power he had during his great six-year stretch. While the Braves would have been more than happy to keep him, the Cubs, who felt they had a legitimate shot at a pennant, made them an offer for Hornsby they couldn't refuse: five players and $200,000 in cash.

Hornsby, playing for his fourth team in four years, did indeed lead the Cubs to their first pennant in 11 years when he put together a monster season in 1929, batting .380 with 39 homers, 149 RBIs, 47 doubles, and 156 runs scored. In 1931 the Cubs made Hornsby their manager, but his angry managing style and strict team rules rubbed the players the wrong way and affected their performance. In the middle of the 1932 season, Hornsby was fired and replaced by Charlie Grimm, who turned the team around in the last two months and won the pennant. The Cubs hated Hornsby so much that they voted not to give him any part of their World Series money. When Hornsby protested to Commissioner Landis—the same guy Hornsby told to stick it five years earlier in the horse-betting affair—Landis sided with the players.

Hornsby moved on to manage the St. Louis Browns for five years (1933–1937) before spending the next 14 years managing in the minors and operating a baseball school. He played very little after the age of 35, but returned to the majors in 1952 and 1953, managing the Browns and Reds. After that he became a scout and coach for the Cubs and Mets until he died in 1963. Rogers Hornsby, the greatest right-handed hitter of all time, was elected to the Hall of Fame in 1942.

CAREER CARDINALS RECORD:

Games	AB	Hits	Runs
1,580	5,881	2,110	1,089
Avg	**HR**	**RBI**	**SB**
.359	193	1,072	118

King, Silver (SP)
(1887–1889)

Charles "Silver" King, thought to be the first sidearm pitcher in baseball history, led the American Association's St. Louis Browns to two league championships in 1887 and 1888, and a strong second-place finish in 1889, winning 111 games in those three years. King, who got his nickname from his light blond hair, went 32–12 during the regular season in 1887, but was only 1–3 in the 15-game World Series against the National League's Wolverines that year as Detroit bested St. Louis, 10 games to five. In 1888 King improved to 45–21 with a 1.64 ERA and 64 complete games as the Browns returned to the World Series, though St. Louis lost again, this time to the New York Giants, six games to four. After going 35–16 in 1889, his last year with the Browns, King jumped to the Players' League in 1890, posting a 30–22 record.

When the Players' League folded after just one season, King signed with Pittsburgh in 1891, becoming the highest-paid player in baseball at $5,000 for one year. Proving the old adage that the more things change, the more they stay the same, Pittsburgh's new high-priced free agent finished with a 14–29 record and he was released. King pitched for the New York Giants in 1892, improving somewhat to a 23–24 record. After he started the 1893 season 3–4 with an 8.63 ERA, King was released and later picked up by Cincinnati, where he struggled to a 5–6 record over the remainder of the year. It was reported that King's struggles in 1893 centered on the newly introduced pitching rubber that was used on the mound for the first time that season. Discouraged, King quit baseball and went to work in his father's bricklaying business. He attempted a comeback in 1896 and 1897, but after a 16–16 record, he retired for good and went back to laying bricks.

CAREER CARDINALS RECORD:

W	L	W%	ERA	SV
111	50	.689	2.71	2
K	**BB**	**SHO**	**IP**	
574	310	10	1,433.7	

LANKFORD, RAY (OF)
(1990–2001, 2004)

The Cardinals drafted Ray Lankford in the third round of the June 1987 amateur draft and brought him to the majors near the end of the 1990 season. He had been drafted by the Cubs the year before, but refused to sign. By 1991 Lankford earned a spot as a regular in the St. Louis outfield. His combination of speed and power enabled the Cardinals to bat him in the leadoff or cleanup spots, depending on their needs and the opposing team's starting pitcher. Lankford had a tendency to suffer through prolonged slumps and also to reel off blistering hot streaks. He had five seasons in which he hit at least 20 homers and stole at least 20 bases. In 1996 he led all National League outfielders in fielding with a .997 average, but did not win a Gold Glove. In 1998, when teammate Mark McGwire hit 70 home runs in the great race with Sammy Sosa, it was Lankford who protected McGwire in the lineup, hitting 31 homers with 105 RBIs and a .293 average. Nagged by various injuries over his last several years, including one that kept him out all of 2003, Lankford retired after the 2004 season.

CAREER CARDINALS RECORD:

Games	AB	Hits	Runs
1,580	5,417	1,479	928
Avg	**HR**	**RBI**	**SB**
.273	228	829	250

MARTIN, PEPPER (OF/3B)
(1928, 1930–1940, 1944)

Johnny "Pepper" Martin, who played his entire 13-year career with St. Louis, was known as "the Wild Horse of the Osage" for his blazing speed and reckless style of play. His aggressive play fit in perfectly with the "Gas House Gang" Cardinals of the mid-1930s, a team full of wacky players who were as comically zany as they were good. If they weren't dropping water balloons on the heads of sportswriters, they were placing smoke bombs on cars, or releasing sneezing powder in hotel lobbies. On the field they could be seen using flashlights in the outfield when the afternoon sun went down while a game was still in progress; there is a famous picture of several of them sitting in front of their dugout posing as if they're rowing a boat.

Pepper Martin

Martin, a four-time All-Star who led the National League in stolen bases three times, was the Gas House Gang's spark plug. He hit over .300 six times with the Cards, but he was at his best in the World Series, hitting .418 in 15 career Series games with 14 runs, seven doubles, and nine RBIs. In the 1931 Series he was a one-man wrecking crew, hitting .500 (12-for-24) with five runs, five stolen bases, four doubles, and a homer as he helped the Cardinals to an upset win against the powerful two-time defending champion Philadelphia A's.

Martin retired after the 1940 season and became a player-manager in the minors for several years before returning for a short time in 1944 to help out during the player shortages during World War II. After retiring a second time in 1944, Martin became a wealthy cattle rancher who served as the director of the Oklahoma State Penitentiary. He was a coach for the Cubs in 1956, then the manager of the Tulsa Oilers in 1965 when he died of a heart attack.

CAREER CARDINALS RECORD:

Games	AB	Hits	Runs
1,189	4,117	1,227	754
Avg	**HR**	**RBI**	**SB**
.298	59	501	146

McGee, Willie (OF)
(1982–1990, 1996–1999)

The New York Yankees drafted Willie McGee in the first round of the January 1977 amateur draft (secondary phase) and kept their speedy outfielder in the minor leagues until 1981, when they traded him to St. Louis for pitcher Bob Sykes. Sykes never played a game for the Yankees while McGee would go on to an 18-year career—13 of them with St. Louis—in which he would hit .295 and collect 2,254 hits in 2,201 games. McGee was named to the All-Star Game four times and won the National League's MVP Award in 1985 when he hit .353 with 114 runs, 18 triples, and 56 stolen bases. For good measure that year, the switch-hitting McGee won a Gold Glove, the Silver Slugger Award, and the first of two National League batting titles as he helped the Cardinals win their second pennant in four years.

After nine years with St. Louis, McGee was traded to the Oakland A's on August 29, 1990, even though he was leading the NL in hitting at the time with a .335 average. He had enough plate appearances in the NL to qualify for the batting title, which he ended up winning, the only time in history a player won a title in one league while toiling in the other league. McGee left Oakland via free agency and spent four years with the Giants and one more with the Red Sox before returning to the Cardinals for the last four years of his career. McGee hit over .300 in 1996 and 1997, but slumped to the .250s in his final two years before retiring after the 1999 season.

CAREER CARDINALS RECORD:

Games	AB	Hits	Runs
1,661	5,734	1,683	760
Avg	**HR**	**RBI**	**SB**
.294	63	678	301

McGwire, Mark (1B)
(1997–2001)

After coming to the Cardinals from Oakland at the 1997 trading deadline, McGwire finished the season with a career-high 58 homers, just three short of Roger Maris's record, and in so doing, he became the first player in history to hit more than 20 homers with two different teams in the same season. Ken Griffey Jr., who had been chasing Maris's record along with McGwire, finished with 56 homers. In 1998, the baseball world again turned its attention to McGwire and Griffey. Would this be the year that Maris's record fell? Although Griffey had another fabulous year, finishing with 56 homers for the second straight year, the real home run race developed between McGwire and Sammy

Sosa of the Cubs. By the end of June, both players had broken the record for homers by June 30. By the end of August, both players had 55 homers. It was a foregone conclusion that one or both of them would break the record. McGwire got there first, lining a laser beam over the left-field fence in Busch Stadium on September 8th; Sosa followed up with his 62nd blast five days later (to significantly less fanfare). With two games left, McGwire crushed four more blasts, finishing at 70 to Sosa's 66. The fan who caught the 70th home run ball auctioned it off for $3 million.

During "the chase," a reporter happened to notice a bottle of powdered supplement, androstenedione, in McGwire's locker. The resulting uproar over McGwire's use of supplements—legal in baseball, but illegal in other sports—opened a Pandora's box that is still consuming the sport to this day. McGwire hit 65 homers the next year, claiming he was no longer taking "andro." After hitting just .187 in 2001, McGwire retired due to eyesight problems. In 2005 he appeared before Congress during a government investigation into steroids in baseball, and lost significant credibility with both Congress and baseball fans by refusing to answer specific questions regarding his own use of steroids. McGwire's 583 career homers will likely land him in the Hall of Fame some day, but it remains to be seen if the steroids controversy will keep him from being a first-ballot inductee. *(See A's bio.)*

CAREER CARDINALS RECORD:

Games	AB	Hits	Runs
545	1,739	469	394
Avg	**HR**	**RBI**	**SB**
.270	220	473	4

MEDWICK, JOE (OF)
(1932–1940, 1947–1948)

Joe "Ducky" Medwick was a three-sport star in high school who received many scholarship offers, but decided on baseball. When the Cardinals signed him to a minor league contract in 1930, Medwick wanted to keep his academic options open, so he played under the assumed name of Mickey King. After he hit .419 in 1930 and .354 in 1931, the Cardinals called him up to St. Louis in 1932, where he hit .349, the first of 11 consecutive .300 seasons. Beginning in 1934, Medwick posted six consecutive seasons of 100+ RBIs, and from 1936 to 1938, he led the National League, averaging nearly 140 RBIs per season. In 1936 he hit 64 doubles, still the NL record. In 1937 he won the National League Triple Crown, batting .374 with 31 homers and 154 RBIs, and capturing the league's MVP Award as well.

Medwick, a 10-time All-Star, is most often remembered for his role in an incident from Game 7 of the 1934 World Series against the Tigers, when he slid hard into third base after hitting a triple off the center-field fence in Detroit. Whether accidentally or intentionally, Tigers third baseman Marv Owen spiked Medwick. While still on the ground, Medwick repeatedly kicked Owen and the two eventually came to blows. After umpire Bill Klem broke up the fistfight, declining to eject either player, Medwick offered to shake hands with Owen, but the Detroit third baseman refused. When Medwick took his position in left field in the bottom of the inning, he was showered with debris, including bottles and various fruits and vegetables. The crowd, already angry because their team trailed 9–0, was getting ugly. As the bombardment increased in intensity, the crowd began to chant, "Take him out! Take him out!" over and over again. Play was halted during the barrage, which only got worse by the minute. Commissioner Landis, who was in attendance, finally summoned the umpires, Medwick, and St. Louis manager Frankie Frisch to his box. Landis, rather than ordering the umpires to declare a forfeit—which would have been the standard response to such an incident—decided that Medwick should be removed from the game for his own safety. The Cardinals won the game, 11–0, but Medwick, because he'd been pulled from the game, lost a chance to set a new record for most hits in a World Series.

In a surprise move, the Cardinals sent Medwick to the Dodgers in mid-1940 for four players and $125,000 cash. Six days later, Medwick suffered a severe beaning by Cardinals pitcher Bob Bowman that affected his play for the rest of his career. On the morning of the beaning, Medwick and Dodgers manager Leo Durocher had exchanged heated words with St. Louis pitcher Bob Bowman in the elevator of Manhattan's New Yorker Hotel. According to Durocher, Bowman, that day's scheduled pitcher, shouted at them, "I'll take care of both you guys! Wait and see!" Later that day, in the bottom of the first inning, the first three Dodgers smashed line-drive hits. When Medwick came to the plate, Bowman drilled him in the temple with a fastball, knocking Medwick unconscious. As Medwick was carried off the field, a furious Durocher had to be restrained from going after Bowman. Dodgers GM Larry MacPhail was also livid, standing in front of the Cardinals' bench and challenging all of them to a fight. It took a police escort to get Bowman safely off the field and back to the hotel. The Brooklyn District Attorney's office looked into the matter but did not file any charges. MacPhail tried unsuccessfully to get Bowman banned for life.

The difference in Medwick's production before and after the beaning was dramatic. In the seven full seasons before the beaning, Medwick averaged about 20 homers, 110 runs, 125 RBIs, 49 doubles, and 10 triples with a .340 average. In the seven seasons after the beaning, Medwick averaged about 6 homers, 49 runs, 60 RBIs, 22 doubles, and three triples with a .307 average. After struggling through 19 at-bats in the 1948 season, Medwick retired at the age of 36, no longer the feared hitter he once was. He was elected to the Hall of Fame in 1968 and died seven years later.

CAREER CARDINALS RECORD:

Games	AB	Hits	Runs
1,216	4,747	1,590	811
Avg	**HR**	**RBI**	**SB**
.335	152	923	28

MIZE, JOHNNY (1B)
(1936–1941)

First baseman Johnny Mize divided his 15-year major league career almost equally among three teams: the Cardinals, Giants, and Yankees. Mize was that rare thing—a high-average hitter who also hit home runs and struck out very little. He is the only player in baseball history to hit more than 50 homers and strike out fewer than 50 times (42) in the same season (1947). After hitting .336 over six minor league seasons, Mize finally got his chance at the big leagues when St. Louis called him up in 1936. Mize hit over .300 in all six of his seasons in St. Louis, including 1939, when he hit .349 to win the NL batting title. He collected 100 or more RBIs in all but his rookie year when he had 93. From 1938 to 1940, Mize was simply dominant, leading the National League all three years in numerous categories: total bases, slugging percentage, extra-base hits, runs created, and OPS. The runner-up for the league's MVP Award in both 1939 and 1940, Mize was a 10-time All-Star.

Mize's contract talks with the Cardinals near the end of his stint with St. Louis offer a glimpse into the negotiation tactics of the era. After leading the league with a .349 average in 1939, Mize felt he should and would get a raise. Instead, St. Louis GM Branch Rickey told him they couldn't justify a raise since his home run production had only increased by one, from 27 to 28. So in 1940, Mize upped his home run total to a Cardinals record of 43 while knocking in 137 runs to win the RBI crown as well. Mize was confident when he went into Rickey's office to talk contract for 1941. "Well," said Rickey, "your batting average went down to .314, putting you fifth in the league, whereas last season you were first with a .349 average." Rickey then asked Mize if he would be willing to take a cut. Mize was furious; he told Rickey what he would be willing to take was a trade. Following the 1941 season, Rickey accommodated the miffed Mize, who had hit a career-low 16 homers, and sent him to the Giants for three players and $50,000.

After a solid season in 1942, Mize went into the Navy for three years during World War II. When he returned, Mize tied Ralph Kiner for the home run titles in 1947 and 1948. When Leo Durocher arrived in 1948, he felt the team was overloaded with slow-footed power hitters and in 1949 he shipped Mize across town to the Yankees. Mize played his last four major league seasons coming off the bench as a role-player for the Yanks. He led the American League in pinch-hits from 1951 to 1953. After sitting for most of the first three games of the 1952 World Series, Mize came off the bench to homer in Game 3, then hit round-trippers in Games 4 and 5 to become the first player in history to sock home runs in three consecutive World Series games. During his four-plus years with the Yankees, Mize collected only 230 hits, but had an astonishing 179 RBIs. "The Big Cat" was elected to the Hall of Fame in 1981. He died in 1993.

CAREER CARDINALS RECORD:

Games	AB	Hits	Runs
854	3,121	1,048	546
Avg	**HR**	**RBI**	**SB**
.336	158	653	14

MUSIAL, STAN (OF/1B)
(1941–1944, 1946–1963)

Stan "The Man" Musial began his career as a pitcher in the Cardinals' minor league system. He went 18–4 for Daytona Beach while hitting .311 and playing the outfield whenever he didn't pitch. After hurting his shoulder late in the 1940 season, Musial was almost released by St. Louis until someone decided to give him a shot as a full-time outfielder. The experiment worked and near the end of the 1941 season he was called up to the big leagues, where he hit .426 in 47 at-bats. By 1942 he was St. Louis's starting left fielder. As the season wore on, Musial began to gel, and the Cardinals began to click as a team, going 43–9 over their last 52 games to edge out Brooklyn by two games for the National League pennant. The Cardinals repeated this in both 1943 and 1944 as Musial won the first of seven batting titles in 1943 and the first of three MVP Awards in 1944. Musial missed the 1945 season after being drafted into the Navy during World War

II, but when he returned in 1946, it was as if he'd never been gone. He set career highs in almost every offensive category as he led the Cardinals to their fourth pennant in five years. The only season the Cardinals didn't win the pennant from 1942 to 1946 was in 1945, the year Musial was in the military. It was during 1946 that Musial switched to first base at the team's request.

During a game in Brooklyn, St. Louis sportswriter Bob Broeg overheard the Dodger fans talking about Musial whenever he came to the plate. "Here comes the man. Here comes the man." After Broeg included the anecdote in his article, the nickname "Stan the Man" was born. From 1946 to 1955, Musial proved to be one of the most durable players in baseball, playing all but 17 games during that 10-year span. In 1948 he slugged a career-high 39 homers and batted .373 as he won his third NL MVP Award. On May 13, 1958, Musial collected his 3,000th career hit. In 1962, at age 41, Musial hit .330, the third-highest average ever for a player over the age of 40. When his average dropped to .255 in 1963, Musial knew it was time to call it quits, ending his career with 3,630 hits, still the fourth-best total in major league history. Musial played in 24 All-Star Games during his 22 seasons (there were two games a year from 1959 to 1962). It's hard to fully appreciate Musial's record until you examine his performance in so many different aspects of the game. For instance, during his long career, Musial led the league in runs created nine times; doubles and times on base eight times each; batting average and OPS seven times each; hits, total bases, on-base percentage, and slugging average six times each; and runs and triples five times each. After retiring, Musial, who was elected to the Hall of Fame in 1969, opened a popular restaurant in St. Louis and worked in the Cardinals' front office.

CAREER CARDINALS RECORD:

Games	AB	Hits	Runs
3,026	10,972	3,630	1,949
Avg	**HR**	**RBI**	**SB**
.331	475	1,951	78

Pujols, Albert (1B/OF) (2001–2005)

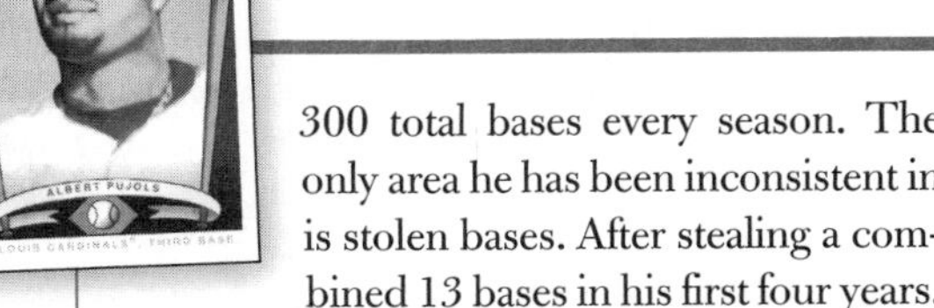

Albert Pujols is not only the best offensive player in the game today, but his career has gotten off to one of the greatest starts in baseball history. If he maintains his current level of play for only five more years—at which point he'll be just 30 years of age—Pujols will be sitting on 400+ homers, 2,000+ hits, and 1,200+ runs and RBIs, all staggering totals. He has been remarkably consistent, batting over .300 every year he's been in the majors. Pujols also has scored 112–137 runs each year, knocked in 117–130 RBIs, and laced 38–51 doubles. His at-bat totals are truly amazing, with 590–592 each year, and he has topped 300 total bases every season. The only area he has been inconsistent in is stolen bases. After stealing a combined 13 bases in his first four years, Pujols swiped 16 in 2005 alone. He's getting better and better every year, and he was finally given official recognition in 2005 when he won his first MVP Award. Fans should watch Pujols while they can, because a player of his caliber only comes along once in a generation.

CAREER CARDINALS RECORD:

Games	AB	Hits	Runs
790	2,954	982	629
Avg	**HR**	**RBI**	**SB**
.332	201	621	29

SCHOENDIENST, RED (2B) (1945–1956, 1961–1963)

Albert "Red" Schoendienst wanted to play baseball, and he wanted it badly, so in 1942 he hitchhiked from his home in Illinois to St. Louis to take part in an open tryout with the Cardinals in Sportsman's Park. Of the 500 hopefuls who tried out that day, only Schoendienst was chosen. Cardinals scout Joe Mathes drove the 19-year-old home to get his father's signature on a contract. The elder Schoendienst, who was busy painting a bridge in the hot sun when the pair arrived, tried to get a bonus out of Mathes, but the scout wouldn't budge, countering with an offer of a ham sandwich and a glass of milk. With World War II raging across the globe, Schoendienst had a great first year in the minors, but he, like every other able-bodied man of draft age in America, knew that someday Uncle Sam would come calling. When Schoendienst did get his notice to report, doctors discovered tuberculosis in his lungs, so he was classified 4-F and allowed to return to playing baseball. After three years in the minors, Schoendienst received another call-up in 1945, this time to the major leagues in St. Louis. Schoendienst had a terrific rookie season, batting .278 with 26 stolen bases, which led the league. Over his next 18 major league seasons, he would steal only 63 more.

He quickly became known as much for his glove as his bat, leading National League second basemen in fielding percentage six times and putting together several long streaks of errorless play. Schoendienst, a seven-time .300 hitter, went to 10 All-Star Games, winning the 1950 edition with a 14th-inning homer at Comiskey Park. After 11-plus seasons in St. Louis, Schoendienst was sent to the Giants as part of a nine-player trade in June 1956 and then to Milwaukee the next year. He played on two pennant-winning Braves teams before returning to St. Louis, where he spent the last three years of his playing career from 1961 to 1963, retiring the same year as Stan Musial. He was a Cardinals coach for a year before taking over the managing reins for 12 years, winning back-to-back pennants in 1967 and 1968 and the World Series in 1967. Following the 1976 season, Schoendienst returned to coaching and was the team's interim manager a couple of times in 1980 and 1990. In 1989 he was elected to the Hall of Fame.

CAREER CARDINALS RECORD:

Games	AB	Hits	Runs
1,795	6,841	1,980	1,025
Avg	**HR**	**RBI**	**SB**
.289	65	651	80

SHERDEL, BILL (SP/RP) (1918–1930, 1932)

Bill Sherdel spent 13-plus seasons with the Cardinals, never dominating on the mound, but establishing a decent career through an assortment of crafty pitches. A free spirit who was given to whistling or singing to himself while pitching, Sherdel arrived in St. Louis in 1918 and helped turn the weak franchise into a respectable one. He was a reliever as well as a starter, leading the National League in saves three times (1920, 1927, and 1928). After going 16–12 in 1926 and helping the Cardinals win their first modern-era pennant,

Sherdel was given the honor of pitching the team's first World Series game since the 1888 American Association team—losing a heartbreaker to Herb Pennock of the Yankees, 2–1. He lost Game 5 as well, 3–2, but St. Louis prevailed in seven games. Sherdel had a better year in 1928 (21–10), the only 20-win season of his career, in which he led the Redbirds to their second World Series in three years, but he again lost two games as the Cardinals were swept by the Yankees. That was Sherdel's last decent year, as he won only 25 games in the remaining four years of his career before retiring in 1932.

CAREER CARDINALS RECORD:

W	L	W%	ERA	SV
153	131	.539	3.64	25
K	BB	SHO	IP	
779	595	11	2,450.7	

SIMMONS, TED (C) (1968–1980)

Ted Simmons was drafted in the first round of the June 1967 amateur draft by the Cardinals and was playing in the major leagues the next year. A switch-hitter—unusual for a catcher—Simmons was tough and durable, as his 21-year career would suggest. A better-than-average hitter, Simmons hit over .300 seven times and drove in 90+ runs eight times. Those were fine numbers for a catcher, a fact that helped to keep him in the lineup, because his defense was porous. He recorded 182 passed balls, the most by any catcher in the 20th century, leading the National League three times in the embarrassing category. An eight-time All-Star—incredible in itself since Johnny Bench was in the league at almost exactly the same time—Simmons hit home runs from both sides of the plate in the same game three times during his career. Simmons had a strong personality and often clashed with manager Whitey Herzog. When Herzog acquired free-agent catcher Darrell Porter in December 1980, Simmons became expendable and was traded to Milwaukee five days later. Simmons helped the Brewers to their only pennant in 1982, hitting 23 homers with 97 RBIs as he helped to mold their pitchers into a respectable staff. As his career got long in the tooth, he found himself playing more DH than catcher. In 1986 he was traded to the Atlanta Braves and finished his career as a utility player for three seasons. After his retirement from the playing field, Simmons became the director of player development for St. Louis. Three years later he became the GM of the Pirates, but left 18 months later after suffering a major heart attack. Simmons took it easy for a few years, and then returned to baseball in 1999, joining the front office of the San Diego Padres.

CAREER CARDINALS RECORD:

Games	AB	Hits	Runs
1,564	5,725	1,704	736
Avg	HR	RBI	SB
.298	172	929	11

SLAUGHTER, ENOS (OF) (1938–1942, 1946–1953)

Enos "Country" Slaughter was one of the greatest hustlers in baseball history . . . on the field, that is. While he didn't steal many bases in his career, he never failed to run out a hit or an out. After hitting .382 to lead the American Association's Columbus Redbirds, Slaughter was called up to the major leagues the next season and stayed there for the next 19 years, including 13 seasons with the Cardinals. Playing well enough to earn a raise from $400 to $600 a month in 1939, Slaughter celebrated by going rabbit hunting with his father. While in the field, Slaughter and his father both contracted tularemia from the infected carcasses. Slaughter became quite ill, and his father died three days later. Still ailing, Slaughter nonetheless reported to spring training on time, fiercely determined to keep his spot on the team.

Slaughter routinely played while hurt, often with broken bones. He once broke a collarbone in an effort to avoid a collision with a teammate in the outfield. Before the bone had set, Slaughter was back in the lineup. On a hard swing, he ripped the wound open and blood spurted all over his uniform. He refused to come out of the game, uttering the line he became famous for: "I'll never quit. They'll have to tear my uniform off me." And he meant it. In 1942 he led the Cardinals to a five-game World Series win over the favored Yankees, providing New York manager Joe McCarthy with his only Series loss as Yankee manager. Following the 1942 season, Slaughter went into the military and played ball to entertain the troops and boost their morale, including a game on Iwo Jima just after it had been taken.

Slaughter hit over .300 10 times during his career (eight times with St. Louis), including 1946 when he also set career highs in homers (18) and RBIs (130). That year he once again led St. Louis into the World Series, this time against the Red Sox, in a Fall Classic that would showcase all his talents and establish his lasting legacy. In Game 4, Slaughter got four hits (including a home run) and scored four runs as he rallied the Cards back to tie the Series at two games apiece. In the sixth inning, the Red Sox had the bases loaded with one out when Boston's Hal Wagner lined a pitch over Slaughter's head. Slaughter raced back and snagged the ball. Rudy York, the runner on third, tagged up and headed home. Then, according to *The New York Times*, "The throw was so impossibly far that it wouldn't even be attempted. But Slaughter, who never gave up on anything, threw York out at the plate." In Game 5, Slaughter was hit on the elbow by a pitch from Joe Dobson, but even though he was in great pain, Slaughter wouldn't give the pitcher the satisfaction of knowing it. The elbow was broken and Slaughter developed a

dangerous blood clot, but still he would not come out of the lineup and he immediately stole second base. In Game 6, with his elbow heavily bandaged, he got a single in the Cardinals' winning rally. Game 7 was tied at 3–3 in the bottom of the eighth. Slaughter led off with a single, but the next two hitters were retired without advancing him into scoring position. So Slaughter felt he had to take matters into his own hands. With Harry "The Hat" Walker, a good contact hitter, at the plate, Slaughter decided to try and steal second. He broke with the pitch and Walker blooped the ball into the outfield. Center fielder Leon Culberson, who had just come into the game as a replacement for the injured Dom DiMaggio, retrieved the ball and threw it to shortstop Johnny Pesky, the cutoff man. Pesky turned to see if Walker would try and advance to second, never thinking for a moment that Slaughter would try to score. Meanwhile, Slaughter, head down and barreling like a freight train, never hesitated for a moment, running right through third-base coach Mike Gonzalez's stop signal. When Slaughter scored the lead run from first base on Walker's single, the St. Louis crowd went nuts. The stunned Red Sox went quietly in the ninth, and the Cardinals were World Champions.

In April of 1954, Slaughter—who bled Cardinals red—was traded to the Yankees for Bill Virdon. When he received the news, Slaughter wept openly in front of his locker. News photos of the sobbing outfielder made it around the world, including the Soviet Union, whose Communist Party magazine, *Soviet Sport,* felt the need to comment on the decadent Americans and their national pastime, criticizing the ". . . flesh peddling in disregard of the player's wishes and rights . . . a typical example of beer and beizbol. The beizbol bosses care nothing about sport or their athletes, but only about profits." After voluntarily playing six more years for the profit-minded Yankees, Athletics, and Braves, Slaughter retired in 1959 and was elected to the Hall of Fame in 1985. He died in 2002.

CAREER CARDINALS RECORD:

Games	AB	Hits	Runs
1,820	6,775	2,064	1,071
Avg	**HR**	**RBI**	**SB**
.305	146	1,148	64

Smith, Lee (RP)
(1990–1993)

After 10-plus years with the Cubs and Red Sox, Lee Smith was traded to St. Louis on May 4, 1990, by Boston for Tom Brunansky. Even though Smith only played three-plus seasons with St. Louis before being traded to the Yankees on August 31, 1993, he left as the team's all-time leader in saves and still holds the top spot today, although Jason Isringhausen is poised to pass him in the very near future. Smith earned 27 saves for the Redbirds over the remainder of the 1990 season, and then put together consecutive years of 47, 43, and 43 for St. Louis before finishing out his career with five other teams. *(See Cubs bio.)*

CAREER CARDINALS RECORD:

W	L	W%	ERA	SV
15	20	.429	2.90	160
K	**BB**	**SHO**	**IP**	
246	68	0	266.7	

SMITH, OZZIE (SS)
(1982–1996)

The San Diego Padres drafted Ozzie Smith in the fourth round of the June 1977 amateur draft. He had been drafted the year before by the Tigers, but refused to sign. It only took Smith a year to make it to the majors and he sizzled from the git-go, stealing 40 bases in his rookie year and playing stellar defense. After winning two Gold Gloves with the Padres, Smith arrived in St. Louis in a trade of renowned shortstops that sent Garry Templeton to San Diego.

Smith, known affectionately as the "Wizard of Oz" for his many incredible defensive gems, ranks among the best defensive shortstops of all time. Ozzie, who would excite the crowd by doing a backflip once a game as he took his position in the field, not only made a habit of getting to balls that many other fielders could not, but he'd also manage to turn them into double plays. By the time he retired, Smith had participated in more double plays than any shortstop in the history of major league baseball. The National League's all-time leader in Gold Gloves (13 consecutive from 1980 to 1992), Smith was also a very successful base stealer, swiping 433 for St. Louis (580 overall) while only being thrown out 102 times (148 overall).

Smith was an expert hit-and-run man and could lay down a bunt with the best of them. He was a tough hitter in the clutch who seldom struck out. In the 1985 NLCS against the Dodgers, Smith came to bat with the score tied 2–2 in the deciding game. The switch-hitting Smith hit a home run in the bottom of the ninth to win the game and series and propel the Cardinals into the World Series. It was the only left-handed home run of his career.

When Smith won his 13th consecutive Gold Glove in 1992, he broke the record held by Willie Mays and Roberto Clemente, who each had 12 in a row. Upon retiring as a player, the good-natured Smith was hired to replace the late Mel Allen as host of *This Week in Baseball.* He was inducted into the Hall of Fame in 2002.

CAREER CARDINALS RECORD:

Games	AB	Hits	Runs
1,990	7,160	1,944	991
Avg	**HR**	**RBI**	**SB**
.272	27	664	433

San Diego Padres

Since 1969

1974 On Opening Day owner Ray Kroc, dismayed at his team's play, gets on the public address system and says, "I have some good news and some bad news: The good news is that we've outdrawn the Dodgers. The bad news is that I've never seen such stupid ballplaying in my life." Inspired perhaps by his candor, Padres home attendance in 1974 shoots up 80 percent over the previous five seasons, although the team wins only 60 games.... **1977** The Padres set a major league record with only six complete games, all by rookie Bob Owchinko.... **1995** Ken Caminiti becomes the first player in major league history to homer from both sides of the plate three times in one season.... **1992** Fred McGriff becomes the first player in history to win home run titles in both the American and National Leagues.

FRANCHISE HISTORY

In 1969, when the American League expanded from 10 to 12 teams with franchises in Kansas City and Seattle, the National League responded with an expansion to Montreal and San Diego. The San Diego team gave the National League a third franchise on the West Coast, easing some of the long-distance travel for the Dodgers and Giants.

The original owner of the San Diego franchise, C. Arnholdt Smith, chose the nickname "Padres" after the Pacific Coast League team he also owned. (That team, which had operated successfully in the city since 1936, had been named after the Catholic padres who ran San Diego's missions during the 18th century.) Smith, a majority shareholder of the United States National Bank, immediately brought in Buzzie Bavasi, former general manager of the Dodgers, and promised him 32 percent ownership if he was successful. Unfortunately, Smith's banking empire crumbled (in the largest bank failure in U.S. history up to that point) and he was convicted of tax evasion. Facing a $27 million tax debt, Smith accepted an offer of $12.5 million for the Padres from grocery store magnate Joe Danzansky. However, this deal fell through when Danzansky wanted to move the team to Washington, D.C., in 1974, but was unable to escape its San Diego stadium lease. Another $12.5 million offer was made by Hollywood Park racetrack owner Marje Everett and songwriter Burt Bacharach, but this deal fell through as well. Throughout the turmoil surrounding the team's IRS problems and aborted sale attempts, Bavasi remained the one constant; he held the position of team president as well as minority owner until he resigned in 1977 to become vice president of the California Angels.

Finally, Ray Kroc, the owner of the McDonald's hamburger empire, made a $12.5 million offer that was accepted and approved. He announced that he was not buying the team to make money, but simply because he loved baseball and wanted to keep the team in San Diego. He ran the Padres for 10 years before his death in 1984, at which time his wife Joan took over. She ran the team for six more years, although she showed little interest in it. In 1987, she announced the sale of the team to Southern California businessman George Argyros (the Seattle Mariners owner) for nearly $50 million, but she called off the deal two months later.

Joan Kroc did finally sell the Padres, in 1990, to a partnership of two suitors headed by Tom Werner, who made his fortune as a TV producer (his credits include *The Cosby Show* and *Roseanne*). The Werner group soon soured on baseball's labor troubles and its escalating player salaries, and sold the team to software magnate John Moores during the 1994 players' strike. Moores had turned a $1,000 investment in his software company in 1980 into $330 million by the mid-1990s. He was a noted philanthropist who had donated tens of millions of dollars to various causes, including $70 million to his alma mater, the University of Houston.

Tony Gwynn

The team, which marks its 38th year in 2006, began play in 1969 in San Diego Stadium, which was originally built for the San Diego Chargers of the NFL. In 1971, it

The Padres beat the Cubs in Game 4 of the 1984 National League playoffs on their way to losing the World Series to Detroit.

was renamed Jack Murphy Stadium in honor of the sportswriter who played a major role in bringing the Padres to San Diego.

Despite sweeping the eventual 1969 World Series champion New York Mets in the first three games of their existence, the Padres ended up in last place in the National League West during their first six years. In 1984, they finally made it to the World Series after defeating the Chicago Cubs in dramatic fashion in the National League Championship Series. However, they were buried, four games to one, by the powerful Detroit Tigers. Their second chance for postseason glory came in 1998, when they appeared in the World Series for a second time. But they were crushed again, this time by the New York Yankees, in four straight.

In 1972, the Padres were last in the league in runs scored with 488. Incredibly, one player, Nate Colbert, knocked in 111 of them.

TEAM NAME HISTORY

Official Names

Padres

Unofficial Names/Nicknames

Pads

STADIUM HISTORY

San Diego Stadium	1969–1970
Jack Murphy Stadium	1971 to mid-1997
(San Diego Stadium renamed)	
Qualcomm Stadium	mid-1997 to 2003
(Jack Murphy Stadium renamed)	
Petco Park	2004–current

YEARLY RECORD, FINISH, & ATTENDANCE FIGURES

Year	League	Record	DIV/LG Finish	Attendance	Avg/Gm
2005	NL West	82–80	1	2,869,787	35,429
2004	NL West	87–75	3	3,016,752	37,244
2003	NL West	64–98	5	2,030,084	25,063
2002	NL West	66–96	5	2,220,601	27,415
2001	NL West	79–83	4	2,378,128	29,360
2000	NL West	76–86	5	2,352,443	29,043
1999	NL West	74–88	4	2,523,538	31,155
1998	NL West	98–64	1	2,555,874	31,554
1997	NL West	76–86	4	2,089,333	25,794
1996	NL West	91–71	1	2,187,886	27,011
1995	NL West	70–74	3	1,041,805	14,470
1994	NL West	47–70	4	953,857	16,734
1993	NL West	61–101	7	1,375,432	16,981
1992	NL West	82–80	3	1,721,406	21,252
1991	NL West	84–78	3	1,804,289	22,275
1990	NL West	75–87	4	1,856,396	22,918
1989	NL West	89–73	2	2,009,031	24,803
1988	NL West	83–78	3	1,506,896	18,604
1987	NL West	65–97	6	1,454,061	17,951
1986	NL West	74–88	4	1,805,716	22,293
1985	NL West	83–79	3	2,210,352	27,288
1984	NL West	92–70	1	1,983,904	24,493
1983	NL West	81–81	4	1,539,815	18,778
1982	NL West	81–81	4	1,607,516	19,846
1981	NL West	41–69	6/6	519,161	9,439
1980	NL West	73–89	6	1,139,026	14,062
1979	NL West	68–93	5	1,456,967	17,987
1978	NL West	84–78	4	1,670,107	20,619
1977	NL West	69–93	5	1,376,269	16,991
1976	NL West	73–89	5	1,458,478	18,231
1975	NL West	71–91	4	1,281,747	15,824
1974	NL West	60–102	6	1,075,399	13,277
1973	NL West	60–102	6	611,826	7,553
1972	NL West	58–95	6	644,273	8,053
1971	NL West	61–100	6	557,513	6,883
1970	NL West	63–99	6	643,679	7,947
1969	NL West	52–110	6	512,970	6,333

MANAGER HISTORY

Manager	Years	W–L	Win %
Preston Gomez	1969–1972	180–316	.363
Don Zimmer	1972–1973	114–190	.375
John McNamara	1974–1977	224–310	.419
Bob Skinner	1977	1–0	1.000
Alvin Dark	1977	48–65	.425
Roger Craig	1978–1979	152–171	.471
Jerry Coleman	1980	73–89	.451
Frank Howard	1981	41–69	.373
Dick Williams	1982–1985	337–311	.520
Steve Boros	1986	74–88	.457
Larry Bowa	1987–1988	81–127	.389
Jack McKeon	1988–1990	193–164	.541
Greg Riddoch	1990–1992	200–194	.508
Jim Riggleman	1992–1994	112–179	.385
Bruce Bochy	1995–2005	853–901	.486

ALL-TIME WIN-LOSS RECORDS VS. ALL OPPONENTS

ALL-TIME	2,693–3,174
Angels	9–7
Astros	257–285
Athletics	5–11
Blue Jays	1–2
Braves	236–301
Brewers	33–24
Cardinals	163–234
Cubs	171–224
Devil Rays	2–4
Diamondbacks	60–73
Dodgers	294–323
Giants	284–327
Indians	2–4
INTERLEAGUE	67–79
Mariners	25–19
Marlins	53–51
Mets	203–200
Nationals	184–213
Orioles	1–2
Phillies	182–215
Pirates	171–227
Rangers	8–8
Reds	239–301
Red Sox	2–4
Rockies	96–97
Royals	4–2
Tigers	1–2
Twins	3–3
White Sox	1–2
Yankees	2–4

Franchise Highlights, Low Points, and Strange Distinctions

1971 The Padres offense was so anemic that starting pitcher Dave Roberts ended the season with a 14–17 record, even though his 2.10 ERA was second best among all National League starters. The Padres scored only 22 runs in Roberts' 17 losses. Teammates such as Enzo Hernandez didn't help; he set a record for the fewest RBIs (12) by a player with more than 500 at-bats (549) in a season.

••••

1972 The first manager Buzzie Bavasi had ever fired in more than 20 years as a major league executive was Preston Gomez, 11 games into the 1972 season.

From June 18 to July 18, starting pitcher Steve Arlin pitched two one-hitters and three two-hitters, but won only three of the games.

Fred Norman won only nine games, but six of them were shutouts. He also beat the pennant-winning Cincinnati Reds four times.

••••

1975 San Diego's four catchers—Fred Kendall, Randy Hundley, Gerry Moses, and Bob Davis—hit only one home run between them the entire year, although Hundley did hit two as a pinch-hitter.

1977 Alvin Dark became the first manager to be fired during spring training since the Cubs sacked Phil Cavaretta in 1954, when he got the axe on March 21. It was the earliest managerial change in major league history.

••••

1978 The All-Star Game held in San Diego allowed fans to watch player workouts the day before the summer classic. More than 30,000 fans attended.

••••

1979 After another disappointing season, when the Padres once again ended up in fifth place, owner Ray Kroc fired manager Roger Craig on the season's last day and replaced him with radio play-by-play announcer Jerry Coleman, a former player who had never managed before.

••••

1984 After 15 consecutive seasons in the lower half of the NL's West Division, the Padres vaulted to first place. San Diego then defeated the Chicago Cubs three games to two in the NLCS, in strange fashion: The first two games were originally scheduled to be played in San Diego and the last three in Chicago. But due to television concerns over Wrigley Field's lack of lights for desired night games, the series was reversed. After losing the first two games in Chicago, San Diego returned home and swept the Cubs to advance to their first World Series.

1988 Tony Gwynn, nursing an injured left hand, was hitting only .246 on July 2, but he managed to hit .367 in his final 73 games, finishing the season at .313—still the lowest average ever for a National League batting champion.

Chub Feeney's resignation is a perfect example of the consequences of acting before thinking. On September 24, Feeney, who was team president (and former National League president as well), was sitting in his private box high above the field at Jack Murphy Stadium when two fans walked through the stands carrying a "Scrub Chub" banner. He directed an obscene gesture at them, creating quite a public relations commotion. He resigned the next day.

During the season, catcher Benito Santiago picked off eight runners and threw out 45 percent (35 of 77) of those trying to steal, including 11 of 17 while throwing from his knees.

• • • •

1989 After stumbling to a 60–63 record through August 19, the Padres turned it around, going 29–10 (.744) the rest of the way. They nearly won the division title, finishing just three games behind the Giants.

Only nine Padres were hit by pitches during the entire season!

1992 Incredibly, San Diego catchers allowed only two passed balls during the entire season.

Gary Sheffield could have won baseball's most coveted prize, the Triple Crown, if he hadn't missed 16 games during the season due to injury. He did win the batting title with a .330 average, but missed winning the home run title by two and fell just nine short of the lead in RBIs.

• • • •

1994 The players' strike that ended the season was very good to the Padres. After a horrendous 10–32 start to the season, they finished with the worst record in the majors, 47–70, including an embarrassing 0–12 record against the Montreal Expos.

• • • •

1995 Tony Gwynn won his sixth batting title with a .368 average despite playing the last 10 weeks of the season with a broken right big toe.

• • • •

1996 The Padres played an amazing 24 extra-inning games, winning 13 of them.

From July 22 through September 8, the Padres played 44 games in 10 different cities and three different countries (U.S., Canada, and Mexico), and managed to compile a decent 26–18 record.

Special Achievements

World Series Results

Year	Opponent	Result	Games
1984	Detroit Tigers	Lost	1–4
1998	NY Yankees	Lost	0–4

World Series Managerial Records

Manager	Series Record	Games Record
Dick Williams	0–1	1–4
Bruce Bochy	0–1	0–4

All-Time Postseason Record

Divisional Playoffs	3–7
League Championship Series	7–4
World Series	1–8

All-Star Games at Jack Murphy Stadium

Year	Date	Winner	Score
1978	July 11	National	7–3
1992	July 14	American	13–6

Hall of Famers Who Played for Team

Famers	Games with San Diego	Years
Dave Winfield	1,117	1973–1980

Hall of Famers Who Managed Team

None

MVP Award Winners

Ken Caminiti	3B	1996

Cy Young Award Winners

Pitcher	Year	W–L	SV	ERA
Randy Jones	1976	22–14	0	2.74
Gaylord Perry	1978	21–6	0	2.73
Mark Davis	1989	4–3	44	1.85

Rookie of the Year Award Winners

Butch Metzger	RP	1976
Benito Santiago	C	1987

Gold Glove Winners

Year	Position	Player
1979	OF	Dave Winfield
1980	SS	Ozzie Smith
	OF	Dave Winfield
1981	SS	Ozzie Smith
1986	OF	Tony Gwynn
1987	OF	Tony Gwynn
1988	C	Benito Santiago
1989	C	Benito Santiago
	OF	Tony Gwynn
1990	C	Benito Santiago
	OF	Tony Gwynn
1991	OF	Tony Gwynn
1995	3B	Ken Caminiti
	OF	Steve Finley
1996	3B	Ken Caminiti
	OF	Steve Finley
1997	3B	Ken Caminiti

Triple Crown Winners

None

Fireman of the Year Award Winners

Rollie Fingers	1977
Rollie Fingers	1978
Rollie Fingers	1980
Mark Davis	1989
Trevor Hoffman	1996
Trevor Hoffman	1998

World Series MVP

None

League Championship Series MVP

Steve Garvey	1984
Sterling Hitchcock	1998

All-Star Game MVP

LaMarr Hoyt	1985

Manager of the Year Award Winners

Bruce Bochy	1996

Batting Champions

Year	Player	Avg
1984	Tony Gwynn	.351
1987	Tony Gwynn	.370
1988	Tony Gwynn	.313
1989	Tony Gwynn	.336
1992	Gary Sheffield	.330
1994	Tony Gwynn	.394

1995	Tony Gwynn	.368
1996	Tony Gwynn	.353
1997	Tony Gwynn	.372

NINE-INNING NO-HITTERS PITCHED

None

20-GAME WINNERS

Year	Pitcher	W–L
1975	Randy Jones	20–12
1976	Randy Jones	22–14
1978	Gaylord Perry	21–6

RETIRED UNIFORM NUMBERS

Number	Player	Position
6	Steve Garvey	1B
19	Tony Gwynn	OF
31	Dave Winfield	OF
35	Randy Jones	SP

TEAM RECORDS—WINS & LOSSES

- Games won in a season: 98 in 1998
- Games lost in a season: 110 in 1969
- Games won in a month: 22 in May 2005
- Games lost in a month: 23 in May 2003
- Consecutive games won: 14 in 1999
- Consecutive games lost: 13 in 1994
- Biggest shutout victory: 13–0 over Cincinnati on August 11, 1991
- Biggest shutout loss: 19–0 to Cubs on May 13, 1969 and to Dodgers on June 28, 1969
- Highest winning percentage: .605 in 1998 (98–64)
- Lowest winning percentage: .321 in 1969 (52–110)

TEAM RECORDS—BATTING

- Highest team batting average: .275 in 1994
- Lowest team batting average: .225 in 1969
- Highest team slugging average: .414 in 2004
- Highest team on-base percentage: .343 in 2004
- Total hits: 1,521 in 2004
- Extra-base hits: 489 in 1998
- Hits in a game: 24 vs. San Francisco on April 19, 1982 and vs. Atlanta on August 12, 2003
- Longest individual hitting streak: 34, Benito Santiago, 1987
- Most .300 hitters in a single season: 3 in 1987
- Home runs: 172 in 1970
- Home runs in a month: 14, Ken Caminiti, August 1996
- Home runs in a game: 6 vs. Cincinnati, July 17, 1998
- Home runs by a rookie: 24, Nate Colbert, 1969
- Home runs by a right-hander: 50, Greg Vaughn, 1998
- Home runs by a left-hander: 35, Fred McGriff, 1992
- Home runs by a switch-hitter: 40, Ken Caminiti, 1996
- Grand slams: 10 in 2001
- Grand slams (individual; season): 4, Phil Nevin, 2001
- Grand slams (individual; career): 6, Phil Nevin
- Triples: 53 in 1979
- Doubles: 304 in 2004
- Singles: 1,105 in 1980
- Walks: 678 in 2001
- Runs scored: 795 in 1997
- Runs scored in a game: 20 vs. Florida on July 27, 1996 and vs. Montreal on May 19, 2001
- Runs scored in an inning: 13 vs. St. Louis on August 24, 1993 (first) and vs. Pittsburgh on May 31, 1994 (second)
- Most batters hit by a pitch: 59 in 1993
- Times shut out: 23 in 1969 and 1976
- Grounded into double plays: 146 in 1996
- Fewest grounded into double plays: 81 in 1978
- Runners left on base: 1,239 in 1980

TEAM RECORDS—BASERUNNING

- Stolen bases: 239 in 1980
- Caught stealing: 91 in 1987

TEAM RECORDS—PITCHING

- Lowest earned run average: 3.22 in 1971
- Complete games: 47 in 1971 and 1976
- Saves: 59 in 1998
- Strikeouts: 1,217 in 1998
- Shutouts: 19 in 1985
- Walks: 715 in 1974
- Hit batsmen: 68 in 2000
- Wild pitches: 73 in 1999

- Consecutive wins (individual): 11, Andy Hawkins, 1985; LaMarr Hoyt, 1985; Kevin Brown, 1998
- Consecutive losses (individual): 11, Gary Ross, 1969
- Strikeouts in a game (individual): 15, Fred Norman, Sept. 15, 1972 and Sterling Hitchcock, August 29, 1998
- Runs allowed in a game: 23 vs. Cubs, May 17, 1977

TEAM RECORDS—FIELDING

- Best fielding average: .983 in 1998 and 2003
- Most errors committed: 189 in 1977
- Fewest errors committed: 102 in 2003
- Most double plays turned: 171 in 1978
- Fewest double plays turned: 126 in 1974

TEAM RECORDS—MISCELLANEOUS

- Number of times league champions: 2
- Number of times finishing last in league: 9
- Largest attendance, single game: 61,707 vs. San Francisco, March 31, 2003
- Largest attendance, doubleheader: 43,473 vs. Philadelphia, June 13, 1976
- Players used in a season: 59 in 2002
- Seasons played: 20 by Tony Gwynn

PRIMARY PITCHING STAFFS

Year	Starter	Starter	Starter	Starter	Starter	Closer	Bullpen	Bullpen	Bullpen
2005	Lawrence	Peavy	Williams	Eaton	Stauffer	Hoffman	Linebrink	Otsuka	Seanez
2004	Lawrence	Eaton	Wells	Peavy	Valdez	Hoffman	Otsuka	Linebrink	Witasick
2003	Lawrence	Eaton	Perez	Peavy	Jarvis	Beck	Matthews	Hackman	Witasick
2002	Lawrence	Tomko	Perez	Peavy	Jones	Hoffman	Fikac	Embree	Reed
2001	Jarvis	Williams	Tollberg	Eaton	Jones	Hoffman	Nunez	Lee	Davey
2000	Clement	Williams	Tollberg	Eaton	Meadows	Hoffman	Walker	Almanzar	Wall
1999	Clement	Williams	Hitchcock	Ashby	Boehringer	Hoffman	Miceli	Reyes	Wall
1998	Brown	Hamilton	Hitchcock	Ashby	Langston	Hoffman	Miceli	Boehringer	Wall
1997	Smith	Hamilton	Hitchcock	Ashby	Valenzuela	Hoffman	Bochtler	Cunnane	Worrell
1996	Tewksbury	Hamilton	Sanders	Ashby	Valenzuela	Hoffman	Worrell	Bochtler	Blair
1995	Benes	Hamilton	Dishman	Ashby	Valenzuela	Hoffman	Florie	Williams	Blair
1994	Benes	Hamilton	Sanders	Ashby	Whitehurst	Hoffman	Martinez	Mauser	Tabaka
1993	Benes	Brocail	Harris	Worrell	Whitehurst	Harris	Hoffman	Taylor	Davis
1992	Benes	Hurst	Harris	Lefferts	Seminara	Myers	Rodriguez	Melendez	Maddux
1991	Benes	Hurst	Harris	Rasmussen	Whitson	Lefferts	Rodriguez	Andersen	Maddux
1990	Benes	Hurst	Show	Rasmussen	Whitson	Lefferts	Rodriguez	Schiraldi	Harris
1989	Terrell	Hurst	Show	Rasmussen	Whitson	Davis	Clements	Harris	Grant
1988	Hawkins	Jones	Show	Rasmussen	Whitson	Davis	McCullers	Leiper	Booker
1987	Hawkins	Jones	Show	Grant	Whitson	McCullers	Davis	Gossage	Booker
1986	Hawkins	Dravecky	Show	Hoyt	Thurmond	Gossage	Lefferts	McCullers	Walter
1985	Hawkins	Dravecky	Show	Hoyt	Thurmond	Gossage	Lefferts	Stoddard	DeLeon
1984	Hawkins	Whitson	Show	Lollar	Thurmond	Gossage	Lefferts	Dravecky	DeLeon
1983	Hawkins	Whitson	Show	Lollar	Dravecky	Lucas	Monge	DeLeon	Sosa
1982	Montefusco	Eichelberger	Welsh	Lollar	Curtis	Lucas	Chiffer	DeLeon	Show
1981	Eichelberger	Mura	Welsh	Lollar	Wise	Lucas	Littlefield	Urrea	Boone
1980	Mura	Curtis	Jones	Lucas	Wise	Fingers	Shirley	Rasmussen	Kinney
1979	Perry	Shirley	Jones	Owchinko	Rasmussen	Fingers	D'Acquisto	Lee	Mura
1978	Perry	Shirley	Jones	Owchinko	Rasmussen	Fingers	D'Acquisto	Lee	Lolich
1977	Freisleben	Shirley	Jones	Owchinko	Griffin	Fingers	Tomlin	Spillner	Sawyer
1976	Freisleben	Strom	Jones	Spillner	Griffin	Metzger	Tomlin	Folkers	Foster
1975	Freisleben	Strom	Jones	Spillner	McIntosh	Frisella	Tomlin	Folkers	Greif
1974	Freisleben	Greif	Jones	Spillner	Arlin	Romo	Tomlin	Hardy	Laxton
1973	Kirby	Greif	Jones	Troedson	Arlin	Caldwell	Ross	Corkins	Romo
1972	Kirby	Greif	Norman	Caldwell	Arlin	Corkins	Schaeffer	Acosta	Ross
1971	Kirby	Roberts	Norman	Phoebus	Arlin	Severinsen	Kelley	Coombs	Miller
1970	Kirby	Roberts	Dobson	Coombs	Corkins	Dukes	Herbel	Willis	Ross
1969	Kirby	Niekro	Santorini	Kelley	Sisk	McCool	Reberger	Baldschun	Ross

PRIMARY STARTING LINEUPS

Year	C	1B	2B	3B	SS	LF	CF	RF
2005	Hernandez	Nevin	Loretta	Burroughs	Greene	Klesko	Roberts	Giles
2004	Hernandez	Nevin	Loretta	Burroughs	Greene	Klesko	Payton	Giles
2003	Bennett	Klesko	Loretta	Burroughs	Vazquez	White	Kotsay	Nady
2002	Lampkin	Klesko	Vazquez	Nevin	Cruz	Gant	Kotsay	Trammell
2001	Davis	Klesko	Jackson	Nevin	Jimenez	Henderson	Kotsay	Trammell
2000	Gonzalez	Klesko	Boone	Nevin	Jackson	Martin	Rivera	Owens
1999	Davis	Joyner	Veras	Nevin	Jackson	Sanders	Rivera	Gwynn
1998	Hernandez	Joyner	Veras	Caminiti	Gomez	Vaughn	Finley	Gwynn
1997	Flaherty	Joyner	Veras	Caminiti	Gomez	Vaughn	Finley	Gwynn
1996	Flaherty	Joyner	Reed	Caminiti	Gomez	Henderson	Finley	Gwynn
1995	Ausmus	Williams	Reed	Caminiti	Cedeno	Nieves	Finley	Gwynn
1994	Ausmus	Williams	Roberts	Shipley	Gutierrez	Plantier	Bell	Gwynn
1993	Higgins	McGriff	Gardner	Sheffield	Gutierrez	Plantier	Bell	Gwynn
1992	Santiago	McGriff	Stillwell	Sheffield	Fernandez	Clark	Jackson	Gwynn
1991	Santiago	McGriff	Roberts	Coolbaugh	Fernandez	Clark	Jackson	Gwynn
1990	Santiago	Clark	Alomar	Pagliarulo	Templeton	Roberts	Carter	Gwynn
1989	Santiago	Clark	Alomar	Salazar	Templeton	Martinez	Gwynn	Kruk
1988	Santiago	Moreland	Alomar	Brown	Templeton	Martinez	Wynne	Gwynn
1987	Santiago	Kruk	Flannery	Ready	Templeton	Martinez	Mack	Gwynn
1986	Kennedy	Garvey	Flannery	Nettles	Templeton	Kruk	Wynne	Gwynn
1985	Kennedy	Garvey	Flannery	Nettles	Templeton	Martinez	McReynolds	Gwynn
1984	Kennedy	Garvey	Wiggins	Nettles	Templeton	Martinez	McReynolds	Gwynn
1983	Kennedy	Garvey	Bonilla	Salazar	Templeton	Wiggins	Jones	Lezcano
1982	Kennedy	Perkins	Flannery	Salazar	Templeton	Richards	Jones	Lezcano
1981	Kennedy	Perkins	Bonilla	Salazar	Smith	Richards	Jones	Lefebvre
1980	Tenace	Montanez	Cash	Rodriguez	Smith	Richards	Mumphrey	Winfield
1979	Tenace	Briggs	Gonzalez	Dade	Smith	Turner	Richards	Winfield
1978	Sweet	Tenace	Gonzalez	Almon	Smith	Richards	Thomas	Winfield
1977	Tenace	Ivie	Champion	Ashford	Almon	Richards	Hendrick	Winfield
1976	Kendall	Ivie	Fuentes	Rader	Hernandez	Turner	Davis	Winfield
1975	Kendall	McCovey	Fuentes	Kubiak	Hernandez	Tolan	Grubb	Winfield
1974	Kendall	McCovey	Thomas	Roberts	Hernandez	Winfield	Grubb	Tolan
1973	Kendall	Colbert	Morales	Roberts	Thomas	Lee	Grubb	Gaston
1972	Kendall	Colbert	Thomas	Roberts	Hernandez	Lee	Jeter	Gaston
1971	Barton	Colbert	Mason	Spiezio	Hernandez	Lee	Gaston	Brown
1970	Cannizzaro	Colbert	Campbell	Spiezio	Arcia	Ferrara	Gaston	Brown
1969	Cannizzaro	Colbert	Arcia	Spiezio	Dean	Ferrara	Gaston	Brown

Top 10 Batting Leaders, Single Season & Career with Team

Games Played: Career with Team

Player	G	PA
1. Tony Gwynn	2,440	10,232
2. Garry Templeton	1,286	4,860
3. Dave Winfield	1,117	4,512
4. Tim Flannery	972	2,838
5. Gene Richards	939	3,805
6. Nate Colbert	866	3,485
7. Terry Kennedy	835	3,239
8. Ryan Klesko	822	3,327
9. Phil Nevin	806	3,297
10. Benito Santiago	789	3,065

At-Bats: Season

Player	AB	Year
1. Steve Finley	655	1996
2. Steve Garvey	654	1985
3. Tony Gwynn	642	1986
Gene Richards	642	1980
5. Joe Carter	634	1990
6. Roberto Alomar	623	1989
7. Tony Fernandez	622	1992
Tony Gwynn	622	1985
9. Mark Loretta	620	2004
10. Steve Finley	619	1998

At-Bats: Career with Team

Player	AB	PA
1. Tony Gwynn	9,288	10,232
2. Garry Templeton	4,512	4,860
3. Dave Winfield	3,997	4,512
4. Gene Richards	3,414	3,805
5. Nate Colbert	3,080	3,485
6. Terry Kennedy	2,987	3,239
7. Phil Nevin	2,928	3,297
8. Benito Santiago	2,872	3,065
9. Ryan Klesko	2,814	3,327
10. Cito Gaston	2,615	2,787

Batting Average: Season

Player	BA	Year
1. Tony Gwynn	.394	1994
2. Tony Gwynn	.372	1997
3. Tony Gwynn	.370	1987
4. Tony Gwynn	.368	1995
5. Tony Gwynn	.358	1993
6. Tony Gwynn	.353	1996
7. Tony Gwynn	.351	1984
8. Tony Gwynn	.338	1999
9. Tony Gwynn	.336	1989
10. Mark Loretta	.335	2004

Batting Average: Career with Team

Player	BA	PA
1. Tony Gwynn	.338	10,232
2. Bip Roberts	.298	2,521
3. Ken Caminiti	.295	2,351
4. Gene Richards	.291	3,805
5. Phil Nevin	.288	3,297
6. Johnny Grubb	.286	2,043
7. Dave Winfield	.284	4,512
8. Ryan Klesko	.278	3,327
9. Steve Finley	.276	2,640
10. Steve Garvey	.275	2,439

Total Hits: Season

Player	H	Year
1. Tony Gwynn	220	1997
2. Tony Gwynn	218	1987
3. Tony Gwynn	213	1984
4. Tony Gwynn	211	1986
5. Mark Loretta	208	2004
6. Tony Gwynn	203	1989
7. Tony Gwynn	197	1985
Tony Gwynn	197	1995
9. Steve Finley	195	1996
10. Gene Richards	193	1980

Total Hits: Career with Team

Player	H	PA
1. Tony Gwynn	3,141	10,232
2. Garry Templeton	1,135	4,860
3. Dave Winfield	1,134	4,512
4. Gene Richards	994	3,805
5. Phil Nevin	842	3,297
6. Terry Kennedy	817	3,239
7. Ryan Klesko	783	3,327
8. Nate Colbert	780	3,485
9. Benito Santiago	758	3,065
10. Bip Roberts	673	2,521

Home Runs: Season

Player	HR	Year
1. Greg Vaughn	50	1998
2. Phil Nevin	41	2001
3. Ken Caminiti	40	1996
4. Nate Colbert	38	1970
Nate Colbert	38	1972
6. Fred McGriff	35	1992
7. Phil Plantier	34	1993
Dave Winfield	34	1979
9. Gary Sheffield	33	1992
10. Fred McGriff	31	1991
Phil Nevin	31	2000

Home Runs: Career with Team

Player	HR	PA
1. Nate Colbert	163	3,485
2. Phil Nevin	156	3,297
3. Dave Winfield	154	4,512
4. Tony Gwynn	135	10,232
5. Ryan Klesko	133	3,327
6. Ken Caminiti	121	2,351
7. Benito Santiago	85	3,065
8. Fred McGriff	84	1,623
9. Steve Finley	82	2,640
Carmelo Martinez	82	2,694

Triples: Season

Player	3B	Year
1. Tony Gwynn	13	1987
2. Gene Richards	12	1978
Gene Richards	12	1981
4. Bill Almon	11	1977
Tony Gwynn	11	1991
Gene Richards	11	1977
7. Willie Davis	10	1976
Tony Gwynn	10	1984
Tony Gwynn	10	1990
Dave Winfield	10	1979
Dave Roberts	10	2005

Triples: Career with Team

Player	3B	PA
1. Tony Gwynn	85	10,232
2. Gene Richards	63	3,805
3. Dave Winfield	39	4,512
4. Garry Templeton	36	4,860

5. Cito Gaston	29	2,787
6. Steve Finley	28	2,640
7. Tim Flannery	25	2,838
8. Luis Salazar	24	2,383
9. Nate Colbert	22	3,485
10. Bip Roberts	21	2,521

DOUBLES: SEASON

Player	2B	Year
1. Tony Gwynn	49	1997
2. Mark Loretta	47	2004
3. Steve Finley	45	1996
4. Terry Kennedy	42	1982
5. Tony Gwynn	41	1993
6. Steve Finley	40	1998
7. Ryan Klesko	39	2002
8. Brian Giles	38	2005
9. Ken Caminiti	37	1996
10. Johnny Grubb	36	1975
Tony Gwynn	36	1987
Bip Roberts	36	1990

DOUBLES: CAREER WITH TEAM

Player	2B	PA
1. Tony Gwynn	543	10,232
2. Garry Templeton	195	4,860
3. Dave Winfield	179	4,512
4. Ryan Klesko	175	3,327
5. Terry Kennedy	158	3,239
Phil Nevin	158	3,297
7. Steve Finley	134	2,640
8. Nate Colbert	130	3,485
9. Ken Caminiti	127	2,351
10. Benito Santiago	124	3,065

EXTRA-BASE HITS: SEASON

Player	XBH	Year
1. Steve Finley	84	1996
2. Greg Vaughn	82	1998
3. Ken Caminiti	79	1996
4. Phil Nevin	72	2001
5. Dave Winfield	71	1979
6. Ryan Klesko	70	2001
Gary Sheffield	70	1992
8. Ryan Klesko	69	2002
Fred McGriff	69	1992
10. Tony Gwynn	68	1997

EXTRA-BASE HITS: CAREER WITH TEAM

Player	XBH	PA
1. Tony Gwynn	763	10,232
2. Dave Winfield	372	4,512
3. Ryan Klesko	320	3,327
4. Phil Nevin	317	3,297
5. Nate Colbert	315	3,485
6. Garry Templeton	274	4,860
7. Ken Caminiti	250	2,351
8. Steve Finley	244	2,640
9. Terry Kennedy	241	3,239
10. Benito Santiago	224	3,065

TOTAL BASES: SEASON

Player	TB	Year
1. Steve Finley	348	1996
2. Greg Vaughn	342	1998
3. Ken Caminiti	339	1996
4. Dave Winfield	333	1979
5. Tony Gwynn	324	1997
6. Gary Sheffield	323	1992
7. Phil Nevin	321	2001
8. Cito Gaston	317	1970
9. Mark Loretta	307	2004
10. Tony Gwynn	301	1987

TOTAL BASES: CAREER WITH TEAM

Player	TB	PA
1. Tony Gwynn	4,259	10,232
2. Dave Winfield	1,853	4,512
3. Garry Templeton	1,531	4,860
4. Phil Nevin	1,474	3,297
5. Nate Colbert	1,443	3,485
6. Ryan Klesko	1,381	3,327
7. Gene Richards	1,321	3,805
8. Terry Kennedy	1,217	3,239
9. Benito Santiago	1,167	3,065
10. Steve Finley	1,098	2,640

RUNS BATTED IN: SEASON

Player	RBI	Year
1. Ken Caminiti	130	1996
2. Phil Nevin	126	2001
3. Tony Gwynn	119	1997
Greg Vaughn	119	1998
5. Dave Winfield	118	1979
6. Joe Carter	115	1990
7. Ryan Klesko	113	2001
8. Nate Colbert	111	1972
9. Phil Nevin	107	2000
10. Fred McGriff	106	1991

RUNS BATTED IN: CAREER WITH TEAM

Player	RBI	PA
1. Tony Gwynn	1,138	10,232
2. Dave Winfield	626	4,512
3. Phil Nevin	573	3,297
4. Ryan Klesko	491	3,327
5. Nate Colbert	481	3,485
6. Garry Templeton	427	4,860
7. Terry Kennedy	424	3,239
8. Ken Caminiti	396	2,351
9. Benito Santiago	375	3,065
10. Carmelo Martinez	337	2,694

RUNS SCORED: SEASON

Player	R	Year
1. Steve Finley	126	1996
2. Tony Gwynn	119	1987
3. Greg Vaughn	112	1998
4. Rickey Henderson	110	1996
5. Ken Caminiti	109	1996
6. Mark Loretta	108	2004
7. Tony Gwynn	107	1986
8. Alan Wiggins	106	1984
9. Ryan Klesko	105	2001
10. Steve Finley	104	1995
Bip Roberts	104	1990
Dave Winfield	104	1977

RUNS SCORED: CAREER WITH TEAM

Player	R	PA
1. Tony Gwynn	1,383	10,232
2. Dave Winfield	599	4,512
3. Gene Richards	484	3,805
4. Ryan Klesko	449	3,327
5. Nate Colbert	442	3,485
6. Garry Templeton	430	4,860
7. Phil Nevin	428	3,297
8. Steve Finley	423	2,640
9. Bip Roberts	378	2,521
10. Ken Caminiti	362	2,351

WALKS: SEASON

Player	BB	Year
1. Jack Clark	132	1989
2. Rickey Henderson	125	1996
Gene Tenace	125	1977
4. Brian Giles	119	2005
5. Fred McGriff	105	1991
Gene Tenace	105	1979
7. Jack Clark	104	1990
8. Gene Tenace	101	1978
9. Willie McCovey	96	1974
Fred McGriff	96	1992

Walks: Career with Team

Player	BB	PA
1. Tony Gwynn	790	10,232
2. Ryan Klesko	468	3,327
3. Dave Winfield	463	4,512
4. Gene Tenace	423	2,094
5. Nate Colbert	350	3,485
6. Gene Richards	338	3,805
7. Carmelo Martinez	327	2,694
8. Phil Nevin	325	3,297
9. Ken Caminiti	298	2,351
10. Tim Flannery	277	2,838
Rickey Henderson	277	1,432

Strikeouts: Season

Player	SO	Year
1. Nate Colbert	150	1970
2. Phil Nevin	147	2001
3. Nate Colbert	146	1973
4. Jack Clark	145	1989
5. Ruben Rivera	143	1999
6. Cito Gaston	142	1970
7. Ruben Rivera	137	2000
8. Fred McGriff	135	1991
9. Damian Jackson	128	2001
10. Nate Colbert	127	1972

Strikeouts: Career with Team

Player	SO	PA
1. Nate Colbert	773	3,485
2. Garry Templeton	684	4,860
3. Phil Nevin	669	3,297
4. Cito Gaston	595	2,787
5. Dave Winfield	585	4,512
6. Benito Santiago	516	3,065
7. Terry Kennedy	508	3,239
8. Ryan Klesko	486	3,327
9. Tony Gwynn	434	10,232
10. Ken Caminiti	419	2,351

Slugging Percentage: Season

Player	SLG	Year
1. Ken Caminiti	.621	1996
2. Greg Vaughn	.597	1998
3. Phil Nevin	.588	2001
4. Gary Sheffield	.580	1992
5. Tony Gwynn	.568	1994
6. Dave Winfield	.558	1979
7. Fred McGriff	.556	1992
8. Tony Gwynn	.547	1997
9. Cito Gaston	.543	1970
Phil Nevin	.543	2000

Slugging Percentage: Career with Team

Player	SLG	PA
1. Ken Caminiti	.540	2,351
2. Phil Nevin	.503	3,297
3. Ryan Klesko	.491	3,327
4. Nate Colbert	.469	3,485
5. Dave Winfield	.464	4,512
6. Tony Gwynn	.459	10,232
7. Steve Finley	.458	2,640
8. Gene Tenace	.422	2,094
9. Steve Garvey	.409	2,439
10. Carmelo Martinez	.408	2,694

On-Base Percentage: Season

Player	OBP	Year
1. Tony Gwynn	.454	1994
2. Tony Gwynn	.447	1987
3. Jack Clark	.441	1990
4. Merv Rettenmund	.432	1977
5. Randy Ready	.423	1987
Brian Giles	.423	2005
7. Willie McCovey	.416	1974
8. Gene Tenace	.415	1977
9. Rickey Henderson	.410	1996
Jack Clark	.410	1989
Tony Gwynn	.410	1984

On-Base Percentage: Career with Team

Player	OBP	PA
1. Gene Tenace	.403	2,094
2. Tony Gwynn	.388	10,232
3. Ken Caminiti	.384	2,351
4. Ryan Klesko	.380	3,327
5. Johnny Grubb	.363	2,043
6. Bip Roberts	.361	2,521
7. Phil Nevin	.359	3,297
8. Dave Winfield	.357	4,512
Gene Richards	.357	3,805
10. Carmelo Martinez	.341	2,694

OPS (On-Base Percentage + Slugging Percentage): Season

Player	OPS	Year
1. Ken Caminiti	1.028	1996
2. Tony Gwynn	1.022	1994
3. Phil Nevin	.976	2001
4. Jack Clark	.974	1990
5. Gary Sheffield	.965	1992
6. Greg Vaughn	.960	1998
7. Tony Gwynn	.958	1987
8. Tony Gwynn	.957	1997
9. Dave Winfield	.953	1979
10. Fred McGriff	.950	1992

OPS (On-Base Percentage + Slugging Percentage): Career with Team

Player	OPS	PA
1. Ken Caminiti	.924	2,351
2. Ryan Klesko	.871	3,327
3. Phil Nevin	.862	3,297
4. Tony Gwynn	.847	10,232
5. Gene Tenace	.825	2,094
6. Dave Winfield	.821	4,512
7. Nate Colbert	.800	3,485
8. Steve Finley	.792	2,640
9. Johnny Grubb	.760	2,043
10. Carmelo Martinez	.748	2,694

Stolen Bases: Season

Player	SB	Year
1. Alan Wiggins	70	1984
2. Alan Wiggins	66	1983
3. Gene Richards	61	1980
4. Ozzie Smith	57	1980
5. Tony Gwynn	56	1987
Gene Richards	56	1977
7. Jerry Mumphrey	52	1980
8. Bip Roberts	46	1990
9. Roberto Alomar	42	1989
10. Tony Gwynn	40	1989
Ozzie Smith	40	1978

Stolen Bases: Career with Team

Player	SB	PA
1. Tony Gwynn	319	10,232
2. Gene Richards	242	3,805
3. Alan Wiggins	171	1,606
4. Bip Roberts	148	2,521
5. Ozzie Smith	147	2,536
6. Dave Winfield	133	4,512
7. Enzo Hernandez	129	2,609
8. Garry Templeton	101	4,860
9. Damian Jackson	100	1,796
10. Luis Salazar	93	2,383

Sacrifice Hits: Season

Player	Sac	Year
1. Ozzie Smith	28	1978
2. Enzo Hernandez	24	1975
3. Ozzie Smith	23	1980
4. Ozzie Smith	22	1979
5. Bill Almon	20	1977
6. Pat Dobson	19	1970
7. Roberto Alomar	17	1989
Andy Ashby	17	1995
Randy Jones	17	1975
10. Roberto Alomar	16	1988
Tito Fuentes	16	1976
Enzo Hernandez	16	1976
Alan Wiggins	16	1983

Sacrifice Hits: Career with Team

Player	Sac	PA
1. Enzo Hernandez	83	2,609
Ozzie Smith	83	2,536
3. Randy Jones	63	639
4. Andy Ashby	60	430
5. Ed Whitson	51	481
6. Andy Benes	48	443
7. Andy Hawkins	46	382
8. Tony Gwynn	45	10,232
9. Garry Templeton	43	4,860
10. Eric Show	40	554

Hit by Pitch: Season

Player	HBP	Year
1. Gene Tenace	13	1977
2. Derek Bell	12	1993
3. Sean Burroughs	11	2003
Al Ferrara	11	1970
Gene Tenace	11	1978
6. Rickey Henderson	10	1996
Ruben Rivera	10	2000
Bobby Tolan	10	1975
9. Sean Burroughs	9	2004
Tim Flannery	9	1985
Carlos Hernandez	9	1998
Mark Loretta	9	2004
Bobby Tolan	9	1974

Hit by Pitch: Career with Team

Player	HBP	PA
1. Gene Tenace	35	2,094
2. Tim Flannery	32	2,838
3. Sean Burroughs	26	1,665
4. Tony Gwynn	24	10,232
5. Nate Colbert	22	3,485
6. Gene Richards	20	3,805
Mark Loretta	20	1,823
8. Bobby Tolan	19	979
9. Al Ferrara	18	873
10. Chris Gomez	17	1,932
Rickey Henderson	17	1,432
Ruben Rivera	17	1,180

Top 10 Pitching Leaders, Single Season & Career with Team

Games Pitched: Season

Player	GP	Year
1. Craig Lefferts	83	1986
2. Rollie Fingers	78	1977
Lance McCullers	78	1987
4. Mike Matthews	77	2003
Butch Metzger	77	1976
6. Larry Hardy	76	1974
Dan Spillner	76	1977
Dave Tomlin	76	1977
9. Greg Harris	73	1990
Scott Linebrink	73	2004
Akinori Otsuka	73	2004
Scott Linebrink	73	2005

Games Pitched: Career with Team

Player	GP	IP
1. Trevor Hoffman	728	786.7
2. Craig Lefferts	375	659.0
3. Eric Show	309	1,603.3
4. Rollie Fingers	265	426.3
5. Randy Jones	264	1,766.0
6. Dave Tomlin	239	315.7
7. Mark Davis	230	308.0
Gary Lucas	230	428.3
9. Lance McCullers	229	392.0
10. Ed Whitson	227	1,354.3

Innings Pitched: Season

Player	IP	Year
1. Randy Jones	315.3	1976
2. Randy Jones	285.0	1975
3. Dave Roberts	269.7	1971
4. Clay Kirby	267.3	1971
5. Randy Jones	263.0	1979
6. Gaylord Perry	260.7	1978
7. Kevin Brown	257.0	1998
8. Randy Jones	253.0	1978
9. Pat Dobson	251.0	1970
10. Steve Arlin	250.0	1972

Innings Pitched: Career with Team

Player	IP
1. Randy Jones	1,766.0
2. Eric Show	1,603.3
3. Ed Whitson	1,354.3
4. Andy Benes	1,235.0
5. Andy Ashby	1,212.0
6. Clay Kirby	1,128.0
7. Andy Hawkins	1,102.7
8. Joey Hamilton	934.7
9. Brian Lawrence	934.0
10. Bruce Hurst	911.7

Batters Faced: Season

Player	BF	Year
1. Randy Jones	1,251	1976
2. Randy Jones	1,124	1975
3. Clay Kirby	1,107	1971
4. Randy Jones	1,088	1979
5. Dave Roberts	1,086	1971
6. Pat Dobson	1,073	1970
7. Steve Arlin	1,072	1972
8. Randy Jones	1,058	1978
9. Gaylord Perry	1,055	1978
10. Kevin Brown	1,032	1998

Batters Faced: Career with Team

Player	BF	IP
1. Randy Jones	7,292	1,766.0
2. Eric Show	6,737	1,603.3

Player		
3. Ed Whitson	5,600	1,354.3
4. Andy Benes	5,163	1,235.0
5. Andy Ashby	5,053	1,212.0
6. Clay Kirby	4,832	1,128.0
7. Andy Hawkins	4,712	1,102.7
8. Joey Hamilton	3,994	934.7
9. Brian Lawrence	3,984	934.0
10. Bruce Hurst	3,730	911.7

Games Started: Season

Player	GS	Year
1. Randy Jones	40	1976
2. Randy Jones	39	1979
3. Steve Arlin	37	1972
Gaylord Perry	37	1978
5. Randy Jones	36	1975
Randy Jones	36	1978
Clay Kirby	36	1971
8. Kevin Brown	35	1998
Bill Greif	35	1974
Andy Hawkins	35	1986
Clay Kirby	35	1969
Bob Shirley	35	1977
Eric Show	35	1985

Games Started: Career with Team

Player	GS	IP
1. Randy Jones	253	1,766.0
2. Eric Show	230	1,603.3
3. Ed Whitson	208	1,354.3
4. Andy Benes	186	1,235.0
5. Andy Ashby	185	1,212.0
6. Andy Hawkins	172	1,102.7
7. Clay Kirby	170	1,128.0
8. Brian Lawrence	146	934.0
9. Joey Hamilton	142	934.7
10. Bruce Hurst	131	911.7
Adam Eaton	131	796.0

Complete Games: Season

Player	CG	Year
1. Randy Jones	25	1976
2. Randy Jones	18	1975
3. Dave Roberts	14	1971
4. Clay Kirby	13	1971
Eric Show	13	1988
6. Steve Arlin	12	1972
7. Steve Arlin	10	1971
Bruce Hurst	10	1989
Fred Norman	10	1972
Gaylord Perry	10	1979

Complete Games: Career with Team

Player	CG	IP
1. Randy Jones	71	1,766.0
2. Eric Show	35	1,603.3
3. Clay Kirby	34	1,128.0
4. Steve Arlin	31	745.0
5. Bruce Hurst	29	911.7
6. Dave Dravecky	23	900.3
7. Ed Whitson	22	1,354.3
8. Andy Hawkins	19	1,102.7
9. Andy Ashby	18	1,212.0
Bill Greif	18	645.0

Games Won: Season

Player	W	Year
1. Randy Jones	22	1976
2. Gaylord Perry	21	1978
3. Randy Jones	20	1975
4. Kevin Brown	18	1998
Andy Hawkins	18	1985
6. Andy Ashby	17	1998
7. La Marr Hoyt	16	1985
Tim Lollar	16	1982
Eric Show	16	1988
Ed Whitson	16	1989

Games Won: Career with Team

Player	W	IP
1. Eric Show	100	1,603.3
2. Randy Jones	92	1,766.0
3. Ed Whitson	77	1,354.3
4. Andy Ashby	70	1,212.0
5. Andy Benes	69	1,235.0
6. Andy Hawkins	60	1,102.7
7. Joey Hamilton	55	934.7
Bruce Hurst	55	911.7
9. Dave Dravecky	53	900.3
10. Clay Kirby	52	1,128.0

Games Lost: Season

Player	L	Year
1. Randy Jones	22	1974
2. Steve Arlin	21	1972
3. Clay Kirby	20	1969
4. Steve Arlin	19	1971
Bill Greif	19	1974
Bobby Jones	19	2001
7. Clay Kirby	18	1973
Bob Shirley	18	1977
9. Matt Clement	17	2000
Bill Greif	17	1973
Joe Niekro	17	1969
Dave Roberts	17	1971

Games Lost: Career with Team

Player	L	IP
1. Randy Jones	105	1,766.0
2. Eric Show	87	1,603.3
3. Clay Kirby	81	1,128.0
4. Andy Benes	75	1,235.0
5. Ed Whitson	72	1,354.3
6. Steve Arlin	62	745.0
Andy Ashby	62	1,212.0
8. Bill Greif	61	645.0
Brian Lawrence	61	934.0
10. Andy Hawkins	58	1,102.7

Winning Percentage: Season

Player	W%	Year
1. Gaylord Perry	.778	1978
Dennis Rasmussen	.778	1988
3. Kevin Brown	.720	1998
4. Jake Peavy	.714	2004
5. Andy Hawkins	.692	1985
6. Adam Eaton	.688	2005
7. La Marr Hoyt	.667	1985
8. Andy Ashby	.654	1998
9. Bruce Hurst	.652	1991
10. Jake Peavy	.650	2005

Winning Percentage: Career with Team

Player	W%	IP
1. Jake Peavy	.597	661.7
2. Bruce Hurst	.591	911.7
3. Joey Hamilton	.556	934.7
4. Eric Show	.535	1,603.3
5. Adam Eaton	.534	796.0
6. Andy Ashby	.530	1,212.0
7. Ed Whitson	.517	1,354.3
8. Dave Dravecky	.515	900.3
9. Greg Harris	.512	673.3
10. Craig Lefferts	.512	659.0

Shutouts: Season

Player	SHO	Year
1. Randy Jones	6	1975
Fred Norman	6	1972
3. Randy Jones	5	1976

4. Steve Arlin	4	1971
Bruce Hurst	4	1990
Bruce Hurst	4	1992
7. 13 tied with . . .	3	——

SHUTOUTS: CAREER WITH TEAM

Player	SHO	IP
1. Randy Jones	18	1,766.0
2. Steve Arlin	11	745.0
Eric Show	11	1,603.3
4. Bruce Hurst	10	911.7
5. Andy Benes	8	1,235.0
6. Andy Hawkins	7	1,102.7
Clay Kirby	7	1,128.0
8. Andy Ashby	6	1,212.0
Dave Dravecky	6	900.3
Dave Freisleben	6	730.0
Fred Norman	6	413.0
Ed Whitson	6	1,354.3

ERA: SEASON

Player	ERA	Year
1. Dave Roberts	2.10	1971
2. Randy Jones	2.24	1975
3. Jake Peavy	2.27	2004
4. Kevin Brown	2.38	1998
5. Ed Whitson	2.60	1990
6. Ed Whitson	2.66	1989
7. Bruce Hurst	2.69	1989
8. Gaylord Perry	2.73	1978
9. Randy Jones	2.74	1976
10. Clay Kirby	2.83	1971

ERA: CAREER WITH TEAM

Player	ERA	IP
1. Trevor Hoffman	2.73	786.7
2. Greg Harris	2.95	673.3
3. Dave Roberts	2.99	500.0
4. Dave Dravecky	3.12	900.3
5. Craig Lefferts	3.24	659.0
6. Bruce Hurst	3.27	911.7
7. Randy Jones	3.30	1,766.0
8. Jake Peavy	3.33	661.7
9. Andy Benes	3.57	1,235.0
10. Bob Shirley	3.58	722.0

EARNED RUNS ALLOWED: SEASON

Player	ER	Year
1. Matt Clement	117	2000
Bill Greif	117	1974
3. Bobby Jones	111	2001
4. Clay Kirby	108	1970
Ed Whitson	108	1987
6. Randy Jones	106	1979
7. Pat Dobson	105	1970
Brian Lawrence	105	2005
9. Joey Hamilton	103	1998
Kevin Jarvis	103	2001
Randy Jones	103	1974

EARNED RUNS ALLOWED: CAREER WITH TEAM

Player	ER	IP
1. Randy Jones	648	1,766.0
2. Eric Show	639	1,603.3
3. Ed Whitson	555	1,354.3
4. Andy Benes	490	1,235.0
5. Andy Ashby	484	1,212.0
6. Andy Hawkins	471	1,102.7
7. Clay Kirby	468	1,128.0
8. Brian Lawrence	426	934.0
9. Joey Hamilton	398	934.7
10. Adam Eaton	384	796.0

STRIKEOUTS: SEASON

Player	K	Year
1. Kevin Brown	257	1998
2. Clay Kirby	231	1971
3. Jake Peavy	216	2005
4. Sterling Hitchcock	194	1999
5. Andy Benes	189	1994
6. Pat Dobson	185	1970
7. Joey Hamilton	184	1996
8. Andy Benes	179	1993
Bruce Hurst	179	1989
10. Clay Kirby	175	1972

STRIKEOUTS: CAREER WITH TEAM

Player	K	IP
1. Andy Benes	1,036	1,235.0
2. Eric Show	951	1,603.3
3. Trevor Hoffman	889	786.7
4. Andy Ashby	829	1,212.0
5. Clay Kirby	802	1,128.0
6. Ed Whitson	767	1,354.3
7. Randy Jones	677	1,766.0
8. Joey Hamilton	639	934.7
9. Jake Peavy	635	661.7
10. Adam Eaton	623	796.0

STRIKEOUTS PER NINE IP: SEASON

Player	K/9	Year
1. Andy Benes	9.87	1994
2. Jake Peavy	9.58	2005
3. Jake Peavy	9.36	2004
4. Kevin Brown	9.00	1998
5. Sterling Hitchcock	8.49	1999
6. Sterling Hitchcock	8.06	1998
7. Joey Hamilton	7.82	1996
8. Clay Kirby	7.78	1971
9. Matt Clement	7.46	2000
10. Jake Peavy	7.21	2003

STRIKEOUTS PER NINE IP: CAREER WITH TEAM

Player	K/9	IP
1. Trevor Hoffman	10.17	786.7
2. Jake Peavy	8.64	661.7
3. Sterling Hitchcock	7.60	649.0
4. Andy Benes	7.55	1,235.0
5. Adam Eaton	7.04	796.0
6 Clay Kirby	6.40	1,128.0
7. Greg Harris	6.18	673.3
8. Andy Ashby	6.16	1,212.0
9. Joey Hamilton	6.15	934.7
10. Bruce Hurst	6.08	911.7

HITS ALLOWED: SEASON

Player	HA	Year
1. Randy Jones	274	1976
2. Randy Jones	263	1978
3. Pat Dobson	257	1970
Randy Jones	257	1979
5. Bobby Jones	250	2001
6. Bill Greif	244	1974
7. Randy Jones	242	1975
8. Gaylord Perry	241	1978
9. Dave Roberts	238	1971
10. Andy Benes	230	1992
Brian Lawrence	230	2002

HITS ALLOWED: CAREER WITH TEAM

Player	HA	IP
1. Randy Jones	1,720	1,766.0
2. Eric Show	1,464	1,603.3
3. Ed Whitson	1,314	1,354.3
4. Andy Ashby	1,186	1,212.0
5. Andy Benes	1,128	1,235.0
6. Andy Hawkins	1,089	1,102.7
7. Clay Kirby	1,026	1,128.0

Player		
8. Brian Lawrence	980	934.0
9. Joey Hamilton	912	934.7
10. Bruce Hurst	835	911.7

Hits Allowed Per Nine IP: Season

Player	H/9	Year
1. Clay Kirby	7.17	1971
2. Jake Peavy	7.18	2005
3. Tim Lollar	7.43	1982
Clay Kirby	7.43	1972
5. Bruce Hurst	7.56	1990
6. Eric Show	7.62	1984
7. Randy Jones	7.64	1975
8. Eric Show	7.71	1988
9. Tim Lollar	7.73	1984
10. Andy Benes	7.80	1993

Hits Allowed Per Nine IP: Career with Team

Player	H/9	IP
1. Trevor Hoffman	6.90	786.7
2. Greg Harris	7.90	673.3
3. Jake Peavy	7.98	661.7
4. Dave Dravecky	8.12	900.3
5. Tim Lollar	8.16	680.7
6. Clay Kirby	8.19	1,128.0
7. Eric Show	8.22	1,603.3
Andy Benes	8.22	1,235.0
9. Bruce Hurst	8.24	911.7
10. Adam Eaton	8.73	667.3

Walks Allowed: Season

Player	BB	Year
1. Matt Clement	125	2000
2. Steve Arlin	122	1972
3. Clay Kirby	120	1970
4. Clay Kirby	116	1972
5. Dave Freisleben	112	1974
6. Joey Hamilton	106	1998
7. Tim Lollar	105	1984
8. Steve Arlin	103	1971
Clay Kirby	103	1971
10. Clay Kirby	100	1969
Bob Shirley	100	1977

Walks Allowed: Career with Team

Player	BB	IP
1. Eric Show	593	1,603.3
2. Clay Kirby	505	1,128.0
3. Randy Jones	414	1,766.0
4. Andy Hawkins	412	1,102.7
5. Andy Benes	402	1,235.0
6. Steve Arlin	351	745.0
7. Ed Whitson	350	1,354.3
8. Dave Freisleben	346	730.0
9. Joey Hamilton	343	934.7
10. Tim Lollar	328	680.7

Walks Allowed Per Nine IP: Season

Player	BB/9	Year
1. La Marr Hoyt	.86	1985
2. David Wells	.92	2004
3. Randy Jones	1.43	1976
4. Kevin Brown	1.72	1998
5. Bobby Jones	1.75	2001
6. Randy Jones	1.77	1975
7. Ed Whitson	1.85	1990
8. Bob Tewksbury	1.87	1996
9. Ed Whitson	1.90	1989
10. Craig Lefferts	1.93	1992

Walks Allowed Per Nine IP: Career with Team

Player	BB/9	IP
1. Randy Jones	2.11	1,766.0
2. Dave Roberts	2.21	500.0
3. Ed Whitson	2.33	1,354.3
4. Bruce Hurst	2.39	911.7
5. Andy Ashby	2.41	1,212.0
6. Brian Lawrence	2.46	934.0
7. Trevor Hoffman	2.49	786.7
8. Craig Lefferts	2.51	659.0
9. Dave Dravecky	2.70	900.3
10. Greg Harris	2.74	673.3

WHIP (Walks + Hits Per Nine IP): Season

Player	WHIP	Year
1. Randy Jones	1.027	1976
2. Jake Peavy	1.044	2005
3. Randy Jones	1.046	1975
4. Kevin Brown	1.066	1998
5. Eric Show	1.082	1988
6. Ed Whitson	1.084	1989
7. La Marr Hoyt	1.094	1985
8. Dave Roberts	1.109	1971
9. Bruce Hurst	1.122	1990
10. Andy Benes	1.135	1991

WHIP (Walks + Hits Per Nine IP): Career with Team

Player	WHIP	IP
1. Trevor Hoffman	1.044	786.7
2. Bruce Hurst	1.181	911.7
3. Greg Harris	1.182	673.3
4. Dave Dravecky	1.202	900.3
5. Randy Jones	1.208	1,766.0
6. Dave Roberts	1.216	500.0
7. Jake Peavy	1.217	661.7
8. Ed Whitson	1.229	1,354.3
9. Andy Benes	1.239	1,235.0
10. Andy Ashby	1.246	1,212.0

Home Runs Allowed: Season

Player	HRA	Year
1. Kevin Jarvis	37	2001
Bobby Jones	37	2001
3. Ed Whitson	36	1987
4. Jake Peavy	33	2003
Woody Williams	33	1999
6. Brett Tomko	31	2002
7. Clay Kirby	30	1973
8. Sterling Hitchcock	29	1998
Sterling Hitchcock	29	1999
Clay Kirby	29	1970

Home Runs Allowed: Career with Team

Player	HRA	IP
1. Eric Show	166	1,603.3
2. Ed Whitson	148	1,354.3
3. Andy Ashby	130	1,212.0
4. Clay Kirby	118	1,128.0
5. Andy Benes	115	1,235.0
6. Randy Jones	110	1,766.0
7. Woody Williams	108	681.0
8. Adam Eaton	101	796.0
9. Sterling Hitchcock	100	649.0
10. Andy Hawkins	99	1,102.7

Saves: Season

Player	SV	Year
1. Trevor Hoffman	53	1998
2. Mark Davis	44	1989
3. Trevor Hoffman	43	2000
Trevor Hoffman	43	2001

Trevor Hoffman	43	2005
6. Trevor Hoffman	42	1996
7. Trevor Hoffman	41	2004
8. Trevor Hoffman	40	1999
9. Trevor Hoffman	38	2002
Randy Myers	38	1992

Saves: Career with Team

Player	SV	IP
1. Trevor Hoffman	434	786.7
2. Rollie Fingers	108	426.3
3. Rich Gossage	83	298.0
4. Mark Davis	78	308.0
5. Craig Lefferts	64	659.0
6. Gary Lucas	49	428.3
7. Randy Myers	38	94.0
8. Lance McCullers	36	392.0
9. Luis DeLeon	31	294.3
10. Gene Harris	23	93.0

Wild Pitches: Season

Player	WP	Year
1. Matt Clement	23	2000
2. Steve Arlin	15	1972
Sterling Hitchcock	15	1999
4. Andy Benes	14	1993
Joey Hamilton	14	1996
6. Clay Kirby	13	1971
Clay Kirby	13	1973
Fred Norman	13	1972
Brent Strom	13	1976
10. Dave Freisleben	12	1974
Al Santorini	12	1969

Wild Pitches: Career with Team

Player	WP	IP
1. Clay Kirby	48	1,128.0
2. Steve Arlin	40	745.0
Trevor Hoffman	40	786.7
4. Sterling Hitchcock	38	649.0
5. Matt Clement	36	399.3
6. Andy Ashby	35	1,212.0
Dave Freisleben	35	730.0
8. Eric Show	34	1,603.3
9. Joey Hamilton	33	934.7
10. Tim Lollar	30	680.7

Hit Batsmen: Season

Player	HB	Year
1. Matt Clement	16	2000
2. Bill Greif	14	1974
3. Joey Hamilton	12	1997
4. Andy Ashby	11	1995
Mike Corkins	11	1973
Joey Hamilton	11	1995
Brian Lawrence	11	2002
Brian Lawrence	11	2003
Jake Peavy	11	2004
Brian Lawrence	11	2005

Hit Batsmen: Career with Team

Player	HB	IP
1. Joey Hamilton	46	934.7
Eric Show	46	1,603.3
3. Brian Lawrence	45	934.0
4. Andy Ashby	37	1,212.0
5. Bill Greif	32	645.0
6. Adam Eaton	31	796.0
7. Jake Peavy	27	661.7
8. Andy Hawkins	26	1,102.7
9. Matt Clement	25	399.3
10. Sterling Hitchcock	24	649.0

Games Finished: Season

Player	GF	Year
1. Rollie Fingers	69	1977
2. Mark Davis	65	1989
3. Rollie Fingers	62	1978
Trevor Hoffman	62	1996
Butch Metzger	62	1976
6. Trevor Hoffman	61	1998
7. Trevor Hoffman	59	1997
Trevor Hoffman	59	2000
9. Randy Myers	57	1992
10. Trevor Hoffman	55	2001

Games Finished: Career with Team

Player	GF	IP
1. Trevor Hoffman	619	786.7
2. Rollie Fingers	218	426.3
3. Craig Lefferts	181	659.0
4. Rich Gossage	157	298.0
5. Mark Davis	146	308.0
6. Gary Lucas	134	428.3
7. Lance McCullers	120	392.0
8. Luis DeLeon	98	294.3
9. Gary Ross	79	382.3
10. Dave Tomlin	74	315.7

Terry Kennedy in Goose Gossage's arms after clinching 1984 National League Championship.

Significant Padres

BENES, ANDY (SP)
(1989–1995)

The San Diego Padres selected Benes as the first overall pick of the June 1988 amateur free-agent draft. After spending just a few months in the minors, he moved up to the major leagues in 1989 and pitched well enough to be named the National League Rookie Pitcher of the Year by *The Sporting News.* Although predicted to be a dominant pitcher in the National League, Benes never quite lived up to expectations and was traded to the Seattle Mariners in 1995 for Ron Villone and Marc Newfield.

CAREER PADRES RECORD:

W	L	W%	ERA	SV
69	75	.479	3.57	0

K	BB	SHO	IP
1,036	402	8	1,235.0

COLBERT, NATE (1B)
(1969–1974)

Nate Colbert came to the Padres from Houston as San Diego's ninth pick in the 1968 expansion draft. The three-time Padres All-Star quickly established himself as one of the National League's top young sluggers. On August 1, 1972, he slammed five homers and drove in 13 runs in a doubleheader against Atlanta. The 13 RBIs smashed the old doubleheader record of 11, and the five homers tied Stan Musial's 1954 record set at Sportsmen's Park in St. Louis (in a game that Colbert, a St. Louis native, had attended as a young boy). Although he was prone to striking out (he whiffed seven consecutive times at one point), Colbert managed to carry the Padres almost single-handedly in 1972 when he drove in 111 of the team's 488 runs. Unfortunately, his power mysteriously vanished and he was traded to the Tigers after the 1974 season. After two dismal sub-.200 campaigns in 1975 and 1976 for three different teams, Colbert retired and was out of baseball at the age of 30.

CAREER PADRES RECORD:

Games	AB	Hits	Runs
866	3,080	780	442

Avg	HR	RBI	SB
.253	163	481	48

FINGERS, ROLLIE (RP)
(1977–1980)

After spending nine seasons with the Athletics and establishing himself as one of baseball's best relievers, Fingers opted for free agency after the 1976 season and signed with the Padres. Although he spent only four seasons in San Diego, Fingers had his best years there in terms of saves, leading the National League with 35 in 1977 and 37 in 1978. In both years he was named the Rolaids Relief Man of the Year and *The Sporting News* Fireman of the Year. On December 8, 1980, he was traded to St. Louis along with Bob Shirley and Gene Tenace for seven players. Four days later, the Cardinals traded him, Ted Simmons, and Pete Vuckovich to the Brewers for four players. *(See A's and Brewers bios.)*

CAREER PADRES RECORD:

W	L	W%	ERA	SV
34	40	.459	3.12	108
K	BB	SHO	IP	
319	134	0	426.3	

GWYNN, TONY (OF)
(1982–2001)

A college star at San Diego State in both baseball and basketball, Gwynn was drafted in the third round of the 1981 amateur draft by the Padres and the 10th round of the NBA draft by the San Diego Clippers (now the Los Angeles Clippers). He chose baseball over basketball, laboring in the San Diego outfield for 20 years, becoming one of those rare players who spend their entire career with the same team. Gwynn debuted with the Padres in July 1982 and hit .289 for the partial season. For the next 19 seasons, he batted over .300. He suffered a terrible half in 1988, but stormed back to finish with a .313 average, the lowest ever to lead the National League. In 1994, one of his finest seasons was unfortunately marred by the players' strike. When play stopped on August 11, Gwynn was hitting .394, the highest average in the National League since Bill Terry hit .401 for the New York Giants in 1930. (Over the last 15 games before the strike, Gwynn went 26-for-60, so many baseball analysts felt he had a shot at .400 that season.)

In 1997, Gwynn won his fourth consecutive batting title, joining Hall of Famers Ty Cobb, Rogers Hornsby, Rod Carew, and Wade Boggs as the only players to win four or more consecutive titles. When he retired after the 2001 season, he held nearly every Padres career hitting record except for home runs. He was the toughest player to strike out in the National League during 10 different seasons. Along the way, he won eight NL batting titles (a record he shares with Honus Wagner), seven Silver Slugger Awards, and five Gold Gloves, and was selected to the All-Star team 15 times. A member of the elite 3,000-hit club, Gwynn was particularly noted for his charitable nature and was honored in 1999 with the Roberto Clemente Award. He will undoubtedly be a first-ballot Hall of Fame selection when he becomes eligible.

CAREER PADRES RECORD:

Games	AB	Hits	Runs
2,440	9,288	3,141	1,383
Avg	HR	RBI	SB
.338	135	1,138	319

HOFFMAN, TREVOR (RP)
(1993–2005)

Trevor Hoffman had spent only a few months with the Florida Marlins as a rookie pitcher when he was traded to San Diego in a five-player deal that sent Gary Sheffield to the Marlins. Over the next 13 seasons, he became one of baseball's best closers ever, surpassing the 400 mark in saves in 2005, all but two of them with the Padres. He was originally an infielder, but converted to pitcher in 1991. His 53 saves in 1998 tied Randy Myers for the National League record at the time. Although he missed almost the entire 2003 season due to injury (he played just nine innings), the four-time All-Star made a big comeback in 2004 with 41 saves and was still going strong in 2005 at the age of 37 when he collected 43 more.

CAREER PADRES RECORD:

W	L	W%	ERA	SV
47	51	.480	2.73	434
K	**BB**	**SHO**	**IP**	
889	218	0	786.7	

JONES, RANDY (SP)
(1973–1980)

The San Diego Padres selected Randy Jones in the fifth round of the 1972 amateur draft. By 1973 the hard-throwing rookie was on the young expansion team's major league roster. After suffering two losing seasons, including 22 losses in 1974, Jones—whose fastball had diminished greatly due to a serious elbow injury—took the advice of his pitching coach and changed his delivery so that he threw across his body, making it harder for hitters to pick up the ball. He also developed a wicked sinkerball, one that dropped as much as a foot as it crossed the plate. These two changes, along with an already masterful control, allowed him to become one of the most dominant pitchers in 1975. He won 20 games and led the National League with a 2.24 ERA.

Because his ease-of-motion fastball now topped out at 75 miles per hour, Jones was able to pitch deep into games; in 1976 he compiled an amazing 315 innings pitched with 25 complete games. After winning 22 games in 1976, he won the National League's Cy Young Award. That same year, he tied Christy Mathewson's NL record by going 68 consecutive innings without issuing a walk. He also became the first National League pitcher in more than 30 years to win at least 20 games and not strike out at least 100 batters. Jones figured prominently in the All-Star Games in 1975 and 1976, stopping the AL in the ninth inning of the 1975 contest and starting and winning the 1976 game. Jones was stellar on defense as well; in 1976, he handled 112 chances without an error, setting a major league record. Unfortunately, in late September 1976, he severed a nerve that could not be repaired. He never again attained the mastery that was the hallmark of his incredible 1975 and 1976 seasons, and he finished his career in 1982 with six consecutive losing seasons, the last two with the Mets. In 1997, the Padres honored Randy Jones by retiring his uniform number, 35.

CAREER PADRES RECORD:

W	L	W%	ERA	SV
92	105	.467	3.30	2
K	**BB**	**SHO**	**IP**	
677	414	18	1,766.0	

NEVIN, PHIL (3B/1B)
(1999–2005)

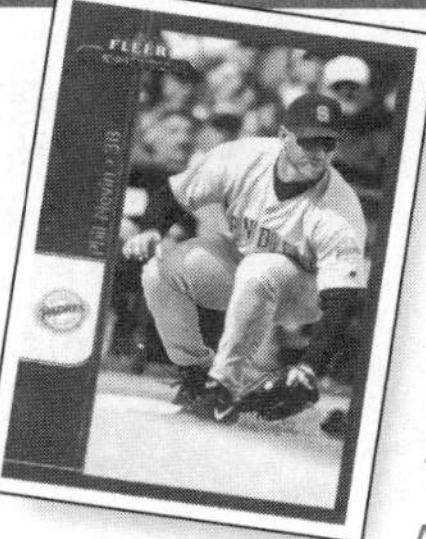

Phil Nevin, primarily a third baseman for the Padres, came to San Diego in a trade with the Angels that sent Andy Sheets to Anaheim just before the 1999 regular season. While not spectacular, he was a very solid performer for the Padres and was creeping into the top 10 of many of San Diego's career hitting categories when the team traded him to the Texas Rangers in July 2005 for pitcher Chan Ho Park.

CAREER PADRES RECORD:

Games	AB	Hits	Runs
733	2,647	770	397
Avg	**HR**	**RBI**	**SB**
.291	147	526	13

PERRY, GAYLORD (SP)
(1978–1979)

Gaylord Perry was traded to the Padres by the Texas Rangers for Dave Tomlin in 1978, just prior to spring training. By the time he came to the Padres, Perry had already spent 16 seasons in the major leagues, so it was assumed that the 40-year-old pitcher's best years were behind him. But the future Hall of Famer responded with a 21–6 record in 1978, winning the NL Cy Young Award and becoming the first pitcher in major league history to win the honor in both leagues. (He had won the award in 1972 with Cleveland, also his first year with that team.) After posting a 12–11 record in 1979, Perry was traded back to the Rangers along with two other players for Willie Montanez. *(See Giants bio.)*

CAREER PADRES RECORD:

W	L	W%	ERA	SV
33	17	.660	2.88	0
K	**BB**	**SHO**	**IP**	
294	133	2	493.3	

RICHARDS, GENE (OF)
(1977–1983)

Drafted as the first pick overall in the 1975 amateur draft, the speedy Richards was the all-time hitting leader of the Padres (.291 career average) until Tony Gwynn came along. As a rookie in 1977, Richards stole 56 bases. In 1980 he joined Ozzie Smith and Jerry Mumphrey as the first trio of teammates to steal over 50 bases each in the same season. Richards was also a stellar defensive outfielder, leading the majors in assists in 1980 with 21. He left San Diego via free agency after the 1983 season, but after one more year of part-time play for the Giants, Richards was released and never played again, out of baseball at the age of 30.

CAREER PADRES RECORD:

Games	AB	Hits	Runs
939	3,414	994	484
Avg	**HR**	**RBI**	**SB**
.291	26	251	242

SANTIAGO, BENITO (C)
(1986–1992)

Benito Santiago was signed by the Padres in September 1982 to an amateur free-agent contract. After four seasons in the minors, he burst onto the major league scene and was named the National League's Rookie of the Year, hitting .300 with 18 homers, 21 stolen bases, and a rookie-record 34-game hitting streak. He had a powerful arm behind the plate and developed a reputation for throwing out runners while kneeling. Considered one of the best catchers in baseball in the late 1980s and early 1990s, Santiago was named to the All-Star team four times and won three Gold Gloves and four Silver Slugger Awards as a member of the Padres. After the 1992 season, Santiago left the Padres via free agency, and by 2005 he was still in the big leagues, having played for nine different teams in 13 years since leaving San Diego. Over that span, Santiago left via free agency every time but one (when he was traded to Pittsburgh in 2004), never being released by a team.

CAREER PADRES RECORD:

Games	AB	Hits	Runs
789	2,872	758	312
Avg	**HR**	**RBI**	**SB**
.264	85	375	62

SHOW, ERIC (SP)
(1981–1990)

An unspectacular but effective major leaguer, Eric Show remains the all-time leader in victories for the San Diego Padres. He spent the first 10 of his 11-year career with the Padres before declaring free agency and playing one final year with the Oakland A's in 1991. He will probably be most remembered for two things: giving up the record-breaking career hit number 4,192 to Pete Rose, and dying from an overdose of cocaine and heroin at the age of 37 on March 16, 1994, two years after his exit from major league baseball.

CAREER PADRES RECORD:

W	L	W%	ERA	SV
100	87	.535	3.59	7
K	**BB**	**SHO**	**IP**	
951	593	11	1,603.3	

TEMPLETON, GARRY (SS)
(1982–1991)

Garry Templeton came to the Padres in a six-player trade that he himself demanded after the 1981 season; the deal sent Ozzie Smith to the Cardinals in an exchange of star shortstops. The moody, switch-hitting Templeton led the Padres to the World Series in 1984, but by and large didn't enjoy the hitting success in San Diego that he had with the Cardinals. His only All-Star appearance as a Padre came in 1985 when, along with four of his teammates, he was named a starter, something that agreed with him (in 1979, he had refused to show up for the All-Star Game because he was named as an alternate). In mid-1991, his hitting skills clearly in decline, Templeton was traded to the New York Mets, where he finished the last few months of his career.

CAREER PADRES RECORD:

Games	AB	Hits	Runs
1,286	4,512	1,135	430
Avg	**HR**	**RBI**	**SB**
.252	43	427	101

WINFIELD, DAVE (OF)
(1973–1980)

Dave Winfield was a star athlete at the University of Minnesota in several sports. He was named the MVP of the 1973 College World Series, finishing with a .400 batting average and a 13–1 record on the mound. He was not only drafted by the Padres, but also by the Atlanta Hawks of the NBA, the Utah Stars of the ABA, and the Minnesota Vikings of the NFL. The six-foot-six Winfield chose baseball and jumped immediately from college to the majors. Playing for the lowly Padres, Winfield became a star and left the team via free agency after the 1980 season, signing a huge 10-year contract with the Yankees. While with the Padres, he was named to the All-Star team four times and won two Gold Gloves. Although he played two more years for the Yankees than he did with San Diego, he chose to enter the Hall of Fame as a member of the Padres, becoming the franchise's first representative in Cooperstown.

CAREER PADRES RECORD:

Games	AB	Hits	Runs
1,117	3,997	1,134	599
Avg	**HR**	**RBI**	**SB**
.284	154	626	133

Petco Park, San Diego's contribution to the urban retro baseball park revival.

San Francisco Giants

Since 1883

1956 Team Ball

1885 First baseman Roger Connor of the Giants hits .371 to lead the National League while second baseman Joe Gerhardt hits just .155, the lowest average ever by a full-time player other than a catcher.... **1904** Giants pitcher Joe McGinnity wins 35 games while teammate Christy Mathewson wins 33, combining for what remains the modern record for two teammates.... **1922** The Giants become the first team ever to win a pennant without a 20-game winner on their staff.... **1930** Bill Terry is the last National League hitter to hit over .400 (he managed to reach .401 for the season) and the Giants as a team hit .319, a 20th-century record.... **1946** The Giants hit 121 home runs, 40 more than their closest competitor, and still manage to finish in last place.... **1993** Dusty Baker wins 103 games as a rookie manager, the most in National League history.

FRANCHISE HISTORY

The San Francisco Giants began play in New York City as the Gothams in 1883. Some sources incorrectly claim that the franchise was transferred from Troy, New York, but in reality the Troy franchise was forced to fold by the National League after the 1882 season; a new franchise was granted to New York, with millionaire John B. Day as the owner. At the time, Day already owned the New York Metropolitans of the American Association. Far from minding that Day owned two major league teams in rival leagues, the leagues believed that his large bank account and love of the game outweighed any possible conflict of interest. (It was common during the 19th century for individuals to own shares in more than one team, and even hold controlling interest in several teams at the same time.) Day had made his fortune in the tobacco business and had come to New York to open a new cigar factory. He was a true baseball fan who once had tried to make it as a pitcher, but, after a miserable tryout with the American Association's Metropolitans, he realized it made more sense to buy the team instead, and within the year he did.

Day jumped at the chance to purchase the new National League franchise for New York City. His two New York teams played right next to each other, their stadium outfields separated by a canvas fence. On many occasions the two teams played at the same time, conveniently allowing fans sitting in the upper bleacher seats to watch both games simultaneously. Day's Metropolitans won the American Association in 1884, but lost the World Series to Providence, three games to none. Day was furious with his Mets for having lost, so in early 1885 he transferred two of his best players, Tim Keefe and Tom 'Dude' Esterbrook, and manager Jim Mutrie to his Gothams team in order to improve their chances in the National League, whose status surpassed that of the American Association. The move predictably

The 1888 edition of the New York Giants.

created an uproar, as the American Association owners felt Day was just using the Mets as a feeder team for the Giants. The American Association quickly moved to revoke Day's charter for the Mets, but Day moved even quicker when he got wind of the league's intentions, selling the Mets to millionaire promoter Erasmus Wiman, owner of the Staten Island railroad ferry, for $25,000. When the league retaliated by kicking the Mets out of the AA, Wiman sued and got an injunction allowing him to remain in the league.

After suffering a beaning in 1905, Giants catcher Roger Bresnahan was the first player to experiment with using a batting helmet.

Meanwhile, Day renamed his team the Giants and put all his efforts into making them the crown jewel of the National League. When the Players' League began play in 1890, Day, who turned down the new entity's offer of becoming league president, suffered so much financial loss that it affected his tobacco business as well. Over the next several years, Day sold off increasing amounts of his team's stock in order to raise operating capital, eventually selling off so much that he lost control of the team. Day also sank further and further into debt by securing loans from several other league owners, both for his team and his factory. Although Day continued to work in the team's front office for another decade, the once-proud millionaire ended up a poor and broken man living in a small apartment, watching his wife sew and wash clothes for the other tenants just to raise food money.

The largest purchaser of Giants stock was Andrew Freedman, a wealthy real estate developer with extensive political connections, who used any means necessary to increase his wealth, including taking kickbacks on city insurance policies. By all accounts, Freedman was a despicable man who was held in contempt by the other league owners, especially those in Brooklyn, the Giants' rival for fans in the New York City area. Freedman had strong connections to the New York City subway authorities, and he used his influence to keep the subway lines from stopping at any station that might be beneficial to the Brooklyn team. By 1902 Freedman was universally hated among fans, players, owners, and many city officials. When his political cronies got swept out of office in 1901, Freedman lost much of his former clout and soon became the target of an orchestrated power play by several groups that forced him to sell his controlling interest to minority owner John Brush for $200,000.

Brush, who made his fortune as the owner of the When Department Stores, convinced John McGraw to become the team's new manager, a position he would hold for more than three decades. It was a sharp departure from the Freedman era, which saw a dozen managers come and go in less than a decade. Brush was the antithesis of Freedman, popular with everyone, including New York celebrities

Christy Mathewson, who won 373 games.

The Catch: Willie Mays runs down Vic Wertz's 435-foot blast in Game One of the 1954 World Series.

such as actor Douglas Fairbanks and stage star Lillian Russell. The team responded well to Brush, winning six pennants in 17 years, after not winning a single pennant for Freedman despite his efforts to acquire star players. When Brush died in 1912, he left the team to his wife and daughters, who controlled the team until 1919, when they sold controlling interest to Charles Stoneham for $750,000, and minority shares to John McGraw and several others.

Stoneham was a wealthy Wall Street stockbroker who benefited from the fact that World War I was raging when he began negotiations to buy the team in 1918. Brush's heirs were operating under the assumption that the current wartime restrictions (such as shorter schedules, travel limitations, etc.) would worsen their financial burden. Charles Stoneham owned the team until his death in 1936, presiding over the team for six pennants and three World Series titles. When Charles died, his son Horace Stoneham took over the team and ran it until 1976. Unlike most baseball owners, Horace Stoneham's only source of income was the team, so he had to watch his nickels and dimes. He couldn't spend the money on big-name talent, which partly explains why his Giants only won five pennants in 41 years.

Horace's Giants suffered under the financial strain of having to compete with the Dodgers and Yankees for New York fans until 1958, when the Dodgers decided to move to the greener grass of California. Horace decided to move with them, giving the National League two West Coast franchises with no other competing teams on the Western seaboard. Horace sold the team in 1976 to Robert Lurie (51 percent) and Bud Herseth (49 percent) for $8 million.

Lurie, the son of real estate tycoon Louis R. Lurie, was worth more than $400 million when he purchased the Giants just to keep them from being sold to a Toronto group. Herseth, a wealthy meatpacker from Arizona, agreed to come in on the deal only so long as the Giants continued to hold their spring training in Phoenix. Lurie, who initially had no intention of being a long-term owner, tried unsuccessfully to sell the team in 1985 for an advertised sale price of $35 million. By the time he eventually sold it to an investment group headed by Peter Magowan in 1992, the team fetched more than $100 million.

Magowan, who had been a member of the Giants' board of directors for a decade when he purchased the team, got his start as the manager of a Safeway store in 1968, then worked his way up to company CEO by 1980. Magowan, who still owns controlling interest in the team, did have a little help from his dad, though, who happened to be the owner of the Safeway chain.

During the 19th century, the Giants were loaded with stars, including 20-game winners Mickey Welch, Tim Keefe, and Amos Rusie, who combined for 11 seasons of 30 or more victories. The 19th century Giants were even more loaded on the hitting side, featuring first baseman Roger Connor (major league baseball's career home run leader before he was surpassed by Babe Ruth in 1921), infielder George Davis (a nine-time .300 hitter for New York), Buck Ewing (considered by most baseball historians to be the greatest player of the 19th century), and outfielders Jim O'Rourke, George Van Haltren (eight-time .300 hitter), and Mike Tiernan (seven-time .300 hitter)—sluggers all.

Yet the Giants won only two pennants during the 19th century, back-to-back titles in 1888 and 1889. Tim Keefe's 19 straight wins in 1888 sealed the NL flag and the Giants went on to defeat the American Association's St. Louis Browns, 6 games to 4 in the post-season championship series, which was more of an exhibition series than a World Series as we know it today. In 1889 the Giants won the pennant by one game on the last day of the season and then defeated the Brooklyn Bridegrooms of the American Association, 6 games to 3 for their second consecutive world title.

After slogging their way through the 1890s and early 1900s with many poor finishes, the Giants returned to prominence in 1904 under third-year manager John McGraw, winning their first pennant since 1889. Leading the way were Iron Man Joe McGinnity (35 wins) and Christy Mathewson (33 wins). McGraw refused, however, to allow his Giants to play the American League's Boston Pilgrims (repeat champions from 1903) in the World Series because he considered the American League to be inferior, even though the Pilgrims (later renamed the Red Sox) dispatched the powerful Honus Wagner–led Pittsburgh Pirates in the 1903 World Series. After putting up with cries

The team leaves the Polo Grounds for the last time on September 29, 1957. A crowd of only 11,606 watched them lose to the Pirates, 9–1.

of "Coward!" from reporters and the American League itself, the Giants manager relented when the Giants again won the NL pennant in 1905 and faced off against the Philadelphia Athletics. The Giants drubbed the A's, 4 games to 1, largely on 31-game winner Christy Mathewson's three shutouts.

The Giants should have won the pennant in 1908 behind Christy Mathewson's 37 victories, but they snatched defeat out of the jaws of victory because of Fred Merkle's baserunning error, dubbed "Merkle's Boner." In an apparent late-season win over the Cubs, Merkle didn't touch second base on the game-ending play, instead joining the on-field celebration of fans and players. The Cubs noticed his gaff, found a baseball somewhere, and proceeded to initiate a force play at second. The umpires ruled in favor of the Cubs, called the game a tie due to the riot-like atmosphere on the field, and then all hell broke lose. When the Cubs and Giants ended the regular season in a dead heat, the game was ordered replayed. The Cubs won the "do-over" sudden-death game on October 8th, beating the Giants by a game for the pennant and defeating Christy Mathewson, the pitcher who should have notched the victory in the original game played on September 23rd.

Rookie Will Clark hit a home run against Nolan Ryan in his first major league at-bat in 1986.

The Giants won the NL pennant three straight years from 1911–1913, but lost the World Series each time, to the A's, Red Sox, and A's, respectively. The Giants routed the NL in 1917 by 10 games, but, once again, lost the World Series, this time to the White Sox in six games. After three straight second-place finishes, the Giants again reached the Fall Classic in 1921 for the first of four-straight World Series berths. In 1921 and 1922, the Giants defeated the Babe Ruth–led Yankees, while in 1923 they fell to the Yankees. In 1924

Barry Bonds

Barry Bonds

the Giants lost in seven games to Walter Johnson and the Washington Senators. The Giants next reached the World Series in 1933 under new manager Bill Terry, who took over the reins in mid-1932 from John McGraw. Carl Hubbell won two games as the Giants repaid the Senators for their 1924 Series loss. The Giants won two more pennants in 1936 and 1937, but each year were bounced by the Yankees in the World Series.

After a 14-year post-season drought, the Giants staged a furious comeback in the last half of the 1951 season to tie the Brooklyn Dodgers at the end of the regular season. In the bottom of the 9th inning of Game 3 of their best-of-three playoffs, Bobby Thomson hit "The Shot Heard 'Round The World" to give the Giants the victory, 5–4. The emotionally drained and physically tired Giants then lost the World Series in six games to the hated Yankees.

Led by the "Say Hey!" kid, Willie Mays, the 1954 Giants won the pennant and then swept the heavily favored Indians in the World Series. After moving to the west coast, the Giants won their first pennant as the San Francisco Giants in 1962, though they lost the Series to the Yankees in seven. It would be 27 years before the Giants would reach the Series again, this time against their cross-bay rivals, the Oakland A's. In the middle of the contest, a powerful earthquake devastated the bay area, disrupting the World Series for a full week before the Giants were finally swept by the A's in four straight. The Giants last appeared in the World Series in 2002 when they lost to the Anaheim Angels in seven games after leading, 3 games to 2.

Recently, the Giants have received more attention from the exploits of one player—Barry Bonds—than they have as a team. First, Bonds broke Mark McGwire's single-season home run record of 70 when he clubbed 73 in 2001, the only year in his career in which he hit more than 49. He is now pursuing Babe Ruth and Hank Aaron on the all time home run charts, but Bonds has been heavily tainted by the steroids scandal. He either denies the accusations of heavy steroid use—or else claims that if he did take steroids given to him by his trainer, he did so unknowingly. Bonds has also testified at secret grand jury hearings regarding IRS and mistress problems. With mounting pressure to investigate Bonds' alleged steroid abuse, it is uncertain if Bonds will indeed finish—or be allowed to finish—his pursuit of Hank Aaron's record of 755 career home runs.

TEAM NAME HISTORY

Official Names

New York Gothams (1883–1884)
New York Giants (1885–1957)
San Francisco Giants (1958–current)

Unofficial Names/Nicknames

Green Stockings (1883–1884 only)

STADIUM HISTORY

Polo Grounds	1883–1888
Oakland Park (two games)	1889
St. George Grounds (25 games)	1889
Manhattan Field	July 8, 1889–1890
Polo Grounds (Brotherhood Park renamed after Players' League team folded)	1891–1957
Seals Stadium	1958–1959
Candlestick Park	1960–1996
3Com Park (Candlestick Park renamed)	1997–1999
Pacific Bell Park	2000–2003
SBC Park	2004–current

YEARLY RECORD, FINISH, & ATTENDANCE FIGURES

Year	League	Record	DIV/LG Finish	Attendance	Avg/Gm
2005	NL West	75–87	3	3,181,023	39,272
2004	NL West	91–71	2	3,256,854	39,718
2003	NL West	100–61	1	3,264,898	40,307
2002	NL West	95–66	2	3,253,203	40,163
2001	NL West	90–72	2	3,311,958	40,888
2000	NL West	97–65	1	3,318,800	40,973
1999	NL West	86–76	2	2,078,399	25,659
1998	NL West	89–74	2	1,925,364	23,770
1997	NL West	90–72	1	1,690,869	20,875
1996	NL West	68–94	4	1,413,922	17,243
1995	NL West	67–77	4	1,241,500	17,243
1994	NL West	55–60	2	1,704,608	28,410
1993	NL West	103–59	2	2,606,354	32,177
1992	NL West	72–90	5	1,560,998	19,272
1991	NL West	75–87	4	1,737,478	21,450
1990	NL West	85–77	3	1,975,528	24,389
1989	NL West	92–70	1	2,059,701	25,428
1988	NL West	83–79	4	1,785,297	22,041
1987	NL West	90–72	1	1,917,168	23,669
1986	NL West	83–79	3	1,528,748	18,873
1985	NL West	62–100	6	818,697	10,107
1984	NL West	66–96	6	1,001,545	12,365
1983	NL West	79–83	5	1,251,530	15,451
1982	NL West	87–75	3	1,200,948	14,827
1981	NL West	56–55	5/3	632,274	11,930
1980	NL West	75–86	5	1,096,115	13,532
1979	NL West	71–91	4	1,456,402	17,980
1978	NL West	89–73	3	1,740,477	21,487
1977	NL West	75–87	4	700,056	8,643
1976	NL West	74–88	4	626,868	7,739
1975	NL West	80–81	3	522,919	6,456
1974	NL West	72–90	5	519,987	6,420
1973	NL West	88–74	3	834,193	10,299
1972	NL West	69–86	5	647,744	8,412
1971	NL West	90–72	1	1,106,043	13,655
1970	NL West	86–76	3	740,720	9,145
1969	NL West	90–72	2	873,603	10,785
1968	NL	88–74	2	837,220	10,336
1967	NL	91–71	2	1,242,480	15,152
1966	NL	93–68	2	1,657,192	20,459
1965	NL	95–67	2	1,546,075	19,087
1964	NL	90–72	4	1,504,364	18,572
1963	NL	88–74	3	1,571,306	19,399
1962	NL	103–62	1	1,592,594	19,422
1961	NL	85–69	3	1,390,679	18,061
1960	NL	79–75	5	1,795,356	23,316
1959	NL	83–71	3	1,422,130	18,469
1958	NL	80–74	3	1,272,625	16,528
1957	NL	69–85	6	653,923	8,493
1956	NL	67–87	6	629,179	8,171
1955	NL	80–74	3	824,112	10,432

YEARLY RECORD, FINISH, & ATTENDANCE FIGURES (CONT.)

Year	League	Record	DIV/LG Finish	Attendance	Avg/Gm
1954	NL	97–57	1	1,155,067	15,198
1953	NL	70–84	5	811,518	10,539
1952	NL	92–62	2	984,940	12,791
1951	NL	98–59	1	1,059,539	13,584
1950	NL	86–68	3	1,008,878	13,275
1949	NL	73–81	5	1,218,446	15,423
1948	NL	78–76	5	1,459,269	18,952
1947	NL	81–73	4	1,600,793	21,063
1946	NL	61–93	8	1,219,873	15,843
1945	NL	78–74	5	1,016,468	13,032
1944	NL	67–87	5	674,483	8,993
1943	NL	55–98	8	466,095	6,053
1942	NL	85–67	3	779,621	9,869
1941	NL	74–79	5	763,098	9,783
1940	NL	72–80	6	747,852	9,840
1939	NL	77–74	5	702,457	9,493
1938	NL	83–67	3	799,633	10,954
1937	NL	95–57	1	926,887	12,358
1936	NL	92–62	1	837,952	10,743
1935	NL	91–62	3	748,748	9,478
1934	NL	93–60	2	730,851	9,745
1933	NL	91–61	1	604,471	7,850
1932	NL	72–82	7	484,868	6,297
1931	NL	87–65	2	812,163	10,412
1930	NL	87–67	3	868,714	11,282
1929	NL	84–67	3	868,806	11,283
1928	NL	93–61	2	916,191	11,899
1927	NL	92–62	3	858,190	11,597
1926	NL	74–77	5	700,362	9,215
1925	NL	86–66	2	778,993	10,250
1924	NL	93–60	1	844,068	10,962
1923	NL	95–58	1	820,780	10,659
1922	NL	93–61	1	945,809	11,972
1921	NL	94–59	1	973,477	12,322
1920	NL	86–68	2	929,609	11,620
1919	NL	87–53	2	708,857	10,273
1918	NL	71–53	2	256,618	4,582
1917	NL	98–56	1	500,264	6,253
1916	NL	86–66	4	552,056	7,078
1915	NL	69–83	8	391,850	5,156
1914	NL	84–70	2	364,313	4,554
1913	NL	101–51	1	630,000	7,778
1912	NL	103–48	1	638,000	8,395
1911	NL	99–54	1	675,000	9,000
1910	NL	91–63	2	511,785	6,478
1909	NL	92–61	3	783,700	10,178
1908	NL	98–56	3	910,000	11,375
1907	NL	82–71	4	538,350	6,992
1906	NL	96–56	2	402,850	5,371
1905	NL	105–48	1	552,700	7,272
1904	NL	106–47	1	609,826	7,260

YEARLY RECORD, FINISH, & ATTENDANCE FIGURES (CONT.)

Year	League	Record	DIV/LG Finish	Attendance	Avg/Gm
1903	NL	84–55	2	579,530	8,279
1902	NL	48–88	8	302,875	4,266
1901	NL	52–85	7	297,650	4,192
1900	NL	60–78	8	190,000	2,695
1899	NL	60–90	10	121,384	1,597
1898	NL	77–73	7	265,414	3,381
1897	NL	83–48	3	390,340	5,698
1896	NL	64–67	7	274,000	4,120
1895	NL	66–65	9	240,000	3,636
1894	NL	88–44	2	387,000	5,650
1893	NL	68–64	5	290,000	4,265
1892	NL	71–80	8	130,566	1,707
1891	NL	71–61	3	210,568	3,097
1890	NL	63–68	6	60,667	899
1889	NL	83–43	1	N/A	N/A
1888	NL	84–47	1	N/A	N/A
1887	NL	68–55	4	N/A	N/A
1886	NL	75–44	3	N/A	N/A
1885	NL	85–27	2	N/A	N/A
1884	NL	62–50	4	N/A	N/A
1883	NL	46–50	6	N/A	N/A

MANAGER HISTORY

Manager	Years	W–L	Win %
John Clapp	1883	46–50	.479
Jim Price	1884	56–42	.571
Monte Ward	1884, 1893–1894	162–116	.583
Jim Mutrie	1885–1891	529–345	.605
Pat Powers	1892	71–80	.470
George Davis	1895, 1900–1901	107–139	.435
Jack Doyle	1895	32–31	.508
Harvey Watkins	1895	18–17	.514
Arthur Irwin	1896	36–53	.404
Bill Joyce	1896–1898	179–122	.595
Cap Anson	1898	9–13	.409
John Day	1899	29–35	.453
Fred Hoey	1899	31–55	.348
Buck Ewing	1900	21–41	.339
Horace Fogel	1902	18–23	.439
Heinie Smith	1902	5–27	.156
John McGraw	1902–1932	2,604–1,801	.591
Bill Terry	1932–1941	823–661	.555
Mel Ott	1942–1948	464–530	.467
Leo Durocher	1948–1955	637–523	.549
Bill Rigney	1956–1960, 1976	406–430	.486
Tom Sheehan	1960	46–50	.479
Alvin Dark	1961–1964	366–277	.569
Herman Franks	1965–1968	367–280	.567
Clyde King	1969–1970	109–95	.534

MANAGER HISTORY (CONT.)

Manager	Years	W–L	Win %
Charlie Fox	1970–1974	348–327	.516
Wes Westrum	1974–1975	118–129	.478
Joe Altobelli	1977–1979	225–239	.485
Dave Bristol	1979–1980	85–98	.464
Frank Robinson	1981–1984	264–277	.488
Danny Ozark	1984	24–32	.429
Jim Davenport	1985	56–88	.389
Roger Craig	1985–1992	586–566	.509
Dusty Baker	1993–2002	840–715	.540
Felipe Alou	2003–2005	266–219	.548

ALL-TIME WIN-LOSS RECORDS VS. ALL OPPONENTS (SINCE 1900)

Opponent	W–L
ALL-TIME	8,823–7,572
Angels	11–5
Astros	343–324
Athletics	24–26
Blue Jays	5–1
Braves	1,086–905
Brewers	37–24
Cardinals	964–898
Cubs	975–900
Devil Rays	3–3
Diamondbacks	76–55
Dodgers	1,059–1,033
Indians	0–3
INTERLEAGUE	78–68
Mariners	9–7
Marlins	67–41
Mets	288–237
Nationals	208–195
Orioles	3–3
Padres	327–284
Phillies	1,089–766
Pirates	1,004–864
Rangers	9–7
Reds	1,108–899
Red Sox	2–1
Rockies	114–79
Royals	2–4
Tigers	4–2
Twins	3–3
White Sox	2–1
Yankees	1–2

The Wild West: Koufax tries to break up fight between John Roseboro and the Giants' Juan Marichal on August 22, 1965.

Franchise Highlights, Low Points, and Strange Distinctions

1888 Tim Keefe of the Giants won 19 consecutive games in 1888 to establish a single-season major league record that still stands. Twenty-four years later, in 1912, Rube Marquard—also of the Giants—tied Keefe's record, although if today's rules for determining the winning pitcher had been in effect, Keefe's streak would have reached 20 games.

....

1895 The Giants finished the season with a 66–65 record (.504), yet placed just ninth in the 12-team National League, the lowest finish ever for a team with a winning record.

....

1897 Bill Joyce of the New York Giants hit four triples in a nine-inning game on May 18, becoming the last player to do so.

....

1900 New York's .928 fielding average in 1900 remains the lowest in the last 110 years of major league play. First baseman Jack Doyle committed 41 errors and third baseman Piano Legs Hickman 86, both modern-era records.

....

1901 The Giants collected a team-record 31 hits on June 9, in a 25–13 victory at Cincinnati, led by outfielder Kip Selbach's 6-for-6 performance.

1903 Giants pitcher Dummy Taylor (a deaf mute) and manager John McGraw (who knew sign language) were once tossed out of a game by umpire Tim Hurst for arguing his calls and using profanity—in sign language. It seems Hurst had a deaf relative who was proficient in signing.

....

1906 The Giants had an impressive season, winning 96 games for a .632 winning percentage, yet they finished a whopping 20 games behind the pennant-winning Cubs, who won 116 games to set an NL record that still stands.

Another oddity that year saw the Pirates finish with a 93–60 record and .608 winning percentage while every other team in the league finished with a sub-.500 record.

....

1911 On May 13, the Giants delighted their home fans by scoring 10 runs in the bottom of the first inning against the St. Louis Cardinals before an out had been made. It's still a major league record.

....

1913 Christy Mathewson of the Giants, the first 20th-century pitcher to collect 300 career wins, pitched an amazing 68 consecutive innings without issuing a single base on balls.

1916 During the season, the Giants had two incredible winning streaks. After getting off to a dismal 2–13 start, the Giants won 17 straight games in May—all on the road—before the Phillies ended their streak. Then, from September 7–30, the Giants reeled off 26 straight wins (with a 1–1 tie game mixed in)—all at home, as part of a 31-game home stand. Despite the combined 43–0 record in the two streaks, the Giants were just 43–66 in the rest of their games, good only for fourth-place in the standings.

• • • •

1923 The New York Giants became the first modern-era team to score in all nine innings of a game when they trashed the Phillies 22–8 on June 1.

• • • •

1924 The Giants became the first team in either the National or American League to win four consecutive pennants. St. Louis of the American Association had won four straight from 1885 to 1888.

The last active major leaguer to be banned for life was Jimmy O'Connell of the 1924 Giants—for his part in a bribe offer to shortstop Heinie Sand of the Philadelphia Phillies.

• • • •

1926 Mel Ott became the youngest player in National League history to get a pinch-hit when he came through in the clutch at the age of 17. Three years later he became the youngest player in major league history to hit at least 40 homers in a season, when he smacked 42 in 1929.

1927–28 Giants pitcher Larry Benton led the league in winning percentage with records of 17–7 (.708) and 25–9 (.735), yet retired as the only pitcher ever to lead twice in winning percentage and still leave baseball with a sub-.500 winning percentage (127–128, .498).

• • • •

1929 The New York Giants became the first major league team to utilize a public address system in their ballpark when they unveiled the new technology in the Polo Grounds on July 5.

• • • •

1935 Freddie Fitzsimmons finished with a 4–8 record, but all four of his wins were shutouts, which tied him for the National League lead in the department. The next year he won 10 games, but none was a shutout.

• • • •

1943 Mel Ott of the Giants placed second in the National League home run race with 18, all of which were hit at the Polo Grounds.

• • • •

1944 Bill Voiselle pitched 313 innings for the Giants, becoming the last rookie in the major leagues to top the 300-inning mark.

1951 In spite of his .219 batting average, Giants catcher Wes Westrum was incredibly productive. With only 79 hits on the season, Westrum slugged 20 home runs and collected 79 RBIs. Amazingly, he also collected 104 walks that season. Westrum also holds a peculiar major league record: He's the only catcher to snag three foul pop-ups in an inning twice in his career.

• • • •

1952 When Giants relief pitcher Hoyt Wilhelm stepped to the plate for his first major league at-bat, he slugged a home run. Over the next 21 seasons of the Hall of Famer's career, he never hit another.

• • • •

1956 During their combined careers, Mickey Mantle and Willie Mays collected a staggering 3,412 RBIs. Incredibly, Mays, with over 1,900 RBIs, never won an RBI crown (and Mantle won only one, in 1956).

• • • •

1959 Willie McCovey collected four hits in his major league debut, tying the record set by Casey Stengel in 1912.

1962 Second baseman Chuck Hiller of the San Francisco Giants hit the National League's first-ever grand slam in World Series play when he connected in the seventh inning off Yankee Marshall Bridges in Game 4 of the Fall Classic.

• • • •

1964 Who was the worst hitter of all time? Pitcher Ron Herbel—who played most of his career with the San Francisco Giants—made a case for himself during his nine-year career when he went hitless in 47 at-bats during his rookie year of 1964. Over his career, Herbel hit .029, going 6-for-206, the lowest all-time by a player with at least 200 career at-bats. His high-water mark came in 1967 when he hit .107.

• • • •

1975 When Juan Marichal's career ended in 1975, he had six 20-win seasons under his belt, but no Cy Young Awards, making him the record holder for most 20-win seasons without winning the top prize for pitchers.

1991 After winning a Gold Glove for his play at third base, San Francisco's Matt Williams turned it around in reverse in 1992, leading all National League third basemen in errors with 23.

• • • •

1994 Four Giants won Gold Gloves (Barry Bonds, Robby Thompson, Matt Williams, and Kirt Manwaring), but strangely enough, outfielder Darren Lewis did not, even though he finished the season without making an error all year. Lewis was riding a consecutive-game errorless streak that had reached 316 games. The streak ended on June 30 of the next year at a major league record 392 games and 938 chances when Lewis made the first error of his major league career.

• • • •

1998 On August 23, Barry Bonds homered against the Marlins, becoming the first player in history to amass at least 400 homers and 400 stolen bases. In 2003, with his final steal of the year, Bonds became the only 500–500 player in major league history.

• • • •

2000 From 1997 to 2000, Jeff Kent, despite missing nearly 60 games due to various injuries, collected 475 RBIs, the most in major league history by a second baseman in a four-year span.

2004 Barry Bonds won the NL batting title with a .362 average, but only 373 at-bats, the fewest ever by a batting champion. When he was chosen as the NL MVP that year, he became not only the oldest MVP in baseball history (at age 40), but also the oldest player of any North American professional sports league to be selected as its MVP. The award was the seventh of his career, leaving him two behind hockey's Wayne Gretzky for the most MVP Awards among the four major sports.

For 50 years Hank Aaron was #1. Forever more he will be no better than #2, because on April 6, San Francisco Giants pitcher David Aardsma made his major league debut, thereby supplanting Aaron as the first player to be listed alphabetically in baseball reference books.

• • • •

2005 On May 2, Giants pitcher Scott Eyre allowed a run in a 9–8 win over the Diamondbacks—without allowing a base runner! How did he do it? Eyre was on the mound when he struck out Arizona's Shawn Green. The Giants' Gold Glove catcher, Mike Matheny, let the third strike get by him for a passed ball and Green reached first. The rules of baseball statistics do not charge a pitcher with having allowed a base runner in the case of a passed ball. Eyre was taken out of the game and the next pitcher allowed a double to Tony Clark, which scored Green. The run was charged to Eyre.

Special Achievements

World Series Results

Year	Opponent	Result	Games
1905	Philadelphia A's	Won	4–1
1911	Philadelphia A's	Lost	2–4
1912	Boston Red Sox	Lost	3–4
1913	Philadelphia A's	Lost	1–4
1917	Chicago White Sox	Lost	2–4
1921	New York Yankees	Won	5–3
1922	New York Yankees	Won	4–0
1923	New York Yankees	Lost	2–4
1924	Washington Senators	Lost	3–4
1933	Washington Senators	Won	4–1
1936	New York Yankees	Lost	2–4
1937	New York Yankees	Lost	1–4
1951	New York Yankees	Lost	2–4
1954	Cleveland Indians	Won	4–0
1962	New York Yankees	Lost	3–4
1989	Oakland A's	Lost	0–4
2002	Anaheim Angels	Lost	3–4

World Series Managerial Records

Manager	Series Record	Games Record
John McGraw	3–6	26–28
Bill Terry	1–2	7–9
Leo Durocher	1–1	6–4
Alvin Dark	0–1	3–4
Roger Craig	0–1	0–4
Dusty Baker	0–1	3–4

All-Time Postseason Record

Divisional Playoffs	5–11
League Championship Series	12–9
World Series	45–53

All-Star Games at New York (when NL was home team) & San Francisco

Year	Date	Winner	Score	Stadium
1934	July 10	American	9–7	Polo Grounds
1942	July 6	American	3–1	Polo Grounds
1961	July 11	National	5–4	Candlestick Park (Game 1)
1984	July 10	National	3–1	Candlestick Park

Hall of Famers Who Played for Team

	Position	Years	Games with New York/ San Francisco
Dave Bancroft	SS	1920–1923, 1930	534
Jake Beckley	1B	1896–1897	63
Roger Bresnahan	C/OF	1902–1908	751
Dan Brouthers	1B	1904	2
Jesse Burkett	OF/SP/RP	1890	101
Steve Carlton	SP	1986	6
Gary Carter	C	1990	92
Orlando Cepeda	1B/OF	1958–1966	1,114
Roger Connor	1B	1883–1889, 1891, 1893–1894	1,120
George Davis	SS/3B	1893–1901, 1903	1,096
Buck Ewing	C/1B/OF	1883–1889, 1891–1892	734
Frankie Frisch	2B/3B	1919–1926	1,000
Burleigh Grimes	SP/RP	1927	39
Gabby Hartnett	C	1941	64
Rogers Hornsby	2B	1927	155
Waite Hoyt	SP/RP	1918, 1932	19
Carl Hubbell	SP/RP	1928–1943	535
Monte Irvin	OF/1B	1949–1955	653
Travis Jackson	SS/3B	1922–1936	1,656
Tim Keefe	SP	1885–1889, 1891	273
Willie Keeler	3B/OF	1892–1893, 1910	40
George Kelly	1B/2B	1915–1917, 1919–1926	1,136
King Kelly	C	1893	20
Tony Lazzeri	3B	1939	13
Fred Lindstrom	3B/OF	1924–1932	1,087
Ernie Lombardi	C	1943–1947	472
Juan Marichal	SP	1960–1973	462
Rube Marquard	SP/RP	1908–1915	239
Christy Mathewson	SP/RP	1900–1916	645
Willie Mays	OF	1951–1952, 1954–1972	2,857
Willie McCovey	1B/OF	1959–1973, 1977–1980	2,256
Joe McGinnity	SP/RP	1902–1908	306
John McGraw	SS	1902–1906	59
Bill McKechnie	3B	1916	71
Joe Medwick	OF	1943–1945	232
Johnny Mize	1B	1942, 1946–1949	655
Joe Morgan	2B	1981–1982	224

Jim O'Rourke	OF/C	1885–1889, 1891–1892, 1904	807
Mel Ott	OF/3B	1926–1947	2,730
Gaylord Perry	SP/RP	1962–1971	376
Edd Roush	OF	1916, 1927–1929	340
Amos Rusie	SP	1890–1898	451
Red Schoendienst	2B	1956–1957	149
Duke Snider	OF	1964	91
Warren Spahn	SP/RP	1965	16
Casey Stengel	OF	1921–1923	177
Bill Terry	1B	1923–1936	1,721
John Ward	SS/OF	1883–1889, 1893–1894	1,070
Mickey Welch	SP	1883–1892	462
Hoyt Wilhelm	RP	1952–1956	319
Hack Wilson	OF	1923–1925	172
Ross Youngs	OF	1917–1926	1,211

HALL OF FAMERS WHO MANAGED TEAM

	Years	Games with New York/ San Francisco
Cap Anson	1898	22
George Davis	1895, 1900–1901	252
Leo Durocher	1948–1955	1,163
Buck Ewing	1900	63
Rogers Hornsby	1927	33
Hughie Jennings	1924–1925	76
John McGraw	1902–1932	4,424
Mel Ott	1942–1948	1,004
Bill Terry	1932–1941	1,496
John Ward	1884, 1893–1894	291

MVP AWARD WINNERS

Carl Hubbell	SP	1933
Carl Hubbell	SP	1936
Willie Mays	OF	1954
Willie Mays	OF	1965
Willie McCovey	1B	1969
Kevin Mitchell	OF	1989
Barry Bonds	OF	1993
Jeff Kent	2B	2000
Barry Bonds	OF	2001
Barry Bonds	OF	2002
Barry Bonds	OF	2003
Barry Bonds	OF	2004

CY YOUNG AWARD WINNERS

Pitcher	Year	W-L	ERA
Mike McCormick	1967	22–10	2.85

ROOKIE OF THE YEAR AWARD WINNERS

Willie Mays	OF	1951
Orlando Cepeda	1B	1958
Willie McCovey	1B	1959
Gary Matthews	OF	1973
John Montefusco	SP	1975

GOLD GLOVE WINNERS

Year	Position	Player
1957	OF	Willie Mays
1958	OF	Willie Mays
1959	OF	Willie Mays
1960	OF	Willie Mays
1961	OF	Willie Mays
1962	3B OF	Jim Davenport Willie Mays
1963	OF	Willie Mays
1964	OF	Willie Mays
1965	OF	Willie Mays
1966	OF	Willie Mays
1967	OF	Willie Mays
1968	OF	Willie Mays
1971	OF	Bobby Bonds
1973	OF	Bobby Bonds
1974	OF	Bobby Bonds
1987	SP	Rick Reuschel
1991	1B 3B	Will Clark Matt Williams
1993	C 2B 3B OF	Kirt Manwaring Robbie Thompson Matt Williams Barry Bonds
1994	3B OF	Matt Williams Barry Bonds
1996	OF	Barry Bonds
1997	1B OF	J.T. Snow Barry Bonds
1998	1B OF	J.T. Snow Barry Bonds
1999	1B	J.T. Snow
2000	1B	J.T. Snow
2003	OF	Jose Cruz
2005	C SS	Mike Matheny Omar Vizquel

TRIPLE CROWN WINNERS

None

FIREMAN OF THE YEAR AWARD WINNERS

Stu Miller	1961
Robb Nen	2001 (tie)

World Series MVP

Dusty Rhodes	1954

League Championship Series MVP

Jeffrey Leonard	1987
Will Clark	1989
Benito Santiago	2002

All-Star Game MVP

Willie Mays	1963
Juan Marichal	1965
Willie Mays	1968
Willie McCovey	1969
Bobby Bonds	1973

Manager of the Year Award Winners

Dusty Baker	1993
Dusty Baker	1997
Dusty Baker	2000

Batting Champions

Year	Player	AVG
1885	Roger Connor	.371
1890	Jack Glasscock	.336
1915	Larry Doyle	.320
1930	Bill Terry	.401
1954	Willie Mays	.345
2002	Barry Bonds	.370
2004	Barry Bonds	.362

Nine-Inning No-Hitters Pitched

Year	Pitcher	Opp.	Score
1891	Amos Rusie	BRK	6–0
1901	Christy Mathewson	STL	5–0
1905	Christy Mathewson	CHC	1–0
1908	George Wiltse	PHI	1–0
1912	Jeff Tesreau	PHI	3–0
1915	Rube Marquard	BRK	2–0
1922	Jesse Barnes	PHI	6–0
1929	Carl Hubbell	PIT	11–0
1963	Juan Marichal	HOU	1–0
1968	Gaylord Perry	STL	1–0
1975	Ed Halicki	NYM	6–0
1976	John Montefusco	ATL	9–0

20-Game Winners

Year	Pitcher	W–L
1883	Mickey Welch	25–23
1884	Mickey Welch	39–21
1885	Mickey Welch Tim Keefe	44–11 32–13
1886	Tim Keefe Mickey Welch	42–20 33–22
1887	Tim Keefe Mickey Welch	35–19 22–15
1888	Tim Keefe Mickey Welch	35–12 26–19
1889	Tim Keefe Mickey Welch	28–13 27–12
1890	Amos Rusie	29–34
1891	Amos Rusie John Ewing	33–20 21–8
1892	Amos Rusie Silver King	31–31 23–24
1893	Amos Rusie	33–21
1894	Amos Rusie Jouett Meekin	36–13 33–9
1895	Amos Rusie	23–23
1896	Jouett Meekin	26–14
1897	Amos Rusie Jouett Meekin Cy Seymour	28–10 20–11 20–14
1898	Cy Seymour Amos Rusie	25–19 20–11
1901	Christy Mathewson	20–17
1903	Joe McGinnity Christy Mathewson	31–20 30–13
1904	Joe McGinnity Christy Mathewson Luther Taylor	35–8 33–12 21–15
1905	Christy Mathewson Leon Ames Joe McGinnity	31–9 22–8 21–15
1906	Joe McGinnity Christy Mathewson	27–12 22–12
1907	Christy Mathewson	24–12
1908	Christy Mathewson	37–11
1909	Christy Mathewson George Wiltse	25–6 20–11
1910	Christy Mathewson	27–9
1911	Christy Mathewson Rube Marquard	26–13 24–7
1912	Rube Marquard Christy Mathewson	26–11 23–12
1913	Christy Mathewson Rube Marquard Jeff Tesreau	25–11 23–10 22–13
1914	Jeff Tesreau Christy Mathewson	26–10 24–13
1917	Ferdie Schupp	21–7
1919	Jess Barnes	25–9
1920	Fred Toney Art Nehf Jess Barnes	21–11 21–12 20–15
1921	Art Nehf	20–10
1928	Larry Benton Fred Fitzsimmons	25–9 20–9
1933	Carl Hubbell	23–12

1934	Hal Schumacher Carl Hubbell	23–10 21–12
1935	Carl Hubbell	23–12
1936	Carl Hubbell	26–6
1937	Carl Hubbell Cliff Melton	22–8 20–9
1944	Bill Voiselle	21–16
1947	Larry Jansen	21–5
1951	Sal Maglie Larry Jansen	23–6 23–11
1954	Johnny Antonelli	21–7
1956	Johnny Antonelli	20–13
1959	Sam Jones	21–15
1962	Jack Sanford	24–7
1963	Juan Marichal	25–8
1964	Juan Marichal	21–8
1965	Juan Marichal	22–13
1966	Juan Marichal Gaylord Perry	25–6 21–8
1967	Mike McCormick	22–10
1968	Juan Marichal	26–9
1969	Juan Marichal	21–11
1970	Gaylord Perry	23–13
1973	Ron Bryant	24–12
1986	Mike Krukow	20–9
1993	John Burkett Bill Swift	22–7 21–8

RETIRED UNIFORM NUMBERS

Number	Player	Position
3	Bill Terry	1B
4	Mel Ott	OF
11	Carl Hubbell	SP
24	Willie Mays	OF
27	Juan Marichal	SP
30	Orlando Cepeda	1B
36	Gaylord Perry	SP
44	Willie McCovey	1B

TEAM RECORDS—WINS & LOSSES

- Games won in a season: 106 in 1904
- Games lost in a season: 100 in 1985
- Games won in a month: 29 in September 1916
- Games lost in a month: 25 in August 1953
- Consecutive games won: 26 in 1916
- Consecutive games lost: 13 in 1902 and 1944
- Biggest shutout victory: 24–0 over Buffalo on May 27, 1885
- Biggest shutout loss: 19–0 to Chicago Cubs on June 7, 1906
- Highest winning percentage: .759 in 1885 (85–27)
- Lowest winning percentage: .353 in 1902 (48–88)

TEAM RECORDS—BATTING

- Highest team batting average: .319 in 1930
- Lowest team batting average: .233 in 1985
- Highest team slugging average: .473 in 1930
- Highest team on-base percentage: .384 in 1887
- Total hits: 1,769 in 1930
- Extra-base hits: 579 in 2001
- Hits in a game: 31 vs. Cincinnati on June 9, 1901
- Longest individual hitting streak: 33, George Davis, 1893
- Most .300 hitters in a single season: 8 in 1921, 1922, 1924, 1930, and 1931
- Home runs: 235 in 2001
- Home runs in a month: 17, Willie Mays, August 1965 and Barry Bonds, May 2001
- Home runs in a game: 8 vs. Milwaukee Braves on April 30, 1961
- Home runs by a rookie: 31, Jim Hart, 1964
- Home runs by a right-hander: 52, Willie Mays, 1965
- Home runs by a left-hander: 73, Barry Bonds, 2001
- Home runs by a switch-hitter: 28, J.T. Snow, 1997
- Grand slams: 8 in 1951
- Grand slams (individual; season): 3 by many players
- Grand slams (individual; career): 16, Willie McCovey
- Triples: 103 in 1911
- Doubles: 314 in 2004
- Singles: 1,279 in 1930
- Walks: 729 in 1970
- Runs scored: 959 in 1930
- Runs scored in a game: 29 vs. Philadelphia Phillies on June 15, 1887
- Runs scored in an inning: 13 (accomplished five times): vs. Philadelphia Phillies on September 8, 1883 (third inning); vs. Cleveland Blues on July 19, 1890 (second inning); vs. St. Louis Cardinals on May 13, 1911 (first inning); vs. St. Louis Cardinals on May 7, 1966 (third inning); vs. San Diego Padres on July 15, 1997 (seventh inning)
- Most batters hit by a pitch: 91 in 1903
- Times shut out: 20 in 1915

- Grounded into double plays: 153 in 1939
- Fewest grounded into double plays: 83 in 1986 and 1990
- Runners left on base: 1,289 in 2004

TEAM RECORDS—BASERUNNING

- Stolen bases: 415 in 1887
- Caught stealing: 114 in 1915

TEAM RECORDS—PITCHING

- Lowest earned run average: 1.72 in 1885
- Complete games: 140 in 1898
- Saves: 50 in 1993
- Strikeouts: 1,089 in 1998
- Shutouts: 25 in 1908
- Walks: 660 in 1946
- Hit batsmen: 100 in 1899
- Wild pitches: 101 in 1884
- Consecutive wins (individual): 24, Carl Hubbell, over 1936 (16) and 1937 (8); in one season: 19, Rube Marquard, 1912
- Consecutive losses (individual): 12, Rube Marquard, 1914
- Strikeouts in a game (individual): 16, Christy Mathewson, October 3, 1904
- Runs allowed in a game: 28 vs. Hartford on May 13, 1876

TEAM RECORDS—FIELDING

- Best fielding average: .987 in 2003
- Most errors committed: 565 in 1892
- Fewest errors committed: 80 in 2003
- Most double plays turned: 183 in 1987
- Fewest double plays turned: 52 in 1883

TEAM RECORDS—MISCELLANEOUS

- Number of times league champions: 20
- Number of times finishing last in league: 6
- Largest attendance, single game: 61,389 vs. Los Angeles Dodgers, September 30, 1999
- Largest attendance, doubleheader: 60,747 vs. Brooklyn Dodgers, May 31, 1937
- Players used in a season: 51 in 1990
- Seasons played: 22 by Mel Ott

PRIMARY PITCHING STAFFS

Year	Starter	Starter	Starter	Starter	Starter	Closer	Bullpen	Bullpen	Bullpen
2005	Lowry	Tomko	Schmidt	Hennessey	Rueter	Walker	Eyre	Christiansen	Fassero
2004	Williams	Tomko	Schmidt	Hermanson	Rueter	Herges	Eyre	Christiansen	Brower
2003	Williams	Foppert	Schmidt	Moss	Rueter	Worrell	Eyre	Nathan	Rodriguez
2002	Hernandez	Ortiz	Schmidt	Jensen	Rueter	Nen	Worrell	Zerbe	Rodriguez
2001	Hernandez	Ortiz	Estes	Gardner	Rueter	Nen	Worrell	Fultz	Rodriguez
2000	Hernandez	Ortiz	Estes	Gardner	Rueter	Nen	Embree	Fultz	Rodriguez
1999	Brock	Ortiz	Estes	Gardner	Rueter	Nen	Embree	Rodriguez	Johnstone
1998	Hershiser	Darwin	Estes	Gardner	Rueter	Nen	Tavarez	Rodriguez	Johnstone
1997	VanLandingham	Fernandez	Estes	Gardner	Rueter	Beck	Tavarez	Rodriguez	Henry
1996	VanLandingham	Fernandez	Watson	Gardner	Leiter	Beck	Dewey	Creek	DeLucia
1995	VanLandingham	Mulholland	Wilson	Portugal	Leiter	Beck	Barton	Bautista	Hook
1994	VanLandingham	Burkett	Swift	Portugal	Torres	Monteleone	Burba	Frey	Beck
1993	Wilson	Burkett	Swift	Black	Hickerson	Beck	Burba	Jackson	Rogers
1992	Wilson	Burkett	Swift	Black	Burba	Beck	Hickerson	Jackson	Brantley
1991	Wilson	Burkett	Robinson	Black	McClellan	Righetti	Oliveras	Downs	Brantley
1990	Wilson	Burkett	Robinson	Garrelts	Reuschel	Brantley	Oliveras	Bedrosian	Thurmond
1989	LaCoss	Downs	Robinson	Garrelts	Reuschel	Lefferts	Brantley	Bedrosian	Gossage
1988	LaCoss	Downs	Robinson	Krukow	Reuschel	Garrelts	Lefferts	Hammaker	Price
1987	LaCoss	Downs	Hammaker	Krukow	Dravecky	Garrelts	Lefferts	Robinson	Gott
1986	LaCoss	Downs	Blue	Krukow	Garrelts	Robinson	Davis	Minton	Berenguer
1985	LaPoint	Hammaker	Blue	Krukow	Gott	Garrelts	Davis	Minton	Williams
1984	Laskey	Robinson	Davis	Krukow	Grant	Minton	Lavelle	Lerch	Williams
1983	Laskey	Breining	Davis	Krukow	Hammaker	Minton	Lavelle	McGaffigan	Barr

PRIMARY PITCHING STAFFS (CONT.)

Year	Starter	Starter	Starter	Starter	Starter	Closer	Bullpen	Bullpen	Bullpen
1982	Laskey	Gale	Martin	Fowlkes	Hammaker	Minton	Lavelle	Holland	Breining
1981	Alexander	Griffin	Whitson	Blue	Ripley	Minton	Lavelle	Holland	Breining
1980	Knepper	Montefusco	Whitson	Blue	Ripley	Minton	Lavelle	Holland	Griffin
1979	Knepper	Montefusco	Halicki	Blue	Curtis	Lavelle	Minton	Borbon	Griffin
1978	Knepper	Montefusco	Halicki	Blue	Barr	Lavelle	Moffitt	Curtis	Williams
1977	Knepper	Montefusco	Halicki	McGlothen	Barr	Lavelle	Moffitt	Heaverlo	Williams
1976	D'Acquisto	Montefusco	Halicki	Dressler	Barr	Moffitt	Lavelle	Heaverlo	Caldwell
1975	Falcone	Montefusco	Halicki	Caldwell	Barr	Moffitt	Lavelle	Heaverlo	Williams
1974	D'Acquisto	Bryant	Bradley	Caldwell	Barr	Moffitt	Sosa	Willoughby	Williams
1973	Marichal	Bryant	Bradley	Willoughby	Barr	Sosa	Moffitt	Carrithers	McMahon
1972	Marichal	Bryant	McDowell	Stone	Barr	Johnson	Moffitt	Carrithers	McMahon
1971	Marichal	Bryant	Perry	Stone	Cumberland	Johnson	Hamilton	Robertson	McMahon
1970	Marichal	Robertson	Perry	Reberger	Pitlock	McMahon	Bryant	Johnson	Davison
1969	Marichal	McCormick	Perry	Bolin	Sadecki	Linzy	Bryant	Herbel	Robertson
1968	Marichal	McCormick	Perry	Bolin	Sadecki	Linzy	Gibbon	Herbel	McDaniel
1967	Marichal	McCormick	Perry	Bolin	Sadecki	Linzy	Henry	Herbel	McDaniel
1966	Marichal	Herbel	Perry	Bolin	Sadecki	Linzy	Priddy	Gibbon	McDaniel
1965	Marichal	Herbel	Perry	Shaw	Sanford	Linzy	Murakami	Bolin	Henry
1964	Marichal	Herbel	Perry	Hendley	Bolin	Shaw	O'Dell	Duffalo	Pierce
1963	Marichal	Sanford	O'Dell	Pierce	Fisher	Bolin	Larsen	Duffalo	Perry
1962	Marichal	Sanford	O'Dell	Pierce	McCormick	Miller	Larsen	Duffalo	Bolin
1961	Marichal	Sanford	Loes	Jones	McCormick	Miller	O'Dell	LeMay	Bolin
1960	Marichal	Sanford	O'Dell	Jones	McCormick	Antonelli	Miller	Loes	Byerly
1959	Antonelli	Sanford	Miller	Jones	McCormick	Worthington	Jones	Fisher	
1958	Antonelli	Gomez	Miller	Monzant	McCormick	Grissom	Worthington	Giel	Johnson
1957	Antonelli	Gomez	Miller	Barclay	Crone	Grissom	Worthington	McCormick	Monzant
1956	Antonelli	Gomez	Worthington	Hearn	Margoneri	Wilhelm	McCall	Grissom	Ridzik
1955	Antonelli	Gomez	Maglie	Hearn	Liddle	Grissom	McCall	Wilhelm	Giel
1954	Antonelli	Gomez	Maglie	Hearn	Liddle	Grissom	McCall	Wilhelm	Corwin
1953	Jansen	Gomez	Maglie	Hearn	Worthington	Wilhelm	Koslo	Grissom	Corwin
1952	Jansen	Koslo	Maglie	Hearn	Lanier	Wilhelm	Spencer	Kennedy	Corwin
1951	Jansen	Koslo	Maglie	Hearn	Jones	Spencer	Gettel	Kennedy	Corwin
1950	Jansen	Koslo	Kennedy	Hearn	Jones	Maglie	Kramer	Hansen	
1949	Jansen	Koslo	Kennedy	Hartung	Jones	Behrman	Higbe	Hansen	
1948	Jansen	Koslo	Poat	Hartung	Jones	Trinkle	Kennedy	Konikowski	Hansen
1947	Jansen	Koslo	Kennedy	Hartung	Iott	Trinkle	Beggs	Jones	Hansen
1946	Voiselle	Koslo	Kennedy	Trinkle	Schumacher	Thompson	Budnick	Kraus	
1945	Voiselle	Feldman	Mungo	Brewer	Hansen	Adams	Emmerich	Fischer	Maglie
1944	Voiselle	Feldman	Pyle	Fischer	Allen	Adams	Seward	Hansen	Polli
1943	Melton	Wittig	Chase	Fischer	Mungo	Adams	Feldman	Sayles	Lohrman
1942	Melton	Schumacher	Carpenter	Hubbell	Lohrman	Adams	Feldman	McGee	Sunkel
1941	Melton	Schumacher	Carpenter	Hubbell	Lohrman	Brown	Adams	Bowman	Wittig
1940	Melton	Schumacher	Gumbert	Hubbell	Lohrman	Brown	Lynn	Joiner	Dean
1939	Melton	Schumacher	Gumbert	Hubbell	Lohrman	Brown	Lynn	Salvo	Coffman
1938	Melton	Schumacher	Gumbert	Hubbell	Lohrman	Coffman	Brown	Castleman	Wittig
1937	Melton	Schumacher	Gumbert	Hubbell	Castleman	Coffman	Smith	Baker	
1936	Smith	Schumacher	Gumbert	Hubbell	Fitzsimmons	Coffman	Gabler	Castleman	
1935	Parmelee	Schumacher	Castleman	Hubbell	Fitzsimmons	Gabler	Stout	Smith	
1934	Parmelee	Schumacher	Bowman	Hubbell	Fitzsimmons	Luque	Bell	Salveson	Smith
1933	Parmelee	Schumacher	Bell	Hubbell	Fitzsimmons	Luque	Spencer	Clark	
1932	Walker	Schumacher	Mooney	Hubbell	Fitzsimmons	Luque	Gibson	Bell	
1931	Walker	Mitchell	Berly	Hubbell	Fitzsimmons	Heving	Morrell	Chaplin	

PRIMARY PITCHING STAFFS (CONT.)

Year	Starter	Starter	Starter	Starter	Starter	Closer	Bullpen	Bullpen	Bullpen
1930	Walker	Mitchell	Donohue	Hubbell	Fitzsimmons	Heving	Pruett	Genewich	Chaplin
1929	Walker	Benton	Henry	Hubbell	Fitzsimmons	Mays	Genewich	Scott	
1928	Genewich	Benton	Aldridge	Hubbell	Fitzsimmons	Faulkner	Walker	Henry	
1927	Grimes	Benton	Barnes	Henry	Fitzsimmons	Clarkson	Songer	Greenfield	
1926	Greenfield	Ring	Barnes	McQuillan	Fitzsimmons	Davies	Scott	McNamara	
1925	Greenfield	Scott	Barnes	Bentley	Nehf	Dean	Huntzinger	Wisner	
1924	McQuillan	Dean	Barnes	Bentley	Nehf	Ryan	Jonnard	Maun	
1923	McQuillan	Scott	Watson	Bentley	Nehf	Ryan	Jonnard	Barnes	
1922	McQuillan	Barnes	Douglas	Ryan	Nehf	Causey	Jonnard	Barnes	
1921	Toney	Barnes	Douglas	Ryan	Nehf	Sallee	Benton	Shea	
1920	Toney	Barnes	Douglas	Benton	Nehf	Winters	Hubbell	Perritt	
1919	Toney	Barnes	Causey	Benton	Nehf	Winters	Dubuc	Perritt	
1918	Perritt	Barnes	Causey	Sallee	Demaree	Anderson	Tesreau	Steele	
1917	Perritt	Schupp	Benton	Sallee	Tesreau	Anderson	Demaree	Smith	
1916	Perritt	Anderson	Benton	Sallee	Tesreau	Schupp	Schauer	Mathewson	
1915	Perritt	Mathewson	Stroud	Marquard	Tesreau	Schupp	Schauer	Ritter	
1914	Demaree	Mathewson	Fromme	Marquard	Tesreau	Schupp	Wiltse	O'Toole	
1913	Demaree	Mathewson	Fromme	Marquard	Tesreau	Crandall	Wiltse	Ames	
1912	Ames	Mathewson	Wiltse	Marquard	Tesreau	Crandall			
1911	Ames	Mathewson	Wiltse	Marquard	Crandall	Raymond	Drucke		
1910	Ames	Mathewson	Wiltse	Drucke	Crandall	Raymond	Marquard	Dickson	
1909	Ames	Mathewson	Wiltse	Raymond	Marquard	Crandall	Klawitter		
1908	Ames	Mathewson	Wiltse	Crandall	McGinnity	Taylor	Malarkey		
1907	Ames	Mathewson	Wiltse	Taylor	McGinnity	Ferguson	Lynch		
1906	Ames	Mathewson	Wiltse	Taylor	McGinnity	Ferguson			
1905	Ames	Mathewson	Wiltse	Taylor	McGinnity	Elliott			
1904	Ames	Mathewson	Wiltse	Taylor	McGinnity				
1903	Cronin	Mathewson	Miller	Taylor	McGinnity				
1902	Evans	Mathewson	Sparks	Taylor	McGinnity	Cronin	Miller	Kennedy	
1901	Phyle	Mathewson	Denzer	Taylor	Hickman	Doheny	Magee		
1900	Carrick	Hawley	Mercer	Doheny	Seymour	Taylor	Mathewson		
1899	Carrick	Meekin	Gettig	Doheny	Seymour	Colcolough			
1898	Rusie	Meekin	Gettig	Doheny	Seymour				
1897	Rusie	Meekin	Sullivan	Doheny	Seymour	Clarke			
1896	Clarke	Meekin	Sullivan	Doheny	Seymour	Campfield			
1895	Clarke	Meekin	Rusie	German					
1894	Clarke	Meekin	Rusie	German	Westervelt				
1893	Baldwin	King	Rusie	German	Crane	Petty			
1892	King	Rusie	Crane						
1891	Ewing	Welch	Rusie	Sharrott	Keefe	Coughlin			
1890	Burkett	Welch	Rusie	Sharrott					
1889	Keefe	Welch	Crane	O'Day		Hatfield			
1888	Keefe	Welch	Crane	Titcomb					
1887	Keefe	Welch	George	Titcomb	Mattimore				
1886	Keefe	Welch					Richardson		
1885	Keefe	Welch	Richardson	Corcoran					
1884	Begley	Welch	Dorgan	Ward					
1883	Ward	Welch	O'Neill						

PRIMARY STARTING LINEUPS

Year	C	1B	2B	3B	SS	LF	CF	RF
2005	Matheny	Snow	Durham	Alfonzo	Vizquel	Feliz	Ellison	Tucker
2004	Pierzynski	Snow	Durham	Alfonzo	Cruz	Bonds	Grissom	Tucker
2003	Santiago	Snow	Durham	Alfonzo	Aurilia	Bonds	Grissom	Cruz
2002	Santiago	Snow	Kent	Bell	Aurilia	Bonds	Shinjo	Sanders
2001	Santiago	Snow	Kent	Feliz	Aurilia	Bonds	Murray	Rios
2000	Estalella	Snow	Kent	Mueller	Aurilia	Bonds	Benard	Burks
1999	Mayne	Snow	Kent	Mueller	Aurilia	Bonds	Benard	Burks
1998	Johnson	Snow	Kent	Mueller	Aurilia	Bonds	Hamilton	Javier
1997	Wilkins	Snow	Kent	Mueller	Vizcaino	Bonds	Hamilton	Hill
1996	Lampkin	Carreon	Scarsone	Williams	Aurilia	Bonds	Benard	Hill
1995	Manwaring	Carreon	Thompson	Williams	Clayton	Bonds	Lewis	Hill
1994	Manwaring	Benzinger	Patterson	Williams	Clayton	Bonds	Lewis	Martinez
1993	Manwaring	Clark	Thompson	Williams	Clayton	Bonds	Lewis	McGee
1992	Manwaring	Clark	Thompson	Williams	Clayton	James	Lewis	McGee
1991	Decker	Clark	Thompson	Williams	Uribe	Mitchell	McGee	Bass
1990	Kennedy	Clark	Thompson	Williams	Uribe	Mitchell	Butler	Kingery
1989	Kennedy	Clark	Thompson	Riles	Uribe	Mitchell	Butler	Maldonado
1988	Melvin	Clark	Thompson	Mitchell	Uribe	Aldrete	Butler	Maldonado
1987	Brenly	Clark	Thompson	Mitchell	Uribe	Leonard	Davis	Maldonado
1986	Brenly	Clark	Thompson	Brown	Uribe	Leonard	Gladden	Davis
1985	Brenly	Green	Trillo	Brown	Uribe	Leonard	Gladden	Davis
1984	Brenly	Thompson	Trillo	Youngblood	LeMaster	Leonard	Gladden	Clark
1983	Brenly	Evans	Wellman	O'Malley	LeMaster	Leonard	Davis	Clark
1982	May	Smith	Morgan	Evans	LeMaster	Wohlford	Davis	Clark
1981	May	Cabell	Morgan	Evans	LeMaster	Herndon	Martin	Clark
1980	May	Ivie	Stennett	Evans	LeMaster	Whitfield	North	Clark
1979	Littlejohn	Ivie	Strain	Evans	LeMaster	Whitfield	North	Clark
1978	Hill	McCovey	Madlock	Evans	LeMaster	Whitfield	Herndon	Clark
1977	Hill	McCovey	Andrews	Madlock	Foli	Evans	Thomas	Clark
1976	Rader	Evans	Perez	Reitz	Speier	Matthews	Herndon	Murcer
1975	Rader	Montanez	Thomas	Ontiveros	Speier	Matthews	Joshua	Murcer
1974	Rader	Kingman	Fuentes	Ontiveros	Speier	Matthews	Maddox	Bonds
1973	Rader	McCovey	Fuentes	Goodson	Speier	Matthews	Maddox	Bonds
1972	Rader	McCovey	Fuentes	Gallagher	Speier	Henderson	Maddox	Bonds
1971	Dietz	McCovey	Fuentes	Gallagher	Speier	Henderson	Mays	Bonds
1970	Dietz	McCovey	Hunt	Gallagher	Lanier	Henderson	Mays	Bonds
1969	Dietz	McCovey	Hunt	Davenport	Lanier	Marshall	Mays	Bonds
1968	Dietz	McCovey	Hunt	Davenport	Lanier	Hart	Mays	Alou
1967	Haller	McCovey	Fuentes	Hart	Lanier	Alou	Mays	Brown
1966	Haller	McCovey	Lanier	Hart	Fuentes	Gabrielson	Mays	Brown
1965	Haller	McCovey	Lanier	Hart	Schofield	Alou	Mays	Alou
1964	Haller	Cepeda	Lanier	Hart	Pagan	McCovey	Mays	Alou
1963	Bailey	Cepeda	Hiller	Davenport	Pagan	McCovey	Mays	Alou
1962	Haller	Cepeda	Hiller	Davenport	Pagan	Kuenn	Mays	Alou
1961	Bailey	McCovey	Amalfitano	Davenport	Pagan	Kuenn	Mays	Alou
1960	Schmidt	McCovey	Blasingame	Davenport	Bressoud	Cepeda	Mays	Kirkland
1959	Landrith	Cepeda	Spencer	Davenport	Bressoud	Brandt	Mays	Kirkland
1958	Schmidt	Cepeda	O'Connell	Davenport	Spencer	Sauer	Mays	Kirkland
1957	Thomas	Lockman	O'Connell	Jablonski	Spencer	Sauer	Mays	Mueller
1956	Sarni	White	Schoendienst	Castleman	Spencer	Brandt	Mays	Mueller
1955	Katt	Harris	Terwilliger	Thompson	Dark	Lockman	Mays	Mueller
1954	Westrum	Lockman	Williams	Thompson	Dark	Irvin	Mays	Mueller

PRIMARY STARTING LINEUPS (CONT.)

Year	C	1B	2B	3B	SS	LF	CF	RF
1953	Westrum	Lockman	Williams	Thompson	Dark	Irvin	Thomson	Mueller
1952	Westrum	Lockman	Williams	Thomson	Dark	Rhodes	Thompson	Mueller
1951	Westrum	Lockman	Stanky	Thompson	Dark	Irvin	Mays	Mueller
1950	Westrum	Gilbert	Stanky	Thompson	Dark	Lockman	Thomson	Mueller
1949	Westrum	Mize	Thompson	Gordon	Kerr	Lockman	Thomson	Marshall
1948	Cooper	Mize	Rigney	Gordon	Kerr	Thomson	Lockman	Marshall
1947	Cooper	Mize	Rigney	Lohrke	Kerr	Gordon	Thomson	Marshall
1946	Cooper	Mize	Blattner	Rigney	Kerr	Gordon	Marshall	Graham
1945	Lombardi	Weintraub	Hausmann	Reyes	Kerr	Gardella	Rucker	Ott
1944	Lombardi	Weintraub	Hausmann	Luby	Kerr	Medwick	Rucker	Ott
1943	Mancuso	Orengo	Witek	Bartell	Jurges	Medwick	Rucker	Ott
1942	Danning	Mize	Witek	Werber	Jurges	Barna	Young	Ott
1941	Danning	Young	Whitehead	Bartell	Jurges	Moore	Rucker	Ott
1940	Danning	Young	Cuccinello	Whitehead	Witek	Moore	Demaree	Ott
1939	Danning	Bonura	Whitehead	Hafey	Jurges	Moore	Demaree	Ott
1938	Danning	McCarthy	Kampouris	Ott	Bartell	Moore	Leiber	Ripple
1937	Danning	McCarthy	Whitehead	Chiozza	Bartell	Moore	Berger	Ott
1936	Mancuso	Leslie	Whitehead	Jackson	Bartell	Moore	Leiber	Ott
1935	Mancuso	Terry	Koenig	Jackson	Bartell	Moore	Leiber	Ott
1934	Mancuso	Terry	Critz	Vergez	Jackson	Moore	Watkins	Ott
1933	Mancuso	Terry	Critz	Vergez	Ryan	Moore	Davis	Ott
1932	Hogan	Terry	Critz	Vergez	Marshall	Moore	Lindstrom	Ott
1931	Hogan	Terry	Hunnefield	Vergez	Jackson	Leach	Ott	Lindstrom
1930	Hogan	Terry	Critz	Lindstrom	Jackson	Leach	Roettger	Ott
1929	Hogan	Terry	Cohen	Lindstrom	Jackson	Leach	Roush	Ott
1928	Hogan	Terry	Cohen	Lindstrom	Jackson	O'Doul	Welsh	Ott
1927	Taylor	Terry	Hornsby	Lindstrom	Jackson	Mueller	Roush	Harper
1926	Florence	Kelly	Frisch	Lindstrom	Jackson	Meusel	Tyson	Youngs
1925	Snyder	Terry	Kelly	Lindstrom	Jackson	Meusel	Southworth	Youngs
1924	Snyder	Kelly	Frisch	Groh	Jackson	Meusel	Wilson	Youngs
1923	Snyder	Kelly	Frisch	Groh	Bancroft	Meusel	O'Connell	Youngs
1922	Snyder	Kelly	Frisch	Groh	Bancroft	Meusel	Stengel	Youngs
1921	Snyder	Kelly	Rawlings	Frisch	Bancroft	Burns	Walker	Youngs
1920	Snyder	Kelly	Doyle	Frisch	Bancroft	Burns	King	Youngs
1919	McCarty	Chase	Doyle	Zimmerman	Fletcher	Burns	Kauff	Youngs
1918	McCarty	Holke	Doyle	Zimmerman	Fletcher	Burns	Kauff	Youngs
1917	Rariden	Holke	Herzog	Zimmerman	Fletcher	Burns	Kauff	Robertson
1916	Rariden	Merkle	Doyle	McKechnie	Fletcher	Burns	Kauff	Robertson
1915	Meyers	Merkle	Doyle	Lobert	Fletcher	Burns	Snodgrass	Robertson
1914	Meyers	Merkle	Doyle	Stock	Fletcher	Burns	Bescher	Robertson
1913	Meyers	Merkle	Doyle	Herzog	Fletcher	Burns	Snodgrass	Murray
1912	Meyers	Merkle	Doyle	Herzog	Fletcher	Devore	Becker	Murray
1911	Meyers	Merkle	Doyle	Devlin	Bridwell	Devore	Snodgrass	Murray
1910	Meyers	Merkle	Doyle	Devlin	Bridwell	Devore	Seymour	Murray
1909	Schlei	Tenney	Doyle	Devlin	Bridwell	McCormick	O'Hara	Murray
1908	Bresnahan	Tenney	Doyle	Devlin	Bridwell	Shannon	Seymour	Donlin
1907	Bresnahan	McGann	Doyle	Devlin	Dahlen	Shannon	Seymour	Browne
1906	Bresnahan	McGann	Gilbert	Devlin	Dahlen	Shannon	Seymour	Browne
1905	Bresnahan	McGann	Gilbert	Devlin	Dahlen	Mertes	Donlin	Browne
1904	Warner	McGann	Gilbert	Devlin	Dahlen	Mertes	Bresnahan	Browne
1903	Warner	McGann	Gilbert	Lauder	Babb	Mertes	Bresnahan	Browne
1902	Bowerman	McGann	Smith	Lauder	Bean	Browne	Brodie	Dunn

Primary Starting Lineups (cont.)

Year	C	1B	2B	3B	SS	LF	CF	RF
1901	Warner	Ganzel	Nelson	Strang	Davis	Selbach	Van Haltren	McBride
1900	Bowerman	Doyle	Gleason	Hickman	Davis	Selbach	Van Haltren	Smith
1899	Warner	Doyle	Gleason	Hartman	Davis	O'Brien	Van Haltren	Foster
1898	Warner	Joyce	Gleason	Hartman	Davis	Tiernan	Van Haltren	McCreery
1897	Warner	Clark	Gleason	Joyce	Davis	Holmes	Van Haltren	Tiernan
1896	Wilson	Clark	Gleason	Davis	Connaughton	Stafford	Van Haltren	Tiernan
1895	Farrell	Doyle	Stafford	Davis	Fuller	Burke	Van Haltren	Tiernan
1894	Farrell	Doyle	Ward	Davis	Fuller	Burke	Van Haltren	Tiernan
1893	Doyle	Connor	Ward	Davis	Fuller	Burke	Stafford	Tiernan
1892	Boyle	Ewing	Burke	Lyons	Fuller	O'Rourke	Lyons	Tiernan
1891	Buckley	Connor	Richardson	Bassett	Glasscock	O'Rourke	Gore	Tiernan
1890	Buckley	Whistler	Bassett	Denny	Glasscock	Hornung	Tiernan	Burkett
1889	Ewing	Connor	Richardson	Whitney	Ward	O'Rourke	Gore	Tiernan
1888	Ewing	Connor	Richardson	Whitney	Ward	O'Rourke	Slattery	Tiernan
1887	Brown	Connor	Richardson	Ewing	Ward	Gillespie	Gore	Dorgan
1886	Ewing	Connor	Gerhardt	Esterbrook	Ward	Gillespie	O'Rourke	Dorgan
1885	Ewing	Connor	Gerhardt	Esterbrook	Ward	Gillespie	O'Rourke	Dorgan
1884	Ewing	McKinnon	Connor	Hankinson	Caskin	Gillespie	Ward	Dorgan
1883	Ewing	Connor	Troy	Hankinson	Caskin	Gillespie	Ward	Dorgan

Top 10 Batting Leaders, Single Season & Career with Team

Games Played: Career with Team

Player	G	PA
1. Willie Mays	2,857	12,012
2. Mel Ott	2,730	11,337
3. Willie McCovey	2,256	8,518
4. Bill Terry	1,721	7,111
5. Barry Bonds	1,720	7,381
6. Travis Jackson	1,656	6,679
7. Larry Doyle	1,622	6,793
8. Jim Davenport	1,501	4,981
9. Whitey Lockman	1,485	6,197
10. Mike Tiernan	1,476	6,716

At-Bats: Season

Player	AB	Year
1. Jo-Jo Moore	681	1935
2. Bobby Bonds	663	1970
3. Hughie Critz	659	1932
4. Tito Fuentes	656	1973
5. George Van Haltren	654	1898
6. Dave Bancroft	651	1922
7. Jo-Jo Moore	649	1936
8. Alvin Dark	647	1953
9. Alvin Dark	646	1951
Freddie Lindstrom	646	1928

At-Bats: Career with Team

Player	AB	PA
1. Willie Mays	10,477	12,012
2. Mel Ott	9,456	11,337
3. Willie McCovey	7,214	8,518
4. Bill Terry	6,428	7,111
5. Travis Jackson	6,086	6,679
6. Larry Doyle	5,995	6,793
7. Mike Tiernan	5,906	6,716
8. Whitey Lockman	5,584	6,197
9. Barry Bonds	5,556	7,381
10. Jo-Jo Moore	5,427	5,848

Batting Average: Season

Player	BA	Year
1. Bill Terry	.401	1930
2. Freddie Lindstrom	.379	1930
3. Bill Terry	.372	1929
4. Roger Connor	.371	1885
5. Barry Bonds	.370	2002
6. Mike Tiernan	.369	1896
7. Jack Doyle	.367	1894
8. Barry Bonds	.362	2004
9. Rogers Hornsby	.361	1927
10. Chief Meyers	.358	1912

Batting Average: Career with Team

Player	BA	PA
1. Bill Terry	.341	7,111
2. George Davis	.332	4,781
3. Ross Youngs	.322	5,333
4. Frankie Frisch	.321	4,447
George Van Haltren	.321	5,465

6. Roger Connor	.319	4,945
7. Freddie Lindstrom	.318	4,617
8. Barry Bonds	.316	7,381
9. Irish Meusel	.314	3,232
10. Shanty Hogan	.311	2,206

TOTAL HITS: SEASON

Player	H	Year
1. Bill Terry	254	1930
2. Freddie Lindstrom	231	1928
Freddie Lindstrom	231	1930
4. Bill Terry	226	1929
5. Bill Terry	225	1932
6. Frankie Frisch	223	1923
7. Mike Donlin	216	1905
8. Bill Terry	213	1931
Bill Terry	213	1934
10. Don Mueller	212	1954

TOTAL HITS: CAREER WITH TEAM

Player	H	PA
1. Willie Mays	3,187	12,012
2. Mel Ott	2,876	11,337
3. Bill Terry	2,193	7,111
4. Willie McCovey	1,974	8,518
5. Mike Tiernan	1,834	6,716
6. Travis Jackson	1,768	6,679
7. Barry Bonds	1,758	7,381
8. Larry Doyle	1,751	6,793
9. Jo-Jo Moore	1,615	5,848
10. George Van Haltren	1,575	5,465

HOME RUNS: SEASON

Player	HR	Year
1. Barry Bonds	73	2001
2. Willie Mays	52	1965
3. Willie Mays	51	1955
Johnny Mize	51	1947
5. Barry Bonds	49	2000
Willie Mays	49	1962
7. Willie Mays	47	1964
Kevin Mitchell	47	1989
9. Barry Bonds	46	1993
Barry Bonds	46	2002
Orlando Cepeda	46	1961

HOME RUNS: CAREER WITH TEAM

Player	HR	PA
1. Willie Mays	646	12,012
2. Barry Bonds	532	7,381
3. Mel Ott	511	11,337
4. Willie McCovey	469	8,518
5. Matt Williams	247	4,497
6. Orlando Cepeda	226	4,528
7. Bobby Thomson	189	4,630
8. Bobby Bonds	186	4,610
9. Will Clark	176	4,878
10. Jeff Kent	175	3,903

TRIPLES: SEASON

Player	3B	Year
1. George Davis	27	1893
2. Larry Doyle	25	1911
3. Roger Connor	22	1887
4. Mike Tiernan	21	1890
Mike Tiernan	21	1895
George Van Haltren	21	1896
7. Roger Connor	20	1886
Buck Ewing	20	1884
Willie Mays	20	1957
Red Murray	20	1912
Bill Terry	20	1931

TRIPLES: CAREER WITH TEAM

Player	3B	PA
1. Mike Tiernan	162	6,716
2. Willie Mays	139	12,012
3. Roger Connor	131	4,945
4. Larry Doyle	117	6,793
5. Bill Terry	112	7,111
6. Buck Ewing	109	3,174
7. George Davis	98	4,781
8. Ross Youngs	93	5,333
9. George Van Haltren	88	5,465
10. Travis Jackson	86	6,679

DOUBLES: SEASON

Player	2B	Year
1. Jeff Kent	49	2001
2. Jack Clark	46	1978
3. Barry Bonds	44	1998
4. Willie Mays	43	1959
Bill Terry	43	1931
6. George Kelly	42	1921
Jeff Kent	42	2002
Bill Terry	42	1932
9. Dave Bancroft	41	1922
Alvin Dark	41	1951
Alvin Dark	41	1953
Jeff Kent	41	2000

DOUBLES: CAREER WITH TEAM

Player	2B	PA
1. Willie Mays	504	12,012
2. Mel Ott	488	11,337
3. Bill Terry	373	7,111
4. Barry Bonds	344	7,381
5. Willie McCovey	308	8,518
6. Travis Jackson	291	6,679
7. Larry Doyle	275	6,793
8. George Burns	267	6,044
9. Jo-Jo Moore	258	5,848
10. Mike Tiernan	256	6,716

EXTRA-BASE HITS: SEASON

Player	XBH	Year
1. Barry Bonds	107	2001
2. Willie Mays	90	1962
3. Barry Bonds	88	1993
Barry Bonds	88	1998
5. Willie Mays	87	1954
Kevin Mitchell	87	1989
7. Willie Mays	82	1955
Willie Mays	82	1959
9. Six tied with . . .	81	——

EXTRA-BASE HITS: CAREER WITH TEAM

Player	XBH	PA
1. Willie Mays	1,289	12,012
2. Mel Ott	1,071	11,337
3. Barry Bonds	917	7,381
4. Willie McCovey	822	8,518
5. Bill Terry	639	7,111
6. Mike Tiernan	524	6,716
7. Travis Jackson	512	6,679
8. Orlando Cepeda	474	4,528
9. Will Clark	462	4,878
10. Larry Doyle	459	6,793

TOTAL BASES: SEASON

Player	TB	Year
1. Barry Bonds	411	2001
2. Bill Terry	392	1930
3. Willie Mays	382	1955
Willie Mays	382	1962
5. Willie Mays	377	1954
6. Bill Terry	373	1932
7. Willie Mays	366	1957
8. Barry Bonds	365	1993

9. Rich Aurilia	364	2001
10. Willie Mays	360	1965
Johnny Mize	360	1947

TOTAL BASES: CAREER WITH TEAM

Player	TB	PA
1. Willie Mays	5,907	12,012
2. Mel Ott	5,041	11,337
3. Barry Bonds	3,780	7,381
4. Willie McCovey	3,779	8,518
5. Bill Terry	3,252	7,111
6. Mike Tiernan	2,732	6,716
7. Travis Jackson	2,636	6,679
8. Larry Doyle	2,461	6,793
9. Orlando Cepeda	2,234	4,528
10. Whitey Lockman	2,216	6,197
Jo-Jo Moore	2,216	5,848

RUNS BATTED IN: SEASON

Player	RBI	Year
1. Mel Ott	151	1929
2. Orlando Cepeda	142	1961
3. Willie Mays	141	1962
4. Johnny Mize	138	1947
5. Barry Bonds	137	2001
6. George Davis	136	1897
George Kelly	136	1924
8. Mel Ott	135	1934
Mel Ott	135	1936
10. Irish Meusel	132	1922

RUNS BATTED IN: CAREER WITH TEAM

Player	RBI	PA
1. Mel Ott	1,860	11,337
2. Willie Mays	1,859	12,012
3. Willie McCovey	1,388	8,518
4. Barry Bonds	1,297	7,381
5. Bill Terry	1,078	7,111
6. Travis Jackson	929	6,679
7. Mike Tiernan	851	6,716
8. George Davis	816	4,781
9. Roger Connor	786	4,945
10. Orlando Cepeda	767	4,528

RUNS SCORED: SEASON

Player	R	Year
1. Mike Tiernan	147	1889
2. Bill Terry	139	1930
3. Mel Ott	138	1929
4. Johnny Mize	137	1947
5. George Van Haltren	136	1896
6. Bobby Bonds	134	1970
7. Rogers Hornsby	133	1927
8. George Gore	132	1889
Mike Tiernan	132	1890
Mike Tiernan	132	1896

RUNS SCORED: CAREER WITH TEAM

Player	R	PA
1. Willie Mays	2,011	12,012
2. Mel Ott	1,859	11,337
3. Barry Bonds	1,406	7,381
4. Mike Tiernan	1,313	6,716
5. Bill Terry	1,120	7,111
6. Willie McCovey	1,113	8,518
7. George Van Haltren	973	5,465
8. Roger Connor	946	4,945
9. Larry Doyle	906	6,793
10. George Burns	877	6,044

WALKS: SEASON

Player	BB	Year
1. Barry Bonds	232	2004
2. Barry Bonds	198	2002
3. Barry Bonds	177	2001
4. Barry Bonds	151	1996
5. Barry Bonds	148	2003
6. Barry Bonds	145	1997
7. Eddie Stanky	144	1950
8. Willie McCovey	137	1970
9. Barry Bonds	130	1998
10. Eddie Stanky	127	1951

WALKS: CAREER WITH TEAM

Player	BB	PA
1. Mel Ott	1,708	11,337
2. Barry Bonds	1,700	7,381
3. Willie Mays	1,394	12,012
4. Willie McCovey	1,168	8,518
5. Mike Tiernan	747	6,716
6. George Burns	631	6,044
7. Darrell Evans	605	4,406
8. Roger Connor	578	4,945
9. Larry Doyle	576	6,793
10. J.T. Snow	565	4,497

STRIKEOUTS: SEASON

Player	SO	Year
1. Bobby Bonds	189	1970
2. Bobby Bonds	187	1969
3. Bobby Bonds	148	1973
4. Dave Kingman	140	1972
5. Matt Williams	138	1990
6. Bobby Bonds	137	1971
Bobby Bonds	137	1972
8. Bobby Bonds	134	1974
9. Jeff Kent	133	1997
Robby Thompson	133	1989

STRIKEOUTS: CAREER WITH TEAM

Player	SO	PA
1. Willie Mays	1,436	12,012
2. Willie McCovey	1,351	8,518
3. Bobby Bonds	1,016	4,610
4. Robby Thompson	987	5,235
5. Mel Ott	896	11,337
6. Matt Williams	872	4,497
7. Barry Bonds	844	7,381
8. J.T. Snow	806	4,497
9. Will Clark	744	4,878
10. Jim Davenport	673	4,981

SLUGGING PERCENTAGE: SEASON

Player	SLG	Year
1. Barry Bonds	.863	2001
2. Barry Bonds	.812	2004
3. Barry Bonds	.799	2002
4. Barry Bonds	.749	2003
5. Barry Bonds	.688	2000
6. Barry Bonds	.677	1993
7. Willie Mays	.667	1954
8. Willie Mays	.659	1955
9. Willie McCovey	.656	1969
10. Barry Bonds	.647	1994

SLUGGING PERCENTAGE: CAREER WITH TEAM

Player	SLG	PA
1. Barry Bonds	.680	7,381
2. Willie Mays	.564	12,012
3. Johnny Mize	.549	2,816

4. Kevin Mitchell	.536	2,516
5. Jeff Kent	.535	3,903
Orlando Cepeda	.535	4,528
7. Mel Ott	.533	11,337
8. Willie McCovey	.524	8,518
9. Bill Terry	.506	7,111
10. Will Clark	.499	4,878

ON-BASE PERCENTAGE: SEASON

Player	OBP	Year
1. Barry Bonds	.609	2004
2. Barry Bonds	.582	2002
3. Barry Bonds	.529	2003
4. Barry Bonds	.515	2001
5. Barry Bonds	.461	1996
6. Eddie Stanky	.460	1950
7. Mel Ott	.458	1930
Barry Bonds	.458	1993
9. Willie McCovey	.453	1969
10. Mike Tiernan	.452	1896

ON-BASE PERCENTAGE: CAREER WITH TEAM

Player	OBP	PA
1. Barry Bonds	.478	7,381
2. Mel Ott	.414	11,337
3. Roger Bresnahan	.403	3,024
4. Roger Connor	.402	4,945
5. Ross Youngs	.399	5,333
6. George Davis	.393	4,781
Bill Terry	.393	7,111
8. Mike Tiernan	.392	6,716
9. Johnny Mize	.389	2,816
Monte Irvin	.389	2,506

OPS (ON-BASE PERCENTAGE + SLUGGING PERCENTAGE): SEASON

Player	OPS	Year
1. Barry Bonds	1.422	2004
2. Barry Bonds	1.381	2002
3. Barry Bonds	1.379	2001
4. Barry Bonds	1.278	2003
5. Barry Bonds	1.136	1993
6. Barry Bonds	1.127	2000
7. Willie McCovey	1.108	1969
8. Mel Ott	1.084	1929
9. Willie Mays	1.078	1954
10. Barry Bonds	1.076	1996

OPS (ON-BASE PERCENTAGE + SLUGGING PERCENTAGE): CAREER WITH TEAM

Player	OPS	PA
1. Barry Bonds	1.159	7,381
2. Willie Mays	.949	12,012
3. Mel Ott	.947	11,337
4. Johnny Mize	.938	2,816
5. Jeff Kent	.903	3,903
6. Willie McCovey	.900	8,518
7. Bill Terry	.899	7,111
8. Kevin Mitchell	.892	2,516
9. Roger Connor	.890	4,945
10. Orlando Cepeda	.887	4,528

STOLEN BASES: SEASON

Player	SB	Year
1. John Ward	111	1887
2. George Davis	65	1897
3. George Burns	62	1914
John Ward	62	1889
5. Josh Devore	61	1911
6. Art Devlin	59	1905
7. Billy North	58	1979
8. Red Murray	57	1910
9. Mike Tiernan	56	1890
10. Eddie Burke	54	1893
Art Devlin	54	1906
Jack Glasscock	54	1890

STOLEN BASES: CAREER WITH TEAM

Player	SB	PA
1. Mike Tiernan	428	6,716
2. George Davis	354	4,781
3. Willie Mays	336	12,012
4. George Burns	334	6,044
5. John Ward	332	4,688
6. George Van Haltren	320	5,465
7. Larry Doyle	291	6,793
8. Art Devlin	266	4,498
9. Bobby Bonds	263	4,610
10. Barry Bonds	255	7,381

SACRIFICE HITS: SEASON

Player	Sac	Year
1. Art Devlin	36	1907
2. Mike Donlin	33	1908
Travis Jackson	33	1928
Cy Seymour	33	1908
5. Dan McGann	30	1903
6. Art Devlin	28	1910
Freddie Lindstrom	28	1926
8. George Hausmann	27	1944
9. Frankie Frisch	26	1921
Billy Gilbert	26	1903
Rogers Hornsby	26	1927
Fred Snodgrass	26	1911

SACRIFICE HITS: CAREER WITH TEAM

Player	Sac	PA
1. Travis Jackson	171	6,679
2. Larry Doyle	169	6,793
3. Art Devlin	157	4,498
4. Bill Terry	137	7,111
5. Art Fletcher	132	5,197
6. Ross Youngs	119	5,333
7. Jim Davenport	111	4,981
8. Mel Ott	109	11,337
9. Dan McGann	104	2,835
10. George Browne	102	3,159
Freddie Lindstrom	102	4,617

HIT BY PITCH: SEASON

Player	HBP	Year
1. Ron Hunt	26	1970
2. Eddie Burke	25	1893
Ron Hunt	25	1968
Ron Hunt	25	1969
5. Charlie Babb	22	1903
6. Billy Gilbert	20	1903
7. Art Fletcher	19	1917
Dan McGann	19	1905
9. Bill Joyce	18	1898
Dan McGann	18	1904

HIT BY PITCH: CAREER WITH TEAM

Player	HBP	PA
1. Art Fletcher	132	5,197
2. Art Devlin	79	4,498
3. Dan McGann	77	2,835
4. Ron Hunt	76	1,661
5. Barry Bonds	73	7,381
6. Robby Thompson	66	5,235
7. Willie McCovey	64	8,518
Mel Ott	64	11,337
9. John Warner	60	2,284
10. Fred Snodgrass	58	3,129

Top 10 Pitching Leaders, Single Season & Career with Team

Games Pitched: Season

Player	GP	Year
1. Jim Brower	89	2004
Julian Tavarez	89	1997
3. Scott Eyre	86	2005
4. Scott Eyre	83	2004
5. Mike Jackson	81	1993
6. Felix Rodriguez	80	2001
Tim Worrell	80	2002
8. Robb Nen	79	2001
9. Mark Dewey	78	1996
Greg Minton	78	1982
Joe Nathan	78	2003
Robb Nen	78	1998

Games Pitched: Career with Team

Player	GP	IP
1. Gary Lavelle	647	980.3
2. Christy Mathewson	634	4,771.7
3. Greg Minton	552	870.3
4. Carl Hubbell	535	3,590.3
5. Randy Moffitt	459	682.3
6. Juan Marichal	458	3,444.0
7. Mickey Welch	427	3,579.0
8. Amos Rusie	426	3,522.7
9. Rod Beck	416	463.0
10. Fred Fitzsimmons	403	2,514.3

Innings Pitched: Season

Player	IP	Year
1. Mickey Welch	557.3	1884
2. Amos Rusie	548.7	1890
3. Tim Keefe	535.0	1886
4. Amos Rusie	532.0	1892
5. Amos Rusie	500.3	1891
6. Mickey Welch	500.0	1886
7. Mickey Welch	492.0	1885
8. Amos Rusie	482.0	1893
9. Tim Keefe	476.7	1887
10. Amos Rusie	444.0	1894

Innings Pitched: Career with Team

Player	IP
1. Christy Mathewson	4,771.7
2. Carl Hubbell	3,590.3
3. Mickey Welch	3,579.0
4. Amos Rusie	3,522.7
5. Juan Marichal	3,444.0
6. Fred Fitzsimmons	2,514.3
7. Hal Schumacher	2,482.3
8. Gaylord Perry	2,294.7
9. Tim Keefe	2,265.0
10. Joe McGinnity	2,151.3

Batters Faced: Season

Player	BF	Year
1. Mickey Welch	2,370	1884
2. Tim Keefe	2,173	1886
3. Mickey Welch	2,151	1886
4. Tim Keefe	1,981	1887
5. Mickey Welch	1,963	1885
6. Mickey Welch	1,829	1883
7. Joe McGinnity	1,814	1903
8. Tim Keefe	1,723	1888
9. Mickey Welch	1,710	1888
10. Tim Keefe	1,704	1889

Batters Faced: Career with Team

Player	BF	IP
1. Christy Mathewson	19,093	4,771.7
2. Carl Hubbell	14,805	3,590.3
3. Juan Marichal	13,958	3,444.0
4. Mickey Welch	13,009	3,579.0
5. Hal Schumacher	10,571	2,482.3
6. Fred Fitzsimmons	10,413	2,514.3
7. Tim Keefe	9,425	2,265.0
8. Gaylord Perry	9,417	2,294.7
9. Joe McGinnity	8,879	2,151.3
10. Hooks Wiltse	8,187	2,053.0

Games Started: Season

Player	GS	Year
1. Mickey Welch	65	1884
2. Tim Keefe	64	1886
3. Amos Rusie	63	1890
4. Amos Rusie	61	1892
5. Mickey Welch	59	1886
6. Amos Rusie	57	1891
7. Tim Keefe	56	1887
8. Mickey Welch	55	1885
9. Amos Rusie	52	1893
Mickey Welch	52	1883

Games Started: Career with Team

Player	GS	IP
1. Christy Mathewson	550	4,771.7
2. Juan Marichal	446	3,444.0
3. Carl Hubbell	431	3,590.3
4. Mickey Welch	412	3,579.0
5. Amos Rusie	403	3,522.7
6. Fred Fitzsimmons	329	2,514.3
Hal Schumacher	329	2,482.3
8. Gaylord Perry	283	2,294.7
9. Kirk Rueter	277	1,614.0
10. Tim Keefe	269	2,265.0

Complete Games: Season

Player	CG	Year
1. Tim Keefe	62	1886
Mickey Welch	62	1884
3. Amos Rusie	58	1892
4. Amos Rusie	56	1890
Mickey Welch	56	1886
6. Mickey Welch	55	1885
7. Tim Keefe	54	1887
8. Amos Rusie	52	1891
9. Amos Rusie	50	1893
10. Tim Keefe	48	1888

Complete Games: Career with Team

Player	CG	IP
1. Christy Mathewson	433	4,771.7
2. Mickey Welch	391	3,579.0
3. Amos Rusie	371	3,522.7
4. Carl Hubbell	260	3,590.3
5. Tim Keefe	252	2,265.0
6. Juan Marichal	244	3,444.0
7. Joe McGinnity	186	2,151.3
8. Jouett Meekin	178	1,741.0
9. Dummy Taylor	156	1,882.3
10. Hooks Wiltse	153	2,053.0

GAMES WON: SEASON

Player	W	Year
1. Mickey Welch	44	1885
2. Tim Keefe	42	1886
3. Mickey Welch	39	1884
4. Christy Mathewson	37	1908
5. Amos Rusie	36	1894
6. Tim Keefe	35	1887
Tim Keefe	35	1888
Joe McGinnity	35	1904
9. Christy Mathewson	33	1904
Jouett Meekin	33	1894
Amos Rusie	33	1891
Amos Rusie	33	1893
Mickey Welch	33	1886

GAMES WON: CAREER WITH TEAM

Player	W	IP
1. Christy Mathewson	372	4,771.7
2. Carl Hubbell	253	3,590.3
3. Juan Marichal	238	3,444.0
Mickey Welch	238	3,579.0
5. Amos Rusie	233	3,522.7
6. Tim Keefe	174	2,265.0
7. Fred Fitzsimmons	170	2,514.3
8. Hal Schumacher	158	2,482.3
9. Joe McGinnity	151	2,151.3
10. Hooks Wiltse	136	2,053.0

GAMES LOST: SEASON

Player	L	Year
1. Amos Rusie	34	1890
2. Amos Rusie	31	1892
3. Bill Carrick	27	1899
Dummy Taylor	27	1901
5. Dad Clarke	24	1896
Ed Crane	24	1892
Silver King	24	1892
8. Amos Rusie	23	1895
Mickey Welch	23	1883
10. Bill Carrick	22	1900
Rube Marquard	22	1914
Mickey Welch	22	1886

GAMES LOST: CAREER WITH TEAM

Player	L	IP
1. Christy Mathewson	188	4,771.7
2. Amos Rusie	163	3,522.7
3. Carl Hubbell	154	3,590.3
4. Mickey Welch	146	3,579.0
5. Juan Marichal	140	3,444.0
6. Hal Schumacher	121	2,482.3
7. Fred Fitzsimmons	114	2,514.3
8. Gaylord Perry	109	2,294.7
9. Dave Koslo	104	1,559.7
10. Dummy Taylor	103	1,882.3

WINNING PERCENTAGE: SEASON

Player	W%	Year
1. Hoyt Wilhelm	.833	1952
2. Sal Maglie	.818	1950
3. Joe McGinnity	.814	1904
4. Carl Hubbell	.812	1936
Hooks Wiltse	.812	1904
6. Doc Crandall	.810	1910
7. Larry Jansen	.808	1947
8. Juan Marichal	.806	1966
Christy Mathewson	.806	1909
10. Mickey Welch	.800	1885

WINNING PERCENTAGE: CAREER WITH TEAM

Player	W%	IP
1. Jason Schmidt	.705	856.3
2. Sal Maglie	.693	1,297.7
3. Tim Keefe	.680	2,265.0
4. Christy Mathewson	.664	4,771.7
5. Jesse Barnes	.656	1,150.3
6. Doc Crandall	.650	1,002.7
7. Art Nehf	.641	1,436.0
8. Fred Toney	.636	880.3
9. Joe McGinnity	.632	2,151.3
10. Juan Marichal	.630	3,444.0

SHUTOUTS: SEASON

Player	SHO	Year
1. Christy Mathewson	11	1908
2. Carl Hubbell	10	1933
Juan Marichal	10	1965
4. Joe McGinnity	9	1904
5. Tim Keefe	8	1888
Juan Marichal	8	1969
Christy Mathewson	8	1902
Christy Mathewson	8	1905
Christy Mathewson	8	1907
Christy Mathewson	8	1909
Jeff Tesreau	8	1914
Jeff Tesreau	8	1915

SHUTOUTS: CAREER WITH TEAM

Player	SHO	IP
1. Christy Mathewson	79	4,771.7
2. Juan Marichal	52	3,444.0
3. Carl Hubbell	36	3,590.3
4. Amos Rusie	29	3,522.7
5. Mickey Welch	28	3,579.0
6. Hal Schumacher	27	2,482.3
Jeff Tesreau	27	1,679.0
Hooks Wiltse	27	2,053.0
9. Joe McGinnity	26	2,151.3
10. Tim Keefe	22	2,265.0

ERA: SEASON

Player	ERA	Year
1. Christy Mathewson	1.14	1909
2. Christy Mathewson	1.28	1905
3. Christy Mathewson	1.43	1908
4. Fred Anderson	1.44	1917
5. Tim Keefe	1.57	1885
6. Joe McGinnity	1.61	1904
7. Carl Hubbell	1.66	1933
Mickey Welch	1.66	1885
9. Tim Keefe	1.74	1888
10. Fred Toney	1.84	1919

ERA: CAREER WITH TEAM

Player	ERA	IP
1. Christy Mathewson	2.12	4,771.7
2. Slim Sallee	2.26	572.7
3. Joe McGinnity	2.38	2,151.3
4. Jeff Tesreau	2.43	1,679.0
5. Red Ames	2.45	1,802.7
6. Hooks Wiltse	2.48	2,053.0
7. Tim Keefe	2.53	2,265.0
8. Pol Perritt	2.58	964.7
9. Al Demaree	2.60	660.0
10. Ferdie Schupp	2.63	561.3

EARNED RUNS ALLOWED: SEASON

Player	ER	Year
1. Bill Carrick	187	1899
2. Amos Rusie	173	1893
3. Amos Rusie	170	1892
4. Jouett Meekin	168	1894
5. Dad Clarke	166	1896

Player		
Mickey Welch	166	1886
7. Tim Keefe	165	1887
8. Amos Rusie	163	1895
9. Amos Rusie	156	1890
10. Mickey Welch	155	1884

EARNED RUNS ALLOWED: CAREER WITH TEAM

Player	ER	IP
1. Carl Hubbell	1,188	3,590.3
2. Amos Rusie	1,133	3,522.7
3. Christy Mathewson	1,125	4,771.7
4. Juan Marichal	1,086	3,444.0
5. Mickey Welch	1,068	3,579.0
6. Fred Fitzsimmons	988	2,514.3
7. Hal Schumacher	926	2,482.3
8. Jouett Meekin	776	1,741.0
9. Kirk Rueter	775	1,614.0
10. Gaylord Perry	755	2,294.7

STRIKEOUTS: SEASON

Player	K	Year
1. Mickey Welch	345	1884
2. Amos Rusie	341	1890
3. Amos Rusie	337	1891
4. Tim Keefe	335	1888
5. Tim Keefe	297	1886
6. Amos Rusie	288	1892
7. Mickey Welch	272	1886
8. Christy Mathewson	267	1903
9. Christy Mathewson	259	1908
10. Mickey Welch	258	1885

STRIKEOUTS: CAREER WITH TEAM

Player	K	IP
1. Christy Mathewson	2,499	4,771.7
2. Juan Marichal	2,281	3,444.0
3. Amos Rusie	1,819	3,522.7
4. Carl Hubbell	1,677	3,590.3
5. Gaylord Perry	1,606	2,294.7
6. Mickey Welch	1,570	3,579.0
7. Tim Keefe	1,302	2,265.0
8. Red Ames	1,169	1,802.7
9. Mike McCormick	1,030	1,822.7
10. Bobby Bolin	977	1,282.3

STRIKEOUTS PER NINE IP: SEASON

Player	K/9	Year
1. Jason Schmidt	10.04	2004
2. Jason Schmidt	9.52	2002
3. Jason Schmidt	9.01	2003
4. Jason Schmidt	8.63	2005
5. Shawn Estes	8.10	1997
6. John Montefusco	7.94	1975
7. Gaylord Perry	7.82	1965
8. Rube Marquard	7.68	1911
Russ Ortiz	7.68	2000
10. Noah Lowry	7.56	2005

STRIKEOUTS PER NINE IP: CAREER WITH TEAM

Player	K/9	IP
1. Jason Schmidt	9.30	856.3
2. Mark Davis	7.77	555.0
3. Shawn Estes	7.23	990.0
4. Sam Jones	7.17	633.0
5. Russ Ortiz	6.93	924.7
6. Bobby Bolin	6.86	1,282.3
7. Jeff Brantley	6.84	505.3
8. Ray Sadecki	6.79	685.3
9. John Montefusco	6.61	1,182.7
10. Scott Garrelts	6.60	959.3

HITS ALLOWED: SEASON

Player	HA	Year
1. Mickey Welch	528	1884
2. Mickey Welch	514	1886
3. Bill Carrick	485	1899
4. Tim Keefe	479	1886
5. Amos Rusie	451	1893
6. Amos Rusie	436	1890
7. Dad Clarke	431	1896
Mickey Welch	431	1883
9. Tim Keefe	428	1887
10. Amos Rusie	426	1894

HITS ALLOWED: CAREER WITH TEAM

Player	HA	IP
1. Christy Mathewson	4,203	4,771.7
2. Carl Hubbell	3,461	3,590.3
3. Mickey Welch	3,307	3,579.0
4. Amos Rusie	3,095	3,522.7
5. Juan Marichal	3,081	3,444.0
6. Fred Fitzsimmons	2,607	2,514.3
7. Hal Schumacher	2,424	2,482.3
8. Gaylord Perry	2,061	2,294.7
9. Joe McGinnity	1,937	2,151.3
10. Tim Keefe	1,914	2,265.0

HITS ALLOWED PER NINE IP: SEASON

Player	H/9	Year
1. Christy Mathewson	6.28	1909
2. Bobby Bolin	6.52	1968
3. Jeff Tesreau	6.56	1912
4. Christy Mathewson	6.57	1908
Tim Keefe	6.57	1888
6. Jason Schmidt	6.59	2003
7. Jason Schmidt	6.60	2004
8. Jeff Tesreau	6.65	1914
9. Juan Marichal	6.68	1966
Ferdie Schupp	6.68	1917

HITS ALLOWED PER NINE IP: CAREER WITH TEAM

Player	H/9	IP
1. Ferdie Schupp	7.07	561.3
2. Jason Schmidt	7.17	856.3
3. Jeff Tesreau	7.24	1,679.0
4. Tim Keefe	7.61	2,265.0
5. Bobby Bolin	7.64	1,282.3
6. Scott Garrelts	7.65	959.3
7. Red Ames	7.70	1,802.7
8. Hoyt Wilhelm	7.88	608.0
9. Amos Rusie	7.91	3,522.7
10. Christy Mathewson	7.93	4,771.7

WALKS ALLOWED: SEASON

Player	BB	Year
1. Amos Rusie	289	1890
2. Amos Rusie	267	1892
3. Amos Rusie	262	1891
4. Amos Rusie	218	1893
5. Cy Seymour	213	1898
6. Amos Rusie	200	1894
7. Ed Crane	189	1892
8. Silver King	174	1892
9. Jouett Meekin	171	1894
10. Cy Seymour	170	1899

WALKS ALLOWED: CAREER WITH TEAM

Player	BB	IP
1. Amos Rusie	1,585	3,522.7

Player		
2. Mickey Welch	1,077	3,579.0
3. Hal Schumacher	902	2,482.3
4. Christy Mathewson	843	4,771.7
5. Carl Hubbell	725	3,590.3
6. Juan Marichal	690	3,444.0
7. Fred Fitzsimmons	670	2,514.3
8. Cy Seymour	652	1,026.0
9. Jouett Meekin	648	1,741.0
10. Red Ames	620	1,802.7

Walks Allowed Per Nine IP: Season

Player	BB/9	Year
1. Christy Mathewson	0.62	1913
2. Christy Mathewson	0.66	1914
3. Christy Mathewson	0.97	1908
Christy Mathewson	0.97	1915
5. Christy Mathewson	0.99	1912
6. John Ward	1.01	1883
7. Juan Marichal	1.05	1966
8. Carl Hubbell	1.06	1934
9. Jesse Barnes	1.07	1919
10. Christy Mathewson	1.11	1911

Walks Allowed Per Nine IP: Career with Team

Player	BB/9	IP
1. Slim Sallee	1.10	572.7
2. Jesse Barnes	1.56	1,150.3
3. Christy Mathewson	1.59	4,771.7
4. Juan Marichal	1.80	3,444.0
5. Carl Hubbell	1.82	3,590.3
6. Rube Benton	1.88	1,012.7
7. Dad Clarke	1.89	747.7
8. Joe McGinnity	1.94	2,151.3
9. Jim Barr	1.95	1,800.3
10. Fred Toney	1.99	880.3

WHIP (Walks + Hits Per Nine IP): Season

Player	WHIP	Year
1. Christy Mathewson	0.828	1909
2. Christy Mathewson	0.837	1908
3. Juan Marichal	0.859	1966
4. Juan Marichal	0.914	1965
5. Christy Mathewson	0.933	1905
6. Tim Keefe	0.937	1888
7. Jason Schmidt	0.953	2003
8. Christy Mathewson	0.962	1907
9. Fred Anderson	0.963	1917
Joe McGinnity	0.963	1904

WHIP (Walks + Hits Per Nine IP): Career with Team

Player	WHIP	IP
1. Christy Mathewson	1.057	4,771.7
2. Slim Sallee	1.079	572.7
3. Juan Marichal	1.095	3,444.0
4. Tim Keefe	1.101	2,265.0
5. Joe McGinnity	1.116	2,151.3
6. Ferdie Schupp	1.129	561.3
7. Hooks Wiltse	1.137	2,053.0
8. Bill Swift	1.139	506.7
9. Jeff Tesreau	1.145	1,679.0
Rube Benton	1.145	1,012.7

Home Runs Allowed: Season

Player	HRA	Year
1. Larry Jansen	36	1949
2. Juan Marichal	34	1962
3. Mike McCormick	33	1961
4. Juan Marichal	32	1966
5. Johnny Antonelli	31	1958
Larry Jansen	31	1950
Bill Voiselle	31	1944
8. Bob Knepper	30	1979
9. Johnny Antonelli	29	1959
Mark Gardner	29	1998

Home Runs Allowed: Career with Team

Player	HRA	IP
1. Juan Marichal	315	3,444.0
2. Carl Hubbell	227	3,590.3
3. Mike McCormick	194	1,822.7
4. Kirk Rueter	189	1,614.0
5. Larry Jansen	186	1,731.0
6. Gaylord Perry	165	2,294.7
7. Fred Fitzsimmons	155	2,514.3
8. Johnny Antonelli	152	1,600.7
9. Mark Gardner	145	951.3
10. Hal Schumacher	139	2,482.3

Saves: Season

Player	SV	Year
1. Rod Beck	48	1993
2. Robb Nen	45	2001
3. Robb Nen	43	2002
4. Robb Nen	41	2000
5. Robb Nen	40	1998
6. Tim Worrell	38	2003
7. Rod Beck	37	1997
Robb Nen	37	1999
9. Rod Beck	35	1996
10. Rod Beck	33	1995

Saves: Career with Team

Player	SV	IP
1. Robb Nen	206	378.3
2. Rod Beck	199	463.0
3. Gary Lavelle	127	980.3
4. Greg Minton	125	870.3
5. Randy Moffitt	83	682.3
6. Frank Linzy	78	531.0
7. Marv Grissom	58	543.3
8. Ace Adams	49	552.7
9. Scott Garrelts	48	959.3
10. Stu Miller	47	804.3

Wild Pitches: Season

Player	WP	Year
1. Mickey Welch	51	1886
2. Tim Keefe	40	1886
3. Mickey Welch	39	1884
Mickey Welch	39	1885
5. Tim Keefe	37	1887
6. Amos Rusie	36	1890
7. Tim Keefe	35	1885
8. Ed Begley	33	1884
Tip O'Neill	33	1883
10. Ed Crane	31	1892

Wild Pitches: Career with Team

Player	WP	IP
1. Mickey Welch	222	3,579.0
2. Tim Keefe	149	2,265.0
3. Amos Rusie	142	3,522.7

Player	HB	IP
4. Christy Mathewson	113	4,771.7
5. Red Ames	107	1,802.7
6. Gaylord Perry	81	2,294.7
7. Jouett Meekin	72	1,741.0
8. Ed Doheny	70	905.0
9. Mike McCormick	64	1,822.7
10. Ed Crane	62	755.3

HIT BATSMEN: SEASON

Player	HB	Year
1. Ed Doheny	37	1899
2. Cy Seymour	32	1898
3. Bill Carrick	23	1899
4. Ed Doheny	22	1900
5. Cy Seymour	21	1897
Cy Seymour	21	1899
7. Ed Doheny	20	1898
Pink Hawley	20	1900
Win Mercer	20	1900
10. Joe McGinnity	19	1903

HIT BATSMEN: CAREER WITH TEAM

Player	HB	IP
1. Ed Doheny	93	905.0
2. Joe McGinnity	84	2,151.3
Cy Seymour	84	1,026.0
4. Dummy Taylor	70	1,882.3
5. Christy Mathewson	59	4,771.7
6. Bobby Bolin	53	1,282.3
Carl Hubbell	53	3,590.3
8. Gaylord Perry	50	2,294.7
9. Tim Keefe	42	2,265.0
10. Bill Carrick	41	743.0

GAMES FINISHED: SEASON

Player	GF	Year
1. Rod Beck	71	1993
Robb Nen	71	2001
3. Robb Nen	67	1998
4. Rod Beck	66	1997
Greg Minton	66	1982
6. Robb Nen	65	2002
7. Robb Nen	64	1999
Tim Worrell	64	2003
9. Robb Nen	63	2000
10. Rod Beck	58	1996

GAMES FINISHED: CAREER WITH TEAM

Player	GF	IP
1. Gary Lavelle	369	980.3
2. Rod Beck	346	463.0
3. Greg Minton	335	870.3
4. Robb Nen	330	378.3
5. Randy Moffitt	254	682.3
6. Ace Adams	218	552.7
7. Frank Linzy	217	531.0
8. Marv Grissom	169	543.3
9. Scott Garrelts	162	959.3
10. Stu Miller	156	804.3

In the 1950's, the Giants were often breathing down the Dodgers' neck.

Significant Giants

BONDS, BARRY (OF)
(1993–2005)

After emerging as a star during his seven years in Pittsburgh, Bonds returned to his hometown of San Francisco, signing a $43 million, seven-year contract. His first season with the Giants seemed to be his statement that he was worth the big money, as he set personal highs in batting average (.336), homers (46), RBIs (123), hits (181), runs scored (129), doubles (38), on-base percentage (.458), and slugging average (.677), winning the NL MVP Award for the third time. Bonds became the first 40–40 man in National League history in 1996. Amazingly, his offensive numbers (except stolen bases) have increased as he's gotten older. From 2000 to 2004, Bonds hit at least 45 homers each year, topping out at 73 blasts in 2001 and shattering Mark McGwire's single-season record. By the end of the 2005 campaign, his career home run total stood at 708, just six behind Babe Ruth and 47 behind Hank Aaron on the all-time list. Through 2005 Bonds had appeared in 13 All-Star Games and won 12 Silver Slugger Awards, eight Gold Gloves, seven MVP Awards, and two batting titles. He's also led the league in on-base average eight times, slugging average seven times, and walks 10 times.

But his recent glory hasn't come without a price, as he became the central player caught up in the steroids scandal. His personal trainer has admitted giving steroids to other players, but not Bonds. Bonds said any steroids he took were by accident, and that he thought they were something else. (Uh-huh. And the forty pounds of extra muscle mass he's added to his frame came from . . . *where?* Reconstituted Gatorade? And his home run production went up 32% the year after hooking up with his trainer because of . . . *more time on the exercycle?*) Whether or not it's ultimately proven that Bonds used steroids, he's already guilty in the public's eye. It's a shame, because he had the raw talent to be one of the best in the history of baseball without using the drugs. *(See Pirates bio.)*

CAREER GIANTS RECORD:

Games	AB	Hits	Runs
1,720	5,556	1,758	1,406
Avg	**HR**	**RBI**	**SB**
.316	532	1,297	255

CEPEDA, ORLANDO (1B/OF)
(1958–1966)

The New York Giants signed Puerto Rican slugger Orlando Cepeda as an amateur free agent before the 1955 season. The son of Pedro "The Bull" Cepeda, a fearsome Puerto Rican slugger, Orlando "The Baby Bull" Cepeda was sent to Virginia to play for an independent team after receiving a contract and a $500 bonus. Upon arriving in Virginia, however, Cepeda had to turn right around and return to Puerto Rico to be by the side of his dying father. He used the $500 bonus money to pay for the funeral. Cepeda talked about giving up baseball and staying in Puerto Rico to be with his mother, but she insisted he return to the United States because that was her husband's dying wish. He returned, and with a vengeance, hitting .393 in 1955, then winning the Northern League Triple Crown in 1956. When spring training broke in 1958, Cepeda was the Giants' first baseman and, after hitting .312 with 25 homers and 96 RBIs, the National League's Rookie of the Year. Over his first seven seasons in San Francisco, Cepeda hit between 24 and 46 homers with 96–142 RBIs each year, and hit over .300 in six of those years, missing only in 1960 when he hit .297.

While working out in the offseason before the 1964 campaign, Cepeda dropped an 80-pound weight on his knee, severely injuring it. Afraid to tell his manager about it, Cepeda kept the injury hidden, but it affected him for the next two years, causing others to accuse him of malingering. After hitting just .176 in early 1965, he finally had surgery on the knee, ending his season. Early in 1966, the Giants decided to move Willie McCovey to first from the outfield, making Cepeda expendable, and he was traded to St. Louis. In 1967 he hit 25 homers with 111 RBIs, leading St. Louis to the NL pennant and World Series title, winning unanimous selection as the league's MVP, the first unanimous selection since Carl Hubbell in 1936. Cepeda spent the last six years of his career bouncing around with Atlanta, Oakland, Boston, and Kansas City before retiring in 1974. In 1975 Cepeda was arrested by federal agents with 160 pounds of marijuana in the trunk of his car at the San Juan, Puerto Rico, airport and spent 10 months incarcerated at Florida's Elgin Air Force Base. His eventual election to the Hall of Fame in 1999 was no doubt delayed for many years because of his conviction as a drug smuggler.

CAREER GIANTS RECORD:

Games	AB	Hits	Runs
1,114	4,178	1,286	652
Avg	**HR**	**RBI**	**SB**
.308	226	767	92

CONNOR, ROGER (1B)
(1883–1889, 1891, 1893–1894)

Roger Connor was a giant of a man for the 19th century, standing 6'3" tall and weighing 220 pounds. It was probably fitting, then, that he was the era's leading home run hitter, clouting 138 career homers, the major league record until Babe Ruth eclipsed it in 1921. After spending three years with the National League's Troy Trojans, Connor went to the New York Gothams when the National League decertified the Troy franchise. Although he led the league only once in home runs, Connor had some individual shots that are worth mentioning. On September 10, 1881, Connor belted the first grand slam in major league history. In 1883, Connor, whose salary was $1,800, hit just one home run for New York, but it was such a prodigious shot that the fans took up a collection and bought him a $500 gold watch. Connor, like several other New York players, was quite tall, and manager Jim Mutrie liked to refer to them as "my giants." The nickname stuck, and in 1885 it became the official team name. Connor's 14 homers paced the Giants as they won the 1888 NL pennant and the World Series against the St. Louis Browns. In 1889 he hit 13 homers and a league-leading 130 RBIs to help the Giants win their second straight pennant, this time knocking off the American Association's Brooklyn nine in the World Series. The 1889 Series was the beginning of the Giants-Dodgers rivalry that thrives to this day.

Like many stars in 1890, Connor jumped to the Players' League, hitting .349 and leading the league in homers with 14, his only home run crown. He returned to the National League after the Players' League folded and played three more years for the Giants, three-plus for St. Louis, and one for Philadelphia. In 18 major league seasons, Connor hit over .300 11 times. He was elected to the Hall of Fame in 1976.

CAREER GIANTS RECORD:

Games	AB	Hits	Runs
1,120	4,346	1,388	946
Avg	**HR**	**RBI**	**SB**
.319	76	786	161

DAVIS, GEORGE (SS/3B)
(1893–1901, 1903)

After an early career as an erratic outfielder with the Cleveland Spiders, switch-hitting George Davis was traded to the Giants for Buck Ewing, one of the best players of the 19th century. With the Giants, Davis moved to the infield, where he became a star. In nine seasons with the team, Davis hit over .300 every year. He had 100+ RBIs three times and scored 100+ runs four times. His best season came in 1897, when he batted .353, scored 112 runs, hit 31 doubles, 10 triples, 10 homers, stole 65 bases, and led the NL with 136 RBIs. Like many New York Giants stars, Davis jumped to the new American League once despicable owner Andrew Freedman took over the team and imposed, among other hardships, a petty system of player fines that were just a disguise for reducing salaries. Davis finished his career with six fine years as a member of the White Sox, collecting nearly 2,700 career hits, an excellent number considering he played much of his career at a time when the seasons were 20–30 games shorter than today. Davis received his call to the Hall of Fame in 1998.

CAREER GIANTS RECORD:

Games	AB	Hits	Runs
1,096	4,303	1,427	838
Avg	**HR**	**RBI**	**SB**
.332	53	816	354

DOYLE, LARRY (2B)
(1907–1916, 1918–1920)

Nicknamed "Laughing" Larry Doyle because of his cheerful disposition, Doyle came to New York in mid-1907 after the Giants paid $4,500 for his contract, a record price at the time for a minor league player. The scrappy second baseman was so well regarded that he eventually became the Giants' captain. Doyle's best year was 1912, when he led the Giants to the NL pennant, batting .330 with 10 homers, 90 RBIs, 98 runs, 36 steals, and 33 doubles, winning the NL MVP Award in the process. In 1915 he won the NL batting title on the last day of the season, collecting four hits to finish at .320.

After hitting over .300 in five of his 10 seasons in New York, Doyle was traded to the Cubs in 1916, but returned in 1918 for three final years with the Giants before retiring in 1920.

CAREER GIANTS RECORD:

Games	AB	Hits	Runs
1,622	5,995	1,751	906
Avg	**HR**	**RBI**	**SB**
.292	67	725	291

EWING, BUCK (C/1B/OF) (1883–1889, 1891–1892)

William "Buck" Ewing, considered by many to be the best player of the 19th century, began his career with three years in Troy. Ewing was among those players transferred to the Gothams when the National League revoked Troy's charter. In nine seasons with the Giants, he hit over .300 eight times. Official baseball scribe Francis Richter wrote in the 1919 *Reach Baseball Guide* that ". . . Ewing in his prime [was] the greatest player of the game from the standpoint of supreme excellence in all departments—batting, catching, fielding, baserunning, throwing, and Baseball brains—a player without a weakness of any kind, physical, mental, or temperamental."

Although he played all nine positions at one time or another during his career, Ewing was best at catcher, a brutal position in baseball's early days. When Ewing played catcher, the term "backstop" had a literal meaning. Shin guards wouldn't be invented for another 20 years; the mask had no or little padding, so taking a ball off the mask was like getting smacked in the face; the padding in the mitts was a joke, so broken fingers were common; and chest protectors weren't often used and did little good when they were. Catchers routinely played many feet behind the batter when no one was on base, preferring to let the ball bounce to them on one hop. With runners on base, however, the catcher had to play up close and take his chances. Also, until 1893, the pitcher's mound was either 45 or 50 feet away instead of the current 60' 6". The position was so demanding and dangerous that no catcher was expected to play every day. In spite of all this, Ewing was so good that he often threw runners out while still in the squatting position behind the plate. He was the team's leader, and in 1888 led the Giants to their first-ever pennant. In the World Series against St. Louis, Ewing hit .346 with two triples and a homer to help New York to their first World Championship.

Ewing, like many other stars, jumped to the Players' League in 1890 when the owners implemented their new cost-savings plan, a salary schedule that ranked players according to their performance and paid them anywhere from $1,500–$2,500. Although the Players' League outdrew both the National League and the American Association, it folded after a year when the investors got cold feet and pulled the cash rug out from under the players.

Ewing returned to the Giants in 1891, but he suffered an arm injury from which he never recovered. He spent his last six seasons almost exclusively at either first base or in the outfield, two positions that required him to throw very little. After being traded to Cleveland in 1893, Ewing had the best year of his career offensively, batting .344 with 117 runs and 122 RBIs, the only time in his career he surpassed 100 in either category. Following two years in Cleveland, Ewing became the player-manager for Cincinnati in 1895. After retiring as a player in 1897, Ewing remained Cincinnati's manager through 1899, and then took over the Giants in 1900, but, like everyone else, he couldn't get along with Giants owner Andrew Freedman so he retired mid-season. Ewing became wealthy through real estate investments, though he didn't get to enjoy a retirement of ease; he developed diabetes and died in 1906, just three days after his 47th birthday. In 1939 Buck Ewing became the first catcher to be enshrined in Cooperstown.

CAREER GIANTS RECORD:

Games	AB	Hits	Runs
734	2,957	905	643
Avg	**HR**	**RBI**	**SB**
.306	47	459	178

FITZSIMMONS, FRED (SP/RP)
(1925–1937)

Freddie "Fat" Fitzsimmons, so nicknamed because of his weight problems, spent 12-plus seasons with the Giants and six-plus seasons with Brooklyn, but only once did he win 20 games (1928). During spring training in 1927, he fell asleep in a rocking chair at the team's hotel and rocked over the fingers of his pitching hand, knocking him out of action for nearly a month. During his time in New York, Fitzsimmons won at least 14 games nine times. Though not a big-name star, he was so consistent for so long that he appears on many of the Giants' top 10 lists for career performances. In mid-1937, with his skills clearly in decline, Fitzsimmons was traded to Brooklyn, where he was a role player. In mid-1943 he was released so that he could take over as manager of the Phillies, a job he held for two years before being fired.

CAREER GIANTS RECORD:

W	L	W%	ERA	SV
170	114	.599	3.54	9
K	**BB**	**SHO**	**IP**	
693	670	21	2,514.3	

FRISCH, FRANKIE (2B/3B)
(1919–1926)

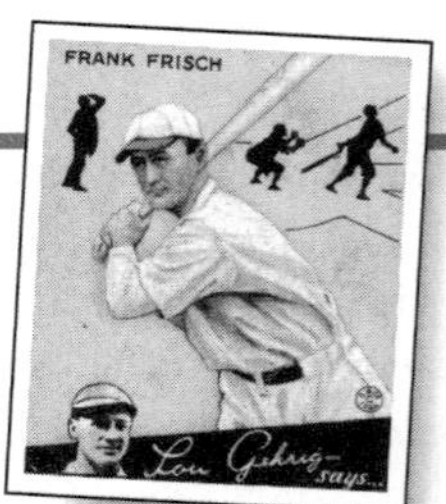

Frankie Frisch was a four-sport star at Fordham University, where he earned the nickname "the Fordham Flash." He was captain of the baseball, basketball, and football teams, and a football All-American. His Fordham baseball coach Art Devlin, a former New York Giant, arranged a tryout for Frisch in the Polo Grounds. John McGraw signed him to a short-term contract after the tryout and took the young second baseman under his wing, much as he had nurtured Christy Mathewson two decades before. McGraw recognized that Frisch had a good head for the game, so he spent time grooming him to be his "assistant manger"—a position Frisch often filled because McGraw sometimes showed up late, or even not at all. Frisch was a feisty player who hit over .300 his last six years with the Giants, sparking them to four consecutive pennants from 1921 to 1924. He never backed down from a battle, even with McGraw. By 1926 the two men had become bitter enemies and McGraw felt threatened by Frisch's new status as "manager in waiting," so he convinced the Giants owner to trade Frisch to St. Louis for an even better second baseman, Rogers Hornsby. *(See Cardinals bio.)*

CAREER GIANTS RECORD:

Games	AB	Hits	Runs
1,000	4,053	1,303	701
Avg	**HR**	**RBI**	**SB**
.321	54	524	224

HUBBELL, CARL (SP/RP) (1928–1943)

Nicknamed "the Meal Ticket," Carl Hubbell played his entire 16-year major league career with New York. Hubbell spent three years in the minor league system of the Detroit Tigers, pitching batting practice every spring, but never in a game. He was told not to throw his screwball, his best pitch. Each spring he was farmed out, so he eventually decided to quit baseball and go to work in the oil business. He told his minor league manager, Claude Robinson, that he would not return to the Detroit organization and if he wasn't sold by the end of the season, he'd quit baseball. Robinson arranged for him to be sold to the Giants, finally giving Hubbell a chance to show off his killer screwball, a pitch he threw so often that his arm actually turned inward.

Hubbell was a winner right from the start, compiling a winning record in each of his first 12 major league seasons, all with the same team, something no other pitcher has ever done. On May 8, 1929, he tossed a no-hitter against Pittsburgh. From July 13–August 1, 1933, Hubbell recorded 46.3 consecutive scoreless innings, exceeded in the 20th century National League by only Orel Hershiser and Don Drysdale. Hubbell won 16 straight games from July 18, 1936, through the end of the season, then reeled off eight straight to begin 1937, giving him 24 consecutive wins before losing to the Dodgers on Memorial Day.

In the five years from 1933 to 1937, Hubbell was the best pitcher in baseball, winning 21 or more games each year. Hubbell is most famously remembered for the 1934 All-Star Game, when he struck out—in succession—five of the best hitters in baseball history: Babe Ruth, Lou Gehrig, Jimmie Foxx, Al Simmons, and Joe Cronin. Hubbell appeared in nine All-Star Games during his career, won two NL MVP Awards (1933 and 1936), and led the league in many different categories over the years. After four straight years in which he collected exactly 11 victories each season, Hubbell fell to 4–4 in 1943 and was released after the season. The Giants' owner, Horace Stoneham, appointed Hubbell to be the team's director of farm clubs, a position he held for 34 years before becoming a scout for the team in 1977 at the age of 74. Hubbell was named to the Hall of Fame in 1947. He died in 1988.

CAREER GIANTS RECORD:

W	L	W%	ERA	SV
253	154	.622	2.98	33
K	**BB**	**SHO**	**IP**	
1,677	725	36	3,590.3	

JACKSON, TRAVIS (SS/3B)
(1922–1936)

Travis "Stonewall" Jackson got his nickname in honor of his impenetrable defense at shortstop. He was also a very good hitter, topping the .300 level six times in his 15-year career, all of which was spent with the Giants. From 1927 to 1929, Jackson was part of an all Hall of Fame infield that included George Kelly at either first or second, Bill Terry at first, Frankie Frisch and Rogers Hornsby at second, Jackson at shortstop, and Freddie Lindstrom at third. Before the major leagues starting naming official All-Star teams in 1933, *The Sporting News* named an All-Star team for a number of years, and Travis Jackson was given shortstop honors in 1927, 1928, and 1929. In 1930 Jackson (.339) was a member of the best-hitting infield in major league history, joining first baseman Bill Terry (.401), second baseman Hughie Critz (.265), and third baseman Freddie Lindstrom (.379). Jackson was elected to the Hall of Fame in 1982 and he died in 1987.

CAREER GIANTS RECORD:

Games	AB	Hits	Runs
1,656	6,086	1,768	833
Avg	**HR**	**RBI**	**SB**
.291	135	929	71

KEEFE, TIM (SP)
(1885–1889, 1891)

TIM KEEFE, P., N.Y.'S
GOODWIN & CO. New York.

Tim Keefe was an intelligent pitcher who knew the weakness of every hitter in the league, according to teammate Mickey Welch, himself a great pitcher. Keefe understood the necessity of changing speeds, and his most effective pitch was the change-up. After pitching in the minor leagues in 1878 and 1879, Keefe joined Troy of the major leagues in 1880. When the Troy team was disbanded following the 1882 season, Keefe went to the New York Metropolitans of the American Association, where he won 78 games in 1883–1884. The Mets' owner, John Day, also owned the New York Gothams franchise. Although Day was generally pleased with his Metropolitans and their 1884 American Association pennant, he recognized that the Gothams had more prestige as a National League team, so he transferred some of the better players from the Mets to the Gothams. (Besides, the Gothams were getting 50¢ admission as an NL team and the Mets only 25¢ as an AA team, both prices set by the league.)

In addition to pitching, Keefe was an entrepreneur, undertaking various ventures during his baseball career. He opened a sporting goods business, designed and sold the Giants their tight black uniforms, designed the Players' League baseball, and provided the league with their required baseballs. Keefe also studied shorthand in preparation for a career after his playing days were over, and his skills earned him the job of secretary of the Brotherhood of Professional Base Ball Players, a benevolent association formed in 1885.

In 1887 Keefe sat out several weeks of the season after one of his pitches nearly killed a batter. Some reports suggest he might have had a nervous breakdown over the incident, but he eventually returned and won 35 games on the season. But his strikeout totals began to decline. During the 1888 season, Keefe recorded 19 straight wins, a single-season record that has never been exceeded, and matched only by fellow Giant Rube Marquard. He won the Triple Crown in 1888 with 35 wins, a 1.74 ERA, and 335 strikeouts. In that year's championship series, Keefe won four games in the Giants' six-games-to-four win over the American Association's St. Louis Browns. After the season he demanded a raise to $4,500, and he got it, making him the highest-paid member of the team. After spending the 1890 season in the Players' League, Keefe returned to the Giants in 1891, but was traded in midseason to the Phillies, where he finished his career in 1893. He was an umpire in 1894 and 1895, but quit after taking abuse at the Polo Grounds, of all places, the field where he had played for so long. Keefe, who was elected to the Hall of Fame in 1964, later coached baseball at Harvard, Princeton, and Tufts.

CAREER GIANTS RECORD:

W	L	W%	ERA	SV
174	82	.680	2.53	1

K	BB	SHO	IP
1,302	580	22	2,265.0

KELLY, GEORGE (1B/2B)
(1915–1917, 1919–1926)

From 1915 to 1919, George "Highpockets" Kelly spent one year in the military and four years on the New York Giants, mostly on the bench next to John McGraw. Kelly, who got his nickname because of his 6'4" frame, took a lot of ribbing over the years for his time spent on the bench, both from other players and the fans. McGraw had taken a special interest in Kelly, and brought him along slowly until the final month of the 1919 season, when he took over for the popular Hal Chase at first base. Kelly was booed initially by fans who didn't know that McGraw had taken the popular Chase out of the lineup because he suspected him of throwing games. When Kelly started the 1921 season with a quick seven homers, the newspapers began to run a daily comparison of him and Babe Ruth, who had hit 54 homers the year before. But Ruth soon ran away from Kelly en route to 59 homers, although Kelly's 23 were good enough to lead the National League.

From 1921 to 1924, the Giants won four straight pennants, with Kelly hitting over .300 each year and logging 468 RBIs. According to John McGraw, Kelly got more "important" hits for the Giants during those four years than any other player. When superstar Bill Terry eventually arrived in 1925, Kelly was moved to second base, becoming baseball's tallest second sacker, though he performed much better than generally predicted. In 1927, however, Rogers Hornsby, the best right-handed hitter in the history of the game, arrived and "Highpockets" was out of a job. Traded to Cincinnati before the 1927 season, Kelly spent four years with the Reds and was playing quite well for the last-place team when they cut him (and his $15,000 salary) to save money. The Cubs picked him up for the pennant drive, but dropped the .331 hitter as soon as they were eliminated. After sitting out the 1931 season, Kelly attempted a comeback in 1932 with Brooklyn, but the attempt lasted only 64 games with a .243 average and he left again, this time for good. Following his playing career, Kelly spent 14 years coaching for the Reds and Braves before returning to his native Bay-area home and scouting for Oakland in the Pacific Coast League. He was elected to the Hall of Fame in 1973 and died in 1984.

CAREER GIANTS RECORD:

Games	AB	Hits	Runs
1,136	4,213	1,270	608

Avg	HR	RBI	SB
.301	123	762	54

LINDSTROM, FREDDIE (3B/OF)
(1924–1932)

The New York Giants signed Freddie Lindstrom right out of high school and brought the 18-year-old up to the majors in 1924. He played against Washington in the Fall Classic that year, becoming the youngest player ever to see World Series action at 18 years, 10 months, and 13 days old. He played errorless defense at third and had 10 hits, including four off Walter Johnson in Game 5. He'll be most remembered, however, for two ground balls that took incredibly weird, high hops over his head and helped the Senators win the Series. Nicknamed the "Boy Wonder," Lindstrom hit over .300 in six consecutive seasons from 1926 to 1931. He was also notable for openly talking back to John McGraw, something almost no player ever did. In 1931, Giants president Charles Stoneham told Lindstrom that he was next in line to be manager of the Giants, and this emboldened the young third baseman, who saw less and less need to be on the same page as McGraw. McGraw, upset at Lindstrom's subversiveness, succeeded in convincing Stoneham that Lindstrom would not make a good manager, and after the 1931 season Bill Terry was named. Lindstrom asked to be traded, but it took until the end of the 1932 season to get a deal worked out with Pittsburgh.

After two years with the Pirates, Lindstrom was traded to the Cubs and helped them win the NL pennant by driving in or scoring the winning run in seven games of a 21-game winning streak the team put together to snare the pennant in most unexpected fashion. (So unexpected was their pennant that the World Series had to open in Detroit instead of Chicago because the Cubs hadn't had time to print their World Series tickets.) After a brief stint with Brooklyn the following year, Lindstrom retired at the age of 30. Lindstrom, elected to the Hall of Fame in 1976, spent several years managing in the minors and two more as a radio announcer in Chicago. He died in 1981.

CAREER GIANTS RECORD:

Games	AB	Hits	Runs
1,087	4,242	1,347	705
Avg	**HR**	**RBI**	**SB**
.318	91	603	80

MARICHAL, JUAN (SP)
(1960–1973)

The New York Giants signed Juan Marichal as an amateur free agent before the 1957 season. By 1960 he made his major league debut—and what a debut it was. In his first start, the Dominican right-hander pitched a one-hit shutout against Philadelphia, and in his next start he four-hit the Pirates. By 1962 he pitched in the first of his nine All-Star Games, and in 1965 he was named the game's MVP. In 1963 he pitched the first no-hitter by a Giants pitcher since Carl Hubbell turned the trick in 1929. Just a few starts later, Marichal hooked up in a classic pitching duel with Warren Spahn, a 16-inning affair won by Marichal 1–0 on Willie Mays' home run. Marichal will forever be remembered for a horrible incident in an August 1965 game against the Dodgers, whom the Giants were battling for the pennant. Early in the game, Marichal threw two knockdown pitches at

Dodger hitters. When Sandy Koufax returned the gesture, knocking down Marichal at the plate, John Roseboro, the Dodgers' catcher, fired the ball back to Koufax, almost hitting Marichal in the ear. An incensed Marichal clubbed Roseboro over the head with his bat, opening a large gash. Marichal received a nine-day suspension and a $1,750 fine, penalties many felt were too lenient. He missed two starts, and then went 3–4 in his last seven decisions of the year as the Giants lost the pennant to the Dodgers by just two games.

During the 1960s, Marichal won 191 games, 27 more than Bob Gibson, his closest competitor, yet he never won a Cy Young. He won 25 games twice (in 1963 and 1966), but both times was bested for the award by Koufax. He went 26–9 in 1968, but was eclipsed by Gibson. Incredibly, the closest he ever came was an eighth-place finish in the 1971 voting. A six-time 20-game winner, Marichal suffered a severe reaction to penicillin, its complications leading to severe back pain and arthritic problems that bothered him the rest of his playing days. After going 17–31 in 1972–1973, Marichal was sold to the Red Sox, where he went 5–1 in nine starts. After Boston released him, Marichal signed as a free agent with the Dodgers, but Los Angeles fans were so outraged it took a special plea from John Roseboro to calm them down. After getting hammered in two games with the Dodgers, Marichal retired, but when he became eligible for Hall of Fame induction, he was passed over his first two years. Roseboro again stood up for Marichal, pleading with sports writers not to let the 1965 incident keep them from voting Marichal to his rightful spot in the Hall. The writers did as Roseboro asked in 1981, and in his induction speech, Marichal thanked Roseboro, who had become Marichal's good friend some years earlier.

CAREER GIANTS RECORD:

W	L	W%	ERA	SV
238	140	.630	2.84	2

K	BB	SHO	IP
2,281	690	52	3,444.0

MARQUARD, RUBE (SP/RP) (1908–1915)

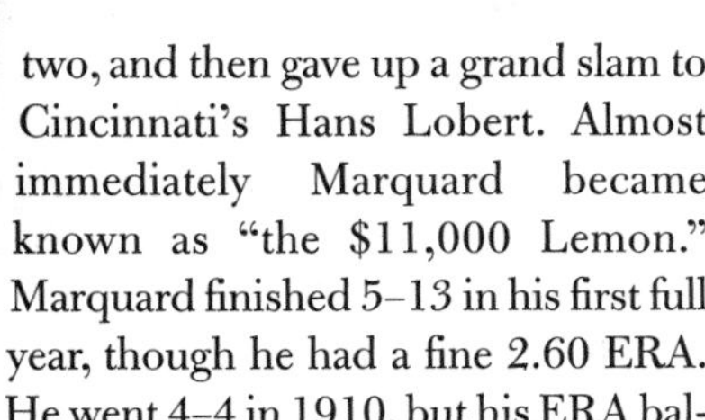

Richard "Rube" Marquard got his nickname because he closely resembled Rube Waddell, another ace pitcher of the era. Marquard was enjoying a terrific year with Indianapolis in 1908 when a number of scouts showed up to watch him pitch. He responded by tossing a perfect game, setting off a bidding war for his services. The Giants outbid the Indians by $500, topping out at $11,000, the highest amount ever paid for a player up to that time. When he arrived in New York shortly thereafter, the media, fans, and players all awaited his debut with much fanfare. When the game started, Marquard hit the first batter, walked the next two, and then gave up a grand slam to Cincinnati's Hans Lobert. Almost immediately Marquard became known as "the $11,000 Lemon." Marquard finished 5–13 in his first full year, though he had a fine 2.60 ERA. He went 4–4 in 1910, but his ERA ballooned to 4.46 and many eyebrows were raised. In 1911, however, Marquard quickly quieted the critics, beginning the year with 19 straight wins, tying Tim Keefe's all-time record for a single-season winning streak. His nickname soon changed to "the $11,000 Beauty," and he ended the season with 24 victories. He won 26 and 23 games the following two years, establishing himself as one of the best pitchers in the game. In 1914, Marquard fell to 12–22, becoming one of the very few pitchers in history to win 20 games one season and lose 20 the next. He tossed a no-hitter against Brooklyn in 1915, but was put on waivers before the end of the season and was picked up by Brooklyn. Although Marquard lasted 10 more years in the majors, in only two of them did he approach his former glory. In 1971 he was elected to the Hall of Fame.

CAREER GIANTS RECORD:

W	L	W%	ERA	SV
103	76	.575	2.85	12
K	BB	SHO	IP	
897	430	16	1,546.0	

MATHEWSON, CHRISTY (SP/RP) (1900–1916)

Christy Mathewson was not only one of the best pitchers in the history of the game, but he was also one of baseball's top goodwill ambassadors. In an era of rough-and-tumble, often vulgar players, Mathewson was a true gentleman who inspired a new breed of fans to embrace the game. He was intelligent and handsome, two qualities that endeared the game to women for the first time and prompted owners to adopt a new marketing promotion—Ladies' Day. Four times during his career, Mathewson won 30 or more games, and in a stretch of 12 consecutive seasons he won at least 22 games. He was particularly superb in the 1905 World Series, pitching three complete-game shutouts against the Philadelphia Athletics—probably the best pitching performance in Series history. In 1913 he had a streak of 68 consecutive innings during which he didn't walk a batter.

Mathewson had his share of hard luck during his career, none worse than 1908 when he was the pitcher during the Merkle's Boner incident, in which a sure win was misplayed into a tie. When the Cubs and Giants replayed the tie game at the end of the season to determine the league champion, Mathewson was again on the mound with the pennant on the line. In the third inning, Mathewson implored center fielder Cy Seymour to play deeper on Joe Tinker, but Seymour refused to back up. Tinker promptly hit a ball over Seymour's head that led to a four-run inning. The Giants lost the replay game—and the pennant—4–2.

Mathewson finished 24–13 in 1914, but began to complain of side pains near the end of the season. In 1915 he had his first losing season since 1902, finishing 8–14 as his ERA ballooned to 3.58, the highest of his career besides his brief rookie season. On July 20, 1916, after compiling only a 3–4 record for New York in 12 games, Mathewson was traded to the Reds so he could become their player-manager. (The Reds and their fans must have been happy to get Mathewson on their team since he had compiled a 64–18 record against them over the years, including 22 straight wins at one point.) He pitched only one game with Cincinnati, recording a win in spite of allowing eight earned runs, and ended his playing career to concentrate solely on managing.

He remained manager of the Reds until 1918 when he left in midseason to join the military during World War I. Mathewson received the rank of captain and joined the troops on the Western Front, where he had the misfortune to come in contact with some poison gas. He returned to the major leagues in 1919 as a coach for the Giants, but in 1921 he was diagnosed as having tuberculosis in both lungs, the result of his earlier gassing. While receiving treatment at Saranac Lake, one of his lungs collapsed. He returned home in 1922 with his doctors ordering complete rest, but by 1923 he could no longer just lie around. Baseball had been his whole life and he wasn't about to let his illness stop him, so he took the job of president of the Boston Braves. He collapsed under the job's strain in 1925 and returned to Saranac Lake, where he died on October 7. Mathewson was one of the Hall of Fame's five original inductees in 1936.

CAREER GIANTS RECORD:

W	L	W%	ERA	SV
372	188	.664	2.12	28

K	BB	SHO	IP
2,499	843	79	4,771.7

MAYS, WILLIE (OF)
(1951–1952, 1954–1972)

Willie Mays was one of baseball's rare talents. The "Say Hey Kid" could do it all: hit for average as well as power, run, throw, and play superb defense. At age 17 Mays signed his first professional contract with the Birmingham Black Barons of the Negro National League. In 1950 he was sold to the New York Giants for $15,000 and made it to the big leagues in 1951, though his beginning was most inauspicious. After going 0–24 to start his career, Mays was sobbing in the clubhouse when manager Leo Durocher came over and told the youngster that he was the best center fielder he had ever seen, and the job was his as long as Durocher was the manager. Sparked by the encouragement, Mays homered off Warren Spahn the next day to begin his turnaround. Spahn later said that he never forgave himself for giving up the homer to Mays because everyone knew the kid was emotionally on the ropes—if he'd gone a few more games without getting a hit, he might have been sent back to the minors, possibly never to return to the majors. As it was, over the last five months of the season, Mays hit .274 with 20 homers and won the NL Rookie of the Year Award.

After playing only 34 games in 1952, Mays was drafted into the military and didn't return to baseball until 1954, when he set the league on fire by batting .345 with 41 homers, 110 RBIs, 119 runs, and winning the NL MVP Award. In the World Series that year he made an over-the-shoulder catch considered by many to be the best in the history of the game, snaring Vic Wertz's 449-foot drive on a dead run. He then quickly whirled and fired the ball to his infield, allowing only one baserunner to advance. The game remained tied at 2–2 when the baserunners were eventually stranded.

Mays was remarkably consistent for many years, driving in more than 100 runs 10 times, scoring more than 100 runs for 12 straight years (1954–1965), and clubbing 660 homers during his career (a total that was second only to Babe Ruth's when Mays retired, and has been surpassed since only by Hank Aaron and Mays' own godson, Barry Bonds). Mays played in 24 All-Star Games during his 22-year career, taking home the game's MVP Award twice (1963 and 1968). He also won two NL MVPs (1954 and 1965) as well as 12 Gold Gloves (he twice caught long drives with his bare hand). Another mark of his incredible consistency was the 300+ total bases he accumulated for 13 consecutive years, from 1954 to 1966.

In May 1972, after more than 20 years with the Giants, Mays was traded to the New York Mets, a team still trying to attract fans by employing ancient baseball gladiators. In 1973, Mays' final season, he was an aching, swollen shadow of his former self, but he did manage to hit .211 in 66 games, and in the World Series he came through with a 12th-inning single to provide the Mets with their margin of victory in Game 2. It would be the last hit of his illustrious career. After being elected to the Hall of Fame in 1979, Mays took a position later the same year with Bally's Casino in Atlantic City and was suspended from involvement in major league baseball by Commissioner Bowie Kuhn until 1985, when new commissioner Peter Ueberoth removed the suspension.

CAREER GIANTS RECORD:

Games	AB	Hits	Runs
2,857	10,477	3,187	2,011
Avg	**HR**	**RBI**	**SB**
.304	646	1,859	336

McCovey, Willie (1B/OF)
(1959–1973, 1977–1980)

Willie "Stretch" McCovey, signed by the New York Giants as an amateur free agent in 1955, was the National League's all-time leading left-handed home run hitter until his total was surpassed by Barry Bonds. He first came to the majors in 1959 and retired in 1980, making him one of the few players in baseball who have played in four different decades. During the span, he slugged 521 home runs, tying him with Ted Williams on the all-time list. Eighteen of McCovey's homers were grand slams, making him second only to Lou Gehrig when McCovey retired.

In his debut game in 1959, McCovey hit two triples and two singles against Hall of Famer Robin Roberts of the Philadelphia Phillies. McCovey played in only 52 games in his rookie year, but he batted .354 with 13 homers and 38 RBIs while putting together a 23-game hitting streak. For his efforts, McCovey was voted the National League Rookie of the Year. His first seven seasons were spent as a platoon player in left field because Orlando Cepeda had a lock on first base. When Cepeda was traded to St. Louis, McCovey took over at first and remained a fixture in the Giants' infield for the next nine years. A six-time All-Star, McCovey joined an elite list in 1969 when he hit two homers in the Summer Classic, becoming just the fourth player to do so, and won the game's MVP honors. At season's end he captured the NL MVP Award after hitting .320 with 45 homers and 126 RBIs, all career highs.

By 1970 the big first baseman began to suffer from an accumulation of injuries, including blurred vision, chronic knee pain, and shoulder and hip trouble. After the 1973 season, McCovey was traded to San Diego. After three modest seasons with the Padres and A's, McCovey returned to the Giants in 1977 at the age of 39, when he led the Giants with 28 homers, 86 RBIs, and 15 game-winning hits, earning the Comeback Player of the Year Award. About all one can say of McCovey's next three years with the Giants was that he "hung on." After retirement, McCovey spent time as an executive with a linen company before joining the Giants' front office in a variety of positions. He was named to the Hall of Fame in 1986.

CAREER GIANTS RECORD:

Games	AB	Hits	Runs
2,256	7,214	1,974	1,113
Avg	**HR**	**RBI**	**SB**
.274	469	1,388	24

McGINNITY, JOE (SP/RP) (1902–1908)

Many people mistakenly assume that Joe "Iron Man" McGinnity's nickname refers to his toughness on the pitching mound (he pitched both games of a doubleheader on numerous occasions, he pitched into his 50s, and he threw many complete games, often on short rest). While all of these things are true, he actually got his nickname because he worked in an iron foundry during the offseason. McGinnity was still just pitching semipro ball in 1898 at the age of 27 when he finally hooked up with Peoria of the Western Association. He had the good fortune to pitch a 21-inning victory that was seen by a fan who knew Brooklyn owner Charles Ebbets personally. Ebbets bought McGinnity's contract, but because Brooklyn was one of the syndicate teams of the time (owners typically held simultaneous stakes in more than one team), McGinnity was sent to Baltimore. Ebbets, of course, had no way of knowing that McGinnity would lead the National League in wins with 28. The next year (1900), McGinnity was sent to Brooklyn when Baltimore left the league; there he equaled his 28-win performance from the year before, reeling off a 10-game win streak.

In 1901 the American League had become a major league and was offering much larger salaries to the players. So McGinnity jumped to the AL, where he won 26 games. Following the 1902 season, Baltimore manager John McGraw decided to part ways with AL president Ban Johnson, so he jumped to the Giants and took a lot of his top talent with him, including McGinnity.

In his first year in New York, McGinnity won 31 games and established the modern-era record for innings pitched with 434. That season he pitched both games of a doubleheader three times, winning all six games. In 1904 he put together a 14-game winning streak that ended with a 12-inning, 1–0 loss to the Cubs, a game in which Chicago pitcher Bob Wicker threw a no-hitter against the Giants for the first nine innings, but was matched zero for zero by McGinnity until the Cubs won it in the 12th.

In the famous "Merkle's Boner" game of 1908, when Fred Merkle failed to touch second base on Al Bridwell's game-winning hit, Johnny Evers supposedly retrieved the ball from the crowd and appealed the play, which ultimately caused the game to be declared a tie instead of a Giants victory. Then, because the Giants and Cubs ended up in a tie at the end of the regular season, they had to replay the infamous game to determine the league winner. The Cubs won the replayed game, and the pennant. McGinnity, however, claimed that the Evers appeal was a sham because McGinnity saw what Evers was trying to do and beat him to the ball, flinging it far into the grandstand in an effort to keep Evers from making an appeal. The replay of the Merkle's Boner game turned out to be 37-year-old McGinnity's last game in the majors. He did, however, have a long and productive minor league career, winning more than 200 games after leaving the bigs. When McGinnity was 54 years old, he pitched 268 innings for Dubuque in the Mississippi Valley League, winning 15 games. After his extensive minor league career, McGinnity became the third-base coach for Brooklyn until he died of cancer in 1929. In 1946 he was elected to the Hall of Fame.

CAREER GIANTS RECORD:

W	L	W%	ERA	SV
151	88	.632	2.38	21

K	BB	SHO	IP
787	464	26	2,151.3

NEN, ROBB (RP)
(1998–2002)

Robb Nen, one of the top relievers in baseball in the 1990s with a 100-mph fastball, was a star for the Marlins when they won the World Series in 1997. When Florida's owner decided to clean house and severely cut player salaries within days of winning the championship, Nen was one of the high-priced players put on the trading block. After coming to the Giants in a swap for Joe Fontenot, Nen proceeded to post five great years in a row, averaging 41 saves a season during that span until a severe shoulder injury ended his career. In 2003, Nen was diagnosed as having a torn labrum, a torn rotator cuff, and damage to his capsule. Any one of these could have put his career in question. Having all three left no question—at 33, he was done. *(See Marlins bio.)*

CAREER GIANTS RECORD:

W	L	W%	ERA	SV
24	25	.490	2.43	206

K	BB	SHO	IP
453	113	0	378.3

O'ROURKE, JIM (OF/C/3B/1B)
(1885–1892, 1904)

Jim O'Rourke's father died when he was a young boy. As a teenager, Jim assumed responsibility for putting food on his family's table. When he was offered his first professional contract, his mother would not let him sign until the team agreed to supply the family with a farm laborer to take his place. When Harry Wright signed him for Boston, he tried to get O'Rourke to change his last name, as the Irish were not held in high regard in Boston at the time. O'Rourke refused, saying he would rather die than give up his father's name. "Orator" Jim O'Rourke acquired his nickname because of his tendency to give ornate answers and make florid speeches about life's daily occurrences. When O'Rourke learned that Louis Sockalexis, an Indian who played for Cleveland, had a clause in his contract that prohibited him from drinking alcohol, O'Rourke observed, "I see that Sockalexis must forego frescoing his tonsils with the cardinal brush; it is so nominated in the contract of the aborigine."

O'Rourke was primarily an outfielder, but he did play 148 or more games at catcher, first, and third in his career. He played in the majors for 23 years, finishing above .300 in 14 seasons. O'Rourke played on eight championship teams and was the league leader in home runs three times (1874, 1875, and 1880). He had the distinction of collecting the first hit in National League history (a single against the Phillies on April 22, 1876). While playing with Boston, O'Rourke became upset with the team's ownership because of a $20-per-season charge for uniforms and a 50¢-per-day charge while on the road for "travel maintenance," so he jumped to the Providence team. This defection caused Boston owner Arthur H. Soden to include the dreaded reserve clause in all of his player contracts, a practice which then spread to all the other teams. Before this, players had been free to sign with any team they chose from year to year.

O'Rourke was already a 13-year veteran when he came to the Giants in 1885. He helped the Giants win the pennant and the World Series in back-to-back seasons in 1888 and 1889. O'Rourke retired as a player in 1893 at the age of 42, then spent one year as an umpire in the National League before taking over as manager of the Bridgeport team of the Connecticut League for 12 years (1897–1908) and as the league's president from 1907–1913. During one of the years he was both manager and league president, O'Rourke got into a spirited argument with an umpire, whereupon he used some choice profanity that was totally out of character for him. After he realized what he had done, he turned to the crowd and announced that President O'Rourke was fining Manager O'Rourke for using profanity.

During a late-season 1904 visit to the Polo Grounds, New York manager John McGraw let the 53-year-old O'Rourke catch the pennant-clinching game for the Giants, even though he hadn't played in 11 years. O'Rourke played well defensively and collected a single in four trips to the plate. O'Rourke had earned a law degree from Yale and in his later life served on various commissions for the city of Bridgeport. On a terribly cold New Year's Day in 1919, he walked into town to meet with a business client, catching pneumonia in the process. Seven days later he was dead. Jim O'Rourke was elected to the Hall of Fame in 1945.

CAREER GIANTS RECORD:

Games	AB	Hits	Runs
807	3,232	966	592
Avg	**HR**	**RBI**	**SB**
.299	21	446	153

OTT, MEL (OF/3B)
(1926–1947)

For more than two decades, Mel Ott was a star in a city of stars. Many New York celebrities who attended Giants games in the Polo Grounds preferred to sit in the right-field bleachers, which were known as "Ottville," to be closer to their favorite player. Ott joined the Giants when he was just 17 years old, never having played a game in the minors. For two years he sat next to John McGraw on the bench, receiving intense personal instruction from the master manager. In 1929, when he was just 20, Ott had one of the best years ever for such a young player: He hit .328 with 42 homers, 151 RBIs, 138 runs scored, and 37 doubles.

He was a terrific outfielder who played the caroms off the wall to perfection, cutting down many runners on the basepaths during his career. Ott had a unique batting style in which he raised his front foot high off the ground as the pitch approached, and then took a powerful swing that was perfectly level. From 1928 to 1945, Ott led the Giants in home runs every year, eventually becoming the first National League player to crack the 500 mark. He was helped by playing at the Polo Grounds with its intimate right-field fence—he hit 323 of his 511 career homers there. In the ten years from 1929 to1938, Ott posted 100 RBIs nine times. Thanks to a discerning eye, he is one of only five players in history to have hit 40 homers in a season and strike out fewer than 40 times. Ott also received a lot of walks, partly out of respect for his power and partly because the Giants often had no one to protect him in the lineup. Six times he led the league in walks, and four times he received five walks in a game, something no other player has accomplished more than twice.

Ott was also one of the most well liked players in the game. Dodgers manager Leo Durocher, chatting with a group of reporters during pregame workouts, once said of Ott and the Giants, "Take a look at that Number Four there. A nicer guy never drew a breath. Take a look at them. See all those guys. Nice guys. Last-place team." Filtered through the media, the comment became the immortal, "Nice guys finish last."

Ott was selected to 12 consecutive All-Star Games beginning in 1934, and in 1942 he took over as the team's player-manager, a position he held through 1947 when he retired as a player. After another year as manager, Ott joined the front office as an assistant to Carl Hubbell, who was running the team's farm system. In 1951, the same year he was enshrined in the Hall of Fame, Ott became the manager of the Oakland Oaks of the PCL. He later took a job in the broadcast booth with the Detroit Tigers for several years before dying from injuries suffered in a car accident in 1958.

CAREER GIANTS RECORD:

Games	AB	Hits	Runs
2,730	9,456	2,876	1,859
Avg	**HR**	**RBI**	**SB**
.304	511	1,860	89

PERRY, GAYLORD (SP/RP) (1962–1971)

The San Francisco Giants signed Gaylord Perry as an amateur free agent in 1958 for a team-record $73,500 bonus. After four years in the minors, Perry was first brought up to San Francisco in 1962, though he bounced back and forth between the minor leagues and San Francisco for a few years because of his tendency to do well in Triple-A, but get smoked in the majors.

After compiling a 24–30 record during his first four years, Perry knew he needed another breaking pitch to make him a complete pitcher, and his slider wasn't progressing very well. He happened to observe pitcher Bob Shaw, a wily veteran, throw a pitch that came in around thigh-high but then broke sharply to ankle-level. Curious, he had Shaw teach him the pitch—a spitball. Perry embraced the new pitch with fervor, practicing all winter long to perfect it. When he used the illegal pitch to become a 20-game winner in 1966, he was sold on his new life of crime. Perry flaunted both his new pitch as well as the rules that forbade it. Detecting Perry's use of foreign substances on the ball became almost a game between him and the umpires, opposing managers and players, and league officials. He would go through a routine on the mound that kept everyone guessing, touching his cap, mouth, belt, pants, shirt and glove, almost like hand signals. Even if he had no intention of throwing a spitter on a particular pitch, he often had the batters convinced they were about to see one. Everyone knew he was throwing a spitter, but he was caught so seldom that no one could figure out how he was applying the substance, be it saliva, grease, Vaseline, or the "spit of the day."

With 314 career wins under his belt, Perry might very well have been baseball's most successful spitball pitcher, even though the pitch was outlawed in 1920. In 1967 Perry was 15–17 with a sparkling 2.61 ERA, but he lost 10 one-run decisions. On September 17, 1968, Perry pitched a no-hitter against Bob Gibson and the Cardinals. When asked about his success, he attributed it to his "super slider." After 10 years with the Giants, Perry was traded to Cleveland for Sam McDowell following the 1971 season. While McDowell went 10–8 for the Giants with a 4.33 ERA in the fewest number of games he'd pitched in a decade, Perry won 24 games for the Indians with a 1.92 ERA, capturing the American League Cy Young Award. After posting 19 wins in 1973, Perry won 21 in 1974, including a 15-game winning streak that was one short of the AL record. Over his last nine years in the majors, Perry played for seven different teams. He returned to the National League in 1978 with the Padres and won the NL Cy Young Award at the age of 40, becoming the first pitcher ever to win the award in both leagues.

In 22 major league seasons, Perry never appeared in a World Series, the second-longest string of postseason futility next to Phil Niekro's 24 seasons. Perry's older brother, Jim, collected 215 major league wins in his own 17-year career. Together the Perry brothers won 529 games, second only to the Niekro brothers, Phil and Joe. They do, however, hold the sibling record for strikeouts (5,110) and shutouts (85). After retiring as a player, Perry returned to North Carolina to take care of his farm. In 1991, he was elected to the Hall of Fame.

CAREER GIANTS RECORD:

W	L	W%	ERA	SV
134	109	.551	2.96	10
K	BB	SHO	IP	
1,606	581	21	2,294.7	

RUSIE, AMOS (SP)
(1890–1895, 1897–1898)

Fireballer Amos Rusie played eight seasons with the Giants in the 1890s and never won fewer than 20 games in any year. Four times he posted more than 30 wins. According to legendary managers Connie Mack and John McGraw, Amos Rusie was easily the fastest pitcher in baseball. He was also the wildest—and those two traits combined to make many hitters literally afraid to stand in the box against him. He was so dominating—terrifying, actually—that in 1893, the pitcher's mound was moved back an additional 18 inches from the plate just because of him.

Rusie first came to the attention of major league personnel in 1889 while pitching for a semipro team in Indianapolis called the "Sturm Avenue Never Sweats." The National League's Boston and Washington teams had come to town to play some exhibition games, including one each against the "Sweats." After Rusie shut out both teams in back-to-back games, the race was on to secure the 18-year-old's services. The winner was Rusie's hometown team, the National League's Indianapolis Hoosiers, a third-year club. After a 12–10 rookie campaign, Rusie was suddenly out of a job when the Indianapolis team folded. The National League, engaged in a bitter war in 1890 with both the Players' League and the American Association, two rival major leagues, realized that New York had to have a showcase team in order to generate the kind of revenue they needed, so a deal was made to transfer several of the star Indianapolis players, including Rusie, to New York.

The baseball fans of 1890 were thoroughly disgusted with the events taking place in baseball's three major leagues, especially the endless shuffling and jumping of players. One bright spot was the emergence of Rusie, with his league-leading 341 strikeouts and 29 wins. Even when the big stars returned to the National League in 1891, Rusie didn't miss a beat, striking out 337 batters and winning 33 games, including a July 31 no-hitter against Brooklyn. After winning 31 more games in 1892, Rusie became a bona fide star, outshining even Roger Connor, Tim Keefe, and Buck Ewing, all of whom had large followings. Rusie inspired stories, poems, skits, and plays; songs, drinks, and books were named after him. The era's leading starlet, actress Lillian Russell, insisted on being introduced to him.

Over the last half of his tenure in New York, Rusie was in a constant battle with management over financial issues. When despised owner Andrew Freedman bought the Giants in 1895, he instituted a series of petty (and phony) player fines in an attempt to reduce player salaries. Rusie was so offended by the fines and Freedman's low-ball offer of $2,500 for his 1896 contract that he sat out the entire year and then sued Freedman for $5,000. At the time, Rusie was a great drawing card, even on the road—and because the other owners had suffered from his absence, they (much to their credit) paid Rusie the $5,000 to get him to return for the 1897 season.

The year off seemed to make Rusie a better pitcher, as he recorded the lowest walk and ERA totals of his career. His strikeout totals were down, too, but that had more to do with the fact that he was making more use of his devastating curveball, which from 60'6" was now his most effective pitch. In 1898, while making a pickoff move to first base, something popped in Rusie's shoulder and his arm immediately went dead. He sat out for the next two years, hoping his arm would come back, but it didn't. In just 22 innings for Cincinnati, Rusie allowed 43 hits and recorded only six strikeouts, compiling an 0–1 record and 8.59 ERA. Rusie's career had effectively ended at the age of 27. When he left baseball, Rusie returned to Indiana and worked in a paper mill, then did some freshwater pearling. After 10 years as a steamfitter in Seattle, Rusie spent eight years as the superintendent of the Polo Grounds before returning to Seattle. Amos "the Hoosier Thunderbolt" Rusie was elected to the Hall of Fame in 1977, his 0–1 Cincinnati stint having given him the qualifying 10 years in the majors needed for Hall of Fame consideration.

CAREER GIANTS RECORD:

W	L	W%	ERA	SV
233	163	.588	2.89	5

K	BB	SHO	IP
1,819	1,585	29	3,522.7

Schumacher, Hal (SP/RP) (1931–1942, 1946)

Right-hander Hal Schumacher was a fine complement to left-hander Carl Hubbell for a dozen years on the Giants. Together throughout the 1930s, they won a combined 358 games, third best all-time for a righty-lefty duo. Schumacher was an intelligent player who had dropped out of college to pursue his dream of playing baseball, but once he started making good money in the major leagues, he resurrected his college education and finally received his diploma from St. Lawrence in June 1933. His graduation fell on an off-day for the Giants, and the entire Giants team traveled with him by train to attend the ceremony. After Schumacher received his diploma, the Giants played an exhibition game against the university, defeating the college nine, 12–4, in front of 9,000 fans and an NBC Radio audience.

Later in his career, on a very hot day in St. Louis, Schumacher passed out from the heat while on the mound. His heart stopped, but he was revived after he was packed in ice. Schumacher, a two-time All-Star, missed three years while serving as an officer on an aircraft carrier during World War II. He returned to baseball in 1946, but after posting a 4–4 record, he retired from the game at the age of 35. Following his playing days, Schumacher spent more than two decades as the executive vice president of the Adirondack Bat Company before going to work for the Little League in Williamsport, Pennsylvania. He died in 1993.

CAREER GIANTS RECORD:

W	L	W%	ERA	SV
158	121	.566	3.36	7

K	BB	SHO	IP
906	902	27	2,482.3

TERRY, BILL (1B)
(1923–1936)

Like most players, Bill Terry liked playing baseball, but he was unsentimental about it. He played more for the money than for a love of the game, and he made no bones about it. "I'm giving this game the best years of my life," he once said. "I'd make any other business pay for that." He was stubborn, with a cold edge that made him hard to like. Forced to go to work unloading freight cars at the age of 13 to help support his mother and siblings, Terry continued to suffer financially even as a young married man, once pawning his wife's wedding ring for grocery money. On one occasion, when he was sold in the minor leagues, he refused to report to his new team, preferring instead to go to work for Standard Oil as the player-manager of their top-flight baseball team, the Polarines, at $300 per week—much more than he could make in the minor leagues.

When the legendary John McGraw saw the young first baseman play, he was determined to make him a member of the Giants. McGraw invited him to his posh suite at his Memphis hotel, where he wined him and dined him before asking him if he'd like to play for New York. Terry bluntly asked McGraw how much he'd be willing to pay. McGraw, who'd never had a player talk to him the way Terry did, was stunned. "Excuse me, Mr. McGraw, if I don't fall all over myself," said Terry, "but the Giants don't mean a thing to me unless you can make it worth my while. I'm doing all right here. I have a nice home and I'm in no hurry to leave it or the job. If I can make much more money going to New York, I'll go." After three weeks of haggling, Terry finally agreed to a $5,000-per-year contract.

After two solid seasons in the minors in which he hit .336 and .377, Terry was brought up to New York in 1923 for three games, then for good in 1924. He got off to a slow start as a platoon player, hitting .239 in his first major league campaign, but after that his average skyrocketed, topping out at .401 in 1930, making him the last National League hitter to break the .400 barrier. For his career he hit .341, 13th on the all-time list. Terry surpassed the .300 mark 11 times.

Over the years, the relationship between Terry and McGraw deteriorated, caused in part by McGraw's ridiculous attempt to cut Terry's salary by $3,000 for hitting .349 the year after hitting .401. Unlike almost every other player, Terry wasn't afraid of McGraw, giving as good as he got, finally exploding on McGraw during a game in 1932. "You've been blaming other people for the mistakes you've been making for 20 years!" Surprisingly, a short time later McGraw asked Terry if he wanted to become the team's manager, and Terry accepted. In 1933 player-manager Terry led the Giants to their first pennant in nine years and a World Series victory over Washington. He won two more pennants in 1936 (his last year as a player) and 1937, but lost the Series each time to the Yankees.

Following the 1941 season, Terry was replaced as manager by Mel Ott, but took a job as the team's farm system director for $30,000 a year. He quit suddenly a year later to return home, leaving baseball with one last parting shot: "I'm not worried about the game. No business in the world has ever made more money with poorer management. It can survive anything." In 1954 he was elected to the Hall of Fame, enduring a longer wait than necessary because of his strained relationship with the voters, baseball's writers. In 1955 his bid to purchase the Giants was rebuffed. He died in 1989.

CAREER GIANTS RECORD:

Games	AB	Hits	Runs
1,721	6,428	2,193	1,120
Avg	**HR**	**RBI**	**SB**
.341	154	1,078	56

TIERNAN, MIKE (OF)
(1887–1899)

"Silent Mike" Tiernan they called him, because he never talked about his accomplishments and rarely ever disputed an umpire's call. Originally a pitcher, he was converted to the outfield only after he demanded it, threatening to leave the game if necessary. His future as an outfielder looked a bit shaky in 1887, though, as on May 16 he committed five errors, still the single-game record for an outfielder. In 1889 he scored a whopping 147 runs in only 122 games, aided by 96 walks, and during his career, he topped the 100-run mark seven times. Tiernan played his entire 13-year career with the Giants, batting over .300 seven times and twice leading the league in homers (1890 and 1891). On June 15, 1887, Tiernan scored six of New York's 29 runs against the Phillies. Following his .255 campaign in 1898, his second consecutive sub-.300 season, Tiernan was released by the Giants, and he was out of baseball for good. After operating a popular restaurant in New York for years, Tiernan died of tuberculosis in 1918 at the age of 51.

CAREER GIANTS RECORD:

Games	AB	Hits	Runs
1,476	5,906	1,834	1,313
Avg	**HR**	**RBI**	**SB**
.311	106	851	428

VAN HALTREN, GEORGE (OF)
(1894–1903)

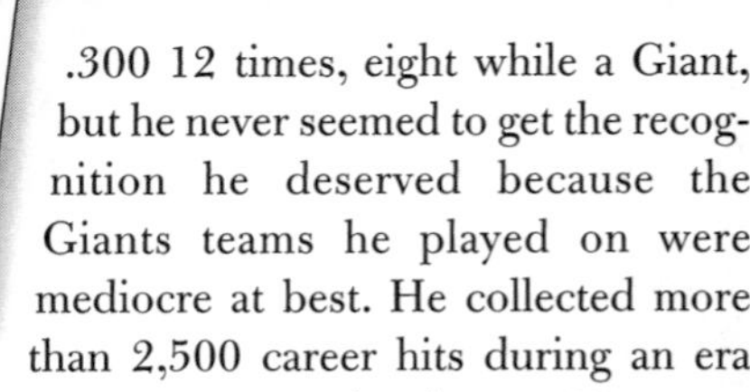

After playing for seven different teams in his first seven years in the major leagues, George "Rip" Van Haltren finally settled in with the Giants, for whom he played the last 10 seasons of his career. Originally a left-handed pitcher, he eventually became an outfielder who "ripped" line drives—hence his nickname. Van Haltren hit over .300 12 times, eight while a Giant, but he never seemed to get the recognition he deserved because the Giants teams he played on were mediocre at best. He collected more than 2,500 career hits during an era when seasons were only about 130 games long. He also topped 1,600 runs in his career, 11 times eclipsing the 100-run mark. Van

Haltren, whose name is sprinkled liberally among the league leaders in many categories throughout his career, probably ranks next to Ron Santo as a player who deserves Hall of Fame consideration, while many lesser players are already enshrined in Cooperstown.

CAREER GIANTS RECORD:

Games	AB	Hits	Runs
1,221	4,906	1,575	973
Avg	**HR**	**RBI**	**SB**
.321	29	604	320

WARD, JOHN (SS/OF) (1883–1889, 1893–1894)

John Montgomery Ward was one of the most important figures in baseball history. As a player, Ward compiled a pitching record of 164–102 primarily in six seasons; as a position player (short, second, and outfield), he played nearly 1,600 additional games, amassing more than 2,100 hits in his career. As a manager, Ward compiled a .563 winning percentage (412–320) in eight seasons, collecting four second-place finishes among his eight campaigns.

During his playing career, in 1885, Ward was instrumental in organizing the Brotherhood of Professional Base Ball Players, baseball's first union, which sought to protect the rights of the players, both individually and collectively. In 1887, as president of the Brotherhood, Ward, who had a law degree from Columbia University, published a lengthy article critical of a number of baseball issues, particularly the reserve clause. Following the 1888 season, Ward went on a world tour with Albert Spalding and a number of other stars. While the group was out of the country, league owners implemented a new salary structure that paid players according to a formula devised by the owners. The new formula, of course, lowered player salaries and then froze them. For more than a year, the players—led by Ward—tried to negotiate the matter with the owners, to no avail. So in 1890, the players—again led by Ward—formed their own circuit called the Players' League, making for three major leagues. The Players' League fared the best of the three entities in terms of attendance, but still lost money, although not as much as the American Association and the National League. After the 1890 season, the backers of the Players' League lost heart for the protracted labor battle and pulled their funding, causing the league to fold. A year later the American Association collapsed as well, and it took years for the National League to recoup its huge losses of 1890.

As for his playing career, Ward's two best years as a pitcher were 1879 and 1880 with the Providence Grays of the National League, when he won 47 and 39 games respectively, including major league baseball's second perfect game, a 5–0 gem over Buffalo on June 17, 1880. When Ward wasn't pitching, he usually played another position, mostly shortstop, second base, or the outfield. His career average was .275; five times he passed the 100-run mark. Ward stole more than 500 bases in his career, collecting 50 or more five times, including a career-best 111 in 1887, although the rules regarding the crediting of stolen bases were different that year. (Base runners were credited with a stolen base whenever they took an extra base on either a hit or an out.)

After the Players' League folded, Ward, who was player-manager of the Brooklyn franchise, was given stock in the National League's Brooklyn team as part of the overall three-league settlement. Later he acquired stock in the New York Giants after winning a bet with one of New York's owners, thus giving him ownership interest in two teams at the same time, not an uncommon thing at the time. (Many of the National League's owners held stock in the Giants, the league's preeminent and most profitable team.) In 1894, at the age of 34, Ward retired from baseball, though he was still an able player. He had just grown weary of dealing with the despicable principal owner of the Giants, Andrew Freedman.

After his playing career was over, Ward became a leading corporate attorney in New York. It was Ward who represented pitcher Amos Rusie in his lawsuit against Freedman for lost salary. Ward continued to keep his finger in baseball over the years, conducting an unsuccessful bid to become NL president in 1909, becoming president and part-owner of the Braves in 1911, and business manager of the Federal League's Brooklyn Tip-Tops in 1913. He was the founder of the Long Island Golf Association and authored several books and many magazine articles on baseball. In 1964 Ward was elected to the Hall of Fame.

CAREER GIANTS RECORD:

Games	AB	Hits	Runs
1,070	4,461	1,245	828
Avg	**HR**	**RBI**	**SB**
.279	17	546	332

WELCH, MICKEY (SP)
(1883–1892)

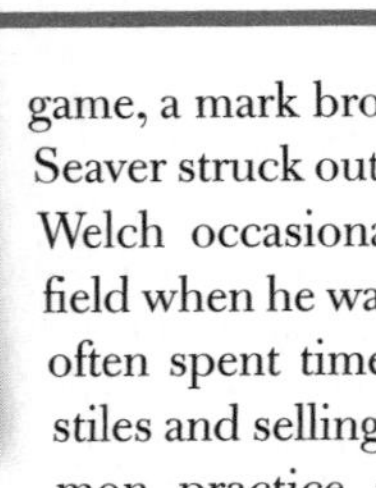

Mickey Welch began his career in the National League by spending three seasons playing for the Troy Trojans. When the team's charter was revoked following the 1882 season, Welch was shuttled to the Gothams (later to become the Giants) by John Day, the man who bought the disbanded team and divided the good players between the two teams he owned, the New York Giants of the NL, and the New York Metropolitans of the AA.

Welch spent the next 10 years with the Giants, winning 25 or more games six times during that span. In 1885, his best year, he went 44–11 with a 1.66 ERA, winning 17 straight games at one point. On August 28, 1884, Welch established a major league record when he fanned nine consecutive batters in a game, a mark broken only when Tom Seaver struck out 10 in a row in 1970. Welch occasionally played the outfield when he wasn't pitching, and he often spent time watching the turnstiles and selling tickets, a fairly common practice at the time. Welch started 549 games in his career, completing an incredible 525 of them, and collecting 308 wins. Following his playing career, Welch was a custodian at the Polo Grounds for many years, and could always be found chatting and reminiscing with the fans. In 1973 he was elected to the Hall of Fame.

CAREER GIANTS RECORD:

W	L	W%	ERA	SV
238	146	.620	2.69	4
K	**BB**	**SHO**	**IP**	
1,570	1,077	28	3,579.0	

WILTSE, HOOKS (SP/RP)
(1904–1914)

Left-hander George "Hooks" Wiltse pitched on the same team as Christy Mathewson for more than a decade, and today they still rank as the second-best lefty-righty combination in major league history with 435 victories, trailing only Warren Spahn and Lew Burdette. In his first season with the Giants, Wiltse had a 12-game winning streak on his way to a 13–3 record. He is one of a handful of pitchers to strike out four batters in an inning, accomplishing the feat on May 15, 1906. His best years were 1908 and 1909, when he won 23 and 20 games respectively, including a no-hitter against the Phillies on July 4, 1908. Hooks got his nickname not from his curveball, as many think, but from the way in which he "hooked" ground balls that were hit at him on the mound. After 11 years in New York, Wiltse jumped to the Brooklyn Tip-Tops, but after going 3–5 in his only season with anyone other than the Giants, his career ended in 1915 right along with the Federal League.

CAREER GIANTS RECORD:

W	L	W%	ERA	SV
136	85	.615	2.48	29
K	**BB**	**SHO**	**IP**	
948	491	27	2,053.0	

YOUNGS, ROSS (OF)
(1917–1926)

Ross Youngs was a speedy outfielder with a powerful arm who scorched the minor leagues in 1916 and 1917, hitting .362 and .346 before being called up to New York at the end of the 1917 season. Youngs, a personal favorite of John McGraw's, hit over .300 in nine of his 10 major league seasons. He played a major role in helping the Giants win four pennants in a row from 1921 to 1924, two of which resulted in World Series titles. In the 1921 World Series he hit a triple and a double in the seventh inning, the first player ever to collect two hits in one inning in World Series play. Youngs also stole home 10 times during his career, and once hit three triples in a game.

In June 1926 Youngs suddenly became ill and had to be hospitalized for what turned out to be a severe urinary tract infection that had begun in his throat and moved to his kidneys. He returned to the team in August, but was under constant medical supervision. He took a turn for the worse after the season, however, and was bedridden for the entire 1927 campaign. In October, Youngs died, and McGraw was devastated, calling him the greatest outfielder he ever saw. During his long career, McGraw kept pictures of only two players in his office—Christy Mathewson and Ross Youngs, who was elected to the Hall of Fame in 1972, barely having fulfilled the required 10-year term in the major leagues.

CAREER GIANTS RECORD:

Games	AB	Hits	Runs
1,211	4,627	1,491	812
Avg	**HR**	**RBI**	**SB**
.322	42	592	153

The Giants under the lights against the Boston Braves in the late 1930s.

Seattle Mariners

Since 1977

1989 Team Ball

1977 The first official Mariners game draws 57,762 fans, an all-time American League record for a night game opener and the highest single-game attendance for an expansion team in a U.S. city.... **1983** The Mariners are so bad (winning only 60 games all year) that the largest crowd of the season—37,807—comes mostly to see a postgame concert by the Beach Boys.... **1991** The Mariners clinch their first-ever winning season (83–79) by beating the White Sox 6–4 on October 4. They help their cause with 39 come-from-behind victories during the season.... **2001** During Seattle's incredible 116-win season, the Mariners are 59–22 on the road, an all-time American League record. Of 26 series away from home, they lose only one and split four.

FRANCHISE HISTORY

The Seattle Mariners began play in 1977 when the American League expanded from 12 teams to 14. The team joined the West Division while the Toronto Blue Jays were assigned to the East Division. One deciding factor in awarding Seattle a franchise was a pending $90 million lawsuit by the city of Seattle against Major League Baseball over the quick departure of the Seattle Pilots to Milwaukee (where the team became known as the Brewers) after a single season in 1969. (In fairness to Major League Baseball, Seattle's ballpark, Sick's Stadium, was far too small and the city failed to approve a new park. In addition, the franchise was in such poor financial condition that the American League had to loan the team $650,000 to stay afloat during the season. The Pilots' owners tried but failed to find local buyers for the team, necessitating the move to Milwaukee.) Once the Kingdome was completed in 1976—primarily for the NFL's Seattle Seahawks—Major League Baseball approved the new franchise in Seattle.

The original owners of the Mariners were a group of seven equal partners, including famed entertainer Danny Kaye. The managing partner was Les Smith, owner of numerous Pacific Northwest radio stations, among other businesses. The original owners held the team until January 1981 when they sold majority interest to Southern California entrepreneur George Argyros, who had made his fortune in real estate and the airline industry. The flamboyant Argyros made many grand statements to the media about how he was going to bring a contender to Seattle and make

> Half of Griffey's 56 homers in 1997 traveled more than 400 feet.

Ken Griffey Jr. scores one of the 1,063 runs he totaled for the Mariners from 1989 to 1999.

the franchise a showcase on the order of the Yankees or Red Sox. He failed so miserably that one local radio station repeatedly played a song parody that mercilessly poked fun at him. He eventually gave up his dream and sold the Mariners to Indianapolis businessman Jeff Smulyan in 1989 for $76 million.

The Mariners enjoyed some minor success under Smulyan's tenure, finishing over .500 for the first time (1991) with the debut of superstar Ken Griffey Jr. Still, operating losses mounted and Smulyan gave up the battle of trying to make a small-market club profitable. He sold the Mariners in June 1992 to Japanese corporate giant Nintendo, but not before a battle within baseball's inner circle. Commissioner Fay Vincent, concerned about foreign ownership, originally nixed the deal, but eventually relented. Nintendo paid $125 million for the team, but continued to lose huge amounts of money—$67 million in the first four years alone—before a winning team and the construction of new Safeco Field turned things around. About the huge early losses suffered by Nintendo, company president Hiroshi Yamauchi explained that since the company had such a heavy presence in Seattle, he felt it was their civic duty to invest in the team, and that profit was not their main motive.

The popular Jay Buhner scalps his father on Jay Buhner Buzz Cut Night in 1999.

On the field, the Mariners did not enjoy the early success realized by their expansion mates, the Blue Jays. In the time it took Toronto to win five division titles, two American League pennants, and two World Series, the Mariners barely managed two winning seasons. In the next decade, however, Seattle's fortunes changed for the better. With the arrival of Ken Griffey Jr., Edgar Martinez, Randy Johnson, Alex Rodriguez, Ichiro Suzuki, and others, the Mariners became a force in the American League. While the Mariners still hadn't made it to the World Series as of the 2005 season, they went to the American League Championship Series in 2001 (losing to the Yankees, 4–1) on the strength of a 116-win season, which set an American League record and tied the nearly century-old major league record held by the Cubs set back in 1906.

TEAM NAME HISTORY

Official Names

Mariners (1977–current)

Unofficial Names/Nicknames:

M's

STADIUM HISTORY

The Kingdome	1977–June 27, 1999
Safeco Field	July 15, 1999–current

YEARLY RECORD, FINISH, & ATTENDANCE FIGURES

Year	League	Record	DIV/LG. Finish	Attendance	Avg/Gm
2005	AL West	69–93	4	2,725,459	33,648
2004	AL West	63–99	4	2,940,731	35,863
2003	AL West	93–69	2	3,268,509	40,352
2002	AL West	93–69	3	3,542,938	43,740
2001	AL West	116–46	1	3,507,326	43,300
2000	AL West	91–71	2	2,914,624	35,983
1999	AL West	79–83	3	2,916,346	36,004
1998	AL West	76–85	3	2,651,511	32,735
1997	AL West	90–72	1	3,192,237	39,410
1996	AL West	85–76	2	2,723,850	33,628
1995	AL West	79–66	1	1,643,203	22,510
1994	AL West	49–63	3	1,104,206	25,096
1993	AL West	82–80	4	2,052,638	25,341
1992	AL West	64–98	7	1,651,367	20,387
1991	AL West	83–79	5	2,052,638	26,517
1990	AL West	77–85	5	1,651,367	18,639
1989	AL West	73–89	6	2,147,905	16,030
1988	AL West	68–93	7	1,509,727	12,622
1987	AL West	78–84	4	1,298,443	14,003
1986	AL West	67–95	7	1,029,045	12,549
1985	AL West	74–88	6	1,128,696	13,599
1984	AL West	74–88	5	870,372	10,745
1983	AL West	60–102	7	813,537	10,044
1982	AL West	76–86	4	1,070,404	13,215
1981	AL West	44–65	6/5	636,276	11,163
1980	AL West	59–103	7	836,204	10,324
1979	AL West	67–95	6	844,447	10,425
1978	AL West	56–104	7	877,440	10,833
1977	AL West	64–98	6	1,338,511	16,525

MANAGER HISTORY

Manager	Years	W–L	Win %
Darrell Johnson	1977–1980	226–362	.384
Maury Wills	1980–1981	26–56	.317
Rene Lachemann	1981–1983	140–180	.438
Del Crandall	1983–1984	93–141	.397
Chuck Cottier	1984–1986	98–119	.452
Marty Martinez	1986	0–1	.000
Dick Williams	1986–1988	159–192	.453
Jimmy Snyder	1988	45–60	.429
Jim Lefebvre	1989–1991	233–253	.479
Bill Plummer	1992	64–98	.395
Lou Piniella	1993–2002	840–711	.542
Bob Melvin	2003–2004	156–168	.481
Mike Hargrove	2005–current	69–93	.426

ALL-TIME WIN-LOSS RECORDS VS. ALL OPPONENTS

Opponent	Record
ALL-TIME	2,149–2,424
Angels	190–211
Astros	3–3
Athletics	162–233
Blue Jays	144–160
Braves	2–1
Brewers	112–115
Cardinals	2–4
Cubs	1–2
Devil Rays	45–30
Diamondbacks	7–5
Dodgers	8–8
Giants	7–9
Indians	133–175
INTERLEAGUE	84–74
Marlins	2–1
Mets	5–1
Nationals	4–5
Orioles	143–174
Padres	19–25
Phillies	5–1
Pirates	3–0
Rangers	212–196
Reds	3–0
Red Sox	133–187
Rockies	12–7
Royals	164–82
Tigers	142–166
Twins	179–164
White Sox	163–181
Yankees	143–176

The Seattle Kingdome is blown to kingdome come on March 26, 2000.

Franchise Highlights, Low Points, and Strange Distinctions

1980 Mike Parrott, the ace of the Mariners in 1979, got the Opening Day start in 1980 and defeated the Toronto Blue Jays 8–6, then proceeded to lose an incredible 16 straight games.

• • • •

1981 Amazingly, only one player in the major leagues hit three homers in one game: Mariner Jeff Burroughs. His three clouts against the Twins on August 15 led the M's to a 6–0 victory.

In the strike-shortened, split season, when major league teams played around 55 games in each half of the season, Gary Gray slugged 13 homers in the first half and none in the second half.

• • • •

1984 Seattle's fortunes changed with the arrival of two talented rookies, Alvin Davis and Mark Langston. Davis had an incredible year in which he set major league rookie records for most intentional walks (16) and game-winning RBIs (13). Langston became the first rookie since Herb Score in 1955 to lead the league in strikeouts, with 204.

The Mariners team was in such a state of irritability and "confused disarray" in August that pitching coach Frank Funk and catcher Bob Kearney actually got into an on-field fistfight. Funk, popular with the pitching staff, was fired by manager Del Crandall, who in turn was fired a week later.

1989 Ken Griffey Jr. was well on his way to winning the American League Rookie of the Year Award when, on July 24, he fell in a shower in a Chicago hotel room and broke his hand. After missing a month, he came back, but struggled to hit even .200 the rest of the way, and he ended up third in the ROY balloting.

• • • •

1989–90 Manager Jim Lefebvre had to contend with so many injuries in his first two seasons at the Mariners' helm (1989–1990) that he used more than 200 different lineups.

• • • •

1992 Rookie left-hander Dave Fleming got bombed in his first start, 9–1 by the Rangers, then proceeded to reel off a club-record nine straight wins.

• • • •

1993 No Mariner hit for the cycle until June 23, in the team's 17th season. Surprisingly, the slow-footed Jay Buhner accomplished the feat against the Oakland A's.

From July 20–28, Ken Griffey Jr. hit home runs in eight consecutive games, tying the major league record held by Don Mattingly and Dale Long.

When Randy Johnson struck out over 300 batters, he became the first left-hander in the majors to accomplish the feat since Steve Carlton did it for Philadelphia in 1972.

1994 Shortly before the July 19 game against Baltimore was to begin in the Kingdome, several 26-pound ceiling tiles fell from the roof. Fearing for the safety of fans and players, the team cancelled the game. During the repair work, three workers were injured and two were killed when their crane bucket fell 250 feet to the stadium floor. After further inspection, it was decided the Kingdome ceiling would need to be repaired before games could again be played in the facility. As a result, the Mariners were forced to play their next 20 games on the road, and because of the season-ending labor stoppage, these were the last 20 games of the season. The resulting 22-day road trip covered a major league record 10,425 miles. The Mariners had just completed a 10-game road trip prior to a five-game homestand before the tile incident, meaning the team played 30 of its last 35 games on the road.

The strike-shortened season might have cost Ken Griffey Jr. a new home-run record. At the end of May he had 22 homers, breaking Mickey Mantle's all-time record for the first two months of a season (20 in 1956), and by the end of June, Griffey had 32 (Ruth had 30 in both 1928 and 1930).

• • • •

1995 That the Mariners made it to the playoffs at all is amazing considering that on August 20, Seattle was 12 1/2 games behind the Angels and had lost Ken Griffey Jr. for 73 games due to injury.

2001 During Seattle's 116-win season, the Mariners didn't lose more than two consecutive games all season until Oakland swept them in a three-game series on September 21–23. The M's also became the first team since the 1948 Cleveland Indians to lead the league in batting average (.288), earned run average (3.54), and fielding average (.986).

• • • •

2004 On September 22, Raul Ibañez tied the American League record for hits in a nine-inning game when he went 6-for-6 against the Angels.

When Ichiro Suzuki collected 262 hits in the 2004 season for a new major league record, it was also his fourth straight 200-hit season, making him the first player in major league history to collect at least 200 hits in his first four seasons in the majors. Suzuki followed it up with 206 hits in 2005 for five straight 200-hit seasons, although his hit total was the lowest of his five-year major league career. His 262 hits in 2004 were also the most ever by a batting champion, as were his 704 at-bats. Suzuki had 127 more hits than the NL batting champion, Barry Bonds—the greatest difference in number of hits between the two leagues' batting champs.

Special Achievements

World Series Results

None

World Series Managerial Records

None

All-Time Postseason Record

Divisional Playoffs	10–7
League Championship Series	5–12
World Series	0–0

All-Star Games at Seattle

Year	Date	Winner	Score	Stadium
1979	July 17	National	7–6	The Kingdome
2001	July 10	American	4–1	Safeco Field

Hall of Famers Who Played for Team

	Position	Years	Games with Seattle
Gaylord Perry	SP	1982–1983	48

Hall of Famers Who Managed Team

None

MVP Award Winners

Ken Griffey Jr.	OF	1997
Ichiro Suzuki	OF	2001

Cy Young Award Winners

Pitcher	Year	W–L	ERA
Randy Johnson	1995	18–2	2.48

Rookie of the Year Award Winners

Alvin Davis	1B	1984
Kazuhiro Sasaki	RP	2000
Ichiro Suzuki	OF	2001

Gold Glove Winners

Year	Position	Player
1987	SP	Mark Langston
1988	SP	Mark Langston
	2B	Harold Reynolds
1989	2B	Harold Reynolds
1990	2B	Harold Reynolds
	OF	Ken Griffey Jr.
1991	OF	Ken Griffey Jr.
1992	OF	Ken Griffey Jr.
1993	SS	Omar Vizquel
	OF	Ken Griffey Jr.
1994	OF	Ken Griffey Jr.
1995	OF	Ken Griffey Jr.
1996	OF	Ken Griffey Jr.
	OF	Jay Buhner
1997	OF	Ken Griffey Jr.
1998	OF	Ken Griffey Jr.
1999	OF	Ken Griffey Jr.
2000	1B	John Olerud
2001	OF	Mike Cameron
	OF	Ichiro Suzuki
2002	1B	John Olerud
	2B	Bret Boone
	OF	Ichiro Suzuki
2003	1B	John Olerud
	2B	Bret Boone
	OF	Mike Cameron
	OF	Ichiro Suzuki
2004	2B	Bret Boone
	OF	Ichiro Suzuki
2005	OF	Ichiro Suzuki

Triple Crown Winners

None

Fireman of the Year Award Winners

None

World Series MVP

None

League Championship Series MVP

None

All-Star Game MVP

None

MANAGER OF THE YEAR AWARD WINNERS

Lou Piniella	1995
Lou Piniella	2001

BATTING CHAMPIONS

Year	Player	Avg
1992	Edgar Martinez	.343
1995	Edgar Martinez	.356
1996	Alex Rodriguez	.358
2001	Ichiro Suzuki	.350
2004	Ichiro Suzuki	.372

NINE-INNING NO-HITTERS PITCHED

Year	Pitcher	Opp.	Score
1990	Randy Johnson	DET	2–0
1993	Chris Bosio	BOS	7–0

20-GAME WINNERS

Year	Pitcher	W–L
1997	Randy Johnson	20–4
2001	Jamie Moyer	20–6
2003	Jamie Moyer	21–7

RETIRED UNIFORM NUMBERS

None

TEAM RECORDS—WINS & LOSSES

- Games won in a season: 116 in 2001
- Games lost in a season: 104 in 1978
- Games won in a month: 20, four times (June 1997 and April/May/August 2001)
- Games lost in a month: 22, August 1977
- Consecutive games won: 15 in 2001
- Consecutive games lost: 14 in 1992
- Biggest shutout victory: 14–0, 3 times (August 7, 1987 vs. Angels; May 15, 2000 vs. Twins; Sept. 16, 2000 vs. Orioles)
- Biggest shutout loss: 15–0 to Minnesota on July 10, 1977
- Highest winning percentage: .716 in 2001 (116–46)
- Lowest winning percentage: .350 in 1978 (56–104)

TEAM RECORDS—BATTING

- Highest team batting average: .288 in 2001
- Lowest team batting average: .240 in 1983
- Highest team slugging average: .485 in 1997
- Highest team on-base percentage: .366 in 1996
- Total hits: 1,637 in 2001
- Extra-base hits: 607 in 1996
- Hits in a game: 24, three times: vs. Minnesota on June 11, 1996, Anaheim on September 22, 2004, and Boston September 3, 1981 (20 innings)
- Longest individual hitting streak: 24, Joey Cora, 1997
- Most .300 hitters in a season: 4 in 1997 and 2001
- Home runs: 264 in 1997
- Home runs in a month: 15, Ken Griffey Jr., May 1994
- Home runs in a game: 7, accomplished four times
- Home runs by a rookie: 27, Alvin Davis, 1984
- Home runs by a righthander: 44, Jay Buhner, 1996
- Home runs by a lefthander: 56, Ken Griffey Jr., 1997 and 1998
- Home runs by a switch-hitter: 19, David Segui, 1998
- Grand slams: 11 in 1996 and 2000
- Grand slams (individual; season): 4, Edgar Martinez, 2000
- Grand slams (individual; career): 12, Ken Griffey Jr.
- Triples: 52 in 1979
- Doubles: 343 in 1996
- Singles: 1,120 in 2001
- Walks: 775 in 2000
- Runs scored: 993 in 1996
- Runs scored in a game: 22 vs. Detroit on April 29, 1999
- Runs scored in an inning: 11 vs. Detroit on April 29, 1999 (fifth inning) and White Sox on May 12, 1997 (seventh inning)
- Most batters hit by a pitch: 75 in 1996
- Times shut out: 15, three times: 1978, 1983, and 1990
- Grounded into double plays: 158 in 1979
- Fewest grounded into double plays: 101 in 1984
- Runners left on base: 1,257 in 2001

TEAM RECORDS—BASERUNNING

- Stolen bases: 174 in 1987 and 2001
- Caught stealing: 82 in 1982

Team Records—Pitching

- Lowest earned run average: 3.54 in 2001
- Complete games: 39 in 1987
- Saves: 56 in 2001
- Strikeouts: 1,207 in 1997
- Shutouts: 15 in 2003
- Walks: 684 in 1999
- Hit batsmen: 72 in 2004
- Wild pitches: 82 in 1991
- Consecutive wins (individual): 10, Paul Abbot and Jamie Moyer, both in 2001
- Consecutive losses (individual): 16, Mike Parrott in 1980
- Strikeouts in a game (individual): 19, Randy Johnson (twice) on June 24, 1997 and August 8, 1997
- Runs allowed in a game: 20 vs. Detroit, April 17, 1993

Team Records—Fielding

- Best fielding average: .989 in 2003
- Most errors committed: 156 in 1986
- Fewest errors committed: 65 in 2003
- Most double plays turned: 191 in 1986
- Fewest double plays turned: 134 in 2002

Team Records—Miscellaneous

- Number of times league champions: 0
- Number of times finishing last in league: 5
- Largest attendance, single game: 57,822 vs. Cleveland, March 31, 1998
- Largest attendance, doubleheader: 32,597 vs. Angels, August 12, 1985
- Players used in a season: 51 in 1999
- Seasons played: 18, Edgar Martinez

Primary Pitching Staffs

Year	Starter	Starter	Starter	Starter	Starter	Closer	Bullpen	Bullpen	Bullpen
2005	Moyer	Pineiro	Franklin	Meche	Sele	Guardado	Putz	Thornton	Mateo
2004	Moyer	Franklin	Meche	Pineiro	Garcia	Guardado	Hasegawa	Villone	Putz
2003	Moyer	Franklin	Meche	Pineiro	Garcia	Hasegawa	Rhodes	Mateo	Nelson
2002	Moyer	Franklin	Baldwin	Pineiro	Garcia	Sasaki	Rhodes	Hasegawa	Nelson
2001	Moyer	Sele	Abbott	Halama	Garcia	Sasaki	Rhodes	Paniagua	Nelson
2000	Moyer	Sele	Abbott	Halama	Garcia	Sasaki	Rhodes	Paniagua	Mesa
1999	Moyer	Fassero	Meche	Halama	Garcia	Mesa	Rodriguez	Paniagua	Cloude
1998	Moyer	Fassero	Cloude	Swift	Johnson	Timlin	Spoljaric	Slocumb	Ayala
1997	Moyer	Fassero	Wolcott	Olivares	Johnson	Charlton	McCarthy	Wells	Ayala
1996	Hitchcock	Wells	Wolcott	Wagner	Mulholland	Charlton	Carmona	Jackson	Ayala
1995	Bosio	Johnson	Belcher	Torres	Benes	Ayala	Nelson	Risley	Wells
1994	Bosio	Johnson	Fleming	Hibbard	Salkeld	Ayala	Gossage	Risley	Davis
1993	Bosio	Johnson	Fleming	Hanson	Leary	Charlton	Nelson	Powell	Henry
1992	Fisher	Johnson	Fleming	Hanson	DeLucia	Schooler	Nelson	Powell	Swan
1991	Holman	Johnson	Krueger	Hanson	DeLucia	Swift	Jackson	Murphy	Swan
1990	Holman	Johnson	Young	Hanson	Swan	Schooler	Jackson	Comstock	Swift
1989	Holman	Johnson	Bankhead	Hanson	Swift	Schooler	Jackson	Reed	Powell
1988	Langston	Moore	Bankhead	Campbell	Swift	Schooler	Jackson	Reed	Scurry
1987	Langston	Moore	Bankhead	Morgan	Guetterman	Nunez	Wilkinson	Trujillo	Reed
1986	Langston	Moore	Swift	Morgan	Wilcox	Young	Huismann	Guetterman	Ladd
1985	Langston	Moore	Swift	Young	Wills	Nunez	Vande Berg	Thomas	Long
1984	Langston	Moore	Beattie	Young	Vande Berg	Stanton	Mirabella	Beard	Nunez
1983	Stoddard	Moore	Beattie	Young	Clark	Caudill	Vande Berg	Stanton	Thomas
1982	Bannister	Moore	Beattie	Perry	Nelson	Caudill	Vande Berg	Andersen	Stanton
1981	Bannister	Abbott	Clay	Gleaton	Parrott	Rawley	Drago	Andersen	Clark
1980	Bannister	Abbott	Honeycutt	Beattie	Parrott	Rawley	McLaughlin	Heaverlo	Roberts
1979	Bannister	Abbott	Honeycutt	Jones	Parrott	McLaughlin	Rawley	Montague	Stein
1978	Mitchell	Abbott	Honeycutt	Colborn	Pole	Romo	Rawley	Todd	House
1977	Wheelock	Abbott	Montague	House	Pole	Romo	Laxton	Kekich	Segui

PRIMARY STARTING LINEUPS

Year	C	1B	2B	3B	SS	LF	CF	RF	DH
2005	Olivo	Sexson	Boone	Beltre	Morse	Winn	Reed	Suzuki	Ibanez
2004	Wilson	Olerud	Boone	Spiezio	Aurilia	Ibanez	Winn	Suzuki	Martinez
2003	Wilson	Olerud	Boone	Cirillo	Guillen	Winn	Cameron	Suzuki	Martinez
2002	Wilson	Olerud	Boone	Cirillo	Guillen	McLemore	Cameron	Suzuki	Martinez
2001	Wilson	Olerud	Boone	Bell	Guillen	Martin	Cameron	Suzuki	Martinez
2000	Wilson	Olerud	McLemore	Bell	Rodriguez	Henderson	Cameron	Buhner	Martinez
1999	Wilson	Segui	Bell	Davis	Rodriguez	Hunter	Griffey	Buhner	Martinez
1998	Wilson	Segui	Cora	Davis	Rodriguez	Hill	Griffey	Buhner	Martinez
1997	Wilson	Sorrento	Cora	Davis	Rodriguez	Cruz	Griffey	Buhner	Martinez
1996	Wilson	Sorrento	Cora	Davis	Rodriguez	Amaral	Griffey	Buhner	Martinez
1995	Wilson	Martinez	Cora	Blowers	Sojo	Amaral	Griffey	Buhner	Martinez
1994	Wilson	Martinez	Amaral	Martinez	Fermin	Anthony	Griffey	Buhner	Jefferson
1993	Valle	Martinez	Amaral	Blowers	Vizquel	Felder	Griffey	Buhner	O'Brien
1992	Valle	O'Brien	Reynolds	Martinez	Vizquel	Mitchell	Griffey	Buhner	Martinez
1991	Valle	O'Brien	Reynolds	Martinez	Vizquel	Briley	Griffey	Buhner	Davis
1990	Valle	O'Brien	Reynolds	Martinez	Vizquel	Leonard	Griffey	Cotto	Davis
1989	Valle	Davis	Reynolds	Presley	Vizquel	Briley	Griffey	Coles	Leonard
1988	Bradley	Davis	Reynolds	Presley	Quinones	Brantley	Cotto	Wilson	Phelps
1987	Bradley	Davis	Reynolds	Presley	Quinones	Bradley	Moses	Kingery	Phelps
1986	Kearney	Davis	Reynolds	Presley	Owen	Bradley	Moses	Tartabull	Phelps
1985	Kearney	Davis	Perconte	Presley	Owen	Bradley	Henderson	Cowens	Thomas
1984	Kearney	Davis	Perconte	Presley	Owen	Bonnell	Henderson	Cowens	Phelps
1983	Sweet	Putnam	Bernazard	Allen	Owen	Henderson	Henderson	Cowens	Zisk
1982	Sweet	Gray	Cruz	Castillo	Cruz	Bochte	Henderson	Cowens	Zisk
1981	Narron	Bochte	Cruz	Randle	Anderson	Paciorek	Simpson	Burroughs	Zisk
1980	Cox	Bochte	Cruz	Cox	Mendoza	Meyer	Beniquez	Roberts	Horton
1979	Cox	Bochte	Cruz	Meyer	Mendoza	Paciorek	Jones	Simpson	Horton
1978	Stinson	Meyer	Cruz	Stein	Reynolds	Bochte	Jones	Roberts	Stanton
1977	Stinson	Meyer	Baez	Stein	Reynolds	Braun	Jones	Lopez	Bernhardt

Top 10 Batting Leaders, Single Season & Career with Team

GAMES PLAYED: CAREER WITH TEAM

Player	G	PA
1. Edgar Martinez	2,055	8,672
2. Ken Griffey Jr.	1,535	6,688
3. Jay Buhner	1,440	5,828
4. Dan Wilson	1,251	4,500
5. Alvin Davis	1,166	4,892
6. Harold Reynolds	1,155	4,593
7. Dave Valle	846	2,834
8. Bret Boone	803	3,467
9. Jim Presley	799	3,175
10. Ichiro Suzuki	796	3,692

AT-BATS: SEASON

Player	AB	Year
1. Ichiro Suzuki	704	2004
2. Ichiro Suzuki	692	2001
3. Alex Rodriguez	686	1998
4. Ichiro Suzuki	679	2003
Ichiro Suzuki	679	2005
6. Ichiro Suzuki	647	2002
7. Willie Horton	646	1979
8. Harold Reynolds	642	1990
9. Phil Bradley	641	1985
10. Ken Griffey Jr.	633	1998

AT-BATS: CAREER WITH TEAM

Player	AB	PA
1. Edgar Martinez	7,213	8,672
2. Ken Griffey Jr.	5,832	6,688
3. Jay Buhner	4,922	5,828
4. Alvin Davis	4,136	4,892
5. Harold Reynolds	4,090	4,593
6. Dan Wilson	4,085	4,500
7. Ichiro Suzuki	3,401	3,692
8. Alex Rodriguez	3,126	3,515
9. Bret Boone	3,119	3,467
10. Jim Presley	2,946	3,175

Batting Average: Season

Player	BA	Year
1. Ichiro Suzuki	.372	2004
2. Alex Rodriguez	.358	1996
3. Edgar Martinez	.356	1995
4. Ichiro Suzuki	.350	2001
5. Edgar Martinez	.343	1992
6. Edgar Martinez	.337	1999
7. Bret Boone	.331	2001
8. Edgar Martinez	.330	1997
9. Edgar Martinez	.327	1996
Ken Griffey Jr.	.327	1991

Batting Average: Career with Team

Player	BA	PA
1. Ichiro Suzuki	.332	3,692
2. Edgar Martinez	.312	8,672
3. Alex Rodriguez	.309	3,515
4. Phil Bradley	.301	2,476
5. Ken Griffey Jr.	.299	6,688
6. Joey Cora	.293	2,317
7. Bruce Bochte	.290	2,770
8. John Olerud	.285	2,976
9. Alvin Davis	.281	4,892
10. Bret Boone	.277	3,467

Total Hits: Season

Player	H	Year
1. Ichiro Suzuki	262	2004
2. Ichiro Suzuki	242	2001
3. Alex Rodriguez	215	1996
4. Alex Rodriguez	213	1998
5. Ichiro Suzuki	212	2003
6. Ichiro Suzuki	208	2002
7. Bret Boone	206	2001
Ichiro Suzuki	206	2005
9. Phil Bradley	192	1985
10. Ken Griffey Jr.	185	1997

Total Hits: Career with Team

Player	H	PA
1. Edgar Martinez	2,247	8,672
2. Ken Griffey Jr.	1,742	6,688
3. Jay Buhner	1,255	5,828
4. Alvin Davis	1,163	4,892
5. Ichiro Suzuki	1,130	3,692
6. Dan Wilson	1,071	4,500
7. Harold Reynolds	1,063	4,593
8. Alex Rodriguez	966	3,515
9. Bret Boone	863	3,467
10. Jim Presley	736	3,175

Home Runs: Season

Player	HR	Year
1. Ken Griffey Jr.	56	1997
Ken Griffey Jr.	56	1998
3. Ken Griffey Jr.	49	1996
4. Ken Griffey Jr.	48	1999
5. Ken Griffey Jr.	45	1993
6. Jay Buhner	44	1996
7. Alex Rodriguez	42	1998
Alex Rodriguez	42	1999
9. Alex Rodriguez	41	2000
10. Jay Buhner	40	1995
Jay Buhner	40	1997
Ken Griffey Jr.	40	1994

Home Runs: Career with Team

Player	HR	PA
1. Ken Griffey Jr.	398	6,688
2. Edgar Martinez	309	8,672
3. Jay Buhner	307	5,828
4. Alex Rodriguez	189	3,515
5. Alvin Davis	160	4,892
6. Bret Boone	143	3,467
7. Jim Presley	115	3,175
8. Ken Phelps	105	1,753
9. Tino Martinez	88	2,139
Dan Wilson	88	4,500

Triples: Season

Player	3B	Year
1. Ichiro Suzuki	12	2005
2. Harold Reynolds	11	1988
3. Phil Bradley	10	1987
4. Ruppert Jones	9	1979
Mark McLemore	9	2001
Harold Reynolds	9	1989
7. Phil Bradley	8	1985
Al Cowens	8	1982
Ruppert Jones	8	1977
Spike Owen	8	1984
Harold Reynolds	8	1987
Ichiro Suzuki	8	2001
Ichiro Suzuki	8	2002
Ichiro Suzuki	8	2003

Triples: Career with Team

Player	3B	PA
1. Harold Reynolds	48	4,593
2. Ichiro Suzuki	41	3,692
3. Ken Griffey Jr.	30	6,688
4. Phil Bradley	26	2,476
5. Spike Owen	23	1,769
6. Ruppert Jones	20	1,919
7. Jay Buhner	19	5,828
Mike Cameron	19	2,528
Dan Meyer	19	2,522
10. Joey Cora	18	2,317

Doubles: Season

Player	2B	Year
1. Alex Rodriguez	54	1996
2. Edgar Martinez	52	1995
Edgar Martinez	52	1996
4. Edgar Martinez	46	1992
Edgar Martinez	46	1998
6. John Olerud	45	2000
7. Ken Griffey Jr.	42	1991
8. Joey Cora	40	1997
Edgar Martinez	40	2001
Alex Rodriguez	40	1997

Doubles: Career with Team

Player	2B	PA
1. Edgar Martinez	514	8,672
2. Ken Griffey Jr.	320	6,688
3. Jay Buhner	231	5,828
4. Alvin Davis	212	4,892
5. Dan Wilson	207	4,500
6. Harold Reynolds	200	4,593
7. Alex Rodriguez	194	3,515
8. Bret Boone	167	3,467
9. John Olerud	164	2,976
10. Jim Presley	147	3,175

Extra-Base Hits: Season

Player	XBH	Year
1. Ken Griffey Jr.	93	1997
2. Ken Griffey Jr.	92	1998
3. Alex Rodriguez	91	1996
4. Ken Griffey Jr.	86	1993
5. Alex Rodriguez	82	1998
6. Edgar Martinez	81	1995
7. Edgar Martinez	80	1996
8. Bret Boone	77	2001
Ken Griffey Jr.	77	1996
Ken Griffey Jr.	77	1999
Alex Rodriguez	77	2000

Extra-Base Hits: Career with Team

Player	XBH	PA
1. Edgar Martinez	838	8,672
2. Ken Griffey Jr.	748	6,688
3. Jay Buhner	557	5,828

4. Alex Rodriguez	396	3,515
5. Alvin Davis	382	4,892
6. Bret Boone	326	3,467
7. Dan Wilson	308	4,500
8. Jim Presley	275	3,175
9. Harold Reynolds	265	4,593
10. John Olerud	238	2,976

TOTAL BASES: SEASON

Player	TB	Year
1. Ken Griffey Jr.	393	1997
2. Ken Griffey Jr.	387	1998
3. Alex Rodriguez	384	1998
4. Alex Rodriguez	379	1996
5. Bret Boone	360	2001
6. Ken Griffey Jr.	359	1993
7. Ken Griffey Jr.	349	1999
8. Ken Griffey Jr.	342	1996
9. Alex Rodriguez	336	2000
10. Bret Boone	333	2003

TOTAL BASES: CAREER WITH TEAM

Player	TB	PA
1. Edgar Martinez	3,718	8,672
2. Ken Griffey Jr.	3,316	6,688
3. Jay Buhner	2,445	5,828
4. Alvin Davis	1,875	4,892
5. Alex Rodriguez	1,753	3,515
6. Dan Wilson	1,568	4,500
7. Ichiro Suzuki	1,503	3,692
8. Bret Boone	1,491	3,467
9. Harold Reynolds	1,410	4,593
10. Jim Presley	1,254	3,175

RUNS BATTED IN: SEASON

Player	RBI	Year
1. Ken Griffey Jr.	147	1997
2. Ken Griffey Jr.	146	1998
3. Edgar Martinez	145	2000
4. Bret Boone	141	2001
5. Ken Griffey	140	1996
6. Jay Buhner	138	1996
7. Ken Griffey Jr.	134	1999
8. Alex Rodriguez	132	2000
9. Alex Rodriguez	124	1998
10. Alex Rodriguez	123	1996

RUNS BATTED IN: CAREER WITH TEAM

Player	RBI	PA
1. Edgar Martinez	1,261	8,672
2. Ken Griffey Jr.	1,152	6,688
3. Jay Buhner	951	5,828

4. Alvin Davis	667	4,892
5. Alex Rodriguez	595	3,515
6. Bret Boone	535	3,467
7. Dan Wilson	508	4,500
8. Jim Presley	418	3,175
9. John Olerud	405	2,976
10. Mike Cameron	344	2,528

RUNS SCORED: SEASON

Player	R	Year
1. Alex Rodriguez	141	1996
2. Alex Rodriguez	134	2000
3. Ichiro Suzuki	127	2001
4. Ken Griffey Jr.	125	1996
Ken Griffey Jr.	125	1997
6. Ken Griffey Jr.	123	1999
Alex Rodriguez	123	1998
8. Edgar Martinez	121	1995
Edgar Martinez	121	1996
10. Ken Griffey Jr.	120	1998

RUNS SCORED: CAREER WITH TEAM

Player	R	PA
1. Edgar Martinez	1,219	8,672
2. Ken Griffey Jr.	1,063	6,688
3. Jay Buhner	790	5,828
4. Alex Rodriguez	627	3,515
5. Alvin Davis	563	4,892
6. Ichiro Suzuki	561	3,692
7. Harold Reynolds	543	4,593
8. Bret Boone	467	3,467
9. Dan Wilson	433	4,500
10. Julio Cruz	402	3,068

WALKS: SEASON

Player	BB	Year
1. Edgar Martinez	123	1996
2. Jay Buhner	119	1997
Edgar Martinez	119	1997
4. Edgar Martinez	116	1995
5. Edgar Martinez	106	1998
6. John Olerud	102	2000
7. Alvin Davis	101	1989
8. Jay Buhner	100	1993
Alex Rodriguez	100	2000
10. John Olerud	98	2002

WALKS: CAREER WITH TEAM

Player	BB	PA
1. Edgar Martinez	1,283	8,672
2. Jay Buhner	788	5,828
3. Ken Griffey Jr.	747	6,688
4. Alvin Davis	672	4,892

5. John Olerud	418	2,976
6. Harold Reynolds	391	4,593
7. Julio Cruz	330	3,068
8. Ken Phelps	317	1,753
9. Bruce Bochte	313	2,770
10. Alex Rodriguez	310	3,515

STRIKEOUTS: SEASON

Player	SO	Year
1. Mike Cameron	176	2002
2. Jay Buhner	175	1997
3. Jim Presley	172	1986
4. Richie Sexson	167	2005
5. Jay Buhner	159	1996
6. Jim Presley	157	1987
Danny Tartabull	157	1986
8. Mike Cameron	155	2001
9. Jay Buhner	146	1992
10. Jay Buhner	144	1993

STRIKEOUTS: CAREER WITH TEAM

Player	SO	PA
1. Jay Buhner	1,375	5,828
2. Edgar Martinez	1,202	8,672
3. Ken Griffey Jr.	984	6,688
4. Dan Wilson	739	4,500
5. Jim Presley	713	3,175
6. Alex Rodriguez	616	3,515
7. Bret Boone	610	3,467
8. Mike Cameron	601	2,528
9. Alvin Davis	549	4,892
10. Phil Bradley	448	2,476

SLUGGING PERCENTAGE: SEASON

Player	SLG	Year
1. Ken Griffey Jr.	.674	1994
2. Ken Griffey Jr.	.646	1997
3. Alex Rodriguez	.631	1996
4. Edgar Martinez	.628	1995
Ken Griffey Jr.	.628	1996
6. Ken Griffey Jr.	.617	1993
7. Ken Griffey Jr.	.611	1998
8. Alex Rodriguez	.607	2000
9. Edgar Martinez	.595	1996
10. Alex Rodriguez	.586	1999

SLUGGING PERCENTAGE: CAREER WITH TEAM

Player	SLG	PA
1. Ken Griffey Jr.	.569	6,688
2. Alex Rodriguez	.561	3,515

3. Edgar Martinez	.515	8,672
4. Jay Buhner	.497	5,828
5. Bret Boone	.478	3,467
6. Tino Martinez	.466	2,139
7. Alvin Davis	.453	4,892
8. Phil Bradley	.449	2,476
9. Mike Cameron	.448	2,528
10. Ichiro Suzuki	.442	3,692

On-Base Percentage: Season

Player	OBP	Year
1. Edgar Martinez	.479	1995
2. Edgar Martinez	.464	1996
3. Edgar Martinez	.456	1997
4. Edgar Martinez	.447	1999
5. Edgar Martinez	.429	1998
6. Alvin Davis	.424	1989
7. Edgar Martinez	.423	2001
Edgar Martinez	.423	2000
9. Alex Rodriguez	.420	2000
10. Ichiro Suzuki	.414	2004

On-Base Percentage: Career with Team

Player	OBP	PA
1. Edgar Martinez	.418	8,672
2. John Olerud	.388	2,976
3. Phil Bradley	.382	2,476
4. Alvin Davis	.381	4,892
5. Ken Griffey Jr.	.380	6,688
6. Ichiro Suzuki	.377	3,692
7. Alex Rodriguez	.374	3,515
8. Bruce Bochte	.370	2,770
9. Jay Buhner	.360	5,828
10. Joey Cora	.355	2,317

OPS (On-Base Percentage + Slugging Percentage): Season

Player	OPS	Year
1. Edgar Martinez	1.107	1995
2. Ken Griffey Jr.	1.076	1994
3. Edgar Martinez	1.059	1996
4. Alex Rodriguez	1.045	1996
5. Ken Griffey Jr.	1.028	1997
6. Alex Rodriguez	1.026	2000
7. Ken Griffey Jr.	1.025	1993
8. Ken Griffey Jr.	1.020	1996
9. Edgar Martinez	1.009	1997
10. Edgar Martinez	1.002	2000

OPS (On-Base Percentage + Slugging Percentage): Career with Team

Player	OPS	PA
1. Ken Griffey Jr.	.948	6,688
2. Alex Rodriguez	.934	3,515
3. Edgar Martinez	.933	8,672
4. Jay Buhner	.857	5,828
5. Alvin Davis	.834	4,892
6. Phil Bradley	.830	2,476
7. John Olerud	.827	2,976
8. Ichiro Suzuki	.819	3,692
9. Bret Boone	.814	3,467
10. Tino Martinez	.801	2,139

Stolen Bases: Season

Player	SB	Year
1. Harold Reynolds	60	1987
2. Julio Cruz	59	1978
3. Ichiro Suzuki	56	2001
4. Julio Cruz	49	1979
5. Julio Cruz	46	1982
Alex Rodriguez	46	1998
7. Julio Cruz	45	1980
8. Brian Hunter	44	1999
9. Julio Cruz	43	1981
10. Phil Bradley	40	1987

Stolen Bases: Career with Team

Player	SB	PA
1. Julio Cruz	290	3,068
2. Harold Reynolds	228	4,593
3. Ichiro Suzuki	190	3,692
4. Ken Griffey Jr.	167	6,688
5. Alex Rodriguez	133	3,515
6. Phil Bradley	107	2,476
7. Mike Cameron	106	2,528
8. Henry Cotto	102	1,732
9. Rich Amaral	97	1,799
10. Mark McLemore	92	1,824

Sacrifice Hits: Season

Player	Sac	Year
1. Larry Milbourne	15	1980
Craig Reynolds	15	1977
3. Harold Reynolds	14	1991
4. Jeff Cirillo	13	2002
Joey Cora	13	1995
Julio Cruz	13	1980
Mario Mendoza	13	1979
Omar Vizquel	13	1989
Omar Vizquel	13	1993
10. Felix Fermin	12	1994
Joe Simpson	12	1980

Sacrifice Hits: Career with Team

Player	Sac	PA
1. Dan Wilson	85	4,500
2. Harold Reynolds	63	4,593
3. Omar Vizquel	53	2,355
4. Julio Cruz	45	3,068
5. Larry Milbourne	39	1,420
6. Joey Cora	37	2,317
7. Dave Valle	30	2,834
8. Rich Amaral	28	1,799
9. Bob Kearney	26	1,067
Spike Owen	26	1,769
Craig Reynolds	26	1,059
Joe Simpson	26	1,329

Hit by Pitch: Season

Player	HBP	Year
1. Dave Valle	17	1993
2. Phil Bradley	12	1985
3. Edgar Martinez	11	1997
4. Mike Cameron	10	2001
Alex Rodriguez	10	1998
6. Bret Boone	9	2001
Jay Buhner	9	1996
Mike Cameron	9	2000
Jeff Cirillo	9	2002
Rob Ducey	9	1998
Edgar Martinez	9	2001
John Marzano	9	1998
Dave Valle	9	1988
Dave Valle	9	1991

Hit by Pitch: Career with Team

Player	HBP	PA
1. Edgar Martinez	89	8,672
2. Dave Valle	60	2,834
3. Jay Buhner	53	5,828
4. Ken Griffey Jr.	47	6,688
5. Bret Boone	33	3,467
6. Phil Bradley	31	2,476
Mike Cameron	31	2,528
Alex Rodriguez	31	3,515
9. Alvin Davis	28	4,892
10. Ichiro Suzuki	27	3,692

Top 10 Pitching Leaders, Single Season & Career with Team

Games Pitched: Season

Player	GP	Year
1. Ed Vande Berg	78	1982
2. Ed Vande Berg	76	1985
3. Mike Jackson	73	1996
4. Mike Jackson	72	1991
Arthur Rhodes	72	2000
6. Bobby Ayala	71	1997
Norm Charlton	71	1997
Jeff Nelson	71	1993
Arthur Rhodes	71	2001
Bill Swift	71	1991

Games Pitched: Career with Team

Player	GP	IP
1. Jeff Nelson	432	447.3
2. Mike Jackson	335	436.7
3. Jamie Moyer	299	1,933.0
4. Bobby Ayala	292	367.0
5. Bill Swift	282	903.7
6. Arthur Rhodes	276	261.0
7. Randy Johnson	274	1,838.3
8. Ed Vande Berg	272	338.3
9. Norm Charlton	249	275.0
10. Mike Schooler	243	267.3

Innings Pitched: Season

Player	IP	Year
1. Mark Langston	272.0	1987
2. Mike Moore	266.0	1986
3. Mark Langston	261.3	1988
4. Randy Johnson	255.3	1993
5. Floyd Bannister	247.0	1982
Mike Moore	247.0	1985
7. Mark Langston	239.3	1986
8. Freddy Garcia	238.7	2001
9. Erik Hanson	236.0	1990
10. Jeff Fassero	234.3	1997
Jamie Moyer	234.3	1998

Innings Pitched: Career with Team

Player	IP
1. Jamie Moyer	1,933.0
2. Randy Johnson	1,838.3
3. Mike Moore	1,457.0
4. Mark Langston	1,197.7
5. Freddy Garcia	1,096.3
6. Erik Hanson	967.3
7. Jim Beattie	944.7
8. Glenn Abbott	904.0
9. Bill Swift	903.7
10. Matt Young	864.3

Batters Faced: Season

Player	BF	Year
1. Mark Langston	1,152	1987
2. Mike Moore	1,145	1986
3. Mark Langston	1,078	1988
4. Mark Langston	1,057	1986
5. Randy Johnson	1,043	1993
6. Floyd Bannister	1,022	1982
7. Mike Moore	1,020	1987
8. Mike Moore	1,016	1985
9. Jeff Fassero	1,010	1997
10. Jamie Moyer	974	1998

Batters Faced: Career with Team

Player	BF	IP
1. Jamie Moyer	8,117	1,933.0
2. Randy Johnson	7,721	1,838.3
3. Mike Moore	6,243	1,457.0
4. Mark Langston	5,126	1,197.7
5. Freddy Garcia	4,660	1,096.3
6. Jim Beattie	4,060	944.7
7. Erik Hanson	4,048	967.3
8. Bill Swift	3,929	903.7
9. Glenn Abbott	3,859	904.0
10. Matt Young	3,747	864.3

Games Started: Season

Player	GS	Year
1. Mike Moore	37	1986
2. Mark Langston	36	1986
3. Floyd Bannister	35	1982
Jeff Fassero	35	1997
Sterling Hitchcock	35	1996
Mark Langston	35	1987
Mark Langston	35	1988
Matt Young	35	1985
9. Eight tied with . . .	34	——

Games Started: Career with Team

Player	GS	IP
1. Jamie Moyer	298	1,933.0
2. Randy Johnson	266	1,838.3
3. Mike Moore	217	1,457.0
4. Mark Langston	173	1,197.7
5. Freddy Garcia	169	1,096.3
6. Jim Beattie	147	944.7
7. Glenn Abbott	146	904.0
8. Erik Hanson	143	967.3
9. Matt Young	127	864.3
10. Joel Piñeiro	123	830.3

Complete Games: Season

Player	CG	Year
1. Mark Langston	14	1987
Mike Moore	14	1985
3. Mike Parrott	13	1979
4. Jim Beattie	12	1984
Mike Moore	12	1987
6. Mike Moore	11	1986
7. Randy Johnson	10	1993
8. Rick Honeycutt	9	1980
Randy Johnson	9	1994
Mark Langston	9	1986
Mark Langston	9	1988
Mike Moore	9	1988
Mike Morgan	9	1986

Complete Games: Career with Team

Player	CG	IP
1. Mike Moore	56	1,457.0
2. Randy Johnson	51	1,838.3
3. Mark Langston	41	1,197.7
4. Jim Beattie	30	944.7
5. Glenn Abbott	28	904.0
6. Floyd Bannister	24	768.3
7. Erik Hanson	21	967.3
Rick Honeycutt	21	560.7
9. Matt Young	19	864.3
10. Jamie Moyer	18	1,933.0

Games Won: Season

Player	W	Year
1. Jamie Moyer	21	2003
2. Randy Johnson	20	1997
Jamie Moyer	20	2001

4. Randy Johnson	19	1993
Mark Langston	19	1987
6. Freddy Garcia	18	2001
Erik Hanson	18	1990
Randy Johnson	18	1995
9. Paul Abbott	17	2001
Dave Fleming	17	1992
Freddy Garcia	17	1999
Mark Langston	17	1984
Mike Moore	17	1985
Jamie Moyer	17	1997
Aaron Sele	17	2000

Games Won: Career with Team

Player	W	IP
1. Jamie Moyer	139	1,933.0
2. Randy Johnson	130	1,838.3
3. Freddy Garcia	76	1,096.3
4. Mark Langston	74	1,197.7
5. Mike Moore	66	1,457.0
6. Erik Hanson	56	967.3
7. Joel Piñeiro	50	830.3
8. Matt Young	45	864.3
9. Glenn Abbott	44	904.0
Gil Meche	44	628.7

Games Lost: Season

Player	L	Year
1. Mike Moore	19	1987
Matt Young	19	1985
3. Matt Young	18	1990
4. Erik Hanson	17	1992
Rick Honeycutt	17	1980
Mike Moore	17	1984
Mike Morgan	17	1986
Mike Morgan	17	1987
Bob Stoddard	17	1983
10. Jim Beattie	16	1984
Ryan Franklin	16	2004
Mike Parrott	16	1980

Games Lost: Career with Team

Player	L	IP
1. Mike Moore	96	1,457.0
2. Jamie Moyer	75	1,933.0
3. Randy Johnson	74	1,838.3
4. Jim Beattie	72	944.7
5. Mark Langston	67	1,197.7
6. Matt Young	66	864.3
7. Glenn Abbott	62	904.0
8. Erik Hanson	54	967.3
9. Floyd Bannister	50	768.3
Freddy Garcia	50	1,096.3
Ryan Franklin	50	811.3

Winning Percentage: Season

Player	W%	Year
1. Randy Johnson	.900	1995
2. Randy Johnson	.833	1997
3. Paul Abbott	.810	2001
4. Jamie Moyer	.773	1997
5. Jamie Moyer	.769	2001
6. Freddy Garcia	.750	2001
Jamie Moyer	.750	2003
Aaron Sele	.750	2001
9. Dave Fleming	.706	1993
10. Randy Johnson	.704	1993

Winning Percentage: Career with Team

Player	W%	IP
1. Jamie Moyer	.650	1,933.0
2. Randy Johnson	.637	1,838.3
3. Freddy Garcia	.603	1,096.3
4. Gil Meche	.550	628.7
5. Joel Piñeiro	.543	830.3
6. Mark Langston	.525	1,197.7
7. Erik Hanson	.509	967.3
8. Bill Swift	.456	903.7
9. Floyd Bannister	.444	768.3
10. Glenn Abbott	.415	904.0

Shutouts: Season

Player	SHO	Year
1. Dave Fleming	4	1992
Randy Johnson	4	1994
3. Floyd Bannister	3	1982
Freddy Garcia	3	2001
Brian Holman	3	1991
Randy Johnson	3	1993
Randy Johnson	3	1995
Mark Langston	3	1987
Mark Langston	3	1988
Mike Moore	3	1988
Jamie Moyer	3	1998

Shutouts: Career with Team

Player	SHO	IP
1. Randy Johnson	19	1,838.3
2. Mark Langston	9	1,197.7
Mike Moore	9	1,457.0
4. Floyd Bannister	7	768.3
5. Jim Beattie	6	944.7
6. Dave Fleming	5	578.3
Brian Holman	5	544.7
Jamie Moyer	5	1,933.0
Matt Young	5	864.3
10. Freddy Garcia	4	1,096.3
Aaron Sele	4	542.7

ERA: Season

Player	ERA	Year
1. Randy Johnson	2.28	1997
2. Randy Johnson	2.48	1995
3. Freddy Garcia	3.05	2001
4. Randy Johnson	3.19	1994
5. Erik Hanson	3.24	1990
Joel Piñeiro	3.24	2002
Randy Johnson	3.24	1993
8. Jamie Moyer	3.27	2003
Matt Young	3.27	1983
10. Jamie Moyer	3.32	2002

ERA: Career with Team

Player	ERA	IP
1. Randy Johnson	3.42	1,838.3
2. Erik Hanson	3.69	967.3
3. Brian Holman	3.73	544.7
4. Floyd Bannister	3.75	768.3
5. Freddy Garcia	3.89	1,096.3
6. Jamie Moyer	3.94	1,933.0
7. Mark Langston	4.01	1,197.7
8. Ryan Franklin	4.10	620.7
9. Joel Piñeiro	4.11	830.3
10. Matt Young	4.13	864.3

Earned Runs Allowed: Season

Player	ER	Year
1. Mark Langston	129	1986
2. Mike Moore	127	1986
3. Mike Moore	121	1987
4. Matt Young	119	1985
5. Joel Piñeiro	118	2005
6. Sterling Hitchcock	117	1996
Mike Moore	117	1984
Jamie Moyer	117	2004
9. Mark Langston	116	1987
10. Jeff Fassero	114	1999

Earned Runs Allowed: Career with Team

Player	ER	IP
1. Jamie Moyer	846	1,933.0
2. Mike Moore	709	1,457.0

Player	K	IP
3. Randy Johnson	698	1,838.3
4. Mark Langston	533	1,197.7
5. Freddy Garcia	474	1,096.3
6. Glenn Abbott	456	904.0
7. Jim Beattie	435	944.7
Bill Swift	435	903.7
9. Erik Hanson	397	967.3
Matt Young	397	864.3

STRIKEOUTS: SEASON

Player	K	Year
1. Randy Johnson	308	1993
2. Randy Johnson	294	1995
3. Randy Johnson	291	1997
4. Mark Langston	262	1987
5. Mark Langston	245	1986
6. Randy Johnson	241	1992
7. Mark Langston	235	1988
8. Randy Johnson	228	1991
9. Randy Johnson	213	1998
10. Erik Hanson	211	1990

STRIKEOUTS: CAREER WITH TEAM

Player	K	IP
1. Randy Johnson	2162	1,838.3
2. Jamie Moyer	1157	1,933.0
3. Mark Langston	1078	1,197.7
4. Mike Moore	937	1,457.0
5. Freddy Garcia	819	1,096.3
6. Erik Hanson	740	967.3
7. Matt Young	597	864.3
8. Joel Piñeiro	571	830.3
9. Floyd Bannister	564	768.3
10. Jim Beattie	563	944.7

STRIKEOUTS PER NINE IP: SEASON

Player	K/9	Year
1. Randy Johnson	12.35	1995
2. Randy Johnson	12.30	1997
3. Randy Johnson	10.86	1993
4. Randy Johnson	10.67	1994
5. Randy Johnson	10.31	1992
6. Randy Johnson	10.19	1991
7. Mark Langston	9.21	1986
8. Mark Langston	8.67	1987
9. Mark Langston	8.16	1984
10. Mark Langston	8.09	1988

STRIKEOUTS PER NINE IP: CAREER WITH TEAM

Player	K/9	IP
1. Randy Johnson	10.58	1,838.3
2. Mark Langston	8.10	1,197.7
3. Jeff Fassero	7.01	598.0
4. Erik Hanson	6.88	967.3
5. Freddy Garcia	6.72	1,096.3
6. Floyd Bannister	6.61	768.3
7. Matt Young	6.22	864.3
8. Joel Piñeiro	6.19	830.3
9. Gil Meche	6.00	628.7
10. Scott Bankhead	5.94	568.3

HITS ALLOWED: SEASON

Player	HA	Year
1. Mike Moore	279	1986
2. Mike Moore	268	1987
3. Sterling Hitchcock	245	1996
Mike Morgan	245	1987
Gaylord Perry	245	1982
6. Mike Morgan	243	1986
7. Mark Langston	242	1987
Matt Young	242	1985
9. Mike Moore	236	1984
10. Jamie Moyer	235	1999

HITS ALLOWED: CAREER WITH TEAM

Player	HA	IP
1. Jamie Moyer	1,921	1,933.0
2. Mike Moore	1,498	1,457.0
3. Randy Johnson	1,414	1,838.3
4. Mark Langston	1,068	1,197.7
5. Freddy Garcia	1,035	1,096.3
6. Bill Swift	1,010	903.7
7. Glenn Abbott	999	904.0
8. Jim Beattie	966	944.7
9. Erik Hanson	949	967.3
10. Matt Young	867	864.3

HITS ALLOWED PER NINE IP: SEASON

Player	H/9	Year
1. Randy Johnson	6.21	1997
2. Randy Johnson	6.52	1993
3. Randy Johnson	6.59	1992
4. Randy Johnson	6.68	1995
5. Randy Johnson	6.75	1991
6. Randy Johnson	6.91	1994
7. Randy Johnson	7.13	1990
8. Freddy Garcia	7.50	2001
9. Mark Langston	7.52	1984
10. Chris Bosio	7.56	1993

HITS ALLOWED PER NINE IP: CAREER WITH TEAM

Player	H/9	IP
1. Randy Johnson	6.92	1,838.3
2. Mark Langston	8.03	1,197.7
3. Freddy Garcia	8.50	1,096.3
4. Floyd Bannister	8.64	768.3
5. Erik Hanson	8.83	967.3
6. Scott Bankhead	8.88	568.3
7. Joel Pineiro	8.93	830.3
8. Jamie Moyer	8.94	1,933.0
9. Gil Meche	8.98	628.7
10. Matt Young	9.03	864.3

WALKS ALLOWED: SEASON

Player	BB	Year
1. Randy Johnson	152	1991
2. Randy Johnson	144	1992
3. Mark Langston	123	1986
4. Randy Johnson	120	1990
5. Mark Langston	118	1984
6. Mark Langston	114	1987
7. Mark Langston	110	1988
8. Matt Young	107	1990
9. Randy Johnson	99	1993
10. Jim Beattie	98	1980

WALKS ALLOWED: CAREER WITH TEAM

Player	BB	IP
1. Randy Johnson	884	1,838.3
2. Mark Langston	575	1,197.7
3. Mike Moore	535	1,457.0
4. Jamie Moyer	480	1,933.0
5. Freddy Garcia	389	1,096.3
6. Jim Beattie	369	944.7
7. Matt Young	365	864.3
8. Bill Swift	304	903.7
9. Erik Hanson	285	967.3
10. Gil Meche	279	628.7

Walks Allowed Per Nine IP: Season

Player	BB/9	Year
1. Jamie Moyer	1.61	1998
2. Jamie Moyer	1.89	2001
Jamie Moyer	1.89	1999
4. Jamie Moyer	1.95	2002
5. Glenn Abbott	2.05	1980
Jamie Moyer	2.05	1997
7. Aaron Sele	2.13	2001
8. Gaylord Perry	2.24	1982
9. Mike Morgan	2.30	1987
10. Jamie Moyer	2.34	2005

Walks Allowed Per Nine IP: Career with Team

Player	BB/9	IP
1. Jamie Moyer	2.23	1,933.0
2. Glenn Abbott	2.29	904.0
3. Scott Bankhead	2.63	568.3
4. Ryan Franklin	2.64	811.3
5. Erik Hanson	2.65	967.3
6. Aaron Sele	2.75	542.7
7. John Halama	2.76	557.0
8. Joel Piñeiro	2.85	830.3
9. Floyd Bannister	2.93	768.3
10. Rick Honeycutt	3.00	560.7

WHIP (Walks + Hits Per Nine IP): Season

Player	WHIP	Year
1. Randy Johnson	1.05	1995
Randy Johnson	1.05	1997
3. Jamie Moyer	1.08	2002
4. Jamie Moyer	1.10	2001
5. Randy Johnson	1.11	1993
6. Freddy Garcia	1.12	2001
7. Mike Moore	1.13	1988
8. Erik Hanson	1.16	1990
9. Jamie Moyer	1.18	1998
10. Randy Johnson	1.19	1994

WHIP (Walks + Hits Per Nine IP): Career with Team

Player	WHIP	IP
1. Jamie Moyer	1.242	1,933.0
2. Randy Johnson	1.250	1,838.3
3. Erik Hanson	1.276	967.3
4. Scott Bankhead	1.279	568.3
5. Floyd Bannister	1.286	768.3
6. Freddy Garcia	1.299	1,096.3
7. Joel Piñeiro	1.309	830.3
8. Ryan Franklin	1.326	811.3
9. Glenn Abbott	1.360	904.0
10. Mark Langston	1.372	1,197.7

Home Runs Allowed: Season

Player	HRA	Year
1. Jamie Moyer	44	2004
2. Scott Bankhead	35	1987
3. Jeff Fassero	34	1999
Ryan Franklin	34	2003
5. Jeff Fassero	33	1998
Ryan Franklin	33	2004
7. Glenn Abbott	32	1977
Floyd Bannister	32	1982
Mark Langston	32	1988
10. Rich DeLucia	31	1991
Freddy Garcia	31	2003

Home Runs Allowed: Career with Team

Player	HRA	IP
1. Jamie Moyer	236	1,933.0
2. Randy Johnson	160	1,838.3
3. Mike Moore	146	1,457.0
4. Mark Langston	133	1,197.7
5. Ryan Franklin	124	811.3
6. Glenn Abbott	123	904.0
7. Freddy Garcia	119	1,096.3
8. Floyd Bannister	95	768.3
9. Joel Piñeiro	92	830.3
10. Jeff Fassero	88	598.0

Saves: Season

Player	SV	Year
1. Kazuhiro Sasaki	45	2001
2. Kazuhiro Sasaki	37	2000
Kazuhiro Sasaki	37	2002
4. Eddie Guardado	36	2005
5. Jose Mesa	33	1999
Mike Schooler	33	1989
7. Mike Schooler	30	1990
8. Bill Caudill	26	1982
Bill Caudill	26	1983
10. Norm Charlton	20	1996

Saves: Career with Team

Player	SV	IP
1. Kazuhiro Sasaki	129	223.3
2. Mike Schooler	98	267.3
3. Norm Charlton	67	275.0
4. Bobby Ayala	56	367.0
5. Eddie Guardado	54	101.7
6. Bill Caudill	52	168.3
7. Shane Rawley	36	377.7
8. Edwin Nuñez	35	328.7
9. Mike Jackson	34	436.7
Jose Mesa	34	149.3

Wild Pitches: Season

Player	WP	Year
1. Matt Young	16	1990
2. Erik Hanson	14	1991
3. Jeff Fassero	13	1997
Randy Johnson	13	1992
Gaylord Perry	13	1982
6. Jeff Fassero	12	1998
Freddy Garcia	12	1999
Randy Johnson	12	1991
9. Paul Abbott	11	2001
Freddy Garcia	11	2003
Mike Morgan	11	1987

Wild Pitches: Career with Team

Player	WP	IP
1. Randy Johnson	66	1,838.3
2. Erik Hanson	43	967.3
3. Freddy Garcia	42	1,096.3
Mike Moore	42	1,457.0
5. Matt Young	36	864.3
6. Mark Langston	34	1,197.7
7. Jeff Fassero	32	598.0
8. Norm Charlton	31	275.0
9. Bill Swift	28	903.7
10. Jim Beattie	26	944.7
Joel Piñeiro	26	830.3

Hit Batsmen: Season

Player	HB	Year
1. Randy Johnson	18	1992
2. Randy Johnson	16	1993
3. Glenn Abbott	12	1977
Randy Johnson	12	1991
Mike Moore	12	1986
Ron Villone	12	2004

7. Freddy Garcia	11	2003
Randy Johnson	11	1998
Jamie Moyer	11	2004
10. Eight tied with . . .	10	—

HIT BATSMEN: CAREER WITH TEAM

Player	HB	IP
1. Randy Johnson	89	1,838.3
2. Jamie Moyer	76	1,933.0
3. Jeff Nelson	43	447.3
4. Bill Swift	40	903.7
5. Freddy Garcia	36	1,096.3
Ryan Franklin	36	811.3
7. Mike Moore	29	1,457.0
Matt Young	29	864.3
9. Mark Langston	26	1,197.7
Joel Piñeiro	26	830.3

GAMES FINISHED: SEASON

Player	GF	Year
1. Bill Caudill	64	1982
2. Kazuhiro Sasaki	63	2001
3. Jose Mesa	60	1999
Mike Schooler	60	1989
5. Kazuhiro Sasaki	58	2000
6. Kazuhiro Sasaki	55	2002
Eddie Guardado	55	2005
8. Bill Caudill	54	1983
9. Edwin Nuñez	53	1985
10. Bobby Ayala	50	1995
Norm Charlton	50	1996

GAMES FINISHED: CAREER WITH TEAM

Player	GF	IP
1. Kazuhiro Sasaki	201	223.3
2. Mike Schooler	197	267.3
3. Bobby Ayala	185	367.0
4. Norm Charlton	149	275.0
5. Mike Jackson	142	436.7
6. Jeff Nelson	139	447.3
7. Edwin Nuñez	128	328.7
8. Shane Rawley	120	377.7
9. Bill Caudill	118	168.3
10. Ed Vande Berg	92	338.3
Shigetoshi Hasegawa	92	278.0

Ichiro Suzuki

Significant Mariners

BOONE, BRET (2B)
(1992–1993, 2001–2005)

The slick-fielding power-hitting second baseman first came to the Mariners via the 1990 amateur draft. By 1992 Boone was on the major league roster, but after two less-than-stellar seasons he was traded by Seattle along with Erik Hanson to Cincinnati for Dan Wilson and Bobby Ayala. After spending seven years in the National League with three different teams, Boone returned for a second stint with the Mariners after becoming a free agent. By now he was a steady, if unspectacular, performer. But once the 2001 season began, Boone played like he never had before, suddenly becoming a home run hitter and Gold Glove fielder. He led the Mariners to their fantastic 116-win season with a .331 average, 37 homers, and 141 RBIs.

This sudden transformation shouldn't have come as a *complete* surprise, however, since Bret is part of a baseball dynasty: His father, catcher Bob Boone *(see Angels bio)*, spent 19 seasons in the majors, following in the footsteps of Bret's grandfather, Ray Boone. (Bret's brother Aaron is also a major league infielder.)

The fiery Bret Boone was named to the American League All-Star team in 2001 and 2003, and won Gold Gloves in 2002, 2003, and 2004. He won the Silver Slugger Award for AL second basemen in 2001 and 2003. After a sudden and mysterious loss of power, and a falling batting average, a sobbing Bret Boone was released by the Mariners in mid-2005. He hooked up with Minnesota for a short time, but was equally as unimpressive (.170 in 14 games with no homers) and released again.

CAREER MARINERS RECORD:

Games	AB	Hits	Runs
803	3,119	863	467
Avg	**HR**	**RBI**	**SB**
.277	143	535	50

BUHNER, JAY (OF)
(1988–2001)

Jay Buhner was, and still remains, one of the most popular Mariners ever. After playing just 32 games for the Yankees in 1987 and 1988, Buhner was traded to Seattle on July 21, 1988 in a deal for Ken Phelps—one of the worst trades in Yankee history, as Phelps soon disappeared from baseball while Buhner went on to play 14 seasons for the Mariners. Buhner, who played with a shaved head, inspired one of the team's most popular promotions: Jay Buhner Buzz Cut Night, in which fans willing to get their hair shaved off before the game got to see it for free.

From 1991 to 1997, Buhner clubbed 224 home runs, three times eclipsing 40 homers and 100 RBIs. In 1995 he set a major league record, compiling a .984 RBI-to-hits ratio by knocking in 121 runs with only 123 hits. Buhner played in the same outfield as Ken Griffey Jr., giving the Mariners a potent 1-2 offensive punch, and he also won a Gold Glove along with Griffey in 1996. Buhner was especially tough in the clutch, typically elevating his game in the playoffs and during pennant runs in the mid- to late 1990s.

CAREER MARINERS RECORD:

Games	AB	Hits	Runs
1,440	3,908	4,922	790
Avg	**HR**	**RBI**	**SB**
.255	307	951	6

DAVIS, ALVIN (1B/DH) (1984–1991)

Alvin Davis was one of the most promising young players ever to arrive in Seattle. He had a remarkable rookie season in 1984, hitting .284 with 27 homers and 116 RBIs, winning the American League Rookie of the Year Award and making the All-Star team in the process. Davis played seven more seasons in Seattle, never quite exceeding or achieving again the success of his rookie year. He was let go after the 1991 season and played a few games for the Angels in 1992 before moving on to Japan, where he finished his career.

CAREER MARINERS RECORD:

Games	AB	Hits	Runs
1,166	4,136	1,163	563
Avg	**HR**	**RBI**	**SB**
.281	160	667	7

GRIFFEY, KEN, JR. (OF) (1989–1999)

One of the brightest young superstars to arrive on the major league scene in the last 50 years, Ken Griffey Jr. (son of 19-year major leaguer Ken Griffey Sr.) made his Mariner debut in 1989 at the tender age of 19. (In 1990, his dad joined the Mariners and the Griffeys became the first father-son tandem to play for the same team at the same time. When Griffey Jr., won the All-Star Game MVP Award in 1992, he joined his father as the only father-son combo to achieve that feat as well.) In his 11 seasons with Seattle, "Junior" was named to the American League All-Star team 10 consecutive times, won 10 consecutive Gold Gloves, seven Silver Slugger Awards, an All-Star Game MVP Award, and the 1997 American League MVP. Griffey Jr. was an outstanding five-tool player—he could hit, hit for power, run, field, and throw. His running, over-the-fence leaping catches became legendary. Griffey Jr., was named to the All-Century Team in 1999, and then voted by fans as one of the top 25 players of the 20th century. He already had 398 homers by the time he was 30 in 1999.

Following the 1999 season, Griffey wanting to be closer to his home in Cincinnati, forced the Mariners to trade him. Just before the 2000 season, the Mariners gave in to his demand and sent him to Cincinnati for Mike Cameron, Brett Tomko, and two minor leaguers. In six seasons with the Reds, Griffey has continued to move up the all-time charts in many categories, but due to a series of major injuries, his progress has been much slower than it was in Seattle. Once mentioned by Hank Aaron as the player most likely to surpass his career home run record, Griffey now sits at 536 homers through 2005, a very unlikely candidate to catch Hammerin' Hank.

CAREER MARINERS RECORD:

Games	AB	Hits	Runs
1,535	5,832	1,742	1,063
Avg	**HR**	**RBI**	**SB**
.292	398	1,152	167

JOHNSON, RANDY (SP)
(1989–1997)

Randy Johnson was one of the most dominating and intimidating pitchers in baseball during his 10-year stretch in Seattle. Acquired on May 25, 1989, in a trade that sent Mark Langston to the Montreal Expos, the erratic Johnson finally found some control and had an almost immediate impact on the Mariners. In 1990, his first full season in Seattle, Johnson threw a no-hitter against Detroit. Using a 100-mph fastball, a sweeping curveball, and a hard biting slider, the left-handed Johnson established the reputation as the pitcher most batters—particularly lefties—hated to face. He won the Cy Young Award in strike-shortened 1995, going 18–2 with a 2.48 ERA and 294 strikeouts. In 1997 he won 20 games for the first time and twice struck out 19 batters in a game. From 1995 through 1997, "the Big Unit" was an incredible 43–6, even though a herniated disk in his back forced him to miss most of the 1996 season. After becoming disgruntled with Seattle management over a variety of issues, most notably his salary, he was traded on July 31, 1998, to Houston (where he pitched only a third of a season before signing with Arizona) for Freddy Garcia, John Halama, and Carlos Guillen. Johnson, a five-time All-Star with the Mariners, left Seattle as the team's all-time leader in games won with 130, a mark since eclipsed by Jamie Moyer. *(See Diamondbacks bio.)*

CAREER MARINERS RECORD:

W	L	W%	ERA	SV
130	74	.637	3.42	2
K	**BB**	**SHO**	**IP**	
2,162	884	19	1,838.3	

LANGSTON, MARK (SP)
(1984–1989)

Mark Langston was picked by the Mariners in the second round of the 1981 amateur draft. When he joined the major league club in 1984, Langston had an immediate impact, winning 17 games in his rookie season. The left-hander led the American League in strikeouts in three of his first four seasons in the majors. In 1987 he was named to the All-Star team and won the first of two Gold Gloves with the Mariners (he has seven overall). In May 1989 the standout Langston was traded to the Montreal Expos for three prospects, among them a young Randy Johnson. The deal was heavily criticized by fans at the time, but it later turned out to be a godsend to the Mariners, as Johnson eventually eclipsed all the records Langston had set while with Seattle.

CAREER MARINERS RECORD:

W	L	W%	ERA	SV
74	67	.525	4.01	0
K	**BB**	**SHO**	**IP**	
1,078	575	9	1,197.7	

MARTINEZ, EDGAR (DH)
(1987–2004)

While Ken Griffey Jr. was highly regarded as a player, "The Edgar" was much more beloved by the fans in Seattle, where he spent his entire 18-year career. The quiet but steady Martinez, who was signed as an amateur free agent on December 19, 1982, began his career as a third baseman, played a little first, but eventually settled in as the team's designated hitter for most of his career. When Martinez led the American League with a .356 batting average in 1995, he became the first right-handed batter since Joe DiMaggio to win two AL batting titles, having won the 1992 crown with a .343 average. In 1996 Martinez became the first hitter since Joe Medwick of the Cardinals in 1937 to hit 50 doubles in consecutive seasons. In the Mariners' first-ever trip to the postseason in 1995, Martinez racked up 12 hits and 10 RBIs in just five games, including an all-time postseason record seven RBIs in Game 4 of the divisional playoffs against the Yankees. Martinez retired after the 2004 season with a .312 career average, five Silver Slugger Awards, two batting titles, and seven All-Star game appearances.

CAREER MARINERS RECORD:

Games	AB	Hits	Runs
2,055	7,213	2,247	1,219

Avg	HR	RBI	SB
.312	309	1,261	49

MOYER, JAMIE (SP)
(1996–2005)

Jamie Moyer came to the Mariners in a July 30, 1996 trade with Boston that sent Darren Bragg to the Red Sox and he's remained with the team ever since. By the close of the 2005 season, Moyer was Seattle's all-time leader in victories. He also holds the distinction of being the only Mariner to have more than one 20-win season, as he accomplished the feat in both 2001 and 2003. Moyer has won numerous awards for his charity and humanitarian work, including the Hutch Award, the Lou Gehrig Memorial Award, and the Roberto Clemente Award (all in 2003).

CAREER MARINERS RECORD:

W	L	W%	ERA	SV
139	75	.650	3.94	0

K	BB	SHO	IP
1,157	480	5	1,933.0

REYNOLDS, HAROLD (2B)
(1983–1992)

The speedy, switch-hitting Reynolds was the second pick overall by the Mariners in the June 1980 amateur draft. Reynolds spent the first 10 years of his 12-year major league career with Seattle, collecting three Gold Gloves in the process. When he was named to his second All-Star team in 1988, he became the first Mariner in history to be selected to the team twice. Reynolds led the league in stolen bases in 1987 with 60, the first time in history a Mariner had led the league in a major offensive category. In so doing, he also became the first player in history to lead the league in steals while batting ninth in the order. After the 1992 season, Reynolds opted for free agency and signed a one-year contract with the Orioles. Since his retirement, he has been a longtime regular on ESPN's *Baseball Tonight.*

CAREER MARINERS RECORD:

Games	AB	Hits	Runs
1,155	4,090	1,063	543
Avg	**HR**	**RBI**	**SB**
.260	17	295	228

RODRIGUEZ, ALEX (SS)
(1994–2000)

The Seattle Mariners chose Alex Rodriguez with the first pick in the first round of the June 1993 amateur draft and he lived up to everyone's wildest expectations. He made his major league debut at the age of 18, and there is now serious talk that, given that early start, he may ultimately establish himself as the all-time home run king, eclipsing Ruth, Bonds, and Aaron. When "A-Rod" won the American League batting title in 1996 with a .358 average, he became the first shortstop to lead the AL in batting since Hall of Famer Lou Boudreau in 1944. In 1998 Rodriguez slugged 42 homers, the most ever by an American League shortstop. With his 46 stolen bases that season, he became the third member of baseball's "40-40" club. Rodriguez was named to the All-Star team four times as a Mariner, won four Silver Slugger Awards, and was consistently in the top 10 of most American League hitting categories. After the 2000 season, Rodriguez signed the largest contract in sports history ($252 million) with the Texas Rangers as a free agent. *(See Rangers bio.)*

CAREER MARINERS RECORD:

Games	AB	Hits	Runs
790	3,126	966	627
Avg	**HR**	**RBI**	**SB**
.309	189	595	133

SASAKI, KAZUHIRO (RP)
(2000–2003)

Given the Japanese ownership of the team, it was only natural that the Seattle Mariners would benefit in a big way from Japanese talent. The first Japanese star to land in Seattle, relief pitcher Kazuhiro Sasaki, was a dominant closer with a wicked, diving breaking pitch that hitters found tough to resist. Sasaki compiled 129 saves in the four years from 2000 to 2003, and was named Rookie of the Year in 2000. He succumbed to homesickness, however, and left his contract early and returned to Japan following the 2003 season.

CAREER MARINERS RECORD:

W	L	W%	ERA	SV
7	16	.304	3.14	129
K	BB	SHO	IP	
242	77	0	223.3	

SUZUKI, ICHIRO (OF)
(2001–2005)

Soon after Kaz Sasaki joined the Mariners bullpen, another Japanese star arrived in Seattle. Ichiro Suzuki burst onto the scene as an immediate sensation. Cries of "Ichiro! Ichiro!" became commonplace not only at Safeco Field, but in parks around the league, as the slight but powerful right fielder established his prowess at the plate and in the field. He routinely scaled the outfield walls to make incredible catches, and made accurate monster throws on the fly from the warning track to his target base. Ichiro led the league in hits in his rookie season (2001) and in 2004 he set the major league record for hits in a season with 262. As good a base stealer as a hitter, he led the league in stolen bases in 2001 with 56, and has never swiped fewer than 31 bags in a season. Ichiro has been named to the All-Star team and won a Gold Glove every year he's been in the league. Ichiro owns two batting titles (2001 and 2004), and in 2001 he won both the Rookie of the Year and MVP Awards (Boston's Fred Lynn is the only other player to win both awards in the same year).

CAREER MARINERS RECORD:

Games	AB	Hits	Runs
796	3,401	1,130	561
Avg	HR	RBI	SB
.332	52	310	190

WILSON, DAN (C)
(1995–2005)

Dan Wilson is another longtime fan favorite in Seattle. After playing in only 48 games for the Cincinnati Reds over two seasons, Wilson was traded to Seattle along with Bobby Ayala for Erik Hanson and Bret Boone after the 1993 season. Though he never hit much, he was the Mariners' primary receiver for a solid decade, an outstanding handler of pitchers, and a steadying force on the team.

CAREER MARINERS RECORD:

Games	AB	Hits	Runs
1,251	4,085	1,071	433
Avg	**HR**	**RBI**	**SB**
.262	88	508	23

Tampa Bay Devil Rays

Since 1998

1998 Rolando Arrojo's 14 wins are the most ever by a pitcher on an American League expansion team in its first season, and ties the major league record set the same season by Arizona's Andy Benes. The rest of Tampa Bay's starters combined for a total of 25 wins.... **1999** When Wade Boggs homers for his 3,000th career hit on August 7, it marks the first time ever that a member of the 3,000-hit club accomplished the feat with a round-tripper.... **2001** Tampa Bay becomes just the second team in history to go an entire season with only one complete game.

FRANCHISE HISTORY

The Tampa Bay Devil Rays franchise came into being on March 9, 1995, the same date as the Arizona Diamondbacks, after a unanimous 28–0 vote by baseball owners approved the expansion. Arizona joined the National League West Division while Tampa Bay joined the American League East. A local group headed by Tampa businessman Vincent J. Naimoli was awarded the franchise after paying a record $130 million fee to Major League Baseball. The Home Shopping Network was also an original investor.

Although Arizona and Tampa Bay joined the major leagues at the same time, the two teams have had remarkably different results on the field. Arizona has spent liberally on free agents in order to win three division titles and one World Series championship in its brief existence, but Tampa Bay has exercised fiscal restraint and escaped the cellar only once. In 2005 Vince Naimoli relinquished control of the team to Stuart Sternberg, a wealthy Wall Street investor. Sternberg originally bought a 48 percent interest in the team in May, then acquired controlling interest as he bought out the other limited partners who had grown weary of dealing with the difficult Naimoli.

On the field, the Devil Rays have had little success, but a number of fading stars (Wade Boggs, Fred McGriff, Roberto Hernandez, and Wilson Alvarez, among others). On August 7, 1999, Boggs provided a franchise highlight when he smacked a home run for his 3,000th hit, the only member of the exclusive group to do so, and he accomplished the feat at Tropicana Field, the cavernous and depressing indoor stadium that is actually located in St. Petersburg, not Tampa Bay. McGriff joined the 400-home run club in 2000, although his historic homer came at Shea Stadium. McGriff is also the only player in major league history besides Frank Robinson to hit at least 200 career homers in both the National and American Leagues.

Wade Boggs embraces his father Win after getting his 3,000th hit on August 7, 1999.

After five consecutive losing seasons, the Devil Rays hired fiery manager Lou Piniella in 2003 to turn things around. After a last-place finish that year, Piniella did lead the team to its only non-last-place finish ever in 2004 with a 70–91 record in 2004, good for fourth place. The Rays, behind young stars Aubrey Huff and Carl Crawford, actually stood at 42–41 during the season, the latest they have ever been over .500. After a dismal return to last-place form in 2005, a disgruntled Piniella resigned, upset over the team's apparent lack of commitment to building a competitive franchise

TEAM NAME HISTORY

Official Names

Devil Rays	(1998–current)

Unofficial Names/Nicknames:

Rays, D-Rays

STADIUM HISTORY

Tropicana Field	1998–current

YEARLY RECORD, FINISH, & ATTENDANCE FIGURES

Year	League	Record	DIV/LG Finish	Attendance	Avg/Gm
2005	AL East	67–95	5	1,141,669	14,095
2004	AL East	70–91	4	1,274,911	15,936
2003	AL East	63–99	5	1,058,695	13,070
2002	AL East	55–106	5	1,065,742	13,157
2001	AL East	62–100	5	1,298,365	16,029
2000	AL East	69–92	5	1,449,673	18,121
1999	AL East	69–93	5	1,562,827	19,294
1998	AL East	63–99	5	2,506,293	30,942

MANAGER HISTORY

Manager	Years	W–L	Win %
Larry Rothschild	1998–2001	205–294	.411
Hal McRae	2001–2002	113–196	.366
Lou Piniella	2003–2005	200–285	.412
Joe Maddon	(Took over beginning in 2006)		

ALL-TIME WIN-LOSS RECORDS VS. ALL OPPONENTS

Opponent	W–L
ALL-TIME	518–775
Angels	28–50
Astros	0–3
Athletics	22–53
Blue Jays	60–71
Braves	4–11
Brewers	2–1
Cardinals	0–3
Cubs	1–2
Diamondbacks	3–0
Dodgers	1–2
Giants	3–3
Indians	23–41
INTERLEAGUE	56–86
Mariners	30–45
Marlins	15–28
Mets	5–7
Nationals	5–7
Orioles	62–69
Padres	4–2
Phillies	8–4
Pirates	2–4
Rangers	32–47
Reds	0–6
Red Sox	44–88
Rockies	3–3
Royals	34–33
Tigers	31–29
Twins	28–38
White Sox	26–37
Yankees	42–88

Franchise Highlights, Low Points, and Strange Distinctions

1998 The Devil Rays' 12 wins in April of 1998 were the most ever by an expansion team for that month.

On May 15, the Devil Rays began a four-game sweep of Baltimore in Camden Yards. This marked the first time ever that an expansion team had swept a four-game series from a defending league or divisional champion in its home park.

When Tampa Bay ended the 1998 season 51 games behind the New York Yankees in the East, it was the widest margin between a divisional champ and the last-place team since divisional play began in 1969.

• • • •

1999 After an impressive tryout and short stint in the minors, 35-year-old Jim Morris made the incredible jump from high school baseball coach to major league relief pitcher for the Rays. The feat was later memorialized in the movie *The Rookie,* starring Dennis Quaid. In five relief appearances in 1999, Morris held opposing batters to a .167 average.

• • • •

2000 Fred McGriff achieved a number of milestones: 400 career homers, 2,000 career hits, and 2,000 games played. He eventually became only the second player in major league history to hit 200 home runs in both leagues (Frank Robinson's the other).

• • • •

2001 Cy Young winner Roger Clemens, then pitching with the Yankees, lost only three games all season, two of them to the Devil Rays.

Carl Crawford goes all out in 2005. The ball fell for a double.

Special Achievements

WORLD SERIES RESULTS

None

WORLD SERIES MANAGERIAL RECORDS

None

ALL-TIME POSTSEASON RECORD

None

ALL-STAR GAMES AT TROPICANA FIELD

None

HALL OF FAMERS WHO PLAYED FOR TEAM

	Position	Years	Games with Tampa Bay
Wade Boggs	3B/DH	1998–1999	213

HALL OF FAMERS WHO MANAGED TEAM

None

MVP AWARD WINNERS

None

CY YOUNG AWARD WINNERS

None

ROOKIE OF THE YEAR AWARD WINNERS

None

GOLD GLOVE WINNERS

None

TRIPLE CROWN WINNERS

None

FIREMAN OF THE YEAR AWARD WINNERS

None

WORLD SERIES MVP

None

LEAGUE CHAMPIONSHIP SERIES MVP

None

ALL-STAR GAME MVP

None

MANAGER OF THE YEAR AWARD WINNERS

None

NINE-INNING NO-HITTERS PITCHED

None

20-GAME WINNERS

None

RETIRED UNIFORM NUMBERS

None

TEAM RECORDS—WINS & LOSSES

- Games won in a season: 70 in 2004
- Games lost in a season: 106 in 2002
- Games won in a month: 20 in June 2004
- Games lost in a month: 21 in June 2003
- Consecutive games won: 12 in 2004
- Consecutive games lost: 15 in 2002
- Biggest shutout victory: 10–0 over Seattle (September 8, 1998) and Montreal (July 12, 2001)
- Biggest shutout loss: 14–0 to Toronto on July 1, 2004
- Highest winning percentage: .435 in 2004 (70–91)
- Lowest winning percentage: .342 in 2002 (55–106)

TEAM RECORDS—BATTING

- Highest team batting average: .274 in 1999 and 2005
- Lowest team batting average: .253 in 2002
- Highest team slugging average: .425 in 2005
- Highest team on-base percentage: .343 in 1999
- Total hits: 1,531 in 1999
- Extra-base hits: 486 in 2005
- Hits in a game: 24 vs. Toronto on June 24, 2004
- Longest individual hitting streak: 18, Quinton McCracken, 1998

- Most .300 hitters in a single season: 1 in 1999, 2003, and 2005
- Home runs: 162 in 2000
- Home runs in a month: 10, Jose Canseco, April 1999 and Aubrey Huff, May 2003
- Home runs in a game: 6 vs. Kansas City on Aug. 10, 2002
- Home runs by a rookie: 21, Jonny Gomes, 2005
- Home runs by a right-hander: 34, Jose Canseco, 1999
- Home runs by a left-hander: 34, Aubrey Huff, 2003
- Home runs by a switch-hitter: 21, Jose Cruz Jr., 2004
- Grand slams: 4 in 2000 and 2001
- Grand slams (individual; season): 2, accomplished by five players
- Grand slams (individual; career): 2, accomplished by six players
- Triples: 46 in 2004
- Doubles: 333 in 2002
- Singles: 1,085 in 1999
- Walks: 558 in 2000
- Runs scored: 772 in 1999
- Runs scored in a game: 19 vs. Toronto on June 24, 2004
- Runs scored in an inning: 11 vs. Seattle on May 28, 2000 (eighth inning)
- Most batters hit by a pitch: 69 in 2005
- Times shut out: 17 in 1998
- Grounded into double plays: 157 in 1999
- Fewest grounded into double plays: 97 in 2004
- Runners left on base: 1,169 in 1999

TEAM RECORDS—BASERUNNING

- Stolen bases: 151 in 2005
- Caught stealing: 73 in 1998

TEAM RECORDS—PITCHING

- Lowest earned run average: 4.35 in 1998
- Complete games: 12 in 2002
- Saves: 45 in 1999
- Strikeouts: 1,055 in 1999
- Shutouts: 8 in 2000
- Walks: 695 in 1999
- Hit batsmen: 95 in 2003
- Wild pitches: 75 in 2001
- Consecutive wins (individual): 7, Mark Hendrickson, 2005
- Consecutive losses (individual): 10, Albie Lopez, 2001
- Strikeouts in a game (individual): 12, Dan Wheeler, September 12, 1999
- Runs allowed in a game: 22 vs. Boston, July 23, 2002

TEAM RECORDS—FIELDING

- Best fielding average: .985 in 1998
- Most errors committed: 139 in 2001
- Fewest errors committed: 94 in 1998
- Most double plays turned: 198 in 1999
- Fewest double plays turned: 139 in 2004 and 2005

TEAM RECORDS—MISCELLANEOUS

- Number of times league champions: 0
- Number of times finishing last in league: 3
- Largest attendance, single game: 45,369 vs. Detroit, March 31, 1998
- Largest attendance, doubleheader: has never played a doubleheader at home
- Players used in a season: 51 in 2003
- Seasons played: 5 by nine players (Flaherty, Hall, Huff, McGriff, Rolls, B. Smith, Winn, Harper, Yan)

PRIMARY PITCHING STAFFS

Year	Starter	Starter	Starter	Starter	Starter	Closer	Bullpen	Bullpen	Bullpen
2005	Kazmir	Hendrickson	Waechter	Fossum	Nomo	Baez	Miller	Harper	Carter
2004	Hendrickson	Zambrano	Brazelton	Bell	Waechter	Baez	Miller	Carter	Harper
2003	Gonzalez	Zambrano	Kennedy	Bell	Sosa	Carter	Colome	Levine	Harper
2002	Sturtze	Wilson	Kennedy	Rupe	Sosa	Yan	Zambrano	Kent	Harper
2001	Sturtze	Wilson	Kennedy	Rupe	Rekar	Yan	Zambrano	Creek	Phelps
2000	Lopez	Trachsel	Yan	Rupe	Rekar	Hernandez	White	Creek	Mecir
1999	Witt	Alvarez	Arrojo	Rupe	Eiland	Hernandez	White	Lopez	Yan
1998	Saunders	Alvarez	Arrojo	Santana	Springer	Hernandez	Mecir	Lopez	Yan

PRIMARY STARTING LINEUPS

Year	C	1B	2B	3B	SS	LF	CF	RF	DH
2005	Hall	Lee	Green	Gonzalez	Lugo	Crawford	Hollins	Huff	Gomes
2004	Hall	Martinez	Sanchez	Huff	Lugo	Crawford	Baldelli	Cruz	Fick
2003	Hall	Lee	Anderson	Rolls	Lugo	Crawford	Baldelli	Huff	Martin
2002	Hall	Cox	Abernathy	Sandberg	Gomez	Crawford	Winn	Grieve	Huff
2001	Flaherty	Cox	Abernathy	Huff	Martinez	Tyner	Williams	Grieve	Vaughn
2000	Flaherty	McGriff	Cairo	Castilla	Martinez	Vaughn	Williams	Guillen	Canseco
1999	Flaherty	McGriff	Cairo	Boggs	Stocker	Trammell	Winn	Martinez	Canseco
1998	Flaherty	McGriff	Cairo	Smith	Stocker	Kelly	McCracken	Martinez	Sorrento

Top 10 Batting Leaders, Single Season & Career with Team

GAMES PLAYED: CAREER WITH TEAM

Player	G	PA
1. Aubrey Huff	736	3,066
2. Fred McGriff	577	2,399
3. Carl Crawford	522	2,298
Toby Hall	522	1,964
5. Randy Winn	519	2,047
6. John Flaherty	471	1,802
7. Julio Lugo	432	1,827
8. Miguel Cairo	389	1,483
9. Steve Cox	378	1,399
10. Ben Grieve	345	1,405

AT-BATS: SEASON

Player	AB	Year
1. Carl Crawford	644	2005
2. Rocco Baldelli	637	2003
3. Aubrey Huff	636	2003
4. Gerald Williams	632	2000
5. Carl Crawford	630	2003
6. Carl Crawford	626	2004
7. Julio Lugo	616	2005
8. Quinton McCracken	614	1998
9. Randy Winn	607	2002
10. Aubrey Huff	600	2004

AT-BATS: CAREER WITH TEAM

Player	AB	PA
1. Aubrey Huff	2,798	3,066
2. Carl Crawford	2,159	2,298
3. Fred McGriff	2,074	2,399
4. Randy Winn	1,836	2,047
5. Toby Hall	1,829	1,964
6. John Flaherty	1,673	1,802
7. Julio Lugo	1,630	1,827
8. Miguel Cairo	1,355	1,483
9. Steve Cox	1,239	1,399
10. Greg Vaughn	1,197	1,404

BATTING AVERAGE: SEASON

Player	BA	Year
1. Aubrey Huff	.313	2002
2. Aubrey Huff	.311	2003
3. Fred McGriff	.310	1999
4. Carl Crawford	.301	2005
5. Randy Winn	.298	2002
6. Aubrey Huff	.297	2004
7. Carl Crawford	.296	2004
8. Miguel Cairo	.295	1999
Julio Lugo	.295	2005
10. Quinton McCracken	.292	1998

BATTING AVERAGE: CAREER WITH TEAM

Player	BA	PA
1. Fred McGriff	.291	2,430
2. Carl Crawford	.289	2,298
3. Aubrey Huff	.288	3,066
4. Julio Lugo	.283	1,827
5. Randy Winn	.279	2,047
6. Miguel Cairo	.275	1,483
7. Toby Hall	.266	1,964
8. Steve Cox	.262	1,399
9. Ben Grieve	.254	1,405
10. John Flaherty	.252	1,802

TOTAL HITS: SEASON

Player	H	Year
1. Aubrey Huff	198	2003
2. Carl Crawford	194	2005
3. Carl Crawford	185	2004
4. Rocco Baldelli	184	2003
5. Julio Lugo	182	2005
6. Randy Winn	181	2002
7. Quinton McCracken	179	1998
8. Aubrey Huff	178	2004
9. Carl Crawford	177	2003
10. Gerald Williams	173	2000

TOTAL HITS: CAREER WITH TEAM

Player	H	PA
1. Aubrey Huff	805	3,066
2. Carl Crawford	623	2,298
3. Fred McGriff	603	2,399
4. Randy Winn	513	2,047
5. Toby Hall	487	1,964
6. Julio Lugo	461	1,827
7. John Flaherty	422	1,802
8. Miguel Cairo	373	1,483
9. Rocco Baldelli	329	1,249
10. Steve Cox	324	1,399

HOME RUNS: SEASON

Player	HR	Year
1. Jose Canseco	34	1999
Aubrey Huff	34	2003
3. Fred McGriff	32	1999
4. Aubrey Huff	29	2004
5. Greg Vaughn	28	2000
Jorge Cantu	28	2005
7. Fred McGriff	27	2000
8. Greg Vaughn	24	2001
9. Aubrey Huff	23	2002
Tino Martinez	23	2004

Home Runs: Career with Team

Player	HR	PA
1. Aubrey Huff	120	3,066
2. Fred McGriff	99	2,399
3. Greg Vaughn	60	1,404
4. Jose Canseco	43	766
5. Steve Cox	39	1,399
6. Toby Hall	36	1,964
7. John Flaherty	35	1,802
8. Ben Grieve	34	1,405
9. Carl Crawford	33	2,298
Bubba Trammell	33	757

Triples: Season

Player	3B	Year
1. Carl Crawford	19	2004
2. Carl Crawford	15	2005
3. Carl Crawford	9	2003
Randy Winn	9	1998
Randy Winn	9	2002
6. Rocco Baldelli	8	2003
Jose Cruz	8	2004
8. Quinton McCracken	7	1998
9. Carl Crawford	6	2002
Jonny Gomes	6	2005
Julio Lugo	6	2005
Randy Winn	6	2001

Triples: Career with Team

Player	3B	PA
1. Carl Crawford	49	2,298
2. Randy Winn	28	2,047
3. Julio Lugo	14	1,827
4. Miguel Cairo	12	1,483
5. Rocco Baldelli	11	1,249
6. Jose Cruz	8	636
Aubrey Huff	8	3,066
Quinton McCracken	8	877
9. Dave Martinez	7	1,058
10. Jonny Gomes	6	438
Kevin Stocker	6	804
Jason Tyner	6	796

Doubles: Season

Player	2B	Year
1. Aubrey Huff	47	2003
2. Julio Lugo	41	2004
3. Jorge Cantu	40	2005
4. Randy Winn	39	2002
5. Quinton McCracken	38	1998
6. Travis Lee	37	2003
7. Julio Lugo	36	2005
8. Carl Crawford	33	2005
Fred McGriff	33	1998
10. Rocco Baldelli	32	2003

Doubles: Career with Team

Player	2B	PA
1. Aubrey Huff	157	3,066
2. Fred McGriff	102	2,399
3. Toby Hall	99	1,964
4. Randy Winn	94	2,047
5. Julio Lugo	90	1,827
6. Carl Crawford	88	2,298
7. John Flaherty	82	1,802
8. Steve Cox	72	1,399
9. Ben Grieve	67	1,405
10. Greg Vaughn	62	1,404

Extra-Base Hits: Season

Player	XBH	Year
1. Aubrey Huff	84	2003
2. Jorge Cantu	69	2005
3. Carl Crawford	63	2005
Fred McGriff	63	1999
5. Randy Winn	62	2002
6. Travis Lee	59	2003
7. Aubrey Huff	58	2004
8. Carl Crawford	56	2004
Greg Vaughn	56	2000
10. Jose Cruz	54	2004

Extra-Base Hits: Career with Team

Player	XBH	PA
1. Aubrey Huff	285	3,066
2. Fred McGriff	202	2,399
3. Carl Crawford	170	2,298
4. Randy Winn	146	2,047
5. Toby Hall	136	1,964
6. Julio Lugo	132	1,827
7. Greg Vaughn	125	1,404
8. John Flaherty	118	1,802
9. Steve Cox	113	1,399
10. Ben Grieve	103	1,405

Total Bases: Season

Player	TB	Year
1. Aubrey Huff	353	2003
2. Carl Crawford	302	2005
3. Jorge Cantu	297	2005
4. Aubrey Huff	296	2004
5. Fred McGriff	292	1999
6. Carl Crawford	282	2004
7. Randy Winn	280	2002
8. Gerald Williams	270	2000
9. Rocco Baldelli	265	2003
10. Fred McGriff	256	2000

Total Bases: Career with Team

Player	TB	PA
1. Aubrey Huff	1,338	3,066
2. Fred McGriff	1,004	2,399
3. Carl Crawford	908	2,298
4. Randy Winn	735	2,047
5. Toby Hall	696	1,964
6. Julio Lugo	663	1,827
7. John Flaherty	611	1,802
8. Greg Vaughn	519	1,404
9. Steve Cox	517	1,399
10. Rocco Baldelli	491	1,249

Runs Batted In: Season

Player	RBI	Year
1. Jorge Cantu	117	2005
2. Aubrey Huff	107	2003
3. Fred McGriff	106	2000
4. Aubrey Huff	104	2004
Fred McGriff	104	1999
6. Jose Canseco	95	1999
7. Aubrey Huff	92	2005
8. Gerald Williams	89	2000
9. Greg Vaughn	82	2001
10. Carl Crawford	81	2005
Fred McGriff	81	1998

Runs Batted In: Career with Team

Player	RBI	PA
1. Aubrey Huff	421	3,066
2. Fred McGriff	359	2,399
3. Toby Hall	228	1,964
4. Carl Crawford	220	2,298
5. John Flaherty	196	1,802
6. Julio Lugo	185	1,827
Greg Vaughn	185	1,404
8. Randy Winn	182	2,047
9. Steve Cox	158	1,399
10. Ben Grieve	153	1,405

Runs Scored: Season

Player	R	Year
1. Carl Crawford	104	2004
2. Carl Crawford	101	2005
3. Aubrey Huff	92	2004
4. Aubrey Huff	91	2003
5. Rocco Baldelli	89	2003

Julio Lugo	89	2005
7. Gerald Williams	87	2000
Randy Winn	87	2002
9. Julio Lugo	83	2004
Greg Vaughn	83	2000

RUNS SCORED: CAREER WITH TEAM

Player	R	PA
1. Aubrey Huff	374	3,066
2. Carl Crawford	308	2,298
3. Fred McGriff	277	2,399
4. Randy Winn	264	2,047
5. Julio Lugo	230	1,827
6. Greg Vaughn	185	1,404
7. Toby Hall	179	1,964
8. Rocco Baldelli	168	1,249
9. Ben Grieve	162	1,405
10. Miguel Cairo	159	1,483

WALKS: SEASON

Player	BB	Year
1. Fred McGriff	91	2000
2. Ben Grieve	87	2001
3. Fred McGriff	86	1999
4. Greg Vaughn	80	2000
5. Fred McGriff	79	1998
6. Jose Cruz	76	2004
7. Greg Vaughn	71	2001
8. Ben Grieve	69	2002
9. Tino Martinez	66	2004
10. Travis Lee	64	2003

WALKS: CAREER WITH TEAM

Player	BB	PA
1. Fred McGriff	305	2,399
2. Aubrey Huff	223	3,066
3. Greg Vaughn	192	1,404
4. Ben Grieve	188	1,405
5. Randy Winn	165	2,047
6. Julio Lugo	150	1,827
7. Steve Cox	130	1,399
8. Dave Martinez	105	1,058
9. Paul Sorrento	103	843
10. Jose Canseco	99	766
Travis Lee	99	1,054

STRIKEOUTS: SEASON

Player	SO	Year
1. Ben Grieve	159	2001
2. Jared Sandberg	139	2002
3. Jose Canseco	135	1999
4. Paul Sorrento	133	1998
5. Greg Vaughn	130	2001
6. Rocco Baldelli	128	2003
Greg Vaughn	128	2000
8. Ben Grieve	121	2002
9. Fred McGriff	120	2000
10. Fred McGriff	118	1998

STRIKEOUTS: CAREER WITH TEAM

Player	SO	PA
1. Fred McGriff	433	2,399
2. Aubrey Huff	387	3,066
3. Randy Winn	347	2,047
4. Greg Vaughn	340	1,404
5. Ben Grieve	321	1,405
6. Carl Crawford	308	2,298
7. Bobby Smith	268	914
8. Julio Lugo	266	1,827
9. John Flaherty	250	1,802
10. Steve Cox	240	1,399

SLUGGING PERCENTAGE: SEASON

Player	SLG	Year
1. Jose Canseco	.563	1999
2. Aubrey Huff	.555	2003
3. Fred McGriff	.552	1999
4. Jonny Gomes	.534	2005
5. Aubrey Huff	.520	2002
6. Greg Vaughn	.499	2000
7. Jorge Cantu	.497	2005
8. Aubrey Huff	.493	2004
9. Carl Crawford	.469	2005
10. Randy Winn	.461	2002

SLUGGING PERCENTAGE: CAREER WITH TEAM

Player	SLG	PA
1. Fred McGriff	.484	2,399
2. Aubrey Huff	.478	3,066
3. Greg Vaughn	.434	1,404
4. Rocco Baldelli	.425	1,249
5. Carl Crawford	.421	2,298
6. Steve Cox	.417	1,399
7. Julio Lugo	.407	1,827
8. Randy Winn	.400	2,047
9. Ben Grieve	.399	1,405
10. Toby Hall	.381	1,964

ON-BASE PERCENTAGE: SEASON

Player	OBP	Year
1. Fred McGriff	.405	1999
2. Steve Cox	.379	2000
3. Fred McGriff	.373	2000
4. Ben Grieve	.372	2001
Jonny Gomes	.372	2005
6. Fred McGriff	.371	1998
7. Jose Canseco	.369	1999
8. Aubrey Huff	.367	2003
9. Greg Vaughn	.365	2000
10. Aubrey Huff	.364	2002

ON-BASE PERCENTAGE: CAREER WITH TEAM

Player	OBP	PA
1. Fred McGriff	.380	2,399
2. John Flaherty	.365	1,802
3. Ben Grieve	.364	1,405
4. Julio Lugo	.346	1,827
5. Aubrey Huff	.342	3,066
Randy Winn	.342	2,047
7. Steve Cox	.340	1,399
8. Greg Vaughn	.335	1,404
9. Rocco Baldelli	.326	1,249
10. Carl Crawford	.320	2,298

OPS (ON BASE PERCENTAGE + SLUGGING PERCENTAGE): SEASON

Player	OPS	Year
1. Fred McGriff	.957	1999
2. Jose Canseco	.931	1999
3. Aubrey Huff	.922	2003
4. Jonny Gomes	.906	2005
5. Aubrey Huff	.884	2002
6. Greg Vaughn	.864	2000
7. Aubrey Huff	.853	2004
8. Steve Cox	.832	2000
9. Fred McGriff	.826	2000
10. Tino Martinez	.823	2004

OPS (ON BASE PERCENTAGE + SLUGGING PERCENTAGE): CAREER WITH TEAM

Player	OPS	PA
1. Fred McGriff	.864	2,399
2. Aubrey Huff	.820	3,066
3. Greg Vaughn	.769	1,404
4. Ben Grieve	.763	1,405
5. Steve Cox	.757	1,399
6. Julio Lugo	.753	1,827
7. Rocco Baldelli	.751	1,249
8. Randy Winn	.742	2,047
9. Carl Crawford	.740	2,298
10. Toby Hall	.684	1,964

Stolen Bases: Season

Player	SB	Year
1. Carl Crawford	59	2004
2. Carl Crawford	55	2003
3. Carl Crawford	46	2005
4. Julio Lugo	39	2005
5. Jason Tyner	31	2001
6. Miguel Cairo	28	2000
7. Rocco Baldelli	27	2003
Randy Winn	27	2002
9. Randy Winn	26	1998
10. Miguel Cairo	22	1999

Stolen Bases: Career with Team

Player	SB	PA
1. Carl Crawford	169	2,298
2. Randy Winn	80	2,047
3. Julio Lugo	70	1,827
4. Miguel Cairo	69	1,483
5. Jason Tyner	46	796
6. Rocco Baldelli	44	1,249
7. Damian Rolls	27	883
8. Joey Gathright	26	275
9. Quinton McCracken	25	877
10. Dave Martinez	22	1,058
Greg Vaughn	22	1404
Gerald Williams	22	934

Sacrifice Hits: Season

Player	Sac	Year
1. Felix Martinez	12	2000
2. Miguel Cairo	11	1998
Randy Winn	11	1998
4. Dave Martinez	10	1999
Nick Green	10	2005
6. Quinton McCracken	9	1998
Gerald Williams	9	2000
8. Brent Abernathy	8	2002
Kevin Stocker	8	1998
10. Miguel Cairo	7	1999
Julio Lugo	7	2003
Julio Lugo	7	2004
Andy Sheets	7	2001

Sacrifice Hits: Career with Team

Player	Sac	PA
1. Miguel Cairo	24	1,483
2. Randy Winn	20	2,047
3. Julio Lugo	17	1,827
4. Carl Crawford	16	2,298
5. Felix Martinez	15	591
Jason Tyner	15	796
7. John Flaherty	14	1,802
Kevin Stocker	14	804
9. Gerald Williams	12	934
10. Brent Abernathy	11	846
Dave Martinez	11	1,058

Hit by Pitch: Season

Player	HBP	Year
1. Jonny Gomes	14	2005
2. Jose Guillen	13	2000
3. Nick Green	11	2005
4. Steve Cox	10	2001
Herb Perry	10	1999
6. Tino Martinez	9	2004
7. Seven tied with ...	8	—

Hit by Pitch: Career with Team

Player	HBP	PA
1. Jose Guillen	23	680
2. Ben Grieve	22	1,405
3. Steve Cox	21	1,399
Toby Hall	21	1,964
Aubrey Huff	21	3,066
6. Rocco Baldelli	16	1,249
Randy Winn	16	2,047
8. Miguel Cairo	15	1,483
Jonny Gomes	15	438
Julio Lugo	15	1,827

Top 10 Pitching Leaders, Single Season & Career with Team

Games Pitched: Season

Player	GP	Year
1. Roberto Hernandez	72	1999
2. Roberto Hernandez	68	2000
Jim Mecir	68	1998
4. Roberto Hernandez	67	1998
Danys Baez	67	2005
6. Doug Creek	66	2001
7. Esteban Yan	64	1998
8. Rick White	63	1999
9. Danys Baez	62	2004
Lance Carter	62	2003

Games Pitched: Career with Team

Player	GP	IP
1. Esteban Yan	266	418.7
2. Travis Harper	210	369.7
3. Roberto Hernandez	207	218.0
4. Jesus Colome	185	250.7
5. Albie Lopez	170	453.7
6. Lance Carter	165	236.7
7. Rick White	145	248.0
8. Doug Creek	140	160.7
9. Victor Zambrano	135	481.7
10. Danys Baez	129	140.3

Innings Pitched: Season

Player	IP	Year
1. Tanyon Sturtze	224.0	2002
2. Rolando Arrojo	202.0	1998
3. Joe Kennedy	196.7	2002
4. Tanyon Sturtze	195.3	2001
5. Paul Wilson	193.7	2002
6. Tony Saunders	192.3	1998
7. Victor Zambrano	188.3	2003
8. Scott Kazmir	186.0	2005
9. Albie Lopez	185.3	2000
10. Mark Hendrickson	183.3	2004

Innings Pitched: Career with Team

Player	IP
1. Bryan Rekar	495.3
2. Victor Zambrano	481.7
3. Tanyon Sturtze	472.0
4. Ryan Rupe	466.7
5. Albie Lopez	453.7
6. Joe Kennedy	448.0
7. Esteban Yan	418.7
8. Paul Wilson	396.0
9. Wilson Alvarez	377.7
10. Travis Harper	369.7

Batters Faced: Season

Player	BF	Year
1. Tanyon Sturtze	1,008	2002
2. Tony Saunders	855	1998
3. Rolando Arrojo	853	1998
4. Paul Wilson	851	2002
5. Joe Kennedy	840	2002
6. Tanyon Sturtze	837	2001
7. Victor Zambrano	836	2003
8. Scott Kazmir	818	2005
9. Bobby Witt	815	1999
10. Mark Hendrickson	803	2004

Batters Faced: Career with Team

Player	BF	IP
1. Bryan Rekar	2,179	495.3
2. Victor Zambrano	2,155	481.7
3. Tanyon Sturtze	2,060	472.0
4. Ryan Rupe	2,056	466.7
5. Albie Lopez	1,981	453.7
6. Joe Kennedy	1,957	448.0
7. Esteban Yan	1,854	418.7
8. Paul Wilson	1,731	396.0
9. Wilson Alvarez	1,666	377.7
10. Travis Harper	1,610	369.7

Games Started: Season

Player	GS	Year
1. Tanyon Sturtze	33	2002
2. Rolando Arrojo	32	1998
Bobby Witt	32	1999
Scott Kazmir	32	2005
5. Tony Saunders	31	1998
Mark Hendrickson	31	2005
7. Mark Hendrickson	30	2004
Joe Kennedy	30	2002
Paul Wilson	30	2002
10. Wilson Alvarez	28	1999
Victor Zambrano	28	2003

Games Started: Career with Team

Player	GS	IP
1. Ryan Rupe	83	466.7
2. Bryan Rekar	79	495.3
3. Joe Kennedy	72	448.0
4. Tanyon Sturtze	65	472.0
5. Wilson Alvarez	63	377.7
6. Mark Hendrickson	61	361.7
Paul Wilson	61	396.0
Victor Zambrano	61	481.7
9. Rolando Arrojo	56	342.7
10. Albie Lopez	44	453.7
Doug Waechter	44	262.7

Complete Games: Season

Player	CG	Year
1. Joe Kennedy	5	2002
2. Albie Lopez	4	2000
Tanyon Sturtze	4	2002
4. Steve Trachsel	3	2000
Bobby Witt	3	1999
6. Rolando Arrojo	2	1998
Rolando Arrojo	2	1999
Jeremi Gonzalez	2	2003
Mark Hendrickson	2	2004
Bryan Rekar	2	2000
Ryan Rupe	2	2002
Tony Saunders	2	1998

Complete Games: Career with Team

Player	CG	IP
1. Joe Kennedy	6	448.0
2. Albie Lopez	5	453.7
3. Rolando Arrojo	4	342.7
Tanyon Sturtze	4	472.0
5. Bryan Rekar	3	495.3
Steve Trachsel	3	137.7
Bobby Witt	3	180.3
Mark Hendrickson	3	361.7
9. Jeremi Gonzalez	2	206.7
Ryan Rupe	2	466.7
Tony Saunders	2	234.3

Games Won: Season

Player	W	Year
1. Rolando Arrojo	14	1998
2. Victor Zambrano	12	2003
3. Albie Lopez	11	2000
Tanyon Sturtze	11	2001
Mark Hendrickson	11	2005
6. Mark Hendrickson	10	2004
Scott Kazmir	10	2005
8. Wilson Alvarez	9	1999
Victor Zambrano	9	2004
10. Six tied with . . .	8	——

Games Won: Career with Team

Player	W	IP
1. Victor Zambrano	35	481.7
2. Albie Lopez	26	453.7
Esteban Yan	26	418.7
4. Ryan Rupe	23	466.7
5. Rolando Arrojo	21	342.7
Mark Hendrickson	21	361.7
7. Travis Harper	20	369.7
8. Tanyon Sturtze	19	472.0
9. Joe Kennedy	18	448.0
Bryan Rekar	18	495.3

Games Lost: Season

Player	L	Year
1. Tanyon Sturtze	18	2002
2. Mark Hendrickson	15	2004
Tony Saunders	15	1998
Bobby Witt	15	1999
5. Wilson Alvarez	14	1998
6. Albie Lopez	13	2000
Bryan Rekar	13	2001
8. 10 tied with . . .	12	——

Games Lost: Career with Team

Player	L	IP
1. Bryan Rekar	37	495.3
Ryan Rupe	37	466.7
3. Joe Kennedy	31	448.0
Albie Lopez	31	453.7

5. Tanyon Sturtze	30	472.0
Esteban Yan	30	418.7
7. Travis Harper	29	369.7
8. Victor Zambrano	27	481.7
9. Wilson Alvarez	26	377.7
Jorge Sosa	26	327.3

Winning Percentage: Season

Player	W%	Year
1. Mark Hendrickson	.579	2005
2. Victor Zambrano	.562	2004
3. Victor Zambrano	.545	2003
4. Rolando Arrojo	.538	1998
5. Scott Kazmir	.526	2005
6. Wilson Alvarez	.500	1999
Rob Bell	.500	2004
Victor Zambrano	.500	2002
9. Tanyon Sturtze	.478	2001
10. Ryan Rupe	.471	1999
Paul Wilson	.471	2001

Winning Percentage: Career with Team

Player	W%	IP
1. Victor Zambrano	.565	481.7
Lance Carter	.565	236.7
3. Rob Bell	.519	249.0
4. Scott Kazmir	.500	219.3
5. Mark Hendrickson	.477	361.7
6. Rolando Arrojo	.467	342.7
7. Esteban Yan	.464	418.7
8. Albie Lopez	.456	453.7
9. Travis Harper	.408	369.7
10. Rick White	.400	248.0

Shutouts: Season

Player	SHO	Year
1. Rolando Arrojo	2	1998
Bobby Witt	2	1999
3. Travis Harper	1	2000
Joe Kennedy	1	2002
Joe Kennedy	1	2003
Albie Lopez	1	2000
Albie Lopez	1	2001
Jorge Sosa	1	2003
Steve Trachsel	1	2000
Doug Waechter	1	2003

Shutouts: Career with Team

Player	SHO	IP
1. Rolando Arrojo	2	342.7
Joe Kennedy	2	448.0
Albie Lopez	2	453.7
Bobby Witt	2	180.3
5. Travis Harper	1	369.7
Jorge Sosa	1	327.3
Steve Trachsel	1	137.7
Doug Waechter	1	262.7

ERA: Season

Player	ERA	Year
1. Rolando Arrojo	3.56	1998
2. Scott Kazmir	3.77	2005
3. Tony Saunders	4.12	1998
4. Albie Lopez	4.13	2000
5. Victor Zambrano	4.21	2003
5. Bryan Rekar	4.41	2000
7. Tanyon Sturtze	4.42	2001
8. Joe Kennedy	4.53	2002
9. Mark Hendrickson	4.81	2004
10. Paul Wilson	4.83	2002

ERA: Career with Team

Player	ERA	IP
1. Rolando Arrojo	4.23	342.7
2. Albie Lopez	4.27	453.7
3. Victor Zambrano	4.47	481.7
4. Tanyon Sturtze	4.58	472.0
5. Wilson Alvarez	4.62	377.7
6. Paul Wilson	4.66	396.0
7. Travis Harper	4.94	369.7
8. Joe Kennedy	4.98	448.0
9. Esteban Yan	5.01	418.7
10. Jorge Sosa	5.17	327.3

Earned Runs Allowed: Season

Player	ER	Year
1. Tanyon Sturtze	129	2002
2. Bobby Witt	117	1999
Mark Hendrickson	117	2005
4. Ryan Rupe	105	2001
5. Paul Wilson	104	2002
6. Joe Kennedy	99	2002
7. Mark Hendrickson	98	2004
Doug Waechter	98	2005
9. Tanyon Sturtze	96	2001
10. Esteban Yan	95	2000

Earned Runs Allowed: Career with Team

Player	ER	IP
1. Ryan Rupe	303	466.7
2. Bryan Rekar	286	495.3
3. Joe Kennedy	248	448.0
4. Tanyon Sturtze	240	472.0
5. Victor Zambrano	239	481.7
6. Esteban Yan	233	418.7
7. Albie Lopez	215	453.7
Mark Hendrickson	215	361.7
9. Paul Wilson	205	396.0
10. Travis Harper	203	369.7

Strikeouts: Season

Player	K	Year
1. Scott Kazmir	174	2005
2. Tony Saunders	172	1998
3. Rolando Arrojo	152	1998
4. Tanyon Sturtze	137	2002
5. Victor Zambrano	132	2003
6. Wilson Alvarez	128	1999
Casey Fossum	128	2005
8. Ryan Rupe	123	2001
Bobby Witt	123	1999
10. Paul Wilson	119	2001

Strikeouts: Career with Team

Player	K	IP
1. Victor Zambrano	372	481.7
2. Esteban Yan	351	418.7
3. Ryan Rupe	348	466.7
4. Bryan Rekar	292	495.3
5. Wilson Alvarez	291	377.7
6. Tanyon Sturtze	285	472.0
7. Paul Wilson	270	396.0
8. Joe Kennedy	264	448.0
9. Albie Lopez	262	453.7
10. Rolando Arrojo	259	342.7

Strikeouts per Nine IP: Season

Player	K/9	Year
1. Scott Kazmir	8.42	2005
2. Tony Saunders	8.05	1998
3. Casey Fossum	7.08	2005
4. Rolando Arrojo	6.77	1998
5. Victor Zambrano	6.31	2003
6. Bobby Witt	6.14	1999
7. Tanyon Sturtze	5.50	2002
8. Paul Wilson	5.16	2002

Player		
9. Tanyon Sturtze	5.07	2001
10. Joe Kennedy	4.99	2002

Strikeouts Per Nine IP: Career with Team

Player	K/9	IP
1. Esteban Yan	7.55	418.7
2. Victor Zambrano	6.95	481.7
3. Wilson Alvarez	6.93	377.7
4. Rolando Arrojo	6.80	342.7
5. Ryan Rupe	6.71	466.7
6. Paul Wilson	6.14	396.0
7. Jorge Sosa	5.88	327.3
8. Travis Harper	5.82	369.7
9. Tanyon Sturtze	5.43	472.0
10. Bryan Rekar	5.31	495.3

Hits Allowed: Season

Player	HA	Year
1. Tanyon Sturtze	271	2002
2. Mark Hendrickson	227	2005
3. Paul Wilson	219	2002
4. Bobby Witt	213	1999
5. Mark Hendrickson	211	2004
6. Joe Kennedy	204	2002
7. Bryan Rekar	200	2000
Tanyon Sturtze	200	2001
9. Albie Lopez	199	2000
10. Rolando Arrojo	195	1998

Hits Allowed: Career with Team

Player	HA	IP
1. Bryan Rekar	583	495.3
2. Tanyon Sturtze	518	472.0
3. Ryan Rupe	501	466.7
4. Joe Kennedy	493	448.0
5. Albie Lopez	490	453.7
6. Esteban Yan	447	418.7
7. Mark Hendrickson	438	361.7
8. Victor Zambrano	430	481.7
9. Paul Wilson	422	396.0
10. Travis Harper	389	369.7

Hits Allowed Per Nine IP: Season

Player	H/9	Year
1. Victor Zambrano	7.88	2003
2. Scott Kazmir	8.32	2005
3. Rolando Arrojo	8.69	1998
4. Tony Saunders	8.94	1998
5. Tanyon Sturtze	9.22	2001
6. Joe Kennedy	9.34	2002
7. Casey Fossum	9.41	2005
8. Albie Lopez	9.66	2000
9. Paul Wilson	10.18	2002
10. Mark Hendrickson	10.36	2004

Hits Allowed Per Nine IP: Career with Team

Player	H/9	IP
1. Victor Zambrano	8.03	481.7
2. Wilson Alvarez	8.79	377.7
3. Jorge Sosa	8.94	327.3
4. Rolando Arrojo	9.38	342.7
5. Travis Harper	9.47	369.7
6. Paul Wilson	9.59	396.0
7. Esteban Yan	9.61	418.7
8. Ryan Rupe	9.66	466.7
9. Albie Lopez	9.72	453.7
10. Scott Kazmir	9.90	448.0

Walks Allowed: Season

Player	BB	Year
1. Tony Saunders	111	1998
2. Victor Zambrano	106	2003
3. Scott Kazmir	100	2005
4. Bobby Witt	96	1999
Victor Zambrano	96	2004
6. Tanyon Sturtze	89	2002
7. Wilson Alvarez	79	1999
Tanyon Sturtze	79	2001
9. Albie Lopez	70	2000
10. Jeremi Gonzalez	69	2003

Walks Allowed: Career with Team

Player	BB	IP
1. Victor Zambrano	288	481.7
2. Wilson Alvarez	183	377.7
3. Tanyon Sturtze	182	472.0
4. Albie Lopez	177	453.7
5. Jorge Sosa	168	327.3
6. Ryan Rupe	161	466.7
7. Esteban Yan	155	418.7
8. Bryan Rekar	146	495.3
9. Dewon Brazelton	142	253.0
10. Tony Saunders	140	234.3
Jesus Colome	140	250.7

Walks Allowed Per Nine IP: Season

Player	BB/9	Year
1. Bryan Rekar	2.02	2000
2. Mark Hendrickson	2.26	2004
3. Mark Hendrickson	2.47	2005
4. Joe Kennedy	2.52	2002
5. Rolando Arrojo	2.90	1998
6. Paul Wilson	3.11	2002
7. Casey Fossum	3.32	2005
8. Albie Lopez	3.40	2000
9. Tanyon Sturtze	3.58	2002
10. Tanyon Sturtze	3.64	2001

Walks Allowed Per Nine IP: Career with Team

Player	BB/9	IP
1. Mark Hendrickson	2.36	361.7
2. Bryan Rekar	2.65	495.3
3. Joe Kennedy	2.73	448.0
4. Doug Waechter	2.95	262.7
5. Travis Harper	2.99	369.7
6. Paul Wilson	3.07	396.0
7. Ryan Rupe	3.10	466.7
8. Rolando Arrojo	3.28	342.7
9. Esteban Yan	3.33	418.7
10. Tanyon Sturtze	3.47	472.0

WHIP (Walks + Hits Per Nine IP): Season

Player	WHIP	Year
1. Rolando Arrojo	1.287	1998
2. Joe Kennedy	1.317	2002
3. Bryan Rekar	1.379	2000
4. Mark Hendrickson	1.402	2004
5. Casey Fossum	1.414	2005
6. Tanyon Sturtze	1.428	2001
7. Victor Zambrano	1.439	2003
8. Albie Lopez	1.451	2000
9. Scott Kazmir	1.462	2005
10. Paul Wilson	1.477	2002

WHIP (Walks + Hits Per Nine IP): Career with Team

Player	WHIP	IP
1. Travis Harper	1.385	369.7
2. Joe Kennedy	1.404	448.0

3. Paul Wilson	1.407	396.0
Rolando Arrojo	1.407	342.7
5. Ryan Rupe	1.419	366.7
6. Doug Waechter	1.424	262.7
7. Esteban Yan	1.438	418.7
8. Wilson Alvarez	1.462	377.7
9. Albie Lopez	1.470	453.7
10. Bryan Rekar	1.472	495.3

Home Runs Allowed: Season

Player	HRA	Year
1. Tanyon Sturtze	33	2002
2. Ryan Rupe	30	2001
3. Paul Wilson	29	2002
Doug Waechter	29	2005
5. Esteban Yan	26	2000
6. Albie Lopez	24	2000
Mark Hendrickson	24	2005
8. Rolando Arrojo	23	1999
Joe Kennedy	23	2002
Tanyon Sturtze	23	2001
Bobby Witt	23	1999

Home Runs Allowed: Career with Team

Player	HRA	IP
1. Ryan Rupe	77	466.7
2. Bryan Rekar	73	495.3
3. Esteban Yan	62	418.7
4. Tanyon Sturtze	60	472.0
5. Joe Kennedy	58	448.0
6. Albie Lopez	55	453.7
Victor Zambrano	55	481.7
Travis Harper	55	369.7
9. Wilson Alvarez	53	377.7
Doug Waechter	53	262.7

Saves: Season

Player	SV	Year
1. Roberto Hernandez	43	1999
2. Danys Baez	41	2005
3. Roberto Hernandez	32	2000
4. Danys Baez	30	2004
5. Lance Carter	26	2003
Roberto Hernandez	26	1998
7. Esteban Yan	22	2001
8. Esteban Yan	19	2002
9. Travis Phelps	5	2001
10. Jesus Colome	3	2004

Saves: Career with Team

Player	SV	IP
1. Roberto Hernandez	101	218.0
2. Danys Baez	71	140.3
3. Esteban Yan	42	418.7
4. Lance Carter	29	236.7
5. Jesus Colome	5	250.7
Travis Phelps	5	99.7
7. Albie Lopez	4	453.7
8. Victor Zambrano	3	481.7
9. Travis Harper	2	369.7
Rick White	2	248.0

Wild Pitches: Season

Player	WP	Year
1. Victor Zambrano	15	2003
2. Tanyon Sturtze	11	2001
3. Rob Bell	10	2004
Victor Zambrano	10	2002
5. Bobby Witt	9	1999
6. Jorge Sosa	8	2003
Casey Fossum	8	2005
8. Eight tied with . . .	7	——

Wild Pitches: Career with Team

Player	WP	IP
1. Victor Zambrano	34	481.7
2. Esteban Yan	25	418.7
3. Ryan Rupe	21	466.7
4. Jesus Colome	20	250.7
5. Tanyon Sturtze	19	472.0
6. Bryan Rekar	16	495.3
7. Travis Harper	15	369.7
Jorge Sosa	15	327.3
9. Rob Bell	13	249.0
Albie Lopez	13	453.7

Hit Batsmen: Season

Player	HB	Year
1. Victor Zambrano	20	2003
2. Rolando Arrojo	19	1998
3. Casey Fossum	18	2005
4. Joe Kennedy	16	2002
Victor Zambrano	16	2004
6. Rolando Arrojo	14	1999
7. Paul Wilson	13	2001
Paul Wilson	13	2002
9. Jeremi Gonzalez	12	2003
Ryan Rupe	12	1999
Dennis Springer	12	1998

Hit Batsmen: Career with Team

Player	HB	IP
1. Victor Zambrano	43	481.7
2. Ryan Rupe	42	466.7
3. Rolando Arrojo	33	342.7
Esteban Yan	33	418.7
5. Joe Kennedy	30	448.0
Paul Wilson	30	396.0
7. Travis Harper	24	369.7
8. Dewon Brazelton	20	253.0
9. Wilson Alvarez	19	377.7
Tanyon Sturtze	19	472.0

Games Finished: Season

Player	GF	Year
1. Roberto Hernandez	66	1999
2. Danys Baez	64	2005
3. Danys Baez	59	2004
4. Roberto Hernandez	58	1998
Roberto Hernandez	58	2000
6. Lance Carter	55	2003
7. Esteban Yan	51	2001
8. Esteban Yan	47	2002
9. Lance Carter	27	2004
10. Jesus Colome	24	2003

Games Finished: Career with Team

Player	GF	IP
1. Roberto Hernandez	182	218.0
2. Esteban Yan	139	418.7
3. Danys Baez	123	140.3
4. Lance Carter	107	236.7
5. Jesus Colome	75	250.7
6. Travis Harper	54	369.7
7. Albie Lopez	36	453.7
Jim Mecir	36	154.3
9. Victor Zambrano	32	481.7
10. Rick White	31	248.0

Significant Devil Rays

CRAWFORD, CARL (OF)
(2002–2005)

Carl Crawford, a rising star, is one of the fastest men in baseball and has become one of the American League's biggest stolen-base threats. Although he's currently just 24 years of age, Crawford has gotten increasingly better as his career has progressed. In 2005 he set career highs in batting average (.301), slugging average (.469), total bases (302), home runs (15), RBIs (81), doubles (33), at-bats (644), and hits (194). His numbers are starting to approach superstar status, a fact recognized by the team's management, which signed him to a long-term contract following the 2005 season.

CAREER DEVIL RAYS RECORD:

Games	AB	Hits	Runs
366	1,515	429	207

Avg	HR	RBI	SB
.283	18	139	123

HERNANDEZ, ROBERTO (RP)
(1998–2000)

After spending seven-plus years, mostly with the White Sox, Hernandez came to the Devil Rays as a free agent following the 1997 season. In the three years from 1998 to 2000, the hard-throwing Hernandez collected 101 saves for the expansion Devil Rays, providing one of the few bright spots on the young team's pitching staff. Following the 2000 season, Hernandez was sent to the Royals, and from 2001 to 2005, he bounced around with four different teams, still a productive pitcher at the age of 40.

CAREER DEVIL RAYS RECORD:

W	L	W%	ERA	SV
8	16	.333	3.43	101

K	BB	SHO	IP
185	97	0	218.0

HUFF, AUBREY (3B/OF/DH/1B) (2000–2005)

The Devil Rays selected Aubrey Huff in the fifth round of the June 1998 amateur draft and brought him up quickly to the majors—as struggling expansion teams tend to do—in 2000. The versatile Huff has proven to be the consummate team player, playing at least 149 games at four different positions. Along with teammate Carl Crawford, Huff has been a consistent performer for the perennially weak Devil Rays, ranking at or near the top of most career offensive categories in the Devil Rays' short history.

CAREER DEVIL RAYS RECORD:

Games	AB	Hits	Runs
582	2,223	655	304
Avg	**HR**	**RBI**	**SB**
.295	98	329	12

MCGRIFF, FRED (1B) (1998–2001, 2004)

In his first tour with Tampa Bay, McGriff hit nearly 100 homers in four fine seasons. An aging "Crime Dog" returned for a second stint with the Devil Rays in 2004, hoping to get the nine homers he needed to make the 500-homer club. But he hit only two to end his season and career with 493. He held many of the Devil Rays hitting records until his numbers were surpassed by Aubrey Huff. Despite a 19-year career in the big leagues, McGriff is only a borderline choice for the Hall of Fame.

CAREER DEVIL RAYS RECORD:

Games	AB	Hits	Runs
577	2,074	603	277
Avg	**HR**	**RBI**	**SB**
.291	99	359	11

Texas Rangers

Since 1961

1976 Team Ball

1966 The long-suffering Washington fans rejoice as the team posts its first winning record at home (42–36), but more important, it wins the season series against the Yankees (10–5) for the first time since 1933.... **1970** On April 6, the Senators lose their eighth straight Presidential Opener, this time to Detroit, 5–0.... **1994** Kenny Rogers pitches a perfect game against the Angels on July 28, 1994, the first American League left-hander ever to perform the feat.... **2001** Rafael Palmeiro hits 47 home runs, becoming only the second player in major league history to hit at least 38 homers a year in at least seven consecutive seasons. The other is Babe Ruth.

FRANCHISE HISTORY

The Texas Rangers were called to the rescue, but not in Texas—at least not initially. When the original Washington Senators moved to Minnesota for the 1961 season and became the Twins, Congress was outraged and threatened to eliminate Major League Baseball's antitrust exemption unless Washington got another team. The American League, still seething from the National League's unilateral expansion move into New York and Houston, quickly jumped on the bandwagon and announced an expansion of their own. Not only would the American League replace the lost Washington team with a new Senators franchise, but they would move into the Los Angeles market and compete with the Dodgers.

Ted Williams tried his hand at managing, with the Senators/Rangers, 1967–72.

Then came the shocker: The American League announced that its two new expansion teams would begin play in 1961, beating the National League—which was set to launch its new teams in 1962—to the punch. The announcement came in the fall of 1960, so the AL had to put its expansion plans on a fast track. When the two leagues held their annual winter meeting in St. Louis on December 5–7,1960, tempers flew. In a contentious meeting, the American League proposed an interesting solution. If the NL wouldn't go into New York, the AL agreed to pass on Los Angeles. Then, according to the AL proposal, each league would consist of nine teams and the two leagues would begin—horror of horrors—interleague play! The Dodgers agreed to the proposal, but every other NL owner voted against it and the expansion war was on.

Among the unsuccessful bidders for the Washington franchise were Rear Admiral John J. Bergen (retired) of the Graham-Paige Corp; Billy Werber, a former major league player who had become an insurance tycoon in Washington; Bob Rodenberg, former owner of the Baltimore Colts football team; and department store executive Jack Blau. But the dubious prize of the replacement Senators franchise went to General Elwood Quesada, head of the Federal Aviation Agency and a World War II hero. Upon purchasing the team, Quesada resigned his position with the FAA at the changeover in administrations when President Kennedy took office on January 20, 1961. Quesada owned the team for just two years before selling his 80 percent share of the team to James M. Johnston, James Lemon, and George Bunker. Johnston became the new chairman of the board. When Johnston died a few years later, Lemon took control of the team and shortly thereafter put the Senators up for sale. Comedian Bob Hope became interested in buying the team and Lemon gave him an option, but Hope eventually passed on the deal, so Lemon sold the team to Bob Short in 1968.

Bob Short was a trucking magnate who at one time owned the NBA's Minneapolis Lakers. He had become heavily involved in Democratic politics and was the Democratic

National Committee Treasurer when he visited Washington in 1968 to raise money for Hubert Humphrey's presidential campaign. While in Washington, he learned that the Senators were for sale. Having sold the Lakers three years before, he was more than window-shopping for a major league baseball team. He had tried to buy the Senators in 1965 without any luck. This time, though, Lemon was ready to sell, and the two came to terms for $9 million. At the press conference announcing his purchase of the team, Short said, "There are plenty of people who wonder why there are boobs like me who would buy this team, which right now looks like a license to lose money. The team now probably isn't worth what I paid for it, but nobody ever lost money selling a big league baseball franchise." That statement would be a harbinger of things to come.

Bob Short's love of the game was eclipsed by his love of the money that could be made from it. Almost from the time he purchased the club, Short was considering possible relocation cities. He eventually decided on Arlington, Texas, and amid resounding cries of "Foul!" in the nation's capital, he moved the team prior to the 1972 season. When it became public that the Senators were moving to Arlington, where they would be rechristened the Texas Rangers, Short was required to pay each of the six Texas League teams $40,000 for invading their territory. He also agreed to play an annual exhibition game between the Rangers and a team of Texas League all-stars. Sportswriter Russ White once commented about Short and his ownership techniques, "Bob Short should be named Minor League Executive of the Year."

The Rangers were to play their games in Turnpike Stadium, a minor league park with a capacity of 20,000. Once it was announced the Senators were moving to Arlington, the name was changed to Arlington Stadium and construction began at the park to increase capacity to 35,000. Another round of construction after the team arrived increased seating capacity to 43,500. In spite of the excitement generated by

Juan Gonzalez won his first home run title at the age of 22.

the arrival of major league baseball, the team didn't have its first sellout until June 27, 1973, when high school phenom David Clyde made his debut on the mound. Short quickly arranged for a 10-year, $7.5 million broadcasting deal. Cynical critics predicted (successfully) that Short would sell the team just as soon as his five-year tax depreciation schedule ran out in 1973. Short's faith in the market for baseball teams paid off: In 1974, he sold the Rangers for a tidy profit to a group of investors led by 36-year-old Bradford G. Corbett.

Corbett had made his fortune in the industrial and commercial plastic piping business after parlaying a $360,000 Small Business Administration loan into $55 million in sales in 1973 alone. Among the minority owners were Amon Carter Jr., former owner of the Fort Worth *Star-Telegram* newspaper, and Eddie Chiles, owner of the world's largest oil-field servicing company. In 1980 Chiles purchased the team from Corbett. When his oil-field business began to decline in the early 1980s, Chiles sold 30 percent interest in the team to Edward Gaylord, an Oklahoma broadcasting and publishing magnate. Along with his 30 percent interest in the Rangers, Gaylord was given first right of refusal to veto any proposed sale of the club.

After vetoing a proposed sale to a Tampa group, Gaylord approved Chiles' $46 million sale of the club in March 1989 to a group headed by George W. Bush, son of sitting U.S. President George Bush, and Edward Rose, a man who made more than $100 million in the stock market betting that certain companies would lose. Although George W. Bush was the front man for the team, he actually owned less than 5 percent. The two largest owners were Roland Betts (11 percent), Bush's classmate at Yale, and Gaylord (10 percent). During the Bush years, the Rangers began play in their current stadium, The Ballpark at Arlington, one of the most beautiful baseball stadiums ever built. In 1998 the Bush group sold the team to Tom Hicks, owner of the NHL's Dallas Stars and more than 400 radio stations, for $250 million, the highest sale price in American League history. (Bush paid only about $500,000—borrowed against his shares in a failed oil company—but pocketed almost $15 million when the team was sold.) Hicks still owns the team today.

On the field, the Rangers for the most part have been a futile team. During the team's 12-year stay in Washington, they finished in the second division 10 times, never finishing higher than fourth place (in 1969). Once in Texas, it would be 25 years before the Rangers even made the playoffs. In 1973, Whitey Herzog, the team's new manager, said, "We need just two players to be a contender—Babe Ruth and Sandy Koufax." They were in first place in the AL West in 1994 (albeit with a losing 52–62 record), when the players went on strike and ended the season. In the Rangers' only three playoff appearances (in 1996, 1998, and 1999), the Yankees brushed them aside each time in the Division Series.

TEAM NAME HISTORY

Official Names

Senators (1961–1971)
Rangers (1972–current)

Unofficial Names/Nicknames

Nats (while in Washington)

STADIUM HISTORY

Griffith Stadium	1961
District of Columbia Stadium	1962–1968
R.F.K. Memorial Stadium (District of Columbia Stadium renamed)	1969–1971
Arlington Stadium	1972–1993
The Ballpark at Arlington	1994–2004
Ameriquest Field in Arlington (The Ballpark at Arlington renamed)	2005–current

YEARLY RECORD, FINISH, & ATTENDANCE FIGURES

Year	League	Record	DIV/LG Finish	Attendance	Avg/Gm
2005	AL West	79–83	3	2,525,221	31,176
2004	AL West	89–73	3	2,513,685	31,033
2003	AL West	71–91	4	2,094,394	25,857
2002	AL West	72–90	4	2,352,397	29,042
2001	AL West	73–89	4	2,831,021	34,525
2000	AL West	71–91	4	2,588,401	31,956
1999	AL West	95–67	1	2,771,469	34,216
1998	AL West	88–74	1	2,927,399	36,141
1997	AL West	77–85	3	2,945,228	36,361
1996	AL West	90–72	1	2,889,020	35,667
1995	AL West	74–70	3	1,985,910	27,582
1994	AL West	52–62	1	2,503,198	39,733
1993	AL West	86–76	2	2,244,616	27,711
1992	AL West	77–85	4	2,198,231	27,139
1991	AL West	85–77	3	2,297,720	28,367
1990	AL West	83–79	3	2,057,911	25,096
1989	AL West	83–79	4	2,043,993	25,234
1988	AL West	70–91	6	1,581,901	19,530
1987	AL West	75–87	6	1,763,053	21,766
1986	AL West	87–75	2	1,692,002	20,889
1985	AL West	62–99	7	1,112,497	13,906
1984	AL West	69–92	7	1,102,471	13,781
1983	AL West	77–85	3	1,363,469	16,833
1982	AL West	64–98	6	1,154,432	14,252
1981	AL West	57–48	2/3	850,076	15,180
1980	AL West	76–85	4	1,198,175	14,977
1979	AL West	83–79	3	1,519,671	18,761
1978	AL West	87–75	2	1,447,963	17,658
1977	AL West	94–68	2	1,250,722	15,441
1976	AL West	76–86	4	1,164,982	14,382
1975	AL West	79–83	3	1,127,924	14,099
1974	AL West	84–76	2	1,193,902	14,924
1973	AL West	57–105	6	686,085	8,470
1972	AL West	54–100	6	662,974	8,610
1971	AL East	63–96	5	655,156	8,088
1970	AL East	70–92	6	824,789	10,183
1969	AL East	86–76	4	918,106	11,335
1968	AL	65–96	10	546,661	6,749
1967	AL	76–85	6	770,868	9,636
1966	AL	71–88	8	576,260	7,388
1965	AL	70–92	8	560,083	6,915
1964	AL	62–100	9	600,106	7,409
1963	AL	56–106	10	535,604	6,695
1962	AL	60–101	10	729,775	9,122
1961	AL	61–100	9	597,287	7,561

MANAGER HISTORY

Manager	Years	W–L	Win %
Mickey Vernon	1961–1963	135–227	.373
Gil Hodges	1963–1967	321–444	.420
Jim Lemon	1968	65–96	.404
Ted Williams	1969–1972	273–364	.429
Whitey Herzog	1973	47–91	.341
Del Wilber	1973	1–0	1.000
Billy Martin	1973–1975	137–141	.493
Frank Lucchesi	1975–1977	142–149	.488
Eddie Stanky	1977	1–0	1.000
Connie Ryan	1977	2–4	.333
Billy Hunter	1977–1978	146–108	.575
Pat Corrales	1978–1980	160–164	.494
Don Zimmer	1981–1982	95–106	.473
Darrell Johnson	1982	26–40	.394
Doug Rader	1983–1985	155–200	.437
Bobby Valentine	1985–1992	581–605	.490
Toby Harrah	1992	32–44	.421
Kevin Kennedy	1993–1994	138–138	.500
Johnny Oates	1995–2001	506–476	.515
Jerry Narron	2001–2002	134–162	.453
Buck Showalter	2003–2005	229–247	.481

ALL-TIME WIN-LOSS RECORDS VS. ALL OPPONENTS

ALL-TIME	3,336–3,807
Angels	323–343
Astros	14–16
Athletics	326–338
Blue Jays	164–158
Braves	2–7
Brewers	152–181
Cardinals	1–2
Cubs	2–1
Devil Rays	47–32
Diamondbacks	10–6
Dodgers	7–9
Giants	7–9
Indians	293–274
INTERLEAGUE	75–83
Mariners	196–212
Marlins	5–4
Mets	1–2
Nationals	2–4
Orioles	216–346
Padres	8–8
Phillies	0–3
Pirates	6–0
Reds	2–4
Red Sox	264–297
Rockies	8–8
Royals	218–244
Tigers	265–312
Twins	291–324
White Sox	273–331
Yankees	233–332

Franchise Highlights, Low Points, and Strange Distinctions

1963 The expansion Senators lost 100 games their first year and 101 their second. On May 22, after a 14–26 start, Manager Mickey Vernon was fired in order for the team to "take a new direction." When Gil Hodges, the new manager, took over the reins, the team responded by going 3–19 in his first 22 games, ultimately losing 106 games on the season.

• • • •

1964 The Senators adopted the slogan, "Get off the floor in '64." It must have inspired the team because they jumped to ninth place in the 10-team league. The team lost 100 games again, keeping their perfect record of 100-loss seasons intact. Their hitting attack was so futile in 1964 that they were shut out in four consecutive home games during September, twice by Cleveland and twice by Detroit.

• • • •

1965 Senators fans had to be conflicted in 1965. Their replacement team set a new record by winning 70 games and losing only 92, the first time in the franchise's five-year history they didn't lose at least 100 games. But the old Senators team—the one that moved to Minnesota and became the Twins—won 102 games and the AL pennant.

1967 The Senators continued their upward trend, winning 76 games, a new club record, and finishing in a sixth-place tie with Baltimore, the defending AL champs. They also played several unusually long games that season. On June 12 the Senators and White Sox played the longest-ever night game up to that time, in both innings and actual time: a 22-inning, 6-hour-and-38-minute epic won by the Senators, 6–5. They also played a 20-inning affair with the Twins (which they won 9–7) and a 19-inning game with Baltimore (a 7–5 loss).

• • • •

1968 The 1968 season has been called the Year of the Pitcher, but Frank Howard did his best to disprove it. From his third at-bat on May 12 until his third at-bat on May 18, Howard stepped to the plate 20 times and hit 10 home runs, a record for a six-game span. One of his homers hit off the rooftop of Detroit's Briggs Stadium. Several others hit buildings outside of Fenway Park and Cleveland's Municipal Stadium. But Howard's heroics were about the only bright spot in Washington's 1968 season. The traditional Presidential Opener in D.C. was delayed two days due to rioting in D.C. over the assassination of Dr. Martin Luther King, and the attendance, for what was normally a sellout, was down 10,000. The Senators also lost more players to military duty than any other team in the majors.

1969 Bringing Ted Williams in as the new manager of the Senators seemed, at season's end, a stroke of brilliance. Not only did the team win 21 more games than the previous season with virtually the same lineup, but he helped the team's hitters across the board to raise their averages, some as many as 80 points from their 1968 totals. Attendance was also up nearly 400,000 to 918,106, the second-highest ever for a team in Washington.

• • • •

1970 From time to time it's been said that the baseball season is too long. The 1970 Washington Senators would probably have agreed that it's exactly 14 games too long. Their last win of the season came on September 17. From September 18 through October 1, the Senators lost 14 straight games to end the year.

Left-hander Darold Knowles compiled 27 saves, but amassed a 2–14 record.

• • • •

1971 Washington fans felt especially cheated. The team had announced that after the season it would be moving to Texas, leaving the nation's capital without a major league team for the first time in 71 years. On September 30, the last game of the season, and apparently the last game in D.C., the Senators were leading the Yankees 7–5, with the visitors down to their last two outs. Suddenly, after being unruly all night, souvenir collectors and demonstrators charged onto the field. They tore up clumps of grass, stole grounds equipment, ripped out seats and other fixtures, and refused to leave the field. Unable to clear the field and restore order, the umpires had no choice but to award the game to the Yankees by forfeit, 9–0. The Senators didn't even have the distinction of winning or losing their final game on the field.

1972 The expected big fan turnout in Texas didn't materialize in 1972 as expected. The players' strike in the spring dampened the enthusiasm among baseball fans everywhere, particularly the Dallas–Fort Worth area. Attendance for the Rangers' home games was up only 7,800 on the year over the 1971 season in D.C. There were other problems as well. Frank Howard, who had hit 44, 48, and 44 homers the three previous years, was a holdout in s pring training. He eventually was given the $120,000 contract he sought (the same salary as the previous year), but by then the psychological damage was done. When owner Bob Short traded Hondo to Detroit on August 31 (for just the waiver price), Howard only had nine homers and 44 RBIs. Manager Ted Williams was so disgusted with his team's last-place finish and its major league-worst 54–100 record that he resigned at the end of the season with a year remaining on his contract.

• • • •

1973 In spite of new manager Whitey Herzog's fresh approach and grand promises for the year, the Rangers finished with the worst record in baseball again (this time 57–105). After going 1–15 in late August and early September, Herzog was fired and replaced by Billy Martin, who boldly predicted the Rangers would be contenders in 1974 and the team would draw 1 million fans (after drawing only 686,000 in 1973). Martin's comments kept the press busy all winter wondering how he was going to pull off the "miracle." When the dust settled after the 1974 season, the Rangers stood in second place, only five games behind the eventual World Series champion Oakland A's. They won 27 more games than in 1973, finishing at 84–76. (Oh, and they also drew 1.2 million in attendance, just as Billy Martin had predicted.) Youngsters Jeff Burroughs and Mike Hargrove copped the AL's MVP and Rookie of the Year Awards, respectively.

• • • •

1974 One of the biggest reasons for the Rangers' turnabout was pitcher Fergie Jenkins. The Chicago Cubs castoff finished with a 25–12 record. Incredibly, he could have won 30. During one nine-game stretch in which he pitched through a sore leg that affected his delivery and strikeout totals, Jenkins was 1–8. For the rest of the season, when he wasn't hurting, the ace was 24–4.

On June 4, the Rangers were playing in Cleveland on "10-Cent Beer Night." The Indians had just tied the score in the bottom of the ninth at 5–5 and had the winning run on third when hundreds of fans jumped the right-field fence and attacked Rangers right fielder Jeff Burroughs and several other players. Nestor Chylak, the umpiring crew chief, was struck on the head. He declared the game forfeited to Texas. Six fans were ultimately arrested and taken to jail.

• • • •

1977 Owner Brad Corbett was so disgusted with his team's play that he publicly called the Rangers "dogs on the field and dogs off the field." He then tearfully announced at a press conference that he was putting his team up for sale. The franchise was so dysfunctional that the Rangers had four different managers in six days! Frank Lucchesi started the year as manager, but spent a week in the hospital after suffering a severe beating at the hands of his backup second baseman, Lenny Randle, during spring training. Randle, upset over losing his starting job to Bump Wills, was fined $25,000, suspended for 30 days, then traded to the Mets. With the Rangers struggling to stay at .500, Corbett announced he was going to "live and die with Frank." On June 22, with the team in Minnesota, he fired Lucchesi and, with a lot of public fanfare, hired Eddie Stanky to take over the team. Stanky flew to Minnesota from his home in Alabama and held a press conference, talking mostly about his "zest" for the game. He managed the Rangers to victory that night. By morning he was gone, back to Alabama, explaining that he was homesick. Coach Connie Ryan took over the team and asked to be named permanent manager, but after three games he was replaced by Bill Hunter.

Once Hunter took over, all the distractions and quibbling ended. The Rangers went 31–9 in Hunter's first 40 games, actually climbing from 10 games back into first place. Although the Rangers ended up second to the Royals, who performed at a blistering pace themselves, they did win 94 games, far and away their best record in Texas.

• • • •

1980 Fergie Jenkins became just the fourth pitcher in history to win 100 games in both the National and American Leagues. Some luster was taken off of his accomplishment, however, when he was arrested in Toronto on August 26 on a charge of possession of narcotics, a misdemeanor. When Jenkins refused to answer Commissioner Bowie Kuhn's questions into the matter, Kuhn suspended the pitcher for most of September. Two weeks later, Jenkins was reinstated when an arbitrator overturned the commissioner's ruling. The whole affair undoubtedly cost Jenkins some votes when he became eligible for Hall of Fame consideration years later.

1982 In a huge public relations foul-up, Manager Don Zimmer actually ran the team for three games in July—after being fired!

• • • •

1986 Reliever Mitch Williams set both a rookie and club record by appearing in 80 games with the Rangers. The following year he broke his own record by appearing in 85 games, more than half of the team's scheduled games.

• • • •

1987 One of the strangest disabled-list stories ever came in the 1987 season. Closer Greg Harris, who had 20 saves in 1986, missed nearly three weeks in August and September with a swollen right elbow—injured not while pitching, but while flicking sunflower seeds to a friend in the stands. In Harris's own words: "I held them on my left hand and flicked them with the middle finger of my right hand. I was getting a few of them up past the first aisle."

• • • •

1988 Bobby Witt began the season 1–5 with a 7.68 ERA and was sent to Oklahoma City for two months to work things out. And work things out he did. When he returned to the Rangers later that year, Witt pitched nine consecutive complete games and won eight of 13 decisions. Despite missing a third of the year, Witt was second in the American League in complete games with 13. Prior to the 1988 season, Witt had only thrown one complete game in 56 starts.

• • • •

1991 From May 12–27, the Rangers won 14 consecutive games and went from sixth place to first. Rookie catcher Ivan Rodriguez, just 19 years old, helped the cause by throwing out 34 of 70 runners attempting to steal (49%), and hitting .264, the highest batting average by a teenage regular since Robin Yount's .267 in 1975.

• • • •

1993 The Rangers set a record with 27 disabled-list stints totaling an incredible 1,373 days.

In 1993, Juan Gonzalez (46), Rafael Palmeiro (37), and Dean Palmer (33) combined for 116 home runs, the most by three teammates since Davey Johnson, Darrell Evans, and Hank Aaron smacked 124 for the Atlanta Braves in 1973. That record has since been eclipsed twice, both times by Colorado. In 1996 Andres Galarraga (47), Ellis Burks (40), and Vinny Castilla (40) teamed up to hit 127 homers, and in 1997 Larry Walker (49), Andres Galarraga (41), and Vinny Castilla (40) hit a combined 130 homers.

• • • •

1995 When the Rangers failed to make the playoffs, it marked the 35th consecutive year of the franchise's post-season drought, 11 in Washington and 24 in Texas. The Rangers were the only American League team never to have made the playoffs through the 1995 season. Even the expansion Toronto Blue Jays and Seattle Mariners, who joined the American League in 1977, both managed to make the playoffs by 1995.

• • • •

1996 Although the Rangers were quickly brushed aside in the Division Series against the Yankees—the first playoff appearance in the team's 36-year existence—there was much to be excited about in 1996. The Rangers were in first (tied or alone) 178 days of the 182-day season. Despite missing 28 games, outfielder Juan Gonzalez set club records with 47 homers and 144 RBIs. His average of 1.07 RBIs per game was the best ratio since Jimmie Foxx averaged 1.17 in 1938. Catcher Ivan Rodriguez had 44 doubles, the most by any catcher in major league history, and his 116 runs were the most by a catcher since Yogi Berra scored the same number in 1950. Finally, Texas led the American League in fielding, setting a new record with 15 consecutive errorless games.

• • • •

1999 The Rangers made the playoffs for the third time in four years, largely on the backs of their potent offense. Four Rangers had more than 100 RBIs and a fifth nearly did. Palmeiro led the way with 148, followed by Juan Gonzalez (128), Ivan Rodriguez (113), and Rusty Greer (101). Todd Zeile just missed with 98.

1999 Ivan Rodriguez won the AL MVP Award, largely on the strength of his hitting (35 homers, 113 RBIs, and 116 runs). He also threw out 54.2 percent of all runners attempting to steal, a major league record.

• • • •

2001 Alex Rodriguez (52) and Rafael Palmeiro (47) became only the fourth pair of teammates in major league history to hit at least 45 homers in the same season when they turned the trick in 2001. The other three were Babe Ruth and Lou Gehrig (twice), and Roger Maris and Mickey Mantle. The feat has never been accomplished in the National League.

During the 2001 season, pitcher Kenny Rogers had a rib that was compressing a nerve in his pitching shoulder. He eventually had surgery—to remove the rib!

Texas-size lighting over The Ballpark at Arlington.

Special Achievements

World Series Results

None

World Series Managerial Records

None

All-Time Postseason Record

Divisional Playoffs	1–9
League Championship Series	0–0
World Series	0–0

All-Star Games at Texas/Washington, D.C.

Year	Date	Winner	Score	Stadium
1962	July 10	National	3–1	District of Columbia Stadium (Washington, D.C.)
1969	July 23	National	9–3	R.F.K. Memorial Stadium (Washington, D.C.)
1995	July 11	National	3–2	The Ballpark in Arlington

Hall of Famers Who Played for Team

	Position	Years	Games with Washington/ Texas
Ferguson Jenkins	SP	1974–75, 1978–81	197
Gaylord Perry	SP	1975–1977, 1980	112
Nolan Ryan	SP	1989–1993	129

Hall of Famers Who Managed Team

	Years	Games with Washington/ Texas
Ted Williams	1969–1972	637

MVP Award Winners

Jeff Burroughs	OF	1974
Juan Gonzalez	OF	1996
Juan Gonzalez	OF	1998
Ivan Rodriguez	C	1999
Alex Rodriguez	SS	2003

Cy Young Award Winners

None

Rookie of the Year Award Winners

Mike Hargrove	1B	1974

Gold Glove Winners

Year	Position	Player
1976	C	Jim Sundberg
1977	C OF	Jim Sundberg Juan Beniquez
1978	C	Jim Sundberg
1979	C 3B	Jim Sundberg Buddy Bell
1980	C 3B	Jim Sundberg Buddy Bell
1981	C 3B	Jim Sundberg Buddy Bell
1982	3B	Buddy Bell
1983	3B	Buddy Bell
1984	3B	Buddy Bell
1990	OF	Gary Pettis
1992	C	Ivan Rodriguez
1993	C	Ivan Rodriguez
1994	C	Ivan Rodriguez
1995	C	Ivan Rodriguez
1996	C	Ivan Rodriguez
1997	C	Ivan Rodriguez
1998	C	Ivan Rodriguez
1999	C 1B	Ivan Rodriguez Rafael Palmeiro
2000	SP C	Kenny Rogers Ivan Rodriguez
2001	C	Ivan Rodriguez
2002	SP SS	Kenny Rogers Alex Rodriguez
2003	SS	Alex Rodriguez
2004	SP	Kenny Rogers
2005	SP 1B	Kenny Rogers Mark Teixeira

Triple Crown Winners

None

Fireman of the Year Award Winners

Jim Kern	1979 (tie)
Jeff Russell	1989

World Series MVP

None

LEAGUE CHAMPIONSHIP SERIES MVP

None

ALL-STAR GAME MVP

Julio Franco	1990
Alfonso Soriano	2004

MANAGER OF THE YEAR AWARD WINNERS

Johnny Oates	1996 (tied)
Buck Showalter	2004

BATTING CHAMPIONS

Year	Player	Avg
1991	Julio Franco	.341

NINE-INNING NO-HITTERS PITCHED

Year	Pitcher	Opp.	Score
1973	Jim Bibby	OAK	6–0
1977	Bert Blyleven	LAA	6–0
1990	Nolan Ryan	OAK	5–0
1991	Nolan Ryan	TOR	3–0
1994	Kenny Rogers	LAA	4–0 (perfect)

20-GAME WINNERS

Year	Pitcher	W–L
1974	Ferguson Jenkins	25–12
1992	Kevin Brown	21–11
1998	Rick Helling	20–7

RETIRED UNIFORM NUMBERS

Number	Player	Position
34	Nolan Ryan	SP
26	Johnny Oates	Mgr

TEAM RECORDS—WINS & LOSSES

- Games won in a season: 95 in 1999
- Games lost in a season: 106 in 1963
- Games won in a month: 21 in September 1978
- Games lost in a month: 24 in August 1961 and August 1973
- Consecutive games won: 14 in 1991
- Consecutive games lost: 15 in 1972
- Biggest shutout victory: 14–0 over Oakland on July 26, 1977
- Biggest shutout loss: 17–0 to Los Angeles Angels on August 23, 1963
- Highest winning percentage: .586 in 1999 (95–67)
- Lowest winning percentage: .346 in 1963 (56–106)

TEAM RECORDS—BATTING

- Highest team batting average: .293 in 1999
- Lowest team batting average: .223 in 1967
- Highest team slugging average: .479 in 1999
- Highest team on-base percentage: .361 in 1999
- Total hits: 1,653 in 1999
- Extra-base hits: 600 in 2005
- Hits in a game: 23 vs. Chicago White Sox on April 2, 1998 and Seattle on June 24, 2004
- Longest individual hitting streak: 28, Gabe Kapler, 2000
- Most .300 hitters in a season: 4 in 1998 and 1999
- Home runs: 260 in 2005
- Home runs in a month: 15 (four times): Frank Howard, May 1968; Juan Gonzalez, July 1996; Rafael Palmeiro, August 1999; Alex Rodriguez, August 2003
- Home runs in a game: 8 vs. Houston on May 21, 2005 and vs. Los Angeles Angels on June 30, 2005
- Home runs by a rookie: 30, Pete Incaviglia, 1986
- Home runs by a right-hander: 57, Alex Rodriguez, 2002
- Home runs by a left-hander: 47, Rafael Palmeiro (twice): 1999 and 2001
- Home runs by a switch-hitter: 43, Mark Texeira, 2005
- Grand slams: 8 in 1999
- Grand slams (individual; season): 3, by four players: Jeff Burroughs, 1973; Larry Parrish, 1982; Rafael Palmeiro, 1999; Hank Blalock, 2004
- Grand slams (individual; career): 7, Juan Gonzalez and Rafael Palmeiro
- Triples: 46 in 1989
- Doubles: 330 in 2000
- Singles: 1,202 in 1980
- Walks: 660 in 1996
- Runs scored: 945 in 1999
- Runs scored in a game: 26 vs. Baltimore on April 19, 1996
- Runs scored in an inning: 16 vs. Baltimore on April 19, 1996 (eighth inning)

TEAM RECORDS—BATTING (CONT.)

- Most batters hit by a pitch: 75 in 2001 and 2003
- Times shut out: 27 in 1972
- Grounded into double plays: 161 in 2000
- Fewest grounded into double plays: 91 in 2004
- Runners left on base: 1,253 in 1996

TEAM RECORDS—BASERUNNING

- Stolen bases: 196 in 1978
- Caught stealing: 91 in 1978

TEAM RECORDS—PITCHING

- Lowest earned run average: 3.31 in 2001
- Complete games: 63 in 1976
- Saves: 52 in 2004
- Strikeouts: 1,112 in 1989
- Shutouts: 17 in 1977
- Walks: 760 in 1987
- Hit batsmen: 81 in 2004
- Wild pitches: 94 in 1986
- Consecutive wins (individual): 12, Bobby Witt in 1990
- Consecutive losses (individual): 10, Bennie Daniels in 1962
- Strikeouts in a game (individual): 21, Tom Cheney, September 12, 1962 (16 innings); 9 innings: 16 (twice) by Nolan Ryan, April 26, 1990 and May 1, 1991
- Runs allowed in a game: 23 vs. Oakland, June 24, 2004

TEAM RECORDS—FIELDING

- Best fielding average: .986 in 1996
- Most errors committed: 191 in 1975
- Fewest errors committed: 87 in 1996
- Most double plays turned: 173 in 1970 and 1975
- Fewest double plays turned: 137 in 1989

TEAM RECORDS—MISCELLANEOUS

- Number of times league champions: 0
- Number of times finishing last in league: 6
- Largest attendance, single game: 50,708 vs. Oakland, July 31, 2004
- Largest attendance, doubleheader: 42,163 vs. Detroit, July 10, 1982
- Players used in a season: 52 in 1992, 2003, and 2004
- Seasons played: 13, Juan Gonzalez

PRIMARY PITCHING STAFFS

Year	Starter	Starter	Starter	Starter	Starter	Closer	Bullpen	Bullpen	Bullpen
2005	Young	Rogers	Park	Astacio	Drese	Cordero	Shouse	Brocail	Loe
2004	Rogers	Drese	Park	Dickey	Benoit	Cordero	Almanzar	Mahay	Shouse
2003	Thomson	Lewis	Valdez	Dickey	Benoit	Urbina	Cordero	Fultz	Shouse
2002	Rogers	Park	Valdez	Burba	Bell	Irabu	Van Poppel	Powell	Alvarez
2001	Rogers	Helling	Davis	Oliver	Bell	Zimmerman	Venafro	Mahomes	Petkovsek
2000	Rogers	Helling	Loaiza	Oliver	Glynn	Wetteland	Zimmerman	Crabtree	Venafro
1999	Sele	Helling	Loaiza	Burkett	Morgan	Wetteland	Zimmerman	Crabtree	Venafro
1998	Sele	Helling	Loaiza	Burkett	Oliver	Wetteland	Gunderson	Crabtree	Patterson
1997	Witt	Hill	Santana	Burkett	Oliver	Wetteland	Gunderson	Hernandez	Patterson
1996	Witt	Hill	Pavlik	Gross	Oliver	Henneman	Cook	Russell	Vosberg
1995	Witt	Rogers	Pavlik	Gross	Tewksbury	Russell	McDowell	Whiteside	Vosberg
1994	Brown	Rogers	Pavlik	Fajardo	Helling	Henke	Carpenter	Whiteside	Oliver
1993	Brown	Rogers	Pavlik	Leibrandt	Ryan	Henke	Patterson	Whiteside	Lefferts
1992	Brown	Guzman	Pavlik	Witt	Ryan	Russell	Rogers	Mathews	Nunez
1991	Brown	Guzman	Boyd	Witt	Ryan	Russell	Rogers	Jeffcoat	Gossage
1990	Brown	Hough	Jeffcoat	Witt	Ryan	Rogers	Arnsberg	Moyer	Mielke
1989	Brown	Hough	Jeffcoat	Witt	Ryan	Russell	Rogers	Guante	Mielke
1988	Kilgus	Hough	Guzman	Witt	Russell	Williams	Vande Berg	McMurtry	Mohorcic
1987	Harris	Hough	Guzman	Witt	Correa	Mohorcic	Williams	Russell	Loynd
1986	Mason	Hough	Guzman	Witt	Correa	Harris	Williams	Russell	Mohorcic

PRIMARY PITCHING STAFFS (CONT.)

Year	Starter	Starter	Starter	Starter	Starter	Closer	Bullpen	Bullpen	Bullpen
1985	Mason	Hough	Hooton	Tanana	Russell	Harris	Schmidt	Stewart	Rozema
1984	Mason	Hough	Darwin	Tanana	Stewart	Schmidt	Jones	Henke	Tobik
1983	Smithson	Hough	Darwin	Tanana	Honeycutt	Jones	Butcher	Schmidt	Tobik
1982	Medich	Hough	Matlack	Tanana	Honeycutt	Darwin	Mirabella	Schmidt	Comer
1981	Medich	Darwin	Matlack	Jenkins	Honeycutt	Kern	Johnson	Hough	Comer
1980	Medich	Perry	Matlack	Jenkins	Comer	Lyle	Johnson	Darwin	Kern
1979	Medich	Alexander	Matlack	Jenkins	Comer	Kern	Lyle	Darwin	Rajsich
1978	Medich	Alexander	Matlack	Jenkins	Ellis	Cleveland	Umbarger	Comer	Barker
1977	Perry	Alexander	Blyleven	Briles	Ellis	Devine	Knowles	Lindblad	Moret
1976	Perry	Umbarger	Blyleven	Briles	Boggs	Hoerner	Foucault	Hargan	Terpko
1975	Perry	Jenkins	Hargan	Hands	Wright	Foucault	Umbarger	Thomas	Kekich
1974	Bibby	Jenkins	Hargan	Brown	Clyde	Foucault	Merritt	Stanhouse	Allen
1973	Bibby	Siebert	Broberg	Merritt	Clyde	Foucault	Gogolewski	Paul	Brown
1972	Bosman	Hand	Broberg	Gogolewski	Paul	Pina	Lindblad	Panther	Cox
1971	Bosman	McLain	Broberg	Gogolewski	Shellenback	Lindblad	Riddleberger	Pina	Cox
1970	Bosman	Cox	Coleman	Brunet	Hannan	Knowles	Shellenback	Pina	Grzenda
1969	Bosman	Cox	Coleman	Moore	Hannan	Higgins	Knowles	Humphreys	Baldwin
1968	Pascual	Bertaina	Coleman	Moore	Hannan	Higgins	Bosman	Humphreys	Baldwin
1967	Pascual	Bertaina	Coleman	Moore	Ortega	Knowles	Cox	Lines	Baldwin
1966	Richert	McCormick	Hannan	Segui	Ortega	Kline	Humphreys	Lines	Cox
1965	Richert	McCormick	Narum	Daniels	Ortega	Kline	Ridzik	Bridges	Koplitz
1964	Osteen	Koch	Narum	Daniels	Stenhouse	Kline	Duckworth	Hannan	Ridzik
1963	Osteen	Rudolph	Cheney	Daniels	Stenhouse	Kline	Duckworth	Roebuck	Burnside
1962	Osteen	Rudolph	Cheney	Daniels	Stenhouse	Kutyna	Hannan	Hamilton	Hobaugh
1961	McClain	Donovan	Hobaugh	Daniels	Burnside	Sisler	Kutyna	Klippstein	Gabler

PRIMARY STARTING LINEUPS

Year	C	1B	2B	3B	SS	LF	CF	RF	DH
2005	Barajas	Teixeira	Soriano	Blalock	Young	Mench	Matthews	Hidalgo	Dellucci
2004	Barajas	Teixeira	Soriano	Blalock	Young	Dellucci	Nix	Matthews	Fullmer
2003	Diaz	Teixeira	Young	Blalock	Rodriguez	Spencer	Christenson	Gonzalez	Palmeiro
2002	Rodriguez	Palmeiro	Young	Perry	Rodriguez	Mench	Rivera	Gonzalez	Greer
2001	Rodriguez	Palmeiro	Young	Lamb	Rodriguez	Catalanotto	Kapler	Ledee	Sierra
2000	Rodriguez	Palmeiro	Alicea	Lamb	Clayton	Greer	Kapler	Ledee	Segui
1999	Rodriguez	Stevens	McLemore	Zeile	Clayton	Greer	Goodwin	Gonzalez	Palmeiro
1998	Rodriguez	Clark	McLemore	Tatis	Elster	Greer	Goodwin	Gonzalez	Stevens
1997	Rodriguez	Clark	McLemore	Palmer	Gil	Greer	Buford	Newson	Gonzalez
1996	Rodriguez	Clark	McLemore	Palmer	Elster	Greer	Hamilton	Gonzalez	Tettleton
1995	Rodriguez	Clark	Frye	Pagliarulo	Gil	McLemore	Nixon	Greer	Gonzalez
1994	Rodriguez	Clark	Frye	Palmer	Lee	Gonzalez	Hulse	Greer	Canseco
1993	Rodriguez	Palmeiro	Strange	Palmer	Lee	Gonzalez	Hulse	Peltier	Franco
1992	Rodriguez	Palmeiro	Newman	Palmer	Thon	Reimer	Gonzalez	Sierra	Downing
1991	Rodriguez	Palmeiro	Franco	Buechele	Huson	Reimer	Pettis	Sierra	Downing
1990	Petralli	Palmeiro	Franco	Buechele	Huson	Incaviglia	Pettis	Sierra	Baines
1989	Kreuter	Palmeiro	Franco	Buechele	Fletcher	Incaviglia	Espy	Sierra	Baines
1988	Petralli	O'Brien	Wilkerson	Buechele	Fletcher	Incaviglia	McDowell	Sierra	Parrish
1987	Slaught	O'Brien	Browne	Buechele	Fletcher	Incaviglia	McDowell	Sierra	Parrish
1986	Slaught	O'Brien	Harrah	Buechele	Fletcher	Ward	McDowell	Incaviglia	Parrish
1985	Slaught	O'Brien	Harrah	Bell	Wilkerson	Ward	McDowell	Parrish	Johnson
1984	Scott	O'Brien	Tolleson	Bell	Wilkerson	Sample	Ward	Parrish	Rivers

PRIMARY STARTING LINEUPS (CONT.)

Year	C	1B	2B	3B	SS	LF	CF	RF	DH
1983	Sundberg	O'Brien	Tolleson	Bell	Dent	Sample	Wright	Parrish	Hostetler
1982	Sundberg	Hostetler	Richardt	Bell	Wagner	Sample	Wright	Parrish	Johnson
1981	Sundberg	Putnam	Wills	Bell	Mendoza	Sample	Rivers	Grubb	Oliver
1980	Sundberg	Putnam	Wills	Bell	Frias	Oliver	Rivers	Grubb	Zisk
1979	Sundberg	Putnam	Wills	Bell	Norman	Sample	Oliver	Zisk	Ellis
1978	Sundberg	Hargrove	Wills	Harrah	Campaneris	Oliver	Beniquez	Bonds	Zisk
1977	Sundberg	Hargrove	Wills	Harrah	Campaneris	Washington	Beniquez	May	Horton
1976	Sundberg	Hargrove	Randle	Howell	Harrah	Clines	Beniquez	Burroughs	Grieve
1975	Sundberg	Spencer	Randle	Howell	Harrah	Hargrove	Moates	Burroughs	Tovar
1974	Sundberg	Hargrove	Nelson	Randle	Harrah	Johnson	Lovitto	Burroughs	Spencer
1973	Suarez	Spencer	Nelson	Fregosi	Harrah	Carty	Harris	Burroughs	Johnson
1972	Billings	Howard	Randle	Nelson	Harrah	Grieve	Lovitto	Ford	
1971	Casanova	Mincher	Cullen	Nelson	Harrah	Howard	Unser	Biittner	
1970	Casanova	Epstein	Cullen	Rodriguez	Brinkman	Howard	Stroud	Maye	
1969	Casanova	Epstein	Allen	McMullen	Brinkman	Howard	Unser	Stroud	
1968	Casanova	Epstein	Allen	McMullen	Hansen	Howard	Unser	Stroud	
1967	Casanova	Epstein	Allen	McMullen	Brinkman	Howard	Stroud	Peterson	
1966	Casanova	Nen	Saverine	McMullen	Brinkman	Howard	Lock	King	
1965	Brumley	Nen	Blasingame	McMullen	Brinkman	Howard	Lock	King	
1964	Brumley	Skowron	Blasingame	Kennedy	Brinkman	Hinton	Lock	King	
1963	Retzer	Osborne	Cottier	Zimmer	Brinkman	Hinton	Lock	King	
1962	Retzer	Bright	Cottier	Johnson	Hamlin	Lock	Piersall	King	
1961	Green	Long	Cottier	O'Connell	Veal	Hinton	Tasby	Woodling	

Top 10 Batting Leaders, Single Season & Career with Team

GAMES PLAYED: CAREER WITH TEAM

Player	G	PA
1. Rafael Palmeiro	1,573	6,767
2. Jim Sundberg	1,512	5,378
3. Ivan Rodriguez	1,479	6,062
4. Juan Gonzalez	1,400	5,925
5. Toby Harrah	1,355	5,407
6. Ruben Sierra	1,190	4,975
7. Frank Howard	1,172	4,744
8. Ed Brinkman	1,143	4,215
9. Rusty Greer	1,027	4,420
10. Buddy Bell	958	4,032

AT-BATS: SEASON

Player	AB	Year
1. Michael Young	690	2004
2. Buddy Bell	670	1979
3. Michael Young	668	2005
4. Michael Young	666	2003
5. Ruben Sierra	661	1991
6. Al Oliver	656	1980
7. Hank Blalock	647	2005
8. Mark Teixeira	644	2005
9. Ruben Sierra	643	1987
10. Ivan Rodriguez	639	1996

AT-BATS: CAREER WITH TEAM

Player	AB	PA
1. Rafael Palmeiro	5,830	6,767
2. Ivan Rodriguez	5,656	6,062
3. Juan Gonzalez	5,435	5,925
4. Jim Sundberg	4,684	5,378
5. Ruben Sierra	4,580	4,975
6. Toby Harrah	4,572	5,407
7. Frank Howard	4,120	4,744
8. Ed Brinkman	3,847	4,215
9. Rusty Greer	3,829	4,420
10. Buddy Bell	3,623	4,032

BATTING AVERAGE: SEASON

Player	BA	Year
1. Julio Franco	.341	1991
2. Mickey Rivers	.333	1980
3. Rusty Greer	.332	1996
Ivan Rodriguez	.332	1999
5. Michael Young	.331	2005
6. Frank Catalanotto	.330	2001
7. Will Clark	.329	1994
Buddy Bell	.329	1980
9. Will Clark	.326	1997
Juan Gonzalez	.326	1999

BATTING AVERAGE: CAREER WITH TEAM

Player	BA	PA
1. Al Oliver	.319	2,263
2. Will Clark	.308	2,604
3. Julio Franco	.307	2,680

4. Alex Rodriguez	.305	2,172
Ivan Rodriguez	.305	6,062
Rusty Greer	.305	4,420
7. Mickey Rivers	.303	2,076
8. Michael Young	.297	3,248
9. Juan Gonzalez	.293	5,925
Mike Hargrove	.293	3,004
Buddy Bell	.293	4,032

Total Hits: Season

Player	H	Year
1. Michael Young	221	2005
2. Michael Young	216	2004
3. Mickey Rivers	210	1980
4. Al Oliver	209	1980
5. Michael Young	204	2003
6. Rafael Palmeiro	203	1991
Ruben Sierra	203	1991
8. Julio Franco	201	1991
Alex Rodriguez	201	2001
10. Buddy Bell	200	1979

Total Hits: Career with Team

Player	H	PA
1. Ivan Rodriguez	1,723	6,062
2. Rafael Palmeiro	1,692	6,767
3. Juan Gonzalez	1,595	5,925
4. Ruben Sierra	1,281	4,975
5. Jim Sundberg	1,180	5,378
6. Toby Harrah	1,174	5,407
7. Rusty Greer	1,166	4,420
8. Frank Howard	1,141	4,744
9. Buddy Bell	1,060	4,032
10. Pete O'Brien	914	3,805

Home Runs: Season

Player	HR	Year
1. Alex Rodriguez	57	2002
2. Alex Rodriguez	52	2001
3. Frank Howard	48	1969
4. Juan Gonzalez	47	1996
Rafael Palmeiro	47	1999
Rafael Palmeiro	47	2001
Alex Rodriguez	47	2003
8. Juan Gonzalez	46	1993
9. Juan Gonzalez	45	1998
10. Frank Howard	44	1968
Frank Howard	44	1970

Home Runs: Career with Team

Player	HR	PA
1. Juan Gonzalez	372	5,925
2. Rafael Palmeiro	321	6,767
3. Frank Howard	246	4,744
4. Ivan Rodriguez	215	6,062
5. Ruben Sierra	180	4,975
6. Alex Rodriguez	156	2,172
7. Dean Palmer	154	3,076
8. Larry Parrish	149	3,547
9. Toby Harrah	124	5,407
Pete Incaviglia	124	2,718

Triples: Season

Player	3B	Year
1. Ruben Sierra	14	1989
2. Chuck Hinton	12	1963
3. David Hulse	10	1993
Ruben Sierra	10	1986
Ed Stroud	10	1968
6. Ed Brinkman	9	1966
Marty Keough	9	1961
Michael Young	9	2003
Michael Young	9	2004
10. Five tied with . . .	8	—

Triples: Career with Team

Player	3B	PA
1. Ruben Sierra	44	4,975
2. Michael Young	35	3,248
3. Chuck Hinton	30	2,202
4. Ivan Rodriguez	28	6,062
5. Ed Brinkman	27	4,215
Jim Sundberg	27	5,378
7. Rusty Greer	25	4,420
Rafael Palmeiro	25	6,767
9. Ed Stroud	24	1,279
10. Toby Harrah	22	5,407
Oddibe McDowell	22	2,265
Del Unser	22	2,345

Doubles: Season

Player	2B	Year
1. Juan Gonzalez	50	1998
2. Rafael Palmeiro	49	1991
3. Ivan Rodriguez	47	1996
4. Ruben Sierra	44	1991
5. Al Oliver	43	1980
Alfonso Soriano	43	2005
7. Buddy Bell	42	1979
Rusty Greer	42	1997
Larry Parrish	42	1984
10. Will Clark	41	1998
Rusty Greer	41	1996
Rusty Greer	41	1999
Todd Zeile	41	1999
Mark Teixeira	41	2005

Doubles: Career with Team

Player	2B	PA
1. Ivan Rodriguez	344	6,062
2. Rafael Palmeiro	321	6,767
3. Juan Gonzalez	320	5,925
4. Rusty Greer	258	4,420
5. Ruben Sierra	257	4,975
6. Jim Sundberg	200	5,378
7. Buddy Bell	197	4,032
8. Toby Harrah	187	5,407
9. Pete O'Brien	161	3,805
10. Frank Howard	155	4,744

Extra-Base Hits: Season

Player	XBH	Year
1. Juan Gonzalez	97	1998
2. Alex Rodriguez	87	2001
Mark Teixeira	87	2005
4. Alex Rodriguez	86	2002
5. Alex Rodriguez	83	2003
6. Juan Gonzalez	82	1996
7. Alfonso Soriano	81	2005
8. Juan Gonzalez	80	1993
Rafael Palmeiro	80	2001
10. Rafael Palmeiro	79	1993

Extra-Base Hits: Career with Team

Player	XBH	PA
1. Juan Gonzalez	713	5,925
2. Rafael Palmeiro	667	6,767
3. Ivan Rodriguez	587	6,062
4. Ruben Sierra	481	4,975
5. Frank Howard	421	4,744
6. Rusty Greer	402	4,420
7. Toby Harrah	333	5,407
8. Buddy Bell	305	4,032
Larry Parrish	305	3,547
10. Dean Palmer	296	3,076

Total Bases: Season

Player	TB	Year
1. Alex Rodriguez	393	2001
2. Alex Rodriguez	389	2002
3. Juan Gonzalez	382	1998
4. Mark Teixeira	370	2005
5. Alex Rodriguez	364	2003
6. Rafael Palmeiro	356	1999
7. Juan Gonzalez	348	1996

8. Ruben Sierra	344	1989
9. Michael Young	343	2005
10. Frank Howard	340	1969

Total Bases: Career with Team

Player	TB	PA
1. Juan Gonzalez	3,073	5,925
2. Rafael Palmeiro	3,026	6,767
3. Ivan Rodriguez	2,768	6,062
4. Ruben Sierra	2,166	4,975
5. Frank Howard	2,074	4,744
6. Rusty Greer	1,831	4,420
7. Toby Harrah	1,777	5,407
8. Jim Sundberg	1,614	5,378
9. Buddy Bell	1,560	4,032
10. Larry Parrish	1,464	3,547

Runs Batted In: Season

Player	RBI	Year
1. Juan Gonzalez	157	1998
2. Rafael Palmeiro	148	1999
3. Juan Gonzalez	144	1996
Mark Teixeira	144	2005
5. Alex Rodriguez	142	2002
6. Alex Rodriguez	135	2001
7. Juan Gonzalez	131	1997
8. Juan Gonzalez	128	1999
9. Frank Howard	126	1970
10. Rafael Palmeiro	123	2001

Runs Batted In: Career with Team

Player	RBI	PA
1. Juan Gonzalez	1,180	5,925
2. Rafael Palmeiro	1,039	6,767
3. Ivan Rodriguez	829	6,062
4. Ruben Sierra	742	4,975
5. Frank Howard	701	4,744
6. Rusty Greer	614	4,420
7. Toby Harrah	568	5,407
8. Larry Parrish	522	3,547
9. Buddy Bell	499	4,032
10. Pete O'Brien	487	3,805

Runs Scored: Season

Player	R	Year
1. Alex Rodriguez	133	2001
2. Alex Rodriguez	125	2002
3. Rafael Palmeiro	124	1993
Alex Rodriguez	124	2003
5. Ivan Rodriguez	116	1996
Ivan Rodriguez	116	1999
7. Rafael Palmeiro	115	1991
8. Juan Gonzalez	114	1999
Michael Young	114	2004
Michael Young	114	2005

Runs Scored: Career with Team

Player	R	PA
1. Rafael Palmeiro	958	6,767
2. Juan Gonzalez	878	5,925
3. Ivan Rodriguez	852	6,062
4. Ruben Sierra	645	4,975
5. Rusty Greer	643	4,420
6. Toby Harrah	631	5,407
7. Frank Howard	544	4,744
8. Jim Sundberg	482	5,378
9. Buddy Bell	471	4,032
10. Michael Young	468	3,248

Walks: Season

Player	BB	Year
1. Frank Howard	132	1970
2. Toby Harrah	113	1985
3. Toby Harrah	109	1977
4. Mike Hargrove	107	1978
Mickey Tettleton	107	1995
6. Rafael Palmeiro	104	2002
7. Mike Hargrove	103	1977
Rafael Palmeiro	103	2000
9. Frank Howard	102	1969
10. Rafael Palmeiro	101	2001

Walks: Career with Team

Player	BB	PA
1. Rafael Palmeiro	805	6,767
2. Toby Harrah	708	5,407
3. Frank Howard	575	4,744
4. Jim Sundberg	544	5,378
5. Rusty Greer	519	4,420
6. Mike Hargrove	435	3,004
7. Pete O'Brien	404	3,805
8. Juan Gonzalez	375	5,925
9. Mark McLemore	358	2,783
10. Buddy Bell	335	4,032
Jeff Burroughs	335	2,908

Strikeouts: Season

Player	SO	Year
1. Pete Incaviglia	185	1986
2. Pete Incaviglia	168	1987
3. Jeff Burroughs	155	1975
Frank Howard	155	1967
5. Dean Palmer	154	1992
Dean Palmer	154	1993
Larry Parrish	154	1987
8. Pete Incaviglia	153	1988
9. Don Lock	151	1963
10. Hank Blalock	149	2004

Strikeouts: Career with Team

Player	SO	PA
1. Juan Gonzalez	1,076	5,925
2. Frank Howard	909	4,744
3. Pete Incaviglia	788	2,718
4. Ivan Rodriguez	763	6,062
5. Dean Palmer	757	3,076
6. Rafael Palmeiro	754	6,767
7. Larry Parrish	715	3,547
8. Jim Sundberg	687	5,378
9. Ruben Sierra	676	4,975
10. Don Lock	592	2,397

Slugging Percentage: Season

Player	SLG	Year
1. Juan Gonzalez	.643	1996
2. Juan Gonzalez	.632	1993
3. Juan Gonzalez	.630	1998
Rafael Palmeiro	.630	1999
5. Alex Rodriguez	.623	2002
6. Alex Rodriguez	.622	2001
7. Juan Gonzalez	.601	1999
8. Alex Rodriguez	.600	2003
9. Juan Gonzalez	.589	1997
10. Mark Teixeira	.575	2005

Slugging Percentage: Career with Team

Player	SLG	PA
1. Alex Rodriguez	.615	2,172
2. Juan Gonzalez	.565	5,925
3. Rafael Palmeiro	.519	6,767
4. Frank Howard	.503	4,744
5. Ivan Rodriguez	.489	6,062
6. Will Clark	.485	2,604
7. Rusty Greer	.478	4,420
8. Ruben Sierra	.473	4,975
9. Hank Blalock	.471	2,205
10. Dean Palmer	.470	3,076

On-Base Percentage: Season

Player	OBP	Year
1. Toby Harrah	.432	1985
2. Will Clark	.431	1994
3. Mike Hargrove	.420	1977
Rafael Palmeiro	.420	1999
5. Frank Howard	.416	1970
6. Mike Epstein	.414	1969
7. Julio Franco	.408	1991
8. Brian Downing	.407	1992
9. Rusty Greer	.405	1997
Rusty Greer	.405	1999

On-Base Percentage: Career with Team

Player	OBP	PA
1. Mike Hargrove	.399	3,004
2. Alex Rodriguez	.395	2,172
Will Clark	.395	2,604
4. Rusty Greer	.387	4,420
5. Julio Franco	.382	2,680
6. Rafael Palmeiro	.378	6,767
7. Frank Howard	.367	4,744
8. Mike Epstein	.365	2,000
9. Mark McLemore	.363	2,783
10. Al Oliver	.358	2,263

OPS (On-Base Percentage + Slugging Percentage): Season

Player	OPS	Year
1. Rafael Palmeiro	1.050	1999
2. Alex Rodriguez	1.021	2001
3. Alex Rodriguez	1.015	2002
4. Juan Gonzalez	1.012	1996
5. Juan Gonzalez	1.000	1993
6. Juan Gonzalez	.997	1998
7. Alex Rodriguez	.995	2003
8. Juan Gonzalez	.980	1999
9. Frank Howard	.976	1969
10. Mike Epstein	.965	1969

OPS (On-Base Percentage + Slugging Percentage): Career with Team

Player	OPS	PA
1. Alex Rodriguez	1.011	2,172
2. Juan Gonzalez	.907	5,925
3. Rafael Palmeiro	.897	6,767
4. Will Clark	.879	2,604
5. Frank Howard	.870	4,744
6. Rusty Greer	.865	4,420
7. Ivan Rodriguez	.831	6,062
8. Al Oliver	.824	2,263
9. Julio Franco	.822	2,680
10. Mike Hargrove	.809	3,004

Stolen Bases: Season

Player	SB	Year
1. Bump Wills	52	1978
2. Dave Nelson	51	1972
3. Otis Nixon	50	1995
4. Cecil Espy	45	1989
5. Bill Sample	44	1983
6. Dave Nelson	43	1973
7. Tom Goodwin	39	1999
8. Tom Goodwin	38	1998
Gary Pettis	38	1990
10. Bobby Bonds	37	1978

Stolen Bases: Career with Team

Player	SB	PA
1. Bump Wills	161	2,962
2. Toby Harrah	153	5,407
3. Dave Nelson	144	2,296
4. Oddibe McDowell	129	2,265
5. Julio Franco	98	2,680
6. Tom Goodwin	93	1,298
7. Chuck Hinton	92	2,202
Bill Sample	92	2,423
9. Cecil Espy	91	994
10. Ruben Sierra	90	4,975

Sacrifice Hits: Season

Player	Sac	Year
1. Bert Campaneris	40	1977
2. Bert Campaneris	25	1978
3. Jim Sundberg	20	1977
4. Nelson Norman	18	1979
5. Jim Sundberg	17	1974
6. Kevin Elster	16	1996
Len Randle	16	1974
8. Scott Fletcher	15	1988
Danny O'Connell	15	1961
Bump Wills	15	1980

Sacrifice Hits: Career with Team

Player	Sac	PA
1. Jim Sundberg	102	5,378
2. Bert Campaneris	65	977
3. Toby Harrah	56	5,407
4. Bump Wills	51	2,962
5. Len Randle	43	2,392
6. Scott Fletcher	39	2,229
Mark McLemore	39	2,783
8. Steve Buechele	38	3,047
9. Dave Nelson	37	2,296
10. Dick Bosman	34	382
Ed Brinkman	34	4,215

Hit by Pitch: Season

Player	HBP	Year
1. Alex Rodriguez	16	2001
2. Alex Rodriguez	15	2003
3. Mark Teixeira	14	2003
4. Mike Epstein	13	1968
Juan Gonzalez	13	1993
6. Scott Fletcher	12	1988
7. Mark Teixeira	11	2005
8. 10 tied with . . .	10	——

Hit by Pitch: Career with Team

Player	HBP	PA
1. Rafael Palmeiro	54	6,767
2. Juan Gonzalez	53	5,925
3. Mike Epstein	45	2,000
4. Alex Rodriguez	41	2,172
5. Ivan Rodriguez	39	6,062
6. Mark Teixeira	35	1,944
7. Mike Hargrove	27	3,004
Pete Incaviglia	27	2,718
Dean Palmer	27	3,076
10. Toby Harrah	26	5,407
Fred Valentine	26	1,489

Top 10 Pitching Leaders, Single Season & Career with Team

Games Pitched: Season

Player	GP	Year
1. Mitch Williams	85	1987
2. Kenny Rogers	81	1992
3. Mitch Williams	80	1986
4. Mike Venafro	77	2000
5. Ron Kline	74	1965
Dale Mohorcic	74	1987
7. Francisco Cordero	73	2003
Greg Harris	73	1986
Kenny Rogers	73	1989
10. Jim Kern	71	1979
Darold Knowles	71	1970
Jeff Russell	71	1989

Games Pitched: Career with Team

Player	GP	IP
1. Kenny Rogers	528	1,909.0
2. Jeff Russell	445	752.7
3. Charlie Hough	344	2,308.0
4. Francisco Cordero	307	348.3
5. Casey Cox	302	747.3
6. Bobby Witt	276	1,680.7
7. Darold Knowles	271	424.0
8. Ron Kline	260	364.7
9. Jim Hannan	248	778.7
John Wetteland	248	253.0

Innings Pitched: Season

Player	IP	Year
1. Fergie Jenkins	328.3	1974
2. Charlie Hough	285.3	1987
3. Fergie Jenkins	270.0	1975
Jon Matlack	270.0	1978
5. Charlie Hough	266.0	1984
6. Kevin Brown	265.7	1992
7. Jim Bibby	264.0	1974
8. Fergie Jenkins	259.0	1979
9. Claude Osteen	257.0	1964
10. Charlie Hough	252.0	1983
Charlie Hough	252.0	1988

Innings Pitched: Career with Team

Player	IP
1. Charlie Hough	2,308.0
2. Kenny Rogers	1,909.0
3. Bobby Witt	1,680.7
4. Fergie Jenkins	1,410.3
5. Kevin Brown	1,278.7
6. Dick Bosman	1,103.3
7. Jose Guzman	1,013.7
8. Rick Helling	1,008.0
9. Jon Matlack	915.0
10. Danny Darwin	872.0

Batters Faced: Season

Player	BF	Year
1. Fergie Jenkins	1,305	1974
2. Charlie Hough	1,231	1987
3. Jim Bibby	1,134	1974
4. Charlie Hough	1,133	1984
5. Fergie Jenkins	1,119	1975
6. Kevin Brown	1,108	1992
7. Jon Matlack	1,097	1978
8. Fergie Jenkins	1,089	1979
9. Claude Osteen	1,070	1964
10. Charlie Hough	1,067	1988

Batters Faced: Career with Team

Player	BF	IP
1. Charlie Hough	9,736	2,308.0
2. Kenny Rogers	8,271	1,909.0
3. Bobby Witt	7,521	1,680.7
4. Fergie Jenkins	5,797	1,410.3
5. Kevin Brown	5,487	1,278.7
6. Dick Bosman	4,582	1,103.3
7. Rick Helling	4,377	1,008.0
8. Jose Guzman	4,330	1,013.7
9. Jon Matlack	3,836	915.0
10. Darren Oliver	3,816	842.7

Games Started: Season

Player	GS	Year
1. Jim Bibby	41	1974
Fergie Jenkins	41	1974
3. Charlie Hough	40	1987
4. Fergie Jenkins	37	1975
Fergie Jenkins	37	1979
6. Joe Coleman	36	1969
Steve Comer	36	1979
Charlie Hough	36	1984
Claude Osteen	36	1964
10. Eight tied with . . .	35	—

Games Started: Career with Team

Player	GS	IP
1. Charlie Hough	313	2,308.0
2. Bobby Witt	269	1,680.7
3. Kenny Rogers	252	1,909.0
4. Fergie Jenkins	190	1,410.3
5. Kevin Brown	186	1,278.7
6. Rick Helling	159	1,008.0
7. Dick Bosman	155	1,103.3
8. Jose Guzman	152	1,013.7
9. Darren Oliver	137	842.7
10. Nolan Ryan	129	840.0

Complete Games: Season

Player	CG	Year
1. Fergie Jenkins	29	1974
2. Fergie Jenkins	22	1975
3. Gaylord Perry	21	1976
4. Jon Matlack	18	1978
5. Charlie Hough	17	1984
6. Fergie Jenkins	16	1978
7. Bert Blyleven	15	1977
Gaylord Perry	15	1975
9. Bert Blyleven	14	1976
Charlie Hough	14	1985

Complete Games: Career with Team

Player	CG	IP
1. Charlie Hough	98	2,308.0
2. Fergie Jenkins	90	1,410.3
3. Gaylord Perry	55	827.3
4. Kevin Brown	40	1,278.7
5. Joe Coleman	36	850.3
6. Bobby Witt	33	1,680.7
7. Jon Matlack	32	915.0

8. Bert Blyleven	29	437.0
9. Claude Osteen	28	638.0
10. Jim Bibby	26	529.0

GAMES WON: SEASON

Player	W	Year
1. Fergie Jenkins	25	1974
2. Kevin Brown	21	1992
3. Rick Helling	20	1998
4. Jim Bibby	19	1974
Aaron Sele	19	1998
6. Charlie Hough	18	1987
Fergie Jenkins	18	1978
Kenny Rogers	18	2004
Aaron Sele	18	1999
10. Six tied with . . .	17	—

GAMES WON: CAREER WITH TEAM

Player	W	IP
1. Charlie Hough	139	2,308.0
2. Kenny Rogers	133	1,909.0
3. Bobby Witt	104	1,680.7
4. Fergie Jenkins	93	1,410.3
5. Kevin Brown	78	1,278.7
6. Rick Helling	68	1,008.0
7. Jose Guzman	66	1,013.7
8. Dick Bosman	59	1,103.3
9. Danny Darwin	55	872.0
10. Darren Oliver	54	842.7

GAMES LOST: SEASON

Player	L	Year
1. Denny McLain	22	1971
2. Jim Bibby	19	1974
Don Rudolph	19	1963
4. Fergie Jenkins	18	1975
Joe McClain	18	1961
Frank Tanana	18	1982
7. Rick Honeycutt	17	1982
8. Dick Bosman	16	1971
Joe Coleman	16	1968
Bennie Daniels	16	1962
Charlie Hough	16	1985
Charlie Hough	16	1988

GAMES LOST: CAREER WITH TEAM

Player	L	IP
1. Charlie Hough	123	2,308.0
2. Bobby Witt	104	1,680.7
3. Kenny Rogers	96	1,909.0
4. Fergie Jenkins	72	1,410.3
5. Dick Bosman	64	1,103.3

7. Jose Guzman	62	1,013.7
8. Bennie Daniels	60	821.3
9. Danny Darwin	52	872.0
10. Rick Helling	51	1,008.0

WINNING PERCENTAGE: SEASON

Player	W%	Year
1. Danny Darwin	.765	1980
2. Rick Helling	.741	1998
3. Dick Bosman	.737	1969
4. Jim Kern	.722	1979
5. Kenny Rogers	.708	1995
6. Darren Oliver	.700	1996
7. Fergie Jenkins	.692	1978
8. Steve Comer	.688	1978
9. Fergie Jenkins	.676	1974
10. Roger Pavlik	.667	1993
Kenny Rogers	.667	2004
Nolan Ryan	.667	1991
Aaron Sele	.667	1999

WINNING PERCENTAGE: CAREER WITH TEAM

Player	W%	IP
1. Kenny Rogers	.581	1,909.0
2. Rick Helling	.571	1,008.0
3. Nolan Ryan	.567	840.0
4. Fergie Jenkins	.564	1,410.3
5. Kevin Brown	.549	1,278.7
6. Roger Pavlik	.547	743.0
7. Doc Medich	.538	790.3
8. Darren Oliver	.535	842.7
9. Charlie Hough	.531	2,308.0
10. Gaylord Perry	.527	827.3

SHUTOUTS: SEASON

Player	SHO	Year
1. Bert Blyleven	6	1976
Fergie Jenkins	6	1974
3. Jim Bibby	5	1974
Bert Blyleven	5	1977
5. Nine tied with . . .	4	—

SHUTOUTS: CAREER WITH TEAM

Player	SHO	IP
1. Fergie Jenkins	17	1,410.3
2. Gaylord Perry	12	827.3
3. Bert Blyleven	11	437.0
Charlie Hough	11	2,308.0
5. Dick Bosman	9	1,103.3
6. Jim Bibby	8	529.0
7. Tom Cheney	7	393.3

Joe Coleman	7	850.3
Doc Medich	7	790.3
10. Kevin Brown	6	1,278.7
Phil Ortega	6	712.3
Nolan Ryan	6	840.0
Kenny Rogers	6	1,909.0

ERA: SEASON

Player	ERA	Year
1. Dick Bosman	2.19	1969
2. Jon Matlack	2.27	1978
3. Dick Donovan	2.40	1961
4. Rick Honeycutt	2.42	1983
5. Pete Richert	2.60	1965
6. Camilo Pascual	2.69	1968
7. Bert Blyleven	2.72	1977
8. Bert Blyleven	2.76	1976
9. Casey Cox	2.78	1969
10. Fergie Jenkins	2.82	1974

ERA: CAREER WITH TEAM

Player	ERA	IP
1. Gaylord Perry	3.26	827.3
2. Dick Bosman	3.35	1,103.3
3. Jon Matlack	3.41	915.0
4. Nolan Ryan	3.43	840.0
5. Claude Osteen	3.46	638.0
6. Joe Coleman	3.51	850.3
7. Fergie Jenkins	3.56	1,410.3
8. Casey Cox	3.67	747.3
9. Charlie Hough	3.68	2,308.0
10. Danny Darwin	3.72	872.0

EARNED RUNS ALLOWED: SEASON

Player	ER	Year
1. Jim Bibby	139	1974
2. Rick Helling	124	2001
3. John Burkett	123	1998
4. Charlie Hough	120	1987
Bobby Witt	120	1996
6. Rick Helling	118	1999
Fergie Jenkins	118	1975
8. Fergie Jenkins	117	1979
John Thomson	117	2003
10. Roger Pavlik	116	1996

EARNED RUNS ALLOWED: CAREER WITH TEAM

Player	ER	IP
1. Charlie Hough	943	2,308.0

Player	K	IP
2. Bobby Witt	906	1,680.7
3. Kenny Rogers	882	1,909.0
4. Fergie Jenkins	558	1,410.3
5. Rick Helling	544	1,008.0
6. Kevin Brown	541	1,278.7
7. Darren Oliver	494	842.7
8. Jose Guzman	439	1,013.7
9. Dick Bosman	411	1,103.3
10. Bennie Daniels	378	821.3
Roger Pavlik	378	743.0

Strikeouts: Season

Player	K	Year
1. Nolan Ryan	301	1989
2. Nolan Ryan	232	1990
3. Fergie Jenkins	225	1974
4. Charlie Hough	223	1987
5. Bobby Witt	221	1990
6. Nolan Ryan	203	1991
7. Pete Richert	195	1966
8. Ed Correa	189	1986
9. Aaron Sele	186	1999
10. Bert Blyleven	182	1977
Joe Coleman	182	1969

Strikeouts: Career with Team

Player	K	IP
1. Charlie Hough	1,452	2,308.0
2. Bobby Witt	1,405	1,680.7
3. Kenny Rogers	1,201	1,909.0
4. Nolan Ryan	939	840.0
5. Fergie Jenkins	895	1,410.3
6. Kevin Brown	742	1,278.7
7. Jose Guzman	715	1,013.7
8. Rick Helling	687	1,008.0
9. Gaylord Perry	575	827.3
10. Dick Bosman	573	1,103.3

Strikeouts Per Nine IP: Season

Player	K/9	Year
1. Nolan Ryan	11.32	1989
2. Nolan Ryan	10.56	1991
3. Nolan Ryan	10.24	1990
4. Bobby Witt	8.96	1990
5. Ed Correa	8.41	1986
6. Aaron Sele	8.17	1999
7. Jim Bibby	7.74	1973
8. Bobby Witt	7.69	1989
9. Bobby Witt	7.64	1988
10. Tom Cheney	7.63	1962

Strikeouts Per Nine IP: Career with Team

Player	K/9	IP
1. Nolan Ryan	10.06	840.0
2. Bobby Witt	7.52	1,680.7
3. Roger Pavlik	6.37	743.0
4. Jose Guzman	6.35	1,013.7
5. Gaylord Perry	6.26	827.3
6. John Burkett	6.19	600.3
7. Rick Helling	6.13	1,008.0
8. Joe Coleman	5.94	850.3
9. Kenny Rogers	5.85	1,713.7
10. Danny Darwin	5.84	872.0

Hits Allowed: Season

Player	HA	Year
1. Fergie Jenkins	286	1974
2. Jon Matlack	265	1980
3. Kevin Brown	262	1992
4. Fergie Jenkins	261	1975
5. Charlie Hough	260	1984
6. Kenny Rogers	257	2000
7. Rick Helling	256	2001
Claude Osteen	256	1964
9. Jim Bibby	255	1974
10. Fergie Jenkins	252	1979
Jon Matlack	252	1978

Hits Allowed: Career with Team

Player	HA	IP
1. Kenny Rogers	1,997	1,909.0
2. Charlie Hough	1,995	2,308.0
3. Bobby Witt	1,649	1,680.7
4. Fergie Jenkins	1,339	1,410.3
5. Kevin Brown	1,322	1,278.7
6. Dick Bosman	1,075	1,103.3
7. Rick Helling	1,054	1,008.0
8. Jose Guzman	983	1,013.7
9. Darren Oliver	972	842.7
10. Jon Matlack	964	915.0

Hits Allowed Per Nine IP: Season

Player	H/9	Year
1. Nolan Ryan	5.31	1991
2. Jim Bibby	6.04	1973
Nolan Ryan	6.04	1990
4. Nolan Ryan	6.09	1989
5. Pete Richert	6.77	1965
6. Bobby Witt	6.92	1988
7. Bert Blyleven	6.94	1977
8. Tom Cheney	6.96	1962
9. Charlie Hough	7.12	1985
10. Pete Richert	7.18	1966

Hits Allowed Per Nine IP: Career with Team

Player	H/9	IP
1. Nolan Ryan	6.35	840.0
2. Charlie Hough	7.78	2,308.0
3. Jim Bibby	7.96	529.0
4. Phil Ortega	8.06	712.3
5. Joe Coleman	8.39	850.3
6. Fergie Jenkins	8.54	1,410.3
7. Gaylord Perry	8.56	827.3
8. Danny Darwin	8.60	872.0
9. Jose Guzman	8.73	1,013.7
10. Dick Bosman	8.77	1,103.3

Walks Allowed: Season

Player	BB	Year
1. Bobby Witt	143	1986
2. Bobby Witt	140	1987
3. Ed Correa	126	1986
Charlie Hough	126	1988
5. Charlie Hough	124	1987
6. Charlie Hough	119	1990
7. Bobby Witt	114	1989
8. Jim Bibby	113	1974
9. Bobby Witt	110	1990
10. Jim Bibby	106	1973

Walks Allowed: Career with Team

Player	BB	IP
1. Bobby Witt	1,001	1,680.7
2. Charlie Hough	965	2,308.0
3. Kenny Rogers	686	1,909.0
4. Kevin Brown	428	1,278.7
5. Jose Guzman	395	1,013.7
6. Rick Helling	381	1,008.0
7. Jim Hannan	378	778.7
8. Darren Oliver	376	842.7
9. Nolan Ryan	353	840.0
10. Roger Pavlik	351	743.0

Walks Allowed Per Nine IP: Season

Player	BB/9	Year
1. Fergie Jenkins	1.23	1974
2. John Burkett	1.43	1997
3. Fergie Jenkins	1.48	1978

Player		
4. Jon Matlack	1.70	1978
5. Gaylord Perry	1.76	1975
6. Dick Bosman	1.82	1969
7. Jon Matlack	1.84	1980
8. Don Rudolph	1.86	1963
9. Fergie Jenkins	1.87	1975
Dick Donovan	1.87	1961

Walks Allowed Per Nine IP: Career with Team

Player	BB/9	IP
1. Fergie Jenkins	2.01	1,410.3
2. Gaylord Perry	2.07	827.3
John Burkett	2.07	600.3
4. Jon Matlack	2.15	915.0
5. Dick Bosman	2.47	1,103.3
6. Claude Osteen	2.54	638.0
7. Steve Hargan	2.69	512.7
8. Frank Tanana	2.76	677.7
9. Casey Cox	2.77	747.3
10. Doc Medich	2.86	790.3

WHIP (Walks + Hits Per Nine IP: Season

Player	WHIP	Year
1. Nolan Ryan	1.006	1991
2. Fergie Jenkins	1.008	1974
3. Dick Bosman	1.010	1969
4. Dick Donovan	1.026	1961
5. Nolan Ryan	1.034	1990
6. Gaylord Perry	1.049	1975
7. Bert Blyleven	1.065	1977
8. Phil Ortega	1.069	1966
9. Pete Richert	1.079	1966
10. Fergie Jenkins	1.080	1978

WHIP (Walks + Hits Per Nine IP): Career with Team

Player	WHIP	IP
1. Nolan Ryan	1.126	840.0
2. Fergie Jenkins	1.173	1,410.3
3. Gaylord Perry	1.181	827.3
4. Dick Bosman	1.249	1,103.3
5. Claude Osteen	1.273	638.0
Phil Ortega	1.273	712.3
7. Joe Coleman	1.282	850.3
Charlie Hough	1.282	2,308.0
9. Frank Tanana	1.290	677.7
10. Jon Matlack	1.293	915.0

Home Runs Allowed: Season

Player	HRA	Year
1. Rick Helling	41	1999
2. Fergie Jenkins	40	1979
3. Rick Helling	38	2001
4. Fergie Jenkins	37	1975
5. Charlie Hough	36	1987
Pete Richert	36	1966
7. Phil Ortega	33	1965
Bobby Witt	33	1997
9. Charlie Hough	32	1986
10. Denny McLain	31	1971
Buster Narum	31	1964

Home Runs Allowed: Career with Team

Player	HRA	IP
1. Charlie Hough	238	2,308.0
2. Kenny Rogers	195	1,909.0
3. Bobby Witt	164	1,680.7
4. Rick Helling	163	1,008.0
5. Fergie Jenkins	161	1,410.3
6. Darren Oliver	107	842.7
7. Jose Guzman	103	1,013.7
8. Phil Ortega	90	712.3
9. Dick Bosman	89	1,103.3
10. Kevin Brown	85	1,278.7
Roger Pavlik	85	743.0

Saves: Season

Player	SV	Year
1. Francisco Cordero	49	2004
2. John Wetteland	43	1999
3. John Wetteland	42	1998
4. Tom Henke	40	1993
5. Jeff Russell	38	1989
6. Francisco Cordero	37	2005
7. John Wetteland	34	2000
8. Mike Henneman	31	1996
John Wetteland	31	1997
10. Jeff Russell	30	1991

Saves: Career with Team

Player	SV	IP
1. John Wetteland	150	253.0
2. Jeff Russell	134	752.7
3. Francisco Cordero	111	348.3
4. Ron Kline	83	364.7
5. Darold Knowles	64	424.0
6. Tom Henke	58	172.3
7. Jim Kern	37	236.3
8. Steve Foucault	35	382.7
9. Mitch Williams	32	274.7
Jeff Zimmerman	32	228.7

Wild Pitches: Season

Player	WP	Year
1. Bobby Witt	22	1986
2. Ed Correa	19	1986
Nolan Ryan	19	1989
4. Frank Bertaina	17	1968
5. Charlie Hough	16	1986
Bobby Witt	16	1988
7. Dennis Higgins	15	1969
8. Pete Broberg	14	1972
Joe Coleman	14	1970
10. Seven tied with...	12	——

Wild Pitches: Career with Team

Player	WP	IP
1. Charlie Hough	99	2,308.0
2. Bobby Witt	95	1,680.7
3. Kevin Brown	52	1,278.7
4. Nolan Ryan	48	840.0
5. Kenny Rogers	47	1,909.0
6. Joe Coleman	43	850.3
7. Roger Pavlik	39	743.0
Jeff Russell	39	752.7
9. Jim Hannan	37	778.7
10. Darren Oliver	36	842.7

Hit Batsmen: Season

Player	HB	Year
1. Charlie Hough	19	1987
2. Chan Ho Park	17	2002
3. Kevin Brown	15	1993
4. Pete Broberg	13	1972
Kevin Brown	13	1991
Chan Ho Park	13	2004
Aaron Sele	13	1998
8. Joe Coleman	12	1968
Charlie Hough	12	1988
Nolan Ryan	12	1992
Aaron Sele	12	1999

Hit Batsmen: Career with Team

Player	HB	IP
1. Charlie Hough	89	2,308.0
2. Kenny Rogers	62	1,909.0
3. Kevin Brown	52	1,278.7
4. Darren Oliver	48	842.7

5. Chan Ho Park	42	380.7
6. Nolan Ryan	34	840.0
7. Joe Coleman	31	850.3
8. Pete Broberg	29	448.7
9. Fergie Jenkins	27	1,410.3
10. Aaron Sele	25	417.7

GAMES FINISHED: SEASON

Player	GF	Year
1. Jeff Russell	66	1989
2. Francisco Cordero	63	2004
Greg Harris	63	1986
4. Tom Henke	60	1993
Francisco Cordero	60	2005
6. John Wetteland	59	1998
John Wetteland	59	1999
8. Ron Kline	58	1965
John Wetteland	58	1997
10. Jim Kern	57	1979
John Wetteland	57	2000

GAMES FINISHED: CAREER WITH TEAM

Player	GF	IP
1. Jeff Russell	251	752.7
2. John Wetteland	233	253.0
3. Ron Kline	202	364.7
4. Francisco Cordero	199	348.3
5. Darold Knowles	173	424.0
6. Steve Foucault	147	382.7
7. Kenny Rogers	128	1,909.0
8. Mitch Williams	121	274.7
9. Tom Henke	115	172.3
10. Dave Schmidt	114	343.7

Nolan Ryan, six strikes away from his 5,000th strikeout, in 1989.

Significant Senators/Rangers

GONZALEZ, JUAN (OF/DH) (1989–1999, 2002–2003)

The Texas Rangers signed the 16-year-old Puerto Rican–born Juan Gonzalez as an amateur free agent in May 1986. By the time he was 19, "Juan-Gone" was playing in the major leagues. At the age of 22 he won his first home run title, slugging 43 in 1992. The following year he won the homer title again with 46. It was also his third straight year with at least 100 RBIs. After two subpar years in 1994 and 1995—thanks to the players' strike, his brother's death, and assorted injury problems—Gonzalez rebounded in 1996 with career highs in average (.314), homers (47), and RBIs (144), despite spending almost the entire month of May on the disabled list. For this performance he was rewarded with the American League MVP Award, beating out Alex Rodriguez of the Mariners in one of the closest votes in MVP history (290–287). He also led the Rangers into the playoffs for the first time in franchise history. In the five-game Division Series against the Yankees, Gonzalez batted .438 and smacked five home runs, but the Rangers lost in four games. Gonzalez's 1997 season was almost identical to 1996; he hit 42 homers with 131 RBIs, despite spending time on the DL again.

Gonzalez won his second MVP Award in 1998, making him one of only 15 players to win the award more than once. He got off to a blazing start, collecting 35 RBIs in April. By the All-Star break he had 101 RBIs, second most in history, and 26 against Kansas City alone. At season's end, Gonzalez had 157 RBIs to go with his 45 homers and a new career-high batting average of .318. He again led the Rangers into the playoffs against the Yankees, but New York swept aside the Rangers in three straight.

In 1999 Gonzalez once more hit for a new career high in average, finishing at .326. He also had 39 homers and 128 RBIs, his seventh 100-RBI season, but he received more attention for his off-field actions. When the fans failed to vote him onto the All-Star team as a starter, Gonzalez threw a fit and stayed home rather than participating as a reserve who was named by the AL manager. For the third time in four years, the Rangers met the Yanks in the playoffs, and for the third straight time, the Yankees sent Texas home early. Texas only scored one run in the three game series, and Gonzalez knocked it in.

After the season, Gonzalez was sent to Detroit in a nine-player trade. He spent a year with Detroit and another with Cleveland before returning to Texas as a free agent for two more seasons, but injuries severely limited his playing time. In 2003 he hit 24 homers in only 82 games, proving he still had the ability if only he could stay healthy. After the 2003 season, Gonzalez left via free agency again, this time landing in Kansas City for a year, but he only hit 5 homers in 33 games in 2004. He signed with Cleveland again for 2005, but he was again unable to play due to injuries, throwing his baseball future into serious doubt.

CAREER RANGERS RECORD:

Games	AB	Hits	Runs
1,400	5,435	1,595	878
Avg	HR	RBI	SB
.293	372	1,180	24

GREER, RUSTY (OF)
(1994–2002)

Rusty Greer was chosen in the 10th round of the June 1990 amateur draft by the Rangers and played four seasons in their minor league system. When he was finally called up in mid-1994, he had a solid year, hitting .314 and finishing third in the AL Rookie of the Year race. A steady and productive player in his first six years with the Rangers, Greer broke the .300 barrier five times, and had 100 runs, 100 RBIs, and 40 doubles three times each. He also excelled defensively; it was his diving catch in the ninth inning that preserved a perfect game for Kenny Rogers. Greer played on all three Rangers playoff teams, though he hit only .111 in the postseason. A series of injuries began to take their toll, however, starting in 2000, and he lost progressively more games each year until his career ended in 2002 after only nine years.

CAREER RANGERS RECORD:

Games	AB	Hits	Runs
1,027	3,829	1,166	643
Avg	**HR**	**RBI**	**SB**
.305	119	614	31

HARRAH, TOBY (SS/3B)
(1969, 1971–1978, 1985–1986)

Originally drafted by the Philadelphia Phillies, Harrah came to the Washington Senators in the 1967 minor league draft and was still with the team when the franchise shifted to Texas in 1972. After making the team for good in his rookie year of 1971, Harrah took over most of the shortstop duties for the Senators, although his hitting left something to be desired (he batted only .230 with two homers for the season). In 1972, the first year the team was in Texas, Harrah started to show some promise at the plate. By 1975, he hit .293 with 20 homers and 93 RBIs. He also had 98 walks and stole 23 bases. Harrah moved to third base in 1977 when the Rangers signed Bert Campaneris and responded with career highs in homers (27), runs (90), and steals (27).

In a game at Yankee Stadium that year, Harrah and Bump Wills hit back-to-back inside-the-park homers, only the second time the feat had ever been accomplished in major league history. Harrah did set two unusual records during his time in Texas. In 1976 he played both games of a doubleheader at shortstop without accepting any fielding chances. In 1977 he played third base in a 17-inning game without having an assist. After slumping badly in 1978, Harrah was traded to Cleveland for their third baseman, Buddy Bell. A three-time All-Star with the Rangers, Harrah returned to the team after retiring as a player and managed in their minor league system two years before joining the major league team as a coach from 1989 to 1992. He then replaced Bobby Valentine as manager in the middle of the 1992 season, guiding Texas to a 32–44 record to finish the season, the only time Harrah would manage in the majors.

CAREER SENATORS/RANGERS RECORD:

Games	AB	Hits	Runs
1,355	4,572	1,174	631
Avg	**HR**	**RBI**	**SB**
.257	124	568	153

HOUGH, CHARLIE (SP)
(1980–1990)

Hough's career was marked by a strange symmetry. After spending 10½ seasons with the Los Angeles Dodgers, the knuckleball pitcher was purchased on July 11, 1980 by the Rangers, the team with which he would spend the next 10½ seasons. While with the Dodgers, Hough had appeared in more than 400 games, but only 14 as a starter. In 1982, Hough's second year in Texas, the Rangers decided to try their veteran reliever in the starting rotation. Over Hough's final 13 years, he would start more than 400 games and relieve only three times, becoming the first pitcher in baseball history to record more than 400 starts and 400 relief appearances in a career. During the six years from 1982 to 1987, Hough, whose lone appearance in the All-Star Game came in 1986, led Texas in wins, complete games, and innings pitched. He also won a higher percentage of his team's games than any other pitcher in the major leagues during that same six-year period. In 1987 Hough, at 39, became the oldest pitcher in American League history to lead the league in starts and innings pitched. The Rangers set a major league record in 1987 with 73 passed balls, and Hough's knuckleball contributed to 65 them. Nearly 43 years old, Hough was granted free-agent status after the 1990 season. He played two more years each with the White Sox and Marlins before retiring.

CAREER RANGERS RECORD:

W	L	W%	ERA	SV
139	123	.531	3.68	1
K	BB	SHO	IP	
1,452	965	11	2,308.0	

HOWARD, FRANK (OF/1B)
(1965–1972)

After seven seasons with the Dodgers, Frank "Hondo" Howard was traded to the Washington Senators as part of a six-player deal that brought pitcher Claude Osteen to Los Angeles. Howard spent the next eight years with the Senators, moving with the team to Texas in 1972. At 6'8" and nearly 300 pounds, Howard is best remembered for his mammoth home runs. Ted Williams called him the strongest man ever to play baseball. During one especially hot streak in May 1968, Howard hit 10 home runs in 20 at-bats over a six-game stretch, including at least one homer each game. In a game at Fenway Park, Howard hit a line drive so hard that when it hit the center-field fence, it rebounded into center fielder Reggie Smith's glove before Howard got to first base. Howard, a four-time All-Star from 1968 to 1971, led the American League in homers twice (1968 and 1970), hitting 44 each time. He slugged 48 in 1969, but lost the home run crown to Harmon Killebrew's 49. Howard's prodigious home runs earned him the nickname "The Capital Punisher." His career with the Rangers ended on August 31, 1972 when he was sold outright to the Detroit Tigers. Howard went on to manage the Padres for two years and the Mets for one.

CAREER SENATORS/RANGERS RECORD:

Games	AB	Hits	Runs
1,172	4,120	1,141	544
Avg	HR	RBI	SB
.277	246	701	5

JENKINS, FERGUSON (SP)
(1974–1975, 1978–1981)

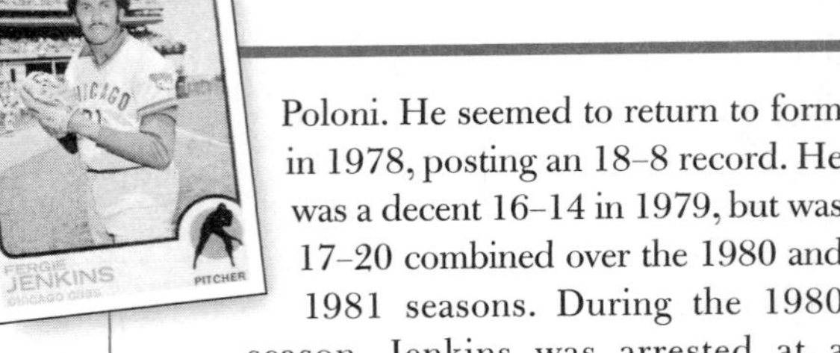

After spending nine seasons in the National League with the Phillies and Cubs, Jenkins was traded to the Rangers after the 1973 season for Bill Madlock and Vic Harris. In his first start as a Ranger in 1974, Jenkins one-hit the defending World Series champion Oakland A's. It was the first of 25 victories he would record that year to go along with a sparkling 2.82 ERA. He was runner-up to Oakland's Catfish Hunter in the Cy Young voting. In 1975, however, Jenkins slipped to 17–18 and was traded after the season to Boston for Juan Beniquez, Steve Barr, and Craig Skok. After compiling a 22–21 record in two mediocre years with the Red Sox, Jenkins was traded back to Texas for John Poloni. He seemed to return to form in 1978, posting an 18–8 record. He was a decent 16–14 in 1979, but was 17–20 combined over the 1980 and 1981 seasons. During the 1980 season, Jenkins was arrested at a Canadian airport and charged with drug possession. After Texas released him in November 1981, Jenkins pitched two more lackluster years for the Cubs before retiring following the 1983 season. *(See Cubs bio.)*

CAREER RANGERS RECORD:

W	L	W%	ERA	SV
93	72	.564	3.56	0
K	BB	SHO	IP	
895	315	17	1,410.3	

PALMEIRO, RAFAEL (OF/DH)
(1989–1993, 1999–2003)

Palmeiro played with the Cubs for three years before being traded to Texas along with Jamie Moyer as part of a nine-player trade that brought Mitch Williams to Chicago. While the Cubs thought the Cuban-born Palmeiro had potential, they were distressed by his lack of power and clutch hitting. In 580 at-bats as a full-time first baseman in 1988, Palmeiro generated only eight homers and 53 RBIs, none of them game winners—a major league record for most at-bats in a season without a single game-winning RBI. With the Rangers, Palmeiro continued to get around 600 at-bats per season, but his power numbers increased only modestly, as he averaged slightly more than 17 homers a year during his first four seasons in Texas. In 1993, his last full season with Texas during his first stint with the team (and his first full season with Jose Canseco as a teammate), Palmeiro's home run production increased dramatically as he hit 39 round-trippers. He also broke the 100-RBI mark for the first time in eight major league seasons.

After a bitter contract dispute with the Texas front office, Palmeiro was granted free agency and signed with Baltimore, where he continued to average 40 homers and 120 RBIs during his five years there. Following five seasons in Baltimore, free-agent Palmeiro returned to Texas for another five-year stint with the Rangers. Amazingly, even as he aged, Palmeiro's power numbers never dropped a bit. On the contrary. During his second tour with the Rangers, Palmeiro averaged 43 homers and 122 RBIs per season. While primarily a first baseman, Palmeiro started seeing more and more time as the team's DH over the next five years. He joined the elite 500-homer club during the 2003 season. During his ten years in Texas, Palmeiro won one Gold Glove, one Silver Slugger Award, and was named to the All-Star team twice.

Following the 2003 season, Palmeiro again declared free agency and signed on with Baltimore for another tour with the Orioles. During the 2005 season, the veteran Oriole rapped his 3,000th hit, joining Hank Aaron, Willie Mays, and Eddie Murray as the only members of both the 3,000-hit and 500-homer clubs. However, he became embroiled in the steroids controversy when he tested positive for steroid use—just months after wagging his finger before Congress and angrily denying ever having used steroids. While Palmeiro certainly has Hall of Fame numbers, it remains to be seen how the steroid scandal will affect his chances of entering Cooperstown.

CAREER RANGERS RECORD:

Games	AB	Hits	Runs
1,573	5,830	1,692	958
Avg	**HR**	**RBI**	**SB**
.290	321	1,039	44

RODRIGUEZ, ALEX (SS) (2001–2003)

Alex Rodriguez spent seven outstanding seasons in Seattle before signing the richest contract in sports history: a $252 million, 10-year deal with the Rangers. The deal set off widespread debate in and out of baseball on the wisdom and ethics of such a large contract, but "A-Rod" has proven that if any player is ever worth such a fortune, he's the one. He was an All-Star each year, won a Silver Slugger Award each year, and collected two Gold Gloves for his shortstop play. He only spent three years in Texas before being traded to the Yankees for second baseman Alfonso Soriano, but while with the Rangers, he put up staggering numbers for a shortstop: He *averaged* 52 home runs, 132 RBIs, 127 runs, and 15 steals, while batting .305. What's hard to believe is that during his three seasons as a Ranger, he won the AL's MVP Award only once (2003)—the year in which he posted his lowest batting average, fewest homers, fewest RBIs, fewest runs, and fewest total bases. The 2001 MVP balloting is even more amazing, given A-Rod's numbers. With a .318 average, 52 homers, 135 RBIs, 133 runs, 18 stolen bases (he was caught only three times), 393 total bases (the 38th-highest total in major league history), Rodriguez finished *sixth* in the voting, a travesty. It makes one wonder if there was some sort of backlash against Rodriguez among MVP Award voters in 2001 over his quarter-billion-dollar contract. *(See Mariners bio.)*

CAREER RANGERS RECORD:

Games	AB	Hits	Runs
485	1,863	569	382
Avg	**HR**	**RBI**	**SB**
.305	156	395	44

RODRIGUEZ, IVAN (C)
(1991–2002)

On July 27, 1988, the Texas Rangers signed 16-year-old Ivan Rodriguez to a free-agent contract. By the time "Pudge" was 19, he took over the regular catching duties for the Rangers, where he proved himself both offensively and defensively. During his 12-year career with the Rangers, Rodriguez threw out nearly half of all runners who tried to steal on him. He made an often-weak pitching staff better just because of his defense, and would often pick runners off base when they strayed too far from the bag. From 1992 to 2001, Rodriguez won 10 consecutive Gold Gloves and was named to the American League All-Star team every year. Joe Torre once called him the best catcher he had ever seen in baseball. Rodriguez's offense was every bit as good as his catching. From 1994 to 1999, he won the Silver Slugger Award as the American League's best-hitting catcher. In 1996 he hit 47 doubles, an all-time record by a catcher. In 1999 he won the AL's MVP Award after batting .332 with 35 homers, 113 RBIs, 116 runs, and 25 stolen bases. His 35 homers set a new AL record by a catcher and his .332 average was the highest by a catcher in the American League since Bill Dickey's .362 in 1936.

After the 2002 season, Rodriguez left Texas via free agency, signing a one-year deal with the Marlins (it paid off, as he led Florida to a World Series victory and was named MVP of the NLCS along the way). He signed a big contract with the Tigers in 2004, but during his two seasons in Detroit, Rodriguez's numbers have started to slip just a bit as age (he'll be 34 in 2006) starts to take its toll.

CAREER RANGERS RECORD:

Games	AB	Hits	Runs
1,479	5,656	1,723	852
Avg	**HR**	**RBI**	**SB**
.305	215	829	80

ROGERS, KENNY (SP)
(1989–1995, 2000–2002, 2004–2005)

Kenny Rogers was drafted in the 39th round of the June 1982 amateur draft by the Rangers after playing only one year of organized baseball, his senior year of high school. He bounced around in the minors for seven years and compiled a 22–38 record before being called up to the Rangers in 1989. He averaged more than 70 appearances a season in relief, including a league-leading 81 in 1992, for his first four years before being converted to a starter in 1993. On July 29, 1994, Rogers pitched a perfect game against the Angels. Following the 1995 season, George Steinbrenner's deep pockets lured Rogers to New York. After pitching for the Yankees, A's, and Mets for four years, Rogers returned to Texas for a second tour of duty in 2000. During the next three seasons, Rogers compiled a 31–28 record for the Rangers before signing a one-year free agent contract with the Twins. Rogers returned to the Rangers for a third stint in 2004 and fashioned a solid 18–9 year, although his ERA climbed to 4.76. In 2005 the 40-year-old Rogers, a three-time Gold Glove winner with Texas, was enjoying a fine year on the field, even being selected to the All-Star Game for just the third time in his career, when he physically assaulted two television cameramen during pregame warm-ups. Commissioner Bud Selig slapped him with a 20-game suspension and controversy dogged him for the rest of the season; after starting 11–4 with a 2.46 ERA, Rogers finished 3–4 the rest of the way, doubling his first-half ERA.

CAREER RANGERS RECORD:

W	L	W%	ERA	SV
133	96	.581	4.16	28
K	BB	SHO	IP	
1,201	686	6	1,909.0	

RUSSELL, JEFF (RP)
(1985–1992, 1995–1996)

Russell came to the Rangers on July 23, 1985, in a trade that sent Buddy Bell to the Cincinnati Reds. Russell had been a starter in his two years with Cincinnati and his first year with Texas, but was converted to middle reliever in 1986. In 1988 he became a starter again for one season, before stepping into the closer's role in 1989. From 1989 to 1992, Russell recorded 106 saves before being traded to Oakland on August 31, 1992 (along with Ruben Sierra and Bobby Witt), for slugger Jose Canseco. After spending 1993 and 1994 with Boston and Cleveland, Russell returned to Texas as a free agent and pitched two more seasons with the Rangers before retiring as the Rangers' career leader in saves with 134. He was later passed by John Wetteland, but is still second on the all-time saves list.

CAREER RANGERS RECORD:

W	L	W%	ERA	SV
42	40	.512	3.73	134
K	BB	SHO	IP	
474	295	0	752.7	

RYAN, NOLAN (SP)
(1989–1993)

On December 7, 1988, Nolan Ryan left the Astros and signed a free-agent contract with Texas, where he pitched the last five seasons of his remarkable 27-year career. With the Rangers, Ryan made the leap from great pitcher to legend. In his first season in Texas, at the age of 42, Ryan went 16–10 with a major league-leading 301 strikeouts—the first 300-strikeout season for him in 12 years—and made the All-Star team. He pitched two complete-game one-hitters and took five different no-hitters into the eighth inning or later, losing two of them in the ninth.

On August 22, 1989, Ryan made Oakland's Rickey Henderson the 5,000th strikeout victim of his career. At the age of 43, Ryan became the oldest pitcher in major league history to throw a no-hitter when he beat Oakland, 5–0, on June 11, 1990. Weeks later he became only the 20th pitcher in history to record 300 wins. In 1991 Ryan was the oldest player in the major leagues, period, when he pitched his seventh no-hitter, beating Toronto 3–0 on May 1. On September 30 he recorded his 5,500th strikeout. Age and nagging injuries finally caught up with him on September 22, 1993, in a game against Seattle, when Ryan walked off the mound for the last time. He retired with 5,714 career strikeouts, nearly 1,600 ahead of Steve Carlton, who is second on the list. In 1999, his first year of eligibility, Ryan became the first Ranger elected to the Hall of Fame. He captured 98.8 percent of the vote, second-best all time behind Tom Seaver. *(See Angels and Astros bios.)*

CAREER RANGERS RECORD:

W	L	W%	ERA	SV
51	39	.567	3.43	0
K	BB	SHO	IP	
939	353	6	840.0	

SIERRA, RUBEN (OF/DH)
(1986–1992, 2000–2001, 2003)

The Texas Rangers signed Sierra as an amateur free agent on November 21, 1982, at the age of 17. He made the majors when he was 20 and immediately became a starter in the Rangers' outfield. In 1987, the 21-year-old Sierra slugged 30 homers with 109 RBIs. Sierra was the runner-up to Robin Yount for the AL MVP Award in 1989 when he batted .306 with 29 homers, 119 RBIs, 101 runs, 35 doubles, 14 triples, and won the Silver Slugger Award. After three more solid seasons with the Rangers, Sierra, a three-time All-Star, was sent to Oakland in a blockbuster trade that brought Jose Canseco to Texas. Eight years later, after he had bounced around either playing for or signing contracts with nine different teams, Sierra was purchased from the Cancun Mexican League club. By then his skills were greatly diminished and he was more of a role player/DH. Sierra left and returned one final time in 2003 before being picked up by the Yankees.

CAREER RANGERS RECORD:

Games	AB	Hits	Runs
1,190	4,580	1,281	645
Avg	HR	RBI	SB
.280	180	742	90

SUNDBERG, JIM (C)
(1974–1983, 1988–1989)

Jim Sundberg was drafted by the Texas Rangers in the first round of the 1973 amateur draft (secondary phase). He played less than a season in Double-A ball before making the jump to the majors, and when he did, he immediately became the starting catcher for Texas. His defensive abilities were incomparable. A two-time All-Star with Texas, Sundberg won six consecutive Gold Gloves from 1976 to 1981—more than any other catcher in history except Johnny Bench (until Ivan Rodriguez came along). Some years he threw out more than half of all runners who tried to steal on him. Sundberg was also remarkably durable, playing all but five of 1,932 games at catcher, and averaging more than 140 games caught in his first 10 seasons in Texas. In 1979 he set a major league record by committing only four errors all year in 150 games caught. After the 1983 season, Sundberg was traded to Milwaukee for Ned Yost. He returned to Texas in 1988 and played another year and a half as a backup catcher before retiring.

CAREER RANGERS RECORD:

Games	AB	Hits	Runs
1,512	4,684	1,180	482
Avg	**HR**	**RBI**	**SB**
.252	60	480	18

WETTELAND, JOHN (RP)
(1997–2000)

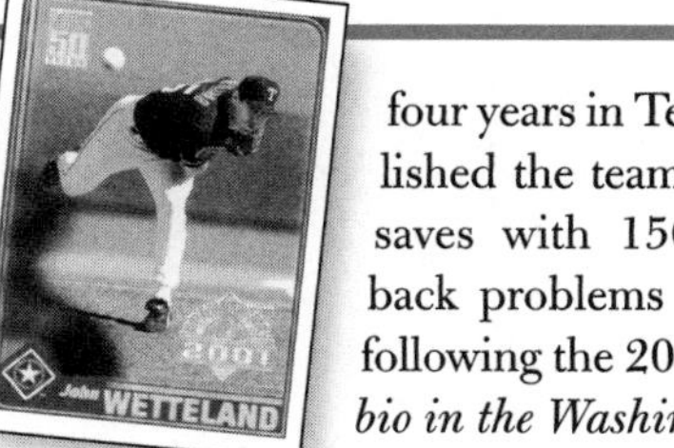

John Wetteland spent eight years with the Dodgers, Expos, and Yankees before coming to Texas as a $23 million free agent prior to the 1997 season. In the five years preceding his arrival in Texas, Wetteland had been one of the top closers in all of baseball (even winning the World Series MVP Award for saving all four victories with the Yankees in 1996). During his four years in Texas, Wetteland established the team's all-time record for saves with 150. Severe, recurring back problems forced him to retire following the 2000 season. *(See Expos bio in the Washington chapter.)*

CAREER RANGERS RECORD:

W	L	W%	ERA	SV
20	12	.625	2.95	150
K	**BB**	**SHO**	**IP**	
248	78	0	253.0	

WITT, BOBBY (SP)
(1986–1992, 1995–1998)

Bobby Witt was originally drafted by Cincinnati in the seventh round of the June 1982 amateur draft, but chose not to sign with the Reds. Three years later he was drafted by the Rangers as the third pick of the first round of the June 1985 amateur draft. In each of his first seven years with Texas, Witt, a fireballer with questionable control, walked almost as many batters as he struck out. He was a streaky pitcher, good and bad, and his career record with Texas (104–104) is a fair reflection of his up-and-down performances. After seven years with Texas, he was traded to Oakland on the trading deadline, along with Jeff Russell and Ruben Sierra, for Jose Canseco. He played just over two seasons in Oakland and then signed with the Florida Marlins as a free agent. After playing less than a year in Florida, Witt was traded back to Texas for Wilson Heredia and Scott Podsednik. By then he had matured further, becoming more of a pitcher rather than a thrower, but a rotator cuff tear and other arm troubles had slowed him down. Witt, who occupies second place on the franchise's career wins and strikeouts lists, was sent to the Cardinals in mid-1998, and played for four more teams in four years before retiring after the 2001 season.

CAREER RANGERS RECORD:

W	L	W%	ERA	SV
104	104	.500	4.85	0

K	BB	SHO	IP
1,405	1,001	5	1,680.7

Toronto Blue Jays

Since 1977

1977 Toronto's paid attendance of 1,701,039 sets an all-time record for a first-year expansion team.... **1984** The Blue Jays win more one-run games (34) than any team in the American League, including an incredible 19 in a row at one point, as they finish second on the season.... **1987** As the Blue Jays thrash Baltimore 18–3 on September 14, the team hits a major league record 10 home runs.... **2003** On September 25, during a 10–8 win over Tampa Bay, Carlos Delgado becomes the 15th player in major league history to hit four homers in one game.

FRANCHISE HISTORY

The Blue Jays franchise was created in 1976, when the American League owners voted to expand by two teams, Toronto and the Seattle Mariners. Toronto became the second Canadian city to field a major league team, following Montreal. One of the team's original owners was a brewery with a popular beer named "Blue." The brewery's owner was hoping the sportswriters of the time would shorten the name in the papers to the "Blues," but it didn't take.

The three primary original owners were Labatt's Brewery (45 percent), Imperial Trust, Ltd. (45 percent), and the Canadian Bank of Commerce (10 percent). Labatt's also owned the Toronto Argonauts of the Canadian Football League. Imperial Trust, Ltd., the outgrowth of R. Howard Webster's fortune, eventually sold their share to Labatt's. In the summer of 1995, Labatt's was purchased by a Belgian brewery, Interbrew, for nearly $3 billion. The owner of Interbrew, Gerald Fauchey, soon put the Blue Jays up for sale, remarking, "Baseball is a very obscure sport in our country." In 2000, Rogers Communications purchased controlling interest (80 percent) in the team for $112 million, while Interbrew and Canadian Bank of Commerce each retained 10 percent.

On April 7, 1977, the Blue Jays played their first home game on a field covered with snow for most of the game; despite battling a wind chill of 10 degrees below zero, they won 9–5 over the White Sox. The Blue Jays quickly reverted to expansion-team form, however, finishing last in the American League East for the first five years of their existence. They did, however, build a strong franchise from within by developing their own players, many of whom quickly rose to prominence in the American League, including Dave Stieb, Jimmy Key, and Tony Fernandez.

The Blue Jays played their home games in Exhibition Stadium, a converted football field, until SkyDome opened on June 19, 1989. This amazing structure, built at a cost of $583 million (including a $100 million retractable roof), included a hotel/restaurant complex that achieved a notoriety of its own beyond its architectural wonder. The hotel, located above the outfield with its windows facing down onto the field, once treated the fans to one of the other national pastimes: During a nationally televised game—and visible to many in the stands—a couple was observed engaging in various sexual activities during the game, blissfully unaware that they had forgotten to close their curtains.

Over the next four full seasons, the Blue Jays averaged nearly 50,000 fans per game. They shattered all previous season attendance records by drawing over 4 million fans a season from 1991 to 1993. The new SkyDome was only partly responsible for the surge in attendance. The other was the fact that the Blue Jays put a winning team on the field. The team won its first division title in 1985, but lost to the

Joe Carter's walk-off home run gives the Blue Jays their second straight World Series title in 1993.

The SkyDome, opened in 1989, was funded mostly by taxpayers.

Royals in the American League Championship Series after leading three games to one. Toronto lost the division by two games in both 1987 and 1988 before winning again in 1989. This time it was the Oakland A's who ousted the Blue Jays from the playoffs. After falling short by two games again in 1990, the Blue Jays won the division title in 1991, only to get knocked out by the Twins.

In 1992, with Jack Morris leading the league with 21 wins, the Blue Jays defeated Oakland for the American League pennant and then won their first-ever World Series by defeating the Atlanta Braves in six games. They repeated as world champions in 1993, defeating the White Sox for the American League pennant and the Phillies in six games for the World Series title. Joe Carter hit a dramatic three-run homer off Mitch Williams in the bottom of the ninth of Game 6 to win it for the Jays, 8–6. As Carter danced around the bases, it marked the first time in major league history that a team trailing in the ninth had won a World Series on a home run.

Since 1993, however, the Blue Jays have fallen on tough times, never finishing higher than third in the division. There were a few individual bright spots during that time: the team had three consecutive Cy Young Award winners (Pat Hentgen in 1996 and Roger Clemens in 1997 and 1998) and, in 2000, six Blue Jays hit 20 or more home runs, led by Tony Batista and Carlos Delgado with 41 each. In a division now dominated by Boston and New York, the future looks dim for Toronto.

TEAM NAME HISTORY

Official Names

Blue Jays

Unofficial Names/Nicknames

Jays

STADIUM HISTORY

Exhibition Stadium	1977–May 28, 1989
SkyDome	June 5, 1989–2004
Rogers Centre (SkyDome renamed)	2005–current

YEARLY RECORD, FINISH, & ATTENDANCE FIGURES

Year	League	Record	DIV/LG Finish	Attendance	Avg/Gm
2005	AL East	80–82	3	2,014,995	24,876
2004	AL East	67–94	5	1,900,041	23,457
2003	AL East	86–76	3	1,799,458	22,216
2002	AL East	78–84	3	1,637,900	20,221
2001	AL East	80–82	3	1,915,438	23,359
2000	AL East	83–79	3	1,705,712	21,058
1999	AL East	84–78	3	2,163,464	26,709
1998	AL East	88–74	3	2,454,303	30,300
1997	AL East	76–86	5	2,589,297	31,967
1996	AL East	74–88	4	2,559,573	31,600
1995	AL East	56–88	5	2,826,483	39,257
1994	AL East	55–60	3	2,907,933	49,287
1993	AL East	95–67	1	4,057,947	50,098
1992	AL East	96–66	1	4,028,318	49,732
1991	AL East	91–71	1	4,001,527	49,402
1990	AL East	86–76	2	3,885,284	47,966
1989	AL East	89–73	1	3,375,883	41,678
1988	AL East	87–75	3	2,595,175	32,039
1987	AL East	96–66	2	2,778,429	34,302
1986	AL East	86–76	4	2,455,477	30.315
1985	AL East	99–62	1	2,468,925	30,862
1984	AL East	89–73	2	2,110,009	26,049
1983	AL East	89–73	4	1,930,415	23,832
1982	AL East	78–84	6	1,275,978	15,753
1981	AL East	37–69	7/7	755,083	14,247
1980	AL East	67–95	7	1,400,327	17,288
1979	AL East	53–109	7	1,431,651	17,675
1978	AL East	59–102	7	1,562,585	19,291
1977	AL East	54–107	7	1,701,052	21,263

MANAGER HISTORY

Manager	Years	W–L	Win %
Roy Hartsfield	1977–1979	166–318	.343
Bobby Mattick	1980–1981	104–164	.388
Bobby Cox	1982–1985	355–292	.549
Jimy Williams	1986–1989	281–241	.538
Cito Gaston	1989–1997	702–650	.519
Mel Queen	1997	4–1	.800
Tim Johnson	1998	88–74	.543
Jim Fregosi	1999–2000	167–159	.512
Buck Martinez	2001–2002	100–115	.465
Carlos Tosca	2002–2004	191–191	.500
John Gibbons	2004–2005	100–112	.472

ALL-TIME WIN-LOSS RECORDS VS. ALL OPPONENTS

Opponent	Record
ALL-TIME	2,258–2,315
Angels	163–154
Astros	0–3
Athletics	143–172
Braves	9–6
Brewers	115–155
Cardinals	2–4
Cubs	4–2
Devil Rays	71–60
Diamondbacks	3–3
Dodgers	3–3
Giants	1–5
Indians	169–159
INTERLEAGUE	74–83
Mariners	160–144
Marlins	4–11
Mets	3–12
Nationals	27–22
Orioles	206–191
Padres	2–1
Phillies	7–8
Pirates	3–0
Rangers	158–164
Reds	2–1
Red Sox	171–223
Rockies	3–0
Royals	155–155
Tigers	184–154
Twins	159–138
White Sox	157–147
Yankees	174–218

The Rocket was a glaring success in his two seasons in Toronto.

Franchise Highlights, Low Points, and Strange Distinctions

1977 Bob Bailor's .310 batting average in 1977 was the highest ever up to that point for a player on a first-year expansion team.

First baseman Doug Ault hit home runs in his first two at-bats in Toronto's first-ever game, a 9–5 win over the White Sox, but hit only two more in his four-year career.

Blue Jays right fielder Otto Velez was named the American League player of the month for April 1977, the Jays' first month in existence.

Starting pitcher Dave Lemanczyk tied the record for wins by a pitcher for a first-year expansion team when he won 13 games for the 1977 team. He won his 13th game on the last day of the season, an 11-inning 2–1 victory over Cleveland in a game in which the Jays collected only two hits.

Rookie left-hander Jerry Garvin picked off an astonishing 22 base runners in 1977, believed to be an unofficial record.

....

1978 From the Department of Jekyll and Hyde Performances: In August the Jays set a franchise record for wins in a month with 16, but followed it up in September with their worst month ever, in which they won only four games.

The 1978 Blue Jays stole only 28 bases all year and were thrown out a whopping 52 times, the only team in the majors to achieve a success rate of less than 50 percent.

....

1981 Of Toronto's 69 losses in the strike-shortened season, 20 were shutouts.

1985 When Jimmy Key defeated the Angels 6–3 on May 1, it was the first win by a left-handed Toronto starter in 614 games dating back to the 1980 season.

Dennis Lamp was perfect in 1985, going 11–0, with all of his wins coming in long relief appearances.

....

1987 When George Bell was named the American League MVP, it was the first time a native of the Dominican Republic had ever won the award.

....

1989 The Blue Jays didn't have a mid-season managerial change until 1989, their 13th year in the league, when they fired Jimy Williams on May 15 after a 12–24 start and replaced him with Cito Gaston who, by the way, became the first black manager to take his team to the playoffs. Gaston's record the remainder of 1989 was 77–49, best in the majors for the last 126 games of the season.

....

1990 The 1990 Blue Jays were so poor at "small ball," that they only had 18 sacrifices, the lowest total in major league history. Their season-long ineptness at this and other basic fundamentals cost them, as they ended up in second place by two games to the Red Sox in the American League East.

In 1990, Toronto rookie Glenallen Hill spent time on the disabled list after suffering severe cuts and scrapes to his feet and knees following a nightmare about spiders.

....

1995 Blue Jays pitchers issued an incredible 24 walks in two back-to-back games against Oakland on April 12–13.

....

1997 On July 12, Roger Clemens faced his former team, the Red Sox, in Fenway Park for the first time and struck out 16 batters in eight innings for a 3–1 win, then went on to win the pitcher's equivalent of the Triple Crown, leading the American League with 21 wins, a 2.05 ERA, and 292 strikeouts.

1998 The very next year, Clemens again won the American League's pitching Triple Crown, this time with 20 wins, a 2.65 ERA, and 271 strikeouts. The two incredible back-to-back seasons would be Clemens' only two years with Toronto.

....

1999 In a six-game span that ended on August 11, Carlos Delgado slugged eight home runs.

....

2001 The Blue Jays homered in 23 straight games during one stretch, shattering the club record.

Fans got an unusual glimpse of dancers performing in the stadum's adjoining SkyDome Hotel during 2004 home opener.

Special Achievements

World Series Results

Year	Opponent	Result	Games
1992	Atlanta	Won	4–2
1993	Philadelphia	Won	4–2

World Series Managerial Records

Manager	Series Record	Games Record
Cito Gaston	2–0	8–4

All-Time Postseason Record

Divisional Playoffs	0–0
League Championship Series	13–16
World Series	8–4

All-Star Games at Toronto

Year	Date	Winner	Score	Stadium
1991	July 9	American	4–2	SkyDome

Hall of Famers Who Played for Team

	Position	Years	Games with Toronto
Paul Molitor	DH	1993–1995	405
Phil Niekro	SP	1987	3
Dave Winfield	DH/OF	1992	156

Hall of Famers Who Managed Team

None

MVP Award Winners

George Bell	OF	1987

Cy Young Award Winners

Pitcher	Year	W–L	ERA
Pat Hentgen	1996	20–10	3.22
Roger Clemens	1997	21–7	2.05
Roger Clemens	1998	20–6	2.65
Roy Halladay	2003	22–7	3.25

Rookie of the Year Award Winners

Alfredo Griffin	SS	1979
Eric Hinske	3B	2002

Gold Glove Winners

Year	Position	Player
1986	SS	Tony Fernandez
	OF	Jesse Barfield
1987	SS	Tony Fernandez
	OF	Jesse Barfield
1988	SS	Tony Fernandez
1989	SS	Tony Fernandez
1990	3B	Kelly Gruber
1991	2B	Roberto Alomar
	OF	Devon White
1992	2B	Roberto Alomar
	OF	Devon White
1993	2B	Roberto Alomar
	OF	Devon White
1994	2B	Roberto Alomar
	OF	Devon White
1995	2B	Roberto Alomar
	OF	Devon White
1999	OF	Shawn Green
2004	OF	Vernon Wells
2005	2B	Orlando Hudson
	OF	Vernon Wells

Triple Crown Winners

None

Fireman of the Year Award Winners

None

World Series MVP

Pat Borders	1992
Paul Molitor	1993

League Championship Series MVP

Roberto Alomar	1992
Dave Stewart	1993

All-Star Game MVP

None

Manager of the Year Award Winners

Bobby Cox	1985

BATTING CHAMPIONS

Year	Player	Avg
1993	John Olerud	.363

NINE-INNING NO-HITTERS PITCHED

Year	Pitcher	Opp.	Score
1990	Dave Stieb	CLE	3–0

20-GAME WINNERS

Year	Pitcher	W–L
1992	Jack Morris	21–6
1996	Pat Hentgen	20–10
1997	Roger Clemens	21–7
1998	Roger Clemens	20–6
2000	David Wells	20–8
2003	Roy Halladay	22–7

RETIRED UNIFORM NUMBERS

None

TEAM RECORDS—WINS & LOSSES

- Games won in a season: 99 in 1985
- Games lost in a season: 109 in 1979
- Games won in a month: 21 in May 2003
- Games lost in a month: 23 in May 1979
- Consecutive games won: 11 in 1987 and 1998
- Consecutive games lost: 12 in 1981
- Biggest shutout victory: 15–0 over Detroit on July 6, 1996
- Biggest shutout loss: 15–0 to New York Yankees on September 25, 1977
- Highest winning percentage: .615 in 1985 (99–62)
- Lowest winning percentage: .327 in 1979 (53–109)

TEAM RECORDS—BATTING

- Highest team batting average: .280 in 1999
- Lowest team batting average: .244 in 1997
- Highest team slugging average: .469 in 2000
- Highest team on-base percentage: .352 in 1999
- Total hits: 1,580 in 1999 and 2003
- Extra-base hits: 593 in 2000
- Hits in a game: 25 vs. Texas on August 9, 1999 and Boston on June 20, 1980
- Longest individual hitting streak: 28, Shawn Green, 1999
- Most .300 hitters in a season: 4 in 1999
- Home runs: 244 in 2000
- Home runs in a month: 12, Carlos Delgado, August 1999, and Jose Cruz Jr., August 2001
- Home runs in a game: 10 vs. Baltimore on September 14, 1987
- Home runs by a rookie: 24, Eric Hinske, 2002
- Home runs by a right-hander: 47, George Bell, 1987
- Home runs by a left-hander: 44, Carlos Delgado, 1999
- Home runs by a switch-hitter: 34, Jose Cruz Jr., 2001
- Grand slams: 9 in 2000
- Grand slams (individual; season): 3, Carlos Delgado, 1997 and Darrin Fletcher, 2000
- Grand slams (individual; career): 9, Carlos Delgado
- Triples: 68 in 1984
- Doubles: 357 in 2003
- Singles: 1,069 in 1984
- Walks: 588 in 1993
- Runs scored: 894 in 2003
- Runs scored in a game: 24 vs. Baltimore on June 26, 1978
- Runs scored in an inning: 11 vs. Seattle on July 20, 1984 (ninth inning) and vs. Chicago White Sox on May 12, 1997 (seventh inning)
- Most batters hit by a pitch: 92 in 1996
- Times shut out: 20 in 1981
- Grounded into double plays: 156 in 1977
- Fewest grounded into double plays: 91 in 1984
- Runners left on base: 1,187 in 1993

TEAM RECORDS—BASERUNNING

- Stolen bases: 193 in 1984
- Caught stealing: 81 in 1982 and 1998

TEAM RECORDS—PITCHING

- Lowest earned run average: 3.31 in 1985
- Complete games: 44 in 1979
- Saves: 60 in 1991
- Strikeouts: 1,154 in 1998
- Shutouts: 17 in 1998
- Walks: 654 in 1995
- Hit batsmen: 76 in 2001
- Wild pitches: 83 in 1993

- Consecutive wins (individual): 15, Roger Clemens in 1998 and Roy Halladay in 2003
- Consecutive losses (individual): 10, Jerry Garvin in 1977 and 1978, and Paul Mirabella in 1980
- Strikeouts in a game (individual): 18, Roger Clemens, August 25, 1998
- Runs allowed in a game: 24 vs. California Angels, August 25, 1979

TEAM RECORDS—FIELDING

- Best fielding average: .986 in 1990
- Most errors committed: 164 in 1977
- Fewest errors committed: 86 in 1990
- Most double plays turned: 206 in 1980
- Fewest double plays turned: 109 in 1992

TEAM RECORDS—MISCELLANEOUS

- Number of times league champions: 2
- Number of times finishing last in league: 4
- Largest attendance, single game: 50,560 vs. Boston, April 8, 2005
- Largest attendance, doubleheader: 48,641 vs. California, July 17, 1989
- Players used in a season: 53 in 1999
- Seasons played: 15, Dave Stieb

PRIMARY PITCHING STAFFS

Year	Starter	Starter	Starter	Starter	Starter	Closer	Bullpen	Bullpen	Bullpen
2005	Chacin	Towers	Lilly	Bush	Halladay	Batista	Schoeneweis	Frasor	Speier
2004	Lilly	Batista	Towers	Halladay	Hentgen	Frasor	Speier	Ligtenberg	Chulk
2003	Lidle	Davis	Escobar	Halladay	Hendrickson	Lopez	Miller	Politte	Tam
2002	Loaiza	Walker	Miller	Halladay	Parris	Escobar	Cassidy	Politte	Heredia
2001	Loaiza	Carpenter	Hamilton	Michalak	Parris	Koch	Quantrill	Borbon	Plesac
2000	Loaiza	Carpenter	Wells	Escobar	Castillo	Koch	Quantrill	Borbon	Frascatore
1999	Hentgen	Carpenter	Wells	Escobar	Hamilton	Koch	Quantrill	Lloyd	Spoljaric
1998	Hentgen	Carpenter	Clemens	Williams	Guzman	Myers	Quantrill	Plesac	Risley
1997	Hentgen	Person	Clemens	Williams	Guzman	Escobar	Quantrill	Plesac	Timlin
1996	Hentgen	Hanson	Quantrill	Flener	Guzman	Timlin	Crabtree	Castillo	Spoljaric
1995	Hentgen	Leiter	Cone	Darwin	Guzman	Castillo	Crabtree	Timlin	Cox
1994	Hentgen	Leiter	Stewart	Stottlemyre	Guzman	Hall	Castillo	Timlin	Williams
1993	Hentgen	Morris	Stewart	Stottlemyre	Guzman	Ward	Castillo	Timlin	Eichhorn
1992	Key	Morris	Wells	Stottlemyre	Guzman	Henke	MacDonald	Hentgen	Ward
1991	Key	Candiotti	Wells	Stottlemyre	Guzman	Henke	Ward	Timlin	Acker
1990	Key	Stieb	Wells	Stottlemyre	Cerutti	Henke	Ward	Wills	Acker
1989	Key	Stieb	Flanagan	Stottlemyre	Cerutti	Henke	Ward	Wills	Wells
1988	Key	Stieb	Flanagan	Stottlemyre	Clancy	Henke	Ward	Cerutti	Wells
1987	Key	Stieb	Cerutti	Johnson	Clancy	Henke	Musselman	Eichhorn	Nunez
1986	Key	Stieb	Cerutti	Alexander	Clancy	Henke	Eichhorn	Lamp	Caudill
1985	Key	Stieb	Leal	Alexander	Clancy	Caudill	Lavelle	Lamp	Acker
1984	Gott	Stieb	Leal	Alexander	Clancy	Jackson	Key	Lamp	Acker
1983	Gott	Stieb	Leal	Alexander	Clancy	Moffitt	McLaughlin	Jackson	Geisel
1982	Gott	Stieb	Leal	Bomback	Clancy	Murray	McLaughlin	Jackson	Garvin
1981	Todd	Stieb	Leal	Bomback	Clancy	McLaughlin	Willis	Jackson	Garvin
1980	Todd	Stieb	Mirabella	Jefferson	Clancy	Garvin	McLaughlin	Barlow	Buskey
1979	Moore	Stieb	Huffman	Lemanczyk	Underwood	Buskey	Lemongello	Freisleben	Jefferson
1978	Garvin	Clancy	Jefferson	Lemanczyk	Underwood	Cruz	Murphy	Willis	Moore
1977	Byrd	Clancy	Jefferson	Lemanczyk	Garvin	Vuckovich	Murphy	Willis	Johnson

PRIMARY STARTING LINEUPS

Year	C	1B	2B	3B	SS	LF	CF	RF	DH
2005	Zaun	Hinske	Hudson	Koskie	Adams	Johnson	Wells	Rios	Hill
2004	Zaun	Delgado	Hudson	Hinske	Gomez	Johnson	Wells	Rios	Phelps
2003	Myers	Delgado	Hudson	Hinske	Woodward	Stewart	Wells	Johnson	Phelps
2002	Huckaby	Delgado	Hudson	Hinske	Woodward	Stewart	Wells	Mondesi	Phelps
2001	Fletcher	Delgado	Bush	Batista	Gonzalez	Stewart	Cruz	Mondesi	Fullmer
2000	Fletcher	Delgado	Bush	Batista	Gonzalez	Stewart	Cruz	Mondesi	Fullmer
1999	Fletcher	Delgado	Bush	Fernandez	Batista	Stewart	Cruz	Green	Greene
1998	Fletcher	Delgado	Grebeck	Sprague	Gonzalez	Stewart	Cruz	Green	Canseco
1997	Santiago	Delgado	Garcia	Sprague	Gonzalez	Cruz	Nixon	Merced	Carter
1996	O'Brien	Olerud	Perez	Sprague	Gonzalez	Carter	Nixon	Green	Delgado
1995	Parrish	Olerud	Alomar	Sprague	Gonzalez	Carter	White	Green	Molitor
1994	Borders	Olerud	Alomar	Sprague	Schofield	Huff	White	Carter	Molitor
1993	Borders	Olerud	Alomar	Sprague	Fernandez	Henderson	White	Carter	Molitor
1992	Borders	Olerud	Alomar	Gruber	Lee	Maldonado	White	Carter	Winfield
1991	Myers	Olerud	Alomar	Gruber	Lee	Maldonado	White	Carter	Mulliniks
1990	Borders	McGriff	Lee	Gruber	Fernandez	Bell	Wilson	Felix	Olerud
1989	Whitt	McGriff	Liriano	Gruber	Fernandez	Bell	Moseby	Felix	Mulliniks
1988	Whitt	McGriff	Lee	Gruber	Fernandez	Bell	Moseby	Barfield	Mulliniks
1987	Whitt	Upshaw	Iorg	Gruber	Fernandez	Bell	Moseby	Barfield	McGriff
1986	Whitt	Upshaw	Garcia	Mulliniks	Fernandez	Bell	Moseby	Barfield	Johnson
1985	Whitt	Upshaw	Garcia	Mulliniks	Fernandez	Bell	Moseby	Barfield	Burroughs
1984	Whitt	Upshaw	Garcia	Mulliniks	Griffin	Collins	Moseby	Bell	Johnson
1983	Whitt	Upshaw	Garcia	Mulliniks	Griffin	Collins	Moseby	Barfield	Johnson
1982	Whitt	Upshaw	Garcia	Mulliniks	Griffin	Bonnell	Moseby	Barfield	Revering
1981	Whitt	Mayberry	Garcia	Ainge	Griffin	Woods	Moseby	Bonnell	Velez
1980	Whitt	Mayberry	Garcia	Howell	Griffin	Bonnell	Moseby	Bailor	Velez
1979	Cerone	Mayberry	Ainge	Howell	Griffin	Woods	Bosetti	Bailor	Carty
1978	Cerone	Mayberry	McKay	Howell	Gomez	Bosetti	Bailor	Velez	Carty
1977	Ashby	Ault	Staggs	Howell	Torres	A. Woods	Bowling	Velez	Fairly

Top 10 Batting Leaders, Single Season & Career with Team

GAMES PLAYED: CAREER WITH TEAM

Player	G	PA
1. Tony Fernandez	1,450	5,900
2. Carlos Delgado	1,423	6,018
3. Lloyd Moseby	1,392	5,799
4. Ernie Whitt	1,218	3,977
5. George Bell	1,181	4,877
6. Rance Mulliniks	1,115	3,470
Willie Upshaw	1,115	4,172
8. Joe Carter	1,039	4,494
9. Jesse Barfield	1,032	3,869
10. Alfredo Griffin	982	3,654

AT-BATS: SEASON

Player	AB	Year
1. Tony Fernandez	687	1986
2. Vernon Wells	678	2003
3. Alfredo Griffin	653	1980
4. Tony Fernandez	648	1988
5. Devon White	642	1991
6. George Bell	641	1986
Devon White	641	1992
8. Shannon Stewart	640	2001
9. Joe Carter	638	1991
10. Roberto Alomar	637	1991

AT-BATS: CAREER WITH TEAM

Player	AB	PA
1. Tony Fernandez	5,335	5,900
2. Lloyd Moseby	5,124	5,799
3. Carlos Delgado	5,008	6,018
4. George Bell	4,528	4,877
5. Joe Carter	4,093	4,494
6. Willie Upshaw	3,710	4,172
7. Damaso Garcia	3,572	3,756
8. Ernie Whitt	3,514	3,977
9. Jesse Barfield	3,463	3,869
10. Shannon Stewart	3,450	3,852

Batting Average: Season

Player	BA	Year
1. John Olerud	.363	1993
2. Carlos Delgado	.344	2000
3. Paul Molitor	.341	1994
4. Paul Molitor	.332	1993
5. Tony Fernandez	.328	1999
6. Roberto Alomar	.326	1993
7. Rance Mulliniks	.324	1984
8. Tony Fernandez	.322	1987
9. Tony Fernandez	.321	1998
10. Darrin Fletcher	.320	2000

Batting Average: Career with Team

Player	BA	PA
1. Roberto Alomar	.307	3,105
2. Shannon Stewart	.301	3,852
3. Tony Fernandez	.297	5,900
4. John Olerud	.293	3,689
5. Damaso Garcia	.288	3,756
6. George Bell	.286	4,877
Shawn Green	.286	2,766
8. Vernon Wells	.285	2,848
9. Carlos Delgado	.282	6,018
10. Rance Mulliniks	.280	3,470

Total Hits: Season

Player	H	Year
1. Vernon Wells	215	2003
2. Tony Fernandez	213	1986
3. Paul Molitor	211	1993
4. Shannon Stewart	202	2001
5. John Olerud	200	1993
6. George Bell	198	1986
7. Carlos Delgado	196	2000
8. Roberto Alomar	192	1993
9. Shawn Green	190	1999
10. Roberto Alomar	188	1991
George Bell	188	1987

Total Hits: Career with Team

Player	H	PA
1. Tony Fernandez	1,583	5,900
2. Carlos Delgado	1,413	6,018
3. Lloyd Moseby	1,319	5,799
4. George Bell	1,294	4,877
5. Joe Carter	1,051	4,494
6. Shannon Stewart	1,040	3,852
7. Damaso Garcia	1,028	3,756
8. Willie Upshaw	982	4,172
9. Jesse Barfield	919	3,869
10. John Olerud	910	3,689

Home Runs: Season

Player	HR	Year
1. George Bell	47	1987
2. Jose Canseco	46	1998
3. Carlos Delgado	44	1999
4. Carlos Delgado	42	2003
Shawn Green	42	1999
6. Tony Batista	41	2000
Carlos Delgado	41	2000
8. Jesse Barfield	40	1986
9. Carlos Delgado	39	2001
10. Carlos Delgado	38	1998

Home Runs: Career with Team

Player	HR	PA
1. Carlos Delgado	336	6,018
2. Joe Carter	203	4,494
3. George Bell	202	4,877
4. Jesse Barfield	179	3,869
5. Lloyd Moseby	149	5,799
6. Ernie Whitt	131	3,977
7. Fred McGriff	125	2,322
8. Jose Cruz	122	2,901
9. Shawn Green	119	2,766
10. Kelly Gruber	114	3,372

Triples: Season

Player	3B	Year
1. Tony Fernandez	17	1990
2. Dave Collins	15	1984
Alfredo Griffin	15	1980
Lloyd Moseby	15	1984
5. Roberto Alomar	11	1991
6. Tony Fernandez	10	1985
Alfredo Griffin	10	1979
Devon White	10	1991
9. Eight tied with . . .	9	—

Triples: Career with Team

Player	3B	PA
1. Tony Fernandez	72	5,900
2. Lloyd Moseby	60	5,799
3. Alfredo Griffin	50	3,654
4. Willie Upshaw	42	4,172
5. Roberto Alomar	36	3,105
6. Devon White	34	2,979
7. George Bell	32	4,877
Shannon Stewart	32	3,852
9. Joe Carter	28	4,494
10. Jesse Barfield	27	3,869

Doubles: Season

Player	2B	Year
1. Carlos Delgado	57	2000
2. John Olerud	54	1993
3. Vernon Wells	49	2003
4. Shawn Green	45	1999
Eric Hinske	45	2003
6. Shannon Stewart	44	2001
7. Carlos Delgado	43	1998
Shannon Stewart	43	2000
9. Joe Carter	42	1991
Carlos Delgado	42	1997
Devon White	42	1993

Doubles: Career with Team

Player	2B	PA
1. Carlos Delgado	343	6,018
2. Tony Fernandez	291	5,900
3. Lloyd Moseby	242	5,799
4. George Bell	237	4,877
5. Joe Carter	218	4,494
Shannon Stewart	218	3,852
7. John Olerud	213	3,689
8. Rance Mulliniks	204	3,470
9. Willie Upshaw	177	4,172
10. Damaso Garcia	172	3,756
Alex Gonzalez	172	3,634

Extra-Base Hits: Season

Player	XBH	Year
1. Carlos Delgado	99	2000
2. Shawn Green	87	1999
Vernon Wells	87	2003
4. George Bell	83	1987
Carlos Delgado	83	1999
6. Carlos Delgado	82	1998
7. Carlos Delgado	81	2003
8. John Olerud	80	1993
9. Joe Carter	78	1991
10. Jesse Barfield	77	1986

Extra-Base Hits: Career with Team

Player	XBH	PA
1. Carlos Delgado	690	6,018
2. George Bell	471	4,877
3. Lloyd Moseby	451	5,799
4. Joe Carter	449	4,494
5. Tony Fernandez	423	5,900
6. Jesse Barfield	368	3,869
7. Willie Upshaw	331	4,172
8. John Olerud	328	3,689
9. Shannon Stewart	323	3,852
10. Ernie Whitt	310	3,977

Total Bases: Season

Player	TB	Year
1. Carlos Delgado	378	2000
2. Vernon Wells	373	2003
3. George Bell	369	1987
4. Shawn Green	361	1999
5. George Bell	341	1986
6. Carlos Delgado	338	2003
7. John Olerud	330	1993
8. Jesse Barfield	329	1986
9. Carlos Delgado	327	1999
10. Paul Molitor	324	1993

Total Bases: Career with Team

Player	TB	PA
1. Carlos Delgado	2,786	6,018
2. George Bell	2,201	4,877
3. Tony Fernandez	2,198	5,900
4. Lloyd Moseby	2,128	5,799
5. Joe Carter	1,934	4,494
6. Jesse Barfield	1,672	3,869
7. Willie Upshaw	1,579	4,172
8. Shannon Stewart	1,541	3,852
9. Ernie Whitt	1,475	3,977
10. John Olerud	1,462	3,689

Runs Batted In: Season

Player	RBI	Year
1. Carlos Delgado	145	2003
2. Carlos Delgado	137	2000
3. George Bell	134	1987
Carlos Delgado	134	1999
5. Shawn Green	123	1999
6. Joe Carter	121	1993
7. Joe Carter	119	1992
8. Kelly Gruber	118	1990
9. Vernon Wells	117	2003
10. Carlos Delgado	115	1998

Runs Batted In: Career with Team

Player	RBI	PA
1. Carlos Delgado	1,058	6,018
2. George Bell	740	4,877
3. Joe Carter	736	4,494
4. Lloyd Moseby	651	5,799
5. Tony Fernandez	613	5,900
6. Jesse Barfield	527	3,869
7. Ernie Whitt	518	3,977
8. Willie Upshaw	478	4,172
9. John Olerud	471	3,689
10. Kelly Gruber	434	3,372

Runs Scored: Season

Player	R	Year
1. Shawn Green	134	1999
2. Paul Molitor	121	1993
3. Vernon Wells	118	2003
4. Carlos Delgado	117	2003
5. Devon White	116	1993
6. Carlos Delgado	115	2000
7. Carlos Delgado	113	1999
8. George Bell	111	1987
9. Devon White	110	1991
10. Roberto Alomar	109	1993
John Olerud	109	1993

Runs Scored: Career with Team

Player	R	PA
1. Carlos Delgado	889	6,018
2. Lloyd Moseby	768	5,799
3. Tony Fernandez	704	5,900
4. George Bell	641	4,877
5. Shannon Stewart	581	3,852
6. Joe Carter	578	4,494
7. Willie Upshaw	538	4,172
8. Jesse Barfield	530	3,869
9. John Olerud	464	3,689
10. Damaso Garcia	453	3,756

Walks: Season

Player	BB	Year
1. Carlos Delgado	123	2000
2. Fred McGriff	119	1989
3. John Olerud	114	1993
4. Carlos Delgado	111	2001
5. Carlos Delgado	109	2003
6. Carlos Delgado	102	2002
7. Fred McGriff	94	1990
8. Roberto Alomar	87	1992
9. Carlos Delgado	86	1999
10. John Olerud	84	1995

Walks: Career with Team

Player	BB	PA
1. Carlos Delgado	827	6,018
2. Lloyd Moseby	547	5,799
3. John Olerud	514	3,689
4. Tony Fernandez	439	5,900
5. Rance Mulliniks	416	3,470
6. Ernie Whitt	403	3,977
7. Willie Upshaw	390	4,172
8. Fred McGriff	352	2,322
9. Jesse Barfield	342	3,869
10. Roberto Alomar	322	3,105

Strikeouts: Season

Player	SO	Year
1. Jose Canseco	159	1998
2. Alex Gonzalez	149	2001
Fred McGriff	149	1988
4. Jesse Barfield	146	1986
Ed Sprague	146	1996
6. Jesse Barfield	143	1985
7. Shawn Green	142	1998
8. Jesse Barfield	141	1987
Carlos Delgado	141	1999
10. Carlos Delgado	139	1996
Carlos Delgado	139	1998

Strikeouts: Career with Team

Player	SO	PA
1. Carlos Delgado	1,242	6,018
2. Lloyd Moseby	1,015	5,799
3. Jesse Barfield	855	3,869
4. Alex Gonzalez	758	3,634
5. Joe Carter	696	4,494
6. Ed Sprague	647	3,527
7. Jose Cruz	635	2,901
8. Willie Upshaw	576	4,172
9. Devon White	572	2,979
10. George Bell	563	4,877

Slugging Percentage: Season

Player	SLG	Year
1. Carlos Delgado	.664	2000
2. George Bell	.605	1987
3. John Olerud	.599	1993
4. Carlos Delgado	.593	2003
5. Carlos Delgado	.592	1998
6. Shawn Green	.588	1999
7. Carlos Delgado	.571	1999
8. Jesse Barfield	.559	1986
9. Brad Fullmer	.558	2000
10. Fred McGriff	.552	1988

Slugging Percentage: Career with Team

Player	SLG	PA
1. Carlos Delgado	.556	6,018
2. Fred McGriff	.530	2,322
3. Shawn Green	.505	2,766
4. George Bell	.486	4,877
5. Jesse Barfield	.483	3,869
6. Vernon Wells	.481	2,848
7. Joe Carter	.473	4,494
8. John Olerud	.471	3,689
9. Jose Cruz	.462	2,901
10. Roberto Alomar	.451	3,105

On-Base Percentage: Season

Player	OBP	Year
1. John Olerud	.473	1993
2. Carlos Delgado	.470	2000
3. Tony Fernandez	.427	1999
4. Carlos Delgado	.426	2003
5. Paul Molitor	.410	1994
6. Roberto Alomar	.408	1993
Carlos Delgado	.408	2001
8. Carlos Delgado	.406	2002
9. Roberto Alomar	.405	1992
10. Paul Molitor	.402	1993

On-Base Percentage: Career with Team

Player	OBP	PA
1. John Olerud	.395	3,689
2. Carlos Delgado	.392	6,018
3. Fred McGriff	.389	2,322
4. Roberto Alomar	.382	3,105
5. Shannon Stewart	.367	3,852
6. Rance Mulliniks	.365	3,470
7. Tony Fernandez	.353	5,900
8. John Mayberry	.352	2,102
9. Shawn Green	.344	2,766
10. Willie Upshaw	.336	4,172

OPS (On-Base Percentage + Slugging Percentage): Season

Player	OPS	Year
1. Carlos Delgado	1.134	2000
2. John Olerud	1.072	1993
3. Carlos Delgado	1.019	2003
4. Carlos Delgado	.978	1998
5. Shawn Green	.972	1999
6. George Bell	.957	1987
7. Carlos Delgado	.955	2002
8. Carlos Delgado	.948	1999
Carlos Delgado	.948	2001
10. Fred McGriff	.930	1990

OPS (On-Base Percentage + Slugging Percentage): Career with Team

Player	OPS	PA
1. Carlos Delgado	.949	6,018
2. Fred McGriff	.919	2,322
3. John Olerud	.866	3,689
4. Shawn Green	.849	2,766
5. Roberto Alomar	.833	3,105
6. Jesse Barfield	.817	3,869
7. Shannon Stewart	.814	3,852
8. George Bell	.811	4,877
Vernon Wells	.811	2,848
10. John Mayberry	.802	2,102

Stolen Bases: Season

Player	SB	Year
1. Dave Collins	60	1984
2. Roberto Alomar	55	1993
3. Damaso Garcia	54	1982
Otis Nixon	54	1996
5. Roberto Alomar	53	1991
6. Shannon Stewart	51	1998
7. Roberto Alomar	49	1992
8. Otis Nixon	47	1997
9. Damaso Garcia	46	1984
10. Lloyd Moseby	39	1984
Lloyd Moseby	39	1987

Stolen Bases: Career with Team

Player	SB	PA
1. Lloyd Moseby	255	5,799
2. Roberto Alomar	206	3,105
3. Damaso Garcia	194	3,756
4. Tony Fernandez	172	5,900
5. Shannon Stewart	163	3,852
6. Devon White	126	2,979
7. Otis Nixon	101	1,039
8. Dave Collins	91	943
9. Jose Cruz	85	2,901
Alex Gonzalez	85	3,634

Sacrifice Hits: Season

Player	Sac	Year
1. Luis Gomez	19	1978
2. Roberto Alomar	16	1991
Alex Gonzalez	16	2000
Alfredo Griffin	16	1979
5. Alex Gonzalez	13	1998
Alfredo Griffin	13	1984
7. Alex Gonzalez	11	1997
Alfredo Griffin	11	1982
Alfredo Griffin	11	1983
10. Eight tied with...	10	—

Sacrifice Hits: Career with Team

Player	Sac	PA
1. Alfredo Griffin	74	3,654
2. Alex Gonzalez	64	3,634
3. Roberto Alomar	39	3,105
4. Lloyd Moseby	38	5,799
5. Tony Fernandez	34	5,900
6. Al Woods	31	2,171
7. Manuel Lee	28	2,357
8. Damaso Garcia	27	3,756
Willie Upshaw	27	4,172
10. Dave McKay	24	999

Hit by Pitch: Season

Player	HBP	Year
1. Shea Hillenbrand	22	2005
2. Reed Johnson	20	2003
3. Carlos Delgado	19	2003
4. Charlie O'Brien	17	1996

Josh Phelps	17	2003
6. Carlos Delgado	16	2001
Reed Johnson	16	2005
8. Carlos Delgado	15	1999
Carlos Delgado	15	2000
Ed Sprague	15	1995
Shannon Stewart	15	1998

HIT BY PITCH: CAREER WITH TEAM

Player	HBP	PA
1. Carlos Delgado	122	6,018
2. Ed Sprague	68	3,527
3. Shannon Stewart	56	3,852
4. Lloyd Moseby	50	5,799
5. Joe Carter	49	4,494
6. Tony Fernandez	48	5,900
Reed Johnson	48	1,478
8. George Bell	35	4,877
Kelly Gruber	35	3,372
10. Alex Gonzalez	32	3,634
John Olerud	32	3,689

Top 10 Pitching Leaders, Single Season & Career with Team

GAMES PITCHED: SEASON

Player	GP	Year
1. Mark Eichhorn	89	1987
2. Paul Quantrill	82	1998
3. Duane Ward	81	1991
4. Paul Quantrill	80	2001
Scott Schoeneweis	80	2005
6. Trever Miller	79	2003
Duane Ward	79	1992
8. Dan Plesac	78	1998
9. Paul Quantrill	77	1997
10. Kelvim Escobar	76	2002

GAMES PITCHED: CAREER WITH TEAM

Player	GP	IP
1. Duane Ward	452	650.7
2. Tom Henke	446	563.0
3. Dave Stieb	439	2,873.0
4. Paul Quantrill	386	517.7
5. Jim Clancy	352	2,204.7
6. Jimmy Key	317	1,695.7
7. David Wells	306	1,148.7
8. Mike Timlin	305	393.3
9. Kelvim Escobar	301	849.0
10. Jim Acker	281	524.3

INNINGS PITCHED: SEASON

Player	IP	Year
1. Dave Stieb	288.3	1982
2. Dave Stieb	278.0	1983
3. Dave Stieb	267.0	1984
4. Jim Clancy	266.7	1982
5. Roy Halladay	266.0	2003
6. Pat Hentgen	265.7	1996
7. Dave Stieb	265.0	1985
8. Roger Clemens	264.0	1997
Pat Hentgen	264.0	1997
10. Doyle Alexander	261.7	1984

INNINGS PITCHED: CAREER WITH TEAM

Player	IP
1. Dave Stieb	2,873.0
2. Jim Clancy	2,204.7
3. Jimmy Key	1,695.7
4. Pat Hentgen	1,636.0
5. Juan Guzman	1,215.7
6. David Wells	1,148.7
7. Todd Stottlemyre	1,139.0
8. Roy Halladay	1,116.3
9. Luis Leal	946.0
10. Chris Carpenter	870.7

BATTERS FACED: SEASON

Player	BF	Year
1. Dave Stieb	1,187	1982
2. Dave Stieb	1,141	1983
3. Jim Clancy	1,100	1982
Pat Hentgen	1,100	1996
5. Dave Lemanczyk	1,092	1977
6. Doyle Alexander	1,090	1985
7. Dave Stieb	1,087	1985
8. Pat Hentgen	1,085	1997
Dave Stieb	1,085	1984
10. Jim Clancy	1,075	1980

BATTERS FACED: CAREER WITH TEAM

Player	BF	IP
1. Dave Stieb	11,965	2,873.0
2. Jim Clancy	9,397	2,204.7
3. Pat Hentgen	7,048	1,636.0
4. Jimmy Key	6,983	1,695.7
5. Juan Guzman	5,209	1,215.7
6. Todd Stottlemyre	4,921	1,139.0
7. David Wells	4,821	1,148.7
8. Roy Halladay	4,680	1,116.3
9. Luis Leal	4,057	946.0
10. Chris Carpenter	3,831	870.7

GAMES STARTED: SEASON

Player	GS	Year
1. Jim Clancy	40	1982
2. Luis Leal	38	1982
Dave Stieb	38	1982
4. Jim Clancy	37	1987
5. Doyle Alexander	36	1985
Jim Clancy	36	1984
Roy Halladay	36	2003
Jimmy Key	36	1987
Dave Stieb	36	1983
Dave Stieb	36	1985

GAMES STARTED: CAREER WITH TEAM

Player	GS	IP
1. Dave Stieb	408	2,873.0
2. Jim Clancy	345	2,204.7
3. Jimmy Key	250	1,695.7

4. Pat Hentgen	238	1,636.0
5. Juan Guzman	195	1,215.7
6. Todd Stottlemyre	175	1,139.0
7. Roy Halladay	159	1,116.3
8. Luis Leal	151	946.0
9. David Wells	138	1,148.7
10. Chris Carpenter	135	870.7

Complete Games: Season

Player	CG	Year
1. Dave Stieb	19	1982
2. Jim Clancy	15	1980
3. Dave Stieb	14	1980
Dave Stieb	14	1983
5. Jerry Garvin	12	1977
Tom Underwood	12	1979
7. Doyle Alexander	11	1984
Jim Clancy	11	1982
Jim Clancy	11	1983
Dave Lemanczyk	11	1977
Dave Lemanczyk	11	1979
Dave Stieb	11	1981
Dave Stieb	11	1984

Complete Games: Career with Team

Player	CG	IP
1. Dave Stieb	103	2,873.0
2. Jim Clancy	73	2,204.7
3. Pat Hentgen	31	1,636.0
4. Jimmy Key	28	1,695.7
5. Luis Leal	27	946.0
6. Doyle Alexander	25	750.0
Dave Lemanczyk	25	575.0
8. Jesse Jefferson	21	666.3
9. Roy Halladay	20	1,116.3
10. Tom Underwood	19	424.7

Games Won: Season

Player	W	Year
1. Roy Halladay	22	2003
2. Roger Clemens	21	1997
Jack Morris	21	1992
4. Roger Clemens	20	1998
Pat Hentgen	20	1996
David Wells	20	2000
7. Roy Halladay	19	2002
Pat Hentgen	19	1993
9. Dave Stieb	18	1990
10. Seven tied with...	17	——

Games Won: Career with Team

Player	W	IP
1. Dave Stieb	175	2,873.0
2. Jim Clancy	128	2,204.7
3. Jimmy Key	116	1,695.7
4. Pat Hentgen	107	1,636.0
5. David Wells	84	1,148.7
6. Roy Halladay	79	1,116.3
7. Juan Guzman	76	1,215.7
8. Todd Stottlemyre	69	1,139.0
9. Kelvim Escobar	58	849.0
10. Luis Leal	51	946.0

Games Lost: Season

Player	L	Year
1. Jerry Garvin	18	1977
Phil Huffman	18	1979
3. Erik Hanson	17	1996
Jesse Jefferson	17	1977
Todd Stottlemyre	17	1990
6. Jim Clancy	16	1980
Jesse Jefferson	16	1978
Dave Lemanczyk	16	1977
Tom Underwood	16	1979
10. Five tied with...	15	——

Games Lost: Career with Team

Player	L	IP
1. Jim Clancy	140	2,204.7
2. Dave Stieb	134	2,873.0
3. Pat Hentgen	85	1,636.0
4. Jimmy Key	81	1,695.7
5. Todd Stottlemyre	70	1,139.0
6. Juan Guzman	62	1,215.7
7. Luis Leal	58	946.0
8. Jesse Jefferson	56	666.3
9. Kelvim Escobar	55	849.0
David Wells	55	1,148.7

Winning Percentage: Season

Player	W%	Year
1. Juan Guzman	.824	1993
2. Jack Morris	.778	1992
3. Roger Clemens	.769	1998
4. Juan Guzman	.762	1992
5. Roy Halladay	.759	2003
6. Roger Clemens	.750	1997
Dave Stieb	.750	1990
Roy Halladay	.750	2005
9. Doyle Alexander	.739	1984
10. Roy Halladay	.731	2002

Winning Percentage: Career with Team

Player	W%	IP
1. Roy Halladay	.648	1,116.3
2. David Wells	.604	1,148.7
3. Jimmy Key	.589	1,695.7
4. Dave Stieb	.566	2,873.0
5. Pat Hentgen	.557	1,636.0
6. John Cerutti	.554	772.3
7. Juan Guzman	.551	1,215.7
8. Kelvim Escobar	.513	849.0
9. Todd Stottlemyre	.496	1,139.0
10. Chris Carpenter	.495	870.7

Shutouts: Season

Player	SHO	Year
1. Dave Stieb	5	1982
2. Dave Stieb	4	1980
Dave Stieb	4	1983
Dave Stieb	4	1988
5. Jim Clancy	3	1982
Jim Clancy	3	1986
Roger Clemens	3	1997
Roger Clemens	3	1998
Pat Hentgen	3	1994
Pat Hentgen	3	1996
Pat Hentgen	3	1997
Dave Lemanczyk	3	1979

Shutouts: Career with Team

Player	SHO	IP
1. Dave Stieb	30	2,873.0
2. Jim Clancy	11	2,204.7
3. Jimmy Key	10	1,695.7
4. Pat Hentgen	9	1,636.0
5. Roy Halladay	8	1,116.3
6. Roger Clemens	6	498.7
7. Chris Carpenter	5	870.7
8. Jesse Jefferson	4	666.3
Todd Stottlemyre	4	1,139.0
10. Six tied with...	3	——

ERA: Season

Player	ERA	Year
1. Roger Clemens	2.05	1997
2. Dave Stieb	2.48	1985

3. Juan Guzman	2.64	1992
4. Roger Clemens	2.65	1998
5. Jimmy Key	2.76	1987
6. Dave Stieb	2.83	1984
7. Juan Guzman	2.93	1996
Dave Stieb	2.93	1990
Roy Halladay	2.93	2002
10. Jimmy Key	3.00	1985

ERA: Career with Team

Player	ERA	IP
1. Tom Henke	2.48	563.0
2. Duane Ward	3.18	650.7
3. Dave Stieb	3.42	2,873.0
Jimmy Key	3.42	1,695.7
5. Doyle Alexander	3.56	750.0
6. Paul Quantrill	3.67	517.7
7. Roy Halladay	3.70	1,116.3
8. John Cerutti	3.87	772.3
9. David Wells	4.06	1,148.7
10. Jim Acker	4.07	524.3

Earned Runs Allowed: Season

Player	ER	Year
1. Erik Hanson	129	1996
2. Jim Clancy	125	1984
3. David Wells	124	1999
4. Cory Lidle	123	2003
5. Chris Carpenter	122	2000
6. Dave Lemanczyk	119	1977
7. Jerry Garvin	114	1977
Pat Hentgen	114	1995
9. Phil Huffman	111	1979
10. Jim Clancy	110	1982
Kelvim Escobar	110	1999

Earned Runs Allowed: Career with Team

Player	ER	IP
1. Dave Stieb	1,091	2,873.0
2. Jim Clancy	1,005	2,204.7
3. Pat Hentgen	778	1,636.0
4. Jimmy Key	645	1,695.7
5. Todd Stottlemyre	555	1,139.0
6. Juan Guzman	550	1,215.7
7. David Wells	518	1,148.7
8. Chris Carpenter	467	870.7
9. Roy Halladay	459	1,116.3
10. Luis Leal	435	946.0

Strikeouts: Season

Player	K	Year
1. Roger Clemens	292	1997
2. Roger Clemens	271	1998
3. Roy Halladay	204	2003
4. Dave Stieb	198	1984
5. Juan Guzman	194	1993
6. Dave Stieb	187	1983
7. Jim Clancy	180	1987
8. Pat Hentgen	177	1996
9. David Wells	169	1999
10. Roy Halladay	168	2002
Ted Lilly	168	2004

Strikeouts: Career with Team

Player	K	IP
1. Dave Stieb	1,658	2,873.0
2. Jim Clancy	1,237	2,204.7
3. Juan Guzman	1,030	1,215.7
4. Pat Hentgen	1,028	1,636.0
5. Jimmy Key	944	1,695.7
6. Roy Halladay	810	1,116.3
7. David Wells	784	1,148.7
8. Kelvim Escobar	744	849.0
9. Duane Ward	671	650.7
10. Todd Stottlemyre	662	1,139.0

Strikeouts Per Nine IP: Season

Player	K/9	Year
1. Roger Clemens	10.39	1998
2. Roger Clemens	9.95	1997
3. Juan Guzman	8.22	1992
4. Kelvim Escobar	7.94	2003
5. Juan Guzman	7.91	1996
6. Juan Guzman	7.90	1993
7. Ted Lilly	7.66	2004
8. Pat Hentgen	7.57	1994
9. Al Leiter	7.52	1995
10. Kelvim Escobar	7.10	2000

Strikeouts Per Nine IP: Career with Team

Player	K/9	IP
1. Tom Henke	10.29	563.0
2. Duane Ward	9.28	650.7
3. Kelvim Escobar	7.89	849.0
4. Juan Guzman	7.63	1,215.7
5. Roy Halladay	6.53	1,116.3
6. Woody Williams	6.44	613.3
7. Chris Carpenter	6.33	870.7
8. David Wells	6.14	1,148.7
9. Paul Quantrill	5.81	517.7
10. Pat Hentgen	5.66	1,636.0

Hits Allowed: Season

Player	HA	Year
1. Dave Lemanczyk	278	1977
2. Dave Stieb	271	1982
3. Doyle Alexander	268	1985
4. David Wells	266	2000
5. Roy Halladay	253	2003
Pat Hentgen	253	1997
7. Jim Clancy	251	1982
8. Luis Leal	250	1982
9. Jim Clancy	249	1984
10. Jerry Garvin	247	1977

Hits Allowed: Career with Team

Player	HA	IP
1. Dave Stieb	2,545	2,873.0
2. Jim Clancy	2,185	2,204.7
3. Pat Hentgen	1,677	1,636.0
4. Jimmy Key	1,624	1,695.7
5. Todd Stottlemyre	1,182	1,139.0
6. David Wells	1,171	1,148.7
7. Roy Halladay	1,103	1,116.3
8. Juan Guzman	1,099	1,215.7
9. Chris Carpenter	984	870.7
10. Luis Leal	968	946.0

Hits Allowed Per Nine IP: Season

Player	H/9	Year
1. Roger Clemens	6.48	1998
2. Juan Guzman	6.73	1992
3. Dave Stieb	6.82	1988
4. Roger Clemens	6.95	1997
5. Dave Stieb	7.00	1985
6. Dave Stieb	7.14	1989
7. Dave Stieb	7.22	1983
8. Jimmy Key	7.24	1987
9. Dave Stieb	7.25	1984
Dave Stieb	7.25	1981

Hits Allowed Per Nine IP: Career with Team

Player	H/9	IP
1. Tom Henke	6.57	563.0
2. Duane Ward	7.32	650.7
3. Dave Stieb	7.97	2,873.0
4. Juan Guzman	8.14	1,215.7
5. Jimmy Key	8.62	1,695.7
6. Woody Williams	8.64	613.3
7. Roy Halladay	8.89	1,116.3
8. Jim Clancy	8.92	2,204.7
9. Kelvim Escobar	8.97	849.0
10. Doyle Alexander	9.02	750.0

Walks Allowed: Season

Player	BB	Year
1. Jim Clancy	128	1980
2. Juan Guzman	110	1993
3. Al Leiter	108	1995
4. Erik Hanson	102	1996
5. Miguel Batista	96	2004
Dave Stieb	96	1985
7. Tom Underwood	95	1979
8. Pat Hentgen	94	1996
9. Dave Stieb	93	1983
10. Jim Clancy	91	1978

Walks Allowed: Career with Team

Player	BB	IP
1. Dave Stieb	1,020	2,873.0
2. Jim Clancy	814	2,204.7
3. Pat Hentgen	599	1,636.0
4. Juan Guzman	546	1,215.7
5. Todd Stottlemyre	414	1,139.0
6. Jimmy Key	404	1,695.7
7. Kelvim Escobar	394	849.0
8. Chris Carpenter	331	870.7
9. Luis Leal	320	946.0
10. Roy Halladay	299	1,116.3

Walks Allowed Per Nine IP: Season

Player	BB/9	Year
1. Roy Halladay	1.08	2003
2. Jimmy Key	1.12	1989
3. David Wells	1.21	2000
4. Josh Towers	1.25	2005
5. Jimmy Key	1.89	1991
Esteban Loaiza	1.89	2001
7. Doyle Alexander	2.03	1984
8. Jimmy Key	2.12	1985
9. David Wells	2.14	1990
10. Jim Clancy	2.15	1988

Walks Allowed Per Nine IP: Career with Team

Player	BB/9	IP
1. Doyle Alexander	2.06	750.0
2. Jimmy Key	2.14	1,695.7
3. David Wells	2.30	1,148.7
4. Roy Halladay	2.41	1,116.3
5. Paul Quantrill	2.50	517.7
6. Tom Henke	2.65	563.0
7. John Cerutti	2.96	772.3
8. Luis Leal	3.04	946.0
9. Dave Stieb	3.20	2,873.0
10. Jerry Garvin	3.25	606.0

WHIP (Walks + Hits Per Nine IP): Season

Player	WHIP	Year
1. Roger Clemens	1.030	1997
2. Jimmy Key	1.057	1987
3. Roy Halladay	1.071	2003
4. Roger Clemens	1.095	1998
5. David Wells	1.111	1990
6. Jimmy Key	1.119	1985
7. Juan Guzman	1.124	1996
8. Dave Stieb	1.135	1984
Doyle Alexander	1.135	1984
10. Dave Stieb	1.137	1983

WHIP (Walks + Hits Per Nine IP): Career with Team

Player	WHIP	IP
1. Tom Henke	1.025	563.0
2. Jimmy Key	1.196	1,695.7
3. Doyle Alexander	1.232	750.0
4. Duane Ward	1.240	650.7
5. Dave Stieb	1.241	2,873.0
6. Roy Halladay	1.256	1,116.3
7. David Wells	1.275	1,148.7
8. Juan Guzman	1.353	1,215.7
9. Jim Clancy	1.360	2,204.7
10. Luis Leal	1.362	946.0

Home Runs Allowed: Season

Player	HRA	Year
1. Woody Williams	36	1998
2. Jerry Garvin	33	1977
3. Pat Hentgen	32	1999
David Wells	32	1999
5. Pat Hentgen	31	1997
Woody Williams	31	1997
7. Chris Carpenter	30	2000
John Cerutti	30	1987
9. Chris Carpenter	29	2001
Dave Stieb	29	1986

Home Runs Allowed: Career with Team

Player	HRA	IP
1. Dave Stieb	224	2,873.0
2. Jim Clancy	219	2,204.7
3. Pat Hentgen	207	1,636.0
4. Jimmy Key	165	1,695.7
5. David Wells	126	1,148.7
6. Juan Guzman	115	1,215.7
Todd Stottlemyre	115	1,139.0
8. Chris Carpenter	111	870.7
9. John Cerutti	110	772.3
10. Luis Leal	101	946.0

Saves: Season

Player	SV	Year
1. Duane Ward	45	1993
2. Kelvim Escobar	38	2002
3. Billy Koch	36	2001
4. Tom Henke	34	1987
Tom Henke	34	1992
6. Billy Koch	33	2000
7. Tom Henke	32	1990
Tom Henke	32	1991
9. Billy Koch	31	1999
Mike Timlin	31	1996
Miguel Batista	31	2005

Saves: Career with Team

Player	SV	IP
1. Tom Henke	217	563.0
2. Duane Ward	121	650.7
3. Billy Koch	100	211.7
4. Kelvim Escobar	58	849.0
5. Mike Timlin	52	393.3
6. Miguel Batista	36	273.3
7. Joey McLaughlin	31	341.0

8. Roy Lee Jackson	30	337.0
9. Randy Myers	28	42.3
10. Darren Hall	20	48.0

WILD PITCHES: SEASON

Player	WP	Year
1. Juan Guzman	26	1993
2. Dave Lemanczyk	20	1977
3. Juan Guzman	14	1992
Al Leiter	14	1995
Jack Morris	14	1993
6. Juan Guzman	13	1994
Erik Hanson	13	1996
Duane Ward	13	1989
9. Miguel Batista	12	2004
Jim Clancy	12	1981
Jim Clancy	12	1987
Pete Vuckovich	12	1977

WILD PITCHES: CAREER WITH TEAM

Player	WP	IP
1. Juan Guzman	88	1,215.7
2. Jim Clancy	82	2,204.7
3. Pat Hentgen	56	1,636.0
4. Dave Stieb	51	2,873.0
Duane Ward	51	650.7
6. David Wells	46	1,148.7
7. Dave Lemanczyk	36	575.0
8. Chris Carpenter	32	870.7
9. Jimmy Key	31	1,695.7

10. John Cerutti	30	772.3
Todd Stottlemyre	30	1,139.0
Roy Halladay	30	1,116.3

HIT BATSMEN: SEASON

Player	HB	Year
1. Chris Carpenter	16	2001
2. Dave Stieb	15	1986
3. Dave Stieb	14	1983
4. Dave Stieb	13	1988
Dave Stieb	13	1989
David Bush	13	2005
7. Roger Clemens	12	1997
Chris Michalak	12	2001
Todd Stottlemyre	12	1991
10. Justin Miller	11	2002
Dave Stieb	11	1981
Dave Stieb	11	1984

HIT BATSMEN: CAREER WITH TEAM

Player	HB	IP
1. Dave Stieb	129	2,873.0
2. Todd Stottlemyre	49	1,139.0
3. Pat Hentgen	41	1,636.0
4. Chris Carpenter	35	870.7
5. Roy Halladay	31	1,116.3
6. Kelvim Escobar	30	849.0
7. Juan Guzman	29	1,215.7
8. Jim Clancy	28	2,204.7

David Wells	28	1,148.7
10. Jim Acker	25	524.3

GAMES FINISHED: SEASON

Player	GF	Year
1. Duane Ward	70	1993
2. Kelvim Escobar	68	2002
3. Tom Henke	62	1987
Billy Koch	62	2000
Miguel Batista	62	2005
6. Tom Henke	58	1990
7. Tom Henke	56	1989
Billy Koch	56	2001
Mike Timlin	56	1996
10. Bill Caudill	51	1985
Tom Henke	51	1986

GAMES FINISHED: CAREER WITH TEAM

Player	GF	IP
1. Tom Henke	386	563.0
2. Duane Ward	266	650.7
3. Mike Timlin	175	393.3
4. Billy Koch	166	211.7
5. Kelvim Escobar	130	849.0
6. Paul Quantrill	125	517.7
7. Joey McLaughlin	123	341.0
8. Mark Eichhorn	105	493.0
9. Roy Lee Jackson	93	337.0
10. Jim Acker	82	524.3

April 9, 1977. The Blue Jays play their first game in Toronto.

Significant Blue Jays

ALOMAR, ROBERTO (2B) (1991–1995)

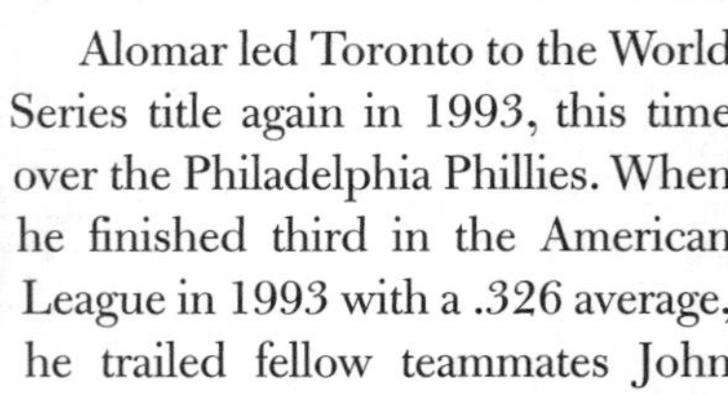

On December 5, 1990, Roberto Alomar was already a young star with the San Diego Padres when he was traded along with Joe Carter to Toronto for established stars Fred McGriff and Tony Fernandez in one of the era's blockbuster deals. Alomar, the brother of catcher Sandy Alomar Jr. and son of major leaguer Sandy Alomar Sr., had great speed (swiping nearly 500 stolen bases for his career, 206 with Toronto), and phenomenal range at second base. He won Gold Gloves all five years he was a Blue Jay (and won a total of 10 Gold Gloves throughout his career). He was also a steady hitter, compiling a .307 average for Toronto and a .300 lifetime average over 17 seasons. One of his more memorable hits was the ninth-inning home run that turned around Game 4 of the 1992 ALCS. The Jays trailed by five runs in the eighth inning before Alomar's two-run shot tied the game, setting the stage for Toronto's 11th-inning victory. He won the MVP Award for the series with a .423 average before leading Toronto to their first World Series title as the Blue Jays defeated the Atlanta Braves. After the season he was honored with the Silver Slugger Award, one of four he would win over his career (but the only one while with Toronto).

Alomar led Toronto to the World Series title again in 1993, this time over the Philadelphia Phillies. When he finished third in the American League in 1993 with a .326 average, he trailed fellow teammates John Olerud and Paul Molitor, the first time in American League history that three members of the same team ended up 1–2–3 in the batting race. Alomar was named to the American League All-Star team in each of his five Toronto seasons (he was an All-Star 12 times over the course of his career). Following the 1995 season, Alomar opted for free agency and signed with the Baltimore Orioles. During his long career, Alomar never played more than three seasons with the same team except for the five years he spent with Toronto, so when he eventually takes his place in the Hall of Fame, it is likely that he will enter as the Blue Jay's first-ever representative in Cooperstown.

CAREER BLUE JAYS RECORD:

Games	AB	Hits	Runs
703	2,706	832	451
Avg	**HR**	**RBI**	**SB**
.307	55	342	206

BARFIELD, JESSE (OF)
(1981–1989)

Jesse Barfield was drafted in the ninth round of the June 1977 amateur draft by the Blue Jays and eventually made it to the majors in late 1981. For the first few years of his Blue Jays career, Barfield was a platoon player in right field who showed good power and a great arm, but his low batting average kept him from becoming a full-time player. By 1985 Barfield became a regular in the lineup and responded with a .289 average and 27 homers. He also stole 22 bases and threw out 22 runners on the base paths, both career highs. In 1986 he led the American League with 40 homers. He also was selected to the All-Star team, and won the Silver Slugger Award as well as the first of two Gold Glove Awards (the other came in 1987). Barfield, a devout Christian, became openly critical of new manager Jimy Williams' policy of eliminating clubhouse prayer before games and his rule against wearing the team logo to charitable religious events. The Blue Jays traded Barfield to the Yankees early in the 1989 season and he finished his career with three-plus mediocre seasons for New York before retiring at age 32.

CAREER BLUE JAYS RECORD:

Games	AB	Hits	Runs
1,032	3,463	919	530
Avg	**HR**	**RBI**	**SB**
.265	179	527	55

BELL, GEORGE (OF)
(1981, 1983–1990)

George Bell was drafted out of the Philadelphia Phillies minor league organization as a Rule V draftee in December 1980. One of the American League's top sluggers of the mid-1980s, Bell set or broke many team records during his nine seasons as a Blue Jay. He had a unique batting style: He rocked back on his feet and then strode into the pitch with tremendous power. He once hit two towering home runs over the roof of Comiskey Park in the same series. In 1987 he won the American League MVP Award after hitting .308, slugging 47 home runs, and collecting 134 RBIs. In 1988, after being made the team's DH because of his failing knees, Bell became the first major leaguer in history to hit three home runs on Opening Day. As a Blue Jay, Bell was selected to the All-Star team twice (1987 and 1990) and won three consecutive Silver Slugger Awards (1985–1987). Because of continued problems with his knees and shoulder, Bell was granted free agency after the 1990 season and signed on with the Cubs. A year later he joined the White Sox for the last two seasons of his career, which ended at age 33 due to rapidly diminishing skills.

CAREER BLUE JAYS RECORD:

Games	AB	Hits	Runs
1,181	4,528	1,294	641
Avg	**HR**	**RBI**	**SB**
.286	202	740	59

CARTER, JOE (OF)
(1991–1997)

A durable player for most of his career, Joe Carter was part of a blockbuster trade in December of 1990 in which the San Diego Padres sent him to Toronto along with Roberto Alomar for Fred McGriff and Tony Fernandez. He had played six years for the Indians and one for the Cubs before landing in San Diego for one season. In the next seven seasons with the Blue Jays, Carter was named to the American League All-Star team five times and he won Silver Slugger Awards in 1991 and 1992. In 1997 he became the ninth player in major league history to have 100 or more RBIs in at least 10 different seasons. The other eight players (Ruth, Goslin, Gehrig, Foxx, Simmons, Musial, Mays, and Aaron) are all in the Hall of Fame. Carter's main claim to fame, however, was his historic home run off the Phillies' Mitch Williams in the bottom of the ninth of Game 6 of the 1993 World Series. The homer marked the first time in World Series history that a team trailing in the bottom of the ninth of the last game won on a walk-off homer, and only the second time a Series had ended with a homer. (Bill Mazeroski's homer in the 1960 World Series came with the game tied at 9–9.) The dramatic blast gave the Blue Jays their second consecutive World Series title. Carter left Toronto via free agency after the 1997 season, but played only one more year for the Orioles and Giants before retiring.

CAREER BLUE JAYS RECORD:

Games	AB	Hits	Runs
1,039	4,093	1,051	578
Avg	**HR**	**RBI**	**SB**
.257	203	736	78

CLANCY, JIM (SP)
(1977–1988)

Jim Clancy was drafted by the Blue Jays out of the Texas Rangers minor league organization as part of the 1976 expansion draft and made Toronto's major league roster in 1977. For the next 12 years he was a mainstay in the early years of the Blue Jays' starting rotation, winning a career-high 16 games in 1982, when he was selected to the American League All-Star team. Clancy left Toronto via free agency after the 1988 season and finished out his career with three seasons in the National League for Houston and Atlanta.

CAREER BLUE JAYS RECORD:

W	L	W%	ERA	SV
128	140	.478	4.10	1
K	**BB**	**SHO**	**IP**	
1,237	814	11	2,204.7	

CLEMENS, ROGER (SP)
(1997–1998)

Though he only spent two years of his long and illustrious career with the Blue Jays, Clemens left a lasting impression on both Toronto's fans and its team record book. In December of 1996, Clemens signed with the Blue Jays as a free agent after 12 years pitching for the Boston Red Sox. "The Rocket" was simply dominant during his two seasons as a Blue Jay, leading the American League both years in wins, strikeouts, and ERA. In 1997 he was 21–7, although the team finished 76–86. For his efforts he was selected to the All-Star team each of his two years in Toronto and was voted the Cy Young Award winner for both 1997 and 1998. When the future Hall of Famer asked to be traded to a championship team, the Blue Jays management obliged during spring training of 1999 by sending him to the Yankees for David Wells, Homer Bush, and Graeme Lloyd. In his four seasons with New York, Clemens won two World Series rings and another Cy Young. *(See Red Sox bio.)*

CAREER BLUE JAYS RECORD:

W	L	W%	ERA	SV
41	13	.759	2.33	0

K	BB	SHO	IP
563	156	6	498.7

DELGADO, CARLOS (1B)
(1993–2004)

The holder of many Toronto hitting records, Carlos Delgado was signed as an amateur free-agent catcher by the Blue Jays in October 1988. Although he got into a couple of games in 1993, he didn't stick with the team until the following season as a part-time player. In 1996, when he moved to first base and became a regular, his career took off like the bombs from his powerful bat. From 1997 through 2004, the tall first baseman never hit fewer than 30 homers in a season and averaged around 120 RBIs during that span, becoming one of the most feared hitters in the league. A two-time All-Star and three-time Silver Slugger Award winner with the Jays, Delgado left Toronto after 12 years to sign as a free agent with the Florida Marlins in 2005. After batting .301 with 33 home runs and 115 RBIs in his only season in Florida, Delgado was traded to the Mets.

CAREER BLUE JAYS RECORD:

Games	AB	Hits	Runs
1,423	5,008	1,413	889

Avg	HR	RBI	SB
.282	336	1,058	9

FERNANDEZ, TONY (SS)
(1983–1990, 1993, 1998–1999, 2001)

Tony Fernandez was signed by the Blue Jays as an amateur free agent in April 1979. After two seasons as a part-time player in 1983 and 1984, Fernandez became a regular beginning in 1985 and shined both offensively and defensively. He won four consecutive Gold Gloves from 1986 to 1989 for his play at shortstop, and four of his five career All-Star appearances were as a Blue Jay. Fernandez hit over .300 in six different seasons with Toronto. After eight years with the team, he was traded along with Fred McGriff to the San Diego Padres for Joe Carter and Roberto Alomar in one of the biggest trades of the era. After two seasons in San Diego and another half season with the Mets, New York traded him back to Toronto in June 1993 for Darrin Jackson. At the end of 1993, Fernandez left Toronto again, this time via free agency, and bounced around for four years with several teams before coming back to Toronto a third time in 1998 as a free agent. He was now a second baseman and hit .321, one point shy of his career high up to that point. In 1999 he moved to third base for the Jays and hit .328, setting a new career mark. He even flirted with .400 for the first half of the season. After 1999, Fernandez signed with the Seibu Lions of the Japanese Pacific League for the 2000 season. He returned for a fourth and final stint with Toronto as a free agent in 2001, the final year of his long career.

CAREER BLUE JAYS RECORD:

Games	AB	Hits	Runs
1,450	5,335	1,583	704
Avg	**HR**	**RBI**	**SB**
.297	60	613	172

GARCIA, DAMASO (2B)
(1980–1986)

The Blue Jays received Damaso Garcia along with Chris Chambliss and Paul Mirabella in a trade with the Yankees for Tom Underwood, Rick Cerone, and Ted Wilborn in November 1979. Garcia immediately moved into the starting second-base spot for the Jays and remained there for the next seven seasons, winning the Silver Slugger Award in 1982 and making the All-Star team twice (1984 and 1985). He was traded to Atlanta before the 1987 season, and finished his career with a year there and another year in Montreal as a part-time player for both teams.

CAREER BLUE JAYS RECORD:

Games	AB	Hits	Runs
902	3,572	1,028	453
Avg	**HR**	**RBI**	**SB**
.288	32	296	194

HENKE, TOM (RP)
(1985–1992)

The hard-throwing Henke became a Blue Jay in January 1985 when Toronto selected him as a free-agent compensation pick from the Texas Rangers. By 1986 he was the Blue Jays' closer; by 1987 he was the top closer in the American League, leading the circuit in saves that year with 34. After eight solid seasons with Toronto, Henke opted for free agency after the 1992 season and signed again with Texas, leaving Toronto as the career leader in many pitching categories. After two years as the closer for Texas and another as the closer for St. Louis, Henke retired with 311 career saves. As of 2006 he is still Toronto's career leader in numerous categories, including ERA, ratio, and saves.

CAREER BLUE JAYS RECORD:

W	L	W%	ERA	SV
29	29	.500	2.48	217

K	BB	SHO	IP
644	166	0	563.0

KEY, JIMMY (SP)
(1984–1992)

Jimmy Key was drafted by the Blue Jays in the June 1982 amateur draft and made the team as a reliever in 1984. In 1985 he moved to the starting rotation and averaged more than 30 starts a year for the next eight seasons. He made the All-Star team twice as a Blue Jay, in 1985 and 1991 (but surprisingly not in 1987, the best season of his career). He led the American League with a 2.76 ERA and held opposing batters to a league-low .221 batting average. He was also runner-up to Roger Clemens for the Cy Young Award. After nine solid seasons with the Blue Jays, Key left the team after the 1992 season via free agency, signing a big contract with the Yankees, where he spent four seasons, two of which were good. After winning the clinching game of the 1996 World Series, Key left New York for Baltimore and had one good season in 1997 (16–10), but retired in mid- season 1998 after winning just six games.

CAREER BLUE JAYS RECORD:

W	L	W%	ERA	SV
116	81	.589	3.42	10

K	BB	SHO	IP
944	404	10	1,695.7

MOSEBY, LLOYD (OF)
(1980–1989)

The Blue Jays selected Moseby as the second pick overall in the June 1978 amateur draft. Though a regular for most of his 10 years in Toronto, he never quite lived up to expectations that he would be a star. Moseby did have exceptional speed, and he still holds the Blue Jays' career record for stolen bases with 255. He made the All-Star team once (1986) and won one Silver Slugger Award (1983). After the 1989 season he left the team as a free agent and signed with Detroit where he finished the last two years of his career.

CAREER BLUE JAYS RECORD:

Games	AB	Hits	Runs
1,392	5,124	1,319	768

Avg	HR	RBI	SB
.257	149	651	255

STEWART, SHANNON (OF)
(1995–2003)

Shannon Stewart was a first-round pick by the Blue Jays in the June 1992 amateur draft and saw his first big league action in 1995. The speedy outfielder became a regular in 1998. From 1999 through 2002, Stewart typically posted 600 at-bats, 40 doubles, 100+ runs, and a .310 average each season. With his numbers on the decline, especially in stolen bases, Stewart was traded to the Minnesota Twins in mid-2003. As a member of the Twins, Stewart has continued to underperform through the 2005 season.

CAREER BLUE JAYS RECORD:

Games	AB	Hits	Runs
855	3,450	1,040	581

Avg	HR	RBI	SB
.301	73	356	163

STIEB, DAVE (SP)
(1979–1992, 1998)

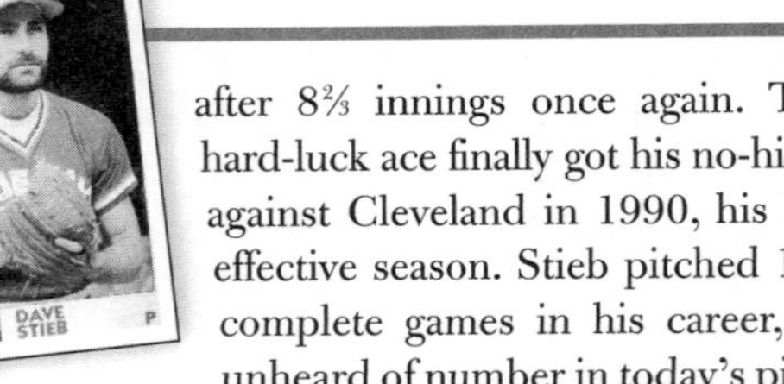

Dave Stieb was selected in the fifth round of the June 1978 amateur draft by the Blue Jays, and, by 1979, was in Toronto's starting lineup. Even though Stieb pitched for an expansion team, he was one of the best pitchers in the game during the 1980s. He was selected to the American League All-Star team seven times. On September 24, 1988, against Cleveland, the tough-luck Stieb came within one strike of pitching Toronto's first-ever no-hitter before Julio Franco's bad-hop single ruined the effort. In his very next start, on September 30, Stieb again was within one strike of a no-hitter before Baltimore pinch-hitter Jim Traber singled to right. Stieb thus became the first pitcher in major league history to lose no-hitters after 8⅔ innings in back-to-back games. In August 1989, Stieb retired the first 26 Yankees he faced before giving up a double and losing his perfect game after 8⅔ innings once again. The hard-luck ace finally got his no-hitter against Cleveland in 1990, his last effective season. Stieb pitched 103 complete games in his career, an unheard of number in today's pitch count-conscious era, along with 30 shutouts. After struggling in 1991 and 1992 to a combined 8–9 record, he left Toronto for the free-agent market but failed in stints with the White Sox and Royals in 1993. After sitting out of baseball for five years, Stieb attempted a comeback with the Blue Jays but was ineffective, compiling a 1–2 record in 50 innings before retiring for good in 1998.

CAREER BLUE JAYS RECORD:

W	L	W%	ERA	SV
175	134	.566	3.42	3

K	BB	SHO	IP
1,658	1,020	30	2,873.0

WARD, DUANE (RP)
(1986–1993, 1995)

Duane Ward came to the Blue Jays in 1986 in a trade with Atlanta for Doyle Alexander. For seven years he and Tom Henke were a potent 1–2 punch out of the Toronto bullpen. Ward was the primary setup man for Henke until the Jays decided to let Henke go to free agency after the 1992 season and install Ward as their new closer. Ward had a fantastic season in 1993, leading the American League with 45 saves. He was the winning pitcher in the last World Series game that year when Joe Carter hit his walk-off home run. During the offseason, however, he developed arm trouble. During 1994 spring training, his sore arm was upgraded to a cartilage tear, which was eventually correctly diagnosed as a torn rotator cuff that ended his career. Ward tried a brief comeback bid in 1995, but, after giving up 10 runs in just over two innings, he called it quits at the age of 31.

CAREER BLUE JAYS RECORD:

W	L	W%	ERA	SV
32	36	.471	3.18	121
K	BB	SHO	IP	
671	278	0	650.7	

WHITT, ERNIE (C)
(1977–1978, 1980–1989)

Ernie Whitt, selected from the Red Sox organization in the 1976 expansion draft, was Toronto's main catcher from 1982 to 1989 and one of the most popular players ever to wear a Blue Jays uniform. He was a solid defensive catcher and deft in his handling of pitchers. Whitt, who had a strong work ethic, posted decent offensive numbers as well, averaging nearly 16 homers a season during that same span. He was selected to the 1985 All-Star team. In December 1989 Whitt was traded with Kevin Batiste to the Atlanta Braves for Ricky Trlicek, and performed as the team's backup for a year, then spent 1991 in the same role with Baltimore before retiring.

CAREER BLUE JAYS RECORD:

Games	AB	Hits	Runs
1,218	3,514	888	424
Avg	HR	RBI	SB
.253	131	518	2

Roberto Alomar demonstrates why he won a gold glove every year he played second for the Jays.

Washington Nationals

Since 1969

1969 On April 17, in just the team's ninth game in existence, pitcher Bill Stoneman hurls a no-hitter against the Phillies, the earliest a no-hitter had ever been pitched in any team's history.... **1979–83** The Expos own the National League's best record (413–341) in this span and are in the race until the final week in all five years. But the team wins only one division title, in strike-shortened 1981.... **1994** When Montreal sweeps its 12-game series with San Diego, it marks only the second season series sweep in National League history. Atlanta did it against Colorado the year before.... **2000** Vladimir Guerrero hits .345 with 44 homers and 123 RBIs, becoming the first National Leaguer and only the fourth player in major league history (joining Jimmie Foxx, Ted Williams, and Joe DiMaggio) to bat at least .300 with 35 homers and 100 RBIs in three straight seasons, all before the age of 25.

FRANCHISE HISTORY

In the wake of Montreal's successful World's Fair, "Expo 67," Major League Baseball was eager to expand to Canada. The franchise awarded to Montreal took "Expos" as its nickname. For its first 36 years, the team was located in Montreal, but before the 2005 season, the Expos moved to Washington, D.C. Major league baseball returned to the nation's capital for the first time since the second Senators team abandoned the city in 1971 (becoming the Texas Rangers). The franchise changed its name to the Nationals, a name once held by no fewer than four previous major league teams in Washington, and also the unofficial and occasional nickname of early Senators teams.

Of the 23 weather-related postponements that occurred in 1971, Montreal was involved in 10 of them.

The first owner of the Expos was Charles Bronfman, the owner of Seagram's Distillery Company. He owned the team for more than two decades, finally selling out in 1991 to a consortium of private citizens and the city of Montreal. The group's leader was Claude Brochu, the chief executive officer of Seagram and Sons, and he became the team's president and lead general partner. In 1999, Major League Baseball approved the transfer of control of the Expos to a group composed of local interests and New York art dealer Jeffrey Loria, who would control 39 percent of the team. Three years later, Loria sold the Expos to Major League Baseball for $120 million and a loan of $38.5 million. That same day he then turned

Mack Jones slides into third during Montreal's inaugural season, 1969.

Thirty years after being named baseball's first black manager, Nationals skipper Frank Robinson tips his hat to the crowd.

around and bought the Florida Marlins for $158.5 million from John Henry, who a month earlier had bought the Boston Red Sox. At the end of the 2005 season, Major League Baseball still owned the franchise, but was looking for a buyer for the team.

The franchise had a losing record for its first 10 years of existence. When the Expos finally pulled off their first winning season in 1979, they did so in style, almost winning the National League East Division title. As it was, the team finished with a 95–65 record, just three games behind the Pirates, who went on to win the World Series. The Expos did make the playoffs in 1981, thanks to the split-season format, but lost to the Dodgers. Perhaps the best year in franchise history was 1994—the Expos had the best record in all of baseball when the players' strike cancelled the remainder of the season.

When the franchise shifted to Washington, D.C., for the 2005 season, the excitement among former Senators fans could hardly be contained, and season ticket sales set records for a D.C. franchise. The team, usually an also-ran in the National League East, surprised almost everyone by picking up momentum as the season wore on. By July 1 the team was sitting atop the NL East standings, trailing only St. Louis for the best record in the National League. But losing months in July (9–18), August (13–15), September (12–15), and October (0–2) consigned the transplanted team, alas, to the cellar.

TEAM NAME HISTORY

Official Names

Expos (1969–2004)
Nationals (2005–current)

Unofficial Names

'Spos (while in Montreal)
Nats (while in Washington)

STADIUM HISTORY

Jarry Park	1969–1976
Olympic Stadium	1977–2004
RFK Stadium	2005–current

Livan Hernandez throws the first pitch of the franchise's new Washington incarnation.

YEARLY RECORD, FINISH, & ATTENDANCE FIGURES

Year	League	Record	DIV/LG Finish	Attendance	Avg/Gm
2005	NL East	81–81	5	2,731,993	33,728
2004	NL East	67–95	5	749,550	9,369
2003	NL East	83–79	4	1,025,639	12,662
2002	NL East	83–79	2	812,045	10,025
2001	NL East	68–94	5	642,745	7,935
2000	NL East	67–95	4	926,272	11,435
1999	NL East	68–94	4	773,277	9,547
1998	NL East	65–97	4	914,909	11,295
1997	NL East	78–84	4	1,497,609	18,489
1996	NL East	88–74	2	1,616,709	19,959
1995	NL East	66–78	5	1,309,618	18,189
1994	NL East	74–40	1	1,276,250	24,543
1993	NL East	94–68	2	1,641,437	20,265
1992	NL East	87–75	2	1,669,127	20,607
1991	NL East	71–90	6	934,742	13,746
1990	NL East	85–77	3	1,373,087	16,952
1989	NL East	81–81	4	1,783,533	22,019
1988	NL East	81–81	3	1,478,659	18,255
1987	NL East	91–71	3	1,850,324	22,844
1986	NL East	78–83	4	1,128,981	14,112
1985	NL East	84–77	3	1,502,494	18,549
1984	NL East	78–83	5	1,606,531	19,834
1983	NL East	82–80	3	2,320,651	28,650
1982	NL East	86–76	3	2,318,292	28,621
1981	NL East	60–48	3/1	1,534,564	27,403
1980	NL East	90–72	2	2,208,175	27,602
1979	NL East	95–65	2	2,102,173	25,953
1978	NL East	76–86	4	1,427,007	17,838
1977	NL East	75–87	5	1,433,757	17,701
1976	NL East	55–107	6	646,704	8,084
1975	NL East	75–87	5	908,292	11,213
1974	NL East	79–82	4	1,019,134	12,739
1973	NL East	79–83	4	1,246,863	15,393
1972	NL East	70–86	5	1,142,145	14,643
1971	NL East	71–90	5	1,290,963	16,137
1970	NL East	73–89	6	1,424,683	17,809
1969	NL East	52–110	6	1,212,608	14,970

MANAGER HISTORY

Manager	Years	W–L	Win %
Gene Mauch	1969–1975	499–627	.443
Karl Kuehl	1976	43–85	.336
Charlie Fox	1976	12–22	.353
Dick Williams	1977–1981	380–347	.523
Jim Fanning	1981–1982, 1984	116–103	.530
Bill Virdon	1983–1984	146–147	.498
Buck Rodgers	1985–1991	520–499	.510
Tom Runnells	1991–1992	68–81	.456
Felipe Alou	1992–2001	691–717	.491
Jeff Torborg	2001	47–62	.431
Frank Robinson	2002–2005	314–334	.485

ALL-TIME WIN-LOSS RECORDS VS. ALL OPPONENTS

ALL-TIME	2,836–3,024
Angels	3–3
Astros	173–222
Athletics	3–3
Blue Jays	22–27
Braves	223–252
Brewers	29–30
Cardinals	264–271
Cubs	276–249
Devil Rays	7–5
Diamondbacks	32–25
Dodgers	171–229
Giants	195–208
Indians	2–1
INTERLEAGUE	81–76
Mariners	5–4
Marlins	91–100
Mets	306–310
Orioles	9–6
Padres	213–184
Phillies	299–315
Pirates	254–281
Rangers	4–2
Reds	179–214
Red Sox	7–8
Rockies	50–58
Royals	5–1
Tigers	4–2
Twins	0–3
White Sox	4–2
Yankees	6–9

Franchise Highlights, Low Points, and Strange Distinctions

1970 Montreal hitters were last in the league in batting average, the pitching staff was last in ERA—and yet, amazingly, the Expos won 21 more games than they had in 1969, their inaugural year.

....

1971 Montreal batters were hit by pitches 78 times. Ron Hunt accounted for 50 of them.

....

1972 During the season, outfielder Ken Singleton was forced to the bench because of severe allergies. It was eventually discovered that the source of his problems was the team's wool, so a special double-knit uniform was made just for him. By the end of 1973, all players on the Expos—as well as all teams in the majors—were outfitted with double-knit uniforms.

....

1974 Bad weather forced the Expos to play an incredible 21 doubleheaders.

....

1978 There were only two 20-game winners in the National League, and both pitched for expansion teams. Gaylord Perry (21–6) pitched for San Diego and won the NL Cy Young Award. Montreal's Ross Grimsley was the other 20-game winner, finishing 20–11.

The Expos lost a whopping 36 one-run games.

....

1980 During one stretch, pitcher Woodie Fryman retired 43 of the 45 batters he faced, accumulating a 24 1/3 consecutive scoreless innings streak.

Of second baseman Rodney Scott's 63 stolen bases, 24 were thefts of third base.

....

1983 When Tim Raines broke the rookie stolen-base record in 1981 with his 71 steals, he did it despite missing 78 games due to the players' strike and a hand injury. In 1983 Raines became the first National League player in history to have more than 70 stolen bases and 70 RBIs in the same season. He finished with 90 steals and 71 RBIs.

....

1990 Rookie second baseman Delino DeShields made his major league debut in dramatic fashion by collecting four hits on Opening Day in St. Louis.

....

1991 On September 13, a 55-ton cement beam fell from Olympic Stadium. Luckily no one was injured because the Expos were on the road, but engineers needed time to assess the facility's safety, forcing the Expos to play the last 26 games of the season on the road. By the time the season ended, Montreal had played 93 road games, a major league record.

Montreal Expos shortstop Wil Cordero in 1994 action.

1992 Manager Felipe Alou became the fifth manager in major league history to manage his own son when Moises Alou joined the team.

• • • •

1994 Before the players' strike ended the season, Montreal had won 20 of their last 23 games, leaving them with the best record in all of baseball. Unfortunately, no playoffs were held that year. Perhaps even more frustrating to Expos fans was the fact that from 1979 through 1994 their team had won 29 more games than any other National League team, but had appeared in the playoffs only once (1981).

• • • •

1995 On September 28, Greg A. Harris became the first pitcher since Elton Chamberlain in 1888 to pitch ambidextrously in a major league game. Normally a right-hander, Harris was allowed to pitch one inning of two-handed relief against Cincinnati by the manager of the Expos, Felipe Alou. After the scoreless inning, which included pitching to two batters left-handed and two batters right-handed, Harris's special-made six-fingered, two-thumbed glove was sent to Cooperstown.

• • • •

1996 Mark Grudzielanek became the first shortstop since Honus Wagner to have at least 200 hits, a .300 average, and 30 steals in one season. In 1997 he smashed the National League record for doubles in a season when he collected 54, bettering Dick Bartell's mark of 48, set in 1932.

• • • •

1997 The Expos were forced to watch two opponents clinch playoff berths at their expense in back-to-back games on September 22 and 23. First the Braves beat them 3–2 in 11 innings to clinch the NL East title, then the Marlins defeated them the next night, 6–3, to win the Wild Card.

During the first year of interleague play, the Expos were tied with the Marlins for the best interleague record at 12–3.

• • • •

1999 Reliever Ugueth Urbina collected 41 saves, an amazing stat considering the team only won 68 games.

• • • •

1999–2000 During the combined seasons of 1999 and 2000, relief pitcher Steve Kline appeared in an incredible 165 games.

Special Achievements

World Series Results

None

World Series Managerial Records

None

All-Time Postseason Record

Divisional Playoffs	3–2
League Championship Series	2–3
World Series	0–0

All-Star Games at Montreal

Year	Date	Winner	Score	Stadium
1982	July 13	National	4–1	Olympic Stadium

Hall of Famers Who Played for Team

	Position	Years	Games with Montreal
Gary Carter	C	1974–1984	1,503
Tony Perez	1B	1977–1979	434

Hall of Famers Who Managed Team

None

MVP Award Winners

None

Cy Young Award Winners

Pitcher	Year	W–L	ERA
Pedro Martinez	1997	17–8	1.90

Rookie of the Year Award Winners

Carl Morton	SP	1970
Andre Dawson	OF	1977

Gold Glove Winners

Year	Position	Player
1973	1B	Mike Jorgensen
1978	OF	Ellis Valentine
1980	C OF	Gary Carter Andre Dawson
1981	C OF	Gary Carter Andre Dawson
1982	C OF	Gary Carter Andre Dawson
1983	OF	Andre Dawson
1984	OF	Andre Dawson
1985	3B OF	Tim Wallach Andre Dawson
1988	3B	Tim Wallach
1989	1B	Andres Galarraga
1990	1B 3B	Andres Galarraga Tim Wallach
1992	OF	Larry Walker
1993	OF OF	Larry Walker Marquis Grissom
1994	OF	Marquis Grissom
2001	SS	Orlando Cabrera

Triple Crown Winners

None

Fireman of the Year Award Winners

Mike Marshall	1973
Jeff Reardon	1985
Ugueth Urbina	1999

World Series MVP

None

League Championship Series MVP

None

All-Star Game MVP

Gary Carter	1981
Gary Carter	1984
Tim Raines	1987

Manager of the Year Award Winners

Buck Rodgers	1987
Felipe Alou	1994

Batting Champions

Year	Player	Avg
1982	Al Oliver	.331
1986	Tim Raines	.334

Nine-Inning No-Hitters Pitched

Year	Pitcher	Opp.	Score
1969	Bill Stoneman	PHI	7–0
1972	Bill Stoneman	NYM	7–0
1981	Charlie Lea	SF	4–0
1991	Dennis Martinez	LAD	2–0

20-GAME WINNERS

Year	Pitcher	W–L
1978	Ross Grimsley	20–11

RETIRED UNIFORM NUMBERS

Number	Player	Position
8	Gary Carter	C
10	Rusty Staub	1B/OF
10	Andre Dawson	OF
30	Tim Raines	OF

TEAM RECORDS—WINS & LOSSES

- Games won in a season: 95 in 1979
- Games lost in a season: 110 in 1969
- Games won in a month: 23 in September 1979
- Games lost in a month: 23 in August 1969 and September 1976
- Consecutive games won: 10 (four times): 1979, 1980, 1997, and 2005
- Consecutive games lost: 20 in 1969
- Biggest shutout victory: 19–0 over Atlanta on July 30, 1978
- Biggest shutout loss: 18–0 to San Francisco on May 24, 2000
- Highest winning percentage: .649 in 1994 (74–40)
- Lowest winning percentage: .321 in 1969 (52–110)

TEAM RECORDS—BATTING

- Highest team batting average: .278 in 1994
- Lowest team batting average: .235 in 1976
- Highest team slugging average: .435 in 1994
- Highest team on-base percentage: .343 in 1994
- Total hits: 1,482 in 1983
- Extra-base hits: 545 in 1997
- Hits in a game: 28 vs. Atlanta on July 30, 1978
- Longest individual hitting streak: 31, Vladimir Guerrero, 1999
- Most .300 hitters in a season: 3 in 1999
- Home runs: 178 in 2000
- Home runs in a month: 13, Vladimir Guerrero, Sept. 2000
- Home runs in a game: 8 vs. Atlanta on July 30, 1978
- Home runs by a rookie: 30, Brad Wilkerson, 2002
- Home runs by a right-hander: 44, Vladimir Guerrero, 2000
- Home runs by a left-hander: 36, Henry Rodriquez, 1996
- Home runs by a switch-hitter: 24, Jose Vidro, 2000
- Grand slams: 9 in 1996
- Grand slams (individual; season): 2, by many players
- Grand slams (individual; career): 7, Gary Carter
- Triples: 61 in 1980
- Doubles: 339 in 1997
- Singles: 1,042 in 1983
- Walks: 695 in 1973
- Runs scored: 741 in 1987 and 1996
- Runs scored in a game: 21 vs. Colorado on April 28, 1996
- Runs scored in an inning: 13 vs. San Francisco on May 7, 1997 (sixth inning)
- Most batters hit by a pitch: 89 in 2005
- Times shut out: 20 in 1972
- Grounded into double plays: 151 in 2001
- Fewest grounded into double plays: 95 in 1993 and 1997
- Runners left on base: 1,232 in 1973

TEAM RECORDS—BASERUNNING

- Stolen bases: 237 in 1980
- Caught stealing: 100 in 1991

TEAM RECORDS—PITCHING

- Lowest earned run average: 3.08 in 1988
- Complete games: 49 in 1971
- Saves: 61 in 1993
- Strikeouts: 1,206 in 1996
- Shutouts: 18 in 1979
- Walks: 716 in 1970
- Hit batsmen: 79 in 2004
- Wild pitches: 71 in 2003
- Consecutive wins (individual): 11, Dennis Martinez, 1989
- Consecutive losses (individual): 10, Steve Renko, 1972
- Strikeouts in a game (individual): 18, Bill Gullickson, September 10, 1980
- Runs allowed in a game: 20 vs. San Diego, May 19, 2001

TEAM RECORDS—FIELDING

- Best fielding average: .985 in 2005
- Most errors committed: 184 in 1969
- Fewest errors committed: 92 in 2005
- Most double plays turned: 193 in 1970
- Fewest double plays turned: 113 in 1992

TEAM RECORDS—MISCELLANEOUS

- Number of times league champions: 0
- Number of times finishing last in league: 3
- Largest attendance, single game: 57,694 vs. Philadelphia, August 15, 1982
- Largest attendance, doubleheader: 59,282 vs. St. Louis, Sept. 16, 1979
- Players used in a season: 55 in 2005
- Seasons played: 13 by Steve Rogers, Tim Wallach, and Tim Raines

PRIMARY PITCHING STAFFS

Year	Starter	Starter	Starter	Starter	Starter	Closer	Bullpen	Bullpen	Bullpen
2005	Hernandez	Loaiza	Patterson	Armas	Drese	Cordero	Majewski	Ayala	Carrasco
2004	Hernandez	Patterson	Day	Kim	Armas	Cordero	Ayala	Tucker	Horgan
2003	Hernandez	Ohka	Day	Vazquez	Vargas	Biddle	Stewart	Eischen	Ayala
2002	Armas	Ohka	Yoshii	Vazquez	Colon	Stewart	Herges	Eischen	Tucker
2001	Armas	Thurman	Yoshii	Vazquez	Reames	Urbina	Stewart	Strickland	Lloyd
2000	Armas	Thurman	Hermanson	Vazquez	Pavano	Kline	Telford	Strickland	Lira
1999	Smith	Thurman	Hermanson	Vazquez	Pavano	Urbina	Telford	Kline	Ayala
1998	Perez	Batista	Hermanson	Vazquez	Pavano	Urbina	Telford	Bennett	Kline
1997	Perez	Martinez	Hermanson	Bullinger	Juden	Urbina	Telford	Veres	Valdes
1996	Fassero	Martinez	Cormier	Urbina	Rueter	Rojas	Dyer	Veres	Daal
1995	Fassero	Martinez	Perez	Henry	Heredia	Rojas	Scott	Shaw	Harris
1994	Fassero	Martinez	Hill	Henry	Rueter	Wetteland	Scott	Shaw	Rojas
1993	Fassero	Martinez	Hill	Nabholz	Rueter	Wetteland	Barnes	Shaw	Rojas
1992	Gardner	Martinez	Hill	Nabholz	Barnes	Wetteland	Fassero	Sampen	Rojas
1991	Gardner	Martinez	Boyd	Nabholz	Barnes	Jones	Fassero	Sampen	Ruskin
1990	Gardner	Martinez	Boyd	Gross	Smith	Burke	Frey	Sampen	Hall
1989	Smith	Martinez	Perez	Gross	Langston	Burke	McGaffigan	Hesketh	Smith
1988	Smith	Martinez	Perez	Dopson	Holman	Burke	McGaffigan	Hesketh	Parrett
1987	Smith	Martinez	Heaton	Sebra	Youmans	Burke	McGaffigan	McClure	Parrett
1986	Smith	Martinez	Tibbs	Hesketh	Youmans	Reardon	McGaffigan	McClure	Burke
1985	Smith	Gullickson	Palmer	Hesketh	Schatzeder	Reardon	Lucas	Roberge	Burke
1984	Smith	Gullickson	Palmer	Lea	Rogers	Reardon	Schatzeder	James	Lucas
1983	Burris	Gullickson	Sanderson	Lea	Rogers	Reardon	Schatzeder	James	Smith
1982	Burris	Gullickson	Sanderson	Lea	Rogers	Reardon	Schatzeder	Fryman	Smith
1981	Burris	Gullickson	Sanderson	Lea	Rogers	Fryman	Sosa	Reardon	Lee
1980	Palmer	Gullickson	Sanderson	Lea	Rogers	Fryman	Norman	Bahnsen	Sosa
1979	Lee	Grimsley	Sanderson	Schatzeder	Rogers	Sosa	Fryman	Bahnsen	Palmer
1978	May	Grimsley	Fryman	Schatzeder	Rogers	Garman	Twitchell	Knowles	Bahnsen
1977	Brown	Bahnsen	Twitchell	Stanhouse	Rogers	Kerrigan	McEnaney	Atkinson	Alcala
1976	Fryman	Carrithers	Warthen	Stanhouse	Rogers	Murray	Kerrigan	Dunning	Taylor
1975	Fryman	Blair	Warthen	Renko	Rogers	Murray	Demola	Scherman	Taylor
1974	Torrez	Blair	McAnally	Renko	Rogers	Taylor	Montague	Walker	Murray
1973	Torrez	Moore	McAnally	Renko	Stoneman	Marshall	Jarvis	Walker	Scott
1972	Torrez	Moore	McAnally	Morton	Stoneman	Marshall	Strohmayer	Walker	Renko
1971	Renko	Strohmayer	McAnally	Morton	Stoneman	Marshall	McGinn	Raymond	Reed
1970	Renko	McGinn	Wegener	Morton	Stoneman	Raymond	Strohmayer	Marshall	Reed
1969	Renko	Robertson	Wegener	Reed	Stoneman	McGinn	Face	Shaw	Waslewski

PRIMARY STARTING LINEUPS

Year	C	1B	2B	3B	SS	LF	CF	RF
2005	Schneider	Johnson	Vidro	Castilla	Guzman	Byrd	Wilkerson	Guillen
2004	Schneider	Wilkerson	Vidro	Batista	Cabrera	Sledge	Chavez	Rivera
2003	Schneider	Cordero	Vidro	Carroll	Cabrera	Wilkerson	Chavez	Guerrero
2002	Barrett	Galarraga	Vidro	Tatis	Cabrera	O'Leary	Wilkerson	Guerrero
2001	Barrett	Stevens	Vidro	Blum	Cabrera	Smith	Bergeron	Guerrero
2000	Widger	Stevens	Vidro	Mordecai	Cabrera	White	Bergeron	Guerrero
1999	Widger	Fullmer	Vidro	Andrews	Cabrera	White	Martinez	Guerrero
1998	Widger	Fullmer	Vidro	Andrews	Grudzielanek	Santangelo	White	Guerrero
1997	Widger	Segui	Lansing	Strange	Grudzielanek	Rodriguez	White	Guerrero
1996	Fletcher	Segui	Lansing	Andrews	Grudzielanek	Rodriguez	White	Alou
1995	Fletcher	Segui	Lansing	Berry	Cordero	Alou	White	Tarasco
1994	Fletcher	Floyd	Lansing	Berry	Cordero	Alou	Grissom	Walker
1993	Fletcher	Colbrunn	DeShields	Berry	Cordero	Alou	Grissom	Walker
1992	Carter	Cianfrocco	DeShields	Wallach	Owen	Alou	Grissom	Walker
1991	Reyes	Galarraga	DeShields	Wallach	Owen	Calderon	Grissom	Walker
1990	Fitzgerald	Galarraga	DeShields	Wallach	Owen	Raines	Martinez	Walker
1989	Santovenia	Galarraga	Foley	Wallach	Owen	Raines	Martinez	Brooks
1988	Santovenia	Galarraga	Foley	Wallach	Rivera	Raines	Nixon	Brooks
1987	Fitzgerald	Galarraga	Law	Wallach	Brooks	Raines	Winningham	Webster
1986	Bilardello	Galarraga	Law	Wallach	Brooks	Raines	Webster	Dawson
1985	Fitzgerald	Driessen	Law	Wallach	Brooks	Raines	Winningham	Dawson
1984	Carter	Francona	Flynn	Wallach	Salazar	Wohlford	Raines	Dawson
1983	Carter	Oliver	Flynn	Wallach	Speier	Raines	Dawson	Cromartie
1982	Carter	Oliver	Flynn	Wallach	Speier	Raines	Dawson	Cromartie
1981	Carter	Cromartie	Scott	Parrish	Speier	Raines	Dawson	Wallach
1980	Carter	Cromartie	Scott	Parrish	Speier	LeFlore	Dawson	Valentine
1979	Carter	Perez	Scott	Parrish	Speier	Cromartie	Dawson	Valentine
1978	Carter	Perez	Cash	Parrish	Speier	Cromartie	Dawson	Valentine
1977	Carter	Perez	Cash	Parrish	Speier	Cromartie	Dawson	Valentine
1976	Foote	Jorgensen	Mackanin	Parrish	Foli	Rivera	White	Unser
1975	Foote	Jorgensen	Mackanin	Parrish	Foli	Bailey	Mangual	Carter
1974	Foote	Jorgensen	Cox	Hunt	Foli	Bailey	Davis	Singleton
1973	Boccabella	Jorgensen	Hunt	Bailey	Foli	Fairly	Woods	Singleton
1972	Boccabella	Jorgensen	Hunt	Bailey	Foli	Singleton	Day	Fairly
1971	Bateman	Fairly	Hunt	Bailey	Wine	Fairey	Day	Staub
1970	Bateman	Fairly	Sutherland	Laboy	Wine	Jones	Phillips	Staub
1969	Brand	Bailey	Sutherland	Laboy	Wine	Jones	Phillips	Staub

Top 10 Batting Leaders, Single Season & Career with Team

iGames Played: Career with Team

Player	G	PA
1. Tim Wallach	1,767	7,174
2. Gary Carter	1,503	6,019
3. Tim Raines	1,452	6,256
4. Andre Dawson	1,443	6,138
5. Warren Cromartie	1,038	4,170
6. Vladimir Guerrero	1,004	4,220
7. Jose Vidro	1,060	4,242
8. Larry Parrish	967	3,735
9. Bob Bailey	951	3,548
Andres Galarraga	951	3,700

At-Bats: Season

Player	AB	Year
1. Warren Cromartie	659	1979
2. Dave Cash	658	1978
3. Mark Grudzielanek	657	1996
4. Marquis Grissom	653	1992
5. Dave Cash	650	1977
6. Mark Grudzielanek	649	1997
7. Tim Raines	647	1982
8. Mike Lansing	641	1996
9. Andre Dawson	639	1979
10. Andre Dawson	633	1983

At-Bats: Career with Team

Player	AB	PA
1. Tim Wallach	6,529	7,174
2. Andre Dawson	5,628	6,138
3. Tim Raines	5,383	6,256
4. Gary Carter	5,303	6,019
5. Warren Cromartie	3,796	4,170
6. Jose Vidro	3,794	4,242
7. Vladimir Guerrero	3,763	4,220
8. Larry Parrish	3,411	3,735
9. Andres Galarraga	3,374	3,700
10. Orlando Cabrera	3,288	3,592

Batting Average: Season

Player	BA	Year
1. Vladimir Guerrero	.345	2000
2. Moises Alou	.339	1994
3. Vladimir Guerrero	.336	2002
4. Tim Raines	.334	1986
5. Al Oliver	.331	1982
6. Tim Raines	.330	1987
Jose Vidro	.330	2000
Vladimir Guerrero	.330	2003
9. Vladimir Guerrero	.324	1998
10. Larry Walker	.322	1994

Batting Average: Career with Team

Player	BA	PA
1. Vladimir Guerrero	.323	4,220
2. Jose Vidro	.302	4,242
3. Tim Raines	.301	6,256
4. Rusty Staub	.295	2,163
5. Rondell White	.293	3,021
6. Moises Alou	.292	2,383
7. Ellis Valentine	.288	2,532
8. Larry Walker	.281	2,690
Mark Grudzielanek	.281	2,112
10. Warren Cromartie	.280	4,170

Total Hits: Season

Player	H	Year
1. Vladimir Guerrero	206	2002
2. Al Oliver	204	1982
3. Vladimir Guerrero	202	1998
4. Mark Grudzielanek	201	1996
5. Jose Vidro	200	2000
6. Vladimir Guerrero	197	2000
7. Tim Raines	194	1986
8. Vladimir Guerrero	193	1999
9. Tim Raines	192	1984
10. Jose Vidro	190	2002

Total Hits: Career with Team

Player	H	PA
1. Tim Wallach	1,694	7,174
2. Tim Raines	1,622	6,256
3. Andre Dawson	1,575	6,138
4. Gary Carter	1,427	6,019
5. Vladimir Guerrero	1,215	4,220
6. Jose Vidro	1,146	4,242
7. Warren Cromartie	1,063	4,170
8. Andres Galarraga	906	3,700
9. Larry Parrish	896	3,735
10. Orlando Cabrera	877	3,592

Home Runs: Season

Player	HR	Year
1. Vladimir Guerrero	44	2000
2. Vladimir Guerrero	42	1999
3. Vladimir Guerrero	39	2002
4. Vladimir Guerrero	38	1998
5. Henry Rodriguez	36	1996
6. Vladimir Guerrero	34	2001
7. Tony Batista	32	2004
Andre Dawson	32	1983
Brad Wilkerson	32	2004
10. Gary Carter	31	1977

Home Runs: Career with Team

Player	HR	PA
1. Vladimir Guerrero	234	4,220
2. Andre Dawson	225	6,138
3. Gary Carter	220	6,019
4. Tim Wallach	204	7,174
5. Bob Bailey	118	3,548
6. Andres Galarraga	115	3,700
7. Jose Vidro	108	4,242
8. Rondell White	101	3,021
9. Larry Parrish	100	3,735
10. Larry Walker	99	2,690

Triples: Season

Player	3B	Year
1. Tim Raines	13	1985
Rodney Scott	13	1980

Mitch Webster	13	1986
4. Andre Dawson	12	1979
5. Vladimir Guerrero	11	2000
Ron LeFlore	11	1980
7. Andre Dawson	10	1983
Tim Raines	10	1986
9. Willie Davis	9	1974
Andre Dawson	9	1977
Marquis Grissom	9	1991
Tim Raines	9	1984

TRIPLES: CAREER WITH TEAM

Player	3B	PA
1. Tim Raines	82	6,256
2. Andre Dawson	67	6,138
3. Vladimir Guerrero	34	4,220
4. Tim Wallach	31	7,174
5. Warren Cromartie	30	4,170
6. Delino DeShields	25	2,406
Mitch Webster	25	1,861
8. Gary Carter	24	6,019
Larry Parrish	24	3,735
10. Bob Bailey	23	3,548
Marquis Grissom	23	2,925
Rondell White	23	3,021
Brad Wilkerson	23	2,690

DOUBLES: SEASON

Player	2B	Year
1. Mark Grudzielanek	54	1997
2. Jose Vidro	51	2000
3. Orlando Cabrera	47	2003
4. Warren Cromartie	46	1979
5. Vladimir Guerrero	45	2001
Mike Lansing	45	1997
Jose Vidro	45	1999
8. Brad Fullmer	44	1998
Larry Walker	44	1994
10. Orlando Cabrera	43	2002
Al Oliver	43	1982
Jose Vidro	43	2002

DOUBLES: CAREER WITH TEAM

Player	2B	PA
1. Tim Wallach	360	7,174
2. Andre Dawson	295	6,138
3. Tim Raines	281	6,256
4. Jose Vidro	278	4,242
5. Gary Carter	274	6,019
6. Vladimir Guerrero	226	4,220
7. Warren Cromartie	222	4,170
8. Orlando Cabrera	214	3,592
9. Larry Parrish	208	3,735
10. Andres Galarraga	180	3,700

EXTRA-BASE HITS: SEASON

Player	XBH	Year
1. Vladimir Guerrero	84	1999
2. Vladimir Guerrero	83	2000
Vladimir Guerrero	83	2001
4. Vladimir Guerrero	82	1998
5. Andres Galarraga	79	1988
Henry Rodriguez	79	1996
7. Andre Dawson	78	1983
Vladimir Guerrero	78	2002
9. Jose Vidro	77	2000
10. Brad Wilkerson	73	2004

EXTRA-BASE HITS: CAREER WITH TEAM

Player	XBH	PA
1. Tim Wallach	595	7,174
2. Andre Dawson	587	6,138
3. Gary Carter	518	6,019
4. Vladimir Guerrero	494	4,220
5. Tim Raines	459	6,256
6. Jose Vidro	397	4,242
7. Larry Parrish	332	3,735
8. Warren Cromartie	312	4,170
9. Andres Galarraga	309	3,700
10. Orlando Cabrera	302	3,592

TOTAL BASES: SEASON

Player	TB	Year
1. Vladimir Guerrero	379	2000
2. Vladimir Guerrero	367	1998
3. Vladimir Guerrero	366	1999
4. Vladimir Guerrero	364	2002
5. Andre Dawson	341	1983
6. Vladimir Guerrero	339	2001
7. Andres Galarraga	329	1988
8. Jose Vidro	327	2000
9. Al Oliver	317	1982
10. Tim Wallach	305	1987

TOTAL BASES: CAREER WITH TEAM

Player	TB	PA
1. Tim Wallach	2,728	7,174
2. Andre Dawson	2,679	6,138
3. Gary Carter	2,409	6,019
4. Tim Raines	2,355	6,256
5. Vladimir Guerrero	2,211	4,220
6. Jose Vidro	1,770	4,242
7. Warren Cromartie	1,525	4,170
8. Andres Galarraga	1,459	3,700
9. Larry Parrish	1,452	3,735
10. Orlando Cabrera	1,333	3,592

RUNS BATTED IN: SEASON

Player	RBI	Year
1. Vladimir Guerrero	131	1999
2. Vladimir Guerrero	123	2000
Tim Wallach	123	1987
4. Andre Dawson	113	1983
5. Vladimir Guerrero	111	2002
6. Tony Batista	110	2004
7. Vladimir Guerrero	109	1998
Al Oliver	109	1982
9. Vladimir Guerrero	108	2001
10. Gary Carter	106	1984

RUNS BATTED IN: CAREER WITH TEAM

Player	RBI	PA
1. Tim Wallach	905	7,174
2. Andre Dawson	838	6,138
3. Gary Carter	823	6,019
4. Vladimir Guerrero	702	4,220
5. Tim Raines	556	6,256
6. Jose Vidro	503	4,242

7. Andres Galarraga	473	3,700
8. Bob Bailey	466	3,548
9. Larry Parrish	444	3,735
10. Hubie Brooks	390	2,670

RUNS SCORED: SEASON

Player	R	Year
1. Tim Raines	133	1983
2. Tim Raines	123	1987
3. Tim Raines	115	1985
4. Brad Wilkerson	112	2004
5. Vladimir Guerrero	108	1998
6. Andre Dawson	107	1982
Vladimir Guerrero	107	2001
8. Vladimir Guerrero	106	2002
Tim Raines	106	1984
10. Andre Dawson	104	1983
Marquis Grissom	104	1993

RUNS SCORED: CAREER WITH TEAM

Player	R	PA
1. Tim Raines	947	6,256
2. Andre Dawson	828	6,138
3. Tim Wallach	737	7,174
4. Gary Carter	707	6,019
5. Vladimir Guerrero	641	4,220
6. Jose Vidro	562	4,242
7. Warren Cromartie	446	4,170
8. Marquis Grissom	430	2,925
9. Andres Galarraga	424	3,700
10. Larry Parrish	421	3,735

WALKS: SEASON

Player	BB	Year
1. Ken Singleton	123	1973
2. Rusty Staub	112	1970
3. Rusty Staub	110	1969
4. Brad Wilkerson	106	2004
5. Bob Bailey	100	1974
6. Bob Bailey	97	1971
Tim Raines	97	1983
8. Delino DeShields	95	1991
9. Tim Raines	93	1989
Ken Singleton	93	1974

WALKS: CAREER WITH TEAM

Player	BB	PA
1. Tim Raines	793	6,256
2. Gary Carter	582	6,019
3. Tim Wallach	514	7,174
4. Bob Bailey	502	3,548
5. Vladimir Guerrero	381	4,220
6. Brad Wilkerson	377	2,690
7. Ron Fairly	370	2,642
8. Jose Vidro	356	4,242
9. Andre Dawson	354	6,138
10. Chris Speier	337	3,289

STRIKEOUTS: SEASON

Player	SO	Year
1. Andres Galarraga	169	1990
2. Brad Wilkerson	161	2002
3. Henry Rodriguez	160	1996
4. Andres Galarraga	158	1989
5. Lee Stevens	157	2001
6. Brad Wilkerson	155	2003
7. Andres Galarraga	153	1988
8. Brad Wilkerson	152	2004
9. Delino DeShields	151	1991
10. Henry Rodriguez	149	1997

STRIKEOUTS: CAREER WITH TEAM

Player	SO	PA
1. Tim Wallach	1,009	7,174
2. Andre Dawson	896	6,138
3. Andres Galarraga	871	3,700
4. Gary Carter	691	6,019
5. Brad Wilkerson	656	2,690
6. Larry Parrish	612	3,735
7. Bob Bailey	607	3,548
8. Tim Raines	569	6,256
9. Rondell White	494	3,021
10. Vladimir Guerrero	484	4,220

SLUGGING PERCENTAGE: SEASON

Player	SLG	Year
1. Vladimir Guerrero	.664	2000
2. Vladimir Guerrero	.600	1999
3. Bob Bailey	.597	1970
4. Vladimir Guerrero	.593	2002
5. Moises Alou	.592	1994
6. Vladimir Guerrero	.589	1998
7. Larry Walker	.587	1994
8. Vladimir Guerrero	.586	2003
9. Vladimir Guerrero	.566	2001
10. Henry Rodriguez	.562	1996

SLUGGING PERCENTAGE: CAREER WITH TEAM

Player	SLG	PA
1. Vladimir Guerrero	.588	4,220
2. Rusty Staub	.497	2,163
3. Moises Alou	.489	2,383
4. Larry Walker	.483	2,690
5. Rondell White	.480	3,021
6. Andre Dawson	.476	6,138
Ellis Valentine	.476	2,532
8. Jose Vidro	.467	4,242
9. Gary Carter	.454	6,019
10. Brad Wilkerson	.452	2,690

ON-BASE PERCENTAGE: SEASON

Player	OBP	Year
1. Mike Jorgensen	.444	1974
2. Tim Raines	.429	1987
3. Vladimir Guerrero	.426	2003
Rusty Staub	.426	1969
5. Ken Singleton	.425	1973
6. Ron Fairly	.422	1973
7. Ron Hunt	.418	1973
8. Vladimir Guerrero	.417	2002
9. Tim Raines	.413	1986
10. Vladimir Guerrero	.410	2000

ON-BASE PERCENTAGE: CAREER WITH TEAM

Player	OBP	PA
1. Rusty Staub	.402	2,163
2. Tim Raines	.391	6,256
3. Vladimir Guerrero	.390	4,220
Ron Hunt	.390	2,140
5. Ron Fairly	.381	2,642

Player	OBP	PA
6. Bob Bailey	.368	3,548
7. Delino DeShields	.367	2,406
8. Brad Wilkerson	.365	2,690
Mike Jorgensen	.365	2,248
10. Jose Vidro	.364	4,242

OPS (On-Base Percentage + Slugging Percentage): Season

Player	OPS	Year
1. Vladimir Guerrero	1.074	2000
2. Vladimir Guerrero	1.012	2003
3. Vladimir Guerrero	1.010	2002
4. Bob Bailey	1.004	1970
5. Moises Alou	.989	1994
6. Larry Walker	.981	1994
7. Vladimir Guerrero	.978	1999
8. Vladimir Guerrero	.960	1998
9. Tim Raines	.955	1987
10. Rusty Staub	.952	1969

OPS (On-Base Percentage + Slugging Percentage): Career with Team

Player	OPS	PA
1. Vladimir Guerrero	.978	4,220
2. Rusty Staub	.899	2,163
3. Larry Walker	.839	2,690
4. Moises Alou	.838	2,383
5. Jose Vidro	.831	4,242
6. Tim Raines	.829	6,256
7. Rondell White	.827	3,021
8. Ron Fairly	.821	2,642
9. Brad Wilkerson	.817	2,690
10. Ellis Valentine	.805	2,532

Stolen Bases: Season

Player	SB	Year
1. Ron LeFlore	97	1980
2. Tim Raines	90	1983
3. Marquis Grissom	78	1992
Tim Raines	78	1982
5. Marquis Grissom	76	1991
6. Tim Raines	75	1984
7. Tim Raines	71	1981
8. Tim Raines	70	1985
Tim Raines	70	1986
10. Rodney Scott	63	1980

Stolen Bases: Career with Team

Player	SB	PA
1. Tim Raines	635	6,256
2. Marquis Grissom	266	2,925
3. Andre Dawson	253	6,138
4. Delino DeShields	187	2,406
5. Rodney Scott	139	1,741
6. Otis Nixon	133	861
7. Vladimir Guerrero	123	4,220
8. Larry Walker	98	2,690
9. Ron LeFlore	97	587
10. Mike Lansing	96	2,828
Mitch Webster	96	1,861

Sacrifice Hits: Season

Player	Sac	Year
1. Larry Lintz	23	1974
2. Steve Rogers	20	1983
3. Tim Foli	17	1974
Tim Foli	17	1975
5. Boots Day	16	1971
Tim Foli	16	1972
Ken Hill	16	1994
Pedro Martinez	16	1996
Scott Sanderson	16	1982
Javier Vazquez	16	2001

Sacrifice Hits: Career with Team

Player	Sac	PA
1. Steve Rogers	101	1,045
2. Javier Vazquez	65	441
3. Dennis Martinez	64	591
4. Tim Foli	62	2,845
5. Bryn Smith	58	469
6. Bill Gullickson	42	443
7. Ken Hill	40	217
Ron Hunt	40	2,140
9. Boots Day	39	1,274
Jeff Fassero	39	264
Scott Sanderson	39	306

Hit by Pitch: Season

Player	HBP	Year
1. Ron Hunt	50	1971
2. Ron Hunt	26	1972
3. F.P. Santangelo	25	1997
4. Ron Hunt	24	1973
5. F.P. Santangelo	23	1998
6. Jose Guillen	19	2005
7. Mack Jones	15	1969
8. Ron Hunt	14	1974
9. Andres Galarraga	13	1989
Mack Jones	13	1970

Hit by Pitch: Career with Team

Player	HBP	PA
1. Ron Hunt	114	2,140
2. Tim Wallach	64	7,174
3. Andre Dawson	62	6,138
4. F.P. Santangelo	61	1,482
5. Andres Galarraga	52	3,700
6. Vladimir Guerrero	50	4,220
7. Rondell White	41	3,021
8. Gary Carter	40	6,019
9. Mark Grudzielanek	35	2,112
10. Jose Vidro	33	4,242

Top 10 Pitching Leaders, Single Season & Career with Team

Games Pitched: Season

Player	GP	Year
1. Mike Marshall	92	1973
2. Graeme Lloyd	84	2001
3. Steve Kline	83	2000
4. Steve Kline	82	1999
5. Luis Ayala	81	2004
Dale Murray	81	1976
7. Anthony Telford	79	1999
Gary Majewski	79	2005
9. Tim Burke	78	1985
Steve Kline	78	1998

Games Pitched: Career with Team

Player	GP	IP
1. Tim Burke	425	600.3
2. Steve Rogers	399	2,837.7
3. Mel Rojas	388	512.3
4. Jeff Reardon	359	506.3
5. Woodie Fryman	297	721.7
6. Ugueth Urbina	296	406.7
7. Anthony Telford	293	361.3
8. Bryn Smith	284	1,400.3
9. Steve Kline	269	250.0
10. Jeff Fassero	262	850.0

Innings Pitched: Season

Player	IP	Year
1. Steve Rogers	301.7	1977
2. Bill Stoneman	294.7	1971
3. Carl Morton	284.7	1970
4. Steve Rogers	281.0	1980
5. Steve Rogers	277.0	1982
6. Steve Renko	275.7	1971
7. Steve Rogers	273.0	1983
8. Ross Grimsley	263.0	1978
9. Livan Hernandez	255.0	2004
10. Steve Rogers	253.7	1974

Innings Pitched: Career with Team

Player	IP
1. Steve Rogers	2,837.7
2. Dennis Martinez	1,609.0
3. Bryn Smith	1,400.3
4. Steve Renko	1,359.3
5. Javier Vazquez	1,229.3
6. Bill Gullickson	1,186.3
7. Bill Stoneman	1,085.3
8. Scott Sanderson	883.0
9. Jeff Fassero	850.0
10. Pedro Martinez	797.3

Batters Faced: Season

Player	BF	Year
1. Bill Stoneman	1,243	1971
2. Steve Rogers	1,235	1977
3. Carl Morton	1,218	1970
4. Steve Renko	1,193	1971
5. Steve Rogers	1,151	1980
6. Steve Rogers	1,125	1983
7. Steve Rogers	1,122	1982
8. Ross Grimsley	1,068	1978
Steve Rogers	1,068	1975
10. Livan Hernandez	1,065	2005

Batters Faced: Career with Team

Player	BF	IP
1. Steve Rogers	11,702	2,837.7
2. Dennis Martinez	6,591	1,609.0
3. Steve Renko	5,850	1,359.3
4. Bryn Smith	5,770	1,400.3
5. Javier Vazquez	5,183	1,229.3
6. Bill Gullickson	4,895	1,186.3
7. Bill Stoneman	4,728	1,085.3
8. Scott Sanderson	3,650	883.0
9. Jeff Fassero	3,576	850.0
10. Charlie Lea	3,291	793.3

Games Started: Season

Player	GS	Year
1. Steve Rogers	40	1977
2. Bill Stoneman	39	1971
3. Steve Rogers	38	1974
4. Carl Morton	37	1970
Steve Renko	37	1971
Steve Rogers	37	1979
Steve Rogers	37	1980
8. Ross Grimsley	36	1978
Steve Rogers	36	1983
Bill Stoneman	36	1969

Games Started: Career with Team

Player	GS	IP
1. Steve Rogers	393	2,837.7
2. Dennis Martinez	233	1,609.0
3. Bryn Smith	193	1,400.3
4. Steve Renko	192	1,359.3
5. Javier Vazquez	191	1,229.3
6. Bill Gullickson	170	1,186.3
7. Bill Stoneman	157	1,085.3
8. Scott Sanderson	136	883.0
9. Dustin Hermanson	122	759.7
10. Charlie Lea	121	793.3
Tony Armas Jr.	121	666.3

Complete Games: Season

Player	CG	Year
1. Bill Stoneman	20	1971
2. Ross Grimsley	19	1978
3. Steve Rogers	17	1977
4. Steve Rogers	14	1980
Steve Rogers	14	1982
6. Pedro Martinez	13	1997
Steve Rogers	13	1979
Steve Rogers	13	1983
Bill Stoneman	13	1972
Mike Torrez	13	1972

Complete Games: Career with Team

Player	CG	IP
1. Steve Rogers	129	2,837.7
2. Bill Stoneman	46	1,085.3
3. Dennis Martinez	41	1,609.0
4. Steve Renko	40	1,359.3
5. Bill Gullickson	31	1,186.3
6. Scott Sanderson	24	883.0
7. Charlie Lea	22	793.3
Carl Morton	22	699.7

Mike Torrez	22	640.7
10. Ross Grimsley	21	455.7
Ernie McAnally	21	623.3

Games Won: Season

Player	W	Year
1. Ross Grimsley	20	1978
2. Steve Rogers	19	1982
3. Carl Morton	18	1970
Bryn Smith	18	1985
5. Bill Gullickson	17	1983
Pedro Martinez	17	1997
Steve Rogers	17	1977
Steve Rogers	17	1983
Bill Stoneman	17	1971
10. 10 tied with . . .	16	——

Games Won: Career with Team

Player	W	IP
1. Steve Rogers	158	2,837.7
2. Dennis Martinez	100	1,609.0
3. Bryn Smith	81	1,400.3
4. Bill Gullickson	72	1,186.3
5. Steve Renko	68	1,359.3
6. Javier Vazquez	64	1,229.3
7. Jeff Fassero	58	850.0
8. Scott Sanderson	56	883.0
9. Charlie Lea	55	793.3
Pedro Martinez	55	797.3

Games Lost: Season

Player	L	Year
1. Steve Rogers	22	1974
2. Bill Stoneman	19	1969
3. Carl Morton	18	1971
4. Steve Rogers	17	1976
5. Balor Moore	16	1973
Steve Renko	16	1974
Jerry Robertson	16	1969
Steve Rogers	16	1977
Bill Stoneman	16	1971
10. Seven tied with...	15	——

Games Lost: Career with Team

Player	L	IP
1. Steve Rogers	152	2,837.7
2. Steve Renko	82	1,359.3
3. Dennis Martinez	72	1,609.0
Bill Stoneman	72	1,085.3
5. Bryn Smith	71	1,400.3
6. Javier Vazquez	68	1,229.3
7. Bill Gullickson	61	1,186.3
8. Woodie Fryman	52	721.7
9. Ernie McAnally	49	623.3
10. Jeff Fassero	48	850.0
Tony Armas Jr.	48	666.3

Winning Percentage: Season

Player	W%	Year
1. Bryn Smith	.783	1985
2. Ken Hill	.762	1994
3. Jeff Parrett	.750	1988
4. Jeff Fassero	.706	1993
5. Steve Rogers	.704	1982
6. Dennis Martinez	.696	1989
7. Jeff Juden	.688	1997
Pedro Martinez	.688	1994
9. Pedro Martinez	.680	1997
10. Dale Murray	.652	1975
Mike Torrez	.652	1974

Winning Percentage: Career with Team

Player	W%	IP
1. Pedro Martinez	.625	797.3
2. Dennis Martinez	.581	1,609.0
3. Charlie Lea	.573	793.3
4. Jeff Fassero	.547	850.0
5. Scott Sanderson	.544	883.0
6. Bill Gullickson	.541	1,186.3
7. Livan Hernandez	.539	734.7
8. Bryn Smith	.533	1,400.3
9. Steve Rogers	.510	2,837.7
10. Woodie Fryman	.495	721.7

Shutouts: Season

Player	SHO	Year
1. Dennis Martinez	5	1991
Carlos Perez	5	1997
Steve Rogers	5	1979
Steve Rogers	5	1983
Bill Stoneman	5	1969
6. Mark Langston	4	1989
Charlie Lea	4	1983
Pedro Martinez	4	1997
Carl Morton	4	1970
Steve Rogers	4	1976
Steve Rogers	4	1977
Steve Rogers	4	1980
Steve Rogers	4	1982
Bill Stoneman	4	1972

Shutouts: Career with Team

Player	SHO	IP
1. Steve Rogers	37	2,837.7
2. Bill Stoneman	15	1,085.3
3. Dennis Martinez	13	1,609.0
4. Woodie Fryman	8	721.7
Charlie Lea	8	793.3
Pedro Martinez	8	797.3
Scott Sanderson	8	883.0
Bryn Smith	8	1,400.3
9. Bill Gullickson	6	1,186.3
Ernie McAnally	6	623.3
Carlos Perez	6	511.3
Steve Renko	6	1,359.3
Javier Vazquez	6	1,229.3
Floyd Youmans	6	496.3

ERA: Season

Player	ERA	Year
1. Pedro Martinez	1.90	1997
2. Dennis Martinez	2.39	1991
Mark Langston	2.39	1989
4. Steve Rogers	2.40	1982
5. Pascual Perez	2.44	1988
6. Dennis Martinez	2.47	1992
Steve Rogers	2.47	1978
8. Mike Marshall	2.66	1973
9. Ken Hill	2.68	1992
10. Dennis Martinez	2.72	1988

ERA: Career with Team

Player	ERA	IP
1. Tim Burke	2.61	600.3
2. Jeff Reardon	2.84	506.3
3. Ken Hill	3.04	556.3
4. Pedro Martinez	3.06	797.3
Dennis Martinez	3.06	1,609.0
6. Dan Schatzeder	3.09	749.7
7. Mel Rojas	3.11	512.3
8. Steve Rogers	3.17	2,837.7
9. Jeff Fassero	3.20	850.0
10. Woodie Fryman	3.24	721.7

Earned Runs Allowed: Season

Player	ER	Year
1. Steve Rogers	126	1974
2. Javier Vazquez	116	1998
3. Steve Renko	115	1971
Bill Stoneman	115	1969

5. Carl Morton	114	1970
Carl Morton	114	1971
7. Livan Hernandez	109	2005
8. Steve Renko	107	1970
9. Bill Stoneman	106	1970
10. Dustin Hermanson	105	2000

Earned Runs Allowed: Career with Team

Player	ER	IP
1. Steve Rogers	1,001	2,837.7
2. Steve Renko	589	1,359.3
3. Javier Vazquez	568	1,229.3
4. Dennis Martinez	547	1,609.0
5. Bryn Smith	511	1,400.3
6. Bill Stoneman	480	1,085.3
7. Bill Gullickson	453	1,186.3
8. Dustin Hermanson	336	759.7
9. Scott Sanderson	327	883.0
10. Tony Armas Jr.	320	666.3

Strikeouts: Season

Player	K	Year
1. Pedro Martinez	305	1997
2. Bill Stoneman	251	1971
3. Javier Vazquez	241	2003
4. Jeff Fassero	222	1996
Pedro Martinez	222	1996
6. Javier Vazquez	208	2001
7. Steve Rogers	206	1977
8. Floyd Youmans	202	1986
9. Javier Vazquez	196	2000
10. Livan Hernandez	186	2004

Strikeouts: Career with Team

Player	K	IP
1. Steve Rogers	1,621	2,837.7
2. Javier Vazquez	1,076	1,229.3
3. Dennis Martinez	973	1,609.0
4. Pedro Martinez	843	797.3
5. Bryn Smith	838	1,400.3
6. Bill Stoneman	831	1,085.3
7. Steve Renko	810	1,359.3
8. Jeff Fassero	750	850.0
9. Bill Gullickson	678	1,186.3
10. Scott Sanderson	603	883.0

Strikeouts Per Nine IP: Season

Player	K/9	Year
1. Pedro Martinez	11.37	1997
2. Javier Vazquez	9.40	2003
3. Pedro Martinez	9.22	1996
4. Mark Langston	8.92	1989
5. Jeff Fassero	8.62	1996
6. John Patterson	8.39	2005
7. Javier Vazquez	8.37	2001
8. Floyd Youmans	8.30	1986
9. Javier Vazquez	8.10	2000
10. Tony Armas Jr.	8.05	2001

Strikeouts Per Nine IP: Career with Team

Player	K/9	IP
1. Pedro Martinez	9.52	797.3
2. Jeff Fassero	7.94	850.0
3. Javier Vazquez	7.88	1,229.3
4. Mel Rojas	7.36	512.3
5. Jeff Reardon	7.07	506.3
6. Bill Stoneman	6.89	1,085.3
7. Tony Armas Jr.	6.81	666.3
8. Mark Gardner	6.75	527.0
9. Dustin Hermanson	6.27	759.7
10. Livan Hernandez	6.26	734.7

Hits Allowed: Season

Player	HA	Year
1. Carl Morton	281	1970
2. Steve Rogers	272	1977
3. Livan Hernandez	268	2005
4. Steve Rogers	258	1983
5. Steve Renko	256	1971
6. Steve Rogers	255	1974
7. Carl Morton	252	1971
8. Steve Rogers	248	1975
9. Steve Rogers	247	1980
Javier Vazquez	247	2000

Hits Allowed: Career with Team

Player	HA	IP
1. Steve Rogers	2,619	2,837.7
2. Dennis Martinez	1,439	1,609.0
3. Bryn Smith	1,310	1,400.3
4. Steve Renko	1,262	1,359.3
5. Javier Vazquez	1,235	1,229.3
6. Bill Gullickson	1,149	1,186.3
7. Bill Stoneman	1,018	1,085.3
8. Scott Sanderson	838	883.0
9. Jeff Fassero	782	850.0
10. Dustin Hermanson	748	759.7

Hits Allowed Per Nine IP: Season

Player	H/9	Year
1. Pedro Martinez	5.89	1997
2. Floyd Youmans	5.96	1986
3. Pascual Perez	6.37	1988
4. Dennis Martinez	6.84	1992
5. Dan Warthen	6.98	1975
6. Mark Langston	7.03	1989
7. Steve Renko	7.25	1973
8. Pedro Martinez	7.30	1995
9. Charlie Lea	7.35	1982
10. Bryn Smith	7.39	1989

Hits Allowed Per Nine IP: Career with Team

Player	H/9	IP
1. Pedro Martinez	7.00	797.3
2. Jeff Reardon	7.39	506.3
3. Mel Rojas	7.52	512.3
4. Chris Nabholz	7.62	535.3
5. Tim Burke	7.75	600.3
6. Dan Schatzeder	7.82	749.7
7. Ken Hill	8.01	556.3
8. Charlie Lea	8.03	793.3
9. Dennis Martinez	8.05	1,609.0
10. Mark Gardner	8.08	527.0

Walks Allowed: Season

Player	BB	Year
1. Bill Stoneman	146	1971
2. Steve Renko	135	1971
3. Carl Morton	125	1970
4. Bill Stoneman	123	1969
5. Floyd Youmans	118	1986
6. Mike Torrez	115	1973
7. Balor Moore	109	1973
Bill Stoneman	109	1970
9. Steve Renko	108	1973
10. Dennis Blair	106	1975

WALKS ALLOWED: CAREER WITH TEAM

Player	BB	IP
1. Steve Rogers	876	2,837.7
2. Steve Renko	624	1,359.3
3. Bill Stoneman	535	1,085.3
4. Dennis Martinez	407	1,609.0
5. Bryn Smith	341	1,400.3
6. Javier Vazquez	331	1,229.3
7. Tony Armas Jr.	328	666.3
8. Mike Torrez	303	640.7
9. Charlie Lea	291	793.3
10. Bill Gullickson	288	1,186.3

WALKS ALLOWED PER NINE IP: SEASON

Player	BB/9	Year
1. Bryn Smith	1.45	1988
2. Bill Gullickson	1.47	1984
3. Bryn Smith	1.66	1985
4. Neal Heaton	1.72	1987
5. Javier Vazquez	1.77	2001
6. Carlos Perez	1.82	1998
7. Bill Lee	1.86	1979
8. Dennis Martinez	1.90	1989
9. Javier Vazquez	1.91	2002
10. Dennis Martinez	1.95	1990

WALKS ALLOWED PER NINE IP: CAREER WITH TEAM

Player	BB/9	IP
1. Carlos Perez	1.92	511.3
2. Bill Gullickson	2.18	1,186.3
3. Bryn Smith	2.19	1,400.3
4. Tomokazu Ohka	2.26	585.0
5. Dennis Martinez	2.28	1,609.0
6. Javier Vazquez	2.42	1,229.3
7. Scott Sanderson	2.45	883.0
8. Livan Hernandez	2.74	734.7
9. Steve Rogers	2.78	2,837.7
10. Pedro Martinez	2.80	797.3

WHIP (WALKS + HITS PER NINE IP): SEASON

Player	WHIP	Year
1. Pedro Martinez	0.932	1997
2. Pascual Perez	0.941	1988
3. Dennis Martinez	1.025	1992
4. Bryn Smith	1.052	1985
5. Dennis Martinez	1.062	1990
6. Bryn Smith	1.066	1988
7. Bryn Smith	1.071	1989
8. Javier Vazquez	1.077	2001
9. Javier Vazquez	1.105	2003
10. Steve Rogers	1.119	1982

WHIP (WALKS + HITS PER IP): CAREER WITH TEAM

Player	WHIP	IP
1. Pedro Martinez	1.089	797.3
2. Dennis Martinez	1.147	1,609.0
3. Jeff Reardon	1.173	506.3
4. Tim Burke	1.176	600.3
5. Bryn Smith	1.179	1,400.3
6. Mel Rojas	1.189	512.3
7. Bill Gullickson	1.211	1,186.3
8. Dan Schatzeder	1.219	749.7
9. Scott Sanderson	1.221	883.0
10. Steve Rogers	1.232	2,837.7

HOME RUNS ALLOWED: SEASON

Player	HRA	Year
1. Javier Vazquez	31	1998
2. Javier Vazquez	28	2002
Javier Vazquez	28	2003
4. Bill Gullickson	27	1984
Livan Hernandez	27	2003
Dennis Martinez	27	1993
Carl Morton	27	1970
Steve Renko	27	1970
9. Six tied with . . .	26	—

HOME RUNS ALLOWED: CAREER WITH TEAM

Player	HRA	IP
1. Javier Vazquez	155	1,229.3
2. Steve Rogers	151	2,837.7
3. Steve Renko	141	1,359.3
4. Dennis Martinez	126	1,609.0
5. Bryn Smith	108	1,400.3
6. Bill Stoneman	99	1,085.3
7. Bill Gullickson	88	1,186.3
8. Scott Sanderson	83	883.0
Tony Armas Jr.	83	666.3
10. Dustin Hermanson	82	759.7

SAVES: SEASON

Player	SV	Year
1. Chad Cordero	47	2005
2. John Wetteland	43	1993
3. Jeff Reardon	41	1985
Ugueth Urbina	41	1999
5. John Wetteland	37	1992
6. Mel Rojas	36	1996
7. Jeff Reardon	35	1986
8. Rocky Biddle	34	2003
Ugueth Urbina	34	1998
10. Mike Marshall	31	1973

SAVES: CAREER WITH TEAM

Player	SV	IP
1. Jeff Reardon	152	506.3
2. Ugueth Urbina	125	406.7
3. Mel Rojas	109	512.3
4. John Wetteland	105	232.3
5. Tim Burke	101	600.3
6. Mike Marshall	75	471.0
7. Chad Cordero	62	168.0
8. Woodie Fryman	52	721.7
9. Rocky Biddle	45	149.7
10. Dale Murray	33	337.0

WILD PITCHES: SEASON

Player	WP	Year
1. Steve Renko	19	1974
2. Ernie McAnally	18	1971
3. Tony Armas Jr.	14	2002
Steve Rogers	14	1977
Mike Torrez	14	1973
6. Zach Day	13	2003
Steve Rogers	13	1975
Mike Wegener	13	1969
9. Dennis Blair	12	1975
Steve Rogers	12	1984

WILD PITCHES: CAREER WITH TEAM

Player	WP	IP
1. Steve Rogers	87	2,837.7
2. Steve Renko	58	1,359.3
3. Ernie McAnally	40	623.3
4. Jeff Fassero	34	850.0
Tony Armas Jr.	34	666.3
6. Bill Stoneman	33	1,085.3
7. Bill Gullickson	30	1,186.3
Charlie Lea	30	793.3
9. Mike Marshall	29	471.0
10. Mike Torrez	28	640.7

Hit Batsmen: Season

Player	HB	Year
1. Bill Stoneman	14	1970
2. Sun-Woo Kim	13	2004
Livan Hernandez	13	2005
4. Jim Bullinger	12	1997
Bill Stoneman	12	1969
6. Dennis Martinez	11	1993
Pedro Martinez	11	1994
Pedro Martinez	11	1995
Javier Vazquez	11	1998
10. Five tied with...	10	——

Hit Batsmen: Career with Team

Player	HB	IP
1. Dennis Martinez	52	1,609.0
2. Steve Rogers	43	2,837.7
3. Bill Stoneman	40	1,085.3
4. Pedro Martinez	34	797.3
5. Livan Hernandez	33	734.7
6. Bryn Smith	31	1,400.3
Javier Vazquez	31	1,229.3
8. Tony Armas Jr.	30	666.3
9. Carl Pavano	29	452.7
10. Woodie Fryman	24	721.7
Mark Gardner	24	527.0
Mel Rojas	24	512.3

Games Finished: Season

Player	GF	Year
1. Mike Marshall	73	1973
2. Mel Rojas	64	1996
3. Ugueth Urbina	62	1999
Chad Cordero	62	2005
5. Ugueth Urbina	59	1998
6. Rocky Biddle	58	2003
Jeff Reardon	58	1984
John Wetteland	58	1992
John Wetteland	58	1993
10. Mike Marshall	56	1972

Games Finished: Career with Team

Player	GF	IP
1. Jeff Reardon	281	506.3
2. Tim Burke	228	600.3
3. Ugueth Urbina	224	406.7
4. Mel Rojas	209	512.3
5. Mike Marshall	192	471.0
6. John Wetteland	159	232.3
7. Woodie Fryman	133	721.7
8. Dale Murray	127	337.0
9. Chad Cordero	106	168.0
10. Elias Sosa	101	229.7

RFK stadium's right-field foul pole gets a touch-up before Opening Day.

Significant Expos/Nationals

CARTER, GARY (C)
(1974–1984, 1992)

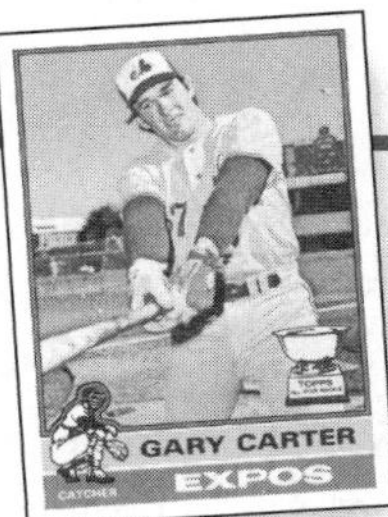

Although Gary "Kid" Carter spent as much time in the outfield as he did behind the plate during his first three years in the majors, he eventually became one of the best backstops of all time, both defensively and offensively. Drafted in the third round of the June 1972 amateur draft, Carter became the Expos' everyday catcher in 1977 when Barry Foote was traded to Philadelphia. In 1978 he established a major league record with just one passed ball in 152 games. Carter consistently ranked at or near the top of most catching categories for many years. In 1980 he finished second to Mike Schmidt for the National League's MVP Award. Carter was selected to the All-Star team a total of 11 times, seven while with Montreal. He was named the All-Star Game MVP twice, in 1981 and 1984, and won three consecutive Gold Gloves from 1980 to 1982. Three of his five Silver Slugger Awards came while with Montreal (1981, 1982, 1984). After the 1984 season, Carter was traded to the New York Mets for four players: Hubie Brooks, Mike Fitzgerald, Herm Winningham, and Floyd Youmans. After five years with the Mets (where he won a World Series ring) and one each with San Francisco and Los Angeles, Carter returned to Montreal in 1992 for the final year of his career. When Carter was elected to the Baseball Hall of Fame in 2003, he was the first Expos representative in Cooperstown. Montreal retired Carter's number 8 in 1993.

CAREER EXPOS RECORD:

Games	AB	Hits	Runs
1,503	5,303	1,427	707
Avg	**HR**	**RBI**	**SB**
.269	220	823	34

CROMARTIE, WARREN (OF/1B)
(1974, 1976–1983)

Selected as the sixth pick of the first round of the June 1973 amateur draft, the talented Cromartie was once regarded as one of the National League's most promising young stars, but he never quite lived up to his billing. Prone to long slumps, Cromartie spent nine basically mediocre seasons with the Expos as an outfielder and first baseman before leaving America after the 1983 season to play in Japan. He returned to the majors in 1991, playing just 69 games with Kansas City before retiring.

CAREER EXPOS RECORD:

Games	AB	Hits	Runs
1,038	3,796	1,063	446
Avg	**HR**	**RBI**	**SB**
.280	60	371	49

DAWSON, ANDRE (OF)
(1976–1986)

What a bargain Andre Dawson turned out to be. Not selected until the 11th round of the June 1975 amateur draft, Dawson became the regular center fielder for the Expos in 1977 and promptly won the league's Rookie of the Year Award. By the end of the 1983 season, Dawson owned the franchise record for hits, doubles, triples, homers, and RBIs. All was not well, however, as the artificial turf at Olympic Stadium was taking its toll on Dawson's knees. During his last three years with Montreal (1984–1986), Dawson missed 20–30 games each year due to knee trouble. Desperately wanting to play on natural grass to prolong his career, he opted for free agency but, possibly as a result of rumored collusion at the time among owners, Dawson found no takers. He signed a contract with the Cubs with the dollar amount left blank, eventually agreeing to just $500,000, far below his market value at the time. He responded with an incredible 1987 season, smacking 49 homers and knocking in 137 runs, winning the league's MVP Award in the process. After six years in Chicago, two more in Boston, and a final two in Florida, Dawson retired with 21 major league seasons under his belt and career stats very close to Hall of Fame caliber. Should he ever be elected to Cooperstown, he would enter as an Expo. Montreal retired his uniform number 10 in 1997.

CAREER EXPOS RECORD:

Games	AB	Hits	Runs
1,443	5,628	1,575	828
Avg	**HR**	**RBI**	**SB**
.280	225	838	253

GALARRAGA, ANDRES (1B/OF)
(1985–1991, 2002)

Galarraga was signed as a undrafted free agent in 1979 but didn't make the major leagues with the Expos until 1985. While he showed some promise early in his Expos career, three straight years of declining batting averages concerned the team and led to his trade to St. Louis after the 1991 season. He eventually rose to prominence as a member of the Colorado Rockies. *(See Rockies bio.)*

CAREER EXPOS RECORD:

Games	AB	Hits	Runs
951	3,374	906	424
Avg	**HR**	**RBI**	**SB**
.269	115	473	56

GUERRERO, VLADIMIR (OF)
(1996–2003)

Signed as a 16-year-old free agent out of the Dominican Republic, Vladimir Guerrero quickly made a name for himself as one of the best players ever to come up in the Montreal system. After winning back-to-back batting titles in the minors in 1995 and 1996, Guerrero skipped Triple-A and jumped right to the majors. Considered the odds-on favorite to win the Rookie of the Year honors, Guerrero instead made several trips to the disabled list and missed about half the year, although he did hit .302. He stormed back in 1998, however, hitting .324 with 38 homers and 109 RBIs. After the 1998 season, Guerrero was rewarded with one of the richest contracts in Expos history and he continued his assault on Montreal's hitting records. In 1999 and 2000, he clubbed more than 40 homers and had 100+ runs and RBIs. He joined Ted Williams, Jimmie Foxx, and Joe DiMaggio as the only players in major league history (and the only National Leaguer) to hit .300 with at least 35 homers and 100 RBIs for three consecutive seasons before the age of 25. In 1999 he put together a 31-game hitting streak, longest by any player in the 1990s. A back injury not only cost Guerrero 50 games during the 2003 season, but ended his streak of five consecutive years with at least 34 homers, and 100+ runs and RBIs. After his rich five-year contract expired following the 2003 season, Guerrero, now firmly established as one of the best players in the game today, left Montreal and signed an even bigger free-agent deal with the Anaheim Angels, where he won the AL MVP Award in 2004. As a member of the Expos, Guerrero was selected to the All-Star team four times and won three Silver Slugger Awards.

CAREER EXPOS RECORD:

Games	AB	Hits	Runs
1,004	3,763	1,215	641
Avg	**HR**	**RBI**	**SB**
.323	234	702	123

MARTINEZ, DENNIS (SP)
(1986–1993)

After spending 10½ seasons as an Oriole, Dennis Martinez was traded to the Expos on June 16, 1986, for Rene Gonzalez. During his 7½ seasons with the Expos, the Nicaraguan-born Martinez, a recovering alcoholic, won 100 games in a sort of "second career" as a mainstay in Montreal's rotation. In 1991, Martinez led the majors in ERA at 2.39 and pitched a perfect game in Dodger Stadium on July 28. For six straight years he pitched more than 220 innings for the Expos. After leaving Montreal for free agency following the 1993 season, Martinez played five more years for Cleveland, Seattle, and Atlanta, retiring in 1998 with 245 wins, the most ever by a Latin American pitcher. During his 23-year career, Martinez was named to the All-Star team four times, three as a member of the Expos.

CAREER EXPOS RECORD:

W	L	W%	ERA	SV
100	72	.581	3.06	1
K	**BB**	**SHO**	**IP**	
973	407	13	1,609.0	

Martinez, Pedro (SP)
(1994–1997)

After playing for the Los Angeles Dodgers for two years, relief pitcher Pedro Martinez was traded to Montreal for second baseman Delino DeShields after the 1993 season. The Expos made Martinez a starter in 1994 and he quickly earned a reputation as a headhunter. In 23 starts that season, Martinez hit 11 batters, was ejected 12 times, and was involved in at least three fights. He lost a perfect-game bid to Cincinnati in the eighth inning after hitting Reggie Sanders with a pitch. On June 3, 1995, Martinez pitched nine perfect innings against San Diego, but the scoreless game went to extra innings and Martinez was pulled after giving up a leadoff hit in the 10th. In 1997 he won the first of his Cy Young Awards when he compiled a 17–8 record with more than 300 strikeouts and an ERA of 1.90. Unable to afford their rising star, the Expos traded him to Boston after the 1997 season for Carl Pavano and Tony Armas Jr. *(See Red Sox bio.)*

CAREER EXPOS RECORD:

W	L	W%	ERA	SV
55	33	.625	3.06	1
K	BB	SHO	IP	
843	248	8	797.3	

Raines, Tim (OF)
(1979–1990, 2001)

Drafted by Montreal in the fifth round of the June 1977 amateur draft, Tim "Rock" Raines was often referred to as the National League's version of Rickey Henderson, a player who built his career largely on speed. After a brief September call-up in 1980, Raines made the team as a regular in 1981. He won the NL stolen base title and set a rookie record for stolen bases with 71 in spite of the strike-shortened season and a September injury that combined to cost him about half the season. Raines was the runner-up to Fernando Valenzuela for Rookie of the Year honors. He then led the league in steals the next three years as well with totals of 78, 90, and 75, and stole 70 more in each of the next two seasons, though he didn't lead the league. Raines made the NL All-Star team his first seven seasons in the major leagues, capping it off with the All-Star Game MVP Award in 1987. Of Raines' 23 major league seasons, 13 were spent with the Expos. He batted over .300 in six of those years, and won the batting title in 1986, when he hit .334. When he retired, Raines' stolen-base success rate of .847 was the highest in major league history. Raines has embarked on a coaching career, and is currently the first-base coach for the White Sox.

CAREER EXPOS RECORD:

Games	AB	Hits	Runs
1,452	5,383	1,622	947
Avg	HR	RBI	SB
.301	96	556	635

REARDON, JEFF (RP)
(1981–1986)

In one of the worst trades in New York Mets history, Jeff Reardon went to Montreal on May 29, 1981, for oft-injured outfielder Ellis Valentine. Reardon came into his own in Montreal and, although he had never earned a save before he became a major leaguer, eventually became the career leader in saves with 367; 152 of those coming during his six years in Montreal. Just before the 1987 season, Reardon was traded away to Minnesota in a deal that the Expos, like the Mets, later came to regret. Reardon had two All-Star appearances with the Expos, in 1985 and 1986. He also won the NL Rolaids Relief Award in 1985 when he collected 41 saves.

CAREER EXPOS RECORD:

W	L	W%	ERA	SV
32	37	.464	2.84	152
K	**BB**	**SHO**	**IP**	
398	178	0	506.3	

ROGERS, STEVE (SP)
(1973–1985)

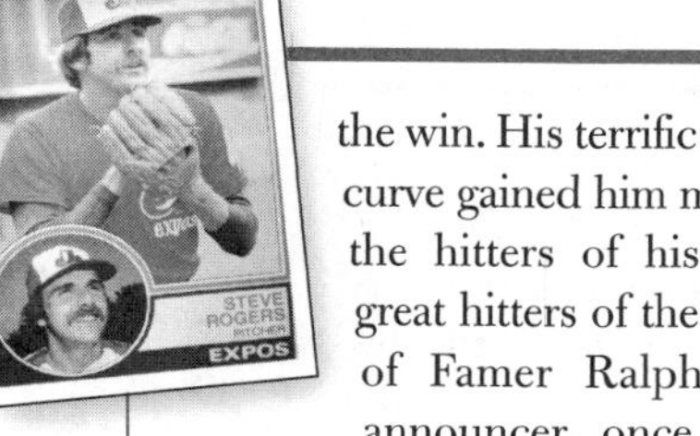

Steve Rogers was the greatest pitcher in Montreal's history, although many would say he never quite lived up to expectations. Originally drafted by the Yankees in 1967, Rogers elected instead to first get a college education, earning a degree in petroleum engineering. Four years later he was drafted by Montreal as the fourth pick of the first round of the 1971 amateur draft (secondary phase). He played his entire 13-year career with the Expos, finishing with 158 wins. His 10–5 record and 1.54 ERA as a rookie in 1973 probably led to those lofty but unrealized expectations. In 1974, his second year in the majors, Rogers started 38 games and was credited with an amazing 37 decisions, going 15–22. Rogers did make the All-Star team five times and had the honor of starting the first All-Star Game in Canada, in which he got credit for the win. His terrific fastball and sharp curve gained him much respect from the hitters of his day—and some great hitters of the past as well. Hall of Famer Ralph Kiner, a Mets announcer, once said of Rogers, "He is the epitome of a thinking man's pitcher." After suffering through two years of serious arm troubles, and dismayed over the booing of hometown fans, the holder of many of Montreal's all-time pitching records was released by the Expos in 1985. Although he signed free-agent contracts with both the Angels and White Sox later in 1985, he never appeared in the majors with either team.

CAREER EXPOS RECORD:

W	L	W%	ERA	SV
158	152	.510	3.17	2
K	**BB**	**SHO**	**IP**	
1,621	876	37	2,837.7	

URBINA, UGUETH (RP)
(1995–2001)

The Montreal Expos signed Ugueth Urbina in 1990 as an amateur free agent out of Venezuela at the age of 16. He made his major league debut with the team in 1995 as the fourth-youngest player in the majors. Urbina made 17 starts for the team in 1996, but thereafter was used exclusively in relief, compiling 125 saves before being traded to the Boston Red Sox at the trading deadline in 2001 for Tomokazu Ohka and Rich Rundles. As a member of the Expos, Urbina made the All-Star team in 1998 and led the National League in saves in 1999 with 41.

CAREER EXPOS RECORD:

W	L	W%	ERA	SV
31	26	.544	3.52	125
K	BB	SHO	IP	
480	182	0	406.7	

VIDRO, JOSE (2B)
(1997–2005)

The Puerto Rican-born Jose Vidro was selected by the Expos in the sixth round of the June 1992 amateur draft. He made his major league debut in 1997 but struggled his first two seasons. By 1999, however, the second baseman had blossomed to become a good fielder and a consistent .300 hitter with some power. He was named to the All-Star team three times (2000, 2002, 2003) and won the Silver Slugger Award in 2003. In 2000 and 2002, Vidro finished in the top three in the National League in hits and doubles, and top seven in batting average.

CAREER EXPOS/NATIONALS RECORD:

Games	AB	Hits	Runs
1,060	3,794	1,146	562
Avg	HR	RBI	SB
.302	108	503	20

WALLACH, TIM (3B)
(1980–1992)

Tim Wallach spent the first 13 of his 17 major league seasons as a member of the Expos. The 10th pick of the first round in the June 1979 amateur draft, Wallach got his first taste of major league action in 1980 when he hit a homer in his first major league at-bat, something he had also done in his first minor league appearance. Not only was Wallach a great defensive third baseman, winning three Gold Gloves, but he could hit with power, five times surpassing the 20-homer mark and twice leading the National League in doubles. Wallach was a five-time All-Star and won two Silver Slugger Awards (1985, 1987). In typical Montreal cost-cutting fashion, Wallach was traded to the Dodgers after the 1992 season for minor leaguer Tim Barker. After four more years of declining production with the Dodgers and Angels, Wallach called it quits in 1996.

CAREER EXPOS RECORD:

Games	AB	Hits	Runs
1,767	6,529	1,694	737
Avg	**HR**	**RBI**	**SB**
.259	204	905	50

WETTELAND, JOHN (RP)
(1992–1994)

During the 1990s, John Wetteland was one of the premier closers in baseball, and he spent three of those years with Montreal. After logging three lackluster seasons with the Dodgers from 1989–1991, Wetteland ran afoul of Los Angeles manager Tommy Lasorda not just for his performance, but for his erratic habits (he insisted on wearing the hat issued to him in spring training for the entire year, regardless of how sweaty and grimy it got) and bizarre declarations (he explored Satanic cults and beliefs before becoming a born-again Christian). He was traded twice during the offseason, first to the Reds and then to the Expos, becoming a closer upon arriving in Montreal. He collected more than 100 saves from 1992 through the strike-shortened 1994 season, and was then traded to the Yankees just before the beginning of the late-starting 1995 season. In 1996, he became the first pitcher to save all four victories of a World Series, a feat that earned him MVP honors as well. *(See Rangers bio.)*

CAREER EXPOS RECORD:

W	L	W%	ERA	SV
17	13	.567	2.32	105
K	**BB**	**SHO**	**IP**	
280	85	0	232.3	

SIGNIFICANT PLAYERS INDEX